THE Prentice Hall AMERICAN WORLD ATLAS

THE *Prentice Hall* AMERICAN WORLD ATLAS

Prentice-Hall, Inc.,
Englewood Cliffs, New Jersey 07632

Edited by
Bill Willett, Cartographic Editor, George Philip and Son Ltd.

Library of Congress Cataloging in Publication Data

Prentice-Hall, inc.
The Prentice-Hall American world atlas.

Includes index.
1. Atlases. I. Title II. Title: American world atlas.
G1021.P6836 1984 912 84-675206
ISBN 0-13-695024-8

The large scale maps of the United States are based on material appearing in the National Atlas of the United States. The material was supplied by the National Cartographic Information Center, U.S. Geological Survey, Reston, Va.

Printed in Hong Kong

10 9 8 7 6 5 4 3 2 1

ISBN 0-13-695024-8

This edition published and distributed by
Prentice-Hall, Inc., Englewood Cliffs, N.J. 07632

Prentice-Hall International, *London*
Prentice-Hall of Australia Pty. Limited, *Sydney*
Prentice-Hall Canada Inc., *Toronto*
Prentice-Hall of India Private Limited, *New Delhi*
Prentice-Hall of Japan, Inc., *Tokyo*
Prentice-Hall Southeast Asia Pte. Ltd., *Singapore*
Whitehall Books Limited, Wellington, *New Zealand*
Editora Prentice-Hall do Brazil Ltda., *Rio de Janeiro*

Preface

As the title suggests, this is a comprehensive atlas both of America and of the World. Unlike many other atlases, all its principal maps are fully physical; that is, they show surface features both by shading and by colored layers that are keyed to scales accompanying each map. This, plus the fact that the cartography is entirely new, makes the American state-by-state map section of the atlas unique.

As in most atlases, the maps contained in the *American World Atlas* have been drawn to a variety of scales. The scale of any individual map is always represented on the map by a stated ratio. For example, 1:1 000 000 means that one inch on the map represents one million inches, or about 16 miles, on the ground. The larger the scale (that is, the smaller the number in the second term of the ratio), the more detail is shown. Thus, for example, the map of North Carolina that appears on page 54 is drawn to 1:2 500 000 and therefore shows more detail about that particular state than does the 1:6 000 000 map of the eastern United States appearing on page 19. The eastern United States map, on the other hand, because of its smaller scale, has the advantage of being able to show North Carolina both in relation to its neighboring states and to the region as a whole. Similarly, on pages 218 and 219 the whole of Japan is shown at a scale of 1:5 000 000, and on the next two pages, the densely populated southern half of Japan, at 1:2 500 000.

In addition to a full range of topographical features, what kinds of details can you expect to find on these maps? By way of illustration, let us take one of the relatively large-scale (1:2 500 000) U.S. state maps. The state boundary appears as a heavy red line, and for added clarity, areas outside the boundary have been tinted neutrally. County boundaries within the state appear as thin pink lines, and the boundaries of other areas, such as national parks, recreation areas, and Indian reservations are clearly defined in green or orange. Primary and secondary highways are shown, as are railroads, airports, and national forests. Of course, all principal cities and towns, as graded by the 1980 U.S. census, are shown, with the state capital and the county seats clearly indicated. And there is much more.

A similar profusion of detail appears on the world maps. On these, it may be noted, the spelling of place names always appears as it is rendered by the natives. Thus the city of Munich, Germany, is rendered as 'München', with 'Munich' appearing in parentheses beneath. In the index, you will find entries under both 'Munich' and 'München'. For countries that do not use a Roman script, place names have been transcribed according to the standard systems adopted by the U.S. and British Geographic Name authorities. For Chinese place names, the modern Pinyin system has been used, with some of the older spellings appearing in parentheses: for example, Beijing (Peking). Both of these spellings appear in the index.

The index itself is divided into two parts: one lists place names in the United States, and the other, place names for the rest of the world. Individual index entries give the place name, followed by the page number of the relevant map, and then by the geographic coordinates which locate the position of the place on the map. For more information about how to use the index, please read the instructions at the beginning of the index section of the atlas.

CONTENTS

XIV-XV Selected References

The World

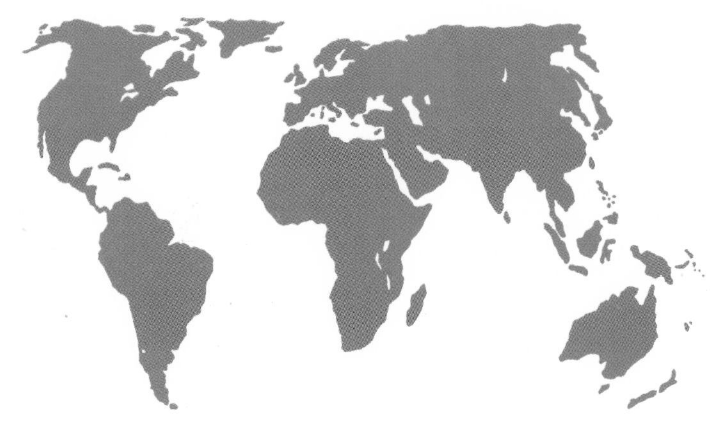

1	**Map Symbols**	
2-3	**The World** *Political*	*1:80 000 000*
4-5	**The World** *Density of Population*	*1:73 200 000*
6-7	**The World**	
	Structure	*1:95 000 000*
	Volcanoes	*1:280 000 000*
	Earthquakes	*1:280 000 000*
8-9	**The World** *Temperature and Ocean Currents, Pressure, Winds and Annual Precipitation*	*1:190 000 000*
10-11	**The World** *Climatic Regions*	*1:120 000 000*
12-13	**Polar Regions** *Arctic Regions* *Antarctic Regions*	*1:35 000 000*

North America

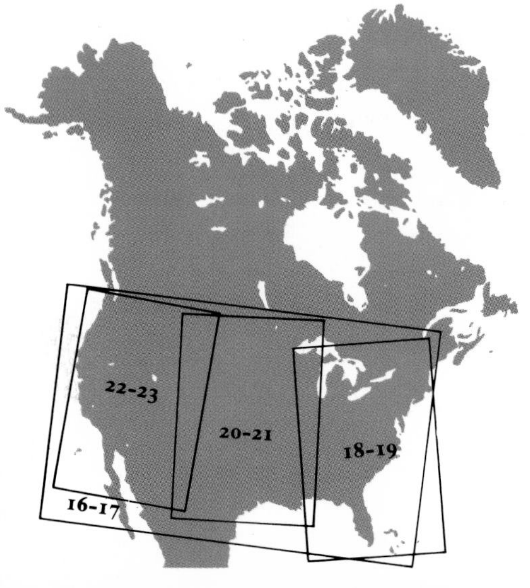

22-23
20-21
18-19
16-17

14	**North America** *Physical*	*1:35 000 000*
15	**North America** *Political*	*1:35 000 000*
16-17	**Continental United States**	*1:12 000 000*
18-19	**Eastern United States**	*1:6 000 000*
20-21	**Middle United States**	*1:6 000 000*
22-23	**Western United States**	*1:6 000 000*

United States

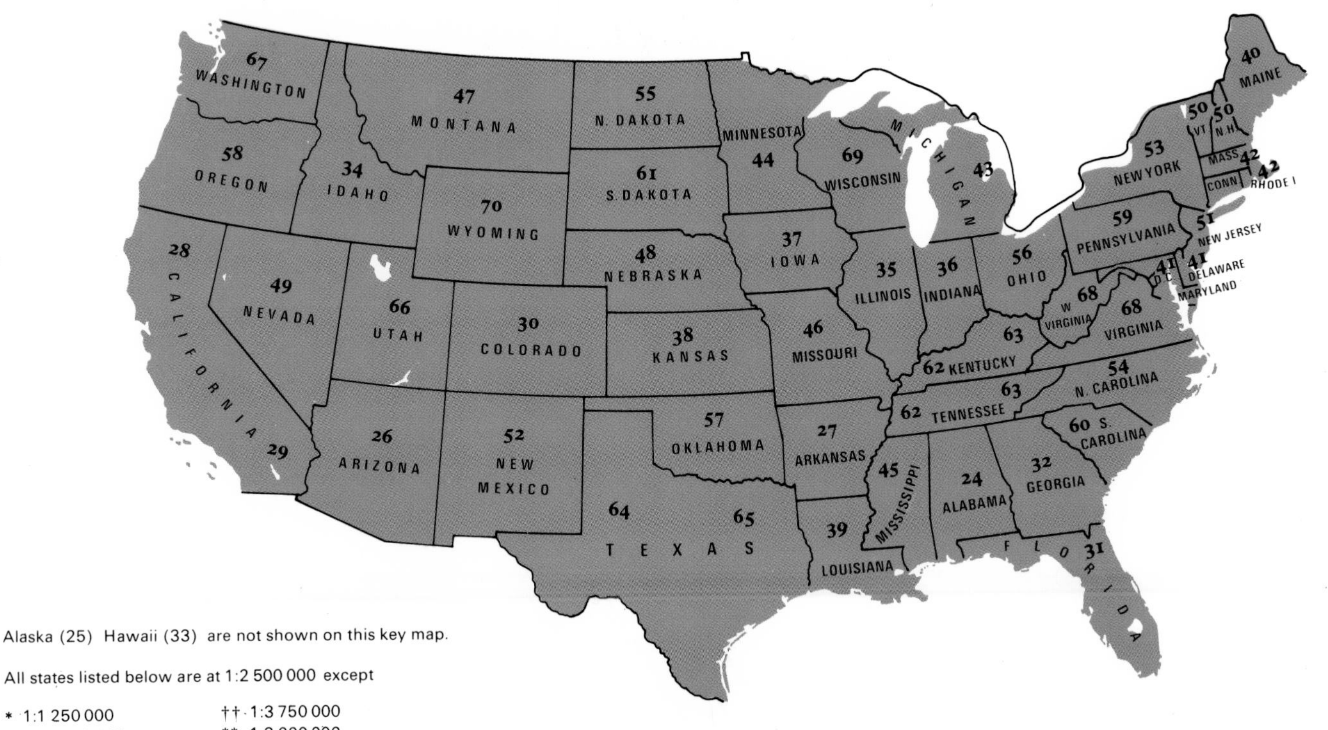
67 WASHINGTON
58 OREGON
34 IDAHO
47 MONTANA
70 WYOMING
55 N. DAKOTA
61 S. DAKOTA
48 NEBRASKA
38 KANSAS
57 OKLAHOMA
64 65 TEXAS
28 CALIFORNIA 29
49 NEVADA
66 UTAH
30 COLORADO
26 ARIZONA
52 NEW MEXICO
44 MINNESOTA
37 IOWA
46 MISSOURI
27 ARKANSAS
39 LOUISIANA
69 WISCONSIN
43 MICHIGAN
35 ILLINOIS
36 INDIANA
56 OHIO
62 63 KENTUCKY
62 63 TENNESSEE
45 MISSISSIPPI
24 ALABAMA
32 GEORGIA
31 FLORIDA
60 S. CAROLINA
54 N. CAROLINA
68 VIRGINIA
68 W VIRGINIA
59 PENNSYLVANIA
53 NEW YORK
51 NEW JERSEY
41 DELAWARE
41 MARYLAND
D.C.
40 MAINE
50 VT
50 N.H.
42 MASS
42 CONN
42 RHODE I

Alaska (25) Hawaii (33) are not shown on this key map.

All states listed below are at 1:2 500 000 except

* 1:1 250 000
† 1:10 000 000
†† 1:3 750 000
** 1:3 000 000

24	Alabama
25	†Alaska
26	Arizona
27	Arkansas
28-29	California
30	Colorado
42	*Connecticut
41	*Delaware
41	*District of Columbia
31	Florida
32	Georgia
33	Hawaii
34	Idaho
35	Illinois
36	Indiana
37	Iowa
38	Kansas
62-63	Kentucky
39	Louisiana
40	Maine
41	*Maryland
42	*Massachusetts
43	Michigan
44	Minnesota
45	Mississippi
46	Missouri
47	††Montana
48	Nebraska
49	Nevada
50	*New Hampshire
51	*New Jersey
52	*New Mexico
53	New York
54	North Carolina
55	North Dakota
56	Ohio
57	Oklahoma
58	Oregon
59	Pennsylvania
42	*Rhode Island
60	South Carolina
61	South Dakota
62-63	Tennessee
64-65	**Texas
66	Utah
50	*Vermont
68	Virginia
67	Washington
68	West Virginia
69	Wisconsin
70	Wyoming
71	Puerto Rico and the Virgin Islands — *1:1 000 000*

Canada

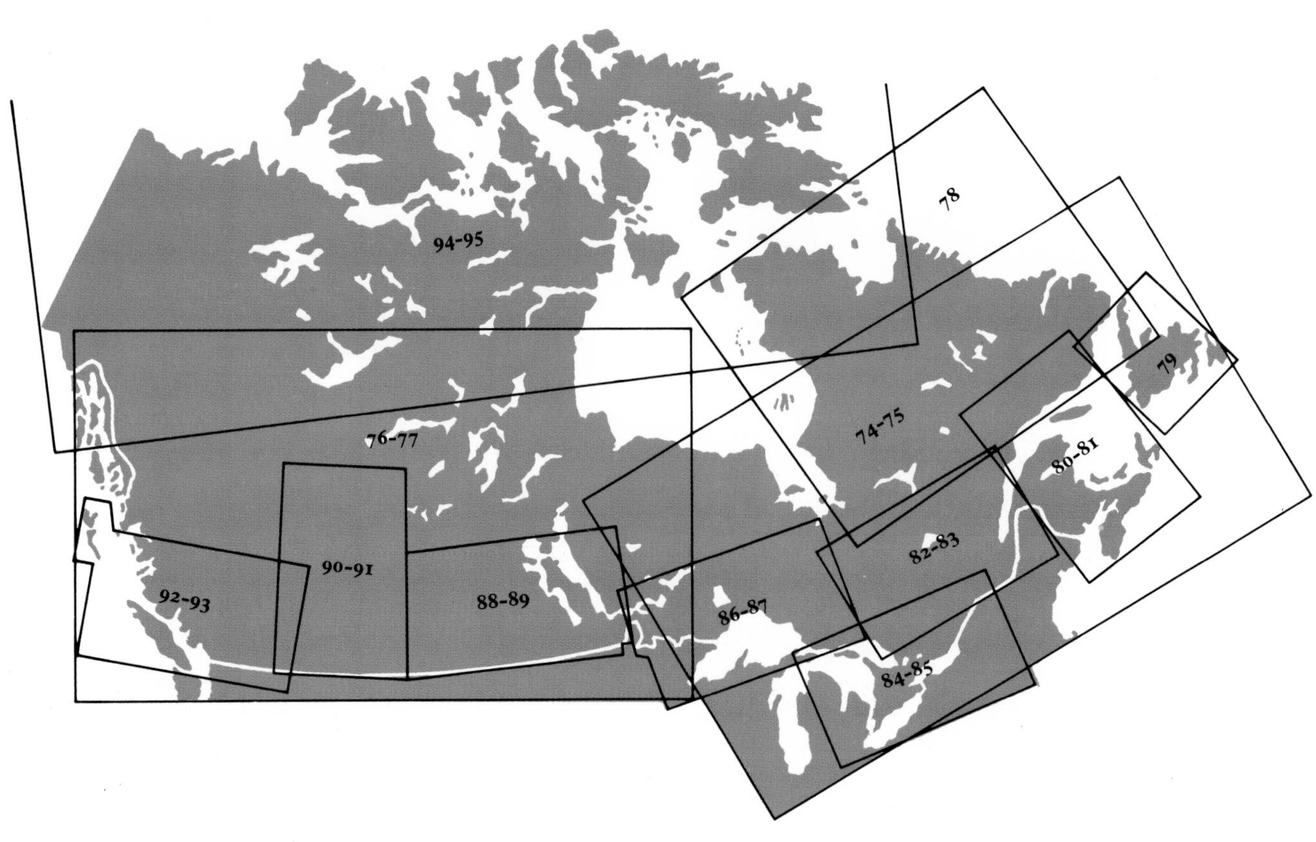

94-95
78
76-77
74-75
79
80-81
90-91
92-93
88-89
86-87
82-83
84-85

72-73	**Canada**	*1:17 500 000*
74-75	**Eastern Canada**	*1:7 000 000*
76-77	**Western Canada**	*1:7 000 000*
78	**Labrador and Québec - North**	*1:7 000 000*
79	**Newfoundland**	*1:2 500 000*
80-81	**Atlantic Provinces**	*1:2 500 000*
82-83	**Québec - South**	*1:2 500 000*
84-85	**Ontario - South**	*1:2 500 000*
86-87	**Central Ontario - Lake Superior**	*1:2 500 000*
88-89	**Manitoba and Saskatchewan - South**	*1:2 500 000*
90-91	**Alberta - South**	*1:2 500 000*
92-93	**British Columbia - South**	*1:2 500 000*
94-95	**Yukon and the Northwest Territories**	*1:10 000 000*

Mexico, Central America and the Caribbean

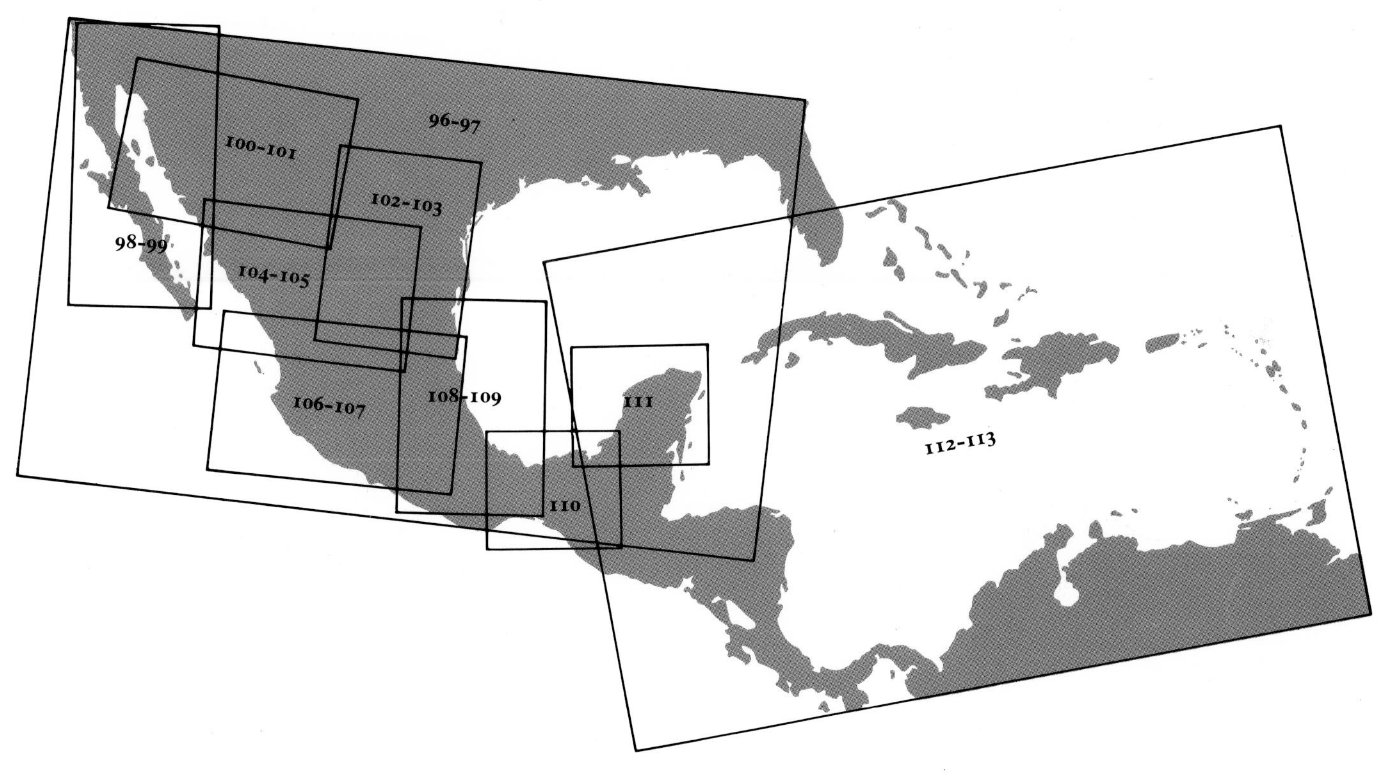
96-97
100-101
102-103
98-99
104-105
106-107
108-109
111
110
112-113

96-97	**Mexico**	*1:8 000 000*
98-99	**Baja California**	*1:2 500 000*
100-101	**Sonora and Chihuahua**	*1:2 500 000*
102-103	**Coahuila, Nuevo León, Tamaulipas and San Luis Potosí**	*1:2 500 000*
104-105	**Nayarit, Sinaloa, Durango, Zacetas and Aguascalientes**	*1:2 500 000*
106-107	**Central Mexico**	*1:2 500 000*
108-109	**Veracruz, Puebla and Oaxaca**	*1:2 500 000*
110	**Tabasco and Chiapas**	*1:2 500 000*
111	**Yucatan, Quintana Roo and Campeche**	*1:2 500 000*
112-113	**Central America and the West Indies**	*1:8 000 000*

South America

114	**South America** *Physical*	*1:30 000 000*
115	**South America** *Political*	*1:30 000 000*
116-117	**South America - North**	*1:16 000 000*
118-119	**South America - North-West**	*1:8 000 000*
120-121	**Eastern Brazil**	*1:8 000 000*
122-123	**South America - West**	*1:8 000 000*
124-125	**Central South America**	*1:8 000 000*
126	**Southern Chile and Argentina**	*1:8 000 000*
127	**The Americas**	*1:60 000 000*
128-129	**The Atlantic Ocean**	*1:45 000 000*

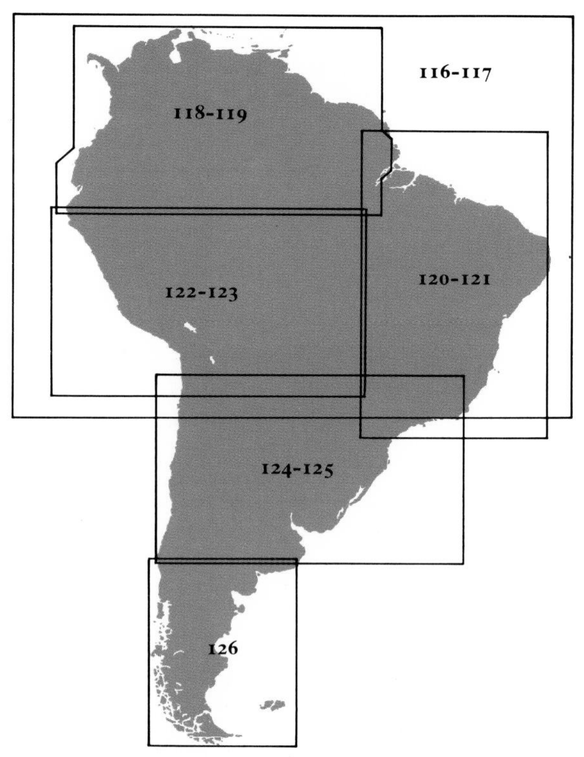

116-117
118-119
120-121
122-123
124-125
126

Europe

130	**Europe** *Physical*	*1:20 000 000*
131	**Europe** *Political*	*1:20 000 000*
132-133	**England and Wales**	*1:2 000 000*
134	**Scotland**	*1:2 000 000*
135	**Ireland**	*1:2 000 000*
136	**British Isles** *Administrative*	*1:4 000 000*
137	**France** *Administrative*	*1:5 000 000*
138-139	**Northern France**	*1:2 500 000*
140-141	**Southern France**	*1:2 500 000*
142-143	**Netherlands, Belgium and Luxembourg**	*1:1 250 000*
144-145	**Central Europe**	*1:5 000 000*
146-147	**West Germany and East Germany**	*1:2 500 000*
148-149	**Switzerland**	*1:1 000 000*
150-151	**Austria, Czechoslovakia and Hungary**	*1:2 500 000*
152	**Poland**	*1:3 000 000*

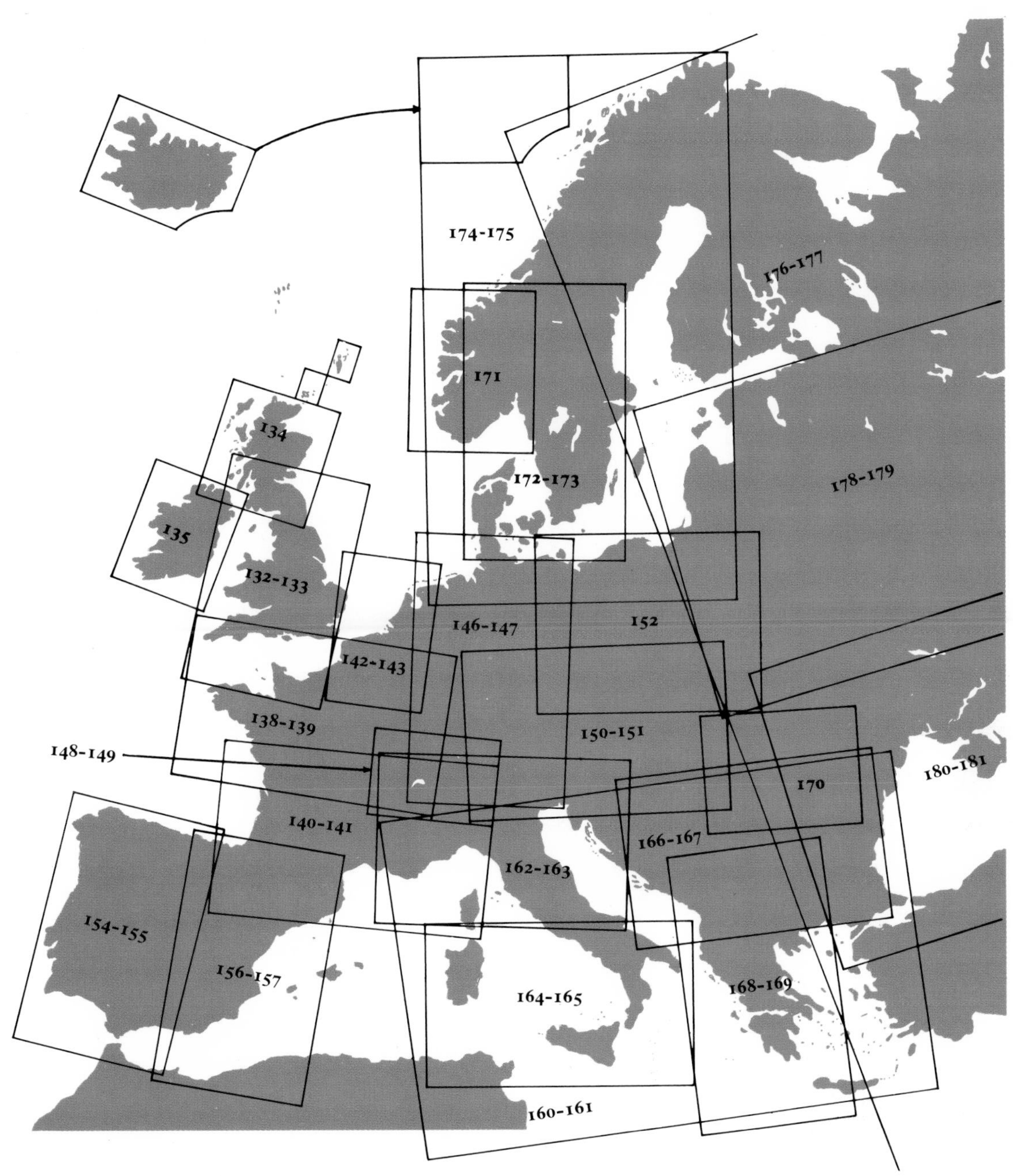
174-175
176-177
171
134
135
172-173
178-179
132-133
146-147
152
142-143
138-139
148-149
150-151
170
180-181
140-141
166-167
162-163
154-155
156-157
168-169
164-165
160-161

153	**Spain and Portugal**	*1:5 000 000*
154-155	**Western Spain and Portugal**	*1:2 500 000*
156-157	**Eastern Spain**	*1:2 500 000*
158-159	**Mediterranean Lands**	*1:10 000 000*
160-161	**Italy and the Balkan States**	*1:5 000 000*
162-163	**Northern Italy and Western Yugoslavia**	*1:2 500 000*
164-165	**Southern Italy**	*1:2 500 000*
166-167	**Eastern Yugoslavia and Bulgaria**	*1:2 500 000*
168-169	**Greece and Albania**	*1:2 500 000*
170	**Romania**	*1:2 500 000*
171	**Southern Norway**	*1:2 500 000*
172-173	**Denmark and Southern Sweden**	*1:2 500 000*
174-175	**Scandinavia and the Baltic Lands**	*1:5 000 000*
176-177	**European Russia and Turkey**	*1:10 000 000*
178-179	**Central European Russia**	*1:5 000 000*
180-181	**Southern European Russia**	*1:5 000 000*

Asia

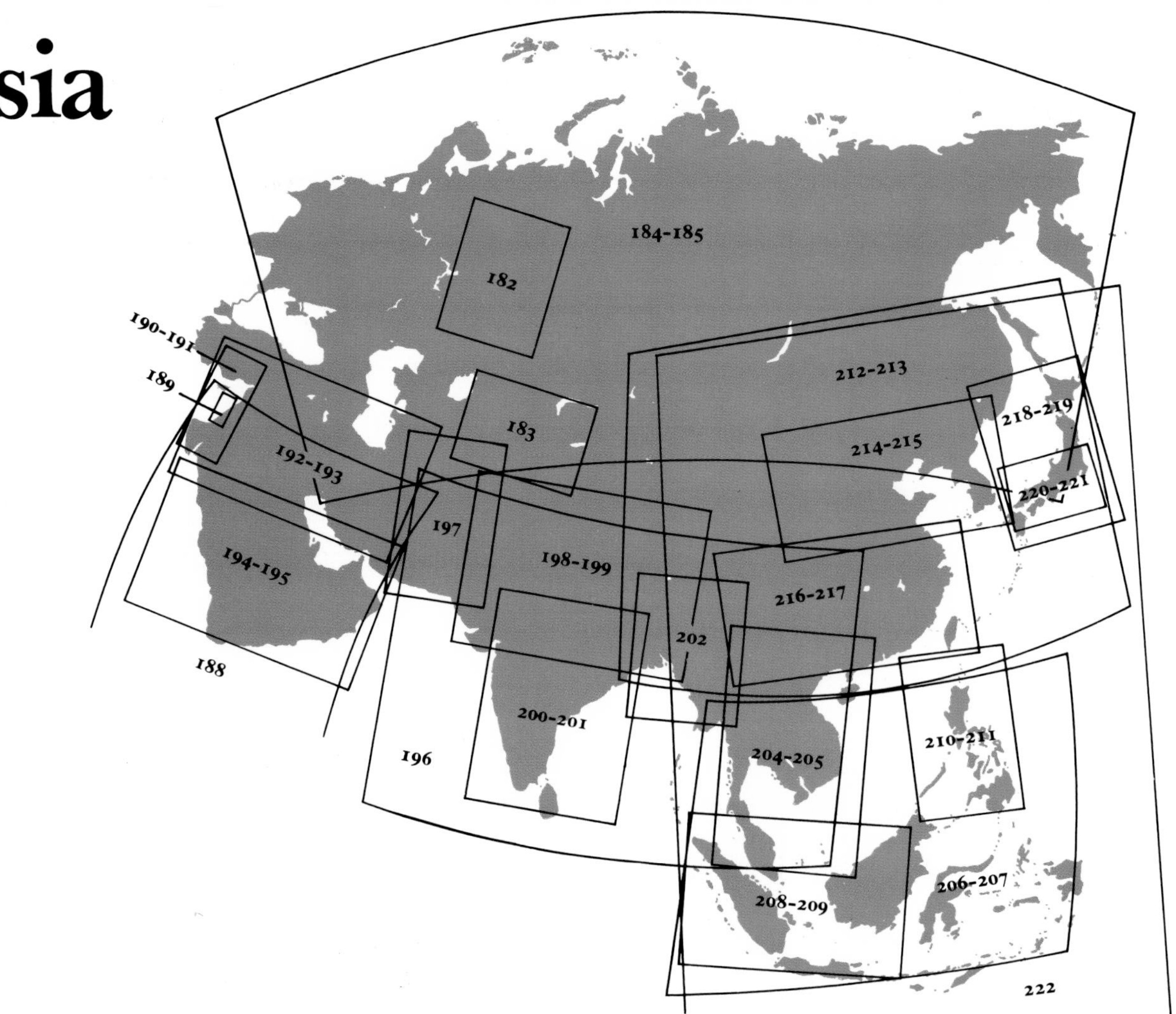

184-185
182
190-191
189
183
192-193
212-213
218-219
214-215
220-221
197
198-199
194-195
216-217
202
188
200-201
196
204-205
210-211
206-207
208-209
222

182	**Southern Urals**	*1:5 000 000*
183	**Tashkent Region**	*1:5 000 000*
184-185	**Union of Soviet Socialist Republics**	*1:20 000 000*
186	**Asia** *Physical*	*1:50 000 000*
187	**Asia** *Political*	*1:50 000 000*
188	**Arabian Peninsula**	*1:15 000 000*
189	**The Holy Land**	*1:1 000 000*
190-191	**The Near East**	*1:2 500 000*
192-193	**The Middle East**	*1:7 000 000*
194-195	**Southern Arabian Peninsula**	*1:7 000 000*
196	**Southern Asia**	*1:20 000 000*
197	**Afghanistan and Pakistan**	*1:7 000 000*
198-199	**The Indo-Gangetic Plain**	*1:6 000 000*
200-201	**Southern India and Sri Lanka**	*1:6 000 000*
202	**Bangladesh, North-Eastern India and Burma**	*1:6 000 000*
203	**Indian Ocean**	*1:50 000 000*
204-205	**Mainland South-East Asia**	*1:6 000 000*
206-207	**Indonesia and the Philippines**	*1:12 500 000*
208-209	**Western Indonesia**	*1:7 000 000*
210-211	**Philippines**	*1:4 000 000*
212-213	**China and Korea**	*1:15 000 000*
214-215	**Northern China and Korea**	*1:6 000 000*
216-217	**Southern China**	*1:6 000 000*
218-219	**Japan**	*1:5 000 000*
220-221	**Southern Japan**	*1:2 500 000*
222	**South-Eastern Asia and Australasia**	*1:45 000 000*

Australia and New Zealand

223	**Australia and New Zealand** *Physical and Political*	*1:40 000 000*
224-225	**Pacific Ocean**	*1:54 000 000*
226	**Pacific Islands**	
227	**Papua New Guinea**	*1:6 500 000*
228-229	**Western Australia**	*1:8 000 000*
230-231	**Eastern Australia**	*1:8 000 000*
232-233	**South-East Australia**	*1:4 000 000*
234	**New Zealand - North Island**	*1:3 500 000*
235	**New Zealand - South Island**	*1:3 500 000*

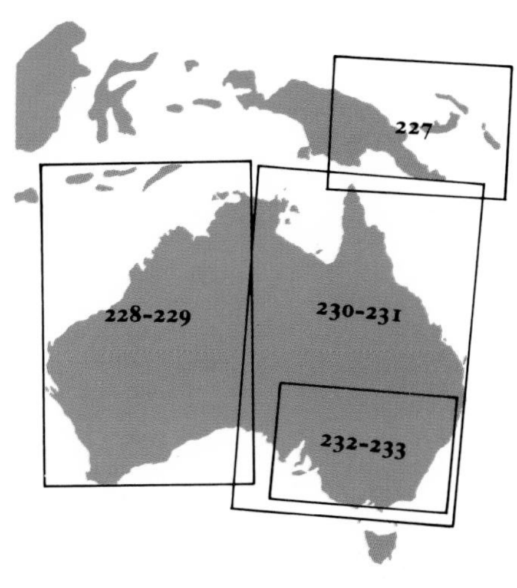

227
228-229
230-231
232-233

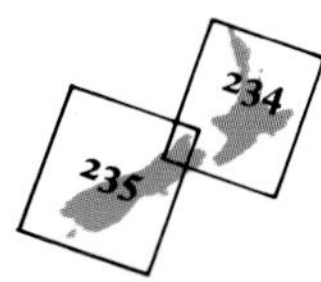

234
235

Africa

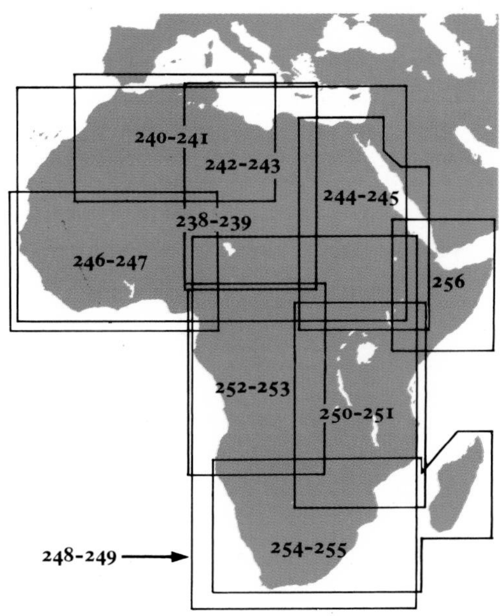

240-241
242-243
244-245
238-239
246-247
256
252-253
250-251
254-255
248-249

236	**Africa** *Physical*	*1:40 000 000*
237	**Africa** *Political*	*1:40 000 000*
238-239	**Northern Africa**	*1:15 000 000*
240-241	**North-West Africa**	*1:8 000 000*
242-243	**Central North Africa**	*1:8 000 000*
244-245	**The Nile Valley**	*1:8 000 000*
246-247	**West Africa**	*1:8 000 000*
248-249	**Central and Southern Africa**	*1:15 000 000*
250-251	**East Africa**	*1:8 000 000*
252-253	**Central Africa**	*1:8 000 000*
254-255	**Southern Africa**	*1:8 000 000*
256	**Horn of Africa**	*1:8 000 000*

Index

United States Index
World Index

Selected References

These selected references are additional to the contents list on the previous pages and are included to take the reader directly to the page required for certain well known and used names. The list includes all country names and names of large geographical features, mountains and seas for example. The page quoted will be the one where the feature appears as a whole and at the largest scale. No U.S. state names are included as they will be found in the alphabetical list in the main contents list.

Adriatic Sea 160-161
Aegean Sea 161
Afghanistan 197
Africa 236-237
Ahaggar Mountains 241
Albania 168
Alberta 76
Aleutian Islands 25
Algeria 240
Alps 144
Altai Mountains 184-185
American Samoa 225
Amundsen Sea 13
Anatolia 177
Andaman Islands 196
Andes 114
Andorra 156
Angola 253
Anguilla 113
Annam 204
Antarctica 13
Antigua 113
Antilles 112-113
Apennines 160
Appalachian Mountains 17
Arabia 188
Arabian Gulf 193
Arabian Sea 203
Aral Sea 184
Arctic Ocean 12
Arctica 12
Argentina 124-126
Armenia 177
Ascension 129
Asia 186-187
Atacama Desert 122
Atlantic Ocean 128-129
Atlas Mountains 240
Australia 223
Austria 150
Azerbaijan 177
Azores 128
Azov, Sea of 180

Baffin Island 95
Bahamas 112-113
Bahrain 193
Baikal, Lake 185
Balearics 156-157
Balkhash, Lake 184
Baltic Sea 175
Bangladesh 202
Barbados 113
Barbuda 113
Barents Sea 184
Basque Provinces 156
Bavaria 147
Beaufort Sea 94
Bechuanaland 254
Belgium 143
Belize 112
Bellingshausen Sea 13
Belorussia 178
Bengal, Bay of 196
Benin 247
Bering Sea 185
Bering Strait 12
Bermuda 128
Bhutan 202
Biscay, Bay of 139
Bismarck Archipelago 227
Bismarck Sea 227
Black Forest 149
Black Sea 180-181
Bolivia 122-123
Borneo 209
Bothnia, Gulf of 174-175
Botswana 254
Brazil 115
British Antarctic Territory 13
British Columbia 76
British Isles 136
Brittany 138
Brunei 209
Bulgaria 167
Burma 202
Burundi 250
Byelorussia 178

California, Gulf of 98-99
Cambodia 204-205
Cameroon 252
Canada 72-73
Canary Islands 240
Cantabrica 156
Cape Province 254
Cape Verde Islands 128
Caribbean Sea 112-113
Caroline Islands 224
Carpathians 145
Carpentaria, Gulf of 230
Caspian Sea 177
Castille 158-159
Caucasus 181
Cayman Islands 112
Celebes 207
Celtic Sea 136
Central African Republic 252
Central America 112
Ceylon 201
Chad 243
Channel Islands 138
Chile 115
China 212-213
Cochin China 205
Cocos Islands 203
Colombia 118
Congo 252
Corsica 141
Costa Rica 112
Crete 169
Crimea 180
Cuba 112
Cyclades 169
Cyprus 190
Czechoslovakia 150-151

Dead Sea 189
Deccan 200
Denmark 173
Djibouti 256
Dodecanese 169
Dominica 113
Dominican Republic 113
Drakensberg 255

East Germany 146-147
East Siberian Sea 185
Ecuador 118
Egypt 244
El Salvador 112
Ellesmere Island 95
England 132-133
English Channel 133
Equatorial Guinea 252
Estonia 180
Ethiopia 188
Europe 130-131

Falkland Islands 126
Faroe Islands 130
Fiji 224
Finland 176
France 137
French Guiana 119
French Polynesia 225

Gabon 252
Galapagos Islands 225
Galilee 189
Gambia 246
Georgia, U.S.S.R. 177
Germany 146-147
Ghana 246-247
Ghats 200-201
Gibraltar 155
Gilbert Islands 224
Gobi 185
Gran Chaco 124
Great Barrier Reef 230
Great Dividing Range 232-233
Great Lakes 17
Great Plains 16
Greater Antilles 112-113
Greece 168-169
Greenland Sea 12
Grenada 113
Guadeloupe 113
Guatemala 112
Guiana 118-119
Guinea 246
Guinea, region 236
Guinea-Bissau 246
Guinea, Gulf of 236
Guyana 119

Haiti 113
Himalayas 198-199
Hindu Kush 197
Hispaniola 113
Holland 142-143
Honduras 112
Hong Kong 217
Honshu 218-219
Hormuz, Strait of 195
Hudson Bay 72-73
Hungary 15

Iceland 174
India 196
Indian Ocean 203
Indo-China 204-205
Indonesia 206-207
Inner Mongolia 214
Ionian Sea 161
Iran 192-193
Iraq 192
Ireland 135
Irish Sea 136
Israel 190-191
Italy 160
Ivory Coast 246

Jamaica 112
Jammu and Kashmir 199
Japan 218-219
Japan, Sea of 218-219
Java 208-209
Java Sea 209
Jordan 192

Kalahari 254
Kamchatka 185
Kampuchea 204-205
Kara Sea 184
Karakoram 199
Kashmir 199
Kazakhstan 184
Kenya 250
Kirgizia 183
Kiribati 224-225
Korea 215
Kuria Muria Islands 195
Kuril Islands 185
Kuwait 192-193
Kyushu 219

Labrador 78
Laccadive Islands 196
Laos 204
Laptev Sea 185

Latvia 178
Lebanon 190
Leeward Islands 113
Lesotho 255
Lesser Antilles 113
Liberia 246
Libya 242
Liechtenstein 149
Lithuania 178
Lion, Golfe du 140
Llanos 118
Lofoten Islands 174
Lower California 98-99
Luxembourg 143
Luzon 210

Macau 217
Madagascar 255
Madeira 240
Malacca, Straits of 205
Malawi 251
Malawi, Lake 251
Malaya 205
Malaysia 208-209
Maldive Islands 203
Mali 238
Malta 160
Manchuria 215
Manitoba 77
Marquesas Islands 225
Marshall Islands 224
Martinique 113
Massif Central 140
Mato Grosso 123
Mauritania 238
Mauritius 203
Mediterranean Sea 158-159
Melanesia 224
Mesopotamia 193
Mexico 96-97
Mexico, Gulf of 97
Micronesia 224
Middle East 192-193
Mindanao 211
Moldavia 180
Monaco 141
Mongolia 185
Montserrat 113
Morocco 240
Mozambique 249
Mozambique Channel 236

Namibia 254
Natal 255
Nauru 224
Nepal 199
Netherlands 142-143
Netherlands Antilles 113
New Brunswick 81
New Caledonia 224
New Siberian Islands 185
New South Wales 231
New Zealand 234-235
Newfoundland 79
Nicaragua 112
Nicobar Islands 196
Niger 238-239
Nigeria 247
Nile Valley 244-245
Normandy 138
North America 14-15
North Korea 215
North Sea 130
North West Territories 94-95
Northern Ireland 135
Northern Territory 223
Norway 174-175
Nova Scotia 81
Novaya Zemlya 184
Nyasa, Lake 251

Okhotsk, Sea of 185
Oman 195
Oman, Gulf of 195
Ontario 72-73
Orange Free State 254
Orkney Islands 134

Pacific Ocean 224-225
Pakistan 197
Palestine 189
Pamirs 183
Pampas 124
Panama 112
Papua New Guinea 227
Paraguay 124-125
Patagonia 126
Persian Gulf 193
Peru 122
Philippines 210-211
Plenty, Bay of 234
Poland 152
Polynesia 225
Portugal 154-155
Prince Edward Island 81
Puerto Rico 113
Pyrenees 156

Qatar 193
Québec 77
Queen Elizabeth Islands 94-95
Queensland 230-231

Red Sea 238-239
Reunion 203
Rocky Mountains 14
Romania 170
Ross Sea 13
Russia 184-185
Rwanda 250
Ryukyu Islands 219

Saarland 147
Sabah 209
Sahara 238-239
St. Helena 129
St. Kitts-Nevis 113
St. Lucia 113
St. Pierre and Miquelon 79
St. Vincent 113
Sakhalin 185
Samaria 189
San Marino 163
São Tomé 236
Sarawak 209
Sardinia 164
Sargasso Sea 128
Saskatchewan 77
Saudi Arabia 188
Saxony 146
Sayan Mountains 185
Scandinavia 174-175
Scotland 134
Selvas 122-123
Senegal 246
Severnaya Zemlya 185
Seychelles 203
Shetland Islands 134
Shikoku 219
Siberia 185
Sicily 164-165
Sierra Leone 246
Sierra Madre 102-103
Sikkim 202
Sinai 191
Singapore 205
Solomon Islands 227
Solomon Sea 227
Somalia 256
South Africa 254-255
South America 114
South Australia 223
South Georgia 129
South Korea 215
South Yemen 194-195
Southern Ocean 13
Soviet Union 184-185
Spain 153
Spitzbergen 12
Sri Lanka 201
Steppes 186
Sudan 239
Suez 191
Sulu Sea 211
Sumatra 208
Sunda Islands 209
Surinam 119
Svalbard 12
Swaziland 255
Sweden 174-175
Switzerland 148-149
Syria 192

Tadzhikstan 183
Taiwan 217
Tanganyika, Lake 250
Tanzania 250-251
Tasmania 230
Thailand 204-205
Thailand, Gulf of 205
The Gulf 193
Tian Shan 184
Tibesti Mountains 243
Tibet 212
Togo 247
Tokelau Islands 224
Tonga 224
Tonkin, Gulf of 204
Transvaal 255
Trinidad and Tobago 113
Tuamotu Archipelago 225
Tubuai Islands 225
Tunisia 241
Turkey 177
Turkmenistan 184
Turks and Caicos Islands 113
Tuvalu 224
Tyrrhenian Sea 160

Uganda 250
Ukraine 176
United Arab Emirates 195
United Kingdom 136
United States of America 16-17
Ural Mountains 184
Uruguay 124-125
U.S.S.R. 184-185
Uzbekistan 184

Vatican 162
Venezuela 118-119
Verkhoyansk Mountains 185
Victoria 232-233
Victoria, Lake 250
Vietnam 204-205
Virgin Islands 113

Wales 132-133
Weddell Sea 13
West Germany 146-147
West Indies 112-113
Western Australia 228-229
Western Sahara 240
Western Samoa 224
White Russia 178
White Sea 176
Windward Islands 113

Yellow Sea 215
Yemen 194
Yucatan 111
Yukon Territory 94
Yugoslavia 160-161

Zagros Mountains 193
Zaïre 248
Zambia 248-249
Zimbabwe 255

Map Symbols

UNITED STATES

Settlements

Settlement symbols in order of size (based on 1980 census)

BALTIMORE NEWARK Allentown Trenton Norristown Bridgeton Quakertown Parkesburg Avondale

Administration

International Boundaries CANADA / UNITED STATES

State Boundaries OHIO / INDIANA

County Boundaries (census areas in Alaska and parishes in Louisiana)

County Names ADDISON

Indian Reservations

National Capital WASHINGTON

State Capitals RICHMOND

County seats have red infills

National Parks, Recreation Areas, Monuments and Seashores

National Forests MARK TWAIN NATIONAL FOREST

Communications

Interstate Highways and Major Turnpikes 95

Other Highways

Railroads

Railroad Tunnels

Transportation Canals

Other Canals

International Airports

Airfields

Passes

Physical Features

Perennial Streams

Intermittent Streams

Perennial Lakes

Intermittent Lakes

Dry Lakes

Swamps and Marshes

Dams with Reservoirs

Waterfalls

Permanent Ice and Glaciers

Elevations in meters ▲ 733

Sea Depths in meters ▼ 329

Height of Lake Surface Above Sea Level in meters 174

Elevation and Depth Tints

(United States and the World)

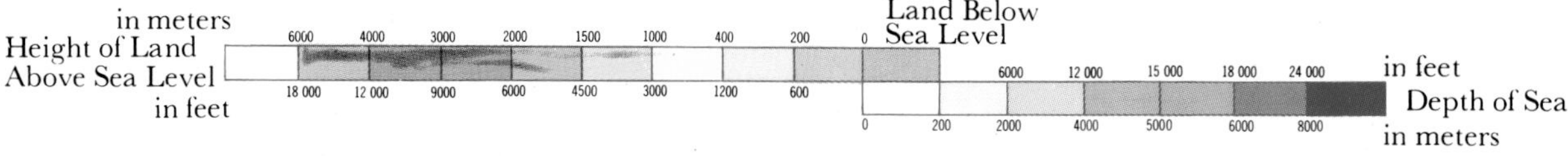

in meters
Height of Land
Above Sea Level
in feet
6000 4000 3000 2000 1500 1000 400 200 0
18 000 12 000 9000 6000 4500 3000 1200 600
Land Below
Sea Level
6000 12 000 15 000 18 000 24 000
0 200 2000 4000 5000 6000 8000
in feet
Depth of Sea
in meters

Some of the maps have different contours to highlight and clarify the principal relief features

WORLD

Settlements

Settlement symbols in order of size

Canada and Mexico

MEXICO **HAMILTON** **Moncton** **Moose Jaw** **Sabinas** **Allende** Sonoyta Miquelon

World

PARIS **Berne** Livorno Brugge *Algeciras* *Fréjus* *Oberammergau* *Thira*

Settlement symbols and type styles vary according to the scale of each map and indicate the importance of towns on the map rather than specific population figures

Ruins or Archæological Sites ∴

Important Ruins in Mexico ■

Wells in Desert

Administration

International Boundaries

International Boundaries (Undefined)

Internal Boundaries

National Parks

National and Provincial Parks in Canada

Country Names

NICARAGUA

Administrative Area Names

KENT

CALABRIA

International boundaries show the *de facto* situation where there are rival claims to territory

Communications

Freeways in Canada and *Autopistas* in Mexico

Trans-Canada Highway

Principal Roads

Other Roads

Trails and Seasonal Roads

Passes

Airfields

Principal Railroads

Other Railroads

Railroads Under Construction

Railroad Tunnels

Principal Canals

Principal Oil Pipelines

Principal Shipping Routes 3386

Physical Features

Perennial Streams

Intermittent Streams

Perennial Lakes

Intermittent Lakes

Swamps and Marshes

Permanent Ice and Glaciers

Elevations in meters ▲ 8848

Sea Depths in meters ▼ 8050

Height of Lake Surface Above Sea Level in meters *1134*

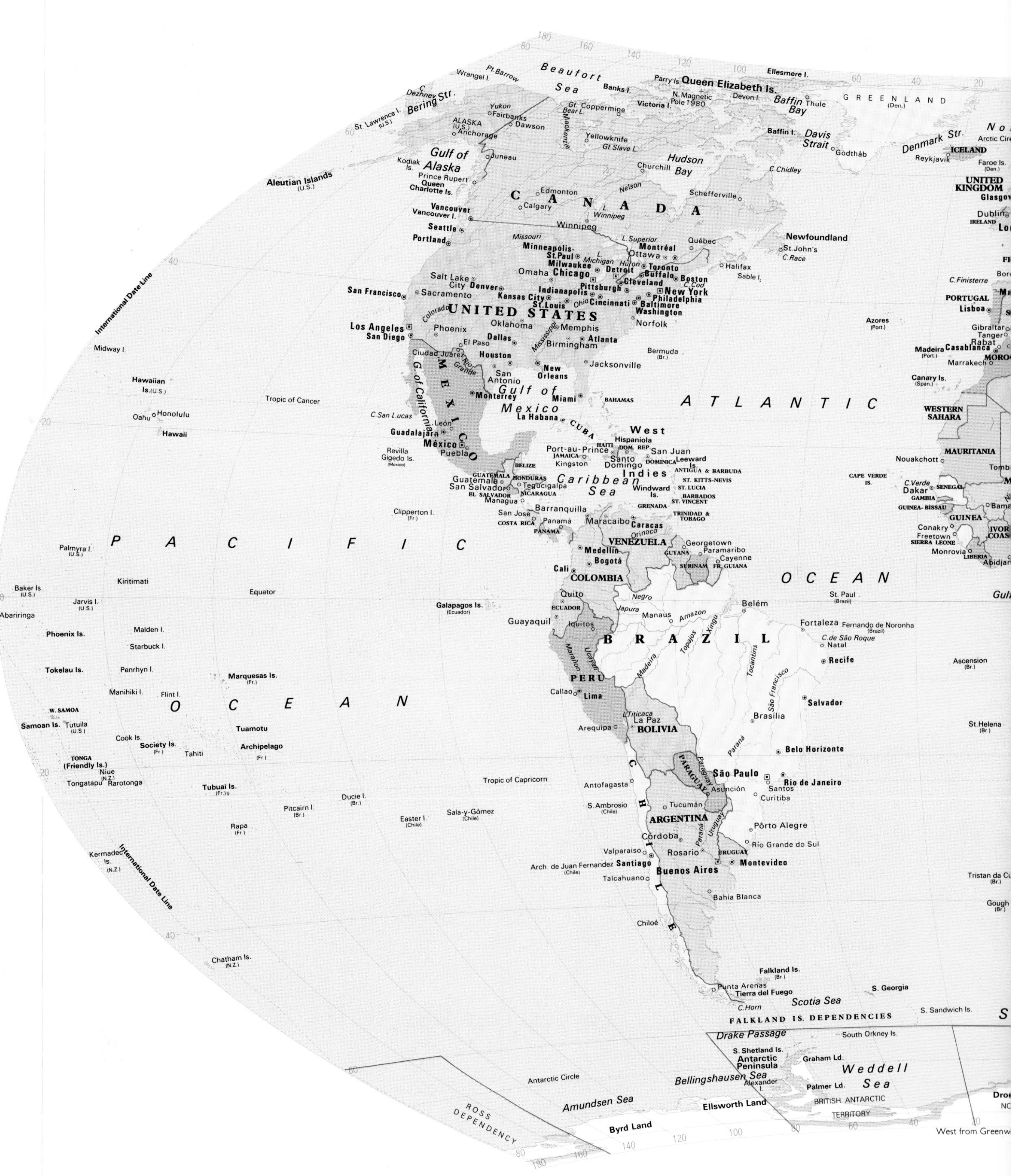
Beaufort Sea
Wrangel I.
Pt. Barrow
C. Dezhnev
Bering Str.
St. Lawrence I. (U.S.)
Yukon
Fairbanks
Dawson
ALASKA (U.S.)
Anchorage
Banks I.
Parry Is.
Queen Elizabeth Is.
Ellesmere I.
N. Magnetic Pole 1980
Victoria I.
Devon I.
Baffin Bay
Thule
GREENLAND (Den.)
Gt. Bear L.
Coppermine
Mackenzie
Yellowknife
Gt. Slave L.
Baffin I.
Davis Strait
Godthåb
Denmark Str.
Arctic Circle
ICELAND
Reykjavik
Faroe Is. (Den.)
Gulf of Alaska
Juneau
Kodiak Is.
Hudson Bay
Churchill
Prince Rupert
Queen Charlotte Is.
Aleutian Islands (U.S.)
C. Chidley
UNITED KINGDOM
Glasgow
Nelson
Edmonton
CANADA
Schefferville
Calgary
L. Winnipeg
Vancouver
Vancouver I.
Winnipeg
Dublin
IRELAND
Seattle
Portland
Missouri
L. Superior
Québec
Newfoundland
Minneapolis-St.Paul
Montréal
St. John's
C. Race
Milwaukee
L. Michigan
Ottawa
Huron
Toronto
Detroit
Buffalo
Halifax
Sable I.
Omaha
Chicago
Salt Lake City
Boston
Denver
Cleveland
C. Cod
C. Finisterre
San Francisco
Sacramento
Indianapolis
Pittsburgh
New York
Kansas City
Philadelphia
St. Louis
Ohio
Cincinnati
Baltimore
Washington
PORTUGAL
Lisboa
Colorado
UNITED STATES
Norfolk
Oklahoma
Mississippi
Memphis
Azores (Port.)
Los Angeles
San Diego
Phoenix
Atlanta
Gibraltar
Tanger
Rabat
Dallas
Birmingham
International Date Line
El Paso
Ciudad Juárez
Madeira (Port.)
Casablanca
Midway I.
Rio Grande
Houston
Bermuda (Br.)
Jacksonville
Marrakech
San Antonio
New Orleans
Hawaiian Is. (U.S.)
MEXICO
Gulf of Mexico
Canary Is. (Span.)
G. of California
Monterrey
Miami
BAHAMAS
ATLANTIC
Tropic of Cancer
C. San Lucas
La Habana
CUBA
WESTERN SAHARA
Oahu
Honolulu
León
West
Hawaii
Guadalajara
Hispaniola
HAITI
DOM. REP.
México
San Juan
Revilla Gigedo Is. (Mexico)
Puebla
Port-au-Prince
JAMAICA
Kingston
Santo Domingo
DOMINICA
Leeward Is.
MAURITANIA
Indies
ANTIGUA & BARBUDA
Nouakchott
BELIZE
Caribbean Sea
ST. KITTS-NEVIS
CAPE VERDE IS.
GUATEMALA
HONDURAS
Guatemala
Tegucigalpa
Windward Is.
ST. LUCIA
C. Verde
Dakar
SENEGAL
GAMBIA
San Salvador
EL SALVADOR
NICARAGUA
BARBADOS
ST. VINCENT
Managua
GRENADA
GUINEA-BISSAU
Clipperton I. (Fr.)
Barranquilla
TRINIDAD & TOBAGO
GUINEA
San José
COSTA RICA
Panamá
PANAMA
Maracaibo
Caracas
Conakry
Freetown
SIERRA LEONE
Orinoco
VENEZUELA
Georgetown
Paramaribo
Monrovia
LIBERIA
Abidjan
Palmyra I. (U.S.)
PACIFIC
Medellín
GUYANA
Cayenne
Bogotá
SURINAM
FR. GUIANA
Cali
COLOMBIA
OCEAN
Kiritimati
Baker Is. (U.S.)
Equator
Negro
Jarvis I. (U.S.)
Quito
Belém
St. Paul (Brazil)
Abariringa
Galapagos Is. (Ecuador)
ECUADOR
Japura
Amazon
Malden I.
Guayaquil
Iquitos
Manaus
Xingu
Fortaleza
Fernando de Noronha (Brazil)
Phoenix Is.
Starbuck I.
BRAZIL
Tapajós
C. de São Roque
Natal
Marañón
Ucayali
Madeira
Tocantins
Recife
Tokelau Is.
Penrhyn I.
Ascension (Br.)
Marquesas Is. (Fr.)
São Francisco
PERU
Manihiki I.
Flint I.
Callao
Lima
OCEAN
Salvador
W. SAMOA
Samoan Is.
Tutuila (U.S.)
L. Titicaca
Brasília
La Paz
BOLIVIA
Tuamotu Archipelago (Fr.)
Arequipa
St. Helena (Br.)
Cook Is.
Society Is. (Fr.)
Tahiti
Paraná
Belo Horizonte
TONGA (Friendly Is.)
Niue (N.Z.)
Tongatapu
Rarotonga
PARAGUAY
Paraguay
São Paulo
Rio de Janeiro
Tropic of Capricorn
Antofagasta
Asunción
Santos
Tubuai Is. (Fr.)
Ducie I. (Br.)
Curitiba
S. Ambrosio (Chile)
Tucumán
Pitcairn I. (Br.)
Easter I. (Chile)
Sala-y-Gómez (Chile)
ARGENTINA
Pôrto Alegre
Rapa (Fr.)
CHILE
Córdoba
Paraná
Uruguay
Rio Grande do Sul
Kermadec Is. (N.Z.)
Valparaiso
Rosario
URUGUAY
Montevideo
Arch. de Juan Fernandez (Chile)
Santiago
Buenos Aires
Tristan da Cunha (Br.)
Talcahuano
Bahia Blanca
Gough (Br.)
Chiloé
Chatham Is. (N.Z.)
Falkland Is. (Br.)
Punta Arenas
S. Georgia
Tierra del Fuego
Scotia Sea
C. Horn
FALKLAND IS. DEPENDENCIES
S. Sandwich Is.
Drake Passage
South Orkney Is.
S. Shetland Is.
Antarctic Peninsula
Graham Ld.
Weddell Sea
Antarctic Circle
Bellingshausen Sea
Alexander I.
Palmer Ld.
Amundsen Sea
Ellsworth Land
BRITISH ANTARCTIC TERRITORY
ROSS DEPENDENCY
Byrd Land
West from Greenwich
180
160
140
120
100
80
60
40
20
0

Projection: *Hammer Equal Area*

ARCTIC OCEAN
Zemlya Frantsa Iosifa
Novaya Zemlya
Barents Sea
Nord Kapp
Murmansk
Kara Sea
Severnaya Zemlya
Laptev Sea
New Siberian Is.
East Siberian Sea
Arctic Circle
Ust Port
Tiksi
Verkhoyansk
Nizhne-Kolymsk
Anadyr
Yenisey
Lena
Vilyuysk
Yakutsk
Arkhangelsk
Salekhard
Ob
UNION OF SOVIET SOCIALIST REPUBLICS
RUSSIAN SOVIET FEDERATIVE SOCIALIST REPUBLIC
Bering Sea
Sea of Okhotsk
Okhotsk
Kamchatka
Petropavlovsk-Kamchatskiy
C.Lopatka
Narvik
FINLAND
SWEDEN
Helsinki
Stockholm
Leningrad
Yaroslavl
Moskva
Perm
Sverdlovsk
Novosibirsk
Omsk
Tomsk
Krasnoyarsk
L.Baykal
Ulan Ude
Irkutsk
Novokuznetsk
Barnaul
Kazan
Ufa
Chelyabinsk
Kuybyshev
Orenburg
Minsk
Voronezh
POLAND
Warszawa
Berlin
Praha
Wien
Kiyev
Kharkov
Lvov
Budapest
Saratov
Volgograd
Rostov
Astrakhan
Volga
Ural
Irtysh
Karaganda
KAZAKHSTAN
L.Balkhash
Ulaanbaatar
MONGOLIA
Sakhalin
Komsomolsk
Khabarovsk
Amur
Kuril Is.
Harbin
Changchun
Shenyang
Vladivostok
Sapporo
Hakodate
UKRAINE
Odessa
ROMANIA
Beograd
YUGOSLAVIA
Bucuresti
BULGARIA
Sofiya
Black Sea
Istanbul
Ankara
TURKEY
Izmir
Athinai
GREECE
ITALY
Roma
Napoli
Sardinia
Sicily
MALTA
Crete
CYPRUS
Mediterranean Sea
Tarabulus
Banghazi
LIBYA
Grozny
Tbilisi
Yerevan
Baku
Tabriz
Caspian Sea
Aral Sea
UZBEKISTAN
TURKMENISTAN
Samarkand
Ashkhabad
Tashkent
KIRGIZIA
Alma Ata
Dushanbe
CHINA
Beijing
Tianjin
Taiyuan
Jinan
Lüda
Qingdao
Pyongyang
N.KOREA
S.KOREA
Soul
Pusan
Sea of Japan
JAPAN
Tokyo
Yokohama
Kyoto
Kobe
Nagoya
Osaka
Kitakyushu
Lanzhou
Xi'an
Huang He
Nanjing
Shanghai
Wuhan
Chengdu
Chongqing
Chang Jiang
Changsha
East China Sea
Ryukyu Is.
Fuzhou
Taibei
TAIWAN (FORMOSA)
Guangzhou
Hong Kong (Br.)
Kunming
Halab
SYRIA
Dimashq
LEB.
Bayrut
ISR.
Tel Aviv-Yafo
JORDAN
Amman
Jerusalem
El Iskandariya
El Qahira
Bur Said
EGYPT
Nile
Aswan
Baghdad
IRAQ
Esfahan
Abadan
Tehran
IRAN (PERSIA)
Mashhad
Shiraz
KUWAIT
BAHRAIN
QATAR
U.A.E.
The Gulf
AFGHANISTAN
Kabul
Rawalpindi
PAKISTAN
Indus
Srinagar
Lahore
XIZANG (TIBET)
Lhasa
Delhi
NEPAL
Katmandu
BHU.
Agra
Kanpur
Lucknow
Ganga
INDIA
Karachi
Ahmadabad
BANGLADESH
Dacca
Calcutta
BURMA
Mandalay
Hanoi
Hainan
VIETNAM
Vientiane
THAILAND
Rangoon
Bangkok
CAMBODIA
Phnom Penh
Phan Bho Ho Chi Minh
South China Sea
Manila
PHILIPPINES
Cebu
Ar Riyad
SAUDI ARABIA
Makkah
Red Sea
OMAN
YEMEN
SOUTH YEMEN
Aden
Gulf of Aden
Socotra (S.Yemen)
Arabian Sea
Bombay
Pune
Nagpur
Bay of Bengal
Hyderabad
Bangalore
Madras
Andaman Is. (India)
Nicobar Is. (India)
Lakshadweep Is.
SRI LANKA (CEYLON)
Colombo
MALDIVES
Dondra Hd.
CHAD
NIGER
L.Chad
Ndjamena
SUDAN
Omdurman
El Khartum
Blue Nile
White Nile
Asmera
DJIBOUTI
ETHIOPIA
Addis Abeba
SOMALI REP.
NIGERIA
CAMEROON
Douala
Yaounde
CENTRAL AFRICAN REPUBLIC
Bangui
GABON
CONGO
Brazzaville
Kinshasa
CABINDA
ZAIRE (CONGO)
Zaire (Congo)
Kisangani
UGANDA
Kampala
KENYA
Nairobi
L.Turkana
Muqdisho
Victoria
RW.
BUR.
Mombasa
Zanzibar
Dar es Salaam
L.Tanganyika
TANZANIA
Kasai
Kananga
Luanda
ANGOLA
Benguela
Lubumbashi
ZAMBIA
Lusaka
L.Malawi
MALAWI
Zomba
Harare
ZIMBABWE
MOZAMBIQUE
Mozambique Chan.
NAMIBIA
Windhoek
BOTSWANA
Gaborone
Pretoria
SWAZ.
Maputo
Johannesburg
SOUTH AFRICA
LES.
Durban
Cape Town
C.of Good Hope
Port Elizabeth
MADAGASCAR
Antananarivo
COMORO IS.
Aldabra
Amirante Is.
SEYCHELLES
MAURITIUS
Reunion (Fr.)
Rodriguez
Chagos Arch. (Br.)
Diego Garcia (Br.)
INDIAN OCEAN
Equator
Tropic of Capricorn
Tropic of Cancer
Cocos (Keeling Is.) (Australia)
Christmas I. (Australia)
MALAYSIA
Kuala Lumpur
PEN. MALAYSIA
BRUNEI
SABAH
SARAWAK
Kuching
SINGAPORE
Medan
Sumatera
Borneo
Sulawesi
Maluku
Banjarmasin
Ujung Pandang
Palembang
INDONESIA
Jakarta
Bandung
Jawa
Surabaya
Sunda Islands
Timor
Timor Sea
Arafura Sea
Irian Jaya
PAPUA NEW GUINEA
Port Moresby
New Ireland
Rabaul
New Britain
SOLOMON IS.
Louisiade Arch.
C.York
Darwin
Cairns
NORTHERN TERRITORY
Townsville
WESTERN AUSTRALIA
QUEENSLAND
Alice Springs
AUSTRALIA
Rockhampton
SOUTH AUSTRALIA
Brisbane
Kalgoorlie
Perth
Fremantle
C.Leeuwin
North West C.
NEW SOUTH WALES
Darling
Newcastle
Sydney
Canberra
Great Australian Bight
Adelaide
VICTORIA
Melbourne
Tasman Sea
TASMANIA
Hobart
Lord Howe I. (Australia)
Norfolk I. (Australia)
North C.
Auckland
North I.
NEW ZEALAND
Wellington
C.Farewell
Christchurch
South I.
Dunedin
Stewart I.
Bounty Is.
Antipodes Is. (N.Z.)
Auckland I. (N.Z.)
Campbell I. (N.Z.)
Macquarie I. (Australia)
PACIFIC OCEAN
Northern Marianas (U.S.)
Wake I. (U.S.)
Guam (U.S.)
Yap
Belau
TRUST TERRITORY OF THE PACIFIC ISLANDS (U.S.)
Truk
Ponape
Caroline Is.
Marshall Is.
KIRIBATI
NAURU
TUVALU
Santa Cruz Is.
VANUATU
Vanua Levu
FIJI
Viti Levu
Suva
New Caledonia (Fr.)
Amsterdam (Fr.)
St.Paul (Fr.)
Pr.Edward Is. (South Africa)
Crozet Is. (Fr.)
Kerguelen (Fr.)
McDonald I. (Australia)
Heard I. (Australia)
SOUTHERN OCEAN
Antarctic Circle
Enderby Land
Wilkes Land
S.Magnetic Pole 1980
Balleny Is.
AUSTRALIAN DEPENDENCY
TERRE ADELIE
Ross Sea
East from Greenwich

THE WORLD : Density of Population

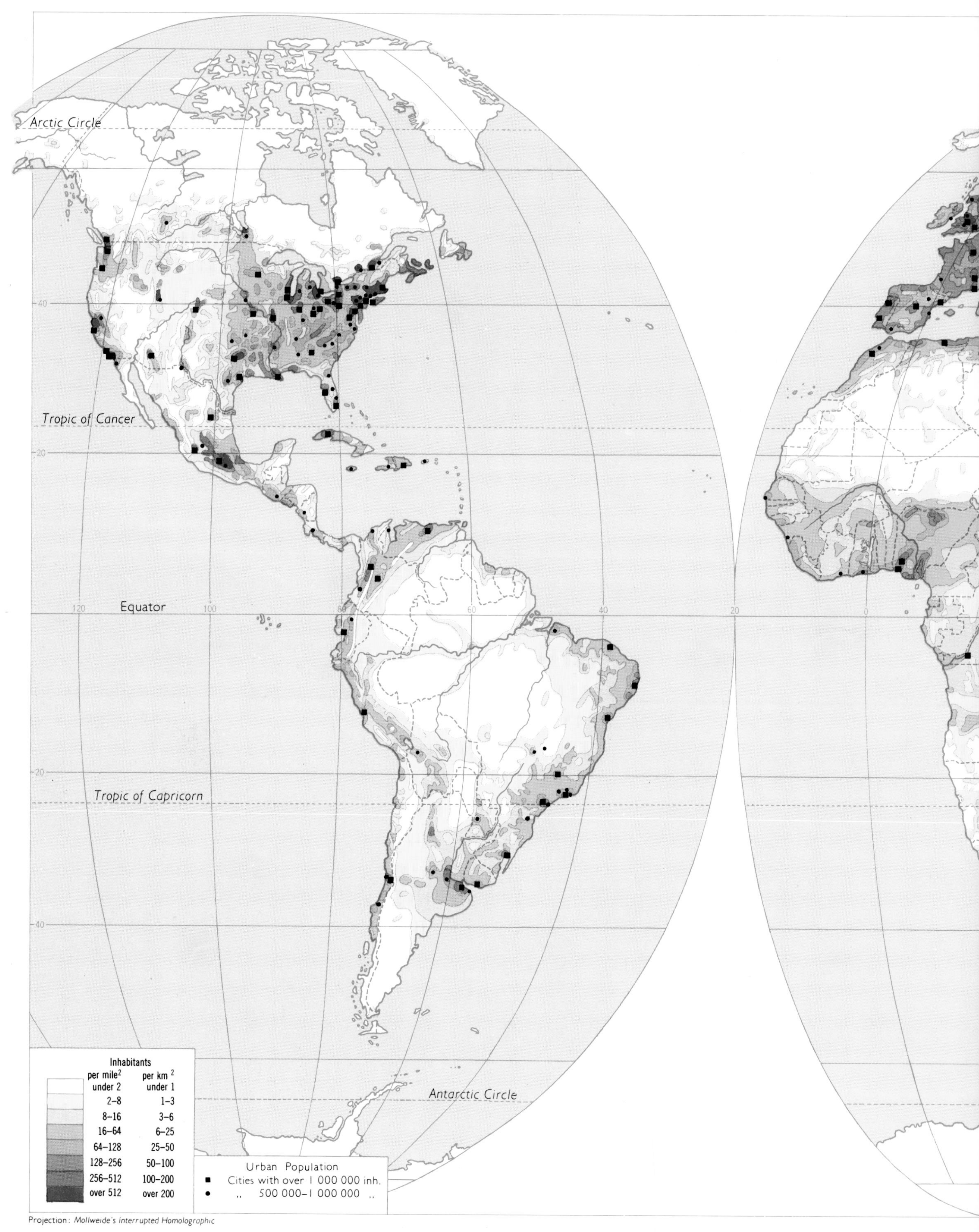

Arctic Circle
Tropic of Cancer
Equator
Tropic of Capricorn
Antarctic Circle
40
20
20
40
120
100
80
60
40
20
0
Inhabitants
per mile²
per km²
under 2
under 1
2–8
1–3
8–16
3–6
16–64
6–25
64–128
25–50
128–256
50–100
256–512
100–200
over 512
over 200
Urban Population
Cities with over 1 000 000 inh.
,, 500 000–1 000 000 ,,

Projection: *Mollweide's Interrupted Homolographic*

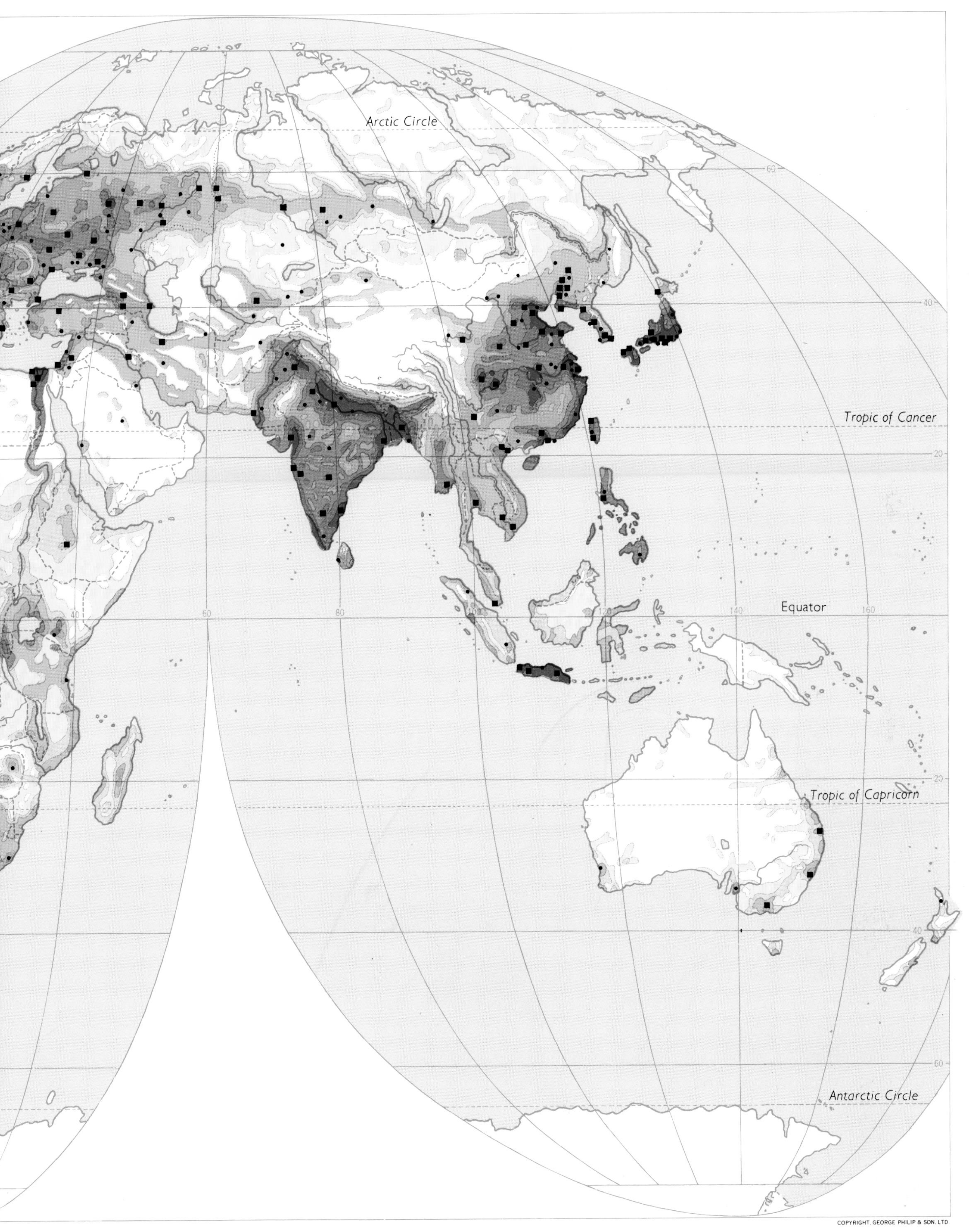
Arctic Circle
Tropic of Cancer
Equator
Tropic of Capricorn
Antarctic Circle
60
40
20
20
40
60
40
60
80
100
120
140
160

6 THE WORLD : Structure, Volcanoes and Earthquakes

STRUCTURE

1: 95 000 000

Structural Regions of the Land

- Pre-Cambrian shields
- Sedimentary cover on Pre-Cambrian shields
- Palæozoic (Caledonian and Hercynian) folding
- Sedimentary cover on Palæozoic folding
- Mesozoic folding
- Sedimentary cover on Mesozoic folding
- Cainozoic folding
- Sedimentary cover on Cainozoic folding
- Intensive Mesozoic and Cainozoic vulcanism
- Oceanic-type crust raised above sea level

Structural Regions of the Oceans

- Regions of continental-type crust
- Limit of continental shelf
- Oceanic marginal troughs
- Mid-oceanic volcanic ridges
- Rift valleys in mid-oceanic ridges
- Principal faults
- Frontal line of overthrust folds

GEOLOGICAL TIME SCALE

Era		System	Orogeny
Cainozoic (Tertiary, Quaternary)		Quaternary	Alpine Folding
		Pliocene	
		Miocene	
		Oligocene	
		Eocene	
		Paleocene	Laramide Folding
Mesozoic (Secondary)		Cretaceous	
		Jurassic	
		Triassic	
Palæozoic (Primary)	Upper	Permian	
		Carboniferous	Hercynian Folding
		Devonian	
	Lower	Silurian	Caledonian Folding
		Ordovician	
		Cambrian	
Pre-Cambrian		Pre-Cambrian	

Millions of years before present: 50, 100, 150, 200, 250, 300, 350, 400, 450, 500, 550, 600

VOLCANOES

Equatorial Scale 1: 280 00

Projection: *Interrupted Mollweide's Homolographic*

- Land volcanoes active since 1700
- Land volcanoes inactive since 1700
- Submarine volcanoes
- Geysers
- Plate boundaries
- Andesite line (boundary b sial continental crust anc oceanic crust in the Paci

1: 95 000 000

Baltic Shield
Urals
Angara Shield
Altai
Alps
Tien Shan
Chinese Shield
Atlas
Hindu Kush
Himalayas
Kunlun Shan
Zagros
Arabian Shield
Great Rift Valley
Indian Shield
Ethiopian Shield
Carlsberg Ridge
Southern Mid-Atlantic Ridge
Mid-Indian Ridge
Australian Shield
Great Divide
Atlantic - Indian Ridge

Projection: *Hammer Equal Area*

ARTHQUAKES

Equatorial Scale 1: 280 000 000

Major Earthquakes

		Nos. killed
1556	Shensi, China	830 000
1730	Hokkaido, Japan	137 000
1737	Calcutta, India	300 000
1755	Lisbon, Portugal	60 000
1868	Ecuador and N. Peru	40 000
1906	Valparaiso, Chile	22 000
1906	San Francisco, U.S.A.	450
1908	Messina, Italy	77 000
1915	Avezzano, Italy	30 000
1920	Kansu, China	180 000
1923	Yokohama, Japan	143 000
1927	Nan Shan, China	200 000
1931	Napier, N. Zealand	250
1932	Kansu, China	70 000
1934	Nepal	11 700
1935	Quetta, Pakistan	30 000
1939	Erzincan, Turkey	30 000
1960	Agadir, Morocco	12 000
1962	Khorasan, Iran	10 000
1963	Skopje, Yugoslavia	1000
1964	Anchorage, Alaska	100
1968	N.E. Iran	12 000
1970	N. Peru	67 000
1972	Managua, Nicaragua	7 000
1974	N. Pakistan	10 000
1976	Tangshan, China	650 000
1976	Lice, Turkey	3 800
1978	Tabas, Iran	11 000
1980	**El Asnam, Algeria**	**20 000**

1906 Principal earthquakes and their dates
Oceanic marginal troughs
Mobile land areas
Submarine zones of mobile land areas
Stable land platforms
Submarine extensions of stable land platforms
Mid-oceanic volcanic ridges
Oceanic platforms

THE WORLD : Temperature and Ocean Currents

1:190 000 000

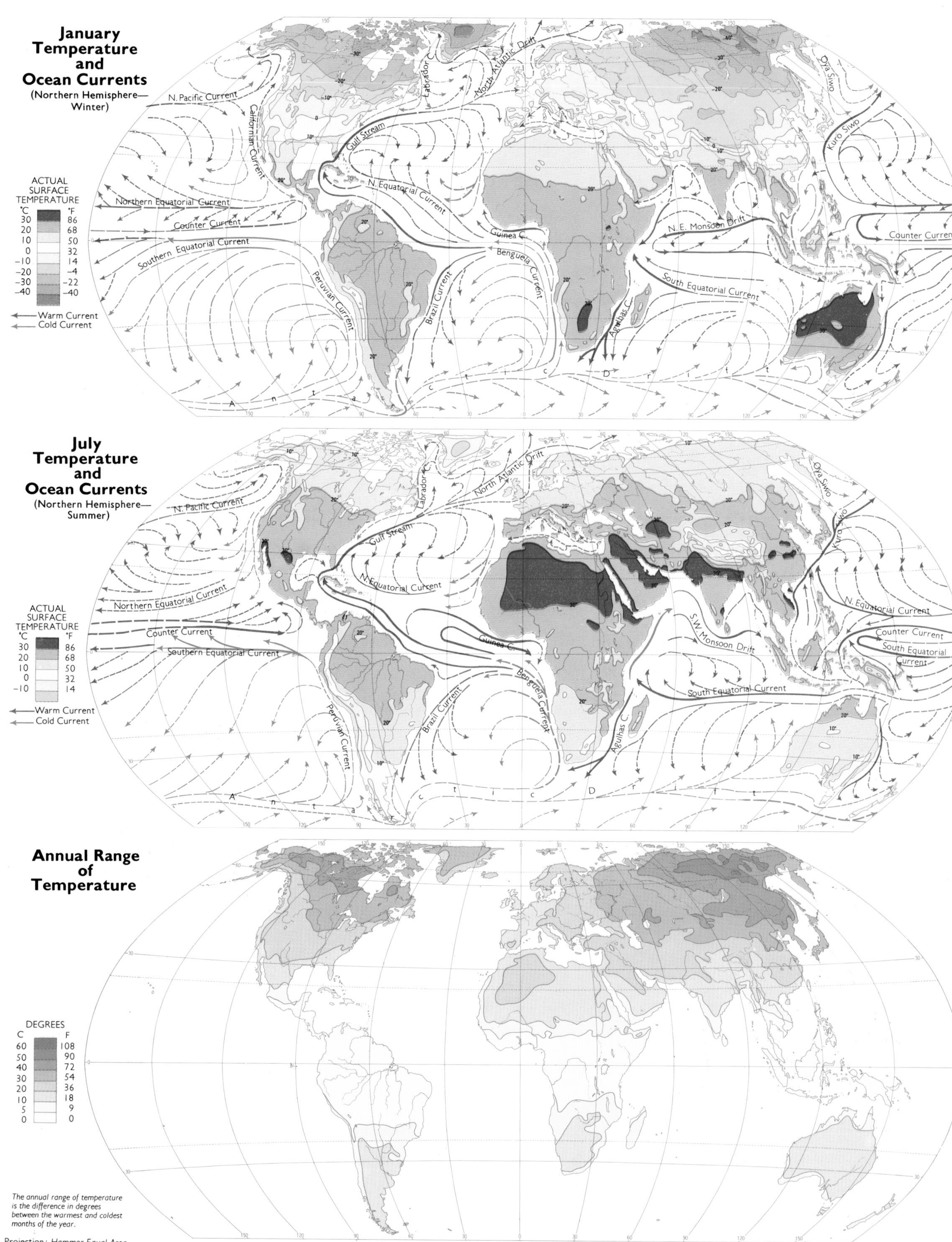

January Temperature and Ocean Currents
(Northern Hemisphere—Winter)
ACTUAL SURFACE TEMPERATURE
°C °F
30 86
20 68
10 50
0 32
−10 14
−20 −4
−30 −22
−40 −40
Warm Current
Cold Current
N. Pacific Current
Californian Current
Labrador C.
North Atlantic Drift
Gulf Stream
N. Equatorial Current
Northern Equatorial Current
Counter Current
Southern Equatorial Current
Guinea C.
Benguela Current
Peruvian Current
Brazil Current
Agulhas C.
N. E. Monsoon Drift
South Equatorial Current
Oya Siwo
Kuro Siwo
Counter Current
A n t a r c t i c D r i f t
July Temperature and Ocean Currents
(Northern Hemisphere—Summer)
ACTUAL SURFACE TEMPERATURE
°C °F
30 86
20 68
10 50
0 32
−10 14
Warm Current
Cold Current
N. Pacific Current
Labrador C.
North Atlantic Drift
Gulf Stream
N. Equatorial Current
Northern Equatorial Current
Counter Current
Southern Equatorial Current
Guinea C.
Benguela Current
Peruvian Current
Brazil Current
Agulhas C.
S.W. Monsoon Drift
South Equatorial Current
N. Equatorial Current
Counter Current
South Equatorial Current
Oya Siwo
Kuro Siwo
A n t a r c t i c D r i f t
Annual Range of Temperature
DEGREES
C F
60 108
50 90
40 72
30 54
20 36
10 18
5 9
0 0
The annual range of temperature is the difference in degrees between the warmest and coldest months of the year.
Projection: Hammer Equal Area

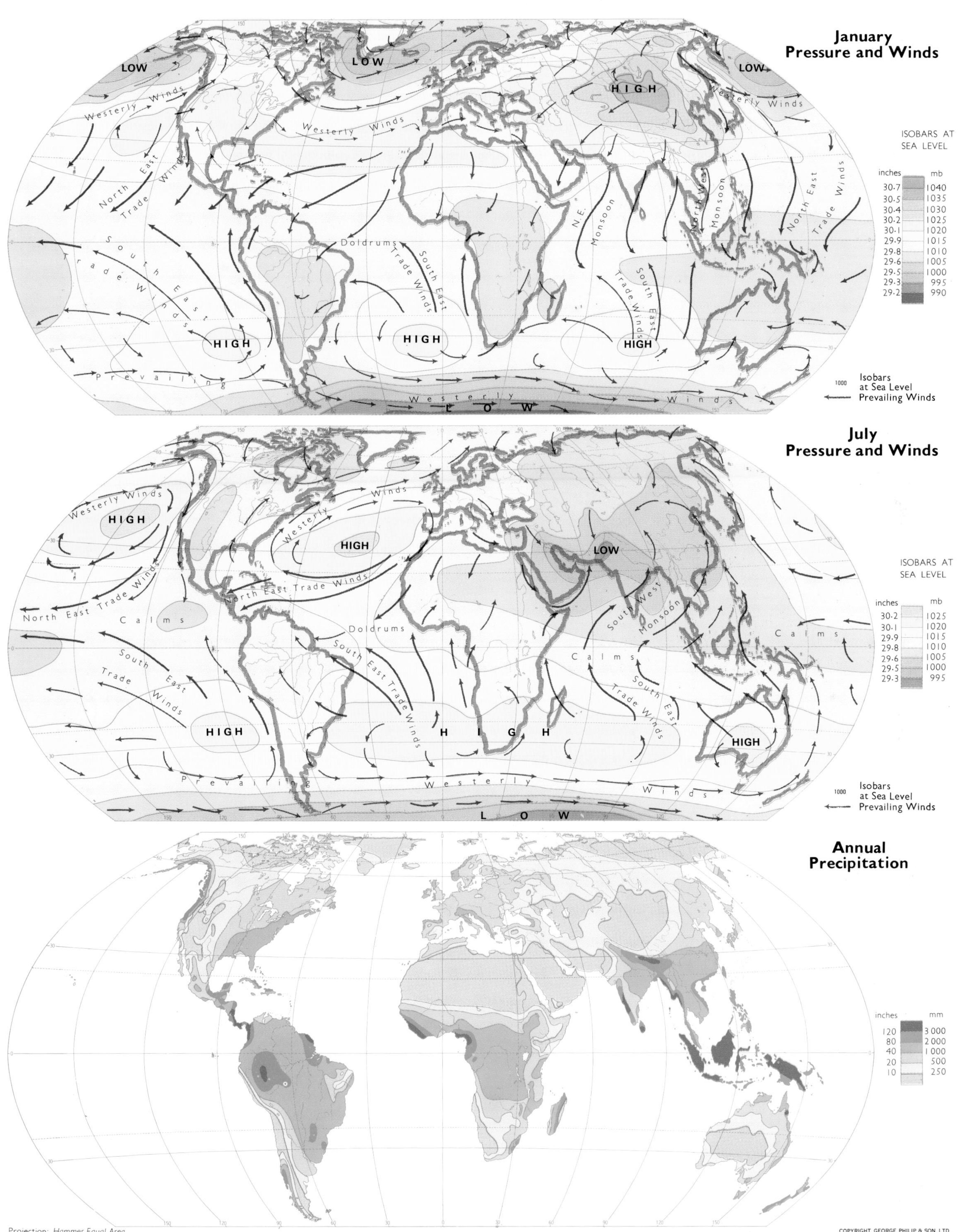
January
Pressure and Winds
LOW
LOW
LOW
HIGH
HIGH
HIGH
HIGH
Westerly Winds
Westerly Winds
North East Trade Winds
South East Trade Winds
Doldrums
N.E. Monsoon
North West Monsoon
Prevailing Westerly Winds
LOW
ISOBARS AT SEA LEVEL
inches mb
30·7 1040
30·5 1035
30·4 1030
30·2 1025
30·1 1020
29·9 1015
29·8 1010
29·6 1005
29·5 1000
29·3 995
29·2 990
1000 Isobars at Sea Level
Prevailing Winds
July
Pressure and Winds
Westerly Winds
HIGH
HIGH
LOW
North East Trade Winds
Calms
Doldrums
South East Trade Winds
South West Monsoon
HIGH
HIGH
HIGH
Prevailing Westerly Winds
LOW
ISOBARS AT SEA LEVEL
inches mb
30·2 1025
30·1 1020
29·9 1015
29·8 1010
29·6 1005
29·5 1000
29·3 995
1000 Isobars at Sea Level
Prevailing Winds
Annual Precipitation
inches mm
120 3 000
80 2 000
40 1 000
20 500
10 250

Projection: *Hammer Equal Area*

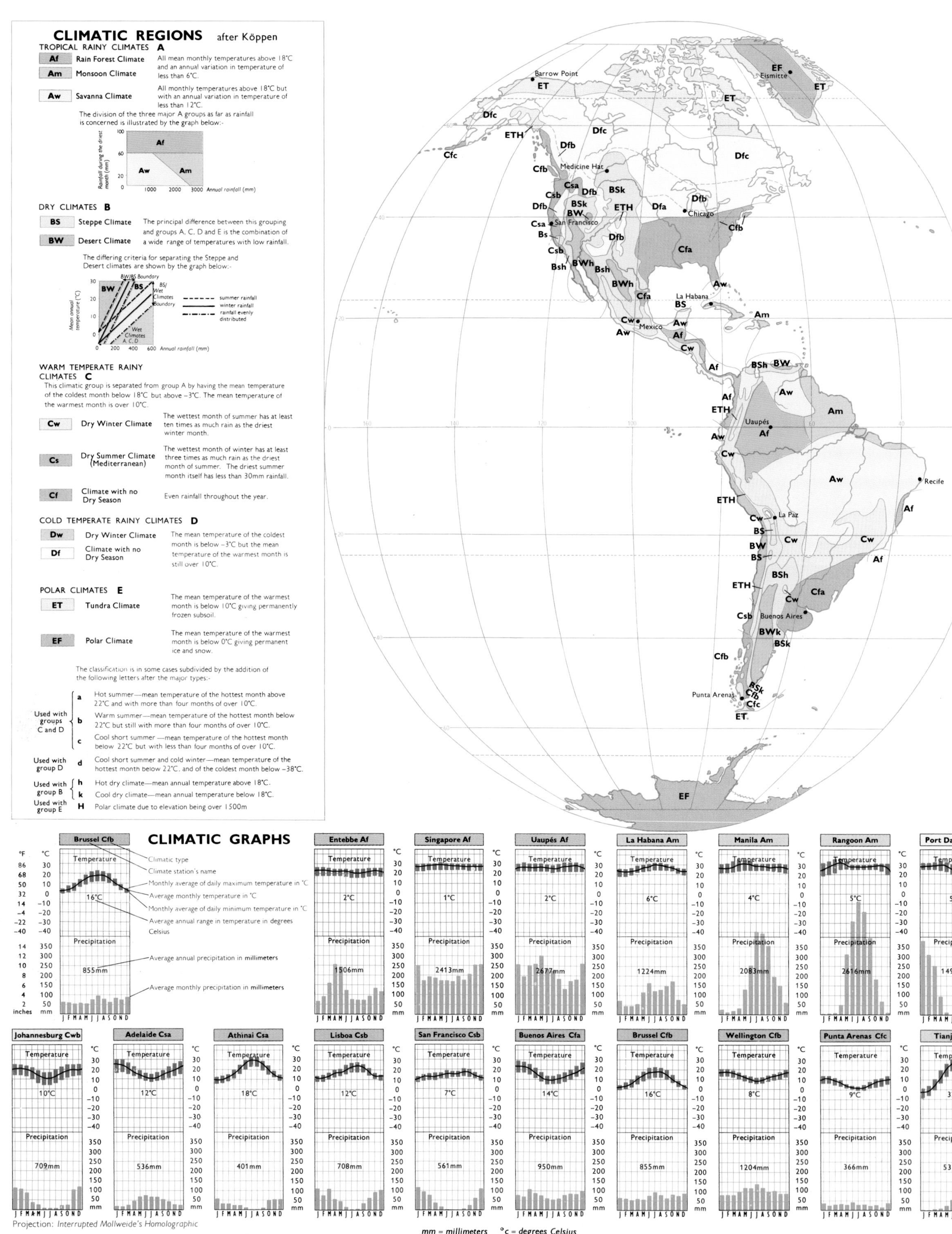
CLIMATIC REGIONS after Köppen
TROPICAL RAINY CLIMATES A
Af Rain Forest Climate
Am Monsoon Climate
All mean monthly temperatures above 18°C and an annual variation in temperature of less than 6°C.
Aw Savanna Climate
All monthly temperatures above 18°C but with an annual variation in temperature of less than 12°C.
The division of the three major A groups as far as rainfall is concerned is illustrated by the graph below:-
Rainfall during the driest month (mm)
Annual rainfall (mm)
DRY CLIMATES B
BS Steppe Climate
BW Desert Climate
The principal difference between this grouping and groups A, C, D and E is the combination of a wide range of temperatures with low rainfall.
The differing criteria for separating the Steppe and Desert climates are shown by the graph below:-
BW/BS Boundary
BS/Wet Climates Boundary
Wet Climates A, C, D
Mean annual temperature (°C)
summer rainfall
winter rainfall
rainfall evenly distributed
Annual rainfall (mm)
WARM TEMPERATE RAINY CLIMATES C
This climatic group is separated from group A by having the mean temperature of the coldest month below 18°C but above −3°C. The mean temperature of the warmest month is over 10°C.
Cw Dry Winter Climate
The wettest month of summer has at least ten times as much rain as the driest winter month.
Cs Dry Summer Climate (Mediterranean)
The wettest month of winter has at least three times as much rain as the driest month of summer. The driest summer month itself has less than 30mm rainfall.
Cf Climate with no Dry Season
Even rainfall throughout the year.
COLD TEMPERATE RAINY CLIMATES D
Dw Dry Winter Climate
Df Climate with no Dry Season
The mean temperature of the coldest month is below −3°C but the mean temperature of the warmest month is still over 10°C.
POLAR CLIMATES E
ET Tundra Climate
The mean temperature of the warmest month is below 10°C giving permanently frozen subsoil.
EF Polar Climate
The mean temperature of the warmest month is below 0°C giving permanent ice and snow.
The classification is in some cases subdivided by the addition of the following letters after the major types:-
Used with groups C and D
a Hot summer—mean temperature of the hottest month above 22°C and with more than four months of over 10°C.
b Warm summer—mean temperature of the hottest month below 22°C but still with more than four months of over 10°C.
c Cool short summer—mean temperature of the hottest month below 22°C but with less than four months of over 10°C.
Used with group D
d Cool short summer and cold winter—mean temperature of the hottest month below 22°C, and of the coldest month below −38°C.
Used with group B
h Hot dry climate—mean annual temperature above 18°C.
k Cool dry climate—mean annual temperature below 18°C.
Used with group E
H Polar climate due to elevation being over 1500m
Barrow Point
Eismitte
Medicine Hat
Chicago
San Francisco
La Habana
Mexico
Uaupés
Recife
La Paz
Buenos Aires
Punta Arenas
CLIMATIC GRAPHS
Climatic type
Climate station's name
Monthly average of daily maximum temperature in °C
Average monthly temperature in °C
Monthly average of daily minimum temperature in °C
Average annual range in temperature in degrees Celsius
Average annual precipitation in millimeters
Average monthly precipitation in millimeters
Temperature
Precipitation
Brussel Cfb 16°C 855mm
Entebbe Af 2°C 1506mm
Singapore Af 1°C 2413mm
Uaupés Af 2°C 2677mm
La Habana Am 6°C 1224mm
Manila Am 4°C 2083mm
Rangoon Am 5°C 2616mm
Johannesburg Cwb 10°C 709mm
Adelaide Csa 12°C 536mm
Athinai Csa 18°C 401mm
Lisboa Csb 12°C 708mm
San Francisco Csb 7°C 561mm
Buenos Aires Cfa 14°C 950mm
Brussel Cfb 16°C 855mm
Wellington Cfb 8°C 1204mm
Punta Arenas Cfc 9°C 366mm
J F M A M J J A S O N D
Projection: Interrupted Mollweide's Homolographic
mm = millimeters °c = degrees Celsius
100 millimeters = approximately 4 inches

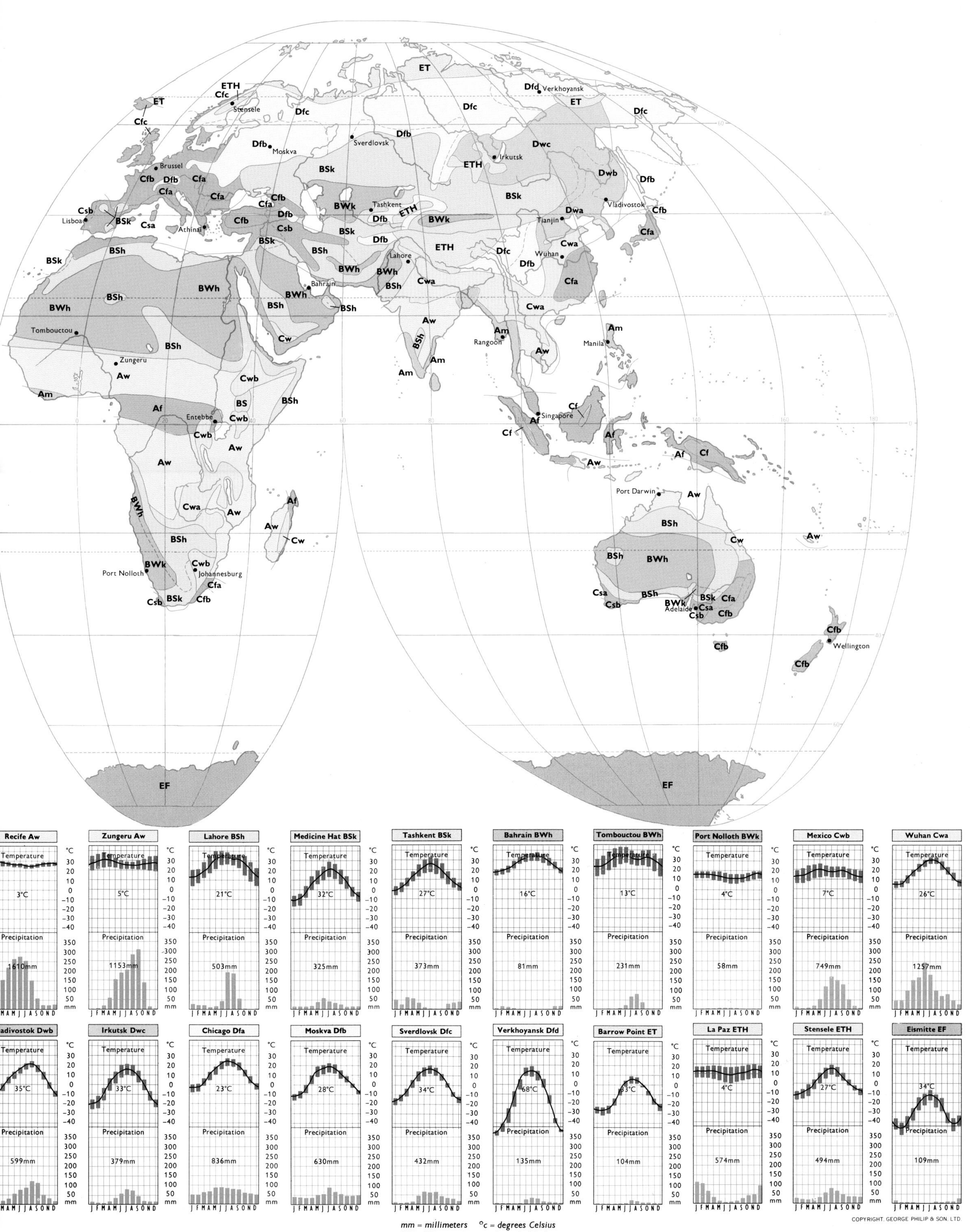
ET
ETH
Cfc
Stensele
Cfc
Dfc
Dfd
Verkhoyansk
ET
Dfc
Dfc
Dfb
Sverdlovsk
Dfb
Moskva
Dwc
Irkutsk
ETH
Brussel
BSk
Dwb
Dfb
Cfb
Dfb
Cfa
Cfa
Cfa
BSk
Vladivostok
Cfb
Cfa
Cfb
BWk
Tashkent
ETH
Csb
Lisboa
BSk
Csa
Athinai
Cfb
Dfb
Dfb
BWk
Tianjin
Dwa
Cfa
Csb
BSk
BSk
Dfb
Cwa
BSk
BSh
BSh
Lahore
ETH
Dfc
Wuhan
Dfb
BWh
BWh
Bahrain
BSh
Cwa
Cfa
BWh
BSh
BWh
BSh
BSh
Cwa
Tombouctou
Aw
Am
Rangoon
Am
Manila
BSh
Cw
BSh
Aw
Zungeru
Aw
Am
Am
Cwb
Am
BS
BSh
Af
Entebbe
Cwb
Cf
Singapore
Af
Cf
Af
Cwb
Aw
Aw
Af
Cf
Aw
Port Darwin
Aw
BWh
Cwa
Af
Aw
Aw
Cw
BSh
BSh
Cw
Aw
BSh
BWh
BWk
Cwb
Port Nolloth
Johannesburg
Cfa
Csb
BSk
Cfb
Csa
Csb
BSh
BWk
BSk
Cfa
Adelaide
Csa
Csb
Cfb
Cfb
Wellington
Cfb
Cfb
EF
EF
Recife Aw
Zungeru Aw
Lahore BSh
Medicine Hat BSk
Tashkent BSk
Bahrain BWh
Tombouctou BWh
Port Nolloth BWk
Mexico Cwb
Wuhan Cwa
Vladivostok Dwb
Irkutsk Dwc
Chicago Dfa
Moskva Dfb
Sverdlovsk Dfc
Verkhoyansk Dfd
Barrow Point ET
La Paz ETH
Stensele ETH
Eismitte EF
Temperature
Precipitation
°C
mm
J F M A M J J A S O N D
3°C
5°C
21°C
32°C
27°C
16°C
13°C
4°C
7°C
26°C
1610mm
1153mm
503mm
325mm
373mm
81mm
231mm
58mm
749mm
1257mm
35°C
33°C
23°C
28°C
34°C
68°C
33°C
4°C
27°C
34°C
599mm
379mm
836mm
630mm
432mm
135mm
104mm
574mm
494mm
109mm

mm = millimeters °c = degrees Celsius
100 millimeters = approximately 4 inches

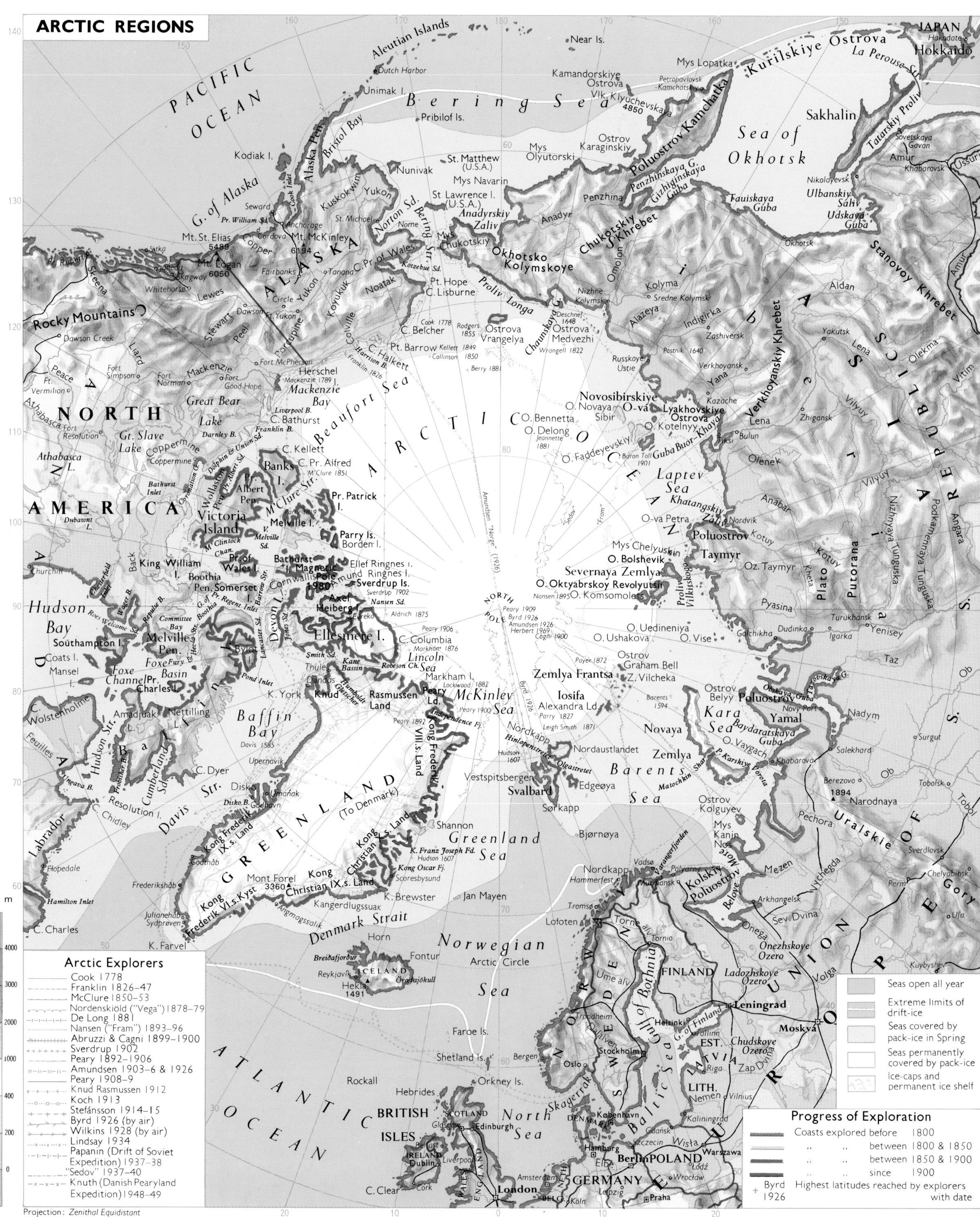
ARCTIC REGIONS
PACIFIC OCEAN
Bering Sea
Sea of Okhotsk
ARCTIC OCEAN
Beaufort Sea
Laptev Sea
Kara Sea
Barents Sea
Greenland Sea
Norwegian Sea
North Sea
Baltic Sea
ATLANTIC OCEAN
Hudson Bay
Baffin Bay
Davis Str.
Denmark Strait
Lincoln Sea
McKinley Sea
NORTH AMERICA
ALASKA
Rocky Mountains
GREENLAND (To Denmark)
ICELAND
BRITISH ISLES
NORWAY
SWEDEN
FINLAND
UNION OF SOVIET SOCIALIST REPUBLICS
EUROPE
JAPAN
Hokkaido
Sakhalin
Kamchatka
Kurilskiye Ostrova
Aleutian Islands
Mt. McKinley 6194
Mt. Logan 6050
Mt. St. Elias 5489
Victoria Island
Banks I.
Ellesmere I.
Baffin I.
Devon I.
Melville I.
Novosibirskiye O-va
Severnaya Zemlya
Zemlya Frantsa Iosifa
Novaya Zemlya
Svalbard
Vestspitsbergen
Jan Mayen
Arctic Circle
NORTH POLE
North Magnetic Pole 1980
Uralskie Gory
Verkhoyanskiy Khrebet
Stanovoy Khrebet
Chukotskiy Khrebet
Arctic Explorers
Cook 1778
Franklin 1826–47
McClure 1850–53
Nordenskiöld ("Vega") 1878–79
De Long 1881
Nansen ("Fram") 1893–96
Abruzzi & Cagni 1899–1900
Sverdrup 1902
Peary 1892–1906
Amundsen 1903–6 & 1926
Peary 1908–9
Knud Rasmussen 1912
Koch 1913
Stefánsson 1914–15
Byrd 1926 (by air)
Wilkins 1928 (by air)
Lindsay 1934
Papanin (Drift of Soviet Expedition) 1937–38
"Sedov" 1937–40
Knuth (Danish Pearyland Expedition) 1948–49
Seas open all year
Extreme limits of drift-ice
Seas covered by pack-ice in Spring
Seas permanently covered by pack-ice
Ice-caps and permanent ice shelf
Progress of Exploration
Coasts explored before 1800
,, ,, between 1800 & 1850
,, ,, between 1850 & 1900
,, ,, since 1900
+ Byrd 1926 Highest latitudes reached by explorers with date
ft m
12,000 4000
9000 3000
6000 2000
3000 1000
1200 400
600 200
0 0
Projection: Zenithal Equidistant

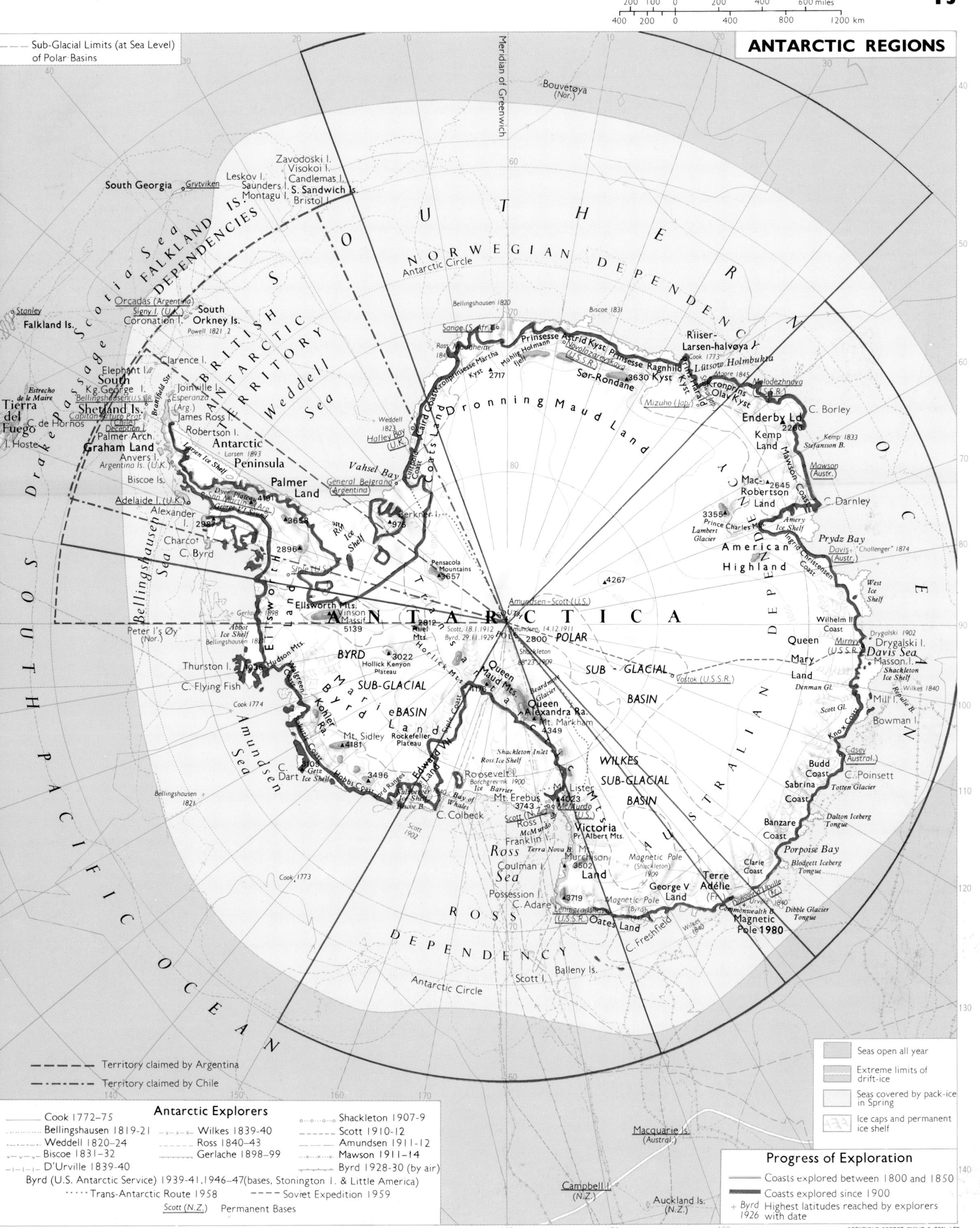
1:35 000 000
200 100 0 200 400 600 miles
400 200 0 400 800 1200 km
ANTARCTIC REGIONS
— — — Sub-Glacial Limits (at Sea Level) of Polar Basins
Meridian of Greenwich
Bouvetøya (Nor.)
South Georgia
Grytviken
Zavodoski I.
Visokoi I.
Candlemas I.
Leskov I.
Saunders I.
Montagu I.
S. Sandwich Is.
Bristol I.
Scotia Sea
FALKLAND IS. DEPENDENCIES
Stanley
Falkland Is.
Orcadas (Argentina)
Signy I. (U.K.)
Coronation I.
South Orkney Is.
Powell 1821-2
Drake Passage
Clarence I.
Elephant I.
South Shetland Is.
Kg. George I.
Bellingshausen (U.S.S.R.)
Capitán Arturo Prat (Chile)
Deception I.
Estrecho de le Maire
Tierra del Fuego
C. de Hornos
I. Hoste
Joinville I.
Esperanza (Arg.)
James Ross I.
Palmer Arch.
Robertson I.
Graham Land
Antarctic Peninsula
Larsen 1893
Larsen Ice Shelf
Anvers I.
Argentina Is. (U.K.)
Biscoe Is.
Adelaide I. (U.K.)
Alexander I.
Charcot I.
C. Byrd
BRITISH ANTARCTIC TERRITORY
Weddell Sea
Weddell 1823
Halley Bay (U.K.)
Palmer Land
Vahsel Bay
General Belgrano (Argentina)
Filchner Ice Shelf
Berkner I.
Pensacola Mountains
Bellingshausen Sea
Ellsworth Land
Ellsworth Mts.
Vinson Massif 5139
Siple (U.S.)
Gerlache 1898
Abbot Ice Shelf
Peter I's Øy (Nor.)
Thurston I.
C. Flying Fish
Hudson Mts.
Cook 1774
Amundsen Sea
BYRD SUB-GLACIAL BASIN
Hollick Kenyon Plateau
Marie Byrd Land
Kohler Ra.
Mt. Sidley 4181
Rockefeller Plateau
C. Dart
Getz Ice Shelf
Hobbs Coast
Edward VII Land
Bay of Whales
C. Colbeck
Bellingshausen 1821
SOUTH PACIFIC OCEAN
Cook 1773
NORWEGIAN DEPENDENCY
Antarctic Circle
Bellingshausen 1820
Biscoe 1831
Sanae (S. Afr.)
Prinsesse Astrid Kyst
Prinsesse Ragnhild Kyst
Novolazarevskaya (U.S.S.R.)
Kronprinsesse Martha Kyst
Mühlig Hofmann fjell
Sør-Rondane
Dronning Maud Land
Caird Coast
Coats Land
Riiser-Larsen-halvøya
Lützow Holmbukta
Kronprins Olav Kyst
Mizuho (Jap.)
Molodezhnaya (U.S.S.R.)
Enderby Ld
C. Borley
Kemp Land
Kemp 1833
Stefansson B.
Mawson Coast
Mawson (Austr.)
Mac. Robertson Land
C. Darnley
Amery Ice Shelf
Prince Charles Mts.
Lambert Glacier
American Highland
Prydz Bay
Davis (Austr.)
Ingrid Christensen Coast
"Challenger" 1874
West Ice Shelf
Wilhelm II Coast
Amundsen-Scott (U.S.)
SOUTH POLE
ANTARCTICA
Trans Antarctic Mts.
Scott, 18.1.1912
Byrd, 29.11.1929
Amundsen, 14.12.1911
Shackleton 88°23' 1909
POLAR SUB-GLACIAL BASIN
Vostok (U.S.S.R.)
Queen Mary Land
Drygalski 1902
Drygalski I.
Mirnyy (U.S.S.R.)
Davis Sea
Masson I.
Shackleton Ice Shelf
Denman Gl.
Wilkes 1840
Mill I.
Bowman I.
Scott Gl.
Knox Coast
Casey (Austral.)
Budd Coast
C. Poinsett
Sabrina Coast
Totten Glacier
Banzare Coast
Dalton Iceberg Tongue
Porpoise Bay
Blodgett Iceberg Tongue
Clarie Coast
AUSTRALIAN DEPENDENCY
WILKES SUB-GLACIAL BASIN
Horlick Mts.
Queen Maud Mts.
Beardmore Glacier
Queen Alexandra Ra.
Mt. Markham
Shackleton Inlet
Ross Ice Shelf
Roosevelt I.
Borchgrevink 1900
Ice Barrier
Mt. Erebus
Ross I.
McMurdo
Scott (N.Z.)
McMurdo (U.S.)
Mt. Lister
Franklin I.
Victoria Land
Pr. Albert Mts.
Terra Nova B.
Mt. Murchison
Ross Sea
Coulman I.
Magnetic Pole (Shackleton) 1909
George V Land
Terre Adélie (Fr.)
Dumont d'Urville (Fr.)
Commonwealth B.
Dibble Glacier Tongue
Magnetic Pole 1980
Possession I.
C. Adare
Magnetic Pole (Byrd)
Leningradskaya (U.S.S.R.)
Oates Land
C. Freshfield
Scott 1902
ROSS DEPENDENCY
Scott I.
Balleny Is.
Antarctic Circle
Macquarie Is. (Austral.)
Campbell I. (N.Z.)
Auckland Is. (N.Z.)
— — — — Territory claimed by Argentina
— · — · — Territory claimed by Chile
Antarctic Explorers
Cook 1772-75
Bellingshausen 1819-21
Weddell 1820-24
Biscoe 1831-32
D'Urville 1839-40
Wilkes 1839-40
Ross 1840-43
Gerlache 1898-99
Shackleton 1907-9
Scott 1910-12
Amundsen 1911-12
Mawson 1911-14
Byrd 1928-30 (by air)
Byrd (U.S. Antarctic Service) 1939-41, 1946-47 (bases, Stonington I. & Little America)
····· Trans-Antarctic Route 1958
— — — Soviet Expedition 1959
Scott (N.Z.) Permanent Bases
Seas open all year
Extreme limits of drift-ice
Seas covered by pack-ice in Spring
Ice caps and permanent ice shelf
Progress of Exploration
Coasts explored between 1800 and 1850
Coasts explored since 1900
+ Byrd 1926 Highest latitudes reached by explorers with date
Projection: Zenithal Equidistant

NORTH AMERICA

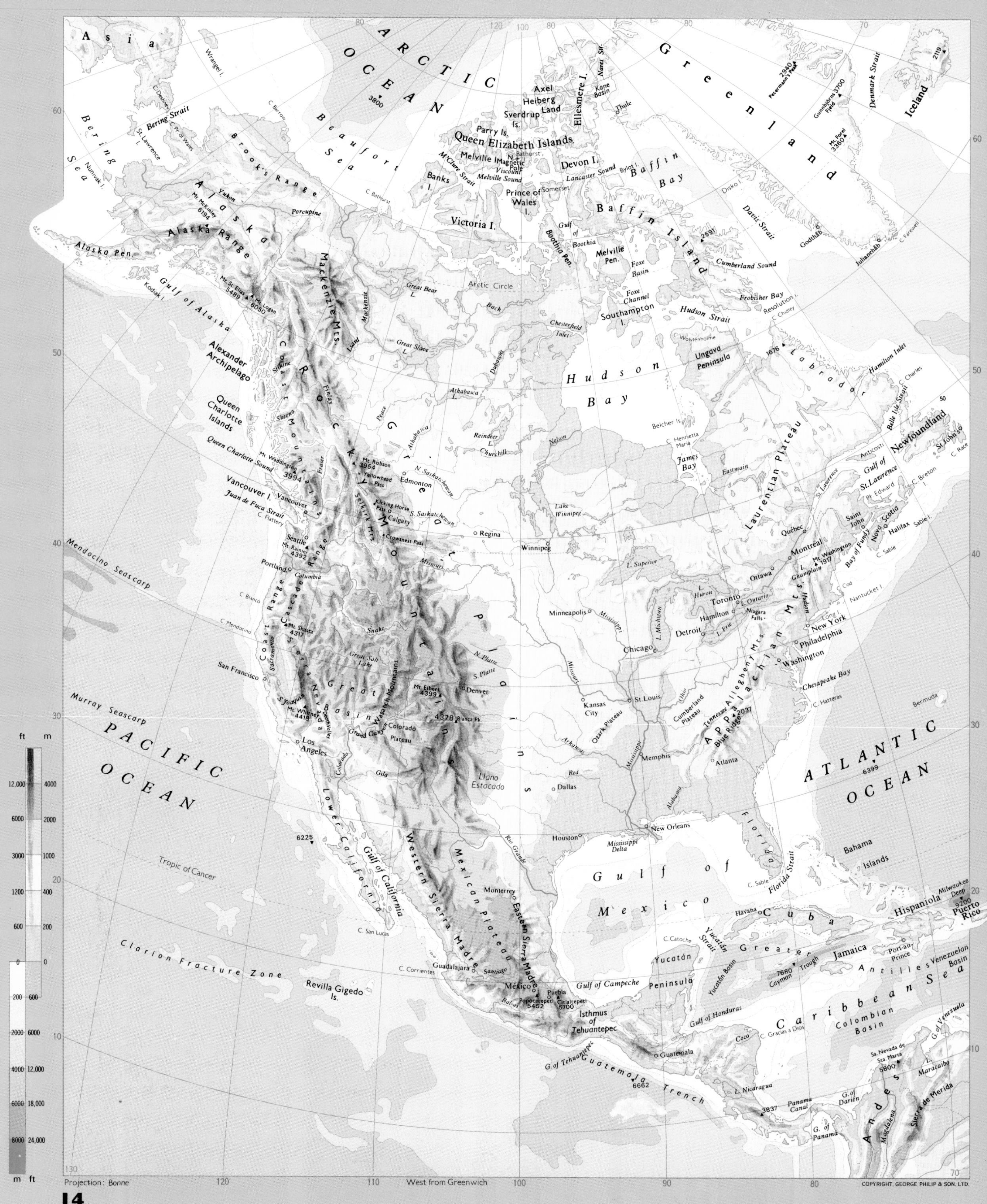
ARCTIC OCEAN
Greenland
Beaufort Sea
Baffin Bay
Hudson Bay
PACIFIC OCEAN
ATLANTIC OCEAN
Gulf of Mexico
Caribbean Sea
Rocky Mountains
Great Plains
Alaska Range
Brook's Range
Mackenzie Mts.
Appalachian Mts.
Laurentian Plateau
Great Basin
Sierra Nevada
Mexican Plateau
Western Sierra Madre
Eastern Sierra Madre
Queen Elizabeth Islands
Baffin Island
Victoria I.
Banks I.
Devon I.
Ellesmere I.
Newfoundland
Cuba
Hispaniola
Jamaica
Puerto Rico
Bahama Islands
Iceland
Bering Strait
Gulf of Alaska
Gulf of California
Gulf of St. Lawrence
Hudson Strait
Davis Strait
Denmark Strait
Florida Strait
Yucatán Peninsula
Isthmus of Tehuantepec
Panama Canal
Guatemala Trench
Clarion Fracture Zone
Murray Seascarp
Mendocino Seascarp
Tropic of Cancer
Arctic Circle
Andes
Projection: Bonne
West from Greenwich
ft m
12,000 4000
6000 2000
3000 1000
1200 400
600 200
0 0
200 600
2000 6000
4000 12,000
6000 18,000
8000 24,000
m ft

● State Capital (U.S.A.)
◎ Provincial or Territorial Capital (Canada)

C.	CONNECTICUT	N.H.	NEW HAMPSHIRE
D.	DELAWARE	N.J.	NEW JERSEY
D.C.	DISTRICT OF COLUMBIA	R.I.	RHODE ISLAND
M.	MARYLAND	VER.	VERMONT
MASS.	MASSACHUSETTS	SPM	ST. PIERRE ET MIQUELON

Projection: *Bonne*

120 110 100 West from Greenwich 90 80

1:35 000 000

200 100 0 200 400 600 miles

400 200 0 400 800 1200 km

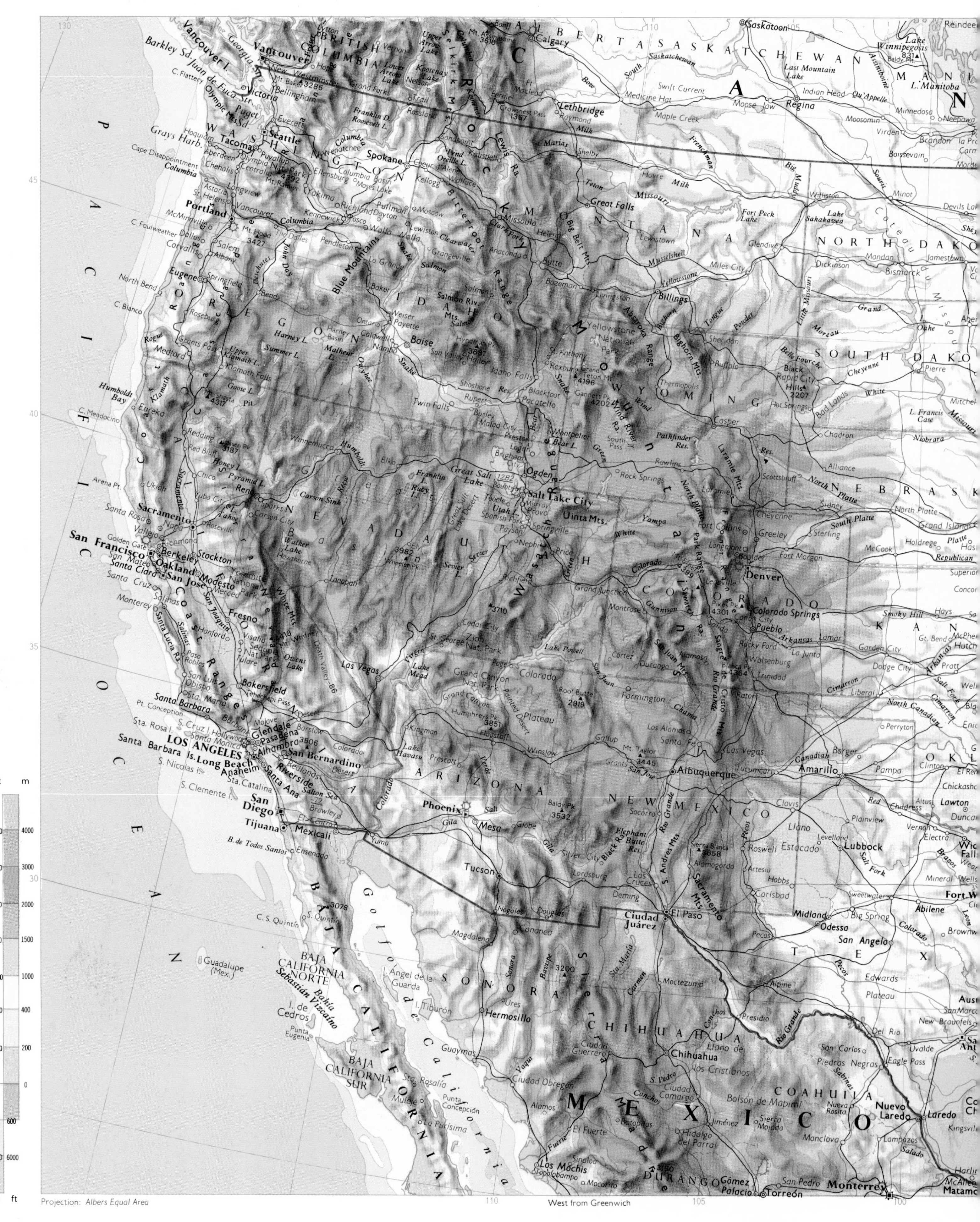

ALBERTA
SASKATCHEWAN
MANITOBA
BRITISH COLUMBIA
Vancouver I.
Vancouver
Victoria
Calgary
Saskatoon
Regina
Lethbridge
Medicine Hat
Swift Current
Moose Jaw
Maple Creek
Lake Winnipegosis
L. Manitoba
Last Mountain Lake
PACIFIC OCEAN
WASHINGTON
OREGON
CALIFORNIA
NEVADA
IDAHO
MONTANA
WYOMING
UTAH
COLORADO
ARIZONA
NEW MEXICO
NORTH DAKOTA
SOUTH DAKOTA
NEBRASKA
KANSAS
TEXAS
MEXICO
SONORA
CHIHUAHUA
COAHUILA
DURANGO
BAJA CALIFORNIA NORTE
BAJA CALIFORNIA SUR
Golfo de California
Seattle
Tacoma
Spokane
Portland
Salem
Eugene
Boise
Missoula
Helena
Great Falls
Butte
Billings
Bismarck
Casper
Cheyenne
Denver
Colorado Springs
Pueblo
Salt Lake City
Ogden
Reno
Sacramento
San Francisco
Oakland
Berkeley
San Jose
Stockton
Fresno
Bakersfield
LOS ANGELES
Long Beach
Pasadena
Glendale
San Bernardino
San Diego
Tijuana
Mexicali
Las Vegas
Phoenix
Mesa
Tucson
Albuquerque
Santa Fe
El Paso
Ciudad Juárez
Amarillo
Lubbock
Midland
Odessa
San Angelo
Abilene
Hermosillo
Chihuahua
Monterrey
Nuevo Laredo
Laredo
Torreón
Great Salt Lake
Lake Powell
Lake Mead
Grand Canyon Nat. Park
Yellowstone National Park
Blue Mountains
Bitterroot Range
Uinta Mts.
Wasatch Range
Coast Ranges
Sierra Nevada
Rocky Mountains
Colorado Plateau
Black Hills
Projection: Albers Equal Area
West from Greenwich

1:12 000 000

50 0 50 100 150 200 250 300 miles

50 0 50 100 150 200 250 300 350 400 450 km

TENNESSEE
NORTH CAROLINA
SOUTH CAROLINA
GEORGIA
ALABAMA
MISSISSIPPI
FLORIDA
MAINE
NEW HAMPSHIRE
CANADA
NASHVILLE
ATLANTA
JACKSONVILLE
Knoxville
Chattanooga
Asheville
Winston-Salem
Greensboro
Durham
Raleigh
Charlotte
Columbia
Wilmington
Charleston
Savannah
Augusta
Macon
Columbus
Montgomery
Birmingham
Mobile
Pensacola
Tallahassee
Orlando
Tampa
St. Petersburg
Miami
Ft. Lauderdale
West Palm Beach
St. Augustine
Daytona Beach
Gainesville
Pamlico Sound
C. Hatteras
C. Fear
C. Canaveral
Portland
Bangor
Augusta
Lewiston
Continuation Eastwards On same scale
GULF OF MEXICO
ATLANTIC OCEAN
BAHAMAS
Grand Bahama I.
Freeport
Great Abaco I.
Little Abaco I.
Projection: Alber's Equal Area with two standard parallels
West from Greenwich
1:6 000 000
50 0 50 100 miles
50 0 50 100 150 km
COPYRIGHT GEORGE PHILIP & SON, LTD.

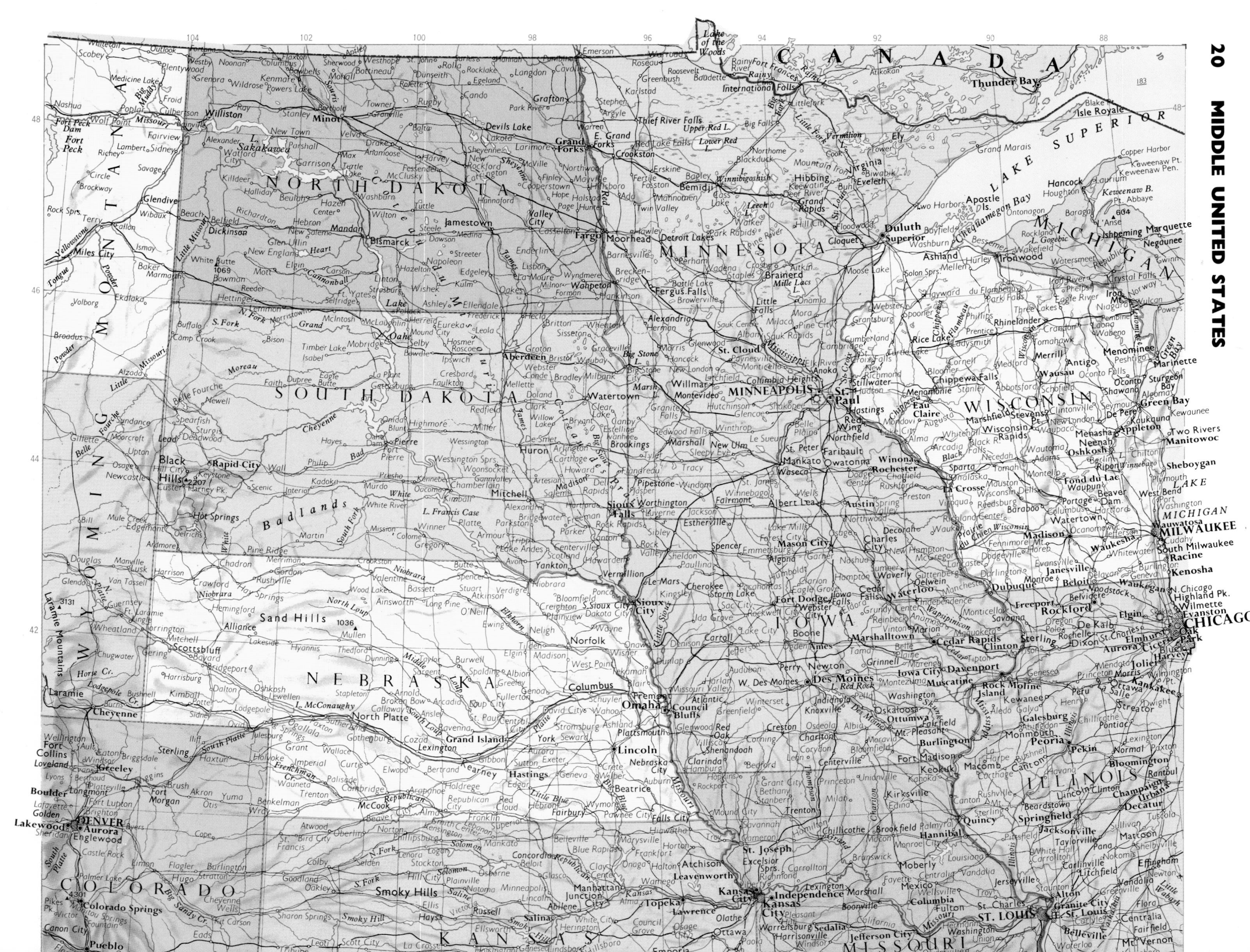

CANADA
LAKE SUPERIOR
LAKE MICHIGAN
MICHIGAN
MINNESOTA
WISCONSIN
IOWA
ILLINOIS
MISSOURI
NORTH DAKOTA
SOUTH DAKOTA
NEBRASKA
KANSAS
MONTANA
WYOMING
COLORADO
CHICAGO
MILWAUKEE
MINNEAPOLIS
St. Paul
Duluth
Thunder Bay
Des Moines
Omaha
Lincoln
ST. LOUIS
Kansas City
DENVER
Cheyenne
Bismarck
Fargo
Pierre
Rapid City
Badlands
Sand Hills
Black Hills
Smoky Hills
Laramie Mountains
Missouri
Mississippi

1:6 000 000

50 0 50 100 miles

50 0 50 100 150 km

OKLAHOMA
ARKANSAS
MISSISSIPPI
TENNESSEE
LOUISIANA
TEXAS
NEW MEXICO
MEXICO
COAHUILA
CHIHUAHUA
GULF OF MEXICO
Llano Estacado
Edwards Plateau
Stockton Plateau
Ouachita Mts.
Boston Mts.
Sangre de Cristo Mts.
Balcones
Mississippi River Delta
Río Bravo del Norte
Oklahoma City
Tulsa
Wichita
Little Rock
Memphis
Jackson
Shreveport
Baton Rouge
New Orleans
Dallas
Fort Worth
Arlington
Houston
San Antonio
Austin
Amarillo
Lubbock
Wichita Falls
Corpus Christi
Laredo
Nuevo Laredo
Brownsville
Continuation Southwards on same scale

Projection: Albers' Equal Area with two standard parallels

West from Greenwich

1:6 000 000

50 0 50 100 miles

50 0 50 100 150 km

BRITISH COLUMBIA
ALBERTA
SASKATCHEWAN
CANADA
WASHINGTON
OREGON
IDAHO
MONTANA
WYOMING
NEVADA
VANCOUVER
SEATTLE
PORTLAND
Salt Lake City
Sacramento
Spokane
Boise
Helena
Casper
Reno
Bighorn Mountains
Blue Mountains
Salmon River Mountains
Clearwater Mountains
Uinta Mountains
Medicine Bow Mts.
Great Sandy Desert
Snake River Plain

COLORADO
NEW MEXICO
ARIZONA
TEXAS
MEXICO
CHIHUAHUA
SONORA
BAJA CALIFORNIA
PACIFIC
OCEAN
Golfo de California
Colorado Plateau
Painted Desert
Grand Canyon
Mogollon Rim
Sonora Desert
Desierto de Altar
Gran Desierto
Mojave Desert
Death Valley
Sangre de Cristo Mts.
San Juan Mts.
Sacramento Mts.
Santa Lucia Range
Sierra de Juarez
Rio Grande
Rio Bravo del Norte
Albuquerque
Santa Fe
El Paso
Ciudad Juárez
Las Cruces
Tucson
PHOENIX
Flagstaff
Yuma
Las Vegas
LOS ANGELES
SAN DIEGO
Tijuana
Mexicali
Nogales
Hermosillo
Chihuahua
Bakersfield
Fresno
Santa Barbara
West from Greenwich
34
32
30
28
108
110
112
114
116
118

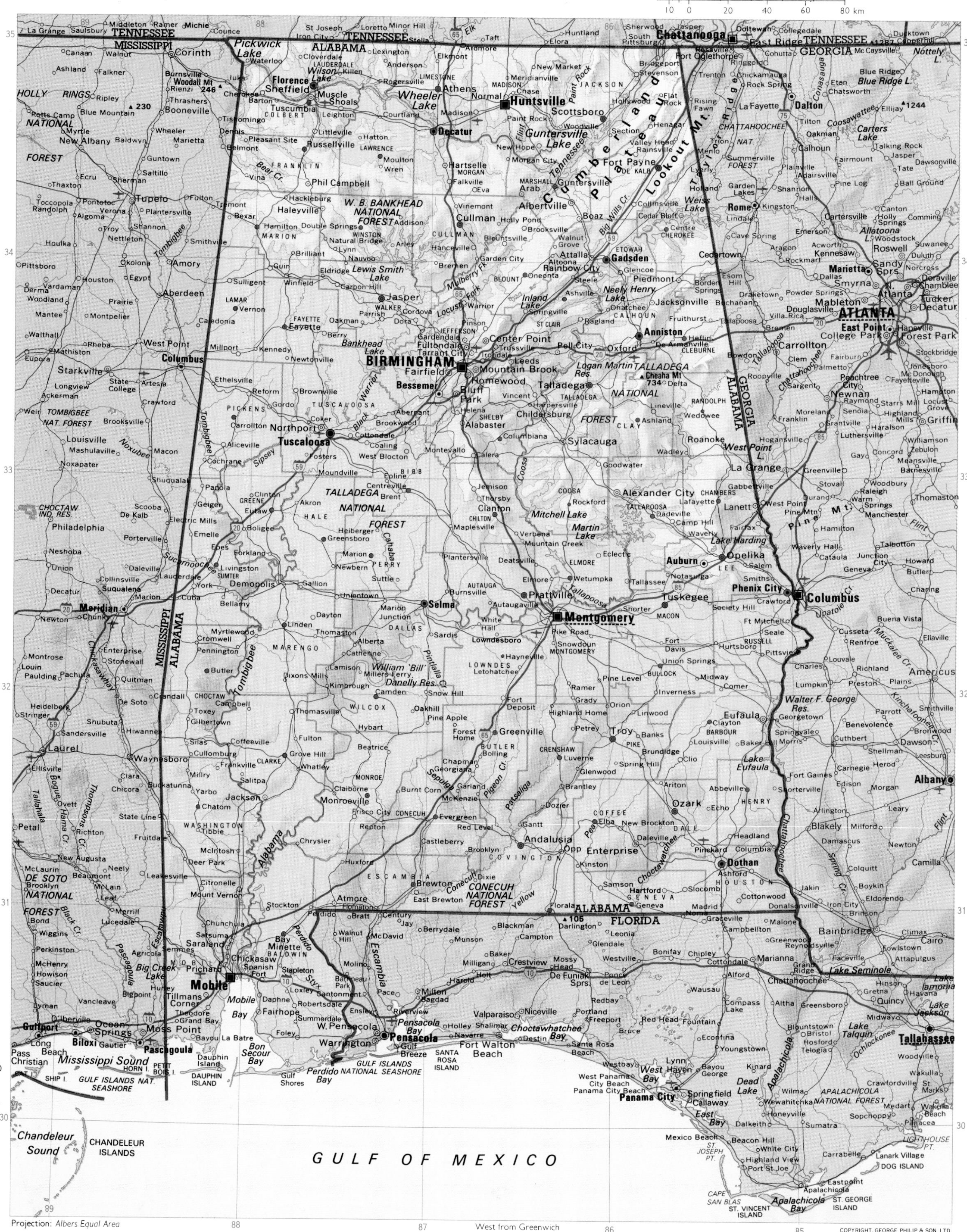

1: 2 500 000
10 0 10 20 30 40 50 miles
10 0 20 40 60 80 km
TENNESSEE
MISSISSIPPI
ALABAMA
GEORGIA
FLORIDA
GULF OF MEXICO
Chattanooga
Huntsville
Florence
Sheffield
Decatur
Gadsden
Anniston
BIRMINGHAM
Tuscaloosa
Montgomery
Selma
Auburn
Opelika
Phenix City
Columbus
Dothan
Mobile
Pensacola
Tallahassee
Panama City
ATLANTA
Meridian
Tupelo
Corinth
Laurel
Biloxi
Gulfport
Pascagoula
Wheeler Lake
Guntersville Lake
Pickwick Lake
Lewis Smith Lake
Cumberland Plateau
Lookout Mt.
W. B. BANKHEAD NATIONAL FOREST
TALLADEGA NATIONAL FOREST
CONECUH NATIONAL FOREST
TOMBIGBEE NAT. FOREST
DE SOTO NATIONAL FOREST
HOLLY SPRINGS NATIONAL FOREST
CHATTAHOOCHEE NAT. FOREST
APALACHICOLA NATIONAL FOREST
Walter F. George Res.
Lake Seminole
Mobile Bay
Mississippi Sound
GULF ISLANDS NATIONAL SEASHORE
Chandeleur Sound
CHANDELEUR ISLANDS
Cheaha Mt 734
Woodall Mt 246
Tombigbee
Alabama
Tallapoosa
Coosa
Black Warrior
Chattahoochee
Apalachicola

Projection: *Albers Equal Area*

West from Greenwich

1:10 000 000

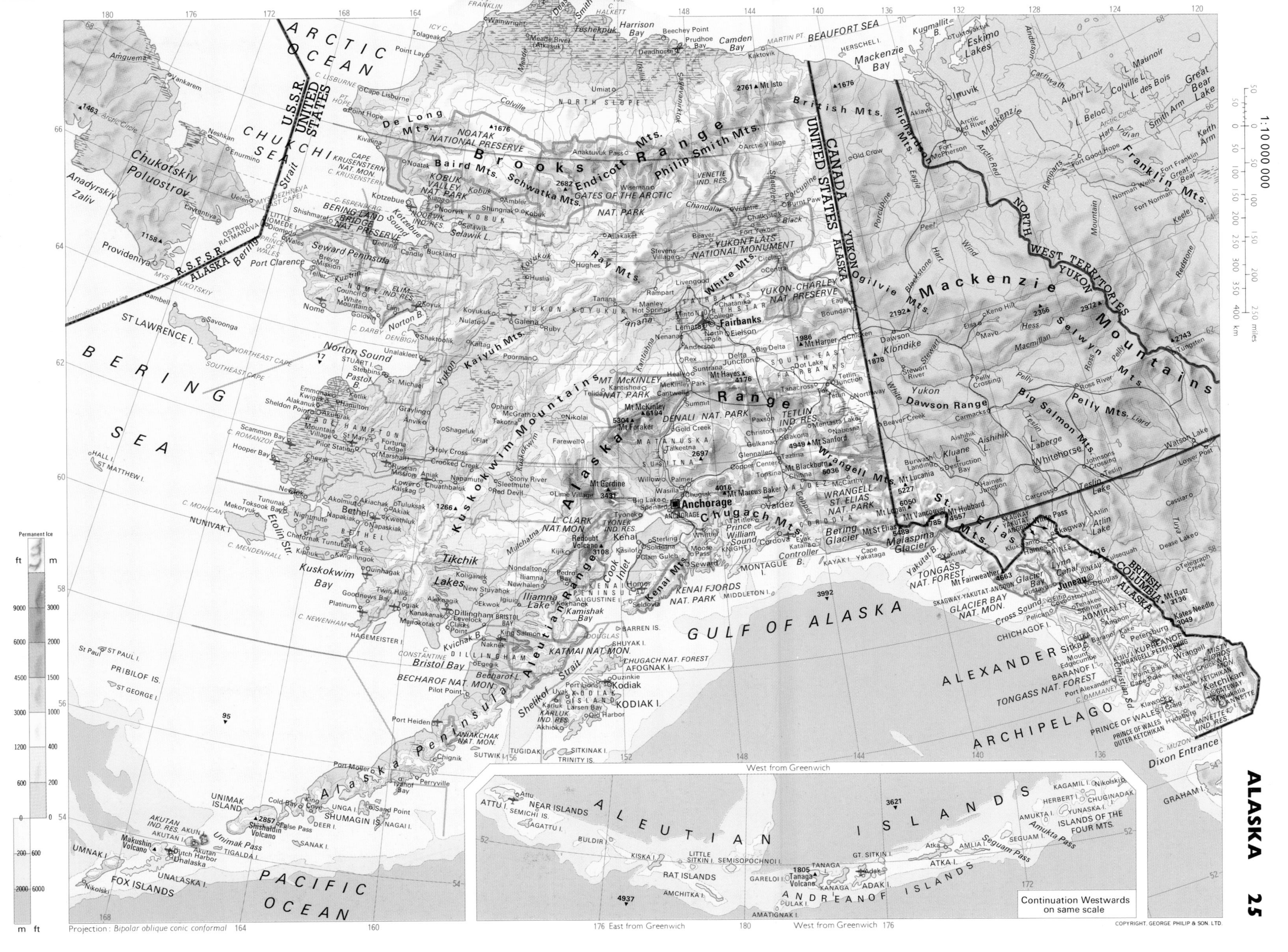

50 0 50 100 150 200 250 miles
50 0 50 100 150 200 250 300 350 400 km
ARCTIC OCEAN
BEAUFORT SEA
CHUKCHI SEA
BERING SEA
GULF OF ALASKA
PACIFIC OCEAN
CANADA
UNITED STATES
YUKON
ALASKA
NORTH WEST TERRITORIES
BRITISH COLUMBIA
U.S.S.R.
R.S.F.S.R.
Brooks Range
Alaska Range
Mackenzie Mountains
Selwyn Mts.
Kuskokwim Mountains
Aleutian Range
Chugach Mts.
Wrangell Mts.
St Elias Mts.
Ogilvie Mts.
Richardson Mts.
British Mts.
Franklin Mts.
Pelly Mts.
Big Salmon Mts.
Dawson Range
White Mts.
Ray Mts.
Baird Mts.
De Long Mts.
Schwatka Mts.
Endicott Mts.
Philip Smith Mts.
Kenai Mts.
Kaiyuh Mts.
Anchorage
Fairbanks
Juneau
Whitehorse
Nome
Kodiak
Bethel
Dawson
Inuvik
Mt McKinley 6194
Mt Logan 6050
Mt St Elias 5489
Mt Sanford
Mt Hayes 4176
Mt Marcus Baker 4016
Mt Isto 2761
Alaska Peninsula
Seward Peninsula
ALEXANDER ARCHIPELAGO
ALEUTIAN ISLANDS
ANDREANOF ISLANDS
RAT ISLANDS
NEAR ISLANDS
FOX ISLANDS
PRIBILOF IS.
ST LAWRENCE I.
NUNIVAK I.
KODIAK I.
UNIMAK ISLAND
UNALASKA I.
Norton Sound
Kotzebue Sound
Bristol Bay
Kuskokwim Bay
Cook Inlet
Prince William Sound
Bering Strait
Chukotskiy Poluostrov
Anadyrskiy Zaliv
DENALI NAT. PARK
GATES OF THE ARCTIC NAT. PARK
KATMAI NAT. MON.
GLACIER BAY NAT. MON.
WRANGELL ST. ELIAS NAT. PARK
KENAI FJORDS NAT. PARK
TONGASS NAT. FOREST
YUKON FLATS NATIONAL MONUMENT
Continuation Westwards on same scale
West from Greenwich
East from Greenwich
Projection: Bipolar oblique conic conformal
COPYRIGHT. GEORGE PHILIP & SON. LTD.
Permanent Ice
m ft

1:2 500 000

10 0 10 20 30 40 50 miles

10 0 20 40 60 80 km

West from Greenwich

Projection: Albers Equal Area

m	0	200	400	1000	1500	2000	3000
ft	0	600	1200	3000	4500	6000	9000

1:2 500 000

10 0 10 20 30 40 50 miles

10 0 20 40 60 80 km

ft 1200 600 0

m 400 200 0

Projection: Albers Equal Area

West from Greenwich

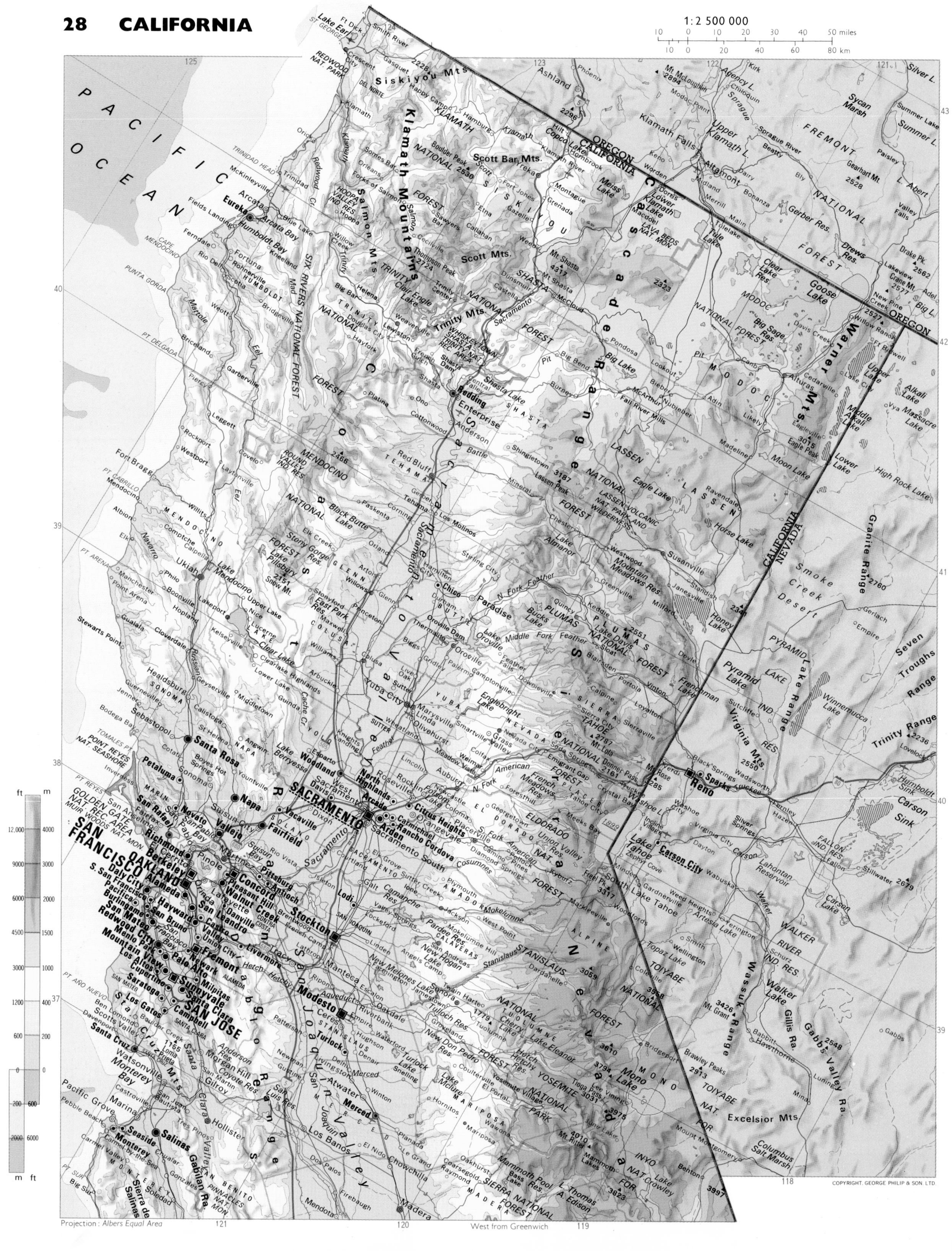
1:2 500 000
10 0 10 20 30 40 50 miles
10 0 20 40 60 80 km
PACIFIC OCEAN
OREGON
CALIFORNIA
NEVADA
Siskiyou Mts
Klamath Mountains
Scott Mts.
Trinity Mts.
Salmon Mts
Cascade Range
Coast Ranges
Sacramento Valley
Sierra Nevada
San Joaquin Valley
Diablo Range
Santa Cruz Mts.
Warner Mts
Smoke Creek Desert
Granite Range
Seven Troughs Range
Trinity Range
Carson Sink
Wassuk Range
Excelsior Mts.
SACRAMENTO
SAN FRANCISCO
OAKLAND
SAN JOSE
Stockton
Modesto
Merced
Reno
Carson City
Redding
Chico
Eureka
Santa Rosa
Salinas
Monterey
Lake Tahoe
Pyramid Lake
Walker Lake
Mono Lake
Goose Lake
Clear Lake
Lake Almanor
Honey Lake
Mt. Shasta 4317
Lassen Peak 3187
Monterey Bay
Projection: Albers Equal Area
West from Greenwich
COPYRIGHT. GEORGE PHILIP & SON LTD.

Coast Ranges
Salinas Valley
Santa Lucia Range
Gabilan Ra.
Sierra de Salinas
San Joaquin Valley
Sierra Nevada
White Mountains
Inyo Mts.
Saline Valley
Panamint Range
Panamint Valley
Death Valley
DEATH VALLEY NATIONAL MONUMENT
Amargosa Range
Amargosa Desert
Pahute Mesa
Cactus Ra.
Silver Peak Ra.
Sarcobatus Flat
Spring Mts.
Nopah Ra.
Temblor Range
San Rafael Mts.
Santa Ynez Mts.
LOS PADRES NATIONAL FOREST
Tehachapi Mts.
Mojave Desert
San Gabriel Mts.
ANGELES NATIONAL FOREST
San Bernardino Mts.
SAN BERNARDINO
Devils Playground
Providence Mts.
Bristol Mts.
Bullion Mts.
Sheep Hole Mts.
Old Woman Mts.
Sonora Desert
Chocolate Mts.
Chuckawalla Mts.
Imperial Valley
Salton Sea
Santa Rosa Mts.
San Jacinto Mts.
Santa Ana Mts.
JOSHUA TREE NAT. MON.
ANZA BORREGO DESERT STATE PARK
CLEVELAND NAT. FOR.
INDIAN RESERVATIONS
KINGS CANYON NATIONAL PARK
SEQUOIA NAT. PARK
SEQUOIA NATIONAL FOREST
SIERRA NATIONAL FOREST
INYO NATIONAL FOREST
Mt. Whitney 4418
Mt. Morgan 4190
Mt. Humphreys 4263
N. Palisade 4341
White Mt. Peak 4341
Telescope Pk. 3366
Mt. Pinos 2692
San Bernardino 3505
San Jacinto 3293
Clark Mt. 2417
Madera
Fresno
Clovis
Sanger
Selma
Hanford
Visalia
Tulare
Porterville
Delano
Wasco
Bakersfield
Oildale
Hillcrest Center
Lancaster
Palmdale
Mojave
Barstow
Victorville
Ridgecrest
San Luis Obispo
Santa Maria
Lompoc
Santa Barbara
Goleta
Ventura
Oxnard
Camarillo
Thousand Oaks
Simi Valley
LOS ANGELES
Burbank
Glendale
Pasadena
Santa Monica
Inglewood
Torrance
LONG BEACH
Anaheim
Fullerton
Garden Grove
Santa Ana
Huntington Beach
Newport Beach
Costa Mesa
Irvine
Ontario
Pomona
Cucamonga
Fontana
San Bernardino
Riverside
Redlands
Palm Springs
Oceanside
Carlsbad
Vista
Escondido
SAN DIEGO
La Mesa
El Cajon
Chula Vista
National City
TIJUANA
MEXICALI
El Centro
Needles
Blythe
Yuma
Santa Barbara Channel
San Pedro Channel
Gulf of Santa Catalina
Outer Santa Barbara Passage
CHANNEL ISLANDS
SANTA CATALINA ISLAND
SAN CLEMENTE ISLAND
SAN NICOLAS ISLAND
PACIFIC OCEAN
UNITED STATES
MEXICO
CALIF.
BAJA CALIFORNIA
CALIFORNIA
NEVADA
ARIZONA
Colorado
Projection: Albers Equal Area
West from Greenwich

1: 2 500 000

NEBRASKA
COLORADO
KANSAS
COLORADO
WYOMING
COLORADO
NEW MEXICO
OKLAHOMA
UTAH
Projection: Albers Equal Area
West from Greenwich
COPYRIGHT GEORGE PHILIP & SON, LTD.

See pages 41-42 for Delaware and Connecticut

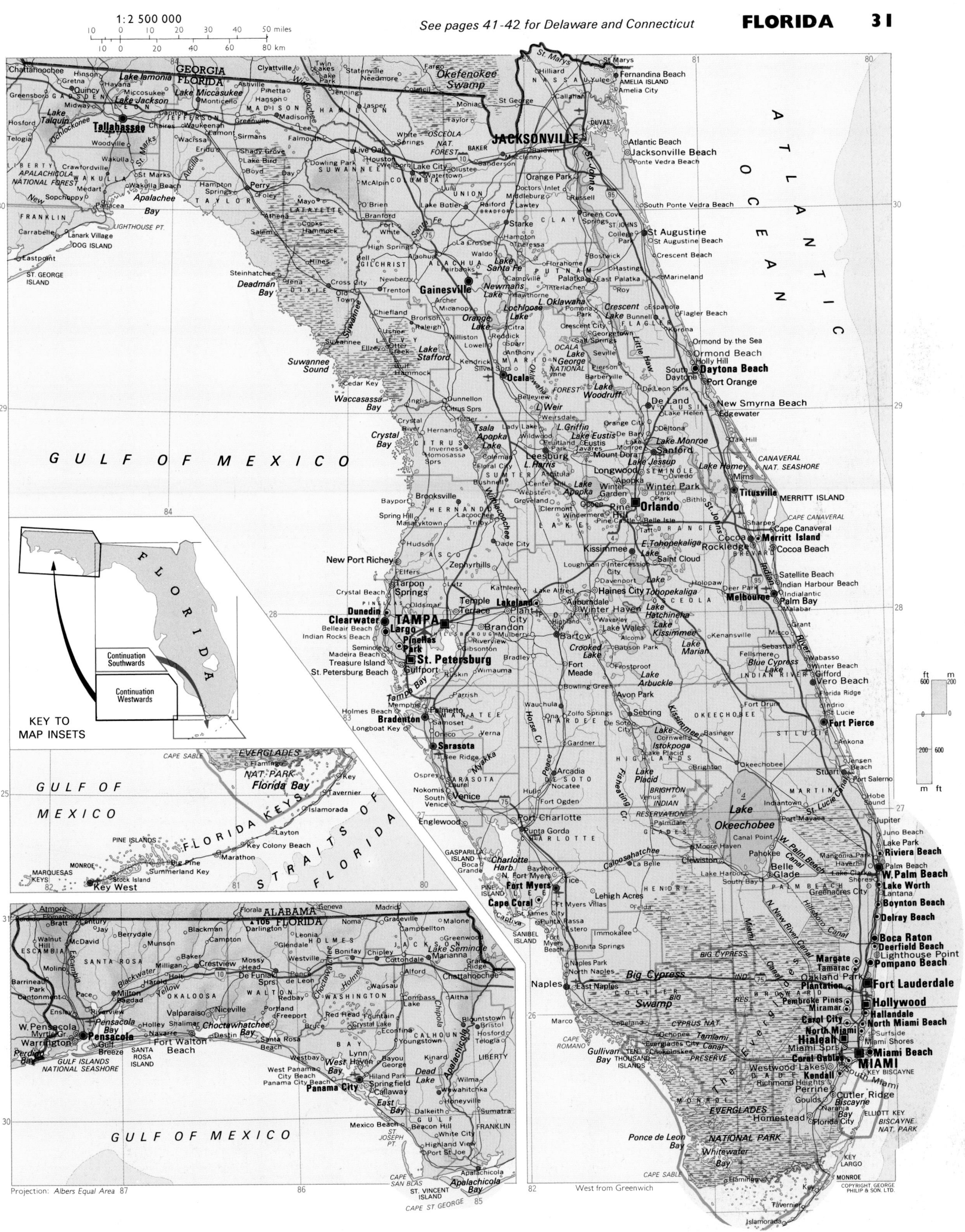
1:2 500 000
10 0 10 20 30 40 50 miles
10 0 20 40 60 80 km
GEORGIA
FLORIDA
ALABAMA
Tallahassee
JACKSONVILLE
Okefenokee Swamp
Apalachee Bay
Gainesville
Ocala
St Augustine
Daytona Beach
Orlando
TAMPA
Clearwater
St. Petersburg
Lakeland
Sarasota
Bradenton
Fort Myers
Cape Coral
Naples
Big Cypress Swamp
Lake Okeechobee
Melbourne
Fort Pierce
W. Palm Beach
Boca Raton
Fort Lauderdale
Hollywood
MIAMI
Miami Beach
Hialeah
ATLANTIC OCEAN
GULF OF MEXICO
STRAITS OF FLORIDA
FLORIDA KEYS
Key West
EVERGLADES NATIONAL PARK
Florida Bay
Pensacola
Panama City
Fort Walton Beach
KEY TO MAP INSETS
Continuation Southwards
Continuation Westwards
FLORIDA
Projection: Albers Equal Area
West from Greenwich
COPYRIGHT GEORGE PHILIP & SON LTD.

1:2 500 000

10 0 10 20 30 40 50 miles

10 0 20 40 60 80 km

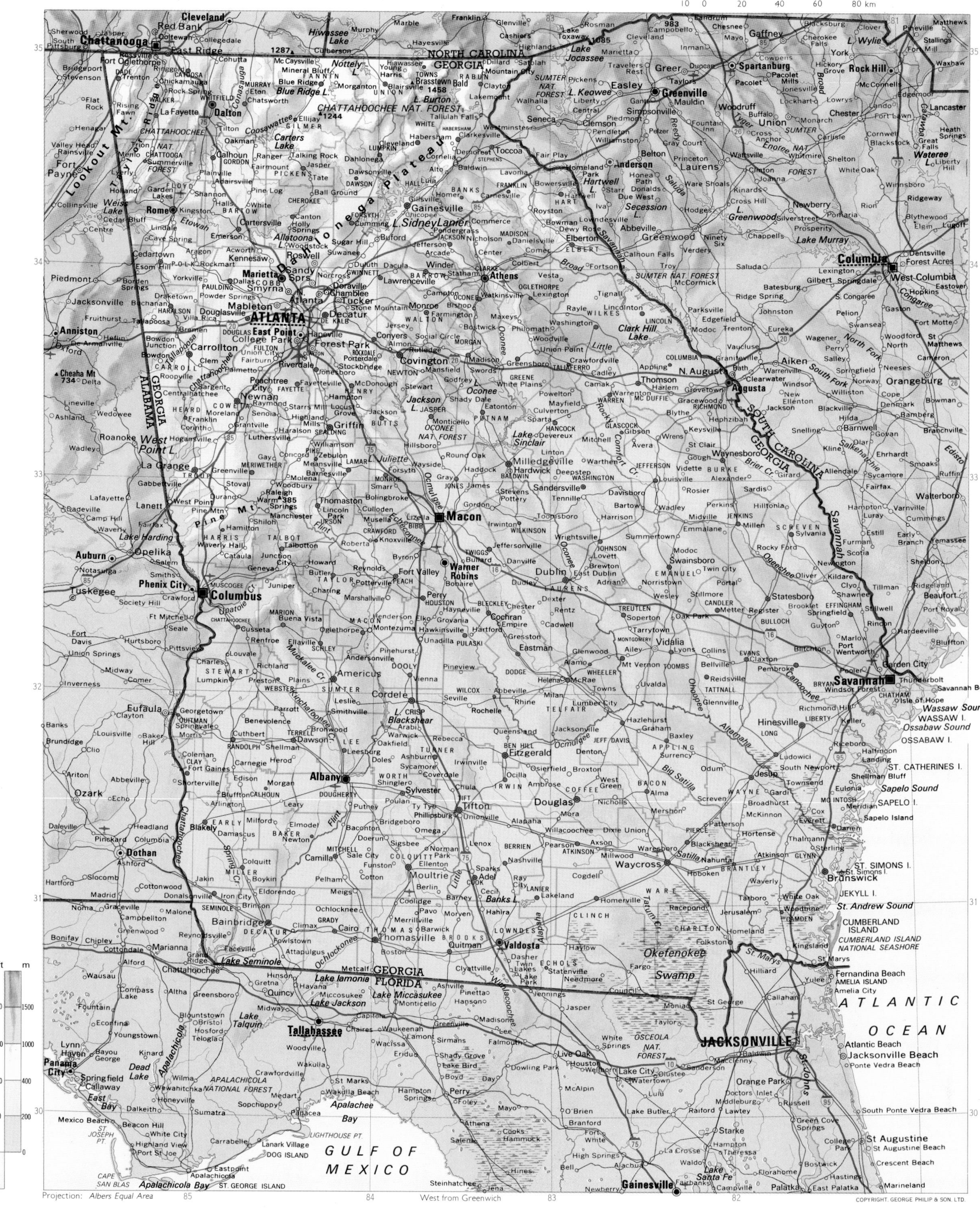

GEORGIA
ALABAMA
FLORIDA
NORTH CAROLINA
SOUTH CAROLINA
ATLANTIC OCEAN
GULF OF MEXICO
ATLANTA
Chattanooga
Macon
Columbus
Augusta
Savannah
Albany
Athens
Jacksonville
Tallahassee
Gainesville
Valdosta
Waycross
Brunswick
Dothan
Columbia
Greenville
Spartanburg
Anderson
Rome
Dalton
Marietta
Griffin
Americus
Tifton
Douglas
Dublin
Milledgeville
Thomasville
Bainbridge
Okefenokee Swamp
Lookout Mt.
Dahlonega Plateau
Pine Mt
CHATTAHOOCHEE NAT. FOREST
OCONEE NAT. FOREST
SUMTER NAT. FOREST
APALACHICOLA NATIONAL FOREST
OSCEOLA NAT. FOREST
CUMBERLAND ISLAND NATIONAL SEASHORE
L. Sidney Lanier
Clark Hill Lake
Lake Seminole
Lake Sinclair
L. Blackshear
West Point L.
Hartwell L.
Apalachee Bay
St. Andrew Sound
Sapelo Sound
Ossabaw Sound
Wassaw Sound
ST. SIMONS I.
JEKYLL I.
CUMBERLAND ISLAND
SAPELO I.
ST. CATHERINES I.
OSSABAW I.
WASSAW I.
AMELIA ISLAND
Savannah
Altamaha
Ocmulgee
Oconee
Ogeechee
Flint
Chattahoochee
Satilla
St. Marys
St. Johns
Apalachicola
Cheaha Mt 734
ft m
4500 1500
3000 1000
1200 400
600 200
0 0
Projection: Albers Equal Area
West from Greenwich
85 84 83 82
35 34 33 32 31 30
COPYRIGHT, GEORGE PHILIP & SON, LTD.

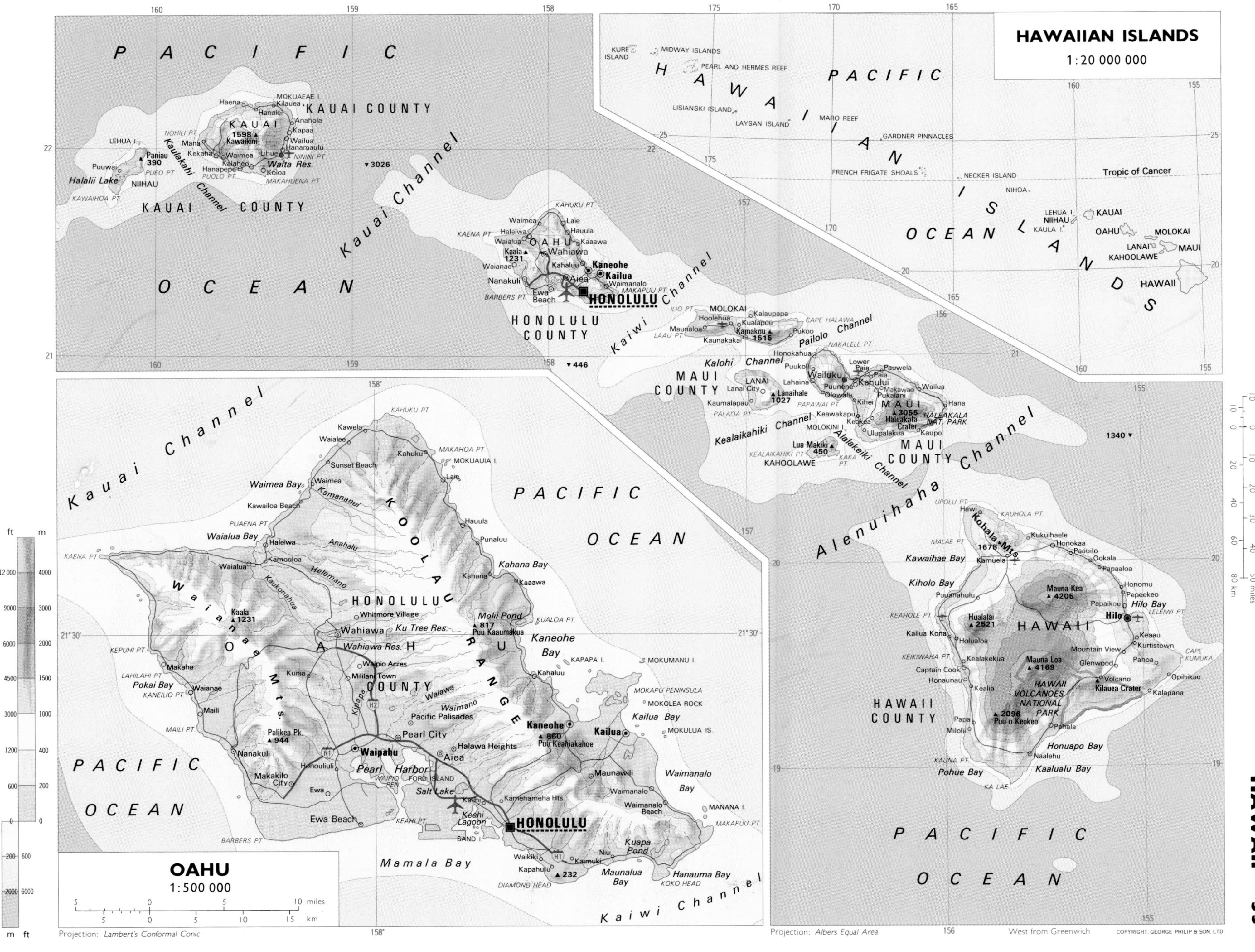
HAWAIIAN ISLANDS
1:20 000 000
KURE ISLAND
MIDWAY ISLANDS
PEARL AND HERMES REEF
LISIANSKI ISLAND
LAYSAN ISLAND
MARO REEF
GARDNER PINNACLES
FRENCH FRIGATE SHOALS
NECKER ISLAND
NIHOA
Tropic of Cancer
LEHUA I.
NIIHAU
KAULA I.
KAUAI
OAHU
MOLOKAI
LANAI
MAUI
KAHOOLAWE
HAWAII
PACIFIC OCEAN
HAWAIIAN ISLANDS
PACIFIC OCEAN
KAUAI COUNTY
KAUAI
1598 Kawaikini
Waita Res.
Paniau 390
NIIHAU
Halalii Lake
Kaulakahi Channel
Kauai Channel
3026
OAHU
HONOLULU
HONOLULU COUNTY
Kaiwi Channel
446
MOLOKAI
Kamakou 1515
Pailolo Channel
Kalohi Channel
LANAI
Lanaihale 1027
MAUI COUNTY
MAUI
Haleakala Crater 3055
HALEAKALA NAT. PARK
Kealaikahiki Channel
Alalakeiki Channel
Lua Makika 450
KAHOOLAWE
Alenuihaha Channel
1340
1:2 500 000
50 miles
80 km
Kohala Mts. 1678
Kawaihae Bay
Kiholo Bay
Mauna Kea 4205
Hualalai 2521
HAWAII
Hilo
Hilo Bay
Mauna Loa 4169
HAWAII VOLCANOES NATIONAL PARK
Kilauea Crater
2096 Puu o Keokeo
HAWAII COUNTY
Honuapo Bay
Kaalualu Bay
Pohue Bay
PACIFIC OCEAN
Projection: Albers Equal Area
West from Greenwich
COPYRIGHT, GEORGE PHILIP & SON, LTD.
Kauai Channel
PACIFIC OCEAN
KOOLAU RANGE
HONOLULU COUNTY
Waianae Mts.
Kaala 1231
Palikea Pk. 944
Puu Kaaumakua 817
Puu Keahiakahoe 860
Wahiawa
Ku Tree Res.
Wahiawa Res.
Pearl City
Waipahu
Pearl Harbor
Aiea
Salt Lake
Keehi Lagoon
Kaneohe
Kailua
Kaneohe Bay
Kailua Bay
Kahana Bay
Waimanalo Bay
HONOLULU
Mamala Bay
Maunalua Bay
Hanauma Bay
Kuapa Pond
Ewa Beach
Waimea Bay
Waialua Bay
Pokai Bay
KAENA PT.
BARBERS PT.
DIAMOND HEAD
KOKO HEAD
MAKAPUU PT.
KAHUKU PT.
Kaiwi Channel
PACIFIC OCEAN
OAHU
1:500 000
10 miles
15 km
Projection: Lambert's Conformal Conic
ft
m
12 000
9000
6000
4500
3000
1200
600
0
600
6000
4000
3000
2000
1500
1000
400
200
0
200
2000

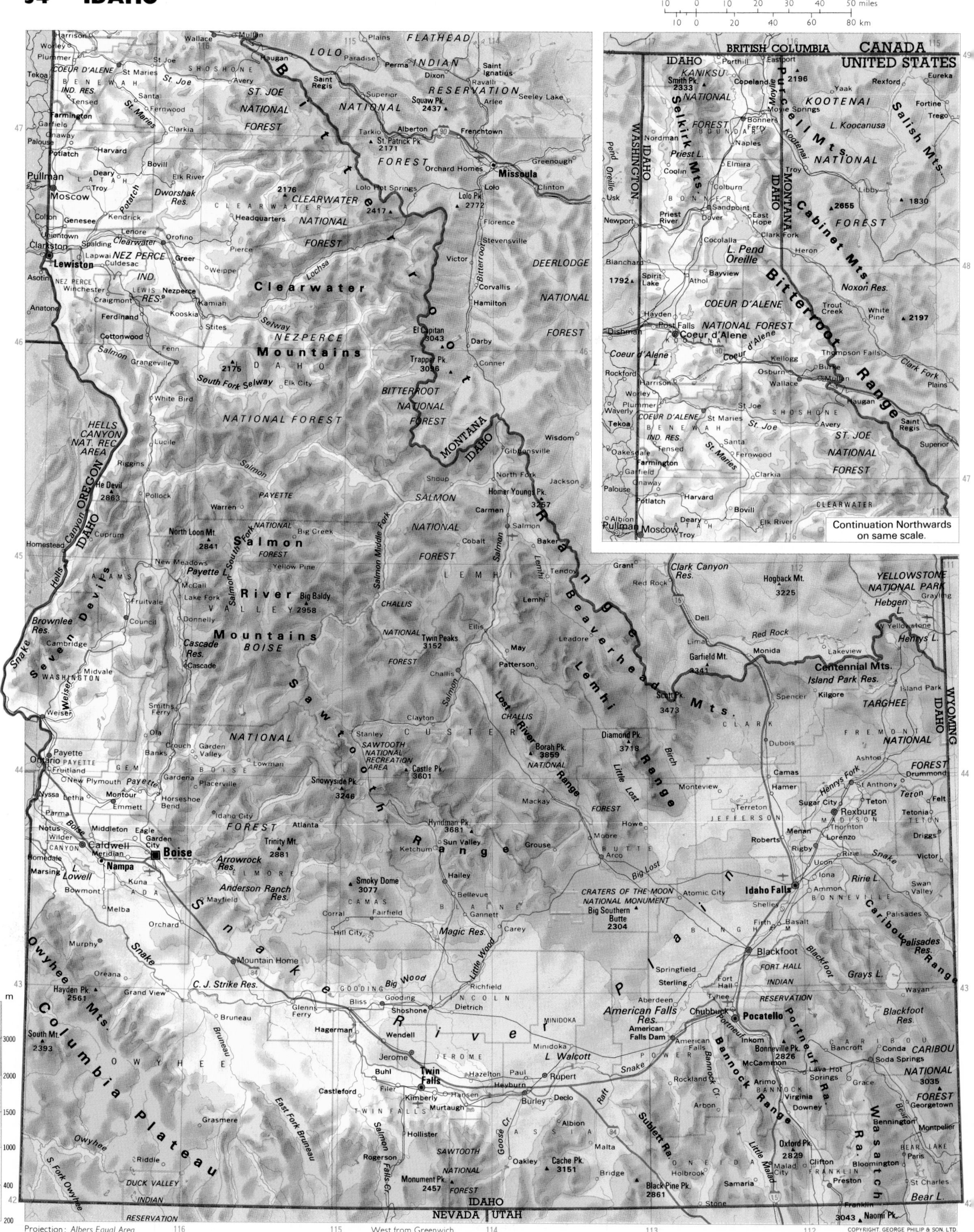
1:2 500 000
10 0 10 20 30 40 50 miles
10 0 20 40 60 80 km
ft m
9000 3000
6000 2000
4500 1500
3000 1000
1200 400
600 200
Continuation Northwards on same scale.
CANADA
UNITED STATES
BRITISH COLUMBIA
IDAHO
MONTANA
WASHINGTON
OREGON
WYOMING
NEVADA
UTAH
Bitterroot Range
Clearwater Mountains
Salmon River Mountains
Sawtooth Range
Beaverhead Mts.
Lemhi Range
Lost River Range
Centennial Mts.
Seven Devils Mts.
Owyhee Mts.
Columbia Plateau
Snake River Plain
Bannock Range
Portneuf Ra.
Wasatch Ra.
Caribou Range
Selkirk Mts.
Purcell Mts.
Cabinet Mts.
Salish Mts.
Boise
Lewiston
Moscow
Pullman
Missoula
Coeur d'Alene
Idaho Falls
Pocatello
Twin Falls
Nampa
Caldwell
Mountain Home
Blackfoot
Rexburg
Sandpoint
Grangeville
Salmon
Challis
Ketchum
Sun Valley
Hailey
Burley
Rupert
Jerome
Shoshone
Gooding
Payette
Weiser
McCall
Cascade
Arco
Mackay
Dubois
Ashton
St Anthony
Montpelier
Preston
Malad City
Soda Springs
American Falls
Borah Pk. 3859
Hyndman Pk. 3681
Castle Pk. 3601
Diamond Pk. 3718
Scott Pk. 3473
He Devil 2863
Big Baldy 2958
Trinity Mt. 2881
Smoky Dome 3077
Hells Canyon Nat. Rec. Area
Craters of the Moon National Monument
Yellowstone National Park
Nez Perce Ind. Res.
Coeur d'Alene Ind. Res.
Fort Hall Indian Reservation
Duck Valley Indian Reservation
Sawtooth National Recreation Area
Dworshak Res.
Cascade Res.
Brownlee Res.
Arrowrock Res.
Anderson Ranch Res.
C. J. Strike Res.
American Falls Res.
Palisades Res.
Island Park Res.
Magic Res.
L. Pend Oreille
Priest L.
Grays L.
Bear L.
Snake
Salmon
Clearwater
Boise
Payette
Weiser
Bruneau
Big Wood
Big Lost
Blackfoot
Henrys Fork
Lochsa
Selway
St. Joe
Kootenai

Projection: *Albers Equal Area* West from Greenwich

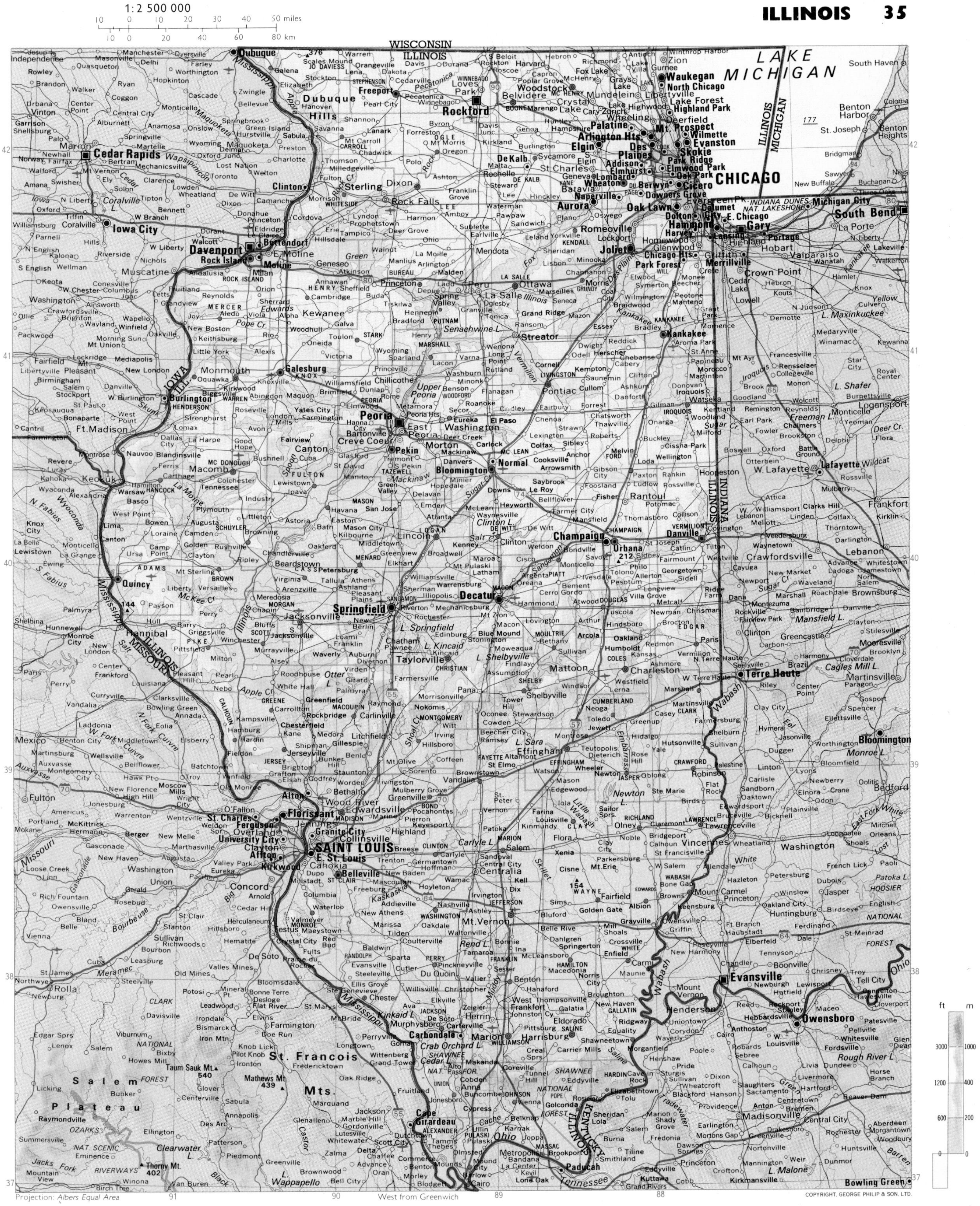

1:2 500 000

10 0 10 20 30 40 50 miles

10 0 20 40 60 80 km

ft m

3000 1000

1200 400

600 200

0 0

Projection: Albers Equal Area

91 90 West from Greenwich 89 88

1:2 500 000

10 0 10 20 30 40 50 miles

10 0 20 40 60 80 km

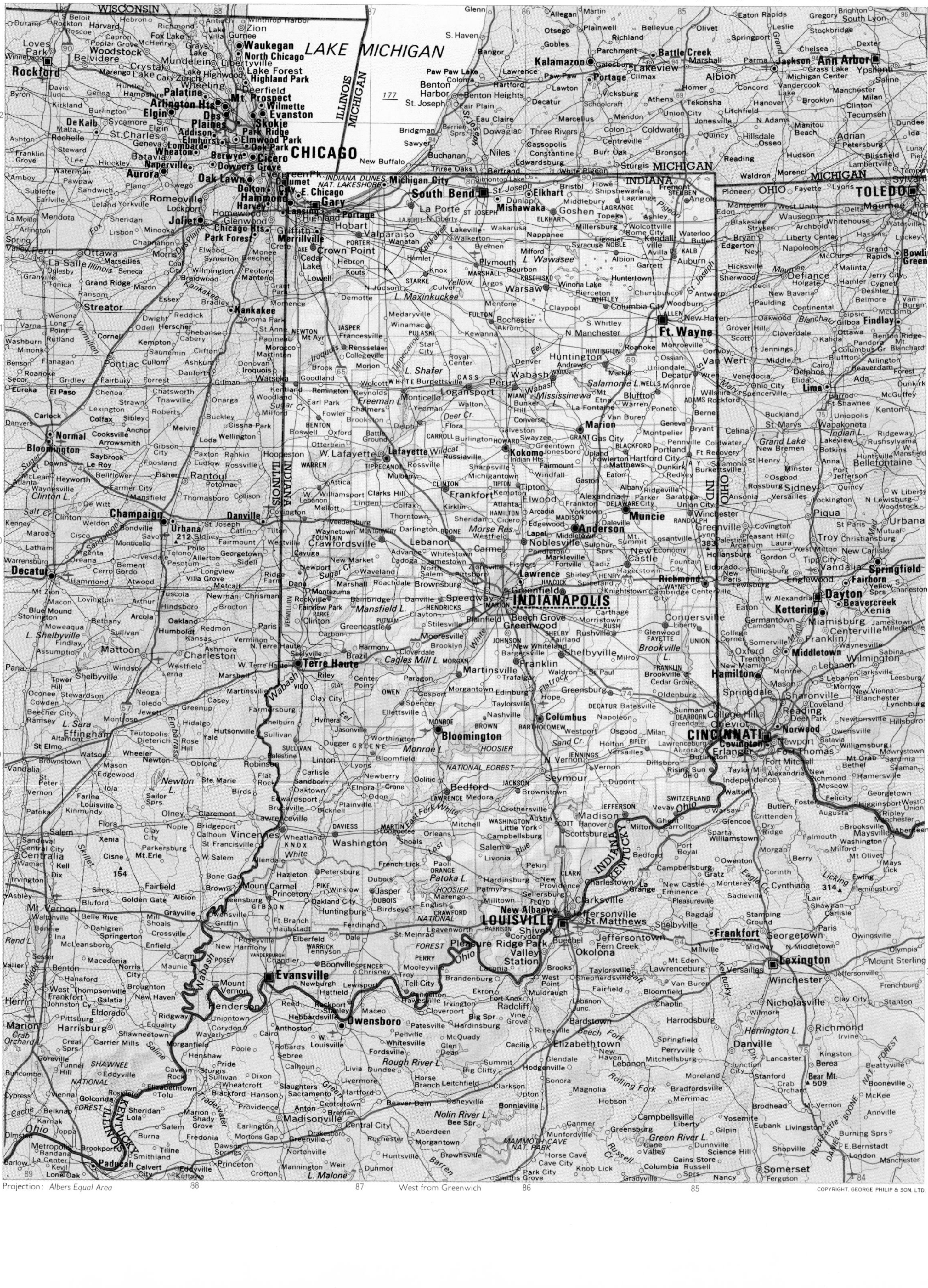

ft m

1200 400

600 200

0 0

Projection: *Albers Equal Area*

West from Greenwich

1:2 500 000

10 0 10 20 30 40 50 miles

10 0 20 40 60 80 km

West from Greenwich

Projection: Albers Equal Area

m: 0, 200, 400

ft: 0, 600, 1200

1:2 500 000

10 0 10 20 30 40 50 miles

10 0 20 40 60 80 km

Projection: Albers Equal Area

West from Greenwich

m ft

1000 3000

400 1200

200 600

1:2 500 000

10 0 10 20 30 40 50 miles

10 0 20 40 60 80 km

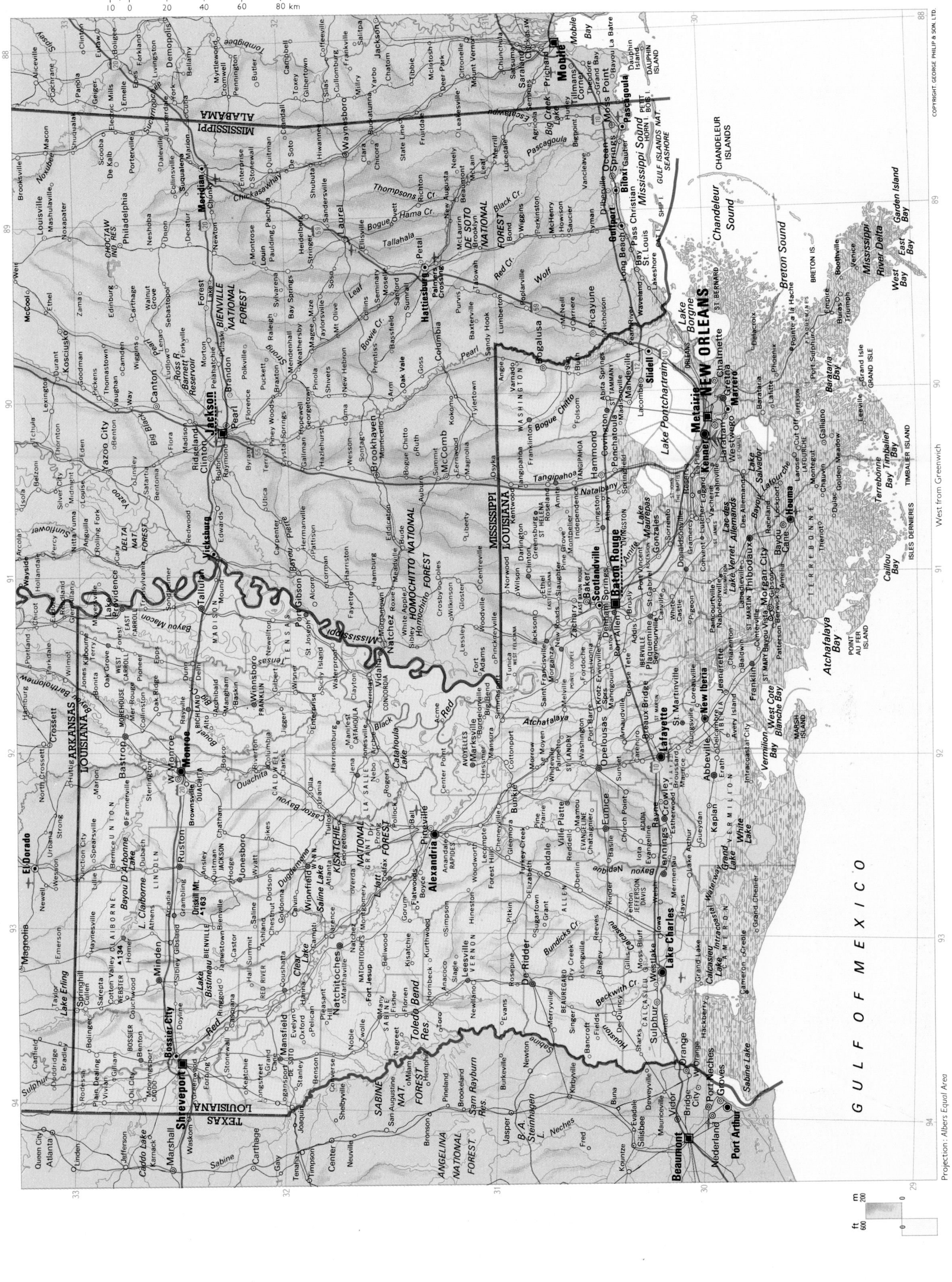

See pages 62-63 for Kentucky

GULF OF MEXICO

West from Greenwich

Projection: Albers Equal Area

ft 600 0 — m 200 0

1:2 500 000

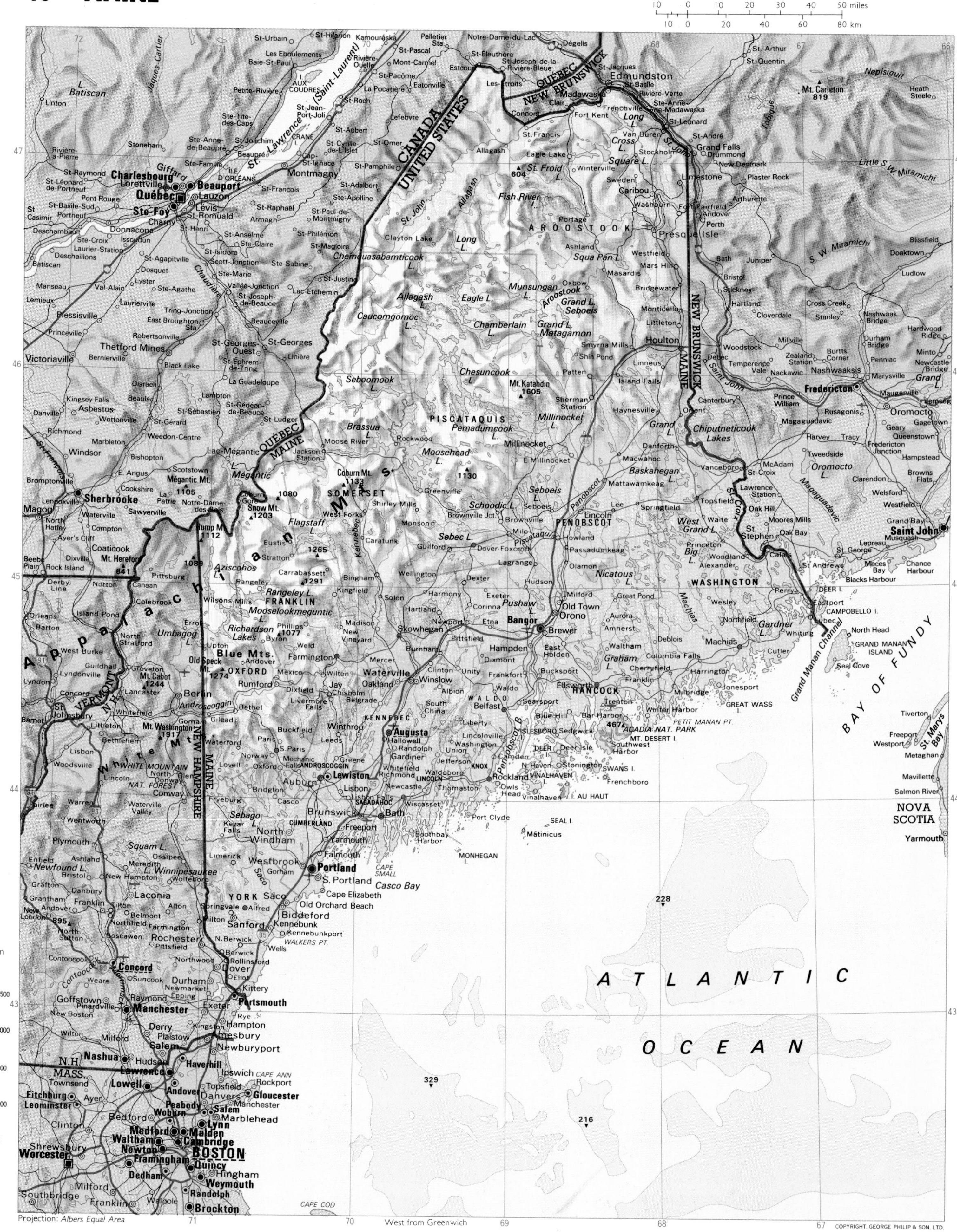
CANADA
UNITED STATES
QUÉBEC
NEW BRUNSWICK
MAINE
NEW HAMPSHIRE
VERMONT
N.H.
MASS.
NOVA SCOTIA
ATLANTIC OCEAN
BAY OF FUNDY
Appalachian Mts
White Mts
AROOSTOOK
PISCATAQUIS
SOMERSET
PENOBSCOT
WASHINGTON
HANCOCK
WALDO
FRANKLIN
OXFORD
KENNEBEC
ANDROSCOGGIN
CUMBERLAND
YORK
Québec
Charlesbourg
Beauport
Ste-Foy
Lévis
Sherbrooke
Edmundston
Fredericton
Saint John
Presque Isle
Houlton
Caribou
Bangor
Augusta
Portland
Lewiston
Waterville
Concord
Manchester
Portsmouth
Lowell
Lawrence
Worcester
BOSTON
Mt. Katahdin 1605
Mt. Washington 1917
Moosehead L.
Chesuncook L.
Sebago L.
Casco Bay
St. Lawrence
Penobscot
Kennebec
Androscoggin
Grand Manan Channel
St. Croix
St. John
Allagash
CAPE COD
CAPE ANN
MT. DESERT I.
ACADIA NAT. PARK
GRAND MANAN ISLAND
CAMPOBELLO I.
MONHEGAN I.
WHITE MOUNTAIN NAT. FOREST

Projection: *Albers Equal Area*

West from Greenwich

1:1 250 000

10 0 10 20 miles

10 0 10 20 30 km

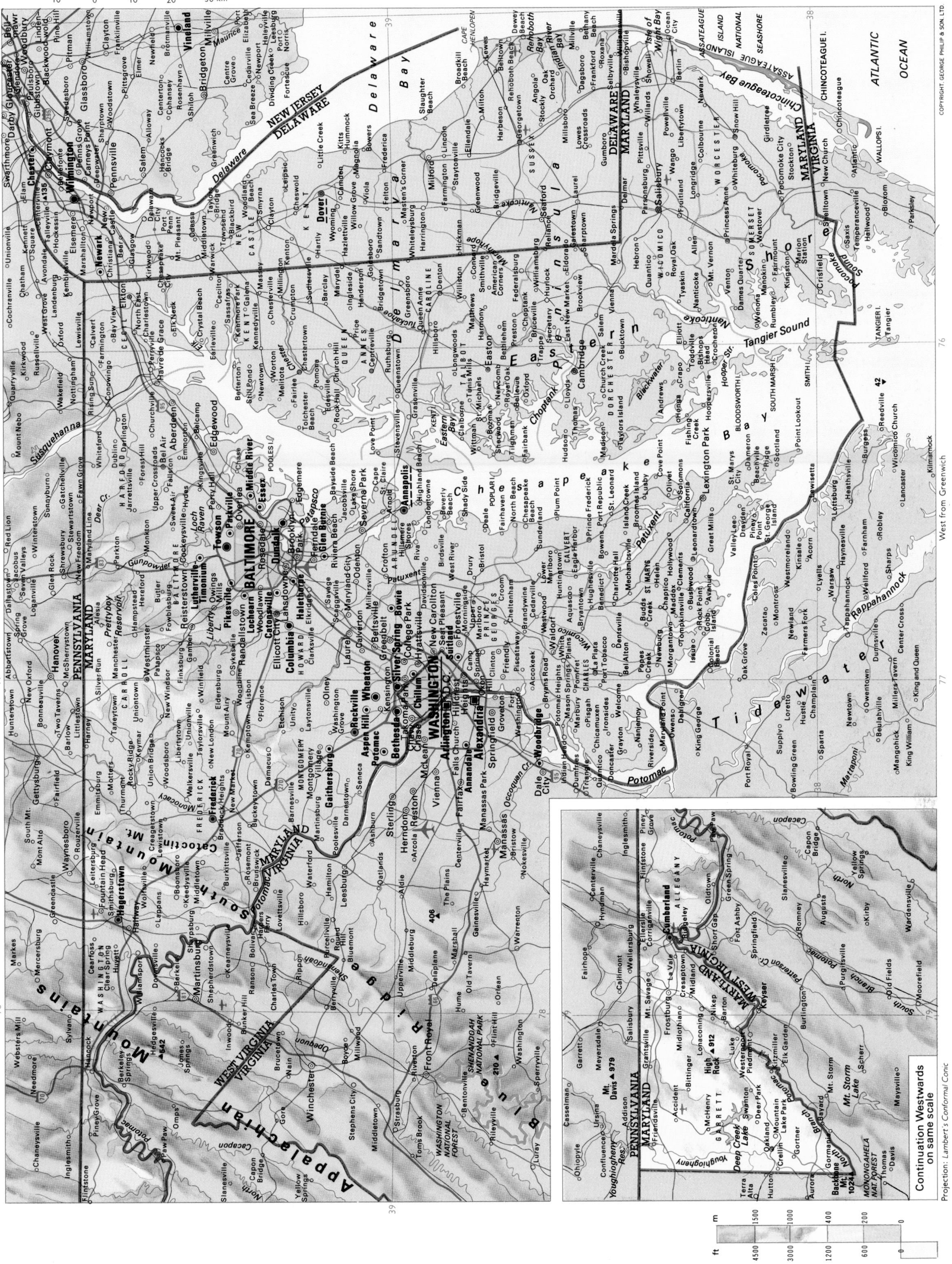

West from Greenwich

Continuation Westwards on same scale

Projection: Lambert's Conformal Conic

m 1500 1000 400 200 0

ft 4500 3000 1200 600 0

1:1 250 000

10 0 10 20 miles

10 0 10 20 30 km

ATLANTIC OCEAN

Massachusetts Bay

Cape Cod Bay

Nantucket Sound

Rhode Island Sound

Block Island Sound

Long Island Sound

m	ft
1000	3000
400	1200
200	600
0	0

Projection: Lambert's Conformal Conic

West from Greenwich

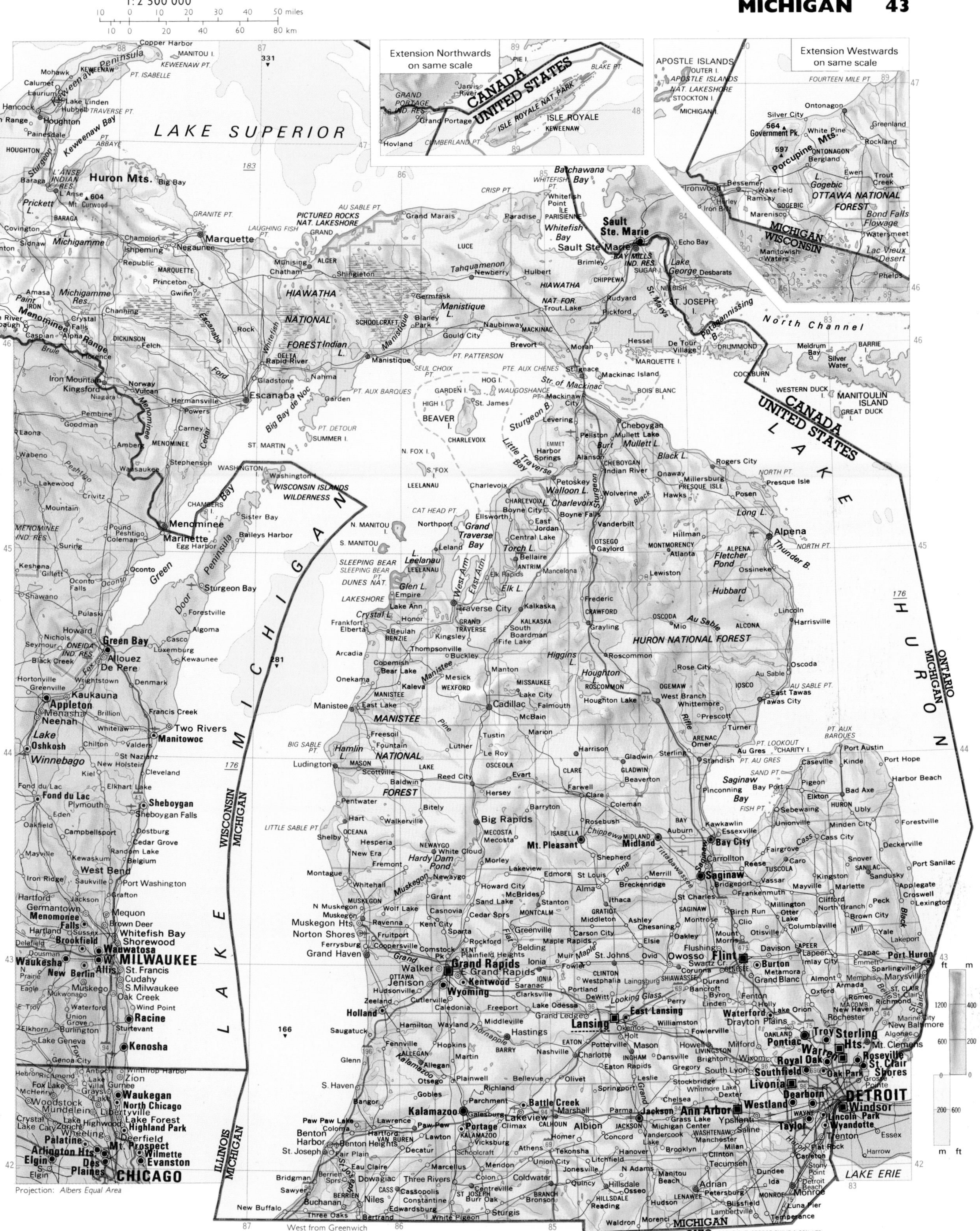
1:2 500 000
10 0 10 20 30 40 50 miles
10 0 20 40 60 80 km
Extension Northwards on same scale
CANADA
UNITED STATES
ISLE ROYALE NAT. PARK
ISLE ROYALE
Extension Westwards on same scale
APOSTLE ISLANDS NAT. LAKESHORE
OTTAWA NATIONAL FOREST
Porcupine Mts.
MICHIGAN
WISCONSIN
LAKE SUPERIOR
Keweenaw Peninsula
Keweenaw Bay
Huron Mts.
PICTURED ROCKS NAT. LAKESHORE
Marquette
HIAWATHA NATIONAL FOREST
HIAWATHA NAT. FOR.
Sault Ste. Marie
Whitefish Bay
North Channel
MANITOULIN ISLAND
Escanaba
Big Bay de Noc
Str. of Mackinac
Menominee
Marinette
Green Bay
Door Peninsula
WISCONSIN ISLANDS WILDERNESS
LAKE MICHIGAN
LAKE HURON
Grand Traverse Bay
SLEEPING BEAR DUNES NAT. LAKESHORE
Traverse City
HURON NATIONAL FOREST
Alpena
Thunder B.
Houghton L.
Cadillac
MANISTEE NATIONAL FOREST
Saginaw Bay
Bay City
Saginaw
Midland
Mt. Pleasant
Big Rapids
Muskegon
Grand Rapids
Lansing
East Lansing
Flint
Port Huron
Kalamazoo
Battle Creek
Jackson
Ann Arbor
DETROIT
Windsor
LAKE ERIE
MILWAUKEE
Racine
Kenosha
Waukegan
CHICAGO
ONTARIO
MICHIGAN
WISCONSIN
MICHIGAN
ILLINOIS
MICHIGAN
MICHIGAN
OHIO
m ft
1200 400
600 200
0 0
200 600
West from Greenwich
Projection: Albers Equal Area

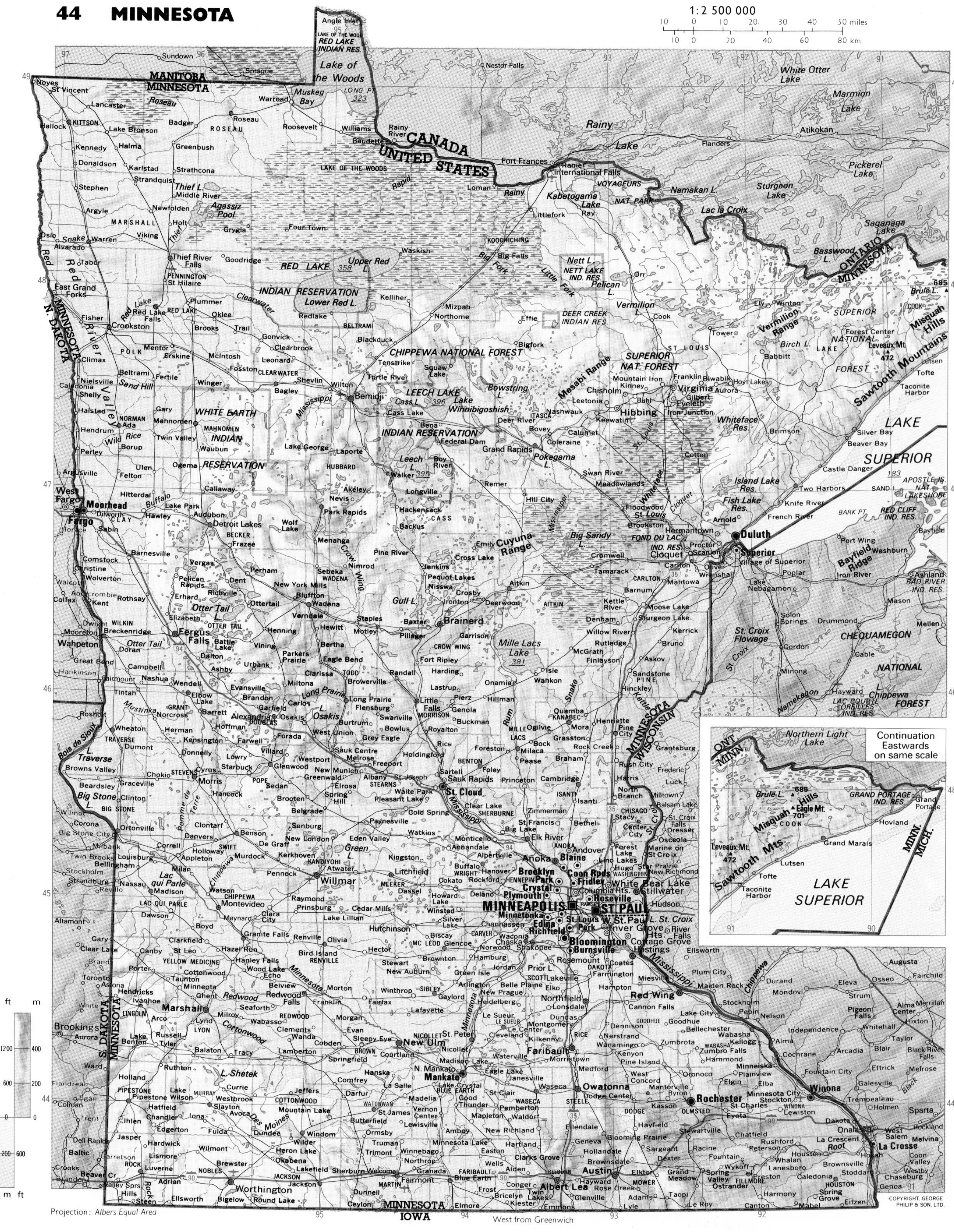

1:2 500 000
10 0 10 20 30 40 50 miles
10 0 20 40 60 80 km
Continuation Eastwards on same scale
LAKE SUPERIOR
CANADA
UNITED STATES
MANITOBA
MINNESOTA
ONTARIO
N. DAKOTA
S. DAKOTA
IOWA
WISCONSIN
MINN.
MICH.
Lake of the Woods
RED LAKE INDIAN RES.
RED LAKE INDIAN RESERVATION
Upper Red L.
Lower Red L.
CHIPPEWA NATIONAL FOREST
SUPERIOR NAT. FOREST
VOYAGEURS NAT. PARK
LEECH LAKE INDIAN RESERVATION
WHITE EARTH INDIAN RESERVATION
Mesabi Range
Cuyuna Range
Sawtooth Mountains
Misquah Hills
Mille Lacs Lake
Mississippi
Minnesota
Red River Valley
Duluth
Superior
Moorhead
Fargo
Brainerd
St. Cloud
MINNEAPOLIS
ST. PAUL
Bloomington
Rochester
Mankato
New Ulm
Winona
La Crosse
Albert Lea
Austin
Owatonna
Faribault
Red Wing
Willmar
Marshall
Worthington
Fergus Falls
Bemidji
Grand Rapids
Hibbing
Virginia
International Falls
ft m
1200 400
600 200
0 0
200 600
m ft
Projection: Albers Equal Area
West from Greenwich
COPYRIGHT, GEORGE PHILIP & SON, LTD.

1:2 500 000

10 0 10 20 30 40 50 miles

10 0 20 40 60 80 km

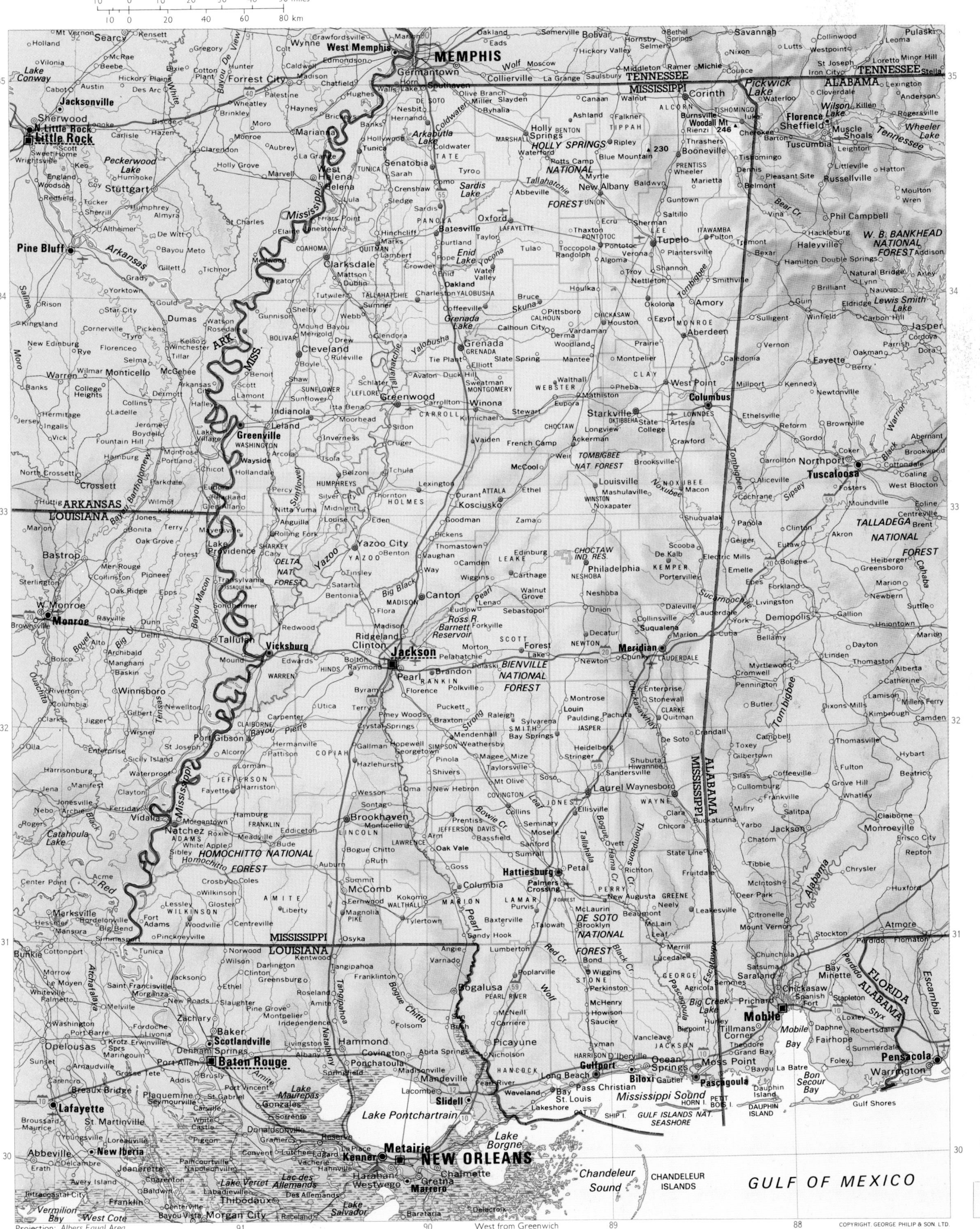
MEMPHIS
West Memphis
Germantown
TENNESSEE
MISSISSIPPI
ALABAMA
ARKANSAS
LOUISIANA
FLORIDA
Corinth
Tupelo
Columbus
Starkville
Greenville
Greenwood
Clarksdale
Cleveland
Grenada
Oxford
Vicksburg
Jackson
Meridian
Hattiesburg
Laurel
Natchez
McComb
Brookhaven
Gulfport
Biloxi
Pascagoula
Mobile
Pensacola
Tuscaloosa
Little Rock
N. Little Rock
Pine Bluff
Monroe
Baton Rouge
Lafayette
NEW ORLEANS
Metairie
Kenner
Slidell
Lake Pontchartrain
Lake Borgne
Lake Maurepas
Mississippi Sound
Mobile Bay
Chandeleur Sound
CHANDELEUR ISLANDS
GULF ISLANDS NAT. SEASHORE
GULF OF MEXICO
HOLLY SPRINGS NATIONAL FOREST
TOMBIGBEE NAT FOREST
BIENVILLE NATIONAL FOREST
HOMOCHITTO NATIONAL FOREST
DE SOTO NATIONAL FOREST
DELTA NAT FOREST
W. B. BANKHEAD NATIONAL FOREST
TALLADEGA NATIONAL FOREST
CHOCTAW IND. RES.
Mississippi
Arkansas
Yazoo
Pearl
Tombigbee
Alabama
Pickwick Lake
Sardis Lake
Arkabutla Lake
Enid Lake
Grenada Lake
Ross R. Barnett Reservoir
Woodall Mt 246
Projection: Albers Equal Area
West from Greenwich
91
90
89
88
35
34
33
32
31
30
ft
m
600
200
0
0

1: 2 500 000

10 0 10 20 30 40 50 miles

10 0 20 40 60 80 km

Projection: Albers Equal Area

West from Greenwich

ft 1200 600 0

m 400 200 0

1:3 750 000

20 0 20 40 60 80 100 miles

20 0 20 40 60 80 100 120 140 160 km

Projection: Albers' Equal Area

West from Greenwich

m 4000 3000 2000 1500 1000 400

ft 12 000 9000 6000 4500 3000 1200

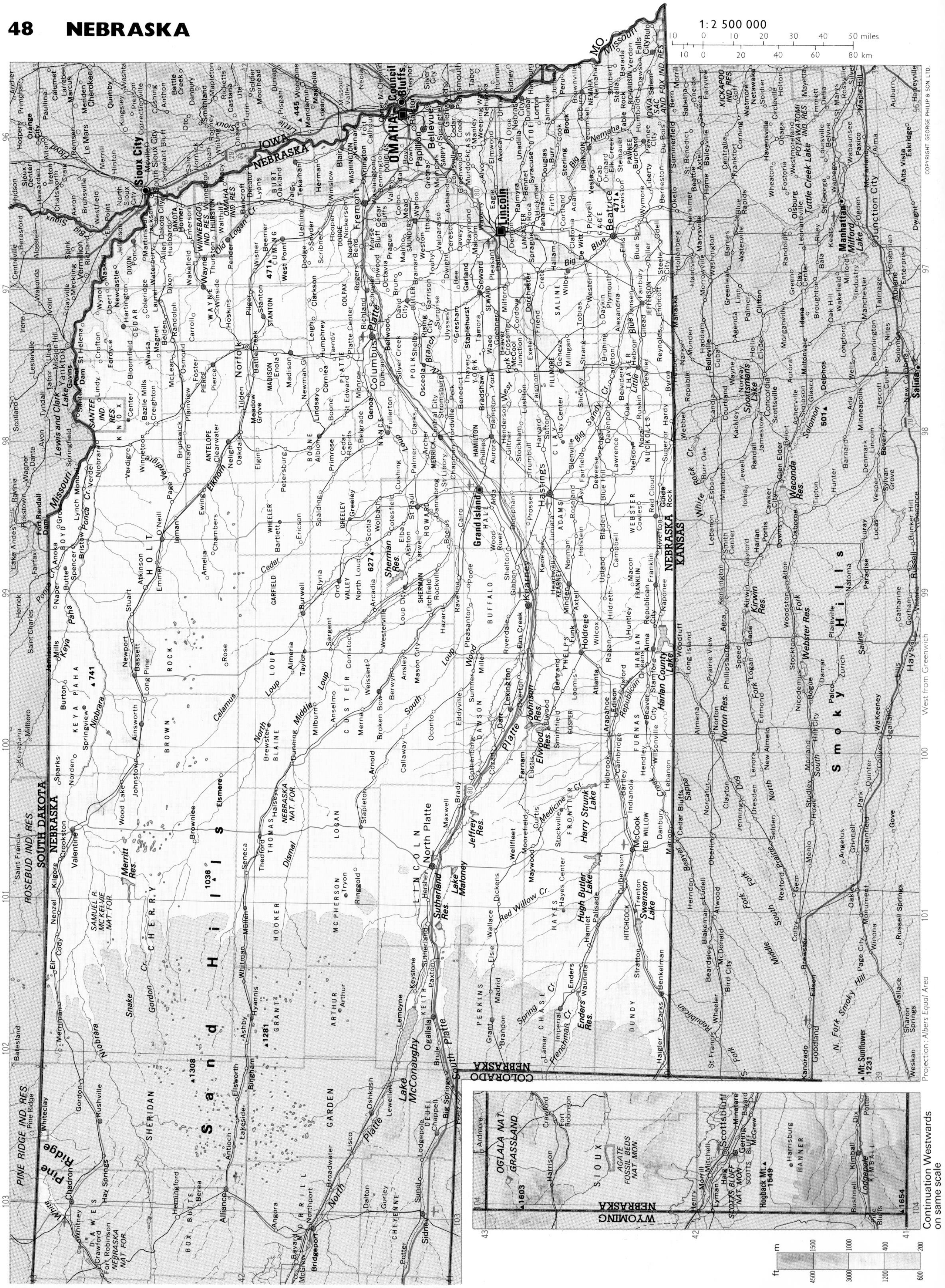

1:2 500 000

10 0 10 20 30 40 50 miles

10 0 20 40 60 80 km

Projection: Albers Equal Area

West from Greenwich

Continuation Westwards on same scale

m	ft
1500	4500
1000	3000
400	1200
200	600

1:2 500 000

10 0 10 20 30 40 50 miles
10 0 20 40 60 80 km

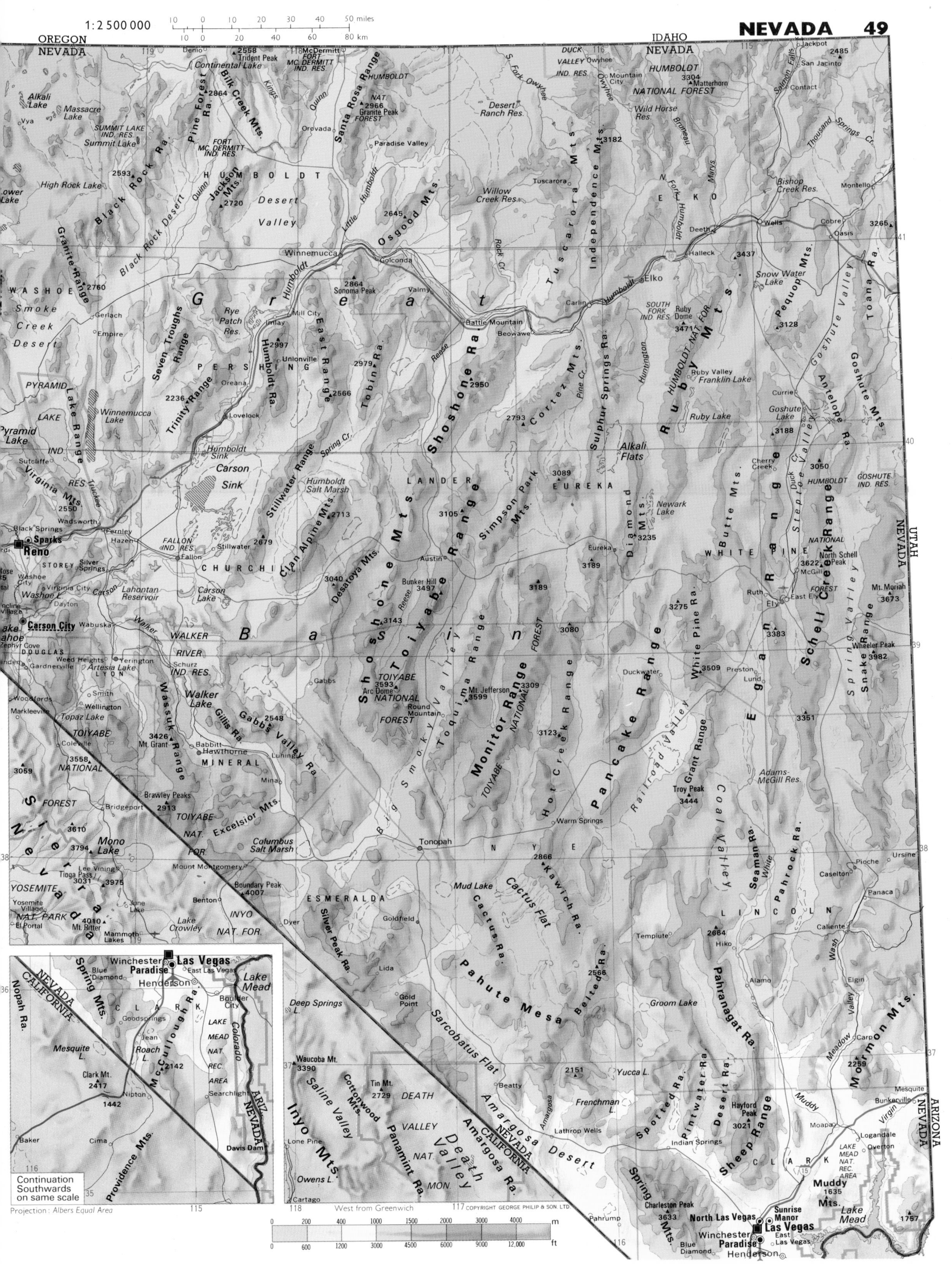
OREGON
NEVADA
IDAHO
NEVADA
UTAH
NEVADA
ARIZONA
NEVADA
Denio
2558 Trident Peak
McDermitt
FORT MC DERMITT IND. RES.
Continental Lake
Bilk Creek Mts.
Pine Forest Ra.
2864
Kings
Quinn
Santa Rosa Range
HUMBOLDT NAT. FOREST
2966 Granite Peak
Orovada
Paradise Valley
S. Fork Owyhee
DUCK VALLEY IND. RES.
Owyhee
Mountain City
HUMBOLDT NATIONAL FOREST
3304 Matterhorn
Jackpot
2485
San Jacinto
Contact
Salmon Falls
Thousand Springs Cr.
Desert Ranch Res.
Wild Horse Res.
Bruneau
Alkali Lake
Massacre Lake
Vya
SUMMIT LAKE IND. RES.
Summit Lake
FORT MC DERMITT IND. RES.
Black Rock Ra.
2593
High Rock Lake
Lower Lake
HUMBOLDT
Jackson Mts.
2720
Desert Valley
Black Rock Desert
Quinn
Little Humboldt
Osgood Mts.
2645
Independence Mts.
3182
Tuscarora Mts.
Tuscarora
Willow Creek Res.
Marys
N. Fork Humboldt
ELKO
Bishop Creek Res.
Montello
Wells
Cobre
Oasis
3265
Deeth
Halleck
3437
Snow Water Lake
Pequop Mts.
Toana Ra.
Granite Range
2760
WASHOE
Smoke Creek Desert
Winnemucca
Golconda
Humboldt
2864 Sonoma Peak
Valmy
Great
Rock Cr.
Elko
Carlin
SOUTH FORK IND. RES.
Ruby Dome 3471
HUMBOLDT NAT. FOR.
Ruby Mts.
3128
Goshute Valley
Gerlach
Empire
Seven Troughs Range
Rye Patch Res.
Imlay
Mill City
East Range
Battle Mountain
Beowawe
2997
Humboldt Ra.
Unionville
PERSHING
Tobin Ra.
2979
Reese
Shoshone Ra.
2950
Cortez Mts.
Sulphur Springs Ra.
Pine Cr.
Huntington
Ruby Valley
Franklin Lake
Currie
Antelope Ra.
Goshute Mts.
PYRAMID LAKE IND. RES.
Lake Range
Winnemucca Lake
Trinity Range
2236
Oreana
Lovelock
2566
2793
Ruby Lake
Goshute Lake
3188
Pyramid Lake
Sutcliffe
Humboldt Sink
Carson Sink
Spring Cr.
Stillwater Range
Humboldt Salt Marsh
Alkali Flats
Cherry Creek
Steptoe Valley
Duck Cr.
3050
HUMBOLDT
GOSHUTE IND. RES.
Virginia Mts.
2550
Truckee
Wadsworth
Black Springs
Sparks
Reno
Fernley
Hazen
FALLON IND. RES.
Stillwater
2679
Clan Alpine Mts.
2713
LANDER
Shoshone Mts.
3105
Toiyabe Range
Simpson Park Mts.
3089
EUREKA
Diamond Mts.
Newark Lake
Butte Mts.
3235
Egan Range
Schell Creek Range
NATIONAL FOREST
North Schell Peak
3622
McGill
STOREY
Silver Springs
Fallon
CHURCHILL
Austin
Eureka
3189
WHITE PINE
Washoe
Washoe L.
Virginia City
Carson
Lahontan Reservoir
Carson Lake
Desatoya Mts.
3040
Bunker Hill 3497
3189
Ruth
East Ely
Ely
3275
Mt. Moriah 3673
Dayton
Carson City
Wabuska
Walker
WALKER RIVER IND. RES.
3143
Basin
FOREST
3080
White Pine Ra.
3383
Spring Valley
Snake Range
Zephyr Cove
Lake Tahoe
DOUGLAS
Weed Heights
Artesia Lake
Yerington
LYON
Schurz
Gardnerville
Gabbs
TOIYABE 3593 Arc Dome NATIONAL FOREST
Round Mountain
Toquima Range
Mt. Jefferson 3599
Monitor Range
3309
Hot Creek Range
Pancake Range
Duckwater
3509
Preston
Lund
Wheeler Peak 3982
Woodfords
Markleeville
Smith
Wellington
Topaz Lake
Walker Lake
Wassuk Range
Gillis Ra.
Gabbs Valley Ra.
2548
Big Smoky Valley
TOIYABE NATIONAL
3123
Railroad Valley
Grant Range
3351
TOIYABE
Coleville
3426 Mt. Grant
Babbitt
Hawthorne
Luning
MINERAL
3558 NATIONAL
3059
Mina
Troy Peak 3444
Coal Valley
Adams-McGill Res.
Sierra Nevada
FOREST
Brawley Peaks 2913
Bridgeport
TOIYABE NAT. FOR.
Excelsior Mts.
Warm Springs
Seaman Ra.
White
Pahrock Ra.
3610
Mono Lake
3794
Columbus Salt Marsh
Tonopah
NYE
Ursine
Pioche
Lee Vining
Tioga Pass 3031
3975
Mount Montgomery
YOSEMITE NAT. PARK
Boundary Peak 4007
2866
Kawich Ra.
Mud Lake
Cactus Flat
Cactus Ra.
Caselton
Panaca
Benton
ESMERALDA
Silver Peak Ra.
Goldfield
LINCOLN
Caliente
Yosemite Village
June Lake
Lake Crowley
INYO NAT. FOR.
Dyer
El Portal
4010 Mt. Ritter
Mammoth Lakes
Tempiute
2664
Hiko
Wash
Pahranagat Ra.
Lida
Pahute Mesa
Belted Ra.
2566
Alamo
Elgin
Gold Point
Groom Lake
Valley
Mormon Mts.
Deep Springs L.
Sarcobatus Flat
Meadow
Carp
Waucoba Mt. 3390
Tin Mt. 2729
DEATH VALLEY
Saline Valley
Cottonwood Mts.
Panamint Ra.
Inyo Mts.
Beatty
2151
Yucca L.
Spotted Ra.
Pintwater Ra.
Desert Ra.
Hayford Peak 3021
Sheep Range
2259
Mesquite
Bunkerville
Virgin
Muddy
Frenchman L.
Amargosa
Lathrop Wells
Amargosa Desert
Amargosa Ra.
CALIFORNIA NEVADA
Death Valley
NAT. MON.
Indian Springs
Moapa
Logandale
Overton
LAKE MEAD NAT. REC. AREA
CLARK
Lone Pine
Owens L.
Cartago
Spring Mts.
Charleston Peak 3633
Muddy Mts. 1635
Lake Mead
1757
Pahrump
North Las Vegas
Sunrise Manor
Las Vegas
Winchester
Paradise
East Las Vegas
Blue Diamond
Henderson
Winchester
Las Vegas
Paradise
East Las Vegas
Henderson
Blue Diamond
Spring Mts.
Lake Mead
Boulder City
NEVADA CALIFORNIA
Nopah Ra.
CLARK
McCullough Ra.
Goodsprings
Jean
Roach L.
2142
LAKE MEAD NAT. REC. AREA
Colorado
Mesquite L.
Clark Mt. 2417
Nipton
1442
Searchlight
ARIZ. NEVADA
Baker
Cima
Providence Mts.
Davis Dam
Continuation Southwards on same scale
119
118
117
116
115
41
40
39
38
37
36
35
Projection: Albers Equal Area
West from Greenwich
0 200 400 1000 1500 2000 3000 4000 m
0 600 1200 3000 4500 6000 9000 12,000 ft

NEW HAMPSHIRE AND VERMONT

1:1 250 000

10 0 10 20 miles

10 0 10 20 30 km

ft	m
4500	1500
3000	1000
1200	400
600	200
0	0

Projection: *Lambert's Conformal Conic* 73 West from Greenwich 72 71

1:1 250 000

10 0 10 20 miles
10 0 10 20 30 km

NEW JERSEY
NEW YORK
PHILADELPHIA
NEWARK
ATLANTIC
OCEAN
LONG ISLAND
Long Island Sound
Delaware Bay
Pine Barrens
Kittatinny Mts.
Pocono Mts.
PENNSYLVANIA
NEW JERSEY
NEW YORK
CONNECTICUT
DELAWARE
MARYLAND
Scranton
Allentown
Bethlehem
Easton
Phillipsburg
Trenton
Camden
Wilmington
Chester
Levittown
Paterson
Clifton
Passaic
Elizabeth
Bayonne
Jersey City
Union City
Yonkers
Mt. Vernon
New Rochelle
Stamford
Bridgeport
Danbury
Norwalk
New Brunswick
Edison
Perth Amboy
Princeton
Lakewood
Asbury Park
Long Branch
Vineland
Millville
Bridgeton
Atlantic City
Ocean City
Cape May
Dover
Raritan Bay
Lower New York Bay
Barnegat Bay
Great Bay
Hudson
Delaware
Lehigh
Raritan
Mullica
Great Egg Harbor
Maurice
STATEN ISLAND
CAPE MAY
CAPE HENLOPEN
SANDY HOOK GATEWAY NAT. REC. AREA
FIRE ISLAND NAT. SEASHORE
DELAWARE WATER GAP NAT. REC. AREA
ft
m
4500
1500
3000
1000
1200
400
600
200
0
0

Projection: *Lambert's Conformal Conic* West from Greenwich

1:2 600 000

10 0 10 20 30 40 50 miles

10 0 20 40 60 80 km

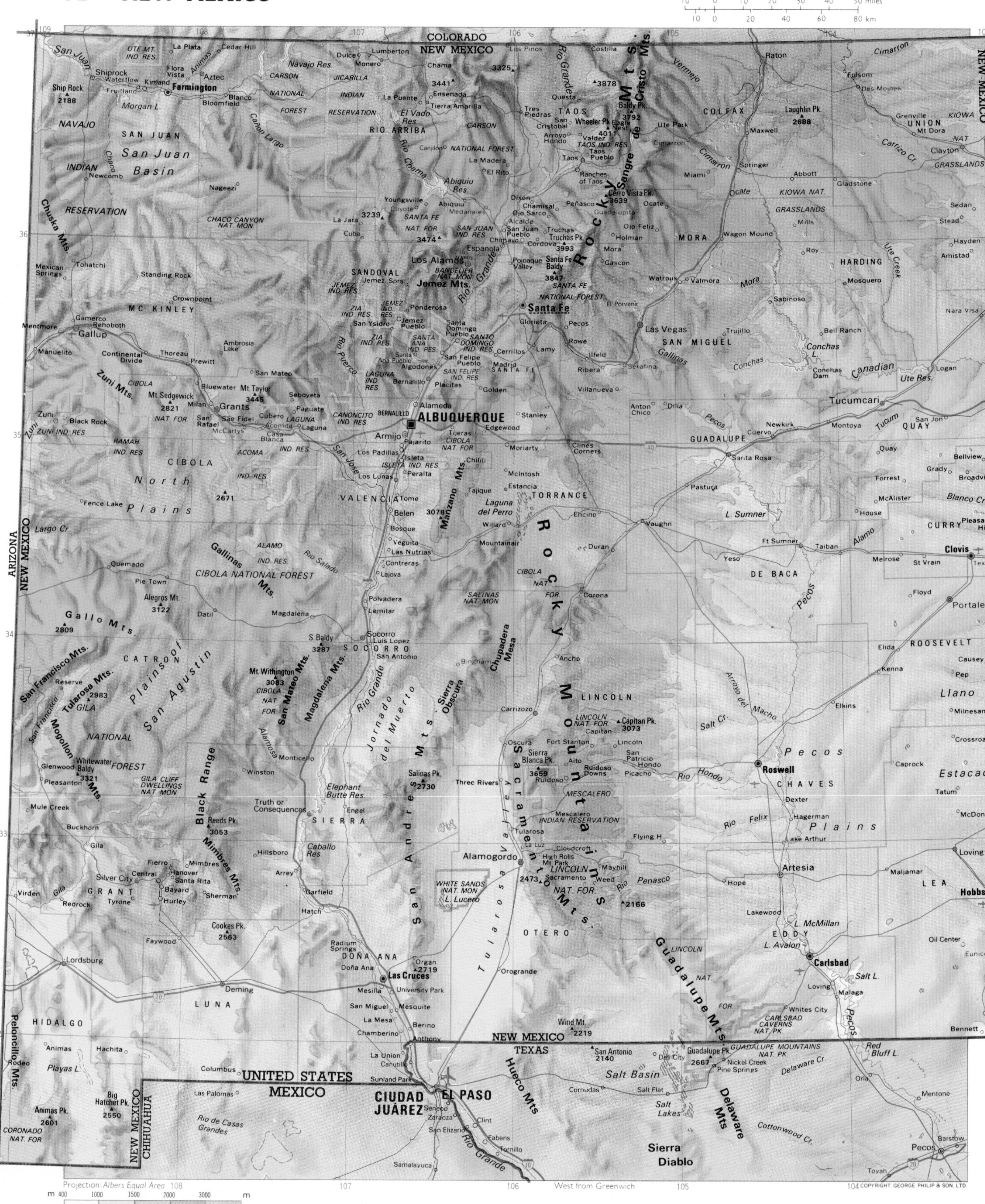

COLORADO
NEW MEXICO
ARIZONA
TEXAS
UNITED STATES
MEXICO
CHIHUAHUA
Rocky Mts.
Sangre de Cristo Mts.
Rocky Mountains
San Juan
San Juan Basin
NAVAJO INDIAN RESERVATION
UTE MT. IND. RES.
Chuska Mts.
Shiprock
Ship Rock 2188
Farmington
Aztec
Bloomfield
Kirtland
Fruitland
Waterflow
Morgan L.
La Plata
Cedar Hill
Flora Vista
Blanco
Navajo Res.
CARSON NATIONAL FOREST
JICARILLA INDIAN RESERVATION
Dulce
Lumberton
Monero
Chama
3441
Ensenada
Tierra Amarilla
La Puente
El Vado Res.
RIO ARRIBA
Los Pinos
3325
Costilla
Questa
3878
Baldy Pk. 3792
Wheeler Pk.
4011
Valdez
TAOS IND. RES.
Taos
Taos Pueblo
Ranches of Taos
Tres Piedras
San Cristobal
Arroyo Hondo
Rio Grande
Vermejo
Raton
Cimarron
Folsom
Des Moines
COLFAX
Laughlin Pk. 2688
Ute Park
Maxwell
Springer
Miami
Grenville
UNION
Mt Dora
KIOWA NAT. GRASSLANDS
Clayton
Carrizo Cr.
Abbott
Gladstone
Sedan
Stead
Hayden
Amistad
Mills
Roy
HARDING
Mosquero
Ute Creek
MORA
Wagon Mound
Ocate
Cerro Vista Pk. 3639
Peñasco
Guadalupita
Ojo Feliz
Holman
Truchas Pk. 3993
Truchas
Cordova
Chimayo
Espanola
Dixon
Chamisal
Ojo Sarco
Alcalde
San Juan Pueblo
SAN JUAN IND. RES.
Canjilon
La Madera
El Rito
Abiquiu Res.
Abiquiu
Medanales
Youngsville
Coyote
SANTA FE NAT. FOR.
3239
3474
La Jara
Cuba
Canon Largo
Nageezi
Chaco
Newcomb
CHACO CANYON NAT. MON.
Tohatchi
Mexican Springs
Standing Rock
Crownpoint
MC KINLEY
Gamerco
Rehoboth
Mentmore
Gallup
Manuelito
Continental Divide
Thoreau
Prewitt
Ambrosia Lake
San Mateo
Los Alamos
BANDELIER NAT. MON.
Jemez Mts.
SANDOVAL
Jemez Sprs.
JEMEZ IND. RES.
ZIA IND. RES.
San Ysidro
Ponderosa
Jemez Pueblo
Santa Domingo Pueblo
SANTO DOMINGO IND. RES.
SANTA ANA IND. RES.
San Felipe Pueblo
SAN FELIPE IND. RES.
Algodones
Bernalillo
Placitas
Cerrillos
Madrid
Lamy
Golden
Pojoaque Valley
Santa Fe Baldy 3847
SANTA FE NATIONAL FOREST
Santa Fe
Glorieta
Pecos
Rowe
Ilfeld
Ribera
Serafina
Villanueva
El Porvenir
Gascon
Mora
Watrous
Valmora
Sabinoso
Las Vegas
Trujillo
SAN MIGUEL
Gallinas
Bell Ranch
Conchas L.
Conchas Dam
Canadian
Nara Visa
Logan
Ute Res.
Tucumcari
San Jon
QUAY
Montoya
Tucum
Newkirk
Cuervo
GUADALUPE
Santa Rosa
Pastura
Anton Chico
Dilia
Pecos
Bellview
Grady
Broadview
Forrest
McAlister
Blanco Cr.
House
CURRY
Pleasant Hill
Clovis
Texico
Melrose
St Vrain
Taiban
Alamo
Ft Sumner
Yeso
DE BACA
L. Sumner
Vaughn
Encino
Duran
Corona
Floyd
Portales
ROOSEVELT
Elida
Kenna
Causey
Pep
Llano
Milnesand
Elkins
Arroyo del Macho
Crossroads
Caprock
Estacado
Tatum
McDonald
Lovington
Hobbs
LEA
Maljamar
Roswell
CHAVES
Pecos Plains
Dexter
Hagerman
Lake Arthur
Artesia
Hope
Lakewood
EDDY
L. McMillan
L. Avalon
Carlsbad
Oil Center
Eunice
Salt L.
Loving
Malaga
Whites City
CARLSBAD CAVERNS NAT. PK.
Bennett
Red Bluff L.
Orla
Mentone
Barstow
Pecos
Toyah
Delaware Cr.
Delaware Mts
Cottonwood Cr.
Guadalupe Pk. 2667
GUADALUPE MOUNTAINS NAT. PK.
Nickel Creek
Pine Springs
Dell City
Salt Basin
Salt Flat
Salt Lakes
Sierra Diablo
Cornudas
Hueco Mts
San Antonio 2140
Guadalupe Mts.
LINCOLN NAT. FOR.
Wind Mt. 2219
2166
Rio Penasco
Mayhill
Weed
Sacramento
Sacramento Mts.
Cloudcroft
High Rolls
Mt Park
2473
Alamogordo
OTERO
Orogrande
Tularosa
Tularosa Valley
Mescalero
MESCALERO INDIAN RESERVATION
Ruidoso
Ruidoso Downs
Alto
Sierra Blanca Pk. 3659
Hondo
San Patricio
Picacho
Rio Hondo
Lincoln
Capitan Pk. 3073
Capitan
Fort Stanton
Oscura
Carrizozo
LINCOLN
Ancho
Three Rivers
Flying H
Rio Felix
Salt Cr.
Chupadera Mesa
Bingham
Sierra Oscura
San Andres Mts.
Salinas Pk. 2730
WHITE SANDS NAT. MON.
L. Lucero
Jornado del Muerto
Elephant Butte Res.
Engel
Truth or Consequences
SIERRA
Caballo Res.
Hillsboro
Arrey
Garfield
Hatch
Radium Springs
DOÑA ANA
Doña Ana
Organ
2719
Las Cruces
Mesilla
University Park
San Miguel
Mesquite
La Mesa
Berino
Chamberino
Anthony
La Union
Canutillo
Sunland Park
CIUDAD JUÁREZ
EL PASO
Senecú
Zaragoza
San Elizario
Clint
Fabens
Tornillo
Samalayuca
Rio Grande
Las Palomas
Rio de Casas Grandes
Columbus
Deming
LUNA
Lordsburg
HIDALGO
Animas
Hachita
Playas L.
Rodeo
Peloncillo Mts.
Big Hatchet Pk. 2550
Animas Pk. 2601
CORONADO NAT. FOR.
Faywood
Cookes Pk. 2563
Silver City
Central
Hanover
Fierro
Santa Rita
Bayard
Hurley
Sherman
Mimbres
Mimbres Mts.
Tyrone
GRANT
Gila
Virden
Redrock
Buckhorn
Mule Creek
Reeds Pk. 3053
Black Range
GILA CLIFF DWELLINGS NAT. MON.
GILA NATIONAL FOREST
Winston
Monticello
Glenwood
Pleasanton
Whitewater Baldy 3321
Mogollon Mts.
San Francisco Mts.
Tularosa Mts.
2983
Reserve
San Francisco
CATRON
Plains of San Agustin
Mt. Withington 3083
CIBOLA NAT. FOR.
San Mateo Mts.
Magdalena Mts.
Rio Grande
Alamosa
S. Baldy 3287
SOCORRO
Socorro
Luis Lopez
San Antonio
Magdalena
Datil
Gallo Mts.
2809
Alegros Mt. 3122
Pie Town
Quemado
Gallinas Mts.
CIBOLA NATIONAL FOREST
ALAMO IND. RES.
Rio Salado
Largo Cr.
Fence Lake
North Plains
2671
CIBOLA
RAMAH IND. RES.
Zuni
ZUNI IND. RES.
Zuni Mts.
Black Rock
Mt. Sedgewick 2821
CIBOLA NAT. FOR.
Bluewater
Mt. Taylor 3445
Milan
Grants
San Rafael
San Fidel
McCartys
Cubero
Seboyeta
Paguate
LAGUNA
Laguna
Acomita
Casa Blanca
ACOMA IND. RES.
LAGUNA IND. RES.
CANONCITO IND. RES.
BERNALILLO
ALBUQUERQUE
Alameda
Armijo
Pajarito
Los Padillas
Isleta
ISLETA IND. RES.
Peralta
Los Lunas
VALENCIA
Tome
Belen
Bosque
Veguita
Las Nutrias
Contreras
Lajoya
Polvadera
Lemitar
Rio Puerco
Rio San Jose
Tijeras
CIBOLA NAT. FOR.
Edgewood
Stanley
Moriarty
Chilili
Manzano Mts.
3078
Tajique
Estancia
McIntosh
Clines Corners
TORRANCE
Laguna del Perro
Willard
Mountainair
SALINAS NAT. MON.
CIBOLA NAT. FOR.

Projection: Albers Equal Area

West from Greenwich

COPYRIGHT GEORGE PHILIP & SON, LTD.

m	400	1000	1500	2000	3000	m
ft	1200	3000	4500	6000	9000	ft

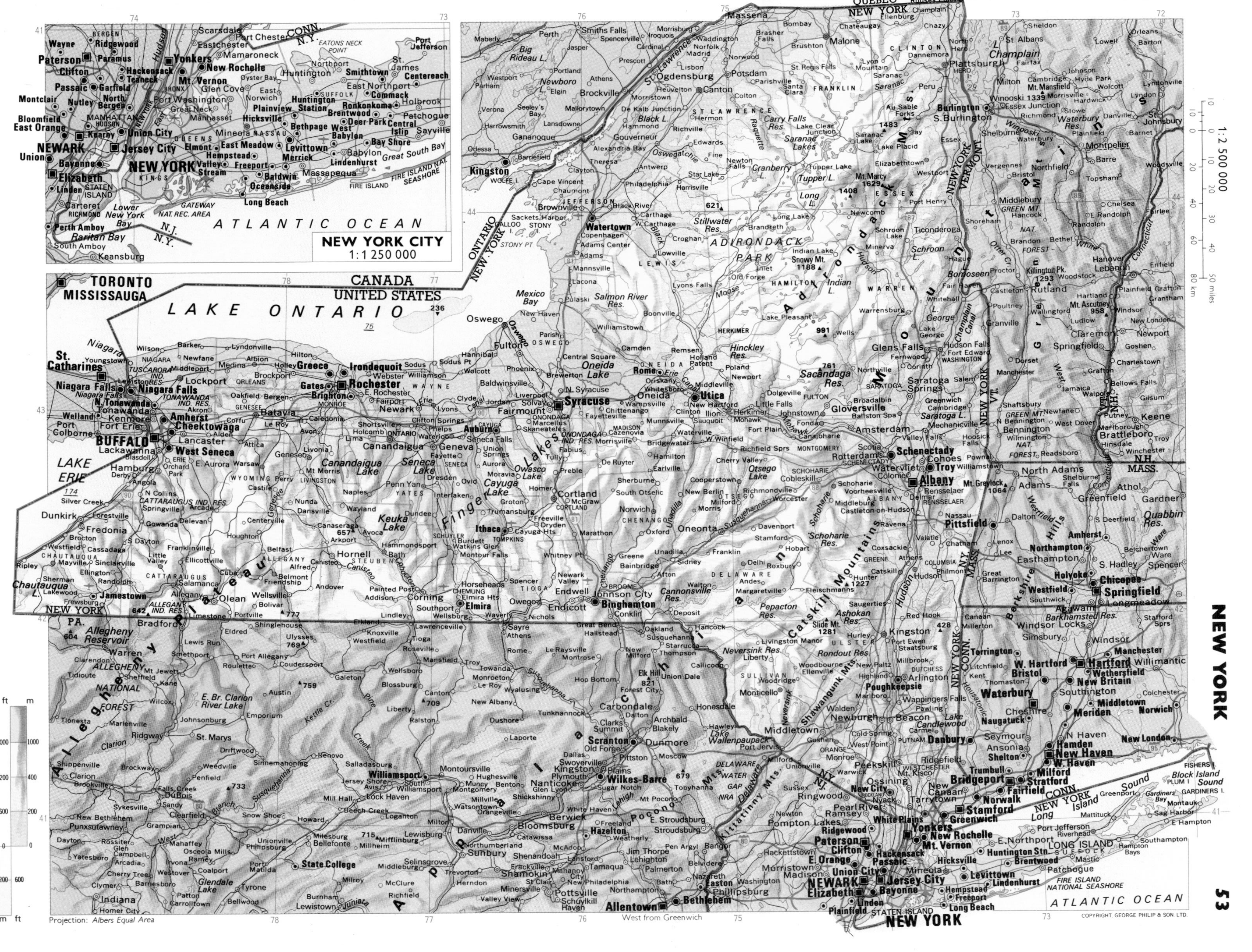
1:2 500 000
10 0 10 20 30 40 50 miles
10 0 20 40 60 80 km
NEW YORK CITY
1:1 250 000
ATLANTIC OCEAN
LAKE ONTARIO
LAKE ERIE
CANADA
UNITED STATES
QUEBEC
NEW YORK
VERMONT
ONTARIO
Adirondack Mts.
Catskill Mountains
Finger Lakes
Allegheny Mts.
Pocono Mts.
Berkshire Hills
Green Mts.
TORONTO
MISSISSAUGA
BUFFALO
Rochester
Syracuse
Albany
NEWARK
Projection: Albers Equal Area
West from Greenwich
COPYRIGHT GEORGE PHILIP & SON LTD.

1: 2 500 000

10 0 10 20 30 40 50 miles

10 0 20 40 60 80 km

Projection: Albers Equal Area

Continuation Westward on same scale

West from Greenwich

m 1500 1000 400 200 0

ft 4500 3000 1200 600 0

m 200 600 2000 6000 ft

1:2 500 000

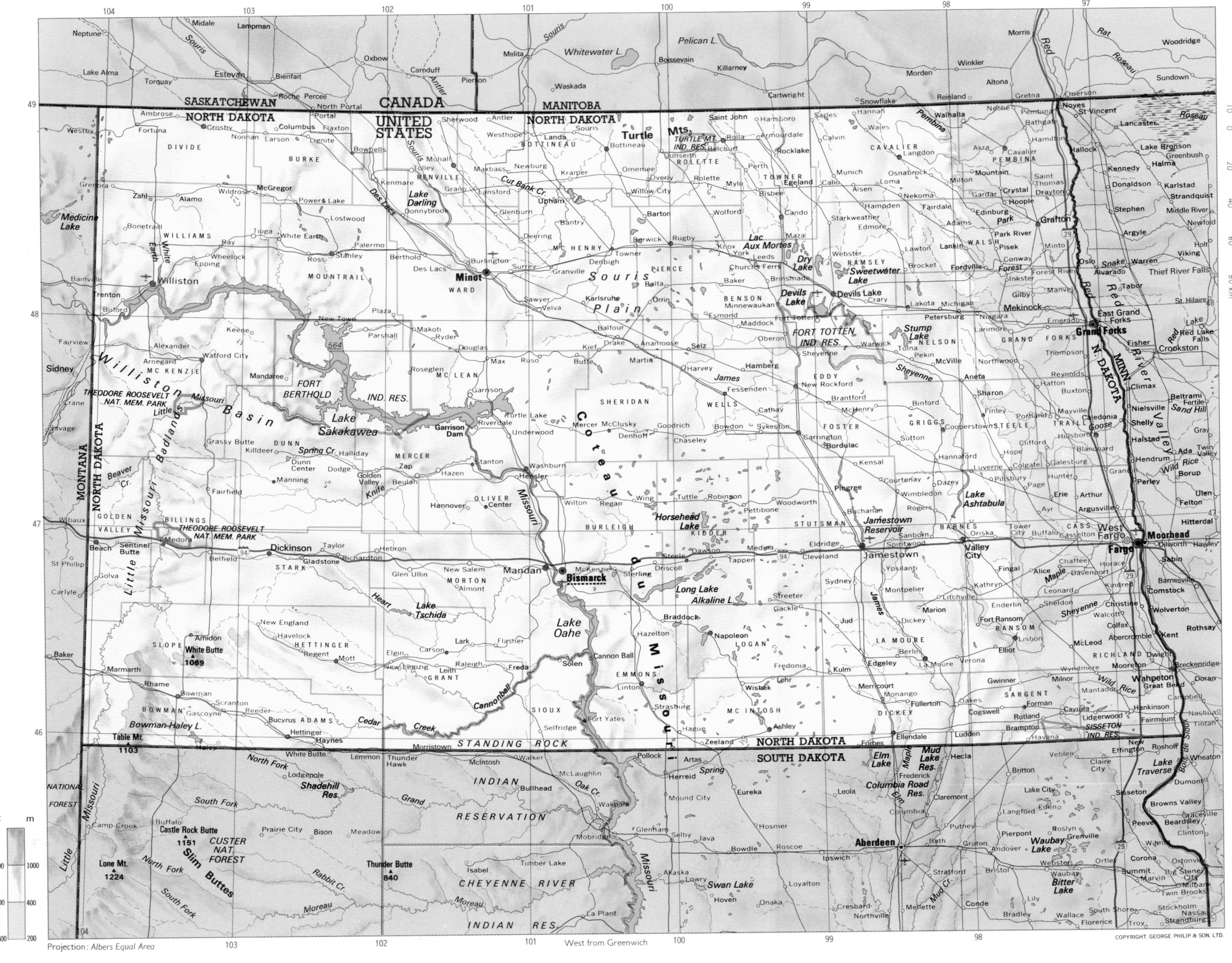
10 0 10 20 30 40 50 miles
10 0 20 40 60 80 km
CANADA
UNITED STATES
SASKATCHEWAN
MANITOBA
NORTH DAKOTA
SOUTH DAKOTA
MONTANA
MINN.
N. DAKOTA
Bismarck
Fargo
Moorhead
West Fargo
Grand Forks
East Grand Forks
Minot
Jamestown
Dickinson
Williston
Mandan
Devils Lake
Valley City
Aberdeen
Lake Sakakawea
Lake Oahe
Garrison Dam
Missouri
Red River Valley
James
Sheyenne
Souris Plain
Coteau du Missouri
Williston Basin
Turtle Mts.
FORT BERTHOLD IND. RES.
TURTLE MT. IND. RES.
FORT TOTTEN IND. RES.
SISSETON IND. RES.
STANDING ROCK INDIAN RESERVATION
CHEYENNE RIVER INDIAN RES.
THEODORE ROOSEVELT NAT. MEM. PARK
CUSTER NAT. FOREST
NATIONAL FOREST
White Butte 1069
Table Mt. 1103
Thunder Butte 840
Castle Rock Butte 1151
Lone Mt. 1224
Slim Buttes
West from Greenwich
Projection: Albers Equal Area
COPYRIGHT. GEORGE PHILIP & SON. LTD.
ft 3000 1200 600
m 1000 400 200

1:2 500 000

10 0 10 20 30 40 50 miles
10 0 20 40 60 80 km
LAKE ERIE
CANADA
UNITED STATES
ONTARIO
OHIO
MICHIGAN
INDIANA
KENTUCKY
PA.
W.VA.
DETROIT
TOLEDO
CLEVELAND
COLUMBUS
CINCINNATI
PITTSBURGH
Lansing
East Lansing
Ann Arbor
Windsor
Akron
Canton
Youngstown
Dayton
Springfield
Mansfield
Lima
Ft. Wayne
Zanesville
Lexington
Frankfort
Charleston
Huntington
Erie
Lake St. Clair
Long Point Bay
PELEE I.
KELLEYS ISLAND
PT. PELEE
Ohio
85
84
83
82
81
80
42
41
40
39
38
ft
m
3000
1000
1200
400
600
200
0
Projection: Albers Equal Area
West from Greenwich
COPYRIGHT, GEORGE PHILIP & SON, LTD.

1:2 500 000

10 0 10 20 30 40 50 miles

10 0 20 40 60 80 km

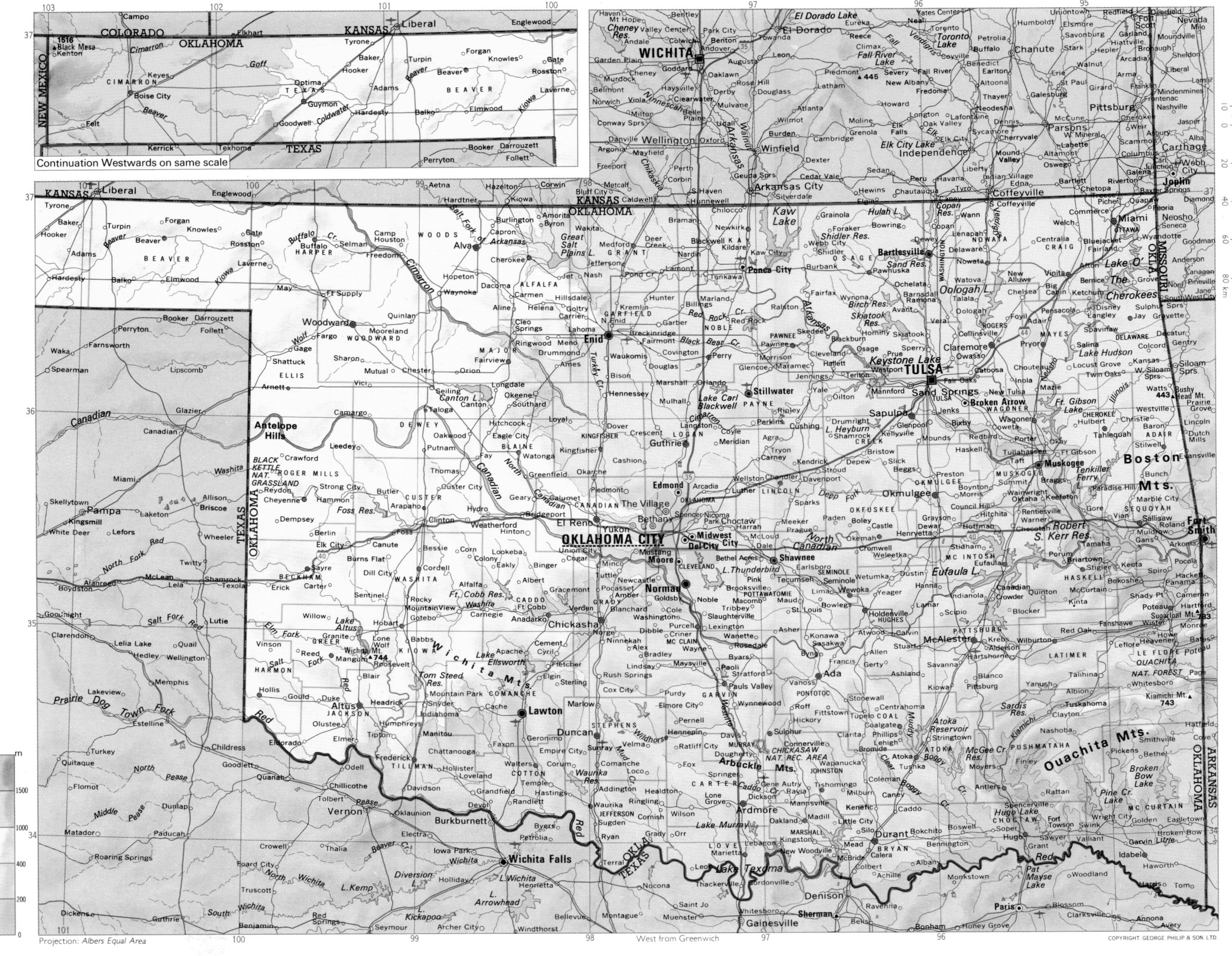
OKLAHOMA
KANSAS
MISSOURI
ARKANSAS
TEXAS
NEW MEXICO
COLORADO
OKLAHOMA CITY
TULSA
WICHITA
Wichita Falls
Lawton
Norman
Enid
Muskogee
Fort Smith
Ouachita Mts.
Boston Mts.
Wichita Mts.
Arbuckle Mts.
Red
Canadian
Cimarron
Arkansas
Lake Texoma
Eufaula L.
Continuation Westwards on same scale
West from Greenwich
Projection: Albers Equal Area
ft 4500 3000 1200 600 0
m 1500 1000 400 200 0

1:2 500 000
10 0 10 20 30 40 50 miles
10 0 20 40 60 80 km
IDAHO
OREGON
WASHINGTON
NEVADA
CALIFORNIA
PACIFIC OCEAN
PORTLAND
Salem
Eugene
Medford
Bend
Columbia Plateau
Great Sandy Desert
Harney Basin
Cascade Range
Coast Ranges
Blue Mts.
Wallowa Mts.
Owyhee Mts.
Steens Mountain
Alvord Desert
Catlow Valley
Klamath Mts.
Siskiyou Mts.
Projection: Albers Equal Area
West from Greenwich
COPYRIGHT GEORGE PHILIP & SON LTD.

See page 42 for Rhode Island

1:2 500 000

10 0 10 20 30 40 50 miles

10 0 20 40 60 80 km

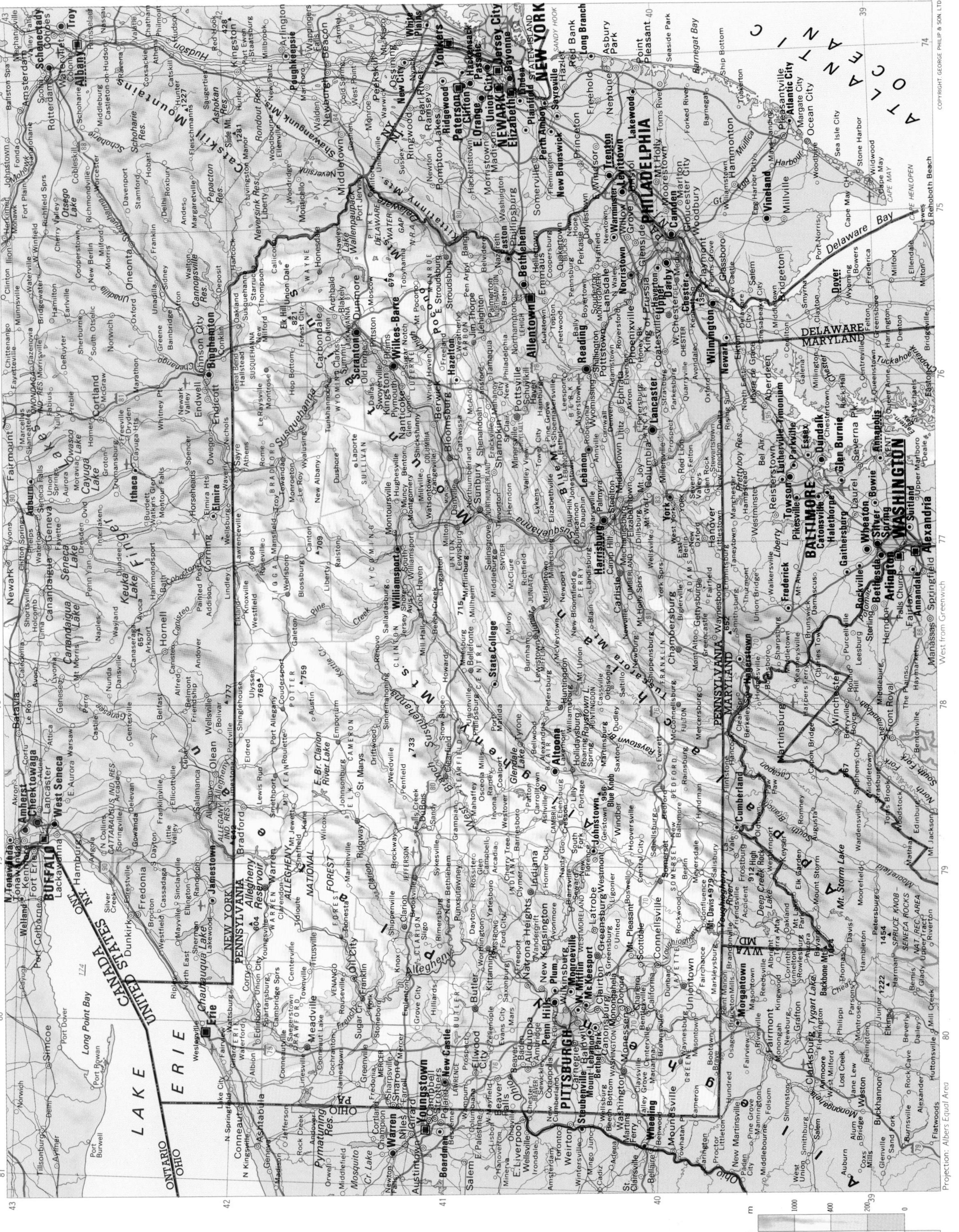

PENNSYLVANIA
NEW YORK
PHILADELPHIA
PITTSBURGH
BALTIMORE
WASHINGTON
DELAWARE
MARYLAND
LAKE ERIE
CANADA
UNITED STATES
ONTARIO
OHIO
ATLANTIC OCEAN
Delaware Bay
Catskill Mountains
Finger Lakes
Allegheny Mountains
Blue Mts.
Harrisburg
Allentown
Scranton
Wilkes-Barre
Erie
Buffalo
Albany
Trenton
Wilmington
Lancaster
Reading
Altoona
Johnstown
Williamsport
State College
Youngstown
Binghamton
Elmira
Ithaca
Susquehanna
West from Greenwich
Projection: Albers Equal Area
COPYRIGHT GEORGE PHILIP & SON LTD.
ft
3000
1200
600
0
m
1000
400
200
0

1:2 500 000

10 0 10 20 30 40 50 miles

10 0 20 40 60 80 km

ATLANTIC OCEAN

West from Greenwich

Projection: Albers Equal Area

m	ft
1500	4500
1000	3000
400	1200
200	600
0	0
200	600

1:2 500 000

10 0 10 20 30 40 50 miles

10 0 20 40 60 80 km

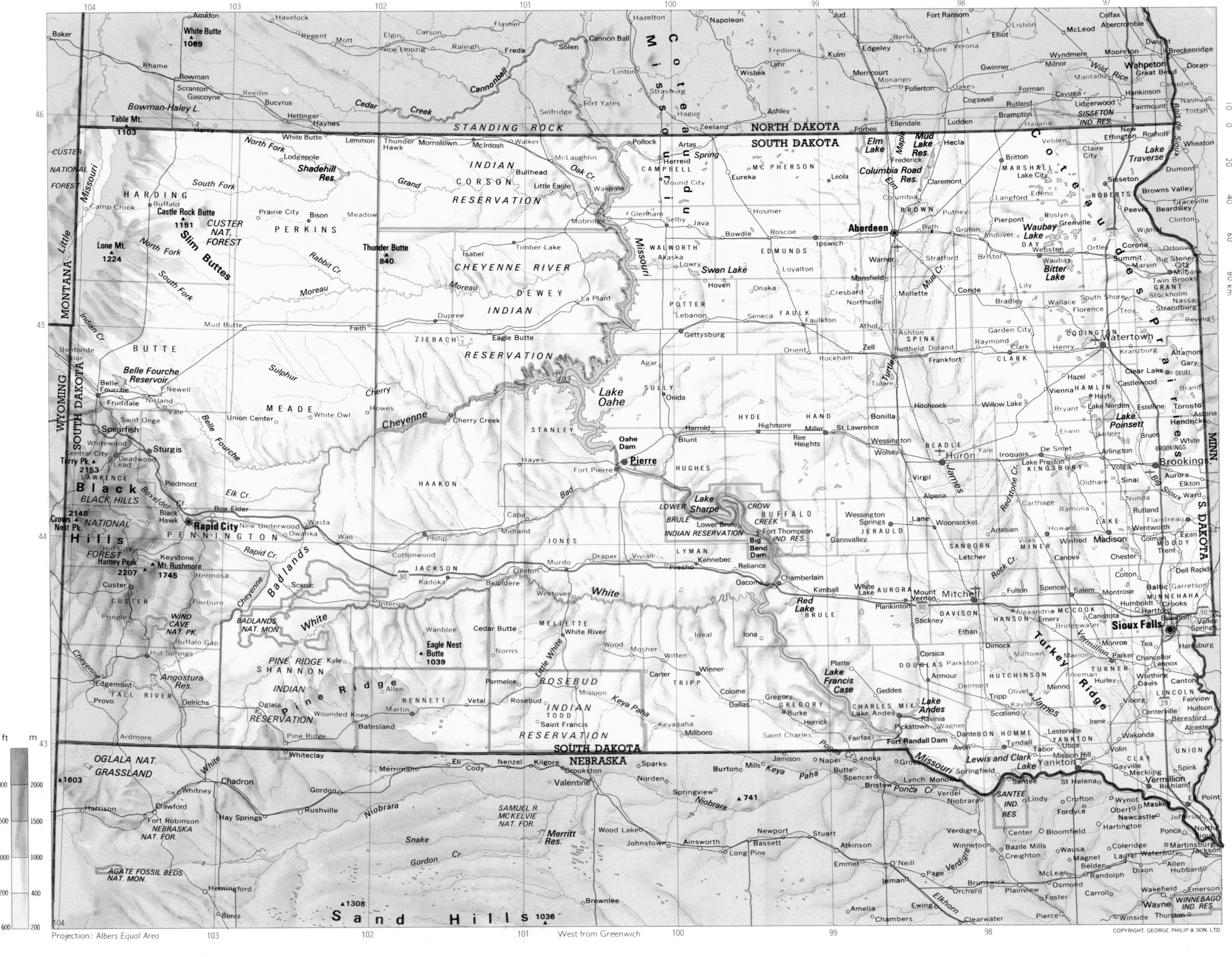
NORTH DAKOTA
SOUTH DAKOTA
MINN.
S. DAKOTA
NEBRASKA
WYOMING
MONTANA
Pierre
Aberdeen
Sioux Falls
Rapid City
Watertown
Brookings
Huron
Mitchell
Yankton
Vermillion
Lake Oahe
Missouri
Lake Francis Case
Lewis and Clark Lake
Black Hills
Badlands
BADLANDS NAT. MON.
STANDING ROCK
CHEYENNE RIVER
PINE RIDGE
ROSEBUD
Coteau des Prairies
Coteau du Missouri
Sand Hills
Projection: Albers Equal Area
West from Greenwich
ft m

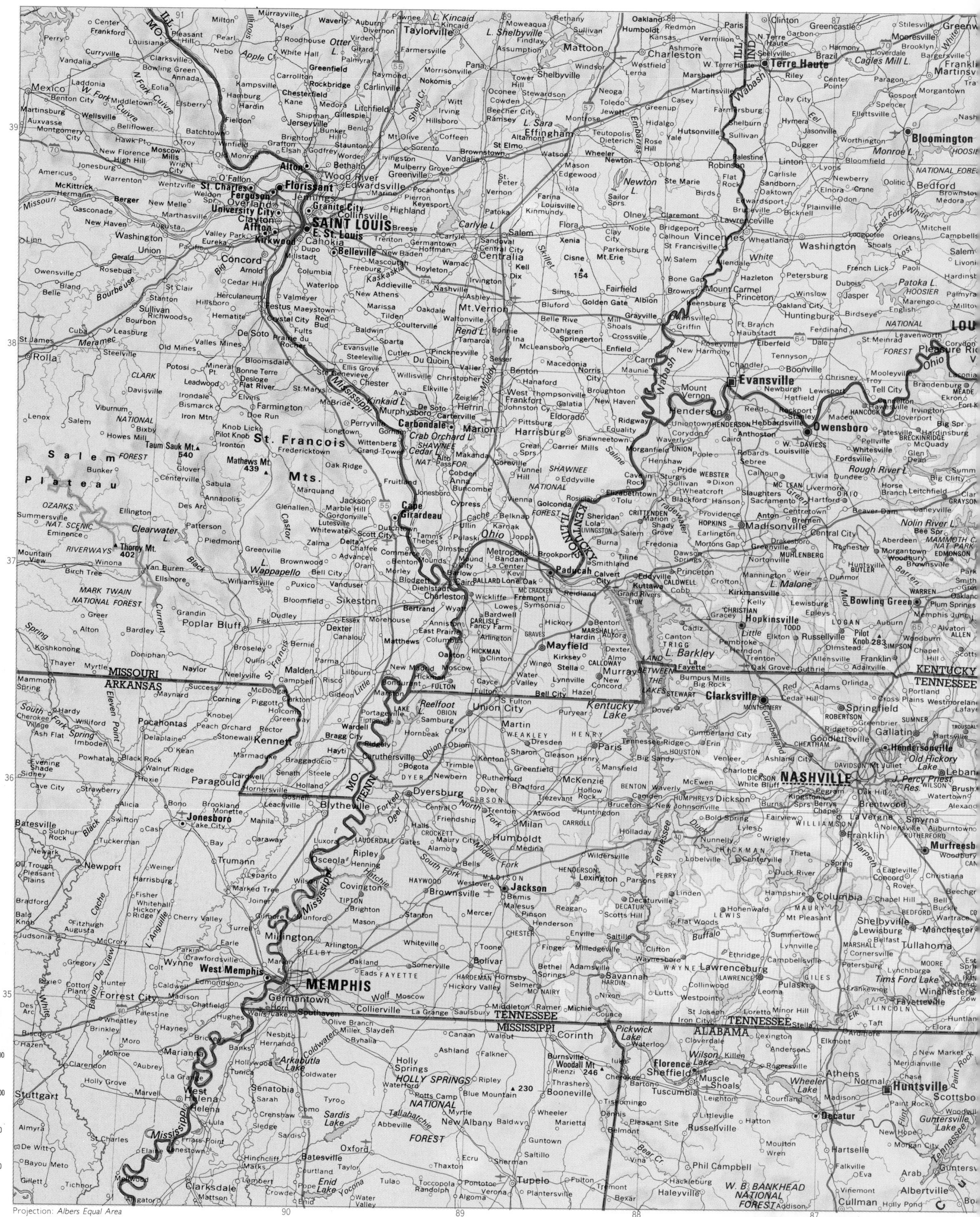
SAINT LOUIS
MEMPHIS
NASHVILLE
Evansville
Terre Haute
Bloomington
Owensboro
Paducah
Clarksville
Huntsville
Jackson
Cape Girardeau
West Memphis
MISSOURI
ARKANSAS
TENNESSEE
MISSISSIPPI
ALABAMA
KENTUCKY
St. Francois Mts.
Salem Plateau
Mississippi
Ohio
Wabash
Tennessee
Cumberland
Kentucky Lake
L. Barkley
Reelfoot L.
MARK TWAIN NATIONAL FOREST
SHAWNEE NATIONAL FOREST
HOLLY SPRINGS NATIONAL FOREST
W. B. BANKHEAD NATIONAL FOREST
LAND BETWEEN THE LAKES
Taum Sauk Mt. 540
Woodall Mt 246
ft
m
4500
1500
3000
1000
1200
400
600
200
0
0
91
90
89
88
87
39
38
37
36
35
Projection: Albers Equal Area

1:2 500 000

10 0 10 20 30 40 50 miles

10 0 20 40 60 80 km

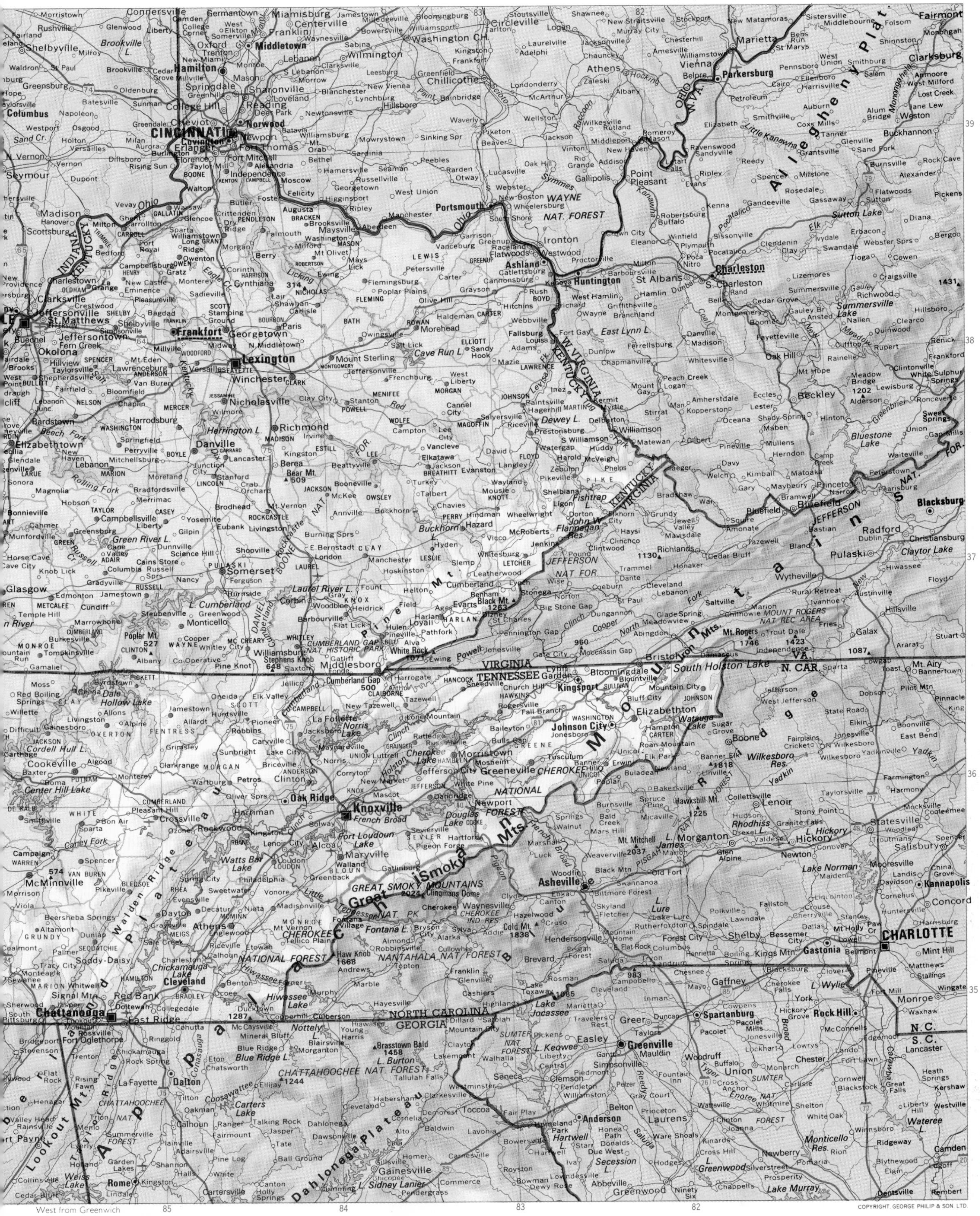

West from Greenwich 85 84 83 82

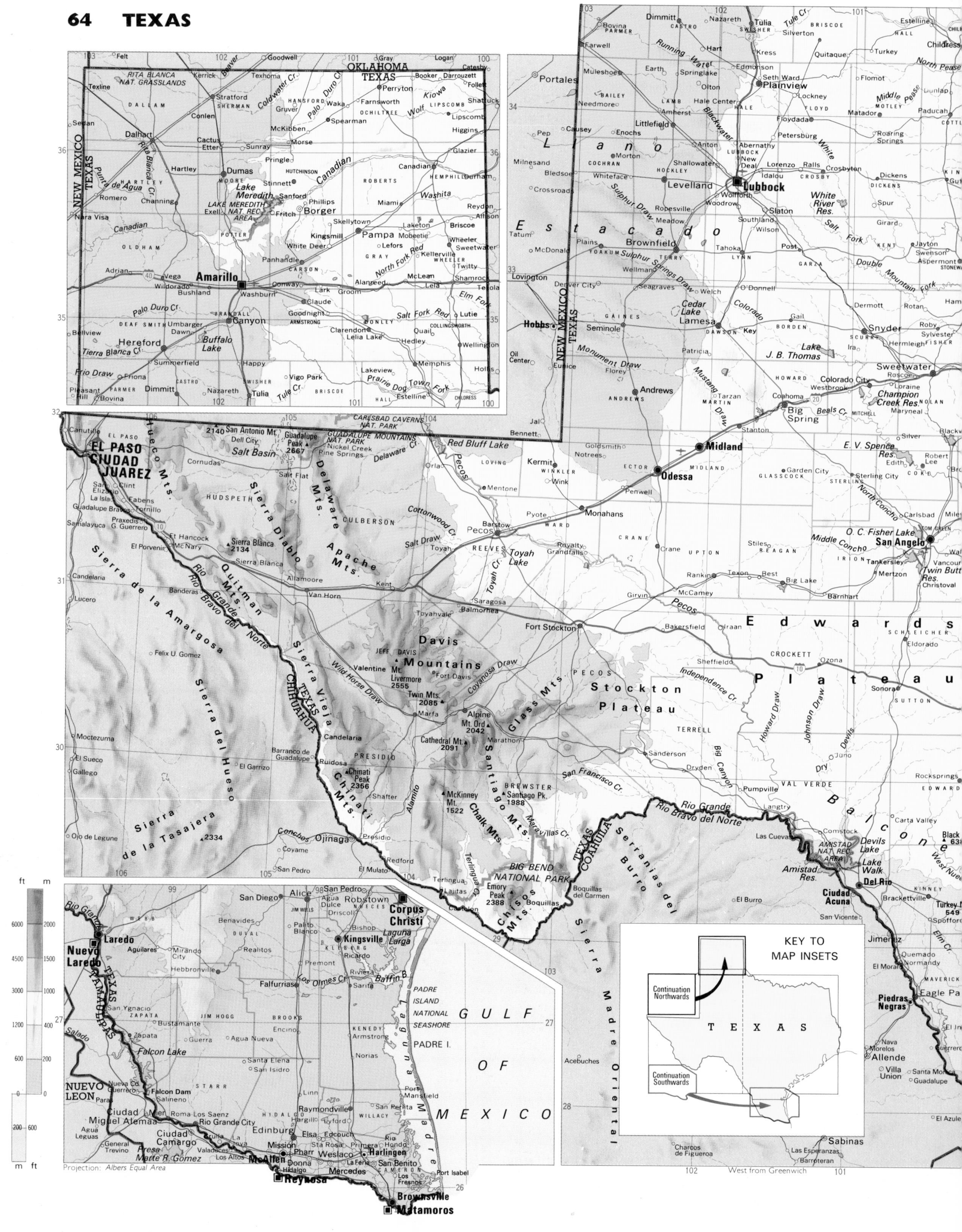

NEW MEXICO
TEXAS
OKLAHOMA
Amarillo
Lubbock
Midland
Odessa
El Paso
Ciudad Juarez
San Angelo
Del Rio
Corpus Christi
Laredo
Nuevo Laredo
Brownsville
Matamoros
McAllen
Reynosa
Llano Estacado
Edwards Plateau
Stockton Plateau
Davis Mountains
Sierra Madre Oriental
Big Bend National Park
GULF OF MEXICO
Padre Island National Seashore
KEY TO MAP INSETS
Continuation Northwards
Continuation Southwards
Projection: Albers Equal Area
West from Greenwich

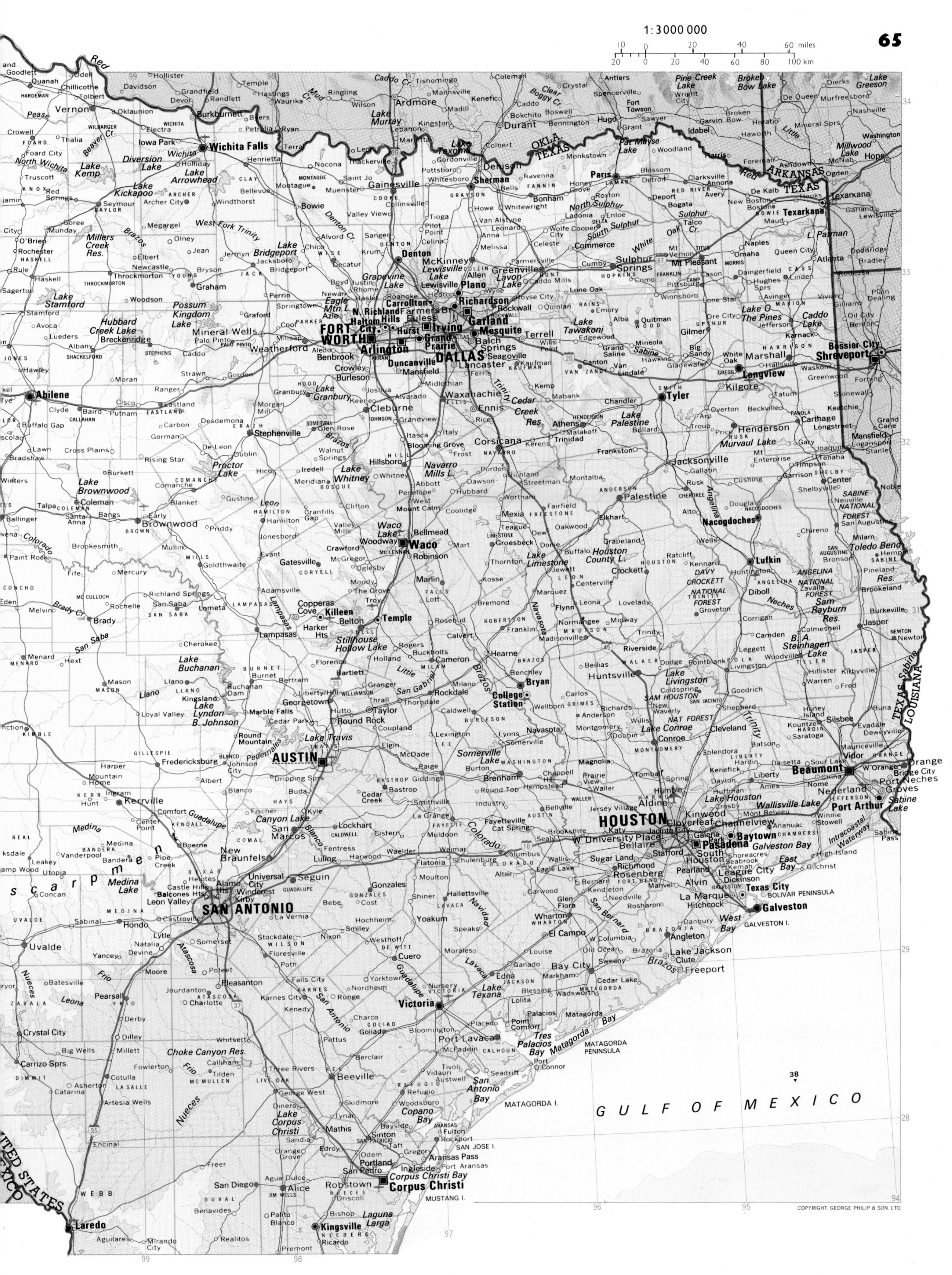
1:3 000 000
10 0 20 40 60 miles
20 0 20 40 60 80 100 km
Wichita Falls
Abilene
Denton
FORT WORTH
Arlington
DALLAS
Garland
Irving
Mesquite
Richardson
Plano
Tyler
Longview
Shreveport
Texarkana
Waco
Temple
Killeen
Bryan
College Station
Lufkin
Nacogdoches
AUSTIN
SAN ANTONIO
HOUSTON
Pasadena
Baytown
Beaumont
Port Arthur
Galveston
Victoria
Corpus Christi
Laredo
Kingsville
GULF OF MEXICO
OKLA.
TEXAS
ARKANSAS
LOUISIANA
UNITED STATES
MEXICO
Red
Brazos
Trinity
Colorado
Sabine
Galveston Bay
Matagorda Bay
Lake Texoma
COPYRIGHT, GEORGE PHILIP & SON, LTD

1:2 500 000

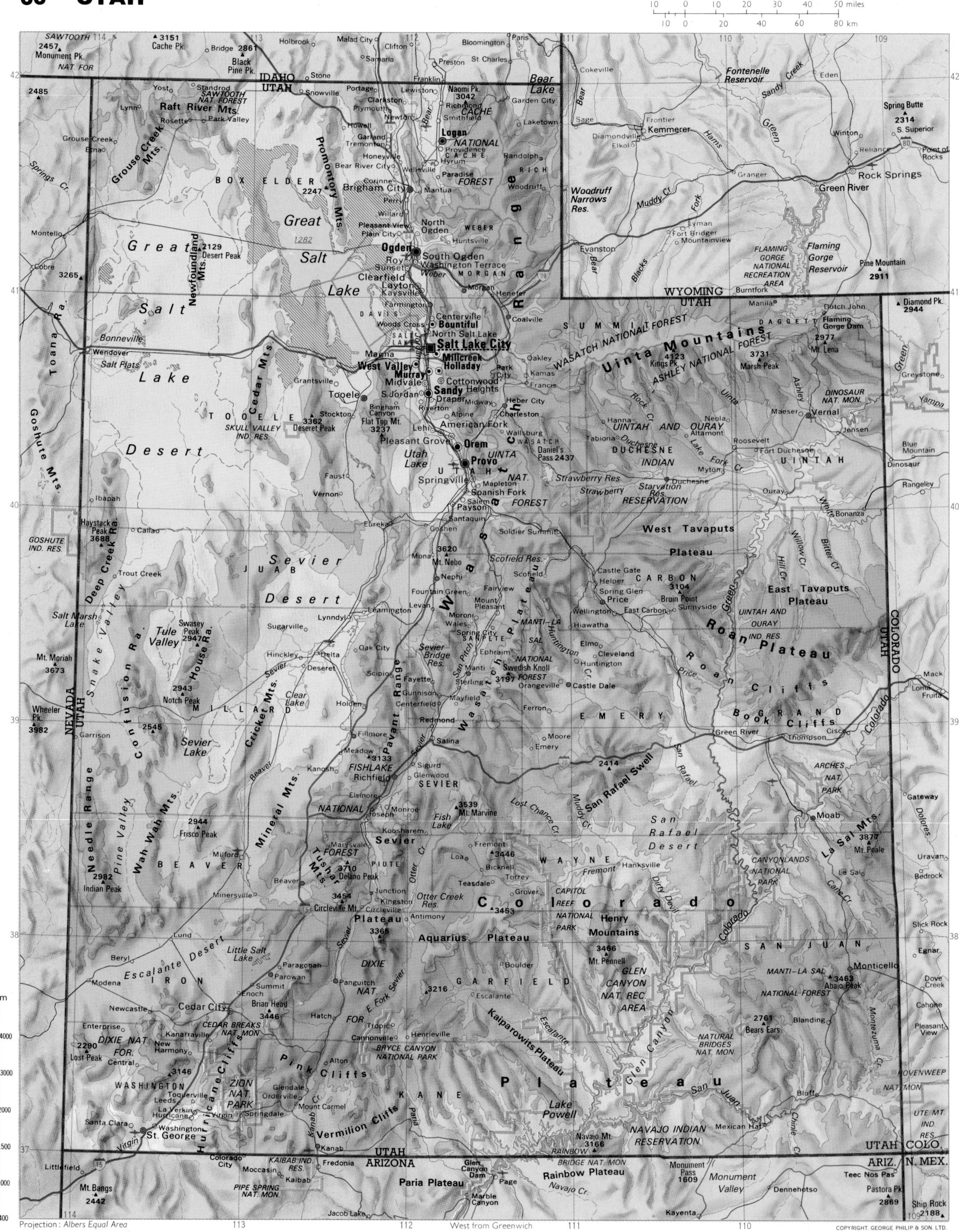

Projection: Albers Equal Area

West from Greenwich

See page 68 for Virginia and page 50 for Vermont

1:2 500 000

10 0 10 20 30 40 50 miles

10 0 20 40 60 80 km

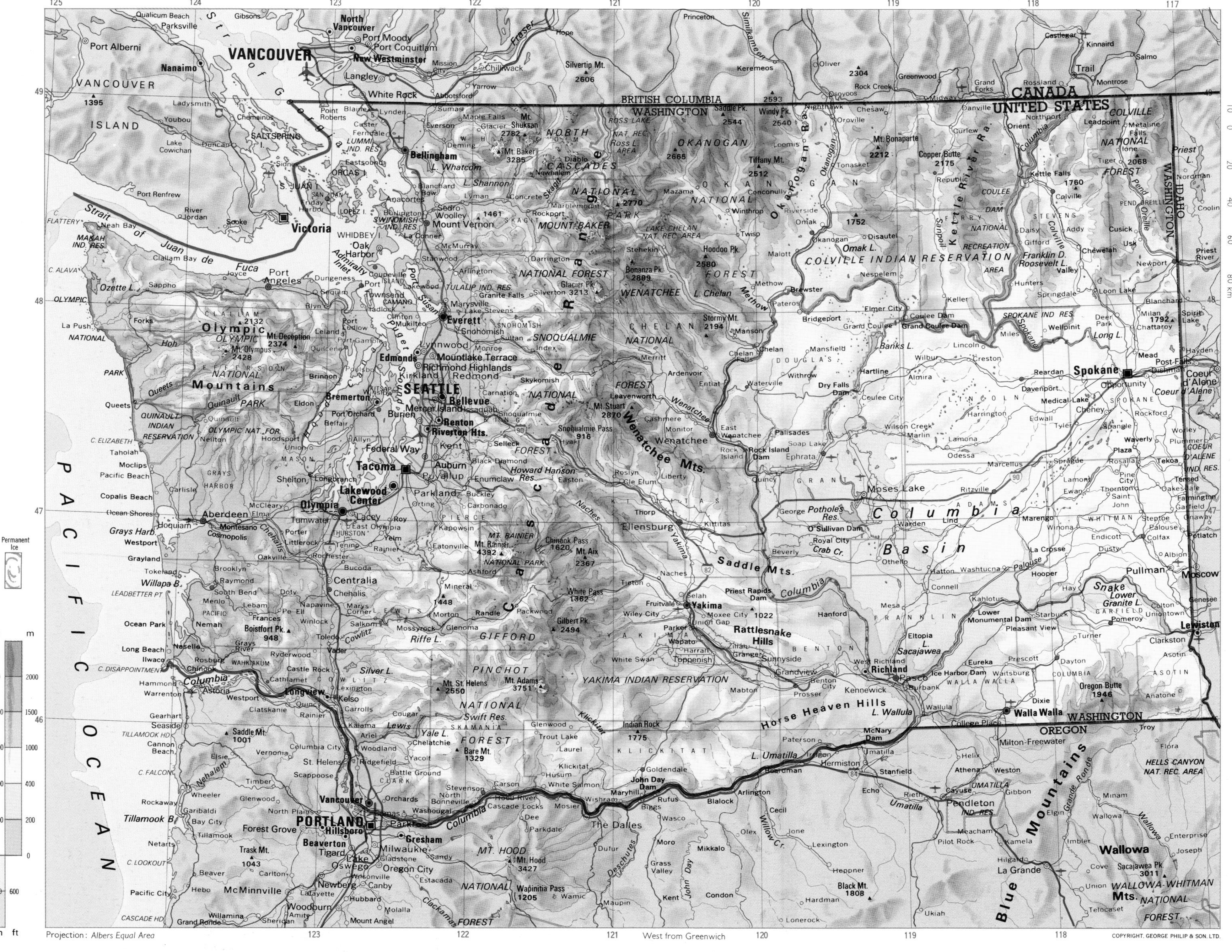
CANADA
UNITED STATES
BRITISH COLUMBIA
WASHINGTON
IDAHO
OREGON
PACIFIC OCEAN
Str. of Georgia
Strait of Juan de Fuca
VANCOUVER ISLAND
VANCOUVER
Victoria
SEATTLE
Tacoma
Olympia
Everett
Bellingham
Spokane
Yakima
Richland
Walla Walla
PORTLAND
Vancouver
Olympic Mountains
Columbia Basin
Blue Mountains
Wenatchee Mts.
Saddle Mts.
Horse Heaven Hills
Puget Sound
Mt. Rainier 4392
Mt. St. Helens 2550
Mt. Adams 3751
Mt. Baker 3285
Mt. Olympus 2428
Mt. Hood 3427
Columbia
Snake
Yakima
Wallowa Mts.
West from Greenwich
Projection: Albers Equal Area
COPYRIGHT, GEORGE PHILIP & SON, LTD.
Permanent Ice
m 2000 1500 1000 400 200 0
ft 6000 4500 3000 1200 600 0
200 600

WEST VIRGINIA AND VIRGINIA

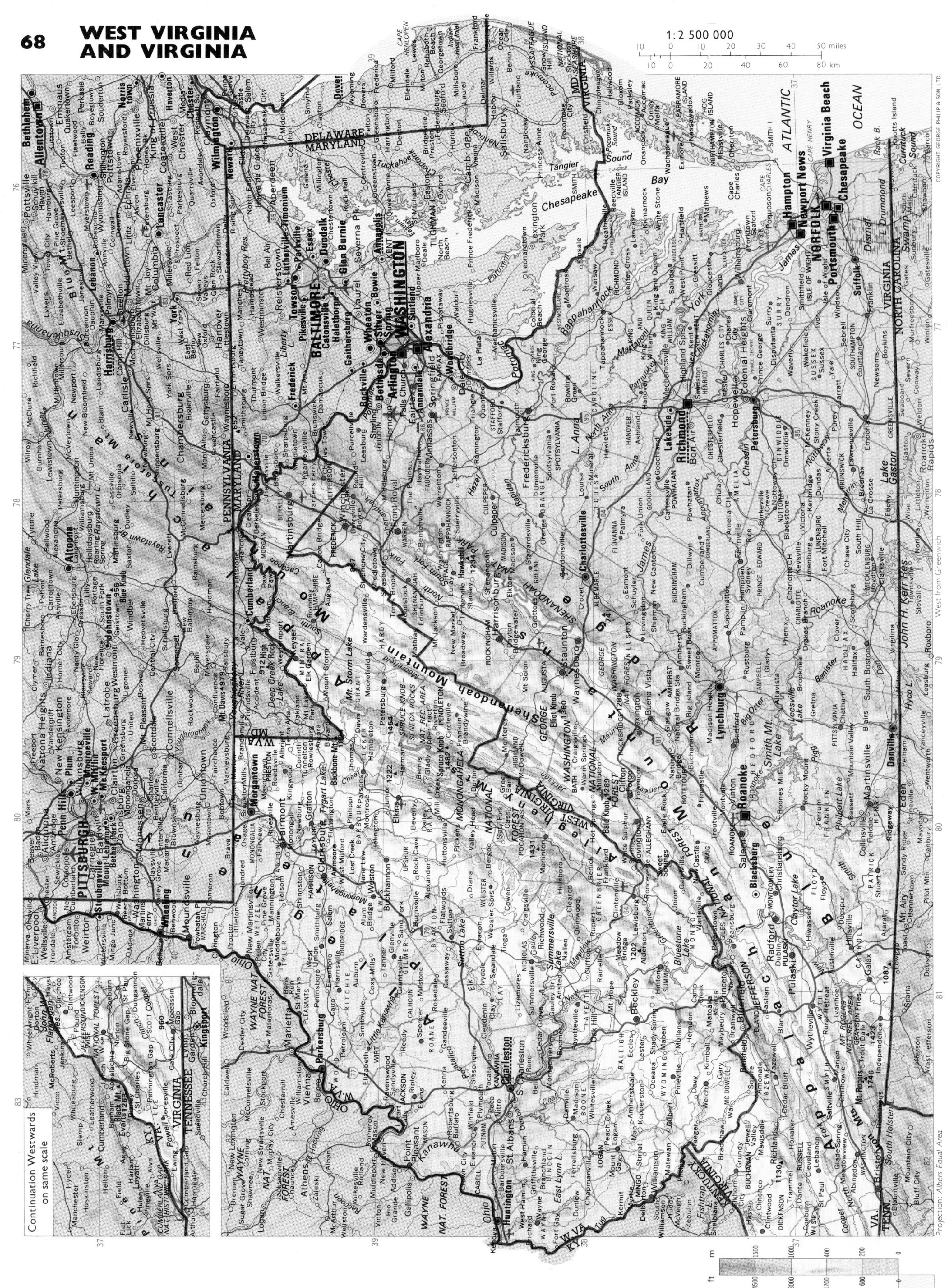

1:2 500 000
10 0 10 20 30 40 50 miles
10 0 20 40 60 80 km
ft m
4500 1500
3000 1000
1200 400
600 200
0 0
Continuation Westwards on same scale
West from Greenwich
Projection: Albers Equal Area
COPYRIGHT GEORGE PHILIP & SON, LTD

1:2 500 000
10 0 10 20 30 40 50 miles
10 0 20 40 60 80 km

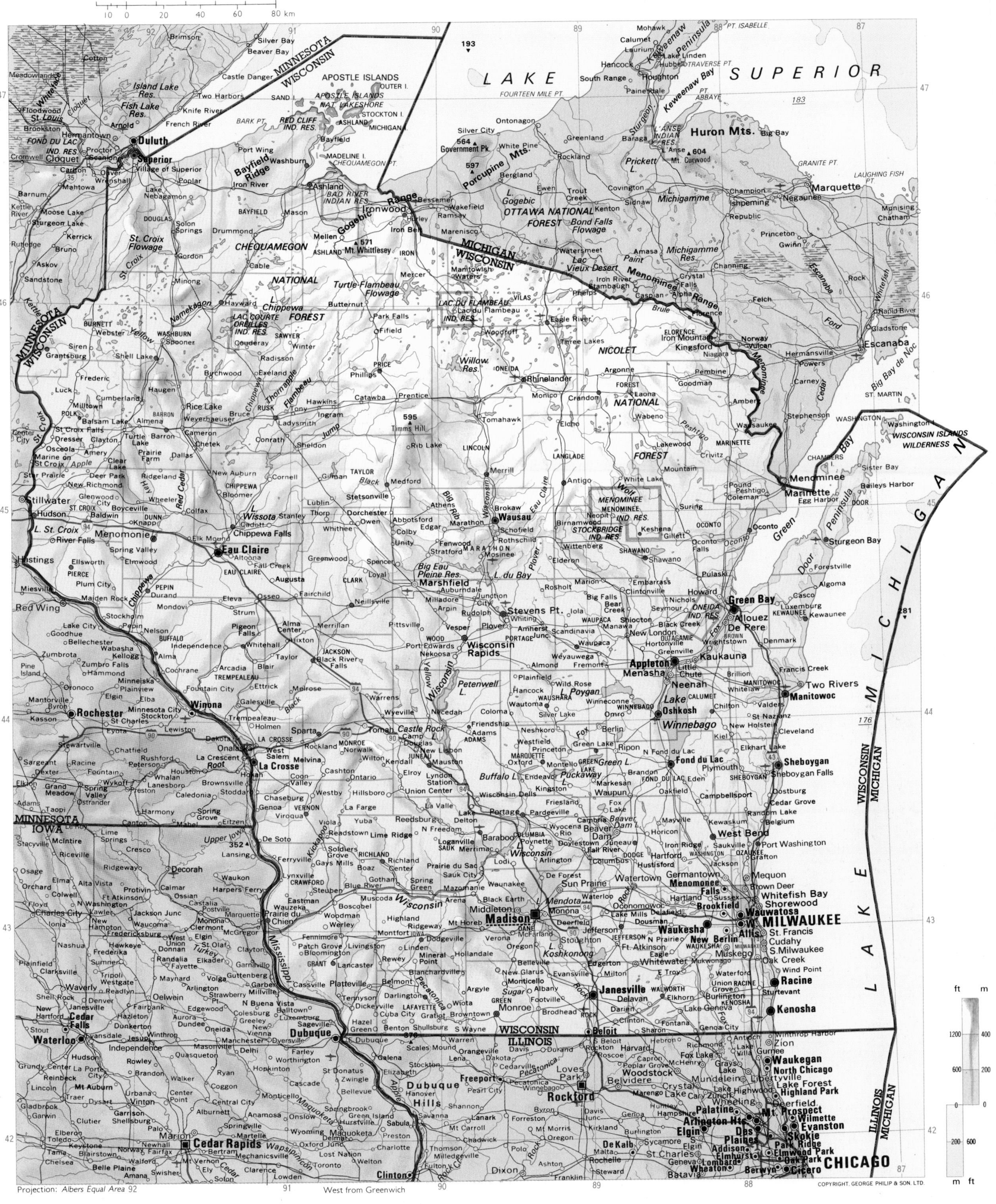
LAKE SUPERIOR
LAKE MICHIGAN
MINNESOTA
WISCONSIN
MICHIGAN
IOWA
ILLINOIS
APOSTLE ISLANDS
APOSTLE ISLANDS NAT. LAKESHORE
RED CLIFF IND. RES.
BAD RIVER INDIAN RES.
CHEQUAMEGON NATIONAL FOREST
NICOLET NATIONAL FOREST
OTTAWA NATIONAL FOREST
MENOMINEE IND. RES.
LAC COURTE OREILLES IND. RES.
LAC DU FLAMBEAU IND. RES.
STOCKBRIDGE IND. RES.
ONEIDA IND. RES.
WISCONSIN ISLANDS WILDERNESS
Huron Mts.
Porcupine Mts.
Gogebic Range
Menominee Range
Keweenaw Peninsula
Keweenaw Bay
Door Peninsula
Green Bay
Big Bay de Noc
Lake Winnebago
L. Poygan
Petenwell L.
Wisconsin
Mississippi
Chippewa
Wolf
Fox
Rock
Duluth
Superior
Ashland
Ironwood
Marquette
Escanaba
Menominee
Marinette
Rhinelander
Wausau
Eau Claire
Chippewa Falls
Stevens Pt.
Wisconsin Rapids
Marshfield
Green Bay
Appleton
Oshkosh
Fond du Lac
Sheboygan
Manitowoc
Two Rivers
La Crosse
Winona
Rochester
Madison
Janesville
Beloit
Waukesha
MILWAUKEE
Racine
Kenosha
Waukegan
Rockford
Dubuque
Cedar Rapids
Waterloo
Elgin
CHICAGO
Projection: Albers Equal Area
West from Greenwich
COPYRIGHT, GEORGE PHILIP & SON, LTD.

1:2 500 000

10 0 10 20 30 40 50 miles

10 0 20 40 60 80 km

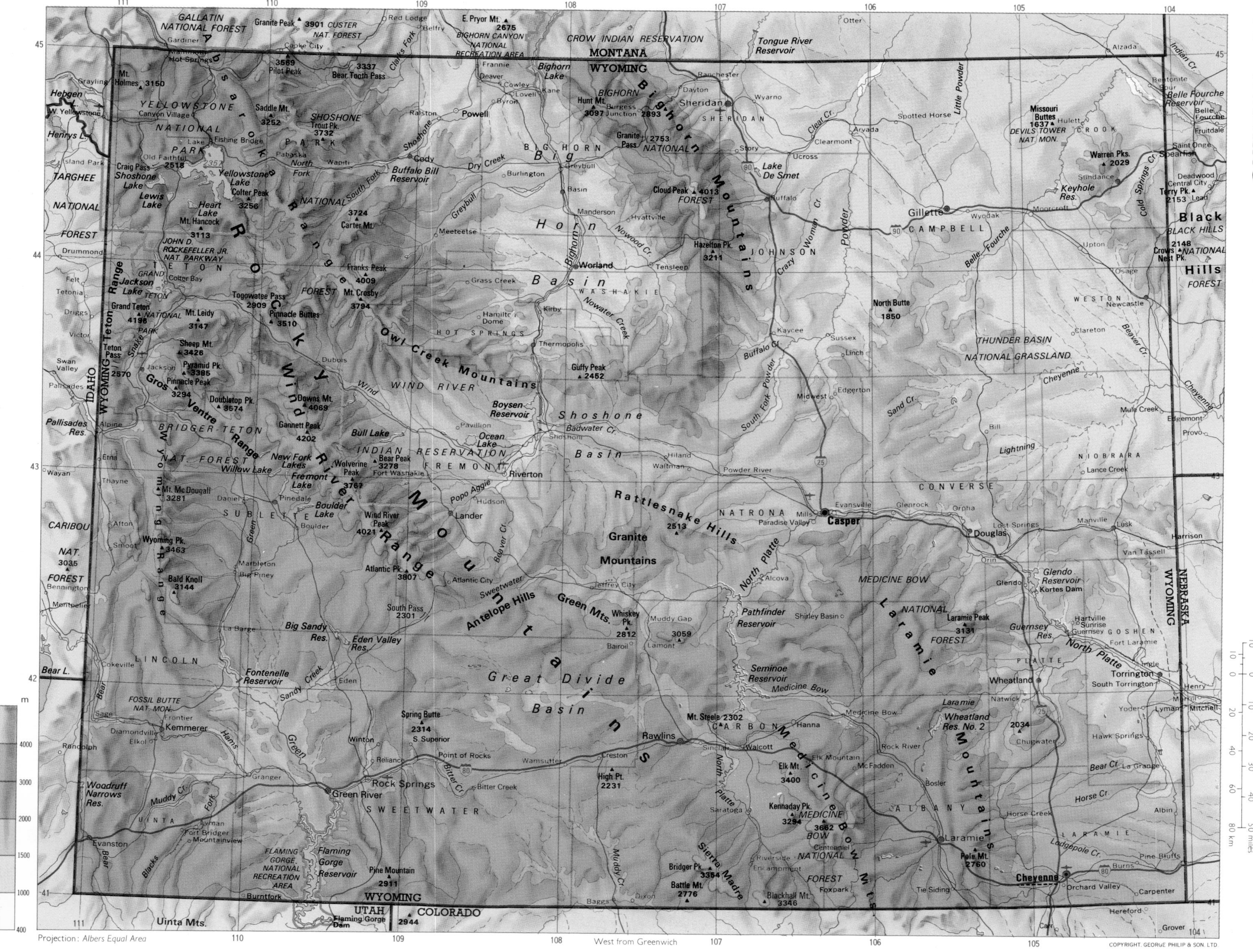
NEBRASKA
WYOMING
MONTANA
WYOMING
IDAHO
WYOMING
UTAH
WYOMING
COLORADO
Cheyenne
Casper
Laramie
Gillette
Sheridan
Buffalo
Douglas
Rawlins
Rock Springs
Green River
Evanston
Kemmerer
Riverton
Lander
Worland
Thermopolis
Cody
Powell
Torrington
Wheatland
Newcastle
Lusk
Bighorn Mountains
Laramie Mountains
Medicine Bow Mts.
Wind River Range
Owl Creek Mountains
Absaroka Range
Teton Range
Wyoming Range
Rocky Mountains
Rattlesnake Hills
Granite Mountains
Green Mts.
Antelope Hills
Sierra Madre
Uinta Mts.
Black Hills
Bighorn Basin
Shoshone Basin
Great Divide Basin
Thunder Basin National Grassland
YELLOWSTONE NATIONAL PARK
Yellowstone Lake
Jackson Lake
Boysen Reservoir
Pathfinder Reservoir
Seminoe Reservoir
Flaming Gorge Reservoir
Fontenelle Reservoir
Keyhole Res.
Buffalo Bill Reservoir
Bighorn Lake
Tongue River Reservoir
Glendo Reservoir
Guernsey Res.
North Platte
Powder
Wind
Green
Bear
Grand Teton 4196
Gannett Peak 4202
Fremont Peak
Cloud Peak 4013
Laramie Peak 3131
Medicine Bow Pk. 3662
Devils Tower Nat. Mon.
Fossil Butte Nat. Mon.
Projection: Albers Equal Area
West from Greenwich
COPYRIGHT GEORGE PHILIP & SON LTD.

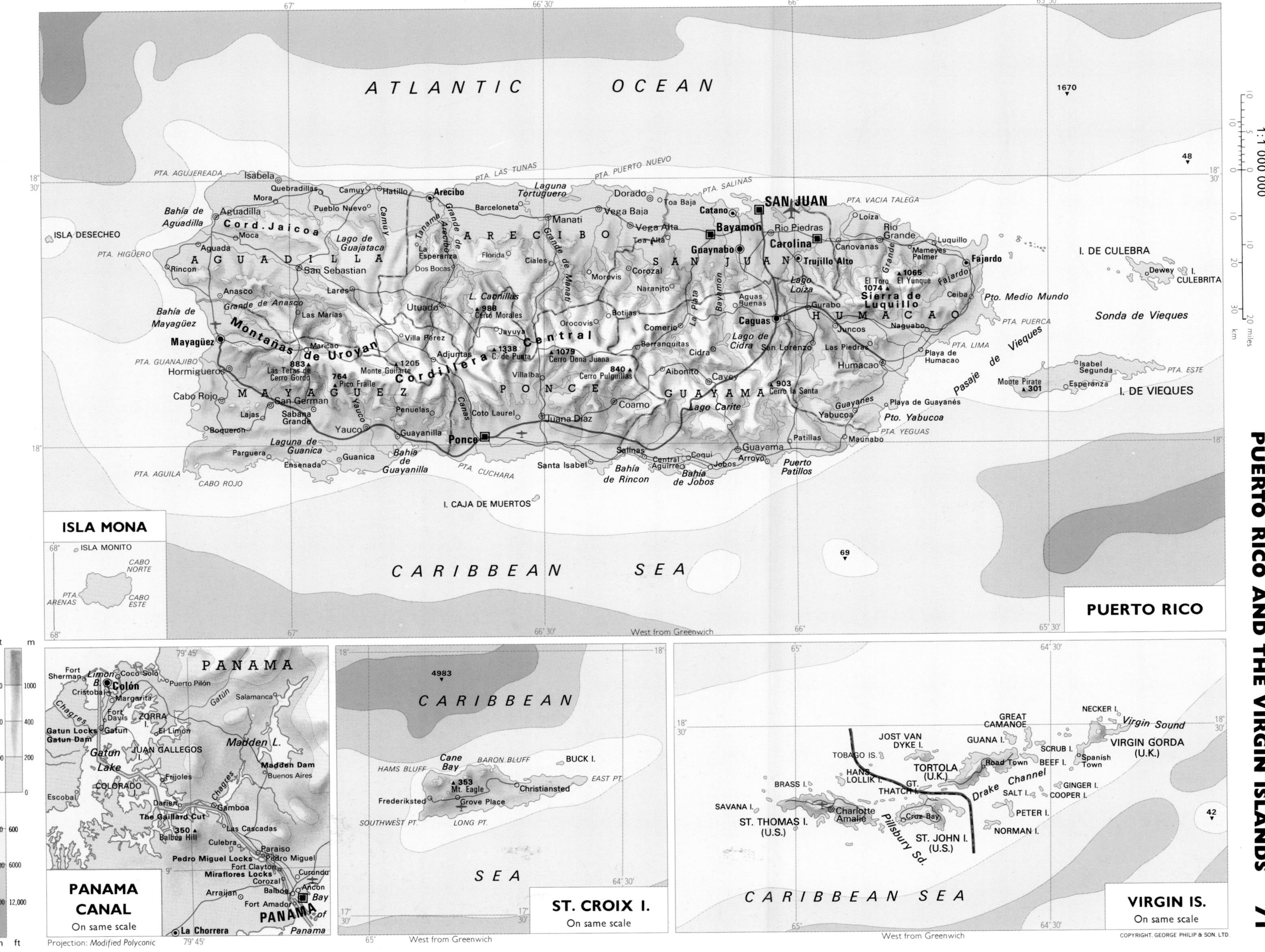
1:1 000 000
miles
km
PUERTO RICO
ATLANTIC OCEAN
CARIBBEAN SEA
SAN JUAN
Bayamon
Carolina
Guaynabo
Caguas
Ponce
Mayagüez
Arecibo
Fajardo
Humacao
Guayama
Cordillera Central
Montañas de Uroyan
Cord. Jaicoa
Sierra de Luquillo
AGUADILLA
ARECIBO
SAN JUAN
HUMACAO
MAYAGUEZ
PONCE
GUAYAMA
I. DE CULEBRA
I. CULEBRITA
I. DE VIEQUES
Sonda de Vieques
Pasaje de Vieques
ISLA DESECHEO
I. CAJA DE MUERTOS
ISLA MONA
ISLA MONITO
CABO NORTE
CABO ESTE
PTA. ARENAS
PANAMA
PANAMA CANAL
On same scale
Colón
Gatun Lake
Madden L.
Madden Dam
Gatun Locks
Gatun Dam
The Gaillard Cut
Pedro Miguel Locks
Miraflores Locks
Balboa
La Chorrera
Bay of Panama
Projection: Modified Polyconic
CARIBBEAN SEA
ST. CROIX I.
On same scale
Christiansted
Frederiksted
Mt. Eagle
VIRGIN IS.
On same scale
VIRGIN GORDA (U.K.)
TORTOLA (U.K.)
ST. JOHN I. (U.S.)
ST. THOMAS I. (U.S.)
Charlotte Amalie
Road Town
Drake Channel
Pillsbury Sd.
Virgin Sound
West from Greenwich
COPYRIGHT. GEORGE PHILIP & SON, LTD.

ARCTIC OCEAN
Beaufort Sea
PACIFIC OCEAN
ALASKA (USA)
YUKON TERRITORY
NORTHWEST TERR
INUVIK REGION
KITIKMEOT REGION
FORT SMITH REGION
KEEWA
BRITISH COLUMBIA
ALBERTA
SASKATCHEWAN
MANITOBA
WASHINGTON
OREGON
IDAHO
MONTANA
WYOMING
NEVADA
CALIFORNIA
NORTH DAKOTA
SOUTH DAKOTA
NEBRASKA
MINNESOTA
UNITED STATES
Banks Island
Victoria Island
Prince of Wales Island
Somerset Island
Queen Elizabeth
Sverdrup Islands
Amundsen Gulf
Coronation Gulf
Queen Maud Gulf
Gulf of Boothia
Viscount Melville Sound
M'Clintock Channel
Great Slave L.
Gr. Bear Lake
Lake Athabasca
Lake Winnipeg
Queen Charlotte Is.
Vancouver I.
Arctic Circle
Anchorage
Fairbanks
Whitehorse
Yellowknife
Edmonton
Calgary
Vancouver
Victoria
Seattle
Spokane
Portland
Saskatoon
Regina
Winnipeg
Prince Albert
Medicine Hat
Lethbridge
Moose Jaw
Duluth
Minneapolis
St. Paul
Salt Lake City
Ogden
Sacramento
San Francisco
Oakland
Berkeley
Richmond
ft
m
12 000
9000
6000
4500
3000
1200
600
200
4000
3000
2000
1500
1000
400
200
0
0
200
600
m
ft

Projection: *Bonne*

West from Greenwich

1:17 500 000
100 0 100 200 300 400 500 miles
100 0 100 200 300 400 500 600 700 800 km
CANADA ADMINISTRATIVE
1:40 000 000
National Capital
Provincial or Territorial Capital
Undemarcated boundary
District boundary
GREENLAND
ALASKA
Arctic Circle
Inuvik Region
Kitikmeot Region
Baffin Region
YUKON TERRITORY
Whitehorse
NORTHWEST TERRITORIES
Fort Smith Region
Yellowknife
Keewatin Region
NEWFOUNDLAND
BRITISH COLUMBIA
ALBERTA
Edmonton
SASKATCHEWAN
MANITOBA
QUEBEC
PRINCE EDWARD ISLAND
Charlottetown
ONTARIO
NEW BRUNSWICK
Fredericton
NOVA SCOTIA
Halifax
Quebec
Victoria
Regina
Winnipeg
Ottawa
Toronto
UNITED STATES
West from Greenwich
Hudson Strait
Ungava Bay
Frobisher Bay
Foxe Basin
Foxe Channel
James Bay
Baffin Bay
Melville Bay
Cumberland Sd.
Resolution I.
C. Chidley
Akpatok I.
Gulf of St. Lawrence
I. d'Anticosti
ATLANTIC OCEAN
ST. PIERRE & MIQUELON (Fr.)
Sable I. (Nova Scotia)
St. John's
Bonavista
C. Race
Gander
C. Harrison
Belle Isle
Schefferville
Churchill Falls
Labrador City
Sept-Îles
Gaspé Pen.
PR. EDWARD I.
Charlottetown
Sydney
C. Breton I.
C. Canso
Halifax
Dartmouth
Bridgewater
Liverpool
Shelburne
C. Sable
Yarmouth
Truro
Moncton
Saint John
Fredericton
NEW BRUNSWICK
MAINE
Bangor
Portland
Lewiston
Augusta
VERMONT
NEW HAMPSHIRE
Manchester
Lowell
MASS.
Boston
Worcester
Springfield
Hartford
CONN.
Providence
RHODE I.
C. Cod
Albany
Utica
Syracuse
Rochester
Buffalo
Elmira
Binghamton
Waterbury
NEW YORK
Québec
MONTRÉAL
Hull
Ottawa
Chicoutimi
Jonquière
Trois-Rivières
Shawinigan
Sherbrooke
Rivière-du-Loup
La Tuque
Kingston
Peterboro
Toronto
Hamilton
Guelph
Kitchener
Brantford
London
Windsor
DETROIT
Toledo
Cleveland
Erie
Chatham
Sarnia
Saginaw
Grand Rapids
Muskegon
Lake Huron
L. Ontario
Lake Erie
Georgian Bay
North Bay
Sudbury
Sault Ste. Marie
Timmins
Cochrane
Hearst
Kapuskasing
Rouyn
Kirkland Lake
Haileybury
Cobalt
Chibougamau
Mistassini
L. Mistassini
Moosonee
Ft. Albany
Attawapiskat
C. Henrietta Maria
Belcher Is.
Sleeper Is.
Ottawa Is.
Mansel I.
Coats I.
Digges Is.
Southampton
Coral Harbour
Nottingham I.
Amadjuak L.
Nettilling L.
Cumberland Peninsula
Prince Charles I.
Bylot I.
Pond Inlet
Clyde
Scott I.
Thule (Qanaq)
Dundas (Thule)
C. York
C. Parry
Inglefield Gulf
Kane Basin
Washington Land
Alert
COPYRIGHT, GEORGE PHILIP & SON, LTD.

N. W TERRITORIES

Lambert's Equivalent Azimuthal

INDIANA OHIO PENNSYLVANIA

1:7 000 000
miles
km
NEWFOUNDLAND
COAST OF LABRADOR
LABRADOR
QUEBEC
NEW BRUNSWICK
NOVA SCOTIA
MAINE
PRINCE EDWARD ISLAND
GULF OF ST. LAWRENCE
ATLANTIC OCEAN
Cabot Strait
Str. of Belle Isle
Bay of Fundy
St. Lawrence
Î. d'Anticosti
Dét. de Jacques-Cartier
Dét. d'Honguedo
Smallwood Reservoir
Churchill Falls
Happy Valley-Goose Bay
North-West River
L. Melville
Mealy Mts.
Labrador City
Sept-Îles
Rés. Manicouagan
Mts. Chic-Chocs
Pén. de Gaspé
Îs. de la Madeleine (Quebec)
Cape Breton Island
Sydney
Glace Bay
New Waterford
Sydney Mines
Halifax
Dartmouth
Truro
New Glasgow
Moncton
Saint John
Fredericton
Charlottetown
Summerside
Campbellton
Dalhousie
Bathurst
Chatham
Newcastle
Edmundston
Rimouski
Rivière-du-Loup
Chicoutimi
Jonquière
Québec
Lévis
Sherbrooke
Thetford Mines
Corner Brook
Stephenville
Gander
Grand Falls
Botwood
Lewisporte
St. John's
Avalon Peninsula
Long Range Mts.
Miquelon
Langlade
St. Pierre
SAINT-PIERRE ET MIQUELON (Fr.)
Sable I. (Nova Scotia)
Yarmouth
Digby
Kentville
Bangor
Augusta
Portland
Lewiston
Auburn
Manchester
Portsmouth
Lowell
Lynn
Gloucester
BOSTON
Brockton
West from Greenwich
COPYRIGHT. GEORGE PHILIP & SON. LTD.

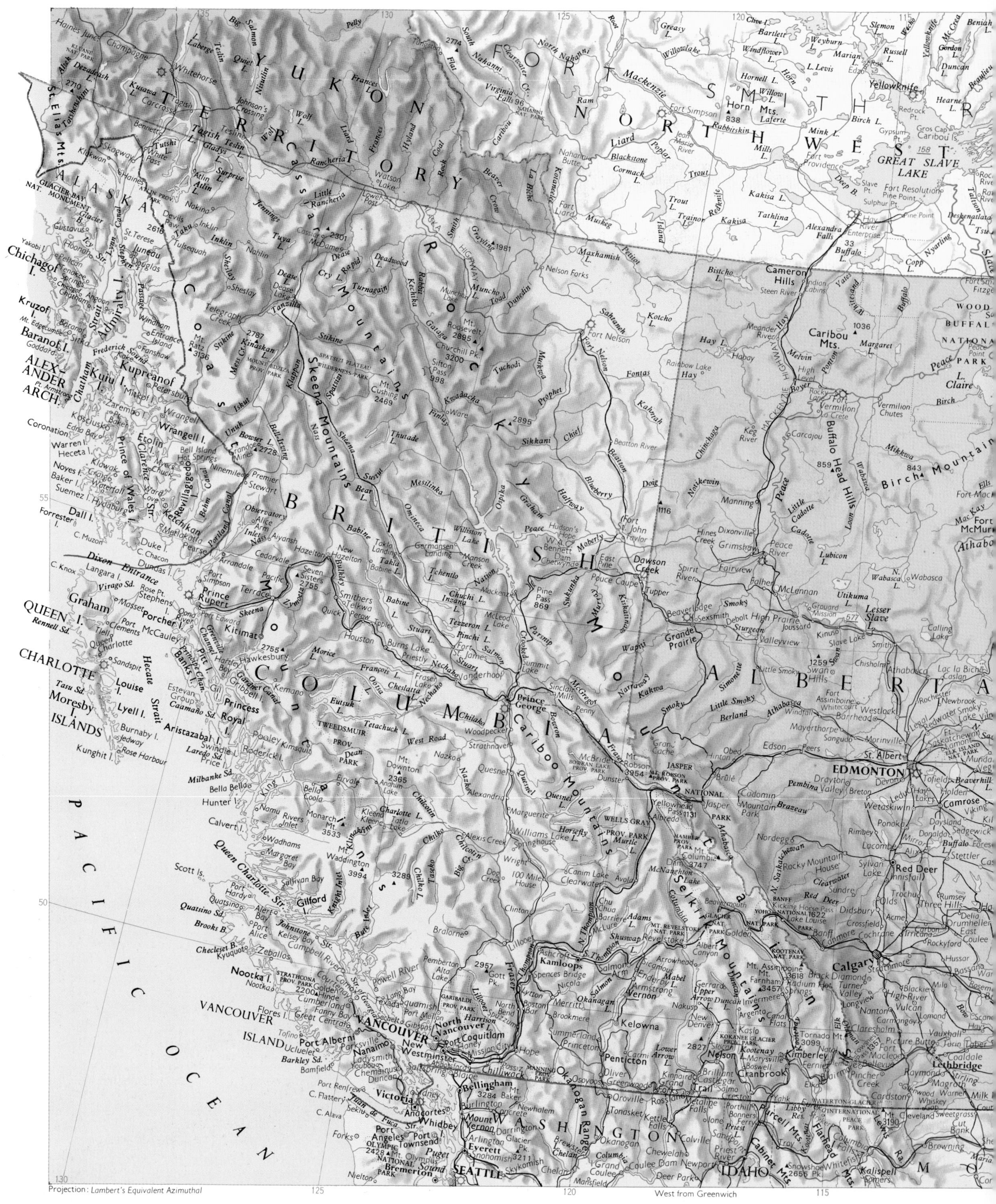
YUKON TERRITORY
NORTH WEST TERRITORIES
BRITISH COLUMBIA
ALBERTA
ALASKA
WASHINGTON
IDAHO
PACIFIC OCEAN
QUEEN CHARLOTTE ISLANDS
VANCOUVER ISLAND
ALEXANDER ARCH.
GREAT SLAVE LAKE
Rocky Mountains
Coast Mountains
Skeena Mountains
Cariboo Mountains
Selkirk Mountains
Cassiar Mountains
Caribou Mts.
Buffalo Head Hills
Birch Mountains
Whitehorse
Yellowknife
Fort Simpson
Fort Nelson
Prince Rupert
Prince George
Dawson Creek
Grande Prairie
EDMONTON
Calgary
Red Deer
Lethbridge
Kamloops
Kelowna
Penticton
VANCOUVER
Victoria
Nanaimo
Port Alberni
SEATTLE
Bellingham
Everett
Juneau
Kitimat
Quesnel
Peace River
Jasper
Banff
Medicine Hat
Cranbrook
Nelson
Trail
Vernon
Hay River
Fort Providence
Fort Resolution
Hinton
Edson
Camrose
Lake Louise
Williams Lake
Terrace
Smithers
Dixon Entrance
Hecate Strait
Queen Charlotte Str.
Juan de Fuca Str.
Graham I.
Moresby I.
Chichagof I.
Baranof I.
Kupreanof I.
Prince of Wales I.
Revillagigedo I.
Mt. Robson 3954
Mt. Waddington 3994
Mt. Baker 3284
Mt. Columbia 3747
Mt. Assiniboine 3618
Mt. Fairweather
WELLS GRAY PROV. PARK
JASPER NATIONAL PARK
BANFF NATIONAL PARK
TWEEDSMUIR PROV. PARK
OLYMPIC NATIONAL PARK
Projection: Lambert's Equivalent Azimuthal
West from Greenwich

1:7 000 000

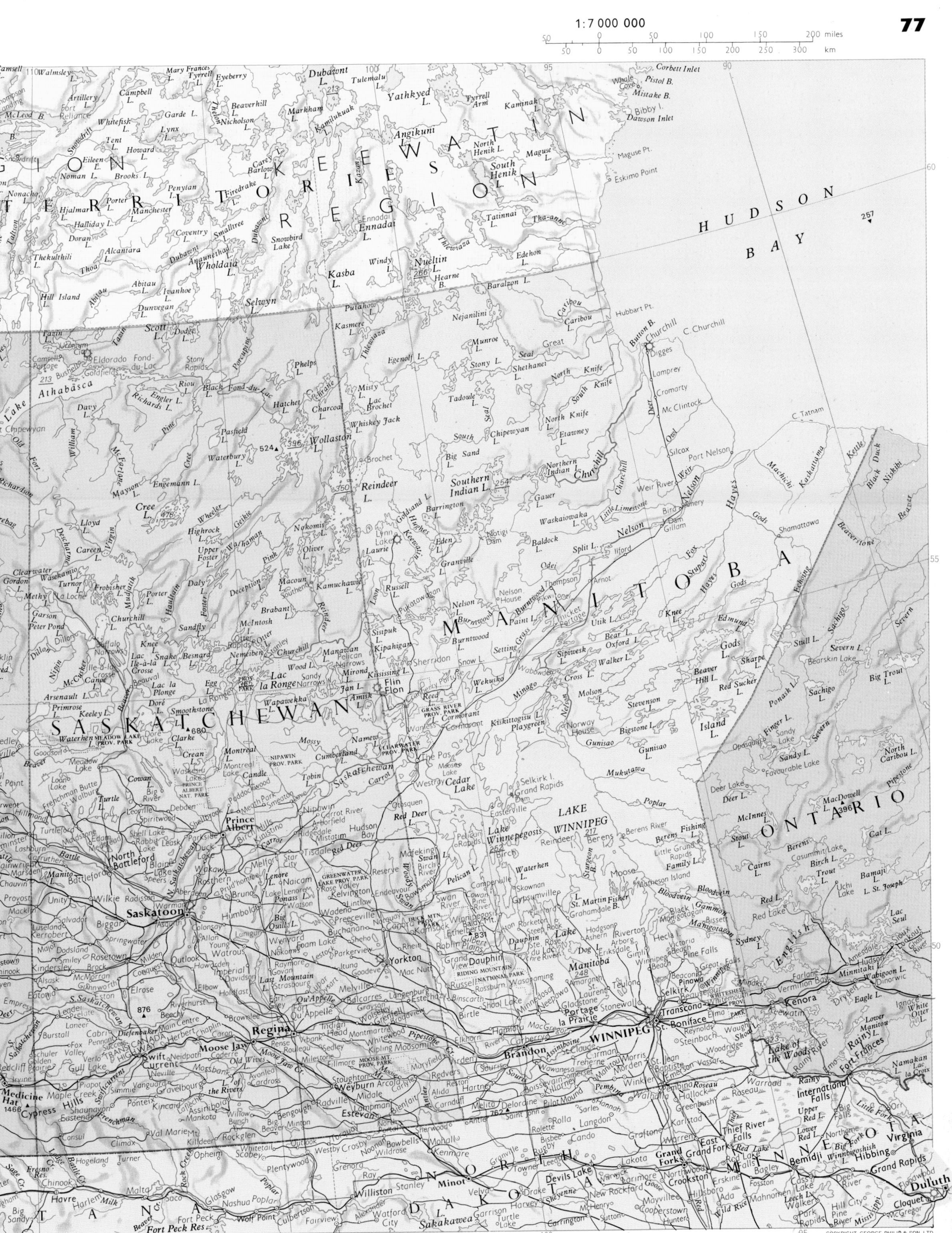
50 0 50 100 150 200 miles
50 0 50 100 150 200 250 300 km
KEEWATIN
REGION
HUDSON
BAY
MANITOBA
SASKATCHEWAN
ONTARIO
LAKE WINNIPEG
MINNESOTA
NORTH DAKOTA
Saskatoon
Prince Albert
North Battleford
Regina
Moose Jaw
Swift Current
Medicine Hat
Yorkton
Brandon
WINNIPEG
Portage la Prairie
Flin Flon
The Pas
Churchill
Kenora
Fort Frances
Grand Forks
Minot
Duluth
Cedar Lake
Lake Winnipegosis
Lake Manitoba
Lake of the Woods
Reindeer L.
Southern Indian L.
Lac la Ronge
Athabasca
Wollaston
Nueltin L.
Cypress Hills
Nelson
Churchill
Saskatchewan

LABRADOR AND QUÉBEC-NORTH

1:7 000 000

50 0 50 100 150 200 miles

50 0 50 100 150 200 250 300 km

Projection: Lambert's Equivalent Azimuthal

West from Greenwich

ft 4500 3000 1200 600 0 200 6000 12 000 ft

m 1500 1000 400 200 0 200 2000 4000 m

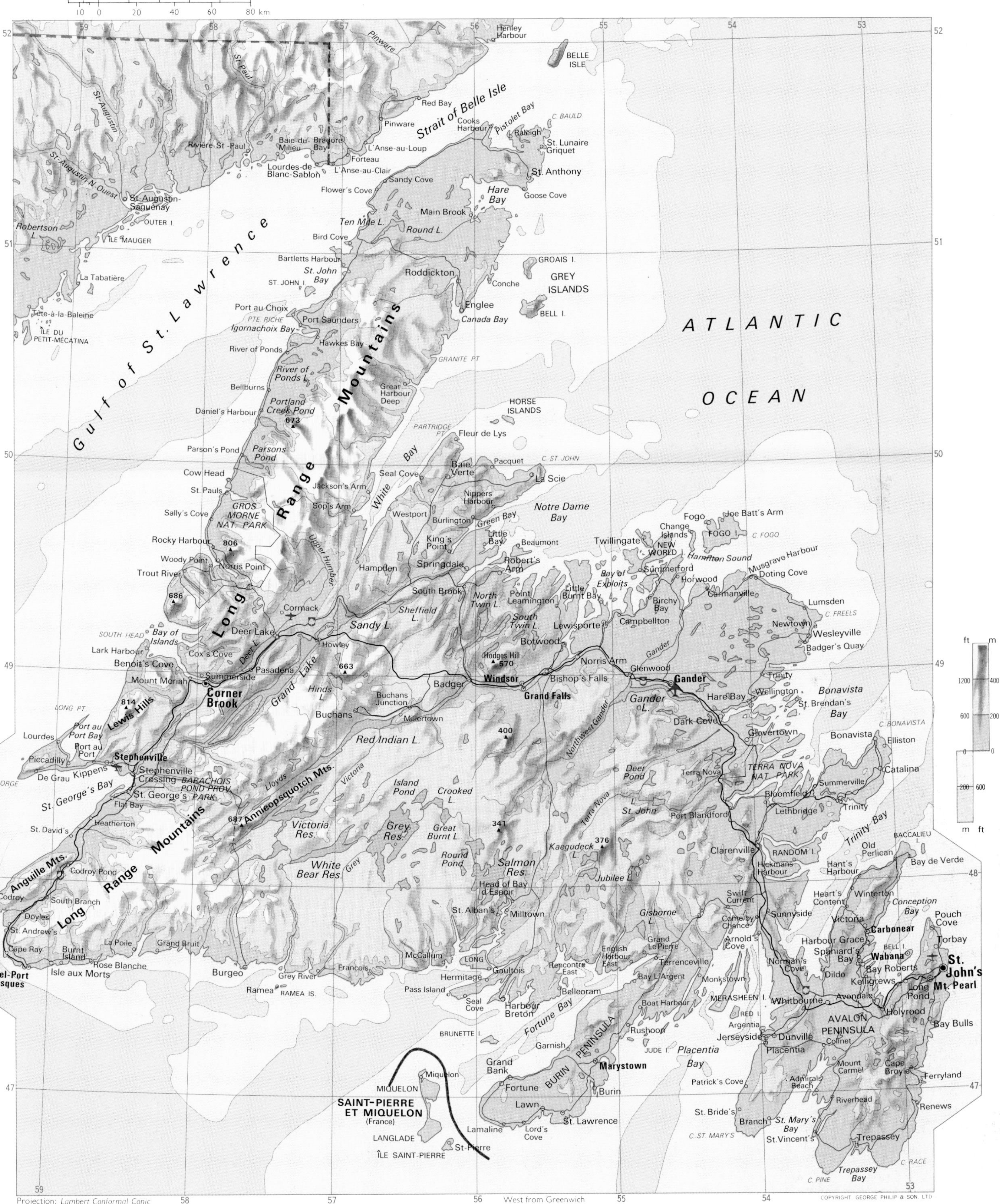
1:2 500 000
50 miles
80 km
Strait of Belle Isle
Gulf of St. Lawrence
Long Range Mountains
ATLANTIC OCEAN
Notre Dame Bay
White Bay
BELLE ISLE
GREY ISLANDS
St. Anthony
Corner Brook
Stephenville
Gander
Grand Falls
Windsor
Carbonear
St. John's
Mt. Pearl
Wabana
Marystown
AVALON PENINSULA
BURIN PENINSULA
Placentia Bay
Fortune Bay
Trinity Bay
Bonavista Bay
Conception Bay
St. George's Bay
Red Indian L.
Grand Lake
Deer Lake
Gander L.
Annieopsquotch Mts.
Anguille Mts.
Lewis Hills
GROS MORNE NAT. PARK
TERRA NOVA NAT. PARK
SAINT-PIERRE ET MIQUELON (France)
MIQUELON
LANGLADE
ÎLE SAINT-PIERRE
Projection: Lambert Conformal Conic
West from Greenwich
COPYRIGHT GEORGE PHILIP & SON LTD

Q U É B E C
GULF OF ST. LAWRENCE
ÎLE D'ANTICOSTI
Détroit de Jacques-Cartier
Détroit D'Honguedo
St. Lawrence (Saint-Laurent)
Péninsule de Gaspé
NOTRE DAME
ÎLES DE MINGAN
Sept-Îles
Port-Cartier
Baie-Comeau
Matane
Gaspé
Percé
Labrador City
Wabush
Gagnon
Mont Wright
Havre-St-Pierre
Natashquan
Kegaska
Musquaro
Gethsémani
Harrington Harbour
Pointe-à-Maurier
Etamamu
Wolf Bay
St-Augustin
Petit-Mécatina
Port-Menier
Baie-Ste-Claire
Baie-du-Renard
Rivière-de-la-Chaloupe
Île d'Anticosti
Jupiter
Salmon
PTE OUEST
PTE SUD
HEATH PT
PTE DU SUD-OUEST
CAP DE GASPÉ
PTE DE MONTS
Moisie
Mingan
Longue-Pointe-de-Mingan
Rivière-St-Jean
Rivière-au-Tonnerre
Magpie
Sheldrake
Rivière-à-la-Chaloupe
Manitou
Rivière-Pigou
Rivière-Ste-Marguerite
Clarke City
Port-Cartier-Ouest
Rivière-Pentecôte
Pointe-aux-Anglais
Baie-Trinité
Godbout
Franquelin
Aguanish
Pointe-Parent
Ste-Anne-des-Monts
Cap-Chat
Les Méchins
Mont-St-Pierre
Madeleine-Centre
Grande-Vallée
Murdochville
Mont Jacques-Cartier 1268
Mount Logan 1149
MONTS CHIC-CHOCS
PARC PROV. DE LA GASPÉSIE
PARC NATIONAL DE FORILLON
PARC PROV. DE MATANE
PARC PROV. DE DUNIÈRE
PARC PROV. DE LA PETITE CASCAPÉDIA
PARC PROV. DE PORT-DANIEL
Amqui
Causapscal
Sayabec
Chandler
Grande-Rivière
Cap d'Espoir
Barachois-de-Malbaie
Douglastown
Wakeham
Cap-des-Rosiers
Rivière-au-Renard
Petit-Cap
Romaine
Nabisipi
Aguanus
Olomane
Caopacho
Nipissis
Wacouno
Toulnustouc Nord-Est
Toulnustouc
Pentecôte
Ste-Marguerite
Pékans
Rochers
St-Jean
Manitou
West Magpie
Atikonak
Little Mecatina
Natashquan-Est
Mistanipisipou
Lac Joseph
Petit lac Joseph
Ashuanipi Lake
L. Ménistouc
L. Opocopa
L. Carheil
Petit Lac Manicouagan
L. Gaillarbois
L. Grandmesnil
Grand Lac Germain
L. Marceau
Grand Lac du Nord
Petit Lac du Nord
Walker L.
L. Pasteur
L. Matamec
L. Fournier
L. Saubosq
Magpie L.
L. Mine
L. Manitou
L. des Eudistes
L. Coupeaux
L. Kleczkowski
L. Buit
L. Allard
Lac Allard
L. Puyjalon
L. Garneau
Sénécal L.
L. Brûlé
Sequart L.
L. Thévet
Atikonak Lake
L. Fleur-de-May
L. Véron
L. Assigny
Eric L.
Seahorse L.
Dumbell L.
L. à l'Eau-Claire
Ritchie L.
L. Caopacho
Lac à l'Aigle
L. Nipisso
L. Bigot
L. Saumur
L. aux Deux-Loutres
L. La Galissonnière
L. De Morhiban
L. de la Robe-Noire
L. Piashti
L. Beetz
L. Costebelle
L. Victor
L. Ménascouagama
L. Le Doré (Lillian L.)
L. Bastille
L. Fonteneau
L. Guinès
L. Arvert
Dominion L.
Minipi L.
L. Fourmont
Joir
L. Le Breton
L. Chenil
L. Briçonnet
L. Cobaz
L. Maryen
L. Montcevelles
L. Du Gas
L. Faride
L. Triquet
L. Noirclair
L. Coacoachou
L. Goyelle
L. Cauchy
L. Watshishou
L. Musquanousse
L. Musquaro
L. D'Auteuil
L. Durocher
L. Paimpont
L. Kégashka
L. Aticonipi
L. Barbel
L. Caron
L. Fortin
L. Broach
L. Bardoux
L. Caotibi
L. Ste-Anne
L. Pentecôte
L. Dionne
L. Nipissis
Waco

1:2 500 000
10 0 10 20 30 40 50 miles
10 0 20 40 60 80 km
NEW BRUNSWICK
NOVA SCOTIA
PRINCE EDWARD ISLAND
CAPE BRETON ISLAND
ÎLES DE LA MADELEINE
MAINE
ATLANTIC OCEAN
Bay of Fundy
Northumberland Strait
Chaleur Bay
Minas Basin
Minas Channel
Chignecto Bay
Miramichi Bay
Egmont Bay
Hillsborough Bay
George Bay
Chedabucto Bay
Bras d'Or Lake
St. Marys Bay
MOUNT CARLETON PROV. PARK
KOUCHIBOUGUAC NAT. PARK
FUNDY NAT. PARK
PRINCE EDWARD ISLAND NAT. PARK
CAPE BRETON HIGHLANDS NAT. PARK
LOUISBOURG NAT. HISTORIC PARK
KEJIMKUJIK NAT. PARK
Fredericton
Saint John
Moncton
Riverview
Dieppe
Bathurst
Campbellton
Dalhousie
Edmundston
Newcastle
Chatham
Oromocto
Sackville
Amherst
Charlottetown
Summerside
Halifax
Dartmouth
Truro
New Glasgow
Stellarton
Antigonish
Sydney
North Sydney
Sydney Mines
New Waterford
Glace Bay
Louisbourg
Yarmouth
Kentville
Windsor
Bridgewater
Lunenburg
Liverpool
Digby
Presque Isle
Houlton
Caribou
St. Stephen
Quispamsis
Springhill
Wolfville
Shelburne
Projection: Bonne
West from Greenwich
COPYRIGHT. GEORGE PHILIP & SON. LTD.

Timmins
Cochrane
Iroquois Falls
Kirkland Lake
Noranda
Rouyn
Amos
Val-d'Or
Malartic
Senneterre
Lebel-sur-Quévillon
Matagami
Chapais
New Liskeard
Haileybury
Cobalt
Lake Timiskaming
Témiscaming
Sudbury
Sturgeon Falls
North Bay
Lake Nipissing
Mattawa
Deep River
Chalk River
Petawawa
Pembroke
Renfrew
Arnprior
Hull
OTTAWA
Buckingham
Gatineau
Maniwaki
Mont-Laurier
Parry Sound
Huntsville
Bracebridge
Gravenhurst
Georgian Bay
ALGONQUIN PROV. PARK
PARC PROV. DE LA VÉRENDRYE
Lake Abitibi
Carleton Place
Cornwall
Projection: Bonne

1:2 500 000
10 0 10 20 30 40 50 miles
10 0 20 40 60 80 km
Baie-du-Poste
PARC PROV. DE MISTASSINI
L. File Axe
L. Waconichi
Chibougamau
L. Chibougamau
R. du Chef
Nestaocano
Mistassibi
Mistassibi Nord-Est
L. Péribonca
Manouane
Outardes
L. Ste-Anne
L. St-Pierre
L. De La Blache
Chute-des-Passes
L. du Goéland
Réservoir Pipmuacan
L. du Brochet
Boucher
Manicouagan
L. Dionne
Godbout
Réservoir Pipmuacan
Franquelin
Godbout
Labrieville
Baie-Comeau
Hauterive
Pointe-Lebel
Chute-aux-Outardes
Ruisseau-Vert
Pointe-aux-Outardes
Betsiamites
Betsiamites
Rivière-Bersimis
Colombier
L. Rouvray
L. Itomamo
Sault aux Cochons
PARC PROV. DE CHIBOUGAMAU
L. Poutrincourt
Bochart
L. Chigoubiche
Ouasiemsca
R. aux Rats
Mistassibi
Péribonca
L. Onatchiway
Chamouchouane
Girardville
Mistassini
Milot
Albanel
Dolbeau
L. Marquette
Normandin
Péribonka
Ste-Monique
Réservoir La Mothe
L. Poulin-de-Courval
L. Moncouche
PARC PROV. DE CHICOUTIMI
Portneuf
St. Lawrence (Saint-Laurent)
Forestville
St-Ulric
Baie-des-Sables
Métis-sur-Mer
Price
St-Noël
Sayabec
Mont-Joli
Luceville
Ste-Angèle-de-Mérici
St-Anaclet
Rimouski
Rimouski-Est
St-Gabriel-de-Rimouski
Ste-Blandine
Rivière-Portneuf
St-Paul-du-Nord
Sault-au-Mouton
N.D.-de la Doré
L'Ascension
St-Cœur-de-Marie
St-Ambroise
St-Félicien
St-Prime
Lac St-Jean
Alma
St-Honoré
Roberval
St-Gédéon
St-Bruno
Arvida
St-Fulgence
Kénogami
Chicoutimi
Saguenay
Chambord
Desbiens
St-Jérôme
Jonquière
Bagotville
La Baie
Grande-Baie
Les Escoumins
ÎLE DU BIC
Bic
Grandes-Bergeronnes
St-Fabien
Rimouski
Sacré-Cœur-de-Jésus
Petit-Saguenay
Tadoussac
Trois-Pistoles
St-Simon-de-Rimouski
Ste-Françoise
PARC PROV. DE RIMOUSKI
Wabano
Windigo
St-Maurice
Trenche
Lac Bouchette
L. Kénogami
L. des Commissaires
Baie-Ste-Catherine
ISLE VERTE
St-Éloi
St-Jean-de-Dieu
St-Georges-de-Cacouna
L'Isle Verte
Squatec
B E C
Van Bruyssel
St-Siméon
Rivière-du-Loup
St-Hubert-de-Témiscouata
Lejeune
Casey
Sanmaur
Vandry
PARC PROV. DES LAURENTIDES
Notre-Dame-du-Portage
St-Antonin
NEW BRUNSW.
Clermont
Andréville
St-Alexandre
Cabano
Notre-Dame-du-Lac
Dégelis
Rapide-Blanc
L. Châteauvert
Lac Édouard
L. Jacques-Cartier
St-Hilarion
La Malbaie
Pointe-au-Pic
Kamouraska
Pelletier Sta.
St-Éleuthère
St-Eusèbe
St-Joseph-de-la-Rivière-Bleue
Green
St-Jacques
Edmundston
St-Basile
Rivière Verte
St-Urbain
St-Pascal
Les Éboulements
Baie-St-Paul
Rivière-Ouelle
Mont-Carmel
Estcourt
Les Étroits
Madawaska
Frenchville
Clair
Kempt Lake
L. Mondonac
Vermilion
La Tuque
L. Batiscan
Jacques-Cartier
ÎLE AUX COUDRES
La Pocatière
St-Pacôme
Eatonville
St-Roch
Connors
Fort Kent
Ste-Anne-de-Madawaska
St-Leonard
Van Buren
Petite-Rivière
St-Francis
St. John
Soldier Pond
L. Wayagamac
Linton
Lefebvre
Dickey
Allagash
Stockholm
St-Jean-Port-Joli
St-Aubert
Eagle Lake
Winterville
Rivière-aux-Rats
PARC PROV. DE PORTNEUF
Batiscan
St-Tite-des-Caps
CRANE I.
St-Omer
PARC PROV. DU ST-MAURICE
L. Devenyns
L. Mékinac
Stoneham
Ste-Anne-de-Beaupré
St-Joachim
Cap-St-Ignace
St-Cyrille-de-L'Islet
St-Pamphile
Caribou
Rivière-à-Pierre
Beaupré
Ste-Famille
ÎLE D'ORLÉANS
Montmagny
St-François
Matawin
St-Raymond
Charlesbourg
Giffard
Loretteville
Beauport
St-Adalbert
Washburn
Lac-aux-Sables
Ste-Thècle
St-Léonard-de-Portneuf
QUÉBEC
Lauzon
Lévis
Ste-Apolline
Portage Lake
Mapleton
Presque Isle
Réservoir Matawin
PARC NAT. DE LA MAURICIE
St-Tite
Pont-Rouge
St-Basile-Sud
Ste-Foy
St-Romuald
St-Raphaël
Armagh
St-Paul-de-Montmigny
Ashland
Westfield
PARC
Grandes Piles
St-Casimir
Portneuf
Charny
St-Henri
St-Anselme
St-Philémon
St-Magloire
St. John
Clayton Lake
Masardis
St-Michel-des-Saints
MASTIGOUCHE
Grand-Mère
Shawinigan
Shawinigan-Sud
Deschambault
Donnacona
Ste-Croix
Issoudun
St-Agapitville
Ste-Claire
Scott-Jonction
Ste-Sabine
St-Justine
Aroostook
PARC PROV. DE JOLIETTE
St-Alexis-des-Monts
Batiscan
Deschaillons
Laurier-Station
Ste-Marie
Chaudière
Eagle L.
St-Paulin
Charette
Cap-de-la-Madeleine
Val-Alain
Dosquet
Ste-Agathe
Vallée-Jonction
Lac-Etchemin
Allagash L.
M A I N E
St-Donat-de-Montcalm
Trois-Rivières
Manseau
Lyster
St-Joseph-de-Beauce
Chamberlain L.
Smyrna Mills
L. Ouareau Rés.
St-Gabriel
St-Côme
Louiseville
Maskinongé
Lemieux
Laurierville
Tring-Jonction
East Broughton Station
Caucomgomoc L.
BAXTER STATE PARK
Oakfield
St-Barthélémy
Lac St-Pierre
Nicolet
Plessisville
Beauceville
East Penobscot
Island Falls
St-Félix-de-Valois
Baieville
Princeville
Robertsonville
St-Georges-Ouest
St-George
Chesuncook L.
Patten
Ste-Agathe-des-Monts
St-Joseph-de-Sorel
Berthierville
Pierreville
Victoriaville
Bernierville
Thetford Mines
St-Éphrem-de-Tring
Linière
Seboomook L.
Mt. Katahdin 1605
Sherman
Rawdon
Joliette
Sorel
St-François-du-Lac
Black Lake
La Guadeloupe
Stacyville
Haynesville
Yamaska
Notre-Dame-du-Bon-Conseil
West Penobscot
Benedicta
Monarda
St-Jacques
Lanoraie
Lavaltrie
St-Ours
Massueville
Disraëli
Seboomook
Millinocket L.
L'Épiphanie
Tracy
Drummondville
Beaulac
Lambton
St-Gédéon-de-Beauce
Pemadumcook L.
St-Jérôme
L'Assomption
St-Guillaume
St-Germain-de-Grantham
Kingsey Falls
St-Gérard
St-Sébastien
Brassua L.
Rockwood
Millinocket
East Millinocket
Mascouche
Repentigny
Contrecoeur
Verchères
Wickham
Asbestos
St-Ludger
Jackman
Kokad-jo
Kingman
Terrebonne
St-Nazaire
Wottonville
Medway
St-Jude
Weedon-Centre
Moosehead L.
White Cap Mt. 1130
Mattawamkeag
Blainville
Rosemère
Pointe-aux-Trembles
Upton
Richmond
Lac-Mégantic
Winn
Caroll
Lachute
LAVAL
St-Eustache
Acton Vale
Marbleton
St-Hyacinthe
Roxton Falls
Windsor
Bishopton
Tumbledown Mt. 1080
Coburn Mt. 1133
Greenville
Schoodic L.
Springfield
MONTRÉAL
LONGUEUIL
Beloeil
St-Pie
Valcourt
E. Angus
Mégantic
Scotstown
Mt. Mégantic 1105
Shirley Mills
Penobscot
Lincoln
Ste-Prudentienne
Bury
Dorion
Lachine
Pointe-Claire
Chambly
Marieville
Granby
Sherbrooke
Bromptonville
Cookshire
La Patrie
Notre-Dame-des-Bois
Brownville Junction
Brownville
Enfield
Beauharnois
Léry
Mercier
Ste-Césaire
St-Luc
Iberville
Bromont
Waterloo
Eastman
Lennoxville
Sawyerville
Snow Mt. 1203
Monson
Dover-Foxcroft
Milo
Howland
Salaberry-de-Valleyfield
St-Jean
St-Rémi
Farnham
Foster
Magog
North Hatley
Waterville
Compton
Rump Mt. 1112
Flagstaff L.
Abbot Village
Guilford
Sangerville
Lagrange
Olamon
Nicatous L.
Napierville
Cowansville
Knowlton
Stratton
Ormstown
Howick
Henryville
L. Memphremagog
Ayer's Cliff
Coaticook
NEW HAMP.
Bingham
Dexter
Bradford
Costigan
St-Anicet
St-Chrysostôme
Bedford
Sutton
Mt. Hereford
Dixville 844
Kennebago Lake
Sugarloaf Mt. 1291
Harmony
Old Town
Great Pond
Huntingdon
Lacolle
Rouses Point
▲972
Beebe Plain
Rock Island
Corrina
Orono
Hemmingford
Philipsburg
Derby Line
Rangeley
Hartland
Bangor
Amherst
Champlain
Richford
N. Troy
Jay Peak 1177
Newport
Rangeley L.
Newport
Carmel
Brewer
Covington
Mooers
Alburg
74
73
West from Greenwich
72
71
70
69
68
50
49
48
47
46
45
COPYRIGHT, GEORGE PHILIP & SON, LTD.

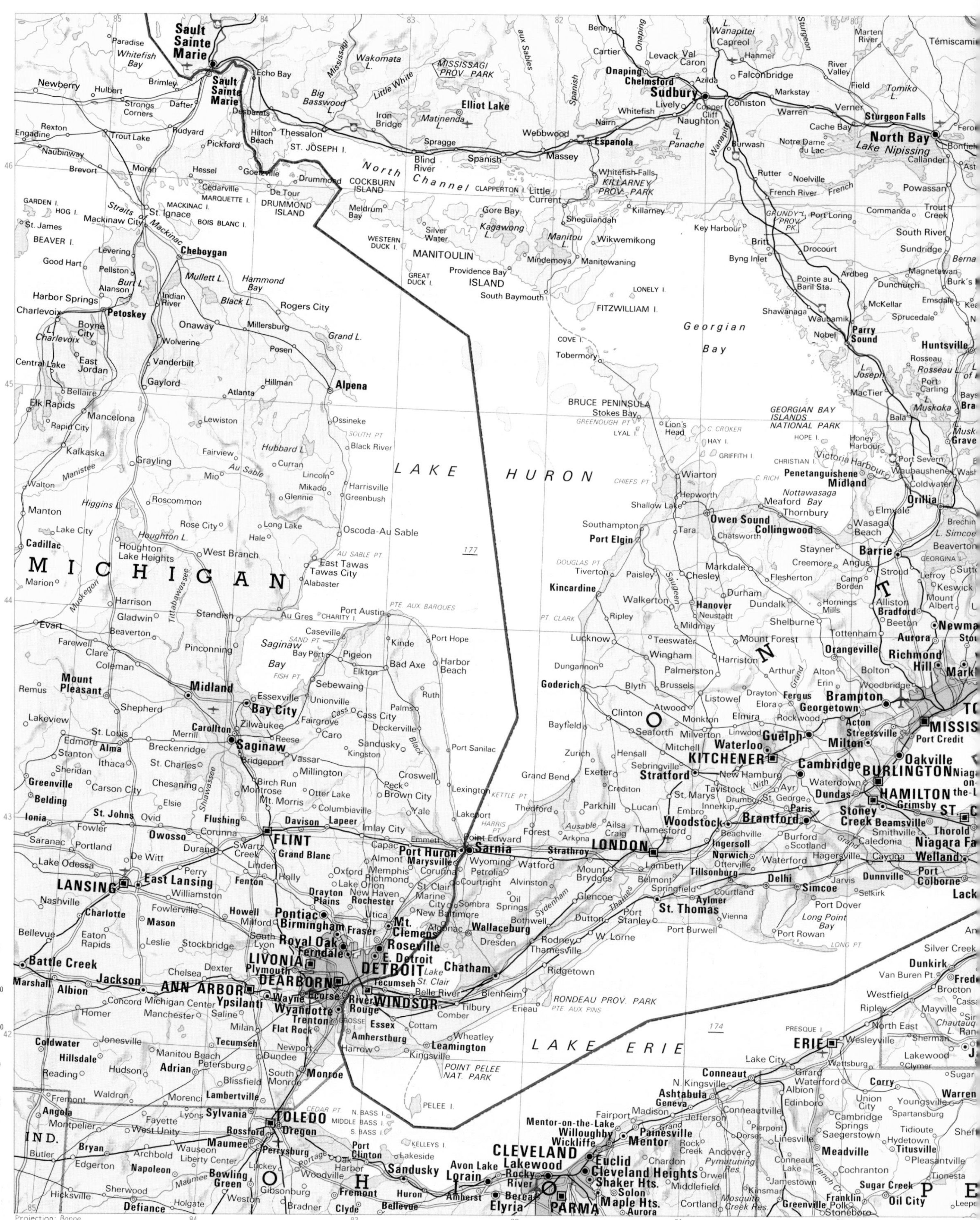
MICHIGAN
LAKE HURON
LAKE ERIE
Georgian Bay
North Channel
Saginaw Bay
Lake Nipissing
Lake St. Clair
Straits of Mackinac
MANITOULIN ISLAND
DRUMMOND ISLAND
COCKBURN ISLAND
ST. JOSEPH I.
BRUCE PENINSULA
GEORGIAN BAY ISLANDS NATIONAL PARK
MISSISSAGI PROV. PARK
KILLARNEY PROV. PARK
RONDEAU PROV. PARK
POINT PELEE NAT. PARK
PELEE I.
IND.
Sault Sainte Marie
Elliot Lake
Espanola
Sudbury
Chelmsford
Onaping
North Bay
Sturgeon Falls
Parry Sound
Huntsville
Penetanguishene
Midland
Orillia
Barrie
Collingwood
Owen Sound
Wiarton
Port Elgin
Kincardine
Goderich
Hanover
Orangeville
Brampton
Georgetown
Milton
Oakville
BURLINGTON
HAMILTON
Guelph
KITCHENER
Waterloo
Cambridge
Stratford
Brantford
Woodstock
LONDON
Ingersoll
St. Thomas
Tillsonburg
Simcoe
Delhi
Welland
Port Colborne
Dunnville
Sarnia
Port Huron
Chatham
WINDSOR
Leamington
Wallaceburg
DETROIT
Dearborn
LIVONIA
Royal Oak
Pontiac
Birmingham
Roseville
ANN ARBOR
Ypsilanti
Jackson
LANSING
East Lansing
FLINT
Saginaw
Bay City
Midland
Mount Pleasant
Alpena
Cheboygan
Petoskey
Gaylord
Cadillac
Battle Creek
Monroe
TOLEDO
Oregon
Sandusky
Lorain
Elyria
CLEVELAND
Lakewood
Euclid
Cleveland Heights
PARMA
Mentor
Ashtabula
Conneaut
ERIE
Meadville
Warren
Oil City
Projection: Bonne
ft
m
4500
3000
1200
600
1500
1000
400
200
0
200
600
174
177

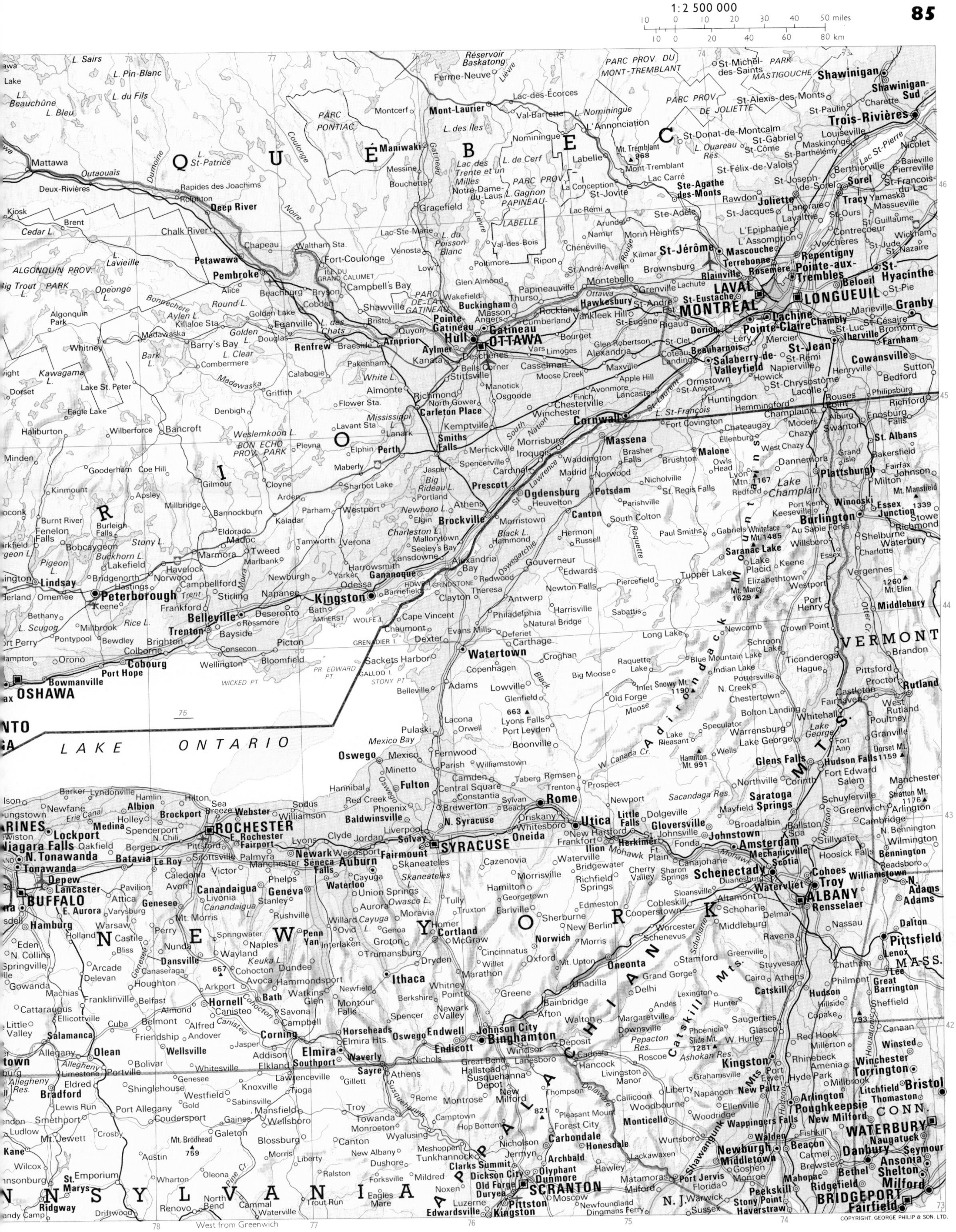

QUÉBEC

ONTARIO

NEW YORK

PENNSYLVANIA

VERMONT

MASS.

CONN.

N. J.

LAKE ONTARIO

Lake Champlain

Adirondack Mountains

APPALACHIAN Mts.

Catskill Mts.

OTTAWA

MONTREAL

LAVAL

LONGUEUIL

Trois-Rivières

Shawinigan

Hull

Gatineau

Kingston

Peterborough

OSHAWA

ROCHESTER

SYRACUSE

BUFFALO

ALBANY

Schenectady

Utica

Rome

Binghamton

SCRANTON

BRIDGEPORT

WATERBURY

Burlington

Plattsburgh

Cornwall

Watertown

Elmira

Ithaca

Poughkeepsie

West from Greenwich

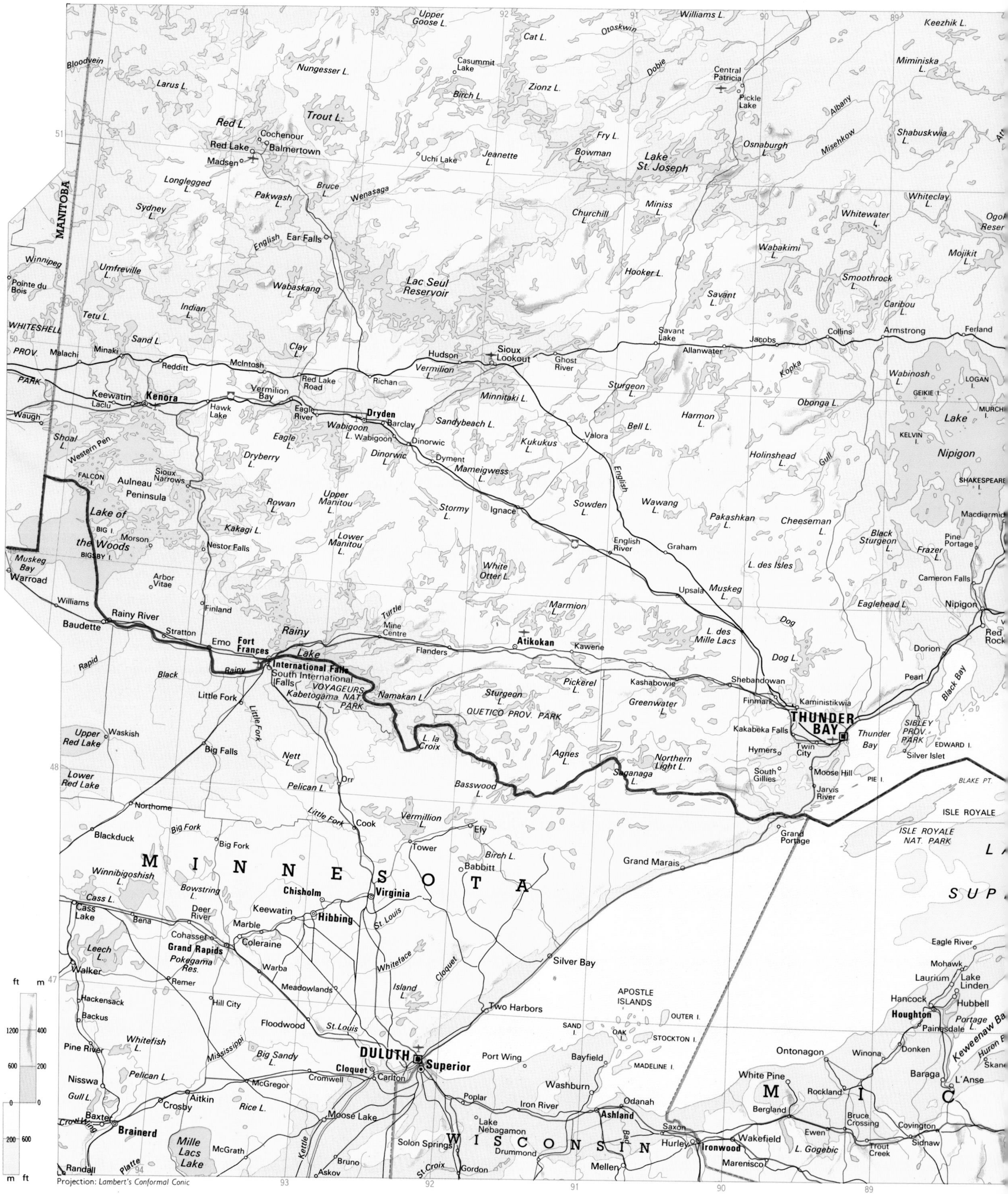

MANITOBA
Red Lake
Balmertown
Cochenour
Lac Seul Reservoir
Lake St. Joseph
Central Patricia
Pickle Lake
Sioux Lookout
Kenora
Dryden
Lake of the Woods
Fort Frances
International Falls
Atikokan
QUETICO PROV. PARK
Lake Nipigon
Nipigon
THUNDER BAY
Grand Portage
ISLE ROYALE
MINNESOTA
Hibbing
Virginia
Chisholm
Grand Rapids
DULUTH
Superior
Two Harbors
Silver Bay
APOSTLE ISLANDS
Ashland
Ironwood
WISCONSIN
Houghton
Hancock
Brainerd
Mille Lacs Lake

Projection: Lambert's Conformal Conic

1:2 500 000

10 0 10 20 30 40 50 miles

10 0 20 40 60 80 km

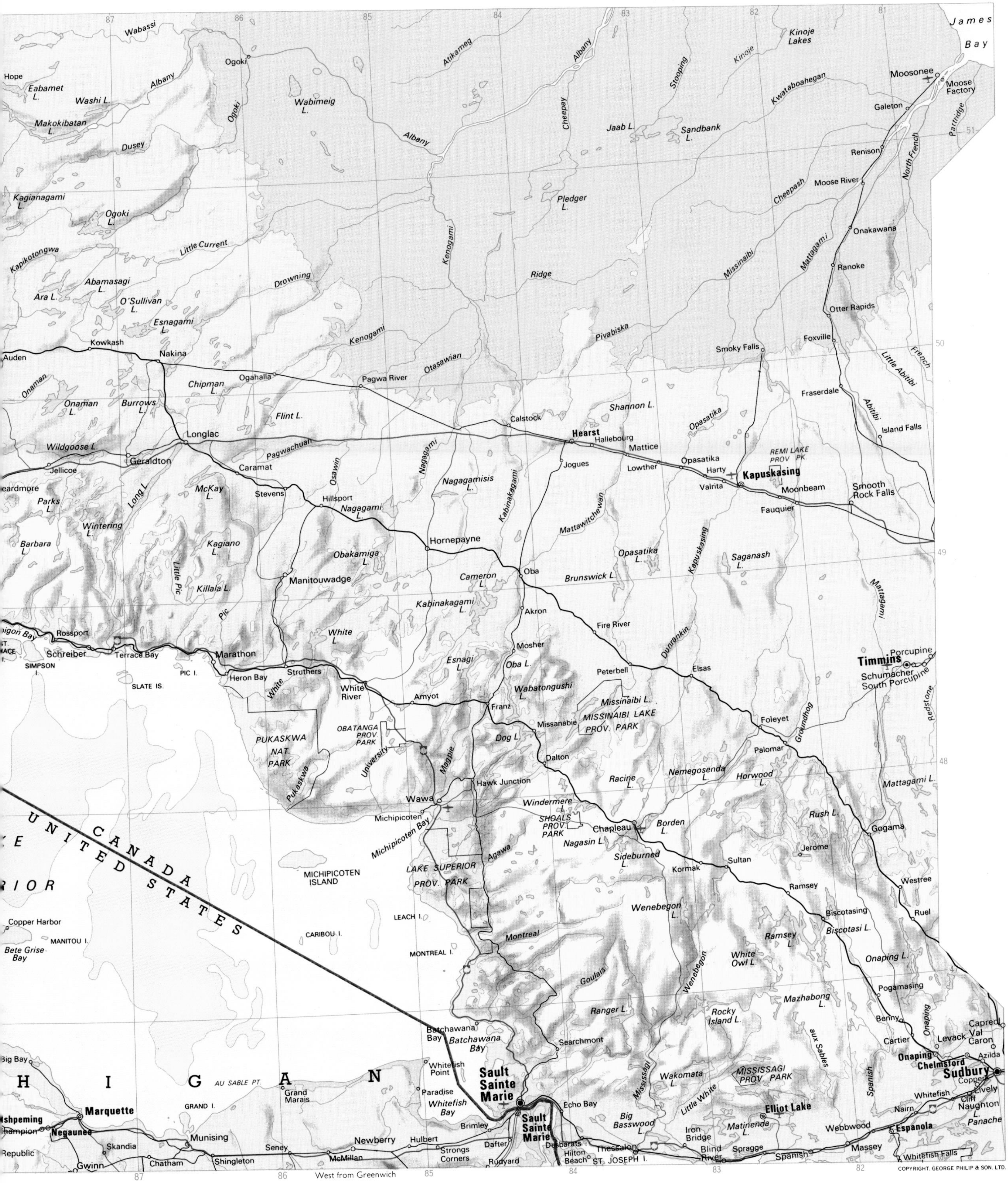

James Bay
Moosonee
Moose Factory
Galeton
Partridge
Renison
North French
Moose River
Onakawana
Ranoke
Otter Rapids
Foxville
Little Abitibi
French
Fraserdale
Abitibi
Island Falls
Smooth Rock Falls
Kinoje Lakes
Kinoje
Kwataboahegan
Stooping
Albany
Cheepay
Jaab L.
Sandbank L.
Cheepash
Missinaibi
Mattagami
Pledger L.
Ridge
Pivabiska
Smoky Falls
Atikameg
Wabimeig L.
Ogoki
Wabassi
Hope
Eabamet L.
Washi L.
Makokibatan L.
Dusey
Kagianagami L.
Ogoki L.
Kapikotongwa
Little Current
Abamasagi L.
Ara L.
O'Sullivan L.
Esnagami L.
Drowning
Kenogami
Otasawian
Auden
Kowkash
Nakina
Onaman
Onaman L.
Chipman L.
Ogahalla
Pagwa River
Burrows L.
Flint L.
Calstock
Shannon L.
Hearst
Hallebourg
Mattice
Opasatika
Lowther
Harty
Kapuskasing
Valrita
Moonbeam
Fauquier
REMI LAKE PROV. PK.
Longlac
Wildgoose L.
Geraldton
Jellicoe
Beardmore
Pagwachuan
Caramat
Nagagami
Osawin
Nagagamisis L.
Kabinakagami
Mattawitchewan
Kapuskasing
Parks L.
Long L.
McKay L.
Stevens
Hillsport
Nagagami L.
Wintering L.
Barbara L.
Kagiano L.
Little Pic
Obakamiga L.
Hornepayne
Opasatika L.
Saganash L.
Manitouwadge
Cameron L.
Oba
Brunswick L.
Killala L.
Pic
Kabinakagami L.
Akron
Fire River
Dunrankin
Mattagami
Nipigon Bay
Rossport
Schreiber
Terrace Bay
ST. IGNACE I.
SIMPSON I.
Marathon
White L.
Mosher
Heron Bay
PIC I.
SLATE IS.
Struthers
Esnagi L.
Oba L.
Peterbell
Elsas
Timmins
Porcupine
Schumacher
South Porcupine
Redstone
White
White River
Amyot
Wabatongushi L.
Missinaibi L.
MISSINAIBI LAKE PROV. PARK
Franz
Missanabie
Foleyet
Groundhog
OBATANGA PROV. PARK
PUKASKWA NAT. PARK
Dog L.
University
Magpie
Dalton
Palomar
Pukaskwa
Hawk Junction
Nemegosenda L.
Racine L.
Horwood L.
Mattagami L.
Wawa
Michipicoten
Windermere L.
SHOALS PROV. PARK
Chapleau
Borden L.
Rush L.
Michipicoten Bay
Nagasin L.
Gogama
Agawa
Sideburned L.
Sultan
Jerome
Kormak
CANADA
UNITED STATES
LAKE SUPERIOR
MICHIPICOTEN ISLAND
LAKE SUPERIOR PROV. PARK
Ramsey
Westree
Wenebegon L.
Biscotasing
Ruel
Copper Harbor
LEACH I.
CARIBOU I.
Ramsey L.
Biscotasi L.
MANITOU I.
Montreal
Bete Grise Bay
MONTREAL I.
White Owl L.
Onaping L.
Wenebegon
Goulais
Pogamasing
Mazhabong L.
Ranger L.
Rocky Island L.
Benny
Onaping
Capreol
aux Sables
Levack
Val Caron
Cartier
Azilda
Batchawana Bay
Batchawana Bay
Searchmont
Onaping
Chelmsford
Big Bay
MICHIGAN
Whitefish Point
AU SABLE PT.
Sault Sainte Marie
MISSISSAGI PROV. PARK
Sudbury
Copper Cliff
Lively
Wakomata L.
Mississagi
Spanish
Grand Marais
Paradise
Whitefish Bay
GRAND I.
Marquette
Echo Bay
Little White
Elliot Lake
Whitefish
Naughton L.
Ishpeming
Champion
Negaunee
Sault Sainte Marie
Big Basswood L.
Nairn
Panache
Munising
Newberry
Hulbert
Brimley
Iron Bridge
Matinenda L.
Webbwood
Espanola
Republic
Skandia
Seney
McMillan
Strongs Corners
Dafter
Desbarats
Thessalon
Blind River
Spragge
Spanish
Massey
Gwinn
Chatham
Shingleton
Rudyard
Hilton Beach
ST. JOSEPH I.
Whitefish Falls

87 86 85 84 83 82 81
51 50 49 48 47

West from Greenwich

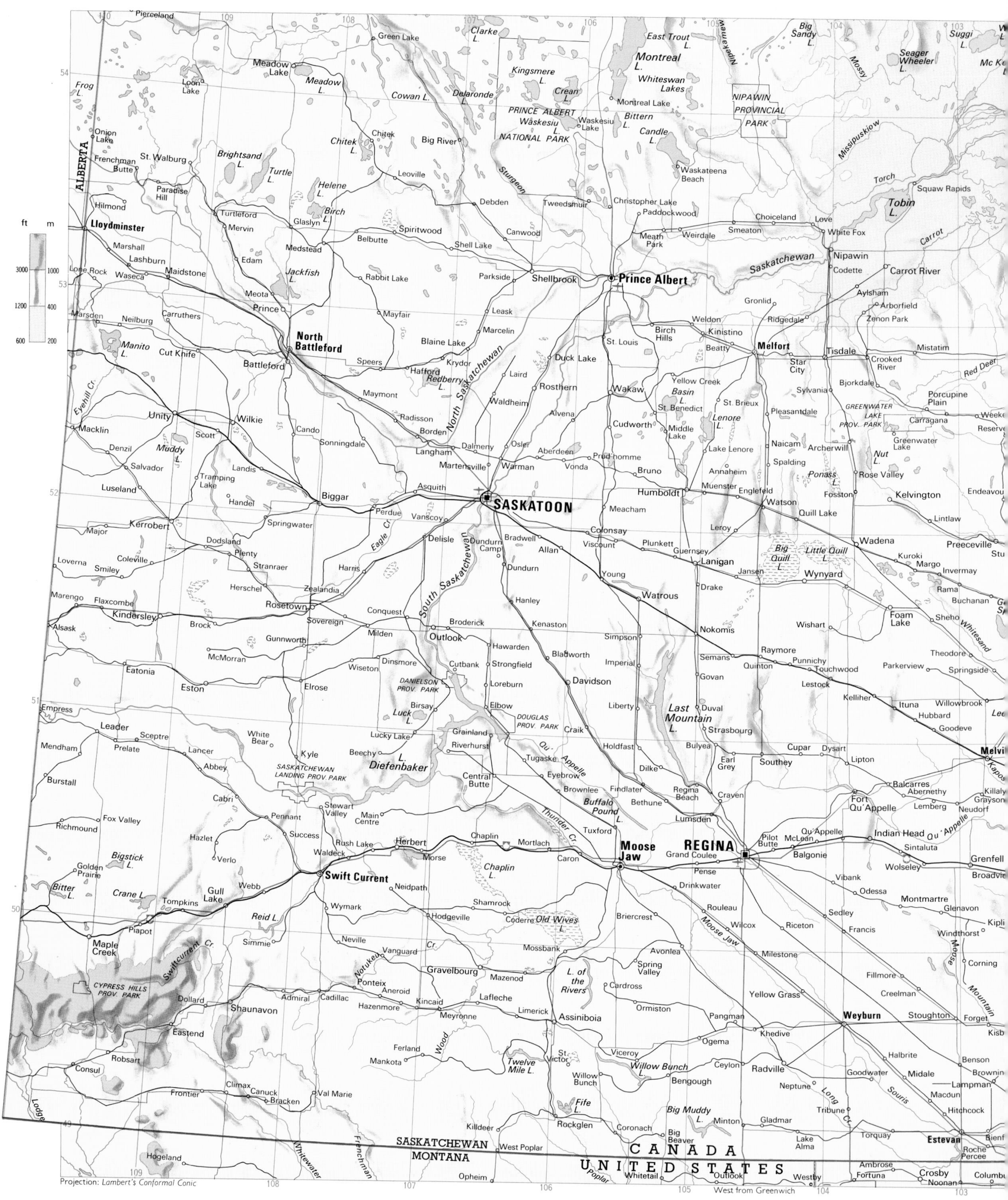
SASKATOON
REGINA
Prince Albert
Moose Jaw
Swift Current
North Battleford
Lloydminster
Melfort
Weyburn
Estevan
Humboldt
ALBERTA
SASKATCHEWAN
MONTANA
CANADA
UNITED STATES
NIPAWIN PROVINCIAL PARK
PRINCE ALBERT NATIONAL PARK
CYPRESS HILLS PROV. PARK
DOUGLAS PROV. PARK
DANIELSON PROV. PARK
SASKATCHEWAN LANDING PROV. PARK
GREENWATER LAKE PROV. PARK
L. Diefenbaker
Last Mountain L.
South Saskatchewan
North Saskatchewan
Saskatchewan
Qu'Appelle
Souris
Projection: Lambert's Conformal Conic
West from Greenwich

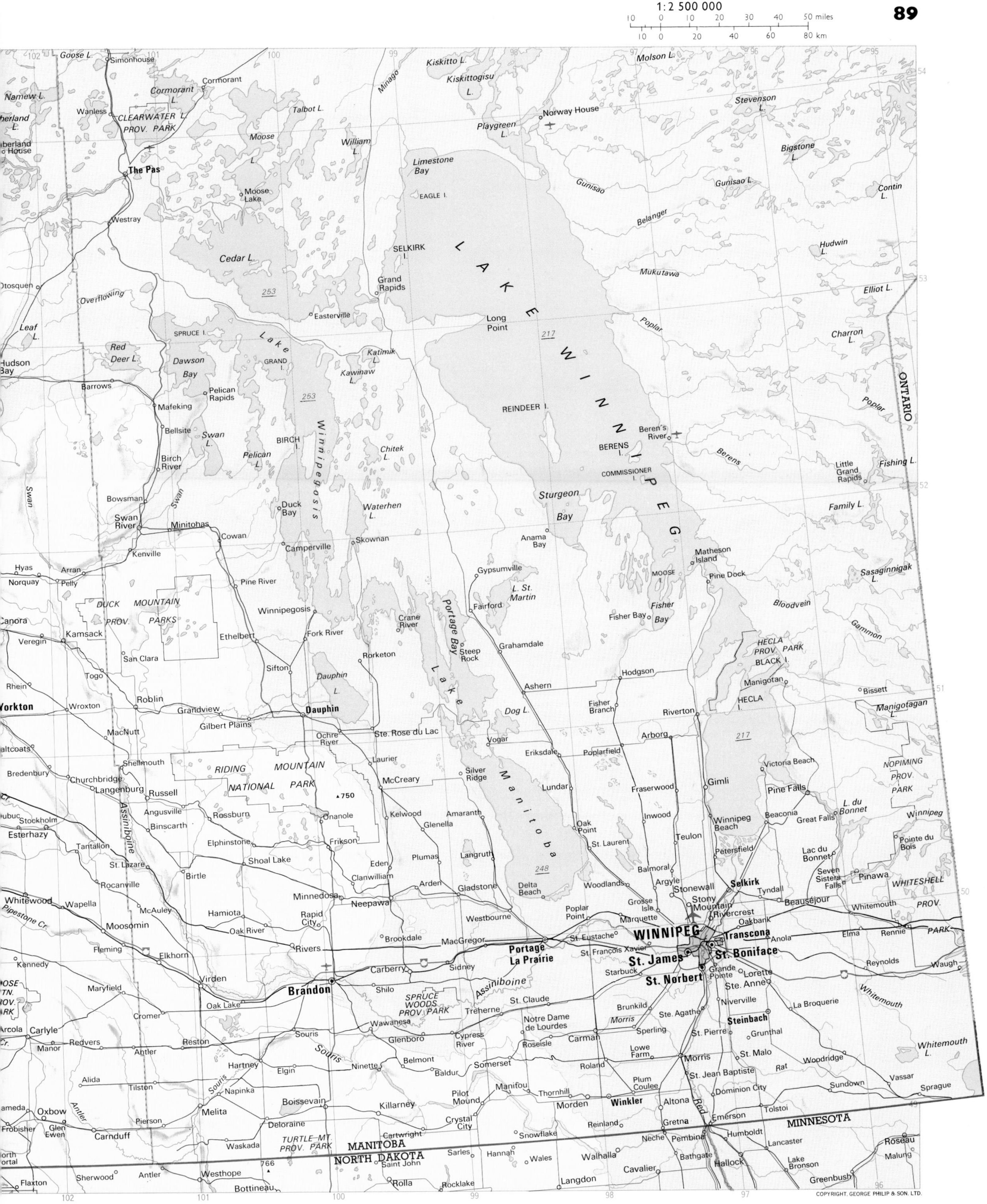
1:2 500 000
10 0 10 20 30 40 50 miles
10 0 20 40 60 80 km
LAKE WINNIPEG
Lake Winnipegosis
Lake Manitoba
ONTARIO
MANITOBA
NORTH DAKOTA
MINNESOTA
WINNIPEG
St. James
St. Boniface
St. Norbert
Transcona
Brandon
Portage La Prairie
Dauphin
The Pas
Selkirk
Steinbach
Winkler
Goose L.
Simonhouse
Cormorant
Cormorant L.
Namew L.
Wanless
CLEARWATER L. PROV. PARK
Talbot L.
Moose L.
Moose Lake
William L.
Westray
Cedar L.
Otosquen
Overflowing
Easterville
Grand Rapids
SELKIRK I.
Limestone Bay
EAGLE I.
Kiskitto L.
Kiskittogisu L.
Minago
Molson L.
Norway House
Playgreen L.
Stevenson L.
Bigstone L.
Gunisao
Gunisao L.
Contin L.
Belanger
Hudwin L.
Mukutawa
Elliot L.
Poplar
Charron L.
Long Point
Leaf L.
Red Deer L.
Hudson Bay
SPRUCE I.
Dawson Bay
GRAND I.
Katimik L.
Kawinaw L.
Barrows
Pelican Rapids
Mafeking
Bellsite
Swan L.
Pelican L.
BIRCH I.
Birch River
Chitek L.
REINDEER I.
Beren's River
BERENS I.
COMMISSIONER I.
Berens
Little Grand Rapids
Fishing L.
Family L.
Swan
Bowsman
Swan River
Minitonas
Cowan
Duck Bay
Waterhen L.
Sturgeon Bay
Anama Bay
Kenville
Camperville
Skownan
Matheson Island
Hyas
Norquay
Arran
Pelly
Pine River
Gypsumville
L. St. Martin
MOOSE I.
Pine Dock
Sasaginnigak L.
DUCK MOUNTAIN PROV. PARKS
Winnipegosis
Fairford
Fisher Bay
Bloodvein
Canora
Kamsack
Veregin
Ethelbert
Fork River
Crane River
Portage Bay
Steep Rock
Grahamdale
Gammon
HECLA PROV. PARK
BLACK I.
San Clara
Togo
Rorketon
Sifton
Dauphin L.
Hodgson
Ashern
Manigotan
Bissett
Rhein
Yorkton
Wroxton
Roblin
Grandview
Gilbert Plains
Dog L.
Fisher Branch
Riverton
HECLA I.
Manigotagan L.
MacNutt
Ochre River
Ste. Rose du Lac
Vogar
Arborg
Saltcoats
Shellmouth
Laurier
Eriksdale
Poplarfield
Victoria Beach
NOPIMING PROV. PARK
Bredenbury
Churchbridge
Langenburg
Russell
RIDING MOUNTAIN NATIONAL PARK
750
McCreary
Silver Ridge
Lundar
Fraserwood
Gimli
Pine Falls
L. du Bonnet
Winnipeg
Assiniboine
Angusville
Rossburn
Onanole
Kelwood
Amaranth
Glenella
Inwood
Winnipeg Beach
Beaconia
Great Falls
Stockholm
Binscarth
Esterhazy
Tantallon
Elphinstone
Frikson
Oak Point
St. Laurent
Teulon
Petersfield
Lac du Bonnet
Pointe du Bois
St. Lazare
Shoal Lake
Eden
Plumas
Langruth
Balmoral
Seven Sisters Falls
Pinawa
WHITESHELL PROV. PARK
Birtle
Clanwilliam
Rocanville
Arden
Gladstone
Argyle
Stonewall
Tyndall
Woodlands
Delta Beach
Whitewood
Wapella
McAuley
Minnedosa
Neepawa
Stony Mountain
Beausejour
Whitemouth
Pipestone Cr.
Hamiota
Rapid City
Westbourne
Grosse Isle
Poplar Point
Marquette
Rivercrest
Oakbank
Moosomin
Oak River
Brookdale
MacGregor
St. Eustache
Anola
Elma
Rennie
Fleming
Elkhorn
Rivers
St. Francois Xavier
Kennedy
Carberry
Sidney
Starbuck
Grande Pointe
Lorette
Reynolds
Waugh
Virden
Maryfield
Shilo
SPRUCE WOODS PROV. PARK
Ste. Anne
Oak Lake
St. Claude
Treherne
Brunkild
Niverville
La Broquerie
Cromer
Wawanesa
Notre Dame de Lourdes
Morris
Ste. Agathe
Carlyle
Arcola
Redvers
Manor
Reston
Souris
Glenboro
Cypress River
Roseisle
Carman
Sperling
St. Pierre
Grunthal
Whitemouth L.
Antler
Hartney
Elgin
Ninette
Belmont
Lowe Farm
St. Malo
Alida
Tilston
Napinka
Baldur
Somerset
Roland
St. Jean Baptiste
Rat
Woodridge
Vassar
Melita
Boissevain
Manitou
Thornhill
Plum Coulee
Dominion City
Sundown
Sprague
Oxbow
Glen Ewen
Frobisher
Pierson
Killarney
Pilot Mound
Morden
Altona
Red
Emerson
Tolstoi
Carnduff
Deloraine
Crystal City
Cartwright
Reinland
Gretna
TURTLE MT. PROV. PARK
Waskada
Snowflake
Neche
Pembina
Humboldt
Lancaster
Roseau
Malung
Sarles
Hannah
Wales
Walhalla
Bathgate
Hallock
Lake Bronson
766
Westhope
Saint John
Cavalier
Flaxton
Sherwood
Rolla
Rocklake
Langdon
Greenbush
Bottineau
102
101
100
99
98
97
96
95
54
53
52
51
50
49
217
253
248
COPYRIGHT, GEORGE PHILIP & SON, LTD.

1: 2 500 000

10 0 10 20 30 40 50 miles

10 0 20 40 60 80 km

SASKATCHEWAN
Fort McMurray
Fort MacKay
Athabasca
Clearwater
Christina
Gordon L.
Garson L.
Winefred L.
Firebag
Mc Clelland L.
Gardiner Lakes
Ells
Mackay
Conklin
Sand
Cold L.
Cold Lake
Medley
Grand Centre
Marie L.
Ardmore
Bonnyville
Muriel L.
Frog L.
Kitscoty
Marwayne
Dewberry
Islay
Vermilion
Elk Point
Derwent
Clandonald
St. Paul
Glendon
Mallaig
Ashmont
Myrnam
Two Hills
Innisfree
Ranfurly
Lavoy
Lac La Biche
Plamondon
Caslan
Kikino
Vilna
Smoky Lake
Saskatchewan
North
Willingdon
Mundare
Vegreville
Beaverhill L.
Tofield
Andrew
Bruderheim
Lamont
Chipman
ELK ISLAND NAT. PARK
North Buck L.
Boyle
Long L.
Newbrook
Waskatenau
Radway
Redwater
Fort Saskatchewan
Sherwood Park
Cooking L.
Beaumont
Calling Lake
Calling L.
Athabasca
Flat L.
Colinton
Rochester
Thorhild
Gibbons
Legal
Bon Accord
Clyde
Westlock
Morinville
Carbondale
St. Albert
EDMONTON
Spruce Grove
Stony Plain
Devon
Mikkwa
Birch
Wabasca
N. Wabasca L.
Wabasca Desmarais
S. Wabasca L.
Peerless Lake
Graham L.
Peerless L.
Muskwa
Muskwa L.
Nipisi L.
LESSER SLAVE LAKE PROV. PARK
Slave Lake
Smith
Hondo
Chisholm
Flatbush
Fawcett
Linaria
Fort Assiniboine
Barrhead
Highridge
Arvilla
Rich Valley
Sandy L.
Onoway
Alberta Beach
Wabamun
Genesee
Pembina
Cherhill
Sanguido
Lac Ste. Anne
Isle L.
Seba Beach
Round Valley
Panny
Loon
Wadlin L.
Utikuma L.
Lesser Slave L.
Canyon Creek
Kinuso
Swan
Swan Hills
Freeman
Lone Pine
Mystery Lake
Mayerthorpe
Evansburg
Chip L.
Wildwood
Cynthia
Hattonford
Blue Ridge
Whitecourt
McLeod
Lubicon Lake
Lubicon L.
Gift Lake
Grouard Mission
Joussard
Faust
Bison L.
Buffalo
South Heart
WINAGAMI LAKE PROV. PARK
Winagami L.
Enilda
High Prairie
Two Creeks
Windfall
MacKay
Peers
Cadotte
Little Cadotte
Kimiwan L.
McLennan
Snipe L.
Fox Creek
Edson
Peace
Peace River
Falher
Donnelly
Little Smoky
Smoky
Manning
North Star
Dixonville
Chinook Valley
Cardinal L.
Grimshaw
Berwyn
Girouxville
Sturgeon L.
Valleyview
Berland
Oped
Hinton
WILLIAM A. SWITZER PROV. PARK
Hotchkiss
Notikewin
Eureka River
Hines Creek
Fairview
Dunvegan
Eaglesham
Wanham
Bad Heart
Teepee Creek
Debolt
Simonette
Wildhay
Brule
Chinchaga
Worsley
Blueberry Mountain
Rycroft
Spirit River
Clairmont
Sexsmith
Grande Prairie
Wapiti
Grovedale
Homestead
Muskeg River
WILLMORE WILDERNESS PARK
2607
Cutbank
Kakwa
Grande Cache
3331
Clear
Doig
Bonanza
Hythe
Bear L.
Lymburn
Beaverlodge
Wembley
Redwillow
Elmworth
Sylvester
Narraway

BRITISH COLUMBIA

MONTANA

WASHINGTON

IDAHO

U. S. A.

Rocky Mountains

Cariboo Mountains

CALGARY

Lethbridge

Medicine Hat

Red Deer

ft	m
9000	3000
6000	2000
4500	1500
3000	1000
1200	400
600	200

West from Greenwich

Projection: Lambert's Conformal Conic

1:2 500 000

10 0 10 20 30 40 50 miles

10 0 20 40 60 80 km

Prince George
Shelley
Penny
Pineview
Red Rock
Stoner
Woodpecker
Hixon
Strathnaver
Dunkley
Moose Heights
Quesnel
Kersley
Alexandria
Castle Rock
Marguerite
Macalister
Williams Lake
150 Mile House
Meldrum Creek
Riske Creek
Hanceville
Springhouse
Big Creek
Gang Ranch
Dog Creek
Wright
Lac la Hache
Forest Grove
Canim Lake
Tatton
Buffalo Creek
100 Mile House
Lone Butte
70 Mile House
Chasm
Clinton
Big Bar Creek
Cache Creek
Ashcroft
Walhachin
Savona
Cherry Creek
Kamloops
Bralorne
Shalalth
Seton Portage
Lillooet
Spences Bridge
Birken
Pemberton
Lytton
Alta Lake
North Bend
Boston Bar
Spuzzum
Yale
Hope
Laidlaw
Cheam View
Agassiz
Harrison Hot Springs
Rosedale
Chilliwack
Sardis
Mission City
Yarrow
Abbotsford
Sumas
Lindell Beach
Squamish
Brackendale
Woodfibre
Britannia Beach
Port Mellon
Bowen Island
North Vancouver
Port Moody
Port Coquitlam
Haney
VANCOUVER
New Westminster
Fort Langley
Langley
White Rock
Blaine
Lynden
Ferndale
Bellingham
Anacortes
Sedro Woolley
Burlington
Mountvernon
Oak Harbor
Stanwood
Arlington
Coupeville
Darrington
VICTORIA
Sooke
Sidney
Chemainus
Crofton
Maple Bay
Fulford Harbour
Dome Creek
Crescent Spur
Lamming Mills
McBride
Dunster
Valemount
Albreda
Wells
Likely
Horsefly
Hendrix Lake
Mahood Falls
Clearwater
Birch Island
Vavenby
Little Fort
Chu Chua
Barrière
Louis Creek
McLure
Black Pines
Rayleigh
Westsyde
Chase
Salmon Arm
Canoe
Sicamous
Enderby
Armstrong
Vernon
Cherryville
Oyama
Kelowna
Okanagan Mission
Wilson Landing
Peachland
Summerland
Penticton
Merritt
Lower Nicola
Nicola
Quilchena
Valleyview
Aspen Grove
Brookmere
Coalmont
Princeton
Hedley
Keremeos
Oliver
Osoyoos
Oroville
Rock Creek
Greenwood
Midway
Grand Forks
Christina
Eholt
Carmi
Beaverdell
Rossland
Warfield
Trail
Fruitvale
Montrose
Castlegar
Kinnaird
Brilliant
Salmo
Nelson
Procter
Boswell
Renata
Edgewood
Fauquier
Burton
Nakusp
Arrow Park
Slocan
Silverton
New Denver
Kaslo
Riondel
Marblehead
Trout Lake
Gerrard
Arrowhead
Revelstoke
Albert Canyon
Glacier
Golden
Parson
Donald
Beavermouth
Lake Louise
Seymour Arm
Avola
Blue River
Mica Creek
Mica Dam
Jasper
Hinton
Obed
Brûlé
Miette Hotsprings
Luscar
Cadomin
Mountain Park
Mercoal
Robb
Foothills
Nordegg
Cynthia
Pembina
Big Horn Dam
Sunwapta Pass
Bow Pass
Kicking Horse Pass
Vermilion Pass
Yellowhead Pass
Red Pass
Lucerne
Snaring
Rocky Mountains
Cariboo Mountains
ALBERTA
WASHINGTON
IDAHO
CANADA
U.S.A.
Mt. Robson 3954
Mt. Columbia 3747
Mt. Chapman 3075
Mt. Sir Sandford 3522
Mt. Templeman 3070
Mt. Garibaldi 2678
Skihist Mt. 2944
Silvertip Mt. 2606
Mt. Baker 3284
Glacier Peak 3211
Mt. Alex Graham 1665
WILLMORE WILDERNESS PARK
WILLIAM A. SWITZER PROV. PARK
JASPER NATIONAL PARK
MT. ROBSON PROV. PARK
BOWRON LAKE PROV. PARK
WELLS GRAY PROVINCIAL PARK
HAMBER PROV. PARK
BANFF NATIONAL PARK
YOHO NATIONAL PARK
GLACIER NAT'L PARK
MT. REVELSTOKE NAT'L PARK
BUGABOO GLACIER PROV. PARK
MONASHEE PROV. PARK
SILVER STAR PROV. PARK
KOKANEE GLACIER PROV. PARK
OKANAGAN MOUNTAIN PROV. PARK
GARIBALDI PROV. PARK
GOLDEN EARS PROV. PARK
MANNING PROV. PARK
CATHEDRAL PROV. PARK
NORTH CASCADES NATIONAL PARK
McNaughton Lake
Shuswap L.
Kamloops L.
Okanagan L.
Upper Arrow Lake
Lower Arrow L.
Kootenay L.
Slocan L.
Duncan L.
Harrison Lake
Quesnel L.
Horsefly L.
Murphy L.
Canim L.
Mahood L.
Sheridan L.
Bonaparte L.
Nicola L.
Adams L.
Mabel L.
Sugar L.
Anderson L.
Seton L.
Lillooet L.
Carpenter L.
Pitt L.
Stave L.
Ross L.
Chelan L.
Osoyoos L.
Fraser
Thompson
North Thompson
South Thompson
Columbia
Clearwater
Adams
Athabasca
Smoky
Kettle
Granby
Okanogan
Sanpoil
Pend Oreille
Kootenay
Tonasket
Riverside
Omak
Okanogan
Conconully
Mazama
Winthrop
Twisp
Carlton
Malott
Nespelem
Republic
Kettle Falls
Colville
Chewelah
Springdale
Newport
Northport
Metaline Falls
Ione
Priest L.
Concrete
Rockport
Marblemount
Newhalem
Hamilton
Maple Falls
Stehekin
Holden
Lucerne
Silverton
COPYRIGHT. GEORGE PHILIP & SON, LTD.

ARCTIC OCEAN
Beaufort Sea
Permanent Polar Ice
Pt. Franklin
Barrow
Pt. Barrow
C. Halkett
Colville
Umiat
Prudhoe Bay
Kaktovik
Martin Pt.
Brooks Range
Mt. Doonerak 2320
Endicott Mts.
Evansville
Wiseman
Allakaket
Mt. Isto 2761
Arctic Village
Herschel I.
Mackenzie Bay
Richards I.
British Mts.
ALASKA (U.S.A.)
Stevens
Beaver
Fort Yukon
Porcupine
Old Crow
Livengood
Fairbanks
Yukon
Tanana
Delta Junction
Eagle
Circle
Chicken
Tanacross
Ogilvie Mts.
Aklavik
Inuvik
Tuktoyaktuk
Eskimo Lakes
Richardson Mts.
Ft. McPherson
Arctic Red River
Peel
Mackenzie
Dawson
Klondike
Mt. Sanford 4949
Wrangell Mts.
Stewart River
Beaver Creek
Elsa
Keno Hill
Mayo
Mackenzie Mountains
Pelly Crossing
Carmacks
YUKON TERRITORY
Mt. Steele 5011
Mt. Logan 6051
Kluane L.
Burwash Landing
Destruction Bay
Haines Junc.
Mt. Kennedy 4236
KLUANE NAT. PARK
Whitehorse
St. Elias Mts.
Yakutat
Carcross
Bennett
Jakes Corner
Johnsons Crossing
Teslin
Atlin
4663
Fairweather
Skagway
Cross Sd.
Chichagof I.
Juneau
Douglas
Admiralty I.
Sitka
Baranof I.
Cassiar Mts.
Cassiar
Dease
Dease Lake
Stikine
Telegraph Creek
Faro
Ross River
Pelly
2965
S. Nahanni
2743
Tungsten
NAHANNI NAT. PARK
Upper Liard
Watson Lake
Nahanni Butte
Liard
Fort Liard
ALASKA HIGHWAY
Ft. Nelson
Mt. Lloyd George 3292
Nelson
Liverpool Bay
C. Bathurst
Franklin Bay
Darnley Bay
Paulatuk
Anderson
Horton
Hornaday
INUVIK REGION
NORTHWEST
Aubry L.
Colville Lake
L. Belot
L. Maunoir
Bluenose L.
Ft. Good Hope
L. des Bois
Smith Arm
Dease Arm
Franklin Mts.
Norman Wells
Ft. Norman
Fort Franklin
Great Bear
Keith Arm
Gt. Bear Lake
157
Echo Bay (Port Radium)
Hottah L.
Wrigley
Mackenzie
Ft. Simpson
Jean Marie River
Liard
L. la Martre
Lac la Martre
Rae Lakes
Snare Lakes
Yellowknife
Rae-Edzo
Yellowknife
Detah
FORT SMITH REGION
Fort Providence
Great Slave L.
156
Hay River
Enterprise
Trout L.
Trout Lake
Petitot
Pine Point
Fort Resolution
Rocher River
Slave
WOOD BUFFALO NAT. PARK
Ft. Smith
Caribou Mts.
Meander River
MACKENZIE HIGHWAY
C. Wrottesley
C. Prince Alfred
Storkerson B.
Banks Island
C. Kellett
Sachs Harbour
Thesiger Bay
C. Lambton
750
Amundsen Gulf
Prince of Wales Str.
Passage Pt.
M'Clure Strait
Borden I.
Prince Gustav Adolf Sea
Brock I.
Mackenzie King I.
Parry Island
Lougheed I.
Prince Patrick I.
Mould Bay
Eglinton I.
Kellett Str.
Blue Hills 1067
Melville I.
Liddon Gulf
Dundas Pen.
C. Hay
Viscount Melville Sound
Stefansson I.
Wynniatt Bay
Prince Albert Pen.
Hadley Bay
Holman
Victoria Island
C. Baring
Prince Albert Sd.
Wollaston Pen.
Dolphin & Union Str.
Read Island
Cambridge Bay
Kent Pen.
Coppermine
Coronation Gulf
Bathurst Inlet
Bathurst Inlet
Coppermine
Takiyuak L.
Burnside
Pelly L.
Contwoyto L.
Point L.
L. de Gras
Back
Aylmer L.
Clinton Colden L.
Reliance
Snowdrift
Nonacho L.
Dubawnt
Wholdaia L.
ft m
12 000 4000
9000 3000
6000 2000
4500 1500
3000 1000
1200 400
600 200
0 0
200 600
m ft
Projection: Bonne
170 160 150 140 130 120 110 70

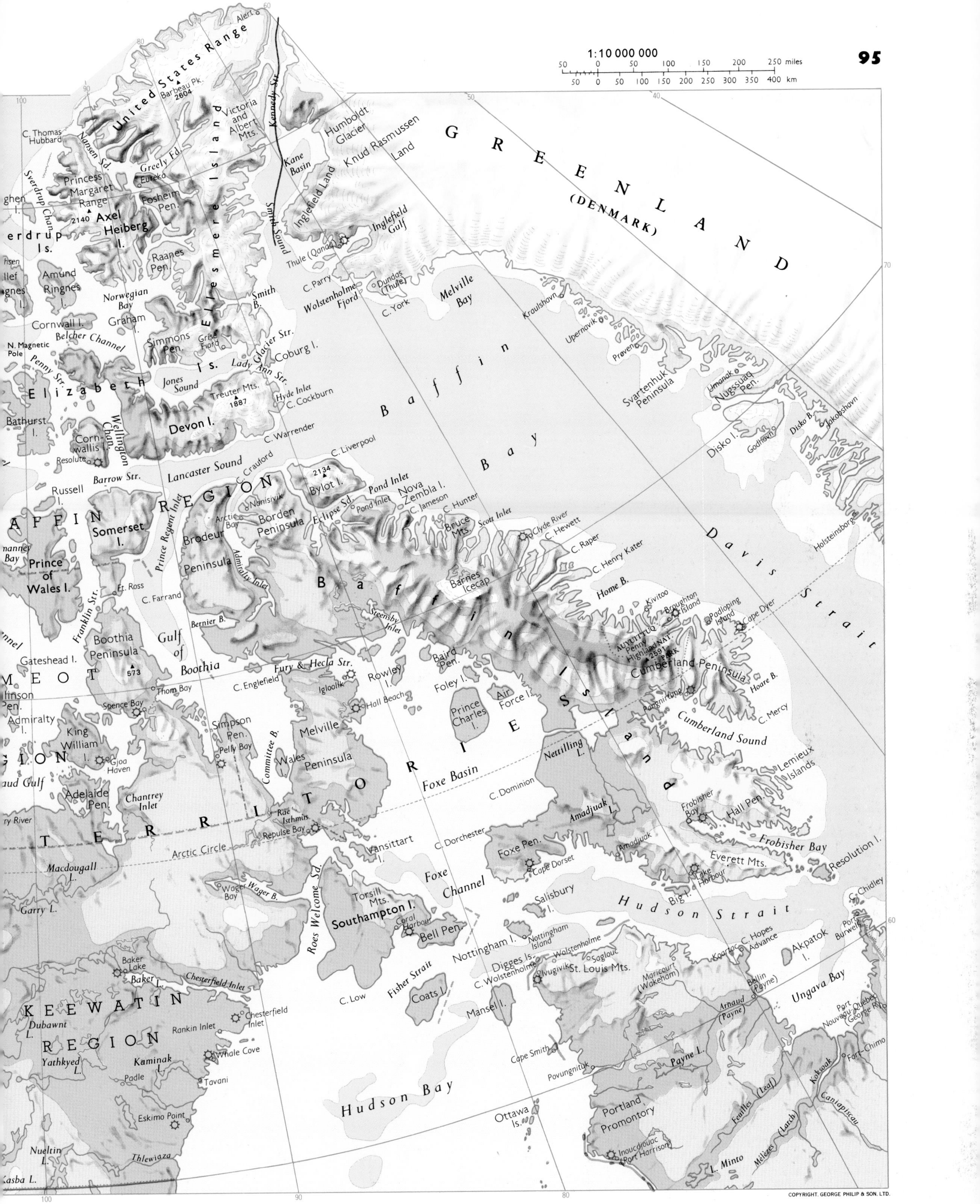

1:10 000 000

50 0 50 100 150 200 250 miles

50 0 50 100 150 200 250 300 350 400 km

GREENLAND
(DENMARK)
Baffin Bay
Davis Strait
Baffin Island
United States Range
Ellesmere Island
Axel Heiberg I.
Devon I.
Lancaster Sound
Gulf of Boothia
Foxe Basin
Foxe Channel
Hudson Strait
Hudson Bay
Ungava Bay
Southampton I.
Melville Peninsula
Cumberland Sound
Frobisher Bay
KEEWATIN REGION
BAFFIN REGION
TERRITORIES
Arctic Circle

PACIFIC OCEAN
Golfo de California
BAJA CALIFORNIA NORTE
BAJA CALIFORNIA SUR
SONORA
CHIHUAHUA
COAHUILA
DURANGO
SINALOA
NAYARIT
JALISCO
COLIMA
MICHOACAN
ZACATECAS
NEW MEXICO
ARIZONA
TIJUANA
MEXICALI
Ensenada
TUCSON
CIUDAD JUÁREZ
EL PASO
Hermosillo
Guaymas
Ciudad Obregón
Navojoa
Los Mochis
Culiacán
Mazatlán
Tepic
GUADALAJARA
CHIHUAHUA
Victoria de Durango
Zacatecas
Aguascalientes
LEÓN
TORREÓN
Saltillo
Monclova
La Paz
Morelia
Colima
Manzanillo
Is. de Revillagigedo (Mexico)
REFERENCE TO NUMBERS
1 Federal District
2 Aguascalientes
3 Guanajuato
4 Hidalgo
5 México
6 Morelos
7 Querétaro
8 Tlaxcala
Projection: Bi-polar oblique Conical Orthomorphic
West from Greenwich

1:8 000 000
50 0 50 100 150 200 miles
50 0 50 100 150 200 250 300 km
ARKANSAS
MISSISSIPPI
ALABAMA
GEORGIA
LOUISIANA
FLORIDA
STATES
Wichita Falls
Denison
Sherman
Paris
Texarkana
Hope
Camden
El Dorado
Greenville
Tuscaloosa
Opelika
Columbus
Selma
Phenix City
Montgomery
McRae
Americus
Cordele
Albany
Tifton
Waycross
Troy
Dothan
Jim Woodruff Res.
Valdosta
Tallahassee
Lake City
Denton
Greenville
Possum Kingdom Res.
FORT WORTH
DALLAS
Ranger
Cleburne
Marshall
Longview
Tyler
Monroe
Tallulah
Vicksburg
Jackson
Meridian
Shreveport
Natchez
Laurel
Hattiesburg
Flomaton
Hillsboro
Corsicana
Palestine
Toledo Bend Res.
Nacogdoches
Brownwood
Waco
Lufkin
Sam Rayburn Res.
Alexandria
McComb
Bogalusa
MOBILE
Pensacola
Panama City
Apalchee Bay
Temple
Jewett
Huntsville
Bryan
Baton Rouge
Hammond
Biloxi
Gulfport
L. Pontchartrain
NEW ORLEANS
Mobile Bay
Breton Sound
C. San Blas
Suwannee
Austin
Navasota
Beaumont
Lake Charles
Lafayette
HOUSTON
Port Arthur
Atchafalaya Bay
Terrebonne B.
Mississippi Delta
Rosenberg
Galveston
Clearwater
SAN ANTONIO
Victoria
Guadalupe
Dilley
Nueces
Alice
Corpus Christi
Laredo
Kingsville
Nuevo Laredo
Zapata
GULF OF MEXICO
Laguna Madre
Camargo
Mc Allen
Harlingen
Brownsville
Presa M.R. Gomez
Reynosa
China
Matamoros
Valle Hermoso
Santa Teresa
Montemorelos
Mendez
Laguna Madre
San Fernando
Linares
Villagrán
Santander-Jiménez
La Pesca
Soto la Marina
TAMAULIPAS
Sierra de Tamaulipas
Ciudad Victoria
Llera
Aldama
Pta. Jerez
Ciudad Mante
Ciudad Madero
Tampico
Altamira
Ciudad de Valles
Pánuco
Laguna de Tamiahua
Tempoal
Ozuluama
C. Rojo
Tantoyuca
Tamazunchale
Chicontepec
Tuxpan
Poza Rica
Papantla
Zimapán
Huichapan
Pachuca
Huauchinango
Nautla
Misantla
Tulancingo
Teziutlán
Jalapa Enríquez
Tula
Zumpango
Zempoala
MÉXICO
Tlaxcala
PUEBLA
Coatepec
Veracruz Llave
Citlaltépetl 5700
Amecameca
Popocatépetl 5452
Orizaba
Córdoba
Alvarado
Tlacotalpan
Cuernavaca
Tehuacán
Cosamaloapan
San Andrés Tuxtla
1879
Coatzacoalcos
Iguala
Acatlán
Tres Valles
Presa Miguel Alemán
Acayucan
Minatitlán
Chilapa
Chilpancingo
Huajuapan de León
Asunción Nochixtlán
Tlaxiaco
Oaxaca
Ocotlán
Ixtepec
Matías Romero
Juchitán
Tehuantepec
Salina Cruz
Golfo de Tehuantepec
Acapulco
Ometepec
Pinotepa Nacional
Jamiltepec
Tututepec
Pta. Maldonado
Miahuatlán
3139
Pochutla
Puerto Escondido
Puerto Ángel
Papagayo
Verde
OAXACA
Sierra Madre del Sur
Golfo de Campeche
Campeche
Champotón
Chenkán
Ciudad del Carmen
Laguna de Términos
Frontera
Paraíso
Comalcalco
La Venta
Cárdenas
TABASCO
Villahermosa
Palizada
Balancán
Macuspana
Tenosique
Palenque
Jesús Carranza
Presa Netzahualcoyotl
Copainalá
Simojovel
Chiapa de Corzo
Ocosingo
San Cristóbal de las Casas
Usumacinta
Tuxtla Gutiérrez
CHIAPAS
Comitán
La Independencia
Lacantún
Arriaga
Tonalá
Sierra Madre
La Concordia
Mar Muerto
Puerto Arista
Pijijiapan
Mapastepec
Motozintla
Huixtla
4247
Tapachula
Isla Desterrada
Isla Pérez
Canal de Yucatán
C. San Antonio
La Esperanza
CUBA
Guane
La Fé
C. Corrientes
Pta. Yalkubul
Río Lagartos
C. Catoche
El Cuyo
Pta. Juárez
Dzilam de Bravo
Progreso
Mérida
Motul
Temax
Izamal
Tizimín
Espita
Valladolid
Puerto Morelos
Isla Cozumel
Cozumel
YUCATÁN
Maxcanú
Sotuta
Uxmal
Ticul
Tekax
Peto
Tenabo
Bolonchenticul
Hopelchén
Vigía Chico
B. de la Ascensión
B. del Espíritu Santo
Felipe Carrillo Puerto
QUINTANA ROO
Bacalar
Banco Chinchorro
Chetumal
B. de Chetumal
Corozal
Ambergris Cay
CAMPECHE
Matamoros
Pital
Concepción
Orange Walk
Hondo
Turneffe Is.
Uaxactún
Tikal
L. Petén Itzá
La Libertad
Flores
San Ignacio
Belize City
Belmopan
BELIZE
Dangriga
Benque Viejo
Golfo de Honduras
Islas de la Bahía
Maya Mts.
Monkey River
San Antonio
Punta Gorda
San Luis
Roatán
Puerto Castilla
Trujillo
Sebol
Livingston
Puerto Barrios
Puerto Cortés
Tela
La Ceiba
L. de Izabel
GUATEMALA
Cobán
Cuchumatanes
Huehuetenango
Motagua
Sa. de las Minas
Zacapa
Chiquimula
San Pedro Sula
HONDURAS
Santa Bárbara
Yoro
Olanchito
Savá
Catacamas
Patuca
Juticalpa
Comayagua
Tegucigalpa
Danlí
Santa Rosa de Copán
El Jaral
L. de Yojoa
La Paz
La Esperanza
Jalapa
Antigua
Totonicapán
San Marcos
Quez.
Sololá
Mazatenango
Retalhuleu
Coatepeque
Ocos
Amatitlán
Utatlán
Salamá
Cuilco
Yuscarán
COPYRIGHT, GEORGE PHILIP & SON, LTD.

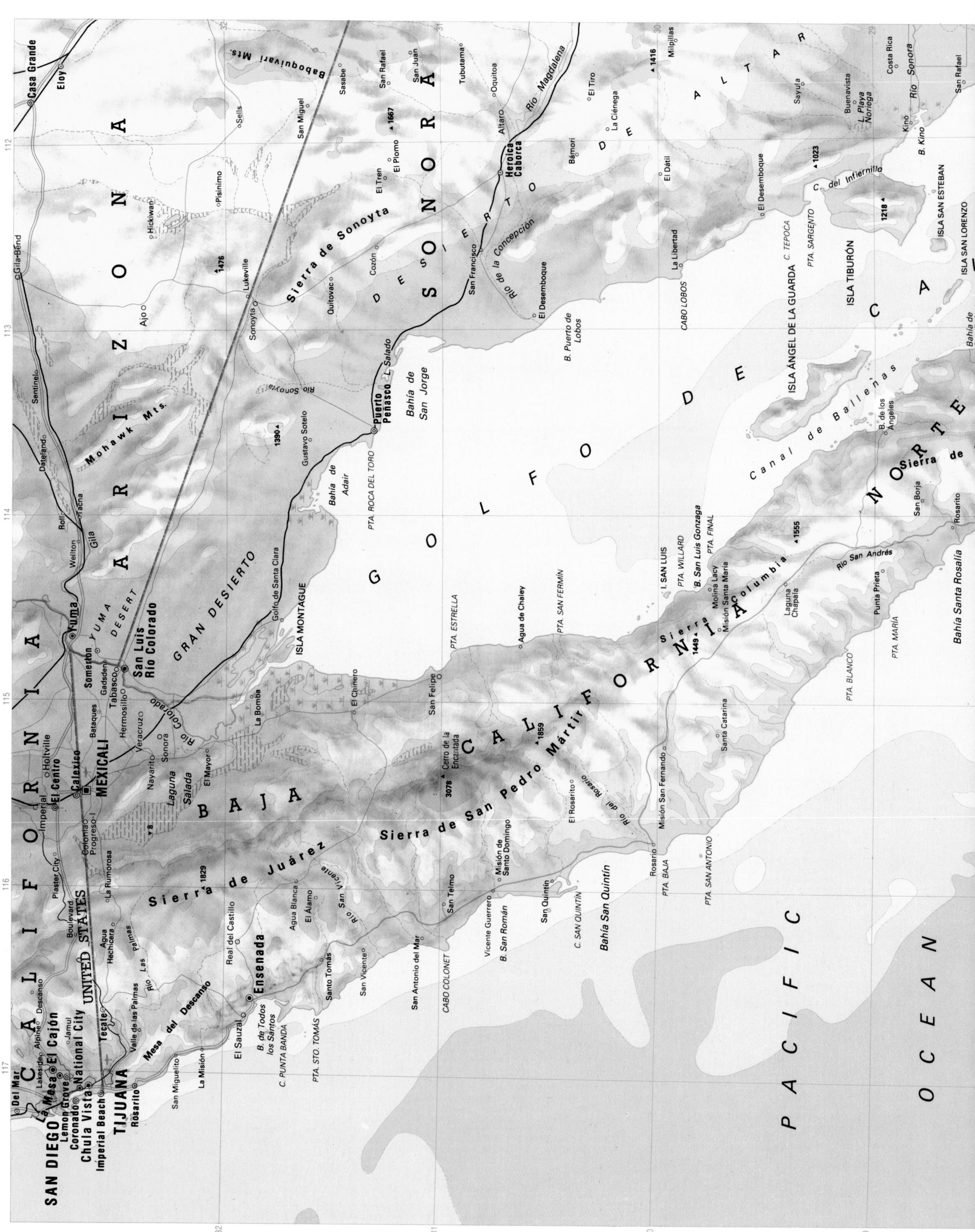

CALIFORNIA
ARIZONA
SONORA
BAJA CALIFORNIA NORTE
GOLFO DE CALIFORNIA
PACIFIC OCEAN
UNITED STATES
DESIERTO DE ALTAR
GRAN DESIERTO
YUMA DESERT
SAN DIEGO
TIJUANA
MEXICALI
Ensenada
Yuma
San Luis Río Colorado
Puerto Peñasco
Heroica Caborca
Casa Grande
Eloy
Gila Bend
Ajo
Sells
Sonoyta
Lukeville
Calexico
El Centro
Imperial
Holtville
Tecate
Rosarito
Chula Vista
National City
El Cajon
La Mesa
Lemon Grove
Coronado
Imperial Beach
Del Mar
Lakeside
Alpine
Descanso
Jamul
Boulevard
Plaster City
La Rumorosa
Colonia Progreso
Laguna Salada
Sierra de Juárez
Sierra de San Pedro Mártir
Cerro de la Encantada
3078
1859
1829
Mesa del Descanso
Valle de las Palmas
San Miguelito
La Misión
El Sauzal
B. de Todos los Santos
C. PUNTA BANDA
PTA. STO. TOMÁS
Santo Tomás
San Vicente
San Antonio del Mar
CABO COLONET
San Telmo
Vicente Guerrero
B. San Román
Misión de Santo Domingo
San Quintín
C. SAN QUINTÍN
Bahía San Quintín
El Rosarito
Río del Rosario
Rosario
PTA. BAJA
PTA. SAN ANTONIO
Misión San Fernando
Santa Catarina
San Felipe
El Chinero
La Bomba
PTA. ESTRELLA
Agua de Chaley
PTA. SAN FERMÍN
I. SAN LUIS
PTA. WILLARD
B. San Luis Gonzaga
PTA. FINAL
Misión Santa María
Molina Lacy
Sierra Columbia
1449
1555
Laguna Chapala
Punta Prieta
PTA. MARÍA
PTA. BLANCO
Bahía Santa Rosalía
Río San Andrés
San Borja
Rosarito
B. de los Ángeles
Canal de Ballenas
Sierra de
ISLA ÁNGEL DE LA GUARDA
ISLA TIBURÓN
ISLA SAN ESTEBAN
ISLA SAN LORENZO
C. del Infiernillo
PTA. SARGENTO
C. TEPOCA
CABO LOBOS
La Libertad
El Desemboque
Bahía de San Jorge
Bahía de Adair
PTA. ROCA DEL TORO
Gustavo Sotelo
1390
ISLA MONTAGUE
Golfo de Santa Clara
Río Colorado
Río Sonoyta
Mohawk Mts.
Sierra de Sonoyta
Baboquivari Mts.
Río Magdalena
Río de la Concepción
Río Sonora
Gila
Wellton
Tacna
Roll
Dateland
Sentinel
Somerton
Gadsden
Tabasco
Hermosillo
Veracruz
Sonora
Nayarito
El Mayor
Bataques
Quitovac
Cozón
El Tren
El Plomo
1667
San Miguel
Sasabe
San Rafael
San Juan
Tubutama
Oquitoa
Altar
Pitiquito
Bámori
El Tiro
La Ciénega
El Dátil
1416
Milpillas
San Francisco
1476
Hickiwan
Pisinimo
Sayula
Buenavista
L. Playa Noriega
Costa Rica
Kino
B. Kino
1023
1218
B. Puerto de Lobos
Real del Castillo
Agua Blanca
El Álamo
Agua Hechicera
Las Palmas

1:2 500 000

10 0 10 20 30 40 50 miles

10 0 20 40 60 80 km

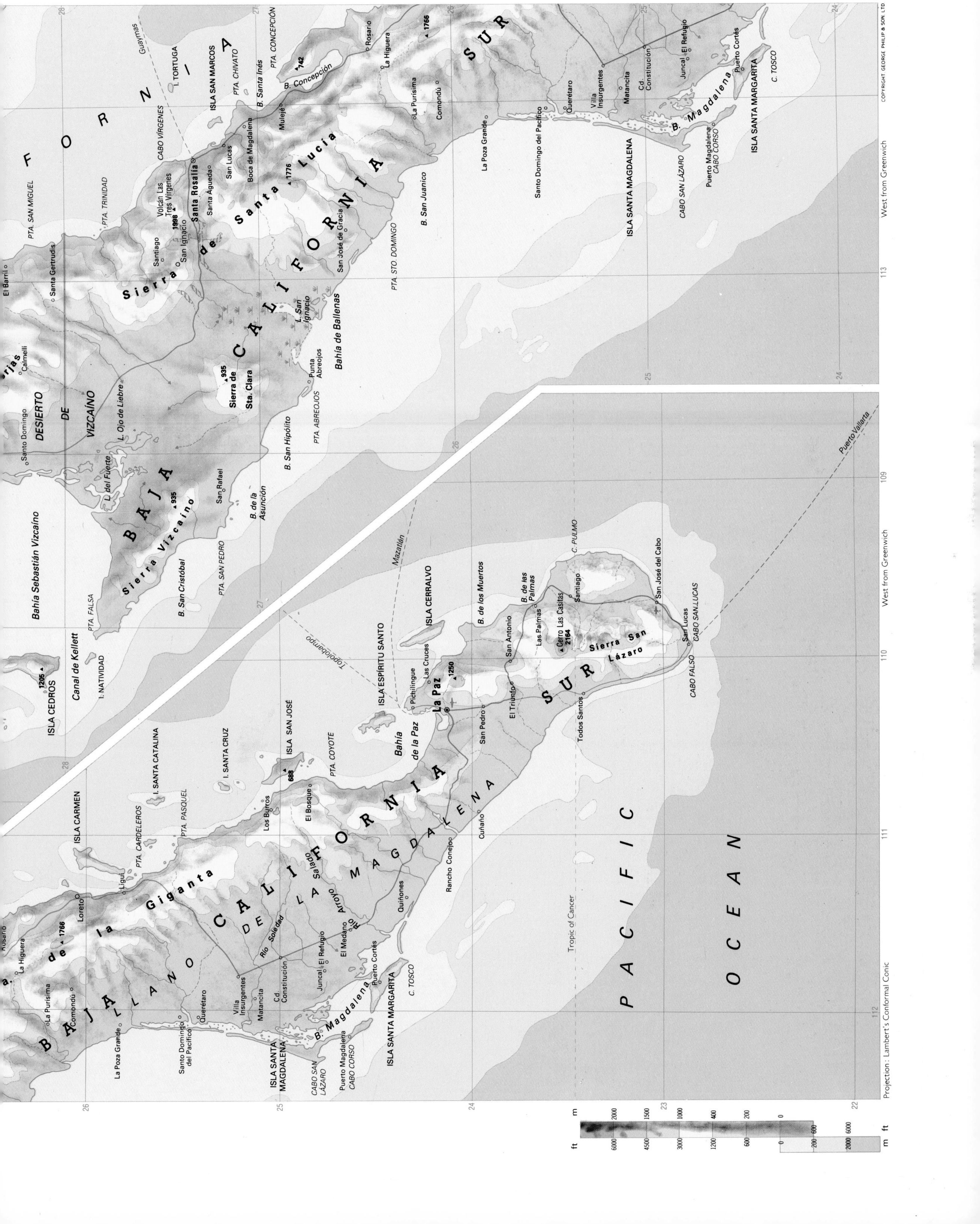

BAJA CALIFORNIA SUR

Sierra de Santa Lucía

DESIERTO DE VIZCAÍNO

Sierra Vizcaíno

Sierra de Sta. Clara

Bahía Sebastián Vizcaíno

Canal de Kellett

ISLA CEDROS

I. NATIVIDAD

PTA. FALSA

B. San Cristóbal

PTA. SAN PEDRO

B. de la Asunción

San Rafael

B. San Hipólito

PTA. ABREOJOS

Punta Abreojos

Bahía de Ballenas

L. San Ignacio

PTA. STO. DOMINGO

B. San Juanico

L. del Fuerte

L. Ojo de Liebre

Santo Domingo

El Barril

Santa Gertrudis

PTA. SAN MIGUEL

PTA. TRINIDAD

Calmelli

Santiago

San Ignacio

Volcán Las Tres Vírgenes

Santa Rosalía

Santa Agueda

San Lucas

Boca de Magdalena

Mulegé

B. Concepción

B. Santa Inés

PTA. CONCEPCIÓN

PTA. CHIVATO

CABO VÍRGENES

ISLA SAN MARCOS

I. TORTUGA

Guaymas

Rosario

La Higuera

La Purísima

Comondú

San José de Gracia

La Poza Grande

Santo Domingo del Pacifico

Querétaro

Villa Insurgentes

Matancita

Cd. Constitución

Juncal

El Refugio

Puerto Cortés

B. Magdalena

ISLA SANTA MAGDALENA

CABO SAN LÁZARO

Puerto Magdalena

CABO CORSO

ISLA SANTA MARGARITA

C. TOSCO

West from Greenwich

LLANO DE LA MAGDALENA

Sierra de la Giganta

Loreto

Ligui

ISLA CARMEN

PTA. CARDELEROS

I. SANTA CATALINA

PTA. PASQUEL

I. SANTA CRUZ

ISLA SAN JOSÉ

PTA. COYOTE

Los Burros

El Bosque

Río Salado

Arroyo

Río Soledad

El Medano

Quiñones

Rancho Conejo

Cuñano

Bahía de la Paz

La Paz

Pichilingue

ISLA ESPÍRITU SANTO

Las Cruces

ISLA CERRALVO

Topolobampo

Mazatlán

B. de los Muertos

San Pedro

El Triunfo

San Antonio

Las Palmas

B. de las Palmas

Cerro Las Casitas

Santiago

C. PULMO

San José del Cabo

Sierra San Lázaro

Todos Santos

San Lucas

CABO SAN LUCAS

CABO FALSO

Puerto Vallarta

Tropic of Cancer

PACIFIC OCEAN

Projection: Lambert's Conformal Conic

m ft

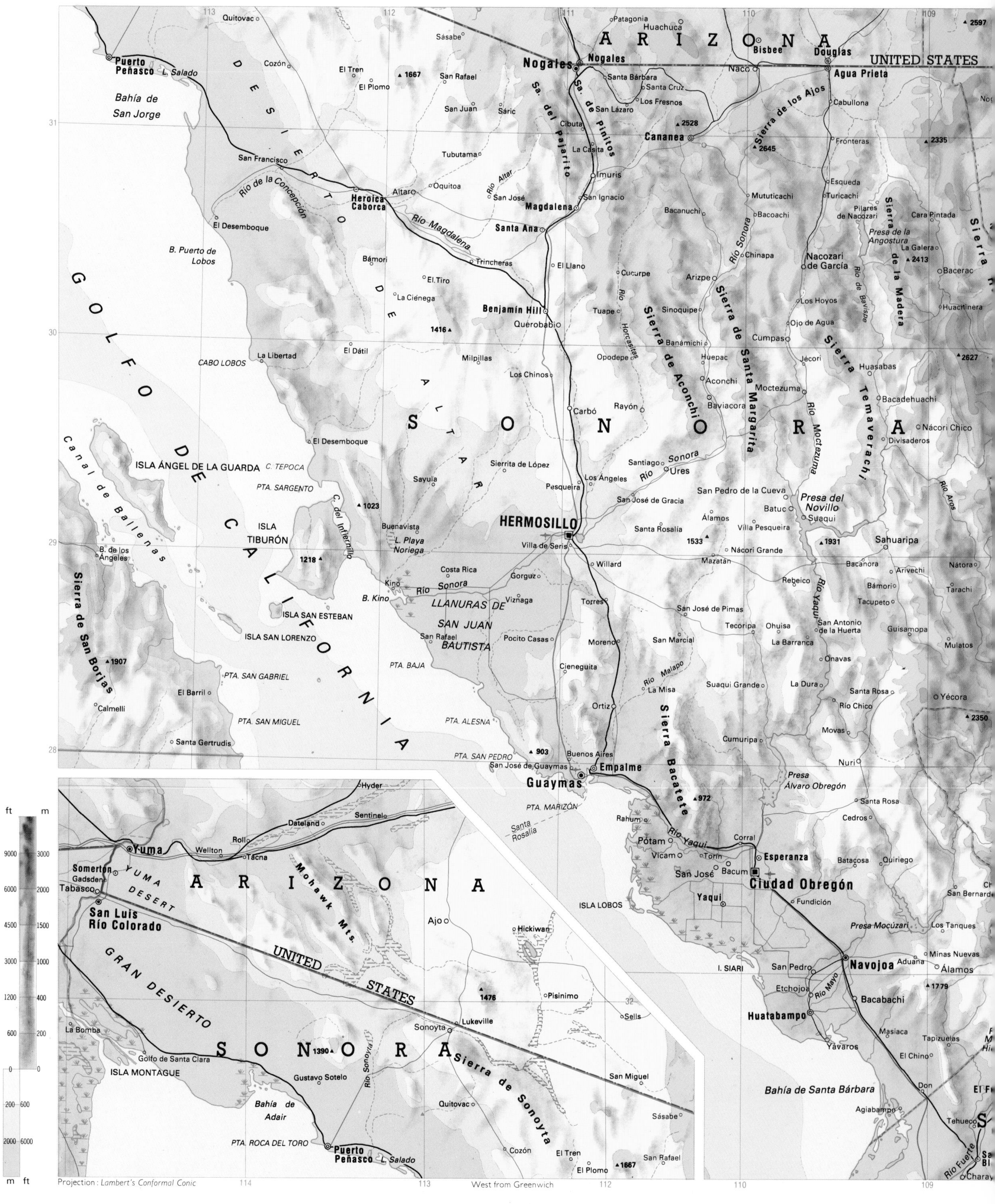
ARIZONA
UNITED STATES
SONORA
GOLFO DE CALIFORNIA
DESIERTO DE ALTAR
Nogales
Hermosillo
Guaymas
Empalme
Ciudad Obregón
Navojoa
Huatabampo
Heroica Caborca
Puerto Peñasco
Magdalena
Santa Ana
Cananea
Agua Prieta
Douglas
Bisbee
Naco
Benjamín Hill
Nacozari de García
Esperanza
Bahía de San Jorge
Bahía de Santa Bárbara
ISLA TIBURÓN
ISLA ÁNGEL DE LA GUARDA
ISLA SAN ESTEBAN
ISLA SAN LORENZO
ISLA LOBOS
Canal de Ballenas
Sierra de San Borjas
Sierra de Aconchi
Sierra de Santa Margarita
Sierra Temaveráchi
Sierra Bacatete
Sierra de los Ajos
Sierra de la Madera
Sa. de Pinitos
Sa. del Pajarito
Río Sonora
Río Yaqui
Río Mayo
Río Magdalena
Río de la Concepción
Presa del Novillo
Presa Álvaro Obregón
Presa Mocúzari
LLANURAS DE SAN JUAN BAUTISTA
Yuma
Somerton
San Luis Río Colorado
GRAN DESIERTO
YUMA DESERT
Mohawk Mts.
Sierra de Sonoyta
Sonoyta
Lukeville
Ajo
Bahía de Adair
Golfo de Santa Clara
ISLA MONTAGUE
ft
m
9000
6000
4500
3000
1200
600
0
200
2000
3000
2000
1500
1000
400
200
600
6000
Projection: Lambert's Conformal Conic
West from Greenwich

1: 2 500 000

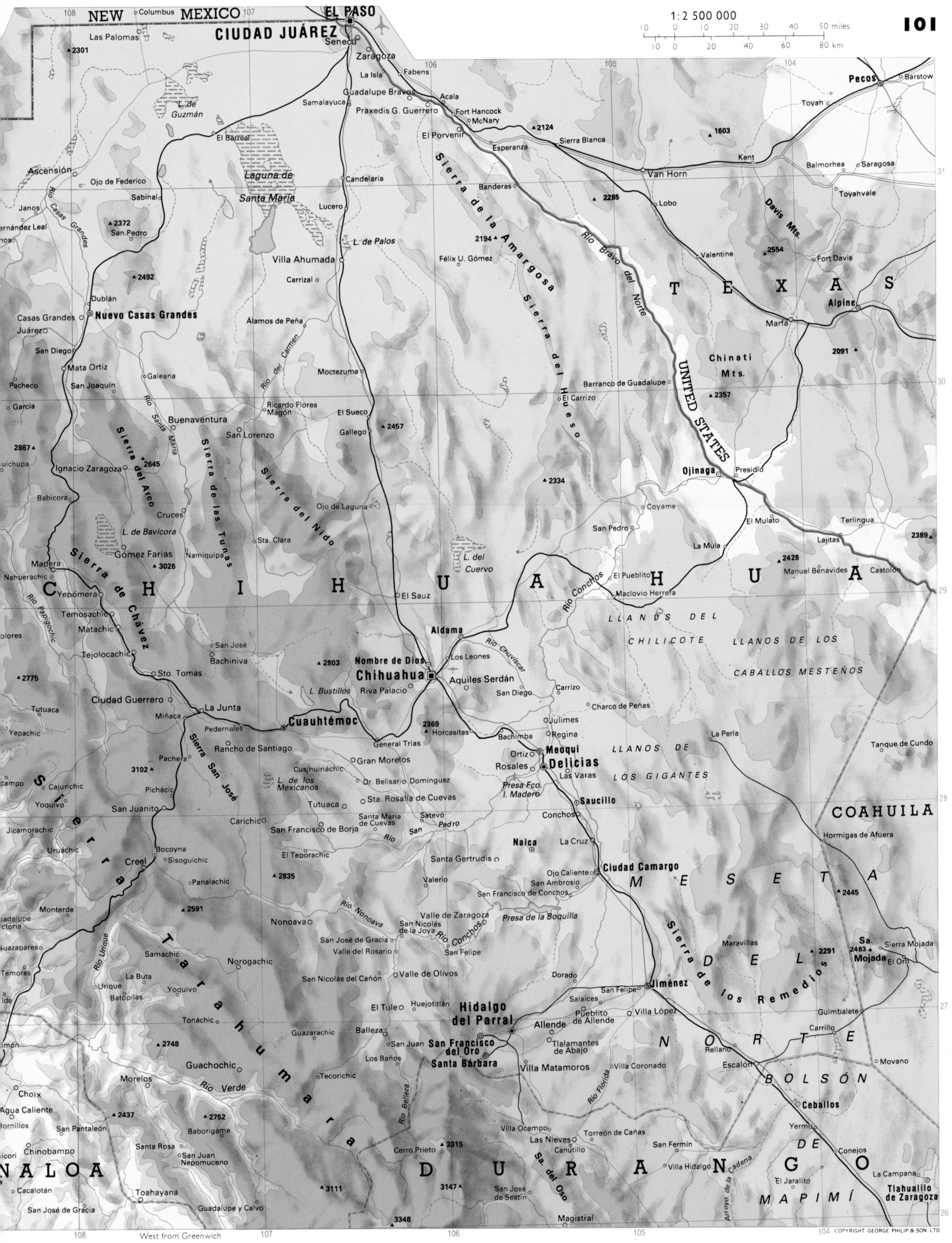

NEW MEXICO
EL PASO
CIUDAD JUÁREZ
TEXAS
UNITED STATES
CHIHUAHUA
COAHUILA
DURANGO
Chihuahua
Sierra de la Amargosa
Sierra del Hueso
Sierra Tarahumara
Sierra de los Remedios
Río Bravo del Norte
Río Conchos
Laguna de Santa María
LLANOS DEL CHILICOTE
LLANOS DE LOS CABALLOS MESTEÑOS
LLANOS DE LOS GIGANTES
MESETA DEL NORTE
BOLSÓN DE MAPIMÍ
Hidalgo del Parral
Ciudad Camargo
Delicias
Cuauhtémoc
Nuevo Casas Grandes
Ojinaga
Jiménez
Davis Mts.
Chinati Mts.
West from Greenwich

COAHUILA, NUEVO LEÓN, TAMAULIPAS AND SAN LUIS POTOSÍ

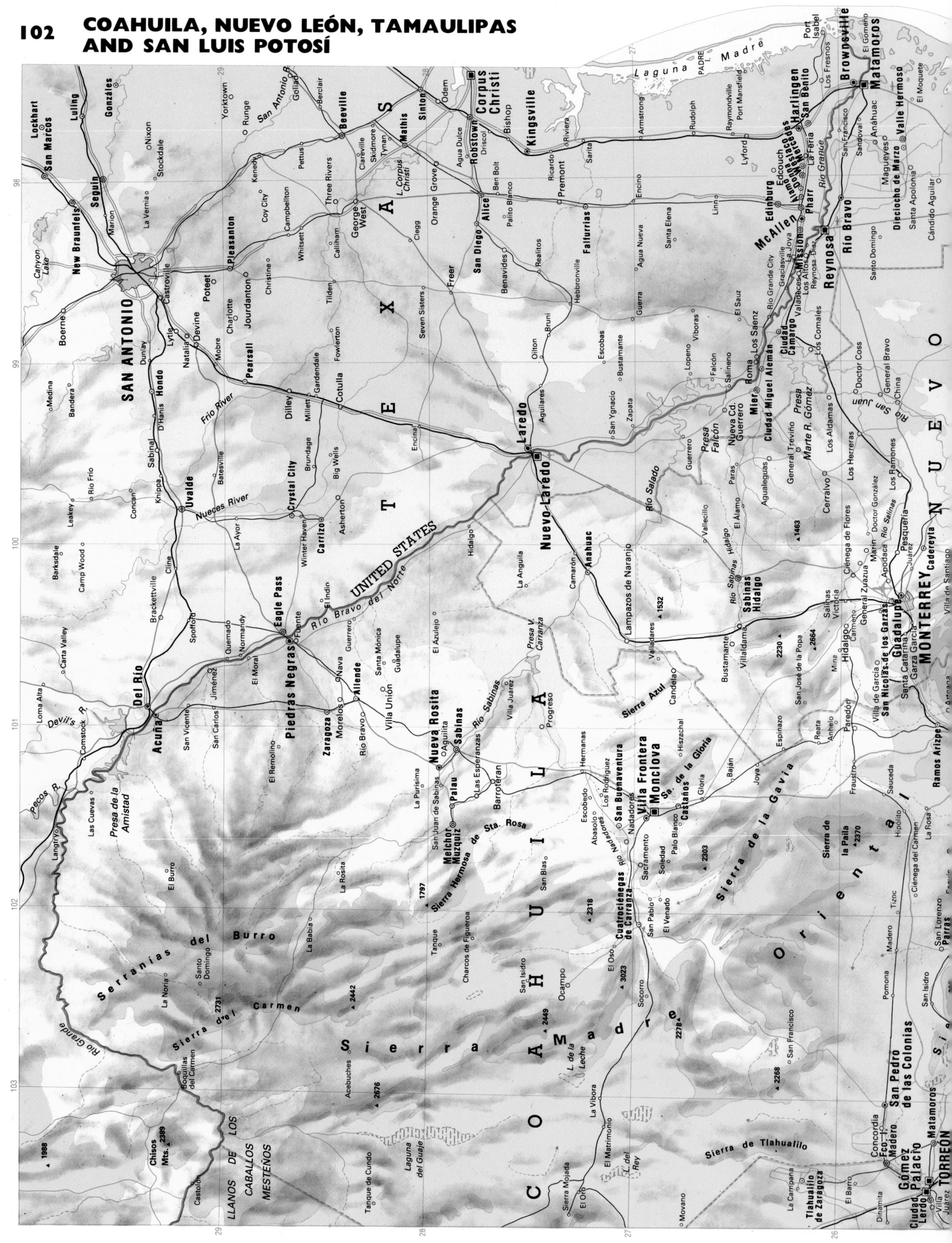

SAN ANTONIO
T E X A S
UNITED STATES
Río Bravo del Norte
Rio Grande
Laredo
Nuevo Laredo
Corpus Christi
Kingsville
Brownsville
Matamoros
McAllen
Reynosa
Harlingen
Eagle Pass
Piedras Negras
Del Río
Acuña
Uvalde
Monclova
MONTERREY
Guadalupe
Nueva Rosita
Sabinas
Torreón
Gómez Palacio
Ciudad Lerdo
San Pedro de las Colonias
Cuatrociénegas de Carranza
C O A H U I L A
N U E V O
Sierra Madre Oriental
Serranías del Burro
Sierra del Carmen
Sierra de la Gavia
Sierra de Tlahualilo
Presa de la Amistad
Presa Falcón
LLANOS DE LOS CABALLOS MESTEÑOS
Laguna Madre
Nueces River
Frio River
Pecos R.
Devil's R.
Río Salado
Río Sabinas
Chisos Mts.

1:2 500 000

10 0 10 20 30 40 50 miles

10 0 20 40 60 80 km

DURANGO
ZACATECAS
SAN LUIS POTOSÍ
TAMAULIPAS
LEÓN
VERACRUZ
HIDALGO
QUERÉTARO
GUANAJUATO
AGUASCALIENTES
JALISCO
Sierra Madre Oriental
Sierra de Tamaulipas
Sierra Esmeralda
Sierra del Bozal
Sierra Catorce
Sierra de Charcas
Sa. de Zacatecas
Sa. de Mazapil
Sa. de la Candelaria
Sierra Gorda
Laguna Madre
Laguna de Tamiahua
Tropic of Cancer
MESA HERRADURA
LLANOS DE LA GRUÑIDORA
SALADO DE SAN LUIS
Ciudad Victoria
Ciudad Madero
TAMPICO
Ciudad Mante
Ciudad de Valles
Matehuala
SAN LUIS POTOSÍ
Zacatecas
Aguascalientes
LEÓN
Guanajuato
GUADALAJARA
Fresnillo
Linares
Montemorelos
General Terán
San Fernando
Rioverde
Cerritos
Ciudad del Maíz
Lagos de Moreno
San Francisco del Rincón
Silao
San Miguel de Allende
Ciudad de Dolores Hidalgo
Tepatitlán de Morelos
Sombrerete
Valparaíso
Jerez de García Salinas
Río Grande
Juan Aldama
Miguel Auza
Concepción del Oro
Salinas de Hidalgo
Charcas
Tula
Jaumave
Xicoténcatl
González
Altamira
Pánuco
Ébano
Tamuín
Tamazunchale
Zimapán
Projection: Lambert's Conformal Conic
West from Greenwich

SONORA
CHIHUAHUA
SINALOA
DURANGO
NAYARIT
JALISCO
GOLFO DE CALIFORNIA
PACIFIC OCEAN
Sierra Madre Occidental
Sierra de Tepehuanes
Los Mochis
Culiacán
Mazatlán
Tepic
Guasave
Guamúchil
El Fuerte
Navolato
El Dorado
Rosario
Escuinapa de Hidalgo
Acaponeta
Tecuala
Tuxpan
Santiago Ixcuintla
Compostela
Ahuacatlán
Ixtlán del Río
Puerto Vallarta
Bahía de Banderas
ISLAS TRES MARÍAS
ISLA MARÍA MADRE
ISLA MARÍA MAGDALENA
ISLA MARÍA CLEOFÁS
ISLA ISABELA
ISLA CERRALVO
ISLA ALTAMURA
ISLA SAN JUANICO
Tropic of Cancer
El Salto
Santiago Papasquiaro
Guanaceví
Tepehuanes
Presa Adolfo López Mateos
Presa Sanalona
Presa Miguel Hidalgo
ft m
9000 3000
6000 2000
4500 1500
3000 1000
1200 400
600 200
0 0
200 600
2000 6000
m ft
Projection: *Lambert's Conformal Conic*

1:2 500 000
10 0 10 20 30 40 50 miles
10 0 20 40 60 80 km

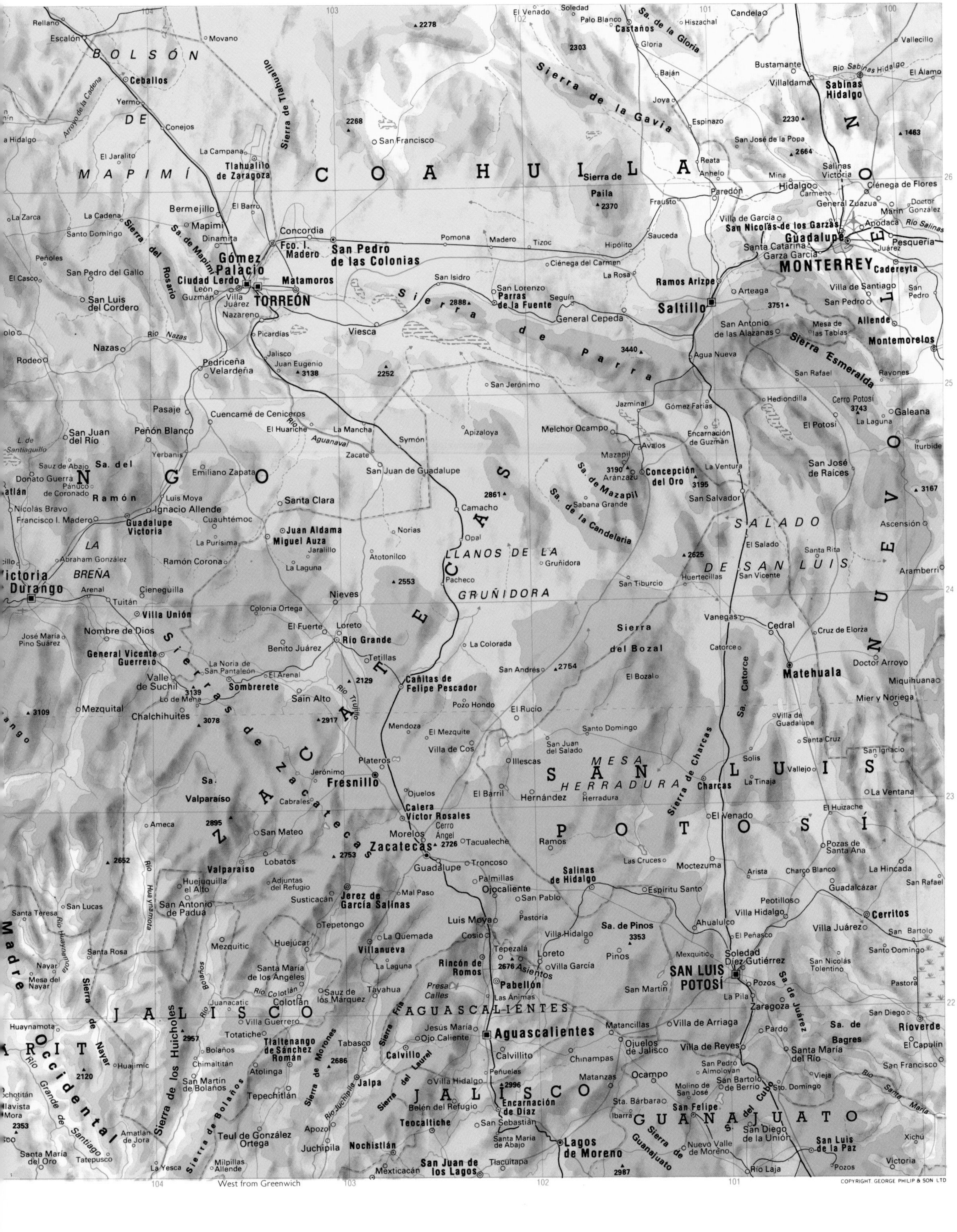

Rellano
Escalón
Movano
BOLSÓN DE MAPIMÍ
Ceballos
Arroyo de la Cadena
Yermo
Conejos
a Hidalgo
El Jaralito
La Campana
Tlahualilo de Zaragoza
Sierra de Tlahualilo
2278
2268
San Francisco
El Venado
Soledad
Palo Blanco
Castaños
Sa. de la Gloria
Hiszachal
Gloria
2303
Sierra de la Gavia
Bajan
Joya
Espinazo
Candela
Bustamante
Villaldama
Río Sabinas Hidalgo
Sabinas Hidalgo
Vallecillo
El Álamo
2230
1483
San José de la Popa
2664
Reata
Anhelo
Salinas Victoria
Mina
Hidalgo
Carmen
Paredón
COAHUILA
Sierra de Paila
2370
Frausto
Ciénega de Flores
General Zuazua
Marín
Doctor González
Apodaca
Río Salinas
Pesquería
Juárez
Villa de García
San Nicolás de los Garzas
Guadalupe
Santa Catarina
Garza García
MONTERREY
Cadereyta
La Zarca
La Cadena
Santo Domingo
Sierra del Rosario
Bermejillo
El Barro
Mapimí
Sa. de Mapimí
Dinamita
Concordia
Fco. I. Madero
San Pedro de las Colonias
Pomona
Madero
Tizoc
Hipólito
Sauceda
Ciénega del Carmen
Peñoles
El Casco
San Pedro del Gallo
Gómez Palacio
Ciudad Lerdo
León Guzmán
Villa Juárez
TORREÓN
Matamoros
San Isidro
San Lorenzo
Parras de la Fuente
Seguín
La Rosa
Ramos Arizpe
Arteaga
Villa de Santiago
San Pedro
San Luis del Cordero
Nazareno
Sierra de Parra
2888
Saltillo
3751
Allende
General Cepeda
San Antonio de las Alazanas
Mesa de las Tablas
Montemorelos
Sierra Esmeralda
Río Nazas
Picardías
Viesca
3440
Agua Nueva
Nazas
Jalisco
Juan Eugenio
3138
Rodeo
Pedriceña
Velardeña
2252
San Jerónimo
San Rafael
Rayones
Jazminal
Gómez Farías
Hediondilla
Cerro Potosí 3743
La Laguna
Galeana
Pasaje
Cuencamé de Ceniceros
Río Aguanaval
El Huarichi
La Mancha
Apizaloya
Melchor Ocampo
Encarnación de Guzmán
El Potosí
San Juan del Río
Peñón Blanco
L. de Santiaguillo
Symón
Zacate
Ávalos
Mazapil
Iturbide
Sauz de Abajo
Sa. del Ramón
Yerbanis
Donato Guerra
Pánuco de Coronado
Emiliano Zapata
San Juan de Guadalupe
3190
Aránzazu
Sa. de Mazapil
Concepción del Oro
3195
La Ventura
San José de Raíces
DURANGO
Luis Moya
Ignacio Allende
Santa Clara
2861
Camacho
Sabana Grande
Sa. de la Candelaria
San Salvador
3167
Nicolás Bravo
Francisco I. Madero
Guadalupe Victoria
Cuauhtémoc
Juan Aldama
Miguel Auza
Norias
SALADO DE SAN LUIS
Ascensión
LA BREÑA
La Purísima
Jaralillo
Opal
LLANOS DE LA GRUÑIDORA
Gruñidora
El Salado
Santa Rita
Abraham González
Ramón Corona
La Laguna
Atotonilco
2625
Huertecillas
San Vicente
Aramberri
Victoria de Durango
Pacheco
2553
San Tiburcio
NUEVO LEÓN
Arenal
Cieneguilla
Tuitán
Nieves
Vanegas
Cedral
Villa Unión
Colonia Ortega
Sierra del Bozal
Cruz de Elorza
José María Pino Suárez
Nombre de Dios
El Fuerte
Loreto
Río Grande
La Colorada
Catorce
General Vicente Guerrero
Benito Juárez
Tetillas
Matehuala
La Noria de San Pantaleón
El Arenal
2129
San Andrés
2754
El Bozal
Sa. de Catorce
Doctor Arroyo
Valle de Súchil
3139
Sombrerete
Cañitas de Felipe Pescador
Río Trujillo
Miquihuana
Lo de Mena
Sain Alto
Pozo Hondo
El Rucio
Mier y Noriega
3109
Mezquital
Chalchihuites
3078
2917
Sierras de Zacatecas
Mendoza
El Mezquite
Santo Domingo
Villa de Guadalupe
San Juan del Salado
Villa de Cos
Santa Cruz
Plateros
Illescas
MESA HERRADURA
Solis
San Ignacio
Sa. Valparaíso
Jerónimo
Fresnillo
Sierra de Charcas
Charcas
La Tinaja
Vallejo
SAN LUIS POTOSÍ
Cabrales
Ojuelos
El Barril
Hernández
Herradura
La Ventana
Calera
Víctor Rosales
El Venado
El Huizache
Ameca
2895
San Mateo
Cerro Ángel
Morelos
Zacatecas
2726
Tacualeche
Ramos
Pozos de Santa Ana
2652
Lobatos
2753
Guadalupe
Troncoso
Las Cruces
Moctezuma
Arista
Charco Blanco
La Hincada
Valparaíso
Río Huaynamota
Huejuquilla el Alto
Adjuntas del Refugio
Palmillas
Ojocaliente
Salinas de Hidalgo
Espíritu Santo
Guadalcázar
San Rafael
San Lucas
San Antonio de Padua
Susticacán
Jerez de García Salinas
Mal Paso
San Pablo
Peotillos
Santa Teresa
Pastoría
Villa Hidalgo
Cerritos
Tepetongo
Luis Moya
Ahualulco
Villa Juárez
San Bartolo
Madre Occidental
Santa Rosa
Mezquitic
Huejúcar
La Quemada
Cosío
Villa Hidalgo
Sa. de Pinos
3353
El Peñasco
Santo Domingo
Villanueva
Tepezalá
Loreto
Soledad Díez Gutiérrez
San Nicolás Tolentino
Nayar
Mesa del Nayar
Sierra de Nayar
Santa María de los Ángeles
Río Bolaños
La Laguna
Rincón de Romos
2676
Asientos
Villa García
Pinos
Mexquitic
SAN LUIS POTOSÍ
Pastora
Río Colotlán
Colotlán
Sauz de los Márquez
Tayahua
Presa Calles
Pabellón
Las Ánimas
San Martín
Pozos
Sa. de Juárez
La Pila
Juanacatic
JALISCO
Villa Guerrero
AGUASCALIENTES
Zaragoza
San Diego
Rioverde
Huaynamota
Totatiche
2957
Tlaltenango de Sánchez Román
Sierra de Morones
Tabasco
Sierra Fría
Jesús María
Ojo Caliente
Aguascalientes
Matancillas
Villa de Arriaga
Pardo
Sa. de Bagres
El Capulín
NAYARIT
Bolaños
Chimaltitán
2686
Calvillo
Calvillito
Ojuelos de Jalisco
Chinampas
Villa de Reyes
Santa María del Río
Huajimic
Sierra de los Huicholes
Atolinga
Peñuelas
Sierra del Laurel
Matanzas
San Pedro Almoloyan
Vieja
San Francisco
2120
San Martín de Bolaños
Sierra de Bolaños
Tepechitlán
Río Juchipila
Jalpa
Villa Hidalgo
2996
Ocampo
Molino de San José
San Bartolo de Berrio
Sierra del Cubo
Sto. Domingo
Río Santa María
Río Grande de Santiago
Chotitlán
Llavista
Mora
2353
Belén del Refugio
JALISCO
Encarnación de Díaz
Sta. Bárbara
Ibarra
San Felipe
GUANAJUATO
Teocaltiche
San Sebastián
Xichú
Amatlán de Jora
Teul de González Ortega
Apozol
Santa María de Abajo
Lagos de Moreno
Sierra de Guanajuato
San Diego de la Unión
San Luis de la Paz
Santa María del Oro
Tatepusco
Juchipila
Nochistlán
Nuevo Valle de Moreno
Milpillas Allende
Mexticacán
San Juan de los Lagos
Tlacuitapa
Río Laja
Victoria
La Yesca
2987
Pozos
104
103
102
101
100
26
25
24
23
22
West from Greenwich

NAYARIT
JALISCO
COLIMA
ZACATECAS
AGUASCALIENTES
GUADALAJARA
Tepic
Puerto Vallarta
Manzanillo
Colima
Aguascalientes
Lago de Chapala
PACIFIC OCEAN
ISLAS TRES MARÍAS
ISLA MARÍA MADRE
ISLA MARÍA MAGDALENA
ISLA MARÍA CLEOFÁS
ISLA SAN JUANICO
ISLA ISABELA
Bahía de Banderas
CABO CORRIENTES
Sierra del Cuale
Sierra de Cacoma
Sierra de Coalcomán
Sierra de los Huicholes
Río Grande de Santiago
Tlaquepaque
Zapopán
Ciudad Guzmán
Tecomán
Armería
Uruapan del Progreso
Zamora de Hidalgo
Ocotlán
La Piedad
Apatzingan
Projection: Lambert's Conformal Conic
West from Greenwich
ft
m
12 000
9000
6000
4500
3000
1200
600
4000
3000
2000
1500
1000
400
200

1:2 500 000

10 0 10 20 30 40 50 miles

10 0 20 40 60 80 km

SAN LUIS POTOSÍ

GUANAJUATO

QUERÉTARO

HIDALGO

VERACRUZ

MÉXICO

TLAXCALA

PUEBLA

MORELOS

D. F.

MICHOACÁN

GUERRERO

OAXACA

Sierra Madre del Sur

Ciudad de Valles

Tamuín

Pánuco

Rioverde

Cárdenas

El Higo

Tempoal

Laguna de Tamiahua

CABO ROJO

I. DEL IDOLO

Tamiahua

Naranjos

Tantoyuca

Cerro Azul

Tuxpan

Álamo

Poza Rica

Papantla de Olarte

Gutiérrez Zamora

Martínez de la Torre

Misantla

Jalapa Enríquez

Coatepec

Córdoba

Orizaba

P. Blanco

Nogales

Cd. Mendoza

Tehuacán

San Felipe

Guanajuato

Silao

Irapuato

Salamanca

Celaya

Valle de Santiago

Moroleón

Uriangato

Yuriria

Acámbaro

Morelia

Zitácuaro

Ciudad Hidalgo

San Miguel de Allende

Dolores Hidalgo

Comonfort

Querétaro

San Juan del Río

Tula de Allende

Pachuca de Soto

Tulancingo

Huauchinango

Teziutlán

Zacatlán

Tizayuca

Ciudad Sahagún

Apan

Apizaco

Tlaxcala

Heroica Huamantla

Tlalnepantla

Atzcapotzalco

MÉXICO

Coyoacán

Xochimilco

Tlalpan

Toluca de Lerdo

Contreras

Texcoco de Mora

Los Reyes

San Martín Texmelucan

Huejotzinco

Cholula de Rivadabia

PUEBLA

Tepeaca

Atlixco

CUERNAVACA

Cuautla Morelos

Jojutla de Juárez

Izúcar de Matamoros

Taxco de Alarcón

Iguala de la Independencia

Ciudad Altamirano

Chilpancingo de los Bravos

Tixtla de Guerrero

Zumpango del Río

Tlapa de Comonfort

Huajuapan de León

Acatlán de Osorio

Tecpán de Galeana

Atoyac de Álvarez

Coyuca de Benítez

ACAPULCO de Juárez

San Marcos

Ometepec

Pinotepa de Don Luis

Putla de Guerrero

Zihuatanejo

Petatlán

Bahía Potosí

Bahía Tequepa

Infiernillo

Río Balsas

PTA. PILARES

PTA. DIAMANTE

Vol. Popocatépetl 5452

Iztaccíhuatl 5326

Nev. de Toluca 4558

Vol. Citlaltépetl 5700

2987

2850

3944

3375

3703

3658

2708

1803

1182

2023

2295

2652

2896

101 100 99 98 97

22 21 20 19 18 17

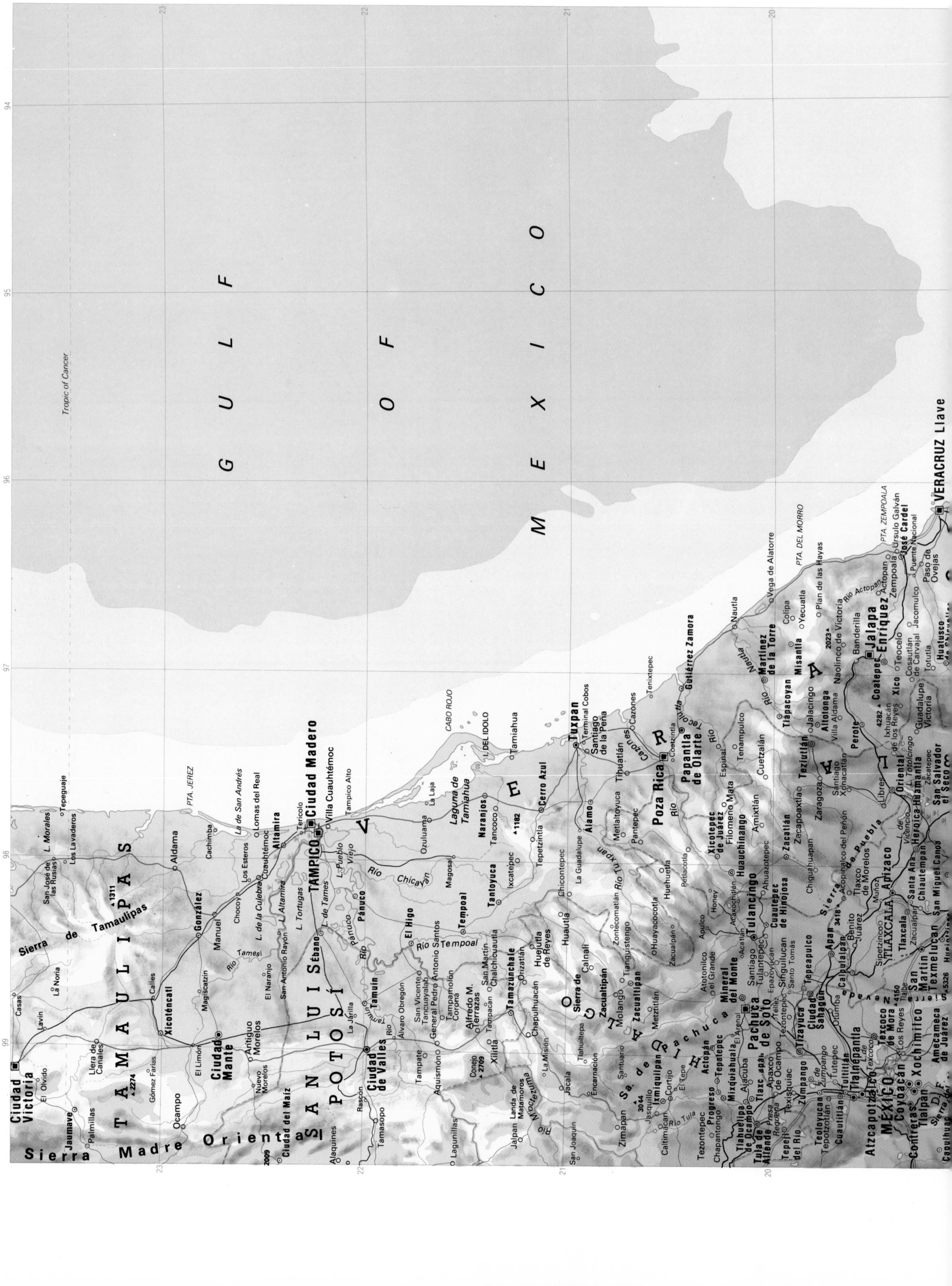

GULF OF MEXICO

Tropic of Cancer

TAMAULIPAS

Sierra de Tamaulipas

Sierra Madre Oriental

SAN LUIS POTOSÍ

VERACRUZ

HIDALGO

PUEBLA

MEXICO

TLAXCALA

Ciudad Victoria
El Olvido
Jaumave
Palmillas
Ocampo
Gómez Farías
Llera de Canales
Lavín
Casas
La Noria
San José de las Rusias
Los Lavaderos
L. Morales
Tepeguaje
Aldama
Cachimba
PTA. JEREZ
La de San Andrés
Lomas del Real
Los Esteros
Cuauhtémoc
Altamira
Tericolo
Ciudad Madero
Villa Cuauhtémoc
Tampico Alto
TAMPICO
L. de la Culebra
L. Altamira
L. Tortugas
L. de Tamesí
L. Pueblo Viejo
Pánuco
Río Pánuco
Río Tamesí
Choco
Manuel
González
Xicoténcatl
Calles
Magiscatzin
El Limón
Ciudad Mante
Antiguo Morelos
Nuevo Morelos
El Naranjo
San Antonio Rayón
Ciudad del Maíz
Ébano
Alaquines
Rascón
Tamasopo
La Jarilla
Ciudad de Valles
Tamuín
Álvaro Obregón
San Vicente Tancuayalab
General Pedro Antonio Santos
Tampamolón Corona
Tampate
Aquismón
Lagunillas
Conejo 2709
El Higo
Río Tempoal
Tempoal
Ozuluama
La Laja
Magosal
Río Chicayán
Laguna de Tamiahua
Naranjos
Tancoco
Tantoyuca
Ixcatepec
Tepetzintla
Cerro Azul
Alfredo M. Terrazas
Tampacán
San Martín Chalchicuautla
Tamazunchale
Orizatlán
Huejutla de Reyes
Xilitla
Chapulhuacán
Jalpan
Landa de Matamoros
La Misión
Río Moctezuma
CABO ROJO
I. DEL ÍDOLO
Tamiahua
Tuxpan
Terminal Cobos
Santiago de la Peña
Álamo
La Guadalupe
Chicontepec
Huautla
Calnali
Zacualtipán
Sierra de
Tianguistengo
Molango
Metztitlán
Tlahuiltepa
Encarnación
Jacala
San Joaquín
Zimapán
Río Tuxpan
Metlaltoyuca
Tihuatlán
Cazones
Río Cazones
Pantepec
Poza Rica
Coatzintla
Papantla de Olarte
Tecolutla
Río Tecolutla
Gutiérrez Zamora
Tenixtepec
Espinal
Tenampulco
Filomeno Mata
Xicotepec de Juárez
Huauchinango
Amixtlán
Cuetzalán
Zacatlán
Zacapoaxtla
Tlapacoyan
Nautla
Río Nautla
Martínez de la Torre
Vega de Alatorre
Colipa
Misantla
Yecuatla
PTA. DEL MORRO
Plan de las Hayas
Tulancingo
Ahuazotepec
Cuautepec de Hinojosa
Acaxochitlán
Honey
Pahuatlán
Huehuetla
Zontecomatlán
Huayacocotla
Zacualpan
Apulco
Atotonilco el Grande
Mineral del Monte
Pachuca de Soto
Actopan
Santiago Tulantepec
Singuilucan
Epazoyucan
Santo Tomás
Tepeapulco
Ciudad Sahagún
Apan
Tizayuca
Zumpango
Tecámac
Ixmiquilpan
Cortijo
El Tepe
Santuario
Tepatepec
Progreso
Mixquiahuala
Tlahuelilpa de Ocampo
Tula de Allende
Río Tula
Caltimacán
Tezontepec
Chapantongo
Tepeji del Río
Tlaxcoapan
Apaxco
Tequixquiac
Tepotzotlán
Teoloyucan
Cuautitlán
Tultitlán
Tlalnepantla
Atzcapotzalco
MÉXICO
Coyoacán
Contreras
Tlalpan
Xochimilco
Texcoco de Mora
Los Reyes
Amecameca de Juárez
Chalco
San Martín Texmelucan
San Salvador el Seco
Calpulalpan
Otumba
Tlaxcala
Apizaco
Zacatelco
Heroica Huamantla
Chiautempan
Santa Ana
Benito Juárez
Tlaxco de Morelos
Acopinalco del Peñón
Sierra de Puebla
Chignahuapan
Zaragoza
Teziutlán
Jalacingo
Altotonga
Villa Aldama
Santiago Xonacatlán
Libres
Oriental
L. de Totolcingo
Perote
Ixhuacán de los Reyes
Coatepec
Xico
Teocelo
Cosautlán de Carvajal
Jalapa Enríquez
Banderilla
Naolinco de Victoria
Río Actopan
Actopan
Zempoala
PTA. ZEMPOALA
Úrsulo Galván
José Cardel
Puente Nacional
Paso de Ovejas
Jacomulco
Totutla
Huatusco
Guadalupe Victoria
VERACRUZ Llave
Iztaccíhuatl
Popocatépetl

94 95 96 97 98 99

20 21 22 23

PACIFIC OCEAN
GOLFO DE TEHUANTEPEC
OAXACA
GUERRERO
PUEBLA
MORELOS
VERACRUZ
Sierra Madre
Sierra de Miahuatlán
Sierra de Juárez
Sierra de Nochixtlan
Sierra de Ixtlán
Sierra de Villa Alta
Sierra de Mixes
Sierra de Tlaxiaco
Sierra de Malinaltepec
Sierra de Zapotitlán
Sierra Tamazulapán
Sa. de Tentzo
Sa. de los Tuxtlas
Sa. de Zongolica
Sa. de Tenango
Coatzacoalcos
Minatitlán
Cosoleacaque
Las Choapas
La Venta
Acayucan
Juan Rodríguez Clara
Isla
Villa Azueta
Loma Bonita
S. Juan Bautista Tuxtepec
Alvarado
Tlacotalpan
Lerdo de Tejada
San Andrés Tuxtla
Santiago Tuxtla
Catemaco
Cosamaloapan de Carpio
Tierra Blanca
Córdoba
Orizaba
Ciudad Serdán
Tehuacán
Tecamachalco
Cd. Mendoza
Nogales
Cuernavaca
Cuautla Morelos
Atlixco
Izúcar de Matamoros
Acatlán de Osorio
Huajuapan de León
Tlapa de Comonfort
Chilpancingo de los Bravos
Iguala de la Independencia
Oaxaca de Juárez
Zaachila
Ocotlán de Morelos
Ejutla de Crespo
Miahuatlán de Porfirio Díaz
Zimatlán de Álvarez
Santa María Asunción Tlaxiaco
Putla de Guerrero
Santiago Pinotepa Nacional
Jamiltepec
Puerto Escondido
San Pedro Pochutla
Puerto Ángel
Salina Cruz
Santo Domingo Tehuantepec
Juchitán de Zaragoza
Ixtepec
Matías Romero
Arriaga
Tonalá
Cintalapa de Figueroa
Presa Netzahualcóyotl
Presa Miguel Alemán
Presa B. Juárez
PTA. ROCA PARTIDA
PTA. MALDONADO
1:2 500 000
10 0 10 20 30 40 50 miles
10 0 20 40 60 80 km
Projection: Lambert's Conformal Conic
West from Greenwich

1:2 500 000

10 0 10 20 30 40 50 miles

10 0 20 40 60 80 km

Projection: *Lambert's Conformal Conic*

West from Greenwich

m	ft
3000	9000
2000	6000
1500	4500
1000	3000
400	1200
200	600
0	0
15	
200	600
2000	6000

1:2 500 000

10 0 10 20 30 40 50 miles

10 0 20 40 60 80 km

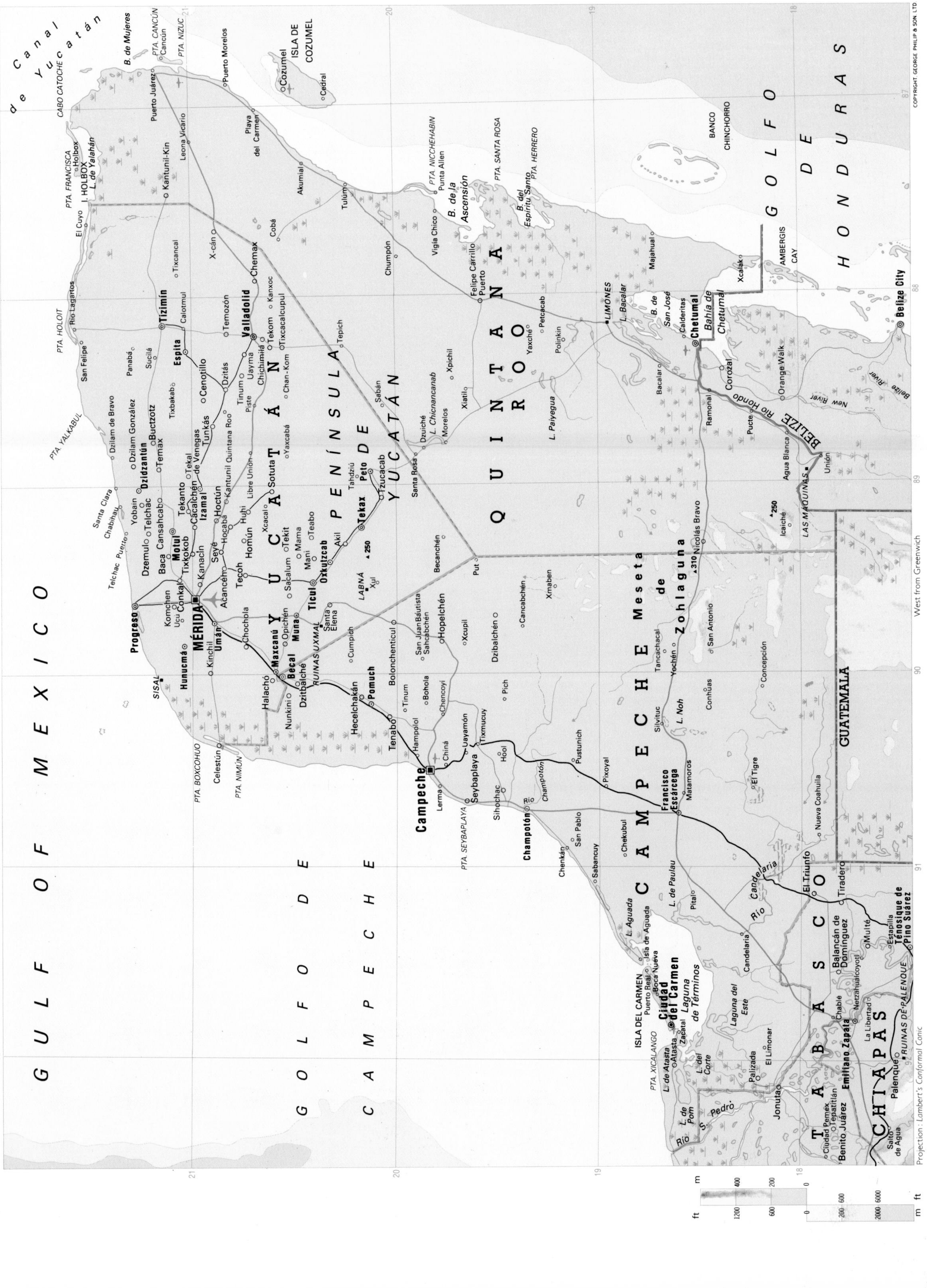

GULF OF MEXICO

GOLFO DE CAMPECHE

Canal de Yucatán

GOLFO DE HONDURAS

PENÍNSULA DE YUCATÁN

YUCATÁN

QUINTANA ROO

CAMPECHE

Meseta de Zohlaguna

TABASCO

CHIAPAS

GUATEMALA

BELIZE

ISLA DE COZUMEL

ISLA DEL CARMEN

BANCO CHINCHORRO

AMBERGIS CAY

MÉRIDA, Progreso, Umán, Hunucmá, Kinchil, Sisal, Celestún, Maxcanú, Halachó, Bécal, Dzitbalché, Nunkiní, Muna, Ticul, Oxkutzcab, Tekax, Peto, Tzucacab, Akil, Tekit, Mama, Teabo, Mani, Sacalum, Opichén, Chochola, Acancéh, Tecoh, Homún, Huhi, Sotuta, Izamal, Motul, Tixkokob, Kanacín, Conkal, Komchen, Ucu, Baca, Cansahcab, Dzemulo, Telchác, Yobain, Dzidzantún, Dzilam González, Dzilam de Bravo, Buctzotz, Temax, Tekanto, Cacalchén, Tekal de Venegas, Tunkás, Cenotillo, Espita, Tizimín, Calotmul, Sucilá, Panabá, Tixbakab, Dzitás, Temozón, Valladolid, Chichimilá, Tekom, Tixcacalcupul, Chan-Kom, Uayma, Tinum, Piste, Kanxoc, Chemax, Tixcancal, X-cán, Kantunil-Kin, Leona Vicario, Puerto Juárez, Cancún, Puerto Morelos, Playa del Carmen, Cozumel, Cedral, Akumal, Tulúm, Cobá, Chumpón, Vigía Chico, Punta Allen, Felipe Carrillo Puerto, Tepich, Sabán, Dzuiché, Morelos, Xiatil, Xpichil, Yaxché, Petcacab, Polinkin, Limones, Bacalar, Chetumal, Calderitas, Corozal, Ramonal, Pucte, Agua Blanca, Unión, Nicolás Bravo, Icaiché, Xcalak, Majahual, Orange Walk, Belize City, San Felipe, Río Lagartos, El Cuyo, Holbox, Santa Clara, Chabihau, Telchac Puerto, Santa Rosa, Becanchén, Put, Xul, Labná, Santa Elena, Cumpich, Bolonchenticul, Hopelchén, Xcupil, Dzibalchén, Cancabchén, Xmaben, San Juan Bautista Sahcabchén, Tinum, Bohola, Chencoyi, Pomuch, Hecelchakán, Tenabo, Hampolol, Chiná, Uayamón, Tixmucuy, Hool, Campeche, Lerma, Seybaplaya, Sihochac, Champotón, Pustunich, Pixoyal, Francisco Escárcega, Matamoros, Silvituc, Tancachacal, Yochén, Conhuas, Concepción, San Antonio, El Tigre, Nueva Coahuila, El Triunfo, Candelaria, Tiradero, Chekubul, San Pablo, Chenkán, Sabancuy, Pital, Isla de Aguada, Ciudad del Carmen, Puerto Real, Boca Nueva, Zacatal, Atasta, Palizada, El Limonar, Jonuta, Balancán de Domínguez, Multé, Estapilla, Tenosique de Pino Suárez, Emiliano Zapata, Chable, La Libertad, Netzahualcoyotl, Palenque, Salto de Agua, Tepatitlán, Ciudad Pemex, Benito Juárez

RUINAS UXMAL, RUINAS DE PALENQUE

L. de Yalahán, L. Chicnancanab, L. Bacalar, L. Paiyegua, L. Noh, L. de Paulau, L. Aguada, Laguna de Términos, Laguna del Este, L. del Corte, L. de Atasta, L. de Pom

B. de Mujeres, B. de la Ascensión, B. del Espíritu Santo, B. de San José, Bahía de Chetumal

PTA. CANCÚN, PTA. NIZUC, CABO CATOCHE, PTA. FRANCISCA, PTA. HOLOIT, PTA. YALKABUL, PTA. NICCHEHABIN, PTA. SANTA ROSA, PTA. HERRERO, PTA. BOXCOHUO, PTA. NIMUN, PTA. SEYBAPLAYA, PTA. XICALANGO

Río Hondo, New River, Belize River, Río Champotón, Río Candelaria, Río S. Pedro

LAS MÁQUINAS

▲250, ▲310

West from Greenwich

Projection: Lambert's Conformal Conic

m	ft
400	1200
200	600
0	0
200	600
2000	6000

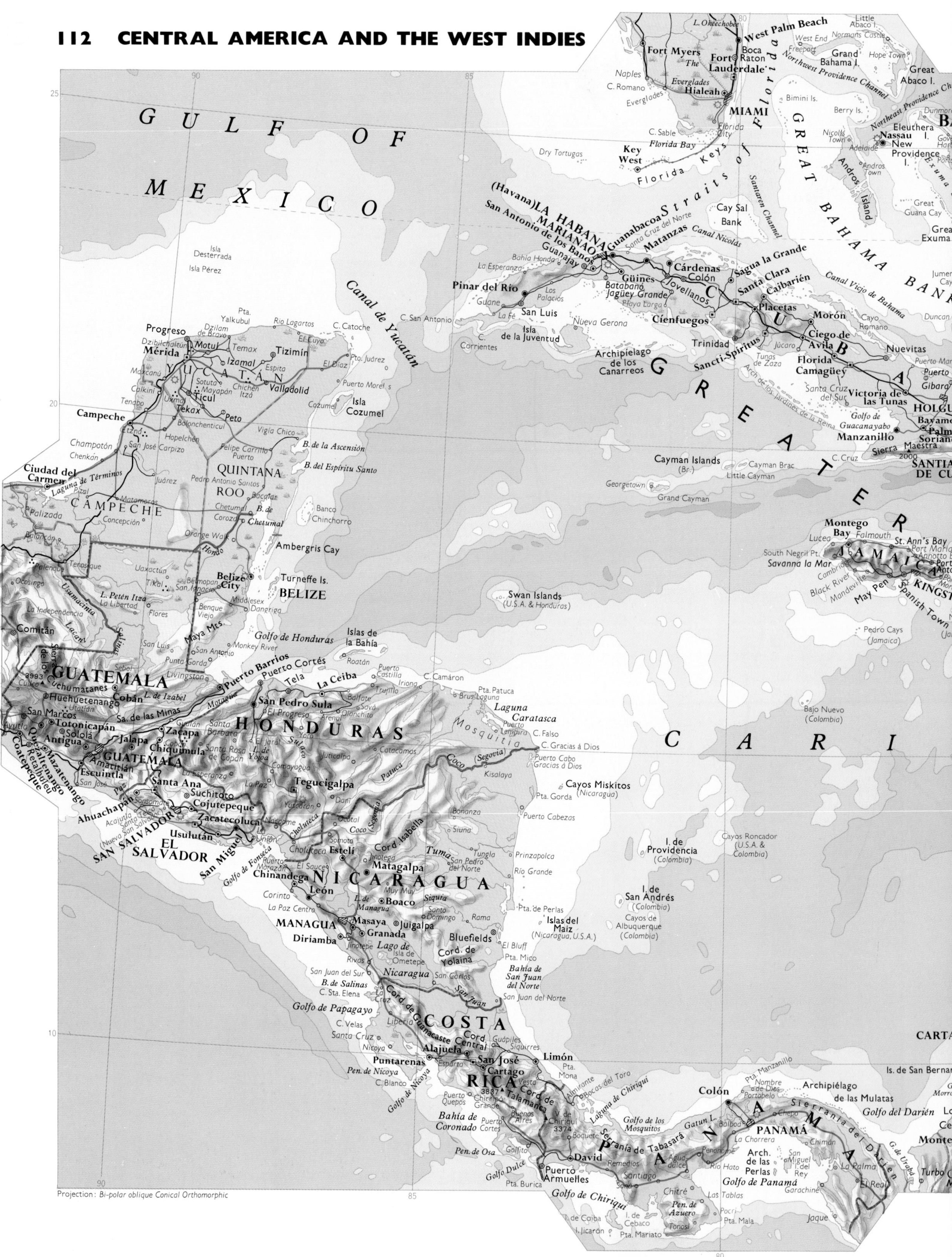
GULF OF MEXICO
Canal de Yucatán
Straits of Florida
GREATER
CARI
West Palm Beach
Fort Myers
Boca Raton
Fort Lauderdale
Naples
C. Romano
Everglades
Hialeah
MIAMI
C. Sable
Florida Bay
Florida City
Key West
Florida Keys
Dry Tortugas
Bimini Is.
Grand Bahama I.
Northwest Providence Channel
Great Abaco I.
Northeast Providence Channel
Berry Is.
Eleuthera I.
Nassau
New Providence I.
Andros Island
Great Guana Cay
Great Exuma I.
GREAT BAHAMA BANK
Canal Viejo de Bahama
Cay Sal Bank
Santaren Channel
Canal Nicolás
(Havana) LA HABANA
MARIANAO
San Antonio de los Baños
Guanabacoa
Guanajay
Matanzas
Cárdenas
Colón
Sagua la Grande
Santa Clara
Caibarién
Pinar del Río
San Luis
Güines
Batabanó
Jagüey Grande
Jovellanos
Cienfuegos
Placetas
Morón
Ciego de Avila
Trinidad
Sancti-Spíritus
Isla de la Juventud
Nueva Gerona
Archipiélago de los Canarreos
C. San Antonio
C. Corrientes
Nuevitas
Florida
Camagüey
Victoria de las Tunas
Golfo de Guacanayabo
Manzanillo
Sierra Maestra
Cayman Islands (Br.)
Cayman Brac
Little Cayman
Georgetown
Grand Cayman
Montego Bay
Falmouth
St. Ann's Bay
Lucea
South Negril Pt.
Savanna la Mar
JAMAICA
Black River
Mandeville
May Pen
Spanish Town
Pedro Cays (Jamaica)
Swan Islands (U.S.A. & Honduras)
Isla Desterrada
Isla Pérez
Progreso
Mérida
Motul
Temax
Tizimín
Izamal
Valladolid
Maxcanú
Ticul
Tekax
Peto
Campeche
Champotón
Isla Cozumel
Cozumel
Vigía Chico
B. de la Ascensión
B. del Espíritu Santo
Felipe Carrillo Puerto
QUINTANA ROO
CAMPECHE
Ciudad del Carmen
Laguna de Términos
Palizada
Chetumal
Banco Chinchorro
Ambergris Cay
Turneffe Is.
Belize City
BELIZE
Belmopan
Tikal
L. Petén Itzá
Flores
Maya Mts.
Golfo de Honduras
Islas de la Bahía
Roatán
Puerto Barrios
Puerto Cortés
Tela
La Ceiba
San Pedro Sula
Comitán
GUATEMALA
Huehuetenango
Cobán
L. de Izabal
San Marcos
Totonicapán
Quezaltenango
Sololá
Antigua
Jalapa
Zacapa
Chiquimula
Escuintla
HONDURAS
Laguna Caratasca
Mosquitia
C. Falso
C. Gracias á Dios
Tegucigalpa
Santa Ana
Suchitoto
Cojutepeque
Zacatecoluca
Usulután
San Miguel
SAN SALVADOR
EL SALVADOR
Golfo de Fonseca
Cayos Miskitos (Nicaragua)
Pta. Gorda
Puerto Cabezas
Estelí
Matagalpa
Chinandega
León
NICARAGUA
MANAGUA
Masaya
Boaco
Juigalpa
Granada
Diriamba
Lago de Nicaragua
Bluefields
Islas del Maíz (Nicaragua, U.S.A.)
I. de Providencia (Colombia)
I. de San Andrés (Colombia)
Cayos Roncador (U.S.A. & Colombia)
Bajo Nuevo (Colombia)
Golfo de Papagayo
COSTA RICA
Liberia
Puntarenas
Alajuela
San José
Cartago
Limón
Pen. de Nicoya
Golfo de Nicoya
Golfo Dulce
Puerto Armuelles
David
Golfo de Chiriquí
Laguna de Chiriquí
Golfo de los Mosquitos
Serranía de Tabasará
Colón
Gatun L.
Balboa
PANAMÁ
PANAMA
Arch. de las Perlas
Golfo de Panamá
Pen. de Azuero
Archipiélago de las Mulatas
Golfo del Darién
Serranía del Darién
Is. de San Bernardo

Projection: *Bi-polar oblique Conical Orthomorphic*

1:8 000 000

50 0 50 100 150 200 miles

50 0 50 100 150 200 250 300 km

ATLANTIC OCEAN
Tropic of Cancer
CARIBBEAN SEA
ANTILLES
HISPANIOLA
HAITI
DOMINICAN REP.
PORT-AU-PRINCE
SANTO DOMINGO
PUERTO RICO (U.S.A.)
SAN JUAN
LESSER ANTILLES
LEEWARD ISLANDS
WINDWARD ISLANDS
ANTIGUA & BARBUDA
ST. KITTS-NEVIS
GUADELOUPE (Fr.)
DOMINICA
MARTINIQUE (Fr.)
ST. LUCIA
ST. VINCENT
BARBADOS
GRENADA
TRINIDAD & TOBAGO
Port of Spain
VENEZUELA
CARACAS
MARACAIBO
BARQUISIMETO
Valencia
Maracay
Barcelona
Ciudad Guayana
Ciudad Bolívar
Cúcuta
Santa Marta
Turks Islands (Br.)
Caicos Islands (Br.)
Great Inagua I.
Acklins I.
Crooked I.
Long I.
West from Greenwich
COPYRIGHT. GEORGE PHILIP & SON. LTD.

SOUTH AMERICA

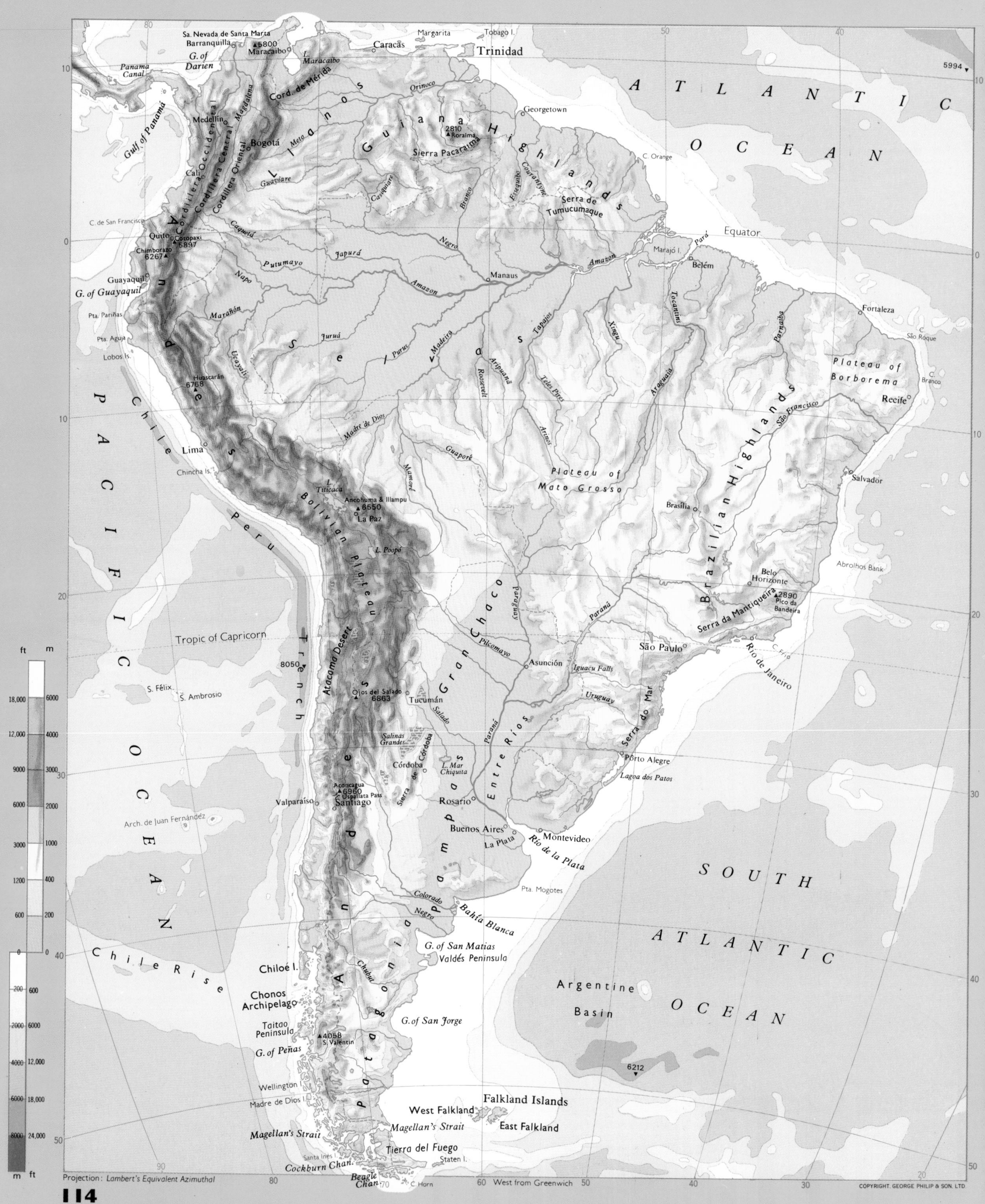

Sa. Nevada de Santa Marta
Barranquilla
5800
Maracaibo
L. Maracaibo
Caracas
Margarita
Tobago I.
Trinidad
G. of Darien
Panama Canal
Cord. de Mérida
Orinoco
Georgetown
ATLANTIC
OCEAN
C. Orange
Gulf of Panamá
Medellín
Bogotá
Llanos
Guiana Highlands
2810 Roraima
Sierra Pacaraima
Serra de Tumucumaque
Cali
Cordillera Occidental
Cordillera Central
Cordillera Oriental
Magdalena
Meta
Guaviare
Casiquiare
Branco
Essequibo
Courantyne
C. de San Francisco
Quito
Cotopaxi 5897
Chimborazo 6267
Caquetá
Equator
Negro
Japurá
Putumayo
Marajó I.
Pará
Belém
Amazon
Manaus
Guayaquil
G. of Guayaquil
Napo
Pta. Pariñas
Marañón
Tocantins
Fortaleza
Pta. Aguja
Juruá
Purus
Madeira
Tapajós
Xingu
Parnaíba
C. São Roque
Lobos Is.
Ucayali
Aripuanã
Roosevelt
Teles Pires
Araguaia
Plateau of Borborema
C. Branco
Huascarán 6768
Recife
Chile
PACIFIC
OCEAN
Madre de Dios
Guaporé
Arinos
São Francisco
Lima
Chincha Is.
Plateau of Mato Grosso
Salvador
Mamoré
L. Titicaca
Ancohuma & Illampu 6550
La Paz
Bolivian Plateau
Brasília
Brazilian Highlands
Peru
L. Poopó
Abrolhos Bank
Belo Horizonte
2890 Pico da Bandeira
Serra da Mantiqueira
Gran Chaco
Paraguay
Paraná
Tropic of Capricorn
Trench
São Paulo
C. Frio
Rio de Janeiro
Pilcomayo
Asunción
Iguaçu Falls
8050
Atacama Desert
S. Félix
S. Ambrosio
Ojos del Salado 6863
Tucumán
Uruguay
Salado
Serra do Mar
Salinas Grandes
Entre Rios
Porto Alegre
Córdoba
L. Mar Chiquita
Sierra de Córdoba
Lagoa dos Patos
Aconcagua 6960
Uspallata Pass
Valparaíso
Santiago
Rosario
Pampas
Arch. de Juan Fernández
Buenos Aires
La Plata
Montevideo
Río de la Plata
SOUTH
ATLANTIC
OCEAN
Pta. Mogotes
Colorado
Negro
Bahía Blanca
Andes
Patagonia
G. of San Matías
Valdés Peninsula
Chile Rise
Chiloé I.
Chubut
Argentine Basin
Chonos Archipelago
G. of San Jorge
Taitao Peninsula
4058 S. Valentín
G. of Peñas
6212
Wellington
Madre de Dios I.
Falkland Islands
West Falkland
East Falkland
Magellan's Strait
Magellan's Strait
Tierra del Fuego
Santa Inés I.
Staten I.
Cockburn Chan.
Beagle Chan.
C. Horn
5994
ft m
18,000 6000
12,000 4000
9000 3000
6000 2000
3000 1000
1200 400
600 200
0 0
200 600
2000 6000
4000 12,000
6000 18,000
8000 24,000
m ft
Projection: Lambert's Equivalent Azimuthal
West from Greenwich
COPYRIGHT, GEORGE PHILIP & SON, LTD.

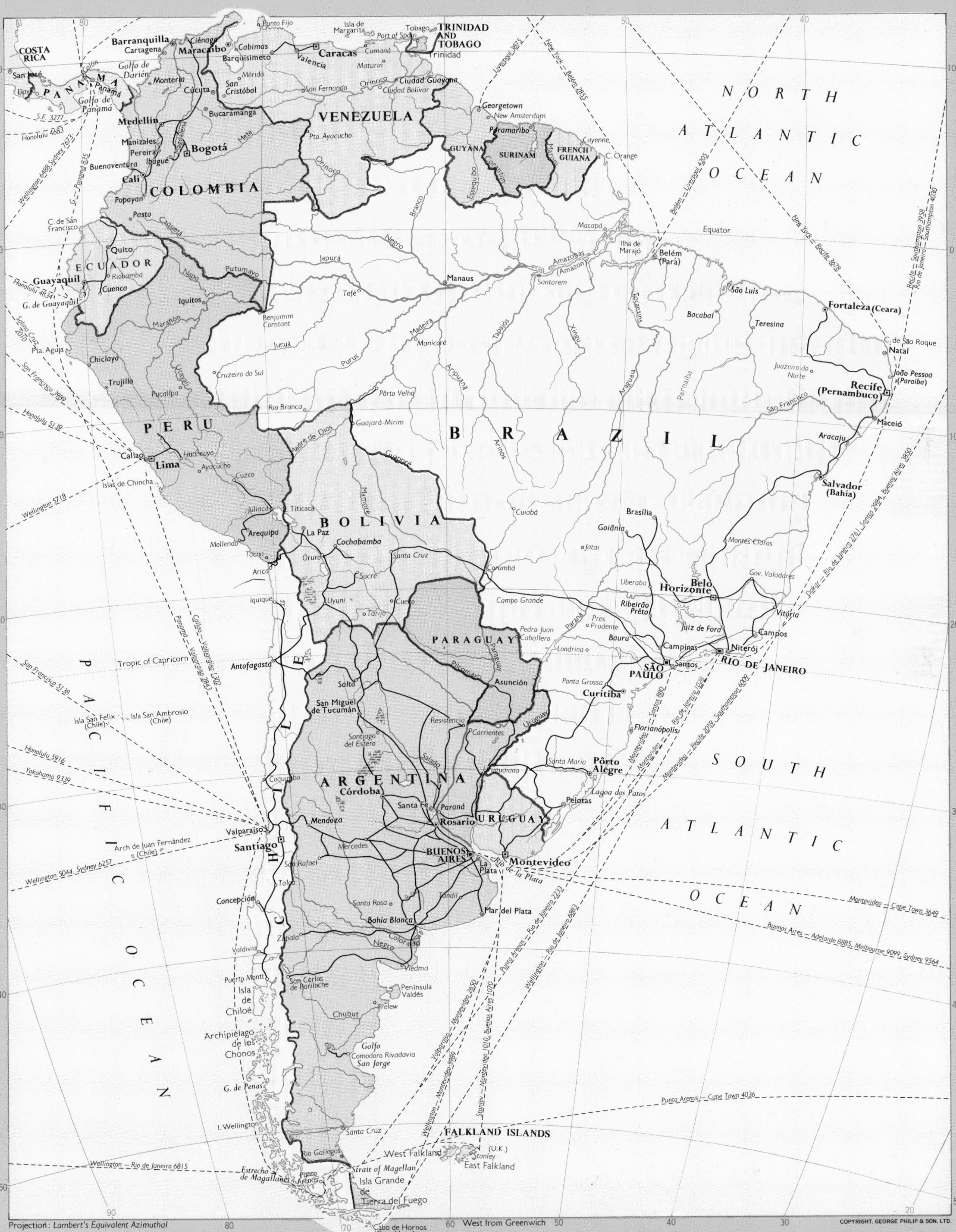

NORTH ATLANTIC OCEAN

SOUTH ATLANTIC OCEAN

PACIFIC OCEAN

COSTA RICA
PANAMA
COLOMBIA
VENEZUELA
TRINIDAD AND TOBAGO
GUYANA
SURINAM
FRENCH GUIANA
ECUADOR
PERU
BRAZIL
BOLIVIA
PARAGUAY
CHILE
ARGENTINA
URUGUAY
FALKLAND ISLANDS (U.K.)

Barranquilla
Cartagena
Maracaibo
Caracas
Valencia
Barquisimeto
Medellín
Bogotá
Cali
Quito
Guayaquil
Cuenca
Iquitos
Lima
Callao
Arequipa
La Paz
Cochabamba
Santa Cruz
Sucre
Antofagasta
Asunción
Salta
San Miguel de Tucumán
Córdoba
Santa Fe
Rosario
Mendoza
Valparaíso
Santiago
Concepción
BUENOS AIRES
La Plata
Montevideo
Mar del Plata
Bahía Blanca
Georgetown
Paramaribo
Cayenne
Manaus
Belém (Pará)
São Luís
Fortaleza (Ceará)
Natal
Recife (Pernambuco)
Maceió
Aracaju
Salvador (Bahia)
Brasília
Goiânia
Belo Horizonte
Vitória
RIO DE JANEIRO
SÃO PAULO
Santos
Curitiba
Florianópolis
Pôrto Alegre
Pelotas
West Falkland
East Falkland
Stanley
Strait of Magellan
Isla Grande de Tierra del Fuego
Cabo de Hornos (Cape Horn)

Equator
Tropic of Capricorn
Amazonas (Amazon)

Projection: *Lambert's Equivalent Azimuthal*

West from Greenwich

1: 30 000 000

100 0 100 200 300 400 500 miles

100 0 200 400 600 800 km

NICARAGUA
COSTA RICA
PANAMA
PACIFIC OCEAN
COLOMBIA
VENEZUELA
ECUADOR
PERU
BOLIVIA
AMAZONAS
RORAIMA
RONDÔNIA
ACRE
ARGENTINA
TRINIDAD & TOBAGO
GRENADA
Barranquilla
Cartagena
Maracaibo
CARACAS
Medellín
BOGOTA
Cali
Quito
Guayaquil
Manaus
LIMA
Callao
Arequipa
La Paz
Cochabamba
Santa Cruz
Sucre
Potosí
Oruro
Iquitos
Cuzco
Panamá
Port of Spain
Ciudad Bolívar
Equator
Milne Edwards Trench
Peru Chile Trench
Krümmel Trench
Cocos Ridge
Sierra Pacaraima
Projection: Sanson-Flamsteed's Sinusoidal
West from Greenwich

1:16 000 000
100 0 100 200 300 400 500 miles
100 0 100 200 300 400 500 600 700 800 km
ATLANTIC OCEAN
Equator
Paramaribo
FR. GUIANA
Cayenne
C.Orange
AMAPÁ
Macapá
C.do Norte
Estuario do Rio Amazonas
Ilha Caviana
Ilha de Marajó
Belém (Pará)
São Luís (Maranhão)
Amazonas (Amazon)
Santarém
P A R Á
MARANHÃO
Teresina
Parnaíba
Fortaleza (Ceará)
Rocas
Fernando de Noronha (Braz.)
CEARÁ
RIO GRANDE DO NORTE
C. de São Roque
Natal
João Pessoa (Paraíba)
PARAÍBA
Campina Grande
RECIFE (Pernambuco)
PERNAMBUCO
PIAUÍ
Maceió
ALAGOAS
SERGIPE
Aracaju
6059
B R A Z I L
BAHIA
GOIÁS
Salvador (Bahia)
Feira de Santana
Ilhéus
Vitória da Conquista
Brasília
DIST. FED.
Goiânia
Anápolis
Planalto do Mato Grosso
MATO GROSSO
MATO GROSSO DO SUL
Planalto Brasil
MINAS GERAIS
Montes Claros
Teófilo Otoni
Gov. Valadares
Belo Horizonte
ESPÍRITO SANTO
Vitória
Campo Grande
Uberaba
Uberlândia
Ribeirão Prêto
SÃO PAULO
Campinas
Juiz de Fora
Campos
Petrópolis
Niterói
RIO DE JANEIRO
Cabo Frio
Trindade (Braz.)
Greenwich

CARIBBEAN SEA
PACIFIC OCEAN
COLOMBIA
VENEZUELA
ECUADOR
PERU
PANAMA
CANAL ZONE (U.S.)
Colón
PANAMÁ
La Chorrera
Arch. de las Perlas
Golfo de Panamá
Golfo del Darién
DARIÉN
Aruba (Neth.)
Curaçao (Neth.)
Bonaire (Neth.)
Willemstad
Is. de Aves (Ven.)
Is. Los Roques
Pta. Gallinas
Cabo de la Vela
Península de la Guajira
GUAJIRA
Ríohacha
Maicao
Santa Marta
Ciénaga
BARRANQUILLA
Sierra Nevada de Santa Marta
5800
ATLÁNTICO
CARTAGENA
Sabanalarga
Valledupar
MAGDALENA
CÉSAR
BOLÍVAR
CÓRDOBA
SUCRE
Montería
Sincelejo
Magangué
Mompós
G. de Morrosquillo
Golfo de Urabá
Turbo
MARACAIBO
Lago de Maracaibo
ZULIA
Golfo de Venezuela
Paraguaná
Punto Fijo
Punta Cardón
Coro
FALCÓN
Puerto Cumarebo
LARA
BARQUISIMETO
Cabimas
Ciudad Ojeda
Valencia
Maracay
CARACAS
La Guaira
Maiquetía
DISTRITO FEDERAL
MIRANDA
Los Teques
ARAGUA
Pto. Cabello
San Felipe
YARACUY
CARABOBO
COJEDES
San Carlos
PORTUGUESA
Guanare
Acarigua
Araure
TRUJILLO
Trujillo
Valera
Boconó
MÉRIDA
Mérida
5007
BARINAS
Barinas
TÁCHIRA
San Cristóbal
Cúcuta
NORTE DE SANTANDER
Ocaña
Pamplona
BUCARAMANGA
SANTANDER
Barrancabermeja
San Gil
APURE
San Fernando de Apure
GUÁRICO
Calabozo
ARAUCA
Arauca
Meta
Orinoco
Puerto Carreño
Puerto Ayacucho
Guaviare
VICHADA
BOYACÁ
Tunja
Sogamoso
Duitama
CUNDINAMARCA
BOGOTÁ
Zipaquirá
Fusagasugá
Girardot
ANTIOQUIA
MEDELLÍN
Bello
Envigado
Rionegro
CHOCÓ
Quibdó
Golfo de Tibugá
Golfo de Cupica
CALDAS
Manizales
RISARALDA
Pereira
QUINDÍO
Armenia
TOLIMA
Ibagué
VALLE
Cali
Palmira
Buga
Tuluá
Buenaventura
B. de Buenaventura
CAUCA
Popayán
HUILA
Neiva
Garzón
NARIÑO
Pasto
Tumaco
Ipiales
META
Villavicencio
San Martín
Ser. de la Macarena
GUAINÍA
VAUPÉS
Mitú
CAQUETÁ
Florencia
Caquetá
PUTUMAYO
Putumayo
AMAZONAS
Apaporis
Leticia
Amazonas
Iquitos
LORETO
Napo
Marañón
Ucayali
ESMERALDAS
Esmeraldas
IMBABURA
Ibarra
CARCHI
Tulcán
Cayambe
5796
QUITO
PICHINCHA
MANABÍ
Manta
Portoviejo
Cotopaxi
5896
Latacunga
Ambato
TUNGURAHUA
Riobamba
CHIMBORAZO
6267
Sangay
5230
GUAYAQUIL
GUAYAS
Golfo de Guayaquil
Isla de Puná
Cuenca
AZUAY
CAÑAR
Machala
EL ORO
Loja
LOJA
ZAMORA CHINCHIPE
MORONA-SANTIAGO
NAPO
PASTAZA
Tumbes
Sullana
PIURA
3934
Japurá
Içana
Negro
Benjamin Constant
Tabatinga
São Paulo de Olivença
Santo Antônio do Içá
Fonte Boa
Solimões
Juruá
Jutaí
Iça
Tefé
Uaupés
AMAZONAS

Projection: Lambert's Equivalent Azimuthal

1: 8 000 000

50 0 50 100 150 200 miles

50 0 100 200 300 km

ATLANTIC OCEAN
TRINIDAD AND TOBAGO
Tobago
Trinidad
Port of Spain
Arima
San Fernando
Scarborough
Galeota Point
The Grenadines
St. George's
GRENADA
La Blanquilla (Ven.)
Los Hermanos (Ven.)
Is. Los Testigos (Ven.)
NUEVA ESPARTA
Margarita
La Asunción
Porlamar
I. Coche
Carúpano
Pen. de Paria
Güiria
Golfo de Paria
Serpent's Mouth
Boca de la Sierpe
Dragon's Mouth
Boca del Dragón
Pen. de Araya
Cumaná
Puerto La Cruz
Barcelona
SUCRE
Caripito
Maturín
MONAGAS
Anaco
Cantaura
Aragua de Barcelona
Zaraza
ANZOÁTEGUI
El Tigre
Tucupita
DELTA AMACURO
Orinoco
Boca Grande
I. Corocoro
Pto. Ordaz
Santo Tomé de Guayana
Soledad
Ciudad Bolívar
Upata
El Palmar
Guri Dam
El Callao
Tumeremo
Serranía Turagua
BOLÍVAR
VENEZUELA
El Dorado
Angel Falls
2560
La Gran Sabana
Mt. Roraima
2772
Sierra Pacaraima
Sa. Tepequem
Sierra Parima
Serra Curupira
Serra do Apiaú
Serra do Mucajaí
RORAIMA
Boa Vista
Caracaraí
Serra Tabatinga
GUYANA
Morawhanna
Charity
Anna Regina
Suddie
Georgetown
Buxton
Mahaicony
New Amsterdam
Port Mourant
Bartica
Mackenzie
Skeldon
Kaieteur Falls
Pakaraima Mts.
Kamoa Mts.
Lethem
Essequibo
Demerara
Berbice
Corentyne
Rupununi
734
Serra Acaraí
SURINAM
Nieuw Nickerie
Paramaribo
Nieuw Amsterdam
Moengo
Albina
Brokopondo
Prof. Dr. Ir. W. J. Van Blommestein Meer
NICKERIE
CORONIE
SARAMACCA
BROKOPONDO
COMMEWIJNE
MAROWIJNE
Wilhelmina Geb.
Julianatop
1280
Apetina
FRENCH GUIANA
St. Laurent
Mana
Iracoubo
Sinnamary
Kourou
Iles du Salut
Cayenne
Rémire
Roura
Régina
St. Georges
Oiapoque
Cabo Orange
Maripasoula
Saül
Camopi
690
Serra Tumucumaque
AMAPÁ
Amapá
Calçoene
I. de Maracá
Macapá
Serra do Navio
Pôrto Grande
Pôrto Santana
Mazagão
Canal do Norte
I. Caviana
Ilha de Marajó
Breves
I. Grande de Gurupá
Almeirim
Bôca do Jari
BRAZIL
Negro
Barcelos
Moura
Manaus
Itacoatiara
Parintins
Óbidos
Alenquer
Monte Alegre
Santarém
Amazonas
Xingu
Altamira
Pôrto de Moz
Trombetas
Tapajós
Madeira
Purus
Coari
Tefé
Codajás
Manacapuru
Maués
Borba
Nova Olinda
Itaituba
Aveiro
Belterra
PARÁ
Arquipélago das Anavilhanas
Uatumã
Urubu
Jari
Branco
Catrimani
Demini
Pôrto Alegre
Novo Aripuanã
West from Greenwich
65
60
55
50
10
5
0

ATLANTIC OCEAN
AMAPÁ
PARÁ
MARANHÃO
PIAUÍ
CEARÁ
RIO GRANDE DO NORTE
PERNAMBUCO
ALAGOAS
BRAZIL
Macapá
Ilha de Marajó
BELÉM (Pará)
Abaetetuba
Bragança
Capanema
Castanhal
Vigia
Soure
Tocantins
Xingu
Marabá
Imperatriz
Tocantinópolis
SÃO LUÍS (Maranhão)
Bacabal
Pedreiras
Caxias
Codó
Parnaíba
TERESINA
Timon
Floriano
Oeiras
Picos
Crateús
Sobral
Camocim
FORTALEZA (Ceará)
Aracati
Mossoró
NATAL
João Pessoa (Paraíba)
Campina Grande
Caruaru
RECIFE (Pernambuco)
Olinda
MACEIÓ
Aracaju
Petrolina
Juazeiro
Crato
Juàzeiro do Norte
Balsas
Carolina
Chapada das Mangabeiras
Serra dos Carajás
Serra do Gurupi
Sa. do Tiracambu
Serra do Estrondo
Serra dos Gradaus
Sa. da Ibiapaba
Sa. das Marrecas
Serra Talhada
Sa. Grande
Parnaíba
Barra
Xique-Xique
Senhor do Bonfim
Jacobina
Paulo Afonso

ATLANTIC OCEAN
ESPÍRITO SANTO
BAHIA
GOIÁS
MINAS GERAIS
SÃO PAULO
RIO DE JANEIRO
PARANÁ
DISTRITO FEDERAL
BRASÍLIA
GOIÂNIA
BELO HORIZONTE
SALVADOR (Bahia)
NITERÓI
RIO DE JANEIRO
SÃO PAULO
SANTO ANDRÉ
SANTOS
CURITIBA
CAMPINAS
CAMPOS
DUQUE DE CAXIAS
SÃO GONÇALO
Vitória
Tropic of Capricorn
West from Greenwich

ft m

6000 2000 · 4500 1500 · 3000 1000 · 1200 400 · 600 200 · 0 0

200 600 · 2000 6000 · 4000 12 000

m ft

Projection: *Lambert's Equivalent Azimuthal*

1:8 000 000

50 0 50 100 150 200 miles

50 0 100 200 300 km

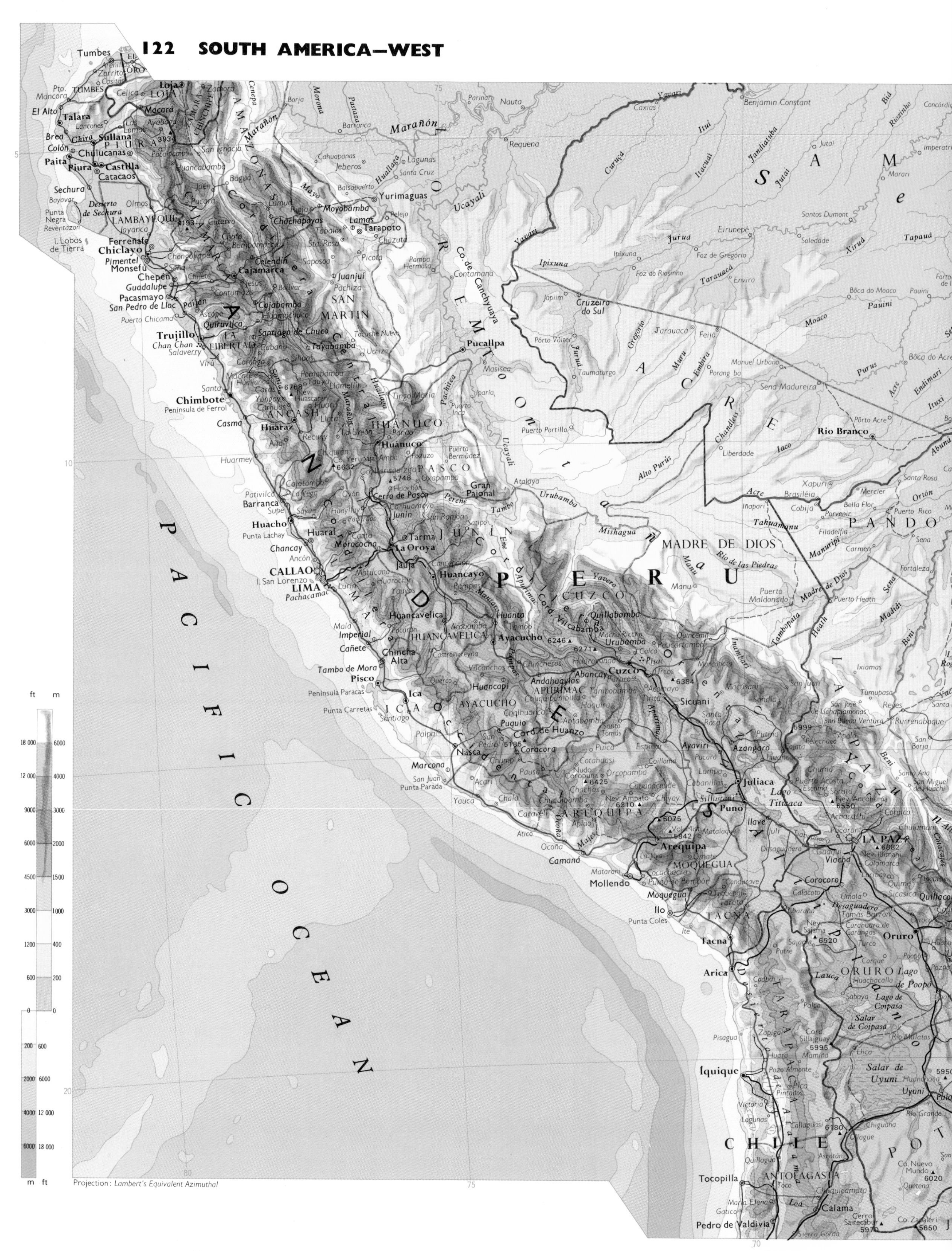
PACIFIC OCEAN
PERU
CHILE
ACRE
LA PAZ
PANDO
MADRE DE DIOS
Tumbes
Talara
Sullana
Paita
Piura
Chiclayo
Trujillo
Chimbote
Huacho
CALLAO
LIMA
Pisco
Ica
Nasca
Arequipa
Mollendo
Moquegua
Ilo
Tacna
Arica
Iquique
Tocopilla
Pedro de Valdivia
Calama
Oruro
Lago Titicaca
Puno
Juliaca
Cuzco
Ayacucho
Huancayo
La Oroya
Cerro de Pasco
Huánuco
Pucallpa
Cajamarca
Chachapoyas
Moyobamba
Yurimaguas
Tarapoto
Requena
Benjamin Constant
Cruzeiro do Sul
Rio Branco
Eirunepé
Marañón
Ucayali
Urubamba
Madre de Dios
Lago de Poopó
Salar de Uyuni
Salar de Coipasa
Desierto de Sechura
ft m
18 000 6000
12 000 4000
9000 3000
6000 2000
4500 1500
3000 1000
1200 400
600 200
0 0
200 600
2000 6000
4000 12 000
6000 18 000
m ft
Projection: Lambert's Equivalent Azimuthal

1:8 000 000

50 0 50 100 150 200 miles

50 0 100 200 300 km

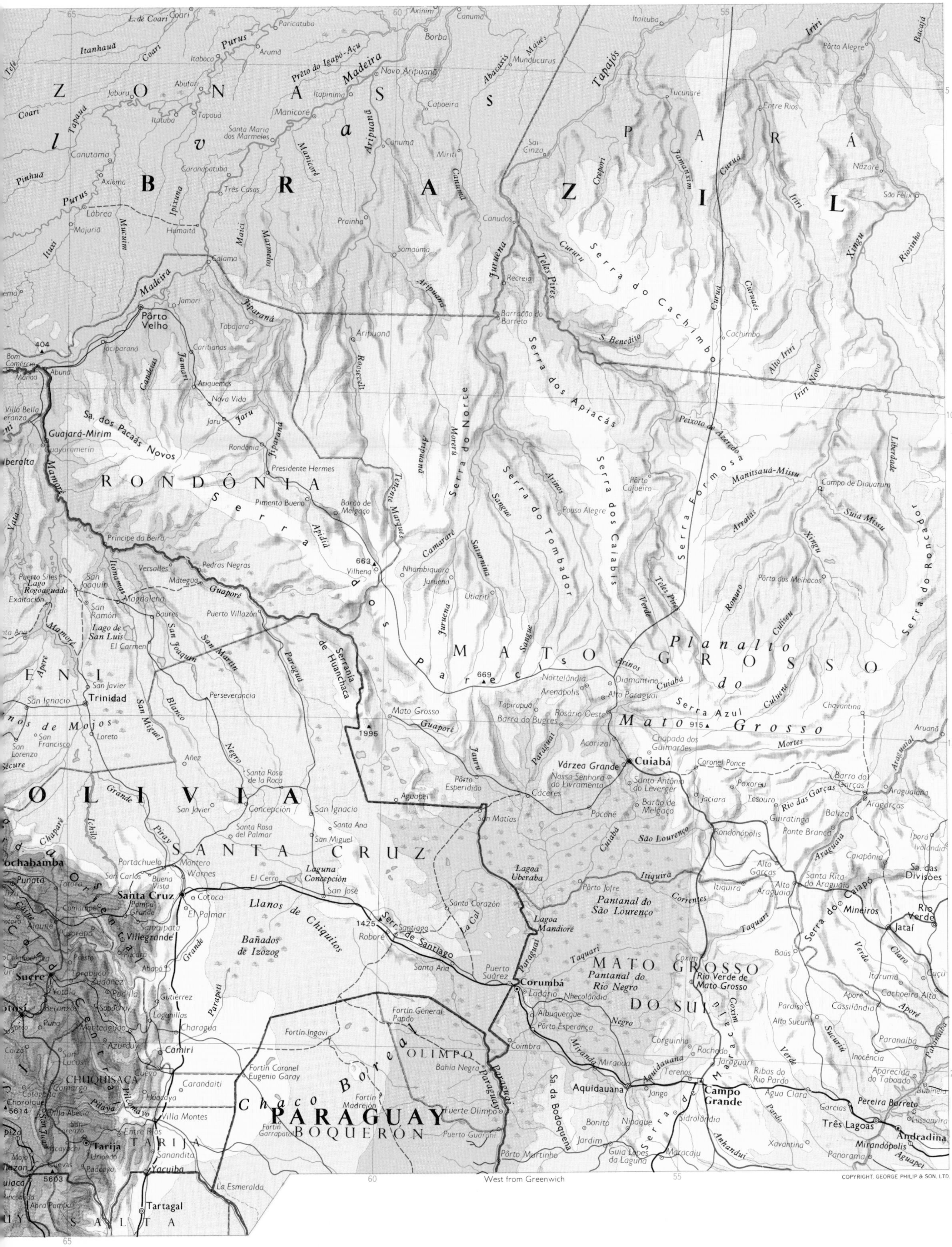

BRAZIL

AMAZONAS

PARÁ

RONDÔNIA

MATO GROSSO

MATO GROSSO DO SUL

BOLIVIA

BENI

SANTA CRUZ

CHUQUISACA

TARIJA

SALTA

PARAGUAY

BOQUERÓN

OLIMPO

Chaco Boreal

Planalto do Mato Grosso

Serra dos Parecís

Serra do Cachimbo

Serra dos Apiacás

Serra do Norte

Serra do Tombador

Serra dos Caiabis

Serra Formosa

Serra do Roncador

Serra Azul

Serra de Maracaju

Serra do Caiapó

Sa. dos Pacaás Novos

Serrania de Huanchaca

Serra de Santiago

Sa. da Bodoquena

Llanos de Chiquitos

Llanos de Mojos

Bañados de Izozog

Pantanal do São Lourenço

Pantanal do Rio Negro

Cordillera Oriental

Cordillera Central

Madeira, Purus, Tapajós, Juruena, Teles Pires, Xingu, Iriri, Curuá, Aripuanã, Roosevelt, Guaporé, Mamoré, Paraguai, Cuiabá, Taquari, São Lourenço, Araguaia, Paraná, Pilcomayo, Grande, Parapetí, Beni, Itonamas, San Miguel, Blanco, Negro, Manicoré, Canumã, Jiparaná, Jamari, Candeias, Arinos, Sangue, Camararé, Ronuro, Culuene, Manitsauá-Missu, Suiá Missu, Liberdade, Rio das Garças, Sucuriú, Verde, Pardo, Anhanduí, Aquidauana, Miranda, Coxim, Itiquira, Correntes, Jauru, Mortes

Pôrto Velho, Guajará-Mirim, Abunã, Humaitá, Lábrea, Manicoré, Borba, Novo Aripuanã, Itaituba, Jacareacanga, Cachimbo, Vilhena, Presidente Hermes, Pimenta Bueno, Ariquemes, Rondônia, Príncipe da Beira, Pedras Negras, Mato Grosso, Cáceres, Cuiabá, Várzea Grande, Rosário Oeste, Diamantino, Alto Paraguai, Rondonópolis, Poxoréu, Barra do Garças, Aragarças, Jataí, Rio Verde, Mineiros, Coxim, Corumbá, Ladário, Aquidauana, Campo Grande, Três Lagoas, Andradina, Pereira Barreto, Ponta Porã, Bela Vista, Porto Murtinho

Trinidad, Santa Cruz, Sucre, Potosí, Cochabamba, Tarija, Camiri, Yacuiba, Villa Montes, Concepción, San Ignacio, San Matías, Puerto Suárez, Roboré, San José, Magdalena, San Joaquín, Riberalta

Fortín General Pando, Fortín Ingavi, Fortín Coronel Eugenio Garay, Bahía Negra, Fuerte Olimpo, Puerto Guaraní, Fortín Madrejón, La Esmeralda, Tartagal

404, 663, 669, 915, 1425, 1995, 5614, 5603

65, 60, 55, 5, 10, 15, 20

West from Greenwich

PACIFIC OCEAN
BOLIVIA
POTOSÍ
TARIJA
BOQUERÓN
PARAGUAY
Gran Chaco
PRESIDENTE HAYES
FORMOSA
CHACO
JUJUY
SALTA
ANTOFAGASTA
ATACAMA
CATAMARCA
TUCUMÁN
SANTIAGO DEL ESTERO
LA RIOJA
SAN JUAN
CÓRDOBA
SANTA FE
CORRIENTES
ENTRE RÍOS
MISIONES
COQUIMBO
MENDOZA
SAN LUIS
LA PAMPA
BUENOS AIRES
NEUQUÉN
CHILE
ANDES
ARGENTINA
Pampa
Cordillera de Domeyko
Desierto de Atacama
Cordillera Oriental
Cordillera Principal
Sierra de Famatina
Salar de Uyuni
Salar de Atacama
Salar de Arizaro
Salinas Grandes
Salinas Ambargasta
Pampa de las Salinas
Mar Chiquita
Iquique
Tocopilla
Calama
Pedro de Valdivia
Mejillones
Antofagasta
Taltal
Chañaral
Copiapó
Vallenar
La Serena
Coquimbo
Ovalle
Illapel
Los Andes
Viña del Mar
VALPARAÍSO
Quillota
SANTIAGO
Puente Alto
San Bernardo
San Antonio
Rancagua
Rengo
San Fernando
Curicó
Talca
Constitución
Linares
Cauquenes
Parral
San Carlos
Chillán
Tomé
Talcahuano
Concepción
Coronel
Lota
Los Angeles
Mulchén
Lebu
Cañete
Angol
Collipulli
Tupiza
Villazón
La Quiaca
Tarija
Yacuiba
Villa Montes
Tartagal
San Ramón de la Nueva Orán
Tabacal
S. Salvador de Jujuy
San Pedro de Jujuy
Salta
Metán
Rosario de la Frontera
SAN MIGUEL DE TUCUMÁN
Tafí Viejo
Concepción
Santiago del Estero
La Banda
Añatuya
Catamarca
La Rioja
San Juan
Mendoza
Godoy Cruz
San Rafael
San Luis
Mercedes
Villa Dolores
Río Cuarto
CÓRDOBA
Cruz del Eje
Deán Funes
Villa María
Rafaela
Esperanza
SANTA FE
Paraná
ROSARIO
San Nicolás de los Arroyos
Pergamino
Junín
Venado Tuerto
Rufino
General Pico
Santa Rosa
Bahía Blanca
Punta Alto
Tres Arroyos
Necochea
Tandil
MAR DEL PLATA
Dolores
Azul
Olavarría
BUENOS AIRES
La Plata
Quilmes
Luján
Campana
Zárate
Concordia
Salto
Paysandú
Concepción del Uruguay
Gualeguaychú
Corrientes
Resistencia
Formosa
ASUNCIÓN
Concepción
Reconquista
Goya
Mercedes
Presidencia Roque Sáenz Peña
Río Paraná
Uruguay
Bermejo
Pilcomayo
Salado
Colorado
Chadileuvú
Projection: Lambert's Equivalent Azimuthal

1:8 000 000
50 0 50 100 150 miles
50 0 50 100 150 200 km
BELO HORIZONTE
Vitória
Vila Velha
ATLANTIC
OCEAN
BRAZIL
GROSSO
DO SUL
SÃO PAULO
PARANÁ
SANTA CATARINA
RIO GRANDE
DO SUL
RIO DE JANEIRO
MISIONES
UAY
Três Lagoas
Andradina
Araçatuba
Mirassol
S. José do Rio Prêto
Bebedouro
Ribeirão Prêto
Passos
Juiz de Fora
Barbacena
Cataguases
Campos
Petrópolis
Nova Friburgo
Macaé
Cabo Frio
Niterói
RIO DE JANEIRO
DUQUE DE CAXIAS
SÃO GONÇALO
Nova Iguaçu
Volta Redonda
Barra Mansa
Taubaté
S. J. dos Campos
Mogi das Cruzes
SÃO PAULO
SANTO ANDRÉ
SANTOS
Guarujá
São Vicente
Jundiaí
CAMPINAS
Piracicaba
Limeira
Rio Claro
Americana
Sorocaba
Bauru
Marília
Presidente Prudente
Londrina
Maringá
Apucarana
Arapongas
Ourinhos
Guaíra
Ponta Grossa
Guarapuava
CURITIBA
Paranaguá
Joinvile
São Francisco do Sul
Blumenau
Itajaí
Brusque
Florianópolis
Ilha de Santa Catarina
Lajes
Tubarão
Laguna
Cabo Santa Marta Grande
Criciúma
Caxias do Sul
Nôvo Hamburgo
São Leopoldo
PÔRTO ALEGRE
Passo Fundo
Erechim
Cruz Alta
Santo Ângelo
Santa Maria
Santa Cruz do Sul
Cachoeira do Sul
Rio Pardo
Alegrete
São Gabriel
Santana do Livramento
Rivera
Bagé
Pelotas
Rio Grande
Lagoa dos Patos
Lagoa Mirim
Lagoa Mangueira
Jaguarão
Melo
Treinta y Tres
Tacuarembó
Minas
Rocha
San Carlos
Maldonado
MONTEVIDEO
Encarnación
Foz do Iguaçu
Iguaçu Falls
Pedro Juan Caballero
Ponta Porã
Tropic of Capricorn
Ilha de São Sebastião
Ilha Comprida
Ilha do Cardoso
Iguape
5304
West from Greenwich
55
50
45
40
25
30
35

1:8 000 000
PACIFIC OCEAN
SOUTH ATLANTIC OCEAN
FALKLAND ISLANDS
(ISLAS MALVINAS)
West Falkland
East Falkland
Stanley
LA PAMPA
BUENOS AIRES
NEUQUÉN
RÍO NEGRO
CHUBUT
SANTA CRUZ
TIERRA DEL FUEGO
ARAUCANIA
LOS LAGOS
Golfo San Matías
Golfo San Jorge
Bahía Grande
Strait of Magellan
Isla Grande de Tierra del Fuego
Archipiélago de los Chonos
Golfo de Penas
Isla de Chiloé
Bahía Blanca
Neuquén
Temuco
Valdivia
Osorno
Puerto Montt
San Carlos de Bariloche
Comodoro Rivadavia
Río Gallegos
Punta Arenas
Ushuaia
Trelew
Rawson
Puerto Madryn
Viedma
Carmen de Patagones
Coihaique
Puerto Aisén
Puerto Natales
Cabo de Hornos
(Cape Horn)
Projection: Lambert's Equivalent Azimuthal
West from Greenwich

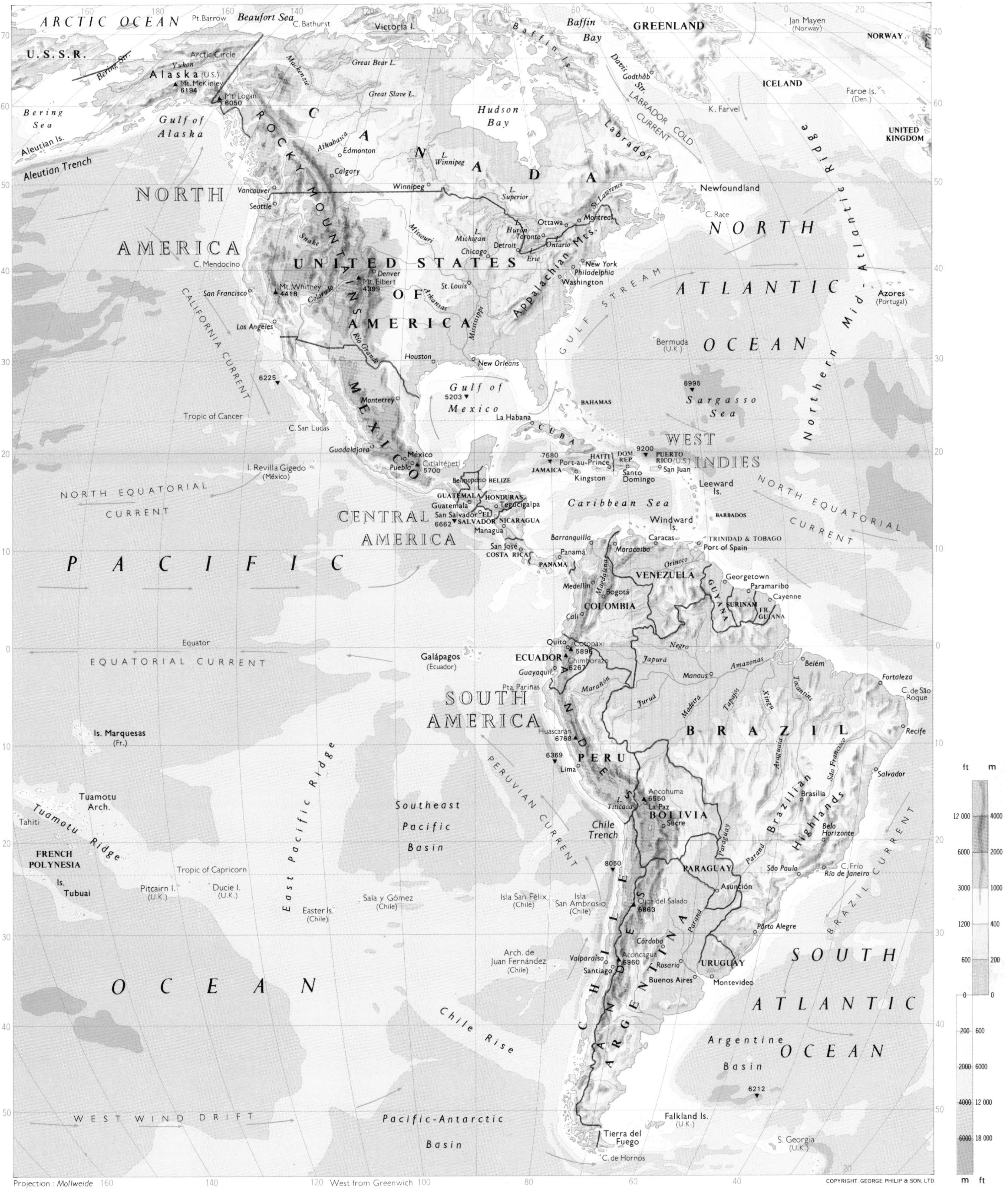
ARCTIC OCEAN
Pt.Barrow
Beaufort Sea
C. Bathurst
Victoria I.
Baffin Is.
Baffin Bay
GREENLAND
Jan Mayen (Norway)
NORWAY
U.S.S.R.
Bering Str.
Arctic Circle
Yukon
Alaska (U.S.)
Mt.McKinley 6194
Mt.Logan 6050
Mackenzie
Great Bear L.
Great Slave L.
Davis Str.
Godthåb
ICELAND
Faroe Is. (Den.)
Bering Sea
Gulf of Alaska
Aleutian Is.
Aleutian Trench
C A N A D A
ROCKY MOUNTAINS
Hudson Bay
LABRADOR COLD CURRENT
Labrador
K. Farvel
UNITED KINGDOM
Athabasca
Edmonton
Calgary
L. Winnipeg
Winnipeg
Vancouver
Seattle
L. Superior
St. Lawrence
Newfoundland
C. Race
NORTH AMERICA
Snake
Missouri
L. Michigan
L. Huron
Ottawa
Montreal
Toronto
Ontario
Erie
Detroit
Chicago
UNITED STATES OF AMERICA
C. Mendocino
Appalachian Mts.
New York
Philadelphia
Washington
NORTH ATLANTIC OCEAN
Northern Mid-Atlantic Ridge
Azores (Portugal)
Mt.Whitney 4418
Mt.Elbert 4399
Denver
San Francisco
Colorado
Arkansas
St. Louis
Mississippi
GULF STREAM
CALIFORNIA CURRENT
Los Angeles
Rio Grande
Houston
New Orleans
Bermuda (U.K.)
6225
Gulf of Mexico
5203
MEXICO
Monterrey
6995
Sargasso Sea
BAHAMAS
Tropic of Cancer
C. San Lucas
La Habana
CUBA
WEST INDIES
Guadalajara
México
Citlaltépetl 5700
Puebla
7680
JAMAICA
HAITI
Port-au-Prince
Kingston
DOM. REP.
Santo Domingo
9200
PUERTO RICO (U.S.)
San Juan
I. Revilla Gigedo (México)
Belmopan
BELIZE
Leeward Is.
NORTH EQUATORIAL CURRENT
GUATEMALA
HONDURAS
Tegucigalpa
Guatemala
San Salvador
EL SALVADOR
6662
NICARAGUA
Managua
Caribbean Sea
Windward Is.
BARBADOS
CENTRAL AMERICA
Barranquilla
Maracaibo
Caracas
TRINIDAD & TOBAGO
Port of Spain
Panamá
San José
COSTA RICA
PANAMA
Orinoco
P A C I F I C
VENEZUELA
Georgetown
Paramaribo
Cayenne
GUYANA
SURINAM
FR. GUIANA
Medellín
Magdalena
Bogotá
COLOMBIA
Cali
Equator
EQUATORIAL CURRENT
Quito
Cotopaxi 5896
ECUADOR
Chimborazo 6267
Guayaquil
Galápagos (Ecuador)
Negro
Japurá
Manaus
Amazonas
Belém
Fortaleza
C. de São Roque
Pta Pariñas
Marañon
Juruá
Madeira
Tapajós
Xingu
Tocantins
SOUTH AMERICA
Huascarán 6768
BRAZIL
Recife
Is. Marquesas (Fr.)
6369
Lima
PERU
ANDES
Araguaia
São Francisco
Salvador
PERUVIAN CURRENT
East Pacific Ridge
Tuamotu Arch.
Tuamotu Ridge
Tahiti
Southeast Pacific Basin
L. Titicaca
Ancohuma 6550
La Paz
BOLIVIA
Sucre
Chile Trench
Brasília
Brazilian Highlands
Belo Horizonte
FRENCH POLYNESIA
Paraguay
Paraná
8050
PARAGUAY
São Paulo
C. Frío
Rio de Janeiro
BRAZIL CURRENT
Tropic of Capricorn
Is. Tubuai
Pitcairn I. (U.K.)
Ducie I. (U.K.)
Sala y Gómez (Chile)
Easter Is. (Chile)
Isla San Félix (Chile)
Isla San Ambrosio (Chile)
Ojos del Salado 6863
Asunción
Pôrto Alegre
Córdoba
Arch. de Juan Fernández (Chile)
Valparaíso
Aconcagua 6960
Santiago
Rosario
URUGUAY
Buenos Aires
Montevideo
SOUTH ATLANTIC OCEAN
O C E A N
Chile Rise
CHILE
ARGENTINA
Argentine Basin
6212
WEST WIND DRIFT
Pacific-Antarctic Basin
Falkland Is. (U.K.)
Tierra del Fuego
C. de Hornos
S. Georgia (U.K.)
ft m
12 000 4000
6000 2000
3000 1000
1200 400
600 200
0 0
200 600
2000 6000
4000 12 000
6000 18 000
m ft

Projection: *Mollweide* 160 140 120 West from Greenwich 100 80 60 40

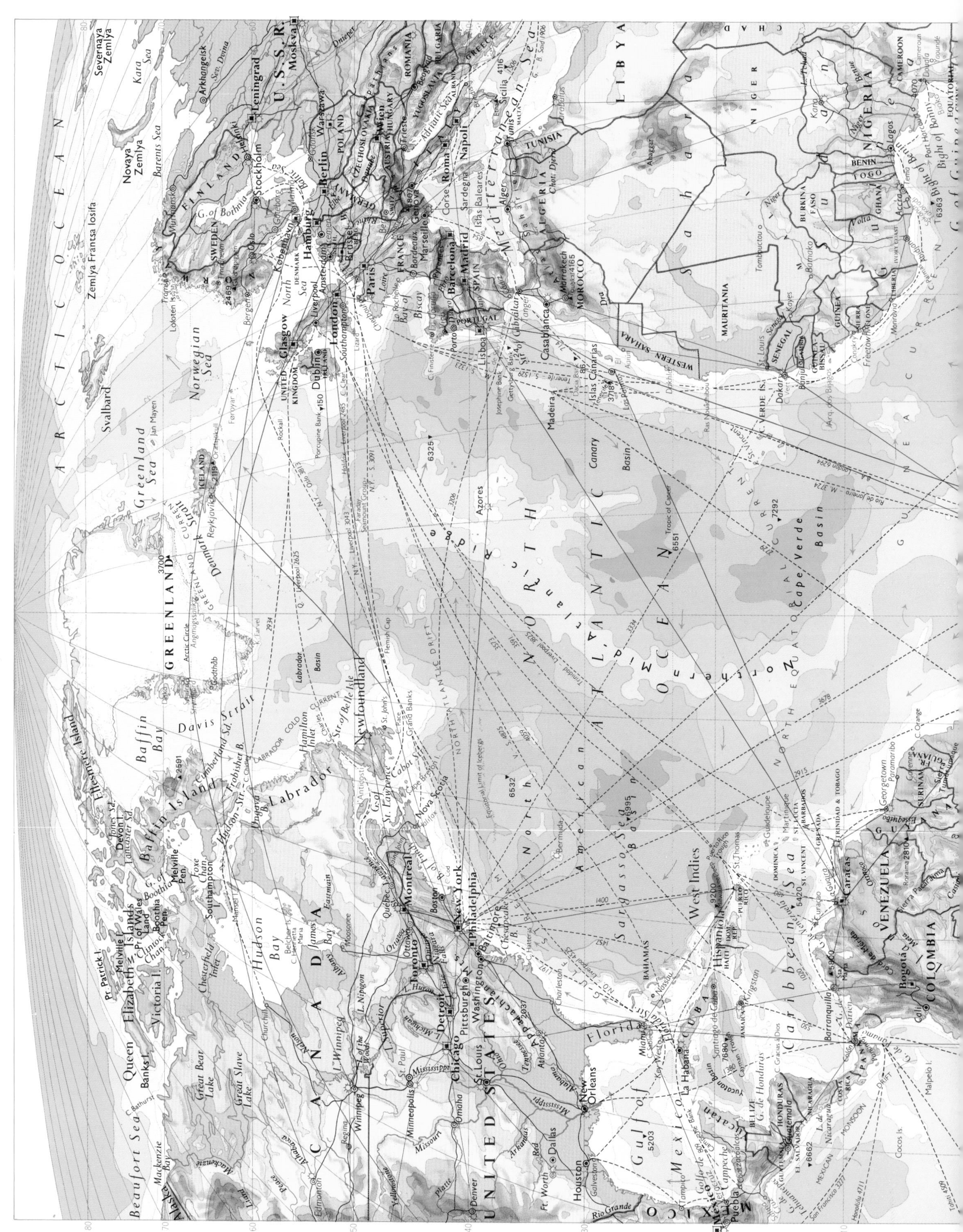

A R C T I C   O C E A N
Greenland Sea
Norwegian Sea
GREENLAND
Baffin Bay
Davis Strait
Labrador Basin
Hudson Bay
C A N A D A
Newfoundland
Labrador
U N I T E D   S T A T E S
Gulf of Mexico
Caribbean Sea
Sargasso Sea
West Indies
Azores
Madeira
Canary Basin
Cape Verde Basin
N O R T H   A T L A N T I C   O C E A N
North American Basin
Northern Atlantic Ridge
Mediterranean Sea
S a h a r a
MOROCCO
ALGERIA
TUNISIA
LIBYA
MAURITANIA
NIGERIA
U.S.S.R.
FINLAND
SWEDEN
UNITED KINGDOM
FRANCE
SPAIN
PORTUGAL
VENEZUELA
COLOMBIA

SOUTH ATLANTIC OCEAN
PACIFIC OCEAN
SOUTHERN OCEAN
BRAZIL
ARGENTINA
BOLIVIA
PERU
PARAGUAY
URUGUAY
ECUADOR
CHILE
FALKLAND IS.
DEPENDENCIES
BRITISH ANTARCTIC TERRITORY
NAMIBIA
SOUTH AFRICA
CONGO
South East Pacific Basin
Brazil Basin
Angola Basin
Cape Basin
Agulhas Basin
Argentine Basin
Southern Mid-Atlantic Ridge
Walvis Ridge
Atlantic Indian Ridge
Antarctic 5385 (Southern Pacific) Basin
Antarctic Basin
Chile Rise
BENGUELA COLD CURRENT
PERUVIAN COLD CURRENT
SOUTH EQUATORIAL CURRENT
BRAZIL CURRENT
CAPE HORN COLD CURRENT
WEST WIND DRIFT
Weddell Sea
Scotia Sea
Ross Sea
Drake Passage
Dronning Maud Land
Ellsworth Land
Byrd Land
Coats Land
Enderby Land
Graham Land
Palmer Land
Antarctic Peninsula
Antarctic Circle
Peter Ist I.
Charcot I.
Tropic of Capricorn
Equatorial Limit of Icebergs
Falkland Is. (Islas Malvinas)
Shag Rocks
Burdwood Bank
South Georgia
South Orkney Is.
South Shetland Is.
South Sandwich Is.
South Sandwich Trench
Tierra del Fuego
Cabo de Hornos
Tristan da Cunha
Gough I.
Bouvetøya
St. Helena
Ascension
Trindade
Martin Vaz
Fernando de Noronha
Abrolhos
Bromley Plateau
Galápagos
S. Ambrosio
Arch. de Juan Fernández
Rio de Janeiro
São Paulo
Santos
Belo Horizonte
Salvador
Recife
Fortaleza
Belém
São Luís
Brasília
Goiânia
Pôrto Alegre
Rio Grande
Montevideo
Buenos Aires
Rosario
Córdoba
Tucumán
Santiago
Valparaíso
Concepción
Puerto Montt
Asunción
La Paz
Arica
Iquique
Antofagasta
Lima
Callao
Quito
Guayaquil
Iquitos
Leticia
Manaus
Cape Town
Lüderitz
Walvisbaai
Swakopmund
Windhoek
Port Nolloth
Luanda
Benguela
Lobito
Namibe
Pointe Noire
Brazzaville
Kinshasa
Annobón
C. Lopez
Pampas
Mato Grosso
Gran Chaco
Patagonia
Brazilian Highlands
Andes
Amazon
Paraná
Paraguay
Madeira
Tocantins
Xingu
Tapajós
Aripuanã
Araguaia
Purus
Negro
Japurá
Putumayo
Ucayali
Marañón
São Francisco
Parnaíba
Jequitinhonha
Grande
Pilcomayo
Salado
Colorado
Chubut
Deseado
Congo
Cunene
Oranje
L. Titicaca
L. Poopó
L. dos Patos
L. Mirim
Río de la Plata
Bahía Blanca
Golfo San Matías
Pen. Valdés
Golfo San Jorge
Isla de Chiloé
Arch. de los Chonos
Pen. de Taitao
G. de Penas
Str. of Magellan
Punta Arenas
I. Sta. Inés
Golfo de Guayaquil
Pta. Pariñas
C. Frio
C. de São Tomé
C. de São Roque
C. Fria
Kaap die Goeie Hoop
Agulhas Bank
Chimborazo 6267
Cotopaxi 5897
Ancohuma 6550
Ojos del Salado 6863
Aconcagua 6960
Llullaillaco 6723
Serra da Mantiqueira 2880
Richards Deep 8050
6369
6866
6537
6027
5755
638
302
5457
892
6013
411
6212
5552
8428
6739
Sydney 7692
Wellington 6488
Madeira – Cape Town 4677
3778
3267
2615
1340
1355
1070
1020
1187
550
m
ft
Projection: Mollweide
Principal Shipping Routes (Distances in Nautical Miles)
Principal Air Routes
Direction of Currents
COPYRIGHT GEORGE PHILIP & SON LTD

EUROPE

Tundra
Ural Mountains
Narodnaya 1894
Telpos Iz 1617
Pechora
Kanin Peninsula
Kola Peninsula
White Sea
Mezen
N. Dvina
Onega
Lapland
Kebnekaise 2123
Scandinavia
Galdhöpiggen 2469
Iceland
Hekla 1491
Oraefa Jökull 2119
Arctic Circle
NORWEGIAN SEA
Lofoten
Vesterålen
North Cape
Nordkinn
L. Inari
Faroe Is.
Fisher Bank
Shetland Is.
Orkney Is.
Rockall
Hebrides
British Isles
Ben Nevis 1347
Great Britain
Ireland
Irish Sea
Snowdon 1085
Valentia I.
C. Clear
Land's End
Thames
ATLANTIC OCEAN
NORTH SEA
Dogger Bank
Heligoland
Lindesnes
Skagerrak
Kattegat
Jutland
Netherlands
English Channel
Brittany
Bay of Biscay
4861
C. Finisterre
Loire
Gironde
Garonne
Seine
Meuse
Ardennes
Eifel
Rhine
Westerwald
Taunus
Hunsrück
Vosges
Black For.
Jura
Weser
Elbe
Harz 1142
Erz Geb.
Sudetes
Moravian Heights
Bohemian For.
Danube
Inn
Central Massif
Mt. Dore 1886
Cevennes
Rhône
G. of Lions
Alps
Mt. Blanc 4807
Po
Pyrenees
Pico de Aneto 3404
Cantabrian Mts.
Old Castile
New Castile
Iberian Peninsula
Sa. de Guadarrama
Sa. da Estrela
Douro
Tagus
Tejo
C. da Roca
Sierra Morena
Guadalquivir
Andalusia
Sa. Nevada
Mulhacén 3478
C. St. Vincent
C. Trafalgar
C. Spartel
Str. of Gibraltar
Er Rif
Maritime Atlas
Plateau of the Shotts
Balearic Is.
MEDITERRANEAN SEA
C. Blanco
C. Bon
Malta
Corsica
Sardinia
Str. of Bonifacio
Ligurian Sea
Tyrrhenian Sea
Tiber
Apennines
Gran Sasso 2914
Vesuvius 1277
Calabria
Str. of Messina
Sicily
Etna 3263
ADRIATIC SEA
Str. of Otranto
Ionian Sea
Ionian Is.
Dinaric Alps
Bakony For.
Plain of Hungary
Drava
Sava
Tisza
Mures
Danube
Carpathians
Tatra 2655
Transylvanian Alps
Wallachia
Morava
Balkans
Balkan Peninsula
Rhodope
Pindus
Morea
5121
C. Matapan
Aegean Sea
Ida 1766
S. of Marmara
Bosporus
Gotland
Mälaren
Vänern
Vättern
Indals
Ume
Torne
G. of Bothnia
BALTIC SEA
G. of Finland
G. of Riga
Finland
L. Ladoga
Svir
L. Onega
Neva
L. Chudskoye
North European Plain
W. Dvina
Niemen
Wisła (Vistula)
Odra (Oder)
Pripyat Marshes
Pripyat (Pripet)
Dniestr (Dniester)
Prut
Bug
Dnepr (Dnieper)
Ukraine
Central Russian Uplands
Rybinsk Res.
Volga
Oka
Don
Kama
Volga Uplands
Obshchi Syrt
Ural
Ob
Tsimlyansk Res.
Manych
CASPIAN SEA
-28
Sea of Azov
Crimea
Str. of Kerch
Kuban
BLACK SEA
2211
Caucasus
Elbrus 5633
Terek
Kura
Rion
Armenia
Ararat 5165
Araks
L. Urmia
L. Van
Tigris
Kurdistan
Euphrates
Anatolia
Kizil Irmak
L. Tuz
Taurus
Erciyas 3770
Cyprus 1951
ft m
12 000 4000
6000 2000
3000 1000
1200 400
600 200
0 0
200 600
2000 6000
4000 12 000
m ft
Projection: Bonne West from Greenwich 0 East from Greenwich
COPYRIGHT, GEORGE PHILIP & SON, LTD.

1:20 000 000
100 0 100 200 300 400 500 miles
100 0 200 400 600 800 km
Projection: Bonne West from Greenwich 0 East from Greenwich
COPYRIGHT. GEORGE PHILIP & SON, LTD.
UNION OF SOVIET SOCIALIST REPUBLICS
R. S. F. S. R.
ATLANTIC OCEAN
NORTH SEA
BALTIC SEA
BLACK SEA
CASPIAN SEA
MEDITERRANEAN SEA
BAY OF BISCAY
ADRIATIC SEA
Tyrrhenian Sea
Ionian Sea
English Channel
Arctic Circle
ICELAND
UNITED KINGDOM
IRELAND
NORWAY
SWEDEN
FINLAND
DENMARK
POLAND
GERMANY
FRANCE
SPAIN
PORTUGAL
ITALY
SWITZERLAND
AUSTRIA
HUNGARY
CZECHOSLOVAKIA
ROMANIA
BULGARIA
YUGOSLAVIA
ALBANIA
GREECE
TURKEY
SYRIA
IRAQ
IRAN (PERSIA)
CYPRUS
MOROCCO
ALGERIA
TUNISIA
MOSKVA
Leningrad
LONDON
PARIS
BERLIN
WARSZAWA
PRAHA
WIEN
BUDAPEST
BUCUREŞTI
ROMA
MADRID
LISBOA
STOCKHOLM
Oslo
KØBENHAVN
ATHINAI
ISTANBUL

NORTH SEA
IRISH SEA
SCOTLAND
Southern Uplands
Pennines
North Channel
Firth of Clyde
Firth of Forth
Solway Firth
NORTHUMBERLAND
TYNE & WEAR
DURHAM
CLEVELAND
CUMBRIA
NORTH YORKSHIRE
HUMBERSIDE
LANCASHIRE
MERSEYSIDE
W. YORKSHIRE
SOUTH YORKSHIRE
CHESHIRE
DERBY
NOTTS
LINCOLN
CLWYD
GWYNEDD
ISLE OF MAN
Edinburgh
Glasgow
Newcastle
Carlisle
Middlesbrough (Teesside)
York
Leeds
Bradford
Hull
Manchester
Liverpool
Sheffield
Nottingham
Lincoln
Derby
Stoke-on-Trent
Belfast
Douglas
Cumbrian Mts.
N. York Moors
Lincoln Wolds
The Wash
Berwick-upon-Tweed
Scarborough
Blackpool
Preston
Chester

1:2 000 000

10 0 10 20 30 40 50 miles

10 0 10 20 30 40 50 60 70 80 km

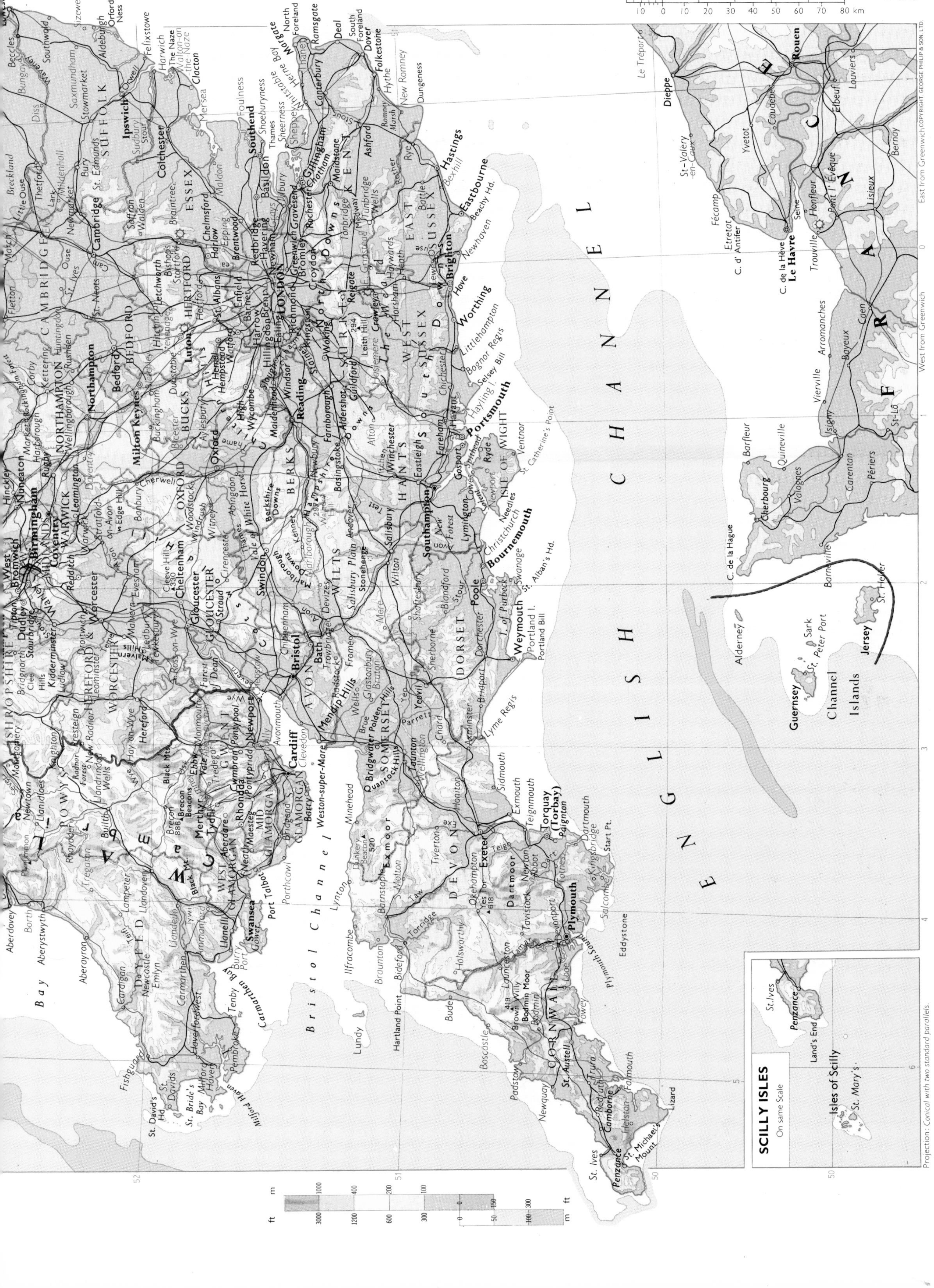

ENGLISH CHANNEL

Bristol Channel

FRANCE

Channel Islands

Alderney

Guernsey

Sark

Jersey

St. Peter Port

St. Helier

CORNWALL

DEVON

DORSET

SOMERSET

AVON

WILTS

HANTS

BERKS

SURREY

WEST SUSSEX

EAST SUSSEX

KENT

ESSEX

SUFFOLK

CAMBRIDGE

NORTHAMPTON

BEDFORD

BUCKS

HERTFORD

OXFORD

WARWICK

GLOUCESTER

HEREFORD & WORCESTER

SHROPSHIRE

POWYS

DYFED

GWENT

WEST GLAMORGAN

MID GLAMORGAN

SOUTH GLAMORGAN

ISLE OF WIGHT

LONDON

Birmingham

Bristol

Cardiff

Swansea

Plymouth

Exeter

Southampton

Portsmouth

Bournemouth

Brighton

Dover

Ipswich

Cambridge

Oxford

Reading

Northampton

Coventry

Le Havre

Rouen

Cherbourg

Dieppe

SCILLY ISLES

On same Scale

Isles of Scilly

St. Mary's

Penzance

St. Ives

Land's End

ft	m
3000	1000
1200	400
600	200
300	100
0	0
50	150
100–300	
ft	m

West from Greenwich

East from Greenwich

Projection: Conical with two standard parallels.

1:2 000 000

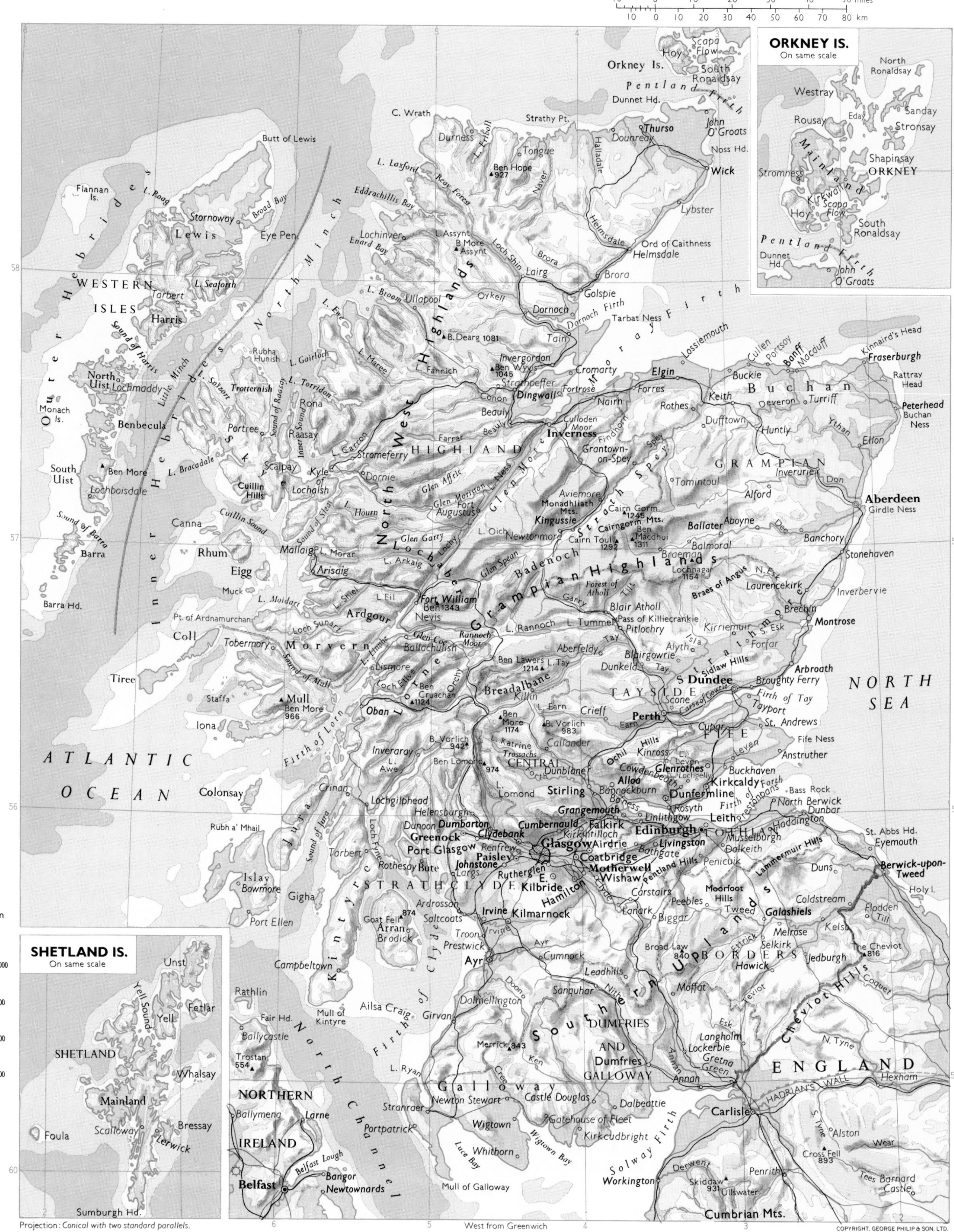
10 0 10 20 30 40 50 miles
10 0 10 20 30 40 50 60 70 80 km
ORKNEY IS.
On same scale
North Ronaldsay
Westray
Sanday
Rousay
Eday
Stronsay
Shapinsay
ORKNEY
Mainland
Stromness
Kirkwall
Hoy
Scapa Flow
South Ronaldsay
Pentland Firth
Dunnet Hd.
John O'Groats
SHETLAND IS.
On same scale
Unst
Yell Sound
Yell
Fetlar
SHETLAND
Whalsay
Mainland
Bressay
Scalloway
Lerwick
Foula
Sumburgh Hd.
ft
m
3000
1000
1200
400
600
200
300
100
0
50
150
100
300
Orkney Is.
Hoy
Scapa Flow
South Ronaldsay
Pentland Firth
Dunnet Hd.
C. Wrath
Strathy Pt.
Thurso
Dounreay
John O'Groats
Noss Hd.
Wick
Durness
L. Hope
Tongue
Ben Hope 927
Naver
Halladale
Lybster
Helmsdale
Ord of Caithness
Brora
Golspie
Lairg
Dornoch
Dornoch Firth
Tarbat Ness
Tain
Butt of Lewis
Flannan Is.
L. Roag
Broad Bay
Stornoway
Lewis
Eye Pen.
WESTERN ISLES
Tarbert
L. Seaforth
Harris
Sound of Harris
Outer Hebrides
North Minch
Little Minch
Inner Hebrides
North Uist
Lochmaddy
Monach Is.
Benbecula
South Uist
Ben More
Lochboisdale
Sound of Barra
Barra
Barra Hd.
L. Laxford
Reay Forest
Eddrachillis Bay
Lochinver
Enard Bay
L. Assynt
B. More Assynt
Loch Shin
Oykell
L. Broom
Ullapool
L. Ewe
B. Dearg 1081
North West Highlands
L. Gairloch
L. Maree
L. Fannich
Rubha Hunish
Trotternish
L. Snizort
L. Torridon
Sound of Raasay
Rona
Raasay
Inner Sound
Portree
Skye
L. Bracadale
Scalpay
Cuillin Hills
Kyle of Lochalsh
Stromeferry
L. Carron
Dornie
Cuillin Sound
Canna
Rhum
Eigg
Muck
Sound of Sleat
L. Hourn
Mallaig
L. Morar
Arisaig
L. Arkaig
Glen Garry
L. Lochy
Lochaber
Glen Affric
Glen Moriston
Fort Augustus
Loch Ness
Glen More
L. Oich
Invergordon
Ben Wyvis 1045
Strathpeffer
Dingwall
Fortrose
Conon
Beauly
Cromarty
Moray Firth
Lossiemouth
Elgin
Forres
Nairn
Culloden Moor
Inverness
Findhorn
Grantown-on-Spey
Spey
Strath Spey
Aviemore
Monadhliath Mts.
Kingussie
Newtonmore
Cairn Gorm 1245
Cairngorm Mts.
Ben Macdhui 1311
Cairn Toul 1292
Badenoch
Glen Spean
HIGHLAND
Farrar
Cullen
Portsoy
Banff
Macduff
Kinnaird's Head
Fraserburgh
Rattray Head
Buckie
Keith
Buchan
Deveron
Turriff
Rothes
Dufftown
Huntly
Peterhead
Buchan Ness
Ythan
Ellon
GRAMPIAN
Tomintoul
Inverurie
Don
Alford
Aberdeen
Girdle Ness
Ballater
Aboyne
Dee
Banchory
Balmoral
Braemar
Lochnagar 1154
Stonehaven
Grampian Highlands
N. Esk
Braes of Angus
Laurencekirk
Inverbervie
Brechin
Montrose
Forest of Atholl
Garry
Tilt
Blair Atholl
Pass of Killiecrankie
Pitlochry
L. Tummel
L. Rannoch
Rannoch Moor
Kirriemuir
S. Esk
Isla
Alyth
Forfar
Strathmore
Blairgowrie
Aberfeldy
Tay
Ben Lawers 1214
L. Tay
Dunkeld
Sidlaw Hills
Arbroath
Dundee
Broughty Ferry
Firth of Tay
Tayport
TAYSIDE
Scone
Carse of Gowrie
Perth
Earn
Crieff
L. Earn
Killin
Breadalbane
NORTH SEA
Cupar
FIFE
St. Andrews
Fife Ness
Anstruther
Leven
Ochil Hills
Kinross
Glenrothes
Lochgelly
Kirkcaldy
Cowdenbeath
Buckhaven
Firth of Forth
Alloa
Dunfermline
Bannockburn
Stirling
Dunblane
Prestonpans
Bass Rock
North Berwick
Dunbar
Rosyth
Grangemouth
Bo'ness
Linlithgow
Leith
Haddington
LOTHIAN
Edinburgh
Musselburgh
Dalkeith
Livingston
Bathgate
Falkirk
Cumbernauld
Kirkintilloch
Glasgow
Airdrie
Coatbridge
Motherwell
Wishaw
Pentland Hills
Penicuik
Lammermuir Hills
St. Abbs Hd.
Eyemouth
Duns
Berwick-upon-Tweed
Holy I.
Moorfoot Hills
Carstairs
Peebles
Tweed
Coldstream
Flodden
Till
Lanark
Biggar
Galashiels
Melrose
Selkirk
Kelso
Ettrick
BORDERS
Jedburgh
The Cheviot 816
Hawick
Teviot
Coquet
Cheviot Hills
Broad Law 840
Southern Uplands
Moffat
Leadhills
Sanquhar
Nith
Esk
Langholm
Lockerbie
Annan
Gretna Green
DUMFRIES AND GALLOWAY
Dumfries
N. Tyne
ENGLAND
Hexham
HADRIAN'S WALL
Carlisle
S. Tyne
Alston
Wear
Cross Fell 893
Tees
Barnard Castle
Penrith
Ullswater
Skiddaw 931
Derwent
Workington
Cumbrian Mts.
Solway Firth
Dalbeattie
Castle Douglas
Gatehouse of Fleet
Kirkcudbright
Galloway
Newton Stewart
Wigtown
Wigtown Bay
Whithorn
Cree
Ken
Merrick 843
Dalmellington
Doon
Cumnock
Ayr
Prestwick
Troon
Irvine
Kilmarnock
Saltcoats
Ardrossan
Hamilton
E. Kilbride
Clyde
Rutherglen
Johnstone
Paisley
Renfrew
Port Glasgow
Greenock
Clydebank
Dumbarton
Dunoon
Helensburgh
Largs
Rothesay
Bute
STRATHCLYDE
Goat Fell 874
Arran
Brodick
Firth of Clyde
Campbeltown
Kintyre
Mull of Kintyre
Ailsa Craig
Girvan
L. Ryan
Stranraer
Portpatrick
Luce Bay
Mull of Galloway
North Channel
Rathlin
Fair Hd.
Ballycastle
Trostan 554
NORTHERN IRELAND
Ballymena
Larne
Belfast Lough
Belfast
Bangor
Newtownards
Islay
Bowmore
Port Ellen
Gigha
Jura
Sound of Jura
Rubh a' Mhail
Colonsay
Tarbert
Loch Fyne
Lochgilphead
Crinan
Inveraray
L. Awe
B. Vorlich 942
Ben Lomond 974
L. Lomond
L. Katrine
Trossachs
CENTRAL
Callander
Forth
Ben More 1174
B. Vorlich 983
Oban
Lorne
Firth of Lorn
Ben Cruachan 1124
Loch Etive
Lismore
Orchy
Ballachulish
Glen Coe
L. Linnhe
Fort William
Ben Nevis 1343
L. Eil
Ardgour
L. Shiel
L. Moidart
Loch Sunart
Morvern
Tobermory
Sound of Mull
Mull
Ben More 966
Iona
Staffa
Tiree
Coll
Pt. of Ardnamurchan
ATLANTIC OCEAN
West from Greenwich
58
57
56
55
59
60

Projection: *Conical with two standard parallels.*

1:2 000 000
10 0 10 20 30 40 50 miles
10 0 10 20 30 40 50 60 70 80 km
ATLANTIC OCEAN
IRISH SEA
North Channel
St. George's Channel
NORTHERN IRELAND
IRELAND
ULSTER
CONNACHT
LEINSTER
MUNSTER
DONEGAL
SLIGO
LEITRIM
MAYO
ROSCOMMON
GALWAY
LONGFORD
CAVAN
MONAGHAN
LOUTH
MEATH
WESTMEATH
DUBLIN
OFFALY
KILDARE
LAOIS
WICKLOW
CARLOW
KILKENNY
WEXFORD
CLARE
LIMERICK
TIPPERARY
WATERFORD
KERRY
CORK
Kintyre
Arran
Campbeltown
Rathlin I.
Mull of Kintyre
Ailsa Craig
Fair Hd.
Giant's Causeway
Portrush
Malin Hd.
Lough Swilly
Carndonagh
Inishowen Pen.
Moville
Buncrana
Lough Foyle
Limavady
Coleraine
Ballycastle
Ballymoney
Trostan 554
Mts. of Antrim
Ballymena
Larne
I. Magee
Stranraer
Portpatrick
Carrickfergus
Belfast L.
Antrim
Bangor
Donaghadee
Newtownards
Belfast
Lisburn
Ards Pen.
Strangford L.
Londonderry
Sperrin Mts.
Sawel 683
Magherafelt
Strabane
Lifford
Cookstown
Lough Neagh 16
Omagh
Dungannon
Irvinestown
Blackwater
Portadown
Lurgan (Craigavon)
Armagh
Banbridge
Downpatrick
Dundrum
Slieve Donard 852
Newcastle
Dundrum Bay
Mourne Mts.
Warrenpoint
Newry
Sl. Gullion 577
Castleblayney
Carlingford L.
Greenore
Dundalk
Dundalk Bay
Enniskillen
L. Erne
Upper L. Erne
Clones
Monaghan
Tory I.
Horn Hd.
Sheep Haven
Bloody Foreland
Gweedore
Errigal 752
Derryveagh Mts.
Letterkenny
Aran I.
Gweebarra B.
Glenties
Finn
Loughros More B.
Bluestack 676
Rossan Pt.
Rathlin O Birne I.
Killybegs
Donegal
Donegal Bay
Ballyshannon
Bundoran
Erne
Sligo B.
Sligo
Collooney
Ox Mts.
L. Allen
Arrow
Leitrim
Boyle
Carrick-on-Shannon
Belturbet
Annalee
Cootehill
Cavan
Carrickmacross
Kingscourt
Louth
Ardee
L. Sheelin
L. Gowna
Granard
Longford
Oldcastle
Ceanannas Mor (Kells)
An Uaimh (Navan)
Drogheda
Balbriggan
Athboy
Trim
Boyne
Mullingar
L. Ree
Inny
Athlone
Swords
Lambay I.
Ireland's Eye
Howth Head
Dublin (Baile Atha Cliath)
Dublin Bay
Dun Laoghaire
Bray
Maynooth
Celbridge
Liffey
Naas
Kippure 754
Poulaphouca Res.
Wicklow Mts.
Wicklow
Wicklow Hd.
Rathdrum
Mizen Hd.
Arklow
Lugnaquillia 923
Shillelagh
Gorey
Tullow
Muine Bheag
Mt. Leinster 796
Slaney
Enniscorthy
Cahore Pt.
Wexford
Wexford Harbour
Rosslare
Greenore Pt.
Tuscar Rock
Carnsore Pt
Saltee Is.
Hook Hd.
Waterford Harbour
New Ross
Barrow
Downpatrick Hd.
Broad Haven
Killala B.
Erris Hd.
Belmullet
Mullet Peninsula
Killala
Ballina
Moy
Blacksod Bay
L. Conn
Nephin 806
Achill Hd.
Achill
Achill I.
Castlebar
Clew Bay
Clare I.
Westport
Croagh Patrick 765
Claremorris
Castlereagh
Killary Harbour
Mweelrea 819
L. Mask
Inishbofin
Robe
Ballinrobe
Roscommon
Suck
Tuam
Twelve Pins
Connemara
Clifden
Slyne Hd.
L. Corrib
Ballinasloe
Clara
Edenderry
Tullamore
Daingean
Brosna
Bog of Allen
Droichead Nua
Kildare
Portarlington
Mountmellick
Port Laoise
Athy
Carlow
Galway
Athenry
Loughrea
Kilkieran B.
Galway Bay
Inishmore
Aran Is.
Slieve Aughty
Shannon
Portumna
Birr
Sl. Bloom
Gort
Hags Hd.
Ennistymon
Liscannor Bay
Mal Bay
Miltown Malbay
Ennis
L. Derg
Roscrea
Killaloe
Ballina
Nenagh
Keeper 694
Ardnacrusha
Templemore
Nore
Thurles
Kilkee
Kilrush
Rineanna
Limerick
Kilkenny
Callan
Loop Hd.
R. Shannon
Foynes
Rathkeale
Golden Vale
Cashel
Tipperary
Listowel
Newcastle
Feale
Kerry Hd.
Fenit
Tralee Bay
Brandon Bay
Tralee
Rath Luirc (Charleville)
Galtymore 920
Galty Mts.
Caher
Slievenamon 722
Carrick-on-Suir
Clonmel
Suir
Comeragh Mts.
Waterford
Tramore
Brandon 953 Mt.
Sl. Mish
Maine
Dingle
Gt. Blasket I.
Newmarket
Mitchelstown
Knockmealdown Mts.
Kanturk
Mallow
Blackwater
Fermoy
Lismore
Dungarvan
Dungarvan Bay
Dunmore Hd.
Dingle Bay
Laune
Killarney
Macgillycuddy's Reeks
Carrauntuohill 1040
Lakes of Killarney
Boggeragh Mts.
Blarney
Cork
Youghal
Youghal Harbour
Valentia Harbour
Valentia I.
Cahirciveen
Kenmare
Macroom
Lee
Midleton
Passage West
Cobh
Skellig Rocks
Ballinskelligs B.
Kenmare River
Caha Mts.
Glengarriff
Bandon
Crosshaven
Kinsale
Cork Harbour
Bantry
Castletown Bearhaven
Bear I.
Clonakilty
Skibbereen
Clonakilty Bay
Old Head of Kinsale
Crow Hd.
Bantry Bay
Skull
Dunmanus Bay
Galley Hd
Mizen Hd.
Baltimore
Fastnet Rock
Clear I.
C. Clear
St. David's Hd.
Towns underlined in Northern Ireland give their names to the Districts in which they stand
The remaining Districts are:—
1 Fermanagh
2 Moyle
3 Newtownabbey
4 North Down
5 Castlereagh
6 Ards
7 Down
8 Newry & Mourne
ft m
3000 1000
1200 400
600 200
300 100
0 0
100 300
200 600
m ft
West from Greenwich
Projection: Conical with two standard parallels.
COPYRIGHT, GEORGE PHILIP & SON, LTD.

1:4 000 000

The DISTRICTS of Northern Ireland have been numbered and can be identified by reference to this table.

1	Londonderry	14	Craigavon
2	Limavady	15	Armagh
3	Coleraine	16	Newry & Mourne
4	Ballymoney	17	Banbridge
5	Moyle	18	Down
6	Larne	19	Lisburn
7	Ballymena	20	Antrim
8	Magherafelt	21	Newtownabbey
9	Cookstown	22	Carrickfergus
10	Strabane	23	North Down
11	Omagh	24	Ards
12	Fermanagh	25	Castlereagh
13	Dungannon	26	Belfast

1	Merseyside
2	Greater Manchester
3	West Yorkshire
4	South Yorkshire
5	West Glamorgan
6	Mid Glamorgan
7	South Glamorgan

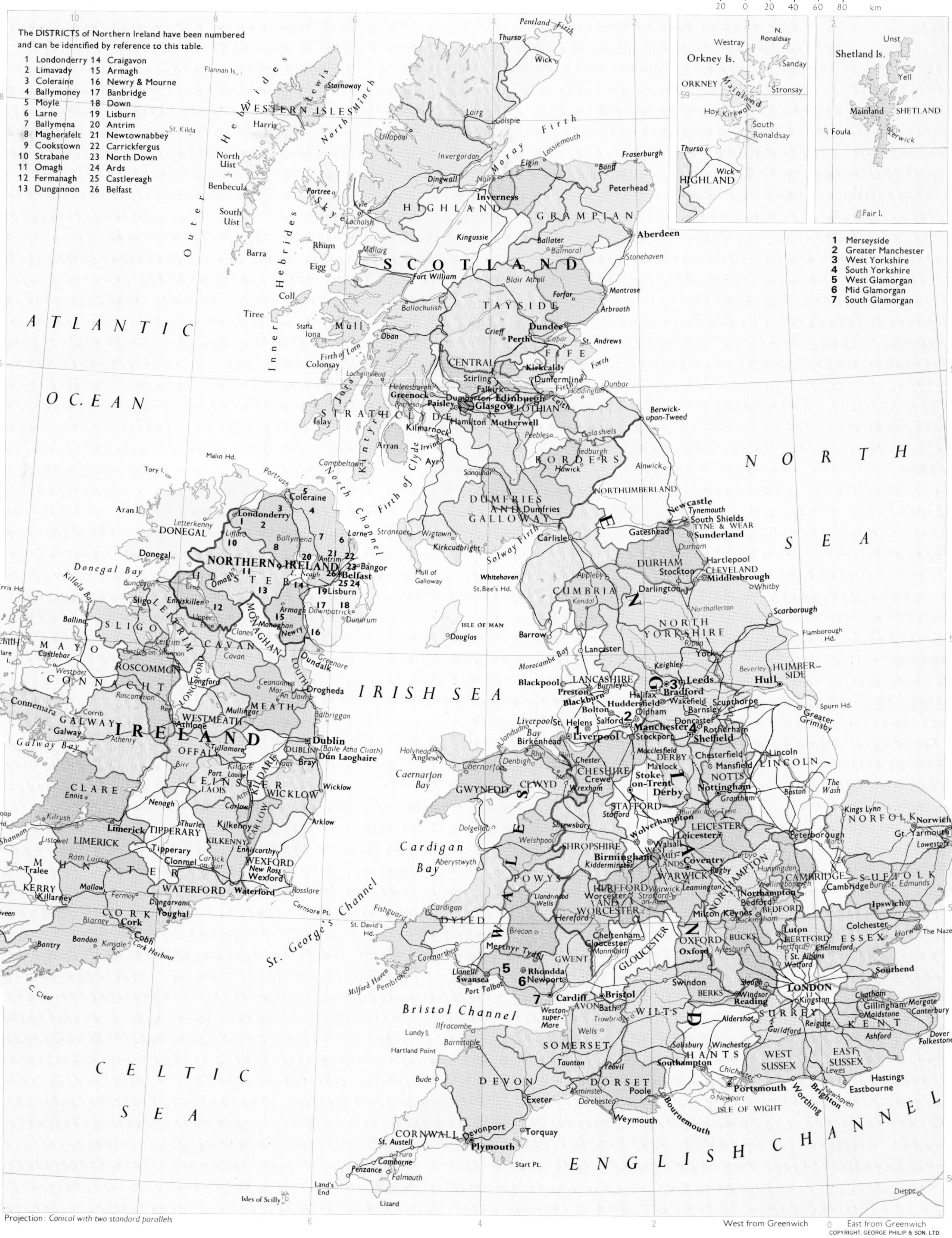

Projection: Conical with two standard parallels

West from Greenwich 0 East from Greenwich

1:5 000 000

25 0 50 100 150 miles

25 0 50 100 150 200 250 km

PARIS REGION

1:2 500 000

- Département boundary
- 4 Département number
- ⊙ Préfecture
- ○ Sous-préfecture

ENGLAND
English Channel
CHANNEL ISLANDS
Alderney
Guernsey
St. Peter Port
Herm
Sark
Jersey
St. Helier
Casquets
Les Minquiers
Golfe de St-Malo
Baie de la Seine
Mer d'Iroise
Ile d'Ouessant
Baie de Bourgneuf
Ile de Noirmoutier
Ile d'Yeu
Belle-Ile
Ile de Groix
Ile de Ré
Ile d'Oléron
Pertuis Breton
Pertuis d'Antioche
Lyme Bay
Exeter
Plymouth
Dartmoor
St. Austell
Falmouth
Penzance
Camborne
Torquay
Weymouth
Southampton
Eastleigh
Bournemouth
Poole
Portsmouth
Isle of Wight
Brighton
Worthing
Hastings
Eastbourne
Bexhill
South Downs
Cherbourg
Le Havre
Rouen
Dieppe
Caen
Rennes
Brest
Quimper
Lorient
Vannes
St. Nazaire
Nantes
Angers
Laval
Le Mans
Tours
Poitiers
Niort
La Rochelle
Rochefort
Saintes
Cognac
Angoulême
Limoges
Cholet
La Roche-sur-Yon
Les Sables-d'Olonne
Châtellerault
St-Brieuc
Fougères
Alençon
Blois
BRETAGNE
NORMANDIE
MAINE
ANJOU
TOURAINE
POITOU
AUNIS
ANGOUMOIS
Collines de Normandie
Collines du Perche
Monts d'Arrée
Montagne Noire
Plateau du Limousin
Loire
Vilaine
Seine
ft
m
12 000
4000
9000
3000
6000
2000
4500
1500
3000
1000
1200
400
600
200
0
0
200
600
2000
6000
m
ft
DÉPARTEMENTS IN THE PARIS AREA
1 Ville de Paris
2 Seine-St-Denis
3 Val-de-Marne
4 Hauts-de-Seine
West from Greenwich
East from Greenwich

Projection: *Conical with two standard parallels*

1:2 500 000

10 0 10 20 30 40 50 miles

10 0 10 20 30 40 50 60 70 80 km

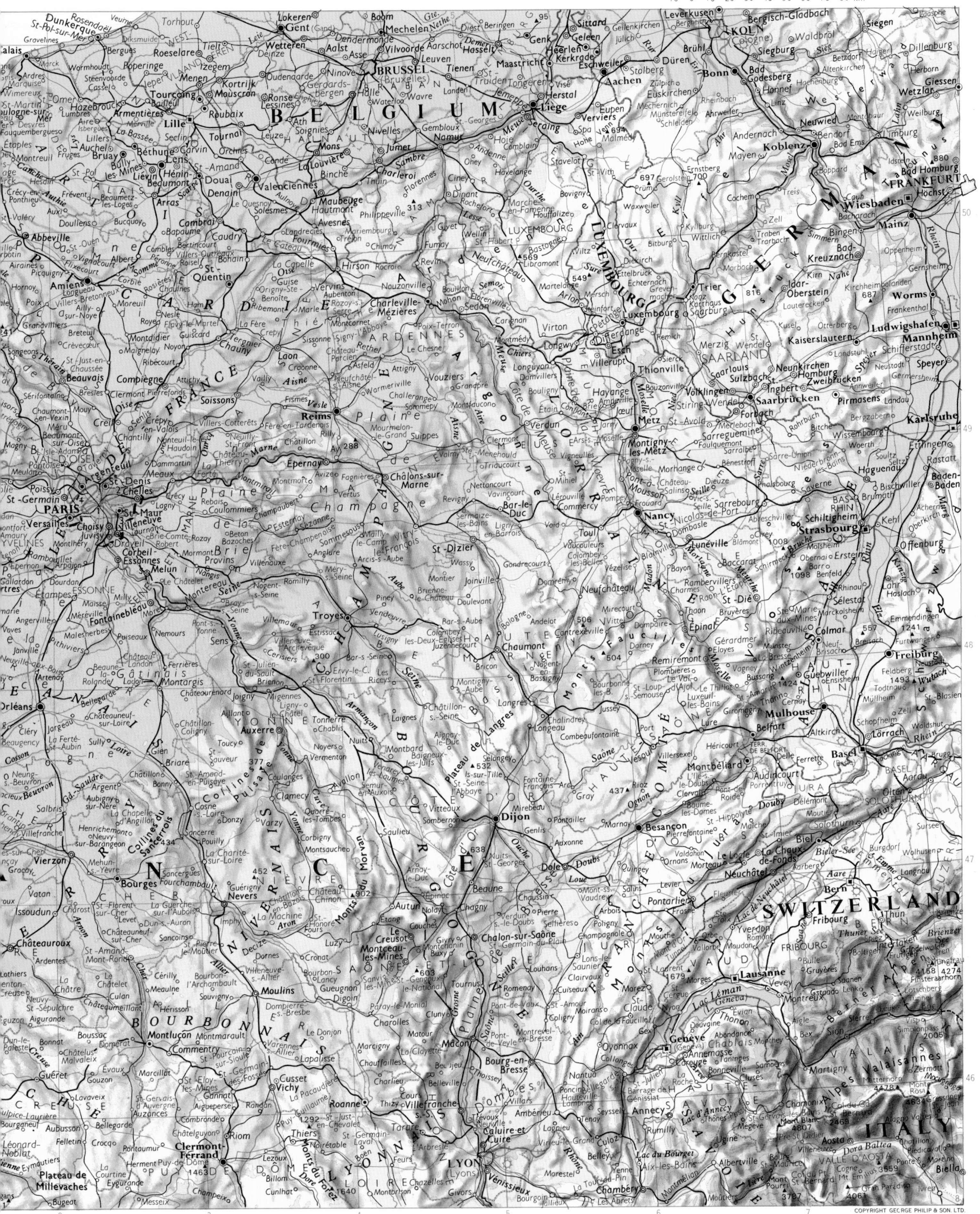
BELGIUM
FRANCE
GERMANY
LUXEMBOURG
SWITZERLAND
ITALY
SAARLAND
ARDENNES
CHAMPAGNE
LORRAINE
BOURGOGNE
BOURBONNAIS
NIVERNAIS
LYONNAIS
PARIS
BRUSSEL (Bruxelles)
Lille
Liège
Luxembourg
Metz
Nancy
Strasbourg
Reims
Dijon
Lyon (Lyons)
Genève
Lausanne
Basel
Bern
Orléans
Bourges
Troyes
Besançon
Mulhouse
Freiburg
Karlsruhe
Mannheim
Wiesbaden
Koblenz
Bonn
Köln (Cologne)
Aachen
Gent
Mechelen
Antwerpen
Amiens
Abbeville
Dunkerque
Calais
Clermont-Ferrand
Saarbrücken
Trier
Mainz
Frankfurt

ATLANTIC
OCEAN
Golfe de
Gascogne
Golf
ANGOUMOIS
AUNIS
SAINTONGE
CHARENTE
CHARENTE-MARITIME
DORDOGNE
HAUTE-VIENNE
CORRÈZE
LOT-ET-GARONNE
GARONNE
LOT
TARN
AVEYRON
HÉRAULT
AUDE
ARIÈGE
HAUTES-PYRÉNÉES
PYRÉNÉES-ORIENTALES
ROUSSILLON
ANDORRA
BÉARN
NAVARRE
NAVARRA
Sierra de la Peña
Sierra de Guara
Plateau de Millevaches
Mts de Lacaune
Causse Méjean
Plaines et seuil du Poitou
Bordeaux
Toulouse
Limoges
Poitiers
La Rochelle
Angoulême
Périgueux
Agen
Montauban
Albi
Rodez
Carcassonne
Narbonne
Perpignan
Béziers
Tarbes
Pau
Bayonne
Biarritz
San Sebastián
Pamplona
Zaragoza
Huesca
Lérida
Gerona
Figueras
Clermont-Ferrand
Moulins
Bourges
Nevers
Châteauroux
Montluçon
Aurillac
Millau
Cholet
Niort
Rochefort
Cognac
Libourne
Bergerac
Cahors
Castres
Mazamet
Dax
Projection: Conical with two standard parallels
West from Greenwich
East from Greenwich
ft
m
12 000
9000
6000
4500
3000
1200
600
4000
3000
2000
1500
1000
400
200
0
200
600
2000
6000
m
ft

1:2 500 000

SWITZERLAND
ITALY
CORSICA
LIGURIAN SEA
Golfo di Génova
MEDITERRANEAN SEA
Lion
Bern
Luzern
Lausanne
Genève
LYON
Grenoble
TORINO
MILANO
GENOVA
Marseille
Toulon
Nice
MONACO
Cannes
Avignon
Aix-en-Provence
Bastia
Ajaccio
Livorno
La Spezia
Parma
Brescia
Bergamo
Novara
Pavia
Alessandria
Asti
Savona
San Remo
Valence
Arles
Nîmes
ILES D'HYÈRES
Elba
Capraia
PROVENCE
SAVOIE
HAUTE-SAVOIE
ALPES-DE-HAUTE-PROVENCE
ALPES-MARITIMES
VAUCLUSE
DRÔME
HAUTE-CORSE
CORSE-DU-SUD

NORTH SEA
WADDENEILANDEN
OSTFRIESISCHE INSELN
WADDENZEE
IJSSELMEER
Markerwaard
Noordoostpolder
Oostelijk-Flevoland
Zuidelijk-Flevoland
Schiermonnikoog
Ameland
Terschelling
Vlieland
Texel
Borkum
Norderney
Juist
Emden
Groningen
Leeuwarden
Drachten
Assen
Emmen
Zwolle
Kampen
Meppel
Hoogeveen
Almelo
Hengelo
Enschede
Nordhorn
Deventer
Apeldoorn
Zutphen
Arnhem
Nijmegen
Amersfoort
Hilversum
Utrecht
AMSTERDAM
Haarlem
Leiden
'S GRAVENHAGE
(DEN HAAG)
(THE HAGUE)
ROTTERDAM
Dordrecht
Den Helder
Alkmaar
Hoorn
Harlingen
Sneek
Delft
Gouda

1:1 250 000
5 0 5 10 15 20 25 miles
5 0 10 20 30 40 km
Projection: Conical with two standard parallels
East from Greenwich
COPYRIGHT, GEORGE PHILIP & SON LTD.
BELGIUM
LUXEMBOURG
GERMANY
FRANCE
BRUSSEL
Antwerpen
Liège
Namur
Charleroi
Mons
Gent
Brugge
Oostende
Lille
Roubaix
Maastricht
Aachen
KÖLN
DÜSSELDORF
ESSEN
DORTMUND
Bonn
Trier
Luxembourg
Eindhoven
Tilburg
Breda
Charleville-Mézières
Valenciennes
Cambrai
St-Quentin
Laon
ft
m

Projection: *Conical with two standard parallels*

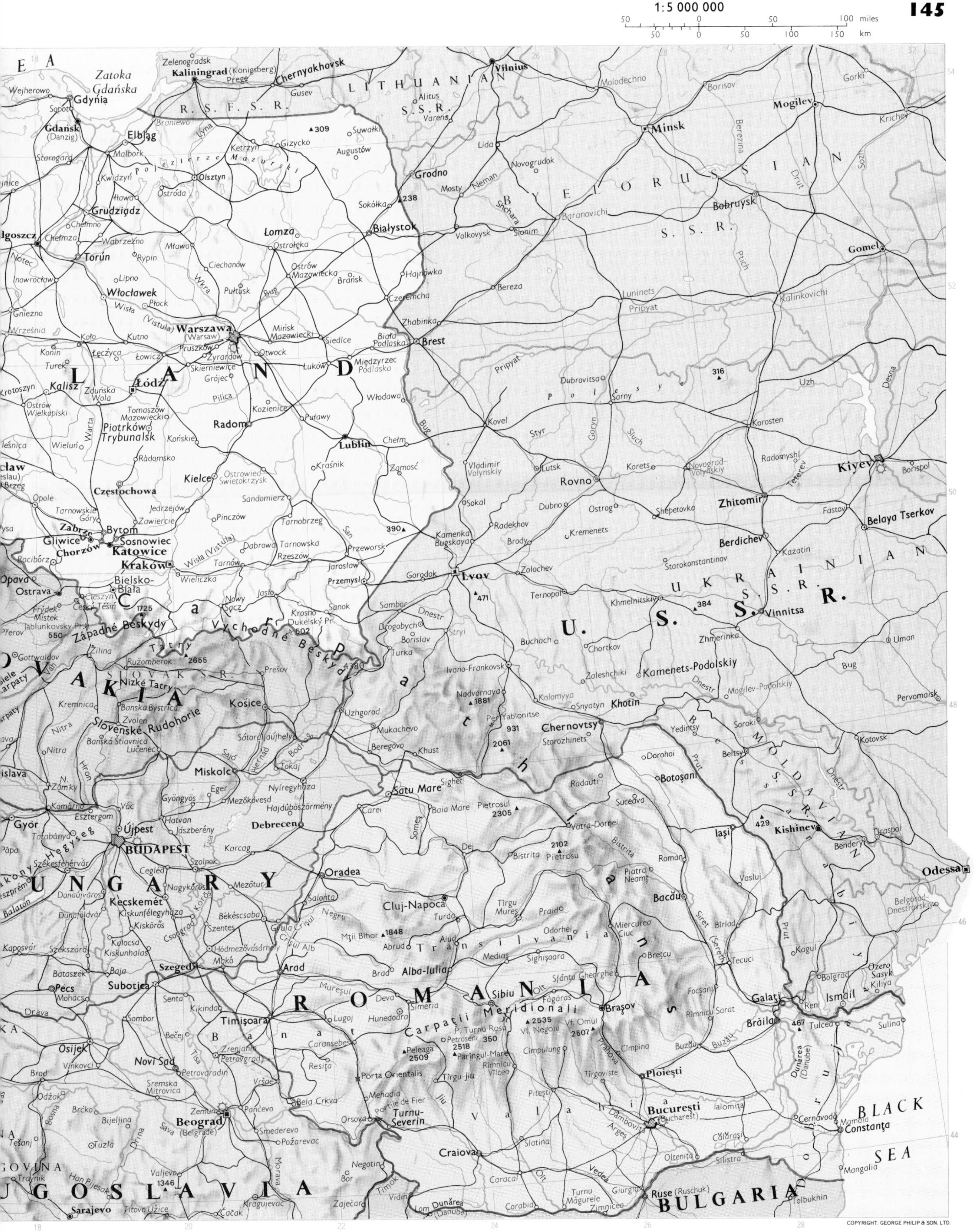
1:5 000 000
miles
km
Zatoka Gdańska
Kaliningrad (Königsberg)
Chernyakhovsk
Gdynia
Gdańsk (Danzig)
Elbląg
R. S. F. S. R.
LITHUANIAN S.S.R.
Vilnius
Molodechno
Borisov
Mogilev
Minsk
Gorki
Krichev
Olsztyn
Grodno
Lida
Novogrudok
BYELORUSSIAN S.S.R.
Bobruysk
Gomel
Grudziądz
Białystok
Baranovichi
Slonim
Volkovysk
Łomza
Toruń
Włocławek
Płock
Warszawa (Warsaw)
Pinsk
Luninets
Pripyat
Kalinkovichi
Brest
Siedlce
Łódź
Lublin
Radom
Kovel
Dubrovitsa
Sarny
Polesye
Korosten
Uzh
Desna
Kielce
Częstochowa
Lutsk
Rovno
Zhitomir
Kiyev
Borispol
Belaya Tserkov
Berdichev
Katowice
Kraków
Lvov
Ternopol
Khmelnitskiy
Vinnitsa
U. S. S. R.
UKRAINIAN S.S.R.
Uman
Ivano-Frankovsk
Kamenets-Podolskiy
Chernovtsy
Khotin
Dnestr
Bug
Pervomaisk
Kotovsk
MOLDAVIAN S.S.R.
Kishinev
Tiraspol
Bendery
Odessa
Tatry
Vysoké Tatry
Nízké Tatry
Západné Beskydy
Východné Beskydy
Carpathians
Košice
Miskolc
Uzhgorod
Mukachevo
Khust
Satu Mare
Debrecen
Oradea
Cluj-Napoca
Iași
Botoșani
Suceava
Bacău
Transilvania
Sibiu
Brașov
Carpații Meridionali
Galați
Brăila
Tulcea
Sulina
Ploiești
București (Bucharest)
Constanța
BLACK SEA
Craiova
Ruse (Ruschuk)
BULGARIA
ROMANIA
Timișoara
Arad
Szeged
Kecskemét
BUDAPEST
Győr
HUNGARY
Pécs
Subotica
Novi Sad
Beograd (Belgrade)
Osijek
Sarajevo
JUGOSLAVIA
Dunărea (Danube)
Bratislava
Ostrava
Gottwaldov

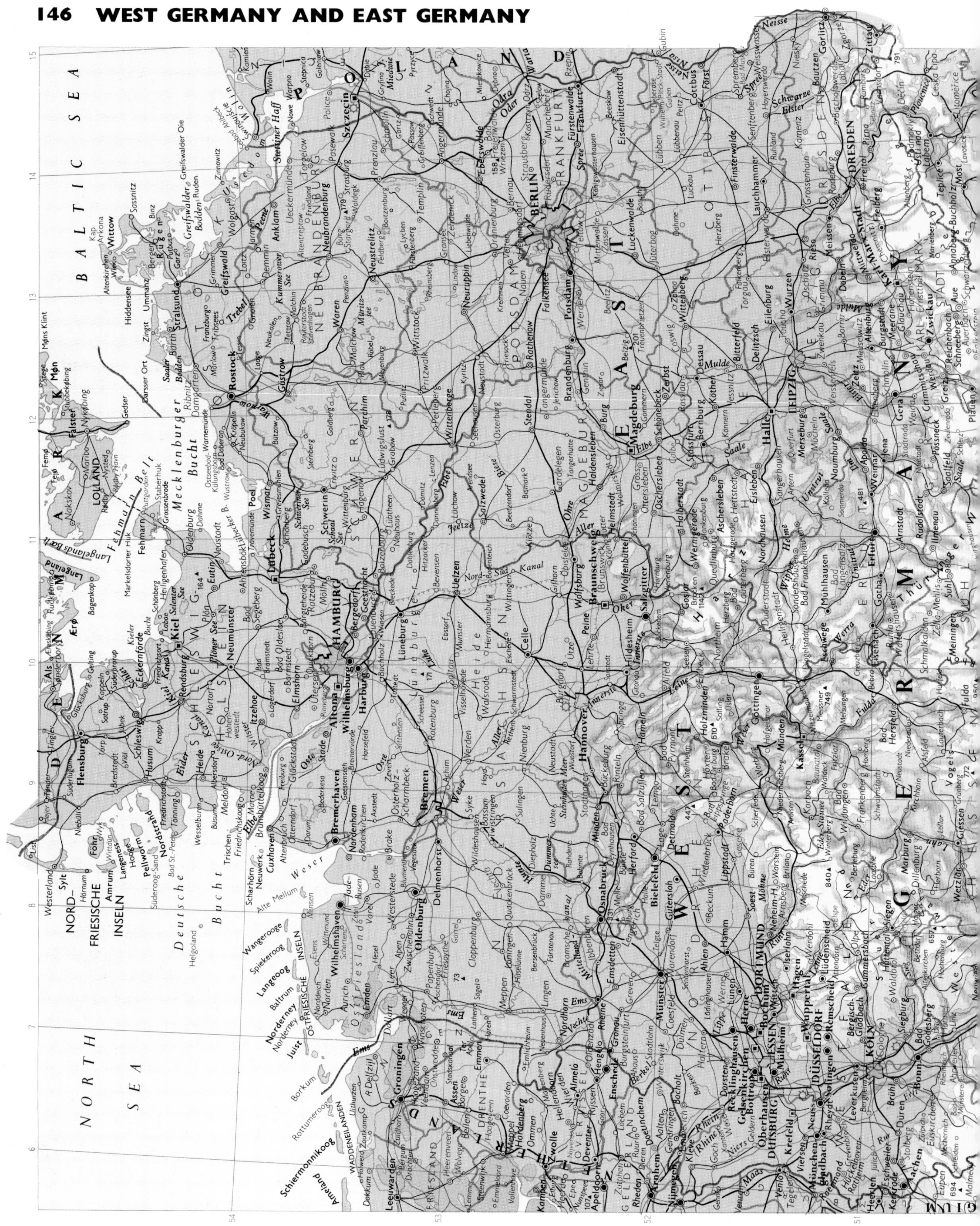

BALTIC SEA
NORTH SEA
NORDFRIESISCHE INSELN
OSTFRIESISCHE INSELN
WADDENEILANDEN
Deutsche Bucht
Mecklenburger Bucht
Stettiner Haff
Fehmarn Belt
Langelands Bælt
Helgoland
Sylt
Föhr
Amrum
Pellworm
Borkum
Juist
Norderney
Langeoog
Spiekeroog
Wangerooge
Rügen
Hiddensee
Fehmarn
Poel
LOLLAND
Falster
Møn
Ærø
Langeland
Als
Flensburg
Kiel
Lübeck
Rostock
Stralsund
Greifswald
Wismar
Schwerin
HAMBURG
Bremen
Bremerhaven
Wilhelmshaven
Emden
Oldenburg
Osnabrück
Münster
Hannover
Braunschweig
Magdeburg
Potsdam
BERLIN
FRANKFURT
Frankfurt
Cottbus
DRESDEN
LEIPZIG
Halle
Erfurt
Weimar
Jena
Gera
Zwickau
Kassel
Göttingen
Bielefeld
DORTMUND
ESSEN
DÜSSELDORF
KÖLN
Bonn
Aachen
Duisburg
Wuppertal
Gelsenkirchen
Bochum
Groningen
Zwolle
Arnhem
Nijmegen
Szczecin
Neubrandenburg
Schleswig
Holstein
Lüneburger Heide
Harz
Thüringer Wald
Elbe
Weser
Ems
Oder
Saale
Mittelland Kanal
Nord-Ostsee Kanal

1:2 500 000

10 0 10 20 30 40 50 miles

10 0 10 20 30 40 50 60 70 80 km

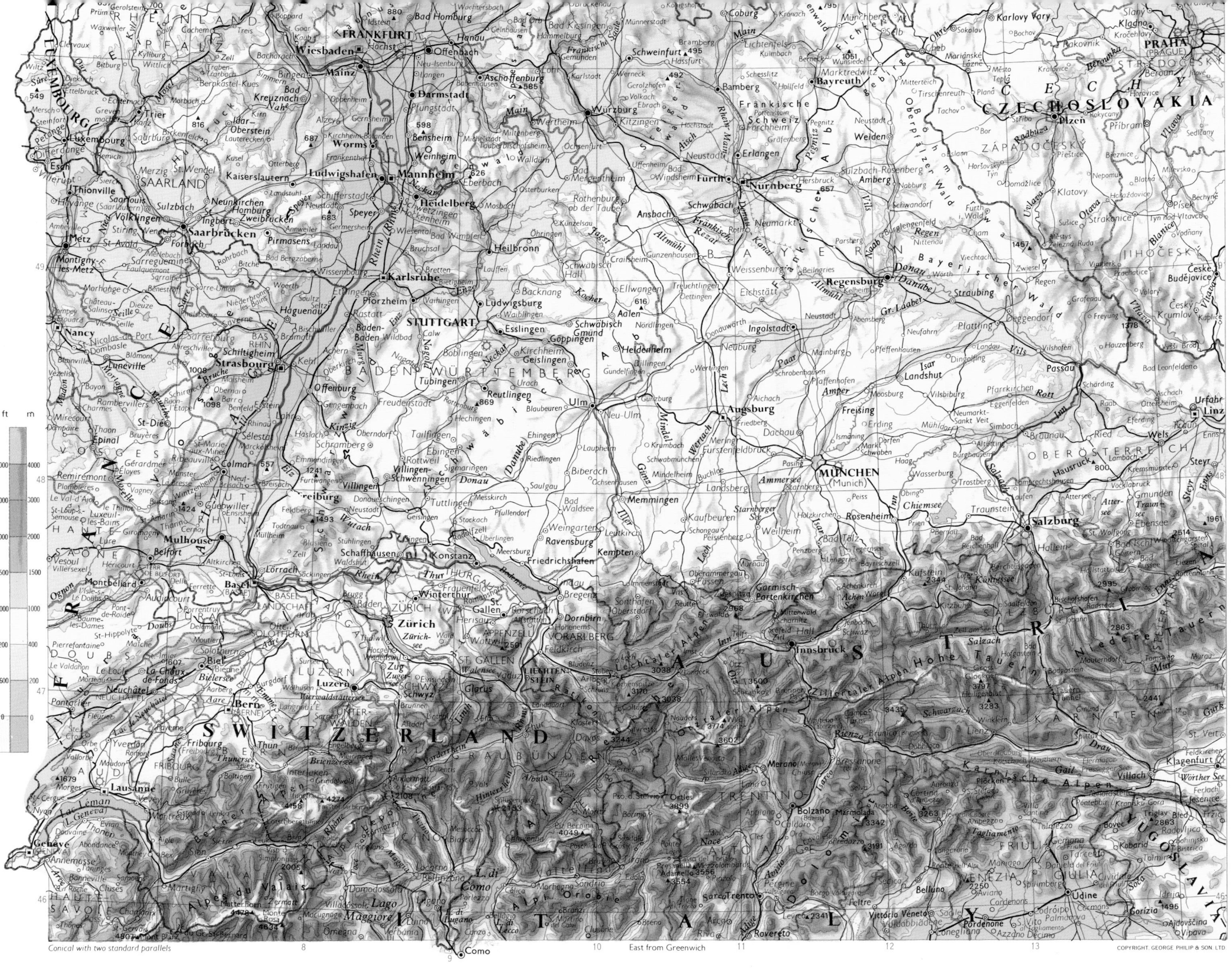
ft m
12 000 4000
9000 3000
6000 2000
4500 1500
3000 1000
1200 400
600 200
0 0
FRANKFURT
Wiesbaden
Mainz
Darmstadt
Mannheim
Heidelberg
Karlsruhe
STUTTGART
Würzburg
Nürnberg
Regensburg
Ingolstadt
Augsburg
Ulm
MÜNCHEN
(Munich)
Salzburg
Linz
Innsbruck
Zürich
Bern
Basel
Strasbourg
Luxembourg
Saarbrücken
Plzeň
PRAHA
(PRAGUE)
CZECHOSLOVAKIA
SWITZERLAND
YUGOSLAVIA
Conical with two standard parallels
East from Greenwich
COPYRIGHT GEORGE PHILIP & SON, LTD

F R A N C E
HAUTE-SAÔNE
DOUBS
JURA
HAUTE-SAVOIE
SAVOIE
HAUT-RHIN
BELFORT
Sundgau
Porte de Bourgogne
Schwarzwald
MULHOUSE
BASEL (BASLE)
BASEL LANDSCHAFT
SOLOTHURN
AARGAU
LUZERN
BERN
FRIBOURG
NEUCHÂTEL
VAUD
VALAIS
OBWALDEN
VALLE D'AOSTA
Franches Montagnes
Mittelland
Berner Oberland
Berner Alpen
Freiburger Alpen
Alpi Pennine
Chablais
Faucigny
Genevois
Emmental
Gruyère
Ober-Aargau
Pays de Gex
Jura Français
Lac de Neuchâtel
Bielersee
Lac Léman (L. Geneva)
Thunersee
Brienzersee
Lac d'Annecy
Lac du Bourget
Montagnes du Lomont
BESANÇON
Vesoul
Lure
Belfort
Montbéliard
Audincourt
Valentigney
Gray
Pontarlier
Porrentruy
Delémont
Moutier
Tramelan
St.-Imier
La Chaux-de-Fonds
Le Locle
Morteau
Neuchâtel
Grenchen
Solothurn
Biel (Bienne)
Olten
Aarau
Langenthal
Burgdorf
BERN (BERNE)
Köniz
Thun
Spiez
Fribourg (Freibourg)
Payerne
Yverdon
Ste-Croix
Vallorbe
LAUSANNE
Morges
Vevey
Montreux
Nyon
Thonon-les-Bains
Evian-les-Bains
GENÈVE (GENEVA)
Annemasse
Oyonnax
St.-Claude
Morez
Bellegarde-s.-V.
Annecy
Rumilly
Belley
Aix-les-Bains
Ugine
Albertville
Chamonix-Mont-Blanc
Martigny
Sion
Sierre
Monthey
Aigle
Bulle
Aosta
Lörrach
Rheinfelden
Pratteln
Liestal
Mont Blanc 4807
Matterhorn (Mte. Cervino) 4478
Monte Rosa 4634
Simplonpass 2005
Dom 4545
Weisshorn 4505
Projection: Conical with two standard parallels

1:1 000 000
5 0 5 10 15 20 25 miles
5 0 10 20 30 40 km
W. GERMANY
BADEN-WÜRTTEMBERG
BAYERN
AUSTRIA
TIROL
VORARLBERG
LIECHTENSTEIN
ITALY
LOMBARDIA
TRENTINO
GRAUBÜNDEN
TICINO
ZÜRICH
THURGAU
SCHAFFHAUSEN
SCHWYZ
ZUG
GLARUS
APPENZELL
ST. GALLEN
Bodensee (L. Constance)
Allgäuer Alpen
Lechtaler Alpen
Bregenzer Wald
Rätikon
Silvretta Gruppe
Unter Engadin
National Park
Oberengadin
Glarner Alpen
Oberland
Lepontine Alpen
Adula-Gruppe
Alpi Retiche
Alpi Orobie
Valtellina
Val Camonica
Valle Seriana
Giudicarie
Ötztaler Alpen
Brianza
Stockach
Singen
Radolfzell
Konstanz
Überlingen
Weingarten
Ravensburg
Friedrichshafen
Tettnang
Wangen i. A.
Leutkirch
Kempten
Isny
Lindau
Lindenberg i.A.
Oberstaufen
Immenstadt i.A.
Sonthofen
Oberstdorf
Füssen
Schongau
Peiting
Marktoberdorf
Schaffhausen
Neuhausen a. Rh.
Kreuzlingen
Frauenfeld
Weinfelden
Romanshorn
Amriswil
Arbon
Rorschach
Winterthur
Bülach
Kloten
Wettingen
Baden
Schlieren
Dübendorf
Uster
Wetzikon
Küsnacht
Kilchberg
Thalwil
Horgen
Männedorf
Wädenswil
Richterswil
Rapperswil
Zug
Cham
Küssnacht
Einsiedeln
Luzern
Schwyz
Altdorf
Glarus
Wil
Uzwil
Flawil
St. Gallen
Gossau
Herisau
Appenzell
Teufen
Altstätten
Bregenz
Lustenau
Dornbirn
Hohenems
Götzis
Rankweil
Feldkirch
Bludenz
Vaduz
Buchs
Churfisten
Walensee
Bad Ragaz
Landquart
Chur
Davos
Klosters
St. Moritz
Landeck
Imst
Zürichsee
Bellinzona
Locarno
Domodóssola
Lago Maggiore
Pallanza
Verbania
Intra
Lugano
Lago di Lugano
Mendrisio
Chiasso
Como
Lago di Como
Varese
Lago di Varese
Lecco
Bergamo
Seriate
Morbegno
Sondrio
Tirano
Chiavenna
Lago d'Iseo
Lago d'Idro
Riva del Garda
Lago di Garda
Gardone Val Trómpia
Vobarno
Clusone
Lovere
Gallarate
Saronno
Cantu
Seregno
Merate
East from Greenwich
8 30′
9
9 30′
10
10 30′
47 30′
47
46 30′
46

DRESDEN
Karl-Marx-Stadt
Erfurt
Weimar
Jena
Gera
Zwickau
Plauen
Hof
Coburg
Bamberg
Bayreuth
Würzburg
Erlangen
Nürnberg
Fürth
Regensburg
Ingolstadt
Augsburg
Ulm
Neu Ulm
Heilbronn
Ludwigsburg
STUTTGART
Esslingen
Göppingen
Aschaffenburg
Fulda
MÜNCHEN
(Munich)
Landshut
Passau
Rosenheim
Salzburg
Linz
Wels
Steyr
Innsbruck
Bregenz
Dornbirn
Feldkirch
Kempten
Friedrichshafen
Memmingen
Garmisch-Partenkirchen
Klagenfurt
Villach
Graz
Leoben
Kapfenberg
Maribor
Ljubljana
Celje
Kranj
Trieste
Udine
Gorizia
Pordenone
Treviso
Vicenza
Trento
Bolzano
Merano
Belluno
Bérgamo
Bréscia
Verona
Rovereto
Schio
Plzeň
PRAHA
(PRAGUE)
Kladno
Most
Chomutov
Teplice
Ústí nad Labem
Děčín
Liberec
Jablonec
Karlovy Vary
Cheb
České Budějovice
Jihlava
Kolín
Labe (Elbe)
Donau
(Danube)
Inn
Vltava
Enns
Mur
Drau
Drava
Sava
GERMANY
AUSTRIA
CZECHOSLOVAKIA
SWITZERLAND
LIECHTENSTEIN
ITALY
YUGOSLAVIA
BAYERN
BADEN-WÜRTTEMBERG
HESSEN
VORARLBERG
TIROL
SALZBURG
KÄRNTEN
STEIERMARK
OBERÖSTERREICH
NIEDERÖSTERREICH
ZÁPADOČESKÝ
JIHOČESKÝ
STŘEDOČESKÝ
SEVEROČESKÝ
VYCHODOČESKÝ
Böhmer Wald
Bayerischer Wald
Thüringer Wald
Erzgebirge
Fichtelgebirge
Fränkische Alb
Schwäbische Alb
Hohe Tauern
Niedere Tauern
Zillertaler Alpen
Ötztaler Alpen
Lechtaler Alpen
Karnische Alpen
Karawanken
Julijske Alpe
Dolomiti
Alpi Orobie
Chiemsee
Ammersee
Starnberger See
Bodensee
Lago di Garda
Wörther See
ft
m
12 000
9000
6000
4500
3000
1200
600
0
4000
3000
2000
1500
1000
400
200
0
Projection: Conical with two standard parallels

East from Greenwich

1: 3 000 000

20 10 0 10 20 30 40 50 60 miles

20 0 20 40 60 80 km

Projection: Conical with two standard parallels

East from Greenwich

m	ft
3000	9000
2000	6000
1500	4500
1000	3000
400	1200
200	600
0	0

1:5 000 000

50 0 50 100 miles

50 0 50 100 150 km

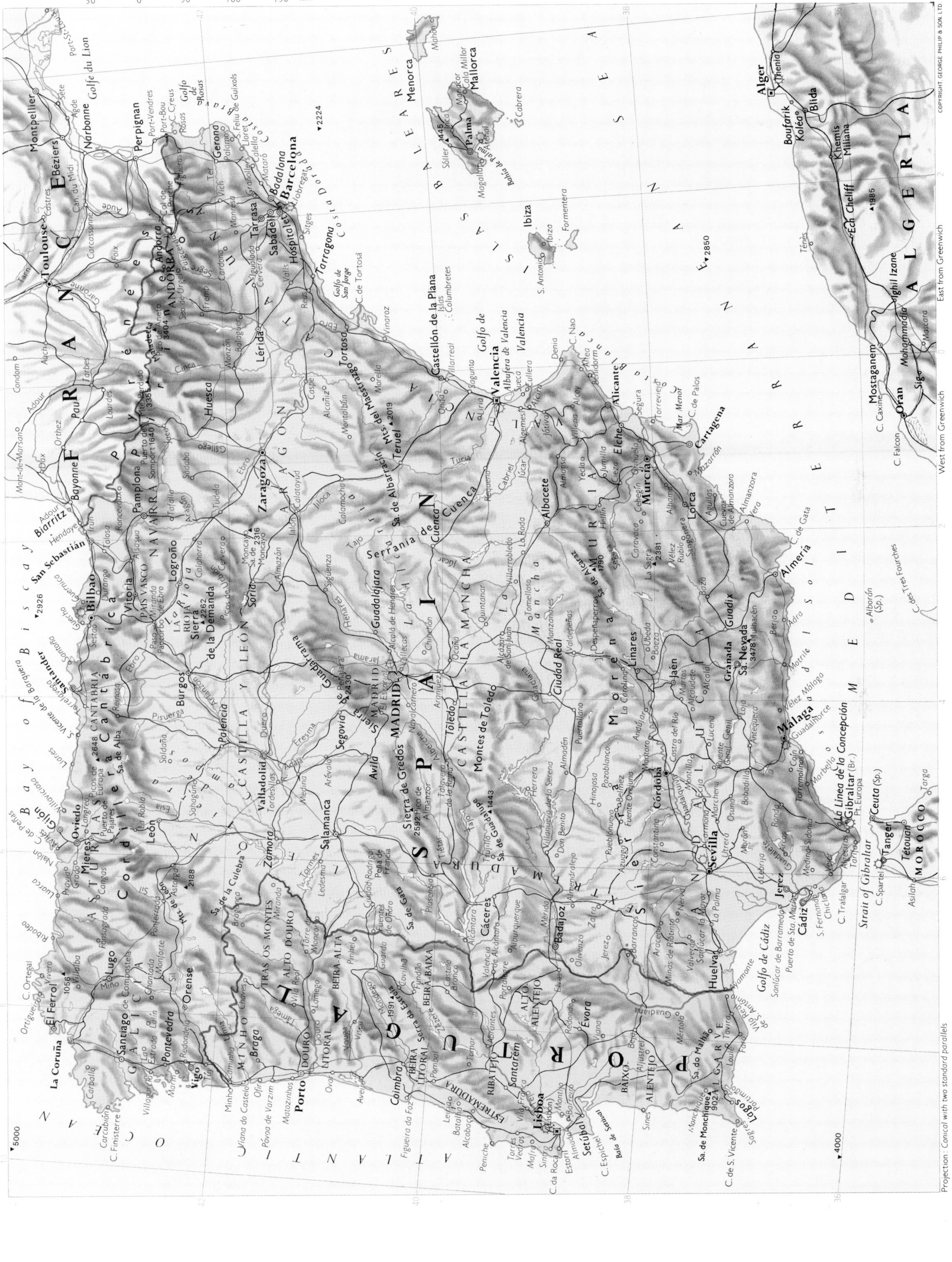

Projection: Conical with two standard parallels

West from Greenwich

East from Greenwich

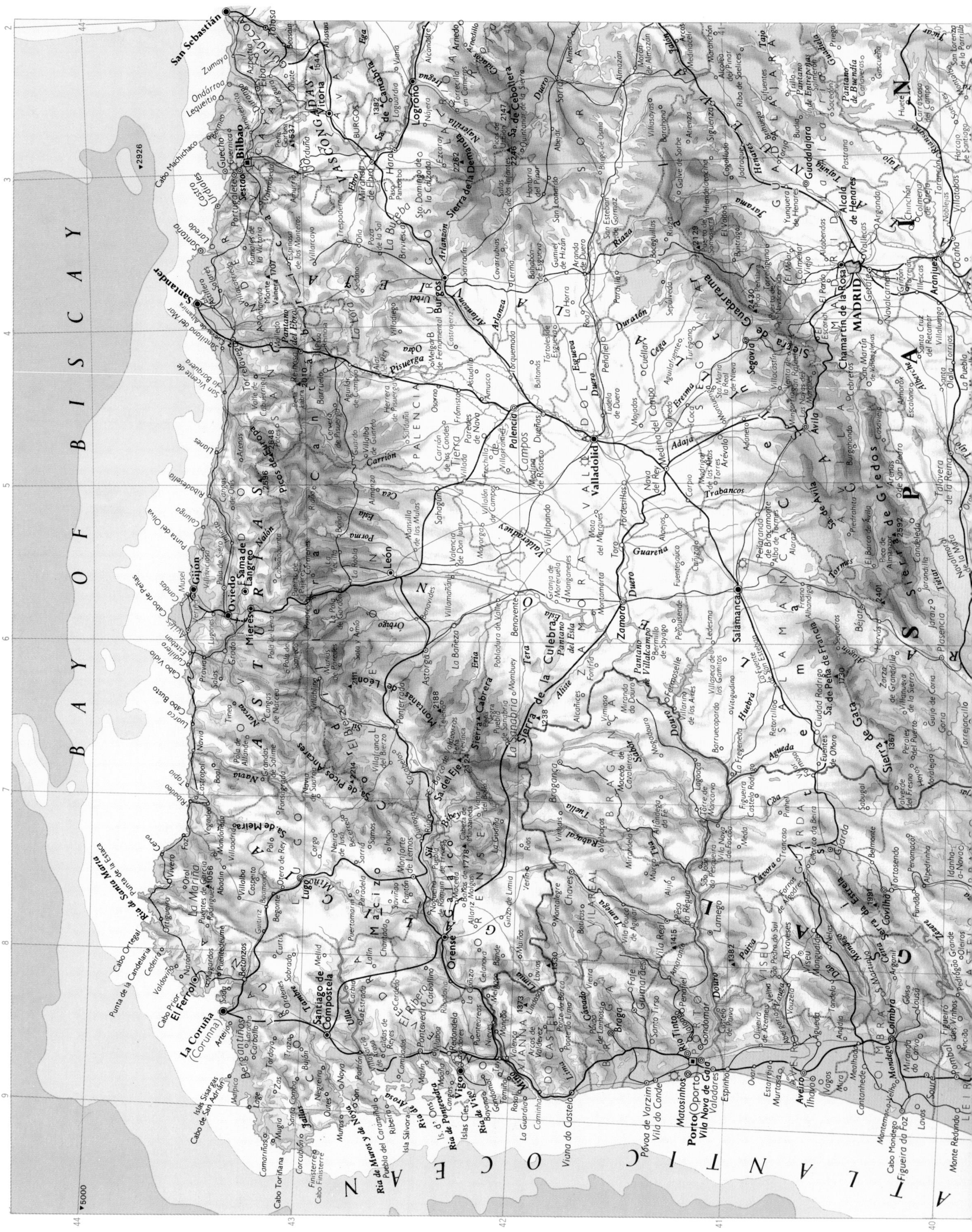
BAY OF BISCAY
ATLANTIC OCEAN
San Sebastián
Bilbao
Santander
Gijón
Oviedo
La Coruña
(Corunna)
El Ferrol
Lugo
Santiago de Compostela
Orense
Vigo
Porto (Oporto)
Vila Nova de Gaia
Braga
Aveiro
Coimbra
Vitoria
Logroño
Burgos
León
Palencia
Valladolid
Zamora
Salamanca
Segovia
Avila
MADRID
Guadalajara
Alcalá de Henares
Aranjuez
Plasencia
Sierra de Gredos
Sierra de Guadarrama
Picos de Europa
Sierra de Gata
Serra da Estrela
Duero
Douro
Miño
Ebro
Tajo
Pisuerga
Esla
Tormes

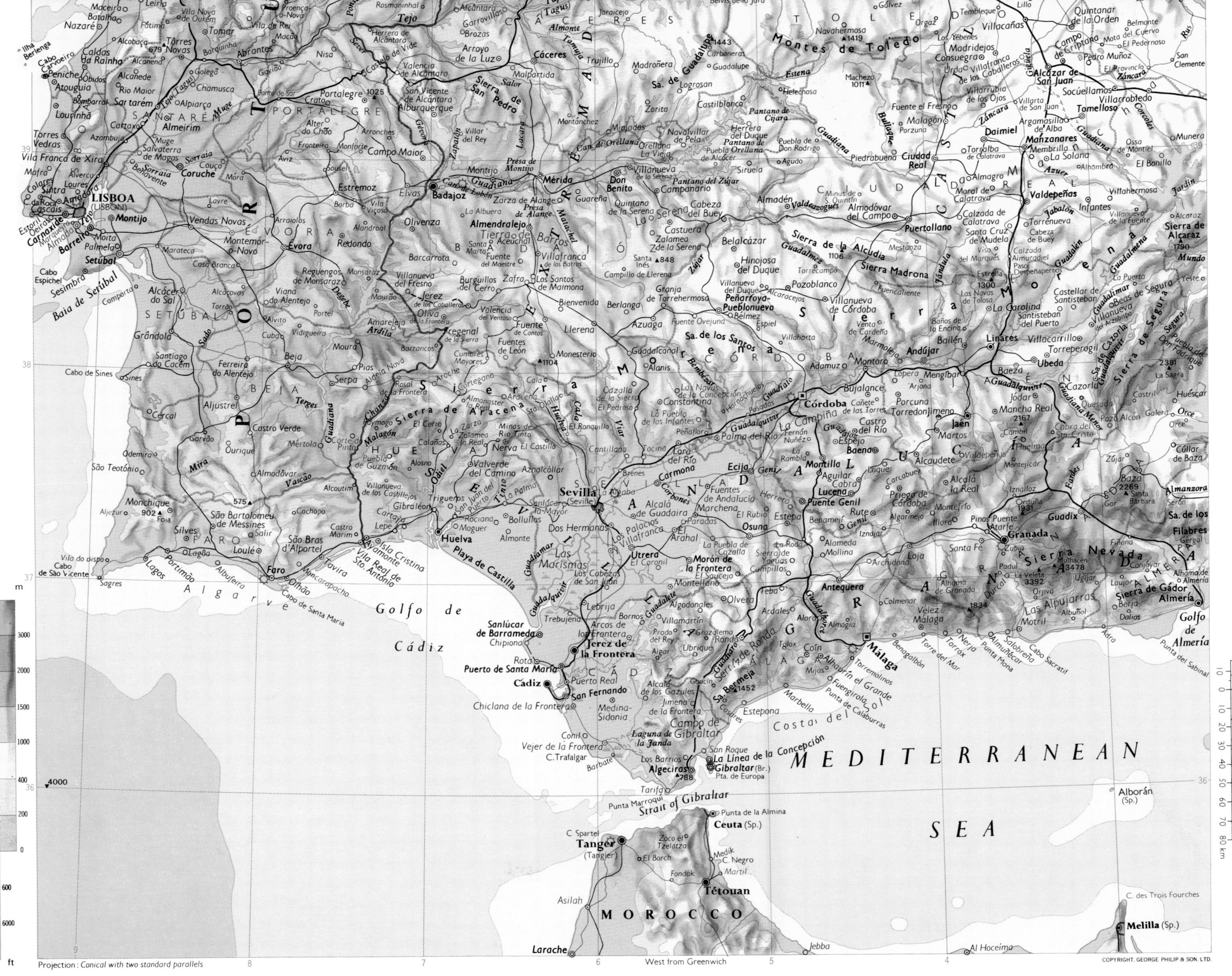
MEDITERRANEAN SEA
MOROCCO
Golfo de Cádiz
Strait of Gibraltar
Golfo de Almería
Algarve
Costa del Sol
Sierra Nevada
Sierra Morena
Montes de Toledo
Sierra de Segura
Sierra Madrona
Sierra de Aracena
Sierra de San Pedro
LISBOA (LISBON)
Setúbal
Évora
Beja
Faro
Badajoz
Mérida
Cáceres
Huelva
Sevilla (Seville)
Córdoba
Jaén
Granada
Málaga
Almería
Cádiz
Jerez de la Frontera
Algeciras
Gibraltar (Br.)
Ceuta (Sp.)
Tanger (Tangier)
Tétouan
Melilla (Sp.)
Alborán (Sp.)
Larache
Ciudad Real
Puertollano
Linares
Úbeda
Baeza
Andújar
Ecija
Osuna
Antequera
Lucena
Marbella
Tavira
Portimão
Lagos
Cabo de São Vicente
Cabo de Sines
Cabo Espichel
Guadalquivir
Guadiana
Tejo
Projection: Conical with two standard parallels
West from Greenwich
COPYRIGHT, GEORGE PHILIP & SON, LTD.
1:2 500 000
10 0 10 20 30 40 50 miles
10 0 10 20 30 40 50 60 70 80 km

BAY OF BISCAY
Golfe de Gascogne
FRANCE
SPAIN
ANDORRA
ROUSSILLON
PYRÉNÉES ORIENTALES
HAUTES PYRÉNÉES
PYRÉNÉES-ATLANTIQUES
BÉARN
NAVARRE
NAVARRA
VASCONGADAS
SANTANDER
BURGOS
SORIA
SEGOVIA
GUADALAJARA
TERUEL
CASTELLÓN
VALENCIA
CUENCA
LÉRIDA
GERONA
BARCELONA
TARRAGONA
HUESCA
ZARAGOZA
BALEARES (BALEARIC ISLANDS)
Menorca (Minorca)
Mallorca (Majorca)
Palma
Mahón
Ciudadela
Toulouse
Montauban
Carcassonne
Narbonne
Béziers
Perpignan
Tarbes
Pau
Bayonne
Biarritz
Lourdes
San Sebastián
Bilbao
Santander
Vitoria
Pamplona
Logroño
Burgos
Zaragoza (Saragossa)
Huesca
Lérida
Tarragona
Reus
Tarrasa
Sabadell
Badalona
Mataró
Gerona
Manresa
Hospitalet de Llobregat
Teruel
Castellón de la Plana
Sagunto
Cuenca
Guadalajara
Alcalá de Henares
MADRID
Aranjuez
Soria
Calatayud
Tudela
Ebro
Duero
Sierra de Guara
Sa. de Alcubierre
Los Monegros
Sierra de la Peña
Montes Universales
Mts. del Maestrazgo
Golfo de San Jorge
Costa Brava
Costa Dorada
Cabo Creus
Islas Columbretes
Pico de Aneto 3404
Causse du Larzac
Mts. de Lacaune
Canal du Midi
Sa. de Cebollera 2147
Sierra de la Demanda 2262
Sa. del Moncayo 2316

1:2 500 000

10 0 10 20 30 40 50 miles

10 0 10 20 30 40 50 60 70 80 km

MEDITERRANEAN SEA

ALGERIA

MOROCCO

ISLAS BALEARES

Projection: Conical with two standard parallels

West from Greenwich

East from Greenwich

ft	m
9000	3000
6000	2000
4500	1500
3000	1000
1200	400
600	200
0	0
600	200
6000	2000
ft	m

LONDON
PARIS
MADRID
ROMA
FRANCE
SPAIN
PORTUGAL
SWITZERLAND
BELGIUM
NETH.
GERMANY
MOROCCO
ALGERIA
TUNISIA
Bay of Biscay
English Channel
MEDITERRANEAN
Tyrrhenian Sea
Ligurian Sea
Islas Baleares
Pyrenees
Cordillera Cantábrica
Sierra Morena
Atlas Saharien
Haut Atlas
Hauts Plateaux
Jabal Nafūsah
Tarābulus
Projection: Conical with two standard parallels.
West from Greenwich 0 East from Greenwich

1:10 000 000

50 0 50 100 150 200 miles

50 0 100 200 300 km

POLAND
Warszawa
Poznań
Łódź
Wrocław
Kraków
Lublin
Radom
Brest
Pinsk
Chernigov
Sumy
Kharkov
Volgograd
Kiyev
Zhitomir
Poltava
Kremenchug
U. S. S. R.
Vinnitsa
Lvov
Dneprodzerzhinsk
Dnepropetrovsk
Kirovograd
Krivoy Rog
Donetsk
Makeyevka
Gorlovka
Voroshilovgrad
Shakhty
Novocherkassk
Rostov
Zaporozhye
Zhdanov
Taganrog
Nikolayev
Kherson
Melitopol
Sea of Azov
Kerch
Krasnodar
Stavropol
Novorossiysk
Odessa
Kishinev
MOLDAVIAN S.S.R.
Chernovtsy
Iaşi
Simferopol
Sevastopol
Karkinitskiy Zaliv
BLACK SEA
CZECHOSLOVAKIA
Ostrava
Bratislava
Košice
Miskolc
Debrecen
HUNGARY
Budapest
Kecskemét
Szeged
Pécs
Oradea
Cluj-Napoca
ROMANIA
Braşov
Galaţi
Brăila
Ploieşti
Bucureşti
Constanţa
Craiova
Timişoara
Arad
Zagreb
Novi Sad
Beograd
Sarajevo
YUGOSLAVIA
Niš
Skopje
Varna
Burgas
Sofiya
BULGARIA
Plovdiv
Edirne
Rhodopi Planina
Stara Planina
ALBANIA
Tirana
Shkodër
Bitola
GREECE
Thessaloníki
Kerkira
Kefallinía
Pátrai
Athínai
Piraievs
Pelopónnisos
Límnos
Lésvos
Khíos
Kikládhes
Náxos
Ródhos
Kríti
Iráklion
Aegean Sea
Dhodhekánisos
İstanbul
Üsküdar
Bursa
Eskişehir
Ankara
TURKEY
Kayseri
İzmir
Konya
Adana
Antalya
Afyon Karahisar
Trabzon
Samsun
Sinop
Batumi
Kuzey Anadolu Dağları
Toros Dağları
Gaziantep
Halab
SYRIA
Ḥamāh
Ḥims
Dimashq
LEBANON
Bayrūt
Tarābulus
CYPRUS
Nicosia
ISRAEL
Tel Aviv-Yafo
Jerusalem
'Ammān
JORDAN
Dead Sea
Ionian Sea
MEDITERRANEAN SEA
Bari
Táranto
Reggio
Banghāzī
Khalīj Surt
Barqa
LIBYA
El Iskandarîya
Bur Sa'id
Ismâ'ilîya
El Qâhira
Tanta
El Suweis
EGYPT
Sinai
COPYRIGHT. GEORGE PHILIP & SON. LTD.

– – – – – Division between Greeks and Turks in Cyprus; Turks to the north.

SWITZERLAND
AUSTRIA
Brenner
Passo del S. Gottardo
Genève
Lyon
Sion
Domodóssola
Matterhorn
Mte. Rosa
Lago Maggiore
Locarno
Lugano
Bernina
Chiavenna
Ortles
Merano
Bolzano
TRENTINO ALTO-ADIGE
Marmolada
Drave
Villach
Klagenfurt
Bleiburg
Maribor
Karawanken
Triglav
Kobarid (Caporetto)
FRIULI VENEZIA GIULIA
Údine
Ljubljana
Celje
Sava
Zagreb
Bjelovar
Annecy
Mt. Blanc
Gr. St. Bernard
V. D'AOSTA
Aosta
Gran Paradiso
Ivrea
Biella
Busto Arsizio
Como
Lecco
Bergamo
L. di Como
Adamello
Trento
Riva
Rovereto
Belluno
Vittório Véneto
Gorízia
Trieste
Postojna
Cerknica
Kočevje
Kupa
Karlovac
Sisak
Chambéry
Aix-les-Bains
Vienne
Voiron
Grenoble
Tournon
Valence
DAUPHINÉ
Moutiers
St. Jean
Modane
Col du Mt. Cenis
Mt. Pelvoux
Briançon
Susa
Chivasso
Torino (Turin)
PIEMONTE
Novara
Vercelli
Casale
Milano (Milan)
LOMBARDIA
Pavia
Bréscia
Lago di Garda
Vicenza
Verona
Pádova (Padua)
VENETO
Treviso
Bassano
Schio
Venézia (Venice)
Chióggia
Golfo di Venézia
Istra
Koper
Rijeka (Fiume)
Rovinj
Pula (Pola)
Rt. Kamenjak
Krk
Cres
Lošinj
Senj
Kvarner
Montelimar
Nyons
Embrun
Pinerolo
Viso
Saluzzo
Asti
Alba
Alessándria
Piacenza
Cremona
Mántova (Mantua)
Po
Adige
Rovigo
Ferrara
Comácchio
Orange
Avignon
Mt. Pelat
Alpes Maritimes
Cúneo
Mondovì
Savona
P. dei Giovi
Génova (Genoa)
Riv. di Ponente
Riv. di Levante
Chiávari
Parma
Réggio
Módena
Bologna
EMILIA ROMAGNA
Mte. Cimone
Imola
Faenza
Forlì
Ravenna
Cesena
Rubicone
Rímini
Digne
Tende
PROVENCE
Verdon
Durance
MONACO
Menton
Monte Carlo
San Remo
Impéria
Grasse
Draguignan
Côte d'Azur
Antibes
Nice
Cannes
Aix
Marseille
Martigues
Toulon
Fréjus
St. Tropez
Îles d'Hyères
LIGURIAN SEA
Golfo di Génova
La Spézia
Massa
Carrara
Pistóia
Prato
Lucca
Pisa
Arno
Firenze (Florence)
Livorno (Leghorn)
Pontedera
Volterra
TOSCANA
Siena
Arezzo
Cortona
SAN MARINO
Urbino
Pésaro
Fano
Senigállia
Ancona
Loreto
MARCHE
Macerata
Fabriano
Civitanova
Perúgia
L. Trasimeno
Assisi
Foligno
Monti Vettore
UMBRIA
San Benedetto
Ascoli Piceno
Spoleto
Terni
Orvieto
L. di Bolsena
Viterbo
Chiusi
Amiata
Grosseto
Orbetello
Mte. Argentario
Civitavécchia
L. di Bracciano
Rieti
Téramo
Gran Sasso
L'Aquila
Pescara
Chieti
Ortona
Lanciano
ABRUZZI
Mt. Amaro
Vasto
Térmoli
ADRIATIC SEA
C. Corse
Capraia
Piombino
Portoferráio
Elba
Bastia
Calvi
Mt. Cinto
CORSE (CORSICA) (Fr.)
Ajaccio
Aléria
Sartène
Pto. Vecchio
Bonifacio
Bouches de Bonifacio
Maddalena
Caprera
Asinara
C. Falcone
Golfo dell'Asinara
Porto Torres
Sássari
Ólbia (Terranova)
Golfo Aranci
Alghero
Bosa
Nuoro
Orosei
SARDEGNA (SARDINIA)
C. Mte. Santo
Mt. Gennargentu
Arbatax
Oristano
Golfo di Oristano
Tirso
Sorgono
Iglésias
Portoscuso
Carbonia
Cágliari
Golfo di Cágliari
C. Carbonara
C. Spartivento
G. di Palmas
Fiora
Tivoli
Campagna
ROMA (Rome)
Ostia
Velletri
Frosinone
Ánzio
Latina
Sabáudia
Terracina
Fondi
Gaeta
Ísole Ponziane
Garigliano
Volturno
Caserta
Aversa
Vesuvio
Ischia
Napoli (Naples)
Torre Annunziata
Capri
Sorrento
Castellammare
Salerno
Sele
Éboli
Nocera
Avellino
Benevento
CAMPANIA
MOLISE
S. Severo
Campobasso
Sannicandro
Monte Gargano
Monte S. Ángelo
Fóggia
G. di Manfredónia
Cerignola
Barletta
Trani
Molfetta
Bari
Andria
Corato
Ofanto
Spinazzola
PUGLIA
Monopoli
Putignano
Matera
Taranto
Potenza
BASILICATA
Agri
Sinni
Golfo di Taranto
Pisciotta
TYRRHENIAN SEA
Corigliano
Cosenza
Crotone
Sambiase
Nicastro
Catanzaro
Squillace
Pizzo
CALABRIA
Palmi
Scilla
Taurianova
Réggio
C. Spartivento
Ustica (It.)
Strómboli
Isole Eólie o Lípari
Salina
Lípari
Vulcano
C. Peloro
Milazzo
Patti
Messina
Str. di Messina
Palermo
Castellammare
Términi
Cefalù
Érice
Trápani
Isole Égadi
Favignana
Segesta
Alcamo
Marsala
Castelvetrano
Selinunte
Menfi
Sciacca
Platani
Caltanissetta
Enna
Mistretta
Monti Nebrodi
Etna
Adrano
Paternò
Giarre
Catánia
Lentini
Augusta
Siracusa (Syracuse)
Piazza
Caltagirone
Favara
Agrigento
Pto. Empédocle
Licata
Salso
Gela
Vittória
Ragusa
Módica
Noto
Íspica
C. Passero
SICILIA
Pantelleria (Ital.)
Gozo
Comino
Valletta
Mdina
MALTA
Lampedusa (Ital.)
MEDIT
La Galite
Skikda
C. de Fer
Annaba
Binzert (Bizerte)
Béja
Tunis
G. de Tunis
C. Bon
Constantine
Nabeul
ALGERIA
TUNISIA
G. de Hammamet
Kairouan
Sousse
Khenchela
Tebessa
Senj
Velebit Planina
Pag
Zadar
Dugi Otok
Gospić
Bihać
Kremen
Gračac
Dinara Planina
Troglav
Šibenik
Split
Brač
Hvar
Vis
Korčula
Lastovo
Palagruža (Yugoslavia)
Drava
Varaždin
HRVATSKA
C. S. Dimitri
Gozo (Ghawdex)
Victoria (Rabat)
Comino (Kemmuna)
St. Pauls Bay
Mosta
Sliema
Mdina
Hamrun
Rabat
Valletta
Luqa
Marsaxlokk
Żurrieq
Birżebbuġa
MALTA
1:1 000 000
10 miles
0 5 15 km
Projection: Conical with two standard parallels

1: 5 000 000

50 0 50 100 miles

50 0 50 100 150 km

HUNGARY
ROMANIA
U.S.S.R.
YUGOSLAVIA
BULGARIA
ALBANIA
GREECE
TURKEY

Transilvania
Carpatii Meridionali
Banat
Valahia
Dobrogea
Stara Planina
Rhodopi Planina
Makedonija
Makedhonia
Thráki
Serbija
Crna Gora
Ipiros
Thessalia
Sterea Ellas
Pelopónnisos
Kikládhes
Dhodhekanisos
Kriti
Anadolu

BLACK SEA
AEGEAN SEA
IONIAN SEA
MEDITERRANEAN SEA
Marmara denizi
Str. of Otranto

Szeged
Arad
Timişoara
Sibiu
Braşov
Galaţi
Brăila
Ploieşti
Bucureşti (Bucharest)
Constanţa
Craiova
Beograd (Belgrade)
Novi Sad
Sarajevo
Niš
Ruse (Ruschuk)
Varna
Burgas
Sofiya (Sofia)
Plovdiv
Pleven
Skopje
Titograd (Podgorica)
Tiranë
Edirne
İstanbul
Üsküdar
Bursa
İzmir (Smyrna)
Thessaloníki
Lárisa
Vólos
Pátrai
Athínai (Athens)
Piraievs (Piraeus)
Iráklion
Ródhos
Bríndisi
Lecce

East from Greenwich

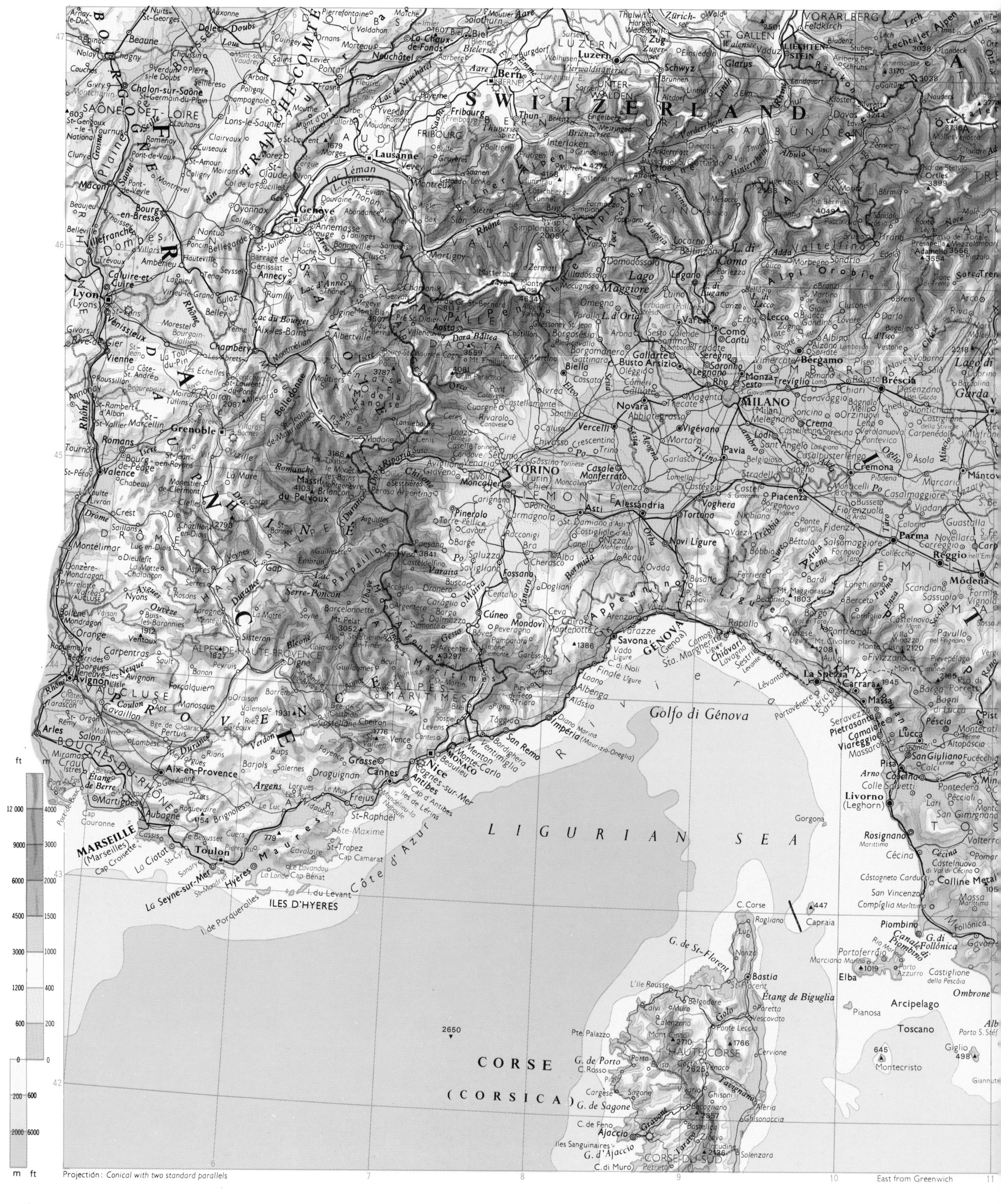
SWITZERLAND
FRANCE
LIGURIAN SEA
Golfo di Génova
CORSE
(CORSICA)
Côte d'Azur
ILES D'HYERES
Riviera
MILANO
(Milan)
TORINO
(Turin)
GENOVA
(Genoa)
Lyon
(Lyons)
MARSEILLE
(Marseilles)
Genève
Lausanne
Bern
Luzern
Zürich
Grenoble
Chambéry
Avignon
Aix-en-Provence
Toulon
Nice
Cannes
Monaco
San Remo
Savona
La Spezia
Livorno
(Leghorn)
Pisa
Lucca
Parma
Piacenza
Cremona
Bergamo
Brescia
Novara
Vercelli
Alessandria
Asti
Cúneo
Bastia
Ajaccio
Elba
Capraia
Montecristo
Arcipelago Toscano
Lago Maggiore
L. di Como
Lago di Garda
Lac Léman
(L. Geneva)
LIECHTENSTEIN
VORARLBERG
Golfo di Génova
ft
m
12 000
9000
6000
4500
3000
1200
600
0
4000
3000
2000
1500
1000
400
200
200
2000
600
6000
m
ft
Projection: Conical with two standard parallels
East from Greenwich
6
7
8
9
10
11
47
46
45
44
43
42

1:2 500 000
10 0 10 20 30 40 50 miles
10 0 10 20 30 40 50 60 70 80 km
HUNGARY
YUGOSLAVIA
AUSTRIA
ITALY
ADRIATIC SEA
Golfo di Venézia
Innsbruck
Graz
Klagenfurt
Villach
Maribor
Ljubljana
Zagreb
Karlovac
Rijeka (Fiume)
Trieste
G. di Trieste
Venézia (Venice)
Pádova (Padua)
Vicenza
Treviso
Mestre
Chióggia
Rovigo
Ferrara
Bologna
Ravenna
Rímini
SAN MARINO
Pésaro
Ancona
Firenze (Florence)
Arezzo
Perúgia
Assisi
Terni
Viterbo
Civitavécchia
ROMA (ROME)
Pescara
Chieti
L'Aquila
Téramo
Ascoli Piceno
Macerata
Fermo
Vasto
Térmoli
Vieste
Monte Sant'Ángelo
Zadar
Šibenik
Split
Brač
Hvar
Vis
Korčula
Lastovo
Mljet
Pelješac
Banja Luka
Bihać
Gospić
Sisak
Varaždin
Nagykanizsa
Zalaegerszeg
Szombathely
Balaton
Udine
Gorízia
Monfalcone
Pordenone
Belluno
Bolzano
Pula
Poreč
Rovinj
Opatija
Krk
Cres
Lošinj
Rab
Pag
Dugi Otok
Kornat
Kvarner
Kvarnerič
Velika Kapela
Velebit Planina
Dinara Planina
Karawanken
Karnische Alpen
Hohe Tauern
Niedere Tauern
Zillertaler Alpen
Julijske Alpe
Bakony Hegység
Bilo Gora
Moslavačka Gora
Kozara
Grmeč Planina
Gran Sasso d'Italia
ABRUZZI
UMBRIA
MARCHE
LAZIO
MOLISE
TOSCANA
EMILIA
VENETO
FRIULI-VENEZIA GIULIA
SLOVENIJA
HRVATSKA
BOSNA
HERCEGOVINA
DALMACIJA
ZALA
SOMOGY
KÄRNTEN
Drava
Sava
Mura
Kupa
Una
Piave
Po
Foci del Po
Tévere (Tiber)
Pescara
Tronto
Metauro
L. Trasimeno
L. di Bolsena
L. di Bracciano
Valli di Comácchio
Laguna Véneta
Tremiti
Pianosa
Palagruža
Susak
Silba
Premuda
Unije
Svetac
Biševo
Sušac
Vis Kanal
Korčulanski Kanal
Lastovski Kanal
Neretvanski Kan.
Hvarski Kanal
Splitski Kan.
Brački Kan.
Rt. Kamenjak
Brionski (Brijuni)
Monte Gargano
Testa del Gargano
L. di Lésina
L. di Varano
Conca del Fucino
2914
2795
2487
2283
2213
2476
1738
1654
1570
1913
2006
1961
1872
1762
1758
1699
1604
1533
1495
1107
1796
1543
1035
1061
1181
978
989
953
3797
3283
3435
3342
3263
3191
2863
2558
2441
2396
2341
2250
2081
1989

CORSE
CORSICA
CORSE-DU-SUD
Iles Sanguinaires
G. d'Ajaccio
C. di Muro
G. de Valinco
Propriano
Sartène
Porto-Vecchio
Iles Cerbicales
Bonifacio
I. de Cavallo
Bouches de Bonifacio
Solenzara
Favone
Zonza
Levie
Maddalena
Santa Teresa Gallura
La Maddalena
Caprera
Asinara
Punta dello Scorno
Golfo dell' Asinara
Costa Smeralda
Coghinas
Tempio Pausania
Calangianus
Golfo Aranci
G. di Ólbia
Ólbia
Tavolara
Porto Tórres
Sorso
Sennori
Sássari
Ósilo
C. dell'Argentiera
Fertilia
Alghero
Ittiri
M. Limbara
L. di Coghinas
Ozieri
Óschiri
Pattada
Buddusò
Posada
Tanaunella
Siniscola
C. Comino
Villanova Monteleone
Bonorva
Tirso
Bitti
Orune
Nùoro
Bosa
Temo
Macomer
Oliena
Dorgali
Golfo di Orosei
SARDEGNA
Ghilarza
L. del Tirso
Fonni
Monti del Gennargentu
1834
C. Mannu
Sorgono
Baunei
C. di Monte Santu
Cabras
Oristano
Laconi
Arbatax
Lanusei
Golfo di Oristano
M. Arci
812
Arborea
Terralba
Ierzu
Nurri
Mandas
Flumendosa
S. Gavino Monreale
Sanluri
Gúspini
Arbus
SARDINIA
C. Pécora
Gonnosfanadiga
Villacidro
1236
M. Linas
Fluminimaggiore
Senorbì
S. Vito
Villaputzu
Muravera
Iglésias
Cixerri
Serramanna
Dolianova
Assémini
Sestu
Sinnai
Pta. Serpeddì
1069
Portoscuso
Gonnesa
Siliqua
Selargius
Quartu Sant'Elena
C. Ferrato
Carloforte
Carbonia
Cágliari
Golfo di Cágliari
San Pietro
1116
Santadi
Serpentara
C. Carbonara
Sant'Antioco
Porto Botte
Pula
Sant' Antíoco
G. di Pálmas
Teulada
C. Spartivento
TYRRHENIAN
SEA
3719
3589
Vatican City
ROMA
(Rome)
Tívoli
Subiaco
Conca del Fucino
Fregene
Palestrina
Tevere (Tiber)
Valmontone
Lido di Ostia (Lido di Roma)
Velletri
Anagni
Alatri
Véroli
Sora
Prática di Mare
Albano Laziale
Frosinone
Ferentino
Cori
Cisterna di Latina
Aprília
Arpino
Monte S. Giov
Latina
Sezze
Ceccano
Cassino
Ánzio
Nettuno
Priverno
Sonnino
Fondi
Pontinia
Liri
1533
Sabáudia
Monte Circeo
541
Terracina
Formia
Gaeta
Minturno
Garigliano
Golfo di Gaeta
Mondragone
Volturno
Zannone
Palmarola
Ponza
283
Ísole Ponziane
Ventotene
Íschia
788
Ustica
C. San Vito
Castellammare del Golfo
G. di Castellammare
Terrasini Favarotta
C. Gallo
PALERMO
Bagheria
Levanzo
Trápani
Érice
1110
Carini
Monreale
Partinico
Misilmeri
Marettimo
Ísole Égadi
Favignana
Alcamo
Paceco
S. Giuseppe Iato
Stagnone
Calatafimi
Salemi
Camporeale
Corleone
1613
Marineo
Marsala
Gibellina
Lercara Friddi
Partanna
Castelvetrano
Bisacquino
Prizzi
Mazara del Vallo
Sambuca di Sicilia
Menfi
Burgio
Mussomeli
Campobello di Mazara
Belice
Sciacca
Caltabellotta
Ribera
Platani
San Cataldo
Racalmuto
Cattólica Eraclea
Raffadali
Siculiana
Aragona
Porto Empédocle
Agrigento
Favara
Naro
Palma di Montechiaro
Campobello di Licata
Sicilian Channel
Iles de la Galite
C. Serrat
C. Blanc
Cani
Bizerte (Binzert)
Plane
Menzel-Bourguiba
Zembra
Mateur
Golfe de Tunis
C. Bon
El Kala
ALGERIA
Tabarka
Tébourba
TUNIS
Halq el Oued
Kelibia
Menzel-Temime
Bou Salem
Béja
Medjerda
Soliman
TUNISIA
Téboursouk
Nabeul
Mellègue
Zaghouan
Hammamet
Pantelleria
836
(It.)
1319
MEDITE
ft
m
9000
3000
6000
2000
4500
1500
3000
1000
1200
400
600
200
0
0
200
600
2000
6000
4000
12,000
Projection: Conical with two standard parallels
East from Greenwich

1:2 500 000

10 0 10 20 30 40 50 miles

10 0 10 20 30 40 50 60 70 80 km

ADRIATIC SEA
IONIAN SEA
Strait of Otranto
G. di Manfredónia
Golfo di Táranto
G. di Salerno
G. di Policastro
Golfo di Sant'Eufémia
Golfo di Squillace
G. di Gióia
Str. di Messina
Golfo di Catánia
Isole Eólie o Lípari (Æolian Is.)
BASILICATA
CALABRIA
ALBANIA
Foggia
Manfredónia
Monte Sant'Ángelo
Barletta
Trani
Bisceglie
Molfetta
Bari
Andria
Altamura
Matera
Monopoli
Fasano
Ostuni
Bríndisi
Táranto
Lecce
Otranto
Gallípoli
C. Santa Maria di Leuca
Potenza
Salerno
Benevento
Avellino
Campobasso
Cosenza
Crotone
Catanzaro
Vibo Valéntia
Réggio di Calábria
Messina
Milazzo
Stromboli
Lípari
Vulcano
Salina
Filicudi
Alicudi
Panarea
Monti Nébrodi
Etna 3340
Catánia
Acireale
Augusta
Siracusa
Ragusa
Módica
Noto
Pachino
C. Passero
Gela
Vittória
Caltagirone
Enna
Piazza Armerina
Taormina
Aspromonte 1956
C. Spartivento
Rossano
Corigliano Cálabro
Cassano Iónio
Castrovillari
Monte Pollino 2271
La Sila 1929
Durrësi (Durazzo)
Tiranë (Tirana)
Vlorë (Valona)
Fieri
Berati
Kérkira (Corfu)
3065
4116

HUNGARY
YUGOSLAVIA
ALBANIA
ADRIATIC SEA
Beograd
(Belgrade)
Novi Sad
Sarajevo
Skopje
Tirana
Timişoara
Arad
Szeged
Pécs
Osijek
Banja Luka
Zenica
Mostar
Dubrovnik
Kragujevac
Niš
Priština
Titograd
Shkodra
Durrësi
Elbasani
Bitola
Ohrid
Prilep
Kumanovo
Leskovac
Vidin
Pernik
Kyustendil
Drobeta-Turnu Severin
Subotica
Zrenjanin
Pančevo
Smederevo
Danube
Drava
Sava
Drina
Morava
Ibar
Tisa
Vardar
Bosna
Neretva
Socijalistička Autonomna Pokrajina Kosovo
Autonomna Pokrajina Vojvodina
Ohridsko Jezero (L. Ohrid)
Prespansko Jezero (L. Prespa)
Skadarsko Jezero
Projection: Conical with two standard parallels
East from Greenwich
ft m
9000 3000
6000 2000
4500 1500
3000 1000
1200 400
600 200
0 0
200 600
2000 6000
m ft

TRANSILVANIA
ROMANIA
BULGARIA
TURKEY
GREECE
U. S. S. R.
UKRAINIAN S.S.R.
BLACK SEA
WALLACHIA
DOBRUDJA
HARGHITA
COVASNA
VRANCEA
BACĂU
VASLUI
GALAŢI
BRĂILA
TULCEA
IALOMIŢA
CĂLĂRAŞI
CONSTANŢA
GIURGIU
TELEORMAN
OLT
DOLJ
VÎLCEA
ARGEŞ
DÎMBOVIŢA
PRAHOVA
BUZĂU
SIBIU
ALBA
MUREŞ
BRAŞOV
KIRKLARELI
EDIRNE
TEKIRDAĞ
ISTANBUL
DRAMA
XANTHI
SERRAI
BUCUREŞTI (Bucharest)
Ploieşti
Piteşti
Craiova
Braşov
Sibiu
Buzău
Brăila
Galaţi
Constanţa
Tulcea
Focşani
Bacău
Bîrlad
Tecuci
Rîmnicu Sărat
Tîrgovişte
Slobozia
Călăraşi
Alexandria
Giurgiu
Olteniţa
Cernavodă
Mangalia
Sulina
Izmail
Reni
Bolgrad
Kagul
Komrat
Artsiz
Kiliya
Vilkovo
Dunărea (Danube)
Dunay (Danube)
Braţul Chilia
Braţul Sulina
Braţul Sfîntu Gheorghe
Lacul Razelm
Muntii Făgăraş
Muntii Ciuc
Muntii Vrancei
Muntii Harghita
Lom
Vratsa
Pleven
Lovech
Svishtov
Ruse (Ruschuk)
Razgrad
Silistra
Tolbukhin
Kolarovgrad (Šumen)
Tŭrgovishte
Tŭrnovo
Gabrovo
Sevlievo
Troyan
Varna
Burgas
Burgaski Zaliv
Sliven
Yambol
Stara Zagora
Kazanlŭk
Plovdiv (Philippopolis)
Pazardzhik
Khaskovo
Kŭrdzhali
Smolyan
Sofiya (Sofia)
Samokov
Blagoevgrad
Petrich
Sredna Gora
Stara Planina (Balkan)
Rodopi
Pirin Planina
Rila
Iskŭr
Yantra
Maritsa
Tundzha
Kamchiya
Golyama Kamchiya
Luda Kamchiya
Osŭm
Vit
Ogosta
Edirne (Adrianople)
Kirklareli
Lüleburgaz
Çorlu
Çatalca
Silivri
Istranca Dağlari
Karadeniz Boğazı (Bosporus)
Üsküdar
Beykoz
Komotini
Xanthi
Dráma
Néstos
Évros
Ergene

YUGOSLAVIA
BULGARIA
ALBANIA
TURKEY
Sofiya
Plovdiv
Stara Zagora
Sliven
Yambol
Pleven
Vratsa
Lovech
Svishtov
Razgrad
Pernik
Blagoevgrad
Edirne
Niš
Priština
Skopje
Kumanovo
Prilep
Bitola
Shkodra
Tirana
Durrësi
Berati
Korça
Vlora (Valona)
Titograd
Thessaloníki
Kavála
Xánthi
Komotiní
Sérrai
Dráma
Kateríni
Lárisa
Vólos
Trikkala
Ioánnina
Kérkira (Corfu)
Thásos
Samothráki
Límnos
Ayíos Evstrátios
Gökçeada
Çanakkale
Saros Körfezi
Thrakikón Pélagos
Thermaïkós Kólpos
Strimonikós Kólpos
Stara Planina
Sredna Gora
Rodopi
Pindus Mountains

1: 2 500 000

10 0 10 20 30 40 50 miles

10 0 10 20 30 40 50 60 70 80 km

AEGEAN SEA
IONIAN SEA
SEA OF CRETE
(Sea of Candia)
KIKLÁDHES
(CYCLADES)
ARKHIPÉLAGOS
DHODHEKÁNISOS
(DODECANESE)
PELOPÓNNISOS KAI DHITIKÍ IPROTIKÍ ÉLLAS
ATTIKÍ
AKARNANÍA
AITOLÍA
KORINTHÍA
ARKADHÍA
MESSINÍA
LAKONÍA
AKHAÏA
FOKÍS
VOIOTÍA
TURKEY
AYDIN
MUĞLA
ATHÍNAI
(ATHENS)
Piraiévs
(Piraeus)
Pátrai
Kórinthos
Corinth Canal
Korinthiakós Kólpos
Saronikós Kólpos
Argolikós Kólpos
Lakonikós Kólpos
Messiniakós Kólpos
Kiparissiakós Kólpos
Pátraikós Kólpos
Kefallinía
(Cephalonia)
Zákinthos
(Zante)
Itháki
(Ithaca)
Levkás
(Santa Maura)
Kíthira
(Cerigo)
Náxos
Páros
Míkonos
Tínos
Ándros
Síros
Kíthnos
Kéa
Sérifos
Sífnos
Mílos
Íos
Thíra
Amorgós
Astipálaia
Ikaría
Khíos
(Chios)
Psará
Skíros
Skópelos
Sámos
Kos
Ródhos
(Rhodes)
Kárpathos
Kásos
Iráklion
(Candia)
Khaniá
(Canea)
Réthimnon
Taïyetos Óros
Párnon Óros
Stenón Kásos
Stenón Karpáthos
Kerme Körfezi
Kuşadasi Körfezi
Mandalya Körfezi
Continuation Eastwards on same scale
East from Greenwich
Projection: Conical with two standard parallels

ft m
9000 3000
6000 2000
4500 1500
3000 1000
1200 400
600 200
0 0
200 600
2000 6000
m ft

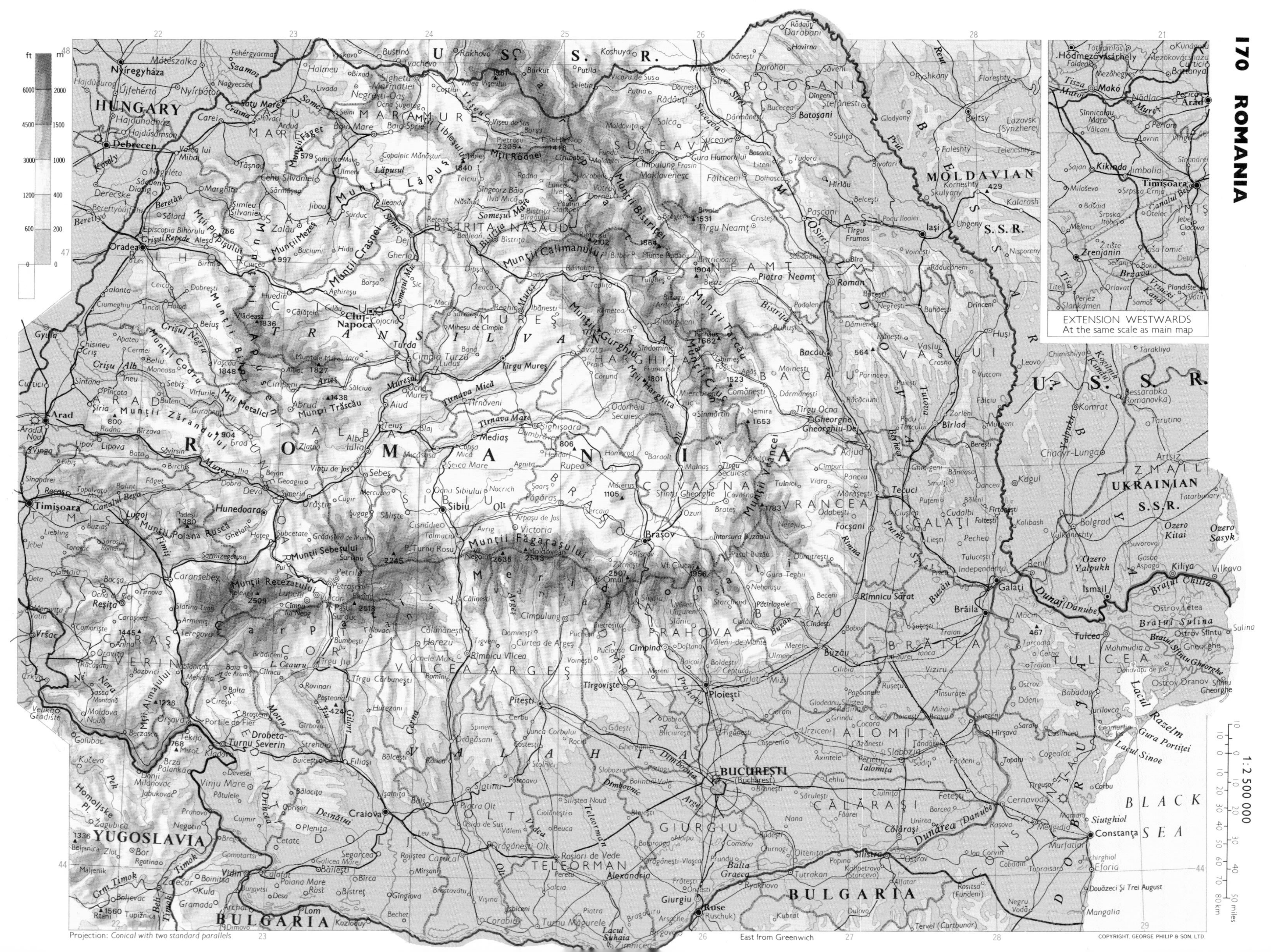
1:2 500 000
50 miles
80 km
EXTENSION WESTWARDS
At the same scale as main map
ROMANIA
BUCUREŞTI
(Bucharest)
HUNGARY
BULGARIA
YUGOSLAVIA
U. S. S. R.
MOLDAVIAN S.S.R.
UKRAINIAN S.S.R.
BLACK SEA
East from Greenwich
Projection: Conical with two standard parallels
COPYRIGHT. GEORGE PHILIP & SON, LTD.

1:2 500 000

10 0 10 20 30 40 50 miles

10 0 10 20 30 40 50 60 70 80 km

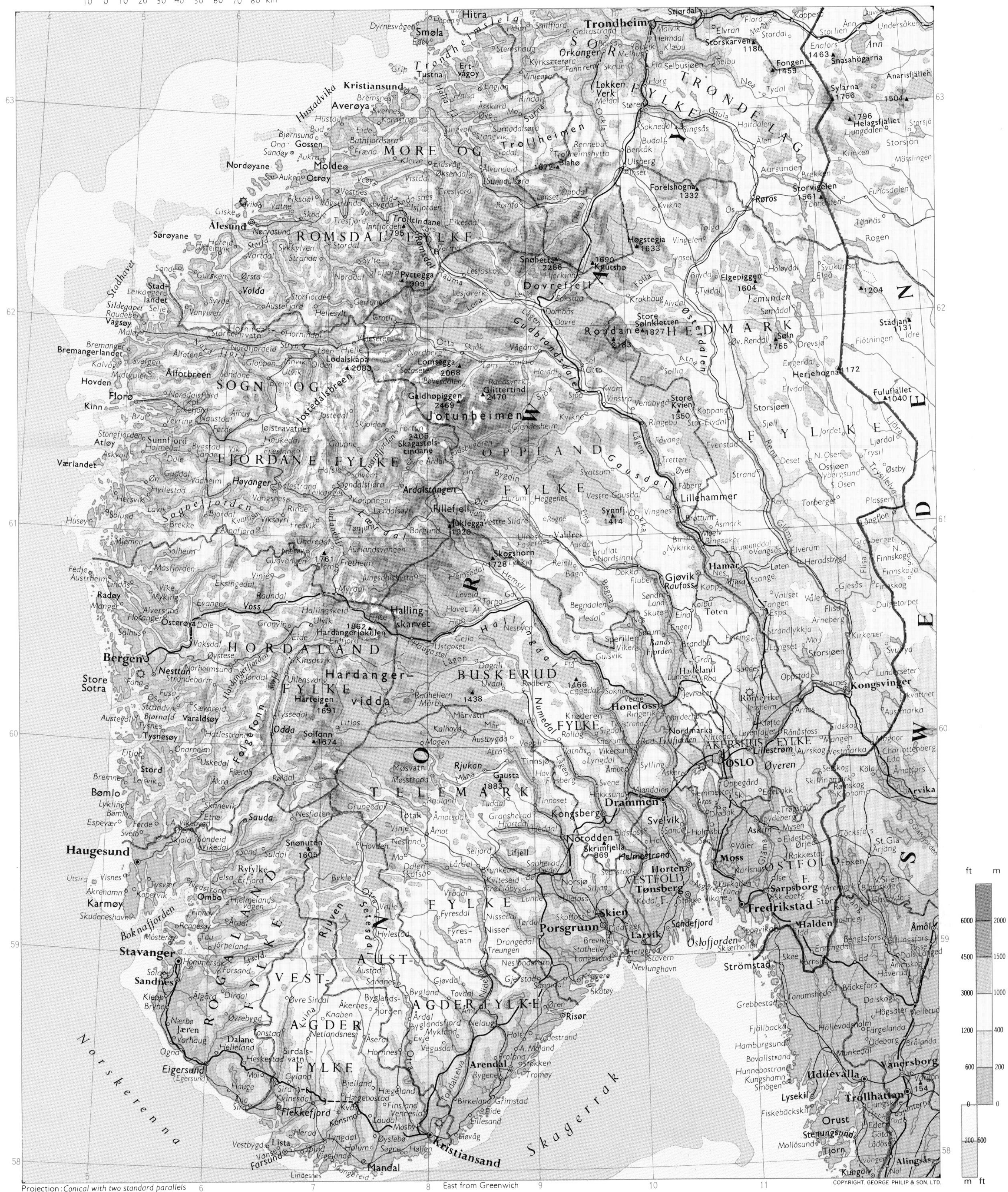
Trondheim
Kristiansund
Molde
Ålesund
MØRE OG ROMSDAL FYLKE
SØR-TRØNDELAG
Trollheimen
Dovrefjell
Snøhetta 2286
Røros
HEDMARK
Rondane
Gudbrandsdalen
Jotunheimen
Galdhøpiggen 2469
Glittertind 2470
SOGN OG FJORDANE FYLKE
Jostedalsbreen
Sognefjorden
Florø
OPPLAND FYLKE
Lillehammer
Hamar
Gjøvik
Bergen
Voss
HORDALAND
Hardangerjøkulen
Hardangervidda
BUSKERUD
Hønefoss
Drammen
OSLO
AKERSHUS FYLKE
Lillestrøm
Kongsvinger
Haugesund
Stavanger
Sandnes
ROGALAND FYLKE
TELEMARK
Kongsberg
Skien
Porsgrunn
Larvik
Tønsberg
VESTFOLD
Sandefjord
Moss
ØSTFOLD
Sarpsborg
Fredrikstad
Halden
AUST-AGDER FYLKE
VEST-AGDER FYLKE
Arendal
Kristiansand
Mandal
Flekkefjord
Eigersund
Skagerrak
Norskerenna
Oslofjorden
Strömstad
Uddevalla
Vänersborg
Trollhättan
Arvika
SWEDEN
Stadhavet
Hitra
Smøla
ft m
6000 2000
4500 1500
3000 1000
1200 400
600 200
0 0
200 600
m ft

Projection: *Conical with two standard parallels*

East from Greenwich

Gulf of Bothnia
Örnsköldsvik
Härnösand
Sundsvall
Hudiksvall
Söderhamn
Gävle
Uppsala
STOCKHOLM
Norrtälje
Södertälje
Västerås
Eskilstuna
Örebro
Karlstad
Falun
Borlänge
Mora
Östersund
Trondheim
Oslo
Drammen
Hamar
Lillehammer
Gjøvik
Kongsberg
Skien
Porsgrunn
Larvik
Tønsberg
Fredrikstad
Sarpsborg
Halden
Moss
Kristiansund
Molde
JÄMTLANDS LÄN
GÄVLEBORGS LÄN
KOPPARBERGS LÄN
VÄRMLANDS LÄN
UPPSALA LÄN
STOCKHOLMS LÄN
VÄSTMANLANDS LÄN
SÖDERMANLANDS LÄN
ÖREBRO LÄN
VÄSTERNORRLANDS LÄN
HEDMARK FYLKE
OPPLAND FYLKE
BUSKERUD FYLKE
TELEMARK FYLKE
ØSTFOLD
VESTFOLD
AKERSHUS FYLKE
SØR TRØNDELAG FYLKE
MØRE OG ROMSDAL FYLKE
Jotunheimen
Dovrefjell
Rondane
Gudbrandsdalen
Hjälmaren
Transtrandsfjällen

1:2 500 000

10 0 10 20 30 40 50 miles

10 0 10 20 30 40 50 60 70 80 km

Projection: Conical with two standard parallels

East from Greenwich

ICELAND
on the same scale as general map
West from 18 Greenwich
Arctic Circle
Vatnajökull
Reykjavík
Akureyri
Keflavík
Akranes
Húsavík
Seyðisfjörður
Hafnarfjörður
NORWEGIAN SEA
Lofoten
Vesterålen
Vestfjorden
Narvik
Tromsø
Hammerfest
Vadsø
Nordkapp
Kiruna
Gällivare
Boden
Luleå
Haparanda
Tornio
Kemi
Rovaniemi
Oulu
Umeå
Skellefteå
Piteå
Lycksele
Bodø
Mo
Mosjøen
Namsos
Steinkjer
Levanger
Trondheim
Kristiansund
Molde
Ålesund
Östersund
Örnsköldsvik
Kramfors
Härnösand
Vaasa
Kokkola
Jakobstad
Kuopio
Jyväskylä
NORRBOTTEN
VÄSTERBOTTEN
N.-TRØNDELAG
SØR-TRØNDELAG
GULF OF BOTHNIA

1:5 000 000

20 10 0 20 40 60 80 100 miles

40 20 0 40 80 120 160 km

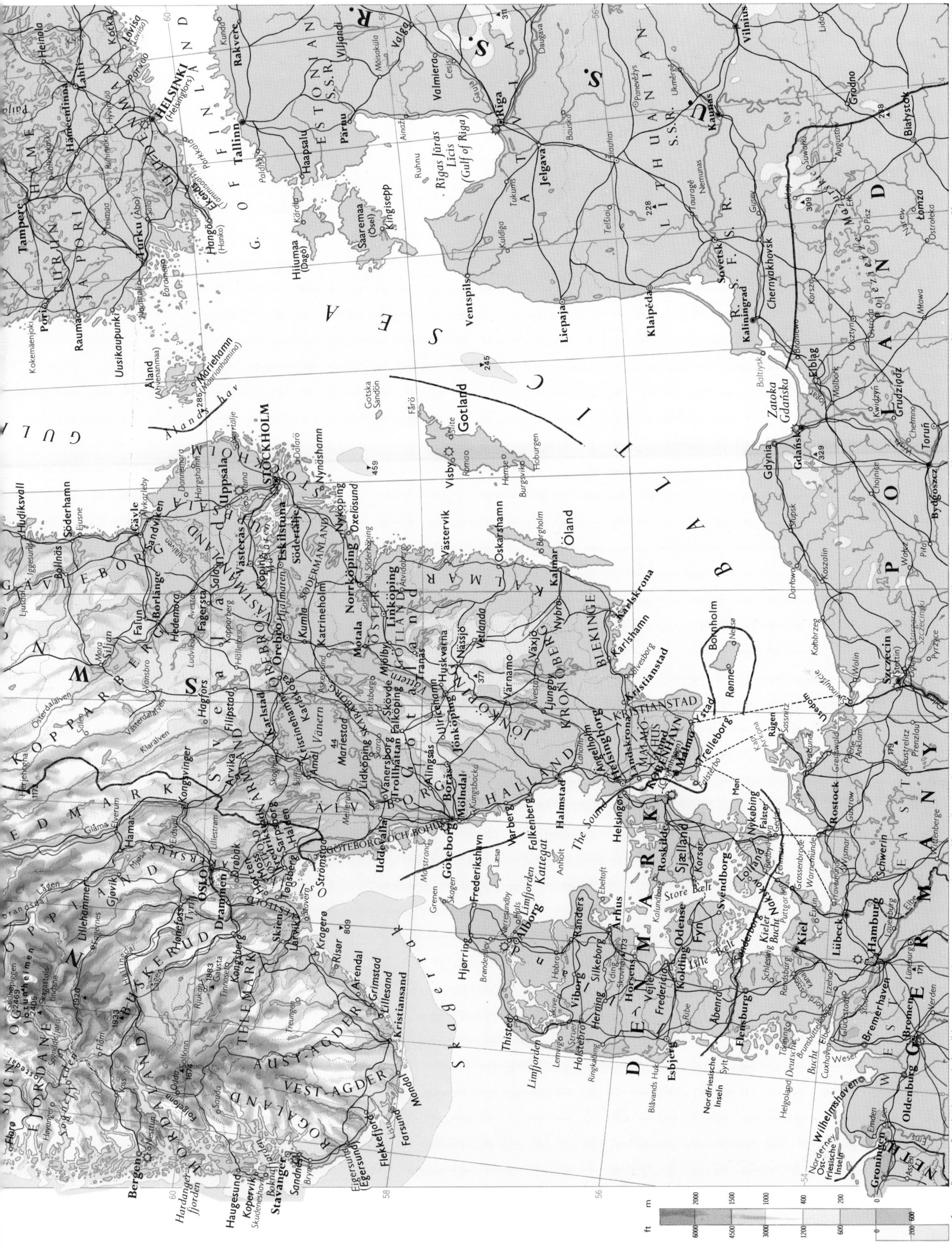

East from Greenwich

Projection: Conical with two standard parallels

m	ft
2000	6000
1500	4500
1000	3000
400	1200
200	600
0	0
200	600

NORWAY
SWEDEN
FINLAND
ESTONIAN S.S.R.
LATVIAN S.S.R.
LITHUANIAN S.S.R.
BYELORUSSIAN S.S.R.
(WHITE RUSSIA)
POLAND
RUSSIAN SOVIET FEDERATIVE SOCIALIST REPUBLIC
KARELIAN A.S.S.R.
Kolskiy Poluostrov
Beloye More (White Sea)
Gulf of Bothnia
G. of Finland
Timanskiy Kryazh
Bolshezemelskaya Tundra
Malozemelskaya Tundra
Severnyye Uvaly
Kolguyev
P-ov. Kanin
Cheshskaya Guba
Pechorskaya Guba
Arctic Circle
Murmansk
Arkhangelsk
(Archangel)
Kotlas
Syktyvkar
Kirov
Perm
Vologda
Yaroslavl
Kostroma
Ivanovo
Gorkiy
Kazan
Ulyanovsk
Kuybyshev
Ufa
Sverdlovsk
Nizhniy Tagil
Orenburg
Penza
Ryazan
Tula
Kaluga
Bryansk
Orel
Smolensk
Vitebsk
Minsk
Mogilev
Gomel
Vilnius
Kaunas
Riga
Tallinn
Helsinki
Stockholm
Turku
Tampere
Leningrad
Novgorod
Pskov
Kalinin
Moskva
(Moscow)
Petrozavodsk
Ladozhskoye Ozero
Onezhskoye Ozero
Cheboksary
Yoshkar Ola
Vladimir
Warszawa
(Warsaw)
Kaliningrad
Brest
Grodno
Bialystok

1 Kabardino-Balkar A.S.S.R.
2 North Ossetian A.S.S.R.
3 Nakhichevan A.S.S.R. (Azer.)
4 Checheno-Ingush A.S.S.R.
CASPIAN SEA
BLACK SEA
MEDITERRANEAN SEA
Levant
Azovskoye More (Sea of Azov)
Zaliv Kara Bogaz Gol
Karagiye Depression
KALMYK A.S.S.R.
Prikaspiyskaya Nizmennost
KAZAKH S.S.R.
Kirgiz Steppe
GEORGIAN S.S.R.
ARMENIAN S.S.R.
AZERBAIJAN S.S.R.
MOLDAVIAN S.S.R.
UKRAINIAN S.S.R.
TURKEY
SYRIA
IRAQ
IRAN (PERSIA)
CYPRUS
LEBANON
ROMANIA
BULGARIA
Bolshoi Kavkaz
Kuzey Anadolu Dağlari
Toros Dağlari
Alborz
Bādiyat ash Sham
KIYEV
KHARKOV
Volgograd (Stalingrad)
Rostov
Odessa
Sevastopol
Krasnodar
Tbilisi
Yerevan
BAKU
Astrakhan
TEHRĀN
Baghdād
Dimashq (Damascus)
Bayrūt (Beirut)
Halab
Ankara
ISTANBUL
İzmir (Smyrna)
BUCUREȘTI (Bucharest)
Trabzon
Tabrīz
Erzurum
Projection: Conical with two standard parallels
Division between Greeks and Turks in Cyprus; Turks to the North.
East from Greenwich
ft m
12 000 4000
6000 2000
3000 1000
1200 400
600 200
0 0
200 600
1000 3000
2000 6000
4000 12 000
m ft
1:10 000 000
100 50 0 50 100 150 200 miles
100 0 100 200 300 km

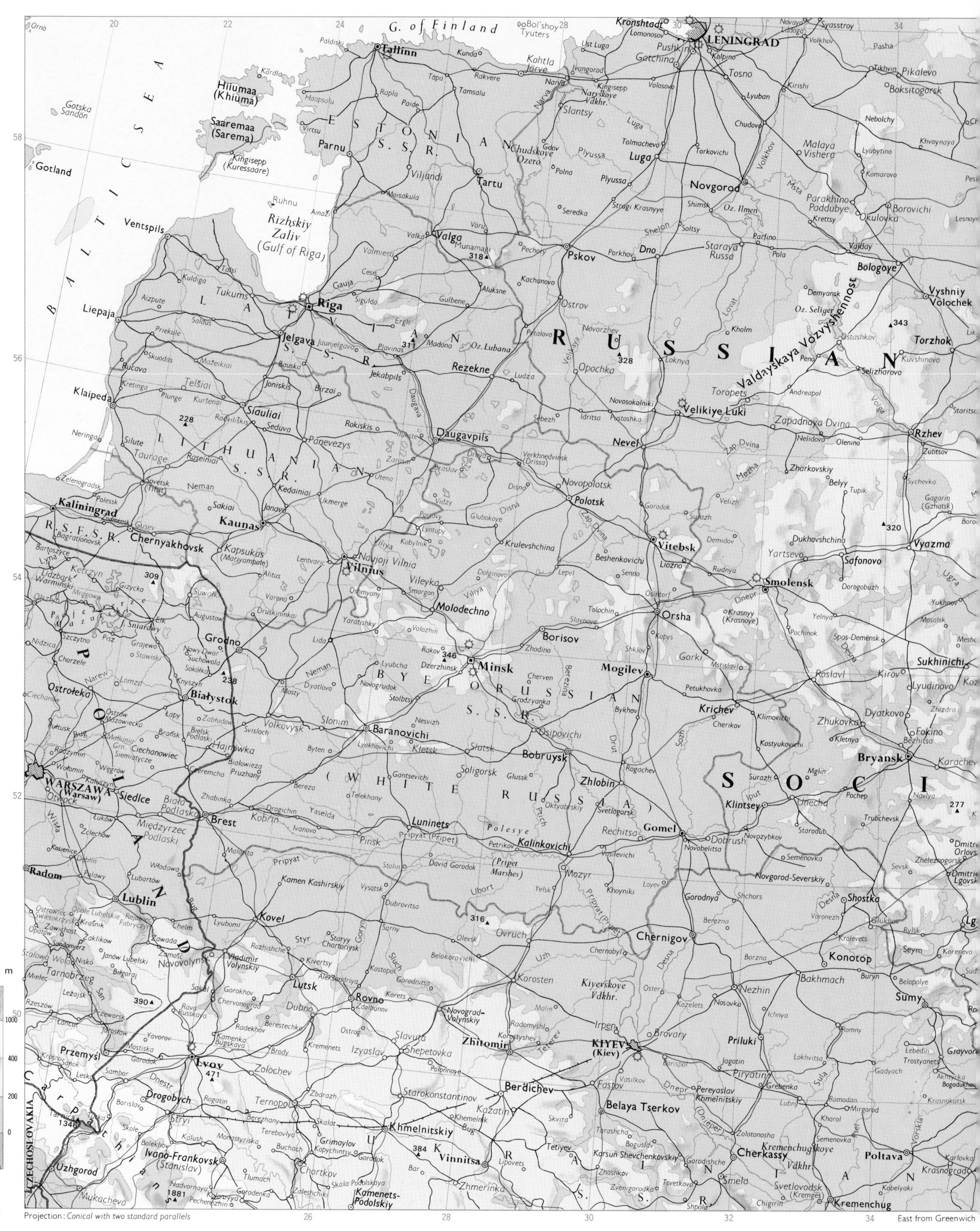
G. of Finland
BALTIC SEA
Rizhskiy Zaliv (Gulf of Riga)
ESTONIAN S.S.R.
LATVIAN S.S.R.
LITHUANIAN S.S.R.
BYELORUSSIAN S.S.R. (WHITE RUSSIA)
RUSSIAN SOVIET
UKRAINIAN S.S.R.
POLAND
R.S.F.S.R.
LENINGRAD
Tallinn
Riga
Vilnius
Minsk
Kiyev (Kiev)
Warszawa (Warsaw)
Kaliningrad
Smolensk
Projection: Conical with two standard parallels
East from Greenwich

1:5 000 000

50 0 50 100 miles

50 0 50 100 150 km

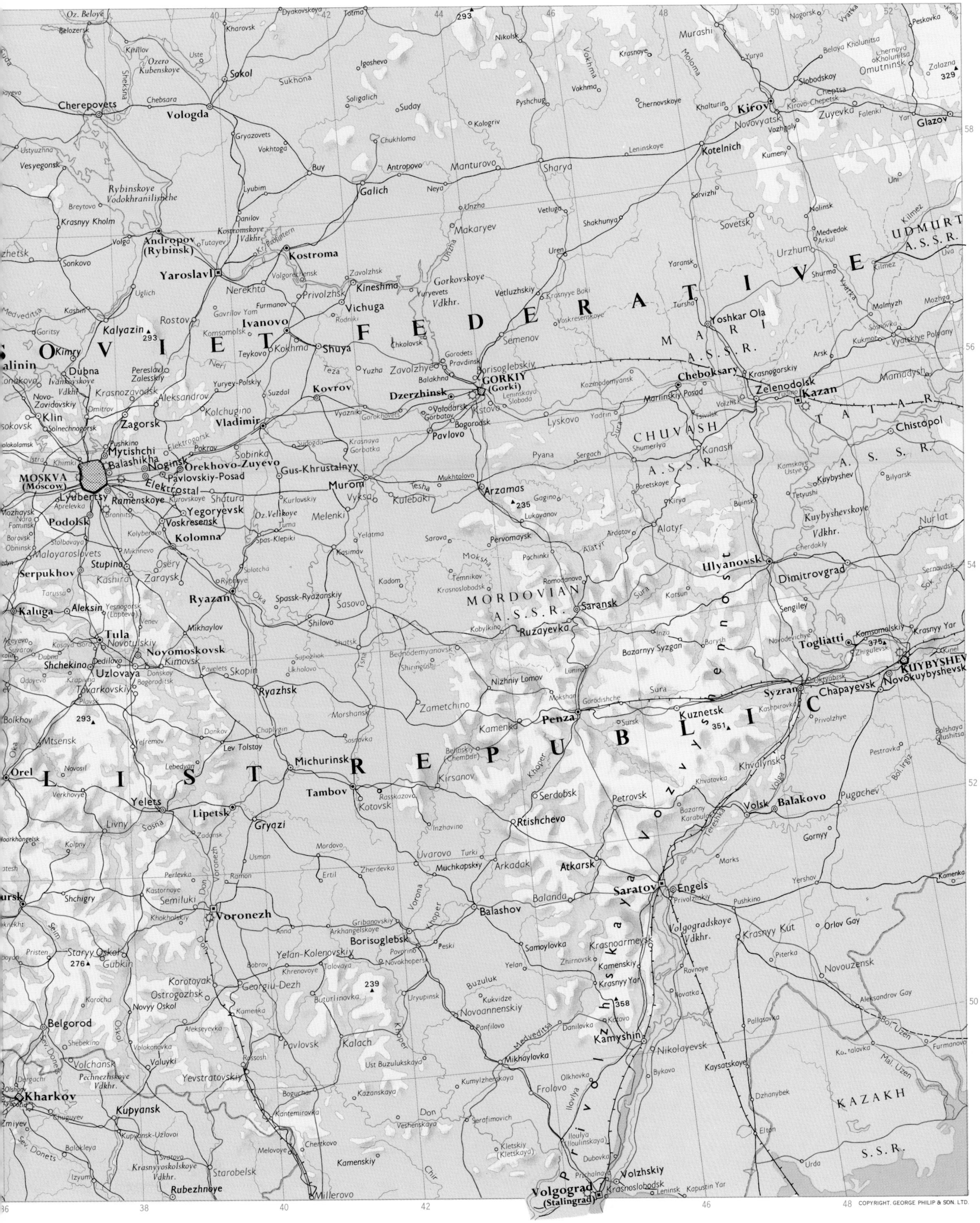

SOVIET FEDERATIVE SOCIALIST REPUBLIC

UDMURT A.S.S.R.

MARI A.S.S.R.

CHUVASH A.S.S.R.

TATAR A.S.S.R.

MORDOVIAN A.S.S.R.

KAZAKH S.S.R.

Vozvyshennost Privolzhskaya

MOSKVA (Moscow)
Kalinin
Yaroslavl
Kostroma
Ivanovo
Vladimir
Andropov (Rybinsk)
Cherepovets
Vologda
Sokol
Galich
Kirov
Kotelnich
Glazov
Omutninsk
Yoshkar Ola
Cheboksary
Kazan
Zelenodolsk
Chistopol
GORKIY (Gorki)
Dzerzhinsk
Kovrov
Murom
Arzamas
Saransk
Ruzayevka
Ulyanovsk
Dimitrovgrad
Togliatti
KUYBYSHEV
Novokuybyshevsk
Syzran
Chapayevsk
Penza
Kuznetsk
Ryazan
Tula
Novomoskovsk
Kaluga
Serpukhov
Podolsk
Kolomna
Orel
Yelets
Lipetsk
Tambov
Michurinsk
Voronezh
Belgorod
Kharkov
Kursk
Saratov
Engels
Balakovo
Volsk
Balashov
Borisoglebsk
Kamyshin
Volgograd (Stalingrad)
Volzhskiy
Millerovo

Rybinskoye Vodokhranilishche

Gorkovskoye Vdkhr.

Kuybyshevskoye Vdkhr.

Volgogradskoye Vdkhr.

38 40 42 44 46 48 50 52

58 56 54 52 50

Lvov
Rovno
Dubno
Korosten
Nezhin
Bakhmach
Sumy
Belgorod
Starvy Oskol
Zhitomir
KIYEV
(Kiev)
Kiyevskoye Vdkhr.
Berdichev
Priluki
Khmelnitskiy
Belaya Tserkov
Kharkov
Ternopol
Vinnitsa
Poltava
Kupyansk
Ivano-Frankovsk
(Stanislav)
Cherkassy
Kremenchugskoye Vdkhr.
Smela
Uman
Kremenchug
Kirovograd
Chernovtsy
Dneprodzerzhinsk
Dnepropetrovsk
Pavlograd
Kramatorsk
Slavyansk
Artemovsk
Konstantinovka
Gorlovka
Makeyevka
Donetsk
(Stalino)
Krivoy Rog
Zaporozhye
Nikopol
Beltsy
Pervomaysk
Kishinev
Tiraspol
Bendery
Nikolayev
Kherson
Odessa
Melitopol
Zhdanov
Berdyansk
Taganrog
Yeysk
U K R A I N I A N S. S. R.
MOLDAVIAN S.S.R.
ROMANIA
Carpathians
Bacău
Iasi
Brașov
Galați
Braila
Ploiești
BUCUREȘTI
(Bucharest)
Constanța
Ismail
Ruse
Varna
Burgas
BULGARIA
Edirne
Kirklareli
AZOVSKOYE
MORE
(Sea of Azov)
Karkinitskiy Zaliv
Dzhankoi
Krymskiy P.-ov.
(Crimea)
Yevpatoriya
Simferopol
Sevastopol
Yalta
Feodosiya
Kerch
Kerchenskiy Proliv
Novorossiysk
Anapa
Gelendzhik
B L A C K   S E A
Nos Kaliakra
İnce-Burnu
Zonguldak
Karadeniz Boğazi
(Bosporus)
İstanbul
Üsküdar
MARMARA DENIZI
(Sea of Marmara)
İzmit
Adapazari
Bursa
Samsun
Sinop
Kuzey Anadolu
T U R K
Ankara
ft
m
12 000
9000
6000
4500
3000
1200
600
0
200
2000
4000
3000
2000
1500
1000
400
200
0
600
6000
m
ft
Projection: Conical with two standard parallels

1:5 000 000
50 0 50 100 miles
50 0 50 100 150 km
Volgograd (Stalingrad)
Volzhskiy
Krasnoslobodsk
Krasnoarmeysk
Kamyshin
Nikolayevsk
Frolovo
Privolzhskaya
Vozyshennost
Volgogradskoye Vdkhr.
Krasnyy Kut
Novouzensk
Novoannenskiy
Uryupinsk
Georgiu-Dezh
Ostrogozhsk
Yelan-Kolenovskiy
Buturlinovka
Pavlovsk
Kalach
Millerovo
Starobelsk
Voroshilovgrad (Lugansk)
Kamensk-Shakhtinskiy
Morozovsk
Belaya Kalitva
Gukovo
Krasnodon
Krasnyy Luch
Rovenki
Snezhnoye
Novoshakhtinsk
Shakhty
Novocherkassk
Rostov
Bataysk
Azov
Tsimlyansk
Volgodonsk
Tsimlyanskoye Vdkhr.
Kotelnikovo
Veselovskoye Vdkhr.
Zernograd
Proletarskaya
Salsk
Oz. Manych-Gudilo
Kushchevskaya
Kanevskaya
Tikhoretsk
Timashevsk
Korenovsk
Krasnodar
Ust-Labinsk
Armavir
Stavropol
Nevinnomyssk
Svetlograd (Petrovskoye)
Blagodarnoye
Elista (Stepnoi)
Ergeni Vozyshennost
KALMYK A.S.S.R.
Astrakhan
Prikaspiyskaya Nizmennost
KAZAKH S.S.R.
Guryev
Akhtubinsk (Petropavlovskiy)
Kapustin Yar
Elton
Dzhanybek
Shungay
Urda
Zelënyy
Makhambet (Yamankhalinka)
Inderborskiy
Kalmykovo
Karsha
Mergenevskiy
Chapayevo
Oz. Chalkar
Dzhambeyty
Aleksandrov Gay
Ural
Bol. Uzen
Mal. Uzen
Krasnyy Yar
CASPIAN SEA
Mangyshlakskiy Zaliv
P-ov. Mangyshlak
O. Kulaly
M. Tyub Karagan
Fort Shevchenko
Shevchenko
Kultay
Tyuleniy
O. Chechen
Kaspiyskiy
Kizlyar
Prikumsk
Zelenokumsk (Vorontsovo-Aleksandrovskoye)
Cherkessk
Mineralnyye Vody
Pyatigorsk
Yessentuki
Kislovodsk
Maykop
Labinsk
Mozdok
CHECHENO-INGUSH A.S.S.R.
Groznyy
Gudermes
Makhachkala
Kaspiysk
Buynaksk
DAGESTAN A.S.S.R.
Derbent
Nalchik
KABARDINO-BALKAR A.S.S.R.
N. OSSETIAN A.S.S.R.
Ordzhonikidze
Beslan
Bolshoy Kavkaz (Caucasus)
Elbrus 5633
Kazbek 5047
Tebulos 4492
Bazar Dyuzi 4466
Baba dag 3629
Sochi
Adler
Gagra
ABKHAZ A.S.S.R.
Sukhumi
Ochamchire
Tkvarcheli
Kutaisi
GEORGIA S.S.R.
Tskhinvali (Staliniri)
Poti
Batumi
ADZHAR A.S.S.R.
Tbilisi
Rustavi
Telavi
Mingechaurskoye Vdkhr.
Kirovabad
AZERBAIJAN S.S.R.
Sumgait
BAKU
Kazi Magomed
Siazan
Leninakan
Kirovakan
ARMENIAN S.S.R.
Yerevan
Ozero Sevan
Aragats 4090
Kars
Trabzon
Rize
Hopa
Doğu Karadeniz Dağlari
East from Greenwich

1:5 000 000

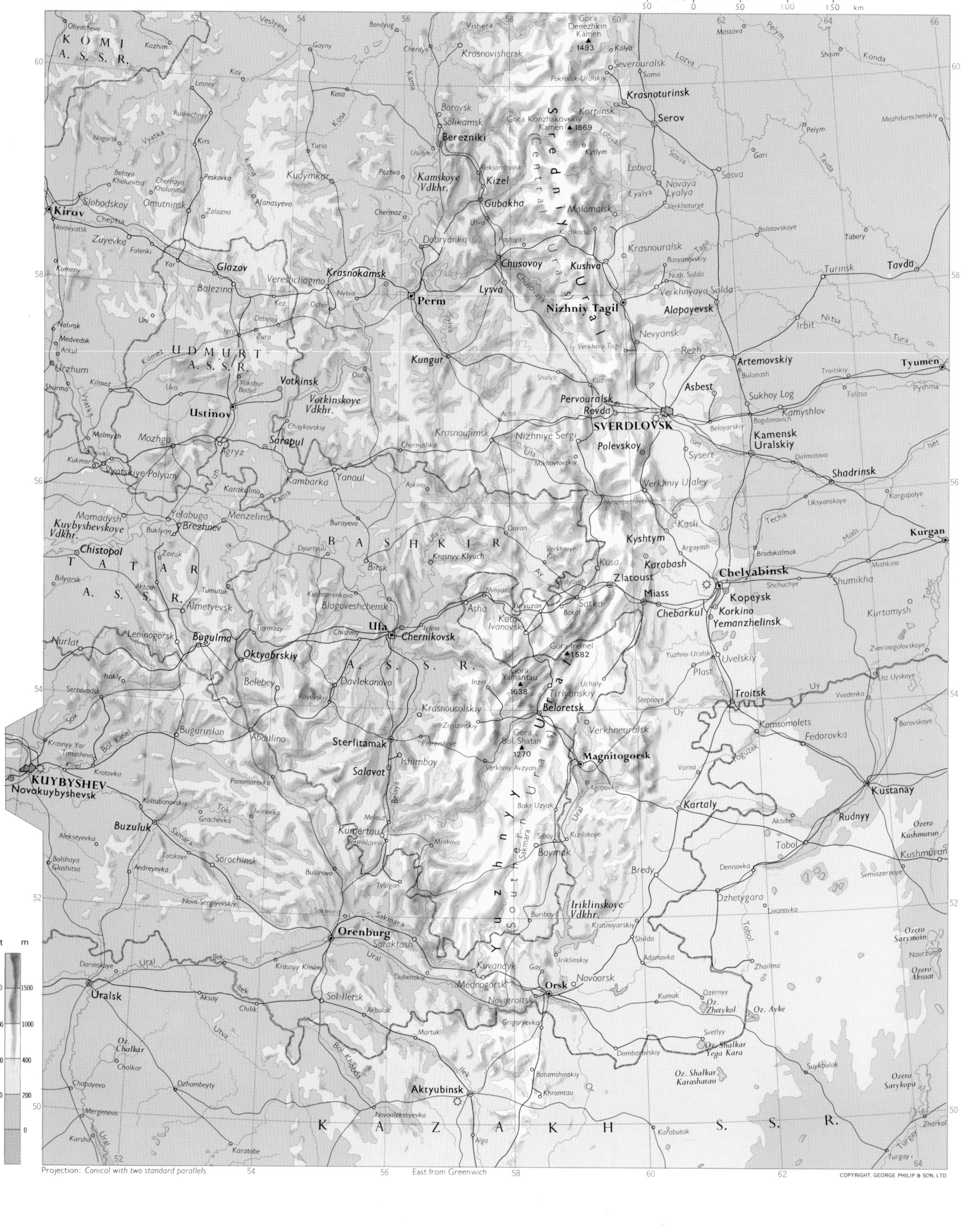

50 0 50 100 miles

50 0 50 100 150 km

KOMI A. S. S. R.

UDMURT A. S. S. R.

TATAR A. S. S. R.

BASHKIR A. S. S. R.

KAZAKH S. S. R.

Srednyiy Ural (Central Urals)

Yuzhnyy Ural (Southern Urals)

Gora Denezhkin Kamen 1493
Gora Konzhakovskiy Kamen 1569
Gora Iremel 1582
Gora Yamantau 1638
Gora Bol. Shatan 1270

Obyachevo, Kazhim, Veslyana, Bondyug, Vishera, Gayny, Cherdyn, Krasnovishersk, Kalya, Severouralsk, Lozva, Pelym, Massava, Shaim, Konda, Pokrovsk-Uralskiy, Sama, Kay, Lesnoy, Kosa, Kama, Krasnoturinsk, Serov, Karpinsk, Borovsk, Solikamsk, Berezniki, Usolye, Rudnichnyy, Nagorsk, Vyatka, Kirs, Yuria, Kytlym, Lobva, Sosva, Gari, Pelym, Tavda, Mezhdurechenskiy, Belaya Kholunitsa, Chernaya Kholunitsa, Peskovka, Kudymkar, Pozhva, Aleksandrovsk, Kamskoye Vdkhr., Kizel, Novaya Lyalya, Lyalya, Verkhoturye, Kirov, Slobodskoy, Omutninsk, Zalazna, Afanasyevo, Chermoz, Gubakha, Malomalsk, Novovyatsk, Cheptsa, Usva, Kachkanar, Bolotovskoye, Tabory, Zuyevka, Falenki, Dobryanka, Pashiya, Krasnouralsk, Tagil, Basyanovskiy, Chusovoy, Kushva, Nizh. Salda, Turinsk, Tavda, Kumeny, Yar, Glazov, Krasnokamsk, Vereshchagino, Balezino, Nytva, Perm, Lysva, Chusovaya, Verkhnyaya Salda, Nizhniy Tagil, Alapayevsk, Ocher, Kez, Debessy, Uni, Igra, Zura, Sylva, Nitsa, Irbit, Nevyansk, Verkhniy Tagil, Rezh, Tura, Nolinsk, Medvedok, Arkul, Kilmez, Urzhum, Kungur, Artemovskiy, Bulanash, Troitskiy, Tyumen, Shurma, Uva, Yakshur Bodya, Votkinsk, Osa, Shalya, Kuzino, Asbest, Sukhoy Log, Talitsa, Pyshma, Votkinskoye Vdkhr., Ustinov, Pervouralsk, Revda, Achit, Kamyshlov, Bogdanovich, Beloyarskiy, Malmyzh, Mozhga, Chaykovskiy, Sarapul, Krasnoufimsk, Nizhniye Sergi, SVERDLOVSK, Kamensk Uralskiy, Polevskoy, Agryz, Chernushka, Iset, Sysert, Dalmatovo, Kukmor, Vyatskiye Polyany, Izh, Ufa, Mikhaylovsk, Yanaul, Karakulino, Kambarka, Askino, Verkhniy Ufaley, Shadrinsk, Kargapolye, Nyazepetrovsk, Uksyanskoye, Mamadysh, Yelabuga, Menzelinsk, Kuybyshevskoye Vdkhr., Brezhnev, Buklyan, Burayevo, Duvan, Kasli, Techa, Miass, Kurgan, Chistopol, Zainsk, Dyurtyuli, Krasnyy Klyuch, Verkhniye Kigi, Kyshtym, Argayash, Karabash, Brodokalmak, Mishkino, Bilyarsk, Aktash, Birsk, Kusa, Chelyabinsk, Shchuchye, Shumikha, Tumutuk, Kushnarenkovo, Blagoveshchensk, Minyar, Ay, Kardyash, Zlatoust, Kopeysk, Almetyevsk, Asha, Yuryuzan, Satka, Bakal, Chebarkul, Korkino, Yemanzhelinsk, Kurtamysh, Tobol, Tuymazy, Iglino, Katav Ivanovsk, Leninogorsk, Bugulma, Chishmy, Chernikovsk, Nurlat, Oktyabrskiy, Yuzhno-Uralsk, Uvelskiy, Zverinogolovskoye, Isakly, Belebey, Davlekanovo, Inzer, Uchaly, Plast, Ust Uyskoye, Uy, Sernovodsk, Rayevskiy, Tirlyanskiy, Stepnoye, Troitsk, Vvedenka, Sok, Krasnousolskiy, Beloretsk, Borovskoye, Buguruslan, Zigazinskiy, Verkhneuralsk, Komsomolets, Krasnyy Yar, Timashevo, Bol. Kinel, Abdulino, Sterlitamak, Petrovskoye, Fedorovka, Kinel, Krotovka, Ishimbay, Verkhniy Avzyan, Magnitogorsk, Toguzak, KUYBYSHEV, Novokuybyshevsk, Ponomarevka, Salavat, Belaya, Varna, Agapovka, Kustanay, Koltubanovskiy, Tok, Ivanovka, Bakr Uzyak, Kartaly, Rudnyy, Buzuluk, Grachevka, Meleuz, Aktobe, Ozero Kushmurun, Alekseyevka, Samara, Kumertau, Yermolayevo, Mrakovo, Sakmara, Sibay, Kizilskoye, Tobol, Kushmurun, Bolshaya Glushitsa, Totskoye, Andreyevka, Sorochinsk, Baymak, Bredy, Denisovka, Semiozernoye, Bulanovo, Tyulgan, Novo-Sergiyevskiy, Iriklinskoye Vdkhr., Buribay, Dzhetygara, Livanovka, Orenburg, Saraktash, Krasnoyarskiy, Shilda, Ozero Sarymoin, Darinskoye, Ural, Ilek, Krasnyy Kholm, Kuvandyk, Iriklinskiy, Adamovka, Zhailma, Naurzum, Ozero Aksuat, Uralsk, Aksay, Dubenskiy, Mednogorsk, Gay, Orsk, Novoorsk, Sol Iletsk, Chilik, Akbulak, Novotroitsk, Kumak, Ozernyy, Oz. Zhetykol, Oz. Ayke, Utva, Martuk, Grigoryevka, Svetlyy, Oz. Chalkar, Chalkar, Bol. Khobda, Oz. Shalkar Yega Kara, Dombarovskiy, Suykbulak, Batamshinskiy, Or, Oz. Shalkar Karashatau, Ozero Sarykopa, Chapayevo, Dzhambeyty, Aktyubinsk, Khromtau, Mergenevo, Novoalekseyevka, Karabutak, Zharkol, Turgay, Karsha, Karatobe, Alga

ft m
4500 1500
3000 1000
1200 400
600 200
0 0

Projection: Conical with two standard parallels — East from Greenwich

1:5 000 000

50 0 50 100 miles

50 0 50 100 150 km

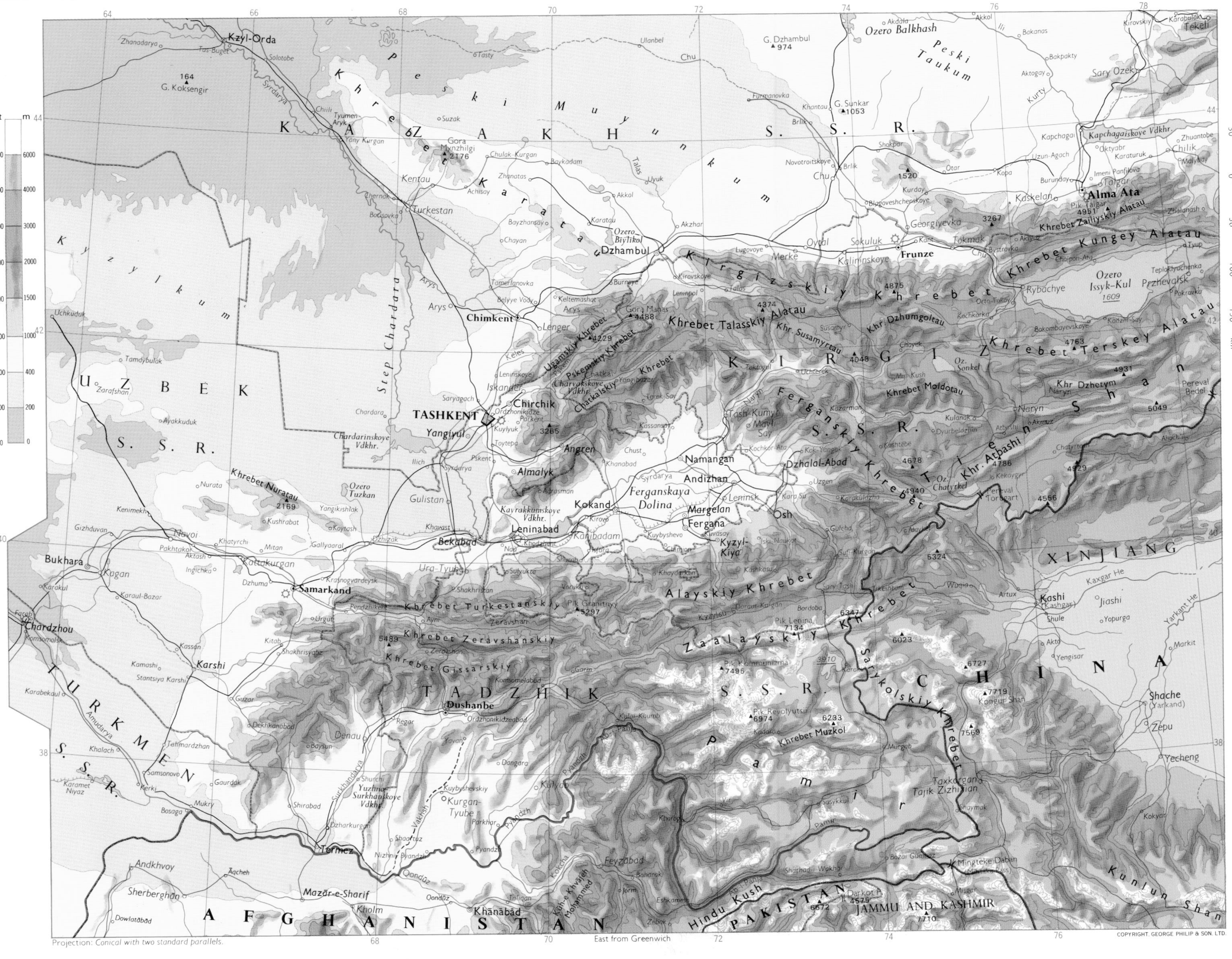
TASHKENT
Chimkent
Chirchik
Yangiyul
Angren
Almalyk
Leninabad
Kokand
Namangan
Andizhan
Fergana
Margelan
Osh
Dzhalal-Abad
Dzhambul
Frunze
Alma Ata
Dushanbe
Samarkand
Bukhara
Karshi
Termez
Chardzhou
Kzyl-Orda
Turkestan
Kashi
Shache
K A Z A K H S. S. R.
K I R G I Z S. S. R.
U Z B E K S. S. R.
T A D Z H I K S. S. R.
T U R K M E N S. S. R.
A F G H A N I S T A N
C H I N A
X I N J I A N G
PAKISTAN
JAMMU AND KASHMIR
Ozero Issyk-Kul
Ozero Balkhash
Peski Taukum
Peski Muyunkum
Kyzylkum
Step Chardara
Ferganskaya Dolina
Kirgizskiy Khrebet
Khrebet Terskey Alatau
Khrebet Kungey Alatau
Alayskiy Khrebet
Zaalayskiy Khrebet
Khrebet Turkestanskiy
Khrebet Zeravshanskiy
Khrebet Gissarskiy
Ferganskiy Khrebet
Khrebet Karatau
Tien Shan
Pamir
Kunlun Shan
Hindu Kush
Amudarya
Syrdarya
Chu
Ili
Naryn
Pik Kommunizma 7495
Pik Lenina 7134
Projection: Conical with two standard parallels.
East from Greenwich
ft 18 000 12 000 9000 6000 4500 3000 1200 600 0
m 6000 4000 3000 2000 1500 1000 400 200 0

R.S.F.S.R.
1. Daghestan A.S.S.R.
2. Kabardino-Balkar A.S.S.R.
3. Mari A.S.S.R.
4. Mordovian A.S.S.R.
5. North Ossetian A.S.S.R.
6. Tatar A.S.S.R.
7. Udmurt A.S.S.R.
8. Chuvash A.S.S.R.
9. Checheno-Ingush A.S.S.R.
AZERBAIJAN
10. Nakhichevan A.S.S.R.
GEORGIA
11. Abkhaz A.S.S.R.
12. Adzhar A.S.S.R.
ft m
12000 4000
6000 2000
3000 1000
1200 400
600 200
0 0
200 600
m ft
NORWAY
SWEDEN
FINLAND
POLAND
DENMARK
TURKEY
IRAN (PERSIA)
IRAQ
AFGHANISTAN
RUSSIAN SOVIET FEDERATIVE S.S.R.
KAZAKH S.S.R.
UZBEK S.S.R.
TURKMEN S.S.R.
KIRGIZ S.S.R.
TADZHIK S.S.R.
BYELORUSSIAN S.S.R.
UKRAINIAN S.S.R.
MOLDAVIAN S.S.R.
LITHUANIAN S.S.R.
LATVIAN S.S.R.
ESTONIAN S.S.R.
GEORGIAN S.S.R.
ARMENIAN S.S.R.
AZERBAIJAN S.S.R.
KARELIAN A.S.S.R.
KARAKALPAK A.S.S.R.
North Sea
Baltic Sea
Gulf of Bothnia
G. of Finland
Barents Sea
Kara Sea
Beloye More
Black Sea
Caspian Sea
Azovskoye More
Aralskoye More
Ozero Balkhash
Zemlya Frantsa Iosifa
Novaya Zemlya
Moskva
Leningrad
Kiyev
Minsk
Riga
Tallinn
Vilnius
Kishinev
Tbilisi
Yerevan
Baku
Tashkent
Alma Ata
Frunze
Dushanbe
Ashkhabad
Sverdlovsk
Novosibirsk
Omsk
Stockholm
Oslo
København
Helsinki
Warszawa
Berlin
Tehrān
Baghdad
Projection: Conical Orthomorphic with two standard parallels
East from Greenwich

1:20 000 000
100 0 100 200 300 400 500 miles
100 0 200 400 600 800 km
Mys Dezhneva (East C.)
St. Lawrence I. (U.S.A.)
Chukotskoye More
Chukotskiy Khrebet
Anadyrskiy Zaliv
Ostrov Vrangelya
East Siberian Sea
Ostrova Medvezhi
Novosibirskiye Ostrova
Ostrov Kotelnyy
Lyakhovskiye Ostrova
Proliv Dmitriya Lapteva
Laptev Sea
OCEAN
Severnaya Zemlya
Ostrov Komsomolets
Ostrov Oktyabrskoy Revolyutsii
Ostrov Bolshevik
Proliv Vilkitskogo
Poluostrov Taymyr
Gory Byrranga
Nordvik
Khatanga
Tiksi
Verkhoyansk
Verkhoyanskiy Khrebet
Khrebet Cherskogo
Srednekolymsk
Kolyma
Koryakskiy Khrebet
Bering Sea
Komandorskiye Ostrova
Poluostrov Kamchatka
Petropavlovsk-Kamchatskiy
Okhotsk
Magadan
Sea of Okhotsk
YAKUT A.S.S.R.
SOCIALIST REPUBLIC
Arctic Circle
Yakutsk
Olekminsk
Vilyuysk
Lena
Aldan
Stanovoy Khrebet
Dzhugdzhur Khrebet
Nikolayevsk-na-Amure
Sakhalin
Sovetskaya Gavan
Yuzhno-Sakhalinsk
Kurilskiye Ostrova
Khabarovsk
Komsomolsk
Blagoveshchensk
Sikhote Alin
Vladivostok
Nakhodka
Ussuriysk
Sea of Japan
Hokkaido
Sapporo
Hakodate
Honshu
Nii-gata
To-yama
Kanazawa
Kirensk
Bratsk
Krasnoyarsk
Nizhneudinsk
Irkutsk
Angarsk
Ulan Ude
Chita
BURYAT A.S.S.R.
Yablonovyy Khrebet
Da Hinggan Ling
Qiqihar
Harbin
Jilin
Changchun
Shenyang
Fushun
Anshan
Dandong
Yingkou
Lüda
Beijing
Zhangjiakou
Baotou
MONGOLIA
Ulaanbaatar (Ulan Bator)
Hangayn Nuruu
Hentiyn Nuruu
GOBI
Hulun Nur
Choybalsan
NORTH KOREA
P'yongyang
Chongjin
SOUTH KOREA
Sŏul
Inch'on
Taejŏn
Pusan
PEOPLE'S REPUBLIC
Boundaries of U.S.S.R.
Boundaries of S.S.R.
Boundaries of A.S.S.R.
COPYRIGHT, GEORGE PHILIP & SON, LTD.

ASIA

PACIFIC OCEAN
ARCTIC OCEAN
INDIAN OCEAN
Bering Sea
Sea of Okhotsk
Sea of Japan
Yellow Sea
East China Sea
South China Sea
Sulu Sea
Celebes Sea
Banda Sea
Arafura Sea
Java Sea
Bay of Bengal
Arabian Sea
G. of Oman
G. of Aden
Red Sea
Caspian Sea
Black Sea
Aral Sea
Mediterranean Sea
Adriatic Sea
Baltic Sea
North Sea
Barents Sea
Kara Sea
Laptev Sea
White Sea
The Gulf
Aleutian Is.
Kurile Is.
Ryukyu Is.
Philippine Is.
Caroline Is.
Palau Is.
Moluccas
Andaman Is.
Nicobar Is.
Laccadive Is.
Maldive Is.
Chagos Arch.
Seychelles
Amirantes
Hokkaido
Honshu
Kyushu
Shikoku
Sakhalin
Formosa
Luzon
Mindanao
Halmahera
Celebes
Borneo
Sumatra
Java
Timor
Flores
Ceram
Bali
New Guinea
Australia
Hainan
Ceylon
Cyprus
Socotra
Iceland
British Isles
Greenland
Svalbard
Novaya Zemlya
Severnaya Zemlya
New Siberian Is.
Wrangel I.
Kolguyev I.
Kola Pen.
Taimyr Peninsula
Kamchatka Peninsula
Malay Peninsula
Somali Peninsula
Scandinavia
Finland
Arctic Circle
Tropic of Cancer
Equator
Ural Mountains
Verkhoyansk Range
Stanovoy Ra.
Yablonovy Ra.
Sayan Mts.
Altai
Tien Shan
Kunlun Shan
Himalaya
Karakoram Ra.
Hindu Kush
Pamirs
Sulaiman Ra.
Elburz Mts.
Caucasus
Taurus Mts.
Carpathians
Western Ghats
Eastern Ghats
Great Khingan Mts.
Sikhote Alin Ra.
Sredinny Ra.
Gydan Ra. (Kolyma)
Central Siberian Plateau
West Siberian Plain
North European Plain
Central Russian Uplands
Turan Plain
Plateau of Tibet
Plateau of Iran
Plateau of Mongolia
Manchurian Plain
Great Plain of China
Tarim Basin
Turfan Basin
Takla Makan
Gobi
Thar
Syrian Desert
Libyan Desert
Great Salt Desert
Arabia
Anatolia
Mesopotamia
Deccan
India
China
Steppe
Lena
Yenisei
Ob
Irtysh
Tobol
Angara
Lower Tunguska
Amur
Sungari
Hwang Ho
Yangtze
Si-kiang
Mekong
Menam
Salween
Irrawaddy
Brahmaputra
Ganga
Indus
Narmada
Godavari
Krishna
Amu Darya
Syr Darya
Tigris
Euphrates
Volga
Ural
Don
Dnepr
Danube
Vistula
Oder
Elbe
Rhine
Nile
N. Dvina
Kolyma
Indigirka
L. Baikal
L. Balkhash
Koko Nor
Lop Nor
Dead Sea
Lake Victoria
Str. of Malacca
Makasar Strait
Sunda Str.
Palk Strait
Bering Str.
La Perouse Str.
Korea Str.
Bosporus
Suez Canal
Sinai Pen.
C. Comorin
Gulf of Mannar
North Cape
C. Chelyuskin
C. Dezhnev
Everest 8848
8611
7495
Elbrus 5633
Ararat 5165
Demavend 5604
Belukha 4506
Kinabalu 4101
Narodnaya 1894
1640
Klyuchevskaya Volcano 4750
Cape Johnson Deep 10 497
11 022
10 554
10 542
7822
Projection: Bonne
East from Greenwich
COPYRIGHT GEORGE PHILIP & SON, LTD.
m
ft
6000
4000
2000
1000
400
200
0
18 000
12 000
6000
3000
1200
600

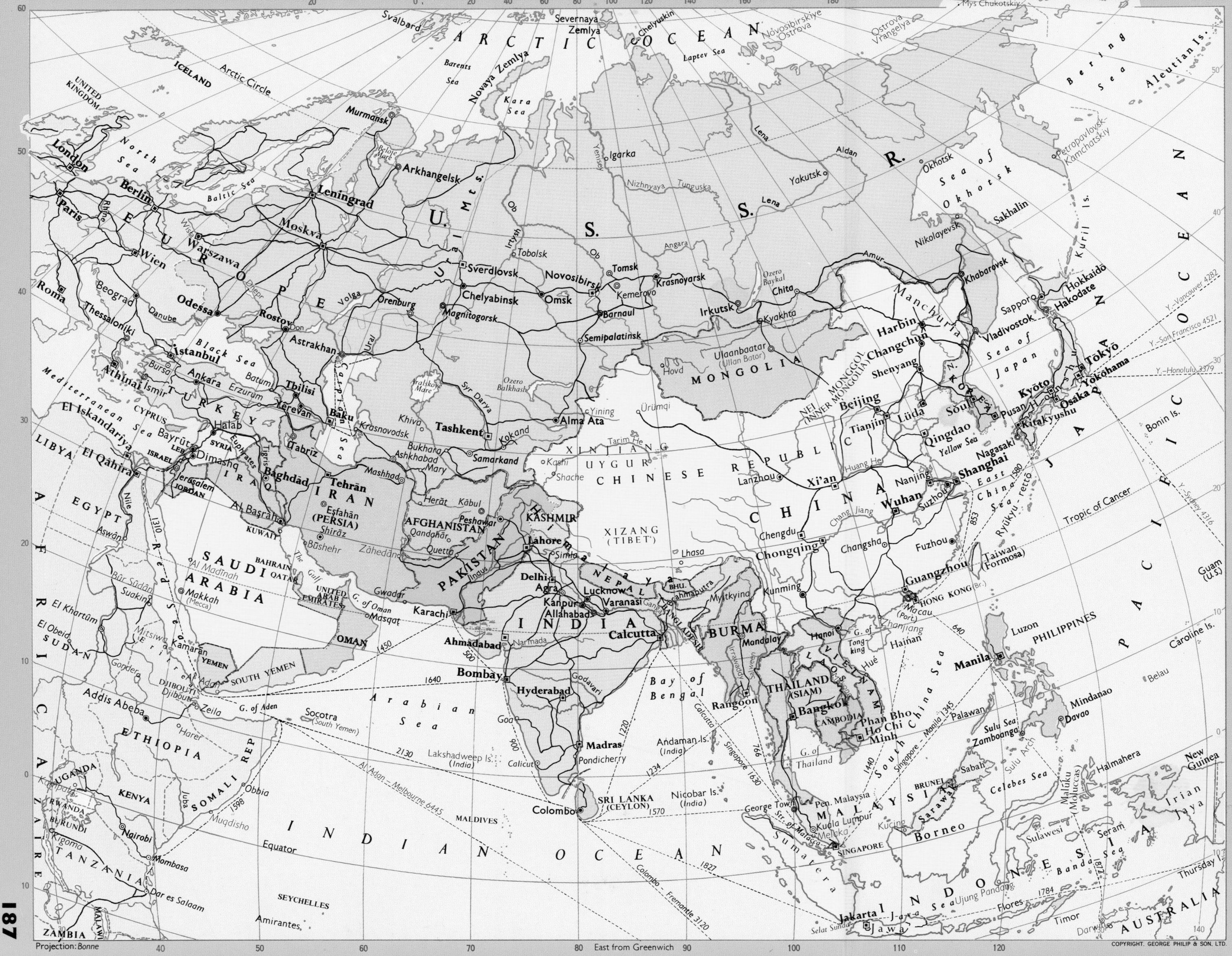

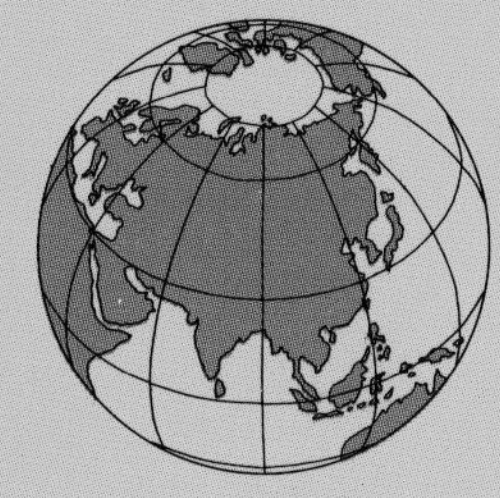

1: 50 000 000

East from Greenwich

0 200 400 600 800 1000 miles

0 200 400 800 1200 1600 km

Projection: Bonne

1:15 000 000

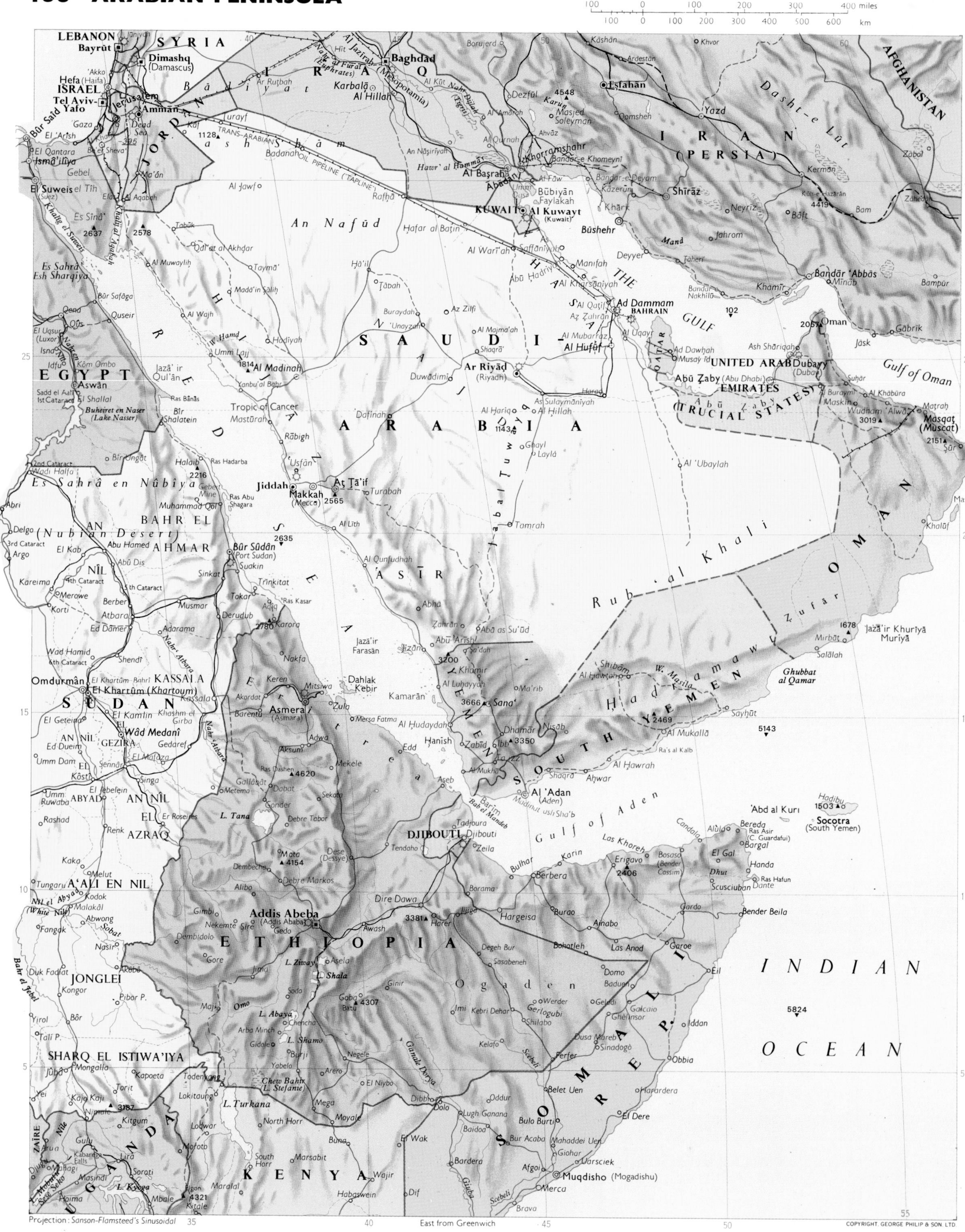
SYRIA
IRAQ
JORDAN
ISRAEL
LEBANON
EGYPT
SUDAN
SAUDI ARABIA
KUWAIT
BAHRAIN
QATAR
UNITED ARAB EMIRATES
(TRUCIAL STATES)
OMAN
YEMEN
SOUTH YEMEN
ETHIOPIA
DJIBOUTI
SOMALI REP.
KENYA
UGANDA
IRAN (PERSIA)
AFGHANISTAN
RED SEA
THE GULF
Gulf of Oman
Gulf of Aden
INDIAN OCEAN
Rub' al Khali
An Nafūd
Tropic of Cancer
Socotra (South Yemen)
Projection: Sanson-Flamsteed's Sinusoidal
East from Greenwich

1:1 000 000

10 5 0 10 20 miles

10 0 10 20 30 km

– – – –	1949–1974 Armistice lines between
....	Israel and the Arab States.

Continuation Southwards
1:2 500 000
0 10 20 miles
0 10 20 30 km

Projection: Conical with two standard parallels

East from Greenwich

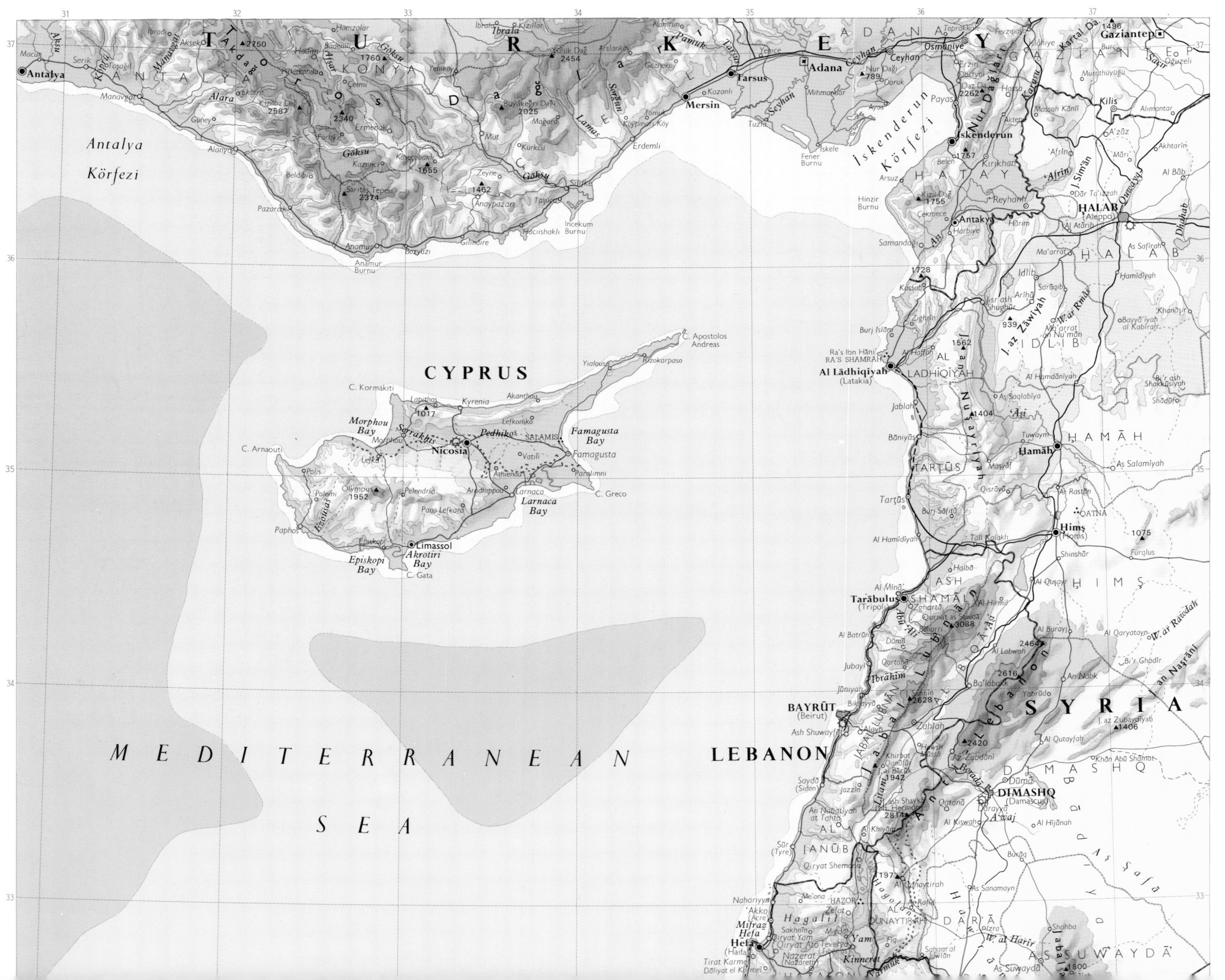
TURKEY
SYRIA
LEBANON
CYPRUS
MEDITERRANEAN SEA
Antalya Körfezi
İskenderun Körfezi
Antalya
Adana
Tarsus
Mersin
İskenderun
Antakya
Gaziantep
Kilis
HALAB (Aleppo)
Hamāh
Hims (Homs)
Al Lādhiqīyah (Latakia)
Tarābulus (Tripoli)
BAYRŪT (Beirut)
DIMASHQ (Damascus)
Şaydā (Sidon)
Şūr (Tyre)
Nicosia
Limassol
Famagusta
Famagusta Bay
Larnaca Bay
Morphou Bay
Episkopi Bay
Akrotiri Bay
Kyrenia
Paphos
C. Apostolos Andreas
C. Greco
C. Arnaouti
C. Kormakiti
C. Gata
Olympus 1952

1:2 500 000

10 0 10 20 30 40 50 miles

10 0 20 40 60 80 km

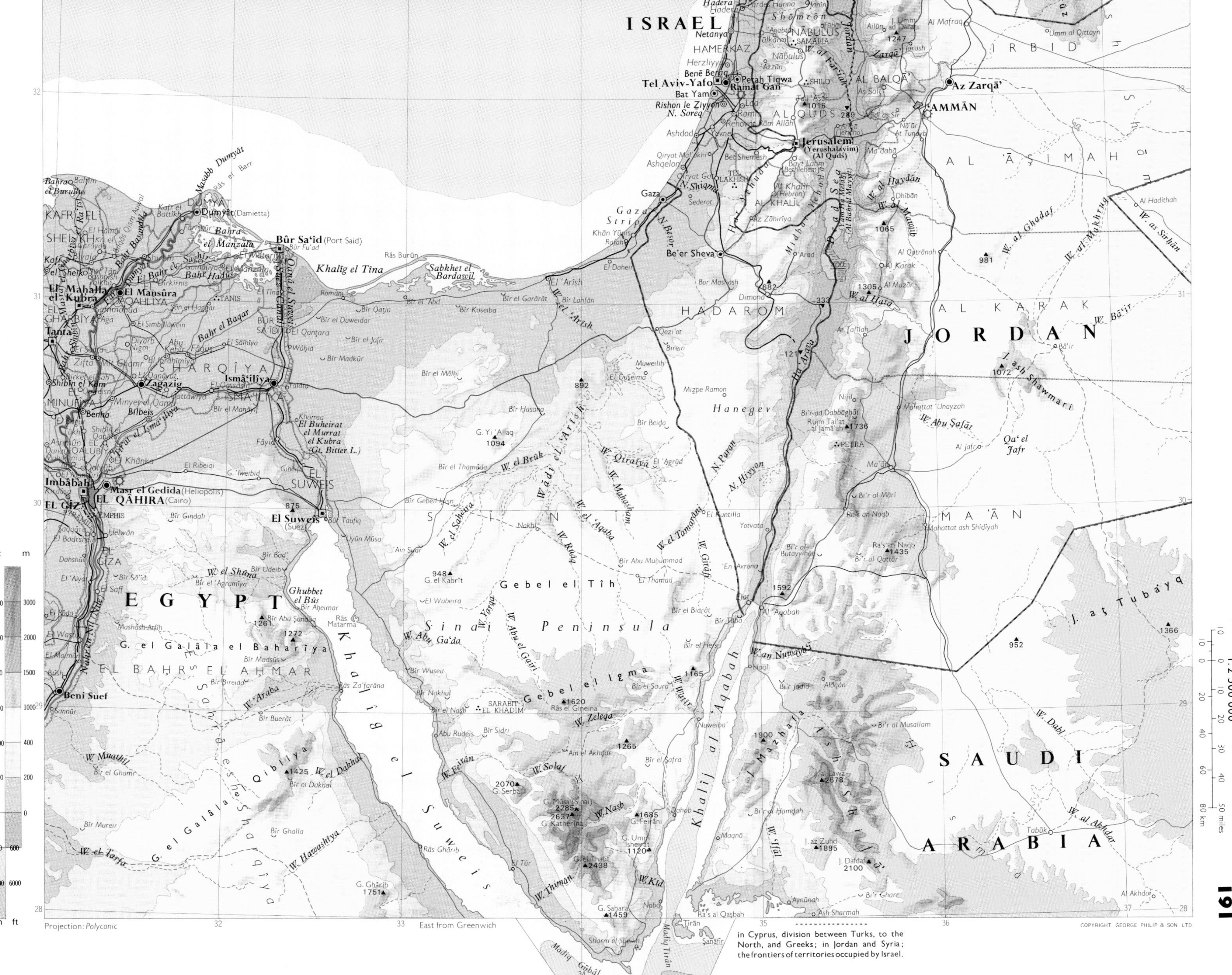
ISRAEL
JORDAN
SAUDI ARABIA
EGYPT
Sinai Peninsula
Gebel el Tîh
Gebel el Igma
Hanegev
HADAROM
HAMERKAZ
AL KARAK
MA'ĀN
AL 'ĀṢIMAH
AL BALQĀ'
IRBID
AL QUDS
Tel Aviv-Yafo
Jerusalem (Yerushalayim) (Al Quds)
'AMMĀN
Az Zarqā'
Gaza
Gaza Strip
Be'er Sheva
Netanya
Ramat Gan
Petah Tiqwa
Bat Yam
Rishon le Ziyyon
Ashdod
Ashqelon
Nābulus
Ma'dabā
Al 'Aqabah
Tabūk
Dead Sea
Khalīj al 'Aqabah
Khalîg el Suweis
Khalîg el Tîna
Sabkhet el Bardawîl
Qanâ el Suweis (Suez Canal)
Bûr Sa'îd (Port Said)
Dumyât (Damietta)
El Mansûra
El Mahalla el Kubra
Tanta
Zagazig
Ismâ'ilîya
El Suweis (Suez)
Masr el Gedîda (Heliopolis)
EL QÂHIRA (Cairo)
Imbâba
EL GÎZA
Beni Suef
Benha
Bilbeis
El 'Arîsh
El Tûr
Sharm el Sheikh
Madîq Tirân
Tirân
Sanâfir
Râs Muhammad
Nahr en Nîl (Nile)
Sahra esh Sharqîya
G. Katherîna 2637
G. Mûsa (Sinai) 2285
J. al Lawz 2578
Jordan
in Cyprus, division between Turks, to the North, and Greeks; in Jordan and Syria; the frontiers of territories occupied by Israel.
East from Greenwich
Projection: Polyconic
COPYRIGHT GEORGE PHILIP & SON, LTD
ft m
9000 3000
6000 2000
4500 1500
3000 1000
1200 400
600 200
0 0
600 200
6000 2000
m ft

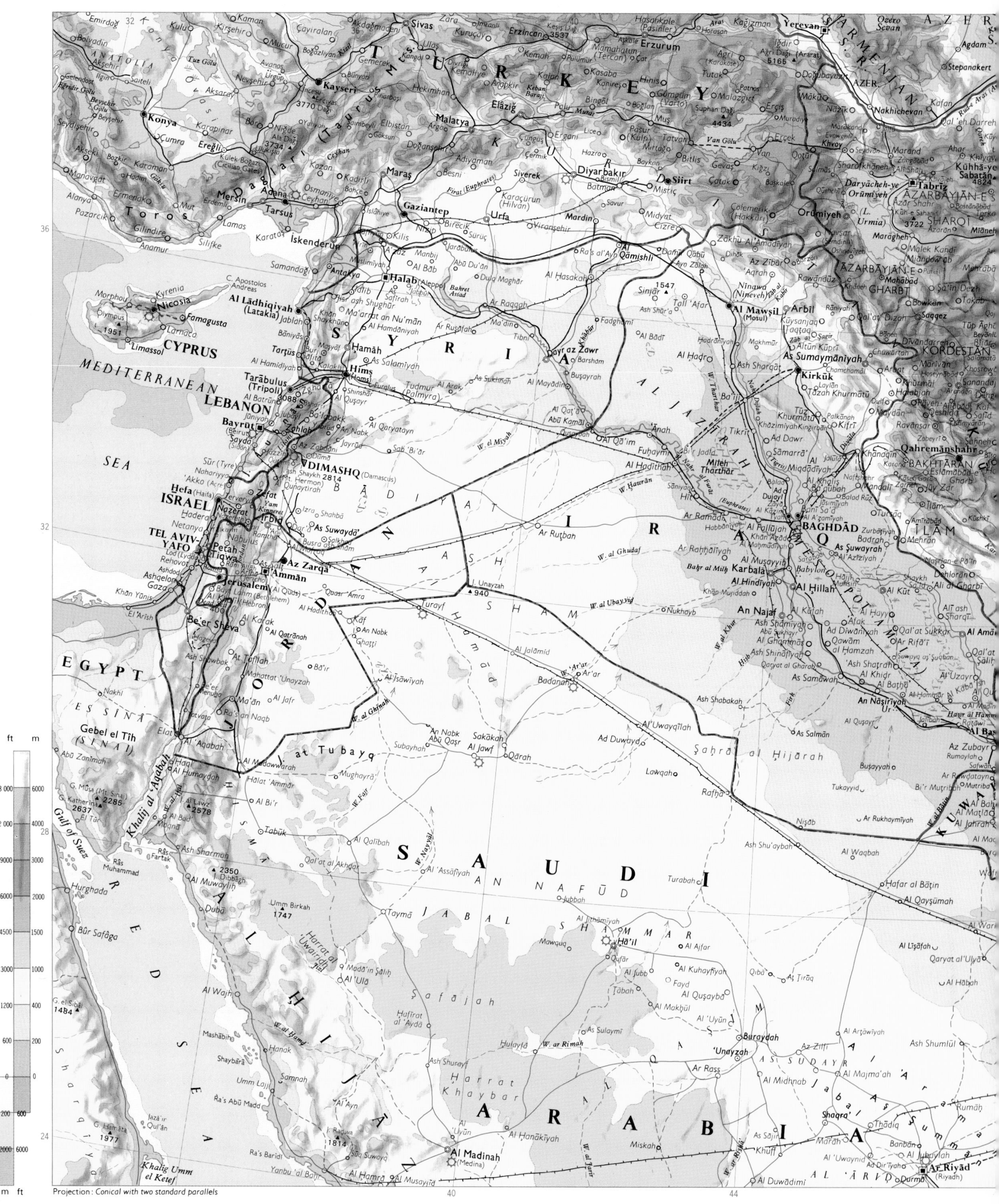

TURKEY
ANATOLIA
Toros
Konya
Kayseri
Sivas
Erzurum
Malatya
Elâzığ
Diyarbakır
Gaziantep
Adana
Mersin
Tarsus
İskenderun
Maraş
Urfa
Mardin
Siirt
Van
Van Gölü
Yerevan
ARMENIAN S.S.R.
AZER.
Nakhichevan
Tabriz
Orūmiyeh
Daryācheh-ye Orūmīyeh
Qahremānshahr
BAKHTARAN
ĪLĀM
KORDESTĀN
CYPRUS
Nicosia
Famagusta
Limassol
MEDITERRANEAN SEA
LEBANON
Bayrūt
Ṭarābulus (Tripoli)
SYRIA
Ḥalab (Aleppo)
Al Lādhiqīyah (Latakia)
Ḥamāh
Ḥimṣ
Dimashq (Damascus)
Dayr az Zawr
Ar Raqqah
Al Qāmishlī
Tudmur (Palmyra)
ISRAEL
Ḥefa (Haifa)
TEL AVIV-YAFO
Jerusalem
Be'er Sheva
JORDAN
'Ammān
Az Zarqā
Al 'Aqabah
IRAQ
BAGHDĀD
Al Mawṣil (Mosul)
Kirkūk
Arbīl
Karbalā
An Najaf
Al Ḥillah
An Nāṣirīyah
Ar Ramādī
Ar Ruṭbah
AL JAZĪRAH
MESOPOTAMIA
KUWAIT
EGYPT
SINAI
Gulf of Suez
Khalīj al 'Aqabah
RED SEA
SAUDI ARABIA
AN NAFŪD
AL ḤIJĀZ
BĀDIYAT ASH SHĀM
Al Madīnah (Medina)
Ar Riyāḍ (Riyadh)
Ḥā'il
Buraydah
Tabūk
Al Jawf
Projection: Conical with two standard parallels
ft
m
18 000
12 000
9000
6000
4500
3000
1200
600
0
200
2000
6000
4000
3000
2000
1500
1000
400
200
0
200
600
6000
m
ft

1:7 000 000

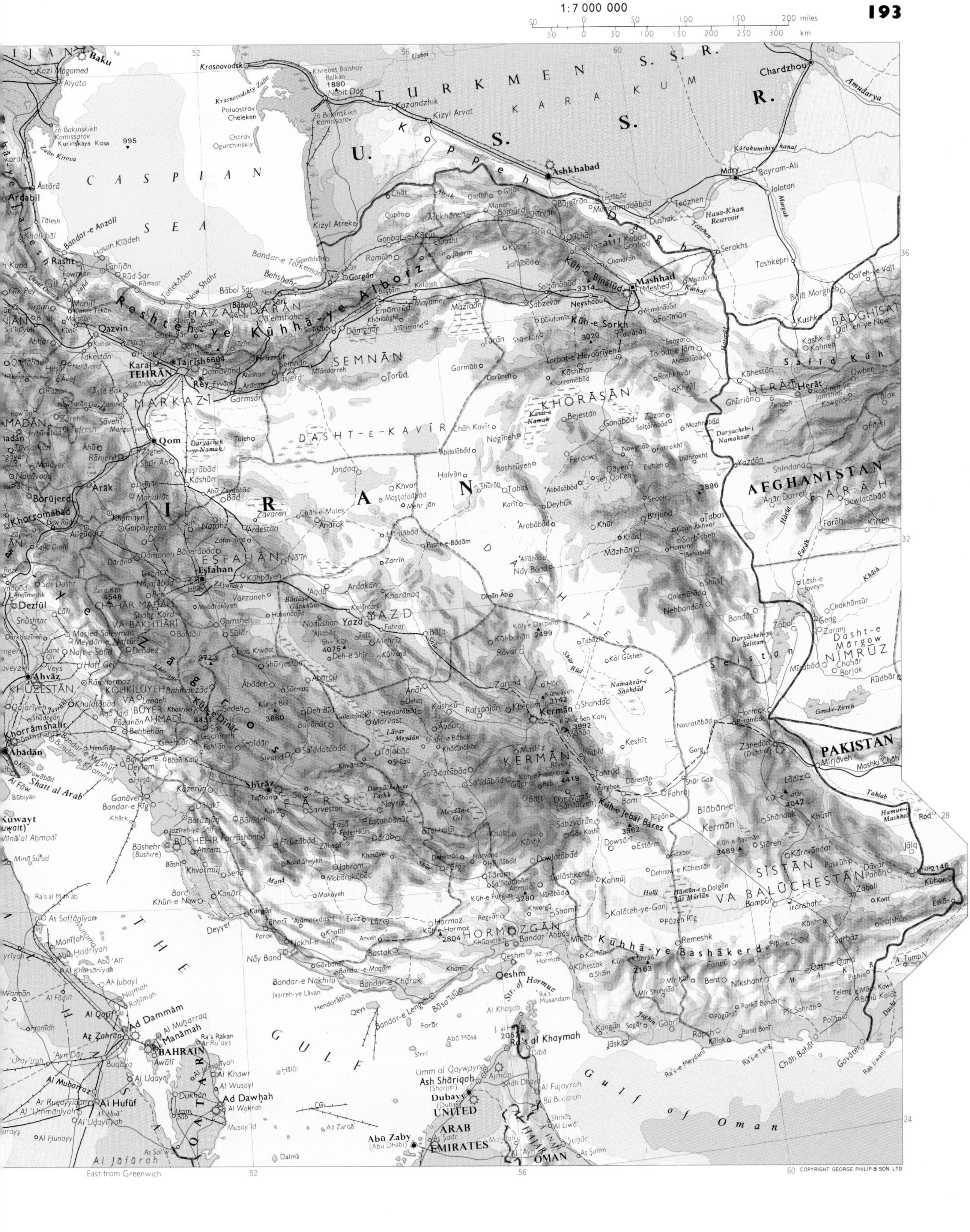

0 50 100 150 200 miles

50 0 50 100 150 200 250 300 km

TURKMEN S.S.R.

U.S.S.R.

KARAKUM

CASPIAN SEA

IRAN

AFGHANISTAN

PAKISTAN

THE GULF

Gulf of Oman

BAHRAIN

QATAR

UNITED ARAB EMIRATES

OMAN

Reshteh-ye Kūhhā-ye Alborz

DASHT-E-KAVĪR

DASHT-E-LUT

Zāgros

Kūhhā-ye Bashākerd

TEHRĀN

Mashhad (Meshed)

Esfahan

Shīrāz

Kermān

Yazd

Ashkhabad

Herāt

East from Greenwich

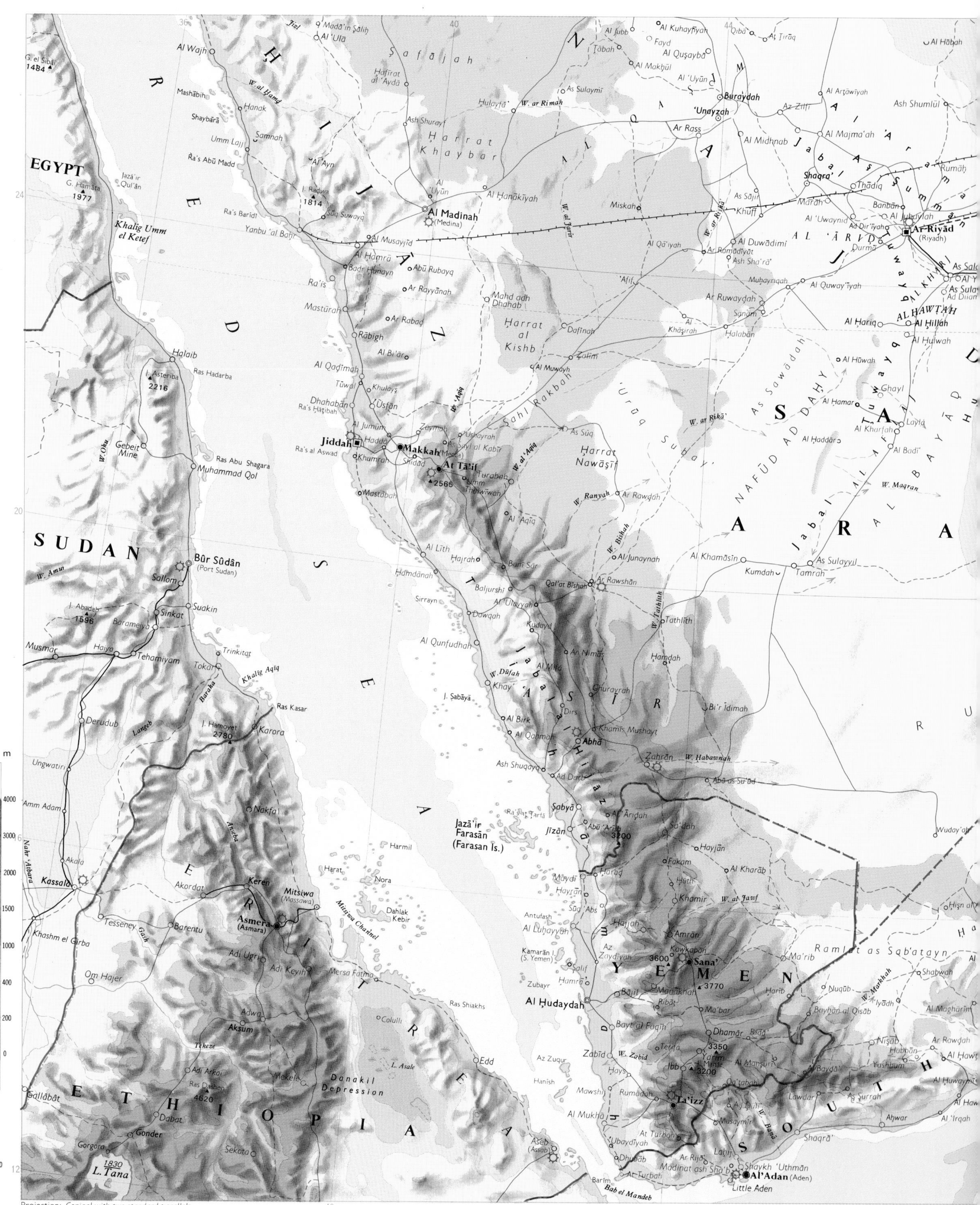
EGYPT
SUDAN
ETHIOPIA
ERITREA
YEMEN
SOUTH
RED SEA
HIJAZ
NAJD
AL 'ARID
ASIR
ARABIA
NAFŪD AD DAHY
Jabal Tuwayq
Jabal al Hijaz
Sahl Rakbah
Harrat Khaybar
Harrat al Kishb
Harrat Nawāṣīf
Ramlat as Sab'atayn
'Urūq Subay'
Al Wajh
Al Madinah
(Medina)
Yanbu 'al Bahr
Badr Hunayn
Mastūrah
Rābigh
Jiddah
Makkah
(Mecca)
At Tā'if
2565
Al Līth
Al Qunfudhah
Abhā
Khamis Mushayt
Jīzān
Jazā'ir Farasān
(Farasān Is.)
Ṣabyā
Sa'dah
3200
Ar Riyād
(Riyadh)
Buraydah
'Unayzah
Ar Rass
Shaqrā'
Al Hawṭah
Al Ḥillah
As Sulayyil
Tamrah
Kumdah
Al Khamāsīn
Tathlīth
Qal'at Bīshah
Ar Rawshān
Zahrān
Najrān
Sanā'
3600
3770
Ma'rib
Al Ḥudaydah
Zabīd
Al Mukhā
Ta'izz
Ibb
3350
3200
Dhamār
Al Bayḍā'
Al 'Adan (Aden)
Little Aden
Shaykh 'Uthmān
Madīnat ash Sha'b
Lahij
Bab el Mandeb
Barim
Kamarān I.
(S. Yemen)
Hanish
Mitsiwa
(Massawa)
Dahlak Kebir
Asmera
(Asmara)
Keren
Akordat
Aksum
Adwa
Mekele
Danakil Depression
L. Asale
Edd
Aseb
(Assab)
Gonder
L. Tana
1830
Ras Dashen
4620
Kassala
Khashm el Girba
Bûr Sûdân
(Port Sudan)
Suakin
Sinkat
Tokar
Halaib
Ras Hadarba
J. Asteriba
2216
G. Ḥamāta
1977
G. el Sibāī
1484
J. Hamoyet
2780
Ras Kasar
Khalig Umm el Ketef
Muhammad Qol
Ras Abu Shagara
Gebeit Mine
ft
m
12 000
9000
6000
4500
3000
1200
600
0
200
2000
4000
4000
3000
2000
1500
1000
400
200
0
600
6000
12 000
m
ft

Projection: Conical with two standard parallels

1:7 000 000

THE GULF
Gulf of Oman
ARABIAN SEA
UNITED ARAB EMIRATES
OMAN
QATAR
BAHRAIN
AR RUB' AL KHALI
Tropic of Cancer
Ad Dammām
Al Manāmah
Ad Dawḥah
Abū Ẓaby
(Abu Dhabi)
Dubayy
(Dubai)
Ash Shāriqah
(Sharjah)
Ra's al Khaymah
Masqaṭ (Muscat)
Al Hufūf
Qeshm
Str. of Hormuz
Ghubbat Ṣawqirah
Khalīj Maṣīrah
Maṣīrah
Kuria Muria Bay
Jazā'ir Khurīyā Murīyā
(Kuria Muria Is.)
(Oman)
Ṣalālah
Ghubbat al Qamar
Al Mukallā
Socotra
(South Yemen)
'Abd al Kūri
(South Yemen)
The Brothers
(South Yemen)
East from Greenwich

1:20 000 000

100 0 100 200 300 400 miles

100 0 100 200 300 400 500 600 km

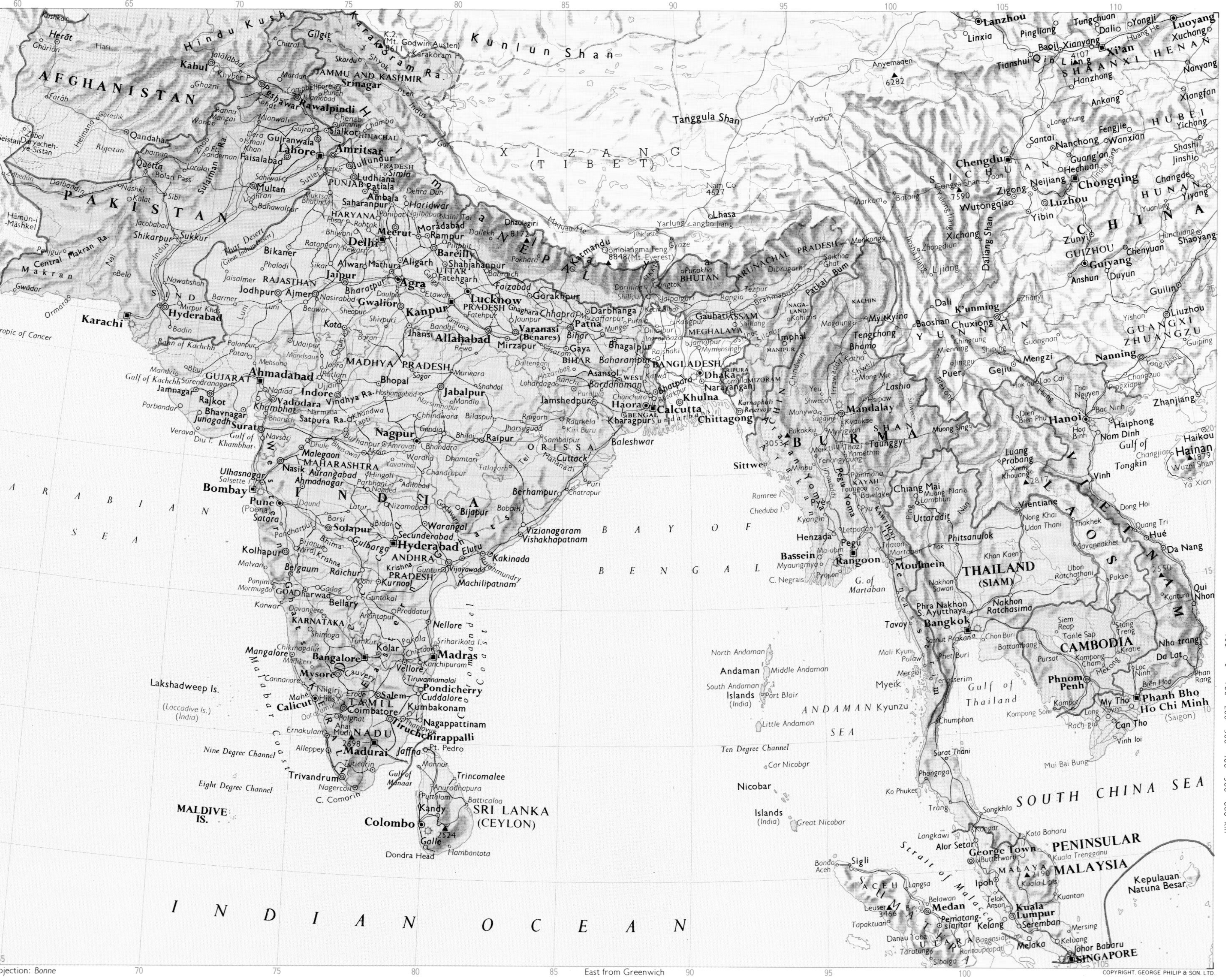
AFGHANISTAN
PAKISTAN
INDIA
NEPAL
BHUTAN
BANGLADESH
BURMA
THAILAND (SIAM)
LAOS
VIETNAM
CAMBODIA
PENINSULAR MALAYSIA
SINGAPORE
SRI LANKA (CEYLON)
MALDIVE IS.
XIZANG (TIBET)
CHINA
ARABIAN SEA
BAY OF BENGAL
INDIAN OCEAN
SOUTH CHINA SEA
ANDAMAN SEA
Gulf of Thailand
Strait of Malacca
Tropic of Cancer
East from Greenwich
Projection: Bonne
COPYRIGHT. GEORGE PHILIP & SON. LTD.
Karachi
Bombay
Delhi
Calcutta
Madras
Colombo
Kabul
Lahore
Dhaka
Rangoon
Bangkok
Hanoi
Kunming
Chengdu
Chongqing
Lhasa
Mandalay
Hyderabad
Bangalore
Tanggula Shan
Kunlun Shan
Karakoram Ra.
Hindu Kush

1:7 000 000

50 0 50 100 150 200 miles

50 0 50 100 150 200 250 300 km

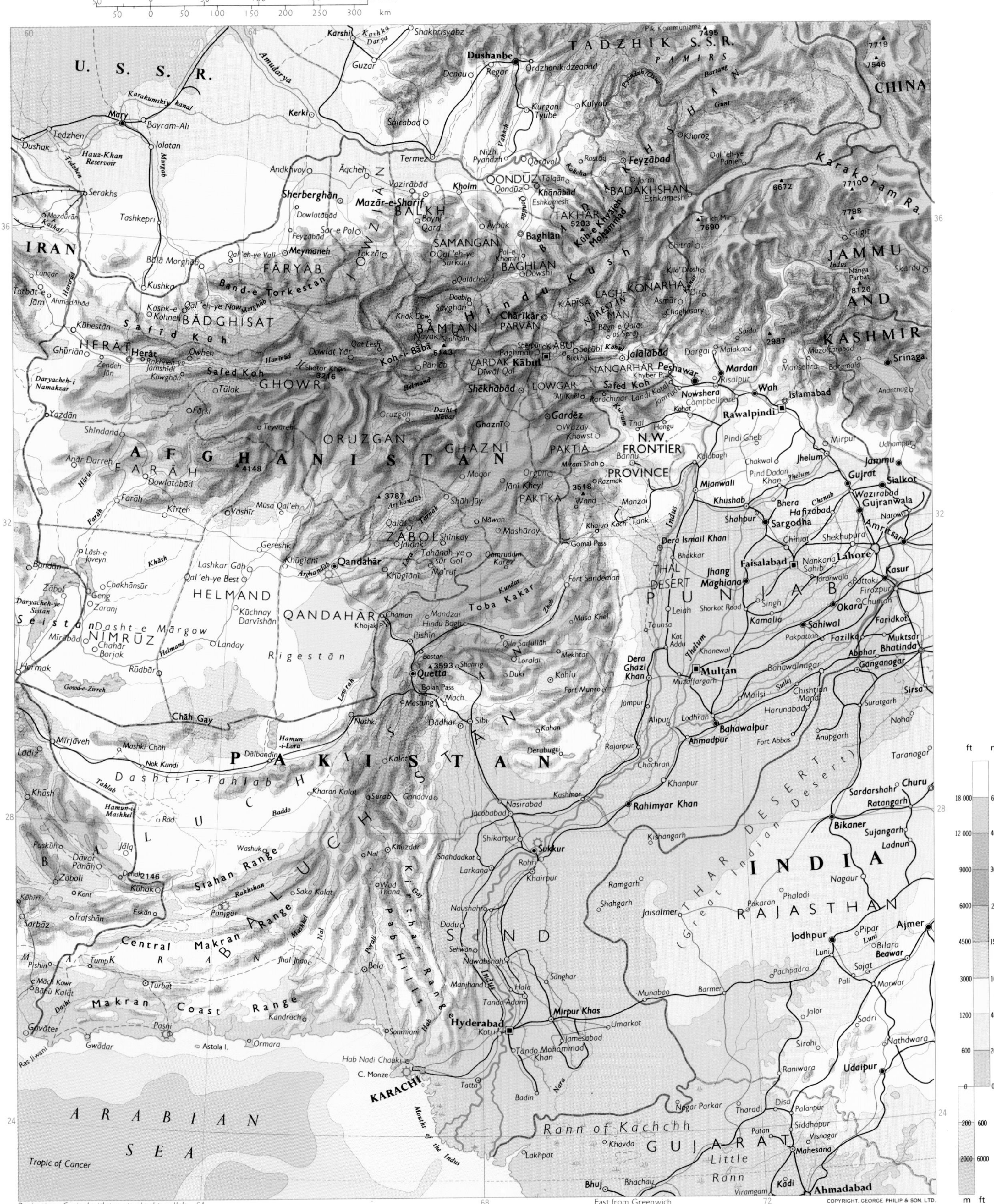
U. S. S. R.
TADZHIK S.S.R.
PAMIRS
CHINA
IRAN
AFGHANISTAN
PAKISTAN
JAMMU AND KASHMIR
INDIA
RAJASTHAN
PUNJAB
SIND
BALUCHISTAN
N.W. FRONTIER PROVINCE
GUJARAT
ARABIAN SEA
Tropic of Cancer
Hindu Kush
Karakoram Ra.
Safīd Kūh
Band-e Torkestan
Safed Koh
Koh-i-Baba
Toba Kakar
Siahan Range
Central Makran Range
Makran Coast Range
Kirthar Range
Pab Hills
Dasht-i-Tahlab
Dasht-e Margow
Rigestān
THAR DESERT (Great Indian Desert)
THAL DESERT
Rann of Kachchh
Little Rann
Mouths of the Indus
Amudarya
Indus
Helmand
Karakumskiy kanal
Hauz-Khan Reservoir
Daryacheh-i Namakzar
Seistan
Gowd-e-Zirreh
Hamun-i-Lora
Hamun-i-Mashkel
Dushanbe
Kabul
Islamabad
Rawalpindi
Peshawar
Lahore
Karachi
Hyderabad
Quetta
Multan
Herāt
Qandahār
Mazār-e-Sharīf
Faisalabad
Sukkur
Bahawalpur
Amritsar
Jodhpur
Ahmadabad
Srinagar
Mary
Termez
Khorog
Feyzābād
Jalālābād
Ghaznī
Gardēz
Chaman
Gwādar
Bikaner
Sialkot
Gujranwala
Mardan
Wah
Kohat
Bannu
Dera Ismail Khan
Dera Ghazi Khan
Jacobabad
Larkana
Nawabshah
Mirpur Khas
Bhuj
Udaipur
Ajmer
Tirich Mir 7690
Nanga Parbat 8126
Pik Kommunizma 7495
Projection: Conical with two standard parallels
East from Greenwich
60 64 68 72 76
36 32 28 24
ft m
18 000 6000
12 000 4000
9000 3000
6000 2000
4500 1500
3000 1000
1200 400
600 200
0 0
200 600
2000 6000
m ft

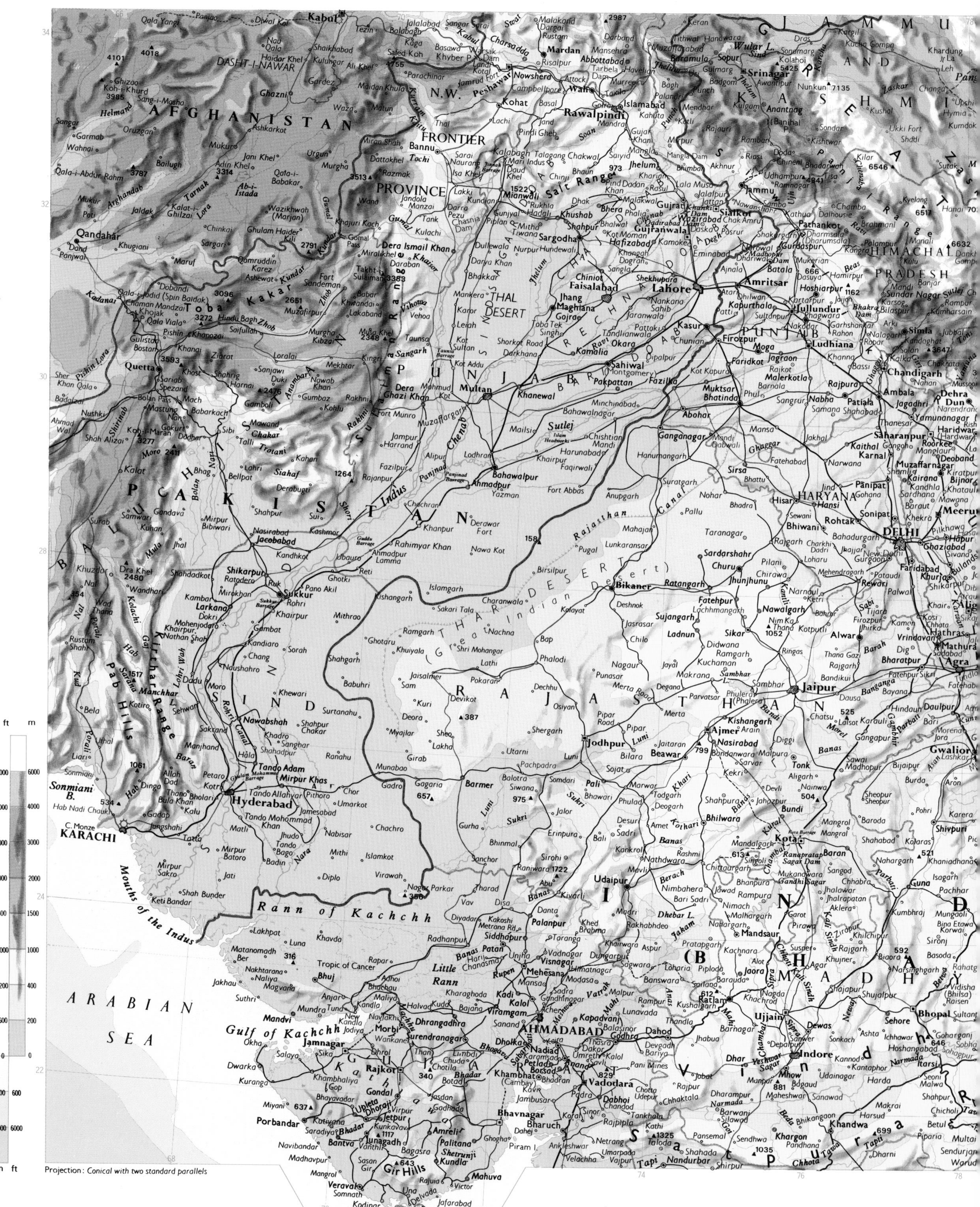
AFGHANISTAN
DASHT-I-NAWAR
N.W. FRONTIER PROVINCE
PAKISTAN
BALUCHISTAN
PUNJAB
SIND
JAMMU AND KASHMIR
HIMACHAL PRADESH
PUNJAB
HARYANA
RAJASTHAN
MADHYA PRADESH
INDIA
GUJARAT
THAR DESERT (Great Indian Desert)
THAL DESERT
ARABIAN SEA
Gulf of Kachchh
Rann of Kachchh
Little Rann
Mouths of the Indus
Sonmiani B.
Tropic of Cancer
Kabul
Jalalabad
Peshawar
Islamabad
Rawalpindi
Srinagar
Jammu
Qandahar
Ghazni
Quetta
Dera Ismail Khan
Dera Ghazi Khan
Multan
Faisalabad
Lahore
Amritsar
Jullundur
Ludhiana
Chandigarh
Simla
Ambala
DELHI
New Delhi
Meerut
Agra
Mathura
Jaipur
Ajmer
Jodhpur
Bikaner
Bahawalpur
Sukkur
Jacobabad
Shikarpur
Larkana
Hyderabad
KARACHI
C. Monze
Nawabshah
Mirpur Khas
Barmer
Udaipur
Kota
Gwalior
Bhopal
Ujjain
Indore
Ratlam
AHMADABAD
Vadodara
Rajkot
Jamnagar
Porbandar
Bhavnagar
Junagadh
Gir Hills
Bhuj
Mandvi
Indus
Chenab
Jhelum
Ravi
Sutlej
Salt Range
Toba Kakar Range
Sulaiman Range
Kirthar Range
Pab Hills
ft
m
18,000
6000
12,000
4000
9000
3000
6000
2000
4500
1500
3000
1000
1200
400
600
200
0
0
200
600
2000
6000
m
ft
Projection: Conical with two standard parallels

Inset map (Jammu and Kashmir):

U.S.S.R.

GILGIT AGENCY

N.W. FRONTIER PROVINCE

Gilgit · Indus · Nanga Parbat · Skardu · Karakoram Range · Deosai Mountains

Zaskar Range · Leh · Kargil · Dras

Muzaffarabad · Baramula · Wular L. · Sopur · Srinagar · Anantnag · Banihal

Abbottabad · Havelian · Murree · Rawalpindi · Islamabad · Kahuta

Punch · Rajauri · Riasi · Ramban · Kishtwar · Doda · Kilar

PUNJAB · Jhelum · Gujrat · Jammu · Sialkot · Wazirabad · Udhampur · Ramnagar

HIMACHAL PRADESH · Chamba · Dalhousie · Kyelang

SODA PLAINS · Aksai Chin · Kunlun Shan · Muztag · Qara Qash

Main map:

CHINESE REPUBLIC

Gangdise Shan · Ngari · Kangri · Mapam Yumco · La'nga Co

XIZANG

Yartung Zangbo Jiang (Brahmaputra) · Xigazê · Lhaze · Gyangzê

Mt. Everest 8848 · Makalu 8481 · Kanchenjunga 8598 · Annapurna 8078 · Dhaulagiri 8172 · Manaslu 8156

NEPAL · Katmandu · Lalitpur · Bhaktapur · Pokhara · Butwal · Gorkha

SIKKIM · Gangtok · Darjeeling · Kalimpong

BHUTAN · Thimphu · Punakha · Tongsa Dzong

ASSAM · Koch Bihar · Brahmaputra · Rangpur · Dhubri

U T T A R P R A D E S H

Moradabad · Rampur · Bareilly · Budaun · Shahjahanpur · Sitapur · Bahraich · Gonda · Faizabad · Basti · Gorakhpur · Lucknow · Kanpur · Rae Bareli · Allahabad · Varanasi (Banaras, Benares) · Mirzapur · Jaunpur · Azamgarh · Ghazipur · Ballia · Deoria

Jhansi · Mahoba · Banda · Fatehpur · Orai · Etawah

M A D H Y A P R A D E S H

Jabalpur · Satna · Rewa · Panna · Chhatarpur · Damoh · Sagar · Bilaspur · Raigarh · Raipur · Sambalpur · Hirakud Dam · Seoni · Balaghat · Mandla

B I H A R

Patna · Gaya · Bhagalpur · Munger · Darbhanga · Muzaffarpur · Chhapra · Arrah · Hazaribag · Ranchi · Dhanbad · Jamshedpur · Bokaro · Daltenganj · Giridih · Deoghar · Purnia · Katihar · Saharsa

WEST BENGAL · Burdwan · Durgapur · Asansol · Krishnanagar · Haora · CALCUTTA · Kharagpur · Midnapur · Behala · Diamond Harbour

BANGLADESH · DHAKA · Rajshahi · Mymensingh · Kushtia · Jessore · Khulna · Barisal · Faridpur · Tangail · Pabna · Bogra · Sirajganj

Sundarbans · Mouths of the Ganga · The Sandheads

1:6 000 000

50 0 50 100 150 miles

50 0 50 100 150 200 250 km

JAMMU AND KASHMIR

On same scale as Main Map

East from Greenwich

NEPAL
UTTAR PRADESH
KANPUR
Lucknow
Allahabad
Varanasi
Agra
Jaipur
Gwalior
Jhansi
Patna
Jabalpur
Bhopal
Indore
Ujjain
Nagpur
Raipur
Cuttack
Bhubaneshwar
Vishakhapatnam
Rajahmundry
Warangal
HYDERABAD
Secunderabad
Solapur
Pune
BOMBAY
Nasik
Aurangabad
Surat
Vadodara
AHMADABAD
Udaipur
Jodhpur
Ajmer
Kota
Gulf of Khambhat
Mahadeo Hills
Maikala Range
Ajanta Range
Kaimur Hills
Gawilgarh Hills
Panna Hills
Balaghat Range
Chilka Lake

1:6 000 000

BAY OF BENGAL
ARABIAN SEA
Gulf of Mannar
Palk Strait
Palk Bay
Coromandel Coast
Malabar Coast
SRI LANKA (CEYLON)
TAMIL NADU
KARNATAKA
KERALA
ANDHRA PRADESH
GOA
MADRAS
BANGALORE
Mysore
Colombo
Trincomalee
Jaffna
Kandy
Madurai
Pondicherry (Puducherry)
Calicut (Kozhikode)
Mangalore
Cochin
Trivandrum
C. Comorin
Adam's Bridge
Nilgiri Hills
Cardamom Hills
East from 80 Greenwich
Projection: Conical with two standard parallels
COPYRIGHT, GEORGE PHILIP & SON, LTD

1:6 000 000

50 0 50 100 150 miles

50 0 50 100 150 200 250 km

ft m

18 000 6000

12 000 4000

9000 3000

6000 2000

4500 1500

3000 1000

1200 400

600 200

0 0

200 600

2000 6000

m ft

Projection: Conical with two standard parallels

East from Greenwich

Equatorial Scale 1:50 000 000

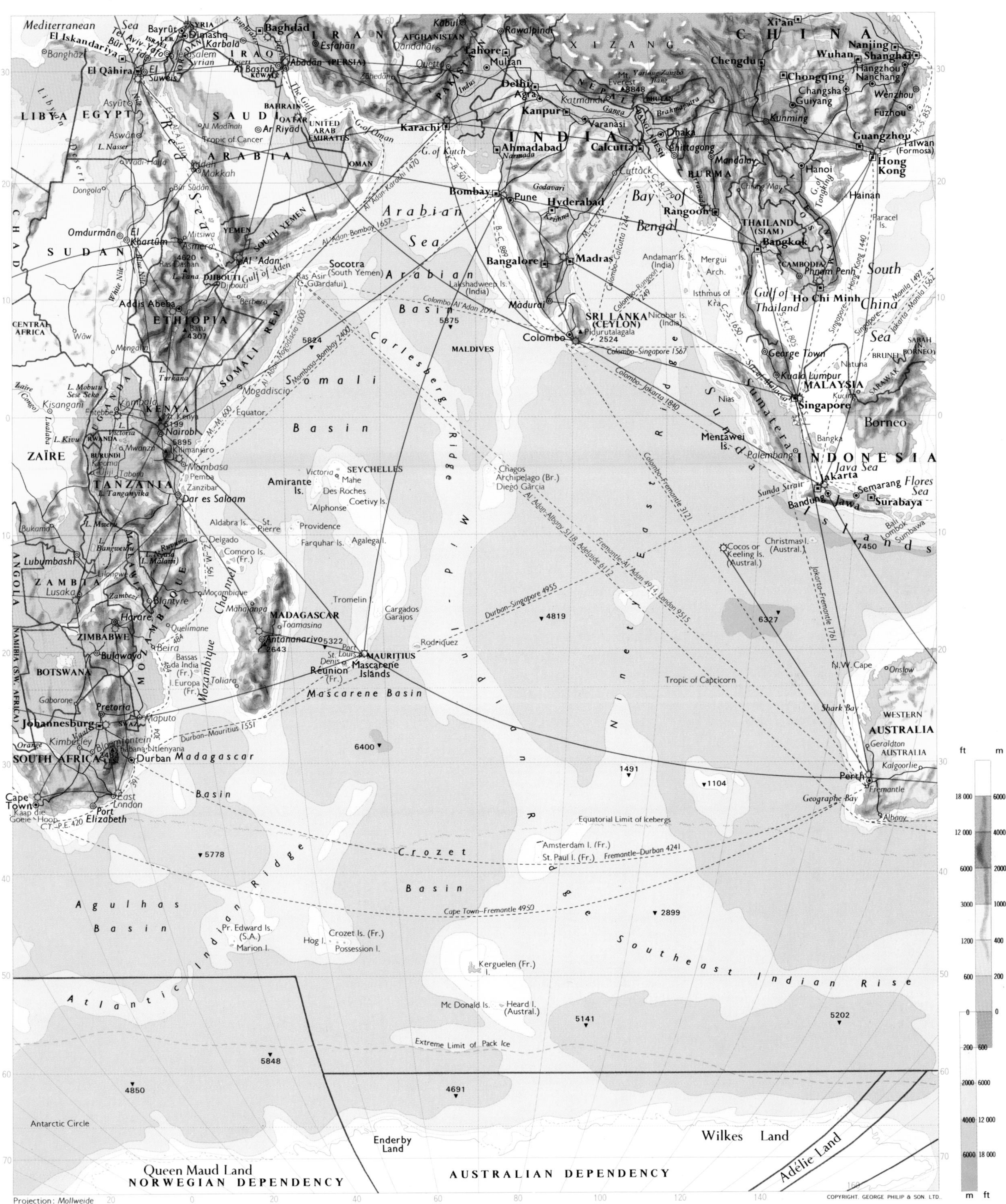
Projection: Mollweide
COPYRIGHT, GEORGE PHILIP & SON, LTD.
Arabian Sea
Bay of Bengal
Somali Basin
Carlesberg Ridge
Mid-Indian Ridge
Ninety East Ridge
Mascarene Basin
Madagascar Basin
Crozet Basin
Agulhas Basin
Atlantic Indian Ridge
Southeast Indian Rise
Tropic of Capricorn
Equatorial Limit of Icebergs
Extreme Limit of Pack Ice
Antarctic Circle
Queen Maud Land
NORWEGIAN DEPENDENCY
AUSTRALIAN DEPENDENCY
Enderby Land
Wilkes Land
Adélie Land
MADAGASCAR
MAURITIUS
SEYCHELLES
MALDIVES
SRI LANKA (CEYLON)
INDIA
INDONESIA
MALAYSIA
WESTERN AUSTRALIA
SOUTH AFRICA
Kerguelen (Fr.)
Amsterdam I. (Fr.)
St. Paul I. (Fr.)
Cocos or Keeling Is. (Austral.)
Christmas I. (Austral.)
Chagos Archipelago (Br.)
Cape Town–Fremantle 4950
Fremantle–Durban 4241
ft m

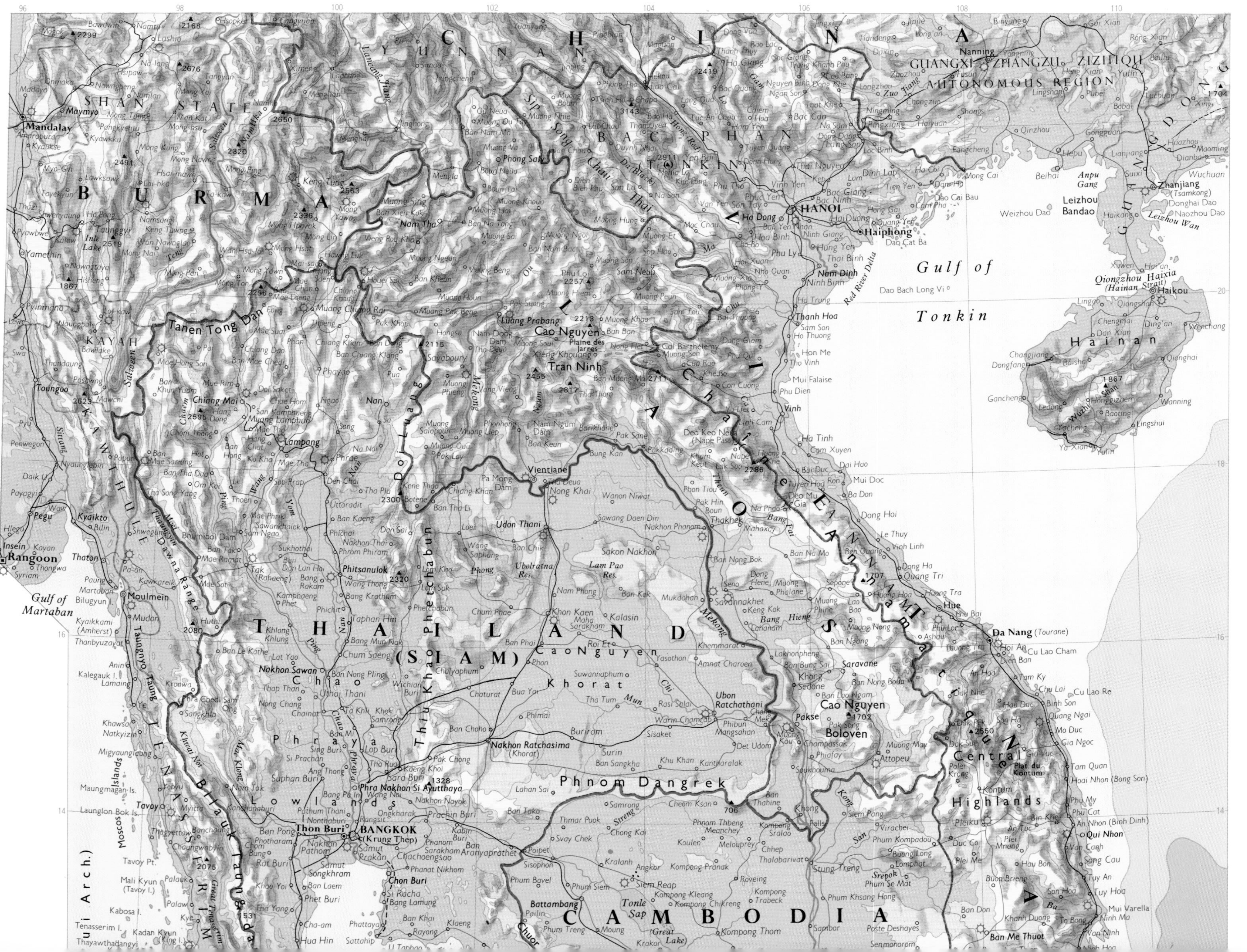

CHINA
YUNNAN
GUANGXI ZHUANGZU ZIZHIQU
GUANGXI ZHUANGZU AUTONOMOUS REGION
Nanning
Zhanjiang (Tsamkong)
Leizhou Bandao
Haikou
Hainan
Gulf of Tonkin
HANOI
Haiphong
Red River Delta
Nam Dinh
Thanh Hoa
Vinh
Hue
Da Nang (Tourane)
Qui Nhon
Central Highlands
Ban Me Thuot
Pakse
Boloven
Saravane
Vientiane
Luang Prabang
Tran Ninh
Plaine des Jarres
Udon Thani
Ubon Ratchathani
Nakhon Ratchasima (Khorat)
Khorat
Phnom Dangrek
Mekong
Tonle Sap (Great Lake)
Battambang
CAMBODIA
LAOS
THAILAND (SIAM)
BANGKOK (Krung Thep)
Thon Buri
Phra Nakhon Si Ayutthaya
Chiang Mai
Lampang
Nakhon Sawan
Phitsanulok
Tanen Tong Dan
Dawna Range
Bilauk Taung
Moulmein
Rangoon
Pegu
Toungoo
Mandalay
Maymyo
Gulf of Martaban
Salween
Sittang
SHAN STATE
KAYAH
BURMA
Lancang Jiang
Tavoy

Gulf of Thailand
SOUTH CHINA SEA
PENINSULAR MALAYSIA
Strait of Malacca
INDONESIA
Kho Khot Kra
(Isthmus of Kra)
Phnom Penh
PHANH BHO HO CHI MINH (Saigon)
Mekong River Delta
Phan Thiet
Con Son Islands
Catwick Islands
Cu Lao Hon
Nakhon Si Thammarat
Songkhla (Singora)
Hat Yai
Phuket
Alur Setar
George Town
Butterworth
Ipoh
Cameron Highlands
Kuala Trengganu
Kota Baharu
Kuantan
Kuala Lumpur
Melaka
Johor Baharu
SINGAPORE
Tanjungpinang
Medan
Kepulauan Anambas
Kepulauan Natuna
Kepulauan Natuna Besar
P. Laut
P. Tioman
BORNEO
SARAWAK
Kucing
Tanjong Datu
East from Greenwich
1:6 000 000
Projection: Conical with two standard parallels
COPYRIGHT GEORGE PHILIP & SON LTD.

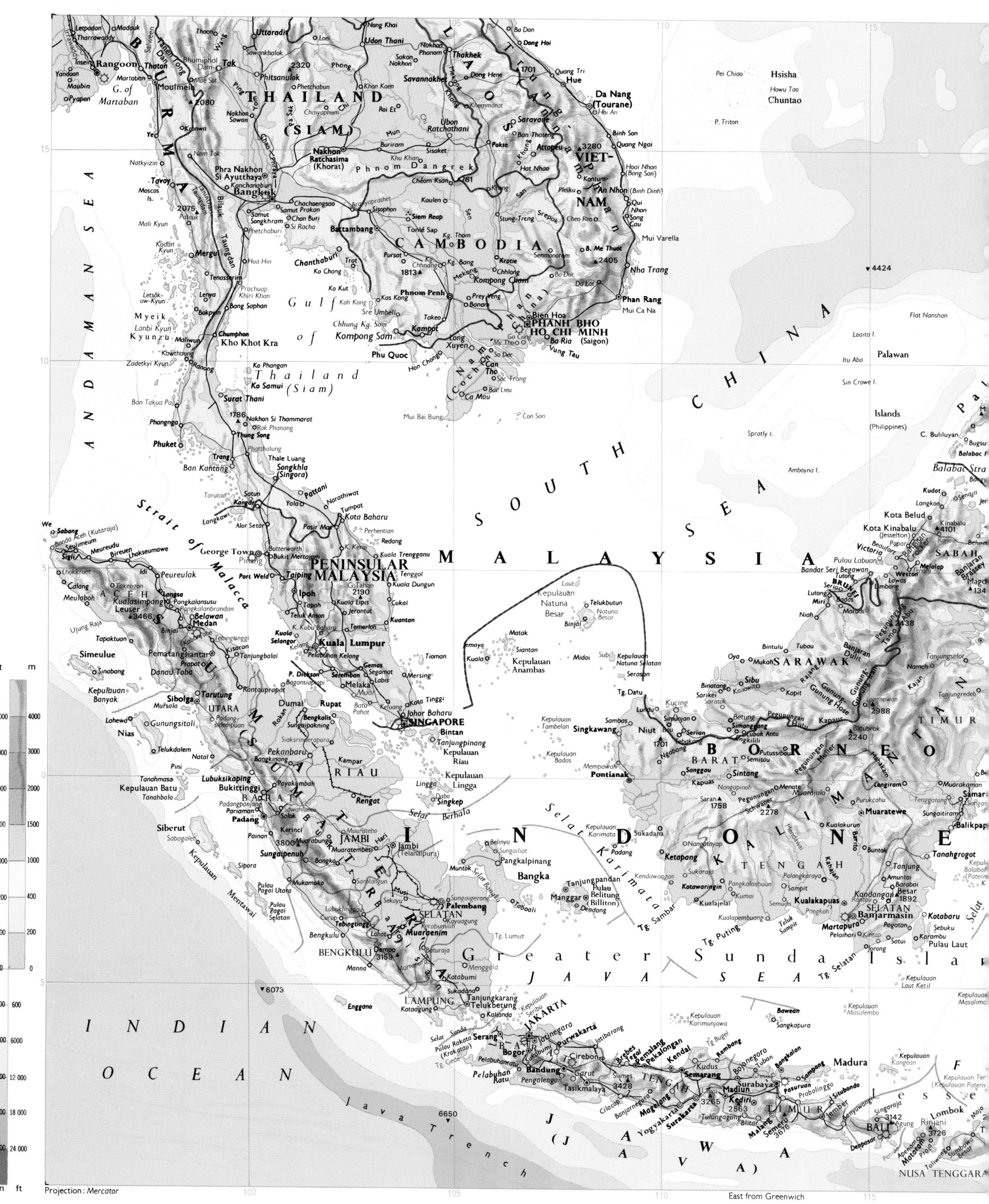

BURMA
Rangoon
Moulmein
G. of Martaban
THAILAND (SIAM)
Bangkok
LAOS
VIET-NAM
Hue
Da Nang (Tourane)
CAMBODIA
Phnom Penh
PHANH BHO HO CHI MINH (Saigon)
Gulf of Thailand (Siam)
ANDAMAN SEA
SOUTH CHINA SEA
Hsisha
Chuntao
Palawan
Spratly I.
Islands (Philippines)
MALAYSIA
PENINSULAR MALAYSIA
Kuala Lumpur
SINGAPORE
Strait of Malacca
George Town
SUMATERA
Medan
Padang
Palembang
Jambi
Bangka
Belitung (Billiton)
Kepulauan Riau
Kepulauan Lingga
Kepulauan Natuna
Kepulauan Anambas
INDONESIA
BORNEO
KALIMANTAN
SARAWAK
SABAH
BRUNEI
Kota Kinabalu (Jesselton)
Pontianak
Banjarmasin
Balikpapan
Greater Sunda Islands
JAVA SEA
JAWA (JAVA)
JAKARTA
Bandung
Semarang
Surabaya
Yogyakarta
Madura
Bali
Lombok
NUSA TENGGARA
Kepulauan Mentawai
Siberut
Nias
Simeulue
Enggano
INDIAN OCEAN
Java Trench
6073
6650
4424
ft
m
12 000
9000
6000
4500
3000
1200
600
0
200
2000
4000
6000
8000
4000
3000
2000
1500
1000
400
200
600
6000
12 000
18 000
24 000
Projection: Mercator
East from Greenwich

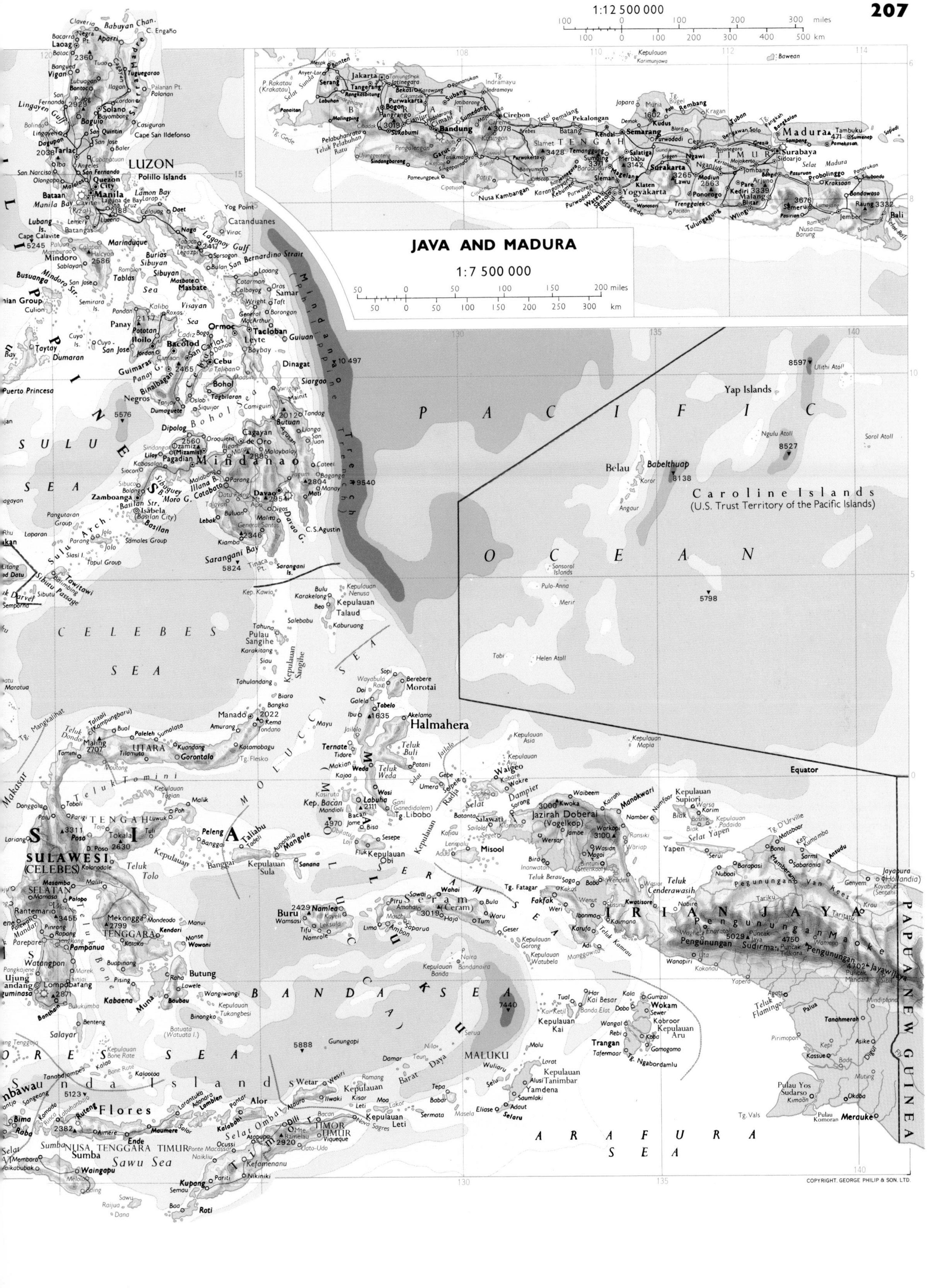

1:12 500 000

100 0 100 200 300 miles

100 0 100 200 300 400 500 km

JAVA AND MADURA

1:7 500 000

50 0 50 100 150 200 miles

50 0 50 100 150 200 250 300 km

LUZON

PHILIPPINES

SULU SEA

Mindanao

CELEBES SEA

PACIFIC OCEAN

Caroline Islands
(U.S. Trust Territory of the Pacific Islands)

Yap Islands

Belau

Halmahera

MOLUCCA SEA

SULAWESI (CELEBES)

BANDA SEA

MALUKU

IRIAN JAYA

PAPUA NEW GUINEA

ARAFURA SEA

FLORES SEA

Nusa Tenggara Timur

Sawu Sea

Equator

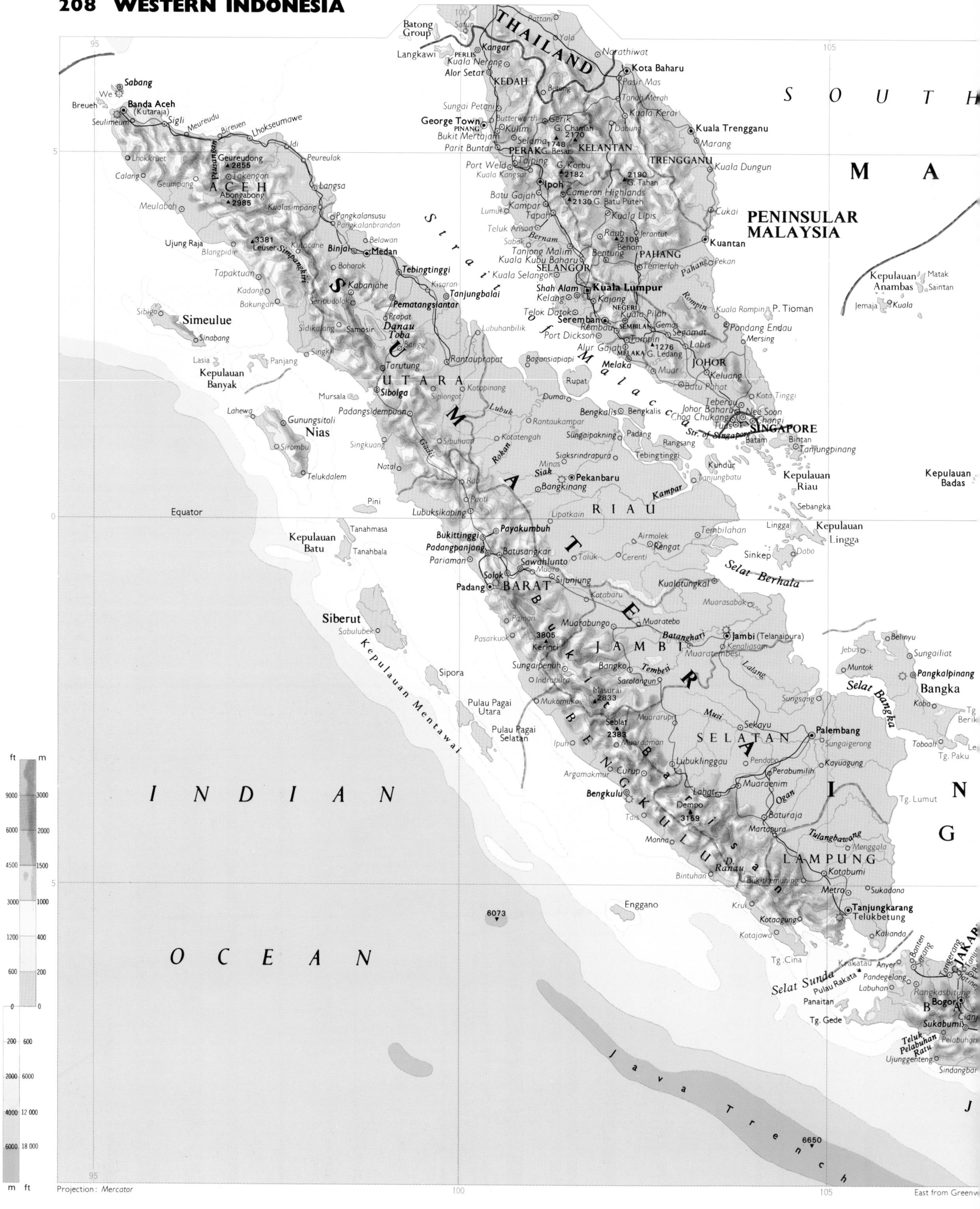

Batong Group
Langkawi
PERLIS
Kangar
Kuala Nerang
Alor Setar
KEDAH
THAILAND
Pattani
Yala
Satun
Narathiwat
Kota Baharu
Pasir Mas
Tanah Merah
Kuala Kerai
Sungai Petani
Butterworth
George Town
PINANG
Bukit Mertajam
Parit Buntar
Kulim
Gerik
G. Chamah
2170
1748
Selama
PERAK
G. Besar
KELANTAN
Dabong
Kuala Trengganu
Marang
TRENGGANU
Kuala Dungun
Port Weld
Kuala Kangsar
Taiping
G. Korbu
2182
2190
G. Tahan
Ipoh
Batu Gajah
Cameron Highlands
2130
G. Batu Puteh
Kampar
Tapah
Lumut
Kuala Lipis
Cukai
Teluk Anson
Bernam
Sabak
Raub
2108
Benom
Jerantut
Kuantan
Tanjong Malim
Kuala Kubu Baharu
Bentung
PAHANG
Temerloh
Pahang
Pekan
SELANGOR
Kuala Selangor
Shah Alam
Kuala Lumpur
Kelang
Kajang
Rompin
Kuala Rompin
P. Tioman
Telok Datok
Seremban
NEGERI
SEMBILAN
Kuala Pilah
Rembau
Gemas
Segamat
Pandang Endau
Mersing
Port Dickson
Tampin
1276
Labis
Alur Gajah
MELAKA
G. Ledang
Melaka
Muar
JOHOR
Keluang
Batu Pahat
Kota Tinggi
Teberau
Johor Baharu
Nee Soon
Choa Chukang
Changi
Tuas
SINGAPORE
Str. of Singapore
PENINSULAR MALAYSIA
S O U T H
M A
Kepulauan Anambas
Matak
Saintan
Jemaja
Kuala
Sabang
We
Breueh
Banda Aceh
(Kutaraja)
Seulimeum
Sigli
Meureudu
Bireuen
Lhokseumawe
Idi
Peureulak
Lhokkruet
Geureudong
2855
Takengon
Peusangan
Calang
Geumpang
ACEH
Abongabong
2985
Langsa
Meulaboh
Kualasimpang
Pangkalansusu
Pangkalanbrandan
Belawan
Ujung Raja
Blangpidie
3381
Leuser
Simpangkiri
Kutacane
Binjai
Medan
Tapaktuan
Bohorok
Tebingtinggi
Kisaran
Kabanjahe
Tanjungbalai
Kadang
Seribudolok
Pematangsiantar
Bakungan
Prapat
Sibigo
Simeulue
Sinabang
Sidikalang
Samosir
Danau Toba
Balige
Lubuhanbilik
Lasia
Panjang
Singkil
Rantauprapat
Kepulauan Banyak
Tarutung
UTARA
Kotapinang
Mursala
Sibolga
Sipongot
Padangsidempuan
Lahewa
Gunungsitoli
Nias
Sirombu
Telukdalem
Singkuang
Natal
Sibuhuan
Gadis
Kotatengah
Rokan
Lubuk
Rantaukampar
Dumai
Rupat
Bagansiapiapi
Strait of Malacca
Bengkalis
Sungaipakning
Padang
Rangsang
Tebingtinggi
Siaksrindrapura
Minas
Siak
Pekanbaru
Bangkinang
Kampar
Batam
Bintan
Tanjungpinang
Kundur
Tanjungbatu
Kepulauan Riau
Kepulauan Badas
Rao
Panti
Pini
Lubuksikaping
Lipatkain
RIAU
Sebangka
Equator
Tanahmasa
Kepulauan Batu
Tanahbala
Bukittinggi
Payakumbuh
Padangpanjang
Batusangkar
Pariaman
Sawahlunto
Taluk
Airmolek
Rengat
Cerenti
Tembilahan
Lingga
Kepulauan Lingga
Singkep
Dabo
Selat Berhala
Solok
Muara
Sijunjung
Padang
BARAT
Kualatungkal
Kotabaru
Muarasabak
Siberut
Sabulubek
Pagai
Muarabungo
Muaratebo
Batanghari
Jambi (Telanaipura)
Pasarkuok
3805
Kerinci
JAMBI
Kenaliasam
Muaratembesi
Sungaipenuh
Bangko
Tembesi
Sarolangun
Indrapura
Sipora
Kepulauan Mentawai
Masurai
2833
Mukomuko
Pulau Pagai Utara
Pulau Pagai Selatan
Seblat
2383
Muararupit
Musi
Sekayu
SELATAN
Palembang
Sungaigerong
Ipuh
Muaraaman
BENGKULU
Lubuklinggau
Pendopo
Argamakmur
Curup
Bengkulu
Prabumulih
Lahat
Muaraenim
Ogan
Dempo
3159
Tais
Baturaja
Manna
Martapura
Tulangbawang
Menggala
LAMPUNG
Ranau
Bintuhan
Kotabumi
Bukitkemuning
Metro
Sukadana
Krui
Tanjungkarang
Telukbetung
Kotaagung
Kalianda
Kotajawa
Enggano
Bukit Barisan
SUMATERA
6073
Tg. Cina
Selat Sunda
Krakatau
Pulau Rakata
Anyer
Pandegelang
Labuhan
Panaitan
Tg. Gede
Banten
Serang
Tangerang
Rangkasbitung
Bogor
Sukabumi
Teluk Pelabuhan Ratu
Pelabuhan
Ujunggenteng
Sindangbar
Belinyu
Jebus
Sungailiat
Muntok
Pangkalpinang
Selat Bangka
Bangka
Sungsang
Koba
Toboali
Tg. Paku
Tg. Lumut
I N D I A N
O C E A N
Java Trench
6650
ft
m
9000
3000
6000
2000
4500
1500
3000
1000
1200
400
600
200
0
200
600
2000
6000
4000
12 000
6000
18 000
95
100
105
5
0
Projection: Mercator
East from Greenw

1:7 000 000
50 0 50 100 150 200 miles
50 0 50 100 150 200 250 300 km
C H I N A S E A
S U L U S E A
M A L A Y S I A
SARAWAK
SABAH
BRUNEI
PHILIPPINES
B O R N E O
K A L I M A N T A N
BARAT
TENGAH
TIMUR
SELATAN
I N D O N E S I A
Greater Sunda Islands
J A V A S E A
F L O R E S S E A
SULAWESI
Selat Makasar
Selat Karimata
Lesser Sunda Islands
JAWA (JAVA)
YOGYAKARTA
NUSA TENGGARA BARAT
Kota Kinabalu (Jesselton)
Kinabalu 4101
Banjaran Crocker
Sandakan
Tawau
Bandar Seri Begawan
Kuala Belait
Miri
G. Mulu 2371
Kapuas
Pegunungan Muller
Pegunungan Schwaner
Kuching
Sibu
Pontianak
Samarinda
Balikpapan
Banjarmasin
Palangkaraya
Peg. Meratus
Tarakan
Kepulauan Natuna
Natuna Besar
Kepulauan Natuna Selatan
Kepulauan Tambelan
Kepulauan Karimata
Pulau Belitung
Kepulauan Balabalangan (Paternoster Is.)
Kepulauan Laut Ketil
Kepulauan Masalembo
Kepulauan Masalima
Kepulauan Karimunjawa
Kepulauan Kangean
Bawean
Madura
Palu
Ujung Pandang
Makale
Parepare
Equator
Bandung
Cirebon
Semarang
Surabaya
Yogyakarta
Surakarta
Malang
Kediri
Madiun
Bali
Denpasar
Lombok
Mataram
Sumbawa
Flores
Tambora 2821
Rinjani 3726
Agung 3142
Nusa Barung
Pulau Laut
D. Sentarum
D. Luar
D. Jempang
Teluk Sampit
Selat Bali
Selat Madura

1:4 000 000

25 0 50 100 miles

25 0 50 100 150 km

Continuation Northwards on same scale

PACIFIC OCEAN

SOUTH CHINA SEA

LUZON

ft	m
9000	3000
6000	2000
4500	1500
3000	1000
1200	400
600	200
0	0
600	200
6000	2000
12 000	4000
18 000	6000
24 000	8000

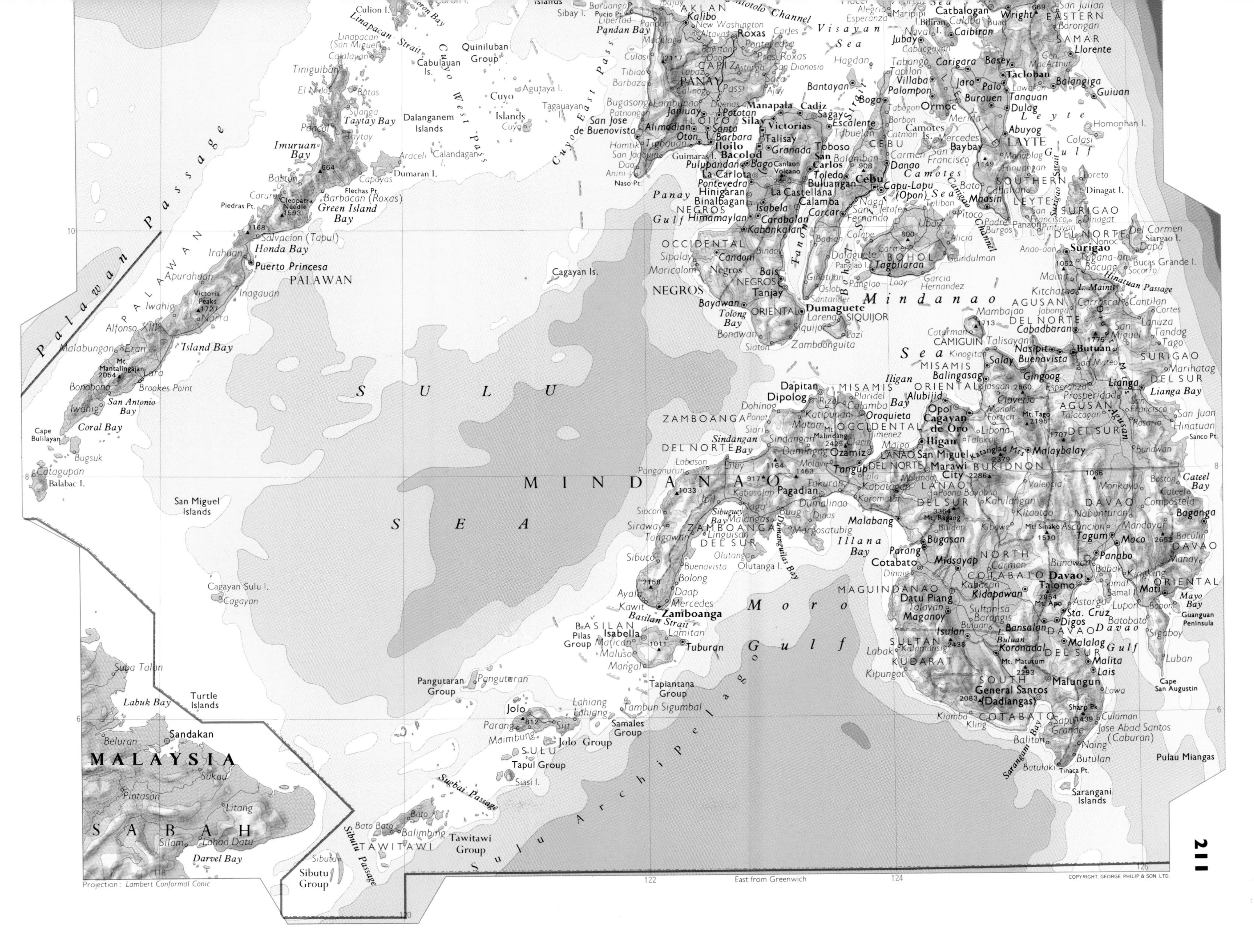
SULU SEA
MINDANAO SEA
Mindanao Sea
Visayan Sea
Moro Gulf
Sulu Archipelago
Leyte Gulf
Surigao Strait
Davao Gulf
Illana Bay
Palawan Passage
Cuyo West Pass
Cuyo East Pass
Basilan Strait
Sibutu Passage
Sugbai Passage
Dumanguilas Bay
Sarangani Bay
Camotes Sea
Canigao Channel
Hinatuan Passage
MALAYSIA
SABAH
PALAWAN
NEGROS
PANAY
BOHOL
SIQUIJOR
CAMIGUIN
BASILAN
SULU
TAWITAWI
Puerto Princesa
Zamboanga
Davao
Cebu
Iloilo
Bacolod
Dumaguete
Cagayan de Oro
Iligan
Cotabato
Butuan
Surigao
Tacloban
Ormoc
Sandakan
Jolo
General Santos (Dadiangas)
Cagayan Sulu I.
Cagayan Is.
Turtle Islands
San Miguel Islands
Balabac I.
Pulau Miangas
Sarangani Islands
Projection: Lambert Conformal Conic
East from Greenwich
COPYRIGHT GEORGE PHILIP & SON LTD

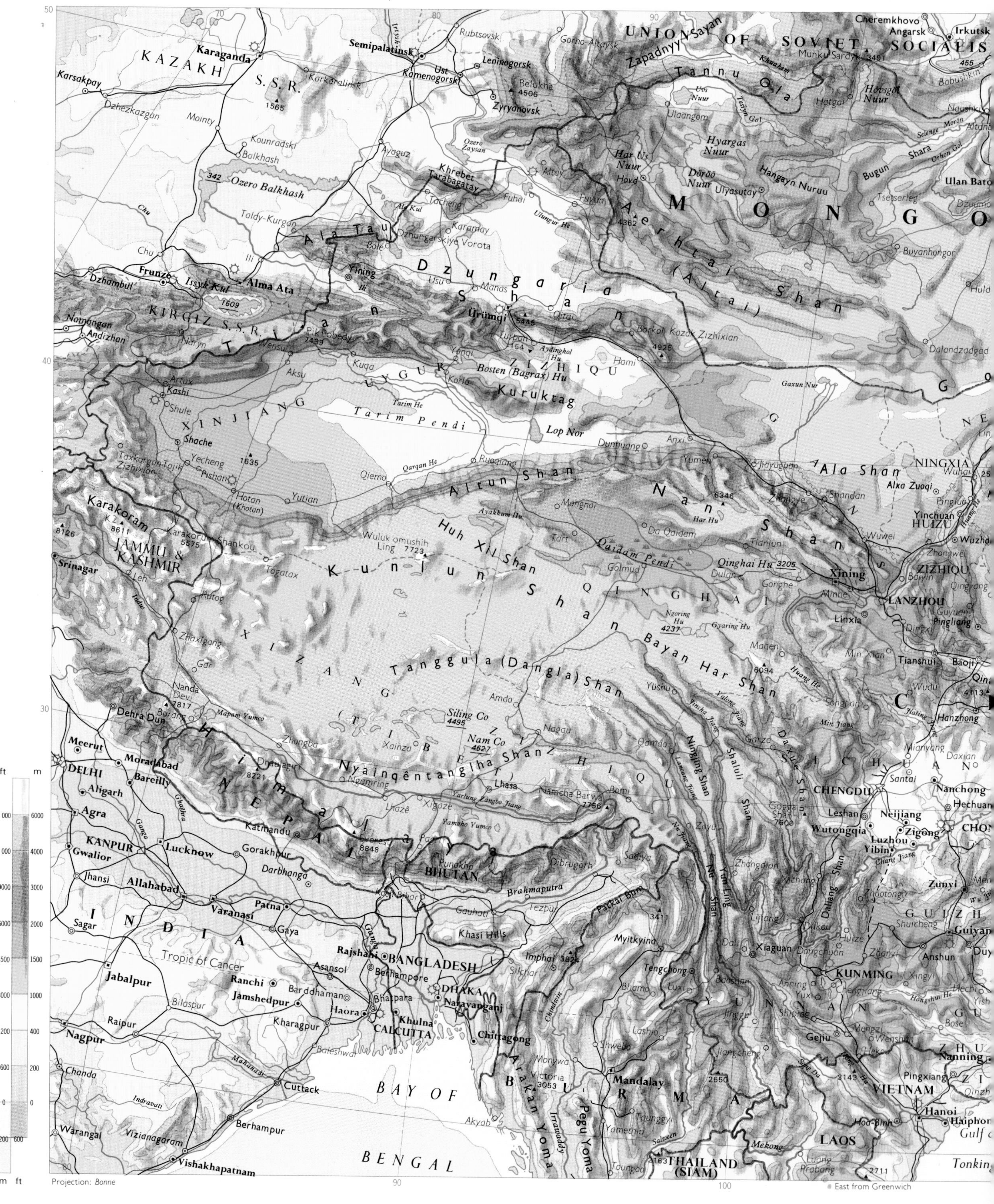
UNION OF SOVIET SOCIALIS
KAZAKH S.S.R.
Karaganda
Semipalatinsk
Ust Kamenogorsk
Leninogorsk
Rubtsovsk
Gorno-Altaysk
Cheremkhovo
Angarsk
Irkutsk
Karsakpay
Dzhezkazgan
Karkaralinsk
Belukha 4506
Zyryanovsk
Mointy
Kounradski
Balkhash
Ozero Balkhash
Ayaguz
Khrebet Tarabagatay
Chu
Taldy-Kurgan
Ala Tau
Ala Kul
Tacheng
Karamay
Dzhungarskiye Vorota
Bole
Yining
Ili
Frunze
Dzhambul
Issyk Kul
Alma Ata
Dzungaria
Usu
Manas
Ürümqi
Qitai
Turpan
Aydingkol Hu
Bosten (Bagrax) Hu
Kuruktag
Hami
Barkol Kazak Zizhixian
KIRGIZ S.S.R.
Namangan
Andizhan
Naryn
Pik Pobedy 7439
Wensu
Aksu
Kuqa
Korla
Yanqi
UYGUR ZIZHIQU
Artux
Kashi
Shule
XINJIANG
Tarim He
Tarim Pendi
Lop Nor
Shache
Yecheng
Pishan
Taxkorgan Tajik Zizhixian
Hotan (Khotan)
Yutian
Qiemo
Qarqan He
Ruoqiang
Altun Shan
Dunhuang
Anxi
Yumen
Jiayuguan
Ala Shan
NINGXIA
Wuhai
Alxa Zuoqi
Yinchuan
HUIZU
Nan Shan
Zhangye
Shandan
Wuwei
Karakoram
K2 8611
Karakoram Shankou
JAMMU & KASHMIR
Srinagar
Leh
Indus
Rutog
Wuluk omushih Ling 7723
Togatax
Kunlun Shan
Huh Xil Shan
Ayakkum Hu
Mangnai
Da Qaidam
Qaidam Pendi
Golmud
Tianjun
Qinghai Hu 3205
Xining
Dulan
Gonghe
QINGHAI
LANZHOU
Linxia
Ngoring Hu 4237
Gyaring Hu
Bayan Har Shan
Maqen
Tianshui
Baoji
XIZANG
Zhaxigang
Gar
Tanggula (Dangla) Shan
Amdo
Nanda Devi 7817
Dehra Dun
Mapam Yumco
Siling Co 4495
Nam Co 4627
Nagqu
Yushu
Zhongba
Xainza
Nyainqêntanglha Shan
Lhasa
Namcha Barwa 7756
Yarlung Zangbo Jiang
Lhazê
Xigazê
Yamzho Yumco
Everest 8848
Himalaya
NEPAL
Katmandu
Punakha
BHUTAN
Meerut
Moradabad
DELHI
Bareilly
Aligarh
Agra
KANPUR
Lucknow
Gwalior
Gorakhpur
Darbhanga
Jhansi
Allahabad
Varanasi
Patna
Gaya
INDIA
Sagar
Tropic of Cancer
Jabalpur
Ranchi
Rajshahi
BANGLADESH
Berhampore
Asansol
Barddhaman
Jamshedpur
Bilaspur
Haora
CALCUTTA
Khulna
DHAKA
Narayanganj
Kharagpur
Raipur
Nagpur
Chittagong
Chanda
Cuttack
Indravati
BAY OF BENGAL
Warangal
Vizianagaram
Berhampur
Vishakhapatnam
Akyab
Brahmaputra
Dibrugarh
Gauhati
Tezpur
Khasi Hills
Imphal
Silchar
Patkai Bum
Myitkyina
Bhamo
Tengchong
Lashio
Shwebo
Monywa
Mandalay
Victoria 3053
Arakan Yoma
Pegu Yoma
Irrawaddy
Salween
Taunggyi
Yamethin
Toungoo
THAILAND (SIAM)
BURMA
LAOS
Mekong
Luang Prabang
VIETNAM
Hanoi
Haiphong
Hoa Binh
Gulf of Tonking
Nanning
Pingxiang
Gejiu
KUNMING
YUNNAN
Xiaguan
Dali
Lijiang
Nu Shan
Yun Ling
Ningjing Shan
Shaluli Shan
Daxue Shan
Gongga Shan 7600
Qamdo
Zayü
Garzê
SICHUAN
CHENGDU
Leshan
Neijiang
Zigong
Wutongqiao
Luzhou
Yibin
Chang Jiang
Zunyi
Guiyang
Anshun
Daliang Shan
Zhaotong
Shuicheng
Min Jiang
Hanzhong
Nanchong
Santai
Mianyang
MONGOLIA
Tannu Ola
Uvs Nuur
Ulaangom
Hyargas Nuur
Har Us Nuur
Hovd
Dörgön Nuur
Uliastay
Hangayn Nuruu
Hövsgöl Nuur
Hatgal
Bugun
Tsetserleg
Ulan Bator
Aerhtai (Altai) Shan
Altay
Fuyun
Fuhai
Ulungur He
Buyanhongor
Dalandzadgad
Gaxun Nur
Projection: Bonne
East from Greenwich

1:15 000 000

100 0 100 200 300 400 miles

100 0 100 200 300 400 500 600 km

Oz. Baykal
REPUBLICS
Chita
Ulan Ude
Yablonovy Khrebet
Bukachacha
Sretensk
Nerchinsk
Olovyannaya
Borzya
Manzhouli
Hailar
Hulun Nur
Buir Nur
Dutulun Shan
Choybalsan
Kerulen
Yilehuli Shan
Blagoveshchensk
Shimanovsk
Svobodny
Aihui
Bureya
Oroqen Zizhiqi
Xiao Hinggan Ling
Nenjiang
Bei'an
Obluchye
Chegdomyn
Komsomolsk
Aleksandrovsk
L. Bolon
Troitskoye
Birobidzhan
Khabarovsk
Amur
Sikhote Alin
Tartarskiy Proliv
Sakhalin
Poronaysk
C. Terpeniya
Dolinsk
Yuzhno-Sakhalinsk
Kholmsk
La Perouse Str.
Wakkanai
Asahigawa
Hokkaido
2290
Kushiro
Otaru
SAPPORO
Muroran
C. Erimo
Hakodate
Tsugaru-kaikyo
Aomori
Hachinohe
Morioka
Akita
Sakata
Ishinomaki
Sendai
Sado
Niigata
Koriyama
Utsunomiya
Wajima
Toyama
Kanazawa
TOKYO
Kawasaki
YOKOHAMA
NAGOYA
Fuji-san
3776
Yokosuka
Shizuoka
Hamamatsu
KYOTO
KOBE
OSAKA
Sakai
Wakayama
Okayama
Hiroshima
Kure
Shimonoseki
Shikoku
Kochi
Matsuyama
KITAKYUSHU
FUKUOKA
Sasebo
Nagasaki
Kumamoto
Kyushu
Kagoshima
Tanega-shima
Honshu
JAPAN
SEA OF JAPAN
Hegang
Jiamusi
Shuangyashan
Yichun
Bikin
Qiqihar
Butha Qi
Arxan
Solon
Anda
Suihua
Mishan
Jixi
Ozero Khanka
Khrebet Sikhote Alin
HARBIN
Shuangcheng
Horqin Youyi Qianqi
(Ulan Hot)
Baicheng
Tao'an
Fuyu
Manchuria
Mudanjiang
Ussuriysk
Artem
Partizansk
Nakhodka
Vladivostok
Jilin
CHANGCHUN
Shuangliao
Siping
Liaoyuan
Dunhua
Songhua Hu
Yanji
Hunchun
Chongjin
Paektu-san
2744
Tonghua
Saynshand
Dzamin Üüd
Erenhot
Abagnar Qi
Linxi
1949
Tongliao
Duolun
Chifeng
Chaoyang
Fuxin
FUSHUN
SHENYANG
Benxi
Liaoyang
Jinzhou
ANSHAN
Yingkou
Dandong
NORTH KOREA
Hungnam
Wonsan
P'YONGYANG
Korea Bay
Liaodong Wan
Liaodong Bandao
LÜDA
Kaesong
SOUL
Inch'on
SOUTH KOREA
Taejon
TAEGU
PUSAN
Masan
Kwangju
1915
Korea Str.
Cheju Do
1950
MONGGOL
NEI MONGOL ZIZHIQU
Da Hinggan Ling
HEILONGJIANG
JILIN
LIAONING
Hohhot
Baotou
Jining
Zhangjiakou
Xuanhua
Chengde
Qinhuangdao
Datong
BEIJING SHI
BEIJING
(Peking)
Tangshan
Baoding
TIANJIN SHI
TIANJIN
Cangzhou
Bo Hai
2894
HEBEI
GREAT WALL
TAIYUAN
Shijiazhuang
Yangquan
Yuci
Fenyang
Taiyue Shan
SHANXI
Dezhou
Huang He
Ye Xian
Yantai
Weihai
Weifang
JINAN
Zibo
QINGDAO
SHANDONG
YELLOW SEA
Handan
Anyang
Changzhi
Linfen
Tai'an
Jining
Xinxiang
Zaozhuang
Lianyungang
Tongchuan
Luoyang
Sanmenxia
Kaifeng
Grand Canal
XI'AN
ZHENGZHOU
HENAN
Shangqiu
Huaibei
Xuzhou
Qingjiang
Yancheng
JIANGSU
Pingdingshan
Nanyang
Shangshui
Fuyang
Hongze Hu
Bengbu
Yangzhou
Taizhou
Changzhou
Nantong
Ankang
Han Shui
Zhumadian
Huainan
Huai He
NANJING
Ma'anshan
Wuxi
Suzhou
SHANGHAI SHI
SHANGHAI
Xiangfan
Dabie Shan
Hefei
ANHUI
Wuhu
Wuxing
Jiaxing
Hangzhou Wan
HUBEI
Zhongxiang
WUHAN
Tongling
Anqing
Hangzhou
Shaoxing
Ningbo
Yichang
Shashi
Huangshi
Tunxi
ZHEJIANG
EAST CHINA SEA
Changde
Yueyang
Dongting Hu
Jiujiang
Poyang Hu
Jingdezhen
Jinhua
Linhai
Yuan Jiang
Yiyang
Nanchang
Shangrao
Qu Xian
Wenzhou
HUNAN
Changsha
Xiangtan
Pingxiang
JIANGXI
Wuyi Shan
2120
Fuzhou
Shaoyang
Hengyang
Jian
Nanping
Min Ch.
Sanming
Fuzhou
Gan Jiang
Ganzhou
Ruijin
FUJIAN
Xing'an
Guilin
Nan Ling
Shaoguan
Longyan
Quanzhou
Zhangzhou
Xiamen
Mei Xian
GUANGDONG
GUANGZHOU
Shantou
Wuzhou
Xi Jiang
Huizhou
Zhaoqing
Foshan
Jiangmen
Macau
(Port.)
HONG KONG (Br.)
Yangjiang
Maoming
Zhanjiang
Qiongzhou Haixia
Haikou
Hainan Dao
1879
Yacheng
Formosa Strait
Jilong
TAIPEI
Taizhong
Jiayi
Yu Shan
3997
TAIWAN
Tainan
Gaoxiong
Pingdong
Sakashima Gunto
Ryūkyū-rettō
Amami-ō-Shima
Okinawa
Naha
Tropic of Cancer
PACIFIC OCEAN
Batan Is.
Babuyan Is.
Pratas
SOUTH CHINA SEA
110
120
130
140
50
40
30
20

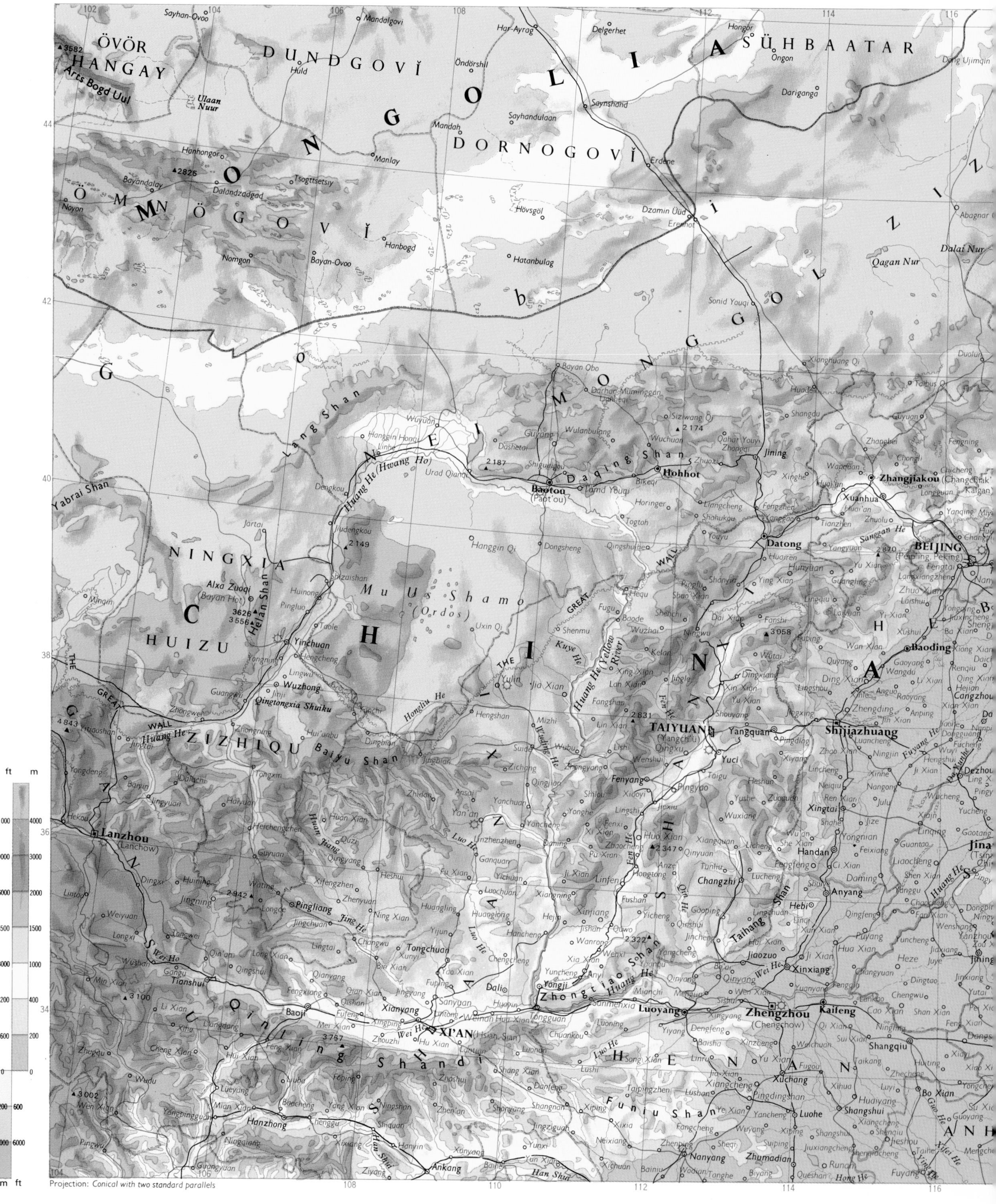
MONGOLIA
ÖVÖR HANGAY
DUNDGOVĬ
SÜHBAATAR
DORNOGOVĬ
ÖMNÖGOVĬ
Arts Bogd Uul
Ulaan Nuur
Mandalgovi
Sayhan-Ovoo
Har-Ayrag
Delgerhet
Hongor
Öndörshil
Huld
Ongon
Dariganga
Saynshand
Sayhandulaan
Mandah
Manlay
Hanhongor
Bayandalay
Dalandzadgad
Tsogttsetsiy
Noyon
Nomgon
Bayan-Ovoo
Hanbogd
Hövsgöl
Hatanbulag
Erdene
Dzamin Üüd
Erenhot
Sonid Youqi
Qagan Nur
Dalai Nur
Abagnar Qi
NEI MONGGOL ZIZHIQU
Bayan Obo
Lang Shan
Yabrai Shan
Hanggin Houqi
Linhe
Wuyuan
Urad Qianqi
Dengkou
Baotou (Pao-t'ou)
Tumd Youqi
Hohhot
Daqing Shan
Guyang
Dashetai
Shiguaigou
Wulanbulang
Wuchuan
Sizwang Qi
Qahar Youyi Zhongqi
Zhuozi
Jining
Huade
Shangdu
Xianghuang Qi
Taibus Qi
Duolun
Guyuan
Zhangbei
Fengning
Zhangjiakou (Changchiak'ou) (Kalgan)
Xuanhua
Datong
Horinger
Togtoh
Liangcheng
Fengzhen
Tianzhen
BEIJING (Pei-p'ing, Peking)
Jartai
Jiudengkou
Hanggin Qi
Dongsheng
NINGXIA HUIZU ZIZHIQU
Alxa Zuoqi (Bayan Hot)
Helan Shan
Mu Us Shamo (Ordos)
Uxin Qi
Yinchuan
Wuzhong
Qingtongxia Shuiku
Huang He (Hwang Ho)
GREAT WALL
Yulin
Shenmu
Fugu
Hequ
Kuye He
Huang He (Yellow River)
Taiyuan (Yangch'ü)
Yangquan
Shijiazhuang
Baoding
HEBEI
SHANXI
SHAANXI
GANSU
HENAN
CHINA
Lanzhou (Lanchow)
Baiyu Shan
Yan'an
Tongchuan
Xianyang
XI'AN (Hsian, Sian)
Baoji
Tianshui
Wei He
Qinling Shandi
Hanzhong
Ankang
Han Shui
Pingliang
Jing He
Luo He
Fen He
Linfen
Changzhi
Taihang Shan
Handan
Xingtai
Anyang
Xinxiang
Jiaozuo
Luoyang
Zhengzhou (Chengchow)
Kaifeng
Shangqiu
Xuchang
Pingdingshan
Luohe
Zhumadian
Nanyang
Funiu Shan
Zhongtiao Shan
Sanmenxia
Dali
Yongji
Dezhou
Jinan
Projection: Conical with two standard parallels

1:6 000 000

50 0 50 100 150 miles

50 0 50 100 150 200 km

Horqin Youyi Qianqi
HARBIN
(Haerhpin)
Jixi
Ozero Khanka
U.S.S.R.
HEILONGJIANG
Zhenlai
Baicheng
Tao'er He
Nen Jiang
Maoxing
Zhaoyuan
Acheng
Shuangcheng
Songhua Jiang
Hulin He
Tuquan
Da'an
Changchunling
Yanshou
Shangzhi
Yimianpo
Linkou
Tao'an
Anguang
Fuyu
Sanchahe
Wuchang
Zhangguangcai Ling
Mudan Jiang
Mudanjiang
Hengdaohezi
Maqiao
Pogranichnyy
Xiachengzi
Suifenhe
Suiyang
Qian Gorlos
Shenjingzi
Benaolaizhao
Songhua
Yushu
Shanhetun
Hailin
Muling
Ning'an
Golenki
Tongyu
Kaoshan
Nong'an
Dehui
Jiutai
Shulan
1690
Dongning
Pokrovka
Jarud Qi
Beizhengzhen
Fulongquan
Gangyao
Dongjingcheng
Jingpo Hu
Luozigou
Ussuriysk
(Voroshilov)
Razdolnoye
Zhanyu
Changling
Wulajie
1949
Xinkai He
Changchun
Jilin
(Kirin, Chilin)
Xinzhan
Emu
Huangsongdian
Chunyang
Artem
Travichanka
Maolin
Huaidezhen
Fanjiatun
Jiaohe
Songhua Hu
Dunhua
Daxinggou
Vladivostok
Bairin Zuoqi
Tongliao
Huaide
Shuangyang
Wangqing
Shixian
Tumen
Hunchun
Slavyanka
2029
Linxi
Bairin Youqi
Kailu
Shuangliao
Lishu
Yitong
Mingyuegue
Yanji
Kraskino
Posyet
Hexigten Qi
Xiliao He
Siping
Liaoyuan
Panshi
Huadian
Helong
Paksikori
Xar Moron He
Laoha He
Bamiancheng
Jargalang
Zhangwu
Xifeng
Dongfeng
Huijia He
Huinan
Erdao Jiang
Antu
Hoeamdong
Unggi
Sosura
Ongniud Qi
Wudanhoolai
Hure Qi
Kangping
Willow Wall
Faku
Kaiyuan
Hailong
Manchuria
Jingyu
1677
Changbai Shan
Hoeryong
Najin
Musan
Pugodong
2020
Xiawa
Liu He
Zhangwu
Liao He
Tieling
Shanchengzhen
Fusong
Puryong
Chongjin
Chifeng
Heishui
Fuxin
Xinlitun
Xinmin
Qingyuan
Huihe
Paektu-san
Yupyongdong
Nanam
Kyongsong
Chuuronjang
2541
Fushun
Linjiang
Weichang
1885
Beipiao
Qinghemen
SHENYANG
(Mukden)
Heishan
Dongbei
Xinbin
Tonghua
Chunggang up
Changbai
Huchang
Hyesan
Hochon
Irhyangdong
Ondaejin
Simpungdong
Ningcheng
Chaoyang
Daling He
Yi Xian
Beizhen
Goubangzi
Liaozhong
Liaoyang
Benxi
Qingshecheng
Inpundong
1845
Ji'an
Manpojin
Kasan-dong
Kapsan
Hapsu
Kilju
Musudan
Longhua
Lingyuan
LIAONING
Panshan
Anping
Huanren
Hun Jiang
Kanggye
Pungsan
Kosongni
Songjin
Chengde
Jinzhou
Niuzhuang
Anshan
Haicheng
Yalu Jiang
Kuup-tong
2522
Pujon-chosuji
Kwangdaegeri
Changhungni
Tanchon
Luanping
Shangbancheng
Jianchang
Jinxi
Tianzhuangtai
Lianshanguan
Kuandian
Supung Sk.
Chosan
Changjin-chosuji
Changjin
Pukchong
Xingcheng
Yingkou
Fengcheng
Pyoktong
Kolo-dong
Sinchang
Sohori
Kuancheng
Liaodong Wan
Gai Xian
Xiuyan
Cao He
Ji'an
Taegwan
NORTH KOREA
Sinhung
Sinpo
Hongwon
Shuangshanzi
Suizhong
Xiongyuecheng
Wafangdian
Liaodong Bandao
1131
Dandong
Sinuiju
Yongampo
Pukchin
Kujang
Oro
Hamhung
Hungnam
Tongchon-ni
Jianchangying
Zunhua
Dongou
Gushan
Chongju
Tokchon
Tongjoson Man
SEA OF JAPAN
Funing
Qinhuangdao
Zhuanghe
Sonchon
Anju
Yonghung
Kowon
Yutian
Fengrun
Luan Xian
Changli
Fu Xian
Sukchon
Unsan
Sinchang
Munchon
Wonsan
Tangshan
Luan He
Leting
Pikou
Sunan
Songchon
Kangdong
Tongyang
Anbyon
Kojo
Wuqing
Hangu
Jin Xian
Korea Bay
P'yongyang
Chunghwa
Koksan
Singosan
Kosong
TIANJIN
(Tientsin, Tienching)
Tanggu
Dagu
Lushun
LÜDA
(Luta)
Chinnampo
Songnim
Sepo-ri
Hoeyang
1638
Kansong
Bo Hai
(Gulf of Chihli)
Suan
Sariwon
Pyonggang
Changdo-ri
Oikou
Chaeryong
Sinmak
Nam-chon
Kumhwa
Hwachon-chosuji
1678
Yangyang
Chumunjin
Cho-do
Changyon
Kumchon
Chorwon
Haeju
Kaesong
Panmunjom
Uijongbu
Chunchon
Hongchon
Kangnung
Ongjin
Yonan
Munsan
Paengnyong-do
Cease Fire Line
Kanghwa
Yongdungpo
SOUL
(Seoul)
Hoengsong
Samchok
Ullung-do
Huang He
Yantai
Penglai
Longkou
Huang Xian
Weihai
Inch'on
Ichon
Yongwol
Wonju
Yoju
Laizhou Wan
Zhaoyuan
Daxindian
Fushan
Muping
Suwon
Osan
Chechon
Ulchin
Huimin
Kenli
Qixia
923
Wendeng
Pyongtaek
Chungju
Yongju
Shanghe
Beizhen
Ye Xian
Shandong Bandao
Rushan
Shidao
Sosan
Chonan
SOUTH KOREA
Yechon
Andong
Yongdok
Qingcheng
Guangrao
Shouguang
Changyi
Laiyang
Haiyang
Nanhuang
Chongju
Yesan
Hongsong
Kongju
Uisong
Chongha
Zhoucun
Zibo
Huantai
Linzi
Weifang
Pingdu
Laixi
Anmyon-do
Taechon
Taejon
Sonsan
Kimchon
Pohang
Tai Shan
Yidu
Fangzi
Anqiu
Lanzhou
Jimo
Nonsan
Yongdong
Yongchon
Kyongju
1524
Boshan
Linqu
Gaomi
Jiao Xian
Chengyang
QINGDAO
(Ch'ingtao)
Kanggyong
Iri
Chonju
Taegu
Ulsan
Laiwu
1108
Kunsan
Kimje
Kochang
Koryong
Chongdo
Miryang
Zhucheng
Jiaozhou Wan
Puan
Hamyang
Tongnae
Xintai
Yishui
Wulian
Chongup
Namwon
1915
Chinju
Masan
Chinhae
PUSAN
Sishui
Mengyin
Rizhao
HUANG HAI
(Yellow Sea)
Sogo-ri
Tamyang
Kwangju
Hadong
Samchonpo
Pingyi
Yi He
Ju Xian
Lijiangcheng
Songjong-ri
Naju
Sunchon
Chungmu
Sasuna
Fei Xian
Tangtou
Andongwei
Mokpo
Posong
Polgyo-ri
Yosu
Korea Strait
Saka
Teng Xian
Linyi
Haizhou Wan
Changhung
Tsushima
Ganyu
Lianyungang
Chindo
Haenam
Izuhara
Tsushima-kaikyo
Zaozhuang
Tancheng
Haizhou
Lianyungang
(Hsinhaihsien)
Iki
Pei Xian
Weishan
Xuzhou
(Hsuchow, Suchow)
Yaowan
Guanyun
Chenjiagang
Xiangshui
Karatsu
Imari
Shuyang
Guannan
Shuanggou
Siyang
Binhai
Suqian
Lianshui
Da Yunhe
Funing
Cheju
Cheju-do
1950
Hallim
Onpyong-ni
Mosulpo
Sogwi-po
JAPAN
Sasebo
Kashima
Omura
Isahaya
Nagasaki
Kuchinotsu
Nakadori-jima
Fukue-jima
Suining
Lingbi
Si Xian
Qingjiang
Huai'an
Hongze Hu
Yancheng
Baoying
JIANGSU
Liuzhuang
Guzhen
Wuhe
Huaiyuan
Bengbu
Fengyang
Gaoyou Hu
Xinghua
Dongtai

118 East from Greenwich 120 122 124 126 128

44 42 40 38 36 34

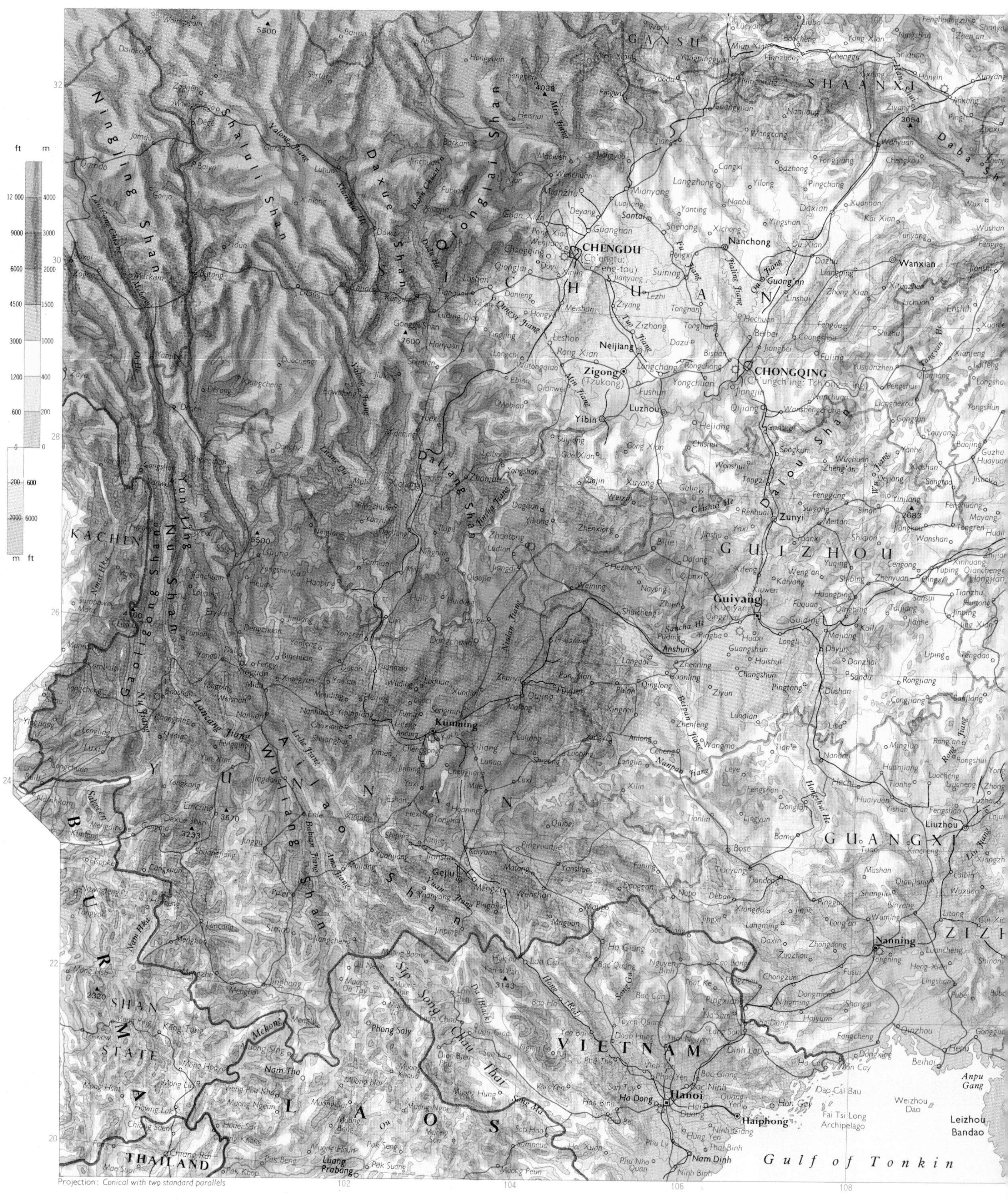
GANSU
SHAANXI
SICHUAN
GUIZHOU
YUNNAN
GUANGXI
KACHIN
SHAN STATE
BURMA
LAOS
VIETNAM
THAILAND
CHENGDU
(Ch'engtu; Tch'eng-tou)
CHONGQING
(Ch'ungch'ing; Tch'ong-k'ing)
Guiyang
(Kueiyang)
Kunming
Nanning
Hanoi
Haiphong
Nanchong
Wanxian
Neijiang
Zigong
(Tzukong)
Yibin
Luzhou
Zunyi
Liuzhou
Gejiu
Luang Prabang
Nam Dinh
Ha Dong
Gulf of Tonkin
Leizhou Bandao
Weizhou Dao
Fai Tsi Long Archipelago
Anpu Gang
Ningjing Shan
Shaluli Shan
Daxue Shan
Qionglai Shan
Daliang Shan
Dalou Shan
Daba Shan
Wuliang Shan
Ailao Shan
Yun Ling
Nu Shan
Gaoligong Shan
Min Jiang
Yalong Jiang
Lancang Jiang
Nu Jiang
Jinsha Jiang
Mekong
Song Ma
Song Da (Black)
Hong (Red)
Gongga Shan
7600
5500
4100
3570
3233
3143
3054
2683
2320
4038
ft
m
12 000
9000
6000
4500
3000
1200
600
0
200
2000
4000
3000
2000
1500
1000
400
200
600
6000
Projection: Conical with two standard parallels
98
100
102
104
106
108
32
30
28
26
24
22
20

1:6 000 000
50 0 50 100 150 miles
50 0 50 100 150 200 250 km
HENAN
JIANGSU
ANHUI
HUBEI
ZHEJIANG
JIANGXI
HUNAN
FUJIAN
GUANGDONG
TAIWAN
(FORMOSA)
SHANGHAI
(Changhai)
NANJING
(Nanking; Nanching)
WUHAN
(Wou-han)
Hankou
Nanchang
Changsha
Hangzhou
(Hangchou; Hangchow)
Fuzhou
(Foochow; Fuchou)
GUANGZHOU
(Kwangchou; Canton)
HONG KONG (U.K.)
Kowloon
VICTORIA
Macau
(Macao)
(Port.)
TAIBEI
(T'aipei)
Jilong
Xiamen
(Hsiamen; Amoy)
Shantou
(Swatow)
Quanzhou
(Ch'uanchou)
Wenzhou
(Wenchow)
Ningbo
(Ningpo)
Suzhou
Wuxi
Changzhou
Zhenjiang
(Chenchiang)
Yangzhou
Nantong
Hefei
Huainan
Bengbu
Wuhu
Anqing
Jiujiang
Jingdezhen
Shangrao
Linchuan
Ganzhou
Shaoguan
Hengyang
Zhuzhou
Xiangtan
Shaoyang
Yichang
(Ich'ang)
Shashi
Xiangfan
Xinyang
Nanyang
Changde
Yiyang
Huangshi
Zhangzhou
Sanming
Nanping
Jinhua
Shaoxing
Jiaxing
Tunxi
Gaoxiong
(Kaohsiung)
Tainan
Taizhong
(Taichung)
Jiayi
Xinzhu
Pingdong
Zhanghua
Guilin
Wuzhou
Zhanjiang
Foshan
Jiangmen
Zhaoqing
Huizhou
Chongming Dao
Zhoushan Dao
Hangzhou Wan
Chang Jiang
Taiwan Strait
Formosa Strait
Luzon Strait
SOUTH CHINA SEA
Tropic of Cancer
Tungsha Tao
Dangan Liedao
Lan Yu
Poyang Hu
Dongting Hu
Dabie Shan
Wuyi Shan
Jiuling Shan
Mufu Shan
Wugong Shan
Taiwan Shan
Xue Shan
Yu Shan
3997
3931
2164
2120
1834
1810
1725
1629
1703
Mazu Dao
Nanri Dao
Nanji Shan
Yuhuan Dao
Taizhou Liedao
Donghai Dao
Naozhou Dao
Leizhou Wan
Honghai Wan
Xinghua Wan
Shangchuan Dao
Xiachuan Dao
Hailing Dao
Gaolan Dao
112
114
116
118
120
122
32
30
28
26
24
22
20
COPYRIGHT. GEORGE PHILIP & SON. LTD.

SEA OF OKHOTSK
SEA OF JAPAN
La Pérouse Strait
(Sōya-Kaikyō)
Sakhalin
Wakkanai
HOKKAIDO
Asahigawa
Kitami
Kushiro
Obihiro
Sapporo
Otaru
Tomakomai
Muroran
Uchiura-Wan
Hakodate
Tsugaru-Kaikyō
Aomori
Hachinohe
TŌHOKU
Morioka
Akita
Sendai
Yamagata
Niigata
Sado
Okushiri-Tō
Rishiri-Tō
U.S.S.R.
CHINA
NORTH KOREA
Vladivostok
Nakhodka
Ussuriysk
Ozero Khanka
Zaliv Petra Velikogo
Chongjin

1: 5 000 000

50 0 50 100 miles

50 0 50 100 150 km

RYUKYU ISLANDS
on same scale
P A C I F I C O C E A N
SOUTH KOREA
Tsushima
Ullung Do
Tok Do
Oki-Shotō
Izu-Shotō
Nansei-Shotō
Sakishima-Guntō
Senkaku-Shotō
Okinawa-Guntō
Amami-Guntō
Ōsumi-Shotō
Tokara-Rettō
Satsunan-Shotō
Gotō-Rettō
Koshiki-Rettō
CHŪGOKU
SHIKOKU
KYŪSHŪ
KINKI
KANTŌ
TOKYO
YOKOHAMA
NAGOYA
KYOTO
ŌSAKA
KOBE
Hiroshima
KITAKYŪSHŪ
Fukuoka
Nagasaki
Kumamoto
Kagoshima
Okinawa-Jima
Naha
Amami-Ō-Shima
Tokuno-Shima
Miyako-Jima
Ishigaki-Shima
Iriomote-Jima
Yaku-Shima
Tane-ga-Shima
Bungo-Suidō
Kii-Suidō
Tosa-Wan
Suruga-Wan
Toyama-wan
Wakasa-Wan
Ōsumi-Kaikyō
Projection: Conical with two standard parallels
East from Greenwich
m ft

SEA OF JAPAN
SOUTH KOREA
HONSHU
Oki-Shotō
Dōgo
Saigō
Daimanji-San
Shimane-Hantō
Jizō-Zaki
Sakaiminato
Matsue
Hirata
Shinji-Ko
Yonago
Yasugi
Izumo
Taisha
Hi-no-Misaki
Kurayoshi
Tottori
Toyooka
Iwami
Daisen
TOTTORI
CHŪGOKU - DISTRICT
Ōda
Sanbe-San
Gōtsu
Hamada
SHIMANE
Chūgoku-Sanchi
Tsuyama
Niimi
OKAYAMA
Shōbara
Miyoshi
Takahashi
Himeji
Aioi
Tatsuno
Nishiwaki
Takasago
Kakogawa
Akashi
Masuda
HIROSHIMA
Okayama
Bizen
Saidaiji
Sōja
Kurashiki
Fuchū
Ibara
Fukuyama
Onomichi
Mihara
Tamano
Kasaoka
Harima-Nada
Awaji-Shima
Sumoto
Shōdo-Shima
Hagi
Mi-Shima
Ōmi-Shima
Tsuno-Shima
Nagato
Hibiki-Nada
YAMAGUCHI
Yamaguchi
Mine
Hōfu
Tokuyama
Iwakuni
Ōtake
Kure
Takehara
Hiroshima-Wan
Aki-Nada
Imabari
Niihama
Saijō
Hiuchi-Nada
Kan'onji
Marugame
Sakaide
Takamatsu
Zentsūji
KAGAWA
Naruto
Tokushima
Komatsujima
Anan
TOKUSHIMA
Shimonoseki
Onoda
Ube
Kudamatsu
Hikari
Suō-Nada
Genkai-Nada
KITAKYŪSHŪ
Nōgata
Yukuhashi
Iizuka
FUKUOKA
Takawa
Nakatsu
Buzen
Usa
Bungotakada
Kunisaki
Kitsuki
Beppu-Wan
Beppu
Ōita
Usuki
Tsukumi
Saiki
Iyo-Nada
Matsuyama
Iyo
Ōzu
Yawatahama
Uwajima
Shikoku-Sanchi
EHIME
KŌCHI
Kōchi
Nankoku
Aki
Susaki
Tosa
Tosa-Wan
Muroto
Muroto-Misaki
SHIKOKU
SHIKOKU - DISTRICT
Nakamura
Sukumo
Tosa-shimizu
Ashizuri-Zaki
Oki-no-Shima
Bungo-Suidō
Hōyo-Kaikyō
Tsushima
Izuhara
Kara-Saki
Kō-Saki
Higasi-Suidō
Iki
Iki-Kaikyō
Karatsu
Imari
Matsuura
Hirado
Hirado-Shima
Ikitsuki-Shima
Sasebo
Takeo
SAGA
Saga
Tosu
Amagi
Kurume
Ōkawa
Yanagawa
Kashima
Ōmuta
Arao
Yamaga
Kikuchi
Ōmura
Isahaya
Nagasaki
NAGASAKI
Kumamoto
Shimabara
Unzen-Dake
Tachibana-Wan
Nomo-Zaki
Hita
Taketa
Aso
Kuju-San
Yufu-Dake
Sobo-San
KUMAMOTO
Takachiho
Uto
Amakusa-Nada
Amakusa-Shotō
Hondo
Shimo-Jima
Kami-Jima
Yatsushiro
Yatsushiro-Kai
Nobeoka
Hyūga
Kyūshū-Sanchi
MIYAZAKI
Hitoyoshi
Minamata
Ushibuka
Naga-Shima
Izumi
Akune
Ōkuchi
Saito
Kobayashi
KYŪSHŪ
KYŪSHŪ - DISTRICT
Miyazaki
Kami-koshiki-Jima
Koshiki-Rettō
Shimo-koshiki-Jima
Sendai
Kushikino
Kokubu
Miyakonojō
Kagoshima
Nichinan
On-Take
Taniyama
Kaseda
Tarumizu
Kanoya
Kushima
Kagoshima-Wan
Satsuma-Hantō
Noma-Saki
Makurazaki
Ibusuki
Shibushi-Wan
Bō-no-Misaki
Kaimon-Dake
Ōsumi-Hantō
Sata-Misaki
Projection: Lambert's Conformal Conic

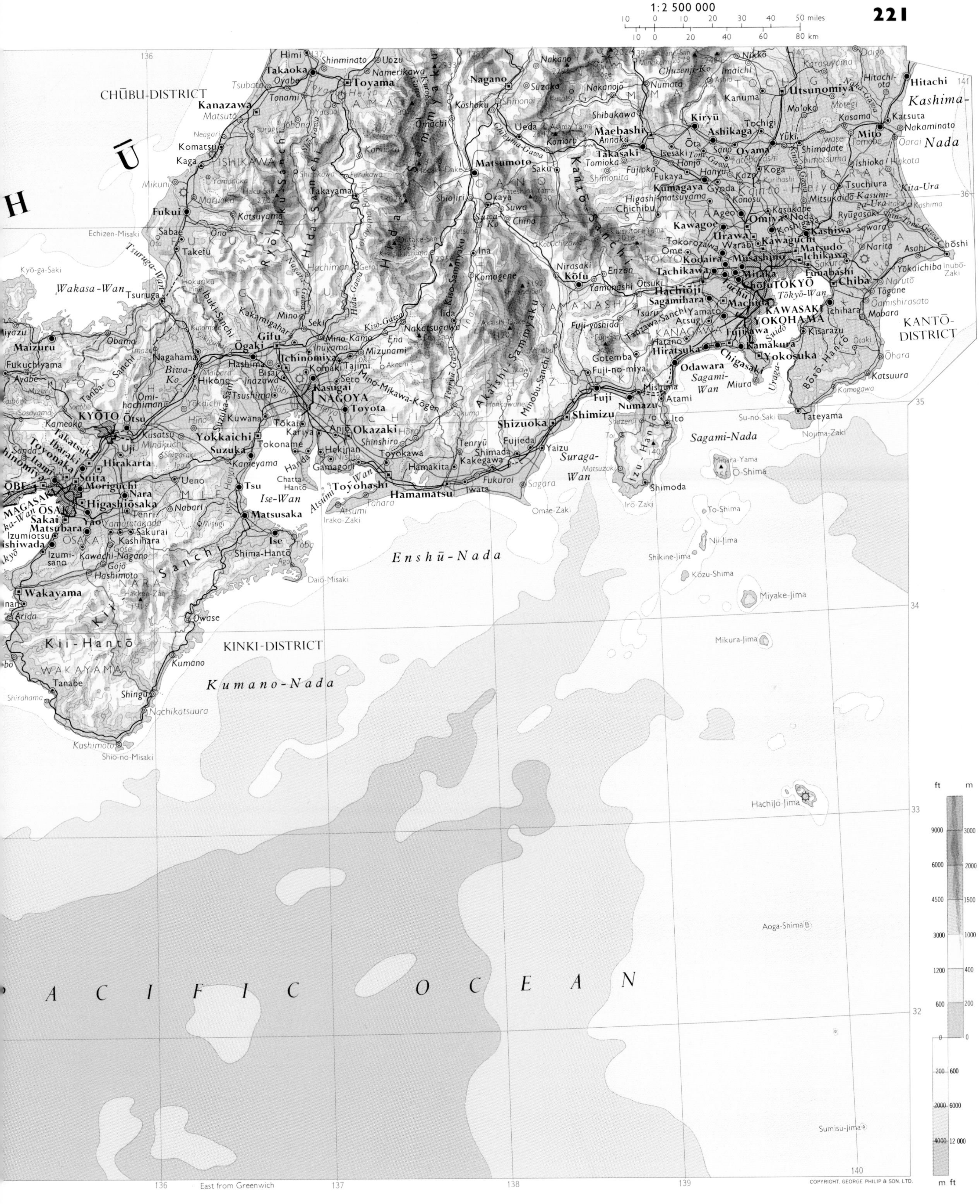

1:2 500 000

10 0 10 20 30 40 50 miles

10 0 20 40 60 80 km

CHŪBU-DISTRICT

KANTŌ-DISTRICT

KINKI-DISTRICT

Enshū-Nada

Kumano-Nada

Sagami-Nada

PACIFIC OCEAN

East from Greenwich

1:45 000 000

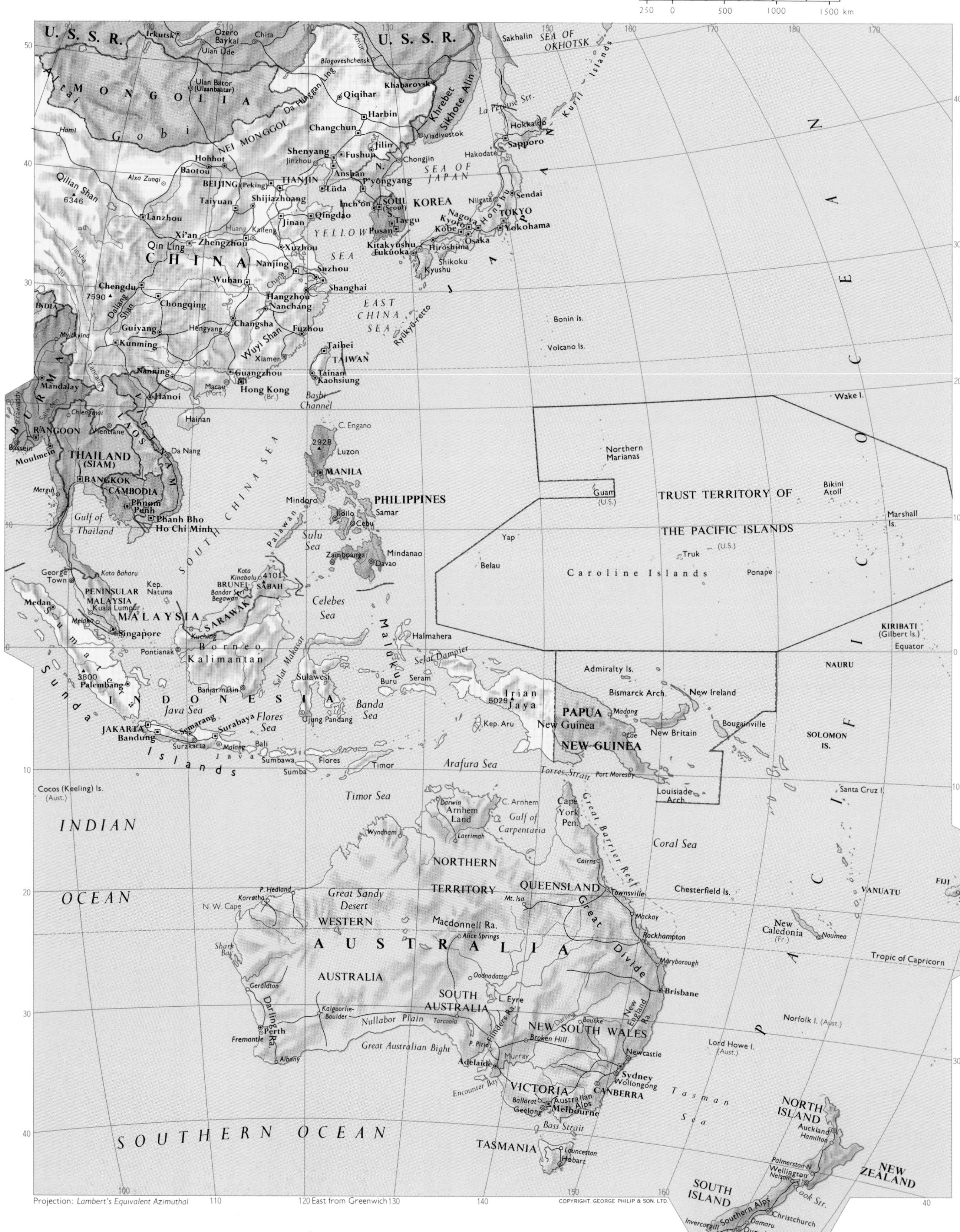
200 0 200 400 600 800 1000 miles
250 0 500 1000 1500 km
U. S. S. R.
Irkutsk
Ozero Baykal
Chita
Ulan Ude
Ulan Bator (Ulaanbaatar)
M O N G O L I A
Altai
Gobi
Hami
Blagoveshchensk
Da Hinggan Ling
Qiqihar
Khabarovsk
Khrebet Sikhote Alin
Sakhalin
SEA OF OKHOTSK
Kuril Islands
La Pérouse Str.
Harbin
NEI MONGGOL
Changchun
Vladivostok
Hokkaido
Sapporo
Hakodate
Jilin
Shenyang
Fushun
Jinzhou
Chongjin
Hohhot
Baotou
Anshan
N. KOREA
SEA OF JAPAN
Alxa Zuoqi
BEIJING (Peking)
TIANJIN
Lüda
P'yongyang
Qilian Shan
6346
Taiyuan
Shijiazhuang
Inch'on
SOUL (Seoul)
S. KOREA
Niigata
Sendai
Honshu
TOKYO
Yokohama
Lanzhou
Jinan
Qingdao
Taegu
Pusan
Nagoya
Kyoto
Kobe
Osaka
Huang
Kaifeng
Xi'an
Qin Ling
Zhengzhou
YELLOW SEA
Kitakyushu
Fukuoka
Hiroshima
Shikoku
Kyushu
Xuzhou
J A P A N
Jinsha
C H I N A
Nanjing
Suzhou
Shanghai
Wuhan
Chang
Chengdu
7590
Hangzhou
Nanchang
EAST CHINA SEA
Ryukyu-retto
INDIA
Chongqing
Daliang Shan
Changsha
Guiyang
Hengyang
Wuyi Shan
Fuzhou
Bonin Is.
Kunming
Myitkyina
Taibei
TAIWAN
Volcano Is.
Xiamen
Nanning
Guangzhou
Tainan
Kaohsiung
Mandalay
Macau (Port.)
Hong Kong (Br.)
Hanoi
Bashi Channel
Wake I.
BURMA
Chiengmai
Hainan
LAOS
Irrawaddy
Salween
RANGOON
Vientiane
C. Engano
2928
Luzon
Bassein
Moulmein
THAILAND (SIAM)
Da Nang
VIETNAM
MANILA
Northern Marianas
BANGKOK
CAMBODIA
Mergui
PHILIPPINES
Mindoro
Samar
Guam (U.S.)
TRUST TERRITORY OF THE PACIFIC ISLANDS (U.S.)
Bikini Atoll
Marshall Is.
Phnom Penh
Phanh Bho Ho Chi Minh
Gulf of Thailand
SOUTH CHINA SEA
Palawan
Iloilo
Cebu
Sulu Sea
Yap
Truk
Mindanao
Zamboanga
Davao
Belau
Caroline Islands
Ponape
George Town
Kota Baharu
Kota Kinabalu
4101
BRUNEI
SABAH
Bandar Seri Begawan
Kep. Natuna
PENINSULAR MALAYSIA
Kuala Lumpur
MALAYSIA
Medan
SARAWAK
Celebes Sea
Melaka
Singapore
Kuching
Maluku
Halmahera
KIRIBATI (Gilbert Is.)
Equator
Pontianak
Borneo
Kalimantan
Selat Makasar
Selat Dampier
NAURU
Sumatera
Sulawesi
Buru
Seram
Admiralty Is.
3800
Palembang
Banjarmasin
Irian Jaya
5029
Bismarck Arch.
New Ireland
Madang
I N D O N E S I A
Java Sea
Banda Sea
PAPUA New Guinea
Sunda Islands
JAKARTA
Bandung
Semarang
Surabaya
Flores Sea
Ujung Pandang
Kep. Aru
Bougainville
Lae
New Britain
SOLOMON IS.
Surakarta
Malang
Bali
Java
Sumbawa
Flores
Timor
Arafura Sea
NEW GUINEA
Sumba
Torres Strait
Port Moresby
Louisiade Arch.
Cocos (Keeling) Is. (Aust.)
Timor Sea
Darwin
Arnhem Land
C. Arnhem
Gulf of Carpentaria
Cape York Pen.
Great Barrier Reef
Santa Cruz I.
INDIAN OCEAN
Wyndham
Larrimah
Coral Sea
NORTHERN TERRITORY
Cairns
QUEENSLAND
Townsville
Chesterfield Is.
VANUATU
FIJI
Suva
P. Hedland
Karratha
Great Sandy Desert
Mt. Isa
N. W. Cape
WESTERN AUSTRALIA
Macdonnell Ra.
Alice Springs
Great Dividing Range
Mackay
Rockhampton
New Caledonia (Fr.)
Noumea
A U S T R A L I A
Shark Bay
Tropic of Capricorn
Maryborough
Oodnadatta
Geraldton
SOUTH AUSTRALIA
L. Eyre
Brisbane
Darling Ra.
Kalgoorlie-Boulder
Nullarbor Plain
Tarcoola
Flinders Ra.
Darling
Bourke
New England Ra.
NEW SOUTH WALES
Norfolk I. (Aust.)
Perth
Fremantle
P. Pirie
Broken Hill
Great Australian Bight
Lord Howe I. (Aust.)
Albany
Adelaide
Murray
Newcastle
Sydney
Wollongong
Encounter Bay
VICTORIA
Australian Alps
CANBERRA
Tasman Sea
Ballarat
Geelong
Melbourne
Bass Strait
NORTH ISLAND
Auckland
Hamilton
SOUTHERN OCEAN
TASMANIA
Launceston
Hobart
Palmerston N.
Wellington
Nelson
NEW ZEALAND
SOUTH ISLAND
Cook Str.
Southern Alps
Christchurch
Invercargill
Oamaru
Dunedin
P A C I F I C O C E A N
120 East from Greenwich

Projection: *Lambert's Equivalent Azimuthal*

AUSTRALIA and NEW ZEALAND

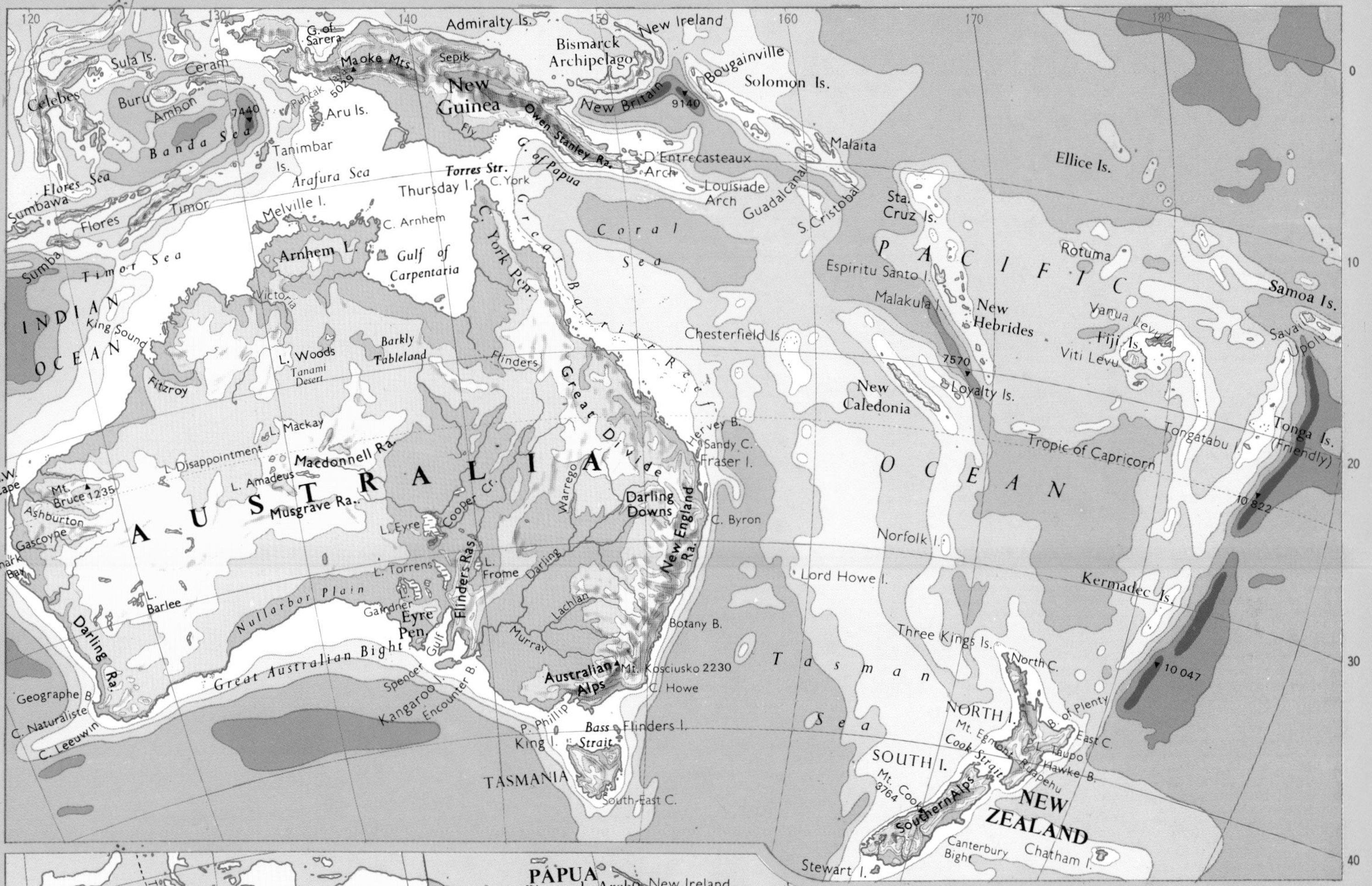

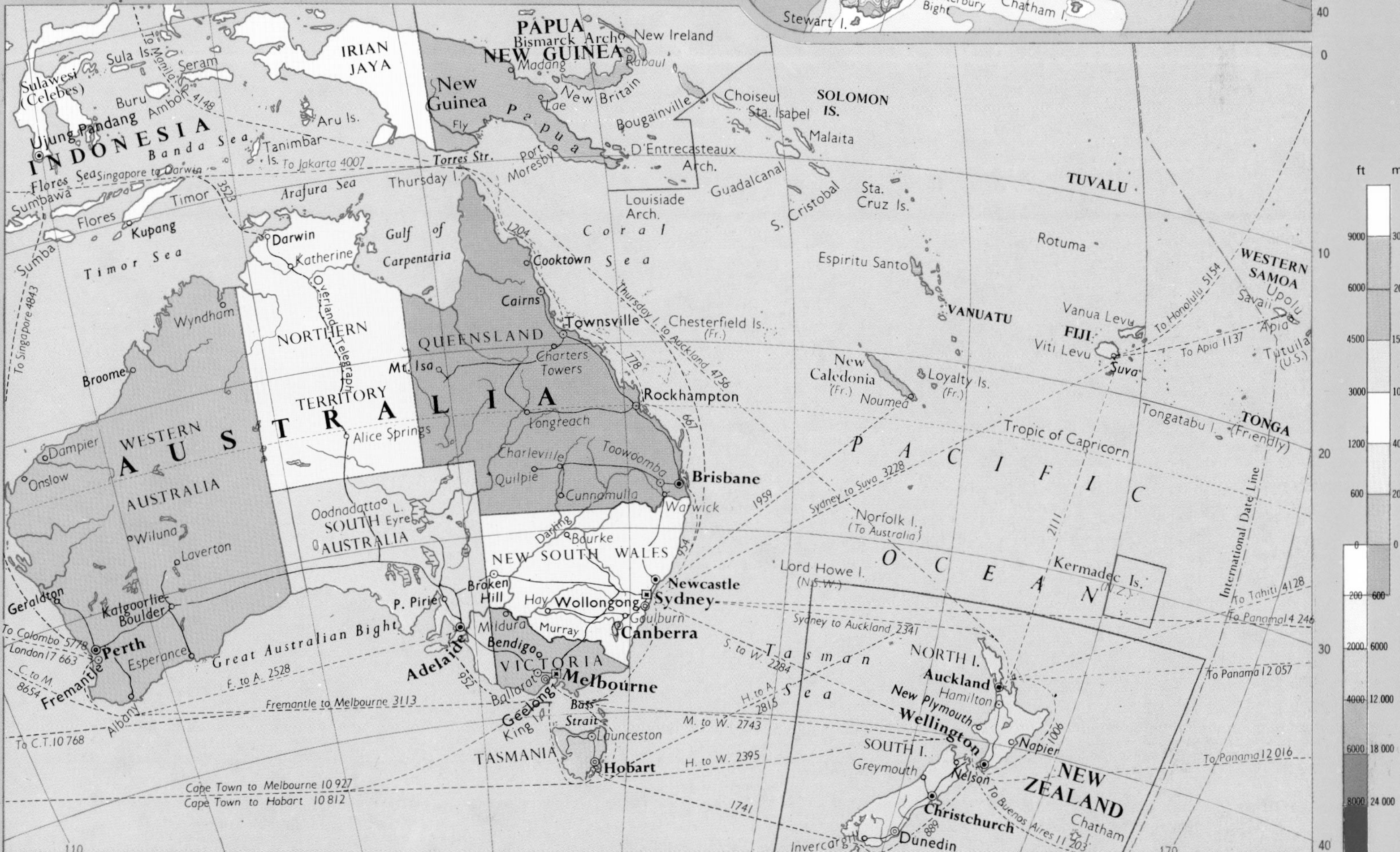

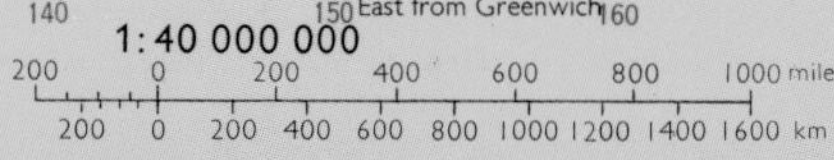

Admiralty Is.
New Ireland
Bismarck Archipelago
G. of Sarera
Maoke Mts.
Sepik
New Guinea
Bougainville
Solomon Is.
Sula Is.
Ceram
Celebes
Buru
Ambon
Banda Sea
7440
Aru Is.
New Britain
9140
Owen Stanley Ra.
Fly
Malaita
Ellice Is.
Tanimbar Is.
Torres Str.
G. of Papua
D'Entrecasteaux Arch.
Flores Sea
Arafura Sea
Thursday I.
C. York
Louisiade Arch.
Guadalcanal
S. Cristobal
Sta. Cruz Is.
Sumbawa
Timor
Flores
Melville I.
C. Arnhem
Coral Sea
Sumba
Timor Sea
Arnhem L.
Gulf of Carpentaria
C. York Pen.
Great Barrier Reef
PACIFIC
Rotuma
Samoa Is.
Espiritu Santo I.
Malakula I.
New Hebrides
Vanua Levu
Fiji Is.
Viti Levu
Savaii
Upolu
INDIAN OCEAN
King Sound
Victoria
L. Woods
Tanami Desert
Barkly Tableland
Flinders
Chesterfield Is.
Fitzroy
7570
Loyalty Is.
New Caledonia
L. Mackay
Great Dividing Range
Hervey B.
Sandy C.
Fraser I.
Tropic of Capricorn
Tongatabu I.
Tonga Is. (Friendly)
N.W. Cape
Mt. Bruce 1235
L. Disappointment
Macdonnell Ra.
L. Amadeus
Musgrave Ra.
AUSTRALIA
Warrego
Darling Downs
OCEAN
Ashburton
Gascoyne
L. Eyre
Cooper Cr.
New England Ra.
C. Byron
Norfolk I.
10 822
Shark Bay
L. Torrens
Flinders Ras.
L. Frome
Darling
Lord Howe I.
Kermadec Is.
L. Barlee
Nullarbor Plain
Gairdner
Eyre Pen.
Lachlan
Botany B.
Three Kings Is.
Darling Ra.
Great Australian Bight
Spencer Gulf
Murray
Australian Alps
Mt. Kosciusko 2230
Tasman Sea
North C.
10 047
Geographe B.
Kangaroo I.
Encounter B.
C. Howe
NORTH I.
B. of Plenty
C. Naturaliste
C. Leeuwin
P. Phillip
Bass Strait
Flinders I.
King I.
Mt. Egmont
East C.
Taupo
Ruapehu
Cook Strait
Hawke B.
TASMANIA
SOUTH I.
Mt. Cook 3764
Southern Alps
NEW ZEALAND
South-East C.
Canterbury Bight
Chatham I.
Stewart I.

PAPUA NEW GUINEA
Bismarck Arch.
New Ireland
IRIAN JAYA
Madang
Rabaul
Sula Is.
Seram
New Guinea
New Britain
Choiseul
SOLOMON IS.
Sulawesi (Celebes)
Buru
Ambon
Lae
Sta. Isabel
Aru Is.
Papua
Bougainville
Malaita
Ujung Pandang
INDONESIA
Banda Sea
Tanimbar Is.
To Jakarta 4007
Fly
Port Moresby
D'Entrecasteaux Arch.
Torres Str.
Flores Sea
Singapore to Darwin
Thursday I.
Arafura Sea
Guadalcanal
TUVALU
Sumbawa
Timor
Louisiade Arch.
S. Cristobal
Sta. Cruz Is.
Flores
Kupang
Darwin
Gulf of Carpentaria
Coral Sea
Rotuma
Sumba
Timor Sea
Katherine
Cooktown
Espiritu Santo
WESTERN SAMOA
To Singapore 4843
Wyndham
Overland Telegraph
Cairns
Townsville
VANUATU
Vanua Levu
FIJI
Viti Levu
Upolu
Savaii
Apia
To Honolulu 5154
To Apia 1137
Tutuila (U.S.)
Suva
NORTHERN TERRITORY
QUEENSLAND
Chesterfield Is. (Fr.)
Thursday I. to Auckland 4756
Broome
Mt Isa
Charters Towers
New Caledonia (Fr.)
Noumea
Loyalty Is. (Fr.)
Rockhampton
AUSTRALIA
Longreach
Tongatabu I.
TONGA (Friendly)
Tropic of Capricorn
Dampier
WESTERN AUSTRALIA
Alice Springs
Toowoomba
Charleville
Quilpie
Cunnamulla
Brisbane
PACIFIC OCEAN
Onslow
Warwick
Sydney to Suva 3228
Oodnadatta
L. Eyre
SOUTH AUSTRALIA
Norfolk I. (To Australia)
Wiluna
Bourke
Darling
Laverton
NEW SOUTH WALES
Lord Howe I. (N.S.W.)
Kermadec Is. (N.Z.)
International Date Line
To Tahiti 4128
To Panama 14 246
Geraldton
Kalgoorlie-Boulder
Broken Hill
Hay
Newcastle
Sydney
Wollongong
P. Pirie
Goulburn
Sydney to Auckland 2341
Murray
Mildura
Canberra
To Colombo 5778
London 17 663
Perth
Fremantle
Esperance
Great Australian Bight
Adelaide
Bendigo
VICTORIA
Melbourne
Tasman Sea
NORTH I.
Auckland
Hamilton
To Panama 12 057
C. to M. 8654
F. to A. 2528
Ballarat
Geelong
S. to W. 2284
H. to A. 2815
New Plymouth
Wellington
Fremantle to Melbourne 3113
Albany
King I.
Bass Strait
M. to W. 2743
Napier
To C.T. 10 768
Launceston
SOUTH I.
TASMANIA
Greymouth
Nelson
To Panama 12 016
Hobart
H. to W. 2395
NEW ZEALAND
Cape Town to Melbourne 10 927
Cape Town to Hobart 10 812
To Buenos Aires 11 203
Christchurch
Chatham
Invercargill
Dunedin

ft m
9000 3000
6000 2000
4500 1500
3000 1000
1200 400
600 200
0 0
200 600
2000 6000
4000 12 000
6000 18 000
8000 24 000
m ft

Projection: Bonne

East from Greenwich
West from Greenwich

1:40 000 000

200 0 200 400 600 800 1000 miles

200 0 200 400 600 800 1000 1200 1400 1600 km

EUROPE
U. S. S. R.
Leningrad
Moskva
Sverdlovsk
Omsk
Tomsk
Novosibirsk
Barnaul
Semipalatinsk
Karaganda
L. Balkhash
Aral Sea
Alma Ata
Tashkent
Samarkand
Irkutsk
Ozero Baykal
Chita
Ulan Ude
Ulaanbaatar
Hovd
Ulyasutay
MONGOLIA
Altai
ASIA
Sea of Okhotsk
Kamchatka
Komandorskie Is. (U.S.S.R.)
Petropavlovsk
Sakhalin
G. of Sakhalin
Blagoveshchensk
Amur
Khabarovsk
Manchuria
Harbin
Changchun
Shenyang
Vladivostok
La Perouse Strait
Kuril Is.
Kuril Trench
10 542
Hakodate
Aleutian Trench
Near I.
7822
KURO SIWO
7168
Emperor Seamount Chain
Sea of Japan
KOREA
JAPAN
Sŏul
Pusan
Kyōto
TOKYO
8412
Yokohama
Nagoya
Ōsaka
Shikoku
Kyūshū
Kitakyūshū
Nagasaki
Japan Trench
10 554
3776
Sendai
Beijing
Tianjin
Jinan
Lüda
Qingdao
Yellow Sea
Lanzhou
Xi'an
Kunlun Shan
CHINA
Nanjing
SHANGHAI
Wuhan
Chongqing
Hangzhou
Changsha
Wenzhou
Fuzhou
Xiamen
East China Sea
Ryūkyū Is.
Taibei
Taiwan (Formosa)
Guangzhou
MACAU (Port.)
HONG KONG
Kunming
Urumqi
XIZANG (TIBET)
Lhasa
Mt. Everest 8848
Himalaya
NEPAL
AFGHANISTAN
Kabul
Srinagar
Lahore
PAKISTAN
Delhi
Agra
Kanpur
Varanasi
Brahmaputra
Ganges
INDIA
Calcutta
BANGLADESH
Chittagong
BURMA
Mandalay
Myitkyina
Cuttack
Hyderabad
Bay of Bengal
Rangoon
Madras
THAILAND (SIAM)
Bangkok
CAMBODIA
VIETNAM
Hanoi
Hainan
Phnom Penh
Phanh Bho Ho Chi Minh (Saigon)
Gulf of Thailand
South China Sea
C. Camau
Andaman Is.
Mergui Arch.
Isthmus of Kra
Nicobar Is.
SRI LANKA
Colombo
PENINSULAR MALAYSIA
George Town
Kuala Lumpur
Melaka
SINGAPORE
Sumatra
Nias
Natuna
Labuan
BRUNEI
SABAH
Kinabalu 4101
SARAWAK
Borneo
Bangka
Palembang
Java Sea
Jakarta
Semarang
Surabaya
Java
Sunda Strait
Sunda Islands
INDONESIA
Bali
Lombok
Sumbawa
Flores
Sumba
Timor
Java Trench
7450
Christmas I. (Austral.)
Cocos (Keeling) Is. (Austral.)
Manila
PHILIPPINES
Mindoro
Palawan
Samar
10 497
Sulu Sea
Mindanao
Mindanao Trench
Celebes Sea
Celebes
Moluccas
Halmahera
Buru
Ceram
Ambon
Ujung Pandang
Banda Sea
Flores Sea
7440
Aru Is.
Tanimbar Is.
Arafura Sea
Torres Strait
Irian
Jaya
5029
PAPUA NEW GUINEA
New Guinea
Madang
Lae
Port Moresby
New Britain
Rabaul
New Ireland
Bismarck Arch.
Admiralty Is.
Dampier Strait
9103
SOLOMON ISLANDS
Honiara
Guadalcanal
Louisiade Arch.
Northern Marianas
Mariana Trench
Guam (U.S.)
11 022
U.S. TRUST TERR. OF THE PACIFIC ISLANDS
Micronesia
Melanesia
Yap
Belau
Fed. States of Micronesia
Truk
Ponape
Caroline Islands
Marshall Is.
Bikini Atoll
Eniwetok Atoll
Jaluit
EQUATORIAL
Butaritari
Gilbert Is.
NAURU
Banaba
Bonin Is.
Volcano Is.
Marcus I.
Marcus Necker Ridge
Wake I. (U.S.)
South Honshū Ridge
6603
Midway Is.
International Date Line
C. Engano
C. Arnhem
Thursday I.
C. York
Darwin
G. of Carpentaria
Ashmore Is.
Wyndham
Katherine
Newcastle Waters
NORTHERN TERRITORY
Cairns
Townsville
Mt. Isa
Coral Sea Islands Territory
Coral Sea
VANUATU
Great Dividing Range
AUSTRALIA
N.W. Cape
Onslow
Alice Springs
Longreach
QUEENSLAND
Rockhampton
Maryborough
Brisbane
Ipswich
WESTERN AUSTRALIA
Shark Bay
Oodnadatta
L. Eyre
SOUTH AUSTRALIA
Geraldton
Kalgoorlie
Perth
Fremantle
Geographe Bay
Albany
Great Australian Bight
K. George Sd.
NEW SOUTH WALES
Darling
Sydney
Newcastle
Katoomba
Wollongong
Canberra
Mt. Kosciusko 2230
Adelaide
Murray
Encounter Bay
VICTORIA
Ballarat
Geelong
Melbourne
Bass Strait
Launceston
TASMANIA
Hobart
AUSTRALIAN CURRENT
Tasman Sea
Lord Howe I. (Aust.)
Lord Howe Rise
Norfolk I. (Aust.)
New Caledonia (Fr.)
Nouméa
Loyalty Is.
Chesterfield Is.
7570
9165
Sta. Cruz Is.
Rotuma
Wallis & Futuna (Fr.)
Vanua Levu
Viti Levu
Suva
FIJI
Tonga Trench
TUVALU (Ellice Is.)
Funafuti
Kermadec Is. (N.Z.)
Kermadec Trench
10 047
10 822
Auckland
Hamilton
NEW ZEALAND
Palmerston N.
Cook Strait
Wellington
Nelson
Mt. Cook 3764
Christchurch
Oamaru
Dunedin
Invercargill
Stewart I.
Chatham Is.
Bounty Is. (N.Z.)
Antipodes Is. (N.Z.)
Auckland Is. (N.Z.)
Macquarie Is. (Austral.)
Campbell I. (N.Z.)
INDIAN OCEAN
Colombo - Fremantle 3120
Al 'Adan - Melbourne 6445
Cape Town - Fremantle 5615
Cape Town - Melbourne 5814
Cape Town - Hobart 5838
F. - A. 1353
S. - A. 1274
H. - W. 1293
Yokohama - Vancouver 4280
Amsterdam I. (Fr.)
St. Paul I. (Fr.)
Mid-Oceanic Ridge
South-East Indian Ridge
Mid-Indian Ridge
Indian-Antarctic Ridge
Crozet Is. (Fr.)
Kerguelen (Fr.)
Heard Is. (Aust.)
ft m
18 000 6000
12 000 4000
6000 2000
3000 1000
600 200
0 0
200 600
2000 6000
4000 12 000
6000 18 000
8000 24 000
m ft
Projection: Mollweide's Homolographic
East from Greenwich
5615 Principal Shipping Routes (Distances in Nautical Miles)

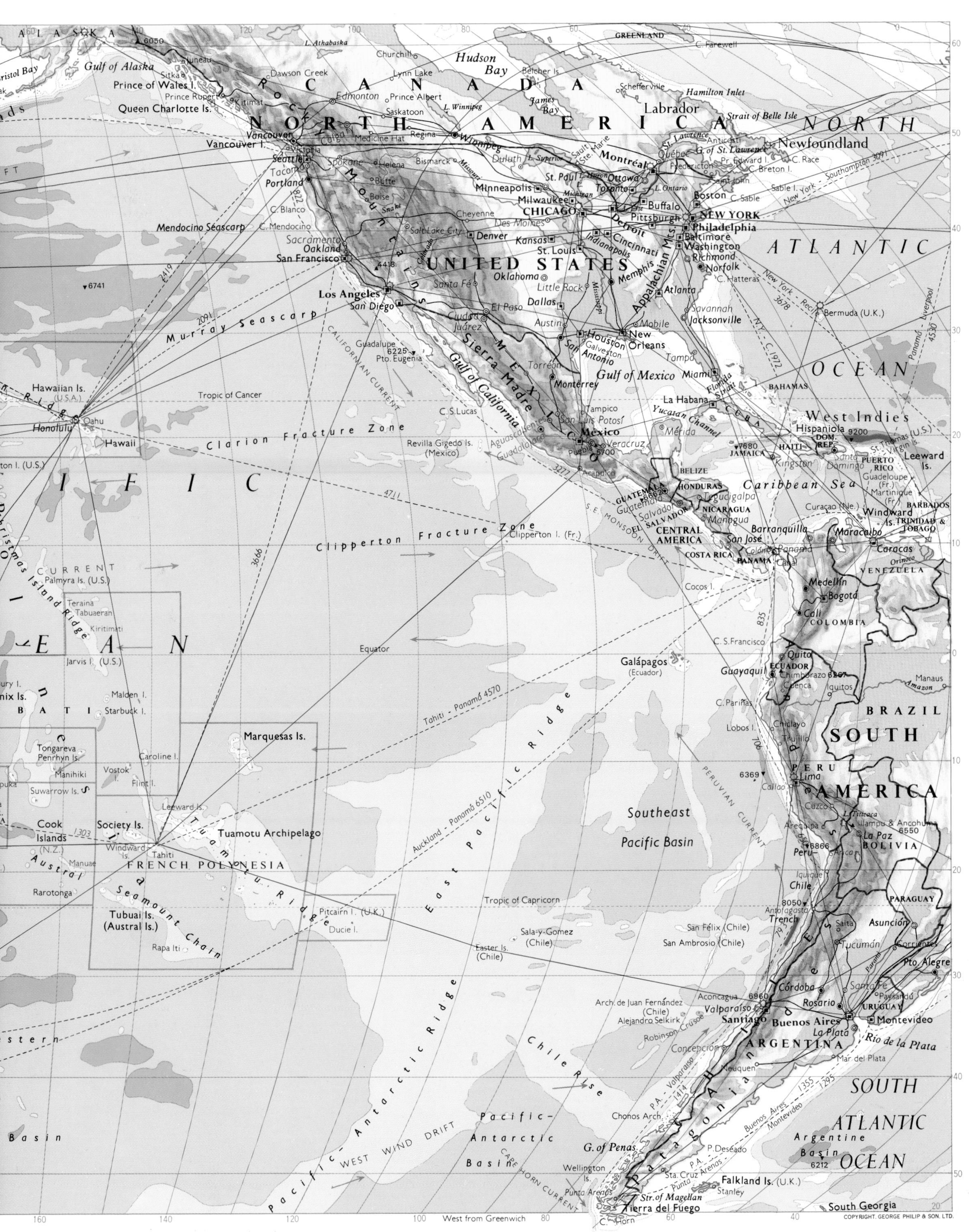
CANADA
NORTH AMERICA
UNITED STATES
MEXICO
Hudson Bay
Labrador
Newfoundland
Gulf of Alaska
Prince of Wales I.
Queen Charlotte Is.
Vancouver I.
Rocky Mountains
Edmonton
Saskatoon
Regina
Winnipeg
Vancouver
Seattle
Portland
Montreal
Ottawa
Toronto
Québec
Minneapolis
Milwaukee
CHICAGO
Detroit
Buffalo
Pittsburgh
Boston
NEW YORK
Philadelphia
Baltimore
Washington
Cincinnati
St. Louis
Denver
Kansas
San Francisco
Oakland
Sacramento
Los Angeles
San Diego
Dallas
Houston
San Antonio
New Orleans
Atlanta
Memphis
Jacksonville
Miami
Appalachian Mts.
ATLANTIC OCEAN
NORTH
Gulf of Mexico
Gulf of California
Sierra Madre
Monterrey
Mexico
Hawaiian Is. (U.S.A.)
Honolulu
Hawaii
Tropic of Cancer
Clarion Fracture Zone
Clipperton Fracture Zone
Murray Seascarp
Mendocino Seascarp
Bermuda (U.K.)
BAHAMAS
La Habana
CUBA
JAMAICA
HAITI
DOM. REP.
Hispaniola
PUERTO RICO
West Indies
Leeward Is.
Windward Is.
Caribbean Sea
BARBADOS
TRINIDAD & TOBAGO
BELIZE
GUATEMALA
HONDURAS
NICARAGUA
EL SALVADOR
CENTRAL AMERICA
COSTA RICA
PANAMA
Barranquilla
Maracaibo
Caracas
VENEZUELA
Medellín
Bogotá
Cali
COLOMBIA
Quito
ECUADOR
Guayaquil
Galápagos (Ecuador)
Equator
BRAZIL
SOUTH AMERICA
PERU
Lima
BOLIVIA
La Paz
Chile
PARAGUAY
Asunción
Córdoba
Rosario
Santiago
Valparaíso
Buenos Aires
Montevideo
URUGUAY
ARGENTINA
Río de la Plata
SOUTH ATLANTIC OCEAN
Argentine Basin
Falkland Is. (U.K.)
South Georgia
Str. of Magellan
Tierra del Fuego
C. Horn
Patagonian Andes
Southeast Pacific Basin
East Pacific Ridge
Pacific-Antarctic Ridge
Pacific-Antarctic Basin
Chile Rise
WEST WIND DRIFT
PERUVIAN CURRENT
CALIFORNIAN CURRENT
Marquesas Is.
Tuamotu Archipelago
Society Is.
Tahiti
FRENCH POLYNESIA
Cook Islands (N.Z.)
Rarotonga
Tubuai Is. (Austral Is.)
Austral Seamount Chain
Tuamotu Ridge
Pitcairn I. (U.K.)
Easter Is. (Chile)
Tropic of Capricorn
Christmas Island Ridge
Palmyra Is. (U.S.)
Jarvis I. (U.S.)
West from Greenwich
COPYRIGHT, GEORGE PHILIP & SON, LTD.

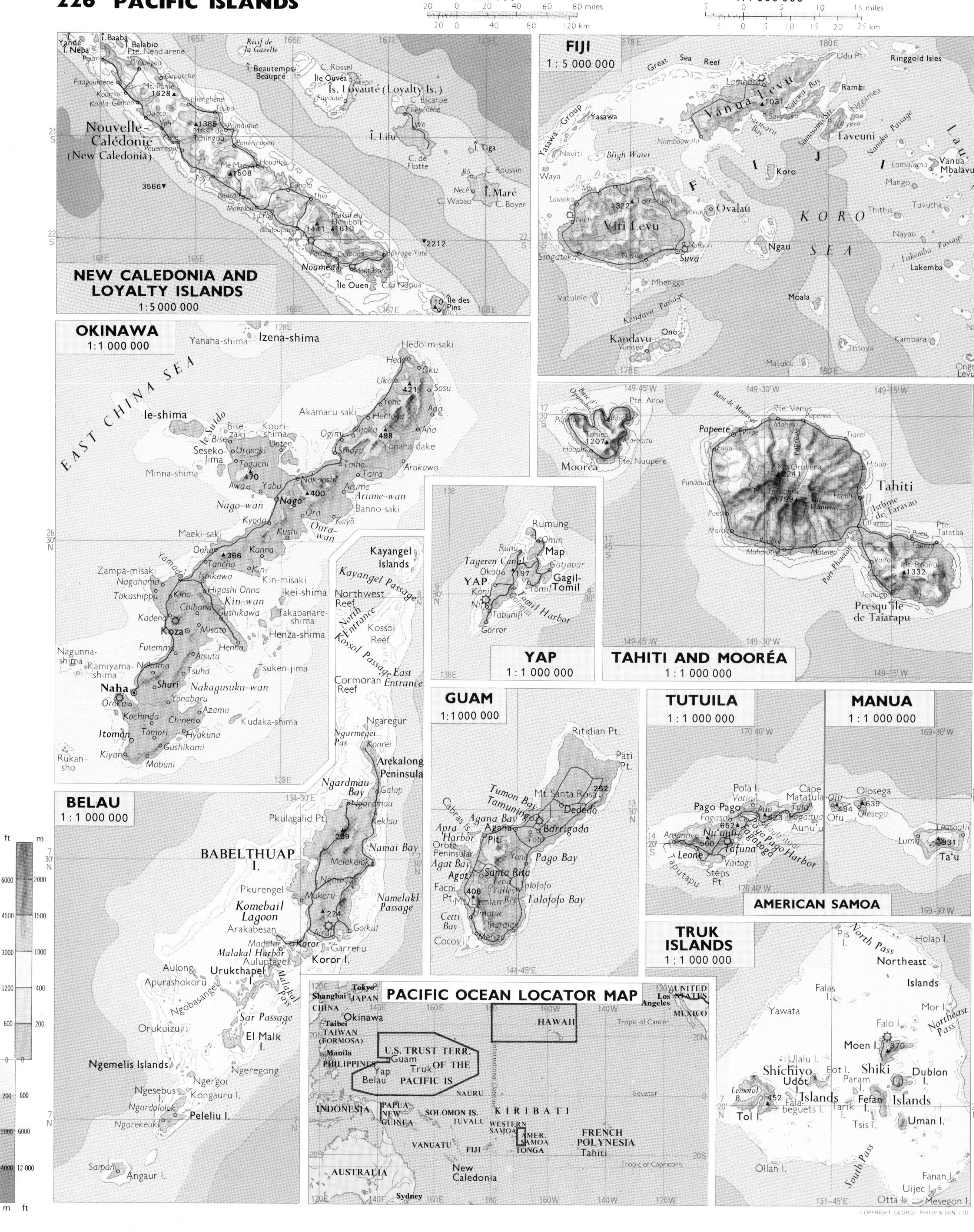

1:5 000 000
20 0 20 40 60 80 miles
20 0 40 80 120 km
1:1 000 000
5 0 5 10 15 miles
5 0 5 10 15 20 25 km
NEW CALEDONIA AND LOYALTY ISLANDS
1:5 000 000
Nouvelle Calédonie (New Caledonia)
Îs. Loyauté (Loyalty Is.)
Î. Ouvéa
Î. Lifu
Î. Maré
Î. Tiga
Île des Pins
Île Ouen
Nouméa
Thio
Bourail
La Foa
Koumac
Poum
Houailou
Mt. Panié
Massif du Humboldt
Récif de la Gazelle
Î. Beautemps-Beaupré
C. Rossel
C. Escarpé
C. de Flotte
C. Roussin
C. Wabao
C. Boyer
Cap Ndoua
Baie de Prony
Î. Baaba
Î. Balabio
Yandé
Î. Neba
FIJI
1 : 5 000 000
Vanua Levu
Viti Levu
Great Sea Reef
Yasawa Group
Yasawa
Naviti
Waya
Bligh Water
Lautoka
Nadi
Singatoka
Suva
Ovalau
Levuka
Koro
Taveuni
Rambi
Ringgold Isles
Udu Pt.
Labasa
Savusavu
Savusavu Bay
Natewa Bay
Somosomo Str.
Nanuku Passage
Lau (Eastern) Group
Vanua Mbalavu
Lomaloma
Mango
Tuvutha
Thithia
Nayau
Lakemba
Lakemba Passage
Moala
Ngau
Mbengga
Vatulele
Kandavu
Kandavu Passage
Ono
Vunisea
Matuku
Totoya
Kambara
Ongea Levu
Namuka
Tomanivi
Nambouwalu
K O R O   S E A
F I J I
OKINAWA
1:1 000 000
EAST CHINA SEA
Yanaha-shima
Izena-shima
Ie-shima
Hedo-misaki
Oku
Sosu
Ada
Aha
Yona
Hentona
Uka
Akamaru-saki
Ogimi
Kijoka
Shioya
Taiho
Taira
Yonaha-dake
Arakawa
Bise
Bise-zaki
Kouri-shima
Unten
Seseko-jima
Urasaki
Toguchi
Minna-shima
Awa
Yabu
Nakaoshi
Nago
Nago-wan
Arume
Arume-wan
Banno-saki
Ora
Oura-wan
Kayo
Kyoda
Kushi
Maeki-saki
Onna
Kanna
Tancha
Kin
Kin-misaki
Zampa-misaki
Nagahama
Takashippu
Kina
Ishikawa
Higashi Onna
Kin-wan
Chibana
Gushikawa
Ikei-shima
Takabanare-shima
Kadena
Koza
Misato
Henza-shima
Henna
Futemma
Atsuta
Nagunna-shima
Kamiyama-shima
Nakama
Tsuha
Tsuken-jima
Naha
Shuri
Nakagusuku-wan
Oroku
Yonabaru
Azama
Kochinda
Chinen
Kudaka-shima
Itoman
Tomori
Hyakuna
Gushikami
Rukan-shō
Kiyan
Mabuni
YAP
1 : 1 000 000
Rumung
Map
Omin
Gatjapar
Gagil-Tomil
Tomil
Tomil Harbor
Tageren Canal
Runu
Okau
Kanif
Nif
Tabunifi
Gorror
TAHITI AND MOORÉA
1 : 1 000 000
Tahiti
Mooréa
Papeete
Pte. Vénus
Papenoo
Tiarei
Hitiaa
Mt. Orohena
Mt. Tetufera
Isthme de Taravao
Taravao
Pte. Tatatua
Presqu'île de Taiarapu
Port Phaeton
Mt. Roonui
Vairao
Teahupoo
Papara
Mataiea
Paea
Punaauia
Faaa
Pirae
Mahina
Baie de Matavai
Tohiea
Pte. Aroa
Pte. Nuupere
Baie d'Opunohu
Papetoai
Haapiti
Afareaitu
BELAU
1 : 1 000 000
Kayangel Islands
Kayangel Passage
Northwest Reef
North Entrance
Kossol Reef
Kossol Passage
East Entrance
Cormoran Reef
Ngaregur
Ngarmegei Pas
Konrei
Arekalong Peninsula
Ngardmau Bay
Galap
Ngardmau
Keklau
Pkulagalid Pt.
Namai Bay
Melekeiok
BABELTHUAP I.
Pkurengel
Komebail Lagoon
Namelakl Passage
Mukeru
Arakabesan
Goikul
Madalai
Malakal Harbor
Koror
Koror I.
Garreru
Aulong
Auluptagel
Urukthapel I.
Malakal Pass
Apurashokoru
Ngobasangel
Sar Passage
Orukuizu
El Malk I.
Ngemelis Islands
Ngeregong
Ngergoi
Ngesebus I.
Kongauru I.
Ngardololok
Peleliu I.
Ngarekeukl
Saipan
Angaur I.
GUAM
1:1 000 000
Ritidian Pt.
Pati Pt.
Tumon Bay
Tamuning
Mt. Santa Rosa
Dededo
Agana Bay
Agana
Barrigada
Cabras Is.
Apra Harbor
Piti
Orote Peninsula
Agat Bay
Agat
Yona
Pago Bay
Santa Rita
Fena Valley Res.
Talofofo
Talofofo Bay
Facpi Pt.
Mt. Lamlam
Umatac
Inarajan
Cetti Bay
Cocos I.
Merizo
TUTUILA
1 : 1 000 000
Pola I.
Vatia
Cape Matatula
Pago Pago
Fagasa
Aua
Nu'uuli
Leone
Tafuna
Pago Pago Harbor
Vaitogi
Aunu'u
Steps Pt.
Taputapu
MANUA
1 : 1 000 000
Olosega
Ofu
Ta'u
Lumā
Leusoalii
AMERICAN SAMOA
TRUK ISLANDS
1 : 1 000 000
Pis I.
North Pass
Holap I.
Northeast Islands
Falas I.
Yawata
Mor I.
Northeast Pass
Falo I.
Moen I.
Ulalu I.
Shichiyo Islands
Eot I.
Udot
Shiki Islands
Dublon I.
Param
Lemotol B.
Fala-beguets I.
Tarik I.
Fefan
Tol I.
Tsis I.
Uman I.
Ollan I.
South Pass
Fanan I.
Uijec I.
Otta I.
Meseglon I.
PACIFIC OCEAN LOCATOR MAP
Tokyo
JAPAN
Shanghai
CHINA
Okinawa
Taibei
TAIWAN (FORMOSA)
Manila
PHILIPPINES
U.S. TRUST TERR. OF THE PACIFIC IS
Guam
Yap
Truk
Belau
NAURU
INDONESIA
PAPUA NEW GUINEA
SOLOMON IS.
TUVALU
KIRIBATI
WESTERN SAMOA
AMER. SAMOA
TONGA
VANUATU
FIJI
FRENCH POLYNESIA
Tahiti
AUSTRALIA
Sydney
New Caledonia
HAWAII
UNITED STATES
Los Angeles
MEXICO
Tropic of Cancer
Equator
Tropic of Capricorn
International Date Line

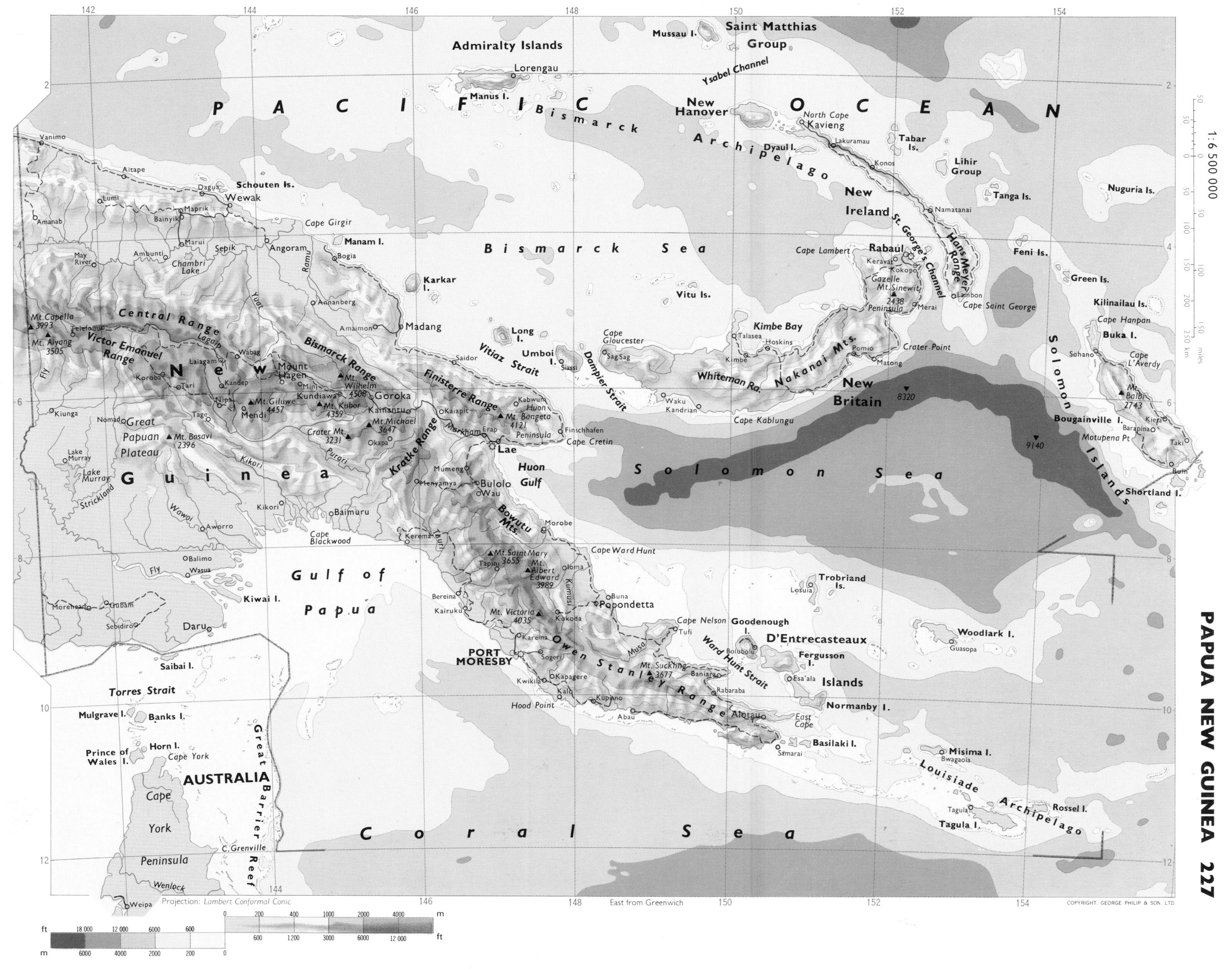
1:6 500 000
50 0 50 100 150 miles
50 0 50 100 150 200 250 km
PACIFIC OCEAN
Bismarck Archipelago
Bismarck Sea
Solomon Sea
Coral Sea
Gulf of Papua
Solomon Islands
Louisiade Archipelago
Admiralty Islands
Manus I.
Lorengau
Mussau I.
Saint Matthias Group
Ysabel Channel
New Hanover
Kavieng
North Cape
Dyaul I.
Lakuramau
Konos
New Ireland
Namatanai
Hans Meyer Range
Tabar Is.
Lihir Group
Tanga Is.
Feni Is.
Green Is.
Nuguria Is.
Kilinailau Is.
Buka I.
Cape Hanpan
Cape L'Averdy
Sohano
Mt. Balbi 2743
Bougainville I.
Motupena Pt
Shortland I.
Kieta
Buin
St. George's Channel
Cape Saint George
Lambon
Rabaul
Kokopo
Kerevat
Gazelle Peninsula
Mt. Sinewit 2438
Merai
Crater Point
Matong
Pomio
Cape Lambert
New Britain
Nakanai Mts.
Kimbe Bay
Hoskins
Talasea
Kimbe
Whiteman Ra.
Cape Kablungu
Kandrian
Waku
Vitu Is.
Cape Gloucester
Sag Sag
Dampier Strait
Umboi I.
Siassi
Long I.
Vitiaz Strait
Karkar I.
Madang
Saidor
Finschhafen
Cape Cretin
Huon Peninsula
Kabwum
Mt. Bangeta 4121
Finisterre Range
Lae
Huon Gulf
Markham
Erap
Kaiapit
Morobe
Bulolo
Wau
Mumeng
Menyamya
Bowutu Mts.
Kratke Range
Mt. Saint Mary 3655
Tapini
Mt. Albert Edward 3989
Ioma
Kokoda
Kumusi
Popondetta
Buna
Cape Ward Hunt
Cape Nelson
Tufi
Ward Hunt Strait
Owen Stanley Range
Mt. Victoria 4035
Mt. Suckling 3677
PORT MORESBY
Sogeri
Karema
Kwikila
Hood Point
Kapagere
Kalo
Kupiano
Abau
Musa
Baniara
Rabaraba
Alotau
East Cape
Samarai
Goodenough I.
Fergusson I.
D'Entrecasteaux Islands
Esa'ala
Bolubolu
Normanby I.
Basilaki I.
Trobriand Is.
Losuia
Woodlark I.
Guasopa
Misima I.
Bwagaoia
Tagula I.
Tagula
Rossel I.
Kairuku
Bereina
Kerema
Tauri
Goroka
Kainantu
Mt. Michael 3647
Okapa
Mt. Wilhelm 4508
Bismarck Range
Mt. Kubor 4359
Kundiawa
Minj
Crater Mt. 3231
Purari
Mount Hagen
Mt. Giluwe 4457
Mendi
Baimuru
Cape Blackwood
Manam I.
Bogia
Amaimon
Annanberg
Cape Girgir
Ramu
Angoram
Schouten Is.
Wewak
Yuat
Sepik
Maprik
Bainyik
Dagua
Chambri Lake
Marui
Ambunti
Wabag
Laiagam
Lagaip
Kandep
Tari
Nipa
Tago
Kikori
Kikori
Kiwai I.
Aworro
Wawoi
Mt. Bosavi 2396
Great Papuan Plateau
Koroba
Nomad
New Guinea
Central Range
Victor Emanuel Range
Telefomin
Mt. Capella 3993
Mt. Aiyang 3505
Lumi
Aitape
Vanimo
Amanab
May River
Fly
Fly
Kiunga
Lake Murray
Lake Murray
Strickland
Balimo
Wasua
Daru
Gubam
Sebidiro
Morehead
Saibai I.
Torres Strait
Mulgrave I.
Banks I.
Horn I.
Cape York
Prince of Wales I.
Cape York Peninsula
AUSTRALIA
Great Barrier Reef
C. Grenville
Wenlock
Weipa
8320
9140
Projection: Lambert Conformal Conic
East from Greenwich
COPYRIGHT GEORGE PHILIP & SON, LTD.
m 0 200 400 1000 2000 4000
ft 600 1200 3000 6000 12 000
ft 18 000 12 000 6000 600
m 6000 4000 2000 200 0

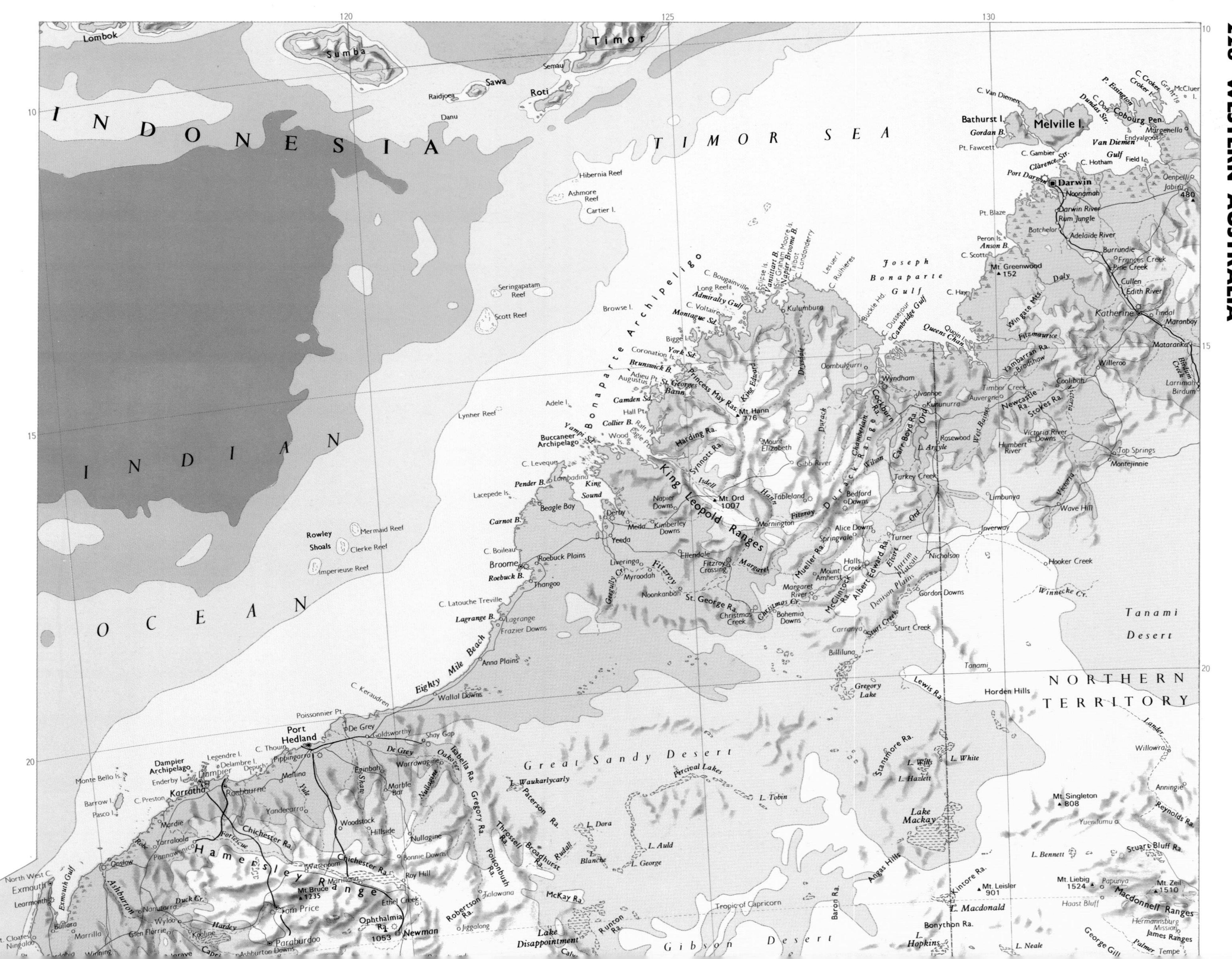
INDONESIA
TIMOR SEA
INDIAN OCEAN
NORTHERN TERRITORY
Tanami Desert
Great Sandy Desert
Gibson Desert
Joseph Bonaparte Gulf
Bonaparte Archipelago
King Leopold Ranges
Hamersley Range
Eighty Mile Beach
Lombok
Sumba
Timor
Sawa
Roti
Melville I.
Bathurst I.
Darwin
Katherine
Wyndham
Kununurra
Derby
Broome
Port Hedland
Karratha
Dampier
Tom Price
Paraburdoo
Newman
Lake Mackay
Lake Disappointment
Mt. Ord 1007
Mt. Bruce 1235

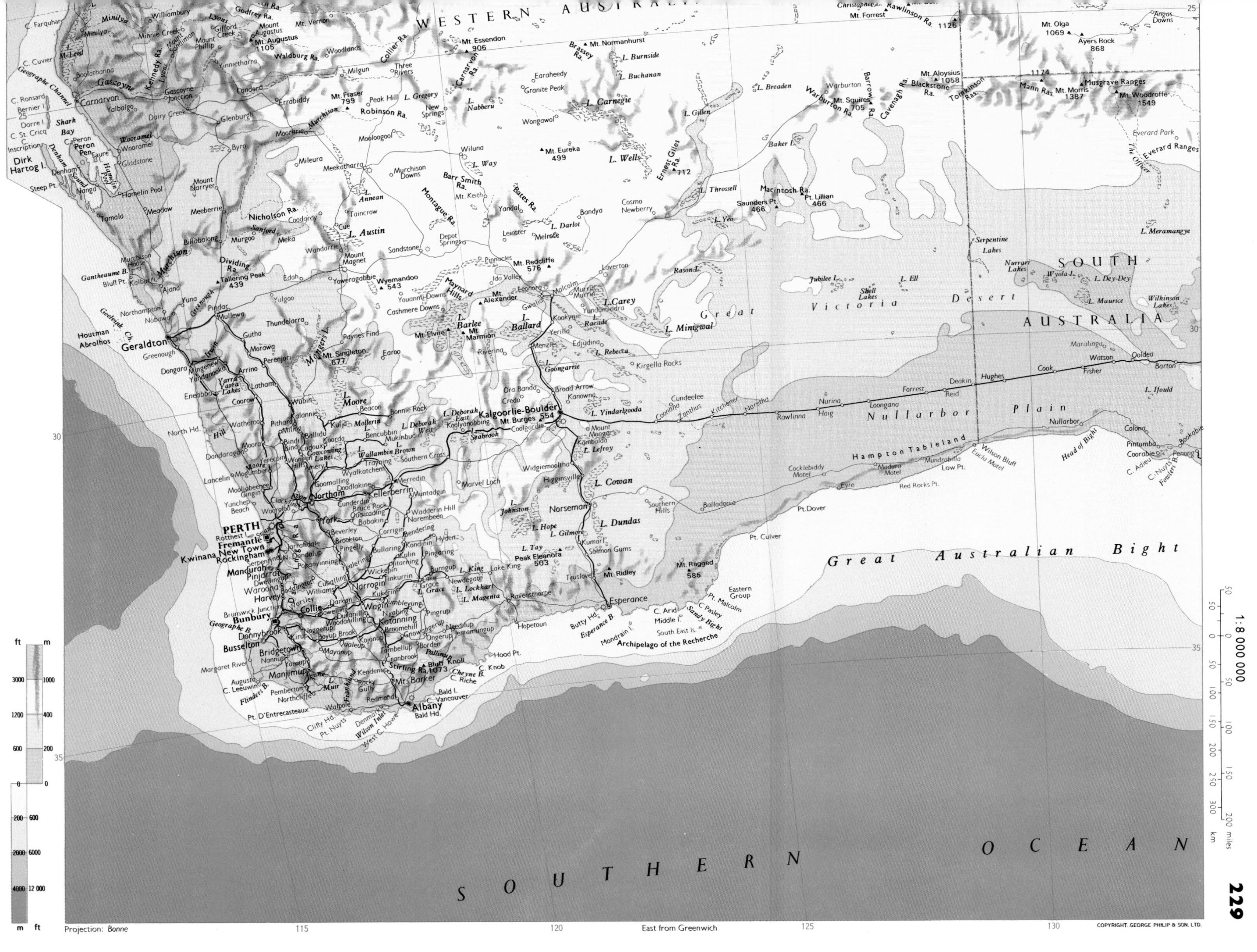

WESTERN AUSTRALIA
SOUTH AUSTRALIA
SOUTHERN OCEAN
Great Australian Bight
Nullarbor Plain
Great Victoria Desert
Hampton Tableland
Archipelago of the Recherche
PERTH
Fremantle
Kwinana New Town
Rockingham
Mandurah
Bunbury
Busselton
Albany
Geraldton
Kalgoorlie-Boulder
Esperance
Norseman
Carnarvon
Northam
York
Narrogin
Collie
Manjimup
Bridgetown
Katanning
Merredin
Southern Cross
Coolgardie
Laverton
Leonora
Menzies
Wiluna
Meekatharra
Cue
Mount Magnet
Dongara
Northampton
Denham
Shark Bay
Dirk Hartog I.
Geographe Channel
Geographe B.
Houtman Abrolhos
Geelvink Ch.
L. Carnegie
L. Wells
L. Barlee
L. Moore
L. Austin
L. Cowan
L. Dundas
L. Lefroy
L. Carey
L. Rebecca
L. Yindarlgooda
L. Ballard
L. Minigwal
L. Throssell
L. Yeo
L. Gillen
L. Breaden
L. Hope
L. Johnston
L. Magenta
L. Grace
L. King
L. Ifould
Mt. Augustus 1105
Mt. Essendon 906
Mt. Fraser 799
Mt. Eureka 499
Mt. Redcliffe 576
Mt. Singleton 677
Mt. Ragged 585
Peak Eleonora 503
Mt. Ridley
Stirling Ra. 1073
Mt. Barker
Mt. Olga 1069
Ayers Rock 868
Mt. Woodroffe 1549
Musgrave Ranges
Mann Ras.
Everard Ranges
Mt. Aloysius 1058
Blackstone Ra.
Rawlinson Ra. 1126
Warburton Ra.
Barrow Ra.
Ernest Giles Ra. 712
Macintosh Ra.
Pt. Lillian 466
Saunders Pt. 466
Eucla Motel
Wilson Bluff
Nullarbor
Cook
Hughes
Forrest
Rawlinna
Kitchener
Zanthus
Ooldea
Watson
Fisher
Barton
Maralinga
Head of Bight
Fowlers Bay
Pt. D'Entrecasteaux
C. Leeuwin
Projection: Bonne
115
120
East from Greenwich
125
130
COPYRIGHT. GEORGE PHILIP & SON. LTD.
ft m
3000 1000
1200 400
600 200
0 0
200 600
2000 6000
4000 12 000
m ft
1:8 000 000
50 0 50 100 150 200 miles
50 0 50 100 150 200 250 300 km

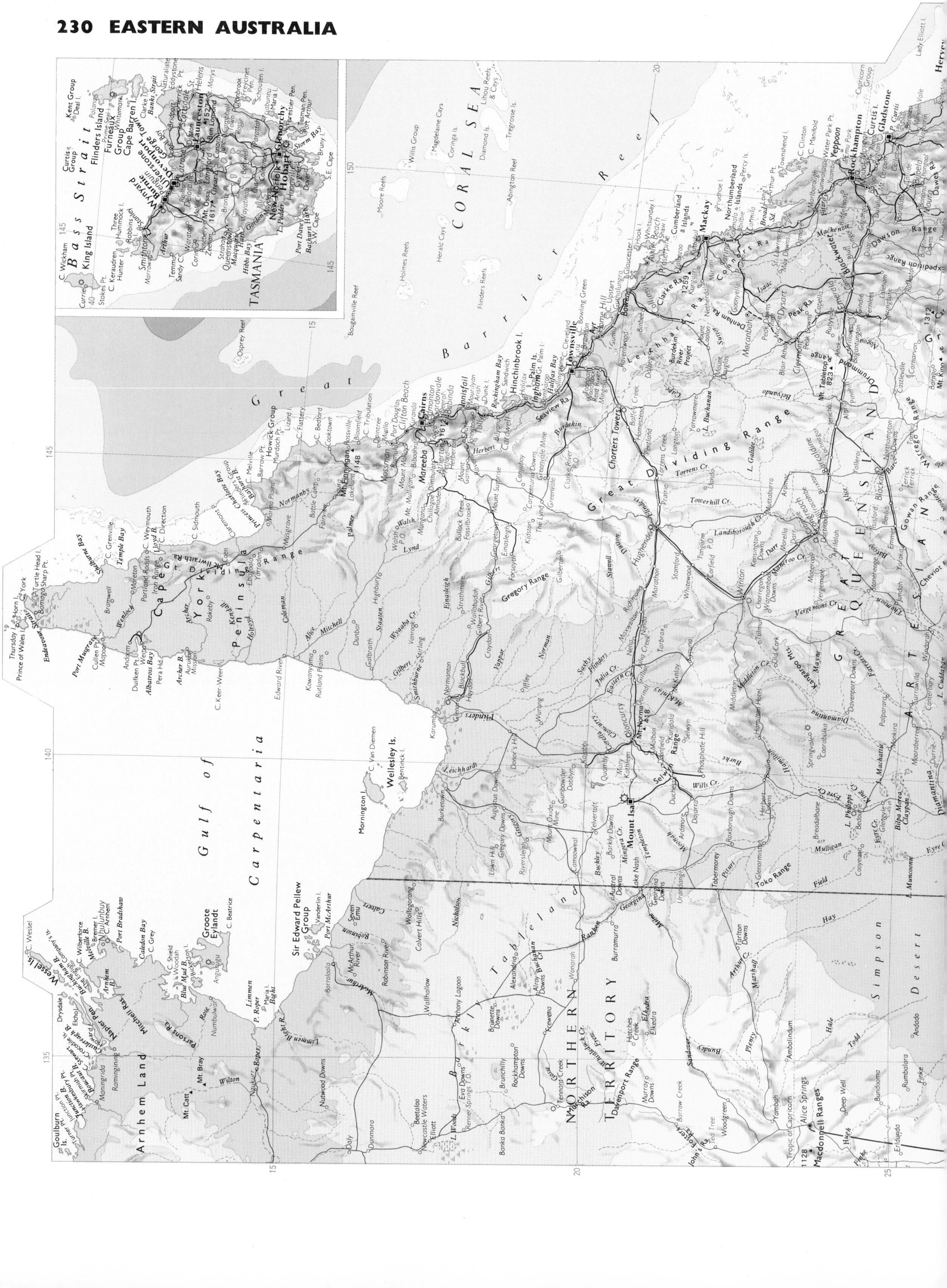
Bass Strait
King Island
Flinders Island
Furneaux Group
Cape Barren I.
Launceston
Devonport
Burnie
Queenstown
Glenorchy
New Norfolk
Hobart
Storm Bay
TASMANIA
CORAL SEA
Great Barrier Reef
Gulf of Carpentaria
Cape York Peninsula
Arnhem Land
Groote Eylandt
Wellesley Is.
Mornington I.
Sir Edward Pellew Group
Barkly Tableland
NORTHERN TERRITORY
QUEENSLAND
Great Dividing Range
Gregory Range
Cairns
Townsville
Mackay
Rockhampton
Gladstone
Mount Isa
Cloncurry
Charters Towers
Hughenden
Winton
Alice Springs
Macdonnell Ranges
Simpson Desert
Tropic of Capricorn

1:8 000 000

50 0 50 100 150 200 miles

50 0 50 100 150 200 250 300 km

Projection: Bonne

East from Greenwich

m	1500	1000	400	200	0	200	2000	4000
ft	4500	3000	1200	600	0	600	6000	12 000

Projection: Alber's Equal area with two standard parallels

1: 4 000 000

20 0 20 40 60 miles

20 0 20 40 60 80 km

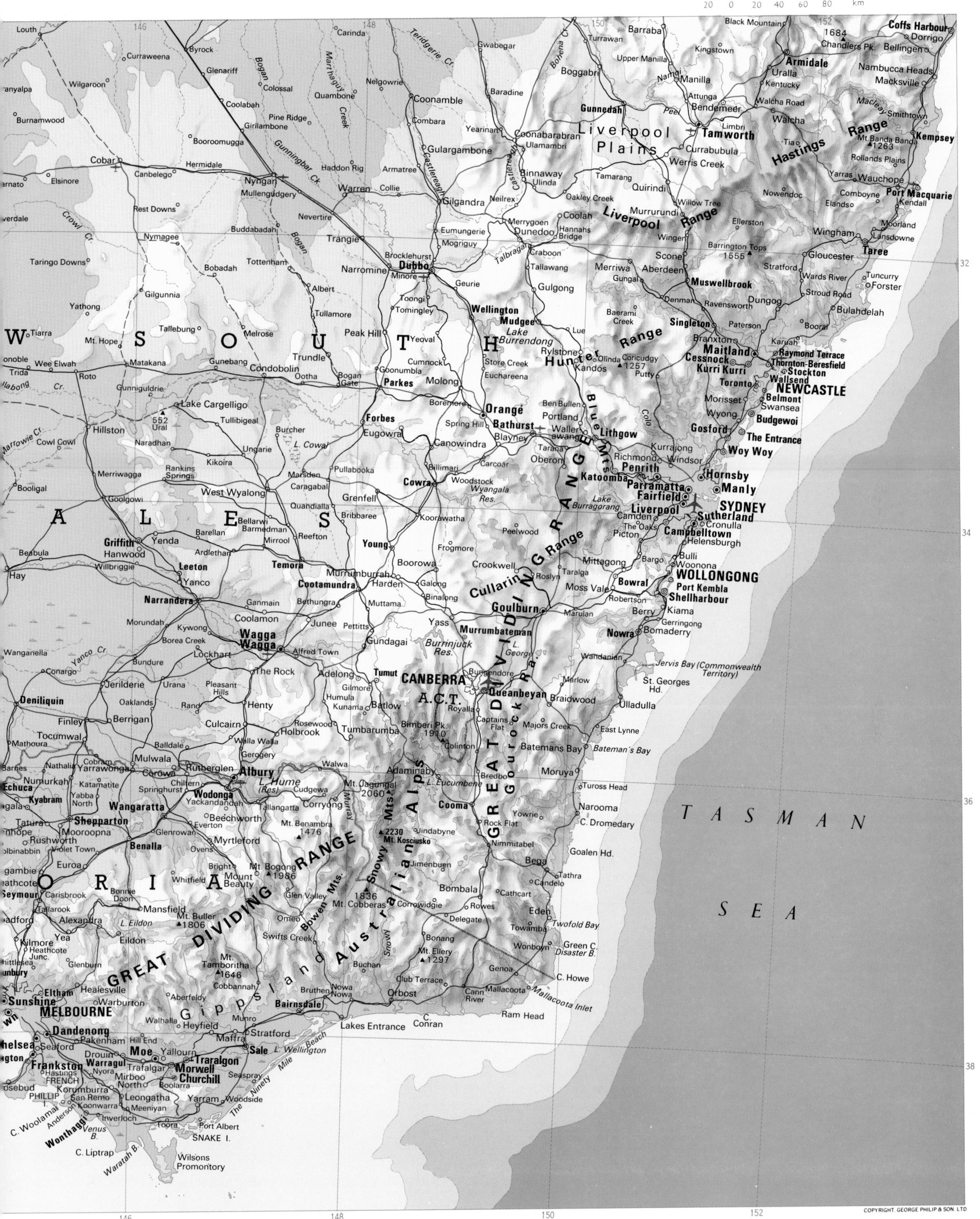

NEW SOUTH WALES
VICTORIA
TASMAN SEA
GREAT DIVIDING RANGE
Liverpool Plains
Liverpool Range
Hastings Range
Hunter Range
Blue Mts.
Cullarin Range
Gourock Ra.
Australian Alps
Snowy Mts.
Bowen Mts.
Gippsland
CANBERRA
A.C.T.
SYDNEY
NEWCASTLE
WOLLONGONG
MELBOURNE
Louth
Byrock
Carinda
Gwabegar
Barraba
Black Mountain
Coffs Harbour
Dorrigo
Bellingen
Chandlers Pk.
1684
Kingstown
Turrawan
Upper Manilla
Manilla
Boggabri
Armidale
Uralla
Kentucky
Nambucca Heads
Macksville
Curraweena
Glenariff
Colossal
Quambone
Nelgowrie
Coonamble
Baradine
Wilgaroon
Coolabah
Pine Ridge
Girilambone
Combara
Gunnedah
Attunga
Bendemeer
Walcha Road
Walcha
Smithtown
Burnamwood
Booroomugga
Yearinan
Coonabarabran
Ulamambri
Tamworth
Currabubula
Werris Creek
Tia
Mt. Banda Banda
1263
Kempsey
Rollands Plains
Cobar
Hermidale
Canbelego
Nyngan
Haddon Rig
Armatree
Gulargambone
Binnaway
Ulinda
Tamarang
Quirindi
Yarras
Wauchope
Port Macquarie
Kendall
Elsinore
Mullengudgery
Warren
Collie
Gilgandra
Neilrex
Oakley Creek
Murrurundi
Willow Tree
Nowendoc
Comboyne
Elandso
Rest Downs
Nevertire
Eumungerie
Mogriguy
Merrygoen
Dunedoo
Coolah
Hannahs Bridge
Ellerston
Wingen
Moorland
Lansdowne
Wingham
Taree
Nymagee
Buddabadah
Trangie
Brocklehurst
Dubbo
Minore
Narromine
Craboon
Tallawang
Barrington Tops
1555
Scone
Aberdeen
Gloucester
Stratford
Wards River
Tuncurry
Forster
Taringo Downs
Tottenham
Bobadah
Albert
Geurie
Merriwa
Gungal
Muswellbrook
Gilgunnia
Toongi
Tomingley
Gulgong
Denman
Ravensworth
Dungog
Stroud Road
Bulahdelah
Yathong
Tullamore
Wellington
Mudgee
Baerami Creek
Singleton
Paterson
Booral
Tiarra
Mt. Hope
Tallebung
Melrose
Peak Hill
Yeoval
Lake Burrendong
Lue
Rylstone
Branxton
Maitland
Karuah
Raymond Terrace
Wee Elwah
Matakana
Gunebang
Condobolin
Trundle
Cumnock
Olinda
Coricudgy
1257
Kandos
Cessnock
Kurri Kurri
Thornton-Beresfield
Stockton
Wallsend
Toronto
Trida
Roto
Ootha
Bogan Gate
Goonumbla
Parkes
Molong
Store Creek
Euchareena
Putty
Gunniguldrie
Lake Cargelligo
Borenore
Orange
Ben Bullen
Portland
Morisset
Belmont
Swansea
Wyong
Budgewoi
552
Ural
Tullibigeal
Forbes
Bathurst
Spring Hill
Blayney
Waller awang
Lithgow
Gosford
The Entrance
Woy Woy
Hillston
Cowl Cowl
Naradhan
Burcher
L. Cowal
Ungarie
Eugowra
Canowindra
Tarana
Oberon
Richmond
Kurrajong
Windsor
Kikoira
Rankins Springs
Merriwagga
Marsden
Pullabooka
Billimari
Carcoar
Katoomba
Penrith
Hornsby
Manly
Parramatta
Fairfield
Booligal
Goolgowi
West Wyalong
Caragabal
Grenfell
Cowra
Woodstock
Wyangala Res.
Lake Burragorang
Liverpool
Sutherland
Cronulla
Camden
The Oaks
Campbelltown
Quandialla
Bribbaree
Koorawatha
Bellarwi
Barmedman
Barellan
Mirrool
Reefton
Peelwood
Picton
Helensburgh
Griffith
Yenda
Ardlethan
Young
Frogmore
Beabula
Hanwood
Willbriggie
Leeton
Temora
Hay
Yanco
Murrumburrah
Boorowa
Crookwell
Mittagong
Bargo
Bulli
Woonona
Harden
Galong
Binalong
Taralga
Roslyn
Moss Vale
Bowral
Port Kembla
Shellharbour
Cootamundra
Bethungra
Muttama
Narrandera
Ganmain
Robertson
Coolamon
Goulburn
Marulan
Berry
Kiama
Gerringong
Bomaderry
Nowra
Morundah
Kywong
Junee
Pettitts
Yass
Murrumbateman
Wagga Wagga
Borea Creek
Alfred Town
Gundagai
Burrinjuck Res.
L. George
Wanganella
Lockhart
Yanco Cr.
Wandandian
Jervis Bay (Commonwealth Territory)
Bundure
The Rock
Adelong
Tumut
Bungendore
Conargo
Jerilderie
Urana
Gilmore
Queanbeyan
Marlow
St. Georges Hd.
Deniliquin
Oaklands
Pleasant Hills
Humula
Kunama
Batlow
Royalla
Braidwood
Ulladulla
Rand
Henty
Berrigan
Culcairn
Rosewood
Holbrook
Tumbarumba
Bimberi Pk.
1910
Captains Flat
Majors Creek
East Lynne
Finley
Tocumwal
Mathoura
Balldale
Walla Walla
Colinton
Batemans Bay
Bateman's Bay
Mulwala
Gerogery
Barnes
Nathalia
Cobram
Yarrawonga
Corowa
Rutherglen
Walwa
Adaminaby
Bredbo
Moruya
Numurkah
Echuca
Katamatite
Chiltern
Albury
L. Hume (Res)
Cudgewa
Mt. Jagungal
2060
L. Eucumbene
Tuross Head
Kyabram
Yabba North
Springhurst
Wodonga
Yackandandah
Tallangatta
Corryong
Cooma
Narooma
Tatura
Shepparton
Wangaratta
Beechworth
Everton
Yowrie
Rock Flat
Mooroopna
Rushworth
Glenrowan
Myrtleford
Mt. Benambra
1476
Jindabyne
C. Dromedary
2230
Mt. Kosciusko
Nimmitabel
Violet Town
Benalla
Ovens
Goalen Hd.
Euroa
Bright
Mt. Bogong
1986
Mount Beauty
Whitfield
Jimenbuen
Bega
Tathra
Candelo
Seymour
Carisbrook
Bonnie Doon
1836
Bombala
Cathcart
Tallarook
Mansfield
Glen Valley
Mt. Cobberas
Corrowidgie
Rowes
Eden
Alexandra
Mt. Buller
1806
L. Eildon
Omeo
Delegate
Towamba
Twofold Bay
Yea
Eildon
Swifts Creek
Bonang
Wonboyn
Green C.
Disaster B.
Kilmore
Heathcote Junc.
Glenburn
Mt. Tamboritha
1646
Mt. Ellery
1297
Genoa
Buchan
C. Howe
Eltham
Healesville
Cobbannah
Club Terrace
Sunshine
Warburton
Aberfeldy
Bruthen
Nowa Nowa
Orbost
Cann River
Mallacoota
Mallacoota Inlet
Walhalla
Munro
Bairnsdale
Ram Head
Heyfield
Stratford
Lakes Entrance
C. Conran
Dandenong
Pakenham
Hill End
Maffra
Sale
L. Wellington
Drouin
Moe
Yallourn
Traralgon
Ninety Mile Beach
Frankston
Hastings
Warragul
Nyora
Trafalgar
Morwell
Churchill
Seaspray
FRENCH I.
Mirboo North
Boolarra
PHILLIP I.
Korumburra
San Remo
Koonwarra
Leongatha
Meeniyan
Yarram
Woodside
C. Woolamai
Anderson
Inverloch
Toora
Port Albert
Wonthaggi
Venus B.
SNAKE I.
C. Liptrap
Waratah B.
Wilsons Promontory
Bogan
Marthaguy Creek
Teridgerie Cr.
Castlereagh
Gunningbar Ck.
Crowl Cr.
Talbragar
Bohena Cr.
Namoi
Peel
Macleay
Colo
Murray
Snowy
Willandra Cr.
Marrowie Cr.
146
148
150
152
32
34
36
38

1:3 500 000

20 0 20 40 60 80 miles

20 0 20 40 60 80 100 120 km

PACIFIC
OCEAN
TASMAN
SEA
C. Reinga
C. Maria van Diemen
North C.
Parengarenga Harb.
Ninety Mile Beach
Rangaunu B.
Doubtless B.
Whangaroa Harb.
Ahipara B.
Cavalli I.
Bay of Islands
C. Brett
Whangaruru Harb.
Poor Knights Island
Hokianga Harb.
Whangarei
Whangarei Harb.
Bream Bay
Hen & Chickens Islands
Dargaville
Needles Point
Great Barrier I.
Lit. Barrier I.
Kawau I.
Hauraki Gulf
Helensville
Takapuna
Devonport
Birkenhead
AUCKLAND
Mt. Roskill
Onehunga
Manukau
Papakura
Coromandel Peninsula
Thames
Mercury B.
Mayor I.
White I.
Waikato
Hamilton
Raglan Harb.
Aotea Harb.
Kawhia Harb.
Albatross Pt.
Tauranga Harb.
Matakana I.
Mt. Maunganui
Bay of Plenty
Whakatane
Rotorua
Tokoroa
L. Tarawera
KAINGAROA STATE FOREST
Raukumara Ra.
C. Runaway
Hicks Bay
East C.
Gisborne
Poverty Bay
Huiarau Ra.
Lake Taupo
Taupo
Taumarunui
North Taranaki Bight
New Plymouth
C. Egmont
Mt. Egmont
Stratford
Opunake
Hawera
South Taranaki Bight
TARANAKI
Kaimanawa Mts.
Ahimanawa Ra.
Kaweka Ra.
Mahia Peninsula
Portland I.
Hawke Bay
Napier
Hastings
Havelock North
C. Kidnappers
HAWKES BAY
Wanganui
Ruahine Ra.
Rangitikei
Feilding
Palmerston North
Dannevirke
Woodville
Levin
Foxton
Tararua Ra.
Puketoi Ra.
Masterton
Castlepoint
C. Turnagain
Kapiti I.
Paraparaumu
Up. Hutt
Lr. Hutt
Petone
Wainuiomata
WELLINGTON
Cook Strait
Palliser Bay
C. Palliser
Aorangi Mts.
Martinborough
Greytown
Carterton
Flat Pt.
C. Farewell
Farewell Spit
Golden Bay
Separation Pt.
D'Urville Island
C. Stephens
Stephens I.
Tasman Bay
Tasman Mts.
Motueka
Nelson
Richmond
Richmond Ra.
Picton
Blenheim
Cloudy B.
Arapawa I.
Lyell Ra.
C. Campbell
2297
1753
1403
1111
2291
2797
2518
1733
1571
983
1775
1760
1875
ft m
9000 3000
6000 2000
3000 1000
1200 400
600 200
0 0
200 600
2000 6000
m ft

Projection: Conical with two standard parallels

East from Greenwich

1:3 500 000

20 0 20 40 60 80 miles

20 0 20 40 60 80 100 120km

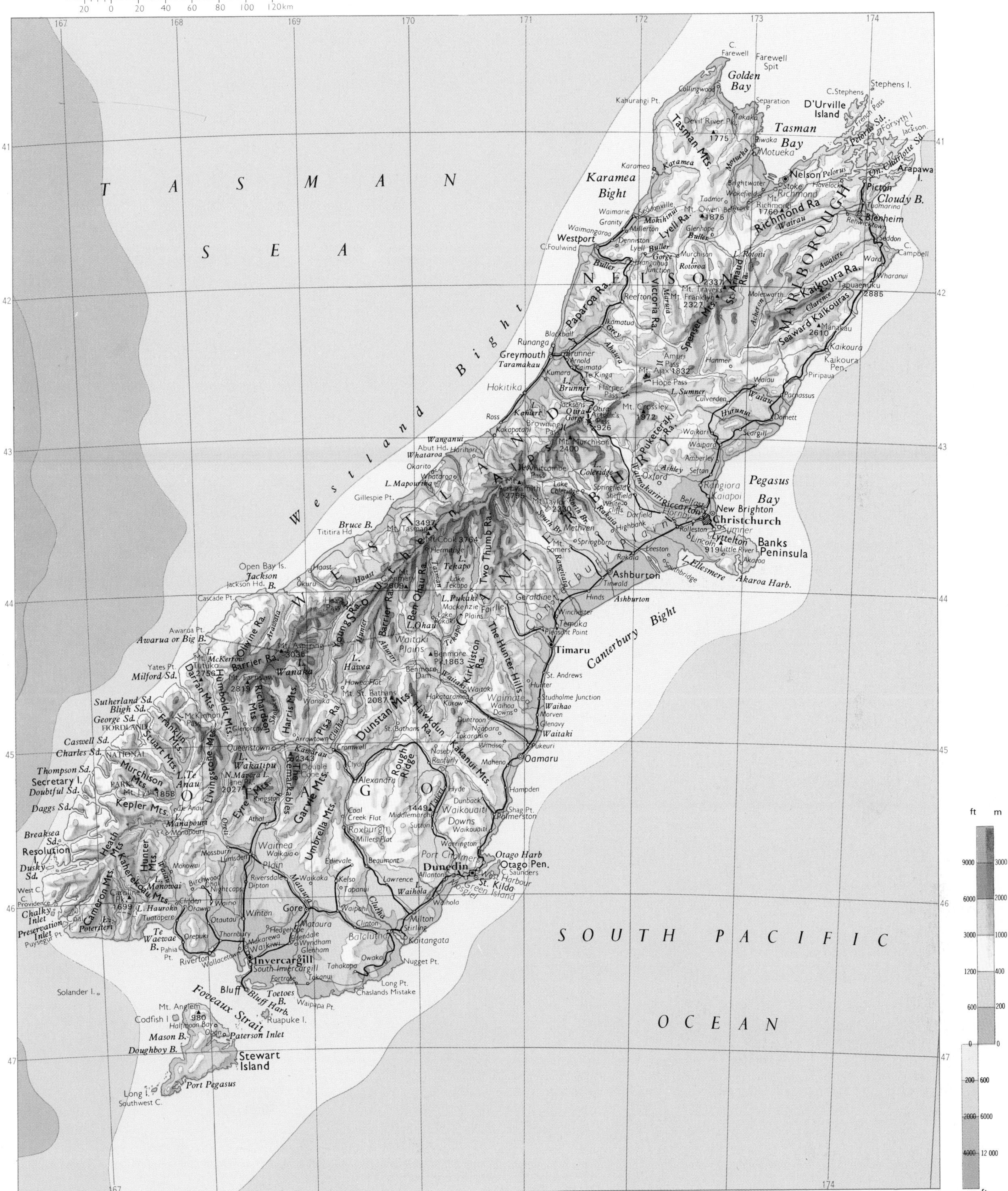
T A S M A N
S E A
Westland Bight
S O U T H P A C I F I C
O C E A N
Golden Bay
Tasman Bay
Karamea Bight
D'Urville Island
Cloudy B.
Pegasus Bay
Canterbury Bight
Banks Peninsula
Foveaux Strait
Stewart Island
NELSON
MARLBOROUGH
WESTLAND
CANTERBURY
OTAGO
SOUTHERN ALPS
Canterbury Plains
Nelson
Blenheim
Picton
Westport
Greymouth
Hokitika
Christchurch
Lyttelton
Ashburton
Timaru
Oamaru
Dunedin
Invercargill
Bluff
Gore
Queenstown
Mt. Cook 3764
Mt. Aspiring 3036
L. Wakatipu
L. Te Anau
L. Manapouri
L. Wanaka
L. Hawea
L. Pukaki
L. Tekapo
L. Ohau
Milford Sd.
Kaikoura
Seward Kaikouras
Kaikoura Ra.
Richmond Ra.
Tasman Mts.
Paparoa Ra.
Victoria Ra.
Spenser Mts.
Dunstan Mts.
Kepler Mts.
Hunter Mts.
Otago Pen.
Stephens I.
C. Farewell
Farewell Spit
Solander I.
Codfish I.
Long I.
Southwest C.
Port Pegasus
Paterson Inlet
ft m
9000 3000
6000 2000
3000 1000
1200 400
600 200
0 0
200 600
2000 6000
4000 12 000
m ft

Projection: *Conical with two standard parallels*

East from Greenwich

AFRICA

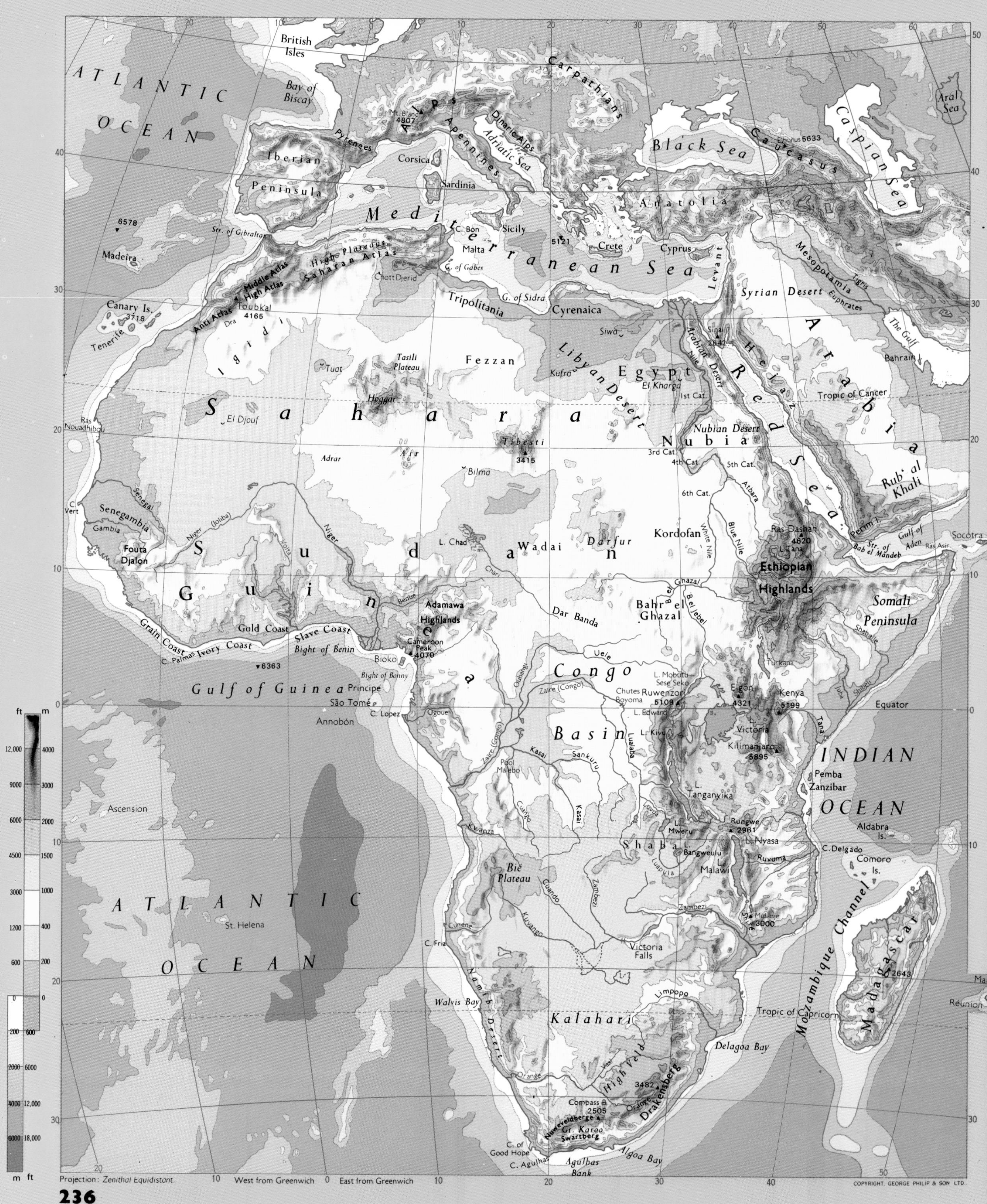
ATLANTIC OCEAN
British Isles
Bay of Biscay
Pyrenees
Iberian Peninsula
Alps
Mt. Blanc 4807
Carpathians
Dinaric Alps
Apennines
Adriatic Sea
Corsica
Sardinia
Black Sea
Caucasus
Elbrus 5633
Caspian Sea
Aral Sea
Mediterranean Sea
Anatolia
Str. of Gibraltar
Madeira
6578
C. Bon
Sicily
Malta
5121
Crete
Cyprus
Levant
Mesopotamia
Tigris
Euphrates
Syrian Desert
High Plateaus
Saharan Atlas
Middle Atlas
High Atlas
Anti Atlas
Toubkal 4165
Chott Djerid
G. of Gabes
G. of Sidra
Tripolitania
Cyrenaica
Canary Is.
3718
Tenerife
Dra
Igidi
Siwa
Sinai 2642
Arabia
The Gulf
Bahrain
Tuat
Tasili Plateau
Fezzan
Libyan Desert
Kufra
Egypt
El Kharga
Arabian Desert
Nile
Hejaz
Red Sea
Tropic of Cancer
Hoggar
Ist Cat.
Ras Nouadhibou
El Djouf
Sahara
Tibesti
3415
Nubian Desert
Nubia
3rd Cat.
4th Cat.
5th Cat.
Adrar
Air
Bilma
Rub' al Khali
Atbara
6th Cat.
C. Vert
Senegal
Senegambia
Gambia
Niger
(Joliba)
Volta
L. Chad
Wadai
Darfur
Kordofan
White Nile
Blue Nile
Ras Dashan 4620
L. Tana
Perim I.
Str. of Bab el Mandeb
Gulf of Aden
Ras Asir
Socotra
Fouta Djalon
Sudan
Guinea
Chari
Ethiopian Highlands
Somali Peninsula
Benue
Adamawa Highlands
Bahr el Ghazal
Bahr el Jebel
Dar Banda
Shabeelle
Grain Coast
Gold Coast
Slave Coast
Ivory Coast
C. Palmas
Bight of Benin
Cameroon Peak 4070
6363
Bioko
Uele
Turkana
Congo
Bight of Bonny
Gulf of Guinea
Principe
São Tomé
C. Lopez
Annobón
Ogooué
Oubangui
Zaïre (Congo)
L. Mobutu Sese Seko
Chutes Boyoma
Ruwenzori 5109
Elgon 4321
Kenya 5199
Juba
Shibeli
Equator
L. Edward
L. Kivu
Victoria
Tana
Basin
Lualaba
Kasai
Sankuru
Pool Malebo
Zaïre (Congo)
Kilimanjaro 5895
INDIAN OCEAN
Pemba
Zanzibar
L. Tanganyika
Ascension
Cuango
Lovua
Kwanza
L. Mweru
Rungwe 2961
L. Nyasa
Aldabra Is.
Shaba
L. Bangweulu
Luapula
Ruvuma
C. Delgado
L. Malawi
Comoro Is.
Bié Plateau
Cuando
Zambezi
ATLANTIC OCEAN
St. Helena
Cunene
Kuvango
Mulanje 3000
Mozambique Channel
Madagascar
C. Fria
Victoria Falls
2643
Namib Desert
Walvis Bay
Limpopo
Tropic of Capricorn
Réunion
Kalahari
Delagoa Bay
High Veld
Vaal
Orange
3482
Drakensberg
Compass B. 2505
Nuweveldberge
Gr. Karoo
Swartberg
C. of Good Hope
C. Agulhas
Agulhas Bank
Algoa Bay
ft
m
12,000
9000
6000
4500
3000
1200
600
0
200
2000
4000
6000
600
6000
12,000
18,000
Projection: Zenithal Equidistant.
West from Greenwich
East from Greenwich
COPYRIGHT. GEORGE PHILIP & SON LTD.

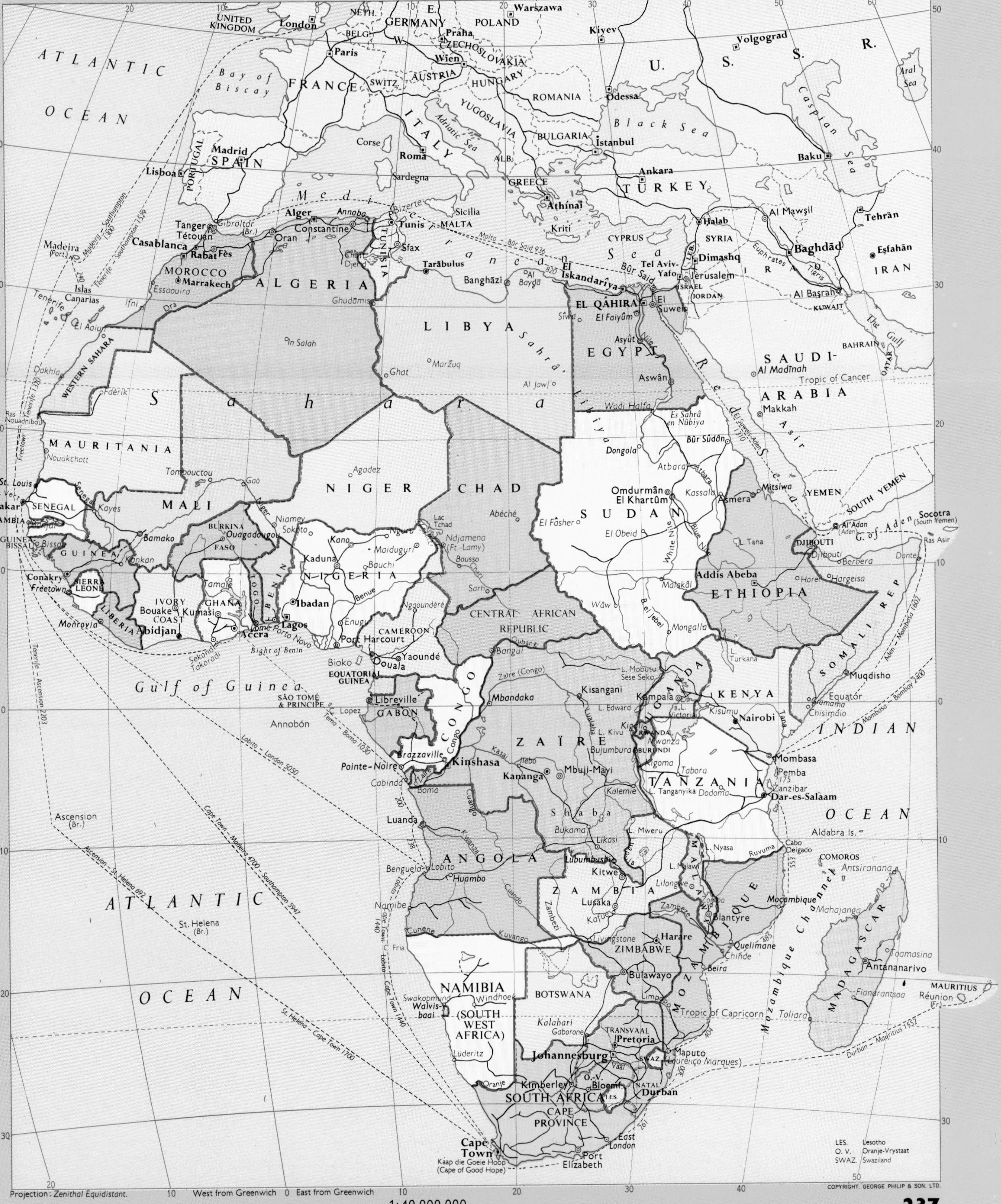

ATLANTIC OCEAN

UNITED KINGDOM
London
NETH.
BELG.
E. GERMANY
W. GERMANY
POLAND
Warszawa
Praha
CZECHOSLOVAKIA
Wien
AUSTRIA
HUNGARY
Kiyev
Volgograd
U. S. S. R.
Aral Sea
Paris
FRANCE
SWITZ.
Bay of Biscay
ROMANIA
Odessa
YUGOSLAVIA
Black Sea
Caspian Sea
Adriatic Sea
BULGARIA
İstanbul
Baku
Corse
ITALY
Roma
ALB.
Madrid
SPAIN
PORTUGAL
Lisboa
Sardegna
GREECE
Ankara
TURKEY
Athínai
Sicilia
MALTA
Mediterranean Sea
Kriti
CYPRUS
Tanger
Tétouan
Gibraltar (Br.)
Alger
Annaba
Bizerte
Tunis
Constantine
Oran
TUNISIA
Sfax
Djerba
Halab
SYRIA
Al Mawşil
Tehrān
Dimashq
Baghdād
Eşfahān
IRAQ
IRAN
Madeira (Port.)
Casablanca
Rabat
Fès
MOROCCO
Marrakech
Essaouira
Islas Canarias
Tenerife
Ifni
Dra
El Aaiun
ALGERIA
Ghudāmis
Tarābulus
Banghāzi
Al Baydā
Iskandarîya
Bûr Saîd
Tel Aviv-Yafo
Jerusalem
ISRAEL
JORDAN
LEB.
Euphrates
Tigris
Al Başrah
KUWAIT
The Gulf
BAHRAIN
QATAR
EL QÂHIRA
El Faiyûm
El Suweis
Sîwa
LIBYA
Sahrâ' Lîbîya
Asyût
EGYPT
Aswân
In Salah
Marzūq
Ghat
Al Jawf
WESTERN SAHARA
Dakhla
Fdérik
Sahara
SAUDI-ARABIA
Al Madīnah
Makkah
Tropic of Cancer
Red Sea
Wadi Halfa
Es Sahrâ en Nûbiya
Bûr Sûdân
Ras Nouadhibou
MAURITANIA
Nouakchott
Dongola
Atbara
Tombouctou
Gao
Agadez
NIGER
CHAD
Mitsiwa
Asmera
YEMEN
SOUTH YEMEN
Socotra (South Yemen)
St. Louis
C. Vert
Dakar
SENEGAL
GAMBIA
Kayes
MALI
Omdurmân
El Khartûm
Kassala
SUDAN
Abéché
Al'Adan (Aden)
Gulf of Aden
Ras Asir
GUINEA BISSAU
Bissau
BURKINA FASO
Ouagadougou
Niamey
Sokoto
Lac Tchad
Ndjamena (Ft.-Lamy)
El Fâsher
El Obeid
DJIBOUTI
Djibouti
Berbera
Dante
GUINEA
Bamako
Kankan
Kano
Maiduguri
Bousso
L. Tana
Conakry
Freetown
SIERRA LEONE
Kaduna
Bauchi
NIGERIA
Harer
Hargeisa
Addis Abeba
ETHIOPIA
IVORY COAST
Bouake
Tamale
GHANA
Kumasi
TOGO
BENIN
Ibadan
Benue
Ngaoundéré
Sarh
Malakâl
Wâw
Bahr el Jebel
White Nile
Blue Nile
Monrovia
LIBERIA
Abidjan
Accra
Lomé
Porto Novo
Lagos
Enugu
Port Harcourt
CAMEROON
CENTRAL AFRICAN REPUBLIC
Bangui
Ubangi
Mongalla
L. Turkana
SOMALI REP.
Sekondi-Takoradi
Bight of Benin
Bioko
Douala
Yaoundé
EQUATORIAL GUINEA
L. Mobutu Sese Seko
UGANDA
Muqdisho
Gulf of Guinea
SÃO TOMÉ & PRINCIPE
C. Lopez
Libreville
GABON
CONGO
Mbandaka
Zaïre (Congo)
Kisangani
Kampala
L. Edward
L. Victoria
Kisumu
KENYA
Nairobi
Tana
Equator
Chisimaio
Annobón
Lualaba
L. Kivu
Kigali
RWANDA
BURUNDI
Bujumbura
Mwanza
INDIAN OCEAN
Brazzaville
Kinshasa
Pointe-Noire
Cabinda
Kasai
Ilebo
ZAÏRE
Kananga
Mbuji-Mayi
Tabora
Kigoma
TANZANIA
Mombasa
Pemba
Zanzibar
Dodoma
Dar-es-Salaam
Boma
Cuango
Kalemie
L. Tanganyika
Ascension (Br.)
Luanda
Kwanza
Shaba
Bukama
Likasi
L. Mweru
Aldabra Is.
Lubumbashi
Kitwe
Nyasa
Ruvuma
Cabo Delgado
COMOROS
Antsiranana
Benguela
Lobito
ANGOLA
Huambo
L. Malawi
Lilongwe
MALAWI
MOZAMBIQUE
Moçambique
ZAMBIA
Lusaka
Kafue
Cuando
Zambeze
Blantyre
Mahajanga
Namibe
Cunene
Kuvango
Livingstone
Harare
ZIMBABWE
Quelimane
Chinde
Beira
Mozambique Channel
MADAGASCAR
Toamasina
Antananarivo
ATLANTIC OCEAN
St. Helena (Br.)
Fria
NAMIBIA (SOUTH WEST AFRICA)
Windhoek
Swakopmund
Walvis-baai
BOTSWANA
Bulawayo
Limpopo
Tropic of Capricorn
Toliara
Fianarantsoa
MAURITIUS
Réunion (Fr.)
Kalahari
Gaborone
TRANSVAAL
Pretoria
Johannesburg
SWAZ.
Maputo (Lourenço Marques)
Vaal
Lüderitz
Oranje
Kimberley
O.-V.
Bloemf.
NATAL
Durban
LES.
SOUTH AFRICA
CAPE PROVINCE
Cape Town
Kaap die Goeie Hoop (Cape of Good Hope)
East London
Port Elizabeth

LES. Lesotho
O. V. Oranje-Vrystaat
SWAZ. Swaziland

Projection: Zenithal Equidistant.
West from Greenwich 0 East from Greenwich

1:40 000 000

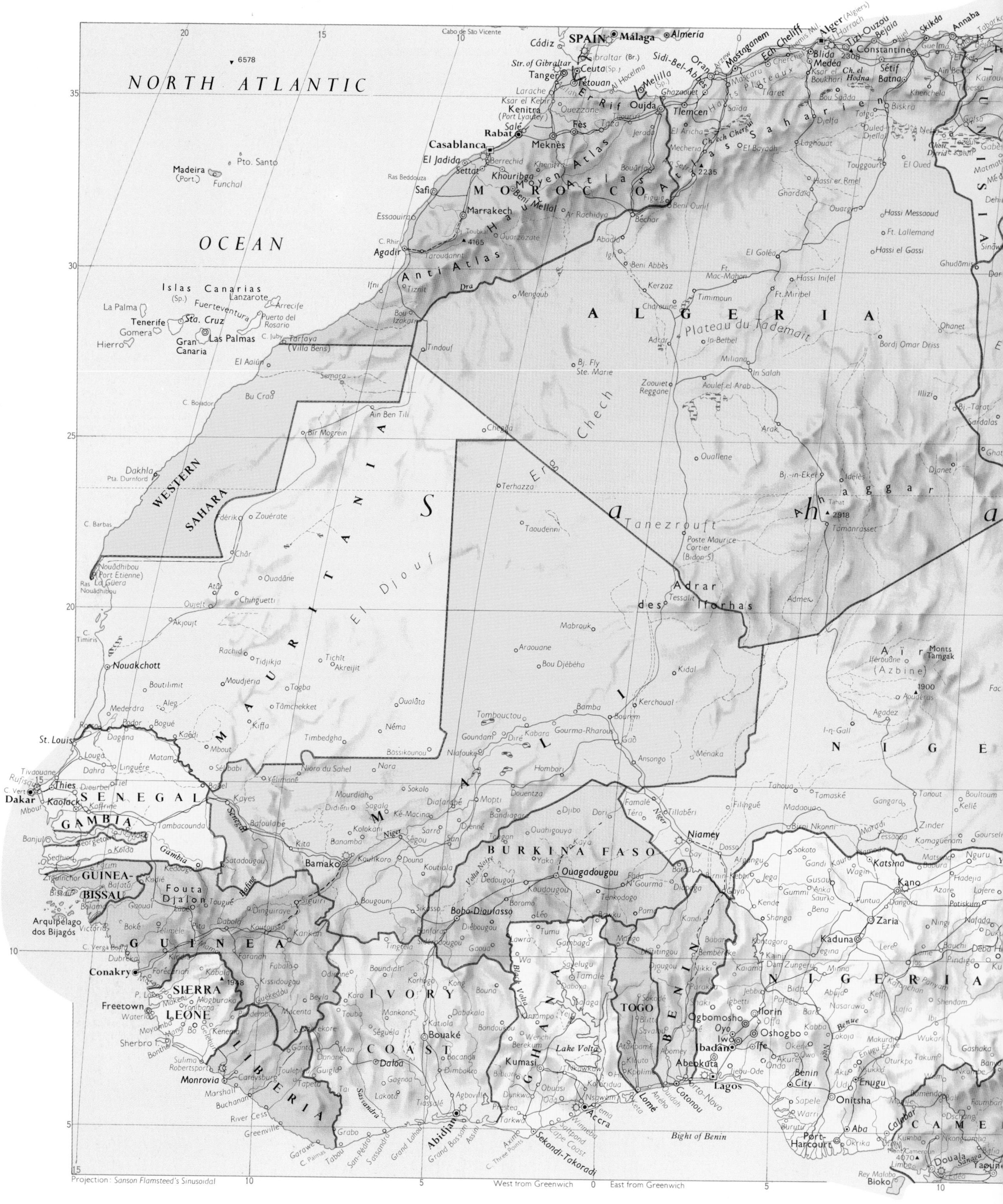
NORTH ATLANTIC
OCEAN
Madeira (Port.)
Pto. Santo
Funchal
Islas Canarias (Sp.)
Lanzarote
Fuerteventura
La Palma
Tenerife
Gomera
Hierro
Gran Canaria
Las Palmas
Sta. Cruz
SPAIN
Málaga
Almería
Cádiz
Str. of Gibraltar
Gibraltar (Br.)
Ceuta (Sp.)
Tanger
Tétouan
Melilla (Sp.)
Oran
Alger (Algiers)
Constantine
Annaba
Skikda
Sidi-Bel-Abbès
Mostaganem
Tlemcen
Oujda
Fès
Meknès
Rabat
Kenitra (Port Lyautey)
Salé
Casablanca
El Jadida
Settat
Khouribga
Safi
Essaouira
Marrakech
Agadir
Beni Mellal
MOROCCO
Moyen Atlas
Haut Atlas
Anti Atlas
Er Rif
Ifni
Tiznit
Tarfaya (Villa Bens)
Tindouf
El Aaiún
Semara
Bu Craa
C. Bojador
Dakhla
WESTERN SAHARA
C. Barbas
Nouâdhibou (Port Etienne)
La Güera
MAURITANIA
Nouakchott
Akjoujt
Atâr
Chinguetti
Ouadâne
Zouérate
F'dérik
Rosso
Tidjikja
Kiffa
Néma
Timbedgha
Kaédi
St. Louis
Dakar
Thies
Kaolack
SENEGAL
GAMBIA
Banjul
Tambacounda
GUINEA-BISSAU
Bissau
Arquipélago dos Bijagós
GUINEA
Conakry
Fouta Djalon
SIERRA LEONE
Freetown
LIBERIA
Monrovia
IVORY COAST
Abidjan
Bouaké
Daloa
Kayes
Bamako
Ségou
Mopti
MALI
Tombouctou
Gao
Kidal
Taoudenni
El Djouf
Erg Chech
Sahara
Tanezrouft
Adrar des Iforhas
ALGERIA
Plateau du Tademaït
Adrar
Timimoun
In Salah
Béchar
El Goléa
Ghardaïa
Ouargla
Hassi Messaoud
Biskra
Djelfa
Laghouat
Sétif
Batna
Touggourt
Ahaggar
Tamanrasset
Djanet
Illizi
Aïr (Azbine)
Agadez
NIGER
Niamey
BURKINA FASO
Ouagadougou
Bobo-Dioulasso
GHANA
Kumasi
Lake Volta
Accra
Sekondi-Takoradi
Tamale
TOGO
Lomé
BENIN
Cotonou
Porto-Novo
NIGERIA
Lagos
Ibadan
Abeokuta
Ogbomosho
Ilorin
Kaduna
Kano
Zaria
Katsina
Sokoto
Enugu
Onitsha
Benin City
Port-Harcourt
Bight of Benin
Douala
Bioko
Projection: Sanson Flamsteed's Sinusoidal
West from Greenwich
East from Greenwich

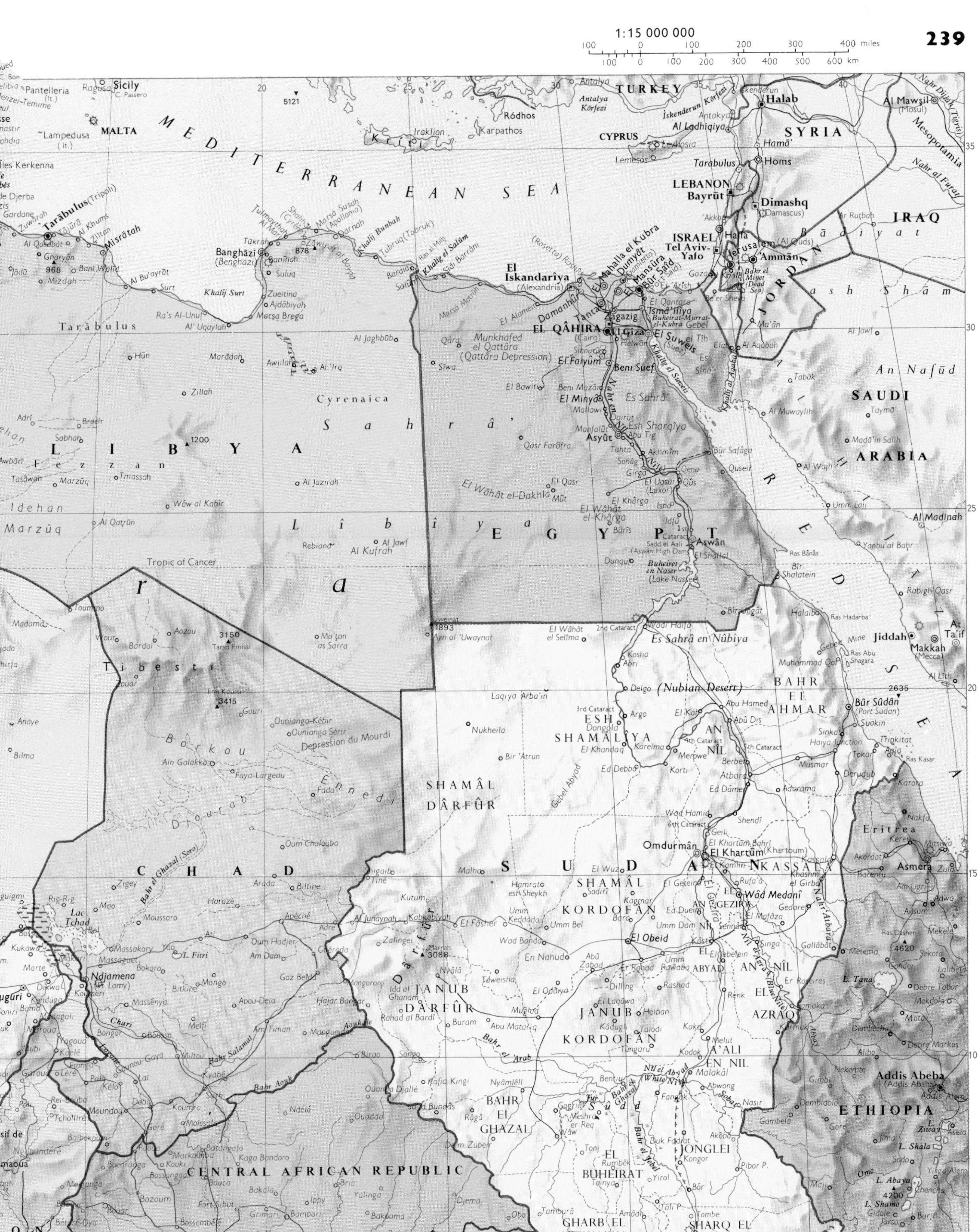
1:15 000 000
100 0 100 200 300 400 miles
100 0 100 200 300 400 500 600 km
MEDITERRANEAN SEA
TURKEY
SYRIA
CYPRUS
LEBANON
ISRAEL
JORDAN
IRAQ
SAUDI ARABIA
MALTA
Sicily
Kriti
LIBYA
EGYPT
CHAD
SUDAN
CENTRAL AFRICAN REPUBLIC
ZAÏRE
KENYA
ETHIOPIA
Eritrea
RED SEA
BAHR EL AHMAR
Sahrâ' Lîbîya
Tibesti
Borkou
Ennedi
Fezzan
Cyrenaica
Es Sahrâ en Nûbiya
(Nubian Desert)
Tropic of Cancer
Tarābulus (Tripoli)
Banghāzī (Benghazi)
El Iskandarîya (Alexandria)
EL QÂHIRA (Cairo)
Bûr Sa'îd
El Suweis (Suez)
Aswân
Asyût
Jerusalem
Tel Aviv-Yafo
Bayrūt
Dimashq (Damascus)
Halab
Homs
'Ammān
Jiddah
Makkah (Mecca)
Omdurmân
El Khartûm (Khartoum)
Bûr Sûdân (Port Sudan)
El Obeid
Wâd Medanî
Asmera
Addis Abeba
Ndjamena (Ft. Lamy)
Bangui
Lac Tchad
L. Tana
L. Turkana
Nîl
Buheiret en Naser (Lake Nasser)
Munkhafed el Qattâra (Qattâra Depression)
Khalîj Surt
An Nafūd
Bādiyat ash Shām
Mesopotamia
SHAMÂL DÂRFÛR
JANUB DÂRFÛR
SHAMÂL KORDOFÂN
JANUB KORDOFÂN
ESH SHAMÂLÎYA
KASSALA
BAHR EL GHAZAL
EL BUHEIRAT
JONGLEI
GHARB EL ISTIWA'IYA
SHARQ EL ISTIWA'IYA
A'ALI EN NIL
15
20
25
30
35

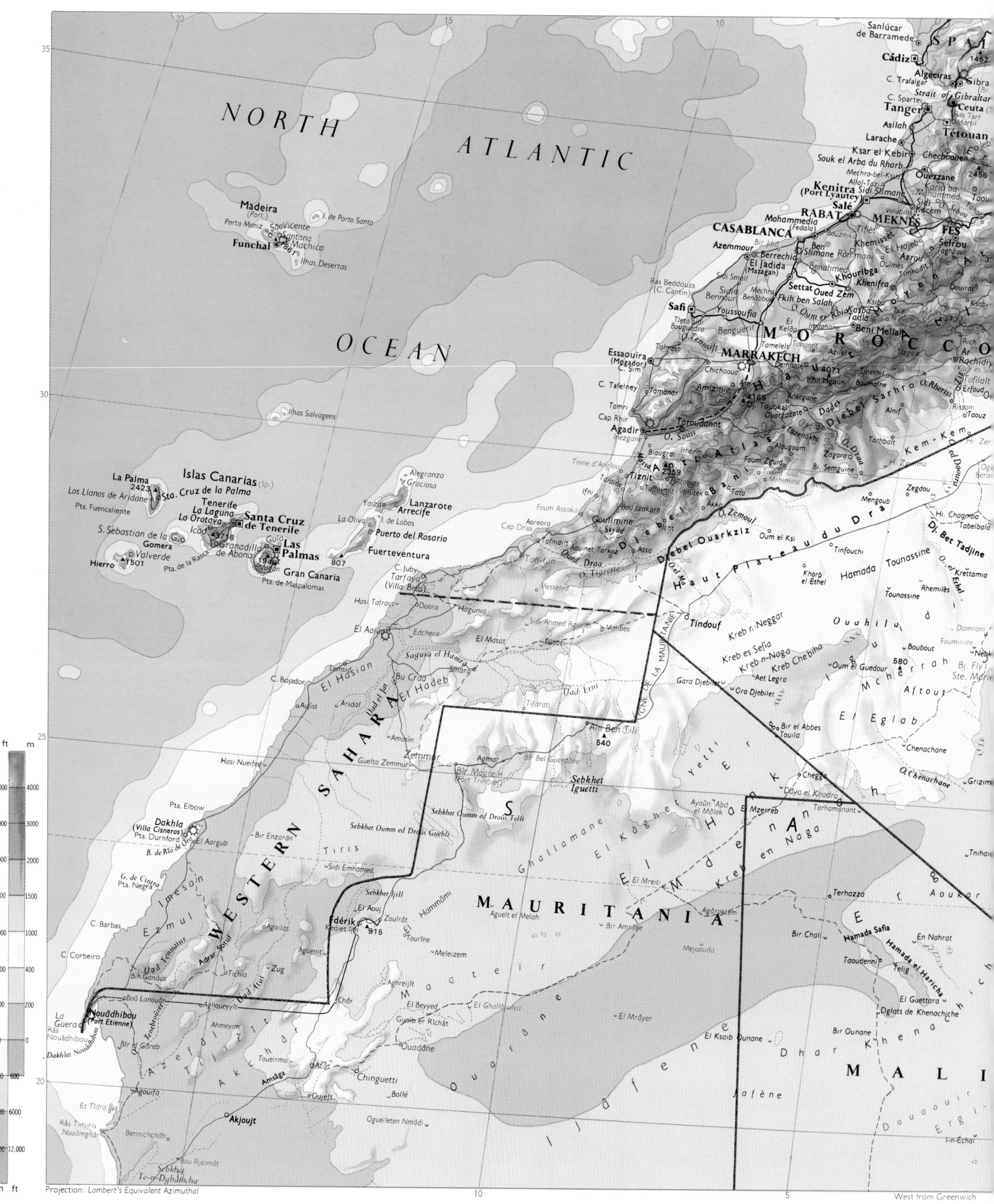
NORTH ATLANTIC OCEAN
Madeira
(Port.)
Porto Moniz
São Vicente
Santana
Machico
Funchal
I. de Porto Santo
Ilhas Desertas
Ilhas Salvagens
Islas Canarias (Sp.)
La Palma
Sta. Cruz de la Palma
Los Llanos de Aridane
Pta. Fuencaliente
Tenerife
La Laguna
La Orotava
Santa Cruz de Tenerife
Icod
S. Sebastian de la G.
Gomera
Valverde
Hierro
Granadilla de Abona
Guía
Las Palmas
Gran Canaria
Pta. de Maspalomas
Alegranza
Graciosa
Lanzarote
Arrecife
Yaiza
La Oliva
I. de Lobos
Puerto del Rosario
Fuerteventura
Sanlúcar de Barrameda
Cádiz
Algeciras
C. Trafalgar
Strait of Gibraltar
C. Spartel
Tanger
Ceuta
Asilah
Larache
Tétouan
Ksar el Kebir
Souk el Arba du Rharb
Chechaouen
Ouezzane
Kenitra (Port Lyautey)
Salé
RABAT
MEKNÈS
FES
Mohammedia (Fedala)
CASABLANCA
Azemmour
Berrechid
El Jadida (Mazagan)
Khemisset
Sefrou
Azrou
Settat
Oued Zem
Khouribga
Khenifra
Ras Beddouza (C. Cantin)
Safi
Youssoufia
Fkih ben Salah
Kasba Tadla
Beni Mellal
Benguerir
MOROCCO
Essaouira (Mogador)
MARRAKECH
C. Sim
C. Tafelney
Tamri
Cap Rhir
Agadir
Inezgane
Taroudannt
O. Sous
Toubkal
4165
Ouarzazate
Djebel Sarhro
Tiznit
Ifni
Goulimine
Tan-tan
Cap Draa
Foum Assaka
Oued Draa
Djebel Bani
Djebel Ouarkziz
Tata
Akka
Foum Zguid
Zagora
Hamada du Draa
Haut Plateau du Draa
Tindouf
C. Juby
Tarfaya (Villa Bens)
Hasi Tafraut
Daora
Hagunia
El Aaiún
Edchera
El Masat
Saguia el Hamra
Smara
Bu Craa
El Hadeb
C. Bojador
El Hasian
Aridal
Auleitis
Amosin
Zemmur
Guelta Zemmur
Hasi Nueifed
WESTERN SAHARA
Pta. Elbow
Dakhla (Villa Cisneros)
Pta. Durnford
B. de Río de Oro
El Aargub
Bir Enzarán
Tiris
Sidi Emhamed
G. de Cintra
Pta. Negra
Imesain
C. Barbas
Ezmul
Adrar Sotuf
C. Corbeiro
Agailás
Zug
Bir Gandús
Tichla
La Güera
Nouâdhibou (Port Etienne)
Râs Nouâdhibou
Dakhlet Nouâdhibou
Boû Lanouâr
Aghoueyyît
Bir el Gâreb
Ahmeyim
Azefal
Akchar
Agouîfa
Et Tîdra
Râs Timirist
Nouâmghâr
Bennichchâb
Akjoujt
Amsâga
Atâr
Ouadâne
Chinguetti
Oujeft
Bollé
Ogueileten Nmâdi
Bou Rjeimât
Sebkhet Te-n-Dghâmcha
Fdérik
Kediet Ijill
Sebkhet Ijill
Zouîrât
915
Tourîne
Meleizem
Aghreijît
Adrar
El Beyyed
Guelb er Richât
El Ghallâouîya
Ouarane
El Mrâyer
El Ksaib Ounane
MAURITANIA
Aguelt el Melah
Bir Amsâne
Mejaouda
Ghallamane
El Mreïti
Agmar
Bir Moghrein (Fort Trinquet)
Sebkhet Oumm ed Droûs Telli
Sebkhet Oumm ed Droûs Guebli
Sebkhet Iguetti
Tifarati
Uad Erni
Aïn Ben Tili
540
Gara Djebilet
Ora Djebilet
Kreb en Naga
Kreb es Sefia
Kreb Chebiha
Aet Legra
Oum el Guedour
580
Ouahila
Mcherrah
Aftout
Eglab
Bir el Abbes
Touila
Chenachane
O. Chenachane
Erg Iguidi
Chegga
Dâya el Khadra
Ayoûn Abd el Mâlek
Mzeïreb
El Hank
El Mreyyé
Hank
Tarhamanant
Terhazza
Taoudenni
Bir Chali
Hamada Safia
En Nahrat
Hamada el Haricha
Telig
El Guettara
Dglats de Khenachiche
Bir Ounane
Khenachich
Dhar
MALI
Jafène
Ijafene
Douaouir
Erg
I-n-Echaï
Aoukar
Tinfouchi
Mengoub
Zegdou
Hi. Chagmba
Tabelbala
Dj. Bet Tadjine
Khorb el Ethel
Hamada Tounassine
Tounassine
Rhemilès
Krettamia
Boubout
Bj. Fly
Ste. Marie
Kem-Kem
Erfoud
Rissani
Taouz
Alnif
Tinerhir
Boumalne
Tafilalt
Rachidiya
Projection: Lambert's Equivalent Azimuthal
West from Greenwich

1:8 000 000

50 0 50 100 150 200 miles

50 0 50 100 150 200 250 300 km

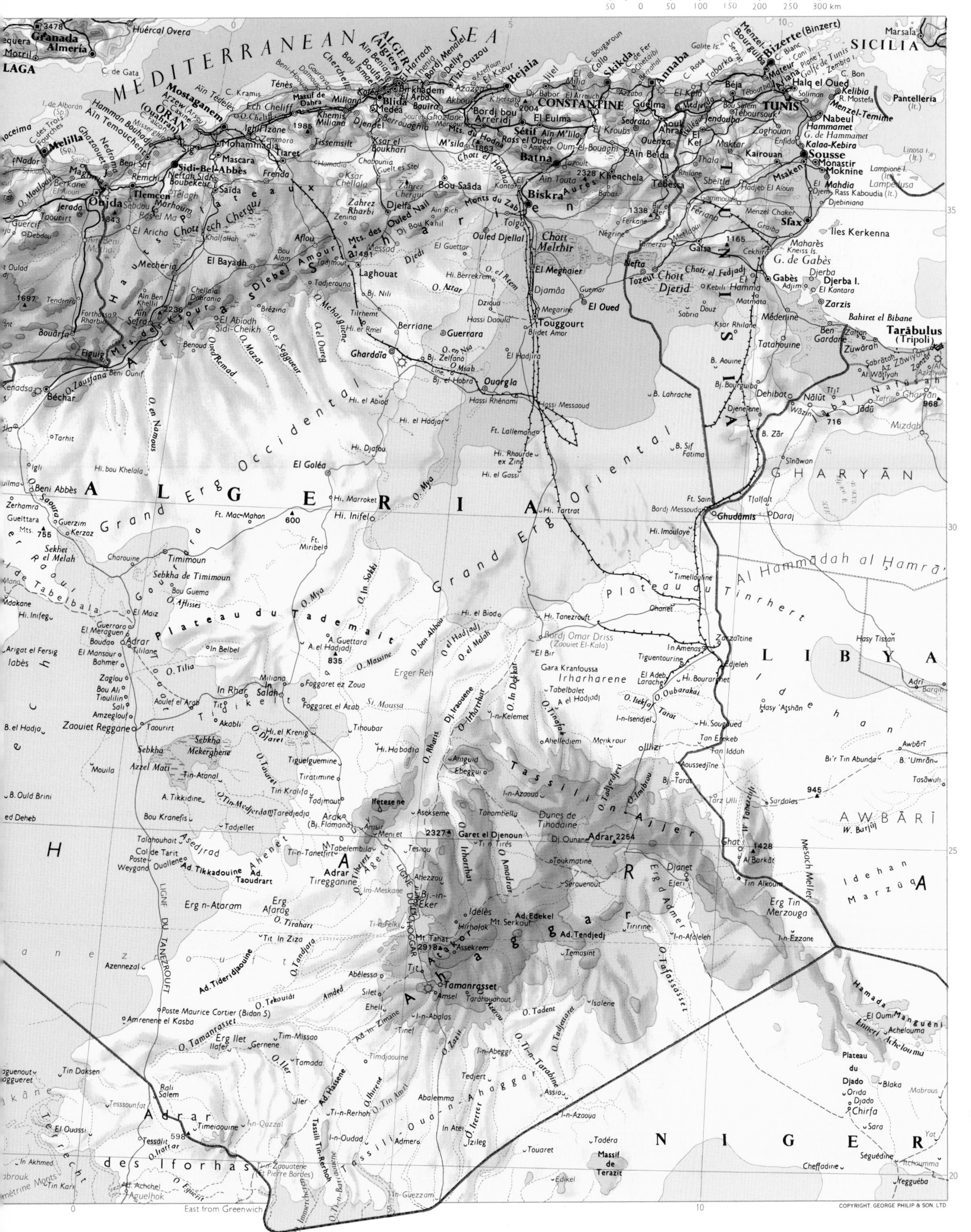

MEDITERRANEAN SEA
SICILIA
ALGERIA
TUNISIA
LIBYA
NIGER
ALGER (Algiers)
ORAN (Ouahran)
CONSTANTINE
TUNIS
Bizerte (Binzert)
Annaba
Skikda
Bejaia
Sétif
Batna
Biskra
Tlemcen
Oujda
Melilla
Mostaganem
Sidi-Bel-Abbès
Blida
Médéa
Sousse
Sfax
Gabès
Djerba I.
Tarābulus (Tripoli)
Touggourt
Ouargla
Ghardaïa
Laghouat
El Goléa
Béchar
Timimoun
Adrar
In Salah
Tamanrasset
Djanet
Ghadāmis
Grand Erg Occidental
Grand Erg Oriental
Plateau du Tademait
Plateau du Tinrhert
Tassili n Ajjer
Ahaggar
Hauts Plateaux
Chott Melrhir
Chott Djerid
Chott ech Chergui
Adrar des Iforhas
Tanezrouft
Al Hammādah al Ḩamrā'
Awbārī
Idehan Marzūq
Gharyān
Pantelleria (It.)
Lampedusa
Iles Kerkenna
Granada
Almería
East from Greenwich
COPYRIGHT. GEORGE PHILIP & SON. LTD.

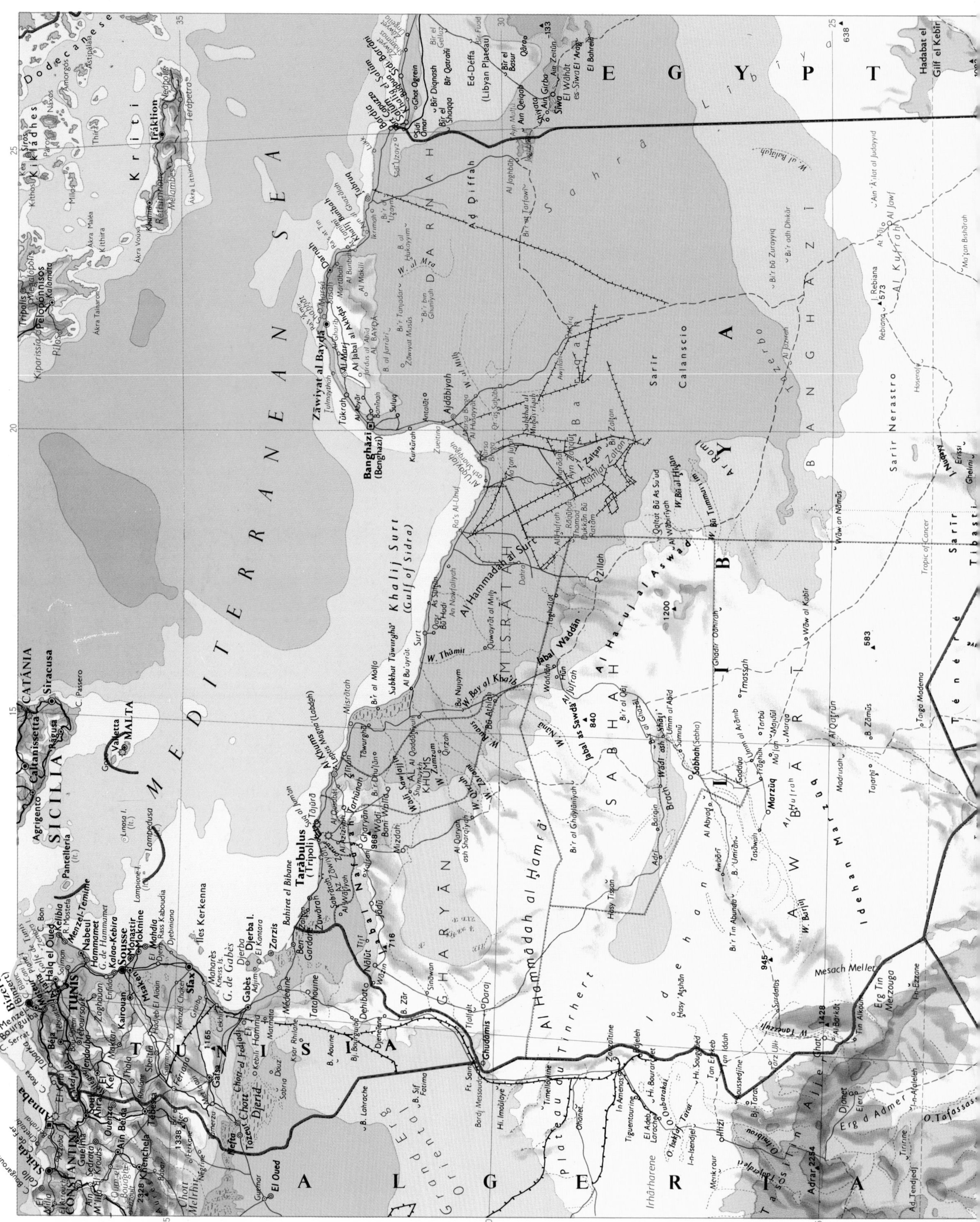
M E D I T E R R A N E A N   S E A
SICILIA
MALTA
Valletta
Kriti
Iráklion
Pelopónnisos
Dodecanese
Kikládhes
CATÁNIA
Siracusa
Caltanissetta
Agrigento
Ragusa
Pantelleria
Lampedusa
Linosa I.
Lampione I.
TUNIS
Bizerte
Sousse
Sfax
Kairouan
Gabès
Djerba I.
Zarzis
Monastir
Mahdia
Îles Kerkenna
G. de Gabès
Chott Djerid
Tozeur
Annaba
CONSTANTINE
El Oued
Ghudāmis
Ṭarābulus (Tripoli)
Al Khums
Mişrātah
Khalij Surt (Gulf of Sidra)
Banghāzī (Benghazi)
Zāwiyat al Bayḑā
Darnah
Ṭubruq
Ajdābiyah
Sabhah (Sebha)
Marzūq
Al Hammādah al Ḩamrā'
Jabal as Sawdā'
Al Haruj al Aswad
Sarir Calanscio
Ed-Deffa (Libyan Plateau)
Siwa
E G Y P T
T U N I S I A
A L G E R I A
L I B Y A
Grand Erg Oriental
Plateau du Tinrhert
Idehan Marzuq
Hadabat el Gilf el Kebir
Tropic of Cancer
Erg d'Admer
Adrar 2254
Mesach Mellet
Erg Tin Merzouga
Sarir Tibasti
Ténéré
Al Kufrah
Sarir Nerastro

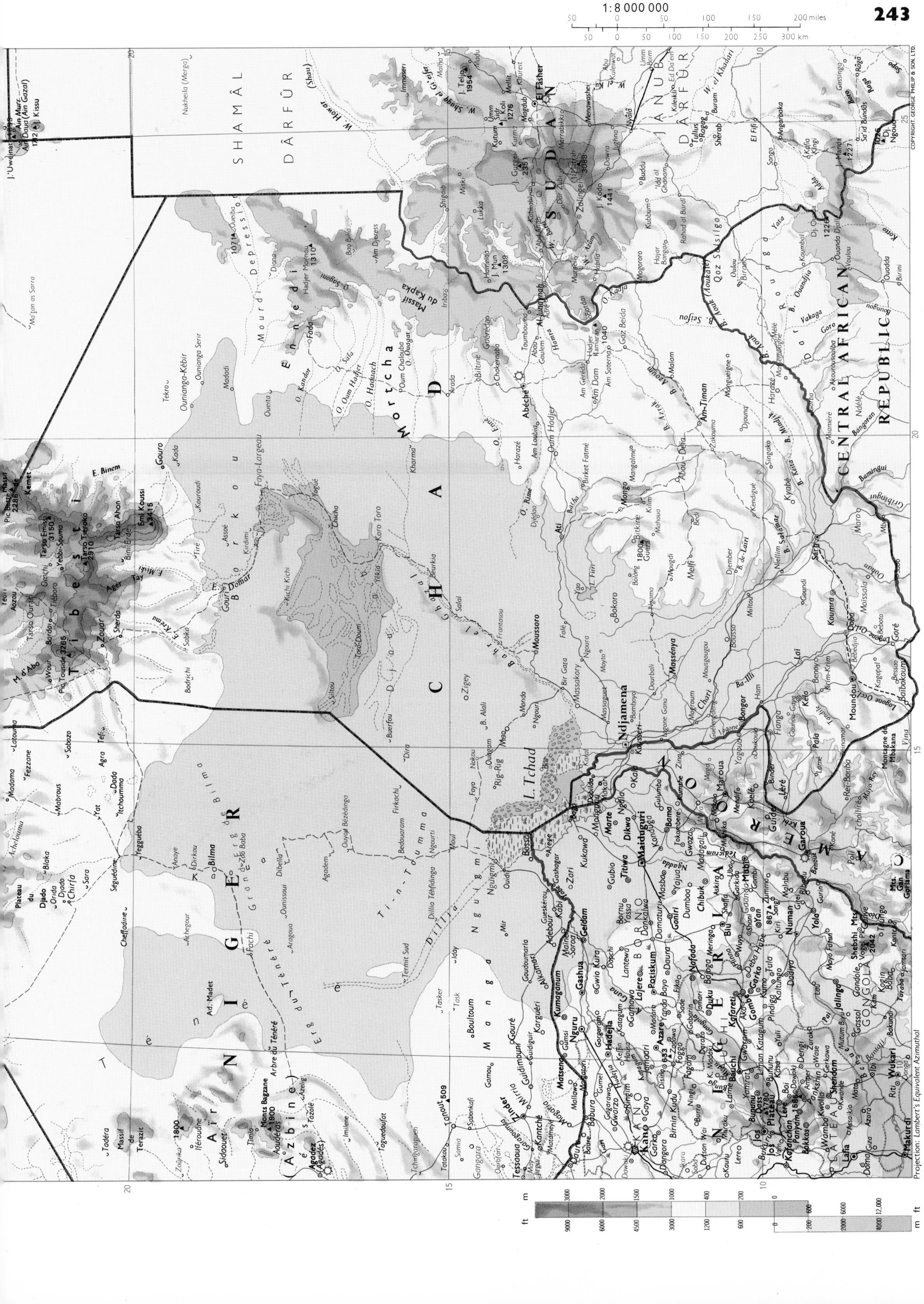

1:8 000 000

50 0 50 100 150 200 miles

50 0 50 100 150 200 250 300 km

NIGER

CHAD

SUDAN

SHAMÂL DÂRFÛR

JANUB DÂRFÛR

CENTRAL AFRICAN REPUBLIC

NIGERIA

CAMEROON

Tibesti

Ennedi

Borkou

Mortcha

Djourab

Bahr el Ghazal

Manga

Ténéré

Erg de Bilma

Aïr (Azbine)

Massif du Kapka

Mourdi Depression

L. Tchad

Ndjamena

Abéché

Faya-Largeau

Moundou

Sarh

Bongor

Mongo

Ati

Am-Timan

El Fasher

Maiduguri

Kano

Agadez

Zinder

Bilma

Emi Koussi 3415

Pic Toussidé 3265

Tarso Emissi 3150

Projection: Lambert's Equivalent Azimuthal

m ft: 3000 9000; 2000 6000; 1500 4500; 1000 3000; 400 1200; 200 600; 0 0; 200 600; 2000 6000; 4000 12,000

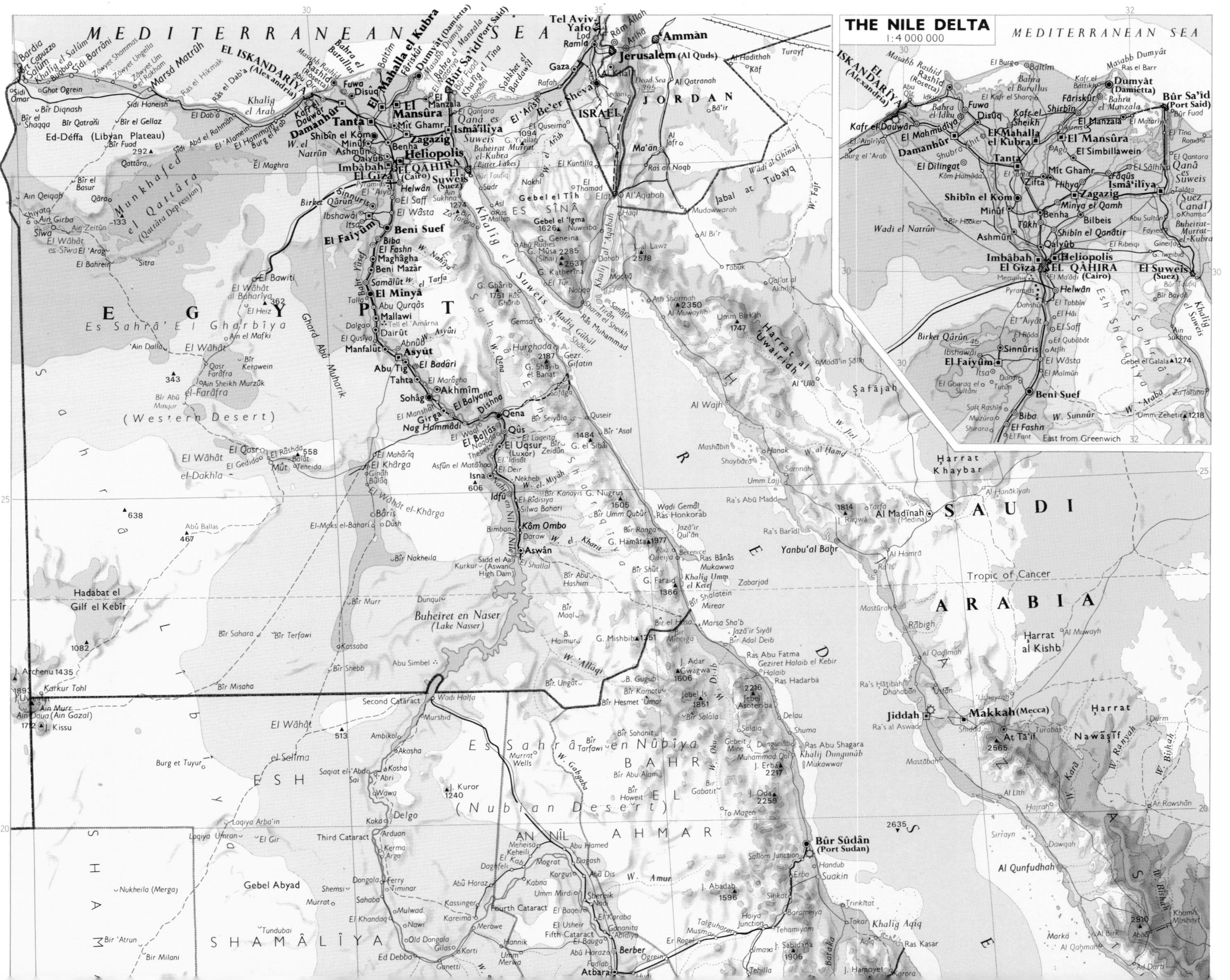
THE NILE DELTA
1:4 000 000
MEDITERRANEAN SEA
EL ISKANDARÎYA (Alexandria)
EL QÂHIRA (Cairo)
Bûr Sa'îd (Port Said)
El Suweis (Suez)
Heliopolis
Dumyât (Damietta)
Rashîd (Rosetta)
East from Greenwich
MEDITERRANEAN SEA
EGYPT
Es Sahrâ' El Gharbîya
(Western Desert)
Khalig el Suweis
SAUDI
ARABIA
JORDAN
ISRAEL
Jerusalem (Al Quds)
Ammân
Tropic of Cancer
Al Madînah (Medina)
Makkah (Mecca)
Jiddah
Bûr Sûdân (Port Sudan)
Aswân
Buheiret en Naser (Lake Nasser)
Es Sahrâ en Nûbîya
(Nubian Desert)
Second Cataract
Third Cataract
Fourth Cataract
Fifth Cataract
Atbara
Berber
Hadabat el Gilf el Kebîr

1:8 000 000

50 0 50 100 150 200 miles

50 0 50 100 150 200 250 300 km

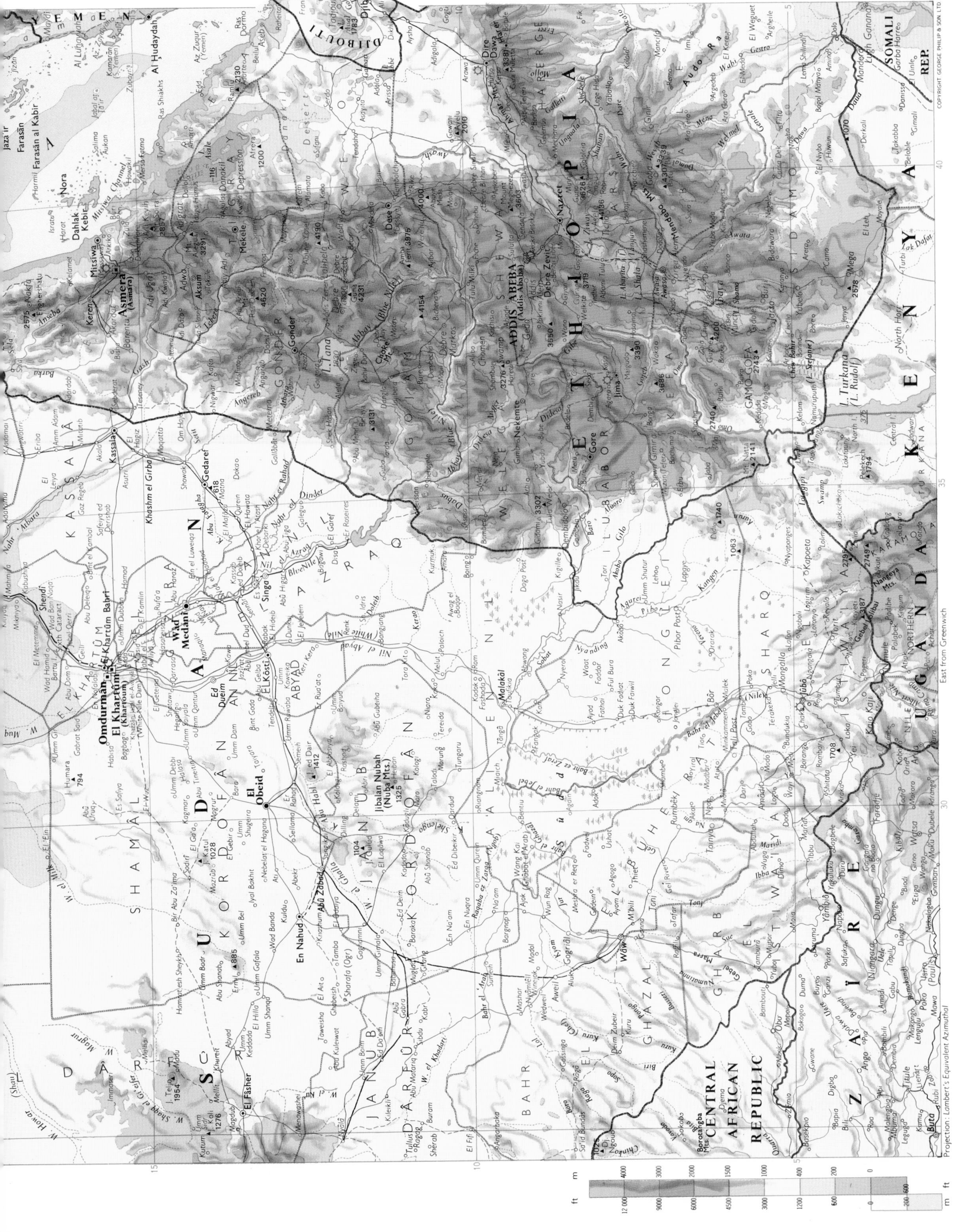

Projection: Lambert's Equivalent Azimuthal

East from Greenwich

m	ft
4000	12 000
3000	9000
2000	6000
1500	4500
1000	3000
400	1200
200	600
0	0
200	600

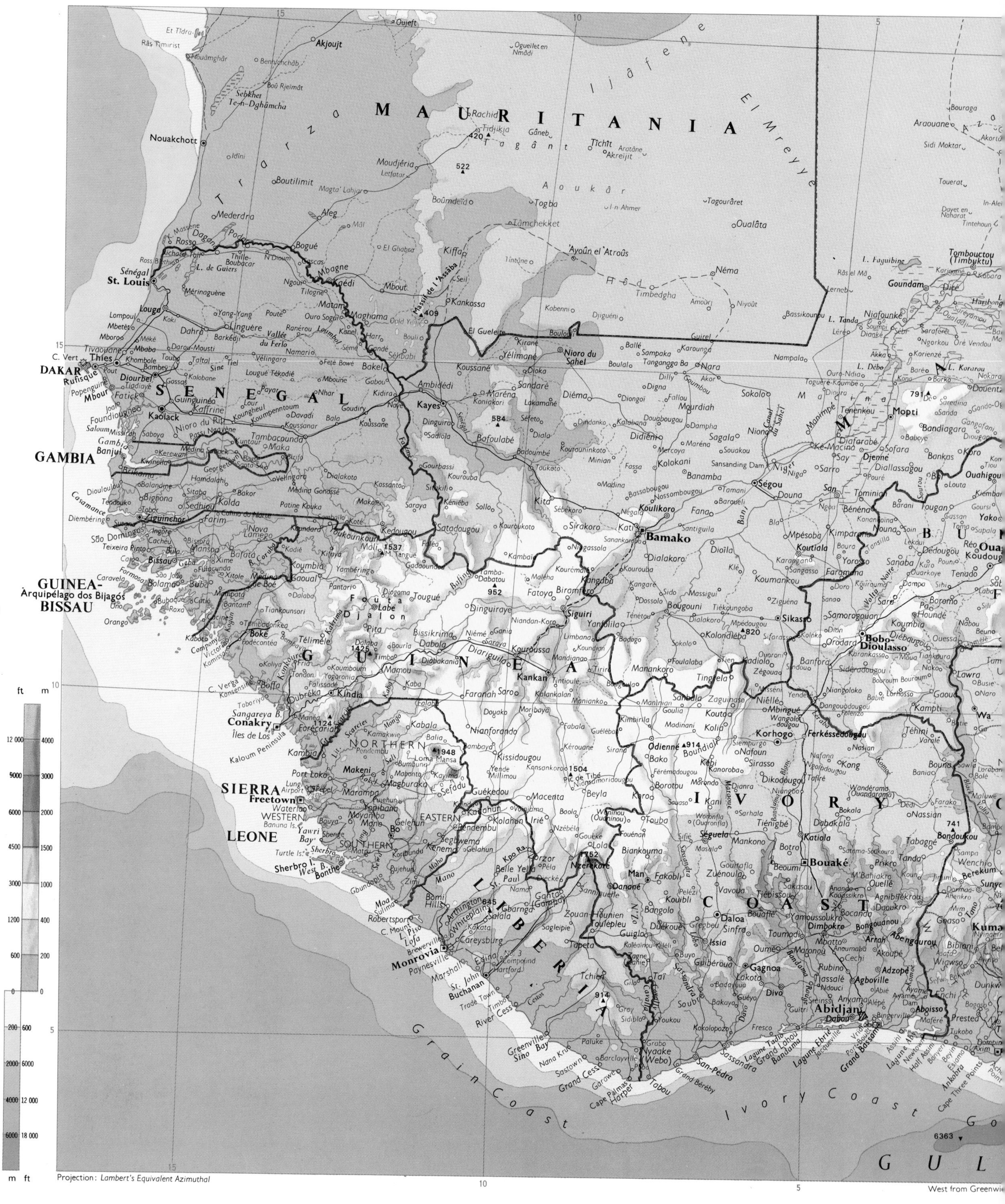
MAURITANIA
SENEGAL
GAMBIA
GUINEA-BISSAU
GUINEA
SIERRA LEONE
LIBERIA
IVORY COAST
Nouakchott
Akjoujt
Boutilimit
Aleg
Kiffa
Tidjikja
Tichit
Néma
'Ayoûn el 'Atroûs
Kaédi
Rosso
St. Louis
DAKAR
Thiès
Rufisque
Diourbel
Kaolack
Banjul
Ziguinchor
Tambacounda
Kayes
Nioro du Sahel
Bamako
Koulikoro
Ségou
Mopti
Tombouctou (Timbuktu)
Goundam
Bissau
Conakry
Kindia
Kankan
Labé
Siguiri
Freetown
Makeni
Bo
Monrovia
Buchanan
Harper
Abidjan
Bouaké
Korhogo
Daloa
Man
San-Pédro
Bobo Dioulasso
Sikasso
Grain Coast
Ivory Coast
Projection: Lambert's Equivalent Azimuthal
West from Greenwich
ft m
12 000 4000
9000 3000
6000 2000
4500 1500
3000 1000
1200 400
600 200
0 0
200 600
2000 6000
4000 12 000
6000 18 000
m ft

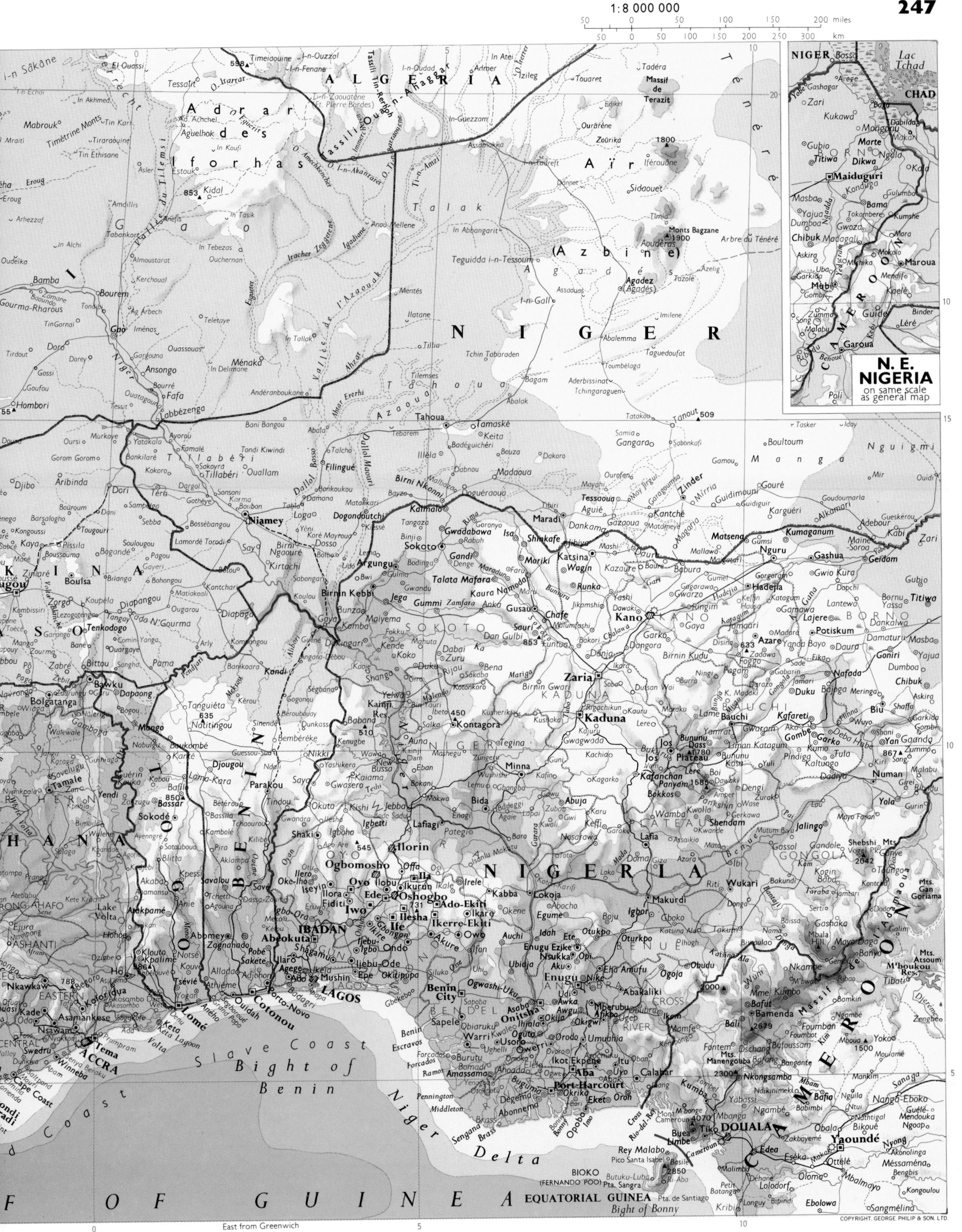

1:8 000 000
50 0 50 100 150 200 miles
50 0 50 100 150 200 250 300 km
ALGERIA
Adrar des Iforhas
Aïr (Azbine)
Massif de Terazit
Ténéré
Talak
Agadès
Tadhoua
Azaouak
NIGER
Manga
Nguigmi
N. E. NIGERIA
on same scale as general map
NIGER
Lac Tchad
CHAD
BORNO
Maiduguri
Kukawa
Dikwa
Bama
Marte
Gubio
Marova
Mubi
Garoua
CAMEROON
Agadez
Tahoua
Tanout
Zinder
Niamey
Dosso
Maradi
Tillabéri
Gao
Bourem
Kidal
Ansongo
Sokoto
Gusau
Katsina
Kano
Zaria
Kaduna
Jos
Plateau
Bauchi
Gombe
Potiskum
Nguru
Hadejia
Azare
Yola
Numan
Jalingo
Minna
Bida
Ilorin
Ogbomosho
Oyo
Oshogbo
IBADAN
Abeokuta
Ilesha
Ife
Ado-Ekiti
Akure
Owo
LAGOS
Ijebu-Ode
Benin City
Sapele
Warri
Onitsha
Asaba
Enugu
Awka
Owerri
Umuahia
Aba
Port Harcourt
Calabar
Makurdi
Lokoja
Abuja
Kontagora
Kainji Res.
Shaki
Kabba
NIGERIA
KADUNA
SOKOTO
KANO
BAUCHI
GONGOLA
BENUE
PLATEAU
NIGER
OYO
ANAMBRA
BENDEL
CROSS RIVER
Shebshi Mts.
Mts. Gan Goriama
Mts. Atsoum
Massif de
Bamenda
Bafoussam
Foumban
Nkongsamba
DOUALA
Buea
Limbe
Tiko
Edea
Yaoundé
Kribi
Ebolowa
Bafia
Mbalmayo
Sangmélina
Rey Malabo
Pico Santa Isabel
BIOKO (FERNANDO POO)
Pta. Sangra
Pta. de Santiago
EQUATORIAL GUINEA
Bight of Bonny
Bight of Benin
Slave Coast
Niger Delta
GULF OF GUINEA
BENIN
Cotonou
Porto-Novo
Parakou
Kandi
Natitingou
Djougou
Abomey
TOGO
Lomé
Sokodé
Bassar
Dapaong
Atakpamé
GHANA
ACCRA
Tema
Tamale
Bolgatanga
Yendi
Cape Coast
Winneba
Keta
Bawku
BURKINA FASO
Ouagadougou
Kaya
Fada N'Gourma
Tenkodogo
Koupéla
Djibo
Dori
East from Greenwich

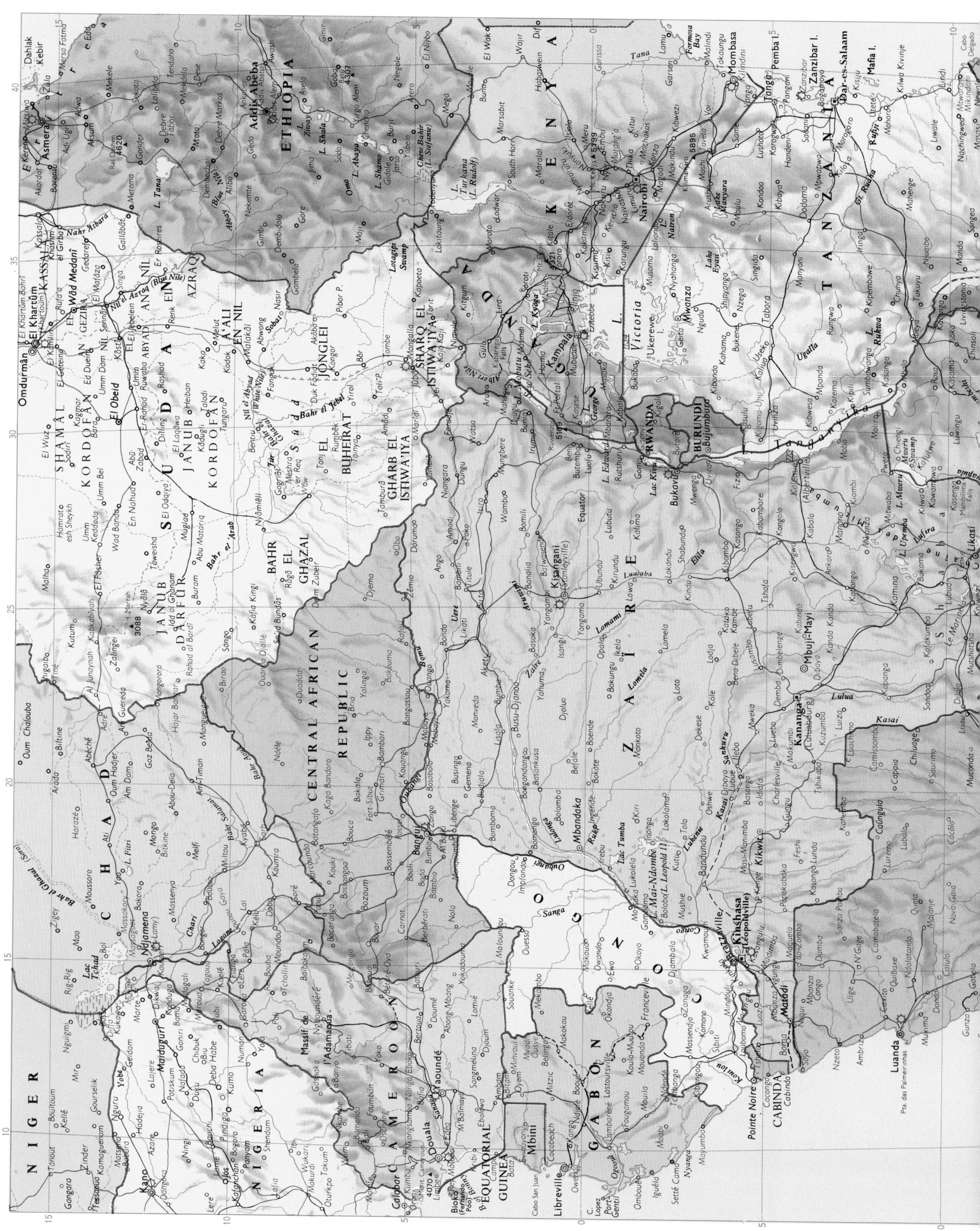
ETHIOPIA
Addis Abeba
KENYA
Nairobi
Mombasa
TANZANIA
Dar-es-Salaam
UGANDA
Kampala
RWANDA
BURUNDI
Bujumbura
L. Victoria
Tanganyika
CHAD
Ndjamena
Lac Tchad
CENTRAL AFRICAN REPUBLIC
Bangui
ZAÏRE
Kisangani
Kinshasa
CONGO
Brazzaville
GABON
Libreville
CAMEROON
Yaoundé
Douala
NIGERIA
Kano
NIGER
EQUATORIAL GUINEA
CABINDA
Luanda
Omdurmân
El Kharṭûm
Pointe Noire
Matadi
Kananga
Mbuji-Mayi

MADAGASCAR

On same scale as General Map

1:15 000 000

0 100 200 300 400 miles

0 100 200 300 400 500 600 km

Projection: Sanson Flamsteed's Sinusoidal

East from Greenwich

Tropic of Capricorn

ATLANTIC OCEAN

INDIAN OCEAN

Mozambique Channel

ZAMBIA

ZIMBABWE

MOZAMBIQUE

MALAWI

BOTSWANA

NAMIBIA (SOUTH WEST AFRICA)

SOUTH AFRICA

TRANSVAAL

ORANJE-VRYSTAAT (O.V.S.)

NATAL

LESOTHO

SWAZILAND

CAPE PROVINCE

Kalahari

Namib Desert

Damaraland

Namaland

Kaokoveld

Caprivi Strip

Harare (Salisbury)

Lusaka

Bulawayo

Maputo (Lourenço Marques)

Beira

Pretoria

Johannesburg

Bloemfontein

Kimberley

Durban

Pietermaritzburg

East London

Port Elizabeth

Cape Town (Kaapstad)

Windhoek

Gaborone

Lilongwe

Antananarivo (Tananarive)

Toliara

Mahajanga

Toamasina

Antsiranana

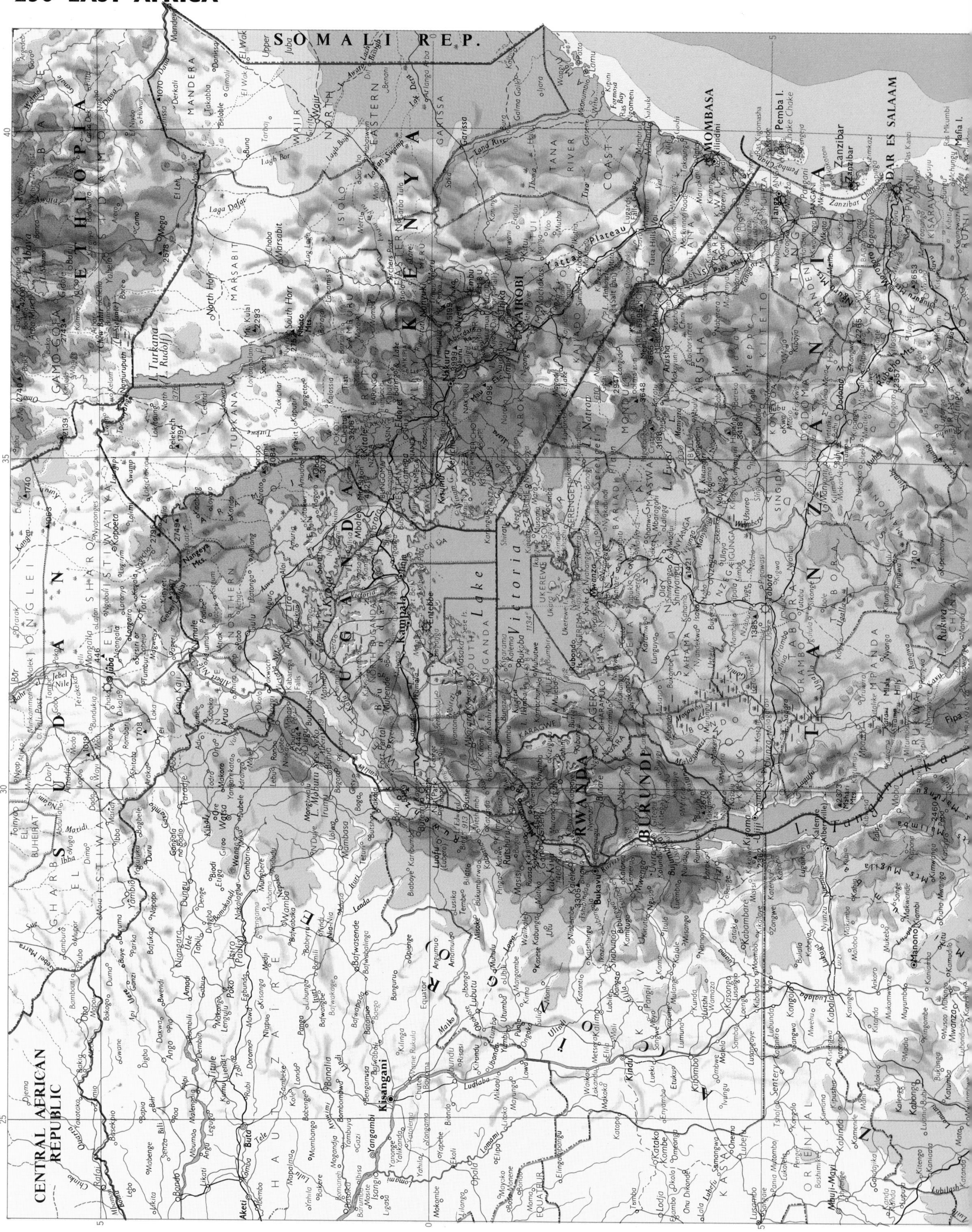

SOMALI REP.

ETHIOPIA

KENYA

UGANDA

RWANDA

BURUNDI

CENTRAL AFRICAN REPUBLIC

NAIROBI

MOMBASA

DAR ES SALAAM

Zanzibar

Pemba I.

Mafia I.

Kampala

Kisangani

Lake Victoria

L. Turkana (L. Rudolf)

L. Tanganyika

1:8 000 000

50 0 50 100 150 200 miles

50 0 100 200 300 km

Projection: Lambert's Equivalent Azimuthal

East from Greenwich

m	ft
6000	18 000
4000	12 000
3000	9000
2000	6000
1500	4500
1000	3000
400	1200
200	600
0	0
200	600
2000	6000

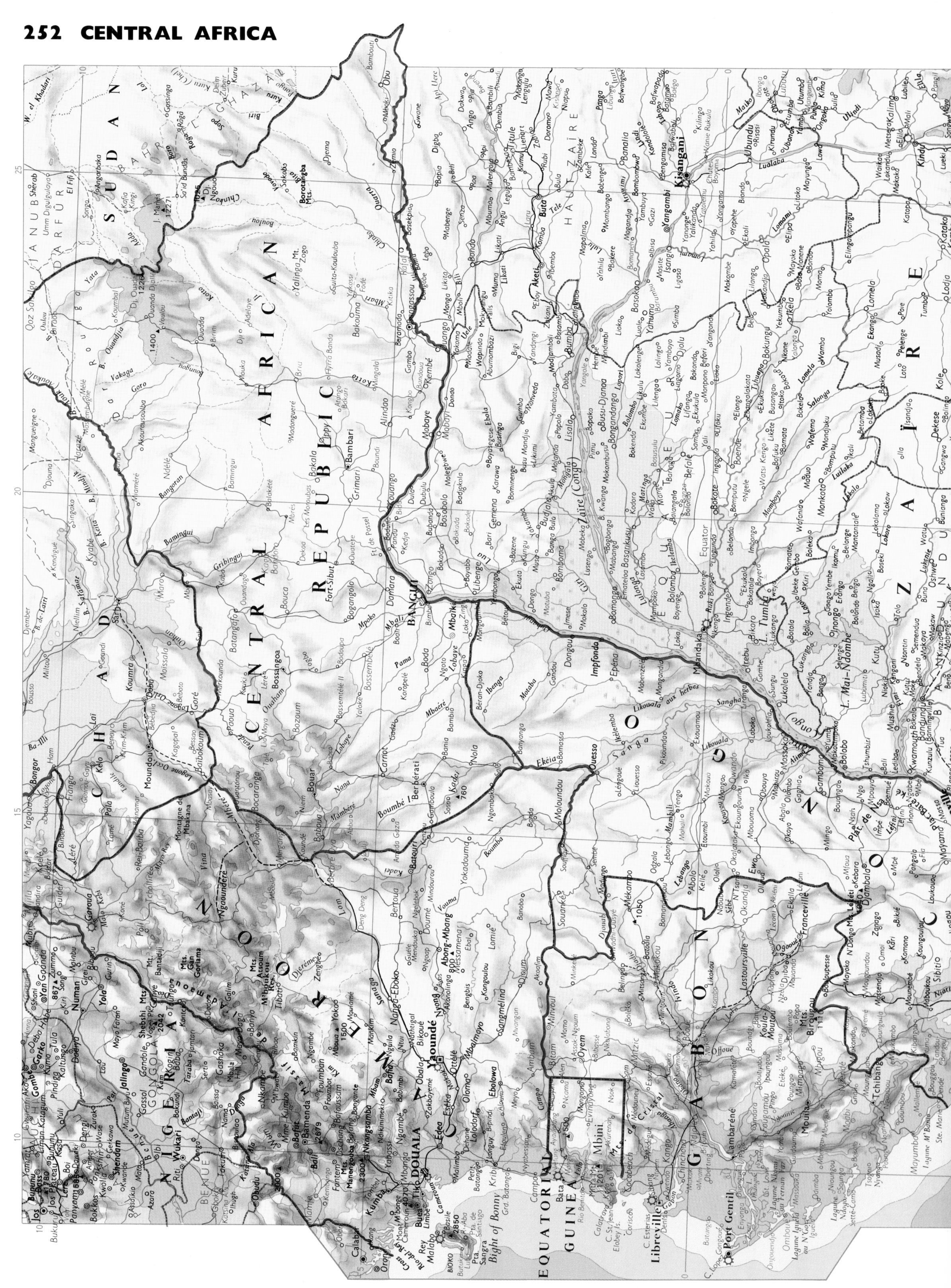
CENTRAL AFRICAN REPUBLIC
CAMEROON
GABON
CONGO
ZAÏRE
EQUATORIAL GUINEA
NIGERIA
CHAD
SUDAN
BANGUI
YAOUNDÉ
DOUALA
Libreville
Port Gentil
Kisangani
Mbandaka
Bight of Bonny

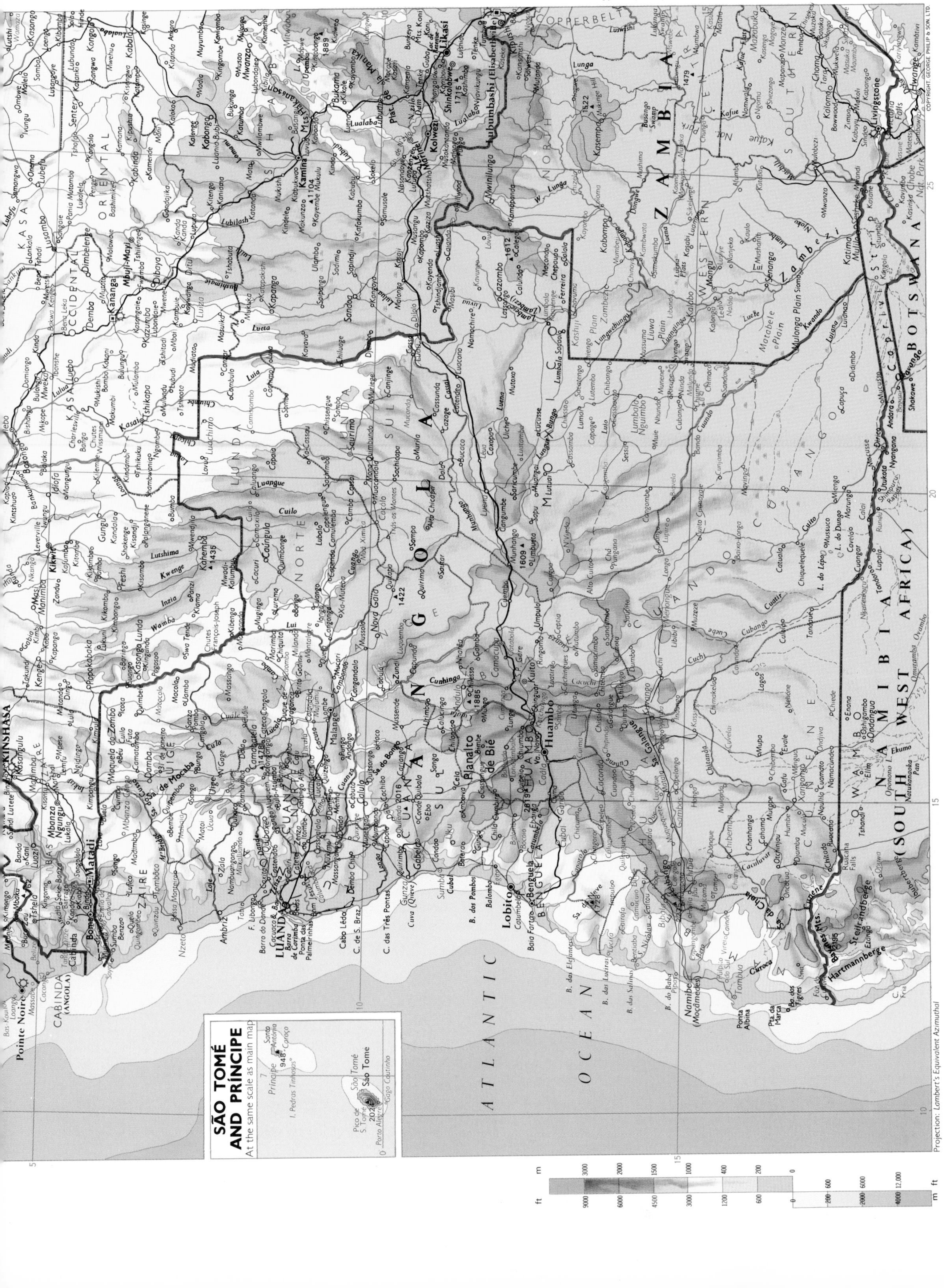

1:8 000 000

50 0 50 100 150 200 miles

50 0 50 100 150 200 250 300 km

SÃO TOMÉ AND PRÍNCIPE

At the same scale as main map

Príncipe
Santo António
948
Coroço
I. Pedras Tinhosas
São Tomé
Pico de S. Tomé
2024
Porto Alegre
Gago Coutinho

ANGOLA
ZAMBIA
ZAIRE
NAMIBIA (SOUTH WEST AFRICA)
BOTSWANA
CABINDA (ANGOLA)
ATLANTIC OCEAN

KINSHASA
LUANDA
Huambo
Lobito
Benguela
Namibe (Moçâmedes)
Lubumbashi (Élisabethville)
Likasi
Kolwezi
Livingstone
Pointe Noire
Matadi

Projection: Lambert's Equivalent Azimuthal

m	3000	2000	1500	1000	400	200	0
ft	9000	6000	4500	3000	1200	600	0

m	0	200	2000	4000
ft	0	600	6000	12,000

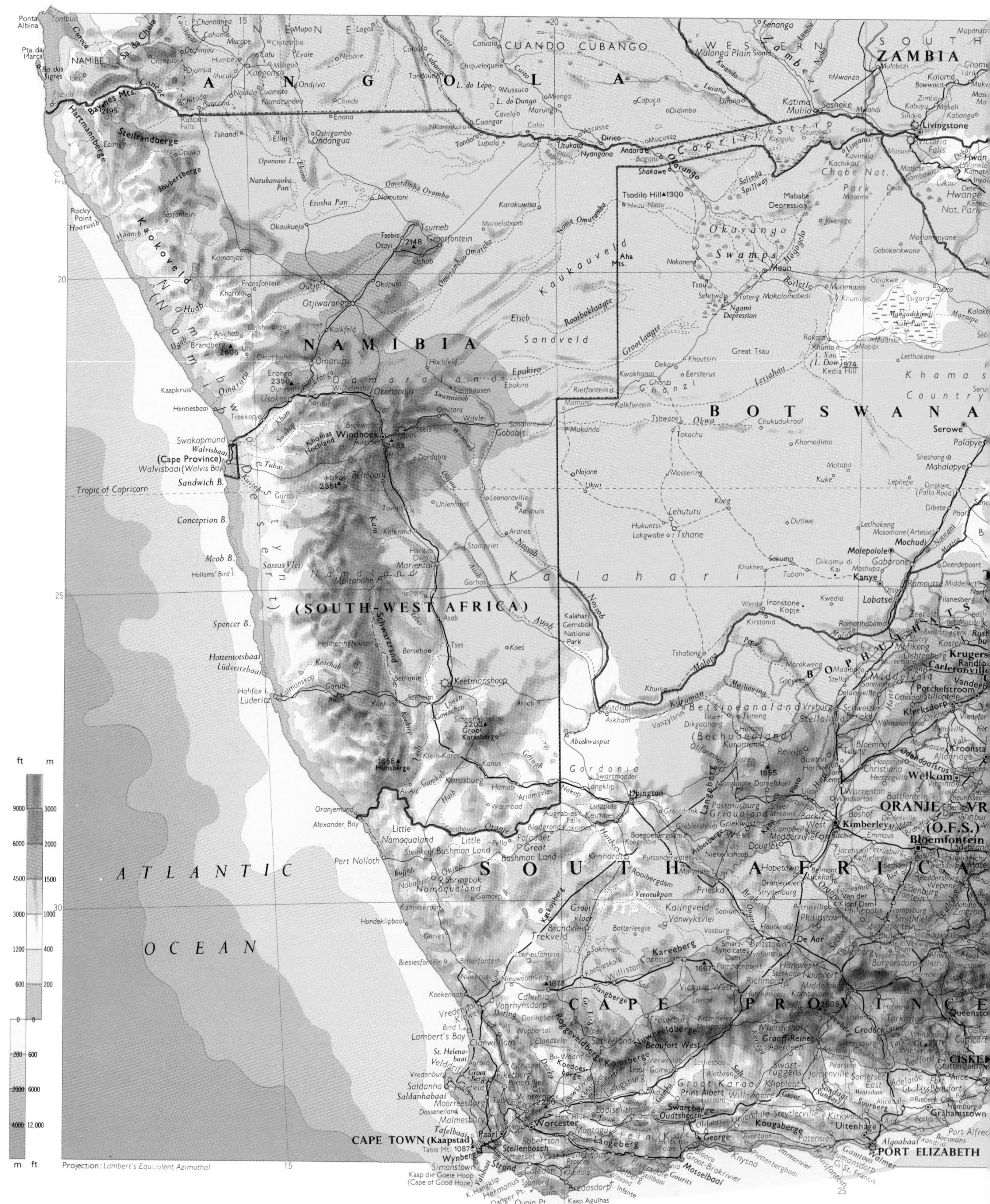

ANGOLA
CUANDO CUBANGO
NAMIBE
ZAMBIA
WESTERN
SOUTH
Livingstone
Victoria Falls
Hwange Nat. Park
Chobe Nat. Park
Caprivi Strip
Katima Mulilo
Sesheke
Okavango Swamps
Maun
Ngami Depression
Makgadikgadi Salt Pan
Tsodilo Hill 1300
Aha Mts.
Kaukauveld
Sandveld
Rooibokkloagte
Ghanzi
BOTSWANA
Serowe
Palapye
Mahalapye
Molepolole
Gaborone
Mochudi
Kanye
Lobatse
Khama's Country
Kalahari
Kalahari Gemsbok National Park
Tshane
Lehututu
Kang
Ruacana Falls
Baynes Mts. 2195
Hartmannberge
Steilrandberge
Joubertberge
Kaokoveld
Namib Desert
Etosha Pan
Tsumeb
Grootfontein
Otavi
2148
Outjo
Otjiwarongo
NAMIBIA
(SOUTH-WEST AFRICA)
Omaruru
Erongo 2350
Brandberg 2606
Damaraland
Okahandja
Windhoek
Khomas Hochland
2483
Gobabis
Swakopmund
Walvisbaai
(Cape Province)
Walvisbaai (Walvis Bay)
Sandwich B.
Tropic of Capricorn
Rehoboth
Hakos 2351
Conception B.
Meob B.
Hollams' Bird I.
Sossus Vlei
Mariental
Maltahöhe
Namaland
Schwarzrand
Spencer B.
Hottentotsbaai
Lüderitzbaai
Halifax I.
Lüderitz
Keetmanshoop
Groot Karasberge
2202
Hunsberge 1655
Karasburg
Oranjemund
Alexander Bay
Little Namaqualand
Port Nolloth
Springbok
Namaqualand
Bushman Land
SOUTH AFRICA
Upington
Gordonia
Kuruman
Vryburg
Betsjoeanaland (Bechuanaland)
BOPHUTHATSWANA
Mafikeng
Lichtenburg
Klerksdorp
Potchefstroom
Kroonstad
Welkom
ORANJE VRYSTAAT (O.F.S.)
Bloemfontein
Kimberley
Griqualand West
Douglas
Prieska
Kenhardt
Hopetown
De Aar
Colesberg
Kareeberg
Carnarvon
Calvinia
Victoria West
Beaufort West
Nuweveldberge
Roggeveldberge
Komsberge
Groot Karoo
Graaff-Reinet
Cradock
Queenstown
CISKEI
Grahamstown
Uitenhage
PORT ELIZABETH
Algoabaai
CAPE PROVINCE
Lambert's Bay
St. Helena-baai
Saldanha
Saldanhabaai
Malmesbury
Tafelbaai
CAPE TOWN (Kaapstad)
Table Mt. 1087
Paarl
Stellenbosch
Worcester
Wynberg
Simonstown
Kaap die Goeie Hoop (Cape of Good Hope)
Hermanus
Danger Pt.
Quoin Pt.
Kaap Agulhas
Swellendam
Mosselbaai
George
Knysna
Oudtshoorn
Swartberge
Langeberg
Klein Karoo
Kougaberge
ATLANTIC
OCEAN
ft
m
9000
3000
6000
2000
4500
1500
3000
1000
1200
400
600
200
0
200
600
2000
6000
4000
12,000
m
ft
15
20
25
30
Projection: Lambert's Equivalent Azimuthal

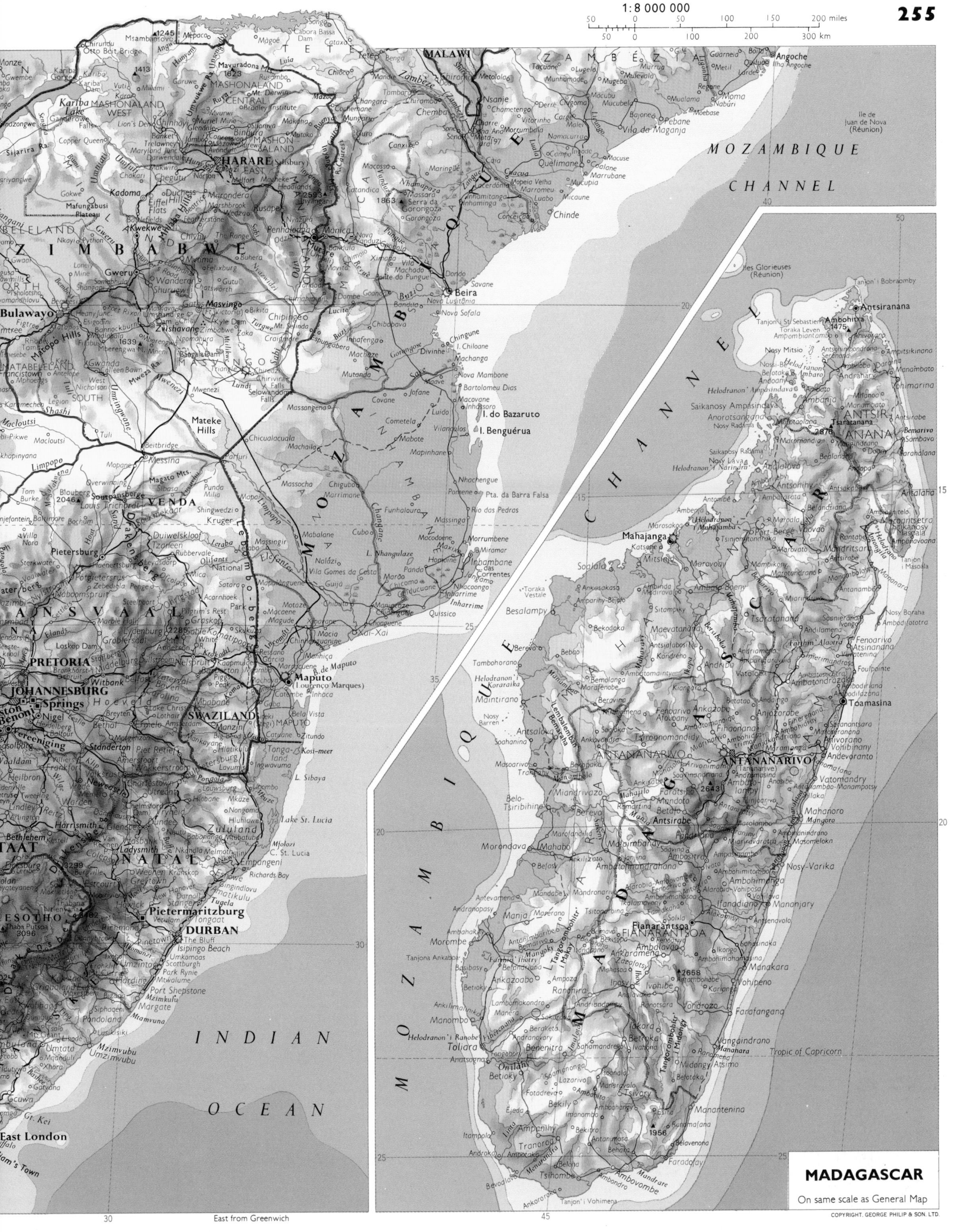

1:8 000 000
50 0 50 100 150 200 miles
50 0 100 200 300 km
ZIMBABWE
MOZAMBIQUE
ZAMBÉZIA
TETE
MALAWI
MASHONALAND CENTRAL
MASHONALAND WEST
MASHONALAND EAST
HARARE
Bulawayo
Gweru
Masvingo
Kadoma
Beira
Chinde
Quelimane
Angoche
Maputo
(Lourenço Marques)
SWAZILAND
PRETORIA
JOHANNESBURG
Springs
Benoni
Pietersburg
Pietermaritzburg
DURBAN
NATAL
East London
INDIAN
OCEAN
MOZAMBIQUE
CHANNEL
I. do Bazaruto
I. Benguérua
Pta. da Barra Falsa
Inhambane
Xai-Xai
Lake St. Lucia
Richards Bay
Port Shepstone
Margate
Mateke Hills
Messina
VENDA
Ile de Juan de Nova (Réunion)
Iles Glorieuses (Réunion)
Antsiranana
Mahajanga
Toamasina
ANTANANARIVO
Antsirabe
Fianarantsoa
Morondava
Toliara
Manakara
Farafangana
Tropic of Capricorn
MADAGASCAR
East from Greenwich

MADAGASCAR

On same scale as General Map

1:8 000 000

50 0 50 100 150 200 miles

50 0 50 100 150 200 250 300 km

Projection: Lambert's Equivalent Azimuthal

East from Greenwich

Index

United States index page 6
World index page 79

Index Introduction

Abbreviations used

A.S.S.R. – *Autonomous Soviet Socialist Republic*
Adr. S. – *Adriatic Sea*
Aeg. S. – *Aegean Sea*
Ala. – *Alabama*
Alta. – *Alberta*
Amer. – *America, American*
Ang. – *Angola*
Arch. – *Archipelago*
Arg. – *Argentina*
Ariz. – *Arizona*
Ark. – *Arkansas*
Atl. Oc. – *Atlantic Ocean*
B. – *Baie, Bahia, Bay, Boca, Bucht, Bugt*
B.C. – *British Columbia*
Br. – *British*
C. – *Cabo, Cap, Cape, Coast, Costa*
C.A.R. – *Central African Republic*
C.H. – *Court House*
C. Prov. – *Cape Province*
Calif. – *California*
Cat. – *Cataract*
Cent. – *Central*
Chan. – *Channel*
Col. – *Colombia*
Colo. – *Colorado*
Conn. – *Connecticut*
Cord. – *Cordillera*
Czech. – *Czechoslovakia*
D.C. – *District of Columbia*
Del. – *Delaware*
Dep. – *Dependency*
Des. – *Desert*
Dist. – *District*
Dj. – *Djebel*
Dom. Rep. – *Dominican Republic*
E. – *East, Eastern*
El Salv. – *El Salvador*
Eq. Guin. – *Equatorial Guinea*
Falk. Is. – *Falkland Is.*
Fd. – *Fjord*
Fed. – *Federal, Federation*
Fla. – *Florida*
Fr. – *France, French*
Fr. Gui. – *French Guiana*
G. – *Golfe, Golfo, Gulf, Guba, Gebel*
Ga. – *Georgia*
Gt. – *Great*
Guat. – *Guatemala*
H.K. – *Hong Kong*
H.P. – *Himachal Pradesh*
Hants. – *Hampshire*
Hd. – *Head*
Hts. – *Heights*
I.(s) – *Ile, Ilha, Insel, Isla Island(s)*
I. of W. – *Isle of Wight*
Ill. – *Illinois*
Ind. Res. – *Indian Reservation*
Ind. – *Indiana*
J. – *Jabal, Jazira*
K. – *Kap. Kapp*
Kans. – *Kansas*
Kep. – *Kepulauan*
Kól. – *Kólpos*
Ky. – *Kentucky*
L. – *Lac, Lacul, Lago, Lagoa, Lake, Limni, Loch, Lough*
La. – *Louisiana*
Lag. – *Laguna*
Ld. – *Land*
Mad. P. – *Madhya Pradesh*
Man. – *Manitoba*
Mass. – *Massachusetts*
Md. – *Maryland*
Mich. – *Michigan*
Minn. – *Minnesota*
Miss. – *Mississippi*
Mo. – *Missouri*
Mozam. – *Mozambique*
Mont. – *Montana*
Mt.(s) – *Mont, Monta, Monti, Muntii, Montaña, Mount, Mountain(s)*
Mys. – *Mysore*
N. – *North, Northern*
N.B. – *New Brunswick*
N.C. – *North Carolina*
N. Dak. – *North Dakota*
N.H. – *New Hampshire*
N.Ire. – *Northern Ireland*
N.J. – *New Jersey*
N. Mex – *New Mexico*
N.S. – *Nova Scotia*
N.S.W. – *New South Wales*
N.W.T. – *North West Territories*
N.Y. – *New York*
N.Z. – *New Zealand*
Nat. For. – *National Forest*
Nat. Park – *National Park*
Nat. Rec. Area – *National Recreation Area*
Nebr. – *Nebraska*
Neth. – *Netherlands*
Nev. – *Nevada*
Newf. – *Newfoundland*
Nic. – *Nicaragua*
Nig. – *Nigeria*
O. – *Oued, Ouadi*
O.F.S. – *Orange Free State*
Okla. – *Oklahoma*
Ont. – *Ontario*
Oreg. – *Oregon*
Os. – *Ostrov*
Oz. – *Ozero*
P. – *Pass, Passo, Pasul, Pulau*
P.E.I. – *Prince Edward Island*
P. Rico – *Puerto Rico*
Pa. – *Pennsylvania*
Pac. Oc. – *Pacific Ocean*
Pak. – *Pakistan*
Papua N.G. – *Papua New Guinea*
Pass. – *Passage*
Pen. – *Peninsula*
Pk. – *Peak*
Plat. – *Plateau*
Port. – *Portugal, Portuguese*
P-ov. – *Poluostrov*
Prov. – *Province, Provincial*
Pt. – *Point*
Pta. – *Ponta, Punta*
Pte. – *Pointe*
Qué. – *Québec*
Queens. – *Queensland*
R. – *Rio, River, Rivière*
R.I. – *Rhode Island*
R.S.F.S.R. – *Russian Soviet Federative Socialist Republic*
Ra.(s) – *Range(s)*
Raj. – *Rajasthan*
Reg. – *Region*
Rep. – *Republic*
Res. – *Reserve, Reservoir, Reservation*
S. – *South, Southern, Sea, Sur*
S.C. – *South Carolina*
S.S.R. – *Soviet Socialist Republic*
S. Africa – *South Africa*
S. Dak. – *South Dakota*
S. Leone – *Sierra Leone*
Sa. – *Serra, Sierra*
Salop. – *Shropshire*
Sask. – *Saskatchewan*
Scot. – *Scotland*
Sd. – *Sound*
Sev. – *Severnaya*
Si. Arabia – *Saudi Arabia*
Sib. – *Siberia*
Sp. – *Spain, Spanish*
Sprgs. – *Springs*
St. – *Saint*
Sta. – *Santa*
Ste. – *Sainte*
Sto. – *Santo*
Str. – *Strait, Stretto*
Switz. – *Switzerland*
Tanz. – *Tanzania*
Tas. – *Tasmania*
Tenn. – *Tennessee*
Terr. – *Territory*
Tex. – *Texas*
Tg. – *Tanjung*
Trin. & Tob. – *Trinidad and Tobago*
U.K. – *United Kingdom*
U.S.A. – *United States of America*
U.S.S.R. – *Union of Soviet Socialist Republics*
Ut. P. – *Uttar Pradesh*
V.S. – *Vozvyshennost*
Va. – *Virginia*
Vdkhr. – *Vodokhranilishche*
Ven. – *Venezuela*
Vf. – *Virful*
Vic. – *Victoria*
Vol. – *Volcano*
Vt. – *Vermont*
Wash. – *Washington*
W. – *West, Western, Wadi*
W. Va. – *West Virginia*
Wis. – *Wisconsin*
Wlkp. – *Wielkopolski*
Worcs. – *Worcestershire*
Wyo. – *Wyoming*
Yorks. – *Yorkshire*
Yug. – *Yugoslavia*

Introduction to Index

The index is divided into two parts for ease of access. The first part gives place names in the United States and the outlying territories of Puerto Rico, the Virgin Islands and the Panama Canal Zone. The second part of the index consists of place names from the rest of the world.

The number in bold type which follows each name in the index refers to the number of the map-page where that feature or place will be found. This is usually the largest scale on which the place or feature appears. Names in the U.S. are indexed to their state, which is not necessarily the largest scale.

The geographical co-ordinates which follow the place name are sometimes only approximate but are close enough for the place name to be located.

A solid square ■ follows the name of a country while an open square □ refers to a first order administrative area (states in the U.S.) A diamond ◇ refers to counties in the U.S. (parishes in Louisiana and census areas in Alaska).

Rivers have been indexed to their mouth or to where they join another river. All river names are followed by the symbol →.

Alphabetical Order

The alphabetical order of names composed of two or more words is governed primarily by the first word and then by the second. This is an example of the rule:

East Tawas
Eastbourne
Easter Is.
Eastern Ghats
Eastmain →.

Physical features composed of a proper name (*Mexico*) and a description (*Gulf of*) are positioned alphabetically by the proper name. The description is positioned after the proper name and is usually abbreviated:

Mexico, G. of
Midi, Canal de
Pacaraima, Sa.

Where a description forms part of a settlement or administrative name however it is always written in full and put in its true alphabetic position:

Lake Placid
Mount Vernon
Sturgeon Bay

Names composed of the definite article (*Le, La, Les, L'*) and a proper name are usually alphabetised by the proper name.

Havre, Le
Spezia, La
Wash, The

This rule does not apply where foreign definite articles have become part of town names in the U.S Index. For example:

La Grange
Le Roy

Names beginning with M', Mc are all indexed as if they were spelled Mac. All names beginning St. are alphabetised under Saint, but Sankt, Sint, Sant', Santa and San are all spelt in full and are alphabetised accordingly.

If the same place name occurs two or more times in the index and all are in the same country, each is followed by the name of the administrative subdivision in which it is located. The names are placed in the alphabetical order of the subdivisions. For example:

Bear L., Alta., Canada
Bear L., B.C., Canada
Bear L., Man., Canada

If the same place name occurs twice or more in the index and the places are in different countries, they will be followed by the country names and the latter in alphabetical order.

Ben Lomond, Australia
Ben Lomond, U.K.

If there is a mixture of these situations, the primary order is fixed by the alphabetical sequence of the countries and the secondary order by that of the country subdivisions. In the latter case the country names are omitted.

Rosario, Arg.
Rosario, Brazil
Rosario, Baja Calif. N., Mexico
Rosario, Baja Calif. S., Mexico
Rosario, Sinaloa, Mexico
Rosario, Paraguay
Rosario, Phil.

Geographical Co-ordinates

In the index, each place name is followed by its geographical co-ordinates which allow the reader to find the place on the map. These co-ordinates give the latitude and the longitude of a particular place.

The latitude (or parallel) is the distance of a point north or south of the Equator measured as an angle with the center of the earth. The Equator is latitude 0°, the North Pole is 90°N, and the South Pole 90°S. On a globe, the lines could be drawn as concentric circles parallel to the Equator, decreasing in diameter from the Equator until they become a point at the poles. On the maps, these lines of latitude are usually represented as lines running across the map from East to West in smooth curves. They are numbered on the sides of the map. North of the Equator the numbers increase northwards, to the south they increase southwards. The degree interval between them depends on the scale of the map. On a large scale map (for example 1:2 500 000), the interval is one degree, but on a small scale map, (for example 1:40 000 000) the interval will be ten degrees.

Lines of longitude (or meridians) cut the latitude lines at right angles on the globe and intersect with one another at the poles. Longitude is measured by an angle at the center of the earth between it and the meridian of origin which runs through Greenwich (0°). It may be a measurement East or West of this line from 0° to 180° in each direction. The longitude line of 180° runs North – South through the Pacific Ocean. On a particular map, the interval between the lines of longitude is always the same as that between the lines of latitude. Normally, the meridians are drawn vertically. They are numbered in the top and bottom margins and a note states East or West from Greenwich.

The unit of measurement for latitude and longitude is the degree, and it is subdivided into 60 minutes. An index entry states the position of a place in degrees and minutes, a space being left between the degrees and minutes. The latitude is followed by N(orth) or S(outh) and the longitude by E(ast) or W(est).

The diagrams below illustrate how the reader has to estimate the required distance from the nearest line of latitude or longitude. In the case of the first diagram, there is one degree, or 60 minutes between the lines and so to find the position of Newport an estimate has to be made. 28 parts of 60 north of the 41 degree latitude line and 19 parts of 60, or 19 minutes west of the 71 degree longitude line. In the case of the second diagram, it is a little more difficult to estimate since there are 10 degrees between the lines. In the example of Anchorage, the reader has to estimate 1 degree 13 minutes north of 60° and 9° 53 minutes west of 140°.

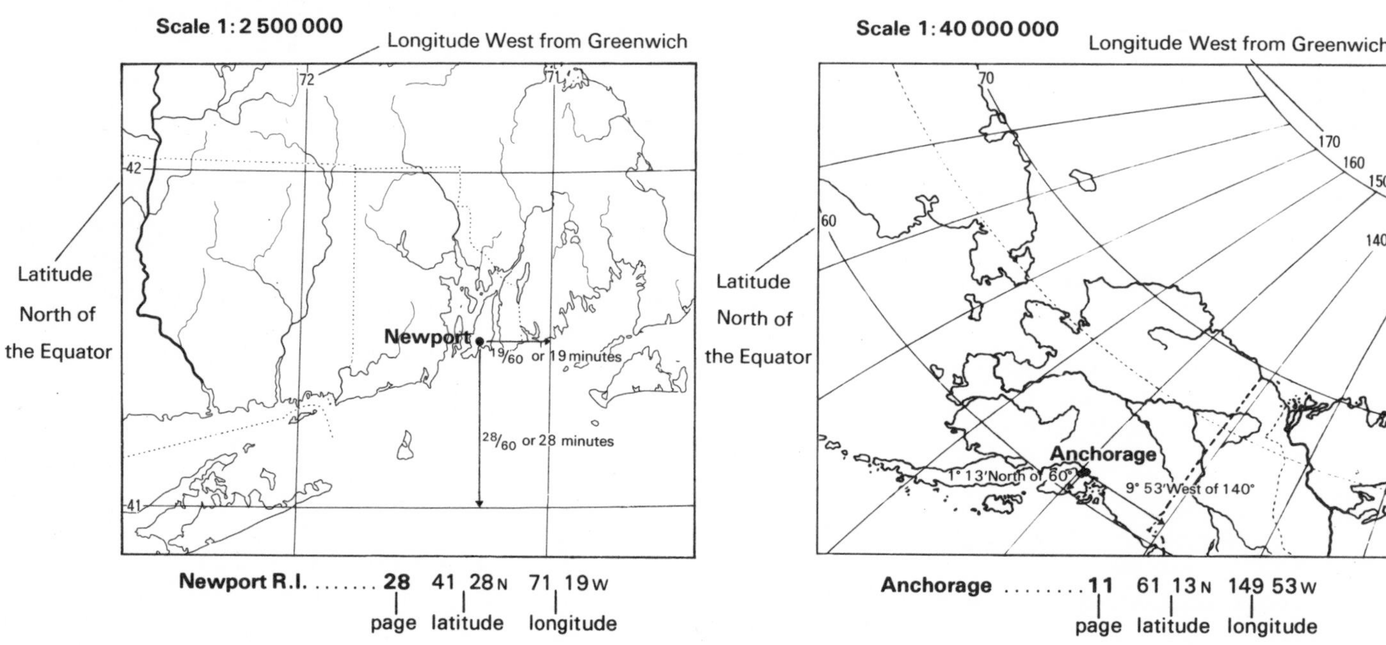

Scale 1:2 500 000
Longitude West from Greenwich
72
71
42
41
Latitude North of the Equator
Newport
19/60 or 19 minutes
28/60 or 28 minutes
Newport R.I. 28 41 28N 71 19W
page latitude longitude
Scale 1:40 000 000
Longitude West from Greenwich
70
170
160
150
140
60
Latitude North of the Equator
Anchorage
1° 13' North of 60°
9° 53' West of 140°
Anchorage 11 61 13N 149 53W
page latitude longitude

Foreign Place Names

The atlas uses the local spellings for most place names, that is the name by which a place or feature is known within the country in which it occurs. For example:

Roma
's-Gravenhage

The English conventional form is usually added in brackets on the map thus:

Roma (Rome)
's-Gravenhage (The Hague)

In the index the English form is cross-referenced to the local spelling:

Rome = Roma
Hague, The = 's-Gravenhage

Spellings of names are in the form given in the latest official lists and generally agree with the rules of the Permanent Committee on Geographical Names and the U.S. Board on Geographic Names.

Where languages do not use Roman alphabets certain rules are used to transcribe these languages into Roman alphabet. These rules are based largely on pronunciation.

The Pronunciation of Foreign Place Names

English speaking people usually have no difficulty in reading and pronouncing correctly American and English place names. However, foreign place name pronunciations may present many problems. Such problems can be minimised by following some simple rules. However, these rules cannot be applied to all situations, and there will be many exceptions.

1. In general, stress each syllable equally, unless your experience suggests otherwise.
2. Pronounce the letter 'a' as a broad 'a' as in 'arm'
3. Pronounce the letter 'e' as a short 'e' as in 'elm'
4. Pronounce the letter 'i' as a cross between a short 'i' and long 'e', as the two 'i's' in 'California'.
5. Pronounce the letter 'o' as an intermediate 'o' as in 'soft'.
6. Pronounce the letter 'u' as an intermediate 'u' as in 'sure'
7. Pronounce consonants hard, except in the Romance-language areas where 'g's are likely to be pronounced softly like 'j' in 'jam'; 'j' itself may be pronounced as 'y'; and 'x's' may be pronounced as 'h'.

Moreover, English has no diacritical marks (accent and pronunciation signs), although some languages do. The following is a brief and general guide to the pronunciation of those most frequently used in the Western European languages.

		Pronunciation as in
French	é	d*a*y and shows that the e is to be pronounced e.g. Orléans.
	è	m*a*re
	î	used over any vowel and does not affect pronunciation; shows contraction of the name, usually ommission of 's' following a vowel.
	ç	's' before 'a', 'o' and 'u'
	¨	over 'e', 'i', and 'u' when they are used with another vowel and shows that each is to be pronounced.
German	ä	f*a*t
	ö	f*u*r
	ü	no English equivalent; like French 't*u*'
Italian	à, é	over vowels and indicates stress.
Portuguese	ã, õ	vowels pronounced nasally.
	ç	bo*ss*
	á	shows stress.
	ô	shows that a vowel has an 'i' or 'u' sound combined with it.
Spanish	ñ	ca*ny*on
	ü	pronounced as *w* and separately from adjoining vowels.
	á	usually indicates that this is a stressed vowel
Swedish	å	l*aw*
	ä	f*a*t
	ö	f*u*r

The problem of place name pronunciation is more difficult where the written form of the name is a transliteration (changing of a letter or letters of one alphabet into corresponding characters of another alphabet or language) from a non-Roman alphabet. Early English-speaking travelers and traders to such countries as China, Japan, and Russia prepared written forms of the names that they heard there. Although not based upon a formal system, many of these written forms have become conventional place name spellings.

More advanced study of particular languages has produced complex transliteration rules. These attempt to retain the nuances of the language concerned. One of the more difficult languages from the standpoint of both transliteration and pronunciation, is Chinese. Following are four examples of place names in three commonly used transliteration systems.

Chinese Postal System	**Wade-Giles (pronunciation)**	**Pinyin**
Peking	Pei-ching (ba-jing)	Beijing
Shanghai	Shang-hai (shäng-hi)	Shanghai
Canton	Kuang-chou (gwäng-jo)	Guangzhou

The Pinyin system, as developed by the Peking government, is the most recent system. It is the one adopted by the U.S. Board on Geographic Names and is used in this atlas. The Postal system contains the conventional place name spellings and does not require diacritical markings. It is listed by the U.S. Board on Geographic Names as an alternative to the Pinyin system for many place names in China.

The Chinese place-name problem is complicated further by actual changes in place-names over the years. For example, Mukden is now known as Shenyang.

In contrast to Chinese, Japanese romanization commonly employs only one diacritical mark, a line over 'o's' and 'u's', which marks these as long vowels. Diacritical marks employed in the romanization of other languages not based on the Roman alphabet (such as Vietnamese and Hindi) are not commonly employed in general reference atlases as yet.

United States Index

A

Abajo Peak **66** 37 51N 109 27W
Abbaye, Pt. **43** 46 58N 88 8W
Abbeville, Ala. **24** 31 34N 85 15W
Abbeville, Ga. **32** 31 59N 83 18W
Abbeville, La. **39** 29 58N 92 8W
Abbeville, Miss. **45** 34 30N 89 30W
Abbeville, S.C. **60** 34 11N 82 23W
Abbeville County ◇ **60** 34 15N 82 30W
Abbotsford **69** 44 57N 90 19W
Abbott, N. Mex. **52** 36 18N 104 16W
Abbott, Tex. **65** 31 53N 97 4W
Abercrombie **55** 46 27N 96 44W
Aberdeen, Idaho **34** 42 57N 112 50W
Aberdeen, Ky. **62** 37 15N 86 41W
Aberdeen, Md. **41** 39 31N 76 10W
Aberdeen, Miss. **45** 33 49N 88 33W
Aberdeen, N.C. **54** 35 8N 79 26W
Aberdeen, S. Dak. **61** 45 28N 98 29W
Aberdeen, Wash. **67** 46 59N 123 50W
Abernant **24** 33 17N 87 12W
Abernathy **64** 33 50N 101 51W
Abert, L. **58** 42 38N 120 14W
Abilene, Kans. **38** 38 55N 97 13W
Abilene, Tex. **65** 32 28N 99 43W
Abingdon, Ill. **35** 40 48N 90 24W
Abingdon, Va. **68** 36 43N 81 59W
Abington, Conn. **42** 41 52N 72 1W
Abington, Mass. **42** 42 6N 70 57W
Abiquiu **52** 36 13N 106 19W
Abiquiu Reservoir **52** 36 16N 106 27W
Abita Springs **39** 30 29N 90 2W
Absaroka Range **70** 44 45N 109 50W
Absarokee **47** 45 31N 109 27W
Absecon **51** 39 26N 74 30W
Acadia National Park **40** 44 20N 68 13W
Acadia Parish ◇ **39** 30 13N 92 22W
Accident **41** 39 38N 79 19W
Accokeek **41** 38 40N 77 2W
Accomac **68** 37 43N 75 40W
Accomack County ◇ **68** 37 45N 75 40W
Achille **57** 33 50N 96 23W
Ackerman **45** 33 19N 89 11W
Ackley **37** 42 33N 93 3W
Acme **39** 31 17N 91 49W
Acoma Indian Reservation **52** 34 45N 107 30W
Acomita **52** 35 3N 107 34W
Acushnet **42** 41 41N 70 55W
Acworth **32** 34 4N 84 41W
Ada, Kans. **38** 39 9N 97 53W
Ada, Minn. **44** 47 18N 96 31W
Ada, Ohio **56** 40 46N 83 49W
Ada, Okla. **57** 34 46N 96 41W
Ada County ◇ **34** 43 30N 116 15W
Adair, Iowa **37** 41 30N 94 39W
Adair, Okla. **57** 36 26N 95 16W
Adair County ◇, Iowa **37** 41 20N 94 30W
Adair County ◇, Ky. **63** 37 5N 85 20W
Adair County ◇, Mo. **46** 40 10N 92 35W
Adair County ◇, Okla. **57** 35 55N 94 45W
Adairsville **32** 34 22N 84 56W
Adairville **62** 36 40N 86 51W
Adak **25** 51 45N 176 45W
Adak I. **25** 51 45N 176 45W
Adams, Ky. **63** 38 3N 82 43W
Adams, Mass. **42** 42 38N 73 7W
Adams, Minn. **44** 43 34N 92 43W
Adams, N. Dak. **55** 48 25N 98 5W
Adams, N.Y. **53** 43 49N 76 1W
Adams, Nebr. **48** 40 28N 96 31W
Adams, Okla. **57** 36 45N 101 5W
Adams, Tenn. **62** 36 35N 87 4W
Adams, Wis. **69** 43 57N 89 49W
Adams Center **53** 43 52N 76 0W
Adams County ◇, Colo. **30** 39 50N 104 10W
Adams County ◇, Idaho **34** 45 0N 116 30W
Adams County ◇, Ill. **35** 40 0N 90 10W
Adams County ◇, Ind. **36** 40 45N 85 0W
Adams County ◇, Iowa **37** 41 0N 94 40W
Adams County ◇, Miss. **45** 31 23N 91 24W
Adams County ◇, N. Dak. **55** 46 0N 102 30W
Adams County ◇, Nebr. **48** 40 30N 98 30W
Adams County ◇, Ohio **56** 38 48N 83 33W
Adams County ◇, Pa. **59** 39 50N 77 14W
Adams County ◇, Wash. **67** 47 0N 118 30W
Adams County ◇, Wis. **69** 43 0N 89 50W
Adams-McGill Reservoir **49** 38 22N 115 7W
Adams Mt. **67** 46 12N 121 30W
Adamstown **59** 40 15N 76 3W
Adamsville, Ohio **56** 40 4N 81 53W
Adamsville, R.I. **42** 41 30N 71 10W
Adamsville, Tenn. **62** 35 14N 88 23W
Adamsville, Tex. **65** 31 18N 98 10W
Addie **54** 35 24N 83 10W
Addieville **35** 38 23N 89 29W
Addington **57** 34 15N 97 58W
Addis **39** 30 21N 91 16W
Addison, Ala. **24** 34 12N 87 11W
Addison, Ill. **35** 41 55N 88 0W
Addison, N.Y. **53** 42 1N 77 14W
Addison, Ohio **56** 38 53N 82 9W
Addison, Vt. **50** 44 8N 73 20W
Addison County ◇ **50** 44 0N 73 15W
Addy **67** 48 21N 117 50W
Adel, Ga. **32** 31 8N 83 25W
Adel, Iowa **37** 41 37N 94 1W
Adel, Oreg. **58** 42 11N 119 54W
Adelanto **29** 34 35N 117 22W
Adelphi **56** 39 28N 82 45W
Adelphia **51** 40 13N 74 15W
Adena **56** 40 13N 80 53W
Adin **28** 41 12N 120 57W
Adirondack Mts. **53** 44 0N 74 0W
Adjuntas **71** 18 10N 66 43W
Admiralty I. **25** 57 30N 134 30W
Admiralty Inlet **67** 48 8N 122 58W
Adobe Creek Reservoir **30** 38 14N 103 17W
Adrian, Ga. **32** 32 33N 82 35W
Adrian, Mich. **43** 41 54N 84 2W
Adrian, Minn. **44** 43 38N 95 56W
Adrian, Mo. **46** 38 24N 94 21W
Adrian, Oreg. **58** 43 45N 117 4W
Adrian, Tex. **64** 35 16N 102 40W
Advance, Ind. **36** 40 0N 86 40W
Advance, Mo. **46** 37 6N 89 55W
Aetna **38** 37 5N 98 58W
Affton **46** 38 33N 90 20W
Afognak I. **25** 58 15N 152 30W
Afton, Calif. **29** 35 2N 116 23W
Afton, Iowa **37** 41 2N 94 12W
Afton, N.Y. **53** 42 14N 75 32W
Afton, Okla. **57** 36 42N 94 58W
Afton, Wyo. **70** 42 44N 110 56W
Agar **61** 44 50N 100 5W
Agassiz Pool **44** 48 20N 95 59W
Agate **30** 39 28N 103 57W
Agate Beach **58** 44 41N 124 4W
Agate Fossil Beds National Monument **48** 42 20N 103 50W
Agattu I. **25** 52 25N 173 35W
Agawam, Mass. **42** 42 5N 72 37W
Agawam, Mont. **47** 48 0N 112 10W
Agency **37** 41 0N 92 18W
Agency L. **58** 42 33N 121 58W
Agenda **38** 39 43N 97 26W
Ages **63** 36 52N 83 21W
Agra, Kans. **38** 39 46N 99 7W
Agra, Okla. **57** 35 54N 96 53W
Agricola **45** 30 48N 88 31W
Agua Dulce **65** 27 47N 97 55W
Agua Fria → **26** 33 23N 112 22W
Agua Nueva **64** 26 54N 98 36W
Aguada **71** 18 23N 67 11W
Aguadilla **71** 18 26N 67 10W
Aguadilla ◇ **71** 18 20N 67 0W
Aguadilla, Bahía de **71** 18 25N 67 10W
Aguas Buenas **71** 18 16N 66 6W
Aguila **26** 33 57N 113 11W
Aguila, Punta **71** 17 57N 67 13W
Aguilar **30** 37 24N 104 39W
Aguilares **64** 27 27N 99 5W
Agujereada, Pta. **71** 18 30N 67 8W
Ahoskie **54** 36 17N 76 59W
Aibonito **71** 18 9N 66 16W
Aiea **33** 21 23N 157 56W
Aiken **60** 33 34N 81 43W
Aiken County ◇ **60** 33 30N 81 40W
Ailey **32** 32 11N 82 34W
Ainsworth, Iowa **37** 41 17N 91 33W
Ainsworth, Nebr. **48** 42 33N 99 52W
Aitkin **44** 46 32N 93 42W
Aitkin County ◇ **44** 46 30N 93 25W
Aix, Mt. **67** 46 47N 121 15W
Ajo **26** 32 22N 112 52W
Akali L. **58** 42 58N 120 2W
Akaska **61** 45 20N 100 7W
Akeley **44** 47 0N 94 44W
Akhiok **25** 56 57N 154 10W
Akiachak **25** 60 55N 161 26W
Akiak **25** 60 55N 161 13W
Akolmiut **25** 60 55N 162 20W
Akra **55** 48 47N 97 44W
Akron, Ala. **24** 32 53N 87 45W
Akron, Colo. **30** 40 10N 103 13W
Akron, Ind. **36** 41 2N 86 1W
Akron, Iowa **37** 42 50N 96 33W
Akron, N.Y. **53** 43 1N 78 30W
Akron, Ohio **56** 41 5N 81 31W
Akron, Pa. **59** 40 9N 76 12W
Akun I. **25** 54 11N 165 32W
Akutan **25** 54 8N 165 46W
Akutan I. **25** 54 7N 165 55W
Akutan Indian Reservation **25** 54 10N 166 0W
Alabama □ **24** 33 0N 87 0W
Alabama → **24** 31 8N 87 57W
Alabaster **24** 33 15N 86 49W
Alachua **31** 29 47N 82 30W
Alachua County ◇ **31** 29 45N 82 20W
Alakunuk **25** 62 41N 164 37W
Alalakeiki Channel **33** 20 30N 156 30W
Alamance County ◇ **54** 36 0N 79 25W
Alameda, Calif. **28** 37 46N 122 15W
Alameda, N. Mex. **52** 35 11N 106 37W
Alameda County ◇ **28** 37 40N 121 50W
Alamito → **64** 29 45N 104 18W
Alamo, Ga. **32** 32 9N 82 47W
Alamo, N. Dak. **55** 48 35N 103 28W
Alamo, Nev. **49** 37 22N 115 10W
Alamo, Tenn. **62** 35 47N 89 7W
Alamo Heights **65** 29 28N 98 28W
Alamo Ind. Res. **52** 34 20N 107 30W
Alamo L. **26** 34 10N 113 35W
Alamogordo **52** 32 54N 105 57W
Alamosa **30** 37 28N 105 52W
Alamosa →, Colo. **30** 37 22N 105 46W
Alamosa →, N. Mex. **52** 33 25N 107 15W
Alamosa County ◇ **30** 37 40N 105 40W
Alamoso → **52** 34 20N 104 10W
Alanreed **64** 35 13N 100 44W
Alanson **43** 45 27N 84 47W
Alapaha **32** 31 23N 83 13W
Alarka **54** 35 21N 83 27W
Alaska □ **25** 64 0N 154 0W
Alaska, Gulf of **25** 59 0N 146 0W
Alaska Peninsula **25** 56 0N 159 0W
Alaska Range **25** 62 0N 149 0W
Alava, C. **67** 48 10N 124 44W
Alba, Mo. **46** 37 14N 94 25W
Alba, Tex. **65** 32 48N 95 38W
Albany, Ga. **32** 31 35N 84 10W
Albany, Ind. **36** 40 18N 85 14W
Albany, Ky. **63** 36 42N 85 8W
Albany, La. **39** 30 30N 90 35W
Albany, Minn. **44** 45 38N 94 34W
Albany, Mo. **46** 40 15N 94 20W
Albany, N.Y. **53** 42 39N 73 45W
Albany, Ohio **56** 39 14N 82 12W
Albany, Okla. **57** 33 53N 96 10W
Albany, Oreg. **58** 44 38N 123 6W
Albany, Tex. **65** 32 44N 99 18W
Albany, Vt. **50** 44 43N 72 23W
Albany County ◇, N.Y. **53** 42 30N 74 0W
Albany County ◇, Wyo. **70** 41 50N 105 40W
Albemarle **54** 35 21N 80 11W
Albemarle County ◇ **68** 38 2N 78 30W
Albemarle Sd. **54** 36 5N 76 0W
Albert, Kans. **38** 38 27N 99 1W
Albert, Okla. **57** 35 14N 98 25W
Albert, Tex. **65** 30 12N 98 36W
Albert City **37** 42 47N 94 57W
Albert Lea **44** 43 39N 93 22W
Alberta, Ala. **24** 32 14N 87 25W
Alberta, Va. **68** 36 52N 77 53W
Alberton **47** 47 0N 114 29W
Albertville, Ala. **24** 34 16N 86 13W
Albertville, Minn. **44** 45 14N 93 39W
Albia **37** 41 2N 92 48W
Albin **70** 41 25N 104 6W
Albion, Calif. **28** 39 14N 123 46W
Albion, Idaho **34** 42 25N 113 35W
Albion, Ill. **35** 38 23N 88 4W
Albion, Ind. **36** 41 24N 85 25W
Albion, Iowa **37** 42 7N 92 59W
Albion, Maine **40** 44 32N 69 27W
Albion, Mich. **43** 42 15N 84 45W
Albion, N.Y. **53** 43 15N 78 12W
Albion, Nebr. **48** 41 42N 98 0W

Albion, Okla. 57 34 40N 95 6W
Albion, Pa. 59 41 53N 80 22W
Albion, Wash. 67 46 48N 117 15W
Albright 68 39 30N 79 39W
Albuquerque 52 35 5N 106 39W
Alburg 50 44 59N 73 18W
Alburnett 37 42 9N 91 37W
Alcalde 52 36 5N 106 3W
Alcester 61 43 1N 96 38W
Alco 27 35 53N 92 22W
Alcoa 63 35 48N 83 59W
Alcolu 60 33 45N 80 13W
Alcoma 31 27 54N 81 29W
Alcona County ◇ 43 44 40N 83 40W
Alcorn 45 31 53N 91 8W
Alcorn County ◇ 45 34 56N 88 31W
Alcova 70 42 34N 106 43W
Alda 48 40 52N 98 28W
Alden, Iowa 37 42 31N 93 23W
Alden, Kans. 38 38 15N 98 19W
Alden, Minn. 44 43 40N 93 34W
Alden, N.Y. 53 42 54N 78 30W
Alder 47 45 19N 112 6W
Alderson 68 37 44N 80 38W
Aldine 65 29 56N 95 23W
Aledo, Ill. 35 41 12N 90 45W
Aledo, Tex. 65 32 42N 97 36W
Alegros Mt. 52 34 9N 108 11W
Aleknagik 25 59 17N 158 36W
Alenuihaha Channel 33 20 30N 156 0W
Alesia 41 39 43N 76 51W
Aleutian Is. 25 52 0N 178 0W
Aleutian Islands ◇ 25 53 0N 176 0W
Aleutian Range 25 60 0N 154 0W
Alex 57 34 55N 97 47W
Alexander, Ga. 32 33 1N 81 53W
Alexander, Iowa 37 42 48N 93 29W
Alexander, Kans. 38 38 28N 99 33W
Alexander, N. Dak. 55 47 51N 103 39W
Alexander, W. Va. 68 38 47N 80 13W
Alexander Archipelago 25 56 0N 136 0W
Alexander City 24 32 56N 85 58W
Alexander County ◇, Ill. 35 37 10N 89 20W
Alexander County ◇, N.C. 54 35 50N 81 10W
Alexandria, Ind. 36 40 16N 85 41W
Alexandria, Ky. 63 38 58N 84 23W
Alexandria, La. 39 31 18N 92 27W
Alexandria, Minn. 44 45 53N 95 22W
Alexandria, Mo. 46 40 27N 91 28W
Alexandria, N.H. 50 43 37N 71 47W
Alexandria, Nebr. 48 40 15N 97 23W
Alexandria, Pa. 59 40 34N 78 6W
Alexandria, S. Dak. 61 43 39N 97 47W
Alexandria, Tenn. 62 36 5N 86 2W
Alexandria, Va. 68 38 48N 77 3W
Alexandria Bay 53 44 20N 75 55W
Alexis 35 41 4N 90 33W
Alfalfa 57 35 13N 98 36W
Alfalfa County ◇ 57 36 45N 98 15W
Alford 31 30 42N 85 24W
Alfred, Maine 40 43 29N 70 43W
Alfred, N.Y. 53 42 16N 77 48W
Alger County ◇ 43 46 20N 86 50W
Algodones 52 35 23N 106 29W
Algoma, Miss. 45 34 11N 89 2W
Algoma, Wis. 69 44 36N 87 26W
Algona 37 43 4N 94 14W
Algonac 43 42 37N 82 32W
Algonquin 35 42 10N 88 18W
Algood 63 36 12N 85 27W
Alhambra 29 34 8N 118 6W
Alice, N. Dak. 55 46 46N 97 33W
Alice, Tex. 65 27 45N 98 5W
Aliceville, Ala. 24 33 8N 88 9W
Aliceville, Kans. 38 38 9N 95 33W
Alicia 27 35 54N 91 5W
Aline 57 36 31N 98 27W
Aliquippa 59 40 37N 80 15W
Alkali Flats 49 40 0N 115 58W
Alkali L. 49 41 42N 119 51W
Alkaline L. 55 46 40N 99 34W
All American Canal 29 32 45N 115 15W
Allagash 40 47 5N 69 3W
Allagash → 40 47 5N 69 3W
Allagash L. 40 46 18N 69 35W
Allakaket 25 66 34N 152 39W
Allamakee County ◇ 37 43 15N 91 20W
Allamoore 64 31 5N 105 0W
Allardt 63 36 23N 84 53W
Allatoona L. 32 34 10N 84 44W
Allegan 43 42 32N 85 51W
Allegan County ◇ 43 42 35N 85 50W
Allegany, N.Y. 53 42 6N 78 30W
Allegany, Oreg. 58 43 26N 124 2W
Allegany County ◇, Md. 41 39 40N 78 40W
Allegany County ◇, N.Y. 53 42 15N 78 0W
Allegany Indian Reservation 53 42 6N 78 55W
Alleghany County ◇, N.C. 54 36 25N 81 10W
Alleghany County ◇, Va. 68 37 50N 80 0W
Allegheny → 59 40 27N 80 1W
Allegheny County ◇ 59 40 25N 80 0W
Allegheny Mts. 68 38 15N 80 10W
Allegheny National Forest 59 41 45N 79 5W
Allegheny Reservoir 59 41 50N 79 0W
Allemands, L. des 39 29 55N 90 35W
Allen, Kans. 38 38 39N 96 10W
Allen, Md. 41 38 17N 75 42W
Allen, Nebr. 48 42 25N 96 51W
Allen, Okla. 57 34 53N 96 25W
Allen, S. Dak. 61 43 17N 101 56W
Allen, Tex. 65 33 6N 96 40W
Allen County ◇, Ind. 36 41 5N 85 5W
Allen County ◇, Kans. 38 37 50N 95 15W
Allen County ◇, Ky. 62 36 45N 86 10W
Allen County ◇, Ohio 56 40 44N 84 6W
Allen Parish ◇ 39 30 37N 92 46W
Allendale, Ill. 35 38 32N 87 43W
Allendale, S.C. 60 33 1N 81 18W
Allendale County ◇ 60 33 0N 81 20W
Allenhurst 51 40 15N 73 59W
Allenspark 30 40 12N 105 32W
Allensville 62 36 43N 87 4W
Allentown, N.J. 51 40 11N 74 35W
Allentown, Pa. 59 40 37N 75 29W
Allerton, Ill. 35 39 55N 87 56W
Allerton, Iowa 37 40 42N 93 22W
Alliance, Nebr. 48 42 6N 102 52W
Alliance, Ohio 56 40 55N 81 6W
Alligator 45 34 6N 90 43W
Allison, Colo. 30 37 2N 107 29W
Allison, Iowa 37 42 45N 92 48W
Allison, Tex. 64 35 36N 100 6W
Allons 63 36 27N 85 21W
Allouez 69 44 27N 88 4W
Alloway 51 39 34N 75 22W
Allyn 67 47 23N 122 50W
Alma, Ark. 27 35 29N 94 13W
Alma, Colo. 30 39 17N 106 4W
Alma, Ga. 32 31 33N 82 28W
Alma, Kans. 38 39 1N 96 17W
Alma, Mich. 43 43 23N 84 39W
Alma, Mo. 46 39 6N 93 33W
Alma, Nebr. 48 40 6N 99 22W
Alma, Wis. 69 44 20N 91 55W
Alma Center 69 44 26N 90 55W
Almanor, L. 28 40 14N 121 9W
Almena 38 39 54N 99 43W
Almeria 48 41 50N 99 31W
Almira 67 47 43N 118 56W
Almo 62 36 42N 88 16W
Almon 32 33 37N 83 56W
Almond, N.C. 54 35 22N 83 34W
Almond, Wis. 69 44 16N 89 25W
Almont, Colo. 30 38 40N 106 51W
Almont, Mich. 43 42 55N 83 3W
Almont, N. Dak. 55 46 44N 101 30W
Almyra 27 34 24N 91 25W
Aloha 58 45 29N 122 52W
Alpaugh 29 35 53N 119 29W
Alpena, Ark. 27 36 18N 93 18W
Alpena, Mich. 43 45 4N 83 27W
Alpena, S. Dak. 61 44 11N 98 22W
Alpena County ◇ 43 45 0N 83 40W
Alpha, Ill. 35 41 12N 90 23W
Alpha, Mich. 43 46 3N 88 23W
Alpha, N.J. 51 40 40N 75 9W
Alpine, Ariz. 26 33 51N 109 9W
Alpine, Ark. 27 34 14N 93 23W
Alpine, Tenn. 63 36 24N 85 13W
Alpine, Tex. 64 30 22N 103 40W
Alpine, Utah 66 40 27N 111 47W
Alpine, Wyo. 70 43 11N 111 3W
Alpine County ◇ 28 38 40N 119 50W
Alsea → 58 44 26N 124 5W
Alsen 55 48 38N 98 42W
Alsey 35 39 34N 90 26W
Alstead 50 43 10N 72 30W
Alta 37 42 40N 95 18W
Alta Vista, Iowa 37 43 12N 92 25W
Alta Vista, Kans. 38 38 52N 96 29W
Altair 65 29 34N 96 27W
Altamaha → 32 31 20N 81 20W
Altamont, Ill. 35 39 4N 88 45W
Altamont, Kans. 38 37 12N 95 18W
Altamont, Mo. 46 39 53N 94 5W
Altamont, Oreg. 58 42 12N 121 44W
Altamont, S. Dak. 61 44 50N 96 42W
Altamont, Tenn. 63 35 26N 85 44W
Altamont, Utah 66 40 22N 110 17W
Altavista 68 37 6N 79 17W
Altha 31 30 34N 85 8W
Altheimer 27 34 19N 91 51W
Alto, Ga. 32 34 28N 83 35W
Alto, La. 39 32 22N 91 52W
Alto, N. Mex. 52 33 23N 105 41W
Alto, Tex. 65 31 39N 95 4W
Alton, Ill. 35 38 53N 90 11W
Alton, Iowa 37 42 59N 96 1W
Alton, Kans. 38 39 28N 98 57W
Alton, Mo. 46 36 42N 91 24W
Alton, Utah 66 37 26N 112 29W
Alton Bay 50 43 27N 71 13W
Altoona, Ala. 24 34 2N 86 20W
Altoona, Iowa 37 41 39N 93 28W
Altoona, Kans. 38 37 32N 95 40W
Altoona, Pa. 59 40 31N 78 24W
Altoona, Wis. 69 44 48N 91 26W
Alturas 28 41 29N 120 32W
Altus 57 34 38N 99 20W
Altus, L. 57 34 53N 99 18W
Alum Bridge 68 39 2N 80 40W
Alva, Ky. 63 36 44N 83 25W
Alva, Okla. 57 36 48N 98 40W
Alvarado, Minn. 44 48 10N 97 0W
Alvarado, Tex. 65 32 24N 97 13W
Alvaton 62 36 53N 86 21W
Alvin, S.C. 60 33 22N 79 48W
Alvin, Tex. 65 29 26N 95 15W
Alvo 48 40 52N 96 23W
Alvord, Iowa 37 43 21N 96 18W
Alvord, Tex. 65 33 22N 97 42W
Alvord Desert 58 42 30N 118 25W
Alvord L. 58 42 23N 118 36W
Alzada 47 45 2N 104 25W
Amador County ◇ 28 38 25N 120 45W
Amagansett 53 40 59N 72 9W
Amana 37 41 48N 91 52W
Amanda 56 39 39N 82 45W
Amargosa → 29 36 14N 116 51W
Amargosa Range 29 36 20N 116 45W
Amarillo 64 35 13N 101 50W
Amasa 43 46 14N 88 27W
Amatignak I. 25 51 16N 179 6W
Amazonia 46 39 53N 94 54W
Amber 57 35 10N 97 53W
Ambler 25 67 5N 157 52W
Amboy, Calif. 29 34 33N 115 45W
Amboy, Ill. 35 41 44N 89 20W
Amboy, Minn. 44 43 53N 94 10W
Ambridge 59 40 36N 80 14W
Ambrose, Ga. 32 31 36N 83 1W
Ambrose, N. Dak. 55 48 57N 103 29W
Ambrosia Lake 52 35 26N 107 54W
Amchitka I. 25 51 32N 179 0 E
Amelia, La. 39 29 40N 91 6W
Amelia, Nebr. 48 42 14N 98 55W
Amelia City 31 30 35N 81 28W
Amelia County ◇ 68 37 21N 77 59W
Amelia Court House 68 37 21N 77 59W
Amelia I. 31 30 40N 81 25W
American Corners 41 38 47N 75 51W
American Falls 34 42 47N 112 51W
American Falls Dam 34 43 0N 113 0W
American Falls Reservoir 34 42 47N 112 52W
American Fork 66 40 23N 111 48W
Americus, Ga. 32 32 4N 84 14W
Americus, Kans. 38 38 30N 96 16W
Americus, Mo. 46 38 47N 91 34W
Amery 69 45 19N 92 22W
Ames, Iowa 37 42 2N 93 37W
Ames, Okla. 57 36 15N 98 11W
Ames, Tex. 65 30 3N 94 45W
Amesbury 42 42 51N 70 56W
Amesville 56 39 24N 81 57W
Amherst, Colo. 30 40 41N 102 10W
Amherst, Maine 40 44 50N 68 22W
Amherst, Mass. 42 42 23N 72 31W
Amherst, N.H. 50 42 52N 71 38W
Amherst, N.Y. 53 42 59N 78 48W
Amherst, Ohio 56 41 24N 82 14W
Amherst, Tex. 64 34 1N 102 25W
Amherst, Va. 68 37 35N 79 3W
Amherst County ◇ 68 37 38N 79 5W
Amherst Junction 69 44 28N 89 19W
Amherstdale 68 37 47N 81 49W
Amidon 55 46 29N 103 19W
Amistad 52 35 55N 103 9W
Amistad National Recreation Area 64 29 32N 101 12W
Amistad Reservoir 64 29 28N 101 4W
Amite 39 30 44N 90 30W
Amite → 39 30 18N 90 34W
Amite County ◇ 45 31 10N 90 49W
Amity, Ark. 27 34 16N 93 28W
Amity, Ind. 36 39 26N 86 0W
Amity, Oreg. 58 45 7N 123 12W
Amlia I. 25 52 4N 173 30W
Ammon 34 43 28N 111 58W
Ammonoosuc → 50 44 10N 72 2W
Amonate 68 37 12N 81 38W
Amoret 46 38 15N 94 35W
Amorita 57 36 56N 98 18W
Amory 45 33 59N 88 29W
Amsden 50 43 25N 72 30W
Amsterdam, N.Y. 53 42 56N 74 11W
Amsterdam, Ohio 56 40 29N 80 56W
Amukta I. 25 52 30N 171 16W
Amukta Pass 25 52 0N 171 0W
Amy 27 33 44N 92 49W
Anacapa I. 29 34 1N 119 26W
Anacoco 39 31 15N 93 21W
Anaconda 47 46 8N 112 57W
Anaconda Ra. 47 45 30N 113 30W
Anacortes 67 48 30N 122 37W
Anadarko 57 35 4N 98 15W
Anahalu → 33 21 37N 158 6W
Anaheim 29 33 50N 117 55W
Anahola 33 22 9N 159 19W
Anahuac 65 29 46N 94 41W
Anaktuvuk Pass 25 68 8N 151 45W
Anamoose 55 47 53N 100 15W
Anamosa 37 42 7N 91 17W
Anandale 39 31 16N 92 27W
Anasco 71 18 17N 67 8W
Anatone 67 46 8N 117 8W
Anceney 47 45 39N 111 21W
Ancho 52 33 56N 105 45W
Anchor 35 40 34N 88 32W
Anchorage 25 61 13N 149 54W
Anchorage ◇ 25 61 0N 150 0W
Ancon 71 8 56N 79 38W
Andale 38 37 48N 97 38W
Andalusia, Ala. 24 31 18N 86 29W
Andalusia, Ill. 35 41 26N 90 43W
Anderson, Ala. 24 34 55N 87 16W
Anderson, Alaska 25 64 25N 149 15W
Anderson, Calif. 28 40 27N 122 18W
Anderson, Ind. 36 40 10N 85 41W
Anderson, Mo. 46 36 39N 94 27W
Anderson, S.C. 60 34 31N 82 39W
Anderson, Tex. 65 30 29N 95 59W
Anderson County ◇, Kans. 38 38 15N 95 15W
Anderson County ◇, Ky. 63 38 0N 85 0W
Anderson County ◇, S.C. 60 34 30N 82 40W
Anderson County ◇, Tenn. 63 36 6N 84 8W
Anderson County ◇, Tex. 65 31 46N 95 38W
Anderson Ranch Reservoir 34 43 22N 115 27W
Anderson Reservoir 28 37 10N 121 38W
Andersonville 32 32 12N 84 9W
Andes 53 42 12N 74 47W
Andes, L. 61 43 11N 98 27W
Andover, Conn. 42 41 44N 72 23W
Andover, Kans. 38 37 43N 97 7W
Andover, Maine 40 44 38N 70 45W
Andover, Mass. 42 42 40N 71 8W
Andover, Minn. 44 45 17N 93 21W
Andover, N.H. 50 43 26N 71 49W
Andover, N.J. 51 40 59N 74 45W
Andover, N.Y. 53 42 10N 77 48W
Andover, Ohio 56 41 36N 80 34W
Andover, S. Dak. 61 45 25N 97 54W
Andreanof Is. 25 51 30N 176 0W
Andrew County ◇ 46 40 0N 94 45W
Andrews, Ind. 36 40 52N 85 36W
Andrews, Md. 41 38 20N 76 10W
Andrews, N.C. 54 35 12N 83 49W
Andrews, S.C. 60 33 27N 79 34W
Andrews, Tex. 64 32 19N 102 33W
Andrews County ◇ 64 32 19N 102 33W
Androscoggin → 40 43 58N 69 52W
Androscoggin County ◇ 40 44 5N 70 10W
Anegam 26 32 22N 112 2W
Aneta 55 47 41N 97 59W
Angeles National Forest 29 33 15N 118 0W
Angelina → 65 30 54N 94 12W
Angelina County ◇ 65 31 21N 94 44W
Angelina National Forest 65 31 7N 94 15W
Angels Camp 28 38 4N 120 32W
Angelus 38 39 11N 100 41W
Angie 39 30 58N 89 49W
Angier 54 35 31N 78 44W
Angle Inlet 44 49 21N 95 4W
Angleton 65 29 10N 95 26W
Angola, Del. 41 38 40N 75 10W
Angola, Ind. 36 41 38N 85 0W
Angola, N.Y. 53 42 38N 79 2W
Angoon 25 57 30N 134 35W
Angora 48 41 51N 103 8W
Angostura Reservoir 61 43 21N 103 26W
Anguilla 45 32 59N 90 50W
Angwin 28 38 34N 122 26W
Aniak 25 61 35N 159 32W
Animas 52 31 57N 108 48W
Animas → 52 36 43N 108 13W
Animas Peak 52 31 35N 108 47W
Anita 37 41 27N 94 46W
Ankeny 37 41 44N 93 36W
Ankona 31 27 21N 80 17W
Anmoore 68 39 16N 80 18W
Ann, C. 42 42 38N 70 35W
Ann Arbor 43 42 17N 83 45W
Anna, Ill. 35 37 28N 89 15W
Anna, Ohio 56 40 24N 84 11W

Anna, Tex. **65** 33 21N 96 33W
Anna, L. **68** 38 4N 77 45W
Annada **46** 39 16N 90 50W
Annandale, Minn. **44** 45 16N 94 8W
Annandale, Va. **68** 38 50N 77 12W
Annapolis, Md. **41** 38 59N 76 30W
Annapolis, Mo. **46** 37 22N 90 42W
Annawan **35** 41 24N 89 55W
Anne Arundel County ◇ **41** 39 0N 76 40W
Annette I. **25** 55 9N 131 28W
Annette Island Indian Reservation **25** 55 5N 131 30W
Anniston, Ala. **24** 33 39N 85 50W
Anniston, Mo. **46** 36 50N 89 20W
Annona **65** 33 35N 94 55W
Annville, Ky. **63** 37 19N 83 58W
Annville, Pa. **59** 40 20N 76 31W
Año Nuevo, Pt. **28** 37 7N 122 19W
Anoka, Minn. **44** 45 12N 93 23W
Anoka, Nebr. **48** 42 57N 98 50W
Anoka County ◇ **44** 45 15N 93 15W
Anselmo **48** 41 37N 99 52W
Ansley, La. **39** 32 24N 92 42W
Ansley, Nebr. **48** 41 18N 99 23W
Anson **65** 32 45N 99 54W
Anson County ◇ **54** 35 0N 80 0W
Ansonia, Conn. **42** 41 21N 73 5W
Ansonia, Ohio **56** 40 13N 84 38W
Ansonville **54** 35 6N 80 7W
Ansted **68** 38 8N 81 6W
Antelope, Kans. **38** 38 26N 96 59W
Antelope, Oreg. **58** 44 55N 120 43W
Antelope County ◇. **48** 42 15N 98 0W
Antelope Cr. → **58** 42 28N 117 13W
Antelope Hills, Okla. **57** 35 55N 99 50W
Antelope Hills, Wyo. **70** 42 20N 108 25W
Antelope Range **49** 40 10N 114 30W
Antelope Reservoir **58** 42 54N 117 14W
Antero, Mt. **30** 38 41N 106 15W
Antero Reservoir **30** 38 56N 105 55W
Anthon **37** 42 23N 95 52W
Anthony, Fla. **31** 29 18N 82 7W
Anthony, Kans. **38** 37 9N 98 2W
Anthony, N. Mex. **52** 32 0N 106 36W
Anthoston **62** 37 46N 87 32W
Antigo **69** 45 9N 89 9W
Antimony **66** 38 7N 112 0W
Antioch, Calif. **28** 38 1N 121 48W
Antioch, Ill. **35** 42 29N 88 6W
Antioch, Nebr. **48** 42 4N 102 35W
Antler **55** 48 59N 101 17W
Antlers **57** 34 14N 95 37W
Antoine **27** 34 2N 93 25W
Anton, Colo. **30** 39 45N 103 13W
Anton, Ky. **62** 37 21N 87 24W
Anton, Tex. **64** 33 49N 102 10W
Anton Chico **52** 35 12N 105 9W
Antonino **38** 38 47N 99 24W
Antonito **30** 37 5N 106 0W
Antrim County ◇ **43** 45 0N 85 10W
Antwerp, N.Y. **53** 44 12N 75 37W
Antwerp, Ohio **56** 41 11N 84 45W
Anvik **25** 62 39N 160 13W
Anza Borrego Desert State Park **29** 33 0N 116 26W
Apache **57** 34 54N 98 22W
Apache County ◇ **26** 35 0N 109 30W
Apache Junction **26** 33 25N 111 33W
Apache L. **26** 33 36N 111 21W
Apache Mts. **64** 31 12N 104 35W
Apache National Forest **26** 33 30N 109 10W
Apache Sitgreaves National Forest **26** 34 30N 110 30W
Apalachee B. **31** 30 0N 84 0W
Apalachicola **31** 29 43N 84 59W
Apalachicola → **31** 29 43N 84 58W
Apalachicola B. **31** 29 40N 85 0W
Apalachicola National Forest **31** 30 10N 85 0W
Apex **54** 35 44N 78 51W
Apishapa → **30** 38 8N 103 57W
Apopka **31** 28 40N 81 31W
Apopka L. **31** 28 38N 81 38W
Apostle Is. **69** 47 0N 90 40W
Apostle Islands Nat. Lakeshore **69** 46 55N 91 0W
Appalachia **68** 36 54N 82 47W
Appalachian Mts. **68** 36 40N 81 45W
Appanoose County ◇ **37** 40 45N 92 50W
Apple →, Ill. **35** 42 11N 90 14W
Apple →, Wis. **69** 45 9N 92 45W
Apple Creek **56** 40 45N 81 51W
Apple Creek → **35** 39 22N 90 37W
Apple Valley **29** 34 32N 117 14W
Applegate, Mich. **43** 43 21N 82 38W
Applegate, Oreg. **58** 42 16N 123 10W
Appleton, Minn. **44** 45 12N 96 1W
Appleton, Wis. **69** 44 16N 88 25W
Appleton City **46** 38 11N 94 2W
Appling **32** 33 33N 82 19W
Appling County ◇ **32** 31 45N 82 15W
Appomattox **68** 37 21N 78 50W
Appomattox → **68** 37 19N 77 17W
Appomattox County ◇ **68** 37 21N 78 50W
Aquarius Mts. **26** 34 45N 113 20W
Aquarius Plateau **66** 38 0N 111 40W
Aquasco **41** 38 35N 76 43W
Arab **24** 34 19N 86 30W
Arabi **32** 31 50N 83 44W
Aragon **32** 34 2N 85 3W
Aransas County ◇ **65** 28 5N 96 28W
Aransas Pass **65** 27 55N 97 9W
Arapaho **57** 35 34N 98 58W
Arapaho National Forest **30** 39 30N 106 15W
Arapahoe, Colo. **30** 38 51N 102 11W
Arapahoe, N.C. **54** 35 2N 76 49W
Arapahoe, Nebr. **48** 40 18N 99 54W
Arapahoe County ◇ **30** 39 40N 104 15W
Ararat **68** 36 36N 80 31W
Arbon **34** 42 27N 112 34W
Arbuckle **28** 39 1N 122 3W
Arbuckle L. **31** 27 42N 81 24W
Arbuckle Mts. **57** 34 20N 97 10W
Arc Dome **49** 38 51N 117 22W
Arcade, Calif. **29** 34 2N 118 15W
Arcade, Ga. **32** 34 5N 83 34W
Arcade, N.Y. **53** 42 32N 78 25W
Arcadia, Fla. **31** 27 13N 81 52W
Arcadia, Ind. **36** 40 11N 86 1W
Arcadia, Iowa **37** 42 5N 95 3W
Arcadia, Kans. **38** 37 38N 94 37W
Arcadia, La. **39** 32 33N 92 55W
Arcadia, Mich. **43** 44 30N 86 14W
Arcadia, Nebr. **48** 41 25N 99 8W
Arcadia, Okla. **57** 35 40N 97 20W
Arcadia, Pa. **59** 40 47N 78 51W
Arcadia, Wis. **69** 44 15N 91 30W
Arcanum **56** 39 59N 84 33W
Arcata **28** 40 52N 124 5W
Arcata B. **28** 40 52N 124 5W
Archbald **59** 41 30N 75 32W
Archbold **56** 41 31N 84 18W
Archdale **54** 35 56N 79 57W
Archer, Fla. **31** 29 32N 82 32W
Archer, Iowa **37** 43 7N 95 45W
Archer, Nebr. **48** 41 10N 98 8W
Archer City **65** 33 36N 98 38W
Archer County ◇ **65** 33 35N 98 40W
Arches National Monument **66** 38 45N 109 25W
Archibald **39** 32 21N 91 47W
Archie, La. **39** 31 35N 91 58W
Archie, Mo. **46** 38 29N 94 21W
Archuleta County ◇ **30** 37 10N 107 0W
Arco, Idaho **34** 43 38N 113 18W
Arco, Minn. **44** 44 23N 96 11W
Arcola, Ill. **35** 39 41N 88 19W
Arcola, Miss. **45** 33 16N 90 53W
Arcola, Mo. **46** 37 33N 93 53W
Arctic Village **25** 68 8N 145 32W
Arden **28** 38 36N 121 33W
Ardenvoir **67** 47 44N 120 22W
Ardmore, Ala. **24** 34 59N 86 52W
Ardmore, Okla. **57** 34 10N 97 8W
Ardmore, S. Dak. **61** 43 1N 103 40W
Arecibo **71** 18 29N 66 43W
Arecibo ◇ **71** 18 20N 66 35W
Aredale **37** 42 50N 93 0W
Arena **69** 43 10N 89 55W
Arena, Pt. **28** 38 57N 123 44W
Arenac County ◇ **43** 44 0N 83 55W
Arenzville **35** 39 53N 90 22W
Argenta **35** 39 59N 88 49W
Argonia **38** 37 16N 97 46W
Argonne **69** 45 40N 88 53W
Argos **36** 41 14N 86 15W
Arguello, Pt. **29** 34 35N 120 39W
Argus Range **29** 36 10N 117 40W
Argusville **55** 47 3N 96 56W
Argyle, Minn. **44** 48 20N 96 49W
Argyle, Wis. **69** 42 42N 89 52W
Ariel **67** 45 57N 122 34W
Arikaree → **48** 40 1N 101 56W
Arimo **34** 42 34N 112 10W
Arion **37** 41 57N 95 27W
Arispe **37** 40 57N 94 13W
Ariton **24** 31 36N 85 43W
Arizona □ **26** 34 0N 112 0W
Arkabutla L. **45** 34 46N 90 8W
Arkadelphia **27** 34 7N 93 4W
Arkansas □ **27** 35 0N 92 0W
Arkansas → **27** 33 47N 91 4W
Arkansas City, Ark. **27** 33 37N 91 12W
Arkansas City, Kans. **38** 37 4N 97 2W
Arkansas County ◇. **27** 34 18N 91 20W
Arkoma **57** 35 21N 94 26W
Arkport **53** 42 24N 77 42W
Arlee **47** 47 10N 114 5W
Arley **24** 34 4N 87 13W
Arlington, Ariz. **26** 33 20N 112 46W
Arlington, Colo. **30** 38 20N 103 21W
Arlington, Ga. **32** 31 26N 84 44W
Arlington, Ill. **35** 41 29N 89 15W
Arlington, Iowa **37** 42 45N 91 40W
Arlington, Kans. **38** 37 54N 98 11W
Arlington, Ky. **62** 36 47N 89 1W
Arlington, Mass. **42** 42 25N 71 9W
Arlington, Minn. **44** 44 36N 94 5W
Arlington, N.Y. **53** 41 42N 73 54W
Arlington, Nebr. **48** 41 27N 96 21W
Arlington, Ohio **56** 40 54N 83 39W
Arlington, Oreg. **58** 45 43N 120 12W
Arlington, S. Dak. **61** 44 22N 97 8W
Arlington, Tenn. **62** 35 18N 89 40W
Arlington, Tex. **65** 32 44N 97 7W
Arlington, Va. **68** 38 53N 77 7W
Arlington, Vt. **50** 43 5N 73 9W
Arlington, Wash. **67** 48 12N 122 8W
Arlington, Wis. **69** 43 20N 89 23W
Arlington Heights **35** 42 5N 87 59W
Arm **45** 31 30N 90 1W
Arma **38** 37 33N 94 42W
Armada **43** 42 51N 82 53W
Armijo **52** 35 4N 106 39W
Armona **29** 36 19N 119 42W
Armour **61** 43 19N 98 21W
Armourdale **55** 48 52N 99 23W
Armstrong, Iowa **37** 43 24N 94 29W
Armstrong, Mo. **46** 39 16N 92 42W
Armstrong, Tex. **64** 26 56N 97 47W
Armstrong County ◇, Pa. **59** 40 45N 79 25W
Armstrong County ◇, Tex. **64** 35 0N 101 20W
Arnaudville **39** 30 24N 91 56W
Arnegard **55** 47 49N 103 27W
Arnett **57** 36 8N 99 46W
Arnold, Md. **41** 39 2N 76 30W
Arnold, Minn. **44** 46 53N 92 5W
Arnold, Mo. **46** 38 26N 90 23W
Arnold, Nebr. **48** 41 26N 100 12W
Arnolds Park **37** 43 22N 95 8W
Arock **58** 42 55N 117 32W
Aroma Park **35** 41 5N 87 48W
Aroostook → **40** 45 48N 67 45W
Aroostook County ◇ **40** 47 0N 69 0W
Arp **65** 32 14N 95 4W
Arpin **69** 44 33N 90 2W
Arraijan **71** 8 56N 79 36W
Arrey **52** 32 48N 107 19W
Arriba **30** 39 17N 103 17W
Arrington **38** 39 28N 95 32W
Arrow Cr. → **47** 47 43N 109 50W
Arrow Rock **46** 39 4N 92 57W
Arrowhead, L. **65** 33 45N 98 25W
Arrowrock Reservoir **34** 43 36N 115 56W
Arrowsmith **35** 40 27N 88 38W
Arroyo **71** 17 58N 66 4W
Arroyo del Macho → **52** 33 49N 104 7W
Arroyo Grande **29** 35 7N 120 35W
Arroyo Hondo **52** 36 32N 105 40W
Artas **61** 45 53N 99 49W
Artesia, Miss. **45** 33 25N 88 39W
Artesia, N. Mex. **52** 32 51N 104 24W
Artesia L. **49** 38 56N 119 22W
Artesia Wells **65** 28 17N 99 17W
Artesian **61** 44 1N 97 55W
Arthur, Ill. **35** 39 43N 88 28W
Arthur, N. Dak. **55** 47 6N 97 13W
Arthur, Nebr. **48** 41 35N 101 41W
Arthur, Tenn. **63** 36 33N 83 40W
Arthur County ◇ **48** 41 30N 101 40W
Artois **28** 39 37N 122 12W
Arvada, Colo. **30** 39 48N 105 5W
Arvada, Wyo. **70** 44 39N 106 8W
Arvin **29** 35 12N 118 50W
Asbury **46** 37 16N 94 36W
Asbury Park **51** 40 13N 74 1W
Ascension Parish ◇. **39** 30 14N 90 55W
Ascutney **50** 43 24N 72 25W
Ash Flat **27** 36 13N 91 37W
Ash Fork **26** 35 13N 112 29W
Ash Grove **46** 37 19N 93 35W
Ashaway **42** 41 25N 71 47W
Ashburn **32** 31 43N 83 39W
Ashburnham **42** 42 38N 71 55W
Ashby, Minn. **44** 46 6N 95 49W
Ashby, Nebr. **48** 42 1N 101 56W
Ashdown **27** 33 40N 94 8W
Ashe County ◇ **54** 36 25N 81 30W
Asheboro **54** 35 43N 79 49W
Asher **57** 34 59N 96 56W
Asherton **65** 28 27N 99 46W
Asherville **38** 39 24N 97 59W
Asheville **54** 35 36N 82 33W
Ashfield **42** 42 32N 72 48W
Ashford, Ala. **24** 31 11N 85 14W
Ashford, Wash. **67** 46 46N 122 2W
Ashkum **35** 40 53N 87 57W
Ashland, Ala. **24** 33 16N 85 50W
Ashland, Ill. **35** 39 53N 90 1W
Ashland, Kans. **38** 37 11N 99 46W
Ashland, Ky. **63** 38 28N 82 38W
Ashland, La. **39** 32 9N 93 6W
Ashland, Maine **40** 46 38N 68 24W
Ashland, Miss. **45** 34 50N 89 11W
Ashland, Mo. **46** 38 47N 92 16W
Ashland, Mont. **47** 45 36N 106 16W
Ashland, N.H. **50** 43 42N 71 38W
Ashland, Nebr. **48** 41 3N 96 23W
Ashland, Ohio **56** 40 52N 82 19W
Ashland, Okla. **57** 34 46N 96 4W
Ashland, Oreg. **58** 42 12N 122 43W
Ashland, Va. **68** 37 46N 77 29W
Ashland, Wis. **69** 46 35N 90 53W
Ashland City **62** 36 17N 87 4W
Ashland County ◇, Ohio **56** 40 52N 82 19W
Ashland County ◇, Wis. **69** 46 35N 90 45W
Ashley, Ill. **35** 38 20N 89 11W
Ashley, Ind. **36** 41 32N 85 4W
Ashley, Mich. **43** 43 11N 84 29W
Ashley, N. Dak. **55** 46 2N 99 22W
Ashley, Ohio **56** 40 25N 82 57W
Ashley → **66** 40 20N 109 17W
Ashley County ◇ **27** 33 14N 91 48W
Ashley National Forest **66** 40 55N 110 0W
Ashmore **35** 39 32N 88 1W
Ashokan Reservoir **53** 41 56N 74 13W
Ashtabula **56** 41 52N 80 47W
Ashtabula County ◇ **56** 41 40N 80 52W
Ashtabula L. **55** 47 2N 98 5W
Ashton, Idaho **34** 44 4N 111 27W
Ashton, Ill. **35** 41 52N 89 13W
Ashton, Iowa **37** 43 19N 95 47W
Ashton, Nebr. **48** 41 15N 98 48W
Ashton, R.I. **42** 41 56N 71 26W
Ashton, S. Dak. **61** 44 59N 98 31W
Ashuelot → **50** 43 0N 72 29W
Ashville, Ala. **24** 33 50N 86 15W
Ashville, Fla. **31** 30 37N 83 39W
Ashville, Pa. **59** 40 34N 78 33W
Ashwood **58** 44 44N 120 45W
Askewville **54** 36 7N 76 57W
Askov **44** 46 12N 92 47W
Asotin **67** 46 20N 117 3W
Asotin County ◇ **67** 46 8N 117 8W
Aspen **30** 39 11N 106 49W
Aspen Hill **41** 39 5N 77 5W
Aspermont **64** 33 8N 100 14W
Assaria **38** 38 41N 97 36W
Assateague I. **41** 38 15N 75 10W
Assateague Island National Seashore **41** 38 15N 75 10W
Assawompset Pond **42** 41 50N 70 55W
Assinippi **42** 42 10N 70 51W
Assonet **42** 41 48N 71 4W
Assumption **35** 39 31N 89 3W
Assumption Parish ◇ **39** 30 0N 91 0W
Astatula **31** 28 43N 81 44W
Astoria, Ill. **35** 40 14N 90 21W
Astoria, Oreg. **58** 46 11N 123 50W
Astoria, S. Dak. **61** 44 34N 96 33W
Atascadero **29** 35 29N 120 40W
Atascosa County ◇ **65** 28 55N 98 33W
Atchafalaya → **39** 29 53N 91 28W
Atchafalaya B. **39** 29 25N 91 25W
Atchison **38** 39 34N 95 7W
Atchison County ◇, Kans. **38** 39 30N 95 15W
Atchison County ◇, Mo. **46** 40 25N 95 25W
Atco **51** 39 46N 74 53W
Athena, Fla. **31** 29 59N 83 30W
Athena, Oreg. **58** 45 49N 118 30W
Athens, Ala. **24** 34 48N 86 58W
Athens, Ga. **32** 33 57N 83 23W
Athens, Ill. **35** 39 58N 89 44W
Athens, La. **39** 32 39N 93 1W
Athens, Mich. **43** 42 5N 85 14W
Athens, N.Y. **53** 42 16N 73 49W
Athens, Ohio **56** 39 20N 82 6W
Athens, Pa. **59** 41 57N 76 31W
Athens, Tenn. **63** 35 27N 84 36W
Athens, Tex. **65** 32 12N 95 51W
Athens, Wis. **69** 45 2N 90 5W
Athens County ◇ **56** 39 20N 82 6W
Athol, Idaho **34** 47 57N 116 42W
Athol, Mass. **42** 42 36N 72 14W
Athol, S. Dak. **61** 45 1N 98 36W
Atka **25** 52 12N 174 12W
Atka I. **25** 52 7N 174 30W
Atkins **27** 35 14N 92 56W
Atkinson, Ga. **32** 31 13N 81 47W
Atkinson, Ill. **35** 41 25N 90 1W
Atkinson, N.C. **54** 34 32N 78 10W
Atkinson, Nebr. **48** 42 32N 98 59W
Atkinson County ◇. **32** 31 15N 82 50W
Atlanta, Ga. **32** 33 45N 84 23W
Atlanta, Idaho **34** 43 48N 115 8W
Atlanta, Ill. **35** 40 16N 89 14W

Atlanta, Ind. **36** 40 13N 86 2W
Atlanta, Kans. **38** 37 26N 96 46W
Atlanta, La. **39** 31 48N 92 45W
Atlanta, Mich. **43** 45 0N 84 9W
Atlanta, Mo. **46** 39 54N 92 29W
Atlanta, Nebr. **48** 40 22N 99 28W
Atlanta, Tex. **65** 33 7N 94 10W
Atlantic, Iowa **37** 41 24N 95 1W
Atlantic, N.C. **54** 34 54N 76 20W
Atlantic Beach **31** 30 20N 81 24W
Atlantic City, N.J. **51** 39 21N 74 27W
Atlantic City, Wyo. **70** 42 30N 108 45W
Atlantic County ◇ **51** 39 30N 74 40W
Atlantic Highlands **51** 40 25N 74 3W
Atlantic Pk. **70** 42 37N 109 0W
Atmore **24** 31 2N 87 29W
Atoka **57** 34 23N 96 8W
Atoka County ◇ **57** 34 25N 96 0W
Atoka Reservoir **57** 34 27N 96 5W
Atomic City **34** 43 27N 112 49W
Atsion **51** 39 44N 74 44W
Attala County ◇ **45** 33 4N 89 35W
Attalla **24** 34 1N 86 6W
Attapulgus **32** 30 45N 84 29W
Attica, Ind. **36** 40 18N 87 15W
Attica, Kans. **38** 37 15N 98 13W
Attica, N.Y. **53** 42 52N 78 17W
Attica, Ohio **56** 41 4N 82 53W
Attleboro **42** 41 57N 71 17W
Attu **25** 52 56N 173 15 E
Attu I. **25** 52 55N 172 55 E
Atwater, Calif. **28** 37 21N 120 37W
Atwater, Minn. **44** 45 8N 94 47W
Atwood, Colo. **30** 40 33N 103 16W
Atwood, Ill. **35** 39 48N 88 28W
Atwood, Kans. **38** 39 48N 101 3W
Atwood, Okla. **57** 34 57N 96 20W
Atwood, Tenn. **62** 35 59N 88 41W
Atwood L. **56** 40 33N 81 13W
Au Gres **43** 44 3N 83 42W
Au Sable **43** 44 25N 83 20W
Au Sable → **43** 44 25N 83 20W
Au Sable Forks **53** 44 27N 73 41W
Au Sable Pt., Alger, Mich. **43** 46 40N 86 8W
Au Sable Pt., Iosco, Mich. **43** 44 20N 83 20W
Auau Channel **33** 20 50N 156 45W
Aubrey **27** 34 43N 90 54W
Aubrey Cliffs **26** 35 45N 113 0W
Auburn, Ala. **24** 32 36N 85 29W
Auburn, Calif. **28** 38 54N 121 4W
Auburn, Ill. **35** 39 36N 89 45W
Auburn, Ind. **36** 41 22N 85 4W
Auburn, Iowa **37** 42 15N 94 53W
Auburn, Kans. **38** 38 54N 95 49W
Auburn, Ky. **62** 36 52N 86 43W
Auburn, Maine **40** 44 6N 70 14W
Auburn, Mass. **42** 42 12N 71 50W
Auburn, Mich. **43** 43 36N 84 4W
Auburn, Miss. **45** 31 22N 90 37W
Auburn, N.Y. **53** 42 56N 76 34W
Auburn, Nebr. **48** 40 23N 95 51W
Auburn, W. Va. **68** 39 6N 80 51W
Auburn, Wash. **67** 47 18N 122 14W
Auburndale, Fla. **31** 28 4N 81 48W
Auburndale, Wis. **69** 44 38N 90 0W
Auburntown **62** 35 57N 86 5W
Aucilla → **31** 30 5N 83 59W
Audrain County ◇ **46** 39 10N 91 50W
Audubon, Iowa **37** 41 43N 94 56W
Audubon, Minn. **44** 46 52N 95 59W
Audubon County ◇ **37** 41 40N 94 50W
Auglaize County ◇ **56** 40 34N 84 12W
Augusta, Ark. **27** 35 17N 91 22W
Augusta, Ga. **32** 33 28N 81 58W
Augusta, Ill. **35** 40 14N 90 57W
Augusta, Kans. **38** 37 41N 96 59W
Augusta, Ky. **63** 38 47N 84 0W
Augusta, Maine **40** 44 19N 69 47W
Augusta, Mo. **46** 38 34N 90 53W
Augusta, Mont. **47** 47 30N 112 24W
Augusta, N.J. **51** 41 8N 74 44W
Augusta, W. Va. **68** 39 18N 78 38W
Augusta, Wis. **69** 44 41N 91 7W
Augusta County ◇ **68** 38 9N 79 4W
Augustine I. **25** 59 22N 153 26W
Aulander **54** 36 14N 77 6W
Aullville **46** 39 1N 93 41W
Ault **30** 40 35N 104 44W
Aurelia **37** 42 43N 95 26W
Aurora, Colo. **30** 39 44N 104 52W
Aurora, Ill. **35** 41 45N 88 19W
Aurora, Ind. **36** 39 4N 84 54W
Aurora, Iowa **37** 42 37N 91 44W
Aurora, Kans. **38** 39 27N 97 32W
Aurora, Ky. **62** 36 47N 88 9W
Aurora, Maine **40** 44 51N 68 20W
Aurora, Minn. **44** 47 32N 92 14W
Aurora, Mo. **46** 36 58N 93 43W
Aurora, N.C. **54** 35 18N 76 47W
Aurora, N.Y. **53** 42 45N 76 42W
Aurora, Nebr. **48** 40 52N 98 0W
Aurora, S. Dak. **61** 44 17N 96 41W
Aurora, W. Va. **68** 39 19N 79 33W
Aurora County ◇ **61** 43 43N 98 29W
Austin, Ark. **27** 35 0N 92 0W
Austin, Ind. **36** 38 45N 85 49W
Austin, Minn. **44** 43 40N 92 58W
Austin, Mont. **47** 46 39N 112 15W
Austin, Nev. **49** 39 30N 117 4W
Austin, Pa. **59** 41 38N 78 6W
Austin, Tex. **65** 30 17N 97 45W
Austin County ◇ **65** 29 57N 96 15W
Austintown **56** 41 6N 80 48W
Austinville **68** 36 51N 80 55W
Austwell **65** 28 23N 96 51W
Autauga County ◇ **24** 32 26N 86 39W
Autaugaville **24** 32 26N 86 39W
Auxvasse **46** 39 1N 91 54W
Auxvasse → **46** 38 41N 91 49W
Ava, Ill. **35** 37 53N 89 30W
Ava, Mo. **46** 36 57N 92 40W
Avalon, Calif. **29** 33 21N 118 20W
Avalon, Miss. **45** 33 39N 90 5W
Avalon, N.J. **51** 39 6N 74 43W
Avalon, L. **52** 32 27N 104 15W
Avant **57** 36 29N 96 4W
Avawatz Mts. **29** 35 40N 116 30W
Avenal **29** 36 0N 120 8W
Avenue **41** 38 16N 76 46W
Avera **32** 33 12N 82 32W
Avery, Idaho **34** 47 15N 115 49W
Avery, Tex. **65** 33 33N 94 47W
Avery County ◇ **54** 36 5N 82 0W
Avery Island **39** 29 55N 91 54W
Avilla, Ind. **36** 41 22N 85 14W
Avilla, Mo. **46** 37 8N 94 8W
Avinger **65** 32 54N 94 33W
Avis **59** 41 11N 77 19W
Avoca, Iowa **37** 41 29N 95 20W
Avoca, Minn. **44** 43 57N 95 39W
Avoca, N.Y. **53** 42 25N 77 25W
Avoca, Nebr. **48** 40 48N 96 7W
Avoca, Tex. **65** 32 52N 99 43W
Avon, Colo. **30** 39 38N 106 31W
Avon, Conn. **42** 41 49N 72 50W
Avon, Ill. **35** 40 40N 90 26W
Avon, Mont. **47** 46 36N 112 36W
Avon, N.C. **54** 35 21N 75 30W
Avon, N.Y. **53** 42 55N 77 45W
Avon, S. Dak. **61** 43 0N 98 4W
Avon Park **31** 27 36N 81 31W
Avondale, Ariz. **26** 33 26N 112 21W
Avondale, Colo. **30** 38 14N 104 21W
Avondale, Pa. **59** 39 50N 75 47W
Avonmore **59** 40 32N 79 28W
Avoyelles Parish ◇ **39** 31 0N 92 0W
Axial **30** 40 17N 107 47W
Axson **32** 31 17N 82 44W
Axtell, Kans. **38** 39 52N 96 15W
Axtell, Nebr. **48** 40 29N 99 8W
Ayden **54** 35 28N 77 20W
Ayer **42** 42 34N 71 35W
Aynor **60** 34 0N 79 12W
Ayr, N. Dak. **55** 47 3N 97 29W
Ayr, Nebr. **48** 40 26N 98 26W
Ayshire **37** 43 2N 94 50W
Aziscohos L. **40** 45 0N 71 0W
Azle **65** 32 54N 97 32W
Aztec, Ariz. **26** 32 49N 113 27W
Aztec, N. Mex. **52** 36 49N 107 59W
Aztec Peak **26** 33 49N 110 54W
Azusa **29** 34 8N 117 52W

B

B. A. Steinhagen L. **65** 30 50N 94 15W
B. Everett Jordan L. **54** 35 30N 79 0W
Babb **47** 48 51N 113 27W
Babbitt, Minn. **44** 47 41N 91 54W
Babbitt, Nev. **49** 38 32N 118 39W
Babbs **57** 34 57N 99 3W
Baboquivari Peak **26** 31 46N 111 36W
Babson Park **31** 27 49N 81 32W
Babylon **53** 40 42N 73 19W
Baca County ◇ **30** 37 15N 102 30W
Back B. **68** 36 35N 75 57W
Backbone Mt. **41** 39 12N 79 28W
Backus **44** 46 49N 94 31W
Bacon County ◇ **32** 31 30N 82 30W
Baconton **32** 31 23N 84 10W
Bad → **61** 44 21N 100 22W
Bad Axe **43** 43 48N 83 0W
Bad River Indian Reservation **69** 46 30N 90 45W
Baden **59** 40 38N 80 14W
Badger, Iowa **37** 42 37N 94 9W
Badger, Minn. **44** 48 47N 96 1W
Badger → **30** 40 17N 103 42W
Badger Pk. **47** 45 40N 106 33W
Badin **54** 35 24N 80 6W
Badin L. **54** 35 25N 80 6W
Badlands **61** 43 55N 102 30W
Badlands National Mounument **61** 43 38N 102 56W
Badwater Cr. → **70** 43 17N 108 8W
Baffin B. **64** 27 18N 97 30W
Bagdad, Ariz. **26** 34 34N 113 11W
Bagdad, Fla. **31** 30 36N 87 2W
Bagdad, Ky. **63** 38 16N 85 3W
Baggs **70** 41 2N 107 39W
Bagley **44** 47 32N 95 24W
Bahama **54** 36 10N 78 53W
Bailey **30** 39 25N 105 29W
Bailey County ◇ **64** 34 0N 102 55W
Baileys Harbor **69** 45 4N 87 8W
Baileyton **63** 36 20N 82 50W
Baileyville **38** 39 51N 96 11W
Bainbridge, Ga. **32** 30 55N 84 35W
Bainbridge, Ind. **36** 39 46N 86 49W
Bainbridge, N.Y. **53** 42 18N 75 29W
Bainbridge, Ohio **56** 39 14N 83 16W
Bainville **47** 48 8N 104 13W
Baird **65** 32 24N 99 24W
Baird Mts. **25** 67 0N 160 0W
Bairoil **70** 42 15N 107 33W
Baker, Calif. **29** 35 16N 116 4W
Baker, Fla. **31** 30 48N 86 41W
Baker, Idaho **34** 45 6N 113 44W
Baker, La. **39** 30 35N 91 10W
Baker, Mont. **47** 46 22N 104 17W
Baker, N. Dak. **55** 48 10N 99 39W
Baker, Okla. **57** 36 52N 101 1W
Baker, Oreg. **58** 44 47N 117 50W
Baker, Mt. **67** 48 47N 121 49W
Baker Butte **26** 34 27N 111 22W
Baker County ◇, Fla. **31** 30 20N 82 15W
Baker County ◇, Ga. **32** 31 20N 84 30W
Baker County ◇, Oreg. **58** 44 40N 117 50W
Baker Hill **24** 31 47N 85 18W
Bakersfield, Calif. **29** 35 23N 119 1W
Bakersfield, Tex. **64** 30 54N 102 18W
Bakersfield, Vt. **50** 44 45N 72 48W
Bala **38** 39 19N 96 57W
Balaton **44** 44 14N 95 52W
Balboa **71** 8 57N 79 34W
Balboa Hill **71** 9 6N 79 44W
Balch Springs **65** 32 43N 96 38W
Balcones Escarpment **64** 29 30N 99 15W
Balcones Heights **65** 29 26N 98 36W
Bald Creek **54** 35 55N 82 25W
Bald Knob, Ark. **27** 35 19N 91 34W
Bald Knob, Va. **68** 37 56N 79 51W
Bald Knoll **70** 42 22N 110 28W
Bald Mt. **58** 43 16N 121 21W
Baldwin, Fla. **31** 30 18N 81 59W
Baldwin, Ga. **32** 34 30N 83 32W
Baldwin, Ill. **35** 38 11N 89 51W
Baldwin, La. **39** 29 50N 91 33W
Baldwin, Mich. **43** 43 54N 85 51W
Baldwin, N. Dak. **55** 47 2N 100 45W
Baldwin, N.Y. **53** 40 39N 73 36W
Baldwin, Pa. **59** 40 23N 79 59W
Baldwin, Wis. **69** 44 58N 92 22W
Baldwin City **38** 38 47N 95 11W
Baldwin County ◇, Ala. **24** 30 53N 87 46W
Baldwin County ◇, Ga. **32** 33 5N 83 10W
Baldwinsville **53** 43 10N 76 20W
Baldwinville **42** 42 37N 72 5W
Baldwyn **45** 34 31N 88 38W
Baldy Peak **26** 33 54N 109 34W
Baldy Pk. **52** 36 38N 105 13W
Balfour **55** 47 57N 100 32W
Balko **57** 36 38N 100 41W
Ball **39** 31 25N 92 25W
Ball Ground **32** 34 20N 84 23W
Ballantine **47** 45 57N 108 9W
Ballard County ◇ **62** 37 0N 89 0W
Ballinger **65** 31 45N 99 57W
Ballston Spa **53** 43 0N 73 51W
Balltown **37** 42 38N 90 51W
Bally **59** 40 24N 75 35W
Balmorhea **64** 30 59N 103 45W
Balsam Lake **69** 45 27N 92 27W
Balta **55** 48 10N 100 2W
Baltic, Conn. **42** 41 37N 72 5W
Baltic, Ohio **56** 40 26N 81 42W
Baltic, S. Dak. **61** 43 46N 96 44W
Baltimore, Md. **41** 39 17N 76 37W
Baltimore, Ohio **56** 39 51N 82 36W
Baltimore County ◇ **41** 39 20N 76 40W
Bamberg **60** 33 18N 81 2W
Bamberg County ◇ **60** 33 10N 81 0W
Bancroft, Idaho **34** 42 43N 111 53W
Bancroft, Iowa **37** 43 18N 94 13W
Bancroft, La. **39** 30 34N 93 41W
Bancroft, Mich. **43** 42 53N 84 4W
Bancroft, Nebr. **48** 42 1N 96 34W
Bandana **62** 37 9N 88 56W
Bandelier National Monument **52** 35 50N 106 25W
Bandera **65** 29 44N 99 5W
Bandera County ◇ **65** 29 48N 99 15W
Bandon **58** 43 7N 124 25W
Bangor, Maine **40** 44 48N 68 46W
Bangor, Mich. **43** 42 18N 86 7W
Bangor, Pa. **59** 40 52N 75 13W
Bangs **65** 31 43N 99 8W
Bangs Mt. **26** 36 48N 113 51W
Banister → **68** 36 42N 78 48W
Banks, Ala. **24** 31 49N 85 51W
Banks, Ark. **27** 33 35N 92 16W
Banks, Idaho **34** 44 5N 116 8W
Banks, Miss. **45** 34 50N 90 14W
Banks County ◇ **32** 34 30N 83 30W
Banks L., Ga. **32** 31 2N 83 6W
Banks L., Wash. **67** 47 47N 119 19W
Bannack **47** 45 10N 112 59W
Banner County ◇ **48** 41 30N 103 40W
Banner Elk **54** 36 10N 81 52W
Banner Hill **63** 36 8N 82 25W
Bannertown **54** 36 29N 80 35W
Banning **29** 33 56N 116 53W
Bannock County ◇ **34** 42 30N 112 10W
Bannock Cr. → **34** 42 53N 112 40W
Bannock Range **34** 42 40N 112 30W
Bantry **55** 48 30N 100 37W
Bapchule **26** 33 12N 111 50W
Bar Harbor **40** 44 23N 68 13W
Baraboo **69** 43 28N 89 45W
Barada **48** 40 13N 95 35W
Baraga **43** 46 47N 88 30W
Baraga County ◇ **43** 46 40N 88 20W
Baranof **25** 57 5N 134 50W
Baranof I. **25** 57 0N 135 0W
Barataria **39** 29 44N 90 8W
Barataria B. **39** 29 20N 89 55W
Barber County ◇ **38** 37 15N 98 40W
Barbers Pt. **33** 21 18N 158 7W
Barberton **56** 41 0N 81 39W
Barberville **31** 29 11N 81 26W
Barbour County ◇, Ala. **24** 31 53N 85 27W
Barbour County ◇, W. Va. **68** 39 9N 80 3W
Barboursville **68** 38 24N 82 18W
Barbourville **63** 36 52N 83 53W
Barceloneta **71** 18 27N 66 32W
Barclay **41** 39 9N 75 52W
Barco **54** 36 24N 75 59W
Bardley **46** 36 42N 91 7W
Bardstown **63** 37 49N 85 28W
Bardwell **62** 36 52N 89 1W
Bare Mt. **67** 45 55N 122 4W
Bargersville **36** 39 31N 86 10W
Baring **46** 40 15N 92 12W
Bark Pt. **69** 46 53N 91 11W
Barker **53** 43 20N 78 33W
Barkhamsted Reservoir **42** 41 53N 72 58W
Barkley, L. **62** 37 1N 88 14W
Barksdale **65** 29 44N 100 2W
Barling **27** 35 20N 94 18W
Barlow **62** 37 3N 89 3W
Barnard, Kans. **38** 39 11N 98 3W
Barnard, Mo. **46** 40 10N 94 50W
Barnard, Vt. **50** 43 43N 72 38W
Barnegat **51** 39 45N 74 14W
Barnegat Bay **51** 39 45N 74 10W
Barnegat Light **51** 39 46N 74 6W
Barnes **38** 39 43N 96 52W
Barnes City **37** 41 31N 92 27W
Barnes County ◇ **55** 47 0N 98 0W
Barnesboro **59** 40 40N 78 47W
Barneston **48** 40 5N 96 38W
Barnesville, Ga. **32** 33 3N 84 9W
Barnesville, Md. **41** 39 13N 77 23W
Barnesville, Minn. **44** 46 39N 96 25W
Barnesville, Ohio **56** 39 59N 81 11W
Barnet **50** 44 18N 72 3W
Barnett **46** 38 23N 92 41W
Barney **32** 31 1N 83 31W
Barnhart **64** 31 8N 101 10W
Barnsdall **57** 36 34N 96 10W
Barnstable **42** 41 42N 70 18W
Barnstable County ◇ **42** 41 40N 70 15W
Barnstaple Harbor **42** 41 43N 70 18W
Barnum **44** 46 30N 92 42W
Barnwell **60** 33 15N 81 23W
Barnwell County ◇ **60** 33 15N 81 30W
Baron **57** 35 55N 94 36W
Barques, Pt. Aux, Huron, Mich. **43** 44 4N 82 58W
Barques, Pt. Aux, Schoolcraft, Mich. **43** 45 48N 86 21W
Barranquitas **71** 18 11N 66 19W
Barre, Mass. **42** 42 25N 72 6W
Barre, Vt. **50** 44 12N 72 30W
Barren → **62** 37 11N 86 37W
Barren County ◇ **62** 37 0N 86 0W
Barren I. **25** 58 55N 152 15W
Barren River L. **62** 36 54N 86 8W
Barrett **44** 45 55N 95 53W
Barrineau Park **31** 30 42N 87 26W
Barrington **42** 41 44N 71 18W
Barron **69** 45 24N 91 51W
Barron County ◇ **69** 45 25N 91 50W
Barrow **25** 71 18N 156 47W

Barrow County ◇ **32** 34 0N 83 40W
Barrow Pt. **25** 71 24N 156 29W
Barry **35** 39 42N 91 2W
Barry County ◇, Mich. **43** 42 35N 85 25W
Barry County ◇, Mo. **46** 36 45N 93 45W
Barryton **43** 43 45N 85 9W
Barstow, Calif. **29** 34 54N 117 1W
Barstow, Tex. **64** 31 28N 103 24W
Bartholomew County ◇ **36** 39 10N 85 55W
Bartlesville **57** 36 45N 95 59W
Bartlett, Kans. **38** 37 3N 95 13W
Bartlett, N.H. **50** 44 5N 71 17W
Bartlett, Nebr. **48** 41 53N 98 33W
Bartlett, Tex. **65** 30 48N 97 26W
Bartlett Reservoir **26** 33 49N 111 38W
Bartley **48** 40 15N 100 18W
Barton, Ala. **24** 34 44N 87 54W
Barton, Md. **41** 39 34N 79 2W
Barton, N. Dak. **55** 48 30N 100 11W
Barton, Vt. **50** 44 45N 72 11W
Barton → **50** 44 53N 72 13W
Barton County ◇, Kans. **38** 38 30N 98 40W
Barton County ◇, Mo. **46** 37 30N 94 20W
Bartonville **35** 40 39N 89 39W
Bartow, Fla. **31** 27 54N 81 50W
Bartow, Ga. **32** 32 53N 82 29W
Bartow County ◇ **32** 34 20N 84 50W
Barwick **32** 30 54N 83 44W
Basalt, Colo. **30** 39 22N 107 2W
Basalt, Idaho **34** 43 19N 112 10W
Basco **35** 40 20N 91 12W
Basile **39** 30 29N 92 36W
Basin, Mont. **47** 46 16N 112 16W
Basin, Wyo. **70** 44 23N 108 2W
Basinger **31** 27 23N 81 2W
Baskahegan L. **40** 45 30N 67 48W
Baskin **39** 32 16N 91 45W
Bass I. **56** 41 40N 82 56W
Bass Lake **28** 37 19N 119 33W
Bassett, Nebr. **48** 42 35N 99 32W
Bassett, Va. **68** 36 46N 79 59W
Bassfield **45** 31 30N 89 45W
Basswood L. **44** 48 7N 91 34W
Bastain **68** 37 9N 81 9W
Bastrop, La. **39** 32 47N 91 55W
Bastrop, Tex. **65** 30 7N 97 19W
Bastrop County ◇ **65** 30 10N 97 20W
Batavia, Ill. **35** 41 51N 88 19W
Batavia, Iowa **37** 41 0N 92 10W
Batavia, N.Y. **53** 43 0N 78 11W
Batavia, Ohio **56** 39 5N 84 11W
Batchtown **35** 39 2N 90 43W
Bates, Ark. **27** 34 55N 94 23W
Bates, Oreg. **58** 44 36N 118 30W
Bates County ◇ **46** 38 15N 94 20W
Batesburg **60** 33 54N 81 33W
Batesland **61** 43 8N 102 6W
Batesville, Ark. **27** 35 46N 91 39W
Batesville, Ind. **36** 39 18N 85 13W
Batesville, Miss. **45** 34 19N 89 57W
Batesville, Tex. **65** 28 58N 99 37W
Bath, Ill. **35** 40 11N 90 8W
Bath, Maine **40** 43 55N 69 49W
Bath, N.C. **54** 35 29N 76 49W
Bath, N.Y. **53** 42 20N 77 19W
Bath, Pa. **59** 40 44N 75 24W
Bath, S.C. **60** 33 31N 81 51W
Bath, S. Dak. **61** 45 28N 98 20W
Bath County ◇, Ky. **63** 38 10N 83 45W
Bath County ◇, Va. **68** 38 0N 79 50W
Bathgate **55** 48 53N 97 29W
Baton Rouge **39** 30 27N 91 11W
Batson **65** 30 15N 94 40W
Batten Kill → **50** 43 6N 73 35W
Battle → **28** 40 21N 122 11W
Battle Creek, Iowa **37** 42 19N 95 36W
Battle Creek, Mich. **43** 42 19N 85 11W
Battle Creek, Nebr. **48** 42 0N 97 36W
Battle Ground, Ind. **36** 40 31N 86 50W
Battle Ground, Wash. **67** 45 47N 122 32W
Battle Lake **44** 46 17N 95 43W
Battle Mountain **49** 40 38N 116 56W
Battle Mt. **70** 41 2N 107 16W
Baudette **44** 48 43N 94 36W
Bauxite **27** 34 33N 92 30W
Bavaria **38** 38 48N 97 45W
Baxley **32** 31 47N 82 21W
Baxter, Iowa **37** 41 49N 93 9W
Baxter, Minn. **44** 46 21N 94 17W
Baxter, Tenn. **63** 36 9N 85 38W
Baxter County ◇ **27** 36 20N 92 23W
Baxter Springs **38** 37 2N 94 44W
Baxterville **45** 31 5N 89 36W
Bay **27** 35 45N 90 34W
Bay City, Mich. **43** 43 36N 83 54W
Bay City, Oreg. **58** 45 31N 123 53W
Bay City, Tex. **65** 28 59N 95 58W
Bay County ◇, Fla. **31** 30 20N 85 45W
Bay County ◇, Mich. **43** 43 45N 84 5W
Bay Mills Indian Reservation **43** 46 25N 84 15W
Bay Minette **24** 30 53N 87 46W
Bay Port **43** 43 51N 83 23W
Bay St. Louis **45** 30 19N 89 20W
Bay Shore **53** 40 43N 73 15W
Bay Springs **45** 31 59N 89 17W
Bay View **41** 39 39N 75 58W
Bayamon **71** 18 24N 66 10W
Bayamon → **71** 18 24N 66 9W
Bayard, Iowa **37** 41 51N 94 33W
Bayard, N. Mex. **52** 32 46N 108 8W
Bayard, Nebr. **48** 41 45N 103 20W
Bayard, W. Va. **68** 39 16N 79 22W
Bayboro **54** 35 9N 76 46W
Bayfield, Colo. **30** 37 14N 107 36W
Bayfield, Wis. **69** 46 49N 90 49W
Bayfield County ◇ **69** 46 25N 91 15W
Bayfield Ridge **69** 46 45N 91 25W
Baylor County ◇ **65** 33 35N 99 16W
Bayonne **51** 40 40N 74 7W
Bayou Bartholomew → **39** 32 43N 92 4W
Bayou Bodcau → **39** 32 13N 93 30W
Bayou Cane **39** 29 37N 90 45W
Bayou D'Arbonne L. **39** 32 43N 92 21W
Bayou De View → **27** 34 48N 91 18W
Bayou Dorcheat → **39** 32 10N 93 25W
Bayou George **31** 30 16N 85 33W
Bayou La Batre **24** 30 24N 88 15W
Bayou Lafourche → **39** 29 5N 90 14W
Bayou Macon → **39** 31 55N 91 33W
Bayou Meto **27** 34 13N 91 31W
Bayou Nepique → **39** 30 11N 92 34W
Bayou Pierre → **45** 31 55N 91 11W
Bayou Vista **39** 29 41N 90 13W
Bayport **31** 28 32N 82 39W
Bayshore **31** 26 43N 81 50W
Bayside **65** 28 6N 97 13W
Bayside Beach **41** 39 8N 76 27W
Baytown **65** 29 43N 94 59W
Bayview **34** 47 59N 116 34W
Bazaar **38** 38 16N 96 32W
Bazile Mills **48** 42 31N 97 53W
Bazine **38** 38 27N 99 42W
Beach **55** 46 58N 104 0W
Beach City **56** 40 39N 81 35W
Beach Haven **51** 39 34N 74 14W
Beachville **41** 38 8N 76 24W
Beachwood **51** 39 56N 74 12W
Beacon, Iowa **37** 41 17N 92 41W
Beacon, N.Y. **53** 41 30N 73 58W
Beacon Hill **31** 29 55N 85 23W
Beadle County ◇ **61** 44 22N 98 13W
Beagle **38** 38 25N 94 57W
Beallsville **56** 39 51N 81 2W
Beals Branch → **64** 32 10N 101 51W
Bear **41** 39 38N 75 39W
Bear → **66** 41 30N 112 8W
Bear Cr. →, Ala. **24** 33 11N 88 5W
Bear Cr. →, Wyo. **70** 41 41N 104 13W
Bear Creek **69** 44 32N 88 44W
Bear L. **66** 41 59N 111 21W
Bear Lake **43** 44 25N 86 9W
Bear Lake County ◇ **34** 42 10N 111 15W
Bear Mt. **63** 37 32N 84 16W
Bear Peak **70** 43 4N 109 13W
Bear River City **66** 41 37N 112 8W
Bear Tooth Pass **70** 44 58N 109 28W
Bearden **27** 33 43N 92 37W
Beardsley, Kans. **38** 39 49N 101 14W
Beardsley, Minn. **44** 45 33N 96 43W
Beardstown **35** 40 1N 90 26W
Bearmouth **47** 46 48N 113 20W
Bearpaw Mts. **47** 48 12N 109 30W
Bears Ears **66** 37 38N 109 51W
Beartooth Ra. **47** 45 5N 109 40W
Beatrice, Ala. **24** 31 44N 87 13W
Beatrice, Nebr. **48** 40 16N 96 45W
Beattie **38** 39 52N 96 25W
Beatty, Nev. **49** 36 54N 116 46W
Beatty, Oreg. **58** 42 27N 121 16W
Beattyville **63** 37 35N 83 42W
Beaufort, N.C. **54** 34 43N 76 40W
Beaufort, S.C. **60** 32 26N 80 40W
Beaufort County ◇, N.C. **54** 35 30N 76 50W
Beaufort County ◇, S.C. **60** 32 20N 80 50W
Beaumont, Calif. **29** 33 56N 116 58W
Beaumont, Miss. **45** 31 10N 88 55W
Beaumont, Tex. **65** 30 5N 94 6W
Beauregard Parish ◇ **39** 30 39N 93 25W
Beaver, Alaska **25** 66 22N 147 24W
Beaver, Kans. **38** 38 38N 98 40W
Beaver, Ohio **56** 39 2N 82 50W
Beaver, Okla. **57** 36 49N 100 31W
Beaver, Oreg. **58** 45 17N 123 49W
Beaver, Pa. **59** 40 42N 80 19W
Beaver, Utah **66** 38 17N 112 38W
Beaver, Wis. **69** 45 8N 88 1W
Beaver → **66** 39 10N 112 57W
Beaver Bay **44** 47 16N 91 18W
Beaver City **48** 40 8N 99 50W
Beaver County ◇, Okla. **57** 36 45N 100 25W
Beaver County ◇, Pa. **59** 40 45N 80 20W
Beaver County ◇, Utah **66** 38 20N 113 10W
Beaver Cr. →, Colo. **30** 40 20N 103 33W
Beaver Cr. →, Mont. **47** 48 27N 107 18W
Beaver Cr. →, N. Dak. **55** 47 20N 103 39W
Beaver Cr. →, Nebr. **48** 40 7N 99 29W
Beaver Cr. →, Tex. **65** 33 53N 98 49W
Beaver Cr. →, Wyo. **70** 42 58N 108 26W
Beaver Creek **44** 43 37N 96 22W
Beaver Crossing **48** 40 47N 97 17W
Beaver Dam, Ky. **62** 37 24N 86 52W
Beaver Dam, Wis. **69** 43 28N 88 50W
Beaver Dam L. **69** 43 31N 88 53W
Beaver Falls **59** 40 46N 80 20W
Beaver I. **43** 45 40N 85 33W
Beaver L. **27** 36 25N 93 51W
Beavercreek **56** 39 43N 84 11W
Beaverdam **56** 40 50N 83 59W
Beaverhead → **47** 45 31N 112 21W
Beaverhead County ◇ **47** 45 5N 113 10W
Beaverhead Mts. **34** 45 0N 113 20W
Beaverton, Mich. **43** 43 53N 84 29W
Beaverton, Mont. **47** 48 26N 107 15W
Beaverton, Oreg. **58** 45 29N 122 48W
Bebe **65** 29 25N 97 38W
Becharof L. **25** 57 56N 156 23W
Bechyn **44** 44 39N 95 5W
Becker County ◇ **44** 46 50N 95 50W
Beckham County ◇ **57** 35 15N 99 40W
Beckley **68** 37 47N 81 11W
Beckville **65** 32 15N 92 27W
Beckwith Cr. → **39** 30 13N 93 13W
Bedford, Ind. **36** 38 52N 86 29W
Bedford, Iowa **37** 40 40N 94 44W
Bedford, Ky. **63** 38 36N 85 19W
Bedford, Mass. **42** 42 29N 71 17W
Bedford, N.H. **50** 42 55N 71 32W
Bedford, Ohio **56** 41 23N 81 32W
Bedford, Pa. **59** 40 1N 78 30W
Bedford, Va. **68** 37 20N 79 31W
Bedford County ◇, Pa. **59** 40 0N 78 30W
Bedford County ◇, Tenn. **62** 35 29N 86 28W
Bedford County ◇, Va. **68** 37 20N 79 31W
Bedias **65** 30 47N 95 57W
Bedrock **30** 38 19N 108 54W
Bee **48** 41 0N 97 4W
Bee County ◇ **65** 28 24N 97 45W
Bee Ridge **31** 27 17N 82 29W
Bee Springs **62** 37 17N 86 17W
Beebe **27** 35 4N 91 53W
Beech Bottom **68** 40 14N 80 39W
Beech Creek **59** 41 5N 77 36W
Beech Fork → **63** 37 46N 85 41W
Beech Grove **36** 39 44N 86 3W
Beecher **35** 41 21N 87 38W
Beecher City **35** 39 11N 88 47W
Beecher Falls **50** 45 1N 71 31W
Beechgrove **62** 35 38N 86 14W
Beeler **38** 38 26N 100 12W
Beemer **48** 41 56N 96 48W
Beersheba Springs **63** 35 28N 85 39W
Beeville **65** 28 24N 97 45W
Beggs **57** 35 45N 96 4W
Bel Air **41** 39 32N 76 21W
Bel Alton **41** 38 28N 76 59W
Belcamp **41** 39 28N 76 14W
Belchertown **42** 42 17N 72 24W
Belcourt **55** 48 50N 99 45W
Belden **48** 42 25N 97 13W
Belding **43** 43 6N 85 14W
Belen **52** 34 40N 106 46W
Belews L. **54** 36 15N 80 5W
Belfair **67** 47 27N 122 50W
Belfast, Maine **40** 44 26N 69 1W
Belfast, N.Y. **53** 42 21N 78 7W
Belfast, Tenn. **62** 35 25N 86 42W
Belfield **55** 46 53N 103 12W
Belfry **47** 45 9N 109 1W
Belgium **69** 43 30N 87 51W
Belgrade, Maine **40** 44 27N 69 50W
Belgrade, Minn. **44** 45 27N 95 0W
Belgrade, Mont. **47** 45 47N 111 11W
Belgrade, Nebr. **48** 41 28N 98 4W
Belhaven **54** 35 33N 76 37W
Belington **68** 39 2N 79 56W
Belknap **35** 37 19N 88 56W
Belknap County ◇ **50** 43 30N 71 30W
Bell **31** 29 45N 82 52W
Bell Buckle **62** 35 35N 86 21W
Bell City, Ky. **62** 36 31N 88 30W
Bell City, Mo. **46** 37 1N 89 49W
Bell County ◇, Ky. **63** 36 45N 83 40W
Bell County ◇, Tex. **65** 31 3N 97 28W
Bell Ranch **52** 35 32N 104 6W
Bellaire, Mich. **43** 44 59N 85 13W
Bellaire, Ohio **56** 40 1N 80 45W
Bellaire, Tex. **65** 29 42N 95 28W
Bellamy **24** 32 27N 88 8W
Belle, Mo. **46** 38 17N 91 43W
Belle, W. Va. **68** 38 14N 81 33W
Belle → **43** 42 43N 82 30W
Belle Fourche **61** 44 40N 103 51W
Belle Fourche → **61** 44 26N 102 18W
Belle Fourche Reservoir **61** 44 44N 103 41W
Belle Glade **31** 26 41N 80 40W
Belle Isle **31** 28 27N 81 21W
Belle Plaine, Iowa **37** 41 54N 92 17W
Belle Plaine, Kans. **38** 37 24N 97 17W
Belle Plaine, Minn. **44** 44 37N 93 46W
Belle Rive **35** 38 14N 88 45W
Belle Valley **56** 39 47N 81 33W
Bellechester **44** 44 22N 92 31W
Bellefontaine **56** 40 22N 83 46W
Bellefonte, Del. **41** 39 47N 75 30W
Bellefonte, Pa. **59** 40 55N 77 47W
Bellemont **26** 35 14N 111 50W
Belleplain **51** 39 11N 74 46W
Belleview **31** 29 4N 82 3W
Belleville, Ill. **35** 38 31N 89 59W
Belleville, Kans. **38** 39 50N 97 38W
Belleville, N.J. **51** 40 47N 74 9W
Belleville, Wis. **69** 42 52N 89 32W
Bellevue, Idaho **34** 43 28N 114 16W
Bellevue, Iowa **37** 42 16N 90 26W
Bellevue, Md. **41** 38 42N 76 11W
Bellevue, Mich. **43** 42 27N 85 1W
Bellevue, Nebr. **48** 41 9N 95 54W
Bellevue, Ohio **56** 41 17N 82 51W
Bellevue, Tex. **65** 33 38N 98 1W
Bellevue, Wash. **67** 47 37N 122 12W
Bellflower, Ill. **35** 40 20N 88 32W
Bellflower, Mo. **46** 39 0N 91 21W
Bellingham, Mass. **42** 42 5N 71 28W
Bellingham, Minn. **44** 45 8N 96 17W
Bellingham, Wash. **67** 48 46N 122 29W
Bellmawr **51** 39 52N 75 5W
Bellmead **65** 31 35N 97 6W
Bellows Falls **50** 43 8N 72 27W
Bellport **53** 40 46N 72 56W
Bells, Tenn. **62** 35 43N 89 5W
Bells, Tex. **65** 33 37N 96 25W
Belltown **41** 38 45N 75 11W
Bellview **52** 34 49N 103 7W
Bellville, Ga. **32** 32 9N 81 59W
Bellville, Tex. **65** 29 57N 96 15W
Bellvue **30** 40 38N 105 10W
Bellwood, La. **39** 31 32N 93 12W
Bellwood, Nebr. **48** 41 21N 97 14W
Bellwood, Pa. **59** 40 36N 78 20W
Belmar **51** 40 11N 74 2W
Belmond **37** 42 51N 93 37W
Belmont, Kans. **38** 37 32N 97 56W
Belmont, Miss. **45** 34 31N 88 13W
Belmont, N.C. **54** 35 14N 81 2W
Belmont, N.H. **50** 43 27N 71 29W
Belmont, N.Y. **53** 42 14N 78 2W
Belmont, Wis. **69** 42 44N 90 20W
Belmont County ◇ **56** 40 1N 81 4W
Belmore **56** 41 9N 83 56W
Beloit, Kans. **38** 39 28N 98 6W
Beloit, Wis. **69** 42 31N 89 2W
Belpre, Kans. **38** 37 57N 99 6W
Belpre, Ohio **56** 39 17N 81 34W
Belt **47** 47 23N 110 55W
Belton, Mo. **46** 38 49N 94 32W
Belton, S.C. **60** 34 31N 82 30W
Belton, Tex. **65** 31 3N 97 28W
Beltrami **44** 47 33N 96 32W
Beltrami County ◇ **44** 47 45N 94 50W
Beltsville **41** 39 2N 76 54W
Belvidere, Ill. **35** 42 15N 88 50W
Belvidere, N.J. **51** 40 50N 75 5W
Belvidere, Nebr. **48** 40 15N 97 33W
Belvidere, S. Dak. **61** 43 50N 101 16W
Belvidere Mt. **50** 44 46N 72 33W
Belview **44** 44 36N 95 20W
Belvue **38** 39 13N 96 11W
Belzoni **45** 33 11N 90 29W
Bement **35** 39 55N 88 34W
Bemidji **44** 47 28N 94 53W
Bemis, Tenn. **62** 35 35N 88 49W
Bemis, W. Va. **68** 38 49N 79 45W
Ben Hill County ◇ **32** 31 45N 83 10W
Ben Lomond, Ark. **27** 33 50N 94 7W
Ben Lomond, Calif. **28** 37 5N 122 5W
Bena **44** 47 21N 94 12W
Benavides **64** 27 36N 98 25W
Benbrook **65** 32 41N 97 28W

Name	Page	Lat.	Long.
Benchley	65	30 45N	96 27W
Bend	58	44 4N	121 19W
Benedict, Kans.	38	37 38N	95 45W
Benedict, Md.	41	38 31N	76 41W
Benedict, Nebr.	48	41 0N	97 36W
Benevolence	32	31 53N	84 44W
Benewah County ◇	34	47 5N	116 35W
Benham	63	36 58N	82 57W
Benjamin	65	33 35N	99 48W
Benkelman	48	40 3N	101 32W
Benld	35	39 6N	89 48W
Bennet	48	40 41N	96 30W
Bennett, Colo.	30	39 46N	104 26W
Bennett, Iowa	37	41 43N	90 59W
Bennett, N.C.	54	35 34N	79 33W
Bennett, N. Mex.	52	32 4N	103 12W
Bennett County ◇	61	43 5N	101 45W
Bennettsville	60	34 37N	79 41W
Bennington, Idaho	34	42 24N	111 19W
Bennington, Kans.	38	39 2N	97 36W
Bennington, N.H.	50	43 0N	71 55W
Bennington, Nebr.	48	41 22N	96 9W
Bennington, Okla.	57	34 0N	96 2W
Bennington, Vt.	50	42 53N	73 12W
Bennington County ◇	50	43 0N	73 10W
Benoit	45	33 39N	91 1W
Bens Run	68	39 28N	81 6W
Benson, Ariz.	26	31 58N	110 18W
Benson, Ill.	35	40 51N	89 7W
Benson, La.	39	31 52N	93 42W
Benson, Minn.	44	45 19N	95 36W
Benson, N.C.	54	35 23N	78 33W
Benson, Vt.	50	43 42N	73 18W
Benson County ◇	55	48 5N	99 25W
Bent County ◇	30	38 0N	103 0W
Bentley	38	37 54N	97 31W
Bentleyville	59	40 7N	80 1W
Benton, Ark.	27	34 34N	92 35W
Benton, Calif.	28	37 48N	118 32W
Benton, Ill.	35	38 0N	88 55W
Benton, Iowa	37	40 42N	94 22W
Benton, Kans.	38	37 47N	97 6W
Benton, Ky.	62	36 52N	88 21W
Benton, La.	39	32 42N	93 44W
Benton, Miss.	45	32 50N	90 16W
Benton, Mo.	46	37 6N	89 34W
Benton, N.H.	50	44 8N	71 55W
Benton, Pa.	59	41 12N	76 23W
Benton, Tenn.	63	35 10N	84 39W
Benton, Wis.	69	42 34N	90 23W
Benton City, Mo.	46	39 8N	91 46W
Benton City, Wash.	67	46 16N	119 29W
Benton County ◇, Ark.	27	36 22N	94 13W
Benton County ◇, Ind.	36	40 35N	87 20W
Benton County ◇, Iowa	37	42 0N	92 0W
Benton County ◇, Minn.	44	45 45N	94 0W
Benton County ◇, Miss.	45	34 50N	89 11W
Benton County ◇, Mo.	46	38 20N	93 15W
Benton County ◇, Oreg.	58	44 30N	123 20W
Benton County ◇, Tenn.	62	36 4N	88 6W
Benton County ◇, Wash.	67	46 25N	119 25W
Benton Harbor	43	42 6N	86 27W
Benton Heights	43	42 7N	86 24W
Benton L.	47	47 40N	111 20W
Benton Ridge	56	41 0N	83 48W
Bentonia	45	32 38N	90 22W
Bentonite Spur	70	44 52N	104 9W
Bentonville, Ark.	27	36 22N	94 13W
Bentonville, Va.	68	38 50N	78 19W
Benwood	68	40 1N	80 44W
Benzie County ◇	43	44 40N	86 0W
Beowawe	49	40 35N	116 29W
Berclair	65	28 32N	97 36W
Berea, Ky.	63	37 34N	84 17W
Berea, Nebr.	48	42 13N	102 59W
Berea, S.C.	60	34 50N	82 25W
Beresford	61	43 5N	96 47W
Bergen	53	43 5N	77 57W
Bergen County ◇	51	41 0N	74 10W
Bergenfield	51	40 54N	73 58W
Berger	46	38 41N	91 20W
Bergland	43	46 36N	89 34W
Bergoo	68	38 29N	80 18W
Bering Glacier	25	60 20N	143 30W
Bering Strait	25	65 30N	169 0W
Berino	52	32 4N	106 37W
Berkeley	28	37 52N	122 16W
Berkeley County ◇, S.C.	60	33 15N	80 0W
Berkeley County ◇, W. Va.	68	39 27N	77 58W
Berkeley Springs	68	39 38N	78 14W
Berks County ◇	59	40 25N	76 0W
Berkshire County ◇	42	42 25N	73 15W
Berkshire Hills	42	42 20N	73 10W
Berlin, Ga.	32	31 4N	83 37W
Berlin, Md.	41	38 20N	75 13W
Berlin, N. Dak.	55	46 23N	98 29W
Berlin, N.H.	50	44 28N	71 11W
Berlin, N.J.	51	39 48N	74 56W
Berlin, Okla.	57	35 27N	99 36W
Berlin, Pa.	59	39 55N	78 57W
Berlin, Wis.	69	43 58N	88 57W
Berlin Heights	56	41 20N	82 30W
Berlin L.	56	41 3N	81 0W
Bern	38	39 58N	95 58W
Bernalillo	52	35 18N	106 33W
Bernalillo County ◇	52	35 0N	106 45W
Bernardston	42	42 40N	72 33W
Bernardsville	51	40 43N	74 34W
Berne	36	40 39N	84 57W
Bernice, La.	39	32 49N	92 39W
Bernice, Okla.	57	36 34N	94 57W
Bernie	46	36 40N	89 58W
Berrien County ◇, Ga.	32	31 15N	83 10W
Berrien County ◇, Mich.	43	42 0N	86 25W
Berrien Springs	43	41 57N	86 20W
Berry, Ala.	24	33 40N	87 36W
Berry, Ky.	63	38 31N	84 23W
Berrydale	31	30 53N	87 3W
Berryessa L.	28	38 31N	122 6W
Berryville, Ark.	27	36 22N	93 34W
Berryville, Va.	68	39 9N	77 59W
Bertha	44	46 16N	95 4W
Berthold	55	48 19N	101 44W
Berthoud	30	40 19N	105 5W
Berthoud Pass	30	39 48N	105 47W
Bertie County ◇	54	36 0N	77 0W
Bertram, Iowa	37	41 57N	91 32W
Bertram, Tex.	65	30 45N	98 3W
Bertrand, Mich.	43	41 47N	86 16W
Bertrand, Mo.	46	36 55N	89 27W
Bertrand, Nebr.	48	40 32N	99 38W
Berwick, Maine	40	43 16N	70 52W
Berwick, N. Dak.	55	48 22N	100 15W
Berwick, Pa.	59	41 3N	76 14W
Berwyn, Ill.	35	41 51N	87 47W
Berwyn, Nebr.	48	41 21N	99 30W
Beryl	66	37 54N	113 40W
Bessemer, Ala.	24	33 24N	86 58W
Bessemer, Mich.	43	46 29N	90 3W
Bessemer, Pa.	59	40 59N	80 30W
Bessemer City	54	35 17N	81 17W
Bessie	57	35 23N	98 59W
Best	64	31 13N	101 37W
Bethalto	35	38 55N	90 2W
Bethany, Ill.	35	39 39N	88 45W
Bethany, Mo.	46	40 16N	94 2W
Bethany, Okla.	57	35 31N	97 38W
Bethany Beach	41	38 32N	75 5W
Bethel, Alaska	25	60 48N	161 45W
Bethel, Conn.	42	41 22N	73 25W
Bethel, Maine	40	44 25N	70 47W
Bethel, Minn.	44	45 24N	93 16W
Bethel, N.C.	54	35 48N	77 22W
Bethel, Ohio	56	38 58N	84 5W
Bethel, Okla.	57	34 22N	94 51W
Bethel, Pa.	59	40 28N	76 18W
Bethel, Vt.	50	43 50N	72 38W
Bethel ◇	25	60 15N	163 0W
Bethel Acres	57	35 22N	97 3W
Bethel Park	59	40 20N	80 1W
Bethel Springs	62	35 14N	88 36W
Bethera	60	33 12N	79 47W
Bethesda, Md.	41	38 59N	77 6W
Bethesda, N.C.	54	35 57N	78 50W
Bethesda, Ohio	56	40 1N	81 4W
Bethlehem, Conn.	42	41 38N	73 13W
Bethlehem, Md.	41	38 45N	75 57W
Bethlehem, N.H.	50	44 17N	71 41W
Bethlehem, Pa.	59	40 37N	75 23W
Bethpage	53	40 44N	73 30W
Bethune, Colo.	30	39 18N	102 26W
Bethune, S.C.	60	34 25N	80 21W
Bettendorf	37	41 32N	90 30W
Betterton	41	39 22N	76 4W
Beulah, Colo.	30	38 5N	104 59W
Beulah, Mich.	43	44 38N	86 6W
Beulah, N. Dak.	55	47 16N	101 47W
Beulahville	54	34 55N	77 46W
Beverly, Kans.	38	39 1N	97 58W
Beverly, Mass.	42	42 33N	70 53W
Beverly, W. Va.	68	38 51N	79 53W
Beverly, Wash.	67	46 50N	119 56W
Beverly Beach	41	38 53N	76 31W
Beverly Hills	29	34 4N	118 25W
Bevier	46	39 45N	92 34W
Bexar	24	34 11N	88 9W
Bexar County ◇	65	29 25N	98 30W
Bexley	56	39 58N	82 56W
Bibb County ◇, Ala.	24	32 57N	87 8W
Bibb County ◇, Ga.	32	32 50N	83 45W
Bicknell, Ind.	36	38 47N	87 19W
Bicknell, Utah	66	38 20N	111 33W
Biddeford	40	43 30N	70 28W
Bieber	28	41 7N	121 8W
Bienville	39	32 22N	92 59W
Bienville National Forest	45	32 10N	89 25W
Bienville Parish ◇	39	32 20N	93 0W
Big →	46	38 28N	90 37W
Big Baldy	34	44 47N	115 13W
Big Bar	28	40 45N	123 15W
Big Bay	43	46 49N	87 44W
Big Bay de Noc	43	45 45N	86 40W
Big Bear City	29	34 16N	116 51W
Big Bear Lake	29	34 15N	116 56W
Big Belt Mts.	47	46 30N	111 25W
Big Bend, Calif.	28	41 1N	121 55W
Big Bend, La.	39	31 5N	91 48W
Big Bend Dam	61	44 1N	99 23W
Big Bend National Park	64	29 20N	103 5W
Big Black →	45	32 3N	91 4W
Big Blue →	38	39 35N	96 34W
Big Bow	38	37 34N	101 34W
Big Cabin	57	36 32N	95 14W
Big Canyon →	64	29 45N	101 48W
Big Chino Wash →	26	34 52N	112 28W
Big Clifty	62	37 33N	86 9W
Big Cr. →	39	32 10N	91 53W
Big Creek	34	45 8N	115 20W
Big Creek L.	24	30 43N	88 20W
Big Cypress Indian Reservation	31	26 20N	81 10W
Big Cypress National Preserve	31	26 0N	81 10W
Big Cypress Swamp	31	26 15N	81 30W
Big Darby →	56	39 37N	82 58W
Big Delta	25	64 10N	145 51W
Big Eau Pleine Reservoir	69	44 44N	89 46W
Big Falls, Minn.	44	48 12N	93 48W
Big Falls, Wis.	69	44 37N	89 1W
Big Flat	27	36 1N	92 24W
Big Fork →	44	48 31N	93 43W
Big Hatchet Peak	52	31 38N	108 24W
Big Hole →	47	45 34N	112 20W
Big Horn Basin	70	44 15N	108 0W
Big Horn County ◇, Mont.	47	45 25N	107 45W
Big Horn County ◇, Wyo.	70	44 45N	108 0W
Big Island	68	37 32N	79 22W
Big L., Calif.	28	41 7N	121 25W
Big L., Maine	40	45 11N	67 41W
Big L., Oreg.	58	42 8N	120 2W
Big Lake, Alaska	25	67 30N	149 27W
Big Lake, Minn.	44	45 20N	93 45W
Big Lake, Tex.	64	31 12N	101 28W
Big Lookout Mt.	58	44 36N	117 17W
Big Lost →	34	43 50N	112 44W
Big Muddy Cr. →	47	48 8N	104 36W
Big Nemaha →	48	40 1N	95 32W
Big Otter →	68	37 7N	79 23W
Big Pine, Calif.	29	37 10N	118 17W
Big Pine, Fla.	31	24 40N	81 21W
Big Piney	70	42 32N	110 7W
Big Rapids	43	43 42N	85 29W
Big Rib →	69	44 56N	89 41W
Big Rock	62	36 35N	87 46W
Big Sable Pt.	43	44 3N	86 1W
Big Sage Reservoir	28	41 35N	120 38W
Big Sandy, Mont.	47	48 11N	110 7W
Big Sandy, Tenn.	62	36 14N	88 5W
Big Sandy, Tex.	65	32 35N	95 7W
Big Sandy →	26	34 19N	113 31W
Big Sandy Cr. →, Colo.	30	38 7N	102 29W
Big Sandy Cr. →, Mont.	47	48 34N	109 48W
Big Sandy Cr. →, Nebr.	48	40 13N	97 18W
Big Sandy L.	44	46 46N	93 17W
Big Sandy Reservoir	70	42 15N	109 26W
Big Satilla →	32	31 27N	82 3W
Big Sheep Mt.	47	47 10N	105 40W
Big Sioux →	61	42 29N	96 27W
Big Smoky Valley	49	38 40N	117 10W
Big Snowy Mts.	47	46 45N	109 30W
Big Southern Butte	34	43 23N	113 1W
Big Spring, Ky.	62	37 48N	86 9W
Big Spring, Tex.	64	32 15N	101 28W
Big Springs	48	41 4N	102 5W
Big Stone City	61	45 18N	96 28W
Big Stone County ◇	44	45 25N	96 15W
Big Stone Gap	68	36 52N	82 47W
Big Sur	28	36 15N	121 48W
Big Swamp →	54	34 28N	78 57W
Big Timber	47	45 50N	109 57W
Big Wells	65	28 34N	99 34W
Big Wood →	34	42 52N	114 54W
Bigelow, Ark.	27	35 0N	92 38W
Bigelow, Minn.	44	43 30N	95 42W
Bigfork, Minn.	44	47 45N	93 39W
Bigfork, Mont.	47	48 4N	114 4W
Biggs, Calif.	28	39 25N	121 43W
Biggs, Oreg.	58	45 40N	120 50W
Biggsville	35	40 51N	90 52W
Bighorn	47	46 10N	107 27W
Bighorn →	47	46 10N	107 28W
Bighorn Canyon Nat. Rec. Area	47	45 10N	108 0W
Bighorn L.	70	44 55N	108 15W
Bighorn Mts.	70	44 25N	107 0W
Bighorn National Forest	70	44 50N	107 25W
Biglerville	59	39 56N	77 15W
Bigpoint	45	30 35N	88 29W
Bijou Cr. →	30	40 17N	104 0W
Bilk Creek Mts.	49	41 50N	118 27W
Bill	70	43 14N	105 16W
Bill Williams →	26	34 18N	114 4W
Bill Williams Mts.	26	35 12N	112 12W
Billerica	42	42 34N	71 16W
Billings, Mo.	46	37 4N	93 33W
Billings, Mont.	47	45 47N	108 30W
Billings, Okla.	57	36 32N	97 27W
Billings County ◇	55	47 0N	103 15W
Billings Heights	47	45 50N	108 28W
Billy Chinook, L.	58	44 33N	121 20W
Biloxi	45	30 24N	88 53W
Biltmore Forest	54	35 34N	82 33W
Binford	55	47 34N	98 21W
Binger	57	35 18N	98 21W
Bingham, Maine	40	45 3N	69 53W
Bingham, N. Mex.	52	33 55N	106 21W
Bingham, Nebr.	48	42 1N	102 5W
Bingham Canyon	66	40 32N	112 9W
Bingham County ◇	34	43 15N	112 30W
Binghamton	53	42 6N	75 55W
Biola	29	36 48N	120 1W
Birch →	34	43 51N	112 43W
Birch L.	44	47 45N	91 51W
Birch Res.	57	36 30N	96 27W
Birch Run	43	43 15N	83 48W
Birch Tree	46	36 59N	91 30W
Birchwood	69	45 40N	91 33W
Bird City	38	39 45N	101 32W
Bird Island	44	44 46N	94 54W
Birds	35	38 50N	87 40W
Birdseye	36	38 19N	86 42W
Birdsville	41	38 54N	76 36W
Birmingham, Ala.	24	33 31N	86 48W
Birmingham, Iowa	37	40 53N	91 57W
Birnamwood	69	44 56N	89 13W
Bisbee, Ariz.	26	31 27N	109 55W
Bisbee, N. Dak.	55	48 37N	99 23W
Biscay	44	44 50N	94 16W
Biscayne National Park	31	25 25N	80 12W
Biscoe, Ark.	27	34 49N	91 25W
Biscoe, N.C.	54	35 22N	79 47W
Bishop, Calif.	29	37 22N	118 24W
Bishop, Ga.	32	33 49N	83 26W
Bishop, Tex.	64	27 35N	97 48W
Bishop Creek Reservoir	49	41 15N	114 55W
Bishops Head	41	38 16N	76 5W
Bishopville, Md.	41	38 22N	75 12W
Bishopville, S.C.	60	34 13N	80 15W
Bismarck, Ark.	27	34 19N	93 10W
Bismarck, Ill.	35	40 16N	87 37W
Bismarck, Mo.	46	37 46N	90 38W
Bismarck, N. Dak.	55	46 48N	100 47W
Bison, Kans.	38	38 31N	99 12W
Bison, Okla.	57	36 12N	97 53W
Bison, S. Dak.	61	45 31N	102 28W
Bistineau, L.	39	32 20N	93 25W
Bitely	43	43 45N	85 52W
Bithlo	31	28 33N	81 6W
Bitter Cr. →, Utah	66	39 59N	109 19W
Bitter Cr. →, Wyo.	70	41 31N	109 27W
Bitter Creek	70	41 33N	108 33W
Bitter L.	61	45 17N	97 19W
Bitterroot →	47	46 52N	114 7W
Bitterroot National Forest	34	45 40N	114 30W
Bitterroot Range	34	46 0N	114 20W
Bittinger	41	39 37N	79 14W
Biwabik	44	47 32N	92 21W
Bixby, Mo.	46	37 40N	91 7W
Bixby, Okla.	57	35 57N	95 53W
Black →, Alaska	25	66 42N	144 42W
Black →, Ariz.	26	33 44N	110 13W
Black →, Ark.	27	35 38N	91 20W
Black →, La.	39	31 16N	91 50W
Black →, Cheboygan, Mich.	43	45 39N	84 31W
Black →, St. Clair, Mich.	43	42 59N	82 27W
Black →, N.C.	54	34 35N	78 16W
Black →, N.Y.	53	43 59N	76 4W
Black →, S.C.	60	33 24N	79 15W
Black →, Caledonia, Vt.	50	44 55N	72 13W
Black →, Windsor, Vt.	50	43 16N	72 27W
Black →, Wis.	69	43 57N	91 22W
Black Bear Cr. →	57	36 25N	96 38W
Black Butte Reservoir	28	39 49N	122 20W
Black Canyon City	26	34 3N	112 5W

Black Canyon of the Gunnison National Monument **30** 38 40N 107 35W
Black Cr. →, Ariz. **26** 35 16N 109 14W
Black Cr. →, Miss. **45** 30 39N 88 39W
Black Creek **69** 44 29N 88 27W
Black Diamond **67** 47 19N 122 0W
Black Earth **69** 43 8N 89 45W
Black Forest **30** 39 0N 104 43W
Black Hawk **61** 44 9N 103 19W
Black Hawk County ◇ **37** 42 25N 92 20W
Black Hills **61** 44 0N 103 45W
Black Hills National Forest **61** 44 10N 103 50W
Black Kettle National Grassland **57** 35 45N 99 45W
Black L., Mich. **43** 45 28N 84 16W
Black L., N.Y. **53** 44 31N 75 36W
Black Mesa, Ariz. **26** 36 30N 110 15W
Black Mesa, Okla. **57** 36 58N 102 58W
Black Mountain **54** 35 37N 82 19W
Black Mt., Ky. **63** 36 54N 82 54W
Black Mt., Oreg. **58** 45 13N 119 17W
Black Mt., Tex. **64** 29 38N 100 20W
Black Mts. **26** 35 30N 114 30W
Black Pine Pk. **34** 42 8N 113 8W
Black Range **52** 33 15N 107 50W
Black River **53** 44 1N 75 48W
Black River Falls **69** 44 18N 90 51W
Black Rock, Ark. **27** 36 7N 91 6W
Black Rock, N. Mex. **52** 35 5N 108 47W
Black Rock Desert **49** 41 10N 118 50W
Black Rock Range **49** 41 20N 119 8W
Black Springs **49** 39 37N 119 51W
Black Squirrel Cr. → **30** 38 14N 104 21W
Black Warrior → **24** 32 32N 87 51W
Blackbird **41** 39 21N 75 40W
Blackburn, Mo. **46** 39 6N 93 29W
Blackburn, Okla. **57** 36 23N 96 38W
Blackburn, Mt. **25** 61 44N 143 26W
Blackduck **44** 47 44N 94 33W
Blackfeet Indian Reservation **47** 48 45N 113 0W
Blackfoot **34** 43 11N 112 21W
Blackfoot →, Idaho **34** 43 8N 112 30W
Blackfoot →, Mont. **47** 46 52N 113 53W
Blackfoot River Reservoir **34** 43 0N 111 43W
Blackford **62** 37 27N 87 56W
Blackford County ◇ **36** 40 30N 85 20W
Blackhall Mt. **70** 41 2N 106 41W
Blackman **31** 30 56N 86 38W
Blacks Fork → **70** 41 25N 109 37W
Blacksburg, S.C. **60** 35 7N 81 31W
Blacksburg, Va. **68** 37 14N 80 25W
Blackshear **32** 31 18N 82 14W
Blackshear L. **32** 31 51N 83 56W
Blackstock **60** 34 34N 81 8W
Blackstone, Mass. **42** 42 1N 71 30W
Blackstone, Va. **68** 37 4N 78 0W
Blackville **60** 33 22N 81 16W
Blackwater **46** 38 59N 92 59W
Blackwater →, Fla. **31** 30 36N 87 2W
Blackwater →, Md. **41** 38 21N 76 1W
Blackwater →, Tex. **64** 33 40N 100 47W
Blackwell, Okla. **57** 36 48N 97 17W
Blackwell, Tex. **64** 32 5N 100 19W
Blackwood **51** 39 48N 75 4W
Bladen **48** 40 19N 98 36W
Bladen County ◇ **54** 34 30N 78 30W
Bladenboro **54** 34 33N 78 48W
Bladsell **53** 42 48N 78 50W
Blain **59** 40 20N 77 31W
Blaine, Minn. **44** 45 10N 93 13W
Blaine, Wash. **67** 48 59N 122 45W
Blaine County ◇, Idaho **34** 43 30N 114 0W
Blaine County ◇, Mont. **47** 48 20N 109 0W
Blaine County ◇, Nebr. **48** 42 0N 100 0W
Blaine County ◇, Okla. **57** 35 50N 98 25W
Blair, Nebr. **48** 41 33N 96 8W
Blair, Okla. **57** 34 47N 99 20W
Blair, Wis. **69** 44 18N 91 14W
Blair County ◇ **59** 40 30N 78 20W
Blairs **68** 36 41N 79 23W
Blairsburg **37** 42 29N 93 39W
Blairsden **28** 39 47N 120 37W
Blairstown, Iowa **37** 41 55N 92 5W
Blairstown, Mo. **46** 38 34N 93 58W
Blairstown, N.J. **51** 40 59N 74 57W
Blairsville, Ga. **32** 34 53N 83 58W
Blairsville, Pa. **59** 40 26N 79 16W
Blake Pt. **43** 48 11N 88 25W
Blakely, Ga. **32** 31 23N 84 56W
Blakely, Pa. **59** 41 28N 75 37W
Blakeman **38** 39 49N 101 7W
Blakesburg **37** 40 58N 92 38W
Blakeslee **56** 41 32N 84 44W
Blalock **58** 45 42N 120 22W
Blanca **30** 37 27N 105 31W
Blanca, Sierra **64** 31 15N 105 26W
Blanca Peak **30** 37 35N 105 29W
Blanchard, Idaho **34** 48 1N 116 59W
Blanchard, Iowa **37** 40 35N 95 13W
Blanchard, N. Dak. **55** 47 21N 97 13W
Blanchard, Okla. **57** 35 8N 97 39W
Blanchard, Wash. **67** 48 36N 122 25W
Blanchard → **56** 41 2N 84 18W
Blanchardville **69** 42 49N 89 52W
Blanchester **56** 39 17N 83 59W
Blanco, N. Mex. **52** 36 43N 107 50W
Blanco, Okla. **57** 34 45N 95 46W
Blanco, Tex. **65** 30 6N 98 25W
Blanco → **65** 29 51N 97 55W
Blanco, C. **58** 42 51N 124 34W
Blanco County ◇ **65** 30 17N 98 25W
Bland, Mo. **46** 38 18N 91 38W
Bland, Va. **68** 37 6N 81 7W
Bland County ◇ **68** 37 6N 81 7W
Blandford **42** 42 11N 72 56W
Blanding **66** 37 37N 109 29W
Blandinsville **35** 40 33N 90 52W
Blaney Park **43** 46 9N 85 55W
Blanket **65** 31 49N 98 47W
Bleckley County ◇ **32** 32 25N 83 15W
Bledsoe **64** 33 38N 103 1W
Bledsoe County ◇ **63** 35 36N 85 11W
Blencoe **37** 41 56N 96 5W
Blewett Falls L. **54** 35 3N 79 54W
Bliss **34** 42 56N 114 57W
Blissfield, Mich. **43** 41 50N 83 52W
Blissfield, Ohio **56** 40 24N 81 58W
Blitchton **32** 32 12N 81 26W
Block I. **42** 41 11N 71 35W
Block Island Sd. **42** 41 15N 71 40W
Blocker **57** 35 4N 95 34W
Blockton **37** 40 37N 94 29W
Blodgett **46** 37 0N 89 32W
Bloodsworth I. **41** 38 10N 76 3W
Bloomer **69** 45 6N 91 29W
Bloomfield, Ind. **36** 39 1N 86 57W
Bloomfield, Iowa **37** 40 45N 92 25W
Bloomfield, Ky. **63** 37 55N 85 19W
Bloomfield, Mo. **46** 36 53N 89 56W
Bloomfield, N.J. **51** 40 48N 74 12W
Bloomfield, N. Mex. **52** 36 43N 107 59W
Bloomfield, Nebr. **48** 42 36N 97 39W
Blooming Grove **65** 32 6N 96 43W
Blooming Prairie **44** 43 52N 93 3W
Bloomingburg **56** 39 36N 83 24W
Bloomingdale **56** 36 34N 82 32W
Bloomington, Idaho **34** 42 11N 111 24W
Bloomington, Ill. **35** 40 28N 89 0W
Bloomington, Ind. **36** 39 10N 86 32W
Bloomington, Minn. **44** 44 50N 93 17W
Bloomington, Tex. **65** 28 39N 96 54W
Bloomington, Wis. **69** 42 53N 90 55W
Bloomsburg **59** 41 0N 76 27W
Bloomsdale **46** 38 1N 90 13W
Bloomville **56** 41 3N 83 1W
Blossburg **59** 41 41N 77 4W
Blossom **65** 33 40N 95 23W
Blount County ◇, Ala. **24** 33 57N 86 28W
Blount County ◇, Tenn. **63** 35 46N 83 58W
Blountstown **31** 30 27N 85 3W
Blountsville **24** 34 5N 86 35W
Blountville **63** 36 32N 82 19W
Bloxom **68** 37 50N 75 38W
Blue → **36** 38 11N 86 19W
Blue Cypress L. **31** 27 44N 80 45W
Blue Diamond **49** 36 3N 115 24W
Blue Earth **44** 43 38N 94 6W
Blue Earth County ◇ **44** 44 5N 94 0W
Blue Eye **46** 36 30N 93 24W
Blue Hill, Maine **40** 44 25N 68 35W
Blue Hill, Nebr. **48** 40 20N 98 27W
Blue Knob **59** 40 17N 78 34W
Blue Lake **28** 40 53N 123 59W
Blue Mesa Reservoir **30** 38 28N 107 20W
Blue Mound, Ill. **35** 39 42N 89 7W
Blue Mound, Kans. **38** 38 5N 95 0W
Blue Mountain, Colo. **30** 40 15N 108 52W
Blue Mountain, Miss. **45** 34 40N 89 2W
Blue Mountain L. **27** 35 2N 93 53W
Blue Mt., Ark. **27** 34 41N 94 3W
Blue Mt., N.H. **50** 44 47N 71 28W
Blue Mt., Pa. **59** 40 30N 76 20W
Blue Mts., Maine **40** 44 50N 70 35W
Blue Mts., Oreg. **58** 45 0N 118 20W
Blue Rapids **38** 39 41N 96 39W
Blue Ridge, Ga. **32** 34 52N 84 20W
Blue Ridge, Va. **68** 36 40N 80 50W
Blue Ridge L. **32** 34 53N 84 17W
Blue River, Oreg. **58** 44 9N 122 20W
Blue River, Wis. **69** 43 11N 90 34W
Blue Springs, Mo. **46** 39 1N 94 17W
Blue Springs, Nebr. **48** 40 9N 96 40W
Blueberry **69** 46 35N 91 55W
Bluefield, Va. **68** 37 15N 81 17W
Bluefield, W. Va. **68** 37 16N 81 13W
Bluejacket **57** 36 48N 95 4W
Bluejoint L. **58** 42 42N 119 38W
Bluestone L. **68** 37 38N 80 53W
Bluewater **52** 35 15N 107 59W
Bluff **66** 37 17N 109 33W
Bluff City, Ark. **27** 33 43N 93 8W
Bluff City, Kans. **38** 37 5N 97 53W
Bluff City, Tenn. **63** 36 28N 82 16W
Bluff Park **24** 33 27N 86 47W
Bluffs **35** 39 45N 90 32W
Bluffton, Ark. **27** 34 54N 93 36W
Bluffton, Ga. **32** 31 31N 84 52W
Bluffton, Ind. **36** 40 44N 85 11W
Bluffton, Minn. **44** 46 28N 95 14W
Bluffton, Ohio **56** 40 54N 83 54W
Bluffton, S.C. **60** 32 14N 80 52W
Bluford **35** 38 20N 88 45W
Blunt **61** 44 31N 99 59W
Bly **58** 42 24N 121 3W
Blyn **67** 48 1N 123 0W
Blythe, Calif. **29** 33 37N 114 36W
Blythe, Ga. **32** 33 17N 82 12W
Blytheville **27** 35 56N 89 55W
Blythewood **60** 34 13N 80 58W
Boardman, Ohio **56** 41 2N 80 40W
Boardman, Oreg. **58** 45 51N 119 43W
Boaz, Ala. **24** 34 12N 86 10W
Boaz, Wis. **69** 43 20N 90 32W
Bobtown **59** 39 46N 79 59W
Boca Grande **31** 26 45N 82 16W
Boca Raton **31** 26 21N 80 5W
Bock **44** 45 47N 93 33W
Bodcaw **27** 33 33N 93 25W
Bode **37** 42 52N 94 17W
Bodega Bay **28** 38 20N 123 3W
Boelus **48** 41 5N 98 43W
Boerne **65** 29 47N 98 44W
Boeuf → **39** 30 36N 92 3W
Bogalusa **39** 30 47N 89 52W
Bogard **46** 39 27N 93 32W
Bogata **65** 33 28N 95 13W
Bogota **62** 36 10N 89 26W
Bogue, Kans. **38** 39 22N 99 41W
Bogue, N.C. **54** 34 42N 77 2W
Bogue Chitto **45** 31 26N 90 27W
Bogue Chitto → **39** 30 34N 89 50W
Bogue Hama Cr. → **45** 31 10N 88 55W
Boiling Springs **54** 35 15N 81 40W
Bois Blanc I. **43** 45 46N 84 27W
Bois D'Arc **46** 37 16N 93 30W
Bois de Sioux → **55** 46 16N 96 36W
Boise **34** 43 37N 116 13W
Boise → **34** 43 49N 117 1W
Boise City **57** 36 44N 102 31W
Boise County ◇ **34** 44 0N 115 45W
Boise National Forest **34** 44 5N 115 30W
Boistfort Pk. **67** 46 29N 123 12W
Bokchito **57** 34 1N 96 9W
Bokoshe **57** 35 11N 94 47W
Bolckow **46** 40 7N 94 50W
Bold Spring **62** 35 58N 87 41W
Boles **27** 34 47N 94 3W
Boley **57** 35 29N 96 29W
Boligee **24** 32 45N 88 2W
Boling **65** 29 16N 95 57W
Bolingbroke **32** 32 57N 83 48W
Bolinger **39** 32 57N 93 41W
Bolivar, Mo. **46** 37 37N 93 25W
Bolivar, N.Y. **53** 42 4N 78 10W
Bolivar, Tenn. **62** 35 12N 89 0W
Bolivar, Mt. **58** 42 51N 123 56W
Bolivar County ◇ **45** 33 50N 90 43W
Bolivar Peninsula **65** 29 27N 94 39W
Bolivia **54** 34 4N 78 9W
Bolling **24** 31 43N 86 42W
Bollinger County ◇ **46** 37 20N 90 0W
Bolton, Miss. **45** 32 21N 90 28W
Bolton, N.C. **54** 34 20N 78 25W
Boma **63** 36 8N 85 41W
Bomarton **65** 33 31N 99 26W
Bombay **53** 44 56N 74 34W
Bomoseen, L. **50** 43 39N 73 13W
Bon Air, Tenn. **63** 35 57N 85 22W
Bon Air, Va. **68** 37 31N 77 34W
Bon Homme County ◇ **61** 43 0N 97 50W
Bon Secour B. **24** 30 15N 87 58W
Bonaire **32** 32 33N 83 36W
Bonanza, Colo. **30** 38 18N 106 8W
Bonanza, Oreg. **58** 42 12N 121 24W
Bonanza, Utah **66** 40 1N 109 11W
Bonanza Pk. **67** 48 14N 120 52W
Bonaparte **37** 40 42N 91 48W
Bonaparte, Mt. **67** 48 45N 119 8W
Bond, Colo. **30** 39 53N 106 42W
Bond, Miss. **45** 30 54N 89 10W
Bond County ◇ **35** 38 50N 89 25W
Bond Falls Flowage **43** 46 30N 89 15W
Bondurant, Iowa **37** 41 42N 93 28W
Bondurant, Ky. **62** 36 31N 89 19W
Bondville **35** 40 7N 88 22W
Bone Gap **35** 38 27N 88 0W
Bonetraill **55** 48 26N 103 51W
Bonham **65** 33 35N 96 11W
Bonifay **31** 30 47N 85 41W
Bonilla **61** 44 35N 98 30W
Bonita **39** 32 55N 91 40W
Bonita Springs **31** 26 21N 81 47W
Bonlee **54** 35 39N 79 25W
Bonne Terre **46** 37 55N 90 33W
Bonneau **60** 33 16N 79 58W
Bonner County ◇ **34** 48 20N 116 30W
Bonners Ferry **34** 48 42N 116 19W
Bonneville County ◇ **34** 43 20N 111 20W
Bonneville Dam **58** 45 33N 121 54W
Bonneville Pk. **34** 42 46N 112 8W
Bonneville Salt Flats **66** 40 45N 113 50W
Bonnie **35** 38 12N 88 54W
Bonnie Doone **54** 35 5N 78 57W
Bonnieville **63** 37 23N 85 54W
Bonny Reservoir **30** 39 37N 102 11W
Bono **27** 35 55N 90 48W
Book Cliffs **66** 39 20N 109 0W
Booker **64** 36 27N 100 32W
Boomer **68** 38 9N 81 17W
Boone, Colo. **30** 38 15N 104 15W
Boone, Iowa **37** 42 4N 93 53W
Boone, N.C. **54** 36 13N 81 41W
Boone, Nebr. **48** 41 38N 97 55W
Boone → **37** 42 19N 93 56W
Boone County ◇, Ark. **27** 36 14N 93 7W
Boone County ◇, Ill. **35** 42 20N 89 50W
Boone County ◇, Ind. **36** 40 5N 86 30W
Boone County ◇, Iowa **37** 42 0N 94 0W
Boone County ◇, Ky. **63** 38 55N 84 45W
Boone County ◇, Mo. **46** 39 0N 92 20W
Boone County ◇, Nebr. **48** 41 40N 98 0W
Boone County ◇, W. Va. **68** 38 4N 81 49W
Boones Mill **68** 37 7N 79 57W
Booneville, Ark. **27** 35 8N 93 55W
Booneville, Ky. **63** 37 29N 83 41W
Booneville, Miss. **45** 34 39N 88 34W
Boonsboro **41** 39 30N 77 39W
Boonton **51** 40 54N 74 25W
Boonville, Calif. **28** 39 1N 123 22W
Boonville, Ind. **36** 38 3N 87 16W
Boonville, Mo. **46** 38 58N 92 44W
Boonville, N.C. **54** 36 14N 80 43W
Boonville, N.Y. **53** 43 29N 75 20W
Boothbay Harbor **40** 43 51N 69 38W
Boothville **39** 29 20N 89 25W
Boqueron **71** 18 2N 67 10W
Boquillas **64** 29 11N 102 58W
Borah Peak **34** 44 8N 113 47W
Bordeaux **62** 36 12N 86 50W
Bordelonville **39** 31 6N 91 55W
Borden County ◇ **64** 32 46N 101 27W
Borden Springs **24** 33 56N 85 28W
Bordentown **51** 40 9N 74 43W
Bordulac **55** 47 23N 98 58W
Borger **64** 35 39N 101 24W
Borgne, L. **39** 30 1N 89 42W
Boron **29** 35 0N 117 39W
Borrego Springs **29** 33 15N 116 23W
Borup **44** 47 11N 96 30W
Boscawen **50** 43 19N 71 37W
Bosco **39** 32 17N 92 5W
Boscobel **69** 43 8N 90 42W
Bosler **70** 41 35N 105 42W
Bosque **52** 34 34N 106 47W
Bosque County ◇ **65** 31 56N 97 39W
Bossier City **39** 32 31N 93 44W
Bossier Parish ◇ **39** 32 42N 93 44W
Boston, Ga. **32** 30 47N 83 47W
Boston, Mass. **42** 42 22N 71 4W
Boston, Tex. **65** 33 27N 94 25W
Boston Bay **42** 42 22N 70 54W
Boston Mts. **27** 35 42N 93 15W
Bostwick, Fla. **31** 29 46N 81 38W
Bostwick, Ga. **32** 33 44N 83 31W
Boswell, Ind. **36** 40 31N 87 23W
Boswell, Okla. **57** 34 2N 95 52W
Boswell, Pa. **59** 40 10N 79 2W
Bosworth **46** 39 28N 93 20W
Botetourt County ◇ **68** 37 32N 79 41W
Botijas **71** 18 15N 66 22W
Botkins **56** 40 28N 84 11W
Bottineau **55** 48 50N 100 27W
Bottineau County ◇ **55** 48 55N 101 0W
Boulder, Colo. **30** 40 1N 105 17W
Boulder, Mont. **47** 46 14N 112 7W
Boulder, Utah **66** 37 55N 111 25W

Boulder, Wyo. **70** 42 45N 109 43W
Boulder City **49** 35 59N 114 50W
Boulder County ◇ **30** 40 10N 105 15W
Boulder Creek **28** 37 7N 122 7W
Boulder L. **70** 42 51N 109 40W
Boulder Peak **28** 41 35N 123 5W
Bound Brook **51** 40 34N 74 32W
Boundary **25** 64 4N 141 6W
Boundary County ◇ **34** 48 45N 116 25W
Boundary Peak **49** 37 51N 118 21W
Bountiful **66** 40 53N 111 53W
Bourbeuse → **46** 38 24N 90 53W
Bourbon, Ind. **36** 41 18N 86 7W
Bourbon, Mo. **46** 38 9N 91 15W
Bourbon County ◇, Kans. **38** 37 45N 94 45W
Bourbon County ◇, Ky. **63** 38 10N 84 15W
Bouse **26** 33 56N 114 0W
Bouse Wash → **26** 34 3N 114 20W
Bovey **44** 47 17N 93 25W
Bovill **34** 46 51N 116 24W
Bovina **64** 34 31N 102 53W
Bow, N.H. **50** 43 10N 71 34W
Bow, Wash. **67** 48 34N 122 24W
Bowbells **55** 48 48N 102 15W
Bowdle **61** 45 27N 99 39W
Bowdoin L. **47** 48 25N 107 41W
Bowdon, Ga. **32** 33 32N 85 15W
Bowdon, N. Dak. **55** 47 28N 99 43W
Bowdon Junction **32** 33 40N 85 9W
Bowen **35** 40 14N 91 4W
Bowens **41** 38 30N 76 8W
Bowers **41** 39 4N 75 24W
Bowersville, Ga. **32** 34 22N 83 5W
Bowersville, Ohio **56** 39 35N 83 44W
Bowie, Ariz. **26** 32 19N 109 29W
Bowie, Colo. **30** 38 55N 107 33W
Bowie, Md. **41** 39 0N 76 47W
Bowie, Tex. **65** 33 34N 97 51W
Bowie County ◇ **65** 33 27N 94 25W
Bowie Cr. → **45** 31 24N 89 27W
Bowlegs **57** 35 9N 96 40W
Bowling Green, Fla. **31** 27 38N 81 50W
Bowling Green, Ky. **62** 36 59N 86 27W
Bowling Green, Mo. **46** 39 21N 91 12W
Bowling Green, Ohio **56** 41 23N 83 39W
Bowling Green, Va. **68** 38 3N 77 21W
Bowlus **44** 45 49N 94 24W
Bowman, Ga. **32** 34 12N 83 2W
Bowman, N. Dak. **55** 46 11N 103 24W
Bowman, S.C. **60** 33 21N 80 41W
Bowman County ◇ **55** 46 2N 103 30W
Bowman-Haley Reservoir **55** 45 59N 103 14W
Bowmont **34** 43 27N 116 32W
Bowring **57** 36 53N 96 7W
Bowstring L. **44** 47 33N 93 55W
Box Butte County ◇ **48** 42 15N 103 0W
Box Elder **61** 44 7N 103 4W
Box Elder County ◇ **66** 41 30N 113 0W
Boxelder Cr. → **61** 45 59N 103 57W
Boxford **42** 42 40N 71 0W
Boxholm **37** 42 10N 94 6W
Boy River **44** 47 10N 94 7W
Boyce, La. **39** 31 23N 92 40W
Boyce, Va. **68** 39 6N 78 4W
Boyceville **69** 45 3N 92 2W
Boyd, Fla. **31** 30 11N 83 37W
Boyd, Minn. **44** 44 51N 95 54W
Boyd, Tex. **65** 33 5N 97 34W
Boyd County ◇, Ky. **63** 38 20N 82 40W
Boyd County ◇, Nebr. **48** 42 50N 98 40W
Boydell **27** 33 22N 91 29W
Boyden **37** 43 12N 96 0W
Boydton **68** 36 40N 78 24W
Boyer → **37** 41 27N 95 55W
Boyero **30** 38 57N 103 16W
Boyertown **59** 40 20N 75 38W
Boyes **47** 45 16N 105 2W
Boyes Hot Springs **28** 38 19N 122 29W
Boykin **32** 31 6N 84 41W
Boykins **68** 36 35N 77 12W
Boyle **45** 33 42N 90 44W
Boyle County ◇ **63** 37 35N 84 55W
Boyne City **43** 45 13N 85 1W
Boyne Falls **43** 45 10N 84 55W
Boynton **57** 35 39N 95 39W
Boynton Beach **31** 26 32N 80 4W
Boys Town **48** 41 16N 96 8W
Boysen Reservoir **70** 43 25N 108 11W
Bozeman **47** 45 41N 111 2W
Bozman **41** 38 46N 76 16W
Bracken County ◇ **63** 38 40N 84 5W
Brackettville **64** 29 19N 100 25W
Braddock **55** 46 34N 100 6W
Braddock Heights **41** 39 25N 77 30W
Braddyville **37** 40 35N 95 2W
Bradenton **31** 27 30N 82 34W
Bradford, Ark. **27** 35 25N 91 27W
Bradford, Ill. **35** 41 11N 89 39W
Bradford, N.H. **50** 43 17N 71 56W
Bradford, Pa. **59** 41 58N 78 38W
Bradford, R.I. **42** 41 24N 71 45W
Bradford, Tenn. **62** 36 5N 88 49W
Bradford, Vt. **50** 43 59N 72 9W
Bradford County ◇, Fla. **31** 30 0N 82 15W
Bradford County ◇, Pa. **59** 41 50N 76 30W
Bradford Mt. **42** 41 59N 73 18W
Bradfordsville **63** 37 30N 85 9W
Bradgate **37** 42 48N 94 25W
Bradley, Ark. **27** 33 6N 93 39W
Bradley, Calif. **29** 35 52N 120 48W
Bradley, Fla. **31** 27 48N 81 59W
Bradley, Ill. **35** 41 9N 87 52W
Bradley, Okla. **57** 34 53N 97 42W
Bradley, S. Dak. **61** 45 5N 97 39W
Bradley County ◇, Ark. **27** 33 27N 92 10W
Bradley County ◇, Tenn. **63** 35 10N 84 53W
Bradner **56** 41 20N 83 26W
Bradshaw, Nebr. **48** 40 53N 97 45W
Bradshaw, Tex. **65** 32 6N 99 54W
Bradshaw, W. Va. **68** 37 21N 81 48W
Brady, Mont. **47** 48 2N 111 51W
Brady, Nebr. **48** 41 1N 100 22W
Brady, Tex. **65** 31 9N 99 20W
Brady Cr. → **65** 31 8N 98 59W
Bragg City **46** 36 16N 89 55W
Braggadocio **46** 36 11N 89 50W
Braggs **57** 35 40N 95 12W
Braham **44** 45 44N 93 10W
Braidwood **35** 41 16N 88 13W
Brainard **48** 41 11N 97 0W
Brainerd **44** 46 22N 94 12W
Braintree **42** 42 13N 71 0W
Braman **57** 36 56N 97 20W
Brampton **55** 46 0N 97 52W
Bramwell **68** 37 20N 81 19W
Branch **27** 35 18N 93 57W
Branch County ◇ **43** 41 50N 85 5W
Branchland **68** 38 13N 82 12W
Branchville, N.J. **51** 41 9N 74 45W
Branchville, S.C. **60** 33 15N 80 49W
Brandenburg **62** 38 0N 86 10W
Brandon, Colo. **30** 38 27N 102 26W
Brandon, Fla. **31** 27 56N 82 17W
Brandon, Iowa **37** 42 19N 92 0W
Brandon, Minn. **44** 45 58N 95 36W
Brandon, Miss. **45** 32 16N 89 59W
Brandon, Nebr. **48** 40 48N 101 55W
Brandon, S. Dak. **61** 43 35N 96 35W
Brandon, Vt. **50** 43 48N 73 6W
Brandon, Wis. **69** 43 44N 88 47W
Brandonville **68** 39 40N 79 37W
Brandreth **53** 43 56N 74 51W
Brandsville **46** 36 39N 91 42W
Brandt **61** 44 40N 96 38W
Brandy Pk. **58** 42 36N 123 53W
Brandywine, Md. **41** 38 42N 76 51W
Brandywine, W. Va. **68** 38 38N 79 15W
Branford, Conn. **42** 41 17N 72 49W
Branford, Fla. **31** 29 58N 82 56W
Branson, Colo. **30** 37 1N 103 53W
Branson, Mo. **46** 36 39N 93 13W
Brantford **55** 47 36N 98 55W
Brantley **24** 31 35N 86 16W
Brantley County ◇ **32** 31 10N 82 0W
Brashear **46** 40 9N 92 23W
Brasher Falls **53** 44 49N 74 47W
Brasstown Bald **32** 34 53N 83 49W
Brassua L. **40** 45 40N 69 55W
Bratt **31** 30 58N 87 26W
Brattleboro **50** 42 51N 72 34W
Brave **59** 39 44N 80 16W
Bravo del Norte, R. → = Grande, R. → **64** 25 57N 97 9W
Brawley **29** 32 59N 115 31W
Brawley Peaks **49** 38 15N 118 55W
Brawley Wash → **26** 32 34N 111 26W
Braxton **45** 32 1N 89 58W
Braxton County ◇ **68** 38 43N 80 39W
Braymer **46** 39 35N 93 48W
Brayton **37** 41 33N 94 56W
Brazil **36** 39 32N 87 8W
Brazoria **65** 29 3N 95 34W
Brazoria County ◇ **65** 29 10N 95 26W
Brazos → **65** 28 53N 95 23W
Brazos County ◇ **65** 30 40N 96 22W
Breathitt County ◇ **63** 37 30N 83 20W
Breaux Bridge **39** 30 16N 91 54W
Breckenridge, Colo. **30** 39 29N 106 3W
Breckenridge, Mich. **43** 43 24N 84 29W
Breckenridge, Minn. **44** 46 16N 96 35W
Breckenridge, Mo. **46** 39 46N 93 48W
Breckenridge, Tex. **65** 32 45N 98 54W
Breckinridge **57** 36 26N 97 44W
Breckinridge County ◇ **62** 37 45N 86 25W
Breda **37** 42 11N 94 59W
Breese **35** 38 37N 89 32W
Bremen, Ala. **24** 33 59N 86 58W
Bremen, Ga. **32** 33 43N 85 9W
Bremen, Ind. **36** 41 27N 86 9W
Bremen, Ky. **62** 37 22N 87 13W
Bremen, Ohio **56** 39 42N 82 26W
Bremer County ◇ **37** 42 50N 92 20W
Bremerton **67** 47 34N 122 38W
Bremond **65** 31 10N 96 41W
Brenham **65** 30 10N 96 24W
Brent **24** 32 56N 87 10W
Brentwood, Calif. **28** 37 56N 121 42W
Brentwood, N.H. **50** 42 58N 71 6W
Brentwood, N.Y. **53** 40 47N 73 15W
Brentwood, Tenn. **62** 36 2N 86 47W
Breton I. **39** 29 13N 89 12W
Breton Sd. **39** 29 35N 89 15W
Brevard **54** 35 14N 82 44W
Brevard County ◇ **31** 28 20N 80 45W
Brevig Mission **25** 65 20N 166 29W
Brevort **43** 46 1N 85 2W
Brewer **40** 44 48N 68 46W
Brewerton **53** 43 14N 76 9W
Brewster, Kans. **38** 39 22N 101 23W
Brewster, Mass. **42** 41 46N 70 5W
Brewster, Minn. **44** 43 42N 95 28W
Brewster, Nebr. **48** 41 56N 99 52W
Brewster, Ohio **56** 40 43N 81 36W
Brewster, Wash. **67** 48 6N 119 47W
Brewster County ◇ **64** 30 0N 103 0W
Brewton, Ala. **24** 31 7N 87 4W
Brewton, Ga. **32** 32 36N 82 48W
Brian Head **66** 37 41N 112 50W
Briartown **57** 35 18N 95 14W
Briceland **28** 40 7N 123 54W
Bricelyn **44** 43 34N 93 49W
Briceville **63** 36 11N 84 11W
Brickeys **27** 34 52N 90 36W
Bridge, Idaho **34** 42 8N 113 20W
Bridge, Oreg. **58** 43 1N 124 0W
Bridge City **65** 30 1N 93 51W
Bridgeboro **32** 31 24N 83 59W
Bridgeport, Ala. **24** 34 57N 85 43W
Bridgeport, Calif. **28** 38 15N 119 14W
Bridgeport, Conn. **42** 41 11N 73 12W
Bridgeport, Ill. **35** 38 43N 87 46W
Bridgeport, Mich. **43** 43 22N 83 53W
Bridgeport, Nebr. **48** 41 40N 103 6W
Bridgeport, Okla. **57** 35 33N 98 23W
Bridgeport, Tex. **65** 33 13N 97 45W
Bridgeport, Wash. **67** 48 0N 119 40W
Bridgeport, L. **65** 33 13N 97 50W
Bridger **47** 45 18N 108 55W
Bridger Peak **70** 41 11N 107 2W
Bridger-Teton National Forest **70** 43 5N 110 5W
Bridgeton, N.C. **54** 35 7N 77 1W
Bridgeton, N.J. **51** 39 26N 75 14W
Bridgetown **41** 39 2N 75 53W
Bridgeville, Calif. **28** 40 25N 123 50W
Bridgeville, Del. **41** 38 45N 75 36W
Bridgewater, Conn. **42** 41 32N 73 22W
Bridgewater, Iowa **37** 41 15N 94 40W
Bridgewater, Maine **40** 46 25N 67 51W
Bridgewater, Mass. **42** 41 59N 70 58W
Bridgewater, N.Y. **53** 42 53N 75 15W
Bridgewater, S. Dak. **61** 43 33N 97 30W
Bridgewater, Va. **68** 38 23N 78 59W
Bridgewater, Vt. **50** 43 35N 72 38W
Bridgman **43** 41 57N 86 33W
Bridgton **40** 44 3N 70 42W
Bridport **50** 43 58N 73 20W
Brier Cr. → **32** 32 44N 81 26W
Brigantine City **51** 39 24N 74 22W
Briggsdale **30** 40 38N 104 20W
Briggsville **27** 34 56N 93 30W
Brigham City **66** 41 31N 112 1W
Brighton, Colo. **30** 39 59N 104 49W
Brighton, Fla. **31** 27 14N 81 6W
Brighton, Ill. **35** 39 2N 90 8W
Brighton, Iowa **37** 41 10N 91 49W
Brighton, Mich. **43** 42 32N 83 47W
Brighton, N.Y. **53** 43 8N 77 34W
Brighton, Tenn. **62** 35 29N 89 43W
Brighton Indian Reservation **31** 27 0N 81 15W
Brightwood **54** 36 10N 79 45W
Brilliant **24** 34 1N 87 46W
Brillion **69** 44 11N 88 4W
Brimfield, Ill. **35** 40 50N 89 53W
Brimfield, Mass. **42** 42 7N 72 12W
Brimley **43** 46 24N 84 34W
Brinkley **27** 34 53N 91 12W
Brinnon **67** 47 41N 122 54W
Brinsmade **55** 48 11N 99 19W
Brinson **32** 30 59N 84 44W
Briscoe **64** 35 35N 100 17W
Briscoe County ◇ **64** 34 28N 101 19W
Bristol, Colo. **30** 38 7N 102 19W
Bristol, Conn. **42** 41 40N 72 57W
Bristol, Fla. **31** 30 26N 84 59W
Bristol, Ind. **36** 41 43N 85 49W
Bristol, Md. **41** 38 47N 76 40W
Bristol, N.H. **50** 43 36N 71 44W
Bristol, Pa. **59** 40 6N 74 51W
Bristol, R.I. **42** 41 40N 71 16W
Bristol, S. Dak. **61** 45 21N 97 45W
Bristol, Tenn. **63** 36 36N 82 11W
Bristol, Va. **68** 36 36N 82 11W
Bristol, Vt. **50** 44 8N 73 5W
Bristol Bay **25** 58 0N 159 0W
Bristol Bay ◇ **25** 59 0N 156 30W
Bristol County ◇, Mass. **42** 41 45N 71 0W
Bristol County ◇, R.I. **42** 41 40N 71 20W
Bristol L. **29** 34 28N 115 41W
Bristol Mts. **29** 34 30N 115 50W
Bristow, Nebr. **48** 42 51N 98 35W
Bristow, Okla. **57** 35 50N 96 23W
Britt **37** 43 6N 93 48W
Britton **61** 45 48N 97 45W
Broad →, Ga. **32** 33 59N 82 39W
Broad →, S.C. **60** 34 1N 81 4W
Broadalbin **53** 43 4N 74 12W
Broadbent **58** 43 1N 124 9W
Broadhurst **32** 31 28N 81 55W
Broadkill Beach **41** 38 47N 75 10W
Broadmoor **30** 38 50N 104 50W
Broadus **47** 45 27N 105 25W
Broadview, Mont. **47** 46 6N 108 53W
Broadview, N. Mex. **52** 34 49N 103 13W
Broadwater **48** 41 36N 102 51W
Broadwater County ◇ **47** 46 25N 111 30W
Broadway **68** 38 37N 78 48W
Broadwell **35** 40 4N 89 27W
Brock **48** 40 29N 95 58W
Brocket **55** 48 13N 98 21W
Brockport **53** 43 13N 77 56W
Brockton, Mass. **42** 42 5N 71 1W
Brockton, Mont. **47** 48 9N 104 55W
Brockway, Mont. **47** 47 18N 105 45W
Brockway, Pa. **59** 41 15N 78 47W
Brocton, Ill. **35** 39 43N 87 56W
Brocton, N.Y. **53** 42 23N 79 26W
Brodhead, Ky. **63** 37 24N 84 25W
Brodhead, Wis. **69** 42 37N 89 22W
Brodnax **68** 36 43N 78 2W
Brogan **58** 44 15N 117 31W
Brokaw **69** 45 2N 89 39W
Broken Arrow **57** 36 3N 95 48W
Broken Bow, Nebr. **48** 41 24N 99 38W
Broken Bow, Okla. **57** 34 2N 94 44W
Broken Bow Lake **57** 34 9N 94 40W
Bromide **57** 34 24N 96 31W
Bronaugh **46** 37 41N 94 28W
Bronson, Fla. **31** 29 27N 82 39W
Bronson, Kans. **38** 37 54N 95 4W
Bronson, Mich. **43** 41 52N 85 12W
Bronson, Tex. **65** 31 21N 94 1W
Bronte **64** 31 53N 100 18W
Bronwood **32** 31 50N 84 22W
Bronx County ◇ **53** 40 50N 73 52W
Brook **36** 40 52N 87 22W
Brook Park **56** 41 24N 80 51W
Brooke County ◇ **68** 40 16N 80 37W
Brookeland **65** 31 10N 94 0W
Brookesmith **65** 31 33N 99 7W
Brookfield, Mass. **42** 42 13N 72 6W
Brookfield, Mo. **46** 39 47N 93 4W
Brookfield, Vt. **50** 44 4N 72 38W
Brookfield, Wis. **69** 43 4N 88 9W
Brookhaven **45** 31 35N 90 26W
Brookings, Oreg. **58** 42 3N 124 17W
Brookings, S. Dak. **61** 44 19N 96 48W
Brookings County ◇ **61** 44 19N 96 48W
Brookland **27** 35 54N 90 35W
Brooklet **32** 32 23N 81 40W
Brookline, Mass. **42** 42 20N 71 7W
Brookline, N.H. **50** 42 44N 71 40W
Brooklyn, Ala. **24** 31 16N 86 46W
Brooklyn, Conn. **42** 41 47N 71 57W
Brooklyn, Ind. **36** 39 32N 86 22W
Brooklyn, Iowa **37** 41 44N 92 27W
Brooklyn, Mich. **43** 42 7N 84 15W
Brooklyn, Miss. **45** 31 3N 89 11W
Brooklyn, Wash. **67** 46 47N 123 31W
Brooklyn Park, Md. **41** 39 14N 76 37W
Brooklyn Park, Minn. **44** 45 6N 93 23W
Brookneal **68** 37 3N 78 57W
Brookport **35** 37 8N 88 38W
Brooks, Ky. **63** 38 4N 85 43W
Brooks, Minn. **44** 47 49N 96 0W
Brooks County ◇, Ga. **32** 30 50N 83 45W
Brooks County ◇, Tex. **64** 27 0N 98 5W
Brooks Range **25** 68 0N 152 0W
Brookshire **65** 29 47N 95 57W
Brookston, Ind. **36** 40 36N 86 52W
Brookston, Minn. **44** 46 52N 92 36W
Brooksville, Fla. **31** 28 33N 82 23W
Brooksville, Ky. **63** 38 41N 84 4W
Brooksville, Miss. **45** 33 14N 88 35W
Brooksville, Okla. **57** 35 12N 96 58W
Brookvale **30** 39 38N 105 26W

Brookview **41** 38 35N 75 48W
Brookville, Ind. **36** 39 25N 85 1W
Brookville, Kans. **38** 38 46N 97 52W
Brookville, N.J. **51** 39 44N 74 18W
Brookville, Pa. **59** 41 10N 79 5W
Brookville L. **36** 39 28N 85 0W
Brookwood **24** 33 17N 87 18W
Broome County ◇ **53** 42 5N 75 45W
Broomes Island **41** 38 25N 76 33W
Broomfield **30** 39 55N 105 5W
Brooten **44** 45 30N 95 8W
Broseley **46** 36 40N 90 15W
Brothers **58** 43 49N 120 36W
Brotmanville **51** 39 33N 75 3W
Broughton, Ill. **35** 37 56N 88 27W
Broughton, Kans. **38** 39 19N 97 3W
Broussard **39** 30 9N 91 58W
Broward County ◇ **31** 26 15N 80 30W
Browerville **44** 46 5N 94 52W
Brown City **43** 43 13N 82 59W
Brown County ◇, Ill. **35** 39 55N 90 45W
Brown County ◇, Ind. **36** 39 10N 86 15W
Brown County ◇, Kans. **38** 39 45N 95 30W
Brown County ◇, Minn. **44** 44 10N 94 50W
Brown County ◇, Nebr. **48** 42 30N 100 0W
Brown County ◇, Ohio **56** 38 55N 83 59W
Brown County ◇, S. Dak. **61** 45 37N 98 19W
Brown County ◇, Tex. **65** 31 43N 98 59W
Brown County ◇, Wis. **69** 44 30N 88 0W
Brown Deer **69** 43 10N 87 58W
Brownell **38** 38 38N 99 45W
Brownfield **64** 33 11N 102 17W
Browning, Ill. **35** 40 8N 90 22W
Browning, Mont. **47** 48 34N 113 1W
Brownlee **48** 42 17N 100 37W
Brownlee Reservoir **34** 44 50N 116 54W
Browns **35** 38 23N 87 59W
Browns Mills **51** 39 58N 74 34W
Browns Valley **44** 45 36N 96 50W
Brownsburg **36** 39 51N 86 24W
Brownsdale **44** 43 45N 92 52W
Brownstown, Ill. **35** 39 0N 88 57W
Brownstown, Ind. **36** 38 53N 86 3W
Brownsville, Ky. **62** 37 12N 86 16W
Brownsville, La. **39** 32 29N 92 9W
Brownsville, Minn. **44** 43 42N 91 17W
Brownsville, Oreg. **58** 44 24N 122 59W
Brownsville, Pa. **59** 40 1N 79 53W
Brownsville, Tenn. **62** 35 36N 89 16W
Brownsville, Tex. **64** 25 54N 97 30W
Browntown **69** 42 35N 89 48W
Brownville, Ala. **24** 33 24N 87 52W
Brownville, Maine **40** 45 18N 69 2W
Brownville, N.Y. **53** 44 0N 75 59W
Brownville, Nebr. **48** 40 24N 95 40W
Brownville Junction **40** 45 21N 69 3W
Brownwood, Mo. **46** 37 5N 89 57W
Brownwood, Tex. **65** 31 43N 98 59W
Brownwood, L. **65** 31 50N 99 0W
Broxton **32** 31 38N 82 53W
Bruce, Fla. **31** 30 28N 85 58W
Bruce, Miss. **45** 33 59N 89 21W
Bruce, S. Dak. **61** 44 26N 96 54W
Bruce, Wis. **69** 45 28N 91 16W
Bruceton **62** 36 3N 88 15W
Bruceton Mills **68** 39 40N 79 38W
Bruceville, Ind. **36** 38 46N 87 25W
Bruceville, Md. **41** 38 40N 75 59W
Bruin Pt. **66** 39 39N 110 21W
Brule **48** 41 6N 101 53W
Brule → **69** 45 57N 88 12W
Brule County ◇ **61** 43 45N 99 0W
Brule L. **44** 46 58N 90 50W
Brumley **46** 38 5N 92 29W
Brundidge **24** 31 43N 85 49W
Bruneau **34** 42 53N 115 48W
Bruneau → **34** 42 56N 115 57W
Bruning **48** 40 20N 97 34W
Bruno, Minn. **44** 46 17N 92 40W
Bruno, Nebr. **48** 41 17N 96 58W
Brunsville **37** 42 49N 96 16W
Brunswick, Ga. **32** 31 10N 81 30W
Brunswick, Maine **40** 43 55N 69 58W
Brunswick, Md. **41** 39 19N 77 38W
Brunswick, Mo. **46** 39 26N 93 8W
Brunswick, Nebr. **48** 42 20N 97 58W
Brunswick, Ohio **56** 41 14N 81 51W
Brunswick County ◇, N.C. **54** 34 0N 78 20W
Brunswick County ◇, Va. **68** 36 46N 77 51W
Brush **30** 40 15N 103 37W
Brush Creek **62** 36 7N 86 2W
Brushton **53** 44 50N 74 31W
Brusly **39** 30 23N 91 14W
Brussels **69** 44 44N 87 37W
Bryan, Ohio **56** 41 28N 84 33W
Bryan, Tex. **65** 30 40N 96 22W
Bryan County ◇, Ga. **32** 32 0N 81 30W
Bryan County ◇, Okla. **57** 34 0N 96 15W
Bryans Road **41** 38 38N 77 4W
Bryant, Ark. **27** 34 36N 92 29W
Bryant, Ind. **36** 40 32N 84 58W
Bryant, S. Dak. **61** 44 35N 97 28W
Bryant Cr. → **46** 36 36N 92 17W
Bryantown **41** 38 36N 76 52W
Bryce Canyon National Park **66** 37 30N 112 10W
Bryson **65** 33 10N 98 23W
Bryson City **54** 35 26N 83 27W
Buchanan, Ga. **32** 33 48N 85 11W
Buchanan, Mich. **43** 41 50N 86 22W
Buchanan, N. Dak. **55** 47 4N 98 50W
Buchanan, Va. **68** 37 32N 79 41W
Buchanan, L. **65** 30 45N 98 25W
Buchanan County ◇, Iowa **37** 42 30N 91 50W
Buchanan County ◇, Mo. **46** 39 40N 94 50W
Buchanan County ◇, Va. **68** 37 17N 82 6W
Buchanan Dam **65** 30 45N 98 25W
Buchon, Pt. **29** 35 15N 120 54W
Buck Grove **37** 41 55N 95 23W
Buck I. **71** 17 46N 64 37W
Buckatunna **45** 31 32N 88 32W
Buckeye, Ariz. **26** 33 22N 112 35W
Buckeye, Iowa **37** 42 25N 93 23W
Buckeystown **41** 39 20N 77 26W
Buckfield **40** 44 17N 70 22W
Buckhannon **68** 39 0N 80 8W
Buckholts **65** 30 52N 97 7W
Buckhorn, Ky. **63** 37 21N 83 28W
Buckhorn, N. Mex. **52** 33 2N 108 42W
Buckhorn L. **63** 37 21N 83 28W
Buckingham, Colo. **30** 40 37N 103 58W
Buckingham, Va. **68** 37 33N 78 33W
Buckingham County ◇ **68** 37 40N 78 40W
Buckland, Alaska **25** 65 59N 161 8W
Buckland, Ohio **56** 40 37N 84 16W
Buckley, Ill. **35** 40 36N 88 2W
Buckley, Mich. **43** 44 30N 85 41W
Buckley, Wash. **67** 47 10N 122 2W
Bucklin, Kans. **38** 37 33N 99 38W
Bucklin, Mo. **46** 39 47N 92 53W
Buckman **44** 45 54N 94 6W
Bucks County ◇ **59** 40 15N 75 10W
Bucks L. **28** 39 54N 121 12W
Buckskin Mts. **26** 34 10N 113 50W
Bucksport **40** 44 34N 68 47W
Bucktown **41** 38 25N 76 3W
Bucoda **67** 46 48N 122 52W
Bucyrus, Kans. **38** 38 44N 94 44W
Bucyrus, N. Dak. **55** 46 4N 102 47W
Bucyrus, Ohio **56** 40 48N 82 59W
Buda, Ill. **35** 41 20N 89 41W
Buda, Tex. **65** 30 5N 97 51W
Budd Lake **51** 40 52N 74 44W
Budds Creek **41** 38 23N 76 51W
Bude **45** 31 28N 90 51W
Buechel **63** 38 12N 85 39W
Buena **51** 39 31N 74 56W
Buena Vista, Colo. **30** 38 51N 106 8W
Buena Vista, Ga. **32** 32 19N 84 31W
Buena Vista, Va. **68** 37 44N 79 21W
Buena Vista County ◇ **37** 42 45N 95 10W
Buena Vista L. **29** 35 12N 119 18W
Buffalo, Kans. **38** 37 42N 95 42W
Buffalo, Minn. **44** 45 10N 93 53W
Buffalo, Mo. **46** 37 39N 93 6W
Buffalo, N. Dak. **55** 46 55N 97 33W
Buffalo, N.Y. **53** 42 53N 78 53W
Buffalo, Okla. **57** 36 50N 99 38W
Buffalo, S.C. **60** 34 43N 81 41W
Buffalo, S. Dak. **61** 45 35N 103 33W
Buffalo, Tex. **65** 31 28N 96 4W
Buffalo, W. Va. **68** 38 37N 81 59W
Buffalo, Wyo. **70** 44 21N 106 42W
Buffalo →, Ark. **27** 36 10N 92 26W
Buffalo →, Minn. **44** 47 6N 96 49W
Buffalo →, Tenn. **62** 36 0N 87 50W
Buffalo Bill Reservoir **70** 44 30N 109 11W
Buffalo Center **37** 43 23N 93 57W
Buffalo County ◇, Nebr. **48** 40 50N 99 0W
Buffalo County ◇, S. Dak. **61** 44 0N 99 5W
Buffalo County ◇, Wis. **69** 44 20N 91 50W
Buffalo Cr. →, Okla. **57** 36 47N 99 15W
Buffalo Cr. →, Wyo. **70** 43 40N 106 30W
Buffalo Creek **30** 39 23N 105 17W
Buffalo Gap, S. Dak. **61** 43 30N 103 19W
Buffalo Gap, Tex. **65** 32 17N 99 50W
Buffalo L., Tex. **64** 34 52N 102 12W
Buffalo L., Wis. **69** 43 47N 89 25W
Buffalo River National Park **27** 36 14N 92 36W
Buford, Ga. **32** 34 10N 84 0W
Buford, N. Dak. **55** 48 0N 103 59W
Buhl **34** 42 36N 114 46W
Buhler **38** 38 8N 97 46W
Buies Creek **54** 35 25N 78 44W
Buladean **54** 36 7N 82 12W
Buldir I. **25** 52 21N 175 56 E
Bull L. **70** 43 13N 109 3W
Bull Mts. **47** 46 8N 109 0W
Bull Shoals L. **27** 36 22N 92 35W
Bullard, Ga. **32** 32 38N 83 30W
Bullard, Tex. **65** 32 8N 95 19W
Bullhead **61** 45 46N 101 5W
Bullion Mts. **29** 34 40N 116 10W
Bullitt County ◇ **63** 38 0N 85 40W
Bulloch County ◇ **32** 32 20N 81 45W
Bullock County ◇ **24** 32 9N 85 43W
Bulls B. **60** 32 59N 79 35W
Bulls Gap **63** 36 15N 83 5W
Bumpus Mills **62** 36 36N 87 50W
Buna **65** 30 26N 93 58W
Bunceton **46** 38 47N 92 48W
Bunch **57** 35 41N 94 46W
Buncombe **35** 37 27N 88 58W
Buncombe County ◇ **54** 35 30N 82 30W
Bundlicks Cr. → **39** 30 36N 92 57W
Bunker **46** 37 27N 91 13W
Bunker Hill, Ill. **35** 39 3N 89 57W
Bunker Hill, Ind. **36** 40 40N 86 6W
Bunker Hill, Kans. **38** 38 53N 98 42W
Bunker Hill, Nev. **49** 39 15N 117 8W
Bunker Hill, Oreg. **58** 43 22N 124 12W
Bunkerville **49** 36 46N 114 8W
Bunkie **39** 30 57N 92 11W
Bunn **54** 35 58N 78 15W
Bunnell **31** 29 28N 81 16W
Buras **39** 29 22N 89 32W
Burbank, Calif. **29** 34 11N 118 19W
Burbank, Okla. **57** 36 42N 96 44W
Burbank, Wash. **67** 46 12N 119 1W
Burchard **48** 40 9N 96 21W
Burden **38** 37 19N 96 45W
Burdett, Kans. **38** 38 12N 99 32W
Burdett, N.Y. **53** 42 25N 76 51W
Burdick **38** 38 34N 96 51W
Bureau County ◇ **35** 41 25N 89 30W
Burgaw **54** 34 33N 77 56W
Burgess Junction **70** 44 46N 107 32W
Burgoon **56** 41 16N 83 15W
Burien **67** 47 28N 122 21W
Burkburnett **65** 34 6N 98 34W
Burke, Idaho **34** 47 31N 115 49W
Burke, S. Dak. **61** 43 11N 99 18W
Burke County ◇, Ga. **32** 33 0N 82 0W
Burke County ◇, N.C. **54** 35 45N 81 40W
Burke County ◇, N. Dak. **55** 48 55N 102 30W
Burkesville **63** 36 48N 85 22W
Burkett **65** 32 0N 99 8W
Burkettsville **56** 40 21N 84 39W
Burkeville, Tex. **65** 31 0N 93 40W
Burkeville, Va. **68** 37 11N 78 12W
Burkittsville **41** 39 22N 77 38W
Burleigh County ◇ **55** 47 0N 100 30W
Burleson **65** 32 33N 97 19W
Burleson County ◇ **65** 30 32N 96 42W
Burley **34** 42 32N 113 48W
Burlingame, Calif. **28** 37 35N 122 21W
Burlingame, Kans. **38** 38 45N 95 50W
Burlington, Colo. **30** 39 18N 102 16W
Burlington, Ill. **35** 42 3N 88 33W
Burlington, Ind. **36** 40 29N 86 24W
Burlington, Iowa **37** 40 49N 91 14W
Burlington, Kans. **38** 38 12N 95 45W
Burlington, Ky. **63** 39 2N 84 43W
Burlington, Mass. **42** 42 30N 71 12W
Burlington, N.C. **54** 36 6N 79 26W
Burlington, N. Dak. **55** 48 17N 101 26W
Burlington, N.J. **51** 40 4N 74 51W
Burlington, Okla. **57** 36 54N 98 25W
Burlington, Vt. **50** 44 29N 73 12W
Burlington, Wash. **67** 48 28N 122 20W
Burlington, Wis. **69** 42 41N 88 17W
Burlington, Wyo. **70** 44 27N 108 26W
Burlington County ◇ **51** 39 50N 74 45W
Burlington Junction **46** 40 27N 95 4W
Burna **62** 37 15N 88 22W
Burnet **65** 30 45N 98 14W
Burnet County ◇ **65** 30 45N 98 15W
Burnett County ◇ **69** 45 50N 92 20W
Burnettsville **36** 40 46N 86 36W
Burney **28** 40 53N 121 40W
Burnham, Maine **40** 44 42N 69 26W
Burnham, Pa. **59** 40 38N 77 34W
Burning Springs **63** 37 15N 83 49W
Burns, Colo. **30** 39 52N 106 53W
Burns, Kans. **38** 38 5N 96 53W
Burns, Oreg. **58** 43 35N 119 3W
Burns, Tenn. **62** 36 3N 87 19W
Burns, Wyo. **70** 41 12N 104 21W
Burns Flat **57** 35 21N 99 10W
Burnside **63** 36 59N 84 36W
Burnsville, Ala. **24** 32 28N 86 53W
Burnsville, Minn. **44** 44 47N 93 17W
Burnsville, Miss. **45** 34 51N 88 19W
Burnsville, N.C. **54** 35 55N 82 18W
Burnsville, W. Va. **68** 38 52N 80 40W
Burnt → **58** 44 22N 117 14W
Burnt Corn **24** 31 33N 87 10W
Burntfork **70** 41 2N 109 59W
Burr **48** 40 33N 96 19W
Burr Oak, Kans. **38** 39 52N 98 18W
Burr Oak, Mich. **43** 41 51N 85 19W
Burrton **38** 38 2N 97 41W
Burt **37** 43 12N 94 13W
Burt County ◇ **48** 41 50N 96 15W
Burt L. **43** 45 28N 84 40W
Burton, Mich. **43** 43 0N 83 40W
Burton, Nebr. **48** 42 55N 99 35W
Burton, Tex. **65** 30 11N 96 42W
Burton, L. **32** 34 50N 83 33W
Burtrum **44** 45 52N 94 41W
Burwell **48** 41 47N 99 8W
Bush **39** 30 36N 89 54W
Bush City **38** 38 13N 95 9W
Bushland **64** 35 11N 102 4W
Bushnell, Fla. **31** 28 40N 82 7W
Bushnell, Ill. **35** 40 33N 90 31W
Bushnell, Nebr. **48** 41 14N 103 54W
Bushong **38** 38 39N 96 15W
Bushton **38** 38 31N 98 24W
Bushwood **41** 38 18N 76 47W
Bushy Head Mt. **57** 36 2N 94 35W
Bussey **37** 41 12N 92 53W
Butler, Ala. **24** 32 5N 88 13W
Butler, Ga. **32** 32 33N 84 14W
Butler, Ind. **36** 41 26N 84 52W
Butler, Ky. **63** 38 47N 84 22W
Butler, Md. **41** 39 35N 76 45W
Butler, Mo. **46** 38 16N 94 20W
Butler, N.J. **51** 41 0N 74 20W
Butler, Okla. **57** 35 38N 99 11W
Butler, Pa. **59** 40 52N 79 54W
Butler County ◇, Ala. **24** 31 50N 86 38W
Butler County ◇, Iowa **37** 42 45N 92 45W
Butler County ◇, Kans. **38** 37 45N 96 45W
Butler County ◇, Ky. **62** 37 10N 86 45W
Butler County ◇, Mo. **46** 36 45N 90 25W
Butler County ◇, Nebr. **48** 41 15N 97 0W
Butler County ◇, Ohio **56** 39 24N 84 34W
Butler County ◇, Pa. **59** 41 0N 80 0W
Butner **54** 36 8N 78 45W
Butte, Mont. **47** 46 0N 112 32W
Butte, N. Dak. **55** 47 50N 100 40W
Butte, Nebr. **48** 42 58N 98 51W
Butte County ◇, Calif. **28** 39 40N 121 45W
Butte County ◇, Idaho **34** 43 50N 113 0W
Butte County ◇, S. Dak. **61** 45 0N 103 30W
Butte Falls **58** 42 33N 122 34W
Butte Mts. **49** 39 50N 115 5W
Butterfield, Minn. **44** 43 58N 94 48W
Butterfield, Mo. **46** 36 45N 93 54W
Butternut **69** 46 1N 90 30W
Buttonwillow **29** 35 24N 119 28W
Butts County ◇ **32** 33 20N 84 0W
Buxton, N.C. **54** 35 16N 75 32W
Buxton, N. Dak. **55** 47 36N 97 6W
Buzzards B. **42** 41 30N 70 45W
Buzzards Bay **42** 41 45N 70 37W
Byars **57** 34 53N 97 3W
Byers, Colo. **30** 39 43N 104 14W
Byers, Kans. **38** 37 48N 98 52W
Byers, Tex. **65** 34 4N 98 11W
Byesville **56** 39 58N 81 32W
Byfield **42** 42 46N 70 57W
Byhalia **45** 34 52N 89 41W
Bylas **26** 33 8N 110 7W
Byng **57** 34 50N 96 42W
Bynum **47** 47 59N 112 19W
Byram **45** 32 11N 90 15W
Byrdstown **63** 36 34N 85 8W
Byron, Ga. **32** 32 39N 83 46W
Byron, Ill. **35** 42 8N 89 15W
Byron, Maine **40** 44 43N 70 38W
Byron, Mich. **43** 42 49N 83 57W
Byron, Minn. **44** 44 2N 92 41W
Byron, Nebr. **48** 40 0N 97 46W
Byron, Okla. **57** 36 54N 98 19W
Byron, Wyo. **70** 44 48N 108 30W

C

C. J. Strike Reservoir **34** 42 59N 115 58W
Caballo Reservoir **52** 32 54N 107 18W
Cabarrus County ◇ **54** 35 20N 80 30W
Cabazon **29** 33 55N 116 47W
Cabell County ◇ **68** 38 26N 82 8W
Cabery **35** 41 0N 88 12W
Cabinet Mts. **47** 45 30N 115 0W
Cable **69** 46 13N 91 17W
Cabo Rojo **71** 18 5N 67 9W
Cabool **46** 37 7N 92 6W
Cabot, Ark. **27** 34 59N 92 1W
Cabot, Vt. **50** 44 23N 72 18W
Cabot, Mt. **50** 44 30N 71 25W
Cabrillo, Pt. **28** 39 21N 123 50W
Cacapon → **68** 39 37N 78 16W
Cache **57** 34 38N 98 38W
Cache →, Ark. **27** 34 43N 91 20W
Cache →, Ill. **35** 37 4N 89 10W
Cache County ◇ **66** 41 40N 111 45W
Cache Cr. → **28** 38 42N 121 42W
Cache la Poudre → **30** 40 25N 104 36W
Cache National Forest **66** 41 45N 111 29W
Cache Peak **34** 42 11N 113 40W
Cactus **64** 36 4N 101 59W
Caddo, Okla. **57** 34 7N 96 16W
Caddo, Tex. **65** 32 43N 98 40W
Caddo → **27** 34 10N 93 3W
Caddo County ◇ **57** 35 10N 98 20W
Caddo Cr. → **57** 34 1N 96 59W
Caddo Gap **27** 34 24N 93 37W
Caddo L. **39** 32 43N 93 55W
Caddo Mills **65** 33 4N 96 14W
Caddo Parish ◇ **39** 32 45N 93 58W
Caddoa **30** 38 4N 102 56W
Cades **60** 33 47N 79 47W
Cadillac **43** 44 15N 85 24W
Cadiz, Ind. **36** 39 57N 85 29W
Cadiz, Ky. **62** 36 52N 87 50W
Cadiz, Ohio **56** 40 22N 81 0W
Cadiz L. **29** 34 18N 115 24W
Cadley **32** 33 32N 82 40W
Cadott **69** 44 57N 91 9W
Cadwell **32** 32 20N 83 3W
Cagles Mill L. **36** 39 30N 86 53W
Caguas **71** 18 14N 66 2W
Cahaba → **24** 32 20N 87 5W
Cahokia **35** 38 34N 90 11W
Cahone **30** 37 39N 108 49W
Caillou B. **39** 29 3N 91 0W
Cains Store **63** 37 8N 84 50W
Cainsville **46** 40 26N 93 47W
Cairo, Ga. **32** 30 52N 84 13W
Cairo, Ill. **35** 37 0N 89 11W
Cairo, Ky. **62** 37 42N 87 39W
Cairo, Mo. **46** 39 31N 92 27W
Cairo, Nebr. **48** 41 0N 98 36W
Cairo, Ohio **56** 40 50N 84 5W
Cairo, W. Va. **68** 39 13N 81 9W
Caja de Muertos, Isla **71** 17 54N 66 31W
Cajon Summit **29** 34 21N 117 27W
Calais **40** 45 11N 67 17W
Calamus → **48** 41 48N 99 9W
Calapooia → **58** 44 38N 123 8W
Calaveras County ◇ **28** 38 15N 120 40W
Calcasieu → **39** 30 5N 93 20W
Calcasieu L. **39** 29 55N 93 18W
Calcasieu Parish ◇ **39** 30 14N 93 23W
Caldwell, Ark. **27** 35 5N 90 49W
Caldwell, Idaho **34** 43 40N 116 41W
Caldwell, Kans. **38** 37 2N 97 37W
Caldwell, Ohio **56** 39 45N 81 31W
Caldwell, Tex. **65** 30 32N 96 42W
Caldwell County ◇, Ky. **62** 37 10N 87 50W
Caldwell County ◇, Mo. **46** 39 40N 94 0W
Caldwell County ◇, N.C. **54** 36 0N 81 30W
Caldwell County ◇, Tex. **65** 29 53N 97 40W
Caldwell Parish ◇ **39** 32 0N 92 0W
Caledonia, Mich. **43** 42 47N 85 31W
Caledonia, Minn. **44** 43 38N 91 30W
Caledonia, Miss. **45** 33 41N 88 20W
Caledonia, N. Dak. **55** 47 28N 96 53W
Caledonia, N.Y. **53** 42 58N 77 51W
Caledonia County ◇ **50** 44 30N 72 10W
Calera, Ala. **24** 33 6N 86 45W
Calera, Okla. **57** 33 52N 96 29W
Calexico **29** 32 40N 115 30W
Calhan **30** 39 2N 104 18W
Calhoun, Ga. **32** 34 30N 84 57W
Calhoun, Ill. **35** 38 39N 88 3W
Calhoun, Ky. **62** 37 32N 87 16W
Calhoun, Mo. **46** 38 28N 93 38W
Calhoun, Tenn. **63** 35 18N 84 45W
Calhoun City **45** 33 51N 89 19W
Calhoun County ◇, Ala. **24** 33 47N 86 0W
Calhoun County ◇, Ark. **27** 33 35N 92 31W
Calhoun County ◇, Fla. **31** 30 30N 85 15W
Calhoun County ◇, Ga. **32** 31 30N 84 35W
Calhoun County ◇, Ill. **35** 39 10N 90 40W
Calhoun County ◇, Iowa **37** 42 25N 94 40W
Calhoun County ◇, Mich. **43** 42 15N 85 0W
Calhoun County ◇, Miss. **45** 33 56N 89 20W
Calhoun County ◇, S.C. **60** 33 45N 80 50W
Calhoun County ◇, Tex. **65** 28 37N 96 38W
Calhoun County ◇, W. Va. **68** 38 55N 81 6W
Calhoun Falls **60** 34 6N 82 36W
Calico Rock **27** 36 7N 92 9W
Caliente, Calif. **29** 35 17N 118 38W
Caliente, Nev. **49** 37 37N 114 31W
Califon **51** 40 42N 74 50W
California, Md. **41** 38 18N 76 32W
California, Mo. **46** 38 38N 92 34W
California, Pa. **59** 40 4N 79 54W
California □ **28** 37 30N 119 30W
California Aqueduct **29** 33 52N 117 12W
California City **29** 35 10N 117 55W
Calio **55** 48 38N 98 56W
Calion **27** 33 20N 92 32W
Calipatria **29** 33 8N 115 31W
Calistoga **28** 38 35N 122 35W
Callahan, Calif. **28** 41 18N 122 48W
Callahan, Fla. **31** 30 34N 81 50W
Callahan County ◇ **65** 32 24N 99 24W
Callao **66** 39 54N 113 43W
Callaway, Fla. **31** 30 8N 85 36W
Callaway, Minn. **44** 46 59N 95 54W
Callaway, Nebr. **48** 41 18N 99 56W
Callaway County ◇ **46** 38 50N 91 50W
Callender **37** 42 22N 94 17W
Callicoon **53** 41 46N 75 3W
Calliham **65** 28 29N 98 21W
Calloway County ◇ **62** 36 40N 88 15W
Calmar **37** 43 11N 91 52W
Caloosahatchee → **31** 26 31N 82 1W
Calpella **28** 39 14N 123 12W
Calpine **28** 39 40N 120 27W
Calumet, Iowa **37** 42 57N 95 33W
Calumet, Mich. **43** 47 14N 88 27W
Calumet, Minn. **44** 47 19N 93 17W
Calumet, Okla. **57** 35 36N 98 7W
Calumet City **35** 41 37N 87 32W
Calumet County ◇ **69** 44 5N 88 10W
Calvert, Md. **41** 39 42N 75 58W
Calvert, Tex. **65** 30 59N 96 40W
Calvert City **62** 37 2N 88 21W
Calvert County ◇ **41** 38 30N 76 35W
Calverton **41** 39 3N 76 56W
Calvin, La. **39** 31 58N 92 47W
Calvin, N. Dak. **55** 48 51N 98 56W
Calvin, Okla. **57** 34 58N 96 15W
Calwa **29** 36 42N 119 46W
Camak **32** 33 27N 82 39W
Camanche **37** 41 47N 90 15W
Camanche Reservoir **28** 38 14N 121 1W
Camano I. **67** 48 0N 122 30W
Camargo **57** 36 1N 99 17W
Camarillo **29** 34 13N 119 2W
Camas, Idaho **34** 44 0N 112 13W
Camas, Wash. **67** 45 35N 122 24W
Camas County ◇ **34** 43 30N 114 50W
Camas Valley **58** 43 2N 123 40W
Cambria, Calif. **29** 35 34N 121 5W
Cambria, Wis. **69** 43 33N 89 7W
Cambria County ◇ **59** 40 30N 78 52W
Cambridge, Idaho **34** 44 34N 116 41W
Cambridge, Ill. **35** 41 18N 90 12W
Cambridge, Iowa **37** 41 54N 93 32W
Cambridge, Kans. **38** 37 19N 96 40W
Cambridge, Mass. **42** 42 22N 71 6W
Cambridge, Md. **41** 38 34N 76 5W
Cambridge, Minn. **44** 45 34N 93 13W
Cambridge, N.Y. **53** 43 2N 73 22W
Cambridge, Nebr. **48** 40 17N 100 10W
Cambridge, Ohio **56** 40 2N 81 35W
Cambridge, Vt. **50** 44 39N 72 53W
Cambridge City **36** 39 49N 85 10W
Cambridge Springs **59** 41 48N 80 4W
Cambridgeport **50** 43 10N 72 35W
Camden, Ala. **24** 31 59N 87 17W
Camden, Ark. **27** 33 35N 92 50W
Camden, Del. **41** 39 7N 75 33W
Camden, Ill. **35** 40 9N 90 46W
Camden, Maine **40** 44 13N 69 4W
Camden, Miss. **45** 32 47N 89 50W
Camden, N.C. **54** 36 20N 76 10W
Camden, N.J. **51** 39 56N 75 7W
Camden, N.Y. **53** 43 20N 75 45W
Camden, Ohio **56** 39 38N 84 39W
Camden, S.C. **60** 34 16N 80 36W
Camden, Tenn. **62** 36 4N 88 6W
Camden, Tex. **65** 30 55N 94 44W
Camden Bay **25** 70 10N 145 15W
Camden County ◇, Ga. **32** 31 0N 81 45W
Camden County ◇, Mo. **46** 38 0N 92 45W
Camden County ◇, N.C. **54** 36 20N 76 15W
Camden County ◇, N.J. **51** 39 45N 75 0W
Camdenton **46** 38 1N 92 45W
Camels Hump **50** 44 19N 72 53W
Cameron, Ariz. **26** 35 53N 111 25W
Cameron, La. **39** 29 48N 93 20W
Cameron, Mo. **46** 39 44N 94 14W
Cameron, Mont. **47** 45 13N 111 41W
Cameron, N.C. **54** 35 20N 79 15W
Cameron, Okla. **57** 35 8N 94 32W
Cameron, S.C. **60** 33 34N 80 43W
Cameron, Tex. **65** 30 51N 96 59W
Cameron, W. Va. **68** 39 50N 80 34W
Cameron, Wis. **69** 45 25N 91 44W
Cameron County ◇, Pa. **59** 41 30N 78 5W
Cameron County ◇, Tex. **64** 26 12N 97 42W
Cameron Parish ◇ **39** 29 58N 93 10W
Camilla **32** 31 14N 84 12W
Camino **28** 38 44N 120 41W
Camp County ◇ **65** 33 0N 94 59W
Camp Creek **68** 37 30N 81 6W
Camp Crook **61** 45 33N 103 59W
Camp Douglas **69** 43 55N 90 16W
Camp Hill, Ala. **24** 32 48N 85 39W
Camp Hill, Pa. **59** 40 14N 76 55W
Camp Houston **57** 36 49N 99 7W
Camp Point **35** 40 3N 91 4W
Camp Springs **41** 38 48N 76 55W
Camp Verde **26** 34 34N 111 51W
Camp Wood **65** 29 40N 100 1W
Campaign **63** 35 46N 85 38W
Campbell, Ala. **24** 31 55N 87 59W
Campbell, Calif. **28** 37 17N 121 57W
Campbell, Minn. **44** 46 6N 96 24W
Campbell, Mo. **46** 36 30N 90 4W
Campbell, Nebr. **48** 40 18N 98 44W
Campbell, Ohio **56** 41 5N 80 37W
Campbell County ◇, Ky. **63** 38 55N 84 20W
Campbell County ◇, S. Dak. **61** 45 55N 100 0W
Campbell County ◇, Tenn. **63** 36 23N 84 7W
Campbell County ◇, Va. **68** 37 15N 79 5W
Campbell County ◇, Wyo. **70** 44 15N 105 30W
Campbellsburg, Ind. **36** 38 39N 86 16W
Campbellsburg, Ky. **63** 38 31N 85 12W
Campbellsport **69** 43 36N 88 17W
Campbellsville, Ky. **63** 37 21N 85 20W
Campbellsville, Tenn. **62** 35 20N 87 8W
Campbellton **31** 30 57N 85 24W
Campion **30** 40 21N 105 5W
Campo **30** 37 6N 102 35W
Campobello **60** 35 7N 82 9W
Campti **39** 31 54N 93 7W
Campton, Fla. **31** 30 53N 86 31W
Campton, Ga. **32** 33 52N 83 43W
Campton, Ky. **63** 37 44N 83 33W
Camptonville **28** 39 27N 121 3W
Campville **31** 29 40N 82 7W
Camuy **71** 18 29N 66 51W
Camuy → **71** 18 29N 66 51W
Canaan, Conn. **42** 42 2N 73 20W
Canaan, Miss. **45** 34 56N 89 8W
Canaan, N.H. **50** 43 40N 72 1W
Canadian, Okla. **57** 35 11N 95 39W
Canadian, Tex. **64** 35 55N 100 23W
Canadian → **57** 35 28N 95 3W
Canadian County ◇ **57** 35 35N 98 0W
Canadys **60** 33 3N 80 37W
Canajoharie **53** 42 54N 74 35W
Canal Fulton **56** 40 53N 81 36W
Canal Point **31** 26 52N 80 38W
Canalou **46** 36 46N 89 41W
Canandaigua **53** 42 54N 77 17W
Canandaigua L. **53** 42 47N 77 19W
Canas, Rio → **71** 18 3N 66 26W
Canaseraga **53** 42 28N 77 45W
Canaveral, C. **31** 28 27N 80 32W
Canaveral National Seashore **31** 28 28N 80 34W
Canby, Calif. **28** 41 27N 120 52W
Canby, Minn. **44** 44 43N 96 16W
Canby, Oreg. **58** 45 16N 122 42W
Candelaria **64** 30 8N 104 41W
Candle **25** 65 55N 161 56W
Candler County ◇ **32** 32 30N 82 0W
Candlewood **51** 40 9N 74 10W
Candlewood, L. **42** 41 30N 73 27W
Cando **55** 48 32N 99 12W
Candor **54** 35 18N 79 45W
Candy Res. **57** 36 32N 96 1W
Cane Bay **71** 17 40N 64 50W
Cane Cr. → **66** 38 35N 109 35W
Cane Valley **63** 37 11N 85 19W
Caney, Kans. **38** 37 1N 95 56W
Caney, Okla. **57** 34 14N 96 13W
Caney Fork → **63** 36 15N 85 57W
Caneyville **62** 37 26N 86 29W
Canfield **27** 33 11N 93 38W
Canisteo **53** 42 16N 77 36W
Canisteo → **53** 42 7N 77 8W
Canistota **61** 43 36N 97 18W
Canjilon **52** 36 29N 106 26W
Canmer **63** 37 17N 85 46W
Cannel City **63** 37 47N 83 17W
Cannelton **36** 37 55N 86 45W
Cannon → **44** 44 35N 92 33W
Cannon Ball **55** 46 25N 100 38W
Cannon Beach **58** 45 54N 123 58W
Cannon County ◇ **62** 35 50N 86 4W
Cannon Falls **44** 44 31N 92 54W
Cannonball → **55** 46 26N 100 35W
Cannonsburg **63** 38 23N 82 42W
Cannonsville Reservoir **53** 42 4N 75 22W
Cannonville **66** 37 34N 112 3W
Canobie Lake **50** 42 49N 71 15W
Canon **32** 34 21N 83 7W
Canon City **30** 38 27N 105 14W
Canon Largo → **52** 36 43N 107 49W
Canoncito Indian Reservation **52** 35 10N 107 0W
Canonsburg **59** 40 16N 80 11W
Canoochee → **32** 31 59N 81 19W
Canova **61** 43 53N 97 30W
Canovanas **71** 18 23N 65 54W
Canterbury **42** 41 41N 71 57W
Canton, Conn. **42** 41 49N 72 54W
Canton, Ga. **32** 34 14N 84 29W
Canton, Ill. **35** 40 33N 90 2W
Canton, Kans. **38** 38 23N 97 26W
Canton, Ky. **62** 36 48N 87 58W
Canton, Mass. **42** 42 9N 71 9W
Canton, Minn. **44** 43 32N 91 56W
Canton, Miss. **45** 32 37N 90 2W
Canton, Mo. **46** 40 8N 91 32W
Canton, N.C. **54** 35 32N 82 50W
Canton, N.Y. **53** 44 36N 75 10W
Canton, Ohio **56** 40 48N 81 23W
Canton, Okla. **57** 36 3N 98 35W
Canton, Pa. **59** 41 39N 76 51W
Canton, S. Dak. **61** 43 18N 96 35W
Canton, Tex. **65** 32 33N 95 52W
Canton L. **57** 36 6N 98 35W
Cantonment **31** 30 37N 87 20W
Cantril **37** 40 39N 92 4W
Cantwell **25** 63 24N 148 57W
Canute **57** 35 25N 99 17W
Canutillo **64** 31 55N 106 36W
Canyon **64** 34 59N 101 55W
Canyon City **58** 44 23N 118 57W
Canyon County ◇ **34** 43 35N 116 50W
Canyon Creek **47** 46 49N 112 16W
Canyon De Chelly National Monument **26** 36 10N 109 20W
Canyon Ferry L. **47** 46 39N 111 44W
Canyon L. **65** 29 52N 98 12W
Canyon Village **70** 44 46N 110 32W
Canyonlands National Park **66** 38 15N 110 0W
Canyonville **58** 42 56N 123 17W
Caonillas, Lago **71** 18 17N 66 39W
Capa **61** 44 7N 100 59W
Capac **43** 43 1N 82 56W
Cape Canaveral **31** 28 24N 80 36W
Cape Charles **68** 37 16N 76 1W
Cape Cod B. **42** 41 50N 70 20W
Cape Cod National Seashore **42** 41 56N 70 6W
Cape Coral **31** 26 33N 81 57W
Cape Elizabeth **40** 43 34N 70 12W
Cape Fear → **54** 33 53N 78 1W
Cape Girardeau **46** 37 19N 89 32W
Cape Girardeau County ◇ **46** 37 25N 89 40W
Cape Hatteras National Seashore **54** 35 30N 75 28W
Cape I. **60** 33 2N 79 21W
Cape Lookout National Seashore **54** 35 45N 76 25W
Cape May **51** 38 56N 74 56W
Cape May County ◇ **51** 39 10N 74 45W
Cape May Court House **51** 39 5N 74 50W
Cape May Point **51** 38 56N 74 58W
Cape Pole **25** 55 58N 133 48W
Cape St. Claire **41** 39 3N 76 25W
Cape Vincent **53** 44 8N 76 20W
Cape Yakataga **25** 60 4N 142 26W
Capitan **52** 33 35N 105 35W
Capitan Pk. **52** 33 36N 105 16W
Capitol Reef National Monument **66** 38 15N 111 10W

Capitol View 60 33 58N 80 55W
Capitola 31 30 27N 84 5W
Capon Bridge 68 39 18N 78 26W
Caprock 52 33 24N 103 43W
Capron, Ill. 35 42 24N 88 44W
Capron, Okla. 57 36 54N 98 35W
Captain Cook 33 19 30N 155 55W
Captiva 31 26 31N 82 11W
Caratunk 40 45 8N 69 59W
Caraway 27 35 46N 90 19W
Carbon, Ind. 36 39 36N 87 6W
Carbon, Iowa 37 41 3N 94 50W
Carbon, Tex. 65 32 16N 98 50W
Carbon County ◇, Mont. 47 45 10N 109 0W
Carbon County ◇, Pa. 59 41 0N 75 50W
Carbon County ◇, Utah 66 39 40N 110 30W
Carbon County ◇, Wyo. 70 42 0N 107 0W
Carbon Hill 24 33 53N 87 32W
Carbonado 67 47 5N 122 3W
Carbondale, Colo. 30 39 24N 107 13W
Carbondale, Ill. 35 37 44N 89 13W
Carbondale, Kans. 38 38 49N 95 41W
Carbondale, Pa. 59 41 35N 75 30W
Cardiff 30 39 31N 107 19W
Cardigan, Mt. 50 43 40N 71 54W
Cardington 56 40 30N 82 54W
Cardwell 46 36 3N 90 17W
Carefree 26 33 50N 111 55W
Carencro 39 30 19N 92 3W
Carey, Idaho 34 43 19N 113 57W
Carey, Ohio 56 40 57N 83 23W
Caribou 40 46 52N 68 1W
Caribou County ◇ 34 42 50N 111 30W
Caribou Nat. Forest 34 42 50N 111 5W
Caribou National Forest 34 42 40N 111 10W
Caribou Range 34 43 10N 111 15W
Carite, Lago 71 18 5N 66 6W
Carl Blackwell, L. 57 36 8N 97 11W
Carl Junction 46 37 11N 94 34W
Carleton, Mich. 43 42 4N 83 24W
Carleton, Nebr. 48 40 18N 97 41W
Carlin 49 40 43N 116 7W
Carlinville 35 39 17N 89 53W
Carlisle, Ark. 27 34 47N 91 45W
Carlisle, Ind. 36 38 58N 87 24W
Carlisle, Iowa 37 41 30N 93 29W
Carlisle, Ky. 63 38 19N 84 1W
Carlisle, Pa. 59 40 12N 77 12W
Carlisle, S.C. 60 34 36N 81 28W
Carlisle, Wash. 67 47 10N 124 6W
Carlisle County ◇ 62 36 50N 89 0W
Carlock 35 40 35N 89 8W
Carlos, Minn. 44 45 58N 95 18W
Carlos, Tex. 65 30 36N 96 5W
Carlsbad, Calif. 29 33 10N 117 21W
Carlsbad, N. Mex. 52 32 25N 104 14W
Carlsbad, Tex. 64 31 36N 100 38W
Carlsbad Caverns National Park 52 32 10N 104 35W
Carlton, Minn. 44 46 40N 92 25W
Carlton, Oreg. 58 45 18N 123 11W
Carlton County ◇ 44 46 35N 92 50W
Carlyle, Ill. 35 38 37N 89 22W
Carlyle, Mont. 47 46 40N 104 4W
Carlyle L. 35 38 37N 89 21W
Carmel, Ind. 36 39 59N 86 8W
Carmel, N.Y. 53 41 26N 73 41W
Carmel-by-the-Sea 28 36 33N 121 55W
Carmel Valley 28 36 29N 121 43W
Carmen, Idaho 34 45 15N 113 54W
Carmen, Okla. 57 36 35N 98 28W
Carmi 35 38 5N 88 10W
Carmichael 28 38 38N 121 19W
Carnation 67 47 39N 121 55W
Carnegie, Ga. 32 31 39N 84 47W
Carnegie, Okla. 57 35 6N 98 36W
Carnegie, Pa. 59 40 24N 80 5W
Carneiro 38 38 44N 98 2W
Carnesville 32 34 22N 83 14W
Carney, Mich. 43 45 35N 87 34W
Carney, Okla. 57 35 48N 97 1W
Carneys Point 51 39 43N 75 28W
Caro 43 43 29N 83 24W
Carol City 31 25 56N 80 16W
Caroleen 54 35 17N 81 48W
Carolina, Puerto Rico 71 18 23N 65 58W
Carolina, U.S.A. 42 41 28N 71 40W
Carolina Beach 54 34 2N 77 54W
Caroline County ◇, Md. 41 38 50N 75 50W
Caroline County ◇, Va. 68 38 3N 77 21W
Carollton 43 43 28N 83 55W
Carp 49 37 7N 114 29W
Carpenter, Iowa 37 43 25N 93 1W
Carpenter, Wyo. 70 41 3N 104 22W
Carpenterville 58 42 13N 124 17W
Carpinteria 29 34 24N 119 31W
Carr 30 40 54N 104 53W
Carr Mt. 50 43 52N 71 50W
Carrabassett 40 45 5N 70 13W
Carrabelle 31 29 51N 84 40W
Carrier 57 36 29N 98 2W
Carrier Mills 35 37 41N 88 38W
Carriere 45 30 37N 89 39W
Carrigain, Mt. 50 44 6N 71 26W
Carrington 55 47 27N 99 8W
Carrizo Cr. → 52 36 55N 103 55W
Carrizo Springs 65 28 31N 99 52W
Carrizozo 52 33 38N 105 53W
Carroll, Iowa 37 42 4N 94 52W
Carroll, Nebr. 48 42 17N 97 12W
Carroll, Ohio 56 39 48N 82 43W
Carroll County ◇, Ark. 27 36 22N 93 34W
Carroll County ◇, Ga. 32 33 30N 85 10W
Carroll County ◇, Ill. 35 42 0N 90 0W
Carroll County ◇, Ind. 36 40 35N 86 35W
Carroll County ◇, Iowa 37 42 0N 94 50W
Carroll County ◇, Ky. 63 38 40N 85 5W
Carroll County ◇, Md. 41 39 30N 77 0W
Carroll County ◇, Miss. 45 33 30N 89 55W
Carroll County ◇, Mo. 46 39 25N 93 30W
Carroll County ◇, N.H. 50 43 50N 71 45W
Carroll County ◇, Ohio 56 40 34N 81 5W
Carroll County ◇, Tenn. 62 36 0N 88 26W
Carroll County ◇, Va. 68 36 55N 80 50W
Carrolls 67 46 4N 122 52W
Carrollton, Ala. 24 33 16N 88 6W
Carrollton, Ga. 32 33 35N 85 5W
Carrollton, Ill. 35 39 18N 90 24W
Carrollton, Ky. 63 38 41N 85 11W
Carrollton, Miss. 45 33 30N 89 55W
Carrollton, Mo. 46 39 22N 93 30W
Carrollton, Ohio 56 40 34N 81 5W
Carrollton, Tex. 65 32 57N 96 55W
Carrolltown 59 40 36N 78 43W
Carry Falls Reservoir 53 44 31N 74 45W
Carson, Calif. 29 33 48N 118 17W
Carson, Iowa 37 41 14N 95 25W
Carson, N. Dak. 55 46 25N 101 34W
Carson, Wash. 67 45 44N 121 49W
Carson → 49 39 45N 118 40W
Carson City 49 39 10N 119 46W
Carson County ◇ 64 35 20N 101 25W
Carson L. 49 39 18N 118 43W
Carson National Forest 52 36 30N 106 15W
Carson Sink 49 39 50N 118 25W
Carta Valley 64 29 48N 100 41W
Cartago 29 36 19N 118 2W
Carter, Ky. 63 38 26N 83 8W
Carter, Okla. 57 35 13N 99 30W
Carter, S. Dak. 61 43 23N 100 12W
Carter County ◇, Ky. 63 38 20N 83 0W
Carter County ◇, Mo. 46 37 0N 91 0W
Carter County ◇, Mont. 47 45 30N 104 30W
Carter County ◇, Okla. 57 34 15N 97 15W
Carter County ◇, Tenn. 63 36 17N 82 10W
Carter Lake 37 41 18N 95 54W
Carter Lake Reservoir 30 40 20N 105 13W
Carter Mt. 70 44 12N 109 25W
Carteret 51 40 34N 74 13W
Carteret County ◇ 54 34 50N 76 30W
Carters L. 32 34 37N 84 40W
Cartersville, Ga. 32 34 10N 84 48W
Cartersville, Va. 68 37 40N 78 6W
Carterville 35 37 46N 89 5W
Carthage, Ark. 27 34 4N 92 33W
Carthage, Ill. 35 40 25N 91 8W
Carthage, Ind. 36 39 44N 85 34W
Carthage, Miss. 45 32 44N 89 32W
Carthage, Mo. 46 37 11N 94 19W
Carthage, N.C. 54 35 21N 79 25W
Carthage, N.Y. 53 43 59N 75 37W
Carthage, S. Dak. 61 44 10N 97 43W
Carthage, Tenn. 63 36 15N 85 57W
Carthage, Tex. 65 32 9N 94 20W
Caruthersville 46 36 11N 89 39W
Carver County ◇ 44 44 50N 93 45W
Carville 39 30 13N 91 6W
Cary, Ill. 35 42 13N 88 14W
Cary, Miss. 45 32 49N 90 56W
Cary, N.C. 54 35 47N 78 46W
Caryville 63 36 18N 84 13W
Casa 27 35 2N 93 3W
Casa Blanca 52 35 3N 107 28W
Casa Grande 26 32 53N 111 45W
Casa Grande Ruins National Monument 26 33 0N 111 30W
Cascade, Colo. 30 38 54N 104 58W
Cascade, Idaho 34 44 31N 116 2W
Cascade, Iowa 37 42 18N 91 1W
Cascade, Mont. 47 47 16N 111 42W
Cascade County ◇ 47 47 20N 111 30W
Cascade Head 58 45 3N 124 1W
Cascade Locks 58 45 40N 121 54W
Cascade Range 58 45 0N 121 45W
Cascade Reservoir 34 44 32N 116 3W
Cascadia 58 44 24N 122 29W
Casco, Maine 40 44 0N 70 31W
Casco, Wis. 69 44 34N 87 37W
Casco B. 40 43 45N 70 0W
Caseville 43 43 56N 83 16W
Casey, Ill. 35 39 18N 87 59W
Casey, Iowa 37 41 31N 94 32W
Casey County ◇ 63 37 20N 85 0W
Cash 27 35 48N 90 56W
Cashie → 54 35 53N 76 49W
Cashiers 54 35 6N 83 6W
Cashion 57 35 48N 97 41W
Cashmere 67 47 31N 120 28W
Cashton 69 43 43N 90 47W
Casmalia 29 34 50N 120 32W
Casnovia 43 43 14N 85 48W
Cason 65 33 2N 94 49W
Casper 70 42 51N 106 19W
Caspian 43 46 4N 88 38W
Caspiana 39 32 17N 93 33W
Cass 68 38 24N 79 55W
Cass → 43 43 23N 83 59W
Cass City 43 43 36N 83 11W
Cass County ◇, Ill. 35 40 0N 90 15W
Cass County ◇, Ind. 36 40 45N 86 20W
Cass County ◇, Iowa 37 41 20N 94 55W
Cass County ◇, Mich. 43 41 50N 86 0W
Cass County ◇, Minn. 44 47 0N 94 10W
Cass County ◇, Mo. 46 38 40N 94 20W
Cass County ◇, N. Dak. 55 47 0N 97 0W
Cass County ◇, Nebr. 48 40 50N 96 10W
Cass County ◇, Tex. 65 33 1N 94 22W
Cass Lake 44 47 23N 94 37W
Cassadaga 53 42 20N 79 19W
Casselton 55 46 54N 97 13W
Cassia County ◇ 34 42 20N 113 30W
Cassoday 38 38 3N 96 38W
Cassopolis 43 41 55N 86 1W
Cassville, Mo. 46 36 41N 93 52W
Cassville, Pa. 59 40 18N 78 2W
Cassville, Wis. 69 42 43N 90 59W
Castaic L. 29 34 32N 118 37W
Castalia, Iowa 37 43 7N 91 41W
Castalia, Ohio 56 41 24N 82 49W
Castana 37 42 4N 95 55W
Castella 28 41 9N 122 19W
Castile 53 42 38N 78 3W
Castle 57 35 28N 96 23W
Castle Dale 66 39 13N 111 1W
Castle Dome Peak 26 33 5N 114 9W
Castle Gate 66 39 44N 110 52W
Castle Hayne 54 34 21N 77 54W
Castle Hills 65 29 32N 98 31W
Castle Peak 30 39 1N 106 52W
Castle Pk. 34 44 1N 114 42W
Castle Rock, Colo. 30 39 22N 104 51W
Castle Rock, Wash. 67 46 17N 122 54W
Castle Rock Butte 61 45 0N 103 27W
Castle Rock L. 69 43 52N 89 57W
Castleberry 24 31 18N 87 1W
Castleford 34 42 31N 114 52W
Castleton 50 43 37N 73 11W
Castleton-on-Hudson 53 42 32N 73 45W
Castlewood 61 44 44N 97 2W
Castolon 64 29 8N 103 31W
Castor 39 32 15N 93 10W
Castor → 46 36 51N 89 44W
Castor Bayou → 39 31 47N 99 22W
Castro County ◇ 64 34 33N 102 19W
Castro Valley 28 37 42N 122 4W
Castroville, Calif. 28 36 46N 121 45W
Castroville, Tex. 65 29 21N 98 53W
Caswell County ◇ 54 36 20N 79 15W
Cat Head Pt. 43 45 11N 85 37W
Cat I. 45 30 14N 89 6W
Cat Spring 65 29 51N 96 20W
Catahoula L. 39 31 31N 92 7W
Catahoula Parish ◇ 39 31 35N 91 58W
Catalina 26 32 30N 110 50W
Catano 71 18 27N 66 7W
Cataract L. 36 39 29N 86 55W
Catarina 65 28 21N 99 37W
Cataula 32 32 39N 84 52W
Catawba 69 45 32N 90 32W
Catawba → 60 34 28N 80 53W
Catawba County ◇ 54 35 40N 81 10W
Catawissa 59 40 57N 76 28W
Cathay 55 47 33N 99 25W
Cathedral City 29 33 47N 116 28W
Cathedral Mt. 64 30 11N 103 40W
Catherine, Ala. 24 32 11N 87 28W
Catherine, Kans. 38 38 56N 99 13W
Cathlamet 67 46 12N 123 23W
Catlettsburg 63 38 25N 82 36W
Catlin 35 40 4N 87 42W
Catlow Valley 58 42 20N 119 5W
Catoctin Mts. 41 39 35N 77 30W
Catonsville 41 39 17N 76 44W
Catoosa 57 36 11N 95 45W
Catoosa County ◇ 32 34 50N 85 10W
Catrima 65 28 21N 99 37W
Catron County ◇ 52 34 0N 108 15W
Catskill 53 42 14N 73 52W
Catskill Mts. 53 42 10N 74 25W
Cattaraugus County ◇ 53 42 30N 78 45W
Cattaraugus Indian Reservation 53 42 30N 79 0W
Caucomgomoc L. 40 46 13N 69 36W
Causey 52 33 53N 103 8W
Cauthron 27 34 55N 94 18W
Cavalier 55 48 48N 97 37W
Cavalier County ◇ 55 48 55N 97 30W
Cave City, Ark. 27 35 57N 91 33W
Cave City, Ky. 63 37 8N 85 58W
Cave Creek 26 33 50N 111 57W
Cave in Rock 35 37 28N 88 10W
Cave Junction 58 42 10N 123 39W
Cave Run L. 63 38 5N 83 25W
Cave Spring 32 34 6N 85 20W
Cawker City 38 39 31N 98 26W
Cayce, Ky. 62 36 33N 89 2W
Cayce, S.C. 60 33 59N 81 4W
Cayey 71 18 7N 66 10W
Cayucos 29 35 27N 120 54W
Cayuga, Ind. 36 39 57N 87 28W
Cayuga, N. Dak. 55 46 4N 97 23W
Cayuga County ◇ 53 43 0N 76 35W
Cayuga Heights 53 42 28N 76 30W
Cayuga L. 53 42 41N 76 41W
Cayuse 58 45 41N 118 33W
Cazenovia 53 42 56N 75 51W
Cearfoss 41 39 0N 77 0W
Cecil, Ga. 32 31 3N 83 24W
Cecil, Oreg. 58 45 37N 119 58W
Cecil County ◇ 41 39 30N 76 0W
Cecilia 63 37 40N 85 57W
Cecilton 41 39 24N 75 52W
Cecilville 28 41 9N 123 8W
Cedar →, Iowa 37 41 17N 91 21W
Cedar →, Mich. 43 45 25N 87 26W
Cedar →, Nebr. 48 41 22N 97 56W
Cedar Bluff, Ala. 24 34 13N 85 37W
Cedar Bluff, Va. 68 37 5N 81 46W
Cedar Bluff Reservoir 38 38 47N 99 43W
Cedar Bluffs, Kans. 38 39 59N 100 34W
Cedar Bluffs, Nebr. 48 41 24N 96 37W
Cedar Breaks National Monument 66 37 40N 112 50W
Cedar Brook 51 39 43N 74 54W
Cedar Butte 61 43 35N 101 1W
Cedar City, Mo. 46 38 36N 92 11W
Cedar City, Utah 66 37 41N 113 4W
Cedar County ◇, Iowa 37 41 45N 91 10W
Cedar County ◇, Mo. 46 37 45N 93 50W
Cedar County ◇, Nebr. 48 42 40N 97 15W
Cedar Cr. → 55 46 8N 101 19W
Cedar Creek, Ark. 27 34 47N 93 51W
Cedar Creek, Nebr. 48 41 2N 96 6W
Cedar Creek, Tex. 65 30 5N 97 30W
Cedar Creek Reservoir 65 32 11N 96 4W
Cedar Falls 37 42 32N 92 27W
Cedar Grove, Ind. 36 39 22N 84 56W
Cedar Grove, N.J. 51 40 51N 74 14W
Cedar Grove, W. Va. 68 38 13N 81 26W
Cedar Grove, Wis. 69 43 34N 87 49W
Cedar Hill, Mo. 46 38 21N 90 39W
Cedar Hill, N. Mex. 52 36 56N 107 53W
Cedar Hill, Tenn. 62 36 33N 87 0W
Cedar Key 31 29 8N 83 2W
Cedar L., Ill. 35 37 37N 89 18W
Cedar L., Tex. 64 32 49N 102 17W
Cedar Lake, Ind. 36 41 22N 87 26W
Cedar Lake, Tex. 65 28 54N 95 38W
Cedar Mills 44 44 57N 94 31W
Cedar Mts. 66 40 10N 112 30W
Cedar Park 65 30 30N 97 49W

Cedar Point **38** 38 16N 96 49W
Cedar Rapids, Iowa **37** 41 59N 91 40W
Cedar Rapids, Nebr. **48** 41 34N 98 9W
Cedar Springs **43** 43 13N 85 33W
Cedar Vale **38** 37 6N 96 30W
Cedaredge **30** 38 54N 107 56W
Cedartown **32** 34 1N 85 15W
Cedarville, Calif. **28** 41 32N 120 10W
Cedarville, Ill. **35** 42 23N 89 38W
Cedarville, Md. **41** 38 40N 76 47W
Cedarville, N.J. **51** 39 18N 75 12W
Cedarwood **30** 37 57N 104 37W
Ceiba **71** 18 16N 65 39W
Celeste **65** 33 18N 96 12W
Celina, Ohio **56** 40 33N 84 35W
Celina, Tenn. **63** 36 33N 85 30W
Celina, Tex. **65** 33 19N 96 47W
Cement **57** 34 56N 98 8W
Centenary **60** 34 2N 79 21W
Centennial Mts. **34** 44 35N 111 55W
Centennial Wash → **26** 33 17N 112 48W
Center, Colo. **30** 37 45N 106 6W
Center, Ga. **32** 34 3N 83 25W
Center, Mo. **46** 39 30N 91 32W
Center, N. Dak. **55** 47 7N 101 18W
Center, Nebr. **48** 42 37N 97 53W
Center, Tex. **65** 31 48N 94 11W
Center Barnstead **50** 43 19N 71 15W
Center City **44** 45 24N 92 49W
Center Cross **68** 37 48N 76 47W
Center Harbor **50** 43 42N 71 27W
Center Hill **31** 28 38N 82 3W
Center Hill L. **63** 36 6N 85 50W
Center Ossipee **50** 43 45N 71 9W
Center Point, Ala. **24** 33 38N 86 41W
Center Point, Ind. **36** 39 25N 87 4W
Center Point, Iowa **37** 42 12N 91 46W
Center Point, La. **39** 31 15N 92 13W
Center Point, Tex. **65** 29 57N 99 2W
Center Sandwich **50** 43 39N 71 25W
Center Strafford **50** 43 17N 71 10W
Centerburg **56** 40 18N 82 42W
Centereach **53** 40 52N 73 6W
Centerfield **66** 39 8N 111 49W
Centerton **51** 39 59N 75 0W
Centertown **46** 38 38N 92 25W
Centerville, Ark. **27** 35 7N 93 10W
Centerville, Calif. **29** 36 44N 119 30W
Centerville, Del. **41** 39 49N 75 37W
Centerville, Ind. **36** 39 49N 85 0W
Centerville, Iowa **37** 40 44N 92 52W
Centerville, Kans. **38** 38 13N 95 1W
Centerville, La. **39** 29 46N 91 26W
Centerville, Mo. **46** 37 26N 90 58W
Centerville, N.C. **54** 36 11N 78 6W
Centerville, N.Y. **53** 42 29N 78 15W
Centerville, Ohio **56** 39 38N 84 8W
Centerville, Crawford, Pa. **59** 41 44N 79 46W
Centerville, Washington, Pa. **59** 40 3N 79 59W
Centerville, S. Dak. **61** 43 7N 96 58W
Centerville, Tenn. **62** 35 47N 87 28W
Centerville, Tex. **65** 31 16N 95 59W
Centerville, Utah **66** 40 55N 111 52W
Centrahoma **57** 34 37N 96 21W
Central, Alaska **25** 65 35N 144 48W
Central, Mich. **43** 47 25N 88 12W
Central, N. Mex. **52** 32 47N 108 9W
Central, S.C. **60** 34 44N 82 47W
Central, Utah **66** 37 25N 113 38W
Central, Cordillera **71** 18 8N 66 35W
Central Aguirre **71** 17 58N 66 14W
Central City, Colo. **30** 39 48N 105 31W
Central City, Ill. **35** 38 33N 89 8W
Central City, Iowa **37** 42 12N 91 32W
Central City, Ky. **62** 37 18N 87 7W
Central City, Nebr. **48** 41 7N 98 0W
Central City, Pa. **59** 40 7N 78 49W
Central City, S. Dak. **61** 44 22N 103 46W
Central Falls **42** 41 54N 71 23W
Central Islip **53** 40 47N 73 12W
Central Lake **43** 45 4N 85 16W
Central Point **58** 42 23N 122 55W
Central Square **53** 43 17N 76 9W
Central Valley **28** 40 41N 122 22W
Centralhatchee **32** 33 22N 85 6W
Centralia, Ill. **35** 38 32N 89 8W
Centralia, Kans. **38** 39 44N 96 8W
Centralia, Mo. **46** 39 13N 92 8W
Centralia, Okla. **57** 36 48N 95 21W
Centralia, Wash. **67** 46 43N 122 58W
Centre **24** 34 9N 85 41W
Centre County ◇ **59** 41 0N 78 0W
Centre Grove **51** 39 20N 75 8W
Centreville, Ala. **24** 32 57N 87 8W
Centreville, Md. **41** 39 3N 76 4W
Centreville, Mich. **43** 41 55N 85 32W
Centreville, Miss. **45** 31 5N 91 4W
Century **31** 30 58N 87 16W
Ceres **28** 37 35N 120 57W
Ceresco **48** 41 3N 96 39W
Cerrillos **52** 35 26N 106 8W
Cerro Gordo **35** 39 53N 88 44W
Cerro Gordo County ◇ **37** 43 5N 93 15W
Cerro Vista Peak **52** 36 14N 105 25W
Ceylon **44** 43 32N 94 38W
Chaco → **52** 36 46N 108 39W
Chaco Canyon National Monument **52** 36 6N 108 0W
Chacuaco → **30** 37 34N 103 38W
Chadbourn **54** 34 19N 78 50W
Chadron **48** 42 50N 103 0W
Chadwick **35** 42 1N 89 53W
Chaffee, Mo. **46** 37 11N 89 40W
Chaffee, N. Dak. **55** 46 46N 97 21W
Chaffee County ◇ **30** 38 45N 106 10W
Chagres → **71** 9 10N 79 40W
Chaires **31** 30 26N 84 7W
Chalk Mts. **64** 29 30N 103 18W
Chalkyitsik **25** 66 39N 143 43W
Challis **34** 44 30N 114 14W
Challis National Forest **34** 44 0N 113 40W
Chalmers **36** 40 40N 86 52W
Chalmette **39** 29 56N 89 58W
Chama, Colo. **30** 37 10N 105 23W
Chama, N. Mex. **52** 36 54N 106 35W
Chama → **52** 36 10N 106 10W
Chamberino **52** 32 3N 106 41W
Chamberlain **61** 43 49N 99 20W
Chamberlain L. **40** 46 14N 69 19W
Chambers, Ariz. **26** 35 11N 109 26W
Chambers, Nebr. **48** 42 12N 98 45W
Chambers County ◇, Ala. **24** 32 54N 85 24W
Chambers County ◇, Tex. **65** 29 47N 94 35W
Chambers I. **69** 45 11N 87 22W
Chambersburg **59** 39 56N 77 40W
Chamblee **32** 33 53N 84 18W
Chamisal **52** 36 10N 105 44W
Chamois **46** 38 41N 91 46W
Champaign **35** 40 7N 88 15W
Champaign County ◇, Ill. **35** 40 10N 88 10W
Champaign County ◇, Ohio **56** 40 7N 83 45W
Champion, Mich. **43** 46 31N 87 58W
Champion, Ohio **56** 41 19N 80 51W
Champion Creek Reservoir **64** 32 17N 100 52W
Champlain **53** 44 59N 73 27W
Champlain, L. **53** 44 40N 73 20W
Champlain Canal **53** 43 30N 73 27W
Chancellor **61** 43 22N 96 59W
Chandalar → **25** 66 37N 146 0W
Chandeleur Is. **39** 29 55N 88 57W
Chandeleur Sd. **39** 29 55N 89 0W
Chandler, Ariz. **26** 33 18N 111 50W
Chandler, Ind. **36** 38 3N 87 22W
Chandler, Minn. **44** 43 56N 95 57W
Chandler, Okla. **57** 35 42N 96 53W
Chandler, Tex. **65** 32 18N 95 29W
Chandlerville **35** 40 3N 90 9W
Chanhassen **44** 44 55N 93 32W
Channahon **35** 41 26N 88 14W
Channel Is. **29** 33 40N 119 15W
Channel Islands National Park **29** 33 30N 119 0W
Channelview **65** 29 47N 95 8W
Channing, Mich. **43** 46 9N 88 5W
Channing, Tex. **64** 35 41N 102 20W
Chanute **38** 37 41N 95 27W
Chapel Hill, Ky. **62** 36 43N 86 18W
Chapel Hill, N.C. **54** 35 55N 79 4W
Chapel Hill, Tenn. **62** 35 38N 86 41W
Chapin **35** 39 46N 90 24W
Chaplin **63** 37 54N 85 13W
Chapman, Ala. **24** 31 40N 86 43W
Chapman, Kans. **38** 38 58N 97 1W
Chapman, Nebr. **48** 41 2N 98 10W
Chapmanville **68** 37 59N 82 1W
Chappaquiddick Island **42** 41 22N 70 30W
Chappell **48** 41 6N 102 28W
Chappell Hill **65** 30 9N 96 15W
Chappells **60** 34 11N 81 52W
Chaptico **41** 38 21N 76 49W
Charco **65** 28 44N 97 37W
Chardon **56** 41 35N 81 12W
Charenton **39** 29 53N 91 32W
Charing **32** 32 28N 84 22W
Chariton **37** 41 1N 93 19W
Chariton → **46** 39 19N 92 58W
Chariton County ◇ **46** 39 30N 93 0W
Charity **46** 37 31N 93 1W
Charity I. **43** 44 2N 83 26W
Charlemont **42** 42 38N 72 52W
Charleroi **59** 40 9N 79 57W
Charles **32** 32 8N 84 50W
Charles → **42** 42 22N 71 3W
Charles, C. **68** 37 7N 75 58W
Charles City, Iowa **37** 43 4N 92 41W
Charles City, Va. **68** 37 21N 77 4W
Charles City County ◇ **68** 37 21N 77 4W
Charles County ◇ **41** 38 30N 77 0W
Charles M. Russell National Wildlife Refuge **47** 47 45N 107 0W
Charles Mill L. **56** 40 45N 82 22W
Charles Mix County ◇ **61** 43 15N 98 42W
Charles Town **68** 39 17N 77 52W
Charleston, Ark. **27** 35 18N 94 5W
Charleston, Ill. **35** 39 30N 88 10W
Charleston, Miss. **45** 34 1N 90 4W
Charleston, Mo. **46** 36 55N 89 21W
Charleston, S.C. **60** 32 46N 79 56W
Charleston, Tenn. **63** 35 17N 84 45W
Charleston, Utah **66** 40 28N 111 28W
Charleston, W. Va. **68** 38 21N 81 38W
Charleston County ◇ **60** 32 50N 80 0W
Charleston Peak **49** 36 16N 115 42W
Charlestown, Ind. **36** 38 27N 85 40W
Charlestown, Md. **41** 39 35N 75 59W
Charlestown, N.H. **50** 43 14N 72 25W
Charlestown, R.I. **42** 41 23N 71 45W
Charlevoix **43** 45 19N 85 16W
Charlevoix, L. **43** 45 16N 85 8W
Charlevoix County ◇ **43** 45 15N 85 10W
Charlo **47** 47 26N 114 10W
Charlotte, Iowa **37** 41 58N 90 28W
Charlotte, Mich. **43** 42 34N 84 50W
Charlotte, N.C. **54** 35 13N 80 51W
Charlotte, Tenn. **62** 36 11N 87 21W
Charlotte, Tex. **65** 28 52N 98 43W
Charlotte Amalie **71** 18 21N 64 56W
Charlotte County ◇, Fla. **31** 26 50N 82 0W
Charlotte County ◇, Va. **68** 37 0N 78 55W
Charlotte Court House **68** 37 3N 78 39W
Charlotte Hall **41** 38 28N 76 45W
Charlotte Harbor **31** 26 50N 82 10W
Charlottesville **68** 38 2N 78 30W
Charlton City **42** 42 9N 71 58W
Charlton County ◇ **32** 30 50N 82 10W
Charter Oak **37** 42 4N 95 36W
Chase, Ala. **24** 34 47N 86 33W
Chase, Kans. **38** 38 21N 98 21W
Chase, Md. **41** 39 22N 76 22W
Chase, Mich. **43** 43 53N 85 38W
Chase City **68** 36 48N 78 28W
Chase County ◇, Kans. **38** 38 15N 96 45W
Chase County ◇, Nebr. **48** 40 30N 101 40W
Chaseburg **69** 43 40N 91 6W
Chaseley **55** 47 27N 99 49W
Chataignier **39** 30 34N 92 19W
Chatanika **25** 65 7N 147 28W
Chateaugay **53** 44 56N 74 5W
Chatfield, Ark. **27** 35 0N 90 24W
Chatfield, Minn. **44** 43 51N 92 11W
Chatfield, Ohio **56** 40 57N 82 57W
Chatham, Ill. **35** 39 40N 89 42W
Chatham, La. **39** 32 18N 92 27W
Chatham, Mass. **42** 41 41N 69 58W
Chatham, Mich. **43** 46 21N 86 56W
Chatham, N.J. **51** 40 44N 74 23W
Chatham, N.Y. **53** 42 21N 73 36W
Chatham, Va. **68** 36 50N 79 24W
Chatham County ◇, Ga. **32** 32 0N 81 10W
Chatham County ◇, N.C. **54** 35 45N 79 10W
Chatom **24** 31 28N 88 16W
Chatsworth, Ga. **32** 34 46N 84 46W
Chatsworth, Ill. **35** 40 45N 88 18W
Chatsworth, Iowa **37** 42 55N 96 31W
Chatsworth, N.J. **51** 39 49N 74 32W
Chattahoochee **31** 30 42N 84 51W
Chattahoochee → **32** 30 54N 84 57W
Chattahoochee County ◇ **32** 32 20N 84 50W
Chattahoochee National Forest **32** 34 50N 84 0W
Chattanooga, Okla. **57** 34 25N 98 39W
Chattanooga, Tenn. **63** 35 3N 85 19W
Chattaroy **67** 47 53N 117 21W
Chattooga County ◇ **32** 34 30N 85 15W
Chaumont **53** 44 4N 76 8W
Chauncey **56** 39 24N 82 8W
Chautauqua **38** 37 1N 96 11W
Chautauqua County ◇, Kans. **38** 37 15N 96 15W
Chautauqua County ◇, N.Y. **53** 42 20N 79 15W
Chautauqua L. **53** 42 10N 79 24W
Chauvin **39** 29 26N 90 36W
Chaves County ◇ **52** 33 15N 104 30W
Chavies **63** 37 21N 83 21W
Chazy **53** 44 53N 73 26W
Cheaha Mt. **24** 33 29N 85 49W
Cheatham County ◇ **62** 36 17N 87 4W
Chebanse **35** 41 0N 87 54W
Cheboygan **43** 45 39N 84 29W
Cheboygan County ◇ **43** 45 20N 84 30W
Checotah **57** 35 28N 95 31W
Cheektowaga **53** 42 54N 78 45W
Cheesman L. **30** 39 13N 105 16W
Chefornak **25** 60 13N 164 12W
Chehalis **67** 46 40N 122 58W
Chehalis → **67** 46 57N 123 50W
Chelan **67** 47 51N 120 1W
Chelan, L. **67** 48 11N 120 30W
Chelan County ◇ **67** 48 0N 120 30W
Chelan Falls **67** 47 48N 119 59W
Chelatchie **67** 45 55N 122 25W
Chelmsford **42** 42 36N 71 21W
Chelsea, Iowa **37** 41 55N 92 24W
Chelsea, Mich. **43** 42 19N 84 1W
Chelsea, Okla. **57** 36 32N 95 26W
Chelsea, Vt. **50** 43 59N 72 27W
Cheltenham **41** 38 42N 76 50W
Chemehuevi Indian Reservation **29** 34 30N 114 25W
Chemquasabamticook L. **40** 46 30N 69 37W
Chemung County ◇ **53** 42 10N 76 45W
Chenango → **53** 42 6N 75 55W
Chenango County ◇ **53** 42 30N 75 40W
Chenes, Pointe aux **43** 45 55N 84 54W
Cheney, Kans. **38** 37 38N 97 47W
Cheney, Wash. **67** 47 30N 117 35W
Cheney Reservoir **38** 37 43N 97 48W
Cheneyville **39** 31 1N 92 17W
Chenoa **35** 40 45N 88 43W
Chenoweth **58** 45 37N 121 13W
Chepachet **42** 41 55N 71 40W
Chequamegon National Forest **69** 46 10N 91 0W
Chequamegon Pt. **69** 46 42N 90 45W
Cheraw, Colo. **30** 38 6N 103 31W
Cheraw, S.C. **60** 34 42N 79 53W
Cheriton **68** 37 17N 75 58W
Cherokee, Ala. **24** 34 45N 87 58W
Cherokee, Iowa **37** 42 45N 95 33W
Cherokee, Kans. **38** 37 21N 94 49W
Cherokee, N.C. **54** 35 29N 83 19W
Cherokee, Okla. **57** 36 45N 98 21W
Cherokee, Tex. **65** 30 59N 98 43W
Cherokee County ◇, Ala. **24** 34 9N 85 41W
Cherokee County ◇, Ga. **32** 34 20N 84 20W
Cherokee County ◇, Iowa **37** 42 45N 95 35W
Cherokee County ◇, Kans. **38** 37 15N 94 45W
Cherokee County ◇, N.C. **54** 35 10N 84 10W
Cherokee County ◇, Okla. **57** 36 0N 95 0W
Cherokee County ◇, S.C. **60** 35 0N 81 40W
Cherokee County ◇, Tex. **65** 31 58N 95 17W
Cherokee Falls **60** 35 4N 81 32W
Cherokee Indian Reservation **54** 35 30N 83 20W
Cherokee L. **63** 36 10N 83 30W
Cherokee National Forest **63** 36 0N 82 40W
Cherokees, Lake O' The **57** 36 28N 95 2W
Cherry → **61** 44 36N 101 30W
Cherry County ◇ **48** 42 30N 101 0W
Cherry Cr. → **30** 39 45N 104 1W
Cherry Creek, Nev. **49** 39 54N 114 53W
Cherry Creek, S. Dak. **61** 44 36N 101 30W
Cherry Creek Lake **30** 39 39N 104 52W
Cherry Hill **51** 39 56N 75 2W
Cherry L. **28** 37 59N 119 55W
Cherry Tree **59** 40 44N 78 48W
Cherry Valley, Ark. **27** 35 24N 90 45W
Cherry Valley, N.Y. **53** 42 48N 74 45W
Cherryfield **40** 44 36N 67 56W
Cherryvale **38** 37 16N 95 33W
Cherryville **54** 35 23N 81 23W
Chesaning **43** 43 11N 84 7W
Chesapeake **68** 36 50N 76 17W
Chesapeake B. **68** 38 0N 76 10W
Chesapeake Beach **41** 38 41N 76 32W
Chesapeake City **41** 39 32N 75 49W
Chesaw **67** 48 57N 119 3W
Chesdin, L. **68** 37 20N 77 40W
Cheshire, Conn. **42** 41 30N 72 54W
Cheshire, Mass. **42** 42 34N 73 10W
Cheshire County ◇ **50** 43 0N 72 15W
Chesilhurst **51** 39 44N 74 52W
Chesnee **60** 35 9N 81 52W
Chester, Ark. **27** 35 41N 94 11W
Chester, Calif. **28** 40 19N 121 14W
Chester, Ga. **32** 32 24N 83 9W

Chester, Ill. **35** 37 55N 89 49W
Chester, Mass. **42** 42 17N 72 59W
Chester, Mont. **47** 48 31N 110 58W
Chester, N.H. **50** 42 55N 71 15W
Chester, N.J. **51** 40 47N 74 42W
Chester, Okla. **57** 36 13N 98 55W
Chester, Pa. **59** 39 51N 75 22W
Chester, S.C. **60** 34 43N 81 12W
Chester, S. Dak. **61** 43 54N 96 56W
Chester, Va. **68** 37 21N 77 27W
Chester, Vt. **50** 43 16N 72 36W
Chester, W. Va. **68** 40 37N 80 34W
Chester → **41** 39 3N 76 16W
Chester County ◇, Pa. **59** 39 59N 75 50W
Chester County ◇, S.C. **60** 34 30N 81 10W
Chester County ◇, Tenn. **62** 35 20N 88 45W
Chesterfield, Ill. **35** 39 15N 90 4W
Chesterfield, N.H. **50** 42 52N 72 28W
Chesterfield, S.C. **60** 34 44N 80 5W
Chesterfield, Va. **68** 37 23N 77 31W
Chesterfield County ◇, S.C. **60** 34 30N 80 10W
Chesterfield County ◇, Va. **68** 37 23N 77 31W
Chesterhill **56** 39 29N 81 52W
Chestertown **41** 39 13N 76 4W
Chesterville **41** 39 17N 75 55W
Chestnut **39** 32 3N 93 1W
Chesuncook L. **40** 46 0N 69 21W
Cheswold **41** 39 13N 75 35W
Chetco → **58** 42 3N 124 16W
Chetek **69** 45 19N 91 39W
Chetopa **38** 37 2N 95 5W
Chevak **25** 61 32N 165 35W
Chevelon Cr. → **26** 34 55N 110 35W
Cheviot **56** 39 10N 84 37W
Chevy Chase **41** 38 59N 77 5W
Chewelah **67** 48 17N 117 43W
Cheyenne, Okla. **57** 35 37N 99 40W
Cheyenne, Wyo. **70** 41 8N 104 49W
Cheyenne → **61** 44 41N 101 18W
Cheyenne Bottoms **38** 38 27N 98 40W
Cheyenne County ◇, Colo. **30** 38 50N 102 35W
Cheyenne County ◇, Kans. **38** 39 45N 101 45W
Cheyenne County ◇, Nebr. **48** 41 15N 103 0W
Cheyenne River Indian Reservation **61** 45 0N 101 0W
Cheyenne Wells **30** 38 49N 102 21W
Chicago **35** 41 53N 87 38W
Chicago Heights **35** 41 30N 87 38W
Chicamuxen **41** 38 33N 77 15W
Chichagof I. **25** 57 30N 135 30W
Chickahominy → **68** 37 14N 76 53W
Chickamauga **32** 34 52N 85 18W
Chickamauga L. **63** 35 6N 85 14W
Chickasaw **24** 30 46N 88 5W
Chickasaw County ◇, Iowa **37** 43 5N 92 20W
Chickasaw County ◇, Miss. **45** 33 54N 89 0W
Chickasaw Nat. Rec. Area **57** 34 26N 97 0W
Chickasawhay → **45** 30 59N 88 44W
Chickasha **57** 35 3N 97 58W
Chicken **25** 64 5N 141 56W
Chico, Calif. **28** 39 44N 121 50W
Chico, Tex. **65** 33 18N 97 48W
Chicopee, Ga. **32** 34 15N 83 51W
Chicopee, Mass. **42** 42 9N 72 37W
Chicopee → **42** 42 9N 72 37W
Chicora **45** 31 34N 88 34W
Chicot **27** 33 12N 91 17W
Chicot County ◇ **27** 33 12N 91 17W
Chidester **27** 33 42N 93 1W
Chiefland **31** 29 29N 82 52W
Chignik **25** 56 18N 158 24W
Chikaskia → **57** 36 37N 97 15W
Childersburg **24** 33 16N 86 21W
Childress **64** 34 25N 100 13W
Childress County ◇ **64** 34 25N 100 15W
Chilhowee **46** 38 36N 93 51W
Chilhowie **68** 36 48N 81 41W
Chilili **52** 34 53N 106 14W
Chillicothe, Ill. **35** 40 55N 89 29W
Chillicothe, Iowa **37** 41 5N 92 32W
Chillicothe, Mo. **46** 39 48N 93 33W
Chillicothe, Ohio **56** 39 20N 82 59W
Chillicothe, Tex. **65** 34 15N 99 31W
Chillum **41** 38 56N 76 58W
Chilmark **42** 41 21N 70 45W
Chilocco **57** 36 59N 97 4W
Chiloquin **58** 42 35N 121 52W
Chilton **69** 44 2N 88 10W
Chilton County ◇ **24** 32 51N 86 38W
Chimayo **52** 36 0N 105 56W
Chimney Rock **30** 37 13N 107 18W
China **65** 30 3N 94 20W
China Grove **54** 35 34N 80 35W
Chinati Mts. **64** 29 55N 104 30W
Chinati Peak **64** 29 57N 104 29W
Chincoteague **68** 37 56N 75 23W
Chincoteague Bay **41** 38 15N 75 15W
Chinle **26** 36 9N 109 33W
Chinle Cr. → **66** 37 12N 109 43W
Chino **29** 34 1N 117 41W
Chino Valley **26** 34 45N 112 27W
Chinook, Mont. **47** 48 35N 109 14W
Chinook, Wash. **67** 46 16N 123 57W
Chinook Pass **67** 46 52N 121 32W
Chinquapin **54** 34 50N 77 49W
Chipley **31** 30 47N 85 32W
Chipola → **31** 30 1N 85 5W
Chippewa →, Mich. **43** 43 35N 84 17W
Chippewa →, Minn. **44** 44 56N 95 44W
Chippewa →, Wis. **69** 44 25N 92 5W
Chippewa, L. **69** 45 57N 91 12W
Chippewa County ◇, Mich. **43** 46 20N 84 40W
Chippewa County ◇, Minn. **44** 45 0N 95 35W
Chippewa County ◇, Wis. **69** 45 5N 91 20W
Chippewa Falls **69** 44 56N 91 24W
Chippewa National Forest **44** 47 45N 94 0W
Chiputneticook Lakes **40** 45 35N 67 35W
Chireno **65** 31 30N 94 21W
Chiricahua Mts. **26** 32 0N 109 15W
Chiricahua National Monument **26** 32 0N 109 20W
Chiricahua Peak **26** 31 51N 109 18W
Chisago County ◇ **44** 45 30N 92 55W
Chisholm, Maine **40** 44 29N 70 12W
Chisholm, Minn. **44** 47 29N 92 53W
Chisos Mts. **64** 29 5N 103 15W
Chistochina **25** 62 34N 144 40W
Chitina **25** 61 31N 144 26W
Chittenango **53** 43 3N 75 52W
Chittenden **50** 43 42N 72 55W
Chittenden County ◇ **50** 44 30N 73 10W
Chivington **30** 38 26N 102 32W
Chloride **26** 35 25N 114 12W
Chocolate Mts., Ariz. **26** 33 15N 114 30W
Chocolate Mts., Calif. **29** 33 15N 115 15W
Chocowinity **54** 35 31N 77 6W
Choctaw **57** 35 31N 97 17W
Choctaw Bluff **24** 31 22N 87 46W
Choctaw County ◇, Ala. **24** 32 0N 88 10W
Choctaw County ◇, Miss. **45** 33 19N 89 11W
Choctaw County ◇, Okla. **57** 34 0N 95 30W
Choctaw Indian Reservation **45** 32 48N 89 7W
Choctawatchee → **31** 30 25N 86 8W
Choctawhatchee B. **31** 30 20N 86 20W
Choke Canyon Res. **65** 28 30N 98 20W
Chokio **44** 45 34N 96 10W
Chokoloskee **31** 25 49N 81 22W
Choptank **41** 38 41N 75 57W
Choptank → **41** 38 38N 76 13W
Choteau **47** 47 49N 112 11W
Chouteau **57** 36 11N 95 21W
Chouteau County ◇ **47** 47 55N 110 30W
Chowan → **54** 36 1N 76 40W
Chowan County ◇ **54** 36 10N 76 40W
Chowchilla **28** 37 7N 120 16W
Chrisman **35** 39 48N 87 41W
Chrisney **36** 38 1N 87 2W
Christian County ◇, Ill. **35** 39 30N 89 15W
Christian County ◇, Ky. **62** 36 50N 87 30W
Christian County ◇, Mo. **46** 37 0N 93 10W
Christian Sd. **25** 55 56N 134 40W
Christiana, Del. **41** 39 40N 75 40W
Christiana, Tenn. **62** 35 43N 86 24W
Christiansburg, Ohio **56** 40 3N 84 2W
Christiansburg, Va. **68** 37 8N 80 25W
Christiansted **71** 17 45N 64 42W
Christie **57** 35 57N 94 42W
Christine **55** 46 35N 96 48W
Christopher **35** 37 59N 89 3W
Christoval **64** 31 12N 100 30W
Chromo **30** 37 2N 106 50W
Chrysler **24** 31 18N 87 42W
Chualar **28** 36 34N 121 31W
Chuathbaluk **25** 61 40N 159 15W
Chubbuck **34** 42 55N 112 28W
Chuckawalla Mts. **29** 33 30N 115 20W
Chugach Mts. **25** 60 45N 147 0W
Chugach National Forest **25** 58 15N 152 45W
Chugiak **25** 61 24N 149 29W
Chuginadak I. **25** 52 50N 169 45W
Chugwater **70** 41 46N 104 50W
Chula, Ga. **32** 31 33N 83 32W
Chula, Mo. **46** 39 55N 93 29W
Chula, Va. **68** 37 23N 77 54W
Chula Vista **29** 32 39N 117 5W
Chunchula **24** 30 55N 88 12W
Chunky **45** 32 20N 88 56W
Chupadera Mesa **52** 34 0N 106 0W
Church Creek **41** 38 30N 76 10W
Church Hill, Md. **41** 39 9N 75 59W
Church Hill, Tenn. **63** 36 31N 82 43W
Church Point **39** 30 24N 92 13W
Churchill County ◇ **49** 39 30N 118 20W
Churchs Ferry **55** 48 16N 99 12W
Churchville **41** 39 34N 76 15W
Churdan **37** 42 9N 94 29W
Churubusco **36** 41 14N 85 19W
Chuska Mts. **52** 36 15N 108 50W
Ciales **71** 18 20N 66 28W
Cibola County ◇ **52** 35 0N 108 0W
Cibola National Forest **52** 35 10N 108 15W
Cicero, Ill. **35** 41 51N 87 45W
Cicero, Ind. **36** 40 8N 86 1W
Cidra **71** 18 11N 66 10W
Cidra, Lago de **71** 18 12N 66 8W
Cima **29** 35 14N 115 30W
Cimarron, Kans. **38** 37 48N 100 21W
Cimarron, N. Mex. **52** 36 31N 104 55W
Cimarron →, N. Mex. **52** 36 15N 104 30W
Cimarron →, Okla. **57** 36 10N 96 17W
Cimarron County ◇ **57** 36 45N 102 30W
Cincinnati, Iowa **37** 40 38N 92 56W
Cincinnati, Ohio **56** 39 6N 84 31W
Circle, Alaska **25** 65 50N 144 4W
Circle, Mont. **47** 47 25N 105 35W
Circleville, Kans. **38** 39 31N 95 52W
Circleville, Ohio **56** 39 36N 82 57W
Circleville, Utah **66** 38 10N 112 16W
Circleville, W. Va. **68** 38 40N 79 30W
Circleville Mt. **66** 38 12N 112 24W
Cisco, Ill. **35** 40 1N 88 44W
Cisco, Tex. **65** 32 23N 98 59W
Cisco, Utah **66** 38 58N 109 19W
Cisne **35** 38 31N 88 26W
Cissna Park **35** 40 34N 87 54W
Cistern **65** 29 49N 97 13W
Citra **31** 29 25N 82 7W
Citronelle **24** 31 6N 88 14W
Citrus County ◇ **31** 28 45N 82 30W
Citrus Heights **28** 38 42N 121 17W
Citrus Springs **31** 29 2N 82 27W
Clackamas → **58** 45 22N 122 36W
Clackamas County ◇ **58** 45 15N 122 15W
Claflin **38** 38 31N 98 32W
Claiborne, Ala. **24** 31 33N 87 31W
Claiborne, Md. **41** 38 50N 76 17W
Claiborne, L. **39** 32 45N 93 0W
Claiborne County ◇, Miss. **45** 31 58N 90 59W
Claiborne County ◇, Tenn. **63** 36 27N 83 34W
Claiborne Parish ◇ **39** 32 48N 93 4W
Clair Engle L. **28** 40 48N 122 46W
Clair Haven **43** 42 36N 82 49W
Claire City **61** 45 52N 97 6W
Clairton **59** 40 18N 79 53W
Clallam Bay **67** 48 15N 124 16W
Clallam County ◇ **67** 48 0N 124 0W
Clam Gulch **25** 60 15N 151 23W
Clan Alpine Mts. **49** 39 40N 117 55W
Clancy **47** 46 28N 111 59W
Clanton **24** 32 51N 86 38W
Clara **45** 31 35N 88 42W
Clara City **44** 44 57N 95 22W
Clare, Iowa **37** 42 35N 94 21W
Clare, Mich. **43** 43 49N 84 46W
Clare County ◇ **43** 44 0N 84 50W
Claremont, Calif. **29** 34 6N 117 43W
Claremont, Ill. **35** 38 43N 87 58W
Claremont, N.H. **50** 43 23N 72 20W
Claremont, S. Dak. **61** 45 40N 98 1W
Claremont, Va. **68** 37 14N 76 58W
Claremore **57** 36 19N 95 36W
Clarence, Iowa **37** 41 53N 91 4W
Clarence, La. **39** 31 49N 93 2W
Clarence, Mo. **46** 39 45N 92 16W
Clarence, Port **25** 65 15N 166 40W
Clarendon, Ark. **27** 34 42N 91 19W
Clarendon, Pa. **59** 41 47N 79 6W
Clarendon, Tex. **64** 34 56N 100 53W
Clarendon County ◇ **60** 33 45N 80 10W
Clareton **70** 43 42N 104 42W
Clarinda **37** 40 44N 95 2W
Clarington **56** 39 46N 80 52W
Clarion, Iowa **37** 42 44N 93 44W
Clarion, Pa. **59** 41 13N 79 23W
Clarion → **59** 41 7N 79 41W
Clarion County ◇ **59** 41 5N 79 40W
Clarissa **44** 46 8N 94 57W
Clarita **57** 34 29N 96 26W
Clark, Mo. **46** 39 17N 92 21W
Clark, N.J. **51** 40 38N 74 18W
Clark, S. Dak. **61** 44 53N 97 44W
Clark Canyon Res. **47** 44 57N 112 56W
Clark County ◇, Ark. **27** 33 55N 93 9W
Clark County ◇, Idaho **34** 44 15N 112 30W
Clark County ◇, Ill. **35** 39 20N 87 45W
Clark County ◇, Ind. **36** 38 30N 85 40W
Clark County ◇, Kans. **38** 37 15N 99 45W
Clark County ◇, Ky. **63** 38 0N 84 10W
Clark County ◇, Mo. **46** 40 25N 91 40W
Clark County ◇, Nev. **49** 36 10N 115 10W
Clark County ◇, Ohio **56** 39 55N 83 49W
Clark County ◇, S. Dak. **61** 44 50N 97 44W
Clark County ◇, Wash. **67** 45 55N 122 25W
Clark County ◇, Wis. **69** 44 40N 90 40W
Clark Fork **34** 48 9N 116 11W
Clark Fork → **34** 48 9N 116 15W
Clark Hill L. **32** 33 40N 82 12W
Clark Mt. **29** 35 32N 115 35W
Clark National Forest **46** 37 40N 92 10W
Clarkdale **26** 34 46N 112 3W
Clarke County ◇, Ala. **24** 31 42N 87 47W
Clarke County ◇, Ga. **32** 34 0N 83 15W
Clarke County ◇, Iowa **37** 41 0N 93 45W
Clarke County ◇, Miss. **45** 32 2N 88 44W
Clarke County ◇, Va. **68** 39 9N 77 59W
Clarkesville **32** 34 37N 83 31W
Clarkfield **44** 44 48N 95 48W
Clarkia **34** 47 1N 116 15W
Clarkrange **63** 36 11N 85 1W
Clarks, La. **39** 32 2N 92 8W
Clarks, Nebr. **48** 41 13N 97 50W
Clarks Fork → **47** 45 32N 108 50W
Clarks Grove **44** 43 46N 93 20W
Clarks Hill **36** 40 15N 86 43W
Clarks Point **25** 58 51N 158 33W
Clarks Summit **59** 41 30N 75 42W
Clarksburg, Calif. **28** 38 25N 121 32W
Clarksburg, Mo. **46** 38 40N 92 40W
Clarksburg, N.J. **51** 40 12N 74 27W
Clarksburg, W. Va. **68** 39 17N 80 30W
Clarksdale, Miss. **45** 34 12N 90 35W
Clarksdale, Mo. **46** 39 49N 94 33W
Clarkson, Ky. **62** 37 30N 86 13W
Clarkson, Nebr. **48** 41 43N 97 7W
Clarkston, Utah **66** 41 55N 112 3W
Clarkston, Wash. **67** 46 25N 117 3W
Clarksville, Ark. **27** 35 28N 93 28W
Clarksville, Ind. **36** 38 17N 85 45W
Clarksville, Iowa **37** 42 47N 92 40W
Clarksville, Md. **41** 39 12N 76 57W
Clarksville, Mich. **43** 42 50N 85 15W
Clarksville, Mo. **46** 39 22N 90 54W
Clarksville, Ohio **56** 39 24N 83 59W
Clarksville, Tenn. **62** 36 32N 87 21W
Clarksville, Tex. **65** 33 37N 95 3W
Clarksville, Va. **68** 36 37N 78 34W
Clarkton **54** 34 29N 78 39W
Clatonia **48** 40 28N 96 51W
Clatskanie **58** 46 6N 123 12W
Clatsop County ◇ **58** 46 0N 123 40W
Claude **64** 35 7N 101 22W
Claxton **32** 32 10N 81 55W
Clay **68** 38 28N 81 5W
Clay Center, Kans. **38** 39 23N 97 8W
Clay Center, Nebr. **48** 40 32N 98 3W
Clay City, Ill. **35** 38 41N 88 21W
Clay City, Ind. **36** 39 17N 87 7W
Clay City, Ky. **63** 37 52N 83 55W
Clay County ◇, Ala. **24** 33 16N 85 50W
Clay County ◇, Ark. **27** 36 19N 90 36W
Clay County ◇, Fla. **31** 30 0N 81 45W
Clay County ◇, Ga. **32** 31 30N 85 0W
Clay County ◇, Ill. **35** 38 45N 88 30W
Clay County ◇, Ind. **36** 39 20N 87 10W
Clay County ◇, Iowa **37** 43 5N 95 10W
Clay County ◇, Kans. **38** 39 20N 97 10W
Clay County ◇, Ky. **63** 37 10N 83 45W
Clay County ◇, Minn. **44** 46 50N 96 30W
Clay County ◇, Miss. **45** 33 36N 88 39W

Clay County ◇, Mo. 46 39 20N 94 20W
Clay County ◇, N.C. 54 35 5N 83 45W
Clay County ◇, Nebr. 48 40 30N 98 0W
Clay County ◇, S. Dak. 61 43 0N 97 0W
Clay County ◇, Tenn. 63 36 33N 85 30W
Clay County ◇, Tex. 65 33 49N 98 12W
Clay County ◇, W. Va. 68 38 28N 81 5W
Clay Springs 26 34 22N 110 18W
Claymont 41 39 48N 75 27W
Claypool, Ariz. 26 33 25N 110 51W
Claypool, Ind. 36 41 8N 85 53W
Claysville 59 40 7N 80 25W
Clayton, Ala. 24 31 53N 85 27W
Clayton, Del. 41 39 17N 75 38W
Clayton, Ga. 32 34 53N 83 23W
Clayton, Idaho 34 44 16N 114 24W
Clayton, Ill. 35 40 2N 90 54W
Clayton, Ind. 36 39 41N 86 31W
Clayton, Iowa 37 42 54N 91 9W
Clayton, Kans. 38 39 44N 100 11W
Clayton, La. 39 31 43N 91 33W
Clayton, Mo. 46 38 39N 90 20W
Clayton, N.C. 54 35 39N 78 28W
Clayton, N.J. 51 39 40N 75 6W
Clayton, N. Mex. 52 36 27N 103 11W
Clayton, N.Y. 53 44 14N 76 5W
Clayton, Okla. 57 34 35N 95 21W
Clayton, Wis. 69 45 20N 92 10W
Clayton County ◇, Ga. 32 33 30N 84 20W
Clayton County ◇, Iowa 37 42 50N 91 20W
Clayton Lake 40 46 36N 69 32W
Claytor L. 68 37 5N 80 35W
Cle Elum 67 47 12N 120 56W
Clear → 26 34 59N 110 38W
Clear Boggy Cr. → 57 34 3N 95 47W
Clear Cr. → 70 44 53N 106 4W
Clear Creek County ◇ 30 39 40N 105 40W
Clear L., Calif. 28 39 2N 122 47W
Clear L., Iowa 37 43 8N 93 26W
Clear L., La. 39 31 53N 93 0W
Clear L., Utah 66 39 7N 112 38W
Clear Lake, Iowa 37 43 8N 93 23W
Clear Lake, Minn. 44 45 27N 94 0W
Clear Lake, Okla. 57 36 41N 100 16W
Clear Lake, S. Dak. 61 44 45N 96 41W
Clear Lake, Wis. 69 45 15N 92 16W
Clear Lake Reservoir 28 41 56N 121 5W
Clear Spring 41 39 39N 77 56W
Clearbrook 44 47 42N 95 26W
Clearco 68 38 6N 80 34W
Clearfield, Iowa 37 40 48N 94 29W
Clearfield, Pa. 59 41 2N 78 27W
Clearfield, Utah 66 41 7N 112 2W
Clearfield County ◇ 59 41 0N 78 35W
Clearlake Highlands 28 38 57N 122 38W
Clearmont, Mo. 46 40 31N 95 2W
Clearmont, Wyo. 70 44 38N 106 23W
Clearwater, Fla. 31 27 58N 82 48W
Clearwater, Kans. 38 37 30N 97 30W
Clearwater, Nebr. 48 42 10N 98 11W
Clearwater →, Idaho 34 46 31N 116 33W
Clearwater →, Minn. 44 47 54N 96 16W
Clearwater County ◇, Idaho 34 46 50N 115 30W
Clearwater County ◇, Minn. 44 47 30N 95 20W
Clearwater L. 46 37 8N 90 47W
Clearwater Mts. 34 46 5N 115 20W
Clearwater National Forest 34 46 40N 115 5W
Cleburne 65 32 21N 97 23W
Cleburne County ◇, Ala. 24 33 39N 85 35W
Cleburne County ◇, Ark. 27 35 30N 92 2W
Clem 32 33 32N 85 1W
Clements, Kans. 38 38 18N 96 44W
Clements, Md. 41 38 18N 76 43W
Clements, Minn. 44 44 23N 95 3W
Clemson 60 34 41N 82 50W
Clendenin 68 38 29N 81 21W
Cleo Springs 57 36 26N 98 29W
Clermont, Fla. 31 28 33N 81 46W
Clermont, Iowa 37 43 0N 91 39W
Clermont, N.J. 51 39 59N 74 48W
Clermont County ◇ 56 39 5N 84 11W
Cleveland, Ga. 32 34 36N 83 46W
Cleveland, Minn. 44 44 19N 93 50W
Cleveland, Miss. 45 33 45N 90 43W
Cleveland, N. Dak. 55 46 54N 99 6W
Cleveland, Ohio 56 41 30N 81 42W
Cleveland, Okla. 57 36 19N 96 28W
Cleveland, S.C. 60 35 4N 82 31W
Cleveland, Tenn. 63 35 10N 84 53W
Cleveland, Tex. 65 30 21N 95 5W
Cleveland, Utah 66 39 21N 110 51W
Cleveland, Va. 68 36 57N 82 9W
Cleveland, Wis. 69 43 55N 87 45W
Cleveland, Mt. 47 48 56N 113 51W
Cleveland County ◇, Ark. 27 33 58N 92 11W
Cleveland County ◇, N.C. 54 35 20N 81 40W
Cleveland County ◇, Okla. 57 35 10N 97 20W
Cleveland Heights 56 41 30N 81 34W
Cleveland National Forest 29 32 45N 116 40W
Clever 46 37 2N 93 28W
Clewiston 31 26 45N 80 56W
Clifford, Mich. 43 43 19N 83 11W
Clifford, N. Dak. 55 47 21N 97 24W
Cliffside 54 35 14N 81 46W
Clifftop 68 38 0N 80 56W
Clifton, Ariz. 26 33 3N 109 18W
Clifton, Colo. 30 39 7N 108 25W
Clifton, Idaho 34 42 11N 112 0W
Clifton, Ill. 35 40 56N 87 56W
Clifton, Kans. 38 39 34N 97 17W
Clifton, N.J. 51 40 53N 74 9W
Clifton, Tenn. 62 35 18N 88 1W
Clifton, Tex. 65 31 47N 97 35W
Clifton Forge 68 37 49N 79 50W
Clifton Springs 53 42 58N 77 8W
Clifty 27 36 14N 93 48W
Climax, Colo. 30 39 22N 106 11W
Climax, Ga. 32 30 53N 84 26W
Climax, Kans. 38 37 43N 96 13W
Climax, Mich. 43 42 14N 85 20W
Climax, Minn. 44 47 37N 96 49W
Clinch → 63 35 53N 84 29W
Clinch County ◇ 32 31 0N 82 45W
Clinchco 68 37 10N 82 22W
Cline 65 29 15N 100 5W
Clines Corners 52 35 1N 105 40W
Clingmans Dome 63 35 34N 83 30W
Clint 64 31 35N 106 14W
Clinton, Ala. 24 32 58N 88 0W
Clinton, Ark. 27 35 36N 92 28W
Clinton, Conn. 42 41 17N 72 32W
Clinton, Ill. 35 40 9N 88 57W
Clinton, Ind. 36 39 40N 87 24W
Clinton, Iowa 37 41 51N 90 12W
Clinton, Ky. 62 36 40N 89 0W
Clinton, La. 39 30 52N 91 1W
Clinton, Maine 40 44 38N 69 30W
Clinton, Mass. 42 42 25N 71 41W
Clinton, Md. 41 38 46N 76 54W
Clinton, Mich. 43 42 4N 83 58W
Clinton, Minn. 44 45 28N 96 26W
Clinton, Miss. 45 32 20N 90 20W
Clinton, Mo. 46 38 22N 93 46W
Clinton, Mont. 47 46 46N 113 43W
Clinton, N.C. 54 35 0N 78 22W
Clinton, N.J. 51 40 38N 74 55W
Clinton, N.Y. 53 43 3N 75 23W
Clinton, Ohio 56 40 56N 81 38W
Clinton, Okla. 57 35 31N 98 58W
Clinton, S.C. 60 34 29N 81 53W
Clinton, Tenn. 63 36 6N 84 8W
Clinton, Wash. 67 47 59N 122 21W
Clinton, Wis. 69 42 34N 88 52W
Clinton County ◇, Ill. 35 38 35N 89 25W
Clinton County ◇, Ind. 36 40 20N 86 30W
Clinton County ◇, Iowa 37 41 55N 90 30W
Clinton County ◇, Ky. 63 36 45N 85 10W
Clinton County ◇, Mich. 43 42 55N 84 40W
Clinton County ◇, Mo. 46 39 35N 94 25W
Clinton County ◇, N.Y. 53 44 50N 73 40W
Clinton County ◇, Ohio 56 39 27N 83 50W
Clinton County ◇, Pa. 59 41 10N 77 50W
Clinton L. 35 40 15N 88 45W
Clintonville, W. Va. 68 37 54N 80 36W
Clintonville, Wis. 69 44 37N 88 46W
Clintwood 68 37 9N 82 28W
Clio, Ala. 24 31 43N 85 37W
Clio, Iowa 37 40 38N 93 27W
Clio, Mich. 43 43 11N 83 44W
Clio, S.C. 60 34 35N 79 33W
Clontarf 44 45 23N 95 40W
Cloquet 44 46 43N 92 28W
Cloquet → 44 46 52N 92 35W
Cloud County ◇ 38 39 30N 97 45W
Cloud Peak 70 44 23N 107 11W
Cloudcroft 52 32 58N 105 45W
Clover, S.C. 60 35 7N 81 14W
Clover, Va. 68 36 50N 78 44W
Cloverdale, Ala. 24 34 56N 87 46W
Cloverdale, Calif. 28 38 48N 123 1W
Cloverdale, Ind. 36 39 31N 86 48W
Cloverdale, Ohio 56 41 1N 84 18W
Cloverleaf 65 29 46N 95 10W
Cloverport 62 37 50N 86 38W
Clovis, Calif. 29 36 49N 119 42W
Clovis, N. Mex. 52 34 24N 103 12W
Clute 65 29 1N 95 24W
Clutier 37 42 4N 92 24W
Clyattville 32 30 42N 83 19W
Clyde, Kans. 38 39 36N 97 24W
Clyde, N.C. 54 35 32N 82 55W
Clyde, N.Y. 53 43 5N 76 52W
Clyde, Ohio 56 41 18N 82 59W
Clyde, Tex. 65 32 24N 99 30W
Clyde, Vt. 50 44 56N 73 0W
Clyde Park 47 45 52N 110 37W
Clymer 59 40 40N 79 1W
Clyo 32 32 29N 81 16W
Co-Operative 63 36 42N 84 37W
Coachella 29 33 41N 116 10W
Coachella Canal 29 32 43N 114 57W
Coahoma 64 32 18N 101 18W
Coahoma County ◇ 45 34 12N 90 35W
Coal City 35 41 17N 88 17W
Coal County ◇ 57 34 40N 96 15W
Coal Grove 56 38 30N 82 39W
Coal Hill 27 35 26N 93 40W
Coaldale 30 38 22N 105 45W
Coalgate 57 34 32N 96 13W
Coaling 24 33 10N 87 20W
Coalinga 29 36 9N 120 21W
Coalmont, Colo. 30 40 34N 106 27W
Coalmont, Tenn. 63 35 20N 85 42W
Coalport 59 40 45N 78 32W
Coalville 66 40 55N 111 24W
Coamo 71 18 5N 66 22W
Coarsegold 28 37 16N 119 42W
Coast Ranges 58 44 0N 123 40W
Coates 44 44 43N 93 2W
Coatesville 59 39 59N 75 50W
Coats, Kans. 38 37 31N 98 50W
Coats, N.C. 54 35 25N 78 40W
Cobalt 34 45 6N 114 14W
Cobb 62 36 59N 87 47W
Cobb County ◇ 32 33 50N 84 40W
Cobb Island 41 38 16N 76 51W
Cobden, Ill. 35 37 32N 89 15W
Cobden, Minn. 44 44 17N 94 51W
Cobleskill 53 42 41N 74 29W
Cobre 49 41 7N 114 24W
Coburg 37 40 55N 95 16W
Coburn Mt. 40 45 28N 70 6W
Cochise 26 32 7N 109 55W
Cochise County ◇ 26 32 0N 109 30W
Cochran 32 32 23N 83 21W
Cochran County ◇ 64 33 37N 102 48W
Cochrane, Ala. 24 33 4N 88 15W
Cochrane, Wis. 69 44 14N 91 50W
Cochranton 59 41 31N 80 3W
Cocke County ◇ 63 35 58N 83 11W
Cockeysville 41 39 29N 76 39W
Coco Solo 71 9 22N 79 53W
Cocoa 31 28 21N 80 44W
Cocoa Beach 31 28 19N 80 37W
Cocolalla 34 48 6N 116 37W
Coconino County ◇ 26 36 0N 112 0W
Coconino National Forest 26 34 45N 111 20W
Coconino Plateau 26 35 45N 112 40W
Cod, C. 42 42 5N 70 10W
Codington County ◇ 61 44 54N 97 7W
Cody, Nebr. 48 42 56N 101 15W
Cody, Wyo. 70 44 32N 109 3W
Coeburn 68 36 57N 82 28W
Coeur d' Alene 34 47 41N 116 46W
Coeur d' Alene Indian Reservation 34 47 10N 116 55W
Coeur d' Alene L. 34 47 32N 116 49W
Coeur d' Alene National Forest 34 47 55N 116 15W
Coeur d'Alene → 34 47 45N 116 0W
Coffee County ◇, Ala. 24 31 23N 85 56W
Coffee County ◇, Ga. 32 31 30N 82 50W
Coffee County ◇, Tenn. 62 35 29N 86 5W
Coffeen 35 39 5N 89 24W
Coffeeville, Ala. 24 31 45N 88 5W
Coffeeville, Miss. 45 33 59N 89 41W
Coffey 46 40 6N 94 0W
Coffey County ◇ 38 38 15N 95 45W
Coffeyville 38 37 2N 95 37W
Cofield 54 36 21N 76 54W
Cogar 57 35 20N 98 8W
Cogdell 32 31 10N 82 43W
Coggon 37 42 17N 91 32W
Cogswell 55 46 7N 97 47W
Cohagen 47 47 3N 106 37W
Cohansey 51 39 21N 75 22W
Cohasset 42 42 14N 70 48W
Cohocton → 53 42 9N 77 6W
Cohoes 53 42 46N 73 42W
Cohutta 32 34 58N 84 57W
Coin 37 40 40N 95 14W
Cokato 44 45 5N 94 11W
Coke County ◇ 64 31 54N 100 29W
Coker 24 33 15N 87 41W
Cokeville 70 42 5N 110 57W
Colbert, Ga. 32 34 2N 83 13W
Colbert, Okla. 57 33 51N 96 30W
Colbert County ◇ 24 34 44N 87 42W
Colbourne 41 38 15N 75 26W
Colburn 34 48 24N 116 32W
Colby, Kans. 38 39 24N 101 3W
Colby, Wis. 69 44 55N 90 19W
Colchester, Conn. 42 41 35N 72 20W
Colchester, Ill. 35 40 25N 90 48W
Colcord 57 36 16N 94 42W
Cold Bay 25 55 12N 162 42W
Cold Mt. 54 35 25N 82 51W
Cold Spring, Minn. 44 45 27N 94 26W
Cold Spring, N.Y. 53 41 25N 73 57W
Cold Springs Cr. → 70 44 32N 104 6W
Coldspring 65 30 36N 95 8W
Coldwater, Kans. 38 37 16N 99 20W
Coldwater, Mich. 43 41 57N 85 0W
Coldwater, Miss. 45 34 41N 89 59W
Coldwater, Ohio 56 40 29N 84 38W
Coldwater → 45 34 10N 90 13W
Coldwater Cr. → 57 36 40N 101 10W
Cole 57 35 8N 97 33W
Cole Camp 46 38 28N 93 12W
Cole County ◇ 46 38 30N 92 15W
Colebrook 50 44 54N 71 30W
Coleman, Fla. 31 28 48N 82 4W
Coleman, Ga. 32 31 40N 84 54W
Coleman, Mich. 43 43 46N 84 35W
Coleman, Okla. 57 34 16N 96 25W
Coleman, Tex. 65 31 50N 99 26W
Coleman, Wis. 69 45 4N 88 2W
Coleman County ◇ 65 31 50N 99 30W
Colerain 54 36 12N 76 46W
Coleraine 44 47 17N 93 27W
Coleridge, N.C. 54 35 39N 79 37W
Coleridge, Nebr. 48 42 30N 97 13W
Coles 45 31 17N 91 2W
Coles County ◇ 35 39 30N 88 15W
Colesburg 37 42 38N 91 12W
Coleville 28 38 34N 119 30W
Colfax, Calif. 28 39 6N 120 57W
Colfax, Ill. 35 40 34N 88 37W
Colfax, Ind. 36 40 12N 86 40W
Colfax, Iowa 37 41 41N 93 14W
Colfax, La. 39 31 31N 92 42W
Colfax, N. Dak. 55 46 28N 96 53W
Colfax, Wash. 67 46 53N 117 22W
Colfax, Wis. 69 45 0N 91 44W
Colfax County ◇, N. Mex. 52 36 30N 104 30W
Colfax County ◇, Nebr. 48 41 30N 97 0W
Colgate 55 47 15N 97 39W
Collbran 30 39 14N 107 58W
College 25 64 52N 147 49W
College Corner 56 39 34N 84 49W
College Heights 27 33 35N 91 48W
College Park, Fla. 31 29 53N 81 21W
College Park, Ga. 32 33 40N 84 27W
College Park, Md. 41 38 59N 76 56W
College Place 67 46 3N 118 23W
College Station 65 30 37N 96 21W
Collegedale 63 35 4N 85 3W
Collegeville 36 40 56N 87 9W
Colleton County ◇ 60 33 0N 80 40W
Collettsville 54 35 56N 81 41W
Colleyville 65 32 53N 97 9W
Collier County ◇ 31 26 0N 81 30W
Collierville 62 35 3N 89 40W
Collin County ◇ 65 33 6N 96 40W
Collingsworth County ◇ 64 35 0N 100 15W
Collins, Ark. 27 33 32N 91 34W
Collins, Ga. 32 32 11N 82 7W
Collins, Iowa 37 41 54N 93 18W
Collins, Miss. 45 31 39N 89 33W
Collins, Mo. 46 37 54N 93 37W
Collinston 39 32 41N 91 52W
Collinsville, Ala. 24 34 16N 85 52W
Collinsville, Conn. 42 41 49N 72 55W
Collinsville, Ill. 35 38 40N 89 59W
Collinsville, Miss. 45 32 30N 88 51W
Collinsville, Okla. 57 36 22N 95 51W
Collinsville, Tex. 65 33 34N 96 55W
Collinsville, Va. 68 36 43N 79 55W
Collinwood 62 35 10N 87 44W
Collison 35 40 14N 87 48W
Collyer 38 39 2N 100 7W
Colman 61 43 59N 96 49W
Colmesneil 65 30 54N 94 25W
Coloma, Calif. 28 38 48N 120 53W
Coloma, Mich. 43 42 11N 86 19W
Coloma, Wis. 69 44 2N 89 31W
Colome 61 43 16N 99 43W

Colón, Panama **71** 9 22N 79 54W
Colon, Mich. **43** 41 57N 85 19W
Colon, N.C. **54** 35 32N 79 2W
Colon, Nebr. **48** 41 18N 96 37W
Colona **30** 38 20N 107 47W
Colonial Beach **68** 38 15N 76 58W
Colonial Heights **68** 37 15N 77 25W
Colonie **53** 42 43N 73 50W
Colony, Kans. **38** 38 4N 95 22W
Colony, Okla. **57** 35 23N 98 41W
Colorado □ **30** 39 30N 105 30W
Colorado →, Oreg. **58** 44 0N 117 30W
Colorado →, Tex. **65** 28 36N 95 59W
Colorado City, Ariz. **26** 36 59N 112 59W
Colorado City, Tex. **64** 32 24N 100 52W
Colorado County ◇ **65** 29 42N 96 33W
Colorado I. **71** 9 12N 79 50W
Colorado Plateau **26** 37 0N 111 0W
Colorado River Aqueduct **29** 33 50N 117 23W
Colorado River Ind. Res. **26** 34 0N 114 25W
Colorado Springs **30** 38 50N 104 49W
Colquitt **32** 31 10N 84 44W
Colquitt County ◇ **32** 31 15N 83 50W
Colrain **42** 42 41N 72 42W
Colstrip **47** 45 53N 106 38W
Colt **27** 35 8N 90 49W
Colter Peak **70** 44 18N 110 7W
Colton, Calif. **29** 34 4N 117 20W
Colton, N.Y. **53** 44 33N 74 56W
Colton, S. Dak. **61** 43 47N 96 56W
Colton, Wash. **67** 46 34N 117 8W
Colts Neck **51** 40 17N 74 11W
Columbia, Ala. **24** 31 18N 85 7W
Columbia, Ill. **35** 38 27N 90 12W
Columbia, Ky. **63** 37 6N 85 18W
Columbia, La. **39** 32 6N 92 5W
Columbia, Md. **41** 39 14N 76 50W
Columbia, Miss. **45** 31 15N 89 50W
Columbia, Mo. **46** 38 57N 92 20W
Columbia, N.C. **54** 35 55N 76 15W
Columbia, N.J. **51** 40 56N 75 6W
Columbia, Pa. **59** 40 2N 76 30W
Columbia, S.C. **60** 34 0N 81 2W
Columbia, S. Dak. **61** 45 37N 98 19W
Columbia, Tenn. **62** 35 37N 87 2W
Columbia → **67** 46 15N 124 5W
Columbia Basin **67** 46 45N 119 5W
Columbia City, Ind. **36** 41 10N 85 29W
Columbia City, Oreg. **58** 45 53N 122 49W
Columbia County ◇, Ark. **27** 33 16N 93 14W
Columbia County ◇, Fla. **31** 30 15N 82 40W
Columbia County ◇, Ga. **32** 33 30N 82 10W
Columbia County ◇, N.Y. **53** 42 10N 73 40W
Columbia County ◇, Oreg. **58** 45 55N 123 0W
Columbia County ◇, Pa. **59** 41 10N 76 20W
Columbia County ◇, Wash. **67** 46 19N 117 59W
Columbia County ◇, Wis. **69** 43 30N 89 20W
Columbia Falls, Maine **40** 44 39N 67 44W
Columbia Falls, Mont. **47** 48 23N 114 11W
Columbia Heights **44** 45 3N 93 15W
Columbia Road Reservoir **61** 45 40N 98 18W
Columbiana, Ala. **24** 33 11N 86 36W
Columbiana, Ohio **56** 40 53N 80 42W
Columbiana County ◇ **56** 40 46N 80 46W
Columbiaville **43** 43 9N 83 25W
Columbine **30** 40 56N 106 59W
Columbus, Ga. **32** 32 28N 84 59W
Columbus, Ind. **36** 39 13N 85 55W
Columbus, Kans. **38** 37 10N 94 50W
Columbus, Ky. **62** 36 46N 89 6W
Columbus, Miss. **45** 33 30N 88 25W
Columbus, Mont. **47** 45 38N 109 15W
Columbus, N.C. **54** 35 15N 82 12W
Columbus, N. Dak. **55** 48 54N 102 47W
Columbus, N. Mex. **52** 31 50N 107 38W
Columbus, Nebr. **48** 41 26N 97 22W
Columbus, Ohio **56** 39 58N 83 0W
Columbus, Tex. **65** 29 42N 96 33W
Columbus, Wis. **69** 43 21N 89 1W
Columbus County ◇ **54** 34 15N 78 45W
Columbus Grove **56** 40 55N 84 4W
Columbus Junction **37** 41 17N 91 22W
Columbus Salt Marsh **49** 38 5N 118 5W
Colusa **28** 39 13N 122 1W
Colusa County ◇ **28** 39 15N 122 15W
Colville **67** 48 33N 117 54W
Colville →, Alaska **25** 70 25N 150 30W
Colville →, Wash. **67** 48 37N 118 5W
Colville Indian Reservation **67** 48 15N 119 0W
Colville National Forest **67** 48 50N 117 15W
Colwell **37** 43 9N 92 36W
Colwich **38** 37 47N 97 32W
Comal County ◇ **65** 29 53N 98 25W
Comanche, Okla. **57** 34 22N 97 58W
Comanche, Tex. **65** 31 54N 98 36W
Comanche County ◇, Kans. **38** 37 15N 99 15W
Comanche County ◇, Okla. **57** 34 40N 98 25W
Comanche County ◇, Tex. **65** 31 55N 98 35W
Comanche National Grassland **30** 37 20N 103 0W
Comer, Ala. **24** 32 2N 85 23W
Comer, Ga. **32** 34 4N 83 8W
Comerio **71** 18 13N 66 14W
Comfort **65** 29 58N 98 55W
Comfrey **44** 44 7N 94 54W
Commack **53** 40 51N 73 18W
Commerce, Ga. **32** 34 12N 83 28W
Commerce, Mo. **46** 37 9N 89 27W
Commerce, Okla. **57** 36 56N 94 53W
Commerce, Tex. **65** 33 15N 95 54W
Commerce City **30** 39 49N 104 56W
Como, Colo. **30** 39 19N 105 54W
Como, Miss. **45** 34 31N 89 56W
Como, Tex. **65** 33 3N 95 28W
Comobabi Mts. **26** 32 0N 111 45W
Compass Lake **31** 30 36N 85 24W
Competition **46** 37 29N 92 26W
Comptche **28** 39 16N 123 35W
Compton, Ark. **27** 36 6N 93 18W
Compton, Calif. **29** 33 54N 118 13W
Comstock, Minn. **44** 46 40N 96 45W
Comstock, Nebr. **48** 41 34N 99 15W
Comstock, Tex. **64** 29 41N 101 10W
Comstock Park **43** 43 2N 85 40W
Conanicut I. **42** 41 32N 71 21W
Conasauga → **32** 34 33N 84 55W
Concan **65** 29 30N 99 43W
Conception, Pt. **29** 34 27N 120 28W
Conception Junction **46** 40 16N 94 42W
Conchas → **52** 35 23N 104 18W
Conchas Dam **52** 35 22N 104 11W
Conchas Lake **52** 35 23N 104 11W
Concho **26** 34 28N 109 36W
Concho → **65** 31 34N 99 43W
Concho County ◇ **65** 31 13N 99 51W
Conconully **67** 48 34N 119 45W
Concord, Calif. **28** 37 59N 122 2W
Concord, Ga. **32** 33 5N 84 27W
Concord, Mass. **42** 42 28N 71 21W
Concord, Md. **41** 38 38N 75 48W
Concord, Mich. **43** 42 11N 84 38W
Concord, Mo. **46** 38 28N 90 23W
Concord, N.C. **54** 35 25N 80 35W
Concord, N.H. **50** 43 12N 71 32W
Concord, Tenn. **63** 35 52N 84 8W
Concord, Vt. **50** 44 26N 71 53W
Concordia, Kans. **38** 39 34N 97 40W
Concordia, Mo. **46** 38 59N 93 34W
Concordia Parish ◇ **39** 31 38N 91 33W
Concrete **67** 48 32N 121 45W
Conda **34** 42 44N 111 32W
Conde **61** 45 9N 98 6W
Condon, Mont. **47** 47 34N 113 45W
Condon, Oreg. **58** 45 14N 120 11W
Conecuh → **31** 30 58N 87 13W
Conecuh County ◇ **24** 31 26N 86 57W
Conecuh National Forest **24** 31 2N 86 45W
Conejos **30** 37 5N 106 1W
Conejos → **30** 37 18N 105 44W
Conejos County ◇ **30** 37 10N 106 10W
Conesville **37** 41 23N 91 21W
Confluence **59** 39 49N 79 21W
Confusion Range **66** 39 20N 113 40W
Congaree → **60** 33 44N 80 38W
Conger **44** 43 37N 93 32W
Congress, Ariz. **26** 34 9N 112 51W
Congress, Ohio **56** 40 56N 82 3W
Conifer **30** 39 31N 105 18W
Conklin **53** 42 2N 75 49W
Conlen **64** 36 14N 102 15W
Conneaut **56** 41 57N 80 34W
Conneaut Lake **59** 41 36N 80 18W
Conneautville **59** 41 45N 80 22W
Connecticut □ **42** 41 30N 72 45W
Connecticut → **42** 41 16N 72 20W
Connell **67** 46 40N 118 52W
Connellsville **59** 40 1N 79 35W
Connemaugh → **59** 40 28N 79 19W
Conner **47** 45 56N 114 7W
Connersville **36** 39 39N 85 8W
Connerville **57** 34 27N 96 38W
Conover **54** 35 42N 81 13W
Conowingo **41** 39 40N 76 11W
Conrad, Iowa **37** 42 14N 92 52W
Conrad, Mont. **47** 48 10N 111 57W
Conrath **69** 45 22N 91 2W
Conroe **65** 30 19N 95 27W
Constantine **43** 41 50N 85 40W
Constantine, C. **25** 58 24N 158 54W
Contact **49** 41 46N 114 45W
Continental **56** 41 6N 84 16W
Continental Divide **52** 35 25N 108 19W
Continental L. **49** 41 54N 118 43W
Contoocock **50** 43 12N 71 45W
Contoocook → **50** 43 27N 71 35W
Contra Costa County ◇ **28** 37 50N 121 50W
Contreras **52** 34 23N 106 49W
Controller B. **25** 60 7N 144 15W
Convent **39** 30 1N 90 50W
Converse, Ind. **36** 40 35N 85 52W
Converse, La. **39** 31 47N 93 42W
Converse County ◇ **70** 43 0N 105 45W
Convoy **56** 40 55N 84 43W
Conway, Ark. **27** 35 5N 92 26W
Conway, Kans. **38** 38 22N 97 47W
Conway, Mo. **46** 37 30N 92 49W
Conway, N.C. **54** 36 26N 77 14W
Conway, N. Dak. **55** 48 14N 97 41W
Conway, N.H. **50** 43 59N 71 7W
Conway, S.C. **60** 33 51N 79 3W
Conway, Tex. **64** 35 13N 101 23W
Conway County ◇ **27** 35 10N 92 38W
Conway L. **27** 34 58N 92 25W
Conway Springs **38** 37 24N 97 39W
Conyers **32** 33 40N 84 1W
Cook **48** 40 31N 96 10W
Cook County ◇, Ga. **32** 31 10N 83 30W
Cook County ◇, Ill. **35** 41 50N 87 45W
Cook County ◇, Minn. **44** 47 50N 90 30W
Cook Inlet **25** 60 0N 152 0W
Cooke City **47** 45 1N 109 56W
Cooke County ◇ **65** 33 38N 97 8W
Cookes Peak **52** 32 32N 107 44W
Cookeville **63** 36 10N 85 30W
Cooks Hammock **31** 29 56N 83 17W
Cooksville **35** 40 33N 88 43W
Cool **65** 32 49N 98 1W
Cooleemee **54** 35 49N 80 33W
Coolidge, Ariz. **26** 32 59N 111 31W
Coolidge, Ga. **32** 31 1N 83 52W
Coolidge, Kans. **38** 38 3N 102 1W
Coolidge, Tex. **65** 31 45N 96 39W
Coolidge Dam **26** 33 0N 110 20W
Coolin **34** 48 29N 116 51W
Coon Rapids, Iowa **37** 41 53N 94 41W
Coon Rapids, Minn. **44** 45 9N 93 19W
Coon Valley **69** 43 42N 91 1W
Cooper, Ky. **63** 36 46N 84 52W
Cooper, Tex. **65** 33 23N 95 42W
Cooper →, S.C. **60** 32 50N 79 56W
Cooper →, Va. **68** 36 40N 82 44W
Cooper County ◇ **46** 38 50N 92 45W
Cooperdale **56** 40 13N 82 4W
Coopersburg **59** 40 31N 75 23W
Cooperstown, N. Dak. **55** 47 27N 98 8W
Cooperstown, N.Y. **53** 42 42N 74 56W
Coopersville **43** 43 4N 85 57W
Coos Bay **58** 43 22N 124 13W
Coos County ◇, N.H. **50** 44 40N 71 15W
Coos County ◇, Oreg. **58** 43 15N 124 0W
Coosa → **24** 32 30N 86 16W
Coosa County ◇ **24** 32 53N 86 13W
Coosawattee → **32** 34 35N 84 55W
Copalis Beach **67** 47 7N 124 10W
Copan **57** 36 54N 95 56W
Copan Res. **57** 36 58N 95 57W
Copano B. **65** 28 5N 97 5W
Copco L. **28** 41 59N 122 20W
Cope, Colo. **30** 39 40N 102 51W
Cope, S.C. **60** 33 23N 81 0W
Copeland, Fla. **31** 25 57N 81 22W
Copeland, Idaho **34** 48 54N 116 23W
Copeland, Kans. **38** 37 33N 100 38W
Copenhagen **53** 43 54N 75 41W
Copiague **53** 40 41N 73 24W
Copiah County ◇ **45** 31 52N 90 24W
Copper → **25** 60 18N 145 3W
Copper Butte **67** 48 42N 118 28W
Copper Center **25** 61 58N 145 18W
Copper Harbor **43** 47 28N 87 53W
Copperas Cove **65** 31 8N 97 54W
Copperhill **63** 35 0N 84 15W
Coqui **71** 17 59N 66 14W
Coquille **58** 43 11N 124 11W
Coquille → **58** 43 7N 124 26W
Coral Gables **31** 25 45N 80 16W
Coralville **37** 41 40N 91 35W
Coralville L. **37** 41 42N 91 33W
Coram, Mont. **47** 48 25N 114 3W
Coram, N.Y. **53** 40 52N 73 0W
Coraopolis **59** 40 31N 80 10W
Corbin, Kans. **38** 37 8N 97 33W
Corbin, Ky. **63** 36 57N 84 6W
Corbin, Mont. **47** 46 23N 112 4W
Corcoran **29** 36 6N 119 33W
Cordele **32** 31 58N 83 47W
Cordell **57** 35 17N 98 59W
Cordova, Ala. **24** 33 46N 87 11W
Cordova, Alaska **25** 60 33N 145 45W
Cordova, Ill. **35** 41 41N 90 19W
Cordova, N. Mex. **52** 36 1N 105 52W
Cordova, Nebr. **48** 40 43N 97 21W
Cordova, S.C. **60** 33 26N 80 55W
Core Banks **54** 34 45N 76 15W
Corfu **53** 42 58N 78 24W
Corinna **40** 44 55N 69 16W
Corinne **66** 41 33N 112 7W
Corinth, Ga. **32** 33 14N 84 57W
Corinth, Ky. **63** 38 30N 84 34W
Corinth, Miss. **45** 34 56N 88 31W
Corinth, N.Y. **53** 43 15N 73 49W
Corinth, W. Va. **68** 39 25N 79 30W
Corn **57** 35 24N 98 48W
Cornelia **32** 34 31N 83 32W
Cornelius **54** 35 29N 80 52W
Cornell, Ill. **35** 41 0N 88 44W
Cornell, Wis. **69** 45 10N 91 9W
Cornersville **62** 35 22N 86 50W
Cornerville **27** 33 51N 91 56W
Corning, Ark. **27** 36 25N 90 35W
Corning, Calif. **28** 39 56N 122 11W
Corning, Iowa **37** 40 59N 94 44W
Corning, Kans. **38** 39 40N 96 2W
Corning, N.Y. **53** 42 9N 77 3W
Corning, Ohio **56** 39 36N 82 5W
Cornish **57** 34 9N 97 36W
Cornlea **48** 41 41N 97 34W
Cornucopia **58** 45 0N 117 12W
Cornudas **64** 31 47N 105 28W
Cornville **26** 34 43N 111 55W
Cornwall, Conn. **42** 41 50N 73 20W
Cornwall, Pa. **59** 40 17N 76 25W
Cornwall, Vt. **50** 43 56N 73 13W
Cornwall Bridge **42** 41 49N 73 22W
Cornwell, Fla. **31** 27 23N 81 6W
Cornwell, S.C. **60** 34 37N 81 10W
Corona, Calif. **29** 33 53N 117 34W
Corona, N. Mex. **52** 34 15N 105 36W
Corona, S. Dak. **61** 45 20N 96 46W
Coronado **29** 32 41N 117 11W
Coronado Nat. Forest **26** 32 10N 110 20W
Corozal, Panama **71** 8 59N 79 34W
Corozal, Puerto Rico **71** 18 21N 66 19W
Corpus Christi **65** 27 47N 97 24W
Corpus Christi, L. **65** 28 2N 97 52W
Corpus Christi B. **65** 27 47N 97 22W
Corral **34** 43 21N 114 57W
Correctionville **37** 42 29N 95 47W
Correll **44** 45 14N 96 10W
Corrigan **65** 31 0N 94 52W
Corriganville **41** 39 45N 78 17W
Corry **59** 41 55N 79 39W
Corryton **63** 36 9N 83 47W
Corsica **61** 43 25N 98 24W
Corsicana **65** 32 6N 96 28W
Corson County ◇ **61** 45 55N 101 0W
Cortez **30** 37 21N 108 35W
Cortez Mts. **49** 40 20N 116 20W
Cortland, N.Y. **53** 42 36N 76 11W
Cortland, Nebr. **48** 40 30N 96 42W
Cortland, Ohio **56** 41 20N 80 44W
Cortland County ◇ **53** 42 35N 76 5W
Corum **57** 34 22N 98 6W
Corunna **43** 42 59N 84 7W
Corvallis, Mont. **47** 46 19N 114 7W
Corvallis, Oreg. **58** 44 34N 123 16W
Corwin **38** 37 5N 98 18W
Corwith **37** 42 59N 93 57W
Corydon, Ind. **36** 38 13N 86 7W
Corydon, Iowa **37** 40 46N 93 19W
Corydon, Ky. **62** 37 44N 87 43W
Coryell County ◇ **65** 31 26N 97 45W
Coshocton **56** 40 16N 81 51W
Coshocton County ◇ **56** 40 16N 81 51W
Cosmopolis **67** 46 57N 123 46W
Cossatot → **27** 33 48N 94 9W
Cost **65** 29 26N 97 32W
Costa Mesa **29** 33 38N 117 55W
Costilla **52** 36 59N 105 32W
Costilla County ◇ **30** 37 15N 105 30W
Cosumnes → **28** 38 16N 121 26W
Cotati **28** 38 20N 122 42W
Coteau des Prairies **61** 44 20N 96 0W
Coteau du Missouri **55** 47 0N 100 0W
Cotesfield **48** 41 22N 98 38W
Coto Laurel **71** 18 3N 66 33W
Cotopaxi **30** 38 22N 105 41W
Cottage Grove **58** 43 48N 123 3W
Cottageville **60** 32 56N 80 29W
Cottle County ◇ **64** 34 0N 100 18W
Cotton, Ga. **32** 31 10N 84 4W
Cotton, Minn. **44** 47 10N 92 28W
Cotton County ◇ **57** 34 15N 98 20W
Cotton Plant **27** 35 0N 91 15W
Cotton Valley **39** 32 49N 93 25W

Cottondale, Ala. 24 33 11N 87 27W
Cottondale, Fla. 31 30 48N 85 23W
Cottonport 39 30 59N 92 3W
Cottonwood, Ala. 24 31 3N 85 18W
Cottonwood, Ariz. 26 34 45N 112 1W
Cottonwood, Calif. 28 40 23N 122 17W
Cottonwood, Idaho 34 46 3N 116 21W
Cottonwood, Minn. 44 44 37N 95 41W
Cottonwood, S. Dak. 61 43 58N 101 54W
Cottonwood ⟶ 44 44 17N 94 25W
Cottonwood County ◇ 44 44 0N 95 10W
Cottonwood Cr. ⟶ 64 31 23N 103 46W
Cottonwood Falls 38 38 22N 96 32W
Cottonwood Heights 66 40 38N 111 49W
Cottonwood Mts. 29 36 50N 117 40W
Cotuit 42 41 37N 70 26W
Cotulla 65 28 26N 99 14W
Couchwood 39 32 46N 93 23W
Couderay 69 45 48N 91 18W
Coudersport 59 41 46N 78 1W
Cougar 67 46 3N 122 18W
Coulee City 67 47 37N 119 17W
Coulee Dam 67 47 58N 118 58W
Coulee Dam Nat. Rec. Area 67 47 48N 119 45W
Coulterville, Calif. 28 37 43N 120 12W
Coulterville, Ill. 35 38 11N 89 36W
Counce 62 35 3N 88 16W
Council, Ga. 32 30 37N 82 31W
Council, Idaho 34 44 44N 116 26W
Council Bluffs 37 41 16N 95 52W
Council Grove 38 38 40N 96 29W
Council Grove Lake 38 38 41N 96 33W
Council Hill 57 35 31N 95 42W
Country Lake 51 39 55N 74 32W
Coupeville 67 48 13N 122 41W
Coupland 65 30 28N 97 23W
Courtenay 55 47 13N 98 34W
Courtland, Ala. 24 34 40N 87 19W
Courtland, Calif. 28 38 20N 121 34W
Courtland, Kans. 38 39 47N 97 54W
Courtland, Minn. 44 44 16N 94 20W
Courtland, Miss. 45 34 14N 89 57W
Courtland, Va. 68 36 43N 77 4W
Courtright Reservoir 29 37 5N 118 58W
Coushatta 39 32 1N 93 21W
Cove, Ark. 27 34 26N 94 25W
Cove, Oreg. 58 45 18N 117 49W
Cove City 54 35 13N 77 19W
Cove Point 41 38 23N 76 24W
Covelo 28 39 48N 123 15W
Coventry, Conn. 42 41 48N 72 23W
Coventry, R.I. 42 41 41N 71 34W
Coverdale 32 31 38N 83 58W
Covington, Ga. 32 33 36N 83 51W
Covington, Ind. 36 40 9N 87 24W
Covington, Ky. 63 39 5N 84 31W
Covington, La. 39 30 29N 90 6W
Covington, Mich. 43 46 33N 88 32W
Covington, Ohio 56 40 7N 84 21W
Covington, Okla. 57 36 18N 97 35W
Covington, Tenn. 62 35 34N 89 39W
Covington, Va. 68 37 47N 79 59W
Covington County ◇, Ala. 24 31 18N 86 29W
Covington County ◇, Miss. 45 31 39N 89 33W
Cow Cr. ⟶ 58 42 57N 123 22W
Cow Head L. 28 41 55N 120 2W
Cowan 62 35 10N 86 1W
Coward 60 33 58N 79 45W
Cowden 35 39 15N 88 52W
Cowdrey 30 40 52N 106 19W
Cowen 68 38 25N 80 34W
Coweta 57 35 57N 95 39W
Coweta County ◇ 32 33 20N 84 50W
Cowles 48 40 10N 98 27W
Cowley 70 44 53N 108 28W
Cowley County ◇ 38 37 15N 96 45W
Cowlic 26 31 48N 111 59W
Cowlitz ⟶ 67 46 6N 122 55W
Cowlitz County ◇ 67 46 5N 122 50W
Cowpens 60 35 1N 81 48W
Cox 32 31 27N 81 34W
Cox City 57 34 43N 97 44W
Coxs Mills 68 39 3N 80 50W
Coxsackie 53 42 21N 73 48W
Coy 27 34 32N 91 53W
Coyanosa Draw ⟶ 64 31 18N 103 6W
Coyle 57 35 57N 97 14W
Coyote 52 36 10N 106 37W
Coyote L. 29 35 4N 116 46W
Coyote Reservoir 28 37 7N 121 33W
Coyville 38 37 41N 95 54W
Cozad 48 40 52N 99 59W
Crab Cr. ⟶ 67 46 49N 119 55W
Crab Orchard, Ky. 63 37 28N 84 30W
Crab Orchard, Nebr. 48 40 20N 96 25W
Crab Orchard L. 35 37 43N 89 9W
Crabtree 58 44 38N 122 54W
Craig, Alaska 25 55 29N 133 9W
Craig, Colo. 30 40 31N 107 33W
Craig, Iowa 37 42 54N 96 19W
Craig, Mo. 46 40 12N 95 23W
Craig, Mont. 47 47 5N 111 58W
Craig, Nebr. 48 41 47N 96 22W
Craig County ◇, Okla. 57 36 45N 95 10W
Craig County ◇, Va. 68 37 25N 80 5W
Craig Pass 70 44 26N 110 43W
Craighead County ◇ 27 35 50N 90 42W
Craigmont 34 46 15N 116 29W
Craigsville, Va. 68 38 5N 79 23W
Craigsville, W. Va. 68 38 20N 80 39W
Cranberry L. 53 44 11N 74 50W
Crandall 45 31 58N 88 32W
Crandon 69 45 34N 88 54W
Crane, Ind. 36 38 54N 86 54W
Crane, Mo. 46 36 54N 93 34W
Crane, Mont. 47 47 35N 104 16W
Crane, Oreg. 58 43 25N 118 35W
Crane, Tex. 64 31 24N 102 21W
Crane County ◇ 64 31 24N 102 21W
Crane Mt. 58 42 4N 120 13W
Cranfills Gap 65 31 46N 97 50W
Cranford 51 40 40N 74 18W
Cranston 42 41 47N 71 26W
Crapo 41 38 18N 76 9W
Crary 55 48 4N 98 38W
Crater L. 58 42 56N 122 6W
Crater Lake 58 42 54N 122 8W
Crater Lake National Park 58 42 55N 122 10W
Craters of the Moon National Monument 34 43 25N 113 30W
Craven County ◇ 54 35 15N 77 10W
Crawford, Ala. 24 32 27N 85 11W
Crawford, Colo. 30 38 42N 107 37W
Crawford, Miss. 45 33 18N 88 37W
Crawford, Nebr. 48 42 41N 103 25W
Crawford, Okla. 57 35 50N 99 48W
Crawford, Tex. 65 31 32N 97 27W
Crawford County ◇, Ark. 27 35 20N 94 18W
Crawford County ◇, Ga. 32 32 50N 84 0W
Crawford County ◇, Ill. 35 39 0N 87 45W
Crawford County ◇, Ind. 36 38 15N 86 25W
Crawford County ◇, Iowa 37 42 0N 95 20W
Crawford County ◇, Kans. 38 37 30N 94 45W
Crawford County ◇, Mich. 43 44 45N 84 40W
Crawford County ◇, Mo. 46 38 0N 91 20W
Crawford County ◇, Ohio 56 40 48N 82 59W
Crawford County ◇, Pa. 59 41 45N 80 0W
Crawford County ◇, Wis. 69 43 15N 90 50W
Crawfordsville, Ark. 27 35 14N 90 20W
Crawfordsville, Ind. 36 40 2N 86 54W
Crawfordsville, Iowa 37 41 12N 91 32W
Crawfordville, Fla. 31 30 11N 84 23W
Crawfordville, Ga. 32 33 33N 82 54W
Crazy Mts. 47 46 12N 110 20W
Crazy Woman Cr. ⟶ 70 44 29N 106 8W
Creagerstown 41 39 37N 77 22W
Creal Springs 35 37 37N 88 50W
Creede 30 37 51N 106 56W
Creedmoor 54 36 7N 78 41W
Creek County ◇ 57 35 50N 96 20W
Creighton, Mo. 46 38 30N 94 4W
Creighton, Nebr. 48 42 28N 97 54W
Crellin 41 39 25N 79 25W
Crenshaw 45 34 30N 90 12W
Crenshaw County ◇ 24 31 43N 86 16W
Creole 39 29 49N 93 7W
Cresaptown 41 39 36N 78 50W
Cresbard 61 45 10N 98 57W
Crescent, Okla. 57 35 57N 97 36W
Crescent, Oreg. 58 43 28N 121 42W
Crescent Beach 31 29 46N 81 15W
Crescent City, Calif. 28 41 45N 124 12W
Crescent City, Fla. 31 29 26N 81 31W
Crescent L. 31 29 28N 81 30W
Cresco 37 43 22N 92 7W
Cresson 59 40 28N 78 36W
Crested Butte 30 38 52N 106 59W
Crestline 56 40 47N 82 44W
Creston, Iowa 37 41 4N 94 22W
Creston, Wash. 67 47 46N 118 31W
Creston, Wyo. 70 41 42N 107 45W
Crestone 30 37 56N 105 47W
Crestview 31 30 46N 86 34W
Crestwood 63 38 19N 85 28W
Crestwood Village 51 39 56N 74 20W
Creswell, N.C. 54 35 53N 76 24W
Creswell, Oreg. 58 43 55N 123 1W
Crete, Ill. 35 41 27N 87 38W
Crete, Nebr. 48 40 38N 96 58W
Creve Coeur 35 40 39N 89 35W
Crewe 68 37 10N 78 8W
Cricket 54 36 11N 81 12W
Cricket Mts. 66 39 0N 112 0W
Criner 57 34 58N 97 34W
Cripple Creek 30 38 45N 105 11W
Crisfield 41 37 59N 75 51W
Crisp County ◇ 32 31 50N 83 50W
Crisp Pt. 43 46 45N 85 16W
Cristobal 71 9 21N 79 55W
Crittenden 63 38 47N 84 36W
Crittenden County ◇, Ark. 27 35 14N 90 20W
Crittenden County ◇, Ky. 62 37 20N 88 5W
Crivitz 69 45 14N 88 1W
Croatan National Forest 54 34 50N 77 5W
Crocheron 41 38 15N 76 3W
Crocker 46 37 57N 92 16W
Crockett 65 31 19N 95 27W
Crockett County ◇, Tenn. 62 35 49N 89 14W
Crockett County ◇, Tex. 64 30 45N 101 30W
Crofton, Ky. 62 37 3N 87 29W
Crofton, Md. 41 39 1N 76 42W
Crofton, Nebr. 48 42 44N 97 30W
Croghan 53 43 54N 75 24W
Cromwell, Ala. 24 32 14N 88 17W
Cromwell, Minn. 44 46 41N 92 53W
Cromwell, Okla. 57 35 22N 96 29W
Crook 30 40 52N 102 48W
Crook County ◇, Oreg. 58 44 10N 120 20W
Crook County ◇, Wyo. 70 44 44N 104 30W
Crooked ⟶ 58 44 32N 121 16W
Crooked Creek 25 61 52N 158 7W
Crooked L. 31 27 48N 81 35W
Crooks 61 43 40N 96 49W
Crookston, Minn. 44 47 47N 96 37W
Crookston, Nebr. 48 42 56N 100 45W
Crooksville 56 39 46N 82 6W
Croom 41 38 45N 76 46W
Cropsey 35 40 37N 88 29W
Crosby, Minn. 44 46 29N 93 58W
Crosby, Miss. 45 31 17N 91 4W
Crosby, N. Dak. 55 48 55N 103 18W
Crosby, Tex. 65 29 55N 95 4W
Crosby, Mt. 70 43 52N 109 20W
Crosby County ◇ 64 33 40N 101 14W
Crosbyton 64 33 40N 101 14W
Cross Anchor 60 34 39N 81 51W
Cross City 31 29 38N 83 7W
Cross County ◇ 27 35 14N 90 47W
Cross Hill 60 34 18N 81 59W
Cross L. 40 47 7N 68 20W
Cross Lake 44 46 40N 94 7W
Cross Plains, Tenn. 62 36 33N 86 42W
Cross Plains, Tex. 65 32 8N 99 11W
Cross Sound 25 56 0N 135 0W
Cross Timbers 46 38 1N 93 14W
Crossett 27 33 8N 91 58W
Crossroads 52 33 31N 103 20W
Crossville, Ill. 35 38 10N 88 4W
Crossville, Tenn. 63 35 57N 85 2W
Croswell 43 43 16N 82 37W
Crothersville 36 38 48N 85 50W
Crouch 34 44 7N 115 58W
Crouse 54 35 25N 81 18W
Crow ⟶ 30 40 23N 104 29W
Crow Agency 47 45 36N 107 28W
Crow Creek Indian Reservation 61 44 3N 99 25W
Crow Indian Reservation 47 45 25N 108 0W
Crow Wing ⟶ 44 46 19N 94 20W
Crow Wing County ◇ 44 46 30N 94 0W
Crowder, Miss. 45 34 11N 90 8W
Crowder, Okla. 57 35 7N 95 40W
Crowell 65 33 59N 99 43W
Crowley, Colo. 30 38 12N 103 51W
Crowley, La. 39 30 13N 92 22W
Crowley, Tex. 65 32 35N 97 22W
Crowley, L. 28 37 35N 118 42W
Crowley County ◇ 30 38 15N 103 45W
Crowley Ridge 27 35 45N 90 45W
Crown City 56 38 36N 82 17W
Crown Point 36 41 25N 87 22W
Crownpoint 52 35 41N 108 9W
Crows Nest Pk. 61 44 3N 103 58W
Croydon Flat 50 43 25N 72 12W
Crozet 68 38 4N 78 42W
Cruger 45 33 19N 90 14W
Crump L. 58 42 17N 119 50W
Crumpton 41 39 14N 75 55W
Cruz Bay 71 18 20N 64 48W
Crystal, Minn. 44 45 3N 93 22W
Crystal, N. Dak. 55 48 36N 97 40W
Crystal ⟶ 30 39 25N 107 14W
Crystal B. 31 28 50N 82 45W
Crystal Bay 49 39 15N 120 0W
Crystal Beach, Fla. 31 28 5N 82 47W
Crystal Beach, Md. 41 39 26N 75 59W
Crystal City, Mo. 46 38 13N 90 23W
Crystal City, Tex. 65 28 41N 99 50W
Crystal Falls 43 46 5N 88 20W
Crystal L. 43 44 40N 86 10W
Crystal Lake, Fla. 31 30 26N 85 42W
Crystal Lake, Ill. 35 42 14N 88 19W
Crystal Lake, Iowa 37 43 13N 93 47W
Crystal River 31 28 54N 82 35W
Crystal Springs 45 31 59N 90 21W
Cuba, Ala. 24 32 26N 88 23W
Cuba, Ill. 35 40 30N 90 12W
Cuba, Kans. 38 39 48N 97 27W
Cuba, Mo. 46 38 4N 91 24W
Cuba, N. Mex. 52 36 1N 107 4W
Cuba, N.Y. 53 42 13N 78 17W
Cuba City 69 42 36N 90 26W
Cubero 52 35 5N 107 31W
Cucamonga 29 34 10N 117 30W
Cuchara, Pta. 71 17 57N 66 42W
Cucharas ⟶ 30 37 55N 104 32W
Cudahy 69 42 58N 87 52W
Cuddeback L. 29 35 18N 117 29W
Cuero 65 29 6N 97 17W
Cuervo 52 35 2N 104 25W
Culberson 54 35 0N 84 9W
Culberson County ◇ 64 31 30N 104 30W
Culbertson, Mont. 47 48 9N 104 31W
Culbertson, Nebr. 48 40 14N 100 50W
Culdesac 34 46 23N 116 40W
Culebra, Isla de 71 18 19N 65 18W
Culebrita, Isla 71 18 19N 65 14W
Cullen 39 32 58N 93 27W
Cullison 38 37 38N 98 54W
Cullman 24 34 11N 86 51W
Cullman County ◇ 24 34 11N 86 51W
Culloden 32 32 52N 84 6W
Cullom 35 40 53N 88 16W
Cullomburg 24 31 43N 88 18W
Cullowhee 54 35 19N 83 11W
Culp Creek 58 43 42N 122 50W
Culpeper 68 38 30N 78 0W
Culpeper County ◇ 68 38 28N 78 0W
Culver, Ind. 36 41 13N 86 25W
Culver, Kans. 38 38 58N 97 46W
Culver, Oreg. 58 44 32N 121 13W
Culverton 32 33 19N 82 54W
Cumberland, Iowa 37 41 16N 94 52W
Cumberland, Ky. 63 36 59N 82 59W
Cumberland, Md. 41 39 39N 78 46W
Cumberland, N.C. 54 35 0N 78 59W
Cumberland, N.J. 51 39 26N 75 14W
Cumberland, Ohio 56 39 51N 81 40W
Cumberland, Va. 68 37 30N 78 15W
Cumberland, Wis. 69 45 32N 92 1W
Cumberland ⟶ 62 37 9N 88 25W
Cumberland, L. 63 36 52N 85 9W
Cumberland City 62 36 23N 87 38W
Cumberland County ◇, Ill. 35 39 15N 88 15W
Cumberland County ◇, Ky. 63 36 45N 85 25W
Cumberland County ◇, Maine 40 43 50N 70 30W
Cumberland County ◇, N.C. 54 35 0N 78 45W
Cumberland County ◇, N.J. 51 39 20N 75 10W
Cumberland County ◇, Pa. 59 40 5N 77 10W
Cumberland County ◇, Tenn. 63 36 0N 85 0W
Cumberland County ◇, Va. 68 37 30N 78 15W
Cumberland Gap 63 36 36N 83 41W
Cumberland Gap Nat. Historic Park 63 36 36N 83 40W
Cumberland Hill 42 41 59N 71 28W
Cumberland I. 32 30 50N 81 25W
Cumberland I. Nat. Seashore 32 30 12N 81 24W
Cumberland Plateau 63 36 0N 85 0W
Cumberland Pt. 43 47 51N 89 14W
Cumby 65 33 8N 95 50W
Cuming County ◇ 48 41 50N 96 40W
Cumming 32 34 12N 84 9W
Cummings 60 32 47N 80 59W
Cundiff 63 36 57N 85 15W
Cunningham 38 37 39N 98 26W
Cupertino 28 37 19N 122 2W
Cuprum 34 45 5N 116 41W
Curecanti Nat. Rec. Area 30 38 24N 107 25W
Curlew, Iowa 37 42 59N 94 44W
Curlew, Wash. 67 48 53N 118 36W
Current ⟶ 27 36 15N 90 55W
Currie, Minn. 44 44 3N 95 40W
Currie, N.C. 54 34 28N 78 6W
Currie, Nev. 49 40 16N 114 45W
Currituck 54 36 27N 76 1W

Currituck County ◇ **54** 36 20N 76 0W
Currituck Sd. **54** 36 20N 75 52W
Curry County ◇, N. Mex. **52** 34 30N 103 15W
Curry County ◇, Oreg. **58** 42 20N 124 20W
Curryville **46** 39 21N 91 21W
Curtin **58** 43 43N 123 12W
Curtis, Ark. **27** 34 0N 93 2W
Curtis, Nebr. **48** 40 38N 100 31W
Curundu **71** 8 59N 79 38W
Cushing, Iowa **37** 42 28N 95 41W
Cushing, Nebr. **48** 41 19N 98 22W
Cushing, Okla. **57** 35 59N 96 46W
Cushing, Tex. **65** 31 49N 94 51W
Cushman, Ark. **27** 35 53N 91 45W
Cushman, Oreg. **58** 43 59N 124 3W
Cusick **67** 48 20N 117 18W
Cusseta **32** 32 18N 84 47W
Custer, Mont. **47** 46 8N 107 33W
Custer, S. Dak. **61** 43 46N 103 36W
Custer, Wash. **67** 48 55N 122 38W
Custer City **57** 35 40N 98 53W
Custer County ◇, Colo. **30** 38 10N 105 20W
Custer County ◇, Idaho **34** 44 0N 114 0W
Custer County ◇, Mont. **47** 46 25N 105 30W
Custer County ◇, Nebr. **48** 41 30N 99 40W
Custer County ◇, Okla. **57** 35 40N 99 0W
Custer County ◇, S. Dak. **61** 43 50N 103 30W
Custer National Forest **47** 45 15N 109 50W
Cut Bank **47** 48 38N 112 20W
Cut Bank Cr. →, Mont. **47** 48 29N 112 14W
Cut Bank Cr. →, N. Dak. **55** 48 10N 100 45W
Cut Off **39** 29 33N 90 20W
Cuthbert **32** 31 46N 84 48W
Cutler, Calif. **29** 36 31N 119 17W
Cutler, Ill. **35** 38 2N 89 34W
Cutler, Maine **40** 44 40N 67 12W
Cutler Ridge **31** 25 35N 80 20W
Cutlerville **43** 42 50N 85 40W
Cuttyhunk I. **42** 41 25N 70 56W
Cuyahoga County ◇ **56** 41 23N 81 43W
Cuyahoga Falls **56** 41 8N 81 29W
Cuyuma → **29** 34 58N 120 38W
Cuyuna Range **44** 46 25N 93 30W
Cyclone **59** 41 50N 78 35W
Cygnes → **46** 38 3N 94 17W
Cygnet **56** 41 14N 83 39W
Cylinder **37** 43 5N 94 33W
Cynthiana **63** 38 23N 84 18W
Cypress **35** 37 22N 89 1W
Cyril **57** 34 54N 98 12W
Cyrus **44** 45 37N 95 44W

D

Dacoma **57** 36 40N 98 34W
Dacula **32** 33 59N 83 54W
Dade City **31** 28 22N 82 11W
Dade County ◇, Fla. **31** 25 30N 80 30W
Dade County ◇, Ga. **32** 35 30N 84 30W
Dade County ◇, Mo. **46** 37 25N 93 50W
Dadeville, Ala. **24** 32 50N 85 46W
Dadeville, Mo. **46** 37 29N 93 41W
Daggett County ◇ **66** 40 55N 109 30W
Dagsboro **41** 38 33N 75 15W
Dahlgren **35** 38 12N 88 41W
Dahlonega **32** 34 32N 83 59W
Dahlonega Plat. **32** 34 10N 84 20W
Dailey **68** 38 48N 79 54W
Daingerfield **65** 33 2N 94 44W
Dairy **58** 42 14N 121 31W
Daisetta **65** 30 7N 94 39W
Daisy, Ark. **27** 34 14N 93 45W
Daisy, Wash. **67** 48 22N 118 10W
Dakota, Ill. **35** 42 23N 89 32W
Dakota, Minn. **44** 43 55N 91 22W
Dakota City, Iowa **37** 42 43N 94 12W
Dakota City, Nebr. **48** 42 25N 96 25W
Dakota County ◇, Minn. **44** 44 45N 93 0W
Dakota County ◇, Nebr. **48** 42 30N 96 30W
Dalark **27** 34 2N 92 53W
Dale, Ind. **36** 38 10N 86 59W
Dale, Okla. **57** 35 24N 97 3W
Dale County ◇ **24** 31 28N 85 39W
Dale Hollow L. **63** 36 32N 85 27W
Daleville, Ala. **24** 31 19N 85 43W
Daleville, Ind. **36** 40 7N 85 33W
Daleville, Miss. **45** 32 34N 88 41W
Dalhart **64** 36 4N 102 31W
Dalkeith **31** 30 0N 85 9W
Dallam County ◇ **64** 36 15N 102 30W
Dallas, Ga. **32** 33 55N 84 51W
Dallas, N.C. **54** 35 19N 81 11W
Dallas, Oreg. **58** 44 55N 123 19W
Dallas, Pa. **59** 41 20N 75 58W
Dallas, S. Dak. **61** 43 14N 99 31W
Dallas, Tex. **65** 32 47N 96 49W
Dallas, Wis. **69** 45 16N 91 51W
Dallas Center **37** 41 41N 93 58W
Dallas City **35** 40 38N 91 10W
Dallas County ◇, Ala. **24** 32 25N 87 1W
Dallas County ◇, Ark. **27** 33 59N 92 38W
Dallas County ◇, Iowa **37** 41 40N 94 0W
Dallas County ◇, Mo. **46** 37 40N 93 0W
Dallas County ◇, Tex. **65** 32 50N 96 50W
Dalton, Ga. **32** 34 46N 84 58W
Dalton, Mass. **42** 42 28N 73 11W
Dalton, Minn. **44** 46 10N 95 55W
Dalton, Nebr. **48** 41 25N 102 58W
Dalton, Ohio **56** 40 48N 81 42W
Dalton, Pa. **59** 41 32N 75 44W
Daly City **28** 37 42N 122 28W
Damar **38** 39 19N 99 35W
Damascus, Ark. **27** 35 22N 92 25W
Damascus, Ga. **32** 31 18N 84 43W
Damascus, Md. **41** 39 17N 77 12W
Damascus, Va. **68** 36 38N 81 47W
Dameron **41** 38 10N 76 22W
Dames Quarter **41** 38 11N 75 54W
Dan → **68** 36 42N 78 50W
Dana, Ind. **36** 39 48N 87 30W
Dana, Iowa **37** 42 6N 94 14W
Dana Point **29** 33 28N 117 42W
Danbury, Conn. **42** 41 24N 73 28W
Danbury, Iowa **37** 42 14N 95 43W
Danbury, N.C. **54** 36 25N 80 12W
Danbury, N.H. **50** 43 32N 71 52W
Danbury, Nebr. **48** 40 3N 100 25W
Danbury, Tex. **65** 29 14N 95 21W
Danby **50** 43 20N 72 59W
Danby L. **29** 34 13N 115 5W
Dandridge **63** 36 1N 83 25W
Dane County ◇ **69** 43 0N 89 29W
Danforth, Ill. **35** 40 49N 87 59W
Danforth, Maine **40** 45 40N 67 52W
Danforth Hills **30** 40 15N 108 0W
Daniel **70** 42 52N 110 4W
Daniel Boone National Forest **63** 37 30N 84 0W
Daniels County ◇ **47** 48 40N 105 20W
Daniel's Pass **66** 40 18N 111 10W
Danielson **42** 41 48N 71 53W
Danielsville **32** 34 8N 83 13W
Dannebrog **48** 41 7N 98 33W
Dannemora **53** 44 43N 73 44W
Dansville, Mich. **43** 42 34N 84 19W
Dansville, N.Y. **53** 42 34N 77 42W
Dante, S. Dak. **61** 43 2N 98 11W
Dante, Va. **68** 36 59N 82 18W
Danvers, Ill. **35** 40 32N 89 11W
Danvers, Mass. **42** 42 34N 70 56W
Danville, Ark. **27** 35 3N 93 24W
Danville, Calif. **28** 37 49N 122 0W
Danville, Ga. **32** 32 37N 83 15W
Danville, Ill. **35** 40 8N 87 37W
Danville, Ind. **36** 39 46N 86 32W
Danville, Iowa **37** 40 52N 91 19W
Danville, Kans. **38** 37 17N 97 54W
Danville, Ky. **63** 37 39N 84 46W
Danville, Ohio **56** 40 27N 82 16W
Danville, Pa. **59** 40 58N 76 37W
Danville, Va. **68** 36 36N 79 23W
Danville, Vt. **50** 44 25N 72 9W
Danville, W. Va. **68** 38 5N 81 50W
Danville, Wash. **67** 48 59N 118 30W
Daphne **24** 30 36N 87 54W
Darby **47** 46 1N 114 11W
Darby, C. **25** 64 19N 162 47W
Dardanelle, Ark. **27** 35 13N 93 9W
Dardanelle, Calif. **28** 38 20N 119 50W
Dardanelle L. **27** 35 14N 93 10W
Dare County ◇ **54** 35 45N 75 40W
Darfur **44** 44 3N 94 50W
Darien, Panama **71** 9 7N 79 46W
Darien, Conn. **42** 41 5N 73 28W
Darien, Ga. **32** 31 23N 81 26W
Darien, Wis. **69** 42 36N 88 43W
Darke County ◇ **56** 40 6N 84 38W
Darling, L. **55** 48 27N 101 35W
Darlington, Fla. **31** 30 57N 86 3W
Darlington, Ind. **36** 40 6N 86 47W
Darlington, La. **39** 30 53N 90 47W
Darlington, Md. **41** 39 38N 76 12W
Darlington, S.C. **60** 34 18N 79 52W
Darlington, Wis. **69** 42 41N 90 7W
Darlington County ◇ **60** 34 20N 80 0W
Darnestown **41** 39 6N 77 18W
Darr **48** 40 49N 99 53W
Darrington **67** 48 15N 121 36W
Darrouzett **64** 36 27N 100 20W
Dasher **32** 30 45N 83 13W
Dassel **44** 45 5N 94 19W
Dateland **26** 32 48N 113 33W
Datil **52** 34 9N 107 51W
Dauphin **59** 40 22N 76 56W
Dauphin County ◇ **59** 40 20N 76 55W
Dauphin I. **24** 30 15N 88 11W
Dauphin Island **24** 30 15N 88 7W
Davenport, Calif. **28** 37 1N 122 12W
Davenport, Fla. **31** 28 10N 81 36W
Davenport, Iowa **37** 41 32N 90 35W
Davenport, N. Dak. **55** 46 43N 97 4W
Davenport, N.Y. **53** 42 28N 74 51W
Davenport, Nebr. **48** 40 19N 97 49W
Davenport, Okla. **57** 35 42N 96 46W
Davenport, Wash. **67** 47 39N 118 9W
Davey **48** 40 59N 96 40W
David **63** 37 36N 82 54W
David City **48** 41 15N 97 8W
Davidson, N.C. **54** 35 30N 80 51W
Davidson, Okla. **57** 34 14N 99 5W
Davidson County ◇, N.C. **54** 35 45N 80 10W
Davidson County ◇, Tenn. **62** 36 10N 86 47W
Davidsonville **41** 38 55N 76 38W
Davie County ◇ **54** 35 50N 80 30W
Daviess County ◇, Ind. **36** 38 40N 87 5W
Daviess County ◇, Ky. **62** 38 40N 87 5W
Daviess County ◇, Mo. **46** 40 0N 94 0W
Davis, Calif. **28** 38 33N 121 44W
Davis, Ill. **35** 42 25N 89 25W
Davis, N.C. **54** 34 48N 76 28W
Davis, Okla. **57** 34 30N 97 7W
Davis, S. Dak. **61** 43 16N 96 59W
Davis, W. Va. **68** 39 8N 79 28W
Davis, Mt. **59** 39 48N 79 10W
Davis City **37** 40 38N 93 49W
Davis County ◇, Iowa **37** 40 45N 92 25W
Davis County ◇, Utah **66** 41 0N 112 5W
Davis Creek **28** 41 44N 120 22W
Davis Dam **26** 35 11N 114 34W
Davis Junction **35** 42 6N 89 6W
Davis Mts. **64** 30 50N 103 55W
Davisboro **32** 32 59N 82 36W
Davison **43** 43 2N 83 31W
Davison County ◇ **61** 43 43N 98 2W
Davisville **46** 37 49N 91 11W
Davy **68** 37 29N 81 39W
Davy Crockett National Forest **65** 31 12N 95 2W
Dawes County ◇ **48** 42 45N 103 0W
Dawn **64** 34 55N 102 12W
Dawson, Ga. **32** 31 46N 84 27W
Dawson, Minn. **44** 44 56N 96 3W
Dawson, N. Dak. **55** 46 52N 99 45W
Dawson, Nebr. **48** 40 8N 95 50W
Dawson, Oreg. **58** 44 22N 123 25W
Dawson, Tex. **65** 31 54N 96 43W
Dawson County ◇, Ga. **32** 34 25N 84 10W
Dawson County ◇, Mont. **47** 47 15N 105 0W
Dawson County ◇, Nebr. **48** 40 50N 99 50W
Dawson County ◇, Tex. **64** 32 44N 101 58W
Dawson Springs **62** 37 10N 87 41W
Dawsonville **32** 34 25N 84 7W
Day **31** 30 12N 83 17W
Day County ◇ **61** 45 20N 97 31W
Daykin **48** 40 21N 97 18W
Dayton, Ala. **24** 32 21N 87 38W
Dayton, Mont. **47** 47 52N 114 17W
Dayton, Nev. **49** 39 14N 119 36W
Dayton, Ohio **56** 39 45N 84 12W
Dayton, Pa. **59** 40 53N 79 15W
Dayton, Tenn. **63** 35 30N 85 1W
Dayton, Tex. **65** 30 3N 94 54W
Dayton, Va. **68** 38 25N 78 56W
Dayton, Wash. **67** 46 19N 117 59W
Dayton, Wyo. **70** 44 53N 107 16W
Daytona Beach **31** 29 13N 81 1W
Dayville **58** 44 28N 119 32W
Dazey **55** 47 11N 98 12W
De Armanville **24** 33 38N 85 45W
De Baca County ◇ **52** 34 15N 104 30W
De Bary **31** 28 54N 81 18W
De Beque **30** 39 20N 108 13W
De Forest **69** 43 15N 89 20W
De Funiak Springs **31** 30 43N 86 7W
De Graff **44** 45 16N 95 28W
De Gray L. **27** 34 13N 93 7W
De Kalb, Ill. **35** 41 56N 88 46W
De Kalb, Miss. **45** 32 46N 88 39W
De Kalb, Tex. **65** 33 31N 94 37W
De Kalb County ◇, Ala. **24** 34 26N 85 43W
De Kalb County ◇, Ga. **32** 33 40N 84 10W
De Kalb County ◇, Ill. **35** 41 50N 88 45W
De Kalb County ◇, Ind. **36** 41 25N 85 0W
De Kalb County ◇, Mo. **46** 39 50N 94 25W
De Kalb County ◇, Tenn. **62** 36 0N 86 0W
De Kalb Junction **53** 44 30N 75 17W
De Land **31** 29 2N 81 18W
De Leon **65** 32 7N 98 32W
De Leon Springs **31** 29 7N 81 21W
De Long Mts. **25** 68 30N 163 0W
De Pere **69** 44 27N 88 4W
De Queen **27** 34 2N 94 21W
De Quincy **39** 30 27N 93 26W
De Ridder **39** 30 51N 93 17W
De Ruyter **53** 42 46N 75 53W
De Smet **61** 44 23N 97 33W
De Smet, L. **70** 44 29N 106 45W
De Soto, Ill. **35** 37 49N 89 14W
De Soto, Kans. **38** 38 59N 94 58W
De Soto, Miss. **45** 31 58N 88 43W
De Soto, Mo. **46** 38 8N 90 34W
De Soto, Wis. **69** 43 25N 91 12W
De Soto City **31** 27 27N 81 24W
De Soto County ◇, Fla. **31** 27 15N 81 45W
De Soto County ◇, Miss. **45** 34 53N 90 1W
De Soto National Forest **45** 31 0N 89 0W
De Soto Parish ◇ **39** 32 2N 93 43W
De Tour Village **43** 46 0N 83 56W
De Witt, Ark. **27** 34 18N 91 20W
De Witt, Ill. **35** 40 11N 88 47W
De Witt, Iowa **37** 41 49N 90 33W
De Witt, Mich. **43** 42 51N 84 34W
De Witt, Nebr. **48** 40 24N 96 55W
De Witt County ◇, Ill. **35** 40 10N 88 55W
De Witt County ◇, Tex. **65** 29 6N 97 17W
Dead L. **31** 30 10N 85 10W
Deadhorse **25** 70 11N 148 27W
Deadman B. **31** 29 30N 83 30W
Deadwood **61** 44 23N 103 44W
Deaf Smith County ◇ **64** 35 0N 102 30W
Deale **41** 38 47N 76 33W
Dearborn, Mich. **43** 42 19N 83 11W
Dearborn, Mo. **46** 39 32N 94 46W
Dearborn County ◇ **36** 39 10N 85 0W
Deary **34** 46 48N 116 32W
Dease Inlet **25** 70 30N 155 0W
Death Valley **29** 36 15N 116 50W
Death Valley Junction **29** 36 20N 116 25W
Death Valley National Monument **29** 36 45N 117 15W
Deatsville **24** 32 37N 86 24W
Deaver **70** 44 54N 108 36W
Deblois **40** 44 45N 68 1W
Decatur, Ala. **24** 34 36N 86 59W
Decatur, Ark. **27** 36 20N 94 28W
Decatur, Ga. **32** 33 47N 84 18W
Decatur, Ill. **35** 39 51N 88 57W
Decatur, Ind. **36** 40 50N 84 56W
Decatur, Mich. **43** 42 7N 85 58W
Decatur, Miss. **45** 32 26N 89 7W
Decatur, Nebr. **48** 42 0N 96 15W
Decatur, Tenn. **63** 35 31N 84 47W
Decatur, Tex. **65** 33 14N 97 35W
Decatur City **37** 40 45N 93 50W
Decatur County ◇, Ga. **32** 31 0N 84 30W
Decatur County ◇, Ind. **36** 39 15N 85 30W
Decatur County ◇, Iowa **37** 40 45N 93 45W
Decatur County ◇, Kans. **38** 39 45N 100 20W
Decatur County ◇, Tenn. **62** 35 35N 88 7W
Decaturville **62** 35 35N 88 7W
Deception, Mt. **67** 47 49N 123 14W
Decherd **62** 35 13N 86 5W
Deckerville **43** 43 32N 82 44W
Declo **34** 42 32N 113 40W
Decorah **37** 43 18N 91 48W
Dedham, Iowa **37** 41 55N 94 49W
Dedham, Mass. **42** 42 15N 71 10W
Deefield **69** 43 3N 89 5W
Deep → **54** 35 36N 79 3W
Deep Cr. → **56** 39 27N 83 0W
Deep Creek L. **41** 39 31N 79 24W
Deep Creek Range **66** 39 50N 113 50W
Deep Fork Canadian → **57** 35 28N 95 50W

Deep River, Conn. 42 41 23N 72 26W
Deep River, Iowa 37 41 35N 92 22W
Deep Springs L. 29 37 20N 118 0W
Deepstep 32 33 1N 82 58W
Deepwater, Mo. 46 38 16N 93 47W
Deepwater, N.J. 51 39 41N 75 29W
Deer 27 35 50N 93 13W
Deer Cr. →, Ind. 36 40 34N 86 41W
Deer Cr. →, Md. 41 39 40N 76 10W
Deer Creek, Ill. 35 40 38N 89 20W
Deer Creek, Okla. 57 36 48N 97 31W
Deer Grove 35 41 37N 89 42W
Deer I., Alaska 25 54 55N 162 18W
Deer I., Maine 40 44 13N 68 41W
Deer Isle 40 44 14N 68 41W
Deer Lodge 47 46 24N 112 44W
Deer Lodge County ◇ 47 46 0N 113 0W
Deer Park, Ala. 24 31 13N 88 19W
Deer Park, Fla. 31 28 6N 80 54W
Deer Park, Md. 41 39 25N 79 18W
Deer Park, N.Y. 53 40 46N 73 20W
Deer Park, Ohio 56 39 13N 84 23W
Deer Park, Wash. 67 47 57N 117 28W
Deer Park, Wis. 69 45 11N 92 23W
Deer River 44 47 20N 93 48W
Deer Trail 30 39 37N 104 2W
Deerfield, Ill. 35 42 10N 87 51W
Deerfield, Kans. 38 37 59N 101 8W
Deerfield, Mo. 46 37 50N 94 30W
Deerfield → 42 42 35N 72 35W
Deerfield Beach 31 26 19N 80 6W
Deering, Alaska 25 66 4N 162 42W
Deering, N. Dak. 55 48 24N 101 3W
Deerlodge National Forest 47 46 20N 113 30W
Deersville 56 40 18N 81 11W
Deerwood 44 46 29N 93 54W
Deeth 49 41 4N 115 17W
Defiance, Iowa 37 41 49N 95 20W
Defiance, Ohio 56 41 17N 84 22W
Defiance County ◇ 56 41 23N 84 32W
Del City 57 35 26N 97 26W
Del Mar 29 32 58N 117 16W
Del Norte 30 37 41N 106 21W
Del Norte County ◇ 28 41 40N 124 0W
Del Rio 64 29 22N 100 54W
Delacroix 39 29 46N 89 45W
Delafield 69 43 4N 88 24W
Delanco 51 40 3N 74 57W
Delano, Calif. 29 35 46N 119 15W
Delano, Minn. 44 45 2N 93 47W
Delano Peak 66 38 22N 112 22W
Delaplaine 27 36 14N 90 44W
Delavan, Ill. 35 40 22N 89 33W
Delavan, Kans. 38 38 40N 96 49W
Delavan, Wis. 69 42 38N 88 39W
Delaware, Ark. 27 35 17N 93 19W
Delaware, Ohio 56 40 18N 83 4W
Delaware, Okla. 57 36 47N 95 39W
Delaware □ 41 39 0N 75 20W
Delaware → 41 39 15N 75 20W
Delaware B. 41 39 0N 75 10W
Delaware City 41 39 35N 75 36W
Delaware County ◇, Ind. 36 40 15N 85 25W
Delaware County ◇, Iowa 37 42 30N 91 20W
Delaware County ◇, N.Y. 53 42 15N 75 0W
Delaware County ◇, Ohio 56 40 18N 83 4W
Delaware County ◇, Okla. 57 36 25N 94 50W
Delaware County ◇, Pa. 59 39 55N 75 23W
Delaware Cr. → 64 32 2N 104 0W
Delaware Mts. 64 31 45N 104 50W
Delaware Water Gap Nat. Rec. Area 51 41 10N 74 55W
Delbarton 68 37 43N 82 11W
Delcambre 39 29 57N 91 58W
Delevan 53 42 29N 78 29W
Delgada, Pt. 28 40 2N 124 5W
Delhi, Calif. 28 37 26N 120 46W
Delhi, Iowa 37 42 26N 91 20W
Delhi, La. 39 32 28N 91 30W
Delhi, N.Y. 53 42 17N 74 55W
Delia 38 39 15N 95 59W
Delight 27 34 2N 93 31W
Dell 47 44 44N 112 42W
Dell City 64 31 56N 105 12W
Dell Rapids 61 43 50N 96 43W
Delmar, Del. 41 38 27N 75 35W
Delmar, Iowa 37 42 0N 90 37W
Delmar, N.Y. 53 42 37N 73 50W
Delmarva Peninsula 41 38 45N 75 45W
Delmont, N.J. 51 39 13N 74 57W
Delmont, S. Dak. 61 43 16N 98 10W
Deloit 37 42 6N 95 19W
Delphi 36 40 36N 86 41W
Delphos, Kans. 38 39 17N 97 46W
Delphos, Ohio 56 40 51N 84 21W
Delray Beach 31 26 28N 80 4W
Delta, Ala. 24 33 26N 85 42W
Delta, Colo. 30 38 44N 108 4W
Delta, Mo. 46 37 12N 89 44W
Delta, Ohio 56 41 34N 84 0W
Delta, Utah 66 39 21N 112 35W
Delta County ◇, Colo. 30 38 50N 107 50W
Delta County ◇, Mich. 43 46 0N 87 0W
Delta County ◇, Tex. 65 33 23N 95 42W
Delta Junction 25 64 2N 145 44W
Delta National Forest 45 32 50N 90 55W
Deltona 31 28 54N 81 16W
Deming, N. Mex. 52 32 16N 107 46W
Deming, Wash. 67 48 50N 122 13W
Demopolis 24 32 31N 87 50W
Demorest 32 34 34N 83 33W
Demotte 36 41 12N 87 12W
Dempsey 57 35 31N 99 49W
Denair 28 37 32N 120 48W
Denbigh 55 48 19N 100 35W
Denbigh, C. 25 64 23N 161 32W
Dendron 68 37 3N 76 56W
Denham 44 46 22N 92 57W
Denham Springs 39 30 29N 90 57W
Denhoff 55 47 29N 100 16W
Denio 49 41 59N 118 38W
Denison, Iowa 37 42 1N 95 21W
Denison, Kans. 38 39 24N 95 38W
Denison, Tex. 65 33 45N 96 33W
Denmark, Kans. 38 39 5N 98 17W
Denmark, S.C. 60 33 19N 81 9W
Denmark, Wis. 69 44 21N 87 50W
Dennard 27 35 46N 92 31W
Dennehotso 26 36 51N 109 51W
Dennis, Kans. 38 37 21N 95 25W
Dennis, Miss. 45 34 34N 88 14W
Dennis Port 42 41 39N 70 8W
Dennison, Minn. 44 44 25N 93 2W
Dennison, Ohio 56 40 24N 81 19W
Dennisville 51 39 12N 74 49W
Dent 44 46 33N 95 43W
Dent County ◇ 46 37 35N 91 30W
Denton, Ga. 32 31 44N 82 42W
Denton, Kans. 38 39 44N 95 16W
Denton, Md. 41 38 53N 75 50W
Denton, Mont. 47 47 19N 109 57W
Denton, N.C. 54 35 38N 80 6W
Denton, Nebr. 48 40 44N 96 51W
Denton, Tex. 65 33 13N 97 8W
Denton County ◇ 65 33 15N 97 10W
Denton Cr. → 65 32 58N 96 57W
Dentsville, Md. 41 38 27N 76 51W
Dentsville, S.C. 60 34 4N 80 58W
Denver, Colo. 30 39 44N 104 59W
Denver, Ind. 36 40 52N 86 5W
Denver, Iowa 37 42 40N 92 20W
Denver, Pa. 59 40 14N 76 8W
Denver City 64 32 58N 102 50W
Denver County ◇ 30 39 45N 105 0W
Deora 30 37 38N 102 56W
Depew 57 35 48N 96 31W
Depoe Bay 58 44 49N 124 4W
Deport 65 33 32N 95 19W
Deposit 53 42 4N 75 25W
Depue 35 41 19N 89 19W
Derby, Conn. 42 41 19N 73 5W
Derby, Iowa 37 40 56N 93 27W
Derby, Kans. 38 37 33N 97 16W
Derby, N.Y. 53 42 41N 78 58W
Derby, Tex. 65 28 46N 99 8W
Derby, Vt. 50 44 57N 72 8W
Derby Line 50 45 0N 72 6W
Derma 45 33 51N 89 17W
Dermott, Ark. 27 33 32N 91 26W
Dermott, Tex. 64 32 51N 101 1W
Dernieres, Isles 39 29 2N 90 50W
Derry 50 42 53N 71 19W
Des Allemands 39 29 49N 90 28W
Des Arc, Ark. 27 34 58N 91 30W
Des Arc, Mo. 46 37 17N 90 38W
Des Lacs 55 48 16N 101 34W
Des Lacs → 55 48 17N 100 20W
Des Moines, Iowa 37 41 35N 93 37W
Des Moines, N. Mex. 52 36 46N 103 50W
Des Moines → 37 40 23N 91 25W
Des Moines County ◇ 37 40 55N 91 10W
Des Plaines 35 42 3N 87 52W
Des Plaines → 35 41 23N 88 15W
Desatoya Mts. 49 39 20N 117 40W
Descanso 29 32 51N 116 37W
Deschutes → 58 45 38N 120 55W
Deschutes County ◇ 58 44 0N 121 30W
Deschutes National Forest 58 43 40N 121 20W
Deschutes-Umatilla Plat. 58 45 0N 119 40W
Desdemona 65 32 16N 98 33W
Desecheo, Isla 71 18 23N 67 29W
Deseret 66 39 17N 112 39W
Deseret Peak 66 40 28N 112 38W
Desert Center 29 33 43N 115 24W
Desert Hot Springs 29 33 58N 116 30W
Desert Peak 66 41 11N 113 22W
Desert Ranch Reservoir 49 41 42N 116 33W
Desert Valley 49 41 10N 118 5W
Desha 27 35 44N 91 41W
Desha County ◇ 27 33 48N 91 16W
Deshler, Nebr. 48 40 9N 97 44W
Deshler, Ohio 56 41 13N 83 54W
Desloge 46 37 51N 90 32W
Destin 31 30 24N 86 30W
Detour, Pt. 43 45 40N 86 40W
Detroit, Mich. 43 42 20N 83 3W
Detroit, Oreg. 58 44 44N 122 9W
Detroit, Tex. 65 33 40N 95 16W
Detroit → 43 42 3N 83 9W
Detroit Beach 43 41 56N 83 19W
Detroit Lakes 44 46 49N 95 51W
Deuel County ◇, Nebr. 48 41 10N 102 20W
Deuel County ◇, S. Dak. 61 44 45N 96 41W
Devereux 32 33 13N 83 5W
Devils Den 29 35 46N 119 58W
Devils L., N. Dak. 55 48 2N 98 58W
Devils L., Tex. 64 29 34N 100 59W
Devils Lake 55 48 7N 98 52W
Devils Playground 29 35 0N 115 50W
Devils Tower National Monument 70 44 48N 104 55W
Devine 65 29 8N 98 54W
Devol 57 34 11N 98 35W
Devon, Kans. 38 37 55N 94 49W
Devon, Mont. 47 48 28N 111 29W
Dew 65 31 36N 96 9W
Dewar 57 35 28N 95 56W
Deweese 48 40 21N 98 8W
Dewey, Puerto Rico 71 18 18N 65 18W
Dewey, Ariz. 26 34 32N 112 15W
Dewey, Okla. 57 36 48N 95 56W
Dewey Beach 41 38 42N 75 5W
Dewey County ◇, Okla. 57 36 0N 99 0W
Dewey County ◇, S. Dak. 61 45 0N 101 0W
Dewey L. 63 37 44N 82 44W
Deweyville 65 30 18N 93 45W
Dewy Rose 32 34 10N 82 57W
Dexter, Ga. 32 32 27N 83 4W
Dexter, Kans. 38 37 11N 96 43W
Dexter, Ky. 62 36 44N 88 17W
Dexter, Maine 40 45 1N 69 18W
Dexter, Mich. 43 42 20N 83 53W
Dexter, Minn. 44 43 43N 92 42W
Dexter, Mo. 46 36 48N 89 57W
Dexter, N. Mex. 52 33 12N 104 22W
Dexter City 56 39 39N 81 28W
Diablo 67 48 43N 121 8W
Diablo, Sierra 64 31 15N 105 0W
Diablo Range 28 37 20N 121 25W
Diagonal 37 40 49N 94 20W
Diamond 46 36 59N 94 19W
Diamond, L. 58 43 10N 122 9W
Diamond Head 33 21 16N 157 49W
Diamond Mts. 49 39 50N 115 30W
Diamond Pk., Colo. 30 40 59N 108 50W
Diamond Pk., Idaho 34 44 9N 113 5W
Diamond Springs 28 38 42N 120 49W
Diamondville 70 41 47N 110 32W
Diana 68 38 34N 80 27W
Dias Creek 51 39 8N 74 53W
Dibble 57 35 2N 97 38W
D'Iberville 45 30 26N 88 54W
Diboll 65 31 11N 94 47W
Dickens, Nebr. 48 40 49N 101 2W
Dickens, Tex. 64 33 37N 100 50W
Dickens County ◇ 64 33 40N 100 50W
Dickenson County ◇ 68 37 10N 82 22W
Dickey 55 46 32N 98 27W
Dickey County ◇ 55 46 2N 98 30W
Dickeyville 69 42 38N 90 36W
Dickinson, N. Dak. 55 46 53N 102 47W
Dickinson, Tex. 65 29 28N 95 3W
Dickinson County ◇, Iowa 37 43 20N 95 10W
Dickinson County ◇, Kans. 38 38 50N 97 10W
Dickinson County ◇, Mich. 43 46 0N 87 50W
Dickson, Okla. 57 34 11N 96 59W
Dickson, Tenn. 62 36 5N 87 23W
Dickson County ◇ 62 36 11N 87 21W
Diehlstadt 46 36 58N 89 26W
Dierks 27 34 7N 94 1W
Dieterich 35 39 4N 88 23W
Dietrich 34 42 55N 114 16W
Difficult 63 36 22N 85 54W
Dighton 38 38 29N 100 28W
Dilia 52 35 12N 105 4W
Dill City 57 35 17N 99 8W
Dillard 32 34 58N 83 23W
Diller 48 40 7N 96 56W
Dilley 65 28 40N 99 10W
Dillingham 25 59 3N 158 28W
Dillingham ◇ 25 58 0N 157 0W
Dillon, Colo. 30 39 37N 106 4W
Dillon, Mont. 47 45 13N 112 38W
Dillon, S.C. 60 34 25N 79 22W
Dillon County ◇ 60 34 20N 79 20W
Dillon L. 56 40 1N 80 4W
Dillon Reservoir 30 39 37N 106 3W
Dillsboro 36 39 1N 85 4W
Dillsburg 59 40 7N 77 2W
Dillwyn 68 37 32N 78 27W
Dimmit County ◇ 65 28 27N 99 46W
Dimmitt 64 34 33N 102 19W
Dimock 61 43 29N 97 59W
Dinero 65 28 14N 97 58W
Dinnebito Wash → 26 35 29N 111 14W
Dinosaur 30 40 15N 109 1W
Dinosaur National Monument 30 40 30N 108 45W
Dinuba 29 36 32N 119 23W
Dinwiddie 68 37 5N 77 35W
Dinwiddie County ◇ 68 37 5N 77 35W
Diomede 25 65 47N 169 0W
Dirty Devil → 66 37 58N 110 24W
Disappointment, C. 67 46 18N 124 5W
Disautel 67 48 22N 119 14W
Dishman 67 47 39N 117 17W
Dismal → 48 41 50N 100 5W
Dismal Swamp 68 36 40N 76 20W
Disney 57 36 29N 95 1W
Disputanta 68 37 8N 77 14W
District of Columbia □ 41 38 54N 77 1W
Divernon 35 39 34N 89 39W
Diversion L. 65 33 49N 98 56W
Divide 47 45 45N 112 45W
Divide County ◇ 55 48 55N 103 30W
Dividing Creek 51 39 16N 75 6W
Dix, Ill. 35 38 27N 88 56W
Dix, Nebr. 48 41 14N 103 29W
Dix → 63 37 49N 84 43W
Dix Hills 53 40 49N 73 22W
Dixfield 40 44 32N 70 28W
Dixie, Ala. 24 31 9N 86 44W
Dixie, Ark. 27 35 5N 91 22W
Dixie, Wash. 67 46 8N 118 9W
Dixie County ◇ 31 29 30N 83 15W
Dixie National Forest 66 37 45N 112 15W
Dixie Union 32 31 20N 82 28W
Dixmont 40 44 41N 69 10W
Dixon, Calif. 28 38 27N 121 49W
Dixon, Ill. 35 41 50N 89 29W
Dixon, Iowa 37 41 45N 90 47W
Dixon, Ky. 62 37 31N 87 41W
Dixon, Mo. 46 37 59N 92 6W
Dixon, Mont. 47 47 19N 114 19W
Dixon, N. Mex. 52 36 12N 105 53W
Dixon, Nebr. 48 42 24N 97 2W
Dixon, Wyo. 70 41 2N 107 32W
Dixon County ◇ 48 42 30N 96 50W
Dixons Mills 24 32 4N 87 47W
Dixville Notch 50 44 50N 71 18W
Dizney 63 36 51N 83 7W
Dobbin 65 30 22N 95 46W
Dobbs Ferry 53 41 1N 73 52W
Dobson 54 36 24N 80 43W
Doctors Inlet 31 30 6N 81 47W
Doddridge 27 33 6N 93 55W
Doddridge County ◇ 68 39 17N 80 44W
Dodge, N. Dak. 55 47 18N 102 12W
Dodge, Nebr. 48 41 43N 96 53W
Dodge, Tex. 65 30 45N 95 24W
Dodge Center 44 44 2N 92 52W
Dodge City 38 37 45N 100 1W
Dodge County ◇, Ga. 32 33 10N 83 10W
Dodge County ◇, Minn. 44 44 0N 92 50W
Dodge County ◇, Nebr. 48 41 30N 96 40W
Dodge County ◇, Wis. 69 43 20N 88 45W
Dodgeville 69 42 58N 90 8W
Dodson, La. 39 32 5N 92 39W
Dodson, Mont. 47 48 24N 108 15W
Doe Run 46 37 45N 90 30W
Doerun 32 31 19N 83 55W
Dog I. 31 29 48N 84 36W
Doland 61 44 54N 98 6W
Doles 32 31 42N 83 53W
Dolgeville 53 43 6N 74 46W
Dolliver 37 43 28N 94 37W
Dolores 30 37 28N 108 30W
Dolores → 66 38 49N 109 17W
Dolores County ◇ 30 37 45N 108 30W
Dolton 35 41 38N 87 36W
Dome, The 50 42 45N 73 12W
Dona Ana 52 32 23N 106 49W

Dona Ana County ◇ **52** 32 20N 107 0W
Dona Juana, Cerro **71** 18 0N 66 0W
Donahue **37** 41 42N 90 41W
Donalds **60** 34 23N 82 21W
Donaldson, Ark. **27** 34 14N 92 55W
Donaldson, Minn. **44** 48 35N 96 53W
Donaldsonville **39** 30 6N 90 59W
Donalsonville **32** 31 3N 84 53W
Doncaster **41** 38 30N 77 15W
Donie **65** 31 29N 96 13W
Doniphan, Kans. **38** 39 38N 95 5W
Doniphan, Mo. **46** 36 37N 90 50W
Doniphan, Nebr. **48** 40 46N 98 22W
Doniphan County ◇ **38** 39 45N 95 0W
Donley County ◇ **64** 35 0N 100 45W
Donna **64** 26 9N 98 4W
Donnan **37** 42 54N 91 53W
Donnelly, Idaho **34** 44 44N 116 5W
Donnelly, Minn. **44** 45 42N 96 1W
Donner Pass **28** 39 19N 120 20W
Donner und Blitzen → **58** 43 17N 118 49W
Donnybrook **55** 48 31N 101 53W
Donora **59** 40 11N 79 52W
Donovan **35** 40 53N 87 37W
Dooly County ◇ **32** 32 10N 83 50W
Doon **37** 43 17N 96 14W
Door County ◇ **69** 45 0N 87 15W
Door Peninsula **69** 44 45N 87 25W
Dora, Ala. **24** 33 44N 87 5W
Dora, Oreg. **58** 43 10N 123 59W
Dorado **71** 18 28N 66 16W
Doran **44** 46 11N 96 29W
Doraville **32** 33 54N 84 17W
Dorchester, N.H. **50** 43 44N 71 56W
Dorchester, Nebr. **48** 40 39N 97 7W
Dorchester, Wis. **69** 45 0N 90 20W
Dorchester County ◇, Md. **41** 38 20N 76 0W
Dorchester County ◇, S.C. **60** 33 10N 80 30W
Dorena **58** 43 43N 122 52W
Dorrance **38** 38 51N 98 35W
Dorris **28** 41 58N 121 55W
Dorset **50** 43 15N 73 6W
Dorton **63** 37 17N 82 35W
Dos Bocas **71** 18 20N 66 40W
Dos Palos **28** 36 59N 120 37W
Dot Lake **25** 63 40N 144 4W
Dothan **24** 31 13N 85 24W
Doty **67** 46 38N 123 17W
Double Mountain Fork Brazos → **64** 33 16N 100 0W
Double Springs **24** 34 9N 87 24W
Doubletop Pk. **70** 43 21N 110 17W
Dougherty, Iowa **37** 42 55N 93 3W
Dougherty, Okla. **57** 34 24N 97 3W
Dougherty County ◇ **32** 31 30N 84 15W
Douglas, Alaska **25** 58 17N 134 24W
Douglas, Ariz. **26** 31 21N 109 33W
Douglas, Ga. **32** 31 31N 82 51W
Douglas, Mass. **42** 42 6N 71 45W
Douglas, N. Dak. **55** 47 51N 101 30W
Douglas, Nebr. **48** 40 36N 96 23W
Douglas, Okla. **57** 36 16N 97 40W
Douglas, Wyo. **70** 42 45N 105 24W
Douglas C. **25** 58 51N 153 15W
Douglas City **28** 40 39N 122 57W
Douglas County ◇, Colo. **30** 39 15N 105 0W
Douglas County ◇, Ga. **32** 33 40N 84 45W
Douglas County ◇, Ill. **35** 39 45N 88 15W
Douglas County ◇, Kans. **38** 38 50N 95 15W
Douglas County ◇, Minn. **44** 45 50N 95 20W
Douglas County ◇, Mo. **46** 36 55N 92 30W
Douglas County ◇, Nebr. **48** 41 15N 96 10W
Douglas County ◇, Nev. **49** 38 55N 119 45W
Douglas County ◇, Oreg. **58** 43 15N 123 0W
Douglas County ◇, S. Dak. **61** 43 25N 98 24W
Douglas County ◇, Wash. **67** 47 50N 119 45W
Douglas County ◇, Wis. **69** 46 25N 91 55W
Douglas L. **63** 35 58N 83 32W
Douglass, Kans. **38** 37 31N 97 1W
Douglass, Tex. **65** 31 40N 94 53W
Douglasville **32** 33 45N 84 45W
Dousman **69** 43 1N 88 29W
Dove Creek **30** 37 46N 108 54W
Dover, Ark. **27** 35 24N 93 7W
Dover, Del. **41** 39 10N 75 32W
Dover, Idaho **34** 48 15N 116 36W
Dover, N.H. **50** 43 12N 70 56W
Dover, N.J. **51** 40 53N 74 34W
Dover, Ohio **56** 40 32N 81 29W
Dover, Okla. **57** 35 59N 97 55W
Dover, Tenn. **62** 36 29N 87 50W
Dover-Foxcroft **40** 45 11N 69 13W
Dow City **37** 41 56N 95 30W
Dowagiac **43** 41 59N 86 6W
Dowling Park **31** 30 15N 83 15W
Downers Grove **35** 41 48N 88 1W
Downey **34** 42 26N 112 7W
Downieville **28** 39 34N 102 50W
Downing **46** 40 29N 92 22W
Downs **35** 40 24N 88 52W
Downs Mt. **70** 43 18N 109 40W
Downsville **41** 39 35N 77 48W
Dows **37** 42 39N 93 30W
Doylestown **69** 43 25N 89 10W
Doyleville **30** 38 25N 106 35W
Doyline **39** 32 32N 93 25W
Dozier **24** 31 10N 86 28W
Dracut **42** 42 40N 71 18W
Dragerton **66** 39 33N 110 25W
Dragoon **26** 32 2N 110 2W
Drain **58** 43 40N 123 19W
Drake, Ariz. **26** 35 0N 112 20W
Drake, Colo. **30** 40 40N 105 20W
Drake, N. Dak. **55** 47 55N 100 23W
Drake Pk. **58** 42 19N 120 7W
Drakes Branch **68** 36 59N 78 36W
Drakesboro **62** 37 13N 87 3W
Drakesville **37** 40 47N 92 31W
Draper, S. Dak. **61** 43 52N 100 30W
Draper, Utah **66** 40 32N 111 52W
Drayden **41** 38 11N 76 28W
Dresden, Kans. **38** 39 38N 100 26W
Dresden, N.Y. **53** 42 41N 76 58W
Dresden, Tenn. **62** 36 18N 88 42W
Dresser **69** 45 20N 92 38W
Drew County ◇ **27** 33 35N 91 40W
Drews Reservoir **58** 42 7N 120 37W
Drexel, Mo. **46** 38 29N 94 37W
Drexel, N.C. **54** 35 45N 81 36W
Driftwood **59** 41 20N 78 8W
Driggs, Ark. **27** 35 14N 93 46W
Driggs, Idaho **34** 43 44N 111 6W
Dripping Springs **65** 30 12N 98 5W
Driscoll, N. Dak. **55** 46 51N 100 9W
Driscoll, Tex. **64** 27 41N 97 45W
Driskill Mt. **39** 32 25N 92 54W
Drummond, Idaho **34** 43 59N 111 20W
Drummond, Mont. **47** 46 40N 113 9W
Drummond, Okla. **57** 36 18N 98 2W
Drummond, Wis. **69** 46 20N 91 15W
Drummond, L. **68** 36 36N 76 28W
Drummond I. **43** 46 1N 83 39W
Drumright **57** 35 59N 96 36W
Drury **41** 38 48N 76 42W
Dry Cr. → **70** 44 31N 108 3W
Dry Creek **39** 30 40N 93 3W
Dry Devils → **64** 29 47N 100 59W
Dry Falls Dam **67** 47 37N 119 19W
Dry L. **55** 48 16N 98 59W
Dry Prong **39** 31 35N 92 32W
Dry Ridge **63** 38 41N 84 35W
Dryden, N.Y. **53** 42 30N 76 18W
Dryden, Tex. **64** 30 3N 102 7W
Du Bay, L. **69** 44 40N 89 39W
Du Bois **48** 40 2N 96 4W
Du Page County ◇ **35** 41 50N 88 5W
Du Quoin **35** 38 1N 89 14W
Dubach **39** 32 42N 92 39W
Dublin, Ga. **32** 32 32N 82 54W
Dublin, Md. **41** 39 39N 76 16W
Dublin, Miss. **45** 34 4N 90 30W
Dublin, N.C. **54** 34 39N 78 43W
Dublin, N.H. **50** 42 52N 72 5W
Dublin, Tex. **65** 32 5N 98 21W
Dublin, Va. **68** 37 6N 80 41W
Dubois, Idaho **34** 44 10N 112 14W
Dubois, Ind. **36** 38 27N 86 48W
Dubois, Pa. **59** 41 7N 78 46W
Dubois, Wyo. **70** 43 33N 109 38W
Dubois County ◇ **36** 38 20N 86 50W
Dubuque **37** 42 30N 90 41W
Dubuque County ◇ **37** 42 30N 90 50W
Dubuque Hills **35** 42 15N 90 0W
Duchesne **66** 40 10N 110 24W
Duchesne → **66** 40 5N 109 41W
Duchesne County ◇ **66** 40 20N 110 30W
Duck → **62** 36 2N 87 52W
Duck Hill **45** 33 38N 89 43W
Duck River **62** 35 43N 87 16W
Duck Valley Indian Reservation **49** 42 0N 116 10W
Ducktown **63** 35 3N 84 23W
Duckwater **49** 38 55N 115 40W
Dudley, Ga. **32** 32 32N 83 5W
Dudley, Mo. **46** 36 46N 90 8W
Dudley, Pa. **59** 40 12N 78 10W
Dudleyville **26** 32 54N 110 42W
Due West **60** 34 20N 82 23W
Dufur **58** 45 27N 121 8W
Dugdemona → **39** 31 47N 92 22W
Dugger **36** 39 4N 87 18W
Duke **57** 34 40N 99 34W
Dukes County ◇ **42** 41 23N 70 31W
Dulac **39** 29 23N 90 42W
Dulce **52** 36 56N 107 0W
Duluth, Ga. **32** 34 0N 84 9W
Duluth, Minn. **44** 46 47N 92 6W
Dumas, Ark. **27** 33 53N 91 29W
Dumas, Tex. **64** 35 52N 101 58W
Dumont **37** 42 45N 92 58W
Dunbar, Nebr. **48** 40 38N 96 1W
Dunbar, Pa. **59** 39 58N 79 37W
Dunbar, W. Va. **68** 38 22N 81 45W
Dunbarton **50** 43 8N 71 38W
Duncan, Ariz. **26** 32 43N 109 6W
Duncan, Nebr. **48** 41 25N 97 30W
Duncan, Okla. **57** 34 30N 97 57W
Duncannon **59** 40 23N 77 2W
Duncanville **65** 32 39N 96 55W
Duncombe **37** 42 28N 94 0W
Dundalk **41** 39 16N 76 32W
Dundas, Minn. **44** 44 26N 93 12W
Dundas, Va. **68** 36 55N 78 1W
Dundee, Iowa **37** 42 35N 91 33W
Dundee, Ky. **62** 37 34N 86 46W
Dundee, Mich. **43** 41 57N 83 40W
Dundee, Minn. **44** 43 51N 95 28W
Dundee, N.Y. **53** 42 32N 76 59W
Dundy County ◇ **48** 40 15N 101 45W
Dunedin **31** 28 1N 82 47W
Dungannon **68** 36 50N 82 28W
Dungeness **67** 48 9N 123 7W
Dunkerton **37** 42 34N 92 10W
Dunkirk, Ind. **36** 40 23N 85 13W
Dunkirk, Mont. **47** 48 29N 111 40W
Dunkirk, N.Y. **53** 42 29N 79 20W
Dunkirk, Ohio **56** 40 48N 83 39W
Dunklin County ◇ **46** 36 20N 90 0W
Dunlap, Ill. **35** 40 52N 89 40W
Dunlap, Ind. **36** 41 39N 85 56W
Dunlap, Iowa **37** 41 51N 95 36W
Dunlap, Kans. **38** 38 35N 96 22W
Dunlap, Tenn. **63** 35 23N 85 23W
Dunlap, Tex. **64** 34 8N 100 18W
Dunlow **68** 38 1N 82 26W
Dunmor **62** 37 4N 86 59W
Dunmore **59** 41 25N 75 38W
Dunn, La. **39** 32 28N 91 35W
Dunn, N.C. **54** 35 19N 78 37W
Dunn Center **55** 47 21N 102 37W
Dunn County ◇, N. Dak. **55** 47 15N 102 35W
Dunn County ◇, Wis. **69** 44 55N 91 50W
Dunnell **44** 43 34N 94 47W
Dunnellon **31** 29 3N 82 28W
Dunning **48** 41 50N 100 6W
Dunnville **63** 37 12N 85 1W
Dunseith **55** 48 50N 100 3W
Dunsmuir **28** 41 13N 122 16W
Duplin County ◇ **54** 34 50N 78 0W
Dupo **35** 38 31N 90 13W
Dupont **36** 38 53N 85 31W
Dupuyer **47** 48 13N 112 30W
Duran **52** 34 28N 105 24W
Durand, Ga. **32** 32 54N 84 51W
Durand, Ill. **35** 42 26N 89 20W
Durand, Mich. **43** 42 55N 83 59W
Durand, Wis. **69** 44 38N 91 58W
Durango **30** 37 16N 107 53W
Durant, Iowa **37** 41 36N 90 54W
Durant, Miss. **45** 33 4N 89 51W
Durant, Okla. **57** 33 59N 96 25W
Durants Neck **54** 36 8N 76 18W
Durbin **68** 38 33N 79 50W
Durham, Conn. **42** 41 29N 72 41W
Durham, Kans. **38** 38 30N 97 15W
Durham, N.C. **54** 35 59N 78 54W
Durham, N.H. **50** 43 8N 70 56W
Durham County ◇ **54** 36 0N 78 55W
Durkee **58** 44 35N 117 30W
Dushore **59** 41 31N 76 24W
Dustin **57** 35 12N 96 1W
Dusty **67** 46 51N 117 38W
Dutch Harbor **25** 53 53N 166 32W
Dutch John **66** 40 55N 109 24W
Dutch Mills **27** 35 52N 94 29W
Dutch Neck **51** 40 17N 74 40W
Dutchess County ◇ **53** 41 45N 73 45W
Dutchtown **46** 37 18N 89 42W
Dutton **47** 47 51N 111 43W
Duval County ◇, Fla. **31** 30 30N 81 30W
Duval County ◇, Tex. **65** 27 50N 98 30W
Duxbury **42** 42 2N 70 40W
Dwight, Ill. **35** 41 5N 88 26W
Dwight, Kans. **38** 38 50N 96 38W
Dwight, Nebr. **48** 41 5N 97 1W
Dworshak Reservoir **34** 46 48N 116 0W
Dyer **62** 36 4N 88 59W
Dyer County ◇ **62** 36 0N 89 25W
Dyersburg **62** 36 3N 89 23W
Dyersville **37** 42 29N 91 8W
Dysart **37** 42 10N 92 18W

E

E. V. Spence Reservoir **64** 31 58N 100 40W
Eads, Colo. **30** 38 29N 102 47W
Eads, Tenn. **62** 35 12N 89 39W
Eagar **26** 34 6N 109 17W
Eagle, Alaska **25** 64 47N 141 12W
Eagle, Colo. **30** 39 39N 106 50W
Eagle, Idaho **34** 43 42N 116 21W
Eagle, Nebr. **48** 40 49N 96 26W
Eagle, Wis. **69** 42 53N 88 29W
Eagle → **30** 39 39N 107 4W
Eagle, Mt. **71** 17 46N 64 49W
Eagle Bend **44** 46 10N 95 2W
Eagle Butte **61** 45 0N 101 10W
Eagle City **57** 35 56N 98 35W
Eagle County ◇ **30** 39 40N 106 50W
Eagle Cr. → **63** 38 36N 85 4W
Eagle Grove **37** 42 40N 93 54W
Eagle Harbor **41** 38 35N 76 40W
Eagle L., Calif. **28** 40 39N 120 45W
Eagle L., Maine **40** 46 20N 69 22W
Eagle Lake, Maine **40** 47 3N 68 36W
Eagle Lake, Minn. **44** 44 10N 93 53W
Eagle Lake, Tex. **65** 29 35N 96 20W
Eagle Mills **27** 33 41N 92 43W
Eagle Mountain **29** 33 49N 115 27W
Eagle Mountain L. **65** 32 53N 97 28W
Eagle Nest **52** 36 33N 105 16W
Eagle Nest Butte **61** 43 27N 101 39W
Eagle Pass **64** 28 43N 100 30W
Eagle Peak **28** 41 17N 120 12W
Eagle Point **58** 42 28N 122 48W
Eagle River **69** 45 55N 89 15W
Eagle Rock **68** 37 38N 79 48W
Eagletail Mts. **26** 33 25N 113 30W
Eagletown **57** 34 2N 94 34W
Eagleville, Calif. **28** 41 19N 120 7W
Eagleville, Mo. **46** 40 28N 93 59W
Eagleville, Tenn. **62** 35 45N 86 39W
Eakly **57** 35 18N 98 34W
Earl, L. **28** 41 50N 124 11W
Earl Park **36** 40 42N 87 25W
Earle **27** 35 16N 90 28W
Earleville **41** 39 24N 75 54W
Earlham **37** 41 30N 94 7W
Earlimart **29** 35 53N 119 16W
Earling **37** 41 28N 95 46W
Earlington **62** 37 16N 87 30W
Earlsboro **57** 35 19N 96 47W
Earlville, Ill. **35** 41 35N 88 55W
Earlville, N.Y. **53** 42 44N 75 33W
Early, Iowa **37** 42 28N 95 9W
Early, Tex. **65** 31 46N 98 58W
Early Branch **60** 32 45N 80 55W
Early County ◇ **32** 31 20N 84 50W
Earth **64** 34 14N 102 24W
Easley **60** 34 50N 82 36W
East → **53** 40 48N 73 48W
East Arm Grand Traverse B. **43** 44 50N 85 30W
East Aurora **53** 42 46N 78 37W
East B., Fla. **31** 30 5N 85 32W
East B., La. **39** 29 0N 89 15W
East B., Tex. **65** 29 30N 94 35W
East Barrington **50** 43 12N 70 59W
East Baton Rouge Parish ◇ **39** 30 30N 91 20W
East Bend **54** 36 13N 80 31W
East Berkshire **50** 44 56N 72 42W
East Berlin **59** 39 56N 76 59W
East Bernard **65** 29 32N 96 4W
East Bernstadt **63** 37 9N 84 12W
East Branch Clarion River L. **59** 41 35N 78 35W
East Brewton **24** 31 5N 87 4W
East Bridgewater **42** 42 2N 70 58W
East Brunswick **51** 40 25N 74 23W
East Canton **56** 40 47N 81 17W
East Carbon **66** 39 35N 110 25W
East Carrell Parish ◇ **39** 32 45N 91 15W
East Charleston **50** 44 49N 72 0W
East Chicago **36** 41 38N 87 27W
East Corinth **50** 44 5N 72 12W
East Dorset **50** 43 13N 73 0W
East Douglas **42** 42 4N 71 43W
East Dublin **32** 32 32N 82 52W
East Dubuque **35** 42 30N 90 39W
East Ely **49** 39 15N 114 53W
East Fairfield **50** 44 47N 72 51W
East Feliciana Parish ◇ **39** 30 47N 91 8W
East Fork Bruneau → **34** 42 34N 115 38W
East Fork Sevier → **66** 38 14N 112 12W
East Fork White → **36** 38 33N 87 14W
East Fultonham **56** 39 51N 82 8W
East Glacier Park **47** 48 27N 113 13W
East Granby **42** 41 57N 72 44W
East Grand Forks **44** 47 56N 97 1W
East Grand Rapids **43** 42 58N 85 37W
East Greenwich **42** 41 40N 71 27W

East Haddam 42 41 27N 72 28W
East Hampton, Conn. 42 41 35N 72 31W
East Hampton, N.Y. 53 40 58N 72 11W
East Hartford 42 41 46N 72 39W
East Haven 42 41 17N 72 52W
East Haverhill 50 44 3N 71 58W
East Helena 47 46 35N 111 56W
East Holden 40 44 44N 68 38W
East Hope 34 48 14N 116 17W
East Jordan 43 45 10N 85 7W
East Kingston 50 42 54N 71 2W
East Lake, Mich. . . . 43 44 15N 86 18W
East Lake, N.C. 54 35 53N 75 58W
East Lansing 43 42 44N 84 29W
East Las Vegas 49 36 6N 115 3W
East Lempster 50 43 13N 72 13W
East Liberty 56 40 20N 83 35W
East Liverpool 56 40 37N 80 35W
East Longmeadow . . 42 42 4N 72 31W
East Lyme 42 41 22N 72 13W
East Lynn L. 68 38 10N 82 23W
East Lynne 46 38 40N 94 14W
East Meadow 53 40 43N 73 34W
East Middlebury . . . 50 43 58N 73 6W
East Millinocket 40 45 38N 68 35W
East Moline 35 41 32N 90 26W
East Naples 31 26 8N 81 46W
East New Market . . . 41 38 36N 75 56W
East Nishnabotna → . 37 40 39N 95 38W
East Northport 53 40 53N 73 20W
East Norwich 53 40 51N 73 32W
East Olympia 67 46 58N 122 50W
East Orange 51 40 46N 74 13W
East Palatka 31 29 39N 81 36W
East Palestine 56 40 50N 80 33W
East Park Reservoir 28 39 37N 122 31W
East Peoria 35 40 40N 89 34W
East Peru 37 41 14N 93 56W
East Petersburg 59 40 6N 76 21W
East Point 32 33 41N 84 27W
East Portal 30 39 54N 105 39W
East Prairie 46 36 47N 89 23W
East Prospect 59 39 58N 76 32W
East Providence 42 41 49N 71 23W
East Pt. 71 17 45N 64 34W
East Randolph 50 43 57N 72 33W
East Range 49 40 30N 117 57W
East Ridge 63 34 59N 85 13W
East Rochester 53 43 7N 77 29W
East Rupert 50 43 16N 73 8W
East St. Louis 35 38 37N 90 9W
East Spring Cr. → . 30 39 30N 102 30W
East Tavaputs Plateau 66 39 40N 109 40W
East Tawas 43 44 17N 83 29W
East Tohopekaliga Lake 31 28 18N 81 15W
East Troy 69 42 47N 88 24W
East Vineland 51 39 30N 74 55W
East Wallingford . . . 50 43 25N 72 54W
East Wareham 42 41 46N 70 40W
East Wenatchee 67 47 25N 120 18W
Eastchester 53 40 57N 73 49W
Eastern Bay 41 38 50N 76 15W
Eastern Shore 41 38 30N 75 50W
Eastham 42 41 50N 69 58W
Easthampton 42 42 16N 72 40W
Eastlake 56 41 40N 81 26W
Eastland 65 32 24N 98 49W
Eastland County ◇ . 65 32 25N 98 50W
Eastman, Ga. 32 32 12N 83 11W
Eastman, Wis. 69 43 10N 91 1W
Easton, Calif. 29 36 39N 119 47W
Easton, Conn. 42 41 15N 73 18W
Easton, Ill. 35 40 14N 89 50W
Easton, Kans. 38 39 21N 95 7W
Easton, Md. 41 38 47N 76 5W
Easton, Minn. 44 43 46N 93 54W
Easton, Mo. 46 39 43N 94 39W
Easton, Pa. 59 40 41N 75 13W
Easton, Wash. 67 47 14N 121 11W
Eastover 60 33 52N 80 41W
Eastpoint 31 29 44N 84 53W
Eastport, Idaho 34 48 59N 116 10W
Eastport, Maine 40 44 56N 67 0W
Eastsound 67 48 42N 122 55W
Eastville 68 37 21N 75 57W
Eaton, Colo. 30 40 32N 104 42W
Eaton, Ind. 36 40 21N 85 21W
Eaton, Ohio 56 39 45N 84 38W
Eaton County ◇ . . . 43 42 35N 84 50W
Eaton Rapids 43 42 31N 84 39W
Eatons Neck Pt. 53 40 57N 73 24W
Eatonton 32 33 20N 83 23W
Eatontown 51 40 19N 74 4W
Eatonville 67 46 52N 122 16W
Eau Claire, Mich. . . 43 41 59N 86 18W
Eau Claire, Wis. . . . 69 44 49N 91 30W
Eau Claire → 69 44 55N 89 35W
Eau Claire County ◇ 69 44 45N 91 20W
Eau Galle 69 44 42N 92 1W
Ebensburg 59 40 29N 78 44W
Ebony 68 36 37N 77 59W
Eccles 68 37 47N 81 16W
Echechonnee → . . . 32 32 39N 83 36W
Echo, Ala. 24 31 29N 85 28W
Echo, Minn. 44 44 37N 95 25W
Echo, Oreg. 58 45 45N 119 12W
Echo Cliffs 26 36 40N 111 35W
Echols County ◇ 32 30 45N 83 0W
Eckley 30 40 7N 102 29W
Eclectic 24 32 38N 86 2W
Econfina 31 30 22N 85 35W
Economy 36 39 59N 85 5W
Ecru 45 34 21N 89 2W
Ector County ◇ 64 31 46N 102 31W
Edcouch 64 26 18N 97 58W
Eddiceton 45 31 30N 90 48W
Eddy County ◇, N. Dak. 55 47 50N 99 0W
Eddy County ◇, N. Mex. 52 32 30N 104 20W
Eddyville, Ill. 35 37 30N 88 35W
Eddyville, Iowa 37 41 9N 92 38W
Eddyville, Ky. 62 37 3N 88 4W
Eddyville, Nebr. . . . 48 41 1N 99 38W
Eden, Miss. 45 32 59N 90 20W
Eden, N.C. 54 36 29N 79 53W
Eden, S. Dak. 61 45 37N 97 25W
Eden, Tex. 65 31 13N 99 51W
Eden, Vt. 50 44 42N 72 33W
Eden, Wis. 69 43 42N 88 22W
Eden, Wyo. 70 42 3N 109 26W
Eden Valley 44 45 19N 94 33W
Eden Valley Reservoir 70 42 14N 109 21W
Edenton 54 36 4N 76 39W
Edesville 41 39 9N 76 13W
Edgar, Nebr. 48 40 22N 97 58W
Edgar, Wis. 69 44 55N 89 59W
Edgar County ◇ . . . 35 39 40N 87 45W
Edgar Springs 46 37 42N 91 52W
Edgard 39 30 3N 90 34W
Edgartown 42 41 23N 70 31W
Edgecombe County ◇ 54 35 50N 77 30W
Edgefield 60 33 47N 81 56W
Edgefield County ◇ 60 33 50N 82 0W
Edgeley 55 46 22N 98 43W
Edgemere 41 39 14N 76 27W
Edgemont, Colo. . . . 30 39 44N 105 8W
Edgemont, S. Dak. . 61 43 18N 103 50W
Edgemoor 60 34 48N 81 1W
Edgerton, Kans. 38 38 46N 95 1W
Edgerton, Minn. . . . 44 43 53N 96 8W
Edgerton, Mo. 46 39 30N 94 38W
Edgerton, Ohio 56 41 27N 84 45W
Edgerton, Wis. 69 42 50N 89 4W
Edgerton, Wyo. 70 43 25N 106 15W
Edgewater 31 28 59N 80 54W
Edgewater Park 51 40 4N 74 54W
Edgewood, Ill. 35 38 55N 88 40W
Edgewood, Ind. 36 39 41N 86 8W
Edgewood, Iowa . . . 37 42 39N 91 24W
Edgewood, Md. 41 39 25N 76 18W
Edgewood, N. Mex. 52 35 4N 106 11W
Edgewood, Tex. 65 32 42N 95 53W
Edina, Minn. 44 44 53N 93 21W
Edina, Mo. 46 40 10N 92 11W
Edinboro 59 41 52N 80 8W
Edinburg, Ill. 35 39 39N 89 23W
Edinburg, Ind. 36 39 21N 85 58W
Edinburg, Miss. 45 32 48N 89 20W
Edinburg, N. Dak. . . 55 48 30N 97 52W
Edinburg, Tex. 64 26 18N 98 10W
Edinburg, Va. 68 38 49N 78 34W
Edison, Ga. 32 31 34N 84 44W
Edison, N.J. 51 40 31N 74 25W
Edison, Nebr. 48 40 17N 99 47W
Edison, Ohio 56 40 33N 82 52W
Edisto → 60 32 29N 80 21W
Edisto Beach 60 32 29N 80 20W
Edisto I. 60 32 35N 80 20W
Edith 64 31 54N 100 37W
Edmond, Kans. 38 39 37N 99 50W
Edmond, Okla. 57 35 39N 97 29W
Edmonds 67 47 49N 122 23W
Edmondson 27 35 6N 90 19W
Edmonson 64 34 17N 101 54W
Edmonson County ◇ 62 37 10N 86 15W
Edmonton 63 36 59N 85 37W
Edmore, Mich. 43 43 25N 85 3W
Edmore, N. Dak. . . . 55 48 25N 98 27W
Edmunds County ◇ 61 45 27N 99 20W
Edna, Kans. 38 37 4N 95 22W
Edna, Tex. 65 28 59N 96 39W
Edon 56 41 33N 84 46W
Edroy 65 27 59N 97 41W
Edson 38 39 20N 101 33W
Edwall 67 47 30N 117 57W
Edwards, Colo. 30 39 39N 106 36W
Edwards, Miss. 45 32 20N 90 36W
Edwards, N.Y. 53 44 20N 75 15W
Edwards → 35 41 9N 90 59W
Edwards Air Force Base 29 34 50N 117 40W
Edwards County ◇, Ill. 35 38 25N 88 5W
Edwards County ◇, Kans. 38 37 50N 99 15W
Edwards County ◇, Tex. 64 30 10N 100 13W
Edwards Plateau . . . 64 30 45N 101 20W
Edwardsburg 43 41 48N 86 6W
Edwardsport 36 38 49N 87 15W
Edwardsville 35 38 49N 89 58W
Eek 25 60 14N 162 2W
Eel →, Calif. 28 40 38N 124 20W
Eel →, Cass, Ind. . 36 40 45N 86 22W
Eel →, Greene, Ind. 36 39 7N 86 57W
Effie 44 47 50N 93 38W
Effingham, Ill. 35 39 7N 88 33W
Effingham, Kans. . . . 38 39 31N 95 24W
Effingham, S.C. 60 34 5N 79 46W
Effingham County ◇, Ga. . . . 32 32 20N 81 15W
Effingham County ◇, Ill. 35 39 5N 88 35W
Effingham Falls 50 43 47N 71 5W
Egan 61 44 0N 96 37W
Egan Range 49 39 35N 114 55W
Egegik 25 58 13N 157 22W
Egeland 55 48 38N 99 6W
Egg Harbor 69 45 3N 87 17W
Egg Harbor City . . . 51 39 32N 74 39W
Egnar 30 37 55N 108 56W
Egypt 45 33 54N 88 44W
Ehrenberg 26 33 36N 114 31W
Ehrhardt 60 33 6N 81 1W
Eitzen 44 43 31N 91 28W
Ekalaka 47 45 53N 104 33W
Ekron 62 37 56N 86 11W
Ekwok 25 59 22N 157 30W
El Cajon 29 32 48N 116 58W
El Campo 65 29 12N 96 16W
El Capitan 47 46 1N 114 23W
El Capitan Reservoir 29 32 53N 116 49W
El Centro 29 32 48N 115 34W
El Cerrito 28 37 55N 122 19W
El Dorado, Ark. . . . 27 33 12N 92 40W
El Dorado, Kans. . . 38 37 49N 96 52W
El Dorado County ◇ 28 38 45N 120 40W
El Indio 64 28 31N 100 19W
El Mirage 26 33 36N 112 19W
El Mirage L. 29 34 39N 117 37W
El Nido 28 37 8N 120 29W
El Paso, Ill. 35 40 44N 89 1W
El Paso, Tex. 64 31 45N 106 29W
El Paso County ◇, Colo. 30 38 50N 104 30W
El Paso County ◇, Tex. 64 31 55N 106 5W
El Portal 28 37 41N 119 47W
El Porvenir 52 35 43N 105 25W
El Reno 57 35 32N 97 57W
El Rio 29 34 14N 119 10W
El Rito 52 36 21N 106 11W
El Toro 71 18 17N 65 50W
El Vado Reservoir . . 52 36 36N 106 44W
El Yunque 71 18 19N 65 50W
Elaine 27 34 19N 90 51W
Elba, Ala. 24 31 25N 86 4W
Elba, Minn. 44 44 5N 92 1W
Elba, Nebr. 48 41 17N 98 34W
Elberfeld 36 38 10N 87 27W
Elberon 37 42 0N 92 19W
Elbert, Colo. 30 39 13N 104 32W
Elbert, Tex. 65 33 15N 99 0W
Elbert, Mt. 30 39 7N 106 27W
Elbert County ◇, Colo. 30 39 20N 104 15W
Elbert County ◇, Ga. 32 34 10N 82 50W
Elberta 43 44 37N 86 14W
Elberton 32 34 7N 82 52W
Elbing 38 38 3N 97 8W
Elbow Lake 44 45 59N 95 58W
Elcho 69 45 26N 89 11W
Elderon 69 44 47N 89 15W
Eldersburg 41 39 24N 76 57W
Eldon, Iowa 37 40 55N 92 13W
Eldon, Mo. 46 38 21N 92 35W
Eldon, Wash. 67 47 33N 123 3W
Eldora, Iowa 37 42 22N 93 5W
Eldora, N.J. 51 39 12N 74 52W
Eldorado, Ill. 35 37 49N 88 26W
Eldorado, Md. 41 38 37N 75 48W
Eldorado, Ohio 56 39 54N 84 41W
Eldorado, Okla. 57 34 28N 99 39W
Eldorado, Tex. 64 30 52N 100 36W
Eldorado National Forest 49 38 50N 120 20W
Eldorado Springs . . . 46 37 52N 94 1W
Eldorendo 32 31 3N 84 39W
Eldred 59 41 58N 78 23W
Eldridge, Ala. 24 33 55N 87 37W
Eldridge, Iowa 37 41 39N 90 35W
Eldridge, Mo. 46 37 50N 92 45W
Eldridge, N. Dak. . . 55 46 54N 98 51W
Eleanor 68 38 32N 81 56W
Eleanor, L. 28 37 59N 119 53W
Electra 65 34 2N 98 55W
Electra L. 30 37 33N 107 48W
Electric Mills 45 32 46N 88 28W
Elephant Butte Reservoir 52 33 9N 107 11W
Eleva 69 44 35N 91 28W
Eleven Point → . . . 27 36 9N 91 5W
Elevenmile Canyon Reservoir 30 38 54N 105 29W
Elfers 31 28 13N 82 43W
Elfin Cove 25 58 12N 136 22W
Elfrida 26 31 41N 109 41W
Elgin, Ill. 35 42 2N 88 17W
Elgin, Iowa 37 42 57N 91 38W
Elgin, Kans. 38 37 0N 96 17W
Elgin, Minn. 44 44 8N 92 15W
Elgin, N. Dak. 55 46 24N 101 51W
Elgin, Nebr. 48 41 59N 98 5W
Elgin, Nev. 49 37 21N 114 32W
Elgin, Okla. 57 34 47N 98 18W
Elgin, Oreg. 58 45 34N 117 55W
Elgin, S.C. 60 34 10N 80 48W
Elgin, Tex. 65 30 21N 97 22W
Eli 48 42 57N 101 29W
Elida, N. Mex. 52 33 57N 103 39W
Elida, Ohio 56 40 47N 84 12W
Elim 25 64 37N 162 15W
Elim Indian Reservation 25 64 40N 162 0W
Eliot 40 43 7N 70 47W
Elizabeth, Colo. 30 39 22N 104 36W
Elizabeth, Ill. 35 42 19N 90 13W
Elizabeth, La. 39 30 52N 92 48W
Elizabeth, Minn. 44 46 23N 96 8W
Elizabeth, N.J. 51 40 40N 74 13W
Elizabeth, W. Va. . . 68 39 4N 81 24W
Elizabeth, C. 67 47 21N 124 19W
Elizabeth City 54 36 18N 76 14W
Elizabeth Islands . . . 42 41 27N 70 47W
Elizabethton 63 36 21N 82 13W
Elizabethtown, Ill. . . 35 37 27N 88 18W
Elizabethtown, Ky. . 63 37 42N 85 52W
Elizabethtown, N.C. 54 34 38N 78 37W
Elizabethtown, N.Y. 53 44 13N 73 36W
Elizabethtown, Pa. . 59 40 9N 76 36W
Elizabethville 59 40 33N 76 49W
Elk 28 39 8N 123 43W
Elk →, Ala. 24 34 46N 87 16W
Elk →, Kans. 38 37 15N 95 41W
Elk →, Md. 41 39 26N 76 1W
Elk →, W. Va. 68 38 21N 81 38W
Elk City, Idaho 34 45 50N 115 26W
Elk City, Kans. 38 37 18N 95 55W
Elk City, Okla. 57 35 25N 99 25W
Elk City Lake 38 37 17N 95 47W
Elk County ◇, Kans. 38 37 30N 96 15W
Elk County ◇, Pa. . . 59 41 35N 78 45W
Elk Cr. → 61 44 15N 102 22W
Elk Creek, Calif. . . . 28 39 36N 122 32W
Elk Creek, Nebr. . . . 48 40 17N 96 8W
Elk Falls 38 37 22N 96 11W
Elk Garden 68 39 23N 79 9W
Elk Grove 28 38 25N 121 22W
Elk Hill 59 41 42N 75 32W
Elk Horn 37 41 36N 95 3W
Elk L. 43 44 50N 85 20W
Elk Mound 69 44 52N 91 42W
Elk Mountain 70 41 41N 106 25W
Elk Mt. 70 41 38N 106 32W
Elk Neck 41 39 31N 75 57W
Elk Park 54 36 10N 81 59W
Elk Point 61 42 41N 96 41W
Elk Rapids 43 44 54N 85 25W
Elk River, Idaho . . . 34 46 47N 116 11W
Elk River, Minn. . . . 44 45 18N 93 35W
Elk Springs 30 40 21N 108 27W
Elk Valley 63 36 29N 84 15W
Elkader 37 42 51N 91 24W
Elkatawa 63 37 34N 83 25W
Elkhart, Ill. 35 40 1N 89 29W
Elkhart, Ind. 36 41 41N 85 58W
Elkhart, Iowa 37 41 48N 93 31W
Elkhart, Kans. 38 37 0N 101 54W
Elkhart, Tex. 65 31 38N 95 35W
Elkhart County ◇ . . 36 41 35N 85 50W
Elkhart Lake 69 43 50N 88 1W
Elkhorn 69 42 40N 88 33W
Elkhorn → 48 41 8N 96 19W
Elkhorn City 63 37 18N 82 21W
Elkin 54 36 15N 80 51W
Elkins, N. Mex. 52 33 42N 104 4W
Elkins, W. Va. 68 38 55N 79 51W
Elkland, Mo. 46 37 27N 93 2W
Elkland, Pa. 59 41 59N 77 19W
Elkmont 24 34 56N 86 58W
Elko, Ga. 32 32 20N 83 42W

Elko, Minn. 44 44 34N 93 19W
Elko, Nev. 49 40 50N 115 46W
Elko County ◇ 49 41 10N 115 20W
Elkol 70 41 43N 110 37W
Elkridge 41 39 13N 76 43W
Elkton, Ky. 62 36 49N 87 9W
Elkton, Md. 41 39 36N 75 50W
Elkton, Mich. 43 43 49N 83 11W
Elkton, Minn. 44 43 40N 92 42W
Elkton, Oreg. 58 43 38N 123 34W
Elkton, S. Dak. 61 44 14N 96 29W
Elkton, Va. 68 38 25N 78 37W
Elkville 35 37 55N 89 14W
Ella 69 44 32N 92 3W
Ellaville 32 32 14N 84 19W
Ellenboro 68 39 16N 81 3W
Ellenburg 53 44 54N 73 48W
Ellendale, Del. 41 38 48N 75 26W
Ellendale, Minn. 44 43 52N 93 18W
Ellendale, N. Dak. 55 46 0N 98 32W
Ellensburg 67 46 59N 120 34W
Ellenton 32 31 11N 83 35W
Ellenville 53 41 43N 74 24W
Ellerbe 54 35 4N 79 46W
Ellettsville 36 39 14N 86 38W
Ellicott City 41 39 16N 76 48W
Ellicottville 53 42 17N 78 40W
Ellijay 32 34 42N 84 29W
Ellington, Conn. 42 41 54N 72 28W
Ellington, Mo. 46 37 14N 90 58W
Ellington, N.Y. 53 42 13N 79 7W
Ellinwood 38 38 21N 98 35W
Elliott, Iowa 37 41 9N 95 10W
Elliott, Md. 41 38 38N 75 59W
Elliott, Miss. 45 33 41N 89 45W
Elliott, N. Dak. 55 46 24N 97 49W
Elliott, S.C. 60 34 6N 80 10W
Elliott County ◇ 63 38 5N 83 5W
Elliott Key 31 25 27N 80 12W
Elliott Knob 68 38 10N 79 19W
Ellis, Idaho 34 44 42N 114 3W
Ellis, Kans. 38 38 56N 99 34W
Ellis, Nebr. 48 40 13N 96 53W
Ellis County ◇, Kans. 38 38 45N 99 15W
Ellis County ◇, Okla. 57 36 20N 99 50W
Ellis County ◇, Tex. 65 32 24N 96 51W
Ellis Grove 35 38 1N 89 55W
Elliston 47 46 33N 112 26W
Ellisville 45 31 36N 89 12W
Elloree 60 33 32N 80 34W
Ellsinore 46 36 56N 90 45W
Ellston 37 40 51N 94 7W
Ellsworth, Kans. 38 38 44N 98 14W
Ellsworth, Maine 40 44 33N 68 25W
Ellsworth, Mich. 43 45 10N 85 15W
Ellsworth, Minn. 44 43 31N 96 1W
Ellsworth, Nebr. 48 42 4N 102 17W
Ellsworth, Wis. 69 44 44N 92 29W
Ellsworth County ◇ 38 38 45N 98 15W
Ellwood City 59 40 52N 80 17W
Ellzey 31 29 19N 82 48W
Elm → 61 44 21N 102 42W
Elm City 54 35 48N 77 52W
Elm Cr. → 65 28 42N 99 59W
Elm Creek 48 40 43N 99 22W
Elm Fork 57 34 53N 99 19W
Elm L. 61 45 51N 98 42W
Elma, Iowa 37 43 15N 92 26W
Elma, Wash. 67 47 0N 123 25W
Elmdale 38 38 22N 96 39W
Elmer, Mo. 46 39 57N 92 39W
Elmer, N.J. 51 39 36N 75 10W
Elmer, Okla. 57 34 29N 99 21W
Elmer City 67 48 0N 118 58W
Elmhurst 35 41 53N 87 56W
Elmira, Idaho 34 48 29N 116 27W
Elmira, N.Y. 53 42 6N 76 48W
Elmira Heights 53 42 8N 76 50W
Elmo, Kans. 38 38 41N 97 14W
Elmo, Mont. 47 47 50N 114 21W
Elmo, Utah 66 39 23N 110 49W
Elmodel 32 31 21N 84 29W
Elmont 53 40 43N 73 43W
Elmore, Ala. 24 32 32N 86 19W
Elmore, Minn. 44 43 30N 94 5W
Elmore City 57 34 37N 97 24W
Elmore County ◇, Ala. 24 32 32N 86 13W
Elmore County ◇, Idaho 34 43 30N 115 30W
Elmwood, Ill. 35 40 47N 89 58W
Elmwood, Nebr. 48 40 50N 96 18W
Elmwood, Wis. 69 44 47N 92 9W
Elmwood Park 35 41 56N 87 49W
Elnora 36 38 53N 87 5W
Elora 62 35 1N 86 21W
Eloy 26 32 45N 111 33W
Elrosa 44 45 34N 94 57W
Elroy 69 43 45N 90 16W
Elsa 64 26 18N 97 59W
Elsah 35 38 57N 90 22W
Elsberry 46 39 10N 90 47W
Elsie, Mich. 43 43 5N 84 23W
Elsie, Nebr. 48 40 51N 101 23W
Elsie, Oreg. 58 45 52N 123 36W
Elsinore 66 38 41N 112 9W
Elsinore L. 29 33 40N 117 21W
Elsinore Lake 29 33 40N 117 20W
Elsmere, Del. 41 39 44N 75 35W
Elsmere, Nebr. 48 42 10N 100 11W
Elsmore 38 37 48N 95 9W
Elsworth, L. 57 34 49N 98 22W
Eltopia 67 46 27N 119 1W
Elverson 59 40 9N 75 50W
Elvins 46 37 50N 90 32W
Elwood, Ill. 35 41 24N 88 7W
Elwood, Ind. 36 40 17N 85 50W
Elwood, Kans. 38 39 45N 94 52W
Elwood, N.J. 51 39 35N 74 43W
Elwood, Nebr. 48 40 36N 99 52W
Elwood Reservoir 48 40 42N 99 55W
Ely, Iowa 37 41 52N 91 35W
Ely, Minn. 44 47 55N 91 51W
Ely, Nev. 49 39 15N 114 54W
Elyria, Kans. 38 38 17N 97 38W
Elyria, Nebr. 48 41 41N 99 0W
Elyria, Ohio 56 41 22N 82 7W
Emanuel County ◇ 32 32 40N 82 20W
Embarras → 35 38 39N 87 37W
Embarrass 69 44 40N 88 42W
Emden 35 40 18N 89 29W
Emelle 24 32 44N 88 19W
Emerado 55 47 55N 97 22W
Emerson, Ark. 27 33 6N 93 11W
Emerson, Ga. 32 34 8N 84 45W
Emerson, Nebr. 48 42 17N 96 44W
Emerson L. 29 34 27N 116 23W
Emery, S. Dak. 61 43 36N 97 37W
Emery, Utah 66 38 55N 111 15W
Emery County ◇ 66 39 0N 110 45W
Emigrant Gap 28 39 19N 120 38W
Emily 44 46 44N 93 58W
Eminece 46 37 9N 91 21W
Eminence 63 38 22N 85 11W
Emlenton 59 41 11N 79 43W
Emmalane 32 32 46N 82 0W
Emmaus 59 40 32N 75 30W
Emmet, Ark. 27 33 44N 93 28W
Emmet, Nebr. 48 42 29N 98 49W
Emmet County ◇, Iowa 37 43 20N 94 40W
Emmet County ◇, Mich. 43 45 30N 84 55W
Emmetsburg 37 43 7N 94 41W
Emmett, Idaho 34 43 52N 116 30W
Emmett, Kans. 38 39 19N 96 3W
Emmett, Mich. 43 42 59N 82 46W
Emmitsburg 41 39 42N 77 20W
Emmonak 25 62 46N 164 30W
Emmons 44 43 30N 93 29W
Emmons County ◇ 55 46 20N 100 10W
Emmorton 41 39 30N 76 20W
Emory 63 32 52N 95 46W
Emory Peak 64 29 15N 103 18W
Empire, Calif. 28 37 38N 120 54W
Empire, Colo. 30 39 46N 105 41W
Empire, Ga. 32 32 21N 83 18W
Empire, La. 39 29 23N 89 36W
Empire, Mich. 43 44 49N 86 4W
Empire, Nev. 49 40 35N 119 21W
Empire City 57 34 25N 98 2W
Empire Reservoir 30 40 16N 104 12W
Emporia, Kans. 38 38 25N 96 11W
Emporia, Va. 68 36 42N 77 32W
Emporium 59 41 31N 78 14W
Encampment 70 41 12N 106 47W
Encinal 65 28 2N 99 21W
Encinitas 29 33 3N 117 17W
Encino, N. Mex. 52 34 39N 105 28W
Encino, Tex. 64 26 56N 98 8W
Enderlin 55 46 38N 97 36W
Enders 48 40 27N 101 32W
Enders Reservoir 48 40 25N 101 31W
Endicott, N.Y. 53 42 6N 76 4W
Endicott, Nebr. 48 40 5N 97 6W
Endicott, Wash. 67 46 56N 117 41W
Endicott Mts. 25 68 0N 152 0W
Endwell 53 42 6N 76 2W
Enfield, Conn. 42 41 58N 72 36W
Enfield, Ill. 35 38 6N 88 20W
Enfield, N.C. 54 36 11N 77 41W
Enfield, N.H. 50 43 39N 72 9W
Enfield Center 50 43 38N 72 8W
Engel 52 33 4N 107 2W
Engelhard 54 35 30N 75 58W
England 27 34 33N 91 58W
Englebright L. 28 39 14N 121 16W
Englewood, Colo. 30 39 39N 104 59W
Englewood, Fla. 31 26 58N 82 21W
Englewood, Kans. 38 37 2N 99 59W
Englewood, Ohio 56 39 53N 84 18W
Englewood, Tenn. 63 35 26N 84 29W
English 36 38 20N 86 28W
English Creek 51 39 20N 74 42W
Englishtown 51 40 18N 74 22W
Enid, Miss. 45 34 7N 89 56W
Enid, Okla. 57 36 24N 97 53W
Enid L. 45 34 9N 89 54W
Enka 54 35 33N 82 39W
Enloe 65 33 26N 95 39W
Ennis, Mont. 47 45 21N 111 44W
Ennis, Tex. 65 32 20N 96 38W
Eno → 54 36 5N 78 50W
Enoch 66 37 47N 113 2W
Enochs 64 33 52N 102 46W
Enola 48 41 54N 97 28W
Enoree → 60 34 26N 81 25W
Enosburg Falls 50 44 55N 72 48W
Ensenada, Puerto Rico 71 17 58N 66 56W
Ensenada, U.S.A. 52 36 44N 106 32W
Ensign 38 37 39N 100 14W
Ensley 31 30 31N 87 16W
Enterprise, Ala. 24 31 19N 85 51W
Enterprise, Calif. 28 40 30N 122 22W
Enterprise, Kans. 38 38 54N 97 7W
Enterprise, La. 39 31 54N 91 53W
Enterprise, Miss. 45 32 10N 88 49W
Enterprise, Oreg. 58 45 25N 117 17W
Enterprise, Utah 66 37 34N 113 43W
Entiat 67 47 40N 120 13W
Enumclaw 67 47 12N 121 59W
Enville 62 35 23N 88 26W
Eolia 46 39 14N 91 1W
Eoline 24 32 59N 87 8W
Epes 24 32 42N 88 7W
Ephraim 66 39 22N 111 35W
Ephrata, Pa. 59 40 11N 76 11W
Ephrata, Wash. 67 47 19N 119 33W
Epleys 62 36 56N 86 56W
Epping, N. Dak. 55 48 17N 103 21W
Epping, N.H. 50 43 2N 71 4W
Epps 39 32 36N 91 29W
Equality 35 37 44N 88 20W
Equinox Mt. 50 43 11N 73 9W
Erath 39 29 58N 92 2W
Erath County ◇ 65 32 13N 98 12W
Erbacon 68 38 31N 80 35W
Erhard 44 46 29N 96 6W
Erick 57 35 13N 99 52W
Ericson 48 41 47N 98 41W
Eridu 31 30 18N 83 45W
Erie, Colo. 30 40 3N 105 3W
Erie, Ill. 35 41 39N 90 5W
Erie, Kans. 38 37 34N 95 15W
Erie, N. Dak. 55 47 7N 97 23W
Erie, Pa. 59 42 8N 80 5W
Erie, L. 56 41 50N 82 0W
Erie Canal 53 43 5N 78 43W
Erie County ◇, N.Y. 53 42 50N 78 45W
Erie County ◇, Ohio 56 41 24N 82 33W
Erie County ◇, Pa. 59 42 0N 80 0W
Erin 62 36 19N 87 42W
Erlanger 63 39 1N 84 36W
Erling, L. 27 33 3N 93 32W
Ernul 54 35 15N 77 4W
Errol 50 44 47N 71 8W
Erskine 44 47 40N 96 0W
Erwin, N.C. 54 35 20N 78 41W
Erwin, S. Dak. 61 44 29N 97 27W
Erwin, Tenn. 63 36 9N 82 25W
Erwinville 39 30 32N 91 24W
Esbon 38 39 49N 98 26W
Escalante 66 37 47N 111 36W
Escalante → 66 37 24N 110 57W
Escalante Desert 66 37 50N 113 20W
Escalon 28 37 48N 121 0W
Escambia → 31 30 32N 87 11W
Escambia County ◇, Ala. 24 31 7N 87 4W
Escambia County ◇, Fla. 31 30 30N 87 30W
Escanaba 43 45 45N 87 4W
Escanaba → 43 45 47N 87 3W
Escatawpa → 45 30 26N 88 33W
Escobal 71 9 9N 79 58W
Escondido 29 33 7N 117 5W
Eskridge 38 38 52N 96 6W
Esmeralda County ◇ 49 37 50N 117 45W
Esmond 55 48 2N 99 46W
Esmont 68 37 50N 78 37W
Esom Hill 32 33 57N 85 23W
Espanola, Fla. 31 29 31N 81 19W
Espanola, N. Mex. 52 35 59N 106 5W
Esparto 28 38 42N 122 1W
Espenberg, C. 25 66 33N 163 36W
Esperanza 71 18 6N 65 28W
Essex, Calif. 29 34 44N 115 15W
Essex, Conn. 42 41 21N 72 24W
Essex, Ill. 35 41 11N 88 11W
Essex, Iowa 37 40 50N 95 18W
Essex, Md. 41 39 19N 76 29W
Essex, Mo. 46 36 50N 89 8W
Essex, Mont. 47 48 17N 113 37W
Essex, N.Y. 53 44 19N 73 21W
Essex County ◇, Mass. 42 42 35N 70 50W
Essex County ◇, N.J. 51 40 45N 74 15W
Essex County ◇, N.Y. 53 44 0N 73 40W
Essex County ◇, Va. 68 37 56N 76 52W
Essex County ◇, Vt. 50 44 45N 71 45W
Essex Junction 50 44 29N 73 7W
Essexville 43 43 37N 83 50W
Estacada 58 45 17N 122 20W
Estancia 52 34 46N 106 4W
Este, Cabo 71 18 5N 67 51W
Este, Punta 71 18 8N 65 16W
Estelline, S. Dak. 61 44 35N 96 54W
Estelline, Tex. 64 34 33N 100 26W
Estellville 51 39 23N 74 45W
Estero 31 26 26N 81 49W
Estes Park 30 40 23N 105 31W
Estherville 37 43 24N 94 50W
Estherwood 39 30 11N 92 28W
Estill 60 32 45N 81 15W
Estill County ◇ 63 37 40N 84 0W
Estill Springs 62 35 16N 86 8W
Etchison 41 39 15N 77 8W
Ethan 61 43 33N 97 59W
Ethel, La. 39 30 47N 91 8W
Ethel, Miss. 45 33 7N 89 28W
Ethel, Mo. 46 39 54N 92 45W
Ethelsville 24 33 25N 88 13W
Ethridge, Mont. 47 48 34N 112 8W
Ethridge, Tenn. 62 35 19N 87 18W
Etna, Calif. 28 41 27N 122 54W
Etna, Maine 40 44 49N 69 7W
Etna, Utah 66 41 40N 113 58W
Etna, Wyo. 70 43 5N 111 0W
Etolin Strait 25 60 20N 165 15W
Eton 32 34 50N 84 46W
Etowah 63 35 20N 84 32W
Etowah → 32 34 15N 85 10W
Etowah County ◇ 24 34 0N 86 0W
Etter 64 36 3N 101 59W
Ettrick 69 44 10N 91 16W
Eubank 63 37 17N 84 40W
Euclid 56 41 34N 81 32W
Eudora, Ark. 27 33 7N 91 16W
Eudora, Kans. 38 38 57N 95 6W
Eufaula, Ala. 24 31 54N 85 9W
Eufaula, Okla. 57 35 17N 95 35W
Eufaula L. 57 35 18N 95 21W
Eugene, Mo. 46 38 21N 92 24W
Eugene, Oreg. 58 44 5N 123 4W
Euless 65 32 50N 97 5W
Eulonia 32 31 32N 81 26W
Eunice, La. 39 30 30N 92 25W
Eunice, N. Mex. 52 32 26N 103 10W
Eupora 45 33 32N 89 16W
Eurcka Springs 27 36 24N 93 44W
Eureka, Calif. 28 40 47N 124 9W
Eureka, Ill. 35 40 43N 89 16W
Eureka, Kans. 38 37 49N 96 17W
Eureka, Mo. 46 38 30N 90 38W
Eureka, Mont. 47 48 53N 115 3W
Eureka, Nev. 49 39 31N 115 58W
Eureka, S.C. 60 33 42N 81 46W
Eureka, S. Dak. 61 45 46N 99 38W
Eureka, Utah 66 39 58N 112 7W
Eureka, Wash. 67 46 18N 118 37W
Eureka County ◇ 49 40 0N 116 10W
Eustis, Fla. 31 28 51N 81 41W
Eustis, Maine 40 45 13N 70 29W
Eustis, Nebr. 48 40 40N 100 2W
Eustis, L. 31 28 50N 81 44W
Eutaw 24 32 50N 87 53W
Eutawville 60 33 24N 80 21W
Eva 24 34 20N 86 46W
Evadale 65 30 21N 94 5W
Evan 44 44 21N 94 50W
Evangeline 39 30 16N 92 34W
Evangeline Parish ◇ 39 30 47N 92 25W
Evans, Colo. 30 40 23N 104 41W
Evans, La. 39 30 59N 93 30W
Evans, W. Va. 68 38 49N 81 47W
Evans, Mt. 30 39 35N 105 39W
Evans City 59 40 46N 80 4W
Evans County ◇ 32 32 10N 81 55W
Evansdale 37 42 30N 92 17W
Evanston, Ill. 35 42 3N 87 41W
Evanston, Ky. 63 37 28N 83 2W
Evanston, Wyo. 70 41 16N 110 58W
Evansville, Ark. 27 35 48N 94 30W
Evansville, Ill. 35 38 5N 89 56W
Evansville, Ind. 36 37 58N 87 35W
Evansville, Minn. 44 46 0N 95 41W
Evansville, Wis. 69 42 47N 89 18W
Evansville, Wyo. 70 42 52N 106 16W
Evant 65 31 29N 98 9W
Evart 43 43 54N 85 2W
Evarts 63 36 52N 83 12W
Eveleth 44 47 28N 92 32W
Evelyn 39 31 59N 93 27W
Evening Shade 27 36 4N 91 37W
Evensville 63 35 34N 84 57W
Everest 38 39 41N 95 26W
Everett, Ga. 32 31 24N 81 38W

Everett, Mass. **42** 42 24N 71 4W
Everett, Pa. **59** 40 1N 78 23W
Everett, Wash. **67** 47 59N 122 12W
Everglades, The **31** 25 50N 81 0W
Everglades City **31** 25 52N 81 23W
Everglades National Park **31** 25 30N 81 0W
Evergreen, Ala. **24** 31 26N 86 57W
Evergreen, Colo. **30** 39 38N 105 19W
Evergreen, Mont. **47** 48 9N 114 13W
Evergreen, N.C. **54** 34 25N 78 54W
Evergreen Park **35** 41 43N 87 41W
Everly **37** 43 10N 95 19W
Everton **46** 37 21N 93 42W
Ewa **33** 21 20N 158 3W
Ewa Beach **33** 21 19N 158 1W
Ewan **67** 47 7N 117 44W
Ewen **43** 46 32N 89 17W
Ewing, Ky. **63** 38 26N 83 52W
Ewing, Mo. **46** 40 6N 91 43W
Ewing, N.J. **51** 40 15N 74 48W
Ewing, Nebr. **48** 42 16N 98 21W
Ewing, Va. **68** 36 38N 83 26W
Excello **46** 39 38N 92 29W
Excelsior Mts. **49** 38 15N 118 10W
Excelsior Springs **46** 39 20N 94 13W
Exell **64** 35 38N 101 59W
Exeter, Calif. **29** 36 18N 119 9W
Exeter, Maine **40** 44 58N 69 9W
Exeter, Mo. **46** 36 40N 93 56W
Exeter, N.H. **50** 42 59N 70 57W
Exeter, Nebr. **48** 40 39N 97 27W
Exeter, R.I. **42** 41 35N 71 32W
Exira **37** 41 35N 94 52W
Exmore **68** 37 32N 75 50W
Eyak **25** 60 32N 145 36W
Eyota **44** 43 59N 92 14W

F

Fabens **64** 31 30N 106 10W
Fabius **53** 42 50N 75 59W
Faceville **32** 30 45N 84 38W
Fair Bluff **54** 34 19N 79 2W
Fair Grove **46** 37 23N 93 9W
Fair Haven, N.J. **51** 40 22N 74 2W
Fair Haven, Vt. **50** 43 36N 73 16W
Fair Oaks **57** 36 17N 95 50W
Fair Plain **43** 42 5N 86 27W
Fair Play, Mo. **46** 37 38N 93 35W
Fair Play, S.C. **60** 34 31N 82 59W
Fairbank, Ariz. **26** 31 43N 110 11W
Fairbank, Iowa **37** 42 38N 92 3W
Fairbank, Md. **41** 38 41N 76 20W
Fairbanks, Alaska **25** 64 51N 147 43W
Fairbanks, Fla. **31** 29 44N 82 16W
Fairbanks North Star ◇ **25** 65 0N 147 0W
Fairborn **56** 39 49N 84 2W
Fairburn, Ga. **32** 33 34N 84 35W
Fairburn, S. Dak. **61** 43 41N 103 13W
Fairbury, Ill. **35** 40 45N 88 31W
Fairbury, Nebr. **48** 40 8N 97 11W
Fairchance **59** 39 49N 79 45W
Fairchild **69** 44 36N 90 58W
Fairdale, Ky. **63** 38 6N 85 46W
Fairdale, N. Dak. **55** 48 30N 98 14W
Fairfax, Ala. **24** 32 48N 85 11W
Fairfax, Calif. **28** 37 59N 122 35W
Fairfax, Iowa **37** 41 55N 91 47W
Fairfax, Minn. **44** 44 32N 94 43W
Fairfax, Mo. **46** 40 20N 95 24W
Fairfax, Okla. **57** 36 34N 96 42W
Fairfax, S.C. **60** 32 59N 81 15W
Fairfax, S. Dak. **61** 43 2N 98 54W
Fairfax, Va. **68** 38 51N 77 18W
Fairfax, Vt. **50** 44 40N 73 1W
Fairfax County ◇ **68** 38 51N 77 18W
Fairfield, Ala. **24** 33 29N 86 55W
Fairfield, Calif. **28** 38 15N 122 3W
Fairfield, Conn. **42** 41 9N 73 16W
Fairfield, Idaho **34** 43 21N 114 44W
Fairfield, Ill. **35** 38 23N 88 22W
Fairfield, Iowa **37** 40 56N 91 57W
Fairfield, Ky. **63** 37 56N 85 23W
Fairfield, Mont. **47** 47 37N 111 59W
Fairfield, N.C. **54** 35 32N 76 14W
Fairfield, N. Dak. **55** 47 11N 103 14W
Fairfield, Nebr. **48** 40 26N 98 6W
Fairfield, Pa. **59** 39 47N 77 22W
Fairfield, Tex. **65** 31 44N 96 10W
Fairfield County ◇, Conn. **42** 41 15N 73 20W
Fairfield County ◇, Ohio **56** 39 43N 82 36W
Fairfield County ◇, S.C. **60** 34 25N 81 10W
Fairgrove **43** 43 32N 83 33W
Fairhaven, Mass. **42** 41 39N 70 55W
Fairhaven, Md. **41** 38 45N 76 34W
Fairhope **24** 30 31N 87 54W
Fairland, Ind. **36** 39 35N 85 52W
Fairland, Okla. **57** 36 45N 94 51W
Fairlee, Md. **41** 39 13N 76 10W
Fairlee, Vt. **50** 43 54N 72 9W
Fairmont, Minn. **44** 43 39N 94 28W
Fairmont, N.C. **54** 34 30N 79 7W
Fairmont, Nebr. **48** 40 38N 97 35W
Fairmont, Okla. **57** 36 21N 97 43W
Fairmont, W. Va. **68** 39 29N 80 9W
Fairmount, Ga. **32** 34 26N 84 42W
Fairmount, Ill. **35** 40 3N 87 56W
Fairmount, Ind. **36** 40 25N 85 39W
Fairmount, Md. **41** 38 6N 75 48W
Fairmount, N. Dak. **55** 46 3N 96 36W
Fairmount, N.Y. **53** 43 5N 76 12W
Fairplains **54** 36 12N 81 9W
Fairplay **30** 39 15N 106 2W
Fairport **53** 43 6N 77 27W
Fairport Harbor **56** 41 45N 81 17W
Fairview, Ill. **35** 40 38N 90 10W
Fairview, Kans. **38** 39 50N 95 44W
Fairview, Mich. **43** 44 44N 84 3W
Fairview, Mont. **47** 47 51N 104 3W
Fairview, N.J. **51** 40 23N 74 5W
Fairview, Okla. **57** 36 16N 98 29W
Fairview, Pa. **59** 42 2N 80 15W
Fairview, S. Dak. **61** 43 13N 96 29W
Fairview, Tenn. **62** 35 59N 87 7W
Fairview, Utah **66** 39 38N 111 26W
Fairview, W. Va. **68** 39 36N 80 15W
Fairview Park **36** 39 41N 87 25W
Fairweather, Mt. **25** 58 55N 137 32W
Faison **54** 35 7N 78 8W
Faith **61** 45 2N 102 2W
Fajardo **71** 18 20N 65 39W
Fajardo → **71** 18 20N 65 39W
Falcon, Colo. **30** 38 56N 104 37W
Falcon, N.C. **54** 35 11N 78 39W
Falcon, C. **58** 45 46N 123 59W
Falcon Reservoir **64** 26 34N 99 10W
Falfurrias **64** 27 14N 98 9W
Falkner **45** 34 51N 88 56W
Falkville **24** 34 22N 86 55W
Fall → **38** 37 24N 95 40W
Fall Branch **63** 36 25N 82 37W
Fall Creek **69** 44 46N 91 17W
Fall River, Kans. **38** 37 36N 96 2W
Fall River, Mass. **42** 41 43N 71 10W
Fall River, Wis. **69** 43 23N 89 3W
Fall River County ◇ **61** 43 10N 103 30W
Fall River Lake **38** 37 39N 96 4W
Fall River Mills **28** 41 3N 121 26W
Fallbrook **29** 33 23N 117 15W
Fallon, Mont. **47** 46 50N 105 8W
Fallon, Nev. **49** 39 28N 118 47W
Fallon County ◇ **47** 46 20N 104 30W
Fallon Indian Reservation **49** 39 25N 118 45W
Falls Church **68** 38 53N 77 10W
Falls City, Nebr. **48** 40 3N 95 36W
Falls City, Oreg. **58** 44 52N 123 26W
Falls City, Tex. **65** 28 59N 98 1W
Falls County ◇ **65** 31 18N 96 54W
Falls Creek **59** 41 9N 78 48W
Fallsburg **63** 38 11N 82 40W
Fallston, Md. **41** 39 31N 76 25W
Fallston, N.C. **54** 35 26N 81 30W
Falmouth, Fla. **31** 30 21N 83 8W
Falmouth, Ky. **63** 38 41N 84 20W
Falmouth, Maine **40** 43 44N 70 14W
Falmouth, Mass. **42** 41 33N 70 37W
Falmouth, Mich. **43** 44 15N 85 5W
Falmouth, Va. **68** 38 20N 77 28W
False Pass **25** 54 51N 163 25W
Falun **38** 38 40N 97 46W
Fancy Farm **62** 36 48N 88 47W
Fannin County ◇, Ga. **32** 34 50N 84 15W
Fannin County ◇, Tex. **65** 33 35N 96 11W
Fanshawe **57** 34 57N 94 55W
Farallon Is. **28** 37 45N 123 10W
Farewell **25** 62 31N 153 54W
Fargo, Ga. **32** 30 41N 82 34W
Fargo, N. Dak. **55** 46 53N 96 48W
Fargo, Okla. **57** 36 22N 99 37W
Faribault **44** 44 18N 93 16W
Faribault County ◇ **44** 43 45N 94 0W
Farina **35** 38 50N 88 46W
Farley **37** 42 27N 91 0W
Farmer City **35** 40 15N 88 39W
Farmers Branch **65** 32 56N 96 54W
Farmersburg **36** 39 15N 87 23W
Farmersville, Calif. **29** 36 18N 119 12W
Farmersville, Ill. **35** 39 27N 89 39W
Farmersville, Tex. **65** 33 10N 96 22W
Farmerville **39** 32 47N 92 24W
Farmingdale **51** 40 12N 74 10W
Farmington, Ark. **27** 36 3N 94 15W
Farmington, Calif. **28** 37 55N 120 59W
Farmington, Del. **41** 38 52N 75 35W
Farmington, Ga. **32** 33 47N 83 26W
Farmington, Ill. **35** 40 42N 90 0W
Farmington, Iowa **37** 40 38N 91 44W
Farmington, Maine **40** 44 40N 70 9W
Farmington, Md. **41** 39 42N 76 4W
Farmington, Minn. **44** 44 38N 93 8W
Farmington, Mo. **46** 37 47N 90 25W
Farmington, Mont. **47** 47 53N 112 10W
Farmington, N.C. **54** 36 1N 80 32W
Farmington, N.H. **50** 43 24N 71 4W
Farmington, N. Mex. **52** 36 44N 108 12W
Farmington, Utah **66** 40 59N 111 53W
Farmington, Wash. **67** 47 5N 117 3W
Farmington → **42** 41 51N 72 38W
Farmville, N.C. **54** 35 36N 77 35W
Farmville, Va. **68** 37 18N 78 24W
Farnam **48** 40 42N 100 13W
Farner **63** 35 9N 84 19W
Farnsworth **64** 36 19N 100 58W
Farragut **37** 40 43N 95 29W
Farrell **59** 41 13N 80 30W
Farwell, Mich. **43** 43 50N 84 52W
Farwell, Minn. **44** 45 45N 95 37W
Farwell, Nebr. **48** 41 13N 98 38W
Farwell, Tex. **64** 34 23N 103 2W
Faucett **46** 39 36N 94 48W
Faulk County ◇ **61** 45 0N 99 0W
Faulkner County ◇ **27** 35 10N 92 16W
Faulkton **61** 45 2N 99 8W
Fauquier County ◇ **68** 38 43N 77 48W
Faust **66** 40 11N 112 24W
Faxon **57** 34 28N 98 35W
Fay **57** 35 49N 98 39W
Fayette, Ala. **24** 33 41N 87 50W
Fayette, Iowa **37** 42 51N 91 48W
Fayette, Miss. **45** 31 43N 91 4W
Fayette, Mo. **46** 39 9N 92 41W
Fayette, N.Y. **53** 42 49N 76 49W
Fayette, Ohio **56** 41 40N 84 20W
Fayette, Utah **66** 39 14N 111 51W
Fayette County ◇, Ala. **24** 33 41N 87 50W
Fayette County ◇, Ga. **32** 33 25N 84 30W
Fayette County ◇, Ill. **35** 39 0N 89 0W
Fayette County ◇, Ind. **36** 39 35N 85 10W
Fayette County ◇, Iowa **37** 42 50N 91 50W
Fayette County ◇, Ky. **63** 38 0N 84 30W
Fayette County ◇, Ohio **56** 39 32N 83 26W
Fayette County ◇, Pa. **59** 40 0N 79 40W
Fayette County ◇, Tenn. **62** 35 15N 89 21W
Fayette County ◇, Tex. **65** 29 54N 96 52W
Fayette County ◇, W. Va. **68** 37 59N 81 9W
Fayetteville, Ark. **27** 36 4N 94 10W
Fayetteville, Ga. **32** 33 27N 84 27W
Fayetteville, N.C. **54** 35 3N 78 53W
Fayetteville, N.Y. **53** 43 2N 76 0W
Fayetteville, Tenn. **62** 35 9N 86 34W
Fayetteville, Tex. **65** 29 54N 96 41W
Fayetteville, W. Va. **68** 38 3N 81 6W
Faywood **52** 32 32N 108 1W
Fear, C. **54** 33 50N 77 58W
Feather → **28** 38 47N 121 36W
Feather Falls **28** 39 36N 121 16W
Federal Dam **44** 47 15N 94 14W
Federal Heights **30** 39 52N 105 1W
Federal Way **67** 47 18N 122 19W
Federalsburg **41** 38 42N 75 47W
Feeding Hills **42** 42 4N 72 41W
Felch **43** 46 0N 87 50W
Felda **31** 26 34N 81 26W
Felicity **56** 38 51N 84 6W
Felix → **52** 33 5N 104 25W
Fellsmere **31** 27 46N 80 36W
Felt, Idaho **34** 43 52N 111 11W
Felt, Okla. **57** 36 34N 102 48W
Felton, Del. **41** 39 1N 75 35W
Felton, Minn. **44** 47 5N 96 30W
Felton, Pa. **59** 39 51N 76 34W
Fence Lake **52** 34 40N 108 40W
Fenn **34** 45 58N 116 16W
Fennimore **69** 42 59N 90 39W
Fennville **43** 42 36N 86 6W
Fenton, Iowa **37** 43 13N 94 26W
Fenton, La. **39** 30 22N 92 55W
Fenton, Mich. **43** 42 48N 83 42W
Fentress **65** 29 45N 97 47W
Fentress County ◇ **63** 36 25N 85 0W
Fenwood **69** 44 52N 90 1W
Ferdinand, Idaho **34** 46 9N 116 24W
Ferdinand, Ind. **36** 38 14N 86 52W
Fergus County ◇ **47** 47 30N 109 10W
Fergus Falls **44** 46 17N 96 4W
Ferguson, Ky. **62** 37 3N 84 36W
Ferguson, Mo. **46** 38 45N 90 18W
Fern Creek **63** 38 9N 85 36W
Fern Ridge L. **58** 44 7N 123 18W
Fernandina Beach **31** 30 40N 81 27W
Ferndale, Calif. **28** 40 35N 124 16W
Ferndale, Md. **41** 39 11N 76 39W
Ferndale, Wash. **67** 48 51N 122 36W
Fernley **49** 39 36N 119 15W
Fernwood, Idaho **34** 47 7N 116 24W
Fernwood, Miss. **45** 31 11N 90 27W
Fernwood, N.Y. **53** 43 16N 73 40W
Ferrellsburg **68** 38 2N 82 6W
Ferriday **39** 31 38N 91 33W
Ferris, Ill. **35** 40 28N 91 10W
Ferris, Tex. **65** 32 32N 96 40W
Ferrisburg **50** 44 12N 73 15W
Ferron **66** 39 5N 111 8W
Ferrum **68** 36 55N 80 1W
Ferry County ◇ **67** 48 30N 118 30W
Ferrysburg **43** 43 5N 86 13W
Ferryville **69** 43 21N 91 6W
Fertile, Iowa **37** 43 16N 93 25W
Fertile, Minn. **44** 47 32N 96 17W
Fessenden **55** 47 39N 99 38W
Festus **46** 38 13N 90 24W
Field **63** 36 54N 83 36W
Fieldon **35** 39 7N 90 30W
Fields **39** 30 32N 93 35W
Fields Landing **28** 40 44N 124 13W
Fierro **52** 32 51N 108 5W
Fife **65** 31 24N 99 22W
Fife Lake **43** 44 35N 85 21W
Fifield **69** 45 53N 90 25W
Filer **34** 42 34N 114 37W
Fillmore, Calif. **29** 34 24N 118 55W
Fillmore, Utah **66** 38 58N 112 20W
Fillmore County ◇, Minn. **44** 43 40N 92 0W
Fillmore County ◇, Nebr. **48** 40 30N 97 40W
Fincastle **68** 37 30N 79 53W
Findlay, Ill. **35** 39 31N 88 45W
Findlay, Ohio **56** 41 2N 83 39W
Fine **53** 44 15N 75 8W
Fingal **55** 46 46N 97 47W
Finger **62** 35 22N 88 36W
Finger Lakes **53** 42 40N 76 30W
Finksburg **41** 39 30N 76 54W
Finley, N. Dak. **55** 47 31N 97 50W
Finley, Okla. **57** 34 20N 95 30W
Finney County ◇ **38** 38 0N 100 40W
Fire I. **53** 40 40N 73 11W
Fire Island National Seashore **53** 40 38N 73 8W
Firebaugh **29** 36 52N 120 27W
First Connecticut L. **50** 45 5N 71 15W
Firth, Idaho **34** 43 18N 112 11W
Firth, Nebr. **48** 40 33N 96 37W
Fischer **65** 29 58N 98 16W
Fish L. **66** 38 33N 111 42W
Fish Lake Reservoir **44** 46 57N 92 17W
Fish Pt. **43** 43 44N 83 31W
Fish River L. **40** 46 50N 68 47W
Fisheating Cr. → **31** 26 57N 81 7W
Fisher, Ark. **27** 35 30N 90 58W
Fisher, Ill. **35** 40 19N 88 21W
Fisher, La. **39** 31 30N 93 28W
Fisher, Minn. **44** 47 48N 96 48W
Fisher → **47** 48 22N 115 19W
Fisher County ◇ **64** 32 45N 100 23W
Fishers **36** 39 57N 86 1W
Fishers I. **53** 41 15N 72 0W
Fishers Peak **30** 37 6N 104 28W
Fishing Bridge **70** 44 29N 110 22W
Fishing Creek **41** 38 20N 76 14W
Fishlake National Forest **66** 38 40N 112 20W
Fishtrap L. **63** 37 25N 82 26W
Fisk **46** 36 47N 90 12W
Fiskdale **42** 42 7N 72 7W
Fitchburg **42** 42 35N 71 48W
Fittstown **57** 34 37N 96 38W
Fitzgerald **32** 31 43N 83 15W
Fitzhugh **27** 35 22N 91 19W
Flagler **30** 39 18N 103 4W
Flagler Beach **31** 29 29N 81 8W
Flagler County ◇ **31** 29 30N 81 20W
Flagstaff **26** 35 12N 111 39W
Flagstaff L., Maine **40** 45 12N 70 19W
Flagstaff L., Oreg. **58** 42 35N 119 45W
Flaherty **62** 37 50N 86 4W
Flambeau → **69** 45 18N 91 14W
Flaming Gorge Dam **66** 40 55N 109 25W
Flaming Gorge National Recreation Area **70** 41 10N 109 25W
Flaming Gorge Reservoir **70** 41 10N 109 25W
Flamingo **31** 25 8N 80 57W
Flanagan **35** 40 53N 88 52W
Flandreau **61** 44 3N 96 36W
Flasher **55** 46 27N 101 14W
Flat **25** 62 28N 158 1W
Flat →, Mich. **43** 42 56N 85 20W
Flat →, N.C. **54** 36 5N 78 49W
Flat Lick **63** 36 50N 83 46W
Flat River **46** 37 51N 90 31W
Flat River Res. **42** 41 42N 71 37W
Flat Rock, Ala. **24** 34 46N 85 42W
Flat Rock, Ill. **35** 38 54N 87 40W

Flat Rock, Mich. **43** 42 6N 83 17W
Flat Top Mt. **66** 40 22N 112 11W
Flat Woods **62** 35 29N 87 50W
Flathead → **47** 47 22N 114 47W
Flathead County ◇ **47** 48 15N 113 30W
Flathead Indian Reservation **47** 47 35N 114 30W
Flathead L. **47** 47 51N 114 8W
Flathead National Forest **47** 47 45N 113 10W
Flatonia **65** 29 41N 97 7W
Flatrock → **36** 39 12N 85 56W
Flattery, C. **67** 48 23N 124 29W
Flatwillow Cr. → **47** 46 56N 107 55W
Flatwoods, Ky. **63** 38 31N 82 43W
Flatwoods, La. **39** 31 24N 92 52W
Flatwoods, W. Va. **68** 38 43N 80 39W
Flaxton **55** 48 54N 102 24W
Flaxville **47** 48 48N 105 11W
Fleetwood **59** 40 27N 75 49W
Fleischmanns **53** 42 10N 74 32W
Fleming **30** 40 41N 102 50W
Fleming County ◇ **63** 38 20N 83 40W
Flemingsburg **63** 38 25N 83 45W
Flemington, N.J. **51** 40 31N 74 52W
Flemington, W. Va. **68** 39 16N 80 8W
Flensburg **44** 45 57N 94 32W
Fletcher, N.C. **54** 35 26N 82 30W
Fletcher, Okla. **57** 34 50N 98 15W
Fletcher Pond **43** 45 1N 83 47W
Flint **43** 43 1N 83 41W
Flint →, Ala. **24** 34 30N 86 30W
Flint →, Ga. **32** 30 57N 84 34W
Flint Hills **38** 38 0N 96 40W
Flintstone **41** 39 42N 78 34W
Flippin **27** 36 17N 92 36W
Flomaton **24** 31 0N 87 16W
Flomot **64** 34 14N 100 59W
Flora, Ill. **35** 38 40N 88 29W
Flora, Ind. **36** 40 33N 86 31W
Flora, Miss. **45** 32 33N 90 19W
Flora, Oreg. **58** 45 54N 117 19W
Flora Vista **52** 36 48N 108 3W
Florahome **31** 29 44N 81 54W
Floral **27** 35 36N 91 45W
Floral City **31** 28 45N 82 17W
Florala **24** 31 0N 86 20W
Florence, Ala. **24** 34 48N 87 41W
Florence, Ariz. **26** 33 2N 111 23W
Florence, Ark. **27** 33 46N 91 39W
Florence, Colo. **30** 38 23N 105 8W
Florence, Kans. **38** 38 15N 96 56W
Florence, Ky. **63** 39 0N 84 38W
Florence, Mass. **42** 42 20N 72 40W
Florence, Md. **41** 39 20N 77 8W
Florence, Miss. **45** 32 9N 90 8W
Florence, Mo. **46** 38 35N 92 59W
Florence, Mont. **47** 46 38N 114 5W
Florence, Oreg. **58** 43 58N 124 7W
Florence, S.C. **60** 34 12N 79 46W
Florence, S. Dak. **61** 45 3N 97 20W
Florence, Tex. **65** 30 51N 97 48W
Florence, Wis. **69** 45 56N 88 15W
Florence County ◇, S.C. **60** 34 0N 79 45W
Florence County ◇, Wis. **69** 45 50N 88 20W
Floresville **65** 29 8N 98 10W
Florey **64** 32 27N 102 36W
Florham Park **51** 40 47N 74 23W
Florida **71** 18 22N 66 34W
Florida □ **31** 28 0N 82 0W
Florida B. **31** 25 0N 80 45W
Florida City **31** 25 27N 80 29W
Florida Keys **31** 24 40N 81 0W
Florida Ridge **31** 27 38N 80 24W
Florien **39** 31 27N 93 28W
Floris **37** 40 52N 92 20W
Florissant, Colo. **30** 38 57N 105 17W
Florissant, Mo. **46** 38 48N 90 20W
Florissant National Monument **30** 38 54N 105 17W
Floyd, Iowa **37** 43 8N 92 44W
Floyd, N. Mex. **52** 34 13N 103 35W
Floyd, Va. **68** 36 55N 80 19W
Floyd → **37** 42 29N 96 23W
Floyd County ◇, Ga. **32** 34 15N 85 10W
Floyd County ◇, Ind. **36** 38 20N 85 55W
Floyd County ◇, Iowa **37** 43 5N 92 45W
Floyd County ◇, Ky. **63** 37 30N 82 45W
Floyd County ◇, Tex. **64** 34 0N 101 15W
Floyd County ◇, Va. **68** 36 58N 80 25W
Floydada **64** 33 59N 101 20W
Flushing, Mich. **43** 43 4N 83 51W
Flushing, Ohio **56** 40 9N 81 4W
Fluvanna County ◇ **68** 37 52N 78 16W
Flying H **52** 33 2N 105 8W
Flynn **65** 31 9N 96 8W
Foard City **65** 33 53N 99 48W
Foard County ◇ **65** 33 59N 99 43W
Foley, Ala. **24** 30 24N 87 41W
Foley, Fla. **31** 30 4N 83 32W
Foley, Minn. **44** 45 40N 93 55W
Folkston **32** 30 50N 82 0W
Follett **64** 36 26N 100 8W
Folsom, La. **39** 30 38N 90 11W
Folsom, N.J. **51** 39 38N 74 51W
Folsom, N. Mex. **52** 36 51N 103 55W
Folsom, W. Va. **68** 39 28N 80 31W
Folsom L. **28** 38 42N 121 9W
Fond du Lac **69** 43 47N 88 27W
Fond du Lac County ◇ **69** 43 40N 88 30W
Fond du Lac Indian Reservation **44** 46 45N 92 40W
Fonda, Iowa **37** 42 35N 94 51W
Fonda, N.Y. **53** 42 57N 74 22W
Fonde **63** 36 36N 83 53W
Fontana, Calif. **29** 34 6N 117 26W
Fontana, Kans. **38** 38 25N 94 51W
Fontana, Wis. **69** 42 33N 88 35W
Fontana L. **54** 35 27N 83 48W
Fontana Village **54** 35 26N 83 50W
Fontanelle **37** 41 17N 94 34W
Fontenelle Reservoir **70** 42 1N 110 3W
Foosland **35** 40 22N 88 26W
Footville **69** 42 40N 89 12W
Forada **44** 45 48N 95 21W
Foraker **57** 36 52N 96 34W
Foraker, Mt. **25** 62 58N 151 24W
Forbes **55** 45 57N 98 47W
Forbing **39** 32 24N 93 44W
Ford **38** 37 38N 99 45W
Ford → **43** 45 41N 87 9W
Ford City, Calif. **29** 35 9N 119 27W
Ford City, Pa. **59** 40 46N 79 32W
Ford County ◇, Ill. **35** 40 30N 88 10W
Ford County ◇, Kans. **38** 37 45N 100 0W
Ford Dry L. **29** 33 37N 114 59W
Ford I. **33** 21 22N 157 58W
Fordland **46** 37 9N 92 57W
Fordoche **39** 30 36N 91 37W
Fordsville **62** 37 38N 86 43W
Fordville **55** 48 13N 97 48W
Fordyce, Ark. **27** 33 49N 92 25W
Fordyce, Nebr. **48** 42 42N 97 22W
Foreman **27** 33 43N 94 24W
Forest, La. **39** 32 47N 91 25W
Forest, Miss. **45** 32 22N 89 29W
Forest, Ohio **56** 40 48N 83 31W
Forest → **55** 48 21N 97 9W
Forest Acres **60** 34 1N 80 58W
Forest Center **44** 47 48N 91 19W
Forest City, Iowa **37** 43 16N 93 39W
Forest City, N.C. **54** 35 20N 81 52W
Forest City, Pa. **59** 41 39N 75 28W
Forest County ◇, Pa. **59** 41 30N 79 10W
Forest County ◇, Wis. **69** 45 35N 88 45W
Forest Dale **50** 43 48N 73 4W
Forest Grove **58** 45 31N 123 7W
Forest Hill, La. **39** 31 3N 92 32W
Forest Hill, Md. **41** 39 35N 76 23W
Forest Home **24** 31 52N 86 50W
Forest Lake **44** 45 17N 92 59W
Forest Park **32** 33 37N 84 22W
Forest River **55** 48 13N 97 28W
Foresthill **28** 39 1N 120 49W
Foreston, Minn. **44** 45 44N 93 43W
Foreston, S.C. **60** 33 38N 80 4W
Forestville, Md. **41** 38 51N 76 52W
Forestville, Mich. **43** 43 40N 82 37W
Forestville, N.Y. **53** 42 28N 79 10W
Forestville, Wis. **69** 44 41N 87 29W
Forgan **57** 36 54N 100 32W
Forge Village **42** 42 35N 71 29W
Fork Union **68** 37 46N 78 16W
Forked Deer → **62** 35 56N 89 35W
Forked River **51** 39 50N 74 12W
Forkland **24** 32 39N 87 53W
Forks **67** 47 57N 124 23W
Forks of Salmon **28** 41 16N 123 19W
Forkville **45** 32 28N 89 40W
Forman **55** 46 7N 97 38W
Forrest, Ill. **35** 40 45N 88 25W
Forrest, N. Mex. **52** 34 48N 103 36W
Forrest City **27** 35 1N 90 47W
Forrest County ◇ **45** 31 10N 89 13W
Forreston **35** 42 8N 89 35W
Forsyth, Ga. **32** 33 2N 83 56W
Forsyth, Mo. **46** 36 41N 93 6W
Forsyth, Mont. **47** 46 16N 106 41W
Forsyth County ◇, Ga. **32** 34 15N 84 5W
Forsyth County ◇, N.C. **54** 36 10N 80 15W
Fort Adams **45** 31 5N 91 33W
Fort Amador **71** 8 56N 79 32W
Fort Apache Indian Reservation **26** 33 45N 110 0W
Fort Atkinson, Iowa **37** 43 9N 91 56W
Fort Atkinson, Wis. **69** 42 56N 88 50W
Fort Barnwell **54** 35 18N 77 20W
Fort Belknap Agency **47** 48 29N 108 45W
Fort Belknap Indian Reservation **47** 48 20N 108 40W
Fort Bend County ◇ **65** 29 34N 95 49W
Fort Benton **47** 47 49N 110 40W
Fort Berthold Indian Reservation **55** 47 45N 102 15W
Fort Bidwell **28** 41 52N 120 9W
Fort Bragg **28** 39 26N 123 48W
Fort Branch **36** 38 15N 87 35W
Fort Bridger **70** 41 19N 110 23W
Fort Calhoun **48** 41 27N 96 2W
Fort Clayton **71** 9 0N 79 35W
Fort Cobb **57** 35 6N 98 26W
Fort Cobb Reservoir **57** 35 10N 98 27W
Fort Collins **30** 40 35N 105 5W
Fort Davis, Panama **71** 9 17N 79 56W
Fort Davis, Ala. **24** 32 15N 85 43W
Fort Davis, Tex. **64** 30 35N 103 54W
Fort Defiance **26** 35 45N 109 5W
Fort Deposit **24** 31 59N 86 35W
Fort Dick **28** 41 52N 124 9W
Fort Dodge **37** 42 30N 94 11W
Fort Drum **31** 27 32N 80 48W
Fort Duchesne **66** 40 17N 109 52W
Fort Edward **53** 43 16N 73 35W
Fort Fairfield **40** 46 46N 67 50W
Fort Gaines **32** 31 36N 85 3W
Fort Garland **30** 37 26N 105 26W
Fort Gay **68** 38 7N 82 36W
Fort Gibson **57** 35 48N 95 15W
Fort Gibson L. **57** 35 52N 95 14W
Fort Hall **34** 43 2N 112 26W
Fort Hall Indian Reservation **34** 43 2N 112 5W
Fort Hancock **64** 31 18N 105 51W
Fort Jennings **56** 40 54N 84 18W
Fort Jesup **39** 31 37N 93 24W
Fort Jones **28** 41 36N 122 51W
Fort Kent **40** 47 15N 68 36W
Fort Klamath **58** 42 42N 122 0W
Fort Knox **63** 37 54N 85 57W
Fort Laramie **70** 42 13N 104 31W
Fort Lauderdale **31** 26 7N 80 8W
Fort Lawn **60** 34 42N 80 54W
Fort Loudoun L. **63** 35 47N 84 15W
Fort Lupton **30** 40 5N 104 49W
Fort McDermitt Ind. Res. **58** 42 0N 117 42W
Fort McDowell Indian Reservation **26** 33 40N 111 50W
Fort Madison **37** 40 38N 91 27W
Fort Meade **31** 27 45N 81 48W
Fort Mill **60** 35 2N 80 57W
Fort Mitchell, Ala. **24** 32 20N 85 1W
Fort Mitchell, Ky. **63** 39 2N 84 34W
Fort Mitchell, Va. **68** 36 55N 78 29W
Fort Mohave Ind. Res. **26** 34 55N 114 35W
Fort Morgan **30** 40 15N 103 48W
Fort Motte **60** 33 44N 80 42W
Fort Myers **31** 26 39N 81 52W
Fort Myers Beach **31** 26 26N 81 52W
Fort Myers Villas **31** 26 34N 81 52W
Fort Oglethorpe **32** 34 57N 85 16W
Fort Payne **24** 34 26N 85 43W
Fort Peck **47** 48 1N 106 27W
Fort Peck Dam **47** 48 0N 106 26W
Fort Peck Indian Reservation **47** 48 30N 105 30W
Fort Peck L. **47** 48 0N 106 26W
Fort Pierce **31** 27 27N 80 20W
Fort Pierre **61** 44 21N 100 22W
Fort Plain **53** 42 56N 74 37W
Fort Randall Dam **61** 43 4N 98 34W
Fort Ransom **55** 46 31N 97 56W
Fort Recovery **56** 40 25N 84 47W
Fort Ripley **44** 46 10N 94 22W
Fort Robinson **48** 42 40N 103 28W
Fort Scott **38** 37 50N 94 42W
Fort Shawnee **56** 40 42N 84 7W
Fort Sherman **71** 9 22N 79 56W
Fort Smith **27** 35 23N 94 25W
Fort Stanton **52** 33 30N 105 31W
Fort Stockton **64** 30 53N 102 53W
Fort Sumner **52** 34 28N 104 15W
Fort Supply **57** 36 35N 99 35W
Fort Thomas **63** 39 5N 84 27W
Fort Thompson **61** 44 3N 99 26W
Fort Totten **55** 47 59N 99 0W
Fort Totten Indian Reservation **55** 47 58N 99 0W
Fort Towson **57** 34 0N 95 10W
Fort Valley **32** 32 33N 83 53W
Fort Walton Beach **31** 30 25N 86 36W
Fort Washakie **70** 43 0N 108 53W
Fort Washington **41** 38 42N 77 3W
Fort Wayne **36** 41 4N 85 9W
Fort White **31** 29 55N 82 43W
Fort Worth **65** 32 45N 97 18W
Fort Yates **55** 46 5N 100 38W
Fort Yukon **25** 66 34N 145 16W
Fort Yuma Indian Reservation **29** 32 45N 114 35W
Fortescue **51** 39 12N 75 12W
Fortine **47** 48 46N 114 54W
Fortsonia **32** 34 1N 82 47W
Fortuna, Calif. **28** 40 36N 124 9W
Fortuna, Mo. **46** 38 34N 92 48W
Fortuna, N. Dak. **55** 48 55N 103 47W
Fortuna Ledge **25** 61 53N 162 5W
Fortville **36** 39 56N 85 51W
Foss Reservoir **57** 35 33N 99 11W
Fossil **58** 45 0N 120 9W
Fossil Butte Nat. Mon. **70** 41 50N 110 27W
Fossil L. **58** 43 19N 120 25W
Fosston **44** 47 35N 95 45W
Foster, Ky. **63** 38 48N 84 13W
Foster, Nebr. **48** 42 16N 97 40W
Foster, Oreg. **58** 44 25N 122 40W
Foster, R.I. **42** 41 47N 71 44W
Foster County ◇ **55** 47 30N 99 0W
Foster L. **58** 42 59N 119 15W
Fosters **24** 33 6N 87 41W
Fostoria, Iowa **37** 43 15N 95 9W
Fostoria, Kans. **38** 39 26N 96 30W
Fostoria, Ohio **56** 41 10N 83 25W
Fouke **27** 33 16N 93 53W
Fount **63** 36 59N 83 50W
Fountain, Colo. **30** 38 41N 104 42W
Fountain, Fla. **31** 30 29N 85 25W
Fountain, Mich. **43** 44 3N 86 11W
Fountain, Minn. **44** 43 45N 92 8W
Fountain, N.C. **54** 35 41N 77 38W
Fountain City, Ind. **36** 39 57N 84 55W
Fountain City, Wis. **69** 44 8N 91 43W
Fountain County ◇ **36** 40 5N 87 15W
Fountain Cr. → **30** 38 15N 104 36W
Fountain Green **66** 39 38N 111 38W
Fountain Head **41** 39 42N 77 42W
Fountain Hill **27** 33 21N 91 51W
Fountain Inn **60** 34 42N 82 12W
Fountain Run **62** 36 18N 85 56W
Four Mountains, Is. of **25** 53 0N 170 0W
Four Oaks **54** 35 27N 78 26W
Four Town **44** 48 17N 95 20W
Fourteen Mile Pt. **43** 47 0N 89 10W
Fowblesburg **41** 39 34N 76 50W
Fowler, Calif. **29** 36 38N 119 41W
Fowler, Colo. **30** 38 8N 104 2W
Fowler, Ind. **36** 40 37N 87 19W
Fowler, Kans. **38** 37 23N 100 12W
Fowler, Mich. **43** 43 0N 84 45W
Fowlerton, Ind. **36** 40 25N 85 34W
Fowlerton, Tex. **65** 28 28N 98 48W
Fowlerville **43** 42 40N 84 4W
Fowlstown **32** 30 48N 84 33W
Fox **57** 34 22N 97 30W
Fox →, Ill. **35** 41 21N 88 50W
Fox →, Wis. **69** 44 32N 88 0W
Fox Is. **25** 54 0N 168 0W
Fox Lake, Ill. **35** 42 24N 88 11W
Fox Lake, Wis. **69** 43 34N 88 55W
Foxboro **42** 42 4N 71 16W
Foxpark **70** 41 5N 106 9W
Foyil **57** 36 26N 95 31W
Frackville **59** 40 47N 76 14W
Framingham **42** 42 17N 71 25W
Frances **67** 46 33N 123 30W
Frances, L. **47** 48 16N 112 13W
Francestown **50** 42 58N 71 48W
Francesville **36** 40 59N 86 53W
Francis, Mont. **47** 46 9N 111 5W
Francis, Okla. **57** 34 52N 96 36W
Francis, Utah **66** 40 37N 111 17W
Francis, L. **50** 45 2N 71 20W
Francis Case, L. **61** 43 4N 98 34W
Francis Creek **69** 44 12N 87 44W
Francis Marion National Forest **60** 33 10N 79 40W
Franconia, Ariz. **26** 34 44N 114 17W
Franconia, N.H. **50** 44 14N 71 44W
Frankenmuth **43** 43 20N 83 44W
Frankewing **62** 35 12N 86 51W
Frankford, Del. **41** 38 31N 75 14W
Frankford, Mo. **46** 39 29N 91 19W
Frankford, W. Va. **68** 37 56N 80 23W
Frankfort, Ind. **36** 40 17N 86 31W
Frankfort, Kans. **38** 39 42N 96 25W
Frankfort, Ky. **63** 38 12N 84 52W
Frankfort, Maine **40** 44 37N 68 53W
Frankfort, Mich. **43** 44 38N 86 14W
Frankfort, Ohio **56** 39 24N 83 11W
Frankfort, S. Dak. **61** 44 53N 98 18W
Franklin, Ariz. **26** 32 41N 109 5W
Franklin, Ga. **32** 33 17N 85 6W
Franklin, Idaho **34** 42 1N 111 48W
Franklin, Ill. **35** 39 37N 90 3W
Franklin, Ind. **36** 39 29N 86 3W
Franklin, Kans. **38** 37 32N 94 42W
Franklin, Ky. **62** 36 43N 86 35W

Franklin, La. **39** 29 48N 91 30W
Franklin, Maine **40** 44 35N 68 14W
Franklin, Mass. **42** 42 5N 71 24W
Franklin, Minn. **44** 47 32N 92 32W
Franklin, N.C. **54** 35 11N 83 23W
Franklin, N.H. **50** 43 27N 71 39W
Franklin, N.J. **51** 41 7N 74 35W
Franklin, N.Y. **53** 42 21N 75 10W
Franklin, Nebr. **48** 40 6N 98 57W
Franklin, Ohio **56** 39 34N 84 18W
Franklin, Pa. **59** 41 24N 79 50W
Franklin, Tenn. **62** 35 55N 86 52W
Franklin, Tex. **65** 31 2N 96 29W
Franklin, Va. **68** 36 41N 76 56W
Franklin, W. Va. **68** 38 39N 79 20W
Franklin, Pt. **25** 70 55N 158 48W
Franklin County ◇, Ala. **24** 34 21N 87 42W
Franklin County ◇, Ark. **27** 35 29N 93 50W
Franklin County ◇, Fla. **31** 29 50N 84 45W
Franklin County ◇, Ga. **32** 34 20N 83 10W
Franklin County ◇, Idaho **34** 42 10N 111 50W
Franklin County ◇, Ill. **35** 38 0N 89 0W
Franklin County ◇, Ind. **36** 39 25N 85 5W
Franklin County ◇, Iowa **37** 42 45N 93 25W
Franklin County ◇, Kans. **38** 38 30N 95 15W
Franklin County ◇, Ky. **63** 38 15N 84 55W
Franklin County ◇, Maine **40** 45 0N 70 30W
Franklin County ◇, Mass. **42** 42 30N 72 35W
Franklin County ◇, Miss. **45** 31 28N 90 54W
Franklin County ◇, Mo. **46** 38 25N 91 0W
Franklin County ◇, N.C. **54** 36 0N 78 20W
Franklin County ◇, N.Y. **53** 44 30N 74 15W
Franklin County ◇, Nebr. **48** 40 15N 99 0W
Franklin County ◇, Ohio **56** 40 0N 83 4W
Franklin County ◇, Pa. **59** 39 56N 77 40W
Franklin County ◇, Tenn. **62** 35 10N 86 1W
Franklin County ◇, Tex. **65** 33 11N 95 13W
Franklin County ◇, Va. **68** 37 0N 80 0W
Franklin County ◇, Vt. **50** 44 50N 72 50W
Franklin County ◇, Wash. **67** 46 30N 119 0W
Franklin D. Roosevelt L. **67** 48 18N 118 9W
Franklin Grove **35** 41 51N 89 18W
Franklin L. **49** 40 25N 115 22W
Franklin Parish ◇ **39** 32 10N 91 43W
Franklin Square **53** 40 43N 73 41W
Franklinton, La. **39** 30 51N 90 9W
Franklinton, N.C. **54** 36 6N 78 27W
Franklinville, N.J. **51** 39 37N 75 5W
Franklinville, N.Y. **53** 42 20N 78 27W
Franks Pk. **70** 43 58N 109 18W
Frankston **65** 32 3N 95 30W
Frankton **36** 40 13N 85 46W
Frankville **24** 31 39N 88 9W
Frannie **70** 44 58N 108 37W
Fraser **30** 39 57N 105 49W
Frazee **44** 46 44N 95 42W
Frazer **47** 48 3N 106 2W
Frazeysburg **56** 40 7N 82 7W
Frazier Park **29** 34 49N 118 56W
Fred **65** 30 34N 94 10W
Freda **55** 46 21N 101 10W
Frederic, Mich. **43** 44 47N 84 45W
Frederic, Wis. **69** 45 40N 92 28W
Frederica **41** 39 1N 75 28W
Frederick, Colo. **30** 40 6N 104 56W
Frederick, Md. **41** 39 25N 77 25W
Frederick, Okla. **57** 34 23N 99 1W
Frederick, S. Dak. **61** 45 50N 98 31W
Frederick County ◇, Md. **41** 39 30N 77 25W
Frederick County ◇, Va. **68** 39 5N 78 13W
Fredericksburg, Iowa **37** 42 58N 92 12W
Fredericksburg, Tex. **65** 30 16N 98 52W
Fredericksburg, Va. **68** 38 18N 77 28W
Fredericktown, Mo. **46** 37 34N 90 18W
Fredericktown, Ohio **56** 40 29N 82 33W
Frederika **37** 42 53N 92 19W
Frederiksted **71** 17 43N 64 53W
Fredonia, Ariz. **26** 36 57N 112 32W
Fredonia, Kans. **38** 37 32N 95 49W
Fredonia, Ky. **62** 37 12N 88 4W
Fredonia, N. Dak. **55** 46 20N 99 6W
Fredonia, N.Y. **53** 42 26N 79 20W
Fredonia, Pa. **59** 41 19N 80 16W
Freeborn County ◇ **44** 43 40N 93 15W
Freeburg, Ill. **35** 38 26N 89 55W
Freeburg, Mo. **46** 38 19N 91 56W
Freedom **57** 36 46N 99 7W
Freehold **51** 40 16N 74 17W
Freel Peak **49** 38 52N 119 54W
Freeland **59** 41 1N 75 54W
Freeman, Mo. **46** 38 37N 94 30W
Freeman, S. Dak. **61** 43 21N 97 26W
Freeman L. **36** 40 42N 86 45W
Freeport, Fla. **31** 30 30N 86 8W
Freeport, Ill. **35** 42 17N 89 36W
Freeport, Kans. **38** 37 12N 97 51W
Freeport, Maine **40** 43 52N 70 6W
Freeport, Mich. **43** 42 46N 85 19W
Freeport, Minn. **44** 45 40N 94 42W
Freeport, N.Y. **53** 40 39N 73 35W
Freeport, Pa. **59** 40 41N 79 41W
Freeport, Tex. **65** 28 57N 95 21W
Freer **65** 27 53N 98 37W
Freesoil **43** 44 7N 86 14W
Freestone County ◇ **65** 31 44N 96 10W
Freeville **53** 42 31N 76 21W
Freistatt **46** 37 1N 93 54W
Fremont, Calif. **28** 37 32N 121 57W
Fremont, Ind. **36** 41 44N 84 56W
Fremont, Iowa **37** 41 13N 92 26W
Fremont, Ky. **62** 36 58N 88 37W
Fremont, Mich. **43** 43 28N 85 57W
Fremont, N.C. **54** 35 33N 77 58W
Fremont, Nebr. **48** 41 26N 96 30W
Fremont, Ohio **56** 41 21N 83 7W
Fremont, Utah **66** 38 27N 111 37W
Fremont, Wis. **69** 44 16N 88 52W
Fremont → **66** 38 24N 110 42W
Fremont County ◇, Colo. **30** 38 30N 105 30W
Fremont County ◇, Idaho **34** 44 15N 111 20W
Fremont County ◇, Iowa **37** 40 45N 95 35W
Fremont County ◇, Wyo. **70** 43 0N 108 30W
Fremont L. **70** 42 57N 109 48W
Fremont National Forest **58** 42 20N 120 50W
French → **59** 45 56N 80 54W
French Broad →, N.C. **54** 35 57N 83 51W
French Broad →, Tenn. **63** 35 58N 83 51W
French Camp, Calif. **28** 37 53N 121 16W
French Camp, Miss. **45** 33 18N 89 24W
French Frigate Shoals **33** 23 45N 166 10W
French Gulch **28** 40 42N 122 38W
French Lick **36** 38 33N 86 37W
French Meadows Res. **28** 39 10N 120 40W
French River **44** 46 54N 91 54W
Frenchboro **40** 44 7N 68 22W
Frenchburg **63** 37 57N 83 38W
Frenchglen **58** 42 50N 118 55W
Frenchman Cr. →, Mont. **47** 48 31N 107 10W
Frenchman Cr. →, Nebr. **48** 40 14N 100 50W
Frenchman L., Calif. **28** 39 54N 120 11W
Frenchman L., Nev. **49** 36 48N 115 56W
Frenchtown, Mont. **47** 47 1N 114 14W
Frenchtown, N.J. **51** 40 32N 75 4W
Frenchville **40** 47 17N 68 23W
Fresno **29** 36 44N 119 47W
Fresno County ◇ **29** 36 40N 120 0W
Fresno Reservoir **47** 48 36N 109 57W
Frewsburg **53** 42 3N 79 10W
Friant **29** 36 59N 119 43W
Friars Point **45** 34 22N 90 38W
Friday Harbor **67** 48 32N 123 1W
Fridley **44** 45 5N 93 16W
Friend, Kans. **38** 38 16N 100 55W
Friend, Nebr. **48** 40 38N 97 17W
Friendly **41** 38 42N 76 59W
Friendship, N.Y. **53** 42 12N 78 8W
Friendship, Tenn. **62** 35 55N 89 14W
Friendship, Wis. **69** 43 58N 89 49W
Friendsville **41** 39 40N 79 24W
Fries **68** 36 43N 80 59W
Friesland **69** 43 35N 89 4W
Frijoles **71** 9 11N 79 48W
Frio → **65** 28 26N 98 11W
Frio County ◇ **65** 28 54N 99 6W
Frio Draw → **64** 34 50N 102 19W
Friona **64** 34 38N 102 43W
Frisco **30** 39 35N 106 6W
Frisco City **24** 31 26N 87 24W
Frisco Peak **66** 38 31N 113 17W
Frissell, Mt. **42** 42 3N 73 28W
Fritch **64** 35 38N 101 36W
Froid **47** 48 20N 104 30W
Fromberg **47** 45 24N 108 54W
Front Range **30** 40 25N 105 45W
Front Royal **68** 38 55N 78 12W
Frontenac **38** 37 27N 94 42W
Frontier **70** 41 49N 110 32W
Frontier County ◇ **48** 40 30N 100 30W
Frost, Minn. **44** 43 35N 93 56W
Frost, Tex. **65** 32 5N 96 49W
Frostburg **41** 39 39N 78 56W
Frostproof **31** 27 45N 81 32W
Fruita **30** 39 9N 108 44W
Fruitdale, Ala. **24** 31 21N 88 25W
Fruitdale, S. Dak. **61** 44 40N 103 42W
Fruithurst **24** 33 44N 85 26W
Fruitland, Idaho **34** 44 0N 116 55W
Fruitland, Iowa **37** 41 21N 91 8W
Fruitland, Md. **41** 38 19N 75 37W
Fruitland, Mo. **46** 37 27N 89 38W
Fruitland, N. Mex. **52** 36 44N 108 24W
Fruitland Park **31** 28 51N 81 54W
Fruitport **43** 43 7N 86 9W
Fruitvale, Colo. **30** 39 5N 108 30W
Fruitvale, Idaho **34** 44 49N 116 26W
Fruitvale, Wash. **67** 46 37N 120 33W
Fryeburg **40** 44 1N 70 59W
Fulda **44** 43 53N 95 36W
Fullerton, Calif. **29** 33 53N 117 56W
Fullerton, N. Dak. **55** 46 10N 98 26W
Fullerton, Nebr. **48** 41 22N 97 58W
Fulton, Ala. **24** 31 47N 87 44W
Fulton, Ark. **27** 33 37N 93 49W
Fulton, Ill. **35** 41 52N 90 11W
Fulton, Kans. **38** 38 1N 94 43W
Fulton, Ky. **62** 36 30N 88 53W
Fulton, Miss. **45** 34 16N 88 25W
Fulton, Mo. **46** 38 52N 91 57W
Fulton, N.Y. **53** 43 19N 76 25W
Fulton, Ohio **56** 40 28N 82 50W
Fulton, S. Dak. **61** 43 44N 97 49W
Fulton, Tex. **65** 28 4N 97 2W
Fulton County ◇, Ark. **27** 36 22N 91 50W
Fulton County ◇, Ga. **32** 33 40N 84 40W
Fulton County ◇, Ill. **35** 40 30N 90 10W
Fulton County ◇, Ind. **36** 41 5N 86 15W
Fulton County ◇, Ky. **62** 36 32N 89 10W
Fulton County ◇, N.Y. **53** 43 10N 74 30W
Fulton County ◇, Ohio **56** 41 33N 84 8W
Fulton County ◇, Pa. **59** 39 55N 78 5W
Fultondale **24** 33 37N 86 48W
Fults **35** 38 10N 90 13W
Fundy, B. of **40** 44 30N 66 30W
Funk **48** 40 28N 99 15W
Funston **32** 31 12N 83 52W
Fuquay-Varina **54** 35 35N 78 48W
Furman **60** 32 41N 81 11W
Furnas County ◇ **48** 40 15N 100 0W

G

Gabbettville **32** 32 57N 85 8W
Gabbs **49** 38 52N 117 55W
Gabbs Valley Range **49** 38 34N 118 0W
Gabilan Range **29** 36 30N 121 15W
Gackle **55** 46 38N 99 9W
Gadsden, Ala. **24** 34 1N 86 1W
Gadsden, Ariz. **26** 32 33N 114 47W
Gadsden, S.C. **60** 33 51N 80 46W
Gadsden County ◇ **31** 30 30N 84 45W
Gaffney **60** 35 5N 81 39W
Gage **57** 36 19N 99 45W
Gage County ◇ **48** 40 20N 96 45W
Gail **64** 32 46N 101 27W
Gaillard, L. **42** 41 21N 72 46W
Gaines County ◇ **64** 32 43N 102 39W
Gainesboro **63** 36 21N 85 39W
Gainesville, Fla. **31** 29 40N 82 20W
Gainesville, Ga. **32** 34 18N 83 50W
Gainesville, Mo. **46** 36 36N 92 26W
Gainesville, Tex. **65** 33 38N 97 8W
Gaithersburg **41** 39 8N 77 12W
Gakona **25** 62 18N 145 18W
Galatia, Ill. **35** 37 51N 88 37W
Galatia, Kans. **38** 38 38N 98 58W
Galax **68** 36 40N 80 56W
Galena, Alaska **25** 64 44N 156 56W
Galena, Ill. **35** 42 25N 90 26W
Galena, Kans. **38** 37 4N 94 38W
Galena, Md. **41** 39 21N 75 53W
Galena, Mo. **46** 36 48N 93 28W
Galena Park **65** 29 44N 95 14W
Galesburg, Ill. **35** 40 57N 90 22W
Galesburg, Kans. **38** 37 28N 95 21W
Galesburg, Mich. **43** 42 17N 85 26W
Galesburg, N. Dak. **55** 47 16N 97 24W
Galestown **41** 38 35N 75 42W
Galesville **69** 44 5N 91 21W
Galeton, Colo. **30** 40 31N 104 35W
Galeton, Pa. **59** 41 44N 77 39W
Galion **56** 40 44N 82 47W
Galiuro Mts. **26** 32 30N 110 20W
Gallatin, Mo. **46** 39 55N 93 58W
Gallatin, Tenn. **62** 36 24N 86 27W
Gallatin, Tex. **65** 31 54N 95 9W
Gallatin → **47** 45 56N 111 30W
Gallatin County ◇, Ill. **35** 37 45N 88 15W
Gallatin County ◇, Ky. **63** 38 45N 84 55W
Gallatin County ◇, Mont. **47** 45 55N 111 15W
Gallatin Gateway **47** 45 35N 111 12W
Gallatin National Forest **47** 45 15N 111 15W
Gallia County ◇ **56** 38 49N 82 12W
Galliano **39** 29 26N 90 18W
Gallinas → **52** 35 0N 104 55W
Gallinas Mts. **52** 34 25N 107 45W
Gallion **24** 32 30N 87 43W
Gallipolis **56** 38 49N 82 12W
Gallman **45** 31 56N 90 23W
Gallo Mts. **52** 34 5N 108 35W
Galloo I. **53** 43 55N 76 25W
Gallup **52** 35 32N 108 45W
Galt, Calif. **28** 38 15N 121 18W
Galt, Iowa **37** 42 42N 93 36W
Galt, Mo. **46** 40 8N 93 23W
Galva, Ill. **35** 41 10N 90 3W
Galva, Iowa **37** 42 30N 95 25W
Galveston, Ind. **36** 40 35N 86 11W
Galveston, Tex. **65** 29 18N 94 48W
Galveston B. **65** 29 36N 94 50W
Galveston County ◇ **65** 29 28N 95 5W
Galveston I. **65** 29 16N 94 51W
Gamaliel, Ark. **27** 36 27N 92 14W
Gamaliel, Ky. **63** 36 38N 85 48W
Gambell **25** 63 47N 171 45W
Gamber **41** 39 28N 76 56W
Gamboa **71** 9 7N 79 42W
Gamerco **52** 35 34N 108 46W
Ganado, Ariz. **26** 35 43N 109 33W
Ganado, Tex. **65** 29 2N 96 31W
Gandeeville **68** 38 42N 81 25W
Gannett **34** 43 22N 114 11W
Gannett Peak **70** 43 11N 109 39W
Gannvalley **61** 44 2N 98 59W
Gans **57** 35 23N 94 42W
Gantt **24** 31 25N 86 29W
Garber **57** 36 26N 97 35W
Garberville **28** 40 6N 123 48W
Garcia **30** 37 0N 105 32W
Gardar **55** 48 35N 97 53W
Garden **43** 45 47N 86 33W
Garden City, Ala. **24** 34 1N 86 45W
Garden City, Ga. **32** 32 6N 81 9W
Garden City, Idaho **34** 43 38N 116 16W
Garden City, Kans. **38** 37 58N 100 53W
Garden City, Mo. **46** 38 34N 94 12W
Garden City, S. Dak. **61** 44 57N 97 35W
Garden City, Tex. **64** 31 52N 101 29W
Garden City, Utah **66** 41 57N 111 24W
Garden County ◇ **48** 41 30N 102 15W
Garden Grove, Calif. **29** 33 47N 117 55W
Garden Grove, Iowa **37** 40 50N 93 36W
Garden I. **43** 45 49N 85 30W
Garden Island B. **39** 29 0N 89 0W
Garden Lakes **32** 34 19N 85 17W
Garden Plain **38** 37 40N 97 41W
Garden Valley **34** 44 6N 115 57W
Gardena **34** 43 58N 116 12W
Gardendale **24** 33 39N 86 49W
Gardi **32** 31 32N 81 48W
Gardiner, Maine **40** 44 14N 69 47W
Gardiner, Mont. **47** 45 2N 110 22W
Gardiner, Oreg. **58** 43 44N 124 7W
Gardiners B. **53** 41 5N 72 5W
Gardiners I. **53** 41 6N 72 6W
Gardner, Colo. **30** 37 47N 105 10W
Gardner, Fla. **31** 27 21N 81 48W
Gardner, Kans. **38** 38 49N 94 56W
Gardner, Mass. **42** 42 34N 71 59W
Gardner L. **40** 44 45N 67 20W
Gardner Pinnacles **33** 25 0N 167 55W
Gardnerville **49** 38 56N 119 45W
Gareloi I. **25** 51 48N 178 48W
Garfield, Ark. **27** 36 27N 93 58W
Garfield, Kans. **38** 38 5N 99 14W
Garfield, Minn. **44** 45 56N 95 30W
Garfield, N.J. **51** 40 52N 74 6W
Garfield, N. Mex. **52** 32 46N 107 16W
Garfield, Wash. **67** 47 1N 117 9W
Garfield County ◇, Colo. **30** 39 30N 108 0W

Garfield County ◇, Mont. 47 47 15N 107 0W
Garfield County ◇, Nebr. 48 41 50N 99 0W
Garfield County ◇, Okla. 57 36 20N 97 45W
Garfield County ◇, Utah 66 37 50N 111 20W
Garfield County ◇, Wash. 67 46 28N 117 36W
Garfield Heights 56 41 26N 81 37W
Garfield Mt. 47 44 31N 112 37W
Garibaldi 58 45 34N 123 55W
Garland, Ala. 24 31 33N 86 50W
Garland, Ark. 27 33 22N 93 43W
Garland, Kans. 38 37 44N 94 37W
Garland, N.C. 54 34 47N 78 24W
Garland, Nebr. 48 40 57N 96 59W
Garland, Tex. 65 32 55N 96 38W
Garland, Utah 66 41 45N 112 10W
Garland County ◇ 27 34 34N 93 10W
Garnavillo 37 42 52N 91 14W
Garner, Iowa 37 43 6N 93 36W
Garner, N.C. 54 35 43N 78 37W
Garnett 38 38 17N 95 14W
Garrard County ◇ 63 37 35N 84 30W
Garretson 61 43 43N 96 30W
Garrett 36 41 21N 85 8W
Garrett County ◇ 41 39 30N 79 20W
Garrison, Iowa 37 42 9N 92 8W
Garrison, Ky. 63 38 36N 83 10W
Garrison, Minn. 44 46 18N 93 50W
Garrison, Mont. 47 46 31N 112 49W
Garrison, N. Dak. 55 47 40N 101 25W
Garrison, Nebr. 48 41 11N 97 10W
Garrison, Tex. 65 31 49N 94 30W
Garrison, Utah 66 38 56N 114 2W
Garrison Dam 55 47 30N 101 25W
Garvin 57 33 57N 94 56W
Garvin County ◇ 57 34 45N 97 20W
Garwin 37 42 6N 92 41W
Garwood 65 29 27N 96 24W
Gary, Ind. 36 41 36N 87 20W
Gary, Minn. 44 47 22N 96 16W
Gary, S. Dak. 61 44 48N 96 27W
Gary, Tex. 65 32 2N 94 22W
Gary, W. Va. 68 37 22N 81 33W
Garza County ◇ 64 33 12N 101 23W
Garza-Little Elm Reservoir 65 33 4N 96 59W
Gas City 36 40 29N 85 37W
Gascon 52 35 53N 105 27W
Gasconade 46 38 40N 91 34W
Gasconade → 46 38 41N 91 33W
Gasconade County ◇ 46 38 25N 91 30W
Gascoyne 55 46 7N 103 5W
Gasparilla I. 31 26 46N 82 16W
Gasquet 28 41 51N 123 58W
Gassaway 68 38 41N 80 47W
Gaston, Ind. 36 40 19N 85 31W
Gaston, N.C. 54 36 30N 77 39W
Gaston, S.C. 60 33 49N 81 5W
Gaston, L. 54 36 30N 77 49W
Gaston County ◇ 54 31 15N 81 10W
Gastonia 54 35 16N 81 11W
Gate 57 36 51N 100 4W
Gate City 68 36 38N 82 35W
Gates, N.C. 54 36 30N 76 46W
Gates, N.Y. 53 43 9N 77 42W
Gates, Oreg. 58 44 45N 122 25W
Gates, Tenn. 62 35 50N 89 24W
Gates County ◇ 54 36 25N 76 40W
Gatesville, N.C. 54 36 24N 76 45W
Gatesville, Tex. 65 31 26N 97 45W
Gateway 30 38 41N 108 59W
Gatliff 63 36 41N 84 1W
Gatlinburg 63 35 43N 83 31W
Gato 30 37 3N 107 12W
Gatun 71 9 16N 79 55W
Gatun Dam 71 9 16N 79 55W
Gatun Lake 71 9 12N 79 55W
Gatun Locks 71 9 16N 79 55W
Gauley → 68 38 10N 81 12W
Gauley Bridge 68 38 10N 81 12W
Gautier 45 30 23N 88 37W
Gavins Point Dam 61 42 51N 97 29W
Gaviota 29 34 29N 120 13W
Gay, Ga. 32 33 6N 84 35W
Gay, Mich. 43 47 14N 88 10W
Gaylord, Kans. 38 39 39N 98 51W
Gaylord, Mich. 43 45 2N 84 41W
Gaylord, Minn. 44 44 33N 94 13W
Gaylordsville 42 41 39N 73 29W
Gays Mills 69 43 19N 90 51W
Gayville 61 42 53N 97 10W
Gazelle 28 41 31N 122 31W
Gearhart 58 46 1N 123 55W
Gearhart Mt. 58 42 30N 120 53W
Geary 57 35 38N 98 19W
Geary County ◇ 38 39 0N 96 45W
Geauga County ◇ 56 41 35N 81 12W
Geddes 61 43 15N 98 42W
Geiger 24 32 52N 88 18W
Geistown 59 40 18N 78 52W
Gem 38 39 26N 100 54W
Gem County ◇ 34 44 0N 116 25W
Gene Autry 57 34 19N 97 2W
Genesee 34 46 33N 116 56W
Genesee → 53 43 16N 77 36W
Genesee County ◇, Mich. 43 43 0N 83 40W
Genesee County ◇, N.Y. 53 43 0N 78 10W
Geneseo, Ill. 35 41 27N 90 9W
Geneseo, Kans. 38 38 31N 98 10W
Geneseo, N.Y. 53 42 48N 77 49W
Geneva, Ala. 24 31 2N 85 52W
Geneva, Ga. 32 32 35N 84 33W
Geneva, Ill. 35 41 53N 88 18W
Geneva, Ind. 36 40 36N 84 58W
Geneva, Iowa 37 42 41N 93 8W
Geneva, Minn. 44 43 49N 93 16W
Geneva, N.Y. 53 42 52N 76 59W
Geneva, Nebr. 48 40 32N 97 36W
Geneva, Ohio 56 41 48N 80 57W
Geneva County ◇ 24 31 6N 85 42W
Genoa, Colo. 30 39 17N 103 30W
Genoa, Ill. 35 42 6N 88 42W
Genoa, Nebr. 48 41 27N 97 44W
Genoa, Ohio 56 41 31N 83 22W
Genoa, Wis. 69 43 35N 91 13W
Genoa City 69 42 30N 88 20W
Genola 44 45 58N 94 7W
Gentry, Ark. 27 36 16N 94 29W
Gentry, Mo. 46 40 20N 94 25W
Gentry County ◇ 46 40 10N 94 25W
George, Iowa 37 43 21N 96 0W
George, Wash. 67 47 5N 119 53W
George, L., Fla. 31 29 17N 81 36W
George, L., Mich. 43 46 27N 84 8W
George, L., N.Y. 53 43 37N 73 33W
George County ◇ 45 30 56N 88 35W
George Washington National Forest 68 38 0N 79 50W
George West 65 28 20N 98 7W
Georgetown, Calif. 28 38 54N 120 50W
Georgetown, Colo. 30 39 42N 105 42W
Georgetown, Del. 41 38 41N 75 23W
Georgetown, Fla. 31 29 23N 81 38W
Georgetown, Ga. 32 31 53N 85 6W
Georgetown, Idaho 34 42 29N 111 22W
Georgetown, Ill. 35 39 59N 87 38W
Georgetown, Ky. 63 38 13N 84 33W
Georgetown, La. 39 31 46N 92 23W
Georgetown, Mass. 42 42 44N 70 59W
Georgetown, Miss. 45 31 52N 90 10W
Georgetown, Ohio 56 38 52N 83 54W
Georgetown, S.C. 60 33 23N 79 17W
Georgetown, Tex. 65 30 38N 97 41W
Georgetown County ◇ 60 33 30N 79 15W
Georgia □ 32 32 50N 83 15W
Georgia, Strait of 67 49 20N 124 0W
Georgia Center 50 44 42N 73 9W
Georgiana 24 31 38N 86 44W
Gerald 46 38 24N 91 20W
Geraldine 47 47 36N 110 16W
Gerber 28 40 4N 122 9W
Gerber Reservoir 58 42 12N 121 8W
Gerdine, Mt. 25 61 35N 152 27W
Gering 48 41 50N 103 40W
Gerlach 49 40 39N 119 21W
Germantown, Ill. 35 38 33N 89 32W
Germantown, Ohio 56 39 38N 84 22W
Germantown, Tenn. 62 35 5N 89 49W
Germantown, Wis. 69 43 14N 88 6W
Geronimo 57 34 29N 98 23W
Gerty 57 34 50N 96 17W
Gettysburg, Pa. 59 39 50N 77 14W
Gettysburg, S. Dak. 61 45 1N 99 57W
Geuda Springs 38 37 7N 97 9W
Geyser 47 47 16N 110 30W
Geyserville 28 38 42N 122 54W
Ghent, Ky. 63 38 44N 85 4W
Ghent, Minn. 44 44 31N 95 54W
Gibbon, Nebr. 48 40 45N 98 51W
Gibbon, Oreg. 58 45 42N 118 21W
Gibbonsville 34 45 33N 113 56W
Gibbstown 51 39 50N 75 18W
Gibsland 39 32 33N 93 3W
Gibson, Ga. 32 33 14N 82 36W
Gibson, La. 39 29 41N 90 59W
Gibson City 35 40 28N 88 22W
Gibson County ◇, Ind. 36 38 20N 87 35W
Gibson County ◇, Tenn. 62 36 0N 89 0W
Gibsonton 31 27 51N 82 23W
Giddings 65 30 11N 96 56W
Gideon 46 36 27N 89 55W
Gifford, Fla. 31 27 40N 80 25W
Gifford, Iowa 37 42 17N 93 5W
Gifford, Wash. 67 48 18N 118 9W
Gifford Pinchot National Forest 67 46 15N 121 55W
Gila 52 32 58N 108 38W
Gila → 26 32 43N 114 33W
Gila Bend 26 32 57N 112 43W
Gila Bend Indian Reservation 26 33 0N 112 30W
Gila Bend Mts. 26 33 10N 113 0W
Gila Cliff Dwellings National Monument 52 33 2N 108 16W
Gila County ◇ 26 33 30N 110 45W
Gila Mts. 26 33 10N 109 50W
Gila National Forest 52 33 30N 108 30W
Gila River Indian Reservation 26 33 15N 112 0W
Gilbert, Ariz. 26 33 21N 111 47W
Gilbert, Iowa 37 42 7N 93 39W
Gilbert, La. 39 32 3N 91 40W
Gilbert, Minn. 44 47 29N 92 28W
Gilbert, S.C. 60 33 56N 81 24W
Gilbert, W. Va. 68 37 37N 81 52W
Gilbert Pk. 67 46 29N 121 25W
Gilbertown 24 31 53N 88 19W
Gilbertville 42 42 19N 72 12W
Gilboa 56 41 1N 83 55W
Gilby 55 48 5N 97 28W
Gilchrist, Oreg. 58 43 29N 121 41W
Gilchrist, Tex. 65 29 31N 94 29W
Gilchrist County ◇ 31 29 45N 82 45W
Gildford 47 48 34N 110 18W
Gilead, Maine 40 44 24N 70 59W
Gilead, Nebr. 48 40 9N 97 25W
Giles County ◇, Tenn. 62 35 10N 86 0W
Giles County ◇, Va. 68 37 20N 80 44W
Gilford Park 51 39 58N 74 8W
Gill 30 40 27N 104 33W
Gillespie 35 39 8N 89 49W
Gillespie County ◇ 65 30 16N 98 52W
Gillett, Ark. 27 34 7N 91 23W
Gillett, Wis. 69 44 54N 88 19W
Gillett Grove 37 43 1N 95 2W
Gillette 70 44 18N 105 30W
Gillham 27 34 10N 94 19W
Gilliam 39 32 50N 93 51W
Gilliam County ◇ 58 47 20N 120 10W
Gillis 39 30 22N 93 12W
Gillis Range 49 38 42N 118 21W
Gillsville 32 34 18N 83 38W
Gilman, Colo. 30 39 32N 106 24W
Gilman, Ill. 35 40 46N 88 0W
Gilman, Iowa 37 41 53N 92 47W
Gilman, Vt. 50 44 23N 71 42W
Gilman, Wis. 69 45 10N 90 48W
Gilman City 46 40 8N 93 53W
Gilmanton 50 43 55N 71 25W
Gilmer 65 32 44N 94 57W
Gilmer County ◇, Ga. 32 34 40N 84 30W
Gilmer County ◇, W. Va. 68 38 56N 80 50W
Gilmore 27 35 25N 90 17W
Gilmore City 37 42 44N 94 27W
Gilpin 63 37 15N 84 53W
Gilpin County ◇ 30 39 50N 105 40W
Gilroy 28 37 1N 121 34W
Gilsum 50 43 3N 72 16W
Giltner 48 40 47N 98 9W
Girard, Ga. 32 33 3N 81 43W
Girard, Ill. 35 39 27N 89 47W
Girard, Kans. 38 37 31N 94 51W
Girard, Ohio 56 41 9N 80 42W
Girard, Pa. 59 42 0N 80 19W
Girard, Tex. 64 33 22N 100 40W
Girdletree 41 38 6N 75 24W
Girvin 64 31 5N 102 24W
Glacier 67 48 53N 121 57W
Glacier Bay 25 58 40N 136 0W
Glacier Bay National Monument 25 58 45N 136 30W
Glacier County ◇ 47 48 50N 112 50W
Glacier Peak 67 48 7N 121 7W
Gladbrook 37 42 11N 92 43W
Glade 38 39 41N 99 19W
Glade Spring 68 36 47N 81 47W
Glades County ◇ 31 26 50N 81 15W
Gladewater 65 32 33N 94 56W
Gladstone, Mich. 43 45 51N 87 1W
Gladstone, Mo. 46 39 13N 94 35W
Gladstone, N. Dak. 55 46 52N 102 34W
Gladstone, N.J. 51 40 43N 74 40W
Gladstone, N. Mex. 52 36 18N 103 58W
Gladstone, Oreg. 58 45 23N 122 36W
Gladwin 43 43 59N 84 29W
Gladwin County ◇ 43 44 0N 84 25W
Glady 68 38 48N 79 43W
Glamis 29 32 55N 115 0W
Glasco 38 39 22N 97 50W
Glascock County ◇ 32 33 15N 82 40W
Glasford 35 40 34N 89 49W
Glasgow, Del. 41 39 38N 75 45W
Glasgow, Ky. 63 37 0N 85 55W
Glasgow, Mo. 46 39 14N 92 51W
Glasgow, Mont. 47 48 12N 106 38W
Glasgow, Va. 68 37 38N 79 27W
Glass Mts. 64 30 30N 103 10W
Glassboro 51 39 42N 75 7W
Glasscock County ◇ 64 31 52N 101 29W
Glastonbury 42 41 43N 72 37W
Glazier 64 36 1N 100 16W
Gleason 62 36 13N 88 37W
Glen, Mont. 47 45 28N 112 43W
Glen, N.H. 50 44 7N 71 11W
Glen Allan 45 33 2N 91 2W
Glen Alpine 54 35 44N 81 47W
Glen Burnie 41 39 10N 76 37W
Glen Campbell 59 40 49N 78 50W
Glen Canyon 66 37 30N 110 40W
Glen Canyon Dam 26 36 57N 111 29W
Glen Canyon National Recreation Area 66 37 15N 111 0W
Glen Cove 53 40 52N 73 38W
Glen Dean 62 37 39N 86 32W
Glen Elder 38 39 30N 98 18W
Glen Flora 65 29 21N 96 12W
Glen Haven 30 40 27N 105 27W
Glen Lyon 59 41 10N 76 5W
Glen Rock 59 39 48N 76 44W
Glen Rose 65 32 14N 97 45W
Glen Ullin 55 46 49N 101 50W
Glenallen 46 37 19N 90 2W
Glenburn 55 48 31N 101 13W
Glencliff 50 43 58N 71 53W
Glencoe, Ala. 24 33 57N 85 56W
Glencoe, Ky. 63 38 43N 84 49W
Glencoe, Minn. 44 44 46N 94 9W
Glencoe, Okla. 57 36 14N 96 56W
Glendale, Ariz. 26 33 32N 112 11W
Glendale, Calif. 29 34 9N 118 15W
Glendale, Fla. 31 30 52N 86 7W
Glendale, Ky. 63 37 36N 85 54W
Glendale, Oreg. 58 42 44N 123 26W
Glendale, Utah 66 37 19N 112 36W
Glendale L. 59 40 42N 78 32W
Glendevey 30 40 48N 105 56W
Glendive 47 47 7N 104 43W
Glendo 70 42 30N 105 2W
Glendo Reservoir 70 42 29N 104 57W
Glendora, Miss. 45 33 50N 90 18W
Glendora, N.J. 51 39 50N 75 4W
Glenham 61 45 32N 100 16W
Glenmont 56 40 31N 82 6W
Glenmora 39 30 59N 92 35W
Glenn, Calif. 28 39 31N 122 1W
Glenn, Mich. 43 42 31N 86 14W
Glenn County ◇ 28 39 40N 122 20W
Glennallen 25 62 7N 145 33W
Glenns Ferry 34 42 57N 115 18W
Glennville 32 31 56N 81 56W
Glenoma 67 46 31N 122 10W
Glenpool 57 35 58N 96 1W
Glenrock 70 42 52N 105 52W
Glens Falls 53 43 19N 73 39W
Glenside 59 40 6N 75 9W
Glenville, Minn. 44 43 34N 93 17W
Glenville, N.C. 54 35 10N 83 8W
Glenville, Nebr. 48 40 30N 98 15W
Glenville, W. Va. 68 38 56N 80 50W
Glenwood, Ala. 24 31 40N 86 10W
Glenwood, Ark. 27 34 20N 93 33W
Glenwood, Ga. 32 32 11N 82 40W
Glenwood, Hawaii 33 19 29N 155 9W
Glenwood, Ill. 35 41 33N 87 37W
Glenwood, Ind. 36 39 37N 85 18W
Glenwood, Iowa 37 41 3N 95 45W
Glenwood, Minn. 44 45 39N 95 23W
Glenwood, N. Mex. 52 33 19N 108 53W
Glenwood, Oreg. 58 45 39N 123 16W
Glenwood, Utah 66 38 46N 111 59W
Glenwood, Wash. 67 46 1N 121 17W
Glenwood City 69 45 4N 92 10W
Glenwood Springs 30 39 33N 107 19W
Glidden 37 42 4N 94 44W
Glide 58 43 18N 123 6W
Globe 26 33 24N 110 47W
Glorieta 52 35 35N 105 46W
Gloster 45 31 12N 91 1W
Gloucester, Mass. 42 42 37N 70 40W
Gloucester, N.J. 51 39 54N 75 8W
Gloucester, Va. 68 37 25N 76 32W
Gloucester County ◇, N.J. 51 39 40N 75 15W
Gloucester County ◇, Va. 68 37 25N 76 32W
Glover, Mo. 46 37 29N 90 42W
Glover, Vt. 50 44 42N 72 12W
Gloversville 53 43 3N 74 21W
Glynn County ◇ 32 31 10N 81 30W
Gnadenhutten 56 40 22N 81 26W
Gobles 43 42 22N 85 53W
Goddard 38 37 39N 97 34W
Godfrey, Ga. 32 33 27N 83 30W
Godfrey, Ill. 35 38 58N 90 11W
Goehner 48 40 50N 97 13W
Goessel 38 38 15N 97 21W
Goff → 57 36 43N 101 29W
Goffs, Calif. 29 34 55N 115 4W
Goffs, Kans. 38 39 40N 95 56W
Goffstown 50 43 1N 71 36W
Gogebic, L. 43 46 30N 89 35W

Gogebic County ◇ . **43** 46 25N 89 45W
Gogebic Range **69** 46 20N 90 20W
Golconda, Ill. **35** 37 22N 88 29W
Golconda, Nev. **49** 40 58N 117 30W
Gold Beach **58** 42 25N 124 25W
Gold Creek **25** 62 46N 149 41W
Gold Hill **58** 42 26N 123 3W
Gold Point **49** 37 21N 117 22W
Goldcreek **47** 46 35N 112 55W
Golden, Ill. **35** 40 7N 91 1W
Golden, Mo. **46** 36 31N 93 39W
Golden, N. Mex. . . . **52** 35 16N 106 13W
Golden, Okla. **57** 34 2N 94 54W
Golden City **46** 37 24N 94 5W
Golden Gate **35** 38 22N 88 12W
Golden Gate National Recreation Area . **28** 37 49N 122 31W
Golden Meadow . . . **39** 29 24N 90 16W
Golden Valley **55** 47 17N 102 4W
Golden Valley County ◇, Mont. . **47** 46 30N 109 15W
Golden Valley County ◇, N. Dak. **55** 47 0N 103 58W
Goldendale **67** 45 49N 120 50W
Goldfield, Iowa **37** 42 44N 93 55W
Goldfield, Nev. **49** 37 42N 117 14W
Goldonna **39** 32 1N 92 54W
Goldsboro, Md. **41** 39 2N 75 47W
Goldsboro, N.C. . . . **54** 35 23N 77 59W
Goldsby **57** 35 9N 97 28W
Goldsmith **64** 31 59N 102 37W
Goldston **54** 35 36N 79 20W
Goldthwaite **65** 31 27N 98 34W
Goleta **29** 34 27N 119 50W
Goliad **65** 28 40N 97 23W
Goliad County ◇ . . . **65** 28 45N 97 25W
Golovin **25** 64 33N 163 2W
Goltry **57** 36 32N 98 9W
Golva **55** 46 44N 103 59W
Gonvick **44** 47 44N 95 31W
Gonzales, Calif. **28** 36 30N 121 26W
Gonzales, La. **39** 30 14N 90 55W
Gonzales, Tex. **65** 29 30N 97 27W
Gonzales County ◇. **65** 29 26N 97 32W
Goochland **68** 37 41N 77 53W
Goochland County ◇ **68** 37 41N 77 53W
Good Hope **35** 40 33N 90 41W
Good Thunder **44** 44 0N 94 4W
Goodell **37** 42 55N 93 37W
Goodhue **44** 44 24N 92 37W
Goodhue County ◇ **44** 44 25N 92 45W
Gooding **34** 42 56N 114 43W
Gooding County ◇ . **34** 43 0N 115 0W
Goodland, Ind. **36** 40 46N 87 18W
Goodland, Kans. . . . **38** 39 21N 101 43W
Goodlett **65** 34 20N 99 53W
Goodlettsville **62** 36 19N 86 43W
Goodman, Miss. . . . **45** 32 58N 89 55W
Goodman, Mo. **46** 36 44N 94 25W
Goodman, Wis. **69** 45 38N 88 21W
Goodnews Bay **25** 59 7N 161 35W
Goodnight **64** 35 2N 101 11W
Goodrich, Colo. **30** 40 20N 104 7W
Goodrich, N. Dak. . **55** 47 29N 100 8W
Goodrich, Tex. **65** 30 36N 94 57W
Goodridge **44** 48 9N 95 48W
Goodsprings **49** 35 50N 115 26W
Goodwater **24** 33 4N 86 3W
Goodwell **57** 36 36N 101 38W
Goodyear **26** 33 26N 112 21W
Goose → **55** 47 28N 96 52W
Goose Creek **60** 32 59N 80 2W
Goose L. **28** 41 56N 120 26W
Gorda, Punta **28** 40 16N 124 22W
Gordo **24** 33 19N 87 54W
Gordon, Ga. **32** 32 54N 83 20W
Gordon, Nebr. **48** 42 48N 102 12W
Gordon, Ohio **56** 39 56N 84 31W
Gordon, Tex. **65** 32 33N 98 22W
Gordon, Wis. **69** 46 15N 91 48W
Gordon County **32** 34 30N 84 50W
Gordon Cr. → **48** 42 49N 100 40W
Gordonsville **68** 38 9N 78 11W
Gordonville, Mo. . . . **46** 37 19N 89 41W
Gordonville, Tex. . . **65** 33 48N 96 51W
Gore **57** 35 32N 95 7W
Gore Mt. **50** 44 55N 71 48W
Goree **65** 33 28N 99 31W
Goreville **35** 37 33N 88 58W
Gorham, Ill. **35** 37 43N 89 29W
Gorham, Kans. **38** 38 53N 99 1W
Gorham, Maine **40** 43 41N 70 26W
Gorham, N.H. **50** 44 23N 71 10W
Gorin **46** 40 22N 92 1W
Gorman **65** 32 12N 98 41W
Gortner **41** 39 20N 79 24W
Gorum **39** 31 26N 92 56W
Goshen, Calif. **29** 36 21N 119 25W
Goshen, Conn. **42** 41 50N 73 14W
Goshen, Ind. **36** 41 35N 85 50W
Goshen, N.J. **51** 39 8N 74 51W
Goshen, N.Y. **53** 41 24N 74 20W
Goshen, Oreg. **58** 43 58N 123 2W
Goshen, Utah **66** 39 57N 111 54W
Goshen County ◇ . . **70** 42 0N 104 10W
Goshute Indian Reservation **49** 39 50N 114 5W
Goshute L. **49** 40 9N 114 42W
Goshute Mts. **49** 40 15N 114 19W
Goshute Valley **49** 40 45N 114 20W
Gosnell **27** 35 58N 89 58W
Gosper County ◇ . . **48** 40 30N 99 50W
Gosport **36** 39 21N 86 40W
Goss **45** 31 21N 89 53W
Gossville **50** 43 12N 71 22W
Gotebo **57** 35 4N 98 53W
Gotham **69** 43 13N 90 18W
Gothenburg **48** 40 56N 100 10W
Gough **32** 33 6N 82 14W
Gould, Ark. **27** 33 59N 91 34W
Gould, Okla. **57** 34 40N 99 47W
Gould City **43** 46 6N 85 42W
Goulds **31** 25 33N 80 23W
Gouverneur **53** 44 20N 75 28W
Govan **60** 33 13N 81 11W
Gove **38** 38 58N 100 29W
Gove County ◇ **38** 38 50N 100 30W
Gowanda **53** 42 28N 78 56W
Gower **46** 39 37N 94 36W
Gowrie **37** 42 17N 94 17W
Grace **34** 42 35N 111 44W
Gracemont **57** 35 11N 98 16W
Graceville, Fla. **31** 30 58N 85 31W
Graceville, Minn. . . . **44** 45 34N 96 26W
Gracewood **32** 33 22N 82 2W
Gracey **62** 36 53N 87 40W
Grady, Ala. **24** 31 59N 86 3W
Grady, Ark. **27** 34 5N 91 42W
Grady, N. Mex. **52** 34 49N 103 19W
Grady County ◇, Ga. **32** 30 50N 84 15W
Grady County ◇, Okla. **57** 35 0N 97 50W
Gradyville **63** 37 4N 85 25W
Graettinger **37** 43 14N 94 45W
Graford **65** 32 56N 98 14W
Grafton, Ill. **35** 38 58N 90 26W
Grafton, Iowa **37** 43 20N 93 4W
Grafton, Mass. **42** 42 12N 71 41W
Grafton, N. Dak. . . . **55** 48 25N 97 25W
Grafton, N.H. **50** 43 34N 71 57W
Grafton, Ohio **56** 41 16N 82 4W
Grafton, Vt. **50** 43 10N 72 37W
Grafton, W. Va. . . . **68** 39 21N 80 2W
Grafton, Wis. **69** 43 19N 87 57W
Grafton County ◇ . . **50** 43 50N 71 45W
Graham, Ga. **32** 31 50N 82 30W
Graham, N.C. **54** 36 5N 79 25W
Graham, Tex. **65** 33 6N 98 35W
Graham, Mt. **26** 32 42N 109 52W
Graham County ◇, Ariz. **26** 33 0N 110 0W
Graham County ◇, Kans. **38** 39 20N 99 45W
Graham County ◇, N.C. **54** 35 20N 83 50W
Graham L. **40** 44 39N 68 24W
Grainfield **38** 39 7N 100 28W
Grainger County ◇ . **63** 36 17N 83 31W
Grainola **57** 36 57N 96 39W
Grambling **39** 32 32N 92 43W
Gramercy **39** 30 4N 90 42W
Grampian **59** 40 58N 78 37W
Granada, Colo. **30** 38 4N 102 19W
Granada, Minn. **44** 43 42N 94 21W
Granbury **65** 32 27N 97 47W
Granby, Colo. **30** 40 5N 105 56W
Granby, Conn. **42** 41 57N 72 47W
Granby, Mo. **46** 36 55N 94 15W
Granby, L. **30** 40 9N 105 52W
Grand →, Mich. . . **43** 43 4N 86 15W
Grand →, Mo. **46** 39 23N 93 7W
Grand →, S. Dak. . **61** 45 40N 100 45W
Grand Bay **24** 30 29N 88 21W
Grand Blanc **43** 42 56N 83 38W
Grand Cane **39** 32 5N 93 49W
Grand Canyon **26** 36 3N 112 9W
Grand Canyon National Park **26** 36 15N 112 30W
Grand Chenier **39** 29 46N 92 58W
Grand Coulee **67** 47 57N 119 0W
Grand Coulee Dam . **67** 47 57N 118 59W
Grand County ◇, Colo. **30** 40 10N 106 15W
Grand County ◇, Utah **66** 39 0N 109 30W
Grand Forks **55** 47 55N 97 3W
Grand Forks County ◇ **55** 47 55N 97 22W
Grand Haven **43** 43 4N 86 13W
Grand I., La. **39** 29 10N 90 0W
Grand I., Mich. **43** 46 31N 86 40W
Grand Island **48** 40 55N 98 21W
Grand Isle, La. **39** 29 14N 90 0W
Grand Isle, Vt. **50** 44 43N 73 18W
Grand Isle County ◇ **50** 44 57N 73 17W
Grand Junction, Colo. **30** 39 4N 108 33W
Grand Junction, Iowa **37** 42 2N 94 14W
Grand L., La. **39** 29 55N 92 47W
Grand L., Maine . . . **40** 45 40N 67 50W
Grand L., Ohio **56** 40 32N 84 25W
Grand Lake, Colo. . . **30** 40 15N 105 49W
Grand Lake, La. . . . **39** 30 2N 93 17W
Grand Lake Matagamon **40** 46 12N 68 47W
Grand Lake Seboeis **40** 46 18N 68 39W
Grand Ledge **43** 42 45N 84 45W
Grand Manan Channel **40** 44 40N 67 0W
Grand Marais, Mich. **43** 46 40N 85 59W
Grand Marais, Minn. **44** 47 45N 90 20W
Grand Meadow **44** 43 42N 92 34W
Grand Mesa **30** 39 0N 108 15W
Grand Mesa National Forest . . **30** 39 20N 107 50W
Grand Portage **44** 47 58N 89 41W
Grand Portage Indian Reservation **44** 47 55N 89 50W
Grand Prairie **65** 32 47N 97 0W
Grand Rapids, Mich. **43** 42 58N 85 40W
Grand Rapids, Minn. **44** 47 14N 93 31W
Grand Rapids, Ohio **56** 41 25N 83 52W
Grand Ridge, Fla. . . **31** 30 43N 85 1W
Grand Ridge, Ill. . . . **35** 41 14N 88 50W
Grand River **37** 40 49N 93 58W
Grand Rivers **62** 37 1N 88 14W
Grand Ronde **58** 45 4N 123 37W
Grand Rounde → . **67** 46 5N 116 59W
Grand Saline **65** 32 41N 95 43W
Grand Teton Mt. . . . **70** 43 44N 110 48W
Grand Teton National Park **70** 43 50N 110 50W
Grand Tower **35** 37 38N 89 30W
Grand Traverse B. . **43** 45 5N 85 35W
Grand Traverse County ◇ **43** 44 40N 85 35W
Grand Valley **30** 39 27N 108 3W
Grand View **34** 42 59N 116 6W
Grand Wash Cliffs . . **26** 36 0N 113 50W
Grande, Rio → . . . **64** 25 58N 97 9W
Grande de Anasco, Rio → **71** 18 16N 67 11W
Grande de Arecibo, Rio → **71** 18 29N 66 43W
Grande de Loiza, Rio → **71** 18 26N 65 53W
Grande de Manati, Rio → **71** 18 29N 66 32W
Grande Ronde → . **58** 46 5N 116 59W
Grandfalls **64** 31 20N 102 51W
Grandfield **57** 34 14N 98 41W
Grandin, Mo. **46** 36 50N 90 50W
Grandin, N. Dak. . . . **55** 47 14N 97 0W
Grandview, Iowa . . . **37** 41 16N 91 11W
Grandview, Mo. **46** 38 53N 94 32W
Grandview, Tex. . . . **65** 32 16N 97 11W
Grandview, Wash. . . **67** 46 15N 119 54W
Grandville **43** 42 54N 85 46W
Granger, Iowa **37** 41 46N 93 49W
Granger, Tex. **65** 30 43N 97 26W
Granger, Wash. **67** 46 21N 120 11W
Granger, Wyo. **70** 41 35N 109 58W
Grangeville **34** 45 56N 116 7W
Granite, Colo. **30** 39 3N 106 16W
Granite, Okla. **57** 34 58N 99 23W
Granite City **35** 38 42N 90 9W
Granite County ◇ . . **47** 46 25N 113 30W
Granite Falls, Minn. **44** 44 49N 95 33W
Granite Falls, N.C. . **35** 48 81 26W
Granite Falls, Wash. **67** 48 5N 121 58W
Granite Mts., Ariz. . **26** 32 20N 113 20W
Granite Mts., Wyo. . **70** 42 45N 107 40W
Granite Pass **70** 44 38N 107 30W
Granite Peak, Mont. **47** 45 10N 109 48W
Granite Peak, Nev. . **49** 41 40N 117 35W
Granite Pt. **43** 46 47N 87 36W
Granite Quarry **54** 35 37N 80 26W
Granite Range **49** 40 55N 119 25W
Graniteville, S.C. . . . **60** 33 34N 81 49W
Graniteville, Vt. **50** 44 8N 72 29W
Grannis **27** 34 14N 94 20W
Grano **55** 48 37N 101 35W
Grant, Colo. **30** 39 28N 105 40W
Grant, Fla. **31** 27 56N 80 32W
Grant, Iowa **37** 41 9N 94 59W
Grant, La. **39** 30 47N 92 57W
Grant, Mich. **43** 43 20N 85 51W
Grant, Mont. **47** 45 1N 113 4W
Grant, Nebr. **48** 40 50N 101 43W
Grant, Okla. **57** 33 57N 95 31W
Grant, Mt. **49** 38 34N 118 48W
Grant City **46** 40 29N 94 25W
Grant County ◇, Ark. **27** 34 19N 92 24W
Grant County ◇, Ind. **36** 40 30N 85 40W
Grant County ◇, Kans. **38** 37 30N 101 15W
Grant County ◇, Ky. **63** 38 35N 84 35W
Grant County ◇, Minn. **44** 45 55N 96 0W
Grant County ◇, N. Dak. **55** 46 15N 101 30W
Grant County ◇, N. Mex. **52** 33 0N 108 30W
Grant County ◇, Nebr. **48** 41 50N 101 45W
Grant County ◇, Okla. **57** 36 50N 97 45W
Grant County ◇, Oreg. **58** 44 30N 119 0W
Grant County ◇, S. Dak. **61** 45 12N 96 47W
Grant County ◇, W. Va. **68** 39 4N 79 4W
Grant County ◇, Wash. **67** 47 10N 119 30W
Grant County ◇, Wis. **69** 42 50N 90 45W
Grant Parish ◇ **39** 31 32N 92 25W
Grant Park **35** 41 14N 87 39W
Grant Range **49** 38 30N 115 25W
Grantham **50** 43 29N 72 8W
Grants **52** 35 9N 107 52W
Grants Pass **58** 42 26N 123 19W
Grantsburg **69** 45 47N 92 41W
Grantsdale **47** 46 12N 114 9W
Grantsville, Md. **41** 39 42N 79 12W
Grantsville, Utah . . . **66** 40 36N 112 28W
Grantsville, W. Va. . . **68** 38 55N 81 6W
Grantville **32** 33 14N 84 50W
Granville, Ill. **35** 41 16N 89 14W
Granville, Mass. **42** 42 4N 72 52W
Granville, N. Dak. . . **55** 48 16N 100 47W
Granville, N.Y. **53** 43 24N 73 16W
Granville, Ohio **56** 40 4N 82 31W
Granville, Vt. **50** 43 58N 72 51W
Granville County ◇. **54** 36 20N 78 40W
Grapeland **65** 31 30N 95 29W
Grapevine L. **65** 32 58N 97 4W
Grasmere **34** 42 23N 115 53W
Grasonville **41** 38 57N 76 13W
Grass Creek **70** 43 56N 108 39W
Grass Lake **43** 42 15N 84 13W
Grass Valley, Calif. . **28** 39 13N 121 4W
Grass Valley, Oreg. . **58** 45 22N 120 47W
Grassrange **47** 47 2N 108 48W
Grasston **44** 45 48N 93 9W
Grassy Butte **55** 47 24N 103 15W
Gratiot **69** 42 35N 90 1W
Gratiot County ◇ . . **43** 43 15N 84 40W
Gratz **63** 38 28N 84 57W
Gravelly **27** 34 53N 93 41W
Graves County ◇ . . . **62** 36 45N 88 40W
Gravette **27** 36 25N 94 27W
Gravity **37** 40 46N 94 45W
Gravois Mills **46** 38 19N 92 49W
Gray, Ga. **32** 33 1N 83 32W
Gray, Iowa **37** 41 49N 94 59W
Gray, Ky. **63** 36 57N 84 0W
Gray, Okla. **57** 36 34N 100 49W
Gray County ◇, Kans. **38** 37 40N 100 20W
Gray County ◇, Tex. **64** 35 26N 100 48W
Gray Court **60** 34 36N 82 7W
Gray Hawk **63** 37 24N 83 56W
Grayland **67** 46 49N 124 6W
Grayling, Alaska . . . **25** 62 57N 160 3W
Grayling, Mich. **43** 44 40N 84 43W
Grays Harbor **67** 46 59N 124 1W
Grays Harbor County ◇ **67** 47 15N 123 45W
Grays L. **34** 43 4N 111 26W
Grays River **67** 46 21N 123 37W
Grayslake **35** 42 21N 88 2W
Grayson, Ky. **63** 38 20N 82 57W
Grayson, Okla. **57** 35 32N 95 51W
Grayson County ◇, Ky. **62** 37 25N 86 20W
Grayson County ◇, Tex. **65** 33 38N 96 36W
Grayson County ◇, Va. **68** 36 40N 81 10W
Graysville **63** 35 27N 85 8W
Grayton **41** 38 26N 77 13W
Grayville **35** 38 16N 88 0W
Great B. **50** 43 5N 70 53W
Great Barrington . . . **42** 42 12N 73 22W
Great Basin **49** 40 0N 117 0W
Great Bay **51** 39 30N 74 25W
Great Bend, Kans. . . **38** 38 22N 98 46W
Great Bend, N. Dak. **55** 46 9N 96 48W

Great Bend, Pa. **59** 41 58N 75 45W
Great Divide Basin . **70** 42 0N 108 0W
Great Egg Harbor → **51** 39 18N 74 40W
Great Falls, Mont. **47** 47 30N 111 17W
Great Falls, S.C. **60** 34 34N 80 54W
Great L. **54** 34 49N 77 2W
Great Miami → **56** 39 7N 84 49W
Great Mills **41** 38 14N 76 30W
Great Neck **53** 40 48N 73 44W
Great Plains Reservoir **30** 38 15N 102 43W
Great Pond **40** 44 57N 68 19W
Great Pt. **42** 41 24N 70 3W
Great Quitticas Pond **42** 41 48N 70 54W
Great Salt L. **66** 41 15N 112 40W
Great Salt Lake Desert **66** 40 50N 113 30W
Great Salt Plains L. **57** 36 45N 98 8W
Great Sand Dunes National Monument **30** 37 48N 105 45W
Great Sandy Desert. **58** 43 35N 120 15W
Great Sitkin I. **25** 52 3N 176 6W
Great Smoky Mts. **63** 35 40N 83 40W
Great Smoky Mts. Nat. Pk. **63** 35 40N 83 40W
Great South Bay **53** 40 40N 73 15W
Great Wass I. **40** 44 29N 67 36W
Greece **53** 43 13N 77 41W
Greeley, Colo. **30** 40 25N 104 42W
Greeley, Iowa **37** 42 35N 91 21W
Greeley, Kans. **38** 38 22N 95 8W
Greeley, Nebr. **48** 41 33N 98 32W
Greeley County ◇, Kans. **38** 38 30N 101 45W
Greeley County ◇, Nebr. **48** 41 30N 98 30W
Greeleyville **60** 33 40N 79 59W
Green **38** 39 26N 97 0W
Green →, Ill. **35** 41 28N 90 23W
Green →, Ky. **62** 37 54N 87 30W
Green →, Utah **66** 38 11N 109 53W
Green B. **69** 46 0N 87 30W
Green Bank, N.J. **51** 39 40N 74 36W
Green Bank, W. Va. **68** 38 25N 79 50W
Green Bay **69** 44 31N 88 0W
Green Camp **56** 40 32N 83 13W
Green City **46** 40 16N 92 57W
Green County ◇, Ky. **63** 37 15N 85 35W
Green County ◇, Wis. **69** 42 45N 89 40W
Green Cove Springs **31** 29 59N 81 42W
Green Creek **51** 39 3N 74 54W
Green Forest **27** 36 20N 93 26W
Green Island **37** 42 9N 90 20W
Green Isle **44** 44 41N 94 1W
Green L., Minn. **44** 45 15N 94 54W
Green L., Wis. **69** 43 49N 89 0W
Green Lake **69** 43 51N 88 58W
Green Lake County ◇ **69** 43 45N 89 0W
Green Mountain National Forest **50** 44 0N 73 0W
Green Mountain Reservoir **30** 39 53N 106 20W
Green Mts. **50** 43 45N 72 45W
Green Peter L. **58** 44 26N 122 37W
Green Pond **60** 32 44N 80 37W
Green Ridge **46** 38 37N 93 25W
Green River, Utah **66** 38 59N 110 10W
Green River, Wyo. **70** 41 32N 109 28W
Green River L. **63** 37 15N 85 15W
Green Sea **60** 34 8N 78 59W
Green Swamp **54** 34 15N 78 25W
Green Valley, Ariz. **26** 31 52N 110 56W
Green Valley, Ill. **35** 40 24N 89 38W
Greenacres City **31** 26 38N 80 7W
Greenback **63** 35 40N 84 10W
Greenbelt **41** 39 0N 76 53W
Greenbrier, Ark. **27** 35 14N 92 23W
Greenbrier, Tenn. **62** 36 26N 86 48W
Greenbrier → **68** 37 39N 80 53W
Greenbrier County ◇ **68** 37 56N 80 23W
Greenbrier Estates **54** 35 42N 78 38W
Greenbush **44** 48 42N 96 11W
Greencastle, Ind. **36** 39 38N 86 52W
Greencastle, Pa. **59** 39 47N 77 44W
Greendale **36** 39 7N 84 52W
Greene, Iowa **37** 42 54N 92 48W
Greene, Maine **40** 44 12N 70 8W
Greene, N.Y. **53** 42 20N 75 46W
Greene County ◇, Ala. **24** 32 50N 87 53W
Greene County ◇, Ark. **27** 36 3N 90 29W
Greene County ◇, Ga. **32** 33 30N 83 5W
Greene County ◇, Ill. **35** 39 20N 90 20W
Greene County ◇, Ind. **36** 39 0N 87 0W
Greene County ◇, Iowa **37** 42 0N 94 25W
Greene County ◇, Miss. **45** 31 10N 88 45W
Greene County ◇, Mo. **46** 37 15N 93 20W
Greene County ◇, N.C. **54** 35 30N 77 40W
Greene County ◇, N.Y. **53** 42 20N 70 0W
Greene County ◇, Ohio **56** 39 41N 83 56W
Greene County ◇, Pa. **59** 39 55N 80 5W
Greene County ◇, Tenn. **63** 36 10N 82 50W
Greene County ◇, Va. **68** 38 18N 78 26W
Greeneville **63** 36 10N 82 50W
Greenfield, Calif. **29** 36 19N 121 15W
Greenfield, Ill. **35** 39 21N 90 12W
Greenfield, Ind. **36** 39 47N 85 46W
Greenfield, Iowa **37** 41 18N 94 28W
Greenfield, Mass. **42** 42 35N 72 36W
Greenfield, Mo. **46** 37 25N 93 51W
Greenfield, N.H. **50** 42 55N 71 51W
Greenfield, Ohio **56** 39 21N 83 23W
Greenfield, Okla. **57** 35 44N 98 23W
Greenfield, Tenn. **62** 36 9N 88 48W
Greenhills **56** 39 16N 84 32W
Greenland, Mich. **43** 46 47N 89 6W
Greenland, N.H. **50** 43 4N 70 50W
Greenleaf **38** 39 44N 96 59W
Greenlee County ◇. **26** 33 0N 109 15W
Greenough **47** 46 55N 113 25W
Greenport **53** 41 6N 72 22W
Greens Pk. **26** 34 5N 109 33W
Greensboro, Ala. **24** 32 42N 87 36W
Greensboro, Fla. **31** 30 34N 84 45W
Greensboro, Ga. **32** 33 35N 83 11W
Greensboro, Md. **41** 38 58N 75 48W
Greensboro, N.C. **54** 36 4N 79 48W
Greensboro, Vt. **50** 44 36N 72 18W
Greensburg, Ind. **36** 39 20N 85 29W
Greensburg, Kans. **38** 37 36N 99 18W
Greensburg, Ky. **63** 37 16N 85 30W
Greensburg, La. **39** 30 50N 90 40W
Greensburg, Pa. **59** 40 18N 79 33W
Greensville County ◇ **68** 36 42N 77 32W
Greentown **36** 40 29N 85 58W
Greenup, Ill. **35** 39 15N 88 10W
Greenup, Ky. **63** 38 35N 82 50W
Greenup County ◇. **63** 38 30N 83 0W
Greenview **35** 40 5N 89 44W
Greenville, Ala. **24** 31 50N 86 38W
Greenville, Calif. **28** 40 8N 120 57W
Greenville, Fla. **31** 30 28N 83 38W
Greenville, Ga. **32** 33 2N 84 43W
Greenville, Ill. **35** 38 53N 89 25W
Greenville, Ky. **62** 37 12N 87 11W
Greenville, Maine **40** 45 28N 69 35W
Greenville, Mich. **43** 43 11N 85 15W
Greenville, Miss. **45** 33 24N 91 4W
Greenville, Mo. **46** 37 8N 90 27W
Greenville, N.C. **54** 35 37N 77 23W
Greenville, N.H. **50** 42 46N 71 49W
Greenville, Ohio **56** 40 6N 84 38W
Greenville, Pa. **59** 41 24N 80 23W
Greenville, S.C. **60** 34 51N 82 24W
Greenville, Tex. **65** 33 8N 96 7W
Greenville, Wis. **69** 44 18N 88 32W
Greenville County ◇ **60** 34 50N 82 20W
Greenwald **44** 45 36N 94 52W
Greenway **27** 36 21N 90 13W
Greenwich, Conn. **42** 41 2N 73 38W
Greenwich, N.J. **51** 39 24N 75 21W
Greenwich, N.Y. **53** 43 5N 73 30W
Greenwich, Ohio **56** 41 2N 82 31W
Greenwood, Ark. **27** 35 13N 94 16W
Greenwood, Del. **41** 38 49N 75 35W
Greenwood, Fla. **31** 30 52N 85 10W
Greenwood, Ind. **36** 39 37N 86 7W
Greenwood, Ky. **63** 36 53N 84 30W
Greenwood, La. **39** 32 27N 93 58W
Greenwood, Miss. **45** 33 31N 90 11W
Greenwood, Nebr. **48** 40 58N 96 27W
Greenwood, S.C. **60** 34 12N 82 10W
Greenwood, Wis. **69** 44 46N 90 36W
Greenwood County ◇, Kans. **38** 37 45N 96 15W
Greenwood County ◇, S.C. **60** 34 10N 82 5W
Greenwood L. **60** 34 11N 81 54W
Greer, Idaho **34** 46 24N 116 11W
Greer, Mo. **46** 36 46N 91 21W
Greer, S.C. **60** 34 56N 82 14W
Greer County ◇ **57** 35 0N 99 35W
Greers Ferry L. **27** 35 32N 92 10W
Greeson L. **27** 34 9N 93 43W
Gregg County ◇ **65** 32 30N 94 44W
Gregory, Ark. **27** 35 9N 91 21W
Gregory, Mich. **43** 42 28N 84 5W
Gregory, S. Dak. **61** 43 14N 99 26W
Gregory, Tex. **65** 27 56N 97 18W
Gregory County ◇ **61** 43 11N 99 18W
Grenada, Calif. **28** 41 39N 122 31W
Grenada, Miss. **45** 33 47N 89 49W
Grenada County ◇ **45** 33 47N 89 49W
Grenada L. **45** 33 50N 89 47W
Grenola **38** 37 21N 96 27W
Grenora **55** 48 37N 103 56W
Grenville, N. Mex. **52** 36 36N 103 37W
Grenville, S. Dak. **61** 45 28N 97 23W
Gres, Pt. au **43** 43 59N 83 41W
Gresham, Nebr. **48** 41 2N 97 24W
Gresham, Oreg. **58** 45 30N 122 26W
Gresham, S.C. **60** 33 56N 79 25W
Gressitt **68** 37 29N 76 43W
Gresston **32** 32 17N 83 15W
Gretna, Fla. **31** 30 37N 84 40W
Gretna, La. **39** 29 55N 90 4W
Gretna, Nebr. **48** 41 8N 96 15W
Gretna, Va. **68** 36 57N 79 22W
Grey Eagle **44** 45 50N 94 45W
Greybull **70** 44 30N 108 3W
Greybull → **70** 44 28N 108 3W
Greylock, Mt. **42** 42 38N 73 10W
Greystone **30** 40 37N 108 41W
Gridley, Calif. **28** 39 22N 121 42W
Gridley, Ill. **35** 40 45N 88 53W
Gridley, Kans. **38** 38 6N 95 53W
Griffin, Ga. **32** 33 15N 84 16W
Griffin, Ind. **36** 38 12N 87 55W
Griffin, L. **31** 28 52N 81 51W
Griffith **36** 41 34N 87 26W
Griffithsville **68** 38 14N 81 59W
Grifton **54** 35 23N 77 26W
Griggs County ◇ **55** 47 34N 98 21W
Griggsville **35** 39 43N 90 43W
Grimes **37** 41 41N 93 47W
Grimes County ◇ **65** 30 29N 95 59W
Grimesland **54** 35 34N 77 11W
Grimsley **63** 36 16N 84 59W
Grinnell, Iowa **37** 41 45N 92 43W
Grinnell, Kans. **38** 39 6N 100 38W
Griswold **37** 41 14N 95 8W
Groesbeck **65** 30 48N 96 31W
Groom **64** 35 12N 101 6W
Groom L. **49** 37 17N 115 48W
Gros Ventre Range . **70** 43 12N 110 22W
Gross **48** 42 57N 98 34W
Grosse Pointe **43** 42 24N 82 56W
Grosse Tete **39** 30 25N 91 26W
Groton, Conn. **42** 41 21N 72 5W
Groton, Mass. **42** 42 37N 71 34W
Groton, N.Y. **53** 42 36N 76 22W
Groton, S. Dak. **61** 45 27N 98 6W
Groton, Vt. **50** 44 12N 72 12W
Grottoes **68** 38 16N 78 50W
Grouse **34** 43 41N 113 37W
Grouse Creek **66** 41 42N 113 53W
Grouse Creek Mts. . **66** 41 30N 113 50W
Grovania **32** 32 22N 83 40W
Grove **57** 36 36N 94 46W
Grove City, Ohio **56** 39 53N 83 6W
Grove City, Pa. **59** 41 10N 80 5W
Grove Hill **24** 31 42N 87 47W
Grove Place **71** 17 43N 64 49W
Groveland, Calif. **28** 37 50N 120 14W
Groveland, Fla. **31** 28 34N 81 51W
Groveland, Mass. **42** 42 46N 71 2W
Groveport **56** 39 51N 82 53W
Grover, Colo. **30** 40 52N 104 14W
Grover, S.C. **60** 33 6N 80 36W
Grover, Utah **66** 38 14N 111 21W
Grover City **29** 35 7N 120 37W
Grover Hill **56** 41 1N 84 29W
Groves **65** 29 57N 93 54W
Grovespring **46** 37 24N 92 37W
Groveton, N.H. **50** 44 36N 71 31W
Groveton, Tex. **65** 31 4N 95 8W
Grovetown **32** 33 27N 82 12W
Growler Mts. **26** 32 15N 113 0W
Growler Wash → **26** 32 40N 113 30W
Grulla **64** 26 16N 98 39W
Grundy **68** 37 17N 82 6W
Grundy Center **37** 42 22N 92 47W
Grundy County ◇, Ill. **35** 41 20N 88 25W
Grundy County ◇, Iowa **37** 42 25N 92 45W
Grundy County ◇, Mo. **46** 40 5N 93 30W
Grundy County ◇, Tenn. **63** 35 26N 85 44W
Gruver, Iowa **37** 43 24N 94 42W
Gruver, Tex. **64** 36 16N 101 24W
Grygla **44** 48 18N 95 37W
Gu Achi **26** 32 20N 112 2W
Guadalupe **26** 33 25N 111 55W
Guadalupe → **65** 28 27N 96 47W
Guadalupe County ◇, N. Mex. **52** 35 0N 104 45W
Guadalupe County ◇, Tex. **65** 29 34N 97 58W
Guadalupe Mts. **52** 32 15N 105 0W
Guadalupe Mts. Nat. Pk. **64** 32 0N 104 30W
Guadalupe Peak **64** 31 50N 104 52W
Guadalupita **52** 36 8N 105 14W
Guajataca, Lago de . **71** 18 24N 66 56W
Gualala **28** 38 46N 123 32W
Guanajibo, Punta **71** 18 10N 67 11W
Guanica **71** 17 59N 66 55W
Guanica, Laguna de **71** 17 58N 66 0W
Guano L. **58** 42 11N 119 32W
Guayama **71** 17 59N 66 7W
Guayama ◇ **71** 18 10N 66 15W
Guayanilla **71** 18 1N 66 47W
Guayanilla, Bahia de **71** 17 55N 66 50W
Guaynabo **71** 18 22N 66 7W
Guerneville **28** 38 30N 123 0W
Guernsey, Iowa **37** 41 39N 92 21W
Guernsey, Wyo. **70** 42 16N 104 45W
Guernsey County ◇ **56** 40 2N 81 35W
Guernsey Reservoir . **70** 42 17N 104 46W
Guerra **64** 26 53N 98 54W
Gueydan **39** 30 2N 92 31W
Guffey **30** 38 45N 105 31W
Guffy Peak **70** 43 29N 107 54W
Guide Rock **48** 40 4N 98 20W
Guilarte, Monte **71** 18 9N 66 46W
Guildhall **50** 44 34N 71 34W
Guilford, Conn. **42** 41 17N 72 41W
Guilford, Maine **40** 45 10N 69 23W
Guilford County ◇ . **54** 36 10N 79 45W
Guin **24** 33 58N 87 55W
Guinda **28** 38 50N 122 12W
Guion **27** 35 56N 91 57W
Gulf Breeze **31** 30 22N 87 9W
Gulf County ◇ **31** 29 50N 85 15W
Gulf Hammock **31** 29 15N 82 43W
Gulf Islands National Seashore **31** 30 10N 87 10W
Gulf Shores **24** 30 17N 87 41W
Gulfport, Fla. **31** 27 44N 82 43W
Gulfport, Miss. **45** 30 22N 89 6W
Gulkana **25** 62 16N 145 23W
Gull L. **44** 46 25N 94 21W
Gullivan B. **31** 25 45N 81 40W
Gumboro **41** 38 28N 75 22W
Gun L. **43** 42 36N 85 31W
Gunnison, Colo. **30** 38 33N 106 56W
Gunnison, Miss. **45** 33 57N 90 57W
Gunnison, Utah **66** 39 9N 111 49W
Gunnison → **30** 39 4N 108 35W
Gunnison County ◇ **30** 38 40N 107 0W
Gunnison National Forest **30** 38 30N 107 0W
Gunnison Peak **30** 38 49N 107 23W
Gunpowder → **41** 39 20N 76 20W
Guntersville **24** 34 21N 86 18W
Guntersville L. **24** 34 25N 86 23W
Guntown **45** 34 27N 88 40W
Gurabo **71** 18 16N 65 58W
Gurdon **27** 33 55N 93 9W
Gurley **48** 41 19N 102 58W
Gurnee **35** 42 22N 87 55W
Gurnet Point **42** 42 1N 70 34W
Gustavus **25** 58 25N 135 44W
Gustine, Calif. **28** 37 16N 121 0W
Gustine, Tex. **65** 31 51N 98 24W
Guthrie, Ky. **62** 36 39N 87 10W
Guthrie, Okla. **57** 35 53N 97 25W
Guthrie, Tex. **64** 33 37N 100 19W
Guthrie Center **37** 41 41N 94 30W
Guthrie County ◇ . **37** 41 40N 94 30W
Guttenberg **37** 42 47N 91 6W
Guyandotte → **68** 38 25N 82 25W
Guyanes → **71** 18 6N 65 50W
Guymon **57** 36 41N 101 29W
Guyton **32** 32 20N 81 24W
Gwinn **43** 46 19N 87 27W
Gwinner **55** 46 14N 97 40W
Gwinnett County ◇ . **32** 34 0N 84 0W
Gypsum, Colo. **30** 39 39N 106 57W
Gypsum, Kans. **38** 38 42N 97 26W

H

Haakon County ◇ **61** 44 25N 101 35W
Habersham **32** 34 36N 83 34W
Habersham County ◇ **32** 34 40N 83 30W
Hachita **52** 31 55N 108 19W
Hackberry, Ariz. **26** 35 22N 113 44W
Hackberry, La. **39** 30 0N 93 17W
Hackensack, Minn. **44** 46 56N 94 31W
Hackensack, N.J. **51** 40 53N 74 3W
Hackett **27** 35 11N 94 25W
Hackettstown **51** 40 51N 74 50W
Hackleburg **24** 34 17N 87 50W
Haddam **38** 39 52N 97 18W
Haddock **32** 33 2N 83 26W
Hadlock **67** 48 2N 122 45W
Hadlyme **42** 41 25N 72 25W
Haena **33** 22 14N 159 34W

Hagemeister I. **25** 58 39N 160 54W
Hagerhill **63** 37 42N 82 48W
Hagerman, Idaho **34** 42 49N 114 54W
Hagerman, N. Mex. **52** 33 7N 104 20W
Hagerstown, Ind. **36** 39 55N 85 10W
Hagerstown, Md. **41** 39 39N 77 43W
Hague, N. Dak. **55** 46 2N 99 59W
Hague, N.Y. **53** 43 45N 73 30W
Hahira **32** 30 59N 83 22W
Hahnville **39** 29 59N 90 25W
Haig **48** 41 53N 103 45W
Haigler **48** 40 1N 101 56W
Hailey **34** 43 31N 114 19W
Haines, Alaska **25** 59 14N 135 26W
Haines, Oreg. **58** 44 55N 117 56W
Haines ◇ **25** 57 0N 135 30W
Haines City **31** 28 7N 81 38W
Hainesport **51** 39 59N 74 50W
Haiwee Reservoir **29** 36 8N 117 57W
Halalii L. **33** 21 52N 160 11W
Halawa, C. **33** 21 10N 156 43W
Halawa Heights **33** 21 23N 157 55W
Halbur **37** 42 0N 94 59W
Haldeman **63** 38 15N 83 19W
Hale, Colo. **30** 39 38N 102 9W
Hale, Mo. **46** 39 36N 93 20W
Hale Center **64** 34 4N 101 51W
Hale County ◇, Ala. **24** 32 42N 87 36W
Hale County ◇, Tex. **64** 34 0N 101 55W
Haleakala Crater **33** 20 43N 156 16W
Haleakala National Park **33** 20 40N 156 15W
Haleiwa **33** 21 36N 158 6W
Halethorpe **41** 39 15N 76 42W
Haley **55** 45 58N 103 7W
Haleyville, Ala. **24** 34 14N 87 37W
Haleyville, N.J. **51** 39 17N 75 2W
Half Way **46** 37 37N 93 15W
Halfmoon Landing **32** 31 42N 81 16W
Halfway **41** 39 37N 77 46W
Halifax, Mass. **42** 41 59N 70 52W
Halifax, N.C. **54** 36 20N 77 35W
Halifax, Va. **68** 36 46N 78 56W
Halifax County ◇, N.C. **54** 36 15N 77 40W
Halifax County ◇, Va. **68** 36 55N 79 0W
Halkett, C. **25** 70 48N 152 11W
Hall **47** 46 35N 113 12W
Hall County ◇, Ga. **32** 34 15N 83 50W
Hall County ◇, Nebr. **48** 40 45N 98 30W
Hall County ◇, Tex. **64** 34 30N 100 35W
Hall I. **25** 60 40N 173 6W
Hall Summit **39** 32 11N 93 18W
Hallam **48** 40 32N 96 47W
Hallandale **31** 25 59N 80 8W
Halleck **49** 40 57N 115 27W
Hallett **57** 36 19N 96 35W
Hallettsville **65** 29 27N 96 57W
Halley **27** 33 32N 91 20W
Halliday **55** 47 21N 102 20W
Halligan Reservoir **30** 40 53N 105 20W
Hallock **44** 48 47N 96 57W
Halls, Ga. **32** 34 18N 84 56W
Halls, Tenn. **62** 35 53N 89 24W
Halls Summit **38** 38 21N 95 41W
Hallstead **59** 41 58N 75 45W
Hallsville, Mo. **46** 39 7N 92 13W
Hallsville, Tex. **65** 32 30N 94 35W
Halltown **46** 37 12N 93 38W
Hallwood **68** 37 53N 75 36W
Halma **44** 48 40N 96 36W
Halsey, Nebr. **48** 41 54N 100 16W
Halsey, Oreg. **58** 44 23N 123 7W
Halstad **44** 47 21N 96 50W
Halstead **38** 38 0N 97 31W
Haltom City **65** 32 48N 97 16W
Hamberg **55** 47 46N 99 31W
Hamblen County ◇ **63** 36 13N 83 18W
Hambleton **68** 39 5N 79 39W
Hamburg, Ark. **27** 33 14N 91 48W
Hamburg, Calif. **28** 41 47N 123 4W
Hamburg, Conn. **42** 41 23N 72 21W
Hamburg, Ill. **35** 39 14N 90 43W
Hamburg, Iowa **37** 40 36N 95 39W
Hamburg, Minn. **44** 44 44N 93 58W
Hamburg, Miss. **45** 31 35N 91 4W
Hamburg, N.J. **51** 41 9N 74 35W
Hamburg, N.Y. **53** 42 43N 78 50W
Hamburg, Pa. **59** 40 33N 75 59W
Hamden **42** 41 23N 72 54W
Hamer **34** 43 56N 112 12W
Hamersville **56** 38 55N 83 59W
Hamilton, Ala. **24** 34 9N 87 59W
Hamilton, Alaska **25** 62 54N 163 53W
Hamilton, Colo. **30** 40 22N 107 37W
Hamilton, Ga. **32** 32 45N 84 53W
Hamilton, Ill. **35** 40 24N 91 21W
Hamilton, Kans. **38** 37 59N 96 10W
Hamilton, Mich. **43** 42 41N 86 0W
Hamilton, Mo. **46** 39 45N 94 0W
Hamilton, Mont. **47** 46 15N 114 10W
Hamilton, N.C. **54** 35 57N 77 12W
Hamilton, N. Dak. **55** 48 48N 97 24W
Hamilton, N.Y. **53** 42 50N 75 33W
Hamilton, Ohio **56** 39 24N 84 34W
Hamilton, Oreg. **58** 44 44N 119 18W
Hamilton, Tex. **65** 31 42N 98 7W
Hamilton, L. **27** 34 26N 93 2W
Hamilton City **28** 39 45N 122 1W
Hamilton County ◇, Fla. **31** 30 30N 83 0W
Hamilton County ◇, Ill. **35** 38 5N 88 30W
Hamilton County ◇, Ind. **36** 40 5N 86 5W
Hamilton County ◇, Iowa **37** 42 20N 93 40W
Hamilton County ◇, Kans. **38** 38 0N 101 45W
Hamilton County ◇, N.Y. **53** 43 30N 74 30W
Hamilton County ◇, Nebr. **48** 40 45N 98 0W
Hamilton County ◇, Ohio **56** 39 13N 84 33W
Hamilton County ◇, Tenn. **63** 35 17N 85 10W
Hamilton County ◇, Tex. **65** 31 40N 98 8W
Hamilton Dome **70** 43 46N 108 35W
Hamler **56** 41 14N 84 2W
Hamlet, Ind. **36** 41 23N 86 35W
Hamlet, N.C. **54** 34 53N 79 42W
Hamlet, Nebr. **48** 40 23N 101 14W
Hamlin, Tex. **64** 32 53N 100 8W
Hamlin, W. Va. **68** 38 17N 82 6W
Hamlin County ◇ **61** 44 40N 97 13W
Hamlin L. **43** 44 3N 86 28W
Hammon **57** 35 38N 99 23W
Hammond, Ill. **35** 39 48N 88 36W
Hammond, Ind. **36** 41 38N 87 30W
Hammond, La. **39** 30 30N 90 28W
Hammond, Minn. **44** 44 13N 92 23W
Hammond, N.Y. **53** 44 27N 75 42W
Hammond, Oreg. **58** 46 12N 123 57W
Hammondsport **53** 42 25N 77 13W
Hammonton **51** 39 39N 74 48W
Hampden, Maine **40** 44 44N 68 51W
Hampden, N. Dak. **55** 48 32N 98 40W
Hampden County ◇ **42** 42 10N 72 35W
Hampden Sydney **68** 37 14N 78 28W
Hampshire, Ill. **35** 42 6N 88 32W
Hampshire, Tenn. **62** 35 36N 87 18W
Hampshire County ◇, Mass. **42** 42 15N 72 35W
Hampshire County ◇, W. Va. **68** 39 18N 78 38W
Hampstead, Md. **41** 39 37N 76 51W
Hampstead, N.C. **54** 34 22N 77 44W
Hampstead, N.H. **50** 42 51N 71 10W
Hampton, Ark. **27** 33 32N 92 28W
Hampton, Conn. **42** 41 47N 72 3W
Hampton, Fla. **31** 29 52N 82 8W
Hampton, Ga. **32** 33 23N 84 17W
Hampton, Iowa **37** 42 45N 93 13W
Hampton, Minn. **44** 44 37N 93 0W
Hampton, N.H. **50** 42 57N 70 50W
Hampton, N.J. **51** 40 42N 74 58W
Hampton, Nebr. **48** 40 53N 97 53W
Hampton, Oreg. **58** 43 40N 120 14W
Hampton, S.C. **60** 32 52N 81 7W
Hampton, Tenn. **63** 36 17N 82 10W
Hampton, Va. **68** 37 2N 76 21W
Hampton Bays **53** 40 53N 72 30W
Hampton County ◇ **60** 32 50N 81 10W
Hampton Springs **31** 30 5N 83 40W
Hams → **70** 41 35N 109 57W
Hams Bluff **71** 17 46N 64 52W
Hana **33** 20 45N 155 59W
Hanaford **35** 37 57N 88 50W
Hanahan **60** 32 55N 80 0W
Hanalei **33** 22 12N 159 30W
Hanamaulu **33** 21 59N 159 22W
Hanapepe **33** 21 55N 159 35W
Hanauma B. **33** 21 15N 157 40W
Hanceville **24** 34 4N 86 46W
Hancock, Iowa **37** 41 24N 95 21W
Hancock, Md. **41** 39 42N 78 11W
Hancock, Mich. **43** 47 8N 88 35W
Hancock, Minn. **44** 45 30N 95 48W
Hancock, N.H. **50** 42 57N 71 58W
Hancock, N.Y. **53** 41 57N 75 17W
Hancock, Vt. **50** 43 56N 72 51W
Hancock, Wis. **69** 44 8N 89 31W
Hancock, Mt. **70** 44 9N 110 25W
Hancock County ◇, Ga. **32** 33 20N 83 0W
Hancock County ◇, Ill. **35** 40 25N 91 10W
Hancock County ◇, Ind. **36** 39 50N 85 45W
Hancock County ◇, Iowa **37** 43 5N 93 45W
Hancock County ◇, Ky. **62** 37 50N 86 45W
Hancock County ◇, Maine **40** 44 30N 68 30W
Hancock County ◇, Miss. **45** 30 17N 89 23W
Hancock County ◇, Ohio **56** 41 2N 83 39W
Hancock County ◇, Tenn. **63** 36 32N 83 13W
Hancock County ◇, W. Va. **68** 40 30N 80 35W
Hancocks Bridge **51** 39 31N 75 28W
Hand County ◇ **61** 44 31N 98 59W
Hanford, Calif. **29** 36 20N 119 39W
Hanford, Wash. **67** 46 37N 119 19W
Hankinson **55** 46 4N 96 54W
Hanksville **66** 38 22N 110 43W
Hanley Falls **44** 44 42N 95 37W
Hanna, Ind. **36** 41 25N 86 47W
Hanna, La. **39** 31 58N 93 21W
Hanna, Okla. **57** 35 12N 95 53W
Hanna, Utah **66** 40 26N 110 48W
Hanna, Wyo. **70** 41 52N 106 34W
Hanna City **35** 40 42N 89 48W
Hannaford **55** 47 19N 98 11W
Hannah **55** 48 58N 98 42W
Hannibal, Mo. **46** 39 42N 91 22W
Hannibal, N.Y. **53** 43 19N 76 35W
Hannover **55** 47 7N 101 26W
Hanover, Ill. **35** 42 15N 90 17W
Hanover, Ind. **36** 38 43N 85 28W
Hanover, Kans. **38** 39 54N 96 53W
Hanover, Mass. **42** 42 7N 70 49W
Hanover, Mich. **43** 42 6N 84 33W
Hanover, Minn. **44** 45 10N 93 40W
Hanover, Mont. **47** 47 7N 109 33W
Hanover, N.H. **50** 43 42N 72 17W
Hanover, N. Mex. **52** 32 48N 108 6W
Hanover, Ohio **56** 40 4N 82 16W
Hanover, Pa. **59** 39 48N 76 59W
Hanover, Va. **68** 37 46N 77 22W
Hanover County ◇ **68** 37 46N 77 29W
Hanoverton **56** 40 45N 80 56W
Hans Lollik I. **71** 18 24N 64 53W
Hansboro **55** 48 57N 99 23W
Hansen **34** 42 32N 114 18W
Hansford County ◇ **64** 36 10N 101 30W
Hanska **44** 44 9N 94 30W
Hanson, Fla. **31** 30 34N 83 21W
Hanson, Ky. **62** 37 25N 87 29W
Hanson County ◇ **61** 43 39N 97 47W
Hanston **38** 38 7N 99 43W
Hapeville **32** 33 40N 84 25W
Happy **64** 34 45N 101 52W
Happy Camp **28** 41 48N 123 23W
Happy Jack **26** 34 45N 111 24W
Harahan **39** 29 56N 90 11W
Haralson **32** 33 14N 84 34W
Haralson County ◇ **32** 33 45N 85 10W
Harbeson **41** 38 43N 75 17W
Harbor Beach **43** 43 51N 82 39W
Harbor Springs **43** 45 26N 85 0W
Harcourt **37** 42 16N 94 11W
Harcuvar Mts. **26** 34 0N 113 30W
Hardee County ◇ **31** 27 30N 81 45W
Hardeeville **60** 32 17N 81 5W
Hardeman County ◇, Tenn. **62** 35 6N 89 0W
Hardeman County ◇, Tex. **65** 34 20N 99 50W
Hardesty **57** 36 37N 101 12W
Hardin, Ill. **35** 39 10N 90 37W
Hardin, Ky. **62** 36 46N 88 18W
Hardin, Mo. **46** 39 16N 93 50W
Hardin, Mont. **47** 45 44N 107 37W
Hardin, Tex. **65** 30 9N 94 44W
Hardin County ◇, Ill. **35** 37 30N 88 15W
Hardin County ◇, Iowa **37** 42 25N 93 15W
Hardin County ◇, Ky. **62** 37 40N 86 0W
Hardin County ◇, Ohio **56** 40 42N 83 47W
Hardin County ◇, Tenn. **62** 35 14N 88 15W
Hardin County ◇, Tex. **65** 30 22N 94 19W
Harding **44** 46 7N 94 2W
Harding, L. **24** 32 40N 85 5W
Harding County ◇, N. Mex. **52** 36 0N 104 0W
Harding County ◇, S. Dak. **61** 45 30N 103 30W
Hardinsburg, Ind. **36** 38 28N 86 17W
Hardinsburg, Ky. **62** 37 47N 86 28W
Hardman **58** 45 10N 119 41W
Hardtner **38** 37 1N 98 39W
Hardwick, Ga. **32** 33 4N 83 14W
Hardwick, Mass. **42** 42 21N 72 12W
Hardwick, Minn. **44** 43 47N 96 12W
Hardwick, Vt. **50** 44 30N 72 22W
Hardy, Ark. **27** 36 19N 91 29W
Hardy, Mont. **47** 47 12N 111 47W
Hardy, Nebr. **48** 40 1N 97 56W
Hardy County ◇ **68** 39 0N 78 50W
Hardy Dam Pond **43** 43 30N 85 37W
Harford County ◇ **41** 39 35N 76 25W
Hargill **64** 26 27N 98 1W
Harker Heights **65** 31 5N 97 40W
Harkers Island **54** 34 42N 76 34W
Harlan, Iowa **37** 41 39N 95 19W
Harlan, Kans. **38** 39 36N 98 46W
Harlan, Ky. **63** 36 51N 83 19W
Harlan County ◇, Ky. **63** 36 50N 83 15W
Harlan County ◇, Nebr. **48** 40 15N 99 30W
Harlan County Lake **48** 40 4N 99 13W
Harlem, Ga. **32** 33 25N 82 19W
Harlem, Mont. **47** 48 32N 108 47W
Harleyville **60** 33 13N 80 27W
Harlingen **64** 26 12N 97 42W
Harlowton **47** 46 26N 109 50W
Harman **68** 38 55N 79 32W
Harmon **35** 41 43N 89 33W
Harmon County ◇ **57** 34 45N 99 50W
Harmony, Ind. **36** 39 32N 87 4W
Harmony, Maine **40** 44 58N 69 33W
Harmony, Md. **41** 38 47N 75 53W
Harmony, Minn. **44** 43 33N 92 1W
Harmony, N.C. **54** 35 58N 80 46W
Harnett County ◇ **54** 35 20N 78 50W
Harney **41** 39 44N 77 13W
Harney, L. **31** 28 45N 81 3W
Harney Basin **58** 43 0N 119 30W
Harney County ◇ **58** 45 0N 119 0W
Harney L. **58** 43 14N 119 8W
Harney Peak **61** 43 52N 103 32W
Harold, Fla. **31** 30 40N 86 53W
Harold, Ky. **63** 37 32N 82 38W
Harper, Iowa **37** 41 22N 92 3W
Harper, Kans. **38** 37 17N 98 1W
Harper, Oreg. **58** 43 52N 117 37W
Harper, Tex. **65** 30 18N 99 15W
Harper, Mt. **25** 64 14N 143 51W
Harper County ◇, Kans. **38** 37 15N 98 0W
Harper County ◇, Okla. **57** 36 50N 99 40W
Harper L. **29** 35 2N 117 17W
Harpers Ferry, Iowa **37** 43 12N 91 9W
Harpers Ferry, W. Va. **68** 39 20N 77 44W
Harpersville **24** 33 21N 86 26W
Harpeth → **62** 36 18N 87 10W
Harquahala Mts. **26** 33 45N 113 20W
Harrah, Okla. **57** 35 29N 97 10W
Harrah, Wash. **67** 46 24N 120 33W
Harrell **27** 33 31N 92 24W
Harrellsville **54** 36 18N 76 48W
Harriman **63** 35 56N 84 33W
Harriman Reservoir **50** 42 48N 72 55W
Harrington, Del. **41** 38 56N 75 35W
Harrington, Maine **40** 44 37N 67 49W
Harrington, Wash. **67** 47 29N 118 15W
Harris, Kans. **38** 38 19N 95 26W
Harris, Minn. **44** 45 35N 92 58W
Harris, Mo. **46** 40 18N 93 21W
Harris, Okla. **57** 33 45N 94 44W
Harris, L. **31** 28 47N 81 49W
Harris County ◇, Ga. **32** 32 40N 84 50W
Harris County ◇, Tex. **65** 29 46N 95 22W
Harrisburg, Ark. **27** 35 34N 90 43W
Harrisburg, Ill. **35** 37 44N 88 32W
Harrisburg, Mo. **46** 39 9N 92 28W
Harrisburg, N.C. **54** 35 19N 80 39W
Harrisburg, Nebr. **48** 41 33N 103 44W
Harrisburg, Oreg. **58** 44 16N 123 10W
Harrisburg, Pa. **59** 40 16N 76 53W
Harrisburg, S. Dak. **61** 43 26N 96 42W
Harrison, Ark. **27** 36 14N 93 7W
Harrison, Ga. **32** 32 50N 82 43W
Harrison, Idaho **34** 47 27N 116 47W
Harrison, Mich. **43** 44 1N 84 48W
Harrison, Mont. **47** 45 42N 111 47W
Harrison, Nebr. **48** 42 41N 103 53W
Harrison Bay **25** 70 40N 151 0W
Harrison County ◇, Ind. **36** 38 10N 86 10W
Harrison County ◇, Iowa **37** 41 40N 95 50W
Harrison County ◇, Ky. **63** 38 25N 84 20W
Harrison County ◇, Miss. **45** 30 30N 89 7W
Harrison County ◇, Mo. **46** 40 20N 94 0W
Harrison County ◇, Ohio **56** 40 18N 81 11W
Harrison County ◇, Tex. **65** 32 33N 94 23W
Harrison County ◇, W. Va. **68** 39 17N 80 30W
Harrisonburg, La. **39** 31 46N 91 49W

Harrisonburg, Va. . . 68 38 27N 78 52W
Harrisonville 46 38 39N 94 21W
Harriston 45 31 44N 91 2W
Harrisville, Mich. . . . 43 44 39N 83 17W
Harrisville, N.Y. . . . 53 44 9N 75 19W
Harrisville, R.I. 42 41 58N 71 41W
Harrisville, W. Va. . 68 39 13N 81 3W
Harrod 56 40 43N 83 56W
Harrodsburg 63 37 46N 84 51W
Harrogate 63 36 35N 83 40W
Harrold 61 44 31N 99 44W
Harry S. Truman
Reservoir 46 38 16N 93 24W
Harry Strunk L. 48 40 23N 100 13W
Hart, Mich. 43 43 42N 86 22W
Hart, Tex. 64 34 23N 102 7W
Hart County ◇, Ga. 32 34 15N 83 0W
Hart County ◇, Ky. 63 37 20N 85 50W
Hart L. 58 42 25N 119 51W
Hart Mt. 58 42 23N 119 53W
Hartfield 68 37 33N 76 27W
Hartford, Ala. 24 31 6N 85 42W
Hartford, Ark. 27 35 1N 94 23W
Hartford, Conn. 42 41 46N 72 41W
Hartford, Ga. 32 32 17N 83 28W
Hartford, Iowa 37 41 28N 93 24W
Hartford, Ky. 62 37 27N 86 55W
Hartford, Mich. 43 42 13N 86 10W
Hartford, S. Dak. . . 61 43 38N 96 57W
Hartford, Tenn. 63 35 49N 83 9W
Hartford, Wis. 69 43 19N 88 22W
Hartford City 36 40 27N 85 22W
Hartford County ◇ . 42 41 45N 72 45W
Hartington 48 42 37N 97 16W
Hartland, Maine 40 44 53N 69 27W
Hartland, Minn. 44 43 48N 93 29W
Hartland, Vt. 50 43 32N 72 24W
Hartland, Wis. 69 43 6N 88 21W
Hartley, Iowa 37 43 11N 95 29W
Hartley, Tex. 64 35 53N 102 24W
Hartley County ◇ . . 64 35 50N 102 30W
Hartline 67 47 41N 119 6W
Hartly 41 39 10N 75 43W
Hartman 30 38 7N 102 13W
Hartsburg 46 38 42N 92 19W
Hartsel 30 39 1N 105 48W
Hartselle 24 34 27N 86 56W
Hartshorne 57 34 51N 95 34W
Hartsville, S.C. 60 34 23N 80 4W
Hartsville, Tenn. . . . 62 36 24N 86 10W
Hartville, Mo. 46 37 15N 92 31W
Hartville, Ohio 56 40 58N 81 20W
Hartville, Wyo. 70 42 20N 104 44W
Hartwell 32 34 21N 82 56W
Hartwell L. 60 34 21N 82 49W
Hartwick 37 41 47N 92 21W
Harvard, Idaho 34 46 55N 116 44W
Harvard, Ill. 35 42 25N 88 37W
Harvard, Nebr. 48 40 37N 98 6W
Harvard, Mt. 30 38 56N 106 19W
Harvey, Ark. 27 34 51N 93 47W
Harvey, Ill. 35 41 36N 87 50W
Harvey, N. Dak. 55 47 47N 99 56W
Harvey Cedars 51 39 43N 74 11W
Harvey County ◇ . . 38 38 0N 97 30W
Harveyville 38 38 47N 95 58W
Harwich 42 41 41N 70 5W
Harwinton 42 41 46N 73 4W
Harwood, Mo. 46 37 57N 94 9W
Harwood, Tex. 65 29 40N 97 30W
Haskell, Ark. 27 34 30N 92 38W
Haskell, Okla. 57 35 50N 95 40W
Haskell, Tex. 65 33 10N 99 44W
Haskell County ◇,
Kans. 38 37 30N 100 45W
Haskell County ◇,
Okla. 57 35 10N 95 10W
Haskell County ◇,
Tex. 65 33 12N 99 45W
Haskins 56 41 28N 83 42W
Haslet 65 32 59N 97 21W
Hassayampa → 26 33 19N 112 42W
Hastings, Fla. 31 29 43N 81 31W
Hastings, Iowa 37 41 1N 95 30W
Hastings, Mich. 43 42 39N 85 17W
Hastings, Minn. 44 44 44N 92 51W
Hastings, Nebr. 48 40 35N 98 23W
Hastings, Okla. 57 34 14N 98 7W
Hasty 30 38 7N 102 58W
Haswell 30 38 27N 103 10W
Hatch, N. Mex. 52 32 40N 107 9W
Hatch, Utah 66 37 39N 112 26W
Hatchie → 62 35 35N 89 53W
Hatchineha, L. 31 28 2N 81 25W
Hatfield, Ark. 27 34 29N 94 23W
Hatfield, Ind. 36 37 54N 87 14W
Hatfield, Mass. 42 42 22N 72 36W
Hatfield, Minn. 44 43 58N 96 12W
Hatfield, Pa. 59 40 17N 75 18W
Hatillo 71 18 29N 66 50W
Hatteras 54 35 13N 75 42W
Hatteras, C. 54 35 14N 75 32W
Hatteras I. 54 35 30N 75 28W
Hattiesburg 45 31 20N 89 17W
Hatton, Ala. 24 34 34N 87 25W
Hatton, N. Dak. . . . 55 47 38N 97 27W
Hatton, Wash. 67 46 47N 118 50W
Haubstadt 36 38 12N 87 34W
Haugan 47 47 23N 115 24W
Haugen 69 45 37N 91 46W
Hauppauge 53 40 50N 73 12W
Hauser 58 43 30N 124 13W
Haut, I. au 40 44 3N 68 38W
Hauula 33 21 37N 157 55W
Havana, Ark. 27 35 7N 93 32W
Havana, Fla. 31 30 37N 84 25W
Havana, Ill. 35 40 18N 90 4W
Havana, Kans. 38 37 6N 95 57W
Havana, N. Dak. . . . 55 45 57N 97 37W
Havasu Cr. → 26 36 19N 112 46W
Havasu L. 26 34 18N 114 8W
Havasupai Indian
Reservation 26 36 15N 112 35W
Havelock, N.C. 54 34 53N 76 54W
Havelock, N. Dak. . 55 46 29N 102 45W
Haven 38 37 54N 97 47W
Havensville 38 39 31N 96 5W
Haverhill, Fla. 31 26 42N 80 7W
Haverhill, Mass. 42 42 47N 71 5W
Haverhill, N.H. 50 44 3N 72 4W
Havertown 59 39 58N 75 18W
Haviland 38 37 37N 99 6W
Havre 47 48 33N 109 41W
Havre de Grace 41 39 33N 76 6W
Haw → 54 35 36N 79 3W
Haw Knob 54 35 19N 84 2W
Hawaii 33 19 30N 155 30W
Hawaii □ 33 20 0N 157 45W
Hawaii County ◇ . . . 33 19 30N 155 30W
Hawaii Volcanoes
National Park 33 19 23N 155 17W
Hawarden 37 43 0N 96 29W
Hawesville 62 37 54N 86 45W
Hawi 33 20 14N 155 50W
Hawk Point 46 38 58N 91 8W
Hawk Springs 70 41 47N 104 16W
Hawkeye 37 42 56N 91 57W
Hawkins, Tex. 65 32 35N 95 12W
Hawkins, Wis. 69 45 31N 90 43W
Hawkins County ◇ . 63 36 24N 83 1W
Hawkinsville 32 32 17N 83 28W
Hawks 43 45 18N 83 53W
Hawksbill 68 38 34N 78 27W
Hawksbill Mt. 54 35 55N 81 53W
Hawley, Minn. 44 46 53N 96 19W
Hawley, Pa. 59 41 28N 75 11W
Hawley, Tex. 65 32 37N 99 49W
Haworth 57 33 51N 94 39W
Hawthorne, Fla. 31 29 36N 82 5W
Hawthorne, Nev. . . . 49 38 32N 118 38W
Haxtun 30 40 39N 102 38W
Hay 67 46 41N 117 55W
Hay → 69 44 59N 91 51W
Hay Springs 48 42 41N 102 41W
Hayden, Ariz. 26 33 0N 110 47W
Hayden, Colo. 30 40 30N 107 16W
Hayden, Idaho 34 47 46N 116 47W
Hayden, N. Mex. . . . 52 35 59N 103 16W
Hayden Peak 34 42 59N 116 40W
Hayes, La. 39 30 7N 92 55W
Hayes, S. Dak. 61 44 23N 101 1W
Hayes, Mt. 25 63 37N 146 43W
Hayes Center 48 40 31N 101 1W
Hayes County ◇ . . . 48 40 30N 101 0W
Hayesville, Iowa . . . 37 41 16N 92 15W
Hayesville, N.C. . . . 54 35 3N 83 49W
Hayfield 44 43 53N 92 51W
Hayfork 28 40 33N 123 11W
Haylow 32 30 50N 82 54W
Haymarket 68 38 49N 77 38W
Haynes, Ark. 27 34 54N 90 47W
Haynes, N. Dak. . . . 55 45 59N 102 28W
Haynesville, La. 39 32 58N 93 8W
Haynesville, Maine . 40 45 50N 67 59W
Hayneville, Ala. 24 32 11N 86 35W
Hayneville, Ga. 32 32 23N 83 37W
Hays 38 38 53N 99 20W
Hays County ◇ 65 29 59N 97 53W
Haysi 68 37 12N 82 18W
Haystack Peak 66 39 50N 113 55W
Haysville 38 37 34N 97 21W
Hayti, Mo. 46 36 14N 89 44W
Hayti, S. Dak. 61 44 40N 97 13W
Hayward, Calif. 28 37 40N 122 5W
Hayward, Minn. 44 43 39N 93 15W
Hayward, Wis. 69 46 1N 91 29W
Haywood 54 35 37N 79 4W
Haywood County ◇,
N.C. 54 35 30N 83 0W
Haywood County ◇,
Tenn. 62 35 36N 89 16W
Hazard, Ky. 63 37 15N 83 12W
Hazard, Nebr. 48 41 6N 99 9W
Hazel, Ky. 62 36 30N 88 20W
Hazel, S. Dak. 61 44 46N 97 23W
Hazel → 68 38 33N 77 51W
Hazel Green 69 42 32N 90 26W
Hazel Run 44 44 45N 95 43W
Hazelton, Idaho 34 42 36N 114 8W
Hazelton, Kans. 38 37 5N 98 24W
Hazelton, N. Dak. . . 55 46 29N 100 17W
Hazelton Peak 70 44 36N 107 3W
Hazelwood 54 35 28N 83 0W
Hazen, Ark. 27 34 47N 91 35W
Hazen, N. Dak. 55 47 18N 101 38W
Hazen, Nev. 49 39 34N 119 3W
Hazlehurst, Ga. 32 31 52N 82 36W
Hazlehurst, Miss. . . . 45 31 52N 90 24W
Hazlet 51 40 25N 74 12W
Hazleton, Ind. 36 38 29N 87 33W
Hazleton, Iowa 37 42 37N 91 54W
Hazleton, Pa. 59 40 57N 75 59W
Hazlettville 41 39 9N 75 40W
He Devil 34 45 21N 116 33W
Headland 24 31 21N 85 21W
Headquarters 34 46 38N 115 48W
Headrick 57 34 38N 99 9W
Healdsburg 28 38 37N 122 52W
Healdton 57 34 14N 97 29W
Healdville 50 43 25N 72 45W
Healy, Alaska 25 63 52N 148 58W
Healy, Kans. 38 38 36N 100 37W
Heard County ◇ . . . 32 33 15N 85 0W
Hearne 65 30 53N 96 36W
Heart → 55 46 46N 100 50W
Heart L. 70 44 16N 110 29W
Heartwell 48 40 34N 98 47W
Heath Springs 60 34 36N 80 40W
Heathsville 68 37 55N 76 29W
Heavener 57 34 53N 94 36W
Hebbardsville 62 37 47N 87 23W
Hebbronville 64 27 18N 98 41W
Heber, Ariz. 26 34 26N 110 36W
Heber, Calif. 29 32 44N 115 32W
Heber City 66 40 31N 111 25W
Heber Springs 27 35 30N 92 2W
Hebgen L. 47 44 52N 111 20W
Hebo 58 45 14N 123 52W
Hebron, Conn. 42 41 39N 72 22W
Hebron, Ill. 35 42 28N 88 26W
Hebron, Ind. 36 41 19N 87 12W
Hebron, Md. 41 38 25N 75 41W
Hebron, N. Dak. 55 46 54N 102 3W
Hebron, N.H. 50 43 42N 71 48W
Hebron, Nebr. 48 40 10N 97 35W
Hebron, Tex. 65 33 2N 96 52W
Hecla 61 45 53N 98 9W
Hector, Ark. 27 35 28N 92 59W
Hector, Minn. 44 44 45N 94 43W
Hedgesville 68 39 31N 77 58W
Hedley 64 34 52N 100 39W
Hedrick 37 41 11N 92 19W
Heflin 24 33 39N 85 35W
Hefner, L. 57 35 35N 97 36W
Heiberger 24 32 46N 87 17W
Heidelberg, Minn. . . 44 44 30N 93 38W
Heidelberg, Miss. . . 45 31 53N 88 59W
Heidrick 63 36 52N 83 54W
Heizer 38 38 25N 98 53W
Helemano → 33 21 35N 158 7W
Helen 41 38 22N 76 42W
Helena, Ala. 24 33 18N 86 51W
Helena, Ark. 27 34 32N 90 36W
Helena, Calif. 28 40 47N 123 8W
Helena, Ga. 32 32 5N 82 55W
Helena, Mont. 47 46 36N 112 2W
Helena National
Forest 47 46 30N 111 30W
Helix 58 45 51N 118 39W
Hell Cr. → 30 39 30N 102 30W
Hellertown 59 40 35N 75 21W
Hells Canyon 58 45 10N 116 50W
Hells Canyon Nat.
Rec. Area 58 45 30N 117 45W
Helmville 47 46 52N 112 58W
Helotes 65 29 35N 98 41W
Helper 66 39 41N 110 51W
Helton 63 36 58N 83 24W
Hematite 46 38 12N 90 29W
Hemet 29 33 45N 116 58W
Hemingford 48 42 19N 103 4W
Hemingway 60 33 45N 79 27W
Hemphill 65 31 20N 93 51W
Hemphill County ◇ . 64 35 55N 100 15W
Hempstead, N.Y. . . . 53 40 43N 73 38W
Hempstead, Tex. . . . 65 30 6N 96 5W
Hempstead
County ◇ 27 33 40N 93 36W
Henagar 24 34 38N 85 46W
Henderson, Ga. 32 32 21N 83 47W
Henderson, Iowa . . . 37 41 8N 95 26W
Henderson, Ky. 62 37 50N 87 35W
Henderson, Md. 41 39 6N 75 47W
Henderson, N.C. . . . 54 36 20N 78 25W
Henderson, Nebr. . . . 48 40 47N 97 49W
Henderson, Nev. 49 36 2N 114 59W
Henderson, Tenn. . . . 62 35 26N 88 38W
Henderson, Tex. 65 32 9N 94 48W
Henderson
County ◇, Ill. 35 40 50N 90 55W
Henderson
County ◇, Ky. . . . 62 37 45N 87 35W
Henderson
County ◇, N.C. . . 54 35 15N 82 30W
Henderson
County ◇, Tenn. . 62 35 39N 88 24W
Henderson
County ◇, Tex. . . 64 32 12N 95 51W
Hendersonville,
N.C. 54 35 19N 82 28W
Hendersonville, S.C. 60 32 48N 80 43W
Hendersonville,
Tenn. 62 36 18N 86 37W
Hendley 48 40 8N 99 58W
Hendricks 44 44 30N 96 25W
Hendricks County ◇ 36 39 45N 86 30W
Hendrum 44 47 16N 96 49W
Hendry County ◇ . . 31 26 30N 81 20W
Henefer 66 41 1N 111 30W
Henlopen, C. 41 38 48N 75 6W
Hennepin, Ill. 35 41 15N 89 21W
Hennepin, Okla. 57 34 31N 97 21W
Hennepin County ◇ 44 45 0N 93 30W
Hennessey 57 36 6N 97 54W
Henniker 50 43 11N 71 50W
Henning, Ill. 35 40 18N 87 42W
Henning, Minn. 44 46 19N 95 27W
Henning, Tenn. 62 35 41N 89 34W
Henrico County ◇ . . 68 37 33N 77 20W
Henrietta 65 33 49N 98 12W
Henriette 44 45 53N 93 7W
Henrieville 66 37 30N 112 0W
Henry, Ill. 35 41 7N 89 22W
Henry, Nebr. 48 41 58N 104 4W
Henry, S. Dak. 61 44 53N 97 28W
Henry, Tenn. 62 36 12N 88 25W
Henry, C. 68 36 56N 76 1W
Henry County ◇,
Ala. 24 31 34N 85 15W
Henry County ◇,
Ga. 32 33 25N 84 5W
Henry County ◇,
Ill. 35 41 20N 90 10W
Henry County ◇,
Ind. 36 39 55N 85 25W
Henry County ◇,
Iowa 37 41 0N 91 30W
Henry County ◇,
Ky. 63 38 25N 85 10W
Henry County ◇,
Mo. 46 38 25N 93 45W
Henry County ◇,
Ohio 56 41 19N 84 2W
Henry County ◇,
Tenn. 62 36 18N 88 19W
Henry County ◇,
Va. 68 36 50N 79 56W
Henry Mts. 66 38 0N 110 50W
Henryetta 57 35 27N 95 59W
Henrys Fork → . . . 34 41 0N 109 39W
Henrys Lake 34 44 36N 111 21W
Henshaw 62 37 37N 88 3W
Henshaw L. 29 33 15N 116 45W
Hensler 55 47 16N 101 5W
Hepburn 37 40 51N 95 1W
Hephzibah 32 33 19N 82 6W
Hepler 38 37 40N 94 58W
Heppner 58 45 21N 119 33W
Herbert I. 25 52 45N 170 7W
Herculaneum 46 38 16N 90 23W
Hereford, Ariz. 26 31 26N 110 6W
Hereford, Colo. 30 40 57N 104 18W
Hereford, Md. 41 39 35N 76 40W
Hereford, Tex. 64 34 49N 102 24W
Herington 38 38 40N 96 57W
Herkimer, Kans. . . . 38 39 54N 96 43W
Herkimer, N.Y. 53 43 2N 74 59W
Herkimer County ◇ 53 43 0N 75 0W
Herman, Minn. 44 45 49N 96 9W
Herman, Nebr. 48 41 40N 96 13W
Hermann 46 38 42N 91 27W
Hermansville 43 45 42N 87 36W
Hermantown 44 46 50N 92 15W
Hermanville 45 31 58N 90 50W
Hermiston 58 45 51N 119 17W
Hermitage, Ark. 27 33 27N 92 10W
Hermitage, Mo. 46 37 56N 93 19W
Hermleigh 64 32 38N 100 46W
Hermon 53 44 28N 75 14W
Hermosa 61 43 50N 103 12W
Hernando, Fla. 31 28 54N 82 23W
Hernando, Miss. . . . 45 34 50N 90 0W
Hernando County ◇ 31 28 35N 82 30W
Herndon, Kans. 38 39 55N 100 47W
Herndon, Ky. 62 36 44N 87 34W
Herndon, Pa. 59 40 43N 76 51W
Herndon, Va. 68 38 58N 77 23W
Herod 32 31 42N 84 26W
Heron 47 48 3N 115 57W
Heron Lake 44 43 48N 95 19W
Herreid 61 45 50N 100 4W
Herrick 61 43 7N 99 11W
Herrin 35 37 48N 89 2W
Herrington L. 63 37 45N 84 44W
Herscher 35 41 3N 88 6W
Hersey 43 43 51N 85 27W

Hershey **48** 41 10N 101 0W
Hertford **54** 36 11N 76 28W
Hertford County ◇ **54** 36 20N 77 0W
Hesperia, Calif. **29** 34 25N 117 18W
Hesperia, Mich. **43** 43 34N 86 3W
Hesperus **30** 37 17N 108 2W
Hessel **43** 46 0N 84 26W
Hessmer **39** 31 3N 92 8W
Hesston **38** 38 8N 97 26W
Hetch Hetchy Aqueduct **28** 37 29N 122 19W
Hetch Hetchy Reservoir **28** 37 57N 119 47W
Hettinger **55** 46 0N 102 42W
Hettinger County ◇ **55** 46 25N 102 30W
Heuvelton **53** 44 37N 75 25W
Hewins **38** 37 3N 96 25W
Hewitt **44** 46 20N 95 5W
Hewlett **68** 37 55N 77 35W
Hext **65** 30 52N 99 32W
Heyburn, L. **57** 35 57N 96 18W
Heyworth **35** 40 19N 88 59W
Hialeah **31** 25 50N 80 17W
Hiattville **38** 37 43N 94 52W
Hiawassee **32** 34 58N 83 46W
Hiawatha, Kans. **38** 39 51N 95 32W
Hiawatha, Utah **66** 39 29N 111 1W
Hiawatha National Forest **43** 46 15N 86 40W
Hibbing **44** 47 25N 92 56W
Hickman, Del. **41** 38 50N 75 42W
Hickman, Ky. **62** 36 34N 89 11W
Hickman, Nebr. **48** 40 37N 96 38W
Hickman County ◇, Ky. **62** 36 40N 89 0W
Hickman County ◇, Tenn. **62** 35 47N 87 28W
Hickok **38** 37 34N 101 14W
Hickory, Ky. **62** 36 48N 88 40W
Hickory, N.C. **54** 35 44N 81 21W
Hickory, L. **54** 35 49N 81 12W
Hickory County ◇ **46** 37 55N 93 15W
Hickory Grove **60** 34 59N 81 25W
Hickory Plains **27** 34 59N 91 44W
Hickory Ridge **27** 35 24N 90 58W
Hickory Valley **62** 35 9N 89 8W
Hicksville, N.Y. **53** 40 46N 73 32W
Hicksville, Ohio **56** 41 18N 84 46W
Hico **65** 31 59N 98 2W
Hidalgo, Ill. **35** 39 9N 88 9W
Hidalgo, Tex. **64** 26 6N 98 16W
Hidalgo County ◇, N. Mex. **52** 32 0N 108 45W
Hidalgo County ◇, Tex. **64** 26 25N 98 10W
Higbee **46** 39 19N 92 31W
Higgins **64** 36 7N 100 2W
Higgins L. **43** 44 29N 84 43W
Higginsport **56** 38 47N 83 58W
Higginsville **46** 39 4N 93 43W
High Bridge **51** 40 40N 74 54W
High Hill **46** 38 53N 91 23W
High I. **43** 45 44N 85 41W
High Island **65** 29 34N 94 24W
High Point **54** 35 57N 80 0W
High Pt., N.J. **51** 41 19N 74 40W
High Pt., Wyo. **70** 41 37N 107 43W
High Rock L., N.C. **54** 35 36N 80 14W
High Rock L., Nev. **49** 41 17N 119 17W
High Rolls **52** 32 57N 105 50W
High Springs **31** 29 50N 82 36W
Highgate Center **50** 44 56N 73 3W
Highland, Calif. **29** 34 8N 117 13W
Highland, Ill. **35** 38 44N 89 41W
Highland, Ind. **36** 41 33N 87 28W
Highland, Kans. **38** 39 52N 95 16W
Highland, N.Y. **53** 41 43N 73 58W
Highland, Wis. **69** 43 5N 90 22W
Highland Beach **41** 38 56N 76 28W
Highland City **31** 27 58N 81 53W
Highland County ◇, Ohio **56** 39 12N 83 37W
Highland County ◇, Va. **68** 38 25N 79 35W
Highland Hills **35** 41 51N 88 1W
Highland Home **24** 31 57N 86 19W
Highland Lakes **51** 41 11N 74 28W
Highland Mills **32** 33 17N 84 17W
Highland Park **35** 42 11N 87 48W
Highland Springs **68** 37 33N 77 20W
Highland View **31** 29 50N 85 19W
Highlands, N.C. **54** 35 3N 83 12W
Highlands, N.J. **51** 40 24N 73 59W
Highlands County ◇ **31** 27 20N 81 20W
Highmore **61** 44 31N 99 27W
Highpoint **45** 33 11N 89 9W
Hightstown **51** 40 16N 74 31W
Highwood **35** 42 12N 87 48W
Highwood Mts. **47** 47 30N 110 30W
Higuero, Punta **71** 18 22N 67 16W
Hiko **49** 37 32N 115 14W
Hiland **70** 43 7N 107 21W
Hiland Park **31** 30 12N 85 33W
Hilda **60** 33 16N 81 15W
Hildreth **48** 40 20N 99 3W
Hilgard **58** 45 21N 118 14W
Hill City, Idaho **34** 43 18N 115 3W
Hill City, Kans. **38** 39 22N 99 51W
Hill City, Minn. **44** 46 59N 93 36W
Hill City, S. Dak. **61** 43 56N 103 35W
Hill County ◇, Mont. **47** 48 40N 110 0W
Hill County ◇, Tex. **65** 32 1N 97 8W
Hill Cr. → **66** 39 55N 109 40W
Hillcrest Center **29** 35 23N 118 57W
Hillcrest Heights **41** 38 50N 76 57W
Hilliard, Fla. **31** 30 41N 81 55W
Hilliard, Ohio **56** 40 2N 83 10W
Hilliards **59** 41 5N 79 50W
Hillister **65** 30 40N 94 23W
Hillman, Mich. **43** 45 4N 83 54W
Hillman, Minn. **44** 46 0N 93 53W
Hillrose **30** 40 20N 103 31W
Hills, Iowa **37** 41 33N 91 32W
Hills, Minn. **44** 43 32N 96 21W
Hills Creek L. **58** 43 43N 122 26W
Hillsboro, Ga. **32** 33 11N 83 38W
Hillsboro, Ill. **35** 39 9N 89 29W
Hillsboro, Kans. **38** 38 21N 97 12W
Hillsboro, Md. **41** 38 55N 75 50W
Hillsboro, Mo. **46** 38 14N 90 34W
Hillsboro, N. Dak. **55** 47 26N 97 3W
Hillsboro, N.H. **50** 43 7N 71 54W
Hillsboro, N. Mex. **52** 32 55N 107 34W
Hillsboro, Ohio **56** 39 12N 83 37W
Hillsboro, Oreg. **58** 45 31N 122 59W
Hillsboro, Tex. **65** 32 1N 97 8W
Hillsboro, W. Va. **68** 38 8N 80 13W
Hillsboro, Wis. **69** 43 39N 90 21W
Hillsboro Canal **31** 26 30N 80 15W
Hillsboro Upper Village **50** 43 9N 71 58W
Hillsborough **54** 36 5N 79 7W
Hillsborough County ◇, Fla. **31** 27 50N 82 20W
Hillsborough County ◇, N.H. **50** 42 50N 71 45W
Hillsdale, Ill. **35** 41 37N 90 11W
Hillsdale, Kans. **38** 38 40N 94 51W
Hillsdale, Mich. **43** 41 56N 84 38W
Hillsdale, Okla. **57** 36 34N 97 59W
Hillsdale County ◇ **43** 41 50N 84 40W
Hillside, Ariz. **26** 34 25N 112 55W
Hillside, N.J. **51** 40 42N 74 13W
Hillsmere Shore **41** 38 56N 76 32W
Hillsville **68** 36 46N 80 44W
Hilltonia **32** 32 53N 81 40W
Hillview **63** 38 5N 85 49W
Hilo **33** 19 44N 155 5W
Hilo B. **33** 19 45N 155 5W
Hilt **28** 41 50N 122 37W
Hilton **53** 43 17N 77 48W
Hilton Head I. **60** 32 13N 80 45W
Hinchcliff **45** 34 19N 90 17W
Hinckley, Ill. **35** 41 46N 88 38W
Hinckley, Minn. **44** 46 1N 92 56W
Hinckley, Utah **66** 39 20N 112 40W
Hinckley Reservoir **53** 43 19N 75 7W
Hindman **63** 37 20N 82 59W
Hinds County ◇ **45** 32 16N 90 25W
Hindsboro **35** 39 41N 88 8W
Hines, Fla. **31** 29 45N 83 14W
Hines, Oreg. **58** 43 34N 119 5W
Hinesburg **50** 44 18N 73 6W
Hineston **39** 31 9N 92 46W
Hinesville **32** 31 51N 81 36W
Hingham, Mass. **42** 42 15N 70 53W
Hingham, Mont. **47** 48 33N 110 25W
Hinsdale, Md. **41** 42 26N 73 8W
Hinsdale, Mont. **47** 48 24N 107 5W
Hinsdale, N.H. **50** 42 47N 72 29W
Hinsdale County ◇ **30** 37 50N 107 20W
Hinson **31** 30 39N 84 25W
Hinton, Iowa **37** 42 38N 96 18W
Hinton, Okla. **57** 35 28N 98 21W
Hinton, W. Va. **68** 37 40N 80 54W
Hiram **56** 41 19N 81 9W
Hitchcock, Okla. **57** 35 58N 98 21W
Hitchcock, S. Dak. **61** 44 38N 98 25W
Hitchcock, Tex. **65** 29 21N 95 1W
Hitchcock County ◇ **48** 40 15N 101 0W
Hitchins **63** 38 17N 82 55W
Hitchita **57** 35 31N 95 44W
Hitterdal **44** 46 59N 96 16W
Hiwannee **45** 31 49N 88 41W
Hiwassee **68** 36 58N 80 43W
Hiwassee → **63** 35 19N 84 47W
Hiwassee L. **54** 35 9N 84 11W
Hixton **69** 44 23N 91 1W
Hobart, Ind. **36** 41 32N 87 15W
Hobart, N.Y. **53** 42 22N 74 40W
Hobart, Okla. **57** 35 1N 99 6W
Hobbs **52** 32 42N 103 8W
Hobe Sound **31** 27 4N 80 8W
Hoberg **46** 37 4N 93 51W
Hobgood **54** 36 2N 77 24W
Hoboken **32** 31 11N 82 8W
Hobson, Ky. **63** 37 25N 85 22W
Hobson, Mont. **47** 47 0N 109 52W
Hobucken **54** 35 15N 76 34W
Hochheim **65** 29 19N 97 17W
Hockessin **41** 39 47N 75 42W
Hocking **56** 39 12N 81 45W
Hocking County ◇ **56** 39 32N 82 25W
Hockley County ◇ **64** 33 35N 102 23W
Hodge **39** 32 17N 92 43W
Hodgeman County ◇ **38** 38 0N 100 0W
Hodgenville **63** 37 34N 85 44W
Hodges **60** 34 17N 82 15W
Hoehne **30** 37 17N 104 23W
Hoffman, Ill. **35** 38 32N 89 16W
Hoffman, Minn. **44** 45 50N 95 48W
Hoffman, N.C. **54** 35 2N 79 33W
Hoffman, Okla. **57** 35 29N 95 51W
Hog I., Mich. **43** 45 48N 85 22W
Hog I., Va. **68** 37 26N 75 42W
Hogansville **32** 33 10N 84 55W
Hogback Mt., Mont. **47** 44 54N 112 7W
Hogback Mt., Nebr. **48** 41 40N 103 42W
Hogeland **47** 48 51N 108 40W
Hoh → **67** 47 45N 124 29W
Hohenwald **62** 35 33N 87 33W
Hoisington **38** 38 31N 98 47W
Hokah **44** 43 46N 91 21W
Hoke County ◇ **54** 35 0N 79 15W
Holbrook, Ariz. **26** 34 54N 110 10W
Holbrook, Idaho **34** 42 10N 112 39W
Holbrook, Mass. **42** 42 9N 71 1W
Holbrook, N.Y. **53** 40 49N 73 5W
Holbrook, Nebr. **48** 40 18N 100 1W
Holcomb, Kans. **38** 37 59N 100 59W
Holcomb, Mo. **46** 36 24N 90 2W
Holcomb, N.Y. **53** 42 54N 77 25W
Holden, Mass. **42** 42 21N 71 52W
Holden, Mo. **46** 38 43N 94 1W
Holden, Utah **66** 39 6N 112 16W
Holdenville **57** 35 5N 96 24W
Holder **31** 28 58N 82 25W
Holderness **50** 43 43N 71 37W
Holdingford **44** 45 44N 94 28W
Holdrege **48** 40 26N 99 23W
Holgate, N.J. **51** 39 33N 74 15W
Holgate, Ohio **56** 41 15N 84 8W
Holladay, Tenn. **62** 35 52N 88 9W
Holladay, Utah **66** 40 40N 111 50W
Holland, Ark. **27** 35 10N 92 16W
Holland, Ga. **32** 34 21N 85 22W
Holland, Iowa **37** 42 24N 92 48W
Holland, Mich. **43** 42 47N 86 7W
Holland, Minn. **44** 44 6N 96 11W
Holland, Mo. **46** 36 3N 89 52W
Holland, Tex. **65** 30 53N 97 24W
Holland Patent **53** 43 15N 75 15W
Hollandale, Minn. **44** 43 46N 93 12W
Hollandale, Miss. **45** 33 10N 90 51W
Hollandale, Wis. **69** 42 53N 89 56W
Hollansburg **56** 39 59N 84 50W
Hollenberg **38** 39 58N 96 59W
Holley, Fla. **31** 30 27N 86 54W
Holley, N.Y. **53** 43 14N 78 2W
Holley, Oreg. **58** 44 21N 122 47W
Holliday **65** 33 49N 98 42W
Hollidaysburg **59** 40 26N 78 24W
Hollis, Ark. **27** 34 52N 93 7W
Hollis, Kans. **38** 39 38N 97 33W
Hollis, Okla. **57** 34 41N 99 55W
Hollister, Calif. **28** 36 51N 121 24W
Hollister, Idaho **34** 42 21N 114 35W
Hollister, Mo. **46** 36 38N 93 12W
Hollister, N.C. **54** 36 15N 77 56W
Hollister, Okla. **57** 34 21N 98 52W
Holliston **42** 42 12N 71 26W
Hollow Rock **62** 36 2N 88 16W
Holloway **44** 45 15N 95 55W
Holly, Colo. **30** 38 3N 102 7W
Holly, Mich. **43** 42 48N 83 38W
Holly Grove **27** 34 36N 91 12W
Holly Hill, Fla. **31** 29 16N 81 3W
Holly Hill, S.C. **60** 33 19N 80 25W
Holly Pond **24** 34 10N 86 37W
Holly Ridge **54** 34 30N 77 33W
Holly Springs, Ga. **32** 34 10N 84 30W
Holly Springs, Miss. **45** 34 46N 89 27W
Holly Springs, N.C. **54** 35 39N 78 50W
Holly Springs National Forest **45** 34 40N 89 5W
Hollywood, Ala. **24** 34 44N 85 59W
Hollywood, Fla. **31** 26 1N 80 9W
Hollywood, Md. **41** 38 21N 76 34W
Hollywood, Miss. **45** 34 45N 90 22W
Holman **52** 36 2N 105 23W
Holmen **69** 43 58N 91 15W
Holmes → **31** 30 30N 85 50W
Holmes, Mt. **70** 44 49N 110 51W
Holmes Beach **31** 27 31N 82 43W
Holmes County ◇, Fla. **31** 30 50N 85 45W
Holmes County ◇, Miss. **45** 33 7N 90 3W
Holmes County ◇, Ohio **56** 40 33N 81 55W
Holmesville **56** 40 38N 81 56W
Holopaw **31** 28 8N 81 5W
Holstein, Iowa **37** 42 29N 95 33W
Holstein, Nebr. **48** 40 28N 98 39W
Holston → **63** 35 58N 83 51W
Holt, Fla. **31** 30 43N 86 45W
Holt, Mich. **43** 42 39N 84 31W
Holt, Minn. **44** 48 18N 96 11W
Holt, Mo. **46** 39 27N 94 21W
Holt County ◇, Mo. **46** 40 5N 95 10W
Holt County ◇, Nebr. **48** 42 30N 98 45W
Holton, Ind. **36** 39 5N 85 23W
Holton, Kans. **38** 39 28N 95 44W
Holtville **29** 32 49N 115 23W
Holualoa **33** 19 37N 155 57W
Holy Cross **25** 62 12N 159 46W
Holyoke, Colo. **30** 40 35N 102 18W
Holyoke, Mass. **42** 42 12N 72 37W
Holyrood **38** 38 35N 98 25W
Home **38** 39 51N 96 31W
Homedale **34** 43 37N 116 56W
Homeland **32** 30 51N 82 1W
Homer, Alaska **25** 59 39N 151 33W
Homer, Ga. **32** 34 20N 83 30W
Homer, La. **39** 32 48N 93 4W
Homer, Mich. **43** 42 9N 84 49W
Homer, N.Y. **53** 42 38N 76 11W
Homer, Nebr. **48** 42 19N 96 29W
Homer City **59** 40 32N 79 10W
Homer Youngs Pk. **47** 45 19N 113 41W
Homerville **32** 31 2N 82 45W
Homestead, Fla. **31** 25 28N 80 29W
Homestead, Oreg. **58** 45 2N 116 51W
Homewood, Ala. **24** 33 29N 86 47W
Homewood, Ill. **35** 41 34N 87 40W
Hominy **57** 36 25N 96 24W
Homochitto National Forest **45** 31 15N 31 20W
Homosassa Springs **31** 28 48N 82 35W
Hon **27** 34 56N 94 11W
Honaker **68** 37 1N 81 59W
Honaunau **33** 19 26N 155 55W
Hondo, N. Mex. **52** 33 24N 105 16W
Hondo, Tex. **65** 29 21N 99 9W
Hondo → **52** 33 20N 104 25W
Honea Path **60** 34 27N 82 24W
Honesdale **59** 41 34N 75 16W
Honey Grove **65** 33 35N 95 55W
Honey Island **65** 30 24N 94 27W
Honey L. **28** 40 15N 120 19W
Honeyville, Fla. **31** 30 3N 85 11W
Honeyville, Utah **66** 41 38N 112 4W
Honga **41** 38 19N 76 14W
Honokaa **33** 20 5N 155 28W
Honokahua **33** 21 0N 156 40W
Honolulu **33** 21 19N 157 52W
Honolulu County ◇ **33** 21 20N 157 50W
Honomu **33** 19 52N 155 7W
Honor **43** 44 40N 86 1W
Honouliuli **33** 21 22N 158 2W
Honuapo B. **33** 19 5N 155 33W
Hood, Mt. **58** 45 23N 121 42W
Hood Canal **67** 47 35N 123 0W
Hood County ◇ **65** 32 27N 97 47W
Hood River **58** 45 43N 121 31W
Hood River County ◇ **58** 45 30N 121 20W
Hoodoo Peak **67** 48 15N 120 19W
Hoodsport **67** 47 24N 123 9W
Hooker **57** 36 52N 101 13W
Hooker County ◇ **48** 41 50N 101 0W
Hooks **65** 33 28N 94 16W
Hooksett **50** 43 5N 71 30W
Hoolehua **33** 21 10N 157 5W
Hoonah **25** 58 7N 135 27W
Hoopa **28** 41 3N 123 41W
Hoopa Valley Indian Reservation **28** 41 10N 123 45W
Hooper, Colo. **30** 37 45N 105 53W
Hooper, Nebr. **48** 41 37N 96 33W
Hooper, Wash. **67** 46 45N 118 9W
Hooper Bay **25** 61 32N 166 6W
Hooper Str. **41** 38 15N 76 5W
Hoopersville **41** 38 16N 76 11W
Hoopeston **35** 40 28N 87 40W
Hoople **55** 48 32N 97 38W
Hoosac Range **42** 42 45N 73 2W
Hoosick Falls **53** 42 54N 73 21W
Hoosier National Forest **36** 38 30N 86 35W
Hoover Dam **26** 36 1N 114 44W
Hoover Reservoir **56** 40 7N 82 53W
Hooversville **59** 40 9N 78 55W
Hop Bottom **59** 41 42N 75 46W
Hopatcong **51** 40 55N 74 40W
Hopatcong, L. **51** 40 57N 74 38W
Hope, Ark. **27** 33 40N 93 36W
Hope, Ind. **36** 39 18N 85 46W
Hope, Kans. **38** 38 41N 97 5W
Hope, N. Dak. **55** 47 19N 97 43W
Hope, N. Mex. **52** 32 49N 104 44W
Hope, R.I. **42** 41 44N 71 34W
Hope Mills **54** 34 59N 78 57W

Hope Valley 42 41 30N 71 43W
Hopedale 35 40 25N 89 25W
Hopeton 57 36 41N 98 40W
Hopewell, Miss. 45 31 57N 90 13W
Hopewell, Va. 68 37 18N 77 17W
Hopi Indian Reservation 26 36 15N 110 30W
Hopkins, Mich. 43 42 37N 85 46W
Hopkins, Mo. 46 40 33N 94 49W
Hopkins, S.C. 60 33 54N 80 53W
Hopkins County ◇, Ky. 62 37 20N 87 30W
Hopkins County ◇, Tex. 65 33 8N 95 36W
Hopkinsville 62 36 52N 87 29W
Hopkinton, Iowa 37 42 21N 91 15W
Hopkinton, Mass. 42 42 14N 71 31W
Hopkinton, N.H. 50 43 12N 71 41W
Hopkinton, R.I. 42 41 28N 71 48W
Hopland 28 38 58N 123 7W
Hoquiam 67 46 59N 123 53W
Horace, Kans. 38 38 29N 101 47W
Horace, N. Dak. 55 46 45N 96 54W
Horatio, Ark. 27 33 56N 94 21W
Horatio, S.C. 60 34 1N 80 33W
Hordville 48 41 5N 97 53W
Horicon 69 43 27N 88 38W
Hormigueros 71 18 8N 67 8W
Horn I. 45 30 14N 88 39W
Horn Lake 45 34 58N 90 2W
Hornbeak 62 36 20N 89 18W
Hornbeck 39 31 20N 93 24W
Hornbrook 28 41 55N 122 33W
Hornell 53 42 20N 77 40W
Hornersville 46 36 3N 90 7W
Hornick 37 42 14N 96 6W
Hornitos 28 37 30N 120 14W
Hornsby 62 35 14N 88 50W
Horry County ◇ 60 33 50N 79 0W
Horse → 30 38 5N 103 19W
Horse Branch 62 37 28N 86 41W
Horse Cave 63 37 11N 85 54W
Horse Cr. →, Fla. 31 27 6N 81 58W
Horse Cr. →, Mo. 46 37 46N 93 53W
Horse Cr. →, Wyo. 70 41 57N 103 58W
Horse Creek 70 41 25N 105 11W
Horse Creek Reservoir 30 38 10N 103 24W
Horse Heaven Hills 67 46 3N 119 30W
Horse L. 28 40 40N 120 31W
Horsehead L. 55 47 3N 99 47W
Horseheads 53 42 10N 76 49W
Horseshoe Bend 34 43 55N 116 12W
Horseshoe Reservoir 26 33 59N 111 42W
Horsetooth Reservoir 30 40 36N 105 10W
Hortense 32 31 20N 81 57W
Horton 38 39 40N 95 32W
Hortonville 69 44 20N 88 38W
Hosford 31 30 23N 84 48W
Hoskins, Nebr. 48 42 7N 97 18W
Hoskins, Oreg. 58 44 41N 123 28W
Hoskinston 63 37 5N 83 24W
Hosmer 61 45 34N 99 28W
Hospers 37 43 4N 95 54W
Hot Creek Range 49 38 40N 116 20W
Hot Spring County ◇ 27 34 14N 92 55W
Hot Springs, Ark. 27 34 31N 93 3W
Hot Springs, Mont. 47 47 37N 114 40W
Hot Springs, N.C. 54 35 54N 82 50W
Hot Springs, S. Dak. 61 43 26N 103 29W
Hot Springs, Va. 68 38 0N 79 50W
Hot Springs County ◇ 70 43 55N 108 30W
Hot Sulphur Springs 30 40 4N 106 6W
Hotchkiss 30 38 48N 107 43W
Hotevilla 26 35 56N 110 41W
Houck 26 35 20N 109 10W
Houghton, Mich. 43 47 7N 88 34W
Houghton, N.Y. 53 42 25N 78 10W
Houghton County ◇ 43 47 0N 88 45W
Houghton L. 43 44 21N 84 44W
Houghton Lake 43 44 18N 84 45W
Houlka 45 34 2N 89 1W
Houlton 40 46 8N 67 51W
Houma 39 29 36N 90 43W
Housatonic 42 42 16N 73 22W
Housatonic → 42 41 10N 73 7W
House 52 34 39N 103 54W
House Range 66 39 30N 113 20W
Houston, Ark. 27 35 2N 92 42W
Houston, Fla. 31 30 15N 82 54W
Houston, Minn. 44 43 46N 91 34W
Houston, Miss. 45 33 54N 89 0W
Houston, Mo. 46 37 22N 91 58W
Houston, Tex. 65 29 46N 95 22W
Houston → 39 30 16N 93 13W
Houston, L. 65 29 55N 95 8W
Houston County ◇, Ala. 24 31 11N 85 14W
Houston County ◇, Ga. 32 32 20N 83 45W
Houston County ◇, Minn. 44 43 35N 91 30W
Houston County ◇, Tenn. 62 36 19N 87 42W
Houston County ◇, Tex. 65 31 19N 95 27W
Houston County L. 65 31 25N 95 35W
Houstonia 46 38 54N 93 22W
Hoven 61 45 15N 99 47W
Hovenweep National Monument 30 37 20N 109 0W
Hovland 44 47 51N 89 58W
Howard, Colo. 30 38 27N 105 50W
Howard, Ga. 32 32 36N 84 23W
Howard, Kans. 38 37 28N 96 16W
Howard, Pa. 59 41 1N 77 40W
Howard, S. Dak. 61 44 1N 97 32W
Howard, Wis. 69 44 33N 88 4W
Howard City 43 43 24N 85 28W
Howard County ◇, Ark. 27 34 7N 94 1W
Howard County ◇, Ind. 36 40 30N 86 10W
Howard County ◇, Iowa 37 43 20N 92 20W
Howard County ◇, Md. 41 39 15N 77 0W
Howard County ◇, Mo. 46 39 10N 92 40W
Howard County ◇, Nebr. 48 41 15N 98 30W
Howard County ◇, Tex. 64 32 15N 101 28W
Howard Draw → 64 30 10N 101 35W
Howard Hanson Reservoir 67 47 17N 121 47W
Howard Lake 44 45 4N 94 4W
Howe, Idaho 34 43 48N 113 0W
Howe, Ind. 36 41 43N 85 25W
Howe, Okla. 57 34 57N 94 38W
Howe, Tex. 65 33 30N 96 37W
Howell, Mich. 43 42 36N 83 56W
Howell, Utah 66 41 48N 112 27W
Howell County ◇ 46 36 45N 91 50W
Howes 61 44 37N 102 3W
Howes Mill 46 37 38N 91 16W
Howison 45 30 40N 89 8W
Howland 40 45 14N 68 40W
Hoxie, Ark. 27 36 3N 90 59W
Hoxie, Kans. 38 39 21N 100 26W
Hoyleton 35 38 27N 89 16W
Hoyt, Colo. 30 40 1N 104 5W
Hoyt, Kans. 38 39 15N 95 43W
Huachuca City 26 31 34N 110 21W
Hualalai 33 19 42N 155 52W
Hualapai Indian Reservation 26 35 45N 113 20W
Hualapai Mts. 26 34 45N 113 45W
Hualapai Peak 26 35 5N 113 54W
Hubbard, Iowa 37 42 18N 93 18W
Hubbard, Nebr. 48 42 23N 96 36W
Hubbard, Oreg. 58 45 11N 122 48W
Hubbard, Tex. 65 31 51N 96 48W
Hubbard County ◇ 44 47 10N 94 50W
Hubbard Creek L. 65 32 50N 98 58W
Hubbard L. 43 44 48N 83 34W
Hubbardton 50 43 42N 73 12W
Hubbell, Mich. 43 47 11N 88 26W
Hubbell, Nebr. 48 40 1N 97 29W
Huber Heights 56 39 50N 84 5W
Huddy 63 37 36N 82 17W
Hudson, Colo. 30 40 4N 104 39W
Hudson, Fla. 31 28 22N 82 42W
Hudson, Iowa 37 42 24N 92 28W
Hudson, Kans. 38 38 6N 98 40W
Hudson, Maine 40 45 0N 68 53W
Hudson, Mass. 42 42 23N 71 34W
Hudson, Md. 41 38 36N 76 15W
Hudson, Mich. 43 41 51N 84 21W
Hudson, N.C. 54 35 51N 81 30W
Hudson, N.H. 50 42 46N 71 26W
Hudson, N.Y. 53 42 15N 73 46W
Hudson, S. Dak. 61 43 8N 96 27W
Hudson, Wis. 69 44 58N 92 45W
Hudson, Wyo. 70 42 54N 108 35W
Hudson → 53 40 42N 74 2W
Hudson, L. 57 36 14N 95 11W
Hudson County ◇ 51 40 45N 74 5W
Hudson Falls 53 43 18N 73 35W
Hudsonville 43 42 52N 85 52W
Hudspeth County ◇ 64 31 30N 105 30W
Hueco Mts. 64 31 53N 105 58W
Huerfano → 30 38 14N 104 15W
Huerfano County ◇ 30 37 40N 104 50W
Huffman 65 30 1N 95 6W
Huger 60 33 6N 79 48W
Hugh Butler L. 48 40 21N 100 39W
Hughes, Alaska 25 66 3N 154 15W
Hughes, Ark. 27 34 57N 90 28W
Hughes County ◇, Okla. 57 35 0N 96 15W
Hughes County ◇, S. Dak. 61 44 30N 100 0W
Hughes Springs 65 33 0N 94 38W
Hughesville, Md. 41 38 32N 76 47W
Hughesville, Mo. 46 38 50N 93 18W
Hughesville, Pa. 59 41 14N 76 44W
Hughson 28 37 36N 120 52W
Hugo, Colo. 30 39 8N 103 28W
Hugo, Okla. 57 34 1N 95 31W
Hugo L. 57 34 3N 95 27W
Hugoton 38 37 11N 101 21W
Hulah L. 57 36 56N 96 5W
Hulbert, Mich. 43 46 21N 85 9W
Hulbert, Okla. 57 35 56N 95 9W
Hulen 63 36 47N 83 31W
Hulett 70 44 41N 104 36W
Hull, Fla. 31 27 7N 81 56W
Hull, Ill. 35 39 43N 91 13W
Hull, Iowa 37 43 11N 96 8W
Hull, Mass. 42 42 18N 70 55W
Humacao 71 18 9N 65 50W
Humacao ◇ 71 18 15N 65 45W
Humansville 46 37 48N 93 35W
Humble 65 30 0N 95 18W
Humboldt, Ariz. 26 34 30N 112 14W
Humboldt, Ill. 35 39 36N 88 19W
Humboldt, Iowa 37 42 44N 94 13W
Humboldt, Kans. 38 37 49N 95 26W
Humboldt, Nebr. 48 40 10N 95 57W
Humboldt, S. Dak. 61 43 39N 97 5W
Humboldt, Tenn. 62 35 50N 88 55W
Humboldt → 49 39 59N 118 36W
Humboldt B. 28 40 45N 124 10W
Humboldt County ◇, Calif. 28 40 50N 124 0W
Humboldt County ◇, Iowa 37 42 50N 94 10W
Humboldt County ◇, Nev. 49 41 20N 118 10W
Humboldt National Forest 49 41 45N 115 30W
Humboldt Peak 30 37 59N 105 33W
Humboldt Range 49 40 20N 118 10W
Humboldt Sink 49 40 1N 118 38W
Humbolt Salt Marsh 49 39 50N 117 55W
Hume 46 38 6N 94 34W
Humeston 37 40 52N 93 30W
Humnoke 27 34 33N 91 45W
Humphrey, Ark. 27 34 25N 91 43W
Humphrey, Nebr. 48 41 42N 97 29W
Humphreys 57 34 33N 99 14W
Humphreys, Mt. 29 37 17N 118 40W
Humphreys County ◇, Miss. 45 33 6N 90 30W
Humphreys County ◇, Tenn. 62 36 5N 87 48W
Humphreys Peak 26 35 21N 111 41W
Hundred 68 39 41N 80 28W
Hungry Horse 47 48 23N 114 4W
Hungry Horse Reservoir 47 48 21N 114 1W
Hunnewell, Kans. 38 37 1N 97 25W
Hunnewell, Mo. 46 39 40N 91 52W
Hunt 65 30 4N 99 20W
Hunt County ◇ 65 33 8N 96 7W
Hunt Mt. 70 44 55N 107 59W
Hunter, Ark. 27 35 3N 91 8W
Hunter, Kans. 38 39 14N 98 24W
Hunter, N. Dak. 55 47 12N 97 13W
Hunter, N.Y. 53 42 13N 74 13W
Hunter, Okla. 57 36 34N 97 40W
Hunterdon County ◇ 51 40 30N 75 0W
Hunters 67 48 7N 118 12W
Huntersville 54 35 25N 80 51W
Huntertown 36 41 14N 85 10W
Huntingburg 36 38 18N 86 57W
Huntingdon, Pa. 59 40 30N 78 1W
Huntingdon, Tenn. 62 36 0N 88 26W
Huntingdon County ◇ 59 40 15N 78 0W
Huntington, Ark. 27 35 5N 94 16W
Huntington, Ind. 36 40 53N 85 30W
Huntington, Mass. 42 42 14N 72 53W
Huntington, N.Y. 53 40 52N 73 26W
Huntington, Oreg. 58 44 21N 117 16W
Huntington, Tex. 65 31 17N 94 34W
Huntington, Utah 66 39 20N 110 58W
Huntington, Vt. 50 44 22N 72 58W
Huntington, W. Va. 68 38 25N 82 27W
Huntington →, Nev. 49 40 37N 115 43W
Huntington →, Utah 66 39 9N 110 55W
Huntington Beach 29 33 40N 118 5W
Huntington County ◇ 36 40 50N 85 30W
Huntington Station 53 40 51N 73 25W
Huntingtown 41 38 37N 76 37W
Huntland 62 35 3N 86 16W
Huntley, Ill. 35 42 10N 88 26W
Huntley, Mont. 47 45 54N 108 19W
Huntley, Nebr. 48 40 13N 99 18W
Huntsville, Ala. 24 34 44N 86 35W
Huntsville, Ark. 27 36 5N 93 44W
Huntsville, Ky. 62 37 10N 86 53W
Huntsville, Mo. 46 39 26N 92 33W
Huntsville, Ohio 56 40 26N 83 48W
Huntsville, Tenn. 63 36 25N 84 29W
Huntsville, Tex. 65 30 43N 95 33W
Huntsville, Utah 66 41 16N 111 46W
Hurley, Miss. 45 30 40N 88 30W
Hurley, Mo. 46 36 56N 93 30W
Hurley, N. Mex. 52 32 42N 108 8W
Hurley, N.Y. 53 41 55N 74 4W
Hurley, S. Dak. 61 43 17N 97 5W
Hurley, Wis. 69 46 27N 90 11W
Hurlock 41 38 38N 75 52W
Huron, Calif. 29 36 12N 120 6W
Huron, Kans. 38 39 38N 95 21W
Huron, Ohio 56 41 24N 82 33W
Huron, S. Dak. 61 44 22N 98 13W
Huron → 43 42 2N 83 11W
Huron, L. 43 44 30N 82 40W
Huron Beach 43 45 30N 84 6W
Huron County ◇, Mich. 43 43 50N 83 0W
Huron County ◇, Ohio 56 41 15N 82 37W
Huron Mts. 43 46 50N 88 0W
Huron National Forest 43 44 30N 84 0W
Hurricane 66 37 11N 113 17W
Hurricane Cliffs 26 36 45N 113 20W
Hurst 65 32 49N 97 9W
Hurstboro 24 32 15N 85 25W
Hurstville 37 42 6N 90 41W
Huslia 25 65 41N 156 24W
Hustisford 69 43 21N 88 36W
Husum 67 45 48N 121 29W
Hutch Mt. 26 34 47N 111 22W
Hutchinson, Kans. 38 38 5N 97 56W
Hutchinson, Minn. 44 44 54N 94 22W
Hutchinson County ◇, S. Dak. 61 43 25N 97 48W
Hutchinson County ◇, Tex. 64 35 50N 101 30W
Hutsonville 35 39 7N 87 40W
Huttig 27 33 2N 92 11W
Hutto 65 30 33N 97 33W
Hutton 35 39 25N 79 28W
Huttonsville 68 38 43N 79 59W
Huxford 24 31 13N 87 28W
Huxley 37 41 54N 93 36W
Huyett 41 39 40N 77 20W
Hyak 67 47 24N 121 24W
Hyannis, Mass. 42 41 39N 70 17W
Hyannis, Nebr. 48 42 0N 101 46W
Hyattsville 41 38 57N 76 56W
Hyattville 70 44 15N 107 36W
Hybart 24 31 50N 87 23W
Hyco L. 54 36 31N 79 3W
Hydaburg 25 55 12N 132 50W
Hyde County ◇, N.C. 54 35 30N 76 20W
Hyde County ◇, S. Dak. 61 44 31N 99 27W
Hyde Park 50 44 36N 72 37W
Hyden 63 37 10N 83 22W
Hydes 41 39 30N 76 29W
Hydro 57 35 33N 98 39W
Hygiene 30 40 11N 105 11W
Hymera 36 39 11N 87 18W
Hyndman 59 39 49N 78 43W
Hyndman Peak 34 43 45N 114 8W
Hyrum 66 41 38N 111 51W
Hysham 47 46 18N 107 14W

I

Iaeger 68 37 28N 81 49W
Iamonia L. 31 30 38N 84 14W
Iatan 46 39 29N 94 59W
Iatt L. 39 31 35N 92 40W
Ibapah 66 40 2N 113 59W
Iberia 46 38 5N 92 18W
Iberia Parish ◇ 39 30 1N 91 49W
Iberville Parish ◇ 39 30 17N 91 14W
Ice Harbor Dam 67 46 15N 118 53W
Icy C. 25 70 20N 161 52W
Ida 43 41 55N 83 34W
Ida County ◇ 37 42 25N 95 30W
Ida Grove 37 42 21N 95 28W
Idabel 57 33 54N 94 50W
Idaho □ 34 45 0N 115 0W
Idaho City 34 43 50N 115 50W
Idaho County ◇ 34 45 35N 115 30W
Idaho Falls 34 43 30N 112 2W
Idaho Springs 30 39 45N 105 31W
Idalia 30 39 42N 102 18W
Idalou 64 33 40N 101 41W
Idana 38 39 22N 97 16W
Idanha 58 44 42N 122 5W
Ideal 61 43 33N 99 54W
Idria 29 36 25N 120 41W
Igiugig 25 59 20N 155 55W
Ignacio 30 37 7N 107 38W
Ihlen 44 43 55N 96 22W
Ilfeld 52 35 25N 105 34W

Iliamna **25** 59 45N 154 55W
Iliamna L. **25** 59 30N 155 0W
Iliff **30** 40 45N 103 4W
Ilio Pt. **33** 21 13N 157 16W
Ilion **53** 43 1N 75 2W
Illinois □ **35** 41 0N 89 0W
Illinois →, Ark. **27** 35 30N 95 5W
Illinois →, Ill. **35** 38 58N 90 28W
Illinois →, Oreg. **58** 42 33N 124 3W
Illiopolis **35** 39 51N 89 15W
Illmo **46** 37 13N 89 30W
Ilwaco **67** 46 19N 124 3W
Imbler **58** 45 28N 117 58W
Imboden **27** 36 12N 91 11W
Imlay **49** 40 40N 118 9W
Imlay City **43** 43 2N 83 5W
Immokalee **31** 26 25N 81 25W
Imnaha → **58** 45 49N 116 46W
Imogene **37** 40 53N 95 29W
Imperial, Calif. **29** 32 51N 115 34W
Imperial, Nebr. **48** 40 31N 101 39W
Imperial, Pt. **26** 36 15N 111 57W
Imperial Beach **29** 32 35N 117 8W
Imperial County ◇ **29** 33 0N 115 20W
Imperial Dam **26** 32 55N 114 25W
Imperial Reservoir **26** 32 53N 114 28W
Imperial Valley **29** 33 0N 115 30W
Ina **35** 38 9N 88 54W
Incline Village **49** 39 10N 119 58W
Independence, Calif. **29** 36 48N 118 12W
Independence, Iowa **37** 42 28N 91 54W
Independence, Kans. **38** 37 14N 95 42W
Independence, Ky. **63** 38 57N 84 33W
Independence, La. **39** 30 38N 90 30W
Independence, Mo. **46** 39 6N 94 25W
Independence, Oreg. **58** 44 51N 123 11W
Independence, Va. **68** 36 37N 81 9W
Independence, Wis. **69** 44 22N 91 25W
Independence County ◇ **27** 35 46N 91 39W
Independence Cr. → **64** 30 27N 101 44W
Independence Mts. **49** 41 20N 116 0W
Independence Pass **30** 39 7N 106 33W
Index **67** 47 50N 121 33W
Indiahoma **57** 34 37N 98 45W
Indialantic **31** 28 6N 80 34W
Indian → **31** 27 10N 80 10W
Indian Cr. → **61** 44 39N 103 19W
Indian Harbour Beach **31** 28 10N 80 35W
Indian Head **41** 38 38N 77 12W
Indian Heights **36** 40 26N 86 10W
Indian L., Mich. **43** 45 59N 86 20W
Indian L., N.Y. **53** 43 42N 74 19W
Indian L., Ohio **56** 40 30N 83 53W
Indian Lake **53** 43 47N 74 16W
Indian Mills **51** 39 48N 74 46W
Indian Peak **66** 38 16N 113 53W
Indian River **43** 45 25N 84 37W
Indian River Bay **41** 38 36N 75 4W
Indian River County ◇ **31** 27 40N 80 45W
Indian Rock **67** 45 59N 120 49W
Indian Rocks Beach **31** 27 53N 82 51W
Indian Springs **49** 36 35N 115 40W
Indian Village **38** 37 5N 95 38W
Indiana **59** 40 37N 79 9W
Indiana □ **36** 40 0N 86 0W
Indiana County ◇ **59** 40 45N 79 0W
Indiana Dunes Nat. Lakeshore **36** 41 40N 87 0W
Indianapolis **36** 39 46N 86 9W
Indianola, Iowa **37** 41 22N 93 34W
Indianola, Miss. **45** 33 27N 90 39W
Indianola, Nebr. **48** 40 14N 100 25W
Indianola, Okla. **57** 35 10N 95 46W
Indiantown **31** 27 1N 80 28W
Indio **29** 33 43N 116 13W
Indrio **31** 27 31N 80 21W
Industry, Ill. **35** 40 20N 90 36W
Industry, Kans. **38** 39 8N 97 10W
Industry, Tex. **65** 29 58N 96 30W
Inez **63** 37 52N 82 32W
Ingalls, Ark. **27** 33 23N 92 9W
Ingalls, Kans. **38** 37 50N 100 27W
Ingham County ◇ **43** 42 35N 84 30W
Ingleside, Md. **41** 39 6N 75 53W
Ingleside, Tex. **65** 27 53N 97 13W
Inglewood **29** 33 58N 118 21W
Inglis **31** 29 2N 82 40W
Ingomar **47** 46 35N 107 23W
Ingram, Tex. **65** 30 5N 99 14W
Ingram, Wis. **69** 45 31N 90 49W
Inkom **34** 42 48N 112 15W
Inkster **55** 48 9N 97 39W
Inland L. **24** 33 50N 86 30W
Inlet **53** 43 45N 74 48W
Inman, Kans. **38** 38 14N 97 47W
Inman, Nebr. **48** 42 23N 98 32W
Inman, S.C. **60** 35 3N 82 5W
Inola **57** 36 9N 95 31W
Intercession City **31** 28 16N 81 31W
Interior **61** 43 44N 101 59W
Interlachen **31** 29 37N 81 53W
Interlaken **53** 42 37N 76 44W
International Falls **44** 48 36N 93 25W
Intervale **50** 44 6N 71 8W
Intracoastal City **39** 29 47N 92 9W
Inver Grove Heights **44** 44 51N 93 1W
Inverness, Ala. **24** 32 1N 85 45W
Inverness, Calif. **28** 38 6N 122 51W
Inverness, Fla. **31** 28 50N 82 20W
Inverness, Miss. **45** 33 21N 90 35W
Inwood **37** 43 19N 96 26W
Inyo County ◇ **29** 36 30N 117 40W
Inyo Mts. **29** 36 40N 118 0W
Inyo National Forest **29** 37 30N 118 15W
Inyokern **29** 35 39N 117 49W
Iola, Ill. **35** 38 50N 88 38W
Iola, Kans. **38** 37 55N 95 24W
Iola, Wis. **69** 44 30N 89 8W
Iona, Idaho **34** 43 32N 111 56W
Iona, Minn. **44** 43 55N 95 47W
Iona, S. Dak. **61** 43 33N 99 26W
Ione, Calif. **28** 38 21N 120 56W
Ione, Oreg. **58** 45 30N 119 50W
Ione, Wash. **67** 48 45N 117 25W
Ionia, Iowa **37** 43 2N 92 27W
Ionia, Kans. **38** 39 40N 98 21W
Ionia, Mich. **43** 42 59N 85 4W
Ionia, Mo. **46** 38 30N 93 19W
Ionia County ◇ **43** 42 55N 85 5W
Iosco County ◇ **43** 44 20N 83 40W
Iota **39** 30 20N 92 30W
Iowa **39** 30 14N 93 1W
Iowa □ **37** 42 15N 93 15W
Iowa → **37** 41 10N 91 1W
Iowa City **37** 41 40N 91 32W
Iowa County ◇, Iowa **37** 41 40N 92 0W
Iowa County ◇, Wis. **69** 43 0N 90 10W
Iowa Falls **37** 42 31N 93 16W
Iowa Park **65** 33 57N 98 40W
Ipava **35** 40 21N 90 19W
Ipswich, Mass. **42** 42 41N 70 50W
Ipswich, S. Dak. **61** 45 27N 99 2W
Ipswich B. **42** 42 41N 70 42W
Ira **64** 32 35N 101 0W
Iraan **64** 30 55N 101 54W
Irasburg **50** 44 18N 73 47W
Iredell **65** 31 59N 97 52W
Iredell County ◇ **54** 35 45N 80 50W
Ireton **37** 42 58N 96 19W
Irion County ◇ **64** 31 15N 101 0W
Iron Belt **69** 46 24N 90 19W
Iron City, Ga. **32** 31 1N 84 49W
Iron City, Tenn. **62** 35 1N 87 35W
Iron County ◇, Mich. **43** 46 15N 88 35W
Iron County ◇, Mo. **46** 37 30N 90 40W
Iron County ◇, Utah **66** 37 50N 113 20W
Iron County ◇, Wis. **69** 46 15N 90 15W
Iron Junction **44** 47 25N 92 36W
Iron Mountain, Mich. **43** 45 49N 88 4W
Iron Mountain, Mo. **46** 37 42N 90 39W
Iron Mts. **45** 36 40N 81 45W
Iron Ridge **69** 43 24N 88 32W
Iron River, Mich. **43** 46 6N 88 39W
Iron River, Wis. **69** 46 34N 91 24W
Irondale, Ala. **24** 33 32N 86 42W
Irondale, Mo. **46** 37 50N 90 41W
Irondale, Ohio **56** 40 34N 80 44W
Irondequoit **53** 43 13N 77 35W
Ironside **58** 44 19N 117 57W
Ironsides **41** 38 30N 77 12W
Ironton, Minn. **44** 46 28N 93 59W
Ironton, Mo. **46** 37 36N 90 38W
Ironton, Ohio **56** 38 32N 82 41W
Ironwood **43** 46 27N 90 9W
Iroquois, Ill. **35** 40 50N 87 35W
Iroquois, S. Dak. **61** 44 22N 97 51W
Iroquois → **36** 41 5N 87 49W
Iroquois County ◇ **35** 40 45N 87 50W
Irrigon **58** 45 54N 119 30W
Irvine, Calif. **29** 33 41N 117 46W
Irvine, Ky. **63** 37 42N 83 58W
Irving, Ill. **35** 39 12N 89 24W
Irving, Tex. **65** 32 49N 96 56W
Irvington, Ill. **35** 38 26N 89 10W
Irvington, Ky. **62** 37 53N 86 17W
Irvona **59** 40 46N 78 33W
Irwin **37** 41 47N 95 12W
Irwin County ◇ **32** 31 40N 83 15W
Irwinton **32** 32 49N 83 10W
Irwinville **32** 31 39N 83 23W
Isabel, Kans. **38** 37 28N 98 33W
Isabel, S. Dak. **61** 45 24N 101 26W
Isabel Segunda **71** 18 9N 65 27W
Isabela **71** 18 30N 67 2W
Isabella County ◇ **43** 43 40N 84 50W
Isabella L. **29** 35 39N 118 28W
Isabelle, Pt. **43** 47 21N 87 56W
Isanti **44** 45 29N 93 15W
Isanti County ◇ **44** 45 30N 93 15W
Isaquah **67** 47 32N 122 2W
Ishpeming **43** 46 29N 87 40W
Isla Vista **29** 34 25N 119 53W
Islamorada **31** 24 56N 80 37W
Island County ◇ **67** 48 10N 122 35W
Island Creek **41** 38 27N 76 35W
Island Falls **40** 46 1N 68 16W
Island Heights **51** 39 57N 74 9W
Island Lake Res. **44** 47 48N 94 19W
Island Park **34** 44 24N 111 19W
Island Park Reservoir **34** 44 25N 111 24W
Island Pond **50** 44 49N 71 53W
Isle **44** 46 8N 93 28W
Isle La Motte **50** 44 52N 73 18W
Isle of Hope **32** 31 58N 81 5W
Isle of Wight **68** 36 54N 76 43W
Isle of Wight Bay **41** 38 22N 75 6W
Isle of Wight County ◇ **68** 36 54N 76 43W
Isle Royale **43** 48 0N 88 54W
Isle Royale National Park **43** 48 0N 88 55W
Islesboro I. **40** 44 19N 68 54W
Isleta **52** 34 55N 106 42W
Isleta Indian Reservation **52** 34 55N 106 45W
Isleton **28** 38 10N 121 37W
Ismay **47** 46 30N 104 48W
Isola **45** 33 16N 90 35W
Israel → **50** 44 29N 71 35W
Issaquena County ◇ **45** 32 54N 91 3W
Issue **41** 38 16N 76 53W
Isto, Mt. **25** 69 12N 143 48W
Istokpoga, L. **31** 27 23N 81 17W
Italy **65** 32 11N 96 53W
Itasca **65** 32 10N 97 9W
Itasca County ◇ **44** 47 25N 93 25W
Itawamba County ◇ **45** 34 16N 88 25W
Ithaca, Mich. **43** 43 18N 84 36W
Ithaca, N.Y. **53** 42 27N 76 30W
Ithaca, Nebr. **48** 41 10N 96 33W
Itkilik → **25** 70 9N 150 56W
Itta Bena **45** 33 30N 90 20W
Iuka, Kans. **38** 37 44N 98 44W
Iuka, Miss. **45** 34 49N 88 12W
Iva **60** 34 19N 82 40W
Ivan **27** 33 55N 92 26W
Ivanhoe, Calif. **29** 36 23N 119 13W
Ivanhoe, Minn. **44** 44 28N 96 15W
Ivanhoe, Va. **68** 36 50N 80 58W
Ivanof Bay **25** 55 54N 159 29W
Ivesdale **35** 39 57N 88 28W
Ivor **68** 36 54N 76 54W
Ivydale **68** 38 32N 81 2W
Ivywild **30** 38 49N 104 51W
Izard County ◇ **27** 36 4N 91 54W

J

J. B. Thomas, L. **64** 32 36N 101 8W
J. Percy Priest Reservoir **62** 36 9N 86 37W
Jacinto City **65** 29 46N 95 13W
Jack County ◇ **65** 33 13N 98 10W
Jackman Station **40** 45 37N 70 15W
Jackpot **49** 41 59N 114 40W
Jacks Fork → **46** 37 12N 91 18W
Jacksboro, Tenn. **63** 36 20N 84 11W
Jacksboro, Tex. **65** 33 13N 98 10W
Jackson, Ala. **24** 31 31N 87 53W
Jackson, Calif. **28** 38 21N 120 46W
Jackson, Ga. **32** 33 20N 83 57W
Jackson, Ky. **63** 37 33N 83 23W
Jackson, La. **39** 30 50N 91 13W
Jackson, Mich. **43** 42 15N 84 24W
Jackson, Minn. **44** 43 37N 95 1W
Jackson, Miss. **45** 32 18N 90 12W
Jackson, Mo. **46** 37 23N 89 40W
Jackson, Mont. **47** 45 23N 113 28W
Jackson, N.C. **54** 36 23N 77 25W
Jackson, N.H. **50** 44 10N 71 11W
Jackson, N.J. **51** 40 6N 74 23W
Jackson, Nebr. **48** 42 27N 96 34W
Jackson, Ohio **56** 39 3N 82 39W
Jackson, S.C. **60** 33 20N 81 47W
Jackson, Tenn. **62** 35 37N 88 49W
Jackson, Wis. **69** 43 19N 88 10W
Jackson, Wyo. **70** 43 29N 110 46W
Jackson County ◇, Ala. **24** 34 40N 86 2W
Jackson County ◇, Ark. **27** 35 37N 91 16W
Jackson County ◇, Colo. **30** 40 45N 106 20W
Jackson County ◇, Fla. **31** 30 45N 85 15W
Jackson County ◇, Ga. **32** 34 10N 83 30W
Jackson County ◇, Ill. **35** 37 45N 89 25W
Jackson County ◇, Ind. **36** 38 55N 86 0W
Jackson County ◇, Iowa **37** 42 10N 90 35W
Jackson County ◇, Kans. **38** 39 20N 95 45W
Jackson County ◇, Ky. **63** 37 25N 84 0W
Jackson County ◇, Mich. **43** 42 15N 84 30W
Jackson County ◇, Minn. **44** 43 40N 95 10W
Jackson County ◇, Miss. **45** 30 32N 88 42W
Jackson County ◇, Mo. **46** 39 0N 94 20W
Jackson County ◇, N.C. **54** 35 20N 83 10W
Jackson County ◇, Ohio **56** 39 3N 82 39W
Jackson County ◇, Okla. **57** 34 30N 99 25W
Jackson County ◇, Oreg. **58** 42 20N 122 45W
Jackson County ◇, S. Dak. **61** 43 45N 101 45W
Jackson County ◇, Tenn. **63** 36 21N 85 39W
Jackson County ◇, Tex. **65** 28 59N 96 39W
Jackson County ◇, W. Va. **68** 38 49N 81 43W
Jackson County ◇, Wis. **69** 44 20N 90 45W
Jackson Junction **37** 43 7N 92 2W
Jackson L., Fla. **31** 30 30N 84 17W
Jackson L., Ga. **32** 33 19N 83 50W
Jackson L., Wyo. **70** 43 52N 110 36W
Jackson Mts. **49** 41 10N 118 30W
Jackson Parish ◇ **39** 32 15N 92 43W
Jackson Reservoir **30** 40 22N 104 6W
Jacksonville, Ala. **24** 33 49N 85 46W
Jacksonville, Ark. **27** 34 52N 92 7W
Jacksonville, Fla. **31** 30 20N 81 39W
Jacksonville, Ga. **32** 31 49N 82 59W
Jacksonville, Ill. **35** 39 44N 90 14W
Jacksonville, N.C. **54** 34 45N 77 26W
Jacksonville, Ohio **56** 39 29N 82 5W
Jacksonville, Oreg. **58** 42 19N 122 57W
Jacksonville, Tex. **65** 31 58N 95 17W
Jacksonville, Vt. **50** 42 47N 72 49W
Jacksonville Beach **31** 30 17N 81 24W
Jacob Lake **26** 36 43N 112 13W
Jacobsville **41** 39 7N 76 31W
Jacumba **29** 32 37N 116 11W
Jaffrey **50** 42 49N 72 2W
Jaicoa, Cord. **71** 18 25N 67 5W
Jakin **32** 31 6N 84 59W
Jal **52** 32 7N 103 12W
Jamaica, Iowa **37** 41 51N 94 18W
Jamaica, Vt. **50** 43 13N 72 46W
James **32** 32 58N 83 29W
James →, Mo. **46** 36 45N 93 30W
James →, S. Dak. **61** 42 52N 97 18W
James →, Va. **68** 36 56N 76 27W
James, L. **54** 35 44N 81 54W
James City **54** 35 5N 77 2W
James City County ◇ **68** 37 16N 76 40W
James Island **60** 32 45N 79 55W
Jamesburg **51** 40 21N 74 27W
Jamesport **46** 39 58N 93 48W
Jamestown, Calif. **28** 37 57N 120 25W
Jamestown, Ind. **36** 39 56N 86 38W
Jamestown, Kans. **38** 39 36N 97 52W
Jamestown, Ky. **63** 36 59N 85 4W
Jamestown, La. **39** 32 21N 93 13W
Jamestown, N. Dak. **55** 46 54N 98 42W
Jamestown, N.Y. **53** 42 6N 79 14W
Jamestown, Ohio **56** 39 39N 83 33W
Jamestown, Pa. **59** 41 29N 80 27W
Jamestown, R.I. **42** 41 30N 71 22W
Jamestown, S.C. **60** 33 17N 79 42W
Jamestown, Tenn. **63** 36 26N 84 56W
Jamestown, Va. **68** 37 13N 76 47W
Jamestown Reservoir **55** 46 56N 98 43W
Jamesville **54** 35 49N 76 54W
Jamieson **58** 44 11N 117 26W
Jamison **48** 43 0N 99 18W
Jane **46** 36 33N 94 18W
Jane Lew **68** 39 7N 80 25W
Janesville, Calif. **28** 40 18N 120 32W
Janesville, Iowa **37** 42 39N 92 28W
Janesville, Minn. **44** 44 7N 93 42W
Janesville, Wis. **69** 42 41N 89 1W
Jansen, Colo. **30** 37 9N 104 32W
Jansen, Nebr. **48** 40 11N 97 5W
Jarratt **68** 36 48N 77 28W
Jarrettsville **41** 39 36N 76 29W
Jarvisburg **54** 36 9N 75 52W
Jasonville **36** 39 10N 87 12W
Jasper, Ala. **24** 33 50N 87 17W
Jasper, Ark. **27** 36 1N 93 11W

Jasper, Fla. 31 30 31N 82 57W
Jasper, Ga. 32 34 28N 84 26W
Jasper, Ind. 36 38 24N 86 56W
Jasper, Minn. 44 43 51N 96 24W
Jasper, Mo. 46 37 20N 94 18W
Jasper, Tenn. 63 35 5N 85 38W
Jasper, Tex. 65 30 56N 94 1W
Jasper County ◇, Ga. 32 33 20N 83 45W
Jasper County ◇, Ill. 35 39 0N 88 10W
Jasper County ◇, Ind. 36 41 0N 87 5W
Jasper County ◇, Iowa 37 41 40N 93 0W
Jasper County ◇, Miss. 45 32 2N 89 2W
Jasper County ◇, Mo. 46 37 10N 94 20W
Jasper County ◇, S.C. 60 32 30N 81 0W
Jasper County ◇, Tex. 65 30 40N 93 54W
Java 61 45 30N 99 53W
Jay, Fla. 31 30 57N 87 9W
Jay, Maine 40 44 30N 70 13W
Jay, N.Y. 53 44 21N 73 45W
Jay, Okla. 57 36 25N 94 48W
Jay County ◇ 36 40 25N 85 0W
Jay Peak 50 44 55N 72 32W
Jayton 64 33 15N 100 34W
Jayuya 71 18 14N 66 36W
Jean, Nev. 49 35 47N 115 20W
Jean, Tex. 65 33 18N 98 37W
Jeanerette 39 29 55N 91 40W
Jeff Davis County ◇, Ga. 32 31 50N 82 45W
Jeff Davis County ◇, Tex. 64 30 55N 104 5W
Jeffers 44 44 3N 95 12W
Jefferson, Colo. 30 39 23N 105 48W
Jefferson, Ga. 32 34 7N 83 35W
Jefferson, Iowa 37 42 1N 94 23W
Jefferson, Maine 40 44 13N 69 27W
Jefferson, Md. 41 39 22N 77 32W
Jefferson, N.C. 54 36 25N 81 28W
Jefferson, Ohio 56 41 44N 80 46W
Jefferson, Okla. 57 36 43N 97 48W
Jefferson, Oreg. 58 44 43N 123 1W
Jefferson, S.C. 60 34 39N 80 23W
Jefferson, S. Dak. 61 42 36N 96 34W
Jefferson, Tex. 65 32 46N 94 21W
Jefferson, Wis. 69 43 0N 88 48W
Jefferson ➝ 47 45 56N 111 31W
Jefferson, Mt. 58 44 41N 121 48W
Jefferson City, Mo. 46 38 34N 92 10W
Jefferson City, Tenn. 63 36 7N 83 30W
Jefferson County ◇, Ala. 24 33 31N 86 48W
Jefferson County ◇, Ark. 27 34 13N 92 1W
Jefferson County ◇, Colo. 30 39 40N 105 15W
Jefferson County ◇, Fla. 31 30 20N 84 0W
Jefferson County ◇, Ga. 32 33 10N 82 25W
Jefferson County ◇, Idaho 34 43 50N 112 20W
Jefferson County ◇, Ill. 35 38 20N 88 55W
Jefferson County ◇, Ind. 36 43 50N 85 25W
Jefferson County ◇, Iowa 37 41 0N 92 0W
Jefferson County ◇, Kans. 38 39 15N 95 30W
Jefferson County ◇, Ky. 63 38 10N 85 40W
Jefferson County ◇, Miss. 45 31 43N 91 4W
Jefferson County ◇, Mo. 46 38 15N 90 30W
Jefferson County ◇, Mont. 47 46 8N 112 0W
Jefferson County ◇, N.Y. 53 44 0N 76 0W
Jefferson County ◇, Nebr. 48 40 15N 97 10W
Jefferson County ◇, Ohio 56 40 25N 80 54W
Jefferson County ◇, Okla. 57 34 10N 97 50W
Jefferson County ◇, Oreg. 58 44 40N 121 10W
Jefferson County ◇, Pa. 59 41 5N 79 0W
Jefferson County ◇, Tenn. 63 36 7N 83 30W
Jefferson County ◇, Tex. 65 29 55N 94 15W
Jefferson County ◇, W. Va. 68 39 17N 77 52W
Jefferson County ◇, Wash. 67 47 50N 123 45W
Jefferson County ◇, Wis. 69 43 0N 88 45W
Jefferson Davis County ◇ 45 31 36N 89 52W
Jefferson Davis Parish ◇ 39 30 14N 92 49W
Jefferson Mt. 49 38 46N 116 55W
Jefferson National Forest 68 37 10N 81 15W
Jefferson Parish ◇ 39 29 44N 90 8W
Jeffersonton 68 38 38N 77 55W
Jeffersontown 63 38 12N 85 35W
Jeffersonville, Ga. 32 32 41N 83 20W
Jeffersonville, Ind. 36 38 17N 85 44W
Jeffersonville, Ky. 63 37 59N 83 51W
Jeffersonville, Ohio 56 39 39N 83 34W
Jeffersonville, Vt. 50 44 40N 72 50W
Jeffrey City 70 42 30N 107 49W
Jeffrey Reservoir 48 40 58N 100 24W
Jekyll I. 32 31 4N 81 25W
Jellico 63 36 53N 84 8W
Jemez Indian Reservation 52 35 40N 106 50W
Jemez Mts. 52 35 45N 106 30W
Jemez Pueblo 52 35 37N 106 44W
Jemez Springs 52 35 46N 106 42W
Jemison 24 32 58N 86 45W
Jena, Fla. 31 29 40N 83 22W
Jena, La. 39 31 41N 92 8W
Jenison 43 42 54N 85 47W
Jenkins, Ky. 63 37 10N 82 38W
Jenkins, Minn. 44 46 39N 94 20W
Jenkins, N.J. 51 39 42N 74 32W
Jenkins County ◇ 32 32 45N 82 0W
Jenks 57 36 1N 95 58W
Jenner 28 38 27N 123 7W
Jennings, Fla. 31 30 36N 83 6W
Jennings, Kans. 38 39 41N 100 18W
Jennings, La. 39 30 13N 92 40W
Jennings, Mo. 46 38 43N 90 16W
Jennings, Okla. 57 36 11N 96 34W
Jennings County ◇ 36 39 0N 85 40W
Jensen 66 40 22N 109 20W
Jensen Beach 31 27 15N 80 14W
Jerauld County ◇ 61 44 0N 98 45W
Jeremy Point 42 41 53N 70 4W
Jerico Springs 46 37 37N 94 1W
Jerimoth Hill 42 41 51N 71 47W
Jermyn 65 33 16N 98 23W
Jerome, Ariz. 26 34 45N 112 7W
Jerome, Ark. 27 33 24N 91 28W
Jerome, Idaho 34 42 44N 114 31W
Jerome County ◇ 34 42 42N 114 15W
Jerry City 56 41 15N 83 36W
Jersey, Ark. 27 33 26N 92 19W
Jersey, Ga. 32 33 43N 83 47W
Jersey City 51 40 44N 74 4W
Jersey County ◇ 35 39 5N 90 20W
Jersey Shore 59 41 12N 77 15W
Jersey Village 65 29 53N 95 34W
Jerseyville 35 39 7N 90 20W
Jerusalem 32 30 58N 81 50W
Jessamine County ◇ 63 37 50N 84 35W
Jessieville 27 34 42N 93 4W
Jessup L. 31 28 43N 81 14W
Jesup, Ga. 32 31 36N 81 53W
Jesup, Iowa 37 42 29N 92 4W
Jet 57 36 40N 98 11W
Jetmore 38 38 4N 99 54W
Jewell, Iowa 37 42 20N 93 39W
Jewell, Kans. 38 39 40N 98 10W
Jewell County ◇ 38 39 45N 98 10W
Jewell Valley 68 37 15N 81 48W
Jewett, Ill. 35 39 13N 88 15W
Jewett, Ohio 56 40 22N 81 2W
Jewett, Tex. 65 31 22N 96 9W
Jewett City 42 41 36N 72 0W
Jicarilla Indian Reservation 52 36 45N 107 0W
Jigger 39 32 2N 91 45W
Jim Hogg County ◇ 64 27 0N 98 45W
Jim Thorpe 59 40 52N 75 44W
Jim Wells County ◇ 65 28 0N 98 0W
Jo Daviess County ◇ 35 42 20N 90 10W
Joanna 60 34 25N 81 49W
Joaquin 65 31 58N 94 3W
Jobos 71 17 58N 66 10W
Jobos, Bahía de 71 17 59N 66 14W
Jocassee, L. 60 34 58N 82 56W
Joes 30 39 39N 102 41W
Johannesburg 29 35 22N 117 38W
John Day 58 44 25N 118 57W
John Day ➝ 58 45 44N 120 39W
John Day Dam 67 45 43N 120 41W
John Day Fossil Buttes Nat. Mon. 58 44 43N 120 21W
John H. Kerr Reservoir 54 36 36N 78 18W
John Martin Reservoir 30 38 4N 102 56W
John Redmond Reservoir 38 38 14N 95 46W
John W. Flanagan Reservoir 68 37 15N 82 22W
Johns I. 60 32 40N 80 10W
Johns Island 60 32 47N 80 7W
Johnson, Kans. 38 37 34N 101 45W
Johnson, Vt. 50 44 38N 72 41W
Johnson City, N.Y. 53 42 7N 75 58W
Johnson City, Tenn. 63 36 19N 82 21W
Johnson City, Tex. 65 30 17N 98 25W
Johnson County ◇, Ark. 27 35 28N 93 28W
Johnson County ◇, Ga. 32 32 45N 82 40W
Johnson County ◇, Ill. 35 37 30N 88 50W
Johnson County ◇, Ind. 36 39 30N 86 5W
Johnson County ◇, Iowa 37 41 40N 91 35W
Johnson County ◇, Kans. 38 38 45N 94 45W
Johnson County ◇, Ky. 63 37 50N 82 50W
Johnson County ◇, Mo. 46 38 45N 93 45W
Johnson County ◇, Nebr. 48 40 20N 96 15W
Johnson County ◇, Tenn. 63 36 29N 81 48W
Johnson County ◇, Tex. 65 32 21N 97 23W
Johnson County ◇, Wyo. 70 44 0N 106 35W
Johnson Draw ➝ 64 30 8N 101 7W
Johnson Reservoir 48 40 42N 99 49W
Johnsonburg, N.J. 51 40 58N 74 53W
Johnsonburg, Pa. 59 41 29N 78 41W
Johnsondale 29 35 58N 118 32W
Johnsonville 60 33 49N 79 27W
Johnston, R.I. 42 41 50N 71 30W
Johnston, S.C. 60 33 50N 81 48W
Johnston City 35 37 49N 88 56W
Johnston County ◇, N.C. 54 35 30N 78 20W
Johnston County ◇, Okla. 57 34 20N 96 40W
Johnstown, Colo. 30 40 20N 104 54W
Johnstown, N.Y. 53 43 0N 74 22W
Johnstown, Nebr. 48 42 34N 100 3W
Johnstown, Ohio 56 40 9N 82 41W
Johnstown, Pa. 59 40 20N 78 55W
Joice 37 43 22N 93 27W
Joiner 27 35 31N 90 9W
Joliet, Ill. 35 41 32N 88 5W
Joliet, Mont. 47 45 29N 108 58W
Jolley 37 42 29N 94 43W
Jones 39 32 58N 91 39W
Jones County ◇, Ga. 32 33 0N 83 30W
Jones County ◇, Iowa 37 42 5N 91 5W
Jones County ◇, Miss. 45 31 36N 89 12W
Jones County ◇, N.C. 54 35 0N 77 30W
Jones County ◇, S. Dak. 61 44 0N 100 50W
Jones County ◇, Tex. 65 32 45N 99 54W
Jonesboro, Ark. 27 35 50N 90 42W
Jonesboro, Ga. 32 33 31N 84 22W
Jonesboro, Ill. 35 37 27N 89 16W
Jonesboro, Ind. 36 40 29N 85 38W
Jonesboro, La. 39 32 15N 92 43W
Jonesboro, Tenn. 63 36 18N 82 29W
Jonesboro, Tex. 65 31 37N 97 53W
Jonesburg 46 38 51N 91 18W
Jonesport 40 44 32N 67 37W
Jonestown, Miss. 45 34 19N 90 27W
Jonestown, Pa. 59 40 25N 76 29W
Jonesville, La. 39 31 38N 91 49W
Jonesville, Mich. 43 41 59N 84 40W
Jonesville, N.C. 54 36 14N 80 51W
Jonesville, S.C. 60 34 50N 81 41W
Jonesville, Va. 68 36 41N 83 7W
Joplin, Mo. 46 37 6N 94 31W
Joplin, Mont. 47 48 34N 110 46W
Joppa 35 37 12N 88 51W
Jordan, Minn. 44 44 40N 93 38W
Jordan, Mont. 47 47 19N 106 55W
Jordan, N.Y. 53 43 4N 76 29W
Jordan ➝ 66 40 49N 112 8W
Jordan Valley 58 42 59N 117 3W
Jornado del Muerto 52 33 15N 106 50W
Joseph, Oreg. 58 45 21N 117 14W
Joseph, Utah 66 38 38N 112 13W
Joseph ➝ 67 46 3N 117 1W
Joseph City 26 34 57N 110 20W
Josephine County ◇ 58 42 20N 123 40W
Joshua 65 32 28N 97 23W
Joshua Tree 29 34 8N 116 19W
Joshua Tree National Monument 29 33 55N 116 0W
Jourdanton 65 28 55N 98 33W
Joy 35 41 12N 90 53W
Joyce 67 48 8N 123 44W
Juab County ◇ 66 39 40N 113 0W
Juan de Fuca, Str of 67 48 18N 124 0W
Juana Diaz 71 18 3N 66 31W
Jud 55 46 32N 98 54W
Judith ➝ 47 47 44N 109 39W
Judith, Pt. 42 41 22N 71 29W
Judith Basin County ◇ 47 46 55N 110 10W
Judith Gap 47 46 41N 109 45W
Judith Mts. 47 47 15N 109 20W
Judsonia 27 35 16N 91 38W
Julesburg 30 40 59N 102 16W
Julesburg Reservoir 30 40 56N 102 38W
Julian, N.C. 54 35 54N 79 39W
Julian, Nebr. 48 40 31N 95 52W
Juliette, L 32 33 2N 83 50W
Jump ➝ 69 45 17N 91 5W
Juncos 71 18 14N 65 55W
Junction, Tex. 65 30 29N 99 46W
Junction, Utah 66 38 14N 112 13W
Junction City, Ga. 32 32 36N 84 28W
Junction City, Kans. 38 39 2N 96 50W
Junction City, Ky. 63 37 35N 84 48W
Junction City, La. 39 33 0N 92 43W
Junction City, Oreg. 58 44 13N 123 12W
Junction City, Wis. 69 44 35N 89 46W
June Lake 28 37 47N 119 4W
Juneau, Alaska 25 58 18N 134 25W
Juneau, Wis. 69 43 24N 88 42W
Juneau ◇ 25 58 30N 134 0W
Juneau County ◇ 69 43 50N 90 10W
Juniata 48 40 35N 98 30W
Juniata ➝ 59 40 24N 77 1W
Juniata County ◇ 59 40 45N 77 5W
Junior 68 38 59N 79 57W
Juniper 32 32 32N 84 36W
Juniper Mts. 26 35 10N 113 0W
Juno 64 30 9N 101 7W
Juno Beach 31 26 52N 80 3W
Juntura 58 43 45N 118 5W
Jupiter 31 26 57N 80 6W
Justice 68 37 35N 81 50W
Justin 65 33 5N 97 18W

K

Ka Lae 33 18 55N 155 41W
Kaaawa 33 21 33N 157 51W
Kaala 33 21 31N 158 9W
Kaalualu B. 33 18 58N 155 37W
Kabetogama L. 44 48 28N 93 1W
Kackley 38 39 42N 97 51W
Kadoka 61 43 50N 101 31W
Kaena Pt. 33 21 35N 158 17W
Kagamil I. 25 53 0N 169 43W
Kahaluu 33 21 28N 157 50W
Kahana 33 21 34N 157 53W
Kahana B. 33 21 35N 157 50W
Kahlotus 67 46 39N 118 33W
Kahoka 46 40 25N 91 44W
Kahoolawe 33 20 33N 156 37W
Kahuku 33 21 41N 157 57W
Kahuku Pt. 33 21 43N 157 59W
Kahului 33 20 54N 156 28W
Kaibab 26 36 54N 112 44W
Kaibab Indian Reservation 26 36 55N 112 40W
Kaibab National Forest 26 36 35N 112 15W
Kaibab Plateau 26 36 45N 112 15W
Kaibito Plateau 26 36 30N 111 15W
Kailua 33 21 24N 157 44W
Kailua B. 33 21 25N 157 40W
Kailua Kona 33 19 39N 155 59W
Kaimuki 33 21 17N 157 48W
Kaiparowits Plateau 66 37 30N 111 20W
Kaiwi Channel 33 21 15N 157 30W
Kaiyuh Mts. 25 64 30N 158 0W
Kaka Pt. 33 20 31N 156 33W
Kake 25 56 59N 133 57W
Kakhonak 25 59 26N 154 51W
Kaktovik 25 70 8N 143 38W
Kalaheo 33 21 56N 159 32W
Kalama 67 46 1N 122 51W
Kalamazoo 43 42 17N 85 35W
Kalamazoo ➝ 43 42 40N 86 10W
Kalamazoo County ◇ 43 42 15N 85 30W
Kalapana 33 19 21N 154 59W
Kalaupapa 33 21 12N 156 59W
Kaleva 43 44 22N 86 1W
Kalida 56 40 59N 84 12W
Kalihi 33 21 20N 157 53W
Kalispell 47 48 12N 114 19W
Kalkaska 43 44 44N 85 11W
Kalkaska County ◇ 43 44 45N 85 5W
Kalohi Channel 33 21 0N 157 0W
Kalona 37 41 29N 91 43W
Kaltag 25 64 20N 158 43W
Kalvesta 38 38 4N 100 18W

Kamakou **33** 21 7N 156 52W
Kamananui → **33** 21 38N 158 4W
Kamas **66** 40 38N 111 17W
Kamehameha
Heights **33** 21 21N 157 52W
Kamela **58** 45 26N 118 24W
Kamiah **34** 46 14N 116 2W
Kamishak Bay **25** 59 15N 153 45W
Kamooloa **33** 21 34N 158 7W
Kampsville **35** 39 18N 90 37W
Kamrar **37** 42 24N 93 44W
Kamuela **33** 20 1N 155 41W
Kanab **66** 37 3N 112 32W
Kanab → **26** 36 24N 112 38W
Kanabec County ◇ . **44** 45 55N 93 20W
Kanaga I. **25** 51 45N 177 22W
Kanarraville **66** 37 32N 113 11W
Kanawha **37** 42 56N 93 48W
Kanawha → **68** 38 50N 82 9W
Kanawha County ◇. **68** 38 21N 81 38W
Kandiyohi County ◇ **44** 45 10N 95 0W
Kane, Ill. **35** 39 11N 90 21W
Kane, Pa. **59** 41 40N 78 49W
Kane, Wyo. **70** 44 51N 108 12W
Kane County ◇, Ill. **35** 41 50N 88 25W
Kane County ◇,
Utah **66** 37 15N 112 0W
Kaneilio Pt. **33** 21 27N 158 12W
Kaneohe **33** 21 25N 157 48W
Kaneohe B. **33** 21 30N 157 50W
Kaniksu National
Forest **34** 48 50N 116 30W
Kankakee **35** 41 7N 87 52W
Kankakee → **35** 41 23N 88 15W
Kankakee County ◇ **35** 41 10N 87 50W
Kannapolis **54** 35 30N 80 37W
Kanopolis **38** 38 43N 98 9W
Kanopolis Lake **38** 38 37N 97 58W
Kanorado **38** 39 20N 102 2W
Kanosh **66** 38 48N 112 26W
Kansas, Ill. **35** 39 33N 87 56W
Kansas, Okla. **57** 36 12N 94 48W
Kansas □ **38** 38 30N 99 0W
Kansas → **38** 39 7N 94 37W
Kansas City, Kans. . **38** 39 7N 94 38W
Kansas City, Mo. ... **46** 39 6N 94 35W
Kantishna → **25** 64 45N 149 58W
Kapaa **33** 22 5N 159 19W
Kapahulu **33** 21 0N 157 0W
Kapapa I. **33** 21 29N 157 48W
Kaplan **39** 30 0N 92 17W
Kapowsin **67** 46 59N 122 13W
Karlsruhe **55** 48 6N 100 37W
Karlstad **44** 48 35N 96 31W
Karluk **25** 57 34N 154 28W
Karluk Indian
Reservation **25** 57 35N 154 20W
Karnack **65** 32 40N 94 10W
Karnak **35** 37 18N 88 58W
Karnes City **65** 28 53N 97 54W
Karnes County ◇ ... **65** 28 49N 97 51W
Karval **30** 38 44N 103 32W
Kasaan **25** 55 32N 132 24W
Kasilof **25** 60 23N 151 18W
Kaskaskia → **35** 37 58N 89 57W
Kasson **44** 44 2N 92 45W
Katahdin, Mt. **40** 45 54N 68 56W
Katalla **25** 60 12N 144 31W
Kathleen **31** 28 7N 82 2W
Kathryn **55** 46 41N 97 58W
Katmai National
Monument **25** 58 20N 155 0W
Katy **65** 29 47N 95 49W
Kauai **33** 22 3N 159 30W
Kauai Channel **33** 21 45N 158 50W
Kauai County ◇.... **33** 22 0N 159 30W
Kaufman **65** 32 35N 96 19W
Kaufman County ◇. **65** 32 35N 96 20W
Kauhola Pt. **33** 20 15N 155 47W
Kaukauna **69** 44 17N 88 17W
Kaukonahua → ... **33** 21 35N 158 7W
Kaula I. **33** 21 40N 160 33W
Kaulakahi Channel . **33** 22 0N 159 55W
Kaumalapau **33** 20 47N 156 59W
Kauna Pt. **33** 19 2N 155 53W
Kaunakakai **33** 21 6N 157 1W
Kaupo **33** 20 38N 156 8W
Kaw City **57** 36 46N 96 50W
Kaw L. **57** 36 50N 96 55W
Kawaihae **33** 20 3N 155 50W
Kawaihae B. **33** 20 0N 155 50W
Kawaihoa Pt. **33** 21 47N 160 12W
Kawaikimi **33** 22 5N 159 29W
Kawailoa Beach **33** 21 37N 158 5W
Kaweah, L. **29** 36 28N 118 52W
Kawela **33** 21 42N 158 1W
Kawkawlin **43** 43 39N 83 57W
Kay County ◇ **57** 36 50N 97 5W
Kayak I. **25** 59 56N 144 23W
Kaycee **70** 43 43N 106 38W
Kayenta **26** 36 44N 110 15W
Kaylor **61** 43 11N 97 50W
Kaysville **66** 41 2N 111 56W
Keaau **33** 19 37N 155 2W
Keahi Pt. **33** 21 19N 157 59W
Keahole Pt. **33** 19 44N 156 4W
Kealaikahiki
Channel **33** 20 35N 156 50W
Kealaikahiki Pt. **33** 20 32N 156 42W
Kealakekua **33** 19 31N 155 55W
Kealia **33** 19 24N 155 53W
Keams Canyon **26** 35 49N 110 12W
Keansburg **51** 40 27N 74 8W
Kearney, Mo. **46** 39 22N 94 22W
Kearney, Nebr. **48** 40 42N 99 5W
Kearney County ◇ . **48** 40 30N 99 0W
Kearneysville **68** 39 23N 77 53W
Kearns **66** 40 39N 112 0W
Kearny, Ariz. **26** 33 3N 110 55W
Kearny, N.J. **51** 40 46N 74 9W
Kearny County ◇ .. **38** 38 0N 101 15W
Kearsarge, Mt. **50** 43 22N 71 50W
Keatchie **39** 32 11N 93 54W
Keating **58** 44 53N 117 35W
Keats **38** 39 14N 96 43W
Keau **33** 19 38N 155 2W
Keawakapu **33** 20 43N 156 27W
Keddie **28** 40 1N 120 58W
Keedysville **41** 39 29N 77 40W
Keefeton **57** 35 36N 95 21W
Keehi Lagoon **33** 21 20N 157 54W
Keene, N. Dak. **55** 47 56N 102 56W
Keene, N.H. **50** 42 56N 72 17W
Keene, Tex. **65** 32 24N 97 20W
Keenesburg **30** 40 7N 104 31W
Keensburg **35** 38 21N 87 52W
Keewatin **44** 47 24N 93 5W
Keikiwaha Pt. **33** 19 31N 155 58W
Keith County ◇ **48** 41 15N 101 40W
Keithsburg **35** 41 6N 90 56W
Keizer **58** 44 57N 123 1W
Kekaha **33** 21 58N 159 43W
Kell **35** 38 30N 88 54W
Keller, Ga. **32** 31 50N 81 15W
Keller, Wash. **67** 48 5N 118 41W
Kellerton **37** 40 43N 94 3W
Kellerville **64** 35 22N 100 30W
Kelley **37** 41 57N 93 40W
Kelleys I. **56** 41 36N 82 42W
Kelliher **44** 47 57N 94 27W
Kellogg, Idaho **34** 47 32N 116 7W
Kellogg, Iowa **37** 41 43N 92 54W
Kellogg, Minn. **44** 44 18N 91 59W
Kelly **62** 36 13N 87 29W
Kellyville **57** 35 57N 96 13W
Kelseyville **28** 38 59N 122 50W
Kelso, Ark. **27** 33 48N 91 16W
Kelso, Wash. **67** 46 9N 122 54W
Kemah **65** 29 33N 95 1W
Kemmerer **70** 41 48N 110 32W
Kemp **65** 32 26N 96 14W
Kemp, L. **65** 33 46N 99 9W
Kemper County ◇ .. **45** 32 46N 88 39W
Kempton, Ill. **35** 40 56N 88 14W
Kempton, Ind. **36** 40 17N 86 14W
Kemptown **41** 39 20N 77 13W
Kenai **25** 60 33N 151 16W
Kenai Mts. **25** 60 0N 150 0W
Kenai Peninsula ... **25** 60 0N 151 0W
Kenai Peninsula ◇ . **25** 59 30N 151 0W
Kenansville, Fla. ... **31** 27 53N 80 59W
Kenansville, N.C. .. **54** 34 58N 77 58W
Kenbridge **68** 36 58N 78 8W
Kendall, Fla. **31** 25 41N 80 19W
Kendall, Kans. **38** 37 56N 101 33W
Kendall, Wis. **69** 43 48N 90 21W
Kendall County ◇,
Ill. **35** 41 35N 88 25W
Kendall County ◇,
Tex. **65** 29 57N 98 48W
Kendall Park **51** 40 25N 74 34W
Kendallville **36** 41 27N 85 16W
Kendleton **65** 29 26N 96 0W
Kendrick, Fla. **31** 29 15N 82 10W
Kendrick, Idaho **34** 46 37N 116 39W
Kendrick, Okla. **57** 35 47N 96 46W
Kenedy **65** 28 49N 97 51W
Kenedy County ◇ .. **64** 27 0N 97 40W
Kenefic **57** 34 9N 96 22W
Kenefick **65** 30 7N 94 52W
Kenesaw **48** 40 37N 98 39W
Kenly **54** 35 36N 78 7W
Kenmare **55** 48 41N 102 5W
Kenmore **53** 42 58N 78 52W
Kenna, N. Mex. **52** 33 51N 103 46W
Kenna, W. Va. **68** 38 41N 81 40W
Kennaday Peak **70** 41 27N 106 31W
Kennard, Nebr. **48** 41 28N 96 12W
Kennard, Tex. **65** 31 22N 95 11W
Kennebec **61** 43 54N 99 52W
Kennebec → **40** 43 45N 69 46W
Kennebec County ◇ **40** 44 20N 69 50W
Kennebunk **40** 43 23N 70 33W
Kennebunkport **40** 43 21N 70 28W
Kennedy, Ala. **24** 33 35N 87 59W
Kennedy, Minn. **44** 48 39N 96 54W
Kennedyville **41** 39 18N 75 58W
Kenner **39** 29 59N 90 15W
Kennesaw **32** 34 1N 84 37W
Kennett **46** 36 14N 90 3W
Kennett Square **59** 39 51N 75 43W
Kennewick **67** 46 12N 119 7W
Kenney **35** 40 6N 89 5W
Keno **58** 42 8N 121 56W
Kenosha **69** 42 35N 87 49W
Kenosha County ◇ . **69** 42 35N 87 50W
Kenova **68** 38 24N 82 35W
Kensal **55** 47 18N 98 44W
Kensett, Ark. **27** 35 14N 91 40W
Kensett, Iowa **37** 43 21N 93 13W
Kensington, Conn. . **42** 41 38N 72 46W
Kensington, Kans. .. **38** 39 46N 99 2W
Kensington, Md. ... **41** 39 2N 77 5W
Kensington, Minn. .. **44** 45 47N 95 42W
Kent, Conn. **42** 41 44N 73 29W
Kent, Iowa **37** 40 57N 94 28W
Kent, Minn. **44** 46 26N 96 41W
Kent, Ohio **56** 41 9N 81 22W
Kent, Oreg. **58** 45 12N 120 42W
Kent, Tex. **64** 31 4N 104 13W
Kent, Wash. **67** 47 23N 122 14W
Kent City **43** 43 12N 85 45W
Kent County ◇,
Del. **41** 39 10N 75 30W
Kent County ◇,
Md. **41** 39 15N 76 0W
Kent County ◇,
Mich. **43** 43 0N 85 35W
Kent County ◇,
R.I. **42** 41 35N 71 40W
Kent County ◇,
Tex. **64** 33 10N 100 45W
Kent I. **41** 38 52N 76 18W
Kentland **36** 40 46N 87 27W
Kentmore Park **41** 39 22N 75 58W
Kenton, Del. **41** 39 14N 75 40W
Kenton, Mich. **43** 46 28N 88 54W
Kenton, Ohio **56** 40 39N 83 37W
Kenton, Okla. **57** 36 54N 102 58W
Kenton, Tenn. **62** 36 12N 89 1W
Kenton County ◇ .. **63** 38 55N 84 32W
Kentucky □ **63** 37 0N 84 0W
Kentucky → **63** 38 41N 85 11W
Kentucky L. **62** 37 1N 88 16W
Kentwood **39** 30 56N 90 31W
Kenyon **44** 44 16N 92 59W
Keo **27** 34 36N 92 1W
Keokea **33** 20 43N 156 22W
Keokuk **37** 40 24N 91 24W
Keokuk County ◇ .. **37** 41 20N 92 10W
Keosauqua **37** 40 44N 91 58W
Keota, Colo. **30** 40 42N 104 5W
Keota, Iowa **37** 41 22N 91 57W
Keota, Okla. **57** 35 15N 94 55W
Keowee L. **60** 34 30N 82 55W
Kepuhi Pt. **33** 21 29N 158 14W
Kerby **58** 42 12N 123 39W
Kerens **65** 32 8N 96 14W
Kerkhoven **44** 45 12N 95 19W
Kerman **29** 36 43N 120 4W
Kermit, Tex. **64** 31 52N 103 6W
Kermit, W. Va. **68** 37 50N 82 24W
Kern → **29** 35 16N 119 18W
Kern County ◇ **29** 35 20N 118 30W
Kernersville **54** 36 7N 80 5W
Kernville **29** 35 45N 118 26W
Kerr County ◇ **65** 27 53N 97 13W
Kerrick, Minn. **44** 46 20N 92 35W
Kerrick, Tex. **64** 36 30N 102 15W
Kerrville **65** 30 3N 99 8W
Kersey **30** 40 23N 104 34W
Kershaw **60** 34 33N 80 35W
Kershaw County ◇ . **60** 34 20N 80 40W
Keshena **69** 44 53N 88 39W
Ketchikan **25** 55 21N 131 39W
Ketchikan
Gateway ◇ **25** 55 30N 131 0W
Ketchum, Idaho **34** 43 41N 114 22W
Ketchum, Okla. **57** 36 32N 95 1W
Kettering **56** 39 41N 84 10W
Kettle → **44** 45 52N 92 46W
Kettle Cr. → **59** 41 18N 77 51W
Kettle Falls **67** 48 37N 118 3W
Kettle River **44** 46 29N 92 53W
Kettle River Range . **67** 48 30N 118 40W
Kettleman City **29** 36 1N 119 58W
Keuka L. **53** 42 30N 77 9W
Kevin **47** 48 45N 111 58W
Kewanee **35** 41 14N 89 56W
Kewanna **36** 41 1N 86 25W
Kewaskum **69** 43 31N 88 14W
Kewaunee **69** 44 27N 87 31W
Kewaunee County ◇ **69** 44 30N 87 40W
Keweenaw B. **43** 47 0N 88 15W
Keweenaw
County ◇ **43** 47 20N 88 5W
Keweenaw Peninsula **43** 47 15N 88 15W
Keweenaw Pt. **43** 47 25N 87 43W
Key **64** 32 44N 101 48W
Key Biscayne **31** 25 42N 80 10W
Key Colony Beach . **31** 24 45N 80 57W
Key Largo **31** 25 5N 80 27W
Key West **31** 24 33N 81 48W
Keya Paha → **48** 42 54N 99 0W
Keya Paha
County ◇ **48** 42 50N 99 40W
Keyapaha **61** 43 7N 100 8W
Keyes **57** 36 49N 102 15W
Keyesport **35** 38 45N 89 17W
Keyhole Reservior .. **70** 44 21N 104 51W
Keymar **41** 39 38N 77 16W
Keyport **51** 40 26N 74 12W
Keyser **68** 39 26N 78 59W
Keystone, Iowa **37** 42 0N 92 12W
Keystone, Nebr. **48** 41 13N 101 35W
Keystone, S. Dak. .. **61** 43 54N 103 25W
Keystone L. **57** 36 15N 96 25W
Keystone Peak **26** 31 53N 111 13W
Keysville, Ga. **32** 33 14N 82 14W
Keysville, Va. **68** 37 2N 78 29W
Keytesville **46** 39 26N 92 56W
Kezar Falls **40** 43 48N 70 53W
Kiamichi → **57** 33 58N 95 14W
Kiamichi Mt. **57** 34 38N 94 35W
Kiana **25** 66 58N 160 26W
Kickapoo → **69** 43 5N 90 53W
Kickapoo, L. **65** 33 40N 98 47W
Kickapoo Indian
Reservation **38** 39 40N 95 50W
Kidder **46** 39 47N 94 6W
Kidder County ◇ ... **55** 47 0N 99 55W
Kief **55** 47 51N 100 31W
Kiel **69** 43 55N 88 2W
Kiester **44** 43 32N 93 43W
Kihei **33** 20 47N 156 28W
Kiholo B. **33** 19 50N 155 55W
Kila **47** 48 7N 114 27W
Kilauea **33** 22 13N 159 25W
Kilauea Crater **33** 19 25N 155 17W
Kilbourne, Ill. **35** 40 9N 90 1W
Kilbourne, La. **39** 33 0N 91 20W
Kildare, Ga. **32** 32 32N 81 27W
Kildare, Okla. **57** 36 48N 97 3W
Kildeer **55** 47 22N 102 45W
Kilgore, Idaho **34** 44 24N 111 54W
Kilgore, Nebr. **48** 42 56N 100 57W
Kilgore, Tex. **65** 32 23N 94 53W
Kilkenny **44** 44 19N 93 34W
Kill Devil Hills **54** 36 1N 75 39W
Killbuck **56** 40 30N 81 59W
Killbuck → **56** 40 30N 81 59W
Killeen **65** 31 7N 97 44W
Killen **24** 34 52N 87 32W
Killingly **42** 41 0N 71 0W
Killingworth **42** 41 21N 72 30W
Kilmarnock **68** 37 43N 76 23W
Kilmichael **45** 33 27N 89 34W
Kim **30** 37 15N 103 21W
Kimball, Nebr. **48** 41 14N 103 40W
Kimball, S. Dak. ... **61** 43 45N 98 57W
Kimball, W. Va. **68** 37 26N 81 30W
Kimball County ◇ .. **48** 41 15N 103 40W
Kimballton **37** 41 38N 95 4W
Kimberly, Idaho **34** 42 32N 114 22W
Kimberly, Oreg. **58** 44 46N 119 39W
Kimble County ◇ .. **65** 30 29N 99 46W
Kimbolton **56** 40 9N 81 34W
Kimbrough **24** 32 2N 87 34W
Kinard **31** 30 16N 85 15W
Kinards **60** 34 23N 81 46W
Kincaid, Ill. **35** 39 35N 89 25W
Kincaid, Kans. **38** 38 5N 95 9W
Kincaid, L. **35** 39 39N 89 29W
Kinchafoonee
Cr. → **32** 31 38N 84 10W
Kinde **43** 43 56N 83 0W
Kinder **39** 30 29N 92 51W
Kindred **55** 46 39N 97 1W
King **54** 36 17N 80 22W
King and Queen
County ◇ **68** 37 40N 76 53W
King and Queen
Court House **68** 37 40N 76 53W
King City, Calif. **29** 36 13N 121 8W
King City, Mo. **46** 40 3N 94 31W
King County ◇,
Tex. **64** 33 37N 100 19W
King County ◇,
Wash. **67** 47 25N 121 40W
King Cove **25** 55 3N 162 19W
King George **68** 38 16N 77 11W
King George
County ◇ **68** 38 16N 77 11W
King of Prussia **59** 40 5N 75 23W
King Salmon **25** 58 42N 156 40W
King William **68** 37 41N 77 1W
King William
County ◇ **68** 37 4,N 77 1W
Kingfield **40** 44 58N 70 9W
Kingfisher **57** 35 52N 97 56W
Kingfisher County ◇ **57** 36 0N 98 0W
Kingman, Ariz. **26** 35 12N 114 4W
Kingman, Kans. **38** 37 39N 98 7W
Kingman County ◇ . **38** 37 30N 98 0W
Kings →, Ark. **27** 36 30N 93 35W
Kings →, Calif. ... **29** 36 3N 119 50W

Kings →, Utah **66** 41 31N 118 8W
Kings Canyon National Park **29** 36 50N 118 40W
Kings County ◇, Calif. **29** 36 0N 119 50W
Kings County ◇, N.Y. **53** 40 37N 73 55W
Kings Mountain **54** 35 15N 81 20W
Kings Peak **66** 40 46N 110 23W
Kings Valley **58** 44 42N 123 26W
Kingsburg **29** 36 31N 119 33W
Kingsbury County ◇ **61** 44 23N 97 33W
Kingsdown **38** 37 32N 99 46W
Kingsford **43** 45 48N 88 4W
Kingsland, Ark. **27** 33 52N 92 18W
Kingsland, Ga. **32** 30 48N 81 41W
Kingsland, Tex. **65** 30 40N 98 26W
Kingsley, Iowa **37** 42 35N 95 58W
Kingsley, Mich. **43** 44 35N 85 32W
Kingsmill **64** 35 29N 101 4W
Kingsport **63** 36 33N 82 33W
Kingston, Ark. **27** 36 3N 93 31W
Kingston, Ga. **32** 34 14N 84 57W
Kingston, Ky. **63** 37 39N 84 15W
Kingston, Mass. **42** 42 0N 70 43W
Kingston, Md. **41** 38 5N 75 46W
Kingston, Mich. **43** 43 25N 83 11W
Kingston, Minn. **44** 45 12N 94 19W
Kingston, Mo. **46** 39 39N 94 2W
Kingston, N.H. **50** 42 56N 71 3W
Kingston, N.Y. **53** 41 56N 73 59W
Kingston, Ohio **56** 39 28N 82 55W
Kingston, Okla. **57** 33 59N 96 45W
Kingston, Pa. **59** 41 16N 75 54W
Kingston, Tenn. **63** 35 52N 84 31W
Kingston, Utah **66** 38 13N 112 11W
Kingston, Wis. **69** 43 42N 89 8W
Kingston Springs **62** 36 6N 87 7W
Kingstree **60** 33 40N 79 50W
Kingsville, Md. **41** 39 27N 76 25W
Kingsville, Mo. **46** 38 45N 94 4W
Kingsville, Tex. **64** 27 31N 97 52W
Kingwood **68** 39 28N 79 41W
Kinkaid L. **35** 37 40N 89 25W
Kinmundy **35** 38 46N 88 51W
Kinnelon **51** 41 0N 74 22W
Kinney **44** 47 31N 92 44W
Kinney County ◇ **64** 29 19N 100 25W
Kinsale **68** 38 2N 76 35W
Kinsley **38** 37 55N 99 25W
Kinston, Ala. **24** 31 13N 86 10W
Kinston, N.C. **54** 35 16N 77 35W
Kinta **57** 35 8N 95 14W
Kinwood **65** 29 55N 95 19W
Kinzua **58** 44 59N 120 3W
Kiowa, Colo. **30** 39 21N 104 28W
Kiowa, Kans. **38** 37 1N 98 29W
Kiowa, Okla. **57** 34 43N 95 54W
Kiowa → **57** 36 46N 99 55W
Kiowa County ◇, Colo. **30** 38 25N 102 50W
Kiowa County ◇, Kans. **38** 37 30N 99 15W
Kiowa County ◇, Okla. **57** 35 0N 99 0W
Kiowa Cr. → **30** 40 20N 104 5W
Kipapa → **33** 21 24N 158 1W
Kipnuk **25** 59 56N 164 3W
Kipp **38** 38 47N 97 27W
Kirby, Ark. **27** 34 15N 93 39W
Kirby, Tex. **65** 29 28N 98 23W
Kirby, Wyo. **70** 43 48N 108 11W
Kirbyville **65** 30 40N 93 54W
Kirk, Colo. **30** 39 37N 102 36W
Kirk, Oreg. **58** 42 45N 121 50W
Kirkland, Ariz. **26** 34 25N 112 43W
Kirkland, Ill. **35** 42 6N 88 51W
Kirkland, Tex. **65** 34 23N 100 4W
Kirkland, Wash. **67** 47 41N 122 13W
Kirkland Junction **26** 34 22N 112 40W
Kirklin **36** 40 12N 86 22W
Kirkman **37** 41 44N 95 16W
Kirkmansville **62** 37 1N 87 15W
Kirksey **62** 36 42N 88 24W
Kirksville **46** 40 12N 92 35W
Kirkwood, Del. **41** 39 34N 75 42W
Kirkwood, Ill. **35** 40 52N 90 45W
Kirkwood, Mo. **46** 38 35N 90 24W
Kiron **37** 42 12N 95 20W
Kirtland **52** 36 44N 108 21W
Kirwin **38** 39 40N 99 7W
Kirwin Reservoir **38** 39 40N 99 8W
Kisatchie **39** 31 25N 93 10W
Kisatchie National Forest **39** 31 45N 92 30W
Kiska I. **25** 51 59N 177 30 E
Kismet **38** 37 12N 100 42W
Kissimmee **31** 28 18N 81 24W
Kissimmee → **31** 27 9N 80 52W
Kissimmee, L. **31** 27 55N 81 17W
Kit Carson **30** 38 46N 102 48W
Kit Carson County ◇ **30** 39 15N 102 30W
Kitsap County ◇ **67** 47 30N 122 45W
Kittanning **59** 40 49N 79 31W
Kittery, Maine **40** 43 5N 70 45W
Kittery, N.H. **50** 43 5N 70 45W
Kittitas **67** 46 59N 120 25W
Kittitas County ◇ **67** 47 10N 120 30W
Kitts Hummock **41** 39 8N 75 25W
Kittson County ◇ **44** 48 50N 96 50W
Kitzmiller **41** 39 23N 79 10W
Kivalina **25** 67 44N 164 33W
Klamath **28** 41 32N 124 2W
Klamath → **28** 41 33N 124 5W
Klamath County ◇ **58** 42 40N 121 40W
Klamath Falls **58** 42 13N 121 46W
Klamath Marsh **58** 43 0N 121 40W
Klamath Mts. **28** 41 50N 123 20W
Klamath National Forest **28** 41 30N 123 20W
Klamath River **28** 41 52N 122 50W
Klawock **25** 55 33N 133 6W
Kleberg County ◇ **64** 27 31N 97 52W
Klein **47** 46 24N 108 33W
Klemme **37** 43 1N 93 36W
Klickitat **67** 45 49N 121 9W
Klickitat County ◇ **67** 45 55N 120 30W
Kline **60** 33 8N 81 21W
Klukwan **25** 59 24N 135 54W
Knapp **69** 44 57N 92 5W
Kneeland **28** 40 45N 123 59W
Knierim **37** 42 27N 94 27W
Knife → **55** 47 17N 101 20W
Knife River **44** 46 57N 91 47W
Knight I. **25** 60 21N 147 45W
Knights Landing **28** 38 48N 121 43W
Knightstown **36** 39 48N 85 32W
Knob Lick, Ky. **63** 37 5N 85 42W
Knob Lick, Mo. **46** 37 41N 90 22W
Knob Noster **46** 38 46N 93 33W
Knobel **27** 36 19N 90 36W
Knott County ◇ **63** 37 20N 83 0W
Knotts Island **54** 36 31N 75 56W
Knowles **57** 36 53N 100 12W
Knox, Ind. **36** 41 18N 86 37W
Knox, N. Dak. **55** 48 20N 99 41W
Knox, Pa. **59** 41 14N 79 32W
Knox City, Mo. **46** 40 9N 92 1W
Knox City, Tex. **65** 33 25N 99 49W
Knox County ◇, Ill. **35** 40 55N 90 10W
Knox County ◇, Ind. **36** 38 40N 87 25W
Knox County ◇, Ky. **63** 36 55N 83 50W
Knox County ◇, Maine **40** 44 5N 69 5W
Knox County ◇, Mo. **46** 40 10N 92 10W
Knox County ◇, Nebr. **48** 42 40N 97 50W
Knox County ◇, Ohio **56** 40 23N 82 29W
Knox County ◇, Tenn. **63** 36 0N 83 0W
Knox County ◇, Tex. **65** 33 35N 99 48W
Knoxville, Ga. **32** 32 47N 83 59W
Knoxville, Ill. **35** 40 55N 90 17W
Knoxville, Iowa **37** 41 19N 93 6W
Knoxville, Pa. **59** 41 57N 77 27W
Knoxville, Tenn. **63** 35 58N 83 55W
Kobuk **25** 66 55N 156 52W
Kobuk ◇ **25** 66 0N 160 0W
Kobuk → **25** 66 54N 160 38W
Kodiak **25** 57 47N 152 24W
Kodiak I. **25** 57 20N 154 0W
Kodiak Island ◇ **25** 57 30N 154 0W
Koehn Dry L. **29** 35 20N 117 53W
Kofa Mts. **26** 33 15N 113 40W
Kohala Mts. **33** 20 5N 155 45W
Koko Head **33** 21 16N 157 43W
Kokomo, Ind. **36** 40 29N 86 8W
Kokomo, Miss. **45** 31 12N 90 0W
Koliganek **25** 59 48N 157 25W
Koloa **33** 21 55N 159 28W
Konawa **57** 34 58N 96 45W
Koochiching County ◇ **44** 48 15N 93 50W
Koolau Range **33** 21 35N 158 0W
Koosharem **66** 38 31N 111 53W
Kooskia **34** 46 9N 115 59W
Kootenai → **34** 49 0N 116 30W
Kootenai County ◇ **34** 47 45N 116 30W
Kootenai National Forest **47** 48 30N 115 40W
Kopperston **68** 37 45N 81 35W
Korona **31** 29 25N 81 12W
Kortes Dam **70** 42 12N 106 52W
Kosciusko **45** 33 4N 89 35W
Kosciusko County ◇ **36** 41 15N 85 50W
Koshkonong **46** 36 36N 91 39W
Koshkonong L. **69** 42 52N 88 58W
Kosse **65** 31 18N 96 38W
Kossuth County ◇ **37** 43 15N 94 10W
Kotlik **25** 63 2N 163 33W
Kotzebue **25** 66 53N 162 39W
Kotzebue Sound **25** 66 20N 163 0W
Kountze **65** 30 22N 94 19W
Kouts **36** 41 19N 87 2W
Koyuk **25** 64 56N 161 9W
Koyukuk **25** 64 53N 157 42W
Koyukuk → **25** 64 55N 157 32W
Kramer **55** 48 42N 100 43W
Kranzburg **61** 44 54N 96 55W
Krebs **57** 34 56N 95 43W
Kremlin **57** 36 33N 97 50W
Kremmling **30** 40 4N 106 24W
Kress **64** 34 22N 101 45W
Krotz Springs **39** 30 32N 91 45W
Krum **65** 33 16N 97 14W
Krusenstern, C. **25** 67 8N 163 45W
Ku Tree Reservoir **33** 21 30N 157 59W
Kualapuu **33** 21 10N 157 2W
Kualoa Pt. **33** 21 31N 157 50W
Kuapa Pond **33** 21 17N 157 43W
Kuiu I. **25** 57 45N 134 10W
Kukuihaele **33** 20 5N 155 35W
Kulm **55** 46 18N 98 57W
Kumukahi, C. **33** 19 31N 154 49W
Kuna **34** 43 30N 116 25W
Kunia **33** 21 28N 158 4W
Kupreanof I. **25** 56 50N 133 30W
Kure I. **33** 28 25N 178 25W
Kurthwood **39** 31 20N 93 10W
Kurtistown **33** 19 36N 155 4W
Kuskokwim → **25** 60 5N 162 25W
Kuskokwim B. **25** 59 45N 162 25W
Kuskokwim Mts. **25** 62 30N 156 0W
Kuttawa **62** 37 4N 88 7W
Kutztown **59** 40 31N 75 47W
Kuzitrin → **25** 65 10N 165 25W
Kvichak B. **25** 58 48N 157 30W
Kwethluk **25** 60 49N 161 26W
Kwigillingok **25** 59 51N 163 8W
Kwiguk **25** 62 46N 164 30W
Kyburz **28** 38 47N 120 18W
Kyle, S. Dak. **61** 43 26N 102 10W
Kyle, Tex. **65** 29 59N 97 53W

L

La Barge **70** 42 16N 110 12W
La Belle, Fla. **31** 26 46N 81 26W
La Belle, Mo. **46** 40 7N 91 55W
La Center **62** 37 4N 88 58W
La Chorrera **71** 8 53N 79 47W
La Conner **67** 48 23N 122 30W
La Crescent **44** 43 50N 91 18W
La Croix L. **44** 48 20N 92 10W
La Crosse, Fla. **31** 29 51N 82 24W
La Crosse, Kans. **38** 38 32N 99 18W
La Crosse, Va. **68** 36 42N 78 6W
La Crosse, Wash. **67** 46 49N 117 53W
La Crosse, Wis. **69** 43 48N 91 15W
La Crosse County ◇ **69** 44 0N 91 0W
La Cygne **38** 38 21N 94 46W
La Esperanza **71** 18 23N 66 45W
La Farge **69** 43 35N 90 38W
La Fayette, Ga. **32** 34 42N 85 17W
La Fayette, Ky. **62** 36 40N 87 40W
La Feria **64** 26 9N 97 50W
La Follette **63** 36 23N 84 7W
La Fontaine **36** 40 40N 85 43W
La Garita **30** 37 50N 106 15W
La Grande **58** 45 20N 118 5W
La Grange, Ark. **27** 34 39N 90 44W
La Grange, Ga. **32** 33 2N 85 2W
La Grange, Ky. **63** 38 25N 85 23W
La Grange, Mo. **46** 40 3N 91 35W
La Grange, N.C. **54** 35 19N 77 47W
La Grange, Tenn. **62** 35 3N 89 15W
La Grange, Tex. **65** 29 54N 96 52W
La Grange, Wyo. **70** 41 38N 104 10W
La Harpe, Ill. **35** 40 35N 90 58W
La Harpe, Kans. **38** 37 55N 95 18W
La Jara, Colo. **30** 37 16N 105 58W
La Jara, N. Mex. **52** 36 5N 106 58W
La Joya **64** 26 14N 98 27W
La Junta **30** 37 59N 103 33W
La Luz **52** 32 59N 105 57W
La Madera **52** 36 23N 106 3W
La Marque **65** 29 23N 94 58W
La Mesa, Calif. **29** 32 46N 117 3W
La Mesa, N. Mex. **52** 32 7N 106 42W
La Moille **35** 41 32N 89 17W
La Moine → **35** 39 59N 90 31W
La Monte **46** 38 46N 93 26W
La Moure **55** 46 21N 98 18W
La Moure County ◇ **55** 46 23N 98 29W
La Palma **26** 32 53N 111 31W
La Pine **58** 43 40N 121 30W
La Place **39** 30 4N 90 29W
La Plant **61** 45 9N 100 39W
La Plata, Md. **41** 38 32N 76 59W
La Plata, Mo. **46** 40 2N 92 29W
La Plata, N. Mex. **52** 36 56N 108 12W
La Plata County ◇ **30** 37 15N 107 50W
La Porte **36** 41 36N 86 43W
La Porte City **37** 42 19N 92 12W
La Porte County ◇ **36** 41 30N 86 45W
La Pryor **65** 28 57N 99 51W
La Puente **52** 36 42N 106 36W
La Push **67** 47 55N 124 38W
La Sal **66** 38 20N 109 15W
La Sal Mts. **66** 38 30N 109 10W
La Salle, Colo. **30** 40 21N 104 42W
La Salle, Ill. **35** 41 20N 89 6W
La Salle, Minn. **44** 44 4N 94 33W
La Salle County ◇, Ill. **35** 41 20N 88 50W
La Salle County ◇, Tex. **65** 28 26N 99 14W
La Salle Parish ◇ **39** 31 41N 92 8W
La Santa, Cerro **71** 18 7N 66 4W
La Union **52** 31 57N 106 40W
La Vale **41** 39 40N 78 48W
La Valle **69** 43 35N 90 8W
La Vergne **62** 36 1N 86 35W
La Verkin **66** 37 12N 113 16W
La Vernia **65** 29 21N 98 7W
La Veta **30** 37 31N 105 0W
La Veta Pass **30** 37 36N 105 13W
Laau Pt. **33** 21 6N 157 19W
Labadieville **39** 29 50N 90 57W
Labette **38** 37 14N 95 11W
Labette County ◇ **38** 37 15N 95 15W
Lac Courte Oreilles Indian Reservation **69** 45 50N 91 15W
Lac du Flambeau **69** 45 58N 89 53W
Lac du Flambeau Indian Reservation **69** 46 0N 89 50W
Lac qui Parle County ◇ **44** 44 55N 96 0W
Lacey **67** 47 7N 122 49W
Lackawanna **53** 42 50N 78 50W
Lackawanna County ◇ **59** 41 30N 75 50W
Laclede County ◇ **46** 37 40N 92 35W
Lacombe **39** 30 19N 89 56W
Lacon **35** 41 2N 89 24W
Lacona, Iowa **37** 41 12N 93 23W
Lacona, N.Y. **53** 43 39N 76 10W
Laconia, Ind. **36** 38 2N 86 5W
Laconia, N.H. **50** 43 32N 71 28W
Lacoochee **31** 28 28N 82 11W
Ladd **35** 41 23N 89 13W
Laddonia **46** 39 15N 91 39W
Ladelle **27** 33 28N 91 48W
Ladoga **36** 39 55N 86 48W
Ladonia **65** 33 25N 95 57W
Ladson **60** 32 59N 80 6W
Lady Lake **31** 28 55N 81 55W
Ladysmith **69** 45 28N 91 12W
Lafayette, Ala. **24** 32 54N 85 24W
Lafayette, Calif. **28** 37 53N 122 7W
Lafayette, Colo. **30** 39 58N 105 12W
Lafayette, Ind. **36** 40 25N 86 54W
Lafayette, La. **39** 30 14N 92 1W
Lafayette, Minn. **44** 44 27N 94 24W
Lafayette, Ohio **56** 40 46N 83 57W
Lafayette, Oreg. **58** 45 15N 123 7W
Lafayette, Tenn. **62** 36 31N 86 2W
Lafayette, Mt. **50** 44 10N 71 38W
Lafayette County ◇, Ark. **27** 33 22N 93 43W
Lafayette County ◇, Fla. **31** 30 0N 83 0W
Lafayette County ◇, Miss. **45** 34 22N 89 31W
Lafayette County ◇, Mo. **46** 39 5N 93 45W
Lafayette County ◇, Wis. **69** 42 35N 90 10W
Lafayette Parish ◇ **39** 30 14N 92 1W
Lafitte **39** 29 40N 90 6W
Lafontaine **38** 37 24N 95 51W
Lafourche Parish ◇ **39** 29 34N 90 23W
Lagrange, Ind. **36** 41 39N 85 25W
Lagrange, Maine **40** 45 11N 68 54W
Lagrange, Ohio **56** 41 14N 82 7W
Lagrange County ◇ **36** 41 35N 85 25W
Laguna **52** 35 2N 107 25W
Laguna Beach **29** 33 33N 117 47W
Laguna Indian Reservation **52** 35 0N 107 20W
Laguna Mts. **29** 33 0N 116 40W
Lahaina **33** 20 53N 156 41W
Lahilahi Pt. **33** 21 28N 158 13W
Lahoma **57** 36 23N 98 5W
Lahontan Reservoir **49** 39 28N 119 4W
Laie **33** 21 39N 157 56W
Laingsburg **43** 42 54N 84 21W
Lair **63** 38 20N 84 18W
Lajas **71** 18 3N 67 4W
Lajitas **64** 29 16N 103 46W
Lajoya **52** 34 21N 106 51W
Lake, Miss. **45** 32 21N 89 20W
Lake, Wyo. **70** 44 33N 110 24W
Lake Alfred **31** 28 6N 81 44W
Lake Andes **61** 43 9N 98 32W
Lake Arthur, La. **39** 30 5N 92 41W

Lake Arthur, N. Mex. **52** 33 0N 104 22W
Lake Benton **44** 44 15N 96 17W
Lake Bird **31** 30 14N 83 37W
Lake Bronson **44** 48 44N 96 40W
Lake Butler **31** 30 1N 82 21W
Lake Charles **39** 30 14N 93 13W
Lake Chelan National Recreation Area **67** 48 25N 120 52W
Lake City, Ark. **27** 35 49N 90 26W
Lake City, Calif. **28** 41 39N 120 13W
Lake City, Colo. **30** 38 2N 107 19W
Lake City, Fla. **31** 30 11N 82 38W
Lake City, Iowa **37** 42 16N 94 44W
Lake City, Kans. **38** 37 21N 98 49W
Lake City, Mich. **43** 44 20N 85 13W
Lake City, Minn. **44** 44 27N 92 16W
Lake City, Pa. **59** 42 1N 80 21W
Lake City, S.C. **60** 33 52N 79 45W
Lake City, S. Dak. **61** 45 44N 97 25W
Lake City, Tenn. **63** 36 13N 84 9W
Lake Clarke Shores **31** 26 39N 80 5W
Lake Clear Junction **53** 44 22N 74 14W
Lake County ◇, Calif. **28** 39 5N 122 45W
Lake County ◇, Colo. **30** 39 10N 106 20W
Lake County ◇, Fla. **31** 28 45N 81 45W
Lake County ◇, Ill. **35** 42 20N 88 0W
Lake County ◇, Ind. **36** 41 25N 87 25W
Lake County ◇, Mich. **43** 44 0N 85 50W
Lake County ◇, Minn. **44** 47 30N 91 20W
Lake County ◇, Mont. **47** 47 40N 114 10W
Lake County ◇, Ohio **56** 41 40N 81 21W
Lake County ◇, Oreg. **58** 44 45N 120 20W
Lake County ◇, S. Dak. **61** 44 0N 97 7W
Lake County ◇, Tenn. **62** 36 23N 89 29W
Lake Crystal **44** 44 6N 94 13W
Lake Delton **69** 43 35N 89 47W
Lake Forest **35** 42 15N 87 50W
Lake Fork **34** 44 50N 116 5W
Lake Fork Cr. → **66** 40 13N 110 7W
Lake Geneva **69** 42 36N 88 26W
Lake George, Colo. **30** 38 59N 105 22W
Lake George, Mich. **43** 43 58N 84 57W
Lake George, Minn. **44** 47 12N 94 59W
Lake George, N.Y. **53** 43 26N 73 43W
Lake Harbor **31** 26 42N 80 48W
Lake Havasu City **26** 34 27N 114 22W
Lake Helen **31** 28 59N 81 14W
Lake Hughes **29** 34 41N 118 26W
Lake Isabella **29** 35 38N 118 28W
Lake Jackson **65** 29 3N 95 27W
Lake Lillian **44** 44 57N 94 53W
Lake Linden **43** 47 11N 88 24W
Lake Lure **54** 35 25N 82 12W
Lake Mead National Recreation Area **26** 36 15N 114 30W
Lake Meredith National Recreation Area **64** 35 50N 101 50W
Lake Mills, Iowa **37** 43 25N 93 32W
Lake Mills, Wis. **69** 43 5N 88 55W
Lake Mohawk **51** 41 1N 74 39W
Lake Monroe **31** 28 50N 81 19W
Lake Nebagamon **69** 46 31N 91 42W
Lake Norden **61** 44 35N 97 13W
Lake Odessa **43** 42 47N 85 8W
Lake of the Woods County ◇ **44** 48 40N 94 50W
Lake Orion **43** 42 47N 83 14W
Lake Oswego **58** 45 25N 122 40W
Lake Ozark **46** 38 12N 92 38W
Lake Park, Fla. **31** 26 48N 80 3W
Lake Park, Ga. **32** 30 41N 83 11W
Lake Park, Iowa **37** 43 27N 95 19W
Lake Park, Minn. **44** 46 53N 96 6W
Lake Placid, Fla. **31** 27 18N 81 22W
Lake Placid, N.Y. **53** 44 17N 73 59W
Lake Pleasant **53** 43 28N 74 25W
Lake Preston **61** 44 22N 97 23W
Lake Providence **39** 32 48N 91 10W
Lake Range **49** 40 10N 119 20W
Lake Ronkonkoma **53** 40 50N 73 6W
Lake Shore **41** 39 7N 76 29W
Lake Stevens **67** 48 1N 122 4W
Lake Toxaway **54** 35 8N 82 56W
Lake View, Iowa **37** 42 18N 95 3W
Lake View, S.C. **60** 34 21N 79 10W
Lake Villa **35** 42 25N 88 5W
Lake Village **27** 33 20N 91 17W
Lake Wales **31** 27 54N 81 35W
Lake Wilson **44** 43 59N 95 57W
Lake Worth **31** 26 37N 80 3W
Lake Zurich **35** 42 12N 88 5W
Lakecreek **58** 42 26N 122 37W
Lakefield **44** 43 41N 95 10W
Lakehurst **51** 40 1N 74 19W
Lakeland, Fla. **31** 28 3N 81 57W
Lakeland, Ga. **32** 31 2N 83 4W
Lakemont **59** 40 28N 78 24W
Lakemount **32** 34 47N 83 25W
Lakeport, Calif. **28** 39 3N 122 55W
Lakeport, Mich. **43** 43 7N 82 30W
Lakeshore, Calif. **29** 37 15N 119 12W
Lakeshore, Miss. **45** 30 15N 89 26W
Lakeside, Ariz. **26** 34 9N 109 58W
Lakeside, Calif. **29** 32 52N 116 55W
Lakeside, Nebr. **48** 42 3N 102 26W
Lakeside, Oreg. **58** 43 35N 124 11W
Lakeside, Va. **68** 37 37N 77 28W
Laketon **64** 35 33N 100 38W
Laketown **66** 41 49N 111 19W
Lakeview, Calhoun, Mich. **43** 42 17N 85 12W
Lakeview, Montcalm, Mich. **43** 43 27N 85 17W
Lakeview, Mont. **47** 44 36N 111 49W
Lakeview, Ohio **56** 40 29N 83 56W
Lakeview, Oreg. **58** 42 11N 120 21W
Lakeview, Tex. **64** 34 40N 100 42W
Lakeville, Conn. **42** 41 58N 73 26W
Lakeville, Ind. **36** 41 31N 86 16W
Lakeville, Mass. **42** 41 50N 70 55W
Lakeville, Minn. **44** 44 39N 93 14W
Lakewood, Colo. **30** 39 44N 105 5W
Lakewood, N.J. **51** 40 6N 74 13W
Lakewood, N. Mex. **52** 32 38N 104 23W
Lakewood, N.Y. **53** 42 6N 79 19W
Lakewood, Ohio **56** 41 29N 81 48W
Lakewood, Wash. **67** 48 9N 122 13W
Lakewood, Wis. **69** 45 18N 88 31W
Lakewood Center **67** 47 11N 122 32W
Lakin **38** 37 57N 101 15W
Lakota, Iowa **37** 43 23N 94 6W
Lakota, N. Dak. **55** 48 2N 98 21W
Lamar, Ark. **27** 35 27N 93 23W
Lamar, Colo. **30** 38 5N 102 37W
Lamar, Mo. **46** 37 30N 94 16W
Lamar, Nebr. **48** 40 34N 101 59W
Lamar, Okla. **57** 35 6N 96 8W
Lamar, S.C. **60** 34 10N 80 4W
Lamar County ◇, Ala. **24** 33 45N 88 7W
Lamar County ◇, Ga. **32** 33 5N 84 10W
Lamar County ◇, Miss. **45** 31 9N 89 25W
Lamar County ◇, Tex. **65** 33 40N 95 33W
Lamb County ◇ **64** 34 0N 102 15W
Lambert, Miss. **45** 34 12N 90 17W
Lambert, Mont. **47** 47 41N 104 37W
Lamberton **44** 44 14N 95 16W
Lambertville, Mich. **43** 41 46N 83 35W
Lambertville, N.J. **51** 40 22N 74 57W
Lame Deer **47** 45 37N 106 40W
Lamesa **64** 32 44N 101 58W
Lamine → **46** 38 59N 92 51W
Lamison **24** 32 7N 87 34W
Lamoille → **50** 44 38N 73 13W
Lamoille County ◇ **50** 44 40N 72 40W
Lamona **67** 47 22N 118 29W
Lamoni **37** 40 37N 93 56W
Lamont, Calif. **29** 35 15N 118 55W
Lamont, Fla. **31** 30 23N 83 49W
Lamont, Kans. **38** 38 7N 96 2W
Lamont, Miss. **45** 33 32N 91 5W
Lamont, Okla. **57** 36 42N 97 30W
Lamont, Wash. **67** 47 12N 117 54W
Lamont, Wyo. **70** 42 13N 107 29W
Lampasas **65** 31 4N 98 11W
Lampasas → **65** 30 59N 97 24W
Lampasas County ◇ **65** 31 5N 98 10W
Lamy **52** 35 29N 105 53W
Lanagan **46** 36 37N 94 27W
Lanai **33** 20 50N 156 55W
Lanai City **33** 20 50N 156 55W
Lanaihale **33** 20 49N 156 53W
Lanark **35** 42 6N 89 50W
Lanark Village **31** 29 53N 84 36W
Lancaster, Calif. **29** 34 42N 118 8W
Lancaster, Kans. **38** 39 34N 95 18W
Lancaster, Ky. **63** 37 37N 84 35W
Lancaster, Minn. **44** 48 52N 96 48W
Lancaster, Mo. **46** 40 31N 92 32W
Lancaster, N.H. **50** 44 29N 71 34W
Lancaster, N.Y. **53** 42 54N 78 40W
Lancaster, Ohio **56** 39 43N 82 36W
Lancaster, Pa. **59** 40 2N 76 19W
Lancaster, S.C. **60** 34 43N 80 46W
Lancaster, Tex. **65** 32 35N 96 45W
Lancaster, Va. **68** 37 46N 76 28W
Lancaster, Wis. **69** 42 51N 90 43W
Lancaster County ◇, Nebr. **48** 40 45N 96 45W
Lancaster County ◇, Pa. **59** 40 0N 76 19W
Lancaster County ◇, S.C. **60** 34 40N 80 40W
Lancaster County ◇, Va. **68** 37 45N 76 30W
Lance Creek **70** 43 2N 104 39W
Land Between The Lakes **62** 36 25N 88 0W
Landa **55** 48 54N 100 55W
Lander **70** 42 50N 108 44W
Lander County ◇ **49** 40 0N 117 0W
Landis **54** 35 33N 80 37W
Landisburg **59** 40 21N 77 19W
Lando **60** 34 46N 81 1W
Landrum **60** 35 11N 82 11W
Lane, Kans. **38** 38 26N 95 5W
Lane, S.C. **60** 33 32N 79 53W
Lane, S. Dak. **61** 44 4N 98 26W
Lane County ◇, Kans. **38** 38 30N 100 30W
Lane County ◇, Oreg. **58** 44 0N 123 0W
Lanesboro, Iowa **37** 42 11N 94 41W
Lanesboro, Mass. **42** 42 31N 73 14W
Lanesboro, Minn. **44** 43 43N 91 58W
Lanett **24** 32 52N 85 12W
Langdon, Kans. **38** 37 51N 98 19W
Langdon, N. Dak. **55** 48 45N 98 22W
Langford **61** 45 36N 97 50W
Langlade County ◇ **69** 45 15N 89 10W
Langley, Ark. **27** 34 19N 93 51W
Langley, Ky. **63** 37 32N 82 47W
Langley, Okla. **57** 36 28N 95 3W
Langlois **58** 42 56N 124 27W
Langston **57** 35 59N 97 18W
Langtry **64** 29 49N 101 34W
L'Anguille → **27** 34 44N 90 40W
Lanier County ◇ **32** 31 0N 83 5W
Lankin **55** 48 19N 97 55W
Lansdale **59** 40 14N 75 17W
Lansdowne **41** 39 15N 76 40W
L'Anse **43** 46 45N 88 27W
L'Anse Indian Reservation **43** 46 45N 88 20W
Lansford, N. Dak. **55** 48 38N 101 23W
Lansford, Pa. **59** 40 50N 75 53W
Lansing, Ill. **35** 41 34N 87 33W
Lansing, Iowa **37** 43 22N 91 13W
Lansing, Kans. **38** 39 15N 94 54W
Lansing, Mich. **43** 42 44N 84 33W
Lantana **31** 26 35N 80 3W
Laona **69** 45 34N 88 40W
Lapeer **43** 43 3N 83 19W
Lapeer County ◇ **43** 43 5N 83 15W
Lapel **36** 40 4N 85 51W
Laporte, Colo. **30** 40 38N 105 8W
Laporte, Minn. **44** 47 13N 94 45W
Laporte, Pa. **59** 41 25N 76 30W
Lappans **41** 39 33N 77 43W
Lapwai **34** 46 24N 116 48W
Laramie **70** 41 19N 105 35W
Laramie → **70** 42 13N 104 33W
Laramie County ◇ **70** 41 15N 104 40W
Laramie Mts. **70** 42 0N 105 30W
Laramie Pk. **70** 42 17N 105 27W
Larchwood **37** 43 27N 96 26W
Laredo, Mo. **46** 40 2N 93 27W
Laredo, Tex. **64** 27 30N 99 30W
Lares **71** 18 18N 66 53W
Larga, L. **65** 27 30N 97 25W
Largo **31** 27 55N 82 47W
Largo Key **31** 25 15N 80 15W
Larimer County ◇ **30** 40 40N 105 20W
Larimore **55** 47 54N 97 38W
Lark, N. Dak. **55** 46 27N 101 24W
Lark, Tex. **64** 35 12N 101 14W
Larkspur **30** 39 14N 104 53W
Larned **38** 38 11N 99 6W
Larose **39** 29 34N 90 23W
Larrabee **37** 42 52N 95 33W
Larsen Bay **25** 57 32N 153 59W
Larson **55** 48 53N 102 52W
Larue **56** 40 35N 83 23W
Larue County ◇ **63** 37 30N 85 40W
Las Animas **30** 38 4N 103 13W
Las Animas County ◇ **30** 37 15N 104 0W
Las Cascadas **71** 9 5N 79 41W
Las Cruces **52** 32 19N 106 47W
Las Marias **71** 18 15N 66 59W
Las Nutrias **52** 34 28N 106 46W
Las Piedras **71** 18 11N 65 52W
Las Tunas, Pta. **71** 18 30N 66 38W
Las Vegas, N. Mex. **52** 35 36N 105 13W
Las Vegas, Nev. **49** 36 10N 115 9W
Lassen County ◇ **28** 40 45N 120 30W
Lassen National Forest **28** 40 30N 121 15W
Lassen Peak **28** 40 29N 121 30W
Lassen Volcanic National Park **28** 40 30N 121 20W
Last Chance **30** 39 44N 103 36W
Lastrup **44** 46 2N 94 4W
Latah County ◇ **34** 46 45N 116 50W
Latham, Ill. **35** 39 58N 89 10W
Latham, Kans. **38** 37 32N 96 38W
Lathrop, Calif. **28** 37 49N 121 16W
Lathrop, Mo. **46** 39 33N 94 20W
Lathrop Wells **49** 36 39N 116 24W
Latimer, Iowa **37** 42 46N 93 22W
Latimer, Kans. **38** 38 44N 96 51W
Latimer County ◇ **57** 34 50N 95 10W
Laton **29** 36 26N 119 41W
Latrobe **59** 40 19N 79 23W
Latta **60** 34 21N 79 26W
Lauderdale **45** 32 31N 88 31W
Lauderdale County ◇, Ala. **24** 34 56N 87 46W
Lauderdale County ◇, Miss. **45** 32 22N 88 42W
Lauderdale County ◇, Tenn. **62** 35 45N 89 23W
Laughing Fish Pt. **43** 46 32N 87 1W
Laughlin Pk. **52** 36 40N 104 10W
Laura **56** 39 59N 84 22W
Laurel, Del. **41** 38 33N 75 34W
Laurel, Fla. **31** 27 8N 82 27W
Laurel, Iowa **37** 41 53N 92 55W
Laurel, Md. **41** 39 6N 76 51W
Laurel, Miss. **45** 31 41N 89 8W
Laurel, Mont. **47** 45 40N 108 46W
Laurel, Nebr. **48** 42 26N 97 6W
Laurel, Wash. **67** 45 57N 121 23W
Laurel Bay **60** 32 27N 80 47W
Laurel County ◇ **63** 37 5N 84 10W
Laurel Hill **54** 34 49N 79 33W
Laurel River L. **63** 36 57N 84 10W
Laureldale, N.J. **51** 39 30N 74 41W
Laureldale, Pa. **59** 40 23N 75 56W
Laurelville **56** 39 28N 82 44W
Laurens, Iowa **37** 42 51N 94 52W
Laurens, S.C. **60** 34 30N 82 1W
Laurens County ◇, Ga. **32** 32 30N 83 0W
Laurens County ◇, S.C. **60** 34 30N 82 0W
Laurinburg **54** 34 47N 79 28W
Laurium **43** 47 14N 88 27W
Lava Beds National Monument **28** 41 40N 121 30W
Lava Hot Springs **34** 42 37N 112 1W
Lavaca **27** 35 20N 94 10W
Lavaca → **65** 28 41N 96 35W
Lavaca County ◇ **65** 29 27N 96 57W
Lavallette **51** 39 58N 74 4W
Laverne **57** 36 43N 99 54W
Lavic L. **29** 34 40N 116 21W
Lavina **47** 46 18N 108 56W
Lavon L. **65** 33 2N 96 28W
Lavonia **32** 34 26N 83 6W
Lawen **58** 43 27N 118 48W
Lawler **37** 43 4N 92 9W
Lawn **65** 32 8N 99 45W
Lawndale **54** 35 25N 81 34W
Lawrence, Ind. **36** 39 50N 86 2W
Lawrence, Kans. **38** 38 58N 95 14W
Lawrence, Mass. **42** 42 43N 71 10W
Lawrence, Mich. **43** 42 13N 86 3W
Lawrence, Nebr. **48** 40 18N 98 16W
Lawrence County ◇, Ala. **24** 34 29N 87 18W
Lawrence County ◇, Ark. **27** 36 0N 91 0W
Lawrence County ◇, Ill. **35** 38 45N 87 45W
Lawrence County ◇, Ind. **36** 38 50N 86 30W
Lawrence County ◇, Ky. **63** 38 5N 82 45W
Lawrence County ◇, Miss. **45** 31 33N 90 7W
Lawrence County ◇, Mo. **46** 37 10N 93 50W
Lawrence County ◇, Ohio **56** 38 32N 82 41W
Lawrence County ◇, Pa. **59** 41 0N 80 15W
Lawrence County ◇, S. Dak. **61** 44 23N 103 44W
Lawrence County ◇, Tenn. **62** 35 14N 87 20W
Lawrenceburg, Ind. **36** 39 6N 84 52W
Lawrenceburg, Ky. **63** 38 2N 84 54W
Lawrenceburg, Tenn. **62** 35 14N 87 20W
Lawrenceville, Ga. **32** 33 57N 83 59W
Lawrenceville, Ill. **35** 38 44N 87 41W
Lawrenceville, N.J. **51** 40 18N 74 44W
Lawrenceville, Pa. **59** 41 59N 77 8W
Lawrenceville, Va. **68** 36 46N 77 51W
Lawson **46** 39 26N 94 12W
Lawtey **31** 30 3N 82 5W
Lawton, Mich. **43** 42 10N 85 50W
Lawton, N. Dak. **55** 48 18N 98 22W
Lawton, Okla. **57** 34 37N 98 25W
Lay **30** 40 32N 107 53W
Laysan I. **33** 25 50N 171 50W
Layton, Fla. **31** 24 50N 80 47W
Layton, N.J. **51** 41 13N 74 50W
Layton, Utah **66** 41 4N 111 58W
Laytonsville **41** 39 13N 77 9W

Laytonville 28 39 41N 123 29W
Lazear 30 38 47N 107 47W
Le Center 44 44 23N 93 44W
Le Claire 37 41 36N 90 21W
Le Flore County ◇ 57 35 0N 94 45W
Le Grand, Calif. 28 37 14N 120 15W
Le Grand, Iowa 37 42 0N 92 47W
Le Loup 38 38 42N 95 10W
Le Mars 37 42 47N 96 10W
Le Moyen 39 30 48N 92 4W
Le Roy, Ill. 35 40 21N 88 46W
Le Roy, Kans. 38 38 5N 95 38W
Le Roy, Mich. 43 44 2N 85 27W
Le Roy, Minn. 44 43 31N 92 30W
Le Roy, N.Y. 53 42 58N 78 0W
Le Roy, Pa. 59 41 41N 76 43W
Le Sueur 44 44 28N 93 55W
Le Sueur County ◇ 44 44 20N 93 45W
Lea County ◇ 52 32 50N 103 30W
Leachville 27 35 56N 90 16W
Lead 61 44 21N 103 46W
Lead Hill, Ark. 27 36 25N 92 55W
Lead Hill, Mo. 46 37 6N 92 38W
Leadbetter Pt. 67 46 39N 124 3W
Leadore 34 44 41N 113 21W
Leadpoint 67 48 55N 117 35W
Leadville 30 39 15N 106 18W
Leadwood 46 37 52N 90 36W
Leaf 45 31 2N 88 48W
Leaf → 45 30 59N 88 44W
League City 65 29 31N 95 6W
Leake County ◇ 45 32 42N 89 38W
Leakesville 45 31 9N 88 33W
Leakey 65 29 44N 99 46W
Leamington 66 39 32N 112 17W
Leary 32 31 29N 84 31W
Leasburg, Mo. 46 38 5N 91 18W
Leasburg, N.C. 54 36 24N 79 10W
Leatherwood 63 37 2N 83 11W
Leavenworth, Ind. 36 38 12N 86 21W
Leavenworth, Kans. 38 39 19N 94 55W
Leavenworth, Wash. 67 47 36N 120 40W
Leavenworth County ◇ 38 39 15N 95 0W
Leavittsburg 56 41 14N 80 53W
Lebam 67 46 34N 123 33W
Lebanon, Conn. 42 41 38N 72 13W
Lebanon, Ind. 36 40 3N 86 28W
Lebanon, Kans. 38 39 49N 98 33W
Lebanon, Ky. 63 37 34N 85 15W
Lebanon, Mo. 46 37 41N 92 40W
Lebanon, N.H. 50 43 39N 72 15W
Lebanon, Nebr. 48 40 3N 100 17W
Lebanon, Ohio 56 39 26N 84 13W
Lebanon, Okla. 57 33 59N 96 55W
Lebanon, Oreg. 58 44 32N 122 55W
Lebanon, Pa. 59 40 20N 76 26W
Lebanon, S. Dak. 61 45 4N 99 46W
Lebanon, Tenn. 62 36 12N 86 18W
Lebanon, Va. 68 36 54N 82 5W
Lebanon County ◇ 59 40 20N 76 25W
Lebanon Junction 63 37 50N 85 44W
Lebanon State Forest 51 39 53N 74 30W
Lebec 29 34 50N 118 52W
Lebo 38 38 25N 95 51W
Lecompte 39 31 6N 92 24W
Ledyard 37 43 25N 94 10W
Lee, Fla. 31 30 25N 83 18W
Lee, Ill. 35 41 48N 88 56W
Lee, Maine 40 45 22N 68 17W
Lee, Mass. 42 42 19N 73 15W
Lee City 63 37 44N 83 20W
Lee County ◇, Ala. 24 32 39N 85 23W
Lee County ◇, Ark. 27 34 46N 90 46W
Lee County ◇, Fla. 31 26 30N 81 45W
Lee County ◇, Ga. 32 31 45N 84 5W
Lee County ◇, Ill. 35 41 45N 89 20W
Lee County ◇, Iowa 37 40 30N 91 30W
Lee County ◇, Ky. 63 37 35N 83 45W
Lee County ◇, Miss. 45 34 16N 88 43W
Lee County ◇, N.C. 54 35 30N 79 10W
Lee County ◇, S.C. 60 34 10N 80 15W
Lee County ◇, Tex. 65 30 17N 96 58W
Lee County ◇, Va. 68 36 45N 83 5W
Lee Vining 28 37 58N 119 7W
Leech L. 44 47 10N 94 24W
Leech Lake Indian Reservation 44 47 20N 94 10W
Leedey 57 35 52N 99 21W
Leeds, Ala. 24 33 33N 86 33W
Leeds, Maine 40 44 18N 70 7W
Leeds, N. Dak. 55 48 17N 99 27W
Leeds, Utah 66 37 14N 113 22W
Leektown 51 39 38N 74 26W
Leelanau County ◇ 43 44 55N 85 50W
Leelanau L. 43 44 55N 85 43W
Lees Summit 46 38 55N 94 23W
Leesburg, Fla. 31 28 49N 81 53W
Leesburg, Ga. 32 31 44N 84 10W
Leesburg, N.J. 51 39 15N 74 59W
Leesburg, Ohio 56 39 21N 83 33W
Leesburg, Va. 68 39 7N 77 34W
Leesport 59 40 27N 75 58W
Leesville, La. 39 31 9N 93 16W
Leesville, Ohio 56 40 27N 81 13W
Leesville L. 68 37 5N 79 25W
Leeville 39 29 15N 90 12W
Leflore 57 34 54N 94 59W
Leflore County ◇ 45 33 30N 90 20W
Lefors 64 35 26N 100 48W
Leggett, Calif. 28 39 52N 123 43W
Leggett, Tex. 65 30 49N 94 52W
Lehi 66 40 24N 111 51W
Lehigh, Iowa 37 42 22N 94 3W
Lehigh, Kans. 38 38 22N 97 18W
Lehigh, Okla. 57 34 28N 96 13W
Lehigh → 59 40 41N 75 12W
Lehigh Acres 31 26 36N 81 39W
Lehigh County ◇ 59 40 40N 75 50W
Lehighton 59 40 50N 75 43W
Lehr 55 46 17N 99 21W
Lehua I. 33 22 1N 160 6W
Leicester, Mass. 42 42 15N 71 55W
Leicester, Vt. 50 43 50N 73 8W
Leidy, Mt. 70 43 44N 110 24W
Leigh 48 41 42N 97 14W
Leighton, Ala. 24 34 42N 87 32W
Leighton, Iowa 37 41 20N 92 47W
Leipsic, Del. 41 39 14N 75 31W
Leipsic, Ohio 56 41 6N 83 59W
Leitchfield 62 37 29N 86 18W
Leitersburg 41 39 42N 77 37W
Leith 55 46 22N 101 38W
Lela 64 35 14N 100 21W
Leland, Ill. 35 41 37N 88 48W
Leland, Iowa 37 43 20N 93 38W
Leland, Mich. 43 45 1N 85 45W
Leland, Miss. 45 33 24N 90 54W
Leland, Oreg. 58 42 38N 123 27W
Leland, Wash. 67 47 53N 122 53W
Leleiwi Pt. 33 19 44N 155 0W
Lelia Lake 64 34 54N 100 46W
Lemay 46 38 32N 90 16W
Lemeta 25 64 52N 147 44W
Lemhi 34 44 52N 113 38W
Lemhi → 34 45 12N 113 53W
Lemhi County ◇ 34 45 0N 114 0W
Lemhi Range 34 44 0N 113 0W
Lemington 50 44 51N 71 36W
Lemitar 52 34 10N 106 55W
Lemmon 61 45 57N 102 10W
Lemon Grove 29 32 45N 117 2W
Lemoore 29 36 18N 119 46W
Lemoyne 48 41 17N 101 49W
Lempster 50 43 15N 72 12W
Lena, Ill. 35 42 23N 89 49W
Lena, Miss. 45 32 36N 89 36W
Lena, Mt. 66 40 50N 109 20W
Lenapah 57 36 51N 95 38W
Lenawee County ◇ 43 41 50N 84 5W
Lennep 47 46 25N 110 33W
Lennox 61 43 21N 96 53W
Lenoir 54 35 55N 81 32W
Lenoir City 63 35 48N 84 16W
Lenoir County ◇ 54 35 10N 77 40W
Lenora 38 39 37N 100 0W
Lenore 34 46 31N 116 33W
Lenox, Ga. 32 31 16N 83 28W
Lenox, Iowa 37 40 53N 94 34W
Lenox, Mass. 42 42 22N 73 17W
Lenox, Mo. 46 37 39N 91 46W
Lenwood 29 34 53N 117 7W
Leola, Ark. 27 34 10N 92 35W
Leola, S. Dak. 61 45 43N 98 56W
Leoma 62 35 10N 87 21W
Leominster 42 42 32N 71 46W
Leon, Iowa 37 40 44N 93 45W
Leon, Kans. 38 37 42N 96 46W
Leon, Okla. 57 33 53N 97 26W
Leon → 65 31 14N 97 28W
Leon County ◇, Fla. 31 30 30N 84 15W
Leon County ◇, Tex. 65 31 16N 95 59W
Leon Valley 65 29 28N 98 38W
Leona, Kans. 38 39 47N 95 19W
Leona, Tex. 65 31 9N 95 58W
Leona → 65 28 45N 99 11W
Leonard, Minn. 44 47 39N 95 16W
Leonard, N. Dak. 55 46 39N 97 15W
Leonard, Tex. 65 33 23N 96 15W
Leonardtown 41 38 17N 76 38W
Leonardville 38 39 22N 96 51W
Leonia 31 30 55N 86 1W
Leoti 38 38 29N 101 21W
Lepanto 27 35 37N 90 20W
Leraysville 59 41 51N 76 11W
Lerna 35 39 25N 88 17W
Leroux Wash → 26 34 50N 110 10W
Leslie, Ark. 27 35 50N 92 34W
Leslie, Ga. 32 31 57N 84 5W
Leslie, Mich. 43 42 27N 84 26W
Leslie County ◇ 63 37 5N 83 25W
Lessley 45 31 10N 91 25W
Lester 68 37 44N 81 18W
Lesterville 61 43 2N 97 35W
Letart Falls 56 38 54N 81 56W
Letcher 61 43 54N 98 8W
Letcher County ◇ 63 37 5N 82 55W
Letha 34 43 54N 116 39W
Letohatchee 24 32 8N 86 29W
Letts 37 41 20N 91 14W
Leucadia 29 33 4N 117 18W
Leupp Corner 26 35 5N 110 52W
Levan 66 39 33N 111 52W
Levelland 64 33 35N 102 23W
Levelock 25 59 7N 156 51W
Levering 43 45 38N 84 47W
Levisa Fork → 63 38 8N 82 37W
Levittown, N.Y. 53 40 44N 73 31W
Levittown, Pa. 59 40 9N 74 51W
Levy County ◇ 31 29 15N 82 45W
Lewellen 48 41 20N 102 9W
Lewes 41 38 46N 75 9W
Lewis, Colo. 30 37 30N 108 40W
Lewis, Iowa 37 41 18N 95 5W
Lewis, Kans. 38 37 56N 99 15W
Lewis → 67 45 51N 122 48W
Lewis and Clark County ◇ 47 47 25N 112 35W
Lewis And Clark L. 48 42 51N 97 29W
Lewis and Clark National Forest 47 47 0N 111 0W
Lewis County ◇, Idaho 34 46 15N 116 29W
Lewis County ◇, Ky. 63 38 30N 83 25W
Lewis County ◇, Mo. 46 40 5N 91 40W
Lewis County ◇, N.Y. 53 43 45N 75 30W
Lewis County ◇, Tenn. 62 35 33N 87 33W
Lewis County ◇, W. Va. 68 39 2N 80 28W
Lewis County ◇, Wash. 67 46 30N 122 0W
Lewis L. 70 44 18N 110 38W
Lewis Range 47 48 5N 113 5W
Lewis Run 59 41 52N 78 40W
Lewis Smith, L. 24 33 56N 87 6W
Lewisburg, Ky. 62 36 59N 86 57W
Lewisburg, Ohio 56 39 51N 84 33W
Lewisburg, Pa. 59 40 58N 76 54W
Lewisburg, Tenn. 62 35 27N 86 48W
Lewisburg, W. Va. 68 37 48N 80 27W
Lewisport 62 37 56N 86 54W
Lewiston, Calif. 28 40 43N 122 48W
Lewiston, Idaho 34 46 25N 117 1W
Lewiston, Maine 40 44 6N 70 13W
Lewiston, Mich. 43 44 53N 84 18W
Lewiston, Minn. 44 43 59N 91 52W
Lewiston, N.C. 54 36 7N 77 10W
Lewiston, N.Y. 53 43 11N 79 3W
Lewiston, Nebr. 48 40 14N 96 25W
Lewiston, Utah 66 41 59N 111 51W
Lewistown, Ill. 35 40 24N 90 9W
Lewistown, Md. 41 39 32N 77 25W
Lewistown, Mo. 46 40 5N 91 49W
Lewistown, Mont. 47 47 4N 109 26W
Lewistown, Pa. 59 40 36N 77 34W
Lewisville, Ark. 27 33 22N 93 35W
Lewisville, Ohio 56 39 46N 81 13W
Lewisville, Tex. 65 33 5N 97 0W
Lexington, Ala. 24 34 58N 87 22W
Lexington, Ga. 32 33 52N 83 7W
Lexington, Ill. 35 40 39N 88 47W
Lexington, Ky. 63 38 3N 84 30W
Lexington, Mich. 43 43 16N 82 32W
Lexington, Miss. 45 33 7N 90 3W
Lexington, Mo. 46 39 11N 93 52W
Lexington, N.C. 54 35 49N 80 15W
Lexington, Nebr. 48 40 47N 99 45W
Lexington, Ohio 56 40 41N 82 35W
Lexington, Okla. 57 35 1N 97 20W
Lexington, Oreg. 58 45 27N 119 42W
Lexington, S.C. 60 33 59N 81 11W
Lexington, Tenn. 62 35 39N 88 24W
Lexington, Tex. 65 30 25N 97 1W
Lexington, Va. 68 37 47N 79 27W
Lexington, Wash. 67 46 11N 122 54W
Lexington County ◇ 60 33 50N 81 10W
Lexington Park 41 38 16N 76 27W
Libby 47 48 23N 115 33W
Liberal, Kans. 38 37 3N 100 55W
Liberal, Mo. 46 37 34N 94 31W
Liberty, Ill. 35 39 53N 91 6W
Liberty, Ind. 36 39 38N 84 56W
Liberty, Kans. 38 37 9N 95 36W
Liberty, Ky. 63 37 19N 84 56W
Liberty, Maine 40 44 24N 69 18W
Liberty, Miss. 45 31 10N 90 49W
Liberty, Mo. 46 39 15N 94 25W
Liberty, N.C. 54 35 51N 79 34W
Liberty, N.Y. 53 41 48N 74 45W
Liberty, Nebr. 48 40 5N 96 29W
Liberty, Pa. 59 41 34N 77 6W
Liberty, S.C. 60 34 48N 82 42W
Liberty, Tex. 65 30 3N 94 48W
Liberty, Wash. 67 47 14N 120 42W
Liberty Center 56 41 27N 84 1W
Liberty County ◇, Fla. 31 30 15N 85 0W
Liberty County ◇, Ga. 32 31 50N 81 30W
Liberty County ◇, Mont. 47 48 40N 111 0W
Liberty County ◇, Tex. 65 30 7N 94 52W
Liberty Hill, S.C. 60 34 29N 80 48W
Liberty Hill, Tex. 65 30 40N 97 55W
Liberty Lake 41 39 23N 76 54W
Libertytown, Frederick, Md. 41 39 30N 77 15W
Libertytown, Worcester, Md. 41 38 18N 75 18W
Libertyville, Ill. 35 42 18N 87 57W
Libertyville, Iowa 37 40 57N 92 3W
Licking 46 37 30N 91 54W
Licking → 63 39 6N 84 30W
Licking County ◇ 56 40 3N 82 24W
Lida 49 37 28N 117 30W
Lidderdale 37 42 8N 94 47W
Lidgerwood 55 46 5N 97 9W
Liebenthal 38 38 39N 99 19W
Lighthouse Point 31 26 15N 80 7W
Lighthouse Pt. 31 29 54N 84 21W
Lightning → 70 43 11N 104 44W
Lignite 55 48 53N 102 34W
Ligon 63 37 22N 82 41W
Ligonier, Ind. 36 41 28N 85 35W
Ligonier, Pa. 59 40 15N 79 14W
Lihue 33 21 59N 159 23W
Likely 28 41 14N 120 30W
Lilbourn 46 36 36N 89 37W
Lillie 39 32 56N 92 39W
Lillington 54 35 24N 78 49W
Lilly 59 40 26N 78 37W
Lily 61 45 11N 97 41W
Lima, Ill. 35 40 11N 91 23W
Lima, Mont. 47 44 38N 112 36W
Lima, N.Y. 53 42 55N 77 37W
Lima, Ohio 56 40 44N 84 6W
Lima, Okla. 57 35 10N 96 36W
Lima, Punta 71 18 11N 65 42W
Lime 58 44 24N 117 19W
Lime Ridge 69 43 28N 90 9W
Lime Springs 37 43 27N 92 17W
Lime Village 25 61 21N 155 28W
Limerick 40 43 41N 70 48W
Limestone, Maine 40 46 55N 67 50W
Limestone, N.Y. 53 42 2N 78 38W
Limestone, Tenn. 63 36 14N 82 38W
Limestone, L. 64 31 25N 96 22W
Limestone County ◇, Ala. 24 34 48N 86 58W
Limestone County ◇, Tex. 65 31 39N 96 31W
Limon 30 39 16N 103 41W
Limon B. 71 9 22N 79 56W
Linch 70 43 37N 106 12W
Lincoln, Ark. 27 35 57N 94 25W
Lincoln, Calif. 28 38 54N 121 17W
Lincoln, Del. 41 38 52N 75 25W
Lincoln, Ill. 35 40 9N 89 22W
Lincoln, Iowa 37 42 16N 92 42W
Lincoln, Kans. 38 39 3N 98 9W
Lincoln, Maine 40 45 22N 68 30W
Lincoln, Mich. 43 44 41N 83 25W
Lincoln, Mo. 46 38 23N 93 20W
Lincoln, Mont. 47 46 58N 112 41W
Lincoln, N.H. 50 44 3N 71 40W
Lincoln, N. Mex. 52 33 30N 105 23W
Lincoln, Nebr. 48 40 49N 96 41W
Lincoln, Wash. 67 47 50N 118 25W
Lincoln City 58 44 57N 124 1W
Lincoln County ◇, Ark. 27 33 56N 91 51W
Lincoln County ◇, Colo. 30 39 0N 103 20W
Lincoln County ◇, Ga. 32 33 45N 82 20W
Lincoln County ◇, Idaho 34 43 0N 114 0W
Lincoln County ◇, Kans. 38 39 0N 98 10W
Lincoln County ◇, Ky. 63 37 25N 84 40W
Lincoln County ◇, Maine 40 44 0N 69 30W
Lincoln County ◇, Minn. 44 44 25N 96 10W
Lincoln County ◇, Miss. 45 31 35N 90 26W
Lincoln County ◇, Mo. 46 39 0N 91 0W
Lincoln County ◇, Mont. 47 48 45N 115 30W
Lincoln County ◇, N.C. 54 35 30N 81 10W
Lincoln County ◇, N. Mex. 52 33 40N 105 30W
Lincoln County ◇, Nebr. 48 41 0N 101 0W

Lincoln County ◇, Nev. **49** 37 20N 115 0W
Lincoln County ◇, Okla. **57** 35 40N 96 50W
Lincoln County ◇, Oreg. **58** 44 40N 123 50W
Lincoln County ◇, S. Dak. **61** 43 21N 96 53W
Lincoln County ◇, Tenn. **62** 35 9N 86 34W
Lincoln County ◇, W. Va. **68** 38 14N 81 59W
Lincoln County ◇, Wash. **67** 47 45N 118 30W
Lincoln County ◇, Wis. **69** 45 20N 89 45W
Lincoln County ◇, Wyo. **70** 42 0N 110 30W
Lincoln National Forest **52** 32 45N 105 40W
Lincoln Parish ◇ **39** 32 32N 92 38W
Lincoln Park, Colo. **30** 38 25N 105 10W
Lincoln Park, Ga. **32** 32 52N 84 20W
Lincoln Park, Mich. **43** 42 15N 83 11W
Lincolnton, Ga. **32** 33 48N 82 29W
Lincolnton, N.C. **54** 35 29N 81 16W
Lincolnville, Kans. **38** 38 30N 96 58W
Lincolnville, Maine **40** 44 17N 69 1W
Lind **67** 46 58N 118 37W
Linda **28** 39 8N 121 34W
Lindale, Ga. **32** 34 11N 85 11W
Lindale, Tex. **65** 32 31N 95 25W
Linden, Ala. **24** 32 18N 87 48W
Linden, Calif. **28** 38 1N 121 5W
Linden, Ind. **36** 40 11N 86 54W
Linden, Mich. **43** 42 49N 83 47W
Linden, N.J. **51** 40 38N 74 15W
Linden, Tenn. **62** 35 37N 87 50W
Linden, Tex. **65** 33 1N 94 22W
Linden, Wis. **69** 42 55N 90 16W
Lindenhurst **53** 40 41N 73 23W
Lindenwold **51** 39 49N 74 59W
Lindley **53** 42 1N 77 8W
Lindon **30** 39 44N 103 24W
Lindsay, Calif. **29** 36 12N 119 5W
Lindsay, Nebr. **48** 41 42N 97 42W
Lindsay, Okla. **57** 34 50N 97 38W
Lindsborg **38** 38 35N 97 40W
Lindy **48** 42 44N 97 44W
Linesville **59** 41 39N 80 26W
Lineville, Ala. **24** 33 19N 85 45W
Lineville, Iowa **37** 40 35N 93 32W
Lingle **70** 42 8N 104 21W
Linn, Kans. **38** 39 41N 97 5W
Linn, Mo. **46** 38 29N 91 51W
Linn, Tex. **64** 26 34N 98 7W
Linn County ◇, Iowa **37** 42 5N 91 35W
Linn County ◇, Kans. **38** 38 15N 94 45W
Linn County ◇, Mo. **46** 39 50N 93 10W
Linn County ◇, Oreg. **58** 44 30N 122 20W
Linn Creek **46** 38 2N 92 43W
Linn Grove **37** 42 53N 95 15W
Linneus, Maine **40** 46 3N 67 52W
Linneus, Mo. **46** 39 53N 93 11W
Lino Lakes **44** 45 12N 93 6W
Linton, Ind. **36** 39 2N 87 10W
Linton, N. Dak. **55** 46 16N 100 14W
Linville **54** 36 4N 81 52W
Linwood, Ala. **24** 31 56N 85 52W
Linwood, Kans. **38** 39 0N 95 2W
Linwood, N.J. **51** 39 21N 74 34W
Linwood, Nebr. **48** 41 25N 96 56W
Lipscomb **64** 36 14N 100 16W
Lipscomb County ◇ **64** 36 15N 100 15W
Lisbon, Ill. **35** 41 29N 88 29W
Lisbon, Maine **40** 44 2N 70 6W
Lisbon, Md. **41** 39 20N 77 4W
Lisbon, N. Dak. **55** 46 27N 97 41W
Lisbon, N.H. **50** 44 13N 71 55W
Lisbon, N.Y. **53** 44 44N 75 19W
Lisbon, Ohio **56** 40 46N 80 46W
Lisbon Falls **40** 44 0N 70 4W
Lisburne, C. **25** 68 53N 166 13W
Lisco **48** 41 30N 102 37W
Liscomb **37** 42 11N 93 0W
Lisianski I. **33** 26 2N 174 0W
Lismore **44** 43 45N 95 57W
Litchfield, Conn. **42** 41 45N 73 11W
Litchfield, Ill. **35** 39 11N 89 39W
Litchfield, Mich. **43** 42 3N 84 46W
Litchfield, Minn. **44** 45 8N 94 32W
Litchfield, Nebr. **48** 41 10N 99 9W
Litchfield County ◇ **42** 41 40N 73 15W
Litchfield Park **26** 33 30N 112 22W
Litchville **55** 46 39N 98 12W
Lititz **59** 40 9N 76 18W
Little →, Ark. **27** 33 45N 94 3W
Little →, Ky. **62** 36 51N 87 58W
Little →, N.C. **54** 35 18N 78 42W
Little →, Tex. **65** 30 51N 96 41W
Little Belt Mts. **47** 46 40N 110 45W
Little Bighorn → **47** 45 44N 107 34W
Little Blue → **38** 39 42N 96 41W
Little Chute **69** 44 17N 88 16W
Little City **57** 34 5N 96 36W
Little Colorado → **26** 36 12N 111 48W
Little Creek **41** 39 10N 75 27W
Little Diomede I. **25** 65 45N 168 56W
Little Eagle **61** 45 40N 100 49W
Little Egg Harbor → **51** 39 35N 74 18W
Little Falls, Minn. **44** 45 59N 94 22W
Little Falls, N.J. **51** 40 53N 74 14W
Little Falls, N.Y. **53** 43 3N 74 51W
Little Fork → **44** 48 31N 93 35W
Little Haw Cr. → **31** 29 23N 81 24W
Little Humboldt → **49** 41 1N 117 43W
Little Kanawha → **68** 39 16N 81 34W
Little Lake **29** 35 56N 117 55W
Little Lost → **34** 43 46N 112 58W
Little Missouri →, Ark. **27** 33 49N 92 54W
Little Missouri →, N. Dak. **55** 47 36N 102 25W
Little Missouri Badlands **55** 47 5N 103 45W
Little Pee Dee → **60** 33 42N 79 11W
Little Powder → **47** 45 28N 105 20W
Little Red → **27** 35 11N 91 27W
Little River **38** 38 24N 98 1W
Little River County ◇ **27** 33 40N 94 8W
Little Rock, Ark. **27** 34 45N 92 17W
Little Rock, S.C. **60** 34 29N 79 24W
Little Rocky Mts. **47** 47 55N 108 30W
Little Sable Pt. **43** 43 38N 86 33W
Little Salt L. **66** 37 55N 112 53W
Little Sioux → **37** 41 48N 96 4W
Little Sitkin **25** 51 57N 178 31 E
Little Snake → **30** 40 27N 108 26W
Little Tallapoosa → **32** 33 18N 85 34W
Little Tennessee → **63** 35 47N 84 16W
Little Traverse B. **43** 45 25N 85 10W
Little Valley **53** 42 15N 78 48W
Little Wabash → **35** 37 55N 88 5W
Little White → **61** 43 40N 100 40W
Little Wood → **34** 42 57N 114 21W
Little York, Ill. **35** 41 1N 90 45W
Little York, Ind. **36** 38 42N 85 54W
Littlefield, Ariz. **26** 36 53N 113 56W
Littlefield, Tex. **64** 33 55N 102 20W
Littlefork **44** 48 24N 93 34W
Littlerock, Calif. **29** 34 31N 117 59W
Littlerock, Wash. **67** 46 54N 123 1W
Littlestown **59** 39 45N 77 5W
Littleton, Colo. **30** 39 37N 105 0W
Littleton, Ill. **35** 40 14N 90 37W
Littleton, Maine **40** 46 14N 67 51W
Littleton, N.C. **54** 36 26N 77 54W
Littleton, N.H. **50** 44 18N 71 46W
Littleton, W. Va. **68** 39 42N 80 32W
Littleton Common **42** 42 33N 71 28W
Littleville **24** 34 36N 87 41W
Live Oak, Calif. **28** 39 17N 121 40W
Live Oak, Fla. **31** 30 18N 82 59W
Live Oak County ◇ **65** 28 20N 98 7W
Livengood **25** 65 32N 148 33W
Livermore, Calif. **28** 37 41N 121 47W
Livermore, Colo. **30** 40 47N 105 16W
Livermore, Iowa **37** 42 52N 94 11W
Livermore, Ky. **62** 37 29N 87 8W
Livermore, Mt. **64** 30 38N 104 11W
Livermore Falls **40** 44 29N 70 11W
Liverpool **53** 43 6N 76 13W
Livia **62** 37 34N 87 6W
Livingston, Ala. **24** 32 35N 88 11W
Livingston, Calif. **28** 37 23N 120 43W
Livingston, Ill. **35** 38 58N 89 46W
Livingston, Ky. **63** 37 17N 84 13W
Livingston, La. **39** 30 30N 90 45W
Livingston, Mont. **47** 45 40N 110 34W
Livingston, N.J. **51** 40 48N 74 19W
Livingston, Tenn. **63** 36 23N 85 19W
Livingston, Tex. **65** 30 43N 94 56W
Livingston, Wis. **69** 42 54N 90 26W
Livingston, L. **65** 30 50N 95 10W
Livingston County ◇, Ill. **35** 40 55N 88 50W
Livingston County ◇, Ky. **62** 37 10N 88 20W
Livingston County ◇, Mich. **43** 42 35N 83 55W
Livingston County ◇, Mo. **46** 39 50N 93 30W
Livingston County ◇, N.Y. **53** 42 40N 77 45W
Livingston Manor **53** 41 54N 74 50W
Livingston Parish ◇ **39** 30 30N 90 45W
Livonia, Ind. **36** 38 33N 86 17W
Livonia, La. **39** 30 34N 91 33W
Livonia, Mich. **43** 42 23N 83 23W
Livonia, Mo. **46** 40 30N 92 42W
Livonia, N.Y. **53** 42 49N 77 40W
Lizard Cr. → **37** 42 30N 94 14W
Lizella **32** 32 48N 83 49W
Lizemores **68** 38 20N 81 11W
Llano **65** 30 45N 98 41W
Llano → **65** 30 39N 98 26W
Llano County ◇ **65** 30 45N 98 41W
Llano Estacado **52** 33 30N 102 40W
Lloyds **41** 38 36N 76 12W
Loa **66** 38 24N 111 39W
Loami **35** 39 40N 89 51W
Lobelville **62** 35 46N 87 47W
Loch Raven **41** 39 26N 76 33W
Lochearn **41** 39 21N 76 43W
Lochloosa L. **31** 29 30N 82 7W
Lochsa → **34** 46 9N 115 36W
Lock Haven **59** 41 8N 77 28W
Lock Springs **46** 39 51N 93 47W
Lockeford **28** 38 10N 121 9W
Lockesburg **27** 33 58N 94 10W
Lockhart, S.C. **60** 34 47N 81 28W
Lockhart, Tex. **65** 29 53N 97 40W
Lockington **56** 40 12N 84 14W
Lockney **64** 34 7N 101 27W
Lockport, Ill. **35** 41 35N 88 3W
Lockport, La. **39** 29 39N 90 33W
Lockport, N.Y. **53** 43 10N 78 42W
Lockridge **37** 40 59N 91 45W
Lockwood **46** 37 23N 93 57W
Loco **57** 34 50N 97 38W
Locust **54** 35 15N 80 25W
Locust Cr. → **46** 39 40N 93 17W
Locust Fork → **24** 33 33N 87 11W
Locust Grove, Ga. **32** 33 21N 84 7W
Locust Grove, Okla. **57** 36 12N 95 10W
Loda **35** 40 31N 88 4W
Lodge → **47** 48 35N 109 12W
Lodge Grass **47** 45 19N 107 22W
Lodgepole, Nebr. **48** 41 9N 102 38W
Lodgepole, S. Dak. **61** 45 48N 102 40W
Lodgepole → **48** 41 2N 102 10W
Lodgepole Cr. → **30** 40 57N 102 23W
Lodi, Calif. **28** 38 8N 121 16W
Lodi, Wis. **69** 43 19N 89 32W
Logan, Iowa **37** 41 39N 95 47W
Logan, Kans. **38** 39 40N 99 34W
Logan, N. Mex. **52** 35 22N 103 25W
Logan, Ohio **56** 39 32N 82 25W
Logan, Utah **66** 41 44N 111 50W
Logan, W. Va. **68** 37 51N 81 59W
Logan County ◇, Ark. **27** 35 18N 93 44W
Logan County ◇, Colo. **30** 40 45N 103 0W
Logan County ◇, Ill. **35** 41 10N 89 20W
Logan County ◇, Kans. **38** 39 0N 101 0W
Logan County ◇, Ky. **62** 36 50N 86 50W
Logan County ◇, N. Dak. **55** 46 28N 99 25W
Logan County ◇, Nebr. **48** 41 30N 100 30W
Logan County ◇, Ohio **56** 40 22N 83 46W
Logan County ◇, Okla. **57** 36 0N 97 30W
Logan County ◇, W. Va. **68** 37 58N 82 0W
Logan Martin Reservoir **24** 33 26N 86 20W
Logandale **49** 36 36N 114 29W
Logansport, Ind. **36** 40 45N 86 22W
Logansport, La. **39** 31 58N 94 0W
Loganton **59** 41 2N 77 19W
Loganville, Ga. **32** 33 50N 83 54W
Loganville, Wis. **69** 43 27N 90 2W
Lohrville **37** 42 17N 94 33W
Loíza **71** 18 26N 65 53W
Loíza, Lago **71** 18 17N 66 0W
Lola **62** 37 19N 88 18W
Lola, Mt. **28** 39 26N 120 22W
Lolita **65** 28 50N 96 33W
Lolo **47** 46 45N 114 5W
Lolo Hot Springs **47** 46 44N 114 32W
Lolo National Forest **47** 47 8N 114 40W
Lolo Peak **47** 46 41N 114 14W
Loma, Colo. **30** 39 12N 108 49W
Loma, Mont. **47** 47 56N 110 30W
Loma, N. Dak. **55** 48 38N 98 32W
Loma Prieta **28** 37 6N 121 50W
Loman **44** 48 31N 93 49W
Lomax **35** 40 41N 91 4W
Lombard **35** 41 53N 88 1W
Lometa **65** 31 13N 98 24W
Lompoc **29** 34 38N 120 28W
Lonaconing **41** 39 34N 78 59W
London, Ark. **27** 35 20N 93 15W
London, Ky. **63** 37 8N 84 5W
London, Ohio **56** 39 53N 83 27W
London Mills **35** 40 43N 90 11W
Londonderry, Ohio **56** 39 16N 82 48W
Londonderry, Vt. **50** 43 14N 72 48W
Londontowne **41** 38 55N 76 33W
Lone Grove **57** 34 11N 97 14W
Lone Mountain **63** 36 24N 83 35W
Lone Mt. **61** 45 23N 103 44W
Lone Oak, Ky. **62** 37 2N 88 40W
Lone Oak, Tex. **65** 33 0N 95 57W
Lone Pine **29** 36 36N 118 4W
Lone Star **65** 32 55N 94 43W
Lone Wolf **57** 34 59N 99 15W
Lonejack **46** 38 52N 94 10W
Lonepine **47** 47 42N 114 38W
Lonerock **58** 45 5N 119 53W
Long B. **60** 33 35N 78 45W
Long Beach, Calif. **29** 33 47N 118 11W
Long Beach, Miss. **45** 30 21N 89 9W
Long Beach, N.Y. **53** 40 35N 73 39W
Long Beach, Wash. **67** 46 21N 124 3W
Long Branch **51** 40 18N 74 0W
Long Branch L. **46** 39 50N 92 30W
Long County ◇ **32** 31 45N 81 45W
Long Creek **58** 44 43N 119 6W
Long I. **53** 40 45N 73 30W
Long Island **38** 39 57N 99 32W
Long Island Sd. **42** 41 10N 73 0W
Long L., Aroostook, Maine **40** 47 13N 68 15W
Long L., Aroostook, Maine **40** 46 43N 69 23W
Long L., Mich. **43** 45 13N 83 29W
Long L., N. Dak. **55** 46 44N 100 6W
Long L., N.Y. **53** 44 1N 74 24W
Long L., Wash. **67** 47 50N 117 51W
Long Lake **53** 43 58N 74 25W
Long Mt. **46** 36 43N 92 31W
Long Pine **48** 42 32N 99 42W
Long Point **35** 41 0N 88 54W
Long Pond **42** 41 48N 70 56W
Long Prairie **44** 45 59N 94 52W
Long Prairie → **44** 46 20N 94 36W
Long Pt **44** 48 59N 94 59W
Long Ridge **63** 38 35N 84 49W
Longboat Key **31** 27 23N 82 39W
Longbranch **67** 47 13N 122 46W
Longdale **57** 36 8N 98 33W
Longford **38** 39 10N 97 20W
Longmeadow **42** 42 3N 72 34W
Longmont **30** 40 10N 105 6W
Longridge **41** 38 16N 75 37W
Longstreet **39** 32 6N 93 57W
Longton **38** 37 23N 96 5W
Longtown **46** 37 40N 89 47W
Longview, Ill. **35** 39 53N 88 4W
Longview, Miss. **45** 33 24N 88 55W
Longview, N.C. **54** 35 44N 81 23W
Longview, Tex. **65** 32 30N 94 44W
Longview, Wash. **67** 46 8N 122 57W
Longville, La. **39** 30 36N 93 14W
Longville, Minn. **44** 46 59N 94 13W
Longwood **31** 28 42N 81 21W
Longwoods **41** 38 52N 76 5W
Lonoke **27** 34 47N 91 54W
Lonoke County ◇ **27** 34 47N 91 54W
Lonsdale **44** 44 29N 93 26W
Loogootee **36** 38 41N 86 55W
Lookeba **57** 35 22N 98 22W
Looking Glass → **43** 42 52N 84 54W
Lookout **28** 41 13N 121 9W
Lookout, C., N.C. **54** 34 35N 76 32W
Lookout, C., Oreg. **58** 45 20N 124 1W
Lookout, Pt. **43** 44 3N 83 35W
Lookout Mountain **63** 34 59N 85 21W
Lookout Mt., Ala. **24** 34 20N 85 45W
Lookout Mt., Oreg. **58** 45 21N 121 31W
Loomis, Nebr. **48** 40 29N 99 31W
Loomis, Wash. **67** 48 49N 119 38W
Loon Lake **67** 48 4N 117 38W
Loose Creek **46** 38 31N 91 57W
Lorain **56** 41 28N 82 11W
Lorain County ◇ **56** 41 14N 82 7W
Loraine, Ill. **35** 40 9N 91 13W
Loraine, Tex. **64** 32 25N 100 43W
Lordsburg **52** 32 21N 108 43W
Lore City **56** 39 59N 81 28W
Loreauville **39** 30 3N 91 44W
Lorenzo, Idaho **34** 43 44N 111 52W
Lorenzo, Tex. **64** 33 40N 101 32W
Loretta **38** 38 39N 99 12W
Loretto **62** 35 5N 87 26W
Lorimor **37** 41 8N 94 3W
Loris **60** 34 4N 78 53W
Lorman **45** 31 49N 91 3W
Lorraine **38** 38 34N 98 19W
Lorton **48** 40 35N 96 1W
Los Alamos, Calif. **29** 34 44N 120 17W
Los Alamos, N. Mex. **52** 35 53N 106 19W
Los Alamos County ◇ **52** 35 55N 106 15W
Los Altos **28** 37 23N 122 7W
Los Angeles **29** 34 4N 118 15W
Los Angeles Aqueduct **29** 35 22N 118 5W
Los Angeles County ◇ **29** 34 20N 118 10W
Los Banos **28** 37 4N 120 51W
Los Fresnos **64** 26 4N 97 29W
Los Gatos **28** 37 14N 121 59W

Los Lunas **52** 34 48N 106 44W
Los Molinos **28** 40 1N 122 6W
Los Olivos **29** 34 40N 120 7W
Los Padillas **52** 34 57N 106 42W
Los Padres National Forest **29** 34 40N 119 40W
Los Pinas → **30** 36 56N 107 36W
Los Pinos **52** 36 59N 106 3W
Losantville **36** 40 2N 85 11W
Lost →, Ind. **36** 38 33N 86 49W
Lost →, Oreg. **58** 41 56N 121 30W
Lost Chance Cr. → **54** 38 32N 110 55W
Lost Creek **68** 39 10N 80 21W
Lost Hills **29** 35 37N 119 41W
Lost Nation **37** 41 58N 90 49W
Lost Peak **66** 37 29N 113 55W
Lost River Range **34** 44 8N 113 47W
Lost Springs, Kans. **38** 38 34N 96 58W
Lost Springs, Wyo. **70** 42 46N 104 56W
Lostwood **55** 48 29N 102 25W
Lothair **47** 48 28N 111 14W
Lott **65** 31 12N 97 2W
Loudon, N.H. **50** 43 16N 71 27W
Loudon, Tenn. **63** 35 45N 84 20W
Loudon County ◇ **63** 35 45N 84 20W
Loudonville **56** 40 38N 82 14W
Loudoun County ◇ **68** 39 5N 77 50W
Loughman **31** 28 14N 81 34W
Louin **45** 32 4N 89 16W
Louisa, Ky. **63** 38 7N 82 36W
Louisa, Va. **68** 38 1N 78 0W
Louisa County ◇, Iowa **37** 41 15N 91 15W
Louisa County ◇, Va. **68** 38 1N 78 0W
Louisana □ **39** 31 0N 93 0W
Louisburg, Kans. **38** 38 37N 94 41W
Louisburg, Minn. **44** 45 10N 96 10W
Louisburg, Mo. **46** 37 46N 93 8W
Louisburg, N.C. **54** 36 6N 78 18W
Louise, Miss. **45** 32 59N 90 35W
Louise, Tex. **65** 29 6N 96 24W
Louisiana **46** 39 27N 91 3W
Louisville, Ala. **24** 31 47N 85 33W
Louisville, Colo. **30** 39 59N 105 8W
Louisville, Ga. **32** 33 0N 82 25W
Louisville, Ill. **35** 38 46N 88 30W
Louisville, Kans. **38** 39 15N 96 18W
Louisville, Ky. **63** 38 15N 85 46W
Louisville, Miss. **45** 33 7N 89 3W
Louisville, Nebr. **48** 41 0N 96 10W
Louisville, Ohio **56** 40 50N 81 16W
Loup → **48** 41 24N 97 19W
Loup City **48** 41 17N 98 58W
Loup County ◇ **48** 41 50N 99 30W
Louvale **32** 32 10N 84 50W
Louviers **30** 39 28N 105 1W
Love County ◇ **57** 34 0N 97 15W
Love Point **41** 39 2N 76 19W
Lovelady **65** 31 8N 95 27W
Loveland, Colo. **30** 40 24N 105 5W
Loveland, Ohio **56** 39 16N 84 16W
Loveland, Okla. **57** 34 18N 98 46W
Loveland Pass **30** 39 40N 105 53W
Lovell, Maine **40** 44 7N 70 54W
Lovell, Wyo. **70** 44 50N 108 24W
Lovelock **49** 40 11N 118 28W
Loves Park **35** 42 19N 89 3W
Lovett **32** 32 38N 82 46W
Lovilia **37** 41 8N 92 55W
Loving **52** 32 17N 104 6W
Loving County ◇ **64** 31 42N 103 36W
Lovingston **68** 37 46N 78 52W
Lovington, Ill. **35** 39 43N 88 38W
Lovington, N. Mex. **52** 32 57N 103 21W
Lowden **37** 41 52N 90 56W
Lowell, Ark. **27** 36 15N 94 8W
Lowell, Fla. **31** 29 20N 82 12W
Lowell, Ind. **36** 41 18N 87 25W
Lowell, Mass. **42** 42 38N 71 19W
Lowell, N.C. **54** 35 16N 81 6W
Lowell, Oreg. **58** 43 55N 122 47W
Lowell, Vt. **50** 44 48N 72 27W
Lowell, L. **34** 43 35N 116 44W
Lower Brule **61** 44 5N 99 34W
Lower Brule Indian Reservation **61** 44 5N 100 0W
Lower Gilmanton **50** 43 24N 71 24W
Lower Granite L. **67** 46 26N 117 14W
Lower Kalskag **25** 61 31N 160 22W
Lower Klamath L. **28** 41 57N 121 42W
Lower L. **28** 41 16N 120 2W
Lower Lake **28** 38 55N 122 37W
Lower Marlboro **41** 38 39N 76 41W
Lower Monumental Dam **67** 46 32N 118 33W
Lower New York B. **51** 40 33N 74 5W
Lower Paia **33** 20 55N 156 23W
Lower Red L. **44** 47 58N 95 0W
Lowes **62** 36 53N 88 46W
Lowes Crossroads **41** 38 34N 75 24W
Lowgap **54** 36 32N 80 52W
Lowland **54** 35 18N 76 35W
Lowman **34** 44 5N 115 37W
Lowmoor **68** 37 47N 79 53W
Lowndes County ◇, Ala. **24** 32 11N 86 35W
Lowndes County ◇, Ga. **32** 30 50N 83 15W
Lowndes County ◇, Miss. **45** 33 30N 88 25W
Lowndesboro **24** 32 17N 86 37W
Lowndesville **60** 34 13N 82 39W
Lowry, Minn. **44** 45 42N 95 31W
Lowry, S. Dak. **61** 45 20N 99 59W
Lowry City **46** 38 8N 93 44W
Lowrys **60** 34 47N 81 14W
Lowville **53** 43 47N 75 29W
Loxley **24** 30 37N 87 45W
Loyal, Okla. **57** 35 59N 98 6W
Loyal, Wis. **69** 44 44N 90 30W
Loyal Valley **65** 30 35N 99 0W
Loyall **63** 36 51N 83 22W
Loyalton, Calif. **28** 39 41N 120 14W
Loyalton, S. Dak. **61** 45 17N 99 17W
Lua Makiki **33** 20 33N 156 37W
Lubbock **64** 33 35N 101 51W
Lubbock County ◇ **64** 33 35N 101 50W
Lubec **40** 44 52N 66 59W
Lublin **69** 45 5N 90 43W
Lucama **54** 35 39N 78 0W
Lucas, Kans. **38** 39 4N 98 32W
Lucas, Ky. **62** 36 53N 86 2W
Lucas, Ohio **56** 40 42N 82 25W
Lucas County ◇, Iowa **37** 41 0N 93 20W
Lucas County ◇, Ohio **56** 41 31N 83 48W
Lucasville **56** 38 53N 82 59W
Luce County ◇ **43** 46 30N 85 30W
Lucedale **45** 30 56N 88 35W
Lucerne **28** 39 6N 122 48W
Lucerne L. **29** 34 31N 116 58W
Lucerne Valley **29** 34 27N 116 57W
Lucero, L. **52** 32 42N 106 27W
Lucile **34** 45 32N 116 18W
Luck **69** 45 35N 92 29W
Luckey **56** 41 27N 83 29W
Ludden **55** 46 1N 98 7W
Ludell **38** 39 52N 100 58W
Ludington **43** 43 57N 86 27W
Ludlow, Calif. **29** 34 43N 116 10W
Ludlow, Colo. **30** 37 20N 104 35W
Ludlow, Ill. **35** 40 23N 88 8W
Ludlow, Mass. **42** 42 10N 72 29W
Ludlow, Miss. **45** 32 34N 89 43W
Ludlow, Mo. **46** 39 39N 93 42W
Ludlow, Vt. **50** 43 24N 72 42W
Ludowici **32** 31 43N 81 45W
Lueders **65** 32 48N 99 37W
Lufkin **65** 31 21N 94 44W
Lugoff **60** 34 13N 80 40W
Luis Lopez **52** 33 59N 106 53W
Lukachukai **26** 36 25N 109 15W
Luke **41** 39 30N 79 5W
Lukeville **26** 31 53N 112 49W
Lula, Ga. **32** 34 23N 83 40W
Lula, Miss. **45** 34 27N 90 29W
Luling **65** 29 41N 97 39W
Lulu **31** 30 7N 82 29W
Lumber → **54** 34 12N 79 10W
Lumber City **32** 31 56N 82 41W
Lumberton, Miss. **45** 31 0N 89 27W
Lumberton, N.C. **54** 34 37N 79 0W
Lumberton, N. Mex. **52** 36 56N 106 56W
Lummi Indian Reservation **67** 48 52N 122 32W
Lumpkin **32** 32 3N 84 48W
Lumpkin County ◇ **32** 34 40N 84 0W
Luna County ◇ **52** 32 15N 107 45W
Lund, Nev. **49** 38 52N 115 0W
Lund, Utah **66** 38 0N 113 26W
Lunenburg, Va. **68** 36 58N 78 16W
Lunenburg, Vt. **50** 44 26N 71 42W
Lunenburg County ◇ **68** 36 58N 78 16W
Luning **49** 38 30N 118 11W
Lupton **26** 35 21N 109 4W
Lupus **46** 38 51N 92 27W
Luquillo **71** 18 23N 65 43W
Luquillo, Sierra de **71** 18 20N 65 47W
Luray, Kans. **38** 39 7N 98 41W
Luray, Mo. **46** 40 27N 91 53W
Luray, S.C. **60** 32 49N 81 14W
Luray, Va. **68** 38 40N 78 28W
Lusby **41** 38 22N 76 26W
Lushton **48** 40 43N 97 44W
Lusk **70** 42 46N 104 27W
Lutcher **39** 30 2N 90 42W
Lutesville **46** 37 18N 89 59W
Luther, Iowa **37** 41 58N 93 49W
Luther, Mich. **43** 44 2N 85 41W
Luther, Okla. **57** 35 40N 97 12W
Luthersville **32** 33 13N 84 45W
Lutherville-Timonium **41** 39 25N 76 38W
Lutie **64** 35 1N 100 13W
Lutsen **44** 47 39N 90 41W
Luttrell **63** 36 12N 83 45W
Lutts **62** 35 9N 87 56W
Lutz **31** 28 9N 82 28W
Luverne, Ala. **24** 31 43N 86 16W
Luverne, Iowa **37** 42 55N 94 5W
Luverne, Minn. **44** 43 39N 96 13W
Luverne, N. Dak. **55** 47 16N 97 55W
Luxemburg, Iowa **37** 42 36N 91 5W
Luxemburg, Wis. **69** 44 33N 87 42W
Luxora **27** 35 45N 89 56W
Luzerne County ◇ **59** 41 10N 76 0W
Lycan **30** 37 37N 102 12W
Lycoming County ◇ **59** 41 20N 77 0W
Lydia **60** 34 17N 80 7W
Lyerly **32** 34 24N 85 24W
Lyford **64** 26 25N 97 48W
Lykens **59** 40 34N 76 42W
Lyle **44** 43 30N 92 57W
Lyles **62** 35 55N 87 21W
Lyman, Miss. **45** 30 30N 89 7W
Lyman, Nebr. **48** 41 55N 104 2W
Lyman, Wash. **67** 48 32N 122 4W
Lyman, Wyo. **70** 41 20N 110 18W
Lyman County ◇ **61** 44 0N 100 0W
Lyman L. **26** 34 22N 109 23W
Lyme **50** 43 48N 72 12W
Lynch, Ky. **63** 36 58N 82 54W
Lynch, Nebr. **48** 42 50N 98 28W
Lynch Station **68** 37 9N 79 18W
Lynchburg, Ohio **56** 39 15N 83 48W
Lynchburg, S.C. **60** 34 3N 80 4W
Lynchburg, Tenn. **62** 35 17N 86 22W
Lynchburg, Va. **68** 37 25N 79 9W
Lynches → **60** 33 50N 79 22W
Lynd **44** 44 23N 95 54W
Lynden **67** 48 57N 122 27W
Lyndon, Ill. **35** 41 43N 89 56W
Lyndon, Kans. **38** 38 37N 95 41W
Lyndon B. Johnson, L. **65** 30 33N 98 20W
Lyndon Station **69** 43 43N 89 54W
Lyndonville, N.Y. **53** 43 20N 78 23W
Lyndonville, Vt. **50** 44 31N 72 1W
Lynn, Ala. **24** 34 3N 87 33W
Lynn, Ind. **36** 40 3N 84 56W
Lynn, Mass. **42** 42 28N 70 57W
Lynn, Utah **66** 41 53N 113 45W
Lynn Canal **25** 58 50N 135 15W
Lynn County ◇ **64** 33 10N 101 48W
Lynn Garden **63** 36 35N 82 34W
Lynn Haven **31** 30 15N 85 39W
Lynndyl **66** 39 31N 112 22W
Lynne **31** 29 12N 81 55W
Lynnville, Ky. **62** 36 34N 88 34W
Lynnville, Tenn. **62** 35 23N 87 0W
Lynnwood **67** 47 49N 122 19W
Lynxville **69** 43 15N 91 2W
Lyon **45** 34 13N 90 33W
Lyon County ◇, Iowa **37** 43 20N 96 10W
Lyon County ◇, Kans. **38** 38 30N 96 10W
Lyon County ◇, Ky. **62** 37 0N 88 5W
Lyon County ◇, Minn. **44** 44 25N 95 50W
Lyon County ◇, Nev. **49** 38 45N 119 10W
Lyon Mountain **53** 44 43N 73 55W
Lyons, Colo. **30** 40 14N 105 16W
Lyons, Ga. **32** 32 12N 82 19W
Lyons, Ind. **36** 38 59N 87 5W
Lyons, Kans. **38** 38 21N 98 12W
Lyons, N.Y. **53** 43 5N 77 0W
Lyons, Nebr. **48** 41 56N 96 28W
Lyons, Ohio **56** 41 42N 84 4W
Lyons, Oreg. **58** 44 47N 122 37W
Lyons, Tex. **65** 30 23N 96 34W
Lyons Falls **53** 43 37N 75 22W
Lytle **65** 29 14N 98 48W
Lytton **37** 42 25N 94 51W

M

Mabank **65** 32 22N 96 6W
Mabel **44** 43 32N 91 46W
Maben **68** 37 38N 81 23W
Mableton **32** 33 49N 84 35W
Mabton **67** 46 13N 120 0W
McAdoo **59** 40 55N 75 59W
McAlester **57** 34 56N 95 46W
McAlister **52** 34 42N 103 47W
McAllen **64** 26 12N 98 14W
McAlpin **31** 30 8N 82 57W
McArthur, Calif. **28** 41 3N 121 24W
McArthur, Ohio **56** 39 15N 82 29W
McBain **43** 44 12N 85 13W
McBee **60** 34 28N 80 15W
McBride, Mo. **46** 37 50N 89 50W
McBride, Okla. **57** 33 54N 96 36W
McBrides **43** 43 21N 85 2W
McCall **34** 44 55N 116 6W
McCallsburg **37** 42 10N 93 23W
McCamey **64** 31 8N 102 14W
McCammon **34** 42 39N 112 12W
McCarthy **25** 61 26N 142 56W
McCartys **52** 35 4N 107 41W
McCaysville **32** 34 59N 84 23W
McClain County ◇ **57** 35 0N 97 30W
McClave **30** 38 8N 102 51W
McCleary **67** 47 3N 123 16W
McClelland **37** 41 20N 95 41W
McClellanville **60** 33 5N 79 28W
Macclenny **31** 30 17N 82 7W
Macclesfield **54** 35 45N 77 40W
McCloud **28** 41 15N 122 8W
McClure, Ohio **56** 41 22N 83 57W
McClure, Pa. **59** 40 42N 77 19W
McClure, L. **28** 37 35N 120 16W
McClusky **55** 47 29N 100 27W
McColl **60** 34 40N 79 33W
McComb, Miss. **45** 31 15N 90 27W
McComb, Ohio **56** 41 7N 83 48W
McConaughy, L. **48** 41 14N 101 40W
McCone County ◇ **47** 47 40N 105 50W
McConnells **60** 34 52N 81 14W
McConnellsburg **59** 39 56N 77 59W
McConnelsville **56** 39 39N 81 51W
McCook **48** 40 12N 100 38W
McCook County ◇ **61** 43 44N 97 23W
McCool **45** 33 12N 89 21W
McCool Junction **48** 40 45N 97 36W
McCormick **60** 33 55N 82 17W
McCormick County ◇ **60** 33 50N 82 15W
McCoy **30** 39 55N 106 44W
McCracken **38** 38 36N 99 33W
McCracken County ◇ **62** 37 5N 88 45W
McCreary County ◇ **63** 37 45N 84 30W
McCrory **27** 35 16N 91 12W
McCulloch County ◇ **65** 31 9N 99 20W
McCune **38** 37 21N 95 1W
McCurtain **57** 35 9N 94 58W
McCurtain County ◇ **57** 34 10N 94 45W
McDade **65** 30 17N 97 14W
McDavid **31** 30 52N 87 19W
McDermitt **49** 41 59N 117 43W
Macdoel **28** 41 50N 122 0W
McDonald, Kans. **38** 39 47N 101 22W
McDonald, N. Mex. **52** 33 9N 103 19W
McDonald, L. **47** 48 35N 113 56W
McDonald County ◇ **46** 36 40N 94 20W
McDonough **32** 33 27N 84 9W
McDonough County ◇ **35** 40 30N 90 40W
McDougal **27** 36 26N 90 23W
McDougall, Mt. **70** 42 54N 110 36W
McDowell **68** 38 20N 79 29W
McDowell County ◇, N.C. **54** 35 40N 82 0W
McDowell County ◇, W. Va. **68** 37 22N 81 33W
McDuffie County ◇ **32** 33 20N 82 25W
Macedonia, Ill. **35** 38 3N 88 42W
Macedonia, Iowa **37** 41 12N 95 25W
Macedonia, Ohio **56** 41 19N 81 31W
Maceo **62** 37 51N 87 0W
McEwen **62** 36 7N 87 38W
McFadden **70** 41 39N 106 8W
McFaddin **65** 28 33N 97 1W
McFall **46** 40 7N 94 13W
McFarland, Calif. **29** 35 41N 119 14W
McFarland, Kans. **38** 39 3N 96 14W
McFarland, Wis. **69** 43 1N 89 17W
McGee Creek Res. **57** 34 22N 95 38W
McGehee **27** 33 38N 91 24W
McGill **49** 39 23N 114 47W
McGrath **25** 62 58N 155 36W
McGraw **53** 42 36N 76 8W
McGregor, Iowa **37** 43 1N 91 11W
McGregor, N. Dak. **55** 48 36N 102 56W
McGregor, Tex. **65** 31 27N 97 24W
McGrew **48** 41 45N 103 25W
McGuffey **56** 40 42N 83 47W
McHenry, Ill. **35** 42 21N 88 16W
McHenry, Md. **41** 39 36N 79 22W
McHenry, Miss. **45** 30 43N 89 8W
McHenry, N. Dak. **55** 47 35N 98 35W
McHenry County ◇, Ill. **35** 42 20N 88 25W
McHenry County ◇, N. Dak. **55** 48 20N 100 45W
Machias **40** 44 43N 67 28W
Machias → **40** 44 43N 67 22W
McIntire **37** 43 26N 92 36W
McIntosh, Ala. **24** 31 16N 88 2W
McIntosh, Minn. **44** 47 38N 95 53W
McIntosh, N. Mex. **52** 34 52N 106 3W
McIntosh, S. Dak. **61** 45 55N 101 21W
McIntosh County ◇, Ga. **32** 31 30N 81 25W

McIntosh County ◇, N. Dak. **55** 46 2N 99 20W
McIntosh County ◇, Okla. **57** 35 20N 95 40W
Mack **30** 39 13N 108 52W
Mackay **34** 43 55N 113 37W
McKean County ◇ **59** 41 50N 78 45W
McKee **63** 37 25N 84 0W
McKee City **51** 39 26N 74 37W
McKee Cr. → **35** 39 46N 90 36W
McKeesport **59** 40 21N 79 52W
McKenney **68** 36 59N 77 43W
McKenzie, Ala. **24** 31 33N 86 43W
McKenzie, N. Dak. **55** 46 50N 100 25W
McKenzie, Tenn. **62** 36 8N 88 31W
McKenzie → **58** 44 7N 123 6W
McKenzie Bridge **58** 44 11N 122 10W
McKenzie County ◇ **55** 47 55N 103 30W
Mackeys **54** 35 56N 76 37W
McKibben **64** 36 8N 101 20W
Mackinac, Straits of **43** 45 50N 84 40W
Mackinac County ◇ **43** 46 5N 85 0W
Mackinac Island **43** 45 51N 84 37W
Mackinaw **35** 40 32N 89 21W
Mackinaw → **35** 40 33N 89 44W
Mackinaw City **43** 45 47N 84 44W
McKinley, Mt. **25** 63 4N 151 0W
McKinley County ◇ **52** 35 30N 108 0W
McKinley Park **25** 63 44N 148 55W
McKinleyville **28** 40 57N 124 6W
McKinney **65** 33 12N 96 37W
McKinney Mt. **64** 29 50N 103 47W
McKinnon **32** 31 25N 81 56W
McKittrick **46** 38 44N 91 27W
Macksburg **37** 41 13N 94 11W
Macksville **38** 37 58N 98 58W
McLain **45** 31 7N 88 50W
McLaughlin **61** 45 49N 100 49W
McLaurin **45** 31 10N 89 13W
McLean, Ill. **35** 40 19N 89 10W
McLean, Nebr. **48** 42 23N 97 28W
McLean, Tex. **64** 35 14N 100 36W
McLean County ◇, Ill. **35** 40 30N 88 50W
McLean County ◇, Ky. **62** 37 30N 87 15W
McLean County ◇, N. Dak. **55** 47 30N 101 0W
McLeansboro **35** 38 6N 88 32W
McLennan County ◇ **65** 31 33N 97 9W
McLeod **55** 46 24N 97 18W
McLeod County ◇ **44** 44 50N 94 15W
McLoud **57** 35 26N 97 6W
McLoughlin, Mt. **58** 42 27N 122 19W
McLouth **38** 39 12N 95 13W
McMillan, L. **52** 32 36N 104 21W
McMinn County ◇ **63** 35 27N 84 36W
McMinnville, Oreg. **58** 45 13N 123 12W
McMinnville, Tenn. **63** 35 41N 85 46W
McMullen County ◇ **65** 28 28N 98 33W
McMurray **67** 48 19N 122 14W
McNab **27** 33 40N 93 50W
McNairy County ◇ **62** 35 10N 88 36W
McNary, Ariz. **26** 34 4N 109 51W
McNary, Tex. **64** 31 15N 105 48W
McNeal **26** 31 36N 109 40W
McNeil **27** 33 21N 93 13W
McNeill **45** 30 40N 89 38W
Macomb, Ill. **35** 40 27N 90 40W
Macomb, Okla. **57** 35 10N 97 0W
Macomb County ◇ **43** 42 40N 83 0W
Macon, Ga. **32** 32 51N 83 38W
Macon, Ill. **35** 39 43N 89 0W
Macon, Miss. **45** 33 7N 88 34W
Macon, Mo. **46** 39 44N 92 28W
Macon, Nebr. **48** 40 13N 98 55W
Macon County ◇, Ala. **24** 32 25N 85 42W
Macon County ◇, Ga. **32** 32 20N 84 0W
Macon County ◇, Ill. **35** 39 50N 89 0W
Macon County ◇, Mo. **46** 39 50N 92 30W
Macon County ◇, N.C. **54** 35 15N 83 30W
Macon County ◇, Tenn. **62** 36 31N 86 2W
Macoupin County ◇ **35** 39 20N 89 55W
McPherson **38** 38 22N 97 40W
McPherson County ◇, Kans. **38** 38 20N 97 40W
McPherson County ◇, Nebr. **48** 41 30N 101 0W
McPherson County ◇, S. Dak. **61** 45 46N 99 0W
McQuady **62** 37 42N 86 31W
McRae, Ark. **27** 35 7N 91 49W
McRae, Ga. **32** 32 4N 82 54W
McRoberts **63** 37 12N 82 40W
McVeigh **63** 37 32N 82 15W
McVeytown **59** 40 30N 77 45W
McVille **55** 47 46N 98 11W
Macwahoc **40** 45 38N 68 16W
Macy **48** 42 7N 96 21W
Mad →, Calif. **28** 40 57N 124 7W
Mad →, Ohio **56** 39 46N 84 12W
Mad →, Vt. **50** 44 18N 72 41W
Madawaska **40** 47 21N 68 20W
Madden Dam **71** 9 13N 79 37W
Madden L. **71** 9 15N 79 35W
Maddock **55** 47 58N 99 32W
Maddox **41** 38 20N 76 48W
Madeira Beach **31** 27 48N 82 48W
Madelia **44** 44 3N 94 25W
Madeline **28** 41 3N 120 28W
Madeline I. **69** 46 49N 90 42W
Madera **29** 36 57N 120 3W
Madera County ◇ **28** 37 15N 119 35W
Madill **57** 34 6N 96 46W
Madison, Ala. **24** 34 42N 86 45W
Madison, Ark. **27** 35 1N 90 43W
Madison, Fla. **31** 30 28N 83 25W
Madison, Ga. **32** 33 36N 83 28W
Madison, Ind. **36** 38 44N 85 23W
Madison, Kans. **38** 38 8N 96 8W
Madison, Maine **40** 44 48N 69 53W
Madison, Md. **41** 38 30N 76 13W
Madison, Minn. **44** 45 1N 96 11W
Madison, Miss. **45** 32 28N 90 7W
Madison, Mo. **46** 39 28N 92 13W
Madison, N.C. **54** 36 23N 79 58W
Madison, N.J. **51** 40 46N 74 25W
Madison, Nebr. **48** 41 50N 97 27W
Madison, Ohio **56** 41 46N 81 3W
Madison, S. Dak. **61** 44 0N 97 7W
Madison, Tenn. **62** 36 16N 86 42W
Madison, Va. **68** 38 23N 78 15W
Madison, W. Va. **68** 38 4N 81 49W
Madison, Wis. **69** 43 4N 89 24W
Madison → **47** 45 56N 111 31W
Madison County ◇, Ala. **24** 34 44N 86 35W
Madison County ◇, Ark. **27** 36 5N 93 44W
Madison County ◇, Fla. **31** 30 30N 83 30W
Madison County ◇, Ga. **32** 34 10N 83 10W
Madison County ◇, Idaho **34** 43 55N 111 50W
Madison County ◇, Ill. **35** 38 50N 89 55W
Madison County ◇, Ind. **36** 40 10N 85 45W
Madison County ◇, Iowa **37** 41 20N 94 0W
Madison County ◇, Ky. **63** 37 40N 84 20W
Madison County ◇, Miss. **45** 32 37N 90 2W
Madison County ◇, Mo. **46** 37 30N 90 20W
Madison County ◇, Mont. **47** 45 12N 112 0W
Madison County ◇, N.C. **54** 35 50N 82 50W
Madison County ◇, N.Y. **53** 43 0N 75 45W
Madison County ◇, Nebr. **48** 41 50N 97 30W
Madison County ◇, Ohio **56** 39 53N 83 27W
Madison County ◇, Tenn. **62** 35 37N 88 49W
Madison County ◇, Tex. **65** 31 0N 96 0W
Madison County ◇, Va. **68** 38 23N 78 15W
Madison Heights **68** 37 25N 79 8W
Madison Lake **44** 44 12N 93 49W
Madison Mills **56** 39 39N 83 20W
Madison Parish ◇ **39** 32 25N 91 11W
Madisonville, Ky. **62** 37 20N 87 30W
Madisonville, La. **39** 30 24N 90 10W
Madisonville, Tenn. **63** 35 31N 84 22W
Madisonville, Tex. **65** 30 57N 95 55W
Madras **58** 44 38N 121 8W
Madre, Laguna **64** 27 0N 97 30W
Madrid, Ala. **24** 31 2N 85 24W
Madrid, Iowa **37** 41 53N 93 49W
Madrid, N. Mex. **52** 35 24N 106 9W
Madrid, N.Y. **53** 44 45N 75 8W
Madrid, Nebr. **48** 40 51N 101 33W
Maeser **66** 40 28N 109 35W
Maeystown **35** 38 13N 90 14W
Magazine **27** 35 9N 93 48W
Magazine Mt. **27** 35 10N 93 41W
Magdalena **52** 34 7N 107 15W
Magdalena Mts. **52** 33 45N 107 15W
Magee **45** 31 52N 89 44W
Magic Reservoir **34** 43 15N 114 22W
Magna **66** 40 42N 112 6W
Magnet **48** 42 27N 97 28W
Magnolia, Ark. **27** 33 16N 93 14W
Magnolia, Del. **41** 39 4N 75 29W
Magnolia, Iowa **37** 41 42N 95 52W
Magnolia, Ky. **63** 37 27N 85 45W
Magnolia, Miss. **45** 31 9N 90 28W
Magnolia, Ohio **56** 40 39N 81 18W
Magnolia, Tex. **65** 30 13N 95 45W
Magoffin County ◇ **63** 37 45N 83 5W
Mahaffey **59** 40 53N 78 44W
Mahanoy City **59** 40 49N 76 9W
Mahaska **38** 39 59N 97 20W
Mahaska County ◇ **37** 41 20N 92 40W
Mahnomen **44** 47 19N 95 58W
Mahnomen County ◇ **44** 47 20N 95 45W
Mahomet **35** 40 12N 88 24W
Mahoning County ◇ **56** 41 6N 80 48W
Mahtowa **44** 46 34N 92 38W
Maiden **54** 35 35N 81 13W
Maiden Rock **69** 44 34N 92 18W
Maili **33** 21 25N 158 11W
Maili Pt **33** 21 24N 158 11W
Maine □ **40** 45 15N 69 15W
Maitland, Maine **40** 40 12N 95 5W
Maitland, Mo. **46** 40 12N 95 5W
Major County ◇ **57** 36 15N 98 30W
Makah Indian Reservation **67** 48 23N 124 29W
Makaha **33** 21 29N 158 13W
Makahoa Pt. **33** 21 41N 157 56W
Makahuena Pt. **33** 21 52N 159 27W
Makakilo City **33** 21 22N 158 5W
Makanda **35** 37 37N 89 13W
Makapuu Pt. **33** 21 19N 157 39W
Makawao **33** 20 52N 156 17W
Makoti **55** 47 58N 101 48W
Makushin Volcano **25** 53 53N 166 55W
Malabar **31** 28 0N 80 34W
Malad City **34** 42 12N 112 15W
Malae Pt. **33** 20 7N 155 53W
Malaga, N. Mex. **52** 32 14N 104 4W
Malaga, Ohio **56** 39 51N 81 9W
Malakoff **65** 32 10N 96 1W
Malaspina Glacier **25** 59 50N 140 30W
Malcolm **48** 40 54N 96 52W
Malcom **37** 41 43N 92 33W
Malden, Ill. **35** 41 25N 89 22W
Malden, Mass. **42** 42 26N 71 4W
Malden, Mo. **46** 36 34N 89 57W
Malesus **62** 35 33N 88 50W
Malheur → **58** 44 4N 116 59W
Malheur County ◇ **58** 45 15N 117 45W
Malheur L. **58** 43 20N 118 48W
Malheur National Forest **58** 44 10N 119 15W
Malibu **29** 34 2N 118 41W
Malin **58** 42 1N 121 24W
Malinta **56** 41 19N 84 2W
Maljamar **52** 32 51N 103 46W
Mallard **37** 42 56N 94 41W
Malmo **48** 41 16N 96 43W
Malone, Fla. **31** 30 57N 85 10W
Malone, N.Y. **53** 44 51N 74 18W
Malone, L. **62** 37 5N 87 2W
Maloney, L. **48** 41 3N 100 48W
Malott **67** 48 17N 119 42W
Maloy **37** 40 40N 94 25W
Malta, Idaho **34** 42 18N 113 22W
Malta, Ill. **35** 41 56N 88 52W
Malta, Mont. **47** 48 21N 107 52W
Malta Bend **46** 39 12N 93 22W
Malvern, Ark. **27** 34 22N 92 49W
Malvern, Iowa **37** 41 0N 95 35W
Malvern, Ohio **56** 40 42N 81 11W
Mamala B. **33** 21 15N 157 55W
Mamaroneck **53** 40 57N 73 44W
Mamayes **71** 18 22N 65 46W
Mammoth **26** 32 43N 110 39W
Mammoth Cave National Park **62** 37 8N 86 13W
Mammoth Hot Springs **70** 44 59N 110 42W
Mammoth Lakes **28** 37 39N 118 59W
Mammoth Pool Reservoir **28** 37 20N 119 19W
Mammoth Spring **27** 36 30N 91 33W
Mamou **39** 30 38N 92 25W
Man **68** 37 45N 81 53W
Mana **33** 22 2N 159 47W
Manahawkin **51** 39 42N 74 16W
Manana I. **33** 21 20N 157 40W
Manasquan **51** 40 8N 74 3W
Manasquan → **51** 40 6N 74 2W
Manassa **30** 37 11N 105 56W
Manassas **68** 38 45N 77 29W
Manatee County ◇ **31** 27 30N 82 30W
Manati **71** 18 26N 66 30W
Manawa **69** 44 28N 88 55W
Mancelona **43** 44 54N 85 4W
Manchester, Calif. **28** 38 58N 123 41W
Manchester, Conn. **42** 41 47N 72 31W
Manchester, Ga. **32** 32 51N 84 37W
Manchester, Iowa **37** 42 29N 91 27W
Manchester, Kans. **38** 39 6N 97 19W
Manchester, Ky. **63** 37 9N 83 46W
Manchester, Mass. **42** 42 35N 70 46W
Manchester, Md. **41** 39 40N 76 53W
Manchester, Mich. **43** 42 9N 84 2W
Manchester, N.H. **50** 42 59N 71 28W
Manchester, Ohio **56** 38 41N 83 36W
Manchester, Tenn. **62** 35 29N 86 5W
Manchester, Vt. **50** 43 10N 73 4W
Mancos **30** 37 21N 108 18W
Mandan **55** 46 50N 100 54W
Mandaree **55** 47 43N 102 41W
Manderson **70** 44 16N 107 58W
Mandeville **39** 30 22N 90 4W
Mangham **39** 32 19N 91 47W
Mangonia Park **31** 26 45N 80 4W
Mangum **57** 34 53N 99 30W
Manhasset **53** 40 48N 73 42W
Manhattan, Kans. **38** 39 11N 96 35W
Manhattan, Mont. **47** 45 51N 111 20W
Manhattan, N.Y. **53** 40 45N 73 59W
Manifest **39** 31 43N 91 58W
Manila, Ark. **27** 35 53N 90 10W
Manila, Utah **66** 40 59N 109 43W
Manilla **37** 41 53N 95 14W
Manistee **43** 44 15N 86 19W
Manistee → **43** 44 15N 86 21W
Manistee County ◇ **43** 44 20N 86 10W
Manistee National Forest **43** 44 0N 86 0W
Manistique **43** 45 57N 86 15W
Manistique → **43** 45 57N 86 15W
Manistique L. **43** 46 15N 85 46W
Manito **35** 40 26N 89 47W
Manitou **57** 34 30N 98 59W
Manitou Beach **43** 41 58N 84 19W
Manitou I. **43** 47 25N 87 37W
Manitou Springs **30** 38 52N 104 55W
Manitowish **69** 46 8N 90 1W
Manitowish Waters **69** 46 9N 89 53W
Manitowoc **69** 44 5N 87 40W
Manitowoc County ◇ **69** 44 10N 87 50W
Mankato, Kans. **38** 39 47N 98 13W
Mankato, Minn. **44** 44 10N 94 0W
Manley **48** 40 55N 96 10W
Manley Hot Springs **25** 65 0N 150 38W
Manlius **35** 41 27N 89 40W
Manly **37** 43 17N 93 12W
Mannford **57** 36 8N 96 24W
Manning, Ark. **27** 34 1N 92 48W
Manning, Iowa **37** 41 55N 95 3W
Manning, N. Dak. **55** 47 14N 102 46W
Manning, S.C. **60** 33 42N 80 13W
Mannington, Ky. **62** 37 8N 87 28W
Mannington, W. Va. **68** 39 32N 80 21W
Manns Harbor **54** 35 53N 75 46W
Mannsville, N.Y. **53** 43 43N 76 4W
Mannsville, Okla. **57** 34 11N 96 53W
Manokin **41** 38 5N 75 55W
Manokotak **25** 58 58N 159 3W
Mansfield, Ark. **27** 35 4N 94 15W
Mansfield, Ga. **32** 33 31N 83 44W
Mansfield, Ill. **35** 40 13N 88 31W
Mansfield, La. **39** 32 2N 93 43W
Mansfield, Mass. **42** 42 2N 71 13W
Mansfield, Mo. **46** 37 6N 92 35W
Mansfield, Ohio **56** 40 45N 82 31W
Mansfield, Pa. **59** 41 48N 77 5W
Mansfield, S. Dak. **61** 45 15N 98 34W
Mansfield, Tenn. **62** 36 11N 88 17W
Mansfield, Tex. **65** 32 34N 97 9W
Mansfield, Wash. **67** 47 49N 119 38W
Mansfield, Mt. **50** 44 33N 72 49W
Mansfield Hollow L. **42** 41 45N 72 11W
Mansfield L. **36** 39 43N 87 4W
Manson, Iowa **37** 42 32N 94 32W
Manson, Wash. **67** 47 53N 120 9W
Mansura **39** 31 4N 92 3W
Mantador **55** 46 10N 96 59W
Manteca **28** 37 48N 121 13W
Mantee **45** 33 44N 89 3W
Manteno **35** 41 15N 87 50W
Manteo **54** 35 55N 75 40W
Manter **38** 37 31N 101 53W
Manti **66** 39 16N 111 38W
Manti-la Sal National Forest **66** 37 50N 109 50W
Mantoloking **51** 40 4N 74 4W
Manton **43** 44 25N 85 24W
Mantorville **44** 44 5N 92 45W
Mantua, Ohio **56** 41 17N 81 14W
Mantua, Utah **66** 41 30N 111 57W
Manuelito **52** 35 24N 109 0W
Manvel **55** 48 5N 97 11W
Manville, N.J. **51** 40 33N 74 35W
Manville, Wyo. **70** 42 47N 104 37W
Many **39** 31 34N 93 29W
Manzanita **58** 45 43N 123 56W
Manzano Mts. **52** 34 40N 106 20W
Manzanola **30** 38 6N 103 52W
Maple →, Iowa **37** 42 0N 95 59W
Maple →, Mich. **43** 42 59N 84 57W
Maple →, N. Dak. **55** 46 56N 96 55W
Maple →, S. Dak. **61** 45 48N 98 38W
Maple Falls **67** 48 56N 122 5W
Maple Hill, Kans. **38** 39 5N 96 2W

Maple Hill, N.C. 54 34 40N 77 42W
Maple Rapids 43 43 6N 84 42W
Maple Shade 51 39 57N 74 58W
Maplesville 24 32 47N 86 52W
Mapleton, Iowa 37 42 10N 95 47W
Mapleton, Kans. 38 38 1N 94 53W
Mapleton, Minn. 44 43 56N 93 57W
Mapleton, Oreg. 58 44 2N 123 52W
Mapleton, Utah 66 40 8N 111 35W
Maquoketa 37 42 4N 90 40W
Maquoketa → 37 42 11N 90 19W
Maquon 35 40 48N 90 10W
Marais des Cygnes → 38 38 2N 94 14W
Maramec 57 36 15N 96 41W
Marana 26 32 27N 111 13W
Marathon, Fla. 31 24 43N 81 5W
Marathon, Iowa 37 42 52N 94 59W
Marathon, N.Y. 53 42 27N 76 2W
Marathon, Tex. 64 30 12N 103 15W
Marathon, Wis. 69 44 56N 89 50W
Marathon County ◇ 69 44 50N 89 45W
Maravillas Cr. → 64 29 34N 102 47W
Marble, Ark. 27 36 8N 93 35W
Marble, Colo. 30 39 4N 107 12W
Marble, N.C. 54 35 10N 83 55W
Marble Canyon 26 36 49N 111 38W
Marble City 57 35 35N 94 49W
Marble Falls 65 30 35N 98 16W
Marble Hill 46 37 18N 89 58W
Marble Rock 37 42 58N 92 52W
Marblehead 42 42 30N 70 51W
Marblemount 67 48 32N 121 26W
Marbleton 70 42 34N 110 7W
Marbury 41 38 35N 77 10W
Marceline 46 39 43N 92 57W
Marcellus, Mich. 43 42 2N 85 49W
Marcellus, N.Y. 53 42 59N 76 20W
Marcellus, Wash. 67 47 14N 118 24W
Marco 31 25 58N 81 44W
Marcola 58 44 10N 122 52W
Marcus 37 42 50N 95 48W
Marcus Baker, Mt. 25 61 26N 147 45W
Marcy, Mt. 53 44 7N 73 56W
Mardela Springs 41 38 28N 75 45W
Marengo, Ill. 35 42 15N 88 37W
Marengo, Ind. 36 38 22N 86 21W
Marengo, Iowa 37 41 48N 92 4W
Marengo, Ohio 56 40 24N 82 49W
Marengo, Wash. 67 47 1N 118 12W
Marengo County ◇ 24 32 18N 87 48W
Marenisco 43 46 23N 89 45W
Marfa 64 30 19N 104 1W
Margaretville 53 42 9N 74 39W
Margarita 71 9 20N 79 55W
Margate 31 26 15N 80 12W
Margate City 51 39 20N 74 30W
Marian, L. 31 27 53N 81 6W
Marianna, Ark. 27 34 46N 90 46W
Marianna, Fla. 31 30 46N 85 14W
Marianna, Pa. 59 40 2N 80 6W
Marias → 47 47 56N 110 30W
Maricao 71 18 11N 66 59W
Maricopa, Ariz. 26 33 4N 112 3W
Maricopa, Calif. 29 35 4N 119 24W
Maricopa County ◇ 26 33 15N 112 30W
Maricopa Indian Reservation 26 33 0N 112 10W
Maricopa Mts. 26 32 0N 112 30W
Marienthal 38 38 29N 101 13W
Marienville 59 41 28N 79 8W
Maries → 46 38 30N 92 1W
Maries County ◇ 46 38 10N 91 55W
Marietta, Ga. 32 33 57N 84 33W
Marietta, Miss. 45 34 30N 88 28W
Marietta, Ohio 56 39 25N 81 27W
Marietta, Okla. 57 33 56N 97 7W
Marietta, S.C. 60 35 1N 82 30W
Marin County ◇ 28 38 0N 122 45W
Marina 28 36 41N 121 48W
Marine 35 38 47N 89 47W
Marine City 43 42 43N 82 30W
Marine on St. Croix 44 45 12N 92 46W
Marineland 31 29 40N 81 13W
Marinette 69 45 6N 87 38W
Marinette County ◇ 69 45 25N 88 10W
Maringouin 39 30 29N 91 31W
Marion, Ala. 24 32 38N 87 19W
Marion, Ark. 27 35 13N 90 12W
Marion, Ill. 35 37 44N 88 56W
Marion, Ind. 36 40 32N 85 40W
Marion, Iowa 37 42 2N 91 36W
Marion, Kans. 38 38 21N 97 1W
Marion, Ky. 62 37 20N 88 5W
Marion, La. 39 32 54N 92 15W
Marion, Mass. 42 41 42N 70 46W
Marion, Mich. 43 44 6N 85 9W
Marion, Miss. 45 32 25N 88 39W
Marion, Mont. 47 48 6N 114 40W
Marion, N.C. 54 35 41N 82 1W
Marion, N. Dak. 55 46 37N 98 20W
Marion, Nebr. 48 40 1N 100 29W
Marion, Ohio 56 40 35N 83 8W
Marion, S.C. 60 34 11N 79 24W
Marion, S. Dak. 61 43 25N 97 16W
Marion, Va. 68 36 50N 81 31W
Marion, Wis. 69 44 39N 88 54W
Marion, L. 60 33 28N 80 10W
Marion County ◇, Ala. 24 34 9N 87 59W
Marion County ◇, Ark. 27 36 14N 92 41W
Marion County ◇, Fla. 31 29 15N 82 0W
Marion County ◇, Ga. 32 32 25N 84 35W
Marion County ◇, Ill. 35 38 40N 88 55W
Marion County ◇, Ind. 36 39 45N 86 10W
Marion County ◇, Iowa 37 41 20N 93 5W
Marion County ◇, Kans. 38 38 20N 97 0W
Marion County ◇, Ky. 63 37 30N 85 15W
Marion County ◇, Miss. 45 31 15N 89 50W
Marion County ◇, Mo. 46 39 50N 91 35W
Marion County ◇, Ohio 56 40 35N 83 8W
Marion County ◇, Oreg. 58 44 50N 122 50W
Marion County ◇, S.C. 60 34 10N 79 20W
Marion County ◇, Tenn. 63 35 5N 85 38W
Marion County ◇, Tex. 65 32 46N 94 21W
Marion County ◇, W. Va. 68 39 29N 80 9W
Marion Junction 24 32 26N 87 14W
Marion Lake 38 38 22N 97 5W
Marion Station 41 38 2N 75 46W
Marionville 46 37 0N 93 38W
Mariposa 28 37 29N 119 58W
Mariposa County ◇ 28 37 30N 120 0W
Marissa 35 38 15N 89 45W
Mark Twain L. 46 39 28N 91 55W
Mark Twain National Forest 46 36 50N 92 0W
Marked Tree 27 35 32N 90 25W
Markesan 69 43 42N 88 59W
Markham 65 28 58N 96 4W
Markle 36 40 50N 85 20W
Markleeville 28 38 42N 119 47W
Markleville 36 39 59N 85 37W
Markleysburg 59 39 44N 79 27W
Marks 45 34 16N 90 16W
Marks Butte 30 40 53N 102 23W
Marksville 39 31 8N 92 4W
Marland 57 36 34N 97 9W
Marlboro, N.J. 51 40 19N 74 15W
Marlboro, N.Y. 53 41 36N 73 59W
Marlboro County ◇ 60 34 40N 79 40W
Marlborough, Conn. 42 41 8N 72 27W
Marlborough, Mass. 42 42 21N 71 33W
Marlborough, N.H. 50 42 54N 72 13W
Marlette 43 43 20N 83 5W
Marlin, Tex. 65 31 18N 96 54W
Marlin, Wash. 67 47 25N 118 59W
Marlinton 68 38 13N 80 6W
Marlow, Ga. 32 32 16N 81 23W
Marlow, N.H. 50 43 9N 72 12W
Marlow, Okla. 57 34 39N 97 58W
Marlton 51 39 54N 74 55W
Marmaduke 27 36 11N 90 23W
Marmarth 55 46 18N 103 54W
Marmora 51 39 16N 74 39W
Marne 37 41 27N 95 6W
Maro Reef 33 25 25N 170 35W
Maroa 35 40 2N 88 57W
Marquand 46 37 26N 90 10W
Marquesas Keys 31 24 35N 82 10W
Marquette, Iowa 37 43 3N 91 11W
Marquette, Kans. 38 38 33N 97 50W
Marquette, Mich. 43 46 33N 87 24W
Marquette County ◇, Mich. 43 46 20N 87 30W
Marquette County ◇, Wis. 69 43 50N 89 25W
Marquette I. 43 45 58N 84 24W
Marquez 65 31 14N 96 15W
Marrero 39 29 54N 90 6W
Marrowbone 63 36 50N 85 30W
Mars 59 40 42N 80 1W
Mars Hill, Maine 40 46 31N 67 52W
Mars Hill, N.C. 54 35 50N 82 33W
Marseilles 35 41 20N 88 43W
Marsh I. 39 29 34N 91 53W
Marsh Pass 26 36 36N 110 35W
Marsh Peak 66 40 43N 109 50W
Marshall = Fortuna Ledge 25 61 53N 162 5W
Marshall, Ark. 27 35 55N 92 38W
Marshall, Ill. 35 39 23N 87 42W
Marshall, Ind. 36 39 51N 87 11W
Marshall, Mich. 43 42 16N 84 58W
Marshall, Mo. 46 39 7N 93 12W
Marshall, N.C. 54 35 48N 82 41W
Marshall, Okla. 57 36 9N 97 38W
Marshall, Tex. 65 32 33N 94 23W
Marshall County ◇, Ala. 24 34 21N 86 18W
Marshall County ◇, Ill. 35 41 0N 89 20W
Marshall County ◇, Ind. 36 41 20N 86 15W
Marshall County ◇, Iowa 37 42 0N 93 0W
Marshall County ◇, Kans. 38 39 45N 96 30W
Marshall County ◇, Ky. 62 36 55N 88 20W
Marshall County ◇, Minn. 44 48 15N 96 15W
Marshall County ◇, Miss. 45 34 46N 89 27W
Marshall County ◇, Okla. 57 34 0N 96 50W
Marshall County ◇, S. Dak. 61 45 48N 97 45W
Marshall County ◇, Tenn. 62 35 27N 86 48W
Marshall County ◇, W. Va. 68 39 50N 80 34W
Marshallberg 54 34 44N 76 31W
Marshallton 41 39 44N 75 39W
Marshalltown 37 42 3N 92 55W
Marshallville, Ga. 32 32 27N 89 56W
Marshallville, Ohio 56 40 54N 81 44W
Marshfield, Mo. 46 37 15N 92 54W
Marshfield, Vt. 50 44 20N 72 20W
Marshfield, Wis. 69 44 40N 90 10W
Marshfield Hills 42 42 9N 70 44W
Marshville 54 35 0N 80 25W
Marshyhope → 41 38 32N 75 45W
Marsing 34 43 33N 116 48W
Marston 46 36 31N 89 37W
Mart 65 31 33N 96 50W
Martelle 37 42 1N 91 22W
Martensdale 37 41 23N 93 45W
Martha's Vineyard 42 41 25N 70 38W
Marthasville 46 38 38N 91 4W
Marthaville 39 31 44N 93 24W
Martin, Mich. 43 42 32N 85 39W
Martin, N. Dak. 55 47 50N 100 7W
Martin, S. Dak. 61 43 11N 101 44W
Martin, Tenn. 62 36 21N 88 51W
Martin County ◇, Fla. 31 27 10N 80 20W
Martin County ◇, Ind. 36 38 40N 86 50W
Martin County ◇, Ky. 63 37 45N 82 30W
Martin County ◇, Minn. 44 43 40N 94 30W
Martin County ◇, N.C. 54 35 45N 77 0W
Martin County ◇, Tex. 64 32 18N 101 58W
Martin L. 24 32 41N 85 55W
Martin Pt. 25 70 8N 143 16W
Martinez 28 38 1N 122 8W
Martinez L. 26 32 59N 114 29W
Martins Ferry 56 40 6N 80 44W
Martinsburg, Md. 41 39 10N 77 28W
Martinsburg, Mo. 46 39 6N 91 39W
Martinsburg, Nebr. 48 42 30N 96 50W
Martinsburg, Ohio 56 40 16N 82 21W
Martinsburg, Pa. 59 40 19N 78 20W
Martinsburg, W. Va. 68 39 27N 77 58W
Martinsville, Ill. 35 39 20N 87 53W
Martinsville, Ind. 36 39 26N 86 25W
Martinsville, Va. 68 36 41N 79 52W
Martinton 35 40 55N 87 44W
Marvel 30 37 7N 108 8W
Marvell 27 34 33N 90 55W
Marvin 61 45 16N 96 55W
Marvine, Mt. 66 38 40N 111 39W
Marydel 41 39 7N 75 45W
Maryhill 67 45 41N 120 49W
Maryland □ 41 39 0N 76 30W
Maryland City 41 39 6N 76 50W
Maryland Line 41 39 43N 76 40W
Maryland Point 41 38 22N 77 14W
Maryneal 64 32 14N 100 27W
Marys → 49 41 4N 115 16W
Marys Corner 67 46 33N 122 49W
Marys Pk. 58 44 30N 123 33W
Marysvale 66 38 27N 112 14W
Marysville, Calif. 28 39 9N 121 35W
Marysville, Kans. 38 39 51N 96 39W
Marysville, Mich. 43 42 54N 82 29W
Marysville, Ohio 56 40 14N 83 22W
Marysville, Pa. 59 40 21N 76 56W
Marysville, Wash. 67 48 3N 122 11W
Maryville, Mo. 46 40 21N 94 52W
Maryville, Tenn. 63 35 46N 83 58W
Masardis 40 46 30N 68 22W
Masaryktown 31 28 27N 82 27W
Mascot 63 36 4N 83 45W
Mascoutah 35 38 29N 89 48W
Mashulaville 45 33 5N 88 45W
Maskell 48 42 41N 96 59W
Mason, Ill. 35 38 57N 88 38W
Mason, Mich. 43 42 35N 84 27W
Mason, N.H. 50 42 45N 71 47W
Mason, Ohio 56 39 22N 84 19W
Mason, Tenn. 62 35 25N 89 32W
Mason, Tex. 65 30 45N 99 14W
Mason, W. Va. 68 39 1N 82 2W
Mason, Wis. 69 46 26N 91 4W
Mason City, Ill. 35 40 12N 89 42W
Mason City, Iowa 37 43 9N 93 12W
Mason City, Nebr. 48 41 13N 99 18W
Mason County ◇, Ill. 35 40 15N 89 50W
Mason County ◇, Ky. 63 38 35N 83 50W
Mason County ◇, Mich. 43 44 0N 86 15W
Mason County ◇, Tex. 65 30 45N 99 15W
Mason County ◇, W. Va. 68 38 50N 82 8W
Mason County ◇, Wash. 67 47 20N 123 10W
Mason Springs 41 38 36N 77 10W
Masontown 68 39 33N 79 48W
Masonville, Colo. 30 40 29N 105 13W
Masonville, Iowa 37 42 29N 91 36W
Massabesic L. 50 43 0N 71 23W
Massac County ◇ 35 37 15N 88 45W
Massachusetts □ 42 42 30N 72 0W
Massachusetts B. 42 42 20N 70 50W
Massacre L. 49 41 39N 119 36W
Massapequa 53 40 41N 73 29W
Massena, Iowa 37 41 15N 94 46W
Massena, N.Y. 53 44 56N 74 54W
Massey 41 39 18N 75 49W
Massillon 56 40 48N 81 32W
Masten's Corner 41 38 57N 75 37W
Masters 30 40 18N 104 15W
Mastic 53 40 47N 72 54W
Matador 64 34 1N 100 49W
Matagorda 65 28 42N 95 58W
Matagorda B. 65 28 40N 96 0W
Matagorda County ◇ 65 29 0N 96 0W
Matagorda I. 65 28 15N 96 30W
Matagorda Peninsula 65 28 38N 96 0W
Matanuska-Susitna ◇ 25 62 30N 150 0W
Matawan 51 40 25N 74 14W
Matewan 68 37 37N 82 10W
Matfield Green 38 38 9N 96 31W
Matheson 30 39 10N 103 59W
Mathews 68 37 26N 76 19W
Mathews, L. 29 33 51N 117 27W
Mathews County ◇ 68 37 26N 76 19W
Mathias 68 38 53N 78 52W
Mathis 65 28 6N 97 50W
Mathiston 45 33 32N 89 7W
Matinicus 40 43 52N 68 54W
Matlock 37 43 15N 95 56W
Matoaka 68 37 25N 81 15W
Mattamuskeet, L. 54 35 30N 76 12W
Mattapoisett 42 41 40N 70 49W
Mattaponi → 68 37 31N 76 47W
Mattawamkeag 40 45 32N 68 21W
Matterhorn 49 41 49N 115 23W
Matthews, Ind. 36 40 23N 85 30W
Matthews, Md. 41 38 49N 75 57W
Matthews, Mo. 46 36 45N 89 35W
Matthews, N.C. 54 35 7N 80 43W
Mattituck 53 40 59N 72 32W
Mattole → 28 40 18N 124 21W
Mattoon, Ill. 35 39 29N 88 23W
Mattoon, Wis. 69 45 1N 89 2W
Mattson 45 34 6N 90 31W
Matunuck 42 41 23N 71 32W
Maud, Okla. 57 35 8N 96 46W
Maud, Tex. 65 33 20N 94 21W
Maui 33 20 48N 156 20W
Maui County ◇ 33 20 45N 156 20W
Mauldin 60 34 47N 82 19W
Maumee 56 41 34N 83 39W
Maumee → 56 41 42N 83 28W
Maumelle, L. 27 34 51N 92 29W
Mauna Kea 33 19 50N 155 28W
Mauna Loa 33 19 30N 155 35W
Maunabo 71 18 1N 65 54W
Maunaloa 33 21 8N 157 13W
Maunalua B. 33 21 15N 157 45W
Maunawili 33 21 23N 157 46W
Maunie 35 38 2N 88 3W
Maupin 58 45 11N 121 5W
Maurepas, L. 39 30 15N 90 30W
Maurice → 51 39 13N 75 2W
Mauriceville 65 30 12N 93 52W
Maury 54 35 29N 77 35W
Maury → 68 37 50N 79 25W
Maury City 62 35 49N 89 14W
Maury County ◇ 62 35 37N 87 2W

Mauston **69** 43 48N 90 5W
Maverick County ◇ **64** 28 55N 100 8W
Mavisdale **68** 37 12N 81 59W
Max **55** 47 49N 101 18W
Maxbass **55** 48 43N 101 9W
Maxeys **32** 33 45N 83 11W
Maxinkuckee, L. **36** 41 12N 86 24W
Maxton **54** 34 44N 79 21W
Maxville **47** 46 28N 113 14W
Maxwell, Calif. **28** 39 17N 122 11W
Maxwell, Iowa **37** 41 53N 93 24W
Maxwell, N. Mex. **52** 36 32N 104 33W
Maxwell, Nebr. **48** 41 5N 100 31W
May, Idaho **34** 44 36N 113 55W
May, Okla. **57** 36 37N 99 45W
May, C. **51** 38 56N 74 58W
Mayaguez **71** 18 13N 67 9W
Mayaguez ◇ **71** 18 10N 67 0W
Mayaguez, Bahia de **71** 18 15N 67 15W
Maybell **30** 40 31N 108 5W
Maybeury **68** 37 22N 81 22W
Mayer **26** 34 24N 112 14W
Mayersville **45** 32 54N 91 3W
Mayes County ◇ **57** 36 15N 95 10W
Mayesville **60** 34 0N 80 12W
Mayetta, Kans. **38** 39 20N 95 43W
Mayetta, N.J. **51** 39 40N 74 18W
Mayfield, Ga. **32** 33 21N 82 48W
Mayfield, Idaho **34** 43 25N 115 54W
Mayfield, Kans. **38** 37 16N 97 33W
Mayfield, Ky. **62** 36 44N 88 38W
Mayfield, Utah **66** 39 7N 111 43W
Mayflower **27** 34 57N 92 26W
Mayhill **52** 32 53N 105 29W
Maynard, Ark. **27** 36 25N 90 54W
Maynard, Iowa **37** 42 47N 91 53W
Maynard, Mass. **42** 42 26N 71 27W
Maynardville **63** 36 15N 83 48W
Mayo, Fla. **31** 30 3N 83 10W
Mayo, S.C. **60** 35 5N 81 52W
Mayodan **54** 36 25N 79 58W
Mays Landing **51** 39 27N 74 44W
Mays Lick **63** 38 31N 83 50W
Maysville, Ky. **63** 38 39N 83 46W
Maysville, Mo. **46** 39 53N 94 22W
Maysville, N.C. **54** 34 54N 77 14W
Maysville, Okla. **57** 34 49N 97 24W
Mayview **46** 39 3N 93 50W
Mayville, Mich. **43** 43 20N 83 21W
Mayville, N. Dak. **55** 47 30N 97 20W
Mayville, N.Y. **53** 42 15N 79 30W
Mayville, Wis. **69** 43 30N 88 33W
Maywood **48** 40 39N 100 37W
Maza **55** 48 22N 99 12W
Mazama **67** 48 36N 120 24W
Mazatzal Mts. **26** 34 0N 111 30W
Mazie, Ky. **63** 38 2N 82 58W
Mazie, Okla. **57** 36 6N 95 22W
Mazomanie **69** 43 11N 89 48W
Mazon **35** 41 14N 88 25W
Meacham **58** 45 31N 118 25W
Mead, Nebr. **48** 41 14N 96 29W
Mead, Okla. **57** 34 0N 96 31W
Mead, Wash. **67** 47 46N 117 21W
Mead, L. **26** 36 1N 114 44W
Meade **38** 37 17N 100 20W
Meade → **25** 70 52N 155 55W
Meade County ◇, Kans. **38** 37 15N 100 20W
Meade County ◇, Ky. **62** 37 55N 86 10W
Meade County ◇, S. Dak. **61** 44 30N 102 30W
Meade River **25** 70 28N 157 24W
Meadow, S. Dak. **61** 45 32N 102 13W
Meadow, Tex. **64** 33 20N 102 12W
Meadow, Utah **66** 38 53N 112 24W
Meadow → **68** 38 12N 80 57W
Meadow Bridge **68** 37 52N 80 51W
Meadow Grove **48** 42 2N 97 44W
Meadow Valley Wash → **49** 36 40N 114 34W
Meadow Vista **28** 39 6N 121 1W
Meadowlands **44** 47 4N 92 44W
Meadows **50** 44 21N 71 28W
Meadowview **68** 36 46N 81 52W
Meadville, Miss. **45** 31 28N 90 54W
Meadville, Mo. **46** 39 47N 93 18W
Meadville, Pa. **59** 41 39N 80 9W
Meagher County ◇ **47** 46 40N 111 0W
Meansville **32** 33 3N 84 18W
Mebane **54** 36 6N 79 16W
Mecca **29** 33 34N 116 5W
Mechanic Falls **40** 44 7N 70 24W
Mechanicsburg, Ill. **35** 39 49N 89 24W
Mechanicsburg, Ohio **56** 40 4N 83 33W
Mechanicsburg, Pa. **59** 40 13N 77 1W
Mechanicsville, Iowa **37** 41 54N 91 16W
Mechanicsville, Md. **41** 38 26N 76 44W
Mechanicsville, Va. **68** 37 36N 77 22W
Mechanicville **53** 42 54N 73 41W
Mecklenburg County ◇, N.C. **54** 35 10N 80 50W
Mecklenburg County ◇, Va. **68** 36 55N 78 20W
Meckling **61** 42 51N 97 4W
Mecosta **43** 43 37N 85 14W
Mecosta County ◇ **43** 43 35N 85 20W
Medanales **52** 36 11N 106 11W
Medart **31** 30 5N 84 23W
Medaryville **36** 41 5N 86 55W
Medfield **42** 42 11N 71 18W
Medford, Mass. **42** 42 25N 71 7W
Medford, Minn. **44** 44 11N 93 15W
Medford, N.J. **51** 39 54N 74 50W
Medford, Okla. **57** 36 48N 97 44W
Medford, Oreg. **58** 42 19N 122 52W
Medford, Wis. **69** 45 9N 90 20W
Medford Lakes **51** 39 52N 74 48W
Media **59** 39 55N 75 23W
Mediapolis **37** 41 0N 91 10W
Medical Lake **67** 47 34N 117 41W
Medicine Bow **70** 41 54N 106 12W
Medicine Bow → **70** 42 0N 106 40W
Medicine Bow Mts. **30** 40 40N 106 0W
Medicine Bow National Forest **70** 42 20N 105 38W
Medicine Cr. →, Mo. **46** 39 43N 93 24W
Medicine Cr. →, Nebr. **48** 40 17N 100 10W
Medicine L. **47** 48 28N 104 24W
Medicine Lake **47** 48 30N 104 30W
Medicine Lodge **38** 37 17N 98 35W
Medicine Lodge → **38** 36 49N 98 20W
Medina, N. Dak. **55** 46 54N 99 18W
Medina, N.Y. **53** 43 13N 78 23W
Medina, Ohio **56** 41 8N 81 52W
Medina, Tenn. **62** 35 48N 88 46W
Medina, Tex. **65** 29 48N 99 15W
Medina → **65** 29 16N 98 29W
Medina County ◇, Ohio **56** 41 8N 81 52W
Medina County ◇, Tex. **65** 29 21N 99 9W
Medina L. **65** 29 32N 98 56W
Medio Mundo, Punta **71** 18 16N 65 37W
Medora, Ill. **35** 39 11N 90 9W
Medora, Ind. **36** 38 49N 86 10W
Medora, N. Dak. **55** 46 55N 103 31W
Medway **42** 42 8N 71 24W
Meeker, Colo. **30** 40 2N 107 55W
Meeker, Okla. **57** 35 30N 96 54W
Meeker County ◇ **44** 45 10N 94 30W
Meeks Bay **28** 39 2N 120 8W
Meeteetse **70** 44 9N 108 52W
Megargel **65** 33 27N 98 56W
Meherrin → **68** 36 26N 76 57W
Meigs **32** 31 4N 84 6W
Meigs County ◇, Ohio **56** 39 3N 82 8W
Meigs County ◇, Tenn. **63** 35 31N 84 47W
Meiss L. **28** 41 52N 122 4W
Mekinock **55** 48 1N 97 22W
Mekoryuk **25** 60 23N 166 11W
Melba **34** 43 23N 116 32W
Melbourne, Ark. **27** 36 4N 91 54W
Melbourne, Fla. **31** 28 5N 80 37W
Melbourne, Iowa **37** 41 57N 93 6W
Melcher **37** 41 14N 93 15W
Melfa **68** 37 39N 75 45W
Melissa **65** 33 17N 96 34W
Melitota **41** 39 16N 76 9W
Mellen **69** 46 20N 90 40W
Mellette **61** 45 9N 98 30W
Mellette County ◇ **61** 43 35N 101 0W
Mellott **36** 40 10N 87 9W
Mellwood **27** 34 12N 90 56W
Melrose, Iowa **37** 40 59N 93 3W
Melrose, Mass. **42** 42 27N 71 4W
Melrose, Minn. **44** 45 40N 94 49W
Melrose, Mont. **47** 45 38N 112 41W
Melrose, N. Mex. **52** 34 26N 103 38W
Melrose, Wis. **69** 44 8N 91 1W
Melstone **47** 46 36N 107 52W
Melvern **38** 38 30N 95 38W
Melvern Lake **38** 38 30N 95 50W
Melville **39** 30 42N 91 45W
Melvin, Ala. **24** 31 56N 88 28W
Melvin, Ill. **35** 40 34N 88 15W
Melvin, Tex. **65** 31 12N 99 35W
Melvin Village **50** 43 42N 71 28W
Melvina **69** 43 48N 90 47W
Memphis, Fla. **31** 27 32N 82 34W
Memphis, Mich. **43** 42 54N 82 46W
Memphis, Mo. **46** 40 28N 92 10W
Memphis, Nebr. **48** 41 6N 96 26W
Memphis, Tenn. **62** 35 8N 90 3W
Memphis, Tex. **64** 34 44N 100 33W
Memphis Junction **62** 36 57N 86 29W
Memphremagog, L. **50** 45 0N 72 12W
Mena **27** 34 35N 94 15W
Menahga **44** 46 45N 95 6W
Menan **34** 43 43N 111 59W
Menard, Mont. **47** 45 59N 111 10W
Menard, Tex. **65** 30 55N 99 47W
Menard County ◇, Ill. **35** 40 0N 89 50W
Menard County ◇, Tex. **65** 30 55N 99 45W
Menasha **69** 44 13N 88 26W
Mendenhall **45** 31 58N 89 52W
Mendenhall, C. **25** 59 45N 166 10W
Mendham **51** 40 47N 74 36W
Mendocino **28** 39 19N 123 48W
Mendocino, C. **28** 40 26N 124 25W
Mendocino, L. **28** 39 12N 123 11W
Mendocino County ◇ **28** 39 20N 123 20W
Mendocino National Forest **28** 39 45N 122 50W
Mendon, Mich. **43** 42 0N 85 27W
Mendon, Mo. **46** 39 36N 93 8W
Mendon, Ohio **56** 40 40N 84 31W
Mendon, Vt. **50** 43 40N 72 54W
Mendota, Calif. **29** 36 45N 120 23W
Mendota, Ill. **35** 41 33N 89 7W
Mendota, L. **69** 43 7N 89 25W
Menifee County ◇ **63** 37 55N 83 35W
Menlo, Ga. **32** 34 29N 85 29W
Menlo, Iowa **37** 41 31N 94 24W
Menlo, Kans. **38** 39 21N 100 43W
Menlo, Wash. **67** 46 38N 123 39W
Menlo Park **28** 37 27N 122 12W
Menno **61** 43 14N 97 34W
Meno **57** 36 23N 98 11W
Menominee **43** 45 6N 87 37W
Menominee → **69** 45 6N 87 36W
Menominee County ◇, Mich. **43** 45 30N 87 40W
Menominee County ◇, Wis. **69** 45 0N 88 45W
Menominee Ind. Reservation **69** 45 0N 88 45W
Menominee Ra. **43** 46 0N 88 10W
Menomonee Falls **69** 43 11N 88 7W
Menomonie **69** 44 53N 91 55W
Mentasta Lake **25** 62 55N 143 45W
Mentmore **52** 35 31N 108 51W
Mentone, Ind. **36** 41 10N 86 2W
Mentone, Tex. **64** 31 42N 103 36W
Mentor, Minn. **44** 47 42N 96 9W
Mentor, Ohio **56** 41 40N 81 21W
Mentor-on-the-Lake **56** 41 43N 81 22W
Mequon **69** 43 14N 87 59W
Mer Rouge **39** 32 47N 91 48W
Meramec → **46** 38 24N 90 21W
Merced **28** 37 18N 120 29W
Merced → **28** 37 21N 120 59W
Merced County ◇ **28** 37 15N 120 30W
Mercedes **64** 26 9N 97 55W
Mercer, Maine **40** 44 41N 69 56W
Mercer, Mo. **46** 40 31N 93 32W
Mercer, N. Dak. **55** 47 29N 100 43W
Mercer, Pa. **59** 41 14N 80 15W
Mercer, Tenn. **62** 35 29N 89 2W
Mercer, Wis. **69** 46 10N 90 4W
Mercer County ◇, Ill. **35** 41 15N 90 40W
Mercer County ◇, Ky. **63** 37 50N 84 50W
Mercer County ◇, Mo. **46** 40 25N 93 30W
Mercer County ◇, N. Dak. **55** 47 15N 102 0W
Mercer County ◇, N.J. **51** 40 15N 74 40W
Mercer County ◇, Ohio **56** 40 33N 84 35W
Mercer County ◇, Pa. **59** 41 15N 80 10W
Mercer County ◇, W. Va. **68** 37 22N 81 6W
Mercer Island **67** 47 35N 122 15W
Mercersburg **59** 39 50N 77 54W
Mercerville **51** 40 14N 74 41W
Mercury **65** 31 28N 99 10W
Meredith, Colo. **30** 39 22N 106 44W
Meredith, N.H. **50** 43 39N 71 30W
Meredith, L. **64** 35 43N 101 33W
Meredith L. **30** 38 12N 103 43W
Meredosia **35** 39 50N 90 34W
Meriden, Conn. **42** 41 32N 72 48W
Meriden, Iowa **37** 42 48N 95 38W
Meriden, Kans. **38** 39 11N 95 34W
Meriden, N.H. **50** 43 36N 72 16W
Meridian, Ga. **32** 31 27N 81 23W
Meridian, Idaho **34** 43 37N 116 24W
Meridian, Miss. **45** 32 22N 88 42W
Meridian, Okla. **57** 35 48N 97 15W
Meridian, Tex. **65** 31 56N 97 39W
Merigold **45** 33 50N 90 43W
Meriwether County ◇ **32** 33 0N 84 40W
Merkel **65** 32 28N 100 1W
Merlin **58** 42 31N 123 25W
Mermentau **39** 30 11N 92 35W
Merna **48** 41 29N 99 46W
Merrick **53** 40 40N 73 33W
Merrick County ◇ **48** 41 15N 98 0W
Merricourt **55** 46 12N 98 46W
Merrill, Iowa **37** 42 43N 96 15W
Merrill, Mich. **43** 43 25N 84 20W
Merrill, Miss. **45** 30 59N 88 43W
Merrill, Oreg. **58** 42 1N 121 36W
Merrill, Wis. **69** 45 11N 89 41W
Merrillan **69** 44 27N 90 50W
Merrillville, Ga. **32** 30 57N 83 53W
Merrillville, Ind. **36** 41 29N 87 20W
Merrimac, Ky. **63** 37 25N 85 8W
Merrimac, Mass. **42** 42 50N 71 0W
Merrimac, Wis. **69** 43 22N 89 37W
Merrimack **50** 42 49N 70 49W
Merrimack → **42** 42 49N 70 49W
Merrimack County ◇ **50** 43 15N 71 45W
Merriman **48** 42 55N 101 42W
Merrimon **54** 34 57N 76 38W
Merritt **67** 47 47N 120 50W
Merritt Island **31** 28 21N 80 42W
Merritt Reservoir **48** 42 38N 100 53W
Merryville **39** 30 45N 93 33W
Mershon **32** 31 28N 82 15W
Mertzon **64** 31 16N 100 49W
Merwin, L. **67** 45 57N 122 33W
Mesa, Ariz. **26** 33 25N 111 50W
Mesa, Colo. **30** 39 10N 108 8W
Mesa, Wash. **67** 46 35N 119 0W
Mesa County ◇ **30** 39 0N 108 30W
Mesa Verde **30** 37 15N 108 45W
Mesa Verde National Park **30** 37 11N 108 29W
Mesabi Range **44** 47 40N 92 45W
Mescalero **52** 33 9N 105 46W
Mescalero Indian Reservation **52** 33 12N 105 40W
Meservey **37** 42 55N 93 29W
Mesick **43** 44 24N 85 43W
Mesilla **52** 32 16N 106 48W
Mesita **30** 37 6N 105 36W
Mesquite, N. Mex. **52** 32 10N 106 42W
Mesquite, Tex. **65** 32 46N 96 36W
Mesquite L. **29** 35 43N 115 35W
Meta **46** 38 19N 92 10W
Metairie **39** 29 58N 90 10W
Metaline Falls **67** 48 52N 117 22W
Metamora, Ill. **35** 40 47N 89 22W
Metamora, Mich. **43** 42 57N 83 17W
Metcalf, Ga. **32** 30 43N 83 59W
Metcalf, Ill. **35** 39 48N 87 48W
Metcalfe County ◇ **63** 37 0N 85 40W
Methow **67** 48 8N 120 0W
Methow → **67** 48 5N 119 55W
Methuen **42** 42 44N 71 11W
Metlakatla **25** 55 8N 131 35W
Metolius **58** 44 35N 121 11W
Metropolis **35** 37 9N 88 44W
Metter **32** 32 24N 82 3W
Metuchen **51** 40 32N 74 22W
Metz **46** 37 59N 94 27W
Mexia **65** 31 41N 96 29W
Mexican Hat **66** 37 9N 109 52W
Mexican Springs **52** 35 47N 108 50W
Mexico, Maine **40** 44 34N 70 33W
Mexico, Mo. **46** 39 10N 91 53W
Mexico B. **53** 43 35N 76 20W
Mexico Beach **31** 29 57N 85 25W
Meyers Chuck **25** 55 45N 132 15W
Meyersdale **59** 39 49N 79 2W
Miami, Ariz. **26** 33 24N 110 52W
Miami, Fla. **31** 25 47N 80 11W
Miami, Mo. **46** 39 19N 93 14W
Miami, N. Mex. **52** 36 21N 104 48W
Miami, Okla. **57** 36 53N 94 53W
Miami, Tex. **64** 35 42N 100 38W
Miami Beach **31** 25 47N 80 8W
Miami Canal **31** 26 30N 80 45W
Miami County ◇, Ind. **36** 40 45N 86 0W
Miami County ◇, Kans. **38** 38 30N 94 45W
Miami County ◇, Ohio **56** 40 9N 84 15W
Miami Shores **31** 25 52N 80 12W
Miami Springs **31** 25 49N 80 17W
Miamisburg **56** 39 38N 84 17W
Micanopy **31** 29 30N 82 17W
Micaville **54** 35 55N 82 13W
Miccasukee, L. **31** 30 33N 83 53W
Micco **31** 27 53N 80 30W
Miccosukee **31** 30 36N 84 3W
Michie **62** 35 3N 88 26W
Michigamme, L. **43** 46 32N 88 5W
Michigamme Res. **43** 46 10N 88 10W
Michigan **55** 48 1N 98 7W
Michigan □ **43** 44 0N 85 0W
Michigan, L. **43** 44 0N 87 0W
Michigan Center **43** 42 14N 84 20W
Michigan City **36** 41 43N 86 54W
Michigan I. **69** 46 53N 90 29W
Michigantown **36** 40 20N 86 24W
Middle Alkali L. **28** 41 27N 120 5W
Middle Concho → **64** 31 27N 100 25W

Middle Fork Feather → **28** 38 33N 121 30W
Middle Fork John Day → **58** 44 45N 119 38W
Middle Fork Salmon → **34** 45 18N 114 36W
Middle Fork Sappa Cr. → **38** 39 42N 100 51W
Middle Loup → **48** 41 17N 98 24W
Middle Pease → **64** 34 15N 100 7W
Middle Point **56** 40 51N 84 27W
Middle River, Md. **41** 39 20N 76 27W
Middle River, Minn. **44** 48 26N 96 10W
Middleberg **57** 35 6N 97 44W
Middleboro **42** 41 54N 70 55W
Middlebourne **68** 39 30N 80 54W
Middleburg, Fla. **31** 30 4N 81 52W
Middleburg, N.Y. **53** 42 36N 74 20W
Middleburg, Pa. **59** 40 47N 77 3W
Middleburg, Va. **68** 38 58N 77 44W
Middlebury, Conn. **42** 41 32N 73 7W
Middlebury, Ind. **36** 41 41N 85 42W
Middlebury, Vt. **50** 44 1N 73 10W
Middlefield, Mass. **42** 42 20N 73 2W
Middlefield, Ohio **56** 41 28N 81 5W
Middleport, N.Y. **53** 43 13N 78 29W
Middleport, Ohio **56** 39 0N 82 3W
Middlesboro **63** 36 36N 83 43W
Middlesex **54** 35 47N 78 12W
Middlesex County ◇, Conn. **42** 41 25N 72 30W
Middlesex County ◇, Mass. **42** 42 20N 71 15W
Middlesex County ◇, N.J. **51** 40 30N 74 25W
Middlesex County ◇, Va. **68** 37 36N 76 36W
Middleton, Idaho **34** 43 42N 116 37W
Middleton, Mass. **42** 42 36N 71 1W
Middleton, Mich. **43** 43 11N 84 43W
Middleton, Tenn. **62** 35 4N 88 53W
Middleton, Wis. **69** 43 6N 89 30W
Middleton I. **25** 59 26N 146 20W
Middletown, Calif. **28** 38 45N 122 37W
Middletown, Conn. **42** 41 34N 72 39W
Middletown, Del. **41** 39 27N 75 43W
Middletown, Ill. **35** 40 11N 89 35W
Middletown, Ind. **36** 40 3N 85 32W
Middletown, Md. **41** 39 27N 77 33W
Middletown, Mo. **46** 39 8N 91 25W
Middletown, N.J. **51** 40 24N 74 8W
Middletown, N.Y. **53** 41 27N 74 25W
Middletown, Ohio **56** 39 31N 84 24W
Middletown, Pa. **59** 40 12N 76 44W
Middletown, R.I. **42** 41 32N 71 17W
Middletown, Va. **68** 39 2N 78 17W
Middletown Springs **50** 43 28N 73 8W
Middleville, Mich. **43** 42 43N 85 28W
Middleville, N.Y. **53** 43 8N 74 58W
Midland, Calif. **29** 33 52N 114 48W
Midland, Md. **41** 39 37N 78 55W
Midland, Mich. **43** 43 37N 84 14W
Midland, Oreg. **58** 42 8N 121 49W
Midland, S. Dak. **61** 44 4N 101 10W
Midland, Tex. **64** 32 0N 102 3W
Midland County ◇, Mich. **43** 43 35N 84 20W
Midland County ◇, Tex. **64** 32 0N 102 0W
Midlothian, Md. **41** 39 40N 78 58W
Midlothian, Tex. **65** 32 30N 97 0W
Midnight **45** 33 3N 90 35W
Midvale, Idaho **34** 44 28N 116 44W
Midvale, Ohio **56** 40 26N 81 23W
Midvale, Utah **66** 40 37N 111 54W
Midville **32** 32 49N 82 14W
Midway, Ala. **24** 32 5N 85 31W
Midway, Fla. **31** 30 30N 84 27W
Midway, Ky. **63** 38 9N 84 41W
Midway, Tex. **65** 31 2N 95 45W
Midway, Utah **66** 40 31N 111 28W
Midway Is. **33** 28 13N 177 22W
Midway Park **54** 34 44N 77 21W
Midwest **70** 43 25N 106 16W
Midwest City **57** 35 27N 97 24W
Miesville **44** 44 36N 92 49W
Miffintown **59** 40 34N 77 24W
Mifflin **56** 40 46N 82 22W
Mifflin County ◇ **59** 40 45N 77 45W
Mifflinburg **59** 40 55N 77 3W
Mikkalo **58** 45 28N 120 14W
Milaca **44** 45 45N 93 39W
Milam **65** 31 26N 93 51W
Milam County ◇ **65** 30 51N 96 59W
Milan, Ga. **32** 32 1N 83 4W
Milan, Ill. **35** 41 27N 90 34W
Milan, Ind. **36** 39 7N 85 8W
Milan, Mich. **43** 42 5N 83 41W
Milan, Minn. **44** 45 7N 95 55W
Milan, Mo. **46** 40 12N 93 7W
Milan, N.H. **50** 44 36N 71 12W
Milan, N. Mex. **52** 35 9N 107 54W
Milan, Ohio **56** 41 18N 82 37W
Milan, Tenn. **62** 35 55N 88 46W
Milan, Wash. **67** 47 58N 117 20W
Milano **65** 30 43N 96 52W
Milbank **61** 45 13N 96 38W
Milbridge **40** 44 32N 67 53W
Milburn, Nebr. **48** 41 43N 99 44W
Milburn, Okla. **57** 34 14N 96 33W
Mildred **38** 38 1N 95 10W
Miles, Tex. **64** 31 36N 100 11W
Miles, Wash. **67** 47 55N 118 18W
Miles City **47** 46 25N 105 51W
Milesburg **59** 40 57N 77 47W
Milford, Calif. **28** 40 10N 120 22W
Milford, Conn. **42** 41 14N 73 3W
Milford, Del. **41** 38 55N 75 26W
Milford, Ga. **32** 31 23N 84 33W
Milford, Ill. **35** 40 38N 87 42W
Milford, Ind. **36** 41 25N 85 51W
Milford, Iowa **37** 43 20N 95 9W
Milford, Kans. **38** 39 10N 96 55W
Milford, Ky. **63** 38 35N 84 9W
Milford, Maine **40** 44 57N 68 39W
Milford, Mass. **42** 42 8N 71 31W
Milford, Mich. **43** 42 35N 83 36W
Milford, Mo. **46** 37 35N 94 9W
Milford, N.H. **50** 42 50N 71 39W
Milford, N.J. **51** 40 34N 75 6W
Milford, N.Y. **53** 42 35N 74 57W
Milford, Nebr. **48** 40 47N 97 3W
Milford, Pa. **59** 41 19N 74 48W
Milford, Utah **66** 38 24N 113 1W
Milford Center **56** 40 11N 83 26W
Milford Lake **38** 39 5N 96 54W
Mililani Town **33** 21 28N 158 1W
Milk → **47** 48 4N 106 19W
Mill → **43** 43 2N 82 35W
Mill City, Nev. **49** 40 41N 118 4W
Mill City, Oreg. **58** 44 45N 122 29W
Mill Creek **68** 38 44N 79 58W
Mill Hall **59** 41 6N 77 29W
Mill Shoals **35** 38 15N 88 21W
Milladore **69** 44 36N 89 51W
Millard **46** 40 7N 92 33W
Millard County ◇ **66** 39 0N 113 0W
Millboro, S. Dak. **61** 43 4N 99 58W
Millboro, Va. **68** 37 59N 79 36W
Millbrook **53** 41 47N 73 42W
Millbury **42** 42 12N 71 46W
Millcreek **66** 40 42N 111 50W
Mille Lacs County ◇ **44** 45 50N 93 45W
Mille Lacs L. **44** 46 15N 93 39W
Milledgeville, Ga. **32** 33 5N 83 14W
Milledgeville, Ill. **35** 41 58N 89 46W
Milledgeville, Ohio **56** 39 36N 83 35W
Milledgeville, Tenn. **62** 35 22N 88 22W
Millen **32** 32 48N 81 57W
Miller, Kans. **38** 38 38N 95 59W
Miller, Miss. **45** 34 55N 89 46W
Miller, Mo. **46** 37 13N 93 50W
Miller, Nebr. **48** 40 56N 99 23W
Miller, S. Dak. **61** 44 31N 98 59W
Miller County ◇, Ark. **27** 33 10N 93 58W
Miller County ◇, Ga. **32** 31 10N 84 45W
Miller County ◇, Mo. **46** 38 15N 92 25W
Millers → **42** 42 35N 72 30W
Millers Creek Res. **65** 33 30N 99 20W
Millers Falls **42** 42 35N 72 30W
Millers Ferry **24** 32 6N 87 22W
Millersburg, Ind. **36** 41 32N 85 42W
Millersburg, Iowa **37** 41 34N 92 10W
Millersburg, Mich. **43** 45 20N 84 4W
Millersburg, Ohio **56** 40 33N 81 55W
Millersburg, Pa. **59** 40 32N 76 58W
Millersport **56** 39 54N 82 32W
Millersville, Md. **41** 39 4N 76 39W
Millersville, Pa. **59** 40 0N 76 22W
Millerton, Iowa **37** 40 51N 93 18W
Millerton, N.Y. **53** 41 57N 73 31W
Millerton L. **29** 37 1N 119 41W
Millett **65** 28 35N 99 12W
Millheim **59** 40 54N 77 29W
Milligan, Fla. **31** 30 45N 86 38W
Milligan, Nebr. **48** 40 30N 97 23W
Millington, Md. **41** 39 16N 75 50W
Millington, Mich. **43** 43 17N 83 32W
Millinocket **40** 45 39N 68 43W
Millinocket L. **40** 45 46N 68 48W
Millis **42** 42 10N 71 22W
Millport **24** 33 34N 88 5W
Millry **24** 31 38N 88 19W
Mills, N. Mex. **52** 36 5N 104 15W
Mills, Nebr. **48** 42 57N 99 27W
Mills, Wyo. **70** 42 50N 106 22W
Mills County ◇, Iowa **37** 41 0N 95 35W
Mills County ◇, Tex. **65** 31 27N 98 34W
Millsboro **41** 38 36N 75 18W
Millstadt **35** 38 28N 90 6W
Millstone **68** 38 48N 81 6W
Milltown, Ind. **36** 38 21N 86 17W
Milltown, S. Dak. **61** 43 25N 97 48W
Milltown, Wis. **69** 45 32N 92 30W
Millville, Del. **41** 38 35N 75 8W
Millville, Iowa **37** 42 42N 91 5W
Millville, Ky. **63** 38 8N 84 49W
Millville, Mass. **42** 42 2N 71 35W
Millville, N.J. **51** 39 24N 75 2W
Millville, Ohio **56** 39 23N 84 39W
Millville, Pa. **59** 41 7N 76 32W
Millwood **32** 31 16N 82 40W
Millwood L. **27** 33 42N 93 58W
Milmay **51** 39 26N 74 52W
Milner **30** 40 29N 107 1W
Milnesand **52** 33 39N 103 20W
Milnor **55** 46 16N 97 27W
Milo, Iowa **37** 41 17N 93 27W
Milo, Maine **40** 45 15N 68 59W
Milo, Mo. **46** 37 45N 94 18W
Milo, Oreg. **58** 42 56N 123 3W
Milolii **33** 19 11N 155 55W
Milpitas **28** 37 26N 121 55W
Milroy, Ind. **36** 39 30N 85 28W
Milroy, Minn. **44** 44 25N 95 33W
Milroy, Pa. **59** 40 43N 77 35W
Milton, Del. **41** 38 47N 75 19W
Milton, Fla. **31** 30 38N 87 3W
Milton, Ill. **35** 39 34N 90 39W
Milton, Iowa **37** 40 41N 92 10W
Milton, Kans. **38** 37 26N 97 46W
Milton, Ky. **63** 38 43N 85 22W
Milton, Mass. **42** 42 15N 71 5W
Milton, N. Dak. **55** 48 38N 98 3W
Milton, N.H. **50** 43 25N 70 59W
Milton, Pa. **59** 41 1N 76 51W
Milton, Vt. **50** 44 38N 73 7W
Milton, W. Va. **68** 38 26N 82 8W
Milton, Wis. **69** 42 47N 88 56W
Milton-Freewater **58** 45 56N 118 23W
Milton Reservoir **30** 40 14N 104 38W
Miltona **44** 46 3N 95 18W
Miltonvale **38** 39 21N 97 27W
Milwaukee **69** 43 2N 87 55W
Milwaukee County ◇ **69** 43 0N 88 0W
Milwaukie **58** 45 27N 122 38W
Mimbres **52** 32 51N 107 59W
Mimbres Mts. **52** 32 50N 107 45W
Mims **31** 28 40N 80 51W
Mina **49** 38 24N 118 7W
Minam **58** 45 38N 117 43W
Minatare **48** 41 49N 103 30W
Minburn **37** 41 45N 94 2W
Minco **57** 35 19N 97 57W
Minden, Iowa **37** 41 28N 95 32W
Minden, La. **39** 32 37N 93 17W
Minden, Nebr. **48** 40 30N 98 57W
Minden, Nev. **49** 38 57N 119 46W
Minden City **43** 43 40N 82 47W
Mindenmines **46** 37 28N 94 35W
Mineola, N.Y. **53** 40 45N 73 39W
Mineola, Tex. **65** 32 40N 95 29W
Miner County ◇ **61** 44 1N 97 36W
Mineral, Calif. **28** 40 21N 121 36W
Mineral, Va. **68** 38 1N 77 55W
Mineral, Wash. **67** 46 43N 122 11W
Mineral Bluff **32** 34 55N 84 17W
Mineral County ◇, Colo. **30** 37 40N 106 50W
Mineral County ◇, Mont. **47** 47 4N 115 0W
Mineral County ◇, Nev. **49** 38 30N 118 25W
Mineral County ◇, W. Va. **68** 39 21N 79 0W
Mineral Mts. **66** 38 30N 112 45W
Mineral Point, Mo. **46** 37 57N 90 44W
Mineral Point, Wis. **69** 42 52N 90 11W
Mineral Springs **27** 33 53N 93 55W
Mineral Wells **65** 32 48N 98 7W
Minersville, Pa. **59** 40 41N 76 16W
Minersville, Utah **66** 38 13N 112 56W
Minerva, N.Y. **53** 43 47N 73 59W
Minerva, Ohio **56** 40 44N 81 6W
Mingo County ◇ **68** 37 43N 82 11W
Mingo Junction **56** 40 19N 80 37W
Minidoka **34** 42 45N 113 29W
Minidoka County ◇ **34** 42 50N 113 38W
Minier **35** 40 26N 89 19W
Minneapolis, Kans. **38** 39 8N 97 42W
Minneapolis, Minn. **44** 44 59N 93 16W
Minnehaha County ◇ **61** 43 40N 96 49W
Minneiska **44** 44 12N 91 52W
Minneola **38** 37 26N 100 1W
Minneota **44** 44 34N 95 59W
Minnesota □ **44** 46 0N 94 15W
Minnesota → **44** 44 54N 93 9W
Minnesota City **44** 44 6N 91 46W
Minnesota Lake **44** 43 51N 93 50W
Minnetonka **44** 44 56N 93 27W
Minnewaukan **55** 48 4N 99 15W
Minong **69** 46 6N 91 49W
Minonk **35** 40 54N 89 2W
Minooka **35** 41 27N 88 16W
Minor Hill **62** 35 4N 87 9W
Minot **55** 48 14N 101 18W
Minster **56** 40 24N 84 23W
Mint Hill **54** 35 13N 80 41W
Minto, Alaska **25** 64 53N 149 11W
Minto, N. Dak. **55** 48 17N 97 22W
Minturn **30** 39 35N 106 26W
Mio **43** 44 39N 84 8W
Miraflores Locks **71** 9 0N 79 36W
Miramar **31** 25 59N 80 15W
Mirando City **64** 27 26N 99 0W
Misenheimer **54** 35 29N 80 17W
Mishawaka **36** 41 40N 86 11W
Misquah Hills **44** 47 50N 90 30W
Misquamicut **42** 41 20N 71 49W
Missaukee County ◇ **43** 44 20N 85 10W
Mission, S. Dak. **61** 43 18N 100 39W
Mission, Tex. **64** 26 13N 98 20W
Mission Hill **61** 42 55N 97 17W
Mission Indian Reservations **29** 33 20N 116 50W
Mission Viejo **29** 33 36N 117 40W
Missiquoi B. **50** 45 5N 73 10W
Missisquoi → **50** 45 0N 73 8W
Mississinewa L. **36** 40 42N 85 52W
Mississippi □ **45** 32 0N 90 0W
Mississippi → **39** 29 9N 89 15W
Mississippi County ◇, Ark. **27** 35 45N 90 5W
Mississippi County ◇, Mo. **46** 36 50N 89 15W
Mississippi River Delta **39** 29 10N 89 15W
Mississippi Sd. **45** 30 20N 89 0W
Missoula **47** 46 52N 114 1W
Missoula County ◇ **47** 47 4N 114 0W
Missouri □ **46** 38 0N 92 0W
Missouri → **46** 38 49N 90 7W
Missouri Buttes **70** 44 37N 104 47W
Missouri City **46** 39 14N 94 18W
Missouri Valley **37** 41 34N 95 53W
Mitchell, Ga. **32** 33 13N 82 42W
Mitchell, Ind. **36** 38 44N 86 28W
Mitchell, Iowa **37** 43 19N 92 53W
Mitchell, Nebr. **48** 41 57N 103 49W
Mitchell, Oreg. **58** 44 34N 120 9W
Mitchell, S. Dak. **61** 43 43N 98 2W
Mitchell, Mt. **54** 35 46N 82 16W
Mitchell County ◇, Ga. **32** 31 15N 84 10W
Mitchell County ◇, Iowa **37** 43 20N 92 45W
Mitchell County ◇, Kans. **38** 39 30N 98 10W
Mitchell County ◇, N.C. **54** 36 5N 82 10W
Mitchell County ◇, Tex. **64** 32 24N 100 52W
Mitchell L. **24** 32 48N 86 27W
Mitchellsburg **63** 37 36N 84 57W
Mitchellville **37** 41 40N 93 22W
Mize **45** 31 52N 89 33W
Mizpah, Minn. **44** 47 55N 94 12W
Mizpah, Mont. **47** 46 14N 105 16W
Moab **66** 38 35N 109 33W
Moapa **49** 36 40N 114 37W
Mobeetie **64** 35 31N 100 26W
Moberly **46** 39 25N 92 26W
Mobile, Ala. **24** 30 41N 88 3W
Mobile, Ariz. **26** 33 3N 112 16W
Mobile B. **24** 30 30N 88 0W
Mobile County ◇ **24** 30 41N 88 3W
Mobridge **61** 45 32N 100 26W
Moca **71** 18 24N 67 10W
Moccasin **26** 36 55N 112 46W
Moccasin Gap **68** 36 38N 82 33W
Mocksville **54** 35 54N 80 34W
Moclips **67** 47 14N 124 13W
Model **30** 37 22N 104 15W
Modena **66** 37 48N 113 56W
Modesto **28** 37 39N 121 0W
Modoc, Ga. **32** 32 37N 82 19W
Modoc, S.C. **60** 33 44N 82 13W
Modoc County ◇ **28** 41 40N 120 50W
Modoc Point **58** 42 27N 121 52W
Moenkopi **26** 36 7N 111 13W
Moenkopi Wash → **26** 35 50N 111 20W
Moffat **30** 37 58N 105 56W
Moffat County ◇ **30** 40 45N 108 10W
Mogollon Mts. **52** 33 25N 108 40W
Mogollon Rim **26** 34 10N 110 50W
Mohall **55** 48 46N 101 31W
Mohave, L. **26** 35 12N 114 34W
Mohave County ◇ **26** 35 0N 114 0W
Mohave Mts. **26** 34 35N 114 10W
Mohawk, Mich. **43** 47 18N 88 21W
Mohawk, N.Y. **53** 43 0N 75 0W
Mohawk → **53** 42 47N 73 41W
Mohawk Mts. **26** 32 30N 113 35W
Mohican → **56** 40 22N 82 9W
Mohican, C. **25** 60 12N 167 25W
Mohicanville Reservoir **56** 40 45N 82 0W
Mohon Pk. **26** 34 57N 113 9W
Mojave **29** 35 3N 118 10W

Mojave → **29** 35 6N 116 4W
Mojave Desert **29** 35 0N 117 20W
Mokane **46** 38 41N 91 53W
Mokapu Peninsula **33** 21 25N 157 45W
Mokelumne → **28** 38 13N 121 28W
Mokelumne Hill **28** 38 18N 120 43W
Mokolea Rock **33** 21 27N 157 44W
Moku Manu **33** 21 29N 157 43W
Mokuaeae I. **33** 22 14N 159 25W
Mokuauia I. **33** 21 40N 157 56W
Mokulua Is. **33** 21 24N 157 42W
Molalla **58** 45 9N 122 35W
Molena **32** 33 1N 84 30W
Molii Pond **33** 21 31N 157 51W
Molina **30** 39 11N 108 4W
Moline, Ill. **35** 41 30N 90 31W
Moline, Kans. **38** 37 22N 96 18W
Molino **31** 30 43N 87 20W
Molokai **33** 21 8N 157 0W
Molokini I. **33** 20 38N 156 30W
Momence **35** 41 10N 87 40W
Mona **66** 39 49N 111 51W
Mona, Isla **71** 18 5N 67 54W
Monadnock, Mt. **50** 42 52N 72 7W
Monahans **64** 31 36N 102 54W
Monango **55** 46 10N 98 36W
Monarch **60** 34 42N 81 34W
Monarch Pass **30** 38 30N 106 20W
Moncks Corner **60** 33 12N 80 1W
Mondamin **37** 41 42N 96 1W
Mondovi **69** 44 34N 91 40W
Monee **35** 41 25N 87 44W
Monero **52** 36 55N 106 52W
Monessen **59** 40 9N 79 54W
Moneta **37** 43 13N 95 24W
Monett **46** 36 55N 93 55W
Monette **27** 35 53N 90 21W
Monhegan I. **40** 43 46N 69 19W
Moniac **32** 30 31N 82 14W
Monico **69** 45 35N 89 9W
Monida **47** 44 34N 112 19W
Moniteau County ◇ **46** 38 35N 92 35W
Monitor **67** 47 29N 120 25W
Monitor Range **49** 38 40N 118 45W
Monkstown **65** 33 48N 95 56W
Monkton **41** 39 35N 76 37W
Monmouth, Ill. **35** 40 55N 90 39W
Monmouth, Oreg. **58** 44 51N 123 14W
Monmouth County ◇ **51** 40 15N 74 15W
Monmouth Junction **51** 40 23N 74 33W
Mono County ◇ **28** 38 0N 119 0W
Mono L. **28** 38 1N 119 1W
Monocacy → **41** 39 13N 77 27W
Monolith **29** 35 7N 118 22W
Monomoy I. **42** 41 36N 69 59W
Monomoy Point **42** 41 33N 70 2W
Monon **36** 40 52N 86 53W
Monona, Iowa **37** 43 3N 91 23W
Monona, Wis. **69** 43 4N 89 20W
Monona County ◇ **37** 42 0N 96 0W
Monongah **68** 39 28N 80 13W
Monongahela **59** 40 12N 79 56W
Monongahela → **59** 40 27N 80 1W
Monongahela National Forest **68** 38 30N 79 57W
Monongalia County ◇ **68** 39 39N 80 1W
Monowi **48** 42 50N 98 20W
Monroe, Ark. **27** 34 44N 91 6W
Monroe, Ga. **32** 33 47N 83 43W
Monroe, Ind. **36** 40 45N 84 56W
Monroe, Iowa **37** 41 31N 93 6W
Monroe, La. **39** 32 30N 92 7W
Monroe, Mich. **43** 41 55N 83 24W
Monroe, N.C. **54** 34 59N 80 33W
Monroe, N.Y. **53** 41 20N 74 11W
Monroe, Nebr. **48** 41 28N 97 36W
Monroe, Ohio **56** 39 27N 84 22W
Monroe, Okla. **57** 34 59N 94 30W
Monroe, Oreg. **58** 44 19N 123 18W
Monroe, S. Dak. **61** 43 29N 97 13W
Monroe, Utah **66** 38 38N 112 7W
Monroe, Va. **68** 37 30N 79 8W
Monroe, Wash. **67** 47 51N 121 58W
Monroe, Wis. **69** 42 36N 89 38W
Monroe, L. **31** 28 50N 81 19W
Monroe City **46** 39 39N 91 44W
Monroe County ◇, Ala. **24** 31 31N 87 20W
Monroe County ◇, Ark. **27** 34 42N 91 19W
Monroe County ◇, Fla. **31** 25 30N 81 0W
Monroe County ◇, Ga. **32** 33 0N 83 55W
Monroe County ◇, Ill. **35** 38 15N 90 10W
Monroe County ◇, Ind. **36** 39 10N 86 30W
Monroe County ◇, Iowa **37** 41 0N 92 50W
Monroe County ◇, Ky. **63** 36 45N 85 45W
Monroe County ◇, Mich. **43** 41 50N 83 35W
Monroe County ◇, Miss. **45** 33 49N 88 33W
Monroe County ◇, Mo. **46** 39 30N 92 0W
Monroe County ◇, N.Y. **53** 43 10N 77 40W
Monroe County ◇, Ohio **56** 39 46N 81 7W
Monroe County ◇, Pa. **59** 41 0N 75 15W
Monroe County ◇, Tenn. **63** 35 31N 84 22W
Monroe County ◇, W. Va. **68** 37 36N 80 33W
Monroe County ◇, Wis. **69** 43 50N 90 40W
Monroe L. **36** 39 1N 86 31W
Monroeton **59** 41 43N 76 29W
Monroeville, Ala. **24** 31 31N 87 20W
Monroeville, Ind. **36** 40 59N 84 52W
Monroeville, Ohio **56** 41 15N 82 42W
Monroeville, Pa. **59** 40 26N 79 45W
Monson **40** 45 17N 69 30W
Mont Alto **59** 39 51N 77 34W
Mont Belvieu **65** 29 51N 94 53W
Mont Ida **38** 38 13N 95 22W
Mont Vernon **50** 42 50N 71 42W
Montague, Calif. **28** 41 44N 122 32W
Montague, Mass. **42** 42 32N 72 32W
Montague, Mich. **43** 43 25N 86 22W
Montague, Tex. **65** 33 42N 97 48W
Montague County ◇ **65** 33 47N 97 44W
Montague I. **25** 60 0N 147 30W
Montalba **65** 31 53N 95 44W
Montana □ **47** 47 0N 110 0W
Montauk **53** 41 3N 71 57W
Montcalm County ◇ **43** 43 15N 85 10W
Montclair **51** 40 49N 74 13W
Monte Vista **30** 37 35N 106 9W
Monteagle **63** 35 15N 85 50W
Montecito **29** 34 26N 119 40W
Montegut **39** 29 28N 90 33W
Montello, Nev. **49** 41 16N 114 12W
Montello, Wis. **69** 43 48N 89 20W
Monterey, Calif. **28** 36 37N 121 55W
Monterey, Ky. **63** 38 25N 84 52W
Monterey, Mass. **42** 42 11N 73 13W
Monterey, Tenn. **63** 36 9N 85 16W
Monterey, Va. **68** 38 25N 79 35W
Monterey B. **28** 36 45N 122 0W
Monterey County ◇ **28** 36 15N 121 20W
Montesano **67** 46 59N 123 36W
Montevallo **24** 33 6N 86 52W
Montevideo **44** 44 57N 95 43W
Monteview **34** 43 56N 112 32W
Montezuma, Ga. **32** 32 18N 84 2W
Montezuma, Ind. **36** 39 48N 87 22W
Montezuma, Iowa **37** 41 35N 92 32W
Montezuma, Kans. **38** 37 36N 100 27W
Montezuma County ◇ **30** 37 20N 108 30W
Montezuma Cr. → **66** 37 17N 109 20W
Montfort **69** 42 58N 90 26W
Montgomery, Ala. **24** 32 23N 86 19W
Montgomery, Ga. **32** 31 57N 81 7W
Montgomery, La. **39** 31 40N 92 53W
Montgomery, Minn. **44** 44 26N 93 35W
Montgomery, Pa. **59** 41 10N 76 53W
Montgomery, Tex. **65** 30 23N 95 42W
Montgomery, W. Va. **68** 38 11N 81 19W
Montgomery Center **50** 44 53N 73 40W
Montgomery City **46** 38 59N 91 30W
Montgomery County ◇, Ala. **24** 32 15N 86 18W
Montgomery County ◇, Ark. **27** 34 34N 93 38W
Montgomery County ◇, Ga. **32** 32 15N 82 35W
Montgomery County ◇, Ill. **35** 39 10N 89 30W
Montgomery County ◇, Ind. **36** 40 5N 86 55W
Montgomery County ◇, Iowa **37** 41 0N 95 10W
Montgomery County ◇, Kans. **38** 37 15N 95 45W
Montgomery County ◇, Ky. **63** 38 0N 83 55W
Montgomery County ◇, Md. **41** 39 15N 77 15W
Montgomery County ◇, Miss. **45** 33 29N 89 44W
Montgomery County ◇, Mo. **46** 38 55N 91 30W
Montgomery County ◇, N.C. **54** 35 20N 79 50W
Montgomery County ◇, N.Y. **53** 42 50N 74 30W
Montgomery County ◇, Ohio **56** 39 45N 84 12W
Montgomery County ◇, Pa. **59** 40 10N 75 10W
Montgomery County ◇, Tenn. **62** 36 32N 87 21W
Montgomery County ◇, Tex. **65** 30 19N 95 27W
Montgomery County ◇, Va. **68** 37 8N 80 25W
Montgomery Village **41** 39 12N 77 13W
Monticello, Ark. **27** 33 38N 91 47W
Monticello, Fla. **31** 30 33N 83 52W
Monticello, Ga. **32** 33 18N 83 40W
Monticello, Ill. **35** 40 1N 88 34W
Monticello, Ind. **36** 40 45N 86 46W
Monticello, Iowa **37** 42 15N 91 12W
Monticello, Ky. **63** 36 50N 84 51W
Monticello, Maine **40** 46 19N 67 51W
Monticello, Minn. **44** 45 18N 93 48W
Monticello, Miss. **45** 31 33N 90 7W
Monticello, Mo. **46** 40 7N 91 43W
Monticello, N. Mex. **52** 33 24N 107 27W
Monticello, N.Y. **53** 41 39N 74 42W
Monticello, Utah **66** 37 52N 109 21W
Monticello, Wis. **69** 42 45N 89 36W
Montmorency County ◇ **43** 45 0N 84 10W
Montour, Idaho **34** 43 55N 116 20W
Montour, Iowa **37** 41 59N 92 43W
Montour County ◇ **59** 41 0N 76 40W
Montour Falls **53** 42 21N 76 51W
Montoursville **59** 41 15N 76 55W
Montoya **52** 35 6N 104 4W
Montpelier, Idaho **34** 42 19N 111 18W
Montpelier, Ind. **36** 40 33N 85 17W
Montpelier, La. **39** 30 41N 90 39W
Montpelier, Miss. **45** 33 43N 88 57W
Montpelier, N. Dak. **55** 46 42N 98 35W
Montpelier, Ohio **56** 41 35N 84 37W
Montpelier, Vt. **50** 44 16N 72 35W
Montrose, Ark. **27** 33 18N 91 30W
Montrose, Colo. **30** 38 29N 107 53W
Montrose, Ill. **35** 39 10N 88 23W
Montrose, Iowa **37** 40 31N 91 25W
Montrose, Mich. **43** 43 11N 83 54W
Montrose, Miss. **45** 32 8N 89 14W
Montrose, Mo. **46** 38 16N 93 59W
Montrose, Pa. **59** 41 50N 75 53W
Montrose, S. Dak. **61** 43 42N 97 11W
Montrose, W. Va. **68** 39 4N 79 49W
Montrose County ◇ **30** 38 30N 108 15W
Montross **68** 38 6N 76 50W
Montvale **68** 37 23N 79 44W
Montville **42** 41 27N 72 8W
Monument, Kans. **38** 39 6N 101 1W
Monument, Oreg. **58** 44 49N 119 25W
Monument Draw → **64** 32 29N 102 20W
Monument Pass **26** 36 58N 110 5W
Monument Pk. **34** 42 7N 114 14W
Monument Valley **26** 37 0N 110 0W
Moodus **42** 41 30N 72 25W
Moody, Mo. **46** 36 32N 91 59W
Moody, Tex. **65** 31 18N 97 21W
Moody County ◇ **61** 44 3N 96 36W
Mooleyville **62** 38 1N 86 28W
Moon L. **28** 41 10N 121 10W
Moorcroft **70** 44 16N 104 57W
Moore, Idaho **34** 43 44N 113 22W
Moore, Mont. **47** 46 59N 109 42W
Moore, Okla. **57** 35 20N 97 29W
Moore, Tex. **65** 29 3N 99 1W
Moore, Utah **66** 38 58N 111 10W
Moore County ◇, N.C. **54** 35 20N 79 20W
Moore County ◇, Tenn. **62** 35 17N 86 22W
Moore County ◇, Tex. **64** 35 55N 101 59W
Moore Haven **31** 26 50N 81 6W
Moore Reservoir **50** 44 20N 71 53W
Moorefield, Nebr. **48** 40 41N 100 24W
Moorefield, W. Va. **68** 39 4N 78 58W
Moorefield → **68** 39 5N 78 59W
Mooreland **57** 36 26N 99 12W
Moorestown **51** 39 58N 74 57W
Mooresville, Ind. **36** 39 37N 86 22W
Mooresville, N.C. **54** 35 35N 80 48W
Mooreton **55** 46 16N 96 53W
Moorhead, Iowa **37** 41 56N 95 51W
Moorhead, Minn. **44** 46 53N 96 45W
Moorhead, Miss. **45** 33 27N 90 30W
Mooringsport **39** 32 41N 93 58W
Moorland **37** 42 26N 94 18W
Moose →, N.Y. **53** 43 38N 75 24W
Moose →, Vt. **50** 44 24N 72 1W
Moose Lake **44** 46 27N 92 46W
Moose Pass **25** 60 29N 149 22W
Moose River **40** 45 39N 70 16W
Moosehead L. **40** 45 38N 69 40W
Mooselookmeguntic L. **40** 44 55N 70 49W
Moosilauke, Mt. **50** 44 3N 71 40W
Moosup **42** 41 43N 71 53W
Mora, Puerto Rico **71** 18 28N 67 2W
Mora, Ga. **32** 31 25N 82 57W
Mora, Minn. **44** 45 53N 93 18W
Mora, N. Mex. **52** 35 58N 105 20W
Mora → **52** 35 35N 104 25W
Mora County ◇ **52** 36 0N 104 0W
Morales **65** 29 8N 96 46W
Moran, Kans. **38** 37 55N 95 10W
Moran, Mich. **43** 46 0N 84 50W
Moran, Tex. **65** 32 33N 99 10W
Moravia, Iowa **37** 40 53N 92 49W
Moravia, N.Y. **53** 42 43N 76 25W
Moreau → **61** 45 18N 100 43W
Morehead **63** 38 11N 83 26W
Morehead City **54** 34 43N 76 43W
Morehouse **46** 36 51N 89 41W
Morehouse Parish ◇ **39** 32 47N 91 48W
Moreland, Ga. **32** 33 17N 84 46W
Moreland, Ky. **63** 37 30N 84 49W
Morenci, Ariz. **26** 33 5N 109 22W
Morenci, Mich. **43** 41 43N 84 13W
Morgan, Ga. **32** 31 32N 84 36W
Morgan, Ky. **63** 38 36N 84 24W
Morgan, Minn. **44** 44 25N 94 56W
Morgan, Utah **66** 41 2N 111 41W
Morgan, Vt. **50** 44 53N 73 2W
Morgan, Mt. **29** 37 31N 118 47W
Morgan City, Ala. **24** 34 28N 86 34W
Morgan City, La. **39** 29 42N 91 12W
Morgan County ◇, Ala. **24** 34 27N 86 56W
Morgan County ◇, Colo. **30** 40 15N 103 50W
Morgan County ◇, Ga. **32** 33 40N 83 25W
Morgan County ◇, Ill. **35** 39 45N 90 10W
Morgan County ◇, Ind. **36** 39 30N 86 25W
Morgan County ◇, Ky. **63** 37 55N 83 15W
Morgan County ◇, Mo. **46** 38 25N 92 50W
Morgan County ◇, Ohio **56** 39 39N 81 51W
Morgan County ◇, Tenn. **63** 36 6N 84 36W
Morgan County ◇, Utah **66** 41 10N 111 45W
Morgan County ◇, W. Va. **68** 39 35N 78 16W
Morgan Hill **28** 37 8N 121 39W
Morgan L. **52** 36 52N 108 41W
Morgan Mill **65** 32 23N 98 10W
Morganfield **62** 37 41N 87 55W
Morganton **54** 35 45N 81 41W
Morgantown, Ind. **36** 39 22N 86 16W
Morgantown, Ky. **62** 37 14N 86 41W
Morgantown, Md. **41** 38 21N 76 58W
Morgantown, Ohio **56** 39 8N 83 12W
Morgantown, W. Va. **68** 39 38N 79 57W
Morganville, Ga. **32** 34 56N 85 27W
Morganville, Kans. **38** 39 28N 97 12W
Morganza **39** 30 44N 91 36W
Moriah Mt. **49** 39 17N 114 12W
Moriarty **52** 34 59N 106 3W
Morland **38** 39 21N 100 5W
Morley, Mich. **43** 43 29N 85 27W
Morley, Mo. **46** 37 3N 89 37W
Mormon L. **26** 34 57N 111 29W
Mormon Lake **26** 34 55N 111 28W
Mormon Mts. **49** 37 0N 114 0W
Morning Sun **37** 41 5N 91 15W
Morningside **41** 38 50N 76 54W
Moro, Ark. **27** 34 48N 90 59W
Moro, Oreg. **58** 45 29N 120 44W
Moro → **27** 33 17N 92 21W
Morocco **36** 40 57N 87 27W
Moroni **66** 39 32N 111 35W
Morovis **71** 18 20N 66 25W
Morral **56** 40 41N 83 13W
Morrill, Kans. **38** 39 56N 95 42W
Morrill, Nebr. **48** 41 58N 103 56W
Morrill County ◇ **48** 41 45N 103 0W
Morrilton **27** 35 9N 92 44W
Morris, Conn. **42** 41 43N 73 15W
Morris, Ga. **32** 31 48N 84 57W
Morris, Ill. **35** 41 22N 88 26W
Morris, Minn. **44** 45 35N 95 55W
Morris, N.Y. **53** 42 33N 75 15W
Morris, Okla. **57** 35 36N 95 51W
Morris County ◇, Kans. **38** 38 30N 96 40W
Morris County ◇, N.J. **51** 40 45N 74 30W
Morris County ◇, Tex. **65** 33 2N 94 44W
Morrison, Ill. **35** 41 49N 89 58W
Morrison, Okla. **57** 36 18N 97 1W
Morrison, Tenn. **63** 35 36N 85 55W
Morrison County ◇ **44** 46 0N 94 10W
Morrisonville **35** 39 25N 89 27W
Morristown, Ariz. **26** 33 51N 112 37W
Morristown, Ind. **36** 39 40N 85 42W
Morristown, Minn. **44** 44 14N 93 27W
Morristown, N.J. **51** 40 48N 74 29W

Place	Map	Lat	Long
Morristown, N.Y.	**53**	44 35N	75 39W
Morristown, S. Dak.	**61**	45 56N	101 43W
Morristown, Tenn.	**63**	36 13N	83 18W
Morrisville, Mo.	**46**	37 29N	93 25W
Morrisville, N.C.	**54**	35 49N	78 50W
Morrisville, N.Y.	**53**	42 53N	75 35W
Morrisville, Vt.	**50**	44 34N	72 36W
Morro Bay	**29**	35 22N	120 51W
Morrow, La.	**39**	30 50N	92 5W
Morrow, Ohio	**56**	39 21N	84 8W
Morrow County ◇, Ohio	**56**	40 33N	82 50W
Morrow County ◇, Oreg.	**58**	45 25N	119 40W
Morrowville	**38**	39 51N	97 10W
Morse	**64**	36 4N	101 29W
Morse Bluff	**48**	41 26N	96 46W
Morse Res.	**36**	40 7N	86 3W
Mortes, L. Aux	**55**	48 20N	99 7W
Morton, Ill.	**35**	40 37N	89 28W
Morton, Minn.	**44**	44 33N	94 59W
Morton, Miss.	**45**	32 21N	89 39W
Morton, Tex.	**64**	33 44N	102 46W
Morton, Wash.	**67**	46 34N	122 17W
Morton County ◇, Kans.	**38**	37 15N	101 45W
Morton County ◇, N. Dak.	**55**	46 45N	101 30W
Mortons Gap	**62**	37 14N	87 28W
Morven, Ga.	**32**	30 57N	83 30W
Morven, N.C.	**54**	34 52N	80 0W
Mosby	**47**	47 0N	107 52W
Mosca	**30**	37 39N	105 52W
Moscow, Idaho	**34**	46 44N	117 0W
Moscow, Kans.	**38**	37 20N	101 12W
Moscow, Ky.	**62**	36 37N	89 2W
Moscow, Ohio	**56**	38 52N	84 14W
Moscow, Pa.	**59**	41 20N	75 31W
Moscow, Tenn.	**62**	35 4N	89 24W
Moscow Mills	**46**	38 57N	90 55W
Moselle	**45**	31 30N	89 17W
Moses Lake	**67**	47 8N	119 17W
Mosheim	**63**	36 11N	82 57W
Mosher	**61**	43 28N	100 18W
Mosier	**58**	45 41N	121 24W
Mosinee	**69**	44 47N	89 43W
Mosquero	**52**	35 47N	103 58W
Mosquito Creek L.	**56**	41 18N	80 46W
Moss	**63**	36 36N	85 37W
Moss Bluff	**39**	30 18N	93 11W
Moss Point	**45**	30 25N	88 30W
Mossy Head	**31**	30 45N	86 19W
Mossyrock	**67**	46 32N	122 29W
Motley	**44**	46 20N	94 40W
Motley County ◇	**64**	34 1N	100 50W
Mott	**55**	46 23N	102 20W
Motters	**41**	39 40N	77 20W
Moulton, Ala.	**24**	34 29N	87 18W
Moulton, Iowa	**37**	40 41N	92 41W
Moulton, Tex.	**65**	29 35N	97 9W
Moultonboro	**50**	43 45N	71 10W
Moultrie	**32**	31 11N	83 47W
Moultrie, L.	**60**	33 20N	80 5W
Moultrie County ◇	**35**	39 40N	88 35W
Mound	**39**	32 21N	91 1W
Mound Bayou	**45**	33 53N	90 44W
Mound City, Ill.	**35**	37 5N	89 10W
Mound City, Kans.	**38**	38 8N	94 49W
Mound City, Mo.	**46**	40 7N	95 14W
Mound City, S. Dak.	**61**	45 44N	100 4W
Mound Valley	**38**	37 12N	95 24W
Moundridge	**38**	38 12N	97 31W
Mounds, Ill.	**35**	37 7N	89 12W
Mounds, Okla.	**57**	35 53N	96 4W
Moundsville	**68**	39 55N	80 44W
Moundville, Ala.	**24**	33 1N	87 37W
Moundville, Mo.	**46**	37 46N	94 27W
Mount Airy, Md.	**41**	39 22N	77 10W
Mount Airy, N.C.	**54**	36 31N	80 37W
Mount Angel	**58**	45 4N	122 48W
Mount Auburn	**37**	42 15N	92 6W
Mount Ayr, Ind.	**36**	40 57N	87 18W
Mount Ayr, Iowa	**37**	40 43N	94 14W
Mount Baker National Forest	**67**	48 10N	121 15W
Mount Blanchard	**56**	40 54N	83 34W
Mount Calm	**65**	31 46N	96 53W
Mount Carmel, Ill.	**35**	38 25N	87 46W
Mount Carmel, Utah	**66**	37 15N	112 40W
Mount Carroll	**35**	42 6N	89 59W
Mount Clemens	**43**	42 35N	82 53W
Mount Desert I.	**40**	44 21N	68 20W
Mount Dora, Fla.	**31**	28 48N	81 38W
Mount Dora, N. Mex.	**52**	36 31N	103 29W
Mount Eaton	**56**	40 42N	81 42W
Mount Eden	**63**	38 3N	85 9W
Mount Edgecumbe	**25**	57 3N	135 21W
Mount Enterprise	**65**	31 55N	94 41W
Mount Erie	**35**	38 31N	88 14W
Mount Etna	**36**	40 45N	85 34W
Mount Gay	**68**	37 51N	82 0W
Mount Gilead, N.C.	**54**	35 13N	80 0W
Mount Gilead, Ohio	**56**	40 33N	82 50W
Mount Holly, N.C.	**54**	35 18N	81 1W
Mount Holly, N.J.	**51**	39 59N	74 47W
Mount Holly Springs	**59**	40 7N	77 12W
Mount Hood National Forest	**58**	45 15N	122 0W
Mount Hope, Kans.	**38**	37 52N	97 40W
Mount Hope, W. Va.	**68**	37 54N	81 10W
Mount Horeb	**69**	43 1N	89 44W
Mount Ida	**27**	34 34N	93 38W
Mount Jackson	**68**	38 45N	78 39W
Mount Jewett	**59**	41 44N	78 39W
Mount Joy	**59**	40 7N	76 30W
Mount Juliet	**62**	36 12N	86 31W
Mount Kisco	**53**	41 12N	73 44W
Mount Laguna	**29**	32 52N	116 25W
Mount Lebanon	**59**	40 23N	80 3W
Mount Liberty	**56**	40 21N	82 38W
Mount McKinley National Park	**25**	63 30N	150 0W
Mount Montgomery	**49**	37 58N	118 20W
Mount Moriah	**46**	40 20N	93 48W
Mount Morris, Ill.	**35**	42 3N	89 26W
Mount Morris, Mich.	**43**	43 7N	83 42W
Mount Morris, N.Y.	**53**	42 44N	77 52W
Mount Olive, Ill.	**35**	39 4N	89 44W
Mount Olive, Miss.	**45**	31 46N	89 39W
Mount Olive, N.C.	**54**	35 12N	78 4W
Mount Olivet	**63**	38 32N	84 2W
Mount Orab	**56**	39 2N	83 55W
Mount Pleasant, Del.	**41**	39 32N	75 43W
Mount Pleasant, Iowa	**37**	40 58N	91 33W
Mount Pleasant, Mich.	**43**	43 36N	84 46W
Mount Pleasant, Pa.	**59**	40 9N	79 33W
Mount Pleasant, S.C.	**60**	32 47N	79 52W
Mount Pleasant, Tenn.	**62**	35 32N	87 12W
Mount Pleasant, Tex.	**65**	33 9N	94 58W
Mount Pleasant, Utah	**66**	39 33N	111 27W
Mount Pocono	**59**	41 7N	75 22W
Mount Prospect	**35**	42 4N	87 56W
Mount Pulaski	**35**	40 1N	89 17W
Mount Rainier National Park	**67**	46 55N	121 50W
Mount Savage	**41**	39 42N	78 53W
Mount Shasta	**28**	41 19N	122 19W
Mount Solon	**68**	38 21N	79 5W
Mount Sterling, Ill.	**35**	39 59N	90 45W
Mount Sterling, Ky.	**63**	38 4N	83 56W
Mount Sterling, Ohio	**56**	39 43N	83 16W
Mount Storm	**68**	39 17N	79 15W
Mount Storm L.	**68**	39 13N	79 16W
Mount Summit	**36**	40 0N	85 23W
Mount Sunapee	**50**	43 19N	72 6W
Mount Trumbull	**26**	36 25N	113 19W
Mount Union, Iowa	**37**	41 3N	91 23W
Mount Union, Pa.	**59**	40 23N	77 53W
Mount Vernon, Ala.	**24**	31 5N	88 1W
Mount Vernon, Ark.	**27**	35 14N	92 8W
Mount Vernon, Ga.	**32**	32 11N	82 36W
Mount Vernon, Ill.	**35**	38 19N	88 55W
Mount Vernon, Ind.	**36**	37 56N	87 54W
Mount Vernon, Iowa	**37**	41 55N	91 23W
Mount Vernon, Ky.	**63**	37 21N	84 21W
Mount Vernon, Md.	**41**	38 47N	77 6W
Mount Vernon, Mo.	**46**	37 6N	93 49W
Mount Vernon, N.Y.	**53**	40 55N	73 50W
Mount Vernon, Ohio	**56**	40 23N	82 29W
Mount Vernon, Oreg.	**58**	44 25N	119 7W
Mount Vernon, S. Dak.	**61**	43 43N	98 16W
Mount Vernon, Tenn.	**63**	35 25N	84 22W
Mount Vernon, Tex.	**65**	33 11N	95 13W
Mount Vernon, Wash.	**67**	48 25N	122 20W
Mount Wolf	**59**	40 4N	76 43W
Mount Zion	**35**	39 46N	88 53W
Mountain, N. Dak.	**55**	48 41N	97 52W
Mountain, Wis.	**69**	45 11N	88 28W
Mountain Brook	**24**	33 30N	86 45W
Mountain City, Ga.	**32**	34 55N	83 23W
Mountain City, Nev.	**49**	41 50N	115 58W
Mountain City, Tenn.	**63**	36 29N	81 48W
Mountain Creek	**24**	32 43N	86 29W
Mountain Grove	**46**	37 8N	92 16W
Mountain Home, Ark.	**27**	36 20N	92 23W
Mountain Home, Idaho	**34**	43 8N	115 41W
Mountain Home, N.C.	**54**	35 23N	82 30W
Mountain Home, Tex.	**65**	30 10N	99 22W
Mountain Iron	**44**	47 32N	92 37W
Mountain Lake	**44**	43 57N	94 56W
Mountain Lake Park	**41**	39 24N	79 23W
Mountain Meadows Reservoir	**28**	40 17N	120 49W
Mountain Park	**57**	34 42N	98 57W
Mountain Pine	**27**	34 34N	93 10W
Mountain View, Ark.	**27**	35 52N	92 7W
Mountain View, Calif.	**28**	37 23N	122 5W
Mountain View, Hawaii	**33**	19 33N	155 7W
Mountain View, Mo.	**46**	37 0N	91 42W
Mountain View, Okla.	**57**	35 6N	98 45W
Mountain Village	**25**	62 5N	163 43W
Mountainair	**52**	34 31N	106 15W
Mountainaire	**26**	35 9N	111 40W
Mountainburg	**27**	35 38N	94 10W
Mountainview	**70**	41 16N	110 20W
Mountlake Terrace	**67**	47 47N	122 19W
Mountrail County ◇	**55**	48 10N	102 30W
Mousie	**63**	37 25N	82 53W
Moville	**37**	42 29N	96 4W
Moweaqua	**35**	39 38N	89 1W
Mower County ◇	**44**	43 40N	92 45W
Mowrystown	**56**	39 2N	83 45W
Moxee City	**67**	46 33N	120 23W
Moyers	**57**	34 19N	95 39W
Moyie Springs	**34**	48 44N	116 11W
Moyie →	**34**	48 43N	116 11W
Muckalee Cr. →	**32**	31 38N	84 9W
Mud →	**62**	37 13N	86 54W
Mud Butte	**61**	45 0N	102 54W
Mud Cr. →, Okla.	**57**	33 55N	97 28W
Mud Cr. →, S. Dak.	**61**	45 11N	98 24W
Mud L.	**49**	37 52N	117 4W
Mud Lake Reservoir	**61**	45 47N	98 15W
Muddy →, Ill.	**35**	37 33N	89 32W
Muddy →, Nev.	**49**	36 31N	114 24W
Muddy Boggy Cr. →	**57**	34 3N	95 47W
Muddy Cr. →, Utah	**66**	38 24N	110 42W
Muddy Cr. →, Wyo.	**70**	41 35N	109 58W
Muddy Creek Reservoir	**30**	37 45N	103 15W
Muddy Gap	**70**	42 21N	107 28W
Muenster	**65**	33 39N	97 23W
Muhlenberg County ◇	**62**	37 10N	87 10W
Muir	**43**	43 0N	84 56W
Muir Woods National Monument	**28**	37 55N	122 35W
Mukilteo	**67**	47 57N	122 18W
Mukwonago	**69**	42 52N	88 20W
Mulberry, Ark.	**27**	35 30N	94 3W
Mulberry, Fla.	**31**	27 54N	81 59W
Mulberry Fork →	**24**	33 33N	87 11W
Mulberry Grove	**35**	38 56N	89 16W
Mulchatna →	**25**	59 40N	157 7W
Muldoon	**65**	29 49N	97 4W
Muldraugh	**63**	37 56N	85 59W
Muldrow	**57**	35 24N	94 36W
Mule Creek, N. Mex.	**52**	33 7N	108 57W
Mule Creek, Wyo.	**70**	43 19N	104 8W
Muleshoe	**64**	34 13N	102 43W
Mulhall	**57**	36 4N	97 25W
Mullan	**34**	47 28N	115 48W
Mullen	**48**	42 3N	101 1W
Mullens	**68**	37 35N	81 23W
Mullett L.	**43**	45 31N	84 31W
Mullett Lake	**43**	45 34N	84 32W
Mullica →	**51**	39 33N	74 25W
Mullin	**65**	31 33N	98 40W
Mullins	**60**	34 12N	79 15W
Mullinville	**38**	37 35N	99 29W
Multnomah County ◇	**58**	45 30N	122 10W
Mulvane	**38**	37 29N	97 15W
Muncie	**36**	40 12N	85 23W
Muncy	**59**	41 12N	76 47W
Munday	**65**	33 27N	99 38W
Mundelein	**35**	42 16N	88 0W
Munden	**38**	39 55N	97 32W
Munford	**62**	35 27N	89 49W
Munfordville	**63**	37 16N	85 54W
Munich	**55**	48 40N	98 50W
Munising	**43**	46 25N	86 40W
Munjor	**38**	38 49N	99 16W
Munnsville	**53**	42 59N	75 35W
Munson	**31**	30 52N	86 52W
Munsungan L.	**40**	46 22N	69 0W
Murdo	**61**	43 53N	100 43W
Murdock, Kans.	**38**	37 37N	97 56W
Murdock, Minn.	**44**	45 13N	95 24W
Murdock, Nebr.	**48**	40 55N	96 17W
Murfreesboro, Ark.	**27**	34 4N	93 41W
Murfreesboro, N.C.	**54**	36 27N	77 6W
Murfreesboro, Tenn.	**62**	35 51N	86 24W
Murphy, Idaho	**34**	43 13N	116 33W
Murphy, N.C.	**54**	35 5N	84 2W
Murphy, Oreg.	**58**	42 21N	123 20W
Murphys Corner	**67**	47 53N	122 12W
Murphysboro	**35**	37 46N	89 20W
Murray, Iowa	**37**	41 3N	93 57W
Murray, Ky.	**62**	36 37N	88 19W
Murray, Utah	**66**	40 40N	111 53W
Murray, L., Okla.	**57**	34 2N	97 3W
Murray, L., S.C.	**60**	34 3N	81 13W
Murray City	**56**	39 31N	82 10W
Murray County ◇, Ga.	**32**	34 50N	84 45W
Murray County ◇, Minn.	**44**	44 0N	95 45W
Murray County ◇, Okla.	**57**	34 30N	97 0W
Murrayville	**35**	39 35N	90 15W
Murrells Inlet	**60**	33 33N	79 2W
Murtaugh	**34**	42 30N	114 10W
Murvaul L.	**65**	32 2N	94 25W
Muscatine	**37**	41 25N	91 3W
Muscatine County ◇	**37**	41 30N	91 0W
Muscle Shoals	**24**	34 45N	87 40W
Muscoda	**69**	43 11N	90 27W
Muscogee County ◇	**32**	32 30N	84 58W
Musconetcong →	**51**	40 36N	75 11W
Muscotah	**38**	39 33N	95 31W
Musella	**32**	32 48N	84 2W
Muskeg B.	**44**	48 55N	95 10W
Muskeget Channel	**42**	41 25N	70 25W
Muskego	**69**	42 55N	88 8W
Muskegon	**43**	43 14N	86 16W
Muskegon →	**43**	43 14N	86 21W
Muskegon County ◇	**43**	43 15N	86 15W
Muskegon Heights	**43**	43 12N	86 16W
Muskingum →	**56**	40 3N	81 59W
Muskingum County ◇	**56**	39 56N	82 1W
Muskogee	**57**	35 45N	95 22W
Muskogee County ◇	**57**	35 40N	95 25W
Mussell Cr. →	**46**	39 26N	92 57W
Musselshell →	**47**	47 21N	107 57W
Musselshell County ◇	**47**	46 35N	108 30W
Mustang	**57**	35 24N	97 42W
Mustang Draw →	**64**	31 58N	102 40W
Mustang I.	**65**	27 52N	97 3W
Mustinka →	**44**	45 45N	96 38W
Mutual, Ohio	**56**	40 5N	83 38W
Mutual, Okla.	**57**	36 14N	99 9W
Muzon, C.	**25**	54 40N	132 42W
Myakka →	**31**	26 56N	82 11W
Myerstown	**59**	40 22N	76 19W
Mylo	**55**	48 38N	99 37W
Myrtle, Miss.	**45**	34 34N	89 7W
Myrtle, Mo.	**46**	36 31N	91 16W
Myrtle, W. Va.	**68**	37 46N	82 12W
Myrtle Beach	**60**	33 42N	78 53W
Myrtle Creek	**58**	43 1N	123 17W
Myrtle Grove	**31**	30 23N	87 17W
Myrtle Point	**58**	43 4N	124 8W
Myrtlewood	**24**	32 16N	87 57W
Mystic, Conn.	**42**	41 21N	71 58W
Mystic, Iowa	**37**	40 47N	92 57W
Mystic Island	**51**	39 34N	74 22W
Myton	**66**	40 12N	110 4W

N

Place	Map	Lat	Long
Naalehu	**33**	19 4N	155 35W
Nabesna	**25**	62 22N	143 0W
Naches	**67**	46 44N	120 42W
Naches →	**67**	46 38N	120 31W
Nacimiento Reservoir	**29**	35 46N	120 53W
Naco	**26**	31 20N	109 57W
Nacogdoches	**65**	31 36N	94 39W
Nacogdoches County ◇	**65**	31 35N	94 40W
Nagai I.	**25**	55 5N	160 0W
Nageezi	**52**	36 16N	107 45W
Nags Head	**54**	35 57N	75 38W
Naguabo	**71**	18 13N	65 44W
Nahant	**42**	42 26N	70 55W
Nahma	**43**	45 50N	86 40W
Nahunta	**32**	31 12N	81 59W
Nakalele Pt.	**33**	21 2N	156 35W
Naknek	**25**	58 44N	157 1W
Nallen	**68**	38 7N	80 53W
Namakan L.	**44**	48 27N	92 36W
Namekagon →	**69**	46 5N	92 6W
Nampa	**34**	43 34N	116 34W
Nanakuli	**33**	21 24N	158 9W

Nance County ◇ **48** 41 25N 98 0W
Nancy **63** 37 4N 84 45W
Nanjemoy **41** 38 27N 77 13W
Nansemond County ◇ **68** 36 45N 76 40W
Nantahala L. **54** 35 10N 83 40W
Nantahala National Forest **54** 35 15N 83 30W
Nanticoke, Md. **41** 38 16N 75 54W
Nanticoke, Pa. **59** 41 12N 76 0W
Nanticoke → **41** 38 16N 75 56W
Nantucket **42** 41 17N 70 6W
Nantucket County ◇ **42** 41 15N 70 5W
Nantucket Harbor **42** 41 17N 70 6W
Nantucket I. **42** 41 16N 70 5W
Nantucket Sd. **42** 41 30N 70 15W
Nanty Glo **59** 40 28N 78 50W
Naomi Peak **66** 41 55N 111 41W
Napa **28** 38 18N 122 17W
Napa County ◇ **28** 38 30N 122 20W
Napaimiut **25** 61 33N 158 42W
Napakiak **25** 60 42N 161 57W
Napaskiak **25** 60 43N 161 55W
Napavine **67** 46 35N 122 54W
Naper **48** 42 58N 99 6W
Naperville **35** 41 46N 88 9W
Naples, Fla. **31** 26 8N 81 48W
Naples, Idaho **34** 48 34N 116 24W
Naples, N.Y. **53** 42 37N 77 24W
Naples, Tex. **65** 33 12N 94 41W
Naples Park **31** 26 17N 81 46W
Napoleanville **39** 29 56N 91 2W
Napoleon, Ind. **36** 39 12N 85 20W
Napoleon, N. Dak. **55** 46 30N 99 46W
Napoleon, Ohio **56** 41 23N 84 8W
Naponee **48** 40 5N 99 9W
Nappanee **36** 41 27N 86 0W
Nara Visa **52** 35 37N 103 6W
Naranja **31** 25 31N 80 26W
Naranjito **71** 18 18N 66 15W
Nardin **57** 36 47N 97 27W
Narka **38** 39 58N 97 25W
Narragansett Bay **42** 41 0N 71 0W
Narragansett Pier **42** 41 26N 71 27W
Narrows **68** 37 20N 80 49W
Naselle **67** 46 22N 123 49W
Nash **57** 36 40N 98 3W
Nash County ◇ **54** 36 0N 78 0W
Nashawena I. **42** 41 26N 70 53W
Nashoba **57** 34 29N 95 13W
Nashua, Iowa **37** 42 57N 92 32W
Nashua, Minn. **44** 46 2N 96 19W
Nashua, Mont. **47** 48 8N 106 22W
Nashua, N.H. **50** 42 45N 71 28W
Nashville, Ark. **27** 33 57N 93 51W
Nashville, Ga. **32** 31 12N 83 15W
Nashville, Ill. **35** 38 21N 89 23W
Nashville, Ind. **36** 39 12N 86 15W
Nashville, Kans. **38** 37 27N 98 25W
Nashville, Mich. **43** 42 36N 85 5W
Nashville, Mo. **46** 37 23N 94 30W
Nashville, N.C. **54** 35 58N 77 58W
Nashville, Ohio **56** 40 36N 82 7W
Nashville, Tenn. **62** 36 10N 86 47W
Nashwauk **44** 47 23N 93 10W
Nassau, Minn. **44** 45 4N 96 26W
Nassau, N.Y. **53** 42 31N 73 37W
Nassau County ◇, Fla. **31** 30 40N 81 45W
Nassau County ◇, N.Y. **53** 40 45N 73 40W
Nassawadox **68** 37 28N 75 52W
Natalbany → **39** 30 20N 90 30W
Natalia **65** 29 11N 98 52W
Natchez, La. **39** 31 41N 93 3W
Natchez, Miss. **45** 31 34N 91 24W
Natchitoches **39** 31 46N 93 5W
Natchitoches Parish ◇ **39** 31 41N 93 3W
Nathrop **30** 38 45N 106 5W
Natick **42** 42 17N 71 21W
National **37** 42 57N 91 17W
National City **29** 32 41N 117 6W
Natoma **38** 39 11N 99 2W
Natrona County ◇ **70** 43 0N 107 0W
Natrona Heights **59** 40 37N 79 44W
Natural Bridge, Ala. **24** 34 6N 87 36W
Natural Bridge, Va. **68** 37 38N 79 33W
Natural Bridge Station **68** 37 37N 79 30W
Naturita **30** 38 14N 108 34W
Natwick **70** 41 58N 105 4W
Naubinway **43** 46 6N 85 27W
Naugatuck **42** 41 30N 73 3W
Nauvoo **35** 40 33N 91 23W
Navajo **26** 35 7N 109 32W
Navajo County ◇ **26** 36 0N 110 20W
Navajo Cr. → **26** 36 59N 111 24W
Navajo Indian Reservation **26** 35 20N 110 0W
Navajo Mt. **66** 37 2N 110 52W
Navajo Reservoir **52** 36 48N 107 36W
Navarre **31** 30 24N 86 52W
Navarro → **28** 39 11N 123 45W
Navarro County ◇ **65** 32 6N 96 28W
Navarro Mills L. **65** 31 57N 96 42W
Navasota **65** 30 23N 96 5W
Navasota → **65** 30 21N 96 10W
Navassa **54** 34 18N 78 0W
Navgatuck → **42** 41 18N 73 7W
Navidad → **65** 28 50N 96 35W
Naylor **46** 36 34N 90 36W
Nazareth, Pa. **59** 40 44N 75 19W
Nazareth, Tex. **64** 34 33N 102 6W
Neah Bay **67** 48 22N 124 37W
Neal **38** 37 50N 96 5W
Near Is. **25** 52 30N 174 0 E
Nebo, Ill. **35** 39 27N 90 47W
Nebo, La. **39** 31 35N 92 9W
Nebo, Mt. **66** 39 49N 111 46W
Nebraska □ **48** 41 30N 99 30W
Nebraska City **48** 40 41N 95 52W
Nebraska National Forest **48** 42 45N 103 10W
Necedah **69** 44 2N 90 4W
Neche **55** 48 59N 97 33W
Neches → **65** 29 58N 93 51W
Necker I. **33** 23 35N 164 42W
Nederland, Colo. **30** 39 58N 105 31W
Nederland, Tex. **65** 29 59N 94 0W
Neebish I. **43** 46 16N 84 9W
Needham **42** 42 17N 71 14W
Needle Range **66** 38 25N 113 55W
Needles **29** 34 51N 114 37W
Needmore, Ga. **32** 30 41N 82 43W
Needmore, Tex. **64** 34 2N 102 45W
Needville **65** 29 24N 95 50W
Neely **45** 31 10N 88 45W
Neely Henry L. **24** 33 55N 86 2W
Neelyville **46** 36 34N 90 30W
Neenah **69** 44 11N 88 28W
Neeses **60** 33 33N 81 7W
Negaunee **43** 46 30N 87 36W
Negreet **39** 31 28N 93 35W
Nehalem → **58** 45 40N 123 56W
Nehawka **48** 40 50N 95 59W
Neillsville **69** 44 34N 90 36W
Neilton **67** 47 25N 123 53W
Nekoma, Kans. **38** 38 28N 99 27W
Nekoma, N. Dak. **55** 48 35N 98 22W
Nekoosa **69** 44 19N 89 54W
Nelhart **47** 46 56N 110 44W
Neligh **48** 42 8N 98 2W
Nelson, Ariz. **26** 35 31N 113 19W
Nelson, Mo. **46** 38 59N 93 3W
Nelson, N.H. **50** 42 58N 72 8W
Nelson, Nebr. **48** 40 12N 98 4W
Nelson, Wis. **69** 44 25N 92 0W
Nelson County ◇, Ky. **63** 37 50N 85 30W
Nelson County ◇, N. Dak. **55** 48 0N 98 5W
Nelson County ◇, Va. **68** 37 50N 78 52W
Nelson Reservoir **47** 48 32N 107 31W
Nemah **67** 46 31N 123 53W
Nemaha, Iowa **37** 42 31N 95 6W
Nemaha, Nebr. **48** 40 20N 95 41W
Nemaha County ◇, Kans. **38** 39 45N 96 0W
Nemaha County ◇, Nebr. **48** 40 20N 95 45W
Nenana **25** 64 34N 149 5W
Nenzel **48** 42 56N 101 6W
Neodesha **38** 37 25N 95 41W
Neoga **35** 39 19N 88 27W
Neola, Iowa **37** 41 27N 95 37W
Neola, Utah **66** 40 26N 110 2W
Neopit **69** 44 59N 88 50W
Neosho **46** 36 52N 94 22W
Neosho → **57** 36 48N 95 18W
Neosho County ◇ **38** 37 30N 95 15W
Neosho Falls **38** 37 59N 95 33W
Neosho Rapids **38** 38 22N 95 59W
Nephi **66** 39 43N 111 50W
Neptune **51** 40 13N 74 2W
Nerstrand **44** 44 20N 93 4W
Nesbit **45** 34 53N 90 1W
Neshkoro **69** 43 58N 89 13W
Neshoba **45** 32 37N 89 8W
Neshoba County ◇ **45** 32 46N 89 7W
Nesmith **60** 33 39N 79 31W
Nespelem **67** 48 10N 118 59W
Ness City **38** 38 27N 99 54W
Ness County ◇ **38** 38 30N 100 0W
Netarts **58** 45 26N 123 57W
Netawaka **38** 39 36N 95 43W
Netcong **51** 40 54N 74 42W
Nett L. **44** 48 7N 93 7W
Nett Lake Indian Reservation **44** 48 5N 93 5W
Nettleton **45** 34 5N 88 37W
Neuse → **54** 35 6N 76 29W
Neuville **65** 31 41N 94 9W
Nevada, Iowa **37** 42 1N 93 27W
Nevada, Mo. **46** 37 51N 94 22W
Nevada □ **49** 39 0N 117 0W
Nevada City **28** 39 16N 121 1W
Nevada County ◇, Ark. **27** 33 36N 93 17W
Nevada County ◇, Calif. **28** 39 15N 121 0W
Neversink → **53** 41 21N 74 42W
Neversink Res. **53** 41 48N 74 42W
Nevis **44** 46 58N 94 51W
New →, Fla. **31** 29 50N 84 40W
New →, W. Va. **68** 38 10N 81 12W
New Albany, Ind. **36** 38 18N 85 49W
New Albany, Kans. **38** 37 34N 95 56W
New Albany, Miss. **45** 34 29N 89 0W
New Albany, Pa. **59** 41 36N 76 27W
New Alluwe **57** 36 37N 95 29W
New Almelo **38** 39 36N 100 7W
New Athens, Ill. **35** 38 19N 89 53W
New Athens, Ohio **56** 40 11N 81 0W
New Auburn, Minn. **44** 44 40N 94 14W
New Auburn, Wis. **69** 45 12N 91 33W
New Augusta **45** 31 12N 89 2W
New Baden **35** 38 32N 89 42W
New Baltimore, Mich. **43** 42 41N 82 44W
New Baltimore, Pa. **59** 39 59N 78 46W
New Bavaria **56** 41 12N 84 10W
New Bedford **42** 41 38N 70 56W
New Berlin, Ill. **35** 39 44N 89 55W
New Berlin, N.Y. **53** 42 37N 75 20W
New Berlin, Wis. **69** 42 59N 88 6W
New Bern **54** 35 7N 77 3W
New Bethlehem **59** 41 0N 79 20W
New Bloomfield, Mo. **46** 38 43N 92 5W
New Bloomfield, Pa. **59** 40 25N 77 11W
New Boston, Ill. **35** 41 10N 91 0W
New Boston, Mass. **42** 42 6N 73 5W
New Boston, N.H. **50** 42 59N 71 41W
New Boston, Ohio **56** 38 45N 82 56W
New Boston, Tex. **65** 33 28N 94 25W
New Braunfels **65** 29 42N 98 8W
New Bremen **56** 40 26N 84 23W
New Britain **42** 41 40N 72 47W
New Brockton **24** 31 23N 85 56W
New Brunswick **51** 40 30N 74 27W
New Buffalo **43** 41 47N 86 45W
New Cambria **38** 38 53N 97 30W
New Canaan **42** 41 9N 73 30W
New Canton **68** 37 42N 78 18W
New Carlisle **56** 39 56N 84 2W
New Carrollton **41** 38 58N 76 53W
New Castle, Colo. **30** 39 34N 107 32W
New Castle, Del. **41** 39 40N 75 34W
New Castle, Ind. **36** 39 55N 85 22W
New Castle, Ky. **63** 38 26N 85 10W
New Castle, Pa. **59** 41 0N 80 21W
New Castle, Va. **68** 37 30N 80 7W
New Castle County ◇ **41** 39 30N 75 40W
New City **53** 41 9N 73 59W
New Concord, Ky. **62** 36 33N 88 9W
New Concord, Ohio **56** 39 59N 81 54W
New Cumberland **68** 40 30N 80 36W
New Deal **64** 33 44N 101 50W
New Don Pedro Reservoir **28** 37 43N 120 24W
New Edinburg **27** 33 46N 92 14W
New Effington **61** 45 51N 96 55W
New Egypt **51** 40 4N 74 32W
New Ellenton **60** 33 28N 81 41W
New England **55** 46 32N 102 52W
New Era **43** 43 34N 86 21W
New Fairfield **42** 41 27N 73 14W
New Florence, Mo. **46** 38 55N 91 27W
New Florence, Pa. **59** 40 23N 79 5W
New Fork Lakes **70** 43 6N 109 57W
New Franklin **46** 39 1N 92 44W
New Freedom **59** 39 44N 76 42W
New Glarus **69** 42 49N 89 38W
New Hampshire □ **50** 44 0N 71 30W
New Hampton, Iowa **37** 43 3N 92 19W
New Hampton, Mo. **46** 40 16N 94 12W
New Hampton, N.H. **50** 43 36N 71 39W
New Hanover County ◇ **54** 34 15N 77 50W
New Harmony, Ind. **36** 38 8N 87 56W
New Harmony, Utah **66** 37 29N 113 19W
New Hartford, Conn. **42** 41 53N 72 59W
New Hartford, Iowa **37** 42 34N 92 37W
New Hartford, N.Y. **53** 43 4N 75 18W
New Haven, Conn. **42** 41 18N 72 55W
New Haven, Ill. **35** 37 55N 88 8W
New Haven, Ind. **36** 41 4N 85 1W
New Haven, Ky. **63** 37 40N 85 36W
New Haven, Mich. **43** 42 44N 82 48W
New Haven, Mo. **46** 38 37N 91 13W
New Haven, N.Y. **53** 43 29N 76 19W
New Haven, W. Va. **68** 38 59N 81 58W
New Haven County ◇ **42** 41 25N 72 50W
New Hebron **45** 31 44N 89 59W
New Hogan L. **28** 38 9N 120 49W
New Holstein **69** 43 57N 88 5W
New Hope, Ala. **24** 34 32N 86 24W
New Hope, Pa. **59** 40 22N 74 57W
New Iberia **39** 30 1N 91 49W
New Ipswich **50** 42 46N 71 51W
New Jersey □ **51** 40 0N 74 30W
New Johnsonville **62** 36 1N 87 58W
New Kensington **59** 40 34N 79 46W
New Kent **68** 37 31N 76 59W
New Kent County ◇ **68** 37 31N 76 59W
New L. **54** 35 39N 76 20W
New Leipzig **55** 46 22N 101 57W
New Lexington **56** 39 43N 82 13W
New Lisbon **69** 43 53N 90 10W
New London, Conn. **42** 41 22N 72 6W
New London, Iowa **37** 40 55N 91 24W
New London, Md. **41** 39 25N 77 16W
New London, Minn. **44** 45 18N 94 56W
New London, Mo. **46** 39 35N 91 24W
New London, N.H. **50** 43 25N 71 59W
New London, Ohio **56** 41 5N 82 24W
New London, Wis. **69** 44 23N 88 45W
New London County ◇ **42** 41 30N 72 15W
New Madison **56** 39 58N 84 43W
New Madrid **46** 36 36N 89 32W
New Madrid County ◇ **46** 36 40N 89 35W
New Market, Ala. **24** 34 55N 86 26W
New Market, Ind. **36** 39 57N 86 55W
New Market, Iowa **37** 40 44N 94 54W
New Market, Md. **41** 39 23N 77 16W
New Market, Tenn. **63** 36 6N 83 33W
New Market, Va. **68** 38 39N 78 40W
New Martinsville **68** 39 39N 80 52W
New Matamoras **56** 39 31N 81 4W
New Meadows **34** 44 58N 116 18W
New Melle **46** 38 43N 90 53W
New Melones L. **28** 37 57N 120 31W
New Mexico □ **52** 34 30N 106 0W
New Miami **56** 39 26N 84 32W
New Milford, Conn. **42** 41 35N 73 25W
New Milford, Pa. **59** 41 52N 75 44W
New Munich **44** 45 38N 94 45W
New Orleans **39** 29 58N 90 4W
New Oxford **59** 39 52N 77 4W
New Paltz **53** 41 45N 74 5W
New Paris **56** 39 51N 84 48W
New Philadelphia, Ohio **56** 40 30N 81 27W
New Philadelphia, Pa. **59** 40 43N 76 7W
New Pine Creek **58** 42 0N 120 18W
New Plymouth **34** 43 58N 116 49W
New Port Richey **31** 28 16N 82 43W
New Prague **44** 44 32N 93 35W
New Preston **42** 41 40N 73 21W
New Princeton **58** 43 15N 118 35W
New Providence **36** 38 28N 85 57W
New Raymer **30** 40 36N 103 51W
New Richland **44** 43 54N 93 30W
New Richmond, Ohio **56** 38 57N 84 17W
New Richmond, Wis. **69** 45 7N 92 32W
New Riegel **56** 41 3N 83 19W
New Roads **39** 30 42N 91 26W
New Rochelle **53** 40 55N 73 47W
New Rockford **55** 47 41N 99 8W
New Salem, Mass. **42** 42 30N 72 20W
New Salem, N. Dak. **55** 46 51N 101 25W
New Sharon **37** 41 28N 92 39W
New Smyrna Beach **31** 29 1N 80 56W
New Straitsville **56** 39 35N 82 14W
New Stuyahok **25** 59 29N 157 20W
New Tazewell **63** 36 27N 83 36W
New Town **55** 47 59N 102 30W
New Tulsa **57** 36 9N 95 48W
New Ulm **44** 44 19N 94 28W
New Underwood **61** 44 6N 102 50W
New Vienna, Iowa **37** 42 33N 91 7W
New Vienna, Ohio **56** 39 19N 83 42W
New Vineyard **40** 44 48N 70 7W
New Virginia **37** 41 11N 93 44W
New Washington **56** 40 58N 82 51W
New Waverly **65** 30 32N 95 29W
New Whiteland **36** 39 33N 86 5W
New Windsor **41** 39 34N 77 9W
New Woodville **57** 33 56N 96 36W
New York **53** 40 43N 74 0W
New York □ **53** 43 0N 75 0W
New York County ◇ **53** 40 45N 73 59W
New York Mills **44** 46 31N 95 22W
New Zion **60** 33 51N 80 2W
Newark, Ark. **27** 35 42N 91 27W
Newark, Calif. **28** 37 32N 122 2W
Newark, Del. **41** 39 41N 75 46W
Newark, Md. **41** 38 15N 75 17W
Newark, N.J. **51** 40 44N 74 10W
Newark, N.Y. **53** 43 3N 77 6W
Newark, Ohio **56** 40 3N 82 24W
Newark, Tex. **65** 33 0N 97 29W
Newark L. **49** 39 42N 115 44W

Name	Page	Lat.	Long.
Newark Valley	**53**	42 14N	76 11W
Newaygo	**43**	43 25N	85 48W
Newaygo County ◇	**43**	43 30N	85 50W
Newberg	**58**	45 18N	122 58W
Newbern, Ala.	**24**	32 36N	87 32W
Newbern, Tenn.	**62**	36 7N	89 16W
Newberry, Fla.	**31**	29 39N	82 37W
Newberry, Ind.	**36**	38 55N	87 1W
Newberry, Mich.	**43**	46 21N	85 30W
Newberry, S.C.	**60**	34 17N	81 37W
Newberry County ◇	**60**	34 20N	81 40W
Newberry Springs	**29**	34 50N	116 41W
Newburg, Md.	**41**	38 22N	76 37W
Newburg, Mo.	**46**	37 55N	91 54W
Newburg, N. Dak.	**55**	48 43N	100 55W
Newburg, Pa.	**59**	40 8N	77 33W
Newburg, W. Va.	**68**	39 23N	79 51W
Newburgh, Ind.	**36**	37 57N	87 24W
Newburgh, N.Y.	**53**	41 30N	74 1W
Newbury	**50**	43 19N	72 3W
Newburyport	**42**	42 49N	70 53W
Newcastle, Calif.	**28**	38 53N	121 8W
Newcastle, Maine	**40**	44 2N	69 32W
Newcastle, Nebr.	**48**	42 39N	96 53W
Newcastle, Okla.	**57**	35 15N	97 36W
Newcastle, Tex.	**65**	33 12N	98 44W
Newcastle, Utah	**66**	37 40N	113 33W
Newcastle, Wyo.	**70**	43 50N	104 11W
Newcomb, Md.	**41**	38 45N	76 12W
Newcomb, N. Mex.	**52**	36 17N	108 42W
Newcomb, N.Y.	**53**	43 58N	74 10W
Newcomerstown	**56**	40 16N	81 36W
Newell, Ark.	**27**	33 10N	92 45W
Newell, Iowa	**37**	42 36N	95 0W
Newell, S. Dak.	**61**	44 43N	103 25W
Newellton	**39**	32 4N	91 14W
Newenham, C.	**25**	58 39N	162 11W
Newfane	**53**	43 17N	78 43W
Newfield	**51**	39 33N	75 1W
Newfolden	**44**	48 21N	96 20W
Newfound L.	**50**	43 40N	71 47W
Newfoundland	**63**	38 8N	83 6W
Newfoundland Mts.	**66**	41 10N	113 20W
Newhalem	**67**	48 40N	121 15W
Newhalen	**25**	59 43N	154 54W
Newhall, Calif.	**29**	34 23N	118 32W
Newhall, Iowa	**37**	41 59N	91 59W
Newington, Conn.	**42**	41 43N	72 45W
Newington, Ga.	**32**	32 35N	81 30W
Newkirk, N. Mex.	**52**	35 4N	104 16W
Newkirk, Okla.	**57**	36 53N	97 3W
Newland	**54**	36 5N	81 56W
Newllano	**39**	31 7N	93 16W
Newman, Calif.	**28**	37 19N	121 1W
Newman, Ill.	**35**	39 48N	87 59W
Newman Grove	**48**	41 45N	97 47W
Newmans L.	**31**	29 40N	82 12W
Newmarket	**50**	43 5N	70 56W
Newnan	**32**	33 23N	84 48W
Newport, Ark.	**27**	35 37N	91 16W
Newport, Del.	**41**	39 43N	75 37W
Newport, Ind.	**36**	39 53N	87 25W
Newport, Ky.	**63**	39 5N	84 30W
Newport, Maine	**40**	44 50N	69 17W
Newport, N.C.	**54**	34 48N	76 52W
Newport, N.H.	**50**	43 22N	72 10W
Newport, N.J.	**51**	39 18N	75 11W
Newport, N.Y.	**53**	43 11N	75 1W
Newport, Nebr.	**48**	42 36N	99 20W
Newport, Oreg.	**58**	44 39N	124 3W
Newport, Pa.	**59**	40 29N	77 8W
Newport, R.I.	**42**	41 29N	71 19W
Newport, Tenn.	**63**	35 58N	83 11W
Newport, Vt.	**50**	44 56N	72 13W
Newport, Wash.	**67**	48 11N	117 3W
Newport Beach	**29**	33 37N	117 56W
Newport County ◇	**42**	41 30N	71 20W
Newport News	**68**	36 59N	76 25W
Newsoms	**68**	36 38N	77 8W
Newtok	**25**	60 56N	164 38W
Newton, Ga.	**32**	31 19N	84 20W
Newton, Ill.	**35**	38 59N	88 10W
Newton, Iowa	**37**	41 42N	93 3W
Newton, Kans.	**38**	38 3N	97 21W
Newton, Mass.	**42**	42 21N	71 12W
Newton, Miss.	**45**	32 19N	89 10W
Newton, N.C.	**54**	35 40N	81 13W
Newton, N.J.	**51**	41 3N	74 45W
Newton, Tex.	**65**	30 51N	93 46W
Newton, Utah	**66**	41 52N	112 0W
Newton County ◇, Ark.	**27**	35 50N	93 13W
Newton County ◇, Ga.	**32**	33 30N	83 50W
Newton County ◇, Ind.	**36**	41 0N	87 25W
Newton County ◇, Miss.	**45**	32 26N	89 7W
Newton County ◇, Mo.	**46**	36 55N	94 20W
Newton County ◇, Tex.	**65**	30 32N	93 49W
Newton Falls, N.Y.	**53**	44 13N	74 59W
Newton Falls, Ohio	**56**	41 11N	80 59W
Newton Grove	**54**	35 14N	78 21W
Newton L.	**35**	38 55N	88 15W
Newtonia	**46**	36 53N	94 11W
Newtonsville	**56**	39 11N	84 5W
Newtonville	**24**	33 33N	87 48W
Newtown, Conn.	**42**	41 25N	73 19W
Newtown, Md.	**41**	39 18N	76 9W
Newtown, Mo.	**46**	40 22N	93 20W
Newtown, Pa.	**59**	40 14N	74 57W
Newville	**59**	40 10N	77 24W
Ney	**56**	41 23N	84 32W
Nez Perce County ◇	**34**	46 10N	116 55W
Nez Perce Indian Reservation	**34**	46 15N	116 30W
Nezperce	**34**	46 14N	116 14W
Nezperce National Forest	**34**	45 50N	115 20W
Niagara	**55**	48 0N	97 54W
Niagara →	**53**	43 16N	79 4W
Niagara County ◇	**53**	43 15N	78 45W
Niagara Falls	**53**	43 5N	79 4W
Niangua	**46**	37 23N	92 50W
Niangua →	**46**	38 58N	92 48W
Niantic	**42**	41 20N	72 11W
Niarada	**47**	47 49N	114 36W
Nicatous L.	**40**	45 5N	68 9W
Nice	**28**	39 7N	122 51W
Niceville	**31**	30 31N	86 30W
Nicholas County ◇, Ky.	**63**	38 20N	84 0W
Nicholas County ◇, W. Va.	**68**	38 17N	80 51W
Nicholasville	**63**	37 53N	84 34W
Nicholls	**32**	31 31N	82 38W
Nichols, Iowa	**37**	41 29N	91 19W
Nichols, N.Y.	**53**	42 1N	76 22W
Nichols, S.C.	**60**	34 14N	79 9W
Nichols, Wis.	**69**	44 40N	88 28W
Nicholson, Ga.	**32**	34 7N	83 26W
Nicholson, Miss.	**45**	30 29N	89 43W
Nickel Creek	**64**	31 55N	104 45W
Nickerson, Kans.	**38**	38 8N	98 5W
Nickerson, Nebr.	**48**	41 32N	96 28W
Nicodemus	**38**	39 24N	99 37W
Nicolet National Forest	**69**	45 35N	88 45W
Nicollet	**44**	44 17N	94 11W
Nicollet County ◇	**44**	44 20N	94 15W
Nicoma Park	**57**	35 30N	97 19W
Nielsville	**44**	47 32N	96 49W
Nighthawk	**67**	48 58N	119 38W
Nightmute	**25**	60 29N	164 44W
Nihoa	**33**	23 6N	161 58W
Niihau	**33**	21 54N	160 9W
Nikep	**41**	39 32N	79 1W
Nikolai	**25**	62 58N	154 10W
Nikolski	**25**	52 56N	168 52W
Niland	**29**	33 14N	115 31W
Niles, Kans.	**38**	38 58N	97 28W
Niles, Mich.	**43**	41 50N	86 15W
Niles, Ohio	**56**	41 11N	80 46W
Nill	**33**	21 19N	157 44W
Nimrod	**44**	46 38N	94 53W
Nimrod L.	**27**	34 57N	93 10W
Ninaview	**30**	37 39N	103 15W
Ninety Six	**60**	34 11N	82 1W
Ninini Pt.	**33**	21 58N	159 20W
Ninnekah	**57**	34 57N	97 56W
Ninnescah →	**38**	37 20N	97 10W
Niobrara	**48**	42 45N	98 2W
Niobrara →	**48**	42 46N	98 3W
Niobrara County ◇	**70**	43 0N	104 25W
Niota	**63**	35 31N	84 33W
Nipomo	**29**	35 3N	120 29W
Nipton	**29**	35 28N	115 16W
Nisland	**61**	44 40N	103 33W
Nisswa	**44**	46 31N	94 17W
Nitro	**68**	38 25N	81 51W
Nitta Yuma	**45**	33 2N	90 51W
Niwot	**30**	40 6N	105 10W
Nixa	**46**	37 3N	93 18W
Nixon, Tenn.	**62**	35 7N	88 16W
Nixon, Tex.	**65**	29 16N	97 46W
Noank	**42**	41 19N	72 1W
Noatak	**25**	67 34N	162 58W
Noble, Ill.	**35**	38 42N	88 14W
Noble, La.	**39**	31 41N	93 41W
Noble, Okla.	**57**	35 8N	97 24W
Noble County ◇, Ind.	**36**	41 25N	85 25W
Noble County ◇, Ohio	**56**	39 45N	81 31W
Noble County ◇, Okla.	**57**	36 20N	97 10W
Nobles County ◇	**44**	43 45N	95 45W
Noblesville	**36**	40 3N	86 1W
Nocatee	**31**	27 10N	81 53W
Nocona	**65**	33 47N	97 44W
Nodaway	**37**	40 56N	94 54W
Nodaway →	**46**	39 54N	94 58W
Nodaway County ◇	**46**	40 20N	94 50W
Noel	**46**	36 33N	94 29W
Nogales	**26**	31 20N	110 56W
Nohili Pt.	**33**	22 4N	159 47W
Nokomis, Fla.	**31**	27 7N	82 27W
Nokomis, Ill.	**35**	39 18N	89 18W
Nolan County ◇	**64**	32 28N	100 25W
Nolensville	**62**	35 57N	86 40W
Nolin River L.	**62**	37 17N	86 15W
Noma	**31**	30 59N	85 37W
Nomans Land	**42**	41 15N	70 49W
Nome, Alaska	**25**	64 30N	165 25W
Nome, Tex.	**65**	30 2N	94 25W
Nome ◇	**25**	64 30N	165 0W
Nondalton	**25**	59 58N	154 51W
Noonan	**55**	48 54N	103 1W
Noorvik	**25**	66 50N	161 3W
Noorvik Indian Reservation	**25**	66 50N	161 5W
Nopah Range	**29**	36 10N	116 10W
Nora	**48**	40 10N	97 58W
Nora Springs	**37**	43 9N	93 1W
Norborne	**46**	39 18N	93 40W
Norcatur	**38**	39 50N	100 11W
Norco	**29**	33 56N	117 33W
Norcross, Ga.	**32**	33 56N	84 13W
Norcross, Minn.	**44**	45 52N	96 12W
Norden	**48**	42 52N	100 5W
Nordheim	**65**	28 55N	97 37W
Nordman	**34**	48 38N	116 57W
Norfolk, Conn.	**42**	41 59N	73 12W
Norfolk, N.Y.	**53**	44 50N	71 1W
Norfolk, Nebr.	**48**	42 2N	97 25W
Norfolk, Va.	**68**	36 51N	76 17W
Norfolk County ◇	**42**	42 10N	71 20W
Norfork	**27**	36 13N	92 17W
Norfork L.	**27**	36 15N	92 14W
Norge	**57**	34 59N	98 0W
Norias	**64**	26 47N	97 47W
Norlina	**54**	36 27N	78 12W
Normal, Ala.	**24**	34 47N	86 34W
Normal, Ill.	**35**	40 31N	88 59W
Norman, Ark.	**27**	34 27N	93 41W
Norman, N.C.	**54**	35 10N	79 43W
Norman, Nebr.	**48**	40 29N	98 48W
Norman, Okla.	**57**	35 13N	97 26W
Norman, L.	**54**	35 26N	80 57W
Norman County ◇	**44**	47 20N	96 30W
Norman Park	**32**	31 16N	83 41W
Normandy	**64**	28 55N	100 36W
Normangee	**65**	31 2N	96 7W
Norphlet	**27**	33 19N	92 40W
Norris, Mont.	**47**	45 34N	111 41W
Norris, S. Dak.	**61**	43 28N	101 12W
Norris, Tenn.	**63**	36 12N	84 4W
Norris City	**35**	37 59N	88 20W
Norris L.	**63**	36 14N	84 6W
Norristown, Ga.	**32**	32 30N	82 30W
Norristown, Pa.	**59**	40 7N	75 21W
North	**60**	33 37N	81 6W
North →	**42**	42 37N	72 44W
North Adams, Mass.	**42**	42 42N	73 7W
North Adams, Mich.	**43**	41 58N	84 32W
North Amherst	**42**	42 25N	72 32W
North Andover	**42**	42 42N	71 8W
North Anna →	**68**	37 48N	77 25W
North Atlanta	**32**	33 52N	84 21W
North Attleboro	**42**	41 59N	71 20W
North Augusta	**60**	33 30N	81 59W
North Beach	**41**	38 43N	76 32W
North Bend, Nebr.	**48**	41 28N	96 47W
North Bend, Oreg.	**58**	43 24N	124 14W
North Bennington	**50**	42 56N	73 15W
North Bergen	**51**	40 48N	74 1W
North Berwick	**40**	43 18N	70 44W
North Bonneville	**67**	45 39N	121 57W
North Branch, Mich.	**43**	43 14N	83 12W
North Branch, Minn.	**44**	45 31N	92 59W
North Branch Elkhorn →	**48**	41 59N	97 27W
North Branch Potomac →	**41**	39 32N	78 35W
North Branch Shenandoah →	**68**	38 59N	78 22W
North Branford	**42**	41 20N	72 46W
North Brookfield	**42**	42 16N	72 5W
North Brunswick	**51**	40 28N	74 28W
North Buena Vista	**37**	42 41N	90 58W
North Butte	**70**	43 54N	105 57W
North Canadian →	**57**	35 16N	95 31W
North Canton	**56**	40 53N	81 24W
North Cape May	**51**	38 59N	74 57W
North Carolina □	**54**	35 30N	80 0W
North Cascades National Park	**67**	48 45N	121 10W
North Channel	**43**	46 5N	83 30W
North Charleston, N.H.	**50**	43 18N	72 24W
North Charleston, S.C.	**60**	32 53N	79 58W
North Chelmsford	**42**	42 38N	71 23W
North Chicago	**35**	42 19N	87 51W
North Chichester	**50**	43 15N	71 22W
North College Hill	**56**	39 13N	84 33W
North Collins	**53**	42 36N	78 56W
North Concho →	**64**	31 27N	100 25W
North Conway	**50**	44 3N	71 8W
North Dakota □	**55**	47 30N	100 15W
North Dartmouth	**42**	41 36N	70 59W
North Dighton	**42**	41 50N	71 10W
North Druid Hills	**32**	33 49N	84 19W
North East, Md.	**41**	39 36N	75 57W
North East, Pa.	**59**	42 13N	79 50W
North East Cape Fear →	**54**	34 11N	77 57W
North Eastham	**42**	41 52N	69 59W
North Easton	**42**	42 4N	71 6W
North English	**37**	41 31N	92 5W
North Enid	**57**	36 26N	97 52W
North Fabius →	**46**	39 54N	91 30W
North Fairfield	**56**	41 6N	82 37W
North Fond du Lac	**69**	43 48N	88 29W
North Fork	**34**	45 25N	113 59W
North Fork American →	**28**	38 57N	120 59W
North Fork Cuivre →	**46**	39 2N	90 59W
North Fork Edisto →	**60**	33 16N	80 54W
North Fork Feather →	**28**	38 33N	121 30W
North Fork Grand →	**61**	45 47N	102 16W
North Fork Humboldt →	**49**	40 56N	115 32W
North Fork John Day →	**58**	44 45N	119 38W
North Fork Moreau →	**61**	45 9N	102 50W
North Fork Red →	**57**	34 24N	99 14W
North Fork Shoshone →	**70**	44 29N	109 18W
North Fork Smoky Hill →	**38**	38 54N	101 18W
North Fork Solomon →	**38**	39 28N	98 26W
North Fork South Platte →	**30**	39 25N	105 10W
North Fort Myers	**31**	26 41N	81 53W
North Fox I.	**43**	45 29N	85 47W
North Freedom	**69**	43 28N	89 52W
North Grafton	**42**	42 14N	71 42W
North Grosvenor Dale	**42**	41 59N	71 54W
North Hampton	**50**	42 57N	70 48W
North Haven, Conn.	**42**	41 23N	72 52W
North Haven, Maine	**40**	44 8N	68 53W
North Hero	**50**	44 49N	73 18W
North Highlands	**28**	38 40N	121 23W
North I.	**60**	33 17N	79 11W
North Judson	**36**	41 13N	86 46W
North Kingsville	**56**	41 54N	80 42W
North Las Vegas	**49**	36 12N	115 7W
North Lewisburg	**56**	40 13N	83 33W
North Liberty, Ind.	**36**	41 32N	86 26W
North Liberty, Iowa	**37**	41 46N	91 35W
North Little Rock	**27**	34 45N	92 16W
North Loon Mt.	**34**	45 7N	115 52W
North Loup	**48**	41 30N	98 46W
North Loup →	**48**	41 17N	98 24W
North Manchester	**36**	41 0N	85 46W
North Manitou I.	**43**	45 7N	86 1W
North Mankato	**44**	44 10N	94 0W
North Miami	**31**	25 54N	80 11W
North Miami Beach	**31**	25 56N	80 10W
North Middletown	**63**	38 9N	84 7W
North Muskegon	**43**	43 15N	86 17W
North Myrtle Beach	**60**	33 48N	78 42W
North Naples	**31**	26 12N	81 48W
North New River Canal	**31**	26 30N	80 30W
North Oaks	**29**	34 25N	118 31W
North Ogden	**66**	41 19N	111 58W
North Olmsted	**56**	41 25N	81 56W
North Palisade	**29**	37 6N	118 31W
North Pease →	**64**	34 15N	100 7W
North Perry	**56**	41 47N	81 9W
North Plains, N. Mex.	**52**	34 45N	108 10W
North Plains, Oreg.	**58**	45 37N	123 0W
North Platte	**48**	41 8N	100 46W
North Platte →	**48**	41 7N	100 42W
North Pole	**25**	64 45N	147 21W
North Powder	**58**	45 2N	117 55W
North Prairie	**69**	42 56N	88 24W
North Providence	**42**	41 50N	71 25W
North Pt., Alpena, Mich.	**43**	45 2N	83 16W
North Pt., Presque Ile, Mich.	**43**	45 22N	83 30W
North Richland Hills	**65**	32 50N	97 14W
North Rim	**26**	36 12N	112 3W
North Salem	**36**	39 52N	86 39W
North Salt Lake	**66**	40 50N	111 55W
North Santiam →	**58**	44 41N	123 0W
North Schell Peak	**49**	39 25N	114 36W
North Sioux City	**61**	42 32N	96 29W
North Slope ◇	**25**	69 0N	154 0W
North Springfield, Pa.	**59**	41 59N	80 26W

North Springfield, Vt. **50** 43 20N 72 32W
North Stonington **42** 41 0N 72 0W
North Stratford **50** 44 45N 71 38W
North Sulphur → **65** 33 23N 95 18W
North Sutton **50** 43 22N 71 56W
North Syracuse **53** 43 8N 76 7W
North Terre Haute **36** 39 31N 87 22W
North Toe → **54** 36 0N 82 16W
North Tonawanda **53** 43 2N 78 53W
North Troy **50** 45 0N 72 24W
North Truro **42** 42 2N 70 5W
North Umpqua → **58** 43 16N 123 27W
North Vernon **36** 39 0N 85 38W
North Wales **59** 40 13N 75 17W
North Washington **37** 43 7N 92 25W
North Wichita → **65** 33 43N 99 29W
North Wildwood **51** 39 0N 74 48W
North Wilkesboro **54** 36 10N 81 9W
North Windham **40** 43 50N 70 26W
Northampton, Mass. **42** 42 19N 72 38W
Northampton, Pa. **59** 40 41N 75 30W
Northampton County ◇, N.C. **54** 36 20N 77 30W
Northampton County ◇, Pa. **59** 40 50N 75 20W
Northampton County ◇, Va. **68** 37 15N 75 55W
Northborough **42** 42 19N 71 39W
Northbridge **42** 42 9N 71 39W
Northeast C. **25** 63 18N 168 42W
Northern Cheyenne Indian Reservation **47** 45 30N 106 40W
Northfield, Maine **40** 44 52N 67 34W
Northfield, Mass. **42** 42 42N 72 27W
Northfield, Minn. **44** 44 27N 93 9W
Northfield, N.H. **50** 43 26N 71 36W
Northfield, N.J. **51** 39 22N 74 33W
Northfield, Vt. **50** 44 9N 72 40W
Northford **42** 41 24N 72 48W
Northglenn **30** 39 53N 104 58W
Northome **44** 47 52N 94 17W
Northport, Ala. **24** 33 14N 87 35W
Northport, Mich. **43** 45 8N 85 37W
Northport, N.Y. **53** 40 54N 73 21W
Northport, Nebr. **48** 41 41N 103 5W
Northport, Wash. **67** 48 55N 117 48W
Northrop **44** 43 44N 94 26W
Northumberland **59** 40 54N 76 48W
Northumberland County ◇, Pa. **59** 40 55N 76 50W
Northumberland County ◇, Va. **68** 37 55N 76 29W
Northview **46** 37 17N 93 0W
Northville, N.Y. **53** 43 13N 74 11W
Northville, S. Dak. **61** 45 9N 98 35W
Northway **25** 62 58N 141 56W
Northwood, Iowa **37** 43 27N 93 13W
Northwood, N. Dak. **55** 47 44N 97 34W
Northwood, N.H. **50** 43 12N 71 9W
Northwye **46** 37 59N 91 46W
Norton, Kans. **38** 39 50N 99 53W
Norton, Mass. **42** 41 58N 71 11W
Norton, Va. **68** 36 56N 82 38W
Norton, Vt. **50** 45 0N 71 48W
Norton B. **25** 64 45N 161 15W
Norton County ◇ **38** 39 45N 99 50W
Norton Reservoir **38** 39 48N 99 56W
Norton Sd. **25** 63 50N 164 0W
Nortonville, Kans. **38** 39 25N 95 20W
Nortonville, Ky. **62** 37 12N 87 27W
Norwalk, Calif. **29** 33 54N 118 5W
Norwalk, Conn. **42** 41 7N 73 22W
Norwalk, Iowa **37** 41 29N 93 41W
Norwalk, Ohio **56** 41 15N 82 37W
Norway, Iowa **37** 41 54N 91 55W
Norway, Kans. **38** 39 42N 97 47W
Norway, Maine **40** 44 13N 70 32W
Norway, Mich. **43** 45 47N 87 55W
Norway, S.C. **60** 33 27N 81 7W
Norwich, Conn. **42** 41 31N 72 5W
Norwich, Kans. **38** 37 27N 97 51W
Norwich, N.Y. **53** 42 32N 75 32W
Norwich, Vt. **50** 43 42N 72 18W
Norwood, Colo. **30** 38 8N 108 20W
Norwood, La. **39** 30 58N 91 6W
Norwood, Mass. **42** 42 12N 71 12W
Norwood, Minn. **44** 44 46N 93 55W
Norwood, Mo. **46** 37 7N 92 24W
Norwood, N.C. **54** 35 14N 80 7W
Norwood, N.Y. **53** 44 45N 75 0W
Norwood, Ohio **56** 39 10N 84 27W
Norwoodville **37** 41 39N 93 33W
Notasulga **24** 32 34N 85 41W
Notch Peak **66** 39 9N 113 25W
Notrees **64** 31 55N 102 45W
Nottely L. **32** 34 58N 84 5W
Nottingham **50** 43 7N 71 6W
Nottoway → **68** 36 33N 76 55W
Nottoway County ◇ **68** 37 8N 78 5W
Nottoway Court House **68** 37 8N 78 5W
Notus **34** 43 43N 116 48W
Novato **28** 38 6N 122 35W
Novinger **46** 40 14N 92 43W
Nowata **57** 36 42N 95 38W
Nowata County ◇ **57** 36 50N 95 40W
Nowater Cr. → **70** 43 57N 108 0W
Nowood Cr. → **70** 44 17N 107 58W
Noxapater **45** 33 1N 89 1W
Noxon Reservoir **47** 47 57N 115 44W
Noxubee → **24** 32 50N 88 10W
Noxubee County ◇ **45** 33 7N 88 34W
Noyes **44** 49 0N 97 12W
Nubieber **28** 41 6N 121 11W
Nuckolls County ◇ **48** 40 15N 98 0W
Nucla **30** 38 16N 108 33W
Nueces → **65** 27 51N 97 30W
Nueces County ◇ **65** 27 47N 97 40W
Nulato **25** 64 43N 158 6W
Nulhegan → **50** 44 45N 71 38W
Numa **37** 40 41N 92 59W
Nunda, N.Y. **53** 42 35N 77 56W
Nunda, S. Dak. **61** 44 10N 97 1W
Nunivak I. **25** 60 10N 166 30W
Nunn **30** 40 42N 104 47W
Nunnelly **62** 35 52N 87 28W
Nursery **65** 28 56N 97 6W
Nutley **51** 40 49N 74 9W
Nutrioso **26** 33 57N 109 13W
Nyack **53** 41 5N 73 55W
Nye County ◇ **49** 37 0N 116 40W
Nyssa **58** 43 53N 117 0W

O

O. C. Fisher L. **64** 31 29N 100 29W
Oacoma **61** 43 48N 99 24W
Oahe, L. **61** 44 27N 100 24W
Oahe Dam **61** 44 27N 100 24W
Oahu **33** 21 28N 157 58W
Oak **48** 40 14N 97 54W
Oak Bluffs **42** 41 27N 70 34W
Oak City, N.C. **54** 35 58N 77 18W
Oak City, Utah **66** 39 22N 112 20W
Oak Cr. →, Ariz. **26** 34 45N 111 55W
Oak Cr. →, S. Dak. **61** 45 35N 100 30W
Oak Creek, Colo. **30** 40 16N 106 57W
Oak Creek, Wis. **69** 42 52N 87 55W
Oak Grove, Ky. **62** 36 40N 87 26W
Oak Grove, La. **39** 32 52N 91 23W
Oak Grove, Mo. **46** 39 0N 94 8W
Oak Harbor, Ohio **56** 41 30N 83 9W
Oak Harbor, Wash. **67** 48 18N 122 39W
Oak Hill, Fla. **31** 28 52N 80 51W
Oak Hill, Kans. **38** 39 15N 97 21W
Oak Hill, Ohio **56** 38 54N 82 35W
Oak Hill, Tenn. **62** 36 5N 86 47W
Oak Hill, W. Va. **68** 37 59N 81 9W
Oak Knolls **29** 34 51N 120 27W
Oak Lawn **35** 41 43N 87 44W
Oak Orchard **41** 38 36N 75 12W
Oak Park, Ga. **32** 32 22N 82 19W
Oak Park, Ill. **35** 41 53N 87 47W
Oak Park, Mich. **43** 42 28N 83 11W
Oak Ridge, La. **39** 32 38N 91 47W
Oak Ridge, Mo. **46** 37 30N 89 44W
Oak Ridge, Tenn. **63** 36 1N 84 16W
Oak Vale **45** 31 26N 89 58W
Oak Valley **38** 37 20N 96 1W
Oak View **29** 34 24N 119 18W
Oakboro **54** 35 13N 80 20W
Oakdale, Calif. **28** 37 46N 120 51W
Oakdale, Ill. **35** 38 16N 89 30W
Oakdale, La. **39** 30 49N 92 40W
Oakdale, Nebr. **48** 42 4N 97 58W
Oakes **55** 46 8N 98 6W
Oakesdale **67** 47 8N 117 15W
Oakfield, Ga. **32** 31 47N 83 58W
Oakfield, N.Y. **53** 43 4N 78 16W
Oakfield, Wis. **69** 43 41N 88 33W
Oakford **35** 40 6N 89 58W
Oakgrove **27** 36 27N 93 26W
Oakhill **24** 31 55N 87 5W
Oakhurst, Calif. **28** 37 19N 119 40W
Oakhurst, N.J. **51** 40 16N 74 1W
Oakland, Ark. **27** 36 28N 92 35W
Oakland, Calif. **28** 37 49N 122 16W
Oakland, Ill. **35** 39 39N 88 2W
Oakland, Iowa **37** 41 19N 95 23W
Oakland, Ky. **62** 37 2N 86 15W
Oakland, Maine **40** 44 33N 69 43W
Oakland, Md. **41** 39 25N 79 24W
Oakland, Miss. **45** 34 3N 89 55W
Oakland, N.J. **51** 41 2N 74 14W
Oakland, Nebr. **48** 41 50N 96 28W
Oakland, Okla. **57** 34 7N 96 49W
Oakland, Oreg. **58** 43 25N 123 18W
Oakland, Pa. **59** 41 57N 75 37W
Oakland, Tenn. **62** 35 14N 89 31W
Oakland City **36** 38 20N 87 21W
Oakland County ◇ **43** 42 35N 83 20W
Oakland Park **31** 26 10N 80 8W
Oaklawn **38** 37 36N 97 18W
Oakley, Idaho **34** 42 15N 113 53W
Oakley, Kans. **38** 39 8N 100 51W
Oakley, Mich. **43** 43 9N 84 10W
Oakley, Utah **66** 40 43N 111 18W
Oakman **24** 33 43N 87 23W
Oakridge **58** 43 45N 122 28W
Oakton **62** 36 40N 89 4W
Oaktown **36** 38 52N 87 27W
Oakville, Conn. **42** 41 36N 73 5W
Oakville, Iowa **37** 41 6N 91 3W
Oakville, Wash. **67** 46 51N 123 14W
Oakwood, Ohio **56** 41 6N 84 23W
Oakwood, Okla. **57** 35 56N 98 42W
Oakwood, Tex. **65** 31 35N 95 51W
Oark **27** 35 41N 93 35W
Oasis **49** 41 2N 114 29W
Oberlin, Kans. **38** 39 49N 100 32W
Oberlin, La. **39** 30 37N 92 46W
Oberlin, Ohio **56** 41 18N 82 13W
Oberon **55** 47 55N 99 13W
Obert **48** 42 41N 97 2W
Obion **62** 36 16N 89 12W
Obion → **62** 35 55N 89 39W
Obion County ◇ **62** 36 20N 89 10W
Oblong **35** 39 0N 87 55W
O'Brien, Fla. **31** 30 2N 82 57W
O'Brien, Oreg. **58** 42 4N 123 42W
O'Brien, Tex. **65** 33 23N 99 51W
O'Brien County ◇ **37** 43 5N 95 35W
Obscura, Sierra **52** 33 45N 106 25W
Ocala **31** 29 11N 82 8W
Ocate **52** 36 11N 105 3W
Ocate → **52** 36 10N 104 30W
Ocean Bluff **42** 42 6N 70 39W
Ocean City, Md. **41** 38 20N 75 5W
Ocean City, N.J. **51** 39 17N 74 35W
Ocean City, Wash. **67** 47 4N 124 10W
Ocean County ◇ **51** 39 50N 74 15W
Ocean L. **70** 43 12N 108 36W
Ocean Park **67** 46 30N 124 3W
Ocean Springs **45** 30 25N 88 50W
Oceana **68** 37 42N 81 38W
Oceana County ◇ **43** 43 40N 86 20W
Oceano **29** 35 6N 120 37W
Oceanport **51** 40 19N 74 3W
Oceanside, Calif. **29** 33 12N 117 23W
Oceanside, N.Y. **53** 40 38N 73 38W
Oceanville **51** 39 28N 74 28W
Ochelata **57** 36 36N 95 59W
Ocheyedan **37** 43 25N 95 32W
Ocheyedan Mound **37** 43 24N 95 31W
Ochiltree County ◇ **64** 36 10N 100 55W
Ochlocknee **32** 30 58N 84 3W
Ochlockonee → **31** 29 59N 84 26W
Ochoco Mts. **58** 44 30N 120 35W
Ochoco National Forest **58** 44 20N 120 15W
Ochopee **31** 25 54N 81 18W
Ocilla **32** 31 36N 83 15W
Ocmulgee → **32** 31 58N 82 33W
Ocoee, Fla. **31** 28 34N 81 33W
Ocoee, Tenn. **63** 35 7N 84 43W
Oconee **35** 39 17N 89 7W
Oconee → **32** 31 58N 82 33W
Oconee, L. **32** 33 28N 83 15W
Oconee County ◇, Ga. **32** 33 50N 83 25W
Oconee County ◇, S.C. **60** 34 45N 83 0W
Oconee National Forest **32** 33 15N 83 45W
Oconomowoc **69** 43 7N 88 30W
Oconto, Nebr. **48** 41 9N 99 46W
Oconto, Wis. **69** 44 53N 87 52W
Oconto → **69** 44 53N 87 50W
Oconto County ◇ **69** 45 0N 88 15W
Oconto Falls **69** 44 52N 88 9W
Ocracoke **54** 35 7N 75 58W
Ocracoke I. **54** 35 10N 75 50W
Octavia **48** 41 21N 97 4W
Odebolt **37** 42 19N 95 15W
Odell, Ill. **35** 41 0N 88 31W
Odell, Nebr. **48** 40 3N 96 48W
Odell, Oreg. **58** 45 38N 121 32W
Odell, Tex. **65** 34 21N 99 25W
Odem **65** 27 57N 97 35W
Oden **27** 34 37N 93 47W
Odenton **41** 39 5N 76 42W
Odessa, Del. **41** 39 27N 75 40W
Odessa, Minn. **44** 45 16N 96 20W
Odessa, Mo. **46** 39 0N 93 57W
Odessa, Tex. **64** 31 52N 102 23W
Odessa, Wash. **67** 47 20N 118 41W
Odon **36** 38 51N 86 59W
O'Donnell **64** 32 58N 101 50W
Odum **32** 31 40N 82 2W
Oelrichs **61** 43 11N 103 14W
Oelwein **37** 42 41N 91 55W
O'Fallon **46** 38 49N 90 42W
Offerle **38** 37 54N 99 33W
Ogallah **38** 38 59N 99 44W
Ogallala **48** 41 8N 101 43W
Ogden, Ark. **27** 33 35N 94 3W
Ogden, Iowa **37** 42 2N 94 2W
Ogden, Kans. **38** 39 7N 96 43W
Ogden, Utah **66** 41 13N 111 58W
Ogdensburg, N.J. **51** 41 5N 74 36W
Ogdensburg, N.Y. **53** 44 42N 75 30W
Ogeechee → **32** 31 50N 81 3W
Ogema **44** 47 6N 95 56W
Ogemaw **27** 33 28N 93 2W
Ogemaw County ◇ **43** 44 15N 84 10W
Ogilvie **44** 45 50N 93 26W
Oglala **61** 43 17N 102 44W
Oglala National Grassland **48** 42 55N 103 45W
Ogle County ◇ **35** 42 0N 89 20W
Oglesby, Ill. **35** 41 18N 89 4W
Oglesby, Tex. **65** 31 25N 97 30W
Oglethorpe **32** 32 18N 84 4W
Oglethorpe County ◇ **32** 33 50N 83 0W
Ohatchee **24** 33 47N 86 0W
Ohio, Colo. **30** 38 34N 106 37W
Ohio, Ill. **35** 41 34N 89 28W
Ohio □ **56** 40 15N 82 45W
Ohio → **62** 36 59N 89 8W
Ohio City **56** 40 46N 84 37W
Ohio County ◇, Ind. **36** 38 55N 85 0W
Ohio County ◇, Ky. **62** 37 30N 86 50W
Ohio County ◇, W. Va. **68** 40 6N 80 34W
Ohioville **59** 40 41N 80 30W
Oil Center **52** 32 30N 103 16W
Oil City, La. **39** 32 45N 93 58W
Oil City, Pa. **59** 41 26N 79 42W
Oil Trough **27** 35 38N 91 28W
Oildale **29** 35 25N 119 1W
Oilmont **47** 48 44N 111 51W
Oilton **57** 36 5N 96 35W
Ojai **29** 34 27N 119 15W
Ojo Feliz **52** 36 4N 105 7W
Ojo Sarco **52** 36 7N 105 47W
Okabena **44** 43 44N 95 19W
Okaloosa County ◇ **31** 30 30N 86 40W
Okanagan Ra. **67** 48 40N 119 45W
Okanogan **67** 48 22N 119 35W
Okanogan → **67** 48 6N 119 44W
Okanogan County ◇ **67** 48 30N 120 0W
Okanogan National Forest **67** 48 30N 120 10W
Okarche **57** 35 44N 97 58W
Okaton **61** 43 53N 100 53W
Okay **57** 35 51N 95 19W
O'Kean **27** 36 10N 90 49W
Okeechobee **31** 27 15N 80 50W
Okeechobee, L. **31** 27 0N 80 50W
Okeechobee County ◇ **31** 27 30N 81 0W
Okeene **57** 36 7N 98 19W
Okefenokee Swamp **32** 30 40N 82 20W
Okemah **57** 35 26N 96 19W
Okemos **43** 42 43N 84 26W
Oketo **38** 39 58N 96 36W
Okfuskee County ◇ **57** 35 25N 96 15W
Oklahoma □ **57** 36 0N 97 0W
Oklahoma City **57** 35 30N 97 30W
Oklahoma County ◇ **57** 35 35N 97 20W
Oklaunion **65** 34 8N 99 9W
Oklawaha → **31** 29 28N 81 41W
Oklawaha, L. **31** 29 30N 81 45W
Oklee **44** 47 50N 95 51W
Okmulgee **57** 35 37N 95 58W
Okmulgee County ◇ **57** 35 40N 96 0W
Okoboji **37** 43 23N 95 8W
Okolona, Ark. **27** 34 0N 93 20W
Okolona, Ky. **63** 38 8N 85 41W
Okolona, Miss. **45** 34 0N 88 45W
Oktaha **57** 35 35N 95 29W
Oktibbeha County ◇ **45** 33 28N 88 49W
Ola, Ark. **27** 35 2N 93 13W
Ola, Idaho **34** 44 11N 116 18W
Olamon **40** 45 7N 68 37W
Olancha **29** 36 17N 118 1W
Olanta **60** 33 56N 79 56W
Olar **60** 33 11N 81 11W
Olathe, Colo. **30** 38 36N 107 59W
Olathe, Kans. **38** 38 53N 94 49W
Olberg **26** 33 6N 111 41W
Old Bridge **51** 40 25N 74 22W
Old Faithful **70** 44 28N 110 50W
Old Forge, N.Y. **53** 43 43N 74 58W
Old Forge, Pa. **59** 41 22N 75 45W
Old Fort **54** 35 38N 82 11W
Old Harbor **25** 57 12N 153 18W
Old Hickory L. **62** 36 18N 86 40W
Old Logan Cr. → **48** 41 37N 96 30W
Old Lyme **42** 41 19N 72 20W
Old Mines **46** 38 1N 90 45W
Old Monroe **46** 38 56N 90 45W
Old Ocean **65** 29 5N 95 45W
Old Orchard Beach **40** 43 31N 70 23W
Old Saybrook **42** 41 18N 72 23W
Old Speck Mt. **40** 44 34N 70 57W
Old Town, Fla. **31** 29 36N 82 59W
Old Town, Maine **40** 44 56N 68 39W

Old Washington **56** 40 2N 81 27W
Old Woman Mts. **29** 34 20N 115 0W
Oldenburg **36** 39 21N 85 12W
Oldham **61** 44 14N 97 19W
Oldham County ◇, Ky. **63** 38 25N 85 30W
Oldham County ◇, Tex. **64** 35 30N 102 30W
Oldsmar **31** 28 2N 82 40W
Oldtown **41** 39 33N 78 37W
Olean, Mo. **46** 38 25N 92 32W
Olean, N.Y. **53** 42 5N 78 26W
Olentangy → **56** 39 58N 83 2W
Olex **58** 45 30N 120 11W
Olive Branch **45** 34 58N 89 50W
Olive Hill **63** 38 18N 83 13W
Olivehurst **28** 39 6N 121 34W
Oliver, Ga. **32** 32 31N 81 32W
Oliver, Wis. **69** 46 40N 92 12W
Oliver County ◇ **55** 47 2N 101 25W
Oliver Springs **63** 36 3N 84 20W
Olivet, Kans. **38** 38 29N 95 45W
Olivet, Md. **41** 38 20N 76 26W
Olivet, Mich. **43** 42 27N 84 56W
Olivet, S. Dak. **61** 43 14N 97 40W
Olivia, Minn. **44** 44 47N 94 59W
Olivia, N.C. **54** 35 22N 79 7W
Olla **39** 31 54N 92 14W
Ollie **37** 41 12N 92 6W
Olmstead, Ill. **35** 37 11N 89 5W
Olmstead, Ky. **62** 36 45N 87 1W
Olmsted County ◇ **44** 44 0N 92 30W
Olney, Ill. **35** 38 44N 88 5W
Olney, Md. **41** 39 9N 77 4W
Olney, Mont. **47** 48 33N 114 35W
Olney, Tex. **65** 33 22N 98 45W
Olney Springs **30** 38 10N 103 57W
Olowalu **33** 20 49N 156 38W
Olpe **38** 38 16N 96 10W
Olsburg **38** 39 26N 96 37W
Olton **64** 34 11N 102 8W
Olustee, Fla. **31** 30 12N 82 26W
Olustee, Okla. **57** 34 33N 99 25W
Olympia **67** 47 3N 122 53W
Olympic Mts. **67** 47 55N 123 45W
Olympic National Forest **67** 47 25N 123 35W
Olympus, Mt. **67** 47 48N 123 43W
Oma **45** 31 44N 90 9W
Omaha, Ark. **27** 36 27N 93 11W
Omaha, Nebr. **48** 41 17N 96 1W
Omaha, Tex. **65** 33 11N 94 45W
Omaha Indian Reservation **48** 42 10N 96 30W
Omak **67** 48 25N 119 31W
Omak L. **67** 48 17N 119 24W
Omega **32** 31 21N 83 36W
Omemee **55** 48 42N 100 22W
Omer **43** 44 3N 83 51W
Ommaney, C. **25** 56 10N 134 40W
Ompompanoosuc → **50** 43 45N 72 14W
Omro **69** 44 2N 88 45W
Ona **31** 27 29N 81 55W
Onaga **38** 39 29N 96 10W
Onaka **61** 45 12N 99 28W
Onalaska **69** 43 53N 91 14W
Onamia **44** 46 4N 93 40W
Onancock **68** 37 43N 75 45W
Onarga **35** 40 43N 88 1W
Onawa **37** 42 2N 96 6W
Onaway, Idaho **34** 46 56N 116 53W
Onaway, Mich. **43** 45 21N 84 14W
Oneco **31** 27 25N 82 31W
Oneida, Ill. **35** 41 4N 90 13W
Oneida, Iowa **37** 42 33N 91 21W
Oneida, Kans. **38** 39 52N 95 56W
Oneida, N.Y. **53** 43 6N 75 39W
Oneida, Tenn. **63** 36 30N 84 31W
Oneida County ◇, Idaho **34** 42 10N 112 30W
Oneida County ◇, N.Y. **53** 43 20N 75 30W
Oneida County ◇, Wis. **69** 45 40N 89 35W
Oneida Indian Reservation **69** 44 25N 88 10W
Oneida L. **53** 43 12N 75 54W
O'Neill **48** 42 27N 98 39W
Onekama **43** 44 22N 86 12W
Oneonta, Ala. **24** 33 57N 86 28W
Oneonta, N.Y. **53** 42 27N 75 4W
Onida **61** 44 42N 100 4W
Onley **68** 37 41N 75 43W
Ono **28** 40 29N 122 37W
Onondaga County ◇ **53** 43 0N 76 15W
Onondaga Indian Reservation **53** 42 55N 76 10W
Onset **42** 41 45N 70 39W
Onslow **37** 42 6N 91 1W
Onslow B. **54** 34 20N 77 15W
Onslow County ◇ **54** 34 50N 77 30W
Ontario, Calif. **29** 34 4N 117 39W
Ontario, Oreg. **58** 44 2N 116 58W
Ontario, Wis. **69** 43 45N 90 35W
Ontario, L. **53** 43 20N 78 0W
Ontario County ◇ **53** 42 50N 77 20W
Ontonagon **43** 46 52N 89 19W
Ontonagon County ◇ **43** 46 40N 89 25W
Ookala **33** 20 1N 155 17W
Oolitic **36** 38 54N 86 31W
Oologah **57** 36 27N 95 43W
Oologah L. **57** 36 26N 95 41W
Ooltewah **63** 35 4N 85 4W
Oostburg **69** 43 37N 87 48W
Opelika **24** 32 39N 85 23W
Opelousas **39** 30 32N 92 5W
Opheim **47** 48 51N 106 24W
Ophir, Alaska **25** 63 10N 156 31W
Ophir, Oreg. **58** 42 34N 124 23W
Opihikao **33** 19 26N 154 53W
Opp **24** 31 17N 86 16W
Opportunity, Mont. **47** 46 6N 112 50W
Opportunity, Wash. **67** 47 39N 117 15W
Optima **57** 36 46N 101 21W
Oquawka **35** 40 56N 90 57W
Oracle **26** 32 37N 110 46W
Oraibi **26** 35 53N 110 37W
Oran **46** 37 5N 89 39W
Orange, Calif. **29** 33 47N 117 51W
Orange, Conn. **42** 41 17N 73 2W
Orange, Mass. **42** 42 35N 72 19W
Orange, Tex. **65** 30 6N 93 44W
Orange, Va. **68** 38 15N 78 7W
Orange City, Fla. **31** 28 57N 81 18W
Orange City, Iowa **37** 43 0N 96 4W
Orange County ◇, Calif. **29** 33 30N 117 45W
Orange County ◇, Fla. **31** 28 30N 81 15W
Orange County ◇, Ind. **36** 38 30N 86 30W
Orange County ◇, N.C. **54** 36 0N 79 10W
Orange County ◇, N.Y. **53** 41 20N 74 15W
Orange County ◇, Tex. **65** 30 12N 93 52W
Orange County ◇, Va. **68** 38 15N 78 7W
Orange County ◇, Vt. **50** 44 0N 72 20W
Orange Cove **29** 36 38N 119 19W
Orange Grove **65** 27 58N 97 56W
Orange Lake **31** 29 25N 82 13W
Orange Park **31** 30 10N 81 42W
Orangeburg **60** 33 30N 80 52W
Orangeburg County ◇ **60** 33 20N 80 30W
Orangevale **28** 38 41N 121 13W
Orangeville, Ill. **35** 42 28N 89 39W
Orangeville, Pa. **59** 41 5N 76 25W
Orangeville, Utah **66** 39 14N 111 3W
Orbisonia **59** 40 15N 77 54W
Orcas **67** 48 36N 122 57W
Orcas I. **67** 48 42N 122 56W
Orchard, Colo. **30** 40 20N 104 7W
Orchard, Idaho **34** 43 19N 116 2W
Orchard, Iowa **37** 43 14N 92 47W
Orchard, Nebr. **48** 42 20N 98 15W
Orchard City **30** 38 50N 107 58W
Orchard Homes **47** 46 55N 114 4W
Orchard Park **53** 42 46N 78 45W
Orchard Valley **70** 41 6N 104 49W
Orchards **67** 45 40N 122 34W
Ord **48** 41 36N 98 56W
Ord, Mt. **64** 30 18N 103 30W
Orderville **66** 37 17N 112 38W
Ordway **30** 38 13N 103 46W
Ore City **65** 32 48N 94 43W
Oreana, Idaho **34** 43 3N 116 24W
Oreana, Ill. **35** 39 56N 88 52W
Oreana, Nev. **49** 40 20N 118 19W
Oregon, Ill. **35** 42 1N 89 20W
Oregon, Mo. **46** 39 59N 95 9W
Oregon, Ohio **56** 41 38N 83 25W
Oregon, Wis. **69** 42 56N 89 23W
Oregon □ **58** 44 0N 121 0W
Oregon Butte **67** 46 7N 117 41W
Oregon Caves National Monument **58** 42 6N 123 24W
Oregon City **58** 45 21N 122 36W
Oregon County ◇ **46** 36 40N 91 25W
Oregon Dunes Nat. Rec. Area **58** 42 3N 123 26W
Orem **66** 40 19N 111 42W
Organ **52** 32 26N 106 36W
Organ Pipe Cactus National Monument **26** 32 0N 113 10W
Orick **28** 41 17N 124 4W
Orient, Iowa **37** 41 12N 94 25W
Orient, Maine **40** 45 49N 67 50W
Orient, S. Dak. **61** 44 54N 99 5W
Orient, Wash. **67** 48 52N 118 12W
Oriental **54** 35 2N 76 42W
Orin **70** 42 39N 105 12W
Orinda **28** 37 53N 122 11W
Orion, Ala. **24** 31 58N 86 0W
Orion, Ill. **35** 41 21N 90 23W
Orion, Okla. **57** 36 13N 98 47W
Oriska **55** 46 56N 97 47W
Oriskany **53** 43 10N 75 20W
Orla **64** 31 50N 103 55W
Orland **28** 39 45N 122 12W
Orlando, Fla. **31** 28 33N 81 23W
Orlando, Okla. **57** 36 9N 97 23W
Orleans, Calif. **28** 41 18N 123 32W
Orleans, Ind. **36** 38 40N 86 27W
Orleans, Mass. **42** 41 47N 69 59W
Orleans, Nebr. **48** 40 8N 99 27W
Orleans, Vt. **50** 44 49N 72 12W
Orleans County ◇, N.Y. **53** 43 15N 78 10W
Orleans County ◇, Vt. **50** 44 45N 72 15W
Orleans Parish ◇ **39** 29 58N 90 4W
Orlinda **62** 36 36N 86 43W
Ormond Beach **31** 29 17N 81 3W
Ormond-by-the-Sea **31** 29 21N 81 4W
Ormsby **44** 43 51N 94 42W
Oro Grande **29** 34 36N 117 20W
Orocovis **71** 18 14N 66 23W
Orofino **34** 46 29N 116 15W
Orogrande **52** 32 24N 106 5W
Orono **40** 44 53N 68 40W
Oronoco **44** 44 10N 92 32W
Orovada **49** 41 34N 117 47W
Oroville, Calif. **28** 39 31N 121 33W
Oroville, Wash. **67** 48 56N 119 26W
Oroville, L. **28** 39 33N 121 29W
Oroville Dam **28** 39 33N 121 29W
Orpha **70** 42 51N 105 30W
Orr, Minn. **44** 48 3N 92 50W
Orr, Okla. **57** 34 2N 97 32W
Orrick **46** 39 13N 94 7W
Orrin **55** 48 6N 100 10W
Orrville **56** 40 50N 81 46W
Orting **67** 47 6N 122 12W
Ortley **61** 45 20N 97 12W
Ortonville **44** 45 19N 96 27W
Orwell **56** 41 32N 80 52W
Osage, Ark. **27** 36 11N 93 24W
Osage, Iowa **37** 43 17N 92 49W
Osage, Okla. **57** 36 19N 96 24W
Osage, W. Va. **68** 39 39N 80 1W
Osage, Wyo. **70** 43 59N 104 25W
Osage → **46** 38 36N 92 57W
Osage Beach **46** 38 9N 92 37W
Osage City, Kans. **38** 38 38N 95 50W
Osage City, Mo. **46** 38 33N 92 2W
Osage County ◇, Kans. **38** 38 40N 95 40W
Osage County ◇, Mo. **46** 38 30N 91 45W
Osage County ◇, Okla. **57** 36 40N 96 30W
Osakis **44** 45 52N 95 9W
Osakis, L. **44** 45 54N 95 7W
Osawatomie **38** 38 31N 94 57W
Osborne **38** 39 26N 98 42W
Osborne County ◇ **38** 39 30N 98 45W
Osburn **34** 47 30N 116 0W
Osceola, Ark. **27** 35 42N 89 58W
Osceola, Iowa **37** 41 2N 93 46W
Osceola, Mo. **46** 38 3N 93 42W
Osceola, Nebr. **48** 41 11N 97 33W
Osceola, Wis. **69** 45 19N 92 42W
Osceola County ◇, Fla. **31** 28 0N 81 0W
Osceola County ◇, Iowa **37** 43 20N 95 35W
Osceola County ◇, Mich. **43** 44 0N 85 20W
Osceola Mills **59** 40 51N 78 16W
Osceola National Forest **31** 30 20N 82 30W
Oscoda **43** 44 26N 83 20W
Oscoda County ◇ **43** 44 40N 84 10W
Oscura **52** 33 29N 106 3W
Osgood, Ind. **36** 39 8N 85 18W
Osgood, Ohio **56** 40 20N 84 30W
Osgood Mts. **49** 41 10N 117 20W
Oshkosh, Nebr. **48** 41 24N 102 21W
Oshkosh, Wis. **69** 44 1N 88 33W
Osierfield **32** 31 40N 83 7W
Oskaloosa, Iowa **37** 41 18N 92 39W
Oskaloosa, Kans. **38** 39 13N 95 19W
Oslo **44** 48 12N 97 8W
Osmond **48** 42 22N 97 36W
Osnabrock **55** 48 40N 98 9W
Osprey **31** 27 12N 82 29W
Ossabaw I. **32** 31 50N 81 5W
Ossabaw Sd. **32** 31 50N 81 6W
Osseo, Mich. **43** 41 53N 84 33W
Osseo, Wis. **69** 44 35N 91 13W
Ossian, Ind. **36** 40 53N 85 10W
Ossian, Iowa **37** 43 9N 91 46W
Ossineke **43** 44 55N 83 26W
Ossining **53** 41 10N 73 55W
Ossipee **50** 43 41N 71 7W
Ossipee L. **50** 43 42N 71 10W
Osterville **42** 41 38N 70 22W
Ostrander **44** 43 37N 92 26W
O'Sullivan Dam **67** 46 59N 119 16W
Oswegatchie → **53** 44 42N 75 30W
Oswego, Ill. **35** 41 41N 88 21W
Oswego, Kans. **38** 37 10N 95 6W
Oswego, N.Y. **53** 43 27N 76 31W
Oswego → **53** 43 27N 76 30W
Oswego County ◇ **53** 43 25N 76 10W
Osyka **45** 31 0N 90 28W
Otero County ◇, Colo. **30** 38 0N 103 45W
Otero County ◇, N. Mex. **52** 32 30N 105 45W
Othello **67** 46 50N 119 10W
Otho **37** 42 25N 94 9W
Otis, Colo. **30** 40 9N 102 58W
Otis, Kans. **38** 38 32N 99 3W
Otis, Mass. **42** 42 12N 73 6W
Otisville **43** 43 10N 83 31W
Oto **37** 42 17N 95 54W
Otoe **48** 40 43N 96 7W
Otoe County ◇ **48** 40 40N 96 0W
Otsego **43** 42 27N 85 42W
Otsego County ◇, Mich. **43** 45 0N 84 40W
Otsego County ◇, N.Y. **53** 42 40N 75 0W
Otsego L. **53** 42 45N 74 52W
Ottawa, Ill. **35** 41 21N 88 51W
Ottawa, Kans. **38** 38 37N 95 16W
Ottawa, Ohio **56** 41 1N 84 3W
Ottawa County ◇, Kans. **38** 39 15N 97 45W
Ottawa County ◇, Mich. **43** 42 50N 86 0W
Ottawa County ◇, Ohio **56** 41 30N 83 9W
Ottawa County ◇, Okla. **57** 36 50N 94 50W
Ottawa National Forest **43** 46 25N 89 15W
Otter **47** 45 12N 106 12W
Otter Cr. →, Utah **66** 38 10N 112 2W
Otter Cr. →, Vt. **50** 44 13N 73 17W
Otter Creek **31** 29 19N 82 46W
Otter Creek Reservoir **66** 38 10N 112 1W
Otter Lake, Ill. **35** 39 28N 89 56W
Otter Lake, Mich. **43** 43 13N 83 28W
Otter Tail → **44** 46 16N 96 36W
Otter Tail County ◇ **44** 46 20N 95 45W
Otter Tail L. **44** 46 24N 95 40W
Otterbein **36** 40 29N 87 6W
Ottertail **44** 46 26N 95 33W
Otterville **46** 38 42N 93 0W
Ottosen **37** 42 54N 94 23W
Ottumwa **37** 41 1N 92 25W
Otway **56** 38 52N 83 11W
Ouachita **27** 33 51N 92 50W
Ouachita → **39** 31 38N 91 49W
Ouachita, L. **27** 34 34N 93 12W
Ouachita County ◇ **27** 33 35N 92 50W
Ouachita Mts. **57** 34 40N 94 25W
Ouachita National Forest **57** 34 50N 94 50W
Ouachita Parish ◇ **39** 32 30N 92 7W
Ouray, Colo. **30** 38 1N 107 40W
Ouray, Utah **66** 40 6N 109 41W
Ouray County ◇ **30** 38 10N 107 45W
Outagamie County ◇ **69** 44 20N 88 30W
Outer I. **69** 47 2N 90 26W
Outer Santa Barbara Passage **29** 33 15N 118 40W
Outlook **47** 48 53N 104 47W
Ouzinkie **25** 57 56N 152 30W
Ovando **47** 47 1N 113 8W
Overbrook **38** 38 47N 95 33W
Overland **46** 38 41N 90 22W
Overland Park, Kans. **38** 38 58N 94 40W
Overland Park, Kans. **38** 38 55N 94 50W
Overlea **41** 39 22N 76 32W
Overly **55** 48 41N 100 9W
Overton, Nebr. **48** 40 44N 99 32W
Overton, Nev. **49** 36 33N 114 27W
Overton, Tex. **65** 32 16N 94 59W
Overton County ◇ **63** 36 23N 85 19W
Ovett **45** 31 29N 89 2W
Ovid, Colo. **30** 40 58N 102 23W
Ovid, Mich. **43** 43 1N 84 22W
Ovid, N.Y. **53** 42 41N 76 49W
Oviedo **31** 28 40N 81 13W
Owanka **61** 44 1N 102 35W
Owasa **37** 42 26N 93 12W
Owasco L. **53** 42 50N 76 31W
Owasso **57** 36 16N 95 51W
Owatonna **44** 44 5N 93 14W
Owego **53** 42 6N 76 16W
Owen **69** 44 57N 90 33W

Owen County ◇, Ind. **36** 39 20N 86 50W
Owen County ◇, Ky. **63** 38 30N 84 50W
Owens → **29** 36 32N 117 59W
Owens L. **29** 36 26N 117 57W
Owensboro **62** 37 46N 87 7W
Owensville, Ark. **27** 34 37N 92 49W
Owensville, Ind. **36** 38 16N 87 41W
Owensville, Mo. **46** 38 21N 91 30W
Owensville, Ohio **56** 39 7N 84 8W
Owenton **63** 38 32N 84 50W
Owings Mills **41** 39 25N 76 47W
Owingsville **63** 38 9N 83 46W
Owl Creek Mts. **70** 43 40N 108 55W
Owls Head **40** 44 5N 69 4W
Owosso **43** 43 0N 84 10W
Owsley County ◇ **63** 37 25N 83 40W
Owyhee **49** 41 57N 116 6W
Owyhee → **58** 43 49N 117 2W
Owyhee, L. **58** 43 38N 117 14W
Owyhee County ◇ **34** 42 45N 116 0W
Owyhee Mts. **34** 42 45N 116 20W
Oxbow **40** 46 25N 68 28W
Oxford, Ala. **24** 33 36N 85 51W
Oxford, Ark. **27** 36 13N 91 56W
Oxford, Colo. **30** 37 10N 107 43W
Oxford, Ind. **36** 40 31N 87 15W
Oxford, Iowa **37** 41 43N 91 47W
Oxford, Kans. **38** 37 17N 97 10W
Oxford, La. **39** 31 56N 93 38W
Oxford, Maine **40** 44 8N 70 30W
Oxford, Mass. **42** 42 7N 71 52W
Oxford, Md. **41** 38 41N 76 11W
Oxford, Mich. **43** 42 49N 83 16W
Oxford, Miss. **45** 34 22N 89 31W
Oxford, N.C. **54** 36 19N 78 35W
Oxford, N.Y. **53** 42 27N 75 36W
Oxford, Nebr. **48** 40 15N 99 38W
Oxford, Ohio **56** 39 31N 84 45W
Oxford, Pa. **59** 39 47N 75 59W
Oxford County ◇ **40** 44 30N 70 30W
Oxford Junction **37** 41 59N 90 57W
Oxford Pk. **34** 42 16N 112 6W
Oxnard **29** 34 12N 119 11W
Oxon Hill **41** 38 48N 76 59W
Oyster Bay **53** 40 52N 73 32W
Ozan **27** 33 51N 93 43W
Ozark, Ala. **24** 31 28N 85 39W
Ozark, Ark. **27** 35 29N 93 50W
Ozark, Mo. **46** 37 1N 93 12W
Ozark County ◇ **46** 36 40N 92 25W
Ozark National Forest **27** 35 40N 93 20W
Ozark Plateau **46** 37 0N 93 0W
Ozark Reservoir **27** 35 30N 94 10W
Ozarks, L. of the **46** 38 12N 92 38W
Ozarks Nat. Scenic Riverways **46** 37 25N 91 12W
Ozaukee County ◇ **69** 43 20N 88 0W
Ozette L. **67** 48 6N 124 38W
Ozona **64** 30 43N 101 12W
Ozone **63** 35 53N 84 49W

P

Paauilo **33** 20 2N 155 22W
Pablo **47** 47 36N 114 7W
Pace **31** 30 36N 87 10W
Pachuta **45** 32 2N 88 53W
Pacific **46** 38 29N 90 45W
Pacific Beach **67** 47 13N 124 12W
Pacific City **58** 45 12N 123 57W
Pacific County ◇ **67** 46 30N 123 55W
Pacific Grove **28** 36 38N 121 56W
Pacific Palisades **33** 21 25N 157 58W
Pacifica **28** 37 36N 122 30W
Packwood, Iowa **37** 41 8N 92 5W
Packwood, Wash. **67** 46 36N 121 40W
Pacolet **60** 34 54N 81 46W
Pacolet Mills **60** 34 55N 81 45W
Paden **57** 35 30N 96 34W
Padre I. **64** 27 10N 97 25W
Padre Island National Seashore **64** 27 0N 97 25W
Padroni **30** 40 47N 103 10W
Paducah, Ky. **62** 37 5N 88 37W
Paducah, Tex. **64** 34 1N 100 18W
Page, Ariz. **26** 36 57N 111 27W
Page, N. Dak. **55** 47 10N 97 34W
Page, Nebr. **48** 42 26N 98 25W
Page, Okla. **57** 34 45N 94 40W
Page City **38** 39 5N 101 9W
Page County ◇, Iowa **37** 40 45N 95 10W
Page County ◇, Va. **68** 38 40N 78 28W
Pageland **60** 34 46N 80 24W
Pagosa Springs **30** 37 16N 107 1W
Paguate **52** 35 8N 107 23W
Pahala **33** 19 12N 155 29W
Pahaska **70** 44 30N 109 58W
Pahoa **33** 19 30N 154 57W
Pahokee **31** 26 50N 80 40W
Pahrump **49** 36 12N 115 59W
Pahute Mesa **49** 37 20N 116 45W
Paia **33** 20 54N 156 22W
Paige **65** 30 13N 97 7W
Pailolo Channel **33** 21 0N 156 40W
Paincourtville **39** 29 59N 91 3W
Painesdale **43** 47 3N 88 40W
Painesville **56** 41 43N 81 15W
Paint → **56** 45 58N 88 15W
Paint Rock, Ala. **24** 34 40N 86 20W
Paint Rock, Tex. **65** 31 31N 99 55W
Paint Rock → **24** 34 28N 86 28W
Painted Desert **26** 36 0N 111 0W
Painted Post **53** 42 10N 77 6W
Paintsville **63** 37 49N 82 48W
Paisley **58** 42 42N 120 32W
Pajarito **52** 34 59N 106 42W
Pala **29** 33 22N 117 5W
Palacios **65** 28 42N 96 13W
Palaoa Pt. **33** 20 44N 156 58W
Palatine **35** 42 7N 88 3W
Palatka **31** 29 39N 81 38W
Palco **38** 39 15N 99 34W
Palen Dry L. **29** 33 46N 115 13W
Palermo, Calif. **28** 39 26N 121 33W
Palermo, N. Dak. **55** 48 21N 102 14W
Palestine, Ark. **27** 34 58N 90 54W
Palestine, Ill. **35** 39 0N 87 37W
Palestine, Ohio **56** 40 3N 84 45W
Palestine, Tex. **65** 31 46N 95 38W
Palestine, L. **65** 32 6N 95 27W
Palikea Pk. **33** 21 26N 158 6W
Palisade, Colo. **30** 39 7N 108 21W
Palisade, Nebr. **48** 40 21N 101 7W
Palisades, Idaho **34** 43 21N 111 13W
Palisades, Wash. **67** 47 25N 119 54W
Palisades Reservoir **34** 43 20N 111 12W
Palito Blanco **64** 27 35N 98 11W
Palm Bay **31** 28 2N 80 35W
Palm Beach **31** 26 43N 80 2W
Palm Beach County ◇ **31** 26 45N 80 20W
Palm Desert **29** 33 43N 116 22W
Palm Springs **29** 33 50N 116 33W
Palmdale, Calif. **29** 34 35N 118 7W
Palmdale, Fla. **31** 26 57N 81 19W
Palmer, Alaska **25** 61 36N 149 7W
Palmer, Iowa **37** 42 38N 94 36W
Palmer, Kans. **38** 39 38N 97 8W
Palmer, Mass. **42** 42 9N 72 20W
Palmer, Nebr. **48** 41 13N 98 15W
Palmer, Tenn. **63** 35 21N 85 34W
Palmer Lake **30** 39 7N 104 55W
Palmers Crossing **45** 31 16N 89 15W
Palmerton **59** 40 48N 75 37W
Palmetto, Fla. **31** 27 31N 82 34W
Palmetto, Ga. **32** 33 31N 84 40W
Palmetto, La. **39** 30 43N 91 55W
Palmyra, Ill. **35** 39 26N 90 0W
Palmyra, Ind. **36** 38 24N 86 7W
Palmyra, Mo. **46** 39 48N 91 32W
Palmyra, N.J. **51** 40 1N 75 1W
Palmyra, Nebr. **48** 40 42N 96 23W
Palmyra, Pa. **59** 40 18N 76 36W
Palmyra, Va. **68** 37 52N 78 16W
Palo **37** 42 4N 91 48W
Palo Alto **28** 37 27N 122 10W
Palo Alto County ◇ **37** 43 5N 94 40W
Palo Duro Cr. → **64** 35 0N 101 55W
Palo Pinto **65** 32 46N 98 18W
Palo Pinto County ◇ **65** 32 45N 98 20W
Palo Verde, Ariz. **26** 33 21N 112 41W
Palo Verde, Calif. **29** 33 26N 114 44W
Palouse **67** 46 55N 117 4W
Palouse → **67** 46 35N 118 13W
Pamlico → **54** 35 20N 76 28W
Pamlico County ◇ **54** 35 10N 76 45W
Pamlico Sd. **54** 35 20N 76 0W
Pampa **64** 35 32N 100 58W
Pamplico **60** 34 0N 79 34W
Pamplin City **68** 37 16N 78 41W
Pamunkey → **68** 37 32N 76 48W
Pana **35** 39 23N 89 5W
Panaca **49** 37 47N 114 23W
Panacea **31** 30 2N 84 23W
Panama, Panama **71** 8 48N 79 55W
Panama, Nebr. **48** 40 36N 96 31W
Panama, Okla. **57** 35 10N 94 40W
Panama, Bay of **71** 8 50N 79 20W
Panama Canal **71** 9 20N 79 55W
Panama City **31** 30 10N 85 40W
Panama City Beach **31** 30 11N 85 48W
Panamint Range **29** 36 20N 117 20W
Panamint Valley **29** 36 15N 117 20W
Pancake Range **49** 38 30N 115 50W
Pandora **56** 40 57N 83 58W
Pangburn **27** 35 26N 91 50W
Panguitch **66** 37 50N 112 26W
Panhandle **64** 35 21N 101 23W
Paniau **33** 21 56N 160 5W
Panola **24** 32 57N 88 16W
Panola County ◇, Miss. **45** 34 19N 89 57W
Panola County ◇, Tex. **65** 32 9N 94 20W
Panora **37** 41 42N 94 22W
Paola **38** 38 35N 94 53W
Paoli, Colo. **30** 40 37N 102 28W
Paoli, Ind. **36** 38 33N 86 28W
Paoli, Okla. **57** 34 50N 97 15W
Paonia **30** 38 52N 107 36W
Papa **33** 19 13N 155 52W
Papaaloa **33** 19 59N 155 13W
Papago Indian Reservation **26** 32 15N 112 0W
Papaikou **33** 19 47N 155 6W
Papawai Pt. **33** 20 47N 156 32W
Papillion **48** 41 9N 96 3W
Papineau **35** 40 58N 87 43W
Paradise, Calif. **28** 39 46N 121 37W
Paradise, Kans. **38** 39 7N 98 55W
Paradise, Mich. **43** 46 38N 85 2W
Paradise, Mont. **47** 47 23N 114 48W
Paradise, Nev. **49** 36 9N 115 10W
Paradise, Utah **66** 41 34N 111 50W
Paradise Hill **57** 35 40N 95 5W
Paradise Valley, Ariz. **26** 33 32N 111 57W
Paradise Valley, Nev. **49** 41 30N 117 32W
Paradise Valley, Wyo. **70** 42 49N 106 23W
Paragon **36** 39 24N 86 34W
Paragonah **66** 37 53N 112 46W
Paragould **27** 36 3N 90 29W
Paraiso **71** 9 3N 79 38W
Paramus **51** 40 55N 74 4W
Parchment **43** 42 20N 85 34W
Pardee Reservoir **28** 38 16N 120 51W
Pardeeville **69** 43 32N 89 18W
Parguera **71** 17 59N 67 3W
Paria → **26** 36 52N 111 36W
Paria Plateau **26** 36 50N 111 50W
Paris, Ark. **27** 35 18N 93 44W
Paris, Idaho **34** 42 14N 111 24W
Paris, Ill. **35** 39 36N 87 42W
Paris, Ky. **63** 38 13N 84 15W
Paris, Maine **40** 44 16N 70 30W
Paris, Mo. **46** 39 29N 92 0W
Paris, Tenn. **62** 36 18N 88 19W
Paris, Tex. **65** 33 40N 95 33W
Parish **53** 43 25N 76 8W
Parishville **53** 44 38N 74 49W
Park **38** 39 7N 100 22W
Park → **55** 48 28N 97 9W
Park City, Kans. **38** 37 48N 97 20W
Park City, Ky. **62** 37 6N 86 3W
Park City, Mont. **47** 45 38N 108 55W
Park City, Utah **66** 40 39N 111 30W
Park County ◇, Colo. **30** 39 0N 105 45W
Park County ◇, Mont. **47** 45 30N 110 30W
Park County ◇, Wyo. **70** 44 30N 109 30W
Park Falls **69** 45 56N 90 27W
Park Forest **35** 41 29N 87 40W
Park Range **30** 40 0N 106 30W
Park Rapids **44** 46 55N 95 4W
Park Ridge, Ill. **35** 42 2N 87 51W
Park Ridge, N.J. **51** 41 2N 74 2W
Park River **55** 48 24N 97 45W
Park Valley **66** 41 49N 113 20W
Parkdale, Ark. **27** 33 7N 91 33W
Parkdale, Colo. **30** 38 29N 105 23W
Parkdale, Oreg. **58** 45 31N 121 36W
Parke County ◇ **36** 39 45N 87 10W
Parker, Ariz. **26** 34 9N 114 17W
Parker, Colo. **30** 39 31N 104 46W
Parker, Kans. **38** 38 18N 95 0W
Parker, S. Dak. **61** 43 24N 97 8W
Parker, Wash. **67** 46 30N 120 28W
Parker City **36** 40 11N 85 12W
Parker County ◇ **65** 32 46N 97 48W
Parker Dam **26** 34 18N 114 8W
Parkers Prairie **44** 46 9N 95 20W
Parkersburg, Ill. **35** 38 36N 88 3W
Parkersburg, Iowa **37** 42 35N 92 47W
Parkersburg, W. Va. **68** 39 16N 81 34W
Parkerville **38** 38 46N 96 40W
Parkesburg **59** 39 58N 75 55W
Parkin **27** 35 16N 90 34W
Parkland **67** 47 9N 122 26W
Parkrose **58** 45 34N 122 33W
Parks, Ark. **27** 34 48N 93 58W
Parks, Nebr. **48** 40 3N 101 44W
Parksley **68** 37 47N 75 39W
Parkston **61** 43 24N 97 59W
Parksville **60** 33 47N 82 13W
Parkton **41** 39 40N 76 40W
Parkville **41** 39 23N 76 33W
Parle, L. qui **44** 45 1N 95 52W
Parlier **29** 36 37N 119 32W
Parma, Idaho **34** 43 47N 116 57W
Parma, Mich. **43** 42 16N 84 36W
Parma, Mo. **46** 36 37N 89 48W
Parma, Ohio **56** 41 23N 81 43W
Parmelee **61** 43 19N 101 2W
Parmer County ◇ **64** 34 38N 102 45W
Parnell, Iowa **37** 41 35N 92 0W
Parnell, Mo. **46** 40 26N 94 37W
Parowan **66** 37 51N 112 50W
Parramore I. **68** 37 32N 75 39W
Parris I. **60** 32 20N 80 41W
Parrish, Ala. **24** 33 44N 87 17W
Parrish, Fla. **31** 27 35N 82 26W
Parrott **32** 31 54N 84 31W
Parshall, Colo. **30** 40 3N 106 11W
Parshall, N. Dak. **55** 47 57N 102 8W
Parsippany **51** 40 52N 74 26W
Parsons, Kans. **38** 37 20N 95 16W
Parsons, Tenn. **62** 35 39N 88 8W
Parsons, W. Va. **68** 39 6N 79 41W
Parsonsburg **41** 38 22N 75 28W
Partridge **38** 37 58N 98 5W
Pasadena, Calif. **29** 34 9N 118 9W
Pasadena, Tex. **65** 29 43N 95 13W
Pascagoula **45** 30 21N 88 33W
Pascagoula → **45** 30 23N 88 37W
Pasco **67** 46 14N 119 6W
Pasco County ◇ **31** 28 20N 82 30W
Pascoag **42** 41 57N 71 42W
Paskenta **28** 39 53N 122 33W
Paso Robles **29** 35 38N 120 41W
Pasquotank County ◇ **54** 36 15N 76 10W
Pass Christian **45** 30 19N 89 15W
Passaconaway **50** 43 59N 71 22W
Passadumkeag **40** 45 11N 68 37W
Passaic, Mo. **46** 38 19N 94 21W
Passaic, N.J. **51** 40 51N 74 7W
Passaic County ◇ **51** 41 0N 74 20W
Passumpsic → **50** 44 18N 72 3W
Pastol B. **25** 63 7N 163 15W
Pastora Peak **26** 36 47N 109 10W
Pastura **52** 34 47N 104 57W
Pat Mayse L. **65** 33 51N 95 33W
Patagonia **26** 31 33N 110 45W
Patapsco **41** 39 32N 76 54W
Patapsco → **41** 39 11N 76 28W
Patch Grove **69** 42 56N 90 58W
Patchogue **53** 40 46N 73 1W
Pateros **67** 48 3N 119 54W
Paterson, N.J. **51** 40 55N 74 11W
Paterson, Wash. **67** 45 56N 119 36W
Patesville **62** 37 47N 86 43W
Pathfinder Reservoir **70** 42 28N 106 51W
Pathfork **63** 36 45N 83 28W
Patillas **71** 18 1N 66 1W
Patillas, Puerto **71** 17 57N 66 0W
Patman, L. **65** 33 19N 94 10W
Patoka **35** 38 45N 89 6W
Patoka L. **36** 38 20N 86 40W
Paton **37** 42 10N 94 16W
Patricia **64** 32 33N 102 1W
Patrick **60** 34 34N 80 3W
Patrick County ◇ **68** 36 55N 80 10W
Patsaliga → **24** 31 22N 86 31W
Patten **40** 46 0N 68 38W
Patterson, Calif. **28** 37 28N 121 8W
Patterson, Ga. **32** 31 23N 82 8W
Patterson, Idaho **34** 44 32N 113 43W
Patterson, La. **39** 29 42N 91 18W
Patterson, Mo. **46** 37 11N 90 33W
Patterson, Pt. **43** 45 58N 85 39W
Pattison **45** 31 53N 90 53W
Patton **59** 40 38N 78 39W
Pattonsburg **46** 40 3N 94 8W
Patuxent → **41** 38 18N 76 25W
Paul **34** 42 36N 113 47W
Paul Spur **26** 31 22N 109 44W
Paulden **26** 34 53N 112 28W
Paulding, Miss. **45** 32 2N 89 2W
Paulding, Ohio **56** 41 8N 84 35W
Paulding County ◇, Ga. **32** 34 0N 84 50W
Paulding County ◇, Ohio **56** 41 8N 84 35W
Paulina **58** 44 8N 119 58W
Paulina Marsh **58** 43 15N 121 0W
Paulina Pk. **58** 43 41N 121 15W
Paulins Kill → **51** 40 55N 75 5W
Paullina **37** 42 59N 95 41W
Pauls Valley **57** 34 44N 97 13W
Paulsboro **51** 39 50N 75 15W
Pauwela **33** 20 56N 156 19W
Pavant Range **66** 39 10N 112 5W
Pavillion **70** 43 15N 108 42W
Pavo **32** 30 58N 83 45W
Paw Creek **54** 35 17N 80 56W
Paw Paw, Mich. **43** 42 13N 85 53W
Paw Paw, W. Va. **68** 39 32N 78 28W
Paw Paw Lake **43** 42 13N 86 16W
Pawcatuck **42** 41 22N 71 52W
Pawhuska **57** 36 40N 96 20W
Pawlet **50** 43 20N 73 12W
Pawling **53** 41 34N 73 36W
Pawnee, Ill. **35** 39 36N 89 35W
Pawnee, Okla. **57** 36 20N 96 48W
Pawnee → **38** 38 10N 99 6W
Pawnee City **48** 40 7N 96 9W
Pawnee County ◇, Kans. **38** 38 10N 99 15W

Pawnee County ◇, Nebr. **48** 40 10N 96 20W
Pawnee County ◇, Okla. **57** 36 20N 96 50W
Pawnee Cr. → **30** 40 34N 103 14W
Pawnee National Grassland **30** 40 40N 104 20W
Pawnee Rock **38** 38 16N 99 1W
Pawpaw **35** 41 41N 88 59W
Pawtucket **42** 41 53N 71 23W
Paxico **38** 39 4N 96 10W
Paxson **25** 63 2N 145 30W
Paxton, Ill. **35** 40 27N 88 6W
Paxton, Mass. **42** 42 19N 71 56W
Paxton, Nebr. **48** 41 7N 101 21W
Payette **34** 44 5N 116 56W
Payette → **34** 44 5N 116 57W
Payette County ◇ . . **34** 44 0N 116 55W
Payette L. **34** 44 55N 116 7W
Payette National Forest **34** 45 10N 115 30W
Payne **56** 41 5N 84 44W
Payne County ◇ . . . **57** 36 5N 97 0W
Paynesville **44** 45 23N 94 43W
Payson, Ariz. **26** 34 14N 111 20W
Payson, Ill. **35** 39 49N 91 15W
Payson, Utah **66** 40 3N 111 44W
Paytes **68** 38 13N 77 49W
Pe Ell **67** 46 34N 123 18W
Pea → **31** 31 1N 85 51W
Pea Ridge **27** 36 27N 94 7W
Peabody, Kans. **38** 38 10N 97 7W
Peabody, Mass. **42** 42 31N 70 56W
Peace → **31** 26 56N 82 6W
Peace Dale **42** 41 27N 71 30W
Peach County ◇ **32** 32 30N 83 50W
Peach Creek **68** 37 53N 81 59W
Peach Orchard **27** 36 17N 90 40W
Peach Springs **26** 35 32N 113 25W
Peachtree City **32** 33 25N 84 35W
Peale, Mt. **66** 38 26N 109 14W
Pearblossom **29** 34 30N 117 55W
Pearce **26** 31 54N 109 49W
Pearisburg **68** 37 20N 80 44W
Pearl, Ill. **35** 39 28N 90 38W
Pearl, Miss. **45** 32 18N 90 12W
Pearl → **45** 30 11N 89 32W
Pearl and Hermes Reef **33** 27 55N 175 45W
Pearl City, Hawaii . . **33** 21 24N 157 59W
Pearl City, Ill. **35** 42 16N 89 50W
Pearl Harbor **33** 21 21N 157 57W
Pearl River, La. **39** 30 23N 89 45W
Pearl River, N.Y. . . **53** 41 4N 74 2W
Pearl River County ◇ **45** 30 40N 89 38W
Pearland **65** 29 34N 95 17W
Pearsall **65** 28 54N 99 6W
Pearson **32** 31 18N 82 51W
Pease **44** 45 42N 93 39W
Pease → **65** 34 12N 99 2W
Pebble Beach **28** 36 34N 121 57W
Pecatonica **35** 42 19N 89 22W
Pecatonica → **35** 42 26N 89 12W
Peck **43** 43 16N 82 49W
Peckerwood L. **27** 34 40N 91 30W
Pecos, N. Mex. **52** 35 35N 105 41W
Pecos, Tex. **64** 31 26N 103 30W
Pecos → **64** 29 42N 101 22W
Pecos County ◇ **64** 30 53N 102 53W
Pecos Plains **52** 33 15N 104 10W
Peculiar **46** 38 43N 94 28W
Pedernales → **65** 30 26N 98 4W
Pedro Bay **25** 59 47N 154 7W
Pedro Miguel **71** 9 2N 79 37W
Pedro Miguel Locks **71** 9 1N 79 36W
Pee Dee → **60** 33 22N 79 16W
Peebles **56** 38 57N 83 24W
Peekskill **53** 41 17N 73 55W
Peerless **47** 48 47N 105 50W
Peetz **30** 40 58N 103 7W
Peever **61** 45 33N 96 57W
Pegram **62** 36 6N 87 3W
Pekin, Ill. **35** 40 35N 89 40W
Pekin, Ind. **36** 38 30N 86 0W
Pekin, N. Dak. **55** 47 48N 98 20W
Pelahatchie **45** 32 19N 89 48W
Pelham, Ga. **32** 31 8N 84 9W
Pelham, Mass. **42** 42 24N 72 24W
Pelham, N.C. **54** 36 31N 79 28W
Pelican, Alaska **25** 57 58N 136 14W
Pelican, La. **39** 31 53N 93 35W
Pelican L. **44** 48 4N 92 55W
Pelican Rapids **44** 46 34N 96 5W
Pelion **60** 33 46N 81 15W
Pell City **24** 33 35N 86 17W
Pella **37** 41 25N 92 55W
Pellston **43** 45 33N 84 47W
Pellville **62** 37 45N 86 49W
Peloncillo Mts. **26** 32 20N 109 0W
Pemadumcook L. . . . **40** 45 42N 68 57W
Pemberton, Minn. . . **44** 44 1N 93 47W
Pemberton, N.J. . . . **51** 39 58N 74 41W
Pemberville **56** 41 25N 83 28W
Pembina **55** 48 58N 97 15W
Pembina → **55** 48 58N 97 14W
Pembina County ◇ . **55** 48 48N 97 37W
Pembine **69** 45 38N 87 59W
Pembroke, Ga. **32** 32 8N 81 37W
Pembroke, Ky. **62** 36 47N 87 21W
Pembroke, Mass. . . . **42** 42 5N 70 48W
Pembroke, N.C. **54** 34 41N 79 12W
Pembroke Pines **31** 26 0N 80 14W
Pemigewasset → . . . **50** 43 26N 71 40W
Pemiscot County ◇ . **46** 36 10N 89 50W
Pen Argyl **59** 40 52N 75 16W
Penacook **50** 43 15N 71 40W
Penalosa **38** 37 43N 98 19W
Penasco **52** 36 10N 105 41W
Peñasco → **52** 32 40N 104 25W
Pend Oreille → **67** 49 4N 117 37W
Pend Oreille County ◇ **67** 48 30N 117 10W
Pend Oreille L. **34** 48 10N 116 21W
Pender **48** 42 7N 96 43W
Pender County ◇ . . . **54** 34 30N 78 0W
Pendergrass **32** 34 10N 83 41W
Pendleton, Ind. **36** 40 0N 85 45W
Pendleton, Oreg. . . . **58** 45 40N 118 47W
Pendleton, S.C. **60** 34 39N 82 47W
Pendleton County ◇, Ky. . . . **63** 38 40N 84 20W
Pendleton County ◇, W. Va. **68** 38 47N 79 17W
Pendroy **47** 48 4N 112 18W
Penelope **65** 31 52N 96 56W
Penfield **59** 41 13N 78 35W
Penn Hills **59** 40 28N 79 52W
Penn Yan **53** 42 40N 77 3W
Pennell, Mt. **66** 37 58N 110 47W
Pennington, Ala. . . . **24** 32 13N 88 3W
Pennington, N.J. . . . **51** 40 19N 74 48W
Pennington County ◇, Minn. . **44** 48 5N 96 0W
Pennington County ◇, S. Dak. **61** 44 0N 103 0W
Pennington Gap **68** 36 46N 83 2W
Pennock **44** 45 9N 95 10W
Penns Grove **51** 39 44N 75 28W
Pennsauken **51** 39 58N 75 3W
Pennsboro **68** 39 17N 80 58W
Pennsburg **59** 40 23N 75 29W
Pennsville **51** 39 39N 75 31W
Pennsylvania □ **59** 40 45N 77 30W
Pennville **36** 40 30N 85 9W
Penobscot → **40** 44 30N 68 48W
Penobscot B. **40** 44 35N 68 50W
Penobscot County ◇ **40** 45 0N 69 0W
Pensacola, Fla. **31** 30 25N 87 13W
Pensacola, Okla. . . . **57** 36 28N 95 7W
Pentwater **43** 43 47N 86 26W
Penuelas **71** 18 4N 66 43W
Penwell **64** 31 45N 102 36W
Peoria, Ariz. **26** 33 35N 112 14W
Peoria, Ill. **35** 40 42N 89 36W
Peoria, Okla. **57** 36 54N 94 41W
Peoria County ◇ . . . **35** 40 45N 89 45W
Peoria Heights **35** 40 45N 89 35W
Peotone **35** 41 20N 87 48W
Pep **52** 33 50N 103 20W
Pepacton Reservoir . **53** 42 5N 74 58W
Pepeekeo **33** 19 51N 155 6W
Pepin **69** 44 27N 92 9W
Pepin County ◇ **69** 44 30N 92 10W
Pepperell **42** 42 40N 71 35W
Pequest → **51** 40 50N 75 5W
Pequop Mts. **49** 40 45N 114 40W
Pequot Lakes **44** 46 36N 94 19W
Peralta **52** 34 50N 106 41W
Perche Cr. → **46** 38 49N 92 24W
Percy **45** 33 7N 90 53W
Perdido **24** 31 0N 87 38W
Perdido → **24** 30 27N 87 23W
Perdido B. **24** 30 20N 87 30W
Perham **44** 46 36N 95 34W
Peridot **26** 33 18N 110 28W
Perkasie **59** 40 22N 75 18W
Perkins **57** 35 58N 97 2W
Perkins County ◇, Nebr. **48** 40 45N 101 45W
Perkins County ◇, S. Dak. **61** 45 30N 102 30W
Perkinston **45** 30 47N 89 8W
Perley **44** 47 11N 96 48W
Perma **47** 47 22N 114 35W
Pernell **57** 34 34N 97 31W
Perquimans County ◇ **54** 36 10N 76 30W
Perrin **65** 33 2N 98 4W
Perrine **31** 25 36N 80 21W
Perris **29** 33 47N 117 14W
Perro, L. del **52** 34 41N 105 58W
Perry, Ark. **27** 35 3N 92 48W
Perry, Fla. **31** 30 7N 83 35W
Perry, Ga. **32** 32 28N 83 44W
Perry, Ill. **35** 39 47N 90 45W
Perry, Iowa **37** 41 51N 94 6W
Perry, Kans. **38** 39 5N 95 24W
Perry, Maine **40** 44 58N 67 5W
Perry, Mich. **43** 42 50N 84 13W
Perry, Mo. **46** 39 26N 91 40W
Perry, N.Y. **53** 42 43N 78 0W
Perry, Okla. **57** 36 17N 97 14W
Perry, S.C. **60** 33 38N 81 19W
Perry, Utah **66** 41 28N 112 2W
Perry County ◇, Ala. **24** 32 38N 87 19W
Perry County ◇, Ark. **27** 35 0N 92 48W
Perry County ◇, Ill. **35** 38 5N 89 20W
Perry County ◇, Ind. **36** 38 5N 86 40W
Perry County ◇, Ky. **63** 37 15N 83 15W
Perry County ◇, Miss. **45** 31 12N 89 2W
Perry County ◇, Mo. **46** 37 45N 89 50W
Perry County ◇, Ohio **56** 39 43N 82 13W
Perry County ◇, Pa. **59** 40 35N 77 5W
Perry County ◇, Tenn. **62** 35 39N 87 50W
Perry Hall **41** 39 25N 76 28W
Perry Lake **38** 39 7N 95 26W
Perrydale **58** 45 3N 123 16W
Perrysburg **56** 41 34N 83 38W
Perrysville **56** 40 40N 82 19W
Perryton **64** 36 24N 100 48W
Perryville, Alaska . . **25** 55 55N 159 9W
Perryville, Ark. **27** 35 0N 92 48W
Perryville, Ky. **63** 37 39N 84 57W
Perryville, Md. **41** 39 34N 76 4W
Perryville, Mo. **46** 37 43N 89 52W
Pershing County ◇ . **49** 40 20N 118 10W
Persia **37** 41 35N 95 33W
Person County ◇ . . . **54** 36 15N 79 0W
Perth, Kans. **38** 37 11N 97 31W
Perth, N. Dak. **55** 48 43N 99 28W
Perth Amboy **51** 40 31N 74 16W
Peru, Ill. **35** 41 20N 89 8W
Peru, Ind. **36** 40 45N 86 4W
Peru, Kans. **38** 37 5N 96 6W
Peru, N.Y. **53** 44 35N 73 32W
Peru, Nebr. **48** 40 29N 95 44W
Peru, Vt. **50** 43 14N 72 54W
Peshtigo → **69** 44 45N 87 40W
Pesotum **35** 39 55N 88 16W
Petal **45** 31 21N 89 16W
Petaluma **28** 38 14N 122 39W
Petenwell L. **69** 44 4N 90 1W
Peterborough **50** 42 53N 71 57W
Petersburg, Alaska . **25** 56 48N 132 58W
Petersburg, Ill. **35** 40 1N 89 51W
Petersburg, Ind. **36** 38 30N 87 17W
Petersburg, Mich. . . **43** 41 54N 83 43W
Petersburg, N. Dak. **55** 48 0N 98 0W
Petersburg, N.J. **51** 39 15N 74 43W
Petersburg, Nebr. . . **48** 41 51N 98 5W
Petersburg, Ohio . . . **56** 40 55N 80 32W
Petersburg, Pa. **59** 40 34N 78 3W
Petersburg, Tenn. . . **62** 35 19N 86 38W
Petersburg, Tex. . . . **64** 33 52N 101 36W
Petersburg, Va. **68** 37 14N 77 24W
Petersburg, W. Va. . **68** 39 1N 79 5W
Petersham **42** 42 29N 72 11W
Peterson, Iowa **37** 42 55N 95 21W
Peterson, Minn. **44** 43 47N 91 50W
Peterstown **68** 37 24N 80 48W
Petersville **63** 38 27N 83 30W
Petit Bois I. **45** 30 12N 88 26W
Petit Manan Pt. **40** 44 24N 67 54W
Petoskey **43** 45 22N 84 57W
Petrey **24** 31 51N 86 13W
Petrified Forest National Park **26** 35 0N 109 30W
Petroleum **68** 39 11N 81 16W
Petroleum County ◇ **47** 47 7N 108 25W
Petrolia, Kans. **38** 37 45N 95 29W
Petrolia, Tex. **65** 34 1N 98 14W
Petros **63** 36 6N 84 27W
Pettibone **55** 47 7N 99 31W
Pettis County ◇ **46** 38 40N 93 15W
Pettus **65** 28 37N 97 48W
Pfeifer **38** 38 43N 99 10W
Pharr **64** 26 12N 98 11W
Pheba **45** 33 35N 88 57W
Phelps, Ky. **63** 37 32N 82 9W
Phelps, N.Y. **53** 42 58N 77 3W
Phelps, Wis. **69** 46 4N 89 5W
Phelps County ◇, Mo. **46** 37 55N 91 45W
Phelps County ◇, Nebr. **48** 40 30N 99 30W
Phelps L. **54** 35 46N 76 27W
Phenix **68** 37 5N 78 45W
Phenix City **24** 32 28N 85 0W
Phil Campbell **24** 34 21N 87 42W
Philadelphia, Miss. . **45** 32 46N 89 7W
Philadelphia, N.Y. . . **53** 44 9N 75 43W
Philadelphia, Pa. . . . **59** 39 57N 75 10W
Philadelphia, Tenn. . **63** 35 41N 84 24W
Philadelphia County ◇ **59** 39 57N 75 10W
Philip **61** 44 2N 101 40W
Philip Smith Mts. . . . **25** 68 0N 148 0W
Philippi **68** 39 9N 80 3W
Philipsburg, Mont. . . **47** 46 20N 113 18W
Philipsburg, Pa. **59** 40 54N 78 13W
Phillips, Maine **40** 44 49N 70 21W
Phillips, Nebr. **48** 40 54N 98 13W
Phillips, Okla. **57** 34 30N 96 12W
Phillips, Tex. **64** 35 42N 101 22W
Phillips, Wis. **69** 45 42N 90 24W
Phillips County ◇, Ark. **27** 34 19N 90 51W
Phillips County ◇, Colo. **30** 40 40N 102 20W
Phillips County ◇, Kans. **38** 39 45N 99 15W
Phillips County ◇, Mont. **47** 48 12N 108 0W
Phillipsburg, Ga. . . . **32** 31 25N 83 30W
Phillipsburg, Kans. . **38** 39 45N 99 19W
Phillipsburg, Mo. . . . **46** 37 33N 92 47W
Phillipsburg, N.J. . . . **51** 40 42N 75 12W
Phillipsburg, Ohio . . **56** 39 54N 84 24W
Philmont **53** 42 15N 73 39W
Philo, Calif. **28** 39 4N 123 26W
Philo, Ill. **35** 40 1N 88 9W
Philomath, Ga. **32** 33 44N 82 59W
Philomath, Oreg. . . . **58** 44 32N 123 22W
Philpott L. **68** 36 47N 80 2W
Phippsburg **30** 40 14N 106 57W
Phoenix, Ariz. **26** 33 27N 112 4W
Phoenix, La. **39** 29 39N 89 56W
Phoenix, N.Y. **53** 43 14N 76 18W
Phoenix, Oreg. **58** 42 16N 122 49W
Phoenixville **59** 40 8N 75 31W
Piatt County ◇ **35** 40 0N 88 35W
Picacho, Ariz. **26** 32 43N 111 30W
Picacho, N. Mex. . . . **52** 33 21N 105 9W
Picayune **45** 30 32N 89 41W
Piceance Cr. → **30** 40 5N 108 14W
Picher **57** 36 59N 94 50W
Pickaway County ◇ . **56** 39 43N 82 59W
Pickens, Ark. **27** 33 51N 91 29W
Pickens, Miss. **45** 32 53N 89 58W
Pickens, Okla. **57** 34 23N 95 2W
Pickens, S.C. **60** 34 53N 82 42W
Pickens, W. Va. **68** 38 39N 80 13W
Pickens County ◇, Ala. **24** 33 16N 88 6W
Pickens County ◇, Ga. **32** 34 30N 84 25W
Pickens County ◇, S.C. **60** 34 50N 82 45W
Pickering **46** 40 27N 94 49W
Pickett County ◇ . . . **63** 36 34N 85 8W
Pickford **43** 46 10N 84 22W
Pickrell **48** 40 23N 96 44W
Pickstown **61** 43 4N 98 32W
Pickwick L. **24** 35 4N 88 15W
Pictured Rocks Nat. Lakeshore **43** 46 30N 86 30W
Pie Town **52** 34 18N 108 9W
Piedmont, Ala. **24** 33 55N 85 37W
Piedmont, Kans. . . . **38** 37 37N 96 22W
Piedmont, Mo. **46** 37 9N 90 42W
Piedmont, Okla. **57** 35 39N 97 44W
Piedmont, S.C. **60** 34 42N 82 28W
Piedmont, S. Dak. . . **61** 44 14N 103 24W
Piedmont L. **56** 40 11N 81 13W
Pierce, Colo. **30** 40 38N 104 45W
Pierce, Idaho **34** 46 30N 115 48W
Pierce, Nebr. **48** 42 12N 97 32W
Pierce City **46** 36 57N 94 0W
Pierce County ◇, Ga. **32** 31 20N 82 10W
Pierce County ◇, N. Dak. **55** 48 0N 100 0W
Pierce County ◇, Nebr. **48** 42 20N 97 40W
Pierce County ◇, Wash. **67** 47 0N 122 0W
Pierce County ◇, Wis. **69** 44 45N 92 25W
Pierceton **36** 41 12N 85 42W
Pierceville **38** 37 53N 100 40W
Piercy **28** 39 59N 123 48W
Pierpont **61** 45 30N 97 50W
Pierre **61** 44 22N 100 21W
Pierron **35** 38 47N 89 36W
Pierson, Fla. **31** 29 14N 81 28W
Pierson, Iowa **37** 42 33N 95 52W
Pierz **44** 45 59N 94 6W
Pigeon, La. **39** 30 4N 91 17W
Pigeon, Mich. **43** 43 50N 83 16W
Pigeon →, Ind. **36** 41 47N 85 49W
Pigeon →, Tenn. . . **63** 36 2N 83 17W
Pigeon Cove **42** 42 41N 70 38W
Pigeon Cr. → **24** 31 20N 86 42W
Pigeon Falls **69** 44 26N 91 13W
Pigeon Forge **63** 35 48N 83 33W
Pigg → **68** 37 0N 79 29W

Piggott **27** 36 23N 90 11W
Pike **68** 39 17N 81 5W
Pike County ◇, Ala. **24** 31 48N 85 58W
Pike County ◇, Ark. **27** 34 14N 93 45W
Pike County ◇, Ga. **32** 33 5N 84 20W
Pike County ◇, Ill. **35** 39 35N 90 50W
Pike County ◇, Ind. **36** 38 25N 87 10W
Pike County ◇, Ky. **63** 37 30N 82 25W
Pike County ◇, Miss. **45** 31 15N 90 27W
Pike County ◇, Mo. **46** 39 20N 91 10W
Pike County ◇, Ohio **56** 39 4N 83 1W
Pike County ◇, Pa. **59** 41 20N 75 0W
Pike National Forest **30** 39 15N 105 20W
Pike Road **24** 32 17N 86 6W
Pikes Peak **30** 38 50N 105 3W
Pikesville **41** 39 23N 76 43W
Piketon **56** 39 4N 83 1W
Pikeville, Ky. **63** 37 29N 82 31W
Pikeville, N.C. **54** 35 30N 77 59W
Pikeville, Tenn. **63** 35 36N 85 11W
Pilger **48** 42 0N 97 3W
Pillager **44** 46 20N 94 28W
Pillsbury **55** 47 13N 97 48W
Pillsbury, L. **28** 39 25N 122 57W
Pillsbury Sd. **71** 18 20N 64 50W
Pilot Grove **46** 38 53N 92 55W
Pilot Knob, Ark. **27** 35 42N 93 57W
Pilot Knob, Ky. **62** 36 50N 86 41W
Pilot Knob, Mo. **46** 37 40N 90 40W
Pilot Mountain **54** 36 23N 80 28W
Pilot Pk. **70** 44 58N 109 53W
Pilot Point, Alaska **25** 57 34N 157 35W
Pilot Point, Tex. **65** 33 24N 96 58W
Pilot Rock **58** 45 29N 118 50W
Pilot Station **25** 61 56N 162 53W
Pima **26** 32 54N 109 50W
Pima County ◇ **26** 32 0N 112 0W
Pinal County ◇ **26** 33 0N 111 15W
Pinas, Mt. **29** 34 50N 119 9W
Pinckard **24** 31 19N 85 33W
Pinckneyville, Ill. **35** 38 5N 89 23W
Pinckneyville, Miss. **45** 31 1N 91 29W
Pinconning **43** 43 51N 83 58W
Pindall **27** 36 4N 92 53W
Pine, Ariz. **26** 34 23N 111 27W
Pine, Oreg. **58** 44 52N 117 5W
Pine → **43** 43 35N 84 8W
Pine Apple **24** 31 52N 87 0W
Pine Barrens **51** 39 30N 74 30W
Pine Bluff **27** 34 13N 92 1W
Pine Bluffs **70** 41 11N 104 4W
Pine Castle **31** 28 28N 81 22W
Pine City, Minn. **44** 45 50N 92 59W
Pine City, Wash. **67** 47 12N 117 31W
Pine County ◇ **44** 46 5N 92 50W
Pine Cr. →, Nev. **49** 40 36N 116 12W
Pine Cr. →, Pa. **59** 41 10N 77 16W
Pine Creek L. **57** 34 7N 95 5W
Pine Flat L. **29** 36 50N 119 20W
Pine Forest Range **49** 41 45N 118 50W
Pine Grove, La. **39** 30 43N 90 45W
Pine Grove, Pa. **59** 40 33N 76 23W
Pine Grove, W. Va. **68** 39 34N 80 41W
Pine Hill, Fla. **31** 28 32N 81 28W
Pine Hill, N.J. **51** 39 47N 74 59W
Pine Is. **31** 26 36N 82 7W
Pine Island **44** 44 12N 92 39W
Pine Knot **63** 36 39N 84 26W
Pine Level **24** 32 4N 86 4W
Pine Log **32** 34 21N 84 44W
Pine Mountain **32** 32 52N 84 51W
Pine Mt., Ga. **32** 34 56N 83 12W
Pine Mt., Ky. **63** 37 0N 83 45W
Pine Mt., Wyo. **70** 41 2N 109 1W
Pine Prairie **39** 30 47N 92 25W
Pine Ridge, S. Dak. **61** 42 30N 102 40W
Pine Ridge, S. Dak. **61** 43 2N 102 33W
Pine Ridge Indian Reservation **61** 43 30N 102 0W
Pine River **44** 46 43N 94 24W
Pine Springs **64** 31 54N 104 49W
Pine Valley **66** 38 20N 113 45W
Pinebluff **54** 35 6N 79 28W
Pinedale, Calif. **29** 36 50N 119 48W
Pinedale, Wyo. **70** 42 52N 109 52W
Pinehurst, Ga. **32** 32 12N 83 46W
Pinehurst, N.C. **54** 35 12N 79 28W
Pineland **65** 31 15N 93 58W
Pinellas County ◇ **31** 28 0N 82 45W
Pinellas Park **31** 27 50N 82 43W
Pines, Lake O The **65** 32 45N 94 30W
Pinetop **26** 34 8N 109 56W
Pinetops **54** 35 46N 77 38W
Pinetown **54** 35 37N 76 52W
Pinetta **31** 30 36N 83 21W
Pineview **32** 32 7N 83 30W
Pineville, Iowa **37** 36 36N 94 23W
Pineville, Ky. **63** 36 46N 83 42W
Pineville, La. **39** 31 19N 92 26W
Pineville, N.C. **54** 35 5N 80 53W
Pineville, S.C. **60** 33 26N 80 1W
Pineville, W. Va. **68** 37 35N 81 32W
Pinewood **60** 33 44N 80 27W
Piney → **46** 37 54N 92 4W
Piney Buttes **47** 47 35N 106 45W
Piney Grove **41** 39 42N 78 24W
Piney Point **41** 38 9N 76 31W
Piney Woods **45** 32 2N 90 0W
Pingree **55** 47 10N 98 55W
Pink **57** 35 18N 97 6W
Pink Cliffs **66** 37 25N 112 20W
Pink Hill **54** 35 3N 77 45W
Pinnacle **54** 36 20N 80 26W
Pinnacle Buttes **70** 43 44N 110 57W
Pinnacle Peak **70** 43 23N 110 32W
Pinnacles National Monument **29** 36 25N 121 12W
Pinola **45** 31 53N 89 58W
Pinole **28** 38 0N 122 17W
Pinon **26** 36 6N 110 14W
Pinson, Ala. **24** 33 41N 86 41W
Pinson, Tenn. **62** 35 29N 88 43W
Pinta, Sierra **26** 32 15N 113 30W
Pintlalla Cr. → **24** 32 21N 86 30W
Pioche **49** 37 56N 114 27W
Pioneer, Iowa **37** 42 39N 94 23W
Pioneer, La. **39** 32 44N 91 26W
Pioneer, Ohio **56** 41 41N 84 33W
Pioneer, Tenn. **63** 36 25N 84 19W
Pipe Creek **65** 29 43N 98 56W
Pipe Spring National Monument **26** 36 50N 112 55W
Pipestone **44** 44 0N 96 19W
Pipestone County ◇ **44** 44 0N 96 15W
Piqua, Kans. **38** 37 56N 95 32W
Piqua, Ohio **56** 40 9N 84 15W
Pirata, Monte **71** 18 6N 65 33W
Piscataquis → **40** 45 15N 68 58W
Piscataquis County ◇ **40** 46 0N 69 0W
Piscataway, Md. **41** 38 42N 76 58W
Piscataway, N.J. **51** 40 34N 74 27W
Pisek **55** 48 19N 97 43W
Pisgah, Iowa **37** 41 50N 95 55W
Pisgah, Md. **41** 38 32N 77 8W
Pisgah Forest **54** 35 15N 82 44W
Pisgah National Forest **54** 35 50N 82 0W
Pisinimo **26** 32 2N 112 19W
Pismo Beach **29** 35 9N 120 38W
Pistol River **58** 42 17N 124 24W
Pit → **28** 40 47N 122 6W
Pitkin, Colo. **30** 38 37N 106 31W
Pitkin, La. **39** 30 56N 92 56W
Pitkin County ◇ **30** 39 10N 106 50W
Pitman **51** 39 44N 75 8W
Pitt County ◇ **54** 35 30N 77 20W
Pittsboro, Ind. **36** 39 52N 86 28W
Pittsboro, Miss. **45** 33 56N 89 20W
Pittsboro, N.C. **54** 35 43N 79 11W
Pittsburg, Calif. **28** 38 2N 121 53W
Pittsburg, Ill. **35** 37 47N 88 51W
Pittsburg, Kans. **38** 37 25N 94 42W
Pittsburg, N.H. **50** 45 3N 71 24W
Pittsburg, Okla. **57** 34 43N 95 52W
Pittsburg, Tex. **65** 33 0N 94 59W
Pittsburg County ◇ **57** 34 50N 95 50W
Pittsburgh **59** 40 26N 80 1W
Pittsfield, Ill. **35** 39 36N 90 49W
Pittsfield, Maine **40** 44 47N 69 23W
Pittsfield, Mass. **42** 42 27N 73 15W
Pittsfield, N.H. **50** 43 18N 71 20W
Pittsfield, Vt. **50** 43 46N 72 48W
Pittsford **50** 43 42N 73 3W
Pittsgrove **51** 39 37N 75 14W
Pittston **59** 41 19N 75 47W
Pittstown **51** 40 36N 74 56W
Pittsview **24** 32 11N 85 10W
Pittsville, Md. **41** 38 24N 75 52W
Pittsville, Mo. **46** 38 50N 93 0W
Pittsville, Wis. **69** 44 27N 90 8W
Pittsylvania County ◇ **68** 36 55N 79 15W
Piute County ◇ **66** 38 20N 112 10W
Pixley **29** 35 58N 119 18W
Placedo **65** 28 41N 96 50W
Placer County ◇ **28** 39 10N 120 30W
Placerville, Calif. **28** 38 44N 120 48W
Placerville, Colo. **30** 38 1N 108 3W
Placerville, Idaho **34** 43 57N 115 57W
Placid, L. **31** 27 15N 81 22W
Placitas **52** 35 18N 106 25W
Plain City **66** 41 18N 112 6W
Plain Dealing **39** 32 54N 93 42W
Plainfield, Conn. **42** 41 41N 71 56W
Plainfield, Ind. **36** 39 42N 86 24W
Plainfield, Iowa **37** 42 51N 92 32W
Plainfield, Mass. **42** 42 0N 72 0W
Plainfield, N.H. **50** 43 32N 72 21W
Plainfield, N.J. **51** 40 37N 74 25W
Plainfield, Vt. **50** 44 17N 72 26W
Plainfield, Wis. **69** 44 13N 89 30W
Plainfield Heights **43** 43 1N 85 37W
Plains, Ga. **32** 32 2N 84 24W
Plains, Kans. **38** 37 16N 100 35W
Plains, Mont. **47** 47 28N 114 53W
Plains, Pa. **59** 41 15N 75 37W
Plains, Tex. **64** 33 11N 102 50W
Plainview, Ark. **27** 35 2N 93 18W
Plainview, Minn. **44** 44 10N 92 10W
Plainview, N.Y. **53** 40 46N 73 29W
Plainview, Nebr. **48** 42 21N 97 47W
Plainview, Tex. **64** 34 11N 101 43W
Plainville, Conn. **42** 41 41N 72 51W
Plainville, Ga. **32** 34 24N 85 2W
Plainville, Ind. **36** 38 48N 87 9W
Plainville, Kans. **38** 39 14N 99 18W
Plainwell **43** 42 27N 85 38W
Plaistow **50** 42 50N 71 6W
Planada **28** 37 16N 120 19W
Plankinton **61** 43 43N 98 29W
Plano, Ill. **35** 41 40N 88 32W
Plano, Tex. **65** 33 1N 96 42W
Plant City **31** 28 1N 82 7W
Plantation **31** 26 8N 80 15W
Plantersville, Ala. **24** 32 40N 86 56W
Plantersville, Miss. **45** 34 12N 88 40W
Plantersville, S.C. **60** 33 33N 79 13W
Plantsite **26** 33 2N 109 21W
Plaquemine **39** 30 17N 91 14W
Plaquemines Parish ◇ **39** 29 29N 89 42W
Plata, Rio de la **71** 18 29N 66 15W
Platina **28** 40 22N 122 53W
Platinum **25** 59 1N 161 49W
Platte **61** 43 23N 98 51W
Platte →, Mo. **46** 39 16N 94 50W
Platte →, Nebr. **48** 41 4N 95 53W
Platte Center **48** 41 32N 97 29W
Platte City **46** 39 22N 94 47W
Platte County ◇, Mo. **46** 39 20N 94 45W
Platte County ◇, Nebr. **48** 41 30N 97 30W
Platte County ◇, Wyo. **70** 42 0N 105 0W
Platteville, Colo. **30** 40 13N 104 49W
Platteville, Wis. **69** 42 44N 90 29W
Plattsburg **46** 39 34N 94 27W
Plattsburgh **53** 44 42N 73 28W
Plattsmouth **48** 41 1N 95 53W
Playa de Guayanés **71** 18 4N 65 49W
Playa de Humacao **71** 18 10N 65 45W
Playas L. **52** 31 51N 108 35W
Plaza, N. Dak. **55** 48 1N 101 58W
Plaza, Wash. **67** 47 19N 117 23W
Pleasant, L. **26** 33 51N 112 16W
Pleasant B. **42** 41 40N 69 57W
Pleasant Dale **48** 40 48N 96 56W
Pleasant Garden **54** 35 58N 79 46W
Pleasant Grove **66** 40 22N 111 44W
Pleasant Hill, Calif. **28** 37 57N 122 4W
Pleasant Hill, Ill. **35** 39 27N 90 52W
Pleasant Hill, La. **39** 31 49N 93 31W
Pleasant Hill, Mo. **46** 38 47N 94 16W
Pleasant Hill, N. Mex. **52** 34 31N 103 4W
Pleasant Hill, Ohio **56** 40 3N 84 21W
Pleasant Hill, Tenn. **63** 35 59N 85 12W
Pleasant Lake **44** 45 30N 94 17W
Pleasant Plains, Ark. **27** 35 33N 91 38W
Pleasant Plains, Ill. **35** 39 52N 89 55W
Pleasant Site **24** 34 33N 88 4W
Pleasant View, Colo. **30** 37 35N 108 46W
Pleasant View, Wash. **67** 46 29N 118 20W
Pleasanton, Iowa **37** 40 35N 93 45W
Pleasanton, Kans. **38** 38 11N 94 43W
Pleasanton, N. Mex. **52** 33 17N 108 53W
Pleasanton, Nebr. **48** 40 58N 99 5W
Pleasanton, Tex. **65** 28 58N 98 29W
Pleasants County ◇ **68** 39 22N 81 12W
Pleasantville, Iowa **37** 41 23N 93 18W
Pleasantville, N.J. **51** 39 24N 74 32W
Pleasantville, Ohio **56** 39 49N 82 32W
Pleasure Ridge Park **63** 38 9N 85 50W
Pleasureville **63** 38 21N 85 7W
Plentywood **47** 48 47N 104 34W
Plevna, Kans. **38** 37 58N 98 19W
Plevna, Mont. **47** 46 25N 104 31W
Plover, Iowa **37** 42 53N 94 38W
Plover, Wis. **69** 44 27N 89 32W
Plover → **69** 44 29N 89 35W
Plum **59** 40 29N 79 47W
Plum City **69** 44 38N 92 11W
Plum I., Mass. **42** 42 45N 70 48W
Plum I., N.Y. **53** 41 11N 72 12W
Plum Point **41** 38 0N 76 0W
Plum Springs **62** 37 0N 86 20W
Plumas County ◇ **28** 40 0N 121 0W
Plumas National Forest **28** 39 50N 120 40W
Plumerville **27** 35 10N 92 38W
Plummer, Idaho **34** 47 20N 116 53W
Plummer, Minn. **44** 47 55N 96 3W
Plush **58** 42 25N 119 54W
Plymouth, Calif. **28** 38 29N 120 51W
Plymouth, Ill. **35** 40 18N 90 58W
Plymouth, Ind. **36** 41 21N 86 19W
Plymouth, Iowa **37** 43 15N 93 7W
Plymouth, Kans. **38** 38 25N 96 20W
Plymouth, Mass. **42** 41 57N 70 40W
Plymouth, Minn. **44** 45 2N 93 27W
Plymouth, N.C. **54** 35 52N 76 43W
Plymouth, N.H. **50** 43 46N 71 41W
Plymouth, Nebr. **48** 40 18N 97 0W
Plymouth, Pa. **59** 41 14N 75 57W
Plymouth, Utah **66** 41 53N 112 9W
Plymouth, Vt. **50** 43 34N 72 45W
Plymouth, W. Va. **68** 38 31N 81 51W
Plymouth, Wis. **69** 43 45N 87 59W
Plymouth Bay **42** 41 57N 70 37W
Plymouth County ◇, Iowa **37** 42 45N 96 10W
Plymouth County ◇, Mass. **42** 41 45N 70 45W
Poca **68** 38 28N 81 49W
Pocahontas, Ark. **27** 36 16N 90 58W
Pocahontas, Ill. **35** 38 50N 89 33W
Pocahontas, Iowa **37** 42 44N 94 40W
Pocahontas County ◇, Iowa **37** 42 45N 94 40W
Pocahontas County ◇, W. Va. **68** 38 10N 80 2W
Pocasset, Mass. **42** 41 41N 70 37W
Pocasset, Okla. **57** 35 12N 97 58W
Pocatalico **68** 38 29N 81 40W
Pocatalico → **68** 38 29N 81 49W
Pocatello **34** 42 52N 112 27W
Pocomoke → **41** 37 58N 75 39W
Pocomoke City **41** 38 5N 75 34W
Pocomoke Sd. **68** 37 50N 75 50W
Pocono Mts. **59** 41 7N 75 22W
Pohue B. **33** 19 0N 155 48W
Poinsett, L. **61** 44 34N 97 5W
Poinsett County ◇ **27** 35 34N 90 43W
Point Arena **28** 38 55N 123 41W
Point au Fer I. **39** 29 18N 91 15W
Point Baker **25** 56 21N 133 37W
Point Comfort **65** 28 41N 96 33W
Point Hope **25** 68 21N 166 47W
Point Lay **25** 69 46N 163 3W
Point Lookout **41** 38 5N 76 18W
Point of Rocks **70** 41 41N 108 47W
Point Pleasant, N.J. **51** 40 5N 74 3W
Point Pleasant, W. Va. **68** 38 51N 82 8W
Point Reyes National Seashore **28** 38 10N 122 55W
Pointblank **65** 30 45N 95 13W
Pointe a la Hache **39** 29 35N 89 48W
Pointe Coupee Parish ◇ **39** 30 36N 91 37W
Pojoaque Valley **52** 35 54N 106 1W
Pokai B. **33** 21 27N 158 12W
Pokegama L. **44** 47 12N 93 35W
Polacca **26** 35 50N 110 23W
Polacca Wash → **26** 35 22N 110 50W
Poland, N.Y. **53** 43 14N 75 4W
Poland, Ohio **56** 41 1N 80 37W
Pole Mt. **70** 41 14N 105 23W
Polk, Nebr. **48** 41 5N 97 46W
Polk, Ohio **56** 40 57N 82 13W
Polk, Pa. **59** 41 22N 79 56W
Polk City **37** 41 46N 93 43W
Polk County ◇, Ark. **27** 34 35N 94 15W
Polk County ◇, Fla. **31** 28 0N 81 45W
Polk County ◇, Ga. **32** 34 0N 85 10W
Polk County ◇, Iowa **37** 41 40N 93 35W
Polk County ◇, Minn. **44** 47 40N 96 30W
Polk County ◇, Mo. **46** 37 35N 93 25W
Polk County ◇, N.C. **54** 35 15N 82 10W
Polk County ◇, Nebr. **48** 41 15N 97 40W
Polk County ◇, Oreg. **58** 44 55N 123 20W
Polk County ◇, Tenn. **63** 35 10N 84 39W
Polk County ◇, Tex. **65** 30 43N 94 56W
Polk County ◇, Wis. **69** 45 30N 92 30W
Polkton **54** 35 1N 80 12W
Polkville, Miss. **45** 32 11N 89 42W
Polkville, N.C. **54** 35 25N 81 39W
Pollock, Idaho **34** 45 19N 116 21W
Pollock, La. **39** 31 32N 92 25W
Pollock, Mo. **46** 40 21N 93 5W
Pollock, S. Dak. **61** 45 55N 100 17W
Pollock Pines **28** 38 46N 120 34W
Pollocksville **54** 35 0N 77 14W
Polo, Ill. **35** 41 59N 89 35W
Polo, Mo. **46** 39 33N 94 3W
Polson **47** 47 41N 114 9W
Polvadera **52** 34 12N 106 55W
Pomaria **60** 34 16N 81 25W
Pomeroy, Iowa **37** 42 33N 94 41W

Pomeroy, Ohio **56** 39 2N 82 2W
Pomeroy, Wash. **67** 46 28N 117 36W
Pomfret, Conn. **42** 41 54N 71 58W
Pomfret, Md. **41** 38 0N 77 0W
Pomme de Terre →, Minn. **44** 45 10N 96 5W
Pomme de Terre →, Mo. **46** 38 11N 93 25W
Pomme de Terre L. **46** 37 54N 93 19W
Pomona, Calif. **29** 34 4N 117 45W
Pomona, Kans. **38** 38 36N 95 27W
Pomona, Md. **41** 39 10N 76 7W
Pomona, Mo. **46** 36 52N 91 55W
Pomona, N.J. **51** 39 29N 74 35W
Pomona Lake **38** 38 39N 95 34W
Pomona Park **31** 29 30N 81 36W
Pompano Beach **31** 26 14N 80 8W
Pompeys Pillar **47** 45 59N 107 57W
Pompton Lakes **51** 41 0N 74 17W
Ponca **48** 42 34N 96 43W
Ponca City **57** 36 42N 97 5W
Ponca Cr. → **48** 42 48N 98 5W
Ponce **71** 18 1N 66 37W
Ponce ◇ **71** 18 10N 66 30W
Ponce de Leon **31** 30 44N 85 56W
Ponce de Leon B. **31** 25 15N 81 10W
Poncha Springs **30** 38 31N 106 5W
Ponchatoula **39** 30 26N 90 26W
Pond Creek **57** 36 40N 97 48W
Pondera County ◇ **47** 48 12N 112 30W
Ponderosa **52** 35 40N 106 40W
Pondosa **28** 41 12N 121 41W
Poneto **36** 40 39N 85 13W
Pontchartrain L. **39** 30 5N 90 5W
Ponte Vedra Beach **31** 30 15N 81 23W
Pontiac, Ill. **35** 40 53N 88 38W
Pontiac, Mich. **43** 42 38N 83 18W
Pontotoc **45** 34 15N 89 0W
Pontotoc County ◇, Miss. **45** 34 15N 89 0W
Pontotoc County ◇, Okla. **57** 34 45N 96 45W
Poole, Ky. **62** 37 38N 87 39W
Poole, Nebr. **48** 40 59N 98 58W
Pooler **32** 32 7N 81 15W
Pooles I. **41** 39 17N 76 16W
Poolesville **41** 39 9N 77 25W
Pope **45** 34 13N 89 57W
Pope County ◇, Ark. **27** 35 28N 92 59W
Pope County ◇, Ill. **35** 37 25N 88 35W
Pope County ◇, Minn. **44** 45 40N 95 25W
Pope Cr. → **35** 41 8N 90 58W
Popejoy **37** 42 36N 93 26W
Popes Creek **41** 38 24N 76 58W
Poplar, Mont. **47** 48 7N 105 12W
Poplar, N.C. **54** 36 4N 82 21W
Poplar, Wis. **69** 46 35N 91 48W
Poplar → **47** 48 5N 105 11W
Poplar Bluff **46** 36 46N 90 24W
Poplar Branch **54** 36 17N 75 53W
Poplar Grove **35** 42 22N 88 49W
Poplar I. **41** 38 46N 76 23W
Poplar Mt. **63** 36 43N 85 3W
Poplar Plains **63** 38 21N 83 41W
Poplarville **45** 30 51N 89 32W
Popo Aggie → **70** 43 1N 108 21W
Poquetanuck **42** 41 29N 72 3W
Poquonock Bridge **42** 41 19N 72 11W
Poquoson **68** 37 8N 76 24W
Porcupine → **25** 66 34N 145 19W
Porcupine Mts. **43** 46 40N 89 40W
Porphyry Pk. **47** 47 14N 109 18W
Port Alexander **25** 56 15N 134 38W
Port Allegany **59** 41 48N 78 17W
Port Allen **39** 30 27N 91 12W
Port Angeles **67** 48 7N 123 27W
Port Aransas **65** 27 50N 97 4W
Port Arthur **65** 29 54N 93 56W
Port Austin **43** 44 3N 83 1W
Port Barre **39** 30 34N 91 57W
Port Charlotte **31** 26 59N 82 6W
Port Chester **53** 41 0N 73 40W
Port Clinton **56** 41 31N 82 56W
Port Clyde **40** 43 56N 69 16W
Port Edwards **69** 44 21N 89 52W
Port Elizabeth **51** 39 19N 74 59W
Port Ewen **53** 41 54N 73 59W
Port Gamble **67** 47 51N 122 35W
Port Gibson **45** 31 58N 90 59W
Port Heiden **25** 56 55N 158 41W
Port Henry **53** 44 3N 73 28W
Port Hope **43** 43 57N 82 43W
Port Hueneme **29** 34 7N 119 12W
Port Huron **43** 42 58N 82 26W
Port Isabel **64** 26 5N 97 12W
Port Jefferson, N.Y. **53** 40 57N 73 3W
Port Jefferson, Ohio **56** 40 20N 84 6W
Port Jervis **53** 41 22N 74 41W
Port Lavaca **65** 28 37N 96 38W
Port Lions **25** 57 52N 152 53W
Port Ludlow **67** 47 56N 122 41W
Port Mansfield **64** 26 34N 97 26W
Port Matilda **59** 40 48N 78 3W
Port Mayaca **31** 26 59N 80 36W
Port Moller **25** 55 59N 160 34W
Port Neches **65** 30 0N 93 59W
Port Norris **51** 39 15N 75 2W
Port Orange **31** 29 9N 80 59W
Port Orchard **67** 47 32N 122 38W
Port Orford **58** 42 45N 124 30W
Port Penn **41** 39 31N 75 35W
Port Republic, Md. **41** 38 30N 76 33W
Port Republic, N.J. **51** 39 31N 74 29W
Port Royal, Ky. **63** 38 33N 85 5W
Port Royal, Va. **68** 38 10N 77 12W
Port Royal Sd. **60** 32 15N 80 40W
Port St. Joe **31** 29 49N 85 18W
Port Salerno **31** 27 9N 80 12W
Port Sanilac **43** 43 26N 82 33W
Port Sulphur **39** 29 29N 89 42W
Port Susan **67** 48 5N 122 15W
Port Tobacco **41** 38 27N 77 2W
Port Townsend **67** 48 7N 122 45W
Port Vincent **39** 30 20N 90 51W
Port Washington, N.Y. **53** 40 50N 73 41W
Port Washington, Ohio **56** 40 20N 81 31W
Port Washington, Wis. **69** 43 23N 87 53W
Port Wentworth **32** 32 9N 81 10W
Port Wing **69** 46 47N 91 23W
Portadale **32** 30 34N 83 54W
Portage, Ind. **36** 41 34N 87 11W
Portage, Maine **40** 46 46N 68 29W
Portage, Mich. **43** 42 12N 85 35W
Portage, Pa. **59** 40 23N 78 41W
Portage, Utah **66** 41 59N 112 14W
Portage, Wis. **69** 43 33N 89 28W
Portage → **56** 41 31N 83 5W
Portage County ◇, Ohio **56** 41 9N 81 15W
Portage County ◇, Wis. **69** 44 25N 89 30W
Portageville **46** 36 26N 89 42W
Portal, Ariz. **26** 31 55N 109 9W
Portal, Ga. **32** 32 33N 81 56W
Portal, N. Dak. **55** 48 59N 102 33W
Portales **52** 34 11N 103 20W
Porter, Minn. **44** 44 38N 96 10W
Porter, Okla. **57** 35 52N 95 31W
Porter, Wash. **67** 46 56N 123 18W
Porter County ◇ **36** 41 25N 87 5W
Porterville, Calif. **29** 36 4N 119 1W
Porterville, Miss. **45** 32 41N 88 28W
Porthill **34** 48 59N 116 30W
Portis **38** 39 34N 98 41W
Portland, Ark. **27** 33 14N 91 31W
Portland, Conn. **42** 41 34N 72 38W
Portland, Fla. **31** 30 31N 86 12W
Portland, Ind. **36** 40 26N 84 59W
Portland, Maine **40** 43 39N 70 16W
Portland, Mich. **43** 42 52N 84 54W
Portland, Mo. **46** 38 43N 91 43W
Portland, N. Dak. **55** 47 30N 97 22W
Portland, Oreg. **58** 45 32N 122 37W
Portland, Tenn. **62** 36 35N 86 31W
Portland, Tex. **65** 27 53N 97 20W
Portneuf → **34** 42 58N 112 35W
Portneuf Range **34** 42 50N 112 0W
Portola **28** 39 49N 120 28W
Portsmouth, N.H. **50** 43 5N 70 45W
Portsmouth, Ohio **56** 38 44N 82 57W
Portsmouth, R.I. **42** 41 36N 71 15W
Portsmouth, Va. **68** 36 50N 76 18W
Portville **53** 42 3N 78 20W
Porum **57** 35 22N 95 16W
Posen **43** 45 16N 83 42W
Posey County ◇ **36** 38 0N 87 50W
Poseyville **36** 38 10N 87 47W
Possum Kingdom L. **65** 32 52N 98 26W
Post, Oreg. **58** 44 10N 120 29W
Post, Tex. **64** 33 12N 101 23W
Post Falls **34** 47 43N 116 57W
Poston **60** 33 53N 79 26W
Postville **37** 43 5N 91 34W
Potagannissing B. **43** 46 5N 83 50W
Potatch → **34** 46 26N 116 47W
Potawatomi Indian Reservation **38** 39 20N 95 52W
Poteau **57** 35 3N 94 37W
Poteau → **57** 35 23N 94 26W
Poteet **65** 29 2N 98 35W
Poth **65** 29 4N 98 5W
Potholes Reservoir **67** 46 59N 119 16W
Potlatch **34** 46 55N 116 54W
Potomac, Ill. **35** 40 18N 87 48W
Potomac, Md. **41** 39 1N 77 13W
Potomac → **41** 38 0N 76 23W
Potomac Heights **41** 38 36N 77 8W
Potosi **46** 37 56N 90 47W
Potsdam **53** 44 40N 74 59W
Pottawatomie County ◇, Kans. **38** 39 20N 96 15W
Pottawatomie County ◇, Okla. **57** 35 10N 97 0W
Pottawattamie County ◇ **37** 41 20N 95 30W
Potter, Kans. **38** 39 26N 95 9W
Potter, Nebr. **48** 41 13N 103 19W
Potter County ◇, Pa. **59** 41 50N 78 0W
Potter County ◇, S. Dak. **61** 45 0N 100 0W
Potter County ◇, Tex. **64** 35 22N 101 50W
Potterville, Ga. **32** 32 31N 84 7W
Potterville, Mich. **43** 42 38N 84 45W
Potts Camp **45** 34 39N 89 18W
Pottsboro **65** 33 46N 96 40W
Pottstown **59** 40 15N 75 39W
Pottsville **59** 40 41N 76 12W
Potwin **38** 37 56N 97 1W
Poughkeepsie **53** 41 42N 73 56W
Poulan **32** 31 31N 83 47W
Poulsbo **67** 47 44N 122 39W
Poultney **50** 43 31N 73 14W
Pound **68** 37 8N 82 36W
Poway **29** 32 58N 117 2W
Powder →, Mont. **47** 46 45N 105 26W
Powder →, Oreg. **58** 44 45N 117 3W
Powder River **70** 43 2N 106 59W
Powder River County ◇ **47** 45 20N 105 40W
Powder Springs **32** 33 52N 84 41W
Powderhorn **30** 38 17N 107 7W
Powell **70** 44 45N 108 46W
Powell → **63** 36 29N 83 52W
Powell Butte **58** 44 15N 121 1W
Powell County ◇, Ky. **63** 37 50N 83 50W
Powell County ◇, Mont. **47** 47 0N 113 0W
Powell L. **66** 36 57N 111 29W
Powellville **41** 38 20N 75 22W
Powelton **32** 33 26N 82 52W
Power County ◇ **34** 42 50N 112 50W
Powers, Mich. **43** 45 41N 87 32W
Powers, Oreg. **58** 42 53N 124 4W
Powers Lake **55** 48 34N 102 39W
Powersville **46** 40 33N 93 15W
Poweshiek County ◇ **37** 41 40N 92 30W
Powhatan, Ark. **27** 36 5N 91 7W
Powhatan, Va. **68** 37 32N 77 55W
Powhatan County ◇ **68** 37 32N 77 55W
Powhatan Point **56** 39 52N 80 49W
Powhattan **38** 39 46N 95 38W
Pownal **50** 42 46N 73 14W
Poygan L. **69** 44 19N 88 50W
Poynette **69** 43 24N 89 24W
Prague, Nebr. **48** 41 19N 96 49W
Prague, Okla. **57** 35 29N 96 41W
Prairie **45** 33 48N 88 40W
Prairie City, Iowa **37** 41 36N 93 14W
Prairie City, Oreg. **58** 44 28N 118 43W
Prairie City, S. Dak. **61** 45 32N 102 48W
Prairie County ◇, Ark. **27** 34 47N 91 35W
Prairie County ◇, Mont. **47** 46 57N 105 30W
Prairie Dog Cr. → **38** 40 0N 99 18W
Prairie Dog Town Ford Red → **64** 34 27N 99 21W
Prairie du Chien **69** 43 3N 91 9W
Prairie du Rocher **35** 38 5N 90 6W
Prairie du Sac **69** 43 17N 89 43W
Prairie Farm **69** 45 14N 91 59W
Prairie Grove **27** 35 59N 94 19W
Prairie Hill **46** 39 31N 92 44W
Prairie Home **46** 38 49N 92 35W
Prairie View, Kans. **38** 39 50N 99 34W
Prairie View, Tex. **65** 30 6N 95 59W
Prairie Village **38** 38 58N 94 38W
Pratt **38** 37 39N 98 44W
Pratt County ◇ **38** 37 35N 98 45W
Prattville **24** 32 28N 86 29W
Preble **53** 42 44N 76 9W
Preble County ◇ **56** 39 45N 84 38W
Premont **64** 27 22N 98 7W
Prentice **69** 45 33N 90 17W
Prentiss **45** 31 36N 89 52W
Prentiss County ◇ **45** 34 39N 88 34W
Prescott, Ariz. **26** 34 33N 112 28W
Prescott, Ark. **27** 33 48N 93 23W
Prescott, Iowa **37** 41 1N 94 37W
Prescott, Kans. **38** 38 4N 94 42W
Prescott, Mich. **43** 44 11N 83 56W
Prescott, Wash. **67** 46 18N 118 19W
Prescott National Forest **26** 34 30N 112 30W
Presho **61** 43 54N 100 3W
Presidential Lakes **51** 39 54N 74 35W
Presidio **64** 29 34N 104 22W
Presidio County ◇ **64** 30 0N 104 0W
Presque Isle, Maine **40** 46 41N 68 1W
Presque Isle, Mich. **43** 45 18N 83 29W
Presque Isle County ◇ **43** 45 15N 84 0W
Preston, Ga. **32** 32 4N 84 32W
Preston, Idaho **34** 42 6N 111 53W
Preston, Iowa **37** 42 3N 90 24W
Preston, Kans. **38** 37 46N 98 33W
Preston, Md. **41** 38 43N 75 55W
Preston, Minn. **44** 43 40N 92 5W
Preston, Nev. **49** 38 55N 115 4W
Preston, Okla. **57** 35 43N 95 59W
Preston City **42** 41 33N 72 57W
Preston County ◇ **68** 39 31N 79 48W
Prestonsburg **63** 37 40N 82 47W
Pretty Prairie **38** 37 47N 98 1W
Prettyboy Reservoir **41** 39 37N 76 43W
Prewitt **52** 35 22N 108 3W
Prewitt Reservoir **30** 40 26N 103 22W
Pribilof Is. **25** 57 0N 170 0W
Price, Md. **41** 39 6N 75 58W
Price, Tex. **65** 32 8N 94 57W
Price, Utah **66** 39 36N 110 49W
Price → **66** 39 10N 110 6W
Price County ◇ **69** 45 45N 90 20W
Prichard, Ala. **24** 30 44N 88 5W
Prichard, W. Va. **68** 38 15N 82 36W
Prichett **30** 37 22N 102 52W
Priddy **65** 31 41N 98 31W
Pride **62** 37 34N 87 53W
Priest → **34** 48 12N 116 54W
Priest L. **34** 48 35N 116 52W
Priest Rapids Dam **67** 46 39N 119 54W
Prieta Loma **28** 37 7N 121 50W
Primghar **37** 43 5N 95 38W
Primrose **48** 41 38N 98 14W
Prince Edward County ◇ **68** 37 15N 78 25W
Prince Frederick **41** 38 33N 76 35W
Prince George **68** 37 13N 77 17W
Prince George County ◇ **68** 37 13N 77 17W
Prince Georges County ◇ **41** 38 45N 76 50W
Prince of Wales, C. **25** 65 36N 168 5W
Prince of Wales I. **25** 55 47N 132 50W
Prince of Wales-Outer Ketchikan ◇ **25** 55 0N 131 30W
Prince William County ◇ **68** 38 45N 77 29W
Prince William Sd. **25** 60 40N 147 0W
Princess Anne **41** 38 12N 75 42W
Princeton, Ark. **27** 33 59N 92 38W
Princeton, Calif. **28** 39 24N 122 1W
Princeton, Ill. **35** 41 23N 89 28W
Princeton, Ind. **36** 38 21N 87 34W
Princeton, Iowa **37** 41 40N 90 20W
Princeton, Kans. **38** 38 29N 95 16W
Princeton, Ky. **62** 37 7N 87 53W
Princeton, Maine **40** 45 13N 67 34W
Princeton, Mass. **42** 42 0N 71 0W
Princeton, Mich. **43** 46 17N 87 29W
Princeton, Minn. **44** 45 34N 93 35W
Princeton, Mo. **46** 40 24N 93 35W
Princeton, N.C. **54** 35 28N 78 10W
Princeton, N.J. **51** 40 21N 74 39W
Princeton, S.C. **60** 34 30N 82 17W
Princeton, W. Va. **68** 37 22N 81 6W
Princeton, Wis. **69** 43 51N 89 8W
Princeville **35** 40 56N 89 46W
Prineville **58** 44 18N 120 51W
Prineville Reservoir **58** 44 7N 120 47W
Pringle, S. Dak. **61** 43 37N 103 36W
Pringle, Tex. **64** 35 57N 101 27W
Prinsburg **44** 44 56N 95 11W
Prior Lake **44** 44 43N 93 25W
Proctor, Colo. **30** 40 48N 102 57W
Proctor, Minn. **44** 46 45N 92 14W
Proctor, Vt. **50** 43 40N 73 2W
Proctor, W. Va. **68** 39 43N 80 49W
Proctor L. **65** 31 58N 98 29W
Proctorsville **50** 43 23N 72 40W
Proctorville **56** 38 26N 82 23W
Promise City **37** 40 45N 93 9W
Promontory Mts. **66** 41 30N 112 30W
Prophetstown **35** 41 40N 89 56W
Prospect, Conn. **42** 41 30N 72 59W
Prospect, Ohio **56** 40 27N 83 11W
Prospect, Oreg. **58** 42 45N 122 29W
Prospect, Pa. **59** 40 54N 80 3W
Prosperity **60** 34 12N 81 32W
Prosser, Nebr. **48** 40 41N 98 34W
Prosser, Wash. **67** 46 12N 119 46W
Protection **38** 37 12N 99 29W
Protem **46** 36 32N 92 51W
Protivin **37** 43 13N 92 6W
Providence, Ky. **62** 37 24N 87 46W
Providence, R.I. **42** 41 49N 71 24W
Providence, Utah **66** 41 43N 111 49W
Providence County ◇ **42** 41 50N 71 40W
Providence Mts. **29** 35 10N 115 15W
Provincetown **42** 42 3N 70 11W
Provo, S. Dak. **61** 43 12N 103 50W
Provo, Utah **66** 40 14N 111 39W
Prowers County ◇ **30** 38 0N 102 30W
Prudence I. **42** 41 37N 71 19W
Prudhoe Bay **25** 70 18N 148 22W

Prue **57** 36 15N 96 15W
Pryor **57** 36 19N 95 19W
Puaena Pt. **33** 21 36N 158 6W
Puckaway L. **69** 43 45N 89 10W
Puckett **45** 32 5N 89 47W
Pueblo **30** 38 16N 104 37W
Pueblo Colorado Wash → **26** 35 5N 110 22W
Pueblo County ◇ **30** 38 15N 104 30W
Pueblo Mt. **58** 42 6N 118 39W
Pueblo Nuevo **71** 18 28N 66 51W
Pueo Pt. **33** 21 54N 160 4W
Puerca, Pta. **71** 18 13N 65 36W
Puerco →, Ariz. **26** 34 54N 110 2W
Puerco →, N. Mex. **52** 34 22N 107 50W
Puerto Nuevo, Pta. **71** 18 30N 66 24W
Puerto Rico ■ **71** 18 15N 66 30W
Puget Sound **67** 47 50N 122 30W
Pukalani **33** 20 51N 156 20W
Pukoo **33** 21 4N 156 48W
Pulaski, Ill. **35** 37 12N 89 10W
Pulaski, Iowa **37** 40 45N 92 12W
Pulaski, N.Y. **53** 43 34N 76 8W
Pulaski, Tenn. **62** 35 12N 87 2W
Pulaski, Va. **68** 37 3N 80 47W
Pulaski, Wis. **69** 44 41N 88 14W
Pulaski County ◇, Ark. **27** 34 45N 92 20W
Pulaski County ◇, Ga. **32** 32 15N 83 30W
Pulaski County ◇, Ill. **35** 37 15N 89 5W
Pulaski County ◇, Ind. **36** 41 0N 86 40W
Pulaski County ◇, Ky. **63** 37 5N 84 35W
Pulaski County ◇, Mo. **46** 37 50N 92 10W
Pulaski County ◇, Va. **68** 37 0N 80 45W
Pullman **67** 46 44N 117 10W
Pumpville **64** 29 53N 101 45W
Punaluu **33** 21 35N 157 53W
Pungo L. **54** 35 42N 76 33W
Punta, Cerro de **71** 18 10N 66 37W
Punta de Agua → **64** 35 32N 102 27W
Punta Gorda **31** 26 56N 82 3W
Punta Rassa **31** 26 26N 81 59W
Punxsatawney **59** 40 57N 78 59W
Puolo Pt. **33** 21 54N 159 36W
Purcell **57** 35 1N 97 22W
Purcell Mts. **47** 48 30N 115 0W
Purcellville **68** 39 8N 77 43W
Purdin **46** 39 57N 93 10W
Purdon **65** 31 57N 96 37W
Purdy, Mo. **46** 36 49N 93 55W
Purdy, Okla. **57** 34 43N 97 35W
Purdy, Va. **68** 36 49N 77 36W
Purgatoire → **30** 38 4N 103 11W
Purvis **45** 31 9N 89 25W
Puryear **62** 36 27N 88 20W
Pushaw L. **40** 44 56N 68 48W
Pushmataha County ◇ **57** 34 25N 95 20W
Put-in Bay **56** 41 39N 82 49W
Putnam, Conn. **42** 41 55N 71 55W
Putnam, Okla. **57** 35 51N 98 58W
Putnam, Tex. **65** 32 22N 99 12W
Putnam County ◇, Fla. **31** 29 35N 81 45W
Putnam County ◇, Ga. **32** 33 20N 83 15W
Putnam County ◇, Ill. **35** 41 10N 89 15W
Putnam County ◇, Ind. **36** 39 40N 86 50W
Putnam County ◇, Mo. **46** 40 30N 93 0W
Putnam County ◇, N.Y. **53** 41 25N 73 45W
Putnam County ◇, Ohio **56** 40 59N 84 12W
Putnam County ◇, Tenn. **63** 36 10N 85 30W
Putnam County ◇, W. Va. **68** 38 32N 81 54W
Putney, Ga. **32** 31 29N 84 8W
Putney, S. Dak. **61** 45 34N 98 11W
Putney, Vt. **50** 42 58N 72 31W
Puu Kaaumakua **33** 21 30N 157 54W
Puu Keahiakahoe **33** 21 23N 157 49W
Puu o Keokeo **33** 19 13N 155 44W
Puuanahulu **33** 19 49N 155 51W
Puukolii **33** 20 56N 156 41W
Puunene **33** 20 53N 156 23W
Puuwai **33** 21 54N 160 12W
Puxico **46** 36 57N 90 10W
Puyallup **67** 47 12N 122 18W
Pymatuning Reservoir **56** 41 30N 80 28W
Pyote **64** 31 32N 103 8W
Pyramid L. **49** 40 1N 119 35W
Pyramid Lake Indian Reservation **49** 40 20N 119 35W
Pyramid Pk. **70** 43 27N 110 28W

Q

Quabbin Reservoir **42** 42 20N 72 20W
Quail **64** 34 55N 100 30W
Quakertown **59** 40 26N 75 21W
Quanah **65** 34 18N 99 44W
Quantico **41** 38 23N 75 44W
Quapaw **57** 36 58N 94 50W
Quarryville **59** 39 54N 76 10W
Quartz Hill **29** 34 39N 118 13W
Quartzsite **26** 33 40N 114 13W
Quay **52** 34 56N 103 45W
Quay County ◇ **52** 35 0N 103 30W
Quebradillas **71** 18 29N 66 56W
Quechee **50** 43 40N 72 25W
Queen Anne **41** 38 55N 75 57W
Queen Annes County ◇ **41** 39 10N 76 0W
Queen City, Mo. **46** 40 25N 92 34W
Queen City, Tex. **65** 33 9N 94 9W
Queen Creek **26** 33 15N 111 35W
Queens County ◇ **53** 40 40N 73 50W
Queensland **32** 31 46N 83 14W
Queenstown **41** 38 59N 76 9W
Queets → **67** 47 33N 124 21W
Quemado **52** 34 20N 108 30W
Quenemo **38** 38 35N 95 30W
Questa **52** 36 42N 105 36W
Quidnet **42** 41 18N 69 58W
Quilcene **67** 47 49N 122 53W
Quimby **37** 42 38N 95 38W
Quinault **67** 47 28N 123 51W
Quinault → **67** 47 21N 124 18W
Quinault Indian Reservation **67** 47 30N 124 5W
Quincy, Calif. **28** 39 56N 120 57W
Quincy, Fla. **31** 30 35N 84 34W
Quincy, Ill. **35** 39 56N 91 23W
Quincy, Mass. **42** 42 15N 71 0W
Quincy, Mich. **43** 41 57N 84 53W
Quincy, Ohio **56** 10 18N 83 58W
Quinebaug **42** 42 1N 71 57W
Quinebaug → **42** 41 33N 72 3W
Quinhagak **25** 59 45N 161 54W
Quinlan, Okla. **57** 36 27N 99 3W
Quinlan, Tex. **65** 32 55N 96 8W
Quinn → **49** 40 53N 119 3W
Quinter **38** 39 4N 100 14W
Quinton **57** 35 7N 95 22W
Quinwood **68** 38 4N 80 42W
Quitaque **64** 34 22N 101 4W
Quitman, Ark. **27** 35 23N 92 13W
Quitman, Ga. **32** 30 47N 83 34W
Quitman, La. **39** 32 21N 92 43W
Quitman, Miss. **45** 32 2N 88 44W
Quitman, Tex. **65** 32 48N 95 27W
Quitman County ◇, Ga. **32** 31 50N 85 0W
Quitman County ◇, Miss. **45** 34 12N 90 17W
Quitman Mts. **64** 31 0N 105 16W
Qulin **46** 36 36N 90 15W
Quonochontaug **42** 41 21N 71 43W

R

Rabbit Cr. → **61** 45 13N 102 10W
Rabun County ◇ **32** 34 50N 83 30W
Raccoon →, Iowa **37** 41 35N 93 37W
Raccoon →, Ohio **56** 40 2N 82 24W
Race Point **42** 42 4N 70 14W
Raceland, Ky. **63** 38 32N 82 44W
Raceland, La. **39** 29 44N 90 36W
Racine **44** 43 48N 92 31W
Radcliff **63** 37 51N 85 57W
Radcliffe **37** 42 20N 93 25W
Radford **68** 37 8N 80 34W
Radisson **69** 45 45N 91 14W
Radium **38** 38 12N 98 56W
Radium Springs **52** 32 30N 106 55W
Radnor **56** 40 23N 83 9W
Raft → **34** 42 37N 113 15W
Raft River Mts. **66** 41 55N 113 25W
Ragan **48** 40 19N 99 15W
Ragland **24** 33 45N 86 9W
Ragley **39** 30 30N 93 15W
Rago **38** 37 26N 98 4W
Rahway **51** 40 37N 74 17W
Raiford **31** 30 4N 82 14W
Railroad Valley **49** 38 25N 115 40W
Rainbow City **24** 33 57N 86 0W
Rainbow Plateau **26** 36 55N 111 0W
Rainelle **68** 37 58N 80 47W
Rainier **67** 46 53N 122 41W
Rainier, Mt. **67** 46 52N 121 46W
Rains County ◇ **65** 32 52N 95 46W
Rainsburg **59** 39 54N 78 30W
Rainsville **24** 34 30N 85 50W
Rainy → **44** 48 50N 94 42W
Rake **37** 43 35N 93 50W
Raleigh, Fla. **31** 29 25N 82 32W
Raleigh, N.C. **54** 35 47N 78 39W
Raleigh, N. Dak. **55** 46 20N 101 20W
Raleigh B. **54** 34 50N 76 15W
Raleigh County ◇ **68** 37 45N 81 10W
Ralls **64** 33 41N 101 24W
Ralls County ◇ **46** 39 30N 91 30W
Ralston, Nebr. **48** 41 12N 96 3W
Ralston, Okla. **57** 36 30N 96 44W
Ralston, Pa. **59** 41 30N 76 57W
Ralston, Wyo. **70** 44 43N 108 52W
Ramah **30** 39 7N 104 10W
Ramer, Ala. **24** 32 3N 86 13W
Ramer, Tenn. **62** 35 4N 88 37W
Ramey **59** 40 48N 78 24W
Ramona, Calif. **29** 33 2N 116 52W
Ramona, Kans. **38** 38 36N 97 4W
Ramona, Okla. **57** 36 32N 95 55W
Ramona, S. Dak. **61** 44 7N 97 13W
Rampart **25** 65 30N 150 10W
Ramsay, Mich. **43** 46 28N 90 0W
Ramsay, Mont. **47** 46 1N 112 42W
Ramseur **54** 35 44N 79 39W
Ramsey, Ill. **35** 39 8N 89 7W
Ramsey, N.J. **51** 41 4N 74 9W
Ramsey County ◇, Minn. **44** 45 0N 93 5W
Ramsey County ◇, N. Dak. **55** 48 15N 98 50W
Ranches of Taos **52** 36 22N 105 37W
Ranchester **70** 44 54N 107 10W
Rancho Cordova **28** 38 36N 121 18W
Rand, Colo. **30** 40 27N 106 11W
Rand, W. Va. **68** 38 17N 81 34W
Randalia **37** 42 52N 91 53W
Randall, Iowa **37** 42 14N 93 35W
Randall, Kans. **38** 39 38N 98 3W
Randall, Minn. **44** 46 5N 94 30W
Randall County ◇ **64** 34 59N 101 55W
Randallstown **41** 39 22N 76 48W
Randle **67** 46 32N 121 57W
Randleman **54** 35 49N 79 48W
Randlett **57** 34 11N 98 28W
Randolph, Iowa **37** 40 52N 95 34W
Randolph, Kans. **38** 39 26N 96 46W
Randolph, Maine **40** 44 14N 69 46W
Randolph, Mass. **42** 42 10N 71 2W
Randolph, Miss. **45** 34 11N 89 10W
Randolph, N.Y. **53** 42 10N 78 59W
Randolph, Nebr. **48** 42 23N 97 22W
Randolph, Utah **66** 41 40N 111 11W
Randolph, Vt. **50** 43 55N 72 40W
Randolph Center **50** 43 55N 72 37W
Randolph County ◇, Ala. **24** 33 20N 85 25W
Randolph County ◇, Ark. **27** 36 20N 91 0W
Randolph County ◇, Ga. **32** 31 45N 84 45W
Randolph County ◇, Ill. **35** 38 0N 89 50W
Randolph County ◇, Ind. **36** 40 10N 85 0W
Randolph County ◇, Mo. **46** 39 25N 92 30W
Randolph County ◇, N.C. **54** 35 40N 79 50W
Randolph County ◇, W. Va. **68** 38 45N 80 0W
Rangeley **40** 44 58N 70 39W
Rangeley L. **40** 44 55N 70 43W
Rangely **30** 40 5N 108 48W
Ranger **65** 32 28N 98 41W
Ranier **44** 48 36N 93 20W
Rankin, Ill. **35** 40 28N 87 54W
Rankin, Tex. **64** 31 13N 101 56W
Rankin County ◇ **45** 32 15N 90 0W
Ransom, Ill. **35** 41 9N 88 39W
Ransom, Kans. **38** 38 38N 99 58W
Ransom County ◇ **55** 46 30N 97 40W
Rantoul, Ill. **35** 40 19N 88 9W
Rantoul, Kans. **38** 38 33N 95 7W
Rapelje **47** 45 58N 109 14W
Rapid → **44** 48 42N 94 26W
Rapid City **61** 44 5N 103 14W
Rapid Cr. → **61** 43 54N 102 37W
Rapid River **43** 45 55N 86 58W
Rapidan → **68** 38 22N 77 37W
Rapides Parish ◇ **39** 31 15N 92 30W
Rappahannock → **68** 37 34N 76 18W
Rappahannock County ◇ **68** 38 40N 78 10W
Raquette → **53** 45 0N 74 42W
Rarden **56** 38 55N 83 12W
Raritan **51** 40 34N 74 38W
Raritan → **51** 40 29N 74 17W
Raritan Bay **51** 40 27N 74 15W
Rat Islands **25** 52 0N 178 0W
Ratcliff **65** 31 24N 95 8W
Rathbun **37** 40 50N 92 50W
Rathbun L. **37** 40 54N 93 5W
Ratliff City **57** 34 25N 97 30W
Raton **52** 36 54N 104 24W
Rattan **57** 34 12N 95 25W
Rattlesnake Cr. → **58** 42 44N 117 47W
Rattlesnake Hills **70** 42 45N 107 10W
Ravalli **47** 47 17N 114 11W
Ravalli County ◇ **47** 46 0N 114 0W
Ravena **53** 42 28N 73 49W
Ravendale **28** 40 48N 120 22W
Ravenel **60** 32 46N 80 15W
Ravenna, Nebr. **48** 41 1N 98 55W
Ravenna, Ohio **56** 41 9N 81 15W
Ravenna, Tex. **65** 33 40N 96 15W
Ravenswood **68** 38 57N 81 46W
Ravenwood **46** 40 22N 94 41W
Ravinia **61** 43 8N 98 26W
Rawlins **70** 41 47N 107 14W
Rawlins County ◇ **38** 39 45N 101 0W
Rawsonville **50** 43 10N 72 50W
Ray, Minn. **44** 48 25N 93 13W
Ray, N. Dak. **55** 48 21N 103 10W
Ray City **32** 31 5N 83 11W
Ray County ◇ **46** 39 20N 94 0W
Ray Mts. **25** 66 0N 152 0W
Rayle **32** 33 48N 82 54W
Raymond, Calif. **28** 37 13N 119 54W
Raymond, Ga. **32** 33 20N 84 43W
Raymond, Ill. **35** 39 19N 89 34W
Raymond, Kans. **38** 38 17N 98 25W
Raymond, Minn. **44** 45 2N 95 14W
Raymond, Miss. **45** 32 16N 90 25W
Raymond, N.H. **50** 43 2N 71 11W
Raymond, Nebr. **48** 40 57N 96 47W
Raymond, S. Dak. **61** 44 55N 97 56W
Raymond, Wash. **67** 46 41N 123 44W
Raymondville, Mo. **46** 37 20N 91 50W
Raymondville, Tex. **64** 26 29N 97 47W
Rayne **39** 30 14N 92 16W
Raystown Branch → **59** 40 27N 77 59W
Raystown L. **59** 40 25N 78 5W
Raytown **46** 39 1N 94 28W
Rayville, La. **39** 32 29N 91 46W
Rayville, Mo. **46** 39 21N 94 4W
Reader **27** 33 46N 93 6W
Reading, Kans. **38** 38 31N 95 58W
Reading, Mass. **42** 42 32N 71 6W
Reading, Mich. **43** 41 50N 84 45W
Reading, Ohio **56** 39 13N 84 26W
Reading, Pa. **59** 40 20N 75 56W
Readland **27** 33 4N 91 13W
Readlyn **37** 42 42N 92 14W
Readsboro **50** 42 46N 72 57W
Readstown **69** 43 27N 90 45W
Reagan **62** 35 31N 88 20W
Reagan County ◇ **64** 31 25N 101 34W
Real County ◇ **65** 29 55N 99 55W
Realitos **64** 27 27N 98 32W
Reardan **67** 47 40N 117 53W
Reasnor **37** 41 35N 93 1W
Rector **27** 36 16N 90 17W
Red →, Ky. **63** 37 51N 84 5W
Red →, La. **39** 31 1N 91 45W
Red →, N. Dak. **55** 49 0N 97 15W
Red →, Tenn. **62** 36 32N 87 22W
Red Bank, N.J. **51** 40 21N 74 5W
Red Bank, Tenn. **63** 35 7N 85 17W
Red Bluff **28** 40 11N 122 15W
Red Bluff L. **52** 31 54N 103 55W
Red Boiling Springs **63** 36 32N 85 51W
Red Bud **35** 38 13N 89 59W
Red Cedar → **69** 44 42N 91 53W
Red Cliff Ind. Reservation **69** 46 50N 90 47W
Red Cloud **48** 40 5N 98 32W
Red Cr. → **45** 30 41N 88 40W
Red Devil **25** 61 46N 157 19W
Red Feather Lakes **30** 40 48N 105 35W
Red Head **31** 30 29N 85 51W
Red Hills **38** 37 40N 98 50W
Red Hook **53** 41 55N 73 53W
Red L., Ariz. **26** 35 40N 114 4W
Red L., S. Dak. **61** 43 44N 99 13W
Red Lake → **44** 47 55N 97 1W
Red Lake County ◇ **44** 47 50N 96 0W
Red Lake Falls **44** 47 53N 96 16W
Red Lake Indian Reservation **44** 48 0N 95 20W
Red Level **24** 31 24N 86 36W
Red Lion, N.J. **51** 39 53N 74 45W
Red Lion, Pa. **59** 39 54N 76 36W
Red Lodge **47** 45 11N 109 15W
Red Mountain **29** 35 37N 117 38W
Red Oak, Iowa **37** 41 1N 95 14W
Red Oak, N.C. **54** 36 2N 77 54W
Red Oak, Okla. **57** 34 57N 95 5W
Red River County ◇ **65** 33 37N 95 3W
Red River Parish ◇ **39** 32 1N 93 21W
Red River Valley **55** 48 0N 96 50W
Red Rock, Ariz. **26** 36 36N 109 3W
Red Rock, Mont. **47** 44 55N 112 50W
Red Rock, Okla. **57** 36 28N 97 11W
Red Rock, L. **37** 41 22N 92 59W
Red Rock Cr. → **57** 36 30N 96 59W
Red Springs, N.C. **54** 34 49N 79 11W
Red Springs, Tex. **65** 33 37N 99 25W

Red Willow County ◇ 48 40 15N 100 30W
Red Willow Cr. → 48 40 13N 100 29W
Red Wing 44 44 34N 92 31W
Redbay 31 30 35N 85 57W
Redbird 57 35 54N 95 36W
Redcliff 30 39 31N 106 22W
Reddell 39 30 40N 92 25W
Reddick, Fla. 31 29 22N 82 12W
Reddick, Ill. 35 41 6N 88 15W
Redding, Calif. 28 40 35N 122 24W
Redding, Iowa 37 40 36N 94 23W
Redding Ridge 42 41 19N 73 21W
Redfield, Ark. 27 34 27N 92 11W
Redfield, Iowa 37 41 35N 94 12W
Redfield, Kans. 38 37 50N 94 53W
Redfield, S. Dak. 61 44 53N 98 31W
Redford 64 29 27N 104 11W
Redkey 36 40 21N 85 9W
Redlake 44 47 53N 95 1W
Redlands 29 34 4N 117 11W
Redmesa 30 37 6N 108 11W
Redmon 35 39 39N 87 52W
Redmond, Oreg. 58 44 17N 121 11W
Redmond, Utah 66 39 0N 111 52W
Redmond, Wash. 67 47 41N 122 7W
Redondo Beach 29 33 50N 118 23W
Redoubt Volcano 25 60 29N 152 45W
Redrock 52 32 41N 108 44W
Redstone 30 39 11N 107 14W
Redstone Cr. → 61 44 4N 98 5W
Redvale 30 38 10N 108 25W
Redwater → 47 48 3N 105 13W
Redwood 45 32 29N 90 48W
Redwood → 44 44 34N 95 5W
Redwood City 28 37 30N 122 15W
Redwood County ◇ 44 44 20N 95 15W
Redwood Cr. → 28 41 18N 124 5W
Redwood Falls 44 44 32N 95 7W
Redwood National Park 28 41 40N 124 5W
Ree Heights 61 44 31N 99 12W
Reece 38 37 48N 96 27W
Reed, Ky. 62 37 51N 87 21W
Reed, Okla. 57 34 54N 99 42W
Reed City 43 43 53N 85 31W
Reeder 55 46 7N 102 57W
Reedley 29 36 36N 119 27W
Reeds 46 37 7N 94 10W
Reeds Pk. 52 33 9N 107 51W
Reeds Spring 46 36 45N 93 23W
Reedsburg 69 43 32N 90 0W
Reedsport 58 43 42N 124 6W
Reedsville, Va. 68 37 51N 76 17W
Reedsville, W. Va. 68 39 31N 79 48W
Reedy 68 38 54N 81 26W
Reedy → 60 28 4N 81 21W
Reelfoot L. 62 36 25N 89 22W
Reese 43 43 27N 83 42W
Reese → 49 40 48N 117 4W
Reeves 39 30 31N 93 3W
Reeves County ◇ 64 31 13N 103 45W
Reform 24 33 23N 88 1W
Refugio 65 28 18N 97 17W
Refugio County ◇ 65 28 14N 97 20W
Regan 55 47 10N 100 32W
Regent 55 46 25N 102 33W
Register 32 32 22N 81 53W
Rehoboth 52 35 32N 108 39W
Rehoboth Bay 41 38 40N 75 6W
Rehoboth Beach 41 38 43N 131 15W
Reidsville, Ga. 32 32 6N 82 7W
Reidsville, N.C. 54 36 21N 79 40W
Reinbeck 37 42 19N 92 36W
Reisterstown 41 39 28N 76 50W
Reliance, Del. 41 38 38N 75 43W
Reliance, S. Dak. 61 43 53N 99 36W
Reliance, Wyo. 70 41 40N 109 12W
Rembert 60 34 6N 80 32W
Rembrandt 37 42 50N 95 10W
Remer 44 47 4N 93 55W
Remington, Ind. 36 40 46N 87 9W
Remington, Va. 68 38 32N 77 49W
Remsen, Iowa 37 42 49N 95 58W
Remsen, N.Y. 53 43 20N 75 11W
Rend Lake 35 38 2N 88 58W
Renfroe 32 32 14N 84 43W
Renick 68 38 1N 80 22W
Reno, Minn. 44 43 36N 91 17W
Reno, Nev. 49 39 31N 119 48W
Reno County ◇ 38 38 0N 98 0W
Renovo 59 41 20N 77 45W
Rensselaer, Ind. 36 40 57N 87 9W
Rensselaer, N.Y. 53 42 38N 73 45W
Rensselaer County ◇ 53 42 40N 73 30W
Rentiesville 57 35 35N 95 30W
Renton 67 47 29N 122 12W
Rentz 32 32 25N 82 59W
Renville 44 44 48N 95 13W
Renville County ◇, Minn. 44 44 45N 95 0W
Renville County ◇, N. Dak. 55 48 37N 101 35W
Renwick 37 42 50N 93 59W
Repton 24 31 25N 87 14W
Republic, Kans. 38 39 55N 97 49W
Republic, Mich. 43 46 25N 87 59W
Republic, Mo. 46 37 7N 93 29W
Republic, Ohio 56 41 8N 83 1W
Republic, Wash. 67 48 39N 118 44W
Republic County ◇ 38 39 45N 97 40W
Republican → 38 39 4N 96 48W
Republican City 48 40 6N 99 13W
Reserve, Kans. 38 39 59N 95 34W
Reserve, La. 39 30 3N 90 33W
Reserve, N. Mex. 52 33 43N 108 45W
Revere, Mass. 42 42 25N 71 1W
Revere, Mo. 46 40 35N 91 41W
Revillo 61 45 1N 96 34W
Rewey 69 42 51N 90 24W
Rexburg 34 43 49N 111 47W
Rexford, Kans. 38 39 28N 100 45W
Rexford, Mont. 47 48 53N 115 13W
Reydon 57 35 39N 99 55W
Reyes, Pt. 28 38 0N 123 0W
Reynolds, Ga. 32 32 33N 84 6W
Reynolds, Ill. 35 41 20N 90 40W
Reynolds, Ind. 36 40 45N 86 52W
Reynolds, N. Dak. 55 47 40N 97 7W
Reynolds, Nebr. 48 40 4N 97 20W
Reynolds County 46 37 20N 91 0W
Reynoldsville 32 30 51N 84 47W
Reynosa Draz 64 26 15N 98 30W
Rhame 55 46 14N 103 39W
Rhea County ◇ 63 35 30N 85 0W
Rhine 32 31 59N 83 12W
Rhinelander 69 45 38N 89 25W
Rhode Island 42 41 30N 71 15W
Rhode Island □ 42 41 40N 71 30W
Rhode Island Sd. 42 41 20N 71 10W
Rhodhiss L. 54 35 47N 81 26W
Rhome 65 33 3N 97 28W
Rib Lake 69 45 19N 90 12W
Ribera 52 35 23N 105 27W
Ricardo 64 27 25N 97 51W
Rice, Calif. 29 34 5N 114 51W
Rice, Minn. 44 45 45N 94 13W
Rice, Tex. 65 32 14N 96 30W
Rice County ◇, Kans. 38 38 25N 98 10W
Rice County ◇, Minn. 44 44 20N 93 15W
Rice Lake 69 45 30N 91 44W
Riceboro 32 31 44N 81 26W
Riceville, Iowa 37 43 22N 92 33W
Riceville, Ky. 63 37 44N 82 55W
Riceville, Tenn. 63 35 23N 84 42W
Rich County ◇ 66 41 30N 111 10W
Rich Fountain 46 38 24N 91 53W
Rich Hill 46 38 6N 94 22W
Rich Square 54 36 16N 77 17W
Richards, Mo. 46 37 54N 94 33W
Richards, Tex. 65 30 32N 95 51W
Richardson 65 32 57N 96 44W
Richardson County ◇ 48 40 15N 95 45W
Richardson Lakes 40 44 46N 70 58W
Richardton 55 46 53N 102 19W
Richey 47 47 39N 105 4W
Richfield, Idaho 34 43 3N 114 9W
Richfield, Kans. 38 37 16N 101 47W
Richfield, Minn. 44 44 53N 93 17W
Richfield, Pa. 59 40 41N 77 7W
Richfield, Utah 66 38 46N 112 5W
Richfield Springs 53 42 51N 74 59W
Richford 50 45 0N 72 40W
Richgrove 29 35 48N 119 7W
Richland, Ga. 32 32 5N 84 40W
Richland, Mich. 43 42 22N 85 27W
Richland, Mo. 46 37 51N 92 26W
Richland, Nebr. 48 41 26N 97 13W
Richland, Oreg. 58 44 46N 117 10W
Richland, S. Dak. 61 42 46N 96 39W
Richland, Tex. 65 31 57N 96 26W
Richland, Wash. 67 46 17N 119 18W
Richland Center 69 43 21N 90 23W
Richland County ◇, Ill. 35 38 45N 88 5W
Richland County ◇, Mont. 47 47 48N 104 40W
Richland County ◇, N. Dak. 55 46 15N 97 0W
Richland County ◇, Ohio 56 40 45N 82 31W
Richland County ◇, S.C. 60 34 10N 81 0W
Richland County ◇, Wis. 69 43 20N 90 30W
Richland Parish ◇ 39 32 22N 91 52W
Richland Springs 65 31 16N 98 57W
Richlands, N.C. 54 34 54N 77 34W
Richlands, Va. 68 37 6N 81 48W
Richmond, Calif. 28 37 56N 122 21W
Richmond, Ill. 35 42 29N 88 18W
Richmond, Ind. 36 39 50N 84 53W
Richmond, Kans. 38 38 24N 95 15W
Richmond, Ky. 63 37 45N 84 18W
Richmond, Maine 40 44 5N 69 48W
Richmond, Mich. 43 42 49N 82 45W
Richmond, Mo. 46 39 17N 93 58W
Richmond, N.H. 50 42 45N 72 18W
Richmond, Tex. 65 29 35N 95 46W
Richmond, Utah 66 41 56N 111 48W
Richmond, Va. 68 37 33N 77 27W
Richmond, Vt. 50 44 24N 72 59W
Richmond County ◇, Ga. 32 33 15N 82 5W
Richmond County ◇, N.C. 54 35 0N 79 45W
Richmond County ◇, N.Y. 53 40 40N 74 15W
Richmond County ◇, Va. 68 37 58N 76 46W
Richmond Heights 31 25 38N 80 23W
Richmond Highlands 67 47 46N 122 21W
Richmond Hill 32 31 56N 81 18W
Richmondville 53 42 38N 74 34W
Richton 45 31 16N 88 56W
Richville, Minn. 44 46 31N 95 38W
Richville, N.Y. 53 44 25N 75 22W
Richwood, Ohio 56 40 26N 83 18W
Richwood, W. Va. 68 38 14N 80 32W
Richwoods 46 38 10N 90 50W
Ricketts 37 42 8N 95 35W
Rico 30 37 42N 108 2W
Riddle, Idaho 34 42 11N 116 7W
Riddle, Oreg. 58 42 57N 123 22W
Ridge 41 38 8N 76 24W
Ridge Farm 35 39 54N 87 39W
Ridge Spring 60 33 51N 81 40W
Ridgecrest 29 35 38N 117 40W
Ridgefield, Conn. 42 41 17N 73 30W
Ridgefield, Wash. 67 45 49N 122 45W
Ridgeland, Miss. 45 32 26N 90 8W
Ridgeland, S.C. 60 32 29N 80 59W
Ridgeland, Wis. 69 45 12N 91 54W
Ridgely 62 36 16N 89 29W
Ridgetop 62 36 24N 86 46W
Ridgeville, Ind. 36 40 18N 85 2W
Ridgeville, S.C. 60 33 6N 80 19W
Ridgeway, Iowa 37 43 18N 91 59W
Ridgeway, Mo. 46 40 23N 93 57W
Ridgeway, Ohio 56 40 31N 83 35W
Ridgeway, S.C. 60 34 18N 80 58W
Ridgeway, Va. 68 36 35N 79 52W
Ridgeway, Wis. 69 43 1N 90 1W
Ridgewood 51 40 59N 74 7W
Ridgway, Colo. 30 38 9N 107 46W
Ridgway, Ill. 35 37 48N 88 16W
Ridgway, Pa. 59 41 25N 78 44W
Rienzi 45 34 46N 88 32W
Riesel 65 31 29N 96 55W
Rieth 58 45 40N 118 54W
Riffe L. 67 46 32N 122 26W
Rifle 30 39 32N 107 47W
Rigby 34 43 40N 111 55W
Riggins 34 45 25N 116 19W
Riley, Ind. 36 39 23N 87 18W
Riley, Kans. 38 39 18N 96 50W
Riley, Oreg. 58 43 32N 119 28W
Riley County ◇ 38 39 20N 96 40W
Rillito 26 32 25N 111 9W
Rimersburg 59 41 3N 79 30W
Rimini 60 33 40N 80 30W
Rinard 37 42 20N 94 29W
Rincon, Puerto Rico 71 18 20N 67 15W
Rincon, U.S.A. 32 32 18N 81 14W
Rincon, Bahia de 71 17 55N 66 20W
Rineyville 63 37 45N 85 58W
Ringgold, Ga. 32 34 55N 85 7W
Ringgold, La. 39 32 20N 93 17W
Ringgold, Nebr. 48 41 31N 100 47W
Ringgold County ◇ 37 40 45N 94 15W
Ringling, Mont. 47 46 16N 110 49W
Ringling, Okla. 57 34 11N 97 36W
Ringoes 51 40 26N 74 52W
Ringsted 37 43 18N 94 31W
Ringwood, N.J. 51 41 7N 74 15W
Ringwood, Okla. 57 36 23N 98 15W
Rio, Ill. 35 41 7N 90 24W
Rio, Wis. 69 43 27N 89 14W
Rio Arriba County ◇ 52 36 30N 106 45W
Rio Blanco 30 39 44N 107 57W
Rio Blanco County ◇ 30 40 0N 108 15W
Rio Dell 28 40 30N 124 6W
Rio Grande, Puerto Rico 71 18 23N 65 50W
Rio Grande, N.J. 51 39 1N 74 53W
Rio Grande, Ohio 56 38 56N 82 21W
Rio Grande City 64 26 23N 98 49W
Rio Grande County ◇ 30 37 40N 106 20W
Rio Grande National Forest 30 37 30N 106 30W
Rio Hondo 64 26 14N 97 35W
Rio Piedras 71 18 24N 66 3W
Rio Vista 28 38 10N 121 42W
Rion 60 34 18N 81 8W
Ripley, Ill. 35 40 1N 90 38W
Ripley, Miss. 45 34 44N 88 57W
Ripley, N.Y. 53 42 16N 79 43W
Ripley, Ohio 56 38 45N 83 51W
Ripley, Okla. 57 36 1N 96 54W
Ripley, Tenn. 62 35 45N 89 32W
Ripley, W. Va. 68 38 49N 81 43W
Ripley County ◇, Ind. 36 39 5N 85 15W
Ripley County ◇, Mo. 46 36 40N 90 50W
Ripon, Calif. 28 37 44N 121 7W
Ripon, Wis. 69 43 51N 88 50W
Rippey 37 41 56N 94 12W
Ririe 34 43 38N 111 47W
Ririe L. 34 43 30N 111 43W
Risco 46 36 33N 89 49W
Rising City 48 41 12N 97 18W
Rising Fawn 32 34 46N 85 32W
Rising Star 65 32 6N 98 58W
Rising Sun, Ind. 36 38 57N 84 51W
Rising Sun, Md. 41 39 42N 76 4W
Rison 27 33 58N 92 11W
Rita Blanca Cr. → 64 35 40N 102 29W
Rita Blanca National Grassland 64 36 20N 102 30W
Ritchie County ◇ 68 39 13N 81 3W
Ritter, Mt. 28 37 41N 119 12W
Rittman 56 40 58N 81 47W
Ritzville 67 47 8N 118 23W
Riva 41 38 57N 76 35W
River Falls 69 44 52N 92 38W
Riverbank 28 37 44N 120 56W
Riverdale, Calif. 29 36 26N 119 52W
Riverdale, Ga. 32 33 34N 84 25W
Riverdale, N. Dak. 55 47 30N 101 22W
Riverdale, Nebr. 48 40 47N 99 10W
Riverhead 53 40 55N 72 40W
Riverside, Calif. 29 33 59N 117 22W
Riverside, Iowa 37 41 29N 91 35W
Riverside, Md. 41 38 22N 77 11W
Riverside, N.J. 51 40 2N 74 58W
Riverside, Oreg. 58 43 32N 118 10W
Riverside, Tex. 65 30 51N 95 24W
Riverside, Wash. 67 48 30N 119 30W
Riverside, Wyo. 70 41 13N 106 47W
Riverside County ◇ 29 33 45N 116 0W
Riverside Reservoir 30 40 20N 104 15W
Riverton, Ill. 35 39 51N 89 33W
Riverton, Iowa 37 40 41N 95 34W
Riverton, Kans. 38 37 5N 94 42W
Riverton, La. 39 32 10N 92 6W
Riverton, Nebr. 48 40 5N 98 46W
Riverton, Oreg. 58 43 10N 124 16W
Riverton, Utah 66 40 31N 111 56W
Riverton, W. Va. 68 38 45N 79 26W
Riverton, Wyo. 70 43 2N 108 23W
Riverton Heights 67 47 28N 122 17W
Riverview 31 27 52N 82 20W
Rivesville 68 39 32N 80 7W
Riviera, Ariz. 26 35 8N 114 32W
Riviera, Tex. 64 27 18N 97 49W
Riviera Beach, Fla. 31 26 47N 80 3W
Riviera Beach, Md. 41 39 10N 76 31W
Roach L. 49 35 41N 115 22W
Roachdale 36 39 51N 86 48W
Roan Cliffs 66 39 20N 109 40W
Roan Cr. → 30 39 20N 108 13W
Roan Mountain 63 36 12N 82 4W
Roan Plateau 66 39 20N 109 20W
Roanaoke I. 54 35 53N 75 39W
Roane County ◇, Tenn. 63 35 52N 84 31W
Roane County ◇, W. Va. 68 38 48N 81 21W
Roanoke, Ala. 24 33 9N 85 22W
Roanoke, Ill. 35 40 48N 89 12W
Roanoke, Ind. 36 40 58N 85 22W
Roanoke, Tex. 65 33 0N 97 10W
Roanoke, Va. 68 37 16N 79 56W
Roanoke → 54 35 57N 76 42W
Roanoke County ◇ 68 37 16N 79 56W
Roanoke Rapids 54 36 28N 77 40W
Roanoke Rapids L. 54 36 29N 77 40W
Roaring Spring 59 40 20N 78 24W
Roaring Springs 64 33 54N 100 52W
Robards 62 37 41N 87 33W
Robbins, N.C. 54 35 26N 79 35W
Robbins, Tenn. 63 36 21N 84 35W
Robbinsville 54 35 19N 83 48W
Robersonville 54 35 50N 77 15W
Robert Lee 64 31 54N 100 29W
Robert S. Kerr Reservoir 57 35 21N 94 47W
Roberta 32 32 43N 84 1W
Roberts, Idaho 34 43 43N 112 8W
Roberts, Ill. 35 40 37N 88 11W
Roberts, Mont. 47 45 22N 109 10W
Roberts County ◇, S. Dak. 61 45 33N 96 57W
Roberts County ◇, Tex. 64 35 55N 100 55W
Robertsdale 24 30 33N 87 43W
Robertson County ◇, Ky. 63 38 30N 84 5W

Robertson County ◇, Tenn. **62** 36 31N 86 53W
Robertson County ◇, Tex. **65** 31 2N 96 29W
Robertsville **51** 40 21N 74 17W
Robeson County ◇ **54** 34 30N 79 10W
Robesonia **59** 40 21N 76 8W
Robinson, Ill. **35** 39 0N 87 44W
Robinson, Kans. **38** 39 49N 95 25W
Robinson, N. Dak. **55** 47 9N 99 47W
Robinson, Tex. **65** 31 28N 97 7W
Robinson, L. **60** 34 30N 80 12W
Robinson Mt. **47** 48 58N 115 25W
Robstown **65** 27 47N 97 40W
Roby, Mo. **46** 37 31N 92 8W
Roby, Tex. **64** 32 45N 100 23W
Roca **48** 40 39N 96 40W
Rochdale **42** 42 12N 71 54W
Rochelle, Ga. **32** 31 57N 83 27W
Rochelle, Ill. **35** 41 56N 89 4W
Rochelle, Tex. **65** 31 14N 99 13W
Rocheport **46** 38 59N 92 34W
Rochester, Ill. **35** 39 45N 89 32W
Rochester, Ind. **36** 41 4N 86 13W
Rochester, Ky. **62** 37 13N 86 53W
Rochester, Mass. **42** 41 44N 70 49W
Rochester, Mich. **43** 42 41N 83 8W
Rochester, Minn. **44** 44 1N 92 28W
Rochester, N.H. **50** 43 18N 70 59W
Rochester, N.Y. **53** 43 10N 77 37W
Rochester, Ohio **56** 41 8N 82 18W
Rochester, Tex. **65** 33 19N 99 51W
Rochester, Vt. **50** 43 51N 72 48W
Rochester, Wash. **67** 46 49N 123 6W
Rock **43** 46 4N 87 10W
Rock → **35** 41 29N 90 37W
Rock Cave **68** 38 50N 80 21W
Rock County ◇, Minn. **44** 43 45N 96 15W
Rock County ◇, Nebr. **48** 42 30N 99 30W
Rock County ◇, Wis. **69** 42 45N 89 10W
Rock Cr. →, Ill. **35** 41 42N 90 3W
Rock Cr. →, Missoula, Mont. **47** 46 43N 113 40W
Rock Cr. →, Valley, Mont. **47** 48 27N 107 6W
Rock Cr. →, Nev. **49** 40 39N 116 55W
Rock Cr. →, Oreg. **58** 45 34N 120 25W
Rock Cr. →, S. Dak. **61** 43 44N 97 58W
Rock Cr. →, Utah **66** 40 17N 110 30W
Rock Creek **56** 41 40N 80 52W
Rock Creek Butte **58** 44 49N 118 7W
Rock Falls, Ill. **35** 41 47N 89 41W
Rock Falls, Iowa **37** 43 13N 93 5W
Rock Hall **41** 39 8N 76 14W
Rock Hill **60** 34 56N 81 1W
Rock Island, Ill. **35** 41 30N 90 34W
Rock Island, Wash. **67** 47 22N 120 8W
Rock Island County ◇ **35** 41 25N 90 30W
Rock Island Dam **67** 47 23N 120 4W
Rock Point **41** 38 16N 76 50W
Rock Rapids **37** 43 26N 96 10W
Rock River **70** 41 44N 105 58W
Rock Spring **32** 34 50N 85 14W
Rock Springs, Mont. **47** 46 49N 106 15W
Rock Springs, Wyo. **70** 41 35N 109 14W
Rock Valley **37** 43 12N 96 18W
Rockaway **58** 45 37N 123 57W
Rockbridge **35** 39 16N 90 12W
Rockbridge County ◇ **68** 37 55N 79 20W
Rockcastle → **63** 36 58N 84 21W
Rockcastle County ◇ **63** 37 20N 84 20W
Rockdale **65** 30 39N 97 0W
Rockdale County ◇ **32** 33 40N 84 0W
Rockford, Ala. **24** 32 53N 86 13W
Rockford, Ill. **35** 42 16N 89 6W
Rockford, Iowa **37** 43 3N 92 57W
Rockford, Mich. **43** 43 7N 85 34W
Rockford, Minn. **44** 45 5N 93 44W
Rockford, Ohio **56** 40 41N 84 39W
Rockford, Wash. **67** 47 27N 117 8W
Rockham **61** 44 55N 98 49W
Rockingham **54** 34 57N 79 46W
Rockingham County ◇, N.C. **54** 36 20N 79 50W
Rockingham County ◇, N.H. **50** 43 0N 71 10W
Rockingham County ◇, Va. **68** 38 27N 78 52W
Rocklake **55** 48 47N 99 15W
Rockland, Idaho **34** 42 34N 112 53W
Rockland, Maine **40** 44 6N 69 7W
Rockland, Mass. **42** 42 8N 70 55W
Rockland, Mich. **43** 46 44N 89 11W
Rockland, Wis. **69** 43 54N 90 55W
Rockland County ◇ **53** 41 10N 74 5W
Rockledge **31** 28 20N 80 43W
Rocklin **28** 38 48N 121 14W
Rockmart **32** 34 0N 85 3W
Rockport, Calif. **28** 39 44N 123 49W
Rockport, Ind. **36** 37 53N 87 3W
Rockport, Mass. **42** 42 39N 70 37W
Rockport, Mo. **46** 40 25N 95 31W
Rockport, Tex. **65** 28 2N 97 3W
Rockport, Wash. **67** 48 29N 121 36W
Rocksprings **64** 30 1N 100 13W
Rockton **35** 42 27N 89 4W
Rockville, Conn. **42** 41 52N 72 28W
Rockville, Ind. **36** 39 46N 87 14W
Rockville, Md. **41** 39 5N 77 9W
Rockville, Mo. **46** 38 4N 94 5W
Rockville, Nebr. **48** 41 7N 98 50W
Rockwall **65** 32 56N 96 28W
Rockwall County ◇ **65** 32 56N 96 28W
Rockwell, Iowa **37** 42 59N 93 11W
Rockwell, N.C. **54** 35 33N 80 25W
Rockwell City **37** 42 24N 94 38W
Rockwood, Maine **40** 45 41N 69 45W
Rockwood, Pa. **59** 39 55N 79 9W
Rockwood, Tenn. **63** 35 52N 84 41W
Rocky **57** 35 9N 99 3W
Rocky → **54** 35 9N 80 4W
Rocky Boy **47** 48 16N 109 47W
Rocky Boys Indian Reservation **47** 48 25N 109 30W
Rocky Comfort Cr. → **32** 32 59N 82 25W
Rocky Ford, Colo. **30** 38 3N 103 43W
Rocky Ford, Ga. **32** 32 40N 81 50W
Rocky Fork **63** 36 2N 82 33W
Rocky Hill **42** 41 40N 72 39W
Rocky Mount, N.C. **54** 35 57N 77 48W
Rocky Mount, Va. **68** 37 12N 79 57W
Rocky Mountain National Park **30** 40 25N 105 45W
Rocky Mts. **30** 39 0N 106 0W
Rocky Point **54** 34 26N 77 53W
Rocky Ridge **41** 39 38N 77 20W
Rocky Top **58** 44 47N 122 17W
Rodeo **52** 31 50N 109 2W
Rodman **37** 43 2N 94 32W
Rodney **37** 42 12N 95 57W
Roebling **51** 40 7N 74 47W
Roeland Park **38** 39 2N 94 39W
Roff **57** 34 38N 96 50W
Roger Mills County ◇ **57** 35 45N 99 45W
Rogers, Ark. **27** 36 20N 94 7W
Rogers, La. **39** 31 32N 92 14W
Rogers, N. Dak. **55** 47 4N 98 12W
Rogers, Nebr. **48** 41 28N 96 55W
Rogers, Tex. **65** 30 56N 97 14W
Rogers, Mt. **68** 36 40N 81 33W
Rogers City **43** 45 25N 83 49W
Rogers County ◇ **57** 36 20N 95 40W
Rogers L. **29** 34 55N 117 50W
Rogerson **34** 42 13N 114 36W
Rogersville, Ala. **24** 34 50N 87 18W
Rogersville, Mo. **46** 37 7N 93 3W
Rogersville, Tenn. **63** 36 24N 83 1W
Roggen **30** 40 10N 104 22W
Rogue → **58** 42 26N 124 26W
Rogue River **58** 42 26N 123 10W
Rogue River Nat. Forest **58** 42 54N 122 22W
Rohnerville **28** 40 34N 124 8W
Rojo, Cabo **71** 17 56N 67 12W
Roland, Iowa **37** 42 10N 93 30W
Roland, Okla. **57** 35 25N 94 31W
Rolette **55** 48 40N 99 51W
Rolette County ◇ **55** 48 55N 99 55W
Rolfe **37** 42 49N 94 31W
Roll **26** 32 45N 113 59W
Rolla, Kans. **38** 37 7N 101 38W
Rolla, Mo. **46** 37 57N 91 46W
Rolla, N. Dak. **55** 48 52N 99 37W
Rolling Fork **45** 32 55N 90 53W
Rolling Fork → **63** 37 55N 85 50W
Roma-Los Saenz **64** 26 24N 99 5W
Romain C. **60** 33 0N 79 22W
Romano C. **31** 25 51N 81 41W
Romanzof C. **25** 61 49N 166 6W
Rome, Ga. **32** 34 15N 85 10W
Rome, Ill. **35** 40 53N 89 30W
Rome, N.Y. **53** 43 13N 75 27W
Rome, Pa. **59** 41 51N 76 21W
Rome City **36** 41 30N 85 23W
Romeo, Colo. **30** 37 10N 105 59W
Romeo, Mich. **43** 42 48N 83 1W
Romeoville **35** 41 39N 88 3W
Romero **64** 35 44N 102 56W
Romney **68** 39 21N 78 45W
Ronan **47** 47 32N 114 6W
Ronceverte **68** 37 45N 80 28W
Rondout Res. **53** 41 50N 74 29W
Ronkonkoma **53** 40 48N 73 7W
Roodhouse **35** 39 29N 90 24W
Roof Butte **26** 36 28N 109 5W
Rooks County ◇ **38** 39 20N 99 15W
Roopville **32** 33 27N 85 8W
Roosevelt, Ariz. **26** 33 41N 111 9W
Roosevelt, Minn. **44** 48 48N 95 6W
Roosevelt, Okla. **57** 34 51N 99 1W
Roosevelt, Utah **66** 40 18N 109 59W
Roosevelt County ◇, Mont. **47** 48 20N 105 20W
Roosevelt County ◇, N. Mex. **52** 34 0N 103 30W
Roosevelt National Forest **30** 40 45N 105 40W
Roper **54** 35 53N 76 37W
Ropesville **64** 33 26N 102 9W
Rosalia **67** 47 14N 117 22W
Rosamond L. **29** 34 50N 118 4W
Rosburg **67** 46 20N 123 38W
Roscoe, Ill. **35** 42 25N 89 1W
Roscoe, S. Dak. **61** 45 27N 99 20W
Roscoe, Tex. **64** 32 27N 100 32W
Roscommon **43** 44 30N 84 35W
Roscommon County ◇ **43** 44 15N 84 40W
Rose **48** 42 9N 99 28W
Rose, Mt. **49** 39 21N 119 55W
Rose Bud **27** 35 20N 92 5W
Rose City **43** 44 25N 84 7W
Rose Creek **44** 43 36N 92 50W
Rose Hill, Ill. **35** 39 6N 88 9W
Rose Hill, Iowa **37** 41 19N 92 28W
Rose Hill, Kans. **38** 37 34N 97 7W
Rose Hill, N.C. **54** 34 50N 78 2W
Rose Pk. **26** 33 25N 109 21W
Roseau **44** 48 51N 95 46W
Roseau → **44** 49 0N 96 30W
Roseau County ◇ **44** 48 45N 95 50W
Roseboro **54** 34 58N 78 31W
Rosebud, Mo. **46** 38 23N 91 25W
Rosebud, Mont. **47** 46 16N 106 27W
Rosebud, S. Dak. **61** 43 14N 100 51W
Rosebud, Tex. **65** 31 4N 96 59W
Rosebud County ◇ **47** 46 30N 106 45W
Rosebud Indian Reservation **61** 43 10N 101 0W
Roseburg **58** 43 13N 123 20W
Rosebush **43** 43 42N 84 46W
Rosedale, Md. **41** 39 19N 76 31W
Rosedale, Miss. **45** 33 51N 91 2W
Rosedale, Okla. **57** 34 55N 97 11W
Rosedale, W. Va. **68** 38 44N 80 57W
Roseglen **55** 47 45N 101 50W
Roseland, La. **39** 30 46N 90 31W
Roseland, Nebr. **48** 40 28N 98 34W
Rosemont **41** 39 20N 77 37W
Rosemount **44** 44 45N 93 8W
Rosenberg **65** 29 34N 95 49W
Rosendale **44** 45 2N 94 43W
Rosenhayn **51** 39 29N 75 8W
Rosepine **39** 30 55N 93 17W
Rosette **66** 41 49N 113 25W
Roseville, Calif. **28** 38 45N 121 17W
Roseville, Ill. **35** 40 44N 90 40W
Roseville, Mich. **43** 42 30N 82 56W
Roseville, Minn. **44** 45 1N 93 10W
Roseville, Ohio **56** 39 49N 82 5W
Roseville, Pa. **59** 41 52N 76 58W
Rosharon **65** 29 21N 95 28W
Rosholt, S. Dak. **61** 45 52N 96 44W
Rosholt, Wis. **69** 44 38N 89 18W
Rosiclare **35** 37 26N 88 21W
Rosier **32** 32 59N 82 15W
Roslyn, S. Dak. **61** 45 30N 97 29W
Roslyn, Wash. **67** 47 13N 120 59W
Rosman **54** 35 9N 82 49W
Ross **55** 48 19N 102 33W
Ross County ◇ **56** 39 20N 82 59W
Ross L. **67** 48 44N 121 4W
Ross Lake National Recreation Area **67** 48 43N 121 4W
Ross R. Barnett Reservoir **45** 32 24N 90 4W
Rossburg **56** 40 17N 84 38W
Rossford **56** 41 36N 83 34W
Rossie **37** 43 1N 95 11W
Rossiter **59** 40 54N 78 56W
Rosston, Ark. **27** 33 36N 93 17W
Rosston, Okla. **57** 36 49N 99 56W
Rossville, Ill. **35** 40 23N 87 40W
Rossville, Ind. **36** 40 25N 86 36W
Rossville, Kans. **38** 39 8N 95 57W
Roswell, Ga. **32** 34 2N 84 22W
Roswell, N. Mex. **52** 33 24N 104 32W
Rotan **64** 32 51N 100 28W
Rothsay **44** 46 28N 96 17W
Rothschild **69** 44 53N 89 37W
Rotterdam **53** 42 48N 74 1W
Rougemont **54** 36 13N 78 56W
Rough River L. **62** 37 37N 86 30W
Roulette **59** 41 47N 78 9W
Round Hill **68** 39 8N 77 46W
Round Lake **44** 43 32N 95 28W
Round Mountain, Nev. **49** 38 43N 117 4W
Round Mountain, Tex. **65** 30 26N 98 21W
Round Oak **32** 33 7N 83 37W
Round Rock, Ariz. **26** 36 31N 109 28W
Round Rock, Tex. **65** 30 31N 97 41W
Round Top **65** 30 4N 96 42W
Round Valley Indian Reservation **28** 39 50N 123 20W
Roundup **47** 46 27N 108 33W
Rouses Point **53** 44 59N 73 22W
Rouseville **59** 41 28N 79 42W
Routt County ◇ **30** 40 30N 107 0W
Routt National Forest **30** 40 45N 107 0W
Rover **62** 35 40N 86 36W
Rowan **37** 42 45N 93 33W
Rowan County ◇, Ky. **63** 38 10N 83 25W
Rowan County ◇, N.C. **54** 35 40N 80 30W
Rowe **52** 35 30N 105 41W
Rowena **65** 31 39N 100 3W
Rowesville **60** 33 22N 80 50W
Rowland **54** 34 32N 79 18W
Rowlesburg **68** 39 21N 79 40W
Rowlett **65** 32 54N 96 34W
Rowley **37** 42 22N 91 51W
Roxana **41** 38 30N 75 10W
Roxboro **54** 36 24N 78 59W
Roxbury, Conn. **42** 41 45N 73 11W
Roxbury, Kans. **38** 38 33N 97 26W
Roxbury, N.Y. **53** 42 17N 74 34W
Roxbury, Vt. **50** 44 8N 72 44W
Roxie **45** 31 30N 91 4W
Roxton **65** 33 33N 95 44W
Roy, Fla. **31** 29 37N 81 29W
Roy, Mont. **47** 47 20N 108 58W
Roy, N. Mex. **52** 35 57N 104 12W
Roy, Utah **66** 41 10N 112 2W
Roy, Wash. **67** 47 0N 122 33W
Royal **37** 43 4N 95 17W
Royal Center **36** 40 52N 86 30W
Royal City **67** 46 54N 119 38W
Royal Oak, Md. **41** 38 44N 76 11W
Royal Oak, Mich. **43** 42 30N 83 9W
Royalston **42** 42 40N 72 12W
Royalton **44** 45 50N 94 18W
Royalty **64** 31 22N 102 52W
Royersford **59** 40 11N 75 33W
Royse City **65** 32 59N 96 20W
Royston **32** 34 17N 83 7W
Rozel **38** 38 12N 99 24W
Ruby, Alaska **25** 64 45N 155 30W
Ruby, S.C. **60** 34 44N 80 11W
Ruby Dome **49** 40 37N 115 28W
Ruby L. **49** 40 10N 115 28W
Ruby Mts. **49** 40 30N 115 20W
Ruby Valley **49** 40 30N 115 21W
Rudolph **69** 44 30N 89 48W
Rudy **27** 35 31N 94 16W
Rudyard, Mich. **43** 46 14N 84 36W
Rudyard, Mont. **47** 48 34N 110 33W
Rufflin **60** 33 0N 80 49W
Rufus **58** 45 42N 120 44W
Rugby **55** 48 22N 100 0W
Ruidosa **64** 29 59N 104 41W
Ruidoso **52** 33 20N 105 41W
Ruidoso Downs **52** 33 20N 105 32W
Rule **65** 33 11N 99 54W
Ruleville **45** 33 44N 90 33W
Rulo **48** 40 3N 95 26W
Rum → **44** 45 11N 93 23W
Rumbley **41** 38 6N 75 51W
Rumford **40** 44 33N 70 33W
Rumney **50** 43 47N 71 48W
Rump Mt. **40** 45 12N 71 4W
Rumson **51** 40 23N 74 0W
Runge **65** 28 53N 97 43W
Runnells **37** 41 31N 93 21W
Runnels County ◇ **65** 31 51N 99 57W
Running Water → **64** 34 0N 101 30W
Rupert, Idaho **34** 42 37N 113 41W
Rupert, Vt. **50** 43 16N 73 13W
Rupert, W. Va. **68** 37 58N 80 41W
Rural Hall **54** 36 15N 80 18W
Rural Retreat **68** 36 54N 81 17W
Rush **63** 38 20N 82 46W
Rush Center **38** 38 28N 99 19W
Rush City **44** 45 41N 92 58W
Rush County ◇, Ind. **36** 39 35N 85 30W
Rush County ◇, Kans. **38** 38 30N 99 15W
Rush Cr. → **30** 38 22N 102 32W
Rush Springs **57** 34 47N 97 58W
Rushford **44** 43 49N 91 46W
Rushmore, Mt. **61** 43 53N 103 28W
Rushville, Ill. **35** 40 7N 90 34W
Rushville, Ind. **36** 39 37N 85 27W
Rushville, Mo. **46** 39 35N 95 1W
Rushville, Nebr. **48** 42 43N 102 28W
Rusk **65** 31 48N 95 9W
Rusk County ◇, Tex. **65** 32 9N 94 48W
Rusk County ◇, Wis. **69** 45 25N 91 10W
Ruskin, Fla. **31** 27 43N 82 26W
Ruskin, Nebr. **48** 40 9N 97 52W

Ruso 55 47 50N 100 56W
Russell, Fla. 31 30 3N 81 45W
Russell, Kans. 38 38 54N 98 52W
Russell County ◇, Ala. 24 32 18N 85 10W
Russell County ◇, Kans. 38 39 0N 98 45W
Russell County ◇, Ky. 63 37 0N 85 0W
Russell County ◇, Va. 68 36 0N 82 0W
Russell Cr. → 63 37 14N 85 30W
Russell Springs, Kans. 38 38 55N 101 11W
Russell Springs, Ky. 63 37 3N 85 5W
Russellville, Ala. 24 34 30N 87 44W
Russellville, Ark. 27 35 17N 93 8W
Russellville, Ky. 62 36 51N 86 53W
Russellville, Mo. 46 38 31N 92 26W
Russellville, Ohio 56 38 52N 83 47W
Russellville, Tenn. 63 36 15N 83 12W
Russian → 28 38 27N 123 8W
Russian Mission 25 61 47N 161 19W
Russiaville 36 40 25N 86 16W
Rustburg 68 37 17N 79 6W
Ruston 39 32 32N 92 38W
Ruth, Miss. 45 31 23N 90 19W
Ruth, Nev. 49 39 17N 114 59W
Rutherford 62 36 8N 88 59W
Rutherford County ◇, N.C. 54 35 20N 81 50W
Rutherford County ◇, Tenn. 62 35 51N 86 24W
Rutherfordton 54 35 22N 81 58W
Ruthsburg 41 39 0N 75 58W
Ruthton 44 44 11N 96 6W
Ruthven 37 43 8N 94 54W
Rutland, Ill. 35 40 59N 89 3W
Rutland, Iowa 37 42 46N 94 18W
Rutland, Mass. 42 42 23N 71 57W
Rutland, N. Dak. 55 46 3N 97 30W
Rutland, Ohio 56 39 3N 82 8W
Rutland, S. Dak. 61 44 5N 96 58W
Rutland, Vt. 50 43 37N 72 58W
Rutland County ◇ 50 43 35N 73 0W
Rutledge, Ga. 32 33 38N 83 37W
Rutledge, Minn. 44 46 16N 92 52W
Rutledge, Tenn. 63 36 17N 83 31W
Ryan, Iowa 37 42 21N 91 29W
Ryan, Okla. 57 34 1N 97 57W
Ryder 55 47 55N 101 40W
Ryderwood 67 46 23N 123 3W
Rye, Ark. 27 33 45N 91 59W
Rye, Colo. 30 37 55N 104 56W
Rye, N.H. 50 43 2N 70 50W
Rye Beach 50 42 59N 70 46W
Rye Patch Reservoir 49 40 28N 118 19W
Ryegate 47 46 18N 109 15W

S

Sabana Grande 71 18 5N 66 58W
Sabetha 38 39 54N 95 48W
Sabin 44 46 47N 96 39W
Sabina 56 39 29N 83 38W
Sabinal 65 29 19N 99 28W
Sabine → 39 29 59N 93 47W
Sabine County ◇ 65 31 20N 93 51W
Sabine L. 39 29 53N 93 51W
Sabine National Forest 65 31 38N 94 0W
Sabine Parish ◇ 39 31 38N 93 39W
Sabine Pass 65 29 44N 93 54W
Sabinoso 52 35 42N 104 24W
Sable, C. 31 25 9N 81 8W
Sabula, Iowa 37 42 4N 90 10W
Sabula, Mo. 46 37 27N 90 42W
Sac → 46 38 1N 93 43W
Sac City 37 42 25N 95 0W
Sac County ◇ 37 42 25N 95 5W
Sacajawea, L. 67 46 20N 118 45W
Sacajawea Peak 58 45 15N 117 17W
Sacandaga Reservoir 53 43 6N 74 16W
Sacaton 26 33 5N 111 44W
Sackets Harbor 53 43 57N 76 7W
Saco, Maine 40 43 30N 70 27W
Saco, Mont. 47 48 28N 107 21W
Saco → 40 43 28N 70 23W
Sacramento, Calif. 28 38 35N 121 29W
Sacramento, Ky. 62 37 25N 87 16W
Sacramento, N. Mex. 52 32 48N 105 34W
Sacramento → 28 38 3N 121 56W
Sacramento County ◇ 28 38 20N 121 20W
Sacramento Mts. 52 32 30N 105 30W
Sacramento South 28 38 32N 121 26W
Sacramento Valley 28 39 30N 122 0W
Sacramento Wash → 26 34 43N 114 28W
Saddle Mt., Oreg. 58 45 58N 123 41W
Saddle Mt., Wyo. 70 44 43N 109 59W
Saddle Mts. 67 46 55N 120 0W
Saddle Peak 67 48 58N 120 9W
Sadieville 63 38 23N 84 32W
Sadorus 35 39 58N 88 21W
Saegerstown 59 41 43N 80 9W
Safford 26 32 50N 109 43W
Sag Harbor 53 41 0N 72 18W
Sagadahoc County ◇ 40 44 0N 70 0W
Sagamore 42 41 45N 70 33W
Sagavanirktok → 25 70 19N 147 53W
Sage 70 41 49N 110 58W
Sage Cr. → 47 47 16N 109 43W
Sagerton 65 33 5N 99 58W
Sageville 37 42 36N 90 43W
Saginaw 43 43 26N 83 56W
Saginaw → 43 43 39N 83 51W
Saginaw B. 43 43 50N 83 40W
Saginaw County ◇ 43 43 20N 84 0W
Saguache 30 38 5N 106 8W
Saguache County ◇ 30 38 10N 106 15W
Saguaro Nat. Monument 26 32 12N 110 38W
Sahuarita 26 31 57N 110 58W
Sailor Springs 35 38 46N 88 22W
St. Albans, Vt. 50 44 49N 73 5W
St. Albans, W. Va. 68 38 23N 81 50W
St. Andrew Sd. 32 31 0N 81 25W
St. Andrews 60 32 47N 80 0W
St. Anne 35 41 1N 87 43W
St. Ansgar 37 43 23N 92 55W
St. Anthony 34 43 58N 111 41W
St. Augustine 31 29 54N 81 19W
St. Augustine Beach 31 29 51N 81 16W
St. Benedict 38 39 53N 96 6W
St. Bernard Parish ◇ 39 29 55N 89 10W
St. Catherines I. 32 31 40N 81 10W
St. Charles, Ark. 27 34 23N 91 8W
St. Charles, Idaho 34 42 7N 111 23W
St. Charles, Ill. 35 41 54N 88 19W
St. Charles, Iowa 37 41 17N 93 49W
St. Charles, Mich. 43 43 18N 84 9W
St. Charles, Minn. 44 43 58N 92 4W
St. Charles, Mo. 46 38 47N 90 29W
St. Charles, S. Dak. 61 43 5N 99 6W
St. Charles, Va. 68 36 48N 83 4W
St. Charles County ◇ 46 38 45N 90 40W
St. Charles Parish ◇ 39 29 59N 90 25W
St. Clair, Ga. 32 33 9N 82 13W
St. Clair, Mich. 43 42 50N 82 30W
St. Clair, Minn. 44 44 5N 93 51W
St. Clair, Mo. 46 38 21N 90 59W
St. Clair, Pa. 59 40 43N 76 12W
St. Clair → 43 42 38N 82 31W
St. Clair, L. 43 42 27N 82 39W
St. Clair County ◇, Ala. 24 33 35N 86 17W
St. Clair County ◇, Ill. 35 38 30N 89 55W
St. Clair County ◇, Mich. 43 43 0N 82 30W
St. Clair County ◇, Mo. 46 38 0N 93 45W
St. Clair Shores 43 42 30N 82 53W
St. Clairsville 56 40 5N 80 54W
St. Cloud, Fla. 31 28 15N 81 17W
St. Cloud, Minn. 44 45 34N 94 10W
St. Croix →, Maine 40 45 4N 67 5W
St. Croix →, Wis. 69 44 45N 92 48W
St. Croix County ◇ 69 45 0N 92 20W
St. Croix Falls 69 45 24N 92 38W
St. Croix Flowage 69 46 15N 91 56W
St. Croix L. 44 44 57N 92 45W
St. David, Ariz. 26 31 54N 110 13W
St. David, Ill. 35 40 30N 90 3W
St. Donatus 37 42 22N 90 33W
St. Edward 48 41 34N 97 52W
St. Elias, Mt. 25 60 18N 140 56W
St. Elias Mts. 25 60 0N 138 0W
St. Elizabeth 46 38 15N 92 16W
St. Elmo 35 39 2N 88 51W
St. Frances 61 43 9N 100 54W
St. Francis, Kans. 38 39 47N 101 48W
St. Francis, Maine 40 47 10N 68 54W
St. Francis, Minn. 44 45 23N 93 22W
St. Francis, Wis. 69 42 58N 87 52W
St. Francis →, Ark. 27 34 38N 90 36W
St. Francis →, Ark. 27 34 40N 90 40W
St. Francis County ◇ 27 35 1N 90 47W
St. Francisville, Ill. 35 38 36N 87 39W
St. Francisville, La. 39 30 47N 91 23W
St. Francois County ◇ 46 37 50N 90 30W
St. Francois Mts. 46 37 30N 90 35W
St. Froid, L. 40 46 57N 68 37W
St. Gabriel 39 30 16N 91 6W
St. Genevieve County ◇ 46 37 50N 90 10W
St. George, Ga. 32 30 31N 82 2W
St. George, Kans. 38 39 12N 96 25W
St. George, S.C. 60 33 11N 80 35W
St. George, Utah 66 37 6N 113 35W
St. George, C. 31 29 40N 85 5W
St. George, Pt. 28 41 47N 124 15W
St. George I., Alaska 25 56 35N 169 35W
St. George I., Fla. 31 29 35N 84 55W
St. George Island 41 38 7N 76 29W
St. Helena, Calif. 28 38 30N 122 28W
St. Helena, Nebr. 48 42 49N 97 15W
St. Helena Parish ◇ 39 30 50N 90 40W
St. Helena Sd. 60 32 15N 80 25W
St. Helens 58 45 52N 122 48W
St. Helens, Mt. 67 46 12N 122 12W
St. Henry 56 40 25N 84 38W
St. Hilaire 44 48 1N 96 14W
St. Ignace 43 45 52N 84 44W
St. Ignatius 47 47 19N 114 6W
St. James, Mich. 43 45 45N 85 31W
St. James, Minn. 44 43 59N 94 38W
St. James, Mo. 46 38 0N 91 37W
St. James, N.Y. 53 40 53N 73 9W
St. James City 31 26 29N 82 5W
St. James Parish ◇ 39 30 1N 90 50W
St. Jo 65 33 42N 97 31W
St. Joe, Ark. 27 36 2N 92 48W
St. Joe, Idaho 34 47 19N 116 21W
St. Joe National Forest 34 47 5N 115 30W
St. John, Kans. 38 38 0N 98 46W
St. John, N. Dak. 55 48 57N 99 43W
St. John, Wash. 67 47 6N 117 35W
St. John → 40 45 12N 66 5W
St. John I. 71 18 20N 64 42W
St. John The Baptist Parish ◇ 39 30 3N 90 33W
St. Johns, Ariz. 26 34 30N 109 22W
St. Johns, Mich. 43 43 0N 84 33W
St. Johns → 31 30 24N 81 24W
St. Johns County ◇ 31 29 45N 81 25W
St. Johnsbury 50 44 25N 72 1W
St. Joseph, Ill. 35 40 7N 88 2W
St. Joseph, La. 39 31 55N 91 14W
St. Joseph, Mich. 43 42 6N 86 29W
St. Joseph, Mo. 46 39 46N 94 50W
St. Joseph, Tenn. 62 35 2N 87 30W
St. Joseph →, Ind. 36 41 5N 85 8W
St. Joseph →, Mich. 43 42 7N 86 29W
St. Joseph County ◇ 36 41 35N 86 15W
St. Joseph Pt. 31 29 52N 85 24W
St. Landry Parish ◇ 39 30 40N 92 0W
St. Lawrence 61 44 31N 98 56W
St. Lawrence County ◇ 53 44 30N 75 0W
St. Lawrence I. 25 63 30N 170 30W
St. Leo 44 44 43N 96 3W
St. Leonard 41 38 28N 76 30W
St. Libory 48 41 5N 98 21W
St. Louis, Mich. 43 43 25N 84 36W
St. Louis, Mo. 46 38 37N 90 12W
St. Louis, Okla. 57 35 5N 96 53W
St. Louis → 44 46 44N 92 9W
St. Louis County ◇, Minn. 44 47 40N 92 20W
St. Louis County ◇, Mo. 46 38 40N 90 25W
St. Louis Park 44 44 57N 93 21W
St. Louisville 56 40 10N 82 25W
St. Lucie 31 27 29N 80 20W
St. Lucie Canal 31 27 10N 80 18W
St. Lucie County ◇ 31 27 25N 80 30W
St. Marie 35 38 56N 88 1W
St. Maries 34 47 19N 116 35W
St. Maries → 34 47 19N 116 33W
St. Marks 31 30 9N 84 12W
St. Marks → 31 30 8N 84 12W
St. Martin I. 43 45 30N 86 46W
St. Martin Parish ◇ 39 30 7N 91 50W
St. Martinville 39 30 7N 91 50W
St. Mary L. 47 48 39N 113 34W
St. Mary Parish ◇ 39 29 48N 91 30W
St. Mary's, Alaska 25 62 4N 163 10W
St. Marys, Ga. 32 30 44N 81 33W
St. Marys, Iowa 37 41 19N 93 44W
St. Marys, Kans. 38 39 12N 96 4W
St. Marys, Mo. 46 37 53N 89 57W
St. Marys, Ohio 56 40 33N 84 24W
St. Marys, Pa. 59 41 26N 78 34W
St. Marys, W. Va. 68 39 23N 81 12W
St. Marys →, Ga. 32 30 43N 81 27W
St. Marys →, Ind. 36 41 5N 85 8W
St. Marys →, Mich. 43 46 0N 83 55W
St. Marys City 41 38 11N 76 26W
St. Marys County ◇ 41 38 15N 76 40W
St. Matthew I. 25 60 24N 172 42W
St. Matthews, Ky. 63 38 15N 85 39W
St. Matthews, S.C. 60 33 40N 80 46W
St. Meinrad 36 38 10N 86 49W
St. Michael 25 63 29N 162 2W
St. Michaels 41 38 47N 76 14W
St. Nazianz 69 44 0N 87 55W
St. Olaf 37 42 56N 91 23W
St. Onge 61 44 33N 103 43W
St. Paris 56 40 8N 83 58W
St. Patrick Peak 47 46 59N 114 51W
St. Paul, Alaska 25 57 7N 170 17W
St. Paul, Ark. 27 35 50N 93 46W
St. Paul, Ind. 36 39 26N 85 38W
St. Paul, Iowa 37 40 46N 91 31W
St. Paul, Kans. 38 37 31N 95 10W
St. Paul, Minn. 44 44 57N 93 6W
St. Paul, Nebr. 48 41 13N 98 27W
St. Paul, Va. 68 36 54N 82 19W
St. Paul I. 25 57 10N 170 15W
St. Pauls 54 34 48N 78 58W
St. Peter, Ill. 35 38 52N 88 51W
St. Peter, Minn. 44 44 20N 93 57W
St. Petersburg 31 27 46N 82 39W
St. Petersburg Beach 31 27 45N 82 45W
St. Phillip 47 46 50N 104 9W
St. Regis 47 47 18N 115 6W
St. Regis Falls 53 44 41N 74 33W
St. Simons I. 32 31 12N 81 15W
St. Stephen 60 33 24N 79 55W
St. Tammany Parish ◇ 39 30 29N 90 2W
St. Thomas, Mo. 46 38 23N 92 13W
St. Thomas, N. Dak. 55 48 37N 97 27W
St. Thomas I. 71 18 20N 64 55W
St. Vincent 44 48 58N 97 14W
St. Vincent I. 31 29 42N 85 3W
St. Vrain 52 34 25N 103 29W
Sakakawea, L. 55 47 30N 101 25W
Salado 27 35 42N 91 36W
Salado, Rio → 52 34 16N 106 52W
Salamanca 53 42 10N 78 43W
Salamonia 36 40 23N 84 52W
Salamonie L. 36 40 46N 85 37W
Sale City 32 31 16N 84 1W
Sale Creek 63 35 23N 85 7W
Salem, Ala. 24 32 36N 85 14W
Salem, Ark. 27 36 22N 91 50W
Salem, Conn. 42 41 0N 72 0W
Salem, Fla. 31 29 53N 83 25W
Salem, Ill. 35 38 38N 88 57W
Salem, Ind. 36 38 36N 86 6W
Salem, Iowa 37 40 51N 91 38W
Salem, Ky. 62 37 16N 88 15W
Salem, Mass. 42 42 31N 70 53W
Salem, Md. 41 38 32N 75 55W
Salem, Mo. 46 37 39N 91 32W
Salem, N.H. 50 42 45N 71 12W
Salem, N.J. 51 39 34N 75 28W
Salem, N.Y. 53 43 10N 73 20W
Salem, Nebr. 48 40 5N 95 43W
Salem, Ohio 56 40 54N 80 52W
Salem, Oreg. 58 44 56N 123 2W
Salem, S. Dak. 61 43 44N 97 23W
Salem, Utah 66 40 3N 111 40W
Salem, Va. 68 37 18N 80 3W
Salem, W. Va. 68 39 17N 80 34W
Salem County ◇ 51 39 40N 75 20W
Salem Plateau 46 37 30N 91 30W
Salemburg 54 35 1N 78 30W
Salida 30 38 32N 106 0W
Salina, Ariz. 26 36 1N 109 52W
Salina, Kans. 38 38 50N 97 37W
Salina, Okla. 57 36 18N 95 9W
Salina, Utah 66 38 58N 111 51W
Salinas, Puerto Rico 71 17 59N 66 18W
Salinas, U.S.A. 28 36 40N 121 39W
Salinas → 28 36 45N 121 48W
Salinas, Punta 71 18 29N 66 11W
Salinas, Sierra de 29 36 20N 121 20W
Salinas Nat. Monument 52 34 6N 106 4W
Salinas Pk. 52 33 22N 106 35W
Salinas Valley 29 36 15N 121 15W
Saline, La. 39 32 10N 92 59W
Saline, Mich. 43 42 10N 83 47W
Saline →, Bradley, Ark. 27 33 10N 92 8W
Saline →, Howard, Ark. 27 33 44N 93 58W
Saline →, Ill. 35 37 35N 88 8W
Saline →, Kans. 38 38 52N 97 30W
Saline County ◇, Ark. 27 34 34N 92 35W
Saline County ◇, Ill. 35 37 45N 88 30W
Saline County ◇, Kans. 38 38 45N 97 40W
Saline County ◇, Mo. 46 39 10N 93 10W
Saline County ◇, Nebr. 48 40 30N 97 10W
Saline L. 39 31 52N 92 54W
Saline Valley 29 36 50N 117 50W
Salineno 64 26 31N 99 7W
Salisbury, Conn. 42 41 59N 73 25W
Salisbury, Mass. 42 42 51N 70 49W
Salisbury, Md. 41 38 22N 75 36W
Salisbury, Mo. 46 39 25N 92 48W
Salisbury, N.C. 54 35 40N 80 29W
Salisbury, N.H. 50 43 22N 71 42W
Salisbury, Pa. 59 39 45N 79 5W
Salisbury, Vt. 50 43 53N 73 6W
Salisbury Heights 50 43 24N 71 44W

Name	Map	Lat.	Long.
Salish Mts.	**47**	45 30N	115 0W
Salitpa	**24**	31 37N	88 1W
Salix	**37**	42 19N	96 17W
Salkehatchie →	**60**	32 37N	80 53W
Salkum	**67**	46 32N	122 38W
Salladasburg	**59**	41 17N	77 14W
Salley	**60**	33 34N	81 18W
Sallisaw	**57**	35 28N	94 47W
Salmon	**34**	45 11N	113 54W
Salmon →	**34**	45 51N	116 47W
Salmon Falls →	**50**	43 12N	70 50W
Salmon Falls Cr. →	**34**	42 43N	114 51W
Salmon Mt.	**50**	45 14N	71 8W
Salmon Mts.	**28**	41 0N	123 0W
Salmon National Forest	**34**	45 10N	114 20W
Salmon River Mts.	**34**	44 50N	115 30W
Salmon River Reservoir	**53**	43 32N	75 55W
Salmon South Fork →	**34**	45 23N	115 31W
Salome	**26**	33 47N	113 37W
Salt →, Ariz.	**26**	33 23N	112 19W
Salt →, Ky.	**63**	38 0N	85 57W
Salt →, Mo.	**46**	39 28N	91 4W
Salt Basin	**64**	31 42N	105 2W
Salt Cr. →, Ill.	**35**	40 8N	89 50W
Salt Cr. →, N. Mex.	**52**	33 30N	104 35W
Salt Draw →	**64**	31 19N	103 28W
Salt Flat	**64**	31 45N	105 5W
Salt Fork	**57**	36 38N	97 35W
Salt Fork Arkansas →	**57**	36 36N	97 3W
Salt Fork Brazos →	**64**	33 16N	100 0W
Salt Fork L.	**56**	40 3N	81 30W
Salt Fork Red →	**57**	34 27N	99 21W
Salt L., Hawaii	**33**	21 21N	157 55W
Salt L., N. Mex.	**52**	32 18N	104 0W
Salt Lake City	**66**	40 45N	111 53W
Salt Lake County ◇	**66**	40 40N	112 0W
Salt Lick	**63**	38 7N	83 37W
Salt Marsh L.	**66**	39 29N	113 55W
Salt River Indian Reservation	**26**	33 35N	111 50W
Salt Springs	**31**	29 21N	81 44W
Salters	**60**	33 36N	79 51W
Saltillo, Miss.	**45**	34 23N	88 41W
Saltillo, Pa.	**59**	40 13N	78 1W
Saltillo, Tenn.	**62**	35 23N	88 13W
Salton Sea	**29**	33 15N	115 45W
Saltville	**68**	36 53N	81 46W
Saluda, N.C.	**54**	35 14N	82 21W
Saluda, S.C.	**60**	34 0N	81 46W
Saluda, Va.	**68**	37 36N	76 36W
Saluda →	**60**	34 1N	81 4W
Saluda County ◇	**60**	34 0N	81 45W
Salus	**27**	35 44N	93 24W
Salvador, L.	**39**	29 43N	90 15W
Salyersville	**63**	37 45N	83 4W
Sam Houston National Forest	**65**	30 32N	95 29W
Sam Rayburn Reservoir	**65**	31 4N	94 5W
Samaria	**34**	42 7N	112 20W
Samburg	**62**	36 23N	89 21W
Samoset	**31**	27 28N	82 33W
Sampson County ◇	**54**	35 0N	78 30W
Samson	**24**	31 7N	86 3W
Samuel R. McKelvie Nat. Forest	**48**	42 40N	101 0W
San Agustin, Plains of	**52**	33 45N	108 15W
San Andreas	**28**	38 12N	120 41W
San Andres Mts.	**52**	33 0N	106 30W
San Angelo	**64**	31 28N	100 26W
San Anselmo	**28**	37 59N	122 34W
San Antonio, Colo.	**30**	37 1N	106 1W
San Antonio, N. Mex.	**52**	33 55N	106 52W
San Antonio, Tex.	**65**	29 25N	98 30W
San Antonio →	**65**	28 30N	96 54W
San Antonio B.	**65**	28 20N	96 45W
San Antonio Mt.	**64**	32 0N	105 30W
San Antonio Reservoir	**29**	35 48N	120 53W
San Ardo	**29**	36 1N	120 54W
San Augustine, Calif.	**29**	34 28N	120 22W
San Augustine, Tex.	**65**	31 32N	94 7W
San Augustine County ◇	**65**	31 30N	94 8W
San Benito	**64**	26 8N	97 38W
San Benito →	**28**	36 53N	121 34W
San Benito County ◇	**29**	36 30N	121 0W
San Bernard →	**65**	28 52N	95 27W
San Bernardino	**29**	34 7N	117 19W
San Bernardino County ◇	**29**	34 45N	116 0W
San Bernardino Mts.	**29**	34 10N	116 45W
San Blas, C.	**31**	29 40N	85 21W
San Bruno	**28**	37 38N	122 25W
San Carlos	**26**	33 21N	110 27W
San Carlos Indian Reservation	**26**	33 25N	110 0W
San Carlos L.	**26**	33 11N	110 32W
San Clemente	**29**	33 26N	117 37W
San Clemente I.	**29**	32 53N	118 29W
San Cristobal	**52**	36 36N	105 39W
San Cristobal Wash →	**26**	32 45N	113 45W
San Diego, Calif.	**29**	32 43N	117 9W
San Diego, Tex.	**65**	27 46N	98 14W
San Diego County ◇	**29**	33 0N	117 15W
San Elizario	**64**	31 35N	106 16W
San Felipe Pueblo	**52**	35 26N	106 27W
San Fernando	**29**	34 17N	118 26W
San Fidel	**52**	35 5N	107 36W
San Francisco	**28**	37 47N	122 25W
San Francisco →	**26**	32 59N	109 22W
San Francisco B.	**28**	37 40N	122 20W
San Francisco County ◇	**28**	37 47N	122 25W
San Francisco Cr. →	**64**	29 53N	102 19W
San Francisco Mts.	**52**	33 45N	108 50W
San Gabriel →	**65**	30 46N	97 1W
San Gabriel Mts.	**29**	34 20N	118 0W
San German	**71**	18 5N	67 3W
San Isabel National Forest	**30**	38 0N	105 2W
San Isidro	**64**	26 43N	98 27W
San Jacinto, Calif.	**29**	33 47N	116 57W
San Jacinto, Nev.	**49**	41 53N	114 47W
San Jacinto County ◇	**65**	30 36N	95 8W
San Jacinto Mts.	**29**	33 45N	116 40W
San Joaquin	**29**	36 36N	120 11W
San Joaquin →	**28**	38 4N	121 51W
San Joaquin County ◇	**28**	37 50N	121 15W
San Joaquin Valley	**28**	37 20N	121 0W
San Jon	**52**	35 6N	103 20W
San Jose, Calif.	**28**	37 20N	121 53W
San Jose, Ill.	**35**	40 18N	89 36W
San Jose →	**52**	34 25N	106 45W
San Jose I.	**65**	27 59N	96 59W
San Juan	**71**	18 28N	66 7W
San Juan ◇	**71**	18 20N	66 10W
San Juan →	**66**	37 16N	110 26W
San Juan Basin	**52**	36 20N	108 10W
San Juan Bautista	**28**	36 51N	121 32W
San Juan Capistrano	**29**	33 30N	117 40W
San Juan County ◇, Colo.	**30**	37 50N	107 40W
San Juan County ◇, N. Mex.	**52**	36 30N	108 30W
San Juan County ◇, Utah	**66**	38 0N	109 30W
San Juan County ◇, Wash.	**67**	48 32N	123 5W
San Juan Cr. →	**29**	35 40N	120 22W
San Juan I.	**67**	48 32N	123 5W
San Juan Indian Reservation	**52**	36 0N	106 10W
San Juan Mts.	**30**	37 30N	107 0W
San Juan National Forest	**30**	37 30N	108 0W
San Juan Pueblo	**52**	36 3N	106 4W
San Leandro	**28**	37 44N	122 9W
San Lorenzo	**71**	18 11N	65 58W
San Lucas	**29**	36 8N	121 1W
San Luis, Ariz.	**26**	32 29N	114 47W
San Luis, Colo.	**30**	37 12N	105 25W
San Luis Cr. →	**30**	37 42N	105 44W
San Luis Obispo	**29**	35 17N	120 40W
San Luis Obispo County ◇	**29**	35 30N	120 30W
San Luis Peak	**30**	37 59N	106 56W
San Luis Reservoir	**28**	37 4N	121 5W
San Luis Rey →	**29**	33 12N	117 24W
San Luis Valley	**30**	37 45N	105 50W
San Manuel	**26**	32 36N	110 38W
San Marcos, Calif.	**29**	33 9N	117 10W
San Marcos, Tex.	**65**	29 53N	97 56W
San Martin	**28**	37 5N	121 37W
San Martin, C.	**29**	35 53N	121 28W
San Mateo, Calif.	**28**	37 34N	122 19W
San Mateo, N. Mex.	**52**	35 20N	107 39W
San Mateo County ◇	**28**	37 30N	122 25W
San Mateo Mts.	**52**	33 45N	107 25W
San Miguel, Calif.	**29**	35 45N	120 42W
San Miguel, N. Mex.	**52**	32 9N	106 44W
San Miguel →	**30**	38 23N	108 48W
San Miguel County ◇, Colo.	**30**	38 0N	108 30W
San Miguel County ◇, N. Mex.	**52**	35 30N	105 0W
San Miguel I.	**29**	34 2N	120 23W
San Nicolas I.	**29**	33 15N	119 30W
San Pablo, Calif.	**28**	37 58N	122 21W
San Pablo, Colo.	**30**	37 9N	105 24W
San Pablo B.	**28**	38 5N	122 20W
San Patricio	**52**	33 25N	105 20W
San Patricio County ◇	**65**	28 2N	97 31W
San Pedro	**65**	27 48N	97 41W
San Pedro →	**26**	32 59N	110 47W
San Pedro Channel	**29**	33 30N	118 25W
San Perlita	**64**	26 30N	97 39W
San Pitch →	**66**	39 3N	111 51W
San Rafael, Calif.	**28**	37 58N	122 32W
San Rafael, N. Mex.	**52**	35 7N	107 53W
San Rafael →	**66**	38 47N	110 7W
San Rafael Mts.	**29**	34 40N	119 50W
San Rafael Swell	**66**	38 45N	110 45W
San Saba	**65**	31 12N	98 43W
San Saba →	**65**	31 15N	98 36W
San Saba County ◇	**65**	31 13N	98 47W
San Sebastian	**71**	18 20N	66 59W
San Simeon	**29**	35 39N	121 11W
San Simon	**26**	32 16N	109 14W
San Simon →	**26**	32 50N	109 39W
San Simon Wash →	**26**	31 45N	112 25W
San Xavier Indian Reservation	**26**	32 10N	111 0W
San Ygnacio	**64**	27 3N	99 26W
San Ysidro	**52**	35 34N	106 46W
Sanak I.	**25**	54 25N	162 40W
Sanborn, Minn.	**44**	44 13N	95 8W
Sanborn, N. Dak.	**55**	46 57N	98 14W
Sanborn County ◇	**61**	44 0N	98 0W
Sanbornville	**50**	43 33N	71 2W
Sand Cr. →, Ind.	**36**	39 3N	85 51W
Sand Cr. →, Wyo.	**70**	43 20N	105 2W
Sand Fork	**68**	38 55N	80 45W
Sand Hill →	**44**	47 36N	96 52W
Sand Hills	**48**	42 10N	101 30W
Sand I., Hawaii	**33**	21 19N	157 53W
Sand I., Wis.	**69**	46 59N	90 58W
Sand Lake	**43**	43 18N	85 31W
Sand Point	**25**	55 20N	160 30W
Sand Pt.	**43**	43 55N	83 24W
Sand Res.	**57**	36 45N	96 10W
Sand Springs	**57**	36 9N	96 7W
Sand Tank Mts.	**26**	32 45N	112 30W
Sandborn	**36**	38 54N	87 11W
Sanders	**26**	35 13N	109 20W
Sanders County ◇	**47**	47 40N	115 30W
Sanderson, Fla.	**31**	30 15N	82 16W
Sanderson, Tex.	**64**	30 9N	102 24W
Sandersville, Ga.	**32**	32 59N	82 48W
Sandersville, Miss.	**45**	31 47N	89 2W
Sandia	**65**	28 1N	97 53W
Sandoval	**35**	38 37N	89 7W
Sandoval County ◇	**52**	35 45N	106 45W
Sandpoint	**34**	48 17N	116 33W
Sandston	**68**	37 31N	77 19W
Sandstone	**44**	46 8N	92 52W
Sandtown	**41**	39 4N	75 44W
Sandusky, Mich.	**43**	43 25N	82 50W
Sandusky, Ohio	**56**	41 27N	82 42W
Sandusky →	**56**	41 27N	83 0W
Sandusky County ◇	**56**	41 21N	83 7W
Sandwich, Ill.	**35**	41 39N	88 37W
Sandwich, Mass.	**42**	41 46N	70 30W
Sandy, Oreg.	**58**	45 24N	122 16W
Sandy, Pa.	**59**	41 6N	78 46W
Sandy, Utah	**66**	40 35N	111 50W
Sandy Cr. →	**70**	41 51N	109 47W
Sandy Hook, Ky.	**63**	38 5N	83 8W
Sandy Hook, Miss.	**45**	31 2N	89 49W
Sandy Hook, N.J.	**51**	40 26N	74 0W
Sandy Ridge	**54**	36 30N	80 6W
Sandy Springs	**32**	33 56N	84 23W
Sandyville	**68**	38 54N	81 40W
Sanford, Colo.	**30**	37 16N	105 54W
Sanford, Fla.	**31**	28 48N	81 16W
Sanford, Maine	**40**	43 27N	70 47W
Sanford, Miss.	**45**	31 29N	89 26W
Sanford, N.C.	**54**	35 29N	79 10W
Sanford, Tex.	**64**	35 42N	101 32W
Sanford, Mt.	**25**	62 13N	144 8W
Sangamon →	**35**	40 7N	90 20W
Sangamon County ◇	**35**	39 45N	89 40W
Sanger, Calif.	**29**	36 42N	119 33W
Sanger, Tex.	**65**	33 22N	97 10W
Sangre de Cristo	**52**	36 40N	105 15W
Sangre de Cristo Mts.	**30**	37 30N	105 20W
Sanibel I.	**31**	26 26N	82 6W
Sanilac County ◇	**43**	43 25N	82 50W
Sanpete County ◇	**66**	39 30N	111 40W
Sanpoil →	**67**	47 57N	118 41W
Sant Joseph County ◇	**43**	41 50N	85 30W
Santa	**34**	47 9N	116 27W
Santa Ana	**29**	33 46N	117 52W
Santa Ana Indian Reservation	**52**	35 26N	106 37W
Santa Ana Mts.	**29**	33 40N	117 30W
Santa Ana Pueblo	**52**	35 26N	106 37W
Santa Anna	**65**	31 45N	99 20W
Santa Barbara	**29**	34 25N	119 42W
Santa Barbara Channel	**29**	34 15N	120 0W
Santa Barbara County ◇	**29**	34 40N	120 0W
Santa Barbara I.	**29**	33 29N	119 2W
Santa Catalina, Gulf of	**29**	33 10N	117 50W
Santa Catalina I.	**29**	33 23N	118 25W
Santa Catalina Mts.	**26**	32 35N	110 50W
Santa Clara, Calif.	**28**	37 21N	121 57W
Santa Clara, N.Y.	**53**	44 38N	74 27W
Santa Clara, Oreg.	**58**	44 6N	123 8W
Santa Clara, Utah	**66**	37 8N	113 39W
Santa Clara →	**29**	34 14N	119 16W
Santa Clara County ◇	**28**	37 15N	121 40W
Santa Clara Valley	**29**	36 50N	121 30W
Santa Cruz	**29**	36 58N	122 1W
Santa Cruz →	**26**	33 20N	112 16W
Santa Cruz County ◇, Ariz.	**26**	31 30N	110 45W
Santa Cruz County ◇, Calif.	**28**	37 0N	122 0W
Santa Cruz I.	**29**	34 1N	119 43W
Santa Cruz Mts.	**28**	37 15N	122 0W
Santa Cruz Wash →	**26**	33 23N	112 12W
Santa Elena	**64**	26 46N	98 29W
Santa Fe	**52**	35 41N	105 57W
Santa Fe →	**31**	29 53N	82 53W
Santa Fe, L.	**31**	29 45N	82 5W
Santa Fe Baldy	**52**	35 50N	105 46W
Santa Fe County ◇	**52**	35 30N	106 0W
Santa Fe Nat. Forest	**52**	36 3N	106 42W
Santa Isabel	**71**	17 58N	66 24W
Santa Lucia Range	**29**	36 0N	121 20W
Santa Margarita L.	**29**	35 20N	120 30W
Santa Maria	**29**	34 57N	120 26W
Santa Maria →	**26**	34 19N	114 31W
Santa Monica	**29**	34 1N	118 29W
Santa Paula	**29**	34 21N	119 4W
Santa Rita, Mont.	**47**	48 42N	112 19W
Santa Rita, N. Mex.	**52**	32 48N	108 4W
Santa Rosa, Calif.	**28**	38 26N	122 43W
Santa Rosa, N. Mex.	**52**	34 57N	104 41W
Santa Rosa, Tex.	**64**	26 16N	97 50W
Santa Rosa Beach	**31**	30 22N	86 14W
Santa Rosa County ◇	**31**	30 45N	87 0W
Santa Rosa I., Calif.	**29**	33 58N	120 6W
Santa Rosa I., Fla.	**31**	30 20N	86 50W
Santa Rosa Mts.	**29**	33 20N	116 15W
Santa Rosa Range	**49**	41 45N	117 40W
Santa Rosa Wash →	**26**	33 0N	112 0W
Santa Ynez →	**29**	35 41N	120 36W
Santa Ynez Mts.	**29**	34 30N	120 0W
Santaquin	**66**	39 59N	111 47W
Sante Genevieve	**46**	37 59N	90 3W
Santee, Calif.	**29**	32 50N	116 58W
Santee, Nebr.	**48**	42 51N	97 50W
Santee →	**60**	33 7N	79 17W
Santee Indian Reservation	**48**	42 50N	97 50W
Santiago Mts.	**64**	29 55N	103 22W
Santiago Peak	**64**	29 47N	103 25W
Santiam Pass	**58**	44 25N	121 55W
Santo Domingo Indian Reservation	**52**	35 30N	106 30W
Santo Domingo Pueblo	**52**	35 31N	106 22W
Sapelo I.	**32**	31 25N	81 12W
Sapelo Island	**32**	31 23N	81 17W
Sapelo Sound	**32**	31 30N	81 10W
Sappa Cr. →	**48**	40 7N	99 39W
Sappho	**67**	48 4N	124 16W
Sappington	**47**	45 48N	111 46W
Sapulpa	**57**	35 59N	96 5W
Sara, L.	**35**	39 8N	88 36W
Saragosa	**64**	31 2N	103 39W
Sarah	**45**	34 34N	90 13W
Saraland	**24**	30 50N	88 4W
Saranac, Mich.	**43**	42 56N	85 13W
Saranac, N.Y.	**53**	44 39N	73 45W
Saranac →	**53**	44 42N	73 27W
Saranac L.	**53**	44 20N	74 10W
Saranac Lake	**53**	44 20N	74 8W
Sarasota	**31**	27 20N	82 32W
Sarasota County ◇	**31**	27 15N	82 20W
Saratoga, Calif.	**28**	37 16N	122 2W
Saratoga, Ind.	**36**	40 14N	84 55W
Saratoga, N.C.	**54**	35 39N	77 47W
Saratoga, Tex.	**65**	30 17N	94 31W
Saratoga, Wyo.	**70**	41 27N	106 49W
Saratoga County ◇	**53**	43 10N	73 50W
Saratoga L.	**53**	43 1N	73 45W
Saratoga Springs	**53**	43 5N	73 47W
Sarcoxie	**46**	37 3N	94 7W
Sardinia	**56**	39 0N	83 49W
Sardis, Ala.	**24**	32 17N	86 59W
Sardis, Ga.	**32**	32 58N	81 46W
Sardis, Miss.	**45**	34 26N	89 55W
Sardis L.	**45**	34 25N	89 48W
Sardis Res.	**57**	34 40N	95 25W
Sarepta	**39**	32 54N	93 27W
Sargeant	**44**	43 48N	92 48W
Sargent, Ga.	**32**	33 26N	84 52W

Sargent, Nebr. **48** 41 39N 99 22W
Sargent County ◇ **55** 46 3N 97 45W
Sargents **30** 38 25N 106 24W
Sarita **64** 27 13N 97 47W
Sarpy County ◇ **48** 41 10N 96 10W
Sartell **44** 45 37N 94 12W
Sasabe **26** 31 29N 111 33W
Sasakwa **57** 34 57N 96 31W
Sassafras **41** 39 22N 75 20W
Sasser **32** 31 43N 84 21W
Satanta **38** 37 26N 100 59W
Satartia **45** 32 40N 90 33W
Satellite Beach **31** 28 10N 80 36W
Satilla → **32** 30 59N 81 29W
Satolah **32** 34 59N 83 11W
Satsuma **24** 30 51N 88 4W
Sauceda Mts. **26** 32 35N 112 35W
Saucier **45** 30 39N 89 8W
Saugatuck **43** 42 40N 86 12W
Saugatuck → **42** 41 7N 73 22W
Saugerties **53** 42 5N 73 57W
Saugus, Calif. **29** 34 25N 118 32W
Saugus, Mass. **42** 42 28N 71 1W
Sauk Centre **44** 45 44N 94 57W
Sauk City **69** 43 17N 89 43W
Sauk County ◇ **69** 43 25N 89 50W
Sauk Rapids **44** 45 35N 94 10W
Saukville **69** 43 23N 87 56W
Saulsbury **62** 35 3N 89 5W
Sault Ste. Marie **43** 46 30N 84 21W
Saunders County ◇ **48** 41 15N 96 40W
Saunemin **35** 40 54N 88 24W
Sauquoit **53** 43 0N 75 16W
Savage, Md. **41** 39 8N 76 50W
Savage, Mont. **47** 47 27N 104 21W
Savana I. **71** 18 21N 65 5W
Savanna, Ill. **35** 42 5N 90 8W
Savanna, Okla. **57** 34 50N 95 51W
Savannah, Ga. **32** 32 5N 81 6W
Savannah, Mo. **46** 39 56N 94 50W
Savannah, Ohio **56** 40 58N 82 22W
Savannah, Tenn. **62** 35 14N 88 15W
Savannah → **60** 32 2N 80 53W
Savannah Beach **32** 32 1N 80 51W
Savonburg **38** 37 45N 95 9W
Savoonga **25** 63 42N 170 29W
Savoy **35** 40 3N 88 15W
Saw Pit **30** 37 56N 108 6W
Sawatch Range **30** 39 0N 106 30W
Sawtooth Mts. **44** 47 30N 91 0W
Sawtooth Nat. Rec. Area **34** 44 0N 114 50W
Sawtooth National Forest **66** 41 50N 113 20W
Sawtooth Range **34** 44 3N 114 58W
Sawyer, Kans. **38** 37 30N 98 41W
Sawyer, Mich. **43** 41 53N 86 35W
Sawyer, N. Dak. **55** 48 5N 101 3W
Sawyer, Okla. **57** 34 1N 95 23W
Sawyer County ◇ **69** 45 50N 91 0W
Sawyers Bar **28** 41 18N 123 7W
Saxapahaw **54** 35 57N 79 19W
Saxonburg **59** 40 45N 79 49W
Saxton, Ky. **63** 36 38N 84 7W
Saxton, Pa. **59** 40 13N 78 15W
Saybrook **35** 40 26N 88 32W
Saylorville L. **37** 41 48N 93 46W
Sayre, Okla. **57** 35 18N 99 38W
Sayre, Pa. **59** 41 59N 76 32W
Sayreville **51** 40 28N 74 22W
Sayville **53** 40 44N 73 5W
Scaggsville **41** 39 8N 76 54W
Scales Mound **35** 42 29N 90 15W
Scammon **38** 37 17N 94 49W
Scammon Bay **25** 61 51N 165 35W
Scandia **38** 39 48N 97 47W
Scandinavia **69** 44 27N 89 9W
Scanlon **44** 46 42N 92 26W
Scappoose **58** 45 45N 122 53W
Scarsdale **53** 40 59N 73 49W
Scarville **37** 43 28N 93 37W
Scenic **61** 43 47N 102 33W
Schaller **37** 42 30N 95 18W
Schell City **46** 38 1N 94 7W
Schell Creek Range **49** 39 25N 114 40W
Schellsburg **59** 40 3N 78 39W
Schenectady **53** 42 49N 73 57W
Schenectady County ◇ **53** 42 50N 74 0W
Schlater **45** 33 39N 90 21W
Schleicher County ◇ **64** 30 52N 100 36W
Schleswig **37** 42 10N 95 26W
Schley County ◇ **32** 32 15N 84 15W
Schoenchen **38** 38 43N 99 20W
Schofield **69** 44 54N 89 36W
Schoharie **53** 42 40N 74 19W
Schoharie → **53** 42 57N 74 18W
Schoharie County ◇ **53** 42 35N 74 30W
Schoharie Res. **53** 42 22N 74 26W
Schoodic L. **40** 45 23N 68 56W
Schoolcraft **43** 42 7N 85 38W
Schoolcraft County ◇ **43** 46 10N 86 15W
Schroon L. **53** 43 47N 73 47W
Schroon Lake **53** 43 50N 73 46W
Schulenburg **65** 29 41N 96 54W
Schurz **49** 38 57N 118 49W
Schuvlkill Haven **59** 40 38N 76 10W
Schuyler, Nebr. **48** 41 27N 97 4W
Schuyler, Va. **68** 37 47N 78 42W
Schuyler County ◇, Ill. **35** 40 10N 90 40W
Schuyler County ◇, Mo. **46** 40 25N 92 30W
Schuyler County ◇, N.Y. **53** 42 20N 76 50W
Schuylkill → **59** 39 53N 75 12W
Schuylkill County ◇ **59** 40 48N 76 50W
Schwatka Mts. **25** 67 20N 156 30W
Science Hill **63** 37 11N 84 38W
Scio, Ohio **56** 40 24N 81 5W
Scio, Oreg. **58** 44 42N 122 51W
Scioto → **56** 38 44N 83 1W
Scioto County ◇ **56** 38 53N 82 59W
Scipio, Okla. **57** 35 3N 95 58W
Scipio, Utah **66** 39 15N 112 6W
Scituate **42** 42 12N 70 44W
Scituate Reservoir **42** 41 45N 71 35W
Scobey **47** 48 47N 105 25W
Scofield **66** 39 44N 111 10W
Scofield Reservoir **66** 39 49N 111 8W
Scooba **45** 32 50N 88 29W
Scotch Plains **51** 40 39N 74 24W
Scotia, Calif. **28** 40 29N 124 6W
Scotia, N.Y. **53** 42 50N 73 58W
Scotia, Nebr. **48** 41 28N 98 42W
Scotia, S.C. **60** 32 41N 81 15W
Scotland, Ark. **27** 35 32N 92 37W
Scotland, Conn. **42** 41 42N 72 7W
Scotland, Md. **41** 38 5N 76 22W
Scotland, S. Dak. **61** 43 9N 97 43W
Scotland County ◇, Mo. **46** 40 25N 92 10W
Scotland County ◇, N.C. **54** 34 50N 79 30W
Scotland Neck **54** 36 8N 77 25W
Scotlandville **39** 30 31N 91 11W
Scott, Ark. **27** 34 42N 92 6W
Scott, Miss. **45** 33 36N 91 5W
Scott, Ohio **56** 40 59N 84 35W
Scott → **28** 41 48N 123 2W
Scott, Mt. **58** 42 56N 122 1W
Scott Bar Mts. **28** 41 50N 123 0W
Scott City, Kans. **38** 38 29N 100 54W
Scott City, Mo. **46** 37 12N 89 30W
Scott County ◇, Ark. **27** 34 54N 94 5W
Scott County ◇, Ill. **35** 39 40N 90 30W
Scott County ◇, Ind. **36** 38 40N 85 45W
Scott County ◇, Iowa **37** 41 35N 90 35W
Scott County ◇, Kans. **38** 38 30N 101 0W
Scott County ◇, Ky. **63** 38 15N 84 35W
Scott County ◇, Minn. **44** 44 40N 93 30W
Scott County ◇, Miss. **45** 32 22N 89 29W
Scott County ◇, Mo. **46** 37 0N 89 35W
Scott County ◇, Tenn. **63** 36 25N 84 29W
Scott County ◇, Va. **68** 36 55N 82 45W
Scott Mts. **28** 41 15N 122 45W
Scott Peak **34** 44 21N 112 49W
Scottdale **59** 40 6N 79 35W
Scotts Bluff County ◇ **48** 41 50N 103 45W
Scotts Bluff National Monument **48** 41 50N 103 40W
Scotts Hill **62** 35 31N 88 15W
Scottsbluff **48** 41 52N 103 40W
Scottsboro **24** 34 40N 86 2W
Scottsburg, Ind. **36** 38 41N 85 47W
Scottsburg, Oreg. **58** 43 39N 123 49W
Scottsburg, Va. **68** 36 45N 78 48W
Scottsdale **26** 33 29N 111 56W
Scottsville, Kans. **38** 39 32N 97 57W
Scottsville, Ky. **62** 36 45N 86 11W
Scottville **43** 43 58N 86 17W
Scranton, Iowa **37** 42 1N 94 33W
Scranton, Kans. **38** 38 47N 95 44W
Scranton, N. Dak. **55** 46 9N 103 9W
Scranton, Pa. **59** 41 25N 75 40W
Screven **32** 31 29N 82 1W
Screven County ◇ **32** 32 45N 81 40W
Scribner **48** 41 40N 96 40W
Scurry **65** 32 31N 96 23W
Scurry County ◇ **64** 32 44N 100 55W
Sea Breeze **51** 39 18N 75 20W
Sea Bright **51** 40 22N 73 59W
Sea Isle City **51** 39 9N 74 42W
Seaboard **54** 36 29N 77 26W
Seabrook, N.H. **50** 42 53N 70 52W
Seabrook, Tex. **65** 29 34N 95 2W
Seadrift **65** 28 25N 96 43W
Seaford, Del. **41** 38 39N 75 37W
Seaford, Va. **68** 37 12N 76 26W
Seaforth **44** 44 29N 95 20W
Seagoville **65** 32 38N 96 32W
Seagraves **64** 32 57N 102 34W
Seagrove **54** 35 33N 79 46W
Seal I. **40** 43 53N 68 45W
Seale **24** 32 18N 85 10W
Sealevel **54** 34 52N 76 23W
Sealy **65** 29 47N 96 9W
Seaman **56** 38 57N 83 34W
Searchlight **49** 35 28N 114 55W
Searcy **27** 35 15N 91 44W
Searcy County ◇ **27** 35 55N 92 38W
Searles L. **29** 35 44N 117 21W
Searsboro **37** 41 35N 92 42W
Searsburg **50** 42 52N 72 58W
Searsport **40** 44 28N 68 56W
Seaside, Calif. **28** 36 37N 121 50W
Seaside, Oreg. **58** 46 0N 123 56W
Seaside Heights **51** 39 55N 74 6W
Seaside Park **51** 39 55N 74 5W
Seat Pleasant **41** 38 54N 76 55W
Seattle **67** 47 36N 122 20W
Seaville **51** 39 12N 74 42W
Sebago L. **40** 43 52N 70 34W
Sebastian **31** 27 49N 80 28W
Sebastian, C. **58** 42 20N 124 26W
Sebastian County ◇ **27** 35 10N 94 10W
Sebastopol, Calif. **28** 38 24N 122 49W
Sebastopol, Miss. **45** 32 34N 89 20W
Sebec L. **40** 45 16N 69 15W
Sebeka **44** 46 38N 95 5W
Sebewaing **43** 43 44N 83 27W
Seboeis **40** 45 22N 68 43W
Seboeis L. **40** 45 28N 68 53W
Seboomook L. **40** 45 56N 69 51W
Seboyeta **52** 35 12N 107 23W
Sebree **62** 37 36N 87 32W
Sebrell **68** 36 47N 77 8W
Sebring **31** 27 30N 81 27W
Secession L. **60** 34 18N 82 39W
Second L. **50** 45 9N 71 10W
Secor **35** 40 45N 89 8W
Secretary **41** 38 37N 75 57W
Section **24** 34 35N 85 59W
Security **30** 38 45N 104 45W
Sedalia, Colo. **30** 39 26N 104 58W
Sedalia, Mo. **46** 38 42N 93 14W
Sedan, Kans. **38** 37 8N 96 11W
Sedan, Minn. **44** 45 35N 95 15W
Sedan, N. Mex. **52** 36 9N 103 8W
Sedgefield **54** 36 1N 79 54W
Sedgewick, Mt. **52** 35 11N 108 6W
Sedgwick, Colo. **30** 40 56N 102 32W
Sedgwick, Kans. **38** 37 55N 97 26W
Sedgwick, Maine **40** 44 18N 68 37W
Sedgwick County ◇, Colo. **30** 40 50N 102 15W
Sedgwick County ◇, Kans. **38** 37 30N 97 20W
Sedona **26** 34 52N 111 46W
Sedro-Woolley **67** 48 30N 122 14W
Seekonk **42** 41 49N 71 20W
Seeley Lake **47** 47 11N 113 29W
Seelyville **36** 39 30N 87 16W
Seguam I. **25** 52 19N 172 30W
Seguam Pass **25** 52 0N 172 30W
Seguin **65** 29 34N 97 58W
Seibert **30** 39 18N 102 53W
Seiling **57** 36 9N 98 56W
Selah **67** 46 39N 120 32W
Selawik **25** 66 36N 160 0W
Selawik L. **25** 66 30N 160 45W
Selby **61** 45 31N 100 2W
Selbyville **41** 38 28N 75 14W
Selden, Kans. **38** 39 33N 100 34W
Selden, N.Y. **53** 40 52N 73 2W
Seldovia **25** 59 26N 151 43W
Selfridge **55** 46 2N 100 56W
Seligman, Ariz. **26** 35 20N 112 53W
Seligman, Mo. **46** 36 31N 93 56W
Selinsgrove **59** 40 48N 76 52W
Selkirk **38** 38 29N 101 32W
Selkirk Mts. **34** 48 30N 116 40W
Selleck **67** 47 23N 121 52W
Sellers **60** 34 17N 79 28W
Sellersburg **36** 38 24N 85 45W
Sells **26** 31 55N 111 53W
Selma, Ala. **24** 32 25N 87 1W
Selma, Ark. **27** 33 42N 91 34W
Selma, Calif. **29** 36 34N 119 37W
Selma, N.C. **54** 35 32N 78 17W
Selma, Oreg. **58** 42 17N 123 37W
Selman **57** 36 48N 99 30W
Selmer **62** 35 10N 88 36W
Selway → **34** 46 9N 115 36W
Selz **55** 47 52N 99 54W
Semichi Is. **25** 52 42N 174 0 E
Seminary **45** 31 34N 89 30W
Seminoe Reservoir **70** 42 9N 106 55W
Seminole, Fla. **31** 27 50N 82 47W
Seminole, Okla. **57** 35 14N 96 41W
Seminole, Tex. **64** 32 43N 102 39W
Seminole, L. **32** 30 43N 84 52W
Seminole County ◇, Fla. **31** 28 40N 81 15W
Seminole County ◇, Ga. **32** 31 0N 84 55W
Seminole County ◇, Okla. **57** 35 10N 96 40W
Semisopochnoi I. **25** 51 55N 179 36 E
Semmes **24** 30 47N 88 16W
Senachwine L. **35** 41 10N 89 20W
Senath **46** 36 8N 90 10W
Senatobia **45** 34 37N 89 58W
Seneca, Ill. **35** 41 19N 88 37W
Seneca, Kans. **38** 39 50N 96 4W
Seneca, Md. **41** 39 5N 77 20W
Seneca, Mo. **46** 36 51N 94 37W
Seneca, Nebr. **48** 42 3N 100 50W
Seneca, Oreg. **58** 44 8N 118 58W
Seneca, S.C. **60** 34 41N 82 57W
Seneca, S. Dak. **61** 45 4N 99 31W
Seneca County ◇, N.Y. **53** 42 45N 76 45W
Seneca County ◇, Ohio **56** 41 7N 83 11W
Seneca Falls **53** 42 55N 76 48W
Seneca L. **53** 42 40N 76 54W
Senecaville L. **56** 39 55N 81 25W
Senoia **32** 33 18N 84 33W
Sentinel, Ariz. **26** 32 52N 113 13W
Sentinel, Okla. **57** 35 9N 99 11W
Sentinel Butte **55** 46 55N 103 51W
Sepulga → **24** 31 11N 86 46W
Sequatchie County ◇ **63** 35 23N 85 23W
Sequim **67** 48 5N 123 6W
Sequoia National Forest **29** 36 0N 118 20W
Sequoia National Park **29** 36 30N 118 30W
Sequoyah County ◇ **57** 35 30N 94 45W
Serafina **52** 35 24N 105 19W
Sergeant Bluff **37** 42 24N 96 22W
Sesser **35** 38 5N 89 1W
Seth Ward **64** 34 13N 101 42W
Seul Choix Pt. **43** 45 55N 85 55W
Seven Devils Mts. **34** 44 45N 116 40W
Seven Springs **54** 35 14N 77 51W
Seven Troughs Range **49** 40 30N 118 40W
Seven Valleys **59** 39 51N 76 46W
Severn **54** 36 31N 77 11W
Severna Park **41** 39 4N 76 33W
Severy **38** 37 37N 96 14W
Sevier → **66** 39 4N 113 6W
Sevier Bridge Reservoir **66** 39 22N 112 2W
Sevier County ◇, Ark. **27** 33 58N 94 10W
Sevier County ◇, Tenn. **63** 35 48N 83 33W
Sevier County ◇, Utah **66** 38 45N 111 50W
Sevier Desert **66** 39 40N 112 45W
Sevier L. **66** 38 54N 113 9W
Sevier Plateau **66** 38 20N 112 10W
Sevierville **63** 35 52N 83 34W
Seville, Fla. **31** 29 19N 81 30W
Seville, Ga. **32** 31 58N 83 36W
Sewanee **63** 35 12N 85 55W
Seward, Alaska **25** 60 7N 149 27W
Seward, Ill. **35** 42 14N 89 22W
Seward, Kans. **38** 38 11N 98 48W
Seward, Nebr. **48** 40 55N 97 6W
Seward, Pa. **59** 40 25N 79 1W
Seward County ◇, Kans. **38** 37 15N 100 45W
Seward County ◇, Nebr. **48** 40 50N 97 10W
Seward Peninsula **25** 65 30N 166 0W
Sewickley **59** 40 32N 80 12W
Seymour, Conn. **42** 41 24N 73 4W
Seymour, Ind. **36** 38 58N 85 53W
Seymour, Iowa **37** 40 45N 93 7W
Seymour, Mo. **46** 37 9N 92 46W
Seymour, Tex. **65** 33 35N 99 16W
Seymour, Wis. **69** 44 31N 88 20W
Seymourville **39** 30 16N 91 14W
Shackelford County ◇ **65** 32 45N 99 18W
Shadehill Reservoir **61** 45 45N 102 12W
Shadow Mt. Nat. Rec. Area **30** 40 7N 105 48W
Shady Cove **58** 42 37N 122 49W
Shady Dale **32** 33 24N 83 36W
Shady Grove, Fla. **31** 30 17N 83 38W
Shady Grove, Ky. **62** 37 20N 87 53W
Shady Point **57** 35 8N 94 40W
Shady Side **41** 38 50N 76 31W
Shady Spring **68** 37 42N 81 6W
Shafer, L. **36** 40 46N 86 46W
Shafter, Calif. **29** 35 30N 119 16W
Shafter, Tex. **64** 29 49N 104 18W
Shaftsbury **50** 43 1N 73 11W
Shageluk **25** 62 41N 159 34W
Shaker Heights **56** 41 29N 81 32W

Shakopee **44** 44 48N 93 32W
Shaktoolik **25** 64 20N 161 9W
Shalimar **31** 30 27N 86 36W
Shallotte **54** 33 58N 78 23W
Shallow Water **38** 38 23N 100 55W
Shallowater **64** 33 36N 102 0W
Shambaugh **37** 40 42N 95 3W
Shamokin **59** 40 47N 76 34W
Shamrock, Okla. **57** 35 56N 96 35W
Shamrock, Tex. **64** 35 13N 100 15W
Shandon **29** 35 39N 120 23W
Shaniko **58** 45 0N 120 45W
Shannon, Ga. **32** 34 20N 85 4W
Shannon, Ill. **35** 42 9N 89 44W
Shannon, Miss. **45** 34 7N 88 43W
Shannon, L. **67** 48 33N 121 45W
Shannon County ◇, Mo. **46** 37 10N 91 20W
Shannon County ◇, S. Dak. **61** 43 15N 102 35W
Shannontown **60** 33 53N 80 21W
Sharkey County ◇ **45** 32 55N 90 53W
Sharon, Conn. **42** 41 53N 73 29W
Sharon, Kans. **38** 37 15N 98 25W
Sharon, Mass. **42** 42 7N 71 11W
Sharon, N. Dak. **55** 47 36N 97 54W
Sharon, Okla. **57** 36 17N 99 20W
Sharon, Pa. **59** 41 14N 80 31W
Sharon, Tenn. **62** 36 14N 88 50W
Sharon, Vt. **50** 43 47N 72 25W
Sharon, Wis. **69** 42 30N 88 44W
Sharon Springs **38** 38 54N 101 45W
Sharonville **56** 39 16N 84 25W
Sharp County ◇ **27** 36 4N 91 37W
Sharpe, L. **61** 44 1N 99 23W
Sharpes **31** 28 26N 80 46W
Sharpsburg, Iowa **37** 40 48N 94 38W
Sharpsburg, Md. **41** 39 28N 77 45W
Sharpsburg, N.C. **54** 35 53N 77 50W
Sharpsville, Ind. **36** 40 23N 86 5W
Sharpsville, Pa. **59** 41 15N 80 29W
Sharptown, Md. **41** 38 0N 75 0W
Sharptown, N.J. **51** 39 40N 75 22W
Shasta **28** 40 36N 122 29W
Shasta, Mt. **28** 41 25N 122 12W
Shasta County ◇ **28** 40 40N 122 0W
Shasta Dam **28** 40 43N 122 25W
Shasta L. **28** 40 43N 122 25W
Shasta National Forest **28** 41 10N 122 20W
Shattuck **57** 36 16N 99 53W
Shaver L. **29** 37 9N 119 18W
Shaw **45** 33 36N 90 47W
Shawangunk Mts. **53** 41 35N 74 30W
Shawano **69** 44 47N 88 36W
Shawano County ◇ **69** 44 45N 88 40W
Shawboro **54** 36 24N 76 6W
Shawhan **63** 38 18N 84 16W
Shawnee, Ga. **32** 32 29N 81 25W
Shawnee, Kans. **38** 39 1N 94 43W
Shawnee, Ohio **56** 39 36N 82 13W
Shawnee, Okla. **57** 35 20N 96 55W
Shawnee County ◇ **38** 39 0N 95 45W
Shawnee National Forest **35** 37 40N 88 20W
Shawneetown **35** 37 42N 88 8W
Sheboygan **69** 43 46N 87 45W
Sheboygan County ◇ **69** 43 45N 87 50W
Sheboygan Falls **69** 43 44N 87 49W
Shedd **58** 44 28N 123 7W
Sheenjek → **25** 66 45N 144 33W
Sheep Hole Mts. **29** 34 10N 117 40W
Sheep Mt. **70** 43 31N 110 28W
Sheep Range **49** 36 35N 115 15W
Sheffield, Ala. **24** 34 46N 87 41W
Sheffield, Ill. **35** 41 21N 89 44W
Sheffield, Iowa **37** 42 54N 93 13W
Sheffield, Mass. **42** 42 5N 73 21W
Sheffield, Tex. **64** 30 41N 101 49W
Shelbiana **63** 37 26N 82 30W
Shelbina **46** 39 47N 92 2W
Shelburn **36** 39 11N 87 24W
Shelburne **50** 44 23N 73 14W
Shelburne Falls **42** 42 36N 72 45W
Shelby, Iowa **37** 41 31N 95 27W
Shelby, Mich. **43** 43 37N 86 22W
Shelby, Miss. **45** 33 57N 90 46W
Shelby, Mont. **47** 48 30N 111 51W
Shelby, N.C. **54** 35 17N 81 32W
Shelby, Nebr. **48** 41 12N 97 26W
Shelby, Ohio **56** 40 53N 82 40W
Shelby County ◇, Ala. **24** 33 15N 86 49W
Shelby County ◇, Ill. **35** 39 25N 88 45W
Shelby County ◇, Ind. **36** 39 30N 85 50W
Shelby County ◇, Iowa **37** 41 40N 95 20W
Shelby County ◇, Ky. **63** 38 10N 85 10W
Shelby County ◇, Mo. **46** 39 50N 92 0W
Shelby County ◇, Ohio **56** 40 17N 84 9W
Shelby County ◇, Tenn. **62** 35 5N 89 55W
Shelby County ◇, Tex. **65** 31 48N 94 11W
Shelbyville, Ill. **35** 39 24N 88 48W
Shelbyville, Ind. **36** 39 31N 85 47W
Shelbyville, Ky. **63** 38 13N 85 14W
Shelbyville, Mo. **46** 39 48N 92 2W
Shelbyville, Tenn. **62** 35 29N 86 28W
Shelbyville, Tex. **65** 31 46N 94 5W
Shelbyville, L. **35** 39 26N 88 46W
Sheldahl **37** 41 52N 93 42W
Sheldon, Iowa **37** 43 11N 95 51W
Sheldon, Mo. **46** 37 40N 94 18W
Sheldon, N. Dak. **55** 46 35N 97 30W
Sheldon, S.C. **60** 32 36N 80 48W
Sheldon, Wis. **69** 45 19N 90 58W
Sheldon Point **25** 62 32N 164 52W
Shelikof Strait **25** 57 30N 155 0W
Shell Lake **69** 45 45N 91 55W
Shell Rock **37** 42 43N 92 35W
Shelley **34** 43 23N 112 7W
Shellman **32** 31 46N 84 37W
Shellman Bluff **32** 31 35N 81 19W
Shellrock → **37** 42 35N 92 25W
Shellsburg **37** 42 6N 91 52W
Shelltown **41** 37 58N 75 40W
Shelly **44** 47 28N 96 49W
Shelton, Conn. **42** 41 19N 73 5W
Shelton, Nebr. **48** 40 47N 98 44W
Shelton, S.C. **60** 34 30N 81 25W
Shelton, Wash. **67** 47 13N 123 6W
Shenandoah, Iowa **37** 40 46N 95 22W
Shenandoah, Pa. **59** 40 49N 76 12W
Shenandoah, Va. **68** 38 29N 78 37W
Shenandoah → **68** 39 19N 77 44W
Shenandoah County ◇ **68** 38 53N 78 30W
Shenandoah Mt. **68** 38 40N 77 15W
Shenandoah National Park **68** 38 35N 78 22W
Shepherd, Mich. **43** 43 32N 84 41W
Shepherd, Mont. **47** 45 57N 108 21W
Shepherd, Tex. **65** 30 31N 95 1W
Shepherdsville **63** 37 59N 85 43W
Sherburn **44** 43 39N 94 43W
Sherburne, N.Y. **53** 42 41N 75 30W
Sherburne, Vt. **50** 43 10N 72 47W
Sherburne County ◇ **44** 45 20N 93 45W
Sheridan, Ark. **27** 34 19N 92 24W
Sheridan, Ill. **35** 41 32N 88 41W
Sheridan, Ind. **36** 40 8N 86 13W
Sheridan, Ky. **62** 37 21N 88 12W
Sheridan, Mo. **46** 40 31N 94 37W
Sheridan, Mont. **47** 45 27N 112 12W
Sheridan, Oreg. **58** 45 6N 123 24W
Sheridan, Wyo. **70** 44 48N 106 58W
Sheridan County ◇, Kans. **38** 39 20N 100 30W
Sheridan County ◇, Mont. **47** 48 48N 104 30W
Sheridan County ◇, N. Dak. **55** 47 45N 100 20W
Sheridan County ◇, Nebr. **48** 42 30N 102 20W
Sheridan County ◇, Wyo. **70** 44 50N 106 45W
Sheridan Lake **30** 38 28N 102 18W
Sherman, Conn. **42** 41 35N 73 30W
Sherman, Ill. **35** 39 54N 89 36W
Sherman, Miss. **45** 34 22N 88 50W
Sherman, N. Mex. **52** 32 45N 107 51W
Sherman, N.Y. **53** 42 10N 79 36W
Sherman, Tex. **65** 33 38N 96 36W
Sherman County ◇, Kans. **38** 39 20N 101 45W
Sherman County ◇, Nebr. **48** 41 15N 99 0W
Sherman County ◇, Oreg. **58** 45 30N 120 40W
Sherman County ◇, Tex. **64** 36 10N 101 58W
Sherman Reservoir **48** 41 18N 98 53W
Sherman Station **40** 45 54N 68 26W
Sherrard **35** 41 19N 90 31W
Sherrill **27** 34 23N 91 57W
Sherwood, Ark. **27** 34 48N 92 16W
Sherwood, Md. **41** 38 46N 76 19W
Sherwood, N. Dak. **55** 48 57N 101 38W
Sherwood, Ohio **56** 41 17N 84 33W
Sherwood, Tenn. **63** 35 5N 85 56W
Shetek, L. **44** 44 7N 95 42W
Shetucket **42** 41 0N 72 0W
Shevlin **44** 47 32N 95 15W
Sheyenne **55** 47 50N 99 7W
Sheyenne → **55** 47 2N 96 50W
Shiawassee County ◇ **43** 42 55N 84 10W
Shickley **48** 40 25N 97 43W
Shickshinny **59** 41 9N 76 9W
Shidler **57** 36 47N 96 40W
Shidler Res. **57** 36 50N 96 40W
Shields **38** 38 37N 100 27W
Shillington **59** 40 18N 75 58W
Shiloh, Ga. **32** 32 49N 84 42W
Shiloh, N.C. **54** 36 17N 76 5W
Shiloh, N.J. **51** 39 28N 75 18W
Shiloh, Ohio **56** 40 58N 82 36W
Shin Pond **40** 46 6N 68 33W
Shiner **65** 29 26N 97 10W
Shinglehouse **59** 41 58N 78 12W
Shingler **32** 31 35N 83 47W
Shingleton **43** 46 21N 86 28W
Shingletown **28** 40 30N 121 53W
Shinnston **68** 39 24N 80 18W
Ship Bottom **51** 39 39N 74 11W
Ship I. **45** 30 13N 88 55W
Ship Rock **52** 36 41N 108 50W
Shipman, Ill. **35** 39 7N 90 3W
Shipman, Va. **68** 37 43N 78 51W
Shippensburg **59** 40 3N 77 31W
Shippenville **59** 41 15N 79 28W
Shiprock **52** 36 47N 108 41W
Shipshewana **36** 41 41N 85 35W
Shirley, Ark. **27** 35 39N 92 19W
Shirley, Ind. **36** 39 53N 85 35W
Shirley, Mass. **42** 42 33N 71 39W
Shirley Basin **70** 42 20N 106 10W
Shirley Mills **40** 45 22N 69 37W
Shishaldin Volcano **25** 54 45N 163 58W
Shishmaref **25** 66 15N 166 4W
Shively **63** 38 12N 85 49W
Shivers **45** 31 48N 89 59W
Shivwits Plateau **26** 36 15N 113 30W
Shoal Cr. →, Ill. **35** 38 28N 89 35W
Shoal Cr. →, Mo. **46** 39 44N 93 32W
Shoals **36** 38 40N 86 47W
Shoemakersville **59** 40 30N 75 58W
Shonto **26** 36 36N 110 39W
Shopville **63** 37 9N 84 29W
Shoreacres **65** 29 36N 95 1W
Shoreham **50** 43 54N 73 19W
Shorewood **69** 43 5N 87 54W
Shorter **24** 32 24N 85 57W
Shorterville **24** 31 34N 85 6W
Shortsville **53** 42 57N 77 14W
Shoshone, Calif. **29** 35 58N 116 16W
Shoshone, Idaho **34** 42 56N 114 25W
Shoshone → **70** 44 52N 108 11W
Shoshone Basin **70** 43 5N 108 5W
Shoshone County ◇ **34** 47 30N 116 0W
Shoshone L. **70** 44 22N 110 43W
Shoshone Mts. **49** 39 20N 117 25W
Shoshone National Forest **70** 44 20N 109 45W
Shoshone Range **49** 40 20N 116 50W
Shoshoni **70** 43 14N 108 7W
Shoup **34** 45 23N 114 17W
Show Low **26** 34 15N 110 2W
Showell **41** 38 24N 75 13W
Shreve **56** 40 41N 82 1W
Shreveport **39** 32 31N 93 45W
Shrewsbury **42** 42 18N 71 43W
Shubert **48** 40 14N 95 41W
Shubuta **45** 31 52N 88 42W
Shuksan, Mt. **67** 48 50N 121 36W
Shullsburg **69** 42 35N 90 13W
Shumagin Is. **25** 55 7N 159 45W
Shungnak **25** 66 52N 157 9W
Shuqualak **45** 32 59N 88 34W
Shutesbury **42** 42 25N 72 25W
Shuyak I. **25** 58 31N 152 30W
Siasconset **42** 41 16N 69 58W
Sibley, Ill. **35** 40 35N 88 23W
Sibley, Iowa **37** 43 24N 95 45W
Sibley, La. **39** 32 33N 93 18W
Sibley, Miss. **45** 31 23N 91 24W
Sibley County ◇ **44** 44 35N 94 15W
Sicily Island **39** 31 51N 91 40W
Sidell **35** 39 55N 87 49W
Sidnaw **43** 46 30N 88 43W
Sidney, Ark. **27** 36 0N 91 40W
Sidney, Ill. **35** 40 1N 88 4W
Sidney, Iowa **37** 40 45N 95 39W
Sidney, Mont. **47** 47 43N 104 9W
Sidney, N.Y. **53** 42 19N 75 24W
Sidney, Nebr. **48** 41 8N 102 59W
Sidney, Ohio **56** 40 17N 84 9W
Sidney Lanier L. **32** 34 10N 84 4W
Sidon **45** 33 25N 90 12W
Sierra Blanca **64** 31 11N 105 22W
Sierra Blanca Peak **52** 33 23N 105 49W
Sierra City **28** 39 34N 120 38W
Sierra County ◇, Calif. **28** 39 40N 121 30W
Sierra County ◇, N. Mex. **52** 33 0N 107 0W
Sierra Madre **70** 41 15N 107 5W
Sierra National Forest **29** 37 15N 119 10W
Sierra Nevada **29** 37 30N 119 0W
Sierra Vista **26** 31 33N 110 18W
Sierraville **28** 39 36N 120 22W
Signal Mountain **63** 35 7N 85 21W
Signal Pk. **26** 33 20N 114 2W
Sigourney **37** 41 20N 92 12W
Sigsbee **32** 31 16N 83 52W
Sigurd **66** 38 50N 111 58W
Sikes **39** 32 5N 92 29W
Sikeston **46** 36 53N 89 35W
Sil Nakya **26** 32 13N 111 49W
Silas **24** 31 46N 88 20W
Siler City **54** 35 44N 79 28W
Siletz **58** 44 43N 123 55W
Silo **57** 34 3N 96 29W
Siloam **32** 33 32N 83 5W
Siloam Springs **27** 36 11N 94 32W
Silsbee **65** 30 21N 94 11W
Silt **30** 39 33N 107 40W
Siltcoos L. **58** 43 53N 124 6W
Silver **64** 32 4N 100 40W
Silver Bay **44** 47 18N 91 16W
Silver Bell **26** 32 23N 111 30W
Silver Bow County ◇ **47** 45 48N 112 45W
Silver Bow Park **47** 46 1N 112 28W
Silver City, Iowa **37** 41 7N 95 39W
Silver City, Mich. **43** 46 50N 89 35W
Silver City, Miss. **45** 33 6N 90 30W
Silver City, N.C. **54** 35 2N 79 12W
Silver City, N. Mex. **52** 32 46N 108 17W
Silver Cliff **30** 38 8N 105 27W
Silver Cr. →, Ariz. **26** 34 44N 110 2W
Silver Cr. →, Oreg. **58** 43 16N 119 13W
Silver Creek, N.Y. **53** 42 33N 79 10W
Silver Creek, Nebr. **48** 41 19N 97 40W
Silver L., Calif. **29** 35 21N 116 7W
Silver L., Harney, Oreg. **58** 43 22N 119 25W
Silver L., Silver, Oreg. **58** 43 6N 120 53W
Silver L., Wash. **67** 46 17N 122 47W
Silver Lake, Kans. **38** 39 6N 95 52W
Silver Lake, Minn. **44** 44 54N 94 12W
Silver Lake, Oreg. **58** 43 8N 121 3W
Silver Lake, Wis. **69** 44 4N 89 14W
Silver Run **41** 39 42N 77 3W
Silver Spring **41** 38 59N 77 2W
Silver Springs, Fla. **31** 29 13N 82 3W
Silver Springs, Nev. **49** 39 25N 119 14W
Silverdale **38** 37 3N 96 54W
Silverstreet **60** 34 13N 81 43W
Silverton, Colo. **30** 37 49N 107 40W
Silverton, N.J. **51** 40 1N 74 10W
Silverton, Oreg. **58** 45 1N 122 47W
Silverton, Tex. **64** 34 28N 101 19W
Silverton, Wash. **67** 48 5N 121 35W
Silvies → **58** 43 34N 119 2W
Simi Valley **29** 34 16N 118 47W
Simla **30** 39 9N 104 5W
Simmesport **39** 30 59N 91 49W
Simms **47** 47 30N 111 56W
Simnasho **58** 44 58N 121 21W
Simonton Lake **36** 41 44N 85 59W
Simpson, Kans. **38** 39 23N 97 56W
Simpson, La. **39** 31 16N 93 1W
Simpson County ◇, Ky. **62** 36 45N 86 35W
Simpson County ◇, Miss. **45** 31 53N 89 58W
Simpson Park Range **49** 39 50N 116 35W
Simpsonville, Ky. **63** 38 13N 85 22W
Simpsonville, S.C. **60** 34 44N 82 15W
Sims **35** 38 22N 88 32W
Simsbury **42** 41 53N 72 48W
Sinai **61** 44 15N 97 3W
Sinclair **70** 41 47N 107 7W
Sinclair, L. **32** 33 8N 83 12W
Sinclairville **53** 42 16N 79 16W
Singer **39** 30 39N 93 25W
Sinking Spring **56** 39 4N 83 23W
Sinnemahoning **59** 41 19N 78 6W
Sinton **65** 28 2N 97 31W
Sioux Center **37** 43 5N 96 11W
Sioux City **37** 42 30N 96 24W
Sioux County ◇, Iowa **37** 43 5N 96 10W
Sioux County ◇, N. Dak. **55** 46 0N 101 0W
Sioux County ◇, Nebr. **48** 42 30N 103 45W
Sioux Falls **61** 43 33N 96 44W
Sioux Rapids **37** 42 53N 95 9W
Sipsey → **24** 33 0N 88 10W
Siren **69** 45 47N 92 24W
Sirmans **31** 30 21N 83 39W
Siskiyou County ◇ **28** 41 40N 122 40W
Siskiyou Mts. **28** 42 0N 122 40W
Siskiyou National Forest **58** 42 20N 124 0W
Sisquoc → **29** 34 54N 120 18W
Sisseton **61** 45 40N 97 3W
Sisseton Indian Reservation **55** 46 0N 126 30W
Sissonville **68** 38 32N 81 38W
Sister Bay **69** 45 11N 87 7W
Sisters **58** 44 18N 121 33W
Sistersville **68** 39 34N 80 59W
Sitka, Alaska **25** 57 3N 135 20W
Sitka, Kans. **38** 37 11N 99 39W
Sitka ◇ **25** 57 0N 135 0W

Sitkinak I. **25** 56 33N 154 10W
Siuslaw → **58** 44 1N 124 8W
Siuslaw National Forest **58** 44 15N 123 50W
Skagit → **67** 48 23N 122 22W
Skagit County ◇ **67** 48 30N 121 30W
Skagway **25** 59 28N 135 19W
Skagway-Yakutat-Angoon ◇ **25** 59 0N 139 0W
Skamania County ◇ **67** 46 0N 122 0W
Skaneateles **53** 42 57N 76 26W
Skedee **57** 36 23N 96 42W
Skellytown **64** 35 34N 101 11W
Skiatook **57** 36 20N 96 0W
Skiatook Res. **57** 36 20N 96 10W
Skidmore, Mo. **46** 40 17N 95 5W
Skidmore, Tex. **65** 28 15N 97 41W
Skillet → **35** 38 5N 88 5W
Skokie **35** 42 3N 87 45W
Skowhegan **40** 44 46N 69 43W
Skull Valley **26** 34 30N 112 41W
Skull Valley Indian Reservation **66** 40 24N 112 45W
Skuna → **45** 33 54N 89 41W
Skunk → **37** 40 42N 91 7W
Skykomish **67** 47 42N 121 22W
Skyland **54** 35 29N 82 32W
Slagle **39** 31 12N 93 8W
Slate Spring **45** 33 44N 89 22W
Slater, Iowa **37** 41 53N 93 41W
Slater, Mo. **46** 39 13N 93 4W
Slaton **64** 33 26N 101 39W
Slaughter **39** 30 43N 91 9W
Slaughter Beach **41** 38 52N 75 18W
Slaughters **62** 37 29N 87 30W
Slaughterville **57** 35 5N 97 20W
Slayden **45** 34 57N 89 27W
Slayton **44** 43 59N 95 45W
Sledge **45** 34 26N 90 13W
Sleeper **46** 37 46N 92 36W
Sleeping Bear Dunes Nat. Lakeshore **43** 44 50N 86 5W
Sleeping Bear Pt. **43** 44 55N 86 3W
Sleepy Eye **44** 44 18N 94 43W
Sleetmute **25** 61 42N 157 10W
Slemp **63** 37 5N 83 6W
Slick **57** 35 47N 96 16W
Slick Rock **30** 38 3N 108 54W
Slide Mt. **53** 42 0N 74 25W
Slidell **39** 30 17N 89 47W
Sligo **59** 41 6N 79 29W
Slim Buttes **61** 45 20N 103 15W
Sloan **37** 42 14N 96 14W
Sloat **28** 39 52N 120 44W
Slocomb **24** 31 7N 85 36W
Slocum **42** 41 32N 71 31W
Slope County ◇ **55** 46 20N 103 30W
Smakover **27** 33 22N 92 44W
Small, C. **40** 43 42N 69 51W
Smarr **32** 32 59N 83 53W
Smarts Mt. **50** 43 48N 72 3W
Smartville **28** 39 13N 121 18W
Smethport **59** 41 49N 78 27W
Smiley **65** 29 16N 97 38W
Smith **49** 38 48N 119 20W
Smith →, Mont. **47** 47 25N 111 29W
Smith →, N.C. **54** 36 27N 79 43W
Smith B. **25** 70 30N 154 20W
Smith Center **38** 39 47N 98 47W
Smith County ◇, Kans. **38** 39 45N 98 45W
Smith County ◇, Miss. **45** 32 1N 89 23W
Smith County ◇, Tenn. **62** 36 5N 86 0W
Smith County ◇, Tex. **65** 32 21N 95 18W
Smith I., Md. **41** 38 0N 76 0W
Smith I., N.C. **54** 33 53N 77 59W
Smith I., Va. **68** 37 9N 75 53W
Smith Mountain L. **68** 37 2N 79 30W
Smith Pk. **34** 48 51N 116 40W
Smith River **28** 41 56N 124 9W
Smithburg, N.J. **51** 40 13N 74 21W
Smithburg, W. Va. **68** 39 17N 80 44W
Smithfield, N.C. **54** 35 31N 78 21W
Smithfield, Nebr. **48** 40 34N 99 45W
Smithfield, Utah **66** 41 50N 111 50W
Smithfield, Va. **68** 36 59N 76 38W
Smithland, Iowa **37** 42 14N 95 56W
Smithland, Ky. **62** 37 9N 88 24W
Smiths **24** 32 32N 85 6W
Smiths Ferry **34** 44 18N 116 5W
Smiths Grove **62** 37 3N 86 12W
Smithsburg **41** 39 39N 77 35W
Smithton **46** 38 41N 93 5W
Smithtown **53** 40 51N 73 12W
Smithville, Ga. **32** 31 54N 84 15W
Smithville, Md. **41** 38 46N 75 45W
Smithville, Miss. **45** 34 4N 88 23W
Smithville, Mo. **46** 39 23N 94 35W
Smithville, Okla. **57** 34 28N 94 39W
Smithville, Tenn. **63** 35 58N 85 49W
Smithville, Tex. **65** 30 1N 97 10W
Smithville, W. Va. **68** 39 4N 81 6W
Smoaks **60** 33 5N 80 49W
Smoke Bend **39** 30 7N 91 1W
Smoke Creek Desert **49** 40 30N 119 40W
Smoky Dome **34** 43 30N 114 56W
Smoky Hill → **38** 39 4N 96 48W
Smoky Hills **38** 39 15N 99 30W
Smolan **38** 38 44N 97 41W
Smoot **70** 42 37N 110 55W
Smyrna, Del. **41** 39 18N 75 36W
Smyrna, Ga. **32** 33 53N 84 31W
Smyrna, Tenn. **62** 35 59N 86 31W
Smyrna Mills **40** 46 8N 68 10W
Smyth County ◇ **68** 36 55N 81 25W
Snake →, Marshall, Minn. **44** 48 26N 97 7W
Snake →, Pine, Minn. **44** 45 49N 92 46W
Snake →, Nebr. **48** 42 47N 100 47W
Snake →, Wash. **67** 46 12N 119 2W
Snake Range **49** 39 0N 114 20W
Snake River Plain **34** 42 50N 114 0W
Snake Valley **66** 39 30N 113 55W
Sneads Ferry **54** 34 33N 77 24W
Sneedville **63** 36 32N 83 13W
Snelling, Calif. **28** 37 31N 120 26W
Snelling, S.C. **60** 33 15N 81 27W
Snohomish **67** 47 55N 122 6W
Snohomish County ◇ **67** 48 0N 121 30W
Snoqualmie **67** 47 31N 121 49W
Snoqualmie National Forest **67** 47 35N 121 20W
Snoqualmie Pass **67** 47 25N 121 25W
Snover **43** 43 28N 82 58W
Snow Hill, Ala. **24** 32 0N 87 0W
Snow Hill, Md. **41** 38 11N 75 24W
Snow Hill, N.C. **54** 35 27N 77 40W
Snow Mt., Calif. **28** 39 23N 122 45W
Snow Mt., Maine **40** 45 18N 70 48W
Snow Shoe **59** 41 2N 77 57W
Snow Water L. **49** 40 48N 114 59W
Snowball **27** 35 55N 92 49W
Snowdoun **24** 32 15N 86 18W
Snowflake **26** 34 30N 110 5W
Snowmass **30** 39 20N 106 59W
Snowmass Mt. **30** 39 8N 107 5W
Snowshoe Pk. **47** 48 13N 115 41W
Snowville **66** 41 58N 112 43W
Snowy Mt. **53** 43 42N 74 23W
Snowyside Pk. **34** 43 57N 114 58W
Snyder, Colo. **30** 40 20N 103 36W
Snyder, Nebr. **48** 41 43N 96 47W
Snyder, Okla. **57** 34 40N 98 57W
Snyder, Tex. **64** 32 44N 100 55W
Snyder County ◇ **59** 40 50N 77 0W
Soap Lake **67** 47 23N 119 29W
Social Circle **32** 33 39N 83 43W
Society Hill, Ala. **24** 32 26N 85 27W
Society Hill, S.C. **60** 34 31N 79 51W
Socorro **52** 34 4N 106 54W
Socorro County ◇ **52** 34 0N 107 0W
Soda L. **29** 35 10N 116 4W
Soda Springs, Calif. **28** 39 20N 120 23W
Soda Springs, Idaho **34** 42 39N 111 36W
Soddy-Daisy **63** 35 17N 85 10W
Sodus **53** 43 14N 77 4W
Sodus Point **53** 43 16N 76 59W
Solano County ◇ **28** 38 20N 121 50W
Soldier, Iowa **37** 41 59N 95 46W
Soldier, Kans. **38** 39 32N 95 58W
Soldier Summit **66** 39 56N 111 5W
Soldiers Grove **69** 43 24N 90 47W
Soldotna **25** 60 29N 151 3W
Soledad **28** 36 26N 121 20W
Solen **55** 46 23N 100 48W
Solomon, Ariz. **26** 32 49N 109 38W
Solomon, Kans. **38** 38 55N 97 22W
Solomon → **38** 38 55N 97 22W
Solomons **41** 38 19N 76 27W
Solon, Iowa **37** 41 48N 91 30W
Solon, Maine **40** 44 57N 69 52W
Solon Springs **69** 46 22N 91 49W
Solvang **29** 34 36N 120 8W
Solvay **53** 43 3N 76 13W
Solway **63** 35 59N 84 11W
Somers, Conn. **42** 41 59N 72 27W
Somers, Iowa **37** 42 23N 94 26W
Somers, Mont. **47** 48 5N 114 13W
Somers Point **51** 39 20N 74 36W
Somerset, Colo. **30** 38 56N 107 28W
Somerset, Ky. **63** 37 5N 84 36W
Somerset, Mass. **42** 41 47N 71 8W
Somerset, Ohio **56** 39 48N 82 18W
Somerset, Pa. **59** 40 1N 79 5W
Somerset, Tex. **65** 29 14N 98 40W
Somerset County ◇, Maine **40** 45 30N 70 0W
Somerset County ◇, Md. **41** 38 10N 75 50W
Somerset County ◇, N.J. **51** 40 35N 74 35W
Somerset County ◇, Pa. **59** 40 0N 79 0W
Somerset Res. **50** 43 0N 72 57W
Somersworth **50** 43 16N 70 52W
Somerton **26** 32 36N 114 43W
Somervell County ◇ **65** 32 14N 97 45W
Somerville, Mass. **42** 42 23N 71 6W
Somerville, N.J. **51** 40 35N 74 38W
Somerville, Ohio **56** 39 34N 84 38W
Somerville, Tenn. **62** 35 15N 89 21W
Somerville, Tex. **65** 30 21N 96 32W
Somerville L. **65** 30 19N 96 31W
Somes Bar **28** 41 23N 123 29W
Sondheimer **39** 32 33N 91 11W
Sonoma **28** 38 18N 122 28W
Sonoma County ◇ **28** 38 30N 123 0W
Sonoma Peak **49** 40 52N 117 36W
Sonora, Calif. **28** 37 59N 120 23W
Sonora, Ky. **63** 37 32N 85 54W
Sonora, Tex. **64** 30 34N 100 39W
Sonora Desert **26** 33 40N 114 15W
Sontag **45** 31 39N 90 12W
Sopchoppy **31** 30 4N 84 29W
Soper **57** 34 2N 95 42W
Soperton **32** 32 23N 82 35W
Sophia **54** 35 50N 79 52W
Sorento **35** 39 1N 89 35W
Sorrento **39** 30 11N 90 51W
Soso **45** 31 45N 89 17W
Souderton **59** 40 19N 75 19W
Souhegan → **50** 42 51N 71 29W
Sour Lake **65** 30 9N 94 25W
Souris **55** 48 55N 100 40W
Souris → **55** 49 0N 100 57W
South → **54** 34 20N 78 3W
South Amboy **51** 40 29N 74 18W
South Anna → **68** 37 48N 77 25W
South Ashburnam **42** 42 37N 71 57W
South Baldy **52** 33 59N 107 11W
South Bay **31** 26 40N 80 43W
South Beloit **35** 42 29N 89 2W
South Bend, Ind. **36** 41 41N 86 15W
South Bend, Wash. **67** 46 40N 123 48W
South Bloomfield **56** 39 43N 82 59W
South Boardman **43** 44 38N 85 17W
South Boston **68** 36 42N 78 54W
South Branch Potomac → **68** 39 32N 78 35W
South Burlington **50** 44 28N 73 13W
South Carolina □ **60** 34 0N 81 0W
South Carver **42** 41 51N 70 54W
South Chaplin **42** 41 46N 72 9W
South Charleston, Ohio **56** 39 50N 83 38W
South Charleston, W. Va. **68** 38 22N 81 44W
South Charlestown **50** 43 12N 72 26W
South China **40** 44 24N 69 34W
South Coffeyville **57** 36 59N 95 37W
South Congaree **60** 33 53N 81 9W
South Dakota □ **61** 44 15N 100 0W
South Dartmouth **42** 41 36N 70 57W
South Daytona **31** 29 10N 81 0W
South Deerfield, Mass. **42** 42 29N 72 37W
South Deerfield, N.H. **50** 43 6N 71 18W
South-East Fairbanks ◇ **25** 64 0N 144 0W
South Easton **42** 42 3N 71 5W
South Egremont **42** 42 10N 73 25W
South Elgin **35** 42 0N 88 18W
South English **37** 41 27N 92 5W
South Fabius → **46** 39 54N 91 30W
South Fork, Colo. **30** 37 40N 106 37W
South Fork, Pa. **59** 40 22N 78 48W
South Fork American → **28** 38 57N 120 59W
South Fork Edisto → **60** 33 16N 80 54W
South Fork Grand → **61** 45 43N 102 17W
South Fork Indian Reservation **49** 40 45N 115 40W
South Fork John Day → **58** 44 28N 119 31W
South Fork Moreau **61** 45 9N 102 50W
South Fork Owyhee → **34** 42 16N 116 53W
South Fork Powder → **70** 43 40N 106 30W
South Fork Republican → **48** 40 3N 101 31W
South Fork Salmon → **34** 45 23N 115 31W
South Fork Sappa Cr. → **38** 39 47N 100 35W
South Fork Selway → **34** 46 10N 115 58W
South Fork Shenandoah → **68** 38 57N 78 12W
South Fork Shoshone → **70** 44 27N 109 14W
South Fork Solomon → **38** 39 28N 98 26W
South Fork Spring → **27** 36 19N 91 30W
South Fox I. **43** 45 25N 85 51W
South Fulton **62** 36 30N 88 52W
South Grand → **46** 38 17N 93 25W
South Greensburg **59** 40 17N 79 33W
South Hadley **42** 42 16N 72 35W
South Hadley Falls **42** 42 14N 72 36W
South Hamilton **42** 42 37N 70 53W
South Haven, Kans. **38** 37 3N 97 24W
South Haven, Mich. **43** 42 24N 86 16W
South Hero **50** 44 39N 73 19W
South Hill **68** 36 44N 78 8W
South Holston L. **63** 36 31N 82 5W
South Houston **65** 29 40N 95 14W
South Hutchinson **38** 38 2N 97 56W
South I. **60** 33 10N 79 14W
South Jacksonville **35** 39 44N 90 12W
South Jordan **66** 40 34N 111 55W
South Junction **58** 44 51N 121 5W
South Lake Tahoe **28** 38 57N 119 59W
South Lancaster **42** 42 27N 71 41W
South Lebanon **56** 39 22N 84 13W
South Loup → **48** 41 4N 98 39W
South Lyon **43** 42 28N 83 39W
South Manitou I. **43** 45 2N 86 8W
South Marsh I. **41** 38 6N 76 2W
South Merrimac **50** 42 49N 71 34W
South Miami **31** 25 42N 80 18W
South Middleboro **42** 41 45N 70 50W
South Mills **54** 36 27N 76 20W
South Milwaukee **69** 42 55N 87 52W
South Mountain **41** 39 30N 77 40W
South Mt. **34** 42 44N 116 54W
South Newport **32** 31 38N 81 24W
South Newtane **50** 42 55N 72 42W
South Ogden **66** 41 12N 112 0W
South Otselic **53** 42 39N 75 47W
South Paris **40** 44 14N 70 31W
South Pekin **35** 40 30N 89 39W
South Pittsburg **63** 35 1N 85 42W
South Platte → **48** 41 7N 100 42W
South Pomfret **50** 43 40N 72 33W
South Ponte Vedra Beach **31** 30 3N 81 20W
South Portland **40** 43 38N 70 15W
South Range **43** 47 4N 88 38W
South River **51** 40 27N 74 23W
South Royalton **50** 43 49N 72 32W
South St. Paul **44** 44 53N 93 2W
South San Francisco **28** 37 39N 122 24W
South Seaville **51** 39 11N 74 46W
South Shore, Ky. **63** 38 43N 82 59W
South Shore, S. Dak. **61** 45 7N 96 56W
South Sioux City **48** 42 28N 96 24W
South Skunk → **37** 41 15N 92 2W
South Stoddard **50** 43 4N 72 7W
South Strafford **50** 43 49N 72 23W
South Sulphur → **65** 33 23N 95 18W
South Superior **70** 41 46N 108 58W
South Torrington **70** 42 3N 104 11W
South Tucson **26** 32 12N 110 58W
South Umpqua → **58** 43 16N 123 27W
South Venice **31** 27 3N 82 25W
South Wayne **69** 42 34N 89 53W
South Weare **50** 43 5N 71 45W
South Webster **56** 38 49N 82 44W
South Wellfleet **42** 41 55N 69 58W
South West City **46** 36 31N 94 37W
South Whitley **36** 41 5N 85 38W
South Williamson **63** 37 40N 82 17W
South Williamsport **59** 41 13N 77 0W
South Windsor **42** 41 49N 72 37W
South Woodstock **50** 43 35N 72 32W
South Yarmouth **42** 41 40N 70 10W
South Zanesville **56** 39 54N 82 2W
Southampton, Mass. **42** 42 14N 72 44W
Southampton, N.Y. **53** 40 53N 72 23W
Southampton County ◇ **68** 36 43N 77 4W
Southard **57** 36 4N 98 29W
Southbeach **58** 44 37N 124 3W
Southbridge **42** 42 5N 72 2W
Southbury **42** 41 29N 73 13W
Southeast C. **25** 62 56N 169 39W
Southern Pines **54** 35 11N 79 24W
Southern Ute Indian Reservation **30** 37 10N 107 30W
Southfield **43** 42 29N 83 17W
Southington **42** 41 36N 72 53W
Southland **64** 33 22N 101 33W
Southport, N.C. **54** 33 55N 78 1W
Southport, N.Y. **53** 42 3N 76 49W
Southwest Harbor **40** 44 17N 68 20W
Southwest Pt. **71** 17 40N 64 55W
Southwick **42** 42 3N 72 46W
Southwood Acres **42** 41 59N 72 32W
Spalding, Idaho **34** 46 27N 116 49W
Spalding, Nebr. **48** 41 42N 98 22W
Spalding County ◇ **32** 33 15N 84 15W
Spanaway **67** 47 6N 122 26W
Spangle **67** 47 26N 117 23W
Spanish Fork **66** 40 7N 111 39W
Spanish Fort **24** 30 40N 87 53W
Sparkman **27** 33 55N 92 51W

Sparks, Ga. **32** 31 11N 83 26W
Sparks, Nebr. **48** 42 56N 100 15W
Sparks, Nev. **49** 39 32N 119 45W
Sparks, Okla. **57** 35 37N 96 50W
Sparland **35** 41 2N 89 26W
Sparlingville **43** 42 58N 82 32W
Sparr **31** 29 20N 82 7W
Sparta, Ga. **32** 33 17N 82 58W
Sparta, Ill. **35** 38 8N 89 42W
Sparta, Ky. **63** 38 41N 84 54W
Sparta, Mich. **43** 43 10N 85 42W
Sparta, Mo. **46** 37 0N 93 5W
Sparta, N.C. **54** 36 30N 81 7W
Sparta, Tenn. **63** 35 56N 85 28W
Sparta, Wis. **69** 43 56N 90 49W
Spartanburg **60** 34 56N 81 57W
Spartanburg County ◇ **60** 34 50N 82 0W
Spartansburg **59** 41 49N 79 41W
Spavinaw **57** 36 23N 95 3W
Speaks **65** 29 15N 96 42W
Spearfish **61** 44 30N 103 52W
Spearman **64** 36 12N 101 12W
Spearsville **39** 32 56N 92 36W
Spearville **38** 37 51N 99 45W
Speed **38** 39 41N 99 25W
Speedway **36** 39 47N 86 15W
Spenard **25** 61 11N 149 55W
Spencer, Idaho **34** 44 22N 112 11W
Spencer, Ind. **36** 39 17N 86 46W
Spencer, Iowa **37** 43 9N 95 9W
Spencer, Mass. **42** 42 15N 71 59W
Spencer, N.C. **54** 35 41N 80 26W
Spencer, N.Y. **53** 42 13N 76 30W
Spencer, Nebr. **48** 42 53N 98 42W
Spencer, Ohio **56** 41 6N 82 8W
Spencer, S. Dak. **61** 43 44N 97 36W
Spencer, Tenn. **63** 35 45N 85 28W
Spencer, W. Va. **68** 38 48N 81 21W
Spencer, Wis. **69** 44 46N 90 18W
Spencer County ◇, Ind. **36** 38 0N 87 0W
Spencer County ◇, Ky. **63** 38 0N 85 20W
Spencerville, Ohio **56** 40 43N 84 21W
Spencerville, Okla. **57** 34 8N 95 21W
Sperry **57** 36 18N 95 59W
Sperryville **68** 38 39N 78 14W
Spiceland **36** 39 50N 85 26W
Spickard **46** 40 14N 93 36W
Spindale **54** 35 22N 81 56W
Spink **61** 42 51N 96 45W
Spink County ◇ **61** 45 0N 98 18W
Spirit L. **37** 43 29N 95 6W
Spirit Lake, Idaho **34** 47 58N 116 52W
Spirit Lake, Iowa **37** 43 26N 95 6W
Spiritwood **55** 46 56N 98 30W
Spiro **57** 35 15N 94 37W
Splendora **65** 30 14N 95 10W
Spofford **64** 29 10N 100 25W
Spokane **67** 47 40N 117 24W
Spokane → **67** 47 54N 118 20W
Spokane County ◇ **67** 47 35N 117 25W
Spokane Indian Reservation **67** 47 57N 118 0W
Spoon → **35** 40 19N 90 4W
Spooner **69** 45 50N 91 53W
Spotswood **51** 40 23N 74 23W
Spotsylvania **68** 38 12N 77 36W
Spotsylvania County ◇ **68** 38 12N 77 36W
Spotted Horse **70** 44 43N 105 50W
Sprague, Nebr. **48** 40 38N 96 45W
Sprague, Wash. **67** 47 18N 117 59W
Sprague → **58** 42 34N 121 51W
Sprague River **58** 42 27N 121 30W
Spray **58** 44 50N 119 48W
Spring **65** 30 5N 95 25W
Spring →, Mo. **46** 37 5N 94 45W
Spring →, S. Dak. **61** 45 45N 100 18W
Spring Butte **70** 41 51N 108 53W
Spring City, Tenn. **63** 35 42N 84 52W
Spring City, Utah **66** 39 29N 111 30W
Spring Cr. →, Ga. **32** 30 54N 84 45W
Spring Cr. →, N. Dak. **55** 47 15N 101 48W
Spring Cr. →, Nebr. **48** 40 20N 101 6W
Spring Cr. →, Nev. **49** 39 55N 117 50W
Spring Glen **66** 39 40N 110 51W
Spring Green **69** 43 11N 90 4W
Spring Grove **44** 43 34N 91 38W
Spring Hill, Ala. **24** 31 42N 85 58W
Spring Hill, Ark. **27** 33 35N 93 39W
Spring Hill, Fla. **31** 28 27N 82 41W
Spring Hill, Iowa **37** 41 25N 93 39W
Spring Hill, Minn. **44** 45 32N 94 50W
Spring Hill, Tenn. **62** 35 45N 86 56W
Spring Hope **54** 35 57N 78 6W
Spring Lake, N.C. **54** 35 10N 78 58W
Spring Lake, N.J. **51** 40 9N 74 2W
Spring Mts. **49** 36 0N 115 45W
Spring Valley, Calif. **29** 32 45N 117 0W
Spring Valley, Ill. **35** 41 20N 89 12W
Spring Valley, Minn. **44** 43 41N 92 23W
Spring Valley, Nev. **49** 39 10N 114 25W
Spring Valley, Wis. **69** 44 51N 92 14W
Springbrook **37** 42 10N 90 29W
Springdale, Ark. **27** 36 11N 94 8W
Springdale, Ohio **56** 39 17N 84 29W
Springdale, Utah **66** 37 10N 113 0W
Springdale, Wash. **67** 48 4N 117 45W
Springer, N. Mex. **52** 36 22N 104 36W
Springer, Okla. **57** 34 19N 97 8W
Springerton **35** 38 11N 88 21W
Springerville **26** 34 8N 109 17W
Springfield, Colo. **30** 37 24N 102 37W
Springfield, Fla. **31** 30 10N 85 37W
Springfield, Ga. **32** 32 22N 81 18W
Springfield, Idaho **34** 43 5N 112 41W
Springfield, Ill. **35** 39 48N 89 39W
Springfield, Ky. **63** 37 41N 85 13W
Springfield, La. **39** 30 26N 90 33W
Springfield, Maine **40** 45 24N 68 8W
Springfield, Mass. **42** 42 6N 72 35W
Springfield, Minn. **44** 44 14N 94 59W
Springfield, Mo. **46** 37 13N 93 17W
Springfield, Nebr. **48** 41 5N 96 8W
Springfield, Ohio **56** 39 55N 83 49W
Springfield, Oreg. **58** 44 3N 123 1W
Springfield, S.C. **60** 33 30N 81 17W
Springfield, S. Dak. **61** 42 49N 97 54W
Springfield, Tenn. **62** 36 31N 86 53W
Springfield, Va. **68** 38 47N 77 11W
Springfield, Vt. **50** 43 18N 72 29W
Springfield, L. **35** 39 46N 89 36W
Springfield Plateau **46** 37 30N 92 45W
Springhill **39** 33 0N 93 28W
Springlake **64** 34 14N 102 18W
Springport **43** 42 22N 84 42W
Springtown **65** 32 58N 97 41W
Springvale, Ga. **32** 31 50N 84 53W
Springvale, Maine **40** 43 28N 70 48W
Springview **48** 42 50N 99 45W
Springville, Ala. **24** 33 46N 86 29W
Springville, Calif. **29** 36 8N 118 49W
Springville, Iowa **37** 42 3N 91 27W
Springville, N.Y. **53** 42 31N 78 40W
Springville, Utah **66** 40 10N 111 37W
Spruce Knob **68** 38 42N 79 32W
Spruce Knob-Seneca Rocks Nat. Rec. Area **68** 38 50N 79 30W
Spruce Pine **54** 35 55N 82 4W
Spur **64** 33 28N 100 52W
Squa Pan L. **40** 46 31N 68 13W
Squam L. **50** 43 45N 71 32W
Square L. **40** 47 3N 68 20W
Squaw Lake **44** 47 38N 94 8W
Squibnocket Point **42** 41 18N 70 47W
Squire **68** 37 14N 81 37W
Squires **46** 36 51N 92 37W
Staatsburg **53** 41 51N 73 56W
Stacy **44** 45 24N 92 59W
Stacyville **37** 43 26N 92 47W
Stafford, Kans. **38** 37 58N 98 36W
Stafford, Tex. **65** 29 37N 95 34W
Stafford, Va. **68** 38 25N 77 25W
Stafford, L. **31** 29 20N 82 29W
Stafford County ◇, Kans. **38** 38 0N 98 45W
Stafford County ◇, Va. **68** 38 25N 77 25W
Stafford Springs **42** 41 57N 72 18W
Stambaugh **43** 46 5N 88 38W
Stamford, Conn. **42** 41 3N 73 32W
Stamford, N.Y. **53** 42 25N 74 38W
Stamford, Nebr. **48** 40 8N 99 36W
Stamford, Tex. **65** 32 57N 99 48W
Stamford, Vt. **50** 42 45N 73 4W
Stamford, L. **65** 33 4N 99 34W
Stamping Ground **63** 38 16N 84 41W
Stamps **27** 33 22N 93 30W
Stanardsville **68** 38 18N 78 26W
Stanberry **46** 40 13N 94 35W
Standing Rock **52** 35 48N 108 22W
Standing Rock Indian Reservation **61** 45 45N 101 10W
Standish, Calif. **28** 40 22N 120 25W
Standish, Mich. **43** 43 59N 83 57W
Standrod **66** 41 59N 113 25W
Stanfield, Ariz. **26** 32 53N 111 58W
Stanfield, Oreg. **58** 45 47N 119 13W
Stanford, Ky. **63** 37 32N 84 40W
Stanford, Mont. **47** 47 9N 110 13W
Stanhope **37** 42 17N 93 48W
Stanislaus → **28** 37 40N 121 14W
Stanislaus County ◇ **28** 37 30N 121 0W
Stanislaus National Forest **28** 38 10N 120 0W
Stanley, Idaho **34** 44 13N 114 56W
Stanley, Kans. **38** 38 51N 94 40W
Stanley, Ky. **62** 37 50N 87 15W
Stanley, La. **39** 31 58N 93 54W
Stanley, N.C. **54** 35 21N 81 6W
Stanley, N. Dak. **55** 48 19N 102 23W
Stanley, N. Mex. **52** 35 9N 105 59W
Stanley, Va. **68** 38 35N 78 30W
Stanley, Wis. **69** 44 58N 90 56W
Stanley County ◇ **61** 44 30N 101 0W
Stanleyville **54** 36 12N 80 17W
Stanly County ◇ **54** 35 20N 80 10W
Stanton, Iowa **37** 40 59N 95 6W
Stanton, Ky. **63** 37 54N 83 52W
Stanton, Mich. **43** 43 18N 85 5W
Stanton, Mo. **46** 38 17N 91 6W
Stanton, N. Dak. **55** 47 19N 101 23W
Stanton, Nebr. **48** 41 57N 97 14W
Stanton, Tenn. **62** 35 28N 89 24W
Stanton, Tex. **64** 32 8N 101 48W
Stanton County ◇, Kans. **38** 37 30N 101 45W
Stanton County ◇, Nebr. **48** 41 50N 97 10W
Stanwood **67** 48 15N 122 23W
Staplehurst **48** 40 58N 97 10W
Staples **44** 46 21N 94 48W
Stapleton **48** 41 29N 100 31W
Star **54** 35 24N 79 47W
Star City, Ark. **27** 33 56N 91 51W
Star City, Ind. **36** 40 58N 86 33W
Star Lake **53** 44 10N 75 2W
Starbuck, Minn. **44** 45 37N 95 32W
Starbuck, Wash. **67** 46 31N 118 7W
Stark **38** 37 42N 95 9W
Stark County ◇, Ill. **35** 41 5N 89 45W
Stark County ◇, N. Dak. **55** 46 55N 102 30W
Stark County ◇, Ohio **56** 40 48N 81 22W
Starke **31** 29 57N 82 7W
Starke County ◇ **36** 41 15N 86 40W
Starks **39** 30 19N 93 40W
Starkville, Colo. **30** 37 8N 104 30W
Starkville, Miss. **45** 33 28N 88 49W
Starkweather **55** 48 27N 98 53W
Starr **60** 34 23N 82 41W
Starr County ◇ **64** 26 30N 98 50W
Starrucca **59** 41 54N 75 28W
Stars Mill **32** 33 19N 84 31W
Starvation Reservoir **66** 40 15N 110 30W
State Center **37** 42 1N 93 10W
State College, Miss. **45** 33 27N 88 47W
State College, Pa. **59** 40 48N 77 52W
State Line **45** 31 26N 88 28W
State Road **54** 36 19N 80 52W
Staten I. **53** 40 35N 74 9W
Statenville **32** 30 42N 83 2W
Statesboro **32** 32 27N 81 47W
Statesville **54** 35 47N 80 53W
Statham **32** 33 58N 83 35W
Staunton, Ill. **35** 39 1N 89 47W
Staunton, Va. **68** 38 9N 79 4W
Stayton **58** 44 48N 122 48W
Staytonville **41** 38 50N 75 32W
Stead **52** 36 6N 103 12W
Steamboat Canyon **26** 35 45N 109 51W
Steamboat Rock **37** 42 25N 93 4W
Steamboat Springs **30** 40 29N 106 50W
Stearns County ◇ **44** 45 35N 94 30W
Stebbins **25** 63 31N 162 17W
Stedman **54** 35 0N 78 41W
Steel, Mt. **70** 41 50N 107 0W
Steele, Ala. **24** 33 56N 86 12W
Steele, Mo. **46** 36 5N 89 50W
Steele, N. Dak. **55** 46 51N 99 55W
Steele City **48** 40 2N 97 2W
Steele County ◇, Minn. **44** 44 0N 93 10W
Steele County ◇, N. Dak. **55** 47 31N 97 50W
Steeleville **35** 38 0N 89 40W
Steelton **59** 40 14N 76 50W
Steelville **46** 37 58N 91 22W
Steen **43** 43 31N 96 16W
Steens Mt. **58** 42 35N 118 40W
Stehekin **67** 48 19N 120 39W
Steinauer **48** 40 12N 96 14W
Steinhatchee **31** 29 40N 83 23W
Stella, Ky. **62** 36 38N 88 24W
Stella, Mo. **46** 36 46N 94 12W
Stella, Nebr. **48** 40 14N 95 46W
Stella, Tenn. **62** 35 2N 87 5W
Stem **54** 36 12N 78 43W
Stephen **44** 48 27N 96 53W
Stephens **27** 33 25N 93 4W
Stephens City **68** 39 5N 78 13W
Stephens County ◇, Ga. **32** 34 35N 83 15W
Stephens County ◇, Okla. **57** 34 30N 97 50W
Stephens County ◇, Tex. **65** 32 45N 98 54W
Stephens Knob **63** 36 37N 84 20W
Stephenson **43** 45 25N 87 36W
Stephenson County ◇ **35** 42 20N 89 40W
Stephenville **65** 32 13N 98 12W
Steptoe **67** 47 0N 117 21W
Steptoe Valley **49** 39 50N 114 45W
Sterling, Alaska **25** 60 32N 150 46W
Sterling, Colo. **30** 40 37N 103 13W
Sterling, Ga. **32** 31 16N 81 34W
Sterling, Idaho **34** 43 2N 112 44W
Sterling, Ill. **35** 41 48N 89 42W
Sterling, Kans. **38** 38 13N 98 12W
Sterling, Mass. **42** 42 26N 71 46W
Sterling, Mich. **43** 44 2N 84 2W
Sterling, N. Dak. **55** 46 49N 100 17W
Sterling, Nebr. **48** 40 28N 96 23W
Sterling, Okla. **57** 34 45N 98 10W
Sterling, Utah **66** 39 12N 111 42W
Sterling, Va. **68** 39 1N 77 26W
Sterling City **64** 31 51N 101 0W
Sterling County ◇ **64** 32 0N 101 0W
Sterling Heights **43** 42 35N 83 0W
Sterling Reservoir **30** 40 47N 103 16W
Sterlington **39** 32 42N 92 5W
Stetsonville **69** 45 4N 90 19W
Steuben County ◇, Ind. **36** 41 40N 85 0W
Steuben County ◇, N.Y. **53** 42 15N 77 20W
Steubens **69** 43 11N 90 52W
Steubenville, Ky. **63** 36 53N 84 48W
Steubenville, Ohio **56** 40 22N 80 37W
Stevens County ◇, Kans. **38** 37 15N 101 20W
Stevens County ◇, Minn. **44** 45 40N 96 0W
Stevens County ◇, Wash. **67** 48 30N 118 0W
Stevens Point **69** 44 31N 89 34W
Stevens Pottery **32** 32 57N 83 17W
Stevens Village **25** 66 1N 149 6W
Stevenson, Ala. **24** 34 52N 85 50W
Stevenson, Wash. **67** 45 42N 121 53W
Stevensville, Md. **41** 38 59N 76 19W
Stevensville, Mont. **47** 46 30N 114 5W
Steward **35** 41 51N 89 1W
Stewardson **35** 39 16N 88 38W
Stewart, Ga. **32** 33 25N 83 52W
Stewart, Minn. **44** 44 43N 94 29W
Stewart, Miss. **45** 33 27N 89 26W
Stewart County ◇, Ga. **32** 32 5N 84 50W
Stewart County ◇, Tenn. **62** 36 20N 87 55W
Stewarts Point **28** 38 39N 123 24W
Stewartstown, N.H. **50** 45 0N 71 31W
Stewartstown, Pa. **59** 39 45N 76 36W
Stewartsville **46** 39 45N 94 30W
Stewartville **44** 43 51N 92 29W
Stickney **61** 43 35N 98 26W
Stidham **57** 35 22N 95 42W
Stigler **57** 35 15N 95 8W
Stiles **64** 31 25N 101 34W
Stilesville **36** 39 38N 86 38W
Still Pond **41** 39 20N 76 3W
Stillhouse Hollow L. **65** 31 2N 97 32W
Stillmore **32** 32 27N 82 13W
Stillwater, Minn. **44** 45 3N 92 49W
Stillwater, Nev. **49** 39 31N 118 33W
Stillwater, Okla. **57** 36 7N 97 4W
Stillwater County ◇ **47** 45 48N 109 15W
Stillwater Range **49** 39 50N 118 5W
Stillwater Reservoir **53** 43 54N 75 3W
Stillwell **32** 32 23N 81 15W
Stilwell, Kans. **38** 38 46N 94 39W
Stilwell, Okla. **57** 35 49N 94 38W
Stinnett **64** 35 50N 101 27W
Stinson Lake **50** 43 51N 71 48W
Stirling City **28** 39 54N 121 32W
Stirrat **68** 37 44N 82 0W
Stites **34** 46 6N 115 59W
Stock Island **31** 24 32N 81 34W
Stockbridge, Ga. **32** 33 33N 84 14W
Stockbridge, Mass. **42** 42 17N 73 19W
Stockbridge, Mich. **43** 42 27N 84 11W
Stockbridge Indian Reservation **69** 44 50N 88 50W
Stockdale **65** 29 14N 97 58W
Stockett **47** 47 21N 111 10W
Stockham **48** 40 43N 97 56W
Stockholm, Maine **40** 47 3N 68 8W
Stockholm, S. Dak. **61** 45 6N 96 48W
Stockholm, Wis. **69** 44 29N 92 16W
Stockland **35** 40 37N 87 36W
Stockly **41** 38 40N 75 20W
Stockport, Iowa **37** 40 51N 91 50W
Stockport, Ohio **56** 39 33N 81 48W
Stockton, Ala. **24** 31 0N 87 52W
Stockton, Calif. **28** 37 58N 121 17W
Stockton, Ill. **35** 42 21N 90 1W
Stockton, Kans. **38** 39 26N 99 16W
Stockton, Md. **41** 38 3N 75 25W
Stockton, Minn. **44** 44 2N 91 46W
Stockton, Mo. **46** 37 42N 93 48W
Stockton, N.J. **51** 40 24N 74 58W
Stockton, Utah **66** 40 27N 112 22W
Stockton I. **69** 46 57N 90 35W
Stockton L. **46** 37 42N 93 46W
Stockton Plateau **64** 30 30N 102 30W
Stockville **48** 40 32N 100 23W
Stoddard **69** 43 40N 91 13W
Stoddard County ◇ **46** 36 50N 90 0W
Stokes County ◇ **54** 36 20N 80 10W

Stone **34** 42 1N 112 42W
Stone County ◇, Ark. **27** 35 52N 92 7W
Stone County ◇, Miss. **45** 30 47N 89 8W
Stone County ◇, Mo. **46** 36 45N 93 25W
Stone Harbor **51** 39 3N 74 45W
Stone Mountain **32** 33 49N 84 10W
Stone Mt. **50** 44 34N 71 40W
Stoneboro **59** 41 20N 80 7W
Stonega **68** 36 57N 82 48W
Stoneham **30** 40 36N 103 40W
Stoner **30** 37 35N 108 19W
Stoneville **54** 36 28N 79 54W
Stonewall, Ark. **27** 36 14N 90 32W
Stonewall, Colo. **30** 37 9N 105 1W
Stonewall, La. **39** 32 17N 93 50W
Stonewall, Miss. **45** 32 8N 88 47W
Stonewall, Okla. **57** 34 39N 96 32W
Stonewall County ◇ **64** 33 8N 100 14W
Stonington, Colo. **30** 37 18N 102 11W
Stonington, Ill. **35** 39 44N 89 12W
Stonington, Maine **40** 44 9N 68 40W
Stony Creek **68** 36 57N 77 24W
Stony Gorge Reservoir **28** 39 35N 122 32W
Stony I. **53** 43 54N 76 20W
Stony Point, Mich. **43** 41 57N 83 16W
Stony Point, N.C. **54** 35 52N 81 3W
Stony Pt. **53** 43 50N 76 18W
Stony Ridge **56** 41 31N 83 30W
Stony River **25** 61 47N 156 35W
Stonyford **28** 39 23N 122 33W
Storey County ◇ **49** 39 30N 119 35W
Storm L. **37** 42 38N 95 13W
Storm Lake **37** 42 39N 95 13W
Stormy Mt. **67** 47 54N 120 21W
Storrs **42** 41 49N 72 15W
Story **70** 44 35N 106 53W
Story City **37** 42 11N 93 36W
Story County ◇ **37** 42 0N 93 25W
Stotesbury **46** 37 59N 94 34W
Stoughton, Mass. **42** 42 8N 71 6W
Stoughton, Wis. **69** 42 55N 89 13W
Stout **37** 42 32N 92 43W
Stoutland **46** 37 49N 92 31W
Stoutsville, Mo. **46** 39 33N 91 51W
Stoutsville, Ohio **56** 39 36N 82 50W
Stovall, Ga. **32** 32 58N 84 51W
Stovall, N.C. **54** 36 27N 78 35W
Stover **46** 38 27N 92 59W
Stowe **50** 44 28N 72 41W
Stowell **65** 29 47N 94 23W
Strafford, Mo. **46** 37 16N 93 7W
Strafford, N.H. **50** 43 19N 71 12W
Strafford County ◇ **50** 43 15N 71 0W
Strandburg **61** 45 3N 96 46W
Strandquist **44** 48 29N 96 27W
Strang **48** 40 25N 97 35W
Strasburg, Colo. **30** 39 44N 104 20W
Strasburg, Mo. **46** 38 46N 94 10W
Strasburg, N. Dak. **55** 46 8N 100 10W
Strasburg, Ohio **56** 40 36N 81 32W
Strasburg, Pa. **59** 39 59N 76 11W
Strasburg, Va. **68** 38 59N 78 22W
Stratford, Calif. **29** 36 11N 119 49W
Stratford, Conn. **42** 41 12N 73 8W
Stratford, Iowa **37** 42 16N 93 56W
Stratford, N.H. **50** 44 42N 71 36W
Stratford, Okla. **57** 34 48N 96 58W
Stratford, S. Dak. **61** 45 19N 98 18W
Stratford, Tex. **64** 36 20N 102 4W
Stratford, Wis. **69** 44 48N 90 4W
Stratham **50** 43 3N 70 55W
Strathcona **44** 48 33N 96 10W
Strathmere **51** 39 12N 74 40W
Strathmore **29** 36 9N 119 4W
Stratton, Colo. **30** 39 19N 102 36W
Stratton, Maine **40** 45 8N 70 26W
Stratton, Nebr. **48** 40 9N 101 14W
Stratton, Vt. **50** 43 4N 72 55W
Stratton Meadows **30** 38 45N 104 48W
Strawberry **27** 35 58N 91 19W
Strawberry →, Ark. **27** 35 53N 91 13W
Strawberry →, Utah **66** 40 10N 110 24W
Strawberry Mt. **58** 44 19N 118 43W
Strawberry Point **37** 42 41N 91 32W
Strawberry Reservoir **66** 40 8N 111 9W
Strawn, Ill. **35** 40 39N 88 24W
Strawn, Tex. **65** 32 33N 98 30W
Streator **35** 41 8N 88 50W
Streeter **55** 46 39N 99 21W
Streetman **65** 31 53N 96 19W
Streetsboro **56** 41 14N 81 21W
Stringer **45** 31 52N 89 16W
Stromsburg **48** 41 7N 97 36W
Strong **27** 33 7N 92 21W
Strong → **45** 31 51N 90 8W
Strong City, Kans. **38** 38 24N 96 32W
Strong City, Okla. **57** 35 40N 99 36W
Stronghurst **35** 40 45N 90 55W
Strongville **56** 41 19N 81 50W
Stroud **57** 35 45N 96 40W
Stroudsburg **59** 40 59N 75 12W
Strum **69** 44 33N 91 24W
Struthers **56** 41 4N 80 39W
Stryker, Mont. **47** 48 41N 114 46W
Stryker, Ohio **56** 41 30N 84 25W
Stuart, Fla. **31** 27 12N 80 15W
Stuart, Iowa **37** 41 30N 94 19W
Stuart, Nebr. **48** 42 36N 99 8W
Stuart, Okla. **57** 34 54N 96 6W
Stuart, Va. **68** 36 38N 80 16W
Stuart, Mt. **67** 47 29N 120 54W
Stuart I. **25** 63 35N 162 30W
Studley **38** 39 21N 100 10W
Stump L. **55** 47 54N 98 24W
Stumpy Point **54** 35 42N 75 44W
Sturgeon **46** 39 14N 92 17W
Sturgeon →, Cheboygan, Mich. **43** 45 24N 84 38W
Sturgeon →, Houghton, Mich. **43** 47 2N 88 30W
Sturgeon B. **43** 45 45N 85 0W
Sturgeon Bay **69** 44 50N 87 23W
Sturgeon Lake **44** 46 23N 92 49W
Sturgis, Ky. **62** 37 33N 87 59W
Sturgis, Mich. **43** 41 48N 85 25W
Sturgis, S. Dak. **61** 44 25N 103 31W
Sturtevant **69** 42 42N 87 54W
Stutsman County ◇ **55** 47 0N 99 0W
Stuttgart **27** 34 30N 91 33W
Styx → **24** 30 31N 87 27W
Sublette, Ill. **35** 41 39N 89 14W
Sublette, Kans. **38** 37 29N 100 51W
Sublette County ◇ **70** 43 0N 110 0W
Sucarnoochee → **24** 32 25N 88 2W
Success **27** 36 27N 90 43W
Success, L. **29** 36 4N 118 55W
Success, Mt. **50** 44 27N 71 5W
Succor Cr. → **34** 43 37N 116 57W
Sudbury **42** 42 23N 71 25W
Sudlersville **41** 39 11N 75 52W
Suffield **42** 41 59N 72 39W
Suffolk **68** 36 44N 76 35W
Suffolk County ◇, Mass. **42** 42 21N 71 5W
Suffolk County ◇, N.Y. **53** 40 50N 73 0W
Sugar →, Ill. **35** 42 26N 89 12W
Sugar →, N.H. **50** 43 24N 72 24W
Sugar City, Colo. **30** 38 14N 103 40W
Sugar City, Idaho **34** 43 52N 111 45W
Sugar Cr. →, Mason, Ill. **35** 40 9N 89 38W
Sugar Cr. →, Ill. **35** 40 50N 87 45W
Sugar Cr. →, Ind. **36** 39 51N 87 21W
Sugar Creek **59** 41 47N 76 27W
Sugar Grove, N.C. **54** 36 15N 81 47W
Sugar Grove, Ohio **56** 39 38N 82 33W
Sugar Hill **32** 34 6N 84 2W
Sugar I. **43** 46 25N 84 12W
Sugar Land **65** 29 37N 95 38W
Sugar Notch **59** 41 12N 75 56W
Sugarloaf Mt. **57** 35 2N 94 28W
Sugartown **39** 30 50N 93 1W
Sugarville **66** 39 28N 112 39W
Sugden **57** 34 5N 97 59W
Suisun B. **28** 38 5N 122 0W
Suisun City **28** 38 15N 122 2W
Suitland **41** 38 51N 76 56W
Sulligent **24** 33 54N 88 8W
Sullivan, Ill. **35** 39 36N 88 37W
Sullivan, Ind. **36** 39 6N 87 24W
Sullivan, Ky. **62** 37 30N 87 57W
Sullivan, Mo. **46** 38 13N 91 10W
Sullivan County ◇, Ind. **36** 39 5N 87 25W
Sullivan County ◇, Mo. **46** 40 10N 93 5W
Sullivan County ◇, N.H. **50** 43 20N 72 15W
Sullivan County ◇, N.Y. **53** 41 45N 74 45W
Sullivan County ◇, Pa. **59** 41 30N 76 35W
Sullivan County ◇, Tenn. **63** 36 32N 82 19W
Sully County ◇ **61** 44 45N 100 0W
Sulphur, La. **39** 30 14N 93 23W
Sulphur, Okla. **57** 34 31N 96 58W
Sulphur →, Ark. **27** 33 7N 93 52W
Sulphur →, S. Dak. **61** 44 45N 102 0W
Sulphur →, Tex. **65** 33 7N 93 52W
Sulphur Draw → **64** 33 12N 102 17W
Sulphur Rock **27** 35 45N 91 30W
Sulphur Springs, Ark. **27** 36 29N 94 28W
Sulphur Springs, Ind. **36** 40 0N 85 27W
Sulphur Springs, Tex. **65** 33 8N 95 36W
Sulphur Springs Draw → **64** 32 12N 101 36W
Sultan **67** 47 52N 121 49W
Sumac **32** 34 53N 84 48W
Sumas **67** 48 59N 122 15W
Sumatra, Fla. **31** 30 1N 84 59W
Sumatra, Mont. **47** 46 37N 107 33W
Summer I. **43** 45 34N 86 39W
Summer L. **58** 42 50N 120 45W
Summer Lake **58** 42 58N 120 47W
Summerdale **24** 30 28N 87 55W
Summerfield, Kans. **38** 39 59N 96 21W
Summerfield, Ohio **56** 39 48N 81 20W
Summerfield, Tex. **64** 34 44N 102 31W
Summerland Key **31** 24 40N 81 27W
Summers County ◇ **68** 37 40N 80 54W
Summersville, Mo. **46** 37 11N 91 40W
Summersville, W. Va. **68** 38 17N 80 51W
Summersville L. **68** 38 13N 80 53W
Summerton **60** 33 36N 80 20W
Summertown, Ga. **32** 32 45N 82 16W
Summertown, Tenn. **62** 35 26N 87 18W
Summerville, Ga. **32** 34 29N 85 21W
Summerville, S.C. **60** 33 1N 80 11W
Summit, Alaska **25** 63 20N 149 7W
Summit, Ill. **35** 41 48N 87 48W
Summit, Ky. **62** 37 34N 86 5W
Summit, Miss. **45** 31 17N 90 28W
Summit, N.J. **51** 40 43N 74 22W
Summit, Okla. **57** 35 40N 95 26W
Summit, Oreg. **58** 44 38N 123 35W
Summit, S. Dak. **61** 45 18N 97 2W
Summit, Utah **66** 37 48N 112 56W
Summit County ◇, Colo. **30** 39 30N 106 0W
Summit County ◇, Ohio **56** 41 8N 81 29W
Summit County ◇, Utah **66** 40 55N 111 0W
Summit L. **49** 41 31N 119 4W
Summit Lake Indian Reservation **49** 41 33N 119 2W
Summit Peak **30** 37 21N 106 42W
Sumner, Iowa **37** 42 51N 92 6W
Sumner, Miss. **45** 33 58N 90 22W
Sumner, Mo. **46** 39 39N 93 15W
Sumner, Nebr. **48** 40 57N 99 31W
Sumner, L. **52** 34 40N 104 25W
Sumner County ◇, Kans. **38** 37 15N 97 20W
Sumner County ◇, Tenn. **62** 36 24N 86 27W
Sumpter **58** 44 45N 118 12W
Sumrall **45** 31 25N 89 33W
Sumter **60** 33 55N 80 21W
Sumter County ◇, Ala. **24** 32 35N 88 11W
Sumter County ◇, Fla. **31** 28 45N 82 10W
Sumter County ◇, Ga. **32** 32 0N 84 10W
Sumter County ◇, S.C. **60** 33 50N 80 30W
Sumter National Forest **60** 34 50N 83 0W
Sun **39** 30 39N 89 54W
Sun → **47** 47 29N 111 19W
Sun City, Ariz. **26** 33 36N 112 17W
Sun City, Calif. **29** 33 42N 117 11W
Sun City, Kans. **38** 37 23N 98 55W
Sun Prairie **69** 43 11N 89 13W
Sun River **47** 47 32N 111 43W
Sun Valley **34** 43 42N 114 21W
Sunapee **50** 43 23N 72 7W
Sunapee L. **50** 43 23N 72 5W
Sunbright **63** 36 15N 84 40W
Sunburg **44** 45 21N 95 14W
Sunburst **47** 48 53N 111 55W
Sunbury, N.C. **54** 36 27N 76 37W
Sunbury, Pa. **59** 40 52N 76 48W
Suncook **50** 43 8N 71 27W
Suncook → **50** 43 8N 71 28W
Sundance **70** 44 24N 104 23W
Sunderland **41** 38 40N 76 36W
Sunflower **45** 33 33N 90 32W
Sunflower → **45** 32 40N 90 40W
Sunflower, Mt. **38** 39 6N 102 2W
Sunflower County ◇ **45** 33 44N 90 33W
Sunland Park **52** 31 50N 106 40W
Sunman **36** 39 14N 85 6W
Sunnyside, Utah **66** 39 34N 110 23W
Sunnyside, Wash. **67** 46 20N 120 0W
Sunnyvale **28** 37 23N 122 2W
Sunol **48** 41 9N 102 46W
Sunray, Okla. **57** 34 25N 97 58W
Sunray, Tex. **64** 36 1N 101 49W
Sunrise **70** 42 20N 104 42W
Sunrise Manor **49** 36 12N 115 3W
Sunset, La. **39** 30 25N 92 4W
Sunset, Utah **66** 41 10N 112 0W
Sunset Beach **33** 21 40N 158 3W
Sunset Crater National Monument **26** 35 20N 111 20W
Suntrana **25** 63 52N 148 51W
Supai **26** 36 15N 112 41W
Superior, Ariz. **26** 33 18N 111 6W
Superior, Iowa **37** 43 26N 94 57W
Superior, Mont. **47** 47 12N 114 53W
Superior, Nebr. **48** 40 1N 98 4W
Superior, Wis. **69** 46 44N 92 6W
Superior, L. **69** 47 0N 90 0W
Superior National Forest **44** 47 40N 92 45W
Suphur Springs Range **49** 40 15N 116 0W
Suqualena **45** 32 27N 88 50W
Sur, Pt. **28** 36 18N 121 54W
Surf City, N.C. **54** 34 26N 77 33W
Surf City, N.J. **51** 39 40N 74 10W
Surfside **31** 25 53N 80 8W
Surfside Beach **60** 33 37N 78 57W
Suring **69** 44 59N 88 22W
Surprise, Ariz. **26** 33 38N 112 19W
Surprise, Nebr. **48** 41 6N 97 19W
Surrency **32** 31 44N 82 12W
Surrey **55** 48 14N 101 6W
Surry, N.H. **50** 43 3N 72 18W
Surry, Va. **68** 37 8N 76 50W
Surry County ◇, N.C. **54** 36 20N 80 45W
Surry County ◇, Va. **68** 37 8N 76 50W
Susank **38** 38 38N 98 46W
Susanville **28** 40 25N 120 39W
Susquehanna → **59** 39 33N 76 5W
Susquehanna County ◇ **59** 41 55N 75 50W
Susquehanna Depot **59** 41 57N 75 36W
Sussex, N.J. **51** 41 13N 74 37W
Sussex, Va. **68** 36 55N 77 17W
Sussex, Wis. **69** 43 8N 88 13W
Sussex, Wyo. **70** 43 42N 106 18W
Sussex County ◇, Del. **41** 38 45N 75 20W
Sussex County ◇, N.J. **51** 41 15N 74 45W
Sussex County ◇, Va. **68** 36 55N 77 17W
Sutcliffe **49** 39 57N 119 36W
Sutherland, Iowa **37** 42 58N 95 29W
Sutherland, Nebr. **48** 41 10N 101 8W
Sutherland Reservoir **48** 41 6N 101 10W
Sutherlin **58** 43 23N 123 19W
Sutter **28** 39 10N 121 45W
Sutter County ◇ **28** 39 0N 121 45W
Sutter Creek **28** 38 24N 120 48W
Suttle **24** 32 32N 87 11W
Sutton, N. Dak. **55** 47 24N 98 27W
Sutton, Nebr. **48** 40 36N 97 52W
Sutton, Vt. **50** 44 39N 72 3W
Sutton, W. Va. **68** 38 40N 80 43W
Sutton County ◇ **64** 30 34N 100 39W
Sutton L. **68** 38 40N 80 41W
Sutwik I. **25** 56 34N 157 12W
Suwanee **32** 34 3N 84 4W
Suwannee **31** 29 20N 83 9W
Suwannee → **31** 29 17N 83 10W
Suwannee County ◇ **31** 30 15N 83 0W
Suwannee Sd. **31** 29 20N 83 15W
Swain **27** 35 51N 93 20W
Swain County ◇ **54** 35 30N 83 20W
Swainsboro **32** 32 36N 82 20W
Swaledale **37** 42 59N 93 19W
Swan L. **61** 45 17N 99 51W
Swan Lake **47** 47 56N 113 51W
Swan Ra. **47** 48 0N 113 45W
Swan Valley **34** 43 27N 111 20W
Swandale **68** 38 30N 80 57W
Swannanoa **54** 35 36N 82 24W
Swanquarter **54** 35 25N 76 20W
Swans I. **40** 44 10N 68 26W
Swansboro **54** 34 39N 77 7W
Swansea **60** 33 44N 81 6W
Swanson L. **48** 40 10N 101 4W
Swanton, Md. **41** 39 27N 79 14W
Swanton, Vt. **50** 44 55N 73 8W
Swanville **44** 45 55N 94 38W
Swartswood **51** 41 8N 74 50W
Swartz Creek **43** 42 58N 83 50W
Swasey Peak **66** 39 23N 113 19W
Swayzee **36** 40 30N 85 50W
Swea City **37** 43 23N 94 19W
Sweatman **45** 33 38N 89 35W
Swedeborg **46** 37 55N 92 20W
Sweden **40** 46 57N 68 8W
Swedesboro **51** 39 45N 75 19W
Swedish Knoll **66** 39 0N 111 0W
Sweeny **65** 29 3N 95 42W
Sweet Air **41** 39 31N 76 32W
Sweet Briar **68** 37 33N 79 4W
Sweet Grass County ◇ **47** 46 0N 110 0W
Sweet Home, Ark. **27** 34 41N 92 15W
Sweet Home, Oreg. **58** 44 24N 122 44W
Sweet Springs **46** 38 58N 93 25W
Sweetgrass **47** 48 59N 111 58W
Sweetwater, Okla. **57** 35 25N 99 55W

Sweetwater, Tenn. 63 35 36N 84 28W
Sweetwater, Tex. 64 32 28N 100 25W
Sweetwater → 70 42 31N 107 2W
Sweetwater County ◇ 70 42 0N 109 0W
Sweetwater L. 55 48 13N 98 50W
Swenson 64 33 13N 100 19W
Swift County ◇ 44 45 15N 95 45W
Swift Reservoir 67 46 4N 122 3W
Swifton 27 35 49N 91 8W
Swink, Colo. 30 38 1N 103 38W
Swink, Okla. 57 34 1N 95 12W
Swinomish Indian Reservation 67 48 23N 122 32W
Swisher 37 41 50N 91 42W
Swisher County ◇ 64 34 32N 101 46W
Swisshome 58 44 4N 123 48W
Switzerland County ◇ 36 38 50N 85 0W
Swords 32 33 33N 83 18W
Swoyerville 59 41 18N 75 53W
Sycamore, Ga. 32 31 40N 83 38W
Sycamore, Ill. 35 41 59N 88 41W
Sycamore, Kans. 38 37 20N 95 43W
Sycamore, Ohio 56 40 57N 83 10W
Sycamore, S.C. 60 33 2N 81 13W
Sycan Marsh 58 42 45N 121 5W
Sydney 55 46 44N 98 46W
Sykeston 55 47 28N 99 24W
Sykesville, Md. 41 39 22N 76 58W
Sykesville, Pa. 59 41 3N 78 50W
Sylacauga 24 33 10N 86 15W
Sylva 54 35 23N 83 13W
Sylvan Grove 38 39 1N 98 24W
Sylvania, Ga. 32 32 45N 81 38W
Sylvania, Ohio 56 41 43N 83 42W
Sylvarena 45 32 1N 89 23W
Sylvester, Ga. 32 31 32N 83 50W
Sylvester, Tex. 64 32 43N 100 15W
Sylvia 38 37 57N 98 25W
Symerton 35 41 20N 88 3W
Symmes → 56 38 26N 82 27W
Symsonia 62 36 55N 88 31W
Syracuse, Ind. 36 41 26N 85 45W
Syracuse, Kans. 38 37 59N 101 45W
Syracuse, Mo. 46 38 40N 92 53W
Syracuse, N.Y. 53 43 3N 76 9W
Syracuse, Nebr. 48 40 39N 96 11W

T

Tabernash 30 39 57N 105 52W
Tabiona 66 40 21N 110 43W
Table Mt., Ariz. 26 32 49N 110 31W
Table Mt., N. Dak. 55 45 57N 103 48W
Table Rock 48 40 11N 96 6W
Table Rock L. 46 36 36N 93 19W
Table Top 26 32 45N 112 8W
Tabor, Iowa 37 40 54N 95 40W
Tabor, Minn. 44 48 5N 96 52W
Tabor, S. Dak. 61 42 57N 97 40W
Tabor City 54 34 10N 78 52W
Tacna 26 32 41N 114 1W
Tacoma 67 47 14N 122 26W
Taconite Harbor 44 47 32N 90 55W
Taft, Calif. 29 35 8N 119 28W
Taft, Fla. 31 28 26N 81 22W
Taft, Okla. 57 35 46N 95 32W
Taft, Tenn. 62 35 1N 86 43W
Taft, Tex. 65 27 59N 97 24W
Tahlequah 57 35 55N 94 58W
Tahoe, L. 49 39 6N 120 2W
Tahoe City 28 39 10N 120 9W
Tahoe National Forest 28 39 20N 120 30W
Tahoka 64 33 10N 101 48W
Taholah 67 47 21N 124 17W
Tahquamenon → 43 46 34N 85 2W
Taiban 52 34 26N 104 1W
Tajique 52 34 45N 106 17W
Takoma Park 41 38 59N 77 0W
Takotna 25 62 59N 156 4W
Talala 57 36 32N 95 42W
Talbert 63 37 25N 83 28W
Talbot County ◇, Ga. 32 32 45N 84 40W
Talbot County ◇, Md. 41 38 45N 76 0W
Talbotton 32 32 41N 84 32W
Talco 65 33 22N 95 6W
Talent 58 42 15N 122 47W
Taliaferro County ◇ 32 33 35N 82 50W
Talihina 57 34 45N 95 3W
Talkeetna 25 62 20N 150 6W
Talking Rock 32 34 31N 84 30W
Talladega 24 33 26N 86 6W
Talladega County ◇ 24 33 26N 86 6W
Talladega National Forest 24 32 55N 87 15W
Tallahala → 45 31 12N 89 5W
Tallahassee 31 30 27N 84 17W
Tallahatchie County ◇ 45 33 58N 90 22W
Tallahtchie → 45 33 33N 90 10W
Tallapoosa 32 33 45N 85 17W
Tallapoosa → 24 32 30N 86 16W
Tallapoosa County ◇ 24 32 50N 85 46W
Tallassee 24 32 32N 85 54W
Talleyville 41 39 48N 75 33W
Tallmadge 56 41 6N 81 27W
Tallula 35 39 56N 89 56W
Tallulah 39 32 25N 91 11W
Tallulah Falls 32 34 44N 83 24W
Talmage, Kans. 38 39 2N 97 16W
Talmage, Nebr. 48 40 32N 96 1W
Taloga 57 36 2N 98 58W
Talowah 45 31 4N 89 26W
Talpa 65 31 47N 99 43W
Talquin, L. 31 30 23N 84 39W
Tama 37 41 58N 92 35W
Tama County ◇ 37 42 5N 92 30W
Tamaha 57 35 20N 94 59W
Tamaqua 59 40 48N 75 58W
Tamarac 31 26 12N 80 10W
Tamarack 44 46 39N 93 8W
Tamaroa 35 38 8N 89 14W
Tamiami Canal 31 25 50N 81 0W
Tamms 35 37 14N 89 16W
Tamora 48 40 54N 97 14W
Tampa, Fla. 31 27 57N 82 27W
Tampa, Kans. 38 38 33N 97 9W
Tampa B. 31 27 50N 82 30W
Tampico 35 41 38N 89 47W
Tamworth 50 43 50N 71 18W
Tanacross 25 63 23N 143 21W
Tanaga I. 25 51 48N 177 53W
Tanaga Volcano 25 51 53N 178 8W
Tanama → 71 18 25N 66 42W
Tanana 25 65 10N 152 4W
Tanana → 25 65 10N 151 58W
Taney County ◇ 46 36 40N 93 0W
Taneytown 41 39 40N 77 11W
Taneyville 46 36 44N 93 2W
Tangent 58 44 33N 123 7W
Tangier I. 68 37 55N 75 59W
Tangier Sd. 41 38 0N 75 57W
Tangipahoa, La. 39 30 52N 90 30W
Tangipahoa → 39 30 15N 90 15W
Tangipahoa Parish ◇ 39 30 30N 90 28W
Tankersley 64 31 21N 100 39W
Tanner 68 38 59N 80 57W
Taopi 44 43 34N 92 38W
Taos 52 36 24N 105 35W
Taos County ◇ 52 36 30N 105 40W
Taos Indian Reservation 52 36 35N 105 25W
Taos Pueblo 52 36 24N 105 33W
Tappahannock 68 37 56N 76 52W
Tappan L. 56 40 22N 81 14W
Tappen 55 46 52N 99 38W
Tar → 54 35 33N 77 6W
Tarboro, Ga. 32 31 1N 81 48W
Tarboro, N.C. 54 35 54N 77 32W
Targhee National Forest 34 44 15N 111 20W
Tarkio, Mo. 46 40 27N 95 23W
Tarkio, Mont. 47 47 1N 114 44W
Tarkio → 46 40 27N 95 23W
Tarlton 56 39 33N 82 47W
Tarnov 48 41 37N 97 30W
Tarpon Springs 31 28 9N 82 45W
Tarrant City 24 33 34N 86 47W
Tarrant County ◇ 65 32 44N 97 7W
Tarryall 30 39 7N 105 29W
Tarryall Cr. → 30 39 5N 105 19W
Tarrytown, Ga. 32 32 19N 82 34W
Tarrytown, N.Y. 53 41 4N 73 52W
Tarzan 64 32 18N 101 58W
Tate 32 34 25N 84 23W
Tate County ◇ 45 34 37N 89 58W
Tatitlek 25 60 52N 146 41W
Tattnall County ◇ 32 32 0N 82 0W
Tatum, N. Mex. 52 33 16N 103 19W
Tatum, Tex. 65 32 19N 94 31W
Tatum Cr. → 32 30 43N 82 32W
Taum Sauk Mt. 46 37 34N 90 44W
Taunton, Mass. 42 41 54N 71 6W
Taunton, Minn. 44 44 36N 96 4W
Taunton Lakes 51 39 51N 74 52W
Tavares 31 28 48N 81 44W
Tavernier 31 25 1N 80 31W
Tawakoni, L. 65 32 49N 95 55W
Tawas City 43 44 16N 83 31W
Taylor, Ariz. 26 34 28N 110 5W
Taylor, Ark. 27 33 6N 93 28W
Taylor, Fla. 31 30 26N 82 18W
Taylor, Mich. 43 42 14N 83 16W
Taylor, Miss. 45 34 16N 89 35W
Taylor, N. Dak. 55 46 54N 102 26W
Taylor, Nebr. 48 41 46N 99 23W
Taylor, Tex. 65 30 34N 97 25W
Taylor, Wis. 69 44 19N 91 7W
Taylor → 30 38 32N 106 55W
Taylor, Mt. 52 35 14N 107 37W
Taylor County ◇, Fla. 31 30 0N 83 30W
Taylor County ◇, Ga. 32 32 35N 84 15W
Taylor County ◇, Iowa 37 40 45N 94 40W
Taylor County ◇, Ky. 63 37 20N 85 20W
Taylor County ◇, Tex. 65 32 21N 99 53W
Taylor County ◇, W. Va. 68 39 21N 80 2W
Taylor County ◇, Wis. 69 45 10N 90 30W
Taylor Mill 63 38 55N 84 32W
Taylor Park Reservoir 30 38 49N 106 36W
Taylor Ridge 32 34 35N 85 12W
Taylors Bridge 41 39 23N 75 36W
Taylors Island 41 38 28N 76 18W
Taylorsville, Ind. 36 39 18N 85 57W
Taylorsville, Ky. 63 38 2N 85 21W
Taylorsville, Md. 41 39 27N 77 8W
Taylorsville, Miss. 45 31 50N 89 26W
Taylorsville, N.C. 54 35 55N 81 11W
Taylorville 35 39 33N 89 18W
Tazewell, Tenn. 63 36 27N 83 34W
Tazewell, Va. 68 37 7N 81 31W
Tazewell County ◇, Ill. 35 40 30N 89 30W
Tazewell County ◇, Va. 68 37 7N 81 31W
Tazlina 25 62 4N 146 27W
Tchula 45 33 11N 90 13W
Tea 61 43 27N 96 50W
Teague 65 31 38N 96 17W
Teaneck 51 40 53N 74 1W
Teasdale 66 38 17N 111 29W
Tecopa 29 35 51N 116 13W
Tecumseh, Mich. 43 42 0N 83 57W
Tecumseh, Nebr. 48 40 22N 96 11W
Tecumseh, Okla. 57 35 15N 96 56W
Tecumseh, Mt. 50 43 57N 71 34W
Teec Nos Pas 26 36 55N 109 6W
Tehachapi 29 35 8N 118 27W
Tehachapi Mts. 29 35 0N 118 30W
Tehachapi Pass 29 35 6N 118 18W
Tehama 28 40 2N 122 7W
Tehama County ◇ 28 40 5N 122 15W
Tejon Pass 29 34 49N 118 53W
Tekamah 48 41 47N 96 13W
Tekoa 67 47 14N 117 4W
Tekonsha 43 42 5N 84 59W
Telescope Pk. 29 36 10N 117 5W
Telfair County ◇ 32 31 55N 83 0W
Telida 25 63 23N 153 16W
Tell City 36 37 57N 86 46W
Teller 25 65 16N 166 22W
Teller County ◇ 30 38 50N 105 10W
Tellico Plains 63 35 22N 84 18W
Telluride 30 37 56N 107 49W
Telocaset 58 45 6N 117 49W
Telogia 31 30 21N 84 49W
Temblor Range 29 35 20N 119 50W
Temecula 29 33 30N 117 9W
Tempe 26 33 25N 111 56W
Temperance 43 41 47N 83 34W
Tempiute 49 37 39N 115 38W
Temple, N.H. 50 42 48N 71 50W
Temple, Okla. 57 34 16N 98 14W
Temple, Tex. 65 31 6N 97 21W
Temple Hill 63 36 53N 85 51W
Temple Terrace 31 28 2N 82 23W
Templeton, Calif. 29 35 33N 120 42W
Templeton, Mass. 42 42 33N 72 4W
Ten Thousand Is. 31 25 55N 81 45W
Tenaha 65 31 57N 94 15W
Tenakee Springs 25 57 47N 135 13W
Tendoy 34 44 57N 113 38W
Tenino 67 46 51N 122 51W
Tenkiller Ferry L. 57 35 35N 95 2W
Tennant 37 41 35N 95 26W
Tennessee 35 40 18N 90 52W
Tennessee □ 62 35 50N 85 30W
Tennessee → 62 37 4N 88 34W
Tennessee Pass 30 39 22N 106 19W
Tennessee Ridge 62 36 19N 87 47W
Tennille 32 32 56N 82 48W
Tennyson, Ind. 36 38 5N 87 7W
Tennyson, Wis. 69 42 41N 90 41W
Tensas → 39 31 38N 91 49W
Tensas Parish ◇ 39 32 0N 91 10W
Tensed 34 47 10N 116 55W
Tensleep 70 44 2N 107 27W
Tenstrike 44 47 39N 94 41W
Terlingua 64 29 19N 103 36W
Terlingua Cr. → 64 29 10N 103 36W
Terlton 57 36 8N 96 29W
Terra Alta 68 39 27N 79 33W
Terra Bella 29 35 58N 119 3W
Terral 57 33 54N 97 57W
Terre Haute 36 39 28N 87 25W
Terrebonne 58 44 21N 121 11W
Terrebonne B. 39 29 5N 90 35W
Terrebonne Parish ◇ 39 29 20N 91 0W
Terrell 65 32 44N 96 17W
Terrell County ◇, Ga. 32 31 50N 84 25W
Terrell County ◇, Tex. 64 30 0N 102 0W
Terreton 34 43 51N 112 26W
Terril 37 43 18N 94 58W
Terry, La. 39 32 56N 91 21W
Terry, Miss. 45 32 6N 90 18W
Terry, Mont. 47 46 47N 105 19W
Terry County ◇ 64 33 11N 102 17W
Terry Pk. 61 44 19N 103 50W
Terryville 42 41 41N 73 3W
Tescott 38 39 1N 97 53W
Teshekpuk L. 25 70 35N 153 26W
Tetlin 25 63 8N 142 31W
Tetlin Indian Reservation 25 63 0N 142 30W
Teton 34 43 53N 111 40W
Teton →, Idaho 34 43 54N 111 51W
Teton →, Mont. 47 47 56N 110 31W
Teton County ◇, Idaho 34 43 55N 111 5W
Teton County ◇, Mont. 47 47 52N 112 20W
Teton County ◇, Wyo. 70 44 0N 110 30W
Teton Pass 70 43 30N 110 57W
Teton Range 70 43 45N 111 0W
Tetonia 34 43 49N 111 10W
Teutopolis 35 39 8N 88 29W
Tewksbury 42 42 37N 71 14W
Texana, L. 65 29 0N 96 35W
Texarkana, Ark. 27 33 26N 94 2W
Texarkana, Tex. 65 33 26N 94 3W
Texas □ 64 31 0N 101 0W
Texas City 65 29 24N 94 54W
Texas County ◇, Mo. 46 37 20N 92 0W
Texas County ◇, Okla. 57 36 45N 101 30W
Texhoma 57 36 30N 101 47W
Texico 52 34 24N 103 3W
Texline 64 36 23N 103 2W
Texola 57 35 12N 99 59W
Texoma, L. 65 33 50N 96 34W
Texon 64 31 13N 101 42W
Thackerville 57 33 48N 97 9W
Thalia 65 33 59N 99 32W
Thalmann 32 31 18N 81 41W
Thames → 42 41 18N 72 5W
Thatcher, Ariz. 26 32 51N 109 46W
Thatcher, Colo. 30 37 33N 104 7W
Thawville 35 40 41N 88 7W
Thaxton 45 34 18N 89 11W
Thayer, Kans. 38 37 29N 95 28W
Thayer, Mo. 46 36 31N 91 33W
Thayer, Nebr. 48 40 58N 97 30W
Thayer County ◇ 48 40 15N 97 40W
Thayne 70 42 55N 111 0W
The Dalles 58 45 36N 121 10W
The Grove 65 31 16N 97 32W
The Plains 68 38 52N 77 47W
The Village 57 35 35N 97 33W
Theba 26 32 55N 112 53W
Thebes 35 37 13N 89 28W
Thedford 48 41 59N 100 35W
Theodore 24 30 33N 88 10W
Theodore Roosevelt L. 26 33 40N 111 10W
Theodore Roosevelt National Memorial Park 55 47 0N 103 25W
Theodosia 46 36 35N 92 39W
Theresa 53 44 13N 75 48W
Theressa 31 29 50N 82 4W
Theriot 39 29 28N 90 45W
Thermal 29 33 39N 116 9W
Thermalito 28 39 31N 121 36W
Thermopolis 70 43 39N 108 13W
Theta 62 35 47N 87 3W
Thibodaux 39 29 48N 90 49W
Thief L. 44 48 30N 95 54W
Thief River Falls 44 48 7N 96 10W
Thielsen, Mt. 58 43 9N 122 4W
Thomas, Md. 41 38 36N 76 18W
Thomas, Okla. 57 35 45N 98 45W
Thomas, W. Va. 68 39 9N 79 30W
Thomas A. Edison, L. 29 37 25N 119 0W
Thomas County ◇, Ga. 32 30 50N 83 55W
Thomas County ◇, Kans. 38 39 20N 101 0W
Thomas County ◇, Nebr. 48 41 50N 100 30W
Thomas Hill Reservoir 46 39 34N 92 39W
Thomasboro 35 40 15N 88 11W
Thomaston, Ala. 24 32 16N 87 38W
Thomaston, Conn. 42 41 41N 73 4W

Thomaston, Ga. **32** 32 53N 84 20W
Thomaston, Maine **40** 44 5N 69 11W
Thomaston Res. **42** 41 42N 73 5W
Thomastown **45** 32 52N 89 40W
Thomasville, Ala. **24** 31 55N 87 44W
Thomasville, Ga. **32** 30 50N 83 59W
Thomasville, N.C. **54** 35 53N 80 5W
Thompson, Iowa **37** 43 22N 93 46W
Thompson, N. Dak. **55** 47 47N 97 6W
Thompson, Pa. **59** 41 52N 75 31W
Thompson, Utah **66** 38 58N 109 43W
Thompson → **46** 39 46N 93 37W
Thompson Falls **47** 47 36N 115 21W
Thompson Pk. **28** 41 0N 123 0W
Thompsons Cr. → **45** 31 10N 88 55W
Thompsonville, Ill. **35** 37 55N 88 46W
Thompsonville, Mich. **43** 44 31N 85 56W
Thomson, Ga. **32** 33 28N 82 30W
Thomson, Ill. **35** 41 58N 90 6W
Thoreau **52** 35 24N 108 13W
Thornapple →, Mich. **43** 42 56N 85 28W
Thornapple →, Wis. **69** 45 28N 91 16W
Thornburg **37** 41 27N 92 20W
Thorndale **65** 30 37N 97 12W
Thornton, Colo. **30** 39 52N 104 58W
Thornton, Idaho **34** 43 45N 111 51W
Thornton, Iowa **37** 42 57N 93 23W
Thornton, Miss. **45** 33 5N 90 19W
Thornton, Tex. **65** 31 25N 96 34W
Thornton, Wash. **67** 47 7N 117 23W
Thorntown **36** 40 8N 86 36W
Thornville **56** 39 54N 82 25W
Thorny Mt. **46** 37 6N 91 10W
Thorp, Wash. **67** 47 4N 120 40W
Thorp, Wis. **69** 44 58N 90 48W
Thorsby **24** 32 55N 86 43W
Thousand Oaks **29** 34 10N 118 50W
Thousand Springs Cr. → **49** 41 17N 113 51W
Thrall **65** 30 35N 97 18W
Thrashers **45** 34 43N 88 32W
Three Forks **47** 45 54N 111 33W
Three Lakes **69** 45 48N 89 10W
Three Oaks **43** 41 48N 86 36W
Three Rivers, Calif. **29** 36 26N 118 54W
Three Rivers, Mich. **43** 41 57N 85 38W
Three Rivers, N. Mex. **52** 33 19N 106 5W
Three Rivers, Tex. **65** 28 28N 98 11W
Three Sisters **58** 44 4N 121 51W
Throckmorton **65** 33 11N 99 11W
Throckmorton County ◇ **65** 33 10N 99 10W
Thunder B. **43** 45 0N 83 20W
Thunder Basin National Grassland **70** 43 45N 105 5W
Thunder Butte **61** 45 19N 101 53W
Thunder Hawk **61** 45 56N 101 58W
Thunderbird, L. **57** 35 14N 97 18W
Thunderbolt **32** 32 3N 81 4W
Thurman **37** 40 49N 95 45W
Thurmont **41** 39 37N 77 25W
Thurston, Nebr. **48** 42 11N 96 42W
Thurston, Ohio **56** 39 50N 82 33W
Thurston County ◇, Nebr. **48** 42 15N 96 40W
Thurston County ◇, Wash. **67** 46 58N 122 59W
Tibble **24** 31 22N 88 15W
Tiber Reservoir **47** 48 19N 111 6W
Tice **31** 26 40N 81 49W
Tichnor **27** 34 8N 91 16W
Ticonderoga **53** 43 51N 73 26W
Tidewater **68** 37 51N 76 42W
Tidioute **59** 41 41N 79 24W
Tie Plant **45** 33 44N 89 47W
Tie Siding **70** 41 5N 105 30W
Tierra Amarilla **52** 36 42N 106 33W
Tierra Blanca Cr. → **64** 34 58N 101 55W
Tieton **67** 46 42N 120 46W
Tiffany **30** 37 2N 107 32W
Tiffany Mt. **67** 48 40N 119 56W
Tiffin, Iowa **37** 41 42N 91 40W
Tiffin, Ohio **56** 41 7N 83 11W
Tift County ◇ **32** 31 30N 83 30W
Tifton **32** 31 27N 83 31W
Tigalda I. **25** 54 6N 165 5W
Tigard **58** 45 26N 122 46W
Tiger **67** 48 42N 117 24W
Tignall **32** 33 52N 82 44W
Tijeras **52** 35 5N 106 23W
Tikchik Lakes **25** 60 0N 159 0W
Tilden, Ill. **35** 38 13N 89 41W
Tilden, Nebr. **48** 42 3N 97 50W
Tilden, Tex. **65** 28 28N 98 33W
Tilghman **41** 38 43N 76 20W
Tiline **62** 37 11N 88 15W
Tillamook **58** 45 27N 123 51W
Tillamook B. **58** 45 30N 123 53W
Tillamook County ◇ **58** 45 20N 123 45W
Tillamook Head **58** 45 57N 124 0W
Tillar **27** 33 43N 91 27W
Tiller **58** 42 56N 122 57W
Tillery, L. **54** 35 12N 80 4W
Tillman **60** 32 28N 81 6W
Tillman County ◇ **57** 34 25N 99 0W
Tillmans Corner **24** 30 46N 88 8W
Tilton, Ga. **32** 34 40N 84 56W
Tilton, Ill. **35** 40 6N 87 38W
Tilton, N.H. **50** 43 27N 71 36W
Timbalier B. **39** 29 3N 90 20W
Timbalier I. **39** 29 3N 90 28W
Timber **58** 45 43N 123 18W
Timber Lake **61** 45 26N 101 5W
Timberlake **54** 36 17N 78 57W
Timbo **27** 35 52N 92 19W
Timken **38** 38 29N 99 11W
Timmonsville **60** 34 8N 79 57W
Timnath **30** 40 32N 104 59W
Timpas **30** 37 49N 103 46W
Timpson **65** 31 54N 94 24W
Tims Ford L. **62** 35 15N 86 10W
Tin Mt. **29** 36 50N 117 10W
Tina **46** 39 32N 93 27W
Tindall **46** 40 10N 93 36W
Tinemaha Reservoir **29** 37 3N 118 13W
Tingley **37** 40 51N 94 12W
Tinmouth **50** 43 26N 73 4W
Tinsley **45** 32 44N 90 28W
Tinsman **27** 33 38N 92 21W
Tintah **44** 46 1N 96 19W
Tioga, N. Dak. **55** 48 24N 102 56W
Tioga, Pa. **59** 41 55N 77 8W
Tioga, Tex. **65** 33 28N 96 55W
Tioga, W. Va. **68** 38 25N 80 40W
Tioga County ◇, N.Y. **53** 42 10N 76 20W
Tioga County ◇, Pa. **59** 41 50N 77 10W
Tioga Pass **28** 37 54N 119 15W
Tionesta **59** 41 30N 79 28W
Tipp City **56** 39 58N 84 11W
Tippah County ◇ **45** 34 44N 88 57W
Tippecanoe → **36** 40 30N 86 45W
Tippecanoe County ◇ **36** 40 25N 86 55W
Tipton, Calif. **29** 36 4N 119 19W
Tipton, Ind. **36** 40 17N 86 2W
Tipton, Iowa **37** 41 46N 91 8W
Tipton, Kans. **38** 39 21N 98 28W
Tipton, Mo. **46** 38 39N 92 47W
Tipton, Okla. **57** 34 30N 99 8W
Tipton County ◇, Ind. **36** 40 20N 86 5W
Tipton County ◇, Tenn. **62** 35 29N 89 43W
Tipton Mt. **26** 35 32N 114 12W
Tiptonville **62** 36 23N 89 29W
Tishomingo, Miss. **45** 34 38N 88 14W
Tishomingo, Okla. **57** 34 14N 96 41W
Tishomingo County ◇ **45** 34 49N 88 12W
Tiskilwa **35** 41 18N 89 30W
Titonka **37** 43 14N 94 3W
Tittabawassee → **43** 43 23N 83 59W
Titus County ◇ **65** 33 9N 94 58W
Titusville, Fla. **31** 28 37N 80 49W
Titusville, Pa. **59** 41 38N 79 41W
Tiverton **42** 41 38N 71 12W
Tivoli **65** 28 27N 96 53W
Toa Alta **71** 18 23N 66 15W
Toa Baja **71** 18 27N 66 15W
Toana Range **49** 40 50N 114 20W
Toano **68** 37 23N 76 48W
Toast **54** 36 30N 80 38W
Tobias **48** 40 25N 97 20W
Tobin Range **49** 40 20N 117 30W
Tobyhanna **59** 41 11N 75 25W
Toccoa **32** 34 35N 83 19W
Toccopola **45** 34 15N 89 14W
Todd County ◇, Ky. **62** 36 50N 87 10W
Todd County ◇, Minn. **44** 46 10N 94 50W
Todd County ◇, S. Dak. **61** 43 5N 101 0W
Toddville **41** 38 18N 76 4W
Tofte **44** 47 35N 90 50W
Togiak **25** 59 4N 160 24W
Togowatee Pass **70** 43 45N 110 4W
Tohatchi **52** 35 52N 108 47W
Tohopekaliga L. **31** 28 12N 81 24W
Toiyabe National Forest **49** 38 40N 117 0W
Toiyabe Range **49** 39 30N 117 0W
Tok **25** 63 20N 142 59W
Tokeland **67** 46 42N 123 59W
Toksook Bay **25** 60 32N 165 0W
Tolbert **65** 34 13N 99 24W
Tolchester Beach **41** 39 13N 76 14W
Toledo, Ill. **35** 39 16N 88 15W
Toledo, Iowa **37** 42 0N 92 35W
Toledo, Ohio **56** 41 39N 83 33W
Toledo, Oreg. **58** 44 37N 123 56W
Toledo, Wash. **67** 46 26N 122 51W
Toledo Bend Reservoir **39** 31 11N 93 34W
Tolland **42** 41 52N 72 22W
Tolland County ◇ **42** 41 45N 72 20W
Tolleson **26** 33 27N 112 16W
Tolley **55** 48 44N 101 50W
Tolna **55** 47 50N 98 26W
Tolono **35** 39 59N 88 16W
Tolu **62** 37 26N 88 15W
Tom **57** 33 44N 94 35W
Tom Green County ◇ **64** 31 28N 100 26W
Tom Steed Res. **57** 34 46N 98 50W
Tomah **69** 43 59N 90 30W
Tomahawk **69** 45 28N 89 44W
Tomales Pt. **28** 38 14N 122 59W
Tomball **65** 30 6N 95 37W
Tombigbee → **24** 31 8N 87 57W
Tombigee National Forest **45** 33 10N 89 0W
Tombstone **26** 31 43N 110 4W
Tome **52** 34 44N 106 44W
Tomichi → **30** 38 31N 106 58W
Tompkins County ◇ **53** 42 30N 76 30W
Tompkinsville, Ky. **63** 36 42N 85 41W
Tompkinsville, Md. **41** 38 18N 76 54W
Toms → **51** 39 57N 74 7W
Toms Brook **68** 38 57N 78 26W
Toms River **51** 39 58N 74 12W
Tonalea **26** 36 19N 110 56W
Tonasket **67** 48 42N 119 26W
Tonawanda **53** 43 1N 78 53W
Tonawanda Indian Reservation **53** 43 5N 78 25W
Tonganoxie **38** 39 7N 95 5W
Tongass National Forest **25** 56 30N 134 0W
Tongue → **47** 46 25N 105 52W
Tongue River Reservoir **47** 45 8N 106 46W
Tonica **35** 41 13N 89 4W
Tonkawa **57** 36 41N 97 18W
Tonopah, Ariz. **26** 33 30N 112 56W
Tonopah, Nev. **49** 38 4N 117 14W
Tonsina **25** 61 39N 145 11W
Tontitown **27** 36 11N 94 14W
Tonto Cr. → **26** 33 45N 111 10W
Tonto National Forest **26** 34 0N 111 20W
Tooele **66** 40 32N 112 18W
Tooele County ◇ **66** 40 25N 113 0W
Toole County ◇ **47** 48 48N 111 50W
Toombs County ◇ **32** 32 10N 82 15W
Toomsboro **32** 32 50N 83 5W
Toone **62** 35 21N 88 57W
Topawa **26** 31 48N 111 51W
Topaz L. **49** 38 41N 119 33W
Topeka, Ind. **36** 41 32N 85 32W
Topeka, Kans. **38** 39 3N 95 40W
Toponas **30** 40 4N 106 48W
Toppenish **67** 46 23N 120 19W
Topsail Beach **54** 34 23N 77 37W
Topsfield, Maine **40** 45 25N 67 44W
Topsfield, Mass. **42** 42 38N 70 57W
Topton, N.C. **54** 35 15N 83 42W
Topton, Pa. **59** 40 30N 75 42W
Toquerville **66** 37 15N 113 17W
Toquima Range **49** 38 55N 116 50W
Torch L. **43** 44 58N 85 18W
Tornillo **64** 31 27N 106 5W
Toro **39** 31 17N 93 33W
Toronto, Iowa **37** 41 54N 90 52W
Toronto, Kans. **38** 37 48N 95 57W
Toronto, Ohio **56** 40 28N 80 36W
Toronto, S. Dak. **61** 44 34N 96 39W
Toronto Lake **38** 37 46N 95 57W
Torrance **29** 33 50N 118 19W
Torrance County ◇ **52** 34 40N 106 0W
Torrey **66** 38 18N 111 25W
Torrington, Conn. **42** 41 48N 73 7W
Torrington, Wyo. **70** 42 4N 104 11W
Tortilla Flat **26** 33 32N 111 23W
Tortuguero, L. **71** 18 28N 66 26W
Toston **47** 46 11N 111 26W
Toughy **48** 41 8N 96 50W
Toulon **35** 41 6N 89 52W
Towanda, Kans. **38** 37 44N 97 0W
Towanda, Pa. **59** 41 46N 76 27W
Towaoc **30** 37 12N 108 44W
Tower **44** 47 48N 92 17W
Tower City, N. Dak. **55** 46 56N 97 40W
Tower City, Pa. **59** 40 35N 76 33W
Tower Hill **35** 39 23N 88 58W
Towner, Colo. **30** 38 28N 102 5W
Towner, N. Dak. **55** 48 21N 100 25W
Towner County ◇ **55** 48 45N 99 10W
Towns **32** 32 0N 82 45W
Towns County ◇ **32** 34 55N 83 45W
Townsend, Del. **41** 39 24N 75 41W
Townsend, Ga. **32** 31 33N 81 31W
Townsend, Mass. **42** 42 40N 71 42W
Townsend, Mont. **47** 46 19N 111 31W
Townshend **50** 43 3N 72 41W
Townsville **54** 36 30N 78 25W
Townville **59** 41 41N 79 53W
Towson **41** 39 24N 76 36W
Toxey **24** 31 55N 88 19W
Toyah **64** 31 19N 103 48W
Toyah Cr. → **64** 31 18N 103 27W
Toyah L. **64** 31 15N 103 20W
Toyahvale **64** 30 57N 103 47W
Tracy, Calif. **28** 37 44N 121 26W
Tracy, Minn. **44** 44 14N 95 37W
Tracy City **63** 35 16N 85 44W
Tradewater → **62** 37 31N 88 3W
Traer **37** 42 12N 92 28W
Trafalgar **36** 39 25N 86 9W
Trail **44** 47 47N 95 42W
Traill County ◇ **55** 47 30N 97 20W
Trammel **68** 37 1N 82 18W
Tramway **54** 35 27N 79 13W
Tranquillity **29** 36 39N 120 15W
Transylvania **39** 32 41N 91 11W
Transylvania County ◇ **54** 35 10N 82 50W
Trappe **41** 38 40N 76 4W
Trapper Pk. **47** 45 54N 114 18W
Trask Mt. **58** 45 22N 123 27W
Traskwood **27** 34 27N 92 39W
Travelers Rest **60** 34 58N 82 27W
Traverse, L. **61** 45 46N 96 38W
Traverse City **43** 44 46N 85 38W
Traverse County ◇ **44** 45 45N 96 25W
Traverse Pt. **43** 47 9N 88 14W
Travis, L. **65** 30 24N 97 55W
Travis County ◇ **65** 30 17N 97 45W
Treasure County ◇ **47** 46 15N 107 20W
Treasure Island **31** 27 46N 82 46W
Treece **38** 37 0N 94 51W
Trego **47** 48 42N 114 52W
Trego County ◇ **38** 38 55N 99 50W
Tremont, Ill. **35** 40 28N 89 29W
Tremont, Miss. **45** 34 14N 88 16W
Tremonton **66** 41 43N 112 10W
Trempealeau **69** 44 0N 91 26W
Trempealeau County ◇ **69** 44 15N 91 20W
Trent **61** 43 54N 96 39W
Trent → **54** 35 5N 77 2W
Trenton, Fla. **31** 29 37N 82 49W
Trenton, Ga. **32** 34 52N 85 31W
Trenton, Ill. **35** 38 36N 89 41W
Trenton, Ky. **62** 36 43N 87 16W
Trenton, Maine **40** 44 27N 68 22W
Trenton, Mich. **43** 42 8N 83 11W
Trenton, Mo. **46** 40 5N 93 37W
Trenton, N.C. **54** 35 4N 77 21W
Trenton, N. Dak. **55** 48 4N 103 51W
Trenton, N.J. **51** 40 14N 74 46W
Trenton, Nebr. **48** 40 11N 101 1W
Trenton, Ohio **56** 39 29N 84 28W
Trenton, S.C. **60** 33 45N 81 51W
Trenton, Tenn. **62** 35 59N 88 56W
Tres Palacios B. **65** 28 30N 96 25W
Tres Piedras **52** 36 39N 105 58W
Tres Pinos **28** 36 48N 121 19W
Treutlen County ◇ **32** 32 25N 82 30W
Trevorton **59** 40 47N 76 41W
Treynor **37** 41 14N 95 36W
Trezevant **62** 36 1N 88 37W
Triangle **68** 38 33N 77 20W
Tribbey **57** 35 7N 97 4W
Tribly **31** 28 28N 82 12W
Tribune **38** 38 28N 101 45W
Trident **47** 45 57N 111 28W
Trident Peak **49** 41 54N 118 25W
Trigg County ◇ **62** 36 50N 87 55W
Trigo Mountans **26** 33 15N 114 40W
Trimble, Mo. **46** 39 28N 94 34W
Trimble, Tenn. **62** 36 12N 89 11W
Trimble County **63** 38 35N 85 20W
Trimont **44** 43 46N 94 43W
Trinchera **30** 37 2N 104 3W
Trinidad, Calif. **28** 41 4N 124 9W
Trinidad, Colo. **30** 37 10N 104 31W
Trinidad, Tex. **65** 32 9N 96 6W
Trinidad Head **28** 41 3N 124 9W
Trinity **65** 30 57N 95 22W
Trinity →, Calif. **28** 41 11N 123 42W
Trinity →, Tex. **65** 29 45N 94 43W
Trinity B. **65** 29 42N 94 55W
Trinity Center **28** 41 0N 122 41W
Trinity County ◇, Calif. **28** 40 40N 123 0W
Trinity County ◇, Tex. **65** 31 4N 95 8W
Trinity Is. **25** 56 33N 154 25W
Trinity Mt. **34** 43 36N 115 26W
Trinity Mts. **28** 40 50N 122 40W
Trinity National Forest **28** 40 40N 123 15W
Trinity Range **49** 40 15N 118 45W
Trinway **56** 40 9N 82 1W
Trion **32** 34 33N 85 19W
Triplett **46** 39 30N 93 12W
Tripoli **37** 42 49N 92 16W
Tripp **61** 43 13N 97 58W

Tripp County ◇ 61 43 20N 100 0W
Triumph 39 29 20N 89 30W
Trona 29 35 46N 117 23W
Tropic 66 37 37N 112 5W
Troup 65 32 9N 95 7W
Troup County ◇ ... 32 33 0N 85 0W
Trousdale 38 37 49N 99 5W
Trousdale County ◇ 62 36 24N 86 10W
Trout Cr. →, Harney, Oreg. ... 58 42 23N 118 3W
Trout Cr. →, Jefferson, Oreg... 58 44 48N 121 3W
Trout Creek, Mich. . 43 46 29N 89 1W
Trout Creek, Mont. 47 47 50N 115 36W
Trout Creek, Utah . 66 39 42N 113 50W
Trout Dale 68 36 42N 81 26W
Trout Lake, Mich... 43 46 12N 85 1W
Trout Lake, Wash. . 67 46 0N 121 32W
Trout Pk. 70 44 36N 109 32W
Troutmans 54 35 42N 80 53W
Troutville 68 37 25N 79 53W
Troy, Ala. 24 31 48N 85 58W
Troy, Idaho 34 46 44N 116 46W
Troy, Ind. 36 37 59N 86 55W
Troy, Kans. 38 39 47N 95 5W
Troy, Mich. 43 42 37N 83 9W
Troy, Miss. 45 34 7N 88 53W
Troy, Mo. 46 38 59N 90 59W
Troy, Mont. 47 48 28N 115 53W
Troy, N.C. 54 35 22N 79 53W
Troy, N.H. 50 42 49N 72 11W
Troy, N.Y. 53 42 44N 73 41W
Troy, Ohio 56 40 2N 84 12W
Troy, Oreg. 58 45 57N 117 27W
Troy, Pa. 59 41 47N 76 47W
Troy, S.C. 60 33 59N 82 17W
Troy, S. Dak. 61 45 2N 96 52W
Troy, Tenn. 62 36 20N 89 10W
Troy, Tex. 65 31 12N 97 18W
Troy, Vt. 50 44 52N 72 25W
Troy Peak 49 38 19N 115 30W
Truchas 52 36 3N 105 49W
Truchas Peak 52 35 58N 105 39W
Truckee 28 39 20N 120 11W
Truckee → 49 39 51N 119 24W
Truesdale 37 42 44N 95 11W
Trufant 43 43 19N 85 21W
Trujillo 52 35 32N 104 42W
Trujillo Alto 71 18 21N 66 1W
Truman 44 43 50N 94 26W
Trumann 27 35 41N 90 31W
Trumansburg 53 42 33N 76 40W
Trumbull, Conn. ... 42 41 15N 73 12W
Trumbull, Nebr. 48 40 41N 98 16W
Trumbull County ◇. 56 41 14N 80 49W
Truro 42 42 0N 70 3W
Truscott 65 33 45N 99 49W
Trussville 24 33 37N 86 35W
Truth or Consequences 52 33 8N 107 15W
Truxton 26 35 29N 113 34W
Tryon, N.C. 54 35 13N 82 14W
Tryon, Nebr. 48 41 33N 100 57W
Tryon, Okla. 57 35 52N 96 58W
Tsala Apopka L. ... 31 28 53N 82 19W
Tschida L. 55 46 36N 101 49W
Tuba City 26 36 8N 111 14W
Tubac 26 31 37N 111 3W
Tuckahoe 51 39 17N 74 45W
Tuckahoe → 41 38 0N 75 0W
Tucker, Ark. 27 34 26N 91 57W
Tucker, Ga. 32 33 51N 84 13W
Tucker County ◇ ... 68 39 9N 79 30W
Tuckerman 27 35 44N 91 12W
Tuckernuck Island . 42 41 18N 70 15W
Tuckerton 51 39 36N 74 20W
Tucson 26 32 13N 110 58W
Tucumcari 52 35 10N 103 44W
Tucumcari Cr. →.. 52 35 20N 103 15W
Tuftonboro 50 43 42N 71 13W
Tug Fork → 68 38 7N 82 36W
Tugidak I. 25 56 30N 154 40W
Tula 45 34 14N 89 22W
Tulalip Indian Reservation 67 48 4N 122 13W
Tulare, Calif. 29 36 13N 119 21W
Tulare, S. Dak. 61 44 44N 98 31W
Tulare County ◇ ... 29 36 10N 118 50W
Tulare Lake Bed ... 29 36 0N 119 48W
Tularosa 52 33 5N 106 1W
Tularosa Mts. 52 33 45N 108 40W
Tularosa Valley 52 32 45N 106 0W
Tule →.......... 29 36 3N 119 50W
Tule Cr. → 64 34 40N 101 14W
Tule L. 28 41 53N 121 30W
Tule River Indian Reservation 29 36 0N 118 50W
Tule Valley 66 39 25N 113 30W
Tulelake 28 41 57N 121 29W
Tulia 64 34 32N 101 46W
Tullahassee 57 35 50N 95 26W
Tullahoma 62 35 22N 86 13W
Tulloch Reservoir .. 28 37 53N 120 36W
Tullos 39 31 49N 92 19W
Tully 53 42 48N 76 7W
Tulsa 57 36 10N 95 55W
Tulsa County ◇ 57 36 0N 95 55W
Tuluksak 25 61 6N 160 58W
Tumwater 67 47 1N 122 54W
Tunica, La. 39 30 56N 91 33W
Tunica, Miss. 45 34 41N 90 23W
Tunica County ◇ ... 45 34 41N 90 23W
Tunis Mills 41 38 49N 76 10W
Tunkhannock 59 41 32N 75 57W
Tunnell Hill 35 37 32N 88 50W
Tunnelton 68 39 24N 79 45W
Tuntutuliak 25 60 22N 162 38W
Tununak 25 60 37N 165 15W
Tuolumne 28 37 58N 120 15W
Tuolumne County ◇ 28 38 0N 120 0W
Tupelo, Miss. 45 34 16N 88 43W
Tupelo, Okla. 57 34 36N 96 26W
Tupper L. 53 44 12N 74 35W
Tupper Lake 53 44 14N 74 28W
Turbeville 60 33 54N 80 1W
Turin 37 42 1N 95 58W
Turkey, Ky. 63 37 29N 83 31W
Turkey, Tex. 64 34 24N 100 54W
Turkey → 37 42 43N 91 2W
Turkey Cr. →..... 57 35 58N 97 56W
Turkey Creek 39 30 53N 92 25W
Turkey Mt. 64 29 22N 100 12W
Turkey Ridge 61 43 25N 97 25W
Turlock 28 37 30N 120 51W
Turlock L. 28 37 37N 120 35W
Turner, Mich. 43 44 9N 83 47W
Turner, Mont. 47 48 51N 108 24W
Turner, Oreg. 58 44 51N 122 57W
Turner, Wash. 67 46 25N 117 51W
Turner County ◇, Ga. 32 31 45N 83 45W
Turner County ◇, S. Dak. 61 43 17N 97 5W
Turners Falls 42 42 36N 72 33W
Turon 38 37 48N 98 26W
Turpin 57 36 52N 100 52W
Turrell 27 35 23N 90 15W
Turtle → 61 44 55N 98 29W
Turtle-Flambeau Flowage 69 46 4N 90 14W
Turtle Lake, N. Dak. 55 47 31N 100 53W
Turtle Lake, Wis. .. 69 45 24N 92 8W
Turtle Mountain Indian Reservation 55 48 58N 99 58W
Turtle Mountains ... 55 48 58N 100 0W
Turtle River 44 47 35N 94 46W
Tuscaloosa 24 33 12N 87 34W
Tuscaloosa County ◇ 24 33 11N 87 27W
Tuscarawas 56 40 24N 81 25W
Tuscarawas County ◇ 56 40 22N 81 26W
Tuscarora 49 41 19N 116 14W
Tuscarora Indian Reservation 53 43 10N 78 55W
Tuscarora Mt. 59 40 55N 77 55W
Tuscarora Mts. 49 41 0N 116 20W
Tuscola, Ill. 35 39 48N 88 17W
Tuscola, Tex. 65 32 12N 99 48W
Tuscola County ◇ .. 43 43 25N 83 20W
Tusculum 63 36 10N 82 46W
Tuscumbia, Ala. 24 34 44N 87 42W
Tuscumbia, Mo. 46 38 14N 92 28W
Tushar Mts. 66 38 20N 112 30W
Tushka 57 34 19N 96 10W
Tuskahoma 57 34 37N 95 17W
Tuskegee 24 32 25N 85 42W
Tustin 43 44 6N 85 28W
Tuttle, N. Dak. 55 47 9N 100 0W
Tuttle, Okla. 57 35 17N 97 49W
Tuttle Creek Lake .. 38 39 15N 96 36W
Tutwiler 45 34 1N 90 26W
Tuweep 26 36 25N 113 4W
Twain Harte 28 38 2N 120 14W
Twentynine Palms .. 29 34 8N 116 3W
Twiggs County ◇ ... 32 32 40N 83 30W
Twin Bridges 47 45 33N 112 20W
Twin Brooks 61 45 12N 96 47W
Twin Buttes Reservoir 64 31 22N 100 32W
Twin City 32 32 35N 82 10W
Twin Falls 34 42 34N 114 28W
Twin Falls County ◇ 34 42 30N 114 45W
Twin Hills 25 59 23N 159 58W
Twin Lakes, Colo. .. 30 39 5N 106 23W
Twin Lakes, Ga. 32 30 43N 83 13W
Twin Lakes, Minn. . 44 43 34N 93 25W
Twin Mountain 50 44 16N 71 32W
Twin Mts. 64 30 25N 103 50W
Twin Oaks 57 36 10N 94 51W
Twin Peaks 34 44 35N 114 29W
Twin Rivers 51 40 15N 74 32W
Twin Valley 44 47 16N 96 16W
Twisp 67 48 22N 120 7W
Twitchell Reservoir . 29 34 59N 120 19W
Twitty 64 35 19N 100 14W
Two Butte → 30 38 2N 102 9W
Two Buttes 30 37 34N 102 24W
Two Buttes Reservoir 30 37 38N 102 32W
Two Harbors 44 47 2N 91 40W
Two Medicine → .. 47 48 29N 112 14W
Two Rivers 69 44 9N 87 34W
Ty Ty 32 31 28N 83 39W
Tyaskin 41 38 18N 75 52W
Tye 65 32 27N 99 52W
Tygart L. 68 39 19N 80 2W
Tyger →.......... 60 34 28N 81 26W
Tygh Valley 58 45 15N 121 10W
Tyhee 34 42 57N 112 28W
Tyler, Tex. 65 32 21N 95 18W
Tyler, Wash. 67 47 26N 117 47W
Tyler County ◇, Tex. 65 30 47N 94 25W
Tyler County ◇, W. Va. 68 39 30N 80 54W
Tylertown 45 31 7N 90 9W
Tymochtee → 56 40 57N 83 16W
Tynan 65 28 10N 97 45W
Tyndall 61 43 0N 97 50W
Tyner 54 36 13N 76 37W
Tyonek 25 61 4N 151 8W
Tyonek Indian Reservation 25 61 5N 151 10W
Tyro, Ark. 27 33 50N 91 43W
Tyro, Kans. 38 37 2N 95 49W
Tyro, Miss. 45 34 35N 89 42W
Tyrone, N. Mex. 52 32 40N 108 22W
Tyrone, Okla. 57 36 57N 101 4W
Tyrone, Pa. 59 40 40N 78 14W
Tyrrell County ◇ .. 54 35 50N 76 10W
Tyson 50 43 27N 72 44W

U

Ubly 43 43 43N 82 56W
Ucon 34 43 36N 111 58W
Udall 38 37 23N 97 7W
Udell 37 40 47N 92 45W
Uehling 48 41 44N 96 30W
Uhrichsville 56 40 24N 81 21W
Uinta →.......... 66 40 14N 109 51W
Uinta County ◇ 70 41 15N 110 30W
Uinta Mts. 66 40 45N 110 30W
Uinta National Forest 66 40 10N 111 20W
Uintah and Ouray Indian Reservation 66 40 15N 110 20W
Uintah County ◇... 66 40 20N 109 30W
Ukiah, Calif. 28 39 9N 123 13W
Ukiah, Oreg. 58 45 8N 118 56W
Ulak I. 25 51 22N 178 57W
Ulen 44 47 5N 96 16W
Ullin 35 37 17N 89 11W
Ulster County ◇ .. 53 41 50N 74 15W
Ulupalakua 33 20 39N 156 24W
Ulysses, Kans. 38 37 35N 101 22W
Ulysses, Nebr. 48 41 4N 97 12W
Ulysses, Pa. 59 41 54N 77 46W
Umatilla 58 45 55N 119 21W
Umatilla → 58 45 55N 119 20W
Umatilla, L. 67 45 53N 119 40W
Umatilla County ◇ . 58 45 40N 118 45W
Umatilla Indian Reservation 58 45 41N 118 31W
Umatilla National Forest 58 45 0N 118 50W
Umbagog L. 50 44 46N 71 3W
Umbarger 64 34 57N 102 7W
Umiat 25 69 22N 152 8W
Umnak I. 25 53 15N 168 20W
Umpire 27 34 17N 94 3W
Umpqua 58 43 22N 123 28W
Umpqua → 58 43 40N 124 12W
Umpqua National Forest 58 43 10N 122 40W
Unadilla, Ga. 32 32 16N 83 44W
Unadilla, N.Y. 53 42 20N 75 19W
Unadilla, Nebr. 48 40 41N 96 16W
Unadilla → 53 42 20N 75 25W
Unalakleet 25 63 52N 160 47W
Unalaska 25 53 53N 166 32W
Unalaska I. 25 53 35N 166 50W
Uncompahgre → .. 30 38 45N 108 6W
Uncompahgre National Forest .. 30 38 30N 108 30W
Uncompahgre Peak . 30 38 4N 107 28W
Uncompahgre Plateau 30 38 20N 108 15W
Underhill Flats 50 44 33N 72 56W
Underwood 55 47 27N 101 9W
Unga I. 25 55 15N 160 40W
Unicoi 63 36 12N 82 21W
Unicoi County ◇ ... 63 36 9N 82 25W
Unimak I. 25 54 45N 164 0W
Unimak Pass 25 54 15N 164 30W
Union, Iowa 37 42 15N 93 4W
Union, La. 39 30 5N 90 54W
Union, Maine 40 44 13N 69 17W
Union, Miss. 45 32 34N 89 7W
Union, Mo. 46 38 27N 91 0W
Union, N.J. 51 40 42N 74 17W
Union, Nebr. 48 40 49N 95 55W
Union, Oreg. 58 45 13N 117 52W
Union, S.C. 60 34 43N 81 37W
Union, W. Va. 68 37 36N 80 33W
Union, Wash. 67 47 22N 123 6W
Union Bridge 41 39 34N 77 11W
Union Center, S. Dak. 61 44 34N 102 40W
Union Center, Wis. . 69 43 41N 90 16W
Union City, Calif. .. 28 37 36N 122 1W
Union City, Ga. 32 33 35N 84 33W
Union City, Ind. ... 36 40 12N 84 49W
Union City, Mich. .. 43 42 4N 85 8W
Union City, N.J. ... 51 40 45N 74 2W
Union City, Ohio ... 56 40 12N 84 48W
Union City, Okla. .. 57 35 23N 97 57W
Union City, Pa. 59 41 54N 79 51W
Union City, Tenn. .. 62 36 26N 89 3W
Union County ◇, Ark. 27 33 12N 92 40W
Union County ◇, Fla. 31 30 0N 82 25W
Union County ◇, Ga. 32 34 50N 84 0W
Union County ◇, Ill. 35 37 30N 89 15W
Union County ◇, Ind. 36 39 35N 84 55W
Union County ◇, Iowa 37 41 0N 94 15W
Union County ◇, Ky. 62 37 40N 87 55W
Union County ◇, Miss. 45 34 29N 89 0W
Union County ◇, N.C. 54 35 0N 80 40W
Union County ◇, N.J. 51 40 40N 74 20W
Union County ◇, N. Mex. 52 36 30N 103 30W
Union County ◇, Ohio 56 40 14N 83 22W
Union County ◇, Oreg. 58 45 15N 118 0W
Union County ◇, Pa. 59 41 0N 77 0W
Union County ◇, S.C. 60 34 45N 81 45W
Union County ◇, S. Dak. 61 42 51N 96 45W
Union County ◇, Tenn. 63 36 15N 83 48W
Union Creek 58 42 55N 122 27W
Union Gap 67 46 33N 120 28W
Union Grove 69 42 41N 88 3W
Union Parish ◇ 39 32 47N 92 24W
Union Park 31 28 34N 81 17W
Union Point 32 33 37N 83 4W
Union Springs, Ala. 24 32 9N 85 43W
Union Springs, N.Y. 53 42 51N 76 42W
Union Star 46 39 59N 94 36W
Union Valley Reservoir 28 38 52N 120 26W
Uniondale, Ind. 36 40 50N 85 15W
Uniondale, N.Y. ... 53 40 43N 73 36W
Uniondale, Pa. 59 41 43N 75 30W
Uniontown, Ala. ... 24 32 27N 87 31W
Uniontown, Kans. .. 38 37 51N 94 59W
Uniontown, Ky. 62 37 47N 87 56W
Uniontown, Md. ... 41 39 36N 77 7W
Uniontown, Pa. 59 39 54N 79 44W
Uniontown, Wash. . 67 46 32N 117 5W
Unionville, Ga. 32 31 26N 83 30W
Unionville, Iowa ... 37 40 49N 92 42W
Unionville, Md. 41 39 28N 77 12W
Unionville, Mich. ... 43 43 39N 83 28W
Unionville, Mo. 46 40 29N 93 1W
Unionville, N.Y. ... 53 41 18N 74 34W
Unionville, Nev. ... 49 40 27N 118 8W
Unionville, Pa. 59 40 55N 77 53W
Unionville, Va. 68 38 16N 77 58W
Uniopolis 56 40 36N 84 5W
United 59 40 13N 79 30W
Unity, Maine 40 44 37N 69 20W
Unity, Md. 41 39 13N 77 5W
Unity, Oreg. 58 44 26N 118 12W
Unity, Wis. 69 44 51N 90 19W
Universal City 65 29 33N 98 17W
University City 46 38 40N 90 20W
University Park 52 32 17N 106 45W
Upatoie → 32 32 22N 84 58W
Upham 55 48 35N 100 44W
Upland, Calif. 29 34 6N 117 39W
Upland, Ind. 36 40 28N 85 30W
Upland, Nebr. 48 40 19N 98 54W
Upolu Pt. 33 20 16N 155 52W
Upper Arlington ... 56 40 0N 83 4W
Upper Crossroads .. 41 39 33N 76 29W
Upper Darby 59 39 58N 75 16W
Upper Iowa → 37 43 29N 91 14W

Upper Klamath L. 58 42 25N 121 55W
Upper L. 28 41 45N 120 9W
Upper Lake 28 39 10N 122 54W
Upper Marlboro 41 38 49N 76 45W
Upper Preoria L. 35 40 52N 89 24W
Upper Red L. 44 48 8N 94 45W
Upper Sandusky 56 40 50N 83 17W
Upper Tract 68 38 47N 79 17W
Upshur County ◇, Tex. 65 32 44N 94 57W
Upshur County ◇, W. Va. 68 39 0N 80 8W
Upson 69 46 22N 90 24W
Upson County ◇ 32 32 50N 84 20W
Upton, Ky. 63 37 28N 85 54W
Upton, Maine 40 44 42N 71 1W
Upton, Mass. 42 42 11N 71 37W
Upton, Wyo. 70 44 6N 104 38W
Upton County ◇ 64 31 15N 102 0W
Urania 39 31 52N 92 18W
Uravan 30 38 22N 108 44W
Urbana, Ark. 27 33 10N 92 27W
Urbana, Ill. 35 40 7N 88 12W
Urbana, Iowa 37 42 13N 91 52W
Urbana, Mo. 46 37 51N 93 10W
Urbana, Ohio 56 40 7N 83 45W
Urbandale 37 41 38N 93 43W
Urbank 44 46 8N 95 31W
Urich 46 38 28N 94 2W
Uroyan, Montanas de 71 18 12N 67 0W
Ursa 35 40 4N 91 22W
Ursine 49 37 59N 114 13W
Usher 31 29 24N 82 49W
Usk 67 48 19N 117 17W
Utah □ 66 39 20N 111 30W
Utah County ◇ 66 40 10N 111 50W
Utah L. 66 40 12N 111 48W
Ute 37 42 3N 95 42W
Ute Creek → 52 35 21N 103 50W
Ute Mountain Indian Reservation 52 36 55N 108 20W
Ute Park 52 36 34N 105 6W
Ute Reservoir 52 35 21N 103 27W
Utica, Kans. 38 38 39N 100 10W
Utica, Miss. 45 32 7N 90 37W
Utica, N.Y. 53 43 6N 75 14W
Utica, Ohio 56 40 14N 82 27W
Utica, S. Dak. 61 42 59N 97 30W
Utleyville 30 37 17N 103 4W
Utopia 65 29 37N 99 32W
Utuado 71 18 16N 66 42W
Uvalda 32 32 2N 82 31W
Uvalde 65 29 13N 99 47W
Uvalde County ◇ 65 29 30N 99 43W
Uwharrie → 54 35 23N 80 3W
Uwharrie National Forest 54 35 20N 80 0W
Uxbridge 42 42 5N 71 38W
Uyak 25 57 38N 154 0W

V

Vacaville 28 38 21N 121 59W
Vacherie 39 30 0N 90 48W
Vacia Talega, Pta. 71 18 26N 65 53W
Vader 67 46 24N 122 58W
Vaiden 45 33 20N 89 45W
Vail, Ariz. 26 32 3N 110 43W
Vail, Colo. 30 39 40N 106 20W
Vail, Iowa 37 42 4N 95 12W
Val Verde County ◇ 64 30 0N 101 0W
Valatie 53 42 25N 73 41W
Valders 69 44 4N 87 53W
Valdese 54 35 44N 81 34W
Valdez, Alaska 25 61 7N 146 16W
Valdez, N. Mex. 52 36 32N 105 35W
Valdez-Cordova ◇ 25 61 0N 144 0W
Valdosta 32 30 50N 83 17W
Vale, Oreg. 58 43 59N 117 15W
Vale, S. Dak. 61 44 37N 103 24W
Valencia County ◇ 52 34 45N 107 0W
Valentine, Ariz. 26 35 23N 113 40W
Valentine, Nebr. 48 42 52N 100 33W
Valentine, Tex. 64 30 35N 104 30W
Valeria 37 41 44N 93 20W
Valhalla 54 36 8N 76 40W
Valier, Ill. 35 38 1N 89 3W
Valier, Mont. 47 48 18N 112 16W
Vallecito 30 37 23N 107 35W
Vallecito Reservoir 30 37 23N 107 34W
Vallejo 28 38 7N 122 14W
Valles Mines 46 38 2N 90 30W
Valley, Nebr. 48 41 19N 96 21W
Valley, Wash. 67 48 11N 117 44W
Valley Center, Calif. 29 33 13N 117 2W
Valley Center, Kans. 38 37 50N 97 22W
Valley City 55 46 55N 98 0W
Valley County ◇, Idaho 34 44 45N 115 30W
Valley County ◇, Mont. 47 48 35N 106 30W
Valley County ◇, Nebr. 48 41 30N 99 0W
Valley Falls, Kans. 38 39 21N 95 28W
Valley Falls, N.Y. 53 42 54N 73 34W
Valley Falls, Oreg. 58 42 29N 120 17W
Valley Falls, R.I. 42 41 54N 71 24W
Valley Grove 68 40 6N 80 34W
Valley Head, Ala. 24 34 34N 85 37W
Valley Head, W. Va. 68 38 33N 80 2W
Valley Lee 41 38 12N 76 31W
Valley Mills 65 31 40N 97 28W
Valley Park 46 38 33N 90 29W
Valley Springs, Calif. 28 38 12N 120 50W
Valley Springs, S. Dak. 61 43 35N 96 28W
Valley Station 63 38 6N 85 52W
Valley Stream 53 40 40N 73 42W
Valley View, Pa. 59 40 39N 76 33W
Valley View, Tex. 65 33 29N 97 10W
Valliant 57 34 0N 95 6W
Valmeyer 35 38 18N 90 19W
Valmora 52 35 49N 104 55W
Valmy 49 40 48N 117 8W
Valparaiso, Fla. 31 30 29N 86 30W
Valparaiso, Ind. 36 41 28N 87 4W
Valparaiso, Nebr. 48 41 5N 96 50W
Valsetz 58 44 50N 123 39W
Van 65 32 31N 95 38W
Van Alstyne 65 33 25N 96 35W
Van Buren, Ark. 27 35 26N 94 21W
Van Buren, Ind. 36 40 37N 85 30W
Van Buren, Ky. 63 37 59N 85 10W
Van Buren, Maine 40 47 10N 67 58W
Van Buren, Mo. 46 37 0N 91 1W
Van Buren, Ohio 56 41 8N 83 39W
Van Buren County ◇, Ark. 27 35 36N 92 28W
Van Buren County ◇, Iowa 37 40 45N 91 55W
Van Buren County ◇, Mich. 43 42 15N 86 0W
Van Buren County ◇, Tenn. 63 35 45N 85 28W
Van Buskirk 69 46 23N 90 9W
Van Horn 64 31 3N 104 50W
Van Meter 37 41 32N 93 57W
Van Tassell 70 42 40N 104 5W
Van Wert, Iowa 37 40 52N 93 48W
Van Wert, Ohio 56 40 52N 84 35W
Van Wert County ◇ 56 40 52N 84 35W
Van Zandt County ◇ 65 32 33N 95 52W
Vance 60 33 26N 80 25W
Vance County ◇ 54 36 15N 78 20W
Vanceboro 40 45 34N 67 26W
Vanceburg 63 38 36N 83 19W
Vancleave 45 30 32N 88 42W
Vancleve 63 37 38N 83 25W
Vancorum 30 38 14N 108 36W
Vancourt 64 31 21N 100 11W
Vancouver 67 45 38N 122 40W
Vancouver, Mt. 25 60 20N 139 41W
Vandalia, Ill. 35 38 58N 89 6W
Vandalia, Mo. 46 39 19N 91 29W
Vandalia, Ohio 56 39 54N 84 12W
Vandemere 54 35 11N 76 41W
Vanderbilt 43 45 9N 84 40W
Vanderburgh County ◇ 36 38 5N 87 35W
Vandergrift 59 40 36N 79 34W
Vanderpool 65 29 45N 99 33W
Vanduser 46 36 59N 89 42W
Vanoss 57 34 46N 96 52W
Vardaman 45 33 53N 89 11W
Varina 37 42 40N 94 54W
Varna 35 41 2N 89 14W
Varnado 39 30 54N 89 50W
Varnville 60 32 51N 81 5W
Vass 54 35 15N 79 17W
Vassar, Kans. 38 38 42N 95 37W
Vassar, Mich. 43 43 22N 83 35W
Vaucluse 60 33 37N 81 49W
Vaughan 45 32 48N 90 3W
Vaughn, Mont. 47 47 33N 111 33W
Vaughn, N. Mex. 52 34 36N 105 13W
Veblen 61 45 52N 97 17W
Veedersburg 36 40 7N 87 16W
Vega 64 35 15N 102 26W
Vega Alta 71 18 25N 66 20W
Vega Baja 71 18 27N 66 23W
Veguita 52 34 31N 106 46W
Velma 57 34 28N 97 40W
Velva 55 48 4N 100 56W
Venango County ◇ 59 41 20N 79 50W
Venedocia 56 40 47N 84 28W
Veneta 58 44 3N 123 21W
Venetie 25 67 1N 146 25W
Venetie Indian Reservation 25 67 20N 146 0W
Venice, Fla. 31 27 6N 82 27W
Venice, La. 39 29 17N 89 22W
Venleer 62 36 14N 87 27W
Ventnor City 51 39 20N 74 29W
Venton 41 38 12N 75 18W
Ventura 29 34 17N 119 18W
Ventura County ◇ 29 34 30N 119 0W
Venus 31 27 4N 81 22W
Vera 57 36 27N 95 53W
Verbena 24 32 45N 86 31W
Verda 39 31 42N 92 46W
Verde → 26 33 33N 111 40W
Verdel 48 42 49N 98 12W
Verden 57 35 5N 98 5W
Verdery 60 34 7N 82 15W
Verdi 49 39 31N 119 59W
Verdigre 48 42 36N 98 2W
Verdigre Cr. → 48 42 42N 98 3W
Verdigris → 57 35 48N 95 19W
Verdon 48 40 9N 95 43W
Vergas 44 46 40N 95 48W
Vergennes 50 44 10N 73 15W
Vermejo → 52 36 25N 104 30W
Vermilion, Ill. 35 39 35N 87 35W
Vermilion, Ohio 56 41 25N 82 22W
Vermilion → 35 41 19N 89 4W
Vermilion B. 39 29 42N 92 0W
Vermilion Cliffs 66 37 10N 112 30W
Vermilion County ◇ 35 40 10N 87 45W
Vermilion L. 44 47 53N 92 26W
Vermilion Parish ◇ 39 29 55N 92 15W
Vermilion Ra. 44 47 50N 92 0W
Vermillion 61 42 47N 96 56W
Vermillion → 61 42 44N 96 53W
Vermillion Bluffs 30 40 50N 108 20W
Vermillion County ◇ 36 39 50N 87 30W
Vermont □ 50 44 0N 73 0W
Verna 31 27 23N 82 16W
Vernal 66 40 27N 109 32W
Verndale 44 46 24N 95 1W
Vernon, Ala. 24 33 45N 88 7W
Vernon, Colo. 30 39 57N 102 19W
Vernon, Conn. 42 41 50N 72 28W
Vernon, Ill. 35 38 48N 89 5W
Vernon, Ind. 36 38 59N 85 36W
Vernon, Tex. 65 34 9N 99 17W
Vernon, Utah 66 40 6N 112 26W
Vernon Center 44 43 58N 94 10W
Vernon County ◇, Mo. 46 37 50N 94 20W
Vernon County ◇, Wis. 69 43 30N 90 50W
Vernon Parish ◇ 39 31 9N 93 16W
Vernonia 58 45 52N 123 11W
Vero Beach 31 27 38N 80 24W
Verona, Miss. 45 34 12N 88 43W
Verona, N.C. 54 34 40N 77 28W
Verona, N. Dak. 55 46 22N 98 4W
Verona, Wis. 69 42 59N 89 32W
Verret, L. 39 29 53N 91 10W
Versailles, Ill. 35 39 53N 90 39W
Versailles, Ind. 36 39 4N 85 15W
Versailles, Ky. 63 38 3N 84 44W
Versailles, Mo. 46 38 26N 92 51W
Versailles, Ohio 56 40 13N 84 29W
Vesper, Kans. 38 39 2N 98 17W
Vesper, Wis. 69 44 29N 89 58W
Vesta, Ga. 32 33 58N 82 56W
Vesta, Nebr. 48 40 21N 96 20W
Vetal 61 43 13N 101 23W
Vevay 36 38 45N 85 4W
Vian 57 35 30N 94 58W
Viborg 61 43 10N 97 5W
Viburnum 46 37 43N 91 8W
Vicco 63 37 13N 83 4W
Vici 57 36 9N 99 18W
Vick 27 33 20N 92 6W
Vicksburg, Mich. 43 42 7N 85 32W
Vicksburg, Miss. 45 32 21N 90 53W
Victor, Colo. 30 38 43N 105 9W
Victor, Idaho 34 43 36N 111 7W
Victor, Iowa 37 41 44N 92 18W
Victor, Mont. 47 46 25N 114 9W
Victoria, Ill. 35 41 2N 90 6W
Victoria, Kans. 38 38 52N 99 9W
Victoria, Tex. 65 28 48N 97 0W
Victoria, Va. 68 36 59N 78 8W
Victoria County ◇ 65 28 45N 96 55W
Victorville 29 34 32N 117 18W
Vidal 29 34 7N 114 31W
Vidalia, Ga. 32 32 13N 82 25W
Vidalia, La. 39 31 34N 91 26W
Vidauri 65 28 26N 97 8W
Vidette 32 33 2N 82 15W
Vidor 65 30 7N 94 1W
Vieja, Sierra 64 30 35N 104 40W
Vienna, Ga. 32 32 6N 83 47W
Vienna, Ill. 35 37 25N 88 54W
Vienna, Md. 41 38 29N 75 50W
Vienna, Mo. 46 38 11N 91 57W
Vienna, S. Dak. 61 44 42N 97 30W
Vienna, W. Va. 68 39 20N 81 33W
Vieques, Isla de 71 18 8N 65 25W
Vieques, Pasaje de 71 18 10N 65 35W
Vieques, Sonda de 71 18 15N 65 15W
Vieux Desert, L. 43 46 8N 89 7W
Vigo County ◇ 36 39 25N 87 25W
Vigo Park 64 34 39N 101 30W
Viking 44 48 13N 96 24W
Vilas, Colo. 30 37 22N 102 27W
Vilas, S. Dak. 61 44 1N 97 36W
Vilas County ◇ 69 46 0N 89 30W
Villa Grove, Colo. 30 38 15N 105 59W
Villa Grove, Ill. 35 39 52N 88 10W
Villa Pérez 71 18 12N 66 47W
Villa Rica 32 33 44N 84 55W
Village of Superior 69 46 40N 92 6W
Villalba 71 18 8N 66 30W
Villanueva 52 35 16N 105 22W
Villard 44 45 43N 95 16W
Villas 51 39 2N 74 56W
Ville Platte 39 30 41N 92 17W
Villegreen 30 37 18N 103 31W
Villisca 37 40 56N 94 59W
Vilonia 27 35 5N 92 13W
Vina 24 34 23N 88 4W
Vinalhaven 40 44 3N 68 50W
Vinalhaven I. 40 44 5N 68 51W
Vincennes 36 38 41N 87 32W
Vincent, Ala. 24 33 23N 86 25W
Vincent, Iowa 37 42 36N 94 1W
Vincentown 51 39 56N 74 45W
Vine Grove 63 37 49N 85 59W
Vineland 51 39 29N 75 2W
Vinemont 24 34 15N 86 52W
Vineyard Haven 42 41 27N 70 36W
Vineyard Sd. 42 41 25N 70 45W
Vining 44 46 16N 95 32W
Vinita 57 36 39N 95 9W
Vinson 57 34 54N 99 52W
Vinton, Calif. 28 39 48N 120 10W
Vinton, Iowa 37 42 10N 92 1W
Vinton, La. 39 30 11N 93 35W
Vinton, Ohio 56 38 59N 82 21W
Vinton County ◇ 56 39 15N 82 29W
Viola, Ark. 27 36 24N 91 59W
Viola, Del. 41 39 5N 75 34W
Viola, Ill. 35 41 12N 90 35W
Viola, Kans. 38 37 29N 97 39W
Viola, Tenn. 63 35 32N 85 52W
Viola, Wis. 69 43 31N 90 40W
Violet 39 29 54N 89 54W
Virden, Ill. 35 39 30N 89 46W
Virden, N. Mex. 52 32 41N 109 0W
Virgil, Kans. 38 37 59N 96 1W
Virgil, S. Dak. 61 44 17N 98 25W
Virgilina 68 36 33N 78 47W
Virgin 66 37 12N 113 11W
Virgin → 49 36 28N 114 21W
Virgin Islands □ 71 18 30N 64 25W
Virginia, Idaho 34 42 30N 112 10W
Virginia, Ill. 35 39 57N 90 13W
Virginia, Minn. 44 47 31N 92 32W
Virginia □ 68 37 30N 78 45W
Virginia Beach 68 36 51N 75 59W
Virginia City, Mont. 47 45 18N 111 56W
Virginia City, Nev. 49 39 19N 119 39W
Virginia Mts. 49 39 50N 119 30W
Viroqua 69 43 34N 90 53W
Visalia 29 36 20N 119 18W
Vista, Calif. 29 33 12N 117 14W
Vista, Mo. 46 37 58N 93 40W
Vivian, La. 39 32 53N 93 59W
Vivian, S. Dak. 61 43 56N 100 18W
Volborg 47 45 51N 105 41W
Volcano 33 19 26N 155 14W
Volga, Iowa 37 42 48N 91 33W
Volga, S. Dak. 61 44 19N 96 56W
Volin 61 42 58N 97 11W
Voluntown 42 41 34N 71 52W
Volusia County ◇ 31 29 0N 81 15W
Vona 30 39 18N 102 45W
Vonore 63 35 36N 84 14W
Voorheesville 53 42 39N 73 56W
Voyageurs Nat. Park 44 48 32N 93 0W
Vulcan 43 45 47N 87 53W
Vulture Mts. 26 33 45N 113 0W
Vya 49 41 35N 119 52W

W

Wabash 36 40 48N 85 49W
Wabash → 36 37 48N 88 2W
Wabash County ◇, Ill. 35 38 30N 87 50W
Wabash County ◇, Ind. 36 40 50N 85 45W
Wabasha 44 44 23N 92 2W
Wabasha County ◇ 44 44 15N 92 15W
Wabasso, Fla. 31 27 45N 80 26W
Wabasso, Minn. 44 44 24N 95 15W
Wabaunsee 38 39 9N 96 21W
Wabaunsee County ◇ 38 39 0N 96 15W
Wabeno 69 45 26N 88 39W
Wabuska 49 39 9N 119 11W

Waccamaw, L. 54 34 18N 78 31W
Waccasassa B. 31 29 10N 82 50W
Wachapreague 68 37 36N 75 42W
Wachusett Reservoir 42 42 24N 71 41W
Wacissa 31 30 22N 83 59W
Waco, Nebr. 48 40 54N 97 28W
Waco, Tex. 65 31 33N 97 9W
Waco L. 65 31 35N 97 12W
Waconda Lake 38 39 29N 98 19W
Waddington 53 44 52N 75 12W
Wade 54 35 10N 78 44W
Wade Hampton ◇ 25 62 0N 164 0W
Wadena 44 46 26N 95 8W
Wadena County ◇ 44 46 30N 95 0W
Wadesboro 54 34 58N 80 5W
Wading River 51 39 38N 74 31W
Wadley, Ala. 24 33 7N 85 34W
Wadley, Ga. 32 32 52N 82 24W
Wadsworth, Nev. 49 39 38N 119 17W
Wadsworth, Ohio 56 41 2N 81 44W
Wadsworth, Tex. 65 28 50N 95 56W
Waelder 65 29 42N 97 18W
Wagener 60 33 39N 81 22W
Wagner 61 43 5N 98 18W
Wagon Mound 52 36 1N 104 42W
Wagon Wheel Gap 30 37 46N 106 49W
Wagoner 57 35 58N 95 22W
Wagoner County ◇ 57 36 0N 95 30W
Wagontire 58 43 15N 119 52W
Wagontire Mt. 58 43 21N 119 53W
Wagram 54 34 54N 79 22W
Wah Wah Mts. 66 38 25N 113 40W
Wahiawa 33 21 30N 158 2W
Wahiawa Reservoir 33 21 30N 158 3W
Wahkiakum County ◇ 67 46 10N 123 30W
Wahkon 44 46 7N 93 31W
Wahoo 48 41 13N 96 37W
Wahpeton 55 46 16N 96 36W
Waialee 33 21 41N 158 1W
Waialua 33 21 34N 158 8W
Waialua B. 33 21 35N 158 5W
Waianae 33 21 27N 158 11W
Waianae Mts. 33 21 30N 158 10W
Waiawa → 33 21 23N 157 59W
Waikiki 33 21 17N 157 50W
Wailua, Kauai, Hawaii 33 22 3N 159 20W
Wailua, Maui, Hawaii 33 20 51N 156 8W
Wailuku 33 20 53N 156 30W
Waimanalo 33 21 21N 157 43W
Waimanalo B. 33 21 20N 157 40W
Waimanalo Beach 33 21 21N 157 42W
Waimano → 33 21 25N 157 58W
Waimea, Kauai, Hawaii 33 21 58N 159 40W
Waimea, Oahu, Hawaii 33 21 39N 158 3W
Waimea B. 33 21 40N 158 5W
Wainwright, Alaska 25 70 38N 160 2W
Wainwright, Okla. 57 35 37N 95 34W
Waipahu 33 21 23N 158 1W
Waipio Acres 33 21 28N 158 1W
Waipio Peninsula 33 21 20N 158 0W
Waita Reservoir 33 21 55N 159 28W
Waite 40 45 20N 67 42W
Waite Park 44 45 33N 94 14W
Waits → 50 43 59N 72 8W
Waitsburg 67 46 16N 118 9W
Waitsfield 50 44 42N 72 50W
Waka 64 36 17N 101 3W
Wakarusa 36 41 32N 86 1W
Wake County ◇ 54 35 40N 78 45W
Wake Forest 54 35 59N 78 30W
WaKeeney 38 39 1N 99 53W
Wakefield, Kans. 38 39 13N 97 1W
Wakefield, Mass. 42 42 30N 71 4W
Wakefield, Mich. 43 46 29N 89 56W
Wakefield, N.H. 50 43 35N 71 4W
Wakefield, Nebr. 48 42 16N 96 52W
Wakefield, R.I. 42 41 26N 71 30W
Wakefield, Va. 68 36 58N 76 59W
Wakita 57 36 53N 97 55W
Wakonda 61 43 0N 97 6W
Wakpala 61 45 40N 100 32W
Wakulla 31 30 14N 84 14W
Wakulla Beach 31 30 6N 84 16W
Wakulla County ◇ 31 30 15N 84 20W
Walcott, Iowa 37 41 35N 90 47W
Walcott, N. Dak. 55 46 33N 96 56W
Walcott, Wyo. 70 41 46N 106 51W
Walcott L. 34 42 40N 113 29W
Walden, Colo. 30 40 44N 106 17W
Walden, N.Y. 53 41 34N 74 11W
Walden Reservoir 30 40 43N 106 17W
Walden Ridge 63 35 30N 85 15W
Waldo, Ark. 27 33 21N 93 18W
Waldo, Fla. 31 29 48N 82 10W
Waldo, Maine 40 44 31N 69 5W
Waldo, Ohio 56 40 28N 83 5W
Waldo County ◇ 40 44 25N 69 0W
Waldoboro 40 44 6N 69 23W
Waldorf, Md. 41 38 38N 76 55W
Waldorf, Minn. 44 43 56N 93 42W
Waldport 58 44 26N 124 4W
Waldron, Ark. 27 34 54N 94 5W
Waldron, Ind. 36 39 27N 85 40W
Waldron, Mich. 43 41 44N 84 25W
Waldwick 51 41 1N 74 7W
Wales, Alaska 25 65 37N 168 5W
Wales, N. Dak. 55 48 54N 98 36W
Wales, Utah 66 39 29N 111 38W
Walford 37 41 53N 91 50W
Walhalla, N. Dak. 55 48 55N 97 55W
Walhalla, S.C. 60 34 46N 83 4W
Walk, L. 64 29 31N 100 59W
Walker, Iowa 37 42 17N 91 47W
Walker, Mich. 43 42 58N 85 46W
Walker, Minn. 44 47 6N 94 35W
Walker, Mo. 46 37 54N 94 14W
Walker, S. Dak. 61 45 55N 101 5W
Walker → 49 38 54N 118 47W
Walker County ◇, Ala. 24 33 50N 87 17W
Walker County ◇, Ga. 32 34 45N 85 15W
Walker County ◇, Tex. 65 30 43N 95 33W
Walker L. 49 38 42N 118 43W
Walker River Indian Reservation 49 39 0N 118 50W
Walkers Pt. 40 43 21N 70 28W
Walkersville 41 39 29N 77 21W
Walkerton 36 41 28N 86 29W
Walkertown 54 36 10N 80 10W
Walkerville 43 43 43N 86 8W
Wall, S. Dak. 61 44 0N 102 8W
Wall, Tex. 64 31 22N 100 18W
Wall Lake 37 42 16N 95 5W
Walla Walla 67 46 4N 118 20W
Walla Walla County ◇ 67 46 18N 118 37W
Wallace, Idaho 34 47 28N 115 56W
Wallace, Kans. 38 38 58N 101 36W
Wallace, N.C. 54 34 44N 77 59W
Wallace, Nebr. 48 40 50N 101 10W
Wallace, S. Dak. 61 45 5N 97 29W
Wallace County ◇ 38 38 50N 101 45W
Walland 63 35 44N 83 49W
Wallenpaupack, L. 59 41 25N 75 15W
Waller 65 30 4N 95 56W
Waller County ◇ 65 30 0N 96 0W
Wallingford, Conn. 42 41 27N 72 50W
Wallingford, Iowa 37 43 19N 94 48W
Wallingford, Vt. 50 43 28N 72 59W
Wallis 65 29 38N 96 4W
Wallisville L. 65 29 57N 94 54W
Walloon L. 43 45 17N 85 0W
Wallowa 58 45 34N 117 32W
Wallowa → 58 45 43N 117 47W
Wallowa County ◇ 58 45 30N 117 10W
Wallowa Mts. 58 45 20N 117 30W
Wallowa-Whitman National Forest 58 45 15N 117 20W
Walls 45 34 58N 90 9W
Wallsburg 66 40 23N 111 25W
Wallula 67 46 5N 118 54W
Wallula, L. 67 46 2N 118 59W
Walnut, Ill. 35 41 33N 89 36W
Walnut, Iowa 37 41 29N 95 13W
Walnut, Kans. 38 37 36N 95 5W
Walnut, Miss. 45 34 57N 88 54W
Walnut, N.C. 54 35 51N 82 44W
Walnut → 38 37 3N 97 0W
Walnut Canyon National Monument 26 35 15N 111 20W
Walnut Cove 54 36 18N 80 9W
Walnut Creek 28 37 54N 122 4W
Walnut Grove, Ala. 24 34 4N 86 18W
Walnut Grove, Miss. 45 32 36N 89 28W
Walnut Grove, Mo. 46 37 25N 93 33W
Walnut Hill 31 30 53N 87 30W
Walnut Ridge 27 36 4N 90 57W
Walnut Springs 65 32 3N 97 45W
Walpole, Mass. 42 42 9N 71 15W
Walpole, N.H. 50 43 5N 72 26W
Walsenburg 30 37 38N 104 47W
Walsh 30 37 23N 102 17W
Walsh County ◇ 55 48 24N 97 45W
Walter F. George Reservoir 24 31 38N 85 4W
Walterboro 60 32 55N 80 40W
Walters 57 34 22N 98 19W
Walterville 58 44 4N 122 48W
Walthall 45 33 37N 89 17W
Walthall County ◇ 45 31 7N 90 9W
Waltham, Maine 40 44 43N 68 20W
Waltham, Mass. 42 42 23N 71 14W
Walthill 48 42 9N 96 30W
Waltman 70 43 4N 107 12W
Walton, Ind. 36 40 40N 86 15W
Walton, Kans. 38 38 7N 97 15W
Walton, Ky. 63 38 52N 84 37W
Walton, N.Y. 53 42 10N 75 8W
Walton County ◇, Fla. 31 30 30N 86 10W
Walton County ◇, Ga. 32 33 45N 83 45W
Waltonville 35 38 13N 89 2W
Walworth County ◇, S. Dak. 61 45 30N 100 0W
Walworth County ◇, Wis. 69 42 40N 88 30W
Wamac 35 38 31N 89 8W
Wamego 38 39 12N 96 18W
Wampsville 53 43 5N 75 42W
Wampum 59 40 54N 80 21W
Wamsutter 70 41 40N 107 58W
Wanamingo 44 44 18N 92 47W
Wanaque 51 41 2N 74 18W
Wanaque Reservoir 51 41 2N 74 18W
Wanatah 36 41 26N 86 54W
Wanblee 61 43 34N 101 40W
Wanchese 54 35 51N 75 38W
Wanda 44 44 19N 95 13W
Wanette 57 34 58N 97 2W
Wango 41 38 20N 75 25W
Wann 57 36 55N 95 48W
Wapakoneta 56 40 34N 84 12W
Wapanucka 57 34 23N 96 26W
Wapato 67 46 27N 120 25W
Wapello 37 41 11N 91 11W
Wapello County ◇ 37 41 0N 92 25W
Wapinitia Pass 58 45 14N 121 42W
Wapiti 70 44 28N 109 26W
Wappapello, L. 46 36 56N 90 17W
Wappingers Falls 53 41 36N 73 55W
Wapsipinicon → 37 41 44N 90 19W
War 68 37 18N 81 41W
Ward 61 44 9N 96 28W
Ward County ◇, N. Dak. 55 48 5N 101 30W
Ward County ◇, Tex. 64 31 32N 103 8W
Wardell 46 36 21N 89 49W
Warden 67 46 58N 119 2W
Wardensville 68 39 5N 78 36W
Wardsville 46 38 29N 92 11W
Ware 42 42 16N 72 14W
Ware → 42 42 11N 72 22W
Ware County ◇ 32 31 10N 82 20W
Ware Shoals 60 34 24N 82 15W
Wareham 42 41 46N 70 43W
Warehouse Point 42 41 56N 72 37W
Waresboro 32 31 15N 82 29W
Warm Springs, Ga. 32 32 53N 84 41W
Warm Springs, Nev. 49 38 10N 116 20W
Warm Springs, Oreg. 58 44 46N 121 16W
Warm Springs, Va. 68 38 3N 79 47W
Warm Springs Indian Reservation 58 45 0N 121 25W
Warm Springs Reservoir 58 43 35N 118 13W
Warner, N.H. 50 43 17N 71 49W
Warner, Okla. 57 35 30N 95 18W
Warner, S. Dak. 61 45 20N 98 30W
Warner Mts. 28 41 40N 120 15W
Warner Robins 32 32 37N 83 36W
Warner Valley 58 42 25N 119 50W
Warr Acres 57 35 31N 97 37W
Warren, Ark. 27 33 37N 92 4W
Warren, Conn. 42 41 0N 73 0W
Warren, Idaho 34 45 16N 115 41W
Warren, Ill. 35 42 29N 90 0W
Warren, Ind. 36 40 41N 85 26W
Warren, Mich. 43 42 30N 83 0W
Warren, Minn. 44 48 12N 96 46W
Warren, N.H. 50 43 56N 71 54W
Warren, Ohio 56 41 14N 80 49W
Warren, Pa. 59 41 51N 79 9W
Warren, R.I. 42 41 43N 71 17W
Warren, Tex. 65 30 37N 94 24W
Warren, Vt. 50 44 7N 72 50W
Warren County ◇, Ga. 32 33 20N 82 40W
Warren County ◇, Ill. 35 40 50N 90 35W
Warren County ◇, Ind. 36 40 20N 87 25W
Warren County ◇, Iowa 37 41 20N 93 35W
Warren County ◇, Ky. 62 37 0N 86 25W
Warren County ◇, Miss. 45 32 21N 90 53W
Warren County ◇, Mo. 46 38 45N 91 10W
Warren County ◇, N.C. 54 36 15N 78 0W
Warren County ◇, N.J. 51 40 50N 75 0W
Warren County ◇, N.Y. 53 43 35N 73 45W
Warren County ◇, Ohio 56 39 26N 84 13W
Warren County ◇, Pa. 59 41 50N 79 15W
Warren County ◇, Tenn. 63 35 41N 85 46W
Warren County ◇, Va. 68 38 55N 78 12W
Warren Grove 51 39 44N 74 22W
Warren Pks. 70 44 29N 104 28W
Warrens 69 44 8N 90 30W
Warrensburg, Ill. 35 39 56N 89 4W
Warrensburg, Mo. 46 38 46N 93 44W
Warrensburg, N.Y. 53 43 29N 73 46W
Warrenton, Ga. 32 33 24N 82 40W
Warrenton, Mo. 46 38 49N 91 9W
Warrenton, N.C. 54 36 24N 78 9W
Warrenton, Oreg. 58 46 10N 123 56W
Warrenton, Va. 68 38 43N 77 48W
Warrenville 60 33 32N 81 48W
Warrick County ◇ 36 38 5N 87 15W
Warrington 31 30 23N 87 17W
Warrior 24 33 49N 86 49W
Warroad 44 48 54N 95 19W
Warsaw, Ill. 35 40 22N 91 26W
Warsaw, Ind. 36 41 14N 85 51W
Warsaw, Ky. 63 38 47N 84 54W
Warsaw, Mo. 46 38 15N 93 23W
Warsaw, N.C. 54 35 0N 78 5W
Warsaw, N.Y. 53 42 45N 78 8W
Warsaw, Va. 68 37 58N 76 46W
Wartburg 63 36 6N 84 36W
Warthen 32 33 6N 82 48W
Wartrace 62 35 32N 86 20W
Warwick, Ga. 32 31 50N 83 57W
Warwick, Mass. 42 42 0N 72 0W
Warwick, Md. 41 39 25N 75 47W
Warwick, N. Dak. 55 47 51N 98 43W
Warwick, N.Y. 53 41 16N 74 22W
Warwick, R.I. 42 41 42N 71 28W
Wasatch County ◇ 66 40 20N 111 15W
Wasatch National Forest 66 40 50N 110 40W
Wasatch Plateau 66 39 20N 111 30W
Wasatch Range 66 40 0N 111 30W
Wasco, Calif. 29 35 36N 119 20W
Wasco, Oreg. 58 45 36N 120 42W
Wasco County ◇ 58 45 15N 121 15W
Waseca 44 44 5N 93 30W
Waseca County ◇ 44 44 0N 93 40W
Washakie County ◇ 70 44 0N 107 40W
Washburn, Ill. 35 40 55N 89 17W
Washburn, Maine 40 46 47N 68 9W
Washburn, Mo. 46 36 35N 93 58W
Washburn, N. Dak. 55 47 17N 101 2W
Washburn, Tex. 64 35 11N 101 34W
Washburn, Wis. 69 46 40N 90 54W
Washburn County ◇ 69 45 50N 91 50W
Washington, Ark. 27 33 47N 93 41W
Washington, Conn. 42 41 39N 73 19W
Washington, D.C. 41 38 54N 77 2W
Washington, Ga. 32 33 44N 82 44W
Washington, Ill. 35 40 42N 89 24W
Washington, Ind. 36 38 40N 87 10W
Washington, Iowa 37 41 18N 91 42W
Washington, Kans. 38 39 49N 97 3W
Washington, Ky. 63 38 37N 83 49W
Washington, La. 39 30 37N 92 4W
Washington, Maine 40 44 16N 69 22W
Washington, Mo. 46 38 33N 91 1W
Washington, N.C. 54 35 33N 77 3W
Washington, N.H. 50 43 11N 72 8W
Washington, N.J. 51 40 46N 74 59W
Washington, Nebr. 48 41 24N 96 13W
Washington, Okla. 57 35 4N 97 29W
Washington, Pa. 59 40 10N 80 15W
Washington, Utah 66 37 8N 113 31W
Washington, Va. 68 38 43N 78 10W
Washington □ 67 47 30N 120 30W
Washington, Mt. 50 44 16N 71 18W
Washington County ◇, Ala. 24 31 22N 88 15W
Washington County ◇, Ark. 27 36 4N 94 10W
Washington County ◇, Colo. 30 40 0N 103 10W
Washington County ◇, Fla. 31 30 30N 85 45W
Washington County ◇, Ga. 32 33 0N 82 50W
Washington County ◇, Idaho 34 44 30N 116 50W
Washington County ◇, Ill. 35 38 20N 89 25W
Washington County ◇, Ind. 36 38 35N 86 5W
Washington County ◇, Iowa 37 41 20N 91 40W
Washington County ◇, Kans. 38 39 45N 97 0W
Washington County ◇, Ky. 63 37 45N 85 10W
Washington County ◇, Maine 40 45 0N 67 30W
Washington County ◇, Md. 41 39 40N 78 0W
Washington County ◇, Minn. 44 45 10N 92 55W

Washington County ◇, Miss. **45** 33 16N 90 53W
Washington County ◇, Mo. **46** 38 0N 90 50W
Washington County ◇, N.C. **54** 35 50N 76 30W
Washington County ◇, N.Y. **53** 43 20N 73 25W
Washington County ◇, Nebr. **48** 41 30N 96 15W
Washington County ◇, Ohio **56** 39 25N 81 27W
Washington County ◇, Okla. **57** 36 40N 95 55W
Washington County ◇, Oreg. **58** 45 30N 123 0W
Washington County ◇, Pa. **59** 40 8N 80 8W
Washington County ◇, R.I. **42** 41 30N 71 40W
Washington County ◇, Tenn. **63** 36 18N 82 29W
Washington County ◇, Tex. **65** 30 10N 96 24W
Washington County ◇, Utah **66** 37 20N 113 30W
Washington County ◇, Va. **68** 36 55N 82 0W
Washington County ◇, Vt. **50** 44 15N 72 40W
Washington County ◇, Wis. **69** 43 20N 88 15W
Washington Court House **56** 39 32N 83 26W
Washington Grove **41** 39 8N 77 11W
Washington I. **69** 45 23N 86 54W
Washington Island **69** 45 24N 86 56W
Washington Parish ◇ **39** 30 51N 90 9W
Washington Terrace **66** 41 11N 111 59W
Washita → **57** 34 8N 96 36W
Washita County ◇ **57** 35 15N 99 0W
Washoe City **49** 39 19N 119 49W
Washoe County ◇ **49** 41 0N 119 40W
Washoe L. **49** 39 16N 119 48W
Washta **37** 42 35N 95 43W
Washtenaw County ◇ **43** 42 15N 83 50W
Washtucna **67** 46 45N 118 19W
Wasilla **25** 61 35N 149 26W
Waskish **44** 48 10N 94 31W
Waskom **65** 32 29N 94 4W
Wassaw I. **32** 31 53N 80 58W
Wassaw Sd. **32** 31 55N 80 55W
Wassuk Range **49** 38 40N 118 50W
Wasta **61** 44 4N 102 27W
Watauga County ◇ **54** 36 15N 81 45W
Watauga L. **63** 36 19N 82 7W
Water Valley, Ky. **62** 36 34N 88 49W
Water Valley, Miss. **45** 34 10N 89 38W
Waterbury, Conn. **42** 41 33N 73 3W
Waterbury, Nebr. **48** 42 27N 96 44W
Waterbury, Vt. **50** 44 20N 72 46W
Waterbury Center **50** 44 22N 72 43W
Wateree → **60** 33 45N 80 37W
Wateree L. **60** 34 20N 80 42W
Waterflow **52** 36 45N 108 27W
Waterford, Calif. **28** 37 38N 120 46W
Waterford, Conn. **42** 41 20N 72 9W
Waterford, Maine **40** 44 14N 70 46W
Waterford, Mich. **43** 42 45N 83 40W
Waterford, Miss. **45** 34 39N 89 28W
Waterford, Pa. **59** 41 57N 79 59W
Waterford, Wis. **69** 42 46N 88 13W
Watergap **63** 37 38N 82 45W
Waterloo, Ala. **24** 34 55N 88 4W
Waterloo, Ark. **27** 33 33N 93 15W
Waterloo, Ill. **35** 38 20N 90 9W
Waterloo, Ind. **36** 41 26N 85 1W
Waterloo, Iowa **37** 42 30N 92 21W
Waterloo, Mont. **47** 45 43N 112 12W
Waterloo, N.Y. **53** 42 54N 76 52W
Waterloo, Wis. **69** 43 11N 88 59W
Waterman **35** 41 46N 88 47W
Waterproof **39** 31 48N 91 23W
Watersmeet **43** 46 16N 89 11W
Waterton-Glacier International Peace Park **47** 48 45N 115 0W
Watertown, Conn. **42** 41 36N 73 7W
Watertown, Fla. **31** 30 11N 82 36W
Watertown, Mass. **42** 42 22N 71 11W
Watertown, N.Y. **53** 43 59N 75 55W
Watertown, S. Dak. **61** 44 54N 97 7W
Watertown, Tenn. **62** 36 6N 86 8W
Watertown, Wis. **69** 43 12N 88 43W
Waterville, Kans. **38** 39 42N 96 45W
Waterville, Maine **40** 44 33N 69 38W
Waterville, Minn. **44** 44 13N 93 34W
Waterville, N.Y. **53** 42 56N 75 23W
Waterville, Ohio **56** 41 30N 83 43W
Waterville, Vt. **50** 44 42N 72 47W
Waterville, Wash. **67** 47 39N 120 4W
Waterville Valley **50** 43 57N 71 31W
Watervliet **53** 42 44N 73 42W
Watford City **55** 47 48N 103 17W
Wathena **38** 39 46N 94 57W
Watkins **44** 45 19N 94 24W
Watkins Glen **53** 42 23N 76 52W
Watkinsville **32** 33 52N 83 25W
Watonga **57** 35 51N 98 25W
Watonwan County ◇ **44** 44 0N 94 40W
Watova **57** 36 37N 95 39W
Watrous **52** 35 48N 104 59W
Watseka **35** 40 47N 87 44W
Watson, Ark. **27** 33 54N 91 15W
Watson, Ill. **35** 39 2N 88 34W
Watson, Minn. **44** 45 1N 95 48W
Watson, Mo. **46** 40 29N 95 40W
Watsontown **59** 41 5N 76 52W
Watsonville **28** 36 55N 121 45W
Watts **57** 36 7N 94 34W
Watts Bar L. **63** 35 37N 84 47W
Wattsburg **59** 42 0N 79 49W
Wattsville **60** 34 31N 82 2W
Watuppa Pond **42** 41 42N 71 6W
Waubay **61** 45 20N 97 18W
Waubay L. **61** 45 25N 97 24W
Waubun **44** 47 11N 95 57W
Wauchula **31** 27 33N 81 49W
Waucoba Mt. **29** 37 1N 118 0W
Waucoma **37** 43 2N 92 1W
Waugoshance Pt. **43** 45 46N 85 1W
Waukee **37** 41 37N 93 53W
Waukeenah **31** 30 25N 83 57W
Waukegan **35** 42 22N 87 50W
Waukesha **69** 43 1N 88 14W
Waukesha County ◇ **69** 43 0N 88 15W
Waukomis **57** 36 17N 97 54W
Waukon **37** 43 16N 91 29W
Waunakee **69** 43 11N 89 27W
Wauneta **48** 40 25N 101 23W
Waupaca **69** 44 21N 89 5W
Waupaca County ◇ **69** 44 25N 89 0W
Waupun **69** 43 38N 88 44W
Waurika **57** 34 10N 98 0W
Waurika Res. **57** 34 10N 98 0W
Wausa **48** 42 30N 97 32W
Wausau, Fla. **31** 30 38N 85 35W
Wausau, Wis. **69** 44 58N 89 38W
Wausaukee **69** 45 23N 87 57W
Wauseon **56** 41 33N 84 8W
Waushara County ◇ **69** 44 10N 89 15W
Wautoma **69** 44 4N 89 18W
Wauwatosa **69** 43 3N 88 0W
Wauzeka **69** 43 5N 90 53W
Waveland, Ind. **36** 39 53N 87 3W
Waveland, Miss. **45** 30 17N 89 23W
Waverley Hall **32** 32 41N 84 44W
Waverly, Ala. **24** 32 44N 85 35W
Waverly, Fla. **31** 27 59N 81 37W
Waverly, Ga. **32** 31 6N 81 43W
Waverly, Ill. **35** 39 36N 89 57W
Waverly, Iowa **37** 42 44N 92 29W
Waverly, Kans. **38** 38 23N 95 36W
Waverly, Ky. **62** 37 43N 87 48W
Waverly, Mo. **46** 39 13N 93 31W
Waverly, N.Y. **53** 42 1N 76 32W
Waverly, Nebr. **48** 40 55N 96 32W
Waverly, Tenn. **62** 36 5N 87 48W
Waverly, Va. **68** 37 2N 77 6W
Waverly, Wash. **67** 47 21N 117 14W
Wawasee, L. **36** 41 24N 85 42W
Wawona **28** 37 32N 119 39W
Waxahachie **65** 32 24N 96 51W
Waxhaw **54** 34 56N 80 45W
Way **45** 32 45N 90 2W
Wayan **34** 42 58N 111 23W
Waycross **32** 31 13N 82 21W
Wayland, Iowa **37** 41 8N 91 40W
Wayland, Ky. **63** 37 27N 82 48W
Wayland, Mass. **42** 42 22N 71 22W
Wayland, Mich. **43** 42 40N 85 39W
Wayland, N.Y. **53** 42 34N 77 35W
Wayne, Kans. **38** 39 43N 97 33W
Wayne, N.J. **51** 40 55N 74 17W
Wayne, Nebr. **48** 42 14N 97 1W
Wayne, Ohio **56** 41 18N 83 29W
Wayne, Okla. **57** 34 55N 97 19W
Wayne, W. Va. **68** 38 13N 82 27W
Wayne County ◇, Ga. **32** 31 30N 82 0W
Wayne County ◇, Ill. **35** 38 25N 88 25W
Wayne County ◇, Ind. **36** 39 50N 85 0W
Wayne County ◇, Iowa **37** 40 45N 93 20W
Wayne County ◇, Ky. **63** 36 45N 84 50W
Wayne County ◇, Mich. **43** 42 15N 83 15W
Wayne County ◇, Miss. **45** 31 40N 88 39W
Wayne County ◇, Mo. **46** 37 5N 90 30W
Wayne County ◇, N.C. **54** 35 20N 78 0W
Wayne County ◇, N.Y. **53** 43 10N 77 0W
Wayne County ◇, Nebr. **48** 42 15N 97 5W
Wayne County ◇, Ohio **56** 40 48N 81 56W
Wayne County ◇, Pa. **59** 41 35N 75 15W
Wayne County ◇, Tenn. **62** 35 10N 87 44W
Wayne County ◇, Utah **66** 38 15N 111 0W
Wayne County ◇, W. Va. **68** 38 13N 82 27W
Wayne National Forest **56** 39 33N 81 4W
Waynesboro, Ga. **32** 33 6N 82 1W
Waynesboro, Miss. **45** 31 40N 88 39W
Waynesboro, Pa. **59** 39 45N 77 35W
Waynesboro, Tenn. **62** 35 19N 87 46W
Waynesboro, Va. **68** 38 4N 78 53W
Waynesburg **59** 39 54N 80 11W
Waynesville, Ill. **35** 40 15N 89 8W
Waynesville, Mo. **46** 37 50N 92 12W
Waynesville, N.C. **54** 35 28N 82 58W
Waynesville, Ohio **56** 39 32N 84 5W
Waynetown **36** 40 5N 87 4W
Waynoka **57** 36 35N 98 53W
Wayside, Ga. **32** 33 4N 83 37W
Wayside, Miss. **45** 33 16N 91 2W
Wayside, Wis. **69** 44 15N 87 57W
Weakley County ◇ **62** 36 14N 88 50W
Weare **50** 43 6N 71 44W
Weatherby **46** 39 55N 94 14W
Weatherford, Okla. **57** 35 32N 98 43W
Weatherford, Tex. **65** 32 46N 97 48W
Weatherly **59** 40 57N 75 50W
Weathersby **45** 31 56N 89 50W
Weaubleau **46** 37 54N 93 32W
Weaverville, Calif. **28** 40 44N 122 56W
Weaverville, N.C. **54** 35 42N 82 34W
Webb, Iowa **37** 42 57N 95 1W
Webb, Miss. **45** 33 57N 90 21W
Webb City, Mo. **46** 37 9N 94 28W
Webb City, Okla. **57** 36 48N 96 42W
Webb County ◇ **65** 27 30N 99 10W
Webber **38** 39 56N 98 2W
Webbville **63** 38 11N 82 52W
Weber → **66** 41 10N 112 10W
Weber County ◇ **66** 41 20N 111 40W
Webster, Fla. **31** 28 37N 82 3W
Webster, Iowa **37** 41 26N 92 10W
Webster, Mass. **42** 42 3N 71 53W
Webster, N. Dak. **55** 48 17N 98 53W
Webster, N.Y. **53** 43 13N 77 26W
Webster, S. Dak. **61** 45 20N 97 31W
Webster, Wis. **69** 45 53N 92 22W
Webster City **37** 42 28N 93 49W
Webster County ◇, Ga. **32** 32 0N 84 35W
Webster County ◇, Iowa **37** 42 25N 94 10W
Webster County ◇, Ky. **62** 37 30N 87 40W
Webster County ◇, Miss. **45** 33 37N 89 17W
Webster County ◇, Mo. **46** 37 15N 92 50W
Webster County ◇, Nebr. **48** 40 15N 98 30W
Webster County ◇, W. Va. **68** 38 29N 80 25W
Webster Parish ◇ **39** 32 40N 93 20W
Webster Reservoir **38** 39 25N 99 26W
Webster Springs **68** 38 29N 80 25W
Wedgefield **60** 33 53N 80 31W
Wedowee **24** 33 19N 85 29W
Weed, Calif. **28** 41 25N 122 23W
Weed, N. Mex. **52** 32 48N 105 31W
Weed Heights **49** 38 59N 119 13W
Weedville **59** 41 17N 78 30W
Weekapaug **42** 41 20N 71 45W
Weeks **39** 29 48N 91 49W
Weekstown **51** 39 37N 74 37W
Weeksville **54** 36 13N 76 10W
Weeping Water **48** 40 52N 96 8W
Weimar, Calif. **28** 39 2N 120 59W
Weimar, Tex. **65** 29 42N 96 47W
Weiner **27** 35 37N 90 54W
Weippe **34** 46 23N 115 56W
Weir, Kans. **38** 37 19N 94 46W
Weir, Ky. **62** 37 7N 87 13W
Weir, Miss. **45** 33 16N 89 18W
Weir, L. **31** 29 0N 81 57W
Weirsdale **31** 28 59N 81 55W
Weirton **68** 40 24N 80 35W
Weiser **34** 44 45N 116 58W
Weiser → **34** 44 14N 116 58W
Weiss L. **24** 34 8N 85 48W
Weissert **48** 41 28N 99 27W
Welch, Okla. **57** 36 52N 95 6W
Welch, Tex. **64** 32 56N 102 8W
Welch, W. Va. **68** 37 26N 81 35W
Welcome, Md. **41** 38 28N 77 8W
Welcome, Minn. **44** 43 40N 94 37W
Welcome, N.C. **54** 35 55N 80 15W
Weld **40** 44 42N 70 25W
Weld County ◇ **30** 40 45N 104 15W
Welda **38** 38 10N 95 18W
Weldon, Ill. **35** 40 7N 88 45W
Weldon, Iowa **37** 40 54N 93 44W
Weldon, N.C. **54** 36 25N 77 36W
Weldon Spring **46** 38 43N 90 41W
Weldona **30** 40 21N 103 58W
Weleetka **57** 35 20N 96 8W
Wellborn **65** 30 32N 96 18W
Wellesley **42** 42 18N 71 18W
Wellfleet, Mass. **42** 41 56N 70 2W
Wellfleet, Nebr. **48** 40 45N 100 44W
Wellington, Colo. **30** 40 42N 105 0W
Wellington, Ill. **35** 40 32N 87 41W
Wellington, Kans. **38** 37 16N 97 24W
Wellington, Maine **40** 45 2N 69 36W
Wellington, Mo. **46** 39 8N 93 59W
Wellington, Nev. **49** 38 45N 119 23W
Wellington, Ohio **56** 41 10N 82 13W
Wellington, Tex. **64** 34 51N 100 13W
Wellington, Utah **66** 39 32N 110 44W
Wellman, Iowa **37** 41 28N 91 50W
Wellman, Tex. **64** 33 3N 102 26W
Wellpinit **67** 47 53N 117 59W
Wells, Kans. **38** 39 5N 97 33W
Wells, Maine **40** 43 20N 70 35W
Wells, Minn. **44** 43 45N 93 44W
Wells, N.Y. **53** 43 24N 74 17W
Wells, Nev. **49** 41 7N 114 58W
Wells, Tex. **65** 31 29N 94 56W
Wells, Vt. **50** 43 25N 73 10W
Wells → **50** 44 10N 72 3W
Wells County ◇, Ind. **36** 40 45N 85 15W
Wells County ◇, N. Dak. **55** 47 35N 99 45W
Wellsboro **59** 41 45N 77 18W
Wellsburg, Iowa **37** 42 26N 92 56W
Wellsburg, N.Y. **53** 42 1N 76 44W
Wellsburg, W. Va. **68** 40 16N 80 37W
Wellsford **38** 37 37N 99 2W
Wellston, Mich. **43** 44 13N 85 58W
Wellston, Ohio **56** 39 7N 82 32W
Wellston, Okla. **57** 35 42N 97 4W
Wellsville, Kans. **38** 38 43N 95 5W
Wellsville, Mo. **46** 39 4N 91 34W
Wellsville, N.Y. **53** 42 7N 77 57W
Wellsville, Ohio **56** 40 36N 80 39W
Wellsville, Pa. **59** 40 3N 76 56W
Wellsville, Utah **66** 41 38N 111 56W
Wellton **26** 32 40N 114 8W
Welsh **39** 30 14N 92 49W
Welton **37** 41 55N 90 36W
Wenatchee **67** 47 25N 120 19W
Wenatchee → **67** 47 27N 120 19W
Wenatchee Mts. **67** 47 15N 120 30W
Wenatchee National Forest **67** 47 55N 120 55W
Wendell, Idaho **34** 42 47N 114 42W
Wendell, Minn. **44** 46 2N 96 6W
Wendell, N.C. **54** 35 47N 78 22W
Wendell, N.H. **50** 43 22N 72 9W
Wenden **26** 33 49N 113 33W
Wendover **66** 40 44N 114 2W
Wenona, Ill. **35** 41 3N 89 3W
Wenona, Md. **41** 38 8N 75 57W
Wentworth, Mo. **46** 36 59N 94 4W
Wentworth, N.C. **54** 36 24N 79 46W
Wentworth, N.H. **50** 43 52N 71 55W
Wentzville **46** 38 49N 90 51W
Weott **28** 40 20N 123 55W
Werley **69** 43 1N 90 46W
Weskan **38** 38 52N 101 57W
Weslaco **64** 26 10N 97 58W
Wesley, Ga. **32** 32 29N 82 20W
Wesley, Iowa **37** 43 5N 93 59W
Wesley, Maine **40** 44 57N 67 40W
Wesleyville **59** 42 9N 80 0W
Wessington **61** 44 27N 98 42W
Wessington Springs **61** 44 5N 98 34W
Wesson, Ark. **27** 33 7N 92 46W
Wesson, Miss. **45** 31 42N 90 24W
West **65** 31 48N 97 6W
West → **50** 42 52N 72 33W
West Acton **42** 42 29N 71 29W
West Alexandria **56** 39 45N 84 32W
West Allis **69** 43 1N 88 0W
West Arlington **50** 43 8N 73 12W
West Arm Grand Traverse B. **43** 44 50N 85 40W
West B., Fla. **31** 30 10N 85 45W
West B., La. **39** 29 3N 89 22W
West B., Tex. **65** 29 14N 95 0W
West Babylon **53** 40 42N 73 21W
West Baton Rouge Parish ◇ **39** 30 27N 91 12W
West Bend, Iowa **37** 42 57N 94 27W
West Bend, Wis. **69** 43 25N 88 11W
West Blocton **24** 33 7N 87 7W
West Boylston **42** 42 22N 71 47W
West Branch, Iowa **37** 41 40N 91 20W
West Branch, Mich. **43** 44 17N 84 14W

West Branch Susquehanna → **59** 40 53N 76 48W
West Bridgewater **42** 42 1N 71 0W
West Brookfield **42** 42 14N 72 9W
West Burke **50** 44 39N 71 59W
West Burlington **37** 40 49N 91 9W
West Campton **50** 43 40N 71 41W
West Canaan **50** 43 40N 72 2W
West Cape May **51** 38 56N 74 56W
West Carroll Parish ◇ **39** 32 30N 92 52W
West Carthage **53** 43 59N 75 37W
West Chester, Iowa **37** 41 20N 91 49W
West Chester, Pa. **59** 39 58N 75 36W
West Columbia, S.C. **60** 34 0N 81 4W
West Columbia, Tex. **65** 29 9N 95 39W
West Concord **44** 44 9N 92 54W
West Cote Blanche B. **39** 29 45N 91 55W
West Covina **29** 34 4N 117 54W
West Creek **51** 39 38N 74 18W
West Cummington **42** 42 29N 72 57W
West Des Moines **37** 41 35N 93 43W
West Dover **50** 42 56N 72 51W
West Dummerston **50** 42 55N 72 38W
West Elk Mts. **30** 38 35N 107 15W
West Elkton **56** 39 35N 84 33W
West End **54** 35 15N 79 34W
West Fairlee **50** 43 54N 72 16W
West Fargo **55** 46 52N 96 54W
West Feliciana Parish ◇ **39** 30 50N 91 23W
West Fork Cuivre → **46** 39 2N 90 59W
West Fork Poplar → **47** 48 31N 105 22W
West Fork Trinity → **65** 32 48N 96 54W
West Forks **40** 45 20N 69 58W
West Frankfort **35** 37 54N 88 55W
West Glacier **47** 48 30N 113 59W
West Grand L. **40** 45 14N 67 51W
West Green **32** 31 37N 82 44W
West Hamlin **68** 38 17N 82 12W
West Hartford **42** 41 45N 72 44W
West Haven **42** 41 17N 72 57W
West Helena **27** 34 33N 90 38W
West Jefferson, N.C. **54** 36 24N 81 30W
West Jefferson, Ohio **56** 39 57N 83 17W
West Kingston **42** 41 29N 71 34W
West Lafayette **36** 40 27N 86 55W
West Lebanon **36** 40 16N 87 23W
West Leipsic **56** 41 7N 84 0W
West Liberty, Iowa **37** 41 34N 91 16W
West Liberty, Ky. **63** 37 55N 83 16W
West Liberty, Ohio **56** 40 15N 83 45W
West Louisville **62** 37 42N 87 17W
West Mansfield **56** 40 24N 83 33W
West Mayfield **59** 40 47N 80 20W
West Memphis **27** 35 9N 90 11W
West Mifflin **59** 40 22N 79 52W
West Milan **50** 44 37N 71 18W
West Milford **68** 39 12N 80 24W
West Millgrove **56** 41 15N 83 30W
West Milton **56** 39 58N 84 20W
West Mineral **38** 37 17N 94 55W
West Monroe **39** 32 31N 92 9W
West Newbury **42** 42 48N 70 0W
West Nishnabotna → **37** 40 39N 95 38W
West Nueces → **65** 29 16N 99 56W
West Okoboji L. **37** 43 23N 95 9W
West Orange **65** 30 5N 93 46W
West Ossipee **50** 43 48N 71 12W
West Palm Beach **31** 26 43N 80 3W
West Palm Beach Canal **31** 26 40N 80 15W
West Panama City Beach **31** 30 13N 85 53W
West Pawlet **50** 43 21N 73 15W
West Pensacola **31** 30 25N 87 16W
West Plains **46** 36 44N 91 51W
West Plymouth **50** 43 45N 71 45W
West Point, Calif. **28** 38 24N 120 32W
West Point, Ga. **32** 32 53N 85 11W
West Point, Ill. **35** 40 15N 91 11W
West Point, Iowa **37** 40 43N 91 27W
West Point, Ky. **63** 37 59N 85 57W
West Point, Miss. **45** 33 36N 88 39W
West Point, N.Y. **53** 41 24N 73 58W
West Point, Nebr. **48** 41 51N 96 43W
West Point, Va. **68** 37 32N 76 48W
West Point L. **24** 33 0N 85 5W
West Richland **67** 46 18N 119 20W
West Rindge **50** 42 47N 72 3W
West River **41** 38 52N 76 31W
West Rutland **50** 43 36N 73 3W
West Sacramento **28** 38 35N 121 32W
West Salem, Ill. **35** 38 31N 88 1W
West Salem, Ohio **56** 40 58N 82 7W
West Salem, Wis. **69** 43 54N 91 5W
West Seneca **53** 42 51N 78 48W
West Siloam Springs **57** 36 12N 94 39W
West Springfield **42** 42 6N 72 38W
West Stewartstown **50** 44 59N 71 32W
West Tavaputs Plateau **66** 39 50N 110 20W
West Terre Haute **36** 39 28N 87 27W
West Thompson Res. **42** 41 57N 71 54W
West Thorton **50** 43 55N 71 42W
West Thumb **70** 44 25N 110 34W
West Tisbury **42** 41 23N 70 41W
West Topsham **50** 44 7N 72 19W
West Union, Iowa **37** 42 57N 91 49W
West Union, Minn. **44** 45 48N 95 5W
West Union, Ohio **56** 38 48N 83 33W
West Union, W. Va. **68** 39 18N 80 47W
West Unity **56** 41 35N 84 26W
West University Place **65** 29 42N 95 26W
West Valley **66** 40 42N 111 58W
West Virginia □ **68** 38 45N 80 30W
West Warwick **42** 41 43N 71 32W
West Winfield **53** 42 53N 75 12W
West Yarmouth **42** 41 39N 70 15W
West Yellowstone **47** 44 40N 111 6W
West York **59** 39 57N 76 46W
Westbay **31** 30 18N 85 52W
Westboro **46** 40 32N 95 19W
Westborough **42** 42 16N 71 37W
Westbrook, Conn. **42** 41 17N 72 27W
Westbrook, Maine **40** 43 41N 70 22W
Westbrook, Minn. **44** 44 3N 95 26W
Westbrook, Tex. **64** 32 21N 101 1W
Westby, Mont. **47** 48 52N 104 3W
Westby, Wis. **69** 43 39N 90 51W
Westchester County ◇ **53** 41 40N 73 45W
Westcliffe **30** 38 9N 105 28W
Westend **29** 35 42N 117 24W
Westerly **42** 41 22N 71 50W
Western **48** 40 24N 97 12W
Western Grove **27** 36 6N 92 57W
Westernport **41** 39 29N 79 3W
Westerville, Nebr. **48** 41 24N 99 23W
Westerville, Ohio **56** 40 8N 82 56W
Westfall **58** 43 59N 117 48W
Westfield, Ill. **35** 39 27N 88 0W
Westfield, Ind. **36** 40 2N 86 8W
Westfield, Iowa **37** 42 45N 96 36W
Westfield, Maine **40** 46 34N 67 55W
Westfield, Mass. **42** 42 7N 72 45W
Westfield, N.J. **51** 40 39N 74 21W
Westfield, N.Y. **53** 42 20N 79 35W
Westfield, Pa. **59** 41 55N 77 32W
Westfield, Wis. **69** 43 53N 89 30W
Westfield → **42** 42 5N 72 35W
Westfir **58** 43 46N 122 31W
Westford **42** 42 35N 71 26W
Westgate **37** 42 46N 92 0W
Westhoff **65** 29 12N 97 28W
Westhope **55** 48 55N 101 1W
Westland **43** 42 15N 83 20W
Westminster, Calif. **29** 33 46N 118 1W
Westminster, Colo. **30** 39 50N 105 2W
Westminster, Mass. **42** 42 33N 71 55W
Westminster, Md. **41** 39 34N 76 59W
Westminster, S.C. **60** 34 40N 83 6W
Westminster, Vt. **50** 43 5N 72 27W
Westmont **59** 40 19N 78 58W
Westmore **50** 44 0N 72 0W
Westmoreland, Kans. **38** 39 24N 96 25W
Westmoreland, N.H. **50** 42 57N 72 25W
Westmoreland, Tenn. **62** 36 34N 86 15W
Westmoreland County ◇, Pa. **59** 40 20N 79 25W
Westmoreland County ◇, Va. **68** 38 6N 76 50W
Westmorland **29** 33 2N 115 37W
Weston, Colo. **30** 37 8N 104 48W
Weston, Mo. **46** 39 25N 94 54W
Weston, Nebr. **48** 41 12N 96 45W
Weston, Oreg. **58** 45 49N 118 26W
Weston, Vt. **50** 43 18N 72 38W
Weston, W. Va. **68** 39 2N 80 28W
Weston, Wis. **69** 44 49N 92 4W
Weston County ◇ **70** 43 55N 104 35W
Westover, Md. **41** 38 7N 75 42W
Westover, Pa. **59** 40 45N 78 40W
Westover, S. Dak. **61** 43 45N 100 40W
Westover, Tenn. **62** 35 37N 88 53W
Westphalia, Mich. **43** 42 56N 84 48W
Westphalia, Mo. **46** 38 26N 92 0W
Westpoint **62** 35 8N 87 32W
Westport, Calif. **28** 39 38N 123 47W
Westport, Conn. **42** 41 9N 73 22W
Westport, Ind. **36** 39 11N 85 34W
Westport, Minn. **44** 45 43N 95 10W
Westport, N.H. **50** 42 49N 72 20W
Westport, N.Y. **53** 44 11N 73 26W
Westport, Okla. **57** 36 8N 96 20W
Westport, Oreg. **58** 46 8N 123 23W
Westport, Wash. **67** 46 53N 124 6W
Westville, Fla. **31** 30 46N 85 51W
Westville, Ill. **35** 40 2N 87 38W
Westville, Okla. **57** 35 58N 94 40W
Westville, S.C. **60** 34 27N 80 36W
Westwego **39** 29 54N 90 8W
Westwood, Calif. **28** 40 18N 121 0W
Westwood, Ky. **63** 38 30N 82 50W
Westwood, Mass. **42** 42 13N 71 14W
Westwood, Md. **41** 38 40N 76 45W
Westwood, N.J. **51** 40 58N 74 2W
Westwood Lakes **31** 25 44N 80 23W
Wet Mts. **30** 38 0N 105 10W
Wethersfield **42** 41 42N 72 40W
Wetmore, Colo. **30** 38 14N 105 5W
Wetmore, Kans. **38** 39 38N 95 49W
Wetumka **57** 35 14N 96 15W
Wetumpka **24** 32 32N 86 13W
Wetzel County ◇ **68** 39 34N 80 41W
Wewahitchka **31** 30 7N 85 12W
Wewoka **57** 35 9N 96 30W
Wexford County ◇ **43** 44 20N 85 40W
Weyauwega **69** 44 19N 88 56W
Weyerhaeuser **69** 45 26N 91 25W
Weymouth **42** 42 13N 70 58W
Whalan **44** 43 44N 91 55W
Whaleysville **41** 38 24N 75 18W
Wharton, N.J. **51** 40 54N 74 35W
Wharton, Ohio **56** 40 52N 83 28W
Wharton, Tex. **65** 29 19N 96 6W
Wharton County ◇ **65** 29 12N 96 16W
Wharton State Forest **51** 39 45N 74 40W
What Cheer **37** 41 24N 92 21W
Whatcom, L. **67** 48 44N 122 20W
Whatcom County ◇ **67** 48 56N 122 0W
Whatley **24** 31 39N 87 42W
Wheat Ridge **30** 39 46N 105 5W
Wheatcroft **62** 37 30N 87 52W
Wheatland, Calif. **28** 39 1N 121 25W
Wheatland, Ind. **36** 38 40N 87 19W
Wheatland, Iowa **37** 41 50N 90 51W
Wheatland, Mo. **46** 37 57N 93 24W
Wheatland, Wyo. **70** 42 3N 104 58W
Wheatland County ◇ **47** 46 30N 109 50W
Wheatland Reservoir No.2 **70** 41 50N 105 38W
Wheatley **27** 34 55N 91 7W
Wheaton, Ill. **35** 41 52N 88 6W
Wheaton, Kans. **38** 39 30N 96 19W
Wheaton, Md. **41** 39 3N 77 3W
Wheaton, Minn. **44** 45 48N 96 30W
Wheeler, Ill. **35** 39 3N 88 19W
Wheeler, Kans. **38** 39 46N 101 43W
Wheeler, Miss. **45** 34 35N 88 37W
Wheeler, Oreg. **58** 45 41N 123 53W
Wheeler, Tex. **64** 35 27N 100 16W
Wheeler, Wis. **69** 45 3N 91 55W
Wheeler County ◇, Ga. **32** 32 5N 82 45W
Wheeler County ◇, Nebr. **48** 41 50N 98 30W
Wheeler County ◇, Oreg. **58** 44 45N 120 0W
Wheeler County ◇, Tex. **64** 35 30N 100 15W
Wheeler L. **24** 34 48N 87 23W
Wheeler Peak, N. Mex. **52** 36 33N 105 25W
Wheeler Peak, Nev. **49** 38 59N 114 19W
Wheeler Ridge **29** 35 0N 118 57W
Wheelersburg **56** 38 44N 82 51W
Wheeling, Ill. **35** 42 8N 87 55W
Wheeling, W. Va. **68** 40 4N 80 43W
Wheelock **55** 48 18N 103 15W
Wheelwright **63** 37 20N 82 43W
Whelen Springs **27** 33 50N 93 7W
Whidbey I. **67** 48 12N 122 17W
Whiskey Pk. **70** 42 18N 107 35W
Whiskeytown-Shasta-Trinity Nat. Rec. Area **28** 40 45N 122 15W
Whispering Pines **54** 35 17N 79 26W
Whitakers **54** 36 6N 77 43W
White, Ga. **32** 34 17N 84 45W
White, S. Dak. **61** 44 26N 96 39W
White →, Ariz. **26** 33 44N 110 13W
White →, Ark. **27** 33 57N 91 5W
White →, Ind. **36** 38 25N 87 45W
White →, Nev. **49** 37 19N 115 8W
White →, S. Dak. **61** 43 42N 99 27W
White →, Tex. **64** 33 14N 100 56W
White →, Utah **66** 40 4N 109 41W
White →, Vt. **50** 43 37N 72 20W
White Apple **45** 31 27N 91 4W
White Bear Lake **44** 45 5N 93 1W
White Bird **34** 45 46N 116 18W
White Bluff **62** 36 6N 87 13W
White Butte, N. Dak. **55** 46 23N 103 18W
White Butte, S. Dak. **61** 45 56N 102 22W
White Canyon **66** 37 49N 110 26W
White Castle **39** 30 10N 91 9W
White City, Fla. **31** 29 53N 85 13W
White City, Kans. **38** 38 48N 96 44W
White City, Ky. **63** 37 35N 85 40W
White City, Oreg. **58** 42 26N 122 51W
White Cloud, Kans. **38** 39 59N 95 18W
White Cloud, Mich. **43** 43 33N 85 46W
White County ◇, Ark. **27** 35 15N 91 44W
White County ◇, Ga. **32** 34 40N 83 45W
White County ◇, Ill. **35** 38 5N 88 10W
White County ◇, Ind. **36** 40 45N 86 50W
White County ◇, Tenn. **63** 35 56N 85 28W
White Deer **64** 35 26N 101 10W
White Earth **55** 48 23N 102 46W
White Earth → **55** 48 9N 102 42W
White Earth Indian Reservation **44** 47 20N 95 45W
White Hall, Ala. **24** 32 20N 86 43W
White Hall, Ill. **35** 39 26N 90 24W
White Haven **59** 41 4N 75 47W
White Horse **51** 40 11N 74 42W
White L. **39** 29 44N 92 30W
White Lake, N.C. **54** 34 39N 78 30W
White Lake, S. Dak. **61** 43 44N 98 43W
White Lake, Wis. **69** 45 10N 88 46W
White Mountain **25** 64 41N 163 24W
White Mountain National Forest **50** 44 10N 71 25W
White Mountain Peak **29** 37 38N 118 15W
White Mts., Alaska **25** 65 30N 146 30W
White Mts., Ariz. **26** 34 0N 109 40W
White Mts., Calif. **29** 37 30N 118 15W
White Mts., N.H. **50** 44 10N 71 20W
White Oak, Ga. **32** 31 2N 81 43W
White Oak, S.C. **60** 34 28N 81 7W
White Oak, Tex. **65** 32 32N 94 52W
White Oak Cr. → **65** 33 14N 94 42W
White Owl **61** 44 36N 102 26W
White Pass **67** 46 38N 121 24W
White Pigeon **43** 41 48N 85 39W
White Pine, Mich. **43** 46 45N 89 35W
White Pine, Mont. **47** 47 45N 115 29W
White Pine, Tenn. **63** 36 7N 83 17W
White Pine County ◇ **49** 39 30N 115 0W
White Pine Range **49** 39 10N 115 20W
White Plains, Ga. **32** 33 28N 83 1W
White Plains, Md. **41** 38 36N 76 55W
White Plains, N.Y. **53** 41 2N 73 46W
White River **61** 43 34N 100 45W
White River Junction **50** 43 39N 72 19W
White River National Forest **30** 39 20N 106 45W
White River Reservoir **64** 33 27N 101 5W
White Rock **63** 36 48N 83 26W
White Rock Cr. → **38** 39 55N 97 50W
White Salmon **67** 45 44N 121 29W
White Sands National Monument **52** 32 46N 106 20W
White Springs **31** 30 20N 82 45W
White Stone **68** 37 39N 76 23W
White Sulphur Springs, Mont. **47** 46 33N 110 54W
White Sulphur Springs, W. Va. **68** 37 48N 80 18W
White Swan **67** 46 23N 120 44W
Whiteburg **41** 38 12N 75 32W
Whiteclay **48** 42 57N 102 33W
Whiteface **64** 33 36N 102 37W
Whiteface → **44** 46 58N 92 48W
Whiteface Reservoir **44** 47 17N 92 11W
Whitefield, Maine **40** 44 10N 69 38W
Whitefield, N.H. **50** 44 23N 71 37W
Whitefish **47** 48 25N 114 20W
Whitefish → **43** 45 55N 86 57W
Whitefish B. **43** 46 40N 84 55W
Whitefish Bay **69** 43 23N 87 54W
Whitefish Point **43** 46 45N 84 59W
Whitefish Pt. **43** 46 46N 84 57W
Whiteford **41** 39 42N 76 21W
Whitehall, Ark. **27** 35 29N 90 44W
Whitehall, Mich. **43** 43 24N 86 21W
Whitehall, Mont. **47** 45 52N 112 6W
Whitehall, N.Y. **53** 43 33N 73 24W
Whitehall, Wis. **69** 44 22N 91 19W
Whitehouse **56** 41 31N 83 48W
Whiteland **36** 39 33N 86 5W
Whitelaw **69** 44 9N 87 49W
Whiteleysburg **41** 38 57N 75 45W
Whiteriver **26** 33 50N 109 58W
Whites City **52** 32 11N 104 22W
Whitesboro, N.Y. **53** 43 7N 75 18W
Whitesboro, Okla. **57** 34 41N 94 53W
Whitesboro, Tex. **65** 33 39N 96 54W

Whitesburg 63 37 7N 82 49W
Whiteside County ◇ 35 41 45N 89 55W
Whitestown 36 40 0N 86 21W
Whitesville, Ky. 62 37 41N 86 52W
Whitesville, W. Va. 68 37 59N 81 32W
Whitetail 47 48 54N 105 10W
Whiteville, La. 39 30 47N 92 9W
Whiteville, N.C. 54 34 20N 78 42W
Whiteville, Tenn. 62 35 20N 89 9W
Whitewater, Colo. 30 38 59N 108 27W
Whitewater, Kans. 38 37 58N 97 9W
Whitewater, Mo. 46 37 14N 89 48W
Whitewater, Mont. 47 48 46N 107 38W
Whitewater, Wis. 69 42 50N 88 44W
Whitewater B. 31 25 15N 81 0W
Whitewater Baldy 52 33 20N 108 39W
Whitewood 61 44 28N 103 39W
Whitewright 65 33 31N 96 24W
Whitfield County ◇ 32 34 50N 84 55W
Whiting, Iowa 37 42 8N 96 9W
Whiting, Kans. 38 39 35N 95 37W
Whiting, Maine 40 44 48N 67 11W
Whiting, N.J. 51 39 57N 74 23W
Whiting, Vt. 50 43 50N 73 12W
Whitinsville 42 42 7N 71 40W
Whitlash 47 48 55N 111 15W
Whitley City 63 36 44N 84 28W
Whitley County ◇, Ind. 36 41 10N 85 30W
Whitley County ◇, Ky. 63 36 45N 84 10W
Whitman, Mass. 42 42 5N 70 56W
Whitman, Nebr. 48 42 3N 101 31W
Whitman County ◇ 67 47 0N 117 30W
Whitmire 60 34 30N 81 37W
Whitmore Lake, Mich. 43 42 20N 83 45W
Whitmore Lake, Mich. 43 42 20N 83 45W
Whitmore Village 33 21 31N 158 1W
Whitnel 54 35 53N 81 32W
Whitney, Nebr. 48 42 47N 103 15W
Whitney, Tex. 65 31 57N 97 19W
Whitney, L. 65 31 52N 97 22W
Whitney, Mt. 29 36 35N 118 18W
Whitney Point 53 42 20N 75 58W
Whitsett 65 28 38N 98 16W
Whittemore, Iowa 37 43 4N 94 26W
Whittemore, Mich. 43 44 14N 83 48W
Whitten 37 42 16N 93 0W
Whittier, Alaska 25 60 47N 148 41W
Whittier, Calif. 29 33 58N 118 3W
Whitwell 63 35 12N 85 31W
Wibaux 47 46 59N 104 11W
Wibaux County ◇ 47 46 50N 104 20W
Wichita 38 37 42N 97 20W
Wichita → 65 34 4N 98 10W
Wichita County ◇, Kans. 38 38 30N 101 20W
Wichita County ◇, Tex. 65 33 57N 98 40W
Wichita Falls 65 33 54N 98 30W
Wichita Mt. 57 34 52N 99 17W
Wichita Mts. 57 34 50N 98 45W
Wickenburg 26 33 58N 112 44W
Wickes 27 34 18N 94 20W
Wickiup Reservoir 58 43 41N 121 41W
Wickliffe, Ky. 62 36 58N 89 5W
Wickliffe, Ohio 56 41 36N 81 28W
Wicomico → 41 38 13N 75 55W
Wicomico County ◇ 41 38 25N 75 45W
Wiggins, Colo. 30 40 14N 104 4W
Wiggins, Leake, Miss. 45 32 42N 89 38W
Wiggins, Stone, Miss. 45 30 51N 89 8W
Wilbarger County ◇ 65 34 9N 99 17W
Wilber 48 40 29N 96 58W
Wilbur, Oreg. 58 43 19N 123 21W
Wilbur, Wash. 67 47 46N 118 42W
Wilburton 57 34 55N 95 19W
Wilcox, Nebr. 48 40 22N 99 10W
Wilcox, Pa. 59 41 35N 78 41W
Wilcox County ◇, Ala. 24 31 59N 87 17W
Wilcox County ◇, Ga. 32 32 0N 83 25W
Wild Horse 30 38 50N 103 0W
Wild Horse Reservoir 49 41 41N 115 51W
Wild Rice →, Minn. 44 47 20N 96 50W
Wild Rice →, N. Dak. 55 46 45N 96 47W
Wild Rose 69 44 11N 89 15W
Wildcat → 36 40 28N 86 52W
Wilder, Idaho 34 43 41N 116 55W
Wilder, Minn. 44 43 50N 95 12W
Wilder, Vt. 50 43 40N 72 15W
Wildersville 62 35 47N 88 22W
Wilderville 58 42 23N 123 28W
Wildhorse → 57 34 32N 97 10W
Wildorado 64 35 13N 102 12W
Wildrose 55 48 38N 103 11W
Wildwood, Fla. 31 28 52N 82 2W
Wildwood, N.J. 51 38 59N 74 50W
Wildwood Crest 51 38 58N 74 50W
Wiley 30 38 10N 102 20W
Wiley City 67 46 33N 120 41W
Wilkes-Barre 59 41 15N 75 53W
Wilkes County ◇, Ga. 32 33 50N 82 45W
Wilkes County ◇, N.C. 54 36 10N 81 10W
Wilkesboro 54 36 9N 81 10W
Wilkesboro Res. 54 36 10N 81 20W
Wilkesville 56 39 5N 82 20W
Wilkin County ◇ 44 46 20N 96 25W
Wilkinsburg 59 40 26N 79 53W
Wilkinson 45 31 13N 91 14W
Wilkinson County ◇, Ga. 32 32 45N 83 10W
Wilkinson County ◇, Miss. 45 31 6N 91 18W
Will County ◇ 35 41 25N 88 0W
Willacoochee 32 31 20N 83 3W
Willacy County ◇ 64 26 29N 97 47W
Willamette → 58 45 39N 122 46W
Willamette National Forest 58 44 20N 122 10W
Willamina 58 45 5N 123 29W
Willapa B. 67 46 40N 124 0W
Willard, Colo. 30 40 33N 103 29W
Willard, Mo. 46 37 18N 93 26W
Willard, N. Mex. 52 34 36N 106 2W
Willard, Ohio 56 41 3N 82 44W
Willard, Utah 66 41 25N 112 2W
Willards 41 38 24N 75 21W
Willcox 26 32 15N 109 50W
Willcox Playa 26 32 8N 109 51W
Willette 63 36 27N 85 52W
Willey 37 41 59N 94 49W
William B. Bankhead National Forest 24 34 10N 87 15W
Williams, Ariz. 26 35 15N 112 11W
Williams, Calif. 28 39 9N 122 9W
Williams, Minn. 44 48 45N 94 54W
Williams → 50 43 12N 72 27W
Williams County ◇, N. Dak. 55 48 20N 103 30W
Williams County ◇, Ohio 56 41 35N 84 37W
Williams Fork → 30 40 28N 107 40W
Williams Fork Reservoir 30 40 0N 106 8W
Williamsburg, Iowa 37 41 40N 92 1W
Williamsburg, Kans. 38 38 29N 95 28W
Williamsburg, Ky. 63 36 44N 84 10W
Williamsburg, Mass. 42 42 23N 72 44W
Williamsburg, Md. 41 38 40N 75 50W
Williamsburg, Ohio 56 39 3N 84 4W
Williamsburg, Pa. 59 40 28N 78 12W
Williamsburg, Va. 68 37 16N 76 43W
Williamsburg County ◇ 60 33 40N 79 40W
Williamsfield 35 40 55N 90 1W
Williamson, Ga. 32 33 11N 84 22W
Williamson, Iowa 37 41 5N 93 15W
Williamson, N.Y. 53 43 14N 77 11W
Williamson, W. Va. 68 37 41N 82 17W
Williamson → 58 42 28N 121 57W
Williamson County ◇, Ill. 35 37 40N 88 55W
Williamson County ◇, Tenn. 62 35 55N 86 52W
Williamson County ◇, Tex. 65 30 38N 97 41W
Williamsport, Ind. 36 40 17N 87 17W
Williamsport, Md. 41 39 37N 77 50W
Williamsport, Ohio 56 39 35N 83 7W
Williamsport, Pa. 59 41 15N 77 0W
Williamston, Mich. 43 42 41N 84 17W
Williamston, N.C. 54 35 51N 77 4W
Williamston, S.C. 60 34 37N 82 29W
Williamstown, Ky. 63 38 38N 84 34W
Williamstown, Mass. 42 42 43N 73 12W
Williamstown, N.J. 51 39 41N 74 59W
Williamstown, N.Y. 53 43 26N 75 53W
Williamstown, W. Va. 68 39 24N 81 27W
Williamsville, Del. 41 38 27N 75 8W
Williamsville, Ill. 35 39 57N 89 33W
Williamsville, Mo. 46 36 58N 90 33W
Williford 27 36 15N 91 21W
Willimantic 42 41 43N 72 13W
Willimantic → 42 41 43N 72 12W
Willingboro 51 40 3N 74 54W
Willis, Kans. 38 39 43N 95 31W
Willis, Tex. 65 30 25N 95 29W
Williston, Fla. 31 29 23N 82 27W
Williston, Md. 41 38 48N 75 52W
Williston, N. Dak. 55 48 9N 103 37W
Williston, S.C. 60 33 24N 81 25W
Williston, Vt. 50 44 25N 73 10W
Williston Basin 47 48 0N 104 30W
Willisville 35 37 59N 89 35W
Willits 28 39 25N 123 21W
Willmar 44 45 7N 95 3W
Willoughby 56 41 39N 81 24W
Willow, Alaska 25 61 45N 150 3W
Willow, Ark. 27 34 8N 92 45W
Willow, Okla. 57 35 3N 99 31W
Willow City 55 48 36N 100 18W
Willow Cr. →, Gilliam, Oreg. 58 45 48N 120 1W
Willow Cr. →, Malheur, Oreg. 58 44 0N 117 13W
Willow Cr. →, Utah 66 40 2N 109 45W
Willow Creek, Calif. 28 40 56N 123 38W
Willow Creek, Mont. 47 45 49N 111 39W
Willow Creek Reservoir 49 41 14N 116 32W
Willow Grove, Del. 41 40 8N 75 6W
Willow Grove, Pa. 59 40 9N 75 7W
Willow L. 70 43 0N 109 52W
Willow Lake 61 44 38N 97 38W
Willow Ranch 28 41 54N 120 21W
Willow Reservoir 69 45 43N 89 51W
Willow River 44 46 19N 92 51W
Willow Springs 46 37 0N 91 58W
Willowbrook 38 38 8N 97 57W
Willowdale 58 44 48N 120 57W
Willowick 56 41 38N 81 28W
Willows 28 39 31N 122 12W
Wills Point 65 32 43N 96 1W
Willshire 56 40 45N 84 48W
Wilma 31 30 9N 84 58W
Wilmar 27 33 38N 91 56W
Wilmer 65 32 35N 96 41W
Wilmette 35 42 5N 87 42W
Wilmington, Del. 41 39 45N 75 33W
Wilmington, Ill. 35 41 18N 88 9W
Wilmington, Mass. 42 42 33N 71 10W
Wilmington, N.C. 54 34 14N 77 55W
Wilmington, Ohio 56 39 27N 83 50W
Wilmington, Vt. 50 42 52N 72 52W
Wilmont 44 43 46N 95 50W
Wilmore, Kans. 38 37 20N 99 13W
Wilmore, Ky. 63 37 52N 84 40W
Wilmot, Ark. 27 33 4N 91 34W
Wilmot, Kans. 38 37 22N 96 53W
Wilmot, S. Dak. 61 45 25N 96 52W
Wilsall 47 45 59N 110 38W
Wilsey 38 38 38N 96 41W
Wilson, Ark. 27 35 34N 90 3W
Wilson, Kans. 38 38 50N 98 29W
Wilson, La. 39 30 55N 91 7W
Wilson, N.C. 54 35 44N 77 55W
Wilson, N.Y. 53 43 19N 78 50W
Wilson, Okla. 57 34 10N 97 26W
Wilson, Tex. 64 33 19N 101 44W
Wilson, Mt. 30 37 50N 107 59W
Wilson County ◇, Kans. 38 37 30N 95 45W
Wilson County ◇, N.C. 54 35 45N 78 0W
Wilson County ◇, Tenn. 62 36 12N 86 18W
Wilson County ◇, Tex. 65 29 8N 98 10W
Wilson Creek 67 47 25N 119 7W
Wilson L. 24 34 48N 87 38W
Wilson Lake 38 38 58N 98 30W
Wilsons Mills 40 44 57N 71 2W
Wilsonville, Nebr. 48 40 7N 100 7W
Wilsonville, Oreg. 58 45 18N 122 46W
Wilton, Ark. 27 33 45N 94 9W
Wilton, Conn. 42 41 12N 73 26W
Wilton, Maine 40 44 36N 70 14W
Wilton, Minn. 44 47 30N 95 0W
Wilton, N. Dak. 55 47 10N 100 47W
Wilton, N.H. 50 42 51N 71 44W
Wilton, Wis. 69 43 49N 90 32W
Wimauma 31 27 43N 82 18W
Wimbledon 55 47 10N 98 28W
Winamac 36 41 3N 86 36W
Winchendon 42 42 41N 72 3W
Winchester, Ark. 27 33 47N 91 29W
Winchester, Idaho 34 46 14N 116 38W
Winchester, Ill. 35 39 38N 90 27W
Winchester, Ind. 36 40 10N 84 59W
Winchester, Ky. 63 38 0N 84 11W
Winchester, N.H. 50 42 46N 72 23W
Winchester, Tenn. 62 35 11N 86 7W
Winchester, Va. 68 39 11N 78 10W
Winchester Bay 58 43 41N 124 10W
Wind → 70 43 12N 108 12W
Wind Cave National Park 61 43 32N 103 17W
Wind Mt. 52 32 2N 105 31W
Wind Point 69 42 47N 87 46W
Wind River Indian Reservation 70 43 20N 109 0W
Wind River Pk. 70 42 42N 109 7W
Wind River Range 70 43 0N 109 30W
Windber 59 40 14N 78 50W
Windcrest 65 29 31N 98 19W
Winder 32 34 0N 83 45W
Windfall 36 40 22N 85 57W
Windham 40 43 49N 70 26W
Windham County ◇, Conn. 42 41 45N 72 0W
Windham County ◇, Vt. 50 43 0N 72 45W
Windom, Kans. 38 38 23N 97 55W
Windom, Minn. 44 43 52N 95 7W
Windom Pk. 30 37 35N 107 35W
Window Rock 26 35 41N 109 3W
Windsor, Colo. 30 40 29N 104 54W
Windsor, Conn. 42 41 50N 72 39W
Windsor, Ill. 35 39 26N 88 36W
Windsor, Mo. 46 38 32N 93 31W
Windsor, N.C. 54 36 0N 76 57W
Windsor, S.C. 60 33 29N 81 31W
Windsor, Va. 68 36 49N 76 45W
Windsor, Vt. 50 43 29N 72 24W
Windsor County ◇ 50 43 35N 72 35W
Windsor Forest 32 31 59N 81 5W
Windsor Hts. 37 41 36N 93 42W
Windsor Locks 42 41 56N 72 38W
Windthorst 65 33 34N 98 26W
Windy Pk. 67 48 56N 119 58W
Winema National Forest 58 43 10N 121 50W
Winfall 54 36 13N 76 28W
Winfield, Ala. 24 33 56N 87 49W
Winfield, Iowa 37 41 7N 91 26W
Winfield, Kans. 38 37 15N 96 59W
Winfield, Md. 41 39 26N 77 4W
Winfield, Mo. 46 39 0N 90 44W
Winfield, S. Dak. 61 44 0N 96 59W
Winfield, W. Va. 68 38 32N 81 54W
Winfred 61 44 0N 97 19W
Wing 55 47 9N 100 17W
Wingate 54 34 59N 80 26W
Winger 44 47 32N 95 59W
Wingo 62 36 39N 88 44W
Winifred 47 47 34N 109 23W
Winigan 46 40 3N 92 54W
Wink 64 31 45N 103 9W
Winkelman 26 32 59N 110 46W
Winkler County ◇ 64 31 52N 103 6W
Winlock 67 46 30N 122 56W
Winn Parish ◇ 39 31 56N 92 38W
Winnabow 54 34 9N 78 6W
Winnebago, Ill. 35 42 16N 89 15W
Winnebago, Minn. 44 43 46N 94 10W
Winnebago, Nebr. 48 42 14N 96 28W
Winnebago, L. 69 44 0N 88 26W
Winnebago County ◇, Ill. 35 42 20N 89 10W
Winnebago County ◇, Iowa 37 43 20N 93 40W
Winnebago County ◇, Wis. 69 44 0N 88 45W
Winnebago Indian Reservation 48 42 15N 96 40W
Winneconne 69 44 7N 88 43W
Winnemucca 49 40 58N 117 44W
Winnemucca L. 49 40 7N 119 21W
Winner 61 43 22N 99 52W
Winneshiek County ◇ 37 43 15N 91 50W
Winnetoon 48 42 31N 97 58W
Winnett 47 47 0N 108 21W
Winnfield 39 31 56N 92 38W
Winnibigoshish, L. 44 47 27N 94 13W
Winnie 65 29 49N 94 23W
Winnipesaukee 50 43 40N 71 20W
Winnipesaukee, L. 50 43 38N 71 21W
Winnisquam L. 50 43 33N 71 31W
Winnsboro, La. 39 32 10N 91 43W
Winnsboro, S.C. 60 34 23N 81 5W
Winnsboro, Tex. 65 32 58N 95 17W
Winona, Kans. 38 39 4N 101 15W
Winona, Minn. 44 44 3N 91 39W
Winona, Miss. 45 33 29N 89 44W
Winona, Mo. 46 37 1N 91 20W
Winona, Wash. 67 46 57N 117 48W
Winona County ◇ 44 44 0N 91 50W
Winona Lake 36 41 14N 85 49W
Winooski 50 44 29N 73 11W
Winooski → 50 44 32N 73 17W
Winside 48 42 11N 97 10W
Winslow, Ariz. 26 35 2N 110 42W
Winslow, Ark. 27 35 48N 94 8W
Winslow, Ind. 36 38 23N 87 13W
Winslow, Maine 40 44 33N 69 37W
Winslow, Nebr. 48 41 37N 96 30W
Winslow, Wash. 67 47 38N 122 31W
Winsted, Conn. 42 41 55N 73 4W
Winsted, Minn. 44 44 58N 94 3W
Winston, N. Mex. 52 33 20N 107 39W
Winston, Oreg. 58 45 7N 123 25W
Winston County ◇, Ala. 24 34 9N 87 24W
Winston County ◇, Miss. 45 33 7N 89 3W
Winston-Salem 54 36 6N 80 15W
Winter 69 45 49N 91 1W
Winter Beach 31 27 43N 80 25W
Winter Garden 31 28 34N 81 35W
Winter Harbor 40 44 24N 68 5W

Winter Haven 31 28 1N 81 44W
Winter Park, Colo. 30 39 53N 105 46W
Winter Park, Fla. 31 28 36N 81 20W
Winters 65 31 58N 99 58W
Winterset 37 41 20N 94 1W
Wintersville 56 40 23N 80 42W
Winterville, Maine 40 46 58N 68 34W
Winterville, N.C. 54 35 32N 77 24W
Winthrop, Ark. 27 33 50N 94 21W
Winthrop, Iowa 37 42 28N 91 44W
Winthrop, Maine 40 44 18N 69 58W
Winthrop, Minn. 44 44 32N 94 22W
Winthrop, Wash. 67 48 28N 120 10W
Winthrop Harbor 35 42 29N 87 50W
Winton, Calif. 28 37 23N 120 37W
Winton, Minn. 44 47 56N 91 48W
Winton, N.C. 54 36 24N 76 56W
Winton, Wyo. 70 41 45N 109 10W
Wiota, Iowa 37 41 24N 94 54W
Wiota, Wis. 69 42 39N 89 57W
Wirt County ◇ 68 39 4N 81 24W
Wisacky 60 34 9N 80 12W
Wiscasset 40 44 0N 69 40W
Wisconsin □ 69 44 45N 89 30W
Wisconsin → 69 43 0N 91 15W
Wisconsin Dells 69 43 38N 89 46W
Wisconsin L. 69 43 19N 89 44W
Wisconsin Rapids 69 44 23N 89 49W
Wisdom 47 45 37N 113 27W
Wise, N.C. 54 36 29N 78 10W
Wise, Va. 68 36 59N 82 35W
Wise County ◇, Tex. 65 33 14N 97 35W
Wise County ◇, Va. 68 37 0N 82 45W
Wise River 47 45 48N 112 57W
Wiseman 25 67 25N 150 6W
Wishek 55 46 16N 99 33W
Wishon Res. 29 36 50N 118 50W
Wishram 67 45 40N 120 58W
Wisner, La. 39 31 59N 91 39W
Wisner, Nebr. 48 41 59N 96 55W
Wissota L. 69 44 56N 91 20W
Wister 57 34 58N 94 43W
Withee 69 44 57N 90 36W
Withington Mt. 52 33 53N 107 29W
Withlacoochee →, Citrus, Fla. 31 29 0N 82 45W
Withlacoochee →, Hamilton, Fla. 31 30 24N 83 10W
Withrow 67 47 42N 119 48W
Witt 35 39 15N 89 21W
Witten 61 43 26N 100 5W
Wittenberg, Mo. 46 37 39N 89 31W
Wittenberg, Wis. 69 44 49N 89 10W
Wittman 41 38 48N 76 18W
Wittmann 26 33 47N 112 32W
Wixom 43 42 32N 83 32W
Woburn 42 42 29N 71 9W
Wolbach 48 41 24N 98 24W
Wolcott, Colo. 30 39 42N 106 40W
Wolcott, Conn. 42 41 36N 72 59W
Wolcott, Ind. 36 40 46N 87 3W
Wolcott, N.Y. 53 43 13N 76 49W
Wolcottville 36 41 32N 85 22W
Wolf 38 38 2N 101 6W
Wolf →, Miss. 45 30 22N 89 18W
Wolf →, Okla. 57 36 34N 99 34W
Wolf →, Tenn. 62 35 10N 89 5W
Wolf →, Wis. 69 44 11N 88 48W
Wolf Cr. → 47 47 37N 109 38W
Wolf Creek, Mont. 47 47 0N 112 4W
Wolf Creek, Oreg. 58 42 42N 123 24W
Wolf Creek Pass 30 37 29N 106 48W
Wolf Lake, Mich. 43 43 15N 86 7W
Wolf Lake, Minn. 44 46 48N 95 21W
Wolf Point 47 48 5N 105 39W
Wolfe City 65 33 22N 96 4W
Wolfe County ◇ 63 37 45N 83 30W
Wolfeboro 50 43 35N 71 13W
Wolfforth 64 33 30N 102 1W
Wolford 55 48 30N 99 42W
Wolfsville 41 39 37N 77 35W
Wolsey 61 44 25N 98 28W
Wolverine 43 45 17N 84 36W
Wolverine Peak 70 42 59N 109 22W
Wolverton 44 46 34N 96 44W
Wonalancet 50 43 44N 71 21W
Wood 61 43 30N 100 29W
Wood → 48 41 2N 98 5W
Wood County ◇, Ohio 56 41 23N 83 39W
Wood County ◇, Tex. 65 32 48N 95 27W
Wood County ◇, W. Va. 68 39 14N 81 34W
Wood County ◇, Wis. 69 44 20N 90 0W
Wood Lake, Minn. 44 44 39N 95 32W
Wood Lake, Nebr. 48 42 38N 100 14W
Wood River, Ill. 35 38 52N 90 5W
Wood River, Nebr. 48 40 49N 98 36W
Woodall Mt. 45 34 47N 88 15W
Woodberry 27 33 35N 92 31W
Woodbine, Ga. 32 30 58N 81 44W
Woodbine, Iowa 37 41 44N 95 43W
Woodbine, Kans. 38 38 48N 96 57W
Woodbine, Ky. 63 36 54N 84 5W
Woodbine, Md. 41 39 22N 77 4W
Woodbine, N.J. 51 39 15N 74 49W
Woodbourne 53 41 46N 74 36W
Woodbridge, Conn. 42 41 21N 73 2W
Woodbridge, Va. 68 38 40N 77 15W
Woodburn, Ind. 36 41 8N 84 51W
Woodburn, Iowa 37 41 1N 93 36W
Woodburn, Ky. 62 36 50N 86 32W
Woodburn, Oreg. 58 45 9N 122 51W
Woodbury, Conn. 42 41 33N 73 13W
Woodbury, Ga. 32 32 59N 84 35W
Woodbury, Ky. 62 37 11N 86 38W
Woodbury, N.J. 51 39 50N 75 9W
Woodbury, Tenn. 62 35 50N 86 4W
Woodbury County ◇ 37 42 25N 96 0W
Woodfin 54 35 38N 82 36W
Woodford, S.C. 60 33 40N 81 7W
Woodford, Vt. 50 42 52N 73 6W
Woodford County ◇, Ill. 35 40 50N 89 10W
Woodford County ◇, Ky. 63 38 0N 84 45W
Woodfords 28 38 47N 119 50W
Woodhull 35 41 11N 90 20W
Woodlake 29 36 25N 119 6W
Woodland, Calif. 28 38 41N 121 46W
Woodland, Ill. 35 40 43N 87 44W
Woodland, Maine 40 45 9N 67 25W
Woodland, Miss. 45 33 47N 89 3W
Woodland, N.C. 54 36 19N 77 12W
Woodland, Tex. 65 33 48N 95 17W
Woodland, Wash. 67 45 54N 122 45W
Woodland Beach 41 39 20N 75 28W
Woodland Park 30 38 57N 105 12W
Woodlawn 41 39 19N 76 44W
Woodman 69 43 7N 90 48W
Woodridge 53 41 43N 74 34W
Woodrow 64 33 27N 101 50W
Woodruff, Kans. 38 39 59N 99 19W
Woodruff, S.C. 60 34 45N 82 2W
Woodruff, Utah 66 41 31N 111 10W
Woodruff, Wis. 69 45 54N 89 42W
Woodruff, L. 31 29 6N 81 24W
Woodruff County ◇ 27 35 9N 91 21W
Woodruff Narrows Reservoir 70 41 31N 111 1W
Woods, L. of the 44 49 0N 94 0W
Woods County ◇ 57 36 45N 98 50W
Woods Cross 66 40 52N 111 58W
Woods Hole 42 41 31N 70 40W
Woodsboro, Md. 41 39 32N 77 19W
Woodsboro, Tex. 65 28 14N 97 20W
Woodsfield 56 39 46N 81 7W
Woodson, Ark. 27 34 32N 92 13W
Woodson, Tex. 65 33 1N 99 3W
Woodson County ◇ 38 37 50N 95 45W
Woodstock, Conn. 42 41 0N 72 0W
Woodstock, Ga. 32 34 6N 84 31W
Woodstock, Ill. 35 42 19N 88 27W
Woodstock, N.H. 50 43 57N 71 42W
Woodstock, Ohio 56 40 10N 83 32W
Woodstock, Va. 68 38 53N 78 30W
Woodstock, Vt. 50 43 37N 72 31W
Woodston 38 39 27N 99 6W
Woodstown 51 39 39N 75 20W
Woodsville 50 44 9N 72 2W
Woodville, Ala. 24 34 38N 86 17W
Woodville, Fla. 31 30 19N 84 15W
Woodville, Ga. 32 33 40N 83 7W
Woodville, Miss. 45 31 6N 91 18W
Woodville, Tex. 65 30 47N 94 25W
Woodward, Iowa 37 41 51N 93 55W
Woodward, Okla. 57 36 26N 99 24W
Woodward County ◇ 57 36 25N 99 15W
Woodway 65 31 30N 97 13W
Woodworth, La. 39 31 9N 92 30W
Woodworth, N. Dak. 55 47 9N 99 23W
Woody Creek 30 39 17N 106 54W
Woolridge 46 38 55N 92 32W
Woolstock 37 42 34N 93 51W
Woonsocket, R.I. 42 42 0N 71 31W
Woonsocket, S. Dak. 61 44 3N 98 17W
Wooster, Ark. 27 35 12N 92 27W
Wooster, Ohio 56 40 48N 81 56W
Worcester, Mass. 42 42 16N 71 48W
Worcester, N.Y. 53 42 36N 74 45W
Worcester, Vt. 50 44 20N 72 40W
Worcester County ◇, Mass. 42 42 25N 72 0W
Worcester County ◇, Md. 41 38 15N 75 20W
Worden, Ill. 35 38 56N 89 50W
Worden, Mont. 47 45 58N 108 10W
Worden, Oreg. 58 42 2N 121 52W
Worland 70 44 1N 107 57W
Worley 34 47 24N 116 55W
Woronoco 42 42 10N 72 50W
Worth 46 40 24N 94 27W
Worth County ◇, Ga. 32 31 30N 83 50W
Worth County ◇, Iowa 37 43 20N 93 15W
Worth County ◇, Mo. 46 40 30N 94 25W
Wortham 65 31 47N 96 28W
Worthing 61 43 20N 96 46W
Worthington, Ind. 36 39 7N 86 59W
Worthington, Iowa 37 42 24N 91 7W
Worthington, Minn. 44 43 37N 95 36W
Worthington, Ohio 56 40 5N 83 1W
Worthington, Pa. 59 40 50N 79 38W
Worton 41 39 17N 76 6W
Wounded Knee 61 43 8N 102 22W
Wrangell 25 56 28N 132 23W
Wrangell I. 25 56 16N 132 12W
Wrangell Mts. 25 61 30N 142 0W
Wrangell-Petersburg ◇ 25 57 0N 134 0W
Wray 30 40 5N 102 13W
Wren, Ala. 24 34 26N 87 18W
Wren, Ohio 56 40 48N 84 47W
Wrens 32 33 12N 82 23W
Wrenshall 44 46 37N 92 23W
Wrentham 42 42 4N 71 20W
Wright 38 37 47N 99 54W
Wright City, Mo. 46 38 50N 91 1W
Wright City, Okla. 57 34 5N 95 0W
Wright County ◇, Iowa 37 42 45N 93 40W
Wright County ◇, Minn. 44 45 10N 94 0W
Wright County ◇, Mo. 46 37 15N 92 30W
Wrightson Mt. 26 31 42N 110 51W
Wrightstown, N.J. 51 40 2N 74 37W
Wrightstown, Wis. 69 44 20N 88 10W
Wrightsville, Ark. 27 34 36N 92 13W
Wrightsville, Ga. 32 32 44N 82 43W
Wrightsville Beach 54 34 12N 77 48W
Wrigley 62 35 54N 87 21W
Wupatki National Monument 26 35 35N 111 20W
Wyaconda 46 40 24N 91 55W
Wyalusing 59 41 40N 76 16W
Wyandot County ◇ 56 40 50N 83 17W
Wyandotte, Mich. 43 42 12N 83 9W
Wyandotte, Okla. 57 36 48N 94 44W
Wyandotte County ◇ 38 39 10N 94 45W
Wyarno 70 44 49N 106 46W
Wyatt, La. 39 32 9N 92 42W
Wyatt, Mo. 46 36 55N 89 13W
Wyeville 69 44 2N 90 23W
Wykoff 44 43 42N 92 16W
Wylie 65 33 1N 96 33W
Wylie, L. 60 35 1N 81 1W
Wymore 48 40 7N 96 40W
Wyndmere 55 46 16N 97 8W
Wynne 27 35 14N 90 47W
Wynnewood 57 34 39N 97 10W
Wynona 57 36 33N 96 20W
Wynot 48 42 45N 97 10W
Wyocena 69 43 30N 89 17W
Wyoconda → 46 40 2N 91 34W
Wyodak 70 44 17N 105 22W
Wyoming, Del. 41 39 7N 75 34W
Wyoming, Ill. 35 41 4N 89 47W
Wyoming, Iowa 37 42 4N 91 0W
Wyoming, Mich. 43 42 54N 85 42W
Wyoming □ 70 43 0N 107 30W
Wyoming County ◇, N.Y. 53 42 40N 78 15W
Wyoming County ◇, Pa. 59 41 30N 76 5W
Wyoming County ◇, W. Va. 68 37 35N 81 32W
Wyoming Pk. 70 42 36N 110 37W
Wyoming Range 70 42 55N 110 52W
Wyomissing 59 40 20N 75 59W
Wythe County ◇ 68 37 0N 81 5W
Wytheville 68 36 57N 81 5W

X

Xenia, Ill. 35 38 38N 88 38W
Xenia, Ohio 56 39 41N 83 56W

Y

Yaak 47 48 50N 115 43W
Yabucoa 71 18 3N 65 53W
Yabucoa, Puerto 71 18 8N 65 48W
Yachats 58 44 19N 124 6W
Yacolt 67 45 51N 122 24W
Yadkin → 54 35 29N 80 9W
Yadkin County ◇ 54 36 10N 80 40W
Yadkinville 54 36 8N 80 39W
Yakima 67 46 36N 120 31W
Yakima → 67 46 15N 119 14W
Yakima County ◇ 67 46 30N 120 30W
Yakima Indian Reservation 67 46 10N 120 30W
Yakutat 25 59 33N 139 44W
Yakutat B. 25 59 45N 140 45W
Yale, Ill. 35 39 7N 88 2W
Yale, Iowa 37 41 47N 94 21W
Yale, Mich. 43 43 8N 82 48W
Yale, Okla. 57 36 7N 96 42W
Yale, S. Dak. 61 44 26N 97 59W
Yale, Va. 68 36 51N 77 17W
Yale L. 67 45 58N 122 20W
Yalobusha → 45 33 33N 90 10W
Yalobusha County ◇ 45 33 59N 89 41W
Yamhill County ◇ 58 45 15N 123 10W
Yampa 30 40 9N 106 55W
Yampa → 30 40 32N 108 59W
Yamsay Mt. 58 42 56N 121 22W
Yancey 65 29 8N 99 9W
Yancey County ◇ 54 35 50N 82 20W
Yanceyville 54 36 24N 79 20W
Yankton 61 42 53N 97 23W
Yankton County ◇ 61 43 0N 97 30W
Yanush 57 34 43N 95 19W
Yaquina Head 58 44 41N 124 5W
Yarbo 24 31 32N 88 17W
Yardville 51 40 11N 74 40W
Yarmouth 40 43 48N 70 11W
Yarnell 26 34 13N 112 45W
Yates Center 38 37 53N 95 44W
Yates City 35 40 47N 90 1W
Yates County ◇ 53 42 40N 77 10W
Yatesboro 59 40 48N 79 20W
Yatesville 32 32 55N 84 9W
Yauco 71 18 2N 66 51W
Yauco, Rio → 71 17 59N 66 49W
Yavapai County ◇ 26 34 30N 112 30W
Yazoo → 45 32 22N 90 54W
Yazoo City 45 32 51N 90 25W
Yazoo County ◇ 45 32 50N 90 25W
Yeager 57 35 9N 96 21W
Yeguas, Punta 71 18 1N 65 50W
Yell County ◇ 27 35 3N 93 24W
Yellow →, Fla. 31 30 30N 87 0W
Yellow →, Ind. 36 41 16N 86 50W
Yellow →, Burnett, Wis. 69 46 1N 92 22W
Yellow →, Chippewa, Wis. 69 44 58N 91 18W
Yellow Jacket 30 37 32N 108 43W
Yellow Medicine County ◇ 44 44 40N 95 45W
Yellow Pine 34 44 58N 115 30W
Yellow Springs 56 39 48N 83 53W
Yellowstone → 47 47 59N 103 59W
Yellowstone County ◇ 47 46 10N 108 0W
Yellowstone L. 70 44 27N 110 22W
Yellowstone National Park 70 44 40N 110 30W
Yellville 27 36 14N 92 41W
Yelm 67 46 57N 122 36W
Yemassee 60 32 41N 80 51W
Yeoman 36 40 40N 86 44W
Yerington 49 38 59N 119 10W
Yermo 29 34 54N 116 50W
Yeso 52 34 26N 104 37W
Yetter 37 42 19N 94 51W
Yoakum 65 29 17N 97 9W
Yoakum County ◇ 64 33 11N 102 50W
Yocona → 45 34 11N 90 10W
Yoder 70 41 55N 104 18W
Yogo Pk. 47 46 56N 110 32W
Yolo County ◇ 28 38 45N 121 50W
Yoncalla 58 43 36N 123 17W
Yonkers 53 40 56N 73 54W
York, Ala. 24 32 29N 88 18W
York, N. Dak. 55 48 19N 99 34W
York, Nebr. 48 40 52N 97 36W
York, Pa. 59 39 58N 76 44W
York, S.C. 60 35 0N 81 12W
York → 68 37 15N 76 23W
York County ◇, Maine 40 43 25N 70 50W
York County ◇, Nebr. 48 40 45N 97 40W
York County ◇, Pa. 59 39 58N 76 44W
York County ◇, S.C. 60 34 55N 81 10W
York County ◇, Va. 68 37 14N 76 30W
York Springs 59 40 0N 77 7W
Yorktown, Ark. 27 34 1N 91 49W
Yorktown, Ind. 36 40 10N 85 30W
Yorktown, Tex. 65 28 59N 97 30W
Yorktown, Va. 68 37 14N 76 30W
Yorkville, Ga. 32 33 55N 84 58W
Yorkville, Ill. 35 41 38N 88 27W
Yosemite 63 37 21N 84 50W
Yosemite National Park 28 37 45N 119 40W

Yosemite Village ... 28 37 45N 119 35W
Yost ... 66 41 58N 113 33W
Youghiogheny → .. 59 40 22N 79 52W
Youghiogheny Reservoir ... 41 39 48N 79 22W
Young County ◇ ... 65 33 12N 98 44W
Young Harris ... 32 34 56N 83 51W
Youngstown, Fla. .. 31 30 22N 85 26W
Youngstown, N.Y. . 53 43 15N 79 3W
Youngstown, Ohio . 56 41 6N 80 39W
Youngsville, La. ... 39 30 3N 92 0W
Youngsville, N.C. .. 54 36 1N 78 29W
Youngsville, N. Mex. ... 52 36 11N 106 34W
Youngsville, Pa. ... 59 41 51N 79 19W
Yountville ... 28 38 24N 122 22W
Ypsilanti, Mich. ... 43 42 14N 83 37W
Ypsilanti, N. Dak... 55 46 47N 98 34W
Yreka ... 28 41 44N 122 38W
Yuba ... 69 43 33N 90 26W
Yuba City ... 28 39 8N 121 37W
Yuba County ◇ ... 28 39 15N 121 30W
Yucca ... 26 34 52N 114 9W
Yucca House National Monument ... 30 37 16N 108 38W
Yucca L. ... 49 36 57N 116 2W
Yucca Valley ... 29 34 8N 116 27W
Yukon ... 57 35 31N 97 45W
Yukon → ... 25 62 32N 163 54W
Yukon-Koyukuk ◇ . 25 65 0N 154 0W
Yulee ... 31 30 38N 81 36W
Yuma, Ariz. ... 26 32 43N 114 37W
Yuma, Colo. ... 30 40 8N 102 43W
Yuma County ◇, Ariz. ... 26 33 30N 114 0W
Yuma County ◇, Colo. ... 30 40 0N 102 20W
Yuma Desert ... 26 32 25N 110 30W
Yunaska I. ... 25 52 38N 170 40W
Yutan ... 48 41 15N 96 24W

Z

Zachary ... 39 30 39N 91 9W
Zahl ... 55 48 34N 103 42W
Zaleski ... 56 39 17N 82 24W
Zalma ... 46 37 9N 90 5W
Zama ... 45 32 59N 89 23W
Zanesville ... 56 39 56N 82 1W
Zap ... 55 47 17N 101 55W
Zapata ... 64 26 55N 99 16W
Zapata County ◇ ... 64 27 0N 99 0W
Zavala County ◇ ... 65 28 57N 99 51W
Zavalla ... 65 31 10N 94 26W
Zearing ... 37 42 10N 93 18W
Zebulon, Ga. ... 32 33 6N 84 21W
Zebulon, Ky. ... 63 37 32N 82 28W
Zebulon, N.C. ... 54 35 49N 78 19W
Zeeland, Mich. ... 43 42 49N 86 1W
Zeeland, N. Dak. .. 55 45 58N 99 50W
Zeigler ... 35 37 54N 89 3W
Zelienople ... 59 40 48N 80 8W
Zell ... 61 44 54N 98 44W
Zenda ... 38 37 27N 98 17W
Zephyr Cove ... 49 39 0N 119 57W
Zephyrhills ... 31 28 14N 82 11W
Zia Indian Reservation ... 52 35 30N 106 50W
Ziebach County ◇ .. 61 45 0N 101 50W
Zillah ... 67 46 24N 120 16W
Zimmerman ... 44 45 37N 93 34W
Zion ... 35 42 27N 87 50W
Zion National Park . 66 37 15N 113 5W
Zion Reservoir ... 26 34 37N 109 29W
Zionsville ... 36 39 57N 86 16W
Zirkel, Mt. ... 30 40 50N 106 40W
Zolfo Springs ... 31 27 30N 81 48W
Zorra I. ... 71 9 18N 79 52W
Zumbro Falls ... 44 44 17N 92 26W
Zumbrota ... 44 44 17N 92 40W
Zuni ... 52 35 4N 108 51W
Zuni → ... 26 34 39N 109 40W
Zuni Indian Reservation ... 52 35 0N 108 50W
Zuni Mts. ... 52 35 10N 108 30W
Zurich ... 38 39 14N 99 26W
Zwingle ... 37 42 18N 90 41W
Zwolle ... 39 31 38N 93 39W

World Index

A

Aachen .... **146** 50 47N 6 4 E
Aadorf .... **149** 47 30N 8 55 E
A'âlâ en Nîl □ ..... **245** 8 50N 29 55 E
Aalen .... **147** 48 49N 10 6 E
Aalsmeer .... **142** 52 17N 4 43 E
Aalst .... **143** 50 56N 4 2 E
Aalten .... **142** 51 56N 6 35 E
Aalter .... **143** 51 5N 3 28 E
Aarau .... **148** 47 23N 8 4 E
Aarberg .... **148** 47 2N 7 16 E
Aardenburg .... **143** 51 16N 3 28 E
Aare → .... **148** 47 33N 8 14 E
Aargau □ .... **148** 47 26N 8 10 E
Aarle .... **143** 51 30N 5 38 E
Aarschot .... **143** 50 59N 4 49 E
Aarsele .... **143** 51 0N 3 26 E
Aartrijke .... **143** 51 7N 3 6 E
Aarwangen .... **148** 47 15N 7 46 E
Aba, China .... **216** 32 59N 101 42 E
Aba, Nigeria .... **247** 5 10N 7 19 E
Aba, Zaïre .... **250** 3 58N 30 17 E
Âbâ, Jazîrat .... **245** 13 30N 32 31 E
Abacaxis → .... **119** 3 54 S 58 47W
Ābādān .... **193** 30 22N 48 20 E
Abade .... **245** 9 22N 38 3 E
Ābādeh .... **193** 31 8N 52 40 E
Abadin **154** 43 21N 7 29W
Abadla **240** 31 2N 2 45W
Abaeté .... **121** 19 9 S 45 27W
Abaeté → .... **121** 18 2 S 45 12W
Abaetetuba .... **120** 1 40 S 48 50W
Abagnar Qi .... **214** 43 52N 116 2 E
Abai .... **125** 25 58 S 55 54W
Abak .... **247** 4 58N 7 50 E
Abakaliki .... **247** 6 22N 8 2 E
Abakan .... **185** 53 40N 91 10 E
Abal Nam .... **244** 25 20N 38 37 E
Abalemma .... **247** 16 12N 7 50 E
Abamasagi L. **87** 50 28N 87 15W
Abancay .... **122** 13 35 S 72 55W
Abanilla **157** 38 12N 1 3W
Abano Terme .... **163** 45 22N 11 46 E
Abapó .... **123** 18 48 S 63 25W
Abarán **157** 38 12N 1 23W
Abariringa I. .... **224** 2 50 S 171 40W
Abarqū .... **193** 31 10N 53 20 E
'Abasān .... **189** 31 19N 34 21 E
Abashiri .... **218** 44 0N 144 15 E
Abashiri-Wan .... **218** 44 0N 144 30 E
Abasolo, Coahuila, Mexico **102** 27 12N 101 24W
Abasolo, Durango, Mexico **105** 25 18N 104 40W
Abasolo, Guanajuato, Mexico **107** 20 27N 101 32W
Abasolo, Tamaulipas, Mexico **103** 24 4N 98 22W
Abau .... **227** 10 11 S 148 46 E
Abaújszántó .... **151** 48 16N 21 12 E
Abay .... **184** 49 38N 72 53 E
Abaya, L. .... **245** 6 30N 37 50 E
Abaza .... **184** 52 39N 90 6 E
Abbadia San Salvatore .... **163** 42 53N 11 40 E
'Abbāsābād .... **193** 33 34N 58 23 E
Abbay = Nîl el Azraq → .... **245** 15 38N 32 31 E
Abbé, L. .... **245** 11 8N 41 47 E
Abbeville .... **139** 50 6N 1 49 E
Abbey **88** 50 44N 108 45W
Abbiategrasso .... **162** 45 23N 8 55 E
Abbieglassie .... **231** 27 15 S 147 28 E
Abbot Ice Shelf .... **13** 73 0 S 92 0W
Abbotsford **93** 49 5N 122 20W
Abbottabad .... **198** 34 10N 73 15 E
Abcoude .... **142** 52 17N 4 59 E
Abd al Kūrī .... **195** 12 5N 52 20 E
Ābdar .... **193** 30 16N 55 19 E
'Abdolābād .... **193** 34 12N 56 30 E
Abdulino .... **182** 53 42N 53 40 E
Abéché .... **243** 13 50N 20 35 E
Abejar **156** 41 48N 2 47W
Abekr .... **245** 12 45N 28 50 E
Abêlessa .... **240** 22 58N 4 47 E
Abengourou **246** 6 42N 3 27W
Åbenrå .... **173** 55 3N 9 25 E
Abensberg .... **147** 48 49N 11 51 E
Abeokuta .... **247** 7 3N 3 19 E
Aber .... **250** 2 12N 32 25 E
Aberaeron **133** 52 15N 4 16W
Aberayron = Aberaeron **133** 52 15N 4 16W
Abercorn = Mbala .... **251** 8 46 S 31 24 E
Abercorn .... **231** 25 12 S 151 5 E
Aberdare **133** 51 43N 3 27W
Aberdare Ra. .... **250** 0 15 S 36 50 E
Aberdeen, Australia **231** 32 9 S 150 56 E
Aberdeen, Canada **88** 52 20N 106 8W
Aberdeen, S. Africa **254** 32 28 S 24 2 E
Aberdeen, U.K. **134** 57 9N 2 6W
Aberdovey **133** 52 33N 4 3W
Aberfeldy, Australia **233** 37 42 S 146 22 E
Aberfeldy, U.K. **134** 56 37N 3 50W
Abergaria-a-Velha **154** 40 41N 8 32W
Abergavenny **133** 51 49N 3 1W
Abernethy **88** 50 45N 103 25W
Aberystwyth **133** 52 25N 4 6W
Abha .... **244** 18 0N 42 34 E
Abhar .... **193** 36 9N 49 13 E
Abhayapuri .... **202** 26 24N 90 38 E
Abidiya .... **244** 18 18N 34 3 E
Abidjan **246** 5 26N 3 58W
Abingdon **133** 51 40N 1 17W
Abington Reef .... **230** 18 0 S 149 35 E
Abitau → **77** 59 53N 109 3W
Abitau L. **77** 60 27N 107 15W
Abitibi → **87** 51 3N 80 55W
Abitibi L. **74** 48 40N 79 40W
Abiy Adi .... **245** 13 39N 39 3 E
Abkhaz A.S.S.R. □ **181** 43 0N 41 0 E
Abkit .... **185** 64 10N 157 10 E
Abminga .... **231** 26 8 S 134 51 E
Abnûb .... **244** 27 18N 31 4 E
Åbo .... **175** 60 28N 22 15 E
Abo, Massif d' .... **241** 21 41N 16 8 E
Abocho .... **247** 7 35N 6 56 E
Abohar .... **198** 30 10N 74 10 E
Aboisso **246** 5 30N 3 5W
Abolo .... **252** 0 8N 14 16 E
Aboméy .... **247** 7 10N 2 5 E
Abondance .... **141** 46 18N 6 42 E
Abong-Mbang .... **252** 4 0N 13 8 E
Abongabong .... **208** 4 15N 96 48 E
Abonnema .... **247** 4 41N 6 49 E
Abony .... **151** 47 12N 20 3 E
Aboso **246** 5 23N 1 57W
Abou-Deïa .... **243** 11 20N 19 20 E
Abou Goulem .... **243** 13 37N 21 38 E
Aboyne **134** 57 4N 2 48W
Abra □ .... **210** 17 35N 120 45 E
Abra de Ilog .... **210** 13 27N 120 44 E
Abra Pampa .... **124** 22 43 S 65 42W
Abraham González **105** 24 14N 104 30W
Abrantes **155** 39 24N 8 7W
Abraveses **154** 40 41N 7 55W
Abreojos, Pta. **99** 26 42N 113 35W
Abreschviller .... **139** 48 39N 7 6 E
Abrets, Les .... **141** 45 32N 5 35 E
Abri, Esh Shamâliya, Sudan .... **244** 20 50N 30 27 E
Abri, Janub Kordofân, Sudan .... **245** 11 40N 30 21 E
Abrolhos, Banka .... **121** 18 0 S 38 0W
Abrud .... **170** 46 19N 23 5 E
Abruzzi □ .... **163** 42 15N 14 0 E
Abū al Khaşīb .... **192** 30 25N 48 0 E
Abū 'Alī .... **193** 27 20N 49 27 E
Abū 'Alī → .... **190** 34 25N 35 50 E
Abu 'Arīsh, Si. Arabia .... **188** 16 53N 42 48 E
Abū 'Arīsh, Si. Arabia .... **194** 16 58N 45 20 E
Abû Ballas .... **244** 24 26N 27 36 E
Abu Deleiq .... **245** 15 57N 33 48 E
Abu Dhabi = Abū Ẓāby .... **195** 24 28N 54 22 E
Abū Dīs, Jordan .... **189** 31 47N 35 16 E
Abû Dis, Sudan .... **244** 19 12N 33 38 E
Abû Dom .... **245** 16 18N 32 25 E
Abū Du'ān .... **192** 36 25N 38 15 E
Abu el Gairi, W. → .... **191** 29 35N 33 30 E
Abû Gabra .... **245** 11 2N 26 50 E
Abu Ga'da, W. → .... **191** 29 15N 32 53 E
Abū Ghaush .... **189** 31 48N 35 6 E
Abû Gubeiha .... **245** 11 30N 31 15 E
Abu Habl, Khawr → .... **245** 12 37N 31 0 E
Abū Ḩadrīyah .... **193** 27 20N 48 58 E
Abu Hamed .... **244** 19 32N 33 13 E
Abu Haraz, An Nîl el Azraq, Sudan .... **245** 14 35N 33 30 E
Abû Haraz, Esh Shamâliya, Sudan .... **244** 19 8N 32 18 E
Abû Higar .... **245** 12 50N 33 59 E
Abū Kamāl .... **192** 34 30N 41 0 E
Abū Madd, Ra's .... **192** 24 50N 37 7 E
Abu Qir .... **244** 31 18N 30 0 E
Abu Qireiya .... **244** 24 5N 35 28 E
Abu Qurqâs .... **244** 28 1N 30 44 E
Abū Raşāş, Ra's .... **195** 20 10N 58 38 E
Abū Rubayq .... **194** 23 44N 39 42 E
Abu Rudeis .... **191** 28 54N 33 11 E
Abu Şafāt, W. → .... **191** 30 24N 36 7 E
Abu Salama .... **244** 27 10N 35 51 E
Abû Simbel .... **244** 22 18N 31 40 E
Abū Şukhayr .... **192** 31 54N 44 30 E
Abu Tig .... **244** 27 4N 31 15 E
Abu Tiga .... **245** 12 47N 34 12 E
Abû Zabad .... **245** 12 25N 29 10 E
Abū Ẓāby .... **195** 24 28N 54 22 E
Abū Zeydābād .... **193** 33 54N 51 45 E
Abufari .... **123** 5 25 S 62 59W
Abuja .... **247** 9 16N 7 2 E
Abukuma-Gawa → **218** 38 6N 140 52 E
Abukuma-Sammyaku .... **218** 37 30N 140 45 E
Abulug .... **210** 18 27N 121 27 E
Abumombazi .... **252** 3 42N 22 10 E
Abunã .... **123** 9 40 S 65 20W
Abunã → .... **123** 9 41 S 65 20W
Abung .... **210** 13 46N 121 26 E
Aburatsu .... **220** 31 34N 131 24 E
Aburo, Mt. .... **250** 2 4N 30 53 E
Abut Hd. .... **235** 43 7 S 170 15 E
Abuya **104** 24 9N 107 4W
Abwong .... **245** 9 2N 32 14 E
Åby .... **173** 58 40N 16 10 E
Aby, Lagune **246** 5 15N 3 14W
Acacías **118** 3 59N 73 46W
Acacoyagua **110** 15 21N 92 39W
Acadia Valley **91** 51 8N 110 13W
Acajutla **112** 13 36N 89 50W
Acala **110** 16 34N 92 48W
Açallândia .... **120** 5 0 S 47 50W
Acámbaro **107** 20 2N 100 44W
Acancéh **111** 20 49N 89 27W
Acanthus .... **168** 40 27N 23 47 E
Acapetagua **110** 15 17N 92 42W
Acaponeta **104** 22 30N 105 22W
Acaponeta, R. → **104** 22 20N 105 37W
Acapulco de Juárez **107** 16 51N 99 55W
Acarai, Serra **119** 1 50N 57 50W
Acaraú .... **120** 2 53 S 40 7W
Acari, Brazil .... **120** 6 31 S 36 38W
Acarí, Peru .... **122** 15 25 S 74 36W
Acarigua **118** 9 33N 69 12W
Acatián, R. → **109** 18 5N 98 19W
Acatic **106** 20 47N 102 53W
Acatlán, Hidalgo, Mexico **107** 20 9N 98 27W
Acatlán, Oaxaca, Mexico **109** 18 32N 96 37W
Acatlán de Juárez **106** 20 26N 103 38W
Acatlán de Osorio **109** 18 12N 98 3W
Acatzingo de Hidalgo **109** 18 39N 97 47W
Acaxochitlán **107** 20 10N 98 12W
Acayucan **109** 17 57N 94 55W
Accéglio .... **162** 44 28N 6 59 E
Accra **247** 5 35N 0 6W
Accrington **132** 53 46N 2 22W
Acebal .... **124** 33 20 S 60 50W
Acebuches **102** 28 15N 102 43W
Aceh □ .... **206** 4 15N 97 30 E
Acerenza .... **165** 40 50N 15 58 E
Acerra .... **165** 40 57N 14 22 E
Aceuchal **155** 38 39N 6 30W
Achacachi .... **122** 16 3 S 68 43W
Achaguas **118** 7 46N 68 14W
Achalpur .... **198** 21 22N 77 32 E
Achao .... **126** 42 28 S 73 30W
Achel .... **143** 51 15N 5 29 E
Acheng .... **215** 45 30N 126 58 E
Achenkirch .... **150** 47 32N 11 45 E
Achensee .... **150** 47 26N 11 45 E
Acher .... **198** 23 10N 72 32 E
Achern .... **147** 48 37N 8 5 E
Acheron → .... **235** 42 16 S 173 4 E
Achill **135** 53 56N 9 55W
Achill Hd. **135** 53 59N 10 15W
Achill I. **135** 53 58N 10 5W
Achill Sound **135** 53 53N 9 55W
Achim .... **146** 53 1N 9 2 E
Achinsk .... **185** 56 20N 90 20 E
Achisay .... **183** 43 35N 68 53 E
Achit .... **182** 56 48N 57 54 E
Achol .... **245** 6 35N 31 32 E
Achotal **109** 17 44N 95 10W
Acireale .... **165** 37 37N 15 9 E
Acklins I. **113** 22 30N 74 0W
Acme **91** 51 33N 113 30W
Acobamba .... **122** 12 52 S 74 35W
Acomayo .... **122** 13 55 S 71 38W
Aconcagua □, Argentina .... **124** 32 50 S 70 0W
Aconcagua □, Chile **124** 32 15 S 70 30W

Aconcagua, Cerro 124 32 39 S 70 0W
Aconchi 100 29 50N 110 12W
Aconchi, Sa. de 100 29 52N 110 26W
Aconquija, Mt. 124 27 0 S 66 0W
Acopiara 120 6 6 S 39 27W
Acopinalco del Peñón 107 19 40N 98 10W
Açores, Is. dos = Azores 128 38 44N 29 0W
Acorizal 123 15 12 S 56 22W
Acquapendente 163 42 45N 11 50 E
Acquasanta 163 42 46N 13 24 E
Acquaviva delle Fonti 165 40 53N 16 50 E
Acqui 162 44 40N 8 28 E
Acre = 'Akko 189 32 55N 35 4 E
Acre □ 122 9 1 S 71 0W
Acre → 122 8 45 S 67 22W
Acri 165 39 29N 16 23 E
Acs 151 47 42N 18 0 E
Actium 168 38 57N 20 45 E
Acton 84 43 38N 80 3W
Acton Vale 83 45 39N 72 34W
Actopán, Hidalgo, Mexico 107 20 16N 98 56W
Actopan, Veracruz, Mexico 108 19 30N 96 37W
Actopan, R. → 108 19 25N 96 20W
Açu 120 5 34 S 36 54W
Acuitzio del Canje 107 19 29N 101 20W
Acula 109 18 31N 95 47W
Aculco 107 20 7N 99 49W
Acuña 102 29 18N 100 55W
Ad Dahnā 195 24 30N 48 10 E
Aḍ Ḍālī' 194 13 42N 44 44 E
Ad Dammām 193 26 20N 50 5 E
Ad Darb 194 18 2N 43 7 E
Ad Dawhah 195 25 15N 51 35 E
Ad Dawr 192 34 27N 43 47 E
Aḍ Ḍiffah 242 30 30N 25 30 E
Ad Dilam 194 23 55N 47 10 E
Ad Dir'īyah 192 24 44N 46 35 E
Ad Dīwānīyah 192 32 0N 45 0 E
Ad Dujayl 192 33 51N 44 14 E
Ad Durūz, J. 191 32 35N 36 40 E
Ada, Ghana 247 5 44N 0 40 E
Ada, Yugoslavia 166 45 49N 20 9 E
Adad 256 9 27N 46 49 E
Adair, B. de 100 31 30N 113 48W
Adaja → 154 41 32N 4 52W
Ådalslinden 172 63 27N 16 55 E
Adam 195 22 15N 57 28 E
Adam, Mt. 126 51 34 S 60 4W
Adamantina 121 21 42 S 51 4W
Adamaoua, Massif de l' 252 7 20N 12 20 E
Adamawa Highlands = Adamaoua, Massif de l' 252 7 20N 12 20 E
Adamello, Mt. 162 46 10N 10 34 E
Adami Tulu 245 7 53N 38 41 E
Adaminaby 231 36 0 S 148 45 E
Adamovka 182 51 32N 59 56 E
Adams 210 18 28N 120 54 E
Adams → 93 51 25N 119 27W
Adam's Bridge 201 9 15N 79 40 E
Adams L. 93 51 10N 119 40W
Adam's Peak 201 6 48N 80 30 E
Adamuz 155 38 2N 4 32W
Adana 177 37 0N 35 16 E
Adana □ 190 37 0N 35 30 E
Adanero 154 40 56N 4 36W
Adapazarı 177 40 48N 30 25 E
Adarama 245 17 10N 34 52 E
Adare, C. 13 71 0 S 171 0 E
Adaut 207 8 8 S 131 7 E
Adavale 231 25 52 S 144 32 E
Adda → 162 45 8N 9 53 E
Addis Ababa = Addis Abeba 245 9 2N 38 42 E
Addis Abeba 245 9 2N 38 42 E
Addis Alem 245 9 0N 38 17 E
Addu Atoll 187 0 30 S 73 0 E
Adebour 247 13 17N 11 50 E
Ādeh 192 37 42N 45 11 E
Adelaide, Australia 232 34 52 S 138 30 E
Adelaide, Bahamas 112 25 0N 77 31W
Adelaide, Madag. 255 32 42 S 26 20 E
Adelaide I. 13 67 15 S 68 30W
Adelaide Pen. 95 68 15N 97 30W
Adelaide River 228 13 15 S 131 7 E
Adelboden 148 46 29N 7 33 E
Adele, I. 228 15 32 S 123 9 E
Adélie, Terre 13 68 0 S 140 0 E
Ademuz 156 40 5N 1 13W
Aden = Al 'Adan 194 12 45N 45 0 E
Aden, G. of 188 13 0N 50 0 E
Adendorp 254 32 25 S 24 30 E
Adgz 240 30 47N 6 30W
Adh Dhayd 195 25 17N 55 53 E
Adhoi 198 23 26N 70 32 E
Adi 207 4 15 S 133 30 E
Adi Daro 245 14 20N 38 14 E
Adi Keyih 245 14 51N 39 22 E
Adi Kwala 245 14 38N 38 48 E
Adi Ugri 245 14 58N 38 48 E
Adieu, C. 229 32 0 S 132 10 E
Adieu Pt. 228 15 14 S 124 35 E
Adigala 245 10 24N 42 15 E
Adige → 163 45 9N 12 20 E
Adigrat 245 14 20N 39 26 E
Adilabad 200 19 33N 78 20 E
Adinkerke 143 51 5N 2 36 E
Adjim 241 33 47N 10 50 E
Adjohon 247 6 41N 2 32 E
Adjud 170 46 7N 27 10 E
Adjumani 250 3 20N 31 50 E
Adjuntas, Presa de las 103 23 57N 98 42W
Adjuntas del Refugio 105 22 39N 103 24W
Adlavik Is. 78 55 2N 57 45W
Adler 181 43 28N 39 52 E
Adliswil 149 47 19N 8 32 E
Admer 241 20 21N 5 27 E
Admer, Erg d' 241 24 0N 9 5 E
Admiral 88 49 43N 108 1W
Admiral's Beach 79 47 1N 53 39W
Admiralty G. 228 14 20 S 125 55 E
Admiralty I. 95 69 25N 101 10W
Admiralty Inlet 95 72 30N 86 0W
Admiralty Is. 227 2 0 S 147 0 E
Ado 247 6 36N 2 56 E
Ado Ekiti 247 7 38N 5 12 E
Adok 245 8 10N 30 20 E
Adola 245 11 14N 41 44 E
Adolfo López Mateos, Presa 104 25 10N 107 24W
Adonara 207 8 15 S 123 5 E
Adoni 201 15 33N 77 18W
Adony 151 47 6N 18 52 E
Adour → 140 43 32N 1 32W
Adra, India 199 23 30N 86 42 E
Adra, Spain 157 36 43N 3 3W
Adrano 165 37 40N 14 49 E
Adrar 240 27 51N 0 11W
Adrasman 183 40 38N 69 58 E
Adré 243 13 40N 22 20 E
Adrī 241 27 32N 13 2 E
Ádria 163 45 4N 12 3 E
Adriatic Sea 158 43 0N 16 0 E
Adua 207 1 45 S 129 50 E
Aduana 100 27 3N 109 0W
Adula 149 46 30N 9 3 E
Adung Long 202 28 7N 97 42 E
Adur 201 9 8N 76 40 E
Advocate Harbour 81 45 20N 64 47W
Adwa 245 14 15N 38 52 E
Adzhar A.S.S.R. □ 181 42 0N 42 0 E
Adzopé 246 6 7N 3 49W
Ægean Sea 159 37 0N 25 0 E
Æolian Is. = Eólie, I. 165 38 30N 14 50 E
Aerht'ai Shan 212 46 40N 92 45 E
Ærø 173 54 52N 10 25 E
Ærøskøbing 173 54 53N 10 24 E
Aesch 148 47 28N 7 36 E
Aëtós 169 37 15N 21 50 E
Afafi, Massif d' 241 22 11N 15 10 E
'Afak 192 32 4N 45 15 E
Afanasyevo 182 58 52N 53 15 E
Afándou 169 36 18N 28 12 E
Afarag, Erg 240 23 50N 2 47 E
Afareaitu 226 17 33 S 149 47W
Afdega 256 6 4N 43 30 E
Affreville = Khemis Miliana 241 36 11N 2 14 E
Afghanistan ■ 197 33 0N 65 0 E
Afgoi 256 2 7N 44 59 E
'Afīf 194 23 53N 42 56 E
Afikpo 247 5 53N 7 54 E
Aflisses, O. → 240 28 40N 0 50 E
Aflou 241 34 7N 2 3 E
Afmadu 256 0 31N 42 4 E
Afogados da Ingàzeira 120 7 45 S 37 39W
Afragola 165 40 54N 14 15 E
Afrera 245 13 16N 41 5 E
Africa 236 10 0N 20 0 E
'Afrīn 190 36 32N 36 50 E
'Afrīn → 190 36 20N 36 35 E
Afşar → 190 37 2N 32 35 E
Aftout 240 26 50N 3 45W
Afuá 120 0 15 S 50 20W
Afula 189 32 37N 35 17 E
Afyonkarahisar 177 38 45N 30 33 E
Aga 244 30 55N 31 10 E
Agadès = Agadez 247 16 58N 7 59 E
Agadez 247 16 58N 7 59 E
Agadir 240 30 28N 9 35W
Agailás 240 22 37N 14 22W
Agana 226 13 28N 144 45 E
Agapa 185 71 27N 89 15 E
Agapovka 182 53 18N 59 8 E
Agar 198 23 40N 76 2 E
Agaro 245 7 50N 36 38 E
Agartala 202 23 50N 91 23 E
Ağāş 170 46 28N 26 15 E
Agassiz 93 49 14N 121 46W
Agats 207 5 33 S 138 0 E
Agawa → 87 47 23N 84 40W
Agbélouvé 247 6 35N 1 14 E
Agboville 246 5 55N 4 15W
Agcogan 210 12 4N 121 57 E
Agdam 181 40 0N 46 58 E
Agdash 181 40 44N 47 22 E
Agde 140 43 19N 3 28 E
Agde, C. d' 140 43 16N 3 28 E
Agdzhabedi 181 40 5N 47 27 E
Agen 140 44 12N 0 38 E
Ageo 221 35 58N 139 36 E
Ager Tay 241 20 0N 17 41 E
Agersø 172 55 13N 11 12 E
Ageyevo 179 54 10N 36 27 E
Agger 173 56 47N 8 13 E
Ággius 164 40 56N 9 4 E
Āgh Kand 193 37 15N 48 4 E
Aghil Mts. 199 36 0N 77 0 E
Aghoueyyît 240 21 10N 15 6W
Agiabampo 100 26 24N 109 8W
Aginskoye 185 51 6N 114 32 E
Agira 165 37 40N 14 30 E
Agly → 140 42 46N 3 3 E
Agnes L. 86 48 15N 91 20W
Agnibilékrou 246 7 10N 3 11W
Agnita 170 45 59N 24 40 E
Agnone 165 41 49N 14 20 E
Ago 221 34 20N 136 51 E
Agofie 247 8 27N 0 15 E
Agogna → 162 45 4N 8 52 E
Agogo 245 7 50N 28 45 E
Agon, France 138 49 2N 1 34W
Agön, Sweden 172 61 34N 17 23 E
Agoo 210 16 20N 120 22 E
Ágordo 163 46 18N 12 2 E
Agout → 140 43 47N 1 41 E
Agra 198 27 17N 77 58 E
Agramunt 156 41 48N 1 6 E
Agreda 156 41 51N 1 55W
Agri → 165 40 13N 16 44 E
Ağri Daği 177 39 50N 44 15 E
Ağri Karakose 177 39 44N 43 3 E
Agrigento 164 37 19N 13 33 E
Agrinion 169 38 37N 21 27 E
Agrópoli 165 40 23N 14 59 E
Agryz 182 56 33N 53 2 E
Agua Blanca, Baja Calif. N., Mexico 98 31 39N 115 54W
Agua Blanca, Chihuahua, Mexico 104 25 49N 106 43W
Agua Blanca, Quintana Roo, Mexico 111 18 2N 88 46W
Água Branca 120 5 50 S 42 40W
Agua Brava, L. de 104 22 10N 105 32W
Agua Caliente 104 26 31N 108 22W
Agua Caliente de Gárate 104 23 9N 106 6W
Água Clara 123 20 25 S 52 45W
Agua de Chaley 98 30 37N 114 43W
Agua Dulce 109 18 8N 94 8W
Agua Hechicera 98 32 28N 116 15W
Agua Nueva, Coahuila, Mexico 103 25 12N 101 6W
Agua Nueva, Sinaloa, Mexico 104 24 5N 106 50W
Agua Preta → 119 1 41 S 63 48W
Agua Prieta 100 31 18N 109 34W
Agua Verde 104 22 54N 105 59W
Aguachica 118 8 19N 73 38W
Aguada, L. 111 18 53N 91 23W
Aguada Cecilio 126 40 51 S 65 51W
Aguadas 118 5 40N 75 38W
Aguadulce 112 8 15N 80 32W
Agualeguas 102 26 18N 99 34W
Aguanaval, R. → 103 25 28N 102 53W
Aguanish 80 50 14N 62 2W
Aguanus → 80 50 13N 62 5W
Aguapeí 123 16 12 S 59 43W
Aguapeí → 121 21 0 S 51 0W
Aguapey → 124 29 7 S 56 36W
Aguaray Guazú → 124 24 47 S 57 19W
Aguarico → 118 0 59 S 75 11W
Aguaruto 104 24 47N 107 29W
Aguas → 156 41 20N 0 30W
Aguas Blancas 124 24 15 S 69 55W
Aguas Calientes, Sierra de 124 25 26 S 66 40W
Águas Formosas 121 17 5 S 40 57W
Aguascalientes 105 21 53N 102 18W
Aguascalientes □ 105 22 0N 102 30W
Agudo 155 38 59N 4 52W
Águeda 154 40 34N 8 27W
Agueda → 154 41 2N 6 56W
Aguié 247 13 31N 7 46 E
Aguilafuente 154 41 13N 4 7W
Aguilar 155 37 31N 4 40W
Aguilar de Campóo 154 42 47N 4 15W
Aguilares 124 27 26 S 65 35W
Aguilas 157 37 23N 1 35W
Aguililla 106 18 44N 102 44W
Aguilita 102 27 55N 101 8W
Aguja, C. de la 118 11 18N 74 12W
Agulaa 245 13 40N 39 40 E
Agulhas, Kaap 254 34 52 S 20 0 E
Agung 209 8 20 S 115 28 E
Agur, Israel 189 31 42N 34 55 E
Agur, Uganda 250 2 28N 32 55 E
Agusan → 211 9 0N 125 30 E
Agusan del Norte □ 211 9 20N 125 10 E
Agusan del Sur □ 211 8 30N 125 30 E
Agustín Codazzi 118 10 2N 73 14W
Agutaya I. 211 11 9N 120 58 E
Agvali 181 42 36N 46 8 E
Aha Mts. 254 19 45 S 21 0 E
Ahaggar 241 23 0N 6 30 E
Ahamansu 247 7 38N 0 35 E
Ahar 192 38 35N 47 0 E
Ahaura → 235 42 21 S 171 34 E
Ahaus 146 52 4N 7 1 E
Ahelledjem 241 26 37N 6 58 E
Ahipara B. 234 35 5 S 173 5 E
Ahiri 200 19 30N 80 0 E
Ahlen 146 51 45N 7 52 E
Ahmad Wal 198 29 18N 65 58 E
Ahmadabad, India 198 23 0N 72 40 E
Aḥmadābād, Khorāsān, Iran 193 35 3N 60 50 E
Aḥmadābād, Khorāsān, Iran 193 35 49N 59 42 E
Aḥmadī 193 27 56N 56 42 E
Ahmadnagar 200 19 7N 74 46 E
Ahmadpur 198 29 12N 71 10 E
Ahmar Mts. 245 9 20N 41 15 E
Ahmedabad = Ahmadabad 198 23 0N 72 40 E
Ahmednagar = Ahmadnagar 200 19 7N 74 46 E
Ahoada 247 5 8N 6 36 E
Ahome 104 25 55N 109 11W
Ahome, Pta. 104 25 59N 109 27W
Ahr → 146 50 33N 7 17 E
Ahram 193 28 52N 51 16 E
Ahrensbök 146 54 0N 10 34 E
Ahrweiler 146 50 31N 7 3 E
Āhū 193 34 33N 50 2 E
Ahuacatlán 104 21 3N 104 29W
Ahuachapán 112 13 54N 89 52W
Ahualulco 103 22 24N 101 10W
Ahualulco de Mercado 106 20 42N 103 59W
Ahuazotepec 108 20 3N 98 9W
Ahuijullo 106 19 6N 103 10W
Ahuriri → 235 44 31 S 170 12 E
Åhus 173 55 56N 14 18 E
Ahvāz 193 31 20N 48 40 E
Ahvenanmaa = Åland 175 60 15N 20 0 E
Ahwar 188 13 30N 46 40 E
Ahzar 247 15 30N 3 20 E
Aiari → 118 1 22N 68 36W
Aichach 147 48 28N 11 9 E
Aichi □ 221 35 0N 137 15 E
Aidone 165 37 26N 14 26 E
Aiello Càlabro 165 39 6N 16 12 E
Aigle 148 46 18N 6 58 E
Aigle, L' 138 48 46N 0 38 E
Aignay-le-Duc 139 47 40N 4 43 E
Aigre 140 45 54N 0 1 E
Aigua 125 34 13 S 54 46W
Aiguebelle, Parc 82 48 30N 78 45W
Aigueperse 140 46 3N 3 13 E
Aigues-Mortes 141 43 35N 4 12 E
Aigues-Mortes, G. d' 141 43 31N 4 3 E
Aiguilles 141 44 47N 6 51 E
Aiguillon 140 44 18N 0 21 E
Aiguillon, L' 140 46 20N 1 16W
Aigurande 140 46 27N 1 49 E
Aihui 213 50 10N 127 30 E
Aija 122 9 50 S 77 45W
Aikawa 218 38 2N 138 15 E
Ailao Shan 216 24 0N 101 20 E
Aillant-sur-Tholon 139 47 52N 3 20 E
Aillik 78 55 11N 59 18W
Ailly-sur-Noye 139 49 45N 2 20 E
Ailsa Craig, Canada 84 43 8N 81 33W
Ailsa Craig, U.K. 134 55 15N 5 7W
'Ailūn 189 32 18N 35 47 E
Aim 185 59 0N 133 55 E
Aimere 207 8 45 S 121 3 E
Aimogasta 124 28 33 S 66 50W
Aimorés 121 19 30 S 41 4W
Ain □ 141 46 5N 5 20 E
Ain → 141 45 45N 5 11 E
Aïn Beïda 241 35 50N 7 29 E
Ain Ben Khellil 241 33 15N 0 49W
Aïn Ben Tili 240 25 59N 9 27W
Aïn Beni Mathar 241 34 1N 2 0W
Aïn Benian 241 36 48N 2 55 E
Ain Dalla 244 27 20N 27 23 E
'Ain el Akhḍar 191 28 50N 33 55 E
Ain el Mafki 244 27 30N 28 15 E
Ain Girba 244 29 20N 25 14 E

Aïn M'lila **241** 36 2N 6 35 E
Ain Qeiqab **244** 29 42N 24 55 E
Aïn-Sefra **241** 32 47N 0 37W
Ain Sheikh Murzûk **244** 26 47N 27 45 E
'Ain Sudr **191** 29 50N 33 6 E
Ain Sukhna **244** 29 32N 32 20 E
Aïn Tédelès **241** 36 0N 0 21 E
Aïn-Témouchent **241** 35 16N 1 8W
Aïn Touta **241** 35 26N 5 54 E
Ain Zeitûn **244** 29 10N 25 48 E
Aïn Zorah **241** 34 37N 3 32W
Ainabo **256** 9 0N 46 25 E
Ainaži **178** 57 50N 24 24 E
Aínos Óros **169** 38 10N 20 35 E
Ainslie, L. **81** 46 8N 61 11W
Aioi **220** 34 48N 134 28 E
Aipe **118** 3 13N 75 15W
Aiquile **123** 18 10 S 65 10W
Aïr **247** 18 30N 8 0 E
Air Force I. **95** 67 58N 74 5W
Air Hitam **205** 1 55N 103 11 E
Airaines **139** 49 58N 1 55 E
Airão **119** 1 56 S 61 22W
Airdrie, Canada **91** 51 18N 114 2W
Airdrie, U.K. **134** 55 53N 3 57W
Aire **139** 50 37N 2 22 E
Aire →, France **139** 49 18N 4 55 E
Aire →, U.K. **132** 53 42N 0 55W
Aire, I. del **156** 39 48N 4 16 E
Aire-sur-l'Adour **140** 43 42N 0 15W
Aireys Inlet **232** 38 29 S 144 5 E
Airlie Beach **230** 20 16 S 148 43 E
Airolo **149** 46 32N 8 37 E
Airvault **138** 46 50N 0 8W
Aisch → **147** 49 46N 11 1 E
Aisen □ **126** 46 30 S 73 0W
Aisne □ **139** 49 42N 3 40 E
Aisne → **139** 49 26N 2 50 E
Aitana, Sierra de **157** 38 35N 0 24W
Aitape **227** 3 11 S 142 22 E
Aitolía Kai Akarnanía □ **169** 38 45N 21 18 E
Aitolikón **169** 38 26N 21 21 E
Aiuaba **120** 6 38 S 40 7W
Aiud **170** 46 19N 23 44 E
Aix-en-Provence **141** 43 32N 5 27 E
Aix-la-Chapelle = Aachen **146** 50 47N 6 4 E
Aix-les-Bains **141** 45 41N 5 53 E
Aix-sur-Vienne **140** 45 48N 1 8 E
Aiyang, Mt. **227** 5 10 S 141 20 E
Aiyansh **76** 55 17N 129 2W
Áíyina **169** 37 45N 23 26 E
Aiyínion **168** 40 28N 22 28 E
Aiyion **169** 38 15N 22 5 E
Aizawl **202** 23 40N 92 44 E
Aizenay **138** 46 44N 1 38W
Aizpute **178** 56 43N 21 40 E
Aizuwakamatsu **218** 37 30N 139 56 E
Ajaccio **141** 41 55N 8 40 E
Ajaccio, G. d' **141** 41 52N 8 40 E
Ajacuba **107** 20 5N 99 8W
Ajaju → **118** 0 59N 72 20W
Ajalpán **109** 18 22N 97 15W
Ajanta Ra. **200** 20 28N 75 50 E
Ajax **85** 43 50N 79 1W
Ajax, Mt. **235** 42 35 S 172 5 E
Ajdâbiyah **241** 30 54N 20 4 E
Ajdovščina **163** 45 54N 13 54 E
Ajibar **245** 10 35N 38 36 E
Ajijic **106** 20 18N 103 17W
Ajka **151** 47 4N 17 31 E
'Ajmān **195** 25 25N 55 30 E
Ajmer **198** 26 28N 74 37 E
Ajoie **148** 47 22N 7 0 E
Ajok **245** 9 15N 28 28 E
Ajos, Sa. de los **100** 30 57N 109 54W
Ajusco, Sa. del **107** 19 10N 99 15W
Ajuy **211** 11 10N 123 1 E
Ajuya **104** 24 7N 106 21W
Akaba **247** 8 10N 1 2 E
Akabira **218** 43 33N 142 5 E
Akabli **240** 26 49N 1 31 E
Akaishi-Dake **221** 35 27N 138 9 E
Akaishi-Sammyaku **221** 35 25N 138 10 E
Akaki Beseka **245** 8 55N 38 45 E
Akala **245** 15 39N 36 13 E
Akanthou **190** 35 22N 33 45 E
Akaroa **235** 43 49 S 172 59 E
Akasha **244** 21 10N 30 32 E
Akashi **220** 34 45N 135 0 E
Akbou **241** 36 31N 4 31 E
Akbulak **182** 51 1N 55 37 E
Akchâr **240** 20 20N 14 28W
Akdağ **190** 37 0N 32 0 E
Akdala **183** 45 2N 74 35 E
Akechi **221** 35 18N 137 23 E
Akelamo **207** 1 35N 129 40 E
Åkernes **171** 58 45N 7 30 E
Akershus fylke □ **171** 60 0N 11 10 E
Akeru → **200** 17 25N 80 0 E
Aketi **252** 2 38N 23 47 E
Akhaïa □ **169** 38 5N 21 45 E
Akhalkalaki **181** 41 27N 43 25 E
Akhaltsikhe **181** 41 40N 43 0 E
Akharnaí **169** 38 5N 23 44 E
Akhelóös → **169** 38 36N 21 14 E
Akhendria **169** 34 58N 25 16 E
Akhéron → **168** 39 20N 20 29 E
Akhladhókambos **169** 37 31N 22 35 E
Akhmîm **244** 26 31N 31 47 E
Akhnur **199** 32 52N 74 45 E
Akhtarīn **190** 36 31N 37 20 E
Akhtopol **167** 42 6N 27 56 E
Akhtubinsk **181** 48 13N 46 7 E
Akhty **181** 41 30N 47 45 E
Akhtyrka **178** 50 25N 35 0 E
Aki **220** 33 30N 133 54 E
Aki-Nada **220** 34 5N 132 40 E
Akiéni **252** 1 11 S 13 53 E
Akil **111** 20 15N 89 21W
Akimiski I. **74** 52 50N 81 30W
Akimovka **180** 46 44N 35 0 E
Åkirkeby **173** 55 4N 14 55 E
Akita **218** 39 45N 140 7 E
Akita □ **218** 39 40N 140 30 E
Akjoujt **246** 19 45N 14 15W
Akka **240** 29 22N 8 9W
Akkeshi **218** 43 2N 144 51 E
'Akko **189** 32 55N 35 4 E
Akkol, Kazakh S.S.R., U.S.S.R. **183** 43 36N 70 45 E
Akkol, Kazakh S.S.R., U.S.S.R. **184** 45 0N 75 39 E
Akköy **169** 37 30N 27 18 E
Akkrum **142** 53 3N 5 50 E
Aklampa **247** 8 15N 2 10 E
Aklan □ **211** 11 50N 122 30 E
Aklavik **94** 68 12N 135 0W
Akmonte **155** 37 13N 6 38W
Akmuz **183** 41 15N 76 10 E
Aknoul **241** 34 40N 3 55W
Akō, Japan **220** 34 45N 134 24 E
Ako, Nigeria **247** 10 19N 10 48 E
Akobo → **245** 7 48N 33 3 E
Akola **198** 20 42N 77 2 E
Akonolinga **247** 3 50N 12 18 E
Akordat **245** 15 30N 37 40 E
Akosombo Dam **247** 6 20N 0 5 E
Akot, India **198** 21 10N 77 10 E
Akot, Sudan **245** 6 31N 30 9 E
Akpatok I. **78** 60 25N 68 8W
Akranes **174** 64 19N 21 58W
Åkrehamn **171** 59 15N 5 10 E
Akreïjit **246** 18 19N 9 11W
Akrítas Venétiko, Ákra **169** 36 43N 21 54 E
Akron **87** 48 55N 84 7W
Akrotíri, Ákra **168** 40 26N 25 27 E
Akrotiri Bay **190** 34 35N 33 10 E
Aksai Chih **199** 35 15N 79 55 E
Aksarka **184** 66 31N 67 50 E
Aksay **182** 51 11N 53 0 E
Aksek **190** 37 2N 31 47 E
Aksenovo Zilovskoye **185** 53 20N 117 40 E
Akstafa **181** 41 7N 45 27 E
Aksu **212** 41 5N 80 10 E
Aksu → **190** 36 54N 30 54 E
Aksuat, Ozero **182** 51 32N 64 34 E
Aksum **245** 14 5N 38 40 E
Aktash, R.S.F.S.R., U.S.S.R. **182** 55 2N 52 7 E
Aktash, Uzbek S.S.R., U.S.S.R. **183** 39 55N 65 55 E
Aktepe **190** 36 42N 36 27 E
Aktogay, Kazakh S.S.R., U.S.S.R. **182** 46 57N 79 40 E
Aktogay, Kazakh S.S.R., U.S.S.R. **183** 44 25N 76 44 E
Aktyubinsk **177** 50 17N 57 10 E
Aktyuz **183** 42 54N 76 7 E
Aku **247** 6 40N 7 18 E
Akula **252** 2 22N 20 12 E
Akumial **111** 20 25N 87 18W
Akune **220** 32 1N 130 12 E
Akure **247** 7 15N 5 5 E
Akureyri **174** 65 40N 18 6W
Akuseki-Shima **219** 29 27N 129 37 E
Akusha **181** 42 18N 47 30 E
Akyab = Sittwe **202** 20 18N 92 45 E
Akzhar **183** 43 8N 71 37 E
Al Abyār **241** 32 9N 20 29 E
Al 'Adan **194** 12 45N 45 0 E
Al Aḥsā **193** 25 50N 49 0 E
Al Ajfar **192** 27 26N 43 0 E
Al Akhḍar **191** 28 4N 37 9 E
Al Akhḍar, W. → **191** 28 36N 36 36 E
Al Amādīyah **192** 37 5N 43 30 E
Al Amārah **192** 31 55N 47 15 E
Al 'Aqabah **189** 29 31N 35 0 E
Al' Aqīq **194** 20 39N 41 25 E
Al Arak **192** 34 38N 38 35 E
Al 'Aramah **192** 25 30N 46 0 E
Al 'Ariḍah **194** 17 3N 43 5 E
Al Arṭāwīyah **192** 26 31N 45 20 E
Al Ashkhara **195** 21 50N 59 30 E
Al 'Āṣimah □ **191** 31 40N 36 30 E
Al' Assāfīyah **192** 28 17N 38 59 E
Al Atārib **190** 36 9N 36 49 E
Al 'Ayn, Oman **195** 24 15N 55 45 E
Al 'Ayn, Si. Arabia **192** 25 4N 38 6 E
Al 'Ayzarīyah **189** 31 47N 35 15 E
Al A'ẓamīyah **192** 33 22N 44 22 E
Al 'Azīzīyah, Iraq **192** 32 54N 45 4 E
Al 'Azīzīyah, Libya **241** 32 30N 13 1 E
Al Bāb **190** 36 23N 37 29 E
Al Bad' **192** 28 28N 35 1 E
Al Bādī, Iraq **192** 35 56N 41 32 E
Al Badī', Si. Arabia **194** 22 0N 46 35 E
Al Baḥrah **192** 29 40N 47 52 E
Al Balqā' □ **191** 32 5N 35 45 E
Al Barkāt **241** 24 56N 10 14 E
Al Bārūk, J. **190** 33 39N 35 40 E
Al Baṣrah **192** 30 30N 47 50 E
Al Baṭḥā **192** 31 6N 45 53 E
Al Batrūn **190** 34 15N 35 40 E
Al Bayāḍ **194** 22 0N 47 0 E
Al Bayḍā' **194** 14 5N 45 42 E
Al Bayḍā □ **242** 32 0N 21 30 E
Al Bāzūrīyah **189** 33 15N 35 16 E
Al Bi'ār **194** 22 39N 39 40 E
Al Biqā □ **190** 34 0N 36 5 E
Al Bi'r **192** 28 51N 36 16 E
Al Bīrah **189** 31 55N 35 12 E
Al Birk **194** 18 13N 41 33 E
Al Bu'ayrāt **241** 31 24N 15 44 E
Al Buqay'ah **189** 32 15N 35 30 E
Al Burayj **190** 34 15N 36 46 E
Al Fallūjah **192** 33 20N 43 55 E
Al Fatk **195** 16 31N 52 41 E
Al Fāw **193** 30 0N 48 30 E
Al Faydamī **195** 16 25N 52 26 E
Al Fujayrah **195** 25 7N 56 18 E
Al Ghadaf, W. → **191** 31 26N 36 43 E
Al Ghammās **192** 31 45N 44 37 E
Al Gharīb **242** 32 35N 21 11 E
Al Ghayḍah, S. Yemen **195** 16 13N 52 11 E
Al Ghayḍah, S. Yemen **195** 14 55N 50 0 E
Al Ghayl **195** 15 30N 50 54 E
Al Hābah **192** 27 10N 47 0 E
Al Ḥadd **195** 22 32N 59 48 E
Al Ḥaddār **194** 21 58N 45 57 E
Al Ḥadīthah, Iraq **192** 34 0N 41 13 E
Al Ḥadīthah, Si. Arabia **192** 31 28N 37 8 E
Al Haffah **190** 35 36N 36 1 E
Al Ḥājānah **190** 33 20N 36 33 E
Al Hajarayn **195** 15 29N 48 20 E
Al Ḥallānīyah **195** 17 30N 56 1 E
Al Ḥāmad **192** 31 30N 39 30 E
Al Ḥamar **194** 22 26N 46 12 E
Al Ḥamdāniyah **190** 35 25N 36 50 E
Al Ḥamidīyah **190** 34 42N 35 57 E
Al Ḥammādah al Ḥamrā' **241** 29 30N 12 0 E
Al Ḥammār **192** 30 57N 46 51 E
Al Ḥamrā' **194** 24 2N 38 55 E
Al Ḥarīq **194** 23 29N 46 27 E
Al Ḥarīr, W. → **189** 32 44N 35 59 E
Al Ḥarūj al Aswad **241** 27 0N 17 10 E
Al Ḥasā, W. → **191** 31 4N 35 29 E
Al Ḥasakah **192** 36 35N 40 45 E
Al Ḥāsikīyah **195** 17 28N 55 36 E
Al Ḥasy **195** 14 3N 48 40 E
Al Ḥawrah **194** 13 50N 47 35 E
Al Ḥawṭah, S. Yemen **194** 16 5N 48 20 E
Al Ḥawṭah, S. Yemen **194** 14 23N 47 24 E
Al Ḥawṭah □ **194** 23 30N 47 0 E
Al Haydān, W. → **191** 31 29N 35 34 E
Al Ḥayy **192** 32 5N 46 5 E
Al Ḥijāz **194** 26 0N 37 30 E
Al Ḥillah, Iraq **192** 32 30N 44 25 E
Al Ḥillah, Si. Arabia **194** 23 35N 46 50 E
Al Hirmil **190** 34 26N 36 24 E
Al Ḥiṣnn **189** 32 29N 35 52 E
Al Hoceïma **240** 35 8N 3 58W
Al Ḥudaydah **194** 14 50N 43 0 E
Al Ḥufrah, Awbārī, Libya **241** 25 32N 14 1 E
Al Ḥufrah, Misrātah, Libya **241** 29 5N 18 3 E
Al Hūfuf **193** 25 25N 49 45 E
Al Ḥulwah **194** 23 24N 46 48 E
Al Ḥumayḍah **192** 29 14N 34 56 E
Al Ḥunayy **193** 25 58N 48 45 E
Al Ḥurayḍah **195** 15 36N 48 12 E
Al Husayyāt **241** 30 24N 20 37 E
Al Hūwah **194** 23 2N 45 48 E
Al Ḥuwaymī **194** 13 23N 44 28 E
Al Irq **242** 29 5N 21 35 E
Al 'Irqah **194** 13 39N 47 22 E
Al Īsāwīyah **192** 30 43N 37 59 E
Al Ittihad = Madīnat ash Sha'b **194** 12 50N 45 0 E
Al Jabal al Akhḍar **242** 32 0N 21 30 E
Al Jafr **191** 30 18N 36 14 E
Al Jaghbūb **242** 29 42N 24 38 E
Al Jahrah **192** 29 25N 47 40 E
Al Jalāmīd **192** 31 20N 39 45 E
Al Jamalīyah **195** 25 37N 51 5 E
Al Janūb □ **190** 33 20N 35 20 E
Al Jawf, Libya **242** 24 10N 23 24 E
Al Jawf, Si. Arabia **192** 29 55N 39 40 E
Al Jazirah, Asia **192** 33 30N 44 0 E
Al Jazirah, Libya **242** 26 10N 21 20 E
Al Jithāmīyah **192** 27 41N 41 43 E
Al Jubayl **193** 27 0N 49 50 E
Al Jubaylah **192** 24 55N 46 25 E
Al Jubb **192** 27 11N 42 17 E
Al Jumūm **194** 21 37N 39 42 E
Al Junaynah **243** 13 27N 22 45 E
Al Kabā'ish **192** 30 58N 47 0 E
Al Kāmil **195** 22 13N 59 12 E
Al Karak **191** 31 11N 35 42 E
Al Karak □ **191** 31 0N 36 0 E
Al Kāẓim Tyah **192** 33 22N 44 12 E
Al Khābūra **195** 23 57N 57 5 E
Al Khalīl **189** 31 32N 35 6 E
Al Khalīl □ **191** 31 35N 35 5 E
Al Khalūf **188** 20 30N 58 13 E
Al Khamāsīn **194** 20 29N 44 46 E
Al Kharāb **194** 16 29N 44 18 E
Al Kharfah **194** 22 0N 46 35 E
Al Kharj **194** 24 0N 47 0 E
Al Khāṣirah **194** 23 30N 43 47 E
Al Khawr **195** 25 41N 51 30 E
Al Khiḍr **192** 31 12N 45 33 E
Al Khiyām **190** 33 20N 35 36 E
Al Khums **241** 32 40N 14 17 E
Al Khums □ **241** 31 20N 14 10 E
Al Kiswah **190** 33 23N 36 14 E
Al Kufrah **242** 24 17N 23 15 E
Al Kuhayfīyah **192** 27 12N 43 3 E
Al Kūt **192** 32 30N 46 0 E
Al Kuwayt **192** 29 30N 47 30 E
Al Labwah **190** 34 11N 36 20 E
Al Lādhiqīyah **190** 35 30N 35 45 E
Al Lādhiqīyah □ **190** 35 45N 36 0 E
Al Lawz, J. **191** 28 40N 35 20 E
Al Lidām **188** 20 33N 44 45 E
Al Līth **194** 20 9N 40 15 E
Al Liwā' **195** 24 31N 56 36 E
Al Lubban **189** 32 9N 35 14 E
Al Luḥayyah **194** 15 45N 42 40 E
Al Madīnah, Iraq **192** 30 57N 47 16 E
Al Madīnah, Si. Arabia **192** 24 35N 39 52 E
Al-Mafraq **189** 32 17N 36 14 E
Al Maghārīm **194** 15 1N 47 49 E
Al Maḥmūdīyah **192** 33 3N 44 21 E
Al Majma'ah **192** 25 57N 45 22 E
Al Makhruq, W. → **191** 31 28N 37 0 E
Al Makḥūl **192** 26 37N 42 39 E
Al Makīlī **242** 32 10N 22 17 E
Al Manā'if **195** 23 49N 51 20 E
Al Manāmāh **195** 26 10N 50 30 E
Al Manṣūrī **194** 14 17N 45 16 E
Al Maqwa' **192** 29 10N 47 59 E
Al Marj **242** 32 25N 20 30 E
Al Maṭlā **192** 29 24N 47 40 E
Al Mawjib, W. → **191** 31 28N 35 36 E
Al Mawṣil **192** 36 15N 43 5 E
Al Mayādin **192** 35 1N 40 27 E
Al Mazār **191** 31 4N 35 41 E
Al Mazra **189** 31 16N 35 31 E
Al Midhnab **192** 25 50N 44 18 E
Al Mīfá **194** 18 54N 41 57 E
Al Minā' **190** 34 24N 35 49 E
Al Miqdādīyah **192** 34 0N 45 0 E
Al Mubarraz **193** 25 30N 49 40 E
Al Muḍaybī **195** 22 34N 58 7 E
Al Mughayrā' **195** 24 5N 53 32 E
Al Muḥarraq **195** 26 15N 50 40 E
Al Mukallā **195** 14 33N 49 2 E
Al Mukhā **194** 13 18N 43 15 E
Al Muladdah **195** 23 45N 57 34 E
Al Musayjīd **192** 24 5N 39 5 E
Al Musayyib **192** 32 40N 44 25 E
Al Muwayliḥ **192** 27 40N 35 30 E
Al Owuho = Otukpa **247** 7 9N 7 41 E
Al Qaddāhīyah **241** 31 15N 15 9 E
Al Qadīmah **194** 22 20N 39 13 E
Al Qaḥmah **194** 18 0N 41 41 E
Al Qā'im **192** 34 21N 41 7 E
Al Qalībah **192** 28 24N 37 42 E
Al Qaryah ash Sharqīyah **241** 30 28N 13 40 E
Al Qaryatayn **190** 34 12N 37 13 E
Al Qaşabát **241** 32 39N 14 1 E
Al Qaṭ'ā **192** 34 40N 40 48 E
Al Qaṭīf **193** 26 35N 50 0 E
Al Qaṭn **195** 15 51N 48 26 E
Al Qatrānah **191** 31 14N 36 26 E
Al Qaṭrūn **241** 24 56N 15 3 E

Al Qayşūmah 192 28 20N 46 7 E
Al Qiblīyah 195 17 30N 56 20 E
Al Quds = Jerusalem 189 31 47N 35 10 E
Al Quds □ 191 31 50N 35 20 E
Al Qunaytirah 190 32 55N 35 45 E
Al Qunfudhah 194 19 3N 41 4 E
Al Qurḥ 195 16 44N 51 29 E
Al Qurnah 192 31 1N 47 25 E
Al Quşayr, Iraq 192 30 39N 45 50 E
Al Quşayr, Syria 190 34 31N 36 34 E
Al Qutayfah 190 33 44N 36 36 E
Al Quwayʻīyah 194 24 3N 45 15 E
Al ʻUbaylah 195 21 59N 50 57 E
Alʻ Uḑaylīyah 193 25 8N 49 18 E
Al ʻUlā 192 26 35N 38 0 E
Al ʻUlayyah 194 19 39N 41 54 E
Al Uqaylah ash Sharqīgah 241 30 12N 19 10 E
Al Uqayr 193 25 40N 50 15 E
Al ʻUwaynid 192 24 50N 46 0 E
Alʼ ʻUwayqīlah 192 30 30N 42 10 E
Al ʻUyūn, Si. Arabia 192 26 30N 43 50 E
Al Uyūn, Si. Arabia 192 24 33N 39 35 E
Al Wajh 192 26 10N 36 30 E
Al Wakrah 195 25 10N 51 40 E
Al Wannān 193 26 55N 48 24 E
Al Waqbah 192 28 48N 45 33 E
Al Wariʻāh 192 27 51N 47 25 E
Al Wātīyah 241 32 28N 11 57 E
Al Wusayl 195 25 29N 51 29 E
Al Yāmūn 189 32 29N 35 14 E
Ala 162 45 46N 11 0 E
Ala Shan 212 40 0N 104 0 E
Alaçati 169 38 16N 26 23 E
Alaejos 154 41 18N 5 13W
Alagna Valsésia 162 45 51N 7 56 E
Alagoa Grande 120 7 3 S 35 35W
Alagoas □ 120 9 0 S 36 0W
Alagoinhas 121 12 7 S 38 20W
Alagón 156 41 46N 1 12W
Alagón → 155 39 44N 6 53W
Alajuela 112 10 2N 84 8W
Alakamisy 255 21 19 S 47 14 E
Alakurtti 176 67 0N 30 30 E
Alalapura 119 2 20N 56 25W
Alalaú → 119 0 30 S 61 9W
Alamagre, L. 103 23 48N 97 48W
Alameda, Canada 89 49 16N 102 17W
Alameda, Spain 155 37 12N 4 39W
Alaminos 210 16 10N 119 59 E
Álamo 108 20 55N 97 41W
Álamos, Sonora, Mexico 100 27 1N 108 56W
Álamos, Sonora, Mexico 100 29 13N 110 8W
Álamos de Peña 101 30 21N 106 44W
Åland, Finland 175 60 15N 20 0 E
Aland, India 200 17 36N 76 35 E
Alandroal 155 38 41N 7 24W
Alandur 201 13 0N 80 15 E
Alange, Presa de 155 38 45N 6 18W
Alanis 155 38 3N 5 43W
Alanya 177 36 38N 32 0 E
Alaotra, Farihinʼ 255 17 30 S 48 30 E
Alapayevsk 182 57 52N 61 42 E
ʻAlāqán 191 29 10N 35 21 E
Alaquines 103 22 8N 99 36W
Alar del Rey 154 42 38N 4 20W
Alara → 190 36 38N 31 39 E
Alaraz 154 40 45N 5 17W
Alaşehir 177 38 23N 28 30 E
Alaska Highway 76 60 0N 130 0W
Alássio 162 44 1N 8 10 E
Alatri 164 41 44N 13 21 E
Alatyr 179 54 45N 46 35 E
Alatyr → 179 54 52N 46 36 E
Alausi 118 2 0 S 78 50W
Álava □ 156 42 48N 2 28W
Alaverdi 181 41 15N 44 37 E
Alawoona 232 34 45 S 140 30 E
ʻAlayh 190 33 46N 35 33 E
Alaykel 183 40 15N 74 25 E
Alayor 156 39 57N 4 8 E
Alayskiy Khrebet 183 39 45N 72 0 E
Alazan → 181 41 5N 46 40 E
Alba 162 44 41N 8 1 E
Alba □ 170 46 10N 23 30 E
Alba de Tormes 154 40 50N 5 30W
Alba Iulia 170 46 8N 23 39 E
Albac 170 46 28N 23 1 E
Albacete 157 39 0N 1 50W
Albacete □ 157 38 50N 2 0W
Albacutya, L. 231 35 45 S 141 58 E
Ålbæk 173 57 36N 10 25 E
Ålbæk Bugt 173 57 35N 10 40 E
Albaida 157 38 51N 0 31W
Albalate de las Nogueras 156 40 22N 2 18W
Albalate del Arzobispo 156 41 6N 0 31W
Albanel 83 48 53N 72 27W
Albanel, L. 78 50 55N 73 12W
Albania ■ 168 41 0N 20 0 E
Albano Laziale 164 41 44N 12 40 E
Albany 229 35 1 S 117 58 E
Albany → 74 52 17N 81 31W
Albardón 124 31 20 S 68 30W
Albarracín 156 40 25N 1 26W
Albarracín, Sierra de 156 40 30N 1 30W
Albatross B. 230 12 45 S 141 30 E
Albatross Pt. 234 38 7 S 174 44 E
Albay □ 210 13 13N 123 33 E
Albegna → 163 42 30N 11 11 E
Albenga 162 44 3N 8 12 E
Alberche → 154 39 58N 4 46W
Alberdi 124 26 14 S 58 20W
Alberes, Mts. 156 42 28N 2 56 E
Alberique 157 39 7N 0 31W
Albersdorf 146 54 8N 9 19 E
Albert, Australia 233 32 22 S 147 30 E
Albert, France 139 50 0N 2 38 E
Albert, L. = Mobutu Sese Seko, L. 250 1 30N 31 0 E
Albert, L. 232 35 30 S 139 10 E
Albert Canyon 93 51 8N 117 41W
Albert Edward, Mt. 227 8 20 S 147 24 E
Albert Edward Ra. 228 18 17 S 127 57 E
Albert Nile → 250 3 36N 32 2 E
Albert Town 113 22 37N 74 33 E
Alberta □ 76 54 40N 115 0W
Alberta Beach 90 53 40N 114 21W
Alberti 124 35 1 S 60 16W
Albertinia 254 34 11 S 21 34 E
Albertirsa 151 47 14N 19 37 E
Albertkanaal 143 51 14N 4 26 E
Alberton 81 46 50N 64 0W
Albertville = Kalemie 250 5 55 S 29 9 E
Albertville 141 45 40N 6 22 E
Albi 140 43 56N 2 9 E
Albina 119 5 37N 54 15W
Albina, Ponta 254 15 52 S 11 44 E
Albino 162 45 47N 9 48 E
Alblasserdam 142 51 52N 4 40 E
Albocácer 156 40 21N 0 1 E
Alböke 173 56 57N 16 47 E
Alborán 155 35 57N 3 0W
Alborea 157 39 17N 1 24W
Ålborg 173 57 2N 9 54 E
Ålborg Bugt 173 56 50N 10 35 E
Alborz, Reshteh-ye Kūhhā-ye 193 36 0N 52 0 E
Albox 157 37 23N 2 8W
Albreda 93 52 35N 119 10W
Albuera, La 155 38 45N 6 49W
Albufeira 155 37 5N 8 15W
Albula → 149 46 38N 9 30 E
Albuñol 157 36 48N 3 11W
Albuquerque 123 19 23 S 57 26W
Albuquerque, Cayos de 112 12 10N 81 50W
Alburno, Mte. 165 40 32N 15 15 E
Alburquerque 155 39 15N 6 59W
Albury 231 36 3 S 146 56 E
Alby 172 62 30N 15 28 E
Alcácer do Sal 155 38 22N 8 33W
Alcaçovas 155 38 23N 8 9W
Alcala 210 17 54N 121 39 E
Alcalá de Chisvert 156 40 19N 0 13 E
Alcalá de Guadaira 155 37 20N 5 50W
Alcalá de Henares 156 40 28N 3 22W
Alcalá de los Gazules 155 36 29N 5 43W
Alcalá la Real 155 37 27N 3 57W
Alcamo 164 37 59N 12 55 E
Alcanadre 156 42 24N 2 7W
Alcanadre → 156 41 43N 0 12W
Alcanar 156 40 33N 0 28 E
Alcanede 155 39 25N 8 49W
Alcanena 155 39 27N 8 40W
Alcañices 154 41 41N 6 21W
Alcañiz 156 41 2N 0 8W
Alcântara, Brazil 120 2 20 S 44 30W
Alcántara, Spain 155 39 41N 6 57W
Alcantara L. 77 60 57N 108 9W
Alcantarilla 157 37 59N 1 12W
Alcaracejos 155 38 24N 4 58W
Alcaraz 157 38 40N 2 29W
Alcaraz, Sierra de 157 38 40N 2 20W
Alcarria, La 156 40 31N 2 45W
Alcaudete 155 37 35N 4 5W
Alcázar de San Juan 157 39 24N 3 12W
Alcira 157 39 9N 0 30W
Alcobaça 155 39 32N 9 0W
Alcobendas 156 40 32N 3 38W
Alcolea del Pinar 156 41 2N 2 28W
Alcora 156 40 5N 0 14W
Alcoutim 155 37 25N 7 28W
Alcoy 157 38 43N 0 30W
Alcubierre, Sierra de 156 41 45N 0 22W
Alcublas 156 39 48N 0 43W
Alcudia 156 39 51N 3 7 E
Alcudia, B. de 156 39 47N 3 15 E
Alcudia, Sierra de la 155 38 34N 4 30W
Aldabra Is. 203 9 22 S 46 28 E
Aldama, Chihuahua, Mexico 101 28 51N 105 54W
Aldama, Tabasco, Mexico 110 18 14N 93 19W
Aldama, Tamaulipas, Mexico 103 22 55N 98 4W
Aldan 185 58 40N 125 30 E
Aldan → 185 63 28N 129 35 E
Aldea, La 107 20 54N 101 29W
Aldeburgh 133 52 9N 1 35 E
Aldeia Nova 155 37 55N 7 24W
Alderney 138 49 42N 2 12W
Aldershot, Canada 81 45 6N 64 31W
Aldershot, U.K. 133 51 15N 0 43W
Aldersyde 76 50 40N 113 53W
Alefa 245 11 55N 36 55 E
Aleg 246 17 3N 13 55W
Alegre 121 20 50 S 41 30W
Alegrete 125 29 40 S 56 0W
Alegria 211 11 47N 124 3 E
Aleisk 184 52 40N 83 0 E
Alejandro Selkirk, I. 225 33 50 S 80 15W
Aleksandriya, Ukraine S.S.R., U.S.S.R. 178 50 37N 26 19 E
Aleksandriya, Ukraine S.S.R., U.S.S.R. 180 48 42N 33 3 E
Aleksandriyskaya 181 43 59N 47 0 E
Aleksandrov 179 56 23N 38 44 E
Aleksandrovac, Srbija, Yugoslavia 166 43 28N 21 3 E
Aleksandrovac, Srbija, Yugoslavia 166 44 28N 21 13 E
Aleksandrovka 180 48 55N 32 20 E
Aleksandrovo 167 43 14N 24 51 E
Aleksandrovsk 182 59 9N 57 33 E
Aleksandrovsk-Sakhaliniskiy 185 50 50N 142 20 E
Aleksandrovskiy Zavod 185 50 40N 117 50 E
Aleksandrovskoye 184 60 35N 77 50 E
Aleksandrów Kujawski 152 52 53N 18 43 E
Aleksandrów Łódźki 152 51 49N 19 17 E
Alekseyevka, R.S.F.S.R., U.S.S.R. 179 50 43N 38 40 E
Alekseyevka, R.S.F.S.R., U.S.S.R. 182 52 35N 51 17 E
Aleksin 179 54 31N 37 9 E
Aleksinac 166 43 31N 21 42 E
Além Paraíba 121 21 52 S 42 41W
Alemania, Argentina 124 25 40 S 65 30W
Alemania, Chile 124 25 10 S 69 55W
Ålen 171 62 51N 11 17 E
Alençon 138 48 27N 0 4 E
Aleppo = Ḩalab 190 36 10N 37 15 E
Aléria 141 42 5N 9 26 E
Alert 95 83 2N 60 0W
Alert Bay 92 50 30N 126 55W
Alès 141 44 9N 4 5 E
Aleşd 170 47 3N 22 22 E
Alesna, Pta. 100 28 14N 111 24W
Alessándria 162 44 54N 8 37 E
Ålestrup 173 56 42N 9 29 E
Ålesund 171 62 28N 6 12 E
Alet-les-Bains 140 43 0N 2 14 E
Aletschhorn 148 46 28N 8 0 E
Aleutian Trench 224 48 0N 180 0 E
Alex Graham, Mt. 93 52 4N 122 52W
Alexander, Mt. 229 28 58 S 120 16 E
Alexander B. 254 28 36 S 16 33 E
Alexander I. 13 69 0 S 70 0W
Alexandra, Australia 231 37 8 S 145 40 E
Alexandra, N.Z. 235 45 14 S 169 25 E
Alexandra Falls 76 60 29N 116 18W
Alexandretta = İskenderun 177 36 32N 36 10 E
Alexandria = El Iskandarîya 244 31 0N 30 0 E
Alexandria, Australia 230 19 5 S 136 40 E
Alexandria, B.C., Canada 93 52 35N 122 27W
Alexandria, Ont., Canada 85 45 19N 74 38W
Alexandria, Romania 170 43 57N 25 24 E
Alexandria, S. Africa 254 33 38 S 26 28 E
Alexandrina, L. 232 35 25 S 139 10 E
Alexandroúpolis 168 40 50N 25 54 E
Alexis → 78 52 33N 56 8W
Alexis Creek 92 52 10N 123 20W
Alfambra 156 40 33N 1 5W
Alfândega da Fé 154 41 20N 6 59W
Alfaro 156 42 10N 1 50W
Alfata 104 24 40N 107 55W
Alfatar 167 43 59N 27 13 E
Alfeld 146 52 0N 9 49 E
Alfenas 125 21 20 S 46 10W
Alfiós → 169 37 40N 21 33 E
Alfonsine 163 44 30N 12 1 E
Alfonso XIII 211 9 15N 117 59 E
Alford 134 57 13N 2 42W
Alfred Town 233 35 8 S 147 30 E
Alfredo M. Terrazas 103 21 28N 98 51W
Alfredton 234 40 41 S 175 54 E
Alfreton 132 53 6N 1 22W
Alfta 172 61 21N 16 4 E
Alga 182 49 53N 57 20 E
Algaba, La 155 37 27N 6 1W
Algar 155 36 40N 5 39W
Ålgård 171 58 46N 5 53 E
Algarinejo 155 37 19N 4 9W
Algarve 155 36 58N 8 20W
Algeciras 155 36 9N 5 28W
Algemesí 157 39 11N 0 27W
Alger 240 36 42N 3 8 E
Algeria ■ 240 35 10N 3 11 E
Alghero 164 40 34N 8 20 E
Algiers = Alger 240 36 42N 3 8 E
Algoabaai 254 33 50 S 25 45 E
Algodonales 155 36 54N 5 24W
Algodor → 154 39 55N 3 53W
Algonquin Prov. Park 85 45 50N 78 30W
Alhama de Almería 157 36 57N 2 34W
Alhama de Aragón 156 41 18N 1 54W
Alhama de Granada 155 37 0N 3 59W
Alhama de Murcia 157 37 51N 1 25W
Alhambra, Canada 91 52 20N 114 40W
Alhambra, Spain 157 38 54N 3 4W
Alhaurín el Grande 155 36 39N 4 41W
Alhucemas = Al Hoceïma 240 35 8N 3 58W
Alhuey 104 25 23N 108 10W
ʻAlī al Gharbī 192 32 30N 46 45 E
Alī ash Sharqī 192 32 7N 46 44 E
Ali Bayramly 181 39 59N 48 52 E
ʻAlī Khēl 197 33 57N 69 43 E
Ali Sahîh 245 11 10N 42 44 E
Alī Shāh 192 38 9N 45 50 E
Ália 164 37 47N 13 42 E
ʻAlīābād, Khorāsān, Iran 193 32 30N 57 30 E
Alīābād, Kordestān, Iran 192 35 4N 46 58 E
ʻAlīābād, Yazd, Iran 193 31 41N 53 49 E
Aliaga 156 40 40N 0 42W
Aliákmon → 168 40 30N 22 36 E
Alianza de Caballeros 103 23 53N 99 12W
Alibag 200 18 38N 72 56 E
Alibo 245 9 52N 37 5 E
Alibunar 166 45 5N 20 57 E
Alicante 157 38 23N 0 30W
Alicante □ 157 38 30N 0 37W
Alice, Canada 85 45 47N 77 14W
Alice, S. Africa 254 32 48 S 26 55 E
Alice →, Queens., Australia 230 24 2 S 144 50 E
Alice →, Queens., Australia 230 15 35 S 142 20 E
Alice, Punta dellʼ 165 39 23N 17 10 E
Alice Arm 76 55 29N 129 31W
Alice Downs 228 17 45 S 127 56 E
Alice Springs 230 23 40 S 133 50 E
Alicedale 254 33 15 S 26 4 E
Alicia 211 9 54N 124 26 E
Alick Cr. → 230 20 55 S 142 20 E
Alicudi, I. 165 38 33N 14 20 E
Alida 89 49 25N 101 55W
Aligarh, Raj., India 198 25 55N 76 15 E
Aligarh, Ut. P., India 198 27 55N 78 10 E
Alīgūdarz 193 33 25N 49 45 E
Alijó 154 41 16N 7 27W
Alimantar 190 36 42N 27 26 E
Alimena 165 37 42N 14 4 E
Alimnía 169 36 16N 27 43 E
Alimodian 211 10 49N 122 26 E
Alindao 252 5 2N 21 13 E
Alingsås 173 57 56N 12 31 E
Alipur 198 29 25N 70 55 E
Alipur Duar 202 26 30N 89 35 E
Aliste → 154 41 34N 5 58W
Alitus 178 54 24N 24 3 E
Alivérion 169 38 24N 24 2 E
Aliwal North 254 30 45 S 26 45 E
Alix 91 52 24N 113 11W
Aljezur 155 37 18N 8 49W
Aljojuca 109 19 6N 97 31W
Aljustrel 155 37 55N 8 10W
Alkamari 247 13 27N 11 10 E
Alken 143 50 53N 5 18 E
Alkmaar 142 52 37N 4 45 E
Allacapan 210 18 15N 121 35 E
Allada 247 6 41N 2 9 E
Allah Dad 198 25 38N 67 34 E
Allahabad 199 25 25N 81 58 E
Allakh-Yun 185 60 50N 137 5 E

Allal Tazi 240 34 30N 6 20W
Allan 88 51 53N 106 4W
Allanche 140 45 14N 2 57 E
Allanmyo 202 19 30N 95 17 E
Allanridge 254 27 45 S 26 40 E
Allansford 232 38 26 S 142 39 E
Allanton 235 45 55 S 170 15 E
Allanwater 86 50 14N 90 10W
Allaqi, Wadi → 244 23 7N 32 47 E
Allard, L. 80 50 32N 63 31W
Allardville 81 47 28N 65 29W
Allariz 154 42 11N 7 50W
Allassac 140 45 15N 1 29 E
Alle 143 49 51N 4 58 E
Allègre 140 45 12N 3 41 E
Allen, Argentina 126 38 58 S 67 50W
Allen, Phil. 210 12 30N 124 17 E
Allen, Bog of 135 53 15N 7 0W
Allen, L. 135 54 12N 8 5W
Allenby Br. = Jisr al Ḩusayn 189 31 53N 35 33 E
Allende, Chihuahua, Mexico 101 26 56N 105 24W
Allende, Coahuila, Mexico 102 28 20N 100 51W
Allende, Nuevo León, Mexico 103 25 17N 100 1W
Allende, Tabasco, Mexico 110 18 21N 92 51W
Allende, Veracruz, Mexico 109 18 4N 94 22W
Allentsteig 150 48 41N 15 20 E
Alleppey 201 9 30N 76 28 E
Aller → 146 52 57N 9 10 E
Alleur 143 50 39N 5 31 E
Allevard 141 45 24N 6 5 E
Alliance, Canada 91 52 26N 111 47W
Alliance, Surinam 119 5 50N 54 50W
Allier □ 140 46 25N 3 0 E
Allier → 139 46 57N 3 4 E
Alliford Bay 92 53 12N 131 58W
Allingåbro 173 56 28N 10 20 E
Allinge 173 55 17N 14 50 E
Allison Harbour 92 51 2N 127 29W
Alliston 84 44 9N 79 52W
Alloa 134 56 7N 3 49W
Allora 231 28 2 S 152 0 E
Allos 141 44 15N 6 38 E
Alluviaq, Fj. 78 59 27N 65 10W
Alma, N.B., Canada 81 45 36N 64 57W
Alma, Qué., Canada 83 48 35N 71 40W
'Almā ash Sha'b 189 33 7N 35 9 E
Alma Ata 183 43 15N 76 57 E
Almada 155 38 40N 9 9W
Almaden, Australia 230 17 22 S 144 40 E
Almadén, Spain 155 38 49N 4 52W
Almagro 155 38 50N 3 45W
Almagro I. 211 11 56N 124 18 E
Almalyk 183 40 50N 69 35 E
Almansa 157 38 51N 1 5W
Almanza 154 42 39N 5 3W
Almanzor, Pico de 154 40 15N 5 18W
Almanzora → 157 37 14N 1 46W
Almarcha, La 156 39 41N 2 24W
Almas 121 11 33 S 47 9W
Almaş, Mţii. 170 44 49N 22 12 E
Almazán 156 41 30N 2 30W
Almazora 156 39 57N 0 3W
Almeirim, Brazil 119 1 30 S 52 34W
Almeirim, Portugal 155 39 12N 8 37W
Almelo 142 52 22N 6 42 E
Almenar 156 41 43N 2 12W
Almenara, Brazil 121 16 11 S 40 42W
Almenara, Spain 156 39 46N 0 14W
Almenara, Sierra de 157 37 34N 1 32W
Almendralejo 155 38 41N 6 26W
Almería 157 36 52N 2 27W
Almería □ 157 37 20N 2 20W
Almería, G. de 157 36 41N 2 28W
Almetyevsk 182 54 53N 52 20 E
Älmhult 173 56 33N 14 8 E
Almirante 134 9 10N 82 30W
Almirante Montt, G. 126 51 52 S 72 50W
Almiropótamos 169 38 16N 24 11 E
Almirós 169 39 11N 22 45 E
Almodôvar 155 37 31N 8 2W
Almodóvar del Campo 155 38 43N 4 10W
Almogia 155 36 50N 4 32W
Almonaster la Real 155 37 52N 6 48W
Almonte 85 45 14N 76 12W
Almonte → 155 39 41N 6 28W
Almora 199 29 38N 79 40 E
Almoradi 157 38 7N 0 46W
Almorox 154 40 14N 4 24W
Almoustarat 247 17 35N 0 8 E
Almuñécar 155 36 43N 3 41W
Almunia de Doña Godina, La 156 41 29N 1 23W
Alnif 240 31 10N 5 8W
Alnwick 132 55 25N 1 42W
Alo, Sa. del 106 19 10N 103 15W
Aloi 250 2 16N 33 10 E
Alon 202 22 12N 95 5 E
Alonsa 77 50 50N 99 0W
Alor 207 8 15 S 124 30 E
Alor Setar 205 6 7N 100 22 E
Alora 155 36 49N 4 46W
Alosno 155 37 33N 7 7W
Alotau 227 10 16 S 150 30 E
Alougoum 240 30 17N 6 56W
Aloysius Mt. 229 26 0 S 128 38 E
Alpedrinha 154 40 6N 7 27W
Alpercatas → 120 6 2 S 44 19W
Alpes-de-Haute-Provence □ 141 44 8N 6 10 E
Alpes-Maritimes □ 141 43 55N 7 10 E
Alpha 230 23 39 S 146 37 E
Alphen 143 51 29N 4 58 E
Alphen aan den Rijn 142 52 7N 4 40 E
Alphonse 203 7 0 S 52 45 E
Alpi Apuane 162 44 7N 10 14 E
Alpi Lepontine 149 46 22N 8 27 E
Alpi Orobie 162 46 7N 10 0 E
Alpi Retiche 149 46 30N 10 0 E
Alpiarça 155 39 15N 8 35W
Alpnach 149 46 57N 8 17 E
Alpoyeca 107 17 40N 98 31W
Alps 144 47 0N 8 0 E
Alpujarras, Las 157 36 55N 3 20W
Alpuyeca 107 18 44N 99 16W
Alrø 173 55 52N 10 5 E
Alroy Downs 230 19 20 S 136 5 E
Alsace 139 48 15N 7 25 E
Alsask 88 51 21N 109 59W
Alsásua 156 42 54N 2 10W
Alsen 172 63 23N 13 56 E
Alsfeld 146 50 44N 9 19 E
Alsónémedi 151 47 20N 19 15 E
Alsten 174 65 58N 12 40 E
Alta, Sierra 156 40 31N 1 30W
Alta Gracia 124 31 40 S 64 30W
Alta Lake 93 50 10N 123 0W
Altaelva → 174 69 46N 23 45 E
Altagracia 118 10 45N 71 30W
Altagracia de Orituco 118 9 52N 66 23W
Altai = Aerht'ai Shan 212 46 40N 92 45 E
Altai Mts. 186 46 40N 92 45 E
Altamachi → 122 16 8 S 66 50W
Altamira, Brazil 119 3 12 S 52 10W
Altamira, Chile 124 25 47 S 69 51W
Altamira, Colombia 118 2 3N 75 47W
Altamira, Mexico 103 22 24N 97 55W
Altamira, Cuevas de 154 43 20N 4 5W
Altamira, L. 103 22 24N 98 0W
Altamirano 110 16 53N 92 9W
Altamura 165 40 50N 16 33 E
Altamura, I. 104 25 0N 108 10W
Altanbulag 212 50 16N 106 30 E
Altar 100 30 43N 111 44W
Altar, Desierto de 100 30 10N 112 0W
Altar, R. → 100 30 39N 111 53W
Altario 91 51 55N 110 9W
Altata, B. de 104 24 38N 107 55W
Altavas 211 11 32N 122 29 E
Altay 212 47 48N 88 10 E
Altdorf 149 46 52N 8 36 E
Alte Mellum 146 53 45N 8 6 E
Altea 157 38 38N 0 2W
Altenberg 146 50 46N 13 47 E
Altenbruch 146 53 48N 8 44 E
Altenburg 146 50 59N 12 28 E
Altenkirchen, E. Germany 146 54 38N 13 20 E
Altenkirchen, W. Germany 146 50 41N 7 38 E
Altenmarkt 150 47 43N 14 39 E
Altenteptow 146 53 42N 13 15 E
Alter do Chão 155 39 12N 7 40W
Altiplano 122 17 0 S 68 0W
Altkirch 139 47 37N 7 15 E
Altmühl → 147 48 54N 11 54 E
Alto Adige = Trentino-Alto Adige □ 162 46 30N 11 0 E
Alto Araguaia 123 17 15 S 53 20W
Alto Chindio 251 16 19 S 35 25 E
Alto Cuchumatanes = Cuchumatanes, Sierra de los 112 15 35N 91 25W
Alto Cuito 253 13 27 S 18 49 E
Alto del Inca 124 24 10 S 68 10W
Alto Garças 123 16 56 S 53 32W
Alto Iriri → 123 8 50 S 53 25W
Alto Ligonha 251 15 30 S 38 11 E
Alto Molocue 251 15 50 S 37 35 E
Alto Paraguai 123 14 30 S 56 31W
Alto Paraná □ 125 25 0 S 54 50W
Alto Parnaíba 120 9 6 S 45 57W
Alto Purús → 122 9 12 S 70 28W
Alto Río Senguerr 126 45 2 S 70 50W
Alto Santo 120 5 31 S 38 15W
Alto Sucuriú 123 19 19 S 52 47W
Alto Turi 120 2 54 S 45 38W
Alton 84 43 54N 80 5W
Alton Downs 231 26 7 S 138 57 E
Altona, Canada 89 49 6N 97 33W
Altona, Germany 146 53 32N 9 56 E
Altopáscio 162 43 50N 10 40 E
Altos 120 5 3 S 42 28W
Altotonga 108 19 46N 97 14W
Altötting 147 48 14N 12 41 E
Altstätten 149 47 22N 9 33 E
Altün Küprī 192 35 45N 44 9 E
Altun Shan 212 38 30N 88 0 E
Alubijid 211 8 35N 124 29 E
Alucra 181 40 22N 38 47 E
Aluksne 178 57 24N 27 3 E
Alùla 256 11 50N 50 45 E
Alupka 180 44 23N 34 2 E
Alushta 180 44 40N 34 25 E
Alusi 207 7 35 S 131 40 E
Alustante 156 40 36N 1 40W
Al'Uzayr 192 31 19N 47 25 E
Alvaiázere 154 39 49N 8 23W
Älvängen 173 57 58N 12 8 E
Alvarado 109 18 46N 95 46W
Alvarado, L. 109 18 45N 95 50W
Alvarães 119 3 12 S 64 50W
Álvaro Obregón, Chiapas, Mexico 110 14 55N 92 23W
Álvaro Obregón, Michoacan, Mexico 107 19 50N 101 5W
Alvaro Obregón, San Luis Potosí, Mexico 103 21 51N 98 56W
Álvaro Obregón, Presa 100 27 52N 109 52W
Alvdal 171 62 6N 10 37 E
Alvear 124 29 5 S 56 30W
Alvena 88 52 31N 106 1W
Alverca 155 38 56N 9 1W
Alveringen 143 51 1N 2 43 E
Alvesta 173 56 54N 14 35 E
Alvie 231 38 14 S 143 30 E
Alvinston 84 42 49N 81 52W
Alvito 155 38 15N 8 0W
Älvros 172 62 3N 14 38 E
Älvsborgs län □ 173 58 30N 12 30 E
Älvsbyn 174 65 40N 21 0 E
Älvsered 173 57 14N 12 51 E
Alwar 198 27 38N 76 34 E
Alwaye 201 10 8N 76 24 E
Alxa Zuoqi 214 38 50N 105 40 E
Alyaskitovyy 185 64 45N 141 30 E
Alyata 181 39 58N 49 25 E
Alyth 134 56 38N 3 15W
Alzano Lombardo 162 45 44N 9 43 E
Alzette → 143 49 45N 6 6 E
Alzey 147 49 48N 8 4 E
Am Dam 243 12 40N 20 35 E
Am Géréda 243 12 53N 21 14 E
Am-Timan 243 11 0N 20 10 E
Amacueca 106 20 1N 103 37W
Amacuro □ 119 8 50N 61 5W
Amacuzac 107 18 35N 99 21W
Amacuzac, R. → 107 17 53N 99 12W
Amadeus, L. 229 24 54 S 131 0 E
Amâdi, Sudan 245 5 29N 30 25 E
Amadi, Zaïre 250 3 40N 26 40 E
Amadjuak 95 64 0N 72 39W
Amadjuak L. 95 65 0N 71 8W
Amado Nervo 104 21 3N 104 56W
Amadora 155 38 45N 9 13W
Amagasaki 221 34 42N 135 20 E
Amager 172 55 37N 12 35 E
Amagi 220 33 25N 130 39 E
Amaimon 227 5 12 S 145 30 E
Amakusa-Nada 220 32 35N 130 5 E
Amakusa-Shotō 220 32 15N 130 10 E
Åmål 172 59 3N 12 42 E
Amalapuram 201 16 35N 81 55 E
Amalfi, Colombia 118 6 55N 75 4W
Amalfi, Italy 165 40 39N 14 34 E
Amaliás 169 37 47N 21 22 E
Amalner 198 21 5N 75 5 E
Amambaí 125 23 5 S 55 13W
Amambaí → 125 23 22 S 53 56W
Amambay □ 125 23 0 S 56 0W
Amambay, Cordillera de 125 23 0 S 55 45W
Amami-Guntō 219 28 16N 129 21 E
Amami-Ō-Shima 219 28 0N 129 0 E
Amana → 119 9 45N 62 39W
Amaná, Lago 119 2 35 S 64 40W
Amanab 227 3 40 S 141 14 E
Amanalco de Becerra 107 19 19N 100 1W
Amándola 163 42 59N 13 21 E
Amangeldy 184 50 10N 65 10 E
Amantea 165 39 8N 16 3 E
Amapá 120 2 5N 50 50W
Amapá □ 120 1 40N 52 0W
Amapa, R. → 109 18 16N 96 17W
Amapari 119 0 37N 51 39W
Amara 245 10 25N 34 10 E
Amarante, Brazil 120 6 14 S 42 50W
Amarante, Portugal 154 41 16N 8 5W
Amarante do Maranhão 120 5 36 S 46 45W
Amaranth 89 50 36N 98 43W
Amarapura 202 21 54N 96 3 E
Amaravati → 201 11 0N 78 15 E
Amareleja 155 38 12N 7 13W
Amargosa 121 13 2 S 39 36W
Amargosa, Sa. de la 101 31 5N 105 50W
Amarnath 200 19 12N 73 22 E
Amaro, Mt. 163 42 5N 14 6 E
Amaro Leite 121 13 58 S 49 9W
Amarpur 199 25 5N 87 0 E
Amassama 247 5 1N 6 2 E
Amatán 110 17 21N 92 45W
Amataurá 118 3 29 S 68 6W
Amatenango del Valle 110 16 31N 92 27W
Amatepec 107 18 39N 100 9W
Amatikulu 255 29 3 S 31 33 E
Amatitlán, Guat. 112 14 29N 90 38W
Amatitlán, Mexico 106 20 50N 103 43W
Amatlán de Cañas 104 20 52N 104 27W
Amatlán de Jora 104 21 23N 104 8W
Amatrice 163 42 38N 13 16 E
Amay 143 50 33N 5 19 E
Amaya, R. → 109 18 9N 96 8W
Amayuca 107 18 42N 98 46W
Amazon = Amazonas → 119 0 5 S 50 0W
Amazonas □, Brazil 122 4 0 S 62 0W
Amazonas □, Peru 122 5 0 S 78 0W
Amazonas □, Venezuela 118 3 30N 66 0W
Amazonas → 119 0 5 S 50 0W
Ambad 200 19 38N 75 50 E
Ambahakily 255 21 36 S 43 41 E
Ambala 198 30 23N 76 56 E
Ambalangoda 201 6 15N 80 5 E
Ambalapulai 201 9 25N 76 25 E
Ambalavao 255 21 50 S 46 56 E
Ambalindum 230 23 23 S 135 0 E
Ambam 252 2 20N 11 15 E
Ambanja 255 13 40 S 48 27 E
Ambarchik 185 69 40N 162 20 E
Ambarijeby 255 14 56 S 47 41 E
Ambaro, Helodranon' 255 13 23 S 48 38 E
Ambartsevo 184 57 30N 83 52 E
Ambasamudram 201 8 43N 77 25 E
Ambato 118 1 5 S 78 42W
Ambato, Sierra de 124 28 25 S 66 10W
Ambato Boeny 255 16 28 S 46 43 E
Ambatofinandrahana 255 20 33 S 46 48 E
Ambatolampy 255 19 20 S 47 35 E
Ambatondrazaka 255 17 55 S 48 28 E
Ambatosoratra 255 17 37 S 48 31 E
Ambenja 255 15 17 S 46 58 E
Amberg 147 49 25N 11 52 E
Ambérieu-en-Bugey 141 45 57N 5 20 E
Amberley 235 43 9 S 172 44 E
Ambert 140 45 33N 3 44 E
Ambidédi 246 14 35N 11 47W
Ambikapur 199 23 15N 83 15 E
Ambikol 244 21 20N 30 50 E
Ambinanindrano 255 20 5 S 48 23 E
Ambjörnarp 173 57 25N 13 17 E
Ambleside 132 54 26N 2 58W
Amblève 143 50 21N 6 10 E
Amblève → 143 50 25N 5 45 E
Ambo, Ethiopia 245 12 20N 37 30 E
Ambo, Peru 122 10 5 S 76 10W
Ambodifototra 255 16 59 S 49 52 E
Ambodilazana 255 18 6 S 49 10 E
Ambohimahasoa 255 21 7 S 47 13 E
Ambohimanga 255 20 52 S 47 36 E
Ambohitra 255 12 30 S 49 10 E
Ambon 207 3 35 S 128 20 E
Amboseli L. 250 2 40 S 37 10 E
Ambositra 255 20 31 S 47 25 E
Ambovombé 255 25 11 S 46 5 E
Amboyna I. 206 7 50N 112 50 E
Ambriz 253 7 48 S 13 8 E
Ambunti 227 4 13 S 142 52 E
Ambur 201 12 48N 78 43 E
Amby 231 26 30 S 148 11 E
Amderma 184 69 45N 61 30 E
Amealco 107 20 11N 100 9W
Ameca, Jalisco, Mexico 106 20 33N 104 2W
Ameca, Zacatecas, Mexico 105 22 56N 104 1W
Ameca, R. → 106 20 41N 105 18W
Amecameca de Juárez 107 19 7N 98 46W
Amela, L. de 106 18 51N 103 46W
Ameland 142 53 27N 5 45 E
Amélia 163 42 34N 12 25 E
Amélie-les-Bains-Palalda 140 42 29N 2 41 E
Amen 185 68 45N 180 0 E
Amendolaro 165 39 58N 16 34 E

America 143 51 27N 5 59 E
American Highland 13 73 0 S 75 0 E
American Samoa ■ 225 14 20 S 170 40W
Americana 125 22 45 S 47 20W
Amersfoort, Neth. 142 52 9N 5 23 E
Amersfoort, S. Africa 255 26 59 S 29 53 E
Amery, Australia 229 31 9 S 117 5 E
Amery, Canada 77 56 34N 94 3W
Amery Ice Shelf 13 69 30 S 72 0 E
Amesdale 77 50 2N 92 55W
Amet Sound 81 45 47N 63 10W
Amfíklia 169 38 38N 22 35 E
Amfilokhía 169 38 52N 21 9 E
Amfípolis 168 40 48N 23 52 E
Ámfissa 169 38 32N 22 22 E
Amga 185 60 50N 132 0 E
Amga → 185 62 38N 134 32 E
Amgu 185 45 45N 137 15 E
Amgun → 185 52 56N 139 38 E
Amherst 81 45 48N 64 8W
Amherst I. 85 44 8N 76 43W
Amherstburg 84 42 6N 83 6W
Amiata, Mte. 163 42 54N 11 40 E
Amiens 139 49 54N 2 16 E
Amigdhalokefáli 169 35 23N 23 30 E
Amili 202 28 25N 95 52 E
Amindaion 168 40 42N 21 42 E
Amīrābād 192 33 20N 46 16 E
Amirante Is. 203 6 0 S 53 0 E
Amisk 91 52 33N 111 4W
Amisk L. 77 54 35N 102 15W
Amistad, Presa de la 102 29 26N 101 3W
Amixtlán 108 20 3N 97 48W
Amizmiz 240 31 12N 8 15W
Åmli 171 58 45N 8 32 E
Amlwch 132 53 24N 4 21W
Amm Adam 245 16 20N 36 1 E
'Ammān 189 31 57N 35 52 E
Ammanford 133 51 48N 4 0W
Ammerån 172 63 9N 16 13 E
Ammerån → 172 63 9N 16 13 E
Ammersee 147 48 0N 11 7 E
Ammerzoden 142 51 45N 5 13 E
Ammi'ad 189 32 55N 35 32 E
Amnat Charoen 204 15 51N 104 38 E
Amnéville 139 49 16N 6 9 E
Amo Jiang → 216 23 0N 101 50 E
Āmol 193 36 23N 52 20 E
Amolonga 107 17 37N 99 20W
Amorebieta 156 43 13N 2 44W
Amorgós 169 36 50N 25 57 E
Amos 82 48 35N 78 5W
Åmot, Buskerud, Norway 171 59 54N 9 54 E
Åmot, Telemark, Norway 171 59 34N 8 0 E
Åmotsdal 171 59 37N 8 26 E
Amour, Djebel 241 33 42N 1 37 E
Ampang 205 3 8N 101 45 E
Ampanihy 255 24 40 S 44 45 E
Ampasindava, Helodranon' 255 13 40 S 48 15 E
Ampasindava, Saikanosy 255 13 42 S 47 55W
Ampato, Nevado 122 15 40 S 71 56W
Ampenan 209 8 35 S 116 13 E
Amper 247 9 25N 9 40 E
Amper → 147 48 30N 11 57 E
Ampère 241 35 44N 5 27 E
Ampezzo 163 46 25N 12 48 E
Amposta 156 40 43N 0 34 E
Ampotaka 255 25 3 S 44 41 E
Ampoza 255 22 20 S 44 44 E
Amqa 189 32 59N 35 10 E
Amqui 80 48 28N 67 27W
Amrān 194 15 41N 43 55 E
Amraoti 198 20 55N 77 45 E
Amreli 198 21 35N 71 17 E
Amrenene el Kasba 240 22 10N 0 30 E
Amriswil 149 47 33N 9 18 E
Amritsar 198 31 35N 74 57 E
Amroha 199 28 53N 78 30 E
Amrum 146 54 37N 8 21 E
Amsel 241 22 47N 5 29 E
Amsterdam 142 52 23N 4 54 E
Amsterdam, I. 203 37 30 S 77 30 E
Amstetten 150 48 7N 14 51 E
Amudarya → 184 43 40N 59 0 E
Amulung 210 17 50N 121 43 E
Amund Ringnes I. 95 78 20N 96 25W
Amundsen Gulf 94 71 0N 124 0W
Amundsen Sea 13 72 0 S 115 0W
Amungen 172 61 10N 15 40 E
Amuntai 209 2 28 S 115 25 E
Amur 256 5 16N 46 30 E
Amur → 185 52 56N 141 10 E
Amurang 207 1 5N 124 40 E
Amuri Pass 235 42 31 S 172 11 E
Amurrio 156 43 3N 3 0W
Amursk 185 50 14N 136 54 E
Amurzet 185 47 50N 131 5 E
Amusco 154 42 10N 4 28W
Amutag 210 12 23N 123 16 E
Amvrakikós Kólpos 169 39 0N 20 55 E
Amvrosiyevka 181 47 43N 38 30 E
Amyot 87 48 29N 84 57W
Amzeglouf 240 26 50N 0 1 E
An 202 19 48N 94 0W
An Bien 205 9 45N 105 0 E
An Hoa 204 15 40N 108 5 E
An Khe 204 13 57N 108 39 E
An Nabatīyah at Tahta 190 33 23N 35 27 E
An Nabk, Si. Arabia 192 31 20N 37 20 E
An Nabk, Syria 190 34 2N 36 44 E
An Nabk Abū Qaṣr 192 30 21N 38 34 E
An Nafūd 192 28 15N 41 0 E
An Najaf 192 32 3N 44 15 E
An Naqb, Ra's 191 29 48N 35 44 E
An Nāqūrah 189 33 7N 35 8 E
An Nāṣirīyah 192 31 0N 46 15 E
An Naṣrānī, J. 190 34 3N 37 20 E
An Nawfaliyah 241 30 54N 17 58 E
An Nhon 204 13 55N 109 7 E
An Nîl □ 244 19 30N 33 0 E
An Nîl el Abyad □ 245 14 0N 32 15 E
An Nîl el Azraq □ 245 12 30N 34 30 E
An Nimāş 194 19 7N 42 8 E
An Nu'ayrīyah 192 27 30N 48 30 E
An Nuşayrīyah, J. 190 35 20N 36 13 E
An Nuwayb'ī, W. → 191 29 18N 34 57 E
An Thoi, Dao 205 9 58N 104 0 E
An Uaimh 135 53 39N 6 40W
Åna-Sira 171 58 17N 6 25 E
Anabar → 185 73 8N 113 36 E
'Anabtā 189 32 19N 35 7 E
Anabuki 220 34 2N 134 11 E
Anaco 119 9 27N 64 28W
Anacuao, Mt. 210 16 16N 121 53 E
Anadia, Brazil 120 9 42 S 36 18W
Anadia, Portugal 154 40 26N 8 27W
Anadolu 177 38 0N 30 0 E
Anadyr 185 64 35N 177 20 E
Anadyr → 185 64 55N 176 5 E
Anadyrskiy Zaliv 185 64 0N 180 0 E
Anáfi 169 36 22N 25 48 E
Anafópoulo 169 36 17N 25 50 E
Anagni 164 41 44N 13 8 E
'Anah 192 34 25N 42 0 E
Anahim Lake 92 52 28N 125 18W
Anahuac, Nuevo León, Mexico 102 27 14N 100 9W
Anáhuac, Tamaulipas, Mexico 102 25 50N 97 48W
Anai Mudi, Mt. 201 10 12N 77 4 E
Anaimalai Hills 201 10 20N 76 40 E
Anajás 120 0 59 S 49 57W
Anajatuba 120 3 16 S 44 37W
Anakapalle 200 17 42N 83 6 E
Anakie 230 23 32 S 147 45 E
Anaklia 181 42 22N 41 35 E
Analalava 255 14 35 S 48 0 E
Anamã 119 3 35 S 61 22W
Anama Bay 89 51 58N 98 4W
Anambar → 198 30 15N 68 50 E
Anambas, Kepulauan 208 3 20N 106 30 E
Anamur 177 36 8N 32 58 E
Anamur Burnu 190 36 2N 32 47 E
Anan 220 33 54N 134 40 E
Anand 198 22 32N 72 59 E
Anandpur 199 21 16N 86 13 E
Anánes 169 36 33N 24 9 E
Anantapur 201 14 39N 77 42 E
Anantnag 199 33 45N 75 10 E
Ananyev 180 47 44N 29 47 E
Anao-aon 211 9 47N 125 25 E
Anapa 180 44 55N 37 25 E
Anápolis 121 16 15 S 48 50W
Anapu → 119 1 53 S 50 53W
Anār 193 30 55N 55 13 E
Anār Darreh 197 32 46N 61 39 E
Anārak 193 33 25N 53 40 E
Anatolia = Anadolu 177 38 0N 30 0 E
Anatsogno 255 23 33 S 43 46 E
Añatuya 124 28 20 S 62 50W
Anauá → 119 0 58N 61 21W
Anaunethad L. 77 60 55N 104 25W
Anavilhanas, Arquipélago das 119 2 42 S 60 45W
Anaye 243 19 15N 12 50 E
Anaypazarı 190 36 20N 33 24 E
Anbyŏn 215 39 1N 127 35 E
Ancash □ 122 9 30 S 77 45W
Ancenis 138 47 21N 1 10W
Ancho, Canal 126 50 0 S 74 20W
Anci 214 39 20N 116 40 E
Ancião 154 39 56N 8 27W
Ancohuma, Nevada 122 16 0 S 68 50W
Ancón 122 11 50 S 77 10W
Ancona 163 43 37N 13 30 E
Ancud 126 42 0 S 73 50W
Ancud, G. de 126 42 0 S 73 0W
Anda, China 213 46 24N 125 19 E
Anda, Phil. 210 16 17N 119 57 E
Andacollo, Argentina 124 37 10 S 70 42W
Andacollo, Chile 124 30 5 S 71 10W
Andado 230 25 25 S 135 15 E
Andahuaylas 122 13 40 S 73 25W
Andalgalá 124 27 40 S 66 30W
Åndalsnes 171 62 35N 7 43 E
Andalucía □ 155 37 35N 5 0W
Andalusia □ = Andalucía □ 155 37 35N 5 0W
Andaman Is. 196 12 30N 92 30 E
Andaman Sea 196 13 0N 96 0 E
Andara 254 18 2 S 21 9 E
Andaraí 121 12 48 S 41 20W
Andeer 149 46 36N 9 26 E
Andelfingen 149 47 36N 8 41 E
Andelot 139 48 15N 5 18 E
Andelys, Les 138 49 15N 1 25 E
Andenne 143 50 30N 5 5 E
Andéranboukane 247 15 26N 3 2 E
Anderlecht 143 50 50N 4 19 E
Anderlues 143 50 25N 4 16 E
Andermatt 149 46 38N 8 35 E
Andernach 146 50 24N 7 25 E
Andernos-les-Bains 140 44 44N 1 6W
Anderslöv 172 55 26N 13 19 E
Anderson → 94 69 42N 129 0W
Anderson, Mt. 255 25 5 S 30 42 E
Anderson L. 93 50 37N 122 25W
Anderstorp 173 57 19N 13 39 E
Andes 122 5 40N 75 53W
Andes, Cord. de los 122 20 0 S 68 0W
Andfjorden 174 69 10N 16 20 E
Andhra, L. 200 18 54N 73 32 E
Andhra Pradesh □ 201 16 0N 79 0 E
Andikíthira 169 35 52N 23 15 E
Andīmeshk 193 32 27N 48 21 E
Andímilos 169 36 47N 24 12 E
Andíparos 169 37 0N 25 3 E
Andípaxoi 169 39 9N 20 13 E
Andípsara 169 38 30N 25 29 E
Andírrion 169 38 24N 21 46 E
Andizhan 183 41 10N 72 0 E
Andkhvoy 197 36 52N 65 8 E
Andoany 255 13 25 S 48 16 E
Andoas 118 2 55 S 76 25W
Andol 200 17 51N 78 4 E
Andong 215 36 40N 128 43 E
Andongwei 215 35 6N 119 20 E
Andorra ■ 156 42 30N 1 30 E
Andorra La Vella 156 42 31N 1 32 E
Andover, Canada 81 46 45N 67 42W
Andover, U.K. 133 51 13N 1 29W
Andradina 121 20 54 S 51 23W
Andrahary, Mt. 255 13 37 S 49 17 E
Andraitx 156 39 39N 2 25 E
Andramasina 255 19 11 S 47 35 E
Andranopasy 255 21 17 S 43 44 E
Andreapol 178 56 40N 32 17 E
Andrespol 152 51 45N 19 34 E
Andreville 83 47 41N 69 44W
Andrew 90 53 53N 112 21W
Andrewilla 231 26 31 S 139 17 E
Andreyevka 182 52 19N 51 55 E
Ándria 165 41 13N 16 17 E
Andriba 255 17 30 S 46 58 E
Andrijevica 166 42 45N 19 48 E
Andrítsaina 169 37 29N 21 52 E
Androka 255 24 58 S 44 2 E
Andropov 179 58 5N 38 50 E
Ándros 169 37 50N 24 57 E
Andros I. 112 24 30N 78 0W
Andros Town 112 24 43N 77 47W
Andrychów 152 49 51N 19 18 E
Andújar 155 38 3N 4 5W
Andulo 253 11 25 S 16 45 E
Aneby 173 57 48N 14 49 E
Anegada, Bahía 126 40 20 S 62 20W
Anegada Passage 113 18 15N 63 45W
Anécho 247 6 12N 1 34 E
Añelo 126 38 20 S 68 45W
Anergane 240 31 4N 7 14W
Aneroid 88 49 43N 107 18W
Aneto, Pico de 156 42 37N 0 40 E
Añez 123 15 40 S 63 10W
Anfu 217 27 21N 114 40 E
Ang Thong 204 14 35N 100 31 E
Angadanan 210 16 45N 121 45 E
Angamos, Punta 124 23 1 S 70 32W
Angangueo, Sa. de 107 19 35N 100 12W
Angara → 185 58 30N 97 0 E
Angarab 245 13 11N 37 7 E
Angarsk 185 52 30N 104 0 E
Angas Downs 229 24 49 S 132 14 E
Angas Hills 228 23 0 S 127 50 E
Angaston 232 34 30 S 139 8 E
Angat 210 14 56N 121 2 E
Ånge 172 62 31N 15 35 E
Ángel, Cerro 105 22 49N 102 34W
Ángel de la Guarda, I. 98 29 20N 113 25W
Angel Falls 119 5 57N 62 30W
Angeles 210 15 9N 120 33 E
Ángeles, Sa. de los 103 23 10N 99 15W
Ängelholm 173 56 15N 12 58 E
Angellala 231 26 24 S 146 54 E
Ängelsberg 172 59 58N 16 0 E
Anger → 245 9 37N 36 6 E
Angereb → 245 13 45N 36 40 E
Ångermanälven → 172 62 40N 18 0 E
Angermünde 146 53 1N 14 0 E
Angers, Canada 82 45 31N 75 29W
Angers, France 138 47 30N 0 35W
Angerville 139 48 19N 2 0 E
Ängesån → 174 66 50N 22 15 E
Anghiari 163 43 32N 12 3 E
Angical 121 12 0 S 44 42W
Angikuni L. 77 62 0N 100 0W
Angkor 204 13 22N 103 50 E
Anglem Mt. 235 46 45 S 167 53 E
Anglés 156 41 57N 2 38 E
Anglesey 132 53 17N 4 20W
Anglet 140 43 29N 1 31W
Angleur 143 50 36N 5 35 E
Angliers 82 47 33N 79 14W
Anglin → 140 46 42N 0 52 E
Anglure 139 48 35N 3 50 E
Angmagssalik 12 65 40N 37 20W
Ango 250 4 10N 26 5 E
Angoche 251 16 8 S 40 0 E
Angoche, I. 251 16 20 S 39 50 E
Angol 124 37 56 S 72 45W
Angola ■ 253 12 0 S 18 0 E
Angoram 227 4 4 S 144 4 E
Angostura 104 25 22N 108 11W
Angostura, Presa de la, Chiapas, Mexico 110 16 10N 92 35W
Angostura, Presa de la, Sonora, Mexico 100 30 30N 109 22W
Angoulême 140 45 39N 0 10 E
Angoumois 140 45 50N 0 25 E
Angra dos Reis 125 23 0 S 44 10W
Angren 183 41 1N 70 12 E
Angtassom 205 11 1N 104 41 E
Angu 250 3 25N 24 28 E
Anguang 215 45 15N 123 45 E
Anguila, La 102 27 29N 100 12W
Anguilla 113 18 14N 63 5W
Anguille Mts. 79 48 0N 59 11W
Anguo 214 38 28N 115 15 E
Angurugu 230 14 0 S 136 25 E
Angus 84 44 19N 79 53W
Angus, Braes of 134 56 51N 3 10W
Angusville 89 50 44N 101 1W
Anhanduí → 125 21 46 S 52 9W
Anhée 143 50 18N 4 53 E
Anhelo 102 26 1N 100 57W
Anholt 173 56 42N 11 33 E
Anhua 217 28 23N 111 12 E
Anhui □ 215 32 0N 117 0 E
Anhwei □ = Anhui □ 215 32 0N 117 0 E
Anichab 254 21 0 S 14 46 E
Anicuns 121 16 28 S 49 58W
Ánidhros 169 36 38N 25 43 E
Anie 247 7 42N 1 8 E
Ånimskog 173 58 53N 12 35 E
Anina 166 45 6N 21 51 E
Anini-y 211 10 25N 121 55 E
Anivorano 255 18 44 S 48 58 E
Anjangaon 198 21 10N 77 20 E
Anjar 198 23 6N 70 10 E
Anjidiv I. 201 14 40N 74 10 E
Anjō 221 34 57N 137 5 E
Anjou 138 47 20N 0 15W
Anjozorobe 255 18 22 S 47 52 E
Anju 215 39 36N 125 40 E
Anka 247 12 13N 5 58 E
Ankaboa, Tanjona 255 21 58 S 43 20 E
Ankang 216 32 40N 109 1 E
Ankara 177 40 0N 32 54 E
Ankaramena 255 21 57 S 46 39 E
Ankazoabo 255 22 18 S 44 31 E
Ankazobe 255 18 20 S 47 10 E
Ankisabe 255 19 17 S 46 29 E
Anklam 146 53 48N 13 40 E
Ankleshwar 198 21 38N 73 3 E
Ankober 245 9 35N 39 40 E
Ankoro 250 6 45 S 26 55 E
Anlong 216 25 2N 105 27 E
Anlu 217 31 15N 113 45 E
Anmyŏn-do 215 36 25N 126 25 E
Ånn 172 63 19N 12 34 E
Anna 179 51 28N 40 23 E
Anna Plains 228 19 17 S 121 37 E
Anna Regina 119 7 10N 58 30W
Annaba 241 36 50N 7 46 E
Annaberg-Buchholz 146 50 34N 12 58 E
Annaheim 88 52 19N 104 49W
Annaka 221 36 19N 138 54 E
Annalee → 135 54 3N 7 15W
Annam = Trung-Phan 204 16 0N 108 0 E
Annamitique, Chaîne 204 17 0N 106 0 E

Annan 134 55 0N 3 17W
Annan → 134 54 58N 3 18W
Annanberg 227 4 52S 144 42E
Annapolis Royal 81 44 44N 65 32W
Annapurna 199 28 34N 83 50E
Annean, L. 229 26 54S 118 14E
Anneberg 173 57 32N 12 6E
Annecy 141 45 55N 6 8E
Annecy, L. d' 141 45 52N 6 10E
Annemasse 141 46 12N 6 16E
Annieopsquotch Mts. 79 48 20N 57 30W
Anning 216 24 55N 102 26E
Anningie 228 21 50S 133 7E
Annobón 237 1 25S 5 36E
Annonay 141 45 15N 4 40E
Annonciation, L' 82 46 25N 74 55W
Annot 141 43 58N 6 38E
Annotto Bay 112 18 17N 77 3W
Annuello 231 34 53S 142 55E
Annweiler 147 49 12N 7 58E
Áno Arkhánai 169 35 16N 25 11E
Áno Porróia 168 41 17N 23 2E
Áno Viánnos 169 35 2N 25 21E
Anola 89 49 53N 96 38W
Anorotsangana 255 13 56S 47 55E
Anping, Hebei, China 214 38 15N 115 30E
Anping, Liaoning, China 215 41 5N 123 30E
Anpu Gang 216 21 25N 109 50E
Anqing 217 30 30N 117 3E
Anqiu 215 36 25N 119 10E
Anren 217 26 43N 113 18E
Ans 143 50 39N 5 32E
Ansai 214 36 50N 109 20E
Ansbach 147 49 17N 10 34E
Anse-au-Clair, L' 79 51 25N 57 5W
Anse au Loup, L' 79 51 32N 56 50W
Anseba → 245 16 0N 38 30E
Anserma 118 5 13N 75 48W
Anseroeul 143 50 43N 3 32E
Anshan 215 41 5N 122 58E
Anshun 216 26 18N 105 57E
Ansirabe 255 19 55S 47 2E
Ansó 156 42 51N 0 48W
Anson B. 228 13 20S 130 6E
Ansongo 247 15 25N 0 35E
Anstruther 134 56 14N 2 40W
Ansudu 207 2 11S 139 22E
Antabamba 122 14 40S 73 0W
Antakya 177 36 14N 36 10E
Antalaha 255 14 57S 50 20E
Antalya 177 36 52N 30 45E
Antalya □ 190 36 50N 32 0E
Antalya Körfezi 177 36 15N 31 30E
Antananarivo 255 18 55S 47 31E
Antananarivo □ 255 19 0S 47 0E
Antanimbaribe 255 21 30S 44 48E
Antarctic Pen. 13 67 0S 60 0W
Antarctica 13 90 0S 0 0E
Antelope 251 21 2S 28 31E
Antenor Navarro 120 6 44S 38 27W
Antequera, Paraguay 124 24 8S 57 7W
Antequera, Spain 155 37 5N 4 33W
Anthemoús 168 40 31N 23 15E
Anthony Lagoon 230 18 0S 135 30E
Anti Atlas 240 30 0N 8 30W
Anti-Lebanon 190 33 40N 36 10E
Antibes 141 43 34N 7 6E
Antibes, C. d' 141 43 31N 7 7E
Anticosti, Î. d' 80 49 30N 63 0W
Antifer, C. d' 138 49 41N 0 10E
Antigonish 75 45 38N 61 58W
Antigua, Guat. 112 14 34N 90 41W
Antigua, W. Indies 113 17 0N 61 50W
Antigua and Barbuda ■ 113 17 20N 61 48W
Antiguo Morelos 103 22 33N 99 5W
Antilla 112 20 40N 75 50W
Antioche, Pertuis d' 140 46 6N 1 20W
Antioquia 118 6 40N 75 55W
Antioquia □ 118 7 0N 75 30W
Antipodes Is. 224 49 45S 178 40E
Antiqe □ 211 11 10N 122 5E
Antler 89 49 34N 101 27W
Antler → 89 49 8N 101 0W
Antofagasta 124 23 50S 70 30W
Antofagasta □ 124 24 0S 69 0W
Antofagasta de la Sierra 124 26 5S 67 20W
Antofalla 124 25 30S 68 5W
Antofalla, Salar de 124 25 40S 67 45W
Antoing 143 50 34N 3 27E
Antongila, Helodrano 255 15 30S 49 50E
Antonibé 255 15 7S 47 24E
Antonibé, Presqu'île d' 255 14 55S 47 20E
Antonina 125 25 26S 48 42W
Antonio Escobedo 106 20 46N 103 57W
Antonovo 181 49 25N 51 42E
Antrain 138 48 28N 1 30W
Antrim 135 54 43N 6 13W
Antrim □ 135 54 55N 6 20W
Antrim, Mts. of 135 54 57N 6 8W
Antrim Plateau 228 18 8S 128 20E
Antrodoco 163 42 25N 13 4E
Antropovo 179 58 26N 42 51E
Antsalova 255 18 40S 44 37E
Antsiranana 255 12 25S 49 20E
Antsohihy 255 14 50S 47 59E
Antsohimbondrona Seranana 255 13 7S 48 48E
Antu 215 42 30N 128 20E
Antufash 194 15 42N 42 25E
Antwerp = Antwerpen 143 51 13N 4 25E
Antwerp 232 36 17S 142 4E
Antwerpen 143 51 13N 4 25E
Antwerpen □ 143 51 15N 4 40E
Anupgarh 198 29 10N 73 10E
Anuradhapura 201 8 22N 80 28E
Anveh 193 27 23N 54 11E
Anvers = Antwerpen 143 51 13N 4 25E
Anvers I. 13 64 30S 63 40W
Anxi, Fujian, China 217 25 2N 118 12E
Anxi, Gansu, China 212 40 30N 95 43E
Anxiang 217 29 27N 112 11E
Anxious B. 231 33 24S 134 45E
Anyama 246 5 30N 4 3W
Anyang 214 36 5N 114 21E
Anyer 208 6 4S 105 53E
Anyi, Jiangxi, China 217 28 49N 115 25E
Anyi, Shanxi, China 214 35 2N 111 2E
Anyuan 217 25 9N 115 21E
Anzah 189 32 22N 35 12E
Anzawr 195 17 28N 52 50E
Anze 214 36 10N 112 12E
Anzhero-Sudzhensk 184 56 10N 86 0E
Ánzio 164 41 28N 12 37E
Anzoátegui □ 119 9 0N 64 30W
Aoga-Shima 221 32 28N 139 46E
Aoiz 156 42 46N 1 22W
Aomori 218 40 45N 140 45E
Aomori □ 218 40 45N 140 40E
Aonla 199 28 16N 79 11E
Aono-Yama 220 34 28N 131 48E
Aorangi Mts. 234 41 28S 175 22E
Aoreora 240 28 51N 10 53W
Aosta 162 45 43N 7 20E
Aoudéras 247 17 45N 8 20E
Aouinet Torkoz 240 28 31N 9 46W
Aoukar 240 23 50N 2 45W
Aouker 246 17 40N 10 0W
Aoulef el Arab 240 26 55N 1 2E
Apa → 124 22 6S 58 2W
Apan 107 19 43N 98 25W
Apango 107 17 44N 99 20W
Apapa 247 6 25N 3 25E
Apaporis → 118 1 23S 69 25W
Aparecida do Taboado 121 20 5S 51 5W
Aparri 210 18 22N 121 38E
Aparurén 119 5 6N 62 8W
Apaseo 107 20 33N 100 41W
Apaseo el Alto 107 20 27N 100 37W
Apateu 170 46 36N 21 47E
Apatin 166 45 40N 19 0E
Apàtity 176 67 34N 33 22E
Apatzingan 106 19 5N 102 21W
Apaxco de Ocampo 107 19 59N 99 10W
Apaxtla de Castrejón 107 18 9N 99 52W
Apayao □ 210 18 10N 121 10E
Apeldoorn 142 52 13N 5 57E
Apeldoornsch Kanal 142 52 29N 6 5E
Apen 146 53 12N 7 47E
Apennines 130 44 20N 10 20E
Apere → 123 13 44S 65 18W
Apia 224 13 50S 171 50W
Apiacás, Serra dos 123 9 50S 57 0W
Apiaú → 119 2 39N 61 12W
Apiaú, Serra do 119 2 30N 62 0W
Apidiá → 123 11 39S 61 11W
Apinajé 121 11 31S 48 18W
Apipilulco 107 18 11N 99 41W
Apiti 234 39 58S 175 54E
Apizaco 107 19 25N 98 9W
Apizaloya 105 24 51N 102 20W
Aplao 122 16 0S 72 40W
Apo, Mt. 211 6 53N 125 14E
Apo East Pass 210 12 40N 120 40E
Apo West Pass 210 12 31N 120 22E
Apodaca 102 25 46N 100 12W
Apodi 120 5 39S 37 48W
Apohaqui 81 45 42N 65 36W
Apolda 146 51 1N 11 30E
Apollo Bay 232 38 45S 143 40E
Apollonia = Marsá Susah 242 32 52N 21 59E
Apollonia 169 36 58N 24 43E
Apolo 122 14 30S 68 30W
Apónguao → 119 4 48N 61 36W
Aporé 123 18 58S 52 1W
Aporé → 121 19 27S 50 57W
Aporema 120 1 14N 50 49W
Apóstoles 125 28 0S 56 0W
Apostolos Andreas, C. 190 35 42N 34 35E
Apostolovo 180 47 39N 33 39E
Apoteri 119 4 2N 58 32W
Apozol 105 21 29N 103 6W
Appelscha 142 52 57N 6 21E
Appennini 165 41 0N 15 0E
Appennino Ligure 162 44 30N 9 0E
Appenzell 149 47 20N 9 25E
Appenzell-Ausser Rhoden □ 149 47 23N 9 23E
Appenzell-Inner Rhoden □ 149 47 20N 9 25E
Appiano 163 46 27N 11 17E
Appingedam 142 53 19N 6 51E
Apple Hill 85 45 13N 74 46W
Appleby 132 54 35N 2 29W
Approuague 119 4 20N 52 0W
Approuague → 119 4 30N 51 57W
Apra Harbor 226 13 27N 144 38E
Aprelevka 179 55 34N 37 4E
Apricena 165 41 47N 15 25E
Aprigliano 165 39 17N 16 19E
Aprília 164 41 38N 12 38E
Apsheronsk 181 44 28N 39 42E
Apsley 85 44 45N 78 6W
Apt 141 43 53N 5 24E
Apuaú 119 2 25S 60 53W
Apucarana 125 23 55S 51 33W
Apulco 107 20 19N 98 20W
Apulia = Púglia □ 165 41 0N 16 30E
Apurahuan 211 9 35N 118 20E
Apure □ 118 7 10N 68 50W
Apure → 118 7 37N 66 25W
Apurímac □ 122 14 0S 73 0W
Apurimac → 122 12 17S 73 56W
Apuseni, Munţii 170 46 30N 22 45E
Aqabah = Al 'Aqabah 189 29 31N 35 0E
'Aqabah, Khalīj al 191 28 15N 33 20E
Āqcheh 197 36 56N 66 11E
'Aqdā 193 32 26N 53 37E
Aqīq 244 18 14N 38 12E
Aqīq, Khalīg 244 18 20N 38 10E
'Aqīq, W. al → 194 20 16N 41 40E
Aqrabā 189 32 9N 35 20E
Aqrah 192 36 46N 43 45E
Aquidauana 123 20 30S 55 50W
Aquidauana → 123 19 44S 56 50W
Aquila 106 18 36N 103 30W
Áquila, L' 163 42 21N 13 24E
Aquiles Serdán 101 28 36N 105 53W
Aquin 113 18 16N 73 24W
Aquismón 103 21 38N 99 2W
Ar Rabaḍ 194 23 11N 39 52E
Ar Rachidiya 241 31 58N 4 20W
Ar Rafīd 189 32 57N 35 52E
Ar Raḥḥālīyah 192 32 44N 43 23E
Ar Ramādī 192 33 25N 43 20E
Ar Ramādīyāt 194 24 18N 43 52E
Ar Raml 241 26 45N 19 40E
Ar Ramthā 189 32 34N 36 0E
Ar Raqqah 192 36 0N 38 55E
Ar Rass 192 25 50N 43 40E
Ar Rastān 190 34 55N 36 43E
Ar Rawḍah, S. Yemen 194 14 28N 47 17E
Ar Rawḍah, Si. Arabia 194 21 16N 42 50E
Ar Rawdah, W. → 190 34 24N 37 30E
Ar Rawshān 194 20 2N 42 36E
Ar Rayyānah 194 23 32N 39 45E
Ar Rifā'i 192 31 50N 46 10E
Ar Rijā' 194 13 1N 44 35E
Ar Riyāḍ 192 24 41N 46 42E
Ar Rmās, W. → 190 35 47N 36 50E
Ar Ru'ays 195 26 8N 51 12E
Ar Rukhaymīyah 192 29 22N 45 38E
Ar Rummān 189 32 9N 35 48E
Ar Ruqayyidah 193 25 21N 49 34E
Ar Ruṣāfah 192 35 52N 36 53E
Ar Ruṭbah 192 33 0N 40 15E
Ar Ruwayḍah 194 23 40N 44 40E
Ara 199 25 35N 84 32E
Ara L. 87 50 33N 87 28W
Arab, Bahr el → 245 9 50N 29 0E
Arab, Khalîg el 244 30 55N 29 0E
'Arabābād 193 33 2N 57 41E
'Arabah, W. → 195 18 5N 51 26E
Arabatskaya Strelka 180 45 40N 35 0E
Arabba 163 46 30N 11 51E
Arabelo 119 4 55N 64 13W
Arabia 186 25 0N 45 0E
Arabian Sea 186 16 0N 65 0E
Aracaju 120 10 55S 37 4W
Aracataca 118 10 38N 74 9W
Aracati 120 4 30S 37 44W
Araçatuba 125 21 10S 50 30W
Araceli 211 10 33N 119 59E
Aracena 155 37 53N 6 38W
Aracena, Sierra de 155 37 50N 6 50W
Araçuaí 121 16 52S 42 4W
Araçuaí → 121 16 46S 42 2W
'Arad, Israel 189 31 15N 35 12E
Arad, Romania 170 46 10N 21 20E
Arad □ 170 46 20N 22 0E
Arada 243 15 0N 20 20E
Aradhippou 190 34 57N 33 36E
Aradu Nou 170 46 8N 21 20E
Arafura Sea 207 9 0S 135 0E
Aragarças 123 15 55S 52 15W
Aragats 181 40 30N 44 15E
Aragón □ 156 41 25N 1 0W
Aragón → 156 42 13N 1 44W
Aragona 164 37 24N 13 36E
Aragua □ 118 10 0N 67 10W
Aragua de Barcelona 119 9 28N 64 49W
Araguacema 120 8 50S 49 20W
Araguaçu 121 12 49S 49 51W
Araguaia → 121 5 21S 48 41W
Araguaiana 123 15 43S 51 51W
Araguaína 120 7 12S 48 12W
Araguari 121 18 38S 48 11W
Araguari → 120 1 15N 49 55W
Araguatins 120 5 38S 48 7W
Araioses 120 2 53S 41 55W
Arak, Algeria 240 25 20N 3 45E
Arāk, Iran 193 34 0N 49 40E
Arakan □ 202 19 0N 94 15E
Arakan Yoma 202 20 0N 94 40E
Arákhova 169 38 28N 22 35E
Arakkonam 201 13 7N 79 43E
Araks = Aras, Rūd-e → 192 39 10N 47 10E
Aral Sea = Aralskoye More 184 44 30N 60 0E
Aralsk 184 46 50N 61 20E
Aralskoye More 184 44 30N 60 0E
Aramă, Mţii. de 170 47 10N 22 30E
Aramac 230 22 58S 145 14E
Arambag 199 22 53N 87 48E
Aramberri 103 24 6N 99 49W
Aran Areh 256 9 2N 43 54E
Aran I. 135 55 0N 8 30W
Aran Is. 135 53 5N 9 42W
Aranda de Duero 156 41 39N 3 42W
Arandān 192 35 23N 46 55E
Arandas 106 20 42N 102 21W
Aranđelovac 166 44 18N 20 27E
Aranga 234 35 44S 173 40E
Arani 201 12 43N 79 19E
Aranjuez 154 40 1N 3 40W
Aranos 254 24 9S 19 7E
Aranzazu, Colombia 118 5 16N 75 30W
Aranzazu, Mexico 105 24 37N 101 29W
Arao 220 32 59N 130 25E
Araouane 246 18 55N 3 30W
Arapari 120 5 34S 49 15W
Arapey Grande → 124 30 55S 57 49W
Arapiraca 120 9 45S 36 39W
Arapongas 125 23 29S 51 28W
Ar'ar 192 30 59N 41 2E
Araracuara 118 0 24S 72 17W
Araranguá 125 29 0S 49 30W
Araraquara 121 21 50S 48 0W
Ararás, Serra das 125 25 0S 53 10W
Ararat 231 37 16S 143 0E
Ararat, Mt. = Ağri Daği 177 39 50N 44 15E
Arari 120 3 28S 44 47W
Araria 199 26 9N 87 33E
Araripe, Chapada do 120 7 20S 40 0W
Araripina 120 7 33S 40 34W
Araruama, Lagoa de 121 22 53S 42 12W
Araruna 120 6 52S 35 44W
Aras, Rūd-e → 192 39 10N 47 10E
Araticu 120 1 58S 49 51W
Arauca 118 7 0N 70 40W
Arauca □ 118 6 40N 71 0W
Arauca → 118 7 24N 66 35W
Arauco 124 37 16S 73 25W
Arauco □ 124 37 40S 73 25W
Araújos 121 19 56S 45 14W
Arauquita 118 7 2N 71 25W
Araure 118 9 34N 69 13W
Arawa 245 9 57N 41 58E
Arawata → 235 44 0S 168 40E
Araxá 121 19 35S 46 55W
Araya, Pen. de 119 10 40N 64 0W
Arayat 210 15 10N 120 46E
Arba Minch 245 6 0N 37 30E
Arbat 192 35 25N 45 35E
Arbatax 164 39 57N 9 42E
Arbaza 185 52 40N 92 30E
Arbedo 149 46 12N 9 3E
Arbīl 192 36 15N 44 5E
Arboga 172 59 24N 15 52E
Arbois 139 46 55N 5 46E
Arboletes 118 8 51N 76 26W
Arbon 149 47 31N 9 26E
Arbor Vitae 86 48 54N 94 18W
Arbore 245 5 3N 36 50E
Arborea 164 39 46N 8 34E
Arborfield 88 53 6N 103 39W

Arborg 89 50 54N 97 13W
Arbrå 172 61 28N 16 22 E
Arbresie, L' 141 45 50N 4 26 E
Arbroath 134 56 34N 2 35W
Arbus 164 39 30N 8 33 E
Arbuzinka 180 47 0N 31 59 E
Arc 139 47 28N 5 34 E
Arc → 141 45 34N 6 12 E
Arcachon 140 44 40N 1 10W
Arcachon, Bassin d' 140 44 42N 1 10W
Arcadia 81 43 50N 66 4W
Arcelia 107 18 17N 100 16W
Arcévia 163 43 29N 12 58 E
Archangel = Arkhangelsk 176 64 40N 41 0 E
Archar 166 43 50N 22 54 E
Archena 157 38 9N 1 16W
Archer → 230 13 28 S 141 41 E
Archer B. 230 13 20 S 141 30 E
Archers Post 250 0 35N 37 35 E
Archerwill 88 52 26N 103 51W
Archidona 155 37 6N 4 22W
Arci, Monte 164 39 47N 8 44 E
Arcidosso 163 42 51N 11 30 E
Arcila = Asilah 240 35 29N 6 0W
Arcis-sur-Aube 139 48 32N 4 10 E
Arckaringa 231 27 56 S 134 45 E
Arckaringa Cr. → 231 28 10 S 135 22 E
Arco 162 45 55N 10 54 E
Arco, Sa. del 101 29 38N 107 35W
Arcola 89 49 40N 102 30W
Arcoona 232 31 2 S 137 1 E
Arcos 156 41 12N 2 16W
Arcos de los Frontera 155 36 45N 5 49W
Arcos de Valdevez 154 41 55N 8 22W
Arcot 201 12 53N 79 20 E
Arcoverde 120 8 25 S 37 4W
Arcs, Les 141 43 27N 6 29 E
Arctic Bay 95 73 1N 85 7W
Arctic Ocean 12 78 0N 160 0W
Arctic Red River 94 67 15N 134 0W
Arda →, Bulgaria 167 41 40N 26 29 E
Arda →, Italy 162 44 53N 9 52 E
Ardabīl 193 38 15N 48 18 E
Ardakān = Sepīdān 193 30 20N 52 5 E
Årdal, Aust-Agder, Norway 171 58 42N 7 48 E
Årdal, Rogaland, Norway 171 59 9N 6 13 E
Ardales 155 36 53N 4 51W
Årdalstangen 171 61 14N 7 43 E
Ardatov 179 54 51N 46 15 E
Ardbeg 84 45 38N 80 5W
Ardea 168 40 58N 22 3 E
Ardèche □ 141 44 42N 4 16 E
Ardèche → 141 44 16N 4 39 E
Ardee 135 53 51N 6 32W
Arden, Man., Canada 89 50 17N 99 16W
Arden, Ont., Canada 85 44 43N 76 56W
Arden Stby. 173 56 46N 9 52 E
Ardennes 143 50 0N 5 10 E
Ardennes □ 139 49 35N 4 40 E
Ardentes 139 46 45N 1 50 E
Ardestān 193 33 20N 52 25 E
Ardgour 134 56 45N 5 25W
Árdhas → 168 41 36N 26 25 E
Ardila → 155 38 12N 7 28W
Ardino 167 41 34N 25 9 E
Ardlethan 231 34 22 S 146 53 E
Ardmore, Australia 230 21 39 S 139 11 E
Ardmore, Canada 90 54 20N 110 29W
Ardnacrusha 135 52 43N 8 38W
Ardnamurchan, Pt. of 134 56 44N 6 14W
Ardoise, L' 81 45 37N 60 45W
Ardooie 143 50 59N 3 13 E
Ardore Marina 165 38 11N 16 10 E
Ardres 139 50 50N 2 0 E
Ardrossan, Australia 232 34 26 S 137 53 E
Ardrossan, U.K. 134 55 39N 4 50W
Ards □ 135 54 35N 5 30W
Ards Pen. 135 54 30N 5 25W
Ardud 170 47 37N 22 52 E
Ardunac 181 41 8N 42 5 E
Åre 172 63 22N 13 15 E
Areia Branca 120 5 0 S 37 0W
Aremark 171 59 15N 11 42 E
Arenal, Durango, Mexico 105 24 3N 104 26W
Arenal, Veracruz, Mexico 109 17 53N 95 46W
Arenales, Cerro 126 47 5 S 73 40W
Arenápolis 123 14 26 S 56 49W
Arenas 154 43 17N 4 50W
Arenas de San Pedro 154 40 12N 5 5W
Arendal 171 58 28N 8 46 E
Arendonk 143 51 19N 5 5 E
Arendsee 146 52 52N 11 27 E
Arenillas 118 3 33 S 80 10W
Arenys de Mar 156 41 35N 2 33 E
Arenzano 162 44 24N 8 40 E
Areópolis 169 36 40N 22 22 E
Arequipa 122 16 20 S 71 30W
Arequipa □ 122 16 0 S 72 50W
Arere 119 0 16 S 53 52W
Arero 245 4 41N 38 50 E
Arès 140 44 47N 1 8W
Arévalo 154 41 3N 4 43W
Arezzo 163 43 28N 11 50 E
Arga → 156 42 18N 1 47W
Argalastí 168 39 13N 23 13 E
Argamakmur 208 3 35 S 102 0 E
Argamasilla de Alba 157 39 8N 3 5W
Arganda 156 40 19N 3 26W
Arganil 154 40 13N 8 3W
Argayash 182 55 29N 60 52 E
Argelès-Gazost 140 43 0N 0 6W
Argelès-sur-Mer 140 42 34N 3 1 E
Argens → 141 43 24N 6 44 E
Argent-sur-Sauldre 139 47 33N 2 25 E
Argenta, Canada 76 50 20N 116 55W
Argenta, Italy 163 44 37N 11 50 E
Argentan 138 48 45N 0 1W
Argentário, Mte. 163 42 23N 11 11 E
Argentat 140 45 6N 1 56 E
Argentera 162 44 23N 6 58 E
Argentera, Monte del 162 44 12N 7 5 E
Argenteuil 139 48 57N 2 14 E
Argentia 79 47 18N 53 58W
Argentiera, C. dell' 164 40 44N 8 8 E
Argentière, Aiguilles d' 148 45 58N 7 2 E
Argentière, L' 141 44 47N 6 33 E
Argentina ■ 126 35 0 S 66 0W
Argentina Is. 13 66 0 S 64 0W
Argentino, L. 126 50 10 S 73 0W
Argenton-Château 138 46 59N 0 27W
Argenton-sur-Creuse 140 46 36N 1 30 E
Argeş □ 170 45 0N 24 45 E
Argeş → 170 44 30N 25 50 E
Arghandab → 197 31 30N 64 15 E
Argo 244 19 28N 30 30 E
Argolikós Kólpos 169 37 20N 22 52 E
Argolís □ 169 37 38N 22 50 E
Argonne 139 49 0N 5 20 E
Árgos 169 37 40N 22 43 E
Árgos Orestikón 168 40 27N 21 26 E
Argostólion 169 38 12N 20 33 E
Arguedas 156 42 11N 1 36W
Argun → 185 53 20N 121 28 E
Argungu 247 12 40N 4 31 E
Argyle 89 50 11N 97 27W
Argyle, L. 228 16 20 S 128 40 E
Argyrádhes 168 39 27N 19 58 E
Århus 173 56 8N 10 11 E
Århus Amtskommune □ 173 56 15N 10 15 E
Aria 234 38 33 S 175 0 E
Ariadnoye 218 45 8N 134 25 E
Ariamsvlei 254 28 9 S 19 51 E
Ariana 241 36 52N 10 12 E
Ariano Irpino 165 41 10N 15 4 E
Ariano nel Polèsine 163 44 56N 12 5 E
Ariari → 118 2 35N 72 47W
Aribinda 247 14 17N 0 52W
Arica, Chile 122 18 32 S 70 20W
Arica, Colombia 118 2 0 S 71 50W
Arichat 81 45 31N 61 1W
Arid, C. 229 34 1 S 123 10 E
Arida 221 34 5N 135 8 E
Ariège □ 140 42 56N 1 30 E
Ariège → 140 43 30N 1 25 E
Arieş → 170 46 24N 23 20 E
Arīḩā 190 35 49N 36 35 E
Arilje 166 43 44N 20 7 E
Arima 113 10 38N 61 17W
Aringay 210 16 26N 120 21 E
Arinos → 123 10 25 S 58 20W
Ario de Rosales 106 19 12N 101 43W
Aripuanã 123 9 25 S 60 30W
Aripuanã → 123 5 7 S 60 25W
Ariquemes 123 9 55 S 63 6W
Arisaig 134 56 55N 5 50W
Arīsh, W. el → 244 31 9N 33 49 E
Arismendi 118 8 29N 68 22W
Arissa 245 11 10N 41 35 E
Arista, Chiapas, Mexico 110 15 56N 93 48W
Arista, San Luis Potosí, Mexico 103 22 39N 100 50W
Aristazabal I. 92 52 40N 129 10W
Arita 220 33 11N 129 54 E
Aritao 210 16 18N 121 2 E
Arivechi 100 28 56N 109 11W
Arivonimamo 255 19 1 S 47 11 E
Ariyalur 201 11 8N 79 8 E
Ariza 220 41 19N 2 3W
Arizaro, Salar de 124 24 40 S 67 50W
Arizona 124 35 45 S 65 25W
Arizpe 100 30 20N 110 10W
Årjäng 172 59 24N 12 8 E
Arjeplog 174 66 3N 18 2 E
Arjona, Colombia 118 10 14N 75 22W
Arjona, Spain 155 37 56N 4 4W
Arjuno 209 7 49 S 112 34 E
Arka 185 60 15N 142 0 E
Arkadak 179 51 58N 43 19 E
Arkadhía □ 169 37 30N 22 20 E
Arkaig, L. 134 56 58N 5 10W
Arkalyk 184 50 13N 66 50 E
Árkathos → 168 39 20N 21 4 E
Arkhángelos 169 36 13N 28 7 E
Arkhangelsk 176 64 40N 41 0 E
Arkhangelskoye 179 51 32N 40 58 E
Arkiko 245 15 33N 39 30 E
Arklow 135 52 48N 6 10W
Árkoi 169 37 24N 26 44 E
Arkona 84 43 4N 81 50W
Arkona, Kap 146 54 41N 13 26 E
Arkösund 173 58 29N 16 56 E
Arkoúdhi 169 38 33N 20 43 E
Arkticheskiy, Mys 185 81 10N 95 0 E
Arkul 182 57 17N 50 3 E
Arlanc 140 45 25N 3 42 E
Arlanza → 154 42 6N 4 9W
Arlanzón → 154 42 3N 4 17W
Arlberg Pass 147 47 9N 10 12 E
Arles 141 43 41N 4 40 E
Arlesheim 148 47 30N 7 37 E
Arlington 255 28 1 S 27 53 E
Arlon 143 49 42N 5 49 E
Arlöv 172 55 38N 13 5 E
Arly 247 11 35N 1 28 E
Armagh, Canada 83 46 41N 70 32W
Armagh, U.K. 135 54 22N 6 40W
Armagh □ 135 54 18N 6 37W
Armagnac 140 43 44N 0 10 E
Armançon → 139 47 59N 3 30 E
Armavir 181 45 2N 41 7 E
Armenia 118 4 35N 75 45W
Armenian S.S.R. □ 181 40 0N 44 0 E
Armeniş 170 45 13N 22 17 E
Armentières 139 50 40N 2 50 E
Armería 106 18 56N 103 58W
Armería, R. → 106 18 52N 103 59W
Armidale 231 30 30 S 151 40 E
Armstrong, B.C., Canada 93 50 25N 119 10W
Armstrong, Ont., Canada 86 50 18N 89 4W
Armstrong Cr. → 228 16 35 S 131 40 E
Armur 200 18 48N 78 16 E
Arnaía 168 40 30N 23 40 E
Arnaouti, C. 190 35 6N 32 17 E
Arnarfjörður 174 65 48N 23 40W
Arnaud → 78 59 59N 69 46W
Arnay-le-Duc 139 47 10N 4 27 E
Arnedillo 156 42 13N 2 14W
Arnedo 156 42 12N 2 5W
Arnemuiden 143 51 30N 3 40 E
Árnes, Iceland 174 66 1N 21 31W
Årnes, Norway 171 60 7N 11 28 E
Arnhem 142 51 58N 5 55 E
Arnhem, C. 230 12 20 S 137 30 E
Arnhem B. 230 12 20 S 136 10 E
Arnhem Land 230 13 10 S 134 30 E
Árnissa 168 40 47N 21 49 E
Arno → 162 43 41N 10 17 E
Arno Bay 232 33 54 S 136 34 E
Arnoldstein 150 46 33N 13 43 E
Arnon → 139 47 13N 2 1 E
Arnot 77 55 56N 96 41W
Arnøy 174 70 9N 20 40 E
Arnprior 85 45 26N 76 21W
Arnsberg 146 51 25N 8 2 E
Arnstadt 146 50 50N 10 56 E
Arntfield 82 48 12N 79 15W
Aro → 119 8 1N 64 11W
Aroab 254 26 41 S 19 39 E
Aroánia Óri 169 37 56N 22 12 E
Aroche 155 37 56N 6 57W
Aroeiras 120 7 31 S 35 41W
Arolla 148 46 2N 7 29 E
Arolsen 146 51 23N 9 1 E
Aron → 139 46 50N 3 27 E
Arona 162 45 45N 8 32 E
Aroroy 210 12 31N 123 24 E
Aros, R. → 100 29 20N 109 58W
Arosa 149 46 47N 9 41 E
Arosa, Ria de → 154 42 28N 8 57W
Arpajon, Cantal, France 140 44 54N 2 28 E
Arpajon, Essonne, France 139 48 37N 2 12 E
Arpino 164 41 40N 13 35 E
Arque 122 17 48 S 66 23W
Arrabury 231 26 45 S 141 0 E
Arraias 121 12 56 S 46 57W
Arraias →, Mato Grosso, Brazil 123 11 10 S 53 35W
Arraias →, Pará, Brazil 120 7 30 S 49 20W
Arraiolos 155 38 44N 7 59W
Arran, Canada 89 51 53N 101 43W
Arran, U.K. 134 55 34N 5 12W
Arrandale 76 54 57N 130 0W
Arras 139 50 17N 2 46 E
Arrats → 140 44 6N 0 52 E
Arreau 140 42 54N 0 22 E
Arrecifes 124 34 6 S 60 9W
Arrée, Mts. d' 138 48 26N 3 55W
Arriaga 110 16 14N 93 54W
Arrilalah P.O. 230 23 43 S 143 54 E
Arrino 229 29 30 S 115 40 E
Arrojado → 121 13 24 S 44 20W
Arromanches-les-Bains 138 49 20N 0 38W
Arronches 155 39 8N 7 16W
Arros → 140 43 40N 0 2W
Arrou 138 48 6N 1 8 E
Arrow, L. 135 54 3N 8 20W
Arrow Park 93 50 6N 117 57W
Arrowhead 93 50 40N 117 55W
Arrowsmith, Mt. 235 43 20 S 170 55 E
Arrowtown 235 44 57 S 168 50 E
Arrowwood 91 50 44N 113 9W
Arroyo de la Luz 155 39 30N 6 38W
Arroyo Salado, R. → 99 24 25N 111 33W
Arroyo Seco 107 21 33N 99 42W
Arroyo Zarco 107 20 7N 99 44W
Års, Denmark 173 56 48N 9 30 E
Ars, France 140 46 13N 1 30W
Ars, Iran 192 37 9N 47 46 E
Ars-sur-Moselle 139 49 5N 6 4 E
Arsenault L. 77 55 6N 108 32W
Arsenev 218 44 10N 133 15 E
Arsi □ 245 7 45N 39 0 E
Arsiero 163 45 49N 11 22 E
Arsikere 201 13 15N 76 15 E
Arsk 179 56 10N 49 50 E
Arslanköy 190 37 0N 34 17 E
Arsuz 190 36 24N 35 51 E
Árta, Greece 169 39 8N 21 2 E
Artá, Spain 156 39 41N 3 21 E
Árta □ 168 39 15N 21 5 E
Arteaga, Coahuila, Mexico 102 25 28N 100 51W
Arteaga, Michoacan, Mexico 106 18 28N 102 25W
Arteche 210 12 30N 125 35 E
Arteijo 154 43 19N 8 29W
Artem, Ostrov 181 40 28N 50 20 E
Artemovsk, R.S.F.S.R., U.S.S.R. 185 54 45N 93 35 E
Artemovsk, Ukraine S.S.R., U.S.S.R. 180 48 35N 38 0 E
Artemovski 181 47 45N 40 16 E
Artemovskiy 182 57 21N 61 54 E
Arten 218 43 22N 132 13 E
Artenay 139 48 5N 1 50 E
Artern 146 51 22N 11 18 E
Artesa de Segre 156 41 54N 1 3 E
Artesia = Mosomane 254 24 2 S 26 19 E
Arth 149 47 4N 8 31 E
Arthez-de-Béarn 140 43 29N 0 38W
Arthington 246 6 35N 10 45W
Arthur 84 43 50N 80 32W
Arthur → 230 41 2 S 144 40 E
Arthur Cr. → 230 22 30 S 136 25 E
Arthur Pt. 230 22 7 S 150 3 E
Arthurette 81 46 47N 67 29W
Arthur's Pass 235 42 54 S 171 35 E
Arthur's Town 113 24 38N 75 42W
Artigas 124 30 20 S 56 30W
Artik 181 40 38N 43 58 E
Artillery L. 77 63 9N 107 52W
Artois 139 50 20N 2 30 E
Artotína 169 38 42N 22 2 E
Artsiz 180 46 4N 29 26 E
Artvin 180 41 14N 41 44 E
Aru, Kepulauan 207 6 0 S 134 30 E
Aru Meru □ 250 3 20 S 36 50 E
Arua 250 3 1N 30 58 E
Aruanã 121 14 54 S 51 10W
Aruba 113 12 30N 70 0W
Arudy 140 43 7N 0 28W
Arumã 119 4 44 S 62 8W
Arumpo 231 33 48 S 142 55 E
Arun → 199 26 55N 87 10 E
Arunachal Pradesh □ 202 28 0N 95 0 E
Arundel 82 45 58N 74 37W
Aruppukkottai 201 9 31N 78 8 E
Arusha 250 3 20 S 36 40 E
Arusha □ 250 4 0 S 36 30 E
Arusha Chini 250 3 32 S 37 20 E
Arut → 209 2 42 S 111 34 E
Aruvi → 201 8 48N 79 53 E
Aruwimi → 250 1 13N 23 36 E
Arvakalu 201 8 20N 79 58 E
Arve → 141 46 11N 6 8 E
Arvert, L. 80 52 18N 61 45W
Arvi 198 20 59N 78 16 E
Arvida 83 48 25N 71 14W
Arvidsjaur 174 65 35N 19 10 E

Arvika 172 59 40N 12 36 E
Arvilla 90 53 59N 114 0W
Arxan 213 47 11N 119 57 E
Arys 183 42 26N 68 48 E
Arys → 183 42 45N 68 15 E
Arzachena 164 41 5N 9 27 E
Arzamas 179 55 27N 43 55 E
Arzew 241 35 50N 0 23W
Arzgir 181 45 18N 44 23 E
Arzignano 163 45 30N 11 20 E
As, Belgium 143 51 1N 5 35 E
Aš, Czech. 150 50 13N 12 12 E
Aş Şadr 195 24 40N 54 41 E
Aş Şafā 190 33 10N 37 0 E
'As Saffānīyah 193 28 5N 48 50 E
Aş Şāfī 189 31 2N 35 28 E
As Safīrah 190 36 5N 37 21 E
Aş Şahm 195 24 10N 56 53 E
As Sājir 192 25 11N 44 36 E
As Salamīyah, Si. Arabia 194 24 12N 47 18 E
As Salamīyah, Syria 190 35 1N 37 2 E
As Salt 189 32 2N 35 43 E
As Sal'w'a 195 24 23N 50 50 E
As Samāwah 192 31 15N 45 15 E
As Samū' 189 31 24N 35 4 E
As Sanamayn 189 33 3N 36 10 E
Aş Saqlabīya 190 35 23N 36 23 E
As Sawādah 194 22 24N 44 28 E
As Sayl al Kabīr 194 21 38N 40 25 E
As Sukhnah 192 34 52N 38 52 E
As Sulaymānīyah 194 24 9N 47 18 E
As Sulaymī 192 26 17N 41 21 E
As Sulayyil 194 20 27N 45 34 E
As Sulṭan 241 31 4N 17 8 E
As Sumaymānīyah 192 35 35N 45 29 E
As Summān 192 25 0N 47 0 E
As Sūq 194 21 54N 42 3 E
Aş Şurrah 194 13 57N 46 14 E
As Suwaydā' 190 32 40N 36 30 E
As Suwaydā' □ 190 32 45N 36 45 E
As Suwayh 195 22 10N 59 33 E
As Suwayq 195 23 51N 57 26 E
As Şuwayrah 192 32 55N 45 0 E
Asab 254 25 30 S 18 0 E
Asaba 247 6 12N 6 38 E
Asafo 246 6 20N 2 40W
Asahi 221 35 43N 140 39 E
Asahi-Gawa → 220 34 36N 133 58 E
Asahigawa 218 43 46N 142 22 E
Asale, L. 245 14 0N 40 20 E
Asama-Yama 221 36 24N 138 31 E
Asamankese 247 5 50N 0 40W
Asansol 199 23 40N 87 1 E
Åsarna 172 62 39N 14 22 E
Asbe Teferi 245 9 4N 40 49 E
Asbesberge 254 29 0 S 23 0 E
Asbest 182 57 0N 61 30 E
Asbestos 75 45 47N 71 58W
Ascensión, Chihuahua, Mexico 101 31 6N 107 59W
Ascensión, Nuevo León, Mexico 103 24 20N 99 55W
Ascensión, B. de la 111 19 40N 87 30W
Ascension I. 129 8 0 S 14 15W
Aschach 150 48 22N 14 2 E
Aschaffenburg 147 49 58N 9 8 E
Aschendorf 146 53 2N 7 22 E
Aschersleben 146 51 45N 11 28 E
Asciano 163 43 14N 11 32 E
Áscoli Piceno 163 42 51N 13 34 E
Áscoli Satriano 165 41 11N 15 32 E
Ascona 149 46 9N 8 46 E
Ascope 122 7 46 S 79 8W
Ascotán 124 21 45 S 68 17W
Ascuncion 211 7 35N 125 45 E
Aseb 245 13 0N 42 40 E
Åseda 173 57 10N 15 20 E
Asedjrad 240 24 51N 1 29 E
Asela 245 8 0N 39 0 E
Asenovgrad 167 42 1N 24 51 E
Aseral 171 58 37N 7 25 E
Asfeld 139 49 27N 4 5 E
Asfûn el Matâ'na 244 25 26N 32 30 E
Åsgårdstrand 171 59 22N 10 27 E
Ash Shamāl □ 190 34 25N 36 0 E
Ash Shāmīyah 192 31 55N 44 35 E
Ash Sha'rā' 194 24 16N 44 11 E
Ash Shāriqah 195 25 23N 55 26 E
Ash Sharmah 191 28 1N 35 16 E
Ash Sharqāt 192 35 27N 43 16 E
Ash Shaṭrah 192 31 30N 46 10 E
Ash Shawbak 192 30 32N 35 34 E
Ash Shawmari, J. 191 30 35N 36 35 E
Ash Shaykh, J. 190 33 25N 35 50 E
Ash Shifā' 191 28 30N 35 30 E
Ash Shiḥr 195 14 45N 49 36 E
Ash Shināfīyah 192 31 35N 44 39 E
Ash Shu'aybah 192 27 53N 44 43 E
Ash Shumlūl 192 26 31N 47 20 E
Ash Shūnah ash Shamālīyah 189 32 37N 35 34 E
Ash Shuqayq 194 17 44N 42 1 E
Ash Shūr'a 192 35 58N 43 13 E
Ash Shurayf 192 25 43N 29 14 E
Ash Shuwayfāt 190 33 45N 35 30 E
Asha 182 55 0N 57 16 E
Ashaira 244 21 40N 40 40 E
Ashanti □ 247 7 30N 1 30W
Ashau 204 16 6N 107 22 E
Ashburton 235 43 53 S 171 48 E
Ashburton → 228 21 40 S 114 56 E
Ashburton, North Branch → 235 43 54 S 171 44 E
Ashburton, South Branch → 235 43 54 S 171 44 E
Ashburton Downs 228 23 25 S 117 4 E
Ashby-de-la-Zouch 132 52 45N 1 29W
Ashcroft 93 50 40N 121 20W
Ashdod 189 31 49N 34 35 E
Ashdot Yaaqov 189 32 39N 35 35 E
Ashern 89 51 11N 98 21W
Asheweig → 74 54 17N 87 12W
Ashford, Australia 231 29 15 S 151 3 E
Ashford, U.K. 133 51 8N 0 53 E
Ashibetsu 218 43 31N 142 11 E
Ashikaga 221 36 28N 139 29 E
Ashio 221 36 38N 139 27 E
Ashizuri-Zaki 220 32 44N 133 0 E
Ashkarkot 198 33 3N 67 58 E
Ashkhabad 184 38 0N 57 50 E
Ashmont 90 54 7N 111 35W
Ashmore Reef 228 12 14 S 123 5 E
Ashmûn 244 30 18N 30 55 E
Ashq'elon 189 31 42N 34 35 E
Ashti 200 18 50N 75 15 E
Ashton 254 33 50 S 20 5 E
Ashton-under-Lyne 132 53 30N 2 8W
Ashuanipi, L. 80 52 45N 66 15W
Ashurst 234 40 16 S 175 45 E
'Āṣi →, Syria 190 36 0N 36 22 E
Ası →, Turkey 190 36 2N 35 57 E
Asia 186 45 0N 75 0 E
Asia, Kepulauan 207 1 0N 131 13 E
Āsīā Bak 193 35 19N 50 30 E
Asiago 163 45 52N 11 30 E
Asidonhoppo 119 3 50N 55 30W
Asientos 105 22 14N 102 6W
Asifabad 200 19 20N 79 24 E
Asike 207 6 39 S 140 24 E
Asilah 240 35 29N 6 0W
Asinara, G. dell' 164 41 0N 8 30 E
Asinara I. 164 41 5N 8 15 E
Asino 184 57 0N 86 0 E
'Asīr □ 194 18 40N 42 30 E
Asir, Ras 236 11 55N 51 10 E
Aska 200 19 2N 84 42 E
Asker 171 59 50N 10 26 E
Askersund 173 58 53N 14 55 E
Askim 171 59 35N 11 10 E
Askino 182 56 5N 56 34 E
Askja 174 65 3N 16 48W
Asl 244 29 33N 32 44 E
Āsmār 197 35 10N 71 27 E
Asmara = Asmera 245 15 19N 38 55 E
Asmera 245 15 19N 38 55 E
Asnœs 172 55 40N 11 0 E
Asni 240 31 17N 7 58W
Aso 220 33 0N 131 5 E
Aso-Zan 220 32 53N 131 6 E
Ásola 162 45 12N 10 25 E
Asoteriba, Jebel 244 21 51N 36 30 E
Aspe 157 38 20N 0 40W
Aspen 81 45 18N 62 3W
Aspen Grove 93 49 57N 120 37W
Aspiring, Mt. 235 44 23 S 168 46 E
Aspres 141 44 32N 5 44 E
Aspromonte 165 38 10N 16 0 E
Aspur 198 23 58N 74 7 E
Asquith 88 52 8N 107 13W
Assa 240 28 35N 9 6W
Assâba 246 16 10N 11 45W
Assam □ 202 26 0N 93 0 E
Assamakka 247 19 21N 5 38 E
Asse 143 50 24N 4 10 E
Assebroek 143 51 11N 3 17 E
Assekrem 241 23 16N 5 49 E
Assémini 164 39 18N 9 0 E
Assen 142 53 0N 6 35 E
Assendelft 142 52 29N 4 45 E
Assenede 143 51 14N 3 46 E
Assens, Fyn, Denmark 173 56 41N 10 3 E
Assens, Fyn, Denmark 173 55 16N 9 55 E
Assesse 143 50 22N 5 2 E
Assigny, L. 80 52 0N 65 20W
Assini 246 5 9N 3 17W
Assiniboia 88 49 40N 105 59W
Assiniboine → 89 49 53N 97 8W
Assis 125 22 40 S 50 20W
Assisi 163 43 4N 12 36 E
Ássos 169 38 22N 20 33 E
Assus 168 39 32N 26 22 E
Assynt, L. 134 58 25N 5 15W
Astaffort 140 44 4N 0 40 E
Astakidha 169 35 53N 26 50 E
Astapa 110 17 46N 92 51W
Astara 177 38 30N 48 50 E
Asten 143 51 24N 5 45 E
Asti 162 44 54N 8 11 E
Astipálaia 169 36 32N 26 22 E
Astorga, Mindanao, Phil. 211 6 54N 125 27 E
Astorga, Panay, Phil. 211 11 15N 122 48 E
Astorga, Spain 154 42 29N 6 8W
Åstorp 172 56 6N 12 55 E
Astorville 84 46 11N 79 17W
Astrakhan 181 46 25N 48 5 E
Astrakhan-Bazàr 177 39 14N 48 30 E
Astudillo 154 42 12N 4 22W
Asturias □ 154 43 15N 6 0W
Asunción 124 25 10 S 57 30W
Asunción, B. de la 99 27 6N 114 11W
Asunción, La 119 11 2N 63 53W
Asunción Nochixtlán 109 17 28N 97 14W
Asunción Tlacolulita 109 16 18N 95 44W
Asutri 245 15 25N 35 45 E
Aswa → 250 3 43N 31 55 E
Aswad, Ras al 194 21 20N 39 0 E
Aswân 244 24 4N 32 57 E
Aswân High Dam = Sadd el Aali 244 23 54N 32 54 E
Asyût 244 27 11N 31 4 E
Asyûti, Wadi → 244 27 11N 31 16 E
Aszód 151 47 39N 19 28 E
At Ṭafīlah 191 30 45N 35 30 E
At Ta'if 194 21 5N 40 27 E
At Tāj 242 24 13N 23 18 E
At Tamīmī 242 32 20N 23 4 E
Aṭ Ṭirāq 192 27 19N 44 33 E
Aṭ Ṭubayq 191 29 30N 37 0 E
Aṭ Ṭur 189 31 47N 35 14 E
At Turbah, S. Yemen 194 12 40N 43 30 E
At Turbah, Yemen 194 13 13N 44 7 E
Aṭ Ṭurrah 189 32 39N 35 59 E
Aṭ Ṭuwayrifah 195 21 30N 49 35 E
Atacama □ 124 27 30 S 70 0W
Atacama, Desierto de 124 24 0 S 69 20W
Atacama, Salar de 124 23 30 S 68 20W
Ataco 118 3 35N 75 23W
Atakor 241 23 27N 5 31 E
Atakpamé 247 7 31N 1 13 E
Atalándi 169 38 39N 22 58 E
Atalaya 122 10 45 S 73 50W
Ataléia 121 18 3 S 41 6W
Atami 221 35 5N 139 4 E
Atankawng 202 25 50N 97 47 E
Atapupu 207 9 0 S 124 51 E
Atâr 240 20 30N 13 5W
Atara 185 63 10N 129 10 E
Ataram, Erg n- 240 23 57N 2 0 E
Atarfe 155 37 13N 3 40W
Atarjea 107 21 23N 99 52W
Atasta 111 18 0N 92 57W
Atasta, L. de 111 18 35N 92 6W
Atasu 184 48 30N 71 0 E
Atauro 207 8 10 S 125 30 E
Atbara 244 17 42N 33 59 E
'Atbara → 244 17 40N 33 56 E
Atbasar 184 51 48N 68 20 E
Atbashi 183 41 10N 75 48 E
Atbashi, Khrebet 183 40 50N 75 30 E
Atebubu 247 7 47N 1 0W
Ateca 156 41 20N 1 49W
Atemajac de Brizuela 106 20 11N 103 42W
Atenango del Río 107 18 5N 99 6W
Atencingo 109 18 30N 98 36W
Atenguillo 106 20 25N 104 31W
Atenguillo, R. → 106 20 25N 104 38W
Atequiza 106 20 24N 103 8W
Aterno → 163 42 11N 13 51 E
Atesine, Alpi 162 46 55N 11 30 E
Atessa 163 42 5N 14 27 E
Ath 143 50 38N 3 47 E
Athabasca 90 54 45N 113 20W
Athabasca → 77 58 40N 110 50W
Athabasca, L. 77 59 15N 109 15W
Athboy 135 53 37N 6 55W
Athenry 135 53 18N 8 45W
Athens = Athínai 169 37 58N 23 46 E
Athens 85 44 38N 75 57W
Atherley 84 44 37N 79 20W
Atherton 230 17 17 S 145 30 E
Athiéme 247 6 37N 1 40 E
Athienou 190 35 3N 33 32 E
Athínai 169 37 58N 23 46 E
Athlone 135 53 26N 7 57W
Athni 200 16 44N 75 6 E
Athol 235 45 30 S 168 35 E
Atholl, Forest of 134 56 51N 3 50W
Atholville 81 47 59N 66 43W
Áthos 168 40 9N 24 22 E
Athus 143 49 34N 5 50 E
Athy 135 53 0N 7 0W
Ati, Chad 243 13 13N 18 20 E
Ati, Sudan 245 13 5N 29 2 E
Atiak 250 3 12N 32 2 E
Atiamuri 234 38 24 S 176 5 E
Atico 122 16 14 S 73 40W
Aticonipi, L. 80 51 52N 59 22W
Atienza 156 41 12N 2 52W
Atikokan 86 48 45N 91 37W
Atikonak → 80 52 51N 65 16W
Atikonak L. 80 52 40N 64 32W
Atimonan 210 14 0N 121 55 E
Atinah, W. → 195 18 23N 53 28 E
Atirampattinam 201 10 28N 79 20 E
Atka 185 60 50N 151 48 E
Atkarsk 179 51 55N 45 2 E
Atlacomulco de Fabela 107 19 48N 99 53W
Atlantic Ocean 128 0 0 20 0W
Atlántico □ 118 10 45N 75 0W
Atlatlahucan 107 18 58N 98 54W
Atlin 76 59 31N 133 41W
Atlin, L. 76 59 26N 133 45W
Atlit 189 32 42N 34 56 E
Atlixco 109 18 54N 98 26W
Atløy 171 61 21N 4 58 E
Atmakur 201 14 37N 79 40 E
Atna → 171 61 44N 10 49 E
Atō 220 34 25N 131 40 E
Atok 210 16 35N 120 41 E
Átokos 169 38 28N 20 49 E
Atolinga 105 21 44N 103 28W
Atotonilco 105 24 15N 102 45W
Atotonilco, L. de 106 20 22N 103 39W
Atotonilco el Alto 106 20 33N 102 31W
Atotonilco el Grande 107 20 17N 98 40W
Atouguia 155 39 20N 9 20W
Atoyac 106 20 1N 103 32W
Atoyac, R. →, Oaxaca, Mexico 109 16 30N 97 31W
Atoyac, R. →, Puebla, Mexico 109 18 10N 98 31W
Atoyac de Álvarez 107 17 12N 100 26W
Atoyatempan 109 18 49N 97 55W
Atrak → 193 37 50N 57 0 E
Ätran 173 57 7N 12 57 E
Atrato → 118 8 17N 76 58W
Atrauli 198 28 2N 78 20 E
Atri 163 42 35N 14 0 E
Atsbi 245 13 52N 39 50 E
Atsoum, Mts. 247 6 41N 12 57 E
Atsugi 221 35 25N 139 21 E
Atsumi 221 34 35N 137 4 E
Atsumi-Wan 221 34 44N 137 13 E
Atsuta 218 43 24N 141 26 E
Attawapiskat 74 52 56N 82 24W
Attawapiskat → 74 52 57N 82 18W
Attawapiskat, L. 74 52 18N 87 54W
Attendorn 146 51 8N 7 54 E
Attersee 150 47 55N 13 32 E
Attert 143 49 45N 5 47 E
Attichy 139 49 25N 3 3 E
Attigny 139 49 28N 4 35 E
Attikamagen L. 78 55 0N 66 30W
Attikí □ 169 38 10N 23 40 E
'Attīl 189 32 23N 35 4 E
Attock 198 33 52N 72 20 E
Attopeu 204 14 48N 106 50 E
Attunga 233 30 55 S 150 50 E
Attur 201 11 35N 78 30 E
Attwood → 86 51 15N 88 30W
Atūd 195 14 53N 48 10 E
Atuel → 124 36 17 S 66 50W
Åtvidaberg 173 58 12N 16 0 E
Atwood 84 43 40N 81 1W
Atzcapotzalco 107 19 28N 99 12W
Aubagne 141 43 17N 5 37 E
Aubange 143 49 34N 5 48 E
Aube □ 139 48 15N 4 0 E
Aube → 139 48 34N 3 43 E
Aubel 143 50 42N 5 51 E
Aubenas 141 44 37N 4 24 E
Aubenton 139 49 50N 4 12 E
Aubigny-sur-Nère 139 47 30N 2 24 E
Aubin 140 44 33N 2 15 E
Aubrac, Mts. d' 140 44 38N 2 58 E
Aubry L. 94 67 23N 126 30W
Auburn Range 231 25 15 S 150 30 E
Aubusson 140 45 57N 2 11 E
Auch 140 43 39N 0 36 E
Auchel 139 50 30N 2 29 E
Auchi 247 7 6N 6 13 E
Auckland 234 36 52 S 174 46 E
Auckland □ 234 38 35 S 177 0 E
Auckland Is. 224 50 40 S 166 5 E
Aude □ 140 43 8N 2 28 E
Aude → 140 43 13N 3 14 E
Audegle 256 1 59N 44 50 E
Auden 87 50 14N 87 53W
Auderghem 143 50 49N 4 26 E
Auderville 138 49 43N 1 57W
Audierne 138 48 1N 4 34W
Audincourt 139 47 30N 6 50 E
Audo Ra. 245 6 20N 41 50 E
Aue 146 50 34N 12 43 E

Auerbach 146 50 30N 12 25 E
Aueti Paraná → 118 1 51 S 65 37W
Auffay 138 49 43N 1 7 E
Aufist 240 25 44N 14 39W
Augathella 231 25 48 S 146 35 E
Augrabies Falls 254 28 35 S 20 20 E
Augsburg 147 48 22N 10 54 E
Augusta 165 37 14N 15 12 E
Augustenborg 173 54 57N 9 53 E
Augustines, L. des 82 47 37N 75 56W
Augustów 152 53 51N 23 0 E
Augustus, Mt. 229 24 20 S 116 50 E
Augustus Downs 230 18 35 S 139 55 E
Augustus I. 228 15 20 S 124 30 E
Aukan 245 15 29N 40 50 E
Aulla 162 44 12N 10 0 E
Aulnay 140 46 2N 0 22W
Aulne → 138 48 17N 4 16W
Aulneau Pen. 86 49 23N 94 29W
Aulnoye 139 50 12N 3 50 E
Ault-Onival 138 50 5N 1 29 E
Aulus-les-Bains 140 42 49N 1 19 E
Aumale 139 49 46N 1 46 E
Aumont-Aubrac 140 44 43N 3 17 E
Auna 247 10 9N 4 42 E
Aundh 200 17 33N 74 23 E
Aunis 140 46 5N 0 50W
Auponhia 207 1 58 S 125 27 E
Aups 141 43 37N 6 15 E
Aur, P. 205 2 35N 104 10 E
Aura 202 26 59N 97 57 E
Auraiya 199 26 28N 79 33 E
Aurangabad, Bihar, India 199 24 45N 84 18 E
Aurangabad, Maharashtra, India 200 19 50N 75 23 E
Auray 138 47 40N 3 0W
Aurès 241 35 8N 6 30 E
Aurich 146 53 28N 7 30 E
Aurilândia 121 16 44 S 50 28W
Aurillac 140 44 55N 2 26 E
Aurlandsvangen 171 60 55N 7 12 E
Auronza 163 46 33N 12 27 E
Aurora, Isabela, Phil. 210 16 59N 121 38 E
Aurora, Quezon, Phil. 210 13 21N 122 31 E
Aurora, S. Africa 254 32 40 S 18 29 E
Aurskog 171 59 55N 11 26 E
Aurukun Mission 230 13 20 S 141 45 E
Aus 254 26 35 S 16 12 E
Ausable → 84 43 19N 81 46W
Aust-Agder fylke □ 171 58 55N 7 40 E
Austad 171 58 58N 7 37 E
Austerlitz = Slavkov 151 49 10N 16 52 E
Austevoll 171 60 5N 5 13 E
Austin, L. 229 27 40 S 118 0 E
Austin Chan. 95 75 35N 103 25W
Austral Downs 230 20 30 S 137 45 E
Austral Is. = Tubuai Is. 225 25 0 S 150 0W
Austral Seamount Chain 225 24 0 S 150 0W
Australia ■ 224 23 0 S 135 0 E
Australian Alps 231 36 30 S 148 30 E
Australian Cap. Terr. □ 231 35 30 S 149 0 E
Australian Dependency □ 13 73 0 S 90 0 E
Austria ■ 150 47 0N 14 0 E
Austvågøy 174 68 20N 14 40 E
Autazes 119 3 35 S 59 8W
Autelbas 143 49 39N 5 52 E
Auterive 140 43 21N 1 29 E
Auteuil, L. d' 80 50 38N 61 17W
Authie → 139 50 22N 1 38 E
Authon 138 48 12N 0 55 E
Autlán de Navarro 106 19 46N 104 22W
Autun 139 46 58N 4 17 E
Auvelais 143 50 27N 4 38 E
Auvergne, Australia 228 15 39 S 130 1 E
Auvergne, France 140 45 20N 3 15 E
Auvézére → 140 45 12N 0 50 E
Auxerre 139 47 48N 3 32 E
Auxi-le-Château 139 50 15N 2 8 E
Auxonne 139 47 10N 5 20 E
Auzances 140 46 2N 2 30 E
Auzat 140 45 27N 3 19 E
Avallon 139 47 30N 3 53 E
Avalon Pen. 79 47 30N 53 20W
Avalos 105 24 44N 101 26W
Avanigadda 201 16 0N 80 56 E
Avaré 125 23 4 S 48 58W
Ávas 168 40 57N 25 56 E
Aveiro, Brazil 119 3 10 S 55 5W
Aveiro, Portugal 154 40 37N 8 38W
Aveiro □ 154 40 40N 8 35W
Āvej 193 35 40N 49 15 E
Avelgem 143 50 47N 3 27 E
Avellaneda 124 34 50 S 58 10W
Avellino 165 40 54N 14 46 E
Avenches 148 46 53N 7 2 E
Averøya 171 63 0N 7 35 E
Aversa 165 40 58N 14 11 E
Aves, I. de 113 15 45N 63 55W
Aves, Is. de 113 12 0N 67 30W
Avesnes-sur-Helpe 139 50 8N 3 55 E
Avesta 172 60 9N 16 10 E
Aveyron □ 140 44 22N 2 45 E
Aveyron → 140 44 7N 1 5 E
Avezzano 163 42 2N 13 24 E
Avgó 169 35 33N 25 37 E
Aviá Terai 124 26 45 S 60 50W
Aviano 163 46 3N 12 35 E
Avigliana 162 45 7N 7 13 E
Avigliano 165 40 44N 15 41 E
Avignon 141 43 57N 4 50 E
Ávila 154 40 39N 4 43W
Ávila □ 154 40 30N 5 0W
Ávila, Sierra de 154 40 40N 5 0W
Avilés 154 43 35N 5 57W
Avionárion 169 38 31N 24 8 E
Avisio → 163 46 7N 11 5 E
Aviz 155 39 4N 7 53W
Avize 139 48 59N 4 0 E
Avoca, Australia 231 37 5 S 143 26 E
Avoca, Ireland 135 52 52N 6 13W
Avoca → 231 35 40 S 143 43 E
Avola, Canada 93 51 45N 119 19W
Avola, Italy 165 36 56N 15 7 E
Avon □ 133 51 30N 2 40W
Avon →, Australia 229 31 40 S 116 7 E
Avon →, Avon, U.K. 133 51 30N 2 43W
Avon →, Hants., U.K. 133 50 44N 1 45W
Avon →, Warwick, U.K. 133 52 0N 2 9W
Avondale, Canada 79 47 25N 53 12W
Avondale, Zimbabwe 251 17 43 S 30 58 E
Avonlea 88 50 0N 105 0W
Avonmore 85 45 10N 74 58W
Avonmouth 133 51 30N 2 42W
Avramov 167 42 45N 26 38 E
Avranches 138 48 40N 1 20W
Avre → 138 48 47N 1 22 E
Avrig 170 45 43N 24 21 E
Avrillé 140 46 28N 1 28W
Avtovac 166 43 9N 18 35 E
Awag el Baqar 245 10 10N 33 10 E
A'waj → 190 33 23N 36 20 E
Awaji 221 34 32N 135 1 E
Awaji-Shima 220 34 30N 134 50 E
'Awālī 195 26 0N 50 30 E
Awantipur 199 33 55N 75 3 E
Awanui 234 35 4 S 173 17 E
Awarja → 200 17 5N 76 15 E
'Awartā 189 32 10N 35 17 E
Awarua Pt. 235 44 15 S 168 5 E
Awasa, L. 245 7 0N 38 30 E
Awash 245 9 1N 40 10 E
Awash → 245 11 45N 41 5 E
Awaso 246 6 15N 2 22W
Awatere → 235 41 37 S 174 10 E
Awbārī 241 26 46N 12 57 E
Awbārī □ 241 26 35N 12 46 E
Awe, L. 134 56 15N 5 15W
Aweil 245 8 42N 27 20 E
Awgu 247 6 4N 7 24 E
Awjilah 242 29 8N 21 7 E
Aworro 227 7 43 S 143 11 E
Ax-les-Thermes 140 42 44N 1 50 E
Axarfjörður 174 66 15N 16 45W
Axel 143 51 16N 3 55 E
Axel Heiberg I. 95 80 0N 90 0W
Axim 246 4 51N 2 15W
Axinim 119 4 2 S 59 22W
Axintele 170 44 37N 26 47 E
Axioma 123 6 45 S 64 31W
Axiós → 168 40 57N 22 35 E
Axmarsbruk 172 61 3N 17 10 E
Axminster 133 50 47N 3 1W
Axocuapán 107 18 30N 98 44W
Axstedt 146 53 26N 8 43 E
Axvall 173 58 23N 13 34 E
Ay 139 49 3N 4 0 E
Ay → 182 56 8N 57 40 E
Ayaantang 252 1 58N 10 24 E
Ayabaca 122 4 40 S 79 53W
Ayabe 221 35 20N 135 20 E
Ayacucho, Argentina 124 37 5 S 58 20W
Ayacucho, Peru 122 13 0 S 74 0W
Ayaguz 184 48 10N 80 0 E
Ayakkuduk 183 41 12N 65 12 E
Ayakudi 201 10 28N 77 56 E
Ayala 211 6 57N 121 57 E
Ayamonte 155 37 12N 7 24W
Ayan 185 56 30N 138 16 E
Ayancık 180 41 57N 34 18 E
Ayapel 118 8 19N 75 9W
Ayas, Adana, Turkey 190 36 46N 35 46 E
Ayas, Ankara, Turkey 180 40 10N 32 14 E
Ayaviri 122 14 50 S 70 35W
Āybak 197 36 15N 68 5 E
Aydim, W. →, Oman 195 18 8N 53 8 E
Aydim, W. →, S. Yemen 195 17 44N 50 50 E
Aye 143 50 14N 5 18 E
Ayenngré 247 8 40N 1 1 E
Ayer's Cliff 83 45 10N 72 3W
Ayers Rock 229 25 23 S 131 5 E
Aygues → 141 44 7N 4 43 E
Ayiá 168 39 43N 22 45 E
Ayía Ánna 169 38 52N 23 24 E
Áyia Marína, Kásos, Greece 169 35 27N 26 53 E
Ayía Marína, Leros, Greece 169 37 11N 26 48 E
Ayía Paraskeví 168 39 14N 26 16 E
Ayía Rouméli 169 35 14N 23 58 E
Ayiássos 169 39 5N 26 23 E
Áyion Óros 168 40 25N 24 6 E
Áyios Andréas 169 37 21N 22 45 E
Áyios Evstrátios 168 39 30N 25 0 E
Áyios Ioannis, Ákra 169 35 20N 25 40 E
Áyios Kiríkos 169 37 34N 26 17 E
Áyios Matthaíos 168 39 30N 19 47 E
Áyios Mírono 169 35 15N 25 1 E
Áyios Nikólaos 169 35 11N 25 41 E
Áyios Pétros 169 38 38N 20 33 E
Áyios Yeóryios 169 37 28N 23 57 E
Aykathonisi 169 37 28N 27 0 E
Ayke, Ozero 182 50 57N 61 36 E
Aykin 176 62 15N 49 56 E
Aylen L. 85 45 37N 77 51W
Aylesbury 133 51 48N 0 49W
Aylmer, Ont., Canada 84 42 46N 80 59W
Aylmer, Qué., Canada 82 45 24N 75 51W
Aylmer L. 94 64 0N 110 8W
Aylsham 88 53 12N 103 49W
'Ayn al Ghazālah 242 32 10N 23 20 E
'Ayn 'Arīk 189 31 54N 35 8 E
'Ayn Zaqqūt 241 29 0N 19 30 E
Ayna 157 38 34N 2 3W
Aynāt 195 16 4N 49 9 E
Ayni 183 39 23N 68 32 E
'Aynūnah 191 28 5N 35 8 E
Ayo el Chico 106 20 32N 102 21W
Ayolas 124 27 10 S 56 59W
Ayom 245 7 49N 28 23 E
Ayon, Ostrov 185 69 50N 169 0 E
Ayora 157 39 3N 1 3W
Ayotitlán 106 19 30N 104 10W
Ayr, Australia 230 19 35 S 147 25 E
Ayr, Canada 84 43 17N 80 27W
Ayr, U.K. 134 55 28N 4 37W
Ayr → 134 55 29N 4 40W
Ayre, Pt. of 132 54 27N 4 21W
Aysha 245 10 50N 42 23 E
Aytos 167 42 42N 27 16 E
Aytoska Planina 167 42 45N 27 30 E
Ayu, Kepulauan 207 0 35N 131 5 E
Ayutla, Guat. 112 14 40N 92 10W
Ayutla, Mexico 106 20 7N 104 22W
Ayutla de los Libres 107 16 54N 99 13W
Ayvalık 177 39 20N 26 46 E
Aywaille 143 50 28N 5 40 E
Az Zabdānī 190 33 43N 36 5 E
Az Zāhirīyah 189 31 25N 34 58 E
Az Zahrān 193 26 10N 50 7 E
Az Zarqā 189 32 5N 36 4 E
Az Zāwiyah 241 32 52N 12 56 E
Az Zāwīyah, J. 190 35 45N 36 35 E
Az Zaydīyah 194 15 20N 43 1 E
Az Zībār 192 36 52N 44 4 E
Az-Zilfī 192 26 12N 44 52 E
Az Zubaydīyah, J. 190 33 45N 37 1 E
Az Zubayr 192 30 20N 47 50 E
Az Zuhd, J. 191 28 20N 35 17 E
Az Zuqur 194 14 0N 42 45 E
Azambuja 155 39 4N 8 51W
Azamgarh 199 26 5N 83 13 E
Azangaro 122 14 55 S 70 13W
Azaouak, Vallée de l' 247 15 50N 3 20 E
Āzār Shahr 192 37 45N 45 59 E
Āzarbāyjān-e Gharbī □ 192 37 0N 44 30 E
Āzarbāyjān-e Sharqī □ 192 37 20N 47 0 E
Azare 247 11 55N 10 10 E
Azay-le-Rideau 138 47 16N 0 30 E
A'zāz 190 36 36N 37 4 E
Azazga 241 36 48N 4 22 E
Azbine = Aïr 247 18 30N 8 0 E
Azefal 240 21 0N 14 45W
Azeffoun 241 36 51N 4 26 E
Azemmour 240 33 20N 9 20W
Azerbaijan S.S.R. □ 181 40 20N 48 0 E
Azezo 245 12 28N 37 15 E
Azilal 240 32 0N 6 30W
Azilda 84 46 33N 81 6W
Azimganj 199 24 14N 88 16 E
Aznalcóllar 155 37 32N 6 17W
Azogues 118 2 35 S 78 0W
Azor 189 32 2N 34 48 E
Azores 128 38 44N 29 0W
Azov 181 47 3N 39 25 E
Azov Sea = Azovskoye More 180 46 0N 36 30 E
Azovskoye More 180 46 0N 36 30 E
Azovy 184 64 55N 64 35 E
Azpeitia 156 43 12N 2 19W
Azrou 240 33 28N 5 19W
Azúa de Compostela 113 18 25N 70 44W
Azuaga 155 38 16N 5 39W
Azuara 156 41 15N 0 53W
Azuay □ 118 2 55 S 79 0W
Azuer → 155 39 8N 3 36W
Azuero, Pen. de 112 7 30N 80 30W
Azul 124 36 42 S 59 43W
Azul, Serra 123 14 50 S 54 50W
Azul, Sa. 102 27 9N 101 0W
Azumbilla 109 18 39N 97 23W
Azurduy 123 19 59 S 64 29W
Azure L. 93 52 23N 120 3W
Azzaba 241 36 48N 7 6 E
Azzano Décimo 163 45 53N 12 46 E
'Azzūn 191 32 10N 35 2 E

B

Ba Don 204 17 45N 106 26 E
Ba Dong 205 9 40N 106 33 E
Ba Ngoi = Cam Lam 205 11 54N 109 10 E
Ba Ria 205 10 30N 107 10 E
Ba Tri 205 10 2N 106 36 E
Ba Xian 214 39 8N 116 22 E
Baa 207 10 50 S 123 0 E
Baaba, Î. 226 20 3 S 164 59 E
Baamonde 154 43 7N 7 44W
Baao 210 13 27N 123 22 E
Baar 149 47 12N 8 32 E
Baarle Nassau 143 51 27N 4 56 E
Baarlo 143 51 20N 6 6 E
Baarn 142 52 12N 5 17 E
Bāb el Māndeb 194 12 35N 43 25 E
Baba 167 42 44N 23 59 E
Baba Burnu 168 39 29N 26 2 E
Baba dag 181 41 0N 48 19W
Bābā Kalū 193 30 7N 50 49 E
Babaçulândia 120 7 13 S 47 46W
Babadag 170 44 53N 28 44 E
Babaeski 167 41 26N 27 6 E
Babahoyo 118 1 40 S 79 30W
Babak 211 7 8N 125 41 E
Babakin 229 32 7 S 118 1 E
Babana 247 10 31N 3 46 E
Babar, Algeria 241 35 10N 7 6 E
Babar, Indonesia 207 8 0 S 129 30 E
Babar, Pakistan 198 31 7N 69 32 E
Babarkach 198 29 45N 68 0 E
Babayevo 179 59 24N 35 55 E
Babenhausen 147 49 57N 8 56 E
Babi Besar, P. 205 2 25N 103 59 E
Babia, La 102 28 34N 102 4W
Babia Gora 152 49 38N 19 38 E
Babian Jiang → 216 22 55N 101 47 E
Babicora 101 29 30N 108 1W
Babile 245 9 16N 42 11 E
Babinda 230 17 20 S 145 56 E
Babine 76 55 22N 126 37W
Babine → 76 55 45N 127 44W
Babine L. 76 54 48N 126 0W
Babo 207 2 30 S 133 30 E
Babócsa 151 46 2N 17 21 E
Bābol 193 36 40N 52 50 E
Bābol Sar 193 36 45N 52 45 E
Baborigame 101 26 27N 107 16W
Baborów 151 50 7N 18 1 E
Baboua 252 5 49N 14 58 E
Babuna 166 41 30N 21 40 E
Babura 247 12 51N 8 59 E
Babusar Pass 199 35 12N 73 59 E
Babušnica 166 43 7N 22 27 E
Babuyan Chan. 210 18 40N 121 30 E
Babuyan I. 210 19 32N 121 57 E
Babuyan Is. 210 19 15N 121 40 E
Babylon 192 32 40N 44 30 E
Bač 166 45 29N 19 17 E
Bac Can 204 22 8N 105 49 E
Bac Giang 204 21 16N 106 11 E
Bac Ninh 204 21 13N 106 4 E
Bac Phan 204 22 0N 105 0 E
Bac Quang 204 22 30N 104 48 E
Baca 111 21 6N 89 25W
Bacabachi 100 26 55N 109 24W
Bacabal 120 4 15 S 44 45W
Bacacay 210 13 18N 123 47 E
Bacadehuachi 100 29 44N 109 10W
Bacajá → 119 3 25 S 51 50W
Bacalar 111 18 43N 88 27W
Bacalar, L. 111 18 43N 88 22W
Bacan 207 8 27 S 126 27 E
Bacan, Kepulauan 207 0 35 S 127 30 E
Bacan, Pulau 207 0 50 S 127 30 E
Bacanora 100 28 59N 109 24W

Bacanuchi **100** 30 39N 110 16W
Bacarès, Le **140** 42 47N 3 3 E
Bacarra **210** 18 15N 120 37 E
Bacatete, Sa. **100** 27 54N 110 19W
Bacău **170** 46 35N 26 55 E
Bacău □ **170** 46 30N 26 45 E
Baccalieu I. **79** 48 8N 52 48W
Baccarat **139** 48 28N 6 42 E
Bacchus Marsh **232** 37 43 S 144 27 E
Bacerac **100** 30 18N 108 50W
Băceşti **170** 46 50N 27 11 E
Bach Long Vi, Dao **204** 20 10N 107 40 E
Bachaquero **118** 9 56N 71 8W
Bacharach **147** 50 3N 7 46 E
Bachelina **184** 57 45N 67 20 E
Bachimba **101** 28 25N 105 41W
Bachiniva **101** 28 45N 107 15W
Bachuma **245** 6 48N 35 53 E
Bačina **166** 43 42N 21 23 E
Back → **94** 65 10N 104 0W
Back Bay **81** 45 3N 66 52W
Bačka Palanka **166** 45 17N 19 27 E
Bačka Topola **166** 45 49N 19 39 E
Bäckefors **173** 58 48N 12 9 E
Bački Petrovac **166** 45 29N 19 32 E
Backnang **147** 48 57N 9 26 E
Backstairs Passage **232** 35 40 S 138 5 E
Baco, Mt. **210** 12 49N 121 10 E
Bacoachi **100** 30 38N 109 56W
Bacolod **211** 10 40N 122 57 E
Bacon **210** 13 3N 124 3 E
Bacoor **210** 14 28N 120 56 E
Bacqueville **138** 49 47N 1 0 E
Bacs-Kiskun □ **151** 46 43N 19 30 E
Bácsalmás **151** 46 8N 19 17 E
Bacuag **211** 9 36N 125 38 E
Bacubirit **104** 25 49N 107 56W
Bacuk **205** 6 4N 102 25 E
Baculin **211** 7 27N 126 35 E
Bacum **100** 27 33N 110 5W
Bād **193** 33 41N 52 1 E
Bad Aussee **150** 47 43N 13 45 E
Bad Bergzabern **147** 49 6N 8 0 E
Bad Bramstedt **146** 53 56N 9 53 E
Bad Doberan **146** 54 6N 11 55 E
Bad Driburg **146** 51 44N 9 0 E
Bad Ems **147** 50 22N 7 44 E
Bad Frankenhausen **146** 51 21N 11 3 E
Bad Freienwalde **146** 52 47N 14 3 E
Bad Godesberg **146** 50 41N 7 4 E
Bad Heart **90** 55 30N 118 18W
Bad Hersfeld **146** 50 52N 9 42 E
Bad Hofgastein **150** 47 17N 13 6 E
Bad Homburg **147** 50 17N 8 33 E
Bad Honnef **146** 50 39N 7 13 E
Bad Ischl **150** 47 44N 13 38 E
Bad Kissingen **147** 50 11N 10 5 E
Bad Kreuznach **147** 49 47N 7 47 E
Bad Langensalza **146** 51 6N 10 40 E
Bad Lauterberg **146** 51 38N 10 29 E
Bad Leonfelden **150** 48 31N 14 18 E
Bad Lippspringe **146** 51 47N 8 46 E
Bad Mergentheim **147** 49 29N 9 47 E
Bad Münstereifel **146** 50 33N 6 46 E
Bad Muskau **146** 51 33N 14 43 E
Bad Nauheim **147** 50 24N 8 45 E
Bad Oeynhausen **146** 52 16N 8 45 E
Bad Oldesloe **146** 53 48N 10 22 E
Bad Orb **147** 50 16N 9 21 E
Bad Pyrmont **146** 51 59N 9 15 E
Bad Ragaz **149** 47 0N 9 30 E
Bad Reichenhall **147** 47 44N 12 53 E
Bad St.-Peter **146** 54 23N 8 32 E
Bad Salzuflen **146** 52 8N 8 44 E
Bad Segeberg **146** 53 58N 10 16 E
Bad Tölz **147** 47 43N 11 34 E
Bad Waldsee **147** 47 56N 9 46 E
Bad Wildungen **146** 51 7N 9 10 E
Bad Wimpfen **147** 49 12N 9 10 E
Bad Windsheim **147** 49 29N 10 25 E
Badagara **201** 11 35N 75 40 E
Badagri **247** 6 25N 2 55 E
Badajós, L. **119** 3 15 S 62 50W
Badajoz **155** 38 50N 6 59W
Badajoz □ **155** 38 40N 6 30W
Badakhshān □ **197** 36 30N 71 0 E
Badalona **156** 41 26N 2 15 E
Badalzai **198** 29 50N 65 35 E
Badampahar **199** 22 10N 86 10 E
Badanah **192** 30 58N 41 30 E
Badarinath **199** 30 45N 79 30 E
Badas **206** 4 33N 114 25 E
Badas, Kepulauan **208** 0 45N 107 5 E
Baddeck **81** 46 6N 60 45W
Baddo → **197** 28 0N 64 20 E
Bade **207** 7 10 S 139 35 E
Bademli **190** 37 1N 32 41 E
Baden, Austria **151** 48 1N 16 13 E
Baden, Switz. **149** 47 28N 8 18 E
Baden-Baden **147** 48 45N 8 15 E
Baden Park **232** 32 8 S 144 12 E
Baden-
Württemberg □ **147** 48 40N 9 0 E
Badgastein **150** 47 7N 13 9 E
Badger **79** 49 0N 56 4W
Badger's Quay **79** 49 7N 53 35W
Bādghīsāt □ **197** 35 0N 63 0 E
Badgom **199** 34 1N 74 45 E
Badhoevedorp **142** 52 20N 4 47 E
Badia Polèsine **163** 45 6N 11 30 E
Badian **211** 9 55N 123 24 E
Badin **197** 24 38N 68 54 E
Badiraguato **104** 25 22N 107 31W
Badnera **198** 20 48N 77 44 E
Badoc **210** 17 56N 120 28 E
Badogo **246** 11 2N 8 13W
Badong **217** 31 1N 110 23 E
Badr Ḩunayn **194** 23 44N 38 46 E
Baduen **256** 7 15N 47 40 E
Badulla **201** 7 1N 81 7 E
Badupi **202** 21 36N 93 27 E
Baena **155** 37 37N 4 20W
Baerami Creek **233** 32 27 S 150 27 E
Baexem **143** 51 13N 5 53 E
Baeza, Ecuador **118** 0 25 S 77 53W
Baeza, Spain **157** 37 57N 3 25W
Bafa Gölü **169** 37 30N 27 29 E
Bafang **247** 5 9N 10 11 E
Bafatá **246** 12 8N 14 40W
Baffin □ **95** 70 0N 80 0W
Baffin B. **95** 72 0N 64 0W
Baffin I. **95** 68 0N 75 0W
Bafia **247** 4 40N 11 10 E
Bafilo **247** 9 22N 1 22 E
Bafing → **246** 13 49N 10 50W
Bafliyūn **192** 36 37N 36 59 E
Baflo **142** 53 22N 6 31 E
Bafoulabé **246** 13 50N 10 55W
Bafoussam **247** 5 28N 10 25 E
Bāfq **193** 31 40N 55 25 E
Bafra **180** 41 34N 35 54 E
Bafra, C. **180** 41 44N 35 58 E
Bāft **193** 29 15N 56 38 E
Bafut **247** 6 6N 10 2 E
Bafwasende **250** 1 3N 27 5 E
Bagabag **210** 16 30N 121 15 E
Bagac **210** 14 36N 120 23 E
Bagac Bay **210** 14 36N 120 20 E
Bagalkot **201** 16 10N 75 40 E
Bagamoyo **250** 6 28 S 38 55 E
Bagamoyo □ **250** 6 20 S 38 30 E
Bagan Datoh **205** 3 59N 100 47 E
Bagan Serai **205** 5 1N 100 32 E
Baganga **211** 7 34N 126 33 E
Bagani **254** 18 7 S 21 41 E
Bagansiapiapi **208** 2 12N 100 50 E
Bagasra **198** 21 30N 71 0 E
Bagata **252** 3 44 S 17 57 E
Bagawi **245** 12 20N 34 18 E
Bagdarin **185** 54 26N 113 36 E
Bagé **125** 31 20 S 54 15W
Bagenalstown =
Muine Bheag **135** 52 42N 6 57W
Bagh **199** 33 59N 73 45 E
Baghdād **192** 33 20N 44 30 E
Bagherhat **202** 22 40N 89 47 E
Bagheria **164** 38 5N 13 30 E
Baghlān **197** 36 12N 69 0 E
Baghlān □ **197** 36 0N 68 30 E
Bagnacavallo **163** 44 25N 11 58 E
Bagnara Cálabra **165** 38 16N 15 49 E
Bagnères-de-Bigorre **140** 43 5N 0 9 E
Bagnères-de-Luchon **140** 42 47N 0 38 E
Bagni di Lucca **162** 44 1N 10 37 E
Bagno di Romagna **163** 43 50N 11 59 E
Bagnoles-de-l'Orne **138** 48 32N 0 25W
Bagnoli di Sopra **163** 45 13N 11 55 E
Bagnolo Mella **162** 45 27N 10 14 E
Bagnols-les-Bains **140** 44 30N 3 40 E
Bagnols-sur-Cèze **141** 44 10N 4 36 E
Bagnorégio **163** 42 38N 12 7 E
Bago **211** 10 32N 122 50 E
Bagolino **162** 45 49N 10 28 E
Bagotville **83** 48 22N 70 54W
Bagrdan **166** 44 5N 21 11 E
Bagres **103** 21 45N 100 16W
Bagua **122** 5 35 S 78 22W
Baguio **210** 16 26N 120 34 E
Bahabón de Esgueva **156** 41 52N 3 43W
Bahadurabad Ghat **202** 25 11N 89 44 E
Bahadurgarh **198** 28 40N 76 57 E
Bahama, Canal
Viejo de **112** 22 10N 77 30W
Bahamas ■ **113** 24 0N 75 0W
Baharampur **199** 24 2N 88 27 E
Baharîya, El Wâhât
al **244** 28 0N 28 50 E
Bahau **205** 2 48N 102 26 E
Bahawalnagar **197** 30 0N 73 15 E
Bahawalpur **197** 29 24N 71 40 E
Baheri **199** 28 45N 79 34 E
Bahi **250** 5 58 S 35 21 E
Bahi Swamp **250** 6 10 S 35 0 E
Bahía = Salvador **121** 13 0 S 38 30W
Bahía □ **121** 12 0 S 42 0W
Bahía, Islas de la **112** 16 45N 86 15W
Bahía Blanca **124** 38 35 S 62 13W
Bahía de Caráquez **118** 0 40 S 80 27W
Bahía de los
Ángeles **98** 28 57N 113 34W
Bahía Honda **112** 22 54N 83 10W
Bahía Laura **126** 48 10 S 66 30W
Bahía Negra **123** 20 5 S 58 5W
Bahir Dar **245** 11 37N 37 10 E
Bahlah **195** 22 58N 57 18 E
Bahmanzād **193** 31 15N 51 47 E
Bahmer **240** 27 32N 0 10W
Bahönye **151** 46 25N 17 28 E
Bahr Aouk → **252** 8 40N 19 0 E
Bahr el Ahmar □ **244** 20 0N 35 0 E
Bahr el Ghazâl □ **245** 7 0N 28 0 E
Bahr el Jebel → **245** 7 30N 30 30 E
Bahr Salamat → **243** 9 20N 18 0 E
Bahr Yûsef → **244** 28 25N 30 35 E
Bahra el Burullus **244** 31 28N 30 48 E
Bahraich **199** 27 38N 81 37 E
Bahrain ■ **195** 26 0N 50 35 E
Bahret Assad **192** 36 0N 38 15 E
Bahror **198** 27 51N 76 20 E
Bāhū Kalāt **193** 25 43N 61 25 E
Bai **246** 13 35N 3 28W
Bai Bung, Mui **205** 8 38N 104 44 E
Bai Duc **204** 18 3N 105 49 E
Bai Thuong **204** 19 54N 105 23 E
Baia Farta **253** 12 40 S 13 11 E
Baia Mare **170** 47 40N 23 35 E
Baia-Sprie **170** 47 41N 23 43 E
Baião **120** 2 40 S 49 40W
Baïbokoum **243** 7 46N 15 43 E
Baicheng **215** 45 38N 122 42 E
Băicoi **170** 45 3N 25 52 E
Baidoa **256** 3 8N 43 30 E
Baie Comeau **80** 49 12N 68 10W
Baie-des-Sables **80** 48 43N 67 54W
Baie-du-Poste **83** 50 24N 73 56W
Baie-du-Renard **80** 49 17N 61 50W
Baie-St-Paul **83** 47 28N 70 32W
Baie-Ste-Anne **81** 47 3N 64 58W
Baie-Ste-Catherine **83** 48 6N 69 44W
Baie-Ste-Claire **80** 49 54N 64 30W
Baie Trinité **80** 49 25N 67 20W
Baie Verte, N.B.,
Canada **81** 46 1N 64 6W
Baie Verte, Newf.,
Canada **79** 49 55N 56 12W
Baieville **83** 46 8N 72 43W
Baignes **140** 45 23N 0 25W
Baigneux-les-Juifs **139** 47 31N 4 39 E
Baihe, China **214** 32 50N 110 5 E
Baihe, Taiwan **217** 23 24N 120 24 E
Ba'ījī **192** 35 0N 43 30 E
Baikal, L. =
Baykal, Oz. **185** 53 0N 108 0 E
Bailadila, Mt. **200** 18 43N 81 15 E
Baile Atha Cliath =
Dublin **135** 53 20N 6 18W
Bailei **245** 6 44N 40 18 E
Bailén **155** 38 8N 3 48W
Băileşti **170** 44 1N 23 20 E
Baileux **143** 50 2N 4 23 E
Bailhongal **201** 15 55N 74 53 E
Bailique, Ilha **120** 1 2N 49 58W
Bailleul **139** 50 44N 2 41 E
Bailundo **253** 12 10 S 15 50 E
Baima **216** 33 0N 100 26 E
Baimuru **227** 7 35 S 144 51 E
Bain-de-Bretagne **138** 47 50N 1 40W
Baing **207** 10 14 S 120 34 E
Bainiu **214** 32 50N 112 15 E
Bainyik **227** 3 40 S 143 4 E
Bā'ir **191** 30 45N 36 55 E
Bā'ir, W. → **191** 30 59N 37 24 E
Baird Pen. **95** 68 55N 76 4W
Bairin Youqi **215** 43 30N 118 35 E
Bairin Zuoqi **215** 43 58N 119 15 E
Bairnsdale **231** 37 48 S 147 36 E
Bais **211** 9 35N 123 7 E
Baise → **140** 44 17N 0 18 E
Baisha **214** 34 20N 112 32 E
Baissa **247** 7 14N 10 38 E
Baitadi **199** 29 35N 80 25 E
Baixa Grande **121** 11 57 S 40 11W
Baiyin **214** 36 45N 104 14 E
Baiyü **216** 31 16N 98 50 E
Baiyu Shan **214** 37 15N 107 30 E
Baiyuda **244** 17 35N 32 7 E
Baj Baj **199** 22 30N 88 5 E
Baja **151** 46 12N 18 59 E
Baja, Pta.,
Baja Calif. N.,
Mexico **98** 29 58N 115 49W
Baja, Pta., Sonora,
Mexico **100** 28 28N 111 45W
Baja California
Norte □ **98** 30 0N 115 0W
Baja California
Sur □ **99** 25 50N 111 50W
Baján **102** 26 32N 101 15W
Bajana **198** 23 7N 71 49 E
Bājgīrān **193** 37 36N 58 24 E
Bājil **194** 15 4N 43 17 E
Bajimba, Mt. **231** 29 17 S 152 6 E
Bajina Bašta **166** 43 58N 19 35 E
Bajmok **166** 45 57N 19 24 E
Bajo Nuevo **112** 15 40N 78 50W
Bajoga **247** 10 57N 11 20 E
Bajool **230** 23 40 S 150 35 E
Bak **151** 46 43N 16 51 E
Bakal **182** 54 56N 58 48 E
Bakala **252** 6 15N 20 20 E
Bakanas **183** 44 50N 76 15 E
Bakar **163** 45 18N 14 32 E
Bakchav **184** 57 1N 82 5 E
Bakel, Neth. **143** 51 30N 5 45 E
Bakel, Senegal **246** 14 56N 12 20W
Baker, Canal **126** 47 45 S 74 45W
Baker, L., Australia **229** 26 54 S 126 5 E
Baker, L., Canada **95** 64 0N 96 0W
Baker I. **224** 0 10N 176 35W
Baker Lake **95** 64 20N 96 3W
Bakers Creek **230** 21 13 S 149 7 E
Baker's Dozen Is. **78** 56 45N 78 45W
Bakhchisaray **180** 44 40N 33 45 E
Bakhmach **178** 51 10N 32 45 E
Bakhtārān □ **194** 34 0N 46 30 E
Bakırköy **167** 40 59N 28 53 E
Bakkafjörður **174** 66 2N 14 48W
Bakkagerði **174** 65 31N 13 49W
Bakony → **151** 47 35N 17 54 E
Bakony Forest =
Bakony Hegység **151** 47 10N 17 30 E
Bakony Hegység **151** 47 10N 17 30 E
Bakori **247** 11 34N 7 25 E
Bakouma **252** 5 40N 22 56 E
Bakov **150** 50 27N 14 55 E
Bakpakty **183** 44 35N 76 40 E
Bakr Uzyak **182** 52 59N 58 38 E
Baku **181** 40 25N 49 45 E
Bakun **210** 16 48N 120 40 E
Bakutis Coast **13** 74 0 S 120 0W
Bakwa-Kenge **253** 4 51 S 22 4 E
Bala, Canada **84** 45 1N 79 37W
Bal'ā, Jordan **189** 32 20N 35 6 E
Bala, L. = Tegid, L. **132** 52 53N 3 38W
Bālā Morghāb **197** 35 35N 63 20 E
Balabac, Str. **206** 7 53N 117 5 E
Balabac I. **211** 8 0N 117 0 E
Balabagh **198** 34 25N 70 12 E
Balabakk **190** 34 0N 36 10 E
Balabalangan,
Kepulauan **209** 2 20 S 117 30 E
Balabio, Î. **226** 20 7 S 164 11 E
Bălăciţa **170** 44 23N 23 8 E
Balad **192** 34 1N 44 9 E
Balad Rūz **192** 33 42N 45 5 E
Bālādeh, Fārs, Iran **193** 29 17N 51 56 E
Baladeh,
Māzandaran, Iran **193** 36 12N 51 48 E
Balaghat **199** 21 49N 80 12 E
Balaghat Ra. **200** 18 50N 76 30 E
Balaguer **156** 41 50N 0 50 E
Balakété **252** 6 56N 19 54 E
Balakhna **179** 56 25N 43 32 E
Balaklava, Australia **232** 34 7 S 138 22 E
Balaklava, U.S.S.R. **180** 44 30N 33 30 E
Balakleya **180** 49 28N 36 55 E
Balakovo **179** 52 4N 47 55 E
Balamban **211** 10 30N 123 43 E
Balancán de
Domínguez **110** 17 48N 91 32W
Balanda **179** 51 30N 44 40 E
Balangiga **211** 11 7N 125 23 E
Balangir **199** 20 43N 83 35 E
Balapur **198** 20 40N 76 45 E
Balashikha **179** 55 49N 37 59 E
Balashov **179** 51 30N 43 10 E
Balasinor **198** 22 57N 73 23 E
Balasore =
Baleshwar **199** 21 35N 87 3 E
Balassagyarmat **151** 48 4N 19 15 E
Balât **244** 25 36N 29 19 E
Balaton **151** 46 50N 17 40 E
Balatonfüred **151** 46 58N 17 54 E
Balatonszentgyörgy **151** 46 41N 17 19 E
Balayan **210** 13 57N 120 44 E
Balazote **157** 38 54N 2 9W
Balbalan **210** 17 27N 121 12 E
Balbi, Mt. **227** 5 55 S 154 58 E
Balboa **112** 9 0N 79 30W
Balbriggan **135** 53 35N 6 10W
Balcarce **124** 38 0 S 58 10W
Balcarres **88** 50 50N 103 35W
Balchik **167** 43 28N 28 11 E
Balclutha **235** 46 15 S 169 45 E
Bald Hd. **229** 35 6 S 118 1 E
Bald I. **229** 34 57 S 118 27 E
Baldock L. **77** 56 33N 97 57W
Baldur **89** 49 23N 99 15W
Bale **163** 45 4N 13 46 E
Bale □ **245** 6 20N 41 30 E
Baleares □ **156** 39 30N 3 0 E
Baleares, Islas **156** 39 30N 3 0 E
Balearic Is. =
Baleares, Islas **156** 39 30N 3 0 E
Baleia, Punta da **121** 17 40 S 39 7W
Balen **143** 51 10N 5 10 E

Băleni **170** 45 48N 27 51 E
Baler **210** 15 46N 121 34 E
Baler Bay **210** 15 50N 121 35 E
Balerna **149** 45 52N 9 0 E
Baleshwar **199** 21 35N 87 3 E
Balezino **182** 58 2N 53 6 E
Balfate **112** 15 48N 86 25W
Balfe's Creek **230** 20 12 S 145 55 E
Balfour **255** 26 38 S 28 35 E
Balfouriyya **189** 32 38N 35 18 E
Balgonie **88** 50 29N 104 16W
Balharshah **200** 19 50N 79 23 E
Bali, Cameroon **247** 5 54N 10 0 E
Bali, Indonesia **209** 8 20 S 115 0 E
Bali □ **206** 8 20 S 115 0 E
Bali, Selat **209** 8 18 S 114 25 E
Balicuatro Is. **210** 12 39N 124 24 E
Baligród **152** 49 20N 22 17 E
Balikesir **177** 39 35N 27 58 E
Balikpapan **209** 1 10 S 116 55 E
Balimbing **211** 5 5N 119 58 E
Balimo **227** 8 6 S 142 57 E
Baling **205** 5 41N 100 55 E
Balintang Channel **210** 19 49N 121 40 E
Balintang Is. **210** 19 58N 122 9 E
Baliton **211** 5 44N 125 14 E
Baliza **123** 16 0 S 52 20W
Baljurshi **194** 19 51N 41 33 E
Balk **142** 52 54N 5 35 E
Balkan Mts. = Stara Planina **167** 43 15N 23 0 E
Balkan Pen. **130** 42 0N 22 0 E
Balkh □ **197** 36 30N 67 0 E
Balkhash **184** 46 50N 74 50 E
Balkhash, Ozero **184** 46 0N 74 50 E
Ballachulish **134** 56 40N 5 10W
Balladonia **229** 32 27 S 123 51 E
Ballara **232** 32 19 S 140 45 E
Ballarat **231** 37 33 S 143 50 E
Ballard, L. **229** 29 20 S 120 10 E
Ballater **134** 57 2N 3 2W
Balldale **233** 35 50 S 146 33 E
Ballenas, B. de **99** 26 45N 113 26W
Ballenas, Canal de **98** 29 10N 113 29W
Balleny Is. **13** 66 30 S 163 0 E
Ballesteros **210** 18 25N 121 31 E
Ballia **199** 25 46N 84 12 E
Ballidu **229** 30 35 S 116 45 E
Ballina, Australia **231** 28 50 S 153 31 E
Ballina, Mayo, Ireland **135** 54 7N 9 10W
Ballina, Tipp., Ireland **135** 52 49N 8 27W
Ballinasloe **135** 53 20N 8 12W
Ballinrobe **135** 53 36N 9 13W
Ballinskelligs B. **135** 51 46N 10 11W
Ballon **138** 48 10N 0 14 E
Ballycastle **135** 55 12N 6 15W
Ballymena **135** 54 53N 6 18W
Ballymena □ **135** 54 53N 6 18W
Ballymoney **135** 55 5N 6 30W
Ballymoney □ **135** 55 5N 6 23W
Ballyshannon **135** 54 30N 8 10W
Balmaceda **126** 46 0 S 71 50W
Balmazújváros **151** 47 37N 21 21 E
Balmertown **86** 51 4N 93 41W
Balmhorn **148** 46 26N 7 42 E
Balmoral, Australia **231** 37 15 S 141 48 E
Balmoral, Canada **89** 50 15N 97 19W
Balmoral, U.K. **134** 57 3N 3 13W
Balombo **253** 12 21 S 14 46 E
Balonne → **231** 28 47 S 147 56 E
Balrampur **199** 27 30N 82 20 E
Balranald **231** 34 38 S 143 33 E
Balş **170** 44 22N 24 5 E
Balsapuerto **122** 5 48 S 76 33W
Balsas **107** 17 59N 99 47W
Balsas →, Goiás, Brazil **120** 9 58 S 47 52W
Balsas →, Maranhão, Brazil **120** 7 15 S 44 35W
Balsas, R. → **106** 17 55N 102 10W
Bålsta **172** 59 35N 17 30 E
Balsthal **148** 47 19N 7 41 E
Balta, Romania **170** 44 54N 22 38 E
Balta, R.S.F.S.R., U.S.S.R. **181** 42 58N 44 32 E
Balta, Ukraine S.S.R., U.S.S.R. **180** 48 2N 29 45 E
Baltanás **154** 41 56N 4 15W
Baltic Sea **175** 56 0N 20 0 E
Baltîm **244** 31 35N 31 10 E
Baltimore **135** 51 29N 9 22W
Baltit **199** 36 15N 74 40 E
Baltrum **146** 53 43N 7 25 E
Baluarte, R. → **104** 22 49N 106 2W
Baluchistan □ **197** 27 30N 65 0 E
Balud **210** 12 2N 123 12 E
Balurghat **199** 25 15N 88 44 E
Balygychan **185** 63 56N 154 12 E
Balzar **118** 2 2 S 79 54W
Bam **193** 29 7N 58 14 E
Bama, China **216** 24 8N 107 12 E
Bama, Nigeria **247** 11 33N 13 41 E
Bamako **246** 12 34N 7 55W
Bamba, Mali **247** 17 5N 1 24W
Bamba, Zaïre **253** 5 45 S 18 23 E
Bambam **210** 15 40N 120 20 E
Bambamarca **122** 6 36 S 78 32W
Bambang **210** 16 23N 121 6 E
Bambari **252** 5 40N 20 35 E
Bambaroo **230** 18 50 S 146 10 E
Bamberg **147** 49 54N 10 53 E
Bambesi **245** 9 45N 34 40 E
Bambey **246** 14 42N 16 28W
Bambili **250** 3 40N 26 0 E
Bambuí **121** 20 1 S 45 58W
Bamenda **247** 5 57N 10 11 E
Bamfield **92** 48 45N 125 10W
Bāmīān □ **197** 35 0N 67 0 E
Bamiancheng **215** 43 15N 124 2 E
Bamicori **104** 26 21N 108 30W
Bamingui **252** 7 34N 20 11 E
Bamkin **247** 6 3N 11 27 E
Bamoa **104** 25 42N 108 21W
Bámori, Sonora, Mexico **100** 28 52N 109 10W
Bámori, Sonora, Mexico **100** 30 22N 112 5W
Bampūr **193** 27 15N 60 21 E
Ban Aranyaprathet **204** 13 41N 102 30 E
Ban Ban **204** 19 31N 103 30 E
Ban Bang Hin **205** 9 32N 98 35 E
Ban Chiang Klang **204** 19 25N 100 55 E
Ban Chik **204** 17 15N 102 22 E
Ban Choho **204** 15 2N 102 9 E
Ban Dan Lan Hoi **204** 17 0N 99 35 E
Ban Don = Surat Thani **205** 9 6N 99 20 E
Ban Don **204** 12 53N 107 48 E
Ban Don, Ao **205** 9 20N 99 25 E
Ban Dong **204** 19 30N 100 59 E
Ban Hong **204** 18 18N 98 50 E
Ban Kaeng **204** 17 29N 100 7 E
Ban Keun **204** 18 22N 102 35 E
Ban Khai **204** 12 46N 101 18 E
Ban Kheun **204** 20 13N 101 7 E
Ban Khlong Kua **205** 6 57N 100 8 E
Ban Khuan Mao **205** 7 50N 99 37 E
Ban Khun Yuam **204** 18 49N 97 57 E
Ban Ko Yai Chim **205** 11 17N 99 26 E
Ban Kok **204** 16 40N 103 40 E
Ban Laem **204** 13 13N 99 59 E
Ban Lao Ngam **204** 15 28N 106 10 E
Ban Le Kathe **204** 15 49N 98 53 E
Ban Mae Chedi **204** 19 11N 99 31 E
Ban Mae Laeng **204** 20 1N 99 17 E
Ban Mae Sariang **204** 18 10N 97 56 E
Ban Mi **204** 15 3N 100 32 E
Ban Muong Mo **204** 19 4N 103 58 E
Ban Na Mo **204** 17 7N 105 40 E
Ban Na San **205** 8 53N 99 52 E
Ban Na Tong **204** 20 56N 101 47 E
Ban Nam Bac **204** 20 38N 102 20 E
Ban Nam Ma **204** 22 2N 101 37 E
Ban Ngang **204** 15 59N 106 11 E
Ban Nong Bok **204** 17 5N 104 48 E
Ban Nong Boua **204** 15 40N 106 33 E
Ban Nong Pling **204** 15 40N 100 10 E
Ban Pak Chan **205** 10 32N 98 51 E
Ban Phai **204** 16 4N 102 44 E
Ban Pong **204** 13 50N 99 55 E
Ban Ron Phibun **205** 8 9N 99 51 E
Ban Sanam Chai **205** 7 33N 100 25 E
Ban Sangkha **204** 14 37N 103 52 E
Ban Tak **204** 17 2N 99 4 E
Ban Tako **204** 14 5N 102 40 E
Ban Tha Dua **204** 17 59N 98 39 E
Ban Tha Li **204** 17 37N 101 25 E
Ban Tha Nun **205** 8 12N 98 18 E
Ban Thahine **204** 14 12N 105 33 E
Ban Xien Kok **204** 20 54N 100 39 E
Ban Yen Nhan **204** 20 57N 106 2 E
Baña, Punta de la **156** 40 33N 0 40 E
Banā, W. → **194** 13 3N 45 24 E
Banaba **224** 0 45 S 169 50 E
Banalia **250** 1 32N 25 5 E
Banam **205** 11 20N 105 17 E
Banamba **246** 13 29N 7 22W
Banámichi **100** 30 1N 110 10W
Banana **230** 24 28 S 150 8 E
Bananal, I. do **121** 11 30 S 50 30W
Banaras = Varanasi **199** 25 22N 83 0 E
Banas →, Gujarat, India **198** 23 45N 71 25 E
Banas →, Mad. P., India **199** 24 15N 81 30 E
Bânâs, Ras **244** 23 57N 35 50 E
Banbān **192** 25 1N 46 35 E
Banbridge **135** 54 21N 6 17W
Banbridge □ **135** 54 21N 6 16W
Banbury **133** 52 4N 1 21W
Banchory **134** 57 3N 2 30W
Bancroft **85** 45 3N 77 51W
Band **170** 46 30N 24 25 E
Band Bonī **193** 25 30N 59 33 E
Band-e Torkestān **197** 35 30N 64 0 E
Band Qīr **193** 31 39N 48 53 E
Banda, Cameroon **252** 3 58N 14 32 E
Banda, India **199** 25 30N 80 26 E
Banda, Kepulauan **207** 4 37 S 129 50 E
Banda, La **124** 27 45 S 64 10W
Banda Aceh **208** 5 35N 95 20 E
Banda Banda, Mt. **231** 31 10 S 152 28 E
Banda Elat **207** 5 40 S 133 5 E
Banda Sea **207** 6 0 S 130 0 E
Bandai-San **218** 37 36N 140 4 E
Bandama → **246** 6 32N 5 30W
Bandān **193** 31 23N 60 44 E
Bandanaira **207** 4 32 S 129 54 E
Bandanwara **198** 26 9N 74 38 E
Bandar = Machilipatnam **201** 16 12N 81 8 E
Bandār 'Abbās **193** 27 15N 56 15 E
Bandar-e Anzalī **193** 37 30N 49 30 E
Bandar-e Chārak **193** 26 45N 54 20 E
Bandar-e Deylam **193** 30 5N 50 10 E
Bandar-e Khomeyni **193** 30 30N 49 5 E
Bandar-e Lengeh **193** 26 35N 54 58 E
Bandar-e Maqām **193** 26 56N 53 29 E
Bandar-e Ma'shur **193** 30 35N 49 10 E
Bandar-e Nakhīlū **193** 26 58N 53 30 E
Bandar-e Rīg **193** 29 29N 50 38 E
Bandar-e Torkeman **193** 37 0N 54 10 E
Bandar Maharani = Muar **205** 2 3N 102 34 E
Bandar Penggaram = Batu Pahat **205** 1 50N 102 56 E
Bandar Seri Begawan **206** 4 52N 115 0 E
Bandawe **251** 11 58 S 34 5 E
Bande, Belgium **143** 50 10N 5 25 E
Bande, Spain **154** 42 3N 7 58W
Bandeira, Pico da **121** 20 26 S 41 47W
Bandeirante **121** 13 41 S 50 48W
Bandera **124** 28 55 S 62 20W
Banderas **101** 31 1N 105 35W
Banderas, B. de **106** 20 40N 105 25W
Banderilla **108** 19 35N 96 56W
Bandia → **200** 19 2N 80 28 E
Bandiagara **246** 14 12N 3 29W
Bandırma **177** 40 20N 28 0 E
Bandon **135** 51 44N 8 45W
Bandon → **135** 51 40N 8 41W
Bandoua **252** 4 39N 21 42 E
Bandula **251** 19 0 S 33 7 E
Bandundu **252** 3 15 S 17 22 E
Bandung **209** 6 54 S 107 36 E
Bandya **229** 27 40 S 122 5 E
Băneasa **170** 45 56N 27 55 E
Bāneh **193** 35 59N 45 53 E
Bañeres **157** 38 44N 0 38W
Banes **113** 21 0N 75 42W
Bañeza, La **154** 42 17N 5 54W
Banff, Canada **91** 51 10N 115 34W
Banff, U.K. **134** 57 40N 2 32W
Banff Nat. Park **91** 51 30N 116 15W
Banfora **246** 10 40N 4 40W
Bang Fai → **204** 16 57N 104 45 E
Bang Hieng → **204** 16 10N 105 10 E
Bang Krathum **204** 16 34N 100 18 E
Bang Lamung **204** 13 3N 100 56 E
Bang Mun Nak **204** 16 2N 100 23 E
Bang Pa In **204** 14 14N 100 35 E
Bang Rakam **204** 16 45N 100 7 E
Bang Saphan **205** 11 14N 99 28 E
Bangala Dam **251** 21 7 S 31 25 E
Bangalore **201** 12 59N 77 40 E
Bangante **247** 5 8N 10 32 E
Bangaon **199** 23 0N 88 47 E
Bangassou **252** 4 55N 23 7 E
Bangeta, Mt. **227** 6 21 S 147 3 E
Banggai **207** 1 40 S 123 30 E
Banggi, P. **206** 7 17N 117 12 E
Banghāzī **241** 32 11N 20 3 E
Banghāzī □ **241** 32 7N 20 4 E
Bangil **209** 7 36 S 112 50 E
Bangjang **245** 11 23N 32 41 E
Bangka, Pulau, Sulawesi, Indonesia **207** 1 50N 125 5 E
Bangka, Pulau, Sumatera, Indonesia **206** 2 0 S 105 50 E
Bangka, Selat **208** 2 30 S 105 30 E
Bangkalan **209** 7 2 S 112 46 E
Bangkinang **208** 0 18N 101 5 E
Bangko **208** 2 5 S 102 9 E
Bangkok **204** 13 45N 100 35 E
Bangladesh ■ **202** 24 0N 90 0 E
Bangolo **246** 7 1N 7 29W
Bangor, N. Ireland, U.K. **135** 54 40N 5 40W
Bangor, Wales, U.K. **132** 53 13N 4 9W
Bangu **252** 0 3 S 19 12 E
Bangued **210** 17 40N 120 37 E
Bangui, C.A.R. **252** 4 23N 18 35 E
Bangui, Phil. **210** 18 32N 120 46 E
Banguru **250** 0 30N 27 10 E
Bangweulu, L. **251** 11 0 S 30 0 E
Bangweulu Swamp **251** 11 20 S 30 15 E
Bani, Dom. Rep. **113** 18 16N 70 22W
Bani, Phil. **210** 16 11N 119 52 E
Bani → **246** 14 30N 4 12W
Bani, Djebel **240** 29 16N 8 0W
Bani Bangou **247** 15 3N 2 42 E
Banī Na'īm **189** 31 31N 35 10 E
Banī Sa'd **192** 33 34N 44 32 E
Banī Sār **194** 20 6N 41 27 E
Banī Suhaylah **189** 31 21N 34 19 E
Bania **246** 9 4N 3 6W
Baniara **227** 9 44 S 149 54 E
Banihal Pass **199** 33 30N 75 12 E
Banīnah **241** 32 0N 20 12 E
Bāniyās **190** 35 10N 36 0 E
Banja Luka **166** 44 49N 17 11 E
Banjar **209** 7 24 S 108 30 E
Banjarmasin **209** 3 20 S 114 35 E
Banjarnegara **209** 7 24 S 109 42 E
Banjul **246** 13 28N 16 40W
Banka Banka **230** 18 50 S 134 0 E
Bankeryd **173** 57 53N 14 6 E
Banket **251** 17 27 S 30 19 E
Bankilaré **247** 14 35N 0 44 E
Bankipore **199** 25 35N 85 10 E
Banks I., B.C., Canada **92** 53 20N 130 0W
Banks I., N.W.T., Canada **94** 73 15N 121 30W
Banks I., Papua N. G. **227** 10 10 S 142 15 E
Banks Pen. **235** 43 45 S 173 15 E
Banks Str. **230** 40 40 S 148 10 E
Bankura **199** 23 11N 87 18 E
Bankya **166** 42 43N 23 8 E
Bann →, Down, U.K. **135** 54 30N 6 31W
Bann →, Londonderry, U.K. **135** 55 10N 6 34W
Banna **210** 17 59N 120 39 E
Bannalec **138** 47 57N 3 42W
Bannang Sata **205** 6 16N 101 16 E
Bannerton **232** 34 42 S 142 47 E
Banningville = Bandundu **252** 3 15 S 17 22 E
Bannockburn, Canada **85** 44 39N 77 33W
Bannockburn, U.K. **134** 56 5N 3 55W
Bannockburn, Zimbabwe **251** 20 17 S 29 48 E
Bannu **197** 33 0N 70 18 E
Bañolas **156** 42 16N 2 44 E
Banon **141** 44 2N 5 38 E
Baños de la Encina **155** 38 10N 3 46W
Baños de Molgas **154** 42 15N 7 40W
Bánovce **151** 48 44N 18 16 E
Bansilan □ **211** 6 40N 121 40 E
Banská Bystrica **151** 48 46N 19 14 E
Banská Štiavnica **151** 48 25N 18 55 E
Bansko **167** 41 52N 23 28 E
Banswara **198** 23 32N 74 24 E
Bantayan **211** 11 10N 123 43 E
Bantayan I. **211** 11 13N 123 44 E
Banten **207** 6 5 S 106 8 E
Banton I. **210** 12 56N 122 4 E
Bantry **135** 51 40N 9 28W
Bantry, B. **135** 51 35N 9 50W
Bantul **209** 7 55 S 110 19 E
Bantva **198** 21 29N 70 12 E
Bantval **201** 12 55N 75 0 E
Banya **167** 42 33N 24 50 E
Banyak, Kepulauan **208** 2 10N 97 10 E
Banyo **247** 6 52N 11 45 E
Banyuls **140** 42 29N 3 8 E
Banyumas **207** 7 32 S 109 18 E
Banyuwangi **209** 8 13 S 114 21 E
Banzare Coast **13** 68 0 S 125 0 E
Banzyville = Mobayi **252** 4 15N 21 8 E
Bao Ha **204** 22 11N 104 21 E
Bao Lac **204** 22 57N 105 40 E
Bao Loc **205** 11 32N 107 48 E
Bao'an **217** 22 27N 114 10 E
Baocheng **216** 33 12N 106 56 E
Baode **214** 39 1N 111 5 E
Baodi **215** 39 38N 117 20 E
Baoding **214** 38 50N 115 28 E
Baoji **214** 34 20N 107 5 E
Baojing **216** 28 45N 109 41 E
Baokang **217** 31 54N 111 12 E
Baoro **252** 5 40N 15 58 E
Baoshan, Shanghai, China **217** 31 27N 121 26 E
Baoshan, Yunnan, China **216** 25 10N 99 5 E
Baotou **214** 40 32N 110 2 E
Baoying **215** 33 17N 119 20 E
Bap **198** 27 23N 72 18 E
Bapatla **201** 15 55N 80 30 E
Bapaume **139** 50 7N 2 50 E
Bāqa el Gharbīyya **189** 32 25N 35 2 E
Bāqerābād **193** 33 2N 51 58 E
Ba'qūbah **192** 33 45N 44 50 E

Baquedano **124** 23 20 S 69 52W
Bar, U.S.S.R. **180** 49 4N 27 40 E
Bar, Yugoslavia **166** 42 8N 19 8 E
Bar Bigha **199** 25 21N 85 47 E
Bar-le-Duc **139** 48 47N 5 10 E
Bar-sur-Aube **139** 48 14N 4 40 E
Bar-sur-Seine **139** 48 7N 4 20 E
Barabai **209** 2 32 S 115 34 E
Barabinsk **184** 55 20N 78 20 E
Barachois-de-Malbaie **80** 48 37N 64 17W
Barachois Pond Prov. Park **79** 48 28N 58 15W
Baracoa **113** 20 20N 74 30W
Baradero **124** 33 52 S 59 29W
Baradine **233** 30 56 S 149 4 E
Barahona, Dom. Rep. **113** 18 13N 71 7W
Barahona, Spain **156** 41 17N 2 39W
Baraka → **244** 18 13N 37 35 E
Barakot **199** 21 33N 84 59 E
Barakpur **199** 22 44N 88 30 E
Barakula **231** 26 30 S 150 33 E
Baralaba **230** 24 13 S 149 50 E
Baralzon L. **77** 60 0N 98 3W
Baramati **200** 18 11N 74 33 E
Baramba **199** 20 25N 85 23 E
Barameiya **244** 18 32N 36 38 E
Baramula **199** 34 15N 74 20 E
Baran **198** 25 9N 76 40 E
Baranoa **118** 10 48N 74 55W
Baranovichi **178** 53 10N 26 0 E
Baranów Sandomierski **152** 50 29N 21 30 E
Baranya □ **151** 46 0N 18 15 E
Barão de Cocais **121** 19 56 S 43 28W
Barão de Grajaú **120** 6 45 S 43 1W
Barão de Melgaço, Mato Grosso, Brazil **123** 16 14 S 55 52W
Barão de Melgaço, Rondônia, Brazil **123** 11 50 S 60 45W
Baraolt **170** 46 5N 25 34 E
Barapasi **207** 2 15 S 137 5 E
Barapina **227** 6 21 S 155 25 E
Barasat **199** 22 46N 88 31 E
Barat Daya, Kepulauan **207** 7 30 S 128 0 E
Baraut **198** 29 13N 77 7 E
Baraya **118** 3 10N 75 4W
Barbacan **211** 10 20N 119 21 E
Barbacena **121** 21 15 S 43 56W
Barbacoas, Colombia **118** 1 45N 78 0W
Barbacoas, Venezuela **118** 9 29N 66 58W
Barbados ■ **113** 13 0N 59 30W
Barbalha **120** 7 19 S 39 17W
Barban **163** 45 5N 14 4 E
Barbara L. **87** 49 20N 87 47W
Barbastro **156** 42 2N 0 5 E
Barbate **155** 36 13N 5 56W
Barbaza **211** 11 12N 122 2 E
Barbeau Pk. **95** 81 54N 75 1W
Barbel, L. **80** 51 55N 68 13W
Barberino di Mugello **163** 44 1N 11 15 E
Barberton **255** 25 42 S 31 2 E
Barbezieux **140** 45 28N 0 9W
Barbosa **118** 5 57N 73 37W
Barbuda I. **113** 17 30N 61 40W
Barca, La **106** 20 17N 102 34W
Barcaldine **230** 23 43 S 145 6 E
Barcarrota **155** 38 31N 6 51W
Barcellona Pozzo di Gotto **165** 38 8N 15 15 E
Barcelona, Spain **156** 41 21N 2 10 E
Barcelona, Venezuela **119** 10 10N 64 40W
Barcelona □ **156** 41 30N 2 0 E
Barcelonette **141** 44 23N 6 40 E
Barcelos **119** 1 0 S 63 0W
Barcin **152** 52 52N 17 55 E
Barclay **86** 49 47N 92 43W
Barcoo → **230** 25 30 S 142 50 E
Barcs **151** 45 58N 17 28 E
Barczewo **152** 53 50N 20 42 E
Barda **181** 40 25N 47 10 E
Barda del Medio **126** 38 45 S 68 11W
Bardai **241** 21 25N 17 0 E
Bardas Blancas **124** 35 49 S 69 45W
Barddhaman **199** 23 14N 87 39 E
Bardejov **151** 49 18N 21 15 E
Bardera **256** 2 20N 42 27 E
Bardi **162** 44 38N 9 43 E
Bardia **242** 31 45N 25 0 E
Bardo **152** 50 31N 16 42 E
Bardoli **198** 21 12N 73 5 E
Bardolino **162** 45 33N 10 43 E
Bardoux, L. **80** 51 9N 67 50W
Bardsey I. **132** 52 46N 4 47W
Bareilly **199** 28 22N 79 27 E
Barellan **233** 34 16 S 146 24 E
Barentin **138** 49 33N 0 58 E
Barenton **138** 48 38N 0 50W
Barents Sea **12** 73 0N 39 0 E
Barentu **245** 15 2N 37 35 E
Barfleur **138** 49 40N 1 17W
Barga **162** 44 5N 10 30 E
Bargal **256** 11 25N 51 0 E
Bargara **230** 24 50 S 152 25 E
Barge **162** 44 43N 7 19 E
Bargnop **245** 9 32N 28 25 E
Bargo **233** 34 18 S 150 35 E
Bargteheide **146** 53 42N 10 13 E
Barguzin **185** 53 37N 109 37 E
Barh **199** 25 29N 85 46 E
Barhaj **199** 26 18N 83 44 E
Barhi **199** 24 15N 85 25 E
Bari, India **198** 26 39N 77 39 E
Bari, Italy **165** 41 6N 16 52 E
Bari Doab **198** 30 20N 73 0 E
Bariadi □ **250** 2 45 S 34 40 E
Barīm **194** 12 39N 43 25 E
Barima → **119** 8 33N 60 25W
Barinas **118** 8 36N 70 15W
Barinas □ **118** 8 10N 69 50W
Baring, C. **94** 70 0N 117 30W
Baringa **252** 0 45N 20 52 E
Baringo **250** 0 47N 36 16 E
Baringo □ **250** 0 55N 36 0 E
Baringo, L. **250** 0 47N 36 16 E
Barinitas **118** 8 45N 70 25W
Baripada **199** 21 57N 86 45 E
Bariri **121** 22 4 S 48 44W
Bârîs **244** 24 42N 30 31 E
Barisal **202** 22 45N 90 20 E
Barisan, Bukit **206** 3 30 S 102 15 E
Barito → **206** 4 0 S 114 50 E
Barjac **141** 44 20N 4 22 E
Barjols **141** 43 34N 6 2 E
Barjūj, Wadi → **241** 25 26N 12 12 E
Bark L. **85** 45 27N 77 51W
Barka = Baraka → **244** 18 13N 37 35 E
Barkam **216** 31 51N 102 28 E
Barkley Sound **92** 48 50N 125 10W
Barkly Downs **230** 20 30 S 138 30 E
Barkly East **254** 30 58 S 27 33 E
Barkly Tableland **230** 17 50 S 136 40 E
Barkly West **254** 28 5 S 24 31 E
Barkol **212** 43 37N 93 2 E
Barkol, Wadi → **244** 17 40N 32 0 E
Barlee, L. **229** 29 15 S 119 30 E
Barletta **165** 41 20N 16 17 E
Barleur, Pointe de **138** 49 42N 1 16W
Barlinek **152** 53 0N 15 15 E
Barlow L. **77** 62 0N 103 0W
Barmedman **231** 34 9 S 147 21 E
Barmer **198** 25 45N 71 20 E
Barmera **232** 34 15 S 140 28 E
Barmouth **132** 52 44N 4 3W
Barmstedt **146** 53 47N 9 46 E
Barnagar **198** 23 7N 75 19 E
Barnard Castle **132** 54 33N 1 55W
Barnato **231** 31 38 S 145 0 E
Barnaul **184** 53 20N 83 40 E
Barnes Icecap **95** 70 0N 73 15W
Barnet **133** 51 37N 0 15W
Barneveld **142** 52 7N 5 36 E
Barneville **138** 49 23N 1 46W
Barngo **230** 25 3 S 147 20 E
Barnsley **132** 53 33N 1 29W
Barnstaple **133** 51 5N 4 3W
Barnwell **91** 49 46N 112 15W
Baro **247** 8 35N 6 18 E
Baro → **245** 8 26N 33 13 E
Baroda = Vadodara **198** 22 20N 73 10 E
Baroda **198** 25 29N 76 35 E
Baron Ra. **228** 23 30 S 127 45 E
Barons **91** 50 0N 113 5W
Barpali **199** 21 11N 83 35 E
Barpathar **202** 26 17N 93 53 E
Barpeta **202** 26 20N 91 10 E
Barqin **241** 27 33N 13 34 E
Barquinha **155** 39 28N 8 25W
Barquísimeto **118** 10 4N 69 19W
Barr **139** 48 25N 7 28 E
Barra, Brazil **120** 11 5 S 43 10W
Barra, U.K. **134** 57 0N 7 30W
Barra, Sd. of **134** 57 4N 7 25W
Barra da Estiva **121** 13 38 S 41 19W
Barra de Navidad, La **106** 19 12N 104 41W
Barra de Tonalá **109** 18 12N 94 7W
Barra do Corda **120** 5 30 S 45 10W
Barra do Dande **253** 8 28 S 13 22 E
Barra do Mendes **121** 11 43 S 42 4W
Barra do Piraí **121** 22 30 S 43 50W
Barra Falsa, Pta. da **255** 22 58 S 35 37 E
Barra Hd. **134** 56 47N 7 40W
Barra Mansa **125** 22 35 S 44 12W
Barraba **231** 30 21 S 150 35 E
Barracão do Barreto **123** 8 48 S 58 24W
Barrackpur = Barakpur **199** 22 44N 88 30 E
Barrafranca **165** 37 22N 14 10 E
Barranca, Lima, Peru **122** 10 45 S 77 50W
Barranca, Loreto, Peru **118** 4 50 S 76 50W
Barranca, La, Querétaro, Mexico **107** 21 20N 99 2W
Barranca, La, Sonora, Mexico **100** 28 35N 109 40W
Barranca del Oro **104** 20 56N 104 29W
Barrancabermeja **118** 7 0N 73 50W
Barrancas, Colombia **118** 10 57N 72 50W
Barrancas, Venezuela **119** 8 55N 62 5W
Barranco de Guadalupe **101** 30 2N 104 44W
Barrancos **155** 38 10N 6 58W
Barranqueras **124** 27 30 S 59 0W
Barranquilla **118** 11 0N 74 50W
Barras, Brazil **120** 4 15 S 42 18W
Barras, Colombia **118** 1 45 S 73 13W
Barraute **82** 48 26N 77 38W
Barre do Bugres **123** 15 0 S 57 11W
Barreal **124** 31 33 S 69 28W
Barrei **256** 6 10N 42 49 E
Barreiras **121** 12 8 S 45 0W
Barreirinha **119** 2 30 S 62 50W
Barreirinhas **120** 2 30 S 42 50W
Barreiro **155** 38 40N 9 6W
Barreiros **120** 8 49 S 35 12W
Barrême **141** 43 57N 6 23 E
Barren, Nosy **255** 18 25 S 43 40 E
Barretos **121** 20 30 S 48 35W
Barrhead **90** 54 10N 114 24W
Barrie **84** 44 24N 79 40W
Barriefield **85** 44 14N 76 28W
Barrier, C. **234** 36 25 S 175 32 E
Barrier Ra., Australia **231** 31 0 S 141 30 E
Barrier Ra., N.Z. **235** 44 5 S 169 42 E
Barrier Reef, Gt. **230** 19 0 S 149 0 E
Barrière **93** 51 12N 120 7W
Barrington L. **77** 56 55N 100 15W
Barrington Passage **81** 43 30N 65 38W
Barrington Tops **231** 32 6 S 151 28 E
Barringur **231** 29 1 S 145 41 E
Barro do Garças **123** 15 54 S 52 16W
Barroteran **102** 27 41N 101 18W
Barrow → **135** 52 10N 6 57W
Barrow Creek **230** 21 30 S 133 55 E
Barrow I. **228** 20 45 S 115 20 E
Barrow-in-Furness **132** 54 8N 3 15W
Barrow Pt. **230** 14 20 S 144 40 E
Barrow Ra. **229** 26 0 S 127 40 E
Barrow Str. **95** 74 20N 95 0W
Barrows **89** 52 50N 101 27W
Barruecopardo **154** 41 4N 6 40W
Barruelo **154** 42 54N 4 17W
Barry **133** 51 23N 3 19W
Barry's Bay **85** 45 29N 77 41W
Barsalogho **247** 13 25N 1 3W
Barsat **199** 36 10N 72 45 E
Barsham **192** 35 21N 40 33 E
Barsi **200** 18 10N 75 50 E
Barsø **173** 55 7N 9 33 E
Barth **146** 54 20N 12 36 E
Barthélemy, Col **204** 19 26N 104 6 E
Bartica **119** 6 25N 58 40W
Bartlett, L. **76** 63 5N 118 20W
Bartletts Harbour **79** 50 57N 57 0W
Bartolomeu Dias **251** 21 10 S 35 8 E
Barton, Australia **229** 30 31 S 132 39 E
Barton, Phil. **211** 10 24N 119 8 E
Barton-upon-Humber **132** 53 41N 0 27W
Bartoszyce **152** 54 15N 20 55 E
Barú, I. de **118** 10 15N 75 35W
Barú, Volcan **112** 8 55N 82 35W
Barumba **250** 1 3N 23 37 E
Baruth **146** 52 3N 13 31 E
Barvaux **143** 50 21N 5 29 E
Barvenkovo **180** 48 57N 37 0 E
Barwani **198** 22 2N 74 57 E
Barycz → **152** 51 42N 16 15 E
Barysh **179** 53 39N 47 8 E
Barzān **192** 36 55N 44 3 E
Bas-Rhin □ **139** 48 40N 7 30 E
Bašaid **166** 45 38N 20 25 E
Bāsa'idū **193** 26 35N 55 20 E
Basal **198** 33 33N 72 13 E
Basankusa **252** 1 5N 19 50 E
Basawa **198** 34 15N 70 50 E
Bascharage **143** 49 34N 5 55 E
Basco **210** 20 27N 121 58 E
Bascuñán, C. **124** 28 52 S 71 35W
Basècles **143** 50 32N 3 39 E
Basel **148** 47 35N 7 35 E
Basel-Stadt □ **148** 47 35N 7 35 E
Baselland □ **148** 47 26N 7 45 E
Basento → **165** 40 21N 16 50 E
Basey **211** 11 17N 125 4 E
Bashaw **91** 52 35N 112 58W
Bāshī **193** 28 41N 51 4 E
Bashkir A.S.S.R. □ **182** 54 0N 57 0 E
Basilaki I. **227** 10 35 S 151 0 E
Basilan **211** 6 35N 122 0 E
Basilan □ **211** 6 33N 122 4 E
Basilan Str. **211** 6 50N 122 0 E
Basildon **133** 51 34N 0 29 E
Basilicata □ **165** 40 30N 16 0 E
Basim = Washim **200** 20 3N 77 0 E
Basin L. **88** 52 38N 105 17W
Basingstoke **133** 51 15N 1 5W
Basirhat **202** 22 40N 88 54 E
Baška **163** 44 58N 14 45 E
Baskatong, Rés. **74** 46 46N 75 50W
Basle = Basel **148** 47 35N 7 35 E
Basmat **200** 19 15N 77 12 E
Basoda **198** 23 52N 77 54 E
Basodino **149** 46 25N 8 28 E
Basoka **250** 1 16N 23 40 E
Basongo **253** 4 15 S 20 20 E
Basque Provinces = Vascongadas **156** 42 50N 2 45W
Basra = Al Başrah **192** 30 30N 47 50 E
Bass River **81** 45 25N 63 47W
Bass Rock **134** 56 5N 2 40W
Bass Str. **230** 39 15 S 146 30 E
Bassano **91** 50 48N 112 20W
Bassano del Grappa **163** 45 45N 11 45 E
Bassar **247** 9 19N 0 57 E
Basse Santa-Su **246** 13 13N 14 15W
Basse-Terre **113** 16 0N 61 40W
Bassecourt **148** 47 20N 7 15 E
Bassée, La **139** 50 31N 2 49 E
Bassein, Burma **202** 16 45N 94 30 E
Bassein, India **200** 19 26N 72 48 E
Basseterre **113** 17 17N 62 43W
Bassevelde **143** 51 15N 3 41 E
Bassi **198** 30 44N 76 21 E
Bassigny **139** 48 0N 5 10 E
Bassikounou **246** 15 55N 6 1W
Bassilly **143** 50 40N 3 56 E
Bassum **146** 52 50N 8 42 E
Båstad **173** 56 25N 12 51 E
Bastak **193** 27 15N 54 25 E
Baştām **193** 36 29N 55 4 E
Bastar **200** 19 15N 81 40 E
Basti **199** 26 52N 82 55 E
Bastia **141** 42 40N 9 30 E
Bastia Umbra **163** 43 4N 12 34 E
Bastide-Puylaurent, La **140** 44 35N 3 55 E
Bastille, L. **80** 51 46N 61 11W
Bastogne **143** 50 1N 5 43 E
Basyanovskiy **182** 58 19N 60 44 E
Bat Yam **189** 32 2N 34 44 E
Bata, Eq. Guin. **252** 1 57N 9 50 E
Bata, Romania **170** 46 1N 22 4 E
Bataan **210** 14 40N 120 25 E
Batabanó **112** 22 40N 82 20W
Batabanó, G. de **112** 22 30N 82 30W
Batac **210** 18 3N 120 34 E
Batacosa **100** 27 32N 109 24W
Batagoy **185** 67 38N 134 38 E
Batak **167** 41 57N 24 12 E
Batalha **155** 39 40N 8 50W
Batam **208** 1 5N 104 3 E
Batama **250** 0 58N 26 33 E
Batamay **185** 63 30N 129 15 E
Batamshinskiy **182** 50 36N 58 16 E
Batan I. **210** 20 30N 121 50 E
Batanes □ **210** 20 40N 121 55 E
Batanes Is. **210** 20 30N 121 50 E
Batang, China **216** 30 1N 99 0 E
Batang, Indonesia **209** 6 55 S 109 45 E
Batangafo **252** 7 25N 18 20 E
Batangas **210** 13 35N 121 10 E
Batangas □ **210** 13 15N 121 5 E
Batanghari **208** 1 36 S 103 37 E
Batanta **207** 0 55 S 130 40 E
Bataques **98** 32 33N 115 4W
Batas **211** 11 10N 119 37 E
Batas I. **211** 11 10N 119 36 E
Batatais **125** 20 54 S 47 37W
Bataysk **181** 47 3N 39 45 E
Batchawana B. **87** 46 53N 84 30W
Batchawana Bay **87** 46 55N 84 37W
Batchelor **228** 13 4 S 131 1 E
Batéké, Plat. **252** 3 30 S 15 45 E
Bateman's B. **231** 35 40 S 150 12 E
Batemans Bay **231** 35 44 S 150 11 E
Bath, N.B., Canada **81** 46 31N 67 36W
Bath, Ont., Canada **85** 44 11N 76 47W
Bath, U.K. **133** 51 22N 2 22W
Batheay **205** 11 59N 104 57 E
Bathgate **134** 55 54N 3 38W
Bathmen **142** 52 15N 6 29 E
Bathurst = Banjul **246** 13 28N 16 40W
Bathurst, Australia **231** 33 25 S 149 31 E
Bathurst, Canada **75** 47 37N 65 43W
Bathurst, C. **94** 70 34N 128 0W
Bathurst B. **230** 14 16 S 144 25 E
Bathurst Harb. **230** 43 15 S 146 10 E
Bathurst I., Australia **228** 11 30 S 130 10 E
Bathurst I., Canada **95** 76 0N 100 30W
Bathurst Inlet **94** 68 10N 108 50W
Batie **246** 9 53N 2 53W
Batiscan **83** 46 30N 72 15W

Batiscan → 83 46 16N 72 15W
Batiscan, L. 83 47 22N 71 55W
Batlow 231 35 31 S 148 9 E
Batna 241 35 34N 6 15 E
Bato, Leyte, Phil. 211 10 13N 124 48 E
Bato, Sulu, Phil. 211 5 15N 120 3 E
Bato Bato 211 5 6N 119 49 E
Batoala 252 0 48N 13 27 E
Batobato 211 6 50N 126 5 E
Batočina 166 44 7N 21 5 E
Batoka 251 16 45 S 27 15 E
Batong, Ko 205 6 32N 99 12 E
Batopilas 101 27 1N 107 44W
Batouri 252 4 30N 14 25 E
Battambang 204 13 7N 103 12 E
Batticaloa 201 7 43N 81 45 E
Battice 143 50 39N 5 50 E
Battipáglia 165 40 38N 15 0 E
Battīr 189 31 44N 35 8 E
Battle, Canada 91 52 58N 110 52W
Battle, U.K. 133 50 55N 0 30 E
Battle → 88 52 43N 108 15W
Battle Camp 230 15 20 S 144 40 E
Battle Harbour 78 52 16N 55 35W
Battlefields 251 18 37 S 29 47 E
Battleford 88 52 45N 108 15W
Battonya 151 46 16N 21 3 E
Batu 245 6 55N 39 45 E
Batu, Kepulauan 208 0 30 S 98 25 E
Batu Caves 205 3 15N 101 40 E
Batu Gajah 205 4 28N 101 3 E
Batu Pahat 205 1 50N 102 56 E
Batuata 207 6 12 S 122 42 E
Batuc 100 29 15N 109 44W
Batulaki 211 5 34N 125 19 E
Batumi 181 41 30N 41 30 E
Baturaja 208 4 11 S 104 15 E
Baturité 120 4 28 S 38 45W
Batusangkar 208 0 27 S 100 35 E
Bau 206 1 25N 110 9 E
Bauang 210 16 31N 120 20 E
Baubau 207 5 25 S 122 38 E
Bauchi 247 10 22N 9 48 E
Bauchi □ 247 10 30N 10 0 E
Baud 138 47 52N 3 1W
Baudour 143 50 29N 3 50 E
Bauer, C. 231 32 44 S 134 4 E
Baugé 138 47 31N 0 8W
Bauhinia Downs 230 24 35 S 149 18 E
Bauld, C. 79 51 38N 55 26W
Baule-Escoublac, La 138 47 18N 2 23W
Bauma 149 47 23N 8 53 E
Baume-les-Dames 139 47 22N 6 22 E
Baunatal 146 51 13N 9 25 E
Baunei 164 40 2N 9 41 E
Baures 123 13 35 S 63 35W
Bauru 125 22 10 S 49 0W
Baús 123 18 22 S 52 47W
Bauska 178 56 24N 25 15 E
Bautzen 146 51 11N 14 25 E
Baux, Les 141 43 45N 4 51 E
Bavānāt 193 30 28N 53 27 E
Bavanište 166 44 49N 20 53 E
Bavaria = Bayern □ 147 49 7N 11 30 E
Båven 172 59 0N 16 56 E
Bavi Sadri 198 24 28N 74 30 E
Baviacora 100 29 43N 110 9W
Bavícora, L. de 101 29 24N 107 50W
Bavispe, R. de → 100 29 15N 109 11W
Bawdwin 202 23 5N 97 20 E
Bawean 209 5 46 S 112 35 E
Bawku 247 11 3N 0 19W
Bawlake 202 19 11N 97 21 E
Bawlf 91 52 55N 112 28W
Bawolung 216 28 50N 101 16 E
Baxoi 216 30 1N 96 50 E
Bay, Laguna de 207 14 20N 121 11 E
Bay Bulls 79 47 19N 52 50W
Bay de Verde 79 48 5N 52 54W
Bay L'Argent 79 47 33N 54 54W
Bay Roberts 79 47 36N 53 16W
Bay View 234 39 25 S 176 50 E
Baya 251 11 53 S 27 25 E
Bayambang 210 15 49N 120 27 E
Bayamo 112 20 20N 76 40W
Bayan Har Shan 212 34 0N 98 0 E
Bayan Hot = Alxa Zuoqi 214 38 50N 105 40 E
Bayan Obo 214 41 52N 109 59 E
Bayan-Ovoo 214 42 55N 106 5 E
Bayana 198 26 55N 77 18 E
Bayanaul 184 50 45N 75 45 E
Bayandalay 214 43 30N 103 29 E
Bayawan 211 9 46N 122 45 E
Baybay 211 10 40N 124 55 E
Bayerischer Wald 147 49 0N 13 0 E
Bayern □ 147 49 7N 11 30 E
Bayeux 138 49 17N 0 42W
Bayfield 84 43 34N 81 42W
Bayḥān al Qisāb 194 15 48N 45 44 E
Baykadam 183 43 48N 69 58 E
Baykal, Oz. 185 53 0N 108 0 E
Baykit 185 61 50N 95 50 E
Baykonur 184 47 48N 65 50 E
Baymak 182 52 36N 58 19 E
Baynes Mts. 254 17 15 S 13 0 E
Bayombong 210 16 30N 121 10 E
Bayon 139 48 30N 6 20 E
Bayona 154 42 6N 8 52W
Bayonne 140 43 30N 1 28W
Bayovar 122 5 50 S 81 0W
Bayram-Ali 184 37 37N 62 10 E
Bayreuth 147 49 56N 11 35 E
Bayrischzell 147 47 39N 12 1 E
Bayrūt 190 33 53N 35 31 E
Bays, L. of 84 45 15N 79 4W
Bayside 85 44 7N 77 30W
Baysun 183 38 12N 67 12 E
Baysville 84 45 9N 79 7W
Bayt al Faqīh 194 14 31N 43 19 E
Bayt Awlá 189 31 37N 35 2 E
Bayt Fajjār 189 31 38N 35 9 E
Bayt Fūrīk 189 32 11N 35 20 E
Bayt Ḥānūn 189 31 32N 34 32 E
Bayt Jālā 189 31 43N 35 11 E
Bayt Lahm 189 31 43N 35 12 E
Bayt Rīma 189 32 2N 35 6 E
Bayt Sāḥūr 189 31 42N 35 13 E
Bayt Ummar 189 31 38N 35 7 E
Bayt 'ūr al Taḥtā 189 31 54N 35 5 E
Baytīn 189 31 56N 35 14 E
Baytūniyā 189 31 54N 35 10 E
Bayyā'īyah al Kabīrah 190 35 44N 37 6 E
Bayzhansay 183 43 14N 69 54 E
Bayzo 247 13 52N 4 35 E
Baza 157 37 30N 2 47W
Bazar Dyuzi 181 41 12N 47 50 E
Bazarny Karabulak 179 52 15N 46 20 E
Bazarnyy Syzgan 179 53 45N 46 40 E
Bazartobe 181 49 26N 51 45 E
Bazaruto, I. do 255 21 40 S 35 28 E
Bazas 140 44 27N 0 13W
Bazhong 216 31 52N 106 46 E
Bazin → 82 47 29N 75 22W
Bazmān, Kūh-e 193 28 4N 60 1 E
Beabula 233 34 26 S 145 9 E
Beachburg 85 45 44N 76 51W
Beachport 232 37 29 S 140 0 E
Beachville 84 43 5N 80 49W
Beachy Head 133 50 44N 0 16 E
Beacon 229 30 26 S 117 52 E
Beaconia 89 50 25N 96 31W
Beagle, Canal 126 55 0 S 68 30W
Beagle Bay 228 16 58 S 122 40 E
Bealanana 255 14 33N 48 44 E
Beale, C. 92 48 47N 125 13W
Beamsville 84 43 12N 79 28W
Béar, C. 140 42 31N 3 8 E
Bear I. 135 51 38N 9 50W
Bear L., Alta., Canada 90 55 9N 119 4W
Bear L., B.C., Canada 76 56 10N 126 52W
Bear L., Man., Canada 77 55 8N 96 0W
Bear River 81 44 34N 65 39W
Beardmore 87 49 36N 87 57W
Beardmore Glacier 13 84 30 S 170 0 E
Béarn, Canada 82 47 17N 79 20W
Béarn, France 140 43 8N 0 36W
Bearskin Lake 74 53 58N 91 2W
Beas de Segura 157 38 15N 2 53W
Beasain 156 43 3N 2 11W
Beata, C. 113 17 40N 71 30W
Beata, I. 113 17 34N 71 31W
Beatrice 251 18 15 S 30 55 E
Beatrice, C. 230 14 20 S 136 55 E
Beatton → 76 56 15N 120 45W
Beatton River 76 57 26N 121 20W
Beatty 88 52 54N 104 48W
Beaucaire 141 43 48N 4 39 E
Beauce, Plaine de la 139 48 10N 1 45 E
Beauceville 83 46 13N 70 46W
Beauchêne, I. 126 52 55 S 59 15W
Beauchûne, L. 82 46 35N 78 55W
Beaudesert 231 27 59 S 153 0 E
Beaufort, Australia 232 37 25 S 143 25 E
Beaufort, Malaysia 206 5 30N 115 40 E
Beaufort Sea 94 72 0N 140 0W
Beaufort West 254 32 18 S 22 36 E
Beaugency 139 47 47N 1 38 E
Beauharnois 83 45 20N 73 52W
Beaujeu 141 46 10N 4 35 E
Beaulac 83 45 50N 71 23W
Beaulieu 140 44 59N 1 50 E
Beaulieu → 76 62 3N 113 11W
Beauly 134 57 29N 4 27W
Beauly → 134 57 26N 4 28W
Beaumaris 132 53 16N 4 7W
Beaumetz-les-Loges 139 50 15N 2 40 E
Beaumont, Belgium 143 50 15N 4 14 E
Beaumont, Alta., Canada 90 53 21N 113 25W
Beaumont, Newf., Canada 79 49 37N 55 41W
Beaumont, Dordogne, France 140 44 45N 0 46 E
Beaumont, Sarthe, France 138 48 13N 0 8 E
Beaumont, N.Z. 235 45 50 S 169 33 E
Beaumont-de-Lomagne 140 43 53N 0 59 E
Beaumont-le-Roger 138 49 4N 0 47 E
Beaumont-sur-Oise 139 49 9N 2 17 E
Beaune 139 47 2N 4 50 E
Beaune-la-Rolande 139 48 4N 2 25 E
Beauport 83 46 52N 71 11W
Beaupré 83 47 3N 70 54W
Beaupréau 138 47 12N 1 0W
Beauraing 143 50 7N 4 57 E
Beauséjour 89 50 5N 96 35W
Beausset, Le 141 43 10N 5 46 E
Beautemps-Beaupré, Î. 226 20 24 S 166 9 E
Beauvais 139 49 25N 2 8 E
Beauval 77 55 9N 107 37W
Beauvoir 138 46 55N 2 1W
Beauvoir-sur-Niort 140 46 12N 0 30W
Beaver →, B.C., Canada 76 59 52N 124 20W
Beaver →, Ont., Canada 74 55 55N 87 48W
Beaver →, Sask., Canada 77 55 26N 107 45W
Beaver Brook Station 81 47 8N 65 36W
Beaver Creek 94 63 0N 141 0W
Beaverdell 93 49 27N 119 6W
Beaverhill L., Alta., Canada 90 53 27N 112 32W
Beaverhill L., Man., Canada 77 54 5N 94 50W
Beaverhill L., N.W.T., Canada 77 63 2N 104 22W
Beaverlodge 90 55 11N 119 29W
Beavermouth 93 51 32N 117 23W
Beaverstone → 74 54 59N 89 25W
Beaverton 84 44 26N 79 9W
Beawar 198 26 3N 74 18 E
Bebedouro 125 21 0 S 48 25W
Beboa 255 17 22 S 44 33 E
Bebra 146 50 59N 9 48 E
Becal 111 20 27N 90 2W
Becanchén 111 19 46N 89 17W
Beccles 133 52 27N 1 33 E
Bečej 166 45 36N 20 3 E
Beceni 170 45 23N 26 48 E
Becerreá 154 42 51N 7 10W
Béchar 241 31 38N 2 18W
Bechyně 150 49 17N 14 29 E
Beckum 146 51 46N 8 3 E
Bécon 138 47 30N 0 50W
Bečva → 151 49 31N 17 40 E
Bédar 157 37 11N 1 59W
Bédarieux 140 43 37N 3 10 E
Bédarrides 141 44 2N 4 54 E
Beddouza, Ras 240 32 33N 9 9W
Bedel, Pereval 183 41 26N 78 26 E
Bedele 245 8 31N 36 23 E
Bederkesa 146 53 37N 8 50 E
Bederwanak 256 9 34N 44 23 E
Bedeso 245 9 58N 40 52 E
Bedford, N.S., Canada 81 44 44N 63 40W
Bedford, Qué., Canada 83 45 7N 72 59W
Bedford, S. Africa 254 32 40 S 26 10 E
Bedford, U.K. 133 52 8N 0 29W
Bedford □ 133 52 4N 0 28W
Bedford, C. 230 15 14 S 145 21 E
Bedford Downs 228 17 19 S 127 20 E
Bedi 243 11 6N 18 33 E
Będków 152 51 36N 19 44 E
Bednja → 163 46 12N 16 25 E
Bednodemyanovsk 179 53 55N 43 15 E
Bedónia 162 44 28N 9 36 E
Bedourie 230 24 30 S 139 30 E
Bedous 140 43 0N 0 36W
Bedretto 149 46 31N 8 31 E
Bedum 142 53 18N 6 36 E
Będzin 152 50 19N 19 7 E
Beebe Plain 83 45 1N 72 9W
Beechey Hd. 93 48 10N 123 30W
Beechworth 231 36 22 S 146 43 E
Beechy 88 50 53N 107 24W
Beek, Gelderland, Neth. 142 51 55N 6 11 E
Beek, Limburg, Neth. 143 50 57N 5 48 E
Beek, Noord-Brabant, Neth. 143 51 32N 5 38 E
Beekbergen 142 52 10N 5 58 E
Beelitz 146 52 14N 12 58 E
Beenleigh 231 27 43 S 153 10 E
Be'er Menuḥa 192 30 19N 35 8 E
Be'er Sheva' 189 31 15N 34 48 E
Be'er Sheva' → 189 31 12N 34 40 E
Be'er Toviyya 189 31 44N 34 42 E
Be'eri 189 31 25N 34 30 E
Be'erotayim 189 32 19N 34 59 E
Beersheba = Be'er Sheva' 189 31 15N 34 48 E
Beerta 142 53 11N 7 6 E
Beerze → 142 51 39N 5 20 E
Beesd 142 51 53N 5 11 E
Beeskow 146 52 9N 14 14 E
Beeston 132 52 55N 1 11W
Beetaloo 230 17 15 S 133 50 E
Beeton 84 44 5N 79 47W
Beetsterzwaag 142 53 4N 6 5 E
Beetz, L. 80 50 34N 62 42W
Beetzendorf 146 52 42N 11 6 E
Befale 252 0 25N 20 45 E
Befotaka 255 23 49 S 47 0 E
Bega 231 36 41 S 149 51 E
Bega, Canalul 166 45 37N 20 46 E
Bégard 138 48 38N 3 18W
Bègles 140 44 45N 0 35W
Begna → 171 60 41N 10 0 E
Begonte 154 43 10N 7 40W
Begusarai 199 25 24N 86 9 E
Behābād 193 32 24N 59 47 E
Behbehān 193 30 30N 50 15 E
Behshahr 193 36 45N 53 35 E
Bei Jiang → 217 23 2N 112 58 E
Bei'an 213 48 10N 126 20 E
Beigang 217 23 38N 120 16 E
Beihai 216 21 28N 109 6 E
Beijing 214 39 55N 116 20 E
Beijing □ 214 39 55N 116 20 E
Beilen 142 52 52N 6 27 E
Beiliu 217 22 41N 110 21 E
Beilngries 147 49 1N 11 27 E
Beilpajah 231 32 54 S 143 52 E
Beilul 245 13 2N 42 20 E
Beipiao 215 41 52N 120 32 E
Beira, Mozam. 251 19 50 S 34 52 E
Beira, Somalia 256 6 57N 47 19 E
Beirut = Bayrūt 190 33 53N 35 31 E
Beiseker 91 51 23N 113 32W
Beit Lāhiyah 189 31 32N 34 30 E
Beitaolaizhao 215 44 58N 125 58 E
Beitbridge 251 22 12 S 30 0 E
Beiuş 170 46 40N 22 21 E
Beizhen, Liaoning, China 215 41 38N 121 54 E
Beizhen, Shandong, China 215 37 20N 118 2 E
Beizhengzhen 215 44 31N 123 30 E
Beja, Portugal 155 38 2N 7 53W
Béja, Tunisia 241 36 43N 9 12 E
Beja □ 155 37 55N 7 55W
Bejaia 241 36 42N 5 2 E
Béjar 154 40 23N 5 46W
Bejestān 193 34 30N 58 5 E
Bekaa = Al Biqā □ 190 34 0N 36 5 E
Bekabad 183 40 13N 69 14 E
Bekasi 207 6 14 S 106 59 E
Békés 151 46 47N 21 9 E
Békés □ 151 46 45N 21 0 E
Békéscsaba 151 46 40N 21 5 E
Bekily 255 24 13 S 45 19 E
Bekkevoort 143 50 57N 4 58 E
Bekoji 245 7 40N 39 17 E
Bekok 205 2 20N 103 7 E
Bekwai 247 6 30N 1 34W
Bela, India 199 25 50N 82 0 E
Bela, Pakistan 197 26 12N 66 20 E
Bela Crkva 166 44 55N 21 27 E
Bela Palanka 166 43 13N 22 17 E
Bela Vista, Brazil 124 22 12 S 56 20W
Bela Vista, Mozam. 255 26 10 S 32 44 E
Bélâbre 140 46 34N 1 8 E
Belalcázar 155 38 35N 5 10W
Belanger → 89 53 27N 97 41W
Belanovica 166 44 15N 20 23 E
Belas 253 8 55 S 13 9 E
Belau Is. 226 7 30N 134 30 E
Belavenona 255 24 50 S 47 4 E
Belawan 208 3 33N 98 32 E
Belaya → 182 56 0N 54 32 E
Belaya, Mt. 245 11 25N 36 8 E
Belaya Glina 181 46 5N 40 48 E
Belaya Kalitva 181 48 13N 40 50 E
Belaya Kholunitsa 179 58 41N 50 13 E
Belaya Tserkov 178 49 45N 30 10 E
Belayan → 209 0 14 S 116 36 E
Belbutte 88 53 22N 107 49W
Belceşti 170 47 19N 27 7 E
Bełchatów 152 51 21N 19 22 E
Belcher Chan. 95 77 15N 95 0W
Belcher Is. 78 56 15N 78 45W
Belchite 156 41 18N 0 43W
Belcourt 82 48 24N 77 21W
Beldibi 190 36 25N 32 26 E
Belebey 182 54 7N 54 7 E
Belém 120 1 20 S 48 30W
Belém de São Francisco 120 8 46 S 38 58W
Belén, Argentina 124 27 40 S 67 5W
Belén, Colombia 118 1 26N 75 56W
Belén, Paraguay 124 23 30 S 57 6W
Belen, Turkey 190 36 31N 36 10 E
Belén del Refugio 106 21 31N 102 25W

Belene **167** 43 39N 25 10 E
Bélesta **140** 42 55N 1 56 E
Belet Uen **256** 4 30N 45 5 E
Belev **179** 53 50N 36 5 E
Belfast, N.Z. **235** 43 27 S 172 39 E
Belfast, S. Africa **255** 25 42 S 30 2 E
Belfast, U.K. **135** 54 35N 5 56W
Belfast □ **135** 54 35N 5 56W
Belfast, L. **135** 54 40N 5 50W
Belfeld **143** 51 18N 6 6 E
Belfort **139** 47 38N 6 50 E
Belfort □ **139** 47 38N 6 52 E
Belgaum **201** 15 55N 74 35 E
Belgioioso **162** 45 9N 9 21 E
Belgium ■ **143** 50 30N 5 0 E
Belgorod **179** 50 35N 36 35 E
Belgorod-Dnestrovskiy **180** 46 11N 30 23 E
Belgrade = Beograd **166** 44 50N 20 37 E
Belgrove **235** 41 27 S 172 59 E
Beli Drim → **166** 42 6N 20 25 E
Beli Manastir **166** 45 45N 18 36 E
Beli Timok → **166** 43 53N 22 14 E
Belice → **164** 37 35N 12 55 E
Belin **140** 44 30N 0 47W
Belinga **252** 1 10N 13 2 E
Belinskiy **179** 53 0N 43 25 E
Belinţ **170** 45 48N 21 54 E
Belinyu **208** 1 35 S 105 50 E
Belitung **209** 3 10 S 107 50 E
Beliu **170** 46 30N 22 0 E
Belize ■ **112** 17 0N 88 30W
Belize Inlet **92** 51 8N 127 20W
Beljanica **166** 44 8N 21 43 E
Belkovskiy, Ostrov **185** 75 32N 135 44 E
Bell → **82** 49 48N 77 38W
Bell Bay **230** 41 6 S 146 53 E
Bell I., Newf., Canada **79** 47 38N 52 58W
Bell I., Newf., Canada **79** 50 46N 55 35W
Bell-Irving → **76** 56 12N 129 5W
Bell L. **86** 49 48N 90 58W
Bell Peninsula **95** 63 50N 82 0W
Bell Ville **124** 32 40 S 62 40W
Bella Bella **92** 52 10N 128 10W
Bella Coola **92** 52 25N 126 40W
Bella Flor **122** 11 9 S 67 49W
Bella Unión **124** 30 15 S 57 40W
Bella Vista, Corrientes, Argentina **124** 28 33 S 59 0W
Bella Vista, Tucuman, Argentina **124** 27 10 S 65 25W
Bellac **140** 46 7N 1 3 E
Bellágio **162** 45 59N 9 15 E
Bellary **201** 15 10N 76 56 E
Bellata **231** 29 53 S 149 46 E
Bellavista **104** 21 34N 104 53W
Bellburns **79** 50 20N 57 32W
Belle-Île **138** 47 20N 3 10W
Belle Isle **79** 51 57N 55 25W
Belle Isle, Str. of **79** 51 30N 56 30W
Belle-Isle-en-Terre **138** 48 33N 3 23W
Belle River **84** 42 18N 82 43W
Belle Yella **246** 7 24N 10 0W
Belledonne **141** 45 30N 6 10 E
Belledune **75** 47 55N 65 50W
Bellegarde, Ain, France **141** 46 4N 5 49 E
Bellegarde, Creuse, France **140** 45 59N 2 18 E
Bellegarde, Loiret, France **139** 48 0N 2 26 E
Bellême **138** 48 22N 0 34 E
Belleoram **79** 47 31N 55 25W
Belleterre **82** 47 25N 78 41W
Belleville, Canada **85** 44 10N 77 23W
Belleville, Rhône, France **141** 46 7N 4 45 E
Belleville, Vendée, France **138** 46 48N 1 28W
Bellevue **91** 49 35N 114 22W
Belley **141** 45 46N 5 41 E
Belleza **101** 26 56N 106 21W
Belleza, R. → **101** 26 58N 106 20W
Bellin **78** 60 0N 70 0W
Bellingen **231** 30 25 S 152 50 E
Bellingshausen **13** 62 0 S 59 0W
Bellingshausen Sea **13** 66 0 S 80 0W
Bellinzona **149** 46 11N 9 1 E
Belliveau Cove **81** 44 23N 66 4W
Bello **118** 6 20N 75 33W
Bellpat **198** 29 0N 68 5 E
Bellpuig **156** 41 37N 1 1 E
Bells Corners **85** 45 19N 75 50W
Bellsite **89** 52 35N 101 4W
Belluno **163** 46 8N 12 13 E
Belly → **91** 49 46N 113 2W
Bélmez **155** 38 17N 5 17W
Belmont, Australia **231** 33 4 S 151 42 E
Belmont, Man., Canada **89** 49 25N 99 27W
Belmont, N.S., Canada **81** 45 25N 63 23W
Belmont, Ont., Canada **84** 42 53N 81 5W
Belmonte, Brazil **121** 16 0 S 39 0W
Belmonte, Portugal **154** 40 21N 7 20W
Belmonte, Spain **156** 39 34N 2 43W
Belmopan **112** 17 18N 88 30W
Belmore **232** 33 34 S 141 13 E
Belmullet **135** 54 13N 9 58W
Belo Horizonte **121** 19 55 S 43 56W
Belo Jardim **120** 8 20 S 36 26W
Belo-sur-Mer **255** 20 42 S 44 0 E
Belo-Tsiribihina **255** 19 40 S 44 30 E
Beloeil **83** 45 34N 73 12W
Belogorsk, R.S.F.S.R., U.S.S.R. **185** 51 0N 128 20 E
Belogorsk, Ukraine S.S.R., U.S.S.R. **180** 45 3N 34 35 E
Belogradchik **166** 43 53N 22 15 E
Belogradets **167** 43 22N 27 18 E
Beloha **255** 25 10 S 45 3 E
Belokorovichi **178** 51 7N 28 2 E
Belomorsk **176** 64 35N 34 30 E
Belonia **202** 23 15N 91 30 E
Belopolye **178** 51 14N 34 20 E
Beloretsk **182** 53 58N 58 24 E
Belot, L. **94** 66 53N 126 16W
Belovo **184** 54 30N 86 0 E
Beloyarskiy **182** 56 45N 61 24 E
Beloye, Oz. **176** 60 10N 37 35 E
Beloye More **176** 66 30N 38 0 E
Beloye Ozero **181** 45 15N 46 50 E
Belozem **167** 42 12N 25 2 E
Belozersk **179** 60 0N 37 30 E
Belpasso **165** 37 37N 15 0 E
Belsele **143** 51 9N 4 6 E
Belsito **164** 37 50N 13 47 E
Beltana **231** 30 48 S 138 25 E
Belterra **119** 2 45 S 55 0W
Beltinci **163** 46 37N 16 20 E
Beltsy **180** 47 48N 28 0 E
Belturbet **135** 54 6N 7 28W
Belukha **184** 49 50N 86 50 E
Beluran **206** 5 48N 117 35 E
Beluša **151** 49 5N 18 27 E
Belušić **166** 43 50N 21 10 E
Belvedere Marittimo **165** 39 37N 15 52 E
Belvès **140** 44 46N 1 0 E
Belvis de la Jara **155** 39 45N 4 57W
Belyando → **230** 21 38 S 146 50 E
Belyy **178** 55 48N 32 51 E
Belyy, Ostrov **184** 73 30N 71 0 E
Belyy Yar **184** 58 26N 84 39 E
Belyye Vody **183** 42 25N 69 50 E
Belzig **146** 52 8N 12 36 E
Bełżyce **152** 51 11N 22 17 E
Bemaraha, Lembalemban' i **255** 18 40 S 44 45 E
Bemarivo **255** 21 45 S 44 45 E
Bemarivo → **255** 15 27 S 47 40 E
Bemavo **255** 21 33 S 45 25 E
Bembéréke **247** 10 11N 2 43 E
Bembesi **251** 20 0 S 28 58 E
Bembesi → **251** 18 57 S 27 47 E
Bembézar → **155** 37 45N 5 13W
Bemmel **142** 51 54N 5 54 E
Ben **193** 32 32N 50 45 E
Ben 'Ammi **189** 33 0N 35 7 E
Ben Bullen **233** 33 12 S 150 2 E
Ben Cruachan **134** 56 26N 5 8W
Ben Dearg **134** 57 47N 4 58W
Ben Gardane **241** 33 11N 11 11 E
Ben Hope **134** 58 24N 4 36W
Ben Lawers **134** 56 33N 4 13W
Ben Lomond, N.S.W., Australia **231** 30 1 S 151 43 E
Ben Lomond, Tas., Australia **230** 41 38 S 147 42 E
Ben Lomond, U.K. **134** 56 12N 4 39W
Ben Luc **205** 10 39N 106 29 E
Ben Macdhui **134** 57 4N 3 40W
Ben Mhor **134** 57 16N 7 21W
Ben More, Central, U.K. **134** 56 23N 4 31W
Ben More, Strathclyde, U.K. **134** 56 26N 6 2W
Ben More Assynt **134** 58 7N 4 51W
Ben Nevis **134** 56 48N 5 0W
Ben Ohau Ra. **235** 44 1 S 170 4 E
Ben Quang **204** 17 3N 106 55 E
Ben Slimane **241** 33 38N 7 7W
Ben Tre **205** 10 3N 106 36 E
Ben Vorlich **134** 56 22N 4 15W
Ben Wyvis **134** 57 40N 4 35W
Bena **247** 11 20N 5 50 E
Bena Dibele **253** 4 4 S 22 50 E
Bena-Leka **253** 5 8 S 22 10 E
Bena-Tshadi **253** 4 40 S 22 49 E
Benadir □ **256** 1 30N 44 30 E
Benagalbón **155** 36 45N 4 15W
Benagerie **231** 31 25 S 140 22 E
Benahmed **240** 33 4N 7 9W
Benalla **231** 36 30 S 146 0 E
Benambra, Mt. **233** 36 31 S 147 34 E
Benamejí **155** 37 16N 4 33W
Bénat, C. **141** 43 5N 6 22 E
Benavente, Portugal **155** 38 59N 8 49W
Benavente, Spain **154** 42 2N 5 43W
Benavides **154** 42 30N 5 54W
Benbecula **134** 57 26N 7 21W
Benbonyathe, Mt. **231** 30 25 S 139 11 E
Bencubbin **229** 30 48 S 117 52 E
Bendel □ **247** 6 0N 6 0 E
Bendela **252** 3 18 S 17 36 E
Bender Beila **256** 9 30N 50 48 E
Bender Merchagno **256** 11 41N 50 34 E
Bendering **229** 32 23 S 118 18 E
Bendery **180** 46 50N 29 30 E
Bendigo **231** 36 40 S 144 15 E
Bendorf **146** 50 26N 7 34 E
Benē Beraq **189** 32 6N 34 51 E
Beneden Knijpe **142** 52 58N 5 59 E
Beneditinos **120** 5 27 S 42 22W
Benedito Leite **120** 7 13 S 44 34W
Bénéna **246** 13 9N 4 17W
Benenitra **255** 23 27 S 45 5 E
Benešŏv **150** 49 46N 14 41 E
Bénestroff **139** 48 54N 6 45 E
Benet **140** 46 22N 0 35W
Benevento **165** 41 7N 14 45 E
Benfeld **139** 48 22N 7 34 E
Benga **251** 16 11 S 33 40 E
Bengal, Bay of **196** 15 0N 90 0 E
Bengbu **217** 32 58N 117 20 E
Benghazi = Banghāzī **241** 32 11N 20 3 E
Bengkalis **208** 1 30N 102 10 E
Bengkulu **208** 3 50 S 102 12 E
Bengkulu □ **206** 3 48 S 102 16 E
Bengough **88** 49 25N 105 10W
Benguela **253** 12 37 S 13 25 E
Benguela □ **253** 13 0 S 13 30 E
Benguerir **240** 32 16N 7 56W
Benguérua, I. **255** 21 58 S 35 28 E
Benguet □ **210** 16 30N 120 40 E
Benha **244** 30 26N 31 8 E
Beni **250** 0 30N 29 27 E
Beni □ **123** 14 0 S 65 0W
Beni → **123** 10 23 S 65 24W
Beni Abbès **240** 30 5N 2 5W
Beni-Haoua **240** 36 30N 1 30 E
Beni Mazâr **244** 28 32N 30 44 E
Beni Mellal **240** 32 21N 6 21W
Beni Ounif **240** 32 0N 1 10W
Beni Saf **241** 35 17N 1 15W
Beni Suef **244** 29 5N 31 6 E
Beniah L. **76** 63 23N 112 17W
Benicarló **156** 40 23N 0 23 E
Benidorm **157** 38 33N 0 9W
Benidorm, Islote de **157** 38 31N 0 9W
Benin ■ **247** 10 0N 2 0 E
Benin, Bight of **247** 5 0N 3 0 E
Benin City **247** 6 20N 5 31 E
Benisa **157** 38 43N 0 3 E
Benito Juárez, Michoacan, Mexico **107** 19 14N 100 28W
Benito Juárez, Tabasco, Mexico **110** 17 50N 92 32W
Benito Juárez, Tlaxcala, Mexico **107** 19 35N 98 24W
Benito Juárez, Zacatecas, Mexico **105** 23 51N 103 21W
Benito Juárez, Presa **109** 16 30N 95 28W
Benjamin Aceval **124** 24 58 S 57 34W
Benjamin Constant **118** 4 40 S 70 15W
Benjamin Hill **100** 30 9N 111 7W
Benkovac **163** 44 2N 15 37 E
Benlidi **230** 24 35 S 144 50 E
Benmore Pk. **235** 44 25 S 170 8 E
Bennebroek **142** 52 19N 4 36 E
Bennekom **142** 52 0N 5 41 E
Bennett **76** 59 56N 134 53W
Bennett, Ostrov **185** 76 21N 148 56 E
Benny **84** 46 47N 81 38W
Bénodet **138** 47 53N 4 7W
Benoit's Cove **79** 49 1N 58 7W
Benoni **255** 26 11 S 28 18 E
Benoud **241** 32 20N 0 16 E
Benoy **243** 8 59N 16 19 E
Bensheim **147** 49 40N 8 38 E
Benson **88** 49 27N 103 1W
Bent **193** 26 20N 59 31 E
Benteng **207** 6 10 S 120 30 E
Bentinck I. **230** 17 3 S 139 35 E
Bentiu **245** 9 10N 29 55 E
Bentley **91** 52 28N 114 4W
Bento Gonçalves **125** 29 10 S 51 31W
Bentu Liben **245** 8 32N 38 21 E
Bentung **205** 3 31N 101 55 E
Benue □ **247** 7 30N 7 30 E
Benue → **247** 7 48N 6 46 E
Benxi **215** 41 20N 123 48 E
Benzdorp **119** 3 44N 54 5W
Beo **207** 4 25N 126 50 E
Beograd **166** 44 50N 20 37 E
Bepan Jiang → **216** 24 55N 106 5 E
Beppu **220** 33 15N 131 30 E
Beppu-Wan **220** 33 18N 131 34 E
Bera **202** 24 5N 89 37 E
Berati **168** 40 43N 19 59 E
Berau → **209** 2 10N 117 42 E
Berau, Teluk **207** 2 30 S 132 30 E
Berber **244** 18 0N 34 0 E
Berbera **256** 10 30N 45 2 E
Berbérati **252** 4 15N 15 40 E
Berberia, C. del **157** 38 39N 1 24 E
Berbice □ **119** 4 0N 58 0W
Berbice → **119** 6 20N 57 32W
Berceto **162** 44 30N 10 0 E
Berchtesgaden **147** 47 37N 12 58 E
Berck-sur-Mer **139** 50 25N 1 36 E
Berdale **256** 7 4N 47 51 E
Berdichev **180** 49 57N 28 30 E
Berdsk **184** 54 47N 83 2 E
Berdyansk **180** 46 45N 36 50 E
Berdyaush **182** 55 9N 59 9 E
Berebere **207** 2 25N 128 45 E
Bereda **256** 11 45N 51 0 E
Bereina **227** 8 39 S 146 30 E
Berekum **246** 7 29N 2 34W
Berenice **244** 24 2N 35 25 E
Berens → **89** 52 25N 97 2W
Berens I. **89** 52 18N 97 18W
Berens River **89** 52 25N 97 0W
Beresford **81** 47 42N 65 42W
Berestechko **178** 50 22N 25 5 E
Bereşti **170** 46 6N 27 50 E
Beretău → **170** 46 59N 21 7 E
Berettyo → **151** 46 59N 21 7 E
Berettyóújfalu **151** 47 13N 21 33 E
Berevo, Mahajanga, Madag. **255** 17 14 S 44 17 E
Berevo, Toliara, Madag. **255** 19 44 S 44 58 E
Bereza **178** 52 31N 24 51 E
Berezhany **178** 49 26N 24 58 E
Berezina → **178** 52 33N 30 14 E
Bereziuk, L. **78** 54 0N 76 18W
Berezna **179** 51 35N 31 46 E
Berezniki **182** 59 24N 56 46 E
Berezovka **180** 47 14N 30 55 E
Berezovo **176** 64 0N 65 0 E
Berg **171** 59 10N 11 18 E
Berga, Spain **156** 42 6N 1 48 E
Berga, Sweden **173** 57 14N 16 3 E
Bergambacht **142** 51 56N 4 48 E
Bérgamo **162** 45 42N 9 40 E
Bergantiños **154** 43 20N 8 40W
Bergedorf **146** 53 28N 10 12 E
Bergeijk **143** 51 19N 5 21 E
Bergen, Germany **146** 54 24N 13 26 E
Bergen, Neth. **142** 52 40N 4 43 E
Bergen, Norway **171** 60 23N 5 20 E
Bergen-op-Zoom **143** 51 30N 4 18 E
Bergerac **140** 44 51N 0 30 E
Bergheim **146** 50 57N 6 38 E
Berghem **142** 51 46N 5 33 E
Bergisch-Gladbach **146** 50 59N 7 9 E
Bergkvara **173** 56 23N 16 5 E
Bergschenhoek **142** 51 59N 4 30 E
Bergsjö **172** 61 59N 17 3 E
Bergues **139** 50 58N 2 24 E
Bergum **142** 53 13N 5 59 E
Bergvik **172** 61 16N 16 50 E
Berhala, Selat **208** 1 0 S 104 15 E
Berhampore = Baharampur **199** 24 2N 88 27 E
Berhampur **200** 19 15N 84 54 E
Berheci → **170** 46 7N 27 19 E
Bering Sea **224** 58 0N 167 0 E
Beringen, Belgium **143** 51 3N 5 14 E
Beringen, Switz. **149** 47 38N 8 34 E
Beringovskiy **185** 63 3N 179 19 E
Berislav **180** 46 50N 33 30 E
Berisso **124** 34 56 S 57 50W
Berja **157** 36 50N 2 56W
Berkane **241** 34 52N 2 20W
Berkel → **142** 52 8N 6 12 E
Berkeley **133** 51 41N 2 28W
Berkhout **142** 52 38N 4 59 E
Berkner I. **13** 79 30 S 50 0W
Berkovitsa **167** 43 16N 23 8 E
Berkshire □ **133** 51 30N 1 20W
Berlaar **143** 51 7N 4 39 E
Berland → **90** 54 0N 116 50W
Berlanga **155** 38 17N 5 50W
Berlare **143** 51 2N 4 0 E
Berleburg **146** 51 3N 8 22 E
Berlenga, Ilhas **155** 39 25N 9 30W
Berlin **146** 52 32N 13 24 E
Bermeja, Sierra **155** 36 30N 5 11W
Bermejillo **105** 25 53N 103 37W
Bermejo →, Formosa, Argentina **124** 26 51 S 58 23W
Bermejo →, San Juan, Argentina **124** 32 30 S 67 30W

Bermen, L. 78 53 35N 68 55W
Bermeo 156 43 25N 2 47W
Bermillo de Sayago 154 41 22N 6 8W
Bermuda ■ 128 32 45N 65 0W
Bern 148 46 57N 7 28 E
Bern □ 148 46 45N 7 40 E
Bernal 107 20 45N 99 57W
Bernalda 165 40 24N 16 44 E
Bernard L. 84 45 45N 79 23W
Bernardo de
Irigoyen 125 26 15 S 53 40W
Bernardo
O'Higgins □ 124 34 15 S 70 45W
Bernasconi 124 37 55 S 63 44W
Bernau,
E. Germany 146 52 40N 13 35 E
Bernau,
W. Germany 147 47 45N 12 20 E
Bernay 138 49 5N 0 35 E
Bernburg 146 51 40N 11 42 E
Berndorf 150 47 59N 16 1 E
Berne = Bern 148 46 57N 7 28 E
Berne = Bern □ 148 46 45N 7 40 E
Berneck 147 51 3N 11 40 E
Berner Alpen 148 46 27N 7 35 E
Bernese Oberland =
Oberland 148 46 30N 7 30 E
Bernier B. 95 71 5N 88 15W
Bernier I. 229 24 50 S 113 12 E
Bernierville 83 46 6N 71 34W
Bernina, P. 149 46 22N 9 54 E
Bernina, Piz 149 46 20N 9 54 E
Bernissart 143 50 28N 3 39 E
Bernkastel-Kues 147 49 55N 7 4 E
Beror Hayil 189 31 34N 34 38 E
Béroubouay 247 10 34N 2 46 E
Beroun 150 49 57N 14 5 E
Berounka → 150 50 0N 13 47 E
Berovo 166 41 38N 22 51 E
Berrahal 241 36 54N 7 33 E
Berre, Étang de 141 43 27N 5 5 E
Berrechid 240 33 18N 7 36W
Berri 232 34 14 S 140 35 E
Berriane 241 32 50N 3 46 E
Berrigan 233 35 38 S 145 49 E
Berriozábal 110 16 48N 93 16W
Berriwillock 232 35 36 S 142 59 E
Berrouaghia 241 36 10N 2 53 E
Berry, Australia 231 34 46 S 150 43 E
Berry, France 139 47 0N 2 0 E
Berry Cr. → 91 50 50N 111 37W
Berry Is. 112 25 40N 77 50W
Bersenbrück 146 52 33N 7 56 E
Berthierville 83 46 5N 73 10W
Bertincourt 139 50 5N 2 58 E
Bertoua 252 4 30N 13 45 E
Bertrand 81 47 45N 65 4W
Bertrange 143 49 37N 6 3 E
Bertrix 143 49 51N 5 15 E
Berufjörður 174 64 48N 14 29W
Beruri 119 3 54 S 61 22W
Berwick, N.B.,
Canada 81 45 47N 65 36W
Berwick, N.S.,
Canada 81 45 3N 64 44W
Berwick-upon-
Tweed 132 55 47N 2 0W
Berwyn 90 56 9N 117 44W
Berwyn Mts. 132 52 54N 3 26W
Berzasca 166 44 39N 21 58 E
Berzence 151 46 12N 17 11 E
Besal 199 35 4N 73 56 E
Besalampy 255 16 43 S 44 29 E
Besançon 139 47 15N 6 0 E
Besar 209 2 40 S 116 0 E
Beshenkovichi 178 55 2N 29 29 E
Beška 166 45 8N 20 6 E
Beskydy 151 49 35N 18 40 E
Beslan 181 43 15N 44 28 E
Besna Kobila 166 42 31N 22 10 E
Besnard L. 77 55 25N 106 0W
Besor, N. → 189 31 28N 34 22 E
Beşparmak Dağı 169 37 32N 27 30 E
Bessa Monteiro 253 7 7 S 13 44 E
Bessarabiya 170 47 0N 28 10 E
Bessarabka 180 46 21N 28 58 E
Bessèges 141 44 18N 4 8 E
Bessin 138 49 21N 1 0W
Bessines-sur-
Gartempe 140 46 6N 1 22 E
Best 143 51 31N 5 23 E
Bet Alfa 189 32 31N 35 25 E
Bet Dagan 189 32 1N 34 49 E
Bet Guvrin 189 31 37N 34 54 E
Bet Ha'Emeq 189 32 58N 35 8 E
Bet Hashitta 189 32 31N 35 27 E
Bet Qeshet 189 32 41N 35 21 E
Bet She'an 189 32 30N 35 30 E
Bet Shemesh 189 31 44N 35 0 E
Bet Tadjine, Djebel 240 29 0N 3 30W
Bet Yosef 189 32 34N 35 33 E
Betafo 255 19 50 S 46 51 E
Betanzos, Bolivia 123 19 34 S 65 27W
Betanzos, Spain 154 43 15N 8 12W
Bétaré Oya 252 5 40N 14 5 E
Bétera 156 39 35N 0 28W
Bethal 255 26 27 S 29 28 E
Bethanie 254 26 31 S 17 8 E
Bethany = Al
'Ayzarīyah 189 31 47N 35 15 E
Bethany, Canada 85 44 11N 78 34W
Bethany, S. Africa 254 29 34 S 25 59 E
Bethlehem = Bayt
Lahm 189 31 43N 35 12 E
Bethlehem 255 28 14 S 28 18 E
Bethulie 254 30 30 S 25 59 E
Bethune, Canada 88 50 43N 105 13W
Béthune, France 139 50 30N 2 38 E
Béthune → 138 49 53N 1 9 E
Bethungra 231 34 45 S 147 51 E
Betijoque 118 9 23N 70 44W
Betim 121 19 58 S 44 7W
Betioky 255 23 48 S 44 20 E
Beton Bazoches 139 48 42N 3 15 E
Betong 205 5 45N 101 5 E
Betoota 230 25 45 S 140 42 E
Betroka 255 23 16 S 46 0 E
Betsiamites 83 48 56N 68 40W
Betsiamites → 83 48 56N 68 38W
Betsiboka → 255 16 3 S 46 36 E
Betsjoeanaland 254 26 30 S 22 30 E
Bettembourg 143 49 31N 6 6 E
Bettiah 199 26 48N 84 33 E
Bèttola 162 44 42N 9 32 E
Betul 198 21 58N 77 59 E
Betung 206 1 24N 111 31 E
Betzdorf 146 50 47N 7 53 E
Beuca 170 44 14N 24 56 E
Beuil 141 44 6N 6 59 E
Bevensen 146 53 5N 10 34 E
Beveren 143 51 12N 4 16 E
Beverley, Australia 229 32 9 S 116 56 E
Beverley, U.K. 132 53 52N 0 26W
Beverlo 143 51 7N 5 13 E
Beverwijk 142 52 28N 4 38 E
Bewdley 85 44 5N 78 19W
Bex 148 46 15N 7 0 E
Beyānlū 192 36 0N 47 51 E
Beyin 246 5 1N 2 41W
Beykoz 167 41 8N 29 7 E
Beyla 246 8 30N 8 38W
Beynat 140 45 8N 1 44 E
Beyneu 177 45 10N 55 3 E
Beypazarı 177 40 10N 31 56 E
Beypore → 201 11 10N 75 47 E
Beyşehir Gölü 177 37 40N 31 45 E
Bezdan 166 45 50N 18 57 E
Bezet 189 33 4N 35 8 E
Bezhetsk 179 57 47N 36 39 E
Bezhitsa 178 53 19N 34 17 E
Béziers 140 43 20N 3 12 E
Bezwada =
Vijayawada 201 16 31N 80 39 E
Bhadarwah 199 32 58N 75 46 E
Bhadra → 201 14 0N 75 20 E
Bhadrakh 199 21 10N 86 30 E
Bhadravati 201 13 49N 75 40 E
Bhagalpur 199 25 10N 87 0 E
Bhainsa 200 19 10N 77 58 E
Bhairab → 202 22 51N 89 34 E
Bhairab Bazar 202 24 4N 90 58 E
Bhakkar 197 31 40N 71 5 E
Bhakra Dam 198 31 30N 76 45 E
Bhamo 202 24 15N 97 15 E
Bhamragarh 200 19 30N 80 40 E
Bhandara 199 21 5N 79 42 E
Bhanrer Ra. 198 23 40N 79 45 E
Bharat = India ■ 196 20 0N 78 0 E
Bharatpur 198 27 15N 77 30 E
Bharuch 198 21 47N 73 0 E
Bhatghar L. 200 18 10N 73 48 E
Bhatiapara Ghat 202 23 13N 89 42 E
Bhatinda 198 30 15N 74 57 E
Bhatkal 201 13 58N 74 35 E
Bhatpara 199 22 50N 88 25 E
Bhattiprolu 201 16 7N 80 45 E
Bhaun 198 32 55N 72 40 E
Bhaunagar =
Bhavnagar 198 21 45N 72 10 E
Bhavani 201 11 27N 77 43 E
Bhavani → 201 11 0N 78 15 E
Bhavnagar 198 21 45N 72 10 E
Bhawanipatna 200 19 55N 80 10 E
Bhera 198 32 29N 72 57 E
Bhilsa = Vidisha 198 23 28N 77 53 E
Bhilwara 198 25 25N 74 38 E
Bhima → 200 16 25N 77 17 E
Bhimavaram 201 16 30N 81 30 E
Bhimbar 199 32 59N 74 3 E
Bhind 199 26 30N 78 46 E
Bhiwandi 200 19 20N 73 0 E
Bhiwani 198 28 50N 76 9 E
Bhola 202 22 45N 90 35 E
Bhongir 200 17 30N 78 56 E
Bhopal 198 23 20N 77 30 E
Bhor 200 18 12N 73 53 E
Bhubaneshwar 199 20 15N 85 50 E
Bhuj 198 23 15N 69 49 E
Bhumibol Dam 204 17 15N 98 58 E
Bhusaval 198 21 3N 75 46 E
Bhutan ■ 202 27 25N 90 30 E
Biá → 118 3 28 S 67 23W
Biafra, B. of =
Bonny, Bight of 247 3 30N 9 20 E
Biak 207 1 10 S 136 6 E
Biała 152 50 24N 17 40 E
Biała →, Białystok,
Poland 152 53 11N 23 4 E
Biała →, Tarnów,
Poland 152 50 3N 20 55 E
Biała Piska 152 53 37N 22 5 E
Biała Podlaska 152 52 4N 23 6 E
Biała Podlaska □ 152 52 0N 23 0 E
Biała Rawska 152 51 48N 20 29 E
Białobrzegi 152 52 27N 21 3 E
Białogard 152 54 2N 15 58 E
Białowieża 152 52 41N 23 49 E
Biały Bór 152 53 53N 16 51 E
Białystok 152 53 10N 23 10 E
Białystok □ 152 53 9N 23 10 E
Biancavilla 165 37 39N 14 50 E
Bīārjmand 193 36 6N 55 53 E
Biaro 207 2 5N 125 26 E
Biarritz 140 43 29N 1 33W
Biasca 149 46 22N 8 58 E
Biba 244 28 55N 31 0 E
Bibai 218 43 19N 141 52 E
Bibala 253 14 44 S 13 24 E
Bibane, Bahiret el 241 33 16N 11 13 E
Bibassé 252 1 27N 11 37 E
Bibbiena 163 43 43N 11 50 E
Bibby I. 77 61 55N 93 0W
Biberach 147 48 5N 9 49 E
Biberist 148 47 11N 7 34 E
Bibey → 154 42 24N 7 13W
Bibiani 246 6 30N 2 8W
Bibile 201 7 10N 81 25 E
Biboohra 230 16 56 S 145 25 E
Bibungwa 250 2 40 S 28 15 E
Bic 83 48 20N 68 41W
Bic, Île du 83 48 24N 68 52W
Bicaj 168 42 0N 20 25 E
Bicaz 170 46 53N 26 5 E
Biccari 165 41 23N 15 12 E
Biche, L. la 90 54 50N 112 3W
Biche, La → 76 59 57N 123 50W
Bichena 245 10 28N 38 10 E
Bickerton I. 230 13 45 S 136 10 E
Bickerton West 81 45 6N 61 44W
Bida, Nigeria 247 9 3N 5 58 E
Bida, Zaïre 252 4 55N 19 56 E
Bidar 200 17 55N 77 35 E
Biddiyā 189 32 7N 35 4 E
Biddū 189 31 50N 35 8 E
Biddwara 245 5 11N 38 34 E
Bideford 133 51 1N 4 13W
Bidon 5 = Poste
Maurice Cortier 240 22 14N 1 2 E
Bidor 205 4 6N 101 15 E
Bidura 232 34 10 S 143 21 E
Bié □ 253 12 30 S 17 0 E
Bié, Planalto de 253 12 0 S 16 0 E
Biebrza → 152 53 13N 22 25 E
Biecz 151 49 44N 21 15 E
Biel 148 47 8N 7 14 E
Bielawa 152 50 43N 16 37 E
Bielé Karpaty 151 49 5N 18 0 E
Bielefeld 146 52 2N 8 31 E
Bielersee 148 47 6N 7 5 E
Biella 162 45 33N 8 3 E
Bielsk Podlaski 152 52 47N 23 12 E
Bielsko-Biała 152 49 50N 19 2 E
Bielsko-Biała □ 151 49 45N 19 15 E
Bien Hoa 205 10 57N 106 49 E
Bienfait 88 49 10N 102 50W
Bienne = Biel 148 47 8N 7 14 E
Bienvenida 155 38 18N 6 12W
Bienvenue 119 3 0N 52 30W
Bienville, L. 78 55 5N 72 40W
Biescas 156 42 37N 0 20W
Biese → 146 52 53N 11 46 E
Biesiesfontein 254 30 57 S 17 58 E
Bietigheim 147 48 57N 9 8 E
Bievre 143 49 57N 5 1 E
Biferno → 165 41 59N 15 2 E
Bifoum 252 0 20 S 10 23 E
Big → 78 54 50N 58 55W
Big B. 78 55 43N 60 35W
Big Bar Creek 93 51 12N 122 7W
Big Basswood L. 84 46 25N 83 23W
Big Beaver 88 49 10N 105 10W
Big Bend 255 26 50 S 32 2 E
Big Bend Res. 91 52 59N 115 30W
Big Cr. → 93 51 42N 122 41W
Big Creek 93 51 43N 123 2W
Big Horn Dam 91 52 20N 116 20W
Big I., N.W.T.,
Canada 95 62 43N 70 43W
Big I., Ont., Canada 86 49 9N 94 40W
Big Muddy L. 88 49 9N 104 51W
Big Pond 81 45 57N 60 32W
Big Quill L. 88 51 55N 104 50W
Big Rideau L. 85 44 40N 76 15W
Big River 88 53 50N 107 0W
Big Sand L. 77 57 45N 99 45W
Big Sandy L. 88 54 27N 104 6W
Big Trout L., Ont.,
Canada 74 53 40N 90 0W
Big Trout L., Ont.,
Canada 85 45 46N 78 37W
Big Valley 91 52 2N 112 46W
Biganos 140 44 39N 0 59W
Biggar, Canada 88 52 4N 108 0W
Biggar, U.K. 134 55 38N 3 31W
Bigge I. 228 14 35 S 125 10 E
Biggenden 231 25 31 S 152 4 E
Bigniba → 82 49 18N 77 20W
Bignona 246 12 52N 16 14W
Bigorre 140 43 6N 0 5 E
Bigot, L. 80 50 50N 65 39W
Bigsby I. 86 49 4N 94 34W
Bigstick L. 88 50 16N 109 20W
Bigstone L. 89 53 42N 95 44W
Bigwa 250 7 10 S 39 10 E
Bihać 163 44 49N 15 57 E
Bihar 199 25 5N 85 40 E
Bihar □ 199 25 0N 86 0 E
Biharamulo 250 2 25 S 31 25 E
Biharamulo □ 250 2 30 S 31 20 E
Biharkeresztes 151 47 8N 21 44 E
Bihor □ 170 47 0N 22 10 E
Bihor, Munţii 170 46 29N 22 47 E
Bijagós,
Arquipélago dos 246 11 15N 16 10W
Bijaipur 198 26 2N 77 20 E
Bijapur, Karnataka,
India 200 16 50N 75 55 E
Bijapur, Mad. P.,
India 200 18 50N 80 50 E
Bījār 192 35 52N 47 35 E
Bijeljina 166 44 46N 19 17 E
Bijelo Polje 166 43 1N 19 45 E
Bijie 216 27 20N 105 16 E
Bijni 202 26 30N 90 40 E
Bijnor 198 29 27N 78 11 E
Bikaner 198 28 2N 73 18 E
Bikapur 199 26 30N 82 7 E
Bikeqi 214 40 43N 111 20 E
Bikfayyā 190 33 55N 35 41 E
Bikin 185 46 50N 134 20 E
Bikin → 218 46 51N 134 2 E
Bikini Atoll 224 12 0N 167 30 E
Bikoro 252 0 48 S 18 15 E
Bikoué 247 3 55N 11 50 E
Bilara 198 26 14N 73 53 E
Bilaspara 202 26 13N 90 14 E
Bilaspur, Mad. P.,
India 199 22 2N 82 15 E
Bilaspur, Punjab,
India 198 31 19N 76 50 E
Bilauk Taung dan 204 13 0N 99 0 E
Bilbao 156 43 16N 2 56W
Bilbeis 244 30 25N 31 34 E
Bilbor 170 47 6N 25 30 E
Bíldudalur 174 65 41N 23 36W
Bileća 166 42 53N 18 27 E
Bilecik 177 40 5N 30 5 E
Biłgoraj 152 50 33N 22 42 E
Bilibino 185 68 3N 166 20 E
Bilibiza 251 12 30 S 40 20 E
Bilin 202 17 14N 97 15 E
Bilir 185 65 40N 131 20 E
Biliran I. 211 11 35N 124 28 E
Bilishti 168 40 37N 21 2 E
Billabalong 229 27 25 S 115 49 E
Billiluna 228 19 37 S 127 41 E
Billingham 132 54 36N 1 18W
Billingsfors 172 58 59N 12 15 E
Billiton Is. =
Belitung 209 3 10 S 107 50 E
Billom 140 45 43N 3 20 E
Bilma 243 18 50N 13 30 E
Bilo Gora 166 45 53N 17 15 E
Biloela 230 24 24 S 150 31 E
Biloku 119 1 50N 58 25W
Bilpa Morea
Claypan 230 25 0 S 140 0 E
Bilthoven 142 52 8N 5 12 E
Biltine 243 14 40N 20 50 E
Bilugyun 202 16 24N 97 32 E
Bilyana 230 18 5 S 145 50 E
Bilyarsk 182 54 58N 50 22 E
Bilzen 143 50 52N 5 31 E
Bima 209 8 22 S 118 49 E
Bimban 244 24 24N 32 54 E
Bimberi Peak 233 35 44 S 148 51 E
Bimbila 247 8 54N 0 5 E
Bimbo 252 4 15N 18 33 E
Bimini Is. 112 25 42N 79 25W
Bin Xian,
Heilongjiang,
China 215 45 42N 127 32 E
Bin Xian, Shaanxi,
China 214 35 2N 108 4 E
Bina-Etawah 198 24 13N 78 14 E
Bināb 193 36 35N 48 41 E

Binalbagan 211 10 12N 122 50 E
Binalong 233 34 40 S 148 39 E
Bīnālūd, Kūh-e 193 36 30N 58 30 E
Binatang 206 2 10N 111 40 E
Binbee 230 20 19 S 147 56 E
Binche 143 50 26N 4 10 E
Binchuan 216 25 42N 100 38 E
Binda, Australia 231 27 52 S 147 21 E
Binda, Zaïre 253 5 52 S 13 14 E
Bindi Bindi 229 30 37 S 116 22 E
Bindle 231 27 40 S 148 45 E
Bindoy 211 9 48N 123 5 E
Bindura 251 17 18 S 31 18 E
Bingara, N.S.W., Australia 231 29 52 S 150 36 E
Bingara, Queens., Australia 231 28 10 S 144 37 E
Bingen 147 49 57N 7 53 E
Bingerville 246 5 18N 3 49W
Binh Dinh = An Nhon 204 13 55N 109 7 E
Binh Khe 204 13 57N 108 51 E
Binh Son 204 15 20N 108 40 E
Binhai 215 34 2N 119 49 E
Binjai 208 3 20N 98 30 E
Binnaway 231 31 28 S 149 24 E
Binongko 207 5 55 S 123 55 E
Binscarth 89 50 37N 101 17W
Bint Jubayl 189 33 8N 35 25 E
Bintan 208 1 0N 104 0 E
Bintulu 206 3 10N 113 0 E
Bintuni 207 2 7 S 133 32 E
Binyamina 189 32 32N 34 56 E
Binyang 216 23 12N 108 47 E
Binz 146 54 23N 13 37 E
Binza 253 4 21 S 15 14 E
Binzert = Bizerte 241 37 15N 9 50 E
Bío Bío □ 124 37 35 S 72 0W
Biograd 163 43 56N 15 29 E
Bioko 252 3 30N 8 40 E
Biokovo 166 43 23N 17 0 E
Biougra 240 30 15N 9 14W
Biq'at Bet Netofa 189 32 49N 35 22 E
Bir 200 19 4N 75 46 E
Bir, Ras 245 12 0N 43 20 E
Bîr Abu Hashim 244 23 42N 34 6 E
Bîr Abu M'nqar 244 26 33N 27 33 E
Bîr Abu Muḥammad 191 29 44N 34 14 E
Bi'r ad Dabbāghāt 191 30 26N 35 32 E
Bîr Adal Deib 244 22 35N 36 10 E
Bi'r al Butayyihāt 191 29 47N 35 20 E
Bi'r al Ḥamḍah 191 28 30N 34 55 E
Bi'r al Malfa 241 31 58N 15 18 E
Bi'r al Mārī 191 30 4N 35 33 E
Bi'r al Musallam 191 28 56N 35 38 E
Bi'r al Qattār 191 29 47N 35 32 E
Bir 'Ali 195 14 1N 48 20 E
Bir Aouine 241 32 25N 9 18 E
Bîr 'Asal 244 25 55N 34 20 E
Bi'r ash Shakkūsīyah 190 35 23N 37 26 E
Bîr Beiḍa 191 30 25N 34 29 E
Bi'r Dhu'fān 241 31 59N 14 32 E
Bîr Diqnash 244 31 3N 25 23 E
Bir el Abbes 240 26 7N 6 9W
Bîr el 'Abd 191 31 2N 33 0 E
Bir el Ater 241 34 46N 8 3 E
Bîr el Basur 244 29 51N 25 49 E
Bîr el Biarât 191 29 30N 34 43 E
Bîr el Duweidar 191 30 56N 32 32 E
Bîr el Garârât 191 31 3N 33 34 E
Bîr el Gellaz 244 30 50N 26 40 E
Bîr el Heisi 191 29 22N 34 36 E
Bîr el Jafir 191 30 50N 32 41 E
Bîr el Mâlḥi 191 30 38N 33 19 E
Bîr el Naṣb 191 29 3N 33 2 E
Bîr el Ṣafra 191 28 45N 34 21 E
Bîr el Saura 191 29 9N 34 30 E
Bîr el Shaqqa 244 30 54N 25 1 E
Bîr el Thamâda 191 30 12N 33 27 E
Bîr Fuad 244 30 35N 26 28 E
Bir Gara 243 13 11N 15 58 E
Bîr Gebeil Ḥiṣn 191 30 2N 33 18 E
Bi'r Ghadīr 190 34 6N 37 3 E
Bi'r Gharr 191 28 7N 35 32 E
Bîr Haimur 244 22 45N 33 40 E
Bîr Ḥasana 191 30 29N 33 46 E
Bi'r Īdimah 194 18 31N 44 12 E
Bi'r Jadīd, Iraq 192 34 1N 42 54 E
Bi'r Jadīd, Si. Arabia 191 29 10N 35 6 E
Bir Jdid 240 33 26N 8 0W
Bîr Kanayis 244 24 59N 33 15 E
Bîr Kaseiba 191 31 0N 33 17 E
Bîr Kerawein 244 27 10N 28 25 E
Bîr Lahfân 191 31 0N 33 51 E
Bir Lahrache 241 32 1N 8 12 E
Bîr Madkûr 191 30 44N 32 33 E
Bîr Maql 244 23 7N 33 40 E
Bîr Misaha 244 22 13N 27 59 E
Bir Mogrein 240 25 10N 11 25W
Bîr Murr 244 23 28N 30 10 E
Bi'r Muṭribah 192 29 54N 47 17 E
Bi'r Nabālā 189 31 52N 35 12 E
Bîr Nakheila 244 24 1N 30 50 E
Bîr Nakhul 191 29 5N 33 16 E
Bîr Qaṭia 191 30 58N 32 45 E
Bîr Qatrani 244 30 55N 26 10 E
Bîr Ranga 244 24 25N 35 15 E
Bîr Sahara 244 22 54N 28 40 E
Bîr Seiyâla 244 26 10N 33 50 E
Bir Semguine 240 30 1N 5 39W
Bîr Shalatein 244 23 5N 35 25 E
Bîr Shebb 244 22 25N 29 40 E
Bîr Shût 244 23 50N 35 15 E
Bîr Sidri 191 28 53N 33 28 E
Bîr Tâba 191 29 29N 34 53 E
Bi'r Tamis 195 16 45N 48 48 E
Bîr Terfawi 244 22 57N 28 55 E
Bîr Umm Qubûr 244 24 35N 34 2 E
Bîr Ungât 244 22 8N 33 48 E
Bîr Wuseit 191 29 14N 33 1 E
Bîr Za'farâna 244 29 10N 32 40 E
Bîr Zāmūs 241 24 16N 15 6 E
Bi'r Zayt 189 31 59N 35 11 E
Bîr Zeidûn 244 25 45N 33 40 E
Bira, Indonesia 207 2 3 S 132 2 E
Bîra, Romania 170 47 2N 27 3 E
Birak Sulaymān 189 31 42N 35 7 E
Biramféro 246 11 40N 9 10W
Birao 252 10 20N 22 47 E
Birawa 250 2 20 S 28 48 E
Bîrca 170 43 59N 23 36 E
Birch Hills 88 52 59N 105 25W
Birch I. 89 52 26N 99 54W
Birch Island 93 51 37N 119 54W
Birch L., Alta., Canada 90 53 19N 111 35W
Birch L., N.W.T., Canada 76 62 4N 116 33W
Birch L., Ont., Canada 86 51 23N 92 18W
Birch L., Sask., Canada 88 53 27N 108 10W
Birch Mts. 76 57 30N 113 10W
Birch River 89 52 24N 101 6W
Birchip 231 35 56 S 142 55 E
Birchiş 170 45 58N 22 9 E
Birchwood 235 45 55 S 167 53 E
Birchy Bay 79 49 21N 54 44W
Bird 77 56 30N 94 13W
Bird Cove 79 51 3N 56 56W
Bird I. = Aves, I. de 113 15 45N 63 55W
Bird I. 254 32 3 S 18 17 E
Birdaard 142 53 18N 5 53 E
Birdlip 133 51 50N 2 7W
Birdsville 230 25 51 S 139 20 E
Birdum 228 15 39 S 133 13 E
Birein 191 30 50N 34 28 E
Bireuen 208 5 14N 96 39 E
Birifo 246 13 30N 14 0W
Birigui 125 21 18 S 50 16W
Birini 252 7 51N 22 24 E
Birken 93 50 28N 122 37W
Birkenfeld 147 49 39N 7 11 E
Birkenhead, N.Z. 234 36 49 S 174 46 E
Birkenhead, U.K. 132 53 24N 3 1W
Birket Qârûn 244 29 30N 30 40 E
Birkfeld 150 47 21N 15 45 E
Birkhadem 241 36 43N 3 3 E
Bîrlad 170 46 15N 27 38 E
Birmingham 133 52 30N 1 55W
Birmitrapur 199 22 24N 84 46 E
Birni Ngaouré 247 13 5N 2 51 E
Birni Nkonni 247 13 55N 5 15 E
Birnin Gwari 247 11 0N 6 45 E
Birnin Kebbi 247 12 32N 4 12 E
Birnin Kudu 247 11 30N 9 29 E
Birobidzhan 185 48 50N 132 50 E
Biron 80 48 12N 66 16W
Birougou, Mts. 252 1 51 S 12 20 E
Birqīn 189 32 27N 35 15 E
Birr 135 53 7N 7 55W
Birrie → 231 29 43 S 146 37 E
Birs → 148 47 24N 7 32 E
Birsay 88 51 6N 106 59W
Birsilpur 198 28 11N 72 15 E
Birsk 182 55 25N 55 30 E
Birtin 170 46 59N 22 31 E
Birtle 89 50 30N 101 5W
Biryuchiy 180 46 10N 35 0 E
Birzai 178 56 11N 24 45 E
Bîrzava 170 46 7N 21 59 E
Bisa 207 1 15 S 127 28 E
Bisáccia 165 41 0N 15 20 E
Bisacquino 164 37 42N 13 13 E
Bisai 221 35 16N 136 44 E
Bisalpur 199 28 14N 79 48 E
Bisbal, La 156 41 58N 3 2 E
Biscarrosse, Étang de 140 44 21N 1 10W
Biscay, B. of 128 45 0N 2 0W
Biscéglie 165 41 14N 16 30 E
Bischofshofen 150 47 26N 13 14 E
Bischofswerda 146 51 8N 14 11 E
Bischofszell 149 47 29N 9 15 E
Bischwiller 139 48 41N 7 50 E
Biscoe Bay 13 77 0 S 152 0W
Biscoe I. 13 66 0 S 67 0W
Biscostasing 87 47 18N 82 9W
Biscotasi L. 87 47 22N 82 1W
Biscucuy 118 9 22N 69 59W
Biševo 163 42 57N 16 3 E
Bisha 245 15 30N 37 31 E
Bishah, W. → 194 21 24N 43 26 E
Bishan 216 29 33N 106 12 E
Bishnupur 199 23 8N 87 20 E
Bishop Auckland 132 54 40N 1 40W
Bishop's Falls 79 49 2N 55 30W
Bishop's Stortford 133 51 52N 0 11 E
Bishopton 83 45 35N 71 35W
Bisignano 165 39 30N 16 17 E
Bisina, L. 250 1 38N 33 56 E
Biskra 241 34 50N 5 44 E
Biskupiec 152 53 53N 20 58 E
Bislig 207 8 15N 126 27 E
Bismarck Arch. 224 2 30 S 150 0 E
Bismarck Ra. 227 5 35 S 145 0 E
Bismarck Sea 227 4 10 S 146 50 E
Bismark 146 52 39N 11 31 E
Biso 250 1 44N 31 26 E
Bison L. 90 57 12N 116 8W
Bīsotūn 192 34 23N 47 26 E
Bispgården 172 63 2N 16 40 E
Bissagos = Bijagós, Arquipélago dos 246 11 15N 16 10W
Bissau 246 11 45N 15 45W
Bissett 89 51 2N 95 41W
Bissikrima 246 10 50N 10 58W
Bistcho L. 76 59 45N 118 50W
Bistreţu 170 43 54N 23 23 E
Bistrica = Ilirska-Bistrica 163 45 34N 14 14 E
Bistriţa 170 47 9N 24 35 E
Bistriţa → 170 46 30N 26 57 E
Bistriţa Năsăud □ 170 47 15N 24 30 E
Bistriţei, Munţii 170 47 15N 25 40 E
Biswan 199 27 29N 81 2 E
Bisztynek 152 54 8N 20 53 E
Bitam 252 2 5N 11 25 E
Bitburg 147 49 58N 6 32 E
Bitche 139 49 2N 7 25 E
Bitkine 243 11 59N 18 13 E
Bitlis 177 38 20N 42 3 E
Bitola 166 41 5N 21 10 E
Bitolj = Bitola 166 41 5N 21 10 E
Bitonto 165 41 7N 16 40 E
Bitter L. = Buheirat-Murrat-el-Kubra 244 30 15N 32 40 E
Bitter L. 88 50 7N 109 48W
Bitterfeld 146 51 36N 12 20 E
Bitterfontein 254 31 0 S 18 32 E
Bittern L., Alta., Canada 91 53 3N 113 5W
Bittern L., Sask., Canada 88 53 56N 105 45W
Bitti 164 40 29N 9 20 E
Bittou 247 11 17N 0 18W
Biu 247 10 40N 12 3 E
Bivolari 170 47 31N 27 27 E
Bivolu 170 47 16N 25 58 E
Biwa-Ko 221 35 15N 136 10 E
Bixad 170 47 56N 23 28 E
Biyang 217 32 38N 113 21 E
Biylikol, Ozero 183 43 5N 70 45 E
Biysk 184 52 40N 85 0 E
Bizana 255 30 50 S 29 52 E
Bizen 220 34 43N 134 8 E
Bizerte 241 37 15N 9 50 E
Bjargtangar 174 65 30N 24 30W
Bjelasica 166 42 50N 19 40 E
Bjelašnica 166 43 43N 18 9 E
Bjelovar 166 45 56N 16 49 E
Bjerringbro 173 56 23N 9 39 E
Björbo 172 60 27N 14 44 E
Bjorkdale 88 52 43N 103 39W
Björneborg 172 59 14N 14 16 E
Bjørnøya 12 74 30N 19 0 E
Bjuv 172 56 5N 12 55 E
Blace 166 43 18N 21 17 E
Blache, L. de la 83 50 5N 69 29W
Blachownia 152 50 49N 18 56 E
Black → = Da → 204 21 15N 105 20 E
Black → 84 44 42N 79 19W
Black B. 86 48 40N 88 25W
Black Creek 92 49 49N 125 7W
Black Diamond 91 50 45N 114 14W
Black Forest = Schwarzwald 147 48 0N 8 0 E
Black I. 89 51 12N 96 30W
Black L. 77 59 12N 105 15W
Black Lake 83 46 1N 71 22W
Black Mt. = Mynydd Du 133 51 45N 3 45W
Black Mountain 233 30 18 S 151 39 E
Black Mts. 133 51 52N 3 5W
Black Pines 93 50 57N 120 15W
Black River 112 18 0N 77 50W
Black Rock 232 32 50 S 138 44 E
Black Rock Pt. 78 60 2N 64 10W
Black Sea 159 43 30N 35 0 E
Black Sturgeon L. 86 49 20N 88 53W
Black Volta → 246 8 41N 1 33W
Blackall 230 24 25 S 145 45 E
Blackball 235 42 22 S 171 26 E
Blackbull 230 17 55 S 141 45 E
Blackburn 132 53 44N 2 30W
Blackfalds 91 52 23N 113 47W
Blackfoot 90 53 17N 110 10W
Blackie 91 50 36N 113 37W
Blackpool 132 53 48N 3 3W
Blacks Harbour 81 45 3N 66 49W
Blacksod B. 135 54 6N 10 0W
Blackstone → 76 61 5N 122 55W
Blackstone Ra. 229 26 0 S 129 0 E
Blackville 81 46 44N 65 50W
Blackwater 230 23 35 S 148 53 E
Blackwater →, Ireland 135 51 55N 7 50W
Blackwater →, U.K. 135 54 31N 6 35W
Blackwater Cr. → 231 25 56 S 144 30 E
Blackwood, C. 227 7 49 S 144 31 E
Bladel 143 51 22N 5 13 E
Bladworth 88 51 22N 106 8W
Blaenau Ffestiniog 132 53 0N 3 57W
Blagaj 166 43 16N 17 55 E
Blagodarnoye 181 45 7N 43 37 E
Blagoevgrad 166 42 2N 23 5 E
Blagoveshchensk, Amur, U.S.S.R. 185 50 20N 127 30 E
Blagoveshchensk, Urals, U.S.S.R. 182 55 1N 55 59 E
Blagoveshchenskoye 183 43 18N 74 12 E
Blain 138 47 29N 1 45W
Blaine Lake 88 52 51N 106 52W
Blainville, Canada 83 45 40N 73 52W
Blainville, France 139 48 33N 6 23 E
Blair Athol 230 22 42 S 147 31 E
Blair Atholl 134 56 46N 3 50W
Blairgowrie 134 56 36N 3 20W
Blairmore 91 49 40N 114 25W
Blaj 170 46 10N 23 57 E
Blâmont 139 48 35N 6 50 E
Blanc, C. 241 37 15N 9 56 E
Blanc, Le 140 46 37N 1 3 E
Blanc, Mont 141 45 48N 6 50 E
Blanca, Bahía 126 39 10 S 61 30W
Blanche, C. 231 33 1 S 134 9 E
Blanche L., S. Austral., Australia 231 29 15 S 139 40 E
Blanche L., W. Austral., Australia 228 22 25 S 123 17 E
Blanco 254 33 55 S 22 23 E
Blanco → 124 30 20 S 68 42W
Blanco, C., C. Rica 112 9 34N 85 8W
Blanco, C., Spain 157 39 21N 2 51 E
Blanco, Pta. 98 29 8N 114 43W
Blanco, R. → 109 18 45N 96 0W
Blanda → 174 65 20N 19 40W
Blandford Forum 133 50 52N 2 10W
Blanes 156 41 40N 2 48 E
Blanice → 150 49 10N 14 5 E
Blankenberge 143 51 20N 3 9 E
Blankenburg 146 51 46N 10 56 E
Blanquefort 140 44 55N 0 38W
Blanquilla, La 119 11 51N 64 37W
Blanquillo 125 32 53 S 55 37W
Blansko 151 49 22N 16 40 E
Blantyre 251 15 45 S 35 0 E
Blaricum 142 52 16N 5 14 E
Blarney 135 51 57N 8 35W
Błaski 152 51 38N 18 30 E
Blatná 150 49 25N 13 52 E
Blatnitsa 167 43 41N 28 32 E
Blato 163 42 56N 16 48 E
Blatten 148 46 20N 7 50 E
Blaubeuren 147 48 24N 9 47 E
Blaydon 132 54 56N 1 47W
Blaye 140 45 8N 0 40W
Blaye-les-Mines 140 44 1N 2 8 E
Blayney 231 33 32 S 149 14 E
Blaze, Pt. 228 12 56 S 130 11 E
Błazowa 152 49 53N 22 7 E
Bleckede 146 53 18N 10 43 E
Bled 163 46 27N 14 7 E
Blednaya, Gora 184 76 20N 65 0 E
Bléharis 143 50 31N 3 25 E
Bleiburg 150 46 35N 14 49 E
Blejeşti 170 44 19N 25 27 E
Blekinge län □ 173 56 20N 15 20 E
Blenheim, Canada 84 42 20N 82 0W
Blenheim, N.Z. 235 41 38 S 173 57 E
Bléone → 141 44 5N 6 0 E
Blerick 143 51 22N 6 9 E
Bletchley 133 51 59N 0 44W
Bleu, L. 82 46 35N 78 24W
Bleymard, Le 140 44 30N 3 42 E
Blida 241 36 30N 2 49 E
Blidet Amor 241 32 59N 5 58 E
Blidö 172 59 37N 18 53 E
Blidsberg 173 57 56N 13 30 E
Bligh Sound 235 44 47 S 167 32 E

Bligh Water .... 226 17 0 S 178 0 E
Blind River 84 46 10N 82 58W
Blinishti .... 168 41 52N 19 58 E
Blinnenhorn .... 149 46 26N 8 19 E
Blissfield 81 46 36N 66 5W
Blitar .... 209 8 5 S 112 11 E
Blitta .... 247 8 23N 1 6 E
Blodgett Iceberg
Tongue .... 13 66 8 S 130 35 E
Bloemendaal .... 142 52 24N 4 39 E
Bloemfontein ...... 254 29 6 S 26 14 E
Bloemhof .... 254 27 38 S 25 32 E
Blois .... 138 47 35N 1 20 E
Blokziji .... 142 52 43N 5 58 E
Blomskog .... 172 59 16N 12 2 E
Blönduós 174 65 40N 20 12W
Błonie .... 152 52 12N 20 37 E
Bloodvein → 89 51 47N 96 43W
Bloody Foreland ... 135 55 10N 8 18W
Bloomfield,
Australia .... 230 15 56 S 145 22 E
Bloomfield, Newf.,
Canada 79 48 23N 53 54W
Bloomfield, Ont.,
Canada 85 43 59N 77 14W
Blora .... 209 6 57 S 111 25 E
Blouberg .... 255 23 8 S 29 0 E
Blubber Bay 92 49 47N 124 37W
Bludenz .... 150 47 10N 9 50 E
Blue Hills 94 75 34N 114 30W
Blue Mts. .... 233 33 40 S 150 0 E
Blue Mud B. .... 230 13 30 S 136 0 E
Blue Nile = An Nîl
el Azraq □ ...... 245 12 30N 34 30 E
Blue Nile = Nîl el
Azraq → .... 245 15 38N 32 31 E
Blue Ridge 90 54 8N 115 22W
Blue River 93 52 6N 119 18W
Blue Stack Mts. 135 54 46N 8 5W
Blueberry → 76 56 45N 120 49W
Blueberry Mountain 90 55 56N 119 9W
Bluefields 112 12 20N 83 50W
Bluenose L. 94 68 30N 119 35W
Blueskin B. .... 235 45 44 S 170 38 E
Bluff, Australia .... 230 23 35 S 149 4 E
Bluff, N.Z. .... 235 46 37 S 168 20 E
Bluff Harbour ...... 235 46 36 S 168 21 E
Bluff Knoll .... 229 34 24 S 118 15 E
Bluff Pt. .... 229 27 50 S 114 5 E
Bluffton 91 52 45N 114 17W
Blumenau .... 125 27 0 S 49 0W
Blumenthal .... 146 53 5N 8 20 E
Blümisalphorn ..... 148 46 30N 7 47 E
Blyberg .... 172 61 9N 14 11 E
Blyth, Australia .... 232 33 49 S 138 28 E
Blyth, Canada 84 43 44N 81 26W
Blyth, U.K. 132 55 8N 1 32W
Bø, Norway .... 171 59 25N 9 3 E
Bo, S. Leone 246 7 55N 11 50W
Bo Duc .... 205 11 58N 106 50 E
Bo Hai .... 215 39 0N 120 0 E
Bō-no-Misaki ...... 220 31 15N 130 13 E
Bo Xian .... 214 33 50N 115 45 E
Boa Esperança 119 3 21N 61 23W
Boa Nova .... 121 14 22 S 40 10W
Boa Viagem .... 120 5 7 S 39 44W
Boa Vista 119 2 48N 60 30W
Boac .... 210 13 27N 121 50 E
Boaco 112 12 29N 85 35W
Bo'ai .... 214 35 10N 113 3 E
Boal 154 43 25N 6 49W
Boali .... 252 4 48N 18 7 E
Boat Harbour 79 47 24N 54 50W
Boatman .... 231 27 16 S 146 55 E
Bobadah .... 231 32 19 S 146 41 E
Bobai .... 216 22 17N 109 59 E
Bobbili .... 200 18 35N 83 30 E
Bóbbio .... 162 44 47N 9 22 E
Bobcaygeon 85 44 33N 78 33W
Böblingen .... 147 48 41N 9 1 E
Bobo-Dioulasso 246 11 8N 4 13W
Boboc .... 170 45 13N 26 59 E
Bobolice .... 152 53 58N 16 37 E
Bobon, Davao, Phil. 211 6 53N 126 19 E
Bobon, Samar, Phil. 210 12 32N 124 34 E
Bobonaza → ...... 118 2 36 S 76 38W
Boboshevo .... 166 42 9N 23 0 E
Bobov Dol .... 166 42 20N 23 0 E
Bóbr → .... 152 52 4N 15 4 E
Bobraomby, Tanjon'
i .... 255 12 40 S 49 10 E
Bobrinets .... 180 48 4N 32 5 E
Bobrov .... 179 51 5N 40 2 E
Bobruysk .... 178 53 10N 29 15 E
Bobures 118 9 15N 71 11W
Boca de Drago 119 11 0N 61 50W
Boca de Magdalena . 99 27 4N 112 9W
Boca de Uracoa 118 9 8N 62 20W
Boca del Río,
Sinaloa, Mexico .. 104 25 18N 108 30W
Boca del Río,
Veracruz, Mexico 108 19 6N 96 6W
Bôca do Acre ...... 122 8 50 S 67 27W
Bôca do Jari .... 119 1 7 S 51 58W
Bôca do Moaco .... 122 7 41 S 68 17W
Boca Grande 119 8 40N 60 40W
Boca Nueva 111 18 42N 91 40W
Bocaiúva .... 121 17 7 S 43 49W
Bocanda 246 7 5N 4 31W
Bocaranga .... 252 7 0N 15 35 E
Bocas del Toro 112 9 15N 82 20W
Boceguillas 156 41 20N 3 39W
Bochart 83 49 10N 73 30W
Bochil 110 16 59N 92 55W
Bochnia .... 152 49 58N 20 27 E
Bocholt, Belgium ... 143 51 10N 5 35 E
Bocholt, Germany .. 146 51 50N 6 35 E
Bochov .... 150 50 9N 13 3 E
Bochum .... 146 51 28N 7 12 E
Bockenem .... 146 52 1N 10 8 E
Boćki .... 152 52 39N 23 3 E
Boconó 118 9 15N 70 16W
Boconó → 118 8 43N 69 34W
Bocoyna 101 27 52N 107 35W
Bocq → .... 143 50 20N 4 55 E
Bocşa Montanã .... 166 45 21N 21 47 E
Boda, C.A.R. .... 252 4 19N 17 26 E
Böda, Sweden ..... 173 57 15N 17 3 E
Bodafors .... 173 57 48N 14 23 E
Bodaybo .... 185 57 50N 114 0 E
Boddington .... 229 32 50 S 116 30 E
Bodegraven .... 142 52 5N 4 46 E
Boden .... 174 65 50N 21 42 E
Bodensee .... 149 47 35N 9 25 E
Bodenteich .... 146 52 49N 10 41 E
Bodhan .... 200 18 40N 77 44 E
Bodinayakkanur .... 201 10 2N 77 10 E
Bodinga .... 247 12 58N 5 10 E
Bodio .... 149 46 23N 8 55 E
Bodmin 133 50 28N 4 44W
Bodmin Moor 133 50 33N 4 36W
Bodø .... 174 67 17N 14 24 E
Bodoquena, Serra
da .... 123 21 0 S 56 50W
Bodoupa .... 252 5 43N 17 36 E
Bodrog → .... 151 48 15N 21 35 E
Bódva → .... 151 48 19N 20 45 E
Boechout .... 143 51 10N 4 30 E
Boegoebergdam .... 254 29 7 S 22 9 E
Boekelo .... 142 52 12N 6 49 E
Boelenslaan .... 142 53 10N 6 10 E
Boembé .... 252 2 54 S 15 39 E
Boën .... 141 45 44N 4 0 E
Boende .... 252 0 24 S 21 12 E
Boertange .... 142 53 1N 7 12 E
Boezinge .... 143 50 54N 2 52 E
Boffa 246 10 16N 14 3W
Bogale .... 202 16 17N 95 24 E
Bogan → .... 231 29 59 S 146 17 E
Bogan Gate .... 231 33 7 S 147 49 E
Bogangolo .... 252 5 34N 18 15 E
Bogantungan .... 230 23 41 S 147 17 E
Bogatić .... 166 44 51N 19 30 E
Bogdanovitch ...... 182 56 47N 62 1 E
Bogense .... 173 55 34N 10 5 E
Boggabilla .... 231 28 36 S 150 24 E
Boggabri .... 231 30 45 S 150 0 E
Boggeragh Mts. 135 52 2N 8 55W
Bogia .... 227 4 9 S 145 0 E
Bognor Regis 133 50 47N 0 40W
Bogø, Denmark .... 173 54 55N 12 2 E
Bogo, Phil. .... 211 11 3N 124 0 E
Bogodukhov .... 178 50 9N 35 33 E
Bogong, Mt. .... 231 36 47 S 147 17 E
Bogor .... 207 6 36 S 106 48 E
Bogoroditsk .... 179 53 47N 38 8 E
Bogorodsk .... 179 56 4N 43 30 E
Bogorodskoye ...... 185 52 22N 140 30 E
Bogoso 246 5 38N 2 3W
Bogota 118 4 34N 74 0W
Bogotol .... 184 56 15N 89 50 E
Bogra .... 202 24 51N 89 22 E
Boguchany .... 185 58 40N 97 30 E
Boguchar .... 181 49 55N 40 32 E
Bogué 246 16 45N 14 10W
Boguslav .... 180 49 47N 30 53 E
Boguszów .... 152 50 45N 16 12 E
Bohain .... 139 49 59N 3 28 E
Bohemia .... 150 50 0N 14 0 E
Bohemia Downs .... 228 18 53 S 126 14 E
Bohemian Forest =
Böhmerwald ..... 147 49 30N 12 40 E
Bohena Cr. → .... 231 30 17 S 149 42 E
Bohinjska Bistrica .. 163 46 17N 14 1 E
Böhmerwald .... 147 49 30N 12 40 E
Bohmte .... 146 52 24N 8 20 E
Bohol, Phil. .... 211 9 50N 124 10 E
Bohol, Somalia ..... 256 5 45N 46 9 E
Bohol Sea .... 207 9 0N 124 0 E
Bohol Str. .... 211 9 45N 123 40 E
Bohola 111 19 50N 90 7W
Bohotleh .... 256 8 20N 46 25 E
Boi .... 247 9 35N 9 27 E
Boi, Pta. de .... 125 23 55 S 45 15W
Boiaçu .... 119 0 27 S 61 46W
Boiano .... 165 41 28N 14 29 E
Boileau, C. .... 228 17 40 S 122 7 E
Boinitsa .... 166 43 58N 22 32 E
Boipeba, I. de ..... 121 13 39 S 38 55W
Bois → .... 121 18 35 S 50 2W
Bois, L. des 94 66 50N 125 9W
Bois, Les .... 148 47 11N 6 50 E
Boischot .... 143 51 3N 4 47 E
Boisdale 81 46 6N 60 30W
Boissevain 89 49 15N 100 5W
Boite → .... 163 46 5N 12 5 E
Boitzenburg .... 146 53 16N 13 36 E
Boizenburg .... 146 53 22N 10 42 E
Bojador C. 240 26 0N 14 30W
Bojana → .... 166 41 52N 19 22 E
Bojanowo .... 152 51 43N 16 42 E
Bojnūrd .... 193 37 30N 57 20 E
Bojonegoro .... 209 7 11 S 111 54 E
Boju .... 247 7 22N 7 55 E
Boka .... 166 45 22N 20 52 E
Boka Kotorska ..... 166 42 23N 18 32 E
Bokada .... 252 4 8N 19 23 E
Bokala 246 8 31N 4 33W
Bokatola .... 252 0 38 S 18 46 E
Boké 246 10 56N 14 17W
Bokhara → .... 231 29 55 S 146 42 E
Bokkos .... 247 9 17N 9 1 E
Boknafjorden ...... 171 59 14N 5 40 E
Bokombayevskoye .. 183 42 10N 76 55 E
Bokoro .... 243 12 25N 17 14 E
Bokote .... 252 0 12 S 21 8 E
Boksitogorsk .... 178 59 32N 33 56 E
Bokungu .... 252 0 35 S 22 50 E
Bol, Chad .... 243 13 30N 15 0 E
Bol, Yugoslavia .... 163 43 18N 16 38 E
Bolama 246 11 30N 15 30W
Bolan Pass .... 197 29 50N 67 20 E
Bolangum .... 232 36 42 S 142 54 E
Bolaños 105 21 41N 103 47W
Bolaños, R. → ... 106 21 12N 104 5W
Bolaños, Sa. de 105 21 30N 103 40W
Bolbec .... 138 49 30N 0 30 E
Boldājī .... 193 31 56N 51 3 E
Boldeşti .... 170 45 3N 26 2 E
Bole, China .... 212 45 11N 81 37 E
Bole, Ethiopia ..... 245 6 36N 37 20 E
Bolekhov .... 178 49 0N 24 0 E
Bolesławiec .... 152 51 17N 15 37 E
Bolgatanga 247 10 44N 0 53W
Bolgrad .... 180 45 40N 28 32 E
Boli .... 245 6 2N 28 48 E
Bolinao .... 210 16 23N 119 54 E
Bolinao C. .... 210 16 23N 119 55 E
Boliney .... 210 17 24N 120 48 E
Bolívar, Argentina .. 124 36 15 S 60 53W
Bolívar, Antioquía,
Colombia 118 5 50N 76 1W
Bolívar, Cauca,
Colombia 118 2 0N 77 0W
Bolívar, Peru ...... 122 7 18 S 77 48W
Bolívar □, Colombia 118 9 0N 74 40W
Bolívar □, Ecuador . 118 1 15 S 79 5W
Bolívar □,
Venezuela 119 6 20N 63 30W
Bolivia ■ .... 123 17 6 S 64 0W
Bolivian Plateau .... 114 20 0 S 67 30W
Boljevac .... 166 43 51N 21 58 E
Bolkhov .... 179 53 25N 36 0 E
Bollène .... 141 44 18N 4 45 E
Bollnäs .... 172 61 21N 16 24 E
Bollon .... 231 28 2 S 147 29 E
Bollstabruk .... 172 63 1N 17 40 E
Bollullos 155 37 19N 6 32W
Bolmen .... 173 56 55N 13 40 E
Bolobo .... 252 2 6 S 16 20 E
Bologna .... 163 44 30N 11 20 E
Bologne .... 139 48 10N 5 8 E
Bologoye .... 178 57 55N 34 0 E
Bolomba .... 252 0 35N 19 0 E
Bolonchenticul 111 20 0N 89 49W
Bolong .... 211 7 6N 122 14 E
Bolotovskoye ...... 182 58 31N 62 28 E
Boloven, Cao
Nguyen .... 204 15 10N 106 30 E
Bolpur .... 199 23 40N 87 45 E
Bolsena .... 163 42 40N 11 58 E
Bolsena, L. di ...... 163 42 35N 11 55 E
Bolshaya Glushitsa . 179 52 28N 50 30 E
Bolshaya Irgiz → .. 179 52 10N 49 10 E
Bolshaya
Khobda → ...... 182 50 56N 54 34 E
Bolshaya Kinel → . 182 53 14N 50 30 E
Bolshaya
Martynovka ...... 181 47 12N 41 46 E
Bolshaya Shatan,
Gora .... 182 53 37N 58 3 E
Bolshaya
Vradiyevka ...... 180 47 50N 30 40 E
Bolshereche .... 184 56 4N 74 45 E
Bolshevik, Ostrov .. 185 78 30N 102 0 E
Bolshezemelskaya
Tundra .... 176 67 0N 56 0 E
Bolshoi Kavkas .... 181 42 50N 44 0 E
Bolshoy Anyuy → . 185 68 30N 160 49 E
Bolshoy Atlym ..... 184 62 25N 66 50 E
Bolshoy Begichev,
Ostrov .... 185 74 20N 112 30 E
Bolshoy
Lyakhovskiy,
Ostrov .... 185 73 35N 142 0 E
Bolshoy Tokmak ... 180 47 16N 35 42 E
Bol'shoy Tyuters,
Ostrov .... 178 59 51N 27 13 E
Bolsward .... 142 53 3N 5 32 E
Boltaña .... 156 42 28N 0 4 E
Boltigen .... 148 46 38N 7 24 E
Bolton, Canada 84 43 54N 79 45W
Bolton, U.K. 132 53 35N 2 26W
Bolu .... 177 40 45N 31 35 E
Bolubolu .... 227 9 21 S 150 20 E
Boluo .... 217 23 3N 114 21 E
Bolvadin .... 177 38 45N 31 4 E
Bolzano .... 163 46 30N 11 20 E
Bom Comércio ..... 123 9 45 S 65 54W
Bom Conselho ..... 120 9 10 S 36 41W
Bom Despacho ..... 121 19 43 S 45 15W
Bom Jesus .... 120 9 4 S 44 22W
Bom Jesus da
Gurguéia, Serra .. 120 9 0 S 43 0W
Bom Jesus da Lapa . 121 13 15 S 43 25W
Boma .... 253 5 50 S 13 4 E
Bomaderry .... 231 34 52 S 150 37 E
Bomandjokou ...... 252 0 34N 14 23 E
Bomassa .... 252 2 12N 16 12 E
Bomba, La 98 31 53N 115 2W
Bombala .... 231 36 56 S 149 15 E
Bombarral 155 39 15N 9 9W
Bombay .... 200 18 55N 72 50 E
Bomboma .... 252 2 25N 18 55 E
Bombombwa .... 250 1 40N 25 40 E
Bomi Hills 246 7 1N 10 38W
Bomili .... 250 1 45N 27 5 E
Bommel .... 142 51 43N 4 26 E
Bomokandi → .... 250 3 39N 26 8 E
Bomongo .... 252 1 27N 18 21 E
Bomu → .... 252 4 40N 23 30 E
Bon, C. .... 241 37 1N 11 2 E
Bon Accord 90 53 50N 113 25W
Bon Echo Prov.
Park 85 45 0N 77 20W
Bon Sar Pa .... 204 12 24N 107 35 E
Bonaduz .... 149 46 49N 9 25 E
Bonaire 113 12 10N 68 15W
Bonampak 110 16 44N 91 5W
Bonang .... 231 37 11 S 148 41 E
Bonanza, Canada ... 90 55 55N 119 49W
Bonanza, Nic. 112 13 54N 84 35W
Bonaparte
Archipelago ..... 228 14 0 S 124 30 E
Bonaparte L. 93 51 15N 120 34W
Boñar 154 42 52N 5 19W
Bonaventure 81 48 5N 65 32W
Bonavista 79 48 40N 53 5W
Bonavista, C. 79 48 42N 53 5W
Bonavista B. 79 48 45N 53 25W
Bonawan .... 211 9 8N 122 55 E
Bondeno .... 163 44 53N 11 22 E
Bondo .... 250 3 55N 23 53 E
Bondoukou 246 8 2N 2 47W
Bondowoso .... 209 7 55 S 113 49 E
Bondyug .... 182 60 29N 55 56 E
Bone, Teluk .... 207 4 10 S 120 50 E
Bone Rate .... 207 7 25 S 121 5 E
Bone Rate,
Kepulauan .... 207 6 30 S 121 10 E
Bonefro .... 165 41 42N 14 55 E
Bo'ness 134 56 0N 3 38W
Bonfield 84 46 14N 79 9W
Bong Son = Hoai
Nhon .... 204 14 28N 109 1 E
Bongabon .... 210 15 38N 121 8 E
Bongabong .... 210 12 45N 121 29 E
Bongandanga ...... 252 1 24N 21 3 E
Bongo .... 252 1 47 S 17 41 E
Bongor .... 243 10 35N 15 20 E
Bongouanou 246 6 42N 4 15W
Bonheiden .... 143 51 1N 4 32 E
Bonifacio .... 141 41 24N 9 10 E
Bonifacio, Bouches
de .... 164 41 12N 9 15 E
Bonilla I. 92 53 28N 130 37W
Bonin Is. .... 224 27 0N 142 0 E
Bonke .... 245 6 5N 37 16 E
Bonn .... 146 50 43N 7 6 E
Bonnat .... 140 46 20N 1 54 E
Bonnechere → 85 45 35N 77 50W
Bonnet, Lac du 89 50 22N 95 55W
Bonnétable .... 138 48 11N 0 25 E
Bonneuil-Matours .. 138 46 41N 0 34 E
Bonneval .... 138 48 11N 1 24 E
Bonneville .... 141 46 5N 6 24 E
Bonney, L. .... 232 37 50 S 140 20 E
Bonnie Doon ...... 233 37 2 S 145 53 E
Bonnie Downs ..... 230 22 7 S 143 50 E
Bonnie Rock .... 229 30 29 S 118 22 E
Bonny, France ..... 139 47 34N 2 50 E
Bonny, Nigeria ..... 247 4 25N 7 13 E
Bonny → .... 247 4 20N 7 10 E
Bonny, Bight of .... 247 3 30N 9 20 E
Bonnyville 90 54 20N 110 45W
Bonobono .... 211 8 40N 117 36 E

Bonoi **207** 1 45 S 137 41 E
Bonorva **164** 40 25N 8 47 E
Bontang **209** 0 10N 117 30 E
Bonthain **207** 5 34 S 119 56 E
Bonthe **246** 7 30N 12 33W
Bontoc **210** 17 7N 120 58 E
Bonyeri **246** 5 1N 2 46W
Bonyhád **151** 46 18N 18 32 E
Bonython Ra. **228** 23 40 S 128 45 E
Boogardie **229** 28 2 S 117 45 E
Bookabie **229** 31 50 S 132 41 E
Boolaboolka, L. **231** 32 38 S 143 10 E
Boolarra **233** 38 20 S 146 20 E
Boolcoomata **232** 31 57 S 140 33 E
Booleroo Centre **232** 32 53 S 138 21 E
Booligal **231** 33 58 S 144 53 E
Boom **143** 51 6N 4 20 E
Boonah **231** 27 58 S 152 41 E
Booral **233** 32 30 S 151 56 E
Boorindal **231** 30 22 S 146 11 E
Booroomugga **233** 31 17 S 146 27 E
Boorowa **231** 34 28 S 148 44 E
Boothia, Gulf of **95** 71 0N 90 0W
Boothia Pen. **95** 71 0N 94 0W
Bootle, Cumbria, U.K. **132** 54 17N 3 24W
Bootle, Merseyside, U.K. **132** 53 28N 3 1W
Booué **252** 0 5 S 11 55 E
Bophuthatswana □ **254** 26 0 S 26 0 E
Boppard **147** 50 13N 7 36 E
Boquerón □ **123** 21 30 S 60 0W
Boquete **112** 8 46N 82 27W
Boquilla, Presa de la **101** 27 31N 105 30W
Boquillas del Carmen **102** 29 17N 102 53W
Bor, Czech. **150** 49 41N 12 45 E
Bôr, Sudan **245** 6 10N 31 40 E
Bor, Sweden **173** 57 9N 14 10 E
Bor, Yugoslavia **166** 44 8N 22 7 E
Bor Mashash **191** 31 7N 34 50 E
Boradā → **190** 33 33N 36 34 E
Borama **256** 9 55N 43 7 E
Borang **245** 4 50N 30 59 E
Borangapara **202** 25 14N 90 14 E
Borås **173** 57 43N 12 56 E
Borāzjān **193** 29 22N 51 10 E
Borba, Brazil **119** 4 12 S 59 34W
Borba, Portugal **155** 38 50N 7 26W
Borbon **211** 10 50N 124 2 E
Borborema, Planalto da **120** 7 0 S 37 0W
Borçka **181** 41 25N 41 41 E
Borculo **142** 52 7N 6 31 E
Bord Khūn-e Now **193** 28 3N 51 28 E
Borda, C. **232** 35 45 S 136 34 E
Bordeaux **140** 44 50N 0 36W
Borden, Australia **229** 34 3 S 118 12 E
Borden, P.E.I., Canada **81** 46 18N 63 47W
Borden, Sask., Canada **88** 52 27N 107 14W
Borden I. **94** 78 30N 111 30W
Borden L. **87** 47 50N 83 17W
Borden Pen. **95** 73 0N 83 0W
Borders □ **134** 55 35N 2 50W
Bordertown **232** 36 19 S 140 45 E
Borðeyri **174** 65 12N 21 6W
Bordighera **162** 43 47N 7 40 E
Bordj bou Arreridj **241** 36 4N 4 45 E
Bordj Bourguiba **241** 32 12N 10 2 E
Bordj el Hobra **241** 32 9N 4 51 E
Bordj Fly Ste. Marie **240** 27 19N 2 32W
Bordj-in-Eker **241** 24 9N 5 3 E
Bordj Menaiel **241** 36 46N 3 43 E
Bordj Messouda **241** 30 12N 9 25 E
Bordj Nili **240** 33 28N 3 2 E
Bordj Omar Driss **241** 28 10N 6 40 E
Bordj Zelfana **241** 32 27N 4 15 E
Bordoba **183** 39 31N 73 16 E
Borea Creek **233** 35 5 S 146 35 E
Borek Wielkopolski **152** 51 54N 17 11 E
Boremore **233** 33 15 S 149 0 E
Borensberg **173** 58 34N 15 17 E
Borgarnes **174** 64 32N 21 55W
Borger **142** 52 54N 6 44 E
Borgerhout **143** 51 12N 4 28 E
Borghamn **173** 58 23N 14 41 E
Borgholm **173** 56 52N 16 39 E
Bórgia **165** 38 50N 16 30 E
Borgloon **143** 50 48N 5 21 E
Borgo San Dalmazzo **162** 44 19N 7 29 E
Borgo San Lorenzo **163** 43 57N 11 21 E
Borgo Valsugano **163** 46 3N 11 27 E
Borgomanero **162** 45 41N 8 28 E
Borgonovo Val Tidone **162** 45 1N 9 28 E
Borgorose **163** 42 12N 13 14 E
Borgosésia **162** 45 43N 8 17 E
Borgvattnet **172** 63 26N 15 48 E
Borikhane **204** 18 33N 103 43 E
Borislav **178** 49 18N 23 28 E
Borisoglebsk **179** 51 27N 42 5 E
Borisoglebskiy **179** 56 28N 43 59 E
Borisov **178** 54 17N 28 28 E
Borisovka **183** 43 15N 68 10 E
Borispol **178** 50 21N 30 59 E
Borja, Peru **118** 4 20 S 77 40W
Borja, Spain **156** 41 48N 1 34W
Borjas Blancas **156** 41 31N 0 52 E
Borken **146** 51 51N 6 52 E
Borkou **243** 18 15N 18 50 E
Borkum **146** 53 36N 6 42 E
Borlänge **172** 60 29N 15 26 E
Borley, C. **13** 66 15 S 52 30 E
Bormida → **162** 44 23N 8 13 E
Bórmio **162** 46 28N 10 22 E
Born **143** 51 2N 5 49 E
Borna **146** 51 8N 12 31 E
Borndiep **142** 53 27N 5 35 E
Borne **142** 52 18N 6 46 E
Bornem **143** 51 6N 4 14 E
Borneo **206** 1 0N 115 0 E
Bornholm **173** 55 10N 15 0 E
Bornholmsgattet **173** 55 15N 14 20 E
Borno □ **247** 12 30N 12 30 E
Bornos **155** 36 48N 5 42W
Bornu Yassa **247** 12 14N 12 25 E
Borobudur **209** 7 36 S 110 13 E
Borodino **178** 55 31N 35 40 E
Borogontsy **185** 62 42N 131 8 E
Boromo **246** 11 45N 2 58W
Boronga Is. **202** 19 58N 93 6 E
Borongan **211** 11 37N 125 26 E
Bororen **230** 24 13 S 151 33 E
Borotangba Mts. **245** 6 30N 25 0 E
Borovan **167** 43 27N 23 45 E
Borovichi **178** 58 25N 33 55 E
Borovsk, Moskva, U.S.S.R. **179** 55 12N 36 24 E
Borovsk, Urals, U.S.S.R. **182** 59 43N 56 40 E
Borovskoye **182** 53 48N 64 12 E
Borrby **173** 55 27N 14 10 E
Borriol **156** 40 4N 0 4W
Borroloola **230** 16 4 S 136 17 E
Borşa **170** 47 41N 24 50 E
Borsod-Abaúj-Zemplén □ **151** 48 20N 21 0 E
Borssele **143** 51 26N 3 45 E
Bort-les-Orgues **140** 45 24N 2 29 E
Borth **133** 52 29N 4 3W
Borujerd **193** 33 55N 48 50 E
Borzhomi **181** 41 48N 43 28 E
Borzna **178** 51 18N 32 26 E
Borzya **185** 50 24N 116 31 E
Bosa **164** 40 17N 8 32 E
Bosaga **183** 37 33N 65 41 E
Bosanska Brod **166** 45 10N 18 0 E
Bosanska Dubica **163** 45 10N 16 50 E
Bosanska Gradiška **166** 45 10N 17 15 E
Bosanska Kostajnica **163** 45 11N 16 33 E
Bosanska Krupa **163** 44 53N 16 10 E
Bosanski Novi **163** 45 2N 16 22 E
Bosanski Šamac **166** 45 3N 18 29 E
Bosansko Grahovo **163** 44 12N 16 26 E
Bosansko Petrovac **163** 44 35N 16 21 E
Bosaso **256** 11 12N 49 18 E
Bosavi, Mt. **227** 6 30 S 142 49 E
Boscastle **133** 50 42N 4 42W
Boscotrecase **165** 40 46N 14 28 E
Bose **216** 23 53N 106 35 E
Boshan **215** 36 28N 117 49 E
Boshoek **254** 25 30 S 27 9 E
Boshof **254** 28 31 S 25 13 E
Boshrūyeh **193** 33 50N 57 30 E
Bosilegrad **166** 42 30N 22 27 E
Boskoop **142** 52 4N 4 40 E
Boskovice **151** 49 29N 16 40 E
Bosna → **166** 45 4N 18 29 E
Bosna i Hercegovina □ **166** 44 0N 18 0 E
Bosnik **207** 1 5 S 136 10 E
Bōsō-Hantō **221** 35 20N 140 20 E
Bosobolo **252** 4 15N 19 50 E
Bosporus = Karadeniz Boğazı **177** 41 10N 29 10 E
Bossangoa **252** 6 35N 17 30 E
Bossekop **174** 69 57N 23 15 E
Bossembélé **252** 5 25N 17 40 E
Bossemtele II **252** 5 41N 16 38 E
Bosso **247** 13 43N 13 19 E
Bostānābād **192** 37 50N 46 50 E
Bosten Hu **212** 41 55N 87 40 E
Boston, Phil. **211** 7 52N 126 22 E
Boston, U.K. **132** 52 59N 0 2W
Boston Bar **93** 49 52N 121 30W
Bosusulu **252** 0 50N 20 45 E
Bosut → **166** 45 20N 19 0 E
Boswell **93** 49 28N 116 45W
Botad **198** 22 15N 71 40 E
Botany Bay **231** 34 0 S 151 14 E
Botene **204** 17 35N 101 12 E
Botevgrad **167** 42 55N 23 47 E
Bothaville **254** 27 23 S 26 34 E
Bothnia, G. of **174** 63 0N 20 0 E
Bothwell, Australia **230** 42 20 S 147 1 E
Bothwell, Canada **84** 42 38N 81 52W
Boticas **154** 41 41N 7 40W
Botletle → **254** 20 10 S 23 15 E
Botolan **210** 15 17N 120 1 E
Botoroaga **170** 44 8N 25 32 E
Botoşani **170** 47 42N 26 41 E
Botoşani □ **170** 47 50N 26 50 E
Botro **246** 7 51N 5 19W
Botswana ■ **254** 22 0 S 24 0 E
Bottrop **146** 51 34N 6 59 E
Botucatu **125** 22 55 S 48 30W
Botwood **79** 49 6N 55 23W
Bou Alam **241** 33 50N 1 26 E
Bou Ali **240** 27 11N 0 4W
Bou Djébéha **246** 18 25N 2 45W
Bou Guema **241** 28 49N 0 19 E
Bou Ismael **241** 36 38N 2 42 E
Bou Izakarn **240** 29 12N 9 46W
Boû Lanouâr **240** 21 12N 16 34W
Bou Saâda **241** 35 11N 4 9 E
Bou Salem **241** 36 45N 9 2 E
Bouaké **246** 7 40N 5 2W
Bouanga **252** 2 7 S 16 8 E
Bouar **252** 6 0N 15 40 E
Bouârfa **241** 32 32N 1 58 E
Bouca **252** 6 45N 18 25 E
Boucau **140** 43 32N 1 29W
Boucaut B. **230** 12 0 S 134 25 E
Boucher → **83** 49 10N 69 6W
Bouches-du-Rhône □ **141** 43 37N 5 2 E
Bouchette **82** 46 12N 75 57W
Bouchier, L. **82** 50 6N 77 48W
Bouda **240** 27 50N 0 27W
Boudenib **241** 31 59N 3 31W
Boudry **148** 46 57N 6 50 E
Boufarik **241** 36 34N 2 58 E
Bougainville C. **228** 13 57 S 126 4 E
Bougainville I. **227** 6 0 S 155 0 E
Bougainville Reef **230** 15 30 S 147 5 E
Bougaroun, C. **241** 37 6N 6 30 E
Bougie = Bejaia **241** 36 42N 5 2 E
Bougouni **246** 11 30N 7 20W
Bouillon **143** 49 44N 5 3 E
Bouïra **241** 36 20N 3 59 E
Boulembo **252** 1 26 S 12 0 E
Bouli **246** 15 17N 12 18W
Boulia **230** 22 52 S 139 51 E
Bouligny **139** 49 17N 5 45 E
Boulogne → **138** 47 12N 1 47W
Boulogne-sur-Gesse **140** 43 18N 0 38 E
Boulogne-sur-Mer **139** 50 42N 1 36 E
Bouloire **138** 47 58N 0 33 E
Bouloupari **226** 21 52 S 166 4 E
Boulsa **247** 12 39N 0 34W
Boultoum **247** 14 45N 10 25 E
Boumalne **240** 31 25N 6 0W
Boun Neua **204** 21 38N 101 54 E
Boun Tai **204** 21 23N 101 58 E
Bouna **246** 9 10N 3 0W
Boundiali **246** 9 30N 6 20W
Bounty I. **224** 48 0 S 178 30 E
Bourail **226** 21 34 S 165 30 E
Bourbon-Lancy **140** 46 37N 3 45 E
Bourbon-l'Archambault **140** 46 36N 3 4 E
Bourbonnais **140** 46 28N 3 0 E
Bourbonne-les-Bains **139** 47 59N 5 45 E
Bourem **247** 17 0N 0 24W
Bourg **140** 45 3N 0 34W
Bourg-Argental **141** 45 18N 4 32 E
Bourg-de-Péage **141** 45 2N 5 3 E
Bourg-en-Bresse **141** 46 13N 5 12 E
Bourg-St.-Andéol **141** 44 23N 4 39 E
Bourg-St.-Maurice **141** 45 35N 6 46 E
Bourg-St.-Pierre **148** 45 57N 7 12 E
Bourganeuf **140** 45 57N 1 45 E
Bourges **139** 47 9N 2 25 E
Bourget **85** 45 26N 75 9W
Bourget, L. du **141** 45 44N 5 52 E
Bourgneuf, B. de **138** 47 3N 2 10W
Bourgneuf-en-Retz **138** 47 2N 1 58W
Bourgneuf-la-Fôret, Le **138** 48 10N 0 59W
Bourgogne **139** 47 0N 4 30 E
Bourgoin-Jallieu **141** 45 36N 5 17 E
Bourgueil **138** 47 17N 0 10 E
Bourke **231** 30 8 S 145 55 E
Bournemouth **133** 50 43N 1 53W
Bourriot-Bergonce **140** 44 7N 0 14W
Bouscat, Le **140** 44 53N 0 32W
Boussac **140** 46 22N 2 13 E
Boussens **140** 43 12N 0 58 E
Bousso **243** 10 34N 16 52 E
Boussu **143** 50 26N 3 48 E
Boutilimit **246** 17 45N 14 40W
Boutonne → **140** 45 55N 0 43 E
Bouvet I. = Bouvetøya **129** 54 26 S 3 24 E
Bouvetøya **129** 54 26 S 3 24 E
Bouznika **240** 33 46N 7 6W
Bouzonville **139** 49 17N 6 32 E
Bova Marina **165** 37 59N 15 56 E
Bovalino Marina **165** 38 9N 16 10 E
Bovec **163** 46 20N 13 33 E
Bovenkarspel **142** 52 41N 5 14 E
Bovigny **143** 50 12N 5 55 E
Bovino **165** 41 15N 15 20 E
Bow → **91** 49 57N 111 41W
Bow Island **91** 49 50N 111 23W
Bow Pass **91** 51 43N 116 30W
Bowden **91** 51 55N 114 2W
Bowelling **229** 33 25 S 116 30 E
Bowen **230** 20 0 S 148 16 E
Bowen Island **93** 49 23N 123 20W
Bowen Mts. **231** 37 0 S 148 0 E
Bowkān **192** 36 31N 46 12 E
Bowland, Forest of **132** 54 0N 2 30W
Bowling Green, C. **230** 19 19 S 147 25 E
Bowman I. **13** 65 0 S 104 0 E
Bowman L. **86** 51 10N 91 25W
Bowmans **232** 34 10 S 138 17 E
Bowmanville **85** 43 55N 78 41W
Bowmore **134** 55 45N 6 18W
Bowral **231** 34 26 S 150 27 E
Bowraville **231** 30 37 S 152 52 E
Bowron → **93** 54 3N 121 50W
Bowron Lake Prov. Park **93** 53 10N 121 5W
Bowser **92** 49 27N 124 40W
Bowser L. **76** 56 30N 129 30W
Bowsman **89** 52 14N 101 12W
Bowutu Mts. **227** 7 45 S 147 10 E
Bowwood **251** 17 5 S 26 20 E
Boxcohuo, Pta. **111** 21 1N 90 20W
Boxholm **173** 58 12N 15 3 E
Boxmeer **143** 51 38N 5 56 E
Boxtel **143** 51 36N 5 20 E
Boyabat **180** 41 28N 34 42 E
Boyabo **252** 3 43N 18 46 E
Boyaca □ **118** 5 30N 72 30W
Boyd L. **78** 52 46N 76 42W
Boyer → **76** 58 27N 115 57W
Boyer, C. **226** 21 37 S 168 6 E
Boyle, Canada **90** 54 35N 112 49W
Boyle, Ireland **135** 53 58N 8 19W
Boylston **81** 45 26N 61 30W
Boyne → **135** 53 43N 6 15W
Boyni Qara **197** 36 20N 67 0 E
Boyolali **209** 7 32 S 110 35 E
Boyoma, Chutes **250** 0 35N 25 23 E
Boyup Brook **229** 33 50 S 116 23 E
Bozal, Sa. del **103** 23 50N 101 30W
Bozburun **169** 36 43N 28 8 E
Bozcaada **168** 39 49N 26 3 E
Bozen = Bolzano **163** 46 30N 11 20 E
Bozene **252** 2 56N 19 12 E
Božepole Wielkopolski **152** 54 33N 17 56 E
Boževac **166** 44 32N 21 24 E
Bozouls **140** 44 28N 2 43 E
Bozoum **252** 6 25N 16 35 E
Bozovici **170** 44 56N 22 1 E
Bozyazı **190** 36 6N 33 0 E
Bra **162** 44 41N 7 50 E
Brabant □ **143** 50 46N 4 30 E
Brabant L. **77** 55 58N 103 43W
Brabrand **173** 56 9N 10 7 E
Brač **163** 43 20N 16 40 E
Bracadale, L. **134** 57 20N 6 30W
Bracciano **163** 42 6N 12 10 E
Bracciano, L. di **163** 42 8N 12 11 E
Bracebridge **84** 45 2N 79 19W
Brach **241** 27 31N 14 20 E
Bracieux **139** 47 30N 1 30 E
Bräcke **172** 62 45N 15 26 E
Bracken **88** 49 11N 108 6W
Brackendale **93** 49 48N 123 8W
Bracki Kanal **163** 43 24N 16 40 E
Brad **170** 46 10N 22 50 E
Brádano → **165** 40 23N 16 51 E
Bradford, Canada **84** 44 7N 79 34W
Bradford, U.K. **132** 53 47N 1 45W
Brădiceni **170** 45 3N 23 4 E
Bradley Institute **251** 17 7 S 31 25 E
Bradore Bay **79** 51 27N 57 18W
Bradshaw **228** 15 21 S 130 16 E
Bradwell **88** 51 57N 106 14W
Brœdstrup **173** 55 58N 9 37 E
Braemar **231** 33 12 S 139 35 E
Braeside **85** 45 28N 76 24W
Braga **154** 41 35N 8 25W
Braga □ **154** 41 30N 8 30W
Bragado **124** 35 2 S 60 27W
Bragança, Brazil **120** 1 0 S 47 2W
Bragança, Portugal **154** 41 48N 6 50W
Bragança □ **154** 41 30N 6 45W
Bragança Paulista **125** 22 55 S 46 32W
Bragg Creek **91** 50 57N 114 35W
Brahmanbaria **202** 23 58N 91 15 E
Brahmani → **199** 20 39N 86 46 E
Brahmaputra → **202** 24 2N 90 59 E
Braich-y-pwll **132** 52 47N 4 46W
Braidwood **231** 35 27 S 149 49 E
Brăila **170** 45 19N 27 59 E
Brăila □ **170** 45 5N 27 30 E
Braine-l'Alleud **143** 50 42N 4 23 E
Braine-le-Comte **143** 50 37N 4 8 E

Braintree **133** 51 53N 0 34 E
Brak → **254** 29 35 S 22 55 E
Brake, Niedersachsen, Germany **146** 53 19N 8 30 E
Brake, Nordrhein-Westfalen, Germany **146** 51 43N 9 12 E
Brakel **142** 51 49N 5 5 E
Bräkne-Hoby **173** 56 14N 15 6 E
Brakwater **254** 22 28 S 17 3 E
Brålanda **173** 58 34N 12 21 E
Bralorne **93** 50 50N 123 45W
Bramberg **147** 50 6N 10 40 E
Bramminge **173** 55 28N 8 42 E
Brämön **172** 62 14N 17 40 E
Brampton **84** 43 45N 79 45W
Bramsche **146** 52 25N 7 58 E
Bramwell **230** 12 8 S 142 37 E
Branch **79** 46 53N 53 57W
Branco → **119** 1 20 S 61 50W
Branco, Cabo **120** 7 9 S 34 47W
Brande **173** 55 57N 9 8 E
Brandenburg **146** 52 24N 12 33 E
Brandfort **254** 28 40 S 26 30 E
Brandon **89** 49 50N 99 57W
Brandon, Mt. **135** 52 15N 10 15W
Brandon B. **135** 52 17N 10 8W
Brandsen **124** 35 10 S 58 15W
Brandval **171** 60 19N 12 1 E
Brandvlei **254** 30 25 S 20 30 E
Brandýs **150** 50 10N 14 40 E
Braniewo **152** 54 25N 19 50 E
Bransfield Str. **13** 63 0 S 59 0W
Brańsk **152** 52 45N 22 50 E
Brantford **84** 43 10N 80 15W
Brantôme **140** 45 22N 0 39 E
Brantville **81** 47 22N 64 58W
Branxholme **231** 37 52 S 141 49 E
Branxton **233** 32 38 S 151 21 E
Branzi **162** 46 0N 9 46 E
Bras d'Or, L. **81** 45 50N 60 50W
Brasil, Planalto **114** 18 0 S 46 30W
Brasiléia **122** 11 0 S 68 45W
Brasília **121** 15 47 S 47 55 E
Brasília Legal **119** 3 49 S 55 36W
Braslav **178** 55 38N 27 0 E
Braslovce **163** 46 21N 15 3 E
Braşov **170** 45 38N 25 35 E
Braşov □ **170** 45 45N 25 15 E
Brass **247** 4 35N 6 14 E
Brass → **247** 4 15N 6 13 E
Brassac-les-Mines **140** 45 24N 3 20 E
Brasschaat **143** 51 19N 4 27 E
Brassey, Banjaran **206** 5 0N 117 15 E
Brassey Ra. **229** 25 8 S 122 15 E
Brassus, Le **148** 46 35N 6 13 E
Bratan = Morozov **167** 42 30N 25 10 E
Bratislava **151** 48 10N 17 7 E
Bratsigovo **167** 42 1N 24 22 E
Bratsk **185** 56 10N 101 30 E
Braţul Chilia → **170** 45 25N 29 20 E
Bratul Sfîntu Gheorghe → **170** 45 0N 29 20 E
Braţul Sulina → **170** 45 10N 29 20 E
Bratunac **166** 44 13N 19 21 E
Braunau **150** 48 15N 13 3 E
Braunschweig **146** 52 17N 10 28 E
Braunton **133** 51 6N 4 9W
Brava **256** 1 20N 44 8 E
Bråviken **172** 58 38N 16 32 E
Bray **135** 53 12N 6 6W
Bray, Mt. **230** 14 0 S 134 30 E
Bray, Pays de **139** 49 46N 1 26 E
Bray-sur-Seine **139** 48 25N 3 14 E
Brazeau → **91** 52 55N 115 14W
Brazil ■ **121** 10 0 S 50 0W
Brazilian Highlands = Brasil, Planalto **114** 18 0 S 46 30W
Brazo Sur → **124** 25 21 S 57 42W
Brazzaville **253** 4 9 S 15 12 E
Brčko **166** 44 54N 18 46 E
Brda → **152** 53 8N 18 8 E
Brea **122** 4 40 S 81 7W
Breadalbane, Australia **230** 23 50 S 139 35 E
Breadalbane, U.K. **134** 56 30N 4 15W
Breaden, L. **229** 25 51 S 125 28 E
Breaksea Sd. **235** 45 35 S 166 35 E
Bream Bay **234** 35 56 S 174 28 E
Bream Head **234** 35 51 S 174 36 E
Bream Tail **234** 36 3 S 174 36 E
Breas **124** 25 29 S 70 24W
Brebes **209** 6 52 S 109 3 E
Brecha, La **104** 25 23N 108 26W
Brechin, Canada **84** 44 32N 79 10W
Brechin, U.K. **134** 56 44N 2 40W
Brecht **143** 51 21N 4 38 E
Brecknock, Pen. **126** 54 35 S 71 30W
Břeclav **151** 48 46N 16 53 E
Brecon **133** 51 57N 3 23W
Brecon Beacons **133** 51 53N 3 27W
Breda **143** 51 35N 4 45 E
Bredaryd **173** 57 10N 13 45 E
Bredasdorp **254** 34 33 S 20 2 E
Bredbo **231** 35 58 S 149 10 E
Bredenbury **89** 50 57N 102 3W
Bredene **143** 51 14N 2 59 E
Bredstedt **146** 54 37N 8 59 E
Bredy **182** 52 26N 60 21 E
Bree **143** 51 8N 5 35 E
Breezand **142** 52 53N 4 49 E
Bregalnica → **166** 41 43N 22 9 E
Bregenz **150** 47 30N 9 45 E
Bregovo **166** 44 9N 22 39 E
Bréhal **138** 48 53N 1 30W
Bréhat, I. de **138** 48 51N 3 0W
Breiðafjörður **174** 65 15N 23 15W
Breil **141** 43 56N 7 31 E
Breisach **147** 48 2N 7 37 E
Brejinho de Nazaré **120** 11 1 S 48 34W
Brejo **120** 3 41 S 42 47W
Brekke **171** 61 1N 5 26 E
Breloux-la-Crèche **140** 46 23N 0 19W
Bremangerlandet **171** 61 51N 5 0 E
Bremen **146** 53 4N 8 47 E
Bremen □ **146** 53 6N 8 46 E
Bremer I. **230** 12 5 S 136 45 E
Bremerhaven **146** 53 34N 8 35 E
Bremervörde **146** 53 28N 9 10 E
Bremnes **171** 59 47N 5 8 E
Bremsnes **171** 63 6N 7 40 E
Breña, La **105** 24 15N 104 20W
Brenes **155** 37 32N 5 54W
Brenner Pass **150** 47 0N 11 30 E
Breno **162** 45 57N 10 20 E
Brent, Canada **85** 46 2N 78 29W
Brent, U.K. **133** 51 33N 0 18W
Brenta → **163** 45 11N 12 18 E
Brentwood **133** 51 37N 0 19 E
Bréscia **162** 45 33N 10 13 E
Breskens **143** 51 23N 3 33 E
Breslau = Wrocław **152** 51 5N 17 5 E
Bresle → **138** 50 4N 1 22 E
Bresles **139** 49 25N 2 13 E
Bressanone **163** 46 43N 11 40 E
Bressay I. **134** 60 10N 1 5W
Bresse, La **139** 48 0N 6 53 E
Bresse, Plaine de **139** 46 50N 5 10 E
Bressuire **138** 46 51N 0 30W
Brest, France **138** 48 24N 4 31W
Brest, U.S.S.R. **178** 52 10N 23 40 E
Bretagne **138** 48 0N 3 0W
Bretçu **170** 46 7N 26 18 E
Breteuil, Eure, France **138** 48 50N 0 53 E
Breteuil, Oise, France **139** 49 38N 2 18 E
Breton **91** 53 7N 114 28W
Breton, Le, L. **80** 51 53N 60 9W
Breton, Pertuis **140** 46 17N 1 25W
Brett, C. **234** 35 10 S 174 20 E
Bretten **147** 49 2N 8 43 E
Breukelen **142** 52 10N 5 0 E
Breves **120** 1 40 S 50 29W
Brevik **171** 59 4N 9 42 E
Brewarrina **231** 30 0 S 146 51 E
Brewster, Kap **12** 70 7N 22 0W
Breyten **255** 26 16 S 30 0 E
Breytovo **179** 58 18N 37 50 E
Brezhnev **182** 55 42N 52 19 E
Brežice **163** 45 54N 15 35 E
Brézina **241** 33 4N 1 14 E
Březnice **150** 49 32N 13 57 E
Breznik **166** 42 44N 22 50 E
Brezno **151** 48 50N 19 40 E
Brezovo **167** 42 21N 25 5 E
Bria **252** 6 30N 21 58 E
Briançon **141** 44 54N 6 39 E
Briare **139** 47 38N 2 45 E
Bribbaree **233** 34 10 S 147 51 E
Bribie I. **231** 27 0 S 152 58 E
Bricon **139** 48 5N 5 0 E
Briçonnet, L. **80** 51 27N 60 10W
Bricquebec **138** 49 28N 1 38W
Bridgend **133** 51 30N 3 35W
Bridgenorth **85** 44 23N 78 23W
Bridgeport **84** 43 29N 80 29W
Bridgetown, Australia **229** 33 58 S 116 7 E
Bridgetown, Barbados **113** 13 0N 59 30W
Bridgetown, Canada **81** 44 55N 65 18W
Bridgewater, Australia **232** 36 36 S 143 59 E
Bridgewater, Canada **81** 44 25N 64 31W
Bridgewater, C. **231** 38 23 S 141 23 E
Bridgnorth **133** 52 33N 2 25W
Bridgwater **133** 51 7N 3 0W
Bridlington **132** 54 6N 0 11W
Bridport, Australia **230** 40 59 S 147 23 E
Bridport, U.K. **133** 50 43N 2 45W
Brie, Plaine de la **139** 48 35N 3 10 E
Brie-Comte-Robert **139** 48 40N 2 35 E
Briec **138** 48 6N 4 0W
Brielle **142** 51 54N 4 10 E
Brienne-le-Château **139** 48 24N 4 30 E
Brienon **139** 48 0N 3 35 E
Brienz **148** 46 46N 8 2 E
Brienzersee **148** 46 44N 7 53 E
Briercrest **88** 50 10N 105 16W
Briey **139** 49 14N 5 57 E
Brig **148** 46 18N 7 59 E
Brigg **132** 53 33N 0 30W
Bright **231** 36 42 S 146 56 E
Brighton, Australia **232** 35 5 S 138 30 E
Brighton, Canada **85** 44 2N 77 44W
Brighton, U.K. **133** 50 50N 0 9W
Brightsand L. **88** 53 36N 108 53W
Brightwater **235** 41 22 S 173 9 E
Brignogan-Plage **138** 48 40N 4 20W
Brignoles **141** 43 25N 6 5 E
Brihuega **156** 40 45N 2 52W
Brikama **246** 13 15N 16 45W
Brilliant **93** 49 19N 117 38W
Brilon **146** 51 23N 8 32 E
Brim **232** 36 3 S 142 27 E
Brîndisi **165** 40 39N 17 55 E
Brinje **163** 45 0N 15 9 E
Brinkworth **232** 33 42 S 138 26 E
Brion, Î. **81** 47 46N 61 26W
Brionne **138** 49 11N 0 43 E
Brionski **163** 44 55N 13 45 E
Brioude **140** 45 18N 3 24 E
Briouze **138** 48 42N 0 23W
Brisbane **231** 27 25 S 153 2 E
Brisbane → **231** 27 24 S 153 9 E
Brisighella **163** 44 14N 11 46 E
Bristol, N.B., Canada **81** 46 28N 67 35W
Bristol, Qué., Canada **82** 45 32N 76 28W
Bristol, U.K. **133** 51 26N 2 35W
Bristol Channel **133** 51 18N 4 30W
Bristol I. **13** 58 45 S 28 0W
Britannia Beach **93** 49 38N 123 12W
British Antarctic Territory □ **13** 66 0 S 45 0W
British Columbia □ **76** 55 0N 125 15W
British Guiana = Guyana ■ **119** 5 0N 59 0W
British Honduras = Belize ■ **112** 17 0N 88 30W
British Isles **130** 55 0N 4 0W
British Mts. **94** 68 50N 140 0W
Brits **255** 25 37 S 27 48 E
Britstown **254** 30 37 S 23 30 E
Britt **84** 45 46N 80 34W
Brittany = Bretagne **138** 48 0N 3 0W
Brive-la-Gaillarde **140** 45 10N 1 32 E
Briviesca **156** 42 32N 3 19W
Brixton **230** 23 32 S 144 57 E
Brlik, Kazakh S.S.R., U.S.S.R. **183** 43 40N 73 49 E
Brlik, Kazakh S.S.R., U.S.S.R. **183** 44 5N 73 31 E
Brlik, R.S.F.S.R., U.S.S.R. **184** 44 0N 74 5 E
Brno **151** 49 10N 16 35 E
Bro **172** 59 31N 17 38 E
Broach = Bharuch **198** 21 47N 73 0 E
Broach, L. **80** 50 45N 67 59W
Broad Arrow **229** 30 23 S 121 15 E
Broad B. **134** 58 14N 6 16W
Broad Haven **135** 54 20N 9 55W
Broad Law **134** 55 30N 3 22W
Broad Sd. **230** 22 0 S 149 45 E
Broadback → **78** 51 21N 78 52W
Broadford **233** 37 14 S 145 4 E
Broadhurst Ra. **228** 22 30 S 122 30 E
Broads, The **132** 52 45N 1 30 E
Broadview **88** 50 22N 102 35W
Broager **173** 54 53N 9 40 E
Broaryd **173** 57 7N 13 15 E
Brochet **77** 57 53N 101 40W
Brochet, L. **77** 58 36N 101 35W
Brochet, L. du **83** 49 40N 69 37W
Brock **88** 51 26N 108 43W
Brock → **82** 50 0N 75 5W
Brock I. **94** 77 52N 114 19W
Brocken **146** 51 48N 10 40 E
Brocklehurst **233** 32 9 S 148 38 E
Brockville **85** 44 35N 75 41W
Brod **166** 41 35N 21 17 E
Brodarevo **166** 43 14N 19 44 E
Broderick **88** 51 30N 106 55W
Brodeur Pen. **95** 72 30N 88 10W
Brodick **134** 55 34N 5 9W
Brodnica **152** 53 15N 19 25 E
Brodokalmak **182** 55 35N 62 6 E
Brody **178** 50 5N 25 10 E
Broechem **143** 51 11N 4 38 E
Broek **142** 52 26N 5 0 E
Broek op Langedijk **142** 52 41N 4 49 E
Broglie **138** 49 0N 0 30 E
Brok **152** 52 43N 21 52 E
Broken Hill = Kabwe **251** 14 30 S 28 29 E
Broken Hill **231** 31 58 S 141 29 E
Brokind **173** 58 13N 15 42 E
Brokopondo **119** 5 3N 54 59W
Brokopondo □ **119** 4 30N 55 30W
Bromfield **133** 52 25N 2 45W
Bromley **133** 51 20N 0 5 E
Bromölla **173** 56 5N 14 28 E
Bromont **83** 45 17N 72 39W
Bromptonville **83** 45 28N 71 57W
Brønderslev **173** 57 16N 9 57 E
Brong-Ahafo □ **246** 7 50N 2 0W
Bronkhorstspruit **255** 25 46 S 28 45 E
Bronnitsy **179** 55 27N 38 10 E
Bronte **165** 37 48N 14 49 E
Bronte Park **230** 42 8 S 146 30 E
Brookdale **89** 50 3N 99 34W
Brookes Point **211** 8 47N 117 50 E
Brookfield **81** 45 15N 63 17W
Brooklyn **81** 44 3N 64 42W
Brookmere **93** 49 52N 120 53W
Brooks **91** 50 35N 111 55W
Brooks B. **92** 50 15N 127 55W
Brooks L. **77** 61 55N 106 35W
Brooloo **231** 26 30 S 152 43 E
Broom, L. **134** 57 55N 5 15W
Broome **228** 18 0 S 122 15 E
Broomehill **229** 33 51 S 117 39 E
Broons **138** 48 20N 2 16W
Broquerie, La **89** 49 25N 96 30W
Brora **134** 58 0N 3 50W
Brora → **134** 58 4N 3 52W
Brösarp **173** 55 43N 14 6 E
Brosna → **135** 53 8N 8 0W
Broşteni **170** 47 14N 25 43 E
Brotas de Macaúbas **121** 12 0 S 42 38W
Brøttum **171** 61 2N 10 34 E
Brou **138** 48 13N 1 11 E
Brouage **140** 45 52N 1 4W
Broughams Gate **232** 30 51 S 140 59 E
Broughton I. **92** 50 47N 126 42W
Broughton Island **95** 67 33N 63 0W
Broughty Ferry **134** 56 29N 2 50W
Broumov **151** 50 35N 16 20 E
Brouwershaven **142** 51 45N 3 55 E
Brouwershavensche Gat **142** 51 46N 3 50 E
Brovary **178** 50 34N 30 48 E
Brovst **173** 57 6N 9 31 E
Brown, Mt. **232** 32 30 S 138 0 E
Brown, Pt. **231** 32 32 S 133 50 E
Brown Willy **133** 50 35N 4 34W
Browning **88** 49 27N 102 38W
Brownlee **88** 50 43N 106 1W
Browns Flats **81** 45 28N 66 8W
Brownsburg **83** 45 41N 74 25W
Brownsweg **119** 5 5N 55 15W
Browse I. **228** 14 7 S 123 33 E
Broye → **148** 46 52N 6 58 E
Brozas **155** 39 37N 6 47W
Bru **171** 61 32N 5 11 E
Bruas **205** 4 30N 100 47 E
Bruay-en-Artois **139** 50 29N 2 33 E
Bruce **91** 53 10N 112 2W
Bruce, Mt. **228** 22 37 S 118 8 E
Bruce B. **235** 43 35 S 169 42 E
Bruce L. **86** 50 49N 93 20W
Bruce Mts. **95** 71 12N 72 15W
Bruce Pen. **84** 45 0N 81 30W
Bruce Rock **229** 31 52 S 118 8 E
Bruche → **139** 48 34N 7 43 E
Bruchsal **147** 49 9N 8 39 E
Bruck an der Leitha **151** 48 1N 16 47 E
Bruck an der Mur **150** 47 24N 15 16 E
Brückenau **147** 50 17N 9 48 E
Bruderheim **90** 53 47N 112 56W
Brue → **133** 51 10N 2 59W
Brugelette **143** 50 35N 3 52 E
Bruges = Brugge **143** 51 13N 3 13 E
Brugg **148** 47 29N 8 11 E
Brugge **143** 51 13N 3 13 E
Brühl **146** 50 49N 6 51 E
Bruinisse **143** 51 40N 4 5 E
Brûlé **90** 53 15N 117 58W
Brûlé, L. **80** 52 30N 63 40W
Brûlon **138** 47 58N 0 15W
Brûly **143** 49 58N 4 32 E
Brumado **121** 14 14 S 41 40W
Brumado → **121** 14 13 S 41 40W
Brumath **139** 48 43N 7 40 E
Brummen **142** 52 5N 6 10 E
Brumunddal **171** 60 53N 10 56 E
Brunchilly **230** 18 50 S 134 30 E
Brunei = Bandar Seri Begawan **206** 4 52N 115 0 E
Brunei ■ **206** 4 50N 115 0 E
Brunette Downs **230** 18 40 S 135 55 E
Brunette I. **79** 47 16N 55 55W
Brunflo **172** 63 5N 14 50 E
Brunico **163** 46 50N 11 55 E
Brünig, P. **148** 46 46N 8 8 E
Brunkeberg **171** 59 26N 8 28 E
Brunkild **89** 49 36N 97 35W
Brunna **172** 59 52N 17 25 E
Brunnen **149** 46 59N 8 37 E

Brunner, L. 235 42 37 S 171 27 E
Brunnsvik 172 60 12N 15 8 E
Bruno 88 52 20N 105 30W
Brunsbüttelkoog 146 53 52N 9 13 E
Brunssum 143 50 57N 5 59 E
Brunswick = Braunschweig 146 52 17N 10 28 E
Brunswick, Pen. de 126 53 30 S 71 30W
Brunswick B. 228 15 15 S 124 50 E
Brunswick Junction 229 33 15 S 115 50 E
Brunswick L. 87 48 58N 83 23W
Bruntál 151 50 0N 17 27 E
Bruny I. 230 43 20 S 147 15 E
Brus Laguna 112 15 47N 84 35W
Brusartsi 166 43 40N 23 5 E
Brusio 149 46 14N 10 8 E
Brusque 125 27 5 S 49 0W
Brussel 143 50 51N 4 21 E
Brussels = Bruxelles 143 50 51N 4 21 E
Brussels 84 43 44N 81 15W
Brustem 143 50 48N 5 14 E
Bruthen 231 37 42 S 147 50 E
Bruxelles 143 50 51N 4 21 E
Bruyères 139 48 10N 6 40 E
Brwinów 152 52 9N 20 40 E
Bryagovo 167 41 58N 25 8 E
Bryan, Mt. 231 33 30 S 139 0 E
Bryanka 181 48 32N 38 45 E
Bryansk 178 53 13N 34 25 E
Bryanskoye 181 44 20N 47 10 E
Bryne 171 58 44N 5 38 E
Bryson 82 45 41N 76 37W
Brza Palanka 166 44 28N 22 27 E
Brzava → 166 45 21N 20 45 E
Brzeg 152 50 52N 17 30 E
Brzeg Din 152 51 16N 16 41 E
Brześć Kujawski 152 52 36N 18 55 E
Brzesko 152 49 59N 20 34 E
Brzeszcze 152 49 59N 19 10 E
Brzeziny 152 51 49N 19 42 E
Brzozów 152 49 41N 22 3 E
Bsharri 190 34 15N 36 0 E
Bū Athlah 241 30 9N 15 39 E
Bū Baqarah 195 25 35N 56 25 E
Bu Craa 240 26 45N 12 50W
Bū Ḥasā 195 23 30N 53 20 E
Bua Yai 204 15 33N 102 26 E
Buabuq 244 31 29N 25 29 E
Buad I. 211 11 40N 124 51 E
Buapinang 207 4 40 S 121 30 E
Buayan 207 6 3N 125 6 E
Buba 246 11 40N 14 59W
Bubanda 252 4 14N 19 38 E
Bubanza 250 3 6 S 29 23 E
Būbiyān 193 29 45N 48 15 E
Bucaramanga 118 7 0N 73 0W
Bucas Grande I. 211 9 40N 125 57 E
Buccaneer Arch. 228 16 7 S 123 20 E
Bucchiánico 163 42 20N 14 10 E
Bucecea 170 47 47N 26 28 E
Buchach 178 49 5N 25 25 E
Buchan, Australia 233 37 30 S 148 12 E
Buchan, U.K. 134 57 32N 2 8W
Buchan Ness 134 57 29N 1 48W
Buchanan, Canada 88 51 40N 102 45W
Buchanan, Liberia 246 5 57N 10 2W
Buchanan, L., Queens., Australia 230 21 35 S 145 52 E
Buchanan, L., W. Austral., Australia 229 25 33 S 123 2 E
Buchans 79 48 50N 56 52W
Buchans Junction 79 48 51N 56 28W
Bucharest = Bucureşti 170 44 27N 26 10 E
Buchholz 146 53 19N 9 51 E
Buchloe 147 48 3N 10 45 E
Buchs 149 47 10N 9 28 E
Buck L. 91 52 59N 114 46W
Buck Lake 91 52 57N 114 47W
Bückeburg 146 52 16N 9 2 E
Buckhaven 134 56 10N 3 2W
Buckhorn L. 85 44 29N 78 23W
Buckie 134 57 40N 2 58W
Buckingham, Canada 82 45 37N 75 24W
Buckingham, U.K. 133 52 0N 0 59W
Buckingham □ 133 51 50N 0 55W
Buckingham B. 230 12 10 S 135 40 E
Buckingham Can. 201 14 0N 80 5 E
Buckinguy 231 31 3 S 147 30 E
Buckland Newton 133 50 45N 2 25W
Buckle Hd. 228 14 26 S 127 52 E
Buckleboo 231 32 54 S 136 12 E
Buco Zau 253 4 46 S 12 33 E
Bucquoy 139 50 9N 2 43 E
Buctouche 81 46 30N 64 45W
Buctzotz 111 21 12N 88 47W
Bucureşti 170 44 27N 26 10 E
Budafok 151 47 26N 19 2 E
Budalin 202 22 20N 95 10 E
Budapest 151 47 29N 19 5 E
Budaun 199 28 5N 79 10 E
Budd Coast 13 68 0 S 112 0 E
Buddabadah 233 31 56 S 147 14 E
Buddusò 164 40 35N 9 18 E
Bude 133 50 49N 4 33W
Budel 143 51 17N 5 34 E
Budeşti 170 44 13N 26 30 E
Budge Budge = Baj Baj 199 22 30N 88 5 E
Budgewoi Lake 231 33 13 S 151 34 E
Búðareyri 174 65 2N 14 13W
Búðir 174 64 49N 23 23W
Budia 156 40 38N 2 46W
Budjala 252 2 50N 19 40 E
Búdrio 163 44 31N 11 31 E
Budva 166 42 17N 18 50 E
Budzyń 152 52 54N 16 59 E
Buea 247 4 10N 9 9 E
Buena Vista 123 17 27 S 63 40W
Buenaventura, Colombia 118 3 53N 77 4W
Buenaventura, Mexico 101 29 51N 107 29W
Buenaventura, B. de 118 3 48N 77 17W
Buenavista, Chiapas, Mexico 110 16 25N 93 50W
Buenavista, Michoacan, Mexico 106 18 8N 102 15W
Buenavista, Sonora, Mexico 100 29 6N 111 47W
Buenavista, Luzon, Phil. 210 13 35N 122 34 E
Buenavista, Mindanao, Phil. 211 8 59N 125 24 E
Buenavista, Zamboanga del S., Phil. 211 7 15N 122 16 E
Buenavista, L. 110 15 49N 93 34W
Buenavista de Cuéllar 107 18 27N 99 25W
Buenavista Tomatlán 106 19 12N 102 36W
Buendía, Pantano de 156 40 25N 2 43W
Buenópolis 121 17 54 S 44 11W
Buenos Aires, Argentina 124 34 30 S 58 20W
Buenos Aires, Colombia 118 1 36N 73 18W
Buenos Aires, C. Rica 112 9 10N 83 20W
Buenos Aires, Mexico 100 28 0N 110 57W
Buenos Aires □ 124 36 30 S 60 0W
Buenos Aires, Lago 126 46 35 S 72 30W
Buesaco 118 1 23N 77 9W
Buey, Pta. 110 18 36N 92 42W
Buffalo → 76 60 5N 115 5W
Buffalo Creek 93 51 44N 121 9W
Buffalo Head Hills 76 57 25N 115 55W
Buffalo L. 91 52 27N 112 54W
Buffalo Narrows 77 55 51N 108 29W
Buffalo Pound L. 88 50 39N 105 30W
Buffels → 254 29 36 S 17 15 E
Bug →, Poland 152 52 31N 21 5 E
Bug →, U.S.S.R. 180 46 59N 31 58 E
Buga 118 4 0N 76 15W
Buganda □ 250 0 0 31 30 E
Buganga 250 0 3 S 32 0 E
Bugasan 211 7 27N 124 14 E
Bugasong 211 11 3N 122 4 E
Bugeat 140 45 36N 1 55 E
Bugel, Tanjung 209 6 26 S 111 3 E
Buggenhout 143 51 1N 4 12 E
Bugojno 166 44 2N 17 25 E
Bugsuk 206 8 15N 117 15 E
Bugue, Le 140 44 55N 0 56 E
Buguey 210 18 17N 121 50 E
Bugulma 182 54 33N 52 48 E
Buguma 247 4 42N 6 55 E
Bugun Shara 212 49 0N 104 0 E
Buguruslan 182 53 39N 52 26 E
Buhăeşti 170 46 47N 27 32 E
Buheirat-Murrat-el-Kubra 244 30 15N 32 40 E
Buhuşi 170 46 41N 26 45 E
Builth Wells 133 52 10N 3 26W
Buinsk 179 55 0N 48 18 E
Buíque 120 8 37 S 37 9W
Buir Nur 213 47 50N 117 42 E
Buis-les-Baronnies 141 44 17N 5 16 E
Buit, L. 80 53 59N 63 13W
Buitenpost 142 53 15N 6 9 E
Buitrago 154 41 0N 3 38W
Bujalance 155 37 54N 4 23W
Buján 154 42 59N 8 36W
Bujanovac 166 42 28N 21 44 E
Bujaraloz 156 41 29N 0 10W
Buje 163 45 24N 13 39 E
Buji 227 9 8 S 142 11 E
Bujumbura 250 3 16 S 29 18 E
Bük, Hungary 151 47 22N 16 45 E
Buk, Poland 152 52 21N 16 30 E
Buka I. 227 5 10 S 154 35 E
Bukachacha 185 52 55N 116 50 E
Bukama 251 9 10 S 25 50 E
Bukavu 250 2 20 S 28 52 E
Bukene 250 4 15 S 32 48 E
Bukhara 183 39 48N 64 25 E
Bukidnon □ 211 8 0N 125 0 E
Bukima 250 1 50 S 33 25 E
Bukit Mertajam 205 5 22N 100 28 E
Bukittinggi 208 0 20 S 100 20 E
Bukkapatnam 201 14 14N 77 46 E
Buklyan 182 55 42N 52 10 E
Bukoba 250 1 20 S 31 49 E
Bukoba □ 250 1 30 S 32 0 E
Bukowno 152 50 17N 19 35 E
Bukuru 247 9 42N 8 48 E
Bukuya 250 0 40N 31 52 E
Bula, Guin.-Biss. 246 12 7N 15 43W
Bula, Indonesia 207 3 6 S 130 30 E
Bulacan 210 13 40N 120 21 E
Bulacan □ 210 15 0N 121 5 E
Bülach 149 47 31N 8 32 E
Bulahdelah 231 32 23 S 152 13 E
Bulalacao 210 12 31N 121 26 E
Bulan 210 12 40N 123 52 E
Bulanash 182 57 16N 62 0 E
Bulandshahr 198 28 28N 77 51 E
Bulanovo 182 52 27N 55 10 E
Bûlâq 244 25 10N 30 38 E
Bulawayo 251 20 7 S 28 32 E
Buldana 198 20 30N 76 18 E
Buldon 211 7 33N 124 25 E
Bulgaria ■ 167 42 35N 25 30 E
Bulgroo 231 25 47 S 143 58 E
Bulgunnia 231 30 10 S 134 53 E
Bulhale 256 5 20N 46 29 E
Bulhar 256 10 25N 44 30 E
Buli, Teluk 207 1 5N 128 25 E
Buliluyan, C. 211 8 20N 117 15 E
Bulki 245 6 11N 36 31 E
Bulkley → 76 55 15N 127 40W
Bull → 92 49 18N 115 18W
Bullange 143 50 24N 6 15 E
Bullaque → 155 38 59N 4 17W
Bullara 228 22 40 S 114 3 E
Bullaring 229 32 30 S 117 45 E
Bullas 157 38 2N 1 40W
Bulle 148 46 37N 7 3 E
Buller → 235 41 44 S 171 36 E
Buller, Mt. 233 37 10 S 146 28 E
Buller Gorge 235 41 40 S 172 10 E
Bulli 231 34 15 S 150 57 E
Bullock Creek 230 17 43 S 144 31 E
Bulloo → 231 28 43 S 142 30 E
Bulloo Downs, Queens., Australia 231 28 31 S 142 57 E
Bulloo Downs, W. Austral., Australia 229 24 0 S 119 32 E
Bulloo L. 231 28 43 S 142 25 E
Bulls 234 40 10 S 175 24 E
Bully-les-Mines 139 50 27N 2 44 E
Bulnes 124 36 42 S 72 19W
Bulo Burti 256 3 50N 45 33 E
Bulo Ghedudo 256 2 52N 43 1 E
Bulolo 227 7 10 S 146 40 E
Bulongo 253 4 45 S 21 30 E
Bulpunga 232 33 47 S 141 45 E
Bulqiza 168 41 30N 20 21 E
Bulsar = Valsad 198 20 40N 72 58 E
Bultfontein 254 28 18 S 26 10 E
Bulu Karakelong 207 4 35N 126 50 E
Buluan, L. 211 6 40N 124 49 E
Buluanga 210 12 14N 119 52 E
Buluangan 211 10 24N 123 20 E
Bulukumba 207 5 33 S 120 11 E
Bulun 185 70 37N 127 30 E
Bulungu 253 6 4 S 21 54 E
Bulusan 210 12 45N 124 8 E
Bulyea 88 50 59N 104 52W
Bumba 252 2 13N 22 30 E
Bumbiri I. 250 1 40 S 31 55 E
Bumhkang 202 26 51N 97 40 E
Bumhpa Bum 202 26 51N 97 14 E
Bumi → 251 17 0 S 28 20 E
Bumtang → 202 26 56N 90 53 E
Buna, Kenya 250 2 58N 39 30 E
Buna, Papua N. G. 227 8 42 S 148 27 E
Bunawan, Agusan del S., Phil. 211 8 12N 125 57 E
Bunawan, Davao del S., Phil. 211 7 14N 125 38 E
Bunazi 250 1 3 S 31 23 E
Bunbah, Khalīj 242 32 20N 23 15 E
Bunbury 229 33 20 S 115 35 E
Buncrana 135 55 8N 7 28W
Bundaberg 231 24 54 S 152 22 E
Bünde 146 52 11N 8 33 E
Bundey → 230 21 46 S 135 37 E
Bundi 198 25 30N 75 35 E
Bundooma 230 24 54 S 134 16 E
Bundoran 135 54 24N 8 17W
Bundukia 245 5 14N 30 55 E
Bundure 233 35 10 S 146 1 E
Bung Kan 204 18 23N 103 37 E
Bungatakada 220 33 35N 131 25 E
Bungendore 233 35 14 S 149 30 E
Bungil Cr. → 230 27 5 S 149 5 E
Bungo-Suidō 220 33 0N 132 15 E
Bungoma 250 0 34N 34 34 E
Bungu 250 7 35 S 39 0 E
Bunia 250 1 35N 30 20 E
Bunji 199 35 45N 74 40 E
Bunnik 142 52 4N 5 12 E
Bunnythorpe 234 40 16 S 175 39 E
Buñol 157 39 25N 0 47W
Bunsbeek 143 50 50N 4 56 E
Bunschoten 142 52 14N 5 22 E
Buntok 209 1 40 S 114 58 E
Bununu 247 9 51N 9 32 E
Bununu Dass 247 10 0N 9 31 E
Bunyu 209 3 35N 117 50 E
Bunza 247 12 8N 4 0 E
Buol 207 1 15N 121 32 E
Buon Brieng 204 13 9N 108 12 E
Buon Me Thuot 204 12 40N 108 3 E
Buong Long 204 13 44N 106 59 E
Buorkhaya, Mys 185 71 50N 132 40 E
Buqayq 193 26 0N 49 45 E
Buqei'a 189 32 58N 35 20 E
Bur Acaba 256 3 12N 44 20 E
Bûr Fuad 244 31 15N 32 20 E
Bur Ghibi 256 3 56N 45 7 E
Bûr Safâga 244 26 43N 33 57 E
Bûr Sa'îd 244 31 16N 32 18 E
Bûr Sûdân 244 19 32N 37 9 E
Bûr Taufiq 244 29 54N 32 32 E
Bura 250 1 4 S 39 58 E
Buran 256 10 14N 48 44 E
Burao 256 9 32N 45 32 E
Burāq 190 33 11N 36 29 E
Burauen 211 10 58N 124 53 E
Buraydah 192 26 20N 44 8 E
Burayevo 182 55 50N 55 24 E
Burç 190 36 59N 37 8 E
Burcher 231 33 30 S 147 16 E
Burdekin → 230 19 38 S 147 25 E
Burdeos Bay 210 14 44N 122 6 E
Burdett 91 49 50N 111 32W
Burdur 177 37 45N 30 22 E
Burdwan = Barddhaman 199 23 14N 87 39 E
Bure 245 10 40N 37 4 E
Bure → 132 52 38N 1 45 E
Bureba, La 156 42 36N 3 24W
Büren, Germany 146 51 33N 8 34 E
Buren, Neth. 142 51 55N 5 20 E
Bureya → 185 49 27N 129 30 E
Burford 84 43 7N 80 27W
Burg, Magdeburg, Germany 146 52 16N 11 50 E
Burg, Schleswig-Holstein, Germany 146 54 25N 11 10 E
Burg el Arab 244 30 54N 29 32 E
Burg et Tuyur 244 20 55N 27 56 E
Burgas 167 42 33N 27 29 E
Burgaski Zaliv 167 42 30N 27 39 E
Burgdorf, Germany 146 52 27N 10 0 E
Burgdorf, Switz. 148 47 3N 7 37 E
Burgenland □ 151 47 20N 16 20 E
Burgeo 79 47 37N 57 38W
Burgersdorp 254 31 0 S 26 20 E
Burges, Mt. 229 30 50 S 121 5 E
Burghausen 147 48 10N 12 50 E
Búrgio 164 37 35N 13 18 E
Bürglen 149 46 53N 8 40 E
Burglengenfeld 147 49 11N 12 2 E
Burgo de Osma 156 41 35N 3 4W
Burgohondo 154 40 26N 4 47W
Burgos, Mexico 103 24 57N 98 47W
Burgos, Ilocos N., Phil. 210 18 31N 120 39 E
Burgos, Pangasinan, Phil. 210 16 4N 119 52 E
Burgos, Spain 156 42 21N 3 41W
Burgos □ 156 42 21N 3 42W
Burgstädt 146 50 55N 12 49 E
Burgsteinfurt 146 52 9N 7 23 E
Burgsvik 173 57 3N 18 19 E
Burguillos del Cerro 155 38 23N 6 35W
Burgundy = Bourgogne 139 47 0N 4 30 E
Burhanpur 198 21 18N 76 14 E
Burhou 138 49 45N 2 15W
Buri Pen. 245 15 25N 39 55 E
Burias 210 12 55N 123 5 E
Burias Pass 210 13 0N 123 15 E
Buribay 182 51 57N 58 10 E
Burica, Pta. 112 8 3N 82 51W
Burigi, L. 250 2 2 S 31 22 E
Burin, Canada 79 47 1N 55 14W
Būrīn, Jordan 189 32 11N 35 15 E
Burin Peninsula 79 47 0N 55 40W
Buriram 204 15 0N 103 0 E
Buriti Alegre 121 18 9 S 49 3W

Buriti Bravo . . . . . . 120 5 50 S 43 50W
Buriti dos Lopes . . . 120 3 10 S 41 52W
Burj Islâm . . . . 190 35 42N 35 46 E
Burj Sâfitâ . . . . 190 34 48N 36 7 E
Burji . . . . 245 5 29N 37 51 E
Burke → . . . . 230 23 12 S 139 33 E
Burke Chan. 92 52 10N 127 30W
Burkina Faso ■ 246 12 0N 1 0W
Burk's Falls 84 45 37N 79 24W
Burleigh Falls 85 44 33N 78 12W
Burlington, Newf., Canada 79 49 45N 56 1W
Burlington, Ont., Canada 84 43 18N 79 45W
Burlyu-Tyube . . . . . . 184 46 30N 79 10 E
Burma ■ . . . . 202 21 0N 96 30 E
Burnaby I. 92 52 25N 131 19W
Burnamwood . . . . . . 233 31 7 S 144 53 E
Burngup . . . . 229 33 2 S 118 42 E
Burnie . . . . 230 41 4 S 145 56 E
Burnley 132 53 47N 2 15W
Burnoye . . . . 183 42 36N 70 47 E
Burns Lake 76 54 20N 125 45W
Burnside → 94 66 51N 108 4W
Burnside, L. . . . . . . 229 25 22 S 123 0 E
Burnt Island 79 47 36N 58 53W
Burnt L. 78 53 35N 64 4W
Burnt River 85 44 41N 78 42W
Burntwood → 77 56 8N 96 34W
Burntwood L. 77 55 22N 100 26W
Burqâ . . . . 189 32 18N 35 11 E
Burqân . . . . 192 29 0N 47 57 E
Burra . . . . 232 33 40 S 138 55 E
Burragorang, L. . . . . 233 33 52 S 150 37 E
Burramurra . . . . 230 20 25 S 137 15 E
Burreli . . . . 168 41 36N 20 1 E
Burren Junction . . . . 231 30 7 S 148 59 E
Burrendong, L. . . . . 233 32 45 S 149 10 E
Burrendong Dam . . . 231 32 39 S 149 6 E
Burriana 156 39 50N 0 4W
Burrinjuck Res. . . . . 231 35 0 S 148 36 E
Burrioncito 104 25 32N 108 26W
Burro, Serranías del 102 28 56N 101 32W
Burrows L. 87 49 57N 86 44W
Burrundie . . . . 228 13 32 S 131 42 E
Burruyacú . . . . 124 26 30 S 64 40W
Burry Port 133 51 41N 4 17W
Bursa . . . . 177 40 15N 29 5 E
Burseryd . . . . 173 57 12N 13 17 E
Burstall 88 50 39N 109 54W
Burton 93 50 0N 117 53W
Burton L. 78 54 45N 78 20W
Burton-upon-Trent . 132 52 48N 1 39W
Burtts Corner 81 46 3N 66 52W
Burtundy . . . . 231 33 45 S 142 15 E
Buru . . . . 207 3 30 S 126 30 E
Buruanga . . . . 211 11 51N 121 53 E
Burullus, Bahra el . . 244 31 25N 31 0 E
Burûm . . . . 195 14 22N 48 59 E
Burûn, Râs . . . . 191 31 14N 33 7 E
Burunday . . . . 183 43 20N 76 51 E
Burundi ■ . . . . 250 3 15 S 30 0 E
Bururi . . . . 250 3 57 S 29 37 E
Burutu . . . . 247 5 20N 5 29 E
Burwash 84 46 14N 80 51W
Burwash Landing . . . 94 61 21N 139 0W
Bury, Canada 83 45 28N 71 30W
Bury, U.K. 132 53 36N 2 19W
Bury St. Edmunds . . 133 52 15N 0 42 E
Buryat A.S.S.R. □ . 185 53 0N 110 0 E
Buryn . . . . 178 51 13N 33 50 E
Burzenin . . . . 152 51 28N 18 47 E
Busalla . . . . 162 44 34N 8 58 E
Busango Swamp . . . . 251 14 15 S 25 45 E
Buşayrah . . . . 192 35 9N 40 26 E
Buşayyah . . . . 192 30 0N 46 10 E
Busca . . . . 162 44 31N 7 29 E
Bushati . . . . 168 41 58N 19 34 E
Bûshehr . . . . 193 28 55N 50 55 E
Bûshehr □ . . . . 193 28 20N 51 45 E
Bushell 77 59 31N 108 45W
Bushenyi . . . . 250 0 35 S 30 10 E
Bushire = Bûshehr . 193 28 55N 50 55 E
Busia □ . . . . 250 0 25N 34 6 E
Busie 246 10 29N 2 22W
Businga . . . . 252 3 16N 20 59 E
Buskerud fylke □ . . 171 60 13N 9 0 E
Busko Zdrój . . . . . . 152 50 28N 20 42 E
Buslei . . . . 256 5 28N 44 25 E
Busoga □ . . . . 250 0 5N 33 30 E
Busovača . . . . 166 44 6N 17 53 E
Busra ash Shām . . . . 191 32 30N 36 25 E
Bussang . . . . 139 47 50N 6 50 E
Busselton . . . . 229 33 42 S 115 15 E
Busseto . . . . 162 44 59N 10 2 E
Bussigny . . . . 148 46 33N 6 33 E
Bussum . . . . 142 52 16N 5 10 E
Bustamante, Nuevo León, Mexico 102 26 33N 100 30W
Bustamante, Tamaulipas, Mexico 103 23 26N 99 47W
Bustamante, B. . . . . 126 45 5 S 66 18W
Bustillos, L. 101 28 33N 106 45W
Busto, C. 154 43 34N 6 28W
Busto Arsizio . . . . . . 162 45 40N 8 50 E
Busu-Djanoa . . . . . . 252 1 43N 21 23 E
Busuanga . . . . 210 12 10N 120 0 E
Büsum . . . . 146 54 7N 8 50 E
Buta . . . . 250 2 50N 24 53 E
Buta, La 101 27 12N 107 38W
Butare . . . . 250 2 31 S 29 52 E
Butaritari . . . . 224 3 30N 174 0 E
Bute, Australia . . . . 232 33 51 S 138 2 E
Bute, U.K. 134 55 48N 5 2W
Bute Inlet 92 50 40N 124 53W
Butedale 92 53 8N 128 42W
Butemba . . . . 250 1 9N 31 37 E
Butembo . . . . 250 0 9N 29 18 E
Butera . . . . 165 37 10N 14 10 E
Bütgenbach . . . . 143 50 26N 6 12 E
Butha Qi . . . . 213 48 0N 122 32 E
Buthidaung . . . . 202 20 52N 92 32 E
Butiaba . . . . 250 1 50N 31 20 E
Butkhāk . . . . 197 34 30N 69 22 E
Butom Odrzánski . . . 152 51 44N 15 48 E
Bütschwil . . . . 149 47 23N 9 5 E
Butterworth . . . . 205 5 24N 100 23 E
Buttfield, Mt. . . . . . 229 24 15 S 128 9 E
Buttle L. 92 49 42N 125 33W
Button B. 77 58 45N 94 23W
Button Is. 78 60 38N 64 40W
Butty Hd. . . . . 229 33 54 S 121 39 E
Butuan . . . . 211 8 57N 125 33 E
Butuku-Luba . . . . . . 247 3 29N 8 33 E
Butulan . . . . 211 5 38N 125 26 E
Butung . . . . 207 5 0 S 122 45 E
Buturlinovka . . . . . . 179 50 50N 40 35 E
Butzbach . . . . 146 50 24N 8 40 E
Bützow . . . . 146 53 51N 11 59 E
Buug . . . . 211 7 40N 123 2 E
Buxar . . . . 199 25 34N 83 58 E
Buxton, Guyana 119 6 48N 58 2W
Buxton, S. Africa . . 254 27 38 S 24 42 E
Buxton, U.K. 132 53 16N 1 54W
Buxy . . . . 139 46 44N 4 40 E
Buy . . . . 179 58 28N 41 28 E
Buyaga . . . . 185 59 50N 127 0 E
Buynaksk . . . . 181 42 48N 47 7 E
Büyük Çekmece . . . 167 41 2N 28 35 E
Büyük Kemikli Burun . . . . 168 40 20N 26 15 E
Büyükeğri Dağ . . . . 190 36 45N 33 33 E
Buzançais . . . . 138 46 54N 1 25 E
Buzău . . . . 170 45 10N 26 50 E
Buzău □ . . . . 170 45 20N 26 30 E
Buzău → . . . . 170 45 10N 27 20 E
Buzău, Pasul . . . . . . 170 45 35N 26 12 E
Buzen . . . . 220 33 35N 131 5 E
Buzet . . . . 163 45 24N 13 58 E
Buzi → . . . . 251 19 50 S 34 43 E
Buziaş . . . . 170 45 38N 21 36 E
Buzuluk . . . . 182 52 48N 52 12 E
Buzuluk → . . . . 179 50 15N 42 7 E
Bwagaoia . . . . 227 10 40 S 152 52 E
Bwana Mkubwe . . . . 251 13 8 S 28 38 E
Byala, Ruse, Bulgaria . . . . 167 43 28N 25 44 E
Byala, Varna, Bulgaria . . . . 167 42 53N 27 55 E
Byala Slatina . . . . . . 167 43 26N 23 55 E
Byam Martin I. 94 75 15N 104 15W
Byandovan, Mys . . . 181 39 45N 49 28 E
Bychawa . . . . 152 51 1N 22 36 E
Byczyna . . . . 152 51 7N 18 12 E
Bydgoszcz . . . . 152 53 10N 18 0 E
Bydgoszcz □ . . . . . . 152 53 16N 17 33 E
Byelorussian S.S.R. □ . . . . 178 53 30N 27 0 E
Bygland . . . . 171 58 50N 7 48 E
Byglandsfjord . . . . . 171 58 40N 7 50 E
Byglandsfjorden . . . 171 58 44N 7 50 E
Bykhov . . . . 178 53 31N 30 14 E
Bykle . . . . 171 59 20N 7 22 E
Bykovo . . . . 181 49 50N 45 25 E
Bylderup . . . . 173 54 57N 9 6 E
Bylot I. 95 73 13N 78 34W
Byng Inlet 84 45 46N 80 33W
Byrd, C. . . . . 13 69 38 S 76 7W
Byrd Land . . . . 13 79 30 S 125 0W
Byrd Sub-Glacial Basin . . . . 13 82 0 S 120 0W
Byro . . . . 229 26 5 S 116 11 E
Byrock . . . . 233 30 40 S 146 27 E
Byron Bay . . . . 231 28 43 S 153 37 E
Byrranga, Gory . . . . 185 75 0N 100 0 E
Byrum . . . . 173 57 16N 11 0 E
Bystrovka . . . . 183 42 47N 75 42 E
Bystrzyca →, Lublin, Poland . . . 152 51 21N 22 46 E
Bystrzyca →, Wrocław, Poland . 152 51 12N 16 55 E
Bystrzyca Kłodzka . . 152 50 19N 16 39 E
Byten . . . . 178 52 50N 25 27 E
Bytom . . . . 152 50 25N 18 54 E
Bytów . . . . 152 54 10N 17 30 E
Byumba . . . . 250 1 35 S 30 4 E
Bzenec . . . . 151 48 58N 17 18 E
Bzura → . . . . 152 52 25N 20 15 E

C

Ca → . . . . 204 18 45N 105 45 E
Ca Mau = Quan Long . . . . 205 9 7N 105 8 E
Ca Mau, Mui = Bai Bung, Mui . . . . . . 205 8 38N 104 44 E
Ca Na . . . . 205 11 20N 108 54 E
Caacupé . . . . 124 25 23 S 57 5W
Caála . . . . 253 12 46 S 15 30 E
Caamano Sd. 92 52 55N 129 25W
Caapiranga . . . . 119 3 18 S 61 13W
Caazapá . . . . 124 26 8 S 56 19W
Caazapá □ . . . . 125 26 10 S 56 0W
Cabadbaran . . . . 211 9 10N 125 38 E
Cabagan . . . . 210 17 26N 121 46 E
Cabalian . . . . 211 10 16N 125 10 E
Caballeria, C. de . . . 156 40 5N 4 5 E
Caballos Mesteños, Llanos de los 101 28 30N 104 0W
Cabana . . . . 122 8 25 S 78 5W
Cabanaconde . . . . . . 122 15 38 S 71 58W
Cabañaquinta 154 43 10N 5 38W
Cabanatuan . . . . 210 15 30N 120 58 E
Cabanes . . . . 156 40 9N 0 2 E
Cabangon . . . . 210 15 10N 120 3 E
Cabanillas . . . . 122 15 36 S 70 28W
Çabano 83 47 40N 68 56W
Cabar . . . . 163 45 36N 14 39 E
Cabarroquis . . . . 210 16 50N 121 30 E
Cabarruyan I. . . . . . 210 16 18N 119 59 E
Cabcaben . . . . 210 14 27N 120 35 E
Cabedelo . . . . 120 7 0 S 34 50W
Cabeza del Buey . . . 155 38 44N 5 13W
Cabildo . . . . 124 32 30 S 71 5W
Cabimas 118 10 23N 71 25W
Cabinda . . . . 253 5 33 S 12 11 E
Cabinda □ . . . . 253 5 0 S 12 30 E
Cabiri . . . . 253 8 52 S 13 39 E
Cables . . . . 229 27 55 S 123 25 E
Cabo Blanco . . . . 126 47 15 S 65 47W
Cabo Corrientes 106 20 25N 105 12W
Cabo Frio . . . . 121 22 51 S 42 3W
Cabo Pantoja . . . . . . 118 1 0 S 75 10W
Cabo Raso . . . . 126 44 20 S 65 15W
Cabonga, Réservoir . 82 47 20N 76 40W
Caboolture . . . . 231 27 5 S 152 58 E
Cabora Bassa Dam . 251 15 20 S 32 50 E
Cabot Strait 75 47 15N 59 40W
Cabra 155 37 30N 4 28W
Cabra del Santo Cristo 157 37 42N 3 16W
Cabrales 105 23 4N 103 10W
Cābras . . . . 164 39 57N 8 30 E
Cabrera, I. . . . . 157 39 8N 2 57 E
Cabrera, Sierra 154 42 12N 6 40W
Cabri 88 50 35N 108 25W
Cabriel → 157 39 14N 1 3W
Cabruta 118 7 50N 66 10W
Cabucgayan . . . . 211 11 29N 124 34 E
Cabuga . . . . 210 17 48N 120 27 E
Cabulauan Is. . . . . . . 211 11 25N 120 8 E
Cabullona 100 31 10N 109 34W
Caburan = Jose Abad Santos . . . . . 211 5 55N 125 39 E
Cabuyaro 118 4 18N 72 49W
Cacabelos 154 42 36N 6 44W
Çacahuamilpa 107 18 41N 99 30W
Čačak . . . . 166 43 54N 20 20 E
Cacalchén 111 20 59N 89 14W
Cacalotán, Sinaloa, Mexico 104 23 4N 105 50W
Cacalotán, Sinaloa, Mexico 104 26 11N 108 23W
Cacao 119 4 33N 52 26W
Cáceres, Brazil . . . . . 123 16 5 S 57 40W
Cáceres, Colombia . 118 7 35N 75 20W
Cáceres, Spain 155 39 26N 6 23W
Cáceres □ 155 39 45N 6 0W
Cache Bay 84 46 22N 80 0W
Cache Creek 93 50 48N 121 19W
Cachepo 155 37 20N 7 49W
Cachéu 246 12 14N 16 8W
Cachi . . . . 124 25 5 S 66 10W
Cachimba 103 22 44N 97 51W
Cachimbo . . . . 123 8 57 S 54 54W
Cachimbo, Serra do 123 9 30 S 55 0W
Cachingues . . . . 253 13 5 S 16 43 E
Cachoeira . . . . 121 12 30 S 39 0W
Cachoeira Alta . . . . . 121 18 48 S 50 58W
Cachoeira de Itapemirim . . . . . . 125 20 51 S 41 7W
Cachoeira do Sul . . . 125 30 3 S 52 53W
Cachoeiro do Arari . 120 1 1 S 48 58W
Cachopo 155 37 20N 7 49W
Cachuela Esperanza 123 10 32 S 65 38W
Cacólo . . . . 253 10 9 S 19 21 E
Cacoma o Vélez, Sa. de 106 20 5N 104 35W
Caconda . . . . 253 13 48 S 15 8 E
Cacongo . . . . 253 5 11 S 12 5 E
Caçu . . . . 121 18 37 S 51 4W
Cacula . . . . 253 14 29 S 14 10 E
Caculé . . . . 121 14 30 S 42 13W
Cacuso . . . . 253 9 25 S 15 45 E
Cadarache, Barrage de . . . . 141 43 42N 5 47 E
Čadca . . . . 151 49 26N 18 45 E
Cadell Cr. → . . . . . 230 22 35 S 141 51 E
Cadena, Arroyo de la → 105 26 7N 104 10W
Cadena, La 105 25 53N 104 12W
Cadenazzo . . . . 149 46 9N 8 57 E
Cader Idris 132 52 43N 3 56W
Cadereyta 102 25 36N 100 0W
Cadereyta de Montes 107 20 42N 99 49W
Cadí, Sierra del . . . . 156 42 17N 1 42 E
Cadibarrawirracanna, L. . . . . 231 28 52 S 135 27 E
Cadillac, Qué., Canada 82 48 14N 78 23W
Cadillac, Sask., Canada 88 49 44N 107 44W
Cadillac, France 140 44 38N 0 20W
Cadiz, Phil. . . . . 211 10 57N 123 15 E
Cádiz, Spain 155 36 30N 6 20W
Cádiz □ 155 36 36N 5 45W
Cádiz, G. de 155 36 40N 7 0W
Cadney Park . . . . 231 27 55 S 134 3 E
Cadomin 91 53 2N 117 20W
Cadotte → 90 56 43N 117 10W
Cadours . . . . 140 43 44N 1 2 E
Cadoux . . . . 229 30 46 S 117 7 E
Caen 138 49 10N 0 22W
Caernarfon 132 53 8N 4 17W
Caernarfon B. 132 53 4N 4 40W
Caernarvon = Caernarfon 132 53 8N 4 17W
Caerphilly 133 51 34N 3 13W
Caesarea . . . . 189 32 30N 34 53 E
Caeté . . . . 121 19 55 S 43 40W
Caetité . . . . 121 13 50 S 42 32W
Cafayate . . . . 124 26 2 S 66 0W
Cafifi 118 5 13N 71 4W
Cafu . . . . 254 16 30 S 15 8 E
Cagayan □ . . . . 210 18 0N 121 50 E
Cagayan → . . . . 210 18 25N 121 42 E
Cagayan de Oro . . . . 211 8 30N 124 40 E
Cagayan Is. . . . . 211 9 40N 121 16 E
Cagayan Sulu I. . . . . 211 7 1N 118 30 E
Cagli . . . . 163 43 32N 12 38 E
Cágliari . . . . 164 39 15N 9 6 E
Cágliari, G. di . . . . . 164 39 8N 9 10 E
Cagnano Varano . . . 165 41 49N 15 47 E
Cagnes-sur-Mer . . . . 141 43 40N 7 9 E
Caguán → . . . . 118 0 8 S 74 18W
Caha Mts. 135 51 45N 9 40W
Cahama . . . . 254 16 17 S 14 19 E
Caher 135 52 23N 7 56W
Cahersiveen 135 51 57N 10 13W
Cahore Pt. 135 52 34N 6 11W
Cahors . . . . 140 44 27N 1 27 E
Cahuapanas . . . . 122 5 15 S 77 0W
Cahuinari → . . . . . . 118 1 21 S 70 44W
Cai Bau, Dao . . . . . . 204 21 10N 107 27 E
Cai Nuoc . . . . 205 8 56N 105 1 E
Caia . . . . 251 17 51 S 35 24 E
Caiabis, Serra dos . . 123 11 30 S 56 30W
Caianda . . . . 251 11 2 S 23 31 E
Caiapó, Serra do . . . 123 17 0 S 52 0W
Caiapônia . . . . 123 16 57 S 51 49W
Caibarién 112 22 30N 79 30W
Caibiran . . . . 211 11 34N 124 35 E
Caicara, Bolívar, Venezuela 118 7 38N 66 10W
Caicara, Monagas, Venezuela 119 9 52N 63 38W
Caicó . . . . 120 6 20 S 37 0W
Caicos Is. 113 21 40N 71 40W
Caicos Passage 113 22 45N 72 45W
Cailloma . . . . 122 15 9 S 71 45W
Caimanero 104 22 52N 106 3W
Caimanero, L. 104 23 0N 106 7W
Caine → . . . . 123 18 23 S 65 21W
Cains → 81 46 40N 65 47W
Caird Coast . . . . 13 75 0 S 25 0W
Cairn Gorm 134 57 7N 3 40W
Cairn Toul 134 57 3N 3 44W
Cairngorm Mts. 134 57 6N 3 42W
Cairns . . . . 230 16 57 S 145 45 E
Cairo = El Qâhira . . 244 30 1N 31 14 E
Cairo Montenotte . . 162 44 23N 8 16 E
Caithness, Ord of . . 134 58 9N 3 37W
Caiundo . . . . 253 15 50 S 17 28 E
Caiza . . . . 123 20 2 S 65 40W
Cajabamba . . . . 122 7 38 S 78 4W
Cajamarca . . . . 122 7 5 S 78 28W
Cajamarca □ . . . . . . 122 6 15 S 78 50W
Cajapió . . . . 120 2 58 S 44 48W
Cajarc . . . . 140 44 29N 1 50 E
Cajatambo . . . . 122 10 30 S 77 2W
Çajàzeiras . . . . 120 6 52 S 38 30W
Čajetina . . . . 166 43 47N 19 42 E
Cajidiocan . . . . 210 12 22N 122 41 E
Çajititlán 106 20 26N 103 19W
Čajniče . . . . 166 43 34N 19 5 E
Cajurichic 101 28 7N 108 11W
Çakirgol . . . . 181 40 33N 39 40 E

Čakovec **163** 46 23N 16 26 E
Cal, La → **123** 17 27 S 58 15W
Cala **155** 37 59N 6 21W
Cala → **155** 37 38N 6 5W
Cala Cadolar, Punta de **157** 38 38N 1 35 E
Calabanga **210** 13 42N 123 17 E
Calabar **247** 4 57N 8 20 E
Calabogie **85** 45 18N 76 43W
Calabozo **118** 9 0N 67 28W
Calábria □ **165** 39 24N 16 30 E
Calaburras, Pta. de **155** 36 30N 4 38W
Calaceite **156** 41 1N 0 11 E
Calacota **122** 17 16 S 68 38W
Calafat **170** 43 58N 22 59 E
Calafate **126** 50 19 S 72 15W
Calahorra **156** 42 18N 1 59W
Calais **139** 50 57N 1 56 E
Calais, Pas de **139** 50 57N 1 20 E
Calalaste, Cord. de **124** 25 0 S 67 0W
Calalayan **211** 11 30N 119 38 E
Calama, Brazil **123** 8 0 S 62 50W
Calama, Chile **124** 22 30 S 68 55W
Calamar, Bolívar, Colombia **118** 10 15N 74 55W
Calamar, Vaupés, Colombia **118** 1 58N 72 32W
Calamarca **122** 16 55 S 68 9W
Calamba, Cavite, Phil. **210** 14 13N 121 10 E
Calamba, Misamis, Phil. **211** 8 35N 123 39 E
Calamba, Negros, Phil. **211** 10 11N 123 17 E
Calamian Group **210** 11 50N 119 55 E
Calamocha **156** 40 50N 1 17W
Calañas **155** 37 40N 6 53W
Calanda **156** 40 56N 0 15W
Calandagan I. **211** 10 39N 120 15 E
Calandula **253** 9 6 S 15 57 E
Calang **208** 4 37N 95 37 E
Calangiánus **164** 40 56N 9 12 E
Calanscio, Sarīr **242** 27 0N 21 30 E
Calapan **210** 13 25N 121 7 E
Calape **211** 9 54N 123 52 E
Călăraşi **170** 44 12N 27 20 E
Călăraşi □ **170** 44 10N 27 0 E
Calasparra **157** 38 14N 1 41W
Calatafimi **164** 37 56N 12 50 E
Calatagan **210** 13 50N 120 38 E
Calatayud **156** 41 20N 1 40W
Calato = Kálathos **169** 36 9N 28 8 E
Calauag **210** 13 55N 122 15 E
Calaug **210** 13 58N 122 17 E
Calavà, C. **165** 38 11N 14 55 E
Calavite, Cape **210** 13 26N 120 20 E
Calavite Pass **210** 13 36N 120 25 E
Calayan **210** 19 16N 121 28 E
Calayan I. **210** 19 20N 121 27 E
Calbayog **210** 12 4N 124 38 E
Calbe **146** 51 57N 11 47 E
Calca **122** 13 22 S 72 0W
Calci **162** 43 44N 10 31 E
Calcutta **199** 22 36N 88 24 E
Caldaro **163** 46 23N 11 15 E
Caldas □ **118** 5 15N 75 30W
Caldas da Rainha **155** 39 24N 9 8W
Caldas de Reyes **154** 42 36N 8 39W
Caldas Novas **121** 17 45 S 48 38W
Calder → **132** 53 44N 1 21W
Caldera **124** 27 5 S 70 55W
Calderitas **111** 18 33N 88 15W
Caledon **254** 34 14 S 19 26 E
Caledon → **254** 30 31 S 26 5 E
Caledon B. **230** 12 45 S 137 0 E
Caledonia, N.S., Canada **81** 45 17N 62 33W
Caledonia, N.S., Canada **81** 44 22N 65 2W
Caledonia, Ont., Canada **84** 43 7N 79 58W
Calella **156** 41 37N 2 40 E
Calemba **254** 16 0 S 15 44 E
Calera, La **124** 32 50 S 71 10W
Calera Víctor Rosales **105** 22 57N 102 42W
Caleta Olivia **126** 46 25 S 67 25W
Calf of Man **132** 54 4N 4 48W
Calgary **91** 51 0N 114 10W
Cali **118** 3 25N 76 35W
Calicut **201** 11 15N 75 43 E
California, Golfo de **99** 28 0N 112 0W
Călimăneşti **170** 45 14N 24 20 E
Călimani, Munţii **170** 47 12N 25 0 E
Călineşti **170** 45 21N 24 18 E
Calingasta **124** 31 15 S 69 30W
Calinog **211** 11 7N 122 32 E
Calintaan **210** 12 35N 120 57 E
Calitri **165** 40 54N 15 25 E
Callabonna, L. **231** 29 40 S 140 5 E
Callac **138** 48 25N 3 27W
Callan **135** 52 33N 7 25W
Callander, Canada **84** 46 13N 79 22W
Callander, U.K. **134** 56 15N 4 14W
Callang **210** 17 2N 121 38 E
Callantsoog **142** 52 50N 4 42 E
Callao **122** 12 0 S 77 0W
Calles **103** 23 3N 98 45W
Calles, Presa **105** 22 9N 102 27W
Callide **230** 24 18 S 150 28 E
Calling L. **90** 55 15N 113 20W
Calling Lake **90** 55 15N 113 12W
Calliope **230** 24 0 S 151 16 E
Callosa de Ensarriá **157** 38 40N 0 8W
Callosa de Segura **157** 38 7N 0 53W
Calmar **90** 53 16N 113 49W
Calmellí **99** 28 14N 113 33W
Calnali **107** 20 55N 98 35W
Calne **132** 51 26N 2 0W
Calola **254** 16 25 S 17 48 E
Calolbon **210** 13 36N 124 6 E
Caloocan **210** 14 39N 120 58 E
Calore → **165** 41 11N 14 28 E
Calotmul **111** 21 1N 88 11W
Caloundra **231** 26 45 S 153 10 E
Calpe **157** 38 39N 0 3 E
Calpulalpan, México, Mexico **107** 20 4N 99 38W
Calpulalpán, Tlaxcala, Mexico **107** 19 35N 98 35W
Calpulalpán de Méndez **109** 17 17N 96 25W
Calstock **87** 49 47N 84 9W
Caltabellotta **164** 37 36N 13 11 E
Caltagirone **165** 37 13N 14 30 E
Caltanissetta **165** 37 30N 14 3 E
Caltimacan **107** 20 32N 99 21W
Calucinga **253** 11 18 S 16 12 E
Caluire-et-Cuire **141** 45 49N 4 51 E
Calulo **253** 10 1 S 14 56 E
Calunda **253** 12 7 S 23 36 E
Caluquembe **253** 13 47 S 14 44 E
Caluso **162** 45 18N 7 52 E
Caluya I. **211** 11 55N 121 34 E
Calvados □ **138** 49 5N 0 15W
Calvert → **230** 16 17 S 137 44 E
Calvert C. **92** 51 25N 127 53W
Calvert Hills **230** 17 15 S 137 20 E
Calvert I. **92** 51 30N 128 0W
Calvert Ra. **228** 24 0 S 122 30 E
Calvillito **105** 21 49N 102 11W
Calvillo **105** 21 51N 102 43W
Calvinia **254** 31 28 S 19 45 E
Calw **147** 48 43N 8 44 E
Calzada Almuradiel **157** 38 32N 3 28W
Calzada de Calatrava **155** 38 42N 3 46W
Cam → **133** 52 21N 0 16 E
Cam Lam **205** 11 54N 109 10 E
Cam Pha **204** 21 7N 107 18 E
Cam Ranh **205** 11 54N 109 12 E
Cam Xuyen **204** 18 15N 106 0 E
Camabatela **253** 8 20 S 15 26 E
Camacã **121** 15 24 S 39 30W
Camaçari **121** 12 41 S 38 18W
Camachigama, L. **82** 47 50N 76 19W
Camacho **105** 24 25N 102 18W
Camacupa **253** 11 58 S 17 22 E
Camaguán **118** 8 6N 67 36W
Camagüey **112** 21 20N 78 0W
Camaiore **162** 43 57N 10 18 E
Camamu **121** 13 57 S 39 7W
Camaná **122** 16 30 S 72 50W
Camanongue **253** 11 24 S 20 17 E
Camaquã → **125** 31 17 S 51 47W
Camararé → **123** 12 15 S 58 55W
Camarat, C. **141** 43 12N 6 41 E
Camaret **138** 48 16N 4 37W
Camargo **123** 20 38 S 65 15 E
Camargue **141** 43 34N 4 34 E
Camariñas **154** 43 8N 9 12W
Camarines Norte □ **210** 14 10N 122 45 E
Camarines Sur □ **210** 13 40N 123 20 E
Camarón, Nuevo León, Mexico **102** 27 18N 100 3W
Camarón, Sinaloa, Mexico **104** 23 19N 106 29W
Camarón, C. **112** 16 0N 85 0W
Camarones, Argentina **126** 44 50 S 65 40W
Camarones, Mexico **103** 24 32N 99 46W
Camarones, B. **126** 44 45 S 65 35W
Camaxilo **253** 8 21 S 18 56 E
Cambados **154** 42 31N 8 49W
Cambamba **253** 8 53 S 14 44 E
Cambará **125** 23 2 S 50 5W
Cambay = Khambhat **198** 22 23N 72 33 E
Cambay, G. of **198** 20 45N 72 30 E
Cambil **157** 37 40N 3 33W
Cambo-les-Bains **140** 43 22N 1 23W
Cambodia ■ **204** 12 15N 105 0 E
Camborne **133** 50 13N 5 18W
Cambrai **139** 50 11N 3 14 E
Cambrian Mts. **133** 52 25N 3 52W
Cambridge, N.B., Canada **81** 45 50N 65 58W
Cambridge, Ont., Canada **84** 43 23N 80 15W
Cambridge, Jamaica **112** 18 18N 77 54W
Cambridge, N.Z. **234** 37 54 S 175 29 E
Cambridge, U.K. **133** 52 13N 0 8 E
Cambridge Bay **94** 69 10N 105 0W
Cambridge Gulf **228** 14 55 S 128 15 E
Cambridgeshire □ **133** 52 12N 0 7 E
Cambrils **156** 41 8N 1 3 E
Cambuci **121** 21 35 S 41 55W
Camden **233** 34 1 S 150 43 E
Camden Sound **228** 15 27 S 124 25 E
Camembert **138** 48 53N 0 10 E
Cámeri **162** 45 30N 8 40 E
Camerino **163** 43 10N 13 4 E
Cameron Falls **86** 49 8N 88 19W
Cameron Highlands **205** 4 27N 101 22 E
Cameron Hills **76** 59 48N 118 0W
Cameron L. **87** 49 1N 84 17W
Cameron Mts. **235** 46 1 S 167 0 E
Cameroon ■ **252** 6 0N 12 30 E
Camerota **165** 40 2N 15 21 E
Cameroun → **247** 4 0N 9 35 E
Cameroun, Mt. **247** 4 13N 9 10 E
Cametá **120** 2 12 S 49 30W
Camiguin □ **211** 9 11N 124 42 E
Camiguin I. **210** 18 56N 121 55 E
Camiling **210** 15 42N 120 24 E
Caminha **154** 41 50N 8 50W
Camino Real de Piaxtla **104** 23 52N 106 39W
Camira Creek **231** 29 15 S 152 58 E
Camiranga **120** 1 48 S 46 17W
Camiri **123** 20 3 S 63 31W
Camissombo **253** 8 7 S 20 38 E
Camoa Mts. **119** 1 30N 59 0W
Camocim **120** 2 55 S 40 50W
Camogli **162** 44 21N 9 9 E
Camooweal **230** 19 56 S 138 7 E
Camopi **119** 3 12N 52 17W
Camopi → **119** 3 10N 52 20W
Camotes Is. **211** 10 40N 124 24 E
Camotes Sea **211** 10 30N 124 15 E
Camotlán **106** 20 58N 104 41W
Camotlán de Miraflores **106** 19 13N 104 14W
Camp Borden **84** 44 18N 79 56W
Campagna **165** 40 40N 15 5 E
Campana **124** 34 10 S 58 55W
Campana, I. **126** 48 20 S 75 20W
Campana, La **105** 26 7N 103 31W
Campanario **155** 38 52N 5 36W
Campania □ **165** 40 50N 14 45 E
Campania I. **92** 53 5N 129 25W
Campbell, C. **235** 41 47 S 174 18 E
Campbell I. **224** 52 30 S 169 0 E
Campbell Island **92** 52 8N 128 12W
Campbell L. **77** 63 14N 106 55W
Campbell River **92** 50 5N 125 20W
Campbell Town **230** 41 52 S 147 30 E
Campbellford **85** 44 18N 77 48W
Campbellpur **198** 33 46N 72 26 E
Campbell's Bay **82** 45 44N 76 36W
Campbellton, N.B., Canada **81** 47 57N 66 43W
Campbellton, Newf., Canada **79** 49 17N 54 56W
Campbelltown **231** 34 4 S 150 49 E
Campbeltown **134** 55 25N 5 36W
Campeche **111** 19 51N 90 32W
Campeche □ **111** 19 0N 90 30W
Campeche, B. de **110** 20 0N 94 0W
Camperdown **231** 38 14 S 143 9 E
Camperville **89** 51 59N 100 9W
Campi Salentina **165** 40 22N 18 2 E
Campidano **164** 39 30N 8 40 E
Campillo de Altobuey **156** 39 36N 1 49W
Campillo de Llerena **155** 38 30N 5 50W
Campillos **155** 37 4N 4 51W
Campiña, La **155** 37 45N 4 45W
Campina Grande **120** 7 20 S 35 47W
Campina Verde **121** 19 31 S 49 28W
Campinas **125** 22 50 S 47 0W
Campine **143** 51 8N 5 20 E
Campli **163** 42 44N 13 40 E
Campo, Cameroon **252** 2 22N 9 50 E
Campo, Spain **156** 42 25N 0 24 E
Campo Belo **121** 20 52 S 45 16W
Campo de Criptana **157** 39 24N 3 7W
Campo de Diauarum **123** 11 12 S 53 14W
Campo de Gibraltar **155** 36 15N 5 25W
Campo Flórido **121** 19 47 S 48 35W
Campo Formoso **120** 10 30 S 40 20W
Campo Grande **123** 20 25 S 54 40W
Campo Maíor, Brazil **120** 4 50 S 42 12W
Campo Maior, Portugal **155** 38 59N 7 7W
Campo Mourão **125** 24 3 S 52 22W
Campo Tencia **149** 46 26N 8 43 E
Campo Túres **163** 46 53N 11 55 E
Campoalegre **118** 2 41N 75 20W
Campobasso **165** 41 34N 14 40 E
Campobello di Licata **164** 37 16N 13 55 E
Campobello di Mazara **164** 37 38N 12 45 E
Campofelice **164** 37 54N 13 53 E
Camporeale **164** 37 53N 13 3 E
Campos **121** 21 50 S 41 20W
Campos, Pta. **106** 19 1N 104 21W
Campos Altos **121** 19 47 S 46 10W
Campos Belos **121** 13 10 S 47 3W
Campos del Puerto **157** 39 26N 3 1 E
Campos Novos **125** 27 21 S 51 50W
Campos Sales **120** 7 4 S 40 23W
Camprodón **156** 42 19N 2 23 E
Campuya → **118** 1 40 S 73 30W
Camrose **91** 53 0N 112 50W
Camsell Portage **77** 59 37N 109 15W
Can Gio **205** 10 25N 106 58 E
Can Tho **205** 10 2N 105 46 E
Canaan → **81** 45 55N 65 47W
Canaan Station **81** 46 15N 65 4W
Canada ■ **72** 60 0N 100 0W
Cañada, La **107** 20 37N 100 19W
Canada B. **79** 50 43N 56 8W
Cañada de Gómez **124** 32 40 S 61 30W
Çanakkale **168** 40 8N 26 30 E
Çanakkale Boğazi **168** 40 0N 26 0 E
Canal Flats **91** 50 10N 115 48W
Canal latéral à la Garonne **140** 44 25N 0 15 E
Canala **226** 21 32 S 165 57 E
Canalejas **124** 35 15 S 66 34W
Canals, Argentina **124** 33 35 S 62 53W
Canals, Spain **157** 38 58N 0 35W
Cananea **100** 30 57N 110 18W
Cañar **118** 2 33 S 78 56W
Cañar □ **118** 2 30 S 79 0W
Canarias, Islas **240** 28 30N 16 0W
Canarreos, Arch. de los **112** 21 35N 81 40W
Canary Is. = Canarias, Islas **240** 28 30N 16 0W
Canastra, Serra da **121** 20 0 S 46 20W
Canatlán **105** 24 31N 104 47W
Cañaveras **156** 40 27N 2 24W
Canavieiras **121** 15 39 S 39 0W
Canbelego **231** 31 32 S 146 18 E
Canberra **231** 35 15 S 149 8 E
Cancabchén **111** 19 23N 89 48W
Cancale **138** 48 40N 1 50W
Canche → **139** 50 31N 1 39 E
Canchyuaya, Cordillera de **122** 7 30 S 74 0W
Cancún **111** 21 8N 86 44W
Cancún, Pta. **111** 21 8N 86 45W
Candala **256** 11 30N 49 58 E
Candarave **122** 17 15 S 70 13W
Candas **154** 43 35N 5 45W
Candé **138** 47 34N 1 0W
Candeias → **123** 8 39 S 63 31W
Candela, Italy **165** 41 8N 15 31 E
Candela, Mexico **102** 26 50N 100 40W
Candela, Sa. de la **104** 25 30N 105 37W
Candelaria, Argentina **125** 27 29 S 55 44W
Candelaria, Campeche, Mexico **111** 18 18N 91 21W
Candelaria, Chihuahua, Mexico **101** 31 7N 106 29W
Candelaria, Phil. **210** 13 56N 121 25 E
Candelaria → **111** 18 38N 91 15W
Candelaria, Pta. de la **154** 43 45N 8 0W
Candelaria, Sa. de la **105** 24 25N 101 45W
Candeleda **154** 40 10N 5 14W
Candelo **231** 36 47 S 149 43 E
Candia = Iráklion **169** 35 20N 25 12 E
Candia, Sea of = Crete, Sea of **169** 36 0N 25 0 E
Cándido Aguilar **102** 25 31N 98 2W
Cândido de Abreu **121** 24 35 S 51 20W
Cândido Mendes **120** 1 27 S 45 43W
Candle L. **88** 53 50N 105 18W
Candlemas I. **13** 57 3 S 26 40W
Cando **88** 52 23N 108 14W
Candon **210** 17 12N 120 27 E
Candoni **211** 9 48N 122 30 E
Canea = Khaniá **169** 35 30N 24 4 E
Canela **120** 10 15 S 48 25W
Canelli **162** 44 44N 8 18 E
Canelones **125** 34 32 S 56 17W
Canet-Plage **140** 42 41N 3 2 E
Cañete, Chile **124** 37 50 S 73 30W
Cañete, Peru **122** 13 8 S 76 30W
Cañete, Spain **156** 40 3N 1 54W
Cañete de las Torres **155** 37 53N 4 19W
Canfranc **156** 42 42N 0 31W
Cangamba **253** 13 40 S 19 54 E
Cangandala **253** 9 45 S 16 33 E
Cangas **154** 42 16N 8 47W
Cangas de Narcea **154** 43 10N 6 32W
Cangas de Onís **154** 43 21N 5 8W
Cangoa **253** 13 8 S 18 30 E

Cangombo **253** 14 24 S 19 59 E
Cangongo **253** 9 24 S 17 30 E
Canguaretama **120** 6 20 S 35 5W
Canguçu **125** 31 22 S 52 43W
Cangxi **216** 31 47N 105 59 E
Cangyuan **216** 23 12N 99 14 E
Cangzhou **214** 38 19N 116 52 E
Canhoca **253** 9 15 S 14 41 E
Cani, I. **241** 36 21N 10 5 E
Canicattì **164** 37 21N 13 50 E
Canicattini **165** 37 1N 15 3 E
Canigao Channel **211** 10 15N 124 42 E
Canim, L. **93** 51 45N 120 50W
Canim Lake **93** 51 47N 120 54W
Canindé **120** 4 22 S 39 19W
Canindé → **120** 6 15 S 42 52W
Canipaan **206** 8 33N 117 15 E
Cañitas de Felipe Pescador **105** 23 36N 102 43W
Cañiza, La **154** 42 13N 8 16W
Cañizal **154** 41 12N 5 22W
Canjáyar **157** 37 1N 2 44W
Canjinge **253** 10 12 S 21 17 E
Çankırı **177** 40 40N 33 37 E
Cankuzo **250** 3 10 S 30 31 E
Canmore **91** 51 7N 115 18W
Cann River **231** 37 35 S 149 7 E
Canna **134** 57 3N 6 33W
Cannanore **201** 11 53N 75 27 E
Cannes **141** 43 32N 7 0 E
Canning **81** 45 9N 64 25W
Canning Town = Port Canning **199** 22 23N 88 40 E
Cannington **85** 44 20N 79 2W
Cannock **132** 52 42N 2 2W
Cannondale, Mt. **230** 25 13 S 148 57 E
Caño Colorado **118** 2 18N 68 22W
Canoe **93** 50 45N 119 13W
Canoe L. **77** 55 10N 108 15W
Canopus **232** 33 29 S 140 42 E
Canora **89** 51 40N 102 30W
Canosa di Púglia **165** 41 13N 16 4 E
Canourgue, Le **140** 44 26N 3 13 E
Canowindra **231** 33 35 S 148 38 E
Cansahcab **111** 21 10N 89 6W
Canso **81** 45 20N 61 0W
Canta **122** 11 29 S 76 37W
Cantabria **106** 19 50N 101 44W
Cantabria □ **154** 43 10N 4 0W
Cantabria, Sierra de **156** 42 40N 2 30W
Cantabrian Mts. = Cantábrica, Cordillera **154** 43 0N 5 10W
Cantábrica, Cordillera **154** 43 0N 5 10W
Cantal □ **140** 45 4N 2 45 E
Cantanhede **154** 40 20N 8 36W
Cantaura **119** 9 19N 64 21W
Çantavieja **156** 40 31N 0 25W
Čantavir **166** 45 55N 19 46 E
Cantera **106** 19 52N 102 25W
Canterbury, Australia **230** 25 23 S 141 53 E
Canterbury, Canada **81** 45 53N 67 29W
Canterbury, U.K. **133** 51 17N 1 5 E
Canterbury □ **235** 43 45 S 171 19 E
Canterbury Bight **235** 44 16 S 171 55 E
Canterbury Plains **235** 43 55 S 171 22 E
Cantilan **211** 9 20N 125 58 E
Cantillana **155** 37 36N 5 50W
Canto do Buriti **120** 8 7 S 42 58W
Cantù **162** 45 44N 9 8 E
Canuck **88** 49 12N 108 13W
Canudos **123** 7 13 S 58 5W
Canumã, Amazonas, Brazil **119** 4 2 S 59 4W
Canumã, Amazonas, Brazil **123** 6 8 S 60 10W
Canumã → **123** 3 55 S 59 10W
Canutama **123** 6 30 S 64 20W
Canutillo **104** 26 22N 105 25W
Canwood **88** 53 22N 106 36W
Canyon Creek **90** 55 22N 115 5W
Canzo **162** 45 54N 9 18 E
Cao Bang **204** 22 40N 106 15 E
Cao He → **215** 40 10N 124 32 E
Cao Lanh **205** 10 27N 105 38 E
Cao Xian **214** 34 50N 115 35 E
Caoayan **210** 17 37N 120 23 E
Caobal **110** 17 38N 93 8W
Caopacho → **80** 51 18N 66 18W
Caopacho, L. **80** 52 0N 66 9W
Cáorle **163** 45 36N 12 51 E
Caotibi, L. **80** 50 45N 67 34W
Cap-aux-Meules **81** 47 23N 61 52W
Cap-aux Meules, Î. du **81** 47 23N 61 54W
Cap-Chat **80** 49 6N 66 40W
Cap-de-la-Madeleine **83** 46 22N 72 31W
Cap-des-Rosiers **80** 48 52N 64 13W
Cap d'Espoir **80** 48 26N 64 20W
Cap-Haïtien **113** 19 40N 72 20W
Cap-Pelé **81** 46 13N 64 18W
Cap-St-Ignace **83** 47 2N 70 28W
Cap St.-Jacques = Vung Tau **205** 10 21N 107 4 E
Capa **204** 22 21N 103 50 E
Capa Stilo **165** 38 25N 16 35 E
Capáccio **165** 40 26N 15 4 E
Capacuaro **106** 19 33N 102 3W
Capaia **253** 8 27 S 20 13 E
Capalonga **210** 14 20N 122 30 E
Capanaparo → **118** 7 1N 67 7W
Capanema **120** 1 12 S 47 11W
Caparo →, Barinas, Venezuela **118** 7 46N 70 23W
Caparo →, Bolívar, Venezuela **119** 7 30N 64 0W
Capatárida **118** 11 11N 70 37W
Capayas **211** 10 28N 119 39 E
Capbreton **140** 43 39N 1 26W
Capdenac **140** 44 34N 2 5 E
Cape → **230** 20 49 S 146 51 E
Cape Barren I. **230** 40 25 S 148 15 E
Cape Breton Highlands Nat. Park **81** 46 50N 60 40W
Cape Breton I. **81** 46 0N 60 30W
Cape Broyle **79** 47 6N 52 57W
Cape Coast **247** 5 5N 1 15W
Cape Dorset **95** 64 14N 76 32W
Cape Dyer **95** 66 30N 61 22W
Cape Jervis **232** 35 40 S 138 5 E
Cape Montague **75** 46 5N 62 25W
Cape Palmas **246** 4 25N 7 49W
Cape Preston **228** 20 51 S 116 12 E
Cape Province □ **254** 32 0 S 23 0 E
Cape Ray **79** 47 38N 59 17W
Cape Scott Prov. Park **92** 50 45N 128 20W
Cape Tormentine **81** 46 8N 63 47W
Cape Town **254** 33 55 S 18 22 E
Cape Verde Is. ■ **128** 17 10N 25 20W
Cape York Peninsula **230** 12 0 S 142 30 E
Capela **120** 10 30 S 37 0W
Capela de Campo **120** 4 40 S 41 55W
Capele **253** 13 39 S 14 53 E
Capelinha **121** 17 42 S 42 31W
Capella **230** 23 2 S 148 1 E
Capella, Mt. **227** 5 4 S 141 8 E
Capelle, La **139** 49 59N 3 50 E
Capenda Camulemba **253** 9 24 S 18 27 E
Capendu **140** 43 11N 2 31 E
Capernaum = Kefar Nahum **189** 32 54N 35 34 E
Capestang **140** 43 20N 3 2 E
Capilla de Guadalupe **106** 20 50N 102 35W
Capim **120** 1 41 S 47 47W
Capim → **120** 1 40 S 47 47W
Capinópolis **121** 18 41 S 49 35W
Capinota **122** 17 43 S 66 14W
Capirato **104** 25 11N 107 38W
Capitachouane → **82** 47 40N 76 47W
Capitán Aracena, I. **126** 54 10 S 71 20W
Capitan Arturo Prat **13** 63 0 S 60 15W
Capitán Pastene **126** 38 13 S 73 1W
Capivara, Serra da **121** 14 35 S 45 0W
Capiz □ **211** 11 35N 122 30 E
Capizzi **165** 37 50N 14 26 E
Çaplan **81** 48 6N 65 40W
Čapljina **166** 43 10N 17 43 E
Capoche → **251** 15 35 S 33 0 E
Capoeira **123** 5 37 S 59 33W
Capolo **253** 10 22 S 14 7 E
Capraia **162** 43 2N 9 50 E
Caprarola **163** 42 21N 12 11 E
Capreol **84** 46 43N 80 56W
Caprera **164** 41 12N 9 28 E
Capri **165** 40 34N 14 15 E
Capricorn Group **230** 23 30 S 151 55 E
Capricorn Ra. **228** 23 20 S 116 50 E
Caprino Veronese **162** 45 37N 10 47 E
Caprivi Strip **254** 18 0 S 23 0 E
Captainganj **199** 26 55N 83 45 E
Captain's Flat **231** 35 35 S 149 27 E
Captieux **140** 44 18N 0 16W
Capu-Lapu **211** 10 20N 123 55 E
Cápua **165** 41 7N 14 15 E
Capul I. **210** 12 26N 124 10 E
Capulhuac **107** 19 27N 99 32W
Caquetá □ **118** 1 0N 74 0W
Caquetá → **118** 1 15 S 69 15W
Cara Pintada **100** 30 35N 108 52W
Carabalan **211** 10 6N 122 57 E
Carabao I. **210** 12 4N 121 56 E
Carabobo **118** 10 2N 68 5W
Carabobo □ **118** 10 10N 68 5W
Caracal **170** 44 8N 24 22 E
Caracaraí **119** 1 50N 61 8W
Caracas **118** 10 30N 66 55W
Caracol **120** 9 15 S 43 22W
Caracollo **122** 17 39 S 67 10W
Carácuaro de Morelos **107** 18 46N 101 2W
Caradoc **232** 30 35 S 143 5 E
Caragabal **233** 33 49 S 147 45 E
Caráglio **162** 44 25N 7 25 E
Carahue **126** 38 43 S 73 12W
Caraí **121** 17 12 S 41 42W
Carajás, Serra dos **120** 6 0 S 51 30W
Caramat **87** 49 37N 86 9W
Caramoan **210** 13 46N 123 52 E
Caranapatuba **123** 6 38 S 62 34W
Carandaiti **123** 20 45 S 63 4W
Carangola **121** 20 44 S 42 5W
Carani **229** 30 57 S 116 28 E
Caransebeş **170** 45 28N 22 18 E
Carantec **138** 48 40N 3 55W
Caraparanã → **118** 1 45 S 73 13W
Carapelle → **165** 41 3N 15 55 E
Caraquet **81** 47 48N 64 57W
Caras **122** 9 3 S 77 47W
Caraş Severin □ **166** 45 10N 22 10 E
Caraşova **166** 45 11N 21 51 E
Caratasca, Laguna **112** 15 20N 83 40W
Caratinga **121** 19 50 S 42 10W
Caraúbas **120** 5 43 S 37 33W
Caravaca **157** 38 8N 1 52W
Caravággio **162** 45 30N 9 39 E
Caravelas **121** 17 45 S 39 15W
Caraveli **122** 15 45 S 73 25W
Caràzinho **125** 28 16 S 52 46W
Carballino **154** 42 26N 8 5W
Carballo **154** 43 13N 8 41W
Carberry **89** 49 50N 99 25W
Carbia **154** 42 48N 8 14W
Carbó **100** 29 42N 110 58W
Carbon **91** 51 30N 113 9W
Carbonara, C. **164** 39 8N 9 30 E
Carbondale **90** 53 45N 113 32W
Carbonear **79** 47 42N 53 13W
Carboneras **157** 37 0N 1 53W
Carboneras, Cerro **107** 18 8N 101 8W
Carboneras de Guadazaón **156** 39 54N 1 50W
Carbonia **164** 39 10N 8 30 E
Carcabuey **155** 37 27N 4 17W
Carcagente **157** 39 8N 0 28W
Carcajou **76** 57 47N 117 6W
Carcans, Étang d' **140** 45 6N 1 7W
Carcar **211** 10 6N 123 38 E
Carcasse, C. **113** 18 30N 74 28W
Carcassonne **140** 43 13N 2 20 E
Carche **157** 38 26N 1 9W
Carchi □ **118** 0 45N 78 0W
Carcoar **233** 33 36 S 149 8 E
Carcross **72** 60 13N 134 45W
Cardabia **228** 23 2 S 113 48 E
Cardamom Hills **201** 9 30N 77 15 E
Cardeleros, Pta. **99** 25 42N 111 13W
Cárdenas, Cuba **112** 23 0N 81 30W
Cárdenas, Guanajuato, Mexico **107** 20 38N 101 13W
Cárdenas, San Luis Potosí, Mexico **103** 21 0N 99 40W
Cárdenas, Tabasco, Mexico **110** 17 59N 93 22W
Cardenete **156** 39 46N 1 41W
Cardiel, L. **126** 48 55 S 71 10W
Cardiff **133** 51 28N 3 11W
Cardigan **133** 52 6N 4 41W
Cardigan B. **133** 52 30N 4 30W
Cardinal **85** 44 47N 75 23W
Cardinal L. **90** 56 14N 117 44W
Cardón, Punta **118** 11 37N 70 14W
Cardona, Spain **156** 41 56N 1 40 E
Cardona, Uruguay **124** 33 53 S 57 18W
Cardoner → **156** 41 41N 1 51 E
Cardross **88** 49 50N 105 40W
Cardston **91** 49 15N 113 20W
Cardwell **230** 18 14 S 146 2 E
Careen L. **77** 57 0N 108 11W
Carei **170** 47 40N 22 29 E
Careiro **119** 3 12 S 59 45W
Careme **209** 6 55 S 108 27 E
Carentan **138** 49 19N 1 15W
Carey, L. **229** 29 0 S 122 15 E
Carey L. **77** 62 12N 102 55W
Careysburg **246** 6 34N 10 30W
Cargados Garajos **203** 17 0 S 59 0 E
Cargèse **141** 42 7N 8 35 E
Carhaix-Plouguer **138** 48 18N 3 36W
Carheil, L. **80** 52 40N 67 5W
Carhuamayo **122** 10 51 S 76 4W
Carhuas **122** 9 15 S 77 39W
Carhué **124** 37 10 S 62 50W
Cariango **253** 10 37 S 15 20 E
Caribal **110** 16 31N 90 42W
Caribbean Sea **113** 15 0N 75 0W
Cariboo → **93** 53 3N 121 20W
Cariboo Mts. **93** 53 0N 121 0W
Caribou →, Man., Canada **77** 59 20N 94 44W
Caribou →, N.W.T., Canada **76** 61 27N 125 45W
Caribou I. **87** 47 22N 85 49W
Caribou Is. **76** 61 55N 113 15W
Caribou L., Man., Canada **77** 59 21N 96 10W
Caribou L., Ont., Canada **86** 50 25N 89 5W
Caribou Mts. **76** 59 12N 115 40W
Carichic **101** 27 56N 107 3W
Carigara **211** 11 18N 124 41 E
Carignan **139** 49 38N 5 10 E
Carignano **162** 44 55N 7 40 E
Carin **256** 10 59N 49 13 E
Carinda **233** 30 28 S 147 41 E
Cariñena **156** 41 20N 1 13W
Carinhanha **121** 14 15 S 44 46W
Carinhanha → **121** 14 20 S 43 47W
Carini **164** 38 9N 13 10 E
Carinola **164** 41 11N 13 58 E
Carinthia □ = Kärnten □ **150** 46 52N 13 30 E
Caripito **119** 10 8N 63 6W
Caritianas **123** 9 20 S 63 6W
Carlbrod = Dimitrovgrad **166** 43 0N 22 48 E
Carlentini **165** 37 15N 15 2 E
Carles **211** 11 34N 123 8 E
Carleton, N.B., Canada **81** 48 5N 66 4W
Carleton, N.S., Canada **81** 44 0N 65 56W
Carleton Place **85** 45 8N 76 9W
Carletonville **254** 26 23 S 27 22 E
Carlingford, L. **135** 54 0N 6 5W
Carlisle **132** 54 54N 2 55W
Carlitte, Pic **140** 42 35N 1 55 E
Carloforte **164** 39 10N 8 18 E
Carlos A. Carrillo **109** 18 17N 95 49W
Carlos Casares **124** 35 32 S 61 20W
Carlos Chagas **121** 17 43 S 40 45W
Carlos Tejedor **124** 35 25 S 62 25W
Carlota, La, Argentina **124** 33 30 S 63 20W
Carlota, La, Phil. **211** 10 25N 122 55 E
Carlow **135** 52 50N 6 58W
Carlow □ **135** 52 43N 6 50W
Carlyle **89** 49 40N 102 20W
Carmacks **94** 62 5N 136 16W
Carmagnola **162** 44 50N 7 42 E
Carman **89** 49 30N 98 0W
Carmangay **91** 50 10N 113 10W
Carmanville **79** 49 23N 54 19W
Carmarthen **133** 51 52N 4 20W
Carmarthen B. **133** 51 40N 4 30W
Carmaux **140** 44 3N 2 10 E
Carmel Mt. **189** 32 45N 35 3 E
Carmelo **124** 34 0 S 58 20W
Carmen, Bolivia **122** 11 40 S 67 51W
Carmen, Colombia **118** 9 43N 75 8W
Carmen, Mexico **102** 25 56N 100 22W
Carmen, Paraguay **125** 27 13 S 56 12W
Carmen, Bohol, Phil. **211** 9 50N 124 12 E
Carmen, Cebu, Phil. **211** 10 35N 124 1 E
Carmen, Mindanao, Phil. **211** 7 13N 124 45 E
Carmen, I. **99** 25 57N 111 12W
Carmen, I. del **111** 18 16N 91 48W
Carmen, L. del **110** 18 17N 93 48W
Carmen, R. del → **101** 30 42N 106 29W
Carmen, Sa. del **102** 29 0N 102 28W
Carmen de Patagones **126** 40 50 S 63 0W
Cármenes **154** 42 58N 5 34W
Carmensa **124** 35 15 S 67 40W
Carmi **93** 49 36N 119 8W
Carmila **230** 21 55 S 149 24 E
Carmona **155** 37 28N 5 42W
Carnarvon, Queens., Australia **230** 24 48 S 147 45 E
Carnarvon, W. Austral., Australia **229** 24 51 S 113 42 E
Carnarvon, S. Africa **254** 30 56 S 22 8 E
Carnarvon Ra., Queens., Australia **230** 25 15 S 148 30 E
Carnarvon Ra., W. Austral., Australia **229** 25 0 S 120 45 E
Carnaxide **155** 38 43N 9 14W
Carndonagh **135** 55 15N 7 16W
Carnduff **89** 49 10N 101 50W
Carnegie, L. **229** 26 5 S 122 30 E
Carnic Alps = Karnische Alpen **150** 46 36N 13 0 E
Carnot **252** 4 59N 15 56 E
Carnot B. **228** 17 20 S 121 30 E
Carnsore Pt. **135** 52 10N 6 20W
Carnwood **91** 53 11N 114 38W
Carolina, Brazil **120** 7 10 S 47 30W
Carolina, S. Africa **255** 26 5 S 30 6 E
Carolina, La **155** 38 17N 3 38W
Caroline **91** 52 5N 114 45W
Caroline I. **225** 9 15 S 150 3W
Caroline Is. **224** 8 0N 150 0 E
Caroline Pk. **235** 45 57 S 167 15 E

Caron 88 50 30N 105 50W
Caron, L. 80 50 57N 67 44W
Caroni → 119 8 21N 62 43W
Caroona 231 31 24 S 150 26 E
Carora 118 10 11N 70 5W
Carovigno 165 40 42N 17 40 E
Carpathians, Mts. 130 49 50N 21 0 E
Carpaţii Meridionali 170 45 30N 25 0 E
Carpenédolo 162 45 22N 10 25 E
Carpentaria, G. of 230 14 0 S 139 0 E
Carpentaria Downs 230 18 44 S 144 20 E
Carpenter L. 93 50 53N 122 37W
Carpentras 141 44 3N 5 2 E
Carpi 162 44 47N 10 52 E
Carpina 120 7 51 S 35 15W
Carpino 165 41 50N 15 51 E
Carpio 154 41 13N 5 7W
Carpolac = Morea 231 36 45 S 141 18 E
Carr Boyd Ra. 228 16 15 S 128 35 E
Carragana 88 52 35N 103 6W
Carranglan 210 15 58N 121 4 E
Carranya 228 19 14 S 127 46 E
Carrara 162 44 5N 10 7 E
Carrascal 211 9 22N 125 56 E
Carrascosa del Campo 156 40 2N 2 45W
Carrauntoohill, Mt. 135 52 0N 9 49W
Carreras 104 25 19N 105 41W
Carretas, Punta 122 14 12 S 76 17W
Carrick-on-Shannon 135 53 57N 8 7W
Carrick-on-Suir 135 52 22N 7 30W
Carrickfergus 135 54 43N 5 50W
Carrickfergus □ 135 54 43N 5 49W
Carrickmacross 135 54 0N 6 43W
Carrieton 231 32 25 S 138 31 E
Carrillo 101 26 54N 103 55W
Carrión → 154 41 53N 4 32W
Carrión de los Condes 154 42 20N 4 37W
Carrizal, Chihuahua, Mexico 101 30 34N 106 39W
Carrizal, Sinaloa, Mexico 104 24 36N 107 14W
Carrizal, Pta. 106 19 5N 104 27W
Carrizal Bajo 124 28 5 S 71 20W
Carrizalillo 124 29 5 S 71 30W
Carrizo 101 28 33N 105 22W
Carron → 134 57 30N 5 30W
Carron, L. 134 57 22N 5 35W
Carrot → 89 53 50N 101 17W
Carrot River 88 53 17N 103 35W
Carrouges 138 48 34N 0 10W
Carruthers 88 52 52N 109 16W
Carse of Gowrie 134 56 30N 3 10W
Carsoli 163 42 7N 13 3 E
Carstairs, Canada 91 51 34N 114 6W
Carstairs, U.K. 134 55 42N 3 41W
Cartagena, Colombia 118 10 25N 75 33W
Cartagena, Spain 157 37 38N 0 59W
Cartago, Colombia 118 4 45N 75 55W
Cartago, C. Rica 112 9 50N 85 52W
Cartaxo 155 39 10N 8 47W
Cartaya 155 37 16N 7 9W
Carteret 138 49 23N 1 47W
Carterton 234 41 2 S 175 31 E
Cartier 84 46 42N 81 33W
Cartier I. 228 12 31 S 123 29 E
Cartwright, Man., Canada 89 49 6N 99 20W
Cartwright, Newf., Canada 78 53 41N 56 58W
Cartwright Sd. 92 53 13N 132 38W
Caruaru 120 8 15 S 35 55W
Carubig 210 12 24N 125 3 E
Carúpano 119 10 39N 63 15W
Caruray 211 10 20N 119 0 E
Carutapera 120 1 13 S 46 1W
Carvalho 119 2 16 S 51 29W
Carvin 139 50 30N 2 57 E
Carvoeiro 119 1 30 S 61 59W
Carvoeiro, Cabo 155 39 21N 9 24W
Casa Branca, Brazil 121 21 46 S 47 4W
Casa Branca, Portugal 155 38 29N 8 12W
Casa de Janos 101 30 44N 108 20W
Casa Nova 120 9 25 S 41 5W
Casablanca, Chile 124 33 20 S 71 25W
Casablanca, Morocco 240 33 36N 7 36W
Casacalenda 165 41 45N 14 50 E
Casal di Principe 165 41 0N 14 8 E
Casalbordino 163 42 10N 14 34 E
Casale Monferrato 162 45 8N 8 28 E
Casalmaggiore 162 44 59N 10 25 E
Casalpusterlengo 162 45 10N 9 40 E
Casamance → 246 12 33N 16 46W
Casamássima 165 40 58N 16 55 E
Casanare → 118 6 2N 69 51W
Casarano 165 40 0N 18 10 E
Casares 155 36 27N 5 16W
Casas 103 23 2N 98 45W
Casas Grandes 101 30 22N 107 57W
Casas Grandes → 101 30 22N 107 31W
Casas Ibañez 157 39 17N 1 30W
Casasimarro 157 39 22N 2 3W
Casatejada 154 39 54N 5 40W
Casavieja 154 40 17N 4 46W
Cascade Pt. 235 44 1 S 168 20 E
Cascais 155 38 41N 9 25W
Cáscina 162 43 40N 10 32 E
Caselle Torinese 162 45 12N 7 39 E
Caserta 165 41 5N 14 20 E
Casey 83 47 53N 74 11W
Cashel 135 52 31N 7 53W
Cashmere Downs 229 28 57 S 119 35 E
Casibare → 118 3 48N 72 18W
Casiguran 210 16 22N 122 7 E
Casiguran Sound 210 16 6N 121 58 E
Casilda 124 33 10 S 61 10W
Casimcea 170 44 45N 28 23 E
Casimiro Castillo 106 19 38N 104 28W
Casino 231 28 52 S 153 3 E
Casiquiare → 118 2 1N 67 7W
Casita, La 100 31 0N 110 52W
Casitas 122 3 54 S 80 39W
Çaslan 90 54 38N 112 31W
Čáslav 150 49 54N 15 22 E
Casma 122 9 30 S 78 20W
Casola Valsenio 163 44 12N 11 40 E
Cásoli 163 42 7N 14 18 E
Caspe 156 41 14N 0 1W
Caspian Sea 177 43 0N 50 0 E
Casquets 138 49 46N 2 15W
Cassá de la Selva 156 41 53N 2 52 E
Cassai 253 10 33 S 21 59 E
Cassamba 253 13 6 S 20 18 E
Cassano Iónio 165 39 47N 16 20 E
Cassel 139 50 48N 2 30 E
Casselman 85 45 19N 75 5W
Cassiar 76 59 16N 129 40W
Cassiar Mts. 76 59 30N 130 30W
Cassilândia 123 19 9 S 51 45W
Cassinga 253 15 5 S 16 4 E
Cassino 164 41 30N 13 50 E
Cassis 141 43 14N 5 32 E
Cassoalala 253 9 30 S 14 22 E
Cassoango 253 13 42 S 20 56 E
Cassunda 253 10 57 S 21 3 E
Cástagneto Carducci 162 43 9N 10 36 E
Castanhal 120 1 18 S 47 55W
Castaños 102 26 47N 101 25W
Casteau 143 50 32N 4 2 E
Castéggio 162 45 1N 9 8 E
Castejón de Monegros 156 41 37N 0 15W
Castel di Sangro 163 41 47N 14 6 E
Castel San Giovanni 162 45 4N 9 25 E
Castel San Pietro 163 44 23N 11 30 E
Castelbuono 165 37 56N 14 4 E
Casteldelfino 162 44 35N 7 4 E
Castelfiorentino 162 43 36N 10 58 E
Castelfranco Emília 162 44 37N 11 2 E
Castelfranco Véneto 163 45 40N 11 56 E
Casteljaloux 140 44 19N 0 6 E
Castellabate 165 40 18N 14 55 E
Castellammare, G. di 164 38 5N 12 55 E
Castellammare del Golfo 164 38 2N 12 53 E
Castellammare di Stábia 165 40 47N 14 29 E
Castellamonte 162 45 23N 7 42 E
Castellana, La 211 10 20N 123 3 E
Castellana Grotte 165 40 53N 17 10 E
Castellane 141 43 50N 6 31 E
Castellaneta 165 40 40N 16 57 E
Castellar de Santisteban 157 38 16N 3 8W
Castelleone 162 45 19N 9 47 E
Castelli 124 36 7 S 57 47W
Castelló de Ampurias 156 42 15N 3 4 E
Castellón □ 156 40 15N 0 5W
Castellón de la Plana 156 39 58N 0 3W
Castellote 156 40 48N 0 15W
Castelltersol 156 41 45N 2 8 E
Castelmáuro 165 41 50N 14 40 E
Castelnau-de-Médoc 140 45 2N 0 48W
Castelnaudary 140 43 20N 1 58 E
Castelnovo ne' Monti 162 44 27N 10 26 E
Castelnuovo di Val di Cécina 162 43 12N 10 54 E
Castelo 121 20 33 S 41 14 E
Castelo Branco 154 39 50N 7 31W
Castelo Branco □ 154 39 52N 7 45W
Castelo de Paiva 154 41 2N 8 16W
Castelo de Vide 155 39 25N 7 27W
Castelo do Piauí 120 5 20 S 41 33W
Castelsarrasin 140 44 2N 1 7 E
Casteltérmini 164 37 32N 13 38 E
Castelvetrano 164 37 40N 12 46 E
Castendo 253 8 39 S 14 12 E
Casterton 231 37 30 S 141 30 E
Castets 140 43 52N 1 6W
Castiglione del Lago 163 43 7N 12 3 E
Castiglione della Pescáia 162 42 46N 10 53 E
Castiglione della Stiviere 162 45 23N 10 30 E
Castiglione Fiorentino 163 43 20N 11 55 E
Castilblanco 155 39 17N 5 5W
Castilla 122 5 12 S 80 38W
Castilla, Playa de 155 37 0N 6 33W
Castilla La Mancha 155 39 30N 3 30W
Castilla La Nueva 155 39 45N 3 20W
Castilla La Vieja 154 41 55N 4 0W
Castilla y Leon 154 42 0N 5 0E
Castillon, Barrage de 141 43 53N 6 33 E
Castillon-en-Couserans 140 42 56N 1 1 E
Castillon-la-Bataille 140 44 51N 0 2W
Castillonès 140 44 39N 0 37 E
Castillos 125 34 12 S 53 52W
Castle Douglas 134 54 57N 3 57W
Castle Mountain 91 51 16N 115 55W
Castle Point 234 40 54 S 176 15 E
Castle Rock 93 52 32N 122 29W
Castlebar 135 53 52N 9 17W
Castleblaney 135 54 7N 6 44W
Castlecliff 234 39 57 S 174 59 E
Castlegar 93 49 20N 117 40W
Castlemaine 231 37 2 S 144 12 E
Castlereagh 135 53 47N 8 30W
Castlereagh □ 135 54 33N 5 53W
Castlereagh → 233 30 12 S 147 32 E
Castlereagh B. 230 12 10 S 135 10 E
Castletown 132 54 4N 4 40W
Castletown Bearhaven 135 51 40N 9 54W
Castlevale 230 24 30 S 146 48 E
Castolón 101 29 8N 103 31W
Castor 91 52 15N 111 50W
Castor → 78 53 24N 78 58W
Castres 140 43 37N 2 13 E
Castricum 142 52 33N 4 40 E
Castries 113 14 0N 60 50W
Castril 157 37 48N 2 46W
Castro, Brazil 125 24 45 S 50 0W
Castro, Chile 126 42 30 S 73 50W
Castro Alves 121 12 46 S 39 33W
Castro del Río 155 37 41N 4 29W
Castro Marim 155 37 13N 7 26W
Castro Urdiales 156 43 23N 3 11W
Castro Verde 155 37 41N 8 4W
Castrojeriz 154 42 17N 4 9W
Castropol 154 43 32N 7 0W
Castroreale 165 38 5N 15 15 E
Castrovillari 165 39 49N 16 11 E
Castrovirreyna 122 13 20 S 75 18W
Castuera 155 38 43N 5 37W
Casummit Lake 86 51 29N 92 22W
Cat Ba, Dao 204 20 50N 107 0 E
Cat I. 113 24 30N 75 30W
Çat L. 86 51 40N 91 50W
Čata 151 47 58N 18 38 E
Catabola 253 12 9 S 17 16 E
Catacamas 112 14 54N 85 56W
Catacáos 122 5 20 S 80 45W
Cataguases 121 21 23 S 42 39W
Catagupan 211 8 1N 116 58 E
Catalão 121 18 10 S 47 57W
Catalina 79 48 31N 53 4W
Catalonia = Cataluña □ 156 41 40N 1 15 E
Cataluña □ 156 41 40N 1 15 E
Catamarca 124 28 30 S 65 50W
Catamarca □ 124 27 0 S 65 50W
Catanauan 210 13 36N 122 19 E
Catanduanes 210 13 50N 124 20 E
Catanduanes Island 210 13 45N 124 15 E
Catanduva 125 21 5 S 48 58W
Catánia 165 37 31N 15 4 E
Catánia, G. di 165 37 25N 15 8 E
Catanzaro 165 38 54N 16 38 E
Catarman, Camiguin, Phil. 211 9 8N 124 40 E
Catarman, N. Samar, Phil. 210 12 28N 124 35 E
Catbalogan 211 11 46N 124 53 E
Cateau, Le 139 50 6N 3 30 E
Cateel 211 7 47N 126 24 E
Cateel Bay 211 7 54N 126 25 E
Catemaco 109 18 25N 95 7W
Catemaco, L. 109 18 25N 95 5W
Catende, Angola 253 11 14 S 21 30 E
Catende, Brazil 120 8 40 S 35 43W
Catete 253 9 6 S 13 43 E
Cathcart, Australia 233 36 52 S 149 24 E
Cathcart, S. Africa 254 32 18 S 27 10 E
Cathedral Prov. Park 93 49 5N 120 0W
Catio 246 11 17N 15 15W
Catismiña 119 4 5N 63 40W
Catita 120 9 31 S 43 1W
Catmon 211 10 43N 124 1 E
Catoche, C. 111 21 35N 87 5W
Catolé do Rocha 120 6 21 S 37 45W
Catorce 103 23 42N 100 54W
Catorce, Sa. 103 23 36N 100 52W
Catral 157 38 10N 0 47W
Catria, Mt. 163 43 28N 12 42 E
Catrimani 119 0 27N 61 41W
Catrimani → 119 0 28N 61 44W
Catt, Mt. 230 13 49 S 134 23 E
Cattólica 163 43 58N 12 43 E
Cattólica Eraclea 164 37 27N 13 24 E
Catu 121 12 21 S 38 23W
Catuala 254 16 25 S 19 2 E
Catumbela 253 12 25 S 13 34 E
Catur 251 13 45 S 35 30 E
Catwick Is. 205 10 0N 109 0 E
Cauayan 210 16 56N 121 46 E
Cauca □ 118 2 30N 76 50W
Cauca → 118 8 54N 74 28W
Caucaia 120 3 40 S 38 35W
Caucasia 118 8 0N 75 12W
Caucasus Mts. = Bolshoi Kavkas 181 42 50N 44 0 E
Cauchy, L. 80 50 36N 60 46W
Caudebec-en-Caux 138 49 30N 0 42 E
Caudete 157 38 42N 1 2W
Caudry 139 50 7N 3 22 E
Caulnes 138 48 18N 2 10W
Caulónia 165 38 23N 16 25 E
Caúngula 253 8 26 S 18 38 E
Cauquenes 124 36 0 S 72 22W
Caura → 119 7 38N 64 53W
Caurés → 119 1 21 S 62 20W
Cauresi → 251 17 8 S 33 0 E
Causapscal 80 48 19N 67 12W
Causapscal, Parc Prov. de 80 48 15N 67 0W
Caussade 140 44 10N 1 33 E
Cauterets 140 42 52N 0 8W
Cautín □ 126 39 0 S 72 30W
Caution C. 92 51 10N 127 47W
Caux, Pays de 138 49 38N 0 35 E
Cava dei Tirreni 165 40 42N 14 42 E
Cávado → 154 41 32N 8 48W
Cavaillon 141 43 50N 5 2 E
Cavalaire-sur-Mer 141 43 10N 6 33 E
Cavalcante 121 13 48 S 47 30W
Cavalerie, La 140 44 0N 3 10 E
Cavalese 163 46 17N 11 29 E
Cavalli Is. 234 35 0 S 173 58 E
Cavallo, Île de 141 41 22N 9 16 E
Cavally → 246 4 22N 7 32W
Cavan 135 54 0N 7 22W
Cavan □ 135 53 58N 7 10W
Cavárzere 163 45 8N 12 6 E
Cavenagh Range 229 26 12 S 127 55 E
Cavendish 231 37 31 S 142 2 E
Caviana, I. 120 0 10N 50 10W
Cavite 210 14 29N 120 55 E
Cavite □ 210 14 15N 120 50 E
Cavour 162 44 47N 7 22 E
Cavtat 166 42 35N 18 13 E
Cawasachouane, L. 82 47 27N 77 45W
Cawkers Well 232 31 41 S 142 57 E
Cawndilla, L. 231 32 30 S 142 15 E
Cawnpore = Kanpur 199 26 28N 80 20 E
Caxias 120 4 55 S 43 20W
Caxias do Sul 125 29 10 S 51 10W
Caxine, C. 240 35 56N 0 27W
Caxito 253 8 30 S 13 30 E
Caxopa 253 11 52 S 20 52 E
Cay Sal Bank 112 23 45N 80 0W
Cayambe 118 0 3N 78 8W
Cayambe, Vol. 118 0 2N 77 59W
Caycuse 92 48 53N 124 22W
Cayenne 119 5 0N 52 18W
Cayenne □ 119 4 0N 53 0W
Cayes, Les 113 18 15N 73 46W
Cayeux-sur-Mer 139 50 10N 1 30 E
Cayley 91 50 27N 113 51W
Caylus 140 44 15N 1 47 E
Cayman Brac 112 19 43N 79 49W
Cayman Is. 112 19 40N 80 30W
Cayo Romano 113 22 0N 78 0W
Cayuga 84 42 59N 79 50W
Cazadero 107 20 19N 99 52W
Cazaje 253 11 2 S 20 45 E
Cazalla de la Sierra 155 37 56N 5 45W
Căzăneşti 170 44 36N 27 3 E
Cazaux et de Sanguinet, Étang de 140 44 29N 1 10W
Cazères 140 43 13N 1 5 E
Çazin 163 44 57N 15 57 E
Çazma 163 45 45N 16 39 E
Čazma → 163 45 35N 16 29 E
Cazombo 253 11 54 S 22 56 E
Cazones 108 20 43N 97 19W
Cazones, R. → 108 20 44N 97 12W
Cazorla, Spain 157 37 55N 3 2W
Cazorla, Venezuela 118 8 1N 67 0W
Cazorla, Sierra de 157 38 5N 2 55W
Cea → 154 42 0N 5 36W
Ceamurlia de Jos 170 44 43N 28 47 E
Ceanannus Mor 135 53 42N 6 53W
Ceará = Fortaleza 120 3 45 S 38 35W
Ceará □ 120 5 0 S 40 0W

Ceará Mirim . . . . . . 120 5 38 S 35 25W
Ceauru, L. . . . . 170 44 58N 23 11 E
Cebaco, I. de 112 7 33N 81 9W
Ceballos 105 26 32N 104 9W
Cebollar . . . . 124 29 10 S 66 35W
Cebollera, Sierra de 156 42 0N 2 30W
Ceboruco, Volcán . . 104 21 9N 104 30W
Cebreros 154 40 27N 4 28W
Cebu . . . . 211 10 18N 123 54 E
Ceccano . . . . 164 41 34N 13 18 E
Cece . . . . 151 46 46N 18 39 E
Cechi 246 6 15N 4 25W
Cecil Plains . . . . 231 27 30 S 151 11 E
Cécina . . . . 162 43 19N 10 33 E
Cécina → . . . . 162 43 19N 10 29 E
Ceclavin 154 39 50N 6 45W
Cedar L., Man.,
Canada 89 53 10N 100 0W
Cedar L., Ont.,
Canada 85 46 2N 78 30W
Cedarvale 76 55 1N 128 22W
Cedeira 154 43 39N 8 2W
Cedral,
Quintana Roo,
Mexico 111 20 20N 86 58W
Cedral,
San Luis Potosí,
Mexico 103 23 50N 100 45W
Cedrino → . . . . 164 40 23N 9 44 E
Cedro . . . . 120 6 34 S 39 3W
Cedros 100 27 43N 109 15W
Cedros, I. 99 28 12N 115 15W
Ceduna . . . . 231 32 7 S 133 46 E
Cedynia . . . . 152 52 53N 14 12 E
Cefalù . . . . 165 38 3N 14 1 E
Cega → 154 41 33N 4 46W
Cegléd . . . . 151 47 11N 19 47 E
Céglie Messápico . . . 165 40 39N 17 31 E
Cehegín 157 38 6N 1 48W
Ceheng . . . . 216 24 58N 105 48 E
Cehu-Silvaniei . . . . . 170 47 24N 23 9 E
Ceiba, La 112 15 40N 86 50W
Ceica . . . . 170 46 53N 22 10 E
Ceira → 154 40 13N 8 16W
Cekhira . . . . 241 34 20N 10 5 E
Çekmece . . . . 190 36 13N 36 7 E
Cela . . . . 253 11 25 S 15 7 E
Celano . . . . 163 42 6N 13 30 E
Celanova 154 42 9N 7 58W
Celaya 107 20 31N 100 37W
Celbridge 135 53 20N 6 33W
Celebes =
Sulawesi □ . . . . . . 207 2 0 S 120 0 E
Celebes Sea . . . . 207 3 0N 123 0 E
Celendín . . . . 122 6 52 S 78 10W
Çelestún 111 20 52N 90 24W
Čelić . . . . 166 44 43N 18 47 E
Celica . . . . 118 4 7 S 79 59W
Celje . . . . 163 46 16N 15 18 E
Celldömölk . . . . 151 47 16N 17 10 E
Celle . . . . 146 52 37N 10 4 E
Celle, La 107 20 14N 101 34W
Celles . . . . 143 50 42N 3 28 E
Celorico da Beira . . . 154 40 38N 7 24W
Cenepa → . . . . 118 4 40 S 78 10W
Cengong . . . . 216 27 13N 108 44 E
Cenis, Col du Mt. . . 141 45 15N 6 55 E
Ceno → . . . . 162 44 4N 10 5 E
Cenon 140 44 50N 0 33W
Cenotillo 111 20 58N 88 37W
Centallo . . . . 162 44 30N 7 35 E
Centenário do Sul . . 121 22 48 S 51 36W
Cento . . . . 163 44 43N 11 16 E
Central . . . . 120 11 8 S 42 8W
Central □, Kenya . . 250 0 30 S 37 30 E
Central □, Malawi . . 251 13 30 S 33 30 E
Central □, U.K. 134 56 10N 4 30W
Central □, Zambia . 251 14 25 S 28 50 E
Central, Cordillera,
Bolivia . . . . 123 18 30 S 64 55W
Central, Cordillera,
Colombia 118 5 0N 75 0W
Central, Cordillera,
C. Rica 112 10 10N 84 5W
Central, Cordillera,
Dom. Rep. 113 19 15N 71 0W
Central, Cordillera,
Peru . . . . 122 7 0 S 77 30W
Central African
Republic ■ . . . . . . 252 7 0N 20 0 E
Central Butte 88 50 48N 106 31W
Central I. . . . . 250 3 30N 36 0 E
Central Makran
Range . . . . 197 26 30N 64 15 E
Central Patricia 86 51 30N 90 9W
Central Ra. . . . . 227 5 0 S 143 0 E
Central Russian
Uplands . . . . 130 54 0N 36 0 E
Central Siberian
Plateau . . . . 186 65 0N 105 0 E
Centreville, N.B.,
Canada 81 46 26N 67 43W
Centreville, N.S.,
Canada 81 44 33N 66 1W
Centúripe . . . . 165 37 37N 14 41 E
Cephalonia =
Kefallinía . . . . 169 38 20N 20 30 E
Čepin . . . . 166 45 32N 18 34 E
Ceprano . . . . 164 41 33N 13 30 E
Ceptura . . . . 170 45 1N 26 21 E
Cepu . . . . 209 7 9 S 111 35 E
Ceram = Seram . . . . 207 3 10 S 129 0 E
Ceram Sea = Seram
Sea . . . . 207 2 30 S 128 30 E
Cerbère . . . . 140 42 26N 3 10 E
Cerbicales, Îles . . . . 141 41 33N 9 22 E
Cerbu . . . . 170 44 46N 24 46 E
Cercal 155 37 48N 8 40W
Cercemaggiore . . . . . 165 41 27N 14 43 E
Cerdaña . . . . 156 42 22N 1 35 E
Cerdedo 154 42 33N 8 23W
Cère → . . . . 140 44 55N 1 49 E
Cerea . . . . 163 45 12N 11 13 E
Cereal 91 51 25N 110 48W
Ceres, Argentina . . . 124 29 55 S 61 55W
Ceres, Brazil . . . . . . 121 15 17 S 49 35W
Ceres, Italy . . . . 162 45 19N 7 22 E
Ceres, S. Africa . . . . 254 33 21 S 19 18 E
Céret . . . . 140 42 30N 2 42 E
Cereté 118 8 53N 75 48W
Cerf, L. de 82 46 16N 75 30W
Cerfontaine . . . . 143 50 11N 4 26 E
Cerignola . . . . 165 41 17N 15 53 E
Cerigo = Kíthira . . . 169 36 9N 23 0 E
Cérilly . . . . 140 46 37N 2 50 E
Cerisiers . . . . 139 48 8N 3 30 E
Cerizay 138 46 50N 0 40W
Cerknica . . . . 163 45 48N 14 21 E
Cermerno . . . . 166 43 35N 20 25 E
Cerna . . . . 170 45 4N 28 17 E
Cerna → . . . . 170 44 45N 24 0 E
Cernavodă . . . . 170 44 22N 28 3 E
Cernay . . . . 139 47 44N 7 10 E
Cernik . . . . 166 45 17N 17 22 E
Cerralvo 102 26 6N 99 37W
Cerralvo, I. 99 24 15N 109 55W
Cerreto Sannita . . . . 165 41 17N 14 34 E
Cerritos 103 22 26N 100 17W
Cerro Agudo 104 25 27N 107 37W
Cerro Azul 108 21 12N 97 44W
Cerro Prieto 104 26 19N 106 11W
Cerro Sombrero . . . . 126 52 45 S 69 15W
Certaldo . . . . 162 43 32N 11 2 E
Cervaro → . . . . 165 41 30N 15 52 E
Cervera . . . . 156 41 40N 1 16 E
Cervera de Pisuerga 154 42 51N 4 30W
Cervera del Río
Alhama 156 42 2N 1 58W
Cérvia . . . . 163 44 15N 12 20 E
Cervignano del
Friuli . . . . 163 45 49N 13 20 E
Cervinara . . . . 165 41 2N 14 36 E
Cervione . . . . 141 42 20N 9 29 E
Cervo 154 43 40N 7 24W
César □ 118 9 0N 73 30W
Cesaro . . . . 165 37 50N 14 38 E
Cesena . . . . 163 44 9N 12 14 E
Cesenático . . . . 163 44 12N 12 22 E
Cēsis . . . . 178 57 17N 25 28 E
Česká Lípa . . . . 150 50 45N 14 30 E
Ceska Socialistická
Republika □ . . . . . 150 49 30N 14 40 E
Česká Třebová . . . . . 151 49 54N 16 27 E
České Budějovice . . 150 48 55N 14 25 E
České Velenice . . . . 150 48 45N 15 1 E
Ceskomoravská
Vrchovina . . . . 150 49 30N 15 40 E
Český Brod . . . . 150 50 4N 14 52 E
Český Krumlov . . . . 150 48 43N 14 21 E
Český Těšín . . . . 151 49 45N 18 39 E
Ceşme . . . . 169 38 20N 26 23 E
Cessnock . . . . 231 32 50 S 151 21 E
Cestas 140 44 44N 0 41W
Cestos → 246 5 40N 9 10W
Cetate . . . . 170 44 7N 23 2 E
Cétin Grad . . . . 163 45 9N 15 45 E
Cetina → . . . . 163 43 26N 16 42 E
Cetinje . . . . 166 42 23N 18 59 E
Çetmi . . . . 190 36 52N 32 38 E
Cetraro . . . . 165 39 30N 15 56 E
Ceuta 240 35 52N 5 18W
Ceva . . . . 162 44 23N 8 3 E
Cévennes . . . . 140 44 10N 3 50 E
Ceyhan . . . . 190 37 4N 35 47 E
Ceyhan → . . . . 177 36 38N 35 8 E
Ceylon = Sri
Lanka ■ . . . . 201 7 30N 80 50 E
Ceylon 88 49 27N 104 36W
Cèze → . . . . 141 44 13N 4 43 E
Cha-am . . . . 204 12 48N 99 58 E
Chá Pungana . . . . . . 253 13 44 S 18 39 E
Chaam . . . . 143 51 30N 4 52 E
Chaati I. 92 53 7N 132 30W
Chabeuil . . . . 141 44 54N 5 1 E
Chabihau 111 21 21N 89 7W
Chablais . . . . 141 46 20N 6 36 E
Chablé 110 17 51N 91 46W
Chablis . . . . 139 47 47N 3 48 E
Chabounia . . . . 241 35 30N 2 38 E
Chacabuco . . . . 124 34 40 S 60 27W
Chacalapa 109 15 52N 95 57W
Chachapoyas . . . . . . 122 6 15 S 77 50W
Chachasp . . . . 122 15 30 S 72 15W
Chachoengsao . . . . . 204 13 42N 101 5 E
Chachro . . . . 198 25 5N 70 15 E
Chaco □ . . . . 124 26 30 S 61 0W
Chad ■ . . . . 243 15 0N 17 15 E
Chad, L. = Tchad,
L. . . . . 243 13 30N 14 30 E
Chadan . . . . 185 51 17N 91 35 E
Chadarinskoye
Vdkhr. . . . . 183 41 0N 68 20 E
Chadileuvú → . . . . . 124 37 46 S 66 0W
Chadiza . . . . 251 14 45 S 32 27 E
Chadyr-Lunga . . . . . 180 46 3N 28 51 E
Chae Hom . . . . 204 18 43N 99 35 E
Chaem → . . . . 204 18 11N 98 38 E
Chaeryŏng . . . . 215 38 24N 125 36 E
Chagda . . . . 185 58 45N 130 38 E
Chagny . . . . 139 46 57N 4 45 E
Chagoda . . . . 178 59 10N 35 15 E
Chagos Arch. . . . . . . 196 6 0 S 72 0 E
Chāh Ākhvor . . . . . . 193 32 41N 59 40 E
Chāh Bahār . . . . 193 25 20N 60 40 E
Chāh-e-Malek . . . . . 193 28 35N 59 7 E
Chāh Gay Hills . . . . 197 29 30N 64 0 E
Chāh Kavīr . . . . 193 31 45N 54 52 E
Chahār Borjak . . . . . 197 30 17N 62 3 E
Chahtung . . . . 202 26 41N 98 10 E
Chahuites 109 16 17N 94 11W
Chaillé-les-Marais . . 140 46 25N 1 2W
Chainat . . . . 204 15 11N 100 8 E
Chaise-Dieu, La . . . . 140 45 20N 3 40 E
Chaitén . . . . 126 42 55 S 72 43W
Chaiya . . . . 205 9 23N 99 14 E
Chaize-le-Vicomte,
La 138 46 40N 1 18W
Chaj Doab . . . . 198 32 15N 73 0 E
Chajari . . . . 124 30 42 S 58 0W
Chakaria . . . . 202 21 45N 92 5 E
Chake Chake . . . . . . 250 5 15 S 39 45 E
Chakhānsūr . . . . 197 31 10N 62 0 E
Chakonipau, L. 78 56 18N 68 30W
Chakradharpur . . . . . 199 22 45N 85 40 E
Chakwadam . . . . 202 27 29N 98 31 E
Chakwal . . . . 197 32 56N 72 53 E
Chala . . . . 122 15 48 S 74 20W
Chalais . . . . 140 45 16N 0 3 E
Chalakudi . . . . 201 10 18N 76 20 E
Chalchihuites 105 23 29N 103 53W
Chalcis = Khalkís . . 169 38 27N 23 42 E
Chaleur B. 81 47 55N 65 30W
Chalhuanca . . . . 122 14 15 S 73 15W
Chalindrey . . . . 139 47 48N 5 26 E
Chaling . . . . 217 26 58N 113 30 E
Chalisgaon . . . . 200 20 30N 75 10 E
Chalk River 85 46 1N 77 27W
Chalkar . . . . 181 50 40N 51 53 E
Chalkar, Ozero . . . . 181 50 50N 51 50 E
Chalky Inlet . . . . 235 46 3 S 166 31 E
Challans 138 46 50N 1 52W
Challapata . . . . 122 18 53 S 66 50W
Challerange . . . . 139 49 18N 4 46 E
Chalna . . . . 199 22 36N 89 35 E
Chalon-sur-Saône . . . 139 46 48N 4 50 E
Chalonnes 138 47 20N 0 45W
Châlons-sur-Marne . 139 48 58N 4 20 E
Châlus . . . . 140 45 39N 0 58 E
Chalyaphum . . . . 204 15 48N 102 2 E
Cham, Germany . . . . 147 49 12N 12 40 E
Cham, Switz. . . . . . . 149 47 11N 8 28 E
Cham, Cu Lao . . . . . 204 15 57N 108 30 E
Chaman . . . . 197 30 58N 66 25 E
Chamartín de la
Rosa 156 40 28N 3 40W
Chamba . . . . 198 32 35N 76 10 E
Chambal → . . . . 199 26 29N 79 15 E
Chamberlain → . . . . 228 15 30 S 127 54 E
Chambéry . . . . 141 45 34N 5 55 E
Chambly 83 45 27N 73 17W
Chambois . . . . 138 48 48N 0 6 E
Chambon-
Feugerolles, Le . . . 141 45 24N 4 18 E
Chambord 83 48 25N 72 6W
Chambri L. . . . . 227 4 15 S 143 10 E
Chamchamal . . . . . . 192 35 32N 44 50 E
Chamela 106 19 32N 105 5W
Chamela, B. 106 19 33N 105 7W
Chamical . . . . 124 30 22 S 66 27W
Chamkar Luong . . . . 205 11 0N 103 45 E
Chamonix . . . . 141 45 55N 6 51 E
Chamouchouane → . 83 48 37N 72 20W
Champa . . . . 199 22 2N 82 43 E
Champagne, Canada 76 60 49N 136 30W
Champagne, France 139 49 0N 4 40 E
Champagne, Plaine
de . . . . 139 49 0N 4 30 E
Champagnole . . . . . . 139 46 45N 5 55 E
Champassak . . . . 204 14 53N 105 52 E
Champaubert . . . . . . 139 48 50N 3 45 E
Champdeniers 140 46 29N 0 25W
Champdoré, L. 78 55 55N 65 49W
Champeix . . . . 140 45 37N 3 8 E
Champion 91 50 14N 113 9W
Champlain 74 46 27N 72 24W
Champneuf 82 48 35N 77 30W
Champotón 111 19 21N 90 43W
Champotón, R. → . . 111 19 21N 90 43W
Chamrajnagar . . . . . . 201 11 52N 76 52 E
Chamusca 155 39 21N 8 29W
Chan Chan . . . . 122 8 7 S 79 0W
Chan-Kom 111 20 33N 88 31W
Chana . . . . 205 6 55N 100 44 E
Chanal 110 16 43N 92 24W
Chañaral . . . . 124 26 23 S 70 40W
Chanārān . . . . 193 36 39N 59 6 E
Chanasma . . . . 198 23 44N 72 5 E
Chancay . . . . 122 11 32 S 77 25W
Chance Harbour 81 45 7N 66 21W
Chancy . . . . 148 46 8N 6 0 E
Chandannagar . . . . . 199 22 52N 88 24 E
Chandausi . . . . 199 28 27N 78 49 E
Chandigarh . . . . 198 30 43N 76 47 E
Chandler, Australia . 231 27 0 S 133 19 E
Chandler, Canada . . 80 48 18N 64 46W
Chandlers Peak . . . . 233 30 15 S 151 48 E
Chandless → . . . . . . 122 9 8 S 69 51W
Chandpur, Bangla. . . 202 23 8N 90 45 E
Chandpur, India . . . . 198 29 8N 78 19 E
Chandrapur . . . . 200 19 57N 79 25 E
Chānf . . . . 193 26 38N 60 29 E
Chang . . . . 198 26 59N 68 30 E
Chang, Ko . . . . 205 12 0N 102 23 E
Chang Jiang → . . . . 217 31 48N 121 10 E
Changa . . . . 199 33 53N 77 35 E
Changanacheri . . . . . 201 9 25N 76 31 E
Changbai . . . . 215 41 25N 128 5 E
Changbai Shan . . . . . 215 42 20N 129 0 E
Ch'angchou =
Changzhou . . . . . . 217 31 47N 119 58 E
Changchun . . . . 215 43 57N 125 17 E
Changchunling . . . . . 215 45 18N 125 27 E
Changde . . . . 217 29 4N 111 35 E
Changdo-ri . . . . 215 38 30N 127 40 E
Change Islands 79 49 40N 54 25W
Changfeng . . . . 217 32 28N 117 10 E
Changhai =
Shanghai . . . . 217 31 15N 121 26 E
Changhua . . . . 217 30 12N 119 12 E
Changhŭng . . . . 215 34 41N 126 52 E
Changhŭngni . . . . . . 215 40 24N 128 19 E
Changjiang . . . . 204 19 20N 108 55 E
Changjin . . . . 215 40 23N 127 15 E
Changjin-chŏsuji . . . 215 40 30N 127 15 E
Changle . . . . 217 25 59N 119 27 E
Changli . . . . 215 39 40N 119 13 E
Changling . . . . 215 44 20N 123 58 E
Changlun . . . . 205 6 25N 100 26 E
Changning, Hunan,
China . . . . 217 26 28N 112 22 E
Changning, Yunnan,
China . . . . 216 24 45N 99 30 E
Changping . . . . 214 40 14N 116 12 E
Changsha . . . . 217 28 12N 113 0 E
Changshan . . . . 217 28 55N 118 27 E
Changshou . . . . 216 29 51N 107 8 E
Changshu . . . . 217 31 38N 120 43 E
Changshun . . . . 216 26 3N 106 25 E
Changtai . . . . 217 24 35N 117 42 E
Changting . . . . 217 25 50N 116 22 E
Changwu . . . . 214 35 10N 107 45 E
Changxing . . . . 217 31 0N 119 55 E
Changyang . . . . 217 30 30N 111 10 E
Changyi . . . . 215 36 40N 119 30 E
Changyŏn . . . . 215 38 15N 125 6 E
Changyuan . . . . 214 35 15N 114 42 E
Changzhi . . . . 214 36 10N 113 6 E
Changzhou . . . . 217 31 47N 119 58 E
Chanhanga . . . . 254 16 0 S 14 8 E
Chanlar . . . . 181 40 25N 46 10 E
Channapatna . . . . . . 201 12 40N 77 15 E
Channel Is. 138 49 30N 2 40W
Channel-Port aux
Basques 79 47 30N 59 9W
Chantada 154 42 36N 7 46W
Chantengo, L. 107 16 38N 99 5W
Chanthaburi . . . . 204 12 38N 102 12 E
Chantilly . . . . 139 49 12N 2 29 E
Chantonnay 138 46 40N 1 3W
Chantrey Inlet 95 67 48N 96 20W
Chanza → 155 37 32N 7 30W
Chao Hu . . . . 217 31 30N 117 30 E
Chao Phraya → . . . . 204 13 32N 100 36 E
Chao Phraya
Lowlands . . . . 204 15 30N 100 0 E
Chao Xian . . . . 217 31 38N 117 50 E
Chao'an . . . . 217 23 42N 116 32 E
Chaocheng . . . . 214 36 4N 115 37 E
Chaoyang,
Guangdong,
China . . . . 217 23 17N 116 30 E
Chaoyang, Liaoning,
China . . . . 215 41 35N 120 22 E
Chapada dos
Guimarães . . . . 123 15 26 S 55 45W
Chapais 82 49 47N 74 51W

Chapala, Mexico **106** 20 18N 103 12W
Chapala, Mozam. **251** 15 50 S 37 35 E
Chapala, L. de **106** 20 15N 103 0W
Chapalilla **104** 21 11N 104 38W
Chapantongo **107** 20 17N 99 25W
Chaparé → **123** 15 58 S 64 42W
Chaparmukh **202** 26 12N 92 31 E
Chaparral **118** 3 43N 75 28W
Chapayevo **181** 50 25N 51 10 E
Chapayevsk **179** 53 0N 49 40 E
Chapeau **82** 45 54N 77 4W
Chapecó **125** 27 14 S 52 41W
Chapelle-d'Angillon, La **139** 47 21N 2 25 E
Chapelle-Glain, La **138** 47 38N 1 11W
Chapeyevo **182** 50 12N 51 10 E
Chapleau **87** 47 50N 83 24W
Chaplin **88** 50 28N 106 40W
Chaplin L. **88** 50 22N 106 36W
Chaplino **180** 48 8N 36 15 E
Chaplygin **179** 53 15N 40 0 E
Chapman, Mt. **93** 51 56N 118 20W
Chapulhuacán **107** 21 10N 98 54W
Chapultenango **110** 17 19N 93 7W
Chapultepec **107** 16 43N 99 36W
Châr **240** 21 32N 12 45 E
Chara **185** 56 54N 118 20 E
Charadai **124** 27 35 S 60 0W
Charagua **123** 19 45 S 63 10W
Charalá **118** 6 17N 73 10W
Charambirá, Punta **118** 4 16N 77 32W
Charaña **122** 17 30 S 69 25W
Charapita **118** 0 37 S 74 21W
Charata **124** 27 13 S 61 14W
Charay **104** 26 1N 108 50W
Charcas **103** 23 8N 101 7W
Charcas, Sa. de **103** 23 10N 101 10W
Charco Blanco **103** 22 38N 100 31W
Charco de Peñas **101** 28 31N 104 59W
Charcoal L. **77** 58 49N 102 22W
Charcos de Figueroa **102** 27 45N 102 11W
Chard **133** 50 52N 2 59W
Chardara **183** 41 16N 67 59 E
Chardara, Step **183** 42 20N 68 0 E
Chardarinskoye Vdkhr. **183** 41 10N 68 15 E
Charduar **202** 26 51N 92 46 E
Chardzhou **183** 39 6N 63 34 E
Charente **140** 45 40N 0 5 E
Charente □ **140** 45 50N 0 16 E
Charente → **140** 45 57N 1 5W
Charente-Maritime □ **140** 45 30N 0 35W
Charentsavan **181** 40 35N 44 41 E
Charette **83** 46 27N 72 56W
Chari → **243** 12 58N 14 31 E
Chārīkār **197** 35 0N 69 10 E
Charité, La **139** 47 10N 3 0 E
Charity **119** 7 24N 58 36W
Charkhari **199** 25 24N 79 45 E
Charkhi Dadri **198** 28 37N 76 17 E
Charleroi **143** 50 24N 4 27 E
Charles L. **77** 59 50N 110 33W
Charlesbourg **83** 46 51N 71 16W
Charleston L. **85** 44 32N 76 0W
Charlestown **255** 27 26 S 29 53 E
Charlesville **253** 5 27 S 20 59 E
Charleville = Rath Luirc **135** 52 21N 8 40W
Charleville **231** 26 24 S 146 15 E
Charleville-Mézières **139** 49 44N 4 40 E
Charlieu **141** 46 10N 4 10 E
Charlo **81** 47 59N 66 17W
Charlotte Amalie **113** 18 22N 64 56W
Charlotte L. **92** 52 12N 125 19W
Charlottenberg **172** 59 54N 12 17 E
Charlottetown **81** 46 14N 63 8W
Charlton **231** 36 16 S 143 24 E
Charlton I. **78** 52 0N 79 20W
Charmes **139** 48 22N 6 17 E
Charny **83** 46 43N 71 15W
Charolles **141** 46 27N 4 16 E
Charost **139** 47 0N 2 7 E
Charouine **241** 29 0N 0 15W
Charre **251** 17 13 S 35 10 E
Charron L. **89** 52 44N 95 15W
Charroux **140** 46 9N 0 25 E
Charsadda **198** 34 7N 71 45 E
Charters Towers **230** 20 5 S 146 13 E
Chartre, La **138** 47 42N 0 34 E
Chartres **138** 48 29N 1 30 E
Charvakskoye Vdkhr. **183** 41 35N 70 0 E
Chascomús **124** 35 30 S 58 0W
Chase **93** 50 50N 119 41W
Chasefu **251** 11 55 S 33 8 E
Chaslands Mistake **235** 46 38 S 169 22 E
Chasm **93** 51 13N 121 30W
Chasovnya-Uchurskaya **185** 57 15N 132 50 E
Chasseneuil-sur-Bonnieure **140** 45 52N 0 29 E
Chāt **193** 37 59N 55 16 E
Châtaigneraie, La **138** 46 38N 0 45W
Chatal Balkan = Udvoy Balkan **167** 42 50N 26 50 E
Château, Le **140** 45 52N 1 12W
Château-Chinon **139** 47 4N 3 56 E
Château d'Oex **148** 46 28N 7 8 E
Château-du-Loir **138** 47 40N 0 25 E
Château-Gontier **138** 47 50N 0 48W
Château-la-Vallière **138** 47 30N 0 20 E
Château-Landon **139** 48 8N 2 40 E
Château-Porcien **139** 49 31N 4 13 E
Château-Renault **138** 47 36N 0 56 E
Château-Salins **139** 48 50N 6 30 E
Château-Thierry **139** 49 3N 3 20 E
Châteaubourg **138** 48 7N 1 25W
Châteaubriant **138** 47 43N 1 23W
Châteaudun **138** 48 3N 1 20 E
Châteaugiron **138** 48 3N 1 30W
Châteauguay, L. **78** 56 26N 70 3W
Châteaulin **138** 48 11N 4 8W
Châteaumeillant **140** 46 35N 2 12 E
Châteauneuf **138** 48 35N 1 15 E
Châteauneuf-du-Faou **138** 48 11N 3 50W
Châteauneuf-sur-Charente **140** 45 36N 0 3W
Châteauneuf-sur-Cher **139** 46 52N 2 18 E
Châteauneuf-sur-Loire **139** 47 52N 2 13 E
Châteaurenard **141** 43 53N 4 51 E
Châteauroux **139** 46 50N 1 40 E
Châteauvert, L. **83** 47 39N 73 56W
Châteaux-Arnoux **141** 44 6N 6 0 E
Châtel-St.-Denis **148** 46 32N 6 54 E
Châtelaillon-Plage **140** 46 5N 1 5W
Châtelard, Le **148** 46 4N 6 57 E
Châtelaudren **138** 48 33N 2 59W
Chatelet **143** 50 24N 4 32 E
Châtelet, Le, Cher, France **140** 46 40N 2 20 E
Châtelet, Le, Seine-et-Marne, France **139** 48 30N 2 47 E
Châtelguyon **140** 45 55N 3 4 E
Châtellerault **138** 46 50N 0 30 E
Châtelus-Malvaleix **140** 46 18N 2 1 E
Chatham, N.B., Canada **81** 47 2N 65 28W
Chatham, Ont., Canada **84** 42 24N 82 11W
Chatham, U.K. **133** 51 22N 0 32 E
Chatham, I. **126** 50 40 S 74 25W
Chatham Head **81** 47 0N 65 33W
Chatham Is. **224** 44 0 S 176 40W
Châtillon, Loiret, France **139** 47 36N 2 44 E
Châtillon, Marne, France **139** 49 5N 3 43 E
Chatillon, Italy **162** 45 45N 7 40 E
Châtillon-Coligny **139** 47 50N 2 51 E
Châtillon-en-Bazois **139** 47 3N 3 39 E
Châtillon-en-Diois **141** 44 41N 5 29 E
Châtillon-sur-Indre **138** 46 59N 1 10 E
Châtillon-sur-Seine **139** 47 50N 4 33 E
Châtillon-sur-Sèvre **138** 46 56N 0 45W
Chatkal → **183** 41 38N 70 1 E
Chatkalskiy Khrebet **183** 41 30N 70 45 E
Chatmohar **199** 24 15N 89 15 E
Chatra **199** 24 12N 84 56 E
Chatrapur **199** 19 22N 85 2 E
Châtre, La **140** 46 35N 1 59 E
Chats, L. des **85** 45 30N 76 20W
Chatsworth, Canada **84** 44 27N 80 54W
Chatsworth, Zimbabwe **251** 19 38 S 31 13 E
Chatta-Hantō **221** 34 45N 136 55 E
Chaturat **204** 15 40N 101 51 E
Chatyrkel, Ozero **183** 40 40N 75 18 E
Chatyrtash **183** 40 55N 76 25 E
Chau Doc **205** 10 42N 105 7 E
Chaudanne, Barrage de **141** 43 51N 6 32 E
Chaudes-Aigues **140** 44 51N 3 1 E
Chaudière → **83** 46 45N 71 17W
Chauffailles **141** 46 13N 4 20 E
Chauk **202** 20 53N 94 49 E
Chaukan Pass **202** 27 8N 97 10 E
Chaulnes **139** 49 48N 2 47 E
Chaumont **139** 48 7N 5 8 E
Chaumont-en-Vexin **139** 49 16N 1 53 E
Chaumont-sur-Loire **138** 47 29N 1 11 E
Chaunay **140** 46 13N 0 9 E
Chauny **139** 49 37N 3 12 E
Chausey, Îs. **138** 48 52N 1 49W
Chaussin **139** 46 59N 5 22 E
Chauvigny **138** 46 34N 0 39 E
Chauvin **91** 52 45N 110 10W
Chaux-de-Fonds, La **148** 47 7N 6 50 E
Chauzingo **107** 18 17N 99 7W
Chavantina **123** 14 40 S 52 21W
Chaves, Brazil **120** 0 15 S 49 55W
Chaves, Portugal **154** 41 45N 7 32W
Chávez, Sa. de **101** 29 17N 107 39W
Chavigny, L. **78** 58 12N 75 8W
Chavuma **253** 13 4 S 22 40 E
Chawang **205** 8 25N 99 30 E
Chayan **183** 43 5N 69 25 E
Chayek **183** 41 55N 74 30 E
Chaykovskiy **182** 56 47N 54 9 E
Chazelles-sur-Lyon **141** 45 39N 4 22 E
Chazuta **122** 6 30 S 76 0W
Cheam View **93** 49 15N 121 40W
Cheb **150** 50 9N 12 28 E
Chebarkul **182** 55 0N 60 25 E
Cheboksary **179** 56 8N 47 12 E
Chebsara **179** 59 10N 38 59 E
Chech, Erg **240** 25 0N 2 15W
Chechaouen **240** 35 9N 5 15W
Chechen, Os. **181** 43 59N 47 40 E
Checheno-Ingush A.S.S.R. □ **181** 43 30N 45 29 E
Chechon **215** 37 8N 128 12 E
Chęciny **152** 50 46N 20 28 E
Checleset B. **92** 50 5N 127 35W
Chedabucto B. **81** 45 25N 61 8W
Cheduba I. **202** 18 45N 93 40 E
Cheepash → **87** 51 3N 80 59W
Cheepay → **87** 51 25N 83 26W
Cheepie **231** 26 33 S 145 1 E
Cheeseman L. **86** 49 27N 89 20W
Chef, R. du → **83** 49 21N 73 25W
Chef-Boutonne **140** 46 7N 0 4W
Chegdomyn **185** 51 7N 133 1 E
Chegga **240** 25 27N 5 40W
Cheiron **141** 43 49N 6 58 E
Cheju Do **215** 33 29N 126 34 E
Chekalin **179** 54 10N 36 10 E
Chekiang = Zhejiang □ **217** 29 0N 120 0 E
Chekubul **111** 18 51N 90 58W
Chel = Kuru, Bahr el → **245** 8 10N 26 50 E
Chela, Sa. da **254** 16 20 S 13 20 E
Cheleken **177** 39 26N 53 7 E
Chelforó **126** 39 0 S 66 33W
Chéliff, O. → **241** 36 0N 0 8 E
Chelkar **184** 47 48N 59 39 E
Chelkar Tengiz, Solonchak **184** 48 0N 62 30 E
Chellala Dahrania **240** 33 2N 0 1 E
Chelles **139** 48 52N 2 33 E
Chełm **152** 51 8N 23 30 E
Chełm □ **152** 51 15N 23 30 E
Chełmek **152** 50 6N 19 16 E
Chełmno **152** 53 20N 18 30 E
Chelmsford **133** 51 44N 0 29 E
Chelmsford Dam **255** 27 55 S 29 59 E
Chełmża **152** 53 10N 18 39 E
Chelsea **233** 38 5 S 145 8 E
Cheltenham **133** 51 55N 2 5W
Chelva **156** 39 45N 1 0W
Chelyabinsk **182** 55 10N 61 24 E
Chelyuskin, C. **186** 77 30N 103 0 E
Chemainus **93** 48 55N 123 42W
Chemax **111** 20 39N 87 56W
Chembar = Belinskiy **179** 53 0N 43 25 E
Chemillé **138** 47 14N 0 45W
Chemnitz = Karl-Marx-Stadt **146** 50 50N 12 55 E
Chen, Gora **185** 65 16N 141 50 E
Chen Xian **217** 25 47N 113 1 E
Chenab → **197** 30 23N 71 2 E
Chenachane, O. → **240** 25 20N 3 20W
Chencha **245** 6 15N 37 32 E
Chenchiang = Zhenjiang **217** 32 11N 119 26 E
Chencoyí **111** 19 48N 90 14W
Chênée **143** 50 37N 5 37 E
Chénéville **82** 45 53N 75 3W
Cheng Xian **214** 33 43N 105 42 E
Chengalpattu **201** 12 42N 79 58 E
Chengbu **217** 26 18N 110 16 E
Chengcheng **214** 35 8N 109 56 E
Chengchou = Zhengzhou **214** 34 45N 113 34 E
Chengde **215** 40 59N 117 58 E
Chengdong Hu **217** 32 15N 116 20 E
Chengdu **216** 30 38N 104 2 E
Chengele **202** 28 47N 96 16 E
Chenggong **216** 24 52N 102 56 E
Chenggu **216** 33 10N 107 21 E
Chengjiang **216** 24 39N 103 0 E
Chengkou **216** 31 54N 108 31 E
Chengwu **214** 34 58N 115 50 E
Chengxi Hu **217** 32 15N 116 10 E
Chengyang **215** 36 18N 120 21 E
Chenil, L. **80** 51 51N 59 41W
Chenjiagang **215** 34 23N 119 47 E
Chenkán **111** 19 9N 90 57W
Chenxi **217** 28 2N 110 12 E
Cheo Reo **204** 13 25N 108 28 E
Cheom Ksan **204** 14 13N 104 56 E
Chepelare **167** 41 44N 24 40 E
Chepén **122** 7 15 S 79 23W
Chépénéhé **226** 20 47 S 167 9 E
Chepes **124** 31 20 S 66 35W
Chepo **112** 9 10N 79 6W
Cheptsa → **179** 58 36N 50 4 E
Cheptulil, Mt. **250** 1 25N 35 35 E
Cher □ **139** 47 10N 2 30 E
Cher → **138** 47 21N 0 29 E
Cheran, India **202** 25 45N 90 44 E
Cherán, Mexico **106** 19 41N 101 57W
Cherasco **162** 44 39N 7 50 E
Cheratte **143** 50 40N 5 41 E
Cherbourg **138** 49 39N 1 40W
Cherchell **241** 36 35N 2 12 E
Cherdakly **179** 54 25N 48 50 E
Cherdyn **182** 60 24N 56 29 E
Cheremkhovo **185** 53 8N 103 1 E
Cherepanovo **184** 54 15N 83 30 E
Cherepovets **179** 59 5N 37 55 E
Chergui, Chott ech **241** 34 21N 0 25 E
Cherhill **90** 53 49N 114 41W
Cherikov **178** 53 32N 31 20 E
Cherkassy **180** 49 27N 32 4 E
Cherkessk **181** 44 15N 42 5 E
Cherlak **184** 54 15N 74 55 E
Chermoz **182** 58 46N 56 10 E
Chernak **183** 43 24N 68 2 E
Chernaya Kholunitsa **182** 58 51N 51 52 E
Cherni **167** 42 35N 23 18 E
Chernigov **178** 51 28N 31 20 E
Chernikovsk **182** 54 48N 56 8 E
Chernobyl **178** 51 13N 30 15 E
Chernogorsk **185** 53 49N 91 18 E
Chernomorskoye **180** 45 31N 32 40 E
Chernovskoye **179** 58 48N 47 20 E
Chernovtsy **180** 48 15N 25 52 E
Chernoye **185** 70 30N 89 10 E
Chernushka **182** 56 29N 56 3 E
Chernyakhovsk **178** 54 36N 21 48 E
Chernyshkovskiy **181** 48 30N 42 13 E
Chernyshovskiy **185** 63 0N 112 30 E
Cherquenco **126** 38 35 S 72 0W
Cherry Creek **93** 50 43N 120 40W
Cherryville **93** 50 15N 118 37W
Cherskiy **185** 68 45N 161 18 E
Cherskogo Khrebet **185** 65 0N 143 0 E
Chertkovo **181** 49 25N 40 19 E
Cherven **178** 53 45N 28 28 E
Cherven-Bryag **167** 43 17N 24 7 E
Chervonograd **178** 50 25N 24 10 E
Cherwell → **133** 51 46N 1 18W
Cheshire □ **132** 53 14N 2 30W
Cheshskaya Guba **176** 67 20N 47 0 E
Cheslatta **92** 53 48N 125 48W
Cheslatta L. **92** 53 49N 125 20W
Chesley **84** 44 17N 81 5W
Chesne, Le **139** 49 30N 4 45 E
Cheste **157** 39 30N 0 41W
Chester, Canada **81** 44 33N 64 15W
Chester, U.K. **132** 53 12N 2 53W
Chesterfield **132** 53 14N 1 26W
Chesterfield, Îles **224** 19 52 S 158 15 E
Chesterfield Inlet **95** 63 30N 90 45W
Chesterton Range **231** 25 30 S 147 27 E
Chesterville **85** 45 6N 75 14W
Chetaibi **241** 37 1N 7 20 E
Chéticamp **81** 46 37N 60 59W
Chetumal **111** 18 30N 88 18W
Chetumal, B. de **111** 18 20N 88 5W
Chetwynd **76** 55 45N 121 36W
Chevanceaux **140** 45 18N 0 14W
Cheviot, The **132** 55 29N 2 8W
Cheviot Hills **132** 55 20N 2 30W
Cheviot Ra. **230** 25 20 S 143 45 E
Chew Bahir **245** 4 40N 36 50 E
Cheylard, Le **141** 44 55N 4 25 E
Cheyne B. **229** 34 35 S 118 50 E
Chezacut **92** 52 24N 124 1W
Chhabra **198** 24 40N 76 54 E
Chhapra **199** 25 48N 84 44 E
Chhata **198** 27 42N 77 30 E
Chhatak **202** 25 5N 91 37 E
Chhatarpur **199** 24 55N 79 35 E
Chhep **204** 13 45N 105 24 E
Chhindwara **199** 22 2N 78 59 E
Chhlong **205** 12 15N 105 58 E
Chhuk **205** 10 46N 104 28 E
Chi → **204** 15 11N 104 43 E
Chiamis **207** 7 20 S 108 21 E
Chiamussu = Jiamusi **213** 46 40N 130 26 E
Chiang Dao **204** 19 22N 98 58 E
Chiang Kham **204** 19 32N 100 18 E
Chiang Khan **204** 17 52N 101 36 E
Chiang Khong **204** 20 17N 100 24 E
Chiang Mai **204** 18 47N 98 59 E
Chiang Saen **204** 20 16N 100 5 E
Chiange **253** 15 35 S 13 40 E
Chiapa de Corzo **110** 16 42N 93 0W
Chiapas □ **110** 16 30N 92 30W
Chiapilla **110** 16 31N 92 44W
Chiaramonte Gulfi **165** 37 1N 14 41 E
Chiaravalle **163** 43 38N 13 17 E
Chiaravalle Centrale **165** 38 41N 16 25 E
Chiari **162** 45 31N 9 55 E
Chiasso **149** 45 50N 9 0 E
Chiatura **181** 42 15N 43 17 E
Chiautla de Tapia **109** 18 17N 98 36W

Chiávari 162 44 20N 9 20 E
Chiavenna 162 46 18N 9 23 E
Chiba 221 35 30N 140 7 E
Chiba □ 221 35 30N 140 20 E
Chibabava 255 20 17 S 33 35 E
Chibatu 207 7 6 S 107 59 E
Chibemba, Cunene, Angola 253 15 48 S 14 8 E
Chibemba, Huila, Angola 254 16 20 S 15 20 E
Chibia 253 15 10 S 13 42 E
Chibougamau 83 49 56N 74 24W
Chibougamau → 82 49 42N 75 57W
Chibougamau, Parc Prov. de 83 49 15N 73 45W
Chibougamau L. 83 49 50N 74 20W
Chibuk 247 10 52N 12 50 E
Chic-Chocs, Mts. 80 48 55N 66 0W
Chic-Chocs, Parc Prov. des 80 48 55N 66 20W
Chicacole = Srikakulam 200 18 14N 83 58 E
Chicagua, L. de 109 15 58N 97 35W
Chicapa de Castro 109 16 26N 94 49W
Chicayán → 108 22 2N 98 1W
Chichaoua 240 31 32N 8 44W
Chicheng 214 40 55N 115 55 E
Chichester 133 50 50N 0 47W
Chichibu 221 36 5N 139 10 E
Ch'ich'ihaerh = Qiqihar 213 47 26N 124 0 E
Chichihualco 107 17 41N 99 39W
Chichimilá 111 20 37N 88 13W
Chiclana de la Frontera 155 36 26N 6 9W
Chiclayo 122 6 42 S 79 50W
Chicnancanab, L. 111 19 54N 88 46W
Chico → 126 50 0 S 68 30W
Chicobi, L. 82 48 53N 78 30W
Chicomo 255 24 31 S 34 6 E
Chicomucelo 110 15 46N 92 16W
Chicontepec 108 20 58N 98 10W
Chicoutimi 75 48 28N 71 5W
Chicoutimi, Parc Prov. de 83 48 30N 70 20W
Chicualacuala 255 22 6 S 31 42 E
Chidambaram 201 11 20N 79 45 E
Chidenguele 255 24 55 S 34 11 E
Chidley C. 78 60 23N 64 26W
Chiede 254 17 15 S 16 22 E
Chiefs Pt. 84 44 41N 81 18W
Chiem Hoa 204 22 12N 105 17 E
Chiemsee 147 47 53N 12 27 E
Chiengi 251 8 45 S 29 10 E
Chiengo 253 13 20 S 21 55 E
Chienti → 163 43 18N 13 45 E
Chieri 162 45 0N 7 50 E
Chiers → 139 49 39N 5 0 E
Chiese → 162 45 8N 10 25 E
Chieti 163 42 22N 14 10 E
Chièvres 143 50 35N 3 48 E
Chifeng 215 42 18N 118 58 E
Chigasaki 221 35 19N 139 24 E
Chigirin 180 49 4N 32 38 E
Chignecto, Cape 81 45 20N 64 57W
Chignecto B. 81 45 30N 64 40W
Chigorodó 118 7 41N 76 42W
Chigoubiche, L. 83 49 7N 73 30W
Chiguahuapan 108 19 48N 98 2W
Chiguana 124 21 0 S 67 58W
Chiha-ri 215 38 40N 126 30 E
Chihuahua 101 28 38N 106 5W
Chihuahua □ 101 28 30N 106 0W
Chiili 183 44 20N 66 15 E
Chik Bollapur 201 13 25N 77 45 E
Chikhli 198 20 20N 76 18 E
Chikmagalur 201 13 15N 75 45 E
Chikodi 201 16 26N 74 38 E
Chikugo 220 33 14N 130 28 E
Chikuma-Gawa → 221 36 59N 138 35 E
Chikwawa 251 16 2 S 34 50 E
Chila 109 17 58N 97 52W
Chila, Boca de 104 21 13N 105 14W
Chilako → 92 53 53N 122 57W
Chilam Chavki 199 35 5N 75 5 E
Chilanga 251 15 33 S 28 16 E
Chilanko → 92 52 7N 123 41W
Chilanko Forks 92 52 7N 124 5W
Chilapa 104 22 5N 105 15W
Chilapa de Álvarez 107 17 36N 99 10W
Chilapilla 110 18 7N 92 42W
Chilas 199 35 25N 74 5 E
Chilco 92 54 3N 123 49W
Chilcotin → 93 51 44N 122 23W
Childers 231 25 15 S 152 17 E
Chile ■ 126 35 0 S 72 0W
Chile Chico 126 46 33 S 71 44W
Chile Rise 225 38 0 S 92 0W
Chilecito 124 29 10 S 67 30W
Chilete 122 7 10 S 78 50W
Chilicote, Llanos del 101 28 52N 104 38W
Chilik, Kazakh S.S.R., U.S.S.R. 182 51 7N 53 55 E
Chilik, Kirgiz S.S.R., U.S.S.R. 183 43 33N 78 17 E
Chililabombwe 251 12 18 S 27 43 E
Chilka L. 199 19 40N 85 25 E
Chilko → 92 52 0N 123 40W
Chilko, L. 92 51 20N 124 10W
Chillagoe 230 17 7 S 144 33 E
Chillán 124 36 40 S 72 10W
Chilliwack 93 49 10N 121 54W
Chilo 198 27 25N 73 32 E
Chiloane, I. 255 20 40 S 34 55 E
Chiloé □ 126 43 0 S 73 0W
Chiloé, I. de 126 42 30 S 73 50W
Chilón 110 17 14N 92 25W
Chilonda 253 11 19 S 16 12 E
Chilpancingo de los Bravos 107 17 33N 99 30W
Chiltepec 110 18 25N 93 5W
Chiltern 233 36 10 S 146 36 E
Chiltern Hills 133 51 44N 0 42W
Chiluage 253 9 30 S 21 50 E
Chilubula 251 10 14 S 30 51 E
Chilumba 251 10 28 S 34 12 E
Chilwa, L. 251 15 15 S 35 40 E
Chimaltitán 105 21 35N 103 50W
Chimán 112 8 45N 78 40W
Chimay 143 50 3N 4 20 E
Chimbay 184 42 57N 59 47 E
Chimborazo 118 1 29 S 78 55W
Chimborazo □ 118 1 0 S 78 40W
Chimbote 122 9 0 S 78 35W
Chimion 183 40 15N 71 32 E
Chimishliya 170 46 34N 28 44 E
Chimkent 183 42 18N 69 36 E
Chimoio 251 19 4 S 33 30 E
Chimpembe 251 9 31 S 29 33 E
Chin □ 202 22 0N 93 0 E
Chin Hills 202 22 30N 93 30 E
Chiná, Campeche, Mexico 111 19 46N 90 30W
China, Nuevo León, Mexico 102 25 42N 99 14W
China ■ 213 30 0N 110 0 E
Chinacota 118 7 37N 72 36W
Chinameca 109 18 1N 94 40W
Chinampas 106 21 50N 101 48W
Chinandega 112 12 35N 87 12W
Chinapa 100 30 27N 110 2W
Chincha Alta 122 13 25 S 76 7W
Chinchaga → 90 58 53N 118 20W
Chinchilla 231 26 45 S 150 38 E
Chinchilla de Monte Aragón 157 38 53N 1 40W
Chinchón 156 40 9N 3 26W
Chinchorro, Banco 111 18 35N 87 22W
Chinchou = Jinzhou 215 41 5N 121 3 E
Chinchoua 252 0 1N 9 48 E
Chinde 255 18 35 S 36 30 E
Chindo 215 34 28N 126 15 E
Chindwin → 202 21 26N 95 15 E
Chineni 199 33 2N 75 15 E
Chinga 251 15 13 S 38 35 E
Chingola 251 12 31 S 27 53 E
Chingole 251 13 4 S 34 17 E
Chingoroi 253 13 37 S 14 1 E
Chinguar 253 12 25 S 16 45 E
Chinguetti 240 20 25N 12 24W
Chingune 255 20 33 S 35 0 E
Chinhae 215 35 9N 128 47 E
Chinhanguanine 255 25 21 S 32 30 E
Chinhoyi 251 17 20 S 30 8 E
Chiniot 197 31 45N 73 0 E
Chínipas 100 27 23N 108 32W
Chinju 215 35 12N 128 2 E
Chinnamanur 201 9 50N 77 24 E
Chinnampo 215 38 52N 125 10 E
Chinnur 200 18 57N 79 49 E
Chino 221 35 59N 138 9 E
Chinobampo 104 26 26N 108 16W
Chinon 138 47 10N 0 15 E
Chinook 91 51 28N 110 59W
Chinook Valley 90 56 29N 117 39W
Chinsali 251 10 30 S 32 2 E
Chintamani 201 13 26N 78 3 E
Chióggia 163 45 13N 12 15 E
Chíos = Khíos 169 38 27N 26 9 E
Chip L. 90 53 40N 115 23W
Chip Lake 90 53 35N 115 20W
Chipata 251 13 38 S 32 28 E
Chipatujah 207 7 45 S 108 0 E
Chipewyan L. 77 58 0N 98 27W
Chipinge 251 20 13 S 32 28 E
Chipiona 155 36 44N 6 26W
Chiplun 200 17 31N 73 34 E
Chipman, Alta., Canada 90 53 42N 112 38W
Chipman, N.B., Canada 81 46 6N 65 53W
Chipman L. 87 49 58N 86 15W
Chipoka 251 13 57 S 34 28 E
Chippenham 133 51 27N 2 7W
Chiprovtsi 166 43 24N 22 52 E
Chiputneticook Lakes 81 45 37N 67 40W
Chiquián 122 10 10 S 77 0W
Chiquihuitlán de Benito Juárez 109 17 59N 96 48W
Chiquilistlán 106 20 12N 103 49W
Chiquimula 112 14 51N 89 37W
Chiquinquira 118 5 37N 73 50W
Chiquitos, Llanos de 123 18 0 S 61 30W
Chir → 181 48 30N 43 0 E
Chirala 201 15 50N 80 26 E
Chiramba 251 16 55 S 34 39 E
Chiran 220 31 22N 130 27 E
Chirawa 198 28 14N 75 42 E
Chirayinkil 201 8 41N 76 49 E
Chirchik 183 41 29N 69 35 E
Chirfa 241 20 55N 12 22 E
Chirgua → 118 8 54N 67 58W
Chiriquí, Golfo de 112 8 0N 82 10W
Chiriquí, Lago de 112 9 10N 82 0W
Chirivira Falls 251 21 10 S 32 12 E
Chirnogi 170 44 7N 26 32 E
Chirpan 167 42 10N 25 19 E
Chirripó Grande, Cerro 112 9 29N 83 29W
Chisamba 251 14 55 S 28 20 E
Chishmy 182 54 35N 55 23 E
Chisholm 90 54 55N 114 10W
Chishtian Mandi 198 29 50N 72 55 E
Chishui 216 28 30N 105 42 E
Chishui He → 216 28 49N 105 50 E
Chisimaio 256 0 22 S 42 32 E
Chisimba Falls 251 10 12 S 30 56 E
Chisineu Criş 170 46 32N 21 37 E
Chisone → 162 44 49N 7 25 E
Chistopol 179 55 25N 50 38 E
Chita, Colombia 118 6 11N 72 28W
Chita, U.S.S.R. 185 52 0N 113 35 E
Chitado 253 17 10 S 14 8 E
Chitapur 200 17 10N 77 5 E
Chitek 88 53 48N 107 45W
Chitek L., Man., Canada 89 52 25N 99 25W
Chitek L., Sask., Canada 88 53 45N 107 47W
Chitembo 253 13 30 S 16 50 E
Chitipa 251 9 41 S 33 19 E
Chitose 218 42 49N 141 39 E
Chitrakot 200 19 10N 81 40 E
Chitral 197 35 50N 71 56 E
Chitravati → 201 14 45N 78 15 E
Chitré 112 7 59N 80 27W
Chittagong 202 22 19N 91 48 E
Chittagong □ 202 24 5N 91 0 E
Chittaurgarh 198 24 52N 74 38 E
Chittoor 201 13 15N 79 5 E
Chittur 201 10 40N 76 45 E
Chiumba 253 12 29 S 16 8 E
Chiume 253 15 3 S 21 14 E
Chiusa 163 46 38N 11 34 E
Chiusi 163 43 1N 11 58 E
Chiva 157 39 27N 0 41W
Chivacoa 118 10 10N 68 54W
Chivasso 162 45 10N 7 52 E
Chivato, Pta. 99 27 5N 111 59W
Chivay 122 15 40 S 71 35W
Chivela 109 16 42N 95 0W
Chivhu 251 19 2 S 30 52 E
Chivilcoy 124 34 55 S 60 0W
Chiwanda 251 11 23 S 34 55 E
Chixi 217 22 0N 112 58 E
Chixoy, R. → 110 16 28N 90 31W
Chizela 251 13 10 S 25 0 E
Chkalov = Orenburg 182 51 45N 55 6 E
Chkolovsk 179 56 50N 43 10 E
Chlumec 150 50 9N 15 29 E
Chmielnik 152 50 37N 20 43 E
Cho Bo 204 20 46N 105 10 E
Cho-do 215 38 30N 124 40 E
Cho Phuoc Hai 205 10 26N 107 18 E
Choba 250 2 30N 38 5 E
Chobe National Park 254 18 0 S 25 0 E
Chochiwŏn 215 36 37N 127 18 E
Chochola 111 20 45N 89 50W
Chocianów 152 51 27N 15 55 E
Chociwel 152 53 29N 15 21 E
Chocó □ 118 6 0N 77 0W
Chocontá 118 5 9N 73 41W
Chocoy 103 22 40N 98 18W
Chodaków 152 52 16N 20 18 E
Chodavaram 200 17 50N 82 57 E
Chodecz 152 52 24N 19 2 E
Chodziez 152 52 58N 16 58 E
Choele Choel 126 39 11 S 65 40W
Choelquoit L. 92 51 42N 124 12W
Chōfu 221 35 39N 139 33 E
Choiceland 88 53 29N 104 29W
Choisy-le-Roi 139 48 45N 2 24 E
Choix 104 26 43N 108 17W
Chojna 152 52 58N 14 25 E
Chojnice 152 53 42N 17 32 E
Chojnów 152 51 18N 15 58 E
Chōkai-San 218 39 6N 140 3 E
Choke Mts. 245 11 18N 37 15 E
Chokurdakh 185 70 38N 147 55 E
Cholet 138 47 4N 0 52W
Cholpon-Ata 183 42 40N 77 6 E
Cholula de Rivadabia 109 19 4N 98 18W
Choluteca 112 13 20N 87 14W
Choluteca → 112 13 0N 87 20W
Chom Bung 204 13 37N 99 36 E
Chom Thong 204 18 25N 98 41 E
Choma 251 16 48 S 26 59 E
Chomen Swamp 245 9 20N 37 10 E
Chomun 198 27 15N 75 40 E
Chomutov 150 50 28N 13 23 E
Chon Buri 204 13 21N 101 1 E
Chon Thanh 205 11 24N 106 36 E
Chonan 215 36 48N 127 9 E
Chone 118 0 40 S 80 0W
Chong Kai 204 13 57N 103 35 E
Chong Mek 204 15 10N 105 27 E
Chong'an 217 27 45N 118 0 E
Chongde 217 30 32N 120 26 E
Chŏngdo 215 35 38N 128 42 E
Chŏngha 215 36 12N 129 21 E
Chongjin 215 41 47N 129 50 E
Chŏngju, N. Korea 215 39 40N 125 5 E
Chŏngju, S. Korea 215 36 39N 127 27 E
Chongli 214 40 58N 115 15 E
Chongming 217 31 38N 121 23 E
Chongoyape 122 6 35 S 79 25W
Chongqing, Sichuan, China 216 29 35N 106 25 E
Chongqing, Sichuan, China 216 30 38N 103 40 E
Chongren 217 27 46N 116 3 E
Chŏngŭp 215 35 35N 126 50 E
Chongzuo 216 22 23N 107 20 E
Chŏnju 215 35 50N 127 4 E
Chonming Dao 217 31 40N 121 30 E
Chonos, Arch. de los 126 45 0 S 75 0W
Chopda 198 21 20N 75 15 E
Chopim → 125 25 35 S 53 5W
Chorbat La 199 34 42N 76 37 E
Chorley 132 53 39N 2 39W
Chorolque, Cerro 124 20 59 S 66 5W
Choroszcz 152 53 10N 22 59 E
Chorregon 230 22 40 S 143 32 E
Chorrera, La 118 0 44 S 73 1W
Chortkov 178 49 2N 25 46 E
Chŏrwŏn 215 38 15N 127 10 E
Chorzele 152 53 15N 20 55 E
Chorzów 152 50 18N 18 57 E
Chos-Malal 124 37 20 S 70 15W
Chosan 215 40 50N 125 47 E
Chōshi 221 35 45N 140 51 E
Choszczno 152 53 7N 15 25 E
Chota 122 6 33 S 78 39W
Chotila 198 22 23N 71 15 E
Chowkham 202 20 52N 97 28 E
Choybalsan 213 48 4N 114 30 E
Christchurch, N.Z. 235 43 33 S 172 47 E
Christchurch, U.K. 133 50 44N 1 33W
Christian I. 84 44 50N 80 12W
Christiana 254 27 52 S 25 8 E
Christiansfeld 173 55 21N 9 29 E
Christiansted 113 17 45N 64 42W
Christie B. 77 62 32N 111 10W
Christina → 90 56 40N 111 3W
Christina, L. 93 49 3N 118 12W
Christmas Cr. → 228 18 29 S 125 23 E
Christmas Creek 228 18 29 S 125 23 E
Christmas I. = Kiritimati 225 1 58N 157 27W
Christmas I. 203 10 30 S 105 40 E
Christopher L. 229 24 49 S 127 42 E
Christopher Lake 88 53 32N 105 48W
Chrudim 150 49 58N 15 43 E
Chrzanów 152 50 10N 19 21 E
Chtimba 251 10 35 S 34 13 E
Chu 183 43 36N 73 42 E
Chu →, U.S.S.R. 183 45 0N 67 44 E
Chu →, Vietnam 204 19 53N 105 45 E
Chu Chua 93 51 22N 120 10W
Chu Lai 204 15 28N 108 45 E
Chu Xian 217 32 19N 118 20 E
Chuadanga 202 23 38N 88 51 E
Ch'uanchou = Quanzhou 217 24 55N 118 34 E
Chuankou 214 34 20N 110 59 E
Chūbu □ 221 36 45N 137 30 E
Chubut □ 126 43 30 S 69 0W
Chubut → 126 43 20 S 65 5W
Chuchi L. 76 55 12N 124 30W
Chudovo 178 59 10N 31 41 E
Chudskoye, Oz. 178 58 13N 27 30 E
Chūgoku □ 220 35 0N 133 0 E
Chūgoku-Sanchi 220 35 0N 133 0 E
Chuguyev 180 49 55N 36 45 E
Chuhuichupa 101 29 38N 108 22W
Chukhloma 179 58 45N 42 40 E
Chukotskiy Khrebet 185 68 0N 175 0 E
Chukotskoye More 185 68 0N 175 0W
Chulak-Kurgan 183 43 46N 69 9 E
Chulman 185 56 52N 124 52 E

Chulucanas **122** 5 8S 80 10W
Chulumani **122** 16 24S 67 31W
Chulym → **184** 57 43N 83 51E
Chum Phae **204** 16 40N 102 6E
Chum Saeng **204** 15 55N 100 15E
Chuma **122** 15 24S 68 56W
Chumar **199** 32 40N 78 35E
Chumbicha **124** 29 0S 66 10W
Chumerna **167** 42 45N 25 55E
Chumikan **185** 54 40N 135 10E
Chumphon **205** 10 35N 99 14E
Chumpi **122** 15 4S 73 46W
Chumpón **111** 19 59N 87 47W
Chumuare **251** 14 31S 31 50E
Chumunjin **215** 37 55N 128 54E
Chuna → **185** 57 47N 94 37E
Chun'an **217** 29 35N 119 3E
Chunchŏn **215** 37 58N 127 44E
Chunchura **199** 22 53N 88 27E
Chunga **251** 15 0S 26 2E
Chunggang-ŭp **215** 41 48N 126 48E
Chunghwa **215** 38 52N 125 47E
Chungju **215** 36 58N 127 58E
Chungmu **215** 34 50N 128 20E
Chungt'iaoshan = Zhongtiao Shan **214** 35 0N 111 10E
Chunian **198** 30 57N 74 0E
Chunya **251** 8 30S 33 27E
Chunya □ **250** 7 48S 33 0E
Chunyang **215** 43 38N 129 23E
Chuquibamba **122** 15 47S 72 44W
Chuquibambilla **122** 14 7S 72 41W
Chuquicamata **124** 22 15S 69 0W
Chuquisaca □ **123** 23 30S 63 30W
Chur **149** 46 52N 9 32E
Churachandpur **202** 24 20N 93 40E
Churchbridge **89** 50 54N 101 54W
Churchill **77** 58 47N 94 11W
Churchill →, Man., Canada **77** 58 47N 94 12W
Churchill →, Newf., Canada **78** 53 19N 60 10W
Churchill, C. **77** 58 46N 93 12W
Churchill Falls **78** 53 36N 64 19W
Churchill L., Ont., Canada **86** 50 50N 91 10W
Churchill L., Sask., Canada **77** 55 55N 108 20W
Churchill Pk. **76** 58 10N 125 10W
Churfisten **149** 47 8N 9 17E
Churintzio **106** 20 9N 102 4W
Churu **198** 28 20N 74 50E
Churwalden **149** 46 47N 9 33E
Chushal **199** 33 40N 78 40E
Chusovaya → **182** 58 18N 56 22E
Chusovoy **182** 58 15N 57 40E
Chust **183** 41 0N 71 13E
Chute-aux-Outardes **83** 49 7N 68 24W
Chute-des-Passes **83** 49 52N 71 16W
Chuuronjang **215** 41 35N 129 40E
Chuvash A.S.S.R.□ **179** 55 30N 47 0E
Chuviscar, R. → **101** 28 32N 105 25W
Chuwârtah **192** 35 43N 45 34E
Chuxiong **216** 25 2N 101 28E
Ci Xian **214** 36 20N 114 25E
Ciacova **170** 45 35N 21 10E
Ciamis **209** 7 20S 108 21E
Cianjur **207** 6 49S 107 8E
Cibadok **207** 6 53S 106 47E
Cibatu **207** 7 8S 107 59E
Cibuta **100** 31 4N 110 54W
Cícero Dantas **120** 10 36S 38 23W
Cidacos → **156** 42 21N 1 38W
Cide **180** 41 53N 33 1E
Ciechanów **152** 52 52N 20 38E
Ciechanów □ **152** 53 0N 20 30E
Ciechanowiec **152** 52 40N 22 31E
Ciechocinek **152** 52 53N 18 45E
Ciego de Avila **112** 21 50N 78 50W
Ciénaga **118** 11 1N 74 15W
Ciénaga de Oro **118** 8 53N 75 37W
Ciénega, La **100** 30 13N 111 55W
Ciénega de Escobar **104** 25 37N 105 45W
Ciénega de Flores **102** 25 57N 100 11W
Ciénega del Carmen **102** 25 51N 101 54W
Cieneguilla **105** 24 3N 104 3W
Cieneguita **100** 28 36N 110 16W
Cienfuegos **112** 22 10N 80 30W
Cieplice Śląskie Zdrój **152** 50 50N 15 40E
Cierp **140** 42 55N 0 40E
Cíes, Islas **154** 42 12N 8 55W
Cieszanów **152** 50 14N 23 8E
Cieszyn **152** 49 45N 18 35E
Cieza **157** 38 17N 1 23W
Cifuentes **156** 40 47N 2 37W
Cihuatlán **106** 19 14N 104 35W
Cihuatlán, R. → **106** 19 10N 104 38W
Cijara, Pantano de **155** 39 18N 4 52W
Cijulang **207** 7 42S 108 27E
Cikajang **207** 7 25S 107 48E
Cikampek **207** 6 23S 107 28E
Cilacap **209** 7 43S 109 0E
Çıldır **181** 41 10N 43 20E
Cili **217** 29 30N 111 8E
Cîlnicu **170** 44 54N 23 4E
Cimahi **207** 6 53S 107 33E
Cimone, Mte. **162** 44 10N 10 40E
Cîmpic Turzii **170** 46 34N 23 53E
Cîmpina **170** 45 10N 25 45E
Cîmpulung, Argeş, Romania **170** 45 17N 25 3E
Cîmpulung, Suceava, Romania **170** 47 32N 25 30E
Cîmpuri **170** 46 0N 26 50E
Cinca → **156** 41 26N 0 21E
Cincer **166** 43 55N 17 5E
Cîndeşti **170** 45 15N 26 42E
Ciney **143** 50 18N 5 5E
Cîngoli **163** 43 23N 13 10E
Cinigiano **163** 42 53N 11 23E
Cintalapa de Figueroa **110** 16 44N 93 43W
Cinto, Mt. **141** 42 24N 8 54E
Ciorani **170** 44 45N 26 25E
Çiotat, La **141** 43 12N 5 36E
Čiovo **163** 43 30N 16 17E
Cipó **120** 11 6S 38 31W
Circeo, Monte **164** 41 14N 13 3E
Cirebon **209** 6 45S 108 32E
Cirencester **133** 51 43N 1 59W
Cireşu **170** 44 47N 22 31E
Cirey-sur-Vezouze **139** 48 35N 6 57E
Ciriè **162** 45 14N 7 35E
Cirò **165** 39 23N 17 3E
Cislău **170** 45 14N 26 20E
Cisna **152** 49 12N 22 20E
Cisnădie **170** 45 42N 24 9E
Cisneros **118** 6 33N 75 4W
Cisterna di Latina **164** 41 35N 12 50E
Cisternino **165** 40 45N 17 26E
Citaré → **119** 1 11N 54 41W
Citeli-Ckaro **181** 41 33N 46 0E
Citlaltépetl, Volcán **108** 19 1N 97 16W
Citrusdal **254** 32 35S 19 0E
Città della Pieve **163** 42 57N 12 0E
Città di Castello **163** 43 27N 12 14E
Città Sant' Angelo **163** 42 32N 14 5E
Cittadella **163** 45 39N 11 48E
Cittaducale **163** 42 24N 12 58E
Cittanova **165** 38 22N 16 5E
Ciuc, Munţii **170** 46 25N 26 5E
Ciucaş **170** 45 31N 25 56E
Ciudad, La **104** 23 40N 105 44W
Ciudad Altamirano **107** 18 20N 100 40W
Ciudad Bolívar **119** 8 5N 63 36W
Ciudad Camargo, Chihuahua, Mexico **101** 27 40N 105 10W
Ciudad Camargo, Tamaulipas, Mexico **102** 26 19N 98 50W
Ciudad Constitucion **99** 25 0N 111 42W
Ciudad Cuauhtemoc **110** 15 37N 92 0W
Ciudad de Dolores Hidalgo **107** 21 10N 100 56W
Ciudad de México **107** 19 24N 99 9W
Ciudad de Valles **103** 21 59N 99 1W
Ciudad del Carmen **111** 18 38N 91 50W
Ciudad del Maíz **103** 22 24N 99 36W
Ciudad Guayana **119** 8 0N 62 30W
Ciudad Guerrero **101** 28 33N 107 30W
Ciudad Guzmán **106** 19 41N 103 29W
Ciudad Hidalgo, Chiapas, Mexico **110** 14 41N 92 9W
Ciudad Hidalgo, Michoacan, Mexico **107** 19 41N 100 34W
Ciudad Juárez **101** 31 44N 106 29W
Ciudad Lerdo **105** 25 32N 103 32W
Ciudad Madero **103** 22 16N 97 50W
Ciudad Mante **103** 22 44N 98 57W
Ciudad Manuel Doblado **106** 20 44N 101 56W
Ciudad Mendoza **109** 18 48N 97 11W
Ciudad Miguel Alemán **102** 26 23N 99 2W
Ciudad Obregón **100** 27 29N 109 56W
Ciudad Ojeda **118** 10 12N 71 19W
Ciudad Pemex **110** 17 52N 92 30W
Ciudad Real **155** 38 59N 3 55W
Ciudad Real □ **155** 38 50N 4 0W
Ciudad Rodrigo **154** 40 35N 6 32W
Ciudad Sahagun **107** 19 52N 98 46W
Ciudad Serdán **109** 18 59N 97 27W
Ciudad Trujillo = Santo Domingo **113** 18 30N 64 54W
Ciudad Victoria **103** 23 44N 99 8W
Ciudadela **156** 40 0N 3 50E
Ciulniţa **170** 44 26N 27 22E
Cividale del Friuli **163** 46 6N 13 25E
Cívita Castellana **163** 42 18N 12 24E
Civitanova Marche **163** 43 18N 13 41E
Civitavécchia **163** 42 6N 11 46E
Civitella del Tronto **163** 42 48N 13 40E
Civray **140** 46 10N 0 17E
Cixerri → **164** 39 20N 8 40E
Cizre **177** 37 19N 42 10E
Clackline **229** 31 40S 116 32E
Clacton-on-Sea **133** 51 47N 1 10E
Clain → **138** 46 47N 0 33E
Clairambault, L. **78** 54 29N 69 0W
Claire **83** 47 15N 68 40W
Claire, L. **76** 58 35N 112 5W
Clairmont **90** 55 16N 118 47W
Clairvaux-les-Lacs **141** 46 35N 5 45E
Claise → **138** 46 56N 0 42E
Clamecy **139** 47 28N 3 30E
Clandonald **90** 53 34N 110 44W
Clanwilliam, Canada **89** 50 22N 99 49W
Clanwilliam, S. Africa **254** 32 11S 18 52E
Clapperton I. **84** 46 0N 82 14W
Clara **135** 53 20N 7 38W
Clara → **230** 19 8S 142 30E
Clare **232** 33 50S 138 37E
Clare □ **135** 52 20N 9 0W
Clare → **135** 53 22N 9 5W
Clare I. **135** 53 48N 10 0W
Claremont Pt. **230** 14 1S 143 41E
Claremorris **135** 53 45N 9 0W
Clarence →, Australia **231** 29 25S 153 22E
Clarence →, N.Z. **235** 42 10S 173 56E
Clarence, I. **126** 54 0S 72 0W
Clarence I. **13** 61 10S 54 0W
Clarence Str. **228** 12 0S 131 0E
Clarence Town **113** 23 6N 74 59W
Clarendon **81** 45 29N 66 26W
Clarenville **79** 48 10N 54 1W
Claresholm **91** 50 0N 113 33W
Clarie Coast **13** 68 0S 135 0E
Clarin **211** 8 12N 123 52E
Clarion Fracture Zone **225** 20 0N 120 0W
Clark, Pt. **84** 44 4N 81 45W
Clarke, I. **230** 40 32S 148 10E
Clarke City **80** 50 12N 66 38W
Clarke L. **88** 54 24N 106 54W
Clarke Ra. **230** 20 45S 148 20E
Clark's Harbour **81** 43 25N 65 38W
Claro → **121** 19 8S 50 40W
Claveria, Cagayan, Phil. **210** 12 54N 123 15E
Claveria, Masbate, Phil. **211** 8 38N 124 55E
Claveria, Mindanao, Phil. **210** 18 37N 121 4E
Clay L. **86** 50 3N 93 30W
Clayette, La **141** 46 17N 4 19E
Clear → **90** 56 11N 119 42W
Clear, C. **135** 51 26N 9 30W
Clear, L. **85** 45 26N 77 12W
Clear I. **135** 51 26N 9 30W
Clearwater **93** 51 38N 120 2W
Clearwater →, Alta., Canada **90** 56 44N 111 23W
Clearwater →, Alta., Canada **91** 52 22N 114 57W
Clearwater →, B.C., Canada **93** 51 38N 120 3W
Clearwater Cr. → **76** 61 36N 125 30W
Clearwater L. **93** 52 15N 120 13W
Clearwater Prov. Park **89** 54 0N 101 0W
Clécy **138** 48 55N 0 29W
Cleethorpes **132** 53 33N 0 2W
Cleeve Cloud **133** 51 56N 2 0W
Clelles **141** 44 50N 5 38E
Clemency **143** 49 35N 5 53E
Clementsport **81** 44 40N 65 37W
Cleopatra Needle **211** 10 7N 118 58E
Clerke Reef **228** 17 22S 119 20E
Clerks Rocks **13** 56 0S 34 30W
Clermont, Australia **230** 22 49S 147 39E
Clermont, Canada **83** 47 41N 70 14W
Clermont, France **139** 49 23N 2 24E
Clermont-en-Argonne **139** 49 5N 5 4E
Clermont-Ferrand **140** 45 46N 3 4E
Clermont-l'Hérault **140** 43 38N 3 26E
Clerval **139** 47 25N 6 30E
Clervaux **143** 50 4N 6 2E
Cléry-Saint-André **139** 47 50N 1 46E
Cles **162** 46 21N 11 4E
Cleveland **231** 27 30S 153 15E
Cleveland □ **132** 54 35N 1 8E
Cleveland, C. **230** 19 11S 147 1E
Clevelândia **125** 26 24S 52 23W
Clevelândia do Norte **119** 3 49N 51 52W
Clew B. **135** 53 54N 9 50W
Clifden, Ireland **135** 53 30N 10 2W
Clifden, N.Z. **235** 46 1S 167 42E
Clifton **231** 27 59S 151 53E
Clifton Beach **230** 16 46S 145 39E
Clifton Hills **231** 27 1S 138 54E
Climax **88** 49 10N 108 20W
Clinton, B.C., Canada **93** 51 6N 121 35W
Clinton, Ont., Canada **84** 43 37N 81 32W
Clinton, N.Z. **235** 46 12S 169 23E
Clinton C. **230** 22 30S 150 45E
Clinton Colden L. **94** 63 58N 107 27W
Clinton Creek **94** 64 25N 140 37W
Clipperton, I. **225** 10 18N 109 13W
Clipperton Fracture Zone **225** 19 0N 122 0W
Clisson **138** 47 5N 1 16W
Clive, Canada **91** 52 28N 113 27W
Clive, N.Z. **234** 39 36S 176 58E
Clive L. **76** 63 13N 118 54W
Cliza **123** 17 36S 65 56W
Cloates, Pt. **228** 22 43S 113 40E
Clocolan **255** 28 55S 27 34E
Clodomira **124** 27 35S 64 14W
Clonakilty **135** 51 37N 8 53W
Clonakilty B. **135** 51 33N 8 50W
Cloncurry **230** 20 40S 140 28E
Cloncurry → **230** 18 37S 140 40E
Clones **135** 54 10N 7 13W
Clonmel **135** 52 22N 7 42W
Cloppenburg **146** 52 50N 8 3E
Clorinda **124** 25 16S 57 45W
Cloudy B. **235** 41 25S 174 10E
Clova **82** 48 7N 75 22W
Cloverdale **81** 46 17N 67 22W
Cloyes **138** 48 0N 1 14E
Cloyne **85** 44 49N 77 11W
Club Terrace **233** 37 35S 148 58E
Cluculz L. **92** 53 53N 123 33W
Cluj □ **170** 46 45N 23 30E
Cluj-Napoca **170** 46 47N 23 38E
Clunes **231** 37 20S 143 45E
Cluny **141** 46 26N 4 38E
Cluses **141** 46 5N 6 35E
Clusone **162** 45 54N 9 58E
Clutha → **235** 46 20S 169 49E
Clwyd □ **132** 53 5N 3 20W
Clwyd → **132** 53 20N 3 30W
Clyde, Canada **90** 54 9N 113 39W
Clyde, N.Z. **235** 45 12S 169 20E
Clyde →, Canada **81** 43 35N 65 27W
Clyde →, U.K. **134** 55 56N 4 29W
Clyde, Firth of **134** 55 20N 5 0W
Clyde River, N.S., Canada **81** 43 38N 65 29W
Clyde River, N.W.T., Canada **95** 70 30N 68 30W
Clydebank **134** 55 54N 4 25W
Cŏa → **154** 41 5N 7 6W
Coacoachou, L. **80** 50 25N 60 14W
Coahuayana **106** 18 44N 103 41W
Coahuayana, R. → **106** 18 41N 103 45W
Coahuila □ **102** 27 20N 102 0W
Coal → **76** 59 39N 126 57W
Coal Creek **91** 49 30N 114 59W
Coal Harbour **92** 50 36N 127 35W
Coal I. **235** 46 8S 166 40E
Coalane **251** 17 48S 37 2E
Coalcomán, Sa. de **106** 18 35N 102 30W
Coalcomán de Matamoros **106** 18 47N 103 9W
Coaldale **91** 49 45N 112 35W
Coalhurst **91** 49 45N 112 56W
Coalmont **93** 49 32N 120 42W
Coalville **132** 52 43N 1 21W
Coapa **110** 15 40N 93 8W
Coapa, L. de **110** 18 23N 93 8W
Coaraci **121** 14 38S 39 32W
Coari **119** 4 8S 63 7W
Coari → **119** 4 30S 63 33W
Coari, L. de **119** 4 15S 63 22W
Coast □ **250** 2 40S 39 45E
Coast Mts. **92** 55 0N 129 0W
Coastal Plains Basin **229** 30 10S 115 30E
Coatbridge **134** 55 52N 4 2W
Coatecas Altas **109** 16 32N 96 40W
Coatepec, México, Mexico **107** 18 54N 99 43W
Coatepec, Veracruz, Mexico **108** 19 27N 96 58W
Coatepeque **112** 14 46N 91 55W
Coaticook **83** 45 10N 71 46W
Coats I. **95** 62 30N 83 0W
Coats Land **13** 77 0S 25 0W
Coatzacoalcos **109** 18 9N 94 25W
Coatzacoalcos, R. → **109** 18 9N 94 24W
Coatzingo **109** 18 37N 98 11W
Coatzintla **108** 20 29N 97 27W
Cobá **111** 20 34N 87 42W
Cobadin **170** 44 5N 28 13E
Cobalt **74** 47 25N 79 42W
Cobán **112** 15 30N 90 21W
Cobar **231** 31 27S 145 48E
Cobaz, L. **80** 51 15N 60 21W
Cobberas, Mt. **233** 36 53S 148 12E
Cobden, Australia **232** 38 20S 143 3E
Cobden, Canada **85** 45 38N 76 53W
Cóbh **135** 51 50N 8 18W
Cobham **231** 30 18S 142 7E
Cobija **122** 11 0S 68 50W
Coboconk **85** 44 39N 78 48W
Cobourg **85** 43 58N 78 10W

Cobourg Pen. **228** 11 20 S 132 15 E
Cobram **231** 35 54 S 145 40 E
Coburg **147** 50 15N 10 58 E
Coburg I. **95** 75 57N 79 26W
Coca **154** 41 13N 4 32W
Coca → **118** 0 29 S 76 58W
Cocachacra **122** 17 5 S 71 45W
Cocagne **81** 46 20N 64 37W
Cocal **120** 3 28 S 41 34W
Cocanada =
Kakinada **200** 16 57N 82 11 E
Cocentaina **157** 38 45N 0 27W
Cocha, La **124** 27 50 S 65 40W
Cochabamba **123** 17 26 S 66 10W
Coche, I. **119** 10 47N 63 56W
Cochem **147** 50 8N 7 7 E
Cochemane **251** 17 0 S 32 54 E
Cochenour **86** 51 5N 93 48W
Cochin **201** 9 59N 76 22 E
Cochin China =
Nam-Phan **205** 10 30N 106 0 E
Cochrane, Alta.,
Canada **91** 51 11N 114 30W
Cochrane, Ont.,
Canada **74** 49 0N 81 0W
Cochrane → **77** 59 0N 103 40W
Cochrane, L. **126** 47 10 S 72 0W
Cockburn **231** 32 5 S 141 0 E
Cockburn, Canal **126** 54 30 S 72 0W
Cockburn, C. **95** 74 52N 79 24W
Cockburn I. **84** 45 55N 83 22W
Cockburn Ra. **228** 15 46 S 128 0 E
Cocklebiddy Motel **229** 32 0 S 126 3 E
Coco → **112** 15 0N 83 8W
Coco, Pta. **118** 2 58N 77 43W
Cocobeach **252** 0 59N 9 34 E
Cocora **170** 44 45N 27 3 E
Côcos **121** 14 10 S 44 33W
Côcos → **121** 12 44 S 44 48W
Cocos I., Guam **226** 13 14N 144 39 E
Cocos I., Pac. Oc. **225** 5 25N 87 55W
Cocos Is. **203** 12 10 S 96 55 E
Cocula, Guerrero,
Mexico **107** 18 14N 99 40W
Cocula, Jalisco,
Mexico **106** 20 23N 103 50W
Cod I. **78** 57 47N 61 47W
Codajás **119** 3 55 S 62 0W
Codera, C. **118** 10 35N 66 4W
Coderre **88** 50 11N 106 31W
Codette **88** 53 16N 104 0W
Codigoro **163** 44 50N 12 5 E
Codó **120** 4 30 S 43 55W
Codogno **162** 45 10N 9 42 E
Codpa **122** 18 50 S 69 44W
Codróipo **163** 45 57N 13 0 E
Codroy **79** 47 53N 59 24W
Codroy Pond **79** 48 4N 58 52W
Codru, Munţii **170** 46 30N 22 15 E
Coe Hill **85** 44 52N 77 50W
Coelemu **124** 36 30 S 72 48W
Coelho Neto **120** 4 15 S 43 0W
Coen **230** 13 52 S 143 12 E
Coeneo de la
Libertad **107** 19 49N 101 35W
Coeroeni → **119** 3 21N 57 31W
Coesfeld **146** 51 56N 7 10 E
Coetivy Is. **203** 7 8 S 56 16 E
Coevorden **142** 52 40N 6 44 E
Coffs Harbour **231** 30 16 S 153 5 E
Cofrentes **157** 39 13N 1 5W
Cogealac **170** 44 36N 28 36 E
Coghinas → **164** 40 55N 8 48 E
Coghinas, L. di **164** 40 46N 9 3 E
Cognac **140** 45 41N 0 20W
Cogne **162** 45 37N 7 21 E
Cogolludo **156** 40 59N 3 10W
Cohuna **231** 35 45 S 144 15 E
Coiba, I. **112** 7 30N 81 40W
Coig → **126** 51 0 S 69 10W
Coihaique **126** 45 30 S 71 45W
Coimbatore **201** 11 2N 76 59 E
Coimbra, Brazil **122** 19 55 S 57 48W
Coimbra, Portugal **154** 40 15N 8 27W
Coimbra □ **154** 40 12N 8 25W
Coín **155** 36 40N 4 48W
Coipasa, L. de **122** 19 12 S 68 7W
Coipasa, Salar de **122** 19 26 S 68 9W
Cojata **122** 15 2 S 69 25W
Cojedes □ **118** 9 20N 68 20W
Cojedes → **118** 8 34N 68 5W
Cojimies **122** 0 20N 80 0W
Cojocna **170** 46 45N 23 50 E
Cojumatlán **106** 20 7N 102 50W
Çojutepequé **112** 13 41N 88 54W
Čoka **166** 45 57N 20 12 E
Colaba Pt. **200** 18 54N 72 47 E
Colac **231** 38 21 S 143 35 E
Colachel = Kolachel **201** 8 10N 77 15 E
Colares **155** 38 48N 9 30W
Colasi **211** 10 43N 125 44 E
Colatina **121** 19 32 S 40 37W
Colbeck, C. **13** 77 6 S 157 48W
Colbinabbin **231** 36 38 S 144 48 E
Colborne **85** 44 0N 77 53W
Colchagua □ **124** 34 30 S 71 0W
Colchester **133** 51 54N 0 55 E
Cold L. **90** 54 33N 110 5W
Cold Lake **90** 54 27N 110 10W
Coldstream **134** 55 39N 2 14W
Coldwater **84** 44 42N 79 40W
Colebrook **230** 42 31 S 147 21 E
Coleman **91** 49 40N 114 30W
Coleman → **230** 15 6 S 141 38 E
Colenso **255** 28 44 S 29 50 E
Coleraine, Australia **231** 37 36 S 141 40 E
Coleraine, U.K. **135** 55 8N 6 40 E
Coleraine □ **135** 55 8N 6 40 E
Coleridge, L. **235** 43 17 S 171 30 E
Coleroon → **201** 11 25N 79 50 E
Colesberg **254** 30 45 S 25 5 E
Coleville **88** 51 43N 109 15W
Colhué Huapi, L. **126** 45 30 S 69 0W
Cólico **162** 46 8N 9 22 E
Coligny **255** 26 17 S 26 15 E
Colima **106** 19 14N 103 43W
Colima □ **106** 19 10N 104 0W
Colima, Nevado de **106** 19 33N 103 38W
Colima, Volcán de **106** 19 31N 103 38W
Colina **124** 33 13 S 70 45W
Colina do Norte **246** 12 28N 15 0W
Colinas, Goiás,
Brazil **121** 14 15 S 48 2W
Colinas, Maranhão,
Brazil **120** 6 0 S 44 10W
Colinet **79** 47 13N 53 33W
Colinton, Australia **233** 35 50 S 149 10 E
Colinton, Canada **90** 54 37N 113 15W
Colipa **108** 19 55N 96 42W
Coll **134** 56 40N 6 35W
Collaguasi **124** 21 5 S 68 45W
Collarada, Peña **156** 42 43N 0 29W
Collarenebri **231** 29 33 S 148 34 E
Colle di Val d'Elsa **163** 43 25N 11 7 E
Colle Salvetti **162** 43 34N 10 27 E
Colle Sannita **165** 41 22N 14 48 E
Collécchio **162** 44 45N 10 10 E
Colleen Bawn **251** 21 0 S 29 12 E
College Bridge **81** 45 59N 64 33W
College Heights **91** 52 28N 113 45W
Collette **75** 46 40N 65 30W
Colleymount **92** 54 2N 126 19W
Collie, N.S.W.,
Australia **233** 31 41 S 148 18 E
Collie, W. Austral.,
Australia **229** 33 22 S 116 8 E
Collier B. **228** 16 10 S 124 15 E
Collier Ra. **229** 24 45 S 119 10 E
Colline Metallifere **162** 43 10N 11 0 E
Collingwood,
Canada **84** 44 29N 80 13W
Collingwood, N.Z. **235** 40 41 S 172 40 E
Collingwood Corner **81** 45 37N 63 56W
Collins **86** 50 17N 89 27W
Collinson Pen. **95** 69 58N 101 24W
Collinsville **230** 20 30 S 147 56 E
Collipulli **124** 37 55 S 72 30W
Collo **241** 36 58N 6 37 E
Collonges **141** 46 9N 5 52 E
Collooney **135** 54 11N 8 28W
Colmar **139** 48 5N 7 20 E
Colmars **141** 44 11N 6 39 E
Colmenar **155** 36 54N 4 20W
Colmenar de Oreja **156** 40 6N 3 25W
Colmenar Viejo **154** 40 39N 3 47W
Colmeneros **106** 18 6N 101 40W
Colne **132** 53 51N 2 11W
Colo → **231** 33 25 S 150 52 E
Cologna Véneta **163** 45 19N 11 21 E
Cologne = Köln **146** 50 56N 6 58 E
Colomb-Béchar =
Béchar **241** 31 38N 2 18W
Colombey-les-Belles **139** 48 32N 5 54 E
Colombey-les-Deux-
Églises **139** 48 13N 4 50 E
Colômbia **121** 20 10 S 48 40W
Colombia ■ **118** 3 45N 73 0W
Colombier, Canada **83** 48 52N 68 51W
Colombier, Switz. **148** 46 58N 6 53 E
Colombo **201** 6 56N 79 58 E
Colón, Argentina **124** 32 12 S 58 10W
Colón, Cuba **112** 22 42N 80 54W
Colón, Mexico **107** 20 48N 100 3W
Colón, Panama **112** 9 20N 79 54W
Colón, Peru **122** 5 0 S 81 0W
Colonella **163** 42 52N 13 50 E
Colonet, C. **98** 30 57N 116 19W
Colonia, Pac. Oc. **226** 9 30N 138 10 E
Colonia, Uruguay **124** 34 25 S 57 50W
Colonia Dora **124** 28 34 S 62 59W
Colonia Ortega **105** 23 58N 103 26W
Colonia Progreso **98** 32 38N 115 40W
Colonne, C. delle **165** 39 2N 17 11 E
Colonsay, Canada **88** 51 59N 105 52W
Colonsay, U.K. **134** 56 4N 6 12W
Colorada, La **105** 23 47N 102 24W
Colorado →,
Argentina **126** 39 50 S 62 8W
Colorado →,
Mexico **98** 31 54N 114 57W
Colorno **162** 44 55N 10 21 E
Colotepec → **109** 15 47N 97 3W
Colotlán **105** 22 6N 103 16W
Colotlán → **105** 22 3N 103 53W
Colquechaca **123** 18 40 S 66 1W
Columbia, C. **12** 83 0N 70 0W
Columbia, Mt. **93** 52 8N 117 20W
Columbia, Sa. **98** 29 38N 114 30W
Columbia L. **91** 50 15N 115 52W
Columbretes, Is. **156** 39 50N 0 50 E
Colunga **154** 43 29N 5 16W
Colville, C. **234** 36 29 S 175 21 E
Colville Lake **94** 67 2N 126 7W
Colwyn Bay **132** 53 17N 3 44W
Coma **245** 8 29N 36 53 E
Comácchio **163** 44 41N 12 10 E
Comala **106** 19 19N 103 45W
Comalcalco **110** 18 16N 93 13W
Comallo **126** 41 0 S 70 5W
Comana **170** 44 10N 26 10 E
Comandante Luis
Piedrabuena **126** 49 59 S 68 54W
Comăneşti **170** 46 25N 26 26 E
Cománja **106** 19 44N 101 42W
Comarapa **123** 17 54 S 64 29W
Comayagua **112** 14 25N 87 37W
Combara **233** 31 10 S 148 22 E
Combeaufontaine **139** 47 38N 5 54 E
Comber **84** 42 14N 82 33W
Combermere **85** 45 22N 77 37W
Combermere Bay **202** 19 37N 93 34 E
Comblain-au-Pont **143** 50 29N 5 35 E
Combles **139** 50 0N 2 50 E
Combourg **138** 48 25N 1 46W
Comboyne **233** 31 34 S 152 27 E
Combronde **140** 45 58N 3 5 E
Combulgurri **228** 15 15 S 127 45 E
Come by Chance **79** 47 51N 54 0W
Comedero **104** 24 37N 106 46W
Comeragh Mts. **135** 52 17N 7 35W
Comet **230** 23 36 S 148 38 E
Comet Vale **229** 29 55 S 121 4 E
Comilla **202** 23 28N 91 10 E
Comines **143** 50 46N 3 0 E
Comino **160** 36 0N 14 20 E
Comino, C. **164** 40 28N 9 47 E
Cómiso **165** 36 57N 14 35 E
Comitán de
Dominguez **110** 16 15N 92 8W
Commanda **84** 45 57N 79 36W
Commentry **140** 46 20N 2 46 E
Commercy **139** 48 46N 5 34 E
Commewijne □ **119** 5 25N 54 45W
Commissaires, L.
des **83** 48 10N 72 16W
Commissioner I. **89** 52 10N 97 16W
Committee B. **95** 68 30N 86 30W
Commonwealth B. **13** 67 0 S 144 0 E
Commoron Cr. → **231** 28 22 S 150 8 E
Communism Pk. =
Kommunizma, Pik **183** 39 0N 72 2 E
Como **162** 45 48N 9 5 E
Como, L. di **162** 46 5N 9 17 E
Comodoro
Rivadavia **126** 45 50 S 67 40W
Comondú **99** 26 3N 111 46W
Comonfort **107** 20 43N 100 46W
Comorin, C. **201** 8 3N 77 40 E
Comorişte **166** 45 10N 21 35 E
Comoro Is. ■ **203** 12 10 S 44 15 E
Comox **92** 49 42N 124 55W
Compeer **91** 51 52N 110 0W
Compiègne **139** 49 24N 2 50 E
Compíglia Maríttima **162** 43 4N 10 37 E
Comporta **155** 38 22N 8 46W
Compostela, Mexico **104** 21 14N 104 55W
Compostela, Phil. **211** 7 40N 126 2 E
Comprida, I. **125** 24 50 S 47 42W
Compton **83** 45 14N 71 49W
Compton Downs **231** 30 28 S 146 30 E
Con Cuong **204** 19 2N 104 54 E
Con Son, Is. **205** 8 41N 106 37 E
Cona Niyeu **126** 41 58 S 67 0W
Conakry **246** 9 29N 13 49W
Conara Junction **230** 41 50 S 147 26 E
Conargo **233** 35 16 S 145 10 E
Concarneau **138** 47 52N 3 56W
Conceição, Brazil **120** 7 33 S 38 31W
Conceição, Mozam. **251** 18 47 S 36 7 E
Conceição da Barra **121** 18 35 S 39 45W
Conceição do
Araguaia **120** 8 0 S 49 2W
Conceição do
Canindé **120** 7 54 S 41 34W
Concepción,
Argentina **124** 27 20 S 65 35W
Concepción, Bolivia **123** 16 15 S 62 8W
Concepción, Chile **124** 36 50 S 73 0W
Concepción, Mexico **111** 18 12N 90 4W
Concepción,
Paraguay **124** 23 22 S 57 26W
Concepción, Peru **122** 11 54 S 75 19W
Concepción □ **124** 37 0 S 72 30W
Concepción, B. **99** 26 39N 111 48W
Concepción, Est. de **126** 50 30 S 74 55W
Concepción, L. **123** 17 20 S 61 20W
Concepción, La =
Ri-Aba **247** 3 28N 8 40 E
Concepción, La **118** 10 30N 71 50W
Concepción, Pta. **99** 26 53N 111 50W
Concepción, R. de
la → **100** 30 32N 113 2W
Concepción de
Buenos Aires **106** 19 58N 103 16W
Concepción del Oro **105** 24 38N 101 25W
Concepción del
Uruguay **124** 32 35 S 58 20W
Conception, La **82** 46 9N 74 42W
Conception B.,
Canada **79** 47 45N 53 0W
Conception B.,
Namibia **254** 23 55 S 14 22 E
Conception I. **113** 23 52N 75 9W
Concession **251** 17 27 S 30 56 E
Concha, La **104** 22 45N 105 34W
Conche **79** 50 55N 55 58W
Conches **138** 48 51N 2 43 E
Conchos **101** 27 58N 105 18W
Conchos →,
Chihuahua,
Mexico **101** 29 35N 104 25W
Conchos →,
Tamaulipas,
Mexico **103** 25 7N 98 32W
Concordia,
Argentina **124** 31 20 S 58 2W
Concórdia, Brazil **118** 4 36 S 66 36W
Concordia,
Coahuila, Mexico **102** 25 47N 103 7W
Concordia, Sinaloa,
Mexico **104** 23 17N 106 4W
Concordia, La **110** 16 5N 92 38W
Concots **140** 44 26N 1 40 E
Condah **232** 37 57 S 141 44 E
Condamine **231** 26 56 S 150 9 E
Condat **140** 45 21N 2 46 E
Condé, Angola **253** 10 50 S 14 37 E
Conde, Brazil **121** 11 49 S 37 37W
Condé, France **139** 50 26N 3 34 E
Condé-sur-Noireau **138** 48 51N 0 33W
Condeúba **121** 14 52 S 42 0W
Condobolin **231** 33 4 S 147 6 E
Condom **140** 43 57N 0 22 E
Condove **162** 45 8N 7 19 E
Conegliano **163** 45 53N 12 18 E
Conejera, I. **157** 39 11N 2 58 E
Conejo, Mt. **103** 21 24N 99 6W
Conejos **105** 26 14N 103 53W
Conflans-en-Jarnisy **139** 49 10N 5 52 E
Confolens **140** 46 2N 0 40 E
Confuso → **124** 25 9 S 57 34W
Congjiang **216** 25 43N 108 52 E
Congleton **132** 53 10N 2 12W
Congnarauya **78** 58 35N 68 1W
Congo = Zaïre → **252** 6 4 S 12 24 E
Congo **120** 7 48 S 36 40W
Congo (Kinshasa) ■
= Zaïre ■ **253** 3 0 S 23 0 E
Congo ■ **252** 1 0 S 16 0 E
Congo Basin **236** 0 10 S 24 30 E
Congonhas **121** 20 30 S 43 52W
Conhuas **111** 18 29N 90 7W
Conil **155** 36 17N 6 10W
Coniston **84** 46 29N 80 51W
Conjeeveram =
Kanchipuram **201** 12 52N 79 45 E
Conjuboy **230** 18 35 S 144 35 E
Conkal **111** 21 4N 89 32W
Conklin **90** 55 38N 111 5W
Conlea **231** 30 7 S 144 35 E
Conn, L. **135** 54 3N 9 15W
Connacht **135** 53 23N 8 40W
Connemara **135** 53 29N 9 45W
Conner **210** 17 48N 121 19 E
Connerré **138** 48 3N 0 30 E
Connors **83** 47 10N 68 52W
Connors Ra. **230** 21 40 S 149 10 E
Conoble **231** 32 55 S 144 33 E
Conon → **134** 57 33N 4 28W
Cononaco → **118** 1 32 S 75 35W
Cononbridge **134** 57 32N 4 30W
Conquest **88** 51 32N 107 14W
Conquet, Le **138** 48 21N 4 46W
Conran, C. **231** 37 49 S 148 44 E
Consecon **85** 44 0N 77 31W
Conselheiro Lafaiete **125** 20 40 S 43 48W
Conselheiro Pena **121** 19 10 S 41 30W
Consort **91** 52 1N 110 46W
Constance =
Konstanz **147** 47 39N 9 10 E
Constance, L. =
Bodensee **149** 47 35N 9 25 E
Constanţa **170** 44 14N 28 38 E
Constanţa □ **170** 44 15N 28 15 E
Constantina **155** 37 51N 5 40W
Constantine **241** 36 25N 6 42 E
Constitución, Chile **124** 35 20 S 72 30W

Constitución, Uruguay 124 42 0 S 57 50W
Consuegra 155 39 28N 3 36W
Consul 88 49 20N 109 30W
Contai 199 21 54N 87 46 E
Contamana 122 7 19 S 74 55W
Contarina 163 45 2N 12 13 E
Contas → 121 14 17 S 39 1W
Contes 141 43 49N 7 19 E
Conthey 148 46 14N 7 18 E
Contin L. 89 53 25N 95 10W
Contla 106 19 45N 103 5W
Contra Costa 255 25 9 S 33 30 E
Contrecoeur 83 45 51N 73 14W
Contreras 107 19 18N 99 17W
Contres 138 47 24N 1 26 E
Contrexéville 139 48 6N 5 53 E
Contumaza 122 7 23 S 78 57W
Contwoyto L. 94 65 42N 110 50W
Convención 118 8 28N 73 21W
Conversano 165 40 57N 17 8 E
Conway = Conwy 132 53 17N 3 50W
Conway = Conwy → 132 53 18N 3 50W
Conway, L. 231 28 17 S 135 35 E
Conwy 132 53 17N 3 50W
Conwy → 132 53 18N 3 50W
Cooch Behar = Koch Bihar 202 26 22N 89 29 E
Coodardy 229 27 15 S 117 39 E
Cook 229 30 37 S 130 25 E
Cook, Bahía 126 55 10 S 70 0W
Cook, Mt. 235 43 36 S 170 9 E
Cook Is. 225 17 0 S 160 0W
Cook Strait 235 41 15 S 174 29 E
Cooke Plains 232 35 23 S 139 34 E
Cookhouse 254 32 44 S 25 47 E
Cooking L. 90 53 26N 113 2W
Cook's Harbour 79 51 36N 55 52W
Cookshire 83 45 25N 71 38W
Cookstown 135 54 40N 6 43W
Cookstown □ 135 54 40N 6 43W
Cooktown 230 15 30 S 145 16 E
Coolabah 231 31 1 S 146 43 E
Cooladdi 231 26 37 S 145 23 E
Coolah 231 31 48 S 149 41 E
Coolamon 231 34 46 S 147 8 E
Coolangatta 231 28 11 S 153 29 E
Coolgardie 229 30 55 S 121 8 E
Coolibah 228 15 33 S 130 56 E
Cooma 231 36 12 S 149 8 E
Coombs 92 49 18N 124 25W
Coonabarabran 231 31 14 S 149 18 E
Coonalpyn 232 35 43 S 139 52 E
Coonamble 231 30 56 S 148 27 E
Coonana 229 31 0 S 123 0 E
Coondapoor 201 13 42N 74 40 E
Coongie 231 27 9 S 140 8 E
Coongoola 231 27 43 S 145 51 E
Cooninie, L. 231 26 4 S 139 59 E
Coonoor 201 11 21N 76 45 E
Coopers Cr. → 231 28 29 S 137 46 E
Coorabie 229 31 54 S 132 18 E
Coorabulka 230 23 41 S 140 20 E
Coorong, The 232 35 50 S 139 20 E
Coorow 229 29 53 S 116 2 E
Cooroy 231 26 22 S 152 54 E
Cootamundra 231 34 36 S 148 1 E
Cootehill 135 54 5N 7 5W
Cooyar 231 26 59 S 151 51 E
Cooyeana 230 24 29 S 138 45 E
Copahue Paso 124 37 49 S 71 8W
Copainala 110 17 4N 93 18W
Copala 107 16 39N 99 5W
Copalillo 107 18 2N 99 7W
Copalita 109 15 57N 96 28W
Copalquín 104 25 29N 107 0W
Copán 112 14 50N 89 9W
Copanatoyac 107 17 15N 98 45W
Copas, Pta. 104 25 31N 109 7W
Copatana 118 2 48 S 67 4W
Cope, Cabo 157 37 26N 1 28W
Cope Cope 232 36 27 S 143 5 E
Copenhagen = København 172 55 41N 12 34 E
Copertino 165 40 17N 18 2 E
Copeville 232 34 47 S 139 51 E
Copiapó 124 27 30 S 70 20W
Copiapó → 124 27 19 S 70 56W
Copley 231 30 36 S 138 26 E
Copp L. 76 60 14N 114 40W
Copparo 163 44 52N 11 49 E
Coppename → 119 5 48N 55 55W
Copper Cliff 84 46 28N 81 4W
Copper Queen 251 17 29 S 29 18 E
Copperbelt □ 251 13 15 S 27 30 E
Coppermine 94 67 50N 115 5W
Coppermine → 94 67 49N 116 4W
Coquet → 132 55 18N 1 45W
Coquilhatville = Mbandaka 252 0 1N 18 18 E
Coquimatlán 106 19 12N 103 48W
Coquimbo 124 30 0 S 71 20W
Coquimbo □ 124 31 0 S 71 0W
Corabia 170 43 48N 24 30 E
Coração de Jesus 121 16 43 S 44 22W
Coracora 122 15 5 S 73 45W
Coradi, Is. 165 40 27N 17 10 E
Coral Bay 211 8 25N 117 20 E
Coral Harbour 95 64 8N 83 10W
Coral Sea 224 15 0 S 150 0 E
Corantijn → 119 5 50N 57 8W
Corato 165 41 12N 16 22 E
Corbeil-Essonnes 139 48 36N 2 26 E
Corbie 139 49 54N 2 30 E
Corbières 140 42 55N 2 35 E
Corbigny 139 47 16N 3 40 E
Corbion 143 49 48N 5 0 E
Corbones → 155 37 36N 5 39W
Corby 133 52 49N 0 31W
Corcoles → 157 39 40N 3 18W
Corcubión 154 42 56N 9 12W
Cordenons 163 45 59N 12 42 E
Cordes 140 44 5N 1 57 E
Cordillera Central Range 210 17 20N 120 57 E
Cordisburgo 121 19 7 S 44 21W
Córdoba, Argentina 124 31 20 S 64 10W
Córdoba, Mexico 109 18 53N 96 56W
Córdoba, Spain 155 37 50N 4 50W
Córdoba □, Argentina 124 31 22 S 64 15W
Córdoba □, Colombia 118 8 20N 75 40W
Córdoba □, Spain 155 38 5N 5 0W
Córdoba, Sierra de 124 31 10 S 64 25W
Cordon 210 16 42N 121 32 E
Corella 156 42 7N 1 48W
Corella → 230 19 34 S 140 47 E
Coremas 120 7 1 S 37 58W
Corentyne → 119 5 50N 57 8W
Corfield 230 21 40 S 143 21 E
Corfu = Kérkira 168 39 38N 19 50 E
Corgo 154 42 56N 7 25W
Corguinho 123 19 53 S 54 52W
Cori 164 41 39N 12 53 E
Coria 154 40 0N 6 33W
Coricudgy, Mt. 233 32 51 S 150 24 E
Corigliano Cálabro 165 39 36N 16 31 E
Coringa Is. 230 16 58 S 149 58 E
Corinna 230 41 35 S 145 10 E
Corinth = Kórinthos 169 37 56N 22 55 E
Corinth, G. of = Korinthiakós Kólpos 169 38 16N 22 30 E
Corinth Canal 169 37 58N 23 0 E
Corinto, Brazil 121 18 20 S 44 30W
Corinto, Nic. 112 12 30N 87 10W
Corj □ 170 45 5N 23 25 E
Cork 135 51 54N 8 30W
Cork □ 135 51 50N 8 50W
Cork Harbour 135 51 46N 8 16W
Corlay 138 48 20N 3 5W
Corleone 164 37 48N 13 16 E
Corleto Perticara 165 40 23N 16 2 E
Çorlu 167 41 11N 27 49 E
Cormack 79 49 18N 57 23W
Cormack L. 76 60 56N 121 37W
Cormóns 163 45 58N 13 29 E
Cormorant 89 54 14N 100 35W
Cormorant L. 89 54 15N 100 50W
Corn Is. = Maiz, Islas del 112 12 15N 83 4W
Cornélio Procópio 125 23 7 S 50 40W
Corner Brook 79 48 57N 57 58W
Corníglio 162 44 29N 10 5 E
Corning 88 49 58N 102 58W
Corno, Monte 163 42 28N 13 34 E
Cornwall, Ont., Canada 85 45 2N 74 44W
Cornwall, P.E.I., Canada 81 46 14N 63 13W
Cornwall □ 133 50 26N 4 40W
Cornwall I. 95 77 37N 94 38W
Cornwallis I. 95 75 8N 95 0W
Corny Pt. 232 34 55 S 137 0 E
Coro 118 11 25N 69 41W
Coroaci 121 18 35 S 42 17W
Coroatá 120 4 8 S 44 0W
Coroban 256 3 58N 42 44 E
Corocoro 122 17 15 S 68 28W
Corocoro, I. 119 8 30N 60 10W
Coroico 122 16 0 S 67 50W
Coromandel, Brazil 121 18 28 S 47 13W
Coromandel, N.Z. 234 36 45 S 175 31 E
Coromandel Coast 201 12 30N 81 0 E
Coromandel Pen. 234 37 0 S 175 45 E
Coromandel Ra. 234 37 0 S 175 40 E
Coron 210 12 0N 120 12 E
Coron Bay 211 11 54N 120 8 E
Coron I. 211 11 55N 120 14 E
Corona 231 31 16 S 141 24 E
Coronach 88 49 7N 105 31W
Coronado, Bahía de 112 9 0N 83 40W
Coronados, G. de los 126 41 40 S 74 0W
Coronation 91 52 5N 111 27W
Coronation Gulf 94 68 25N 110 0W
Coronation I. 13 60 45 S 46 0W
Coronation Is. 228 14 57 S 124 55 E
Coronda 124 31 58 S 60 56W
Coronel 124 37 0 S 73 10W
Coronel Bogado 124 27 11 S 56 18W
Coronel Dorrego 124 38 40 S 61 10W
Coronel Fabriciano 121 19 31 S 42 38W
Coronel Murta 121 16 37 S 42 11W
Coronel Oviedo 124 25 24 S 56 30W
Coronel Ponce 123 15 34 S 55 1W
Coronel Pringles 124 38 0 S 61 30W
Coronel Suárez 124 37 30 S 61 52W
Coronel Vidal 124 37 28 S 57 45W
Coroneo 107 20 8N 100 20W
Corongo 122 8 30 S 77 53W
Coronie □ 119 5 55N 56 20W
Coropuna, Nevado 122 15 30 S 72 41W
Çorovoda 168 40 31N 20 14 E
Corowa 231 35 58 S 146 21 E
Corozal 118 9 19N 75 18W
Corps 141 44 50N 5 56 E
Corpus 125 27 10 S 55 30W
Corque 122 18 20 S 67 41W
Corral, Chile 126 39 52 S 73 26W
Corral, Mexico 100 27 37N 109 59W
Corral de Almaguer 156 39 45N 3 10W
Corréggio 162 44 46N 10 47 E
Corrente 120 10 27 S 45 10W
Corrente → 121 13 8 S 43 28W
Correntes → 123 17 38 S 55 8W
Correntes, C. das 255 24 6 S 35 34 E
Correntina 121 13 20 S 44 39W
Corrèze □ 140 45 20N 1 45 E
Correze → 140 45 10N 1 28 E
Corrib, L. 135 53 5N 9 10W
Corrientes 124 27 30 S 58 45W
Corrientes □ 124 28 0 S 57 0W
Corrientes →, Argentina 124 30 42 S 59 38W
Corrientes →, Peru 122 3 43 S 74 35W
Corrientes, C., Mexico 106 20 25N 105 42W
Corrientes, C., Colombia 118 5 30N 77 34W
Corrientes, C., Cuba 112 21 43N 84 30W
Corrigin 229 32 20 S 117 53 E
Corrowidgie 233 36 56 S 148 50 E
Corryong 233 36 12 S 147 53 E
Corse 141 42 0N 9 0 E
Corse, C. 141 43 1N 9 25 E
Corse-du-Sud □ 141 41 45N 9 0 E
Corsica = Corse 141 42 0N 9 0 E
Corso, C. 99 24 39N 112 11W
Cortazar 107 20 29N 100 56W
Corté 141 42 19N 9 11 E
Corte, L. de 111 18 32N 91 59W
Corte do Pinto 155 37 42N 7 29W
Cortegana 155 37 52N 6 49W
Cortes 211 9 17N 126 11 E
Cortijo 107 20 35N 99 10W
Cortina d'Ampezzo 163 46 32N 12 9 E
Cortona 163 43 16N 12 0 E
Coruche 155 38 57N 8 30W
Çorum 177 40 30N 34 57 E
Corumbá 123 19 0 S 57 30W
Corumbá → 121 18 19 S 48 55W
Corumbá de Goiás 121 16 0 S 48 50W
Corumbaíba 121 18 9 S 48 34W
Coruña, La 154 43 20N 8 25W
Coruña, La □ 154 43 10N 8 30W
Corund 170 46 30N 25 13 E
Corunna = Coruña, La 154 43 20N 8 25W
Corunna 84 42 53N 82 26W
Corvette, L. de la 78 53 25N 74 3W
Cosalá 104 24 23N 106 41W
Cosalapa 109 18 35N 96 38W
Cosamaloapan de Carpio 109 18 22N 95 48W
Cosautlán de Carvajal 108 19 20N 96 59W
Coscomatepec de Bravo 109 19 4N 97 2W
Cosenza 165 39 17N 16 14 E
Coşereni 170 44 38N 26 35 E
Cosío 105 22 21N 102 18W
Cosmo Newberry 229 28 0 S 122 54 E
Cosne-sur-Loire 139 47 24N 2 54 E
Cosoleacaque 109 18 0N 94 37W
Cospeito 154 43 12N 7 34W
Cosquín 124 31 15 S 64 30W
Cossato 162 45 34N 8 10 E
Cossé-le-Vivien 138 47 57N 0 54W
Cosson → 139 47 30N 1 15 E
Costa Blanca 157 38 25N 0 10W
Costa Brava 156 41 30N 3 0 E
Costa del Sol 155 36 30N 4 30W
Costa Dorada 156 40 45N 1 15 E
Costa Rica 100 28 55N 111 36W
Costa Rica ■ 112 10 0N 84 0W
Costa Smeralda 164 41 5N 9 35 E
Costebelle, L. 80 50 19N 62 23W
Costigliole d'Asti 162 44 48N 8 11 E
Coştiui 170 47 53N 24 2 E
Coswig 146 51 52N 12 31 E
Cotabato 211 7 14N 124 15 E
Cotabena 232 31 42 S 138 11 E
Cotacajes → 122 16 0 S 67 1W
Cotagaita 124 20 45 S 65 40W
Cotahuasi 122 15 12 S 72 50W
Cotaxtla → 109 19 2N 96 8W
Côte, La 148 46 25N 6 15 E
Côte d'Azur 141 43 25N 6 50 E
Côte d'Or 139 47 10N 4 50 E
Côte-d'Or □ 139 47 30N 4 50 E
Côte-St.-André, La 141 45 24N 5 15 E
Coteau Landing 83 45 15N 74 13W
Cotegipe 121 12 2 S 44 15W
Cotentin 138 49 30N 1 30W
Côtes de Meuse 139 49 15N 5 22 E
Côtes-du-Nord □ 138 48 25N 2 40W
Cotiella 156 42 31N 0 19 E
Cotija de la Paz 106 19 49N 102 43W
Cotina → 166 43 36N 18 50 E
Cotoca 123 17 49 S 63 3W
Cotonou 247 6 20N 2 25 E
Cotopaxi □ 118 0 5 S 78 55W
Cotopaxi, Vol. 122 0 40 S 78 30W
Cotronei 165 39 9N 16 45 E
Cotswold Hills 133 51 42N 2 10W
Cottam 84 42 8N 82 45W
Cottbus 146 51 44N 14 20 E
Cottbus □ 146 51 43N 13 30 E
Coubre, Pte. de la 140 45 42N 1 15W
Couches 139 46 53N 4 30 E
Couço 155 38 59N 8 17W
Coudres, Île aux 83 47 24N 70 23W
Couedic, C. du 232 36 5 S 136 40 E
Couëron 138 47 13N 1 44W
Couesnon → 138 48 38N 1 32W
Couhe-Vérac 140 46 18N 0 12 E
Coulanges 139 47 30N 3 30 E
Coulman I. 13 73 35 S 170 0 E
Coulommiers 139 48 50N 3 3 E
Coulon → 141 43 51N 5 0 E
Coulonge → 82 45 52N 76 46W
Coulonges 140 46 28N 0 35W
Coupeaux, L. 80 51 27N 63 58W
Courantyne → 122 5 55N 57 5W
Courcelles 143 50 28N 4 22 E
Courçon 140 46 15N 0 50W
Couronne, C. 141 43 19N 5 3 E
Cours 141 46 7N 4 19 E
Coursan 140 43 14N 3 4 E
Courseulles 138 49 20N 0 29W
Court-St.-Etienne 143 50 38N 4 34 E
Courtenay 92 49 45N 125 0W
Courtine, La 140 45 43N 2 16 E
Courtland 84 42 51N 80 38W
Courtrai = Kortrijk 143 50 50N 3 17 E
Courtright 84 42 49N 82 28W
Courville 138 48 28N 1 15 E
Coutances 138 49 3N 1 28W
Couterne 138 48 30N 0 25W
Coutras 140 45 3N 0 8W
Coutts 91 49 0N 111 57W
Couture, L. 78 60 7N 75 20W
Couvet 148 46 57N 6 38 E
Couvin 143 50 3N 4 29 E
Covarrubias 156 42 4N 3 31W
Covasna 170 45 50N 26 10 E
Covasna □ 170 45 50N 26 0 E
Cove I. 84 45 17N 81 44W
Coveñas 118 9 24N 75 44W
Coventry 133 52 25N 1 31W
Coventry L. 77 61 15N 106 15W
Covilhã 154 40 17N 7 31W
Cow Head 79 49 55N 57 48W
Cowal, L. 231 33 40 S 147 25 E
Cowan 89 52 5N 100 45W
Cowan, L. 229 31 45 S 121 45 E
Cowan L. 88 54 0N 107 15W
Cowangie 231 35 12 S 141 26 E
Cowansville 83 45 14N 72 46W
Cowarie 231 27 45 S 138 15 E
Cowcowing Lakes 229 30 55 S 117 20 E
Cowdenbeath 134 56 7N 3 20W
Cowell 232 33 39 S 136 56 E
Cowes 133 50 45N 1 18W
Cowichan L. 92 48 53N 124 17W
Cowl Cowl 233 33 36 S 145 18 E
Cowley 91 49 34N 114 5W
Cowra, N.S.W., Australia 231 33 49 S 148 42 E
Cowra, N.S.W., Australia 231 33 50 S 148 41 E
Cox I. 92 50 48N 128 36W
Coxcatlán 109 18 16N 97 9W
Coxim 123 18 30 S 54 55W
Coxim → 123 18 34 S 54 46W
Cox's Bazar 202 21 26N 91 59 E
Cox's Cove 79 49 7N 58 5W
Coyame 101 29 28N 105 6W
Coyoacán 107 19 20N 99 10W
Coyote, Pta. 99 24 44N 110 45W
Coyotitán 104 23 47N 106 35W
Coyuca, de L. 107 16 57N 100 5W
Coyuca de Benítez 107 17 2N 100 4W
Coyuca de Catalán 107 18 20N 100 39W

Coyuquilla 107 17 24N 101 2W
Cozón 100 31 18N 112 29W
Cozumel 111 20 31N 86 55W
Cozumel, I. de 111 20 25N 86 55W
Craboon 231 32 3S 149 30E
Cracow = Kraków 152 50 4N 19 57E
Cracow 231 25 17S 150 17E
Cracroft Is. 92 50 32N 126 25W
Cradock 254 32 8S 25 36E
Craigavon = Lurgan 135 54 28N 6 20W
Craigmore 251 20 28S 32 50E
Craigmyle 91 51 40N 112 15W
Craik 88 51 3N 105 49W
Crailsheim 147 49 7N 10 5E
Craiova 170 44 21N 23 48E
Cramsie 230 23 20S 144 15E
Cranberry Portage 77 54 35N 101 23W
Cranbrook, Tas., Australia 230 42 0S 148 5E
Cranbrook, W. Austral., Australia 229 34 18S 117 33E
Cranbrook, Canada 91 49 30N 115 46W
Crane I. 83 47 4N 70 33W
Crane L. 88 50 5N 109 5W
Crane River 89 51 30N 99 14W
Craon 138 47 50N 0 58W
Craonne 139 49 27N 3 46E
Crapaud 81 46 14N 63 30W
Craponne 140 45 20N 3 51E
Crasna 170 46 32N 27 51E
Crasna → 170 47 44N 22 35E
Crasnei, Munţii 170 47 0N 23 20E
Crater Mt. 227 6 37S 145 7E
Crater Pt. 227 5 25S 152 9E
Crateús 120 5 10S 40 39W
Crati → 165 39 41N 16 30E
Crato, Brazil 120 7 10S 39 25W
Crato, Portugal 155 39 16N 7 39W
Crau 141 43 32N 4 40E
Crauford, C. 95 73 44N 84 51W
Craven 88 50 42N 104 49W
Craven, L. 78 54 20N 76 56W
Cravo Norte 118 6 18N 70 12W
Cravo Norte → 118 6 18N 70 12W
Crawley 133 51 7N 0 10W
Crean L. 88 54 5N 106 9W
Crécy-en-Brie 139 48 50N 2 53E
Crécy-en-Ponthieu 139 50 15N 1 53E
Crediton 84 43 17N 81 33W
Credo 229 30 28S 120 45E
Cree →, Canada 77 58 57N 105 47W
Cree →, U.K. 134 54 51N 4 24W
Cree L. 77 57 30N 106 30W
Creel 101 27 45N 107 38W
Creelman 88 49 49N 103 18W
Creemore 84 44 19N 80 6W
Creil 139 49 15N 2 34E
Crema 162 45 21N 9 40E
Cremona, Canada 91 51 33N 114 29W
Cremona, Italy 162 45 8N 10 2E
Crepaja 166 45 1N 20 38E
Crepori → 123 5 42S 57 8W
Crépy 139 49 37N 3 32E
Crépy-en-Valois 139 49 14N 2 54E
Cres 163 44 58N 14 25E
Crescent Spur 93 53 34N 120 42W
Crescentino 162 45 11N 8 7E
Crespino 163 44 59N 11 51E
Crespo 124 32 2S 60 19W
Cressy 231 38 2S 143 40E
Crest 141 44 44N 5 2E
Cresta, Mt. 210 17 17N 122 6E
Creston 91 49 10N 116 31W
Creswick 232 37 25S 143 58E
Crete = Kríti 169 35 15N 25 0E
Crete, La 76 58 11N 116 24W
Crete, Sea of 169 36 0N 25 0E
Cretin, C. 227 6 40S 147 53E
Creus, C. 156 42 20N 3 19E
Creuse □ 140 46 0N 2 0E
Creuse → 140 47 0N 0 34E
Creusot, Le 139 46 50N 4 24E
Creuzburg 146 51 3N 10 15E
Crevalcore 163 44 41N 11 10E
Crèvecœur-le-Grand 139 49 37N 2 5E
Crevillente 157 38 12N 0 48W
Crewe 132 53 6N 2 28W
Crib Point 231 38 22S 145 13E
Criciúma 125 28 40S 49 23W
Crieff 134 56 22N 3 50W
Crikvenica 163 45 11N 14 40E
Crimea = Krymskiy P-ov. 180 45 0N 34 0E
Crimmitschau 146 50 48N 12 23E
Crimson Lake 91 52 27N 115 2W
Crimson Lake Prov. Park 91 52 28N 114 54W
Crinan 134 56 6N 5 34W
Cristal, Mts. de 252 0 30N 10 30E
Cristalândia 120 10 36S 49 11W
Cristeşti 170 47 15N 26 33E
Cristino Castro 120 8 49S 44 13W
Crişul Alb → 166 46 42N 21 17E
Crişul Negru → 170 46 38N 22 26E
Crişul Repede → 170 46 55N 20 59E
Crivitz 146 53 35N 11 39E
Crixás 121 14 27S 49 58W
Crna Gora 166 42 10N 21 30E
Crna Gora □ 166 42 40N 19 20E
Crna Reka → 166 41 33N 21 59E
Crna Trava 166 42 49N 22 19E
Crni Drim → 166 41 17N 20 40E
Crni Timok → 166 43 53N 22 15E
Çrnoljeva Planina 166 42 20N 21 0E
Črnomelj 163 45 33N 15 10E
Croaghpatrick 135 53 46N 9 40W
Croatia = Hrvatska □ 166 45 20N 18 0E
Crocker, Banjaran 206 5 40N 116 30E
Crocker I. 229 11 12S 132 32E
Crocodile = Krokodil → 255 25 26S 32 0E
Crocodile Is. 230 12 3S 134 58E
Crocq 140 45 52N 2 21E
Crofton 93 48 52N 123 38W
Croisette, C. 141 43 13N 5 20E
Croisic, Le 138 47 18N 2 30W
Croisic, Pte. du 138 47 19N 2 31W
Croix, La, L. 86 48 20N 92 15W
Croker, C., Australia 228 10 58S 132 35E
Croker, C., Canada 84 44 58N 80 59W
Cromarty, Canada 77 58 3N 94 9W
Cromarty, U.K. 134 57 40N 4 2W
Cromer, Canada 89 49 44N 101 14W
Cromer, U.K. 132 52 56N 1 18E
Cromwell 235 45 3S 169 14E
Cronat 139 46 43N 3 40E
Cronulla 231 34 3S 151 8E
Crooked → 76 54 50N 122 54W
Crooked I. 113 22 50N 74 10W
Crooked Island Passage 113 23 0N 74 30W
Crooked L. 79 48 24N 56 17W
Crooked River 88 52 51N 103 44W
Crookwell 231 34 28S 149 24E
Cross → 247 4 42N 8 21E
Cross Creek 81 46 19N 66 43W
Cross Fell 132 54 44N 2 29W
Cross L. 77 54 45N 97 30W
Cross River □ 247 6 0N 8 0E
Crossfield 91 51 25N 114 0W
Crosshaven 135 51 48N 8 19W
Crossley, Mt. 235 42 50S 172 5E
Crotone 165 39 5N 17 6E
Crow → 76 59 41N 124 20W
Crow Hd. 135 51 34N 10 9W
Crowl Creek 233 32 0S 145 30E
Crows Nest 231 27 16S 152 4E
Crowsnest Pass 91 49 40N 114 40W
Croydon, Australia 230 18 13S 142 14E
Croydon, U.K. 133 51 18N 0 5W
Crozet Is. 203 46 27S 52 0E
Crozon 138 48 15N 4 30W
Cruces 101 29 26N 107 24W
Cruillas 103 24 45N 98 31W
Cruz, C. 112 19 50N 77 50W
Cruz, La, C. Rica 112 11 4N 85 39W
Cruz, La, Chihuahua, Mexico 101 27 52N 105 12W
Cruz, La, Sinaloa, Mexico 104 23 55N 106 54W
Cruz, La, Tamaulipas, Mexico 103 24 6N 99 10W
Cruz Alta 125 28 45S 53 40W
Cruz Grande 107 16 44N 99 8W
Cruz das Almas 121 12 0S 39 6W
Cruz de Elorza 103 23 49N 100 29W
Cruz de Malta 120 8 15S 40 20W
Cruz de Piedra 104 23 51N 105 16W
Cruz del Eje 124 30 45S 64 50W
Cruzeiro 121 22 33S 45 0W
Cruzeiro do Oeste 125 23 46S 53 4W
Cruzeiro do Sul 122 7 35S 72 35W
Cry L. 76 58 45N 129 0W
Crystal Brook 231 33 21S 138 12E
Crystal City 89 49 9N 98 57W
Csongrád 151 46 43N 20 12E
Csongrád □ 151 46 32N 20 15E
Csorna 151 47 38N 17 18E
Csurgo 151 46 16N 17 9E
Cu Lao Hon 205 10 54N 108 18E
Cua Rao 204 19 16N 104 27E
Cuácua → 251 17 54S 37 0E
Cuajinicuilapa 107 16 28N 98 25W
Cualac 107 17 46N 98 37W
Cuale, Sa. del 106 20 23N 105 15W
Cuamato 254 17 2S 15 7E
Cuamba 251 14 45S 36 22E
Cuando → 253 14 0S 19 30E
Cuando Cubango □ 254 16 25S 20 0E
Cuangar 254 17 36S 18 39E
Cuango 253 6 15S 16 42E
Cuanza → 236 9 2S 13 30E
Cuanza Norte □ 253 8 50S 14 30E
Cuanza Sul □ 253 10 50S 14 50E
Cuarto → 124 33 25S 63 2W
Cuatotolapan 109 18 8N 95 18W
Cuatrociénegas de Carranza 102 26 59N 102 5W
Cuauhtémoc, Chihuahua, Mexico 101 28 25N 106 52W
Cuauhtémoc, Colima, Mexico 106 19 20N 103 36W
Cuauhtémoc, Durango, Mexico 105 24 24N 103 40W
Cuauhtémoc, Tamaulipas, Mexico 103 22 32N 98 6W
Cuautepec de Hinojosa 107 20 2N 98 18W
Cuautitlán, Jalisco, Mexico 106 19 26N 104 23W
Cuautitlán, México, Mexico 107 19 40N 99 11W
Cuautla 106 20 11N 104 21W
Cuautla Morelos 107 18 48N 98 57W
Cuba 155 38 10N 7 54W
Cuba ■ 112 22 0N 79 0W
Cubal 253 12 26S 14 3E
Cuballing 229 32 50S 117 10E
Cubango → 254 18 50S 22 25E
Cubanja 253 14 49S 21 20E
Cubia 253 15 58S 21 42E
Cubo, Sa. del 107 21 32N 100 57W
Cuchi 253 14 37S 16 58E
Cuchilla, Sa. de la 107 18 10N 101 15W
Cuchillo-Có 126 38 20S 64 37W
Cuchivero → 118 7 40N 65 57W
Cuchumatanes, Sierra de los 112 15 35N 91 25W
Cucuí 118 1 12N 66 50W
Cucurpe 100 30 20N 110 43W
Cucurrupí 118 4 23N 76 56W
Cúcuta 118 7 54N 72 31W
Cudalbi 170 45 46N 27 41E
Cuddalore 201 11 46N 79 45E
Cuddapah 201 14 30N 78 47E
Cuddapan, L. 230 25 45S 141 26E
Cudgewa 231 36 10S 147 42E
Cudillero 154 43 33N 6 9W
Cudworth 88 52 30N 105 44W
Cue 229 27 25S 117 54E
Cuéllar 154 41 23N 4 21W
Cuemba 253 11 50S 17 42E
Cuenca, Ecuador 118 2 50S 79 9W
Cuenca, Spain 156 40 5N 2 10W
Cuenca □ 156 40 0N 2 0W
Cuenca, Serranía de 156 39 55N 1 50W
Cuencamé de Ceniceros 105 24 53N 103 42W
Cuerámaro 107 20 37N 101 43W
Cuerda del Pozo, Pantano de la 156 41 51N 2 44W
Cuernavaca 107 18 55N 99 15W
Cuers 141 43 14N 6 5E
Cuervo, L. del 101 29 17N 105 57W
Cuesmes 143 50 26N 3 56E
Cuetzalán 108 20 2N 97 31W
Cuevas, Cerro 123 22 0S 65 12W
Cuevas del Almanzora 157 37 18N 1 58W
Cuevo 122 20 15S 63 30W
Cugir 170 45 48N 23 25E
Cuiabá 123 15 30S 56 0W
Cuiabá → 123 17 5S 56 36W
Cuicatlán 109 17 48N 96 58W
Cuichapa 109 17 59N 94 15W
Cuilco 112 15 24N 91 58W
Cuillin Hills 134 57 14N 6 15W
Cuillin Sd. 134 57 4N 6 20W
Cuima 253 13 25S 15 45E
Cuiseaux 141 46 30N 5 22E
Cuité 120 6 29S 36 9W
Cuitláhuac 109 18 49N 96 43W
Cuito → 254 18 1S 20 48E
Cuito Cuanavale 253 15 10S 19 10E
Cuitzeo 107 19 59N 101 9W
Cuitzeo, L. de 107 19 55N 101 5W
Cuiuni → 119 0 45S 63 7W
Cujmir 170 44 13N 22 57E
Cukai 205 4 13N 103 25E
Culaba 211 11 40N 124 32E
Culan 140 46 34N 2 20E
Culasi 211 11 26N 122 3E
Culauan 211 5 58N 125 40E
Culburra 232 35 50S 139 58E
Culcairn 231 35 41S 147 3E
Culebra, Sierra de la 154 41 55N 6 20W
Culebra. L. de la 103 22 28N 98 20W
Culemborg 142 51 58N 5 14E
Culgoa 232 35 44S 143 6E
Culgoa → 231 29 56S 146 20E
Culiacán 104 24 48N 107 24W
Culiacán → 104 24 31N 107 41W
Culiacancito 104 24 50N 107 32W
Culion 211 11 54N 120 1E
Culiseu → 123 12 14S 53 17W
Cúllar de Baza 157 37 35N 2 34W
Cullarin Range 231 34 30S 149 30E
Cullen, Australia 228 13 58S 131 54E
Cullen, U.K. 134 57 45N 2 50W
Cullen Pt. 230 11 57S 141 54E
Cullera 157 39 9N 0 17W
Culloden Moor 134 57 29N 4 7W
Culoz 141 45 47N 5 46E
Culpataro 232 33 40S 144 22E
Culuene → 123 12 56S 52 51W
Culver, Pt. 229 32 54S 124 43E
Culverden 235 42 47S 172 49E
Cuma 253 12 52S 15 5E
Cumali 169 36 42N 27 28E
Cumaná 119 10 30N 64 5W
Cumare 118 0 49N 72 32W
Cumari 121 18 16S 48 11W
Cumberland, B.C., Canada 92 49 40N 125 0W
Cumberland, Ont., Canada 85 45 29N 75 24W
Cumberland, Qué., Canada 82 45 30N 75 24W
Cumberland House 89 53 58N 102 16W
Cumberland Is. 230 20 35S 149 10E
Cumberland L. 89 54 3N 102 18W
Cumberland Pen. 95 67 0N 64 0W
Cumberland Sd. 95 65 30N 66 0W
Cumborah 231 29 40S 147 45E
Cumbres Mayores 155 38 4N 6 39W
Cumbria □ 132 54 35N 2 55W
Cumbrian Mts. 132 54 30N 3 0W
Cumbum 201 15 40N 79 10E
Cuminá → 119 1 30S 56 0W
Cuminapanema → 119 1 9S 54 54W
Cummins 231 34 16S 135 43E
Cumnock, Australia 231 32 59S 148 46E
Cumnock, U.K. 134 55 27N 4 18W
Cumpas 100 30 2N 109 48W
Cumpich 111 20 15N 89 57W
Cumshewa Inlet 92 53 3N 131 50W
Cumuripa 100 28 8N 109 53W
Cuñaño 99 23 54N 110 47W
Cuncumén 124 31 53S 70 38W
Cundeelee 229 30 43S 123 26E
Cunderdin 229 31 37S 117 12E
Cundinamarca □ 118 5 0N 74 0W
Cunduacán 110 18 4N 93 10W
Cunene □ 253 16 30S 15 0E
Cunene → 254 17 20S 11 50E
Cúneo 162 44 23N 7 31E
Cunhinga 253 12 11S 16 47E
Cunillera, I. 157 38 59N 1 13E
Cunjamba 253 15 27S 20 10E
Cunlhat 140 45 38N 3 32E
Cunnamulla 231 28 2S 145 38E
Cuorgnè 162 45 23N 7 39E
Cupar, Canada 88 50 57N 104 10W
Cupar, U.K. 134 56 20N 3 0W
Cupareo 107 20 14N 101 1W
Çupica, Golfo de 118 6 25N 77 30W
Ćuprija 166 43 57N 21 26E
Cuquío 106 20 55N 103 2W
Curaçá 120 8 59S 39 54W
Curaçao 113 12 10N 69 0W
Curacautín 126 38 26S 71 53W
Curahuara de Carangas 122 17 52S 68 26W
Curanilahue 124 37 29S 73 28W
Curaray → 118 2 20S 74 5W
Curatabaca 119 6 19N 62 51W
Cure → 139 47 40N 3 41E
Curepto 124 35 8S 72 1W
Curiapo 122 8 33N 61 5W
Curicó 124 34 55S 71 20W
Curicó □ 124 34 50S 71 15W
Curicuriari → 118 0 14S 66 48W
Curimatá 120 10 2S 44 17W
Curiplaya 118 0 16N 74 52W
Curitiba 125 25 20S 49 10W
Currabubula 231 31 16S 150 44E
Currais Novos 120 6 13S 36 30W
Curralinho 120 1 45S 49 46W
Curranyalpa 233 30 53S 144 39E
Curraweena 233 30 47S 145 54E
Currawilla 230 25 10S 141 20E
Currie 230 39 56S 143 53E
Currie, Mt. 255 30 29S 29 21E
Cursole 256 2 14N 45 25E
Curtea de Argeş 170 45 12N 24 42E
Curtis 154 43 7N 8 4W
Curtis Group 230 39 30S 146 37E
Curtis I. 230 23 35S 151 10E
Curuá →, Pará, Brazil 119 2 24S 54 5W
Curuá →, Pará, Brazil 123 5 23S 54 22W
Curuá, I. 120 0 48N 50 10W
Curuaés → 123 7 30S 54 45W
Curuápanema → 119 2 25S 55 2W
Curuçá 120 0 43S 47 50W
Curuguaty 125 24 31S 55 42W
Çürüksu Çayi → 177 37 27N 27 11E
Curup 208 4 26S 102 13E

Curupira, Serra **119** 1 25N 64 30W
Cururu → **123** 7 12 S 58 3W
Cururupu **120** 1 50 S 44 50W
Curuzú Cuatiá **124** 29 50 S 58 5W
Curvelo **121** 18 45 S 44 27W
Curyo **232** 35 50 S 142 47 E
Cushing, Mt. **76** 57 35N 126 57W
Cusihuiriáchic **101** 28 14N 106 50W
Cusna, Monte **162** 44 13N 10 25 E
Cusset **140** 46 8N 3 28 E
Cusson, Pte. **78** 60 23N 77 46W
Custodio **103** 22 39N 99 58W
Cut Knife **88** 52 45N 109 1W
Cutbank **88** 51 18N 106 51W
Cutbank → **90** 54 43N 118 32W
Cutervo **122** 6 25 S 78 55W
Cutral-Có **126** 38 58 S 69 15W
Cutro **165** 39 1N 16 58 E
Cuttaburra → **231** 29 43 S 144 22 E
Cuttack **199** 20 25N 85 57 E
Cutzamala de
Pinzón **107** 18 28N 100 34W
Cuvelai **253** 15 44 S 15 50 E
Cuvier, C. **229** 23 14 S 113 22 E
Cuvier I. **234** 36 27 S 175 50 E
Cuxhaven **146** 53 51N 8 41 E
Cuyabeno **118** 0 16 S 75 53W
Cuyapo **210** 15 46N 120 40 E
Cuyo **211** 10 50N 121 5 E
Cuyo East Pass **211** 11 0N 121 28 E
Cuyo I. **211** 10 51N 121 2 E
Cuyo West Pass **211** 11 0N 120 30 E
Cuyuni → **119** 6 23N 58 41W
Cuyutlán **106** 18 55N 104 4W
Cuyutlán, L. **106** 19 0N 104 10W
Cuzco, Bolivia **122** 20 0 S 66 50W
Cuzco, Peru **122** 13 32 S 72 0W
Çuzco □ **122** 13 31 S 71 59W
Čvrsnica **166** 43 36N 17 35 E
Cwmbran **133** 51 39N 3 0W
Cyangugu **250** 2 29 S 28 54 E
Cybinka **152** 52 12N 14 46 E
Cyclades =
Kikládhes **169** 37 20N 24 30 E
Cygnet **230** 43 8 S 147 1 E
Cynthia **90** 53 17N 115 25W
Cypress Hills **77** 49 40N 109 30W
Cypress Hills Prov.
Park **88** 49 40N 109 30W
Cypress River **89** 49 34N 99 5W
Cyprus ■ **190** 35 0N 33 0 E
Cyrene = Shaḥḥāt **242** 32 48N 21 54 E
Czaplinek **152** 53 34N 16 14 E
Czar **91** 52 27N 110 50W
Czarna →,
Piotrkow Trybunalski,
Poland **152** 51 18N 19 55 E
Czarna →,
Tarnobrzeg,
Poland **152** 50 3N 21 21 E
Czarna Woda **152** 53 51N 18 6 E
Czarne **152** 53 42N 16 58 E
Czarnków **152** 52 55N 16 38 E
Czechoslovakia ■ **151** 49 0N 17 0 E
Czechowice-
Dziedzice **152** 49 54N 18 59 E
Czeladz **152** 50 16N 19 2 E
Czempiń **152** 52 9N 16 33 E
Czeremcha **152** 52 31N 23 21 E
Czersk **152** 53 46N 17 58 E
Czerwieńsk **152** 52 1N 15 13 E
Czerwionka **152** 50 7N 18 37 E
Częstochowa **152** 50 49N 19 7 E
Częstochowa □ **152** 50 45N 19 0 E
Człopa **152** 53 6N 16 6 E
Człuchów **152** 53 41N 17 22 E
Czyzew **152** 52 48N 22 19 E

D

Da → **204** 21 15N 105 20 E
Da Hinggan Ling **213** 48 0N 121 0 E
Da Lat **205** 11 56N 108 25 E
Da Nang **204** 16 4N 108 13 E
Da Qaidam **212** 37 50N 95 15 E
Da Yunhe → **215** 34 25N 120 5 E
Da'an **215** 45 30N 124 7 E
Daap **211** 7 4N 122 12 E
Daarlerveen **142** 52 26N 6 34 E
Dab'a, Râs el **244** 31 3N 28 31 E
Daba Shan **216** 32 0N 109 0 E
Dabai **247** 11 25N 5 15 E
Dabajuro **118** 11 2N 70 40W
Dabakala **246** 8 15N 4 20W
Dabaro **256** 6 21N 48 43 E
Dabbūrīya **189** 32 42N 35 22 E
Dabeiba **118** 7 1N 76 16W
Dabhoi **198** 22 10N 73 20 E
Dąbie, Konin,
Poland **152** 52 5N 18 50 E
Dąbie, Szczecin,
Poland **152** 53 27N 14 45 E
Dabie Shan **217** 31 20N 115 20 E
Dabl, W. → **191** 29 5N 36 16 E
Dabo **208** 0 30 S 104 33 E
Dabola **246** 10 50N 11 5W
Dabou **246** 5 20N 4 23W
Daboya **247** 9 30N 1 20W
Dabrowa Górnicza **152** 50 15N 19 10 E
Dabrowa Tarnówska **152** 50 10N 20 59 E
Dąbrówno **152** 53 27N 20 2 E
Dabu **217** 24 22N 116 41 E
Dabung **205** 5 23N 102 1 E
Dabus → **245** 10 48N 35 10 E
Dacato → **245** 7 25N 42 40 E
Dacca = Dhaka **202** 23 43N 90 26 E
Dacca □ =
Dhaka □ **202** 24 25N 90 25 E
Dachau **147** 48 16N 11 27 E
Dadanawa **119** 2 50N 59 30W
Daday **180** 41 28N 33 27 E
Dades, Oued → **240** 30 58N 6 44W
Dadiya **247** 9 35N 11 24 E
Dadra and Nagar
Haveli □ **198** 20 5N 73 0 E
Dadri = Charkhi
Dadri **198** 28 37N 76 17 E
Dadu **197** 26 45N 67 45 E
Dadu He → **216** 29 31N 103 46 E
Dăeni **170** 44 51N 28 10 E
Daet **210** 14 2N 122 55 E
Dafang **216** 27 9N 105 39 E
Dafdaf, J. **191** 28 16N 35 35 E
Dagana **246** 16 30N 15 35W
Dagash **244** 19 19N 33 25 E
Dagestan
A.S.S.R. □ **181** 42 30N 47 0 E
Dagestanskiye Ogni **181** 42 6N 48 12 E
Dagg Sd. **235** 45 23 S 166 45 E
Daghfeli **244** 19 18N 32 40 E
Dagu **215** 38 59N 117 40 E
Dagua **227** 3 27 S 143 20 E
Daguan **216** 27 43N 103 56 E
Dagupan **210** 16 3N 120 20 E
Dahab **191** 28 31N 34 31 E
Dahlak Kebir **245** 15 50N 40 10 E
Dahlenburg **146** 53 11N 10 43 E
Dahme,
E. Germany **146** 51 51N 13 25 E
Dahme,
W. Germany **146** 54 13N 11 5 E
Dahod **198** 22 50N 74 15 E
Dahomey =
Benin ■ **247** 10 0N 2 0 E
Dahong Shan **217** 31 25N 113 0 E
Dahra **246** 15 22N 15 30W
Dahra, Massif de **240** 36 7N 1 21 E
Dahy, Nafūd ad **194** 22 0N 45 25 E
Dai Hao **204** 18 1N 106 25 E
Dai-Sen **220** 35 22N 133 32 E
Dai Shan **217** 30 25N 122 10 E
Dai Xian **214** 39 4N 112 58 E
Daicheng **214** 38 42N 116 38 E
Daigo **221** 36 46N 140 21 E
Daimanji-San **220** 36 14N 133 20 E
Daimiel **157** 39 5N 3 35W
Daingean **135** 53 18N 7 15W
Dainkog **216** 32 30N 97 58 E
Daintree **230** 16 20 S 145 20 E
Daiō-Misaki **221** 34 15N 136 45 E
Dairût **244** 27 34N 30 43 E
Daisetsu-Zan **218** 43 30N 142 57 E
Daitari **199** 21 10N 85 46 E
Daito **220** 35 19N 132 58 E
Dajarra **230** 21 42 S 139 30 E
Dajia **217** 24 22N 120 37 E
Dajin Chuan → **216** 31 16N 101 59 E
Dak Dam **204** 12 20N 107 21 E
Dak Nhe **204** 15 28N 107 48 E
Dak Pek **204** 15 4N 107 44 E
Dak Song **205** 12 19N 107 35 E
Dak Sui **204** 14 55N 107 43 E
Dakar **246** 14 34N 17 29W
Dakhla **240** 23 50N 15 53W
Dakhla, El Wâhât
el- **244** 25 30N 28 50 E
Dakhovskaya **181** 44 13N 40 13 E
Dakingari **247** 11 37N 4 1 E
Dakor **198** 22 45N 73 11 E
Dakoro **247** 14 31N 6 46 E
Đakovica **166** 42 22N 20 26 E
Đakovo **166** 45 19N 18 24 E
Dala **253** 11 3 S 20 17 E
Dalaba **246** 10 42N 12 15W
Dalachi **214** 36 48N 105 0 E
Dalaguete **211** 9 46N 123 32 E
Dalai Nur **214** 43 20N 116 45 E
Dālakī **193** 29 26N 51 17 E
Dalandzadgad **214** 43 27N 104 30 E
Dalanganem Is. **211** 10 40N 120 17 E
Dālbandīn **197** 29 0N 64 23 E
Dalbeattie **134** 54 55N 3 50W
Dalbosjön **173** 58 40N 12 45 E
Dalby, Australia **231** 27 10 S 151 17 E
Dalby, Sweden **172** 55 40N 13 22 E
Dale **171** 61 22N 5 23 E
Dalen, Neth. **142** 52 42N 6 46 E
Dalen, Norway **171** 59 26N 8 0 E
Dalet **202** 19 59N 93 51 E
Daletme **202** 21 36N 92 46 E
Dalfsen **142** 52 31N 6 16 E
Dalga **244** 27 39N 30 41 E
Dalgān **193** 27 31N 59 19 E
Dalgaranger, Mt. **229** 27 50 S 117 5 E
Dalhousie, Canada **81** 48 5N 66 26W
Dalhousie, India **198** 32 38N 76 0 E
Dalhousie East **81** 44 43N 64 48W
Dalhousie West **81** 44 43N 65 13W
Dali, Shaanxi, China **214** 34 48N 109 58 E
Dali, Yunnan, China **216** 25 40N 100 10 E
Daliang Shan **216** 28 0N 102 45 E
Dalias **157** 36 49N 2 52W
Daling He → **215** 40 55N 121 40 E
Dāliyat el Karmel **189** 32 43N 35 2 E
Dalj **166** 45 29N 18 59 E
Dalkeith **134** 55 54N 3 5W
Dallarnil **231** 25 19 S 152 2 E
Dallol **245** 14 14N 40 17 E
Dalmacija □ **166** 43 20N 17 0 E
Dalmatia =
Dalmacija □ **166** 43 20N 17 0 E
Dalmatovo **182** 56 16N 62 56 E
Dalmellington **134** 55 20N 4 25W
Dalmeny **88** 52 20N 106 46W
Dalnegorsk **218** 44 32N 135 33 E
Dalneretchensk **185** 45 50N 133 40 E
Daloa **246** 7 0N 6 30W
Dalou Shan **216** 28 15N 107 0 E
Dalsjöfors **173** 57 46N 13 5 E
Dalskog **173** 58 44N 12 18 E
Daltenganj **199** 24 0N 84 4 E
Dalton **87** 48 11N 84 1W
Dalton Iceberg
Tongue **13** 66 15 S 121 30 E
Dalupiri I.,
Cagayan, Phil. **210** 19 5N 121 12 E
Dalupiri I.,
N. Samar, Phil. **210** 12 25N 124 16 E
Dalvík **174** 65 58N 18 32W
Daly → **228** 13 35 S 130 19 E
Daly L. **77** 56 32N 105 39W
Daly Waters **230** 16 15 S 133 24 E
Dam Doi **205** 8 50N 105 12 E
Dam Ha **204** 21 21N 107 36 E
Daman **198** 20 25N 72 57 E
Daman □ **198** 20 25N 72 58 E
Dāmaneh **193** 33 1N 50 29 E
Damanhûr **244** 31 0N 30 30 E
Damanzhuang **214** 38 5N 116 35 E
Damar **207** 7 7 S 128 40 E
Damara **252** 4 58N 18 42 E
Damaraland **254** 21 0 S 17 0 E
Damascus =
Dimashq **190** 33 30N 36 18 E
Damaturu **247** 11 45N 11 55 E
Damāvand **193** 35 47N 52 0 E
Damāvand, Qolleh-
ye **193** 35 56N 52 10 E
Damba **253** 6 44 S 15 20 E
Dame Marie **113** 18 36N 74 26W
Dāmghān **193** 36 10N 54 17 E
Dămienesti **170** 46 44N 27 1 E
Damietta = Dumyât **244** 31 24N 31 48 E
Daming **214** 36 15N 115 6 E
Damīr Qābū **192** 36 58N 41 51 E
Dāmīya **189** 32 6N 35 34 E
Dammarie **139** 48 20N 1 30 E
Dammartin **139** 49 3N 2 41 E
Dammastock **149** 46 38N 8 24 E
Damme **146** 52 32N 8 12 E
Damodar → **199** 23 17N 87 35 E
Damoh **199** 23 50N 79 28 E
Damous **241** 36 31N 1 42 E
Dampier **228** 20 41 S 116 42 E
Dampier, Selat **207** 0 40 S 131 0 E
Dampier Arch. **228** 20 38 S 116 32 E
Dampier Str. **227** 5 50 S 148 0 E
Damqawt **195** 16 34N 52 50 E
Damrei, Chuor
Phnum **205** 11 30N 103 0 E
Damville **138** 48 51N 1 5 E
Damvillers **139** 49 20N 5 21 E
Dan-Gulbi **247** 11 40N 6 15 E
Dana **207** 11 0 S 122 52 E
Dana, Lac **78** 50 53N 77 20W
Danakil Depression **245** 12 45N 41 0 E
Danao, Cebu, Phil. **211** 10 31N 124 1 E
Danao, Sorsogon,
Phil. **210** 12 44N 123 51 E
Dand **198** 31 28N 65 32 E
Dandaragan **229** 30 40 S 115 40 E
Dandeldhura **199** 29 20N 80 35 E
Dandenong **231** 38 0 S 145 15 E
Dandong **215** 40 10N 124 20 E
Danfeng **214** 33 45N 110 25 E
Dangan Liedao **217** 22 2N 114 8 E
Dangara **183** 38 6N 69 22 E
Danger Is. =
Pukapuka **225** 10 53 S 165 49W
Danger Pt. **254** 34 40 S 19 17 E
Dangla **245** 11 18N 36 56 E
Dangora **247** 11 30N 8 7 E
Dangrek, Phnom **204** 14 15N 105 0 E
Dangshan **214** 34 27N 116 22 E
Dangtu **217** 31 32N 118 25 E
Dangyang **217** 30 52N 111 44 E
Daniel's Harbour **79** 50 13N 57 35W
Danielskull **254** 28 11 S 23 33 E
Danielson Prov.
Park **88** 51 16N 106 50W
Danilov **179** 58 16N 40 13 E
Danilovgrad **166** 42 38N 19 9 E
Danilovka **179** 50 25N 44 12 E
Daning **214** 36 28N 110 45 E
Danissa **250** 3 15N 40 58 E
Danja **247** 11 21N 7 30 E
Danje-ia-Menha **253** 9 32 S 14 39 E
Ḍank **195** 23 33N 56 16 E
Dankalwa **247** 11 52N 12 12 E
Dankama **247** 13 20N 7 44 E
Dankov **179** 53 20N 39 5 E
Danleng **216** 30 1N 103 31 E
Danlí **112** 14 4N 86 35W
Dannemora **172** 60 12N 17 51 E
Dannenberg **146** 53 7N 11 4 E
Dannevirke **234** 40 12 S 176 8 E
Dannhauser **255** 28 0 S 30 3 E
Danot **256** 7 33N 45 17 E
Danshui **217** 25 12N 121 25 E
Danskin **92** 53 59N 125 47W
Dantan **199** 21 57N 87 20 E
Dante **188** 10 25N 51 16 E
Danube → **170** 45 20N 29 40 E
Danubyu **202** 17 15N 95 35 E
Danukandi **202** 23 32N 90 43 E
Danyang **217** 32 0N 119 31 E
Danzhai **216** 26 11N 107 48 E
Danzig = Gdańsk **152** 54 22N 18 40 E
Dao, Antiqe, Phil. **211** 10 30N 121 57 E
Dao, Capiz, Phil. **211** 11 24N 122 41 E
Dão → **154** 40 20N 8 11W
Dao Xian **217** 25 36N 111 31 E
Daocheng **216** 29 0N 100 10 E
Daora **240** 27 5N 12 59W
Daoud = Aïn Beïda **241** 35 50N 7 29 E
Daoulas **138** 48 22N 4 17W
Dapa **211** 9 46N 126 3 E
Dapitan **211** 8 39N 123 25 E
Dapong **247** 10 55N 0 16 E
Daqing Shan **214** 40 40N 111 0 E
Daqu Shan **217** 30 25N 122 20 E
Dar es Salaam **250** 6 50 S 39 12 E
Dar Mazār **193** 29 14N 57 20 E
Dār Ta'izzah **190** 36 20N 36 52 E
Dar'ā **189** 32 36N 36 7 E
Dar'ā □ **190** 32 55N 36 10 E
Dārāb **193** 28 50N 54 30 E
Darabani **170** 48 10N 26 39 E
Daraj **241** 30 10N 10 28 E
Dārān **193** 32 59N 50 24 E
Daraut Kurgan **183** 39 33N 72 11 E
Daravica **166** 42 32N 20 8 E
Daraw **244** 24 22N 32 51 E
Dārayyā **190** 33 28N 36 15 E
Darazo **247** 11 1N 10 24 E
Darband **198** 34 20N 72 50 E
Darband, Kūh-e **193** 31 34N 57 8 E
Darbhanga **199** 26 15N 85 55 E
Darburruk **256** 9 44N 44 31 E
Darda **166** 45 40N 18 41 E
Dardanelles =
Çanakkale Boğazi **168** 40 0N 26 0 E
Daré, Le, L. =
Lillian L. **80** 51 17N 61 23W
Dārestān **193** 29 9N 58 42 E
Darfield **235** 43 29 S 172 7 E
Darfo **162** 45 52N 10 11 E
Dargai **197** 34 25N 71 55 E
Dargan Ata **184** 40 29N 62 10 E
Dargaville **234** 35 57 S 173 52 E
Darhan Muminggan
Lianheqi **214** 41 40N 110 28 E
Dari **245** 5 48N 30 26 E
Darién, G. del **118** 9 0N 77 0W
Darién, Serranía del **118** 8 30N 77 30W
Dariganga **214** 45 21N 113 45 E
Darinskoye **182** 51 20N 51 44 E
Darjeeling =
Darjiling **199** 27 3N 88 18 E
Darjiling **199** 27 3N 88 18 E
Dark Cove **79** 48 47N 54 13W
Darkan **229** 33 20 S 116 43 E
Darke Peak **232** 33 27 S 136 12 E
Darkhazīneh **193** 31 54N 48 39 E
Darkot Pass **199** 36 45N 73 26 E
Darling → **231** 34 4 S 141 54 E
Darling Downs **231** 27 30 S 150 30 E
Darling Ra. **229** 32 30 S 116 0 E
Darlington **132** 54 33N 1 33W
Darlot, L. **229** 27 48 S 121 35 E
Darłowo **152** 54 25N 16 25 E
Dărmăneşti **170** 46 21N 26 33 E
Darmstadt **147** 49 51N 8 40 E
Darnah **242** 32 40N 22 35 E
Darnah □ **242** 31 0N 23 40 E
Darnall **255** 29 23 S 31 18 E

Darnétal 138 49 25N 1 10 E
Darney 139 48 5N 6 0 E
Darnick 232 32 48 S 143 38 E
Darnley, C. 13 68 0 S 69 0 E
Darnley B. 94 69 30N 123 30W
Daroca 156 41 9N 1 25W
Darr 230 23 13 S 144 7 E
Darr → 230 23 39 S 143 50 E
Darran Mts. 235 44 37 S 167 59 E
Darror → 188 10 30N 50 0 E
Darsana 202 23 35N 88 48 E
Darsi 201 15 46N 79 44 E
Darsser Ort 146 54 29N 12 31 E
Dart → 133 50 24N 3 36W
Dart, C. 13 73 6 S 126 20W
Dartmoor, Australia 232 37 56 S 141 19 E
Dartmoor, U.K. 133 50 36N 4 0W
Dartmouth, Australia 230 23 31 S 144 44 E
Dartmouth, Canada 81 44 40N 63 30W
Dartmouth, U.K. 133 50 21N 3 35W
Dartmouth → 80 48 53N 64 34W
Dartmouth, L. 231 26 4 S 145 18 E
Dartuch, C. 156 39 55N 3 49 E
Daru 227 9 3 S 143 13 E
Daruvar 166 45 35N 17 14 E
Darvaza 184 40 11N 58 24 E
Darvel, Teluk 207 4 50N 118 20 E
Darwha 198 20 15N 77 45 E
Darwin 228 12 25 S 130 51 E
Darwin, Mt. 126 0 10 S 69 55W
Darwin River 228 12 50 S 130 58 E
Daryapur 198 20 55N 77 20 E
Dās 195 25 20N 53 30 E
Dashetai 214 41 0N 109 5 E
Dashkesan 181 40 40N 46 0 E
Dasht 193 37 17N 56 7 E
Dasht → 197 25 10N 61 40 E
Dasht-i-Nawar 198 33 52N 68 0 E
Daska 198 32 20N 74 20 E
Dassa-Zoume 247 7 46N 2 14 E
Dasseneiland 254 33 25 S 18 3 E
Dasserat, L. 82 48 16N 79 25W
Datça 169 36 46N 27 40 E
Datia 199 25 39N 78 27 E
Datian 217 25 40N 117 50 E
Datong, Anhui, China 217 30 48N 117 44 E
Datong, Shanxi, China 214 40 6N 113 18 E
Dattapur = Dhamangaon 198 20 45N 78 15 E
Datu, Tanjung 209 2 5N 109 39 E
Datu Piang 211 7 2N 124 30 E
Daugava → 178 57 4N 24 3 E
Daugavpils 178 55 53N 26 32 E
Daulatabad 200 19 57N 75 15 E
Daule 118 1 56 S 79 56W
Daule → 118 2 10 S 79 52W
Daulnay 81 47 25N 65 28W
Daulpur 198 26 45N 77 59 E
Daun 147 50 10N 6 53 E
Daund 200 18 26N 74 40 E
Dauphin 89 51 9N 100 5W
Dauphin L. 89 51 20N 99 45W
Dauphiné 141 45 15N 5 25 E
Dauqa 244 19 30N 41 0 E
Daura, Borno, Nigeria 247 11 31N 11 24 E
Daura, Kaduna, Nigeria 247 13 2N 8 21 E
Dausa 198 26 52N 76 20 E
Davangere 201 14 25N 75 55 E
Davao 211 7 0N 125 40 E
Davao □ 211 7 0N 125 55 E
Davao, G. of 211 6 30N 125 48 E
Davao del Sur □ 211 6 30N 125 25 E
Davao Oriental □ 211 7 10N 126 30 E
Dāvar Panāh 193 27 25N 62 15 E
Davenport Downs 230 24 8 S 141 7 E
Davenport Ra. 230 20 28 S 134 0 E
David 112 8 30N 82 30W
David Gorodok 178 52 4N 27 8 E
Davidson 88 51 16N 105 59W
Davis 13 68 34 S 17 55 E
Davis Inlet 78 55 50N 60 59W
Davis Sea 13 66 0 S 92 0 E
Davis Str. 95 65 0N 58 0W
Davlekanovo 182 54 13N 55 3 E
Davos 149 46 48N 9 49 E
Davy L. 77 58 53N 108 18W
Dawa → 245 4 11N 42 6 E
Dawaki, Bauchi, Nigeria 247 9 25N 9 33 E
Dawaki, Kano, Nigeria 247 12 5N 8 23 E
Dawes Ra. 230 24 40 S 150 40 E
Dawna Range 202 16 30N 98 30 E
Dawnyein 202 15 54N 95 36 E
Dawqah 194 19 36N 40 54 E
Dawson 94 64 10N 139 30W
Dawson, I. 126 53 50 S 70 50W
Dawson B. 89 52 53N 100 49W
Dawson Creek 76 55 45N 120 15W
Dawson Inlet 77 61 50N 93 25W
Dawson Range 230 24 30 S 149 48 E
Dawu 216 30 55N 101 10 E
Dawwah 195 20 33N 58 48 E
Dax 140 43 44N 1 3W
Daxi 217 24 52N 121 20 E
Daxian 216 31 15N 107 23 E
Daxin 216 22 50N 107 11 E
Daxindian 215 37 30N 120 50 E
Daxinggou 215 43 25N 129 40 E
Daxue Shan, Sichuan, China 216 30 30N 101 30 E
Daxue Shan, Yunnan, China 216 23 42N 99 48 E
Dayao 216 25 43N 101 20 E
Daye 217 30 6N 114 58 E
Dayi 216 30 41N 103 29 E
Daylesford 232 37 21 S 144 9 E
Dayong 217 29 11N 110 30 E
Dayr Abū Sa'īd 189 32 30N 35 42 E
Dayr al-Ghuṣūn 189 32 21N 35 4 E
Dayr az Zawr 192 35 20N 40 5 E
Dayr Dirwān 189 31 55N 35 15 E
Daysland 91 52 50N 112 20W
Dayu 217 25 24N 114 22 E
Daz Dağ 190 36 49N 36 20 E
Dazhu 216 30 41N 107 15 E
Dazu 216 29 40N 105 42 E
De Aar 254 30 39 S 24 0 E
De Bilt 142 52 6N 5 11 E
De Grau 79 48 29N 59 9W
De Grey 228 20 12 S 119 12 E
De Grey → 228 20 12 S 119 13 E
De Koog 142 53 6N 4 46 E
De Morhiban, L. 80 51 50N 62 54W
De Panne 143 51 6N 2 34 E
De Rijp 142 52 33N 4 51 E
Dead Sea 189 31 30N 35 30 E
Deadwood L. 76 59 10N 128 30W
Deakin 229 30 46 S 128 0 E
Deal 133 51 13N 1 25 E
Deal I. 230 39 30 S 147 20 E
Dealesville 254 28 41 S 25 44 E
De'an 217 29 21N 115 46 E
Dean → 92 52 49N 126 58W
Dean, Forest of 133 51 50N 2 35W
Dean Chan. 92 52 30N 127 15W
Deán Funes 124 30 20 S 64 20W
Dease → 76 59 56N 128 32W
Dease Arm 94 66 52N 119 37W
Dease L. 76 58 40N 130 5W
Dease Lake 76 58 25N 130 6W
Deauville 138 49 23N 0 2 E
Deba Habe 247 10 14N 11 20 E
Debaltsevo 180 48 22N 38 26 E
Debao 216 23 21N 106 46 E
Debar 166 41 31N 20 30 E
Debden 88 53 30N 106 50W
Debdou 241 33 59N 3 0W
Debec 81 46 4N 67 41W
Debert 81 45 26N 63 28W
Debessy 182 57 39N 53 49 E
Dębica 152 50 2N 21 25 E
Dęblin 152 51 34N 21 50 E
Debno 152 52 44N 14 41 E
Débo, L. 246 15 14N 4 15W
Debolt 90 55 12N 118 1W
Deborah East, L. 229 30 45 S 119 0 E
Deborah West, L. 229 30 45 S 118 50 E
Debrc 166 44 38N 19 53 E
Debre Birhan 245 9 41N 39 31 E
Debre Markos 245 10 20N 37 40 E
Debre May 245 11 20N 37 25 E
Debre Sina 245 9 51N 39 50 E
Debre Tabor 245 11 50N 38 26 E
Debre Zebit 245 11 48N 38 30 E
Debrecen 151 47 33N 21 42 E
Dečani 166 42 30N 20 10 E
Decazeville 140 44 34N 2 15 E
Deccan 200 18 0N 79 0 E
Decelles, Rés. 82 47 42N 78 8W
Déception, B. 78 62 8N 74 41W
Deception, Mt. 232 30 42 S 138 16 E
Deception I. 13 63 0 S 60 15W
Deception L. 77 56 33N 104 13W
Dechang 216 27 25N 102 11 E
Děčín 150 50 47N 14 12 E
Decize 139 46 50N 3 28 E
Decollatura 165 39 2N 16 21 E
Deda 170 46 56N 24 50 E
Dedaye 202 16 24N 95 53 E
Dedéagach = Alexandroúpolis 168 40 50N 25 54 E
Dedemsvaart 142 52 36N 6 28 E
Dedilovo 179 53 59N 37 50 E
Dédougou 246 12 30N 3 25W
Deduru Oya 201 7 32N 79 50 E
Dedza 251 14 20 S 34 20 E
Dee →, Scotland, U.K. 134 57 4N 2 7W
Dee →, Wales, U.K. 132 53 15N 3 7W
Deep B. 76 61 15N 116 35W
Deep Lead 232 37 0 S 142 43 E
Deep Well 230 24 20 S 134 0 E
Deepwater 231 29 25 S 151 51 E
Deer → 77 58 23N 94 13W
Deer, L. 79 49 6N 57 35W
Deer Lake, Newf., Canada 79 49 11N 57 27W
Deer Lake, Ont., Canada 77 52 36N 94 20W
Deer Pond 79 48 30N 54 45W
Deeral 230 17 14 S 145 55 E
Deerdepoort 254 24 37 S 26 27 E
Deerlijk 143 50 51N 3 22 E
Deganya 189 32 43N 35 34 E
Dêgê 216 31 44N 98 39 E
Degebe → 155 38 13N 7 29W
Degeh Bur 256 8 11N 43 31 E
Dégelis 83 47 30N 68 35W
Degema 247 4 50N 6 48 E
Degersheim 149 47 23N 9 12 E
Deggendorf 147 48 49N 12 59 E
Degollado 106 20 28N 102 9W
Deh Bīd 193 30 39N 53 11 E
Deh-e Shīr 193 31 29N 53 45 E
Dehaj 193 30 42N 54 53 E
Dehak 197 27 11N 62 37 E
Dehdez 193 31 43N 50 17 E
Dehestān 193 28 30N 55 35 E
Dehgolān 192 35 17N 47 25 E
Dehibat 241 32 0N 10 47 E
Dehiwala 201 6 50N 79 51 E
Dehlorān 192 32 41N 47 16 E
Dehnow-e Kūhestān 193 27 58N 58 32 E
Dehra Dun 198 30 20N 78 4 E
Dehri 199 24 50N 84 15 E
Dehua 217 25 26N 118 14 E
Dehui 215 44 30N 125 40 E
Deinze 143 50 59N 3 32 E
Dej 170 47 10N 23 52 E
Deje 172 59 35N 13 29 E
Dejiang 216 28 18N 108 7 E
Dekemhare 245 15 6N 39 0 E
Dekese 252 3 24 S 21 24 E
Dekhkanabad 183 38 21N 66 30 E
Dekoa 252 6 19N 19 4 E
Del Carmen 211 9 50N 126 0 E
Delai 244 17 21N 36 6 E
Delareyville 254 26 41 S 25 26 E
Delaronde L. 88 54 3N 107 3W
Delburne 91 52 12N 113 14W
Delčevo 166 41 58N 22 46 E
Delegate 231 37 4 S 148 56 E
Delémont 148 47 22N 7 20 E
Delft 142 52 1N 4 22 E
Delft I. 201 9 30N 79 40 E
Delfzijl 142 53 20N 6 55 E
Delgado, C. 251 10 45 S 40 40 E
Delgerhet 214 45 50N 110 30 E
Delgo 244 20 6N 30 40 E
Delhi, Canada 84 42 51N 80 30W
Delhi, India 198 28 38N 77 17 E
Deli Jovan 166 44 13N 22 9 E
Delia 91 51 38N 112 23W
Delice → 177 39 45N 34 15 E
Delicias 101 28 13N 105 28W
Delījān 193 33 59N 50 40 E
Delisle 88 51 55N 107 8W
Delitzsch 146 51 32N 12 22 E
Delle 139 47 30N 7 2 E
Dellys 241 36 57N 3 57 E
Delmenhorst 146 53 3N 8 37 E
Delmiro Gouveia 120 9 24 S 38 6W
Delnice 163 45 23N 14 50 E
Delong, Ostrova 185 76 40N 149 20 E
Deloraine, Australia 230 41 30 S 146 40 E
Deloraine, Canada 89 49 15N 100 29W
Delorme, L. 78 54 31N 69 52W
Delphi 169 38 28N 22 30 E
Delportshoop 254 28 22 S 24 20 E
Delsbo 172 61 48N 16 32 E
Delta Amacuro □ 119 8 30N 61 30W
Delta Beach 89 50 11N 98 19W
Delungra 231 29 39 S 150 51 E
Delvina 168 39 59N 20 4 E
Delvinákion 168 39 57N 20 32 E
Demak 209 6 53 S 110 38 E
Demanda, Sierra de la 156 42 15N 3 0W
Demba 253 5 28 S 22 15 E
Demba Chio 253 9 41 S 13 41 E
Dembecha 245 10 32N 37 30 E
Dembi 245 8 5N 36 25 E
Dembia 250 3 33N 25 48 E
Dembidolo 245 8 34N 34 50 E
Demer → 143 50 57N 4 42 E
Demerara □ 119 6 0N 58 30W
Demetrias 168 39 22N 23 1 E
Demidov 178 55 16N 31 30 E
Demini → 119 0 46 S 62 56W
Demmin 146 53 54N 13 2 E
Demnate 240 31 44N 6 59W
Demonte 162 44 18N 7 18 E
Dempo, Mt. 208 4 2 S 103 15 E
Demyansk 178 57 40N 32 27 E
Den Burg 142 53 3N 4 47 E
Den Chai 204 17 59N 100 4 E
Den Dungen 143 51 41N 5 22 E
Den Haag = 's-Gravenhage 142 52 7N 4 17 E
Den Ham 142 52 28N 6 30 E
Den Helder 142 52 57N 4 45 E
Den Hulst 142 52 36N 6 16 E
Den Oever 142 52 56N 5 2 E
Denain 139 50 20N 3 22 E
Denau 183 38 16N 67 54 E
Denbigh, Canada 85 45 8N 77 15W
Denbigh, U.K. 132 53 12N 3 26W
Dendang 209 3 7 S 107 56 E
Dender → 143 51 2N 4 6 E
Denderhoutem 143 50 53N 4 2 E
Denderleeuw 143 50 54N 4 5 E
Dendermonde 143 51 2N 4 5 E
Deneba 245 9 47N 39 10 E
Denekamp 142 52 22N 7 1 E
Denezhkin Kamen, Gora 182 60 25N 59 32 E
Deng Deng 252 5 12N 13 31 E
Deng Xian 217 32 34N 112 4 E
Dengchuan 216 25 59N 100 3 E
Denge 247 12 52N 5 21 E
Dengfeng 214 34 25N 113 2 E
Dengi 247 9 25N 9 55 E
Dengkou 214 40 18N 106 55 E
Denham 229 25 56 S 113 31 E
Denham Ra. 230 21 55 S 147 46 E
Denham Sd. 229 25 45 S 113 15 E
Denia 157 38 49N 0 8 E
Denial B. 231 32 14 S 133 32 E
Deniliquin 231 35 30 S 144 58 E
Denison Plains 228 18 35 S 128 0 E
Denisovka 182 52 28N 61 46 E
Denizli 177 37 42N 29 2 E
Denman 233 32 24 S 150 42 E
Denman Glacier 13 66 45 S 99 25 E
Denman Island 92 49 33N 124 48W
Denmark 229 34 59 S 117 25 E
Denmark ■ 173 55 30N 9 0 E
Denmark Str. 128 66 0N 30 0W
Denpasar 206 8 45 S 115 14 E
D'Entrecasteaux Is. 227 9 0 S 151 0 E
D'Entrecasteaux Pt. 229 34 50 S 115 57 E
Dents du Midi 148 46 10N 6 56 E
Denu 247 6 4N 1 8 E
Denzil 88 52 14N 109 39W
Deoband 198 29 42N 77 43 E
Deobhog 200 19 53N 82 44 E
Deogarh 199 21 32N 84 45 E
Deoghar 199 24 30N 86 42 E
Deolali 200 19 58N 73 50 E
Deoli = Devli 198 25 50N 75 20 E
Deoria 199 26 31N 83 48 E
Deosai Mts. 199 35 40N 75 0 E
Departure Bay 92 49 13N 123 57W
Deping 215 37 25N 116 58 E
Depot Springs 229 27 55 S 120 3 E
Deputatskiy 185 69 18N 139 54 E
Dêqên 216 28 34N 98 51 E
Deqing 217 23 8N 111 42 E
Dera Ghazi Khan 197 30 5N 70 43 E
Dera Ismail Khan 197 31 50N 70 50 E
Derbent 174 42 5N 48 15 E
Derby, Australia 228 17 18 S 123 38 E
Derby, U.K. 132 52 55N 1 28W
Derby □ 132 52 55N 1 28W
Derecske 151 47 20N 21 33 E
Derg → 135 54 42N 7 26W
Derg, L. 135 53 0N 8 20W
Dergachi 179 50 9N 36 11 E
Dermantsi 167 43 8N 24 17 E
Deroche 93 49 12N 122 4W
Dêrong 216 28 44N 99 9 E
Derrinallum 232 37 57 S 143 15 E
Derry = Londonderry 135 55 0N 7 20W
Derryveagh Mts. 135 55 0N 8 40W
Derudub 244 17 31N 36 7 E
Derval 138 47 40N 1 41W
Dervéni 169 38 8N 22 25 E
Derventa 166 44 59N 17 55 E
Derwent 90 53 41N 110 58W
Derwent →, Derby, U.K. 132 52 53N 1 17W
Derwent →, N. Yorks., U.K. 132 53 45N 0 57W
Derwent Water, L. 132 54 35N 3 9W
Desaguadero →, Argentina 124 34 30 S 66 46W
Desaguadero →, Bolivia 122 18 24 S 67 5W
Desaguadero →, Peru 122 16 35 S 69 5W
Desbarats 84 46 20N 83 56W
Desbiens 83 48 25N 71 57W
Descanso, Mesa del. 98 32 15N 116 45W
Deschaillons 83 46 32N 72 7W
Deschambault 83 46 39N 71 56W
Descharme → 77 56 51N 109 13W
Deschênes, Ont., Canada 85 45 25N 75 49W

Deschênes, Qué., Canada 82 45 23N 75 48W
Dese 245 11 5N 39 40 E
Deseado, C. 126 52 45 S 74 42W
Desenzano del Gardo 162 45 28N 10 32 E
Deseronto 85 44 12N 77 3W
Désirade, I. 113 16 18N 61 3W
Deskenatlata L. 76 60 55N 112 3W
Desmarais 90 55 56N 113 49W
Desmaraisville 82 49 32N 76 9W
Desméloizes 82 48 57N 79 29W
Desna → 178 50 33N 30 32 E
Desnătui → 170 44 15N 23 27 E
Desolación, I. 126 53 0 S 74 0W
Desolation Sound Prov. Marine Park 92 50 5N 124 25W
Despeñaperros, Paso 157 38 24N 3 30W
Despotovac 166 44 6N 21 30 E
Dessau 146 51 49N 12 15 E
Dessel 143 51 15N 5 7 E
Dessye = Dese 245 11 5N 39 40 E
D'Estrees B. 232 35 55 S 137 45 E
Destruction Bay 94 61 15N 138 48W
Desuri 198 25 18N 73 35 E
Desvrès 139 50 40N 1 48 E
Det Udom 204 14 54N 105 5 E
Deta 166 45 24N 21 13 E
Dete 251 18 38 S 26 50 E
Detinja → 166 43 51N 19 45 E
Detmold 146 51 55N 8 50 E
Deurne, Belgium 143 51 12N 4 24 E
Deurne, Neth. 143 51 27N 5 49 E
Deutsche Bucht 146 54 10N 7 51 E
Deutschlandsberg 150 46 49N 15 14 E
Deux-Loutres, L. aux 80 51 31N 62 28W
Deux-Sèvres □ 138 46 35N 0 20W
Deva 170 45 53N 22 55 E
Devakottai 201 9 55N 78 45 E
Devaprayag 199 30 13N 78 35 E
Devastation Chan. 92 53 40N 128 50W
Dévaványa 151 47 2N 20 59 E
Deveci Daği 180 40 10N 36 0 E
Devecser 151 47 6N 17 26 E
Deventer 142 52 15N 6 10 E
Devenyns, L. 83 47 5N 73 50W
Deveron → 134 57 40N 2 31W
Devesel 170 44 28N 22 41 E
Devgad, I. 201 14 48N 74 5 E
Devgadh Bariya 198 22 40N 73 55 E
Devil River Pk. 235 40 56 S 172 37 E
Devils Paw 76 58 47N 134 0W
Devil's Pt. 201 9 26N 80 6 E
Devin 167 41 44N 24 24 E
Devizes 133 51 21N 2 0W
Devli 198 25 50N 75 20 E
Devnya 167 43 13N 27 33 E
Devolii → 168 40 57N 20 15 E
Devon 90 53 24N 113 44W
Devon I. 95 75 10N 85 0W
Devonport, Australia 230 41 10 S 146 22 E
Devonport, N.Z. 234 36 49 S 174 49 E
Devonport, U.K. 133 50 23N 4 11W
Devonshire □ 133 50 50N 3 40W
Dewas 198 22 59N 76 3 E
Dewberry 90 53 35N 110 32W
Dewetsdorp 254 29 33 S 26 39 E
Dewsbury 132 53 42N 1 38W
Dexing 217 28 46N 117 30 E
Dey-Dey, L. 229 29 12 S 131 4 E
Deyang 216 31 3N 104 27 E
Deyhūk 193 33 15N 57 30 E
Deyyer 193 27 55N 51 55 E
Dezadeash L. 76 60 28N 136 58W
Dezfūl 193 32 20N 48 30 E
Dezhneva, Mys 185 66 5N 169 40W
Dezhou 214 37 26N 116 18 E
Dháfni 169 37 48N 22 1 E
Dhahab → 190 36 5N 37 30 E
Dhahaban 194 21 58N 39 3 E
Dhahiriya = Az Zāhirīyah 191 31 25N 34 58 E
Dhahran = Az Zahrān 193 26 10N 50 7 E
Dhaka 202 23 43N 90 26 E
Dhaka □ 202 24 25N 90 25 E
Dhamangaon 198 20 45N 78 15 E
Dhamar 194 14 30N 44 20 E
Dhamási 168 39 43N 22 11 E
Dhampur 199 29 19N 78 33 E
Dhamtari 199 20 42N 81 35 E
Dhanbad 199 23 50N 86 30 E
Dhankuta 199 26 55N 87 40 E
Dhanora 199 20 20N 80 22 E
Dhar 198 22 35N 75 26 E
Dharampur, Gujarat, India 200 20 32N 73 17 E
Dharampur, Mad. P., India 198 22 13N 75 18 E
Dharamsala = Dharmsala 198 32 16N 76 23 E
Dharapuram 201 10 45N 77 34 E
Dharmapuri 201 12 10N 78 10 E
Dharmavaram 201 14 29N 77 44 E
Dharmsala 198 32 16N 76 23 E
Dharwad 201 15 22N 75 15 E
Dhaulagiri 199 28 39N 83 28 E
Dhebar, L. 198 24 10N 74 0 E
Dhenkanal 199 20 45N 85 35 E
Dhenoúsa 169 37 8N 25 48 E
Dheskáti 168 39 55N 21 49 E
Dhespotikó 169 36 57N 24 58 E
Dhestina 169 38 25N 22 31 E
Dhībān 191 31 30N 35 46 E
Dhidhimótikhon 168 41 22N 26 29 E
Dhikti 169 35 8N 25 22 E
Dhilianáta 169 38 15N 20 34 E
Dhílos 169 37 23N 25 15 E
Dhimitsána 169 37 36N 22 3 E
Dhírfis 169 38 40N 23 54 E
Dhodhekánisos 169 36 35N 27 0 E
Dhokós 169 37 20N 23 20 E
Dholiana 168 39 54N 20 32 E
Dholka 198 22 44N 72 29 E
Dhomokós 169 39 10N 22 18 E
Dhoraji 198 21 45N 70 37 E
Dhoxáton 168 41 9N 24 16 E
Dhragonísi 169 37 27N 25 29 E
Dhrangadhra 198 22 59N 71 31 E
Dhriopís 169 37 25N 24 35 E
Dhrol 198 22 33N 70 25 E
Dhubāb 194 12 56N 43 25 E
Dhuburi 202 26 2N 89 59 E
Dhula 188 15 10N 47 30 E
Dhulasar 202 21 52N 90 14 E
Dhule 198 20 58N 74 50 E
Dhupdhara 202 26 10N 91 4 E
Dhurm → 244 20 18N 42 53 E
Di Linh 205 11 35N 108 4 E
Di Linh, Cao Nguyen 205 11 30N 108 0 E
Día 169 35 26N 25 13 E
Diablerets, Les 148 46 22N 7 10 E
Diafarabé 246 14 9N 4 57W
Diala 246 14 10N 10 0W
Dialakoro 246 12 18N 7 54W
Diallassagou 246 13 47N 3 41W
Diamante 124 32 5 S 60 40W
Diamante → 124 34 30 S 66 46W
Diamante, Pta. 107 16 47N 99 52W
Diamantina 121 18 17 S 43 40W
Diamantina → 231 26 45 S 139 10 E
Diamantino 123 14 30 S 56 30W
Diamond City 91 49 48N 112 51W
Diamond Harbour 199 22 11N 88 14 E
Diamond Is. 230 17 25 S 151 5 E
Diana B. 78 61 20N 70 0W
Dianbai 217 21 33N 111 0 E
Diancheng 217 21 30N 111 4 E
Diano Marina 162 43 55N 8 3 E
Dianópolis 121 11 38 S 46 50W
Dianra 246 8 45N 6 14W
Diapaga 247 12 5N 1 46 E
Diapangou 247 12 5N 0 10 E
Diapur 232 36 19 S 141 29 E
Diariguila 246 10 35N 10 2W
Dībā 195 25 45N 56 16 E
Dibaya 253 6 30 S 22 57 E
Dibaya-Lubue 253 4 12 S 19 54 E
Dibbi 245 4 10N 41 52 E
Dibble Glacier Tongue 13 66 8 S 134 32 E
Dibete 254 23 45 S 26 32 E
Dibrugarh 202 27 29N 94 55 E
Dickson 184 73 40N 80 5 E
Dicomano 163 43 53N 11 30 E
Didam 142 51 57N 6 8 E
Didesa, W. → 245 10 2N 35 32 E
Didiéni 246 13 53N 8 6W
Didsbury 91 51 35N 114 10W
Didwana 198 27 23N 17 36 E
Die 141 44 47N 5 22 E
Diébougou 246 11 0N 3 15W
Dieciocho de Marzo 102 25 41N 97 50W
Diefenbaker L. 77 51 0N 106 55W
Diego Garcia 203 7 50 S 72 50 E
Diekirch 143 49 52N 6 10 E
Diélette 138 49 33N 1 52W
Diéma 246 14 32N 9 12W
Diémbéring 246 12 29N 16 47W
Diemen 142 52 21N 4 58 E
Dien Ban 204 15 53N 108 16 E
Dien Bien 204 21 20N 103 0 E
Dien Khanh 205 12 15N 109 6 E
Diepenbeek 143 50 54N 5 25 E
Diepenheim 142 52 12N 6 33 E
Diepenveen 142 52 18N 6 9 E
Diepholz 146 52 37N 8 22 E
Diepoldsau 149 47 23N 9 40 E
Dieppe, Canada 81 46 6N 64 45W
Dieppe, France 138 49 54N 1 4 E
Dieren 142 52 3N 6 6 E
Diessen 143 51 29N 5 10 E
Diessenhofen 149 47 42N 8 46 E
Diest 143 50 58N 5 4 E
Dietikon 149 47 24N 8 24 E
Dieulefit 141 44 32N 5 4 E
Dieuze 139 48 49N 6 43 E
Diever 142 52 51N 6 19 E
Differdange 143 49 31N 5 54 E
Diffun 210 16 36N 121 33 E
Dig 198 27 28N 77 20 E
Digba 250 4 25N 25 48 E
Digboi 202 27 23N 95 38 E
Digby 81 44 38N 65 50W
Digby Neck 81 44 30N 66 5W
Digges 77 58 40N 94 0W
Digges Is. 78 62 40N 77 50W
Dighinala 202 23 15N 92 5 E
Diglur 200 18 34N 77 33 E
Digne 141 44 5N 6 12 E
Digoin 140 46 29N 3 58 E
Digos 211 6 45N 125 20 E
Digranes 174 66 4N 14 44 E
Digras 200 20 6N 77 45 E
Digul → 207 7 7 S 138 42 E
Dīhōk 192 36 55N 38 57 E
Dijlah, Nahr → 192 31 0N 47 25 E
Dijle → 143 50 58N 4 41 E
Dijon 139 47 20N 5 0 E
Dikala 245 4 45N 31 28 E
Dikkil 245 11 8N 42 20 E
Dikomu di Kai 254 24 58 S 24 36 E
Diksmuide 143 51 2N 2 52 E
Dikson = Dickson 184 73 40N 80 5 E
Dikwa 247 12 4N 13 30 E
Dila 245 6 21N 38 22 E
Dilbeek 143 50 51N 4 17 E
Dildo 79 47 34N 53 33W
Dili 207 8 39 S 125 34 E
Dilizhan 181 40 46N 44 57 E
Dilj 166 45 29N 18 1 E
Dilke 88 50 52N 105 15W
Dillenburg 146 50 44N 8 17 E
Dilling 245 12 3N 29 35 E
Dillingen 147 48 32N 10 29 E
Dillon 77 55 56N 108 35W
Dillon → 77 55 56N 108 56W
Dilolo 253 10 28 S 22 18 E
Dilsen 143 51 2N 5 44 E
Dilston 230 41 22 S 147 10 E
Dimapur 202 25 54N 93 45 E
Dimas 104 23 43N 106 47W
Dimasalang 210 12 12N 123 51 E
Dimashq 190 33 30N 36 18 E
Dimashq □ 190 33 30N 36 30 E
Dimbelenge 253 5 33 S 23 7 E
Dimbokro 246 6 45N 4 46W
Dimboola 231 36 28 S 142 7 E
Dîmbovița □ 170 45 0N 25 30 E
Dîmbovița → 170 44 14N 26 13 E
Dîmbovnic → 170 44 28N 25 18 E
Dimbulah 230 17 8 S 145 4 E
Dimitrovgrad, Bulgaria 167 42 5N 25 35 E
Dimitrovgrad, U.S.S.R. 179 54 14N 49 39 E
Dimitrovgrad, Yugoslavia 166 43 0N 22 48 E
Dimitrovo = Pernik 166 42 35N 23 2 E
Dimo 245 5 19N 29 10 E
Dimona 189 31 2N 35 1 E
Dimovo 166 43 43N 22 50 E
Dinagat 211 10 10N 125 40 E
Dinaig 211 7 11N 124 10 E
Dinajpur 202 25 33N 88 43 E
Dinalupihan 210 14 52N 120 28 E
Dinamita 105 25 43N 103 38W
Dinan 138 48 28N 2 2W
Dīnān Āb 193 32 4N 56 49 E
Dinant 143 50 16N 4 55 E
Dinapur 199 25 38N 85 5 E
Dinara Planina 163 44 0N 16 30 E
Dinard 138 48 38N 2 6W
Dinaric Alps = Dinara Planina 163 44 0N 16 30 E
Dinas 211 7 38N 123 20 E
Dinder, Nahr ed → 245 14 6N 33 40 E
Dindi → 201 16 24N 78 15 E
Dindigul 201 10 25N 78 0 E
Ding Xian 214 38 30N 114 59 E
Dingalan 210 15 18N 121 25 E
Dingalan Bay 210 15 18N 121 25 E
Dingbian 214 37 35N 107 32 E
Dingelstädt 146 51 19N 10 19 E
Dinghai 217 30 1N 122 6 E
Dingle 135 52 9N 10 17W
Dingle B. 135 52 3N 10 20W
Dingnan 217 24 45N 115 0 E
Dingo 230 23 38 S 149 19 E
Dingolfing 147 48 38N 12 30 E
Dingras 210 18 6N 120 42 E
Dingtao 214 35 5N 115 35 E
Dinguiraye 246 11 18N 10 49W
Dingwall, Canada 81 46 54N 60 28W
Dingwall, U.K. 134 57 36N 4 26W
Dingxi 214 35 30N 104 33 E
Dingxiang 214 38 30N 112 58 E
Dingyuan 217 32 32N 117 41 E
Dinh, Mui 205 11 22N 109 1 E
Dinh Lap 204 21 33N 107 6 E
Dinhata 202 26 8N 89 27 E
Dinkel → 142 52 30N 6 58 E
Dinokwe 254 23 29 S 26 37 E
Dinorwic 86 49 41N 92 30W
Dinorwic L. 86 49 37N 92 33W
Dinosaur Prov. Park 91 50 47N 111 30W
Dinslaken 143 51 34N 6 41 E
Dinsmore 88 51 20N 107 26W
Dinsor 256 2 24N 42 59 E
Dintel → 143 51 39N 4 22 E
Dinteloord 143 51 38N 4 22 E
Dinxperlo 142 51 52N 6 30 E
Dio 173 56 37N 14 15 E
Dionne, L. 80 49 26N 67 55W
Diósgyőr 151 48 7N 20 43 E
Diosig 170 47 18N 22 2 E
Diourbel 246 14 39N 16 12W
Dipaculao 210 15 51N 121 32 E
Diphu Pass 202 28 9N 97 20 E
Diplo 198 24 35N 69 35 E
Dipolog 211 8 36N 123 20 E
Dipșa 170 46 58N 24 27 E
Dipton 235 45 54 S 168 22 E
Dir 197 35 8N 71 59 E
Diré 246 16 20N 3 25W
Dire Dawa 245 9 35N 41 45 E
Diriamba 112 11 51N 86 19W
Dirico 253 17 50 S 20 42 E
Dirk Hartog I. 229 25 50 S 113 5 E
Dirkou 243 19 1N 12 53 E
Dirranbandi 231 28 33 S 148 17 E
Dirs 194 18 32N 42 5 E
Disa, India 198 24 18N 72 10 E
Disa, Sudan 245 12 5N 34 15 E
Disappointment L. 228 23 20 S 122 40 E
Disaster B. 231 37 15 S 150 0 E
Discovery B. 231 38 10 S 140 40 E
Disentis 149 46 42N 8 50 E
Dishna 244 26 9N 32 32 E
Disina 247 11 35N 9 50 E
Disko 12 69 45N 53 30W
Disko Bugt 12 69 10N 52 0W
Disko I. 95 69 30N 54 30W
Disna 178 55 32N 28 11 E
Disna → 178 55 34N 28 12 E
Dison 143 50 37N 5 51 E
Disraëli 83 45 54N 71 21W
Disteghil Sar 199 36 20N 75 12 E
Distrito Federal □, Brazil 121 15 45 S 47 45W
Distrito Federal □, Mexico 107 19 15N 99 10W
Distrito Federal □, Venezuela 118 10 30N 66 55W
Disūq 244 31 8N 30 35 E
Ditu 253 5 23 S 21 27 E
Diu 198 20 45N 70 58 E
Diuata Mts. 211 9 0N 125 50 E
Dīvāndarreh 192 35 55N 47 2 E
Dives → 138 49 18N 0 7W
Dives-sur-Mer 138 49 18N 0 8W
Divi Pt. 201 15 59N 81 9 E
Divichi 181 41 15N 48 57 E
Dividing Ra. 229 27 45 S 116 0 E
Divinópolis 121 20 10 S 44 54W
Divisaderos 100 29 33N 109 14W
Divisões, Serra dos 121 17 0 S 51 0W
Divnoye 181 45 55N 43 21 E
Divo 246 5 48N 5 15W
Dīwāl Kol 197 34 23N 67 52 E
Dixonville 90 56 32N 117 40W
Dixville 83 45 4N 71 46W
Diyarbakir 177 37 55N 40 18 E
Djado 241 21 4N 12 14 E
Djado, Plateau du 241 21 29N 12 21 E
Djakarta = Jakarta 207 6 9 S 106 49 E
Djamâa 241 33 32N 5 59 E
Djamba 254 16 45 S 13 58 E
Djambala 252 2 32 S 14 30 E
Djanet 241 24 35N 9 32 E
Djaul I. 227 2 58 S 150 57 E
Djawa = Jawa 207 7 0 S 110 0 E
Djebiniana 241 35 1N 11 0 E
Djédaa 243 13 31N 18 34 E
Djelfa 241 34 40N 3 15 E
Djema 250 6 3N 25 15 E
Djember 243 10 25N 17 50 E
Djendel 241 36 15N 2 25 E
Djeneïene 241 31 45N 10 9 E
Djenné 246 14 0N 4 30W
Djenoun, Garet el 241 25 4N 5 31 E
Djerba 241 33 52N 10 51 E
Djerba, Île de 241 33 50N 10 48 E
Djerid, Chott 241 33 42N 8 30 E
Djiba 252 1 20 S 13 9 E
Djibo 247 14 9N 1 35W
Djibouti 245 11 30N 43 5 E
Djibouti ■ 245 12 0N 43 0 E
Djolu 252 0 35N 22 5 E
Djougou 247 9 40N 1 45 E
Djoum 252 2 41N 12 35 E
Djourab 243 16 40N 18 50 E
Djugu 250 1 55N 30 35 E
Djúpivogur 174 64 39N 14 17W

Djursholm 172 59 25N 18 6 E
Djursland 173 56 27N 10 45 E
Dmitriev-Lgovskiy 178 52 10N 35 0 E
Dmitriya Lapteva, Proliv 185 73 0N 140 0 E
Dmitrov 179 56 25N 37 32 E
Dmitrovsk-Orlovskiy 178 52 29N 35 10 E
Dneiper = Dnepr → 180 46 30N 32 18 E
Dnepr → 180 46 30N 32 18 E
Dneprodzerzhinsk 180 48 32N 34 37 E
Dneprodzerzhinskoye Vdkhr. 180 49 0N 34 0 E
Dnepropetrovsk 180 48 30N 35 0 E
Dneprorudnoye 180 47 21N 34 58 E
Dnestr → 180 46 18N 30 17 E
Dnestrovski = Belgorod 179 50 35N 36 35 E
Dniester = Dnestr → 180 46 18N 30 17 E
Dno 178 57 50N 29 58 E
Doabi 197 36 1N 69 32 E
Doaktown 81 46 33N 66 8W
Doan Hung 204 21 30N 105 10 E
Doba 243 8 40N 16 50 E
Dobbiaco 163 46 44N 12 13 E
Dobbyn 230 19 44 S 139 59 E
Dobczyce 152 49 52N 20 25 E
Döbeln 146 51 7N 13 10 E
Doberai, Jazirah 207 1 25 S 133 0 E
Dobie → 86 51 41N 90 29W
Dobiegniew 152 52 59N 15 45 E
Doblas 124 37 5 S 64 0W
Dobo 207 5 45 S 134 15 E
Doboj 166 44 46N 18 6 E
Dobra, Konin, Poland 152 51 55N 18 37 E
Dobra, Szczecin, Poland 152 53 34N 15 20 E
Dobra, Dîmbovita, Romania 170 44 52N 25 40 E
Dobra, Hunedoara, Romania 170 45 54N 22 36 E
Dobre Miasto 152 53 58N 20 26 E
Dobrinishta 167 41 49N 23 34 E
Dobříš 150 49 46N 14 10 E
Dobrodzień 152 50 45N 18 25 E
Dobropole 180 48 25N 37 2 E
Dobruja 170 44 30N 28 15 E
Dobrush 179 52 28N 30 19 E
Dobryanka 182 58 27N 56 25 E
Dobrzyń nad Wisła 152 52 39N 19 22 E
Dobtong 245 6 25N 31 40 E
Doc, Mui 204 17 58N 106 30 E
Doce → 121 19 37 S 39 49W
Doctor Arroyo 103 23 40N 100 11W
Doctor Belisario Domínguez 101 28 9N 106 29W
Doctor Coss 102 25 55N 99 11W
Doctor González 102 25 52N 99 57W
Doctor Mora 107 21 7N 100 18W
Doda 199 33 10N 75 34 E
Dodecanese = Dhodhekánisos 169 36 35N 27 0 E
Dodewaard 142 51 55N 5 39 E
Dodge L. 77 59 50N 105 36W
Dodo 245 5 10N 29 57 E
Dodola 245 6 59N 39 11 E
Dodoma 250 6 8 S 35 45 E
Dodoma □ 250 6 0 S 36 0 E
Dodona 168 39 40N 20 46 E
Dodsland 88 51 50N 108 45W
Doesburg 142 52 1N 6 9 E
Doetinchem 142 51 59N 6 18 E
Doftana 170 45 11N 25 45 E
Dog → 86 48 32N 89 39W
Dog Creek 93 51 35N 122 14W
Dog L., Man., Canada 89 51 2N 98 31W
Dog L., Ont., Canada 86 48 18N 89 30W
Dog L., Ont., Canada 87 48 17N 84 8W
Doğanbey 169 37 40N 27 10 E
Dogger Bank 130 54 50N 2 0 E
Dogliani 162 44 35N 7 55 E
Dōgo 220 36 15N 133 16 E
Dōgo-San 220 35 2N 133 13 E
Dogondoutchi 247 13 38N 4 2 E
Dogran 198 31 48N 73 35 E
Doguéraoua 247 14 0N 5 31 E
Dohinog 211 8 32N 123 12 E
Doi 207 2 14N 127 49 E
Doi Luang 204 18 30N 101 0 E
Doi Saket 204 18 52N 99 9 E
Doig → 76 56 25N 120 40W
Dois Irmãos, Sa. 120 9 0 S 42 30W
Dojransko Jezero 166 41 13N 22 44 E
Dokka 171 60 49N 10 7 E
Dokka → 171 61 7N 10 0 E
Dokkum 142 53 20N 5 59 E
Dokkumer Ee → 142 53 18N 5 52 E
Dokri 198 27 25N 68 7 E
Dol-de-Bretagne 138 48 34N 1 47W
Dolbeau 83 48 53N 72 18W
Dole 139 47 7N 5 31 E
Doleib, Wadi → 245 12 10N 33 15 E
Dolgellau 132 52 44N 3 53W
Dolgelley = Dolgellau 132 52 44N 3 53W
Dolginovo 178 54 39N 27 29 E
Dolianova 164 39 23N 9 11 E
Dolinskaya 180 48 6N 32 46 E
Dolj □ 170 44 10N 23 30 E
Dollard 88 49 37N 108 35W
Dollart 142 53 20N 7 10 E
Dolna Banya 167 42 18N 23 44 E
Dolni Dŭbnik 167 43 24N 24 26 E
Dolo, Ethiopia 245 4 11N 42 3 E
Dolo, Italy 163 45 25N 12 4 E
Dolomites = Dolomiti 163 46 30N 11 40 E
Dolomiti 163 46 30N 11 40 E
Dolores, Argentina 124 36 20 S 57 40W
Dolores, Mexico 101 28 53N 108 27W
Dolores, Phil. 210 12 2N 125 29 E
Dolores, Uruguay 124 33 34 S 58 15W
Đolovo 166 44 55N 20 52 E
Dolphin and Union Str. 94 69 5N 114 45W
Dolphin C. 126 51 10 S 59 0W
Dolsk 152 51 59N 17 3 E
Dom 148 46 6N 7 50 E
Dom Joaquim 121 18 57 S 43 16W
Dom Pedrito 125 31 0 S 54 40W
Dom Pedro 120 4 59 S 44 27W
Doma 247 8 25N 8 18 E
Domasi 251 15 15 S 35 22 E
Domat Ems 149 46 50N 9 27 E
Domazlice 150 49 28N 13 0 E
Dombarovskiy 182 50 46N 59 32 E
Dombasle 139 48 38N 6 21 E
Dombes 141 46 3N 5 0 E
Dombóvár 151 46 21N 18 9 E
Dombrád 151 48 13N 21 54 E
Domburg 143 51 34N 3 30 E
Dome Creek 93 53 44N 121 1W
Domérat 140 46 21N 2 32 E
Domett 235 42 53 S 173 12 E
Domeyko 124 29 0 S 71 0W
Domeyko, Cordillera 124 24 30 S 69 0W
Domfront 138 48 37N 0 40W
Dominador 124 24 21 S 69 20W
Dominica ■ 113 15 20N 61 20W
Dominica Passage 113 15 10N 61 20W
Dominican Rep. ■ 113 19 0N 70 30W
Dominion 81 46 13N 60 1W
Dominion, C. 95 65 30N 74 28W
Dominion City 89 49 9N 97 9W
Dominion L. 80 52 40N 61 45W
Domiongo 253 4 37 S 21 15 E
Dömitz 146 53 9N 11 13 E
Domme 140 44 48N 1 12 E
Dommel → 143 51 30N 5 20 E
Domo 256 7 50N 47 10 E
Domodóssola 162 46 6N 8 19 E
Dompaire 139 48 14N 6 14 E
Dompierre-sur-Besbre 140 46 31N 3 41 E
Dompim 246 5 10N 2 5W
Domrémy 139 48 26N 5 40 E
Domsjö 172 63 16N 18 41 E
Domville, Mt. 231 28 1 S 151 15 E
Domvraína 169 38 15N 22 59 E
Domžale 163 46 9N 14 35 E
Don 100 26 26N 109 2W
Don →, India 201 16 20N 76 15 E
Don →, England, U.K. 132 53 41N 0 51W
Don →, Scotland, U.K. 134 57 14N 2 5W
Don →, U.S.S.R. 181 47 4N 39 18 E
Don, C. 228 11 18 S 131 46 E
Don Benito 155 38 53N 5 51W
Don Duong 205 11 51N 108 35 E
Don Pen. 92 52 25N 128 12W
Dona Ana 251 17 25 S 35 5 E
Donaghadee 135 54 38N 5 32W
Donald, Australia 231 36 23 S 143 0 E
Donald, Canada 93 51 29N 117 10W
Donalda 91 52 35N 112 34W
Donato Guerra 105 24 38N 104 38W
Donau → 145 48 10N 17 0 E
Donaueschingen 147 47 57N 8 30 E
Donauwörth 147 48 42N 10 47 E
Donawitz 150 47 22N 15 4 E
Doncaster 132 53 31N 1 9W
Dondo, Angola 253 9 45 S 14 25 E
Dondo, Mozam. 251 19 33 S 34 46 E
Dondo, Zaïre 252 4 11N 21 39 E
Dondo, Teluk 207 0 29N 120 30 E
Dondra Head 201 5 55N 80 40 E
Donegal 135 54 39N 8 8W
Donegal □ 135 54 53N 8 0W
Donegal B. 135 54 30N 8 35W
Donets → 181 47 33N 40 55 E
Donetsk 180 48 0N 37 45 E
Dong Ba Thin 205 12 8N 109 13 E
Dong Dang 204 21 54N 106 42 E
Dong Giam 204 19 25N 105 31 E
Dong Ha 204 16 55N 107 8 E
Dong Hene 204 16 40N 105 18 E
Dong Hoi 204 17 29N 106 36 E
Dong Jiang → 217 23 6N 114 0 E
Dong Khe 204 22 26N 106 27 E
Dong Ujimqin Qi 214 45 32N 116 55 E
Dong Van 204 23 16N 105 22 E
Dong Xoai 205 11 32N 106 55 E
Donga 247 7 45N 10 2 E
Dong'an 217 26 23N 111 12 E
Dongara 229 29 14 S 114 57 E
Dongargarh 199 21 10N 80 40 E
Dongbei 215 42 0N 125 0 E
Dongchuan 216 26 8N 103 1 E
Dongen 143 51 38N 4 56 E
Donges 138 47 18N 2 4W
Dongfang 204 18 50N 108 33 E
Dongfeng 215 42 40N 125 34 E
Donggala 207 0 30 S 119 40 E
Donggan 216 23 22N 105 9 E
Donggou 215 39 52N 124 10 E
Dongguan 217 22 58N 113 44 E
Dongguang 214 37 50N 116 30 E
Donghai Dao 217 21 0N 110 15 E
Dongjingcheng 215 44 0N 129 10 E
Donglan 216 24 30N 107 21 E
Dongliu 217 30 13N 116 55 E
Dongmen 216 22 20N 107 48 E
Dongning 215 44 2N 131 5 E
Dongnyi 216 28 3N 100 15 E
Dongo 253 14 36 S 15 48 E
Dongola 244 19 9N 30 22 E
Dongou 252 2 0N 18 5 E
Dongping 214 35 55N 116 20 E
Dongshan 217 23 43N 117 30 E
Dongsheng 214 39 50N 110 0 E
Dongshi 217 24 18N 120 49 E
Dongtai 217 32 51N 120 21 E
Dongting Hu 217 29 18N 112 45 E
Dongxiang 217 28 11N 116 34 E
Dongxing 216 21 34N 108 0 E
Dongyang 217 29 13N 120 15 E
Dongzhi 217 30 9N 117 0 E
Donington, C. 232 34 45 S 136 0 E
Donja Stubica 163 45 59N 16 0 E
Donji Dušnik 166 43 12N 22 5 E
Donji Miholjac 166 45 45N 18 10 E
Donji Milanovac 166 44 28N 22 6 E
Donji Vakuf 166 44 8N 17 24 E
Donjon, Le 140 46 22N 3 48 E
Donkin 81 46 11N 59 52W
Donnaconna 83 46 41N 71 41W
Donnelly 90 55 44N 117 6W
Donnelly's Crossing 234 35 42 S 173 38 E
Donnybrook 229 33 34 S 115 48 E
Donor's Hill 230 18 42 S 140 33 E
Donque 253 15 28 S 14 6 E
Donskoy 179 53 55N 38 15 E
Donsol 210 12 54N 123 36 E
Donya Lendava 163 46 35N 16 25 E
Donzère-Mondragon 141 44 28N 4 43 E
Donzère-Mondragon, Barrage de 141 44 13N 4 42 E
Donzy 139 47 20N 3 6 E
Doon → 134 55 26N 4 41W
Doorn 142 52 2N 5 20 E
Dor 189 32 37N 34 55 E
Dora, L. 228 22 0 S 123 0 E
Dora Báltea → 162 45 11N 8 5 E
Dora Riparia → 162 45 5N 7 44 E
Dorada, La 118 5 30N 74 40W
Dorado 101 27 8N 105 21W
Doran L. 77 61 13N 108 6W
Dorat, Le 140 46 14N 1 5 E
Dorchester, Canada 81 45 54N 64 31W
Dorchester, U.K. 133 50 42N 2 28W
Dorchester, C. 95 65 27N 77 27W
Dorchester Crossing 81 46 10N 64 34W
Dordogne □ 140 45 5N 0 40 E
Dordogne → 140 45 2N 0 36W
Dordrecht, Neth. 142 51 48N 4 39 E
Dordrecht, S. Africa 254 31 20 S 27 3 E
Dore → 140 45 50N 3 35 E
Doré, Le, L. 80 51 17N 61 23W
Dore, Mt. 140 45 32N 2 50 E
Doré L. 77 54 46N 107 17W
Doré Lake 77 54 38N 107 36W
Dores do Indaiá 121 19 27 S 45 36W
Dorfen 147 48 16N 12 10 E
Dorgali 164 40 18N 9 35 E
Dori 247 14 3N 0 2W
Doring → 254 31 54 S 18 39 E
Dorion, Ont., Canada 86 48 47N 88 39W
Dorion, Qué., Canada 83 45 23N 74 3W
Dormaa-Ahenkro 246 7 15N 2 52W
Dormo, Ras 245 13 14N 42 35 E
Dornach 148 47 29N 7 37 E
Dornberg 163 55 45N 13 50 E
Dornbirn 150 47 25N 9 45 E
Dornes 139 46 48N 3 18 E
Dornoch 134 57 52N 4 0W
Dornoch Firth 134 57 52N 4 0W
Dornogovĭ □ 214 44 0N 110 0 E
Doro 247 16 9N 0 51W
Dorog 151 47 42N 18 45 E
Dorogobuzh 178 54 50N 33 18 E
Dorohoi 170 47 56N 26 30 E
Döröö Nuur 212 48 0N 93 0 E
Dorr 193 33 17N 50 38 E
Dorre I. 229 25 13 S 113 12 E
Dorrigo 231 30 20 S 152 44 E
Dorset 85 45 14N 78 54W
Dorset □ 133 50 48N 2 25W
Dorsten 146 51 40N 6 55 E
Dortmund 146 51 32N 7 28 E
Doruk 190 36 53N 35 45 E
Dorum 146 53 40N 8 33 E
Doruma 250 4 42N 27 33 E
Dorūneh 193 35 10N 57 18 E
Dos Bahías, C. 126 44 58 S 65 32W
Dos Hermanas 155 37 16N 5 55W
Dosquet 83 46 28N 71 32W
Dosso 247 13 0N 3 13 E
Doting Cove 79 49 27N 53 57W
Dottignies 143 50 44N 3 19 E
Douai 139 50 21N 3 4 E
Douala 247 4 0N 9 45 E
Douaouir 240 20 45N 3 0W
Douarnenez 138 48 6N 4 21W
Douăzeci Şi Trei August 170 43 55N 28 40 E
Double Island Pt. 231 25 56 S 153 11 E
Doubrava → 150 49 40N 15 30 E
Doubs □ 139 47 10N 6 20 E
Doubs → 139 46 53N 5 1 E
Doubtful Sd. 235 45 20 S 166 49 E
Doubtless B. 234 34 55 S 173 26 E
Doudeville 138 49 43N 0 47 E
Doué 138 47 11N 0 20W
Douentza 246 14 58N 2 48W
Douglas, Canada 85 45 31N 76 56W
Douglas, S. Africa 254 29 4 S 23 46 E
Douglas, U.K. 132 54 9N 4 29W
Douglas Chan. 92 53 40N 129 20W
Douglas Pt. 84 44 19N 81 37W
Douglas Prov. Park 88 51 3N 106 28W
Douglastown, N.B., Canada 80 48 46N 64 24W
Douglastown, N.B., Canada 81 47 1N 65 30W
Douirat 241 33 2N 4 11W
Doukáton, Ákra 169 38 34N 20 30 E
Doulevant 139 48 22N 4 53 E
Doullens 139 50 10N 2 20 E
Doumé 252 4 15N 13 25 E
Douna 246 13 13N 6 0W
Dounan 217 23 41N 120 26 E
Dounguila 252 2 53 S 11 58 E
Dounreay 134 58 34N 3 44W
Dour 143 50 24N 3 46 E
Dourada, Serra 121 13 10 S 48 45W
Dourados 125 22 9 S 54 50W
Dourados → 125 21 58 S 54 18W
Dourdan 139 48 30N 2 0 E
Douro → 154 41 8N 8 40W
Douvaine 141 46 19N 6 16 E
Douz 241 33 25N 9 0 E
Douze → 140 43 54N 0 30W
Dove → 132 52 51N 1 36W
Dover, Australia 230 43 18 S 147 2 E
Dover, U.K. 133 51 7N 1 19 E
Dover, Pt. 229 32 32 S 125 32 E
Dover, Str. of 138 51 0N 1 30 E
Dovey → 133 52 32N 4 0W
Dovre 171 61 58N 9 15 E
Dovrefjell 171 62 15N 9 33 E
Dow Rūd 193 33 28N 49 4 E
Dowa 251 13 38 S 33 58 E
Dowager I. 92 52 25N 128 22W
Dowgha'i 193 36 54N 58 32 E
Dowlat Yār 197 34 30N 65 45 E
Dowlatābād, Farāh, Afghan. 197 32 47N 62 40 E
Dowlatābād, Fāryāb, Afghan. 197 36 26N 64 55 E
Dowlatābād, Iran 193 28 20N 56 40W
Down □ 135 54 20N 6 0W
Downham Market 133 52 36N 0 22 E
Downpatrick 135 54 20N 5 43W
Downpatrick Hd. 135 54 20N 9 21W
Downton, Mt. 92 52 42N 124 52W
Dowsārī 193 28 25N 57 59 E
Dowshī 197 35 35N 68 43 E
Doyles 79 47 50N 59 12W
Dozois, Rés. 82 47 30N 77 5W
Draa, C. 240 28 47N 11 0W
Draa, Oued → 240 30 29N 6 1W
Drac → 141 45 13N 5 41 E
Drachten 142 53 7N 6 5 E
Drăgăneşti 170 44 9N 24 32 E
Drăgăneşti-Viaşca 170 44 5N 25 33 E
Dragaš 166 42 5N 20 35 E

Drăgăsani **170** 44 39N 24 17 E
Dragina **166** 44 30N 19 25 E
Dragocvet **166** 44 0N 21 15 E
Dragoman, Prokhod **166** 43 0N 22 53 E
Dragonera, I. **156** 39 35N 2 19 E
Dragovishtitsa **166** 42 22N 22 39 E
Draguignan **141** 43 30N 6 27 E
Drake, Australia **231** 28 55 S 152 25 E
Drake, Canada **88** 51 45N 105 1W
Drake Passage **13** 58 0 S 68 0W
Drakensberg **255** 31 0 S 28 0 E
Dráma **168** 41 9N 24 10 E
Dráma □ **168** 41 20N 24 0 E
Drammen **171** 59 42N 10 12 E
Drangajökull **174** 66 9N 22 15W
Drangedal **171** 59 6N 9 3 E
Dranov, Ostrov **170** 44 55N 29 30 E
Dras **199** 34 25N 75 48 E
Drau = Drava → **166** 45 33N 18 55 E
Drava → **166** 45 33N 18 55 E
Draveil **139** 48 41N 2 25 E
Dravograd **163** 46 36N 15 5 E
Drawa → **152** 52 52N 15 59 E
Drawno **152** 53 13N 15 46 E
Drawsko Pomorskie **152** 53 35N 15 50 E
Drayton **84** 43 46N 80 40W
Drayton Valley **90** 53 12N 114 58W
Dreibergen **142** 52 3N 5 17 E
Dren **166** 43 8N 20 44 E
Drenthe □ **142** 52 52N 6 40 E
Drentsche Hoofdvaart **142** 52 39N 6 4 E
Dresden, Canada **84** 42 35N 82 11W
Dresden, Germany **146** 51 2N 13 45 E
Dresden □ **146** 51 12N 14 0 E
Dreux **138** 48 44N 1 23 E
Drezdenko **152** 52 50N 15 49 E
Driel **142** 51 57N 5 49 E
Driffield **132** 54 0N 0 25W
Drin i zi → **168** 41 37N 20 28 E
Drina → **166** 44 53N 19 21 E
Drincea → **170** 44 20N 22 55 E
Drînceni **170** 46 49N 28 10 E
Drini → **168** 42 20N 20 0 E
Drinjača → **166** 44 15N 19 8 E
Drinkwater **88** 50 18N 105 8W
Driva → **171** 62 33N 9 38 E
Drivstua **171** 62 26N 9 47 E
Drniš **163** 43 51N 16 10 E
Drøbak **171** 59 39N 10 39 E
Drobin **152** 52 42N 19 58 E
Drocourt **84** 45 46N 80 21W
Drogheda **135** 53 45N 6 20W
Drogichin **178** 52 15N 25 8 E
Drogobych **178** 49 20N 23 30 E
Drohiczyn **152** 52 24N 22 39 E
Droichead Nua **135** 53 11N 6 50W
Droitwich **133** 52 16N 2 10W
Drôme □ **141** 44 38N 5 15 E
Drôme → **141** 44 46N 4 46 E
Dromedary, C. **231** 36 17 S 150 10 E
Dronero **162** 44 29N 7 22 E
Dronfield **230** 21 12 S 140 3 E
Dronne → **140** 45 2N 0 9W
Dronning Maud Land **13** 72 30 S 12 0 E
Dronninglund **173** 57 10N 10 19 E
Dronrijp **142** 53 11N 5 39 E
Dropt → **140** 44 35N 0 6W
Drosendorf **150** 48 52N 15 37 E
Drouin **233** 38 10 S 145 53 E
Drouzhba **167** 43 15N 28 0 E
Drowning → **87** 50 54N 84 34W
Drumbo **84** 43 16N 80 35W
Drumheller **91** 51 25N 112 40W
Drummond **81** 47 2N 67 41W
Drummond Pt. **231** 34 9 S 135 16 E
Drummond Ra. **230** 23 45 S 147 10 E
Drummondville **83** 45 55N 72 25W
Drunen **143** 51 41N 5 8 E
Druskininkai **178** 54 3N 23 58 E
Drut → **178** 53 3N 30 42 E
Druten **142** 51 53N 5 36 E
Druya **178** 55 45N 27 28 E
Druzhina **185** 68 14N 145 18 E
Drvar **163** 44 21N 16 23 E
Drvenik **163** 43 27N 16 3 E
Drwęca → **152** 53 0N 18 42 E
Dryanovo **167** 42 59N 25 28 E
Dryberry L. **86** 49 33N 93 53W
Dryden **86** 49 47N 92 50W
Drygalski I. **13** 66 0 S 92 0 E
Drysdale → **228** 13 59 S 126 51 E
Drysdale I. **230** 11 41 S 136 0 E
Drzewiczka → **152** 51 36N 20 36 E
Dschang **247** 5 32N 10 3 E
Du Gas, L. **80** 51 55N 75 12W
Du Gué → **78** 57 21N 70 45W
Duaringa **230** 23 42 S 149 42 E
Duarte **107** 21 5N 101 31W
Ḍubā **192** 27 10N 35 40 E
Dubai = Dubayy **195** 25 18N 55 20 E
Dubawnt → **77** 64 33N 100 6W
Dubawnt, L. **77** 63 4N 101 42W
Dubayy **195** 25 18N 55 20 E
Dubbeldam **142** 51 47N 4 43 E
Dubbo **231** 32 11 S 148 35 E
Dubele **250** 2 56N 29 35 E
Dübendorf **149** 47 24N 8 37 E
Dubenskiy **182** 51 27N 56 38 E
Dubica **163** 45 11N 16 48 E
Dublān **101** 30 26N 107 55W
Dublin **135** 53 20N 6 18W
Dublin □ **135** 53 24N 6 20W
Dublin B. **135** 53 18N 6 5W
Dublon I. **226** 7 23N 151 53 E
Dubna, R.S.F.S.R., U.S.S.R. **179** 54 8N 36 59 E
Dubna, R.S.F.S.R., U.S.S.R. **179** 56 44N 37 10 E
Dubno **178** 50 25N 25 45 E
Dubossary **180** 47 15N 29 10 E
Dubossary Vdkhr. **180** 47 30N 29 0 E
Dubovka **181** 49 5N 44 50 E
Dubovskoye **181** 47 28N 42 46 E
Dubrajpur **199** 23 48N 87 25 E
Dubréka **246** 9 46N 13 31W
Dubreuilville **87** 48 21N 84 32W
Dubrovitsa **178** 51 31N 26 35 E
Dubrovnik **166** 42 39N 18 6 E
Dubrovskoye **185** 58 55N 111 10 E
Dubuc **89** 50 41N 102 28W
Dubulu **252** 4 18N 20 16 E
Duchang **217** 29 18N 116 12 E
Duchess, Australia **230** 21 20 S 139 50 E
Duchess, Canada **91** 50 43N 111 55W
Ducie I. **225** 24 40 S 124 48W
Duck Bay **89** 52 10N 100 9W
Duck Cr. → **228** 22 37 S 116 53 E
Duck Lake **88** 52 50N 106 16W
Duck Mt. Prov. Parks **89** 51 45N 101 0W
Düdelange **143** 49 29N 6 5 E
Duderstadt **146** 51 30N 10 15 E
Dudhnai **202** 25 59N 90 47 E
Düdingen **148** 46 52N 7 12 E
Dudinka **185** 69 30N 86 13 E
Dudley **133** 52 30N 2 5W
Dudna → **200** 19 17N 76 54 E
Dudo **256** 9 20N 50 12 E
Dudub **256** 6 55N 46 43 E
Duenas, Phil. **211** 11 4N 122 37 E
Dueñas, Spain **154** 41 52N 4 33W
Dueodde **173** 54 59N 15 4 E
Dueré **121** 11 20 S 49 17W
Duero → **154** 41 8N 8 40W
Dūfah, W. → **194** 18 45N 41 49 E
Duff Is. **224** 9 53 S 167 8 E
Duffel **143** 51 6N 4 30 E
Dufftown **134** 57 26N 3 9W
Dufourspitz **148** 45 56N 7 52 E
Dufrost, Pte. **78** 60 4N 77 39W
Dugi **163** 44 0N 15 0 E
Dugiuma **256** 1 15N 42 34 E
Dugo Selo **163** 45 51N 16 18 E
Duifken Pt. **230** 12 33 S 141 38 E
Duisburg **146** 51 27N 6 42 E
Duitama **118** 5 50N 73 2W
Duiveland **143** 51 38N 4 0 E
Duiwelskloof **255** 23 42 S 30 10 E
Dukati **168** 40 16N 19 32 E
Dūkdamīn **193** 35 59N 57 43 E
Dukelský průsmyk **151** 49 25N 21 42 E
Dukhān **195** 25 25N 50 50 E
Dukhovshchina **178** 55 15N 32 27 E
Duki **197** 30 14N 68 25 E
Dukla **152** 49 30N 21 35 E
Duku, Bauchi, Nigeria **247** 10 43N 10 43 E
Duku, Sokoto, Nigeria **247** 11 11N 4 55 E
Dulag **211** 10 57N 125 2 E
Dulce → **124** 30 32 S 62 33W
Dulce, Golfo **112** 8 40N 83 20W
Dulf **192** 35 7N 45 51 E
Dŭlgopol **167** 43 3N 27 22 E
Dulit, Banjaran **206** 3 15N 114 30 E
Duliu **214** 39 2N 116 55 E
Dullewala **198** 31 50N 71 25 E
Dülmen **146** 51 49N 7 18 E
Dulovo **167** 43 48N 27 9 E
Dulq Maghār **192** 36 22N 38 39 E
Dululu **230** 23 48 S 150 15 E
Dum Dum **199** 22 39N 88 33 E
Dum Hadjer **243** 13 18N 19 41 E
Dūmā, Lebanon **190** 34 12N 35 50 E
Dūmā, Syria **190** 33 34N 36 24 E
Dumaguete **211** 9 17N 123 15 E
Dumai **208** 1 35N 101 28 E
Dumalinao **211** 7 49N 123 23 E
Dumanguilas Bay **211** 7 34N 123 4 E
Dumaran **211** 10 33N 119 50 E
Dumbarton **134** 55 58N 4 35W
Dumbea **226** 22 10 S 166 27 E
Dumbell L. **80** 52 28N 65 45W
Dumbleyung **229** 33 17 S 117 42 E
Dumbo **253** 14 6 S 17 24 E
Dumbrăveni **170** 46 14N 24 34 E
Dumfries **134** 55 4N 3 37W
Dumfries & Galloway □ **134** 55 0N 4 0W
Dumingag **211** 8 20N 123 20 E
Dumka **199** 24 12N 87 15 E
Dümmersee **146** 52 30N 8 21 E
Dumoine → **82** 46 13N 77 51W
Dumoine L. **82** 46 55N 77 55W
Dumraon **199** 25 33N 84 8 E
Dumyât **244** 31 24N 31 48 E
Dumyât, Masabb **244** 31 28N 31 51 E
Dun Laoghaire **135** 53 17N 6 9W
Dun-le-Palestel **140** 46 18N 1 39 E
Dun-sur-Auron **139** 46 53N 2 33 E
Duna → **151** 45 51N 18 48 E
Dunaföldvár **151** 46 50N 18 57 E
Dunaj → **151** 48 5N 17 10 E
Dunajec → **152** 50 15N 20 44 E
Dunajska Streda **151** 48 0N 17 37 E
Dunapatai **151** 46 39N 19 4 E
Dunărea → **170** 45 30N 8 15 E
Dunaszekcsö **151** 46 6N 18 45 E
Dunaújváros **151** 47 0N 18 57 E
Dunav → **166** 44 47N 21 20 E
Dunavtsi **166** 43 57N 22 53 E
Dunay **218** 42 52N 132 22 E
Dunback **235** 45 23 S 170 36 E
Dunbar, Australia **230** 16 0 S 142 22 E
Dunbar, U.K. **134** 56 0N 2 32W
Dunblane **134** 56 10N 3 58W
Duncan **93** 48 45N 123 40W
Duncan, L. **78** 53 29N 77 58W
Duncan Dam **93** 50 15N 116 56W
Duncan L. **76** 62 51N 113 58W
Duncan Town **112** 22 15N 75 45W
Dunchurch **84** 45 39N 79 51W
Dundalk, Canada **84** 44 10N 80 24W
Dundalk, Ireland **135** 54 1N 6 25W
Dundalk Bay **135** 53 55N 6 15W
Dundas, Canada **84** 43 17N 79 59W
Dundas, Greenland **95** 77 0N 69 0W
Dundas, L. **229** 32 35 S 121 50 E
Dundas I. **76** 54 30N 130 50W
Dundas Pen. **94** 74 50N 111 36W
Dundas Str. **228** 11 15 S 131 35 E
Dundee, S. Africa **255** 28 11 S 30 15 E
Dundee, U.K. **134** 56 29N 3 0W
Dundgovĭ □ **214** 45 10N 106 0 E
Dundoo **231** 27 40 S 144 37 E
Dundrum **135** 54 17N 5 50W
Dundrum B. **135** 54 12N 5 40W
Dundurn **88** 51 49N 106 30W
Dundurn Camp **88** 51 51N 106 34W
Dundwara **199** 27 48N 79 9 E
Dunedin **235** 45 50 S 170 33 E
Dunedin → **76** 59 30N 124 5W
Dunfermline **134** 56 5N 3 28W
Dungannon, Canada **84** 43 51N 81 36W
Dungannon, U.K. **135** 54 30N 6 47W
Dungannon □ **135** 54 30N 6 55W
Dungarpur **198** 23 52N 73 45 E
Dungarvan **135** 52 6N 7 40W
Dungarvan Bay **135** 52 5N 7 35W
Dungarvon → **81** 46 49N 65 54W
Dungeness **133** 50 54N 0 59 E
Dungo, L. do **254** 17 15 S 19 0 E
Dungog **231** 32 22 S 151 46 E
Dungu **250** 3 40N 28 32 E
Dungunâb **244** 21 10N 37 9 E
Dungunâb, Khalij **244** 21 5N 37 12 E
Dunhinda Falls **201** 7 5N 81 6 E
Dunhua **215** 43 20N 128 14 E
Dunhuang **212** 40 8N 94 36 E
Dunière, Parc Prov. de **80** 48 45N 66 41W
Dunières **141** 45 13N 4 20 E
Dunk I. **230** 17 59 S 146 29 E
Dunkeld, Australia **232** 37 40 S 142 22 E
Dunkeld, U.K. **134** 56 34N 3 36W
Dunkerque **139** 51 2N 2 20 E
Dunkery Beacon **133** 51 15N 3 37W
Dunkirk = Dunkerque **139** 51 2N 2 20 E
Dunkley **93** 53 17N 122 28W
Dunkuj **245** 12 50N 32 49 E
Dunkwa, Central, Ghana **246** 6 0N 1 47W
Dunkwa, Central, Ghana **247** 5 30N 1 0W
Dúnleary = Dun Laoghaire **135** 53 17N 6 9W
Dunmanus B. **135** 51 31N 9 50W
Dunmara **230** 16 42 S 133 25 E
Dunmore **91** 49 58N 110 36W
Dunmore Hd. **135** 52 10N 10 35W
Dunmore Town **112** 25 30N 76 39W
Dunnet Hd. **134** 58 38N 3 22W
Dunnville **84** 42 54N 79 36W
Dunolly **231** 36 51 S 143 44 E
Dunoon **134** 55 57N 4 56W
Dunqul **244** 23 26N 31 37 E
Dunrankin → **87** 48 47N 82 51W
Duns **134** 55 47N 2 20W
Dunstable **133** 51 53N 0 31W
Dunstan Mts. **235** 44 53 S 169 35 E
Dunster **93** 53 8N 119 50W
Duntroon **235** 44 51 S 170 40 E
Dunvegan **90** 55 55N 118 36W
Dunvegan L. **77** 60 8N 107 10W
Dunville **79** 47 16N 53 54W
Duolun **214** 42 12N 116 28 E
Duong Dong **205** 10 13N 103 58 E
Duparquet **82** 48 30N 79 14W
Duparquet, L. **82** 48 28N 79 16W
Dupax **210** 16 17N 121 5 E
Dupuy **82** 48 50N 79 21W
Duqm **195** 19 39N 57 42 E
Duque de Caxias **121** 22 45 S 43 19W
Duque de York, I. **126** 50 37 S 75 25W
Dūrā **189** 31 31N 35 1 E
Dura, La **100** 28 22N 109 34W
Durack → **228** 15 33 S 127 52 E
Durack Range **228** 16 50 S 127 40 E
Durance → **141** 43 55N 4 45 E
Durango **156** 43 13N 2 40W
Durango □ **104** 24 50N 104 50W
Durango, Sa. de **105** 23 35N 104 50W
Duranillin **229** 33 30 S 116 45 E
Duratón → **154** 41 37N 4 7W
Durazno **124** 33 25 S 56 31W
Durazzo = Durrësi **168** 41 19N 19 28 E
Durban, France **140** 43 0N 2 49 E
Durban, S. Africa **255** 29 49 S 31 1 E
Durbo **256** 11 37N 50 20 E
Dúrcal **155** 37 0N 3 34W
Đurđevac **166** 46 2N 17 3 E
Düren **146** 50 48N 6 30 E
Durg **199** 21 15N 81 22 E
Durgapur **199** 23 30N 87 20 E
Durham, Canada **84** 44 10N 80 49W
Durham, U.K. **132** 54 47N 1 34W
Durham □ **132** 54 42N 1 45W
Durham Bridge **81** 46 7N 66 36W
Durham Downs **231** 26 6 S 141 47 E
Ḍurmā **194** 24 37N 46 8 E
Durmitor **158** 43 10N 19 0 E
Durness **134** 58 34N 4 45W
Durocher, L. **80** 50 52N 61 12W
Durrësi **168** 41 19N 19 28 E
Durrie **230** 25 40 S 140 15 E
Durtal **138** 47 40N 0 18W
Duru **250** 4 14N 28 50 E
D'Urville, Tanjung **207** 1 28 S 137 54 E
D'Urville I. **235** 40 50 S 173 55 E
Dusa Mareb **256** 5 30N 46 15 E
Dusey → **87** 51 11N 86 21W
Dûsh **244** 24 35N 30 41 E
Dushak **184** 37 13N 60 1 E
Dushan **216** 25 48N 107 30 E
Dushanbe **183** 38 33N 68 48 E
Dusheti **181** 42 10N 44 42 E
Dusky Sd. **235** 45 47 S 166 30 E
Dussejour, C. **228** 14 45 S 128 13 E
Düsseldorf **146** 51 15N 6 46 E
Dussen **142** 51 44N 4 59 E
Duszniki-Zdrój **152** 50 24N 16 24 E
Dutlwe **254** 23 58 S 23 46 E
Dutsan Wai **247** 10 50N 8 10 E
Dutton **84** 42 39N 81 30W
Dutton → **230** 20 44 S 143 10 E
Duval **88** 51 9N 104 59W
Duvan **182** 55 42N 57 54 E
Duved **172** 63 24N 12 55 E
Duvno **166** 43 42N 17 13 E
Duyun **216** 26 18N 107 29 E
Duzdab = Zāhedān **193** 29 30N 60 50 E
Dve Mogili **167** 43 35N 25 55 E
Dvina, Sev. → **176** 64 32N 40 30 E
Dvinsk = Daugavpils **178** 55 53N 26 32 E
Dvinskaya Guba **176** 65 0N 39 0 E
Dvor **163** 45 4N 16 22 E
Dvorce **151** 49 50N 17 34 E
Dvur Králové **150** 50 27N 15 50 E
Dwarka **198** 22 18N 69 8 E
Dwellingup **229** 32 43 S 116 4 E
Dwight **85** 45 20N 79 1W
Dyakovskoya **179** 60 5N 41 12 E
Dyatkovo **178** 53 40N 34 27 E
Dyatlovo **178** 53 28N 25 28 E
Dyer Plateau **13** 70 45 S 65 30W
Dyerbeldzhin **183** 41 13N 74 54 E
Dyfed □ **133** 52 0N 4 30W
Dyje → **151** 48 37N 16 56 E
Dyle → **143** 50 58N 4 41 E
Dyment **86** 49 37N 92 18W
Dynevor Downs **231** 28 10 S 144 20 E
Dynów **152** 49 50N 22 11 E
Dysart **88** 50 57N 104 2W
Dyurtyuli **182** 55 9N 54 4 E
Dzamin Üüd **214** 43 50N 111 58 E
Dzemul **111** 21 12N 89 18W
Dzerzhinsk, Byelorussian S.S.R., U.S.S.R. **178** 53 40N 27 1 E
Dzerzhinsk, R.S.F.S.R., U.S.S.R. **179** 56 14N 43 30 E

Dzhalal-Abad **183** 40 56N 73 0 E
Dzhalinda **185** 53 26N 124 0 E
Dzhambeyty **181** 50 16N 52 35 E
Dzhambul **183** 42 54N 71 22 E
Dzhambul, Gora **183** 44 54N 73 0 E
Dzhankoi **180** 45 40N 34 20 E
Dzhanybek **181** 49 25N 46 50 E
Dzhardzhan **185** 68 10N 124 10 E
Dzharkurgan **183** 37 31N 67 25 E
Dzhelinde **185** 70 0N 114 20 E
Dzhetygara **182** 52 11N 61 12 E
Dzhetym, Khrebet **183** 41 30N 77 0 E
Dzhezkazgan **184** 47 44N 67 40 E
Dzhikimde **185** 59 1N 121 47 E
Dzhizak **183** 40 6N 67 50 E
Dzhugdzur, Khrebet **185** 57 30N 138 0 E
Dzhuma **183** 39 42N 66 40 E
Dzhumgoltau, Khrebet **183** 42 15N 74 30 E
Dzhungarskiye Vorota **184** 45 0N 82 0 E
Dzhvari **181** 42 42N 42 4 E
Działdowo **152** 53 15N 20 15 E
Działoszyce **152** 50 22N 20 20 E
Działoszyn **152** 51 6N 18 50 E
Dzibalchén **111** 19 31N 89 45W
Dzidzantún **111** 21 15N 89 3W
Dzierzgoń **152** 53 58N 19 20 E
Dzierzoniów **152** 50 45N 16 39 E
Dzilam de Bravo **111** 21 24N 88 53W
Dzilam González **111** 21 17N 88 56W
Dzioua **241** 33 14N 5 14 E
Dzitás **111** 20 51N 88 31W
Dzitbalché **111** 20 19N 90 3W
Dziwnów **152** 54 2N 14 45 E
Dzuiché **111** 19 54N 88 48W
Dzungaria **212** 44 10N 88 0 E
Dzungarian Gates = Dzhungarskiye Vorota **184** 45 0N 82 0 E
Dzuumod **212** 47 45N 106 58 E

E

Eabamet, L. **87** 51 30N 87 46W
Eagle → **78** 53 36N 57 26W
Eagle Cr. → **88** 52 20N 107 30W
Eagle I. **89** 53 40N 98 55W
Eagle L., B.C., Canada **92** 51 55N 124 23W
Eagle L., Ont., Canada **86** 49 42N 93 13W
Eagle Lake **85** 45 8N 78 29W
Eagle Pt. **228** 16 11 S 124 23 E
Eagle River **86** 49 47N 93 12W
Eaglehead L. **86** 49 2N 89 12W
Eaglesham **90** 55 47N 117 53W
Ealing **133** 51 30N 0 19W
Ear Falls **86** 50 38N 93 13W
Earaheedy **229** 25 34 S 121 29 E
Earl Grey **88** 50 57N 104 43W
Earls Cove **92** 49 45N 124 0W
Earltown **81** 45 35N 63 8W
Earn → **134** 56 20N 3 19W
Earn, L. **134** 56 23N 4 14W
Earnslaw, Mt. **235** 44 32 S 168 27 E
Earoo **229** 29 34 S 118 22 E
East Angus **83** 45 30N 71 40W
East Bay **81** 46 1N 60 25W
East Beskids = Vychodné Beskydy **151** 49 30N 22 0 E
East Broughton Station **83** 46 14N 71 5W
East C., N.Z. **234** 37 42 S 178 35 E
East C., Papua N. G. **227** 10 13 S 150 53 E
East Chezzetcook **81** 44 43N 63 14W
East China Sea **213** 30 5N 126 0 E
East Coast Bays **234** 36 40 S 174 40 E
East Coulee **91** 51 23N 112 27W
East Falkland **126** 51 30 S 58 30W
East Germany ■ **146** 52 0N 12 0 E
East Indies **206** 0 0 120 0 E
East Kilbride **134** 55 46N 4 10W
East London **255** 33 0 S 27 55 E
East Lynne **233** 35 35 S 150 16 E
East Main = Eastmain **78** 52 10N 78 30W
East Pacific Ridge **225** 15 0 S 110 0W
East Pakistan = Bangladesh ■ **202** 24 0N 90 0 E
East Pine **76** 55 48N 120 12W
East Pt. **81** 46 27N 61 58W
East Retford **132** 53 19N 0 55W
East Schelde → = Oosterschelde **143** 51 33N 4 0 E
East Siberian Sea **185** 73 0N 160 0 E
East Sussex □ **133** 51 0N 0 20 E
East Thurlow I. **92** 50 24N 125 25W
East Toorale **231** 30 27 S 145 28 E
East Trout L. **88** 54 22N 105 5W
Eastbourne, N.Z. **234** 41 19 S 174 55 E
Eastbourne, U.K. **133** 50 46N 0 18 E
Eastend **88** 49 32N 108 50W
Easter Islands **225** 27 0 S 109 0W
Eastern □, Kenya **250** 0 0 38 30 E
Eastern □, Uganda **250** 1 50N 33 45 E
Eastern Cr. → **230** 20 40 S 141 35 E
Eastern Ghats **201** 14 0N 78 50 E
Eastern Group = Lau **226** 17 0 S 178 30W
Eastern Group **229** 33 30 S 124 30 E
Eastern Province □ **246** 8 15N 11 0W
Eastern Samar □ **211** 11 40N 125 40 E
Easterville **89** 53 8N 99 49W
Eastleigh **133** 50 58N 1 21W
Eastmain **78** 52 10N 78 30W
Eastmain → **78** 52 27N 78 26W
Eastman **83** 45 18N 72 19W
Eatonia **88** 51 13N 109 25W
Eatonville **83** 47 20N 69 41W
Eau Claire **119** 3 30N 53 40W
Eau-Claire, L. à l', Newf., Canada **80** 52 36N 65 50W
Eau Claire, L. a l', Qué., Canada **78** 56 10N 74 25W
Eauze **140** 43 53N 0 7 E
Ebagoola **230** 14 15 S 143 12 E
Eban **247** 9 40N 4 50 E
Ebangalakata **252** 0 29 S 21 29 E
Ébano **103** 22 13N 98 24W
Ebbw Vale **133** 51 47N 3 12W
Ebebiyín **252** 2 9N 11 20 E
Ebeggui **241** 26 2N 6 0 E
Ebel **252** 0 7N 11 5 E
Ebensee **150** 47 48N 13 46 E
Eberbach **147** 49 27N 8 59 E
Eberswalde **146** 52 49N 13 50 E
Ebetsu **218** 43 7N 141 34 E
Ebian **216** 29 11N 103 13 E
Ebikon **149** 47 5N 8 21 E
Ebingen **147** 48 13N 9 1 E
Ebino **220** 32 2N 130 48 E
Ebnat-Kappel **149** 47 16N 9 7 E
Eboli **165** 40 39N 15 2 E
Ebolowa **247** 2 55N 11 10 E
Eboulements, Les **83** 47 28N 70 21W
Ebrach **147** 49 50N 10 30 E
Ébrié, Lagune **246** 5 12N 4 26W
Ebro → **156** 40 43N 0 54 E
Ebro, Pantano del **154** 43 0N 3 58W
Ebstorf **146** 53 2N 10 23 E
Ecaussines-d'Enghien **143** 50 35N 4 11 E
Eceabat **168** 40 11N 26 21 E
Éceuillé **138** 47 10N 1 19 E
Ech Cheliff **241** 36 10N 1 20 E
Echallens **148** 46 38N 6 38 E
Echelles, Les **141** 45 27N 5 45 E
Echeng **217** 30 23N 114 50 E
Echigo-Sammyaku **219** 36 50N 139 50 E
Echizen-Misaki **221** 35 59N 135 57 E
Echmiadzin **181** 40 12N 44 19 E
Echo Bay, N.W.T., Canada **94** 66 5N 117 55W
Echo Bay, Ont., Canada **84** 46 29N 84 4W
Echoing → **77** 55 51N 92 5W
Échouani, L. **82** 47 46N 75 42W
Echt **143** 51 7N 5 52 E
Echternach **143** 49 49N 6 25 E
Echuca **231** 36 10 S 144 20 E
Ecija **155** 37 30N 5 10W
Eckernförde **146** 54 26N 9 50 E
Eckville **91** 52 21N 114 22W
Eclipse Is. **228** 13 54 S 126 19 E
Eclipse Sd. **95** 72 38N 79 0W
Écommoy **138** 47 50N 0 17 E
Ecoporanga **121** 18 23 S 40 50W
Écorce, L. de l' **82** 47 5N 76 24W
Écos **139** 49 9N 1 35 E
Écouché **138** 48 42N 0 10W
Ecuador ■ **118** 2 0 S 78 0W
Ecuandureo **106** 20 10N 102 11W
Ecueils, Pte. aux **78** 59 47N 77 50W
Ecum Secum **81** 44 58N 62 8W
Ed **173** 58 55N 11 55 E
Ed Dabbura **244** 17 40N 34 15 E
Ed Dâmer **244** 17 27N 34 0 E
Ed Debba **244** 18 0N 30 51 E
Ed-Déffa **244** 30 40N 26 30 E
Ed Deim **245** 10 10N 28 20 E
Ed Dueim **245** 14 0N 32 10 E
Edah **229** 28 16 S 117 10 E
Edam, Canada **88** 53 11N 108 46W
Edam, Neth. **142** 52 31N 5 3 E
Edapally **201** 11 19N 78 3 E
Eday **134** 59 11N 2 47W
Edberg **91** 52 47N 112 47W
Edd **245** 14 0N 41 38 E
Eddrachillis B. **134** 58 16N 5 10W
Eddystone **133** 50 11N 4 16W
Eddystone Pt. **230** 40 59 S 148 20 E
Ede, Neth. **142** 52 4N 5 40 E
Ede, Nigeria **247** 7 45N 4 29 E
Édea **247** 3 51N 10 9 E
Edegem **143** 51 10N 4 27 E
Edehon L. **77** 60 25N 97 15W
Edekel, Adrar **241** 23 56N 6 47 E
Eden, Australia **231** 37 3 S 149 55 E
Eden, Canada **89** 50 23N 99 28W
Eden → **132** 54 57N 3 2W
Eden L. **77** 56 38N 100 15W
Edenburg **254** 29 43 S 25 58 E
Edendale **235** 46 19 S 168 48 E
Edenderry **135** 53 21N 7 3W
Edenville **255** 27 37 S 27 34 E
Eder → **146** 51 15N 9 25 E
Ederstausee **146** 51 11N 9 0 E
Edge Hill **133** 52 7N 1 28W
Edgecumbe **234** 37 59 S 176 47 E
Edgeøya **12** 77 45N 22 30 E
Edgerton **91** 52 45N 110 27W
Edgewater **91** 50 42N 116 5W
Edgewood **93** 49 47N 118 8W
Edhessa **168** 40 48N 22 5 E
Edievale **235** 45 49 S 169 22 E
Edina **246** 6 0N 10 10W
Edinburgh **134** 55 57N 3 12W
Edirne **167** 41 40N 26 34 E
Edithburgh **232** 35 5 S 137 43 E
Edjeleh **241** 28 38N 9 50 E
Edjudina **229** 29 48 S 122 23 E
Edmonton, Australia **230** 17 2 S 145 46 E
Edmonton, Canada **90** 53 30N 113 30W
Edmund L. **77** 54 45N 93 17W
Edmundston **81** 47 23N 68 20W
Edolo **162** 46 10N 10 21 E
Edsbyn **172** 61 23N 15 49 E
Edsel Ford Ra. **13** 77 0 S 143 0W
Edsele **172** 63 25N 16 32 E
Edson **90** 53 35N 116 28W
Eduardo Castex **124** 35 50 S 64 18W
Edward → **231** 35 0 S 143 30 E
Edward, L. **250** 0 25 S 29 40 E
Edward I. **86** 48 22N 88 37W
Edward VII Pen. **13** 80 0 S 150 0W
Edzo **76** 62 49N 116 4W
Eefde **142** 52 10N 6 13 E
Eekloo **143** 51 11N 3 33 E
Eel River Crossing **81** 48 1N 66 25W
Eelde **142** 53 8N 6 34 E
Eem → **142** 52 16N 5 20 E
Eems → **142** 53 26N 6 57 E
Eems Kanaal **142** 53 18N 6 46 E
Eenrum **142** 53 22N 6 28 E
Eernegem **143** 51 8N 3 2 E
Eerste Valthermond **142** 52 53N 6 58 E
Ef'e, Nahal **189** 31 9N 35 13 E
Eferding **150** 48 18N 14 1 E
Eferi **241** 24 30N 9 28 E
Effretikon **149** 47 25N 8 42 E
Eforie Sud **170** 44 1N 28 37 E
Ega → **156** 42 19N 1 55W
Égadi, Ísole **164** 37 55N 12 16 E
Eganville **85** 45 32N 77 5W
Egenolf L. **77** 59 3N 100 0W
Eger = Cheb **150** 50 9N 12 28 E
Eger **151** 47 53N 20 27 E
Eger → **151** 47 38N 20 50 E
Egersund **171** 58 26N 6 1 E
Egg L. **77** 55 5N 105 30W
Eggenburg **150** 48 38N 15 50 E
Eggenfelden **147** 48 24N 12 46 E
Eggiwil **148** 46 52N 7 47 E
Egherta **256** 2 4N 43 11 E
Éghezée **143** 50 35N 4 55 E
Eginbah **228** 20 53 S 119 47 E
Egito **253** 12 4 S 13 58 E
Égletons **140** 45 24N 2 3 E
Eglington I. **94** 75 48N 118 30W
Eglisau **149** 47 35N 8 31 E
Egmond-aan-Zee **142** 52 37N 4 38 E
Egmont **92** 49 45N 123 56W
Egmont, C. **234** 39 16 S 173 45 E
Egmont, Mt. **234** 39 17 S 174 5 E
Egmont B. **81** 46 29N 64 6W
Eğridir **177** 37 52N 30 51 E
Eğridir Gölü **177** 37 53N 30 50 E
Egtved **173** 55 38N 9 18 E
Éguas → **121** 13 26 S 44 14W
Egume **247** 7 30N 7 14 E
Éguzon **140** 46 27N 1 33 E
Egvekinot **185** 66 19N 179 50W
Egyek **151** 47 39N 20 52 E
Egypt ■ **244** 28 0N 31 0 E
Eha Amufu **247** 6 30N 7 46 E
Ehime □ **220** 33 30N 132 40 E
Ehingen **147** 48 16N 9 43 E
Eholt **93** 49 10N 118 34W
Ehrwald **150** 47 24N 10 56 E
Eibar **156** 43 11N 2 28W
Eibergen **142** 52 6N 6 39 E
Eichstatt **147** 48 53N 11 12 E
Eida **171** 60 32N 6 43 E
Eider → **146** 54 19N 8 58 E
Eidsvold **231** 25 25 S 151 12 E
Eifel **147** 50 10N 6 45 E
Eiffel Flats **251** 18 20 S 30 0 E
Eigg **134** 56 54N 6 10W
Eighty Mile Beach **228** 19 30 S 120 40 E
Eil **256** 8 0N 49 50 E
Eil, L. **134** 56 50N 5 15W
Eil Malk **226** 7 10N 134 23 E
Eildon **233** 37 14 S 145 55 E
Eildon, L. **231** 37 10 S 146 0 E
Eileen L. **77** 62 16N 107 37W
Eilenburg **146** 51 28N 12 38 E
Ein el Luweiqa **245** 14 5N 33 50 E
Einasleigh **230** 18 32 S 144 5 E
Einasleigh → **230** 17 30 S 142 17 E
Einbeck **146** 51 48N 9 50 E
Eindhoven **143** 51 26N 5 30 E
Einsiedeln **149** 47 7N 8 46 E
Eire ■ **135** 53 0N 8 0W
Eiríksjökull **174** 64 46N 20 24W
Eirlandsche Gat **142** 53 12N 4 54 E
Eirunepé **122** 6 35 S 69 53W
Eisden **143** 50 59N 5 42 E
Eisenach **146** 50 58N 10 18 E
Eisenberg **146** 50 59N 11 50 E
Eisenerz **150** 47 32N 14 54 E
Eisenhüttenstadt **146** 52 9N 14 41 E
Eisenkappel **150** 46 29N 14 36 E
Eisenstadt **151** 47 51N 16 31 E
Eiserfeld **146** 50 50N 7 59 E
Eisfeld **146** 50 25N 10 54 E
Eisleben **146** 51 31N 11 31 E
Ejby **173** 55 25N 9 56 E
Eje, Sierra del **154** 42 24N 6 54W
Ejea de los Caballeros **156** 42 7N 1 9W
Ejutla de Crespo **109** 16 34N 96 44W
Ekalla **252** 1 27 S 14 0 E
Ekanga **252** 2 23 S 23 14 E
Ekawasaki **220** 33 13N 132 46 E
Ekeren **143** 51 17N 4 25 E
Eket **247** 4 38N 7 56 E
Eketahuna **234** 40 38 S 175 43 E
Ekhínos **168** 41 16N 25 1 E
Ekibastuz **184** 51 50N 75 10 E
Ekimchan **185** 53 0N 133 0W
Ekoli **250** 0 23 S 24 13 E
Eksel **143** 51 9N 5 24 E
Eksere **190** 36 48N 32 0 E
Eksjö **173** 57 40N 14 58W
Ekwan → **74** 53 12N 82 15W
Ekwan Pt. **74** 53 16N 82 7W
El Aaiún **240** 27 9N 13 12W
El Aargub **240** 23 37N 15 52W
El Aat **189** 32 50N 35 45 E
El Abiodh-Sidi-Cheikh **241** 32 53N 0 31 E
El Adde **256** 2 35N 46 9 E
El 'Agrûd **191** 30 14N 34 24 E
El Aïoun **241** 34 33N 2 30W
El 'Aiyat **244** 29 36N 31 15 E
El Alamein **244** 30 48N 28 58 E
El Álamo, Baja Calif. N., Mexico **98** 31 34N 116 2W
El Álamo, Nuevo León, Mexico **102** 26 29N 99 46W
El Alto **122** 4 15 S 81 14W
El 'Aqaba, W. → **191** 30 7N 33 54 E
El 'Arag **244** 28 40N 26 20 E
El Arahal **155** 37 15N 5 33W
El Arba **240** 36 37N 3 12 E
El Arenal, Hidalgo, Mexico **107** 20 14N 98 54W
El Arenal, Zacatecas, Mexico **105** 23 39N 103 27W
El Aricha **241** 34 13N 1 10W
El Arîhā **189** 31 52N 35 27 E
El Arish, Australia **230** 17 35 S 146 1 E
El 'Arîsh, Egypt **191** 31 8N 33 50 E
El 'Arîsh, W. → **191** 31 8N 33 47 E
El Arrouch **241** 36 37N 6 53 E
El Asnam = Ech Cheliff **241** 36 10N 1 20 E
El Astillero **154** 43 24N 3 49W
El Azulejo **102** 28 0N 100 24W
El Badâri **244** 27 4N 31 25 E
El Bahrein **244** 28 30N 26 25 E
El Ballâs **244** 26 2N 32 43 E
El Balyana **244** 26 10N 32 3 E
El Banco **118** 9 0N 73 58W
El Baqeir **244** 18 40N 33 40 E
El Barco de Ávila **154** 40 21N 5 31W
El Barco de Valdeorras **154** 42 23N 7 0W
El Barreal **101** 31 17N 107 10W
El Barretal **103** 24 5N 99 10W
El Barril, Baja Calif. N., Mexico **99** 28 18N 112 55W
El Barril, San Luis Potosí, Mexico **103** 23 2N 102 8W
El Barrio **104** 24 49N 107 22W

El Barro 105 25 50N 103 24W
El Bauga 244 18 18N 33 52 E
El Baúl 118 8 57N 68 17W
El Bawiti 244 28 25N 28 45 E
El Bayadh 241 33 40N 1 1 E
El Bayo 109 18 59N 95 58W
El Bierzo 154 42 45N 6 30W
El Bluff 112 11 59N 83 40W
El Bolsón 126 41 55 S 71 30W
El Bonillo 157 38 57N 2 35W
El Bosque, Baja Calif. S., Mexico 99 24 52N 110 48W
El Bosque, Chiapas, Mexico 110 17 4N 92 44W
El Bozal 103 23 37N 101 25W
El Brûk, W. → 191 30 15N 33 50 E
El Buheirat □ 245 7 0N 30 0 E
El Bur 256 4 40N 46 37 E
El Burro 102 29 16N 101 55W
El Caín 126 41 38 S 68 19W
El Callao 119 7 18N 61 50W
El Camp 156 41 5N 1 10 E
El Capulín 103 21 2N 100 19W
El Carmen, Bolivia 123 13 40 S 63 55W
El Carmen, Venezuela 118 1 16N 66 52W
El Carrizo 101 29 58N 105 16W
El Casco 105 25 34N 104 35W
El Castillo 155 37 41N 6 19W
El Cerro, Bolivia 123 17 30 S 61 40W
El Cerro, Spain 155 37 45N 6 57W
El Chamal 103 23 56N 97 54W
El Chinero 98 31 24N 115 5W
El Chino 100 26 36N 108 59W
El Cocuy 118 6 25N 72 27W
El Corcovado 126 43 25 S 71 35W
El Coronil 155 37 5N 5 38W
El Cuy 126 39 55 S 68 25W
El Cuyo 111 21 31N 87 41W
El Dab'a 244 31 0N 28 27 E
El Daheir 191 31 13N 34 10 E
El Dambahaddo 256 3 17N 46 40 E
El Dátil 100 30 7N 112 15W
El Deir 244 25 25N 32 20 E
El Dere, Ethiopia 256 5 6N 43 5 E
El Dere, Somalia 256 3 50N 47 8 E
El Dere, Somalia 256 5 22N 46 11 E
El Desemboque 100 29 30N 112 27W
El Dilingat 244 30 50N 30 31 E
El Diviso 118 1 22N 78 14W
El Djem 241 35 18N 10 42 E
El Djouf 246 20 0N 11 30 E
El Doctor 107 20 51N 99 35W
El Dorado, Mexico 104 24 17N 107 21W
El Dorado, Venezuela 119 6 55N 61 37W
El Eglab 240 26 20N 4 30W
El Encinal 103 24 24N 98 22W
El Escorial 154 40 35N 4 7W
El Espino 110 18 18N 92 50W
El Eulma 241 36 9N 5 42 E
El Faiyûm 244 29 19N 30 50 E
El Fâsher 245 13 33N 25 26 E
El Fashn 244 28 50N 30 54 E
El Ferrol 154 43 29N 8 15W
El Fifi 245 10 4N 25 0 E
El Fud 256 7 15N 42 52 E
El Fuerte, Sinaloa, Mexico 104 26 25N 108 39W
El Fuerte, Zacatecas, Mexico 105 23 50N 103 6W
El Gal 256 10 58N 50 20 E
El Gebir 245 13 40N 29 40 E
El Gedida 244 25 40N 28 30 E
El Geteina 245 14 50N 32 27 E
El Gezira □ 245 15 0N 33 0 E
El Gineina, Râs 191 29 4N 33 54 E
El Gîza 244 30 0N 31 10 E
El Goléa 241 30 30N 2 50 E
El Gomeño 102 25 53N 97 20W
El Grullo 106 19 48N 104 13W
El Guayabal 109 17 32N 95 20W
El Guettar 241 34 5N 4 38 E
El Hadeb 240 25 51N 13 0W
El Hadjira 241 32 36N 5 30 E
El Hagiz 245 15 15N 35 50 E
El Hajeb 240 33 43N 5 13W
El Hammam 244 30 52N 29 25 E
El Hammâmi 240 23 3N 11 30W
El Hamurre 217 7 13N 48 54 E
El Hank 240 24 30N 7 0W
El Hasian 240 26 20N 14 0W
El Hawata 245 13 25N 34 42 E
El Heiz 244 27 50N 28 40 E
El Higo 108 21 46N 98 28W
El Huariche 103 24 51N 103 9W
El Huizache 103 22 55N 100 25W
El 'Idisât 244 25 30N 32 35 E
El Igma, G. 191 29 10N 34 0 E
El Iskandarîya 244 31 0N 30 0 E
El Jadida 240 33 11N 8 17W
El Jaralito 105 26 7N 104 10W
El Juile 109 17 44N 94 59W
El Kab 244 19 27N 32 46 E
El Kabrît, G. 191 29 42N 33 16 E
El Kala 241 36 50N 8 30 E
El Kalâa 240 32 4N 7 27W
El Kamlin 245 15 3N 33 11 E
El Kantara, Algeria 241 35 14N 5 45 E
El Kantara, Tunisia 241 33 45N 10 58 E
El Karaba 244 18 32N 33 41 E
El Kef 241 36 12N 8 47 E
El Khandaq 244 18 30N 30 30 E
El Khârga 244 25 30N 30 33 E
El Khartûm 245 15 31N 32 35 E
El Khartûm □ 245 16 0N 33 0 E
El Khartûm Bahrî 245 15 40N 32 31 E
El-Khroubs 241 36 10N 6 55 E
El Khureiba 244 28 3N 35 10 E
El Kseur 241 36 46N 4 49 E
El Ksiba 240 32 45N 6 1W
El Kuntilla 191 30 1N 34 45 E
El Laqeita 244 25 50N 33 15 E
El Laurel 109 18 14N 95 22W
El Leiya 245 16 15N 35 28 E
El Limón, Jalisco, Mexico 106 19 49N 104 11W
El Limón, Sonora, Mexico 101 26 56N 108 28W
El Limón, Tamaulipas, Mexico 103 22 11N 98 43W
El Limonar 111 18 10N 91 56W
El Llano 100 30 22N 111 6W
El Mafâza 245 13 38N 34 30 E
El Mahalla el Kubra 244 31 0N 31 0 E
El Mahârîq 244 25 35N 30 35 E
El Mahmûdîya 244 31 10N 30 32 E
El Maitén 126 42 3 S 71 10W
El Maiz 240 28 19N 0 9W
El-Maks el-Bahari 244 24 30N 30 40 E
El Manshâh 244 26 26N 31 50 E
El Mansour 240 27 47N 0 14W
El Mansûra 244 31 0N 31 19 E
El Mantico 119 7 38N 62 45W
El Manzala 244 31 10N 31 50 E
El Marâgha 244 26 35N 31 10 E
El Masid 245 15 15N 33 0 E
El Matariya 244 31 15N 32 0 E
El Matrimonio 102 27 7N 103 9W
El Mayor 98 32 5N 115 13W
El Medano 99 24 37N 111 33W
El Meghaier 241 33 55N 5 58 E
El Meraguen 240 28 0N 0 7W
El Metemma 245 16 50N 33 10 E
El Mezquite 105 23 20N 102 37W
El Miamo 119 7 39N 61 46W
El Milagro 124 30 59 S 65 59W
El Milia 241 36 51N 6 13 E
El Minyâ 244 28 7N 30 33 E
El Molar 156 40 42N 3 45W
El Moquete 102 25 39N 97 34W
El Moral 102 28 51N 100 39W
El Mreyye 246 18 0N 6 0W
El Mulato 101 29 22N 104 10W
El Naranjo 103 22 30N 98 38W
El Nido 211 11 10N 119 25 E
El Obeid 245 13 8N 30 10 E
El Ocotito 107 17 15N 99 34W
El Olvido 103 23 35N 99 13W
El Oro 102 27 15N 103 30W
El Oro □ 118 3 30 S 79 50W
El Oro de Hidalgo 107 19 48N 100 8W
El Oso 102 27 6N 102 11W
El Oued 241 33 20N 6 58 E
El Palmar, Bolivia 123 17 50 S 63 9W
El Palmar, Venezuela 119 7 58N 61 53W
El Palmito 104 25 11N 106 59W
El Panadés 156 41 10N 1 30 E
El Papayo 107 17 2N 100 17W
El Pardo 154 40 31N 3 47W
El Pedernoso 157 39 29N 2 45W
El Pedroso 155 37 51N 5 45W
El Peñasco 103 22 20N 100 57W
El Plomo 100 31 15N 112 4W
El Pobo de Dueñas 156 40 46N 1 39W
El Porvenir 101 31 15N 105 51W
El Potosí 103 24 51N 100 19W
El Pozo 104 24 56N 107 16W
El Pozole 104 22 56N 105 55W
El Prat de Llobregat 156 41 18N 2 3 E
El Progreso 112 15 26N 87 51W
El Provencío 157 39 23N 2 35W
El Pueblito 101 29 6N 105 7W
El Qâhira 244 30 1N 31 14 E
El Qanțara 191 30 52N 32 20 E
El Qasr 244 25 44N 28 42 E
El Quelite 104 23 32N 106 28W
El Quseima 191 30 40N 34 15 E
El Qusîya 244 27 29N 30 44 E
El Râshda 244 25 36N 28 57 E
El Recodo 104 23 24N 106 14W
El Refugio 99 24 49N 111 44W
El Refugio de Suchitlán 106 20 28N 105 32W
El Remolino 102 28 44N 101 7W
El Ribero 154 42 30N 8 30W
El Rîdisiya 244 24 56N 32 51 E
El Ronquillo 155 37 44N 6 10W
El Rosarito 98 30 26N 115 21W
El Rubio 155 37 22N 5 0W
El Rucio 105 23 23N 102 5W
El Saff 244 29 34N 31 16 E
El Saheira, W. → 191 30 5N 33 25 E
El Salado 103 24 18N 100 52W
El Salitre 104 25 51N 106 7W
El Salto 104 23 47N 105 22W
El Salvador ■ 112 13 50N 89 0W
El Sancejo 155 37 4N 5 6W
El Sauce 112 13 0N 86 40W
El Sauz 101 29 3N 106 15W
El Sauzal 98 31 54N 116 41W
El Shallal 244 24 0N 32 53 E
El Simbillawein 244 30 48N 31 13 E
El Sombrero 118 9 23N 67 3W
El Sueco 101 29 54N 106 24W
El Suweis 244 29 58N 32 31 E
El Tamarâni, W. → 191 30 7N 34 43 E
El Tambor 104 25 7N 105 26W
El Tejar 109 19 3N 96 10W
El Tepe 107 20 26N 99 10W
El Teporachic 101 27 49N 106 46W
El Thabt, G. 191 28 17N 34 1 E
El Thamad 191 29 40N 34 28 E
El Tigre, Mexico 111 18 16N 90 33W
El Tigre, Venezuela 119 8 44N 64 15W
El Tîh, G. 191 29 40N 33 50 E
El Tîna, Khalîg 191 31 10N 32 40 E
El Tiro 100 30 19N 111 45W
El Tocuyo 118 9 47N 69 48W
El Tofo 124 29 22 S 71 18W
El Tránsito 124 28 52 S 70 17W
El Tren 100 31 15N 112 11W
El Triunfo, Baja Calif. S., Mexico 99 23 47N 110 8W
El Triunfo, Tabasco, Mexico 110 17 56N 91 9W
El Tuito 106 20 19N 105 22W
El Tule 101 27 3N 106 16W
El Tûr 191 28 14N 33 36 E
El Turbio 126 51 45 S 72 5W
El Uinle 256 3 4N 41 42 E
El Uqsur 244 25 41N 32 38 E
El Vado 156 41 2N 3 18W
El Valle 104 25 31N 107 52W
El Vallés 156 41 35N 2 20 E
El Venado 102 26 47N 101 56W
El Venando 103 22 56N 101 6W
El Vigía 118 8 38N 71 39W
El Wabeira 191 29 34N 33 6 E
El Wak, Kenya 250 2 49N 40 56 E
El Wak, Somalia 256 2 44N 41 1 E
El Waqf 244 25 45N 32 15 E
El Wâsta 244 29 19N 31 12 E
El Weguet 245 5 28N 42 17 E
El Zape 104 25 46N 105 47W
Elafónisos 169 36 29N 22 56 E
Elaho → 92 50 7N 123 23W
Elaine 232 37 44 S 144 2 E
Elamanchili 200 17 33N 82 50 E
Elands 233 31 37 S 152 20 E
Elandsvlei 254 32 19 S 19 31 E
Élassa 169 35 18N 26 21 E
Elassón 168 39 53N 22 12 E
Elat 189 29 30N 34 56 E
Eláthia 169 38 37N 22 46 E
Elâzığ 177 38 37N 39 14 E
Elba 162 42 48N 10 15 E
Elbasani 168 41 9N 20 9 E
Elbasani-Berati □ 168 40 58N 20 0 E
Elbe → 146 53 50N 9 0 E
Elbeuf 138 49 17N 1 2 E
Elbing = Elbląg 152 54 10N 19 25 E
Elbląg 152 54 10N 19 25 E
Elbląg □ 152 54 15N 19 30 E
Elbow 88 51 7N 106 35W
Elbow → 91 51 3N 114 2W
Elbrus 181 43 21N 42 30 E
Elburg 142 52 26N 5 50 E
Elburz Mts. = Alborz, Reshteh-ye Kūhhā-ye 193 36 0N 52 0 E
Elche 157 38 15N 0 42W
Elche de la Sierra 157 38 27N 2 3W
Elcho I. 230 11 55 S 135 45 E
Elda 157 38 29N 0 47W
Eldorado, Argentina 125 26 28 S 54 43W
Eldorado, Ont., Canada 85 44 35N 77 31W
Eldorado, Sask., Canada 77 59 35N 108 30W
Eldoret 250 0 30N 35 17 E
Elefantes → 255 24 10 S 32 40 E
Elefantes, G. 126 46 28 S 73 49W
Elektrogorsk 179 55 56N 38 50 E
Elektrostal 179 55 41N 38 32 E
Elele 247 5 5N 6 50 E
Elena 167 42 55N 25 53 E
Elephant I. 13 61 0 S 55 0W
Elephant Pass 201 9 35N 80 25 E
Elesbão Veloso 120 6 13 S 42 8W
Eleshnitsa 167 41 52N 23 36 E
Eleuthera 112 25 0N 76 20W
Elevsís 169 38 4N 23 26 E
Elevtheroúpolis 168 40 52N 24 20 E
Elgepiggen 171 62 10N 11 21 E
Elgeyo-Marakwet □ 250 0 45N 35 30 E
Elgg 149 47 29N 8 52 E
Elgin, Man., Canada 89 49 27N 100 16W
Elgin, N.B., Canada 75 45 48N 65 10W
Elgin, Ont., Canada 85 44 36N 76 13W
Elgin, U.K. 134 57 39N 3 20W
Elgon, Mt. 250 1 10N 34 30 E
Eliase 207 8 21 S 130 48 E
Elikón, Mt. 169 38 18N 22 45 E
Elin Pelin 167 42 40N 23 36 E
Elisabethville = Lubumbashi 251 11 40 S 27 28 E
Eliseu Martins 120 8 13 S 43 42W
Elista 181 46 16N 44 14 E
Elizabeth 232 34 42 S 138 41 E
Elizondo 156 43 12N 1 30W
Ełk 152 53 50N 22 21 E
Elk →, Canada 91 49 11N 115 14W
Ełk →, Poland 152 53 41N 22 28 E
Elk Island Nat. Park 90 53 35N 112 59W
Elk Lake 74 47 40N 80 25W
Elk Lakes Prov. Park 91 50 30N 115 10W
Elk Point 90 53 54N 110 55W
Elkedra 230 21 9 S 135 33 E
Elkedra → 230 21 8 S 136 22 E
Elkford 91 49 52N 114 53W
Elkhorn 89 49 59N 101 14W
Elkhotovo 181 43 19N 44 15 E
Elkhovo 167 42 10N 26 40 E
Elko 91 49 20N 115 10W
Ell, L. 229 29 13 S 127 46 E
Ellecom 142 52 2N 6 6 E
Ellef Ringnes I. 95 78 30N 102 2W
Ellendale 228 17 56 S 124 48 E
Ellerston 233 31 49 S 151 20 E
Ellery, Mt. 231 37 28 S 148 47 E
Ellesmere I. 95 79 30N 80 0W
Ellesworth Land 13 76 0 S 89 0W
Ellezelles 143 50 44N 3 42 E
Ellice Is. = Tuvalu ■ 224 8 0 S 178 0 E
Elliot, Australia 230 17 33 S 133 32 E
Elliot, S. Africa 255 31 22 S 27 48 E
Elliot L. 89 52 54N 95 18W
Elliot Lake 84 46 25N 82 35W
Elliston 79 48 38N 53 3W
Ellon 134 57 21N 2 5W
Ellore = Eluru 200 16 48N 81 8 E
Ells → 90 57 18N 111 40W
Ellsworth Land 13 76 0 S 89 0W
Ellsworth Mts. 13 78 30 S 85 0W
Ellwangen 147 48 57N 10 9 E
Elm 149 46 54N 9 10 E
Elma 89 49 52N 95 55W
Elmalı 177 36 44N 29 56 E
Elmina 247 5 5N 1 21W
Elmira 84 43 36N 80 33W
Elmore 231 36 30 S 144 37 E
Elmsdale 81 44 58N 63 30W
Elmshorn 146 53 44N 9 40 E
Elmvale 84 44 35N 79 52W
Elmworth 90 55 3N 119 37W
Elne 140 42 36N 2 58 E
Elnora 91 51 59N 113 12W
Elora 84 43 41N 80 26W
Elorza 118 7 3N 69 31W
Elos 169 36 46N 22 43 E
Elota 104 23 58N 106 42W
Elota, R. → 104 23 52N 106 56W
Éloyes 139 48 6N 6 36 E
Elphin 85 44 55N 76 37W
Elphinstone 89 50 32N 100 30W
Elrose 88 51 12N 108 0W
Elsa 94 63 55N 135 29W
Elsas 87 48 32N 82 55W
Elsinore = Helsingør 172 56 2N 12 35 E
Elsinore 233 31 35 S 145 11 E
Elspe 146 51 10N 8 1 E
Elspeet 142 52 17N 5 48 E
Elst 142 51 55N 5 51 E
Elster → 146 51 25N 11 57 E
Elsterwerda 146 51 27N 13 32 E
Elten 142 51 52N 6 9 E
Eltham, Australia 233 37 43 S 145 12 E
Eltham, N.Z. 234 39 26 S 174 19 E
Elton 181 49 5N 46 52 E
Eluanbi 217 21 51N 120 50 E
Eluru 200 16 48N 81 8 E
Elvas 155 38 50N 7 10W
Elven 138 47 44N 2 36W
Elverum 171 60 53N 11 34 E
Elvire → 228 17 51 S 128 11 E
Elvo → 162 45 23N 8 21 E
Elvran 171 63 24N 11 3 E

Ely .... 133 52 24N 0 16 E
Elyashiv .... 189 32 23N 34 55 E
Elyrus .... 169 35 15N 23 45 E
Elz → .... 147 48 21N 7 45 E
Emådalen .... 172 61 20N 14 44 E
Emāmrūd .... 193 36 30N 55 0 E
Emba .... 184 48 50N 58 8 E
Emba → .... 177 46 38N 53 14 E
Embarcación .... 124 23 10 S 64 0W
Embarras Portage .. 77 58 27N 111 28W
Embetsu .... 218 44 44N 141 47 E
Embira → .... 122 7 19 S 70 15W
Embóna .... 169 36 13N 27 51 E
Embrach .... 149 47 30N 8 36 E
Embro 84 43 9N 80 54W
Embrun .... 141 44 34N 6 30 E
Embu .... 250 0 32 S 37 38 E
Embu □ .... 250 0 30 S 37 35 E
Emden .... 146 53 22N 7 12 E
'Emeq Yizre'el .... 189 32 35N 35 12 E
Emerald .... 230 23 32 S 148 10 E
Emeril 78 47 26N 75 47W
Emerson 89 49 0N 97 10W
Emi Koussi .... 241 20 0N 18 55 E
Emilia-Romagna □ . 162 44 33N 10 40 E
Emiliano Martínez .. 104 25 26N 105 14W
Emiliano Zapata, Chiapas, Mexico . 110 17 45N 91 46W
Emiliano Zapata, Durango, Mexico . 105 24 26N 103 54W
Emiliano Zapata, Michoacan, Mexico 106 20 2N 102 35W
Emiliano Zapata, Morelos, Mexico . 107 18 50N 99 11W
Emilius, Mte. .... 162 45 41N 7 23 E
Eminabad .... 198 32 2N 74 8 E
Emine, Nos .... 167 42 40N 27 56 E
Emlichheim .... 146 52 37N 6 51 E
Emmaboda .... 173 56 37N 15 32 E
Emme → .... 148 47 0N 7 42 E
Emmeloord .... 142 52 44N 5 46 E
Emmen .... 142 52 48N 6 57 E
Emmendingen .... 147 48 7N 7 51 E
Emmental .... 148 47 0N 7 35 E
Emmer-Compascuum .... 142 52 49N 7 2 E
Emmerich .... 146 51 50N 6 12 E
Emmet .... 230 24 45 S 144 30 E
Emo 86 48 38N 93 50W
Emöd .... 151 47 57N 20 47 E
Emona .... 167 42 43N 27 53 E
Empalme 100 27 58N 110 51W
Empangeni .... 255 28 50 S 31 52 E
Empedrado .... 124 28 0 S 58 46W
Emperor Seamount Chain .... 224 40 0N 170 0 E
Empoli .... 162 43 43N 10 57 E
Empress 91 50 57N 110 0W
Emptinne .... 143 50 19N 5 8 E
Ems → .... 146 52 37N 9 26 E
Emsdale 84 45 32N 79 19W
Emsdetten .... 146 52 11N 7 31 E
Emu, Australia .... 232 36 44 S 143 26 E
Emu, China .... 215 43 40N 128 6 E
Emu Park .... 230 23 13 S 150 50 E
'En 'Avrona .... 191 29 43N 35 0 E
En Gedi .... 189 31 28N 35 25 E
En Gev .... 189 32 47N 35 38 E
En Harod .... 189 32 33N 35 22 E
'En Kerem .... 189 31 47N 35 6 E
En Nahud .... 245 12 45N 28 25 E
Ena .... 221 35 25N 137 25 E
Ena-San .... 221 35 26N 137 36 E
Enafors .... 172 63 17N 12 20 E
Enambú 118 1 1N 70 17W
Enana .... 254 17 30 S 16 23 E
Enånger .... 172 61 30N 17 9 E
Enaratoli .... 207 3 55 S 136 21 E
Enard B. 134 58 5N 5 20W
Encajonado, R. → 110 16 59N 93 46W
Encantada, Cerro de la 98 31 0N 115 24W
Encantadas, Serra .. 125 30 40 S 53 0W
Encanto, C. .... 207 15 45N 121 38 E
Encarnación, Mexico 107 20 53N 99 13W
Encarnación, Paraguay .... 125 27 15 S 55 50W
Encarnación de Díaz 106 21 31N 102 14W
Encarnación de Guzmán 103 24 50N 101 3W
Enchi 246 5 53N 2 48W
Encontrados 118 9 3N 72 14W
Encounter B. .... 232 35 45 S 138 45 E
Encrucijada 110 18 18N 93 31W
Encruzilhada .... 121 15 31 S 40 54W
Endako 92 54 6N 125 2W
Ende .... 207 8 45 S 121 40 E
Endeavour 88 52 10N 102 39W
Endeavour Str. .... 230 10 45 S 142 0 E
Endelave .... 173 55 46N 10 18 E
Enderbury I. .... 224 3 8 S 171 5W
Enderby 93 50 35N 119 10W
Enderby I. .... 228 20 35 S 116 30 E
Enderby Land .... 13 66 0 S 53 0 E
Endimari → .... 122 8 46 S 66 7W
Endröd .... 151 46 55N 20 47 E
Endyalgout I. .... 228 11 40 S 132 35 E
Ene → .... 122 11 10 S 74 18W
Enewatak .... 224 11 30N 162 15 E
Enez .... 168 40 45N 26 5 E
Enfida .... 241 36 6N 10 28 E
Enfield, Canada 81 44 56N 63 32W
Enfield, U.K. 133 51 39N 0 4W
Engadin .... 149 46 45N 10 10 E
Engaño, C., Dom. Rep. 113 18 30N 68 20W
Engaño, C., Phil. .... 210 18 35N 122 23 E
Engelberg .... 149 46 48N 8 26 E
Engels .... 179 51 28N 46 6 E
Engemann L. 77 58 0N 106 55W
Enger .... 171 60 35N 10 20 E
Enggano .... 208 5 20 S 102 40 E
Enghien .... 143 50 37N 4 2 E
Engil 240 33 12N 4 32W
Engkilili .... 206 1 3N 111 42 E
England □ 131 53 0N 2 0W
Englee 79 50 45N 56 5W
Englefeld 88 52 10N 104 39W
Englefield .... 232 37 21 S 141 48 E
Englefield, C. 95 69 49N 85 34W
Englehart 74 47 49N 79 52W
Engler L. 77 59 8N 106 52W
English →, Ont., Canada 86 49 12N 91 5W
English →, Ont., Canada 86 50 35N 93 30W
English Bazar = Ingraj Bazar .... 199 24 58N 88 10 E
English Channel 138 50 0N 2 0W
English Harbour East 79 47 38N 54 54W
English River 86 49 14N 91 0W
Enilda 90 55 25N 116 18W
Enipévs → .... 168 39 22N 22 17 E
Enkhuizen .... 142 52 42N 5 17 E
Enköping .... 172 59 37N 17 4 E
Enle .... 216 24 0N 101 9 E
Enna .... 165 37 34N 14 15 E
Ennadai 77 61 8N 100 53W
Ennadai L. 77 61 0N 101 0W
Ennedi .... 243 17 15N 22 0 E
Enngonia .... 231 29 21 S 145 50 E
Ennis 135 52 51N 8 59W
Enniscorthy 135 52 30N 6 35W
Enniskillen 135 54 20N 7 40W
Ennistimon 135 52 56N 9 18W
Enns .... 150 48 12N 14 28 E
Enns → .... 150 48 14N 14 32 E
Enping .... 217 22 16N 112 21 E
Enrile .... 210 17 34N 121 42 E
Enriquillo, L. 113 18 20N 72 5W
Ens .... 142 52 38N 5 50 E
Enschede .... 142 52 13N 6 53 E
Ensenada, Argentina .... 124 34 55 S 57 55W
Ensenada, Mexico .. 98 31 52N 116 37W
Ensenada, La .... 126 41 12 S 72 33W
Enshi .... 216 30 18N 109 29 E
Enshū-Nada .... 221 34 27N 137 38 E
Ensisheim .... 139 47 50N 7 20 E
Entebbe .... 250 0 4N 32 28 E
Enter .... 142 52 17N 6 35 E
Enterprise 76 60 47N 115 45W
Entiako L. 92 53 13N 125 31W
Entlebuch .... 148 46 59N 8 4 E
Entre Ríos, Bolivia . 124 21 30 S 64 25W
Entre Rios, Bahia, Brazil .... 121 11 56 S 38 5W
Entre Rios, Pará, Brazil .... 123 5 24 S 54 21W
Entre Ríos □ .... 124 30 30 S 58 30W
Entrecasteaux, Pt. d' 234 34 50 S 115 56 E
Entrepeñas, Pantano de 156 40 34N 2 42W
Enugu .... 247 6 20N 7 30 E
Enugu Ezike .... 247 7 0N 7 29 E
Envermeières .... 138 49 54N 1 16 E
Envermeu .... 138 49 53N 1 15 E
Envigado 118 6 10N 75 35W
Envira .... 122 7 18 S 70 13W
Enz → .... 147 49 1N 9 6 E
Enza → .... 162 44 54N 10 31 E
Enzan .... 221 35 42N 138 44 E
Eólie, I. .... 165 38 30N 14 50 E
Epanomí .... 168 40 25N 22 59 E
Epazoyucan 107 20 2N 98 38W
Epe, Neth. .... 142 52 21N 5 59 E
Epe, Nigeria .... 247 6 36N 3 59 E
Epéna .... 252 1 22N 17 29 E
Épernay .... 139 49 3N 3 56 E
Épernon .... 139 48 35N 1 40 E
Ephesus .... 169 37 50N 27 33 E
Epidaurus Limera .. 169 36 46N 23 0 E
Epila 156 41 36N 1 17W
Épinac-les-Mines .. 139 46 59N 4 31 E
Épinal .... 139 48 10N 6 27 E
Epiphanie, L' 83 45 51N 73 29W
Epira 119 5 5N 57 20W
Episcopia Bihorulu . 170 47 12N 21 55 E
Episkopi .... 190 34 40N 32 54 E
Episkopi Bay .... 190 34 35N 32 50 E
Epitálion .... 169 37 37N 21 30 E
Epping .... 133 51 42N 0 8 E
Epukiro .... 254 21 40 S 19 9 E
Equatorial Guinea ■ .... 252 2 0 S 8 0 E
Equeipa 119 5 22N 62 43W
Er Rahad .... 245 12 45N 30 32 E
Er Rif 240 35 1N 4 1W
Er Roseires .... 245 11 55N 34 30 E
Er Yébigué .... 241 22 30N 17 30 E
Eran .... 211 9 4N 117 42 E
Erandol .... 198 20 56N 75 20 E
Erap .... 227 6 37 S 146 51 E
Erāwadī Myit → = Irrawaddy → .... 202 15 50N 95 6 E
Erba, Italy .... 162 45 49N 9 12 E
Erba, Sudan .... 244 19 5N 36 51 E
Ercha .... 185 69 45N 147 20 E
Erciyaş Daği .... 177 38 30N 35 30 E
Erdao Jiang → .... 215 43 0N 127 0 E
Erdemli .... 190 36 36N 34 19 E
Erdene .... 214 44 13N 111 10 E
Erding .... 147 48 18N 11 55 E
Erdre → 138 47 13N 1 32W
Erebato → 119 5 54N 64 16W
Erebus, Mt. .... 13 77 35 S 167 0 E
Erechim .... 125 27 35 S 52 15W
Ereğli, Turkey .... 177 41 15N 31 30 E
Ereğli, Turkey .... 177 37 31N 34 4 E
Erei, Monti .... 165 37 20N 14 20 E
Erembodegem .... 143 50 56N 4 4 E
Erenhot .... 214 43 48N 111 59 E
Eresma → 154 41 26N 40 45W
Eressós .... 169 39 11N 25 57 E
Erfenis Dam .... 254 28 30 S 26 50 E
Erfjord .... 171 59 20N 6 14 E
Erfoud 241 31 30N 4 15W
Erft → .... 146 51 11N 6 44 E
Erfurt .... 146 50 58N 11 2 E
Erfurt □ .... 146 51 10N 10 30 E
Erğene → .... 167 41 1N 26 22 E
Ergeni Vozyshennost .... 181 47 0N 44 0 E
Ergli .... 178 56 54N 25 38 E
Eria → 154 42 3N 5 44W
Eriba .... 245 16 40N 36 10 E
Eriboll, L. 134 58 28N 4 41W
Eric 78 51 56N 65 45W
Eric L. 80 51 55N 65 36W
Erica .... 142 52 43N 6 56 E
Érice .... 164 38 4N 12 34 E
Erie, L. 84 42 15N 81 0W
Erieau 84 42 16N 81 57W
Erigavo .... 256 10 35N 47 20 E
Erikoúsa .... 168 39 55N 19 14 E
Eriksdale 89 50 52N 98 7W
Erikslund .... 172 62 31N 15 54 E
Erímanthos .... 169 37 57N 21 50 E
Erimo-misaki .... 218 41 50N 143 15 E
Erin 84 43 45N 80 7W
Eriswil .... 148 47 5N 7 46 E
Erithraí .... 169 38 13N 23 20 E
Eritrea □ .... 245 14 0N 41 0 E
Erjas → 155 39 40N 7 1W
Erlandson, L. 78 57 3N 68 28W
Erlangen .... 147 49 35N 11 0 E
Erldunda .... 230 25 14 S 133 12 E
Erlin .... 217 23 55N 120 21 E
Ermelo, Neth. .... 142 52 18N 5 35 E
Ermelo, S. Africa .. 255 26 31 S 29 59 E
Ermenak .... 190 36 38N 33 0 E
Ermióni .... 169 37 23N 23 15 E
Ermoúpolis = Síros . 169 37 28N 24 57 E
Ernakulam = Cochin .... 201 9 59N 76 22 E
Erne → 135 54 30N 8 16W
Erne, Lough 135 54 26N 7 46W
Ernée 138 48 18N 0 56W
Ernest Giles Ra. .... 229 27 0 S 123 45 E
Ernstberg .... 147 50 14N 6 46 E
Erode .... 201 11 24N 77 45 E
Eromanga .... 231 26 40 S 143 11 E
Erongarícuaro 106 19 35N 101 43W
Erongo .... 254 21 39 S 15 58 E
Erp .... 143 51 36N 5 37 E
Erquelinnes .... 143 50 19N 4 8 E
Erquy 138 48 38N 2 29W
Erquy, Cap d' 138 48 39N 2 29W
Err, Piz d' .... 149 46 34N 9 43 E
Errabiddy .... 229 25 25 S 117 5 E
Erramala Hills .... 201 15 30N 78 15 E
Errer → .... 245 7 32N 42 35 E
Errigal, Mt. 135 55 2N 8 8W
Erris Hd. 135 54 19N 10 0W
Erseka .... 168 40 22N 20 40 E
Erskine 91 52 20N 112 53W
Erstein .... 139 48 25N 7 38 E
Erstfeld .... 149 46 50N 8 38 E
Ertil .... 179 51 55N 40 50 E
Ertvågøy .... 171 63 13N 8 26 E
Ertvelde .... 143 51 11N 3 45 E
Eruwa .... 247 7 33N 3 26 E
Ervy-le-Châtel .... 139 48 2N 3 55 E
Eryuan .... 216 26 7N 99 57 E
Erzgebirge .... 146 50 25N 13 0 E
Erzin, Turkey .... 190 36 57N 36 11 E
Erzin, U.S.S.R. .... 185 50 15N 95 10 E
Erzincan .... 177 39 46N 39 30 E
Erzurum .... 177 39 57N 41 15 E
Es Sahrâ' Esh Sharqîya .... 244 26 0N 33 30 E
Es Sînâ' .... 244 29 0N 34 0 E
Es Sûkî .... 245 13 20N 33 58 E
Esa'ala .... 227 9 45 S 150 49 E
Esambo .... 250 3 48 S 23 30 E
Esan-Misaki .... 218 41 40N 141 10 E
Esashi, Hokkaidō, Japan .... 218 44 56N 142 35 E
Esashi, Hokkaidō, Japan .... 218 41 52N 140 7 E
Esbjerg .... 173 55 29N 8 29 E
Escada .... 120 8 22 S 35 8W
Escalente .... 211 10 50N 123 33 E
Escalón 101 26 45N 104 20W
Escalona 154 40 9N 4 29W
Escarparda Pt. .... 210 18 31N 122 13 E
Escarpé, C. .... 226 20 41 S 167 13 E
Escaut → .... 143 51 2N 3 45 E
Esch-sur-Alzette .... 143 49 32N 6 0 E
Eschallens .... 148 46 39N 6 38 E
Eschede .... 146 52 44N 10 13 E
Escholzmatt .... 148 46 55N 7 56 E
Eschwege .... 146 51 10N 10 3 E
Eschweiler .... 146 50 49N 6 14 E
Escobedo 102 27 13N 101 21W
Escoma .... 122 15 40 S 69 8W
Escondida, La 103 24 6N 99 55W
Escoumins, Les 83 48 21N 69 24W
Escuinapa de Hidalgo 104 22 51N 105 48W
Escuintla 112 14 20N 90 48W
Eséka .... 247 3 41N 10 44 E
Esens .... 146 53 40N 7 35 E
Esera → .... 156 42 6N 0 15 E
Eşfahān .... 193 33 0N 53 0 E
Esfīdeh .... 193 33 39N 59 46 E
Esgueva → 154 41 40N 4 43W
Esh Sham = Dimashq .... 190 33 30N 36 18 E
Esh Shamâlîya □ .... 244 19 0N 29 0 E
Eshan .... 216 24 11N 102 24 E
Eshkamesh .... 197 36 23N 69 19 E
Eshowe .... 255 28 50 S 31 30 E
Eshta' ol .... 189 31 47N 35 0 E
Esiama 246 4 56N 2 25W
Esino → .... 163 43 39N 13 22 E
Esk →, Dumf. & Gall., U.K. 134 54 58N 3 4W
Esk →, N. Yorks., U.K. 132 54 27N 0 36W
Eskān .... 197 26 48N 63 9 E
Esker 78 53 53N 66 25W
Eskifjörður 174 65 3N 13 55W
Eskilstuna .... 172 59 22N 16 32 E
Eskimo Lakes 94 69 15N 132 17W
Eskimo Pt. 77 61 10N 94 15W
Eskişehir .... 177 39 50N 30 35 E
Esla → 154 41 29N 6 3W
Esla, Pantano del 154 41 29N 6 3W
Eslāmābād-e Gharb . 192 34 10N 46 30 E
Eslöv .... 172 55 50N 13 20 E
Esmeralda, I. .... 126 48 55 S 75 25W
Esmeralda, La .... 124 22 16 S 62 33W
Esmeralda, Sa. 103 25 8N 100 30W
Esmeraldas 118 1 0N 79 40W
Esmeraldas □ 118 0 40N 79 30W
Esmeraldas → 118 0 58N 79 38W
Esnagami L. 87 50 19N 86 51W
Esnagi L. 87 48 36N 84 33W
Esneux .... 143 50 32N 5 33 E
Espada, Pta. 118 12 5N 71 7W
Espalion .... 140 44 32N 2 47 E
Espalmador, I. .... 157 38 47N 1 26 E
Espanola 84 46 15N 81 46W
Espardell, I. del .... 157 38 48N 1 29 E
Esparraguera .... 156 41 33N 1 52 E
Esparta 112 9 59N 84 40W
Espejo 155 37 40N 4 34W
Esperança .... 120 7 1 S 35 51W
Esperance .... 229 33 45 S 121 55 E
Esperance B. .... 229 33 48 S 121 55 E
Esperantinópolis .... 120 4 53 S 44 53W
Esperanza, Antarct. 13 65 0 S 55 0W
Esperanza, Santa Cruz, Argentina .... 126 51 1 S 70 49W
Esperanza, Santa Fe, Argentina .... 124 31 29 S 61 3W
Esperanza, Canada . 92 49 52N 126 43W
Esperanza, Puebla, Mexico 109 18 52N 97 24W

Esperanza, Sonora, Mexico 100 27 35N 109 56W
Esperanza, Masbate, Phil. 211 11 45N 124 3 E
Esperanza, Mindanao, Phil. 211 8 43N 125 36 E
Esperanza, La, Argentina 126 40 26 S 68 32W
Esperanza, La, Cuba 112 22 46N 83 44W
Esperanza, La, Hond. 112 14 15N 88 10W
Esperanza Inlet 92 49 51N 126 55W
Espéraza 140 42 56N 2 14 E
Espevœr 171 59 35N 5 7 E
Espichel, C. 155 38 22N 9 16W
Espiel 155 38 11N 5 1W
Espigão, Serra do 125 26 35 S 50 30W
Espinal, Colombia 118 4 9N 74 53W
Espinal, Mexico 108 20 16N 97 24W
Espinar 122 14 51 S 71 24W
Espinazo 102 26 16N 101 6W
Espinazo, Sierra del = Espinhaço, Serra do 121 17 30 S 43 30W
Espinhaço, Serra do 121 17 30 S 43 30W
Espinho 154 41 1N 8 38W
Espinilho, Serra do 125 28 30 S 55 0W
Espino 118 8 34N 66 1W
Espinosa de los Monteros 154 43 5N 3 34W
Espírito Santo □ 121 20 0 S 40 45W
Espíritu Santo 105 22 36N 101 27W
Espíritu Santo, B. del 111 19 20N 87 35W
Espíritu Santo, I. 99 24 30N 110 22W
Espita 111 21 1N 88 19W
Esplanada 121 11 47 S 37 57W
Espluga de Francolí 156 41 24N 1 7 E
Espuña, Sierra 157 37 51N 1 35W
Espungabera 255 20 29 S 32 45 E
Esqueda 100 30 46N 109 31W
Esquel 126 42 55 S 71 20W
Esquina 124 30 0 S 59 30W
Essaouira 240 31 32N 9 42W
Essarts, Les 138 46 47N 1 12W
Essebie 250 2 58N 30 40 E
Essen, Belgium 143 51 28N 4 28 E
Essen, Germany 146 51 28N 6 59 E
Essequibo □ 119 7 0N 59 0W
Essequibo → 119 6 50N 58 30W
Essex 84 42 10N 82 49W
Essex □ 133 51 48N 0 30 E
Esslingen 147 48 43N 9 19 E
Essonne □ 139 48 30N 2 20 E
Essvik 172 62 18N 17 24 E
Est, Î. de l' 81 47 37N 61 23W
Estaca, Pta. del 154 43 46N 7 42W
Estadilla 156 42 4N 0 16 E
Estados, I. de Los 126 54 40 S 64 30W
Estagel 140 42 47N 2 40 E
Eşţahbānāt 193 29 8N 54 4 E
Estância 120 11 16 S 37 26W
Estapilla 110 17 33N 91 24W
Estārm 193 28 21N 58 21 E
Estarreja 154 40 45N 8 35W
Estats, Pic d' 156 42 40N 1 24 E
Estavayer-le-Lac 148 46 51N 6 51 E
Estcourt, Canada 83 47 28N 69 14W
Estcourt, S. Africa 255 28 58 S 29 53 E
Este 163 45 12N 11 40 E
Este, L. del 111 18 25N 91 49W
Esteban 154 43 33N 6 5W
Estelí 112 13 9N 86 22W
Estella 156 42 40N 2 0W
Estena → 155 39 23N 4 44W
Estepa 155 37 17N 4 52W
Estepona 155 36 24N 5 7W
Esterhazy 89 50 37N 102 5W
Esternay 139 48 44N 3 33 E
Esterri de Aneu 156 42 38N 1 5 E
Estevan 88 49 10N 102 59W
Estevan Group 92 53 3N 129 38W
Estevan Sd. 92 53 5N 129 34W
Estipac 106 20 22N 103 44W
Estissac 139 48 16N 3 48 E
Eston 88 51 8N 108 40W
Estonian S.S.R. □ 178 58 30N 25 30 E
Estoril 155 38 42N 9 23W
Estouk 247 18 14N 1 2 E
Estrada, La 154 42 43N 8 27W
Estrêla, Serra da 154 40 10N 7 45W
Estrella 157 38 25N 3 35W
Estrella, Pta. 98 30 57N 114 45W
Estremoz 155 38 51N 7 39W
Estrondo, Serra do 120 7 20 S 48 0W
Esztergom 151 47 47N 18 44 E
Et Tîdra 246 19 45N 16 20W
Eţ Ţîra 189 32 14N 34 56 E
Étables-sur-Mer 138 48 38N 2 51W
Etadunna 231 28 43 S 138 38 E
Etah 199 27 35N 78 40 E
Étain 139 49 13N 5 38 E
Etalle 143 49 40N 5 36 E
Etamamu 80 50 18N 59 59W
Étampes 139 48 26N 2 10 E
Étang 139 46 52N 4 10 E
Étang-du-Nord 81 47 22N 61 57W
Etanga 254 17 55 S 13 0 E
Étaples 139 50 30N 1 39 E
Etawah 199 26 48N 79 6 E
Etawney L. 77 57 50N 96 50W
Etchojoa 100 26 55N 109 38W
Eteh 247 7 2N 7 28 E
Éthe 143 49 35N 5 35 E
Ethel, Oued el → 240 28 31N 3 37W
Ethel Creek 228 23 5 S 120 11 E
Ethelbert 89 51 32N 100 25W
Ethiopia ■ 188 8 0N 40 0 E
Ethiopian Highlands 236 10 0N 37 0 E
Etive, L. 134 56 30N 5 12W
Etna 165 37 45N 15 0 E
Etne 171 59 40N 5 56 E
Etoile 251 11 33 S 27 30 E
Etosha Pan 254 18 40 S 16 30 E
Etoumbi 252 0 1 S 14 57 E
Étrépagny 138 49 18N 1 36 E
Étretat 138 49 42N 0 12 E
Étroits, Les 83 47 24N 68 54W
Etropole 167 42 50N 24 0 E
Ettelbruck 143 49 51N 6 5 E
Etten 143 51 34N 4 38 E
Ettlingen 147 48 58N 8 25 E
Ettrick Water 134 55 31N 2 55W
Etuku 250 3 42 S 25 45 E
Etzatlán 106 20 46N 104 5W
Etzikom 91 49 29N 111 6W
Eu 138 50 3N 1 26 E
Euboea = Évvoia 169 38 30N 24 0 E
Euchareena 233 32 57 S 149 6 E
Euclides da Cunha 120 10 31 S 39 1W
Eucumbene, L. 231 36 2 S 148 40 E
Eudistes, L. des 80 50 30N 65 15W
Eudunda 232 34 12 S 139 7 E
Eugowra 231 33 22 S 148 24 E
Eulo 231 28 10 S 145 3 E
Eumungerie 233 31 56 S 148 36 E
Eupen 143 50 37N 6 3 E
Euphrates = Furāt, Nahr al → 192 31 0N 47 25 E
Eure □ 138 49 6N 1 0 E
Eure → 138 49 18N 1 12 E
Eure-et-Loir □ 138 48 22N 1 30 E
Eureka 95 80 0N 85 56W
Eureka, Mt. 229 26 35 S 121 35 E
Eureka River 90 56 27N 118 44W
Eurelia 232 32 33 S 138 35 E
Euroa 231 36 44 S 145 35 E
Europa, Picos de 154 43 10N 4 49W
Europa, Pta. de 155 36 3N 5 21W
Europa Pt. = Europa, Pta. de 155 36 3N 5 21W
Europe 130 50 0N 20 0 E
Europoort 142 51 57N 4 10 E
Euskirchen 146 50 40N 6 45 E
Eutin 146 54 7N 10 38 E
Eutsuk L. 92 53 20N 126 45W
Eva 119 3 9 S 59 56W
Eva Downs 230 18 1 S 134 52 E
Évain 82 48 14N 79 8W
Eval 189 32 15N 35 15 E
Evale 254 16 33 S 15 44 E
Evanger 171 60 39N 6 7 E
Evans Head 231 29 7 S 153 27 E
Evans L. 78 50 50N 77 0W
Evansburg 90 53 36N 114 59W
Évaux-les-Bains 140 46 12N 2 29 E
Evaz 193 27 46N 53 59 E
Even Yahuda 189 32 16N 34 53 E
Evensk 185 62 12N 159 30 E
Evenstad 171 61 25N 11 7 E
Everard, L. 231 31 30 S 135 0 E
Everard Ras. 229 27 5 S 132 28 E
Everdale 233 31 52 S 144 46 E
Evere 143 50 52N 4 25 E
Everest, Mt. 199 28 5N 86 58 E
Evergem 143 51 7N 3 43 E
Everrett Mts. 95 62 45N 67 12W
Everton 233 36 25 S 146 33 E
Evesham 133 52 6N 1 57W
Evian-les-Bains 141 46 24N 6 35 E
Evinayong 252 1 26N 10 35 E
Évinos → 169 38 27N 21 40 E
Evisa 141 42 15N 8 48 E
Evje 171 58 36N 7 51 E
Évora 155 38 33N 7 57W
Évora □ 155 38 33N 7 50W
Evowghlī 192 38 43N 45 13 E
Évreux 138 49 0N 1 8 E
Evritanía □ 169 39 5N 21 30 E
Évron 138 48 10N 0 24W
Évros □ 168 41 10N 26 0 E
Evrótas → 169 36 50N 22 40 E
Évvoia 169 38 30N 24 0 E
Évvoia □ 169 38 40N 23 40 E
Ewe, L. 134 57 49N 5 38W
Ewo 252 0 48 S 14 45 E
Exaltación 123 13 10 S 65 20W
Excideuil 140 45 20N 1 4 E
Exe → 133 50 38N 3 27W
Exeter, Canada 84 43 21N 81 29W
Exeter, U.K. 133 50 43N 3 31W
Exloo 142 52 53N 6 52 E
Exmes 138 48 45N 0 10 E
Exmoor 133 51 10N 3 59W
Exmouth, Australia 228 21 54 S 114 10 E
Exmouth, U.K. 133 50 37N 3 26W
Exmouth G. 228 22 15 S 114 15 E
Expedition Range 230 24 30 S 149 12 E
Exploits, B. of 79 49 20N 55 0W
Exshaw 91 51 3N 115 9W
Extremadura □ 155 39 30N 6 5W
Exuma Sound 112 24 30N 76 20W
Eyasi, L. 250 3 30 S 35 0 E
Eyeberry L. 77 63 8N 104 43W
Eyebrow 88 50 48N 106 9W
Eyehill Cr. → 91 52 14N 110 0W
Eyemouth 134 55 53N 2 5W
Eygurande 140 45 40N 2 26 E
Eyjafjörður 174 66 15N 18 30W
Eymet 140 44 40N 0 25 E
Eymoutiers 140 45 40N 1 45 E
Eyrarbakki 174 63 52N 21 9W
Eyre 229 32 15 S 126 18 E
Eyre (North), L. 231 28 30 S 137 20 E
Eyre (South), L. 231 29 18 S 137 25 E
Eyre Cr. → 230 26 40 S 139 0 E
Eyre Mts. 235 45 25 S 168 25 E
Eyre Pen. 231 33 30 S 137 17 E
Eyvānkī 193 35 24N 51 56 E
Eyzies, Les 140 44 56N 1 1 E
Ez Zeidab 244 17 25N 33 55 E
Ezcaray 156 42 19N 3 0W
Ezequiel Montes 107 20 40N 99 53W
Ezine 168 39 48N 26 12 E
Ezmul 240 22 15N 15 40W
Ezousas → 190 34 44N 32 27 E

F

Fåborg 173 55 6N 10 15 E
Fabre 82 47 12N 79 22W
Fabriano 163 43 20N 12 52 E
Făcăeni 170 44 32N 27 53 E
Facatativá 118 4 49N 74 22W
Fachi 243 18 6N 11 34 E
Facture 140 44 39N 0 58W
Fada 243 17 13N 21 34 E
Fada-n-Gourma 247 12 10N 0 30 E
Fadd 151 46 28N 18 49 E
Faddeyevskiy, Ostrov 185 76 0N 150 0 E
Fadghāmī 192 35 53N 40 52 E
Fadlab 244 17 42N 34 2 E
Faenza 163 44 17N 11 53 E
Fafa 247 15 22N 0 48 E
Fafe 154 41 27N 8 11W
Fagam 247 11 1N 10 1 E
Făgăras 170 45 48N 24 58 E
Făgăras, Munţii 170 45 40N 24 40 E
Fagatogo 226 14 17 S 170 41W
Fågelsjö 172 61 50N 14 35 E
Fagerhult 173 57 8N 15 40 E
Fagersta 172 60 1N 15 46 E
Făget 170 45 52N 22 10 E
Făget, Munţii 170 47 40N 23 10 E
Fagnano, L. 126 54 30 S 68 0W
Fagnano Castello 165 39 31N 16 4 E
Fagnières 139 48 58N 4 20 E
Fahlīān 193 30 11N 51 28 E
Fahr 195 12 26N 54 8 E
Fahraj, Kermān, Iran 193 29 0N 59 0 E
Fahraj, Yazd, Iran 193 31 46N 54 36 E
Faido 149 46 29N 8 48 E
Faillon, L. 82 48 21N 76 39W
Fair Harbour 92 50 4N 127 10W
Fair Hd. 135 55 14N 6 10W
Faire 210 17 53N 121 34 E
Fairfield 233 33 53 S 150 57 E
Fairford 89 51 37N 98 38W
Fairlie 235 44 5 S 170 49 E
Fairmont Hot Springs 76 50 20N 115 56W
Fairvale 81 45 25N 66 0W
Fairview, Australia 230 15 31 S 144 17 E
Fairview, Canada 90 56 5N 118 25W
Faisalabad 197 31 30N 73 5 E
Faizabad 199 26 45N 82 10 E
Faizpur 198 21 14N 75 49 E
Fakam 194 16 38N 43 49 E
Fakfak 207 3 0 S 132 15 E
Fakiya 167 42 10N 27 6 E
Fakobli 246 7 23N 7 23W
Fakse 172 55 15N 12 8 E
Fakse B. 172 55 11N 12 15 E
Fakse Ladeplads 172 55 11N 12 9 E
Faku 215 42 32N 123 21 E
Falaise 138 48 54N 0 12W
Falaise, Mui 204 19 6N 105 45 E
Falakrón Óros 168 41 15N 23 58 E
Falam 202 23 0N 93 45 E
Falces 156 42 24N 1 48W
Fălciu 170 46 17N 28 7 E
Falcón □ 118 11 0N 69 50W
Falcon, C. 240 35 50N 0 50W
Falcón, Presa 102 26 35N 99 10W
Falcon I. 86 49 23N 94 45W
Falconara Marittima 163 43 37N 13 23 E
Falconbridge 84 46 35N 80 45W
Faléa 246 12 16N 11 17W
Falenki 182 58 22N 51 35 E
Faleshty 180 47 32N 27 44 E
Falher 90 55 44N 117 15W
Falkenberg, Germany 146 51 34N 13 13 E
Falkenberg, Sweden 173 56 54N 12 30 E
Falkensee 146 52 35N 13 6 E
Falkenstein 146 50 27N 12 24 E
Falkirk 134 56 0N 3 47W
Falkland, East, I. 126 51 40 S 58 30W
Falkland, West, I. 126 51 40 S 60 0W
Falkland Is. 126 51 30 S 59 0W
Falkland Is. Dependency □ 13 57 0 S 40 0W
Falkland Sd. 126 52 0 S 60 0W
Falkonéra 169 36 50N 23 52 E
Falköping 173 58 12N 13 33 E
Falmouth, Jamaica 112 18 30N 77 40W
Falmouth, U.K. 133 50 9N 5 5W
Falsa, Pta. 99 27 51N 115 3W
False Divi Pt. 201 15 43N 80 50 E
Falset 156 41 7N 0 50 E
Falso, C., Hond. 112 15 12N 83 21W
Falso, C., Mexico 99 22 52N 109 58W
Falster 173 54 45N 11 55 E
Falsterbo 172 55 23N 12 50 E
Fălticeni 170 47 21N 26 20 E
Falun 172 60 37N 15 37 E
Famagusta 190 35 8N 33 55 E
Famagusta Bay 190 35 15N 34 0 E
Famatina, Sierra de 124 27 30 S 68 0W
Family L. 89 51 54N 95 27W
Fan Xian 214 35 55N 115 38 E
Fana, Mali 246 13 0N 6 56W
Fana, Norway 171 60 16N 5 20 E
Fanárion 168 39 24N 21 47 E
Fandriana 255 20 14 S 47 21 E
Fang 204 19 55N 99 13 E
Fang Xian 217 32 3N 110 40 E
Fangchang 217 31 5N 118 4 E
Fangcheng, Guangxi Zhuangzu, China 216 21 42N 108 21 E
Fangcheng, Henan, China 217 33 18N 112 59 E
Fangliao 217 22 22N 120 38 E
Fangshan 214 38 3N 111 25 E
Fangzi 215 36 33N 119 10 E
Fani i Madh → 168 41 56N 20 16 E
Fanjiatun 215 43 40N 125 0 E
Fannich, L. 134 57 40N 5 0W
Fannūj 193 26 35N 59 38 E
Fanny Bay 92 49 27N 124 48W
Fanø, Denmark 173 55 25N 8 25 E
Fano, Italy 163 43 50N 13 0 E
Fanshi 214 39 12N 113 20 E
Fao = Al Fāw 193 30 0N 48 30 E
Faqirwali 198 29 27N 73 0 E
Far Mt. 92 52 47N 125 20W
Fara in Sabina 163 42 13N 12 44 E
Farab 183 39 9N 63 36 E
Faradje 250 3 50N 29 45 E
Faradofay 255 25 2 S 47 0 E
Farafangana 255 22 49 S 47 50 E
Farâfra, El Wâhât el- 244 27 15N 28 20 E
Farāh 197 32 20N 62 7 E
Farāh □ 197 32 25N 62 10 E
Farahalana 255 14 26 S 50 10 E
Faraid, Gebel 244 23 33N 35 19 E
Faramana 246 11 56N 4 45W
Faranah 246 10 3N 10 45W
Farasān, Jazā'ir 194 16 45N 41 55 E
Faratsiho 255 19 24 S 46 57 E
Farbarachi 256 2 30N 45 30 E
Fardes → 157 37 35N 3 0W
Fareham 133 50 52N 1 11W
Farewell, C. 235 40 29 S 172 43 E
Farewell C. = Farvel, Kap 12 59 48N 43 55W
Farewell Spit 235 40 35 S 173 0 E
Fari'a → 189 32 12N 35 27 E
Faride, L. 80 50 58N 59 55W
Faridkot 198 30 44N 74 45 E
Faridpur 202 23 15N 89 55 E
Färila 172 61 48N 15 50 E
Farim 246 12 27N 15 9W
Farīmān 193 35 40N 59 49 E
Farina 231 30 3 S 138 15 E
Faringe 172 59 55N 18 7 E
Farinha → 120 6 51 S 47 30W
Fariske 190 36 37N 32 32 E
Fârîskûr 244 31 20N 31 43 E

Farmakonisi 169 37 17N 27 8 E
Farnborough 133 51 17N 0 46W
Farne Is. 132 55 38N 1 37W
Farnham 83 45 17N 72 59W
Faro, Brazil 119 2 10 S 56 39W
Faro, Canada 94 62 11N 133 22W
Faro, Portugal 155 37 2N 7 55W
Faro □ 155 37 12N 8 10W
Faroe Is. 130 62 0N 7 0W
Farquhar, C. 229 23 50 S 113 36 E
Farquhar Is. 203 11 0 S 52 0 E
Farrand, C. 95 71 45N 90 0W
Farrar → 134 57 30N 4 30W
Farrars Cr. → 230 25 35 S 140 43 E
Farrāshband 193 28 57N 52 5 E
Farrell Flat 232 33 48 S 138 48 E
Farrokhī 193 33 50N 59 31 E
Farrukhabad-cum-Fatehgarh 199 27 30N 79 32 E
Fars □ 193 29 30N 55 0 E
Fársala 168 39 17N 22 23 E
Fārsī 197 33 47N 63 15 E
Farsø 173 56 46N 9 19 E
Farsund 171 58 5N 6 55 E
Fartak, Ra's, S. Yemen 195 15 38N 52 15 E
Fartak, Râs, Si. Arabia 192 28 5N 34 34 E
Fartura, Serra da 125 26 21 S 52 52W
Faru 247 12 48N 6 12 E
Fārūj 193 37 14N 58 14 E
Farum 172 55 49N 12 21 E
Farvel, Kap 12 59 48N 43 55W
Fāryāb □ 197 36 0N 65 0 E
Fasā 193 29 0N 53 39 E
Fasano 165 40 50N 17 20 E
Fashoda 245 9 50N 32 2 E
Fastnet Rock 135 51 22N 9 37W
Fastov 178 50 7N 29 57 E
Fatagar, Tanjung 207 2 46 S 131 57 E
Fatehgarh 199 27 25N 79 35 E
Fatehpur, Raj., India 198 28 0N 74 40 E
Fatehpur, Ut. P., India 199 25 56N 81 13 E
Fatesh 179 52 8N 35 57 E
Fatick 246 14 19N 16 27W
Fatima, Canada 81 47 24N 61 53W
Fátima, Portugal 155 39 37N 8 39W
Fatoya 246 11 37N 9 10W
Faucille, Col de la 141 46 22N 6 2 E
Faucilles, Monts 139 48 5N 5 50 E
Faulquemont 139 49 3N 6 36 E
Fauquembergues 139 50 36N 2 5 E
Fauquier, B.C., Canada 93 49 52N 118 5W
Fauquier, Ont., Canada 87 49 18N 82 3W
Faure I. 229 25 52 S 113 50 E
Făurei 170 45 6N 27 19 E
Fauresmith 254 29 44 S 25 17 E
Faust 90 55 19N 115 38W
Fauvillers 143 49 51N 5 40 E
Fåvang 171 61 27N 10 11 E
Favara 164 37 19N 13 39 E
Favignana 164 37 56N 12 18 E
Favignana, I. 164 37 56N 12 18 E
Favone 141 41 47N 9 26 E
Favourable Lake 74 52 50N 93 39W
Fawcett 90 54 32N 114 5W
Fawn → 74 52 22N 88 20W
Faxaflói 174 64 29N 23 0W
Faya-Largeau 243 17 58N 19 6 E
Fayaoué 226 20 38 S 166 33 E
Fayd 192 27 1N 42 52 E
Fayence 141 43 38N 6 42 E
Fayón 156 41 15N 0 20 E
Fazenda Libongo 253 8 24 S 13 24 E
Fazenda Nova 121 16 11 S 50 48W
Fazilka 198 30 27N 74 2 E
Fazilpur 198 29 18N 70 29 E
Fdérik 240 22 40N 12 45W
Fé, La 112 22 2N 84 15W
Feale → 135 52 26N 9 40W
Featherston 234 41 6 S 175 20 E
Featherstone 251 18 42 S 30 55 E
Fécamp 138 49 45N 0 22 E
Fedala = Mohammedia 240 33 44N 7 21W
Federación 124 31 0 S 57 55W
Fedeshkūh 193 28 49N 53 50 E
Fedjadj, Chott el 241 33 52N 9 14 E
Fedje 171 60 47N 4 43 E
Fedorovka 182 53 38N 62 42 E
Fefan I. 226 7 21N 151 51 E
Fehérgyarmat 151 48 0N 22 30 E
Fehmarn 146 54 26N 11 10 E
Fei Xian 215 35 18N 117 59 E
Feijó 122 8 9 S 70 21W
Feilding 234 40 13 S 175 35 E
Feira de Santana 121 12 15 S 38 57W
Feirân, W. → 191 28 39N 33 12 E
Feirâni, G. 191 28 31N 34 19 E
Feixiang 214 36 30N 114 45 E
Fejér □ 151 47 9N 18 30 E
Fejø 172 54 55N 11 30 E
Fekete → 151 45 47N 18 15 E
Felanitx 157 39 28N 3 9 E
Feldbach 150 46 57N 15 52 E
Feldberg, E. Germany 146 53 20N 13 26 E
Feldberg, W. Germany 147 47 51N 7 58 E
Feldkirch 150 47 15N 9 37 E
Feldkirchen 150 46 44N 14 6 E
Felipe Carrillo Puerto 111 19 35N 88 3W
Félix U. Gómez 101 30 35N 105 50W
Felixlândia 121 18 47 S 44 55W
Felixstowe 133 51 58N 1 22 E
Felletin 140 45 53N 2 11 E
Feltre 163 46 1N 11 55 E
Femø 172 54 58N 11 53 E
Femunden 171 62 10N 11 53 E
Fen He → 214 35 36N 110 42 E
Fenelon Falls 85 44 32N 78 45W
Fener Burnu 190 36 32N 35 21 E
Feneroa 245 13 5N 39 3 E
Feng Xian, Jiangsu, China 214 34 43N 116 35 E
Feng Xian, Shaanxi, China 214 33 54N 106 40 E
Fengári 168 40 25N 25 32 E
Fengcheng, Jiangxi, China 217 28 12N 115 48 E
Fengcheng, Liaoning, China 215 40 28N 124 5 E
Fengdu 216 29 55N 107 41 E
Fengfeng 214 36 28N 114 8 E
Fenggang 216 27 57N 107 47 E
Fenghua 217 29 40N 121 25 E
Fenghuang 216 27 57N 109 29 E
Fenghuangzui 216 33 30N 109 23 E
Fengjie 216 31 5N 109 36 E
Fengkai 217 23 24N 111 30 E
Fengle 217 31 29N 112 29 E
Fengning 214 41 10N 116 33 E
Fengqing 216 24 38N 99 55 E
Fengqiu 214 35 2N 114 25 E
Fengrun 215 39 48N 118 8 E
Fengshan, Guangxi Zhuangzu, China 216 24 39N 109 15 E
Fengshan, Guangxi Zhuangzu, China 216 24 31N 107 3 E
Fengtai, Anhui, China 217 32 50N 116 40 E
Fengtai, Beijing, China 214 39 50N 116 18 E
Fengxian 217 30 55N 121 26 E
Fengxiang 214 34 29N 107 25 E
Fengxin 217 28 41N 115 18 E
Fengyang 217 32 51N 117 29 E
Fengyi 216 25 37N 100 20 E
Fengzhen 214 40 25N 113 2 E
Feni Is. 227 4 0 S 153 40 E
Fenit 135 52 17N 9 51W
Fenny 202 22 55N 91 32 E
Feno, C. de 141 41 58N 8 33 E
Fenoarivo Afovoany 255 18 26 S 46 34 E
Fenoarivo Atsinanana 255 17 22 S 49 25 E
Fens, The 132 52 45N 0 2 E
Fenxi 214 36 40N 111 31 E
Fenyang 214 37 18N 111 48 E
Fenyi 217 27 45N 114 47 E
Feodosiya 180 45 2N 35 28 E
Fer, C. de 241 37 3N 7 10 E
Ferdows 193 33 58N 58 2 E
Fère, La 139 49 40N 3 20 E
Fère-Champenoise 139 48 45N 4 0 E
Fère-en-Tardenois 139 49 10N 3 30 E
Ferentino 164 41 42N 13 14 E
Ferfer 256 5 4N 45 9 E
Fergana 183 40 23N 71 19 E
Ferganskaya Dolina 183 40 50N 71 30 E
Ferganskiy Khrebet 183 41 0N 73 50 E
Fergus 84 43 43N 80 24W
Fergusson I. 227 9 30 S 150 45 E
Fériana 241 34 59N 8 33 E
Feričanci 166 45 32N 18 0 E
Ferintosh 91 52 46N 112 58W
Ferkane 241 34 37N 7 26 E
Ferkéssédougou 246 9 35N 5 6W
Ferlach 150 46 32N 14 18 E
Ferland, Ont., Canada 86 50 19N 88 27W
Ferland, Sask., Canada 88 49 27N 106 57W
Ferlo, Vallée du 246 15 15N 14 15W
Fermanagh □ 135 54 21N 7 40W
Ferme-Neuve 82 46 42N 75 27W
Fermo 163 43 10N 13 42 E
Fermoselle 154 41 19N 6 27W
Fermoy 135 52 4N 8 18W
Fernán Nuñéz 155 37 40N 4 44W
Fernández 124 27 55 S 63 50W
Fernández Leal 101 30 51N 108 17W
Fernando de Noronha 120 4 0 S 33 10W
Fernando Póo = Bioko 252 3 30N 8 40 E
Fernandópolis 121 20 16 S 50 14W
Fernie 91 49 30N 115 5W
Fernlees 230 23 51 S 148 7 E
Feroke 201 11 9N 75 46 E
Feronia 84 46 22N 79 19W
Ferozepore = Firozpur 198 30 55N 74 40 E
Férrai 168 40 53N 26 10 E
Ferrandina 165 40 30N 16 28 E
Ferrara 163 44 50N 11 36 E
Ferrato, C. 164 39 18N 9 39 E
Ferreira do Alentejo 155 38 4N 8 6W
Ferreñafe 122 6 42 S 79 50W
Ferret, C. 140 44 38N 1 15W
Ferrette 139 47 30N 7 20 E
Ferrières 139 48 5N 2 48 E
Ferriete 162 44 40N 9 30 E
Ferrol, Pen. de 122 9 10 S 78 35W
Ferros 121 19 14 S 43 2W
Ferryland 79 47 2N 52 53W
Ferté, La 139 48 57N 3 6 E
Ferté-Bernard, La 138 48 10N 0 40 E
Ferté-Mace, La 138 48 35N 0 21W
Ferté-St.-Aubin, La 139 47 42N 1 57 E
Ferté-Vidame, La 138 48 37N 0 53 E
Fertília 164 40 37N 8 13 E
Fertöszentmiklós 151 47 35N 16 53 E
Fès 240 34 0N 5 0W
Feschaux 143 50 9N 4 54 E
Feshi 253 6 8 S 18 10 E
Feteşti 170 44 22N 27 51 E
Fetlar 134 60 36N 0 52W
Feuerthalen 149 47 37N 8 38 E
Feuilles → 78 58 47N 70 4W
Feuilles, B. aux 78 58 55N 69 20W
Feurs 141 45 45N 4 13 E
Fevzipaşa 190 37 6N 36 37 E
Feyẕābād, Badākhshān, Afghan. 197 37 7N 70 33 E
Feyẕābād, Fāryāb, Afghan. 197 36 17N 64 52 E
Fezzan 236 27 0N 15 0 E
Ffestiniog 132 52 58N 3 56W
Fiambalá 124 27 45 S 67 37W
Fianarantsoa 255 21 26 S 47 5 E
Fianarantsoa □ 255 19 30 S 47 0 E
Fianga 243 9 55N 15 9 E
Fibiş 170 45 57N 21 26 E
Fichtelgebirge 147 50 10N 12 0 E
Ficksburg 255 28 51 S 27 53 E
Fidenza 162 44 51N 10 3 E
Fiditi 247 7 45N 3 53 E
Field 84 46 31N 80 1W
Field → 230 23 48 S 138 0 E
Field I. 228 12 5 S 132 23 E
Fieri 168 40 43N 19 33 E
Fiesch 148 46 25N 8 12 E
Fife □ 134 56 13N 3 2W
Fife L. 88 49 14N 105 53W
Fife Ness 134 56 17N 2 35W
Fifth Cataract 244 18 22N 33 50 E
Figeac 140 44 37N 2 2 E
Figline Valdarno 163 43 37N 11 28 E
Figtree 251 20 22 S 28 20 E
Figueira Castelo Rodrigo 154 40 57N 6 58W
Figueira da Foz 154 40 7N 8 54W
Figueiró dos Vinhos 154 39 55N 8 16W
Figueras 156 42 18N 2 58 E
Figuig 241 32 5N 1 11W
Fihaonana 255 18 36 S 47 12 E
Fiherenana 255 18 29 S 48 24 E
Fiherenana → 255 23 19 S 43 37 E
Fiji ■ 226 17 20 S 179 0 E
Fika 247 11 15N 11 13 E
Filabres, Sierra de los 157 37 13N 2 20W
Filadelfia, Bolivia 122 11 20 S 68 46W
Filadélfia, Brazil 120 7 21 S 47 30W
Filadélfia, Italy 165 38 47N 16 17 E
Fil'akovo 151 48 17N 19 50 E
File Axe, L. 83 50 18N 73 34W
Filey 132 54 13N 0 18W
Filiaşi 170 44 32N 23 31 E
Filiátes 168 39 38N 20 16 E
Filiatrá 169 37 9N 21 35 E
Filicudi 165 38 35N 14 33 E
Filim 195 20 37N 58 12 E
Filiouri → 168 41 15N 25 40 E
Filipów 152 54 11N 22 37 E
Filipstad 172 59 43N 14 9 E
Filisur 149 46 41N 9 40 E
Fillmore 88 49 50N 103 25W
Filomeno Mata 108 20 12N 97 42W
Filottrano 163 43 28N 13 20 E
Fils, L. du 82 46 37N 78 7W
Filyos 180 41 34N 32 4 E
Final, Pta. 98 29 47N 114 19W
Finale Lígure 162 44 10N 8 21 E
Finale nell' Emília 163 44 50N 11 18 E
Fiñana 157 37 10N 2 50W
Finch 85 45 11N 75 7W
Findhorn → 134 57 38N 3 38W
Findlater 88 50 47N 105 24W
Finger L. 92 53 33N 124 18W
Fíngõe 251 15 12 S 31 50 E
Finistère □ 138 48 20N 4 0W
Finisterre 154 42 54N 9 16W
Finisterre, C. 154 42 50N 9 19W
Finisterre Ra. 227 6 0 S 146 30 E
Finke 230 25 34 S 134 35 E
Finke → 230 27 0 S 136 10 E
Finland 86 48 51N 93 55W
Finland ■ 176 63 0N 27 0 E
Finland, G. of 176 60 0N 26 0 E
Finlay → 76 57 0N 125 10W
Finley 231 35 38 S 145 35 E
Finmark 86 48 35N 89 45W
Finn → 135 54 50N 7 55W
Finnigan, Mt. 230 15 49 S 145 17 E
Finniss 232 35 24 S 138 48 E
Finniss, C. 231 33 8 S 134 51 E
Finnmark fylke □ 174 69 30N 25 0 E
Finschhafen 227 6 33 S 147 50 E
Finse 171 60 36N 7 30 E
Finsteraarhorn 148 46 31N 8 10 E
Finsterwalde 146 51 37N 13 42 E
Finsterwolde 142 53 12N 7 6 E
Fiora → 163 42 20N 11 35 E
Fiordland National Park 235 45 0 S 167 50 E
Fiorenzuola d'Arda 162 44 56N 9 54 E
Fīq 189 32 46N 35 41 E
Fire River 87 48 47N 83 21W
Firebag → 90 57 45N 111 21W
Firedrake L. 77 61 25N 104 30W
Firenze 163 43 47N 11 15 E
Firk → 192 30 59N 44 34 E
Firminy, Aveyron, France 140 44 32N 2 19 E
Firminy, Loire, France 141 45 23N 4 18 E
Firozabad 199 27 10N 78 25 E
Firozpur 198 30 55N 74 40 E
Fīrūzābād 193 28 52N 52 35 E
Fīrūzkūh 193 35 50N 52 50 E
Firvale 92 52 27N 126 13W
Fish → 254 28 7 S 17 45 E
Fisher 229 30 30 S 131 0 E
Fisher B. 89 51 35N 97 13W
Fisher Bay 89 51 29N 97 18W
Fisher Branch 89 51 5N 97 13W
Fisher Str. 95 63 15N 83 30W
Fishguard 133 51 59N 4 59W
Fishing L. 89 52 10N 95 24W
Fismes 139 49 20N 3 40 E
Fitero 156 42 4N 1 52W
Fitjar 171 59 55N 5 17 E
Fitri, L. 243 12 50N 17 28 E
Fitz Hugh Sd. 92 51 40N 127 55W
Fitz Roy 126 47 0 S 67 0W
Fitzgerald 76 59 51N 111 36W
Fitzmaurice → 228 14 45 S 130 5 E
Fitzroy →, Queens., Australia 230 23 32 S 150 52 E
Fitzroy →, W. Austral., Australia 228 17 31 S 123 35 E
Fitzroy Crossing 228 18 9 S 125 38 E
Fitzwilliam I. 84 45 30N 81 45W
Fiume = Rijeka 163 45 20N 14 21 E
Fiumefreddo Brúzio 165 39 14N 16 4 E
Five Islands 81 45 23N 64 6W
Fivizzano 162 44 12N 10 11 E
Fizi 250 4 17 S 28 55 E
Fjœra 171 59 52N 6 22 E
Fjellerup 173 56 29N 10 34 E
Fjerritslev 173 57 5N 9 15 E
Fkih ben Salah 240 32 32N 6 45W
Flå, Buskerud, Norway 171 60 25N 9 28 E
Flå, Sør-Trøndelag, Norway 171 63 13N 10 18 E
Flaherty I. 78 56 15N 79 15W
Flamborough Hd. 132 54 8N 0 4W
Flamingo, Teluk 207 5 30 S 138 0 E
Flanders = Flandres 143 51 10N 3 15 E
Flanders 86 48 44N 92 5W
Flandre Occidental □ 143 51 0N 3 0 E
Flandre Orientale □ 143 51 0N 4 0 E
Flandres 143 51 10N 3 15 E
Flandres, Plaines des 143 51 10N 3 15 E
Flåsjön 174 64 5N 15 40 E
Flat → 76 61 51N 128 0W
Flat Bay 79 48 24N 58 36W
Flat L. 90 54 38N 112 54W
Flatbush 90 54 42N 114 9W
Flatey, Barðastrandarsýsla, Iceland 174 66 10N 17 52W

Flatey, Suður-þingeyjarsýsla, Iceland **174** 65 22N 22 56W
Flattery, C. **230** 14 58 S 145 21 E
Flavy-le-Martel **139** 49 43N 3 12 E
Flawil **149** 47 26N 9 11 E
Flaxcombe **88** 51 29N 109 36W
Flechas Pt. **211** 10 22N 119 34 E
Flèche, La **138** 47 42N 0 5W
Fleetwood **132** 53 55N 3 1W
Flekkefjord **171** 58 18N 6 39 E
Flémalle **143** 50 36N 5 28 E
Fleming **89** 50 4N 101 31W
Flensborg Fjord **173** 54 50N 9 40 E
Flensburg **146** 54 46N 9 28 E
Flers **138** 48 47N 0 33W
Flesherton **84** 44 16N 80 33W
Flesko, Tanjung **207** 0 29N 124 30 E
Fletton **133** 52 34N 0 13W
Fleur de Lys **79** 50 7N 56 8W
Fleur-de-May, L. **80** 52 0N 65 5W
Fleurance **140** 43 52N 0 40 E
Fleurier **148** 46 54N 6 35 E
Fleurus **143** 50 29N 4 32 E
Flims **149** 46 50N 9 17 E
Flin Flon **77** 54 46N 101 53W
Flinders → **230** 17 36 S 140 36 E
Flinders B. **229** 34 19 S 115 19 E
Flinders Group **230** 14 11 S 144 15 E
Flinders I. **230** 40 0 S 148 0 E
Flinders Ranges **231** 31 30 S 138 30 E
Flinders Reefs **230** 17 37 S 148 31 E
Flint **132** 53 15N 3 7W
Flint, I. **225** 11 26 S 151 48W
Flint L. **87** 49 52N 85 53W
Flinton **231** 27 55 S 149 32 E
Fliseryd **173** 57 6N 16 15 E
Flix **156** 41 14N 0 32 E
Flixecourt **139** 50 0N 2 5 E
Flobecq **143** 50 44N 3 45 E
Flodden **132** 55 37N 2 8W
Flora **171** 63 27N 11 22 E
Florac **140** 44 20N 3 37 E
Florânia **120** 6 8 S 36 49W
Floreffe **143** 50 26N 4 46 E
Florence = Firenze **163** 43 47N 11 15 E
Florence **81** 46 16N 60 16W
Florence, L. **231** 28 53 S 138 9 E
Florennes **143** 50 15N 4 35 E
Florensac **140** 43 23N 3 28 E
Florenville **143** 49 40N 5 19 E
Flores, Brazil **120** 7 51 S 37 59W
Flores, Guat. **112** 16 59N 89 50W
Flores, Indonesia **207** 8 35 S 121 0 E
Flores I. **92** 49 20N 126 10W
Flores Sea **206** 6 30 S 124 0 E
Floresta **120** 8 40 S 37 26W
Floriano **120** 6 50 S 43 0W
Florianópolis **125** 27 30 S 48 30W
Florida, Cuba **112** 21 32N 78 14W
Florida, Uruguay **125** 34 7 S 56 10W
Florida, R. → **101** 27 43N 105 10W
Florídia **165** 37 6N 15 9 E
Floridsdorf **151** 48 14N 16 22 E
Flórina **168** 40 48N 21 26 E
Flórina □ **168** 40 45N 21 20 E
Florø **171** 61 35N 5 1 E
Flower Sta. **85** 45 10N 76 41W
Flower's Cove **79** 51 14N 56 46W
Flüela Pass **149** 46 45N 9 57 E
Fluk **207** 1 42 S 127 44 E
Flumen → **156** 41 43N 0 9W
Flumendosa → **164** 39 26N 9 38 E
Fluminimaggiore **164** 39 25N 8 30 E
Flushing = Vlissingen **143** 51 26N 3 34 E
Fluviá → **156** 42 12N 3 7 E
Fly → **224** 8 25 S 143 0 E
Flying Fish, C. **13** 72 6 S 102 29W
Foam Lake **88** 51 40N 103 32W
Foča **166** 43 31N 18 47 E
Focşani **170** 45 41N 27 15 E
Fogang **217** 23 52N 113 30 E
Foggaret el Arab **240** 27 13N 2 49 E
Foggaret ez Zoua **240** 27 20N 2 53 E
Fóggia **165** 41 28N 15 31 E
Foggo **247** 11 21N 9 57 E
Foglia → **163** 43 55N 12 54 E
Fogo **79** 49 43N 54 17W
Fogo, C. **79** 49 40N 54 0W
Fogo I. **79** 49 40N 54 5W
Fohnsdorf **150** 47 12N 14 40 E
Föhr **146** 54 40N 8 30 E
Foia **155** 37 19N 8 37W
Foins, L. aux **82** 47 5N 78 11W
Foix **140** 42 58N 1 38 E
Foix □ **140** 43 0N 1 30 E
Fojnica **166** 43 59N 17 51 E
Fokino **178** 53 30N 34 22 E
Fokís □ **169** 38 30N 22 15 E
Fokstua **171** 62 7N 9 17 E
Folda, Nord-Trøndelag, Norway **174** 64 41N 10 50 E
Folda, Nordland, Norway **174** 67 38N 14 50 E
Földeák **151** 46 19N 20 30 E
Folégandros **169** 36 40N 24 55 E
Foley I. **95** 68 32N 75 5W
Foleyet **87** 48 15N 82 25W
Folgefonn **171** 60 3N 6 23 E
Foligno **163** 42 58N 12 40 E
Folkestone **133** 51 5N 1 11 E
Follónica **162** 42 55N 10 45 E
Follónica, Golfo di **162** 42 50N 10 40 E
Fond-du-Lac **77** 59 19N 107 12W
Fond-du-Lac → **77** 59 17N 106 0W
Fondi **164** 41 21N 13 25 E
Fonfría **154** 41 37N 6 9W
Fongen **171** 63 11N 11 38 E
Fonni **164** 40 5N 9 16 E
Fonsagrada **154** 43 8N 7 4W
Fonseca, G. de **112** 13 10N 87 40W
Fontaine **81** 46 51N 64 58W
Fontaine-Française **139** 47 32N 5 21 E
Fontainebleau **139** 48 24N 2 40 E
Fontana, L. **126** 44 55 S 71 30W
Fontas → **76** 58 14N 121 48W
Fonte Boa **118** 2 33 S 66 0W
Fontem **247** 5 32N 9 52 E
Fontenay-le-Comte **140** 46 28N 0 48W
Fonteneau, L. **80** 51 55N 61 30W
Fontur **174** 66 23N 14 32W
Fonyód **151** 46 44N 17 33 E
Foochow = Fuzhou **217** 26 5N 119 16 E
Foothills **91** 53 4N 116 47W
Foping **214** 33 41N 108 0 E
Foppiano **162** 46 21N 8 24 E
Föra **173** 57 1N 16 51 E
Forbach **139** 49 10N 6 52 E
Forbes **231** 33 22 S 148 0 E
Forbesganj **199** 26 17N 87 18 E
Forcados **247** 5 26N 5 26 E
Forcados → **247** 5 25N 5 19 E
Forcall → **156** 40 51N 0 16W
Forcalquier **141** 43 58N 5 47 E
Forchheim **147** 49 42N 11 4 E
Forclaz, Col de la **148** 46 3N 7 1 E
Førde **171** 61 27N 5 53 E
Fording **91** 50 12N 114 52W
Ford's Bridge **231** 29 41 S 145 29 E
Forécariah **246** 9 28N 13 10W
Forel, Mt. **12** 66 52N 36 55W
Foremost **91** 49 26N 111 34W
Forenza **165** 40 50N 15 50 E
Forest, Belgium **143** 50 49N 4 20 E
Forest, Canada **84** 43 6N 82 0W
Forest Grove **93** 51 46N 121 5W
Forestburg **91** 52 35N 112 1W
Forestier Pen. **230** 43 0 S 148 0 E
Forestville **83** 48 48N 69 2W
Forez, Mts. du **140** 45 40N 3 50 E
Forfar **134** 56 40N 2 53W
Forges-les-Eaux **139** 49 37N 1 30 E
Forget **88** 49 39N 102 52W
Forillon, Parc National **80** 48 46N 64 12W
Fork River **89** 51 31N 100 1W
Forlì **163** 44 14N 12 2 E
Formazza **162** 46 23N 8 26 E
Formby Pt. **132** 53 33N 3 7W
Formentera **157** 38 43N 1 27 E
Formentor, C. de **156** 39 58N 3 13 E
Fórmia **164** 41 15N 13 34 E
Formiga **121** 20 27 S 45 25W
Formigine **162** 44 37N 10 51 E
Formiguères **140** 42 37N 2 5 E
Formosa = Taiwan ■ **217** 23 30N 121 0 E
Formosa, Argentina **124** 26 15 S 58 10W
Formosa, Brazil **121** 15 32 S 47 20W
Formosa □ **124** 25 0 S 60 0W
Formosa, Serra **123** 12 0 S 55 0W
Formosa Bay **250** 2 40 S 40 20 E
Formoso → **121** 10 34 S 49 56W
Fornells **156** 40 3N 4 7 E
Fornos de Algodres **154** 40 38N 7 32W
Fornovo di Taro **162** 44 42N 10 7 E
Forres **134** 57 37N 3 38W
Forrest, Vic., Australia **231** 38 33 S 143 47 E
Forrest, W. Austral., Australia **229** 30 51 S 128 6 E
Forrest, Mt. **229** 24 48 S 127 45 E
Forrières **143** 50 8N 5 17 E
Fors **172** 60 14N 16 20 E
Forsa **172** 61 44N 16 55 E
Forsand **171** 58 54N 6 5 E
Forsayth **230** 18 33 S 143 34 E
Forserum **173** 57 42N 14 30 E
Forshaga **172** 59 33N 13 29 E
Forskacka **172** 60 39N 16 54 E
Forsmo **172** 63 16N 17 11 E
Forst **146** 51 43N 14 37 E
Forster **231** 32 12 S 152 31 E
Forsyth I. **235** 40 58 S 174 5 E
Forsythe **82** 48 14N 76 26W
Fort Albany **74** 52 15N 81 35W
Fort Assiniboine **90** 54 20N 114 45W
Fort Augustus **134** 57 9N 4 40W
Fort Beaufort **254** 32 46 S 26 40 E
Fort Chimo **78** 58 6N 68 15W
Fort Chipewyan **77** 58 42N 111 8W
Fort-Coulonge **82** 45 50N 76 45W
Fort-de-France **113** 14 36N 61 2W
Fort de Possel = Possel **252** 5 5N 19 10 E
Fort Frances **86** 48 36N 93 24W
Fort Fraser **92** 54 4N 124 33W
Fort George **78** 53 50N 79 0W
Fort Good-Hope **94** 66 14N 128 40W
Fort Hertz = Putao **202** 27 28N 97 30 E
Fort Hope **87** 51 30N 88 0W
Fort Jameson = Chipata **251** 13 38 S 32 28 E
Fort Lallemand **241** 31 13N 6 17 E
Fort-Lamy = Ndjamena **243** 12 10N 14 59 E
Fort Langley **93** 49 10N 122 35W
Fort Liard **76** 60 14N 123 30W
Fort Liberté **113** 19 42N 71 51W
Fort Mackay **90** 57 12N 111 41W
Fort McKenzie **78** 57 20N 69 0W
Fort Macleod **91** 49 45N 113 30W
Fort MacMahon **241** 29 43N 1 45 E
Fort McMurray **90** 56 44N 111 7W
Fort McPherson **94** 67 30N 134 55W
Fort Miribel **241** 29 25N 2 55 E
Fort Nelson **76** 58 50N 122 44W
Fort Nelson → **76** 59 32N 124 0W
Fort Norman **94** 64 57N 125 30W
Fort Pierre Bordes = Ti-n-Zaouaténe **241** 20 0N 2 55 E
Fort Portal **250** 0 40N 30 20 E
Fort Providence **76** 61 3N 117 40W
Fort Qu'Appelle **88** 50 45N 103 50W
Fort Resolution **76** 61 10N 113 40W
Fort Rixon **251** 20 2 S 29 17 E
Fort Roseberry = Mansa **251** 11 13 S 28 55 E
Fort Ross **95** 72 0N 94 14W
Fort Rousset **252** 0 29 S 15 55 E
Fort Rupert, B.C., Canada **92** 50 42N 127 23W
Fort Rupert, Qué., Canada **78** 51 30N 78 40W
Fort Saint **241** 30 19N 9 31 E
Fort St. James **76** 54 30N 124 10W
Fort St. John **76** 56 15N 120 50W
Fort Sandeman **197** 31 20N 69 31 E
Fort Saskatchewan **90** 53 40N 113 15W
Fort Severn **74** 56 0N 87 40W
Fort Shevchenko **181** 43 40N 51 20 E
Fort-Sibut **252** 5 46N 19 10 E
Fort Simpson **76** 61 45N 121 15W
Fort Smith **76** 60 0N 111 51W
Fort Smith Region □ **94** 63 0N 120 0W
Fort Trinquet = Bir Mogrein **240** 25 10N 11 25W
Fort Vermilion **76** 58 24N 116 0W
Fort William **134** 56 48N 5 8W
Fortaleza, Bolivia **122** 12 6 S 66 49W
Fortaleza, Brazil **120** 3 45 S 38 35W
Forteau **78** 51 28N 56 58W
Forth, Firth of **134** 56 5N 2 55W
Forthassa Rharbia **240** 32 52N 1 18W
Fortín **109** 18 54N 97 0W
Fortin, L. **80** 50 50N 67 46W
Fortín Coronel Eugenio Garay **123** 20 31 S 62 8W
Fortín Garrapatal **123** 21 27 S 61 30W
Fortín General Pando **123** 19 45 S 59 47W
Fortín Madrejón **123** 20 45 S 59 52W
Fortín Uno **126** 38 50 S 65 18W
Fortore → **163** 41 55N 15 17 E
Fortrose, N.Z. **235** 46 38 S 168 45 E
Fortrose, U.K. **134** 57 35N 4 10W
Fortuna **157** 38 11N 1 7W
Fortune **79** 47 4N 55 50W
Fortune B. **79** 47 30N 55 22W
Fos **141** 43 26N 4 56 E
Foshan **217** 23 4N 113 5 E
Fosheim Pen. **95** 80 0N 85 0W
Fossacesia **163** 42 15N 14 30 E
Fossano **162** 44 33N 7 40 E
Fosses-la-Ville **143** 50 24N 4 41 E
Fossilbrook **230** 17 47 S 144 29 E
Fossombrone **163** 43 41N 12 49 E
Fosston **88** 52 12N 103 49W
Foster **83** 45 17N 72 30W
Foster → **77** 55 47N 105 49W
Fosters Ra. **230** 21 35 S 133 48 E
Fougamou **252** 1 16 S 10 30 E
Fougères **138** 48 21N 1 14W
Foul Pt. **201** 8 35N 81 18 E
Foulness I. **133** 51 36N 0 55 E
Foulness Pt. **133** 51 36N 0 59 E
Foulpointe **255** 17 41 S 49 31 E
Foum Assaka **240** 29 8N 10 24W
Foum Zguid **240** 30 2N 6 59W
Foumban **247** 5 45N 10 50 E
Foundiougne **246** 14 5N 16 32W
Fourchambault **139** 47 0N 3 3 E
Fourchu **81** 45 43N 60 17W
Fourmies **139** 50 1N 4 2 E
Fourmont, L. **80** 52 5N 60 27W
Fournás **169** 39 3N 21 52 E
Fournier, L. **80** 51 33N 65 25W
Foúrnoi **169** 37 36N 26 32 E
Fours **139** 46 50N 3 42 E
Fouta Djalon **246** 11 20N 12 10W
Foux, Cap-à- **113** 19 43N 73 27W
Foveaux Str. **235** 46 42 S 168 10 E
Fowey **133** 50 20N 4 39W
Fowlers B. **229** 31 59 S 132 34 E
Fownhope **133** 52 0N 2 37W
Fox → **77** 56 3N 93 18W
Fox Creek **90** 54 24N 116 48W
Fox Valley **88** 50 30N 109 25W
Foxe Basin **95** 66 0N 77 0W
Foxe Chan. **95** 65 0N 80 0W
Foxe Pen. **95** 65 0N 76 0W
Foxen **172** 59 25N 11 55 E
Foxhol **142** 53 10N 6 43 E
Foxton **234** 40 29 S 175 18 E
Foxville **87** 50 4N 81 38W
Foyle, Lough **135** 55 6N 7 8W
Foynes **135** 52 37N 9 5W
Foz **154** 43 33N 7 20W
Fóz do Cunene **254** 17 15 S 11 48 E
Foz do Gregório **122** 6 47 S 70 44W
Foz do Iguaçu **125** 25 30 S 54 30W
Foz do Riosinho **122** 7 11 S 71 50W
Fraga **156** 41 32N 0 21 E
Fraire **143** 50 16N 4 31 E
Frameries **143** 50 24N 3 54 E
Frampol **152** 50 41N 22 40 E
Franca **121** 20 33 S 47 30W
Francavilla al Mare **163** 42 25N 14 16 E
Francavilla Fontana **165** 40 32N 17 35 E
France ■ **138** 47 0N 3 0 E
Frances **232** 36 41 S 140 55 E
Frances → **76** 60 16N 129 10W
Frances L. **76** 61 23N 129 30W
Francés Viejo, C. **113** 19 40N 70 0W
Franceville **252** 1 40 S 13 32 E
Franche-Comté **139** 46 30N 5 50 E
Franches Montagnes **148** 47 10N 7 0 E
Francis **88** 50 6N 103 52W
Francisca, Pta. **111** 21 34N 87 21W
Francisco de Orellana **118** 0 28 S 76 58W
Francisco Escárcega **111** 18 37N 90 43W
Francisco I. Madero, Coahuila, Mexico **102** 25 45N 103 20W
Francisco I. Madero, Durango, Mexico **105** 24 26N 104 18W
Francisco I. Madero, Presa **101** 28 10N 105 37W
Francisco Sáo **121** 16 28 S 43 30W
Franciso González Villarreal **102** 25 22N 97 53W
Francistown **255** 21 7 S 27 33 E
Francofonte **165** 37 13N 14 50 E
François, Canada **79** 47 35N 56 45W
François, Mart. **113** 14 38N 60 57W
François L. **92** 54 0N 125 30W
Francorchamps **143** 50 27N 5 57 E
Franeker **142** 53 12N 5 33 E
Frankado **245** 12 30N 43 12 E
Frankenberg **146** 51 3N 8 47 E
Frankenthal **147** 49 32N 8 21 E
Frankenwald **147** 50 18N 11 36 E
Frankford **85** 44 12N 77 36W
Frankfort **255** 27 17 S 28 30 E
Frankfurt □ **146** 52 30N 14 0 E
Frankfurt am Main **147** 50 7N 8 40 E
Frankfurt an der Oder **146** 52 50N 14 31 E
Fränkische Alb **147** 49 20N 11 30 E
Fränkische Rezal → **147** 49 11N 11 1 E
Fränkische Saale → **147** 50 30N 9 42 E
Fränkische Schweiz **147** 49 45N 11 10 E
Frankland → **229** 35 0 S 116 48 E
Franklin B. **94** 69 45N 126 0W
Franklin I. **13** 76 10 S 168 30 E
Franklin Mts., Canada **94** 65 0N 125 0W
Franklin Mts., N.Z. **235** 44 55 S 167 45 E
Franklin River **92** 49 7N 124 48W
Franklin Str. **95** 72 0N 96 0W
Franklyn Mt. **235** 42 4 S 172 42 E
Frankston **231** 38 8 S 145 8 E
Frankton Junc. **234** 37 47 S 175 16 E
Franquelin **80** 49 18N 67 54W
Fränsta **172** 62 30N 16 11 E
Frantsa Iosifa, Zemlya **184** 82 0N 55 0 E
Franz **87** 48 25N 84 30W
Franz Josef Land = Frantsa Iosifa, Zemlya **184** 82 0N 55 0 E

Franzburg **146** 54 9N 12 52 E
Frascati **164** 41 48N 12 41 E
Fraser →, B.C., Canada **93** 49 7N 123 11W
Fraser →, Newf., Canada **78** 56 39N 62 10W
Fraser, Mt. **229** 25 35 S 118 20 E
Fraser I. **231** 25 15 S 153 10 E
Fraser Lake **92** 54 0N 124 50W
Fraserburg **254** 31 55 S 21 30 E
Fraserburgh **134** 57 41N 2 0W
Fraserdale **87** 49 55N 81 37W
Frasertown **234** 38 58 S 177 28 E
Fraserwood **89** 50 38N 97 13W
Frashëri **168** 40 23N 20 26 E
Frasne **139** 46 50N 6 10 E
Frauenfeld **149** 47 34N 8 54 E
Fraustro **102** 25 55N 101 8W
Fray Bentos **124** 33 10 S 58 15W
Frazer L. **86** 49 15N 88 40W
Frazier Downs **228** 18 48 S 121 42 E
Frechilla **154** 42 8N 4 50W
Fredericia **173** 55 34N 9 45 E
Fredericton **81** 45 57N 66 40W
Fredericton Junc. **81** 45 41N 66 40W
Frederikshavn **173** 57 28N 10 31 E
Frederikssund **172** 55 50N 12 3 E
Frederiksted **113** 17 43N 64 53W
Fredrikstad **171** 59 13N 10 57 E
Freels, C. **79** 49 15N 53 30W
Freeman → **90** 54 19N 114 47W
Freeport, Bahamas **112** 26 30N 78 47W
Freeport, Canada **81** 44 15N 66 20W
Freetown **246** 8 30N 13 17W
Frégate, L. **74** 53 15N 74 45W
Fregenal de la Sierra **155** 38 10N 6 39W
Fregene **164** 41 50N 12 12 E
Fregeneda, La **154** 40 58N 6 54W
Fréhel, C. **138** 48 40N 2 20W
Frei **171** 63 4N 7 48 E
Freiberg **146** 50 55N 13 20 E
Freibourg = Fribourg **148** 46 49N 7 9 E
Freiburg, Baden-W., Germany **147** 48 0N 7 52 E
Freiburg, Niedersachsen, Germany **146** 53 49N 9 17 E
Freiburger Alpen **148** 46 37N 7 10 E
Freire **126** 38 54 S 72 38W
Freirina **124** 28 30 S 71 10W
Freising **147** 48 24N 11 47 E
Freistadt **150** 48 30N 14 30 E
Freital **146** 51 0N 13 40 E
Fréjus **141** 43 25N 6 44 E
Fremantle **229** 32 7 S 115 47 E
French →, Ont., Canada **84** 46 2N 80 34W
French →, Ont., Canada **87** 50 40N 80 59W
French Guiana ■ **119** 4 0N 53 0W
French I. **233** 38 20 S 145 22 E
French River **84** 46 2N 80 34W
French Terr. of Afars & Issas = Djibouti ■ **245** 12 0N 43 0 E
Frenchman Butte **88** 53 35N 109 38W
Frenda **241** 35 2N 1 1 E
Fresco → **123** 7 15 S 51 30W
Freshfield, C. **13** 68 25 S 151 10 E
Fresnay **138** 48 17N 0 1 E
Fresnillo **105** 23 10N 102 53W
Fresno Alhandiga **154** 40 42N 5 37W
Freudenstadt **147** 48 27N 8 25 E
Freux **143** 49 59N 5 27 E
Frévent **139** 50 15N 2 17 E
Frew → **230** 20 0 S 135 38 E
Frewena **230** 19 25 S 135 25 E
Freycinet Pen. **230** 42 10 S 148 25 E
Freyung **147** 48 48N 13 33 E
Fria **246** 10 27N 13 38W
Fria, C. **254** 18 0 S 12 0 E
Fría, La **118** 8 13N 72 15W
Fría, Sa. del **105** 22 0N 102 45W
Frías **124** 28 40 S 65 5W
Fribourg **148** 46 49N 7 9 E
Fribourg □ **148** 46 40N 7 0 E
Frick **148** 47 31N 8 1 E
Fridafors **173** 56 25N 14 39 E
Friedberg, Bayern, Germany **147** 48 21N 10 59 E
Friedberg, Hessen, Germany **147** 50 21N 8 46 E
Friedland **146** 53 40N 13 33 E
Friedrichshafen **147** 47 39N 9 29 E
Friedrichskoog **146** 54 1N 8 52 E
Friedrichsort **146** 54 24N 10 11 E
Friedrichstadt **146** 54 23N 9 6 E
Friendly, Is. = Tonga ■ **224** 19 50 S 174 30W
Friesach **150** 46 57N 14 24 E
Friesack **146** 52 43N 12 35 E
Friesche Wad **142** 53 22N 5 44 E
Friesland □ **142** 53 5N 5 50 E
Friesoythe **146** 53 1N 7 51 E
Frikson **89** 50 30N 99 55W
Frillesås **173** 57 20N 12 12 E
Frinnaryd **173** 57 55N 14 50 E
Frisian Is. **146** 53 30N 6 0 E
Fristad **173** 57 50N 13 0 E
Fritsla **173** 57 33N 12 47 E
Fritzlar **146** 51 8N 9 19 E
Friuli-Venezia Giulia □ **163** 46 0N 13 0 E
Friville-Escarbotin **139** 50 5N 1 33 E
Frobisher **89** 49 12N 102 26W
Frobisher B. **95** 62 30N 66 0W
Frobisher Bay **95** 63 44N 68 31W
Frobisher L. **77** 56 20N 108 15W
Frog L. **90** 53 55N 110 20W
Frogmore **233** 34 15 S 148 52 E
Froid-Chapelle **143** 50 9N 4 19 E
Frolovo **181** 49 45N 43 40 E
Frombork **152** 54 21N 19 41 E
Frome **133** 51 16N 2 17W
Frome, L. **231** 30 45 S 139 45 E
Frome Downs **232** 31 13 S 139 45 E
Fromentine **138** 46 53N 2 9W
Frómista **154** 42 16N 4 25W
Fronteira **155** 39 3N 7 39W
Fronteiras **120** 7 5 S 40 37W
Frontera **110** 18 32N 92 38W
Frontera Comalapa **110** 15 42N 92 6W
Fronteras **100** 30 56N 109 31W
Frontier **88** 49 12N 108 34W
Frontignan **140** 43 27N 3 45 E
Frosinone **164** 41 38N 13 20 E
Frosolone **165** 41 34N 14 27 E
Frostisen **174** 68 14N 17 10 E
Frouard **139** 48 47N 6 8 E
Frövi **172** 59 28N 15 24 E
Frøya **171** 63 43N 8 40 E
Fruges **139** 50 30N 2 8 E
Fruitvale **93** 49 7N 117 33W
Frumoasa **170** 46 28N 25 48 E
Frunze **183** 42 54N 74 46 E
Fruška Gora **166** 45 7N 19 30 E
Frutal **121** 20 0 S 49 0W
Frutigen **148** 46 35N 7 38 E
Fry L. **86** 51 14N 91 19W
Frýdek-Místek **151** 49 40N 18 20 E
Frýdlant, Severočeský, Czech. **150** 50 56N 15 9 E
Frýdlant, Severomoravsky, Czech. **151** 49 35N 18 20 E
Fryvaldov = Jeseník **151** 50 0N 17 8 E
Fthiótis □ **169** 38 50N 22 25 E
Fu Jiang → **216** 30 0N 106 16 E
Fu Xian, Liaoning, China **215** 39 38N 121 58 E
Fu Xian, Shaanxi, China **214** 36 0N 109 20 E
Fu'an **217** 27 11N 119 36 E
Fubian **216** 31 17N 102 22 E
Fucécchio **162** 43 44N 10 51 E
Fucheng **214** 37 50N 116 10 E
Fuchū, Hiroshima, Japan **220** 34 34N 133 14 E
Fūchū, Tōkyō, Japan **221** 35 40N 139 29 E
Fuchuan **217** 24 50N 111 5 E
Fuchun Jiang → **217** 30 5N 120 5 E
Fúcino, Conca del **163** 42 1N 13 31 E
Fuding **217** 27 20N 120 12 E
Fuencaliente **155** 38 25N 4 18W
Fuengirola **155** 36 32N 4 41W
Fuente **102** 28 40N 100 32W
Fuente Álamo, Murcia, Spain **157** 37 42N 1 6W
Fuente Alamo, Albacete, Spain **157** 38 44N 1 24W
Fuente de Cantos **155** 38 15N 6 18W
Fuente de San Esteban, La **154** 40 49N 6 15W
Fuente del Maestre **155** 38 31N 6 28W
Fuente el Fresno **155** 39 14N 3 46W
Fuente Ovejuna **155** 38 15N 5 25W
Fuentes de Andalucía **155** 37 28N 5 20W
Fuentes de Ebro **156** 41 31N 0 38W
Fuentes de León **155** 38 5N 6 32W
Fuentes de Oñoro **154** 40 33N 6 52W
Fuentesaúco **154** 41 15N 5 30W
Fuerte → **104** 25 54N 109 22W
Fuerte, L. del **99** 27 45N 114 15W
Fuerte Olimpo **124** 21 0 S 57 51W
Fufeng **214** 34 22N 108 0 E
Fuga I. **210** 18 52N 121 20 E
Fŭget, Munţii **170** 45 50N 22 9 E
Fughmah **195** 16 9N 49 26 E
Fugløysund **174** 70 15N 20 20 E
Fugong **216** 27 5N 98 47 E
Fugou **214** 34 3N 114 25 E
Fugu **214** 39 2N 111 3 E
Fuhai **212** 47 2N 87 25 E
Fuḩaymī **192** 34 16N 42 10 E
Fuji **221** 35 9N 138 39 E
Fuji-no-miya **221** 35 10N 138 40 E
Fuji-San **221** 35 22N 138 44 E
Fuji-yoshida **221** 35 30N 138 46 E
Fujian □ **217** 26 0N 118 0 E
Fujieda **221** 34 52N 138 16 E
Fujioka **221** 36 15N 139 5 E
Fujisawa **221** 35 22N 139 29 E
Fukaya **221** 36 12N 139 12 E
Fukien = Fujian □ **217** 26 0N 118 0 E
Fukuchiyama **221** 35 19N 135 9 E
Fukue-Shima **219** 32 40N 128 45 E
Fukui **221** 36 0N 136 10 E
Fukui □ **221** 36 0N 136 12 E
Fukuma **220** 33 46N 130 28 E
Fukuoka **220** 33 39N 130 21 E
Fukuoka □ **220** 33 30N 131 0 E
Fukuroi **221** 34 45N 137 55 E
Fukushima **218** 37 44N 140 28 E
Fukushima □ **218** 37 30N 140 15 E
Fukuyama **220** 34 35N 133 20 E
Fulda **146** 50 32N 9 41 E
Fulda → **146** 51 27N 9 40 E
Fulford Harbour **93** 48 47N 123 27W
Fuling **216** 29 40N 107 20 E
Fulongquan **215** 44 20N 124 42 E
Fuluälven **172** 61 18N 13 4 E
Fulufjället **172** 61 32N 12 41 E
Fumay **139** 50 0N 4 40 E
Fumel **140** 44 30N 0 58 E
Fumin **216** 25 10N 102 20 E
Funabashi **221** 35 45N 140 0 E
Funafuti **224** 8 30 S 179 0 E
Fundación **118** 10 31N 74 11W
Fundão, Brazil **121** 19 55 S 40 24W
Fundão, Portugal **154** 40 8N 7 30W
Fundición **100** 27 20N 109 43W
Fundy, B. of **81** 45 0N 66 0W
Fundy Nat. Park **81** 45 35N 65 10W
Funing, Hebei, China **215** 39 53N 119 12 E
Funing, Jiangsu, China **215** 33 45N 119 50 E
Funing, Yunnan, China **216** 23 35N 105 45 E
Funiu Shan **214** 33 30N 112 20 E
Funsi **246** 10 21N 1 54W
Funtua **247** 11 30N 7 18 E
Fuping, Hebei, China **214** 38 48N 114 12 E
Fuping, Shaanxi, China **214** 34 42N 109 10 E
Fuqing **217** 25 41N 119 21 E
Fuquan **216** 26 40N 107 27 E
Fur **173** 56 50N 9 0 E
Furano **218** 43 21N 142 23 E
Furāt, Nahr al → **192** 31 0N 47 25 E
Fürg **193** 28 18N 55 13 E
Furkapass **149** 46 34N 8 35 E
Furmanov **179** 57 10N 41 9 E
Furmanovka **183** 44 17N 72 57 E
Furmanovo **181** 49 42N 49 25 E
Furnas, Reprêsa de **121** 20 50 S 45 0W
Furneaux Group **230** 40 10 S 147 50 E
Furness, Pen. **132** 54 12N 3 10W
Furqlus **190** 34 36N 37 8 E
Fürstenau **146** 52 32N 7 40 E
Fürstenberg **146** 53 11N 13 9 E
Fürstenfeld **150** 47 3N 16 3 E
Fürstenfeldbruck **147** 48 10N 11 15 E
Fürstenwalde **146** 52 20N 14 3 E
Fürth **147** 49 29N 11 0 E
Furth im Wald **147** 49 19N 12 51 E
Furtwangen **147** 48 3N 8 14 E
Furudal **172** 61 10N 15 11 E
Furukawa **221** 38 34N 140 58 E
Furusund **172** 59 40N 18 55 E
Fury and Hecla Str. **95** 69 56N 84 0W
Fusa **171** 60 12N 5 37 E
Fusagasuga **118** 4 21N 74 22W
Fuscaldo **165** 39 25N 16 1 E
Fushan, Shandong, China **215** 37 30N 121 15 E
Fushan, Shanxi, China **214** 35 58N 111 51 E
Fushë Arrëzi **168** 42 4N 20 2 E
Fushun, Liaoning, China **215** 41 50N 123 56 E
Fushun, Sichuan, China **216** 29 13N 104 52 E
Fusio **149** 46 27N 8 40 E
Fusong **215** 42 20N 127 15 E
Füssen **147** 47 35N 10 43 E
Fusui **216** 22 40N 107 56 E
Futago-Yama **220** 33 35N 131 36 E
Futrono **126** 40 8 S 72 24W
Futuna **224** 14 25 S 178 20 E
Fuwa **244** 31 12N 30 33 E
Fuxin **215** 42 5N 121 48 E
Fuyang, Anhui, China **217** 33 0N 115 48 E
Fuyang, Zhejiang, China **217** 30 5N 119 57 E
Fuyang He → **214** 38 12N 117 0 E
Fuying Dao **217** 26 34N 120 9 E
Fuyu **215** 45 12N 124 43 E
Fuyuan **216** 25 40N 104 16 E
Füzesgyarmat **151** 47 6N 21 14 E
Fuzhou **217** 26 5N 119 16 E
Fylde **132** 53 50N 2 58W
Fyn **173** 55 20N 10 30 E
Fyne, L. **134** 56 0N 5 20W
Fyns Amtskommune □ **173** 55 15N 10 30 E
Fyresvatn **171** 59 6N 8 10 E

G

Gaanda **247** 10 10N 12 27 E
Gabarin **247** 11 8N 10 27 E
Gabarouse **81** 45 50N 60 9W
Gabas → **140** 43 46N 0 42W
Gabela **253** 11 0 S 14 24 E
Gabès **241** 33 53N 10 2 E
Gabès, Golfe de **241** 34 0N 10 30 E
Gabgaba, W. → **244** 22 10N 33 5 E
Gabin **152** 52 23N 19 41 E
Gabon ■ **252** 0 10 S 10 0 E
Gaborone **254** 24 45 S 25 57 E
Gābrīk **193** 25 44N 58 28 E
Gabriola I. **93** 49 9N 123 47W
Gabro **256** 6 18N 43 16 E
Gabrovo **167** 42 52N 25 19 E
Gacé **138** 48 49N 0 20 E
Gāch Sār **193** 36 7N 51 19 E
Gachsārān **193** 30 15N 50 45 E
Gacko **166** 43 10N 18 33 E
Gadag **201** 15 30N 75 45 E
Gadamai **245** 17 11N 36 10 E
Gadap **198** 25 5N 67 28 E
Gadarwara **199** 22 50N 78 50 E
Gadebusch **146** 53 41N 11 6 E
Gadein **245** 8 10N 28 45 E
Gadhada **198** 22 0N 71 35 E
Gadmen **149** 46 45N 8 16 E
Gádor, Sierra de **157** 36 57N 2 45W
Gadwal **201** 16 10N 77 50 E
Gadyach **178** 50 21N 34 0 E
Gadzi **252** 4 47N 16 42 E
Găeşti **170** 44 48N 25 19 E
Gaeta **164** 41 12N 13 35 E
Gaeta, G. di **164** 41 0N 13 25 E
Gafsa **241** 32 24N 8 43 E
Gagarin **178** 55 38N 35 0 E
Gagetown **81** 45 46N 66 10W
Gagil-Tomil, I. **226** 9 31N 138 12 E
Gagino **179** 55 15N 45 1 E
Gagliano del Capo **165** 39 50N 18 23 E
Gagnef **172** 60 36N 15 5 E
Gagnoa **246** 6 56N 5 16W
Gagnon **80** 51 50N 68 5W
Gagnon, L., N.W.T., Canada **77** 62 3N 110 27W
Gagnon, L., Qué., Canada **82** 46 7N 75 7W
Gagra **181** 43 20N 40 10 E
Gahini **250** 1 50 S 30 30 E
Gahmar **199** 25 27N 83 49 E
Gai Xian **215** 40 22N 122 20 E
Gaibanda **202** 25 20N 89 36 E
Gaïdhouronísi **169** 34 53N 25 41 E
Gail → **150** 46 36N 13 53 E
Gaillac **140** 43 54N 1 54 E
Gaillarbois, L. **80** 52 0N 67 27W
Gaillon **138** 49 10N 1 20 E
Gaima **227** 8 20 S 142 59 E
Gaimán **126** 43 10 S 65 25W
Gainsborough **132** 53 23N 0 46W
Gairdner L. **231** 31 30 S 136 0 E
Gairloch, L. **134** 57 43N 5 45W
Gais **149** 47 22N 9 27 E
Gaj **166** 45 28N 17 3 E
Gakuch **199** 36 7N 73 45 E
Gal Laghet **256** 4 9N 47 10 E
Gal Oya Res. **201** 7 5N 81 30 E
Gal Tardo **256** 3 34N 45 58 E
Galachipa **202** 22 8N 90 26 E
Galahad **91** 52 31N 111 56W
Galán, Cerro **124** 25 55 S 66 52W
Galana → **250** 3 9 S 40 8 E
Galangue **253** 13 42 S 16 9 E
Galangue, Serra **253** 14 18 S 15 52 E
Galanta **151** 48 11N 17 45 E
Galápagos **225** 0 0 89 0W
Galashiels **134** 55 37N 2 50W
Galatás **169** 37 30N 23 26 E
Galatea **234** 38 24 S 176 45 E
Galaţi **170** 45 27N 28 2 E
Galaţi □ **170** 45 45N 27 30 E
Galatina **165** 40 10N 18 10 E
Galátone **165** 40 8N 18 3 E
Galaxídhion **169** 38 22N 22 23 E
Galbraith **230** 16 25 S 141 30 E
Galcaio **188** 6 30N 47 30 E
Galdhøpiggen **171** 61 38N 8 18 E
Galeana, Chihuahua, Mexico **101** 30 7N 107 38W

Galeana, Nuevo León, Mexico **103** 24 50N 100 4W
Galela **207** 1 50N 127 49 E
Galera **157** 37 45N 2 33W
Galera, La **100** 30 21N 108 50W
Galera, Pta. **126** 39 59 S 73 43W
Galera Point **113** 10 8N 61 0W
Galeton **87** 51 8N 80 55W
Galgasc **256** 0 11N 41 38 E
Galheirão → **121** 12 23 S 45 5W
Galheiros **121** 13 18 S 46 25W
Gali **181** 42 37N 41 46 E
Galicea Mare **170** 44 4N 23 19 E
Galich **179** 58 23N 42 12 E
Galiche **167** 43 34N 23 50 E
Galicia □ **154** 42 43N 7 45W
Galilee = Hagalil **189** 32 53N 35 18 E
Galilee, L. **230** 22 20 S 145 50 E
Galissonnière, La, L. **80** 51 25N 62 0W
Galite, Is. de la **241** 37 30N 8 59 E
Gallarate **162** 45 40N 8 48 E
Gallardon **139** 48 32N 1 42 E
Galle **201** 6 5N 80 10 E
Gallega, La **104** 25 49N 105 8W
Gallego **101** 29 49N 106 22W
Gállego → **156** 41 39N 0 51W
Gallegos → **126** 51 35 S 69 0W
Galley Hd. **135** 51 32N 8 56W
Galliate **162** 45 27N 8 44 E
Gallinas, Pta. **118** 12 28N 71 40W
Gallipoli = Gelibolu **168** 40 28N 26 43 E
Gallípoli **165** 40 8N 18 0 E
Gällivare **174** 67 9N 20 40 E
Gallo, C. **164** 38 13N 13 19 E
Gallocanta, Laguna de **156** 40 58N 1 30W
Galloway **134** 55 0N 4 25W
Galloway, Mull of **134** 54 38N 4 50W
Gallur **156** 41 52N 1 19W
Gallyaaral **183** 40 2N 67 35 E
Gal'on **189** 31 38N 34 51 E
Galong **231** 34 37 S 148 34 E
Galtström **172** 62 10N 17 30 E
Galtür **150** 46 58N 10 11 E
Galty Mts. **135** 52 22N 8 10W
Galtymore **135** 52 22N 8 12W
Galvarino **126** 38 24 S 72 47W
Galve de Sorbe **156** 41 13N 3 10W
Gálvez, Argentina **124** 32 0 S 61 14W
Gálvez, Spain **155** 39 42N 4 16W
Galway **135** 53 16N 9 4W
Galway □ **135** 53 16N 9 3W
Galway B. **135** 53 10N 9 20W
Gam → **204** 21 55N 105 12 E
Gamagori **221** 34 50N 137 14 E
Gamari, L. **245** 11 32N 41 40 E
Gamawa **247** 12 10N 10 31 E
Gamay **210** 12 23N 125 18 E
Gamay Bay **210** 12 21N 125 21 E
Gamba **253** 11 42 S 17 14 E
Gambaga **247** 10 30N 0 28W
Gambat **198** 27 17N 68 26 E
Gambela **245** 8 14N 34 38 E
Gambia ■ **246** 13 25N 16 0W
Gambia → **246** 13 28N 16 34W
Gambier, C. **228** 11 56 S 130 57 E
Gambier I. **93** 49 30N 123 23W
Gambier Is. **232** 35 3 S 136 30 E
Gambo **252** 4 39N 22 16 E
Gamboli **198** 29 53N 68 24 E
Gamboma **252** 1 55 S 15 52 E
Gamboula **252** 4 8N 15 9 E
Gamlakarleby = Kokkola **174** 63 50N 23 8 E
Gammon → **89** 51 24N 95 44W
Gammouda **241** 35 3N 9 39 E
Gamoda-Saki **220** 33 50N 134 45 E
Gamu-Gofa □ **245** 5 40N 36 40 E
Gan **140** 43 12N 0 27W
Gan Gan **126** 42 30 S 68 10W
Gan Goriama, Mts. **247** 7 44N 12 45 E
Gan Jiang → **217** 29 15N 116 0 E
Gan Shemu'el **189** 32 28N 34 56 E
Gan Yavne **189** 31 48N 34 42 E
Gananoque **85** 44 20N 76 10W
Ganaveh **193** 29 35N 50 35 E
Gand = Gent **143** 51 2N 3 42 E
Ganda **253** 13 2 S 14 40 E
Gandak → **199** 25 39N 85 13 E
Gandara **210** 12 1N 124 49 E
Gandava **197** 28 32N 67 32 E
Gander **79** 48 58N 54 35W
Gander → **79** 49 16N 54 30W
Gander L. **79** 48 58N 54 35W
Ganderowe Falls **251** 17 20 S 29 10 E
Gandesa **156** 41 3N 0 26 E
Gandhi Sagar **198** 24 40N 75 40 E
Gandi **247** 12 55N 5 49 E
Gandía **157** 38 58N 0 9W
Gandino **162** 45 50N 9 52 E
Gandole **247** 8 28N 11 35 E
Gandu **121** 13 45 S 39 30W
Ganedidalem = Gani **207** 0 48 S 128 14 E
Ganetti **244** 18 0N 31 10 E
Gang Ranch **93** 51 33N 122 20W
Ganga → **199** 23 20N 90 30 E
Ganga, Mouths of the **199** 21 30N 90 0 E
Ganganagar **198** 29 56N 73 56 E
Gangapur **198** 26 32N 76 49 E
Gangara **247** 14 35N 8 29 E
Gangaw **202** 22 5N 94 5 E
Gangawati **201** 15 30N 76 36 E
Gangdisê Shan **199** 31 20N 81 0 E
Ganges = Ganga → **199** 23 20N 90 30 E
Ganges **140** 43 56N 3 42 E
Gangoh **198** 29 46N 77 18 E
Gangtok **202** 27 20N 88 37 E
Gangu **214** 34 40N 105 15 E
Gangyao **215** 44 12N 126 37 E
Gani **207** 0 48 S 128 14 E
Ganj **199** 27 45N 78 57 E
Gannat **140** 46 7N 3 11 E
Ganquan **214** 36 20N 109 20 E
Gänserdorf **151** 48 20N 16 43 E
Ganshui **216** 28 40N 106 40 E
Gansu □ **214** 36 0N 104 0 E
Ganta **246** 7 15N 8 59W
Gantheaume, C. **232** 36 4 S 137 32 E
Gantheaume B. **229** 27 40 S 114 10 E
Gantsevichi **178** 52 49N 26 30 E
Ganyem **207** 2 46 S 140 12 E
Ganyu **215** 34 50N 119 8 E
Ganyushkino **181** 46 35N 49 20 E
Ganzhou **217** 25 51N 114 56 E
Gao □ **247** 18 0N 1 0 E
Gao Xian **216** 28 21N 104 32 E
Gao'an **217** 28 26N 115 17 E
Gaohe **217** 22 46N 112 57 E
Gaohebu **217** 30 43N 116 49 E
Gaokeng **217** 27 40N 113 58 E
Gaolan Dao **217** 21 55N 113 10 E
Gaoligong Shan **216** 24 45N 98 45 E
Gaomi **215** 36 20N 119 42 E
Gaoping **214** 35 45N 112 55 E
Gaotang **214** 36 50N 116 15 E
Gaoua **246** 10 20N 3 8W
Gaoual **246** 11 45N 13 25W
Gaoxiong **217** 22 38N 120 18 E
Gaoyang **214** 38 40N 115 45 E
Gaoyou **217** 32 47N 119 26 E
Gaoyou Hu **215** 32 45N 119 20 E
Gaoyuan **215** 37 8N 117 58 E
Gaozhou **217** 21 58N 110 50 E
Gap **141** 44 33N 6 5 E
Gapan **210** 15 19N 120 57 E
Gar **212** 32 10N 79 58 E
Garachiné **112** 8 0N 78 12W
Garad **256** 6 57N 49 24 E
Garanhuns **120** 8 50 S 36 30W
Garawe **246** 4 35N 8 0W
Garba Harre **256** 3 19N 42 13 E
Garba Tula **250** 0 30N 38 32 E
Garbagududu **256** 6 12N 43 50 E
Garça **121** 22 14 S 49 37W
Garças → **120** 8 43 S 39 41W
Garças, Rio das → **123** 15 54 S 52 16W
Garchitorena **210** 13 52N 123 40 E
Garcia **101** 29 59N 108 20W
García de la Cadena **106** 21 9N 103 28W
Garcia Hernandez **211** 9 37N 124 18 E
Garcias **123** 20 34 S 52 13W
Gard **256** 9 30N 49 6 E
Gard □ **141** 44 2N 4 10 E
Gard → **141** 43 51N 4 37 E
Garda, L. di **162** 45 40N 10 40 E
Gardanne **141** 43 27N 5 27 E
Garde L. **77** 62 50N 106 13W
Gardelegen **146** 52 32N 11 21 E
Gardēz **197** 33 37N 69 9 E
Gardhíki **169** 38 50N 21 55 E
Gardiner Ls. **90** 57 32N 112 30W
Gardner Canal **92** 53 27N 128 8W
Gardno, Jezioro **152** 54 40N 17 7 E
Gare Tigre **119** 4 58N 53 9W
Garešnica **166** 45 36N 16 56 E
Garéssio **162** 44 12N 8 1 E
Gargaliánoi **169** 37 4N 21 38 E
Gargano, Mte. **165** 41 43N 15 43 E
Gargans, Mt. **140** 45 37N 1 39 E
Gargouna **247** 15 56N 0 13 E
Garhshankar **198** 31 13N 76 11 E
Gari **182** 59 26N 62 21 E
Garibaldi, Mt. **93** 49 51N 123 0W
Garibaldi Prov. Park **93** 49 50N 122 40W
Garies **254** 30 32 S 17 59 E
Garigliano → **164** 41 13N 13 44 E
Garissa **250** 0 25 S 39 40 E
Garissa □ **250** 0 20 S 40 0 E
Garkida **247** 10 27N 12 36 E
Garko **247** 11 45N 8 53 E
Garlasco **162** 45 11N 8 55 E
Garm **183** 39 0N 70 20 E
Garmab, Afghan. **198** 32 50N 65 12 E
Garmāb, Iran **193** 35 25N 56 45 E
Garmisch-Partenkirchen **147** 47 30N 11 5 E
Garmsār **193** 35 20N 52 25 E
Garneau, L. **80** 51 43N 63 22W
Garnish **79** 47 14N 55 22W
Garo Hills **199** 25 30N 90 30 E
Garob **254** 26 37 S 16 0 E
Garoe **256** 8 25N 48 33 E
Garonne → **140** 45 2N 0 36W
Garoua **247** 9 19N 13 21 E
Garrel **146** 52 58N 7 59 E
Garrigues **140** 43 40N 3 30 E
Garrovillas **155** 39 40N 6 33W
Garrucha **157** 37 11N 1 49W
Garry → **134** 56 47N 3 47W
Garry L. **95** 65 58N 100 18W
Garsen **250** 2 20 S 40 5 E
Garson → **77** 56 20N 110 1W
Garson L. **90** 56 19N 110 2W
Gartempe → **140** 46 47N 0 49 E
Gartz **146** 53 12N 14 23 E
Garu **247** 10 55N 0 11W
Garut **209** 7 14 S 107 53 E
Garvão **155** 37 42N 8 21W
Garvie Mts. **235** 45 30 S 168 50 E
Garwa = Garoua **247** 9 19N 13 21 E
Garwa **199** 24 11N 83 47 E
Garwolin **152** 51 55N 21 38 E
Garz **146** 54 17N 13 21 E
Garza García **102** 25 40N 100 24W
Garzê **216** 31 39N 99 58 E
Garzón **118** 2 10N 75 40W
Gas-San **218** 38 32N 140 1 E
Gasan **210** 13 19N 121 51 E
Gasan Kuli **184** 37 40N 54 20 E
Gascogne **140** 43 45N 0 20 E
Gascogne, G. de **156** 44 0N 2 0W
Gascons **80** 48 11N 64 51W
Gascony = Gascogne **140** 43 45N 0 20 E
Gascoyne → **229** 24 52 S 113 37 E
Gascoyne Junc. T.O. **229** 25 2 S 115 17 E
Gascueña **156** 40 18N 2 31W
Gash, Wadi → **245** 16 48N 35 51 E
Gashaka **247** 7 20N 11 29 E
Gasherbrum **199** 35 40N 76 40 E
Gashua **247** 12 54N 11 0 E
Gaspé **80** 48 52N 64 30W
Gaspé, Baie de **80** 48 46N 64 17W
Gaspé, C. **80** 48 48N 64 7W
Gaspé, Pén. de **80** 48 45N 65 40W
Gaspésie, Parc Prov. de la **80** 48 55N 65 50W
Gasselte **142** 52 58N 6 48 E
Gasselternijveen **142** 52 59N 6 51 E
Gássino Torinese **162** 45 8N 7 50 E
Gassol **247** 8 34N 10 25 E
Gastoúni **169** 37 51N 21 15 E
Gastoúri **168** 39 34N 19 54 E
Gastre **126** 42 20 S 69 15W
Gata, C. **190** 34 34N 33 2 E
Gata, C. de **157** 36 41N 2 13W
Gata, Sierra de **154** 40 20N 6 45W
Gataga → **76** 58 35N 126 59W
Gătaia **166** 45 26N 21 30 E
Gatchina **178** 59 35N 30 9 E
Gateshead **132** 54 57N 1 37W
Gateshead I. **95** 70 36N 100 26W
Gaths **251** 20 2 S 30 32 E
Gatico **124** 22 29 S 70 20W
Gâtinais **139** 48 5N 2 40 E
Gâtine, Hauteurs de **140** 46 35N 0 45W
Gatineau, Ont., Canada **85** 45 29N 75 39W
Gatineau, Qué., Canada **82** 45 29N 75 38W
Gatineau → **82** 45 27N 75 42W
Gatineau, Parc de la **82** 45 40N 76 0W
Gatooma **251** 18 20 S 29 52 E
Gattaran **210** 18 4N 121 38 E
Gattinara **162** 45 37N 8 22 E
Gatun, L. **112** 9 7N 79 56W
Gaucín **155** 36 31N 5 19W
Gauer L. **77** 57 0N 97 50W
Gauhati **202** 26 10N 91 45 E
Gauja → **178** 57 10N 24 16 E
Gaula → **171** 63 21N 10 14 E
Gaultois **79** 47 36N 55 54W
Gaurain-Ramecroix **143** 50 36N 3 30 E
Gaurdak **183** 37 50N 66 4 E
Gausta **171** 59 50N 8 37 E
Gāv Koshī **193** 28 38N 57 12 E
Gavá **156** 41 18N 2 0 E
Gāvakān **193** 29 37N 53 10 E
Gavarnie **140** 42 44N 0 3W
Gavāter **193** 25 10N 61 31 E
Gāvbandī **193** 27 12N 53 4 E
Gavdhopoúla **169** 34 56N 24 0 E
Gávdhos **169** 34 50N 24 5 E
Gavere **143** 50 55N 3 40 E
Gavia, Sa. de la **102** 26 15N 101 15W
Gavião **155** 39 28N 7 56W
Gävle **172** 60 40N 17 9 E
Gävleborgs län □ **172** 61 30N 16 15 E
Gavorrano **162** 42 55N 10 49 E
Gavray **138** 48 55N 1 20W
Gavrilov Yam **179** 57 18N 39 49 E
Gávrion **169** 37 54N 24 44 E
Gawachab **254** 27 4 S 17 55 E
Gawai **202** 27 56N 97 30 E
Gawilgarh Hills **198** 21 15N 76 45 E
Gawler **232** 34 30 S 138 42 E
Gaxun Nur **212** 42 22N 100 30 E
Gay **182** 51 27N 58 27 E
Gaya, India **199** 24 47N 85 4 E
Gaya, Niger **247** 11 52N 3 28 E
Gaya, Nigeria **247** 11 57N 9 0 E
Gayndah **231** 25 35 S 151 32 E
Gayny **182** 60 18N 54 19 E
Gayot, L. **78** 55 50N 70 50W
Gaysin **180** 48 57N 28 25 E
Gayvoron **180** 48 22N 29 52 E
Gaza **189** 31 30N 34 28 E
Gaza □ **255** 23 10 S 32 45 E
Gaza Strip **189** 31 29N 34 25 E
Gazaoua **247** 13 32N 7 55 E
Gāzbor **193** 28 5N 58 51 E
Gazelle Pen. **227** 4 40 S 152 0 E
Gazi **250** 1 3N 24 30 E
Gaziantep **177** 37 6N 37 23 E
Gazli **184** 40 14N 63 24 E
Gbarnga **246** 7 19N 9 13W
Gbekebo **247** 6 20N 4 56 E
Gboko **247** 7 17N 9 4 E
Gbongan **247** 7 28N 4 20 E
Gcuwa **255** 32 20 S 28 11 E
Gdańsk **152** 54 22N 18 40 E
Gdańsk □ **152** 54 10N 18 30 E
Gdańska, Zatoka **152** 54 30N 19 20 E
Gdov **178** 58 48N 27 55 E
Gdynia **152** 54 35N 18 33 E
Ge'a **189** 31 38N 34 37 E
Geary **81** 45 46N 66 29W
Gebe **207** 0 5N 129 25 E
Gebeit Mine **244** 21 3N 36 29 E
Gebel Mûsa **244** 28 32N 33 59 E
Gecha **245** 7 30N 35 18 E
Gedaref **245** 14 2N 35 28 E
Gede, Tanjung **208** 6 46 S 105 12 E
Gedera **189** 31 49N 34 46 E
Gedinne **143** 49 59N 4 56 E
Gedo **245** 9 2N 37 25 E
Gèdre **140** 42 47N 0 2 E
Gedser **173** 54 35N 11 55 E
Gedser Odde **173** 54 30N 11 58 E
Geel **143** 51 10N 4 59 E
Geelong **231** 38 10 S 144 22 E
Geelvink Chan. **229** 28 30 S 114 0 E
Geer → **143** 50 51N 5 42 E
Geestenseth **146** 53 31N 8 51 E
Geesthacht **146** 53 25N 10 20 E
Geffen **142** 51 44N 5 28 E
Geidam **247** 12 57N 11 57 E
Geikie → **77** 57 45N 103 52W
Geikie I. **86** 50 0N 88 35W
Geili **245** 16 1N 32 37 E
Geilo **171** 60 32N 8 14 E
Geinica **151** 48 51N 20 55 E
Geisingen **147** 47 55N 8 37 E
Geislingen **147** 48 37N 9 51 E
Geita **250** 2 48 S 32 12 E
Geita □ **250** 2 50 S 32 10 E
Gejiu **216** 23 20N 103 10 E
Gel → **245** 7 5N 29 10 E
Gel River **245** 7 5N 29 10 E
Gela **165** 37 6N 14 18 E
Gela, Golfo di **165** 37 0N 14 8 E
Geladi **256** 6 59N 46 30 E
Gelderland □ **142** 52 5N 6 10 E
Geldermalsen **142** 51 53N 5 17 E
Geldern **146** 51 32N 6 18 E
Geldrop **143** 51 25N 5 32 E
Geleen **143** 50 57N 5 49 E
Gelehun **246** 8 20N 11 40W
Gelendzhik **180** 44 33N 38 10 E
Gelib **256** 0 29N 42 46 E
Gelibolu **168** 40 28N 26 43 E
Gelnhausen **147** 50 12N 9 12 E
Gelsenkirchen **146** 51 30N 7 5 E
Gelting **146** 54 43N 9 53 E
Gem **91** 50 57N 112 11W
Gemas **205** 2 37N 102 36 E
Gembloux **143** 50 34N 4 43 E
Gemena **252** 3 13N 19 48 E
Gemert **143** 51 33N 5 41 E
Gemona del Friuli **163** 46 16N 13 7 E
Gemsa **244** 27 39N 33 35 E
Gemünden **147** 50 3N 9 43 E
Genale, Ethiopia **245** 6 0N 39 30 E
Genale, Somalia **256** 1 48N 44 42 E
Genappe **143** 50 37N 4 30 E
Gençay **140** 46 23N 0 23 E
Gendringen **142** 51 52N 6 21 E
Gendt **142** 51 53N 5 59 E
Geneina, Gebel **244** 29 2N 33 55 E
Genemuiden **142** 52 38N 6 2 E

General Acha **124** 37 20 S 64 38W
General Alvear, Buenos Aires, Argentina **124** 36 0 S 60 0W
General Alvear, Mendoza, Argentina **124** 35 0 S 67 40W
General Artigas **124** 26 52 S 56 16W
General Belgrano **124** 36 35 S 58 47W
General Bravo **102** 25 48N 99 10W
General Cabrera **124** 32 53 S 63 52W
General Carrera, L. **126** 46 35 S 72 0W
General Cepeda **102** 25 23N 101 27W
General Conesa **126** 40 6 S 64 25W
General Escobedo **104** 25 30N 105 15W
General Galeana **104** 25 29N 105 17W
General Guido **124** 36 40 S 57 50W
General Juan Madariaga **124** 37 0 S 57 0W
General La Madrid **124** 37 17 S 61 20W
General Lorenzo Vintter **126** 40 45 S 64 26W
General Luna **210** 13 41N 122 10 E
General MacArthur **211** 11 18N 125 28 E
General Martin Miguel de Güemes **124** 24 50 S 65 0W
General Paz **124** 27 45 S 57 36W
General Pedro Antonio Santos **103** 21 36N 98 58W
General Pico **124** 35 45 S 63 50W
General Pinedo **124** 27 15 S 61 20W
General Pinto **124** 34 45 S 61 50W
General Sampaio **120** 4 2 S 39 29W
General Santos **211** 6 5N 125 14 E
General Terán **103** 25 16N 99 41W
General Tinio **210** 15 39N 121 10 E
General Toshevo **167** 43 42N 28 6 E
General Treviño **102** 26 14N 99 29W
General Trias **101** 28 21N 106 22W
General Viamonte **124** 35 1 S 61 3W
General Vicente Guerrero **105** 23 45N 103 59W
General Villegas **124** 35 0 S 63 0W
General Vintter, L. **126** 43 55 S 71 40W
General Zuazua **102** 25 54N 100 7W
Generoso, Mte. **149** 45 56N 9 2 E
Genesee **90** 53 21N 114 20W
Geneva = Genève **148** 46 12N 6 9 E
Geneva, L. = Léman, Lac **148** 46 26N 6 30 E
Genève **148** 46 12N 6 9 E
Genève □ **148** 46 10N 6 10 E
Geng **197** 32 22N 61 28 E
Gengenbach **147** 48 25N 8 0 E
Gengma **216** 23 32N 99 20 E
Genichesk **180** 46 12N 34 50 E
Genil → **155** 37 42N 5 19W
Génissiat, Barrage de **141** 46 1N 5 48 E
Genk **143** 50 58N 5 32 E
Genkai-Nada **220** 34 0N 130 0 E
Genlis **139** 47 15N 5 12 E
Gennargentu, Mti. del **164** 40 0N 9 10 E
Gennep **143** 51 41N 5 59 E
Gennes **138** 47 20N 0 17W
Genoa = Génova **162** 44 24N 8 56 E
Genoa **231** 37 29 S 149 35 E
Genoa → **126** 44 55 S 70 5W
Génova **162** 44 24N 8 56 E
Génova, Golfo di **162** 44 0N 9 0 E
Gent **143** 51 2N 3 42 E
Gentbrugge **143** 51 3N 3 47 E
Genthin **146** 52 24N 12 10 E
Gentio do Ouro **120** 11 25 S 42 30W
Geographe B. **229** 33 30 S 115 15 E
Geographe Chan. **229** 24 30 S 113 0 E
Geokchay **181** 40 42N 47 43 E
Georga, Zemlya **184** 80 30N 49 0 E
George **254** 33 58 S 22 29 E
George →, Qué., Canada **75** 58 49N 66 10W
George →, Qué., Canada **78** 49 21N 67 59W
George, L., N.S.W., Australia **231** 35 10 S 149 25 E
George, L., S. Austral., Australia **232** 37 25 S 140 0 E
George, L., W. Austral., Australia **228** 22 45 S 123 40 E
George, L., Uganda **250** 0 5N 30 10 E
George B. **81** 45 45N 61 45W
George River = Port Nouveau-Québec **78** 58 30N 65 59W
George Sound **235** 44 52 S 167 25 E
George Town, Australia **230** 41 5 S 146 49 E
George Town, Bahamas **112** 23 33N 75 47W
George Town, Malaysia **205** 5 25N 100 15 E
George V Coast **13** 69 0 S 148 0 E
George VI Sound **13** 71 0 S 68 0W
Georgetown, Australia **230** 18 17 S 143 33 E
Georgetown, Ont., Canada **84** 43 40N 79 56W
Georgetown, P.E.I., Canada **81** 46 13N 62 24W
Georgetown, Cayman Is. **112** 19 20N 81 24W
Georgetown, Gambia **246** 13 30N 14 47W
Georgetown, Guyana **119** 6 50N 58 12W
Georgi Dimitrov **167** 42 15N 23 54 E
Georgi Dimitrov, Yazovir **167** 42 37N 25 18 E
Georgia, Str. of **92** 49 25N 124 0W
Georgian B. **84** 45 15N 81 0W
Georgian S.S.R. □ **181** 42 0N 43 0 E
Georgievsk **181** 44 12N 43 28 E
Georgina → **230** 23 30 S 139 47 E
Georgina Downs **230** 21 10 S 137 40 E
Georgina I. **84** 44 22N 79 17W
Georgiu-Dezh **179** 51 3N 39 30 E
Georgiyevka **183** 43 3N 74 43 E
Gera **146** 50 53N 12 11 E
Gera □ **146** 50 45N 11 45 E
Geraardsbergen **143** 50 45N 3 53 E
Geral, Serra, Bahia, Brazil **121** 14 0 S 41 0W
Geral, Serra, Goiás, Brazil **120** 11 15 S 46 30W
Geral, Serra, Sta. Catarina, Brazil **125** 26 25 S 50 0W
Geral de Goiás, Serra **121** 12 0 S 46 0W
Geral do Paranã Serra **121** 15 0 S 47 30W
Geraldine **235** 44 5 S 171 15 E
Geraldton, Australia **229** 28 48 S 114 32 E
Geraldton, Canada **87** 49 44N 86 59W
Geranium **232** 35 23 S 140 11 E
Gérardmer **139** 48 3N 6 50 E
Gerede **180** 40 45N 32 10 E
Gereshk **197** 31 47N 64 35 E
Gérgal **157** 37 7N 2 31W
Gerik **205** 5 25N 101 0 E
Gerizim **189** 32 13N 35 15 E
Gerlachovka **151** 49 11N 20 7 E
Gerlogubi **256** 6 53N 45 3 E
Germain, Grand L. **80** 51 12N 66 41W
German Planina **166** 42 20N 22 0 E
Germansen Landing **76** 55 43N 124 40W
Germany, East ■ **146** 52 0N 12 0 E
Germany, West ■ **146** 52 0N 9 0 E
Germersheim **147** 49 13N 8 20 E
Germiston **255** 26 15 S 28 10 E
Gernsheim **147** 49 44N 8 29 E
Gero **221** 35 48N 137 14 E
Gerolstein **147** 50 12N 6 40 E
Gerolzhofen **147** 49 54N 10 21 E
Gerona **156** 41 58N 2 46 E
Gerona □ **156** 42 11N 2 30 E
Gérouville **143** 49 37N 5 26 E
Gerrard **93** 50 30N 117 17W
Gerringong **233** 34 46 S 150 47 E
Gers □ **140** 43 35N 0 38 E
Gers → **140** 44 9N 0 39 E
Gersfeld **146** 50 27N 9 57 E
Gersoppa Falls **201** 14 12N 74 46 E
Geseke **146** 51 38N 8 29 E
Geser **207** 3 50 S 130 54 E
Gesso → **162** 44 24N 7 33 E
Gestro, Wabi → **245** 4 12N 42 2 E
Gesves **143** 50 24N 5 4 E
Getafe **154** 40 18N 3 44W
Gethsémani **78** 50 13N 60 40W
Getz Ice Shelf **13** 75 0 S 130 0W
Geul → **143** 50 53N 5 43 E
Geureudong, Mt. **208** 4 13N 96 42 E
Geurie **233** 32 22 S 148 50 E
Gévaudan **140** 44 40N 3 40 E
Gevgelija **166** 41 9N 22 30 E
Gévora → **155** 38 53N 6 57W
Gex **141** 46 21N 6 3 E
Geyikli **168** 39 50N 26 12 E
Geysir **174** 64 19N 20 18W
Ghâbat el Arab = Wang Kai **245** 9 3N 29 23 E
Ghaghara → **199** 25 45N 84 40 E
Ghalat **195** 21 6N 58 53 E
Ghalla, Wadi el → **245** 10 25N 27 32 E
Ghallamane **240** 23 15N 10 0W
Ghana ■ **247** 6 0N 1 0W
Ghansor **199** 22 39N 80 1 E
Ghanzi **254** 21 50 S 21 34 E
Ghanzi □ **254** 21 50 S 21 45 E
Gharb el Istiwa'iya □ **245** 5 0N 30 0 E
Gharbîya, Es Sahrâ el **244** 27 40N 26 30 E
Ghard Abû Muharik **244** 26 50N 30 0 E
Ghardaïa **241** 32 20N 3 37 E
Ghârib, G. **244** 28 6N 32 54 E
Ghârib, Râs **244** 28 6N 33 18 E
Gharm, W. → **195** 19 57N 57 38 E
Gharyān **241** 32 10N 13 0 E
Gharyān □ **241** 30 35N 12 0 E
Ghat **241** 24 59N 10 11 E
Ghatal **199** 22 40N 87 46 E
Ghatampur **199** 26 8N 80 13 E
Ghatprabha → **201** 16 15N 75 20 E
Ghaṭṭī **192** 31 16N 37 31 E
Ghawdex = Gozo **160** 36 0N 14 13 E
Ghayl **194** 21 40N 46 20 E
Ghayl Bā Wazīr **195** 14 47N 49 22 E
Ghazal, Bahr el →, Chad **243** 15 0N 17 0 E
Ghazâl, Bahr el →, Sudan **245** 9 31N 30 25 E
Ghazaouet **241** 35 8N 1 50W
Ghaziabad **198** 28 42N 77 26 E
Ghazipur **199** 25 38N 83 35 E
Ghaznī **197** 33 30N 68 28 E
Ghaznī □ **197** 32 10N 68 20 E
Ghedi **162** 45 24N 10 16 E
Ghelari **170** 45 38N 22 45 E
Ghèlinsor **256** 6 28N 46 39 E
Ghent = Gent **143** 51 2N 3 42 E
Gheorghe Gheorghiu-Dej **170** 46 17N 26 47 E
Gheorgheni **170** 46 43N 25 41 E
Ghergani **170** 44 37N 25 37 E
Gherla **170** 47 0N 23 57 E
Ghilarza **164** 40 8N 8 50 E
Ghisonaccia **141** 42 1N 9 26 E
Ghizao **198** 33 20N 65 44 E
Ghizar → **199** 36 15N 73 43 E
Ghod → **200** 18 30N 74 35 E
Ghogha **198** 21 40N 72 20 E
Ghost River **86** 50 12N 91 30W
Ghot Ogrein **244** 31 10N 25 20 E
Ghotaru **198** 27 20N 70 1 E
Ghotki **198** 28 5N 69 21 E
Ghowr □ **197** 34 0N 64 20 E
Ghudaf, W. al → **192** 32 56N 43 30 E
Ghudāmis **241** 30 11N 9 29 E
Ghughri **199** 22 39N 80 41 E
Ghugus **200** 19 58N 79 12 E
Ghulam Mohammad Barrage **198** 25 30N 68 20 E
Ghurayrah **194** 18 37N 42 41 E
Ghūrīān **197** 34 17N 61 25 E
Gia Dinh **205** 10 49N 106 42 E
Gia Lai = Pleiku **204** 13 57N 108 0 E
Gia Nghia **205** 12 0N 107 42 E
Gia Ngoc **204** 14 50N 108 58 E
Gia Vuc **204** 14 42N 108 34 E
Giamama **256** 0 4N 42 44 E
Gian **207** 5 45N 125 20 E
Giannutri **162** 42 16N 11 5 E
Giant Mts. = Krkonoše **150** 50 50N 15 35 E
Giant's Causeway **135** 55 15N 6 30W
Giarabub = Al Jaghbūb **242** 29 42N 24 38 E
Giarre **165** 37 44N 15 10 E
Giaveno **162** 45 3N 7 20 E
Gibara **112** 21 9N 76 11W
Gibb River **228** 16 26 S 126 26 E
Gibbons **90** 53 50N 113 20W
Gibe → **245** 7 20N 37 36 E
Gibellina **164** 37 48N 13 0 E
Gibraléon **155** 37 23N 6 58W
Gibraltar **155** 36 7N 5 22W
Gibraltar, Str. of **155** 35 55N 5 40W
Gibson Des. **228** 24 0 S 126 0 E
Gibsons **93** 49 24N 123 32W
Giddalur **201** 15 20N 78 57 E
Gidole **245** 5 40N 37 25 E
Gien **139** 47 40N 2 36 E
Giessen **146** 50 34N 8 40 E
Gieten **142** 53 0N 6 46 E
Gīfān **193** 37 54N 57 28 E
Gifatin, Geziret **244** 27 10N 33 50 E
Giffard **83** 46 51N 71 12W
Gifford Creek **229** 24 3 S 116 16 E
Gifhorn **146** 52 29N 10 32 E
Gift Lake **90** 55 53N 115 49W
Gifu **221** 35 30N 136 45 E
Gifu □ **221** 35 40N 137 0 E
Gigant **181** 46 28N 41 20 E
Giganta, Sa. de la **99** 26 18N 111 39W
Gigantes, Llanos de los **101** 28 9N 104 45W
Gigen **167** 43 40N 24 28 E
Gigha **134** 55 42N 5 45W
Giglei **256** 5 25N 45 20 E
Giglio **162** 42 20N 10 52 E
Gigmoto **210** 13 47N 124 23 E
Gignac **140** 43 39N 3 32 E
Gigüela → **157** 39 8N 3 44W
Gijón **154** 43 32N 5 42W
Gil I. **92** 53 12N 129 15W
Gīlān □ **193** 37 0N 50 0 E
Gilău **170** 46 45N 23 23 E
Gilbert → **230** 16 35 S 141 15 E
Gilbert, Mt. **92** 50 52N 124 16W
Gilbert Is. = Kiribati ■ **224** 1 0N 176 0 E
Gilbert Plains **89** 51 9N 100 28W
Gilbert River **230** 18 9 S 142 52 E
Gilberton **230** 19 16 S 143 35 E
Gilbués **120** 9 50 S 45 21W
Gilf el Kebîr, Hadabat el **244** 23 50N 25 50 E
Gilford I. **92** 50 40N 126 30W
Gilgandra **231** 31 43 S 148 39 E
Gilgil **250** 0 30 S 36 20 E
Gilgit **199** 35 50N 74 15 E
Gilgit → **199** 35 44N 74 37 E
Gilgunnia **233** 32 26 S 146 2 E
Gilindire **190** 36 8N 33 19 E
Giljeva Planina **166** 43 9N 20 0 E
Gillam **77** 56 20N 94 40W
Gilleleje **172** 56 8N 12 19 E
Gillen, L. **229** 26 11 S 124 38 E
Gilles, L. **231** 32 50 S 136 45 E
Gillespies Pt. **235** 43 24 S 169 49 E
Gilliat **230** 20 40 S 141 28 E
Gillies Bay **92** 49 42N 124 29W
Gillingham **133** 51 23N 0 34 E
Gilly **143** 50 25N 4 29 E
Gilmore **231** 35 20 S 148 12 E
Gilmore, L. **229** 32 29 S 121 37 E
Gilmour **85** 44 48N 77 37W
Gilo → **245** 8 10N 33 15 E
Gilort → **170** 44 38N 23 32 E
Giluwe, Mt. **227** 6 8 S 143 52 E
Gilze **143** 51 32N 4 57 E
Gimbi **245** 9 3N 35 42 E
Gimigliano **165** 38 58N 16 32 E
Gimli **77** 50 40N 97 0W
Gimo **172** 60 11N 18 12 E
Gimone → **140** 44 0N 1 6 E
Gimont **140** 43 38N 0 52 E
Gimzo **189** 31 56N 34 56 E
Gin → **201** 6 5N 80 7 E
Gin Gin **231** 25 0 S 151 58 E
Ginâh **244** 25 21N 30 30 E
Ginatilan **211** 9 34N 123 19 E
Gindie **230** 23 44 S 148 8 E
Gineta, La **157** 39 8N 2 1W
Gingin **229** 31 22 S 115 54 E
Gîngiova **170** 43 54N 23 50 E
Gingoog **211** 8 50N 125 7 E
Ginir **245** 7 6N 40 40 E
Ginosa **165** 40 35N 16 45 E
Ginzo de Limia **154** 42 3N 7 47W
Giohar **256** 2 48N 45 30 E
Gióia, G. di **165** 38 30N 15 50 E
Gióia del Colle **165** 40 49N 16 55 E
Gióia Táuro **165** 38 26N 15 53 E
Gioiosa Iónica **165** 38 20N 16 19 E
Gióna, Óros **169** 38 38N 22 14 E
Giovi, Passo dei **162** 44 33N 8 57 E
Giovinazzo **165** 41 10N 16 40 E
Gir Hills **198** 21 0N 71 0 E
Girab **198** 26 2N 70 38 E
Girâfi, W. → **191** 29 58N 34 39 E
Giraltovce **151** 49 7N 21 32 E
Girardot **118** 4 18N 74 48W
Girardville **83** 49 0N 72 32W
Girdle Ness **134** 57 9N 2 2W
Giresun **177** 40 55N 38 30 E
Girga **244** 26 17N 31 55 E
Girgir, C. **227** 3 50 S 144 35 E
Giridih **199** 24 10N 86 21 E
Girifalco **165** 38 49N 16 25 E
Girilambone **231** 31 16 S 146 57 E
Giro **247** 11 7N 4 42 E
Giromagny **139** 47 44N 6 50 E
Gironde □ **140** 44 45N 0 30W
Gironde → **140** 45 32N 1 7W
Gironella **156** 42 2N 1 53 E
Girouxville **90** 55 45N 117 20W
Giru **230** 19 30 S 147 5 E
Girvan **134** 55 15N 4 50W
Gisborne **234** 38 39 S 178 5 E
Gisborne L. **79** 47 48N 54 49W
Gisenyi **250** 1 41 S 29 15 E
Giske **171** 62 30N 6 3 E
Gislaved **173** 57 19N 13 32 E
Gisors **139** 49 15N 1 47 E
Gissarskiy, Khrebet **183** 39 0N 69 0 E
Gistel **143** 51 9N 2 59 E
Giswil **148** 46 50N 8 11 E
Gitega **250** 3 26 S 29 56 E
Gits **143** 51 0N 3 6 E
Giuba → **188** 1 30N 42 35 E
Giubiasco **149** 46 11N 9 1 E
Giugliano in Campania **165** 40 55N 14 12 E
Giulianova **163** 42 45N 13 58 E
Giurgeni **170** 44 45N 27 48 E
Giurgiu **170** 43 52N 25 57 E
Giv'at Brenner **189** 31 52N 34 47 E
Giv'atayim **189** 32 4N 34 49 E
Give **173** 55 51N 9 13 E
Givet **139** 50 8N 4 49 E

Givors **141** 45 35N 4 45 E
Givry, Belgium **143** 50 23N 4 2 E
Givry, France **139** 46 41N 4 46 E
Giyon **245** 8 33N 38 1 E
Giza = El Gîza **244** 30 0N 31 10 E
Gizhduvan **183** 40 6N 64 41 E
Gizhiga **185** 62 3N 160 30 E
Gizhiginskaya, Guba **185** 61 0N 158 0 E
Giżycko **152** 54 2N 21 48 E
Gizzeria **165** 38 57N 16 10 E
Gjegjan **168** 41 58N 20 3 E
Gjerstad **171** 58 54N 9 0 E
Gjirokastra **168** 40 7N 20 10 E
Gjoa Haven **95** 68 38N 95 53W
Gjøl **173** 57 4N 9 42 E
Gjøvik **171** 60 47N 10 43 E
Glace Bay **81** 46 11N 59 58W
Glacier Nat. Park **93** 51 15N 117 30W
Glacier Str. **95** 76 12N 79 15W
Gladmar **88** 49 10N 104 27W
Gladstone, S. Austral., Australia **231** 33 15 S 138 22 E
Gladstone, W. Austral., Australia **229** 25 57 S 114 17 E
Gladstone, Canada **89** 50 13N 98 57W
Gladys L. **76** 59 50N 133 0W
Glafsfjorden **172** 59 30N 12 37 E
Głagów Małapolski **151** 50 10N 21 56 E
Glåma **174** 65 48N 23 0W
Glåma → **171** 59 12N 10 57 E
Glamoč **163** 44 3N 16 51 E
Glan **173** 58 37N 16 0 E
Glanerbrug **142** 52 13N 6 58 E
Glarner Alpen **149** 46 50N 9 0 E
Glärnisch **149** 47 0N 9 0 E
Glarus **149** 47 3N 9 4 E
Glarus □ **149** 47 0N 9 5 E
Glasgow **134** 55 52N 4 14W
Glaslyn **88** 53 22N 108 21W
Glastonbury **133** 51 9N 2 42W
Glatt → **149** 47 28N 8 32 E
Glattfelden **149** 47 33N 8 30 E
Glauchau **146** 50 50N 12 33 E
Glazov **179** 58 9N 52 40 E
Gleisdorf **150** 47 6N 15 44 E
Gleiwitz = Gliwice **152** 50 22N 18 41 E
Glen Affric **134** 57 15N 5 0W
Glen Afton **234** 37 37 S 175 4 E
Glen Almond **82** 45 42N 75 29W
Glen Coe **132** 56 40N 5 0W
Glen Ewen **89** 49 12N 102 1W
Glen Garry **134** 57 3N 5 7W
Glen Gowrie **232** 31 4 S 143 10 E
Glen Innes **231** 29 44 S 151 44 E
Glen Massey **234** 37 38 S 175 2 E
Glen Mor **134** 57 12N 4 37 E
Glen Moriston **134** 57 10N 4 58W
Glen Orchy **134** 56 27N 4 52W
Glen Spean **134** 56 53N 4 40W
Glen Valley **231** 36 54 S 147 28 E
Glénans, Îles. de **138** 47 42N 4 0W
Glenariff **233** 30 50 S 146 33 E
Glenavon **88** 50 12N 103 8W
Glenavy **235** 44 54 S 171 7 E
Glenboro **89** 49 33N 99 17W
Glenburgh **229** 25 26 S 116 6 E
Glenburn **233** 37 27 S 145 26 E
Glencoe, Canada **84** 42 45N 81 43W
Glencoe, S. Africa **255** 28 11 S 30 11 E
Glendale, Canada **81** 45 49N 61 18W
Glendale, Zimbabwe **251** 17 22 S 31 5 E
Glendon **90** 54 15N 111 10W
Glenelg **232** 34 58 S 138 31 E
Glenelg → **231** 38 4 S 140 59 E
Glenella **89** 50 33N 99 11W
Glenflorrie **228** 22 55 S 115 59 E
Glengarriff **135** 51 45N 9 33W
Glengyle **230** 24 48 S 139 37 E
Glenham **235** 46 26 S 168 52 E
Glenhope **235** 41 40 S 172 39 E
Glenmary, Mt. **235** 44 0 S 169 55 E
Glenmorgan **231** 27 14 S 149 42 E
Glenorchy, S. Austral., Australia **232** 31 55 S 139 46 E
Glenorchy, Tas., Australia **230** 42 49 S 147 18 E
Glenorchy, Vic., Australia **232** 36 55 S 142 41 E
Glenore **230** 17 50 S 141 12 E
Glenormiston **230** 22 55 S 138 50 E
Glenreagh **231** 30 2 S 153 1 E
Glenrothes **134** 56 12N 3 11W
Glenrowan **233** 36 29 S 146 13 E
Glenroy **232** 37 13 S 140 48 E
Glenties **135** 54 48N 8 18W
Glenwood, Alta., Canada **91** 49 21N 113 31W
Glenwood, Newf., Canada **79** 49 0N 54 58W
Gletsch **149** 46 34N 8 22 E
Glina **163** 45 20N 16 6 E
Glinojeck **152** 52 49N 20 21 E
Glittertind **171** 61 40N 8 32 E
Gliwice **152** 50 22N 18 41 E
Glodeanu Siliştea **170** 44 50N 26 48 E
Glödnitz **150** 46 53N 14 7 E
Glodyany **170** 47 45N 27 31 E
Gloggnitz **150** 47 41N 15 56 E
Głogów **152** 51 37N 16 5 E
Głogowek **152** 50 21N 17 53 E
Gloria **102** 26 41N 101 23W
Gloria, La **118** 8 37N 73 48W
Gloria, Sa. de la **102** 26 45N 101 10W
Glorieuses, Îles **255** 11 30 S 47 20 E
Glossop **132** 53 27N 1 56W
Gloucester, Australia **231** 32 0 S 151 59 E
Gloucester, U.K. **133** 51 52N 2 15W
Gloucester, C. **227** 5 26 S 148 21 E
Gloucester I. **230** 20 0 S 148 30 E
Gloucestershire □ **133** 51 44N 2 10W
Glovertown **75** 48 40N 54 3W
Główno **152** 51 59N 19 42 E
Głubczyce **152** 50 13N 17 52 E
Glubokiy **181** 48 35N 40 25 E
Glubokoye **178** 55 10N 27 45 E
Glŭbovo **167** 42 8N 25 55 E
Głuchołazy **152** 50 19N 17 24 E
Glücksburg **146** 54 48N 9 34 E
Glückstadt **146** 53 46N 9 28 E
Gluepot **232** 33 45 S 140 0 E
Glukhov **178** 51 40N 33 58 E
Glussk **178** 52 53N 28 41 E
Glyngøre **173** 56 46N 8 52 E
Gmünd, Kärnten, Austria **150** 46 54N 13 31 E
Gmünd, Niederösterreich, Austria **150** 48 45N 15 0 E
Gmunden **150** 47 55N 13 48 E
Gnali **252** 2 34 S 11 18 E
Gnarp **172** 62 3N 17 16 E
Gnesta **172** 59 3N 17 17 E
Gniew **152** 53 50N 18 50 E
Gniewkowo **152** 52 54N 18 25 E
Gniezno **152** 52 30N 17 35 E
Gnjilane **166** 42 28N 21 29 E
Gnoien **146** 53 58N 12 41 E
Gnosjö **173** 57 22N 13 43 E
Gnowangerup **229** 33 58 S 117 59 E
Go Cong **205** 10 22N 106 40 E
Gō-no-ura **220** 33 44N 129 40 E
Go Quao **205** 9 43N 105 17 E
Goa, India **201** 15 33N 73 59 E
Goa, Phil. **210** 13 42N 123 29 E
Goa □ **201** 15 33N 73 59 E
Goalen Hd. **231** 36 33 S 150 4 E
Goalpara **202** 26 10N 90 40 E
Goalundo Ghat **199** 23 50N 89 47 E
Goaso **246** 6 48N 2 30W
Goat Fell **134** 55 37N 5 11W
Goba **245** 7 1N 39 59 E
Gobabis **254** 22 30 S 19 0 E
Gobernador Gregores **126** 48 46 S 70 15W
Gobi **214** 44 0N 111 0 E
Gobichettipalayam **201** 11 31N 77 21 E
Gobō, Japan **221** 33 53N 135 10 E
Gobo, Sudan **245** 5 40N 31 10 E
Goch **146** 51 40N 6 9 E
Gochas **254** 24 59 S 18 55 E
Godavari → **200** 16 25N 82 18 E
Godavari Point **200** 17 0N 82 20 E
Godbout **80** 49 20N 67 38W
Godbout → **80** 49 19N 67 36W
Godda **199** 24 50N 87 13 E
Goddua **241** 26 26N 14 19 E
Godech **166** 43 1N 23 4 E
Godegård **173** 58 43N 15 8 E
Goderich **84** 43 45N 81 41W
Goderville **138** 49 38N 0 22 E
Godham **95** 60 55N 60 40W
Godhavn **12** 69 15N 53 38W
Godhra **198** 22 49N 73 40 E
Godinlave **256** 5 54N 46 38 E
Gödöllö **151** 47 38N 19 25 E
Godoy Cruz **124** 32 56 S 68 52W
Gods → **77** 56 22N 92 51W
Gods L. **77** 54 40N 94 15W
Godthåb **12** 64 10N 51 35W
Godwin Austen = K2, Mt. **199** 35 58N 76 32 E
Goeie Hoop, Kaap die **254** 34 24 S 18 30 E
Goéland, L. au **82** 49 50N 76 48W
Goeree **142** 51 50N 4 0 E
Goes **143** 51 30N 3 55 E
Gogama **87** 47 35N 81 43W
Gogango **230** 23 40 S 150 2 E
Gogolin **152** 50 30N 18 0 E
Gogra = Ghaghara → **199** 25 45N 84 40 E
Gogriâl **245** 8 30N 28 8 E
Goiana **120** 7 33 S 34 59W
Goianésia **121** 15 18 S 49 7W
Goiânia **121** 16 43 S 49 20W
Goiás **121** 15 55 S 50 10W
Goiás □ **120** 12 10 S 48 0W
Goiatuba **121** 18 1 S 49 23W
Goirle **143** 51 31N 5 4 E
Góis **154** 40 10N 8 6W
Goisern **150** 47 38N 13 38 E
Gojam □ **245** 10 55N 36 30 E
Gojeb, Wabi → **245** 7 12N 36 40 E
Gojō **221** 34 21N 135 42 E
Gojra **198** 31 10N 72 40 E
Gokak **201** 16 11N 74 52 E
Gokarannath **199** 27 57N 80 39 E
Gokarn **201** 14 33N 74 17 E
Gökçeada **168** 40 10N 25 50 E
Göksu → **190** 36 19N 34 5 E
Gokurt **198** 29 40N 67 26 E
Gola **199** 28 3N 80 32 E
Golaghat **202** 26 30N 94 0 E
Golakganj **199** 26 8N 89 52 E
Golan Heights = Hagolan **189** 33 0N 35 45 E
Golāshkerd **193** 27 59N 57 16 E
Golaya Pristen **180** 46 29N 32 32 E
Golchikha **12** 71 45N 83 30 E
Gold Coast, Australia **231** 28 0 S 153 25 E
Gold Coast, W. Afr. **247** 4 0N 1 40W
Gold River **92** 49 46N 126 3 E
Goldach **149** 47 28N 9 28 E
Gołdap **152** 54 19N 22 18 E
Goldau **149** 47 3N 8 33 E
Goldberg **146** 53 34N 12 6 E
Golden **93** 51 20N 117 59W
Golden Bay **235** 40 40 S 172 50 E
Golden Ears Prov. Park **93** 49 30N 122 25W
Golden Hinde **92** 49 40N 125 44W
Golden Lake **85** 45 34N 77 21W
Golden Prairie **88** 50 13N 109 37W
Golden Rock **201** 10 45N 78 48 E
Golden Vale **135** 52 33N 8 17W
Goldfields **77** 59 28N 108 29W
Goldsand L. **77** 57 2N 101 8W
Goldsworthy **228** 20 21 S 119 30 E
Golegã **155** 39 24N 8 29W
Goleniów **152** 53 35N 14 50 E
Golestānak **193** 30 36N 54 14 E
Golfito **112** 8 41N 83 5W
Golfo Aranci **164** 41 0N 9 35 E
Golfo de Santa Clara **100** 31 45N 114 33W
Golija, Crna Gora, Yugoslavia **166** 43 5N 18 45 E
Golija, Srbija, Yugoslavia **166** 43 22N 20 15 E
Golina **152** 52 15N 18 4 E
Göllersdorf **151** 48 29N 16 7 E
Golo → **141** 42 31N 9 32 E
Golol **256** 3 38N 43 49 E
Golovanevsk **180** 48 25N 30 30 E
Golpāyegān **193** 33 27N 50 18 E
Golra **198** 33 37N 72 56 E
Golspie **134** 57 58N 3 58W
Golub Dobrzyń **152** 53 7N 19 2 E
Golubac **166** 44 38N 21 38 E
Golungo Alto **253** 9 8 S 14 46 E
Golyam Perelik **167** 41 36N 24 33 E
Golyama Kamchiya → **167** 43 10N 27 55 E
Goma, Rwanda **250** 2 11 S 29 18 E
Goma, Zaïre **250** 1 37 S 29 10 E
Gomati → **199** 25 32N 83 11 E
Gombari **250** 2 45N 29 3 E
Gombe **247** 10 19N 11 2 E
Gombe → **250** 4 38 S 31 40 E
Gombi **247** 10 12N 12 30 E
Gomel **178** 52 28N 31 0 E
Gómez Farias, Chihuahua, Mexico **101** 29 17N 107 44W
Gómez Farias, Coahuila, Mexico **103** 24 57N 101 2W
Gómez Farias, Jalisco, Mexico **106** 19 47N 103 29W
Gómez Farías, Tamaulipas, Mexico **103** 23 3N 99 9W
Gómez Palacio **105** 25 34N 103 30W
Gomīshān **193** 37 4N 54 6 E
Gommern **146** 52 5N 11 47 E
Gomogomo **207** 6 39 S 134 43 E
Gomotartsi **166** 44 6N 22 57 E
Gompa = Ganta **246** 7 15N 8 59W
Gomphoi **168** 39 31N 21 27 E
Goms **148** 46 30N 8 15 E
Gonābād **193** 34 15N 58 45 E
Gonaïves **113** 19 20N 72 42W
Gonâve, G. de la **113** 19 29N 72 42W
Gonâve, Î. de la **113** 18 45N 73 0W
Gonbab-e Kāvūs **193** 37 20N 55 25 E
Gönc **151** 48 28N 21 14 E
Gonda **199** 27 9N 81 58 E
Gondal **198** 21 58N 70 52 E
Gonder **245** 12 39N 37 30 E
Gonder □ **245** 12 55N 37 30 E
Gondia **199** 21 23N 80 10 E
Gondola **251** 19 10 S 33 37 E
Gondomar, Portugal **154** 41 10N 8 35W
Gondomar, Spain **154** 42 7N 8 45W
Gondrecourt-le-Château **139** 48 26N 5 30 E
Gong Xian **216** 28 23N 104 47 E
Gong'an **217** 30 7N 112 12 E
Gongcheng **217** 24 50N 110 49 E
Gongga Shan **216** 29 40N 101 55 E
Gongguan **216** 21 48N 109 36 E
Gonghe **212** 36 18N 100 32 E
Gongola □ **247** 8 0N 12 0 E
Gongola → **247** 9 30N 12 4 E
Gongolgon **231** 30 21 S 146 54 E
Gongshan **216** 27 43N 98 29 E
Gongtan **216** 28 55N 108 20 E
Goniadz **152** 53 30N 22 44 E
Goniri **247** 11 30N 12 15 E
Gonjo **216** 30 52N 98 17 E
Gonnesa **164** 39 17N 8 27 E
Gónnos **168** 39 52N 22 29 E
Gonnosfanadiga **164** 39 30N 8 39 E
Gonzaga **210** 18 16N 122 0 E
González **103** 22 48N 98 25W
González Chaves **124** 38 2 S 60 5W
Good Hope, C. of = Goeie Hoop, Kaap die **254** 34 24 S 18 30 E
Good Hope Mt. **92** 51 9N 124 10W
Good Spirit L. **88** 51 34N 102 40W
Goode **231** 31 58 S 133 45 E
Goodenough I. **227** 9 20 S 150 15 E
Gooderham **85** 44 54N 78 21W
Goodeve **88** 51 4N 103 10W
Goodooga **231** 29 3 S 147 28 E
Goodsoil **77** 54 24N 109 13W
Goodwater **88** 49 24N 103 42W
Goole **132** 53 42N 0 52W
Goolgowi **231** 33 58 S 145 41 E
Goolwa **232** 35 30 S 138 47 E
Goomalling **229** 31 15 S 116 49 E
Goombalie **231** 29 59 S 145 26 E
Goonalga **232** 31 45 S 143 37 E
Goonda **251** 19 48 S 33 57 E
Goondiwindi **231** 28 30 S 150 21 E
Goongarrie **229** 30 2 S 121 8 E
Goonumbla **233** 32 59 S 148 11 E
Goonyella **230** 21 47 S 147 58 E
Goor **142** 52 13N 6 33 E
Gooray **231** 28 25 S 150 2 E
Goose → **78** 53 20N 60 35W
Goose Bay **78** 53 15N 60 20W
Goose Cove **79** 51 18N 55 38W
Goose I. **92** 51 57N 128 26W
Goose L. **89** 54 28N 101 30W
Gooty **201** 15 7N 77 41 E
Gopalganj, Bangla. **202** 23 1N 89 50 E
Gopalganj, India **199** 26 28N 84 30 E
Goppenstein **148** 46 23N 7 46 E
Göppingen **147** 48 42N 9 40 E
Gor **157** 37 23N 2 58W
Góra, Leszno, Poland **152** 51 40N 16 31 E
Góra, Płock, Poland **152** 52 39N 20 6 E
Góra Kalwaria **152** 51 59N 21 14 E
Gorakhpur **199** 26 47N 83 23 E
Goražde **166** 43 38N 18 58 E
Gorbatov **179** 56 12N 43 2 E
Gorbea, Peña **156** 43 1N 2 50W
Gorda, Punta **112** 14 20N 83 10W
Gorda, Sa. **107** 21 0N 100 20W
Gordan B. **228** 11 35 S 130 10 E
Gordon **231** 32 7 S 138 20 E
Gordon → **230** 42 27 S 145 30 E
Gordon, I. **126** 54 55 S 69 30W
Gordon Downs **228** 18 48 S 128 33 E
Gordon L., Alta., Canada **90** 56 30N 110 25W
Gordon L., N.W.T., Canada **76** 63 5N 113 11W
Gordon River **229** 34 10 S 117 15 E
Gordonia **254** 28 13 S 21 10 E
Gordonvale **230** 17 5 S 145 50 E
Gore, Australia **231** 28 17 S 151 30 E
Goré, Chad **243** 7 59N 16 31 E
Gore, Ethiopia **245** 8 12N 35 32 E
Gore, N.Z. **235** 46 5 S 168 58 E
Gore Bay **84** 45 57N 82 28W
Gorey **135** 52 41N 6 18W
Gorg **193** 29 29N 59 43 E
Gorgān **193** 36 50N 54 29 E
Gorgona **162** 43 27N 9 52 E
Gorgona, I. **122** 3 0N 78 10W
Gorgora **245** 12 15N 37 17 E
Gorguz **100** 28 56N 111 10W
Gori **181** 42 0N 44 7 E
Gorinchem **142** 51 50N 4 59 E
Gorinhatã **121** 19 15 S 49 45W
Goritsy **179** 57 4N 36 43 E
Gorízia **163** 45 56N 13 37 E
Górka **152** 51 39N 16 58 E

Gorki = Gorkiy **179** 56 20N 44 0 E
Gorki **178** 54 17N 30 59 E
Gorkiy **179** 56 20N 44 0 E
Gorkovskoye Vdkhr. **179** 57 2N 43 4 E
Gørlev **172** 55 30N 11 15 E
Gorlice **152** 49 35N 21 11 E
Görlitz **146** 51 10N 14 59 E
Gorlovka **180** 48 19N 38 5 E
Gorna Dzhumayo = Blagoevgrad **166** 42 2N 23 5 E
Gorna Oryakhovitsa **167** 43 7N 25 40 E
Gornja Radgona **163** 46 40N 16 2 E
Gornja Tuzla **166** 44 35N 18 46 E
Gornji Grad **163** 46 20N 14 52 E
Gornji Milanovac **166** 44 0N 20 29 E
Gornji Vakuf **166** 43 57N 17 34 E
Gorno Ablanovo **167** 43 37N 25 43 E
Gorno-Altaysk **184** 51 50N 86 5 E
Gorno Slinkino **184** 60 5N 70 0 E
Gornyatski **176** 67 32N 64 3 E
Gornyi **218** 44 57N 133 59 E
Gornyy **179** 51 50N 48 30 E
Gorodenka **180** 48 41N 25 29 E
Gorodets **179** 56 38N 43 28 E
Gorodishche, R.S.F.S.R., U.S.S.R. **179** 53 13N 45 40 E
Gorodishche, Ukraine S.S.R., U.S.S.R. **180** 49 17N 31 27 E
Gorodnitsa **178** 50 46N 27 19 E
Gorodnya **178** 51 55N 31 33 E
Gorodok, Byelorussian S.S.R., U.S.S.R. **178** 55 30N 30 3 E
Gorodok, Ukraine S.S.R., U.S.S.R. **178** 49 46N 23 32 E
Goroka **227** 6 7 S 145 25 E
Goroke **232** 36 43 S 141 29 E
Gorokhov **178** 50 30N 24 45 E
Gorokhovets **179** 56 13N 42 39 E
Gorom Gorom **247** 14 26N 0 14W
Goromonzi **251** 17 52 S 31 22 E
Gorongose → **255** 20 30 S 34 40 E
Gorongoza **251** 18 44 S 34 2 E
Gorongoza, Sa. da **251** 18 27 S 34 2 E
Gorontalo **207** 0 35N 123 5 E
Goronyo **247** 13 29N 5 39 E
Górowo Iławeckie **152** 54 17N 20 30 E
Gorredijk **142** 53 0N 6 3 E
Gorron **138** 48 25N 0 50W
Gorssel **142** 52 12N 6 12 E
Gort **135** 53 4N 8 50W
Gorumahisani **199** 22 20N 86 24 E
Gorzkowice **152** 51 13N 19 36 E
Gorzno **152** 53 12N 19 38 E
Gorzów Śląski **152** 51 3N 18 22 E
Gorzów Wielkopolski **152** 52 43N 15 15 E
Gorzów Wielkopolski □ **152** 52 45N 15 30 E
Goschen I. **92** 53 48N 130 33W
Göschenen **149** 46 40N 8 36 E
Gose **221** 34 27N 135 44 E
Gosford **231** 33 23 S 151 18 E
Goshen, Canada **81** 45 23N 61 59W
Goshen, S. Africa **254** 25 50 S 25 0 E
Goshogawara **218** 40 48N 140 27 E
Goslar **146** 51 55N 10 23 E
Gospič **163** 44 35N 15 23 E
Gosport **133** 50 48N 1 8W
Gossau **149** 47 25N 9 15 E
Gosse → **230** 19 32 S 134 37 E
Gostivar **166** 41 48N 20 57 E
Gostyń **152** 51 50N 17 3 E
Gostynin **152** 52 26N 19 29 E
Göta älv → **173** 57 42N 11 54 E
Göteborg **173** 57 43N 11 59 E
Gotemba **221** 35 18N 138 56 E
Götene **173** 58 32N 13 30 E
Gotha **146** 50 56N 10 42 E
Gotland **173** 57 30N 18 33 E
Gotse Delchev **167** 41 43N 23 46 E
Gōtsu **220** 35 0N 132 14 E
Göttingen **146** 51 31N 9 55 E
Gottwaldov **151** 49 14N 17 40 E
Goubangzi **215** 41 20N 121 52 E
Gouda **142** 52 1N 4 42 E
Goudiry **246** 14 15N 12 45W
Gough I. **129** 40 10 S 9 45W
Gough L. **91** 52 2N 112 28W
Gouin Rés. **82** 48 35N 74 40W
Gouitafla **246** 7 30N 5 53W
Goula Touila **240** 21 50N 1 57W
Goulais → **87** 46 43N 84 27W
Goulburn **231** 34 44 S 149 44 E
Goulburn Is. **230** 11 40 S 133 20 E
Goulia **246** 10 1N 7 11W
Goulimine **240** 28 56N 10 0W
Goulmina **240** 31 41N 4 57W
Gouménissa **168** 40 56N 22 37 E
Gounou-Gaya **243** 9 38N 15 31 E
Goúra **169** 37 56N 22 20 E
Gourara **240** 29 0N 0 30 E
Gouraya **240** 36 31N 1 56 E
Gourdon **140** 44 44N 1 23 E
Gouré **247** 14 0N 10 10 E
Gouri **243** 19 36N 19 36 E
Gourits → **254** 34 21 S 21 52 E
Gourma Rharous **247** 16 55N 1 50W
Gournay-en-Bray **139** 49 29N 1 44 E
Gourock Ra. **231** 36 0 S 149 25 E
Goursi **246** 12 42N 2 37W
Gouvêa **121** 18 27 S 43 44W
Gouzon **140** 46 12N 2 14 E
Govan **88** 51 20N 105 0W
Governador Valadares **121** 18 15 S 41 57W
Governor's Harbour **112** 25 10N 76 14W
Gowan Ra. **230** 25 0 S 145 0 E
Gower, The **133** 51 35N 4 10W
Gowna, L. **135** 53 52N 7 35W
Gowrie, Carse of **134** 56 30N 3 10W
Goya **124** 29 10 S 59 10W
Goyder Lagoon **231** 27 3 S 138 58 E
Goyelle, L. **80** 50 47N 60 45W
Goyllarisquisga **122** 10 31 S 76 24W
Goz Beïda **243** 12 10N 21 20 E
Goz Regeb **245** 16 3N 35 33 E
Gozdnica **152** 51 28N 15 4 E
Gözneköy **190** 36 58N 34 33 E
Gozo **160** 36 0N 14 13 E
Graaff-Reinet **254** 32 13 S 24 32 E
Grabow, Germany **146** 53 17N 11 31 E
Grabów, Poland **152** 51 31N 18 7 E
Grabs **149** 47 11N 9 27 E
Gračac **163** 44 18N 15 57 E
Gračanica **166** 44 43N 18 18 E
Graçay **139** 47 10N 1 50 E
Grace, L. (North) **229** 33 10 S 118 20 E
Grace, L. (South) **229** 33 15 S 118 25 E
Gracefield **82** 46 6N 76 3W
Grachevka **182** 52 55N 52 52 E
Gracias a Dios, C. **112** 15 0N 83 10W
Gradačac **166** 44 52N 18 26 E
Gradaús **120** 7 43 S 51 11W
Gradaús, Serra dos **120** 8 0 S 50 45W
Gradeška Planina **166** 41 30N 22 15 E
Gradets **167** 42 46N 26 30 E
Grado, Italy **163** 45 40N 13 20 E
Grado, Spain **154** 43 23N 6 4W
Gradule **231** 28 32 S 149 15 E
Graeca, Lacul **170** 44 5N 26 10 E
Graénalon, L. **174** 64 10N 17 20W
Grafenau **147** 48 51N 13 24 E
Gräfenberg **147** 49 39N 11 15 E
Grafton **231** 29 38 S 152 58 E
Gragnano **165** 40 42N 14 30 E
Graham **86** 49 20N 90 30W
Graham → **76** 56 31N 122 17W
Graham Bell, Os. **184** 80 5N 70 0 E
Graham I., B.C., Canada **92** 53 40N 132 30W
Graham I., N.W.T., Canada **95** 77 25N 90 30W
Graham L. **90** 56 35N 114 33W
Graham Land **13** 65 0 S 64 0W
Grahamdale **89** 51 23N 98 30W
Grahamstown **254** 33 19 S 26 31 E
Grahovo **166** 42 40N 18 40 E
Graïba **241** 34 30N 10 13 E
Graide **143** 49 58N 5 4 E
Graie, Alpi **162** 45 30N 7 10 E
Grain Coast **246** 4 20N 10 0W
Grainland **88** 50 59N 106 33W
Grajaú **120** 5 50 S 46 4W
Grajaú → **120** 3 41 S 44 48W
Grajewo **152** 53 39N 22 30 E
Gramada **166** 43 49N 22 39 E
Gramat **140** 44 48N 1 43 E
Grammichele **165** 37 12N 14 37 E
Grámmos, Óros **168** 40 18N 20 47 E
Grampian □ **134** 57 0N 3 0W
Grampian Mts. **134** 56 50N 4 0W
Grampians, The **231** 37 0 S 142 20 E
Gran → **119** 4 1N 55 30W
Gran Altiplanicie Central **126** 49 0 S 69 30W
Gran Chaco **124** 25 0 S 61 0W
Gran Desierto **100** 32 15N 114 30W
Gran Morelos **101** 28 15N 106 30W
Gran Paradiso **162** 45 33N 7 17 E
Gran Sabana, La **119** 5 30N 61 30W
Gran Sasso d'Italia **163** 42 25N 13 30 E
Granada, Nic. **112** 11 58N 86 0W
Granada, Phil. **211** 10 40N 123 2 E
Granada, Spain **157** 37 10N 3 35W
Granada □ **155** 37 18N 3 0W
Granard **135** 53 47N 7 30W
Granby **83** 45 25N 72 45W
Granby → **93** 49 2N 118 27W
Grand → **84** 42 51N 79 34W
Grand Bahama **112** 26 40N 78 30W
Grand Bank **79** 47 6N 55 48W
Grand Bassam **246** 5 10N 3 49W
Grand Bay **81** 45 18N 66 12W
Grand Bend **84** 43 19N 81 45W
Grand Béréby **246** 4 38N 6 55W
Grand-Bourge **113** 15 53N 61 19W
Grand Bruit **79** 47 40N 58 14W
Grand Calumet, Île du **82** 45 44N 76 41W
Grand Canal = Yun Ho → **215** 39 10N 117 10 E
Grand Cayman **112** 19 20N 81 20W
Grand Centre **90** 54 25N 110 13W
Grand Cess **246** 4 40N 8 12W
Grand-Combe, La **141** 44 13N 4 2 E
Grand Coulee **88** 50 26N 104 49W
Grand Erg de Bilma **243** 18 30N 14 0 E
Grand Erg Occidental **241** 30 20N 1 0 E
Grand Erg Oriental **241** 30 0N 6 30 E
Grand Falls **81** 48 56N 55 40W
Grand Forks **93** 49 0N 118 30W
Grand-Fougeray **138** 47 44N 1 43W
Grand Harbour **81** 44 41N 66 46W
Grand I. **89** 52 51N 100 0W
Grand L., N.B., Canada **81** 45 57N 66 7W
Grand L., Newf., Canada **78** 53 40N 60 30W
Grand L., Newf., Canada **79** 49 0N 57 30W
Grand Lac Victoria **74** 47 35N 77 35W
Grand Lahou **246** 5 10N 5 0W
Grand le Pierre **79** 47 41N 54 47W
Grand-Leez **143** 50 35N 4 45 E
Grand-Lieu, Lac de **138** 47 6N 1 40W
Grand-Luce, Le **138** 47 52N 0 28 E
Grand Manan I. **81** 44 45N 66 52W
Grand Marais **86** 47 45N 90 25W
Grand Mère **83** 46 36N 72 40W
Grand Piles **83** 46 40N 72 40W
Grand Popo **247** 6 15N 1 57 E
Grand-Pressigny, Le **138** 46 55N 0 48 E
Grand Rapids **89** 53 12N 99 19W
Grand St.-Bernard, Col. du **148** 45 53N 7 11 E
Grand Santi **119** 4 20N 54 24W
Grand View **89** 51 10N 100 42W
Grandas de Salime **154** 43 13N 6 53W
Grande →, Jujuy, Argentina **124** 24 20 S 65 2W
Grande →, Mendoza, Argentina **124** 36 52 S 69 45W
Grande →, Bolivia **123** 15 51 S 64 39W
Grande →, Bahia, Brazil **120** 11 30 S 44 30W
Grande →, Minas Gerais, Brazil **121** 20 6 S 51 4W
Grande →, Mexico **109** 17 43N 96 56W
Grande →, Spain **157** 39 6N 0 48W
Grande →, Venezuela **119** 8 36N 61 39W
Grande, B. **126** 50 30 S 68 20W
Grande, Coxilha **125** 28 18 S 51 30W
Grande, I. **121** 23 9 S 44 14W
Grande, La → **78** 53 50N 79 0W
Grande, Serra, Goiás, Brazil **120** 11 15 S 46 30W
Grande, Serra, Piauí, Brazil **120** 8 0 S 45 0W
Grande-Anse **81** 47 48N 65 11W
Grande Baie **83** 48 19N 70 52W
Grande Baleine, R. de la → **78** 55 16N 77 47W
Grande Cache **90** 53 53N 119 8W
Grande-Cascapédia **80** 48 15N 65 54W
Grande de Santiago, R. → **104** 21 36N 105 26W
Grande Dixence, Barr. de la **148** 46 5N 7 23 E
Grande-Entrée **81** 47 30N 61 40W
Grande-Motte, La **141** 43 23N 4 3 E
Grande Pointe **89** 49 46N 97 3W
Grande Prairie **90** 55 10N 118 50W
Grande-Rivière **80** 48 26N 64 30W
Grande-Saulde → **139** 47 22N 1 55 E
Grande-Vallée **80** 49 14N 65 8W
Grandes-Bergeronnes **83** 48 16N 69 35W
Grandeza, La **110** 15 32N 92 14W
Grandmesnil, L. **80** 51 19N 67 33W
Grandoe Mines **76** 56 29N 129 54W
Grândola **155** 38 12N 8 35W
Grandpré **139** 49 20N 4 50 E
Grandson **148** 46 49N 6 39 E
Grandvilliers **139** 49 40N 1 57 E
Graneros **124** 34 5 S 70 45W
Granet, L. **82** 47 47N 77 31W
Grangemouth **134** 56 1N 3 43W
Grängesberg **172** 60 6N 15 1 E
Granite Peak **229** 25 40 S 121 20 E
Granite Pt. **79** 50 31N 56 17W
Granitnyy, Pik **183** 39 32N 70 20 E
Granity **235** 41 39 S 171 51 E
Granja **120** 3 7 S 40 50W
Granja de Moreruela **154** 41 48N 5 44W
Granja de Torrehermosa **155** 38 19N 5 35W
Gränna **173** 58 1N 14 28 E
Granollers **156** 41 39N 2 18 E
Gransee **146** 53 0N 13 10 E
Grant, I. **228** 11 10 S 132 52 E
Grantham **132** 52 55N 0 39W
Grantown-on-Spey **134** 57 19N 3 36W
Granville **138** 48 50N 1 35W
Granville L. **77** 56 18N 100 30W
Grao de Gandía **157** 39 0N 0 7W
Gras, L. de **94** 64 30N 110 30W
Graskop **255** 24 56 S 30 49 E
Gräsö **172** 60 28N 18 35 E
Grass → **77** 56 3N 96 33W
Grass River Prov. Park **77** 54 40N 100 50W
Grassano **165** 40 38N 16 17 E
Grasse **141** 43 38N 6 56 E
Grasset, L. **82** 49 55N 78 10W
Grassmere **231** 31 24 S 142 38 E
Grassy Lake **91** 49 49N 111 43W
Graubünden □ **149** 46 45N 9 30 E
Graulhet **140** 43 45N 1 58 E
Graus **156** 42 11N 0 20 E
Gravatá **120** 8 10 S 35 29W
Grave **142** 51 46N 5 44 E
Grave, Pte. de **140** 45 34N 1 4W
's-Graveland **142** 52 15N 5 7 E
Gravelbourg **88** 49 50N 106 35W
Gravelines **139** 51 0N 2 10 E
's-Gravendeel **142** 51 47N 4 37 E
's-Gravenhage **142** 52 7N 4 17 E
Gravenhurst **84** 44 52N 79 20W
's-Gravenpolder **143** 51 28N 3 54 E
's-Gravensande **142** 52 0N 4 9 E
Gravesend, Australia **231** 29 35 S 150 20 E
Gravesend, U.K. **133** 51 25N 0 22 E
Gravina di Púglia **165** 40 48N 16 25 E
Gravois, Pointe-à- **113** 16 15N 73 56W
Gravone → **141** 41 58N 8 45 E
Gray **139** 47 27N 5 35 E
Grayling → **76** 59 21N 125 0W
Grayson **88** 50 45N 102 40W
Graz **150** 47 4N 15 27 E
Grazalema **155** 36 46N 5 23W
Grdelica **166** 42 55N 22 3 E
Greasy L. **76** 62 55N 122 12W
Great Abaco I. **112** 26 25N 77 10W
Great Australia Basin **230** 26 0 S 140 0 E
Great Australian Bight **229** 33 30 S 130 0 E
Great Bahama Bank **112** 23 15N 78 0W
Great Barrier I. **234** 36 11 S 175 25 E
Great Barrier Reef **230** 18 0 S 146 50 E
Great Bear → **94** 65 0N 124 0W
Great Bear L. **94** 65 30N 120 0W
Great Blasket I. **135** 52 5N 10 30W
Great Britain **130** 54 0N 2 15W
Great Burnt L. **79** 48 20N 56 20W
Great Bushman Land **254** 29 20 S 19 20 E
Great Central **92** 49 20N 125 10W
Great Central L. **92** 49 22N 125 10W
Great Dividing Ra. **233** 23 0 S 146 0 E
Great Duck I. **84** 45 40N 82 57W
Great Exuma I. **112** 23 30N 75 50W
Great Falls **89** 50 27N 96 1W
Great Fish →, C. Prov., S. Africa **254** 33 28 S 27 5 E
Great Fish →, C. Prov., S. Africa **254** 31 30 S 20 16 E
Great Guana Cay **112** 24 0N 76 20W
Great Harbour Deep **79** 50 25N 56 32W
Great I. **77** 58 53N 96 35W
Great Inagua I. **113** 21 0N 73 20W
Great Indian Desert = Thar Desert **198** 28 0N 72 0 E
Great Lake **230** 41 50 S 146 40 E
Great Orme's Head **132** 53 20N 3 52W
Great Ouse → **132** 52 47N 0 22 E
Great Palm I. **230** 18 45 S 146 40 E
Great Papuan Plateau **227** 6 30 S 142 25 E
Great Ruaha → **250** 7 56 S 37 52 E
Great Sandy Desert **228** 21 0 S 124 0 E
Great Scarcies → **246** 9 0N 13 0W
Great Sea Reef **226** 16 15 S 179 0 E
Great Slave L. **76** 61 23N 115 38W
Great Stour = Stour → **133** 51 15N 1 20 E
Great Victoria Des. **229** 29 30 S 126 30 E
Great Wall **214** 38 30N 109 30 E
Great Whernside **132** 54 9N 1 59W
Great Winterhoek **254** 33 7 S 19 10 E
Great Yarmouth **132** 52 40N 1 45 E
Greater Antilles **113** 17 40N 74 0W

Greater London □ **133** 51 30N 0 5W
Greater Manchester □ **132** 53 30N 2 15W
Greater Sunda Is. **206** 7 0 S 112 0 E
Grebbestad **173** 58 42N 11 15 E
Grebenka **178** 50 9N 32 22 E
Greco, C. **190** 34 57N 34 5 E
Greco, Mte. **164** 41 48N 14 0 E
Gredos, Sierra de **154** 40 20N 5 0W
Greece ■ **168** 40 0N 23 0 E
Greely Fd. **95** 80 30N 85 0W
Green → **81** 47 18N 68 9W
Green B. **79** 49 45N 55 55W
Green C. **231** 37 13 S 150 1 E
Green Hd. **229** 30 5 S 114 56 E
Green Is. **227** 4 35 S 154 10 E
Green Island **235** 45 55 S 170 26 E
Green Island Bay **211** 10 12N 119 22 E
Green Lake **88** 54 17N 107 47W
Greenland □ **12** 66 0N 45 0W
Greenland Sea **12** 73 0N 10 0W
Greenock **134** 55 57N 4 46W
Greenore **135** 54 2N 6 8W
Greenore Pt. **135** 52 15N 6 20W
Greenough → **229** 28 51 S 114 38 E
Greenough Pt. **84** 44 58N 81 26W
Greenville **246** 5 1N 9 6W
Greenwater L. **86** 48 34N 90 26W
Greenwater Lake **88** 52 30N 103 31W
Greenwater Lake Prov. Park **88** 52 32N 103 30W
Greenwich **133** 51 28N 0 0 E
Greenwood **93** 49 10N 118 40W
Greenwood, Mt. **228** 13 48 S 130 4 E
Gregório → **122** 6 50 S 70 46W
Gregory → **230** 17 53 S 139 17 E
Gregory, L., S. Austral., Australia **231** 28 55 S 139 0 E
Gregory, L., W. Austral., Australia **229** 25 38 S 119 58 E
Gregory Downs **230** 18 35 S 138 45 E
Gregory Ra., Queens., Australia **230** 19 30 S 143 40 E
Gregory Ra., W. Austral., Australia **228** 21 20 S 121 12 E
Greiffenberg **146** 53 6N 13 57 E
Greifswald **146** 54 6N 13 23 E
Greifswalder Bodden **146** 54 12N 13 35 E
Greifswalder Oie **146** 54 15N 13 55 E
Grein **150** 48 14N 14 51 E
Greiner Wald **150** 48 30N 15 0 E
Greiz **146** 50 39N 12 12 E
Gremikha **176** 67 50N 39 40 E
Grenå **173** 56 25N 10 53 E
Grenada ■ **113** 12 10N 61 40W
Grenade **140** 43 47N 1 17 E
Grenadines **113** 12 40N 61 20W
Grenchen **148** 47 12N 7 24 E
Grenen **173** 57 44N 10 40 E
Grenfell, Australia **231** 33 52 S 148 8 E
Grenfell, Canada **88** 50 30N 102 56W
Grenoble **141** 45 12N 5 42 E
Grenville **82** 45 37N 74 36W
Grenville, C. **230** 12 0 S 143 13 E
Grenville Chan. **92** 53 40N 129 46W
Gréoux-les-Bains **141** 43 45N 5 52 E
Gresik **209** 7 13 S 112 38 E
Grèssoney St. Jean **162** 45 49N 7 47 E
Gretna **89** 49 1N 97 34W
Gretna Green **134** 55 0N 3 3W
Grevelingen Krammer **142** 51 44N 4 0 E
Greven **146** 52 7N 7 36 E
Grevená **168** 40 4N 21 25 E
Grevená □ **168** 40 2N 21 25 E
Grevenbroich **146** 51 6N 6 32 E
Grevenmacher **143** 49 41N 6 26 E
Grevesmühlen **146** 53 51N 11 10 E
Grevie **173** 56 22N 12 46 E
Grey →, Canada **79** 47 34N 57 6W
Grey →, N.Z. **235** 42 27 S 171 12 E
Grey, C. **230** 13 0 S 136 35 E
Grey Is. **79** 50 50N 55 35W
Grey Range **231** 27 0 S 143 30 E
Grey Res. **79** 48 20N 56 30W
Grey River **79** 47 35N 57 6W
Greymouth **235** 42 29 S 171 13 E
Greytown, N.Z. **234** 41 5 S 175 29 E
Greytown, S. Africa **255** 29 1 S 30 36 E
Gribanovskiy **179** 51 28N 41 50 E
Gribbell I. **92** 53 23N 129 0W
Griekwastad **254** 28 49 S 23 15 E
Griffith, Australia **231** 34 18 S 146 2 E
Griffith, Canada **85** 45 15N 77 10W
Griffith I. **84** 44 50N 80 55W
Grigoryevka **182** 50 48N 58 18 E
Grijalva, R. → **110** 18 36N 92 39W
Grijpskerk **142** 53 16N 6 18 E
Grillby **172** 59 38N 17 15 E
Grimari **252** 5 43N 20 6 E
Grimaylov **178** 49 20N 26 5 E
Grimbergen **143** 50 56N 4 22 E
Grimma **146** 51 14N 12 44 E
Grimmen **146** 54 6N 13 2 E
Grimsby, Canada **84** 43 12N 79 34W
Grimsby, U.K. **132** 53 35N 0 5W
Grimselpass **149** 46 34N 8 23 E
Grímsey **174** 66 33N 18 0W
Grimshaw **90** 56 10N 117 40W
Grimstad **171** 58 22N 8 35 E
Grindelwald **148** 46 38N 8 2 E
Grindsted **173** 55 46N 8 55 E
Grindstone I. **85** 44 43N 76 14W
Grindu **170** 44 44N 26 50 E
Griñón **154** 40 13N 3 51W
Grintavec **163** 46 22N 14 32 E
Grip **171** 63 16N 7 37 E
Griqualand East **255** 30 30 S 29 0 E
Griqualand West **254** 28 40 S 23 30 E
Grise Fiord **95** 76 25N 82 57W
Grisolles **140** 43 49N 1 19 E
Grisons = Graubünden □ **149** 46 45N 9 30 E
Grisslehamn **172** 60 5N 18 49 E
Grita, La **118** 8 8N 71 59W
Grivegnée **143** 50 37N 5 36 E
Griz Nez, C. **139** 50 50N 1 35 E
Grmeč Planina **163** 44 43N 16 16 E
Groais I. **79** 50 55N 55 35W
Groblersdal **255** 25 15 S 29 25 E
Grobming **150** 47 27N 13 54 E
Grocka **166** 44 40N 20 42 E
Gródek **152** 53 6N 23 40 E
Grodkow **152** 50 43N 17 21 E
Grodno **178** 53 42N 23 52 E
Grodzisk Mázowiecki **152** 52 7N 20 37 E
Grodzisk Wielkopolski **152** 52 15N 16 22 E
Grodzyanka **178** 53 31N 28 42 E
Groenlo **142** 52 2N 6 37 E
Groesbeek **142** 51 47N 5 58 E
Groix **138** 47 38N 3 29W
Groix, I. de **138** 47 38N 3 28W
Grójec **152** 51 50N 20 58 E
Grolloo **142** 52 56N 6 41 E
Gronau, Niedersachsen, Germany **146** 52 5N 9 47 E
Gronau, Nordrhein-Westfalen, Germany **146** 52 13N 7 2 E
Grong **174** 64 25N 12 8 E
Groningen, Neth. **142** 53 15N 6 35 E
Groningen, Surinam **119** 5 48N 55 28W
Groningen □ **142** 53 16N 6 40 E
Groninger Wad **142** 53 27N 6 30 E
Gronlid **88** 53 6N 104 28W
Grönskåra **173** 57 5N 15 43 E
Gronsveld **143** 50 49N 5 44 E
Groot → **254** 33 45 S 24 36 E
Groot Berg → **254** 32 47 S 18 8 E
Groot-Brakrivier **254** 34 2 S 22 18 E
Groot Karoo **254** 32 35 S 23 0 E
Groote Eylandt **230** 14 0 S 136 40 E
Grootebroek **142** 52 41N 5 13 E
Grootfontein **254** 19 31 S 18 6 E
Grootlaagte → **254** 20 55 S 21 27 E
Gros C. **76** 61 59N 113 32W
Gros-Morne **80** 49 15N 65 34W
Gros Morne Nat. Park **79** 49 40N 57 50W
Grosa, P. **157** 39 6N 1 36 E
Grósio **162** 46 18N 10 17 E
Grosne → **141** 46 42N 4 56 E
Gross Glockner **150** 47 5N 12 40 E
Gross Ottersleben **146** 52 5N 11 33 E
Grosse Isle **89** 50 4N 97 27W
Grossenbrode **146** 54 21N 11 4 E
Grossenhain **146** 51 17N 13 32 E
Grosses-Roches **80** 48 57N 67 5W
Grosseto **162** 42 45N 11 7 E
Grossgerungs **150** 48 34N 14 57 E
Groswater B. **78** 54 20N 57 40W
Grote Gette → **143** 50 51N 5 6 E
Grote Nete → **143** 51 8N 4 34 E
Grottáglie **165** 40 32N 17 25 E
Grottaminarda **165** 41 5N 15 4 E
Grottammare **163** 42 59N 13 52 E
Grouard Mission **90** 55 33N 116 9W
Grouin, Pointe du **138** 48 43N 1 51W
Groundhog → **87** 48 45N 82 58W
Grouw **142** 53 5N 5 51 E
Grovedale **90** 55 3N 118 52W
Grožnjan **163** 45 22N 13 43 E
Groznyy **181** 43 20N 45 45 E
Grubbenvorst **143** 51 25N 6 9 E
Grubišno Polje **166** 45 44N 17 12 E
Grudovo **167** 42 21N 27 10 E
Grudusk **152** 53 3N 20 38 E
Grudziądz **152** 53 30N 18 47 E
Gruissan **140** 43 8N 3 7 E
Grumo Áppula **165** 41 2N 16 43 E
Grums **172** 59 22N 13 5 E
Grünberg **146** 50 37N 8 55 E
Grundy Prov. Pk. **84** 45 58N 80 30W
Grungedal **171** 59 44N 7 43 E
Gruñidora **105** 24 12N 101 56W
Gruñidora, Llanos de la **105** 24 10N 102 10W
Grunthal **89** 49 24N 96 51W
Gruyères **148** 46 35N 7 4 E
Gruža **166** 43 54N 20 46 E
Gryazi **179** 52 30N 39 58 E
Gryazovets **179** 58 50N 40 10 E
Grybów **152** 49 36N 20 55 E
Grycksbo **172** 60 40N 15 29 E
Gryfice **152** 53 55N 15 13 E
Gryfino **152** 53 16N 14 29 E
Gryfow Sl. **152** 51 2N 15 24 E
Grythyttan **172** 59 41N 14 32 E
Grytviken **13** 53 50 S 37 10W
Gstaad **148** 46 28N 7 18 E
Gua Musang **205** 4 53N 101 58 E
Guacanayabo, G. de **112** 20 40N 77 20W
Guacara **118** 10 14N 67 53W
Guachípas → **124** 25 40 S 65 30W
Guachiría → **118** 5 27N 70 36W
Guadajoz → **155** 37 50N 4 51W
Guadalajara, Mexico **106** 20 40N 103 20W
Guadalajara, Spain **156** 40 37N 3 12W
Guadalajara □ **156** 40 47N 3 0W
Guadalcanal, Solomon Is. **224** 9 32 S 160 12 E
Guadalcanal, Spain **155** 38 5N 5 52W
Guadalcázar **103** 22 37N 100 24W
Guadalén → **155** 38 5N 3 32W
Guadales **124** 34 30 S 67 55W
Guadalete → **155** 36 35N 6 13W
Guadalhorce → **155** 36 41N 4 27W
Guadalimar → **157** 38 5N 3 28W
Guadalmena → **157** 38 19N 2 56W
Guadalmez → **155** 38 46N 5 4W
Guadalope → **156** 41 15N 0 3W
Guadalquivir → **155** 36 47N 6 22W
Guadalupe = Guadeloupe ■ **113** 16 20N 61 40W
Guadalupe, Brazil **120** 6 44 S 43 47W
Guadalupe, Coahuila, Mexico **102** 28 9N 100 36W
Guadalupe, Nuevo León, Mexico **102** 25 41N 100 15W
Guadalupe, Zacatecas, Mexico **105** 22 45N 102 31W
Guadalupe, Spain **155** 39 27N 5 17W
Guadalupe, Sierra de **155** 39 28N 5 30W
Guadalupe Bravos **101** 31 23N 106 7W
Guadalupe I. **225** 29 0N 118 50W
Guadalupe Victoria, Chihuahua, Mexico **101** 27 31N 108 29W
Guadalupe Victoria, Durango, Mexico **105** 24 27N 104 7W
Guadalupe Victoria, Puebla, Mexico **108** 19 18N 97 18W
Guadalupe y Calvo **101** 26 6N 106 58W
Guadarrama, Sierra de **154** 41 0N 4 0W
Guadeloupe ■ **113** 16 20N 61 40W
Guadeloupe, La **83** 45 57N 70 56W
Guadeloupe Passage **113** 16 50N 62 15W
Guadiamar → **155** 36 55N 6 24W
Guadiana → **155** 37 14N 7 22W
Guadiana Menor → **157** 37 56N 3 15W
Guadiaro → **155** 36 17N 5 17W
Guadiato → **155** 37 48N 5 5W
Guadiela → **156** 40 22N 2 49W
Guadix **157** 37 18N 3 11W
Guafo, Boca del **126** 43 35 S 74 0W
Guafo, I. **126** 43 35 S 74 50W
Guainía □ **118** 2 30N 69 0W
Guainía → **118** 2 1N 67 7W
Guaíra **125** 24 5 S 54 10W
Guaira, La **118** 10 36N 66 56W
Guaitecas, Islas **126** 44 0 S 74 30W
Guajará-Mirim **123** 10 50 S 65 20W
Guaje, L. del **102** 28 0N 103 14W
Guajira □ **118** 11 30N 72 30W
Guajira, Pen. de la **118** 12 0N 72 0W
Gualaceo **118** 2 54 S 78 47W
Gualán **112** 15 8N 89 22W
Gualdo Tadino **163** 43 14N 12 46 E
Gualeguay **124** 33 10 S 59 14W
Gualeguaychú **124** 33 3 S 59 31W
Gualicho, Salina **126** 40 25 S 65 20W
Gualjaina **126** 42 45 S 70 30W
Guam **224** 13 27N 144 45 E
Guamá **120** 1 37 S 47 29W
Guamá → **120** 1 29 S 48 30W
Guamblin, I. **126** 44 50 S 75 0W
Guaminí **124** 37 1 S 62 28W
Guamote **118** 1 56 S 78 43W
Guampí, Sierra de **119** 6 0N 65 35W
Guamúchil **104** 25 28N 108 6W
Guan Xian **216** 31 2N 103 38 E
Guanabacoa **112** 23 8N 82 18W
Guanacaste, Cordillera del **112** 10 40N 85 4W
Guanacevi **104** 25 56N 105 57W
Guanahani = San Salvador **113** 24 0N 74 40W
Guanajay **112** 22 56N 82 42W
Guanajuato **107** 21 1N 101 15W
Guanajuato □ **107** 21 0N 101 0W
Guanajuato, Sa. de **107** 21 15N 101 20W
Guanambi **121** 14 13 S 42 47W
Guanare **118** 8 42N 69 12W
Guanare → **118** 8 13N 67 46W
Guandacol **124** 29 30 S 68 40W
Guane **112** 22 10N 84 7W
Guang'an **216** 30 28N 106 35 E
Guangchang **217** 26 50N 116 21 E
Guangde **217** 30 54N 119 25 E
Guangdong □ **217** 23 0N 113 0 E
Guangfeng **217** 28 20N 118 15 E
Guanghan **216** 30 58N 104 17 E
Guanghua **217** 32 22N 111 38 E
Guangji **217** 29 52N 115 30 E
Guangling **214** 39 47N 114 22 E
Guangning **217** 23 40N 112 22 E
Guangrao **215** 37 5N 118 25 E
Guangshun **216** 26 8N 106 21 E
Guanguan Peninsula **211** 6 50N 126 19 E
Guangwu **214** 37 48N 105 57 E
Guangxi Zhuangzu Zizhiqu □ **216** 24 0N 109 0 E
Guangyuan **216** 32 26N 105 51 E
Guangze **217** 27 30N 117 12 E
Guangzhou **217** 23 5N 113 10 E
Guanhães **121** 18 47 S 42 57W
Guanipa → **119** 9 56N 62 26W
Guanling **216** 25 56N 105 35 E
Guannan **215** 34 8N 119 21 E
Guanta **119** 10 14N 64 36W
Guantánamo **113** 20 10N 75 14W
Guantao **214** 36 42N 115 25 E
Guanyang **217** 25 30N 111 8 E
Guanyun **215** 34 20N 119 18 E
Guapí **118** 2 36N 77 54W
Guápiles **112** 10 10N 83 46W
Guaporé → **123** 11 55 S 65 4W
Guaqui **122** 16 41 S 68 54W
Guara, Sierra de **156** 42 19N 0 15W
Guarabira **120** 6 51 S 35 29W
Guaranda **118** 1 36 S 79 0W
Guarapari **121** 20 40 S 40 30W
Guarapuava **125** 25 20 S 51 30W
Guaratinguetá **125** 22 49 S 45 9W
Guaratuba **125** 25 53 S 48 38W
Guarda **154** 40 32N 7 20W
Guarda □ **154** 40 40N 7 20W
Guardafui, C. = Asir, Ras **236** 11 55N 51 10 E
Guardamar del Segura **157** 38 5N 0 39W
Guardavalle **165** 38 31N 16 30 E
Guardia, La **154** 41 56N 8 52W
Guardiagrele **163** 42 11N 14 11 E
Guardo **154** 42 47N 4 50W
Guareña **155** 38 51N 6 6W
Guareña → **154** 41 29N 5 23W
Guaria □ **124** 25 45 S 56 30W
Guárico □ **118** 8 40N 66 35W
Guarrojo → **118** 4 6N 70 42W
Guarujá **125** 24 2 S 46 25W
Guarus **121** 21 44 S 41 20W
Guasave **104** 25 34N 108 27W
Guascama, Pta. **118** 2 32N 8 24W
Guasdualito **118** 7 15N 70 44W
Guasipati **119** 7 28N 61 54W
Guasopa **227** 9 12 S 152 56 E
Guastalla **162** 44 55N 10 40 E
Guatemala **112** 14 40N 90 22W
Guatemala ■ **112** 15 40N 90 30W
Guatire **118** 10 28N 66 32W
Guaviare → **118** 4 3N 67 44W
Guaxupé **125** 21 10 S 47 5W
Guayabero → **118** 2 36N 72 47W
Guayameo **107** 18 12N 101 19W
Guayaneco, Arch. **126** 47 45 S 75 10W
Guayaquil **118** 2 15 S 79 52W
Guayaquil, G. de **118** 3 10 S 81 0W
Guayaramerín **123** 10 48 S 65 23W
Guayas → **118** 1 23N 74 50W
Guaymas **100** 27 56N 110 54W
Guazapares **101** 27 22N 108 15W
Guazárachic **101** 26 57N 106 43W
Guazhou **217** 32 17N 119 21 E
Guba **251** 10 38 S 26 27 E
Gubakha **182** 58 52N 57 36 E
Gûbâl, Madîq **244** 27 30N 34 0 E
Gubam **227** 8 39 S 141 53 E
Gubat **210** 12 55N 124 7 E
Gúbbio **163** 43 20N 12 34 E
Gubin **152** 51 57N 14 43 E
Gubio **247** 12 30N 12 42 E
Gubkin **179** 51 17N 37 32 E

Guča 166 43 46N 20 15 E
Gudalur 201 11 30N 76 29 E
Gudata 181 43 7N 40 10 E
Gudenå 173 56 27N 9 40 E
Gudermes 181 43 24N 46 5 E
Gudhjem 173 55 12N 14 58 E
Gudiña, La 154 42 4N 7 8W
Gudivada 201 16 30N 81 3 E
Gudiyattam 201 12 57N 78 55 E
Gudur 201 14 12N 79 55 E
Guebwiller 139 47 55N 7 12 E
Guecho 156 43 21N 2 59W
Guéguen, L. 82 48 6N 77 13W
Guékédou 246 8 40N 10 5W
Guelma 241 36 25N 7 29 E
Guelph 84 43 35N 80 20W
Guelt es Stel 241 35 12N 3 1 E
Guelttara 240 29 23N 2 10W
Guemar 241 33 30N 6 49 E
Guémené-Penfao 138 47 38N 1 50W
Guémené-sur-Scorff 138 48 4N 3 13W
Güémez 103 23 56N 99 0W
Guéné 247 11 44N 3 16 E
Güepi 118 0 9 S 75 10W
Guer 138 47 54N 2 8W
Güer Aike 126 51 39 S 69 35W
Güera, La 240 20 51N 17 0W
Guera Pk. 243 11 55N 18 12 E
Guérande 138 47 20N 2 26W
Guerche, La 138 47 57N 1 16W
Guerche-sur-l'Aubois, La 139 46 58N 2 56 E
Guercif 241 34 14N 3 21W
Guéréda 243 14 31N 22 5 E
Guéret 140 46 11N 1 51 E
Guérigny 139 47 6N 3 10 E
Guernica 156 43 19N 2 40W
Guernsey, Canada 88 51 53N 105 11W
Guernsey, U.K. 138 49 30N 2 35W
Guerrara, Oasis, Algeria 241 32 51N 4 22 E
Guerrara, Saoura, Algeria 240 28 5N 0 8W
Guerrero, Coahuila, Mexico 102 28 20N 100 23W
Guerrero, Tamaulipas, Mexico 102 26 47N 99 20W
Guerrero □ 107 17 40N 100 0W
Guerzim 240 29 39N 1 40W
Gueugnon 141 46 36N 4 4 E
Gügher 193 29 28N 56 27 E
Guglia, P. dal 149 46 28N 9 45 E
Guglionesi 165 41 55N 14 54 E
Gui Jiang → 217 23 30N 111 15 E
Gui Xian 216 23 8N 109 35 E
Guia Lopes da Laguna 125 21 26 S 56 7W
Guichi 217 30 39N 117 27 E
Guider 247 9 56N 13 57 E
Guidimouni 247 13 42N 9 31 E
Guiding 216 26 34N 107 11 E
Guidong 217 26 7N 113 57 E
Guiglo 246 6 45N 7 30W
Guigues 82 47 28N 79 26W
Guijá 255 24 27 S 33 0 E
Guijo de Coria 154 40 6N 6 28W
Guildford 133 51 14N 0 34W
Guilin 217 25 18N 110 15 E
Guillaume-Delisle, L. 78 56 15N 76 17W
Guillaumes 141 44 5N 6 52 E
Guillestre 141 44 39N 6 40 E
Guilvinec 138 47 48N 4 17W
Guimarães, Brazil 120 2 9 S 44 42W
Guimarães, Portugal 154 41 28N 8 24W
Guimaras 211 10 35N 122 37 E
Guimba 210 15 40N 120 46 E
Guimbalete 101 27 2N 103 44W
Guindulman 211 9 46N 124 29 E
Guinea ■ 246 10 20N 10 0W
Guinea, Gulf of 247 3 0N 2 30 E
Guinea-Bissau ■ 246 12 0N 15 0W
Güines 112 22 50N 82 0W
Guines, L. 80 52 8N 61 25W
Guingamp 138 48 34N 3 10W
Guinobatan 210 13 11N 123 36 E
Guiom 211 11 59N 123 44 E
Guipavas 138 48 26N 4 29W
Guiping 217 23 21N 110 2 E
Guipúzcoa □ 156 43 12N 2 15W
Guir, O. → 241 31 29N 2 17W
Guiratinga 123 16 21 S 53 45W
Güiria 119 10 32N 62 18W
Guisamopa 100 28 37N 109 6W
Guiscard 139 49 40N 3 0 E
Guise 139 49 52N 3 35 E
Guitiriz 154 43 11N 7 50W
Guiuan 211 11 5N 125 55 E
Guixi 217 28 16N 117 15 E
Guiyang, Guizhou, China 216 26 32N 106 40 E
Guiyang, Hunan, China 217 25 46N 112 42 E
Guizhou □ 216 27 0N 107 0 E
Gujan-Mestras 140 44 38N 1 4W
Gujarat □ 198 23 20N 71 0 E
Gujiang 217 27 11N 114 47 E
Gujranwala 197 32 10N 74 12 E
Gujrat 197 32 40N 74 2 E
Gukovo 181 48 1N 39 58 E
Gulargambone 233 31 20 S 148 30 E
Gulbarga 200 17 20N 76 50 E
Gulbene 178 57 8N 26 52 E
Gulcha 183 40 19N 73 26 E
Guledagudda 201 16 3N 75 48 E
Gulf, The 193 27 0N 50 0 E
Gulgong 231 32 20 S 149 49 E
Gulin 216 28 1N 105 50 E
Gulistan, Pakistan 198 30 30N 66 35 E
Gulistan, U.S.S.R. 183 40 29N 68 46 E
Gull → 86 49 45N 89 0W
Gull L. 91 52 34N 114 0W
Gull Lake 88 50 10N 108 29W
Gullegem 143 50 51N 3 13 E
Gullringen 173 57 48N 15 44 E
Gulma 247 12 40N 4 23 E
Gulmarg 199 34 3N 74 25 E
Gulnare 232 33 27 S 138 27 E
Gulpen 143 50 49N 5 53 E
Gülpinar 168 39 32N 26 10 E
Gulshad 184 46 45N 74 25 E
Gulsvik 171 60 24N 9 38 E
Gulu 250 2 48N 32 17 E
Gulwe 250 6 30 S 36 25 E
Gulyaypole 180 47 45N 36 21 E
Gum Lake 231 32 42 S 143 9 E
Gumaca 210 13 55N 122 6 E
Gumal → 198 31 40N 71 50 E
Gumbaz 198 30 2N 69 0 E
Gumel 247 12 39N 9 22 E
Gumiel de Hizán 156 41 46N 3 41W
Gumlu 230 19 53 S 147 41 E
Gumma □ 221 36 30N 138 20 E
Gummersbach 146 51 2N 7 32 E
Gummi 247 12 4N 5 9 E
Gümüşhaciköy 180 40 50N 35 18 E
Gumzai 207 5 28 S 134 42 E
Guna 198 24 40N 77 19 E
Guna Mt. 245 11 50N 37 40 E
Gundagai 231 35 3 S 148 6 E
Gundelfingen 147 48 33N 10 22 E
Gundih 209 7 10 S 110 56 E
Gundlakamma → 201 15 30N 80 15 E
Gunebang 233 33 1 S 146 38 E
Güney 190 36 40N 31 52 E
Gungal 233 32 17 S 150 32 E
Gungu 253 5 43 S 19 20 E
Gunisao → 89 53 56N 97 53W
Gunisao L. 89 53 33N 96 15W
Gunnedah 231 30 59 S 150 15 E
Gunniguldrie 233 33 12 S 146 8 E
Gunningbar Cr. → 231 31 14 S 147 6 E
Guntakal 201 15 11N 77 27 E
Guntong 205 4 36N 101 3 E
Guntur 201 16 23N 80 30 E
Gunungapi 207 6 45 S 126 30 E
Gunungsitoli 208 1 15N 97 30 E
Gunupur 200 19 5N 83 50 E
Günz → 147 48 27N 10 16 E
Gunza 253 10 50 S 13 50 E
Günzburg 147 48 27N 10 16 E
Gunzenhausen 147 49 6N 10 45 E
Guo He → 217 32 59N 117 10 E
Guoyang 214 33 32N 116 12 E
Gupis 199 36 15N 73 20 E
Gura Humorului 170 47 35N 25 53 E
Gura-Teghii 170 45 30N 26 25 E
Gurag 245 8 20N 38 20 E
Gurdaspur 198 32 5N 75 31 E
Gurdzhaani 181 41 43N 45 52 E
Gurgaon 198 28 27N 77 1 E
Gurghiu, Munţii 170 46 41N 25 15 E
Gurguéia → 120 6 50 S 43 24W
Gurha 198 25 12N 71 39 E
Guri Dam 119 7 50N 62 52W
Gurk → 150 46 35N 14 31 E
Gurkha 199 28 5N 84 40 E
Gurley 231 29 45 S 149 48 E
Gurué 255 15 25 S 36 58 E
Gurun 205 5 49N 100 27 E
Gurupá 120 1 25 S 51 35W
Gurupá, I. Grande de 119 1 25 S 51 45W
Gurupi 121 11 43 S 49 4W
Gurupi → 120 1 13 S 46 6W
Gurupi, Serra do 120 5 0 S 47 30W
Guryev 181 47 5N 52 0 E
Gus-Khrustalnyy 179 55 42N 40 44 E
Gusau 247 12 12N 6 40 E
Gusev 178 54 35N 22 10 E
Gushan 215 39 50N 123 35 E
Gushi 217 32 11N 115 41 E
Gushiago 247 9 55N 0 15W
Gushikawa 226 26 22N 127 52 E
Gusinje 166 42 35N 19 50 E
Gúspini 164 39 32N 8 38 E
Gusselby 172 59 38N 15 14 E
Güssing 151 47 3N 16 20 E
Gustanj 163 46 36N 14 49 E
Gustavo Sotelo 100 31 36N 113 38W
Güstrow 146 53 47N 12 12 E
Gusum 173 58 16N 16 30 E
Guta = Kalárovo 151 47 54N 18 0 E
Gütersloh 146 51 54N 8 25 E
Gutha 229 28 58 S 115 55 E
Guthalongra 230 19 52 S 147 50 E
Gutian 217 26 32N 118 43 E
Gutiérrez 123 19 25 S 63 34W
Gutiérrez Zamora 108 20 27N 97 5W
Guttannen 149 46 38N 8 18 E
Guyana ■ 119 5 0N 59 0W
Guyang 214 41 0N 110 5 E
Guyenne 140 44 30N 0 40 E
Guyra 231 30 15 S 151 40 E
Guysborough 81 45 23N 61 30W
Guyuan, Hebei, China 214 41 37N 115 40 E
Guyuan, Ningxia Huizu, China 214 36 0N 106 20 E
Guzar 183 38 36N 66 15 E
Guzhang 216 28 42N 109 58 E
Guzhen 217 33 22N 117 18 E
Guzmán, L. de 101 31 20N 107 30W
Gwa 202 17 36N 94 34 E
Gwaai 251 19 15 S 27 45 E
Gwabegar 231 30 31 S 149 0 E
Gwadabawa 247 13 28N 5 15 E
Gwādar 197 25 10N 62 18 E
Gwagwada 247 10 15N 7 15 E
Gwalia 229 28 54 S 121 20 E
Gwalior 198 26 12N 78 10 E
Gwanda 251 20 55 S 29 0 E
Gwandu 247 12 30N 4 41 E
Gwane 250 4 45N 25 48 E
Gwaram 247 10 15N 10 25 E
Gwarzo 247 12 20N 8 55 E
Gwda → 152 53 3N 16 44 E
Gweebarra B. 135 54 52N 8 21W
Gweedore 135 55 4N 8 15W
Gwent □ 133 51 45N 2 55W
Gweru 251 19 28 S 29 45 E
Gwi 247 9 0N 7 10 E
Gwio Kura 247 12 40N 11 2 E
Gwol 246 10 58N 1 59W
Gwoza 247 11 5N 13 40 E
Gwydir → 231 29 27 S 149 48 E
Gwynedd □ 132 53 0N 4 0W
Gyaring Hu 212 34 50N 97 40 E
Gydanskiy P-ov. 184 70 0N 78 0 E
Gyland 171 58 24N 6 45 E
Gympie 231 26 11 S 152 38 E
Gyobingauk 202 18 13N 95 39 E
Gyoda 221 36 10N 139 30 E
Gyoma 151 46 56N 20 50 E
Gyöngyös 151 47 48N 20 0 E
Györ 151 47 41N 17 40 E
Györ-Sopron □ 151 47 40N 17 20 E
Gypsum Palace 232 32 37 S 144 9 E
Gypsum Pt. 76 61 53N 114 35W
Gypsumville 89 51 45N 98 40W
Gyttorp 172 59 31N 14 58 E
Gyula 151 46 38N 21 17 E
Gzhatsk = Gagarin 178 55 38N 35 0 E

H

Ha 'Arava 189 30 50N 35 20 E
Ha Coi 204 21 26N 107 46 E
Ha Dong 204 20 58N 105 46 E
Ha Giang 204 22 50N 104 59 E
Ha Tien 205 10 23N 104 29 E
Ha Tinh 204 18 20N 105 54 E
Ha Trung 204 20 0N 105 50 E
Haacht 143 50 59N 4 37 E
Haag 147 48 11N 12 12 E
Haaksbergen 142 52 9N 6 45 E
Haaltert 143 50 55N 4 1 E
Haamstede 143 51 42N 3 45 E
Haapamäki 174 62 18N 24 28 E
Haapsalu 178 58 56N 23 30 E
Haarlem 142 52 23N 4 39 E
Haast 235 43 51 S 169 1 E
Haast → 235 43 50 S 169 2 E
Haast P. 235 44 6 S 169 21 E
Haastrecht 142 52 0N 4 47 E
Hab Nadi Chauki 198 25 0N 66 50 E
Habana, La 112 23 8N 82 22W
Ḩabarūt 195 17 18N 52 44 E
Habaswein 250 1 2N 39 30 E
Ḩabawnah, W. → 194 17 57N 44 58 E
Habay 76 58 50N 118 44W
Habay-la-Neuve 143 49 44N 5 38 E
Habbān 194 14 21N 47 5 E
Habbānīyah 192 33 17N 43 29 E
Habiganj 202 24 24N 91 30 E
Hablingbo 173 57 12N 18 16 E
Habo 173 57 55N 14 6 E
Haboro 218 44 22N 141 42 E
Haccourt 143 50 44N 5 40 E
Hachenburg 146 50 40N 7 49 E
Hachijō-Jima 221 33 5N 139 45 E
Hachinohe 218 40 30N 141 29 E
Hachiōji 221 35 40N 139 20 E
Hachŏn 215 41 29N 129 2 E
Hachy 143 49 42N 5 41 E
Hacıishaklı 190 36 12N 33 39 E
Hadali 198 32 16N 72 11 E
Hadarba, Ras 244 22 4N 36 51 E
Hadarom □ 191 31 0N 35 0 E
Ḩaḑbaram 195 17 27N 55 15 E
Hadd, Ras al 195 22 35N 59 50 E
Ḩaddā 194 21 27N 39 34 E
Haddington 134 55 57N 2 48W
Haddon Rig 233 31 27 S 147 52 E
Haded Plain 256 9 46N 48 2 E
Hadejia 247 12 30N 10 5 E
Hadejia → 247 12 50N 10 51 E
Haden 231 27 13 S 151 54 E
Ḩadera 189 32 27N 34 55 E
Ḩadera, N. → 189 32 28N 34 52 E
Haderslev 173 55 15N 9 30 E
Hadhra 244 20 10N 41 5 E
Hadhramaut = Ḩaḑramawt 195 15 30N 49 30 E
Hadım 190 36 58N 32 26 E
Hadjeb El Aïoun 241 35 21N 9 32 E
Hadong 215 35 5N 127 44 E
Ḩaḑramawt 195 15 30N 49 30 E
Ḩaḑramawt, W. → 195 16 0N 48 53 E
Ḩadrānīyah 192 35 38N 43 14 E
Hadrians Wall 132 55 0N 2 30W
Hadsten 173 56 19N 10 3 E
Hadsund 173 56 44N 10 8 E
Haeju 215 38 3N 125 45 E
Haenam 215 34 34N 126 35 E
Haerhpin = Harbin 215 45 48N 126 40 E
Hafar al Bāţin 192 28 25N 46 0 E
Hafford 88 52 43N 107 21W
Ḩafirat al 'Aydā 192 26 26N 39 12 E
Ḩafit 195 23 59N 55 49 E
Hafizabad 198 32 5N 73 40 E
Haflong 202 25 10N 93 5 E
Hafnarfjörður 174 64 4N 21 57W
Hafun, Ras 188 10 29N 51 30 E
Hagalil 189 32 53N 35 18 E
Hagari → 201 15 40N 77 0 E
Hagdan 211 11 20N 123 54 E
Hagen 146 51 21N 7 29 E
Hagenow 146 53 25N 11 10 E
Hagensborg 92 52 23N 126 32W
Hagersville 84 42 58N 80 3W
Hagetmau 140 43 39N 0 37W
Hagfors 172 60 3N 13 45 E
Häggenås 172 63 24N 14 55 E
Hagi, Iceland 174 65 28N 23 25W
Hagi, Japan 220 34 30N 131 22 E
Hagolan 189 33 0N 35 45 E
Hagonoy 210 14 50N 120 44 E
Hags Hd. 135 52 57N 9 30W
Hague, C. de la 138 49 44N 1 56W
Hague, The = 's-Gravenhage 142 52 7N 4 17 E
Haguenau 139 48 49N 7 47 E
Hai □ 250 3 10 S 37 10 E
Hai Duong 204 20 56N 106 19 E
Hai'an, Guangdong, China 217 20 18N 110 11 E
Hai'an, Jiangsu, China 217 32 37N 120 27 E
Haicheng, Fujian, China 217 24 23N 117 48 E
Haicheng, Liaoning, China 215 40 50N 122 45 E
Haidar Khel 198 33 58N 68 38 E
Haifa = Ḩefa 189 32 46N 35 0 E
Haifeng 217 22 58N 115 10 E
Haig 229 30 55 S 126 10 E
Haiger 146 50 44N 8 12 E
Haikang 217 20 52N 110 8 E
Haikou 204 20 1N 110 16 E
Ḩā'il 192 27 28N 41 45 E
Hailakandi 202 24 42N 92 34 E
Hailar 213 49 10N 119 38 E
Haileybury 74 47 30N 79 38W
Hailin 215 44 37N 129 30 E
Hailing Dao 217 21 35N 111 47 E
Hailong 215 42 32N 125 40 E
Haimen, Guangdong, China 217 23 15N 116 38 E
Haimen, Jiangsu, China 217 31 52N 121 10 E
Haimen, Zhejiang, China 217 28 40N 121 24 E
Hainan 204 19 0N 110 0 E
Hainan Dao 204 19 0N 109 0 E
Hainaut □ 143 50 30N 4 0 E
Hainburg 151 48 9N 16 56 E
Haines Junction 76 60 45N 137 30W
Hainfeld 150 48 3N 15 48 E
Haining 217 30 28N 120 40 E
Haiphong 204 20 47N 106 41 E
Haiti ■ 113 19 0N 72 30W

Haiya Junction 244 18 20N 36 21 E
Haiyan 217 30 28N 120 58 E
Haiyang 215 36 47N 121 9 E
Haiyuan, Guangxi Zhuangzu, China 216 22 8N 107 35 E
Haiyuan, Ningxia Huizu, China 214 36 35N 105 52 E
Haizhou 215 34 37N 119 7 E
Haizhou Wan 215 34 50N 119 20 E
Haja 207 3 19 S 129 37 E
Hajar Bangar 243 10 40N 22 45 E
Hajdú-Bihar □ 151 47 30N 21 30 E
Hajdúböszörmény 151 47 40N 21 30 E
Hajdúdurog 151 47 48N 21 30 E
Hajdúhadház 151 47 40N 21 40 E
Hajdúnánás 151 47 50N 21 26 E
Hajdúsámson 151 47 37N 21 42 E
Hajdúszoboszló 151 47 27N 21 22 E
Hajiganj 202 23 15N 90 50 E
Hajipur 199 25 45N 85 13 E
Ḥajjah 194 15 42N 43 36 E
Ḥājjī Muḩsin 192 32 35N 45 29 E
Ḥājjīābād, Eşfahan, Iran 193 33 41N 54 50 E
Ḥājjīābād, Hormozgān, Iran 193 28 19N 55 55 E
Hajówka 152 52 47N 23 35 E
Ḥajrah 194 20 14N 41 3 E
Haka 202 22 39N 93 37 E
Hakansson, Mts. 251 8 40 S 25 45 E
Håkantorp 173 58 18N 12 55 E
Hakataramea 235 44 43 S 170 30 E
Ḥakkan 195 20 22N 58 47 E
Hakken-Zan 221 34 10N 135 54 E
Hakodate 218 41 45N 140 44 E
Hakota 221 36 5N 140 30 E
Haku-San 221 36 9N 136 46 E
Hakui 219 36 53N 136 47 E
Hakun 202 26 46N 95 42 E
Hala 197 25 43N 68 20 E
Ḥalab 190 36 10N 37 15 E
Ḥalab □ 190 36 10N 37 10 E
Ḥalaban 194 23 29N 44 23 E
Ḥalabjah 192 35 10N 45 58 E
Halachó 111 20 29N 90 5W
Halaib 244 22 12N 36 30 E
Halanzy 143 49 33N 5 44 E
Hālat' Ammār 192 29 10N 36 4 E
Halbā 190 34 34N 36 6 E
Halbe 244 19 40N 42 15 E
Halberstadt 146 51 53N 11 2 E
Halbrite 88 49 30N 103 33W
Halcombe 234 40 8 S 175 30 E
Halcon, Mt. 210 13 0N 121 30 E
Halden 171 59 9N 11 23 E
Haldensleben 146 52 17N 11 30 E
Haldwani 199 29 31N 79 30 E
Hale → 230 24 56 S 135 53 E
Halen 143 50 57N 5 6 E
Half Assini 246 5 1N 2 50W
Half Island Cove 81 45 21N 61 12W
Halfmoon Bay 235 46 50 S 168 5 E
Halfway → 76 56 12N 121 32W
Ḥalḩul 189 31 35N 35 7 E
Hali, Si. Arabia 244 18 40N 41 15 E
Hali, Yemen 188 18 30N 41 30 E
Haliburton 85 45 3N 78 30W
Halicarnassus 169 37 3N 27 30 E
Halifax, Australia 230 18 32 S 146 22 E
Halifax, Canada 81 44 38N 63 35W
Halifax, U.K. 132 53 43N 1 51W
Halifax B. 230 18 50 S 147 0 E
Halifax I. 254 26 38 S 15 4 E
Halīl → 193 27 40N 58 30 E
Halin 256 9 6N 48 37 E
Halkirk 91 52 17N 112 9W
Hall 150 47 17N 11 30 E
Hall Beach 95 68 46N 81 12W
Hall Pen. 95 63 30N 66 0W
Hall Pt. 228 15 40 S 124 23 E
Hallabro 173 56 22N 15 5 E
Hallands län □ 173 56 50N 12 50 E
Hallands Väderö 173 56 27N 12 34 E
Hallandsås 173 56 22N 13 0 E
Halle, Belgium 143 50 44N 4 13 E
Halle, Halle, Germany 146 51 29N 12 0 E
Halle, Nordrhein-Westfalen, Germany 146 52 4N 8 20 E
Halle □ 146 51 28N 11 58 E
Hallebourg 87 49 40N 83 31W
Hällefors 172 59 47N 14 31 E
Hallein 150 47 40N 13 5 E
Hällekis 173 58 38N 13 27 E
Hallett 231 33 25 S 138 55 E
Hällevadsholm 173 58 35N 11 33 E
Halley Bay 13 75 31 S 26 36W
Hallia → 200 16 55N 79 20 E
Halliday L. 77 61 21N 108 56W
Hallim 215 33 24N 126 15 E
Hallingskeid 171 60 40N 7 17 E
Hällnäs 174 64 19N 19 36 E
Halls Creek 228 18 16 S 127 38 E
Hallsberg 172 59 5N 15 7 E
Hallstahammar 172 59 38N 16 15 E
Hallstatt 150 47 33N 13 38 E
Hallstavik 172 60 5N 18 37 E
Halmahera 207 0 40N 128 0 E
Halmeu 170 47 57N 23 2 E
Halmstad 173 56 41N 12 52 E
Halq el Oued 241 36 53N 10 18 E
Hals 173 56 59N 10 18 E
Halsa 171 63 3N 8 14 E
Halsafjorden 171 63 5N 8 10 E
Hälsingborg = Helsingborg 172 56 3N 12 42 E
Haltdalen 171 62 56N 11 8 E
Haltern 146 51 44N 7 10 E
Halul 195 25 40N 52 40 E
Ḥalvān 193 33 57N 56 15 E
Ham 139 49 45N 3 4 E
Ham Tan 205 10 40N 107 45 E
Ham Yen 204 22 4N 105 3 E
Hamab 254 28 7 S 19 16 E
Hamad 245 15 20N 33 32 E
Hamada 220 34 56N 132 4 E
Hamadān 193 34 52N 48 32 E
Hamadān □ 193 35 0N 49 0 E
Hamadia 241 35 28N 1 57 E
Hamāh 190 35 5N 36 40 E
Ḥamāh □ 190 35 10N 37 0 E
Hamakita 221 34 45N 137 47 E
Hamamatsu 221 34 45N 137 45 E
Hamar 171 60 48N 11 7 E
Hamarøy 174 68 5N 15 38 E
Hamâta, Gebel 244 24 17N 35 0 E
Hamber Prov. Park 93 52 20N 118 0W
Hamburg 146 53 32N 9 59 E
Hamburg □ 146 53 30N 10 0 E
Ḥamḍ, W. al → 192 24 55N 36 20 E
Ḥamḍah 194 19 2N 43 36 E
Ḥamdānah 194 19 59N 40 34 E
Hämeen lääni □ 175 61 24N 24 10 E
Hämeenlinna 174 61 0N 24 28 E
Hamélé 246 10 56N 2 45W
Hamelin Pool 229 26 22 S 114 20 E
Hamelin Pool Bay 229 26 10 S 114 5 E
Hameln 146 52 7N 9 24 E
Hamer Koke 245 5 15N 36 45 E
Hamerkaz □ 191 32 15N 34 55 E
Hamersley Ra. 228 22 0 S 117 45 E
Hamhung 215 39 54N 127 30 E
Hami 212 42 55N 93 25 E
Ḥamīdīyah 190 35 57N 37 5 E
Hamilton, Australia 231 37 45 S 142 2 E
Hamilton, Canada 84 43 15N 79 50W
Hamilton, N.Z. 234 37 47 S 175 19 E
Hamilton, U.K. 134 55 47N 4 2W
Hamilton → 230 23 30 S 139 47 E
Hamilton Hotel 230 22 45 S 140 40 E
Hamilton Inlet 75 54 0N 57 30W
Hamilton Sound 79 49 35N 54 15W
Hamiota 89 50 11N 100 38W
Hamley Bridge 232 34 17 S 138 35 E
Hamm 146 51 40N 7 49 E
Hammam Bouhadjar 241 35 23N 0 58W
Hammamet 241 36 24N 10 38 E
Hammamet, G. de 241 36 10N 10 48 E
Hammarstrand 172 63 7N 16 20 E
Hamme 143 51 6N 4 8 E
Hamme-Mille 143 50 47N 4 43 E
Hammel 173 56 16N 9 52 E
Hammelburg 147 50 7N 9 54 E
Hammeren 173 55 18N 14 47 E
Hammerfest 174 70 39N 23 41 E
Hamneda 173 56 41N 13 51 E
Hamoir 143 50 25N 5 32 E
Hamont 143 51 15N 5 32 E
Hamoyet, Jebel 244 17 33N 38 2 E
Hampden, Canada 79 49 33N 56 51W
Hampden, N.Z. 235 45 18 S 170 50 E
Hampolol 111 19 56N 90 24W
Hampshire □ 133 51 3N 1 20W
Hampshire Downs 133 51 10N 1 10W
Hampstead 81 45 37N 66 5W
Hampton, N.B., Canada 81 45 32N 65 51W
Hampton, Ont., Canada 85 43 58N 78 45W
Hampton Tableland 229 32 0 S 127 0 E
Ḥamrā' 194 15 3N 43 0 E
Hamrat esh Sheykh 245 14 38N 27 55 E
Hamtik 211 10 42N 121 59 E
Hamyang 215 35 32N 127 42 E
Hamzalar 190 37 7N 32 33 E
Han Jiang → 217 23 25N 116 40 E
Han Shui → 217 30 35N 114 18 E
Hanak 192 25 32N 37 0 E
Hanamaki 218 39 23N 141 7 E
Hanang 250 4 30 S 35 25 E
Hanau 147 50 8N 8 56 E
Hanbogd 214 43 11N 107 10 E
Hanceville 93 51 55N 123 2W
Hancheng 214 35 31N 110 25 E
Hanchuan 217 30 40N 113 50 E
Handa, Japan 221 34 53N 137 0 E
Handa, Somalia 256 10 37N 51 2 E
Handan 214 36 35N 114 28 E
Handel 88 52 4N 108 42W
Handen 172 59 12N 18 12 E
Handeni 250 5 25 S 38 2 E
Handeni □ 250 5 30 S 38 0 E
Handlová 151 48 45N 18 35 E
Handub 244 19 15N 37 16 E
Handwara 199 34 21N 74 20 E
Handzame 143 51 2N 3 0 E
Hanegev 189 30 50N 35 0 E
Haney 93 49 12N 122 40W
Hang Chat 204 18 20N 99 21 E
Hang Dong 204 18 41N 98 55 E
Hangang → 215 37 50N 126 30 E
Hangayn Nuruu 212 47 30N 100 0 E
Hangchou = Hangzhou 217 30 18N 120 11 E
Hanggin Houqi 214 40 58N 107 4 E
Hanggin Qi 214 39 52N 108 50 E
Hangklip, K. 254 34 26 S 18 48 E
Hangö 175 59 50N 22 57 E
Hangu, China 215 39 18N 117 53 E
Hangu, Pakistan 197 33 30N 71 10 E
Hangzhou 217 30 18N 120 11 E
Hangzhou Wan 217 30 15N 120 45 E
Hanhongor 214 43 55N 104 28 E
Ḥanīdh 193 26 35N 48 38 E
Ḥanīsh J. 194 13 45N 42 46 E
Haniska 151 48 37N 21 15 E
Hanita 189 33 5N 35 10 E
Hanjiang 217 25 26N 119 6 E
Hanko 175 59 59N 22 57 E
Hankou 217 30 35N 114 30 E
Hanle 199 32 42N 79 4 E
Hanley 88 51 38N 106 26W
Hanmer 84 46 39N 80 56W
Hanmer Springs 235 42 32 S 172 50 E
Hann → 228 17 26 S 126 17 E
Hann, Mt. 228 16 0 S 126 0 E
Hanna 91 51 40N 111 54W
Hannah B. 74 51 40N 80 0W
Hannahs Bridge 233 31 55 S 149 41 E
Hannik 244 18 12N 32 20 E
Hannover 146 52 23N 9 43 E
Hannut 143 50 40N 5 4 E
Hanö 173 56 2N 14 50 E
Hanöbukten 173 55 35N 14 30 E
Hanoi 204 21 5N 105 55 E
Hanover = Hannover 146 52 23N 9 43 E
Hanover, Canada 84 44 9N 81 2W
Hanover, S. Africa 254 31 4 S 24 29 E
Hanover, I. 126 51 0 S 74 50W
Hanpan, C. 227 5 0 S 154 35 E
Hans Meyer Ra. 227 4 20 S 152 55 E
Hanshou 217 28 56N 111 50 E
Hansi 198 29 10N 75 57 E
Hansjö 172 61 10N 14 40 E
Hanson, L. 231 31 0 S 136 15 E
Hant's Harbour 79 48 1N 53 16W
Hantsport 81 45 4N 64 11W
Hanyang 217 30 35N 114 2 E
Hanyin 216 32 54N 108 28 E
Hanyū 221 36 10N 139 32 E
Hanyuan 216 29 21N 102 40 E
Hanzhong 216 33 10N 107 1 E
Hanzhuang 215 34 33N 117 23 E
Haora 199 22 37N 88 20 E
Haoxue 217 30 3N 112 24 E
Haparanda 174 65 52N 24 8 E
Hapert 143 51 22N 5 15 E
Happy Valley 78 53 15N 60 20W
Hapsu 215 41 13N 128 51 E
Hapur 198 28 45N 77 45 E
Ḥaql 191 29 10N 35 0 E
Haquira 122 14 14 S 72 12W
Har 207 5 16 S 133 14 E
Har-Ayrag 214 45 47N 109 16 E
Har Hu 212 38 20N 97 38 E
Har Us Nuur 212 48 0N 92 0 E
Har Yehuda 189 31 35N 34 57 E
Ḥaraḍ, Si. Arabia 195 24 22N 49 0 E
Ḥaraḍ, Yemen 194 16 26N 43 5 E
Haramsøya 171 62 39N 6 12 E
Haranomachi 218 37 38N 140 58 E
Harardera 256 4 33N 47 38 E
Harare 251 17 43 S 31 2 E
Ḥarāsīs, Jiddat al 195 19 30N 56 0 E
Harat 245 16 5N 39 26 E
Harazé, Chad 243 9 57N 20 48 E
Harazé, Chad 243 14 20N 19 12 E
Harbin 215 45 48N 126 40 E
Harbiye 190 36 10N 36 8 E
Harboør 173 56 38N 8 10 E
Harbour Breton 79 47 29N 55 50W
Harbour Grace 79 47 40N 53 22W
Harburg 146 53 27N 9 58 E
Hårby 173 55 13N 10 7 E
Harcourt 81 46 27N 65 15W
Harda 198 22 27N 77 5 E
Hardangerfjorden 171 60 15N 6 0 E
Hardangerjøkulen 171 60 30N 7 0 E
Hardangervidda 171 60 20N 7 20 E
Hardap Dam 254 24 32 S 17 50 E
Hardegarijp 142 53 13N 5 57 E
Harden 233 34 32 S 148 24 E
Hardenberg 142 52 34N 6 37 E
Harderwijk 142 52 21N 5 38 E
Hardey → 228 22 45 S 116 8 E
Harding 255 30 35 S 29 55 E
Harding Ra. 228 16 17 S 124 55 E
Hardisty 91 52 40N 111 18W
Hardoi 199 27 26N 80 6 E
Hardwar = Haridwar 198 29 58N 78 9 E
Hardwicke I. 92 50 27N 125 50W
Hardwicke Island 92 50 26N 125 55W
Hardwood Ridge 81 46 10N 66 1W
Hardy, Pen. 126 55 30 S 68 20W
Hare B. 79 51 15N 55 45W
Hare Bay 79 48 51N 54 1W
Hare Gilboa 189 32 31N 35 25 E
Hare Meron 189 32 59N 35 24 E
Harelbeke 143 50 52N 3 20 E
Haren, Germany 146 52 47N 7 18 E
Haren, Neth. 142 53 11N 6 36 E
Harer 245 9 20N 42 8 E
Harerge □ 245 7 12N 42 0 E
Hareto 245 9 23N 37 6 E
Harfleur 138 49 30N 0 10 E
Hargeisa 256 9 30N 44 2 E
Harghita □ 170 46 30N 25 30 E
Harghita, Mţii 170 46 25N 25 35 E
Hargshamn 172 60 12N 18 30 E
Hari → 208 1 16 S 104 5 E
Ḥarīb 194 14 56N 45 30 E
Haricha, Hamada el 240 22 40N 3 15W
Haridwar 198 29 58N 78 9 E
Harihar 201 14 32N 75 44 E
Hārim 190 36 14N 36 29 E
Harima-Nada 220 34 30N 134 35 E
Haringhata → 202 22 0N 89 58 E
Haringvliet 142 51 48N 4 10 E
Haripad 201 9 14N 76 28 E
Harīrūd → 193 34 20N 62 30 E
Harlech 132 52 52N 4 7W
Harlingen 142 53 11N 5 25 E
Harmånger 172 61 55N 17 20 E
Harmil 245 16 30N 40 10 E
Harmon L. 86 49 56N 90 13W
Härnön 172 62 36N 18 0 E
Härnösand 172 62 38N 18 0 E
Haro 156 42 35N 2 55W
Haro Str. 93 48 30N 123 15W
Harp L. 78 55 5N 61 50W
Harpanahalli 201 14 47N 76 2 E
Harper 246 4 25N 7 43W
Harplinge 173 56 45N 12 45 E
Harrand 198 29 28N 70 3 E
Harrat Khaibar 244 25 45N 40 0 E
Harrat Nawāsīf 244 21 30N 42 0 E
Harricana → 82 50 56N 79 32W
Harrington Harbour 80 50 31N 59 30W
Harris, Canada 88 51 44N 107 35W
Harris, U.K. 134 57 50N 6 55W
Harris, Sd. of 134 57 44N 7 6W
Harris L. 231 31 10 S 135 10 E
Harris Mts. 235 44 49 S 168 49 E
Harris Pt. 84 43 6N 82 9W
Harrismith 255 28 15 S 29 8 E
Harrison, C. 78 54 55N 57 55W
Harrison Hot Springs 93 49 18N 121 47W
Harrison L. 93 49 33N 121 50W
Harriston 84 43 57N 80 53W
Harrogate 132 53 59N 1 32W
Harrow, Canada 84 42 2N 82 55W
Harrow, U.K. 133 51 35N 0 15W
Harrowsmith 85 44 24N 76 40W
Harsefeld 146 53 26N 9 31 E
Harsīn 192 35 12N 46 34 E
Harskamp 142 52 8N 5 46 E
Harstad 174 68 48N 16 30 E
Hart, L. 231 31 10 S 136 25 E
Hartbees → 254 28 45 S 20 32 E
Hartberg 150 47 17N 15 58 E
Hartell 91 50 36N 114 14W
Hartland 81 46 20N 67 32W
Hartland Pt. 133 51 2N 4 32W
Hartlepool 132 54 42N 1 11W
Hartley 251 18 10 S 30 14 E
Hartley Bay 92 53 25N 129 15W
Hartmannberge 254 17 0 S 13 0 E
Hartney 89 49 30N 100 35W
Harty 87 49 29N 82 41W
Harunabad 198 29 35N 73 8 E
Harur 201 12 3N 78 29 E
Harvand 193 28 25N 55 43 E
Harvey, Australia 229 33 5 S 115 54 E
Harvey, Canada 81 45 43N 67 1W
Harwich 133 51 56N 1 18 E
Haryana □ 198 29 0N 76 10 E
Harz 146 51 40N 10 40 E
Harzé 143 50 27N 5 40 E
Harzgerode 146 51 38N 11 8 E

Hasaheisa **245** 14 44N 33 20 E
Hasan Kīādeh **193** 37 24N 49 58 E
Ḥasanābād **193** 32 8N 52 44 E
Hasani **244** 25 0N 37 8 E
Hasanpur **198** 28 43N 78 17 E
Haselünne **146** 52 40N 7 30 E
Hasharon **189** 32 12N 34 49 E
Hashefela **189** 31 30N 34 43 E
Hashima **221** 35 20N 136 40 E
Hashimoto **221** 34 19N 135 37 E
Hashtjerd **193** 35 52N 50 40 E
Ḥāsik **195** 17 22N 55 17 E
Håsjö **172** 63 1N 16 5 E
Haslach **147** 48 16N 8 7 E
Hasle **173** 55 11N 14 44 E
Haslev **172** 55 18N 11 57 E
Hasparren **140** 43 24N 1 18W
Hassa **190** 36 48N 36 29 E
Hasselt, Belgium **143** 50 56N 5 21 E
Hasselt, Neth. **142** 52 36N 6 6 E
Hassene, Adrar **240** 21 0N 4 0 E
Hassfurt **147** 50 2N 10 30 E
Hassi Berrekrem **241** 33 45N 5 16 E
Hassi bou Khelala **241** 30 17N 0 18W
Hassi Daoula **241** 33 4N 5 38 E
Hassi Djafou **241** 30 55N 3 35 E
Hassi el Abiod **241** 31 47N 3 37 E
Hassi el Biod **241** 28 30N 6 0 E
Hassi el Gassi **241** 30 52N 6 5 E
Hassi el Hadjar **241** 31 28N 4 45 E
Hassi er Rmel **241** 32 56N 3 17 E
Hassi Imoulaye **241** 29 54N 9 10 E
Hassi Inifel **241** 29 50N 3 41 E
Hassi Marroket **241** 30 10N 3 0 E
Hassi Messaoud **241** 31 43N 6 8 E
Hassi Rhénami **241** 31 50N 5 58 E
Hassi Tartrat **241** 30 5N 6 28 E
Hassi Zerzour **240** 30 51N 3 56W
Hastière-Lavaux **143** 50 13N 4 49 E
Hastings, Australia **233** 38 18 S 145 12 E
Hastings, Canada **85** 44 18N 77 57W
Hastings, N.Z. **234** 39 39 S 176 52 E
Hastings, U.K. **133** 50 51N 0 36 E
Hastings Ra. **231** 31 15 S 152 14 E
Hästveda **173** 56 17N 13 55 E
Hat Yai **205** 7 1N 100 27 E
Hatanbulag **214** 43 8N 109 5 E
Hatano **221** 35 22N 139 14 E
Hatay □ **190** 36 25N 36 15 E
Hatches Creek **230** 20 56 S 135 12 E
Hatchet L. **77** 58 36N 103 40W
Haţeg **170** 45 36N 22 55 E
Haţeg, Mţii. **170** 45 25N 23 0 E
Hatert **142** 51 49N 5 50 E
Hateruma-Shima **219** 24 3N 123 47 E
Hatfield P.O. **231** 33 54 S 143 49 E
Hatgal **212** 50 26N 100 9 E
Hathras **198** 27 36N 78 6 E
Hato de Corozal **118** 6 11N 71 45W
Hato Mayor **113** 18 46N 69 15W
Hattah **231** 34 48 S 142 17 E
Hattem **142** 52 28N 6 4 E
Hattonford **90** 53 46N 115 42W
Hatvan **151** 47 40N 19 45 E
Hau Bon = Cheo Reo **204** 13 25N 108 28 E
Hau Duc **204** 15 20N 108 13 E
Haug **171** 60 23N 10 26 E
Haugastøl **171** 60 30N 7 50 E
Haugesund **171** 59 23N 5 13 E
Hauhungaroa Ra. **234** 38 42 S 175 40 E
Haulerwijk **142** 53 4N 6 20 E
Haultain → **77** 55 51N 106 46W
Haungpa **202** 25 29N 96 7 E
Hauraki Gulf **234** 36 35 S 175 5 E
Hauran **189** 32 50N 36 15 E
Hausruck **150** 48 6N 13 30 E
Haut Atlas **240** 32 30N 5 0W
Haut-Rhin □ **139** 48 0N 7 15 E
Haut Zaïre □ **250** 2 20N 26 0 E
Haute-Corse □ **141** 42 30N 9 30 E
Haute-Garonne □ **140** 43 28N 1 30 E
Haute-Loire □ **140** 45 5N 3 50 E
Haute-Marne □ **139** 48 10N 5 20 E
Haute-Saône □ **139** 47 45N 6 10 E
Haute-Savoie □ **141** 46 0N 6 20 E
Haute-Vienne □ **140** 45 50N 1 10 E
Hauterive **83** 49 10N 68 16W
Hautes-Alpes □ **141** 44 42N 6 20 E
Hautes Fagnes **143** 50 34N 6 6 E
Hautes-Pyrénées □ **140** 43 0N 0 10 E
Hauteville **141** 45 58N 5 36 E
Hautmont **139** 50 15N 3 55 E
Hautrage **143** 50 29N 3 46 E
Hauts-de-Seine □ **139** 48 52N 2 15 E
Hauts Plateaux **241** 34 14N 1 0 E
Hauzenberg **147** 48 39N 13 38 E
Havana = Habana, La **112** 23 8N 82 22W
Havant **133** 50 51N 0 59W
Havdhem **173** 57 10N 18 20 E
Have, La → **81** 44 14N 64 20W
Havelange **143** 50 23N 5 15 E
Havelian **198** 34 2N 73 10 E
Havelock, N.B., Canada **81** 46 2N 65 24W
Havelock, Ont., Canada **85** 44 26N 77 53W
Havelock, N.Z. **235** 41 17 S 173 48 E
Havelte **142** 52 46N 6 14 E
Haverfordwest **133** 51 48N 4 59W
Haveri **201** 14 53N 75 24 E
Havering **133** 51 33N 0 20 E
Håverud **173** 58 50N 12 28 E
Havîrna **170** 48 4N 26 43 E
Havlíčkův Brod **150** 49 36N 15 33 E
Havneby **173** 55 5N 8 34 E
Havre, Le **138** 49 30N 0 5 E
Havre-Aubert **81** 47 12N 61 56W
Havre Aubert, Î. **81** 47 13N 61 57W
Havre-aux-Maisons, Î. **81** 47 25N 61 47W
Havre-St.-Pierre **80** 50 18N 63 33W
Hawaiian Is. **225** 20 30N 156 0W
Hawaiian Ridge **225** 24 0N 165 0W
Hawarden **88** 51 25N 106 36W
Hawea Flat **235** 44 40 S 169 19 E
Hawea Lake **235** 44 28 S 169 19 E
Hawera **234** 39 35 S 174 19 E
Hawick **134** 55 25N 2 48W
Hawk Junction **87** 48 5N 84 38W
Hawk Lake **86** 49 48N 93 59W
Hawkdun Ra. **235** 44 53 S 170 5 E
Hawke B. **234** 39 25 S 177 20 E
Hawker **232** 31 59 S 138 22 E
Hawkes Bay **79** 50 36N 57 10W
Hawke's Bay □ **234** 39 45 S 176 35 E
Hawkesbury **74** 45 37N 74 37W
Hawkesbury I. **92** 53 37N 129 3W
Hawkesbury Pt. **230** 11 55 S 134 5 E
Hawkwood **231** 25 45 S 150 50 E
Hawrān **189** 32 45N 36 15 E
Hawsh Mūssá **190** 33 45N 35 55 E
Hawzen **245** 13 58N 39 28 E
Hay, Australia **231** 34 30 S 144 51 E
Hay, U.K. **133** 52 4N 3 9W
Hay →, Australia **230** 25 14 S 138 0 E
Hay →, Canada **76** 60 50N 116 26W
Hay, C., Australia **228** 14 5 S 129 29 E
Hay, C., Canada **94** 74 25N 113 0W
Hay Cove **81** 45 45N 60 44W
Hay I. **84** 44 53N 80 58W
Hay L. **76** 58 50N 118 50W
Hay Lakes **91** 53 12N 113 2W
Hay River **76** 60 51N 115 44W
Hayachine-San **218** 39 34N 141 29 E
Hayange **139** 49 20N 6 2 E
Hayato **220** 31 40N 130 43 E
Haydon **230** 18 0 S 141 30 E
Haye-Descartes, La **138** 46 58N 0 42 E
Haye-du-Puits, La **138** 49 17N 1 33W
Hayes → **77** 57 3N 92 12W
Hayjān **194** 16 40N 44 5 E
Haymā' **195** 19 56N 56 19 E
Haynan **195** 15 50N 48 18 E
Ḥayrān **194** 16 8N 43 5 E
Hays, Canada **91** 50 6N 111 48W
Ḥays, Yemen **194** 13 56N 43 29 E
Hayward's Heath **133** 51 0N 0 5W
Ḥayy **195** 20 46N 58 18 E
Haẓafon □ **190** 32 40N 35 20 E
Hazarām, Kūh-e **193** 29 30N 57 18 E
Hazaribag **199** 23 58N 85 26 E
Hazaribag Road **199** 24 12N 85 57 E
Hazebrouck **139** 50 42N 2 31 E
Hazelton **76** 55 20N 127 42W
Hazenmore **88** 49 42N 107 8W
Hazerswoude **142** 52 5N 4 36 E
Ḥaẓeva **192** 30 48N 35 15 E
Hazlet **88** 50 24N 108 36W
Hazlett, L. **228** 21 30 S 128 48 E
Ḥaẓor **189** 33 2N 35 32 E
He Xian, Anhui, China **217** 31 45N 118 20 E
He Xian, Guangxi Zhuangzu, China **217** 24 27N 111 30 E
Head of Bay d'Espoir **79** 47 56N 55 45W
Head of Bight **229** 31 30 S 131 25 E
Head of St. Margarets Bay **81** 44 41N 63 55W
Headlands **251** 18 15 S 32 2 E
Healesville **231** 37 35 S 145 30 E
Heanor **132** 53 1N 1 20W
Heard I. **203** 53 0 S 74 0 E
Hearne B. **77** 60 10N 99 10W
Hearne L. **76** 62 20N 113 10W
Hearst **87** 49 40N 83 41W
Heart's Content **79** 47 54N 53 27W
Heath → **122** 12 31 S 68 38W
Heath Mts. **235** 45 39 S 167 9 E
Heath Pt. **80** 49 8N 61 40W
Heath Steele **81** 47 17N 66 5W
Heathcote **233** 36 56 S 144 45 E
Heatherton **79** 48 17N 58 45W
Hebei □ **214** 39 0N 116 0 E
Hebel **231** 28 58 S 147 47 E
Hebert **88** 50 30N 107 10W
Hebi **214** 35 57N 114 7 E
Hebrides, Inner Is. **134** 57 20N 6 40W
Hebrides, Outer Is. **134** 57 30N 7 40W
Hebron = Al Khalīl **189** 31 32N 35 6 E
Hebron, N.S., Canada **81** 43 53N 66 5W
Hebron, Newf., Canada **78** 58 5N 62 30W
Hebron Fd. **78** 58 9N 62 45W
Heby **172** 59 56N 16 53 E
Hecate I. **92** 51 42N 128 0W
Hecate Str. **92** 53 10N 130 30W
Hecelchakán **111** 20 10N 90 8W
Hechi **216** 24 40N 108 2 E
Hechingen **147** 48 20N 8 58 E
Hechtel **143** 51 8N 5 22 E
Hechuan **216** 30 2N 106 12 E
Hecla I. **89** 51 10N 96 43W
Heddal **171** 59 36N 9 9 E
Hédé, France **138** 48 18N 1 49W
Hede, Sweden **172** 62 23N 13 30 E
Hedemora **172** 60 18N 15 58 E
Hedgehope **235** 46 12 S 168 34 E
Hediondilla **103** 24 58N 100 42W
Hedley **93** 49 22N 120 4W
Hedley B. **94** 73 0N 108 0W
Hedmark fylke □ **171** 61 17N 11 40 E
Hedo **226** 26 52N 128 15 E
Hedrum **171** 59 7N 10 5 E
Heeg **142** 52 58N 5 37 E
Heegermeer **142** 52 56N 5 32 E
Heemskerk **142** 52 31N 4 40 E
Heemstede **142** 52 22N 4 37 E
Heer **143** 50 50N 5 43 E
Heerde **142** 52 24N 6 2 E
's Heerenburg **142** 51 53N 6 16 E
Heerenveen **142** 52 57N 5 55 E
Heerhugowaard **142** 52 40N 4 51 E
Heerlen **143** 50 55N 6 0 E
Heers **143** 50 45N 5 18 E
Heesch **142** 51 44N 5 32 E
Heestert **143** 50 47N 3 25 E
Heeze **143** 51 23N 5 35 E
Ḥefa **189** 32 46N 35 0 E
Ḥefa □ **190** 32 40N 35 0 E
Hefei **217** 31 52N 117 18 E
Hegang **213** 47 20N 130 19 E
Hegyalja **151** 48 25N 21 25 E
Heichengzhen **214** 36 24N 106 3 E
Heide **146** 54 10N 9 7 E
Heidelberg, Germany **147** 49 23N 8 41 E
Heidelberg, C. Prov., S. Africa **254** 34 6 S 20 59 E
Heidelberg, Trans., S. Africa **255** 26 30 S 28 23 E
Heidenheim **147** 48 40N 10 10 E
Heigun-To **220** 33 47N 132 14 E
Heijing **216** 25 22N 101 44 E
Heilbron **255** 27 16 S 27 59 E
Heilbronn **147** 49 8N 9 13 E
Heiligenblut **150** 47 2N 12 51 E
Heiligenhafen **146** 54 21N 10 58 E
Heiligenstadt **146** 51 22N 10 9 E
Heilungkiang □ **142** 48 0N 128 0 E
Heim **171** 63 26N 9 5 E
Heino **142** 52 26N 6 14 E
Heinola **175** 61 13N 26 2 E
Heinsch **143** 49 42N 5 44 E
Heinsun **202** 25 52N 95 35 E
Heirnkut **202** 25 14N 94 44 E
Heishan **215** 41 40N 122 5 E
Heishui, Liaoning, China **215** 42 8N 119 30 E
Heishui, Sichuan, China **216** 32 4N 103 2 E
Heisler **91** 52 41N 112 13W
Heist **143** 51 20N 3 15 E
Heist-op-den-Berg **143** 51 5N 4 44 E
Hejaz = Al Ḥijāz **194** 26 0N 37 30 E
Hejian **214** 38 25N 116 5 E
Hejiang **216** 28 43N 105 46 E
Hejin **214** 35 35N 110 42 E
Hekelegem **143** 50 55N 4 7 E
Hekinan **221** 34 52N 137 0 E
Hekla **174** 63 56N 19 35W
Hekou, Gansu, China **214** 36 10N 103 28 E
Hekou, Guangdong, China **217** 23 13N 112 45 E
Hel **152** 54 37N 18 47 E
Helagsfjället **172** 62 54N 12 25 E
Helan Shan **214** 39 0N 105 55 E
Helchteren **143** 51 4N 5 22 E
Helden **143** 51 19N 6 0 E
Helechosa **155** 39 22N 4 53W
Helene L. **88** 53 33N 108 12W
Helensburgh, Australia **233** 34 11 S 151 1 E
Helensburgh, U.K. **134** 56 0N 4 44W
Helensville **234** 36 41 S 174 29 E
Ḥelez **189** 31 36N 34 39 E
Helgasjön **173** 57 0N 14 50 E
Helgeroa **171** 59 0N 9 45 E
Helgoland **146** 54 10N 7 51 E
Heligoland = Helgoland **146** 54 10N 7 51 E
Heliopolis **244** 30 6N 31 17 E
Hellebœk **172** 56 4N 12 32 E
Helleland **171** 58 33N 6 7 E
Hellendoorn **142** 52 24N 6 27 E
Hellevoetsluis **142** 51 50N 4 8 E
Hellín **157** 38 31N 1 40W
Helmand □ **197** 31 20N 64 0 E
Helmand → **197** 31 12N 61 34 E
Helme → **146** 51 40N 11 20 E
Helmond **143** 51 29N 5 41 E
Helmsdale **134** 58 7N 3 40W
Helmstedt **146** 52 16N 11 0 E
Helnæs **173** 55 9N 10 0 E
Helong **215** 42 40N 129 0 E
Helsingborg **172** 56 3N 12 42 E
Helsinge **172** 56 2N 12 12 E
Helsingfors **175** 60 15N 25 3 E
Helsingør **172** 56 2N 12 35 E
Helsinki **175** 60 15N 25 3 E
Helska, Mierzeja **152** 54 45N 18 40 E
Helston **133** 50 7N 5 17W
Helvellyn **132** 54 31N 3 1W
Helvoirt **143** 51 38N 5 14 E
Helwân **244** 29 50N 31 20 E
Hemavati → **201** 12 30N 76 20 E
Hemford **81** 44 30N 64 47W
Hemmingford **83** 45 3N 73 35W
Hemse **173** 57 15N 18 22 E
Hemsö **172** 62 43N 18 5 E
Hen & Chickens Is. **234** 35 58 S 174 45 E
Henan □ **214** 34 0N 114 0 E
Henares → **156** 40 24N 3 30W
Henashi-Misaki **218** 40 37N 139 51 E
Hendaye **140** 43 23N 1 47W
Henderson **124** 36 18 S 61 43W
Henderson, Mt. **92** 54 16N 128 4W
Hendījān **193** 30 14N 49 43 E
Hendon **231** 28 5 S 151 50 E
Hendorf **170** 46 4N 24 55 E
Hendrix Lake **93** 52 5N 120 48W
Heng Xian **216** 22 40N 109 17 E
Hengcheng **214** 38 18N 106 28 E
Hengdaohezi **215** 44 52N 129 0 E
Hengelo, Gelderland, Neth. **142** 52 3N 6 19 E
Hengelo, Overijssel, Neth. **142** 52 16N 6 48 E
Hengfeng **217** 28 12N 115 48 E
Hengshan, Hunan, China **217** 27 16N 112 45 E
Hengshan, Shaanxi, China **214** 37 58N 109 5 E
Hengshui **214** 37 41N 115 40 E
Hengyang, Hunan, China **217** 26 52N 112 33 E
Hengyang, Hunan, China **217** 26 59N 112 22 E
Hénin-Beaumont **139** 50 25N 2 58 E
Henley Harbour **79** 52 2N 55 51W
Hennan, L. **172** 62 3N 55 46 E
Hennebont **138** 47 49N 3 19W
Hennenman **254** 27 59 S 27 1 E
Hennigsdorf **146** 52 38N 13 13 E
Henrichemont **139** 47 20N 2 30 E
Henrietta, Ostrov **185** 77 6N 156 30 E
Henrietta Maria C. **74** 55 9N 82 20W
Henry Kater, C. **95** 69 8N 66 30W
Henryville **83** 45 8N 73 11W
Hensall **84** 43 26N 81 30W
Hentiyn Nuruu **213** 48 30N 108 30 E
Henty **231** 35 30 S 147 0 E
Henzada **202** 17 38N 95 26 E
Hephaestia **168** 39 55N 25 14 E
Heping **217** 24 29N 115 0 E
Hepu **216** 21 40N 109 12 E
Hepworth **84** 44 37N 81 9W
Heqing **216** 26 37N 100 11 E
Hequ **214** 39 20N 111 15 E
Herad **171** 58 8N 6 47 E
Héraðsflói **174** 65 42N 14 12W
Héraðsvötn → **174** 65 45N 19 25W
Herald Cays **230** 16 58 S 149 9 E
Herāt **197** 34 20N 62 7 E
Herāt □ **197** 35 0N 62 0 E
Hérault □ **140** 43 34N 3 15 E
Hérault → **140** 43 17N 3 26 E
Herbault **138** 47 36N 1 8 E
Herbert → **230** 18 31 S 146 17 E
Herbert Downs **230** 23 7 S 139 9 E
Herbert Inlet **92** 49 20N 125 58W
Herberton **230** 17 20 S 145 25 E
Herbiers, Les **138** 46 52N 1 0W
Herbignac **138** 47 27N 2 18W
Herborn **146** 50 40N 8 19 E
Herby **152** 50 45N 18 50 E
Hercegnovi **166** 42 30N 18 33 E
Hercegovina = Bosna i Hercegovina □ **166** 44 0N 18 0 E
Herðubreið **174** 65 11N 16 21W

Hereford 133 52 4N 2 42W
Hereford, Mt. 83 45 5N 71 36W
Hereford and Worcester □ 133 52 10N 2 30W
Herefoss 171 58 32N 8 23 E
Herekino 234 35 18 S 173 11 E
Herent 143 50 54N 4 40 E
Herentals 143 51 12N 4 51 E
Herenthout 143 51 8N 4 45 E
Herfølge 172 55 26N 12 9 E
Herford 146 52 7N 8 40 E
Héricourt 139 47 32N 6 45 E
Heriot Bay 92 50 7N 125 13W
Herisau 149 47 22N 9 17 E
Hérisson 140 46 32N 2 42 E
Herk → 143 50 56N 5 12 E
Herkenbosch 143 51 9N 6 4 E
Herm 138 49 30N 2 28W
Hermagor-Pressegger See 150 46 38N 13 23 E
Hermanas 102 27 14N 101 14W
Hermannsburg 146 52 49N 10 6 E
Hermannsburg Mission 228 23 57 S 132 45 E
Hermanus 254 34 27 S 19 12 E
Herment 140 45 45N 2 24 E
Hermidale 231 31 30 S 146 42 E
Hermitage, Canada 79 47 33N 55 56W
Hermitage, N.Z. 235 43 44 S 170 5 E
Hermite, I. 126 55 50 S 68 0W
Hermon, Mt. = Ash Shaykh, J. 190 33 25N 35 50 E
Hermosa de Santa Rosa, Sa. 102 27 50N 101 45W
Hermosillo, Baja Calif. N., Mexico 98 32 27N 114 56W
Hermosillo, Sonora, Mexico 100 29 4N 110 58W
Hernad → 151 47 56N 21 8 E
Hernandarias 125 25 20 S 54 40W
Hernández 103 23 2N 102 2W
Hernando 124 32 28 S 63 40W
Herne, Belgium 143 50 44N 4 2 E
Herne, Germany 146 51 33N 7 12 E
Herne Bay 133 51 22N 1 8 E
Herning 173 56 8N 8 58 E
Heroica Caborca 100 30 37N 112 6W
Heroica Huamantla 107 19 19N 97 56W
Heron Bay 87 48 40N 86 25W
Herradura 103 23 1N 101 45W
Herradura, Mesa 103 23 4N 101 43W
Herrera 155 37 26N 4 55W
Herrera de Alcántar 155 39 39N 7 25W
Herrera de Pisuerga 154 42 35N 4 20W
Herrera del Duque 155 39 10N 5 3W
Herrero, Pta. 111 19 17N 87 27W
Herrick 230 41 5 S 147 55 E
Herring Cove 81 44 34N 63 34W
Herrljunga 173 58 5N 13 1 E
Hersbruck 147 49 30N 11 25 E
Herschel 88 51 38N 108 21W
Herschel, I. 94 69 35N 139 5W
Herseaux 143 50 43N 3 15 E
Herselt 143 51 3N 4 53 E
Herstal 143 50 40N 5 38 E
Hersvik 171 61 10N 4 53 E
Hertford 133 51 47N 0 4W
Hertford □ 133 51 51N 0 5W
's-Hertogenbosch 143 51 42N 5 17 E
Hertzogville 254 28 9 S 25 30 E
Hervás 154 40 16N 5 52W
Herve 143 50 38N 5 48 E
Hervey Bay 230 25 3 S 153 5 E
Herwijnen 142 51 50N 5 7 E
Herzberg, Cottbus, Germany 146 51 40N 13 13 E
Herzberg, Niedersachsen, Germany 146 51 38N 10 20 E
Herzele 143 50 53N 3 53 E
Herzliyya 189 32 10N 34 50 E
Herzogenbuchsee 148 47 11N 7 42 E
Herzogenburg 150 48 17N 15 41 E
Ḥeṣār, Fārs, Iran 193 29 52N 50 16 E
Ḥeṣār, Markazī, Iran 193 35 49N 49 24 E
Hesdin 139 50 21N 2 0 E
Hesel 146 53 18N 7 36 E
Heshui 214 36 0N 108 0 E
Heshun 214 37 22N 113 32 E
Heskestad 171 58 28N 6 22 E
Hesperange 143 49 35N 6 10 E
Hesse = Hessen □ 146 50 40N 9 20 E
Hessen □ 146 50 40N 9 20 E
Hettstedt 146 51 39N 11 30 E
Heugem 143 50 49N 5 42 E
Heule 143 50 51N 3 15 E
Heusden, Belgium 143 51 2N 5 17 E
Heusden, Neth. 142 51 44N 5 8 E
Hève, C. de la 138 49 30N 0 5 E
Heverlee 143 50 52N 4 42 E
Heves □ 151 47 50N 20 0 E
Hevron → 189 31 12N 34 42 E
Hewett, C. 95 70 16N 67 45W
Hex River 254 33 30 S 19 35 E
Hexham 132 54 58N 2 7W
Hexi, Yunnan, China 216 24 9N 102 38 E
Hexi, Zhejiang, China 217 27 58N 119 38 E
Hexigten Qi 215 43 18N 117 30 E
Ḥeydarābād 193 30 33N 55 38 E
Heyfield 233 37 59 S 146 47 E
Heysham 132 54 5N 2 53W
Heythuysen 143 51 15N 5 55 E
Heyuan 217 23 39N 114 40 E
Heywood 231 38 8 S 141 37 E
Heze 214 35 14N 115 20 E
Hezhang 216 27 8N 104 41 E
Hi-no-Misaki 220 35 26N 132 38 E
Hibben I. 92 53 0N 132 18W
Hibbs B. 230 42 35 S 145 15 E
Hibernia Reef 228 12 0 S 123 23 E
Hibiki-Nada 220 34 0N 130 0 E
Hickmans Harbour 79 48 6N 53 44W
Hicks Bay 234 37 34 S 178 21 E
Hicks Pt. 231 37 49 S 149 17 E
Hida 170 47 10N 23 19 E
Hida-Gawa → 221 35 26N 137 3 E
Hida-Sammyaku 221 36 30N 137 40 E
Hida-Sanchi 221 36 10N 137 0 E
Hidaka 220 35 30N 134 44 E
Hidaka-Sammyaku 218 42 35N 142 45 E
Hidalgo, Coahuila, Mexico 102 27 47N 99 52W
Hidalgo, Guerrero, Mexico 107 16 55N 98 39W
Hidalgo, Nuevo León, Mexico 102 25 59N 100 27W
Hidalgo, Tamaulipas, Mexico 103 24 15N 99 26W
Hidalgo □ 107 20 30N 99 0W
Hidalgo del Parral 101 26 56N 105 40W
Hidalgo Yalalag 109 17 11N 96 11W
Hidalgotitlán 109 17 47N 94 38W
Hiddensee 146 54 30N 13 6 E
Hidrolândia 121 17 0 S 49 15W
Hieflau 150 47 36N 14 46 E
Hiendelaencina 156 41 5N 3 0W
Hienghène 226 20 41 S 164 56 E
Higashi-matsuyama 221 36 2N 139 25 E
Higashiajima-San 218 37 40N 140 10 E
Higashiōsaka 221 34 40N 135 37 E
Higasi-Suidō 220 34 0N 129 30 E
Higginsville 229 31 42 S 121 38 E
High Atlas = Haut Atlas 240 32 30N 5 0W
High I., Newf., Canada 75 56 40N 61 10W
High I., Newf., Canada 78 52 28N 55 40W
High Level 76 58 31N 117 8W
High Prairie 90 55 30N 116 30W
High River 91 50 30N 113 50W
High Tatra 151 49 30N 20 0 E
High Wycombe 133 51 37N 0 45W
Highbury 230 16 25 S 143 9 E
Highland □ 134 57 30N 5 0W
Highridge 90 54 3N 114 8W
Highrock L. 77 57 5N 105 32W
Higüay 113 18 37N 68 42W
Higuera, La 99 26 20N 111 49W
Hihya 244 30 40N 31 36 E
Hiiumaa 178 58 50N 22 45 E
Híjar 156 41 10N 0 27W
Ḥijāz □ 194 24 0N 40 0 E
Hijāz, Jabal al 194 19 45N 41 55 E
Hiji 220 33 22N 131 32 E
Hijken 142 52 54N 6 30 E
Hijo = Tagum 211 7 33N 125 53 E
Hikari 220 33 58N 131 58 E
Hiketa 220 34 13N 134 24 E
Hikone 221 35 15N 136 10 E
Hilawng 202 21 23N 93 48 E
Hilda 91 50 28N 110 3W
Hildburghhausen 147 50 24N 10 43 E
Hilden 81 45 18N 63 18W
Hildesheim 146 52 9N 9 55 E
Hill → 229 30 23 S 115 3 E
Hill End 233 38 1 S 146 9 E
Hill Island L. 77 60 30N 109 50W
Hill Spring 91 49 17N 113 38W
Hillared 173 57 37N 13 10 E
Hillegom 142 52 18N 4 35 E
Hillerød 172 55 56N 12 19 E
Hillerstorp 173 57 20N 13 52 E
Hilli 202 25 17N 89 1 E
Hillingdon 133 51 33N 0 29W
Hillmond 88 53 26N 109 41W
Hillsborough 113 12 28N 61 28W
Hillsborough B. 81 46 8N 63 5W
Hillside 228 21 45 S 119 23 E
Hillsport 87 49 27N 85 34W
Hillston 231 33 30 S 145 31 E
Hilton Beach 84 46 15N 83 53W
Hilvarenbeek 143 51 29N 5 8 E
Hilversum 142 52 14N 5 10 E
Himachal Pradesh □ 198 31 30N 77 0 E
Himalaya, Mts. 186 29 0N 84 0 E
Himamaylan 211 10 6N 122 52 E
Himara 168 40 8N 19 43 E
Hime-Jima 220 33 43N 131 40 E
Himeji 220 34 50N 134 40 E
Himi 221 36 50N 137 0 E
Himmerland 173 56 45N 9 30 E
Ḥimş 190 34 40N 36 45 E
Ḥims □ 190 34 30N 37 0 E
Hinatuan 211 8 23N 126 20 E
Hinatuan Passage 211 9 45N 125 47 E
Hincada, La 103 22 40N 100 7W
Hinche 113 19 9N 72 1W
Hinchinbrook I. 230 18 20 S 146 15 E
Hinckley 133 52 33N 1 21W
Hindås 173 57 42N 12 27 E
Hindaun 198 26 44N 77 5 E
Hindmarsh L. 231 36 5 S 141 55 E
Hindol 199 20 40N 85 10 E
Hinds 235 43 59 S 171 36 E
Hinds L. 79 48 58N 57 0W
Hindsholm 173 55 30N 10 40 E
Hindu Bagh 197 30 56N 67 50 E
Hindu Kush 183 36 0N 71 0 E
Hindupur 201 13 49N 77 32 E
Hines Creek 90 56 20N 118 40W
Hinganghat 198 20 30N 78 52 E
Hingeon 143 50 32N 4 59 E
Hingoli 200 19 41N 77 15 E
Hinigaran 211 10 16N 122 50 E
Hinlopenstretet 12 79 35N 18 40 E
Hinna = Imi 245 6 28N 42 10 E
Hinna 247 10 25N 11 35 E
Hino 221 35 0N 136 15 E
Hinojosa del Duque 155 38 30N 5 9W
Hinokage 220 32 39N 131 24 E
Hinterrhein → 149 46 40N 9 25 E
Hinton 90 53 26N 117 34W
Hinuangan 211 10 25N 125 12 E
Hinwil 149 47 18N 8 51 E
Hinzır Burnu 190 36 19N 35 46 E
Hipólito 102 25 41N 101 26W
Hippolytushoef 142 52 54N 4 58 E
Hirado 220 33 22N 129 33 E
Hirado-Shima 220 33 20N 129 30 E
Hirakarta 221 34 48N 135 40 E
Hirakud 199 21 32N 83 51 E
Hirakud Dam 199 21 32N 83 45 E
Hirata 220 35 24N 132 49 E
Hiratsuka 221 35 19N 139 21 E
Hirhafok 241 23 49N 5 45 E
Hîrlău 170 47 23N 27 0 E
Hiromi 220 33 13N 132 36 E
Hiroo 218 42 17N 143 19 E
Hirosaki 218 40 34N 140 28 E
Hiroshima 220 34 24N 132 30 E
Hiroshima □ 220 34 50N 133 0 E
Hiroshima-Wan 220 34 5N 132 20 E
Hirsholmene 173 57 30N 10 36 E
Hirson 139 49 55N 4 4 E
Hîrşova 170 44 40N 27 59 E
Hirtshals 173 57 36N 9 57 E
Hisar 198 29 12N 75 45 E
Hisb → 192 31 45N 44 17 E
Ḥismá 191 28 30N 36 0 E
Ḥisn al 'Abr 194 16 8N 47 14 E
Ḥişn al Qarn 195 15 8N 49 7 E
Hispaniola 113 19 0N 71 0W
Hiszachal 102 26 46N 101 8W
Hīt 192 33 38N 42 49 E
Hita 220 33 20N 130 58 E
Hitachi 221 36 36N 140 39 E
Hitachiota 221 36 30N 140 30 E
Hitchcock 88 49 14N 103 7W
Hitchin 133 51 57N 0 16W
Hitoyoshi 220 32 13N 130 45 E
Hitra 171 63 30N 8 45 E
Hitzacker 146 53 9N 11 1 E
Hiuchi-Nada 220 34 5N 133 20 E
Hixon 93 53 25N 122 35W
Ḥiyyon, N. → 189 30 25N 35 10 E
Hjalmar L. 77 61 33N 109 25W
Hjälmare kanal 172 59 20N 15 59 E
Hjälmaren 172 59 18N 15 40 E
Hjartdal 171 59 37N 8 41 E
Hjerkinn 171 62 13N 9 33 E
Hjørring 173 57 29N 9 59 E
Hjorted 173 57 37N 16 19 E
Hjortkvarn 173 58 54N 15 26 E
Hko-ut 202 20 58N 98 2 E
Hkyenhpa 202 27 43N 97 25 E
Hlaingbwe 202 17 8N 97 50 E
Hlinsko 150 49 45N 15 54 E
Hlohovec 151 48 26N 17 49 E
Hlwaze 202 18 54N 96 37 E
Hňak 12 70 40N 52 10W
Ho 247 6 37N 0 27 E
Ho Chi Minh City = Phanh Bho Ho Chi Minh 205 10 58N 106 40 E
Ho Thuong 204 19 32N 105 48 E
Hoa Binh 204 20 50N 105 20 E
Hoa Da 205 11 16N 108 40 E
Hoa Hiep 205 11 34N 105 51 E
Hoai Nhon 204 14 28N 109 1 E
Hoare B. 95 65 17N 62 30W
Hobart 230 42 50 S 147 21 E
Hobbs Coast 13 74 50 S 131 0W
Hobo 118 2 35N 75 30W
Hoboken 143 51 11N 4 21 E
Hobro 173 56 39N 9 46 E
Hobscheid 143 49 42N 5 57 E
Hobson L. 93 52 35N 120 15W
Hoburgen 173 56 55N 18 7 E
Hocabá 111 20 49N 89 15W
Hochdorf 149 47 10N 8 17 E
Hochschwab 150 47 35N 15 0 E
Höchst 147 50 6N 8 33 E
Höchstadt 147 49 42N 10 48 E
Hockenheim 147 49 18N 8 33 E
Hoctún 111 20 52N 89 12W
Hodaka-Dake 221 36 17N 137 39 E
Hodges Hill 79 49 4N 55 53W
Hodgeville 88 50 7N 106 58W
Hodgson 89 51 13N 97 36W
Hódmezővásárhely 151 46 28N 20 22 E
Hodna, Chott el 241 35 30N 5 0 E
Hodna, Monts du 241 35 52N 4 42 E
Hodonín 151 48 50N 17 10 E
Hoeamdong 215 42 30N 130 16 E
Hoëdic 138 47 21N 2 52W
Hoegaarden 143 50 47N 4 53 E
Hoek van Holland 142 52 0N 4 7 E
Hoeksche Waard 142 51 46N 4 25 E
Hoenderloo 142 52 7N 5 52 E
Hoengsŏng 215 37 29N 127 59 E
Hoensbroek 143 50 55N 5 55 E
Hoeryong 215 42 30N 129 45 E
Hoeselt 143 50 51N 5 29 E
Hoëveld 255 26 30 S 30 0 E
Hoeven 143 51 35N 4 35 E
Hoeyang 215 38 43N 127 36 E
Hof, Germany 147 50 18N 11 55 E
Hof, Iceland 174 64 33N 14 40W
Höfðakaupstaður 174 65 50N 20 19W
Hofgeismar 146 51 29N 9 23 E
Hofors 172 60 31N 16 15 E
Hofsjökull 174 64 49N 18 48W
Hofsós 174 65 53N 19 26W
Hōfu 220 34 3N 131 34 E
Hogan Group 230 39 13 S 147 1 E
Hogarth, Mt. 230 21 50 S 137 0 E
Hogenakai Falls 201 12 6N 77 50 E
Högfors 172 59 58N 15 3 E
Hōgo-Kaikyō 220 33 20N 131 58 E
Högsäter 173 58 38N 12 5 E
Högsby 173 57 10N 16 1 E
Högsjö 172 59 4N 15 44 E
Hogsty Reef 113 21 41N 73 48W
Hohe Rhön 147 50 24N 9 58 E
Hohe Tauern 150 47 11N 12 40 E
Hohe Venn 143 50 30N 6 5 E
Hohenau 151 48 36N 16 55 E
Hohenems 150 47 22N 9 42 E
Hohenstein-Ernstthal 146 50 48N 12 43 E
Hohenwestedt 146 54 6N 9 30 E
Hohhot 214 40 52N 111 40 E
Hohoe 247 7 8N 0 32 E
Hoi An 204 15 30N 108 19 E
Hoi Xuan 204 20 25N 105 9 E
Højer 173 54 58N 8 42 E
Hōjō 220 33 58N 132 46 E
Hok 173 57 31N 14 16 E
Hökensås 173 58 0N 14 5 E
Hökerum 173 57 51N 13 16 E
Hokianga Harbour 234 35 31 S 173 22 E
Hokitika 235 42 42 S 171 0 E
Hokkaidō □ 218 43 30N 143 0 E
Hokksund 171 59 44N 9 59 E
Hol-Hol 245 11 20N 42 50 E
Holbæk 172 55 43N 11 43 E
Holberg 92 50 40N 128 0W
Holbox 111 21 33N 87 20W
Holbox, I. 111 21 33N 87 15W
Holbrook 231 35 42 S 147 18 E
Holden 90 53 13N 112 11W
Holder 232 34 21 S 140 0 E
Holderness 132 53 45N 0 5W
Holdfast 88 50 58N 105 25W
Holdich 126 45 57 S 68 13W
Hole 171 60 6N 10 12 E
Hole-Narsipur 201 12 48N 76 16 E
Holešov 151 49 20N 17 35 E
Holguín 112 20 50N 76 20W
Holíč 151 48 49N 17 10 E
Holinshead L. 86 49 39N 89 40W
Hollabrunn 150 48 34N 16 5 E
Hollams Bird I. 254 24 40 S 14 30 E
Hollandsch Diep 143 51 41N 4 30 E
Hollandsch IJssel → 142 51 55N 4 34 E
Höllen 171 58 6N 7 49 E
Holleton 229 31 55 S 119 0 E
Hollfeld 147 49 56N 11 18 E

Hollick Kenyon Plateau 13 82 0 S 110 0W
Hollum 142 53 26N 5 38 E
Holm 172 62 40N 16 40 E
Holman 94 70 44N 117 44W
Hólmavík 174 65 42N 21 40W
Holmedal 171 61 22N 5 11 E
Holmegil 172 59 10N 11 44 E
Holmes Reefs 230 16 27 S 148 0 E
Holmestrand 171 59 31N 10 14 E
Holmsbu 171 59 32N 10 27 E
Holmsjön 172 62 26N 15 20 E
Holmsland Klit 173 56 0N 8 5 E
Holmsund 174 63 41N 20 20 E
Holod 170 46 49N 22 8 E
Holoit, Pta. 111 21 37N 88 8W
Holon 189 32 2N 34 47 E
Holroyd → 230 14 10 S 141 36 E
Holstebro 173 56 22N 8 37 E
Holsteinsborg 95 66 40N 53 30W
Holsworthy 133 50 48N 4 21W
Holt 174 63 33N 19 48W
Holte 172 55 50N 12 29 E
Holten 142 52 17N 6 26 E
Holton 78 54 31N 57 12W
Holum 171 58 6N 7 32 E
Holwerd 142 53 22N 5 54 E
Holy I., England, U.K. 132 55 42N 1 48W
Holy I., Wales, U.K. 132 53 17N 4 37W
Holyhead 132 53 18N 4 38W
Holyrood 79 47 27N 53 8W
Holzkirchen 147 47 53N 11 42 E
Holzminden 146 51 49N 9 31 E
Homa Bay 250 0 36 S 34 30 E
Homa Bay □ 250 0 50 S 34 30 E
Homalin 202 24 55N 95 0 E
Homand 193 32 28N 59 37 E
Homathko → 92 51 0N 124 56W
Homberg 146 51 2N 9 20 E
Hombori 247 15 20N 1 38W
Homburg 147 49 19N 7 21 E
Home B. 95 68 40N 67 10W
Home Hill 230 19 43 S 147 25 E
Homestead, Australia 230 20 20 S 145 40 E
Homestead, Canada 90 55 31N 119 22W
Homnabad 200 17 45N 77 11 E
Homoine 255 23 55 S 35 8 E
Homoljske Planina 166 44 10N 21 45 E
Homonhan I. 211 10 44N 125 43 E
Homorod 170 46 5N 25 15 E
Homs = Ḩimş 190 34 40N 36 45 E
Homún 111 20 44N 89 17W
Hon Chong 205 10 25N 104 30 E
Hon Me 204 19 23N 105 56 E
Hon Quan 205 11 40N 106 50 E
Honan = Henan □ 214 34 0N 114 0 E
Honbetsu 218 43 7N 143 37 E
Honda 118 5 12N 74 45W
Honda Bay 211 9 53N 118 49 E
Hondeklipbaai 254 30 19 S 17 17 E
Hondo, Canada 90 55 4N 114 2W
Hondo, Japan 220 32 27N 130 12 E
Hondo, R. → 111 18 29N 88 19W
Honduras ■ 112 14 40N 86 30W
Honduras, Golfo de 112 16 50N 87 0W
Honey 108 20 15N 98 13W
Honey Harbour 84 44 52N 79 49W
Honfleur 138 49 25N 0 13 E
Hong → 204 20 17N 106 34 E
Hong Gai 204 20 57N 107 5 E
Hong He → 217 32 25N 115 35 E
Hong Kong ■ 217 22 11N 114 14 E
Hong'an 217 31 20N 114 40 E
Hongchŏn 215 37 44N 127 53 E
Honghai Wan 217 22 40N 115 0 E
Honghu 217 29 50N 113 30 E
Hongjiang 216 27 7N 109 59 E
Hongliu He → 214 38 0N 109 50 E
Hongor 214 45 45N 112 50 E
Hongsa 204 19 43N 101 20 E
Hongshui He → 216 23 48N 109 30 E
Hongsŏng 215 36 37N 126 38 E
Hongtong 214 36 16N 111 40 E
Honguedo, Détroit d' 80 49 15N 64 0W
Hongwon 215 40 0N 127 56 E
Hongya 216 29 57N 103 22 E
Hongyuan 216 32 51N 102 40 E
Hongze Hu 217 33 15N 118 35 E
Honiara 224 9 27 S 159 57 E
Honiton 133 50 48N 3 11W
Honjō, Akita, Japan 218 39 23N 140 3 E
Honjō, Gumma, Japan 221 36 14N 139 11 E
Honkawane 221 35 5N 138 5 E
Honkorâb, Ras 244 24 35N 35 10 E
Honshū 219 36 0N 138 0 E
Hontoria del Pinar 156 41 50N 3 10W
Hood, Pt. 229 34 23 S 119 34 E
Hood Pt. 227 10 4 S 147 45 E
Hooge 146 54 31N 8 36 E
Hoogerheide 143 51 26N 4 20 E
Hoogeveen 142 52 44N 6 30 E
Hoogeveensche Vaart 142 52 42N 6 12 E
Hoogezand 142 53 11N 6 45 E
Hooghly → = Hughli → 199 21 56N 88 4 E
Hooghly-Chinsura = Chunchura 199 22 53N 88 27 E
Hoogkerk 142 53 13N 6 30 E
Hooglede 143 50 59N 3 5 E
Hoogstraten 143 51 24N 4 46 E
Hoogvliet 142 51 52N 4 21 E
Hook Hd. 135 52 8N 6 57W
Hook I. 230 20 4 S 149 0 E
Hook of Holland = Hoek van Holland 142 52 0N 4 7 E
Hooker Creek 228 18 23 S 130 38 E
Hooker L. 86 50 35N 91 1W
Hool 111 19 31N 90 27W
Hoopstad 254 27 50 S 25 55 E
Hoorn 142 52 38N 5 4 E
Hopà 181 41 28N 41 30 E
Hope 93 49 25N 121 25 E
Hope, L. 231 28 24 S 139 18 E
Hope I., B.C., Canada 92 50 55N 127 53W
Hope I., Ont., Canada 84 44 55N 80 11W
Hope Town 112 26 35N 76 57W
Hopedale 78 55 28N 60 13W
Hopefield 254 33 3 S 18 22 E
Hopei = Hebei □ 214 39 0N 116 0 E
Hopelchén 111 19 46N 89 51W
Hopen 171 63 27N 8 2 E
Hopes Advance, C. 78 61 4N 69 34W
Hopetoun, Vic., Australia 231 35 42 S 142 22 E
Hopetoun, W. Austral., Australia 229 33 57 S 120 7 E
Hopetown 254 29 34 S 24 3 E
Hopewell 81 45 29N 62 42W
Hopewell Cape 81 45 51N 64 35W
Hopin 202 24 58N 96 30 E
Hopkins, L. 228 24 15 S 128 35 E
Hoptrup 173 55 11N 9 28 E
Hōrai 221 34 58N 137 32 E
Horazdovice 150 49 19N 13 42 E
Horcajo de Santiago 156 39 50N 3 1W
Horcasitas 101 28 22N 105 50W
Horcasitas, R. → 100 29 6N 110 53W
Hordaland fylke □ 171 60 25N 6 15 E
Horden Hills 228 20 40 S 130 20 E
Hordio 256 10 33N 51 6 E
Horezu 170 45 6N 24 0 E
Horgen 149 47 15N 8 35 E
Horgoš 166 46 10N 20 0 E
Horice 150 50 21N 15 39 E
Horinger 214 40 28N 111 48 E
Horlick Mts. 13 84 0 S 102 0W
Hormigas de Afuera 101 27 46N 103 56W
Hormoz 193 27 35N 55 0 E
Hormoz, Jaz. ye 193 27 8N 56 28 E
Hormuz Str. 193 26 30N 56 30 E
Horn, Austria 150 48 39N 15 40 E
Horn, Ísafjarðarsýsla, Iceland 174 66 28N 22 28W
Horn, Suður-Múlasýsla, Iceland 174 65 10N 13 31W
Horn, Neth. 143 51 12N 5 57 E
Horn → 76 61 30N 118 1W
Horn, Cape = Hornos, Cabo de 126 55 50 S 67 30W
Horn Head 135 55 13N 8 0W
Horn I. 230 10 37 S 142 17 E
Horn Mts. 76 62 15N 119 15W
Hornachuelos 155 37 50N 5 14W
Hornaday → 94 69 19N 123 48W
Hornavan 174 66 15N 17 30 E
Hornbœk 172 56 5N 12 26 E
Hornburg 146 52 2N 10 36 E
Hornby 235 43 33 S 172 33 E
Horncastle 132 53 13N 0 8W
Horndal 172 60 18N 16 23 E
Hornell L. 76 62 20N 119 25W
Hornepayne 87 49 14N 84 48W
Hornindal 171 61 58N 6 30 E
Hornings Mills 84 44 9N 80 12W
Hornnes 171 58 34N 7 45 E
Hornos, Cabo de 126 55 50 S 67 30W
Hornoy 139 49 50N 1 54 E
Hornsby 231 33 42 S 151 2 E
Hornsea 132 53 55N 0 10W
Hornslandet 172 61 35N 17 37 E
Hornslet 173 56 18N 10 19 E
Hornu 143 50 26N 3 50 E
Hörnum 146 54 44N 8 18 E
Horobetsu 218 42 24N 141 6 E
Horovice 150 49 48N 13 53 E
Horqin Youyi Qianqi 215 46 5N 122 3 E
Horqueta 124 23 15 S 56 55W
Horqueta, La 119 7 55N 60 20W
Horra, La 154 41 44N 3 53W
Horred 173 57 22N 12 28 E
Horse Is. 79 50 15N 55 50W
Horsefly 93 52 20N 121 25W
Horsefly L. 93 52 25N 121 0W
Horsens 173 55 52N 9 51 E
Horsens Fjord 173 55 50N 10 0 E
Horsham, Australia 231 36 44 S 142 13 E
Horsham, U.K. 133 51 4N 0 20W
Horšovský Týn 150 49 31N 12 58 E
Horst 143 51 27N 6 3 E
Horten 171 59 25N 10 32 E
Hortobágy → 151 47 30N 21 6 E
Horton → 94 69 56N 126 52W
Hörvik 173 56 2N 14 45 E
Horw 149 47 1N 8 19 E
Horwood 79 49 27N 54 32W
Horwood, L. 87 48 5N 82 20W
Hosaina 245 7 30N 37 47 E
Hosdurga 201 13 49N 76 17 E
Hose, Gunung-Gunung 206 2 5N 114 6 E
Ḩoseynābād, Khuzestān, Iran 193 32 45N 48 20 E
Hoseynābād, Kordestān, Iran 192 35 33N 47 8 E
Hoshangabad 198 22 45N 77 45 E
Hoshiarpur 198 31 30N 75 58 E
Hosingen 143 50 1N 6 6 E
Hoskins 227 5 29 S 150 27 E
Hososhima 220 32 26N 131 40 E
Hospental 149 46 37N 8 34 E
Hospet 201 15 15N 76 20 E
Hospitalet, L' 140 42 36N 1 47 E
Hospitalet de Llobregat 156 41 21N 2 6 E
Hoste, I. 126 55 0 S 69 0W
Hostens 140 44 30N 0 40W
Hostotipaquillo 106 21 4N 104 4W
Hot 204 18 8N 98 29 E
Hotan 212 37 25N 79 55 E
Hotazel 254 27 17 S 23 0 E
Hotchkiss → 90 57 2N 117 28W
Hotham, C. 228 12 2 S 131 18 E
Hoting 174 64 8N 16 15 E
Hotolishti 168 41 10N 20 25 E
Hottah L. 94 65 4N 118 30W
Hotte, Massif de la 113 18 30N 73 45W
Hottentotsbaai 254 26 8 S 14 59 E
Hotton 143 50 16N 5 26 E
Houailou 226 21 17 S 165 38 E
Houat 138 47 24N 2 58W
Houdan 139 48 48N 1 35 E
Houdeng-Goegnies 143 50 29N 4 10 E
Houei Sai 204 20 18N 100 26 E
Houffalize 143 50 8N 5 48 E
Houghton-le-Spring 132 54 51N 1 28W
Houhora 234 34 49 S 173 9 E
Houille → 143 50 8N 4 50 E
Houndé 246 11 34N 3 31W
Hourtin 140 45 11N 1 4W
Hourtin, Étang d' 140 45 10N 1 6W
Houston 76 54 25N 126 39W
Houten 142 52 2N 5 10 E
Houthalen 143 51 2N 5 23 E
Houthem 143 50 48N 2 57 E
Houthulst 143 50 59N 3 20 E
Houtman Abrolhos 229 28 43 S 113 48 E
Houyet 143 50 11N 5 1 E
Hov 173 55 55N 10 15 E
Hova 173 58 53N 14 14 E
Høvåg 171 58 10N 8 16 E
Hovd 212 48 2N 91 37 E
Hovden 171 59 33N 7 22 E
Hove 133 50 50N 0 10W
Hoveyzeh 193 31 27N 48 4 E
Hovmantorp 173 56 47N 15 7 E
Hövsgöl 214 43 37N 109 39 E
Hövsgöl Nuur 212 51 0N 100 30 E
Hovsta 172 59 22N 15 15 E
Howakil 245 15 10N 40 16 E
Howar, Wadi → 245 17 30N 27 8 E
Howard 231 25 16 S 152 32 E
Howard I. 230 12 10 S 135 24 E
Howard L. 77 62 15N 105 57W
Howatharra 229 28 29 S 114 33 E
Howe, C. 231 37 30 S 150 0 E
Howe I. 85 44 16N 76 17W
Howe Sd. 93 49 35N 123 15W
Howick, Canada 83 45 11N 73 51W
Howick, N.Z. 234 36 54 S 174 56 E
Howick, S. Africa 255 29 28 S 30 14 E
Howick Group 230 14 20 S 145 30 E
Howitt, L. 231 27 40 S 138 40 E
Howley 79 49 12N 57 2W
Howrah = Haora 199 22 37N 88 20 E
Howth Hd. 135 53 21N 6 0W
Höxter 146 51 45N 9 26 E
Hoy I. 134 58 50N 3 15W
Hoya 146 52 47N 9 10 E
Hoyerswerda 146 51 26N 14 14 E
Hoyleton 232 34 2 S 138 34 E
Hoyos 154 40 9N 6 45W
Hpawlum 202 27 12N 98 12 E
Hpettintha 202 24 14N 95 23 E
Hpizow 202 26 57N 98 24 E
Hrádec Králové 150 50 15N 15 50 E
Hrádek 151 48 46N 16 16 E
Hranice 151 49 34N 17 45 E
Hron → 151 47 49N 18 45 E
Hrubieszów 152 50 49N 23 51 E
Hrubý Nizký Jeseník 151 50 7N 17 10 E
Hrvatska 163 45 20N 16 0 E
Hrvatska □ 166 45 20N 18 0 E
Hsenwi 202 23 22N 97 55 E
Hsiamen = Xiamen 217 24 25N 118 4 E
Hsipaw 202 22 37N 97 18 E
Htawgaw 202 25 57N 98 23 E
Hu Xian 214 34 8N 108 42 E
Hua Hin 204 12 34N 99 58 E
Hua Xian, Henan, China 214 35 30N 114 30 E
Hua Xian, Shaanxi, China 214 34 30N 109 48 E
Hua'an 217 25 1N 117 32 E
Huacana, La 106 18 58N 101 49W
Huacao 107 20 2N 101 1W
Huacaya 123 20 45 S 63 43W
Huacheng 217 24 4N 115 37 E
Huachínera 100 30 9N 108 55W
Huachínera, Sa. 100 30 16N 108 45W
Huacho 122 11 10 S 77 35W
Huachón 122 10 35 S 76 0W
Huade 214 41 55N 113 59 E
Huadian 215 43 0N 126 40 E
Huahuapan 104 24 31N 105 57W
Huai He → 217 33 0N 118 30 E
Huai Yot 205 7 45N 99 37 E
Huai'an, Hebei, China 214 40 30N 114 20 E
Huai'an, Jiangsu, China 215 33 30N 119 10 E
Huaide 215 43 30N 124 40 E
Huaidezhen 215 43 48N 124 50 E
Huaihua 216 27 32N 109 57 E
Huaiji 217 23 55N 112 12 E
Huainan 217 32 38N 116 58 E
Huaining 217 30 24N 116 40 E
Huairen 214 39 48N 113 20 E
Huairou 214 40 20N 116 35 E
Huaiyang 214 33 40N 114 52 E
Huaiyuan, Anhui, China 215 32 55N 117 10 E
Huaiyuan, Guangxi Zhuangzu, China 216 24 31N 108 22 E
Huajianzi 215 41 23N 125 20 E
Huajimic 104 21 42N 104 20W
Huajimic, Sa. 104 22 54N 105 3W
Huajintepec 107 16 36N 98 14W
Huajuapán de León 109 17 48N 97 46W
Hualahuises 103 24 53N 99 41W
Hualian 217 23 59N 121 37 E
Hualicori 104 22 44N 105 21W
Huallaga → 122 5 0 S 75 30W
Huallanca 122 8 50 S 77 56W
Huamachuco 122 7 50 S 78 5W
Huambo 253 12 42 S 15 54 E
Huambo □ 253 13 0 S 16 0 E
Huamuxtitlán 107 17 49N 98 34W
Huan Jiang → 214 34 28N 109 0 E
Huan Xian 214 36 33N 107 7 E
Huancabamba 122 5 10 S 79 15W
Huancane 122 15 10 S 69 44W
Huancapi 122 13 40 S 74 0W
Huancavelica 122 12 50 S 75 5W
Huancavelica □ 122 13 0 S 75 0W
Huancayo 122 12 5 S 75 12W
Huanchaca 122 20 15 S 66 40W
Huanchaca, Serranía de 123 14 30 S 60 39W
Huandacareó 107 19 59N 101 17W
Huang Hai 215 35 0N 123 0 E
Huang He → 215 37 55N 118 50 E
Huang Xian 215 37 38N 120 30 E
Huangchuan 217 32 15N 115 10 E
Huanggang 217 30 29N 114 52 E
Huangling 214 35 34N 109 15 E
Huanglong 214 35 30N 109 59 E
Huanglongtan 217 32 40N 110 33 E
Huangmei 217 30 5N 115 56 E
Huangpi 217 30 50N 114 22 E
Huangping 216 26 52N 107 54 E
Huangshi 217 30 10N 115 3 E
Huangsongdian 215 43 45N 127 25 E
Huangyan 217 28 38N 121 19 E
Huangyangsi 216 26 33N 111 39 E
Huaning 216 24 17N 102 56 E
Huaniqueo de Morales 107 19 54N 101 26W
Huanjiang 216 24 50N 108 18 E
Huanta 122 12 55 S 74 20W
Huantai 215 36 58N 117 56 E
Huánuco 122 9 55 S 76 15W
Huánuco □ 122 9 55 S 76 14W
Huanuni 122 18 16 S 66 51W

Huanzo, Cordillera de 122 14 35 S 73 20W
Huapango, L. 107 20 0N 99 42W
Huaping 216 26 46N 101 25 E
Huaral 122 11 32 S 77 13W
Huaraz 122 9 30 S 77 32W
Huari 122 9 14 S 77 14W
Huarmey 122 10 5 S 78 5W
Huarochiri 122 12 9 S 76 15W
Huarocondo 122 13 26 S 72 14W
Huarong 217 29 29N 112 30 E
Huasabas 100 29 47N 109 18W
Huascarán 122 9 8 S 77 36W
Huascarán, Nevado 122 9 7 S 77 37W
Huasco 124 28 30 S 71 15W
Huasco → 124 28 27 S 71 13W
Huatabampo 100 26 50N 109 38W
Huatusco de Chicuellar 108 19 9N 96 57W
Huauchinango 108 20 12N 98 3W
Huautla 107 17 51N 100 5W
Huautla de Jiménez 109 18 8N 96 51W
Huaxi 216 26 25N 106 40 E
Huayacocotla 108 20 33N 98 29W
Huayin 214 34 35N 110 5 E
Huayllay 122 11 3 S 76 21W
Huaynamota 104 21 56N 104 31W
Huaynamota, R. → 104 21 51N 104 42W
Huayuan 216 28 37N 109 29 E
Huazhou 217 21 33N 110 33 E
Huazuntlán 109 18 9N 94 47W
Hubbard 88 51 8N 103 22W
Hubbards 81 44 38N 64 4W
Hubbart Pt. 77 59 21N 94 41W
Hubei □ 217 31 0N 112 0 E
Hubli-Dharwad = Dharwad 201 15 22N 75 15 E
Huchang 215 41 25N 127 2 E
Hückelhoven-Ratheim 146 51 6N 6 13 E
Huczwa → 152 50 49N 23 58 E
Huddersfield 132 53 38N 1 49W
Hudi 244 17 43N 34 18 E
Hudiksvall 172 61 43N 17 10 E
Hudson 86 50 6N 92 9W
Hudson Bay 89 52 51N 102 23W
Hudson Hope 76 56 0N 121 54W
Hudson Mts. 13 74 32 S 99 20W
Hudson Str. 95 62 0N 70 0W
Hudwin L. 89 53 12N 95 41W
Hue 204 16 30N 107 35 E
Huebra → 154 41 2N 6 48W
Huechucuicui, Pta. 126 41 48 S 74 2W
Huedin 170 46 52N 23 2 E
Huehuetán 110 15 1N 92 22W
Huehuetenango 112 15 20N 91 28W
Huehuetla 107 20 28N 98 3W
Huehuetlán 109 18 44N 98 10W
Huejotitlán 101 27 4N 106 12W
Huejúcar 105 22 21N 103 13W
Huejuquilla el Alto 105 22 36N 103 52W
Huejutla de Reyes 107 21 8N 98 25W
Huelgoat 138 48 22N 3 46W
Huelma 157 37 39N 3 28W
Huelva 155 37 18N 6 57W
Huelva □ 155 37 40N 7 0W
Huelva → 155 37 27N 6 0W
Huentelauquén 124 31 38 S 71 33W
Huepac 100 29 54N 110 10W
Huércal Overa 157 37 23N 1 57W
Huerta, La 106 19 28N 104 39W
Huerta, Sa. de la 124 31 10 S 67 30W
Huertas, C. de las 157 38 21N 0 24W
Huertecillas 103 24 4N 100 9W
Huerva → 156 41 39N 0 52W
Huesca 156 42 8N 0 25W
Huesca □ 156 42 20N 0 1 E
Huéscar 157 37 44N 2 35W
Huesco, Sa. del 101 30 15N 105 15W
Huetamo de Núñez 107 18 35N 100 53W
Huete 156 40 10N 2 43W
Hueyapán de Ocampo 109 18 7N 95 9W
Hugh → 230 25 1 S 134 1 E
Hughenden 230 20 52 S 144 10 E
Hughes 229 30 42 S 129 31 E
Hughli → 199 21 56N 88 4 E
Huhi 111 20 43N 89 10W
Hui Xian, Gansu, China 214 33 50N 106 4 E
Hui Xian, Henan, China 214 35 27N 113 12 E
Hui'an 217 25 1N 118 43 E
Hui'anbu 214 37 28N 106 38 E
Huiarau Ra. 234 38 45 S 176 55 E
Huichang 217 25 32N 115 45 E
Huichapan 107 20 23N 99 39W
Huicholes, Sa. de los 105 21 56N 103 53W
Huidong 216 26 34N 102 35 E
Huifa He → 215 43 0N 127 50 E
Huíla 253 15 4 S 13 32 E
Huila □ 118 2 30N 75 45W
Huila, Nevado del 118 3 0N 76 0W
Huilai 217 23 0N 116 18 E
Huili 216 26 35N 102 17 E
Huimanguillo 110 17 51N 93 23W
Huimilpan 107 20 22N 100 17W
Huimin 215 37 27N 117 28 E
Huinan 215 42 40N 126 2 E
Huinca Renancó 124 34 51 S 64 22W
Huining 214 35 38N 105 0 E
Huinong 214 39 5N 106 35 E
Huiroa 234 39 15 S 174 30 E
Huise 143 50 54N 3 36 E
Huishui 216 26 7N 106 38 E
Huisne → 138 47 59N 0 11 E
Huissen 142 51 57N 5 57 E
Huiting 214 34 5N 116 5 E
Huitong 216 26 51N 109 45 E
Huitupán 110 17 13N 92 39W
Huitziltepec 107 17 49N 99 28W
Huitzuco de los Figueroa 107 18 18N 99 21W
Huixtla 110 15 9N 92 28W
Huize 216 26 24N 103 15 E
Huizen 142 52 18N 5 14 E
Huizhou 217 23 0N 114 23 E
Hukou 217 29 45N 116 21 E
Hukuntsi 254 23 58 S 21 45 E
Hula 245 6 33N 38 30 E
Ḩulayfā' 192 25 58N 40 45 E
Huld 214 45 5N 105 30 E
Hulda 189 31 50N 34 51 E
Hulin He → 215 45 0N 122 10 E
Hull, Canada 82 45 25N 75 44W
Hull, U.K. 132 53 45N 0 20W
Hull → 132 53 43N 0 25W
Hulst 143 51 17N 4 2 E
Hultsfred 173 57 30N 15 52 E
Hulun Nur 213 49 0N 117 30 E
Humahuaca 124 23 10 S 65 25W
Humaitá, Brazil 123 7 35 S 63 1W
Humaitá, Paraguay 124 27 2 S 58 31W
Humansdorp 254 34 2 S 24 46 E
Humbe 254 16 40 S 14 55 E
Humber → 132 53 40N 0 10W
Humberside □ 132 53 50N 0 30W
Humbert River 228 16 30 S 130 45 E
Humboldt 88 52 15N 105 9W
Humboldt Gletscher 12 79 30N 62 0W
Humboldt Mts. 235 44 30 S 168 15 E
Humbolt, Massif du 226 21 53 S 166 25 E
Hume, L. 231 36 0 S 147 0 E
Humenné 151 48 55N 21 50 E
Humpata 253 15 2 S 13 24 E
Humpolec 150 49 31N 15 20 E
Humula 233 35 30 S 147 46 E
Hūn 241 29 2N 16 0 E
Hun Jiang → 215 40 50N 125 38 E
Húnaflói 174 65 50N 20 50W
Hunan □ 217 27 30N 112 0 E
Hunchun 215 42 52N 130 28 E
Hundested 172 55 58N 11 52 E
Hundred and Fifty Mile House 93 52 7N 121 57W
Hundred Mile House 93 51 38N 121 18W
Hunedoara 170 45 40N 22 50 E
Hunedoara □ 170 45 50N 22 54 E
Hünfeld 146 50 40N 9 47 E
Hung Yen 204 20 39N 106 4 E
Hungary ■ 151 47 20N 19 20 E
Hungary, Plain of 130 47 0N 20 0 E
Hungerford 231 28 58 S 144 24 E
Hŭngnam 215 39 49N 127 45 E
Huni Valley 246 5 33N 1 56W
Hunsberge 254 27 45 S 17 12 E
Hunsrück 147 49 30N 7 0 E
Hunstanton 132 52 57N 0 30 E
Hunsur 201 12 16N 76 16 E
Hunte → 146 52 30N 8 19 E
Hunter 235 44 36 S 171 2 E
Hunter → 235 44 21 S 169 27 E
Hunter, C. 95 71 42N 72 30W
Hunter Hills, The 235 44 26 S 170 46 E
Hunter I., Australia 230 40 30 S 144 45 E
Hunter I., Canada 92 51 55N 128 0W
Hunter Mts. 235 45 43 S 167 25 E
Hunter Ra. 231 32 45 S 150 15 E
Hunters Road 251 19 9 S 29 49 E
Hunterton 231 26 12 S 148 30 E
Hunterville 234 39 56 S 175 35 E
Huntingdon, Canada 83 45 6N 74 10W
Huntingdon, U.K. 133 52 20N 0 11W
Huntly, N.Z. 234 37 34 S 175 11 E
Huntly, U.K. 134 57 27N 2 48W
Huntsville 84 45 20N 79 14W
Hunucmá 111 21 1N 89 52W
Hunyani → 251 15 57 S 30 39 E
Hunyuan 214 39 42N 113 42 E
Hunza → 199 35 54N 74 20 E
Huo Xian 214 36 36N 111 42 E
Huon, G. 227 7 0 S 147 30 E
Huon Pen. 227 6 20 S 147 30 E
Huong Hoa 204 16 37N 106 45 E
Huong Khe 204 18 13N 105 41 E
Huonville 230 43 0 S 147 5 E
Huoqiu 217 32 20N 116 12 E
Huoshan, Anhui, China 217 32 28N 118 30 E
Huoshan, Anhui, China 217 31 25N 116 20 E
Huoshao Dao 217 22 40N 121 30 E
Hupeh □ = Hubei □ 217 31 0N 112 0 E
Hupel 93 50 37N 118 44W
Ḩūr 193 30 50N 57 7 E
Hurbanovo 151 47 51N 18 11 E
Hure Qi 215 42 45N 121 45 E
Hurezani 170 44 49N 23 40 E
Hurghada 244 27 15N 33 50 E
Huron, L. 84 45 0N 83 0W
Hurso 245 9 35N 41 33 E
Hurum, Buskerud, Norway 171 59 36N 10 23 E
Hurum, Oppland, Norway 171 61 9N 8 46 E
Hurunui → 235 42 54 S 173 18 E
Hurup 173 56 46N 8 25 E
Húsavík 174 66 3N 17 21W
Huşi 170 46 41N 28 7 E
Huskvarna 173 57 47N 14 15 E
Husøy 171 61 3N 4 44 E
Hussar 91 51 3N 112 41W
Hustopéce 151 48 57N 16 43 E
Husum, Germany 146 54 27N 9 3 E
Husum, Sweden 172 63 21N 19 12 E
Ḩūth 194 16 14N 43 58 E
Hutte Sauvage, L. de la 78 56 15N 64 45W
Huttenberg 150 46 56N 14 33 E
Hüttental 146 50 52N 8 1 E
Hutton, Mt. 231 25 51 S 148 20 E
Huttwil 148 47 7N 7 50 E
Huwun 245 4 23N 40 6 E
Ḩuwwārah 189 32 9N 35 15 E
Huy 143 50 31N 5 15 E
Hvaler 171 59 4N 11 1 E
Hvammur 174 65 13N 21 49W
Hvar 163 43 11N 16 28 E
Hvarski Kanal 163 43 15N 16 35 E
Hvítá 174 64 40N 21 5W
Hvítá → 174 64 0N 20 58W
Hvítárvatn 174 64 37N 19 50W
Hvitsten 171 59 35N 10 42 E
Hwachon-chosuji 215 38 5N 127 50 E
Hwang Ho = Huang He → 215 37 55N 118 50 E
Hwange 251 18 18 S 26 30 E
Hwange Nat. Park 254 19 0 S 26 30 E
Hwekum 202 26 7N 95 22 E
Hyargas Nuur 212 49 0N 93 0 E
Hyas 89 51 54N 102 16W
Hybo 172 61 49N 16 15 E
Hyde 235 45 18 S 170 16 E
Hyde In. 95 75 2N 80 0W
Hyde Park 119 6 30N 58 16W
Hyden 229 32 24 S 118 53 E
Hyderabad, India 200 17 22N 78 29 E
Hyderabad, Pakistan 197 25 23N 68 24 E
Hyères 141 43 8N 6 9 E
Hyères, Îles d' 141 43 0N 6 28 E
Hyesan 215 41 20N 128 10 E
Hyland → 76 59 52N 128 12W
Hylestad 171 59 6N 7 29 E
Hyltebruk 173 56 59N 13 15 E
Hymers 86 48 18N 89 43W
Hymia 199 33 40N 78 2 E
Hyōgo □ 220 35 15N 135 0 E
Hythe, Canada 90 55 20N 119 33W
Hythe, U.K. 133 51 4N 1 5 E
Hyūga 220 32 25N 131 35 E
Hyvinge = Hyvinkää 175 60 38N 24 50 E
Hyvinkää 175 60 38N 24 50 E

I

I-n-Azaoua 241 20 45N 7 31 E
I-n-Échaï 240 20 10N 2 5W
I-n-Gall 247 16 51N 7 1 E
I-n-Tabedog 240 19 48N 1 11 E
Iabès, Erg 240 27 30N 2 2W
Iaco → 122 9 3 S 68 34W
Iacobeni 170 47 25N 25 20 E
Iaçu 121 12 45 S 40 13W
Iakora 255 23 6 S 46 40 E
Ialomiţa □ 170 44 30N 27 30 E
Ialomiţa → 170 44 42N 27 51 E
Ian L. 92 53 50N 132 45W
Ianca 170 45 6N 27 29 E
Iara 170 46 31N 23 35 E
Iaşi 170 47 10N 27 40 E
Iaşi □ 170 47 20N 27 0 E
Iauaretê 118 0 36N 69 12W
Iba 210 15 22N 120 0 E
Ibadan 247 7 22N 3 58 E
Ibagué 118 4 20N 75 20W
Ibaiti 121 23 50 S 50 10W
Ibajay 211 11 49N 122 10 E
Iballja 168 42 12N 20 0 E
Ibăneşti 170 46 45N 24 50 E
Ibar → 166 43 43N 20 45 E
Ibara 220 34 36N 133 28 E
Ibaraki 221 34 49N 135 34 E
Ibaraki □ 221 36 10N 140 10 E
Ibarra, Ecuador 118 0 21N 78 7W
Ibarra, Mexico 107 21 31N 101 32W
Ibba 245 4 49N 29 2 E
Ibba, Bahr el 245 5 30N 28 55 E
Ibbenbüren 146 52 16N 7 41 E
Ibembo 250 2 35N 23 35 E
Ibera, Laguna 124 28 30 S 57 9W
Iberian Peninsula 130 40 0N 5 0W
Iberville 83 45 19N 73 17W
Iberville, Lac d' 78 55 55N 73 15W
Iberville, Mt. d' 78 58 50N 63 50W
Ibi 247 8 15N 9 44 E
Ibiá 121 19 30 S 46 30W
Ibicaraí 121 14 51 S 39 36W
Ibicuí 121 14 51 S 39 59W
Ibicuy 124 33 55 S 59 10W
Ibioapaba, Sa. da 120 4 0 S 41 30W
Ibipetuba 120 11 0 S 44 32W
Ibitiara 121 12 39 S 42 13W
Ibiza 157 38 54N 1 26 E
Íblei, Monti 165 37 15N 14 45 E
Ibn Hāni', Ra's 190 35 35N 35 43 E
Ibo 251 12 22 S 40 40 E
Ibonma 207 3 29 S 133 31 E
Ibotirama 121 12 13 S 43 12W
Ibradi 190 37 4N 31 35 E
Ibrāhīm → 190 34 4N 35 38 E
Ibrala 190 37 9N 33 30 E
'Ibrī 195 23 14N 56 30 E
Ibriktepe 168 41 2N 26 33 E
Ibshawâi 244 29 21N 30 40 E
Ibu 207 1 35N 127 33 E
Ibuki-Sanchi 221 35 25N 136 18 E
Iburg 146 52 10N 8 3 E
Ibusuki 220 31 12N 130 40 E
Icá 122 14 0 S 75 48W
Ica □ 122 14 20 S 75 30W
Iça → 122 2 55 S 67 58W
Icabarú 119 4 20N 61 45W
Icabarú → 119 4 45N 62 15W
Icaiche 111 18 5N 89 10W
Içana 118 0 21N 67 19W
Içana → 118 0 26N 67 19W
Icatu 120 2 46 S 44 4W
İçel □ 190 36 45N 34 0 E
Iceland ■ 174 65 0N 19 0W
Icha 185 55 30N 156 0 E
Ich'ang = Yichang 217 30 40N 111 20 E
Ichchapuram 200 19 10N 84 40 E
Ichihara 221 35 28N 140 5 E
Ichikawa 221 35 44N 139 55 E
Ichilo → 123 15 57 S 64 50W
Ichinohe 218 40 13N 141 17 E
Ichinomiya, Gifu, Japan 221 35 18N 136 48 E
Ichinomiya, Kumamoto, Japan 220 32 58N 131 5 E
Ichinoseki 218 38 55N 141 8 E
Ichnya 178 50 52N 32 24 E
Ichŏn 215 37 17N 127 27 E
Icht 240 29 6N 8 54W
Ichtegem 143 51 5N 3 1 E
Icó 120 6 24 S 38 51W
Icoraci 120 1 18 S 48 28W
Ida Valley 229 28 42 S 120 29 E
Idaga Hamus 245 14 13N 39 48 E
Idah 247 7 5N 6 40 E
Idanha-a-Nova 154 39 50N 7 15W
Idar-Oberstein 147 49 43N 7 19 E
Idd el Ghanam 243 11 30N 24 19 E
Iddan 256 6 10N 48 55 E
Idehan 241 27 10N 11 30 E
Idehan Marzūq 241 24 50N 13 51 E
Idelès 241 23 50N 5 53 E
Idfû 244 25 0N 32 49 E
Ídhi Óros 169 35 15N 24 45 E
Ídhra 169 37 20N 23 28 E
Idi 208 5 2N 97 37 E
Idiofa 253 4 55 S 19 42 E
Idkerberget 172 60 22N 15 15 E
Idku, Bahra el 244 31 18N 30 18 E
Idlib 190 35 55N 36 36 E
Idlib □ 190 35 45N 36 45 E
Idna 189 31 34N 34 58 E
Idolo, I. del 108 21 25N 97 27W
Idrija 163 46 0N 14 5 E
Idritsa 178 56 25N 28 30 E
Idstein 147 50 13N 8 17 E
Idutywa 255 32 8 S 28 18 E
Ieper 143 50 51N 2 53 E
Ierápetra 169 35 0N 25 44 E
Ierissós 168 40 22N 23 52 E
Ierissóu Kólpos 168 40 27N 23 57 E
Ierzu 164 39 48N 9 32 E
Ieshima-Shotō 220 34 40N 134 32 E
Iesi 163 43 32N 13 12 E

Ifach, Punta **157** 38 38N 0 5 E
'Ifāl, W. → **191** 28 7N 35 3 E
Ifanadiana **255** 21 19 S 47 39 E
Ife **247** 7 30N 4 31 E
Iférouâne **247** 19 5N 8 24 E
Iffley **230** 18 53 S 141 12 E
Ifni **240** 29 29N 10 12W
Ifon **247** 6 58N 5 40 E
Iforas, Adrar des **247** 19 40N 1 40 E
Ifrane **240** 33 33N 5 7W
Ifugao □ **210** 16 40N 121 10 E
Iga **221** 34 45N 136 10 E
Iganga **250** 0 37N 33 28 E
Igara Paraná → **118** 2 9 S 71 47W
Igarapava **121** 20 3 S 47 47W
Igarapé Açu **120** 1 4 S 47 33W
Igarapé-Mirim **120** 1 59 S 48 58W
Igarka **185** 67 30N 86 33 E
Igatimi **125** 24 5 S 55 40W
Igatpuri **200** 19 40N 73 35 E
Igbetti **247** 8 44N 4 8 E
Igbo-Ora **247** 7 29N 3 15 E
Igboho **247** 8 53N 3 50 E
Iggesund **172** 61 39N 17 10 E
Ighil Izane **241** 35 44N 0 31 E
Iglene **240** 22 57N 4 58 E
Iglésias **164** 39 19N 8 27 E
Igli **240** 30 25N 2 19W
Iglino **182** 54 50N 56 26 E
Igloolik **95** 69 20N 81 49W
Igma **240** 29 9N 6 24W
Igma, Gebel el **244** 28 55N 34 0 E
Ignace **86** 49 30N 91 40W
Ignacio Allende **105** 24 28N 104 1W
Ignacio de la Llave **109** 18 43N 95 59W
Ignacio Zaragoza **101** 29 40N 107 43W
Igornachoix Bay **79** 50 40N 57 25W
Igoshevo **179** 59 25N 42 35 E
Igoumenítsa **168** 39 32N 20 18 E
Igra **182** 57 33N 53 7 E
Iguaçu → **125** 25 36 S 54 36W
Iguaçu, Cat. del **125** 25 41 S 54 26W
Iguala de la
Independencia **107** 18 21N 99 32W
Igualada **156** 41 37N 1 37 E
Igualapa **107** 16 44N 98 36W
Igualatlaco, Sa. de **107** 17 35N 99 45W
Iguape **121** 24 43 S 47 33W
Iguassu =
Iguaçu → **125** 25 36 S 54 36W
Iguatu **120** 6 20 S 39 18W
Iguéla **252** 2 0 S 9 16 E
Iguig **210** 17 45N 121 44 E
Igunga □ **250** 4 20 S 33 45 E
Iheya-Shima **219** 27 4N 127 58 E
Ihiala **247** 5 51N 6 55 E
Ihosy **255** 22 24 S 46 8 E
Ihotry, L. **255** 21 56 S 43 41 E
Ii-Shima **219** 26 43N 127 47 E
Iida **221** 35 35N 137 50 E
Iisalmi **174** 63 32N 27 10 E
Iiyama **219** 36 51N 138 22 E
Iizuka **220** 33 38N 130 42 E
Ijâfene **240** 20 40N 8 0W
Ijebu-Igbo **247** 6 56N 4 1 E
Ijebu-Ode **247** 6 47N 3 58 E
IJmuiden **142** 52 28N 4 35 E
IJssel → **142** 52 35N 5 50 E
IJsselmeer **142** 52 45N 5 20 E
IJsselmuiden **142** 52 34N 5 57 E
IJsselstein **142** 52 1N 5 2 E
Ijuí → **125** 27 58 S 55 20W
Ijūin **220** 31 37N 130 24 E
IJzendijke **143** 51 19N 3 37 E
IJzer → **143** 51 9N 2 44 E
Ik → **182** 55 55N 52 36 E
Ikale **247** 7 40N 5 37 E
Ikare **247** 7 32N 5 40 E
Ikaría **169** 37 35N 26 10 E
Ikast **173** 56 8N 9 10 E
Ikawa **221** 35 13N 138 15 E
Ikeda **220** 34 1N 133 48 E
Ikeja **247** 6 36N 3 23 E
Ikela **252** 1 6 S 23 6 E
Ikenge **252** 0 8 S 18 8 E
Ikerre-Ekiti **247** 7 25N 5 19 E
Ikhtiman **167** 42 27N 23 48 E
Iki **220** 33 45N 129 42 E
Iki-Kaikyō **220** 33 40N 129 45 E
Ikimba L. **250** 1 30 S 31 20 E
Ikire **247** 7 23N 4 15 E
Ikitsuki-Shima **220** 33 23N 129 26 E
Ikom **247** 6 0N 8 42 E
Ikopa → **255** 16 45 S 46 40 E
Ikot Ekpene **247** 5 12N 7 40 E
Ikrimah **242** 32 2N 23 41 E
Ikungu **250** 1 33 S 33 42 E
Ikuno **220** 35 10N 134 48 E
Ikurun **247** 7 54N 4 40 E
Ila **247** 8 0N 4 39 E
Ilagan **210** 17 7N 121 53 E
Ilam, Iran **192** 33 0N 46 0 E
Ilam, Nepal **199** 26 58N 87 58 E
Ilanskiy **185** 56 14N 96 3 E
Ilanz **149** 46 46N 9 12 E
Ilaro **247** 6 53N 3 3 E
Iława **152** 53 36N 19 34 E
Ilayangudi **201** 9 34N 78 37 E
Ilbilbie **230** 21 45 S 149 20 E
Île-à-la Crosse **77** 55 27N 107 53W
Île-à-la-Crosse, Lac **77** 55 40N 107 45W
Île-Bouchard, L' **138** 47 7N 0 26 E
Île-de-France **139** 49 0N 2 20 E
Île-sur-le-Doubs, L' **139** 47 26N 6 34 E
Ilebo **253** 4 17 S 20 55 E
Ileje □ **251** 9 30 S 33 25 E
Ilek **182** 51 32N 53 21 E
Ilek → **182** 51 30N 53 22 E
Ilero **247** 8 0N 3 20 E
Îles, L. des **82** 46 50N 75 18W
Ilesha, Oyo, Nigeria **247** 7 37N 4 40 E
Ilesha, Oyo, Nigeria **247** 8 57N 3 28 E
Ilford **77** 56 4N 95 35W
Ilfov □ **170** 44 20N 26 0 E
Ilfracombe,
Australia **230** 23 30 S 144 30 E
Ilfracombe, U.K. **133** 51 13N 4 8W
Ilha Grande **119** 0 27 S 65 2W
Ilha Grande, Baía
da **121** 23 9 S 44 30W
Ílhavo **154** 40 33N 8 43W
Ilhéus **121** 14 49 S 39 2W
Ili → **183** 45 53N 77 10 E
Ilia **170** 45 57N 22 40 E
Ilia □ **169** 37 45N 21 35 E
Iliatenco **107** 17 58N 98 40W
Ilich **183** 40 50N 68 27 E
Iligan **211** 8 12N 124 13 E
Iligan Bay **211** 8 25N 124 5 E
Ilíkí, L. **169** 38 24N 23 15 E
Ilin I. **210** 12 14N 121 5 E
Iliodhrómia **168** 39 12N 23 50 E
Ilirska-Bistrica **163** 45 34N 14 14 E
Ilkal **201** 15 57N 76 8 E
Ilkeston **132** 52 59N 1 19W
Illana B. **211** 7 35N 123 45 E
Illapel **124** 32 0 S 71 10W
'Illār **189** 32 23N 35 7 E
Ille **140** 42 40N 2 37 E
Ille-et-Vilaine □ **138** 48 10N 1 30W
Iller → **147** 48 23N 9 58 E
Illescas, Mexico **103** 23 13N 102 7W
Illescas, Spain **154** 40 8N 3 51W
Illiers **138** 48 18N 1 15 E
Illimani **122** 16 30 S 67 50W
Illium = Troy **168** 39 57N 26 12 E
Illizi **241** 26 31N 8 32 E
Illora **155** 37 17N 3 53W
Illukotat → **78** 60 48N 78 11W
Ilm → **146** 51 7N 11 45 E
Ilmen, Oz. **178** 58 15N 31 10 E
Ilmenau **146** 50 41N 10 55 E
Ilo **122** 17 40 S 71 20W
Ilobu **247** 7 45N 4 25 E
Ilocos Norte □ **210** 18 10N 120 45 E
Ilocos Sur □ **210** 17 20N 120 35 E
Iloilo **211** 10 45N 122 33 E
Iloilo □ **211** 11 0N 122 40 E
Ilok **166** 45 15N 19 20 E
Ilora **247** 7 45N 3 50 E
Ilorin **247** 8 30N 4 35 E
Iloulya **181** 49 15N 44 2 E
Ilovatka **179** 50 30N 45 50 E
Ilovlya → **181** 49 14N 43 54 E
Iłowa **152** 51 30N 15 10 E
Ilubabor □ **245** 7 25N 35 0 E
Ilukste **178** 55 55N 26 20 E
Ilva Mică **170** 47 17N 24 40 E
Ilwaki **207** 7 55 S 126 30 E
Ilyichevsk **180** 46 10N 30 35 E
Iłża **152** 51 10N 21 15 E
Iłżanka → **152** 51 14N 21 48 E
Imabari **220** 34 4N 133 0 E
Imaichi **221** 36 43N 139 46 E
Imala **104** 24 53N 107 13W
Imaloto → **255** 23 27 S 45 13 E
Imandra, Oz. **176** 67 30N 33 0 E
Imari **220** 33 15N 129 52 E
Imasa **244** 18 0N 36 12 E
Imathía □ **168** 40 30N 22 15 E
Imbâbah **244** 30 5N 31 12 E
Imbabura □ **118** 0 30N 78 45W
Imbaimadai **119** 5 44N 60 17W
Imdahane **240** 32 8N 7 0W
imeni 26 Bakinskikh
Komissarov,
Azerbaijan,
U.S.S.R. **177** 39 19N 49 12 E
imeni 26 Bakinskikh
Komissarov,
Turkmen S.S.R.,
U.S.S.R. **177** 39 22N 54 10 E
Imeni Panfilova **183** 43 23N 77 7 E
Imeni Poliny
Osipenko **185** 52 30N 136 29 E
Imeri, Serra **118** 0 50N 65 25W
Imerimandroso **255** 17 26 S 48 35 E
Imesan **240** 22 54N 15 30W
Imi **245** 6 28N 42 10 E
Imishly **181** 39 49N 48 4 E
Imitek **240** 29 43N 8 10W
Immenstadt **147** 47 34N 10 13 E
Immingham **132** 53 37N 0 12W
Imo □ **247** 5 15N 7 20 E
Imola **163** 44 20N 11 42 E
Imotski **166** 43 27N 17 12 E
Imperatriz,
Amazonas, Brazil **122** 5 18 S 67 11W
Imperatriz,
Maranhão, Brazil **120** 5 30 S 47 29W
Impéria **162** 43 52N 8 0 E
Imperial, Canada **88** 51 21N 105 28W
Imperial, Peru **122** 13 4 S 76 21W
Imperieuse Reef **228** 17 36 S 118 50 E
Impfondo **252** 1 40N 18 0 E
Imphal **202** 24 48N 93 56 E
Imphy **139** 46 56N 3 15 E
İmroz = Gökçeada **168** 40 10N 25 50 E
Imst **150** 47 15N 10 44 E
Imuris **100** 30 47N 110 52W
Imuruan B. **211** 10 40N 119 10 E
In Belbel **240** 27 55N 1 12 E
In Delimane **247** 15 52N 1 31 E
In Rhar **240** 27 10N 1 59 E
In Salah **240** 27 10N 2 32 E
In Tallak **247** 16 19N 3 15 E
Ina **221** 35 50N 138 0 E
Ina-Bonchi **221** 35 45N 137 58 E
Inagauan **211** 9 33N 118 39 E
Inajá **120** 8 54 S 37 49W
Inangahua Junc. **235** 41 52 S 171 59 E
Inanwatan **207** 2 10 S 132 14 E
Iñapari **122** 11 0 S 69 40W
Inari **174** 68 54N 27 5 E
Inawashiro-Ko **218** 37 29N 140 6 E
Inazawa **221** 35 15N 136 47 E
Inca **156** 39 43N 2 54 E
Incaguasi **124** 29 12 S 71 5W
İnce-Burnu **180** 42 7N 34 56 E
İncekum Burnu **190** 36 13N 33 57 E
Inchon **215** 37 27N 126 40 E
Incio **154** 42 39N 7 21W
Incomáti → **255** 25 46 S 32 43 E
Incudine, L' **141** 41 50N 9 12 E
Inda Silase **245** 14 10N 38 15 E
Indalsälven → **172** 62 36N 17 30 E
Indaparapeo **107** 19 47N 100 58W
Indaw **202** 24 15N 96 5 E
Indbir **245** 8 7N 37 52 E
Inde **104** 25 54N 105 13W
Independence Fjord **12** 82 10N 29 0W
Independência **120** 5 23 S 40 19W
Independencia, La **110** 16 31N 91 47W
Independența **170** 45 25N 27 42 E
Inderborskiy **181** 48 30N 51 42 E
India ■ **196** 20 0N 78 0 E
Indian-Antarctic
Ridge **224** 49 0 S 120 0 E
Indian Cabins **76** 59 52N 117 40W
Indian Harbour **78** 54 27N 57 13W
Indian Head **88** 50 30N 103 41W
Indian L. **86** 50 14N 94 5W
Indian Ocean **203** 5 0 S 75 0 E
Indiapora **121** 19 57 S 50 17W
Indiga **176** 67 50N 48 50 E
Indigirka → **185** 70 48N 148 54 E
Inđija **166** 45 6N 20 7 E
Indonesia ■ **206** 5 0 S 115 0 E
Indore **198** 22 42N 75 53 E
Indramayu **209** 6 20 S 108 19 E
Indravati → **200** 19 20N 80 20 E
Indre □ **139** 46 50N 1 39 E
Indre → **138** 47 16N 0 19 E
Indre-et-Loire □ **138** 47 12N 0 40 E
Indungo **253** 14 48 S 16 17 E
Indus → **197** 24 20N 67 47 E
Indus, Mouth of the **197** 24 0N 68 0 E
İnebolu **177** 41 55N 33 40 E
Inés, Mt. **126** 48 30 S 69 40W
Ineu **170** 46 26N 21 51 E
Inezgane **240** 30 25N 9 29W
Infanta **210** 14 45N 121 39 E
Infante, Kaap **254** 34 27 S 20 51 E
Infantes **157** 38 43N 3 1W
Inferior, L. **109** 16 20N 94 10W
Infiernillo **106** 18 18N 101 55W
Infiernillo, Canal del **100** 29 9N 112 15W
Infiernillo, Presa del **106** 18 35N 101 50W
Infiesto **154** 43 21N 5 21W
Inganda **252** 0 5 S 20 57 E
Ingapirca **118** 2 38 S 78 56W
Ingelmunster **143** 50 56N 3 16 E
Ingende **252** 0 12 S 18 57 E
Ingeniero Jacobacci **126** 41 20 S 69 36W
Ingenio Santa Ana **124** 27 25 S 65 40W
Ingersoll **84** 43 4N 80 55W
Ingham **230** 18 43 S 146 10 E
Ingichka **183** 39 47N 65 58 E
Ingleborough **132** 54 11N 2 23W
Inglefield G. **95** 77 30N 67 0W
Inglewood, Queens.,
Australia **231** 28 25 S 151 2 E
Inglewood, Vic.,
Australia **231** 36 29 S 143 53 E
Inglewood, N.Z. **234** 39 9 S 174 14 E
Ingólfshöfði **174** 63 48N 16 39W
Ingolstadt **147** 48 45N 11 26 E
Ingomar **81** 43 34N 65 22W
Ingonish **81** 46 42N 60 18W
Ingonish Beach **81** 46 38N 60 25W
Ingore **246** 12 24N 15 48W
Ingraj Bazar **199** 24 58N 88 10 E
Ingrid Christensen
Coast **13** 69 30 S 76 0 E
Inguarán **107** 18 57N 101 35W
Inguarán, Sa. de **107** 18 50N 101 30W
Ingul → **180** 46 50N 32 15 E
Ingulec **180** 47 42N 33 14 E
Ingulets → **180** 46 41N 32 48 E
Inguri → **181** 42 38N 41 35 E
Inhaca, I. **255** 26 1 S 32 57 E
Inhafenga **255** 20 36 S 33 53 E
Inhambane **255** 23 54 S 35 30 E
Inhambane □ **255** 22 30 S 34 20 E
Inhambupe **121** 11 47 S 38 21W
Inhaminga **251** 18 26 S 35 0 E
Inharrime **255** 24 30 S 35 0 E
Inharrime → **255** 24 30 S 35 0 E
Inhuma **120** 6 40 S 41 42W
Inhumas **121** 16 22 S 49 30W
Iniesta **157** 39 27N 1 45W
Inini □ **119** 4 0N 53 0W
Inírida → **118** 3 55N 67 52W
Inishbofin **135** 53 35N 10 12W
Inishmore **135** 53 8N 9 45W
Inishowen **135** 55 14N 7 15W
Injune **231** 25 53 S 148 32 E
Inkerman **81** 47 40N 64 49W
Inklin **76** 58 56N 133 5W
Inklin → **76** 58 50N 133 10W
Inle L. **202** 20 30N 96 58 E
Inn → **147** 48 35N 13 28 E
Innamincka **231** 27 44 S 140 46 E
Inner Hebrides **134** 57 0N 6 30W
Inner Mongolia =
Nei Monggol
Zizhiqu □ **214** 42 0N 112 0 E
Inner Sound **134** 57 30N 5 55W
Innerkip **84** 43 13N 80 42W
Innerkirchen **148** 46 43N 8 14 E
Innerste → **146** 52 45N 9 40 E
Innetalling I. **78** 56 0N 79 0W
Innisfail, Australia **230** 17 33 S 146 5 E
Innisfail, Canada **91** 52 0N 113 57W
Innisfree **90** 53 22N 111 32W
In'no-shima **220** 34 19N 133 10 E
Innsbruck **150** 47 16N 11 23 E
Inny → **135** 53 30N 7 50W
Ino **220** 33 33N 133 26 E
Inocência **121** 19 47 S 51 48W
Inongo **252** 1 55 S 18 30 E
Inoni **252** 3 4 S 15 39 E
Inoucdjouac **78** 58 25N 78 15W
Inowrocław **152** 52 50N 18 12 E
Inpundong **215** 41 25N 126 34 E
Inquisivi **122** 16 50 S 67 10W
Ins **148** 47 1N 7 7 E
Inscription, C. **229** 26 25 S 112 59 E
Insein **202** 16 50N 96 5 E
Însurăţei **170** 44 50N 27 40 E
Inta **176** 66 5N 60 8 E
Intata Reach **92** 53 38N 125 30W
Intendente Alvear **124** 35 12 S 63 32W
Interlaken **148** 46 41N 7 50 E
Intiyaco **124** 28 43 S 60 5W
Intragna **149** 46 11N 8 42 E
Intutu **118** 3 32 S 74 48W
Inubo-Zaki **221** 35 42N 140 52 E
Inútil, B. **126** 53 30 S 70 15W
Inuvik **94** 68 16N 133 40W
Inuvik □ **94** 70 0N 130 0W
Inuyama **221** 35 23N 136 56 E
Inveraray **134** 56 13N 5 5W
Inverbervie **134** 56 50N 2 17W
Invercargill **235** 46 24 S 168 24 E
Inverell **231** 29 45 S 151 8 E
Invergordon **134** 57 41N 4 10W
Inverleigh **232** 38 6 S 144 3 E
Invermay **88** 51 48N 103 9W
Invermere **91** 50 30N 116 2W
Inverness, Canada **81** 46 15N 61 19W
Inverness, U.K. **134** 57 29N 4 12W
Inverurie **134** 57 15N 2 21W
Inverway **228** 17 50 S 129 38 E
Investigator Group **231** 34 45 S 134 20 E
Investigator Str. **232** 35 30 S 137 0 E
Inwood **89** 50 30N 97 30W
Inya **184** 50 28N 86 37 E
Inyanga **251** 18 12 S 32 40 E
Inyangani **251** 18 5 S 32 50 E
Inyantue **251** 18 30 S 26 40 E
Inywa **202** 23 56N 96 17 E
Inza **179** 53 55N 46 25 E
Inzer **182** 54 14N 57 34 E
Inzhavino **179** 52 22N 42 30 E
Iō-Jima **219** 30 48N 130 18 E

Place	Page	Lat.	Long.
Ioánnina	168	39 42N	20 47 E
Ioánnina □	168	39 39N	20 57 E
Ioma	227	8 19 S	147 52 E
Ion Corvin	170	44 7N	27 50 E
Iona, Canada	81	45 58N	60 48W
Iona, U.K.	134	56 20N	6 25W
Ionian Is. = Iónioi Nísoi	169	38 40N	20 0 E
Ionian Sea	159	37 30N	17 30 E
Iónioi Nísoi	169	38 40N	20 0 E
Iori →	181	41 3N	46 17 E
Íos	169	36 41N	25 20 E
Ipala	250	4 30 S	32 52 E
Ipameri	121	17 44 S	48 9W
Iparía	122	9 17 S	74 29W
Ipáti	169	38 52N	22 14 E
Ipatovo	181	45 45N	42 50 E
Ipel →	151	48 10N	19 35 E
Ipiales	118	0 50N	77 37W
Ipiaú	121	14 8 S	39 44W
Ipil	211	7 47N	122 35 E
Ipin = Yibin	216	28 45N	104 32 E
Ipirá	121	12 10 S	39 44W
Ipiranga	118	3 13 S	65 57W
Ípiros □	168	39 30N	20 30 E
Ipixuna	122	7 0 S	71 40W
Ipixuna →, Amazonas, Brazil	122	7 11 S	71 51W
Ipixuna →, Amazonas, Brazil	123	5 45 S	63 2W
Ipoh	205	4 35N	101 5 E
Iporá	121	11 23 S	50 40W
Ippy	252	6 5N	21 7 E
Ipsala	168	40 55N	26 23 E
Ipsárion Óros	168	40 40N	24 40 E
Ipswich, Australia	231	27 35 S	152 40 E
Ipswich, U.K.	133	52 4N	1 9 E
Ipu	120	4 23 S	40 44W
Ipueiras	120	4 33 S	40 43W
Ipupiara	121	11 49 S	42 37W
Iput →	178	52 26N	31 2 E
Iquique	122	20 19 S	70 5W
Iquitos	118	3 45 S	73 10W
Irabu-Jima	219	24 50N	125 10 E
Iracoubo	119	5 30N	53 10W
Īrafshān	193	26 42N	61 56 E
Irahuan	211	9 48N	118 41 E
Iráklia	169	36 50N	25 28 E
Iráklion	169	35 20N	25 12 E
Iráklion □	169	35 10N	25 10 E
Irako-Zaki	221	34 35N	137 1 E
Irala	125	25 55 S	54 35W
Iramba □	250	4 30 S	34 30 E
Iran ■	193	33 0N	53 0 E
Iran, Gunung-Gunung	206	2 20N	114 50 E
Iranamadu Tank	201	9 23N	80 29 E
Īrānshahr	193	27 15N	60 40 E
Irapa	119	10 34N	62 35W
Irapuato	107	20 41N	101 28W
Iraq ■	192	33 0N	44 0 E
Irarrar, O. →	240	20 0N	1 30 E
Irati	125	25 25 S	50 38W
Irbid	189	32 35N	35 48 E
Irbid □	191	32 15N	36 35 E
Irbit	182	57 41N	63 3 E
Irebu	252	0 40 S	17 46 E
Irecê	120	11 18 S	41 52W
Iregua →	156	42 27N	2 24 E
Ireland ■	135	53 0N	8 0W
Ireland's Eye	135	53 25N	6 4W
Irele	247	7 40N	5 40 E
Iremel, Gora	182	54 33N	58 50 E
Ireng →	119	3 33N	59 51W
Iret	185	60 3N	154 20 E
Irhârharene	241	27 37N	7 30 E
Irharrhar, O. →	241	28 3N	6 15 E
Irherm	240	30 7N	8 18W
Irhil Mgoun	240	31 30N	6 28W
Irhyangdong	215	41 15N	129 30 E
Iri	215	35 59N	127 0 E
Irian Jaya □	207	4 0 S	137 0 E
Iriba	243	15 7N	22 15 E
Irid, Mt.	210	14 47N	121 19 E
Irié	246	8 15N	9 10W
Iriga	210	13 25N	123 25 E
Iriklinskiy	182	51 39N	58 38 E
Iriklinskoye Vdkhr.	182	52 0N	59 0 E
Iringa	250	7 48 S	35 43 E
Iringa □	250	7 48 S	35 43 E
Irinjalakuda	201	10 21N	76 14 E
Iriomote-Jima	219	24 19N	123 48 E
Iriona	112	15 57N	85 11W
Iriri →	119	3 52 S	52 37W
Iriri Novo →	123	8 46 S	53 22W
Irish Republic ■	135	53 0N	8 0 E
Irish Sea	132	54 0N	5 0W
Irkeshtam	183	39 41N	73 55 E
Irkineyeva	185	58 30N	96 49 E
Irkutsk	185	52 18N	104 20 E
Irma	91	52 55N	111 14W
Irō-Zaki	221	34 36N	138 51 E
Iroise, Mer d'	138	48 15N	4 45W
Iron Baron	231	32 58 S	137 11 E
Iron Bridge	84	46 17N	83 14W
Iron Gate = Portile de Fier	170	44 42N	22 30 E
Iron Knob	231	32 46 S	137 8 E
Iron Springs	91	49 56N	112 41W
Ironbridge	133	52 38N	2 29W
Ironstone Kopje	254	25 17 S	24 5 E
Iroquois	85	44 51N	75 19W
Iroquois Falls	74	48 46N	80 41W
Irosin	210	12 42N	124 2 E
Irpen	178	50 30N	30 15 E
Irrara Cr. →	231	29 35 S	145 31 E
Irrawaddy □	202	17 0N	95 0 E
Irrawaddy →	202	15 50N	95 6 E
Irsina	165	40 45N	16 15 E
Irtysh →	184	61 4N	68 52 E
Irumu	250	1 32N	29 53 E
Irún	156	43 20N	1 52W
Irurzun	156	42 55N	1 50W
Irvine, Canada	91	49 57N	110 16W
Irvine, U.K.	134	55 37N	4 40W
Irvinestown	135	54 28N	7 38W
Irwin →	229	29 15 S	114 54 E
Irwin, Pt.	229	35 5 S	116 55 E
Irymple	231	34 14 S	142 8 E
Is-sur-Tille	139	47 30N	5 10 E
Isa	247	13 14N	6 24 E
Isaac →	230	22 55 S	149 20 E
Isabela	211	10 12N	122 59 E
Isabela □	210	17 0N	122 0 E
Isabela, I.	104	21 51N	105 55W
Isabela, La	113	19 58N	71 2W
Isabella	211	6 40N	122 10 E
Isabella, Cord.	112	13 30N	85 25W
Isabella Ra.	228	21 0 S	121 4 E
Isachsen	95	78 47N	103 30W
Ísafjarðardjúp	174	66 10N	23 0W
Ísafjörður	174	66 5N	23 9W
Isagarh	198	24 48N	77 51 E
Isahaya	220	32 52N	130 2 E
Isaka	250	3 56 S	32 59 E
Isakly	182	54 8N	51 32 E
Isana →	118	0 26N	67 19W
Isangi	252	0 52N	24 10 E
Isar →	147	48 49N	12 58 E
Isarco →	163	46 57N	11 18 E
Ísari	169	37 22N	22 0 E
Isbergues	139	50 36N	2 24 E
Isbiceni	170	43 45N	24 40 E
Iscayachi	123	21 31 S	65 3W
Íschia	164	40 45N	13 51 E
Iscuandé	118	2 28N	77 59W
Isdell →	228	16 27 S	124 51 E
Ise	221	34 25N	136 45 E
Ise-Heiya	221	34 40N	136 30 E
Ise-Wan	221	34 43N	136 43 E
Isefjord	172	55 53N	11 50 E
Iseltwald	148	46 43N	7 58 E
Isenthal	149	46 55N	8 34 E
Iseo	162	45 40N	10 3 E
Iseo, L. d'	162	45 45N	10 3 E
Iseramagazi	250	4 37 S	32 10 E
Isère □	141	45 15N	5 40 E
Isère →	141	44 59N	4 51 E
Iserlohn	146	51 22N	7 40 E
Isérnia	165	41 35N	14 12 E
Isesaki	221	36 19N	139 12 E
Iset →	182	56 36N	66 24 E
Iseyin	247	8 0N	3 36 E
Isfara	183	40 7N	70 38 E
Isherton	119	2 20N	59 25W
Ishigaki-Shima	219	24 20N	124 10 E
Ishikari-Gawa →	218	43 15N	141 23 E
Ishikari-Sammyaku	218	43 30N	143 0 E
Ishikari-Wan	218	43 25N	141 1 E
Ishikawa	226	26 25N	127 48 E
Ishikawa □	221	36 30N	136 30 E
Ishim	184	56 10N	69 30 E
Ishim →	184	57 45N	71 10 E
Ishimbay	182	53 28N	56 2 E
Ishinomaki	218	38 32N	141 20 E
Ishioka	221	36 11N	140 16 E
Ishizuchi-Yama	220	33 45N	133 6 E
Ishkashim	183	36 44N	71 37 E
Ishkuman	199	36 30N	73 50 E
Ishmi	168	41 33N	19 34 E
Ishurdi	202	24 9N	89 3 E
Isigny-sur-Mer	138	49 19N	1 6W
Isil Kul	184	54 55N	71 16 E
Isiolo	250	0 24N	37 33 E
Isiolo □	250	2 30N	37 30 E
Isipingo Beach	255	30 0 S	30 57 E
Isiro	250	2 53N	27 40 E
Isisford	230	24 15 S	144 21 E
Iskander	183	41 36N	69 41 E
Iskele	190	36 34N	35 23 E
Iskenderun	177	36 32N	36 10 E
Iskenderun Körfezi	177	36 40N	35 50 E
Iski-Naukat	183	40 16N	72 36 E
Iskilip	180	40 50N	34 20 E
Iskŭr →	167	43 45N	24 25 E
Iskŭr, Yazovir	167	42 23N	23 30 E
Iskut →	76	56 45N	131 49W
Isla	109	18 4N	95 33W
Isla →	134	56 32N	3 20W
Isla, La	101	31 30N	106 12W
Isla Cristina	155	37 13N	7 17W
Isla de Aguada	111	18 47N	91 28W
İslâhiye	190	37 0N	36 35 E
Islamabad	197	33 40N	73 10 E
Islamkot	198	24 42N	70 13 E
Islampur	200	17 2N	74 20 E
Island →	76	60 25N	121 12W
Island Bay	211	9 6N	118 10 E
Island Falls	87	49 35N	81 20W
Island L.	77	53 47N	94 25W
Island Lagoon	231	31 30 S	136 40 E
Island Pt.	229	30 20 S	115 1 E
Island Pond	79	48 25N	56 23W
Islands, B. of, Canada	79	49 11N	58 15W
Islands, B. of, N.Z.	234	35 15 S	174 6 E
Islay, Canada	90	53 24N	110 33W
Islay, U.K.	134	55 46N	6 10W
Isle →	140	44 55N	0 15W
Isle-Adam, L'	139	49 6N	2 14 E
Isle aux Morts	79	47 35N	59 0W
Isle-Jourdain, L', Gers, France	140	43 36N	1 5 E
Isle-Jourdain, L', Vienne, France	140	46 13N	0 31 E
Isle L.	90	53 38N	114 44W
Isle of Wight □	133	50 40N	1 20W
Isle Pierre	92	53 57N	123 16W
Isle Verte, L'	83	48 1N	69 20W
Isles, L. des	86	49 10N	89 40W
Ismail	180	45 22N	28 46 E
Ismâ'ilîya	244	30 37N	32 18 E
Ismaning	147	48 14N	11 41 E
Isna	244	25 17N	32 30 E
Isogstalo	199	34 15N	78 46 E
Isola del Gran Sasso d'Italia	163	42 30N	13 40 E
Ísola del Liri	164	41 39N	13 32 E
Ísola della Scala	162	45 16N	11 0 E
Ísola di Capo Rizzuto	165	38 56N	17 5 E
Isparta	177	37 47N	30 30 E
Isperikh	167	43 43N	26 50 E
Íspica	165	36 47N	14 53 E
Ispir	181	40 40N	40 50 E
Israel ■	189	32 0N	34 50 E
Issano	119	5 49N	59 26W
Isseka	229	28 30 S	114 35 E
Issia	246	6 33N	6 33W
Issoire	140	45 32N	3 15 E
Issoudun, Canada	83	46 35N	71 38W
Issoudun, France	139	46 57N	2 0 E
Issyk-Kul, Ozero	183	42 25N	77 15 E
Ist	163	44 17N	14 47 E
Istaihah	195	23 19N	54 4 E
İstanbul	177	41 0N	29 0 E
Istiaía	169	38 57N	23 9 E
Istmina	118	5 10N	76 39W
Istok	166	42 45N	20 24 E
Istra, U.S.S.R.	179	55 55N	36 50 E
Istra, Yugoslavia	163	45 10N	14 0 E
Istranca Dağları	167	41 48N	27 30 E
Istres	141	43 31N	4 59 E
Istria = Istra	163	45 10N	14 0 E
Isulan	211	6 30N	124 29 E
Itá	124	25 29 S	57 21W
'Itāb	195	15 20N	51 29 E
Itabaiana, Paraíba, Brazil	120	7 18 S	35 19W
Itabaiana, Sergipe, Brazil	120	10 41 S	37 37W
Itabaianinha	120	11 16 S	37 47W
Itaberaba	121	12 32 S	40 18W
Itaberaí	121	16 2 S	49 48W
Itabira	121	19 37 S	43 13W
Itabirito	121	20 15 S	43 48W
Itaboca	119	4 50 S	62 40W
Itabuna	121	14 48 S	39 16W
Itacajá	120	8 19 S	47 46W
Itacaunas →	120	5 21 S	49 8W
Itacoatiara	119	3 8 S	58 25W
Itacuaí →	122	4 20 S	70 12W
Itaguaçu	121	19 48 S	40 51W
Itaguari →	121	14 11 S	44 40W
Itaguatins	120	5 47 S	47 29W
Itaim →	120	7 2 S	42 2W
Itainópolis	120	7 24 S	41 31W
Itaituba	119	4 10 S	55 50W
Itajaí	125	27 50 S	48 39W
Itajubá	121	22 24 S	45 30W
Itajuípe	121	14 41 S	39 22W
Itaka	251	8 50 S	32 49 E
Itako	221	35 56N	140 33 E
Italy ■	160	42 0N	13 0 E
Itamataré	120	2 16 S	46 24W
Itambacuri	121	18 1 S	41 42W
Itambé	121	15 15 S	40 37W
Itampolo	255	24 41 S	43 57 E
Itanhauã →	119	4 45 S	63 48W
Itanhém	121	17 9 S	40 20W
Itano	220	34 7N	134 28 E
Itapaci	121	14 57 S	49 34W
Itapagé	120	3 41 S	39 34W
Itaparica, I. de	121	12 54 S	38 42W
Itapebi	121	15 56 S	39 32W
Itapecuru-Mirim	120	3 24 S	44 20W
Itaperuna	121	21 10 S	41 54W
Itapetinga	121	15 15 S	40 15W
Itapetininga	125	23 36 S	48 7W
Itapeva	125	23 59 S	48 59W
Itapicuru →, Bahia, Brazil	120	11 47 S	37 32W
Itapicuru →, Maranhão, Brazil	120	2 52 S	44 12W
Itapinima	123	5 25 S	60 44W
Itapipoca	120	3 30 S	39 35W
Itapiranga	119	2 45 S	58 1W
Itapiúna	120	4 33 S	38 57W
Itaporanga	120	7 18 S	38 0W
Itapuá □	125	26 40 S	55 40W
Itapuranga	121	15 40 S	49 59W
Itaquari	121	20 20 S	40 25W
Itaquatiara	122	2 58 S	58 30W
Itaquí	124	29 8 S	56 30W
Itararé	125	24 6 S	49 23W
Itarsi	198	22 36N	77 51 E
Itarumã	121	18 42 S	51 25W
Itatí	124	27 16 S	58 15W
Itatira	120	4 30 S	39 37W
Itatuba	123	5 46 S	63 20W
Itatupa	119	0 37 S	51 12W
Itaueira	120	7 36 S	43 2W
Itaueira →	120	6 41 S	42 55W
Itaúna	121	20 4 S	44 34W
Itbayat	210	20 47N	121 51 E
Itbayat I.	210	20 46N	121 50 E
Itchen →	133	50 57N	1 20W
Ite	122	17 55 S	70 57W
Itéa	169	38 25N	22 25 E
Ithaca = Itháki	169	38 25N	20 40 E
Itháki	169	38 25N	20 40 E
Itinga	121	16 36 S	41 47W
Itiquira	123	17 12 S	54 7W
Itiquira →	123	17 18 S	56 44W
Itiruçu	121	13 31 S	40 9W
Itiúba	120	10 43 S	39 51W
Ito	221	34 58N	139 5 E
Itoigawa	219	37 2N	137 51 E
Itomamo, L.	83	49 11N	70 28W
Itoman	226	26 7N	127 40 E
Iton →	138	49 9N	1 12 E
Itonamas →	122	12 28 S	64 24W
Itsa	244	29 15N	30 47 E
Itsukaichi	220	34 22N	132 22 E
Itsuki	220	32 24N	130 50 E
Íttiri	164	40 38N	8 32 E
Itu, Brazil	125	23 17 S	47 15W
Itu, Nigeria	247	5 10N	7 58 E
Ituaçu	121	13 50 S	41 18W
Ituango	118	7 4N	75 45W
Ituiutaba	121	19 0 S	49 25W
Itumbiara	121	18 20 S	49 10W
Ituna	88	51 10N	103 24W
Itunge Port	251	9 40 S	33 55 E
Ituni	119	5 28N	58 15W
Itupiranga	120	5 9 S	49 20W
Iturama	121	19 44 S	50 11W
Iturbe	124	23 0 S	65 25W
Ituri →	250	1 40N	27 1 E
Ituribe	103	24 44N	99 54W
Iturup, Ostrov	185	45 0N	148 0 E
Ituverava	121	20 20 S	47 47W
Ituxi →	123	7 18 S	64 51W
Ituyuro →	124	22 40 S	63 50W
Itxlahuacán del Río	106	20 52N	103 18W
Itzehoe	146	53 56N	9 31 E
Ivaí →	125	23 18 S	53 42W
Ivalo	174	68 38N	27 35 E
Ivalojoki →	174	68 40N	27 40 E
Ivangorod	178	59 37N	28 40 E
Ivangrad	166	42 51N	19 52 E
Ivanhoe, N.S.W., Australia	231	32 56 S	144 20 E
Ivanhoe, N. Terr., Australia	228	15 41 S	128 41 E
Ivanhoe L.	77	60 25N	106 30W
Ivanić Grad	163	45 41N	16 25 E
Ivanjica	166	43 35N	20 12 E
Ivanjšcice	163	46 12N	16 13 E
Ivankoyskoye Vdkhr.	179	56 37N	36 32 E
Ivano-Frankovsk	178	48 40N	24 40 E
Ivanovka	182	52 34N	53 23 E
Ivanovo, Byelorussian S.S.R., U.S.S.R.	178	52 7N	25 29 E
Ivanovo, R.S.F.S.R., U.S.S.R.	179	57 5N	41 0 E
Ivato	255	20 37 S	47 10 E
Ivaylovgrad	167	41 32N	26 8 E
Ivdel	176	60 42N	60 24 E
Ivindo →	252	0 9 S	12 9 E
Ivinheima →	125	23 14 S	53 42W
Iviza = Ibiza	157	38 54N	1 26 E
Ivohibe	255	22 31 S	46 57 E

Ivolândia 121 16 34 S 50 51W
Ivory Coast ■ 246 7 30N 5 0W
Ivösjön 173 56 8N 14 25 E
Ivrea 162 45 30N 7 52 E
Ivugivik 78 62 24N 77 55W
Iwahig, Palawan, Phil. 206 8 36N 117 32 E
Iwahig, Palawan, Phil. 211 9 19N 118 5 E
Iwai-Jima 220 33 47N 131 58 E
Iwaizumi 218 39 50N 141 45 E
Iwaki 219 37 4N 140 55 E
Iwakuni 220 34 15N 132 8 E
Iwami 220 35 32N 134 15 E
Iwamizawa 218 43 12N 141 46 E
Iwanai 218 42 58N 140 30 E
Iwase 221 36 21N 140 6 E
Iwata 221 34 42N 137 51 E
Iwate □ 218 39 30N 141 30 E
Iwate-San 218 39 51N 141 0 E
Iwo 247 7 39N 4 9 E
Iwonicz-Zdrój 152 49 37N 21 47 E
Iwungu 253 5 16 S 19 17 E
Ixaltepec 109 16 30N 95 3W
Ixcatepec 108 21 12N 97 57W
Ixhuacan de los Reyes 108 19 35N 97 4W
Ixiamas 122 13 50 S 68 5W
Ixmiquilpan 107 20 29N 99 14W
Ixopo 255 30 11 S 30 5 E
Ixtacomitán 110 17 25N 93 6W
Ixtapa 110 16 48N 92 55W
Ixtapa → 107 18 23N 100 42W
Ixtapa, Pta. 107 17 39N 101 40W
Ixtapán de la Sal 107 18 50N 99 41W
Ixtepec 109 16 34N 95 6W
Ixtlahuaca 107 19 34N 99 46W
Ixtlahuacán 106 19 1N 103 45W
Ixtlán 106 20 11N 102 24W
Ixtlán, Sa. de 109 17 25N 96 40W
Ixtlán del Río 104 21 2N 104 22W
'Iyādh 194 14 59N 46 51 E
Iyo 220 33 45N 132 45 E
Iyo-mishima 220 33 58N 133 30 E
Iyo-Nada 220 33 40N 132 20 E
Izabel, L. de 112 15 30N 89 10W
Izamal 111 20 56N 89 1W
Izberbash 181 42 35N 47 52 E
Izbica 152 50 53N 23 10 E
Izbica Kujawska 152 52 25N 18 30 E
Izegem 143 50 55N 3 12 E
Izena-Shima 226 26 56N 127 56 E
Izgrev 167 43 36N 26 58 E
Izh → 182 55 58N 52 38 E
Izhevsk = Ustinov 182 56 51N 53 14 E
Izkī 195 22 56N 27 46 E
İzmir 177 38 25N 27 8 E
İzmit 177 40 45N 29 50 E
Iznajar 155 37 15N 4 19W
Iznalloz 157 37 24N 3 30W
Izobil'nyy 181 45 25N 41 44 E
Izola 163 45 32N 13 39 E
Izozog, Bañados de 123 18 48 S 62 10W
Izra 189 32 51N 36 15 E
Iztochni Rodopi 167 41 45N 25 30 E
Izu-Hantō 221 34 45N 139 0 E
Izu-Shotō 219 34 30N 140 0 E
Izúcar de Matamoros 109 18 36N 98 28W
Izuhara 220 34 12N 129 17 E
Izumi 220 32 5N 130 22 E
Izumi-sano 221 34 23N 135 18 E
Izumiotsu 221 34 30N 135 24 E
Izumo 220 35 20N 132 46 E
Izyaslav 178 50 5N 26 50 E
Izyum 180 49 12N 37 19 E

J

J.F. Rodrigues 120 2 55 S 50 20W
Jaab L. 87 51 10N 82 58W
Jaba, Ethiopia 245 6 20N 35 7 E
Jaba', Jordan 189 32 20N 35 13 E
Jabal el Awliya 245 15 10N 32 31 E
Jabal Lubnān 190 33 45N 35 40 E
Jabalón → 155 38 53N 4 5W
Jabalpur 199 23 9N 79 58 E
Jabālyah 189 31 32N 34 27 E
Jabbūl 192 36 4N 37 30 E
Jablah 190 35 20N 36 0 E
Jablanac 163 44 42N 14 56 E
Jablonec 150 50 43N 15 10 E
Jablonica 151 48 37N 17 26 E
Jabłonowo 152 53 23N 19 10 E
Jaboatão 120 8 7 S 35 1W
Jabonga 211 9 20N 125 32 E
Jaboticabal 125 21 15 S 48 17W
Jabukovac 166 44 22N 22 21 E
Jaburu 123 5 30 S 64 0W
Jaca 156 42 35N 0 33W
Jacala 107 21 1N 99 11W
Jacaré → 120 10 3 S 42 13W
Jacareí 125 23 20 S 46 0W
Jacarèzinho 125 23 5 S 50 0W
Jáchymov 150 50 22N 12 55 E
Jaciara 123 15 59 S 54 57W
Jacinto 121 16 10 S 40 17W
Jaciparaná 123 9 15 S 64 23W
Jackfish L. 88 53 9N 108 29W
Jackson 231 26 39 S 149 39 E
Jackson, C. 235 40 59 S 174 20 E
Jackson Bay 235 43 58 S 168 42 E
Jacksons 235 42 46 S 171 32 E
Jackson's Arm 79 49 52N 56 47W
Jacmel 113 18 14N 72 32W
Jacobabad 197 28 20N 68 29 E
Jacobina 120 11 11 S 40 30W
Jacobs 86 50 15N 89 50W
Jacob's Well 189 32 13N 35 13 E
Jacomulco 108 19 20N 96 44W
Jacona 106 19 57N 102 16W
Jacques-Cartier 83 45 31N 73 29W
Jacques-Cartier → 83 46 40N 71 45W
Jacques Cartier, Dét. de 78 50 0N 63 30W
Jacques-Cartier, L. 83 47 35N 71 13W
Jacques-Cartier, Mt. 80 48 57N 66 0W
Jacquet River 81 47 55N 66 0W
Jacqueville 246 5 12N 4 25W
Jacuí → 125 30 2 S 51 15W
Jacundá → 120 1 57 S 50 26W
Jade 146 53 22N 8 14 E
Jadebusen 146 53 30N 8 15 E
Jadoigne 143 50 43N 4 52 E
Jadotville = Likasi 251 10 55 S 26 48 E
Jadovnik 166 43 20N 19 45 E
Jadów 152 52 28N 21 38 E
Jadraque 156 40 55N 2 55W
Jādū 241 32 0N 12 0 E
Jaén, Peru 122 5 25 S 78 40W
Jaén, Spain 155 37 44N 3 43W
Jaén □ 155 37 50N 3 30W
Jaerens Rev 171 58 45N 5 45 E
Jafène 240 20 35N 5 30W
Jaffa = Tel Aviv-Yafo 189 32 4N 34 48 E
Jaffa, C. 232 36 58 S 139 40 E
Jaffna 201 9 45N 80 2 E
Jagadhri 198 30 10N 77 20 E
Jagadishpur 199 25 30N 84 21 E
Jagdalpur 200 19 3N 82 0 E
Jagersfontein 254 29 44 S 25 27 E
Jagst → 147 49 14N 9 11 E
Jagtial 200 18 50N 79 0 E
Jaguaquara 121 13 32 S 39 58W
Jaguariaíva 125 24 10 S 49 50W
Jaguaribe 120 5 53 S 38 37W
Jaguaribe → 120 4 25 S 37 45W
Jaguaruana 120 4 50 S 37 47W
Jagüey Grande 112 22 35N 81 7W
Jagungal, Mt. 233 36 8 S 148 22 E
Jahangirabad 198 28 19N 78 4 E
Jahrom 193 28 30N 53 31 E
Jaicós 120 7 21 S 41 8W
Jailolo 207 1 5N 127 30 E
Jailolo, Selat 207 0 5N 129 5 E
Jaintiapur 202 25 8N 92 7 E
Jaipur 198 27 0N 75 50 E
Jājarm 193 36 58N 56 27 E
Jajce 166 44 19N 17 17 E
Jajpur 199 20 53N 86 22 E
Jakarta 207 6 9 S 106 49 E
Jakobshavn 95 68 0N 51 0W
Jakobstad 174 63 40N 22 43 E
Jakupica 166 41 45N 21 22 E
Jalacingo 108 19 48N 97 18W
Jalalabad, Afghan. 197 34 30N 70 29 E
Jalalabad, India 199 27 41N 79 42 E
Jalalpur Jattan 198 32 38N 74 11 E
Jalapa, Guat. 112 14 39N 89 59W
Jalapa, Mexico 110 17 43N 92 49W
Jalapa del Marques 109 16 26N 95 25W
Jalapa Enríquez 108 19 32N 96 55W
Jalaun 199 26 8N 79 25 E
Jalcocotán 104 21 28N 105 7W
Jaldak 197 31 58N 66 43 E
Jaleaca de Catalán 107 17 26N 99 51W
Jales 121 20 10 S 50 33W
Jaleswar 199 26 38N 85 48 E
Jalgaon, Maharashtra, India 198 21 2N 76 31 E
Jalgaon, Maharashtra, India 198 21 0N 75 42 E
Jalhay 143 50 33N 5 58 E
Jalībah 192 30 35N 46 32 E
Jalingo 247 8 55N 11 25 E
Jalisco, Coahuila, Mexico 103 25 13N 103 26W
Jalisco, Nayarit, Mexico 104 21 27N 104 54W
Jalisco □ 106 20 20N 103 40W
Jalkot 199 35 14N 73 24 E
Jallas → 154 42 54N 9 8W
Jallumba 232 36 55 S 141 57 E
Jalna 200 19 48N 75 38 E
Jalón → 156 41 47N 1 4W
Jalostotitlán 106 21 12N 102 28W
Jalpa 105 21 38N 102 58W
Jalpa de Méndez 110 18 11N 93 4W
Jalpaiguri 202 26 32N 88 46 E
Jalpan 107 21 14N 99 29W
Jalq 197 27 35N 62 46 E
Jaltemba, B. 104 21 5N 105 16W
Jaltenango 110 15 55N 92 43W
Jaltepec, R. → 109 17 26N 94 59W
Jaluit I. 224 6 0N 169 30 E
Jalūlā 192 34 16N 45 10 E
Jamaari 247 11 44N 9 53 E
Jamaica ■ 112 18 10N 77 30W
Jamalpur, Bangla. 202 24 52N 89 56 E
Jamalpur, India 199 25 18N 86 28 E
Jamalpurganj 199 23 2N 88 1 E
Jamanxim → 123 4 43 S 56 18W
Jamapa, R. → 109 19 2N 96 8W
Jamari 123 8 45 S 63 27W
Jamari → 123 8 27 S 63 30W
Jamay 106 20 18N 102 43W
Jambe 207 1 15 S 132 10 E
Jambes 143 50 27N 4 52 E
Jambi 208 1 38 S 103 30 E
Jambi □ 208 1 30 S 102 30 E
Jambusar 198 22 3N 72 51 E
James B. 87 51 30N 80 0W
James Range 228 24 10 S 132 30 E
James River 81 45 35N 62 7W
James Ross I. 13 63 58 S 57 50W
Jameson, C. 95 72 5N 74 14W
Jamestown, Australia 231 33 10 S 138 32 E
Jamestown, S. Africa 254 31 6 S 26 45 E
Jamīlābād 193 34 24N 48 28 E
Jamiltepec 109 16 17N 97 49W
Jamkhaudi 200 16 30N 75 15 E
Jammā'īn 189 32 8N 35 12 E
Jammalamadugu 201 14 51N 78 25 E
Jammerbugt 173 57 15N 9 20 E
Jammu 198 32 43N 74 54 E
Jammu & Kashmir □ 199 34 25N 77 0 E
Jamnagar 198 22 30N 70 6 E
Jamner 198 20 45N 75 52 E
Jamoigne 143 49 41N 5 24 E
Jampur 197 29 39N 70 40 E
Jamrud 197 33 59N 71 24 E
Jamshedpur 199 22 44N 86 12 E
Jamtara 199 23 59N 86 49 E
Jämtlands län □ 172 62 40N 13 50 E
Jamuna → 202 23 51N 89 45 E
Jamurki 202 24 9N 90 2 E
Jan Kemp 254 27 55 S 24 51 E
Jan L. 77 54 56N 102 55W
Jan Mayen Is. 12 71 0N 9 0W
Janaúba 121 15 48 S 43 19W
Janaucu, I. 120 0 30N 50 10W
Jand 198 33 30N 72 6 E
Janda, Laguna de la 155 36 15N 5 45W
Jandaia 121 17 6 S 50 7W
Jandaq 193 34 3N 54 22 E
Jandiatuba → 118 3 28 S 68 42W
Jandola 198 32 20N 70 9 E
Jandowae 231 26 45 S 151 7 E
Jandrain-Jandrenouilles 143 50 40N 4 58 E
Jándula → 155 38 3N 4 6W
Jane Pk. 235 45 15 S 168 20 E
Janga 247 10 5N 1 0W
Jango 123 20 27 S 55 29W
Jangoon 200 17 44N 79 5 E
Janhtang Ga 202 26 32N 96 38 E
Jānī Kheyl 197 32 46N 68 24 E
Janikowo 152 52 45N 18 7 E
Janīn 189 32 28N 35 18 E
Janinà = Ioánnina □ 168 39 39N 20 57 E
Janiuay 211 10 58N 122 30 E
Janja 166 44 40N 19 17 E
Janjevo 166 42 35N 21 19 E
Janjina 166 42 58N 17 25 E
Janos 101 30 54N 108 10W
Jánoshalma 151 46 18N 19 21 E
Jánosháza 151 47 8N 17 12 E
Jánossomorja 151 47 47N 17 11 E
Janów 152 50 44N 19 27 E
Janów Lubelski 152 50 48N 22 23 E
Janów Podlaski 152 52 11N 23 11 E
Janowiec Wielkopolski 152 52 45N 17 30 E
Jansen 88 51 54N 104 45W
Januária 121 15 25 S 44 25W
Janub Dârfûr □ 245 11 0N 25 0 E
Janub Kordofân □ 245 12 0N 30 0 E
Janville 139 48 10N 1 50 E
Janzé 138 47 55N 1 28W
Jaora 198 23 40N 75 10 E
Japan ■ 219 36 0N 136 0 E
Japan, Sea of 218 40 0N 135 0 E
Japan Trench 224 32 0N 142 0 E
Japen = Yapen 207 1 50 S 136 0 E
Japurá → 118 3 8 S 64 46W
Jaque 118 7 27N 78 8W
Jaques-Cartier, Détroit de 80 50 0N 63 30W
Jarābulus 192 36 49N 38 1 E
Jaraguá 121 15 45 S 49 20W
Jaraguari 123 20 9 S 54 35W
Jaraicejo 155 39 40N 5 49W
Jaraiz 154 40 4N 5 45W
Jaral del Progreso 107 20 22N 101 4W
Jaralillo 105 24 16N 103 1W
Jarama → 156 40 2N 3 39W
Jaramillo 126 47 10 S 67 7W
Jarandilla 154 40 8N 5 39W
Jaranwala 197 31 15N 73 26 E
Jarash 189 32 17N 35 54 E
Jarauçu → 119 1 48 S 52 22W
Jardas al 'Abīd 242 32 18N 20 59 E
Jardim 124 21 28 S 56 2W
Jardín → 157 38 50N 2 10W
Jardines de la Reina, Is. 112 20 50N 78 50W
Jargalang 215 43 5N 122 55 E
Jargeau 139 47 50N 2 1 E
Jari → 119 1 9 S 51 54W
Jarilla, La 103 22 3N 98 50W
Jaripitio 107 20 49N 101 18W
Jarīr, W. al → 192 25 38N 42 30 E
Jarmen 146 53 56N 13 20 E
Jarnac 140 45 40N 0 11W
Jarny 139 49 9N 5 53 E
Jaro 211 11 11N 124 47 E
Jarocin 152 51 59N 17 29 E
Jaroměr 150 50 22N 15 52 E
Jarosław 152 50 2N 22 42 E
Järpås 173 58 23N 12 57 E
Järpen 172 63 21N 13 26 E
Jarrahdale 229 32 24 S 116 5 E
Jarres, Plaine des 204 19 27N 103 10 E
Jarso 245 5 15N 37 30 E
Jartai 214 39 45N 105 48 E
Jaru 123 10 26 S 62 27W
Jaru → 123 10 5 S 61 59W
Jarud Qi 215 44 28N 120 50 E
Jarvis 84 42 53N 80 6W
Jarvis I. 225 0 15 S 159 55W
Jarvis River 86 48 7N 89 21W
Jarvornik 151 50 23N 17 2 E
Jarwa 199 27 38N 82 30 E
Jaša Tomić 166 45 26N 20 50 E
Jasaan 211 8 39N 124 45 E
Jasien 152 51 46N 15 0 E
Jāsimīyah 192 33 45N 44 41 E
Jasin 205 2 20N 102 26 E
Jāsk 193 25 38N 57 45 E
Jasło 152 49 45N 21 30 E
Jason, Is. 126 51 0 S 61 0W
Jasper, Alta., Canada 91 52 55N 118 5W
Jasper, Ont., Canada 85 44 50N 75 56W
Jasper Nat. Park 91 52 50N 118 8W
Jasquillo 107 20 38N 99 12W
Jassy = Iaşi 170 47 10N 27 40 E
Jastrebarsko 163 45 41N 15 39 E
Jastrowie 152 53 26N 16 49 E
Jastrzębie Zdrój 152 49 57N 18 35 E
Jászapáti 151 47 32N 20 10 E
Jászárokszállás 151 47 39N 20 1 E
Jászberény 151 47 30N 19 55 E
Jászkiser 151 47 27N 20 20 E
Jászladány 151 47 23N 20 10 E
Jataí 121 17 58 S 51 48W
Jatapu → 119 2 13 S 58 17W
Jatatè, R. → 110 16 15N 91 17W
Jati 198 24 20N 68 19 E
Jatibarang 209 6 28 S 108 18 E
Jatinegara 207 6 13 S 106 52 E
Játiva 157 39 0N 0 32W
Jatobal 120 4 35 S 49 33W
Jatt 189 32 24N 35 2 E
Jáu, Angola 253 15 12 S 13 31 E
Jaú, Brazil 125 22 10 S 48 30W
Jaú → 119 1 54 S 61 26W
Jauaperí → 119 1 26 S 61 35W
Jauche 143 50 41N 4 57 E
Jauja 122 11 45 S 75 15W
Jaumave 103 23 25N 99 23W
Jaunjelgava 178 56 35N 25 0 E
Jaunpur 199 25 46N 82 44 E
Jauru → 123 16 22 S 57 46W
Java = Jawa 207 7 0 S 110 0 E
Java Sea 209 4 35 S 107 15 E
Java Trench 224 10 0 S 110 0W
Javadi Hills 201 12 40N 78 40 E
Jávea 157 38 48N 0 10 E
Javhlant = Ulyasutay 212 47 56N 97 28 E
Javier, I. 126 47 5 S 74 25W
Javla 200 17 18N 75 9 E
Javron 138 48 25N 0 25W
Jawa 207 7 0 S 110 0 E

Jawf, W. al → 194 15 50N 45 30 E
Jawor 152 51 4N 16 11 E
Jaworzno 152 50 13N 19 11 E
Jaya, Puncak 207 3 57 S 137 17 E
Jayanca 122 6 24 S 79 50W
Jayanti 202 26 45N 89 40 E
Jayapura 207 2 28 S 140 38 E
Jayawijaya, Pegunungan 207 5 0 S 139 0 E
Jayrūd 192 33 49N 36 44 E
Jazīreh-ye Shīf 193 29 4N 50 54 E
Jazminal 103 24 52N 101 24W
Jazzīn 190 33 31N 35 35 E
Jean Marie River 76 61 32N 120 38W
Jean Rabel 113 19 50N 73 5W
Jeanette, Ostrov 185 76 43N 158 0 E
Jeanette L. 86 51 5N 92 5W
Jebba, Morocco 240 35 11N 4 43W
Jebba, Nigeria 247 9 9N 4 48 E
Jebel Qerri 245 16 16N 32 50 E
Jeberos 122 5 15 S 76 10W
Jécori 100 29 58N 109 45W
Jedburgh 134 55 28N 2 33W
Jedlicze 152 49 43N 21 40 E
Jedlnia-Letnisko 152 51 25N 21 19 E
Jędrzejów 152 50 35N 20 15 E
Jedwabne 152 53 17N 22 18 E
Jedway 92 52 17N 131 14W
Jeetze → 146 53 9N 11 6 E
Jega 247 12 15N 4 23 E
Jekabpils 178 56 29N 25 57 E
Jelenia Góra 152 50 50N 15 45 E
Jelenia Góra □ 152 51 0N 15 30 E
Jelgava 178 56 41N 23 49 E
Jelica 166 43 50N 20 17 E
Jelli 245 5 25N 31 45 E
Jellicoe 87 49 40N 87 30W
Jelšava 151 48 37N 20 15 E
Jemaja 208 3 5N 105 45 E
Jemaluang 205 2 16N 103 52 E
Jemappes 143 50 27N 3 54 E
Jember 209 8 11 S 113 41 E
Jembongan 206 6 45N 117 20 E
Jemeppe 143 50 37N 5 30 E
Jemnice 150 49 1N 15 34 E
Jemseg 81 45 50N 66 7W
Jena 146 50 56N 11 33 E
Jenbach 150 47 24N 11 47 E
Jendouba 241 36 29N 8 47 E
Jennings → 76 59 38N 132 5W
Jenny 173 57 47N 16 35 E
Jepara 209 7 40 S 109 14 E
Jeparit 231 36 8 S 142 1 E
Jequié 121 13 51 S 40 5W
Jequitaí → 121 17 4 S 44 50W
Jequitinhonha 121 16 30 S 41 0W
Jequitinhonha → 121 15 51 S 38 53W
Jerada 241 34 17N 2 10W
Jerantut 205 3 56N 102 22 E
Jerécuaro 107 20 9N 100 31W
Jérémie 113 18 40N 74 10W
Jeremoabo 120 10 4 S 38 21W
Jerez, Pta. 103 22 54N 97 46W
Jerez de García Salinas 105 22 39N 103 0W
Jerez de la Frontera 155 36 41N 6 7W
Jerez de los Caballeros 155 38 20N 6 45W
Jericho = Arīḩā 190 35 49N 36 35 E
Jericho = El Arīhā 189 31 52N 35 27 E
Jericho 230 23 38 S 146 6 E
Jerichow 146 52 30N 12 2 E
Jerilderie 231 35 20 S 145 41 E
Jerome 87 47 37N 82 14W
Jerónimo 105 23 8N 103 10W
Jerrobert 88 51 56N 109 8W
Jersey, I. 138 49 13N 2 7W
Jerseyside 79 47 16N 53 58W
Jerusalem 189 31 47N 35 10 E
Jervis B. 231 35 8 S 150 46 E
Jervis Inlet 92 50 0N 123 57W
Jesenice 163 46 28N 14 3 E
Jeseník 151 50 0N 17 8 E
Jesenké 151 48 20N 20 10 E
Jesselton = Kota Kinabalu 209 6 0N 116 4 E
Jessnitz 146 51 42N 12 19 E
Jessore 202 23 10N 89 10 E
Jesús 122 7 15 S 78 25W
Jesús Carranza 109 17 26N 95 2W
Jesús María, Argentina 124 30 59 S 64 5W
Jesús María, Aguascalientes, Mexico 105 21 4N 102 41W
Jesús María, Jalisco, Mexico 106 20 37N 102 7W
Jetafe 211 10 9N 124 9 E
Jetpur 198 21 45N 70 10 E
Jette 143 50 53N 4 20 E
Jevnaker 171 60 15N 10 26 E
Jeyḩūnābād 193 34 58N 48 59 E
Jeypore 200 18 50N 82 38 E
Jeziorak, Jezioro 152 53 40N 19 35 E
Jeziorany 152 53 58N 20 46 E
Jeziorka → 152 51 59N 20 57 E
Jhajjar 198 28 37N 76 42 E
Jhal Jhao 197 26 20N 65 35 E
Jhalakati 202 22 39N 90 12 E
Jhalawar 198 24 40N 76 10 E
Jhang Maghiana 197 31 15N 72 22 E
Jhansi 199 25 30N 78 36 E
Jharia 199 23 45N 86 26 E
Jharsuguda 199 21 56N 84 5 E
Jhelum 197 33 0N 73 45 E
Jhelum → 198 31 20N 72 10 E
Jhunjhunu 198 28 10N 75 30 E
Ji Xian, Hebei, China 214 37 35N 115 30 E
Ji Xian, Henan, China 214 35 22N 114 5 E
Ji Xian, Shanxi, China 214 36 7N 110 40 E
Jia Xian, Henan, China 214 33 59N 113 12 E
Jia Xian, Shaanxi, China 214 38 12N 110 28 E
Jiading 217 31 22N 121 15 E
Jiahe 217 25 38N 112 19 E
Jiali 217 23 12N 120 10 E
Jialing Jiang → 216 29 30N 106 20 E
Jiamusi 213 46 40N 130 26 E
Ji'an, Jiangxi, China 217 27 6N 114 59 E
Ji'an, Jilin, China 215 41 5N 126 10 E
Jianchang 215 40 55N 120 35 E
Jianchangying 215 40 10N 118 50 E
Jianchuan 216 26 38N 99 55 E
Jiande 217 29 23N 119 15 E
Jiangbei 216 29 40N 106 34 E
Jiangcheng 216 22 36N 101 52 E
Jiangdi 216 26 57N 103 37 E
Jiange 216 32 4N 105 32 E
Jiangjin 216 29 14N 106 14 E
Jiangkou 216 27 40N 108 49 E
Jiangle 217 26 42N 117 23 E
Jiangling 217 30 25N 112 12 E
Jiangmen 217 22 32N 113 0 E
Jiangshan 217 28 40N 118 37 E
Jiangsu □ 215 33 0N 120 0 E
Jiangxi □ 217 27 30N 116 0 E
Jiangyin 217 31 54N 120 17 E
Jiangyong 217 25 20N 111 22 E
Jiangyou 216 31 44N 104 43 E
Jianhe 216 26 37N 108 31 E
Jianli 217 29 46N 112 56 E
Jianning 217 26 50N 116 50 E
Jian'ou 217 27 3N 118 17 E
Jianshi 216 30 37N 109 38 E
Jianshui 216 23 36N 102 43 E
Jianyang, Fujian, China 217 27 20N 118 5 E
Jianyang, Sichuan, China 216 30 24N 104 33 E
Jiao Xian 215 36 18N 120 1 E
Jiaohe, Hebei, China 214 38 2N 116 20 E
Jiaohe, Jilin, China 215 43 40N 127 22 E
Jiaoling 217 24 41N 116 12 E
Jiaozhou Wan 215 36 5N 120 10 E
Jiaozuo 214 35 16N 113 12 E
Jiashan 217 32 46N 117 59 E
Jiawang 215 34 28N 117 26 E
Jiaxiang 214 35 25N 116 20 E
Jiaxing 217 30 49N 120 45 E
Jiayi 217 23 30N 120 24 E
Jiayu 217 29 55N 113 55 E
Jibão, Serra do 121 14 48 S 45 0W
Jibiya 247 13 5N 7 12 E
Jibou 170 47 15N 23 17 E
Jibuti = Djibouti ■ 245 12 0N 43 0 E
Jicamorachic 101 27 54N 108 19W
Jicarón, I. 112 7 10N 81 50W
Jičín 150 50 25N 15 28 E
Jiddah 194 21 29N 39 10 E
Jieshou 217 33 18N 115 22 E
Jiexiu 214 37 2N 111 55 E
Jieyang 217 23 35N 116 21 E
Jifnā 189 31 58N 35 13 E
Jihlava 150 49 28N 15 35 E
Jihlava → 150 48 55N 16 36 E
Jihočeský □ 150 49 8N 14 35 E
Jihomoravský □ 151 49 5N 16 30 E
Jijel 241 36 52N 5 50 E
Jijiga 256 9 20N 42 50 E
Jijona 157 38 34N 0 30W
Jikamshi 247 12 12N 7 45 E
Jilin 215 43 44N 126 30 E
Jilin □ 215 44 0N 124 0 E
Jiloca → 156 41 21N 1 39W
Jilong 217 25 8N 121 42 E
Jilotepec de Abasolo 107 19 58N 99 32W
Jilotlán de los Dolores 106 19 12N 103 13W
Jílove 150 49 52N 14 29 E
Jima 245 7 40N 36 47 E
Jimbolia 170 45 47N 20 43 E
Jimena de la Frontera 155 36 27N 5 24W
Jimenbuen 233 36 42 S 148 53 E
Jiménez, Chihuahua, Mexico 101 27 8N 104 54W
Jiménez, Coahuila, Mexico 102 29 2N 100 41W
Jimenez, Phil. 211 8 20N 123 50 E
Jimo 215 36 23N 120 30 E
Jin Jiang → 217 28 24N 115 48 E
Jin Xian, Hebei, China 214 38 2N 115 2 E
Jin Xian, Liaoning, China 215 38 55N 121 42 E
Jinan 214 36 38N 117 1 E
Jincheng 214 35 29N 112 50 E
Jinchuan 216 31 30N 102 3 E
Jind 198 29 19N 76 22 E
Jindabyne 231 36 25 S 148 35 E
Jindrichuv Hradeç 150 49 10N 15 2 E
Jing He → 214 34 27N 109 4 E
Jing Shan 217 31 20N 111 35 E
Jing Xian, Anhui, China 217 30 38N 118 25 E
Jing Xian, Hunan, China 216 26 33N 109 40 E
Jing'an 217 28 50N 115 17 E
Jingbian 214 37 20N 108 30 E
Jingchuan 214 35 20N 107 20 E
Jingde 217 30 15N 118 27 E
Jingdezhen 217 29 20N 117 11 E
Jingdong 216 24 23N 100 47 E
Jinggu 216 23 35N 100 41 E
Jinghai 214 38 55N 116 55 E
Jinghong 216 22 0N 100 45 E
Jingjiang 217 32 2N 120 16 E
Jingle 214 38 20N 111 55 E
Jingmen 217 31 0N 112 10 E
Jingning 214 35 30N 105 43 E
Jingpo Hu 215 43 55N 128 55 E
Jingshan 217 31 1N 113 7 E
Jingtai 214 37 10N 104 6 E
Jingxi 216 23 8N 106 27 E
Jingxing 214 38 2N 114 8 E
Jingyang 214 34 30N 108 50 E
Jingyu 215 42 25N 126 45 E
Jingyuan 214 36 30N 104 40 E
Jingziguan 214 33 15N 111 0 E
Jinhua 217 29 8N 119 38 E
Jining, Nei Mongol Zizhiqu, China 214 41 5N 113 0 E
Jining, Shandong, China 214 35 22N 116 34 E
Jinja 250 0 25N 33 12 E
Jinjang 205 3 13N 101 39 E
Jinji 214 37 58N 106 8 E
Jinjiang, Fujian, China 217 24 43N 118 33 E
Jinjiang, Yunnan, China 216 26 14N 100 34 E
Jinjie 216 23 15N 107 18 E
Jinjini 246 7 26N 3 42W
Jinkou 217 30 20N 114 8 E
Jinmen Dao 217 24 25N 118 25 E
Jinning 216 24 38N 102 38 E
Jinotega 112 13 6N 85 59W
Jinotepe 112 11 50N 86 10W
Jinping, Guizhou, China 216 26 41N 109 10 E
Jinping, Yunnan, China 216 22 45N 103 18 E
Jinsha 216 27 29N 106 12 E
Jinsha Jiang → 216 28 50N 104 36 E
Jinshan 217 30 54N 121 10 E
Jinshi 217 29 40N 111 50 E
Jintan 217 31 42N 119 36 E
Jintotolo Channel 211 11 48N 123 5 E
Jinxi, Jiangxi, China 217 27 56N 116 45 E
Jinxi, Liaoning, China 215 40 52N 120 50 E
Jinxian 217 28 26N 116 17 E
Jinxiang 214 35 5N 116 22 E
Jinyun 217 28 35N 120 5 E
Jinzhai 217 31 40N 115 53 E
Jinzhou 215 41 5N 121 3 E
Jiparaná → 123 8 3 S 62 52W
Jipijapa 118 1 0 S 80 40W
Jiquilpan de Juárez 106 19 59N 102 43W
Jiquipilas 110 16 40N 93 39W
Jiquipilco 107 19 32N 99 36W
Jirwān 195 23 27N 50 53 E
Jishan 214 35 34N 110 58 E
Jishou 216 28 21N 109 43 E
Jishui 217 27 12N 115 8 E
Jisr al Ḩusayn 189 31 53N 35 33 E
Jisr ash Shughūr 190 35 49N 36 18 E
Jitarning 229 32 48 S 117 57 E
Jitotol 110 17 2N 92 52W
Jitra 205 6 16N 100 25 E
Jiu → 170 44 40N 23 25 E
Jiudengkou 214 39 56N 106 40 E
Jiujiang, Guangdong, China 217 22 50N 113 0 E
Jiujiang, Jiangxi, China 217 29 42N 115 58 E
Jiuling Shan 217 28 40N 114 40 E
Jiulong 216 28 57N 101 31 E
Jiutai 215 44 10N 125 50 E
Jiuxiangcheng 217 33 12N 114 50 E
Jiuxincheng 214 39 17N 115 59 E
Jiuyuhang 217 30 18N 119 56 E
Jixi, Anhui, China 217 30 5N 118 34 E
Jixi, Heilongjiang, China 215 45 20N 130 50 E
Jiyang 215 37 0N 117 12 E
Jīz', W. → 195 16 12N 52 14 E
Jize 214 36 54N 114 56 E
Jizera → 150 50 10N 14 43 E
Jizl Wadi 244 25 30N 38 30 E
Jizō-Zaki 220 35 34N 133 20 E
Joaçaba 125 27 5 S 51 31W
Joachín 109 18 38N 96 14W
Joaíma 121 16 39 S 41 2W
João 120 2 46 S 50 59W
João Amaro 121 12 46 S 40 22W
João Câmara 120 5 32 S 35 48W
João Pessoa 120 7 10 S 34 52W
João Pinheiro 121 17 45 S 46 10W
Joaquim Távora 121 23 30 S 49 58W
Joaquín V. González 124 25 10 S 64 0W
Jobourg, Nez de 138 49 41N 1 57W
Jocotepec 106 20 18N 103 26W
Jocotitlán 107 19 42N 99 48W
Jódar 157 37 50N 3 21W
Jodhpur 198 26 23N 73 8 E
Joe Batt's Arm 79 49 44N 54 10W
Joensuu 176 62 37N 29 49 E
Jœuf 139 49 12N 6 1 E
Joffre, Mt. 91 50 32N 115 13W
Joggins 81 45 42N 64 27W
Jogjakarta = Yogyakarta 209 7 49 S 110 22 E
Jogues 87 49 36N 83 45W
Jōhana 221 36 30N 136 57 E
Johannesburg 255 26 10 S 28 2 E
Johansfors 173 56 42N 15 32 E
Jōhen 220 32 58N 132 32 E
John o' Groats 134 58 39N 3 3W
Johnson's Crossing 76 60 29N 133 18W
Johnsonville 234 41 13 S 174 48 E
Johnston, L. 229 32 25 S 120 30 E
Johnston Falls = Mambilima Falls 251 10 31 S 28 45 E
Johnston I. 225 17 10N 169 8W
Johnstone Str. 92 50 28N 126 0W
Johor Baharu 205 1 28N 103 46 E
Joigny 139 48 0N 3 20 E
Joinvile 125 26 15 S 48 55 E
Joinville 139 48 27N 5 10 E
Joinville I. 13 65 0 S 55 30W
Joir → 80 51 59N 60 12W
Jojutla de Juarez 107 18 37N 99 11W
Jokkmokk 174 66 35N 19 50 E
Jökulsá á Dal → 174 65 40N 14 16W
Jökulsá Fjöllum → 174 66 10N 16 30W
Jolalpán 109 18 19N 98 50W
Jolfā, Āzarbājān-e Sharqī, Iran 192 38 57N 45 38 E
Jolfā, Eşfahan, Iran 193 32 58N 51 37 E
Joliette 83 46 3N 73 24W
Joliette, Parc. Prov. de 83 46 30N 74 0W
Jolo 211 6 0N 121 0 E
Jolo Group 211 6 0N 121 9 E
Jomalig 210 14 42N 122 22 E
Jombang 207 7 33 S 112 14 E
Jomda 216 31 28N 98 12 E
Jome 207 1 16 S 127 30 E
Jomfruland 173 58 52N 9 36 E
Jomulco 104 21 5N 104 25W
Jonacapa 107 20 26N 99 32W
Jonacatepec 107 18 41N 98 48W
Jönåker 173 58 44N 16 40 E
Jonava 178 55 8N 24 12 E
Jones 210 16 33N 121 42 E
Jones Sound 95 76 0N 85 0W
Jonglei 245 6 25N 30 50 E
Jonglei □ 245 7 30N 32 30 E
Joniskis 178 56 13N 23 35 E
Jönköping 173 57 45N 14 10 E
Jönköpings län □ 173 57 30N 14 30 E
Jonquière 83 48 27N 71 14W
Jonsberg 173 58 30N 16 48 E
Jonsered 173 57 45N 12 10 E
Jonzac 140 45 27N 0 28W
Jordan ■ 191 31 0N 36 0 E
Jordan → 189 31 48N 35 32 E
Jordan, L. 81 44 5N 65 14W
Jordan Falls 81 43 49N 65 14W
Jordânia 121 15 55 S 40 11W
Jordanów 152 49 41N 19 49 E
Jorge, C. 126 51 40 S 75 35W
Jorhat 202 26 45N 94 12 E
Jorm 197 36 50N 70 52 E
Jörn 174 65 4N 20 1 E

Jorong **209** 3 58 S 114 56 E
Jørpeland **171** 59 3N 6 1 E
Jorquera → **124** 28 3 S 69 58W
Jos **247** 9 53N 8 51 E
Jošanička Banja **166** 43 24N 20 47 E
Jose Abad Santos **211** 5 55N 125 39 E
José Batlle y
Ordóñez **125** 33 20 S 55 10W
José Cardel **108** 19 22N 96 22W
José de San Martín **126** 44 4 S 70 26W
José Maria Pino
Suárez **105** 23 51N 104 28W
Jose Panganiban **210** 14 17N 122 41 E
Joseni **170** 46 42N 25 29 E
Joseph, L., Newf.,
Canada **80** 52 45N 65 18W
Joseph, L., Ont.,
Canada **84** 45 10N 79 44W
Joseph, Petit lac **80** 52 36N 65 5W
Joseph Bonaparte
G. **228** 14 35 S 128 50 E
Josselin **138** 47 57N 2 33W
Jostedal **171** 61 35N 7 15 E
Jotunheimen **171** 61 35N 8 25 E
Joure **142** 52 58N 5 48 E
Joussard **90** 55 22N 115 50W
Jovellanos **112** 22 40N 81 10W
Jovellar **210** 13 4N 123 36 E
Jowai **202** 25 26N 92 12 E
Jowzjān □ **197** 36 10N 66 0 E
Joy B. **78** 61 30N 72 0W
Joya **102** 26 26N 101 8W
Joya, La **122** 16 43 S 71 52W
Joya, L. de la **110** 15 55N 93 40W
Joyeuse **141** 44 29N 4 16 E
Józefów **152** 52 10N 21 11 E
Ju Xian **215** 36 35N 118 20 E
Juáez **101** 30 19N 108 5W
Juan Aldama **105** 24 19N 103 21W
Juan Bautista
Alberdi **124** 34 26 S 61 48W
Juan de Fuca Str. **92** 48 15N 124 0W
Juan de Nova **255** 17 3 S 43 45 E
Juan Eugenio **103** 25 9N 103 19W
Juan Fernández,
Arch. de **225** 33 50 S 80 0W
Juan José Castelli **124** 25 27 S 60 57W
Juan L. Lacaze **124** 34 26 S 57 25W
Juan Perez Sd. **92** 52 32N 131 30W
Juan Rodríguez
Clará **109** 18 0N 95 25W
Juanacatic **105** 22 1N 103 40W
Juanacatlán **106** 20 31N 103 10W
Juanjuí **122** 7 10 S 76 45W
Juárez, Argentina **124** 37 40 S 59 43W
Juárez, Chiapas,
Mexico **110** 17 39N 93 10W
Juárez,
Nuevo León,
Mexico **102** 25 39N 100 5W
Juárez, Sa. de,
Baja Calif. N.,
Mexico **98** 32 0N 115 50W
Juárez, Sa. de,
Oaxaca, Mexico **109** 17 45N 96 35W
Juárez, Sa. de,
San Luis Potosí,
Mexico **103** 22 5N 100 40W
Juatinga, Ponta de **121** 23 17 S 44 30W
Juàzeiro **120** 9 30 S 40 30W
Juàzeiro do Norte **120** 7 10 S 39 18W
Jubay **211** 11 33N 124 18 E
Jubayl **190** 34 5N 35 39 E
Jubbah **192** 28 2N 40 56 E
Jubbulpore =
Jabalpur **199** 23 9N 79 58 E
Jübek **146** 54 31N 9 24 E
Jubga **181** 44 19N 38 48 E
Jubilee L., Australia **229** 29 0 S 126 50 E
Jubilee L., Canada **79** 48 3N 55 11W
Júcar → **157** 39 5N 0 10W
Júcaro **112** 21 37N 78 51W
Juchipila **105** 21 25N 103 7W
Juchitán de
Zaragoza **109** 16 26N 95 1W
Juchitlán, Guerrero,
Mexico **107** 16 37N 98 52W
Juchitlán, Jalisco,
Mexico **106** 21 5N 103 3W
Juchitlán, Jalisco,
Mexico **106** 20 5N 104 7W
Judaea = Har
Yehuda **189** 31 35N 34 57 E
Jude I. **79** 47 15N 54 49W
Judenburg **150** 47 12N 14 38 E
Judique **81** 45 52N 61 30W
Jufari → **119** 1 13 S 62 0W
Jugoslavia =
Yugoslavia ■ **161** 44 0N 20 0 E
Juigalpa **112** 12 6N 85 26W
Juillac **140** 45 20N 1 19 E
Juist **146** 53 40N 7 0 E
Juiz de Fora **121** 21 43 S 43 19W
Jujuy □ **124** 23 20 S 65 40W
Juli **122** 16 10 S 69 25W
Julia Cr. → **230** 20 0 S 141 11 E
Julia Creek **230** 20 39 S 141 44 E
Juliaca **122** 15 25 S 70 10W
Julian Alps =
Julijske Alpe **163** 46 15N 14 1 E
Julian L. **78** 54 25N 77 57W
Julianakanaal **143** 51 6N 5 52 E
Julianatop **119** 3 40N 56 30W
Julianehåb **12** 60 43N 46 0W
Jülich **146** 50 55N 6 20 E
Julierpass **149** 46 28N 9 32 E
Julijske Alpe **163** 46 15N 14 1 E
Julimes **101** 28 25N 105 27W
Jullundur **198** 31 20N 75 40 E
Julu **214** 37 15N 115 2 E
Jumbo **251** 17 30 S 30 58 E
Jumentos Cays **113** 23 0N 75 40 E
Jumet **143** 50 27N 4 25 E
Jumilla **157** 38 28N 1 19W
Jumla **199** 29 15N 82 13 E
Jumna =
Yamuna → **198** 25 30N 81 53 E
Junagadh **198** 21 30N 70 30 E
Junaynah **194** 22 33N 46 18 E
Juncal **99** 24 50N 111 47W
Junction B. **230** 11 52 S 133 55 E
Junction Pt. **230** 12 5 S 133 50 E
Jundah **230** 24 46 S 143 2 E
Jundiaí **125** 24 30 S 47 0W
Junee **231** 34 53 S 147 35 E
Jungapeo **107** 19 27N 100 29W
Jungfrau **148** 46 32N 7 58 E
Junglinster **143** 49 43N 6 15 E
Jungshahi **198** 24 52N 67 44 E
Junín, Argentina **124** 34 33 S 60 57W
Junín, Peru **122** 11 12 S 76 0W
Junín □ **122** 11 30 S 75 0W
Junín de los Andes **126** 39 45 S 71 0W
Juniper **81** 46 33N 67 13W
Jūniyah **190** 33 59N 35 38 E
Junnar **200** 19 12N 73 58 E
Junquera, La **156** 42 25N 2 53 E
Junta, La,
Chihuahua,
Mexico **101** 28 28N 107 20W
Junta, La, Oaxaca,
Mexico **109** 18 29N 96 39W
Juparanã, Lagoa **121** 19 16 S 40 8W
Jupiter → **80** 49 29N 63 37W
Juquiá **121** 24 19 S 47 38W
Jur, Nahr el → **245** 8 45N 29 15 E
Jura, Europe **139** 46 35N 6 5 E
Jura, U.K. **134** 56 0N 5 50W
Jura □ **139** 46 47N 5 45 E
Jura, Sd. of **134** 55 57N 5 45W
Jura Suisse **148** 47 10N 7 0 E
Jurado **118** 7 7N 77 46W
Jurilovca **170** 44 46N 28 52 E
Jurong **217** 31 57N 119 9 E
Juruá → **118** 2 37 S 65 44W
Juruena **123** 13 0 S 58 10W
Juruena → **123** 7 20 S 58 3W
Juruti **119** 2 9 S 56 4W
Juskatla **92** 53 37N 132 18W
Jussey **139** 47 50N 5 55 E
Justo Daract **124** 33 52 S 65 12W
Jutaí **122** 5 11 S 68 54W
Jutaí → **118** 2 43 S 66 57W
Jüterbog **146** 52 0N 13 6 E
Juticalpa **112** 14 40N 86 12W
Jutland = Jylland **173** 56 25N 9 30 E
Jutphaas **142** 52 2N 5 6 E
Juventino Rosas **107** 20 39N 101 0W
Juventud, I. de la **112** 21 40N 82 40W
Juvigny-sous-
Andaine **138** 48 32N 0 30W
Juvisy **139** 48 43N 2 23 E
Jūy Zar **192** 33 50N 46 18 E
Juye **214** 35 22N 116 5 E
Juzennecourt **139** 48 10N 4 48 E
Jylland **173** 56 25N 9 30 E
Jyväskylä **174** 62 14N 25 50 E

K

K2, Mt. **199** 35 58N 76 32 E
Kaala-Gomén **226** 20 40 S 164 25 E
Kaap die Goeie
Hoop **254** 34 24 S 18 30 E
Kaap Plato **254** 28 30 S 24 0 E
Kaapkruis **254** 21 43 S 14 0 E
Kaapstad = Cape
Town **254** 33 55 S 18 22 E
Kaatsheuvel **143** 51 39N 5 2 E
Kabacan **211** 7 8N 124 49 E
Kabaena **207** 5 15 S 122 0 E
Kabala **246** 9 38N 11 37W
Kabale **250** 1 15 S 30 0 E
Kabalo **250** 6 0 S 27 0 E
Kabambare **250** 4 41 S 27 39 E
Kabango **251** 8 35 S 28 30 E
Kabanjahe **208** 3 6N 98 30 E
Kabankalan **211** 9 59N 122 49 E
Kabara **246** 16 40N 2 50W
Kabardinka **180** 44 40N 37 57 E
Kabardino-Balkar-
A.S.S.R. □ **181** 43 30N 43 30 E
Kabare **207** 0 4 S 130 58 E
Kabarega Falls **250** 2 15N 31 30 E
Kabasalan **211** 7 47N 122 44 E
Kabba **247** 7 50N 6 3 E
Kabe **220** 34 31N 132 31 E
Kabi **247** 13 30N 12 35 E
Kabin Buri **204** 13 57N 101 43 E
Kabinakagami → **87** 50 25N 84 20W
Kabinakagami L. **87** 48 54N 84 25W
Kabīr, Zab al **192** 36 0N 43 0 E
Kabkabīyah **243** 13 50N 24 0 E
Kablungu, C. **227** 6 20 S 150 1 E
Kabna **244** 19 6N 32 40 E
Kabo **252** 7 35N 18 38 E
Kabompo **251** 13 36 S 24 14 E
Kabondo **251** 8 58 S 25 40 E
Kabongo **250** 7 22 S 25 33 E
Kabou **247** 9 28N 0 55 E
Kaboudia, Rass **241** 35 13N 11 10 E
Kabra **230** 23 25 S 150 25 E
Kabūd Gonbad **193** 37 5N 59 45 E
Kabugao **210** 18 2N 121 11 E
Kābul **197** 34 28N 69 11 E
Kābul □ **197** 34 30N 69 0 E
Kabul → **197** 33 55N 72 14 E
Kabunga **250** 1 38 S 28 3 E
Kaburuang **207** 3 50N 126 30 E
Kabushiya **245** 16 54N 33 41 E
Kabwe **251** 14 30 S 28 29 E
Kabwum **227** 6 11 S 147 15 E
Kačanik **166** 42 13N 21 12 E
Kachanovo **178** 57 25N 27 38 E
Kachchh, Gulf of **198** 22 50N 69 15 E
Kachchh, Rann of **198** 24 0N 70 0 E
Kachebera **251** 13 50 S 32 50 E
Kachin □ **202** 26 0N 97 30 E
Kachira, L. **250** 0 40 S 31 7 E
Kachiry **184** 53 10N 75 50 E
Kachisi **245** 9 40N 37 50 E
Kachkanar **182** 58 42N 59 33 E
Kachot **205** 11 30N 103 3 E
Kackar **181** 40 45N 41 10 E
Kadaingti **202** 17 37N 97 32 E
Kadaiyanallur **201** 9 3N 77 22 E
Kadan Kyun **206** 12 30N 98 20 E
Kadanai → **198** 31 22N 65 45 E
Kadarkút **151** 46 13N 17 39 E
Kade **247** 6 7N 0 56W
Kadi **198** 23 18N 72 23 E
Kadina **232** 34 0 S 137 43 E
Kadiri **201** 14 12N 78 13 E
Kadiyevka =
Stakhanov **181** 48 35N 38 40 E
Kadom **179** 54 37N 42 30 E
Kaduna **247** 10 30N 7 21 E
Kaduna □ **247** 11 0N 7 30 E
Kadzhi-Say **183** 42 8N 77 10 E
Kaédi **246** 16 9N 13 28W
Kaegudeck L. **79** 48 7N 55 12W
Kaelé **247** 10 7N 14 27 E
Kaeng Khoï **204** 14 35N 101 0 E
Kaeo **234** 35 6 S 173 49 E
Kaesŏng **215** 37 58N 126 35 E
Kāf **192** 31 25N 37 29 E
Kafakumba **253** 9 38 S 23 46 E
Kafan **177** 39 18N 46 15 E
Kafanchan **247** 9 40N 8 20 E
Kafareti **247** 10 25N 11 12 E
Kaffrine **246** 14 8N 15 36W
Kafia Kingi **252** 9 20N 24 25 E
Kafinda **251** 12 32 S 30 20 E
Kafirévs, Ákra **169** 38 9N 24 38 E
Kafr 'Ayn **189** 32 3N 35 7 E
Kafr el Dauwâr **244** 31 8N 30 8 E
Kafr el Sheikh **244** 31 15N 30 50 E
Kafr Kammā **189** 32 44N 35 26 E
Kafr Kannā **189** 32 45N 35 20 E
Kafr Mālik **189** 32 0N 35 18 E
Kafr Mandā **189** 32 49N 35 15 E
Kafr Quaddūm **189** 32 14N 35 7 E
Kafr Rā'ī **189** 32 23N 35 9 E
Kafr Şīr **189** 33 19N 35 23 E
Kafr Yāsīf **189** 32 58N 35 10 E
Kafue **251** 15 46 S 28 9 E
Kafue Flats **251** 15 40 S 27 25 E
Kafulwe **251** 9 0 S 29 1 E
Kaga, Afghan. **198** 34 14N 70 10 E
Kaga, Japan **221** 36 16N 136 15 E
Kaga Bandoro **252** 7 0N 19 10 E
Kagaki L. **86** 49 13N 93 52W
Kagan **183** 39 43N 64 33 E
Kagawa □ **220** 34 15N 134 0 E
Kagawong L. **84** 45 54N 82 15W
Kagera □ **250** 2 0 S 31 30 E
Kagera → **250** 0 57 S 31 47 E
Kagianagami L. **87** 50 57N 87 50W
Kagiano L. **87** 49 16N 86 26W
Kagoshima **220** 31 35N 130 33 E
Kagoshima □ **220** 31 30N 130 30 E
Kagoshima-Wan **220** 31 25N 130 40 E
Kagul **180** 45 50N 28 15 E
Kahak **193** 36 6N 49 46 E
Kahama **250** 4 8 S 32 30 E
Kahama □ **250** 3 50 S 32 0 E
Kahang **205** 2 12N 103 32 E
Kahayan → **209** 3 40 S 114 0 E
Kahe **250** 3 30 S 37 25 E
Kahemba **253** 7 18 S 18 55 E
Kaherekoau Mts. **235** 45 45 S 167 15 E
Kahil, Djebel bou **241** 34 26N 4 0 E
Kahilangan **211** 7 48N 124 48 E
Kahniah → **76** 58 15N 120 55W
Kahnūj **193** 27 55N 57 40 E
Kahurangi, Pt. **235** 40 50 S 172 10 E
Kahuta **198** 33 35N 73 24 E
Kai, Kepulauan **207** 5 55 S 132 45W
Kai Besar **207** 5 35 S 133 0 E
Kai-Ketil **207** 5 45 S 132 40 E
Kai Xian **216** 31 11N 108 21 E
Kaiama **247** 9 36N 4 1 E
Kaiapit **227** 6 18 S 146 18 E
Kaiapoi **235** 42 24 S 172 40 E
Kaibara **221** 35 8N 135 5 E
Kaieteur Falls **119** 5 1N 59 10W
Kaifeng **214** 34 48N 114 21 E
Kaihua **217** 29 12N 118 20 E
Kaiingveld **254** 30 0 S 22 0 E
Kaikohe **234** 35 25 S 173 49 E
Kaikoura **235** 42 25 S 173 43 E
Kaikoura Pen. **235** 42 25 S 173 43 E
Kaikoura Ra. **235** 41 59 S 173 41 E
Kailahun **246** 8 18N 10 39W
Kailashahar **202** 24 19N 92 0 E
Kaili **216** 26 33N 107 59 E
Kailu **215** 43 38N 121 18 E
Kaimana **207** 3 39 S 133 45 E
Kaimanawa Mts. **234** 39 15 S 175 56 E
Kaimata **235** 42 34 S 171 28 E
Kaimganj **199** 27 33N 79 24 E
Kaimon-Dake **220** 31 11N 130 32 E
Kaimur Hill **199** 24 30N 82 0 E
Kainan **220** 34 9N 135 12 E
Kainantu **227** 6 18 S 145 52 E
Kaingaroa Forest **234** 38 24 S 176 30 E
Kainji Res. **247** 10 1N 4 40 E
Kaipara Harbour **234** 36 25 S 174 14 E
Kaiping **217** 22 23N 112 42 E
Kaipokok B. **78** 54 54N 59 47W
Kairana **198** 29 24N 77 15 E
Kaironi **207** 0 47 S 133 40 E
Kairouan **241** 35 45N 10 5 E
Kairuku **227** 8 51 S 146 35 E
Kaiserslautern **147** 49 30N 7 43 E
Kaitaia **234** 35 8 S 173 17 E
Kaitangata **235** 46 17 S 169 51 E
Kaithal **198** 29 48N 76 26 E
Kaitu → **198** 33 10N 70 30 E
Kaiyang **216** 27 4N 106 59 E
Kaiyuan, Liaoning,
China **215** 42 28N 124 1 E
Kaiyuan, Yunnan,
China **216** 23 40N 103 12 E
Kajaani **174** 64 17N 27 46 E
Kajabbi **230** 20 0 S 140 1 E
Kajana = Kajaani **174** 64 17N 27 46 E
Kajang **205** 2 59N 101 48 E
Kajiado **250** 1 53 S 36 48 E
Kajiado □ **250** 2 0 S 36 30 E
Kajiki **220** 31 44N 130 40 E
Kajo Kaji **245** 3 58N 31 40 E
Kakabeka Falls **86** 48 24N 89 37W
Kakamega **250** 0 20N 34 46 E
Kakamega □ **250** 0 20N 34 46 E
Kakamigahara **221** 35 28N 136 48 E
Kakanj **166** 44 9N 18 7 E
Kakanui Mts. **235** 45 10 S 170 30 E
Kake **220** 34 36N 132 19 E
Kakegawa **221** 34 45N 138 1 E
Kakeroma-Jima **219** 28 8N 129 14 E
Kakhib **181** 42 28N 46 34 E
Kakhovka **180** 46 40N 33 15 E
Kakhovskoye
Vdkhr. **180** 47 5N 34 16 E
Kakinada **200** 16 57N 82 11 E
Kakisa → **76** 61 3N 118 10W
Kakisa L. **76** 60 56N 117 43W
Kakogawa **220** 34 46N 134 51 E
Kakwa → **90** 54 37N 118 28W
Kāl Gūsheh **193** 30 59N 58 12 E
Kal Safīd **192** 34 52N 47 23 E
Kala **247** 12 2N 14 40 E
Kala Oya → **201** 8 20N 79 45 E
Kala Shank'ou **199** 35 42N 78 20 E
Kalaa-Kebira **241** 35 59N 10 32 E
Kalabagh **197** 33 0N 71 28 E
Kalabahi **207** 8 13 S 124 31 E
Kalabáka **168** 39 42N 21 39 E
Kalabo **253** 14 58 S 22 40 E
Kalach **179** 50 22N 41 0 E
Kalach na Donu **181** 48 43N 43 32 E
Kaladar **85** 44 37N 77 5W

Kalagua Is. **210** 14 30N 122 55 E
Kalahari **254** 24 0 S 21 30 E
Kalahari Gemsbok Nat. Park **254** 25 30 S 20 30 E
Kalai-Khumb **183** 38 28N 70 46 E
Kālak **193** 25 29N 59 22 E
Kalakamati **255** 20 40 S 27 25 E
Kalakan **185** 55 15N 116 45 E
Kalakh **192** 34 55N 36 10 E
K'alak'unlun Shank'ou **199** 35 33N 77 46 E
Kalam **199** 35 34N 72 30 E
Kalama **250** 2 52 S 28 35 E
Kalamansig **211** 6 33N 124 3 E
Kalamariá **168** 40 33N 22 55 E
Kalamata **169** 37 3N 22 10 E
Kalamb **200** 18 3N 74 48 E
Kalambo Falls **251** 8 37 S 31 35 E
Kálamos, Attiki, Greece **169** 38 17N 23 52 E
Kálamos, Pelopónnisos, Greece **169** 38 37N 20 55 E
Kalamoti **169** 38 15N 26 4 E
Kalangadoo **232** 37 34 S 140 41 E
Kalannie **229** 30 22 S 117 5 E
Kalāntarī **193** 32 10N 54 8 E
Kalao **207** 7 21 S 121 0 E
Kalaotoa **207** 7 20 S 121 50 E
Kälarne **172** 62 59N 16 8 E
Kalárovo **151** 47 54N 18 0 E
Kalasin **204** 16 26N 103 30 E
Kalat **197** 29 8N 66 31 E
Kalāteh **193** 36 33N 55 41 E
Kalāteh-ye-Ganj **193** 27 31N 57 55 E
Kálathos **169** 36 9N 28 8 E
Kalaus → **181** 45 40N 44 7 E
Kalávrita **169** 38 3N 22 8 E
Kalaw **202** 20 38N 96 34 E
Kalbān **195** 20 18N 58 38 E
Kalbarri **229** 27 40 S 114 10 E
Kalecik **180** 40 4N 33 26 E
Kalehe **250** 2 6 S 28 50 E
Kalema **250** 1 12 S 31 55 E
Kalemie **250** 5 55 S 29 9 E
Kalemyo **202** 23 11N 94 4 E
Kalety **152** 50 35N 18 52 E
Kalewa **202** 23 10N 94 15 E
Kálfafellsstaður **174** 64 11N 15 53W
Kalgan = Zhangjiakou **214** 40 48N 114 55 E
Kalgoorlie-Boulder **229** 30 40 S 121 22 E
Kaliakra, Nos **167** 43 21N 28 30 E
Kalianda **208** 5 50 S 105 45 E
Kalibo **211** 11 43N 122 22 E
Kaliganj Town **199** 22 25N 89 8 E
Kalima **250** 2 33 S 26 32 E
Kalimantan Barat □ **209** 0 0 110 30 E
Kalimantan Selatan □ **209** 2 30 S 115 30 E
Kalimantan Tengah □ **209** 2 0 S 113 30 E
Kalimantan Timur □ **209** 1 30N 116 30 E
Kálimnos **169** 37 0N 27 0 E
Kalimpong **199** 27 4N 88 35 E
Kalinadi → **201** 14 50N 74 7 E
Kalinga □ **210** 17 30N 121 20 E
Kalinin **179** 56 55N 35 55 E
Kaliningrad **178** 54 42N 20 32 E
Kalininskoye **183** 42 50N 73 49 E
Kalinkovichi **178** 52 12N 29 20 E
Kalinovik **166** 43 31N 18 29 E
Kalipetrovo **167** 44 5N 27 14 E
Kaliro **250** 0 56N 33 30 E
Kalirrákhi **168** 40 40N 24 35 E
Kalisz **152** 51 45N 18 8 E
Kalisz □ **152** 51 30N 18 0 E
Kalisz Pomorski **152** 53 17N 15 55 E
Kaliua **250** 5 5 S 31 48 E
Kaliveli Tank **201** 12 5N 79 50 E
Kalix → **174** 65 50N 23 11 E
Kalka **198** 30 46N 76 57 E
Kalkaroo **232** 31 12 S 143 54 E
Kalkfeld **254** 20 57 S 16 14 E
Kalkfontein **254** 22 4 S 20 57 E
Kalkrand **254** 24 1 S 17 35 E
Kallakkurichchi **201** 11 44N 79 1 E
Kållandsö **173** 58 40N 13 5 E
Kallia **189** 31 46N 35 30 E
Kallidaikurichi **201** 8 38N 77 31 E
Kallinge **173** 56 15N 15 18 E
Kallithéa **169** 37 55N 23 41 E
Kallmeti **168** 41 51N 19 41 E
Kallonís, Kólpos **169** 39 10N 26 10 E
Kalmalo **247** 13 40N 5 20 E
Kalmar **173** 56 40N 16 20 E
Kalmar län □ **173** 57 25N 16 0 E
Kalmar sund **173** 56 40N 16 25 E
Kalmthout **143** 51 23N 4 29 E
Kalmyk A.S.S.R. □ **181** 46 5N 46 1 E
Kalmykovo **181** 49 0N 51 47 E
Kalna **199** 23 13N 88 25 E
Kalo **227** 10 1 S 147 48 E
Kalocsa **151** 46 32N 19 0 E
Kalofer **167** 42 37N 24 59 E
Kaloko **250** 6 47 S 25 48 E
Kalol, Gujarat, India **198** 22 37N 73 31 E
Kalol, Gujarat, India **198** 23 15N 72 33 E
Kalolímnos **169** 37 4N 27 8 E
Kalomo **251** 17 0 S 26 30 E
Kalonerón **169** 37 20N 21 38 E
Kalpi **199** 26 8N 79 47 E
Kalrayan Hills **201** 11 45N 78 40 E
Kalsubai **200** 19 35N 73 45 E
Kaltbrunn **149** 47 13N 9 2 E
Kaltungo **247** 9 48N 11 19 E
Kalu **198** 25 5N 67 39 E
Kaluga **179** 54 35N 36 10 E
Kalulushi **251** 12 50 S 28 3 E
Kalundborg **172** 55 41N 11 5 E
Kalush **178** 49 3N 24 23 E
Kałuszyn **152** 52 13N 21 52 E
Kalutara **201** 6 35N 80 0 E
Kalwaria **152** 49 53N 19 41 E
Kalya **182** 60 15N 59 59 E
Kalyan, Australia **232** 34 55 S 139 49 E
Kalyan, India **198** 20 30N 74 3 E
Kalyazin **179** 57 15N 37 55 E
Kama, Burma **202** 19 1N 95 4 E
Kama, Zaïre **250** 3 30 S 27 5 E
Kama → **182** 55 45N 52 0 E
Kamachumu **250** 1 37 S 31 37 E
Kamae **220** 32 48N 131 56 E
Kamaing **202** 25 26N 96 35 E
Kamaishi **218** 39 16N 141 53 E
Kamakura **221** 35 19N 139 33 E
Kamalia **198** 30 44N 72 42 E
Kamamaung **202** 17 21N 97 40 E
Kamandorskiye Ostrava **185** 55 0N 167 0 E
Kamapanda **251** 12 5 S 24 0 E
Kamaran **194** 15 21N 42 35 E
Kamashi **183** 38 51N 65 23 E
Kamativi **251** 18 15 S 27 27 E
Kamba **247** 11 50N 3 45 E
Kambalda **229** 31 10 S 121 37 E
Kambam **201** 9 45N 77 16 E
Kambar **198** 27 37N 68 1 E
Kambarka **182** 56 15N 54 11 E
Kambia **246** 9 3N 12 53W
Kambolé **251** 8 47 S 30 48 E
Kambove **251** 10 51 S 26 33 E
Kambuie **253** 6 59 S 22 19 E
Kamchatka, P-ov. **185** 57 0N 160 0 E
Kamen **184** 53 50N 81 30 E
Kamen Kashirskiy **178** 51 39N 24 56 E
Kamen-Rybolov **218** 44 46N 132 2 E
Kamenets-Podolskiy **180** 48 45N 26 10 E
Kamenica, Srbija, Yugoslavia **166** 43 27N 22 27 E
Kamenica, Srbija, Yugoslavia **166** 44 25N 19 40 E
Kamenice **150** 49 18N 15 2 E
Kamenjak, Rt **163** 44 47N 13 55 E
Kamenka, R.S.F.S.R., U.S.S.R. **176** 65 58N 44 0 E
Kamenka, R.S.F.S.R., U.S.S.R. **179** 53 10N 44 5 E
Kamenka, R.S.F.S.R., U.S.S.R. **179** 50 47N 39 20 E
Kamenka, Ukraine S.S.R., U.S.S.R. **180** 49 3N 32 6 E
Kamenka Bugskaya **178** 50 8N 24 16 E
Kamenka Dneprovskaya **180** 47 29N 34 14 E
Kameno **167** 42 34N 27 18 E
Kamenolomini **181** 47 40N 40 14 E
Kamensk-Shakhtinskiy **181** 48 23N 40 20 E
Kamensk Uralskiy **182** 56 25N 62 2 E
Kamenskiy, R.S.F.S.R., U.S.S.R. **179** 50 48N 45 25 E
Kamenskiy, R.S.F.S.R., U.S.S.R. **181** 49 20N 41 15 E
Kamenskoye **185** 62 45N 165 30 E
Kamenyak **167** 43 24N 26 57 E
Kamenz **146** 51 17N 14 7 E
Kameoka **221** 35 0N 135 35 E
Kameyama **221** 34 51N 136 27 E
Kami **168** 42 17N 20 18 E
Kami-Jima **220** 32 27N 130 20 E
Kami-koshiki-Jima **220** 31 50N 129 52 E
Kamień Krajeński **152** 53 32N 17 32 E
Kamień Pomorski **152** 53 57N 14 43 E
Kamienna → **152** 51 6N 21 47 E
Kamienna Góra **152** 50 47N 16 2 E
Kamiensk **152** 51 12N 19 29 E
Kamiita **220** 34 6N 134 22 E
Kamilukuak, L. **77** 62 22N 101 40W
Kamina **251** 8 45 S 25 0 E
Kaminak L. **77** 62 10N 95 0W
Kaministikwia **86** 48 32N 89 35W
Kaminoyama **218** 38 9N 140 17 E
Kamioka **221** 36 25N 137 15 E
Kamituga **250** 3 2 S 28 10 E
Kamloops **93** 50 40N 120 20W
Kamloops L. **93** 50 45N 120 40W
Kamnik **163** 46 14N 14 37 E
Kamo, Japan **218** 37 39N 139 3 E
Kamo, N.Z. **234** 35 42 S 174 20 E
Kamo, U.S.S.R. **181** 40 21N 45 7 E
Kamogawa **221** 35 5N 140 5 E
Kamoke **198** 32 4N 74 4 E
Kamouraska **83** 47 34N 69 52W
Kamp → **150** 48 23N 15 42 E
Kampala **250** 0 20N 32 30 E
Kampar **205** 4 18N 101 9 E
Kampar → **208** 0 30N 103 8 E
Kampen **142** 52 33N 5 53 E
Kamperland **143** 51 34N 3 43 E
Kamphaeng Phet **204** 16 28N 99 30 E
Kampolombo, L. **251** 11 37 S 29 42 E
Kampong To **205** 6 3N 101 13 E
Kampot **205** 10 36N 104 10 E
Kamptee **198** 21 9N 79 19 E
Kampti **246** 10 7N 3 25W
Kampuchea = Cambodia ■ **204** 12 15N 105 0 E
Kampung → **207** 5 44 S 138 24 E
Kampung Air Putih **205** 4 15N 103 10 E
Kampung Jerangau **205** 4 50N 103 10 E
Kampung Raja **205** 5 45N 102 35 E
Kampungbaru = Tolitoli **207** 1 5N 120 50 E
Kamrau, Teluk **207** 3 30 S 133 36 E
Kamsack **89** 51 34N 101 54W
Kamskoye Ustye **179** 55 10N 49 20 E
Kamskoye Vdkhr. **176** 58 0N 56 0 E
Kamuchawie L. **77** 56 18N 101 59W
Kamui-Misaki **218** 43 20N 140 21 E
Kāmyārān **192** 34 47N 46 56 E
Kamyshin **179** 50 10N 45 24 E
Kamyshlov **182** 56 50N 62 43 E
Kamyzyak **181** 46 4N 48 10 E
Kan **202** 22 25N 94 5 E
Kanaaupscow **78** 54 2N 76 30W
Kanaaupscow → **78** 53 39N 77 9W
Kanacín **111** 20 56N 89 34W
Kanagawa □ **221** 35 20N 139 20 E
Kanagi **218** 40 54N 140 27 E
Kanairiktok → **78** 55 2N 60 18W
Kanakapura **201** 12 33N 77 28 E
Kanália **168** 39 30N 22 53 E
Kananga **253** 5 55 S 22 18 E
Kanash **179** 55 30N 47 32 E
Kanastraíon, Ákra **168** 39 57N 23 45 E
Kanata **85** 45 20N 75 59W
Kanazawa **221** 36 30N 136 38 E
Kanbalu **202** 23 12N 95 31 E
Kanchanaburi **204** 14 2N 99 31 E
Kanchenjunga **199** 27 50N 88 10 E
Kanchipuram **201** 12 52N 79 45 E
Kańczuga **151** 49 59N 22 25 E
Kanda Kanda **253** 6 52 S 23 48 E
Kandalaksha **176** 67 9N 32 30 E
Kandalakshkiy Zaliv **176** 66 0N 35 0 E
Kandangan **209** 2 50 S 115 20 E
Kandanos **169** 35 19N 23 44 E
Kandavu **226** 19 0 S 178 15 E
Kandavu Passage **226** 18 45 S 178 0 E
Kandep **227** 5 54 S 143 32 E
Kander → **148** 46 33N 7 38 E
Kandersteg **148** 46 30N 7 40 E
Kandhíla **169** 37 46N 22 22 E
Kandhkot **198** 28 16N 69 8 E
Kandhla **198** 29 18N 77 19 E
Kandi, Benin **247** 11 7N 2 55 E
Kandi, India **199** 23 58N 88 5 E
Kandla **198** 23 0N 70 10 E
Kandos **231** 32 45 S 149 58 E
Kandrian **227** 6 14 S 149 37 E
Kandy **201** 7 18N 80 43 E
Kane Basin **95** 79 1N 73 0W
Kane Bassin **12** 79 30N 68 0W
Kanevskaya **181** 46 3N 39 3 E
Kanfanar **163** 45 7N 13 50 E
Kangaba **246** 11 56N 8 25W
Kangān, Fārs, Iran **193** 27 50N 52 3 E
Kangān, Hormozgān, Iran **193** 25 48N 57 28 E
Kangar **205** 6 27N 100 12 E
Kangaroo I. **232** 35 45 S 137 0 E
Kangaroo Mts. **230** 23 25 S 142 0 E
Kangavar **193** 34 40N 48 0 E
Kangding **216** 30 2N 101 57 E
Kăngdong **215** 39 9N 126 5 E
Kangean, Kepulauan **209** 6 55 S 115 23 E
Kangerdlugsuak **12** 68 10N 32 20W
Kanggyee **215** 41 0N 126 35 E
Kanggyŏng **215** 36 10N 127 0 E
Kanghwa **215** 37 45N 126 30 E
Kangnŭng **215** 37 45N 128 54 E
Kango **252** 0 11N 10 5 E
Kangoya **253** 9 55 S 22 48 E
Kangping **215** 42 43N 123 18 E
Kangpokpi **202** 25 8N 93 58 E
Kangyidaung **202** 16 56N 94 54 E
Kanhangad **201** 12 21N 74 58 E
Kanheri **200** 19 13N 72 50 E
Kani **246** 8 29N 6 36W
Kaniama **250** 7 30 S 24 12 E
Kaniapiskau → **78** 56 40N 69 30W
Kaniapiskau L. **78** 54 10N 69 55W
Kanibadam **183** 40 17N 70 25 E
Kanin, P-ov. **176** 68 0N 45 0 E
Kanin Nos, Mys **176** 68 45N 43 20 E
Kanina **168** 40 23N 19 30 E
Kaniva **231** 36 22 S 141 18 E
Kanjiža **166** 46 3N 20 4 E
Kanjut Sar **199** 36 7N 75 25 E
Kankan **246** 10 23N 9 15W
Kanker **200** 20 10N 81 40 E
Kankunskiy **185** 57 37N 126 8 E
Kanmuri-Yama **220** 34 30N 132 4 E
Kannabe **220** 34 32N 133 23 E
Kannauj **199** 27 3N 79 56 E
Kano **247** 12 2N 8 30 E
Kano □ **247** 11 45N 9 0 E
Kan'onji **220** 34 7N 133 39 E
Kanoroba **246** 9 7N 6 8W
Kanowit **206** 2 14N 112 20 E
Kanowna **229** 30 32 S 121 31 E
Kanoya **220** 31 25N 130 50 E
Kanpetlet **202** 21 10N 93 59 E
Kanpur **199** 26 28N 80 20 E
Kansenia **251** 10 20 S 26 0 E
Kansk **185** 56 20N 95 37 E
Kansŏng **215** 38 24N 128 30 E
Kansu = Gansu □ **214** 36 0N 104 0 E
Kant **183** 42 53N 74 51 E
Kantang **205** 7 25N 99 31 E
Kantché **247** 13 31N 8 30 E
Kanté **247** 9 57N 1 3 E
Kantemirovka **181** 49 43N 39 55 E
Kantharalak **204** 14 39N 104 39 E
Kantō □ **221** 36 15N 139 30 E
Kantō-Heiya **221** 36 0N 139 30 E
Kantō-Sanchi **221** 35 59N 138 50 E
Kantu-long **202** 19 57N 97 36 E
Kantunil **111** 20 48N 89 2W
Kantunil-Kin **111** 21 7N 87 28W
Kanturk **135** 52 10N 8 55W
Kanuma **221** 36 34N 139 42 E
Kanus **254** 27 50 S 18 39 E
Kanxoc **111** 20 6N 88 4W
Kanye **254** 25 0 S 25 28 E
Kanzenze **251** 10 30 S 25 12 E
Kanzi, Ras **250** 7 1 S 39 33 E
Kaohsiung = Gaoxiong **217** 22 38N 120 18 E
Kaokoveld **254** 18 20 S 13 37 E
Kaolack **246** 14 5N 16 8W
Kaoshan **215** 44 38N 124 50 E
Kaouar **243** 19 5N 12 52 E
Kapadvanj **198** 23 5N 73 0 E
Kapagere **227** 9 46 S 147 42 E
Kapanga **253** 8 30 S 22 40 E
Kapatagan **211** 7 52N 123 44 E
Kapchagai **183** 43 51N 77 14 E
Kapchagaiskoye Vdkhr. **183** 43 45N 77 50 E
Kapellen **143** 51 19N 4 25 E
Kapéllo, Ákra **169** 36 9N 23 3 E
Kapema **251** 10 45 S 28 22 E
Kapfenberg **150** 47 26N 15 18 E
Kapia **253** 4 17 S 19 46 E
Kapikotongwa → **87** 50 39N 86 43W
Kapiri Mposhi **251** 13 59 S 28 43 E
Kāpīsā □ **197** 35 0N 69 20 E
Kapiskau → **74** 52 47N 81 55W
Kapit **206** 2 0N 112 55 E
Kapiti I. **234** 40 50 S 174 56 E
Kapka, Massif du **243** 15 7N 21 45 E
Kaplice **150** 48 42N 14 30 E
Kapoe **205** 9 34N 98 32 E
Kapoeta **245** 4 50N 33 35 E
Kápolnásnyék **151** 47 16N 18 41 E
Kaponga **234** 39 29 S 174 9 E
Kapos → **151** 46 44N 18 30 E
Kaposvár **151** 46 25N 17 47 E
Kaposvar Cr. → **88** 50 31N 101 55W
Kappeln **146** 54 37N 9 56 E
Kapps **254** 22 32 S 17 18 E
Kaprije **163** 43 42N 15 43 E
Kaprijke **143** 51 13N 3 38 E
Kapsan **215** 41 4N 128 19 E
Kapsukas **178** 54 33N 23 19 E
Kapuas **209** 3 10 S 114 5 E
Kapuas → **209** 0 25 S 109 20 E
Kapuas Hulu, Pegunungan **206** 1 30N 113 30 E
Kapulo **251** 8 18 S 29 15 E
Kapunda **232** 34 20 S 138 56 E
Kapurthala **198** 31 23N 75 25 E
Kapuskasing **87** 49 25N 82 30W
Kapuskasing → **87** 49 49N 82 0W
Kapustin Yar **181** 48 37N 45 40 E
Kaputar, Mt. **231** 30 15 S 150 10 E

Kaputir 250 2 5N 35 28 E
Kapuvár 151 47 36N 17 1 E
Kara, Turkey 169 36 58N 27 30 E
Kara, U.S.S.R. 184 69 10N 65 0 E
Kara Bogaz Gol, Zaliv 177 41 0N 53 30 E
Kara Burun 169 38 41N 26 28 E
Kara Kalpak A.S.S.R. □ 184 43 0N 60 0 E
Kara-Saki 220 34 41N 129 30 E
Kara Sea 184 75 0N 70 0 E
Kara Su 183 40 44N 72 53 E
Karabash 182 55 29N 60 14 E
Karabekaul 183 38 30N 64 8 E
Karabük 180 41 12N 32 37 E
Karabulak 183 44 54N 78 30 E
Karaburuni 168 40 25N 19 20 E
Karabutak 182 49 59N 60 14 E
Karachala 181 39 45N 48 53 E
Karachayevsk 181 43 50N 42 0 E
Karachev 178 53 10N 35 5 E
Karachi 197 24 53N 67 0 E
Karád, Hungary 151 46 41N 17 51 E
Karad, India 200 17 15N 74 10 E
Karadeniz Boğazı 177 41 10N 29 10 E
Karaga 247 9 58N 0 28W
Karaganda 184 49 50N 73 10 E
Karagayly 184 49 26N 76 0 E
Karaginskiy, Ostrov 185 58 45N 164 0 E
Karagiye Depression 177 43 27N 51 45 E
Karagwe □ 250 2 0 S 31 0 E
Karaikal 201 10 59N 79 50 E
Karaikkudi 201 10 0N 78 45 E
Karaitivu, I. 201 9 45N 79 52 E
Karaj 193 35 48N 51 0 E
Karak 205 3 25N 102 2 E
Karakas 184 48 20N 83 30 E
Karakitang 207 3 14N 125 28 E
Karakoram Pass 199 35 33N 77 50 E
Karakoram Ra. 199 35 30N 77 0 E
Karakul, Tadzhik S.S.R., U.S.S.R. 183 39 2N 73 33 E
Karakul, Uzbek S.S.R., U.S.S.R. 183 39 22N 63 50 E
Karakuldzha 183 40 39N 73 26 E
Karakulino 182 56 1N 53 43 E
Karakum, Peski 184 39 30N 60 0 E
Karal 243 12 50N 14 46 E
Karalon 185 57 5N 115 50 E
Karaman 177 37 14N 33 13 E
Karamay 212 45 30N 84 58 E
Karambu 209 3 53 S 116 6 E
Karamea 235 41 14 S 172 6 E
Karamea → 235 41 13 S 172 26 E
Karamea Bight 235 41 22 S 171 40 E
Karamet Niyaz 183 37 45N 64 34 E
Karamoja □ 250 3 0N 34 15 E
Karamsad 198 22 35N 72 50 E
Karand 192 34 16N 46 15 E
Karanganyar 209 7 38 S 109 37 E
Karanja 198 20 29N 77 31 E
Karapiro 234 37 53 S 175 32 E
Karasburg 254 28 0 S 18 44 E
Karasino 184 66 50N 86 50 E
Karasu → 190 36 37N 36 27 E
Karasuk 184 53 44N 78 2 E
Karasuyama 221 36 39N 140 9 E
Karatau 183 43 10N 70 28 E
Karatau, Khrebet 183 43 30N 69 30 E
Karativu 201 8 22N 79 47 E
Karatobe 182 49 44N 53 30 E
Karatoya → 202 24 7N 89 36 E
Karaturuk 183 43 35N 78 0 E
Karaul-Bazar 183 39 30N 64 48 E
Karauli 198 26 30N 77 4 E
Karávi 169 36 49N 23 37 E
Karawa 252 3 18N 20 17 E
Karawang 209 6 30 S 107 15 E
Karawanken 150 46 30N 14 40 E
Karazhal 184 48 2N 70 49 E
Karbalā 192 32 36N 44 3 E
Kårböle 172 61 59N 15 22 E
Karcag 151 47 19N 20 57 E
Karcha → 199 34 45N 76 10 E
Karda 185 55 0N 103 16 E
Kardhámila 169 38 35N 26 5 E
Kardhítsa 168 39 23N 21 54 E
Kardhítsa □ 168 39 15N 21 50 E
Kärdla 178 58 50N 22 40 E
Kareeberge 254 30 50 S 22 0 E
Kareima 244 18 30N 31 49 E
Karelian A.S.S.R. □ 176 65 30N 32 30 E
Karema 227 9 12 S 147 18 E
Kārevāndar 193 27 53N 60 44 E
Kargapolye 182 55 57N 64 24 E
Kargasok 184 59 3N 80 53 E
Kargat 184 55 10N 80 15 E
Kargı 180 41 11N 34 30 E
Kargil 199 34 32N 76 12 E
Kargopol 176 61 30N 38 58 E
Kargowa 152 52 5N 15 51 E
Karguéri 247 13 27N 10 30 E
Karia ba Mohammed 240 34 22N 5 12W
Kariaí 168 40 14N 24 19 E
Karīān 193 26 57N 57 14 E
Kariba 251 16 28 S 28 50 E
Kariba Gorge 251 16 30 S 28 50 E
Kariba Lake 251 16 40 S 28 25 E
Karibib 254 21 0 S 15 56 E
Karimata, Kepulauan 209 1 25 S 109 0 E
Karimata, Selat 209 2 0 S 108 40 E
Karimnagar 200 18 26N 79 10 E
Karimunjawa, Kepulauan 209 5 50 S 110 30 E
Karin 256 10 50N 45 52 E
Káristos 169 38 1N 24 29 E
Karīt 193 33 29N 56 55 E
Kariya 221 34 58N 137 1 E
Karkal 201 13 15N 74 56 E
Karkar I. 227 4 40 S 146 0 E
Karkaralinsk 184 49 26N 75 30 E
Karkinitskiy Zaliv 180 45 56N 33 0 E
Karkur 189 32 29N 34 57 E
Karkur Tohl 244 22 5N 25 5 E
Karl Libknekht 178 51 40N 35 35 E
Karl-Marx-Stadt 146 50 50N 12 55 E
Karl-Marx-Stadt □ 146 50 45N 13 0 E
Karla, L. = Voiviïs Límni 168 39 30N 22 45 E
Karlino 152 54 3N 15 53 E
Karlobag 163 44 32N 15 5 E
Karlovac 163 45 31N 15 36 E
Karlovka 180 49 29N 35 8 E
Karlovy Vary 150 50 13N 12 51 E
Karlsborg 173 58 33N 14 33 E
Karlshamn 173 56 10N 14 51 E
Karlskoga 172 59 22N 14 33 E
Karlskrona 173 56 10N 15 35 E
Karlsruhe 147 49 3N 8 23 E
Karlstad 172 59 23N 13 30 E
Karlstadt 147 49 57N 9 46 E
Karmøy 171 59 15N 5 15 E
Karnal 198 29 42N 77 2 E
Karnali → 199 29 0N 83 20 E
Karnaphuli Res. 202 22 40N 92 20 E
Karnataka □ 201 13 15N 77 0 E
Karnische Alpen 150 46 36N 13 0 E
Kärnten □ 150 46 52N 13 30 E
Karo 246 12 16N 3 18W
Karoi 251 16 48 S 29 45 E
Karomatan 211 7 55N 123 44 E
Karonga 251 9 57 S 33 55 E
Karoonda 232 35 1 S 139 59 E
Káros 169 36 54N 25 40 E
Karousádhes 168 39 47N 19 45 E
Kárpathos 169 35 37N 27 10 E
Karpáthos, Stenón 169 36 0N 27 30 E
Karpinsk 182 59 45N 60 1 E
Karpogory 176 63 59N 44 27 E
Karrebœk 172 55 12N 11 39 E
Kars 180 40 40N 43 5 E
Karsakpay 184 47 55N 66 40 E
Karsha 181 49 45N 51 35 E
Karshi 183 38 53N 65 48 E
Karsiyang 199 26 56N 88 18 E
Karst 163 45 35N 14 0 E
Karsun 179 54 14N 46 57 E
Kartal Dağları 190 37 4N 36 55 E
Kartál Óros 168 41 15N 25 13 E
Kartaly 182 53 3N 60 40 E
Kartapur 198 31 27N 75 32 E
Kartuzy 152 54 22N 18 10 E
Karuah 233 32 37 S 151 56 E
Karufa 207 3 50 S 133 20 E
Karumba 230 17 31 S 140 50 E
Karumo 250 2 25 S 32 50 E
Karumwa 250 3 12 S 32 38 E
Karungu 250 0 50 S 34 10 E
Karup 173 56 19N 9 10 E
Karur 201 10 59N 78 2 E
Karviná 151 49 53N 18 25 E
Karwi 199 25 12N 80 57 E
Kasache 251 13 25 S 34 20 E
Kasai 220 34 55N 134 52 E
Kasai → 253 3 30 S 16 10 E
Kasai Occidental □ 253 6 0 S 22 0 E
Kasai Oriental □ 250 5 0 S 24 30 E
Kasaji 251 10 25 S 23 27 E
Kasama, Japan 221 36 23N 140 16 E
Kasama, Zambia 251 10 16 S 31 9 E
Kasan-dong 215 41 18N 126 55 E
Kasane 254 17 34 S 24 50 E
Kasanga 251 8 30 S 31 10 E
Kasangulu 253 4 33 S 15 15 E
Kasaoka 220 34 30N 133 30 E
Kasaragod 201 12 30N 74 58 E
Kasat 202 15 56N 98 13 E
Kasba 202 23 45N 91 2 E
Kasba L. 77 60 20N 102 10W
Kasba Tadla 240 32 36N 6 17W
Kaseda 220 31 25N 130 19 E
Kāseh Garān 192 34 5N 46 2 E
Kasempa 251 13 30 S 25 44 E
Kasenga 251 10 20 S 28 45 E
Kasese 250 0 13N 30 3 E
Kasewa 251 14 28 S 28 53 E
Kasganj 199 27 48N 78 42 E
Kashabowie 86 48 40N 90 26W
Kāshān 193 34 5N 51 30 E
Kashi 212 39 30N 76 2 E
Kashihara 221 34 27N 135 46 E
Kashima, Ibaraki, Japan 221 35 58N 140 38 E
Kashima, Saga, Japan 220 33 7N 130 6 E
Kashima-Nada 221 36 0N 140 45 E
Kashimbo 251 11 12 S 26 19 E
Kashin 179 57 20N 37 36 E
Kashipur, Orissa, India 200 19 16N 83 3 E
Kashipur, Ut. P., India 199 29 15N 79 0 E
Kashira 179 54 45N 38 10 E
Kashiwa 221 35 52N 139 59 E
Kashiwazaki 219 37 22N 138 33 E
Kashk-e Kohneh 197 34 55N 62 30 E
Kashkasu 183 39 54N 72 44 E
Kāshmar 193 35 16N 58 26 E
Kashmir 199 34 0N 76 0 E
Kashmor 197 28 28N 69 32 E
Kashpirovka 179 53 0N 48 30 E
Kashun Noerh = Gaxun Nur 212 42 22N 100 30 E
Kasimov 179 54 55N 41 20 E
Kasinge 250 6 15 S 26 58 E
Kasiruta 207 0 25 S 127 12 E
Kaskattama → 77 57 3N 90 4W
Kaskelan 183 43 20N 76 35 E
Kaskinen 174 62 22N 21 15 E
Kaskö 174 62 22N 21 15 E
Kasli 182 55 53N 60 46 E
Kaslo 93 49 55N 116 55W
Kasmere L. 77 59 34N 101 10W
Kasongan 209 2 0 S 113 23 E
Kasongo 250 4 30 S 26 33 E
Kasongo Lunda 253 6 35 S 16 49 E
Kásos 169 35 20N 26 55 E
Kasos, Stenón 169 35 30N 26 30 E
Kaspi 181 41 54N 44 17 E
Kaspichan 167 43 18N 27 11 E
Kaspiysk 181 42 52N 47 40 E
Kaspiyskiy 181 45 22N 47 23 E
Kassab 190 35 55N 35 59 E
Kassab ed Doleib 245 13 30N 33 35 E
Kassaba 244 22 40N 29 55 E
Kassala 245 16 0N 36 0 E
Kassalâ □ 245 15 20N 36 26 E
Kassan 183 39 2N 65 35 E
Kassándra 168 40 0N 23 30 E
Kassansay 183 41 15N 71 31 E
Kassel 146 51 19N 9 32 E
Kassinger 244 18 46N 31 51 E
Kassue 207 6 58 S 139 21 E
Kastamonu 177 41 25N 33 43 E
Kastav 163 45 22N 14 20 E
Kastélli 169 35 29N 23 38 E
Kastéllion 169 35 12N 25 20 E
Kastellorizon = Megiste 159 36 8N 29 34 E
Kastellou, Ákra 169 35 30N 27 15 E
Kasterlee 143 51 15N 4 59 E
Kastlösa 173 56 26N 16 25 E
Kastóri 169 37 10N 22 17 E
Kastoría 168 40 30N 21 19 E
Kastoría □ 168 40 30N 21 15 E
Kastorías, L. 168 40 30N 21 20 E
Kastornoye 179 51 55N 38 2 E
Kastós 169 38 35N 20 55 E
Kástron 168 39 50N 25 2 E
Kastrosikiá 169 39 6N 20 36 E
Kasugai 221 35 12N 136 59 E
Kasukabe 221 35 58N 139 49 E
Kasulu 250 4 37 S 30 5 E
Kasulu □ 250 4 37 S 30 5 E
Kasumi 220 35 38N 134 38 E
Kasumiga-Ura 221 36 0N 140 25 E
Kasumkent 181 41 47N 48 15 E
Kasungu 251 13 0 S 33 29 E
Kasur 197 31 5N 74 25 E
Kata 185 58 46N 102 40 E
Kataba 251 16 5 S 25 10 E
Katako Kombe 250 3 25 S 24 20 E
Katákolon 169 37 38N 21 19 E
Katale 250 4 52 S 31 7 E
Katamatite 231 36 6 S 145 41 E
Katanda, Kivu, Zaïre 250 0 55 S 29 21 E
Katanda, Shaba, Zaïre 250 7 52 S 24 13 E
Katangi 199 21 56N 79 50 E
Katanglad Mts. 211 8 6N 124 54 E
Katangli 185 51 42N 143 14 E
Katapakishi 253 8 15 S 22 49 E
Katastári 169 37 50N 20 45 E
Katav Ivanovsk 182 54 45N 58 12 E
Katavi Swamp 250 6 50 S 31 10 E
Katchiungo 253 12 35 S 16 13 E
Kateríni 168 40 18N 22 37 E
Katherîna 191 28 31N 33 57 E
Katherîna, Gebel 244 28 30N 33 57 E
Katherine 228 14 27 S 132 20 E
Kathiawar 198 22 20N 71 0 E
Kathua 199 32 23N 75 30 E
Kati 246 12 41N 8 4W
Katihar 199 25 34N 87 36 E
Katima Mulilo 254 17 28 S 24 13 E
Katimbira 251 12 40 S 34 0 E
Katimik L. 89 52 53N 99 21W
Katingan = Mendawai → 209 3 30 S 113 0 E
Katiola 246 8 10N 5 10W
Katipunan 211 8 31N 123 17 E
Katkopberg 254 30 0 S 20 0 E
Katlanovo 166 41 52N 21 40 E
Katmandu 199 27 45N 85 20 E
Kato Akhaïa 169 38 8N 21 33 E
Káto Stavros 168 40 39N 23 43 E
Katol 198 21 17N 78 38 E
Katompe 250 6 2 S 26 23 E
Katonga → 250 0 34N 31 50 E
Katoomba 231 33 41 S 150 19 E
Katowice 152 50 17N 19 5 E
Katowice □ 152 50 10N 19 0 E
Katrine, L. 134 56 15N 4 30W
Katrineholm 172 59 9N 16 12 E
Katsepe 255 15 45 S 46 15 E
Katsina Ala → 247 7 10N 9 20 E
Katsumoto 220 33 51N 129 42 E
Katsuta 221 36 25N 140 31 E
Katsuura 221 35 10N 140 20 E
Katsuyama 221 36 3N 136 30 E
Kattakurgan 183 39 55N 66 15 E
Kattegatt 173 57 0N 11 20 E
Katumba 250 7 40 S 25 17 E
Katungu 250 2 55 S 40 3 E
Katwa 199 23 30N 88 5 E
Katwijk-aan-Zee 142 52 12N 4 24 E
Katy 152 51 2N 16 45 E
Kaub 147 50 5N 7 46 E
Kaufbeuren 147 47 50N 10 37 E
Kaukauveld 254 20 0 S 20 15 E
Kauliranta 174 66 27N 23 41 E
Kaunas 178 54 54N 23 54 E
Kaunghein 202 25 41N 95 26 E
Kaura Namoda 247 12 37N 6 33 E
Kautokeino 174 69 0N 23 4 E
Kavacha 185 60 16N 169 51 E
Kavadarci 166 41 26N 22 3 E
Kavaja 168 41 11N 19 33 E
Kavalerovo 218 44 15N 135 4 E
Kavali 201 14 55N 80 1 E
Kavála 168 40 57N 24 28 E
Kavála □ 168 41 5N 24 30 E
Kavála Kólpos 168 40 50N 24 25 E
Kavār 193 29 11N 52 44 E
Kavarna 167 43 26N 28 22 E
Kavieng 227 2 36 S 150 51 E
Kavkaz, Bolshoi 181 42 50N 44 0 E
Kavoúsi 169 35 7N 25 51 E
Kaw 119 4 30N 52 15W
Kawa 245 13 42N 32 34 E
Kawachi-Nagano 221 34 28N 135 31 E
Kawagama L. 85 45 18N 78 45W
Kawagoe 221 35 55N 139 29 E
Kawaguchi 221 35 52N 139 45 E
Kawakawa 234 35 23 S 174 6 E
Kawambwa 251 9 48 S 29 3 E
Kawanoe 220 34 1N 133 34 E
Kawarau 235 45 3 S 168 45 E
Kawardha 199 22 0N 81 17 E
Kawasaki 221 35 35N 139 42 E
Kawau I. 234 36 25 S 174 52 E
Kawene 86 48 45N 91 15W
Kawerau 234 38 7 S 176 42 E
Kawhia Harbour 234 38 5 S 174 51 E
Kawinawl 89 52 50N 99 30W
Kawio, Kepulauan 207 4 30N 125 30 E
Kawit 211 6 57N 121 58 E
Kawkabān 194 15 30N 43 54 E
Kawkareik 202 16 33N 98 14 E
Kawlin 202 23 47N 95 41 E
Kawthoolei □ = Kawthule □ 202 18 0N 97 30 E
Kawthule □ 202 18 0N 97 30 E
Kawya 202 24 50N 94 58 E
Kay 182 59 57N 52 59 E
Kaya 247 13 4N 1 10W
Kayah □ 202 19 15N 97 15 E
Kayan 202 16 54N 96 34 E
Kayan → 209 2 55N 117 35 E
Kayankulam 201 9 10N 76 33 E
Kayapa 210 16 22N 120 53 E
Kayeli 207 3 20 S 127 10 E
Kayes, Congo 253 4 25 S 11 41 E
Kayes, Mali 246 14 25N 11 30W
Kayima 246 8 54N 11 15W
Kayl 143 49 29N 6 2 E
Kayoa 207 0 1N 127 28 E
Kayomba 251 13 11 S 24 2 E
Kayoro 247 11 0N 1 28W
Kayrakkumskoye Vdkhr. 183 40 20N 70 0 E

Kayrunnera **231** 30 40 S 142 30 E
Kaysatskoye **181** 49 47N 46 49 E
Kayseri **177** 38 45N 35 30 E
Kayuagung **208** 3 24 S 104 50 E
Kazachinskoye **185** 56 16N 107 36 E
Kazachye **185** 70 52N 135 58 E
Kazakh S.S.R. □ **183** 50 0N 70 0 E
Kazan **179** 55 48N 49 3 E
Kazanci **190** 36 29N 32 51 E
Kazanlı **190** 36 49N 34 43 E
Kazanlúk **167** 42 38N 25 20 E
Kazanskaya **181** 49 50N 41 10 E
Kazarman **183** 41 24N 73 59 E
Kazatin **180** 49 45N 28 50 E
Kazbek **181** 42 42N 44 30 E
Kāzerūn **193** 29 38N 51 40 E
Kazhim **182** 60 21N 51 33 E
Kazi Magomed **181** 40 3N 49 0 E
Kazimierz Dolny **152** 51 19N 21 57 E
Kazimierza Wielka **152** 50 15N 20 30 E
Kazincbarcika **151** 48 17N 20 36 E
Kazo **221** 36 7N 139 36 E
Kaztalovka **181** 49 47N 48 43 E
Kazu **202** 25 27N 97 46 E
Kazumba **253** 6 25 S 22 5 E
Kazuno **218** 40 10N 140 45 E
Kazym → **184** 63 54N 65 50 E
Kcynia **152** 53 0N 17 30 E
Ke-hsi Mansam **202** 21 56N 97 50 E
Ké-Macina **246** 13 58N 5 22W
Kéa **169** 37 35N 24 22 E
Kearney **84** 45 33N 79 13W
Keban **177** 38 50N 38 50 E
Kébi **246** 9 18N 6 37W
Kebili **241** 33 47N 9 0 E
Kebnekaise **174** 67 53N 18 33 E
Kebri Dehar **256** 6 45N 44 17 E
Kebumen **209** 7 42 S 109 40 E
Kecel **151** 46 31N 19 16 E
Kechika → **76** 59 41N 127 12W
Kecskemét **151** 46 57N 19 42 E
Kedada **245** 5 25N 35 58 E
Kedainiai **178** 55 15N 24 2 E
Kedgwick **81** 47 40N 67 20W
Kedia Hill **254** 21 28 S 24 37 E
Kediri **209** 7 51 S 112 1 E
Kédougou **246** 12 35N 12 10W
Kedzierzyn **152** 50 20N 18 12 E
Keefers **76** 50 0N 121 40W
Keeley L. **77** 54 54N 108 8W
Keeling Is. = Cocos Is. **203** 12 10 S 96 55 E
Keene **85** 44 15N 78 10W
Keeper Hill **135** 52 46N 8 17W
Keer-Weer, C. **230** 14 0 S 141 32 E
Keerbergen **143** 51 1N 4 38 E
Keeten Mastgat **143** 51 36N 4 0 E
Keetmanshoop **254** 26 35 S 18 8 E
Keewatin **86** 49 46N 94 34W
Keewatin □ **77** 63 20N 95 0W
Keewatin → **77** 56 29N 100 46W
Keezhik L. **86** 51 45N 88 30W
Kefa □ **245** 6 55N 36 30 E
Kefallinía **169** 38 20N 20 30 E
Kefamenanu **207** 9 28 S 124 29 E
Kefar 'Eqron **189** 31 52N 34 49 E
Kefar Ḥasīdim **189** 32 47N 35 5 E
Kefar Naḥum **189** 32 54N 35 34 E
Kefar Sava **189** 32 11N 34 54 E
Kefar Szold **189** 33 11N 35 39 E
Kefar Vitkin **189** 32 22N 34 53 E
Kefar Yehezqel **189** 32 34N 35 22 E
Kefar Yona **189** 32 20N 34 54 E
Kefar Zekharya **189** 31 43N 34 57 E
Kefar Zetim **189** 32 48N 35 27 E
Keffi **247** 8 55N 7 43 E
Keflavík **174** 64 2N 22 35W
Keg River **76** 57 54N 117 55W
Kegahka **80** 50 9N 61 18W
Kegalla **201** 7 15N 80 21 E
Kégashka, L. **80** 50 20N 61 25W
Keglo, B. **78** 58 40N 66 0W
Kehl **147** 48 34N 7 50 E
Keighley **132** 53 52N 1 54W
Keimoes **254** 28 41 S 21 0 E
Keita **247** 14 46N 5 56 E
Keith, Australia **232** 36 6 S 140 20 E
Keith, U.K. **134** 57 33N 2 58W
Keith Arm **94** 64 20N 122 15W
Kejimkujik Nat. Park **81** 44 25N 65 25W
Kekaygyr **183** 40 42N 75 32 E
Kekri **198** 26 0N 75 10 E
Kël **185** 69 30N 124 10 E
Kelamet **245** 16 0N 38 30 E
Kelan **214** 38 43N 111 31 E
Kelang **205** 3 2N 101 26 E
Kelani Ganga → **201** 6 58N 79 50 E
Kelantan → **205** 6 13N 102 14 E
Këlcyra **168** 40 22N 20 12 E
Keles → **183** 41 1N 68 37 E
Kelheim **147** 48 58N 11 57 E
Kelibia **241** 36 50N 11 3 E
Kellé **252** 0 8 S 14 38 E
Kellerberrin **229** 31 36 S 117 38 E
Kellett, Canal de **99** 27 59N 115 12W
Kellett C. **94** 72 0N 126 0W
Kellett Str. **94** 75 45N 117 30W
Kelligrews **79** 47 30N 53 1W
Kelliher **88** 51 16N 103 44W
Kelloselkä **174** 66 56N 28 53 E
Kells = Ceanannus Mor **135** 53 42N 6 53W
Kélo **243** 9 10N 15 45 E
Kelowna **93** 49 50N 119 25W
Kelsey Bay **92** 50 25N 126 0W
Kelso, N.Z. **235** 45 54 S 169 15 E
Kelso, U.K. **134** 55 36N 2 27W
Keltemashat **183** 42 25N 70 8 E
Keluang **205** 2 3N 103 18 E
Kelvin I. **86** 49 51N 88 40W
Kelvington **88** 52 10N 103 30W
Kelwood **89** 50 37N 99 28W
Kem **176** 65 0N 34 38 E
Kem → **176** 64 57N 34 41 E
Kem-Kem **240** 30 40N 4 30W
Kema **207** 1 22N 125 8 E
Kemano **92** 53 35N 128 0W
Kemapyu **202** 18 49N 97 19 E
Kemasik **205** 4 25N 103 27 E
Kembé **252** 4 36N 21 54 E
Kembolcha **245** 11 2N 39 42 E
Kemenets-Podolskiy **180** 48 40N 26 40 E
Kemerovo **184** 55 20N 86 5 E
Kemi älv = Kemijoki → **174** 65 47N 24 32 E
Kemijärvi **174** 66 43N 27 22 E
Kemijoki → **174** 65 47N 24 32 E
Kemmel **143** 50 47N 2 50 E
Kemmuna = Comino **160** 36 0N 14 20 E
Kemp Coast **13** 69 0 S 55 0 E
Kempsey **231** 31 1 S 152 50 E
Kempt, L. **83** 47 25N 74 22W
Kempten **147** 47 42N 10 18 E
Kemptown **81** 45 28N 63 5W
Kemptville **85** 45 0N 75 38W
Kenadsa **240** 31 48N 2 26W
Kenaston **88** 51 30N 106 17W
Kendal, Indonesia **209** 6 56 S 110 14 E
Kendal, U.K. **132** 54 19N 2 44W
Kendall **231** 31 35 S 152 44 E
Kendall → **230** 14 4 S 141 35 E
Kendari **207** 3 50 S 122 30 E
Kendawangan **209** 2 32 S 110 17 E
Kende **247** 11 30N 4 12 E
Kendenup **229** 34 30 S 117 38 E
Kendervicës, Mal e. **168** 40 15N 19 52 E
Kendrapara **199** 20 35N 86 30 E
Kene Thao **204** 17 44N 101 10 E
Kenema **246** 7 50N 11 14W
Keng Kok **204** 16 26N 105 12 E
Keng Tawng **202** 20 45N 98 18 E
Kengani **252** 2 59 S 17 36 E
Kenge **253** 4 50 S 17 4 E
Kengeja **250** 5 26 S 39 45 E
Kenhardt **254** 29 19 S 21 12 E
Kenimekh **183** 40 16N 65 7 E
Kenitra **240** 34 15N 6 40W
Kenli **215** 37 30N 118 20 E
Kenmare **135** 51 52N 9 35W
Kenmare → **135** 51 40N 10 0W
Kennebecasis → **81** 45 19N 66 4W
Kennedy, Canada **89** 50 1N 102 21W
Kennedy, Zimbabwe **251** 18 52 S 27 10 E
Kennedy, Mt. **94** 81 2N 78 55W
Kennedy I. **92** 54 3N 130 11W
Kennedy L. **92** 49 3N 125 32W
Kennedy Ra. **229** 24 45 S 115 10 E
Kennet → **133** 51 24N 0 58W
Kennetcook **81** 45 11N 63 44W
Kenneth Ra. **229** 23 50 S 117 8 E
Keno Hill **94** 63 57N 135 18W
Kénogami **83** 48 25N 71 15W
Kenogami → **87** 51 6N 84 28W
Kénogami, L. **83** 48 20N 71 23W
Kenora **86** 49 47N 94 29W
Kensington **81** 46 28N 63 34W
Kensington Downs **230** 22 31 S 144 19 E
Kent □ **133** 51 12N 0 40 E
Kent Group **230** 39 30 S 147 20 E
Kent Junction **81** 46 35N 65 20W
Kent Pen. **94** 68 30N 107 0W
Kentau **183** 43 32N 68 36 E
Kentucky **233** 30 45 S 151 28 E
Kentville **81** 45 6N 64 29W
Kenville **89** 52 0N 101 20W
Kenya ■ **250** 1 0N 38 0 E
Kenya, Mt. **250** 0 10 S 37 18 E
Kenzou **252** 4 10N 15 2 E
Keo Neua, Deo **204** 18 23N 105 10 E
Kep, Cambodia **205** 10 29N 104 19 E
Kep, Vietnam **204** 21 24N 106 16 E
Kep-i-Gjuhës **168** 40 28N 19 15 E
Kepi **207** 6 32 S 139 19 E
Kepice **152** 54 16N 16 51 E
Kepler Mts. **235** 45 25 S 167 20 E
Kępno **152** 51 18N 17 58 E
Kerala □ **201** 11 0N 76 15 E
Kerama-Rettō **219** 26 5N 127 15 E
Keran **199** 34 35N 73 59 E
Kerang **231** 35 40 S 143 55 E
Keratéa **169** 37 48N 23 58 E
Keraudren, C. **228** 19 58 S 119 45 E
Keravat **227** 4 17 S 152 2 E
Kerch **180** 45 20N 36 20 E
Kerchenskiy Proliv **180** 45 10N 36 30 E
Kerchoual **247** 17 12N 0 20 E
Kerem Maharal **189** 32 39N 34 59 E
Kerema **227** 7 58 S 145 50 E
Keremeos **93** 49 13N 119 50W
Keren **245** 15 45N 38 28 E
Kerewan **246** 13 29N 16 10W
Kerguelen **203** 48 15 S 69 10 E
Keri **169** 37 40N 20 49 E
Keri Kera **245** 12 21N 32 42 E
Kericho **250** 0 22 S 35 15 E
Kericho □ **250** 0 30 S 35 15 E
Kerikeri **234** 35 12 S 173 59 E
Kerinci **208** 1 40 S 101 15 E
Kerkdriel **142** 51 47N 5 20 E
Kerkenna, Îles **241** 34 48N 11 11 E
Kerki **183** 37 50N 65 12 E
Kerkinítis, Límni **168** 41 12N 23 10 E
Kérkira **168** 39 38N 19 50 E
Kerkrade **143** 50 53N 6 4 E
Kerma **244** 19 33N 30 32 E
Kermadec Is. **224** 30 0 S 178 15W
Kermadec Trench **224** 30 30 S 176 0W
Kermān **193** 30 15N 57 1 E
Kermān □ **193** 30 0N 57 0 E
Kermānshāh = Qahremānshahr **194** 34 23N 47 0 E
Kerme Körfezi **169** 36 55N 27 50 E
Kermen **167** 42 30N 26 16 E
Kerns **149** 46 54N 8 17 E
Keroh **205** 5 43N 101 1 E
Kerrobert **77** 52 0N 109 11W
Kerry □ **135** 52 7N 9 35W
Kerry Hd. **135** 52 26N 9 56W
Kersa **245** 9 28N 41 48 E
Kersley **93** 52 49N 122 25W
Kerteminde **173** 55 28N 10 39 E
Kertosono **209** 7 38 S 112 9 E
Kerulen → **213** 48 48N 117 0 E
Kerzaz **241** 29 29N 1 37W
Kerzers **148** 46 59N 7 12 E
Kesagami → **74** 51 40N 79 45W
Kesagami L. **74** 50 23N 80 15W
Keşan **168** 40 49N 26 38 E
Kesch, Piz **149** 46 38N 9 53 E
Kesennuma **218** 38 54N 141 35 E
Keshit **193** 29 43N 58 17 E
Kessel, Belgium **143** 51 8N 4 38 E
Kessel, Neth. **143** 51 17N 6 3 E
Kessel-Lo **143** 50 53N 4 43 E
Kestell **255** 28 17 S 28 42 E
Kestenga **176** 66 0N 31 50 E
Kesteren **142** 51 56N 5 34 E
Keswick, Canada **84** 44 15N 79 28W
Keswick, U.K. **132** 54 35N 3 9W
Keszthely **151** 46 50N 17 15 E
Ket → **184** 58 55N 81 32 E
Keta **247** 5 49N 1 0 E
Ketapang **209** 1 55 S 110 0 E
Kete Krachi **247** 7 46N 0 1W
Ketef, Khalîg Umm el **244** 23 40N 35 35 E
Ketelmeer **142** 52 36N 5 46 E
Keti Bandar **198** 24 8N 67 27 E
Ketri **198** 28 1N 75 50 E
Kętrzyn **152** 54 7N 21 22 E
Kettering **133** 52 24N 0 44W
Kettle →, B.C., Canada **93** 48 41N 118 7W
Kettle →, Man., Canada **77** 56 40N 89 34W
Kettle Pt. **84** 43 13N 82 1W
Kety **152** 49 51N 19 16 E
Key Harbour **84** 45 50N 80 45W
Kez **182** 57 55N 53 46 E
Kezhma **185** 58 59N 101 9 E
Kežmarok **151** 49 10N 20 28 E
Khabarovo **184** 69 30N 60 30 E
Khabarovsk **185** 48 30N 135 5 E
Khabr **193** 28 51N 56 22 E
Khābūr → **192** 35 0N 40 30 E
Khachmas **181** 41 31N 48 42 E
Khachrod **198** 23 25N 75 20 E
Khadari, W. el → **245** 10 29N 27 15 E
Khadro **198** 26 11N 68 50 E
Khadyzhensk **181** 44 26N 39 32 E
Khadzhilyangar **199** 35 45N 79 20 E
Khagaria **199** 25 30N 86 32 E
Khaibar **244** 25 49N 39 16 E
Khaipur, Bahawalpur, Pakistan **198** 29 34N 72 17 E
Khaipur, Hyderabad, Pakistan **198** 27 32N 68 49 E
Khair **198** 27 57N 77 46 E
Khairabad **199** 27 33N 80 47 E
Khairagarh **199** 21 27N 81 2 E
Khairpur **197** 27 32N 68 49 E
Khāk Dow **197** 34 57N 67 16 E
Khakhea **254** 24 48 S 23 22 E
Khalach **183** 38 4N 64 52 E
Khalafābād **193** 30 54N 49 24 E
Khalfallah **241** 34 20N 0 16 E
Khalfūt **195** 15 52N 52 10 E
Khalilabad **199** 26 48N 83 5 E
Khalīlī **193** 27 38N 53 17 E
Khalkhāl **193** 37 37N 48 32 E
Khálki **168** 39 36N 22 30 E
Khalkidhikí □ **168** 40 25N 23 20 E
Khalkís **169** 38 27N 23 42 E
Khalmer-Sede = Tazovskiy **184** 67 30N 78 44 E
Khalmer Yu **176** 67 58N 65 1 E
Khalturin **179** 58 40N 48 50 E
Kham Keut **204** 18 15N 104 43 E
Khamaria **199** 23 10N 80 52 E
Khamas Country **254** 21 45 S 26 30 E
Khambhaliya **198** 22 14N 69 41 E
Khambhat **198** 22 23N 72 33 E
Khamgaon **198** 20 42N 76 37 E
Khamilonísion **169** 35 50N 26 15 E
Khamīr, Iran **193** 26 57N 55 36 E
Khamir, Yemen **194** 16 0N 44 0 E
Khamīs Mushayṭ **194** 18 18N 42 44 E
Khammam **200** 17 11N 80 6 E
Khamsa **191** 30 27N 32 23 E
Khān Abū Shāmat **190** 33 39N 36 53 E
Khān Azād **192** 33 7N 44 22 E
Khān Mujiddah **192** 32 21N 43 48 E
Khān Shaykhūn **192** 35 26N 36 38 E
Khān Yūnis **189** 31 21N 34 18 E
Khānābād, Afghan. **197** 36 45N 69 5 E
Khanabad, U.S.S.R. **183** 40 59N 70 38 E
Khānaqīn **192** 34 23N 45 25 E
Khanāṣir **190** 35 45N 37 30 E
Khānbāghī **193** 36 10N 55 25 E
Khandrá **169** 35 3N 26 8 E
Khandwa **198** 21 49N 76 22 E
Khandyga **185** 62 42N 135 35 E
Khāneh **192** 36 41N 45 8 E
Khanewal **197** 30 20N 71 55 E
Khanh Duong **204** 12 44N 108 44 E
Khaniá **169** 35 30N 24 4 E
Khaniá □ **169** 35 30N 24 0 E
Khanion Kólpos **169** 35 33N 23 55 E
Khanka, Ozero **185** 45 0N 132 24 E
Khanna **198** 30 42N 76 16 E
Khanpur **197** 28 42N 70 35 E
Khantau **183** 44 13N 73 48 E
Khanty-Mansiysk **184** 61 0N 69 0 E
Khapalu **199** 35 10N 76 20 E
Khapcheranga **185** 49 42N 112 24 E
Kharagpur **199** 22 20N 87 25 E
Kharaij **244** 21 25N 41 0 E
Kharan Kalat **197** 28 34N 65 21 E
Kharānaq **193** 32 20N 54 45 E
Kharda **200** 18 40N 75 34 E
Khardung La **199** 34 20N 77 43 E
Khârga, El Wâhât el **244** 25 10N 30 35 E
Khargon **198** 21 45N 75 40 E
Kharit, Wadi el → **244** 24 26N 33 3 E
Khārk, Jazireh **193** 29 15N 50 28 E
Kharkov **180** 49 58N 36 20 E
Kharmanli **167** 41 55N 25 55 E
Kharovsk **179** 59 56N 40 13 E
Khartoum = El Khartûm **245** 15 31N 32 35 E
Khasan **218** 42 25N 130 40 E
Khasavyurt **181** 43 16N 46 40 E
Khāsh **193** 28 15N 61 15 E
Khashm el Girba **245** 14 59N 35 58 E
Khashuri **181** 41 58N 43 35 E
Khasi Hills **202** 25 30N 91 30 E
Khaskovo **167** 41 56N 25 30 E
Khatanga **185** 72 0N 102 20 E
Khatanga → **185** 72 55N 106 0 E
Khatangskiy, Zaliv **12** 66 0N 112 0 E
Khatauli **198** 29 17N 77 43 E
Khātūnābād **193** 35 30N 51 40 E
Khatyrchi **183** 40 2N 65 58 E
Khatyrka **185** 62 3N 175 15 E
Khavast **183** 40 10N 68 49 E
Khawlaf, Ra's **195** 12 40N 54 7 E
Khay' **194** 18 45N 41 24 E
Khaybar, Harrat **192** 25 45N 40 0 E
Khaydarken **183** 39 57N 71 20 E
Khāzimiyah **192** 34 46N 43 37 E
Khazzân Jabal el Awliyâ **245** 15 24N 32 20 E
Khe Bo **204** 19 8N 104 41 E
Khe Long **204** 21 29N 104 46 E
Khed, Maharashtra, India **200** 17 43N 73 27 E
Khed, Maharashtra, India **200** 18 51N 73 56 E
Khedive **88** 49 37N 104 31W
Khekra **198** 28 52N 77 20 E
Khemarak Phouminville **205** 11 37N 102 59 E

Khemelnik 180 49 33N 27 58 E
Khemis Miliana 241 36 11N 2 14 E
Khemissèt 240 33 50N 6 1W
Khemmarat 204 16 10N 105 15 E
Khenāmān 193 30 27N 56 29 E
Khenchela 241 35 28N 7 11 E
Khenifra 240 32 58N 5 46W
Kherrata 241 36 27N 5 13 E
Khérson, Greece 168 41 5N 22 47 E
Kherson, U.S.S.R. 180 46 35N 32 35 E
Khersónisos Akrotíri 169 35 30N 24 10 E
Kheta → 185 71 54N 102 6 E
Khiliomódhion 169 37 48N 22 51 E
Khilok 185 51 30N 110 45 E
Khimki 179 55 50N 37 20 E
Khingan 186 47 0N 119 30 E
Khíos 169 38 27N 26 9 E
Khirbat Qanāfār 190 33 39N 35 43 E
Khisar-Momina Banya 167 42 30N 24 44 E
Khiuma = Hiiumaa 178 58 50N 22 45 E
Khiva 184 41 30N 60 18 E
Khīyāv 192 38 30N 47 45 E
Khlebarovo 167 43 37N 26 15 E
Khlong Khlung 204 16 12N 99 43 E
Khmelnitskiy 180 49 23N 27 0 E
Khmer Rep. = Cambodia ■ 204 12 15N 105 0 E
Khoai, Hon 205 8 26N 104 50 E
Khodzhent 183 40 14N 69 37 E
Khojak P. 197 30 55N 66 30 E
Khok Kloi 205 8 17N 98 19 E
Khok Pho 205 6 43N 101 6 E
Khokholskiy 179 51 35N 38 40 E
Kholm, Afghan. 197 36 45N 67 40 E
Kholm, U.S.S.R. 178 57 10N 31 15 E
Kholmsk 185 47 40N 142 5 E
Khomas Hochland 254 22 40 S 16 0 E
Khomayn 193 33 40N 50 7 E
Khon Kaen 204 16 30N 102 47 E
Khong 204 14 7N 105 51 E
Khong Sedone 204 15 34N 105 49 E
Khonu 185 66 30N 143 12 E
Khoper → 179 49 30N 42 20 E
Khor el 'Atash 245 13 20N 34 15 E
Khóra 169 37 3N 21 42 E
Khóra Sfakion 169 35 15N 24 9 E
Khorāsān □ 193 34 0N 58 0 E
Khorat = Nakhon Ratchasima 204 14 59N 102 12 E
Khorat, Cao Nguyen 204 15 30N 102 50 E
Khorb el Ethel 240 28 30N 6 17W
Khorixas 254 20 16 S 14 59 E
Khorog 183 37 30N 71 36 E
Khorol 180 49 48N 33 15 E
Khorramābād, Khorāsān, Iran 193 35 6N 57 57 E
Khorramābād, Lorestān, Iran 193 33 30N 48 25 E
Khorrāmshahr 193 30 29N 48 15 E
Khosravī 193 30 48N 51 28 E
Khosrowābād, Khuzestān, Iran 193 30 10N 48 25 E
Khosrowābād, Kordestān, Iran 192 35 31N 47 38 E
Khosūyeh 193 28 32N 54 26 E
Khotin 180 48 31N 26 27 E
Khouribga 240 32 58N 6 57W
Khowai 202 24 5N 91 40 E
Khoyniki 178 51 54N 29 55 E
Khrami → 181 41 30N 45 0 E
Khrenovoye 179 51 4N 40 16 E
Khristianá 169 36 14N 25 13 E
Khromtau 182 50 17N 58 27 E
Khtapodhiá 169 37 24N 25 34 E
Khu Khan 204 14 42N 104 12 E
Khudrah, W. → 195 18 10N 50 20 E
Khuff 192 24 55N 44 53 E
Khūgīānī, Qandahar, Afghan. 197 31 34N 66 32 E
Khugiani, Qandahar, Afghan. 197 31 28N 65 14 E
Khulayş 194 22 9N 39 19 E
Khulna 202 22 45N 89 34 E
Khulna □ 202 22 25N 89 35 E
Khulo 181 41 33N 42 19 E
Khumago 254 20 26 S 24 32 E
Khumrah 194 21 22N 39 13 E
Khūnsorkh 193 27 9N 56 7 E
Khunzakh 181 42 35N 46 42 E
Khūr 193 32 55N 58 18 E
Khurai 198 24 3N 78 23 E
Khuraydah 195 15 33N 48 18 E
Khurayş 193 25 6N 48 2 E
Khūrīyā Mūrīyā, Jazā 'ir 195 17 30N 55 58 E
Khurja 198 28 15N 77 58 E
Khūsf 193 32 46N 58 53 E
Khushab 197 32 20N 72 20 E
Khuzdar 197 27 52N 66 30 E
Khūzestān □ 193 31 0N 49 0 E
Khvājeh 192 38 9N 46 35 E
Khvājeh Moḩammad, Kūh-e 197 36 22N 70 17 E
Khvalynsk 179 52 30N 48 2 E
Khvānsār 193 29 56N 54 8 E
Khvatovka 179 52 24N 46 32 E
Khvor 193 33 45N 55 0 E
Khvorgū 193 27 34N 56 27 E
Khvormūj 193 28 40N 51 30 E
Khvoy 192 38 35N 45 0 E
Khvoynaya 178 58 58N 34 28 E
Khyber Pass 197 34 10N 71 8 E
Kiabukwa 251 8 40 S 24 48 E
Kiadho → 200 19 37N 77 40 E
Kiama 231 34 40 S 150 50 E
Kiamba 211 6 2N 124 46 E
Kiambi 250 7 15 S 28 0 E
Kiambu 250 1 8 S 36 50 E
Kiangsi = Jiangxi □ 217 27 30N 116 0 E
Kiangsu = Jiangsu □ 215 33 0N 120 0 E
Kiáton 169 38 2N 22 43 E
Kibæk 173 56 2N 8 51 E
Kibanga Port 250 0 10N 32 58 E
Kibangou 252 3 26 S 12 22 E
Kibara 250 2 8 S 33 30 E
Kibare, Mts. 250 8 25 S 27 10 E
Kibawe 211 7 34N 125 0 E
Kibombo 250 3 57 S 25 53 E
Kibondo 250 3 35 S 30 45 E
Kibondo □ 250 4 0 S 30 55 E
Kibumbu 250 3 32 S 29 45 E
Kibungu 250 2 10 S 30 32 E
Kibuye, Burundi 250 3 39 S 29 59 E
Kibuye, Rwanda 250 2 3 S 29 21 E
Kibwesa 250 6 30 S 29 58 E
Kibwezi 250 2 27 S 37 57 E
Kičevo 166 41 34N 20 59 E
Kichiga 185 59 50N 163 5 E
Kicking Horse Pass 93 51 28N 116 16W
Kīd, W. → 191 28 9N 34 27 E
Kidal 247 18 26N 1 22 E
Kidapawan 211 7 1N 125 3 E
Kidderminster 133 52 24N 2 13W
Kidete 250 6 25 S 37 17 E
Kidira 246 14 28N 12 13W
Kidnappers, C. 234 39 38 S 177 5 E
Kidston 230 18 52 S 144 8 E
Kidugallo 250 6 49 S 38 15 E
Kiel 146 54 16N 10 8 E
Kiel Kanal = Nord-Ostsee Kanal 146 54 15N 9 40 E
Kielce 152 50 52N 20 42 E
Kielce □ 152 50 40N 20 40 E
Kieldrecht 143 51 17N 4 11 E
Kieler Bucht 146 54 30N 10 30 E
Kien Binh 205 9 55N 105 19 E
Kien Tan 205 10 7N 105 17 E
Kienge 251 10 30 S 27 30 E
Kiessé 247 13 29N 4 1 E
Kieta 227 6 12 S 155 36 E
Kiev = Kiyev 178 50 30N 30 28 E
Kifār 'Aşyūn 189 31 39N 35 7 E
Kiffa 246 16 37N 11 24W
Kifisiá 169 38 4N 23 49 E
Kifissós → 169 38 35N 23 20 E
Kifrī 192 34 45N 45 0 E
Kigali 250 1 59 S 30 4 E
Kigarama 250 1 1 S 31 50 E
Kiglapait Mts. 78 57 6N 61 22W
Kigoma □ 250 5 0 S 30 0 E
Kigoma-Ujiji 250 4 55 S 29 36 E
Kigomasha, Ras 250 4 58 S 38 58 E
Kihee 231 27 23 S 142 37 E
Kihikihi 234 38 2 S 175 22 E
Kii-Hantō 221 34 0N 135 45 E
Kii-Sanchi 221 34 20N 136 0 E
Kii-Suidō 220 33 40N 135 0 E
Kikaiga-Shima 219 28 19N 129 59 E
Kikinda 166 45 50N 20 30 E
Kikino 90 54 27N 112 8W
Kikkatla 92 53 47N 130 25W
Kikládhes 169 37 20N 24 30 E
Kikládhes □ 169 37 0N 25 0 E
Kikoira 233 33 39 S 146 40 E
Kikori 227 7 25 S 144 15 E
Kikori → 227 7 38 S 144 20 E
Kikuchi 220 32 59N 130 47 E
Kikwit 253 5 5 S 18 45 E
Kila' Drosh 197 35 33N 71 52 E
Kilafors 172 61 14N 16 36 E
Kilakkarai 201 9 12N 78 47 E
Kílalki 169 36 15N 27 35 E
Kilchberg 149 47 18N 8 33 E
Kilcoy 231 26 59 S 152 30 E
Kildala Arm 92 53 50N 128 29W
Kildare 135 53 10N 6 50W
Kildare □ 135 53 10N 6 50W
Kilembe 253 5 42 S 19 55 E
Kilifi 250 3 40 S 39 48 E
Kilifi □ 250 3 30 S 39 40 E
Kilimanjaro 250 3 7 S 37 20 E
Kilimanjaro □ 250 4 0 S 38 0 E
Kilinailau, Is. 227 4 45 S 155 20 E
Kilindini 250 4 4 S 39 40 E
Kilis 190 36 50N 37 10 E
Kiliya 180 45 28N 29 16 E
Kilju 215 40 57N 129 25 E
Kilkee 135 52 41N 9 40W
Kilkenny 135 52 40N 7 17W
Kilkenny □ 135 52 35N 7 15W
Kilkieran B. 135 53 18N 9 45W
Kilkís 168 40 58N 22 57 E
Kilkís □ 168 41 5N 22 50 E
Killala 135 54 13N 9 12W
Killala B. 135 54 20N 9 12W
Killala L. 87 49 5N 86 32W
Killaloe 135 52 48N 8 28W
Killaloe Sta. 85 45 33N 77 25W
Killaly 88 50 45N 102 50W
Killam 91 52 47N 111 51W
Killarney, Australia 231 28 20 S 152 18 E
Killarney, Man., Canada 89 49 10N 99 40W
Killarney, Ont., Canada 84 45 55N 81 30W
Killarney, Ireland 135 52 2N 9 30W
Killarney, Lakes of 135 52 0N 9 30W
Killarney Prov. Park 84 46 2N 81 35W
Killary Harbour 135 53 38N 9 52W
Killdeer 88 49 6N 106 22W
Killiecrankie, Pass of 134 56 44N 3 46W
Killin 134 56 28N 4 20W
Killinek I. 78 60 24N 64 37W
Killíni, Ilía, Greece 169 37 55N 21 8 E
Killíni, Korinthía, Greece 169 37 54N 22 25 E
Killybegs 135 54 38N 8 26W
Kilmar 82 45 46N 74 37W
Kilmarnock 134 55 36N 4 30W
Kilmez 182 56 58N 50 55 E
Kilmez → 182 56 58N 50 28 E
Kilmore 231 37 25 S 144 53 E
Kilondo 251 9 45 S 34 20 E
Kilosa 250 6 48 S 37 0 E
Kilosa □ 250 6 48 S 37 0 E
Kilrush 135 52 39N 9 30W
Kilsmo 172 59 6N 15 35 E
Kilwa □ 251 9 0 S 39 0 E
Kilwa Kisiwani 251 8 58 S 39 32 E
Kilwa Kivinje 251 8 45 S 39 25 E
Kilwa Masoko 251 8 55 S 39 30 E
Kimaam 207 7 58 S 138 53 E
Kimamba 250 6 45 S 37 10 E
Kimba 231 33 8 S 136 23 E
Kimbe 227 5 33 S 150 11 E
Kimbe B. 227 5 15 S 150 30 E
Kimberley, Australia 232 32 50 S 141 4 E
Kimberley, Canada 91 49 40N 115 59W
Kimberley, S. Africa 254 28 43 S 24 46 E
Kimberley Downs 228 17 24 S 124 22 E
Kimchaek 215 40 40N 129 10 E
Kimchŏn 215 36 11N 128 4 E
Kími 169 38 38N 24 6 E
Kimiwan L. 90 55 45N 116 55W
Kimje 215 35 48N 126 45 E
Kímolos 169 36 48N 24 37 E
Kimovsk 179 54 0N 38 29 E
Kimparana 246 12 48N 5 0W
Kimry 179 56 55N 37 15 E
Kimsquit 92 52 45N 126 57W
Kimstad 173 58 35N 15 58 E
Kimvula 253 5 44 S 15 58 E
Kinabalu 205 6 3N 116 14 E
Kínaros 169 36 59N 26 15 E
Kinaskan L. 76 57 38N 130 8W
Kincaid 88 49 40N 107 0W
Kincardine 84 44 10N 81 40W
Kinchil 111 20 55N 89 57W
Kinda, Kasai Or., Zaïre 251 9 18 S 25 4 E
Kinda, Shaba, Zaïre 253 4 47 S 21 48 E
Kindersley 88 51 30N 109 10W
Kindia 246 10 0N 12 52W
Kindu 250 2 55 S 25 50 E
Kinel 182 53 15N 50 40 E
Kineshma 179 57 30N 42 5 E
Kinesi 250 1 25 S 33 50 E
King, L. 229 33 10 S 119 35 E
King, Mt. 230 25 10 S 147 30 E
King Cr. → 230 24 35 S 139 30 E
King Edward → 228 14 14 S 126 35 E
King Frederick VI land = Kong Frederik VI.s Kyst 12 63 0N 43 0W
King George B. 126 51 30 S 60 30W
King George I. 13 60 0 S 60 0W
King George Is. 78 57 20N 78 25W
King I. = Kadan Kyun 206 12 30N 98 20 E
King I., Australia 230 39 50 S 144 0 E
King I., Canada 92 52 10N 127 40W
King Leopold Ranges 228 17 30 S 125 45 E
King Sd. 228 16 50 S 123 20 E
King William I. 95 69 10N 97 25W
King William's Town 254 32 51 S 27 22 E
Kingaroy 231 26 32 S 151 51 E
Kingcome Inlet 92 50 56N 126 29W
Kingirbān 192 34 40N 44 54 E
Kingisepp, Estonia, U.S.S.R. 178 58 15N 22 30 E
Kingisepp, R.S.F.S.R., U.S.S.R. 178 59 25N 28 40 E
Kingking 211 7 9N 125 54 E
King's Lynn 132 52 45N 0 25 E
King's Point 79 49 35N 56 11W
Kingsbridge 133 50 17N 3 46W
Kingscote 232 35 40 S 137 38 E
Kingscourt 135 53 55N 6 48W
Kingsey Falls 83 45 51N 72 4W
Kingsgate 91 49 1N 116 11W
Kingsmere L. 88 54 6N 106 27W
Kingston, N.S., Canada 81 44 59N 64 57W
Kingston, Ont., Canada 85 44 14N 76 30W
Kingston, Jamaica 112 18 0N 76 50W
Kingston, N.Z. 235 45 20 S 168 43 E
Kingston South East 232 36 51 S 139 55 E
Kingston-upon-Thames 133 51 23N 0 20W
Kingstown, Australia 233 30 29 S 151 6 E
Kingstown, St. Vinc. 113 13 10N 61 10W
Kingsville 84 42 2N 82 45W
Kingussie 134 57 5N 4 2W
Kinistino 88 52 57N 105 2W
Kinkala 253 4 18 S 14 49 E
Kinki □ 221 33 30N 136 0 E
Kinkora 81 46 19N 63 36W
Kinleith 234 38 20 S 175 56 E
Kinmount 85 44 48N 78 45W
Kinn 171 61 34N 4 45 E
Kinna 173 57 32N 12 42 E
Kinnaird 93 49 17N 117 39W
Kinnairds Hd. 134 57 40N 2 0W
Kinnared 173 57 2N 13 7 E
Kinneret 189 32 44N 35 34 E
Kinneret, Yam 189 32 45N 35 35 E
Kino 100 28 49N 111 55W
Kino, B. 100 28 47N 111 58W
Kinogitan 211 9 0N 124 48 E
Kinoje → 74 52 8N 81 25W
Kinoje Lakes 87 51 35N 81 48W
Kinomoto 221 35 30N 136 13 E
Kinoni 250 0 41 S 30 28 E
Kinrooi 143 51 9N 5 45 E
Kinross 134 56 13N 3 25W
Kinsale 135 51 42N 8 31W
Kinsale, Old Hd. of 135 51 37N 8 32W
Kinsarvik 171 60 22N 6 43 E
Kinshasa 253 4 20 S 15 15 E
Kintampo 247 8 5N 1 41W
Kintap 209 3 51 S 115 13 E
Kintore Ra. 228 23 15 S 128 47 E
Kintyre 134 55 30N 5 35W
Kintyre, Mull of 134 55 17N 5 55W
Kinu 202 22 46N 95 37 E
Kinu-Gawa → 221 35 36N 139 57 E
Kinushseo → 74 55 15N 83 45W
Kinuso 90 55 20N 115 25W
Kinyangiri 250 4 25 S 34 37 E
Kinzig → 147 48 37N 7 49 E
Kióni 169 38 27N 20 41 E
Kiosk 85 46 6N 78 53W
Kipahigan L. 77 55 20N 101 55W
Kipanga 250 6 15 S 35 20 E
Kiparissía 169 37 15N 21 40 E
Kiparissiakós Kólpos 169 37 25N 21 25 E
Kipawa 82 46 47N 78 59W
Kipawa, Parc de 82 47 0N 78 50W
Kipawa L. 82 46 50N 79 0W
Kipembawe 250 7 38 S 33 27 E
Kipengere Ra. 251 9 12 S 34 15 E
Kipili 250 7 28 S 30 32 E
Kipini 250 2 30 S 40 32 E
Kipling 88 50 6N 102 38W
Kippens 79 48 33N 58 38W
Kippure 135 53 11N 6 23W
Kipungot 211 6 24N 124 4 E
Kipushi 251 11 48 S 27 12 E
Kirandul 200 18 33N 81 10 E
Kiratpur 198 29 32N 78 12 E
Kirchberg 148 47 5N 7 35 E
Kirchhain 146 50 49N 8 54 E
Kirchheim 147 48 38N 9 20 E
Kirchheim-Bolanden 147 49 40N 8 0 E
Kirchschlag 151 47 30N 16 19 E
Kirensk 185 57 50N 107 55 E
Kirgella Rocks 229 30 5 S 122 50 E
Kirgiz S.S.R. □ 183 42 0N 75 0 E
Kirgiziya Steppe 177 50 0N 55 0 E
Kiri 252 1 29 S 19 0 E
Kiri Buru 199 22 0N 85 0 E
Kiribati ■ 224 1 0N 176 0 E
Kırıkhan 190 36 31N 36 21 E
Kırıkkale 176 39 51N 33 32 E
Kirikopuni 234 35 50 S 174 1 E
Kirillov 179 59 51N 38 14 E
Kirin = Jilin 215 43 44N 126 30 E

Kirin □ = Jilin □ **215** 44 0N 124 0 E
Kirindi → **201** 6 15N 81 20 E
Kirishi **178** 59 28N 31 59 E
Kirishima-Yama **220** 31 58N 130 55 E
Kiritimati **225** 1 58N 157 27W
Kirkcaldy **134** 56 7N 3 10W
Kirkcudbright **134** 54 50N 4 3W
Kirkee **200** 18 34N 73 56 E
Kirkenœr **171** 60 27N 12 3 E
Kirkenes **174** 69 40N 30 5 E
Kirkfield **85** 44 34N 78 59W
Kirkintilloch **134** 55 57N 4 10W
Kirkjubœjarklaustur **174** 63 47N 18 4W
Kirkland Lake **74** 48 9N 80 2W
Kırklareli **167** 41 44N 27 15 E
Kirkliston Ra. **235** 44 25 S 170 34 E
Kirkūk **192** 35 30N 44 21 E
Kirkwall **134** 58 59N 2 59W
Kirkwood **254** 33 22 S 25 15 E
Kirlampudi **200** 17 12N 82 12 E
Kirn **147** 49 46N 7 29 E
Kirov, R.S.F.S.R., U.S.S.R. **178** 54 3N 34 20 E
Kirov, R.S.F.S.R., U.S.S.R. **182** 58 35N 49 40 E
Kirovabad **181** 40 45N 46 20 E
Kirovakan **181** 40 48N 44 30 E
Kirovo **183** 40 26N 70 36 E
Kirovo-Chepetsk **179** 58 28N 50 0 E
Kirovograd **180** 48 35N 32 20 E
Kirovsk, R.S.F.S.R., U.S.S.R. **176** 67 48N 33 50 E
Kirovsk, Turkmen S.S.R., U.S.S.R. **184** 37 42N 60 23 E
Kirovsk, Ukraine S.S.R., U.S.S.R. **181** 48 35N 38 30 E
Kirovski **181** 45 51N 48 11 E
Kirovskiy, Kamchatka, U.S.S.R. **185** 54 27N 155 42 E
Kirovskiy, Kazakh S.S.R., U.S.S.R. **183** 44 52N 78 12 E
Kirovskiy, R.S.F.S.R., U.S.S.R. **218** 45 7N 133 30 E
Kirovskoye **183** 42 39N 71 35 E
Kirriemuir, Canada **77** 51 56N 110 20W
Kirriemuir, U.K. **134** 56 41N 3 0W
Kirs **182** 59 21N 52 14 E
Kirsanov **179** 52 35N 42 40 E
Kırşehir **177** 39 14N 34 5 E
Kirstonia **254** 25 30 S 23 45 E
Kirtachi **247** 12 52N 2 30 E
Kīrteh **197** 32 15N 63 0 E
Kirthar Range **197** 27 0N 67 0 E
Kiruna **174** 67 52N 20 15 E
Kirundu **250** 0 50 S 25 35 E
Kirup **229** 33 40 S 115 50 E
Kirya **179** 55 5N 46 45 E
Kiryū **221** 36 24N 139 20 E
Kisa **173** 58 0N 15 39 E
Kisaga **250** 4 30 S 34 23 E
Kisalaya **112** 14 40N 84 3W
Kisambo **253** 6 25 S 18 14 E
Kisámou, Kólpos **169** 35 30N 23 38 E
Kisanga **250** 2 30N 26 35 E
Kisangani **250** 0 35N 25 15 E
Kisantu **253** 5 7 S 15 5 E
Kisar **207** 8 5 S 127 10 E
Kisaran **208** 3 0N 99 37 E
Kisarawe **250** 6 53 S 39 0 E
Kisarawe □ **250** 7 3 S 39 0 E
Kisarazu **221** 35 23N 139 55 E
Kisbér **151** 47 30N 18 0 E
Kisbey **88** 49 39N 102 40W
Kiselevsk **184** 54 5N 86 39 E
Kishanganga → **199** 34 18N 73 28 E
Kishanganj **199** 26 3N 88 14 E
Kishangarh **198** 27 50N 70 30 E
Kishi **247** 9 1N 3 52 E
Kishinev **180** 47 0N 28 50 E
Kishiwada **221** 34 28N 135 22 E
Kishon **189** 32 49N 35 2 E
Kishorganj **202** 24 26N 90 40 E
Kishtwar **199** 33 20N 75 48 E
Kisii **250** 0 40 S 34 45 E
Kisii □ **250** 0 40 S 34 45 E
Kisiju **250** 7 23 S 39 19 E
Kısır, Dağ **181** 41 0N 43 5 E
Kisizi **250** 1 0 S 29 58 E
Kiskatinaw → **76** 56 8N 120 10W
Kiskitto L. **89** 54 16N 98 30W
Kiskittogisu L. **89** 54 13N 98 20W
Kiskomárom = Zalakomár **151** 46 33N 17 10 E
Kiskörös **151** 46 37N 19 20 E
Kiskundorozsma **151** 46 16N 20 5 E
Kiskunfelégyháza **151** 46 42N 19 53 E
Kiskunhalas **151** 46 28N 19 37 E
Kiskunmajsa **151** 46 30N 19 48 E
Kislovodsk **181** 43 50N 42 45 E
Kiso-Gawa → **221** 35 20N 136 45 E
Kiso-Sammyaku **221** 35 45N 137 45 E
Kisofukushima **221** 35 52N 137 43 E
Kisoro **250** 1 17 S 29 48 E
Kispest **151** 47 27N 19 9 E
Kissidougou **246** 9 5N 10 0W
Kississing L. **77** 55 10N 101 20W
Kistanje **163** 43 58N 15 55 E
Kisterenye **151** 48 3N 19 50 E
Kisújszállás **151** 47 12N 20 50 E
Kisuki **220** 35 17N 132 54 E
Kisumu **250** 0 3 S 34 45 E
Kisvárda **151** 48 14N 22 4 E
Kiswani **250** 4 5 S 37 57 E
Kiswere **251** 9 27 S 39 30 E
Kita **246** 13 5N 9 25W
Kita-Ura **221** 36 0N 140 34 E
Kitab **183** 39 7N 66 52 E
Kitaibaraki **219** 36 50N 140 45 E
Kitakami **218** 39 20N 141 10 E
Kitakami-Gawa → **218** 38 25N 141 19 E
Kitakami-Sammyaku **218** 39 30N 141 30 E
Kitakata **218** 37 39N 139 52 E
Kitakyūshū **220** 33 50N 130 50 E
Kitale **250** 1 0N 35 0 E
Kitami **218** 43 48N 143 54 E
Kitami-Sammyaku **218** 44 22N 142 43 E
Kitangiri, L. **250** 4 5 S 34 20 E
Kitano-Kaikyō **220** 34 17N 134 58 E
Kitaotao **211** 7 40N 125 1 E
Kitaya **251** 10 38 S 40 8 E
Kitcharao **211** 9 27N 125 36 E
Kitchener, Australia **229** 30 55 S 124 8 E
Kitchener, Canada **84** 43 27N 80 29W
Kitega = Gitega **250** 3 26 S 29 56 E
Kitengo **250** 7 26 S 24 8 E
Kiteto □ **250** 5 0 S 37 0 E
Kitgum **250** 3 17N 32 52 E
Kíthira **169** 36 9N 23 0 E
Kíthnos **169** 37 26N 24 27 E
Kitikmeot □ **94** 70 0N 110 0W
Kitimat **92** 54 3N 128 38W
Kitimat Arm **92** 53 55N 128 42W
Kitimat Ranges **92** 54 0N 129 15W
Kitiyab **245** 17 13N 33 35 E
Kítros **168** 40 22N 22 34 E
Kitscoty **90** 53 20N 110 20W
Kitsuki **220** 33 25N 131 37 E
Kittakittaooloo, L. **231** 28 3 S 138 14 E
Kittertoksoak, I. **78** 58 50N 65 50W
Kitui **250** 1 17 S 38 0 E
Kitui □ **250** 1 30 S 38 25 E
Kitwe **251** 12 54 S 28 13 E
Kitzbühel **150** 47 27N 12 24 E
Kitzingen **147** 49 44N 10 9 E
Kivarli **198** 24 33N 72 46 E
Kivitoo **95** 67 56N 64 52W
Kivotós **168** 40 13N 21 26 E
Kivu □ **250** 3 10 S 27 0 E
Kivu, L. **250** 1 48 S 29 0 E
Kiwai I. **227** 8 35 S 143 30 E
Kiyev **178** 50 30N 30 28 E
Kiyevskoye Vdkhr. **178** 51 0N 30 0 E
Kizel **182** 59 3N 57 40 E
Kiziguru **250** 1 46 S 30 23 E
Kizil Dağ **190** 36 19N 35 57 E
Kızıl Irmak → **180** 39 15N 36 0 E
Kizil Jilga **199** 35 26N 78 50 E
Kizil Yurt **181** 43 13N 46 54 E
Kızılcahamam **180** 40 30N 32 30 E
Kızıllar **190** 37 8N 33 36 E
Kizilöz Dağ **190** 36 44N 32 21 E
Kizilskoye **182** 52 44N 58 54 E
Kizimkazi **250** 6 28 S 39 30 E
Kizlyar **181** 43 51N 46 40 E
Kizyl-Arvat **184** 38 58N 56 15 E
Kjellerup **173** 56 17N 9 25 E
Kladanj **166** 44 14N 18 42 E
Kladnica **166** 43 23N 20 2 E
Kladno **150** 50 10N 14 7 E
Kladovo **166** 44 36N 22 33 E
Klaeng **204** 12 47N 101 39 E
Klagenfurt **150** 46 38N 14 20 E
Klagshamn **172** 55 32N 12 53 E
Klagstorp **172** 55 22N 13 23 E
Klaipeda **178** 55 43N 21 10 E
Klangklang **202** 22 41N 93 26 E
Klanjec **163** 46 3N 15 45 E
Klappan → **76** 58 0N 129 43W
Klaten **209** 7 43 S 110 36 E
Klatovy **150** 49 23N 13 18 E
Klawer **254** 31 44 S 18 36 E
Klazienaveen **142** 52 44N 7 0 E
Kłecko **152** 52 38N 17 25 E
Kleczew **152** 52 22N 18 9 E
Kleczkowski, L. **80** 50 48N 63 27W
Kleena Kleene **92** 52 0N 124 59W
Klein-Karas **254** 27 33 S 18 7 E
Klein Karoo **254** 33 45 S 21 30 E
Kleindale **92** 49 38N 123 58W
Kleine Gette → **143** 50 51N 5 6 E
Kleine Nete → **143** 51 12N 4 46 E
Klekovača **163** 44 25N 16 32 E
Klemtu **76** 52 35N 128 55W
Klenovec, Czech. **151** 48 36N 19 54 E
Klenovec, Yugoslavia **166** 41 32N 20 49 E
Klerksdorp **254** 26 51 S 26 38 E
Kleszczele **152** 52 35N 23 19 E
Kletnya **178** 53 23N 33 12 E
Kletsk **178** 53 5N 26 45 E
Kletskiy **181** 49 20N 43 0 E
Kleve **146** 51 46N 6 10 E
Klimovichi **178** 53 36N 32 0 E
Klin **179** 56 20N 36 48 E
Klinaklini → **92** 51 21N 125 40W
Kling **211** 5 58N 124 42 E
Klintsey **178** 52 50N 32 10 E
Klipplaat **254** 33 0 S 24 22 E
Klisura **167** 42 40N 24 28 E
Klitmøller **173** 57 3N 8 30 E
Kljajićevo **166** 45 45N 19 17 E
Ključ **163** 44 32N 16 48 E
Kłobuck **152** 50 55N 18 55 E
Kłodawa **152** 52 15N 18 55 E
Kłodzko **152** 50 28N 16 38 E
Kloetinge **143** 51 30N 3 56 E
Klondike **94** 64 0N 139 26W
Kloosterzande **143** 51 22N 4 1 E
Klosi **168** 41 28N 20 10 E
Klosterneuburg **151** 48 18N 16 19 E
Klosters **149** 46 52N 9 52 E
Kloten **149** 47 27N 8 35 E
Klotz, L. **78** 60 32N 73 40W
Klötze **146** 52 38N 11 9 E
Klouto **247** 6 57N 0 44 E
Kluane L. **94** 61 15N 138 40W
Kluczbork **152** 50 58N 18 12 E
Klundert **143** 51 40N 4 32 E
Klyuchevskaya, Guba **185** 55 50N 160 30 E
Knaresborough **132** 54 1N 1 29W
Knee L., Man., Canada **77** 55 3N 94 45W
Knee L., Sask., Canada **77** 55 51N 107 0W
Kneïss, I. **241** 34 22N 10 18 E
Knesselare **143** 51 9N 3 26 E
Knewstubb L. **92** 53 33N 124 55W
Knezha **167** 43 30N 24 5 E
Knić **166** 43 53N 20 45 E
Knight Inlet **92** 50 45N 125 40W
Knighton **133** 52 21N 3 2W
Knin **163** 44 1N 16 17 E
Knittelfeld **150** 47 13N 14 51 E
Knjaževac **166** 43 35N 22 18 E
Knob, C. **229** 34 32 S 119 16 E
Knockmealdown Mts. **135** 52 16N 8 0W
Knokke **143** 51 20N 3 17 E
Knossos **169** 35 16N 25 10 E
Knowlton **83** 45 13N 72 31W
Knox, C. **92** 54 11N 133 5W
Knox Coast **13** 66 30 S 108 0 E
Knud Rasmussen Land **95** 79 0N 60 0W
Knurów **152** 50 13N 18 38 E
Knutshø **171** 62 18N 9 41 E
Knysna **254** 34 2 S 23 2 E
Knyszyn **152** 53 20N 22 56 E
Ko Kha **204** 18 11N 99 24 E
Kō-Saki **220** 34 5N 129 13 E
Ko Tao **205** 10 6N 99 48 E
Koartac **78** 60 55N 69 40W
Koba, Aru, Indonesia **207** 6 37 S 134 37 E
Koba, Bangka, Indonesia **208** 2 26 S 106 14 E
Kobarid **163** 46 15N 13 30 E
Kobayashi **220** 31 56N 130 59 E
Kobdo = Hovd **212** 48 2N 91 37 E
Kōbe **221** 34 45N 135 10 E
Kobelyaki **180** 49 11N 34 9 E
København **172** 55 41N 12 34 E
Kōbi-Sho **219** 25 56N 123 41 E
Koblenz, Germany **147** 50 21N 7 36 E
Koblenz, Switz. **148** 47 37N 8 14 E
Kobo, Ethiopia **245** 12 2N 39 56 E
Kobo, Zaïre **253** 4 54 S 17 9 E
Kobrin **178** 52 15N 24 22 E
Kobroor, Kepulauan **207** 6 10 S 134 30 E
Kobuchizawa **221** 35 52N 138 19 E
Kobuleti **181** 41 55N 41 45 E
Kobylin **152** 51 43N 17 12 E
Kobyłka **152** 52 21N 21 10 E
Kobylkino **179** 54 8N 43 56 E
Kobylnik **178** 54 58N 26 39 E
Kočane **166** 43 12N 21 52 E
Kočani **166** 41 55N 22 25 E
Koçarlı **169** 37 45N 27 43 E
Koceljevo **166** 44 28N 19 50 E
Kočevje **163** 45 39N 14 50 E
Koch Bihar **202** 26 22N 89 29 E
Kochang **215** 35 41N 127 55 E
Kochas **199** 25 15N 83 56 E
Kocher → **147** 49 14N 9 12 E
Kocheya **185** 52 32N 120 42 E
Kōchi **220** 33 30N 133 35 E
Kōchi □ **220** 33 40N 133 30 E
Kōchi-Heiya **220** 33 28N 133 30 E
Kochiu = Gejiu **216** 23 20N 103 10 E
Kochkor-Ata **183** 41 1N 72 29 E
Kochkorka **183** 42 13N 75 46 E
Kock **152** 51 38N 22 27 E
Kodaira **221** 35 44N 139 29 E
Koddiyar Bay **201** 8 33N 81 15 E
Kodinar **198** 20 46N 70 46 E
Kodori → **181** 42 47N 41 10 E
Koekelare **143** 51 5N 2 59 E
Koersel **143** 51 3N 5 17 E
Koes **254** 26 0 S 19 15 E
Kofiau **207** 1 11 S 129 50 E
Köflach **150** 47 4N 15 5 E
Koforidua **247** 6 3N 0 17W
Kōfu **221** 35 40N 138 30 E
Koga **221** 36 11N 139 43 E
Kogaluk → **78** 56 12N 61 44W
Kogan **231** 27 2 S 150 40 E
Kogin Baba **247** 7 55N 11 35 E
Koh-i-Bābā **197** 34 30N 67 0 E
Koh-i-Khurd **198** 33 30N 65 59 E
Kohat **197** 33 40N 71 29 E
Kohima **202** 25 35N 94 10 E
Kohkīlūyeh va Būyer Aḩmadi □ **193** 31 30N 50 30 E
Kohler Ra. **13** 77 0 S 110 0W
Kohtla Järve **178** 59 20N 27 20 E
Kohukohu **234** 35 22 S 173 38 E
Koin-dong **215** 40 28N 126 18 E
Kojetin **151** 49 21N 17 20 E
Kojima **220** 34 30N 133 50 E
Kōjo, Japan **220** 34 33N 133 55 E
Kojŏ, N. Korea **215** 38 58N 127 58 E
Kojonup **229** 33 48 S 117 10 E
Kojūr **193** 36 23N 51 43 E
Kok Yangak **183** 41 2N 73 12 E
Koka **244** 20 5N 30 35 E
Kokand **183** 40 30N 70 57 E
Kokanee Glacier Prov. Park **93** 49 47N 117 10W
Kokas **207** 2 42 S 132 26 E
Kokava **151** 48 35N 19 50 E
Kokchetav **184** 53 20N 69 25 E
Kokemäenjoki → **175** 61 32N 21 44 E
Kokerite **119** 7 12N 59 35W
Kokhma **179** 56 55N 41 18 E
Kokiri **235** 42 29 S 171 25 E
Kokkola **174** 63 50N 23 8 E
Koko **247** 11 28N 4 29 E
Kokoda **227** 8 54 S 147 47 E
Kokolopozo **246** 5 8N 6 5W
Kokonau **207** 4 43 S 136 26 E
Kokopo **227** 4 22 S 152 19 E
Kokoro **247** 14 12N 0 55 E
Koksan **215** 38 46N 126 40 E
Koksengir, Gora **183** 44 21N 65 6 E
Kokstad **255** 30 32 S 29 29 E
Kokubu **220** 31 44N 130 46 E
Kokuora **185** 71 35N 144 50 E
Kola, Indonesia **207** 5 35 S 134 30 E
Kola, U.S.S.R. **176** 68 45N 33 8 E
Kola Pen. = Kolskiy Poluostrov **176** 67 30N 38 0 E
Kolachel **201** 8 10N 77 15 E
Kolahoi **199** 34 12N 75 22 E
Kolahun **246** 8 15N 10 4W
Kolaka **207** 4 3 S 121 46 E
Kolar **201** 13 12N 78 15 E
Kolar Gold Fields **201** 12 58N 78 16 E
Kolarovgrad **167** 43 18N 26 55 E
Kolašin **166** 42 50N 19 31 E
Kolby Kås **173** 55 48N 10 32 E
Kolchugino **179** 56 17N 39 22 E
Kolda **246** 12 55N 14 57W
Kolding **173** 55 30N 9 29 E
Kole **252** 3 16 S 22 42 E
Koléa **241** 36 38N 2 46 E
Kolepom = Yos Sudarso, Pulau **207** 8 0 S 138 30 E
Kolguyev, Ostrov **176** 69 20N 48 30 E
Kolham **142** 53 11N 6 44 E
Kolhapur **200** 16 43N 74 15 E
Kolia **246** 9 46N 6 28W
Kolín **150** 50 2N 15 9 E
Kolind **173** 56 21N 10 34 E
Kölleda **146** 51 11N 11 14 E
Koḷḷegal **201** 12 9N 77 9 E
Kolleru L. **200** 16 40N 81 10 E
Kollum **142** 53 17N 6 10 E
Kolmanskop **254** 26 45 S 15 14 E
Köln **146** 50 56N 6 58 E
Kolno **152** 53 25N 21 56 E
Koło **152** 52 14N 18 40 E
Kołobrzeg **152** 54 10N 15 35 E
Kologriv **179** 58 48N 44 25 E
Kolokani **246** 13 35N 7 45W
Kolomna **179** 55 8N 38 45 E
Kolomyya **180** 48 31N 25 2 E
Kolondiéba **246** 11 5N 6 54W
Kolonodale **207** 2 3 S 121 25 E
Kolosib **202** 24 15N 92 45 E

Kolpashevo 184 58 20N 83 5 E
Kolpino 178 59 44N 30 39 E
Kolpny 179 52 12N 37 10 E
Kolskiy Poluostrov 176 67 30N 38 0 E
Kolskiy Zaliv 176 69 23N 34 0 E
Koltubanovskiy 182 52 57N 52 2 E
Kolubara → 166 44 35N 20 15 E
Kolumna 152 51 36N 19 14 E
Koluszki 152 51 45N 19 46 E
Kolwezi 251 10 40 S 25 25 E
Kolyberovo 179 55 15N 38 40 E
Kolyma → 185 69 30N 161 0 E
Kolymskoye, Okhotsko 185 63 0N 157 0 E
Kôm Ombo 244 24 25N 32 52 E
Komagene 221 35 44N 137 58 E
Komaki 221 35 17N 136 55 E
Komárno 151 47 49N 18 5 E
Komárom 151 47 43N 18 7 E
Komárom □ 151 47 35N 18 20 E
Komarovo 178 58 38N 33 40 E
Komatipoort 255 25 25 S 31 55 E
Komatsu 221 36 25N 136 30 E
Komatsujima 220 34 0N 134 35 E
Kombissiri 247 12 4N 1 20W
Kombo 252 0 20 S 12 22 E
Kombori 246 13 26N 3 56W
Kombóti 169 39 6N 21 5 E
Komchen 111 21 6N 89 40W
Komebail Lagoon 226 7 25N 134 25 E
Komen 163 45 49N 13 45 E
Komenda 247 5 4N 1 28W
Komi A.S.S.R. □ 182 64 0N 55 0 E
Komiža 163 43 3N 16 11 E
Komló 151 46 15N 18 16 E
Kommamur Canal 201 16 0N 80 25 E
Kommunarsk 181 48 30N 38 45 E
Kommunizma, Pik 183 39 0N 72 2 E
Komnes 171 59 30N 9 55 E
Komodo 207 8 37 S 119 20 E
Komoé 246 5 12N 3 44W
Komono 252 3 10 S 13 20 E
Komoran, Pulau 207 8 18 S 138 45 E
Komoro 221 36 19N 138 26 E
Komotini 168 41 9N 25 26 E
Komovi 166 42 41N 19 39 E
Kompong Bang 205 12 24N 104 40 E
Kompong Cham 205 12 0N 105 30 E
Kompong Chhnang 205 12 20N 104 35 E
Kompong Chikreng 204 13 5N 104 18 E
Kompong Kleang 204 13 6N 104 8 E
Kompong Luong 205 11 49N 104 48 E
Kompong Pranak 204 13 35N 104 55 E
Kompong Som 205 10 38N 103 30 E
Kompong Som, Chhung 205 10 50N 103 32 E
Kompong Speu 205 11 26N 104 32 E
Kompong Sralao 204 14 5N 105 46 E
Kompong Thom 204 12 35N 104 51 E
Kompong Trabeck, Cambodia 204 13 6N 105 14 E
Kompong Trabeck, Cambodia 205 11 9N 105 28 E
Kompong Trach 205 11 25N 105 48 E
Kompong Tralach 205 11 54N 104 47 E
Komrat 180 46 18N 28 40 E
Komsberge 254 32 40 S 20 45 E
Komsomolabad 183 38 50N 69 55 E
Komsomolets 182 53 45N 62 2 E
Komsomolets, Ostrov 185 80 30N 95 0 E
Komsomolsk, R.S.F.S.R., U.S.S.R. 179 57 2N 40 20 E
Komsomolsk, R.S.F.S.R., U.S.S.R. 185 50 30N 137 0 E
Komsomolsk, Turkmen S.S.R., U.S.S.R. 183 39 2N 63 36 E
Komsomolskiy 179 53 30N 49 30 E
Konakovo 179 56 52N 36 45 E
Konarhá □ 197 35 30N 71 3 E
Konārī 193 28 13N 51 36 E
Konch 199 26 0N 79 10 E
Kondagaon 200 19 35N 81 35 E
Kondakovo 185 69 36N 152 0 E
Konde 250 4 57 S 39 45 E
Kondiá 168 39 49N 25 10 E
Kondinin 229 32 34 S 118 8 E
Kondo 253 5 35 S 13 0 E
Kondoa 250 4 55 S 35 50 E
Kondoa □ 250 5 0 S 36 0 E
Kondopaga 176 62 12N 34 17 E
Kondratyevo 185 57 22N 98 15 E
Konduga 247 11 35N 13 26 E
Kondukur 201 15 12N 79 57 E
Koné 226 21 4 S 164 52 E
Konevo 176 62 8N 39 20 E
Kong 246 8 54N 4 36W
Kong → 204 13 32N 105 58 E
Kong, Koh 205 11 20N 103 0 E
Kong Christian IX.s Land 12 68 0N 36 0W
Kong Christian X.s Land 12 74 0N 29 0W
Kong Franz Joseph Fd. 12 73 20N 24 30W
Kong Frederik IX.s Land 12 67 0N 52 0W
Kong Frederik VI.s Kyst 12 63 0N 43 0W
Kong Frederik VIII.s Land 12 78 30N 26 0W
Kong Oscar Fjord 12 72 20N 24 0W
Konga 173 56 30N 15 6 E
Kongbo 252 4 44N 21 23 E
Kongeå 173 55 24N 9 39 E
Kongju 215 36 30N 127 0 E
Kongkemul 209 1 52N 112 11 E
Konglu 202 27 13N 97 57 E
Kongolo, Kasai Or., Zaïre 250 5 26 S 24 49 E
Kongolo, Shaba, Zaïre 250 5 22 S 27 0 E
Kongoussi 247 13 19N 1 32W
Kongsberg 171 59 39N 9 39 E
Kongsvinger 171 60 12N 12 2 E
Kongwa 250 6 11 S 36 26 E
Koni 251 10 40 S 27 11 E
Koni, Mts. 251 10 36 S 27 10 E
Koniecpol 152 50 46N 19 40 E
Königsberg = Kaliningrad 178 54 42N 20 32 E
Königshofen 147 50 18N 10 29 E
Königslutter 146 52 14N 10 50 E
Königswusterhausen 146 52 19N 13 38 E
Konin 152 52 12N 18 15 E
Konin □ 152 52 15N 18 30 E
Konispoli 168 39 42N 20 10 E
Kónitsa 168 40 5N 20 48 E
Köniz 148 46 56N 7 25 E
Konjic 166 43 42N 17 58 E
Konjice 163 46 20N 15 28 E
Konkiep 254 26 49 S 17 15 E
Konkouré → 246 9 50N 13 42W
Könnern 146 51 40N 11 45 E
Konnur 201 16 14N 74 49 E
Kono 246 8 30N 11 5W
Konolfingen 148 46 54N 7 38 E
Konongo 247 6 40N 1 15W
Konos 227 3 10 S 151 44 E
Konosha 176 61 0N 40 5 E
Kōnosu 221 36 3N 139 31 E
Konotop 178 51 12N 33 7 E
Końskie 152 51 15N 20 23 E
Konsmo 171 58 16N 7 23 E
Konstantinovka 180 48 32N 37 39 E
Konstantinovski 181 47 33N 41 10 E
Konstantynów Łódźki 152 51 45N 19 20 E
Konstanz 147 47 39N 9 10 E
Kont 193 26 55N 61 50 E
Kontagora 247 10 23N 5 27 E
Kontich 143 51 8N 4 26 E
Kontum 204 14 24N 108 0 E
Kontum, Plat. du 204 14 30N 108 0 E
Konya 177 37 52N 32 35 E
Konyin 202 22 58N 94 42 E
Konz 147 49 41N 6 36 E
Konza 250 1 45 S 37 7 E
Konzhakovskiy Kamen, Gora 182 59 38N 59 8 E
Koocanusa, L. 91 49 20N 115 15W
Kookynie 229 29 17 S 121 22 E
Kooline 228 22 57 S 116 20 E
Kooloonong 231 34 48 S 143 10 E
Koolyanobbing 229 30 48 S 119 36 E
Koondrook 231 35 33 S 144 8 E
Koorawatha 231 34 2 S 148 33 E
Koorda 229 30 48 S 117 35 E
Koostatak 77 51 26N 97 26W
Kootenay L. 93 49 45N 116 50W
Kootenay Nat. Park 91 51 0N 116 0W
Kopa 183 43 31N 75 50 E
Kopanovka 181 47 28N 46 50 E
Kopaonik Planina 166 43 10N 21 50 E
Kopargaon 200 19 51N 74 28 E
Kópavogur 174 64 6N 21 55W
Koper 163 45 31N 13 44 E
Kopervik 171 59 17N 5 17 E
Kopeysk 182 55 7N 61 37 E
Kopi 231 33 24 S 135 40 E
Köping 172 59 31N 16 3 E
Kopiste 163 42 48N 16 42 E
Kopka → 86 50 4N 89 1W
Kopliku 168 42 15N 19 25 E
Köpmanholmen 172 63 10N 18 35 E
Koppal 201 15 23N 76 5 E
Koppang 171 61 34N 11 3 E
Kopparbergs län □ 172 61 20N 14 15 E
Kopperå 171 63 24N 11 50 E
Koppio 232 34 26 S 135 51 E
Koppom 172 59 43N 12 10 E
Koprivlen 167 41 36N 23 53 E
Koprivnica 163 46 12N 16 45 E
Koprivshtitsa 167 42 40N 24 19 E
Köprü → 190 36 48N 31 11 E
Kopychintsy 178 49 7N 25 58 E
Kopys 178 54 20N 30 17 E
Korab 166 41 44N 20 40 E
Korakiána 168 39 42N 19 45 E
Koraput 200 18 50N 82 40 E
Korba 199 22 20N 82 45 E
Korbach 146 51 17N 8 50 E
Korbu, G. 205 4 41N 101 18 E
Korça 168 40 37N 20 50 E
Korça □ 168 40 40N 20 50 E
Korčula 163 42 57N 17 8 E
Korčulanski Kanal 163 43 3N 16 40 E
Kord Kūy 193 36 48N 54 7 E
Kord Sheykh 193 28 31N 52 53 E
Kordestān □ 192 36 0N 47 0 E
Korea, North ■ 215 40 0N 127 0 E
Korea, South ■ 215 36 0N 128 0 E
Korea Bay 215 39 0N 124 0 E
Korea Strait 186 34 0N 129 30 E
Koregaon 200 17 40N 74 10 E
Korenevo 178 51 27N 34 55 E
Korenovsk 181 45 30N 39 22 E
Korets 178 50 40N 27 5 E
Korgus 244 19 16N 33 29 E
Korhogo 246 9 29N 5 28W
Koribundu 246 7 41N 11 46W
Korim 207 0 58 S 136 10 E
Korinthía □ 169 37 50N 22 35 E
Korinthiakós Kólpos 169 38 16N 22 30 E
Kórinthos 169 37 56N 22 55 E
Korioumé 246 16 35N 3 0W
Kōriyama 218 37 24N 140 23 E
Korkino 182 54 54N 61 23 E
Korla 212 41 45N 86 4 E
Kormack 87 47 38N 82 59W
Kormakiti, C. 190 35 23N 32 56 E
Körmend 151 47 5N 16 35 E
Kornat 163 43 50N 15 20 E
Korneshty 180 47 21N 28 1 E
Korneuburg 151 48 20N 16 20 E
Kornsjø 171 58 57N 11 39 E
Kornstad 171 62 59N 7 27 E
Koro, Fiji 226 17 19 S 179 23 E
Koro, Ivory C. 246 8 32N 7 30W
Koro, Mali 246 14 1N 2 58W
Koro Sea 226 17 30 S 179 45W
Koro Toro 243 16 5N 18 30 E
Koroba 227 5 44 S 142 47 E
Koroc → 78 58 50N 65 50W
Korocha 179 50 55N 37 30 E
Korogwe 250 5 5 S 38 25 E
Korogwe □ 250 5 0 S 38 20 E
Koroit 231 38 18 S 142 24 E
Koronadal 211 6 12N 125 1 E
Korong Vale 232 36 22 S 143 45 E
Koróni 169 36 48N 21 57 E
Korónia, Limni 168 40 47N 23 37 E
Koronís 169 37 12N 25 35 E
Koronowo 152 53 19N 17 55 E
Koror 207 7 20N 134 28 E
Körös → 151 46 43N 20 12 E
Köröstarcsa 151 46 53N 21 3 E
Korosten 178 50 57N 28 25 E
Korotoyak 179 51 1N 39 2 E
Korraraika, Helodranon' i 255 17 45 S 43 57 E
Korsakov 185 46 36N 142 42 E
Korshunovo 185 58 37N 110 10 E
Korsun Shevchenkovskiy 180 49 26N 31 16 E
Korsze 152 54 11N 21 9 E
Kortemark 143 51 2N 3 3 E
Kortessem 143 50 52N 5 23 E
Korti 244 18 6N 31 33 E
Kortrijk 143 50 50N 3 17 E
Korumburra 233 38 26 S 145 50 E
Korwai 198 24 7N 78 5 E
Koryakskiy Khrebet 185 61 0N 171 0 E
Koryŏng 215 35 44N 128 15 E
Kos 169 36 50N 27 15 E
Kosa, Ethiopia 245 7 50N 36 50 E
Kosa, U.S.S.R. 182 59 56N 55 0 E
Kosa → 182 60 11N 55 10 E
Kosaya Gora 179 54 10N 37 30 E
Koschagyl 177 46 40N 54 0 E
Kościan 152 52 5N 16 40 E
Kościerzyna 152 54 8N 17 59 E
Kosciusko, Mt. 231 36 27 S 148 16 E
Köseçobanlı 190 36 30N 33 9 E
Kösély → 151 47 25N 21 5 E
Kosgi 200 16 58N 77 43 E
Kosha 244 20 50N 30 30 E
Koshigaya 221 35 54N 139 48 E
K'oshih = Kashi 212 39 30N 76 2 E
Koshiki-Rettō 220 31 45N 129 49 E
Kōshoku 221 36 38N 138 6 E
Koshtëbë 183 41 5N 74 15 E
Kosi 198 27 48N 77 29 E
Kosi-meer 255 27 0 S 32 50 E
Košice 151 48 42N 21 15 E
Kosjerić 166 44 0N 19 55 E
Koslan 176 63 28N 48 52 E
Kosŏng 215 38 40N 128 22 E
Kosovo, Pokrajina 166 42 40N 21 5 E
Kosovska-Mitrovica 166 42 54N 20 52 E
Kostajnica 163 45 17N 16 30 E
Kostamuksa 176 62 34N 32 44 E
Kostanjevica 163 45 51N 15 27 E
Kostelec 151 50 14N 16 35 E
Kostenets 167 42 15N 23 52 E
Koster 254 25 52 S 26 54 E
Kôstî 245 13 8N 32 43 E
Kostolac 166 44 37N 21 15 E
Kostopol 178 50 51N 26 22 E
Kostroma 179 57 50N 40 58 E
Kostromskoye Vdkhr. 179 57 52N 40 49 E
Kostrzyn, Gorzow Wlkp. Poland 152 52 35N 14 39 E
Kostrzyn, Poznań, Poland 152 52 24N 17 14 E
Kostyukovichi 178 53 20N 32 4 E
Koszalin 152 53 50N 16 8 E
Koszalin □ 152 53 40N 16 10 E
Kőszeg 151 47 23N 16 33 E
Kot Addu 197 30 30N 71 0 E
Kot Moman 198 32 13N 73 0 E
Kota 198 25 14N 75 49 E
Kota Baharu 205 6 7N 102 14 E
Kota Belud 206 6 21N 116 26 E
Kota Kinabalu 209 6 0N 116 4 E
Kota Tinggi 205 1 44N 103 53 E
Kotaagung 208 5 38 S 104 29 E
Kotabaru 209 3 20 S 116 20 E
Kotabumi 208 4 49 S 104 54 E
Kotagede 209 7 54 S 110 26 E
Kotamobagu 207 0 57N 124 31 E
Kotaneelee → 76 60 11N 123 42W
Kotawaringin 209 2 28 S 111 27 E
Kotchandpur 202 23 24N 89 1 E
Kotcho L. 76 59 7N 121 12W
Kotel 167 42 52N 26 26 E
Kotelnich 179 58 20N 48 10 E
Kotelnikovo 181 47 38N 43 8 E
Kotelnyy, Ostrov 185 75 10N 139 0 E
Kothagudam 200 17 30N 80 40 E
Kothapet 200 19 21N 79 28 E
Köthen 146 51 44N 11 59 E
Kothi 199 24 45N 80 40 E
Kotiro 198 26 17N 67 13 E
Kotka 175 60 28N 26 58 E
Kotlas 176 61 15N 47 0 E
Kotlenska Planina 167 42 56N 26 30 E
Kotli 198 33 30N 73 55 E
Kotmul 199 35 32N 75 10 E
Kotohira 220 34 11N 133 49 E
Kotonkoro 247 11 3N 5 58 E
Kotor 166 42 25N 18 47 E
Kotor Varoš 166 44 38N 17 22 E
Kotoriba 163 46 23N 16 48 E
Kotovo 179 50 22N 44 45 E
Kotovsk 180 47 45N 29 35 E
Kotputli 198 27 43N 76 12 E
Kotri 197 25 22N 68 22 E
Kotri → 200 19 15N 80 35 E
Kótronas 169 36 38N 22 29 E
Kötschach-Mauthen 150 46 41N 13 1 E
Kottayam 201 9 35N 76 33 E
Kottur 201 10 34N 76 56 E
Kotuy → 185 71 54N 102 6 E
Kouango 252 5 0N 20 10 E
Kouchibouguac Nat. Park 81 46 50N 65 20W
Koudekerke 143 51 29N 3 33 E
Koudougou 246 12 10N 2 20W
Koufonísi 169 34 56N 26 8 E
Koufonísia 169 36 57N 25 35 E
Kougaberge 254 33 48 S 23 50 E
Kouibli 246 7 15N 7 14W
Kouilou → 253 4 10 S 12 5 E
Kouki 252 7 22N 17 3 E
Koula Moutou 252 1 15 S 12 25 E
Koulen 204 13 50N 104 40 E
Koulikoro 246 12 40N 7 50W
Koumac 226 20 33 S 164 17 E
Koumala 230 21 38 S 149 15 E
Koumankou 246 11 58N 6 6W
Koumbia, Guinea 246 11 48N 13 29W
Koumbia, Upp. Volta 246 11 10N 3 50W
Koumboum 246 10 25N 13 0W
Koumpenntoum 246 13 59N 14 34W
Koumra 243 8 50N 17 35 E
Koundara 246 12 29N 13 18W
Koundé 252 6 7N 14 38 E
Kounradskiy 184 46 59N 75 0 E
Koupéla 247 12 11N 0 21W
Kourizo, Passe de 241 22 28N 15 27 E
Kourou 119 5 9N 52 39W
Kouroussa 246 10 45N 9 45W
Koussané 246 14 53N 11 14W
Kousseri 243 12 0N 14 55 E
Koutiala 246 12 25N 5 23W
Kouto 246 9 53N 6 25W
Kouvé 247 6 25N 1 25 E
Kovačica 166 45 5N 20 38 E
Kovdor 176 67 34N 30 24 E

Kovel 178 51 10N 24 20 E
Kovic, B. 78 61 35N 77 36W
Kovilpatti 201 9 10N 77 50 E
Kovin 166 44 44N 20 59 E
Kovrov 179 56 25N 41 25 E
Kovur, Andhra Pradesh, India 200 17 3N 81 39 E
Kovur, Andhra Pradesh, India 201 14 30N 80 1 E
Kowal 152 52 32N 19 7 E
Kowalewo Pomorskie 152 53 10N 18 52 E
Kowghān 197 34 12N 63 2 E
Kowkash 87 50 20N 87 12W
Kowloon 217 22 20N 114 15 E
Kowŏn 215 39 26N 127 14 E
Koyabuti 207 2 36 S 140 37 E
Kōyama 220 31 20N 130 56 E
Köypınarı Köy 190 36 42N 34 16 E
Koytash 183 40 11N 67 19 E
Koyulhisar 180 40 20N 37 52 E
Koza 226 26 19N 127 46 E
Kozáni 168 40 19N 21 47 E
Kozáni □ 168 40 18N 21 45 E
Kozara 163 45 0N 17 0 E
Kozarac 163 44 58N 16 48 E
Kozelsk 178 54 2N 35 48 E
Kozhikode = Calicut 201 11 15N 75 43 E
Kozhva 176 65 10N 57 0 E
Koziegłowy 152 50 37N 19 8 E
Kozienice 152 51 35N 21 34 E
Kozje 163 46 5N 15 35 E
Kozle 152 50 20N 18 8 E
Kozloduy 167 43 45N 23 42 E
Kozlovets 167 43 30N 25 20 E
Koźmin 152 51 48N 17 27 E
Kozmodemyansk 179 56 20N 46 36 E
Kōzu-Shima 221 34 13N 139 10 E
Kozuchów 152 51 45N 15 31 E
Kpabia 247 9 10N 0 20W
Kpalimé 247 6 57N 0 44 E
Kpandae 247 8 30N 0 2W
Kpessi 247 8 4N 1 16 E
Kra, Isthmus of = Kra, Kho Khot 205 10 15N 99 30 E
Kra, Kho Khot 205 10 15N 99 30 E
Kra Buri 205 10 22N 98 46 E
Krabbendijke 143 51 26N 4 7 E
Krabi 205 8 4N 98 55 E
Kragan 209 6 43 S 111 38 E
Kragerø 171 58 52N 9 25 E
Kragujevac 166 44 2N 20 56 E
Krajenka 152 53 18N 16 59 E
Krakatau = Rakata, Pulau 208 6 10 S 105 20 E
Krakor 204 12 32N 104 12 E
Kraków 152 50 4N 19 57 E
Kraków □ 151 50 0N 20 0 E
Kraksaan 209 7 43 S 113 23 E
Kråkstad 171 59 39N 10 55 E
Kralanh 204 13 35N 103 25 E
Králiky 151 50 6N 16 45 E
Kraljevo 166 43 44N 20 41 E
Kralovice 150 49 59N 13 29 E
Královský Chlmec 151 48 27N 22 0 E
Kralupy 150 50 13N 14 20 E
Kramatorsk 180 48 50N 37 30 E
Kramfors 172 62 55N 17 48 E
Kramis, C. 241 36 26N 0 45 E
Krångede 172 63 9N 16 10 E
Kraniá 168 39 53N 21 18 E
Kranídhion 169 37 20N 23 10 E
Kranj 163 46 16N 14 22 E
Kranjska Gora 163 46 29N 13 48 E
Krapina 163 46 10N 15 52 E
Krapina → 163 45 50N 15 50 E
Krapivna 179 53 58N 37 10 E
Krapkowice 152 50 29N 17 56 E
Krasavino 176 60 58N 46 29 E
Krashyy Klyuch 182 55 23N 56 39 E
Kraskino 185 42 44N 130 48 E
Kraslice 150 50 19N 12 31 E
Krasnaya Gorbatka 179 55 52N 41 45 E
Krasnaya Polyana 181 43 40N 40 13 E
Kraśnik 152 50 55N 22 5 E
Kraśnik Fabryczny 152 50 58N 22 11 E
Krasnoarmeisk 180 48 18N 37 11 E
Krasnoarmeysk, R.S.F.S.R., U.S.S.R. 179 51 0N 45 42 E
Krasnoarmeysk, R.S.F.S.R., U.S.S.R. 181 48 30N 44 25 E
Krasnodar 181 45 5N 39 0 E
Krasnodon 181 48 17N 39 44 E
Krasnodonetskaya 181 48 5N 40 50 E
Krasnogorskiy 179 56 10N 48 28 E
Krasnograd 180 49 27N 35 27 E
Krasnogvardeysk 183 39 46N 67 16 E
Krasnogvardeyskoye 181 45 52N 41 33 E
Krasnogvardyesk 180 45 32N 34 16 E
Krasnokamsk 182 58 4N 55 48 E
Krasnokutsk 178 50 10N 34 50 E
Krasnoperekopsk 180 46 0N 33 54 E
Krasnorechenskiy 218 44 41N 135 14 E
Krasnoselkupsk 184 65 20N 82 10 E
Krasnoslobodsk, R.S.F.S.R., U.S.S.R. 179 54 25N 43 45 E
Krasnoslobodsk, R.S.F.S.R., U.S.S.R. 181 48 42N 44 33 E
Krasnoturinsk 182 59 46N 60 12 E
Krasnoufimsk 182 56 57N 57 46 E
Krasnouralsk 182 58 21N 60 3 E
Krasnousolskiy 182 53 54N 56 27 E
Krasnovishersk 182 60 23N 57 3 E
Krasnovodsk 177 40 0N 52 52 E
Krasnoyarsk 185 56 8N 93 0 E
Krasnoyarskiy 182 51 58N 59 55 E
Krasnoye = Krasnyy 178 54 25N 31 30 E
Krasnoye, Kalmyk A.S.S.R., U.S.S.R. 181 46 16N 45 0 E
Krasnoye, R.S.F.S.R., U.S.S.R. 179 59 15N 47 40 E
Krasnozavodsk 179 56 27N 38 25 E
Krasny Liman 180 48 58N 37 50 E
Krasny Sulin 181 47 52N 40 8 E
Krasnystaw 152 50 57N 23 5 E
Krasnyy 178 54 25N 31 30 E
Krasnyy Kholm, R.S.F.S.R., U.S.S.R. 179 58 10N 37 10 E
Krasnyy Kholm, R.S.F.S.R., U.S.S.R. 182 51 35N 54 9 E
Krasnyy Kut 179 50 50N 47 0 E
Krasnyy Luch 181 48 13N 39 0 E
Krasnyy Profintern 179 57 45N 40 27 E
Krasnyy Yar, Kalmyk A.S.S.R., U.S.S.R. 181 46 43N 48 23 E
Krasnyy Yar, R.S.F.S.R., U.S.S.R. 179 53 30N 50 22 E
Krasnyy Yar, R.S.F.S.R., U.S.S.R. 179 50 42N 44 45 E
Krasnyye Baki 179 57 8N 45 10 E
Krasnyyoskolskoye Vdkhr. 180 49 30N 37 30 E
Kraszna → 151 48 0N 22 20 E
Kratie 204 12 32N 106 10 E
Kratke Ra. 227 6 45 S 146 0 E
Kratovo 166 42 6N 22 10 E
Krau 207 3 19 S 140 5 E
Kravanh, Chuor Phnum 205 12 0N 103 32 E
Krawang 207 6 19N 107 18 E
Krefeld 146 51 20N 6 32 E
Krémaston, Límni 169 38 52N 21 30 E
Kremenchug 180 49 5N 33 25 E
Kremenchugskoye Vdkhr. 180 49 20N 32 30 E
Kremenets 180 50 8N 25 43 E
Kremenica 166 40 55N 21 25 E
Kremennaya 180 49 1N 38 10 E
Kremges = Svetlovodsk 178 49 2N 33 13 E
Kremikovtsi 167 42 46N 23 28 E
Kremmen 146 52 45N 13 1 E
Kremnica 151 48 45N 18 50 E
Krems 150 48 25N 15 36 E
Kremsmünster 150 48 3N 14 8 E
Kretinga 178 55 53N 21 15 E
Krettamia 240 28 47N 3 27W
Krettsy 178 58 15N 32 30 E
Kreuzberg 147 50 22N 9 58 E
Kreuzlingen 149 47 38N 9 10 E
Kribi 247 2 57N 9 56 E
Krichem 167 42 8N 24 28 E
Krichev 178 53 45N 31 50 E
Krim 163 45 53N 14 30 E
Krimpen 142 51 55N 4 34 E
Krionéri 169 38 20N 21 35 E
Krishna → 200 15 57N 80 59 E
Krishnagiri 201 12 32N 78 16 E
Krishnanagar 199 23 24N 88 33 E
Krishnaraja Sagara 201 12 20N 76 30 E
Kristiansand 171 58 9N 8 1 E
Kristianstad 173 56 2N 14 9 E
Kristiansund 171 63 7N 7 45 E
Kristiinankaupunki 174 62 16N 21 21 E
Kristinehamn 172 59 18N 14 13 E
Kristinestad 174 62 16N 21 21 E
Kríti 169 35 15N 25 0 E
Kritsá 169 35 10N 25 41 E
Kriva → 166 42 5N 21 47 E
Kriva Palanka 166 42 11N 22 19 E
Krivaja → 166 44 27N 18 9 E
Krivelj 166 44 8N 22 5 E
Krivoy Rog 180 47 51N 33 20 E
Križevci 163 46 3N 16 32 E
Krk 163 45 8N 14 40 E
Krka → 163 45 50N 15 30 E
Krkonoše 150 50 50N 15 35 E
Krnov 151 50 5N 17 40 E
Krobia 152 51 47N 16 59 E
Kročehlavy 150 50 8N 14 9 E
Krøderen 171 60 9N 9 49 E
Krokawo 152 54 47N 18 9 E
Krokeaí 169 36 53N 22 32 E
Krokodil → 255 25 26 S 32 0 E
Krokom 172 63 20N 14 30 E
Krolevets 178 51 35N 33 20 E
Kroměříz 151 49 18N 17 21 E
Krommenie 142 52 30N 4 46 E
Krompachy 151 48 54N 20 52 E
Kromy 178 52 40N 35 48 E
Kronach 147 50 14N 11 19 E
Kronobergs län □ 173 56 45N 14 30 E
Kronprins Olav Kyst 13 69 0 S 42 0 E
Kronprinsesse Märtha Kyst 13 73 30 S 10 0 E
Kronshtadt 178 60 5N 29 45 E
Kroonstad 254 27 43 S 27 19 E
Kröpelin 146 54 4N 11 48 E
Kropotkin, R.S.F.S.R., U.S.S.R. 181 45 28N 40 28 E
Kropotkin, R.S.F.S.R., U.S.S.R. 185 59 0N 115 30 E
Kropp 146 54 24N 9 32 E
Krościenko 152 49 29N 20 25 E
Krośniewice 152 52 15N 19 11 E
Krosno 152 49 42N 21 46 E
Krosno □ 152 49 35N 22 0 E
Krosno Odrzańskie 152 52 3N 15 7 E
Krotoszyn 152 51 42N 17 23 E
Krotovka 182 53 18N 51 10 E
Krraba 168 41 13N 20 0 E
Krško 163 45 57N 15 30 E
Krstača 166 42 57N 20 8 E
Kruger Nat. Park 255 24 0 S 31 40 E
Krugersdorp 255 26 5 S 27 46 E
Kruiningen 143 51 27N 4 2 E
Kruis, Kaap 254 21 55 S 13 57 E
Kruishoutem 143 50 54N 3 32 E
Kruisland 143 51 34N 4 25 E
Kruja 168 41 32N 19 46 E
Krulevshchina 178 55 5N 27 45 E
Kruma 168 42 14N 20 28 E
Krumbach 147 48 15N 10 22 E
Krumovgrad 167 41 29N 25 38 E
Krung Thep = Bangkok 204 13 45N 100 35 E
Krupanj 166 44 25N 19 22 E
Krupina 151 48 22N 19 5 E
Krupinica → 151 48 15N 18 52 E
Kruševac 166 43 35N 21 28 E
Kruševo 166 41 23N 21 19 E
Kruszwica 152 52 40N 18 20 E
Krydor 88 52 47N 107 4W
Krylbo 172 60 7N 16 15 E
Krymsk Abinsk 180 44 50N 38 0 E
Krymskiy P-ov. 180 45 0N 34 0 E
Krynica 152 49 25N 20 57 E
Krynica Morska 152 54 23N 19 28 E
Krynki 152 53 17N 23 43 E
Krzepice 152 50 58N 18 50 E
Krzeszów 152 50 24N 22 21 E
Krzeszowice 152 50 8N 19 37 E
Krzna → 152 51 59N 22 47 E
Krzywiń 152 51 58N 16 50 E
Krzyz 152 52 52N 16 0 E
Ksabi 241 32 51N 4 13W
Ksar Chellala 241 35 13N 2 19 E
Ksar el Boukhari 241 35 51N 2 52 E
Ksar el Kebir 240 35 0N 6 0W
Ksar es Souk = Ar Rachidiya 241 31 58N 4 20W
Ksar Rhilane 241 33 0N 9 39 E
Ksour, Mts. des 241 32 45N 0 30W
Kstovo 179 56 12N 44 13 E
Kuala 208 2 55N 105 47 E
Kuala Berang 205 5 5N 103 1 E
Kuala Dungun 205 4 45N 103 25 E
Kuala Kangsar 205 4 46N 100 56 E
Kuala Kelawang 205 2 56N 102 5 E
Kuala Kerai 205 5 30N 102 12 E
Kuala Kubu Baharu 205 3 34N 101 39 E
Kuala Lipis 205 4 10N 102 3 E
Kuala Lumpur 205 3 9N 101 41 E
Kuala Nerang 205 6 16N 100 37 E
Kuala Pilah 205 2 45N 102 15 E
Kuala Rompin 205 2 49N 103 29 E
Kuala Selangor 205 3 20N 101 15 E
Kuala Terengganu 205 5 20N 103 8 E
Kualajelai 209 2 58 S 110 46 E
Kualakapuas 209 2 55 S 114 20 E
Kualakurun 209 1 10 S 113 50 E
Kualapembuang 209 3 14 S 112 38 E
Kualasimpang 208 4 17N 98 3 E
Kuancheng 215 40 37N 118 30 E
Kuandang 207 0 56N 123 1 E
Kuandian 215 40 45N 124 45 E
Kuangchou = Guangzhou 217 23 5N 113 10 E
Kuantan 205 3 49N 103 20 E
Kuba 181 41 21N 48 32 E
Kuban → 180 45 20N 37 30 E
Kubenskoye, Oz. 179 59 40N 39 25 E
Kuberle 181 47 0N 42 20 E
Kubokawa 220 33 12N 133 8 E
Kubor, Mt. 227 6 10 S 144 44 E
Kubrat 167 43 49N 26 31 E
Kučevo 166 44 30N 21 40 E
Kucha Gompa 199 34 25N 76 56 E
Kuchaman 198 27 13N 74 47 E
Kuchenspitze 150 47 7N 10 12 E
Kuchino-eruba-Jima 219 30 28N 130 12 E
Kuchino-Shima 219 29 57N 129 55 E
Kuchinotsu 220 32 36N 130 11 E
Kucing 209 1 33N 110 25 E
Kuçove = Qytet Stalin 168 40 47N 19 57 E
Kücük Kuyu 168 39 35N 26 27 E
Kud → 198 26 5N 66 20 E
Kudalier → 200 18 35N 79 48 E
Kudamatsu 220 34 0N 131 52 E
Kudara 183 38 25N 72 39 E
Kudat 206 6 55N 116 55 E
Kudayd 194 19 21N 41 48 E
Kudremukh, Mt. 201 13 15N 75 20 E
Kudus 209 6 48 S 110 51 E
Kudymkar 182 59 1N 54 39 E
Kueiyang = Guiyang 216 26 32N 106 40 E
Kufrinjah 189 32 20N 35 41 E
Kufstein 150 47 35N 12 11 E
Kugaluk, B. 78 59 10N 78 40W
Kugong I. 78 56 18N 79 50W
Kūh-e Dīnār 193 30 40N 51 0 E
Kūh-e-Hazārām 193 29 35N 57 20 E
Kūhak 197 27 12N 63 10 E
Kūhbonān 193 31 23N 56 19 E
Kūhestak 193 26 47N 57 2 E
Kūhestān 197 34 39N 61 12 E
Kūhīn 193 35 13N 48 25 E
Kūhīrī 193 26 55N 61 2 E
Kuhnsdorf 150 46 37N 14 38 E
Kūhpāyeh, Eşfahan, Iran 193 32 44N 52 20 E
Kūhpāyeh, Kermān, Iran 193 30 35N 57 15 E
Kui Buri 205 12 3N 99 52 E
Kuinre 142 52 47N 5 51 E
Kuito 253 12 22 S 16 55 E
Kujang 215 39 57N 126 1 E
Kuji 218 40 11N 141 46 E
Kujū-San 220 33 5N 131 15 E
Kujukuri-Heiya 221 35 45N 140 30 E
Kukavica 166 42 48N 21 57 E
Kukawa 247 12 58N 13 27 E
Kukerin 229 33 13 S 118 0 E
Kukësi 168 42 5N 20 20 E
Kukësi □ 168 42 25N 20 15 E
Kukmor 182 56 11N 50 54 E
Kukukus L. 86 49 47N 91 41W
Kukup 205 1 20N 103 27 E
Kukvidze 179 50 40N 43 15 E
Kula, Bulgaria 166 43 52N 22 36 E
Kula, Yugoslavia 166 45 37N 19 32 E
Kulai 205 1 44N 103 35 E
Kulal, Mt. 250 2 42N 36 57 E
Kulaly, O. 181 45 0N 50 0 E
Kulanak 183 41 22N 75 30 E
Kulasekarappattinam 201 8 20N 78 0 E
Kuldiga 178 56 58N 21 59 E
Kuldja = Yining 212 43 58N 81 10 E
Kuldu 245 12 50N 28 30 E
Kulebaki 179 55 22N 42 25 E
Kulen Vakuf 163 44 35N 16 2 E
Kulgam 199 33 36N 75 2 E
Kuli 181 42 2N 47 12 E
Kulim 205 5 22N 100 34 E
Kulin 229 32 40 S 118 2 E
Kulja 229 30 28 S 117 18 E
Küllük 169 37 12N 27 36 E
Kulmbach 147 50 6N 11 27 E
Kulsary 177 46 59N 54 1 E
Kultay 181 45 5N 51 40 E
Kulti 199 23 43N 86 50 E
Kulumbura 228 13 55 S 126 35 E
Kulunda 184 52 35N 78 57 E
Kulungar 198 34 0N 69 2 E
Kūlvand 193 31 21N 54 35 E
Kulwin 231 35 0 S 142 42 E
Kulyab 183 37 55N 69 50 E
Kum Tekei 184 43 10N 79 30 E
Kuma 220 33 39N 132 54 E
Kuma → 181 44 55N 47 0 E
Kumaganum 247 13 8N 10 38 E
Kumagaya 221 36 9N 139 22 E
Kumai 209 2 44 S 111 43 E
Kumak 182 51 10N 60 8 E
Kumamba, Kepulauan 207 1 36 S 138 45 E
Kumamoto 220 32 45N 130 45 E
Kumamoto □ 220 32 55N 130 55 E

Kumano **221** 33 54N 136 5 E
Kumano-Nada **221** 33 47N 136 20 E
Kumanovo **166** 42 9N 21 42 E
Kumara **235** 42 37 S 171 12 E
Kumarkhali **202** 23 51N 89 15 E
Kumarl **229** 32 47 S 121 33 E
Kumasi **246** 6 41N 1 38W
Kumba **247** 4 36N 9 24 E
Kumbakonam **201** 10 58N 79 25 E
Kumbarilla **231** 27 15 S 150 55 E
Kumbo **247** 6 15N 10 36 E
Kumbukkan Oya → **201** 6 35N 81 40 E
Kŭmchŏn **215** 38 10N 126 29 E
Kumdah **194** 20 23N 45 5 E
Kumdok **199** 33 32N 78 10 E
Kume-Shima **219** 26 20N 126 47 E
Kumeny **179** 58 10N 49 47 E
Kumertau **182** 52 46N 55 47 E
Kŭmhwa **215** 38 17N 127 28 E
Kumi **250** 1 30N 33 58 E
Kumkale **168** 40 0N 26 13 E
Kumla **172** 59 8N 15 10 E
Kummerower See **146** 53 47N 12 52 E
Kumo **247** 10 1N 11 12 E
Kumon Bum **202** 26 30N 97 15 E
Kumotori-Yama **221** 35 51N 138 57 E
Kumta **201** 14 29N 74 25 E
Kumtorkala **181** 43 2N 46 50 E
Kumusi → **227** 8 16 S 148 13 E
Kumylzhenskaya **181** 49 51N 42 38 E
Kunágota **151** 46 26N 21 3 E
Kunama **231** 35 35 S 148 4 E
Kunashir, Ostrov **185** 44 0N 146 0 E
Kunda **178** 59 30N 26 34 E
Kundiawa **227** 6 2 S 145 1 E
Kundip **229** 33 42 S 120 10 E
Kundla **198** 21 21N 71 25 E
Kundur **208** 3 8 S 107 48 E
Kungala **231** 29 58 S 153 7 E
Kungälv **173** 57 53N 11 59 E
Kungey Alatau, Khrebet **183** 42 50N 77 0 E
Kunghit I. **92** 52 6N 131 3W
Kungrad **184** 43 6N 58 54 E
Kungsbacka **173** 57 30N 12 5 E
Kungu **252** 2 47N 19 12 E
Kungur **182** 57 25N 56 57 E
Kungurri **230** 21 3 S 148 46 E
Kungyangon **202** 16 27N 96 20 E
Kunhar → **199** 34 20N 73 30 E
Kunhegyes **151** 47 22N 20 36 E
Kunimi-Dake **220** 32 33N 131 1 E
Kuningan **209** 6 59 S 108 29 E
Kunisaki **220** 33 33N 131 45 E
Kunlara **232** 34 54 S 139 55 E
Kunlong **202** 23 20N 98 50 E
Kunlun Shan **212** 36 0N 86 30 E
Kunmadaras **151** 47 28N 20 45 E
Kunming **216** 25 1N 102 41 E
Kunnamkulam **201** 10 38N 76 7 E
Kunrade **143** 50 53N 5 57 E
Kunsan **215** 35 59N 126 45 E
Kunshan **217** 31 22N 120 58 E
Kunszentmárton **151** 46 50N 20 20 E
Kununurra **228** 15 40 S 128 50 E
Kunwarara **230** 22 55 S 150 9 E
Kunya-Urgenoh **184** 42 19N 59 10 E
Künzelsau **147** 49 17N 9 41 E
Kuopio **174** 62 53N 27 35 E
Kuopion lääni □ **174** 63 25N 27 10 E
Kupa → **163** 45 28N 16 24 E
Kupang **207** 10 19 S 123 39 E
Kupiano **227** 10 4 S 148 14 E
Kupres **166** 44 1N 17 15 E
Kupyansk **180** 49 52N 37 35 E
Kupyansk-Uzlovoi **180** 49 45N 37 34 E
Kuqa **212** 41 35N 82 30 E
Kur → **202** 26 50N 91 0 E
Kura → **181** 39 50N 49 20 E
Kurahashi-Jima **220** 34 8N 132 31 E
Kuranda **230** 16 48 S 145 35 E
Kurashiki **220** 34 40N 133 50 E
Kurayoshi **220** 35 26N 133 50 E
Kurday **183** 43 21N 74 59 E
Kurduvadi **200** 18 8N 75 29 E
Kŭrdzhali **167** 41 38N 25 21 E
Kure **220** 34 14N 132 32 E
Kuressaare = Kingisepp **178** 58 15N 22 30 E
Kurgaldzhino **184** 50 35N 70 20 E
Kurgan **182** 55 26N 65 18 E
Kurgan-Tyube **183** 37 50N 68 47 E
Kurganinsk **181** 44 54N 40 34 E
Kurgannaya = Kurganinsk **181** 44 54N 40 34 E
Kuria Maria Is. = Khūrīyā Mūrīyā, Jazā 'ir **195** 17 30N 55 58 E
Kuria Muria B. **195** 17 40N 55 45 E
Kurichchi **201** 11 36N 77 35 E
Kuridala **230** 21 16 S 140 29 E
Kurigram **202** 25 49N 89 39 E
Kurihashi **221** 36 8N 139 42 E
Kuril Is. = Kurilskiye Ostrova **185** 45 0N 150 0 E
Kuril Trench **224** 44 0N 153 0 E
Kurilsk **185** 45 14N 147 53 E
Kurilskiye Ostrova **185** 45 0N 150 0 E
Kuringen **143** 50 56N 5 18 E
Kurino **220** 31 57N 130 43 E
Kürkcü **190** 36 34N 33 39 E
Kurkur **244** 23 50N 32 0 E
Kurkūrah **241** 31 30N 20 1 E
Kurla **200** 19 5N 72 52 E
Kurlovskiy **179** 55 25N 40 40 E
Kurmuk **245** 10 33N 34 21 E
Kurnool **201** 15 45N 78 0 E
Kuro-Shima, Kagoshima, Japan **219** 30 50N 129 57 E
Kuro-Shima, Okinawa, Japan **219** 24 14N 124 1 E
Kurobe-Gawe → **221** 36 55N 137 25 E
Kurogi **220** 33 12N 130 40 E
Kuroki **88** 51 52N 103 29W
Kurovskoye **179** 55 35N 38 55 E
Kurow, N.Z. **235** 44 44 S 170 29 E
Kurów, Poland **152** 51 23N 22 12 E
Kurrajong **231** 33 33 S 150 42 E
Kurram → **197** 32 36N 71 20 E
Kurri Kurri **231** 32 50 S 151 28 E
Kursavka **181** 44 29N 42 32 E
Kuršenai **178** 56 1N 23 3 E
Kursk **179** 51 42N 36 11 E
Kuršumlija **166** 43 9N 21 19 E
Kuršumlijska Banja **166** 43 3N 21 11 E
Kurtamysh **182** 54 55N 64 27 E
Kurty → **183** 44 16N 76 42 E
Kuru, Bahr el → **245** 8 10N 26 50 E
Kuruktag **212** 41 0N 89 0 E
Kuruman **254** 27 28 S 23 28 E
Kurume **220** 33 15N 130 30 E
Kurunegala **201** 7 30N 80 23 E
Kurupukari **119** 4 43N 58 37W
Kurya **185** 61 15N 108 10 E
Kusa **182** 55 20N 59 29 E
Kuşada Körfezı **169** 37 56N 27 0 E
Kuşadası **169** 37 52N 27 15 E
Kusatsu, Gumma, Japan **221** 36 37N 138 36 E
Kusatsu, Shiga, Japan **221** 34 58N 135 57 E
Kusawa L. **76** 60 20N 136 13W
Kusel **147** 49 31N 7 25 E
Kushchevskaya **181** 46 33N 39 35 E
Kushikino **220** 31 44N 130 16 E
Kushima **220** 31 29N 131 14 E
Kushimoto **221** 33 28N 135 47 E
Kushiro **218** 43 0N 144 25 E
Kushiro → **218** 42 59N 144 23 E
Kūshk **193** 28 46N 56 51 E
Kushka **184** 35 20N 62 18 E
Kūshkī, Īlām, Iran **192** 33 31N 47 13 E
Kūshkī, Khorāsān, Iran **193** 37 2N 57 26 E
Kūshkū **193** 27 19N 53 28 E
Kushmurun **182** 52 27N 64 36 E
Kushmurun, Ozero **182** 52 40N 64 48 E
Kushnarenkovo **182** 55 6N 55 22 E
Kushol **199** 33 40N 76 36 E
Kushrabat **183** 40 18N 66 32 E
Kushtia **202** 23 55N 89 5 E
Kushum → **181** 49 0N 50 20 E
Kushva **182** 58 18N 59 45 E
Küsnacht **149** 47 19N 8 35 E
Kussharo-Ko **218** 43 38N 144 21 E
Küssnacht **149** 47 5N 8 26 E
Kustanay **182** 53 10N 63 35 E
Kusu **220** 33 16N 131 9 E
Kut, Ko **205** 11 40N 102 35 E
Kutacane **208** 3 50N 97 50 E
Kütahya **177** 39 30N 30 2 E
Kutaisi **181** 42 19N 42 40 E
Kutaraja = Banda Aceh **208** 5 35N 95 20 E
Kutch, Gulf of = Kachchh, Gulf of **198** 22 50N 69 15 E
Kutch, Rann of = Kachchh, Rann of **198** 24 0N 70 0 E
Kutina **163** 45 29N 16 48 E
Kutiyana **198** 21 36N 70 2 E
Kutjevo **166** 45 23N 17 55 E
Kutkai **202** 23 27N 97 56 E
Kutkashen **181** 40 58N 47 47 E
Kutná Hora **150** 49 57N 15 16 E
Kutno **152** 52 15N 19 23 E
Kuttabul **230** 21 5 S 148 48 E
Kutu **252** 2 40 S 18 11 E
Kutum **245** 14 10N 24 40 E
Kúty **151** 48 40N 17 3 E
Kuŭp-tong **215** 40 45N 126 1 E
Kuurne **143** 50 51N 3 18 E
Kuvandyk **182** 51 28N 57 21 E
Kuvango **253** 14 28 S 16 20 E
Kuvasay **183** 40 18N 71 59 E
Kuvshinovo **178** 57 2N 34 11 E
Kuwait = Al Kuwayt **192** 29 30N 47 30 E
Kuwait ■ **192** 29 30N 47 30 E
Kuwana **221** 35 0N 136 43 E
Kuybyshev, R.S.F.S.R., U.S.S.R. **179** 53 8N 50 6 E
Kuybyshev, R.S.F.S.R., U.S.S.R. **184** 55 27N 78 19 E
Kuybyshevo, Ukraine S.S.R., U.S.S.R. **180** 47 25N 36 40 E
Kuybyshevo, Uzbek S.S.R., U.S.S.R. **183** 40 20N 71 15 E
Kuybyshevskiy **183** 37 52N 68 44 E
Kuybyshevskoye Vdkhr. **179** 55 2N 49 30 E
Kuye He → **214** 38 23N 110 46 E
Kūyeh **192** 38 45N 47 57 E
Kuylyuk **183** 41 14N 69 17 E
Kūysanjaq **192** 36 5N 44 38 E
Kuyto, Oz. **176** 64 40N 31 0 E
Kuyumba **185** 60 58N 96 59 E
Kuzey Anadolu Dağlari **177** 41 30N 35 0 E
Kuzhitturai **201** 8 18N 77 11 E
Kuzino **182** 57 1N 59 27 E
Kuzmin **166** 45 2N 19 25 E
Kuznetsk **179** 53 12N 46 40 E
Kuzomen **176** 66 22N 36 50 E
Kvænangen **174** 70 5N 21 15 E
Kvam **171** 61 40N 9 42 E
Kvamsøy **171** 61 7N 6 28 E
Kvareli **181** 41 27N 45 47 E
Kvarner **163** 44 50N 14 10 E
Kvarnerič **163** 44 43N 14 37 E
Kvernes **171** 63 1N 7 44 E
Kvillsfors **173** 57 24N 15 29 E
Kvine → **171** 58 17N 6 56 E
Kvinesdal **171** 58 19N 6 57 E
Kviteseid **171** 59 24N 8 29 E
Kwabhaga **255** 30 51 S 29 0 E
Kwadacha → **76** 57 28N 125 38W
Kwakhanai **254** 21 39 S 21 16 E
Kwakoegron **119** 5 12N 55 25W
Kwale, Kenya **250** 4 15 S 39 31 E
Kwale, Nigeria **247** 5 46N 6 26 E
Kwale □ **250** 4 15 S 39 10 E
Kwamouth **252** 3 9 S 16 12 E
Kwando → **254** 18 27 S 23 32 E
Kwangdaeri **215** 40 31N 127 32 E
Kwangju **215** 35 9N 126 54 E
Kwango → **252** 3 14 S 17 22 E
Kwangsi-Chuang = Guangxi Zhuangzu Zizhiqu □ **216** 24 0N 109 0 E
Kwangtung = Guangdong □ **217** 23 0N 113 0 E
Kwara □ **247** 8 0N 5 0 E
Kwataboahegan → **87** 51 9N 80 50W
Kwatisore **207** 3 18 S 134 50 E
Kweichow = Guizhou □ **216** 27 0N 107 0 E
Kwekwe **251** 18 58 S 29 48 E
Kwidzyn **152** 53 44N 18 55 E
Kwikila **227** 9 49 S 147 38 E
Kwimba □ **250** 3 0 S 33 0 E
Kwinana New Town **229** 32 15 S 115 47 E
Kwinitsa **92** 54 19N 129 22W
Kwisa → **152** 51 34N 15 24 E
Kwoka **207** 0 31 S 132 27 E
Kya-in-Seikkyi **202** 16 2N 98 8 E
Kyabé **243** 9 30N 19 0 E
Kyabra Cr. → **231** 25 36 S 142 55 E
Kyabram **231** 36 19 S 145 4 E
Kyaiklat **202** 16 25N 95 40 E
Kyaikmaraw **202** 16 23N 97 44 E
Kyaikthin **202** 23 32N 95 40 E
Kyaikto **204** 17 20N 97 3 E
Kyakhta **185** 50 30N 106 25 E
Kyangin **202** 18 20N 95 20 E
Kyaukhnyat **202** 18 15N 97 31 E
Kyaukse **202** 21 36N 96 10 E
Kyauktaw **202** 20 51N 92 59 E
Kyawkku **202** 21 48N 96 56 E
Kybybolite **232** 36 53 S 140 55 E
Kyeintali **202** 18 0N 94 29 E
Kyenjojo **250** 0 40N 30 37 E
Kyidaunggan **202** 19 53N 96 12 E
Kyle **88** 50 50N 108 2W
Kyle Dam **251** 20 15 S 31 0 E
Kyle of Lochalsh **134** 57 17N 5 43W
Kyll → **147** 49 48N 6 42 E
Kyllburg **147** 50 2N 6 35 E
Kyneton **231** 37 10 S 144 29 E
Kynoch Inlet **92** 52 45N 128 0W
Kynuna **230** 21 37 S 141 55 E
Kyō-ga-Saki **221** 35 45N 135 15 E
Kyoga, L. **250** 1 35N 33 0 E
Kyogle **231** 28 40 S 153 0 E
Kyongju **215** 35 51N 129 14 E
Kyŏngsŏng **215** 41 35N 129 36 E
Kyōto **221** 35 0N 135 45 E
Kyōto □ **221** 35 15N 135 45 E
Kyren **185** 51 45N 101 45 E
Kyrenia **190** 35 20N 33 20 E
Kyritz **146** 52 57N 12 25 E
Kyshtym **182** 55 42N 60 34 E
Kystatyam **185** 67 20N 123 10 E
Kytal Ktakh **185** 65 30N 123 40 E
Kytlym **182** 59 30N 59 12 E
Kyu-hkok **202** 24 4N 98 4 E
Kyulyunken **185** 64 10N 137 5 E
Kyunhla **202** 23 25N 95 15 E
Kyuquot **92** 50 3N 127 25W
Kyurdamir **181** 40 25N 48 3 E
Kyūshū **220** 33 0N 131 0 E
Kyūshū □ **220** 33 0N 131 0 E
Kyūshū-Sanchi **220** 32 35N 131 17 E
Kyustendil **166** 42 16N 22 41 E
Kyusyur **185** 70 39N 127 15 E
Kywong **231** 34 58 S 146 44 E
Kyzyl **185** 51 50N 94 30 E
Kyzyl-Kiya **183** 40 16N 72 8 E
Kyzylkum, Peski **182** 42 30N 65 0 E
Kyzylsu → **183** 39 11N 72 2 E
Kzyl-Orda **183** 44 48N 65 28 E

L

Laa **151** 48 43N 16 23 E
Laaber → **147** 49 0N 12 3 E
Laage **146** 53 55N 12 21 E
Laasphe **146** 50 56N 8 23 E
Laba → **181** 45 11N 39 42 E
Labak **211** 6 32N 124 5 E
Laban **202** 25 52N 96 40 E
Labason **211** 8 4N 122 31 E
Labastide **140** 43 28N 2 39 E
Labastide-Murat **140** 44 39N 1 33 E
Labbézenga **247** 15 2N 0 48 E
Labdah = Leptis Magna **241** 32 40N 14 12 E
Labe = Elbe → **146** 53 50N 9 0 E
Labé **246** 11 24N 12 16W
Laberec → **151** 48 37N 21 58 E
Laberge, L. **76** 61 11N 135 12W
Labig Pt. **210** 18 25N 122 25 E
Labin **163** 45 5N 14 8 E
Labinsk **181** 44 40N 40 48 E
Labis **205** 2 22N 103 2 E
Labiszyn **152** 52 57N 17 54 E
Labná **111** 20 9N 89 33W
Labo **210** 14 9N 122 51 E
Laboe **146** 54 25N 10 13 E
Laboka **252** 0 19N 11 32 E
Labouheyre **140** 44 13N 0 55W
Laboulaye **124** 34 10 S 63 30W
Labra, Peña **154** 43 3N 4 26W
Labrador, Coast of □ **75** 53 20N 61 0W
Labrador City **80** 52 57N 66 55W
Lábrea **123** 7 15 S 64 51W
Labrède **140** 44 41N 0 32W
Labrieville **83** 49 18N 69 34W
Labuan, Pulau **206** 5 21N 115 13 E
Labuha **207** 0 30 S 127 30 E
Labuhan **207** 6 22 S 105 50 E
Labuhanbajo **207** 8 28 S 120 1 E
Labuissière **143** 50 19N 4 11 E
Labuk, Telok **206** 6 10N 117 50 E
Labutta **202** 16 9N 94 46 E
Labytnangi **176** 66 39N 66 21 E
Łabżenica **152** 53 18N 17 15 E
Lac Allard **80** 50 33N 63 24W
Lac-au-Saumon **80** 48 25N 67 22W
Lac-aux-Sables **83** 46 51N 72 24W
Lac Bouchette **83** 48 16N 72 11W
Lac Carré **83** 46 7N 74 29W
Lac-des-Écorces **82** 46 34N 75 22W
Lac du Bonnet **89** 50 15N 96 4W
Lac Édouard **83** 47 40N 72 16W
Lac-Etchemin **83** 46 24N 70 30W
Lac la Biche **90** 54 45N 111 58W
Lac la Hache **93** 51 49N 121 27W
Lac la Martre **94** 63 8N 117 16W
Lac-Mégantic **83** 45 35N 70 53W
Lac-Rémi **82** 46 1N 74 46W
Lac-Ste-Marie **82** 45 57N 75 57W
Lac Seul **77** 50 28N 92 0W
Lac Thien **204** 12 25N 108 11 E
Lacanau, Étang de **140** 44 58N 1 7W
Lacanau-Médoc **140** 44 59N 1 5W
Lacantúm, R. → **110** 16 36N 90 39W
Lacara → **155** 38 55N 6 25W
Lacaune **140** 43 43N 2 40 E
Lacaune, Mts. de **140** 43 43N 2 50 E
Laccadive Is. = Lakshadweep Is. **196** 10 0N 72 30 E
Lacepede B. **232** 36 40 S 139 40 E
Lacepede Is. **228** 16 55 S 122 0 E
Lacerdónia **251** 18 3 S 35 35 E
Lachay, Pta. **122** 11 17 S 77 44W
Lachen, India **202** 27 46N 88 36 E

Lachen, Switz. 149 47 12N 8 51 E
Lachhmangarh 198 27 50N 75 4 E
Lachi 198 33 25N 71 20 E
Lachine 83 45 30N 73 40W
Lachlan → 231 34 22 S 143 55 E
Lachute 83 45 39N 74 21W
Laclu 86 49 46N 94 41W
Lacolle 83 45 5N 73 22W
Lacombe 91 52 30N 113 44W
Láconi 164 39 54N 9 4 E
Lacq 140 43 25N 0 35W
Lacub 210 17 40N 120 53 E
Ladakh Ra. 199 34 0N 78 0 E
Ladário 123 19 1 S 57 35W
Lądekzdrój 152 50 21N 16 53 E
Ládhon → 169 37 40N 21 50 E
Ladik 180 40 57N 35 58 E
Ladismith 254 33 28 S 21 15 E
Lādīz 193 28 55N 61 15 E
Ladnun 198 27 38N 74 25 E
Ladoga, L. = Ladozhskoye Ozero 176 61 15N 30 30 E
Ladon 139 48 0N 2 30 E
Ladozhskoye Ozero 176 61 15N 30 30 E
Ladrillero, G. 126 49 20 S 75 35W
Lady Ann Str. 95 75 40N 79 50W
Lady Grey 254 30 43 S 27 13 E
Ladybrand 254 29 9 S 27 29 E
Ladysmith, Canada 92 49 0N 123 49W
Ladysmith, S. Africa 255 28 32 S 29 46 E
Lae 227 6 40 S 147 2 E
Laem Ngop 205 12 10N 102 26 E
Laem Pho 205 6 55N 101 19 E
Lœsø 173 57 15N 10 53 E
Lœsø Rende 173 57 20N 10 45 E
Laferte → 76 61 53N 117 44W
Lafia 247 8 30N 8 34 E
Lafiagi 247 8 52N 5 20 E
Laflamme → 82 49 17N 77 9W
Lafleche 88 49 45N 106 40W
Lafon 245 5 5N 32 29 E
Laforce 82 47 32N 78 44W
Laforsen 172 61 56N 15 3 E
Lagaip → 227 5 4 S 142 52 E
Lagan →, Sweden 173 56 56N 13 58 E
Lagan →, U.K. 135 54 35N 5 55W
Lagangilang 210 17 37N 120 44 E
Lagarfljót → 174 65 40N 14 18W
Lagarto 120 10 54 S 37 41W
Lagawe 210 16 49N 121 6 E
Lage, Germany 146 52 0N 8 47 E
Lage, Spain 154 43 13N 9 0W
Lage-Mierde 143 51 25N 5 9 E
Lågen →, Oppland, Norway 171 61 8N 10 25 E
Lågen →, Vestfold, Norway 171 59 3N 10 5 E
Lägerdorf 146 53 53N 9 35 E
Laghmān □ 197 34 20N 70 0 E
Laghouat 241 33 50N 2 59 E
Lagnieu 141 45 55N 5 20 E
Lagny 139 48 52N 2 40 E
Lago 165 39 9N 16 8 E
Lago Posadas 126 47 30 S 71 40W
Lago Ranco 126 40 19 S 72 30W
Lagôa 155 37 8N 8 27W
Lagoaça 154 41 11N 6 44W
Lagodekhi 181 41 50N 46 22 E
Lagónegro 165 40 8N 15 45 E
Lagonoy Gulf 210 13 50N 123 50 E
Lagos, Nigeria 247 6 25N 3 27 E
Lagos, Portugal 155 37 5N 8 41W
Lagos, R. de los → 106 21 18N 102 32W
Lagos de Moreno 106 21 21N 101 55W
Lagrange 228 18 45 S 121 43 E
Lagrange B. 228 18 38 S 121 42 E
Laguardia 156 42 33N 2 35W
Laguépie 140 44 8N 1 57 E
Laguna 125 28 30 S 48 50W
Laguna □ 210 14 10N 121 20 E
Laguna, La, Nuevo León, Mexico 103 24 50N 100 6W
Laguna, La, Zacatecas, Mexico 105 22 17N 102 48W
Laguna, La, Zacatecas, Mexico 105 24 15N 103 8W
Laguna Chapala 98 29 24N 114 22W
Laguna de la Janda 155 36 15N 5 45W
Laguna Larga 106 20 24N 101 56W
Laguna Limpia 124 26 32 S 59 45W
Lagunas, Chile 124 21 0 S 69 45W
Lagunas, Peru 122 5 10 S 75 35W
Lagunillas, Bolivia 123 19 38 S 63 43W
Lagunillas, Mexico 103 21 34N 99 35W
Lahad Datu 207 5 0N 118 20 E
Lahan Sai 204 14 25N 102 52 E
Lahanam 204 16 16N 105 16 E
Laharpur 199 27 43N 80 56 E
Lahat 208 3 45 S 103 30 E
Lahe 202 26 20N 95 26 E
Lahewa 208 1 22N 97 12 E
Lahiang Lahiang 211 6 1N 121 23 E
Laḩij 194 13 4N 44 53 E
Lahijan 193 37 10N 50 6 E
Lahn → 147 50 52N 8 35 E
Laholm 173 56 30N 13 2 E
Laholmsbukten 173 56 30N 12 45 E
Lahore 197 31 32N 74 22 E
Lahpongsel 202 27 7N 98 25 E
Lahr 147 48 20N 7 52 E
Lahti 175 60 58N 25 40 E
Lahtis = Lahti 175 60 58N 25 40 E
Laï 243 9 25N 16 18 E
Lai Chau 204 22 5N 103 3 E
Lai-hka 202 21 16N 97 40 E
Laiagam 227 5 33 S 143 30 E
Lai'an 217 32 28N 118 30 E
Laibin 216 23 42N 109 14 E
Laidlaw 93 49 20N 121 36W
Laidley 231 27 39 S 152 20 E
Laifeng 217 29 27N 109 20 E
Laignes 139 47 50N 4 20 E
Laikipia □ 250 0 30N 36 30 E
Laingsburg 254 33 9 S 20 52 E
Laird 88 52 43N 106 35W
Lairg 134 58 1N 4 24W
Lais 211 6 20N 125 39 E
Laishui 214 39 23N 115 45 E
Laiwu 215 36 15N 117 40 E
Laixi 215 36 50N 120 31 E
Laiyang 215 36 59N 120 45 E
Laiyuan 214 39 20N 114 40 E
Laizhou Wan 215 37 30N 119 30 E
Laja, La 108 21 41N 97 43W
Laja, R. de la → 107 20 55N 100 46W
Lajere 247 11 58N 11 25 E
Lajes, Rio Grande d. N., Brazil 120 5 41 S 36 14W
Lajes, Sta. Catarina, Brazil 125 27 48 S 50 20W
Lajilla del Norte 103 23 56N 98 40W
Lajinha 121 20 9 S 41 37W
Lajitas 101 29 15N 103 47W
Lajkovac 166 44 27N 20 14 E
Lajosmizse 151 47 3N 19 32 E
Lak Sao 204 18 11N 104 59 E
Lakaband 198 31 2N 69 15 E
Lakar 207 8 15 S 128 17 E
Lake Alma 88 49 9N 104 12W
Lake Cargelligo 231 33 15 S 146 22 E
Lake Coleridge 235 43 17 S 171 30 E
Lake Cowichan 92 48 49N 124 3W
Lake Grace 229 33 7 S 118 28 E
Lake Harbour 95 62 50N 69 50W
Lake King 229 33 5 S 119 45 E
Lake Lenore 88 52 24N 104 59W
Lake Louise 91 51 30N 116 10W
Lake Murray 227 6 48 S 141 29 E
Lake Nash 230 20 57 S 138 0 E
Lake River 74 54 30N 82 31W
Lake St. Peter 85 45 18N 78 2W
Lake Superior Prov. Park 87 47 45N 84 45W
Lake Tekapo 235 44 0 S 170 30 E
Lake Varley 229 32 48 S 119 30 E
Lakefield 85 44 25N 78 16W
Lakes Entrance 231 37 50 S 148 0 E
Lakhaniá 169 35 58N 27 54 E
Lákhi 169 35 24N 23 57 E
Lakhipur, Assam, India 202 24 48N 93 0 E
Lakhipur, Assam, India 202 26 2N 90 18 E
Lakhonpheng 204 15 54N 105 34 E
Lakhpat 198 23 48N 68 47 E
Laki 174 64 4N 18 14W
Lakitusaki → 74 54 21N 82 25W
Lakonía □ 169 36 55N 22 30 E
Lakonikós Kólpos 169 36 40N 22 40 E
Lakota 246 5 50N 5 30W
Laksefjorden 174 70 45N 26 50 E
Lakselv 174 70 2N 24 56 E
Lakshadweep Is. 196 10 0N 72 30 E
Laksham 202 23 14N 91 8 E
Lakshmeshwar 201 15 9N 75 28 E
Lakshmikantapur 199 22 5N 88 20 E
Lakshmipur 202 22 58N 90 50 E
Lakuramau 227 2 54 S 151 15 E
Lal-lo 210 18 12N 121 40 E
Lala 211 7 59N 123 46 E
Lala Musa 198 32 40N 73 57 E
Lalago 250 3 28 S 33 58 E
Lalapanzi 251 19 20 S 30 15 E
Lalganj 199 25 52N 85 13 E
Lalibela 245 12 2N 39 2 E
Lalin, China 215 45 12N 127 0 E
Lalín, Spain 154 42 40N 8 5W
Lalin He → 215 45 32N 125 40 E
Lalinde 140 44 50N 0 44 E
Lalitpur 199 24 42N 78 28 E
Lam 204 21 21N 106 31 E
Lam Pao Res. 204 16 50N 103 15 E
Lama Kara 247 9 30N 1 15 E
Lamaipum 202 25 40N 97 57 E
Lamaline 79 46 52N 55 49W
Lamarque 126 39 24 S 65 40W
Lamas 122 6 28 S 76 31W
Lamas → 190 36 33N 34 15 E
Lamastre 141 44 59N 4 35 E
Lambach 150 48 6N 13 51 E
Lamballe 138 48 29N 2 31W
Lambaréné 252 0 41 S 10 12 E
Lambasa 226 16 30 S 179 10 E
Lambay I. 135 53 30N 6 0W
Lambayeque □ 122 6 45 S 80 0W
Lambert, C. 227 4 11 S 151 31 E
Lambert Glacier 13 71 0 S 70 0 E
Lambesc 141 43 39N 5 16 E
Lambeth 84 42 54N 81 18W
Lámbia 169 37 52N 21 53 E
Lambon 227 4 45 S 152 48 E
Lambro → 162 45 8N 9 32 E
Lambton 83 45 50N 71 5W
Lambton, C. 94 71 5N 123 9W
Lambunao 211 11 3N 122 29 E
Lame 247 45 35N 106 40W
Lamego 154 41 5N 7 52W
Lamèque 81 47 45N 64 38W
Lameroo 232 35 19 S 140 33 E
Lamía 169 38 55N 22 26 E
Lamitan 211 6 39N 122 8 E
Lammermuir Hills 134 55 50N 2 40W
Lamming Mills 93 53 20N 120 15W
Lamon Bay 210 14 30N 122 20 E
Lamongan 209 7 7 S 112 25 E
Lamont 90 53 46N 112 50W
Lampa 122 15 22 S 70 22W
Lampang 204 18 16N 99 32 E
Lampaul 138 48 28N 5 7W
Lampazos de Naranjo 102 27 1N 100 31W
Lampedusa 160 35 36N 12 40 E
Lampeter 133 52 6N 4 6W
Lampione 241 35 33N 12 20 E
Lampman 88 49 25N 102 50W
Lamprechtshausen 150 48 0N 12 58 E
Lamprey 77 58 33N 94 8W
Lampung □ 208 5 30 S 104 30 E
Lamu, Burma 202 19 14N 94 10 E
Lamu, Kenya 250 2 16 S 40 55 E
Lamu □ 250 2 0 S 40 45 E
Lamud 122 6 10 S 77 57W
Lamut 210 16 39N 121 14 E
Lan Xian 214 38 15N 111 35 E
Lan Yu 217 22 5N 121 35 E
Lana, R. de la → 109 17 49N 95 9W
Lanak La 199 34 27N 79 32 E
Lanaken 143 50 53N 5 39 E
Lanak'o Shank'ou = Lanak La 199 34 27N 79 32 E
Lanao, L. 211 7 52N 124 15 E
Lanao del Norte □ 211 8 0N 124 10 E
Lanao del Sur □ 211 7 40N 124 15 E
Lanark, Canada 85 45 1N 76 22W
Lanark, U.K. 134 55 40N 3 48W
Lancang 216 22 36N 99 58 E
Lancang Jiang → 216 21 40N 101 10 E
Lancashire □ 132 53 40N 2 30W
Lancaster, Canada 85 45 10N 74 30W
Lancaster, U.K. 132 54 3N 2 48W
Lancaster Sd. 95 74 13N 84 0W
Lancer 88 50 48N 108 53W
Lanchow = Lanzhou 214 36 1N 103 52 E
Lanciano 163 42 15N 14 22 E
Lanco 126 39 24 S 72 46W
Lancones 122 4 30 S 80 30W
Lancun 215 36 25N 120 10 E
Łancut 152 50 10N 22 13 E
Lancy 148 46 12N 6 8 E
Landa de Matamoros 107 21 13N 99 20W
Landau, Bayern, Germany 147 48 41N 12 41 E
Landau, Rhld-Pfz., Germany 147 49 12N 8 7 E
Landay 197 30 31N 63 47 E
Landeck 150 47 9N 10 34 E
Landen 143 50 45N 5 3 E
Lander → 228 22 0 S 132 0 E
Landerneau 138 48 28N 4 17W
Landeryd 173 57 7N 13 15 E
Landes □ 140 43 57N 0 48W
Landes, Les 140 44 20N 1 0W
Landete 156 39 56N 1 25W
Landi Kotal 197 34 7N 71 6 E
Landis 88 52 12N 108 27W
Landivisiau 138 48 31N 4 6W
Landor 229 25 10 S 116 54 E
Landquart 149 46 58N 9 32 E
Landquart → 149 46 50N 9 47 E
Landrecies 139 50 7N 3 40 E
Landrienne 82 48 30N 77 50W
Land's End 133 50 4N 5 43W
Landsberg 147 48 3N 10 52 E
Landsborough Cr. → 230 22 28 S 144 35 E
Landsbro 173 57 24N 14 56 E
Landshut 147 48 31N 12 10 E
Landskrona 172 55 53N 12 50 E
Landstuhl 147 49 25N 7 34 E
Landvetter 173 57 41N 12 17 E
Laneffe 143 50 17N 4 30 E
Lang Bay 92 49 45N 124 21W
Lang Qua 204 22 16N 104 27 E
Lang Shan 214 41 0N 106 30 E
Lang Son 204 21 52N 106 42 E
Lang Suan 205 9 57N 99 4 E
La'nga Co 199 30 45N 81 15 E
Långadhás 168 40 46N 23 2 E
Langádhia 169 37 43N 22 1 E
Långan → 172 63 19N 14 44 E
Langar 193 35 23N 60 25 E
Langara I. 92 54 14N 133 1W
Langatabbetje 119 4 59N 54 28W
Langdai 216 26 6N 105 21 E
Langdorp 143 50 59N 4 52 E
Langeac 140 45 7N 3 29 E
Langeais 138 47 20N 0 24 E
Langeb Baraka → 244 17 28N 36 50 E
Langeberge, C. Prov., S. Africa 254 28 15 S 22 33 E
Langeberge, C. Prov., S. Africa 254 33 55 S 21 40 E
Langeland 173 54 56N 10 48 E
Langemark 143 50 55N 2 55 E
Langen 147 49 59N 8 40 E
Langenburg 89 50 51N 101 43W
Langeness 146 54 34N 8 35 E
Langenlois 150 48 29N 15 40 E
Langenthal 148 47 13N 7 47 E
Langeoog 146 53 44N 7 33 E
Langeskov 173 55 22N 10 35 E
Langesund 171 59 0N 9 45 E
Langham 88 52 22N 106 58W
Länghem 173 57 36N 13 14 E
Langhirano 162 44 39N 10 16 E
Langholm 134 55 9N 2 59W
Langidoon 232 31 36 S 142 2 E
Langjökull 174 64 39N 20 12W
Langkawi, P. 205 6 25N 99 45 E
Langkon 206 6 30N 116 40 E
Langlade 79 46 50N 56 20W
Langley 93 49 7N 122 39W
Langnau 148 46 56N 7 47 E
Langogne 140 44 43N 3 50 E
Langon 140 44 33N 0 16W
Langøya 174 68 45N 14 50 E
Langres 139 47 52N 5 20 E
Langres, Plateau de 139 47 45N 5 3 E
Langruth 89 50 23N 98 40W
Langsa 208 4 30N 97 57 E
Långsele 172 63 12N 17 4 E
Långshyttan 172 60 27N 16 2 E
Langtao 202 27 15N 97 34 E
Langting 202 25 31N 93 7 E
Langu 205 6 53N 99 47 E
Languedoc 140 43 58N 4 0 E
Langwies 149 46 50N 9 44 E
Langxi 217 31 10N 119 12 E
Langxiangzhen 214 39 43N 116 8 E
Langzhong 216 31 38N 105 58 E
Lanigan 88 51 51N 105 2W
Lankao 214 34 48N 114 50 E
Lannemezan 140 43 8N 0 23 E
Lannilis 138 48 35N 4 32W
Lannion 138 48 46N 3 29W
Lanoraie 83 45 58N 73 13W
Lanouaille 140 45 24N 1 9 E
Lanping 216 26 28N 99 15 E
Lansdowne, Australia 231 31 48 S 152 30 E
Lansdowne, Canada 85 44 24N 76 1W
Lansdowne House 74 52 14N 87 53W
Lanshan 217 25 24N 112 10 E
Lanslebourg 141 45 17N 6 52 E
Lanta Yai, Ko 205 7 35N 99 3 E
Lantian 214 34 11N 109 20 E
Lanus 124 34 44 S 58 27W
Lanusei 164 39 53N 9 31 E
Lanuza 211 9 14N 126 4 E
Lanxi 217 29 13N 119 28 E
Lanz I. 92 50 49N 128 41W
Lanzhou 214 36 1N 103 52 E
Lanzo Torinese 162 45 16N 7 29 E
Lanzville 92 49 15N 124 5W
Lao → 165 39 45N 15 45 E
Lao Bao 204 16 35N 106 30 E
Lao Cai 204 22 30N 103 57 E
Laoag 210 18 7N 120 34 E
Laoang 210 12 32N 125 8 E
Laoha He → 215 43 25N 120 35 E
Laois □ 135 53 0N 7 20W
Laon 139 49 33N 3 35 E
Laos ■ 204 17 45N 105 0 E
Lapa 125 25 46 S 49 44W
Lapalisse 140 46 15N 3 38 E
Laparan 207 6 0N 120 0 E
Lapithos 190 35 21N 33 11 E
Lapland = Lappland 174 68 7N 24 0 E
Lapog 210 17 45N 120 27 E

Lapovo 166 44 10N 21 2 E
Lappland 174 68 7N 24 0 E
Laprida 124 37 34 S 60 45W
Laptev Sea 185 76 0N 125 0 E
Lapuş, Munţii 170 47 20N 23 50 E
Lăpusul → 170 47 25N 23 40 E
Łapy 152 52 59N 22 52 E
Lār, Āzarbājān-e Sharqī, Iran 192 38 30N 47 52 E
Lār, Fārs, Iran 193 27 40N 54 14 E
Lara, Australia 232 38 2 S 144 26 E
Lara, Phil. 211 8 48N 117 52 E
Lara □ 118 10 10N 69 50W
Larabanga 246 9 16N 1 56W
Laracha 154 43 15N 8 35W
Larache 240 35 10N 6 5W
Laragne-Monteglin 141 44 18N 5 49 E
Laranjeiras 120 10 48 S 37 10W
Laranjeiras do Sul 125 25 23 S 52 23W
Larantuka 207 8 21 S 122 55 E
Larap 210 14 18N 122 39 E
Larat 207 7 0 S 132 0 E
Lårdal 171 59 25N 8 10 E
Larde 251 16 28 S 39 43 E
Larder Lake 74 48 5N 79 40W
Lárdhos, Ákra 169 36 4N 28 10 E
Laredo 156 43 26N 3 28W
Laredo Sd. 92 52 30N 128 53W
Laren 142 52 16N 5 14 E
Larena 211 9 15N 123 35 E
Largentière 141 44 34N 4 18 E
Largs 134 55 48N 4 51W
Lari 162 43 34N 10 35 E
Lariang 207 1 26 S 119 17 E
Lārīn 193 35 55N 52 19 E
Larino 165 41 48N 14 54 E
Lárisa 168 39 49N 22 28 E
Lárisa □ 168 39 39N 22 24 E
Lark Harbour 79 49 6N 58 23W
Larkana 197 27 32N 68 18 E
Larkollen 171 59 20N 10 41 E
Larnaca 190 35 0N 33 35 E
Larnaca Bay 190 34 53N 33 45 E
Larne 135 54 52N 5 50W
Larochette 143 49 47N 6 13 E
Larrimah 228 15 35 S 133 12 E
Larrys River 81 45 13N 61 23W
Larsen Ice Shelf 13 67 0 S 62 0W
Larus L. 86 51 17N 94 40W
Larvik 171 59 4N 10 0 E
Laryak 184 61 15N 80 0 E
Larzac, Causse du 140 44 0N 3 17 E
Las Ánimas 105 22 6N 102 16W
Las Anod 256 8 26N 47 19 E
Las Blancos 157 37 38N 0 49W
Las Brenãs 124 27 5 S 61 7W
Las Cabezas de San Juan 155 37 0N 5 58W
Las Casitas, Cerro 99 23 31N 109 53W
Las Choapas 109 17 55N 94 7W
Las Coloradas 126 39 34 S 70 36W
Las Cruces, Baja Calif. S., Mexico 99 24 12N 110 8W
Las Cruces, Chiapas, Mexico 110 16 34N 93 52W
Las Cruces, San Luis Potosí, Mexico 103 22 44N 101 20W
Las Cuevas 102 29 38N 101 19W
Las Esperanzas 102 27 44N 101 20W
Las Flores 124 36 10 S 59 7W
Las Heras 124 32 51 S 68 49W
Las Herreras 104 25 10N 105 31W
Las Higueras 104 25 56N 108 59W
Las Horquetas 126 48 14 S 71 11W
Las Jicamas 107 20 16N 101 22W
Las Khoreh 256 11 10N 48 20 E
Las Lajas 126 38 30 S 70 25W
Las Lomas 122 4 40 S 80 10W
Las Lomitas 124 24 43 S 60 35W
Las Maquinas 111 17 59N 88 57W
Las Margaritas 110 16 19N 91 59W
Las Marismas 155 37 5N 6 20W
Las Mercedes 118 9 7N 66 24W
Las Mesas 107 17 0N 99 30W
Las Navas de la Concepción 155 37 56N 5 30W
Las Navas de Tolosa 155 38 18N 3 38W
Las Nieves 104 26 24N 105 22W
Las Palmas, Argentina 124 27 8 S 58 45W
Las Palmas, Canary Is. 240 28 7N 15 26W
Las Palmas, Mexico 99 23 42N 109 43W
Las Palmas → 98 32 31N 116 58W
Las Palomas 101 31 44N 107 37W
Las Piedras 125 34 44 S 56 14W
Las Pipinas 124 35 30 S 57 19W
Las Plumas 126 43 40 S 67 15W
Las Rosas, Argentina 124 32 30 S 61 35W
Las Rosas, Mexico 110 16 24N 92 23W
Las Tablas, Mexico 103 22 15N 99 52W
Las Tablas, Panama 112 7 49N 80 14W
Las Termas 124 27 29 S 64 52W
Las Tres Vírgenes, Volcán 99 27 27N 112 34W
Las Truchas 106 17 57N 102 13W
Las Varas, Chihuahua, Mexico 101 28 11N 105 20W
Las Varas, Nayarit, Mexico 104 21 10N 105 10W
Las Varillas 124 31 50 S 62 50W
Las Vigas 107 16 46N 99 14W
Lascano 125 33 35 S 54 12W
Lascaux 140 45 5N 1 10 E
Lashburn 88 53 10N 109 40W
Lashio 202 22 56N 97 45 E
Lashkar 198 26 10N 78 10 E
Lashkar Gāh 197 31 35N 64 21 E
Łasin 152 53 30N 19 2 E
Lasíthi □ 169 35 5N 25 50 E
Lask 152 51 34N 19 8 E
Łaskarzew 152 51 48N 21 36 E
Laško 163 46 10N 15 16 E
Lasqueti 92 49 30N 124 21W
Lasqueti I. 92 49 29N 124 16W
Lassance 121 17 54 S 44 34W
Lassay 138 48 27N 0 30W
Last Mountain L. 88 51 5N 105 14W
Lastoursville 252 0 55 S 12 38 E
Lastovo 163 42 46N 16 55 E
Lastovski Kanal 163 42 50N 17 0 E
Lat Yao 204 15 45N 99 48 E
Latacunga 118 0 50 S 78 35W
Latakia = Al Lādhiqīyah 190 35 30N 35 45 E
Latchford 74 47 20N 79 50W
Laterza 165 40 38N 16 47 E
Latham 229 29 44 S 116 20 E
Lathen 146 52 51N 7 21 E
Latiano 165 40 33N 17 43 E
Latina 164 41 26N 12 53 E
Latisana 163 45 47N 13 1 E
Latium = Lazio □ 163 42 10N 12 30 E
Latorica → 151 48 28N 21 50 E
Latouche Treville, C. 228 18 27 S 121 49 E
Latrobe 230 41 14 S 146 30 E
Latrónico 165 40 5N 16 0 E
Latrun 189 31 50N 34 58 E
Latulipe 82 47 26N 79 2W
Latur 200 18 25N 76 40 E
Latvian S.S.R. □ 178 56 50N 24 0 E
Lau 226 17 0 S 178 30W
Lauca → 122 19 9 S 68 10W
Lauchhammer 146 51 35N 13 48 E
Laudal 171 58 15N 7 30 E
Lauenburg 146 53 23N 10 33 E
Läufelfingen 148 47 24N 7 52 E
Laufen 148 47 25N 7 30 E
Lauffen 147 49 4N 9 9 E
Laugarbakki 174 65 20N 20 55W
Laujar 157 37 0N 2 54W
Launceston, Australia 230 41 24 S 147 8 E
Launceston, U.K. 133 50 38N 4 21W
Laune → 135 52 5N 9 40W
Laupheim 147 48 13N 9 53 E
Laur 210 15 35N 121 11 E
Laura, Queens., Australia 230 15 32 S 144 32 E
Laura, S. Austral., Australia 232 33 10 S 138 18 E
Laureana di Borrello 165 38 28N 16 5 E
Laurel, Sa. del 105 21 40N 102 40W
Laurencekirk 134 56 50N 2 30W
Laurentian Plat. 78 52 0N 70 0W
Laurentides, Parc Prov. des 83 47 45N 71 15W
Lauria 165 40 3N 15 50 E
Laurie L. 77 56 35N 101 57W
Laurier 89 50 53N 99 33W
Laurier-Station 83 46 32N 71 38W
Laurierville 83 46 18N 71 39W
Lausanne 148 46 32N 6 38 E
Laut 209 4 45N 108 0 E
Laut, Pulau 209 3 40 S 116 10 E
Laut Ketil, Kepulauan 209 4 45 S 115 40 E
Lautaro 126 38 31 S 72 27W
Lauterbach 146 50 39N 9 23 E
Lauterbrunnen 148 46 36N 7 55 E
Lauterecken 147 49 38N 7 35 E
Lautoka 226 17 37 S 177 27 E
Lauwe 143 50 47N 3 12 E
Lauwers 142 53 32N 6 23 E
Lauwers Zee 142 53 21N 6 13 E
Lauzon 83 46 48N 71 10W
Lavadores 154 42 14N 8 41W
Lavagna 162 44 18N 9 22 E
Laval, Canada 83 45 35N 73 45W
Laval, France 138 48 4N 0 48W
Lavalle 124 28 15 S 65 15W
Lavaltrie 83 45 53N 73 17W
Lavandou, Le 141 43 8N 6 22 E
Lavant Sta. 85 45 3N 76 42W
Lávara 168 41 19N 26 22 E
Lavardac 140 44 12N 0 20 E
Lavaur 140 43 30N 1 49 E
Lavaux 148 46 30N 6 45 E
Lavaveix 140 46 5N 2 8 E
Lavelanet 140 42 57N 1 51 E
Lavello 165 41 4N 15 47 E
Laverendrye Prov. Park 74 46 15N 17 15W
Laverlochère 82 47 26N 79 18W
Lavers Hill 232 38 40 S 143 25 E
Laverton 229 28 44 S 122 29 E
Lavi 189 32 47N 35 25 E
Lavieille, L. 85 45 51N 78 14W
Lavik 171 61 6N 5 25 E
Lavillètte 81 47 16N 65 18W
Lavín 103 23 32N 98 54W
Lávkos 169 39 9N 23 14 E
Lavos 154 40 6N 8 49W
Lavoy 90 53 27N 111 52W
Lavras 121 21 20 S 45 0W
Lavre 155 38 46N 8 22W
Lavrentiya 185 65 35N 171 0W
Lávrion 169 37 40N 24 4 E
Lavumisa 255 27 20 S 31 55 E
Lawa 211 6 12N 125 41 E
Lawa-an 211 11 51N 125 5 E
Lawas 206 4 55N 115 25 E
Lawdar 194 13 53N 45 52 E
Lawele 207 5 16 S 123 3 E
Lawksawk 202 21 15N 96 52 E
Lawn 79 46 57N 55 35W
Lawn Hill 230 18 36 S 138 33 E
Lawqar 192 29 49N 42 45 E
Lawra 246 10 39N 2 51W
Lawrence Station 81 45 26N 67 11W
Lawrencetown 81 44 53N 65 10W
Lawu 209 7 40 S 111 13 E
Laxford, L. 134 58 25N 5 10W
Layht, Ra's 195 12 38N 53 25 E
Laylá 194 22 10N 46 40 E
Laylān 192 35 18N 44 31 E
Layon → 138 47 20N 0 45W
Laysan I. 225 25 30N 167 0W
Laza 202 26 30N 97 38 E
Lazarevac 166 44 23N 20 17 E
Lázaro Cárdenas, Presa 104 25 36N 105 3W
Lazi 211 9 8N 123 38 E
Lazio □ 163 42 10N 12 30 E
Lazo 218 43 25N 133 55 E
Łazy 152 50 27N 19 24 E
Lea → 133 51 30N 0 10W
Leach 205 12 21N 103 46 E
Leach I. 87 47 28N 84 57W
Leader 88 50 50N 109 30W
Leadhills 134 55 25N 3 47W
Leaf L. 89 53 1N 102 8W
Lealui 253 15 10 S 23 2 E
Leamington, Canada 84 42 3N 82 36W
Leamington, U.K. 133 52 18N 1 32W
Le'an 217 27 22N 115 48 E
Leandro Norte Alem 125 27 34 S 55 15W
Learmonth 228 22 13 S 114 10 E
Leask 88 53 5N 106 45W
Łeba 152 54 45N 17 32 E
Łeba → 152 54 46N 17 33 E
Lebane 166 42 56N 21 44 E
Lebango 252 0 39N 14 21 E
Lebanon ■ 190 34 0N 36 0 E
Lebbeke 143 51 0N 4 8 E
Lebedin 178 50 35N 34 30 E
Lebedyan 179 53 0N 39 10 E
Lebel-sur-Quévillon 82 49 3N 76 59W
Lebombo-berge 255 24 30 S 32 0 E
Lębork 152 54 33N 17 46 E
Lebrija 155 36 53N 6 5W
Łebsko, Jezioro 152 54 40N 17 25 E
Lebu 124 37 40 S 73 47W
Lecce 165 40 20N 18 10 E
Lecco 162 45 50N 9 27 E
Lecco, L. di 162 45 51N 9 22 E
Lécera 156 41 13N 0 43W
Lech 150 47 13N 10 9 E
Lech → 147 48 44N 10 56 E
Lechang 217 25 10N 113 20 E
Leche, L. de la 102 27 14N 102 53W
Lechtaler Alpen 150 47 15N 10 30 E
Lectoure 140 43 56N 0 38 E
Łeczna 152 51 18N 22 53 E
Łeczyca 152 52 5N 19 15 E
Ledbury 133 52 3N 2 25W
Lede 143 50 58N 3 59 E
Ledeberg 143 51 2N 3 45 E
Ledeč 150 49 41N 15 18 E
Ledesma 154 41 6N 5 59W
Ledong 204 18 41N 109 5 E
Leduc 90 53 15N 113 30W
Ledyczek 152 53 33N 16 59 E
Lee → 135 51 50N 8 30W
Leech L. 88 51 5N 102 28W
Leeds 132 53 48N 1 34W
Leek, Neth. 142 53 10N 6 24 E
Leek, U.K. 132 53 7N 2 2W
Leende 143 51 21N 5 33 E
Leer 146 53 13N 7 29 E
Leerdam 142 51 54N 5 6 E
Leersum 142 52 0N 5 26 E
Leeston 235 43 45 S 172 19 E
Leeton 231 34 33 S 146 23 E
Leeuwarden 142 53 15N 5 48 E
Leeuwin, C. 229 34 20 S 115 9 E
Leeward Is., Atl. Oc. 113 16 30N 63 30W
Leeward Is., Pac. Oc. 225 16 0 S 147 0W
Lefebvre 83 47 12N 69 49W
Léfini 252 2 55 S 15 39 E
Lefka 190 35 6N 32 51 E
Lefkoniko 190 35 18N 33 44 E
Lefroy 84 44 16N 79 34W
Lefroy, L. 229 31 21 S 121 40 E
Łeg → 152 50 42N 21 50 E
Legal 90 53 55N 113 35W
Legazpi 210 13 10N 123 45 E
Legendre I. 228 20 22 S 116 55 E
Légère 81 47 25N 64 56W
Leghorn = Livorno 162 43 32N 10 18 E
Legion 251 21 25 S 28 30 E
Legionowo 152 52 25N 20 50 E
Léglise 143 49 48N 5 32 E
Legnago 163 45 10N 11 19 E
Legnano 162 45 35N 8 55 E
Legnica 152 51 12N 16 10 E
Legnica □ 152 51 30N 16 0 E
Legrad 163 46 17N 16 51 E
Legume 231 28 20 S 152 19 E
Leh 199 34 9N 77 35 E
Lehliu 170 44 29N 26 20 E
Lehrte 146 52 22N 9 58 E
Lehututu 254 23 54 S 21 55 E
Lei Shui → 217 26 55N 112 35 E
Leiah 197 30 58N 70 58 E
Leibnitz 150 46 47N 15 34 E
Leibo 216 28 11N 103 34 E
Leicester 133 52 39N 1 9W
Leicester □ 133 52 40N 1 10W
Leichhardt → 230 17 35 S 139 48 E
Leichhardt Ra. 230 20 46 S 147 40 E
Leiden 142 52 9N 4 30 E
Leiderdorp 142 52 9N 4 32 E
Leidschendam 142 52 5N 4 24 E
Leie → 143 51 2N 3 45 E
Leigh → 232 38 18 S 144 30 E
Leignon 143 50 16N 5 7 E
Leikanger 171 61 10N 6 52 E
Leiktho 202 19 13N 96 35 E
Leine → 146 52 20N 9 50 E
Leinster 229 27 51 S 120 36 E
Leinster □ 135 53 0N 7 10W
Leinster, Mt. 135 52 38N 6 47W
Leipzig 146 51 20N 12 23 E
Leipzig □ 146 51 20N 12 30 E
Leiria 155 39 46N 8 53W
Leiria □ 155 39 46N 8 53W
Leisler, Mt. 228 23 23 S 129 20 E
Leith 134 55 59N 3 10W
Leith Hill 133 51 10N 0 23W
Leitha → 151 48 0N 16 35 E
Leitrim 135 54 0N 8 5W
Leitrim □ 135 54 8N 8 0W
Leiyang 217 26 27N 112 45 E
Leiza 156 43 5N 1 55W
Leizhou Wan 217 20 50N 110 20 E
Lejeune 83 47 46N 68 34W
Lek → 142 52 0N 6 0 E
Lekáni 168 41 10N 24 35 E
Leke 143 51 2N 2 54 E
Lekhainá 169 37 57N 21 16 E
Lekkerkerk 142 51 54N 4 41 E
Leksula 207 3 46 S 126 31 E
Leland Lakes 77 60 0N 110 59W
Leleque 126 42 28 S 71 0W
Lelu 202 19 4N 95 30 E
Lelystad 142 52 30N 5 25 E
Lema 247 12 58N 4 13 E
Léman, Lac 148 46 26N 6 30 E
Lemberg 88 50 44N 103 12W
Lemelerveld 142 52 26N 6 20 E
Lemera 250 3 0 S 28 55 E
Lemery 210 13 51N 120 56 E
Lemfu 253 5 18 S 15 13 E
Lemgo 146 52 2N 8 52 E
Lemieux 83 46 18N 72 7W
Lemieux, L. 82 50 19N 74 38W
Lemieux Is. 95 63 40N 64 20W
Lemmer 142 52 51N 5 43 E
Lemoine, L. 82 48 0N 78 0W
Lempdes 140 45 22N 3 17 E
Lemsid 240 26 33N 13 51W
Lemvig 173 56 33N 8 20 E
Lemyethna 202 17 36N 95 9 E
Lena → 185 72 52N 126 40 E
Lenartovce 151 48 18N 20 19 E
Lencloître 138 46 50N 0 20 E

Lençóis **121** 12 35 S 41 24W
Lendeh **193** 30 58N 50 25 E
Lendelede **143** 50 53N 3 16 E
Lendinara **163** 45 4N 11 37 E
Lengau de Vaca, Pta. **124** 30 14 S 71 38W
Lenger **183** 42 12N 69 54 E
Lengerich **146** 52 12N 7 50 E
Lenggong **205** 5 6N 100 58 E
Lenggries **147** 47 41N 11 34 E
Lengyeltóti **151** 46 40N 17 40 E
Lenhovda **173** 57 0N 15 16 E
Lenin **181** 48 20N 40 56 E
Lenina, Pik **183** 39 20N 72 55 E
Leninabad **183** 40 17N 69 37 E
Leninakan **181** 40 47N 43 50 E
Leningrad **178** 59 55N 30 20 E
Leningradskaya **13** 69 50 S 160 0 E
Lenino **180** 45 17N 35 46 E
Leninogorsk, Kazakh S.S.R., U.S.S.R. **184** 50 20N 83 30 E
Leninogorsk, R.S.F.S.R., U.S.S.R. **182** 54 36N 52 30 E
Leninpol **183** 42 29N 71 55 E
Leninsk, R.S.F.S.R., U.S.S.R. **181** 48 40N 45 15 E
Leninsk, R.S.F.S.R., U.S.S.R. **181** 46 10N 43 46 E
Leninsk, Uzbek S.S.R., U.S.S.R. **183** 40 38N 72 15 E
Leninsk-Kuznetskiy **184** 54 44N 86 10 E
Leninskaya Sloboda **179** 56 7N 44 29 E
Leninskoye, R.S.F.S.R., U.S.S.R. **179** 58 23N 47 3 E
Leninskoye, R.S.F.S.R., U.S.S.R. **185** 47 56N 132 38 E
Leninskoye, Uzbek S.S.R., U.S.S.R. **183** 41 45N 69 23 E
Lenk **148** 46 27N 7 28 E
Lenkoran **177** 39 45N 48 50 E
Lenmalu **207** 1 45 S 130 15 E
Lenne → **146** 51 25N 7 30 E
Lennox, I. **126** 55 18 S 66 50W
Lennoxville **83** 45 22N 71 51W
Leno **162** 45 24N 10 14 E
Lenore L. **88** 52 30N 104 59W
Lens, Belgium **143** 50 33N 3 54 E
Lens, France **139** 50 26N 2 50 E
Lens St. Remy **143** 50 39N 5 7 E
Lensk **185** 60 48N 114 55 E
Lenskoye **180** 45 3N 34 1 E
Lent **142** 51 52N 5 52 E
Lenti **151** 46 37N 16 33 E
Lentini **165** 37 18N 15 0 E
Lentvaric **178** 54 39N 25 3 E
Lenzburg **148** 47 23N 8 11 E
Lenzen **146** 53 6N 11 26 E
Lenzerheide **149** 46 44N 9 34 E
Léo **246** 11 3N 2 2W
Leoben **150** 47 22N 15 5 E
Leominster **133** 52 15N 2 43W
Léon, France **140** 43 53N 1 18W
León, Mexico **107** 21 7N 101 40W
León, Nic. **112** 12 20N 86 51W
León, Spain **154** 42 38N 5 34W
León □ **154** 42 40N 5 55W
León, Montañas de **154** 42 30N 6 18W
Léon Guzmán **105** 25 31N 103 39W
Leona Vicario **111** 21 0N 87 11W
Leonel, Mte. **148** 46 15N 8 5 E
Leonforte **165** 37 39N 14 22 E
Leongatha **231** 38 30 S 145 58 E
Leonídhion **169** 37 9N 22 52 E
Leonora **229** 28 49 S 121 19 E
Leonora Downs **232** 32 29 S 142 5 E
Léopold II, Lac = Mai-Ndombe, L. **252** 2 0 S 18 20 E
Leopoldina **121** 21 28 S 42 40W
Leopoldo Bulhões **121** 16 37 S 48 46W
Leopoldsburg **143** 51 7N 5 13 E
Léopoldville = Kinshasa **253** 4 20 S 15 15 E
Leoville **88** 53 39N 107 33W
Lépa, L. do **254** 17 0 S 19 0 E
Lepe **155** 37 15N 7 12W
Lepel **178** 54 50N 28 40 E
Lepellé → **78** 59 58N 72 24W
Lepikha **185** 64 45N 125 55 E
Leping **217** 28 47N 117 7 E
Lepontino, Alpi **162** 46 22N 8 27 E
Lepreau **81** 45 10N 66 28W
Lepsény **151** 47 0N 18 15 E
Leptis Magna **241** 32 40N 14 12 E
Lequeitio **156** 43 20N 2 32W
Lercara Friddi **164** 37 42N 13 36 E
Lerdo de Tejada **109** 18 37N 95 31W
Léré, C.A.R. **252** 6 46N 17 25 E
Léré, Chad **243** 9 39N 14 13 E
Lere, Nigeria **247** 9 43N 9 18 E
Leribe **255** 28 51 S 28 3 E
Lérici **162** 44 4N 9 58 E
Lérida **156** 41 37N 0 39 E
Lérida □ **156** 42 6N 1 0 E
Lérins, Is. de **141** 43 31N 7 3 E
Lerma, Mexico **111** 19 48N 90 36W
Lerma, Spain **154** 42 0N 3 47W
Lerma → **106** 20 13N 102 46W
Léros **169** 37 10N 26 50 E
Lérouville **139** 48 50N 5 30 E
Leroy **88** 52 0N 104 44W
Leroy, L. **78** 55 10N 67 15W
Lerwick **134** 60 10N 1 10W
Léry **83** 45 21N 73 48W
Les **170** 46 58N 21 50 E
Lesbos, I. = Lésvos **169** 39 10N 26 20 E
Leshan **216** 29 33N 103 41 E
Leshukonskoye **176** 64 54N 45 46 E
Lésina, L. di **163** 41 53N 15 25 E
Lesja **171** 62 7N 8 51 E
Lesjaverk **171** 62 12N 8 34 E
Lesko **152** 49 30N 22 23 E
Leskov I. **13** 56 0 S 28 0W
Leskovac **166** 43 0N 21 58 E
Leskoviku **168** 40 10N 20 34 E
Leslieville **91** 52 23N 114 36W
Lesna **152** 51 0N 15 15 E
Lesneven **138** 48 35N 4 20W
Lešnica **166** 44 39N 19 20 E
Lesnoy **182** 59 47N 52 9 E
Lesnoye **178** 58 15N 35 18 E
Lesopilnoye **218** 46 44N 134 20 E
Lesotho ■ **255** 29 40 S 28 0 E
Lesozavodsk **185** 45 30N 133 29 E
Lesparre-Médoc **140** 45 18N 0 57W
Lessay **138** 49 14N 1 30W
Lesse → **143** 50 15N 4 54 E
Lesser Antilles **113** 15 0N 61 0W
Lesser Slave L. **90** 55 30N 115 25W
Lesser Slave Lake Prov. Park **90** 55 26N 114 49W
Lessines **143** 50 42N 3 50 E
Lestock **88** 51 19N 103 59W
Lesuer I. **228** 13 50 S 127 17 E
Lésvos **169** 39 10N 26 20 E
Leszno **152** 51 50N 16 30 E
Leszno □ **152** 51 45N 16 30 E
Letchworth **133** 51 58N 0 13W
Letea, Ostrov **170** 45 18N 29 20 E
Lethbridge, Alta., Canada **91** 49 45N 112 45W
Lethbridge, Newf., Canada **79** 48 22N 53 52W
Lethem **119** 3 20N 59 50W
Lethero **232** 33 33 S 142 30 E
Leti, Kepulauan **207** 8 10 S 128 0 E
Letiahau → **254** 21 16 S 24 0 E
Leticia **118** 4 9 S 70 0W
Leting **215** 39 23N 118 55 E
Letlhakeng **254** 24 0 S 24 59 E
Letpadan **202** 17 45N 95 45 E
Letpan **202** 19 28N 94 10 E
Letterkenny **135** 54 57N 7 42W
Leu **170** 44 10N 24 0 E
Léua **253** 11 34 S 20 32 E
Leucate **140** 42 56N 3 3 E
Leucate, Étang de **140** 42 50N 3 0 E
Leuk **148** 46 19N 7 37 E
Leukerbad **148** 46 24N 7 36 E
Leupegem **143** 50 50N 3 36 E
Leuser, G. **208** 3 46N 97 12 E
Leutkirch **147** 47 49N 10 1 E
Leuven **143** 50 52N 4 42 E
Leuze, Hainaut, Belgium **143** 50 36N 3 37 E
Leuze, Namur, Belgium **143** 50 33N 4 54 E
Lev Tolstoy **179** 53 13N 39 29 E
Levack **84** 46 38N 81 23W
Levádhia **169** 38 27N 22 54 E
Levanger **171** 63 45N 11 19 E
Levani **168** 40 40N 19 28 E
Levant, I. du **141** 43 3N 6 28 E
Lévanto **162** 44 10N 9 37 E
Levanzo **164** 38 0N 12 19 E
Leven **134** 56 12N 3 0W
Leven, L. **134** 56 12N 3 22W
Leven, Toraka **255** 12 30 S 47 45 E
Levens **141** 43 50N 7 12 E
Leveque C. **228** 16 20 S 123 0 E
Leverano **165** 40 16N 18 0 E
Leverkusen **146** 51 2N 6 59 E
Leverville **253** 4 50 S 18 44 E
Levet **139** 46 56N 2 22 E
Levice **151** 48 13N 18 35 E
Levico **163** 46 0N 11 18 E
Levie **141** 41 40N 9 7 E
Levier **139** 46 58N 6 8 E
Levin **234** 40 37 S 175 18 E
Lévis **83** 46 48N 71 9W
Levis, L. **76** 62 37N 117 58W
Levítha **169** 37 0N 26 28 E
Levka, Bulgaria **167** 41 52N 26 15 E
Lévka, Greece **169** 35 18N 24 3 E
Levkás **169** 38 40N 20 43 E
Levkímmi **168** 39 25N 20 3 E
Levkôsia = Nicosia **190** 35 10N 33 25 E
Levoča **151** 49 2N 20 35 E
Levroux **139** 47 0N 1 38 E
Levski **167** 43 21N 25 10 E
Levskigrad **167** 42 38N 24 47 E
Levuka **226** 17 34 S 179 0 E
Lewe **202** 19 38N 96 7 E
Lewes **133** 50 53N 0 2 E
Lewin Brzeski **152** 50 45N 17 37 E
Lewis **134** 58 10N 6 40W
Lewis, Butt of **134** 58 30N 6 12W
Lewis Hills **79** 48 48N 58 30W
Lewis Ra. **228** 20 3 S 128 50 E
Lewisporte **79** 49 15N 55 3W
Lewisville **81** 46 6N 64 46W
Leye **216** 24 48N 106 29 E
Leyre → **140** 44 39N 1 1W
Leysin **148** 46 21N 7 0 E
Leyte **211** 11 0N 125 0 E
Leyte Gulf **211** 10 50N 125 25 E
Lezajsk **152** 50 16N 22 25 E
Lezay **140** 46 17N 0 0 E
Lezha **168** 41 47N 19 42 E
Lezhi **216** 30 19N 104 58 E
Lézignan-Corbières **140** 43 13N 2 43 E
Lezoux **140** 45 49N 3 21 E
Lgov **178** 51 42N 35 16 E
Lhasa **212** 29 25N 90 58 E
Lhazê **212** 29 5N 87 38 E
Lhokkruet **208** 4 55N 95 24 E
Lhokseumawe **208** 5 10N 97 10 E
Lhuntsi Dzong **202** 27 39N 91 10 E
Li **204** 17 48N 98 57 E
Li Shui → **217** 29 24N 112 1 E
Li Xian, Gansu, China **214** 34 10N 105 5 E
Li Xian, Hebei, China **214** 38 30N 115 35 E
Li Xian, Hunan, China **217** 29 36N 111 42 E
Li Xian, Sichuan, China **216** 31 23N 103 13 E
Lia-Moya **252** 6 54N 16 17 E
Liádhoi **169** 36 50N 26 11 E
Lian **210** 14 3N 120 39 E
Lian Xian **217** 24 51N 112 22 E
Liancheng **217** 25 42N 116 40 E
Lianga **211** 8 38N 126 6 E
Lianga Bay **211** 8 37N 126 12 E
Liangcheng, Nei Mongol Zizhiqu, China **214** 40 28N 112 25 E
Liangcheng, Shandong, China **215** 35 32N 119 37 E
Liangdang **214** 33 56N 106 18 E
Lianghekou **216** 29 11N 108 44 E
Liangping **216** 30 38N 107 47 E
Lianhua **217** 27 3N 113 54 E
Lianjiang, Fujian, China **217** 26 12N 119 27 E
Lianjiang, Guangdong, China **217** 21 40N 110 20 E
Lianping **217** 24 26N 114 30 E
Lianshan **217** 24 38N 112 8 E
Lianshanguan **215** 40 53N 123 43 E
Lianshui **215** 33 42N 119 20 E
Lianyuan **217** 27 40N 111 38 E
Lianyungang **215** 34 40N 119 11 E
Liao He → **215** 41 0N 121 50 E
Liaocheng **214** 36 28N 115 58 E
Liaodong Bandao **215** 40 0N 122 30 E
Liaodong Wan **215** 40 20N 121 10 E
Liaoning □ **215** 42 0N 122 0 E
Liaoyang **215** 41 15N 122 58 E
Liaoyuan **215** 42 58N 125 2 E
Liaozhong **215** 41 23N 122 50 E
Liapádhes **168** 39 42N 19 40 E
Liard → **76** 61 51N 121 18W
Liari **198** 25 37N 66 30 E
Líbano **118** 4 55N 75 4W
Libau = Liepaja **178** 56 30N 21 0 E
Libenge **252** 3 40N 18 55 E
Liberdade **122** 10 5 S 70 20W
Liberdade → **123** 9 40 S 52 17W
Liberec **150** 50 47N 15 7 E
Liberia **112** 10 40N 85 30W
Liberia ■ **246** 6 30N 9 30W
Libertad, Panay, Phil. **211** 11 46N 121 55 E
Libertad, Tablas, Phil. **210** 12 27N 122 0 E
Libertad, Venezuela **118** 8 20N 69 37W
Libertad, La, Guat. **112** 16 47N 90 7W
Libertad, La, Chiapas, Mexico **110** 17 41N 91 43W
Libertad, La, Sonora, Mexico **100** 29 55N 112 43W
Libertad, La □ **122** 8 0 S 78 30W
Liberty **88** 51 8N 105 26W
Libiaz **151** 50 7N 19 21 E
Libibi **253** 14 42 S 17 44 E
Libin **143** 49 59N 5 15 E
Libmanan **210** 13 42N 123 4 E
Libo **216** 25 22N 107 53 E
Libobo, Tanjung **207** 0 54 S 128 28 E
Libohava **168** 40 3N 20 10 E
Libona **211** 8 20N 124 44 E
Libonda **253** 14 28 S 23 12 E
Libourne **140** 44 55N 0 14W
Libramont **143** 49 55N 5 23 E
Librazhdi **168** 41 12N 20 22 E
Libre Unión **111** 20 42N 88 49W
Libres **108** 19 28N 97 41W
Libreville **252** 0 25N 9 26 E
Libya ■ **242** 27 0N 17 0 E
Libyan Desert **236** 25 0N 25 0 E
Libyan Plateau = Ed-Déffa **244** 30 40N 26 30 E
Licantén **124** 35 55 S 72 0W
Licata **164** 37 6N 13 55 E
Licheng **214** 36 28N 113 20 E
Lichfield **132** 52 40N 1 50W
Lichinga **251** 13 13 S 35 11 E
Lichtaart **143** 51 13N 4 55 E
Lichtenburg **254** 26 8 S 26 8 E
Lichtenfels **147** 50 7N 11 4 E
Lichtenvoorde **142** 51 59N 6 34 E
Lichtervelde **143** 51 2N 3 9 E
Lichuan, Hubei, China **216** 30 18N 108 57 E
Lichuan, Jiangxi, China **217** 27 18N 116 55 E
Licosa, Punta **165** 40 15N 14 53 E
Lida **178** 53 53N 25 15 E
Liddon Gulf **94** 75 3N 113 0W
Lidhult **173** 56 50N 13 27 E
Lidingö **172** 59 22N 18 8 E
Lidköping **173** 58 31N 13 14 E
Lidlidda **210** 17 15N 120 31 E
Lido, Italy **163** 45 25N 12 23 E
Lido, Niger **247** 12 54N 3 44 E
Lido di Roma = Óstia, Lido di **164** 41 43N 12 17 E
Lidzbark **152** 53 15N 19 49 E
Lidzbark Warminski **152** 54 7N 20 34 E
Liebenwalde **146** 52 51N 13 23 E
Lieberose **146** 51 59N 14 18 E
Liebling **170** 45 36N 21 20 E
Liechtenstein ■ **147** 47 8N 9 35 E
Liederkerke **143** 50 52N 4 5 E
Liège **143** 50 38N 5 35 E
Liège □ **143** 50 32N 5 35 E
Liegnitz = Legnica **152** 51 12N 16 10 E
Liempde **143** 51 35N 5 23 E
Lienart **250** 3 3N 25 31 E
Lienyünchiangshih = Lianyungang **215** 34 40N 119 11 E
Lienz **150** 46 50N 12 46 E
Liepaja **178** 56 30N 21 0 E
Lier **143** 51 7N 4 34 E
Lierneux **143** 50 17N 5 47 E
Lieshout **143** 51 31N 5 36 E
Liesţa **170** 45 38N 27 34 E
Liestal **148** 47 29N 7 44 E
Liévin **139** 50 24N 2 47 E
Lièvre → **82** 45 31N 75 26W
Liezen **150** 47 34N 14 15 E
Liffey → **135** 53 21N 6 20W
Lifford **135** 54 50N 7 30W
Liffré **138** 48 12N 1 30W
Lifjell **171** 59 27N 8 45 E
Lifudzin **218** 44 21N 134 58 E
Ligao **210** 13 14N 123 32 E
Lightning Ridge **231** 29 22 S 148 0 E
Lignano **163** 45 42N 13 8 E
Ligny-en-Barrois **139** 48 36N 5 20 E
Ligny-le-Châtel **139** 47 54N 3 45 E
Ligoúrion **169** 37 37N 23 2 E
Ligua, La **124** 32 30 S 71 16W
Ligueil **138** 47 2N 0 49 E
Ligui **99** 25 43N 111 16W
Liguria □ **162** 44 30N 9 0 E
Ligurian Sea **162** 43 20N 9 0 E
Lihir Group **227** 3 0 S 152 35 E
Lihou Reefs and Cays **230** 17 25 S 151 40 E
Lijiang **216** 26 55N 100 20 E
Likasi **251** 10 55 S 26 48 E
Likati **252** 3 20N 24 0 E
Likely **93** 52 37N 121 35W
Likhoslavl **178** 57 12N 35 30 E
Likhovski **181** 48 10N 40 10 E
Likokou **252** 0 12 S 12 48 E
Likoma I. **251** 12 3 S 34 45 E
Likumburu **251** 9 43 S 35 8 E
Liling **217** 27 42N 113 29 E
Lille, Belgium **143** 51 15N 4 50 E
Lille, France **139** 50 38N 3 3 E
Lille Bœlt **173** 55 20N 9 45 E
Lillebonne **138** 49 30N 0 32 E
Lillehammer **171** 61 8N 10 30 E
Lillers **139** 50 35N 2 28 E

Lillesand **171** 58 15N 8 23 E
Lilleshall **133** 52 45N 2 22W
Lillestrøm **171** 59 58N 11 5 E
Lillian L. **80** 51 17N 61 23W
Lillian Point, Mt. **229** 27 40 S 126 6 E
Lillo **156** 39 45N 3 20W
Lillooet **93** 50 44N 121 57W
Lillooet → **93** 49 15N 121 57W
Lillooet L. **93** 50 18N 122 35W
Lilongwe **251** 14 0 S 33 48 E
Liloy **211** 8 4N 122 39 E
Lim → **166** 43 0N 19 40 E
Lima, Indonesia **207** 3 37 S 128 4 E
Lima, Peru **122** 12 0 S 77 0W
Lima, Sweden **172** 60 55N 13 20 E
Lima □ **122** 12 3 S 77 3W
Lima → **154** 41 41N 8 50W
Limages **82** 45 20N 75 16W
Liman **181** 45 45N 47 12 E
Limanowa **152** 49 42N 20 22 E
Limassol **190** 34 42N 33 1 E
Limavady **135** 55 3N 6 58W
Limavady □ **135** 55 0N 6 55W
Limay → **126** 39 0 S 68 0W
Limay Mahuida **124** 37 10 S 66 45W
Limbang **209** 4 42N 115 6 E
Limbara, Monti **164** 40 50N 9 10 E
Limbdi **198** 22 34N 71 51 E
Limbe **247** 4 1N 9 10 E
Limbourg **143** 50 37N 5 56 E
Limbri **231** 31 3 S 151 5 E
Limbueta **253** 12 30 S 18 42 E
Limbunya **228** 17 14 S 129 50 E
Limburg **147** 50 22N 8 4 E
Limburg □, Belgium **143** 51 2N 5 25 E
Limburg □, Neth. **143** 51 20N 5 55 E
Limedsforsen **172** 60 52N 13 25 E
Limeira **125** 22 35 S 47 28W
Limenária **168** 40 38N 24 32 E
Limerick, Canada **88** 49 39N 106 16W
Limerick, Ireland **135** 52 40N 8 38W
Limerick □ **135** 52 30N 8 50W
Limestone → **77** 56 31N 94 7W
Limestone B. **89** 53 50N 98 53W
Limfjorden **173** 56 55N 9 0 E
Limia → **154** 41 41N 8 50W
Limmared **173** 57 34N 13 20 E
Limmat → **149** 47 26N 8 20 E
Limmen **142** 52 34N 4 42 E
Limmen Bight **230** 14 40 S 135 35 E
Limmen Bight → **230** 15 7 S 135 44 E
Límni **169** 38 43N 23 18 E
Límnos **168** 39 50N 25 5 E
Limoeiro **120** 7 52 S 35 27W
Limoeiro do Norte **120** 5 5 S 38 0W
Limoges, Canada **85** 45 20N 75 15W
Limoges, France **140** 45 50N 1 15 E
Limón, C. Rica **112** 10 0N 83 2W
Limón, Mexico **110** 18 26N 93 16W
Limone Piemonte **162** 44 12N 7 32 E
Limones **111** 18 58N 88 12W
Limousin **140** 46 0N 1 0 E
Limousin, Plateaux du **140** 46 0N 1 0 E
Limoux **140** 43 4N 2 12 E
Limpopo → **255** 25 15 S 33 30 E
Limuru **250** 1 2 S 36 35 E
Lin Xian **214** 37 57N 110 58 E
Lin'an **217** 30 15N 119 42 E
Linapacan **211** 11 30N 119 52 E
Linapacan I. **211** 11 27N 119 49 E
Linapacan Str. **211** 11 37N 119 56 E
Linares, Chile **124** 35 50 S 71 40W
Linares, Colombia **118** 1 23N 77 31W
Linares, Mexico **103** 24 52N 99 34W
Linares, Spain **157** 38 10N 3 40W
Linares □ **124** 36 0 S 71 0W
Linaria **90** 54 19N 114 8W
Línas Mte. **164** 39 25N 8 38 E
Lincang **216** 23 58N 100 1 E
Lincheng **214** 37 25N 114 30 E
Linchuan **217** 27 57N 116 15 E
Lincoln, Argentina **124** 34 55 S 61 30W
Lincoln, Canada **84** 43 10N 79 29W
Lincoln, N.Z. **235** 43 38 S 172 30 E
Lincoln, U.K. **132** 53 14N 0 32W
Lincoln □ **132** 53 14N 0 32W
Lincoln Sea **12** 84 0N 55 0W
Lincoln Wolds **132** 53 20N 0 5W
Lincolnville **81** 45 30N 61 33W
Lindås, Norway **171** 60 44N 5 9 E
Lindås, Sweden **173** 56 38N 15 35 E
Lindau **147** 47 33N 9 41 E
Linde → **142** 52 50N 5 57 E
Lindell Beach **93** 49 2N 122 1W
Linden, Canada **91** 51 36N 113 28W
Linden, Guyana **122** 6 0N 58 10W
Lindenheuvel **143** 50 59N 5 48 E
Linderöd **172** 55 56N 13 47 E
Linderödsåsen **172** 55 53N 13 53 E
Lindesberg **172** 59 36N 15 15 E
Lindesnes **171** 57 58N 7 3 E
Lindi **251** 9 58 S 39 38 E
Lindi □ **251** 9 40 S 38 30 E
Lindi → **250** 0 33N 25 5 E
Lindoso **154** 41 52N 8 11W
Lindow **146** 52 58N 12 58 E
Lindsay **85** 44 22N 78 43W
Línea de la Concepción, La **155** 36 15N 5 23W
Linfen **214** 36 3N 111 30 E
Ling Xian, Hunan, China **217** 26 29N 113 48 E
Ling Xian, Shandong, China **214** 37 22N 116 30 E
Lingao **204** 19 56N 109 42 E
Lingayen **210** 16 1N 120 14 E
Lingayen G. **210** 16 10N 120 15 E
Lingbi **215** 33 33N 117 33 E
Lingchuan, Guangxi Zhuangzu, China **217** 25 26N 110 21 E
Lingchuan, Shanxi, China **214** 35 45N 113 12 E
Lingen **146** 52 32N 7 21 E
Lingga **208** 0 12 S 104 37 E
Lingga, Kepulauan **208** 0 10 S 104 30 E
Linghed **172** 60 48N 15 55 E
Lingling **217** 26 17N 111 37 E
Lingqiu **214** 39 28N 114 22 E
Lingshan **216** 22 25N 109 18 E
Lingshi **214** 36 48N 111 48 E
Lingshou **214** 38 20N 114 20 E
Lingshui **204** 18 27N 110 0 E
Lingtai **214** 35 0N 107 40 E
Linguéré **246** 15 25N 15 5W
Linguisan **211** 7 30N 122 27 E
Lingwu **214** 38 6N 106 20 E
Lingyuan **215** 41 10N 119 15 E
Lingyun **216** 25 2N 106 35 E
Linh Cam **204** 18 31N 105 31 E
Linhai **217** 28 50N 121 8 E
Linhares **121** 19 25 S 40 4W
Linhe **214** 40 48N 107 20 E
Linière **83** 46 4N 70 32W
Linjiang **215** 41 50N 127 0 E
Link L. **92** 52 25N 127 40W
Linköping **173** 58 28N 15 36 E
Linkou **215** 45 15N 130 18 E
Linli **217** 29 27N 111 30 E
Linlithgow **134** 55 58N 3 38W
Linnhe, L. **134** 56 36N 5 25W
Linosa, I. **241** 35 51N 12 50 E
Linqi **214** 35 45N 113 52 E
Linqing **214** 36 50N 115 42 E
Linqu **215** 36 25N 118 30 E
Linru **214** 34 11N 112 52 E
Lins **125** 21 40 S 49 44W
Linshui **216** 30 21N 106 57 E
Lintao **214** 35 18N 103 52 E
Linth → **147** 47 7N 9 7W
Linthal **149** 46 54N 9 0 E
Lintlaw **88** 52 4N 103 14W
Linton **83** 47 15N 72 16W
Lintong **214** 34 20N 109 10 E
Linville **231** 26 50 S 152 11 E
Linwood **84** 43 35N 80 43W
Linwu **217** 25 19N 112 31 E
Linxe **140** 43 56N 1 13W
Linxi **215** 43 36N 118 2 E
Linxia **212** 35 36N 103 10 E
Linxiang **217** 29 28N 113 23 E
Linyanti → **254** 17 50 S 25 5 E
Linyi **215** 35 5N 118 21 E
Linz, Austria **150** 48 18N 14 18 E
Linz, Germany **146** 50 33N 7 18 E
Linzhenzhen **214** 36 30N 109 59 E
Linzi **215** 36 50N 118 20 E
Lion, G. du **140** 43 0N 4 0 E
Lion-d'Angers, Le **138** 47 37N 0 43W
Lioni **165** 40 52N 15 10 E
Lion's Den **251** 17 15 S 30 5 E
Lion's Head **74** 44 58N 81 15W
Liouesso **252** 1 2N 15 43 E
Liozno **178** 55 0N 30 50 E
Lipa **210** 13 57N 121 10 E
Lipali **251** 15 50 S 35 50 E
Lípari **165** 38 26N 14 58 E
Lípari, Is. **165** 38 30N 14 50 E
Lipetsk **179** 52 37N 39 35 E
Lipiany **152** 53 2N 14 58 E
Liping **216** 26 15N 109 7 E
Lipkany **180** 48 14N 26 48 E
Lipljan **166** 42 31N 21 7 E
Lipnik **151** 49 32N 17 36 E
Lipno **152** 52 49N 19 15 E
Lipova **166** 46 8N 21 42 E
Lipovcy Manzovka **218** 44 12N 132 26 E
Lipovets **180** 49 12N 29 1 E
Lippe → **146** 51 39N 6 38 E
Lippstadt **146** 51 40N 8 19 E
Lipsko **152** 51 9N 21 40 E
Lipsói **169** 37 19N 26 50 E
Lipton **88** 50 54N 103 51W
Liptovsky Svaty Milkulaš **151** 49 6N 19 35 E
Liptrap C. **231** 38 50 S 145 55 E
Lipu **217** 24 30N 110 22 E
Lira **250** 2 17N 32 57 E
Liri → **164** 41 25N 13 52 E
Liria **156** 39 37N 0 35W
Lisala **252** 2 12N 21 38 E
Lisboa **155** 38 42N 9 10W
Lisboa □ **155** 39 0N 9 12W
Lisbon = Lisboa **155** 38 42N 9 10W
Lisburn **135** 54 30N 6 9W
Liscannor, B. **135** 52 57N 9 24W
Liscia → **164** 41 11N 9 9 E
Lishe Jiang → **216** 24 15N 101 35 E
Lishi **214** 37 31N 111 8 E
Lishu **215** 43 20N 124 18 E
Lishui, Jiangsu, China **217** 31 38N 119 2 E
Lishui, Zhejiang, China **217** 28 28N 119 54 E
Lisianski I. **224** 26 2N 174 0W
Lisichansk **180** 48 55N 38 30 E
Lisieux **138** 49 10N 0 12 E
Lisle-sur-Tarn **140** 43 52N 1 49 E
Lismore, Australia **231** 28 44 S 153 21 E
Lismore, Ireland **135** 52 8N 7 58W
Lisse **142** 52 16N 4 33 E
List **146** 55 1N 8 26 E
Lista **171** 58 7N 6 39 E
Lister, Mt. **13** 78 0 S 162 0 E
Liston **231** 28 39 S 152 6 E
Listowel, Canada **84** 43 44N 80 58W
Listowel, Ireland **135** 52 27N 9 30W
Lit-et-Mixe **140** 44 2N 1 15W
Litang, Guangxi Zhuangzu, China **216** 23 12N 109 8 E
Litang, Sichuan, China **216** 30 1N 100 17 E
Litang, Malaysia **207** 5 27N 118 31 E
Litang Qu → **216** 28 4N 101 32 E
Litani →, Lebanon **189** 33 20N 35 14 E
Litani →, Surinam **189** 3 40N 54 0W
Litchfield **232** 36 18 S 142 52 E
Liteni **170** 47 32N 26 32 E
Lithgow **231** 33 25 S 150 8 E
Líthinon, Ákra **169** 34 55N 24 44 E
Lithuanian S.S.R. □ **178** 55 30N 24 0 E
Litija **163** 46 3N 14 50 E
Litókhoron **168** 40 8N 22 34 E
Litoměřice **150** 50 33N 14 10 E
Litomysl **151** 49 52N 16 20 E
Litschau **150** 48 58N 15 4 E
Little Abaco I. **112** 26 50N 77 30W
Little Abitibi → **87** 50 29N 81 32W
Little Aden **194** 12 45N 44 52 E
Little Andaman I. **196** 10 40N 92 15 E
Little Barrier I. **234** 36 12 S 175 8 E
Little Bay **79** 49 36N 55 57W
Little Bow → **91** 49 53N 112 29W
Little Burnt Bay **79** 49 25N 55 5W
Little Bushman Land **254** 29 10 S 18 10 E
Little Cadotte → **90** 56 41N 117 6W
Little Cayman, I. **112** 19 41N 80 3W
Little Churchill → **77** 57 30N 95 22W
Little Current **84** 45 55N 82 0W
Little Current → **87** 50 57N 84 36W
Little Dover **81** 45 15N 61 3W
Little Fort **93** 51 26N 120 13W
Little Grand Rapids **89** 52 0N 95 29W
Little Inagua I. **113** 21 40N 73 50W
Little Minch **134** 57 35N 6 45W
Little Namaqualand **254** 29 0 S 17 9 E
Little Narrows **81** 45 59N 60 59W
Little Ouse → **133** 52 25N 0 50 E
Little Pic → **87** 48 48N 86 37W
Little Quill L. **88** 51 55N 104 5W
Little Rann **198** 23 25N 71 25 E
Little River **235** 43 45 S 172 49 E
Little Ruaha → **250** 7 57 S 37 53 E
Little Smoky → **90** 54 44N 117 11W
Little White → **84** 46 23N 83 20W
Littlehampton **133** 50 48N 0 32W
Liu He → **215** 40 55N 121 35 E
Liu Jiang → **216** 23 55N 109 30 E
Liuba **214** 33 38N 106 55 E
Liucheng **216** 24 38N 109 14 E
Liugou **215** 40 57N 118 15 E
Liuhe **215** 42 17N 125 43 E
Liuheng Dao **217** 29 40N 122 5 E
Liukang Tenggaja **207** 6 45 S 118 50 E
Liuli **251** 11 3 S 34 38 E
Liuwa Plain **253** 14 20 S 22 30 E
Liuyang **217** 28 10N 113 37 E
Liuzhou **216** 24 22N 109 22 E
Liuzhuang **215** 33 12N 120 18 E
Livada **170** 47 52N 23 5 E
Livadherón **168** 40 2N 21 57 E
Livanovka **182** 52 6N 61 59 E
Livarot **138** 49 0N 0 9 E
Lively **84** 46 26N 81 9W
Liveringa **228** 18 3 S 124 10 E
Liverpool, Australia **231** 33 54 S 150 58 E
Liverpool, Canada **81** 44 5N 64 41W
Liverpool, U.K. **132** 53 25N 3 0W
Liverpool, C. **95** 73 38N 78 6W
Liverpool Bay **94** 70 0N 128 0W
Liverpool Plains **231** 31 15 S 150 15 E
Liverpool Ra. **231** 31 50 S 150 30 E
Livingston **112** 15 50N 88 50W
Livingstone **251** 17 46 S 25 52 E
Livingstone Memorial **251** 12 20 S 30 18 E
Livingstone Mts., N.Z. **235** 45 15 S 168 9 E
Livingstone Mts., Tanzania **251** 9 40 S 34 20 E
Livingstonia **251** 10 38 S 34 5 E
Livno **166** 43 50N 17 0 E
Livny **179** 52 30N 37 30 E
Livorno **162** 43 32N 10 18 E
Livramento **125** 30 55 S 55 30W
Livramento do Brumado **121** 13 39 S 41 50W
Livron-sur-Drôme **141** 44 46N 4 51 E
Liwale **251** 9 48 S 37 58 E
Liwale □ **251** 9 0 S 38 0 E
Liwiec → **152** 52 36N 21 34 E
Lixi **216** 26 23N 101 59 E
Lixoúrion **169** 38 14N 20 24 E
Liyang **217** 31 26N 119 28 E
Lizard I. **230** 14 42 S 145 30 E
Lizard Pt. **133** 49 57N 5 11W
Lizarda **120** 9 36 S 46 41W
Lizzano **165** 40 23N 17 25 E
Ljig **166** 44 13N 20 18 E
Ljubija **163** 44 55N 16 35 E
Ljubinje **166** 42 58N 18 5 E
Ljubljana **163** 46 4N 14 33 E
Ljubno **163** 46 25N 14 46 E
Ljubovija **166** 44 11N 19 22 E
Ljubuški **166** 43 12N 17 34 E
Ljung **173** 58 1N 13 3 E
Ljungan → **172** 62 18N 17 23 E
Ljungaverk **172** 62 30N 16 5 E
Ljungby **173** 56 49N 13 55 E
Ljusdal **172** 61 46N 16 3 E
Ljusnan → **172** 61 12N 17 8 E
Ljusne **172** 61 13N 17 7 E
Ljutomer **163** 46 31N 16 11 E
Llagostera **156** 41 50N 2 54 E
Llamellín **122** 9 0 S 76 54W
Llancanelo, Salina **124** 35 40 S 69 8W
Llandeilo **133** 51 53N 4 0W
Llandovery **133** 51 59N 3 49W
Llandrindod Wells **133** 52 15N 3 23W
Llandudno **132** 53 19N 3 51W
Llanelli **133** 51 41N 4 11W
Llanes **154** 43 25N 4 50W
Llangollen **132** 52 58N 3 10W
Llanidloes **133** 52 28N 3 31W
Llano Grande **104** 23 27N 105 5W
Llanos **122** 5 0N 71 35W
Llanquihue □ **126** 41 30 S 73 0W
Llanquihue, L. **126** 41 10 S 75 50W
Llave, La **107** 20 28N 99 59W
Llera de Canales **103** 23 19N 99 1W
Llerena **155** 38 17N 6 0W
Llica **122** 19 52 S 68 16W
Llico **124** 34 46 S 72 5W
Llobregat → **156** 41 19N 2 9 E
Llorente **211** 11 25N 125 33 E
Lloret de Mar **156** 41 41N 2 53 E
Lloyd B. **230** 12 45 S 143 27 E
Lloyd L. **77** 57 22N 108 57W
Lloydminster **88** 53 17N 110 0W
Lloyds → **79** 48 35N 57 15W
Lluchmayor **157** 39 29N 2 53 E
Llullaillaco, volcán **124** 24 43 S 68 30W
Lo **143** 50 59N 2 45 E
Lo → **204** 21 18N 105 25 E
Lo de Mena **105** 23 32N 103 42W
Lo de Vega **104** 26 12N 108 35W
Loa → **124** 21 26 S 70 41W
Loano **162** 44 8N 8 14 E
Loay **211** 9 36N 124 1 E
Lobatos **105** 22 49N 103 24W
Lobatse **254** 25 12 S 25 40 E
Löbau **146** 51 5N 14 42 E
Lobaye → **252** 3 41N 18 35 E
Lobbes **143** 50 21N 4 16 E
Lobenstein **146** 50 25N 11 39 E
Lobería **124** 38 10 S 58 40W
Łobez **152** 53 38N 15 39 E
Lobito **253** 12 18 S 13 35 E
Lobo **210** 13 39N 121 13 E
Lobón, Canal de **155** 38 50N 6 55W
Lobos **124** 35 10 S 59 0W
Lobos, C. **100** 29 55N 112 46W
Lobos, Is. **114** 6 57 S 80 45W
Lobos, I. **100** 27 20N 110 36W
Lobos de Tierra, I. **122** 6 27 S 80 52W
Lobstick L. **78** 54 0N 65 0W
Lobva **182** 59 10N 60 30 E
Lobva → **182** 59 8N 60 48 E
Loc Binh **204** 21 46N 106 54 E
Loc Ninh **205** 11 50N 106 34 E
Locarno **149** 46 10N 8 47 E
Lochaber **134** 56 55N 5 0W
Lochcarron **134** 57 25N 5 30W

Loche, La **77** 56 29N 109 26W
Lochem **142** 52 9N 6 26 E
Loches **138** 47 7N 1 0 E
Lochgelly **134** 56 7N 3 18W
Lochgilphead **134** 56 2N 5 37W
Lochinver **134** 58 9N 5 15W
Lochnagar, Australia **230** 23 33 S 145 38 E
Lochnagar, U.K. **134** 56 57N 3 14W
Łochów **152** 52 33N 21 42 E
Lochy → **134** 56 52N 5 3W
Lock **231** 33 34 S 135 46 E
Lockeport **81** 43 47N 65 4W
Lockerbie **134** 55 7N 3 21W
Lockhart **233** 35 14 S 146 40 E
Lockhart, L. **229** 33 15 S 119 3 E
Lockington **232** 36 16 S 144 34 E
Locle, Le **148** 47 3N 6 44 E
Locminé **138** 47 54N 2 51W
Locri **165** 38 14N 16 14 E
Locronan **138** 48 7N 4 15W
Loctudy **138** 47 50N 4 12W
Lod **189** 31 57N 34 54 E
Lodalskåpa **171** 61 47N 7 13 E
Lodeinoye Pole **176** 60 44N 33 33 E
Lodève **140** 43 44N 3 19 E
Lodgepole **91** 53 6N 115 19W
Lodhran **198** 29 32N 71 30 E
Lodi **162** 45 19N 9 30 E
Lodja **250** 3 30 S 23 23 E
Lodosa **156** 42 25N 2 4W
Lödöse **173** 58 2N 12 9 E
Lodwar **250** 3 10N 35 40 E
Łódź **152** 51 45N 19 27 E
Łódź □ **152** 51 45N 19 27 E
Loei **204** 17 29N 101 35 E
Loenen **142** 52 7N 6 1 E
Loengo **250** 4 48 S 26 30 E
Lofer **150** 47 35N 12 41 E
Lofoten **174** 68 30N 15 0 E
Lofsdalen **172** 62 10N 13 20 E
Lofsen → **172** 62 7N 13 57 E
Loftahammar **173** 57 54N 16 41 E
Logan, Mount **80** 48 53N 66 38W
Logan I. **86** 50 7N 88 27W
Loggieville **81** 47 4N 65 23W
Logo **245** 5 20N 30 18 E
Logroño **156** 42 28N 2 27W
Logrosán **155** 39 20N 5 32W
Løgstør **173** 56 58N 9 14 E
Lohardaga **199** 23 27N 84 45 E
Lohja **175** 60 12N 24 5 E
Lohr **147** 50 0N 9 35 E
Loi-kaw **202** 19 40N 97 17 E
Loimaa **175** 60 50N 23 5 E
Loir → **138** 47 33N 0 32W
Loir-et-Cher □ **138** 47 40N 1 20 E
Loire □ **141** 45 40N 4 5 E
Loire → **138** 47 16N 2 10W
Loire-Atlantique □ **138** 47 25N 1 40W
Loiret □ **139** 47 58N 2 10 E
Loitz **146** 53 58N 13 8 E
Loja, Ecuador **122** 3 59 S 79 16W
Loja, Spain **155** 37 10N 4 10W
Loja □ **118** 4 0 S 79 13W
Loji **207** 1 38 S 127 28 E
Loka **245** 4 13N 31 0 E
Lokandu **250** 2 30 S 25 45 E
Løken **171** 59 48N 11 29 E
Lokeren **143** 51 6N 3 59 E
Lokhvitsa **178** 50 25N 33 18 E
Lokichokio **250** 4 19N 34 13 E
Lokitaung **250** 4 12N 35 48 E
Lokka **174** 67 49N 27 45 E
Løkken **173** 57 22N 9 41 E
Løkken Verk **172** 63 7N 9 43 E
Loknya **178** 56 49N 30 4 E
Lokoja **247** 7 47N 6 45 E
Lokolama **252** 2 35 S 19 50 E
Lol → **245** 9 13N 26 30 E
Lola **246** 7 52N 8 29W
Lolibai, Gebel **245** 3 50N 33 0 E
Lolimi **245** 4 35N 34 0 E
Loliondo **250** 2 2 S 35 39 E
Lolland **173** 54 45N 11 30 E
Lollar **146** 50 39N 8 43 E
Lolodorf **247** 3 16N 10 49 E
Lom **167** 43 48N 23 12 E
Lom → **166** 43 45N 23 15 E
Lom Kao **204** 16 53N 101 14 E
Lom Sak **204** 16 47N 101 15 E
Loma, La **104** 24 46N 107 43W
Loma Bonita **109** 18 7N 95 53W
Lomami → **250** 0 46N 24 16 E
Lomas de Zamóra **124** 34 45 S 58 25W
Lomas del Real **103** 22 30N 97 54W
Lombadina **228** 16 31 S 122 54 E
Lombardia □ **162** 45 35N 9 45 E
Lombardy = Lombardia □ **162** 45 35N 9 45 E
Lombe **253** 9 27 S 16 13 E
Lombez **140** 43 29N 0 55 E
Lomblen **207** 8 30 S 123 32 E
Lombok **209** 8 45 S 116 30 E
Lomé **247** 6 9N 1 20 E
Lomela **252** 2 19 S 23 15 E
Lomela → **252** 1 30 S 22 50 E
Lomello **162** 45 5N 8 46 E
Lomié **252** 3 13N 13 38 E
Lomma **172** 55 43N 13 6 E
Lomme → **143** 50 8N 5 10 E
Lommel **143** 51 14N 5 19 E
Lomond **91** 50 24N 112 36W
Lomond, L. **134** 56 8N 4 38W
Lomonosov **178** 59 57N 29 53 E
Lomphat **204** 13 30N 106 59 E
Lompobatang **207** 5 24 S 119 56 E
Lomsegga **171** 61 49N 8 21 E
Łomza **152** 53 10N 22 2 E
Łomza □ **152** 53 0N 22 30 E
Lonavale **200** 18 46N 73 29 E
Loncoche **126** 39 20 S 72 50W
Loncopuè **126** 38 4 S 70 37W
Londa **201** 15 30N 74 30 E
Londe, La **141** 43 8N 6 14 E
Londerzeel **143** 51 0N 4 19 E
Londiani **250** 0 10 S 35 33 E
Londinières **138** 49 50N 1 25 E
London, Canada **84** 42 59N 81 15W
London, U.K. **133** 51 30N 0 5W
London, Greater □ **133** 51 30N 0 5W
Londonderry, Canada **81** 45 29N 63 36W
Londonderry, U.K. **135** 55 0N 7 20W
Londonderry □ **135** 55 0N 7 20W
Londonderry, C. **228** 13 45 S 126 55 E
Londonderry, I. **126** 55 0 S 71 0W
Londrina **125** 23 18 S 51 10W
Londuimbale **253** 12 15 S 15 19 E
Lone Butte **93** 51 33N 121 12W
Lone Pine **90** 54 18N 115 7W
Lone Rock **88** 53 3N 109 53W
Lonely I. **84** 45 34N 81 28W
Long Beach **92** 49 1N 125 40W
Long Cr. → **88** 49 7N 102 59W
Long Eaton **132** 52 54N 1 16W
Long I., Australia **230** 22 8 S 149 53 E
Long I., Bahamas **113** 23 20N 75 10W
Long I., N.W.T., Canada **78** 54 50N 79 20W
Long I., Newf., Canada **79** 47 34N 55 59W
Long I., Papua N. G. **227** 5 20 S 147 5 E
Long L., Alta., Canada **90** 54 22N 112 46W
Long L., Ont., Canada **87** 49 30N 86 50W
Long Pt., Man., Canada **89** 53 2N 98 25W
Long Pt., Newf., Canada **79** 48 47N 58 46W
Long Pt., Ont., Canada **84** 42 35N 80 2W
Long Pt., N.Z. **235** 46 34 S 169 36 E
Long Point B. **84** 42 40N 80 10W
Long Range Mts. **79** 49 30N 57 30W
Long Reach **81** 45 28N 66 5W
Long Reef **228** 13 55 S 125 45 E
Long Str. **12** 70 0N 175 0 E
Long Thanh **205** 10 47N 106 57 E
Long Xian **214** 34 55N 106 55 E
Long Xuyen **205** 10 19N 105 28 E
Longa, Angola **253** 14 42 S 18 32 E
Longá, Greece **169** 36 53N 21 55 E
Long'an **216** 23 10N 107 40 E
Longarone **163** 46 15N 12 18 E
Longburn **234** 40 23 S 175 35 E
Longchang **216** 29 18N 105 15 E
Longchi **216** 29 25N 103 24 E
Longchuan, Guangdong, China **217** 24 5N 115 17 E
Longchuan, Yunnan, China **216** 24 23N 97 58 E
Longde **214** 35 30N 106 20 E
Longeau **139** 47 47N 5 20 E
Longford, Australia **230** 41 32 S 147 3 E
Longford, Ireland **135** 53 43N 7 50W
Longford □ **135** 53 42N 7 45W
Longguan **214** 40 45N 115 30 E
Longhua **215** 41 18N 117 45 E
Longhui **217** 27 7N 111 2 E
Longido **250** 2 43 S 36 42 E
Longiram **209** 0 5 S 115 45 E
Longkou, Jiangxi, China **217** 26 8N 115 10 E
Longkou, Shandong, China **215** 37 40N 120 18 E
Longlac **87** 49 45N 86 25W
Longlegged L. **86** 50 46N 94 8W
Longli **216** 26 25N 106 58 E
Longlier **143** 49 52N 5 27 E
Longlin **216** 24 47N 105 20 E
Longling **216** 24 37N 98 39 E
Longmen **217** 23 40N 114 18 E
Longming **216** 22 59N 107 7 E
Longnan **217** 24 55N 114 47 E
Longnawan **209** 1 51N 114 55 E
Longobucco **165** 39 27N 16 37 E
Longone → **243** 10 0N 15 40 E
Longquan **217** 28 7N 119 10 E
Longreach **230** 23 28 S 144 14 E
Longshan **216** 29 29N 109 25 E
Longsheng **216** 25 48N 110 0 E
Longton **230** 20 58 S 145 55 E
Longtown **133** 51 58N 2 59W
Longué **138** 47 22N 0 8W
Longue-Pointe-de-Mingan **80** 50 16N 64 9W
Longueau **139** 49 52N 2 21 E
Longueuil **83** 45 32N 73 30W
Longuyon **139** 49 27N 5 35 E
Longview **91** 50 32N 114 10W
Longvilly **143** 50 2N 5 50 E
Longwy **139** 49 30N 5 45 E
Longxi **214** 34 53N 104 40 E
Longyou **217** 29 1N 119 8 E
Longzhou **216** 22 22N 106 50 E
Lonigo **163** 45 23N 11 22 E
Löningen **146** 52 43N 7 44 E
Lonja → **163** 45 30N 16 40 E
Lonkin **202** 25 39N 96 22 E
Lonquimay **126** 38 26 S 71 14W
Lons-le-Saunier **139** 46 40N 5 31 E
Lønstrup **173** 57 29N 9 47 E
Lookout, C. **74** 55 18N 83 56W
Loolmalasin **250** 3 0 S 35 53 E
Loon →, Alta., Canada **90** 57 8N 115 3W
Loon →, Man., Canada **77** 55 53N 101 59W
Loon Lake **88** 54 2N 109 10W
Loon-op-Zand **143** 51 38N 5 5 E
Loongana **229** 30 52 S 127 5 E
Loop Hd. **135** 52 34N 9 55W
Loosduinen **142** 52 3N 4 14 E
Lop Buri **204** 14 48N 100 37 E
Lop Nor = Lop Nur **212** 40 20N 90 10 E
Lop Nur **212** 40 20N 90 10 E
Lopare **166** 44 39N 18 46 E
Lopatin **181** 43 50N 47 35 E
Lopatina, G. **185** 50 47N 143 10 E
Lopaye **245** 6 37N 33 40 E
Lopera **155** 37 56N 4 14W
Lopez **210** 13 53N 122 15 E
Lopez, C. **252** 0 47 S 8 40 E
Lopez I. **252** 0 50 S 8 47 E
Loppersum **142** 53 20N 6 44 E
Lopphavet **174** 70 27N 21 15 E
Lora →, Afghan. **197** 32 0N 67 15 E
Lora →, Norway **171** 62 8N 8 42 E
Lora, Hamun-i- **197** 29 38N 64 58 E
Lora, La **154** 42 45N 4 0W
Lora Cr. → **231** 28 10 S 135 22 E
Lora del Río **155** 37 39N 5 33W
Loralai **197** 30 20N 68 41 E
Lorca **157** 37 41N 1 42W
Lord Howe I. **224** 31 33 S 159 6 E
Lord Howe Ridge **224** 30 0 S 162 30 E
Lord's Cove **79** 46 53N 55 40W
Loreburn **88** 51 13N 106 36W
Lorengau **227** 2 1 S 147 15 E
Loreto, Bolivia **123** 15 13 S 64 40W
Loreto, Brazil **120** 7 5 S 45 10W
Loreto, Italy **163** 43 26N 13 36 E
Loreto, Baja Calif. S., Mexico **99** 26 1N 111 21W
Loreto, Zacatecas, Mexico **105** 22 16N 101 58W
Loreto, Zacatecas, Mexico **105** 23 51N 103 0W
Loreto □ **118** 5 0 S 75 0W
Loreto Aprutina **163** 42 24N 13 59 E
Lorette **89** 49 44N 96 52W
Loretteville **83** 46 51N 71 21W
Lorgues **141** 43 28N 6 22 E
Lorica **118** 9 14N 75 49W
Lorient **138** 47 45N 3 23W
Lorn **134** 56 26N 5 10W
Lorn, Firth of **134** 56 20N 5 40W
Lorne, Australia **231** 38 33 S 143 59 E
Lorne, Canada **81** 47 53N 66 8W
Lörrach **147** 47 36N 7 38 E
Lorraine **139** 49 0N 6 0 E
Lorrainville **82** 47 21N 79 23W
Los, Îles de **246** 9 30N 13 50W
Los Aldamas **102** 26 3N 99 11W
Los Altos **102** 26 10N 98 25W
Los Andes **124** 32 50 S 70 40W
Los Angeles, Chile **124** 37 28 S 72 23W
Los Ángeles, Mexico **100** 29 27N 110 46W
Los Antiguos **126** 46 35 S 71 40W
Los Baños **101** 26 49N 106 18W
Los Barrios **155** 36 11N 5 30W
Los Blancos **124** 23 40 S 62 30W
Los Burros **99** 25 3N 110 50W
Los Chinos **100** 29 47N 111 6W
Los Comales **102** 26 8N 98 56W
Los Corchos **104** 21 48N 105 26W
Los Esteros **103** 22 31N 98 8W
Los Fresnos **100** 31 12N 110 35W
Los Hermanos **119** 11 45N 84 25W
Los Herreras **102** 25 55N 99 24W
Los Hornillos **104** 26 28N 108 27W
Los Hoyos **100** 30 10N 109 47W
Los Lagos **126** 39 51 S 72 50W
Los Lavaderos **103** 23 29N 98 2W
Los Leones **101** 28 45N 105 57W
Los Lomas **122** 4 40 S 80 10W
Los Menucos **126** 40 50 S 68 10W
Los Mochis **104** 25 45N 108 57W
Los Monegros **156** 41 29N 0 13W
Los Monos **126** 46 1 S 69 36W
Los Naranjos **109** 18 21N 96 10W
Los Palacios **112** 22 35N 83 15W
Los Palacios y Villafranca **155** 37 10N 5 55W
Los Ramones **102** 25 42N 99 37W
Los Reyes **107** 19 12N 98 54W
Los Reyes de Salgado **106** 19 35N 102 29W
Los Ríos □ **118** 1 30 S 79 25W
Los Rodríguez **102** 27 9N 101 21W
Los Roques **118** 11 50N 66 45W
Los Santos de Maimona **155** 38 27N 6 22W
Los Tanques **100** 27 12N 108 54W
Los Tepames **106** 19 6N 103 37W
Los Teques **118** 10 21N 67 2W
Los Testigos **119** 11 23N 63 6W
Los Vilos **124** 32 10 S 71 30W
Los Yébenes **155** 39 36N 3 55W
Losada → **118** 2 12N 73 55W
Loshkalakh **185** 62 45N 147 20 E
Łosice **152** 52 13N 22 43 E
Lošinj **163** 44 30N 14 30 E
Losser **142** 52 16N 7 1 E
Lossiemouth **134** 57 43N 3 17W
Losuia **227** 8 30 S 151 4 E
Lot □ **140** 44 39N 1 40 E
Lot → **140** 44 18N 0 20 E
Lot-et-Garonne □ **140** 44 22N 0 30 E
Lota **124** 37 5 S 73 10W
Løten **171** 60 51N 11 21 E
Loṭfābād **193** 37 32N 59 20 E
Lothian □ **134** 55 50N 3 0W
Lothiers **139** 46 42N 1 33 E
Lotschbergtunnel **148** 46 26N 7 43 E
Lottefors **172** 61 25N 16 24 E
Lotzwil **148** 47 12N 7 48 E
Loubomo **252** 4 9 S 12 47 E
Loudéac **138** 48 11N 2 47W
Loudi **217** 27 42N 111 59 E
Loudima **252** 4 6 S 13 5 E
Loudun **138** 47 0N 0 5 E
Loué **138** 47 59N 0 9W
Loue → **139** 47 1N 5 27 E
Louga **246** 15 45N 16 5W
Loughborough **132** 52 46N 1 11W
Lougheed **91** 52 44N 111 33W
Lougheed I. **94** 77 26N 105 6W
Loughrea **135** 53 11N 8 33W
Loughros More B. **135** 54 48N 8 30W
Louhans **141** 46 38N 5 12 E
Louis Creek **93** 51 8N 120 7W
Louis Trichardt **255** 23 0 S 29 43 E
Louis XIV, Pte. **78** 54 37N 79 45W
Louisbourg **81** 45 55N 60 0W
Louisbourg Nat. Historic Park **81** 45 58N 60 20W
Louisdale **81** 45 36N 61 4W
Louise I. **92** 52 55N 131 50W
Louiseville **83** 46 20N 72 56W
Louisiade Arch. **227** 11 10 S 153 0 E
Loukouo **252** 3 38 S 14 39 E
Loulay **140** 46 3N 0 30W
Loulé **155** 37 9N 8 0W
Lount L. **77** 50 10N 94 20W
Louny **150** 50 20N 13 48 E
Loupe, La **138** 48 29N 1 1 E
Loups Marins, Lacs des **78** 56 30N 73 45W
Lourdes, Canada **79** 48 39N 59 0W
Lourdes, France **140** 43 6N 0 3W
Lourdes-du-Blanc-Sablon **79** 51 24N 57 12W
Lourenço **119** 2 30N 51 40W
Lourenço-Marques = Maputo **255** 25 58 S 32 32 E
Loures **155** 38 50N 9 9W
Lourinhã **155** 39 14N 9 17W
Louroux-Béconnais, Le **138** 47 30N 0 55W
Lousã **154** 40 7N 8 14W
Louth, Australia **233** 30 30 S 145 8 E
Louth, Ireland **135** 53 47N 6 33W
Louth, U.K. **132** 53 23N 0 0 E
Louth □ **135** 53 55N 6 30W
Loutrá Aidhipsoú **169** 38 54N 23 2 E
Loutráki **169** 38 0N 22 57 E
Louvain = Leuven **143** 50 52N 4 42 E
Louveigné **143** 50 32N 5 42 E
Louvière, La **143** 50 27N 4 10 E

Louviers **138** 49 12N 1 10 E
Lovat → **178** 58 14N 30 28 E
Lovćen **166** 42 23N 18 51 E
Love **88** 53 29N 104 10W
Lovech **167** 43 8N 24 42 E
Lóvere **162** 45 50N 10 4 E
Loverna **88** 51 40N 110 0W
Loviisa = Lovisa **175** 60 28N 26 12 E
Lovios **154** 41 55N 8 4W
Lovisa **175** 60 28N 26 12 E
Lovosice **150** 50 30N 14 2 E
Lovran **163** 45 18N 14 15 E
Lovrin **170** 45 58N 20 48 E
Lövstabukten **172** 60 35N 17 45 E
Low **82** 45 50N 76 0W
Low, C. **95** 63 7N 85 18W
Low L. **78** 55 54N 67 5W
Low Pt. **229** 32 25 S 127 25 E
Lowa **250** 1 25 S 25 47 E
Lowa → **250** 1 24 S 25 51 E
Lowe Farm **89** 49 21N 97 35W
Lower Arrow L. **93** 49 40N 118 5W
Lower Austria = Niederösterreich □ **150** 48 25N 15 40 E
Lower Hutt **234** 41 10 S 174 55 E
Lower Manitou L. **86** 49 15N 93 0W
Lower Neguac **75** 47 20N 65 10W
Lower Nicola **93** 50 12N 120 54W
Lower Post **76** 59 58N 128 30W
Lower West Pubnico **81** 43 38N 65 48W
Lower Wood Harbour **81** 43 31N 65 44W
Lowestoft **133** 52 29N 1 44 E
Łowicz **152** 52 6N 19 55 E
Lowther **87** 49 32N 83 2W
Loxton **232** 34 28 S 140 31 E
Loyalty Is. = Loyauté, Is. **226** 21 0 S 167 30 E
Loyang = Luoyang **214** 34 40N 112 26 E
Loyauté, Is. **226** 21 0 S 167 30 E
Loyev **178** 51 56N 30 46 E
Loyoro **250** 3 22N 34 14 E
Lož **163** 45 43N 30 14 E
Lozère □ **140** 44 35N 3 30 E
Loznica **166** 44 32N 19 14 E
Lozovaya **180** 49 0N 36 20 E
Lozva → **182** 59 36N 62 20 E
Luachimo **253** 7 23 S 20 48 E
Luacono **253** 11 15 S 21 37 E
Lualaba → **250** 0 26N 25 20 E
Luampa **251** 15 4 S 24 20 E
Lu'an **217** 31 45N 116 29 E
Luan Chau **204** 21 38N 103 24 E
Luan He → **215** 39 20N 119 5 E
Luan Xian **215** 39 40N 118 40 E
Luancheng, Guangxi Zhuangzu, China **216** 22 48N 108 55 E
Luancheng, Hebei, China **214** 37 53N 114 40 E
Luanda **253** 8 50 S 13 15 E
Luanda □ **253** 9 0 S 13 10 E
Luang Prabang **204** 19 52N 102 10 E
Luang Thale **205** 7 30N 100 15 E
Luangwa Valley **251** 13 30 S 31 30 E
Luanne **215** 40 55N 117 40 E
Luanping **215** 40 53N 117 23 E
Luanshya **251** 13 3 S 28 28 E
Luapula □ **251** 11 0 S 29 0 E
Luapula → **251** 9 26 S 28 33 E
Luarca **154** 43 32N 6 32W
Luashi **251** 10 50 S 23 36 E
Luau **253** 10 40 S 22 10 E
Luba **210** 17 19N 120 42 E
Lubaczów **152** 50 10N 23 8 E
Lubalo **253** 9 10 S 19 15 E
Luban, Phil. **211** 6 26N 126 13 E
Lubań, Poland **152** 51 5N 15 15 E
Lubana, Ozero **178** 56 45N 27 0 E
Lubang **210** 13 52N 120 7 E
Lubang Is. **210** 13 50N 120 12 E
Lubango **253** 14 55 S 13 30 E
Lubao **210** 14 56N 120 36 E
Lubartów **152** 51 28N 22 42 E
Lubawa **152** 53 30N 19 48 E
Lubbeek **143** 50 54N 4 50 E
Lübben **146** 51 56N 13 54 E
Lübbenau **146** 51 49N 13 59 E
Lübeck **146** 53 52N 10 41 E
Lübecker Bucht **146** 54 3N 11 0 E
Lubefu **250** 4 47 S 24 27 E
Lubefu → **250** 4 10 S 23 0 E
Lubero = Luofu **250** 0 10 S 29 15 E
Lubicon L. **90** 56 23N 115 56W
Lubicon Lake **90** 56 22N 115 52W
Lubień Kujawski **152** 52 23N 19 9 E
Lubin **152** 51 24N 16 11 E
Lublin **152** 51 12N 22 38 E
Lublin □ **152** 51 5N 22 30 E
Lubliniec **152** 50 43N 18 45 E
Lubnān, J. **190** 33 50N 35 45 E
Lubny **178** 50 3N 32 58 E
Lubon **152** 52 21N 16 51 E
Lubongola **250** 2 35 S 27 50 E
Lubotin **151** 49 17N 20 53 E
Lubraniec **152** 52 33N 18 50 E
Lubsko **152** 51 45N 14 57 E
Lübtheen **146** 53 18N 11 4 E
Lubuagan **210** 17 21N 121 10 E
Lubudi → **251** 9 0 S 25 35 E
Lubuk Antu **206** 1 3N 111 50 E
Lubuklinggau **208** 3 15 S 102 55 E
Lubuksikaping **208** 0 10N 100 15 E
Lubumbashi **251** 11 40 S 27 28 E
Lubunda **250** 5 12 S 26 41 E
Lubungu **251** 14 35 S 26 24 E
Lubutu **250** 0 45 S 26 30 E
Luc, Le **141** 43 23N 6 21 E
Luc An Chau **204** 22 6N 104 43 E
Luc-en-Diois **141** 44 36N 5 28 E
Lucala **253** 9 7 S 15 58 E
Lucan **84** 43 11N 81 24W
Lucapa **253** 8 20 S 21 45 E
Lucban **210** 14 6N 121 33 E
Lucca **162** 43 50N 10 30 E
Luce Bay **134** 54 45N 4 48W
Lucea **112** 18 25N 78 10W
Lucena, Phil. **210** 13 56N 121 37 E
Lucena, Spain **155** 37 27N 4 31W
Lucena del Cid **156** 40 9N 0 17W
Lučenec **151** 48 18N 19 42 E
Lucens **148** 46 43N 6 51 E
Lucera **165** 41 30N 15 20 E
Lucerne = Luzern **149** 47 3N 8 18 E
Lucerne **93** 52 52N 118 33W
Lucero **101** 30 49N 106 30W
Luceville **83** 48 32N 68 22W
Luchena → **157** 37 44N 1 50W
Lucheng **214** 36 20N 113 11 E
Lucheringo → **251** 11 43 S 36 17 E
Lüchow **146** 52 58N 11 8 E
Luchuan **217** 22 21N 110 12 E
Lucie → **119** 13 51 S 12 35 E
Lucira **253** 14 0 S 12 35 E
Luck L. **88** 51 5N 107 5W
Luckau **146** 51 50N 13 43 E
Luckenwalde **146** 52 5N 13 11 E
Lucknow, Canada **84** 43 57N 81 31W
Lucknow, India **199** 26 50N 81 0 E
Lucky Lake **88** 50 59N 107 8W
Luçon **140** 46 28N 1 10W
Lucusse **253** 12 32 S 20 48 E
Lüda **215** 38 50N 121 40 E
Luda Kamchiya → **167** 43 3N 27 29 E
Ludbreg **163** 46 15N 16 38 E
Lüdenscheid **146** 51 13N 7 37 E
Lüderitz **254** 26 41 S 15 8 E
Ludewe □ **251** 10 0 S 34 50 E
Ludhiana **198** 30 57N 75 56 E
Ludian **216** 27 10N 103 33 E
Luding Qiao **216** 29 53N 102 12 E
Lüdinghausen **146** 51 46N 7 28 E
Ludlow, Canada **81** 46 29N 66 21W
Ludlow, U.K. **133** 52 23N 2 42W
Ludus **170** 46 29N 24 5 E
Ludvika **172** 60 8N 15 14 E
Ludwigsburg **147** 48 53N 9 11 E
Ludwigshafen **147** 49 27N 8 27 E
Ludwigslust **146** 53 19N 11 28 E
Ludza **178** 56 32N 27 43 E
Lue **233** 32 38 S 149 50 E
Luebo **253** 5 21 S 21 23 E
Lueki **250** 3 20 S 25 48 E
Luena, Angola **253** 12 13 S 19 51 E
Luena, Zaïre **251** 9 28 S 25 43 E
Luena, Zambia **251** 10 40 S 30 25 E
Luepa **119** 5 43N 61 31W
Lüeyang **214** 33 22N 106 10 E
Lufeng, Guangdong, China **217** 22 57N 115 38 E
Lufeng, Yunnan, China **216** 25 0N 102 5 E
Lufico **253** 6 24 S 13 23 E
Lufupa **251** 10 37 S 24 56 E
Luga **178** 58 40N 29 55 E
Luga → **178** 59 40N 28 18 E
Lugang **217** 24 4N 120 23 E
Lugano **149** 46 0N 8 57 E
Lugano, L. di **149** 46 0N 9 0 E
Lugansk = Voroshilovgrad **181** 48 38N 39 15 E
Lugard's Falls **250** 3 6 S 38 41 E
Lugela **251** 16 25 S 36 43 E
Lugenda → **251** 11 25 S 38 33 E
Lugh Ganana **256** 3 48N 42 34 E
Lugnaquilla **135** 52 58N 6 28W
Lugnvik **172** 62 56N 17 55 E
Lugo, Italy **163** 44 25N 11 53 E
Lugo, Spain **154** 43 2N 7 35W
Lugo □ **154** 43 0N 7 30W
Lugoj **166** 45 42N 21 57 E
Lugones **154** 43 26N 5 50W
Lugovoye **183** 42 55N 72 43 E
Luhe **217** 32 19N 118 50 E
Luhe → **146** 53 18N 10 11 E
Luhuo **216** 31 21N 100 48 E
Luiana **254** 17 25 S 22 59 E
Luino **162** 46 0N 8 42 E
Luís Correia **120** 3 0 S 41 35W
Luís Gonçalves **120** 5 37 S 50 25W
Luis Moya, Durango, Mexico **105** 24 32N 103 57W
Luis Moya, Zacatecas, Mexico **105** 22 25N 102 15W
Luitpold Coast **13** 78 30 S 32 0W
Luize **253** 7 40 S 22 30 E
Luizi **250** 6 0 S 27 25 E
Luján **124** 34 45 S 59 5W
Lujiang **217** 31 20N 117 15 E
Lukala **253** 5 31 S 14 32 E
Lukanga Swamps **251** 14 30 S 27 40 E
Lukenie → **252** 3 0 S 18 50 E
Lukhisaral **199** 25 11N 86 5 E
Lŭki **167** 41 50N 24 43 E
Lukk **242** 32 1N 24 46 E
Lukolela, Equateur, Zaïre **252** 1 10 S 17 12 E
Lukolela, Kasai Or., Zaïre **250** 5 23 S 24 32 E
Lukosi **251** 18 30 S 26 30 E
Lukovit **167** 43 13N 24 11 E
Łuków **152** 51 55N 22 23 E
Lukoyanov **179** 55 2N 44 29 E
Lule älv → **174** 65 35N 22 10 E
Luleå **174** 65 35N 22 10 E
Lüleburgaz **167** 41 23N 27 22 E
Luliang **216** 25 0N 103 40 E
Lulong **215** 39 53N 118 51 E
Lulonga → **252** 1 0N 19 0 E
Lulua → **253** 6 30 S 22 50 E
Luluabourg = Kananga **253** 5 55 S 22 18 E
Luma **226** 14 15 S 169 32W
Lumai **253** 13 13 S 21 25 E
Lumajang **209** 8 8 S 113 13 E
Lumbala Kaquengue **253** 12 39 S 22 34 E
Lumbala N'guimbo **253** 14 18 S 21 18 E
Lumbres **139** 50 40N 2 5 E
Lumbwa **250** 0 12 S 35 28 E
Lumby **76** 50 10N 118 50W
Lumding **202** 25 46N 93 10 E
Lumi **227** 3 30 S 142 2 E
Lummen **143** 50 59N 5 12 E
Lumsden, Newf., Canada **79** 49 19N 53 37W
Lumsden, Sask., Canada **88** 50 39N 104 52W
Lumsden, N.Z. **235** 45 44 S 168 27 E
Lumut **205** 4 13N 100 37 E
Lumut, Tg. **208** 3 50 S 105 58 E
Luna, Luzon, Phil. **210** 18 18N 121 21 E
Luna, Luzon, Phil. **210** 16 51N 120 23 E
Lunan **216** 24 40N 103 18 E
Lunavada **198** 23 8N 73 37 E
Lunca **170** 47 22N 25 1 E
Lund, Canada **92** 49 59N 124 45W
Lund, Sweden **172** 55 44N 13 12 E
Lunda Norte □ **253** 8 0 S 20 0 E
Lunda Sul □ **253** 10 0 S 20 0 E
Lundar **89** 50 42N 98 2W
Lundazi **251** 12 20 S 33 7 E
Lundbreck **91** 49 35N 114 10W
Lunde **171** 59 17N 9 5 E
Lunderskov **173** 55 29N 9 19 E
Lundi → **251** 21 43 S 32 34 E
Lundu **206** 1 40N 109 50 E
Lundy **133** 51 10N 4 41W
Lune → **132** 54 0N 2 51W
Lüneburg **146** 53 15N 10 23 E
Lüneburg Heath = Lüneburger Heide **146** 53 0N 10 0 E
Lüneburger Heide **146** 53 0N 10 0 E
Lunel **141** 43 39N 4 9 E
Lünen **146** 51 36N 7 31 E
Lunenburg **81** 44 22N 64 18W
Lunéville **139** 48 36N 6 30 E
Lunga → **251** 14 34 S 26 25 E
Lungern **148** 46 48N 8 10 E
Lungi Airport **246** 8 40N 13 17W
Lunglei **202** 22 55N 92 45 E
Lungngo **202** 21 57N 93 36 E
Luni **198** 26 0N 73 6 E
Lūni → **198** 24 41N 71 14 E
Luninets **178** 52 15N 26 50 E
Lunino **179** 53 35N 45 6 E
Lunner **171** 60 19N 10 35 E
Lunsemfwa → **251** 14 54 S 30 12 E
Lunsemfwa Falls **251** 14 30 S 29 6 E
Lunteren **142** 52 5N 5 38 E
Luo He → **214** 34 35N 110 20 E
Luocheng **216** 24 48N 108 53 E
Luochuan **214** 35 45N 109 26 E
Luoci **216** 25 19N 102 18 E
Luodian **216** 25 24N 106 43 E
Luoding **217** 22 45N 111 40 E
Luodong **217** 24 41N 121 46 E
Luofu **250** 0 10 S 29 15 E
Luohe **214** 33 32N 114 2 E
Luojiang **216** 31 18N 104 33 E
Luonan **214** 34 5N 110 10 E
Luoning **214** 34 35N 111 40 E
Luoshan **217** 32 13N 114 30 E
Luotian **217** 30 46N 115 22 E
Luoyang **214** 34 40N 112 26 E
Luoyuan **217** 26 28N 119 30 E
Luozi **253** 4 54 S 14 0 E
Luozigou **215** 43 42N 130 18 E
Lupeni **170** 45 21N 23 13 E
Lupilichi **251** 11 47 S 35 13 E
Lupire **253** 14 36 S 19 29 E
Łupków **151** 49 15N 22 4 E
Lupoing **216** 24 53N 104 21 E
Lupon **211** 6 54N 126 0 E
Luquan **216** 25 35N 102 25 E
Luque, Paraguay **124** 25 19 S 57 25W
Luque, Spain **155** 37 35N 4 16W
Lure **139** 47 40N 6 30 E
Luremo **253** 8 30 S 17 50 E
Lurgan **135** 54 28N 6 20W
Luribay **122** 17 6 S 67 39W
Lurin **122** 12 17 S 76 52W
Lusaka **251** 15 28 S 28 16 E
Lusambo **250** 4 58 S 23 28 E
Lusangaye **250** 4 54 S 26 0 E
Luscar **91** 53 4N 117 24W
Luseland **88** 52 5N 109 24W
Lushan, Henan, China **214** 33 45N 112 55 E
Lushan, Sichuan, China **216** 30 12N 102 52 E
Lushih **214** 34 3N 111 3 E
Lushnja **168** 40 55N 19 41 E
Lushoto **250** 4 47 S 38 20 E
Lushoto □ **250** 4 45 S 38 20 E
Lushui **216** 25 58N 98 44 E
Lüshun **215** 38 45N 121 15 E
Lusignan **140** 46 26N 0 8 E
Lusigny-sur-Barse **139** 48 16N 4 15 E
Lussac-les-Châteaux **140** 46 24N 0 43 E
Lussanvira **121** 20 42 S 51 7W
Luta = Lüda **215** 38 50N 121 40 E
Lutembo **253** 13 26 S 21 16 E
Luton **133** 51 53N 0 24W
Lutong **206** 4 28N 114 0 E
Lutry **148** 46 31N 6 42 E
Lutsk **178** 50 50N 25 15 E
Lutuai **253** 12 41 S 20 7 E
Lützow Holmbukta **13** 69 10 S 37 30 E
Luvo **253** 5 51 S 14 5 E
Luvua **251** 8 48 S 25 17 E
Luvua → **250** 6 50 S 27 30 E
Luwegu → **251** 8 31 S 37 23 E
Luwuk **207** 0 56 S 122 47 E
Luxembourg **143** 49 37N 6 9 E
Luxembourg □ **143** 49 58N 5 30 E
Luxembourg ■ **143** 50 0N 6 0 E
Luxeuil-les-Bains **139** 47 49N 6 24 E
Luxi, Hunan, China **217** 28 20N 110 7 E
Luxi, Yunnan, China **216** 24 40N 103 55 E
Luxi, Yunnan, China **216** 24 27N 98 36 E
Luxor = El Uqsur **244** 25 41N 32 38 E
Luy → **140** 43 39N 1 9W
Luy-de-Béarn → **140** 43 39N 0 48W
Luy-de-France → **140** 43 39N 0 48W
Luyi **214** 33 50N 115 35 E
Luyksgestel **143** 51 17N 5 20 E
Luz, La **106** 20 27N 102 44W
Luz-St-Sauveur **140** 42 53N 0 1 E
Luza **176** 60 39N 47 10 E
Luzern **149** 47 3N 8 18 E
Luzern □ **148** 47 2N 7 55 E
Luzhai **216** 24 29N 109 42 E
Luzhou **216** 28 52N 105 20 E
Luziânia **121** 16 20 S 48 0W
Luzilândia **120** 3 28 S 42 22W
Luzon **210** 16 0N 121 0 E
Luzon Strait **210** 21 0N 122 0 E
Luzy **139** 46 47N 3 58 E
Luzzi **165** 39 28N 16 17 E
Lvov **178** 49 50N 24 0 E
Lwówek **152** 52 28N 16 10 E
Lwówek Śląski **152** 51 7N 15 38 E
Lyakhovichi **178** 53 2N 26 32 E
Lyakhovskiye, Ostrova **185** 73 40N 141 0 E
Lyaki **181** 40 34N 47 22 E
Lyal I. **84** 44 57N 81 24W
Lyall Mt. **235** 45 16 S 167 32 E
Lyallpur = Faisalabad **197** 31 30N 73 5 E
Lyalya → **182** 59 9N 61 29 E
Lyaskovets **167** 43 6N 25 44 E
Lychen **146** 53 13N 13 20 E
Lyckeby **173** 56 12N 15 37 E
Lycksele **174** 64 38N 18 40 E
Lycosura **169** 37 20N 22 3 E
Lydda = Lod **189** 31 57N 34 54 E
Lydenburg **255** 25 10 S 30 29 E
Lyell **235** 41 48 S 172 4 E
Lyell I. **92** 52 40N 131 35W
Lyell Range **235** 41 38 S 172 20 E
Lygnern **173** 57 30N 12 15 E
Lykling **171** 59 42N 5 12 E

Lymburn **90** 55 21N 119 47W
Lyme Regis........ **133** 50 44N 2 57W
Lymington.... .... **133** 50 46N 1 32W
Łyńa → .... **152** 54 37N 21 14 E
Lynd → .... **230** 16 28 S 143 18 E
Lynd Ra........... **231** 25 30 S 149 20 E
Lyndhurst .... **231** 30 15 S 138 18 E
Lyndon → .... **229** 23 29 S 114 6 E
Lyngdal, Aust-Agder, Norway .... **171** 58 8N 7 7 E
Lyngdal, Buskerud, Norway .... **171** 59 54N 9 32 E
Lynher Reef .... **228** 15 27 S 121 55 E
Lynn Lake......... **77** 56 51N 101 3W
Lynton **133** 51 14N 3 50W
Lyntupy .... **178** 55 4N 26 23 E
Lynx L. **77** 62 25N 106 15W
Lyø .... **173** 55 3N 10 9 E
Lyon .... **141** 45 46N 4 50 E
Lyonnais .... **141** 45 45N 4 15 E
Lyons = Lyon ..... **141** 45 46N 4 50 E
Lyrestad........... **173** 58 48N 14 4 E
Lys → .... **139** 50 39N 2 24 E
Lysá .... **150** 50 11N 14 51 E
Lysekil .... **173** 58 17N 11 26 E
Lyskovo .... **179** 56 0N 45 3 E
Lyss .... **148** 47 4N 7 19 E
Lyster............. **83** 46 22N 71 37W
Lysva .... **182** 58 7N 57 49 E
Lysvik .... **172** 60 1N 13 9 E
Lyttelton .... **235** 43 35 S 172 44 E
Lytton **93** 50 13N 121 31W
Lyuban............ **178** 59 16N 31 18 E
Lyubcha........... **178** 53 46N 26 1 E
Lyubertsy .... **179** 55 39N 37 50 E
Lyubim .... **179** 58 20N 40 39 E
Lyubimets .... **167** 41 50N 26 5 E
Lyuboml .... **178** 51 11N 24 4 E
Lyubotin .... **180** 50 0N 36 0 E
Lyubytino .... **178** 58 50N 33 16 E
Lyudinovo......... **178** 53 52N 34 28 E

M

Ma → .... **204** 19 47N 105 56 E
Ma-Me-O Beach ... **91** 52 58N 113 59W
Mā'ad............. **189** 32 37N 35 36 E
Ma'adaba.......... **191** 30 43N 35 47 E
Maamba........... **254** 17 17 S 26 28 E
Ma'ān............. **191** 30 12N 35 44 E
Ma'ān □ .... **191** 30 0N 36 0 E
Ma'anshan......... **217** 31 44N 118 29 E
Maarheeze......... **143** 51 19N 5 36 E
Maarn .... **142** 52 3N 5 22 E
Ma'arrat........... **190** 36 2N 36 49 E
Ma'arrat an Nu'mān **190** 35 43N 36 43 E
Maarssen .... **142** 52 9N 5 2 E
Maartensdijk....... **142** 52 9N 5 10 E
Maas → .... **142** 51 45N 4 32 E
Maasbracht .... **143** 51 9N 5 54 E
Maasbree.......... **143** 51 22N 6 3 E
Maasdam .... **142** 51 48N 4 34 E
Maasdijk .... **142** 51 58N 4 13 E
Maaseik .... **143** 51 6N 5 45 E
Maasland .... **142** 51 57N 4 16 E
Maasniel .... **143** 51 12N 6 1 E
Maassluis .... **142** 51 56N 4 16 E
Maastricht .... **143** 50 50N 5 40 E
Maave .... **255** 21 4 S 34 47 E
Ma'bar .... **194** 14 48N 44 17 E
Mabaruma......... **119** 8 10N 59 50W
Mabein............ **202** 23 29N 96 37 E
Mabel L. **93** 50 35N 118 43W
Mabenge .... **250** 4 15N 24 12 E
Maberly **85** 44 50N 76 32W
Mabian............ **216** 28 47N 103 37 E
Mablethorpe .... **132** 53 21N 0 14 E
Maboma .... **250** 2 30N 28 10 E
Mabou **81** 46 4N 61 29W
Maboukou......... **252** 3 39 S 12 31 E
Mabrouk **247** 19 29N 1 15W
Mabungo .... **256** 0 49N 42 35 E
Mac Bac .... **205** 9 46N 106 7 E
Macachín .... **124** 37 10 S 63 43W
McAdam **81** 45 36N 67 20W
Macaé .... **121** 22 20 S 41 43W
Macaíba .... **120** 5 51 S 35 21W
Macajuba .... **121** 12 9 S 40 22W
Macalelon .... **210** 13 45N 122 8 E
Macalister **93** 52 27N 122 24W
Macamic **82** 48 45N 79 0W
Macão **155** 39 35N 7 59W
Macapá **119** 0 5N 51 4W
Macará............ **118** 4 23 S 79 57W
Macarani .... **121** 15 33 S 40 24W
Macarena, Serranía de la **118** 2 45N 73 55W
Macarthur .... **232** 38 5 S 142 0 E
McArthur → ...... **230** 15 54 S 136 40 E
McArthur River .... **230** 16 27 S 136 7 E
Macas............. **118** 2 19 S 78 7W
Macate .... **122** 8 48 S 78 7W
Macau .... **120** 5 0 S 36 40W
Macaúbas .... **121** 13 2 S 42 42W
McAuley **89** 50 16N 101 23W
Macaya → **118** 0 59N 72 20W
McBride........... **93** 53 20N 120 19W
McCallum **79** 47 38N 56 14W
Maccan **81** 45 43N 64 15W
McCauley I. **92** 53 40N 130 15W
McClelland L. **90** 57 29N 111 20W
Macclesfield **132** 53 16N 2 9W
McClintock **77** 57 50N 94 10W
McClintock Ra. .... **228** 18 44 S 127 38 E
McClure Str........ **94** 75 0N 119 0W
McCreary **89** 50 46N 99 29W
McCusker → **77** 55 32N 108 39W
McDame **76** 59 44N 128 59W
Macdiarmid **86** 49 26N 88 8W
McDonald Is. ...... **203** 54 0 S 73 0 E
Macdonald L. ...... **228** 23 30 S 129 0 E
Macdonnell Ranges **228** 23 40 S 133 0 E
McDouall Peak .... **231** 29 51 S 134 55 E
Macdougall L. **95** 66 0N 98 27W
McDougalls Well ... **232** 31 8 S 141 15 E
MacDowell L. **74** 52 15N 92 45W
Macduff **134** 57 40N 2 30W
Macdun **88** 49 19N 103 16W
Maceda **154** 42 16N 7 39W
Macedonia = Makedhonía □ ... **168** 40 39N 22 0 E
Macedonia = Makedonija □ ... **166** 41 53N 21 40 E
Maceió .... **120** 9 40 S 35 41W
Maceira **155** 39 41N 8 55W
Macenta **246** 8 35N 9 32W
Macerata .... **163** 43 19N 13 28 E
Maces Bay......... **81** 45 6N 66 29W
McFarlane → **77** 59 12N 107 58W
Macfarlane, L. ..... **231** 32 0 S 136 40 E
Macgillycuddy's Reeks **135** 52 2N 9 45W
MacGregor **89** 49 57N 98 48W
McGregor → **76** 55 10N 122 0W
McGregor L. **91** 50 25N 112 52W
McGregor Ra. ..... **231** 27 0 S 142 45 E
Māch Kowr .... **193** 25 48N 61 28 E
Machacalis......... **121** 17 5 S 40 45W
Machado = Jiparaná → ..... **123** 8 3 S 62 52W
Machagai .... **124** 26 56 S 60 2W
Machakos .... **250** 1 30 S 37 15 E
Machakos □ .... **250** 1 30 S 37 15 E
Machala .... **118** 3 20 S 79 57W
Machanga .... **255** 20 59 S 35 0 E
Machattie, L. ...... **230** 24 50 S 139 48 E
Machava .... **255** 25 54 S 32 28 E
Machece .... **251** 19 15 S 35 32 E
Machecoul......... **138** 47 0N 1 49W
Machelen.......... **143** 50 55N 4 26 E
Macheng .... **217** 31 12N 115 2 E
Machevna .... **185** 61 20N 172 20 E
Machezo **155** 39 21N 4 20W
Machichaco, Cabo .. **156** 43 28N 2 47W
Machichi → **77** 57 3N 92 6W
Machida........... **221** 35 28N 139 23 E
Machilipatnam ..... **201** 16 12N 81 8 E
Machine, La .... **139** 46 54N 3 27 E
Machiques......... **118** 10 4N 72 34W
Machona, L. **110** 18 20N 93 40W
Machupicchu....... **122** 13 8 S 72 30W
Machynlleth **133** 52 36N 3 51W
Maciejowice .... **152** 51 36N 21 26 E
McIlwraith Ra...... **230** 13 50 S 143 20 E
Măcin............. **170** 45 16N 28 8 E
Macina **246** 14 50N 5 0W
McIntosh **86** 49 57N 93 36W
McIntosh L. **77** 55 45N 105 0W
Macintyre → ...... **231** 28 37 S 150 47 E
McIntyre B. **92** 54 5N 132 0W
Macizo Galaico **154** 42 30N 7 30W
Mackay, Australia .. **230** 21 8 S 149 11 E
Mackay, Canada ... **90** 53 39N 115 35W
Mackay → **90** 57 10N 111 38W
Mackay, L. .... **228** 22 30 S 129 0 E
McKay L. **87** 49 37N 86 25W
McKay Ra. .... **229** 23 0 S 122 30 E
McKellar **84** 45 30N 79 55W
Mackenzie, Canada . **76** 55 20N 123 5W
Mackenzie, Guyana . **119** 6 0N 58 17W
Mackenzie →, Australia .... **230** 23 38 S 149 46 E
Mackenzie →, Canada........... **94** 69 10N 134 20W
Mackenzie Bay..... **94** 69 0N 137 30W
Mackenzie City = Linden **122** 6 0N 58 10W
Mackenzie Highway **76** 58 0N 117 15W
Mackenzie King I. .. **94** 77 45N 111 0W
McKenzie L. **88** 54 12N 102 30W
Mackenzie Mts. **94** 64 0N 130 0W
Mackenzie Plains .. **235** 44 10 S 170 25W
McKerrow L. ...... **235** 44 25 S 168 5 E
McKinlay.......... **230** 21 16 S 141 18 E
McKinlay → ...... **230** 20 50 S 141 28 E
McKinley Sea **12** 84 0N 10 0W
Mackinnon Road ... **250** 3 40 S 39 1 E
Mackintosh Ra. .... **229** 27 39 S 125 32 E
Macklin **88** 52 20N 109 56W
Macksville .... **231** 30 40 S 152 56 E
McLaren Vale ..... **232** 35 13 S 138 31 E
Maclean .... **231** 29 26 S 153 16 E
McLean **88** 50 31N 104 4W
Maclean Str........ **95** 77 30N 103 30W
Maclear .... **255** 31 2 S 28 23 E
Macleay → .... **231** 30 56 S 153 0 E
McLennan......... **90** 55 42N 116 50W
McLeod → **90** 54 9N 115 42W
MacLeod, B. **77** 62 53N 110 0W
McLeod L. .... **234** 24 9 S 113 47 E
MacLeod Lake **76** 54 58N 123 0W
M'Clintock Chan. .. **94** 72 0N 102 0W
Maclovio Herrera .. **101** 29 5N 105 8W
McLure **93** 51 2N 120 13W
McMorran......... **88** 51 19N 108 42W
McMurdo Sd. ...... **13** 77 0 S 170 0 E
McMurray = Fort McMurray **90** 56 44N 111 7W
McNaughton L. **93** 52 0N 118 10W
MacNutt **89** 51 5N 101 36W
Maco .... **211** 7 20N 125 50 E
Macocolo.......... **253** 6 47 S 16 8 E
Macodoene .... **255** 23 32 S 35 5 E
Macomer .... **164** 40 16N 8 48 E
Mâcon .... **141** 46 19N 4 50 E
Macondo .... **253** 12 37 S 23 46 E
Macossa........... **251** 17 55 S 33 56 E
Macoun L. **77** 56 32N 103 40W
Macovane .... **255** 21 30 S 35 0 E
Macpherson Ra..... **231** 28 15 S 153 15 E
Macquarie Harbour . **230** 42 15 S 145 23 E
Macquarie Is. ...... **224** 54 36 S 158 55 E
MacRobertson Land **13** 71 0 S 64 0 E
Macroom **135** 51 54N 8 57W
Macroy .... **228** 20 53 S 118 2 E
MacTier **84** 45 8N 79 47W
Macubela.......... **251** 16 53 S 37 49 E
Macugnaga .... **162** 45 57N 7 58 E
Macuiza........... **251** 18 7 S 34 29 E
Macujer **118** 0 24N 73 10W
Macun .... **190** 36 56N 30 51 E
Macusani .... **122** 14 4 S 70 29W
Macuse............ **251** 17 45 S 37 10 E
Macuspana **110** 17 46N 92 36W
Macusse .... **254** 17 48 S 20 23 E
Madadi .... **243** 18 28N 20 45 E
Madagali .... **247** 10 56N 13 33 E
Madagascar ■ ..... **255** 20 0 S 47 0 E
Madā'in Sālih ..... **192** 26 46N 37 57 E
Madalag........... **211** 11 32N 122 18 E
Madama........... **241** 22 0N 13 40 E
Madame I. **81** 45 30N 60 58W
Madan .... **167** 41 30N 24 57 E
Madanapalle .... **201** 13 33N 78 28 E
Madang .... **227** 5 12 S 145 49 E
Madaoua .... **247** 14 5N 6 27 E
Madara .... **247** 11 45N 10 35 E
Madaripur .... **202** 23 19N 90 15 E
Madauk .... **202** 17 56N 96 52 E
Madawaska **85** 45 30N 77 55W
Madawaska → **85** 45 27N 76 21W
Madaya .... **202** 22 12N 96 10 E
Madbar .... **245** 6 17N 30 45 E
Maddalena .... **164** 41 15N 9 23 E
Maddalena, La ..... **164** 41 13N 9 25 E
Maddaloni......... **165** 41 4N 14 23 E
Made .... **143** 51 41N 4 49 E
Madeira **240** 32 50N 17 0W
Madeira → .... **119** 3 22 S 58 45W
Madeira Park **92** 49 37N 124 0W
Madeleine → **80** 49 15N 65 19W
Madeleine, Îs. de la **81** 47 30N 61 40W
Madeleine-Centre .. **80** 49 15N 65 22W
Madera **101** 29 12N 108 7W
Madera, Sa. de la .. **100** 30 25N 109 7W
Madero **102** 25 42N 102 13W
Madgaon .... **201** 15 12N 73 58 E
Madha .... **200** 18 0N 75 30 E
Madhubani .... **199** 26 21N 86 7 E
Madhumati → .... **202** 22 53N 89 52 E
Madhya Pradesh □ . **198** 21 50N 81 0 E
Madian............ **217** 33 0N 116 6 E
Madidi → .... **122** 12 32 S 66 52W
Madikeri .... **201** 12 30N 75 45 E
Madimba, Angola .. **253** 6 36 S 14 23 E
Madimba, Zaïre .... **253** 5 0 S 15 0 E
Ma'din .... **192** 35 45N 39 36 E
Madīnat ash Sha'b . **194** 12 50N 45 0 E
Madingou .... **252** 4 10 S 13 33 E
Madîq Gûbâl ...... **191** 27 47N 33 55 E
Madîq Tirân ...... **191** 27 55N 34 30 E
Madirovalo .... **255** 16 26 S 46 32 E
Madista .... **254** 21 15 S 25 6 E
Madiun .... **209** 7 38 S 111 32 E
Madley............ **133** 52 3N 2 51W
Madoc **85** 44 30N 77 28W
Madol............. **245** 9 3N 27 45 E
Madon → .... **139** 48 36N 6 6 E
Madona .... **178** 56 53N 26 5 E
Madonie, Le .... **164** 37 50N 13 50 E
Madrakah, Ra's al .. **195** 19 0N 57 50 E
Madras = Tamil Nadu □ .... **201** 11 0N 77 0 E
Madras............ **201** 13 8N 80 19 E
Madre, L. **103** 25 0N 97 40W
Madre, Sa. **110** 16 48N 94 32W
Madre, Sierra ...... **210** 17 0N 122 0 E
Madre de Dios □... **122** 12 0 S 70 15W
Madre de Dios → . **122** 10 59 S 66 8W
Madre de Dios, I. .. **126** 50 20 S 75 10W
Madre del Sur, Sa. . **107** 17 0N 100 0W
Madre Occidental, Sa. **104** 25 0N 105 0W
Madre Oriental, Sa. **103** 22 0N 99 30W
Madri .... **198** 24 16N 73 32 E
Madrid **154** 40 25N 3 45W
Madrid □ **154** 40 30N 3 45W
Madridejos **155** 39 28N 3 33W
Madrigal de las Altas Torres **154** 41 5N 5 0W
Madrona, Sierra.... **155** 38 27N 4 16W
Madroñera **155** 39 26N 5 42W
Madsen **86** 50 58N 93 55W
Madu .... **245** 14 37N 26 4 E
Madura, Selat...... **209** 7 30 S 113 20 E
Madura Motel ..... **229** 31 55 S 127 0 E
Madurai........... **201** 9 55N 78 10 E
Madurantakam..... **201** 12 30N 79 50 E
Madzhalis .... **181** 42 9N 47 47 E
Mae Chan .... **204** 20 9N 99 52 E
Mae Hong Son..... **204** 19 16N 98 1 E
Mae Khlong → .... **204** 13 24N 100 0 E
Mae Phrik .... **204** 17 27N 99 7 E
Mae Ramat .... **204** 16 58N 98 31 E
Mae Rim .... **204** 18 54N 98 57 E
Mae Sot .... **204** 16 43N 98 34 E
Mae Suai .... **204** 19 39N 99 33 E
Mae Tha .... **204** 18 28N 99 8 E
Maebaru .... **220** 33 33N 130 12 E
Maebashi.......... **221** 36 24N 139 4 E
Maella .... **156** 41 8N 0 7 E
Măeruş............ **170** 45 53N 25 31 E
Maesteg........... **133** 51 36N 3 40W
Maestra, Sierra..... **112** 20 15N 77 0W
Maestrazgo, Mts. del.............. **156** 40 30N 0 25W
Maestre de Campo I. .... **210** 12 56N 121 42 E
Maevatanana ...... **255** 16 56N 46 49 E
Ma'fan .... **241** 25 56N 14 29 E
Mafeking **89** 52 40N 101 10W
Maféré **246** 5 30N 3 2W
Mafeteng .... **254** 29 51 S 27 15 E
Maffe .... **143** 50 21N 5 19 E
Maffra .... **231** 37 53 S 146 58 E
Mafia .... **250** 7 45 S 39 50 E
Mafikeng .... **254** 25 50 S 25 38 E
Mafra, Brazil ...... **125** 26 10 S 50 0W
Mafra, Portugal **155** 38 55N 9 20W
Mafungabusi Plateau **251** 18 30 S 29 8 E
Magadan .... **185** 59 38N 150 50 E
Magadi............ **250** 1 54 S 36 19 E
Magadi, L. .... **250** 1 54 S 36 19 E
Magaguadavic...... **81** 45 42N 67 12W
Magaguadavic → .. **81** 45 7N 66 54W
Magaguadavic L. .. **81** 45 43N 67 12W
Magaliesburg ...... **255** 26 1 S 27 32 E
Magallanes .... **210** 12 50N 123 50 E
Magallanes □ ...... **126** 52 0 S 72 0W
Magallanes, Estrecho de...... **126** 52 30 S 75 0W
Magangué **118** 9 14N 74 45W
Maganoy .... **211** 6 51N 124 31 E
Mağara............ **190** 36 43N 33 52 E
Magaria .... **247** 13 4N 9 5 E
Magburaka **246** 8 47N 12 0W
Magdalena, Argentina .... **124** 35 5 S 57 30W
Magdalena, Bolivia . **123** 13 13 S 63 57W
Magdalena, Malaysia .... **206** 4 25N 117 55 E
Magdalena, Jalisco, Mexico.......... **106** 20 55N 103 57W
Magdalena, Sonora, Mexico.......... **100** 30 38N 110 57W
Magdalena □ **118** 10 0N 74 0W
Magdalena → **118** 11 6N 74 51W
Magdalena, B. **99** 24 35N 112 0W
Magdalena, I. ...... **126** 44 40 S 73 0W
Magdalena, Llano de la **99** 25 0N 111 25W
Magdalena, R. → . **100** 30 48N 112 32W
Magdalena, Sa. de la............... **104** 24 45N 105 13W
Magdalena Apasco . **109** 17 13N 96 49W
Magdalena Tequisistlán...... **109** 16 22N 95 15W
Magdeburg .... **146** 52 8N 11 36 E
Magdeburg □ ...... **146** 52 20N 11 30 E
Magdelaine Cays ... **230** 16 33 S 150 18 E
Magdi'el........... **189** 32 10N 34 54 E
Magdub .... **245** 13 42N 25 5 E

Magee, I. **135** 54 48N 5 44W
Magelang **209** 7 29 S 110 13 E
Magellan's Str. = Magallanes, Estrecho de **126** 52 30 S 75 0W
Magenta, Australia **232** 33 51 S 143 34 E
Magenta, Italy **162** 45 28N 8 53 E
Magenta, L. **229** 33 30 S 119 2 E
Maggea **232** 34 28 S 140 2 E
Maggia **149** 46 15N 8 42 E
Maggia → **149** 46 18N 8 36 E
Maggiorasca, Mte. **162** 44 33N 9 29 E
Maggiore, L. **162** 46 0N 8 35 E
Maghama **246** 15 32N 12 57W
Maghâr **189** 32 54N 35 24 E
Magherafelt **135** 54 44N 6 37W
Maghnia **241** 34 50N 1 43W
Magione **163** 43 10N 12 12 E
Magiscatzin **103** 22 48N 98 42W
Magistral **104** 25 59N 105 24W
Maglaj **166** 44 33N 18 7 E
Magliano in Toscana **163** 42 36N 11 18 E
Máglie **165** 40 8N 18 17 E
Magnac-Laval **140** 46 13N 1 11 E
Magnetawan **84** 45 40N 79 39W
Magnetic Pole (North) **12** 76 12N 100 12W
Magnetic Pole (South) **13** 68 48 S 139 30 E
Magnisía □ **168** 39 15N 22 45 E
Magnitogorsk **182** 53 27N 59 4 E
Magnor **171** 59 56N 12 15 E
Magny-en-Vexin **139** 49 9N 1 47 E
Magog **83** 45 18N 72 9W
Magoro **250** 1 45N 34 12 E
Magosa = Famagusta **190** 35 8N 33 55 E
Magosal **108** 21 34N 97 59W
Magoye **251** 16 1 S 27 30 E
Magpie **80** 50 19N 64 30W
Magpie →, Ont., Canada **87** 47 56N 84 50W
Magpie →, Qué., Canada **80** 50 19N 64 27W
Magpie L. **80** 51 0N 64 41W
Magrath **91** 49 25N 112 50W
Magro → **157** 39 11N 0 25W
Magrur, Wadi → **245** 16 5N 26 30 E
Magsingal **210** 17 41N 120 25 E
Magu □ **250** 2 31 S 33 28 E
Maguan **216** 23 0N 104 21 E
Maguarinho, C. **120** 0 15 S 48 30W
Magueyes **102** 25 44N 97 47W
Maguindanao □ **211** 7 5N 124 0 E
Maguse L. **77** 61 40N 95 10W
Maguse Pt. **77** 61 20N 93 50W
Magwe **202** 20 10N 95 0 E
Maha Sarakham **204** 16 12N 103 16 E
Mahābād **192** 36 50N 45 45 E
Mahabaleshwar **200** 17 58N 73 43 E
Mahabharat Lekh **199** 28 30N 82 0 E
Mahabo **255** 20 23 S 44 40 E
Mahad **200** 18 6N 73 29 E
Mahaddei Uen **256** 2 58N 45 32 E
Mahadeo Hills **198** 22 20N 78 30 E
Mahadeopur **200** 18 48N 80 0 E
Mahagi **250** 2 20N 31 0 E
Mahaicony **119** 6 36N 57 48W
Mahajamba → **255** 15 33 S 47 8 E
Mahajamba, Helodranon' i **255** 15 24 S 47 5 E
Mahajan **198** 28 48N 73 56 E
Mahajanga □ **255** 17 0 S 47 0 E
Mahajilo → **255** 19 42 S 45 22 E
Mahakam → **209** 0 35 S 117 17 E
Mahalapye **254** 23 1 S 26 51 E
Maḩallāt **193** 33 55N 50 30 E
Māhān **193** 30 5N 57 18 E
Mahanadi → **199** 20 20N 86 25 E
Mahanoro **255** 19 54 S 48 48 E
Mahaplag **211** 10 35N 124 57 E
Maharashtra □ **200** 20 30N 75 30 E
Maharès **241** 34 32N 10 29 E
Mahari Mts. **250** 6 20 S 30 0 E
Mahasham, W. → **191** 30 15N 34 10 E
Mahasolo **255** 19 7 S 46 22 E
Mahatta River **92** 50 22N 127 47W
Mahattat ash Shīdīyah **191** 29 55N 35 55 E
Mahattat 'Unayzah **191** 30 30N 35 47 E
Mahaweli → **201** 8 30N 81 15 E
Mahaxay **204** 17 22N 105 12 E
Mahbes **240** 27 10N 9 50W
Mahbubabad **200** 17 42N 80 2 E
Mahbubnagar **200** 16 45N 77 59 E
Maḩḑah **195** 24 24N 55 59 E
Mahdia, Guyana **119** 5 13N 59 8W
Mahdia, Tunisia **241** 35 28N 11 0 E
Mahé, Ind. Oc. **203** 5 0 S 55 30 E
Mahé, India **201** 11 42N 75 34 E
Mahe, Kashmir **199** 33 10N 78 32 E
Mahendra Giri **201** 8 20N 77 30 E
Mahendraganj **202** 25 20N 89 45 E
Mahenge **251** 8 45 S 36 41 E
Maheno **235** 45 10 S 170 50 E
Mahesana **198** 23 39N 72 26 E
Mahia Pen. **234** 39 9 S 177 55 E
Mahirija **241** 34 0N 3 16W
Mahlaing **202** 21 6N 95 39 E
Mahmiya **245** 17 12N 33 43 E
Mahmud Kot **198** 30 16N 71 0 E
Mahmudia **170** 45 5N 29 5 E
Mahoba **199** 25 15N 79 55 E
Mahón **156** 39 53N 4 16 E
Mahone Bay **75** 44 30N 64 20W
Mahood Falls **93** 51 50N 120 38W
Mahood L. **93** 51 50N 120 23W
Mahuta **247** 11 32N 4 58 E
Mai-Ndombe, L. **252** 2 0 S 18 20 E
Mai-Sai **204** 20 20N 99 55 E
Maibara **221** 35 19N 136 17 E
Maicao **118** 11 23N 72 13W
Maicasagi → **82** 49 58N 76 33W
Maïche **139** 47 16N 6 48 E
Maici → **123** 6 30 S 61 43W
Maicurú → **119** 2 14 S 54 17W
Máida **165** 38 51N 16 21 E
Maidan Khula **198** 33 36N 69 50 E
Maidenhead **133** 51 31N 0 42W
Maidi **245** 16 20N 42 45 E
Maidstone, Canada **88** 53 5N 109 20W
Maidstone, U.K. **133** 51 16N 0 31 E
Maiduguri **247** 12 0N 13 20 E
Maignelay **139** 49 32N 2 30 E
Maigo **211** 8 10N 123 57 E
Maigualida, Sierra **119** 5 30N 65 10W
Maigudo **245** 7 30N 37 8 E
Maijdi **202** 22 48N 91 10 E
Maikala Ra. **199** 22 0N 81 0 E
Mailly-le-Camp **139** 48 41N 4 12 E
Mailsi **198** 29 48N 72 15 E
Maimbung **211** 5 56N 121 2 E
Main →, Germany **147** 50 0N 8 18 E
Main →, U.K. **135** 54 49N 6 20W
Main-à-Dieu **81** 46 0N 59 51W
Main Brook **79** 51 11N 56 1W
Main Centre **88** 50 35N 107 21W
Mainburg **147** 48 37N 11 49 E
Maine **138** 48 0N 0 0 E
Maine → **135** 52 10N 9 40W
Maine-et-Loire □ **138** 47 31N 0 30W
Maïne-Soroa **247** 13 13N 12 2 E
Maingkwan **202** 26 15N 96 37 E
Mainit **211** 9 32N 125 32 E
Mainit, L. **211** 9 31N 125 30 E
Mainkaing **202** 24 48N 95 16 E
Mainland, Orkney, U.K. **134** 59 0N 3 10W
Mainland, Shetland, U.K. **134** 60 15N 1 22W
Mainpuri **199** 27 18N 79 4 E
Maintenon **139** 48 35N 1 35 E
Maintirano **255** 18 3 S 44 1 E
Mainvault **143** 50 39N 3 43 E
Mainz **147** 50 0N 8 17 E
Maipú **124** 36 52 S 57 50W
Maiquetía **118** 10 36N 66 57W
Maira → **162** 44 49N 7 38 E
Mairabari **202** 26 30N 92 22 E
Maire, Le, Est. de **126** 54 50 S 65 0W
Mairipotaba **121** 17 18 S 49 28W
Maisí **113** 20 17N 74 9W
Maisi, Pta. de **113** 20 10N 74 10W
Maisonnette **81** 47 49N 65 0W
Maisse **139** 48 24N 2 21 E
Maissin **143** 49 58N 5 10 E
Maitland, N.S.W., Australia **231** 32 33 S 151 36 E
Maitland, S. Austral., Australia **232** 34 23 S 137 40 E
Maitland, Canada **81** 45 19N 63 30W
Maitland Bridge **81** 44 27N 65 12W
Maiyema **247** 12 5N 4 25 E
Maiyuan **217** 25 34N 117 28 E
Maiz, Islas del **112** 12 15N 83 4W
Maizuru **221** 35 25N 135 22 E
Majagual **118** 8 33N 74 38W
Majahual **111** 18 43N 87 43W
Majalengka **209** 6 50 S 108 13 E
Majari → **119** 3 29N 60 58W
Majd el Kurūm **189** 32 56N 35 15 E
Majene **207** 3 38 S 118 57 E
Majes → **122** 16 40 S 72 44W
Majevica Planina **166** 44 45N 18 50 E
Maji **245** 6 12N 35 30 E
Majiang **216** 26 28N 107 32 E
Major **88** 51 52N 109 37W
Majorca, I. = Mallorca **156** 39 30N 3 0 E
Majors Creek **233** 35 33 S 149 45 E
Majuriã **123** 7 30 S 64 55W
Maka **246** 13 40N 14 10W
Makak **247** 3 36N 11 0 E
Makakou **252** 0 11 S 12 12 E
Makale **207** 3 6 S 119 51 E
Makamba **250** 4 8 S 29 49 E
Makarewa **235** 46 20 S 168 21 E
Makarikari = Makgadikgadi Salt Pans **254** 20 40 S 25 45 E
Makarovo **185** 57 40N 107 45 E
Makarska **166** 43 20N 17 2 E
Makaryev **179** 57 52N 43 50 E
Makasar = Ujung Pandang **207** 5 10 S 119 20 E
Makasar, Selat **207** 1 0 S 118 20 E
Makat **177** 47 39N 53 19 E
Makedhonía □ **168** 40 39N 22 0 E
Makedonija □ **166** 41 53N 21 40 E
Makeni **246** 8 55N 12 5W
Makeyevka **180** 48 0N 38 0 E
Makgadikgadi Salt Pans **254** 20 40 S 25 45 E
Makhachkala **181** 43 0N 47 30 E
Makhambet **181** 47 43N 51 40 E
Makharadze **181** 41 55N 42 2 E
Makhmūr **192** 35 46N 43 35 E
Makhyah, W. → **195** 17 40N 49 1 E
Makian **207** 0 20N 127 20 E
Makindu **250** 2 18 S 37 50 E
Makinsk **184** 52 37N 70 26 E
Makkah **194** 21 30N 39 54 E
Makkovik **78** 55 10N 59 10W
Makkum **142** 53 3N 5 25 E
Maklakovo **185** 58 16N 92 29 E
Makó **151** 46 14N 20 33 E
Makok **252** 0 1 S 9 35 E
Makokibatan L. **87** 51 17N 87 20W
Makokou **252** 0 40N 12 50 E
Makongo **250** 3 25N 26 17 E
Makoro **250** 3 10N 29 59 E
Makoua **252** 0 5 S 15 50 E
Maków Mazowiecki **152** 52 52N 21 6 E
Maków Podhal **152** 49 43N 19 45 E
Makrá **169** 36 15N 25 54 E
Makran **197** 26 13N 61 30 E
Makran Coast Range **197** 25 40N 64 0 E
Makrana **198** 27 2N 74 46 E
Mákri **168** 40 52N 25 40 E
Maksimkin Yar **184** 58 42N 86 50 E
Maktar **241** 35 48N 9 12 E
Mākū **192** 39 15N 44 31 E
Makum **202** 27 30N 95 23 E
Makumbi **253** 5 50 S 20 43 E
Makunda **254** 22 30 S 20 7 E
Makurazaki **220** 31 15N 130 20 E
Makurdi **247** 7 43N 8 35 E
Makūyeh **193** 28 7N 53 9 E
Makwassie **254** 27 17 S 26 0 E
Mal **202** 26 51N 88 45 E
Mal B. **135** 52 50N 9 30W
Mal i Gjalicës së Lumës **168** 42 2N 20 25 E
Mal i Gribës **168** 40 17N 19 45 E
Mal i Nemërçkës **168** 40 15N 20 15 E
Mal i Tomorit **168** 40 42N 20 11 E
Mal Paso **105** 22 37N 102 46W
Mala **122** 12 40 S 76 38W
Mala, Pta. **112** 7 28N 80 2W
Mala Kapela **163** 44 45N 15 30 E
Malaban **210** 14 21N 121 0 E
Malabang **211** 7 36N 124 3 E
Malabar Coast **201** 11 0N 75 0 E
Malabrigo Pt. **210** 13 36N 121 15 E
Malabungan **211** 9 3N 117 38 E
Malacca, Str. of **205** 3 0N 101 0 E
Malachi **86** 49 56N 94 59W
Malacky **151** 48 27N 17 0 E
Málaga, Colombia **118** 6 42N 72 44W
Málaga, Spain **153** 36 43N 4 23W
Málaga □ **155** 36 38N 4 58W
Malagarasi **250** 5 5 S 30 50 E
Malagarasi → **250** 5 12 S 29 47 E
Malagón **155** 39 11N 3 52W
Malagón → **155** 37 35N 7 29W
Malaimbandy **255** 20 20 S 45 36 E
Malakâl **245** 9 33N 31 40 E
Malakand **197** 34 40N 71 55 E
Malalag **211** 6 36N 125 24 E
Malam **243** 11 27N 20 59 E
Malamyzh **185** 50 0N 136 50 E
Malang **209** 7 59 S 112 45 E
Malangas **211** 7 37N 123 1 E
Malanje **253** 9 36 S 16 17 E
Malanje □ **253** 9 30 S 16 0 E
Malapo → **100** 27 54N 110 48W
Mälaren **172** 59 30N 17 10 E
Malargüe **124** 35 32 S 69 30W
Malartic **82** 48 9N 78 9W
Malartic, L. **82** 48 15N 78 5W
Malatya **177** 38 25N 38 20 E
Malawi ■ **251** 13 0 S 34 0 E
Malawi, L. **251** 12 30 S 34 30 E
Malay **211** 11 54N 121 55 E
Malay Pen. **205** 7 25N 100 0 E
Malaya Belozërka **180** 47 12N 34 56 E
Malaya Vishera **178** 58 55N 32 25 E
Malaya Viska **180** 48 39N 31 36 E
Malaybalay **211** 8 5N 125 7 E
Malāyer **193** 34 19N 48 51 E
Malaysia ■ **206** 5 0N 110 0 E
Malazgirt **177** 39 10N 42 33 E
Malbaie, La **83** 47 40N 70 10W
Malbon **230** 21 5 S 140 17 E
Malbooma **231** 30 41 S 134 11 E
Malbork **152** 54 3N 19 1 E
Malca Dube **256** 6 47N 42 4 E
Malcésine **162** 45 46N 10 48 E
Malchin **146** 53 43N 12 44 E
Malchow **146** 53 29N 12 25 E
Malcolm **229** 28 51 S 121 25 E
Malcolm, Pt. **229** 33 48 S 123 45 E
Malcolm I. **92** 50 38N 127 0W
Malczyce **152** 51 14N 16 29 E
Maldegem **143** 51 14N 3 26 E
Malden I. **225** 4 3 S 155 1W
Maldives ■ **196** 7 0N 73 0 E
Maldon **232** 37 0 S 144 6 E
Maldonado **125** 35 0 S 55 0W
Maldonado, Pta. **107** 16 20N 98 35W
Malé, Italy **162** 46 20N 10 55 E
Malé, Mexico **110** 15 28N 92 15W
Malé Karpaty **151** 48 30N 17 20 E
Maléa, Ákra **169** 36 28N 23 7 E
Malebo, Pool **236** 4 17 S 15 20 E
Malegaon **198** 20 30N 74 38 E
Malei **251** 17 12 S 36 58 E
Malek Kandī **192** 37 9N 46 6 E
Malela, Bas Zaïre, Zaïre **253** 5 59 S 12 37 E
Malela, Kivu, Zaïre **250** 4 22 S 26 8 E
Malema **251** 14 57 S 37 20 E
Målerås **173** 56 54N 15 34 E
Malerkotla **198** 30 32N 75 58 E
Máles **169** 35 6N 25 35 E
Malesherbes **139** 48 15N 2 24 E
Maleshevska Planina **166** 41 38N 23 7 E
Malestroit **138** 47 49N 2 25W
Malfa **165** 38 35N 14 50 E
Malgobek **181** 43 30N 44 34 E
Malgomaj **174** 64 40N 16 30 E
Malgrat **156** 41 39N 2 46 E
Mali **246** 12 10N 12 20W
Mali ■ **247** 15 0N 2 0W
Mali Hka → **202** 25 42N 97 30 E
Mali Kanal **166** 45 36N 19 24 E
Maligaya **210** 12 59N 121 30 E
Maligne L. **91** 52 40N 117 31W
Malih → **189** 32 20N 35 34 E
Malik **207** 0 39 S 123 16 E
Malili **207** 2 42 S 121 6 E
Malimba, Mts. **250** 7 30 S 29 30 E
Malin **178** 50 46N 29 3 E
Malinaltepec **107** 17 3N 98 40W
Malinaltepec, Sa. de **107** 17 10N 98 30W
Malindang, Mt. **211** 8 13N 123 38 E
Malindi **250** 3 12 S 40 5 E
Malines = Mechelen **143** 51 2N 4 29 E
Maling **207** 1 0N 121 0 E
Malinyi **251** 8 56 S 36 0 E
Malipo **216** 23 7N 104 42 E
Maliqi **168** 40 45N 20 48 E
Malita **211** 6 19N 125 39 E
Maljenik **166** 43 59N 21 55 E
Malkapur, Maharashtra, India **198** 20 53N 73 58 E
Malkapur, Maharashtra, India **200** 16 57N 76 17 E
Małkinia Górna **152** 52 42N 22 5 E
Malko Tŭrnovo **167** 41 59N 27 31 E
Mallacoota **233** 37 40 S 149 40 E
Mallacoota Inlet **231** 37 34 S 149 40 E
Mallaig, Canada **90** 54 13N 111 22W
Mallaig, U.K. **134** 57 0N 5 50W
Mallala **232** 34 26 S 138 30 E
Mallawan **199** 27 4N 80 12 E
Mallawi **244** 27 44N 30 44 E
Malleco □ **126** 38 10 S 72 20W
Mallemort **141** 43 44N 5 11 E
Málles Venosta **162** 46 42N 10 32 E
Mállia **169** 35 17N 25 27 E
Mallig **210** 17 8N 121 42 E
Mallorca **156** 39 30N 3 0 E
Mallorytown **85** 44 29N 75 53W
Mallow **135** 52 8N 8 40W
Malmbäck **173** 57 34N 14 28 E
Malmberget **174** 67 11N 20 40 E
Malmédy **143** 50 25N 6 2 E
Malmesbury **254** 33 28 S 18 41 E
Malmö **172** 55 36N 12 59 E
Malmöhus län □ **172** 55 45N 13 30 E
Malmslätt **173** 58 27N 15 33 E
Malmyzh **179** 56 31N 50 41 E
Malnaş **170** 46 2N 25 49 E
Malo Konare **167** 42 12N 24 24 E
Maloarkhangelsk **179** 52 28N 36 30 E
Maloca **119** 0 43N 55 57W
Maloja **149** 46 25N 9 35 E
Maloja, P. **149** 46 23N 9 42 E
Malolos **210** 14 50N 120 49 E
Malomalsk **182** 58 45N 59 53 E
Malombe L. **251** 14 40 S 35 15 E

Malomir . . . . **167** 42 16N 26 30 E
Malong . . . . **216** 25 24N 103 34 E
Malonga . . . . **253** 10 24 S 23 10 E
Malorad . . . . **167** 43 28N 23 41 E
Malorita . . . . **178** 51 50N 24 3 E
Maloyaroslovets . . . . **179** 55 2N 36 20 E
Malozemelskaya Tundra . . . . **176** 67 0N 50 0 E
Malpartida **155** 39 26N 6 30W
Malpaso **110** 17 13N 93 36W
Malpelo **122** 4 3N 81 35W
Malpica **154** 43 19N 8 50W
Malprabha → . . . . . **201** 16 20N 76 5 E
Malta . . . . **120** 6 54 S 37 31W
Malta ■ . . . . **160** 35 50N 14 30 E
Malta Channel . . . . . **164** 36 40N 14 0 E
Maltahöhe . . . . **254** 24 55 S 17 0 E
Malters . . . . **148** 47 3N 8 11 E
Malton **132** 54 9N 0 48W
Maluku . . . . **207** 1 0 S 127 0 E
Maluku □ . . . . **207** 3 0 S 128 0 E
Maluku, Kepulauan . **207** 3 0 S 128 0 E
Malumfashi . . . . **247** 11 48N 7 39 E
Malung . . . . **172** 60 42N 13 44 E
Malungun . . . . **211** 6 16N 125 14 E
Maluso . . . . **211** 6 33N 121 53 E
Malvalli . . . . **201** 12 28N 77 8 E
Malvan . . . . **201** 16 2N 73 30 E
Malvern **133** 52 7N 2 19W
Malvern Hills **133** 52 0N 2 19W
Malvik . . . . **171** 63 25N 10 40 E
Malvinas, Is. = Falkland Is. . . . . . . **126** 51 30 S 59 0W
Malya . . . . **250** 3 5 S 33 38 E
Malybay . . . . **183** 43 30N 78 25 E
Malyy Lyakhovskiy, Ostrov . . . . **185** 74 7N 140 36 E
Mama, Mexico **111** 20 29N 89 22W
Mama, U.S.S.R. . . . . **185** 58 18N 112 54 E
Mamadysh . . . . **179** 55 44N 51 23 E
Mamaia . . . . **170** 44 18N 28 37 E
Mamaku . . . . **234** 38 5 S 176 8 E
Mamanguape . . . . . . **120** 6 50 S 35 4W
Mamasa . . . . **207** 2 55 S 119 20 E
Mambajao . . . . **211** 9 15N 124 43 E
Mambasa . . . . **250** 1 22N 29 3 E
Mamberamo → . . . **207** 2 0 S 137 50 E
Mambilima Falls . . . **251** 10 31 S 28 45 E
Mambirima . . . . **251** 11 25 S 27 33 E
Mambo . . . . **250** 4 52 S 38 22 E
Mambrui . . . . **250** 3 5 S 40 5 E
Mamburao . . . . **210** 13 13N 120 39 E
Mameigwess L., Ont., Canada **74** 52 35N 87 50W
Mameigwess L., Ont., Canada **86** 49 34N 91 49W
Mamer . . . . **143** 49 38N 6 2 E
Mamers . . . . **138** 48 21N 0 22 E
Mamfe . . . . **247** 5 50N 9 15 E
Māmī, Ra's . . . . **195** 12 32N 54 30 E
Mamiña . . . . **122** 20 5 S 69 14W
Mámmola . . . . **165** 38 23N 16 13 E
Mamoré → . . . . **123** 10 23 S 65 53W
Mamou **246** 10 15N 12 0W
Mamparang Mts. . . . **210** 16 21N 121 28 E
Mampatá **246** 11 54N 14 53W
Mampong **247** 7 6N 1 26W
Mamry, Jezioro . . . . **152** 54 5N 21 50 E
Mamuil Malal, Paso **126** 39 35 S 71 28W
Mamuju . . . . **207** 2 41 S 118 50 E
Ma'mūl . . . . **195** 18 8N 55 16 E
Man **246** 7 30N 7 40W
Man → . . . . **200** 17 31N 75 32 E
Man, I. of **132** 54 15N 4 30W
Man Na . . . . **202** 23 27N 97 19 E
Man Tun . . . . **202** 23 52N 98 38 E
Mana **119** 5 45N 53 55W
Mana →, Fr. Gui. . **119** 5 45N 53 55W
Måna →, Norway . **171** 59 55N 8 50 E
Manaar, Gulf of = Mannar, G. of . . . **201** 8 30N 79 0 E
Manabí □ . . . . **118** 0 40 S 80 5W
Manacacías → **118** 4 23N 72 4W
Manacapuru . . . . **119** 3 16 S 60 37W
Manacapuru → . . . . **119** 3 18 S 60 37W
Manacor . . . . **156** 39 34N 3 13 E
Manado . . . . **207** 1 29N 124 51 E
Manage . . . . **143** 50 31N 4 15 E
Managua **112** 12 6N 86 20W
Managua, L. **112** 12 20N 86 30W
Manaia . . . . **234** 39 33 S 174 8 E
Manakara . . . . **255** 22 8 S 48 1 E
Manakau Mt. . . . . . . **235** 42 15 S 173 42 E
Manākhah . . . . **194** 15 5N 43 44 E
Manam I. . . . . **227** 4 5 S 145 0 E
Manambao → . . . . . **255** 17 35 S 44 0 E
Manambato . . . . **255** 13 43 S 49 7 E
Manambolo → . . . . **255** 19 18 S 44 22 E
Manambolosy . . . . . . **255** 16 2 S 49 40 E
Mananara . . . . **255** 16 10 S 49 46 E
Mananara → . . . . . . **255** 23 21 S 47 42 E
Mananjary . . . . **255** 21 13 S 48 20 E
Manantenina . . . . **255** 24 17 S 47 19 E
Manaos = Manaus . **119** 3 0 S 60 0W
Manapala . . . . **211** 10 58N 123 5 E
Manapire → **118** 7 42N 66 7W
Manapouri . . . . **235** 45 34 S 167 39 E
Manapouri, L. . . . . . **235** 45 32 S 167 32 E
Manar → . . . . **200** 18 50N 77 20 E
Manār, Jabal . . . . **194** 14 2N 44 17 E
Manas, China . . . . . . **212** 44 17N 85 56 E
Manas, Somalia . . . . **256** 2 57N 43 28 E
Manas, Gora . . . . **183** 42 22N 71 2 E
Manaslu, Mt. . . . . . . **199** 28 33N 84 33 E
Manaung . . . . **202** 18 45N 93 40 E
Manaus . . . . **119** 3 0 S 60 0W
Manavgat . . . . **190** 36 47N 31 26 E
Manavgat → . . . . . . **190** 36 43N 31 27 E
Manawan L. **77** 55 24N 103 14W
Manawatu → . . . . . **234** 40 28 S 175 12 E
Manay . . . . **211** 7 17N 126 33 E
Manbij . . . . **192** 36 31N 37 57 E
Mancha, La, Mexico **103** 24 52N 102 47W
Mancha, La, Spain . **157** 39 10N 2 54W
Mancha Real **155** 37 48N 3 39W
Manche □ **138** 49 10N 1 20W
Manchegorsk . . . . . . **176** 67 40N 32 40 E
Manchester **132** 53 30N 2 15W
Manchester L. **77** 61 28N 107 29W
Manchuria = Dongbei . . . . **215** 42 0N 125 0 E
Manciano . . . . **163** 42 35N 11 30 E
Mancifa . . . . **245** 6 53N 41 50 E
Mancora, Pta. . . . . . . **122** 4 9 S 81 1W
Mand → . . . . **193** 28 20N 52 30 E
Manda, Chunya, Tanzania . . . . **250** 6 51 S 32 29 E
Manda, Ludewe, Tanzania . . . . **251** 10 30 S 34 40 E
Mandaguari . . . . **125** 23 32 S 51 42W
Mandah . . . . **214** 44 27N 108 2 E
Mandal . . . . **171** 58 2N 7 25 E
Mandalay . . . . **202** 22 0N 96 4 E
Mandale = Mandalay . . . . **202** 22 0N 96 4 E
Mandalgovi . . . . **214** 45 45N 106 10 E
Mandalī . . . . **192** 33 43N 45 28 E
Mandalya Körfezi . . **169** 37 15N 27 20 E
Mandaon . . . . **210** 12 13N 123 17 E
Mandapeta . . . . **200** 16 47N 81 56 E
Mandar, Teluk . . . . . **207** 3 35 S 119 15 E
Mandas . . . . **164** 39 40N 9 8 E
Mandasor = Mandsaur . . . . **198** 24 3N 75 8 E
Mandayar . . . . **211** 7 34N 126 14 E
Mandelieu-la-Napoule . . . . **141** 43 34N 6 57 E
Mandera . . . . **250** 3 55N 41 53 E
Mandera □ . . . . **250** 3 30N 41 0 E
Manderfeld . . . . **143** 50 20N 6 20 E
Mandi . . . . **198** 31 39N 76 58 E
Mandinga, L. **109** 19 0N 96 4W
Mandioli . . . . **207** 0 40 S 127 20 E
Mandioré, L. . . . . . . **123** 18 8 S 57 33W
Mandji I. = Lopez I. . . . . **252** 0 50 S 8 47 E
Mandla . . . . **199** 22 39N 80 30 E
Mandø . . . . **173** 55 18N 8 33 E
Mandoto . . . . **255** 19 34 S 46 17 E
Mandoúdhion . . . . . . **169** 38 48N 23 29 E
Mandra . . . . **198** 33 23N 73 12 E
Mandráki . . . . **169** 36 36N 27 11 E
Mandrare → . . . . . . **255** 25 10 S 46 30 E
Mandritsara . . . . **255** 15 50 S 48 49 E
Mandsaur . . . . **198** 24 3N 75 8 E
Mandurah . . . . **229** 32 36 S 115 48 E
Mandúria . . . . **165** 40 25N 17 38 E
Mandvi . . . . **198** 22 51N 69 22 E
Mandya . . . . **201** 12 30N 77 0 E
Mandzai . . . . **198** 30 55N 67 6 E
Mané **247** 12 59N 1 21W
Maneh . . . . **193** 37 39N 57 7 E
Manengouba, Mts. . **247** 5 0N 9 50 E
Maner → . . . . **200** 18 30N 79 40 E
Maneroo . . . . **230** 23 22 S 143 53 E
Maneroo Cr. → . . . **230** 23 21 S 143 53 E
Manfalût . . . . **244** 27 20N 30 52 E
Manfred . . . . **231** 33 19 S 143 45 E
Manfredónia . . . . **165** 41 40N 15 55 E
Manfredónia, G. di . **165** 41 30N 16 10 E
Manga, Brazil . . . . . . **121** 14 46 S 43 56W
Manga, Niger . . . . . . **247** 15 0N 14 0 E
Manga, Upp. Volta . **247** 11 40N 1 4W
Mangabeiras, Chapada das . . . . . **120** 10 0 S 46 30W
Mangal . . . . **211** 6 25N 121 58 E
Mangalagiri . . . . **201** 16 26N 80 36 E
Mangaldai . . . . **202** 26 26N 92 2 E
Mangalia . . . . **170** 43 50N 28 35 E
Mangalore, Australia . . . . **233** 36 56 S 145 10 E
Mangalore, India . . . **201** 12 55N 74 47 E
Manganeses **154** 41 45N 5 43W
Mangaon . . . . **200** 18 15N 73 20 E
Mange . . . . **252** 0 54N 20 30 E
Manger . . . . **171** 60 38N 5 3 E
Manggar . . . . **209** 2 50 S 108 10 E
Manggawitu . . . . **207** 4 8 S 133 32 E
Mangin Range . . . . . **202** 24 15N 95 45 E
Mangkalihat, Tanjung . . . . **209** 1 2N 118 59 E
Mangla Dam . . . . **199** 33 9N 73 44 E
Manglares, C. **118** 1 36N 79 2W
Manglaur . . . . **198** 29 44N 77 49 E
Mangnai . . . . **212** 37 52N 91 43 E
Mango . . . . **247** 10 20N 0 30 E
Mangoky → . . . . . . **255** 21 29 S 43 41 E
Mangole . . . . **207** 1 50 S 125 55 E
Mangombe . . . . **250** 1 20 S 26 48 E
Mangonui . . . . **234** 35 1 S 173 32 E
Mangualde **154** 40 38N 7 48W
Mangueigne . . . . **243** 10 30N 21 15 E
Mangueira, Lagoa da . . . . **125** 33 0 S 52 50W
Manguéni, Hamada . **241** 22 35N 12 40 E
Mangyshlak P-ov. . . **181** 44 30N 52 30 E
Mangyshlakskiy Zaliv . . . . **181** 44 40N 50 50 E
Manhiça . . . . **255** 25 23 S 32 49 E
Manhuaçu . . . . **121** 20 15 S 42 2W
Manhumirim . . . . **121** 20 22 S 41 57W
Maní, Colombia **118** 4 49N 72 17W
Mani, Mexico **111** 20 23N 89 24W
Mania → . . . . **255** 19 42 S 45 22 E
Maniago . . . . **163** 46 11N 12 40 E
Manica e Sofala □ . . **255** 19 10 S 33 45 E
Manicaland □ . . . . . . **251** 19 0 S 32 30 E
Manicoré . . . . **123** 5 48 S 61 16W
Manicoré → . . . . . . **123** 5 51 S 61 19W
Manicouagan → . . . **83** 49 30N 68 30W
Manicouagan, Rés. . **78** 51 5N 68 40W
Manicouagan L. **80** 51 25N 68 15W
Manīfah . . . . **193** 27 44N 49 0 E
Manifold . . . . **230** 22 41 S 150 40 E
Manifold, C. . . . . **230** 22 41 S 150 50 E
Maniganggo . . . . **216** 31 56N 99 10 E
Manigotagan **89** 51 6N 96 18W
Manigotagan L. **89** 50 52N 95 37W
Manihiki . . . . **225** 10 24 S 161 1W
Manika, Plat. de la . **251** 10 0 S 25 5 E
Manikganj . . . . **202** 23 52N 90 0 E
Manila . . . . **210** 14 40N 121 3 E
Manila Bay . . . . **210** 14 0N 120 0 E
Manilla . . . . **231** 30 45 S 150 43 E
Manimpé **246** 14 11N 5 28W
Manipur □ . . . . **202** 25 0N 94 0 E
Manipur → . . . . **202** 23 45N 94 20 E
Manisa . . . . **177** 38 38N 27 30 E
Manito L. **88** 52 43N 109 43W
Manitoba □ **89** 55 30N 97 0W
Manitoba, L. **89** 51 0N 98 45W
Manitou, Man., Canada **89** 49 15N 98 32W
Manitou, Qué., Canada **80** 50 18N 65 15W
Manitou → **80** 50 18N 65 15W
Manitou L., Ont., Canada **77** 49 15N 93 0W
Manitou L., Ont., Canada **84** 45 51N 82 0W
Manitou L., Qué., Canada **78** 50 55N 65 17W
Manitoulin I. **84** 45 40N 82 30W
Manitouwadge **87** 49 8N 85 48W
Manitowaning **84** 45 46N 81 49W
Manitsauá-Missu → **123** 10 58 S 53 20W
Maniwaki **82** 46 23N 75 58W
Manizales **118** 5 5N 75 32W
Manja . . . . **255** 21 26 S 44 20 E
Manjakandriana . . . . **255** 18 55 S 47 47 E
Manjeri . . . . **201** 11 7N 76 11 E
Manjhand . . . . **197** 25 50N 68 10 E
Manjil . . . . **193** 36 46N 49 30 E
Manjimup . . . . **229** 34 15 S 116 6 E
Manjra → . . . . **200** 18 49N 77 52 E
Mankayan . . . . **210** 16 52N 120 47 E
Mankayana . . . . **255** 26 38 S 31 6 E
Mankono **246** 8 1N 6 10W
Mankota **88** 49 25N 107 5W
Manlay . . . . **214** 44 9N 107 0 E
Manlleu . . . . **156** 42 2N 2 17 E
Manly . . . . **231** 33 48 S 151 17 E
Manmad . . . . **200** 20 18N 74 28 E
Mann Ranges, Mts. . **229** 26 6 S 130 5 E
Manna . . . . **208** 4 25 S 102 55 E
Mannahill . . . . **231** 32 25 S 140 0 E
Mannar . . . . **201** 9 1N 79 54 E
Mannar, G. of . . . . . **201** 8 30N 79 0 E
Mannar I. . . . . **201** 9 5N 79 45 E
Mannargudi . . . . **201** 10 45N 79 51 E
Mannduque □ . . . . . **210** 13 18N 122 0 E
Männedorf . . . . **149** 47 15N 8 43 E
Mannheim . . . . **147** 49 28N 8 29 E
Manning **90** 56 53N 117 39W
Manning Park **93** 49 4N 120 47W
Manning Prov. Park **93** 49 5N 120 45W
Mannu → . . . . **164** 39 15N 9 32 E
Mannu, C. . . . . **164** 40 2N 8 24 E
Mannum . . . . **232** 34 50 S 139 20 E
Mannville **90** 53 20N 111 10W
Mano **246** 8 3N 12 2W
Manoa . . . . **123** 9 40 S 65 27W
Manokwari . . . . **207** 0 54 S 134 0 E
Manolás . . . . **169** 38 4N 21 21 E
Manolo Fortich . . . . **211** 8 28N 124 50 E
Manombo . . . . **255** 22 57 S 43 28 E
Manono . . . . **250** 7 15 S 27 25 E
Manor **89** 49 36N 102 5W
Manosque . . . . **141** 43 49N 5 47 E
Manotick **85** 45 13N 75 41W
Manouane, L. **83** 47 33N 74 6W
Manouane L. **78** 50 45N 70 45W
Manpojin . . . . **215** 41 6N 126 24 E
Manresa . . . . **156** 41 48N 1 50 E
Mans, Le . . . . **138** 48 0N 0 10 E
Mansa, Gujarat, India . . . . **198** 23 27N 72 45 E
Mansa, Punjab, India . . . . **198** 30 0N 75 27 E
Mansa, Zambia . . . . **251** 11 13 S 28 55 E
Mansalay . . . . **210** 12 31N 121 26 E
Manseau **83** 46 22N 72 0W
Mansehra . . . . **198** 34 20N 73 15 E
Mansel I. **78** 62 0N 80 0W
Mansfield, Australia **231** 37 4 S 146 6 E
Mansfield, U.K. **132** 53 8N 1 12W
Mansi . . . . **202** 24 48N 95 52 E
Mansidão . . . . **120** 10 43 S 44 2W
Mansilla de las Mulas **154** 42 30N 5 25W
Mansle . . . . **140** 45 52N 0 9 E
Manso → . . . . **121** 13 50 S 47 0W
Mansoa **246** 12 0N 15 20W
Manson Creek **76** 55 37N 124 32W
Mansoura . . . . **241** 36 1N 4 31 E
Manta . . . . **118** 1 0 S 80 40W
Manta, B. de . . . . . . **118** 0 54 S 80 44W
Mantalingajan, Mt. . **211** 8 55N 117 45 E
Mantare . . . . **250** 2 42 S 33 13 E
Mantecal **118** 7 34N 69 17W
Mantena . . . . **121** 18 47 S 40 59W
Mantes-la-Jolie . . . . **139** 49 0N 1 41 E
Manthani . . . . **200** 18 40N 79 35 E
Manthelan . . . . **138** 47 9N 0 47 E
Mantiqueira, Serra da . . . . **125** 22 0 S 44 0W
Mantorp . . . . **173** 58 21N 15 20 E
Mántova . . . . **162** 45 20N 10 42 E
Mänttä . . . . **174** 62 0N 24 40 E
Mantua = Mántova . **162** 45 20N 10 42 E
Mantung . . . . **232** 34 35 S 140 3 E
Manturovo . . . . **179** 58 30N 44 30 E
Manu . . . . **122** 12 10 S 70 51W
Manu → . . . . **122** 12 16 S 70 55W
Manua Is. . . . . **226** 14 13 S 169 35W
Manuae . . . . **225** 19 30 S 159 0W
Manuel **103** 22 44N 98 19W
Manuel Alves → . . . **121** 11 19 S 48 28W
Manuel Alves Grande → . . . . . . **120** 7 27 S 47 35W
Manuel Benavides . . **101** 29 8N 103 55W
Manuel Urbano . . . . **122** 8 53 S 69 18W
Manuels **81** 47 3N 64 59W
Manui . . . . **207** 3 35 S 123 5 E
Manukau . . . . **234** 37 1 S 174 55 E
Manukau Harbour . . **234** 37 3 S 174 45 E
Manunui . . . . **234** 38 54 S 175 21 E
Manuripi → . . . . **122** 11 6 S 67 36W
Manus I. . . . . **227** 2 0 S 147 0 E
Manvi . . . . **201** 15 57N 76 59 E
Manwath . . . . **200** 19 19N 76 32 E
Many Island L. **91** 50 8N 110 3W
Manyara, L. . . . . **250** 3 40 S 35 50 E
Manyberries **91** 49 24N 110 42W
Manych → . . . . **181** 47 15N 40 0 E
Manych-Gudilo, Oz. **181** 46 24N 42 38 E
Manyonga → . . . . . **250** 4 10 S 34 15 E
Manyoni . . . . **250** 5 45 S 34 55 E
Manyoni □ . . . . **250** 6 30 S 34 30 E
Manzai . . . . **197** 32 12N 70 15 E
Manzala, Bahra el . . **244** 31 10N 31 56 E
Manzanares **157** 39 0N 3 22W
Manzaneda, Cabeza de **154** 42 12N 7 15W
Manzanillo, Cuba . . **112** 20 20N 77 31W
Manzanillo, Mexico . **106** 19 3N 104 20W
Manzanillo, Pta. **112** 9 30N 79 40W
Manzarīyeh . . . . **193** 34 53N 50 50 E
Manzhouli . . . . **213** 49 35N 117 25 E
Manzini . . . . **255** 26 30 S 31 25 E
Mao . . . . **243** 14 4N 15 19 E
Maoke, Pegunungan **207** 3 40 S 137 30 E
Maolin . . . . **215** 43 58N 123 30 E
Maoming . . . . **217** 21 50N 110 54 E
Maowen . . . . **216** 31 41N 103 49 E
Maoxing . . . . **215** 45 28N 124 40 E
Mapam Yumco . . . . . **199** 30 45N 81 28 E
Mapastepec **110** 15 26N 92 54W
Mapia, Kepulauan . . **207** 0 50N 134 20 E
Mapimí **105** 25 49N 103 51W
Mapimi, Bolson de, Coahuila, Mexico . **101** 27 30N 103 30W
Mapimí, Bolsón de, Durango, Mexico . **105** 26 30N 104 0W
Mapimí, Sa. de **105** 25 45N 103 45W
Maping . . . . **217** 31 34N 113 32 E

Mapinga 250 6 40 S 39 12 E
Mapinhane 255 22 20 S 35 0 E
Mapire 119 7 45N 64 42W
Maple Bay 93 48 48N 123 37W
Maple Creek 88 49 55N 109 29W
Maprik 227 3 44 S 143 3 E
Mapuca 201 15 36N 73 46 E
Mapuera → 119 1 5 S 57 2W
Maputing Baybay 210 12 45N 123 20 E
Maputo 255 25 58 S 32 32 E
Maputo, B. de 255 25 50 S 32 45 E
Maqiaohe 215 44 40N 130 30 E
Maqnā 191 28 25N 34 50 E
Maqran, W. → 194 20 55N 47 12 E
Maqteïr 240 21 50N 11 40W
Maqueda Channel 210 13 42N 124 1 E
Maquela do Zombo 253 6 0 S 15 15 E
Maquinchao 126 41 15 S 68 50W
Mâr → 171 59 59N 8 46 E
Mar, Serra do 125 25 30 S 49 0W
Mar Chiquita, L. 124 30 40 S 62 50W
Mar del Plata 124 38 0 S 57 30W
Mar Menor, L. 157 37 40N 0 45W
Mara, Guyana 119 6 0N 57 36W
Mara, India 202 28 11N 94 14 E
Mara, Tanzania 250 1 30 S 34 32 E
Mara □ 250 1 45 S 34 20 E
Maraâ 118 1 52 S 65 25W
Marabá 120 5 20 S 49 5W
Maracá, I. de 120 2 10N 50 30W
Maracaibo 118 10 40N 71 37W
Maracaibo, Lago de 118 9 40N 71 30W
Maracaju 125 21 38 S 55 9W
Maracajú, Serra de 123 23 57 S 55 1W
Maracanã 120 0 46 S 47 27W
Maracás 121 13 26 S 40 18W
Maracay 118 10 15N 67 28W
Marādah 241 29 15N 19 15 E
Maradi 247 13 29N 8 10 E
Maradun 247 12 35N 6 18 E
Marāgheh 192 37 30N 46 12 E
Maragogipe 121 12 46 S 38 55W
Maragondon 210 14 16N 120 44 E
Marāh 192 25 0N 45 35 E
Marajó, B. de 120 1 0 S 48 30W
Marajó, Ilha de 120 1 0 S 49 30W
Marākand 192 38 51N 45 16 E
Maralal 250 1 0N 36 38 E
Maralinga 229 30 13 S 131 32 E
Marama 232 35 10 S 140 10 E
Marampa 246 8 45N 12 28W
Maramureş □ 170 47 45N 24 0 E
Maran 205 3 35N 102 45 E
Maranboy 228 14 40 S 132 39 E
Maranchón 156 41 6N 2 15W
Marand 192 38 30N 45 45 E
Marang 205 5 12N 103 13 E
Maranguape 120 3 55 S 38 50W
Maranhão = São Luís 120 2 39 S 44 15W
Maranhão □ 120 5 0 S 46 0W
Marano, L. di 163 45 42N 13 13 E
Maranoa → 231 27 50 S 148 37 E
Marañón → 122 4 30 S 73 35W
Marão 255 24 18 S 34 2 E
Marapi → 119 0 37N 55 58W
Marari 122 5 43 S 67 47W
Maraş 177 37 37N 36 53 E
Mărăşeşti 170 45 52N 27 14 E
Maratea 165 39 59N 15 43 E
Marateca 155 38 34N 8 40W
Marathókambos 169 37 43N 26 42 E
Marathon, Australia 230 20 51 S 143 32 E
Marathon, Canada 87 48 44N 86 23W
Marathón, Greece 169 38 11N 23 58 E
Maratua 209 2 10N 118 35 E
Maraú 121 14 6 S 39 0W
Maravatío 107 19 54N 100 27W
Maravillas 101 27 22N 104 29W
Marawi City 211 8 0N 124 21 E
Marāwih 195 24 18N 53 18 E
Marbella 155 36 30N 4 57W
Marble Bar 228 21 9 S 119 44 E
Marblehead 93 50 15N 116 58W
Marbleton 83 45 37N 71 35W
Marburg 146 50 49N 8 36 E
Marby 172 63 7N 14 18 E
Marcal → 151 47 41N 17 32 E
Marcali 151 46 35N 17 25 E
Marcapata 122 13 31 S 70 52W
Marcaria 162 45 7N 10 34 E
Marceau, L. 80 51 25N 66 41W
Marcelin 88 52 55N 106 47W
March 133 52 33N 0 5 E
Marchal 253 5 16 S 14 58 E
Marchand = Rommani 240 33 31N 6 40W
Marché 140 46 0N 1 20 E
Marche □ 163 43 22N 13 10 E
Marche-en-Famenne 143 50 14N 5 19 E
Marchena 155 37 18N 5 23W
Marches = Marche □ 163 43 22N 13 10 E
Marciana Marina 162 42 44N 10 12 E
Marcianise 165 41 3N 14 16 E
Marcigny 141 46 17N 4 2 E
Marcillac-Vallon 140 44 29N 2 27 E
Marcillat 140 46 12N 2 38 E
Marcinelle 143 50 24N 4 26 E
Marck 139 50 57N 1 57 E
Marckolsheim 139 48 10N 7 30 E
Marcona 122 15 10 S 75 0W
Marcos Juárez 124 32 42 S 62 5W
Marcus 224 24 0N 153 45 E
Marcus Necker Ridge 224 20 0N 175 0 E
Mardan 197 34 20N 72 0 E
Mardie 228 21 12 S 115 59 E
Mardin 177 37 20N 40 43 E
Maré, Î. 226 21 30 S 168 0 E
Marechal Deodoro 120 9 43 S 35 54W
Maree L. 134 57 40N 5 30W
Mareeba 230 16 59 S 145 28 E
Marek = Stanke Dimitrov 166 42 17N 23 9 E
Marek 207 4 41 S 120 24 E
Maremma 162 42 45N 11 15 E
Maréna 246 14 0N 7 20W
Marenberg 163 46 38N 15 13 E
Marengo 88 51 29N 109 47W
Marennes 140 45 49N 1 7W
Marenyi 250 4 22 S 39 8 E
Marerano 255 21 23 S 44 52 E
Maréttimo 164 37 58N 12 5 E
Mareuil-sur-Lay 140 46 32N 1 14W
Marganets 180 47 40N 34 40 E
Margaree Forks 81 46 20N 61 5W
Margaret Bay 92 51 20N 126 35W
Margaret L. 76 58 56N 115 25W
Margarita, Isla de 119 11 0N 64 0W
Margaritas 110 15 33N 93 6W
Margarítion 168 39 22N 20 26 E
Margaritovo 218 43 25N 134 45 E
Margate, S. Africa 255 30 50 S 30 20 E
Margate, U.K. 133 51 23N 1 24 E
Margelan 183 40 27N 71 42 E
Margeride, Mts. de la 140 44 43N 3 38 E
Margherita 202 27 16N 95 40 E
Margherita di Savola 165 41 25N 16 5 E
Marghita 170 47 22N 22 22 E
Margo 88 51 49N 103 20W
Margonin 152 52 58N 17 5 E
Margosatubig 211 7 34N 123 10 E
Marguerite 93 52 30N 122 25W
Marhoum 241 34 27N 0 11W
Māri' 190 36 29N 37 10 E
Mari, A.S.S.R. □ 179 56 30N 48 0 E
Maria 80 48 10N 65 59W
María, Pta. 98 28 55N 114 32W
María Cleofás, I. 104 21 16N 106 14W
María Elena 124 22 18 S 69 40W
María Grande 124 31 45 S 59 55W
Maria I., N. Terr., Australia 230 14 52 S 135 45 E
Maria I., Tas., Australia 230 42 35 S 148 0 E
María Madre, I. 104 21 35N 106 33W
María Magdalena 104 21 25N 106 24W
Maria van Diemen, C. 234 34 29 S 172 40 E
Mariager 173 56 40N 10 0 E
Mariager Fjord 173 56 42N 10 19 E
Mariakani 250 3 50 S 39 27 E
Marian L. 76 63 0N 116 15W
Mariana Trench 224 13 0N 145 0 E
Marianao 112 23 8N 82 24W
Mariani 202 26 39N 94 19 E
Mariannelund 173 57 37N 15 35 E
Mariánské Lázně 150 49 48N 12 41 E
Mariato, Punta 112 7 12N 80 52W
Mariazell 150 47 47N 15 19 E
Ma'rib 194 15 25N 45 21 E
Maribo 173 54 48N 11 30 E
Maribor 163 46 36N 15 40 E
Maricaban I. 210 13 39N 120 53 E
Maricalom 211 9 42N 122 25 E
Marico → 254 23 35 S 26 57 E
Maricourt 78 56 34N 70 49W
Marīdī 245 4 55N 29 25 E
Maridi, Wadi → 245 6 15N 29 21 E
Marié → 118 0 27 S 66 26W
Marie-Galante 113 15 56N 61 16W
Marie L. 90 54 38N 110 18W
Mariefred 172 59 15N 17 12 E
Mariehamn 175 60 5N 19 55 E
Marienberg, Germany 146 50 40N 13 10 E
Marienberg, Neth. 142 52 30N 6 35 E
Marienbourg 143 50 6N 4 31 E
Mariental 254 24 36 S 18 0 E
Mariestad 173 58 43N 13 50 E
Marieville 83 45 26N 73 10W
Marignane 141 43 25N 5 13 E
Marihatag 211 8 48N 126 18 E
Mariinsk 184 56 10N 87 20 E
Mariinskiy Posad 179 56 10N 47 45 E
Marília 125 22 13 S 50 0W
Marillana 228 22 37 S 119 16 E
Marimba 253 8 28 S 17 8 E
Marín, Mexico 102 25 52N 100 3W
Marín, Spain 154 42 23N 8 42W
Mariña, La 154 43 30N 7 40W
Marina di Cirò 165 39 22N 17 8 E
Marina Plains 230 14 37 S 143 57 E
Marinduque 210 13 25N 122 0 E
Marinel, Le 251 10 25 S 25 17 E
Marineo 164 37 57N 13 23 E
Maringá 125 23 26 S 52 2W
Marinha Grande 155 39 45N 8 56W
Marion Bay 232 35 12 S 136 59 E
Marion I. 203 47 0 S 38 0 E
Maripa 119 7 26N 65 9W
Maripasoula 119 3 40N 54 4W
Maripipi I. 211 11 47N 124 19 E
Mariscal Estigarribia 124 22 3 S 60 40W
Maritime Alps = Maritimes, Alpes 162 44 10N 7 10 E
Maritimes, Alpes 162 44 10N 7 10 E
Maritsa, Bulgaria 167 42 1N 25 50 E
Maritsá, Greece 169 36 22N 28 10 E
Maritsa → 167 42 15N 24 0 E
Marīvān 192 35 30N 46 25 E
Mariyampole = Kapsukas 178 54 33N 23 19 E
Marizón, Pta. 100 27 51N 110 52W
Marka 244 18 14N 41 19 E
Markah, W. → 194 14 59N 46 36 E
Markam 216 29 42N 98 38 E
Markapur 201 15 44N 79 19 E
Markaryd 173 56 28N 13 35 E
Markazī □ 193 35 0N 49 30 E
Markdale 84 44 19N 80 39W
Marke 143 50 48N 3 14 E
Markelsdorfer Huk 146 54 33N 11 0 E
Marken 142 52 26N 5 12 E
Markerville 91 52 7N 114 10W
Markerwaard 142 52 33N 5 15 E
Market Drayton 132 52 55N 2 30W
Market Harborough 133 52 29N 0 55W
Markham 84 43 52N 79 16W
Markham → 227 6 41 S 147 2 E
Markham I. 12 84 0N 0 45W
Markham L. 77 62 30N 102 35W
Markham Mt. 13 83 0 S 164 0 E
Marki 152 52 20N 21 2 E
Markoupoulon 169 37 53N 23 57 E
Markovac 166 44 14N 21 7 E
Markovo 185 64 40N 169 40 E
Markoye 247 14 39N 0 2 E
Marks 179 51 45N 46 50 E
Markstay 84 46 29N 80 32W
Markt Schwaben 147 48 14N 11 49 E
Marktredwitz 147 50 1N 12 2 E
Marla 231 27 19 S 133 33 E
Marlbank 85 44 26N 77 6W
Marlborough 230 22 46 S 149 52 E
Marlborough □ 235 41 45 S 173 33 E
Marlborough Downs 133 51 25N 1 55W
Marle 139 49 43N 3 47 E
Marlow 146 54 8N 12 34 E
Marly-le-Grand 148 46 47N 7 10 E
Marmagao 201 15 25N 73 56 E
Marmande 140 44 30N 0 10 E
Marmara 180 40 35N 27 38 E
Marmara, Sea of = Marmara Denizi 177 40 45N 28 15 E
Marmara Denizi 177 40 45N 28 15 E
Marmelos → 123 6 6 S 61 46W
Marmion L. 86 48 55N 91 20W
Marmion Mt. 229 29 16 S 119 50 E
Marmolada, Mte. 163 46 25N 11 55 E
Marmolejo 155 38 3N 4 13W
Marmora 85 44 28N 77 41W
Marnay 139 47 20N 5 48 E
Marne 146 53 57N 9 1 E
Marne □ 139 49 0N 4 10 E
Marne → 139 8 23N 18 36 E
Marnueli 181 41 30N 44 48 E
Maro 243 8 30N 19 0 E
Maroa 118 2 43N 67 33W
Maroala 255 15 23 S 47 59 E
Maroantsetra 255 15 26 S 49 44 E
Maromandia 255 14 13 S 48 5 E
Marondera 251 18 5 S 31 42 E
Maroni → 119 4 0N 52 0W
Marónia 168 40 53N 25 24 E
Maroochydore 231 26 29 S 153 5 E
Maroona 231 37 27 S 142 54 E
Maros → 151 46 15N 20 13 E
Marosakoa 255 15 26 S 46 38 E
Marostica 163 45 44N 11 40 E
Maroua 247 10 40N 14 20 E
Marovoay 255 16 6 S 46 39 E
Marowijne □ 119 4 0N 55 0W
Marowijne → 119 5 45N 53 58W
Marquard 254 28 40 S 27 28 E
Marqueira 155 38 41N 9 9W
Marquelia 107 16 36N 98 48W
Marqués, R. del → 106 18 50N 102 4W
Marquesas Is. 225 9 30 S 140 0W
Marquette 89 50 4N 97 44W
Marquette, L. 83 48 54N 73 54W
Marquise 139 50 50N 1 40 E
Marra, Gebel 245 7 20N 27 35 E
Marracuene 255 25 45 S 32 35 E
Marradi 163 44 5N 11 37 E
Marrakech 240 31 9N 8 0W
Marrawah 230 40 55 S 144 42 E
Marrecas, Serra das 120 9 0 S 41 0W
Marree 231 29 39 S 138 1 E
Marrilla 228 22 31 S 114 25 E
Marrimane 255 22 58 S 33 34 E
Marronne → 140 45 4N 1 56 E
Marroquí, Punta 155 36 0N 5 37W
Marrowie Creek 231 33 23 S 145 40 E
Marrubane 251 18 0 S 37 0 E
Marrum 142 53 19N 5 48 E
Marrupa 251 13 8 S 37 30 E
Marsa Brega 241 30 24N 19 37 E
Marsá Matrûh 244 31 19N 27 9 E
Marsá Susah 242 32 52N 21 59 E
Marsabit 250 2 18N 38 0 E
Marsabit □ 250 2 45N 37 45 E
Marsala 164 37 48N 12 25 E
Marsaxlokk 160 35 47N 14 32 E
Marsciano 163 42 54N 12 20 E
Marsden, Australia 231 33 47 S 147 32 E
Marsden, Canada 88 52 51N 109 49W
Marsdiep 142 52 58N 4 46 E
Marseillan 140 43 23N 3 31 E
Marseille 141 43 18N 5 23 E
Marseilles = Marseille 141 43 18N 5 23 E
Marshall, Canada 88 53 11N 109 47W
Marshall, Liberia 246 6 8N 10 22W
Marshall → 230 22 59 S 136 59 E
Marshall Is. 224 9 0N 171 0 E
Marshūn 193 36 19N 49 23 E
Mársico Nuovo 165 40 26N 15 43 E
Marsoui 80 49 13N 66 4W
Märsta 172 59 37N 17 52 E
Marstal 173 54 51N 10 30 E
Marstrand 173 57 53N 11 35 E
Marta → 163 42 14N 11 42 E
Martaban 202 16 30N 97 35 E
Martaban, G. of 202 16 5N 96 30 E
Martagne 138 46 59N 0 57W
Martano 165 40 14N 18 18 E
Martapura, Kalimantan, Indonesia 209 3 22 S 114 47 E
Martapura, Sumatera, Indonesia 208 4 19 S 104 22 E
Marte 247 12 23N 13 46 E
Marte R. Gomez, Presa 102 26 10N 99 0W
Martel 140 44 57N 1 37 E
Martelange 143 49 49N 5 43 E
Marten River 84 46 44N 79 49W
Martensville 88 52 17N 106 40W
Martés, Sierra 157 39 20N 1 0W
Marthaguy Creek → 233 30 16 S 147 35 E
Martigné-Ferchaud 138 47 50N 1 20W
Martigny 148 46 6N 7 3 E
Martigues 141 43 24N 5 4 E
Martil 240 35 36N 5 15W
Martin 151 49 6N 18 48 E
Martín → 156 41 18N 0 19W
Martina 149 46 53N 10 28 E
Martina Franca 165 40 42N 17 20 E
Martinborough 234 41 14 S 175 29 E
Martínez de la Torre 108 20 4N 97 3W
Martinho Campos 121 19 20 S 45 13W
Martinique 113 14 40N 61 0W
Martinique Passage 113 15 15N 61 0W
Martínon 169 38 35N 23 15 E
Martinópolis 125 22 11 S 51 12W
Martinsberg 150 48 22N 15 9 E
Marton 234 40 4 S 175 23 E
Martorell 156 41 28N 1 56 E
Martos 155 37 44N 3 58W
Martre, L., La 94 63 0N 118 0W
Martūbah 242 32 35N 22 46 E
Martuk 182 50 46N 56 31 E
Martuni 181 40 9N 45 10 E
Maru 247 12 22N 6 22 E
Marudi 206 4 11N 114 19 E
Ma'ruf 197 31 30N 67 6 E
Marugame 220 34 15N 133 40 E
Marúggio 165 40 20N 17 33 E
Marui 227 4 4 S 143 2 E
Maruim 120 10 45 S 37 5W
Marulan 231 34 43 S 150 3 E
Marum 142 53 9N 6 16 E
Marunga 254 17 28 S 20 2 E
Marungu, Mts. 250 7 30 S 30 0 E
Maruoka 221 36 9N 136 16 E
Marvast 193 30 30N 54 15 E
Mårvatn 171 60 8N 8 14 E
Marvejols 140 44 33N 3 19 E
Marwar 198 25 43N 73 45 E
Marwayne 90 53 32N 110 20W
Mary 184 37 40N 61 50 E

Mary Frances L. **77** 63 19N 106 13W
Mary Kathleen **230** 20 44 S 139 48 E
Maryborough = Port Laoise **135** 53 2N 7 20W
Maryborough, Queens., Australia **231** 25 31 S 152 37 E
Maryborough, Vic., Australia **231** 37 0 S 143 44 E
Maryen, L. **80** 51 20N 60 28W
Maryfield **89** 49 50N 101 35W
Maryland Jc. **251** 17 45 S 30 31 E
Maryport **132** 54 43N 3 30W
Mary's Harbour **78** 52 18N 55 51W
Marystown **79** 47 10N 55 10W
Marysville, B.C., Canada **91** 49 35N 116 0W
Marysville, N.B., Canada **81** 45 59N 66 35W
Maryvale **231** 28 4 S 152 12 E
Marzo, Punta **118** 6 50N 77 42W
Marzūq **241** 25 53N 13 57 E
Masada = Mesada **189** 31 20N 35 19 E
Masahunga **250** 2 6 S 33 18 E
Masai **205** 1 29N 103 55 E
Masai Steppe **250** 4 30 S 36 30 E
Masaka **250** 0 21 S 31 45 E
Masalembo, Kepulauan **209** 5 35 S 114 30 E
Masalima, Kepulauan **209** 5 4 S 117 5 E
Masamba **207** 2 30 S 120 15 E
Masan **215** 35 11N 128 32 E
Masanasa **157** 39 25N 0 25W
Masasi **251** 10 45 S 38 52 E
Masasi □ **251** 10 45 S 38 50 E
Masaya **112** 12 0N 86 7W
Masba **247** 10 35N 13 1 E
Masbate **210** 12 21N 123 36 E
Masbate, I. **210** 12 21N 123 36 E
Masbate Pass **210** 12 30N 123 35 E
Mascara **241** 35 26N 0 6 E
Mascarene Is. **203** 22 0 S 55 0 E
Mascota **106** 20 32N 104 49W
Mascota, Sa. de **106** 20 40N 104 35W
Mascouche **83** 45 45N 73 36W
Masela **207** 8 9 S 129 51 E
Maseru **254** 29 18 S 27 30 E
Mashaba **251** 20 2 S 30 29 E
Mashābih **192** 25 35N 36 30 E
Mashan **216** 23 40N 108 11 E
Masherbrum **199** 35 38N 76 18 E
Mashhad **193** 36 20N 59 35 E
Mashi **247** 13 0N 7 54 E
Mashiki **220** 32 51N 130 53 E
Mashīz **193** 29 56N 56 37 E
Mashkel, Hamun-i- **197** 28 30N 63 0 E
Mashki Chāh **197** 29 5N 62 30 E
Mashonaland Central □ **255** 17 30 S 31 0 E
Mashonaland East □ **255** 18 0 S 32 0 E
Mashonaland West □ **255** 17 30 S 29 30 E
Mashtaga **181** 40 35N 50 0 E
Masi **174** 69 26N 23 40 E
Masi Manimba **253** 4 40 S 17 54 E
Masiaca **100** 26 45N 109 18W
Masindi **250** 1 40N 31 43 E
Masindi Port **250** 1 43N 32 2 E
Masinloc **210** 15 32N 119 57 E
Maşīrah, Khalīj **195** 20 10N 58 10 E
Maşīrah, Tur'at **195** 20 30N 58 40 E
Masisea **122** 8 35 S 74 22W
Masisi **250** 1 23 S 28 49 E
Masjed Soleyman **193** 31 55N 49 18 E
Mask, L. **135** 53 36N 9 24W
Maski **201** 15 56N 76 46 E
Maskinongé **83** 46 14N 73 1W
Maslen Nos **167** 42 18N 27 48 E
Maslinica **163** 43 24N 16 13 E
Maşna'ah **195** 14 27N 48 17 E
Masnou **156** 41 28N 2 20 E
Masoala, Tanjon' i **255** 15 59 S 50 13 E
Masoarivo **255** 19 3 S 44 19 E
Masohi **207** 3 20 S 128 55 E
Masomeloka **255** 20 17 S 48 37 E
Mason B. **235** 46 55 S 167 45 E
Masqat **195** 23 37N 58 36 E
Massa, Congo **252** 3 45 S 15 29 E
Massa, Italy **162** 44 2N 10 7 E
Massa, O. → **240** 30 2N 9 40W
Massa Marittima **162** 43 3N 10 52 E
Massada **189** 33 41N 35 36 E
Massafra **165** 40 35N 17 8 E
Massaguet **243** 12 28N 15 26 E
Massah Kānlī **190** 36 42N 36 39 E
Massakory **243** 13 0N 15 49 E
Massangena **255** 21 34 S 33 0 E
Massapê **120** 3 31 S 40 19W
Massarosa **162** 43 53N 10 17 E
Massat **140** 42 53N 1 21 E
Massava **182** 60 40N 62 6 E
Massawa = Mitsiwa **245** 15 35N 39 25 E
Massénya **243** 11 21N 16 9 E
Masset **92** 54 2N 132 10W
Masset Inlet **92** 53 43N 132 20W
Massey **84** 46 12N 82 5W
Massiac **140** 45 15N 3 11 E
Massif Central **140** 45 30N 2 21 E
Massinga **255** 23 15 S 35 22 E
Masson **82** 45 32N 75 25W
Masson I. **13** 66 10 S 93 20 E
Massueville **83** 45 55N 72 56W
Mastaba **244** 20 52N 39 30 E
Mastābah **194** 20 49N 39 26 E
Mastanli = Momchilgrad **167** 41 33N 25 23 E
Masterton **234** 40 56 S 175 39 E
Mastigouche, Parc **83** 46 33N 73 41W
Mástikho, Ákra **169** 38 10N 26 2 E
Mastuj **199** 36 20N 72 36 E
Mastung **197** 29 50N 66 56 E
Mastūrah **194** 23 7N 38 52 E
Masuda **220** 34 40N 131 51 E
Masuika **253** 7 37 S 22 32 E
Masvingo **251** 20 8 S 30 49 E
Masvingo □ **251** 21 0 S 31 30 E
Maswa □ **250** 3 30 S 34 0 E
Maşyāf **190** 35 4N 36 20 E
Mata de São João **121** 12 31 S 38 17W
Mata Ortiz **101** 30 8N 108 4W
Matabeleland North □ **251** 19 0 S 28 0 E
Matabeleland South □ **251** 21 0 S 29 0 E
Mataboor **207** 1 41 S 138 3 E
Matachel → **155** 38 50N 6 17W
Matachewan **74** 47 56N 80 39W
Matachic **101** 28 51N 107 45W
Matacuni → **119** 3 2N 65 16W
Matadi **253** 5 52 S 13 31 E
Matagalpa **112** 13 0N 85 58W
Matagami **82** 49 45N 77 34W
Matagami, L. **82** 49 50N 77 40W
Mataguinao **210** 12 5N 124 55 E
Matak, P. **205** 3 18N 106 16 E
Matakana **231** 32 59 S 145 54 E
Matala **253** 14 46 S 15 4 E
Matalaque **122** 16 26 S 70 49W
Matale **201** 7 30N 80 37 E
Matam, Phil. **211** 8 25N 123 19 E
Matam, Senegal **246** 15 34N 13 17W
Matamata **234** 37 48 S 175 47 E
Matamec, L. **80** 50 21N 65 58W
Matameye **247** 13 26N 8 28 E
Matamoros, Campeche, Mexico **111** 18 35N 90 38W
Matamoros, Coahuila, Mexico **102** 25 32N 103 15W
Matamoros, Tamaulipas, Mexico **102** 25 53N 97 30W
Ma'ţan as Sarra **243** 21 45N 22 0 E
Matancillas **107** 21 53N 101 38W
Matancita **99** 25 9N 111 59W
Matandu → **251** 8 45 S 34 19 E
Matane **80** 48 50N 67 33W
Matane → **80** 48 50N 67 35W
Matane, Parc Prov. de **80** 48 40N 67 0W
Matang **216** 23 30N 104 7 E
Matankari **247** 13 46N 4 1 E
Matanzas, Cuba **112** 23 0N 81 40W
Matanzas, Mexico **107** 21 37N 101 38W
Matapan, C. = Taínaron, Ákra **169** 36 22N 22 27 E
Matapédia **81** 48 0N 66 59W
Matapédia, L. **80** 48 35N 67 35W
Matara **201** 5 58N 80 30 E
Mataram **209** 8 41 S 116 10 E
Matarani **122** 77 0 S 72 10W
Mataranka **228** 14 55 S 133 4 E
Matarma, Râs **191** 30 27N 32 44 E
Mataró **156** 41 32N 2 29 E
Matarraña → **156** 41 14N 0 22 E
Mataruška Banja **166** 43 40N 20 45 E
Matata **234** 37 54 S 176 48 E
Matatiele **255** 30 20 S 28 49 E
Mataura **235** 46 11 S 168 51 E
Mataura → **235** 46 34 S 168 44 E
Matawin → **83** 46 54N 72 56W
Matawin, Rés. **83** 46 46N 73 50W
Matchi-Manitou, L. **82** 48 0N 77 4W
Mategua **123** 13 1 S 62 48W
Matehuala **103** 23 39N 100 39W
Mateira **121** 18 54 S 50 30W
Mateke Hills **251** 21 48 S 31 0 E
Matélica **163** 43 15N 13 0 E
Matera **165** 40 40N 16 37 E
Mátészalka **151** 47 58N 22 20 E
Matetsi **251** 18 12 S 26 0 E
Mateur **241** 37 0N 9 40 E
Matfors **172** 62 21N 17 2 E
Matha **140** 45 52N 0 20W
Matheson Island **89** 51 45N 96 56W
Mathoura **233** 35 50 S 144 55 E
Mathura **198** 27 30N 77 40 E
Mati **211** 6 55N 126 15 E
Mati → **168** 41 40N 20 0 E
Matías Romero **109** 16 53N 95 2W
Matibane **251** 14 49 S 40 45 E
Matican **211** 6 39N 121 53 E
Matillas, L. **110** 18 2N 92 42W
Matima **254** 20 15 S 24 26 E
Matinenda L. **84** 46 22N 82 57W
Matlock **132** 53 8N 1 32W
Matmata **241** 33 37N 9 59 E
Matna **245** 13 49N 35 10 E
Matnog **210** 12 35N 124 5 E
Mato → **119** 7 9N 65 7W
Mato, Serrania de **118** 6 25N 65 25W
Mato Grosso □ **123** 14 0 S 55 0W
Mato Grosso, Planalto do **123** 15 0 S 59 57W
Matochkin Shar **184** 73 10N 56 40 E
Matong **227** 5 36 S 151 50 E
Matopo Hills **251** 20 36 S 28 20 E
Matopos **251** 20 20 S 28 29 E
Matosinhos **154** 41 11N 8 42W
Matour **141** 46 19N 4 29 E
Matrah **195** 23 37N 58 30 E
Matsena **247** 13 5N 10 5 E
Matsesta **181** 43 34N 39 51 E
Matsubara **221** 34 33N 135 34 E
Matsudo **221** 35 47N 139 54 E
Matsue **220** 35 25N 133 10 E
Matsumae **218** 41 26N 140 7 E
Matsumoto **221** 36 15N 138 0 E
Matsusaka **221** 34 34N 136 32 E
Matsutō **221** 36 31N 136 34 E
Matsuura **220** 33 20N 129 49 E
Matsuyama **220** 33 45N 132 45 E
Matsuzaki **221** 34 43N 138 50 E
Mattagami → **87** 50 43N 81 29W
Mattagami L. **87** 47 54N 81 35W
Mattancheri **201** 9 50N 76 15 E
Mattawa **74** 46 20N 78 45W
Mattawitchewan → **87** 49 52N 83 12W
Matterhorn **148** 45 58N 7 39 E
Mattersburg **151** 47 44N 16 24 E
Matthew Town **113** 20 57N 73 40W
Matthew's Ridge **119** 7 37N 60 10W
Mattice **87** 49 40N 83 20W
Mattmar **172** 63 18N 13 45 E
Matuba **255** 24 28 S 32 49 E
Matucana **122** 11 55 S 76 25W
Matuku **226** 19 10 S 179 44 E
Matun **198** 33 22N 69 58 E
Maturín **119** 9 45N 63 11W
Matutum, Mt. **211** 6 22N 125 5 E
Matveyev Kurgan **181** 47 35N 38 47 E
Mau **199** 25 56N 83 33 E
Mau Escarpment **250** 0 40 S 36 0 E
Mau Ranipur **199** 25 16N 79 8 E
Mauban **210** 14 12N 121 44 E
Maubeuge **139** 50 17N 3 57 E
Maubourguet **140** 43 29N 0 1 E
Maud, Pt. **228** 23 6 S 113 45 E
Maude **231** 34 29 S 144 18 E
Maudheim **13** 71 5 S 11 0W
Maués **119** 3 20 S 57 45W
Maugerville **81** 45 52N 66 27W
Maule □ **124** 36 5 S 72 30W
Mauléon-Licharre **140** 43 14N 0 54W
Maullín **126** 41 38 S 73 37W
Maulvibazar **202** 24 29N 91 42 E
Maumere **207** 8 38 S 122 13 E
Maun **254** 20 0 S 23 26 E
Maungaturoto **234** 36 6 S 174 23 E
Maungdow **202** 20 50N 92 21 E
Maunoir, L. **94** 67 30N 124 55W
Maure-de-Bretagne **138** 47 53N 2 0W
Maures **141** 43 15N 6 15 E
Mauriac **140** 45 13N 2 19 E
Maurice L. **229** 29 30 S 131 0 E
Mauriceville **234** 40 45 S 175 42 E
Mauricie, Parc Nat. de la **83** 46 45N 73 0W
Mauritania ■ **240** 20 50N 10 0W
Mauritius ■ **203** 20 0 S 57 0 E
Mauron **138** 48 9N 2 18W
Maurs **140** 44 43N 2 12 E
Mauterndorf **150** 47 9N 13 40 E
Mauvezin **140** 43 44N 0 53 E
Mauzé-sur-le-Mignon **140** 46 12N 0 41W
Mavaca → **119** 2 31N 65 11W
Mavelikara **201** 9 14N 76 32 E
Mavillette **81** 44 6N 66 11W
Mavinga **253** 15 50 S 20 21 E
Mavli **198** 24 45N 73 55 E
Mavqi'im **189** 31 38N 34 32 E
Mavrova **168** 40 26N 19 32 E
Mavuradonha Mts. **251** 16 30 S 31 30 E
Mawa **250** 2 45N 26 40 E
Mawana **198** 29 6N 77 58 E
Mawand **198** 29 33N 68 38 E
Mawk Mai **202** 20 14N 97 37 E
Mawlaik **202** 23 40N 94 26 E
Mawlawkho **202** 17 50N 97 38 E
Mawquq **192** 27 25N 41 8 E
Mawshij **194** 13 43N 43 17 E
Mawson Base **13** 67 30 S 62 53 E
Mawson Coast **13** 68 30 S 63 0 E
Maxcanú **111** 20 35N 89 59W
Maxela **107** 18 2N 99 35W
Maxhamish L. **76** 59 50N 123 17W
Maxixe **255** 23 54 S 35 17 E
Maxville **85** 45 17N 74 51W
Maxwell **234** 39 51 S 174 49 E
Maxwelton **230** 20 43 S 142 41 E
May Downs **230** 22 38 S 148 55 E
May Pen **112** 17 58N 77 15W
May River **227** 4 19 S 141 58 E
Maya, Indonesia **209** 1 10 S 109 35 E
Maya, Spain **156** 43 12N 1 29W
Maya → **185** 54 31N 134 41 E
Mayaguana **113** 22 30N 72 44W
Mayahi **247** 13 58N 7 40 E
Mayals **156** 41 22N 0 30 E
Mayama **252** 3 51 S 14 54 E
Mayāmey **193** 36 24N 55 42 E
Mayanalán **107** 18 9N 99 26W
Mayang **216** 27 53N 109 49 E
Mayarí **113** 20 40N 75 41W
Mayavaram = Mayuram **201** 11 3N 79 42 E
Maychew **245** 12 50N 39 31 E
Maydān **192** 34 55N 45 37 E
Maydena **230** 42 45 S 146 30 E
Maydī **194** 16 19N 42 48 E
Maydos **168** 40 13N 26 20 E
Mayen **147** 50 18N 7 10 E
Mayenne **138** 48 20N 0 38W
Mayenne □ **138** 48 10N 0 40W
Mayenne → **138** 47 30N 0 32W
Mayerthorpe **90** 53 57N 115 8W
Mayfair **88** 52 58N 107 36W
Maykop **181** 44 35N 40 25 E
Mayli-Say **183** 41 17N 72 24 E
Maymont **88** 52 34N 107 42W
Maymyo **204** 22 2N 96 28 E
Maynard Hills **229** 28 35 S 119 50 E
Mayne **93** 48 52N 123 17W
Mayne → **230** 23 40 S 141 55 E
Maynooth **135** 53 22N 6 38W
Mayo **94** 63 38N 135 57W
Mayo □ **135** 53 47N 9 7W
Mayo →, Argentina **126** 45 45 S 69 45W
Mayo →, Mexico **100** 26 45N 109 47W
Mayo →, Peru **122** 6 38 S 76 15W
Mayo Bay **211** 6 56N 126 22 E
Mayoko **252** 2 18 S 12 49 E
Mayon Volcano **210** 13 15N 123 41 E
Mayor I. **234** 37 16 S 176 17 E
Mayorga **154** 42 10N 5 16W
Mayoyao **210** 16 59N 121 14 E
Mayraira Pt. **210** 18 39N 120 51 E
Mayskiy **181** 43 47N 44 2 E
Mayson L. **77** 57 55N 107 10W
Maythalūn **189** 32 21N 35 16 E
Mayu **207** 1 30N 126 30 E
Mayumba **252** 3 25 S 10 39 E
Mayuram **201** 11 3N 79 42 E
Mayya **185** 61 44N 130 18 E
Mazabuka **251** 15 52 S 27 44 E
Mazagán = El Jadida **240** 33 11N 8 17W
Mazagão **119** 0 7 S 51 16W
Mazamet **140** 43 30N 2 20 E
Mazamitia **106** 19 55N 103 2W
Mazán **118** 3 30 S 73 0W
Māzandarān □ **193** 36 30N 52 0 E
Mazapa de Madero **110** 15 23N 92 11W
Mazapil **105** 24 38N 101 34W
Mazapil, Sa. de **105** 24 35N 101 30W
Mazar, O. → **241** 31 50N 1 36 E
Mazar-e Sharīf **197** 36 41N 67 0 E
Mazara del Vallo **164** 37 40N 12 34 E
Mazarredo **126** 47 10 S 66 50W
Mazarrón **157** 37 38N 1 19W
Mazarrón, Golfo de **157** 37 27N 1 19W
Mazaruni → **119** 6 25N 58 35W
Mazatan **100** 29 0N 110 8W
Mazatenango **112** 14 35N 91 30W
Mazatlán **104** 23 13N 106 25W
Mažeikiai **178** 56 20N 22 20 E
Mazenod **88** 49 52N 106 13W
Mazhabong L. **87** 46 58N 82 30W
Mazhafa, J. **191** 28 52N 35 5 E
Māzhān **193** 32 30N 59 0 E
Mazīnān **193** 36 19N 56 56 E
Mazoe **251** 16 42 S 33 7 E
Mazowe **251** 17 28 S 30 58 E
Mazrûb **245** 14 0N 29 20 E
Mazu Dao **217** 26 10N 119 55 E
Mazurian Lakes = Mazurski, Pojezierze **152** 53 50N 21 0 E
Mazurski, Pojezierze **152** 53 50N 21 0 E
Mazzarino **165** 37 19N 14 12 E
Mba **226** 17 33 S 177 41 E
Mbaba **246** 14 59N 16 44W
Mbabane **255** 26 18 S 31 6 E

Mbagne **246** 16 6N 14 47W
M'bahiakro **246** 7 33N 4 19W
Mbaïki **252** 3 53N 18 1 E
Mbakana, Mt. de **252** 7 57N 15 6 E
Mbala **251** 8 46 S 31 24 E
Mbale **250** 1 8N 34 12 E
Mbalmayo **247** 3 33N 11 33 E
Mbamba Bay **251** 11 13 S 34 49 E
Mbandaka **252** 0 1N 18 18 E
Mbanga **247** 4 30N 9 33 E
Mbanza Congo **253** 6 18 S 14 16 E
Mbanza Ngungu **253** 5 12 S 14 53 E
Mbarara **250** 0 35 S 30 40 E
Mbatto **246** 6 28N 4 22W
Mbengga **226** 18 23 S 178 8 E
Mbenkuru → **251** 9 25 S 39 50 E
Mberengwa **251** 20 29 S 29 57 E
Mberengwa N. **251** 20 37 S 29 55 E
Mberubu **247** 6 10N 7 38 E
Mbesuma **251** 10 0 S 32 2 E
Mbeya **251** 8 54 S 33 29 E
Mbeya □ **250** 8 15 S 33 30 E
Mbigou **252** 1 53 S 11 56 E
Mbinga **251** 10 50 S 35 0 E
Mbinga □ **251** 10 50 S 35 0 E
Mbini □ **252** 1 30N 10 0 E
Mboki **245** 5 19N 25 58 E
Mboli **252** 4 8N 23 9 E
Mboro **246** 15 9N 16 54W
Mboune **246** 14 42N 13 34W
Mbouomo **252** 0 52 S 15 4 E
Mbour **246** 14 22N 16 54W
Mbout **246** 16 1N 12 38W
Mbozi □ **251** 9 0 S 32 50 E
Mbrés **252** 6 40N 19 48 E
Mbuji-Mayi **250** 6 9 S 23 40 E
Mbulu **250** 3 45 S 35 30 E
Mbulu □ **250** 3 52 S 35 33 E
Mburucuyá **124** 28 1 S 58 14W
Mcherrah **240** 27 0N 4 30W
Mchinja **251** 9 44 S 39 45 E
Mchinji **251** 13 47 S 32 58 E
Mdennah **240** 24 37N 6 0W
Mdina **160** 35 51N 14 25 E
Meacham **88** 52 6N 105 45W
Meachen **91** 49 38N 116 17W
Meadow **229** 26 35 S 114 40 E
Meadow L. **88** 54 7N 108 20W
Meadow Lake **88** 54 10N 108 26W
Meadow Lake Prov. Park **77** 54 27N 109 0W
Meaford **84** 44 36N 80 35W
Meaghers Grant **81** 44 55N 63 15W
Mealhada **154** 40 22N 8 27W
Mealy Mts. **75** 53 10N 58 0W
Meander River **76** 59 2N 117 42W
Meares I. **92** 49 12N 125 50W
Mearim → **120** 3 4 S 44 35W
Meath □ **135** 53 32N 6 40W
Meath Park **88** 53 27N 105 22W
Meatian **232** 35 34 S 143 21 E
Meaulne **140** 46 36N 2 36 E
Meaux **139** 48 58N 2 50 E
Mebechi-Gawa → **218** 40 31N 141 31 E
Mecanhelas **251** 15 12 S 35 54 E
Mecatina, Little → **80** 52 10N 60 40W
Mécatina, Petit- → **80** 50 40N 59 30W
Mecaya → **118** 0 29N 75 11W
Mecayapan **109** 18 13N 94 50W
Mecca = Makkah **194** 21 30N 39 54 E
Mechara **245** 8 36N 40 20 E
Mechelen, Antwerpen, Belgium **143** 51 2N 4 29 E
Mechelen, Limburg, Belgium **143** 50 58N 5 41 E
Mecheria **241** 33 35N 0 18W
Mechernich **146** 50 35N 6 39 E
Mechetinskaya **181** 46 45N 40 32 E
Méchins, Les **80** 48 59N 66 59W
Mechra Benâbbou **240** 32 39N 7 48W
Mecidiye **168** 40 38N 26 32 E
Mecitözü **180** 40 32N 35 17 E
Meconta **251** 14 59 S 39 50 E
Meda, Australia **228** 17 22 S 123 59 E
Meda, Portugal **154** 40 57N 7 18W
Medak **200** 18 1N 78 15 E
Medan **208** 3 40N 98 38 E
Médanos **126** 38 50 S 62 42W
Medanosa, Pta. **126** 48 8 S 66 0W
Medawachchiya **201** 8 30N 80 30 E
Medéa **241** 36 12N 2 50 E
Mededa **166** 43 44N 19 15 E
Médégué **252** 0 37N 10 8 E
Medeiros Neto **121** 17 20 S 40 14W
Medel, Pic **149** 46 34N 8 55 E
Medellín **118** 6 15N 75 35W
Medemblik **142** 52 46N 5 8 E
Médenine **241** 33 21N 10 30 E
Mederdra **246** 17 0N 15 38W
Medgidia **170** 44 15N 28 19 E
Medi **245** 5 4N 30 42 E
Media Agua **124** 31 58 S 68 25W
Media Luna **124** 34 45 S 66 44W
Mediaş **170** 46 9N 24 22 E
Medias Aguas **109** 17 40N 95 2W
Medicina **163** 44 29N 11 38 E
Medicine Hat **91** 50 0N 110 45W
Medina = Al Madīnah **192** 24 35N 39 52 E
Medina, Brazil **121** 16 15 S 41 29W
Medina, Colombia **118** 4 30N 73 21W
Medina de Ríoseco **154** 41 53N 5 3W
Medina del Campo **154** 41 18N 4 55W
Medina-Sidonia **155** 36 28N 5 57W
Medinaceli **156** 41 12N 2 30W
Medinipur **199** 22 25N 87 21 E
Mediterranean Sea **158** 35 0N 15 0 E
Medjerda, O. → **241** 37 7N 10 13 E
Medley **90** 54 25N 110 16W
Mednogorsk **182** 51 24N 57 37 E
Médoc **140** 45 10N 0 56W
Médouneu **252** 0 57N 10 47 E
Medport = Marsaxlokk **160** 35 47N 14 32 E
Medstead **88** 53 19N 108 5W
Meductic **81** 46 0N 67 29W
Medulin **163** 44 49N 13 55 E
Medveda **166** 42 50N 21 32 E
Medveditsa →, R.S.F.S.R., U.S.S.R. **179** 49 35N 42 41 E
Medveditsa →, R.S.F.S.R., U.S.S.R. **179** 57 5N 37 30 E
Medvedok **179** 57 20N 50 1 E
Medvezhi, Ostrava **185** 71 0N 161 0 E
Medvezhyegorsk **176** 63 0N 34 25 E
Medway →, Canada **81** 44 8N 64 36W
Medway →, U.K. **133** 51 28N 0 45 E
Medyn **179** 54 58N 35 52 E
Medzev **151** 48 43N 20 55 E
Medzilaborce **151** 49 17N 21 52 E
Meeberrie **229** 26 57 S 115 51 E
Meekatharra **229** 26 32 S 118 29 E
Meeniyan **233** 38 35 S 146 0 E
Meer **143** 51 27N 4 45 E
Meerane **146** 50 51N 12 30 E
Meerbeke **143** 50 50N 4 3 E
Meerhout **143** 51 7N 5 4 E
Meerle **143** 51 29N 4 48 E
Meersburg **147** 47 42N 9 16 E
Meerssen **143** 50 53N 5 50 E
Meerut **198** 29 1N 77 42 E
Meeuwen **143** 51 6N 5 31 E
Mega **245** 3 57N 38 19 E
Megálo Khorío **169** 36 27N 27 24 E
Megálo Petalí **169** 38 0N 24 15 E
Megalópolis **169** 37 25N 22 7 E
Meganísi **169** 38 39N 20 48 E
Mégantic, L. **83** 45 32N 70 53W
Mégantic, Mt. **83** 45 28N 71 9W
Mégara **169** 37 58N 23 22 E
Megarine **241** 33 14N 6 2 E
Megdhova → **169** 39 10N 21 45 E
Mégève **141** 45 51N 6 37 E
Meghalaya □ **202** 25 50N 91 0 E
Meghezez, Mt. **245** 9 18N 39 26 E
Meghna → **202** 22 50N 90 50 E
Megiddo **189** 32 36N 35 11 E
Mégiscane → **82** 48 29N 75 38W
Mégiscane, L. **82** 48 35N 75 55W
Megiste **159** 36 8N 29 34 E
Mehadia **170** 44 56N 22 23 E
Mehaigne → **143** 50 32N 5 13 E
Mehaïguene, O. → **241** 32 15N 2 59 E
Mehedinţi □ **170** 44 40N 22 45 E
Meheisa **244** 19 38N 32 57 E
Mehndawal **199** 26 58N 83 5 E
Mehr Jān **193** 33 50N 55 6 E
Mehrābād **192** 36 53N 47 55 E
Mehrān **192** 33 7N 46 10 E
Mehrīz **193** 31 35N 54 28 E
Mehun-sur-Yèvre **139** 47 10N 2 13 E
Mei Jiang → **217** 24 25N 116 35 E
Mei Xian, Guangdong, China **217** 24 16N 116 6 E
Mei Xian, Shaanxi, China **214** 34 18N 107 55 E
Meia Ponte → **121** 18 32 S 49 36W
Meicheng **217** 29 29N 119 16 E
Meichengzhen **217** 28 9N 111 40 E
Meichuan **217** 30 8N 115 31 E
Meiganga **252** 6 30N 14 25 E
Meighen I. **95** 80 0N 99 30W
Meijel **143** 51 21N 5 53 E
Meiktila **202** 20 53N 95 54 E
Meilen **149** 47 16N 8 39 E
Meiningen **146** 50 32N 10 25 E
Meio → **121** 13 36 S 44 7W
Me'ir Shefeya **189** 32 35N 34 58 E
Meira, Sierra de **154** 43 15N 7 15W
Meiringen **148** 46 43N 8 12 E
Meishan **216** 30 3N 103 23 E
Meissen **146** 51 10N 13 29 E
Meissner **146** 51 13N 9 51 E
Meitan **216** 27 45N 107 29 E
Méjean, Causse **140** 44 15N 3 30 E
Mejillones **124** 23 10 S 70 30W
Meka **229** 27 25 S 116 48 E
Mékambo **252** 1 2N 13 50 E
Mekdela **245** 11 24N 39 10 E
Mekele **245** 13 33N 39 30 E
Mekhtar **197** 30 30N 69 15 E
Mékinac, L. **83** 47 3N 72 41W
Meknès **240** 33 57N 5 33W
Meko **247** 7 27N 2 52 E
Mekong → **205** 9 30N 106 15 E
Mekongga **207** 3 39 S 121 15 E
Melagiri Hills **201** 12 20N 77 30 E
Melah, Sebkhet el **241** 29 20N 1 30W
Melaka **205** 2 15N 102 15 E
Melalap **206** 5 10N 116 5 E
Mélambes **169** 35 8N 24 40 E
Melanesia **224** 4 0 S 155 0 E
Melapalaiyam **201** 8 39N 77 44 E
Melawi → **209** 0 5N 111 29 E
Melbourne **231** 37 50 S 145 0 E
Melchor Muzquiz **102** 27 53N 101 31W
Melchor Ocampo **105** 24 51N 101 39W
Méldola **163** 44 7N 12 3 E
Meldorf **146** 54 5N 9 5 E
Meldrum Bay **84** 45 56N 83 6W
Meldrum Creek **93** 52 6N 122 21W
Mêle-sur-Sarthe, Le **138** 48 31N 0 22 E
Meleden **256** 10 25N 49 51 E
Melegnano **162** 45 21N 9 20 E
Melenci **166** 45 32N 20 20 E
Melenki **179** 55 20N 41 37 E
Meleuz **182** 52 58N 55 55 E
Mélèzes → **78** 57 40N 69 29W
Melfi, Chad **243** 11 0N 17 59 E
Melfi, Italy **165** 41 0N 15 33 E
Melfort, Canada **88** 52 50N 104 37W
Melfort, Zimbabwe **251** 18 0 S 31 25 E
Melgaço **154** 42 7N 8 15W
Melgar de Fernamental **154** 42 27N 4 17W
Melhus **171** 63 17N 10 18 E
Melick **143** 51 10N 6 1 E
Melide **149** 45 57N 8 57 E
Meligalá **169** 37 15N 21 59 E
Melilla **241** 35 21N 2 57W
Melilot **189** 31 22N 34 37 E
Melipilla **124** 33 42 S 71 15W
Mélissa Óros **169** 37 32N 26 4 E
Melita **89** 49 15N 101 0W
Mélito di Porto Salvo **165** 37 55N 15 47 E
Melitopol **180** 46 50N 35 22 E
Melk **150** 48 13N 15 20 E
Mellan-Fryken **172** 59 45N 13 10 E
Mellansel **174** 63 25N 18 17 E
Melle, Belgium **143** 51 0N 3 49 E
Melle, France **140** 46 14N 0 10W
Melle, Germany **146** 52 12N 8 20 E
Mellègue, O. → **241** 36 32N 8 51 E
Mellerud **173** 58 41N 12 28 E
Mellid **154** 42 55N 8 1W
Mellit **245** 14 7N 25 34 E
Mellizo Sur, Cerro **126** 48 33 S 73 10W
Mellrichstadt **147** 50 26N 10 19 E
Melnik, Bulgaria **167** 41 30N 23 25 E
Mělník, Czech. **150** 50 22N 14 23 E
Melo **125** 32 20 S 54 10W
Melolo **207** 9 53 S 120 40 E
Melouprey **204** 13 48N 105 16 E
Melovoye **181** 49 25N 40 5 E
Melrhir, Chott **241** 34 25N 6 24 E
Melrose, N.S.W., Australia **231** 32 42 S 146 57 E
Melrose, W. Austral., Australia **229** 27 50 S 121 15 E
Melrose, U.K. **134** 53 35N 2 44W
Mels **149** 47 3N 9 25 E
Melsele **143** 51 13N 4 17 E
Melsungen **146** 51 8N 9 34 E
Melton Mowbray **132** 52 46N 0 52W
Melun **139** 48 32N 2 39 E
Melur **201** 10 2N 78 23 E
Melut **245** 10 30N 32 13 E
Melville **88** 50 55N 102 50W
Melville, C. **230** 14 11 S 144 30 E
Melville, L. **78** 53 30N 60 0W
Melville B. **230** 12 0 S 136 45 E
Melville Bugt **95** 75 30N 63 0W
Melville I., Australia **228** 11 30 S 131 0 E
Melville I., Canada **94** 75 30N 112 0W
Melville Pen. **95** 68 0N 84 0W
Melvin → **76** 59 11N 117 31W
Mélykút **151** 46 11N 19 25 E
Memaliaj **168** 40 25N 19 58 E
Memba **251** 14 11 S 40 30 E
Memboro **207** 9 30 S 119 30 E
Membrilla **157** 38 59N 3 21W
Memel = Klaipeda **178** 55 43N 21 10 E
Memel **255** 27 38 S 29 36 E
Memmingen **147** 47 59N 10 12 E
Mempawah **209** 0 30N 109 5 E
Memphrémagog, L. **83** 45 8N 72 17W
Mena → **245** 5 40N 40 50 E
Menai Strait **132** 53 14N 4 10W
Ménaka **247** 15 59N 2 18 E
Menaldum **142** 53 13N 5 40 E
Menamurtee **232** 31 25 S 143 11 E
Menan = Chao Phraya → **204** 13 32N 100 36 E
Menarandra → **255** 25 17 S 44 30 E
Ménascouagama, L. **80** 51 13N 61 52W
Menate **209** 0 12 S 113 3 E
Mendawai → **209** 3 30 S 113 0 E
Mende **140** 44 31N 3 30 E
Mendebo Mts. **245** 7 0N 39 22 E
Méndez **103** 25 7N 98 34W
Mendez Nunez **210** 14 8N 120 54 E
Mendham **88** 50 46N 109 40W
Mendhar **199** 33 35N 74 10 E
Mendi, Ethiopia **245** 9 47N 35 4 E
Mendi, Papua N. G. **227** 6 11 S 143 39 E
Mendip Hills **133** 51 17N 2 40W
Mendocino Seascarp **225** 41 0N 140 0W
Mendoza, Argentina **124** 32 50 S 68 52W
Mendoza, Mexico **105** 23 20N 102 42W
Mendoza □ **124** 33 0 S 69 0W
Mendrisio **149** 45 52N 8 59 E
Mene Grande **118** 9 49N 70 56W
Menen **143** 50 47N 3 7 E
Menéndez, L. **126** 42 40 S 71 51W
Menfi **164** 37 36N 12 57 E
Mengcheng **217** 33 18N 116 31 E
Mengdingjie **216** 23 31N 98 58 E
Mengeš **163** 46 24N 14 35 E
Menggala **208** 4 30 S 105 15 E
Menghai **216** 21 49N 100 55 E
Mengíbar **155** 37 58N 3 48W
Mengjin **214** 34 55N 112 45 E
Mengla **216** 21 20N 101 25 E
Menglian **216** 22 21N 99 27 E
Mengoub **240** 29 49N 5 26W
Mengshan **217** 24 14N 110 55 E
Mengyin **215** 35 40N 117 58 E
Mengzhe **216** 22 2N 100 15 E
Mengzi **216** 23 20N 103 22 E
Menihek **78** 54 28N 56 36W
Menihek L. **78** 54 0N 67 0W
Menin = Menen **143** 50 47N 3 7 E
Menindee **231** 32 20 S 142 25 E
Menindee, L. **231** 32 20 S 142 25 E
Meningie **232** 35 35 S 139 0 E
Ménistouc, L. **80** 52 52N 66 29W
Menongue **253** 14 48 S 17 52 E
Menorca **156** 40 0N 4 0 E
Mentakab **205** 3 29N 102 21 E
Mentawai, Kepulauan **208** 2 0 S 99 0 E
Menton **141** 43 50N 7 29 E
Menyamya **227** 7 10 S 145 59 E
Menzel-Bourguiba **241** 39 9N 9 49 E
Menzel Chaker **241** 35 0N 10 26 E
Menzel-Temime **241** 36 46N 11 0 E
Menzelinsk **182** 55 53N 53 1 E
Menzies **229** 29 40 S 120 58 E
Me'ona **189** 33 1N 35 15 E
Meoqui **101** 28 17N 105 29W
Meota **88** 53 2N 108 27W
Mepaco **251** 15 57 S 30 48 E
Meppel **142** 52 42N 6 12 E
Meppen **146** 52 41N 7 20 E
Mequinenza **156** 41 22N 0 17 E
Merabéllou, Kólpos **169** 35 10N 25 50 E
Merai **227** 4 52 S 152 19 E
Meramangye, L. **229** 28 25 S 132 13 E
Meran = Merano **163** 46 40N 11 10 E
Merano **163** 46 40N 11 10 E
Merasheen I. **79** 47 25N 54 15W
Merate **162** 45 42N 9 23 E
Merauke **207** 8 29 S 140 24 E
Merbabu **209** 7 30 S 110 40 E
Merbein **231** 34 10 S 142 2 E
Merca **256** 1 48N 44 50 E
Mercadal **156** 39 59N 4 5 E
Mercato Saraceno **163** 43 57N 12 11 E
Mercedes, Buenos Aires, Argentina **124** 34 40 S 59 30W
Mercedes, Corrientes, Argentina **124** 29 10 S 58 5W
Mercedes, San Luis, Argentina **124** 33 40 S 65 21W
Mercedes, Camarines N., Phil. **210** 14 7N 123 1 E
Mercedes, Leyte, Phil. **211** 10 41N 124 24 E
Mercedes, Zamboanga del S., Phil. **211** 6 57N 122 9 E
Mercedes, Uruguay **124** 33 12 S 58 0W
Merceditas **124** 28 20 S 70 35W
Mercer **234** 37 16 S 175 5 E
Merchtem **143** 50 58N 4 14 E
Mercier, Bolivia **122** 10 42 S 68 5W

Mercier, Canada **83** 45 19N 73 45W
Mercoal **90** 53 10N 117 5W
Mercy C. **95** 65 0N 63 30W
Merdrignac **138** 48 11N 2 27W
Mere **143** 50 55N 3 58 E
Meredith C. **126** 52 15 S 60 40W
Meregh **256** 3 46N 47 18 E
Merei **170** 45 7N 26 43 E
Merelbeke **143** 51 0N 3 45 E
Méréville **139** 48 20N 2 5 E
Merga = Nukheila **244** 19 1N 26 21 E
Mergenevo **182** 49 56N 51 18 E
Mergenevsky **181** 49 59N 51 15 E
Mergui Arch. = Myeik Kyunzu **204** 11 30N 97 30 E
Meribah **232** 34 43 S 140 51 E
Mérida, Mexico **111** 20 58N 89 37W
Merida, Phil. **211** 10 55N 124 32 E
Mérida, Spain **155** 38 55N 6 25W
Mérida, Venezuela **118** 8 24N 71 8W
Mérida □ **118** 8 30N 71 10W
Mérida, Cord. de **114** 9 0N 71 0W
Merigomish **81** 45 38N 62 26W
Mering **147** 48 15N 11 0 E
Meriruma **119** 1 15N 54 50W
Merke **183** 42 52N 73 11 E
Merksem **143** 51 16N 4 25 E
Merksplas **143** 51 22N 4 52 E
Merlebach **139** 49 5N 6 52 E
Merlerault, Le **138** 48 41N 0 16 E
Mermaid Reef **228** 17 6 S 119 36 E
Mern **172** 55 3N 12 3 E
Merowe **244** 18 29N 31 46 E
Merredin **229** 31 28 S 118 18 E
Merrick **134** 55 8N 4 30W
Merrickville **85** 44 55N 75 50W
Merritt **93** 50 10N 120 45W
Merriwa **231** 32 6 S 150 22 E
Merriwagga **231** 33 47 S 145 43 E
Merry I. **78** 55 29N 77 31W
Merrygoen **231** 31 51 S 149 12 E
Mersa Fatma **245** 14 57N 40 17 E
Mersch **143** 49 44N 6 7 E
Merseburg **146** 51 20N 12 0 E
Mersey →, Canada **81** 44 2N 64 43W
Mersey →, U.K. **132** 53 20N 2 56W
Merseyside □ **132** 53 25N 2 55W
Mersin **177** 36 51N 34 36 E
Mersing **205** 2 25N 103 50 E
Merta **198** 26 39N 74 4 E
Mertert **143** 49 43N 6 29 E
Merthyr Tydfil **133** 51 45N 3 23W
Mértola **155** 37 40N 7 40 E
Mertzig **143** 49 51N 6 1 E
Méru, France **139** 49 13N 2 8 E
Meru, Kenya **250** 0 3N 37 40 E
Meru, Tanzania **250** 3 15 S 36 46 E
Meru □ **250** 0 3N 37 46 E
Merville, Canada **92** 49 48N 125 3W
Merville, France **139** 50 38N 2 38 E
Mervin **88** 53 20N 108 53W
Méry-sur-Seine **139** 48 31N 3 54 E
Merzifon **180** 40 53N 35 32 E
Merzig **147** 49 26N 6 37 E
Merzouga, Erg Tin **241** 24 0N 11 4 E
Mesa de las Tablas **103** 25 14N 100 25W
Mesa del Nayar **104** 22 16N 104 35W
Mesach Mellet **241** 24 30N 11 30 E
Mesada **189** 31 20N 35 19 E
Mesagne **165** 40 34N 17 48 E
Mesaras, Kólpos **169** 35 6N 24 47 E
Meschede **146** 51 20N 8 17 E
Mesfinto **245** 13 20N 37 22 E
Mesgouez, L. **78** 51 20N 75 0W
Meshchovsk **178** 54 22N 35 17 E
Meshed = Mashhad **193** 36 20N 59 35 E
Mesilinka → **76** 56 6N 124 30W
Meslay-du-Maine **138** 47 58N 0 33W
Mesocco **149** 46 23N 9 12 E
Mesolóngion **169** 38 21N 21 28 E
Mesopotamia = Al Jazirah **192** 33 30N 44 0 E
Mesoraca **165** 39 5N 16 47 E
Mésou Volímais **169** 37 53N 20 35 E
Mess Cr. → **76** 57 55N 131 14W
Messac **138** 47 49N 1 50W
Messad **241** 34 8N 3 30 E
Messalo → **251** 12 25 S 39 15 E
Méssaména **247** 3 48N 12 49 E
Messancy **143** 49 36N 5 49 E
Messeix **140** 45 37N 2 33 E
Messeue **169** 37 12N 21 58 E
Messier, Canal **126** 48 20 S 74 33W
Messina, Italy **165** 38 10N 15 32 E
Messina, S. Africa **255** 22 20 S 30 0 E
Messina, Str. di **165** 38 5N 15 35 E
Messine **82** 46 14N 76 2W
Messíni **169** 37 4N 22 1 E
Messínia □ **169** 37 10N 22 0 E
Messiniakós, Kólpos **169** 36 45N 22 5 E
Messkirch **147** 47 59N 9 7 E
Mesta → **167** 41 30N 24 0 E
Mestà, Ákra **169** 38 16N 25 53 E
Mestanza **155** 38 35N 4 4W
Město Teplá **150** 49 59N 12 52 E
Mestre **163** 45 30N 12 13 E
Mestre, Espigão **121** 12 30 S 46 10W
Městys Zelezná Ruda **150** 49 8N 13 15 E
Meta □ **118** 3 30N 73 0W
Meta → **118** 6 12N 67 28W
Metalici, Munţii **170** 46 15N 22 50 E
Metán **124** 25 30 S 65 0W
Metangula **251** 12 40 S 34 50 E
Metapa **110** 14 50N 92 11W
Metauro → **163** 43 50N 13 3 E
Meteghan **81** 44 11N 66 10W
Metema **245** 12 56N 36 13 E
Metengobalame **251** 14 49 S 34 30 E
Metepec, México, Mexico **107** 19 15N 99 36W
Metepec, Puebla, Mexico **109** 18 56N 98 33W
Méthana **169** 37 35N 23 23 E
Methóni **169** 36 49N 21 42 E
Methven **235** 43 38 S 171 40 E
Methy L. **77** 56 28N 109 30W
Métis-sur-Mer **80** 48 40N 67 59W
Metkovets **167** 43 37N 23 10 E
Metković **166** 43 6N 17 39 E
Metlaltoyuca **108** 20 44N 97 51W
Metlaoui **241** 34 24N 8 24 E
Metlatonoc **107** 17 11N 98 20W
Metlika **163** 45 40N 15 20 E
Metro **208** 5 5 S 105 20 E
Métsovon **168** 39 48N 21 12 E
Mettet **143** 50 19N 4 41 E
Mettuppalaiyam **201** 11 18N 76 59 E
Mettur **201** 11 48N 77 47 E
Metulla **189** 33 17N 35 34 E
Metz **139** 49 8N 6 10 E
Metztitlán **107** 20 36N 98 45W
Meulaboh **208** 4 11N 96 3 E
Meulan **139** 49 0N 1 52 E
Meung-sur-Loire **139** 47 50N 1 40 E
Meureudu **208** 5 19N 96 10 E
Meurthe → **139** 48 47N 6 9 E
Meurthe-et-Moselle □ **139** 48 52N 6 0 E
Meuse □ **139** 49 8N 5 25 E
Meuse → **143** 50 45N 5 41 E
Meuselwitz **146** 51 3N 12 18 E
Mexborough **132** 53 29N 1 18W
Mexcaltitán **104** 21 55N 105 31W
Mexcaltitán, L. **104** 21 54N 105 30W
Mexiana, I. **120** 0 0 49 30W
Mexicalcingo **107** 19 21N 99 7W
Mexicali **98** 32 40N 115 29W
Mexicanos, L. de los **101** 28 9N 106 57W
México □ **107** 19 20N 99 30W
Mexico ■ **97** 20 0N 100 0W
Mexico, G. of **97** 25 0N 90 0W
Mexquitic **103** 22 16N 101 7W
Mexticacán **106** 21 13N 102 43W
Meyenburg **146** 53 19N 12 15 E
Meymac **140** 45 32N 2 10 E
Meymaneh **197** 35 53N 64 38 E
Meyrargues **141** 43 38N 5 32 E
Meyronne **88** 49 39N 106 50W
Meyrueis **140** 44 12N 3 27 E
Meyssac **140** 45 3N 1 40 E
Mezcala **107** 17 56N 99 37W
Mezcala, R. → **107** 17 58N 99 42W
Mezdra **167** 43 12N 23 42 E
Mèze **140** 43 27N 3 36 E
Mezen **176** 65 50N 44 20 E
Mezen → **176** 66 11N 43 59 E
Mézenc **141** 44 55N 4 11 E
Mezeş, Munţii **170** 47 5N 23 5 E
Mezha → **178** 55 50N 31 45 E
Mezhdurechenskiy **182** 59 36N 65 56 E
Mézidon **138** 49 5N 0 1W
Mézilhac **141** 44 49N 4 21 E
Mézin **140** 44 4N 0 16 E
Mezöberény **151** 46 49N 21 3 E
Mezöfalva **151** 46 55N 18 49 E
Mezöhegyes **151** 46 19N 20 49 E
Mezökövácsháza **151** 46 25N 20 57 E
Mezökövesd **151** 47 49N 20 35 E
Mézos **140** 44 5N 1 10W
Mezötúr **151** 47 0N 20 41 E
Mezquital **105** 23 29N 104 23W
Mezquital del Oro **106** 21 10N 103 23W
Mezquitic **105** 22 23N 103 41W
Mezzolombardo **162** 46 13N 11 5 E
Mgeta **251** 8 22 S 36 6 E
Mglin **178** 53 2N 32 50 E
Mhlaba Hills **251** 18 30 S 30 30 E
Mhow **198** 22 33N 75 50 E
Mi-Shima **220** 34 46N 131 9 E
Miacatlán **107** 18 46N 99 22W
Miagna, L. **109** 16 1N 97 50W
Miahuatlán, Sa. de **109** 16 10N 96 30W
Miahuatlán de Porfirio Díaz **109** 16 20N 96 36W
Miajadas **155** 39 9N 5 54W
Miallo **230** 16 28 S 145 22 E
Mian Xian **214** 33 10N 106 32 E
Mianchi **214** 34 48N 111 48 E
Mīāndow āb **192** 37 0N 46 5 E
Miandrivazo **255** 19 31 S 45 29 E
Mīāneh **192** 37 30N 47 40 E
Mianning **216** 28 32N 102 9 E
Mianwali **197** 32 38N 71 28 E
Mianyang, Hubei, China **217** 30 25N 113 25 E
Mianyang, Sichuan, China **216** 31 22N 104 47 E
Mianzhu **216** 31 22N 104 7 E
Miaoli **217** 24 37N 120 49 E
Miarinarivo **255** 18 57 S 46 55 E
Miass **182** 54 59N 60 6 E
Miass → **182** 56 6N 64 30 E
Miasteczko Kraj **152** 53 7N 17 1 E
Miastko **152** 54 0N 16 58 E
Mica Creek **93** 52 2N 118 35W
Micăsasa **170** 46 7N 24 7 E
Michael, Mt. **227** 6 27 S 145 22 E
Michalovce **151** 48 47N 21 58 E
Michelstadt **147** 49 40N 9 0 E
Michipicoten **87** 47 55N 84 55W
Michipicoten B. **87** 47 53N 84 53W
Michipicoten I. **87** 47 40N 85 40W
Michoacán □ **106** 19 10N 101 50W
Michurin **167** 42 9N 27 51 E
Michurinsk **179** 52 58N 40 27 E
Miclere **230** 22 34 S 147 32 E
Mico, Pta. **112** 12 0N 83 30W
Micronesia **224** 11 0N 160 0 E
Mid Glamorgan □ **133** 51 40N 3 25W
Mid-Indian Ridge **224** 40 0 S 75 0 E
Mid-Oceanic Ridge **224** 42 0 S 90 0 E
Midai, P. **205** 3 0N 107 47 E
Midale **88** 49 25N 103 20W
Middagsfjället **172** 63 27N 12 19 E
Middelbeers **143** 51 28N 5 15 E
Middelburg, Neth. **143** 51 30N 3 36 E
Middelburg, C. Prov., S. Africa **254** 31 30 S 25 0 E
Middelburg, Trans., S. Africa **255** 25 49 S 29 28 E
Middelfart **173** 55 30N 9 43 E
Middelharnis **142** 51 46N 4 10 E
Middelkerke **143** 51 11N 2 49 E
Middelrode **143** 51 41N 5 26 E
Middle Andaman I. **196** 12 30N 92 30 E
Middle Lake **88** 52 29N 105 18W
Middle Musquodoboit **81** 45 3N 63 9W
Middlemarch **235** 45 30 S 170 9 E
Middlesbrough **132** 54 35N 1 14W
Middlesex **112** 17 2N 88 31W
Middleton, Australia **230** 22 22 S 141 32 E
Middleton, Canada **81** 44 57N 65 4W
Middlewood **81** 44 14N 64 34W
Midelt **240** 32 46N 4 44W
Midhirst **234** 39 17 S 174 18 E
Midi, Canal du **140** 43 45N 1 21 E
Midi d'Ossau **156** 42 50N 0 25W
Midland, Australia **231** 31 54 S 115 59 E
Midland, Canada **84** 44 45N 79 50W
Midlands □ **251** 19 40 S 29 0 E
Midleton **135** 51 52N 8 12W
Midongy, Tangorombohitr' i **255** 23 30 S 47 0 E
Midongy Atsimo **255** 23 35 S 47 1 E
Midour → **140** 43 54N 0 30W
Midouze → **140** 43 48N 0 51W
Midsayap **211** 7 12N 124 32 E
Midu **216** 25 18N 100 30 E
Midway **93** 49 1N 118 48W
Midway Is. **224** 28 13N 177 22W
Midwolda **142** 53 12N 6 52 E
Midzur **166** 43 24N 22 40 E
Mie □ **221** 34 30N 136 10 E
Miechów **152** 50 21N 20 5 E
Miedwie, Jezioro **152** 53 17N 14 54 E
Międzybód **152** 51 25N 17 34 E
Międzychód **152** 52 35N 15 53 E
Międzylesie **152** 50 8N 16 40 E
Międzyrzec Podlaski **152** 51 58N 22 45 E
Międzyrzecz **152** 52 26N 15 35 E
Międzyzdroje **152** 53 56N 14 26 E
Miejska **152** 51 39N 16 58 E
Miélan **140** 43 27N 0 19 E
Mielec **152** 50 15N 21 25 E
Mienga **254** 17 12 S 19 48 E
Mier **102** 26 26N 99 9W
Mier y Noriega **103** 23 25N 100 7W
Miercurea Ciuc **170** 46 21N 25 48 E
Mieres **154** 43 18N 5 48W
Mierlo **143** 51 27N 5 37 E
Mieroszów **152** 50 40N 16 11 E
Mieso **245** 9 15N 40 43 E
Mieszkowice **152** 52 47N 14 30 E
Miette Hotsprings **90** 53 8N 117 46W
Mifraz Ḥefa **190** 32 52N 35 0 E
Migdāl **189** 32 51N 35 30 E
Migdal Afeq **189** 32 5N 34 58 E
Migennes **139** 47 58N 3 31 E
Migliarino **163** 44 45N 11 56 E
Miguel Alemán, Presa **109** 18 15N 96 32W
Miguel Alves **120** 4 11 S 42 55W
Miguel Auza **105** 24 18N 103 25W
Miguel Calmon **120** 11 26 S 40 36W
Miguel Hidalgo, Presa **104** 26 30N 108 34W
Mihara **220** 34 24N 133 5 E
Mihara-Yama **221** 34 43N 139 23 E
Mihmandar **190** 36 51N 35 20 E
Mijares → **156** 39 55N 0 1W
Mijas **155** 36 36N 4 40W
Mikese **250** 6 48 S 37 55 E
Mikha-Tskhakaya **181** 42 15N 42 7 E
Mikhailovka **180** 47 36N 35 16 E
Mikhaylov **179** 54 14N 39 0 E
Mikhaylovgrad **167** 43 27N 23 16 E
Mikhaylovka, Azerbaijan, U.S.S.R. **181** 41 31N 48 52 E
Mikhaylovka, R.S.F.S.R., U.S.S.R. **179** 50 3N 43 5 E
Mikhaylovski **182** 56 27N 59 7 E
Mikhnevo **179** 55 4N 37 59 E
Miki, Hyōgo, Japan **220** 34 48N 134 59 E
Miki, Kagawa, Japan **220** 34 12N 134 7 E
Mikínai **169** 37 43N 22 46 E
Mikindani **251** 10 15 S 40 2 E
Mikkeli **175** 61 43N 27 15 E
Mikkelin lääni □ **174** 61 56N 28 0 E
Mikkwa → **90** 58 25N 114 46W
Mikniya **245** 17 0N 33 45 E
Mikołajki **152** 53 49N 21 37 E
Mikołów **151** 50 10N 18 50 E
Míkonos **169** 37 30N 25 25 E
Mikrí Préspa, Límni **168** 40 47N 21 3 E
Mikrón Dhérion **168** 41 19N 26 6 E
Mikstat **152** 51 32N 17 59 E
Mikulov **151** 48 48N 16 39 E
Mikumi **250** 7 26 S 37 0 E
Mikun **176** 62 20N 50 0 E
Mikuni **221** 36 13N 136 9 E
Mikuni-Tōge **221** 36 50N 138 50 E
Mikura-Jima **221** 33 52N 139 36 E
Milagro **118** 2 11 S 79 36W
Milagros **210** 12 13N 123 30 E
Milan = Milano **162** 45 28N 9 10 E
Milang, S. Austral., Australia **231** 32 2 S 139 10 E
Milang, S. Austral., Australia **232** 35 24 S 138 58 E
Milange **251** 16 3 S 35 45 E
Milano **162** 45 28N 9 10 E
Milâs **177** 37 20N 27 50 E
Milazzo **165** 38 13N 15 13 E
Milden **88** 51 29N 107 32W
Mildmay **84** 44 3N 81 7W
Mildura **231** 34 13 S 142 9 E
Mile **216** 24 28N 103 20 E
Miléai **168** 39 20N 23 9 E
Mileh Tharthār **192** 34 0N 43 15 E
Miles **231** 26 40 S 150 9 E
Milestone **88** 49 59N 104 31W
Mileto **165** 38 37N 16 3 E
Miletto, Mte. **165** 41 26N 14 23 E
Miletus **169** 37 20N 27 33 E
Mileura **229** 26 22 S 117 20 E
Milevsko **150** 49 27N 14 21 E
Milford Haven **133** 51 43N 5 2W
Milford Haven, B. **133** 51 40N 5 10W
Milford Sd. **235** 44 41 S 167 47 E
Milford Station **81** 45 3N 63 26W
Milgun **229** 25 6 S 118 18 E
Milḥ, Baḥr al **192** 32 40N 43 35 E
Miliana, Aïn Salah, Algeria **240** 27 20N 2 32 E
Miliana, Médéa, Algeria **241** 36 20N 2 15 E
Milicz **152** 51 31N 17 19 E
Miling **229** 30 30 S 116 17 E
Militello in Val di Catània **165** 37 16N 14 46 E
Milk → **91** 49 0N 110 33W
Milk, Wadi el → **244** 17 55N 30 20 E
Milk River **91** 49 10N 112 5W
Mill **143** 51 41N 5 48 E
Mill I. **13** 66 0 S 101 30 E
Mill Village **81** 44 9N 64 39W
Millau **140** 44 8N 3 4 E
Millbridge **85** 44 41N 77 36W
Millbrook **85** 44 10N 78 29W
Mille Lacs, L. des **86** 48 45N 90 35W
Millerand **81** 47 13N 61 59W
Millerovo **181** 48 57N 40 28 E
Miller's Flat **235** 45 39 S 169 23 E
Millerton **235** 41 39 S 171 54 E
Millertown **79** 48 49N 56 33W
Millet **91** 53 6N 113 28W
Millevaches, Plateau de **140** 45 45N 2 0 E
Millicent **232** 37 34 S 140 21 E
Millingen **142** 51 52N 6 2 E

Millmerran 231 27 53 S 151 16 E
Mills L. 76 61 30N 118 20W
Millstream 81 48 2N 67 2W
Milltown, N.B., Canada 81 45 10N 67 18W
Milltown, Newf., Canada 79 47 54N 55 46W
Milltown Malbay 135 52 51N 9 25W
Millville 81 46 8N 67 12W
Milly 139 48 24N 2 28 E
Milna 163 43 20N 16 28 E
Milne → 230 21 10 S 137 33 E
Milo 91 50 34N 112 53W
Mílos 169 36 44N 24 25 E
Miloševo 166 45 42N 20 20 E
Miłosław 152 52 12N 17 32 E
Milot 83 48 54N 71 49W
Milparinka P.O. 231 29 46 S 141 57 E
Milpas Viejas 104 22 22N 105 28W
Milpillas 100 29 55N 111 29W
Milpillas Allende 105 21 17N 103 43W
Miltenberg 147 49 41N 9 13 E
Milton, N.S., Canada 81 44 4N 64 45W
Milton, Ont., Canada 84 43 31N 79 53W
Milton, Canada 84 43 33N 79 53W
Milton, N.Z. 235 46 7 S 169 59 E
Milton, U.K. 134 57 18N 4 32W
Milton Keynes 133 52 3N 0 42W
Miltou 243 10 14N 17 26 E
Milverton 84 43 34N 80 55W
Mim 246 6 57N 2 33W
Miminegash 81 46 53N 64 14W
Miminiska L. 86 51 35N 88 37W
Mimizan 140 44 12N 1 13W
Mimon 150 50 38N 14 43 E
Mimongo 252 1 11 S 11 36 E
Mimoso 121 15 10 S 48 5W
Min Jiang →, Fujian, China 217 26 0N 119 35 E
Min Jiang →, Sichuan, China 216 28 45N 104 40 E
Min-Kush 183 41 4N 74 28 E
Min Xian 214 34 25N 104 0 E
Mina 102 26 1N 100 32W
Mina Pirquitas 124 22 40 S 66 30W
Mīnā Su'ud 192 28 45N 48 28 E
Mīnā'al Aḥmadī 193 29 5N 48 10 E
Mīnāb 193 27 10N 57 1 E
Miñaca 101 28 27N 107 26W
Minago → 89 54 33N 98 59W
Minakami 221 36 49N 138 59 E
Minaki 86 49 59N 94 40W
Minakuchi 221 34 58N 136 10 E
Minamata 220 32 10N 130 30 E
Minas 125 34 20 S 55 10W
Minas, Sierra de las 112 15 9N 89 31W
Minas Basin 81 45 20N 64 12W
Minas Channel 81 45 15N 64 45W
Minas de Rio Tinto 155 37 42N 6 35W
Minas de San Quintín 155 38 49N 4 23W
Minas Gerais □ 121 18 50 S 46 0W
Minas Novas 121 17 15 S 42 36W
Minas Nuevas 100 27 5N 108 58W
Minatitlán, Colima, Mexico 106 19 22N 104 4W
Minatitlán, Veracruz, Mexico 109 17 59N 94 31W
Minbu 202 20 10N 94 52 E
Minbya 202 20 22N 93 16 E
Mincio → 162 45 4N 10 59 E
Mindanao 211 8 0N 125 0 E
Mindanao Sea = Bohol Sea 207 9 0N 124 0 E
Mindanao Trench 207 8 0N 128 0 E
Mindel → 147 48 31N 10 23 E
Mindelheim 147 48 4N 10 30 E
Mindemoya 84 45 44N 82 10W
Minden, Canada 85 44 55N 78 43W
Minden, Germany 146 52 18N 8 45 E
Mindiptana 207 5 55 S 140 22 E
Mindon 202 19 21N 94 44 E
Mindoro 210 13 0N 121 0 E
Mindoro Occidental □ 210 13 0N 120 55 E
Mindoro Oriental □ 210 13 0N 121 5 E
Mindoro Strait 210 12 30N 120 30 E
Mindouli 253 4 12 S 14 28 E
Mine 220 34 12N 131 7 E
Mine, L. 80 50 51N 64 43W
Mine Centre 86 48 45N 92 37W
Minegan, Îles de 80 50 12N 63 35W
Minehead 133 51 12N 3 29W
Mineiros 123 17 34 S 52 34W
Mineral de Angangueo 107 19 37N 100 18W
Mineral del Monte 107 20 8N 98 40W
Mineralnyye Vody 181 44 2N 43 8 E
Minervino Murge 165 41 6N 16 4 E
Mingan 80 50 20N 64 0W
Mingan → 80 50 18N 63 59W
Mingary 232 32 8 S 140 45 E
Mingechaur 181 40 45N 47 0 E
Mingechaurskoye Vdkhr. 181 40 56N 47 20 E
Mingela 230 19 52 S 146 38 E
Mingenew 229 29 12 S 115 21 E
Mingera Cr. → 230 20 38 S 138 10 E
Minggang 217 32 24N 114 3 E
Mingin 202 22 50N 94 30 E
Minglanilla 156 39 34N 1 38W
Minglun 216 25 10N 108 21 E
Mingorria 154 40 45N 4 40W
Mingxi 217 26 18N 117 12 E
Mingyuegue 215 43 2N 128 50 E
Minhou 217 26 0N 119 15 E
Minićevo 166 43 42N 22 18 E
Minigwal L. 229 29 31 S 123 14 E
Minilya 229 23 55 S 114 0 E
Minilya → 229 23 45 S 114 0 E
Mininera 232 37 37 S 142 58 E
Minipi, L. 80 52 25N 60 45W
Miniss L. 86 50 48N 90 50W
Minitonas 89 52 5N 101 2W
Minj 227 5 54 S 144 37 E
Mink L. 76 61 54N 117 40W
Minlaton 232 34 45 S 137 35 E
Minna 247 9 37N 6 30 E
Minnedosa 89 50 14N 99 50W
Minnesund 171 60 23N 11 14 E
Minnie Creek 229 24 3 S 115 42 E
Minnitaki L. 86 49 57N 92 10W
Mino 221 35 32N 136 55 E
Miño → 154 41 52N 8 40W
Mino-Kamo 221 35 23N 137 2 E
Mino-Mikawa-Kōgen 221 35 10N 137 23 E
Minoa 169 35 6N 25 45 E
Minobu 221 35 22N 138 26 E
Minobu-Sanchi 221 35 14N 138 20 E
Minorca = Menorca 156 40 0N 4 0 E
Minore 231 32 14 S 148 27 E
Minqin 214 38 38N 103 20 E
Minqing 217 26 15N 118 50 E
Minquiers, Les 138 48 58N 2 8W
Minsen 146 53 43N 7 58 E
Minsk 178 53 52N 27 30 E
Mińsk Mazowiecki 152 52 10N 21 33 E
Minstrel Island 92 50 37N 126 18W
Mintaka Pass 199 37 0N 74 58 E
Minthami 202 23 55N 94 16 E
Minto 81 46 5N 66 5W
Minto, L. 78 57 13N 75 0W
Minton 88 49 10N 104 35W
Mintoum 252 0 27N 12 16 E
Minturno 164 41 15N 13 43 E
Minûf 244 30 26N 30 52 E
Minusinsk 185 53 50N 91 20 E
Minutang 202 28 15N 96 30 E
Minvoul 252 2 9N 12 8 E
Minwakh 195 16 48N 48 6 E
Minya el Qamh 244 30 31N 31 21 E
Minyar 182 55 4N 57 33 E
Minyip 232 36 29 S 142 36 E
Mionica 166 44 14N 20 6 E
Miquelon 82 49 25N 76 27W
Miquelon, I. 79 47 1N 56 20W
Miquihuana 103 23 34N 99 47W
Mir 247 14 5N 11 59 E
Mir-Bashir 181 40 20N 46 58 E
Mīr Kūh 193 26 22N 58 55 E
Mīr Shahdād 193 26 15N 58 29 E
Mira, Canada 81 46 2N 59 58W
Mira, Italy 163 45 26N 12 9 E
Mira, Portugal 154 40 26N 8 44W
Mira →, Canada 81 46 2N 59 58W
Mira →, Colombia 118 1 36N 79 1W
Mira →, Portugal 155 37 43N 8 47W
Mira por vos Cay 113 22 9N 74 30W
Mīrābād 197 30 25N 61 50 E
Mirabella Eclano 165 41 3N 14 59 E
Miracema do Norte 120 9 33 S 48 24W
Mirador 120 6 22 S 44 22W
Miraflores 118 1 25N 72 13W
Miraj 200 16 50N 74 45 E
Miram 230 21 15 S 148 55 E
Miram Shah 197 33 0N 70 2 E
Miramar, Argentina 124 38 15 S 57 50W
Miramar, Mozam. 255 23 50 S 35 35 E
Miramas 141 43 33N 4 59 E
Mirambeau 140 45 23N 0 35W
Miramichi, Little S.W. → 81 46 58N 65 38W
Miramichi, N.W. → 81 46 57N 65 55W
Miramichi, S.W. → 81 46 58N 65 38W
Miramichi B. 81 47 15N 65 0W
Miramont-de-Guyenne 140 44 37N 0 21 E
Miranda 123 20 10 S 56 15W
Miranda □ 118 10 15N 66 25W
Miranda → 123 19 25 S 57 20W
Miranda de Ebro 156 42 41N 2 57W
Miranda do Corvo 154 40 6N 8 20W
Miranda do Douro 154 41 30N 6 16W
Mirande 140 43 31N 0 25 E
Mirandela 154 41 32N 7 10W
Mirandola 162 44 53N 11 2 E
Mirandópolis 125 21 9 S 51 6W
Mirango 251 13 32 S 34 58 E
Mirano 163 45 29N 12 6 E
Mirassol 125 20 46 S 49 28W
Mirbāṭ 195 17 0N 54 45 E
Mirboo North 233 38 24 S 146 10 E
Mirear 244 23 15N 35 41 E
Mirebeau, Côte-d'Or, France 139 47 25N 5 20 E
Mirebeau, Vienne, France 138 46 49N 0 10 E
Mirecourt 139 48 20N 6 10 E
Mirgorod 178 49 58N 33 37 E
Miri 206 4 23N 113 59 E
Miriam Vale 230 24 20 S 151 33 E
Mirim, Lagoa 125 32 45 S 52 50W
Mirimire 118 11 10N 68 43W
Miriti 123 6 15 S 59 0W
Mirnyy, Antarct. 13 66 33 S 93 1 E
Mirnyy, U.S.S.R. 185 62 33N 113 53 E
Miroč 166 44 32N 22 16 E
Mirond L. 77 55 6N 102 47W
Mirosławiec 152 53 20N 16 5 E
Mirpur 199 33 32N 73 56 E
Mirpur Bibiwari 198 28 33N 67 44 E
Mirpur Khas 197 25 30N 69 0 E
Mirpur Sakro 198 24 33N 67 41 E
Mirria 247 13 43N 9 7 E
Mirror 91 52 30N 113 7W
Mîrşani 170 44 1N 23 59 E
Mirsk 152 50 58N 15 23 E
Miryang 215 35 31N 128 44 E
Mirzaani 181 41 24N 46 5 E
Mirzapur 199 25 10N 82 34 E
Mirzapur-cum-Vindhyachal = Mirzapur 199 25 10N 82 34 E
Misa, La 100 28 23N 110 32W
Misamis Occidental □ 211 8 20N 123 42 E
Misamis Oriental □ 211 8 45N 125 0 E
Misantla 108 19 56N 96 50W
Misawa 218 40 41N 141 24 E
Miscou Centre 81 47 57N 64 34W
Miscou I. 81 47 57N 64 31W
Miscouche 81 46 26N 63 52W
Misehkow → 86 51 26N 89 11W
Mish'āb, Ra'as al 192 28 15N 48 43 E
Mishagua → 122 11 12 S 72 58W
Mishan 213 45 37N 131 48 E
Mishbih, Gebel 244 22 38N 34 44 E
Mishima 221 35 10N 138 52 E
Mishkino 182 55 20N 63 55 E
Mishmar Ayyalon 189 31 52N 34 57 E
Mishmar Ha' Emeq 189 32 37N 35 7 E
Mishmar Ha Negev 189 31 22N 34 48 E
Mishmar Ha Yarden 189 33 0N 35 36 E
Mishmi Hills 202 29 0N 96 0 E
Misilmeri 164 38 2N 13 25 E
Misima I. 227 10 40 S 152 45 E
Misión, La, Baja Calif. N., Mexico 98 32 6N 116 53W
Misión, La, Hidalgo, Mexico 107 21 6N 99 8W
Misión de Santo Domingo 98 30 43N 115 56W
Misión Fagnano 126 54 32 S 67 17W
Misión San Fernando 98 29 59N 115 17W
Misión Santa María 98 29 43N 114 35W
Misiones □, Argentina 125 27 0 S 55 0W
Misiones □, Paraguay 124 27 0 S 56 0W
Miskah 192 24 49N 42 56 E
Miskitos, Cayos 112 14 26N 82 50W
Miskolc 151 48 7N 20 50 E
Misoke 250 0 42 S 28 2 E
Misool 207 1 52 S 130 10 E
Misrātah 241 32 24N 15 3 E
Misrātah □ 241 29 0N 16 0 E
Missanabie 87 48 20N 84 6W
Missão Velha 120 7 15 S 39 10W
Missinaibi → 87 50 43N 81 29W
Missinaibi L. 87 48 23N 83 40W
Missinaibi Lake Prov. Park 87 48 25N 83 30W
Mission City 93 49 10N 122 15W
Missipuskiow → 88 53 53N 103 18W
Missisa L. 74 52 20N 85 7W
Missisicabi → 78 51 14N 79 31W
Mississagi → 84 46 15N 83 9W
Mississagi Prov. Park 84 46 30N 82 40W
Mississauga 84 43 32N 79 35W
Mississippi L. 85 45 5N 76 10W
Missour 240 33 3N 4 0W
Mistake B. 77 62 8N 93 0W
Mistanipisipou → 80 51 32N 61 50W
Mistaouac, L. 82 49 25N 78 41W
Mistassibi → 83 48 53N 72 13W
Mistassibi Nord-Est → 83 49 31N 71 56W
Mistassini 83 48 53N 72 12W
Mistassini → 83 48 42N 72 20W
Mistassini, Parc. Prov. de 83 50 20N 74 0W
Mistassini L. 78 51 0N 73 30W
Mistastin L. 75 55 57N 63 20W
Mistatim 88 52 52N 103 22W
Mistelbach 151 48 34N 16 34 E
Misterbianco 165 37 32N 15 0 E
Mistretta 165 37 56N 14 20 E
Misty L. 77 58 53N 101 40W
Misugi 221 34 31N 136 16 E
Misumi 220 32 37N 130 27 E
Mît Ghamr 244 30 42N 31 12 E
Mita, Pta. 104 20 47N 105 33W
Mitaka 221 35 40N 139 33 E
Mitan 183 40 0N 66 35 E
Mitatib 245 15 59N 36 12 E
Mitchell, Australia 231 26 29 S 147 58 E
Mitchell, Canada 84 43 28N 81 12W
Mitchell → 230 15 12 S 141 35 E
Mitchell L. 93 52 52N 120 37W
Mitchelstown 135 52 16N 8 18W
Mitchinamécus, Rés. 82 47 19N 75 9W
Mitha Tiwana 198 32 13N 72 6 E
Míthimna 168 39 20N 26 12 E
Mitiamo 232 36 12 S 144 15 E
Mitilíni 169 39 6N 26 35 E
Mitilinoí 169 37 42N 26 56 E
Mitla, L. 107 17 3N 100 25W
Mito 221 36 20N 140 30 E
Mitsinjo 255 16 1 S 45 52 E
Mitsiwa 245 15 35N 39 25 E
Mitsiwa Channel 245 15 30N 40 0 E
Mitsukaidō 221 36 1N 139 59 E
Mittagong 231 34 28 S 150 29 E
Mittelland 148 46 50N 7 23 E
Mittelland Kanal 146 52 23N 7 45 E
Mittenwalde 146 52 16N 13 33 E
Mitterteich 147 49 57N 12 15 E
Mittweida 146 50 59N 13 0 E
Mitú 118 1 8N 70 3W
Mituas 118 3 52N 68 49W
Mitumba 250 7 8 S 31 2 E
Mitumba, Chaîne des 250 6 0 S 29 0 E
Mitwaba 251 8 2 S 27 17 E
Mityana 250 0 23N 32 2 E
Mitzic 252 0 45N 11 40 E
Miura 221 35 12N 139 40 E
Mixes, Sa. de 109 16 45N 95 30W
Mixquiahuala 107 20 14N 99 13W
Mixteco, R. → 109 18 11N 98 30W
Mixtlán 106 20 26N 104 25W
Miyagi □ 218 38 15N 140 45 E
Miyâh, W. el →, Egypt 244 25 0N 33 23 E
Miyah, W. el →, Syria 192 34 44N 39 57 E
Miyake-Jima 221 34 0N 139 30 E
Miyako 218 39 40N 141 59 E
Miyako-Jima 219 24 45N 125 20 E
Miyako-Rettō 219 24 24N 125 0 E
Miyakonojō 220 31 40N 131 5 E
Miyanojō 220 31 54N 130 27 E
Miyanoura-Dake 219 30 20N 130 31 E
Miyata 220 33 49N 130 42 E
Miyazaki 220 31 56N 131 30 E
Miyazaki □ 220 32 30N 131 30 E
Miyazu 221 35 35N 135 10 E
Miyi 216 26 47N 102 9 E
Miyoshi 220 34 48N 132 51 E
Miyun 214 40 28N 116 50 E
Miyun Sk. 215 40 30N 117 0 E
Mizamis = Ozamis 211 8 15N 123 50 E
Mizdah 241 31 30N 13 0 E
Mizen Hd., Cork, Ireland 135 51 27N 9 50W
Mizen Hd., Wicklow, Ireland 135 52 52N 6 4W
Mizhi 214 37 47N 110 12 E
Mizil 170 44 59N 26 29 E
Mizoram □ 202 23 30N 92 40 E
Mizpe Ramon 189 30 34N 34 49 E
Mizuho, Antarct. 13 70 30 S 41 0 E
Mizuho, Japan 221 35 6N 135 17 E
Mizunami 221 35 22N 137 15 E
Mizusawa 218 39 8N 141 8 E
Mjöbäck 173 57 28N 12 53 E
Mjölby 173 58 20N 15 10 E
Mjømna 171 60 55N 4 55 E
Mjörn 173 57 55N 12 25 E
Mjøsa 171 60 48N 11 0 E
Mkata 250 5 45 S 38 20 E
Mkokotoni 250 5 55 S 39 15 E
Mkomazi 250 4 40 S 38 7 E
Mkulwe 251 8 37 S 32 20 E
Mkumbi, Ras 250 7 38 S 39 55 E
Mkushi 251 14 25 S 29 15 E
Mkushi River 251 13 32 S 29 45 E
Mkuze → 255 27 45 S 32 30 E
Mladá Boleslav 150 50 27N 14 53 E
Mladenovac 166 44 28N 20 44 E

Mlala Hills . . . . **250** 6 50 S 31 40 E
Mlange . . . . **251** 16 2 S 35 33 E
Mlava → . . . . **166** 44 45N 21 13 E
Mława . . . . **152** 53 9N 20 25 E
Mliništa . . . . **163** 44 15N 16 50 E
Mljet . . . . **166** 42 43N 17 30 E
Mljetski Kanal . . . . . **166** 42 48N 17 35 E
Młynąry . . . . **152** 54 12N 19 46 E
Mme . . . . **247** 6 18N 10 14 E
Mo . . . . **171** 59 28N 7 50 E
Mo i Rana . . . . **174** 66 15N 14 7 E
Moa . . . . **207** 8 0 S 128 0 E
Moa → . . . . **246** 6 59N 11 36 E
Moabi . . . . **252** 2 24 S 10 59 E
Moaco → . . . . **122** 7 41 S 68 18W
Moala . . . . **226** 18 36 S 179 53 E
Moalie Park . . . . **231** 29 42 S 143 3 E
Moaña **154** 42 18N 8 43W
Moba . . . . **250** 7 0 S 29 48 E
Mobara . . . . **221** 35 25N 140 18 E
Mobārakābād . . . . . . **193** 28 24N 53 20 E
Mobārakīyeh . . . . **193** 35 5N 51 47 E
Mobaye . . . . **252** 4 25N 21 5 E
Mobayi . . . . **252** 4 15N 21 8 E
Moberly → **76** 56 12N 120 55W
Mobutu Sese Seko,
L. . . . . **250** 1 30N 31 0 E
Moc Chau . . . . **204** 20 50N 104 38 E
Moc Hoa . . . . **205** 10 46N 105 56 E
Mocaba, Sa. de . . . . **253** 7 12 S 15 0 E
Mocabe Kasari . . . . . **251** 9 58 S 26 12 E
Mocajuba . . . . **120** 2 35 S 49 30W
Moçambique . . . . **251** 15 3 S 40 42 E
Moçâmedes =
Namibe . . . . **253** 15 7 S 12 11 E
Mocapra → **118** 7 56N 66 46W
Mocha, I. . . . . **126** 38 22 S 73 56W
Mochicahui **104** 25 56N 108 56W
Mochudi . . . . **254** 24 27 S 26 7 E
Mocimboa da Praia . **251** 11 25 S 40 20 E
Mociu . . . . **170** 46 46N 24 3 E
Möckeln . . . . **173** 56 40N 14 15 E
Mocoa **118** 1 7N 76 35W
Mococa . . . . **125** 21 28 S 47 0W
Mocorito **104** 25 29N 107 55W
Moctezuma,
Chihuahua,
Mexico **101** 30 12N 106 26W
Moctezuma,
San Luis Potosí,
Mexico **103** 22 45N 101 5W
Moctezuma, Sonora,
Mexico **100** 29 48N 109 42W
Moctezuma → **100** 29 9N 109 40W
Mocuba . . . . **251** 16 54 S 36 57 E
Mocúzari, Presa **100** 27 15N 109 5W
Moda . . . . **202** 24 22N 96 29 E
Modalen . . . . **171** 60 49N 5 48 E
Modane . . . . **141** 45 12N 6 40 E
Modasa . . . . **198** 23 30N 73 21 E
Modave . . . . **143** 50 27N 5 18 E
Modder → . . . . **254** 29 2 S 24 37 E
Modderrivier . . . . **254** 29 2 S 24 38 E
Módena . . . . **162** 44 39N 10 55 E
Módica . . . . **165** 36 52N 14 45 E
Modigliana . . . . **163** 44 9N 11 48 E
Modjamboli . . . . **252** 2 28N 22 6 E
Modlin . . . . **152** 52 24N 20 41 E
Mödling . . . . **151** 48 5N 16 17 E
Modo . . . . **245** 5 31N 30 33 E
Modra . . . . **151** 48 19N 17 20 E
Modriča . . . . **166** 44 57N 18 17 E
Moe . . . . **231** 38 12 S 146 19 E
Moebase . . . . **251** 17 3 S 38 41 E
Moëlan-sur-Mer **138** 47 49N 3 38W
Moengo **119** 5 45N 54 20W
Moergestel . . . . **143** 51 33N 5 11 E
Moësa → . . . . **149** 46 12N 9 10 E
Moffat **134** 55 20N 3 27W
Moga . . . . **198** 30 48N 75 8 E
Mogadishu =
Muqdisho . . . . **256** 2 2N 45 25 E
Mogador =
Essaouira **240** 31 32N 9 42W
Mogadouro **154** 41 22N 6 47W
Mogami → . . . . **218** 38 45N 140 0 E
Mogaung . . . . **202** 25 20N 97 0 E
Møgeltønder . . . . **173** 54 57N 8 48 E
Mogente **157** 38 52N 0 45W
Mogho . . . . **245** 4 54N 40 16 E
Mogi das Cruzes . . . **125** 23 31 S 46 11W
Mogi-Guaçu → . . . . **125** 20 53 S 48 10W
Mogi-Mirim . . . . **125** 22 29 S 47 0W
Mogielnica . . . . **152** 51 42N 20 41 E
Mogilev . . . . **178** 53 55N 30 18 E
Mogilev-Podolskiy . . **180** 48 20N 27 40 E
Mogilno . . . . **152** 52 39N 17 55 E
Mogincual . . . . **251** 15 35 S 40 25 E
Mogliano Véneto . . . **163** 45 33N 12 15 E
Mogocha . . . . **185** 53 40N 119 50 E
Mogoi . . . . **207** 1 55 S 133 10 E
Mogok . . . . **202** 23 0N 96 40 E
Mogone **109** 16 59N 95 3W
Mogriguy . . . . **233** 32 3 S 148 40 E
Moguer **155** 37 15N 6 52W
Mogumber . . . . **229** 31 2 S 116 3 E
Mohács . . . . **151** 45 58N 18 41 E
Mohaka → . . . . **234** 39 7 S 177 12 E
Moḥammadābād . . . **193** 37 52N 59 5 E
Mohammadia . . . . . . **241** 35 33N 0 3 E
Mohammedia **240** 33 44N 7 21W
Moheda . . . . **173** 57 1N 14 35 E
Mohinora, Sa. **104** 25 55N 106 45W
Möhne → . . . . **146** 51 29N 7 57 E
Mohnyin . . . . **202** 24 47N 96 22 E
Moholm . . . . **173** 58 37N 14 5 E
Mohon . . . . **139** 49 45N 4 44 E
Mohoro . . . . **250** 8 6 S 39 8 E
Moia . . . . **245** 5 3N 28 2 E
Moidart, L. **134** 56 47N 5 40W
Moinabad . . . . **200** 17 44N 77 16 E
Moindou . . . . **226** 21 42 S 165 41 E
Moineşti . . . . **170** 46 28N 26 31 E
Mointy . . . . **184** 47 10N 73 18 E
Moira → **85** 44 21N 77 24W
Moirans . . . . **141** 45 20N 5 33 E
Moirans-en-
Montagne . . . . **141** 46 26N 5 43 E
Moíres . . . . **169** 35 4N 24 56 E
Moisakula . . . . **178** 58 3N 25 12 E
Moisie **80** 50 12N 66 1W
Moisie → **80** 50 14N 66 5W
Moissac . . . . **140** 44 7N 1 5 E
Moïssala . . . . **243** 8 21N 17 46 E
Moita **155** 38 38N 8 58W
Mojácar **157** 37 6N 1 55W
Mojada, Sa. **101** 27 16N 103 46W
Mojados **154** 41 26N 4 40W
Mojiang . . . . **216** 23 37N 101 35 E
Mojikit L. **86** 50 40N 88 15W
Mojo, Bolivia . . . . . . **124** 21 48 S 65 33W
Mojo, Ethiopia . . . . . **245** 8 35N 39 5 E
Mojokerto . . . . **209** 7 28 S 112 26 E
Mojos, Llanos de . . . **123** 15 0 S 65 0W
Moju → . . . . **120** 1 40 S 48 25W
Mokai . . . . **234** 38 32 S 175 56 E
Mokambo . . . . **251** 12 25 S 28 20 E
Mokameh . . . . **199** 25 24N 85 55 E
Mokau → . . . . **234** 38 35 S 174 35 E
Mokhós . . . . **169** 35 16N 25 27 E
Mokhotlong . . . . **255** 29 22 S 29 2 E
Mokihinui → . . . . . . **235** 41 33 S 171 58 E
Moknine . . . . **241** 35 35N 10 58 E
Mokpalin . . . . **202** 17 26N 96 53 E
Mokra Gora . . . . **166** 42 50N 20 30 E
Mokronog . . . . **163** 45 57N 15 9 E
Moksha → . . . . **179** 54 45N 41 53 E
Mokshan . . . . **179** 53 25N 44 35 E
Mol . . . . **143** 51 11N 5 5 E
Mola, C. de la . . . . . **156** 39 40N 4 20 E
Mola di Bari . . . . **165** 41 3N 17 5 E
Molango **107** 20 47N 98 43W
Moláoi . . . . **169** 36 49N 22 56 E
Molat . . . . **163** 44 15N 14 50 E
Molave . . . . **211** 8 5N 123 30 E
Molchanovo . . . . **184** 57 40N 83 50 E
Mold **132** 53 10N 3 10W
Moldava nad
Bodvou . . . . **151** 48 38N 21 0 E
Moldavia =
Moldova . . . . **170** 46 30N 27 0 E
Moldavian S.S.R. □ **180** 47 0N 28 0 E
Molde . . . . **171** 62 45N 7 9 E
Moldotau, Khrebet . **183** 41 35N 75 0 E
Moldova . . . . **170** 46 30N 27 0 E
Moldova Nouă . . . . . **166** 44 45N 21 41 E
Moldoveanu . . . . **170** 45 36N 24 45 E
Molepolole . . . . **254** 24 28 S 25 28 E
Moléson . . . . **148** 46 33N 7 1 E
Molesworth . . . . **235** 42 5 S 173 16 E
Molfetta . . . . **165** 41 12N 16 35 E
Molina de Aragón . . **156** 40 46N 1 52W
Molina Lacy **98** 29 45N 114 24W
Molinella . . . . **163** 44 38N 11 40 E
Molino de San José . **107** 21 38N 101 16W
Molinos . . . . **124** 25 28 S 66 15W
Moliro . . . . **250** 8 12 S 30 30 E
Molise □ . . . . **163** 41 45N 14 30 E
Moliterno . . . . **165** 40 14N 15 50 E
Mollahat . . . . **199** 22 56N 89 48 E
Mölle . . . . **172** 56 17N 12 31 E
Molledo **154** 43 8N 4 6W
Mollendo . . . . **122** 17 0 S 72 0W
Mollerin, L. . . . . **229** 30 30 S 117 35 E
Mollerusa . . . . **156** 41 37N 0 54 E
Mollina **155** 37 8N 4 38W
Mölln . . . . **146** 53 37N 10 41 E
Mölltorp . . . . **173** 58 30N 14 26 E
Mölndal . . . . **173** 57 40N 12 3 E
Molo . . . . **202** 23 22N 96 53 E
Molochansk . . . . **180** 47 15N 35 35 E
Molochnaya → . . . . **180** 47 0N 35 30 E
Molodechno . . . . **178** 54 20N 26 50 E
Moloma → . . . . **179** 58 20N 48 15 E
Molong . . . . **231** 33 5 S 148 54 E
Molopo → . . . . **254** 28 30 S 20 13 E
Mólos . . . . **169** 38 47N 22 37 E
Molotov = Perm . . . **182** 58 0N 57 10 E
Moloundou . . . . **252** 2 8N 15 15 E
Molsheim . . . . **139** 48 33N 7 29 E
Molson L. **89** 54 22N 96 40W
Molteno . . . . **254** 31 22 S 26 22 E
Molu . . . . **207** 6 45 S 131 40 E
Molucca Sea . . . . **209** 4 0 S 124 0 E
Moluccas = Maluku **207** 1 0 S 127 0 E
Molundo . . . . **211** 7 57N 124 23 E
Moma, Mozam. . . . . **251** 16 47 S 39 4 E
Moma, Zaïre . . . . . . **250** 1 35 S 23 52 E
Momba . . . . **232** 30 58 S 143 30 E
Mombaça . . . . **120** 5 43 S 39 45W
Mombasa . . . . **250** 4 2 S 39 43 E
Mombetsu . . . . **218** 44 21N 143 22 E
Mombil . . . . **202** 27 46N 98 6 E
Mombuey **154** 42 3N 6 20W
Momchilgrad . . . . **167** 41 33N 25 23 E
Momi . . . . **250** 1 42 S 27 0 E
Momignies . . . . **143** 50 2N 4 10 E
Mompog Pass . . . . . . **210** 13 34N 122 13 E
Mompós **118** 9 14N 74 26W
Møn . . . . **173** 54 57N 12 15 E
Mona, Canal de la . . **113** 18 30N 67 45W
Mona, I. **113** 18 5N 67 54W
Mona, Pta. **112** 9 37N 82 36W
Mona, Punta **155** 36 43N 3 45W
Mona Quimbundo . . **253** 9 55 S 19 58 E
Monach Is. **134** 57 32N 7 40W
Monaco ■ . . . . **141** 43 46N 7 23 E
Monadhliath Mts. . . **134** 57 10N 4 4W
Monagas □ **119** 9 20N 63 0W
Monaghan **135** 54 15N 6 58W
Monaghan □ **135** 54 10N 7 0W
Monapo . . . . **251** 14 56 S 40 19 E
Monarch **91** 49 48N 113 7W
Monarch Mt. **76** 51 55N 125 57W
Monashee Prov.
Park **93** 50 30N 118 15W
Monastier-sur-
Gazeille, Le . . . . . **140** 44 57N 3 59 E
Monastir = Bitola . . **166** 41 5N 21 10 E
Monastir . . . . **241** 35 50N 10 49 E
Monastyriska . . . . . . **178** 49 8N 25 14 E
Moncada, Phil. . . . . . **210** 15 44N 120 34 E
Moncada, Spain **156** 39 30N 0 24W
Moncada, La **107** 20 16N 100 48W
Moncalieri . . . . **162** 45 0N 7 40 E
Moncalvo . . . . **162** 45 3N 8 15 E
Moncão **154** 42 4N 8 27W
Moncarapacho **155** 37 5N 7 46W
Moncayo, Sierra del **156** 41 48N 1 50W
Mönchengladbach . . **146** 51 12N 6 23 E
Monchique **155** 37 19N 8 38W
Monclova **102** 26 54N 101 25W
Moncontour **138** 48 22N 2 38W
Moncouche, L. **83** 48 45N 70 42W
Moncoutant **138** 46 43N 0 35W
Moncton **81** 46 7N 64 51W
Mondego → **154** 40 9N 8 52W
Mondego, Cabo **154** 40 11N 8 54W
Mondeodo . . . . **207** 3 34 S 122 9 E
Mondo . . . . **243** 13 47N 15 32 E
Mondolfo . . . . **163** 43 45N 13 8 E
Mondonac, L. **83** 47 24N 73 58W
Mondoñedo **154** 43 25N 7 23W
Mondovì . . . . **162** 44 23N 7 49 E
Mondragon, France . **141** 44 13N 4 44 E
Mondragon, Phil. . . . **211** 12 31N 124 45 E
Mondragone . . . . **164** 41 8N 13 52 E
Mondrain I. . . . . **229** 34 9 S 122 14 E
Monduli □ . . . . **250** 3 0 S 36 0 E
Monemvasía . . . . **169** 36 41N 23 3 E
Monesterio **155** 38 6N 6 15W
Monestier-de-
Clermont . . . . **141** 44 55N 5 38 E
Monêtier-les-Bains,
Le . . . . **141** 44 58N 6 30 E
Monfalcone . . . . **163** 45 49N 13 32 E
Monflanquin . . . . **140** 44 32N 0 47 E
Monforte **155** 39 6N 7 25W
Monforte de Lemos . **154** 42 31N 7 33W
Mong Hta . . . . **202** 19 50N 98 35 E
Mong Ket . . . . **202** 23 8N 98 22 E
Mong Kung . . . . **202** 21 35N 97 35 E
Mong Kyawt . . . . **202** 19 56N 98 45 E
Mong Nai . . . . **202** 20 32N 97 46 E
Mong Ping . . . . **202** 21 22N 99 2 E
Mong Pu . . . . **202** 20 55N 98 44 E
Mong Ton . . . . **202** 20 17N 98 45 E
Mong Tung . . . . **202** 22 2N 97 41 E
Mong Yai . . . . **202** 22 21N 98 3 E
Monga . . . . **252** 4 12N 22 49 E
Mongalla . . . . **245** 5 8N 31 42 E
Mongers, L. . . . . **229** 29 25 S 117 5 E
Monghyr = Munger **199** 25 23N 86 30 E
Mongla . . . . **202** 22 8N 89 35 E
Mongngaw . . . . **202** 22 47N 96 59 E
Mongo, Chad . . . . . . **243** 12 14N 18 43 E
Mongó, Eq. Guin. . . . **252** 1 52N 10 10 E
Mongolia ■ . . . . **212** 47 0N 103 0 E
Mongomo . . . . **252** 1 38N 11 19 E
Mongonu . . . . **247** 12 40N 13 32 E
Mongororo . . . . **243** 12 3N 22 26 E
Mongrove, Pta. **106** 17 56N 102 11W
Mongu . . . . **253** 15 16 S 23 12 E
Môngua . . . . **254** 16 43 S 15 20 E
Monistrol . . . . **140** 45 57N 3 38 E
Monistrol-St-Loire . . **141** 45 17N 4 11 E
Monitor **91** 51 58N 110 34W
Monkayo . . . . **211** 7 50N 126 0 E
Monkey Bay . . . . **251** 14 7 S 35 1 E
Mońki . . . . **152** 53 23N 22 48 E
Monkira . . . . **230** 24 46 S 140 30 E
Monkoto . . . . **252** 1 38 S 20 35 E
Monkstown **79** 47 35N 54 26W
Monkton **84** 43 35N 81 5W
Monmouth **133** 51 48N 2 43W
Monmouth Mt. **92** 51 0N 123 47W
Monópoli . . . . **165** 40 57N 17 18 E
Monor . . . . **151** 47 21N 19 27 E
Monóvar **157** 38 28N 0 53W
Monowai . . . . **235** 45 53 S 167 31 E
Monowai, L. . . . . **235** 45 53 S 167 25 E
Monqoumba . . . . **252** 3 33N 18 40 E
Monreal del Campo **156** 40 47N 1 20W
Monreale . . . . **164** 38 6N 13 16 E
Monrovia **246** 6 18N 10 47W
Mons . . . . **143** 50 27N 3 58 E
Monsaraz **155** 38 28N 7 22W
Monse . . . . **207** 4 0 S 123 10 E
Monsefú . . . . **122** 6 52 S 79 52W
Monségur . . . . **140** 44 38N 0 4 E
Monsélice . . . . **163** 45 16N 11 46 E
Monster . . . . **142** 52 1N 4 10 E
Mont-Carmel **83** 47 26N 69 52W
Mont-de-Marsan . . . **140** 43 54N 0 31W
Mont d'Or, Tunnel . **139** 46 45N 6 18 E
Mont Dore . . . . **226** 22 16 S 166 34 E
Mont-Dore, Le . . . . . **140** 45 35N 2 50 E
Mont-Joli **83** 48 37N 68 10W
Mont Laurier **82** 46 35N 75 30W
Mont-Louis **80** 49 15N 65 44W
Mont St-Pierre **80** 49 13N 65 49W
Mont-sous-Vaudrey . **139** 46 58N 5 36 E
Mont-St-Michel, Le . **138** 48 40N 1 30W
Mont-sur-
Marchienne . . . . . . **143** 50 23N 4 24 E
Mont-Tremblant **82** 46 13N 74 36W
Mont Tremblant
Prov. Park **83** 46 30N 74 30W
Montabaur . . . . **146** 50 26N 7 49 E
Montagnac . . . . **140** 43 29N 3 28 E
Montagnana . . . . **163** 45 13N 11 29 E
Montagu . . . . **254** 33 45 S 20 8 E
Montagu I. . . . . **13** 58 25 S 26 20W
Montague **81** 46 10N 62 39W
Montague, I. **98** 31 45N 114 48W
Montague Ra. . . . . . **229** 27 15 S 119 30 E
Montague Sd. . . . . . . **228** 14 28 S 125 20 E
Montaigu **138** 46 59N 1 18W
Montalbán **156** 40 50N 0 45W
Montalbano di
Elicona . . . . **165** 38 1N 15 0 E
Montalbano Iónico . **165** 40 17N 16 33 E
Montalbo **156** 39 53N 2 42W
Montalcino . . . . **163** 43 4N 11 30 E
Montalegre **154** 41 49N 7 47W
Montalto di Castro . **163** 42 20N 11 36 E
Montalto Uffugo . . . **165** 39 25N 16 9 E
Montamarta **154** 41 39N 5 49W
Montaña, Peru . . . . . **122** 6 0 S 73 0W
Montana, Switz. . . . . **148** 46 19N 7 29 E
Montánchez **155** 39 15N 6 8W
Montañita **118** 1 22N 75 28W
Montargis . . . . **139** 48 0N 2 43 E
Montauban . . . . **140** 44 0N 1 21 E
Montbard . . . . **139** 47 38N 4 20 E
Montbéliard . . . . **139** 47 31N 6 48 E
Montblanch . . . . **156** 41 23N 1 4 E
Montbrison . . . . **141** 45 36N 4 3 E
Montcalm, Pic de . . . **140** 42 40N 1 25 E
Montceau-les-Mines **139** 46 40N 4 23 E
Montcerf **82** 46 32N 76 3W
Montcevelles, L. . . . **80** 51 7N 60 38W
Montchanin . . . . **162** 46 47N 4 30 E
Montcornet . . . . **139** 49 40N 4 0 E
Montcuq . . . . **140** 44 21N 1 13 E
Montdidier . . . . **139** 49 38N 2 35 E
Monte Albán **109** 17 2N 96 46W
Monte Alegre . . . . . . **119** 2 0 S 54 0W
Monte Alegre de
Goiás . . . . **121** 13 14 S 47 10W
Monte Alegre de
Minas . . . . **121** 18 52 S 48 52W
Monte Azul . . . . **121** 15 9 S 42 53W
Monte Bello Is. . . . . **228** 20 30 S 115 45 E
Monte-Carlo . . . . **141** 43 46N 7 23 E
Monte Carmelo . . . . **121** 18 43 S 47 29W
Monte Caseros . . . . . **124** 30 10 S 57 50W
Monte Comán . . . . . **124** 34 40 S 67 53W
Monte Cristi **113** 19 52N 71 39W
Monte Dinero . . . . . . **126** 52 18 S 68 33W
Monte Lindo → . . . **124** 23 56 S 57 12W
Monte Quemado . . . **124** 25 53 S 62 41W
Monte Redondo **154** 39 53N 8 50W
Monte San Giovanni **164** 41 39N 13 33 E
Monte San Savino . . **163** 43 20N 11 42 E
Monte Sant' Ángelo **165** 41 42N 15 59 E

Monte Santu, C. di **164** 40 5N 9 42 E
Monteagudo, Argentina **125** 27 14 S 54 8W
Monteagudo, Bolivia **123** 19 49 S 63 59W
Montealegre **157** 38 48N 1 17W
Montebello **82** 45 40N 74 55W
Montebelluna **163** 45 47N 12 3 E
Montebourg **138** 49 30N 1 20W
Montecastrilli **163** 42 40N 12 30 E
Montecatini Terme **162** 43 55N 10 48 E
Montecristi **118** 1 0 S 80 40W
Montecristo **162** 42 20N 10 20 E
Montefalco **163** 42 53N 12 38 E
Montefiascone **163** 42 31N 12 2 E
Montefrío **155** 37 20N 4 0W
Montegnée **143** 50 38N 5 31 E
Montego Bay **112** 18 30N 78 0W
Montegranaro **163** 43 13N 13 38 E
Montehanin **139** 46 46N 4 44 E
Monteiro **120** 7 48 S 37 2W
Monteith **232** 35 11 S 139 23 E
Montejicar **157** 37 33N 3 30W
Montejinnie **228** 16 40 S 131 38 E
Montelíbano **118** 8 5N 75 29W
Montélimar **141** 44 33N 4 45 E
Montella **165** 40 50N 15 0 E
Montellano **155** 36 59N 5 36W
Montelupo Fiorentino **162** 43 44N 11 2 E
Montemor-o-Novo **155** 38 40N 8 12W
Montemor-o-Velho **154** 40 11N 8 40W
Montemorelos **103** 25 12N 99 49W
Montendre **140** 45 16N 0 26W
Montenegro = Crna Gora □ **166** 42 40N 19 20 E
Montenegro **125** 29 39 S 51 29W
Montenero di Bisaccia **163** 42 0N 14 47 E
Montepuez **251** 13 8 S 38 59 E
Montepuez → **251** 12 32 S 40 27 E
Montepulciano **163** 43 5N 11 46 E
Monterde **101** 27 33N 108 3W
Montereale **163** 42 31N 13 13 E
Montereau **139** 48 22N 2 57 E
Montería **118** 8 46N 75 53W
Montero **123** 17 20 S 63 15W
Monteros **124** 27 11 S 65 30W
Monterotondo **163** 42 3N 12 36 E
Monterrey **102** 25 40N 100 19W
Montes Altos **120** 5 50 S 47 4W
Montes Claros **121** 16 30 S 43 50W
Montesárchio **165** 41 5N 14 37 E
Montescaglioso **165** 40 34N 16 40 E
Montesilvano **163** 42 30N 14 8 E
Montevarchi **163** 43 30N 11 32 E
Montevideo **125** 34 50 S 56 11W
Montfaucon, Haute-Loire, France **141** 45 11N 4 20 E
Montfaucon, Meuse, France **139** 49 16N 5 8 E
Montfort **143** 51 7N 5 58 E
Montfort-l'Amaury **139** 48 47N 1 49 E
Montfort-sur-Meu **138** 48 8N 1 58W
Montgenèvre **141** 44 56N 6 42 E
Montgomery = Sahiwal **197** 30 45N 73 8 E
Montgomery **133** 52 34N 3 9W
Montguyon **140** 45 12N 0 12W
Monthey **148** 46 15N 6 56 E
Monticelli d'Ongina **162** 45 3N 9 56 E
Montichiari **162** 45 28N 10 29 E
Montier **139** 48 30N 4 45 E
Montignac **140** 45 4N 1 10 E
Montignies-sur-Sambre **143** 50 24N 4 29 E
Montigny-les-Metz **139** 49 7N 6 10 E
Montigny-sur-Aube **139** 47 57N 4 45 E
Montijo **155** 38 52N 6 39W
Montijo, Presa de **155** 38 55N 6 26W
Montilla **155** 37 36N 4 40W
Montlhéry **139** 48 39N 2 15 E
Montluçon **140** 46 22N 2 36 E
Montmagny **83** 46 58N 70 34W
Montmarault **140** 46 19N 2 57 E
Montmartre **88** 50 14N 103 27W
Montmédy **139** 49 30N 5 20 E
Montmélian **141** 45 30N 6 4 E
Montmirail **139** 48 51N 3 30 E
Montmoreau-St-Cybard **140** 45 23N 0 8 E
Montmorency **75** 46 53N 71 11W
Montmorillon **140** 46 26N 0 50 E
Montmort **139** 48 55N 3 49 E
Monto **230** 24 52 S 151 6 E
Montoire **138** 47 45N 0 52 E
Montório al Vomano **163** 42 35N 13 38 E
Montoro **155** 38 1N 4 27W
Montpellier **140** 43 37N 3 52 E
Montpezat-de-Quercy **140** 44 15N 1 30 E
Montpon **140** 45 2N 0 11 E
Montréal, Canada **83** 45 31N 73 34W
Montréal, France **140** 43 13N 2 8 E
Montreal → **87** 47 14N 84 39W
Montreal I. **87** 47 19N 84 44W
Montreal L. **88** 54 20N 105 45W
Montreal Lake **88** 54 3N 105 46W
Montredon-Labessonnie **140** 43 45N 2 18 E
Montréjeau **140** 43 6N 0 35 E
Montrésor **138** 47 10N 1 10 E
Montreuil **139** 50 27N 1 45 E
Montreuil, L. **82** 50 12N 77 40W
Montreuil-Bellay **138** 47 8N 0 9W
Montreux **148** 46 26N 6 55 E
Montrevault **138** 47 17N 1 2W
Montrevel-en-Bresse **141** 46 21N 5 8 E
Montrichard **138** 47 20N 1 10 E
Montrose, Canada **93** 49 5N 117 35W
Montrose, U.K. **134** 56 43N 2 28W
Monts, Pte. des **80** 49 20N 67 12W
Monts-sur-Guesnes **138** 46 55N 0 13 E
Montsalvy **140** 44 41N 2 30 E
Montsant, Sierra de **156** 41 17N 1 0 E
Montsauche **139** 47 13N 4 0 E
Montsech, Sierra del **156** 42 0N 0 45 E
Montseny **156** 41 55N 2 25W
Montserrat, Spain **156** 41 36N 1 49 E
Montserrat, W. Indies **113** 16 40N 62 10W
Montuenga **154** 41 3N 4 38W
Montuiri **156** 39 34N 2 59 E
Monveda **252** 2 52N 21 30 E
Monyo **202** 17 59N 95 30 E
Monywa **202** 22 7N 95 11 E
Monza **162** 45 35N 9 15 E
Monze **251** 16 17 S 27 29 E
Monze, C. **197** 24 47N 66 37 E
Monzón **156** 41 52N 0 10 E
Mook **142** 51 46N 5 54 E
Mo'oka **221** 36 26N 140 1 E
Moolawatana **231** 29 55 S 139 45 E
Mooleulooloo **232** 31 36 S 140 32 E
Mooliabeenee **229** 31 20 S 116 2 E
Mooloogool **229** 26 2 S 119 5 E
Moomin, Cr. → **231** 29 44 S 149 20 E
Moonah → **230** 22 3 S 138 33 E
Moonbeam **87** 49 20N 82 10W
Moonie **231** 27 46 S 150 20 E
Moonie → **231** 29 19 S 148 43 E
Moonta **232** 34 6 S 137 32 E
Moora **229** 30 37 S 115 58 E
Mooraberree **230** 25 13 S 140 54 E
Moorarie **229** 25 56 S 117 35 E
Moore → **229** 31 22 S 115 30 E
Moore, L. **229** 29 50 S 117 35 E
Moore Reefs **230** 16 0 S 149 5 E
Mooréa **226** 17 30 S 149 50W
Moores Mill **81** 45 18N 67 17W
Moorfoot Hills **134** 55 44N 3 8W
Moorland **233** 31 46 S 152 38 E
Mooroopna **231** 36 25 S 145 22 E
Moorreesburg **254** 33 6 S 18 38 E
Moorslede **143** 50 54N 3 4 E
Moosburg **147** 48 28N 11 57 E
Moose → **87** 51 20N 80 25W
Moose Creek **85** 45 15N 74 58W
Moose Factory **87** 51 16N 80 32W
Moose Heights **93** 53 4N 122 31W
Moose Hill **86** 48 15N 89 29W
Moose I. **89** 51 42N 97 10W
Moose Jaw **88** 50 24N 105 30W
Moose Jaw Cr. → **88** 50 34N 105 18W
Moose L. **89** 53 46N 100 8W
Moose Lake **89** 53 43N 100 20W
Moose Mountain Cr. → **88** 49 13N 102 12W
Moose Mountain Prov. Park **89** 49 48N 102 25W
Moose River **87** 50 48N 81 17W
Moosomin **89** 50 9N 101 40W
Moosonee **73** 51 17N 80 39W
Mopipi **254** 21 6 S 24 55 E
Mopoi **250** 5 6N 26 54 E
Mopti **246** 14 30N 4 0W
Moqatta **245** 14 38N 35 50 E
Moquegua **122** 17 15 S 70 46W
Moquegua □ **122** 16 50 S 70 55W
Mór **151** 47 25N 18 12 E
Mora, Mexico **104** 21 32N 104 48W
Móra, Portugal **155** 38 55N 8 10W
Mora, Sweden **172** 61 2N 14 38 E
Mora de Ebro **156** 41 6N 0 38 E
Mora de Rubielos **156** 40 15N 0 45W
Mora la Nueva **156** 41 7N 0 39 E
Morača → **166** 42 20N 19 9 E
Morada Nova **120** 5 7 S 38 23W
Morada Nova de Minas **121** 18 37 S 45 22W
Moradabad **199** 28 50N 78 50 E
Morafenobe **255** 17 50 S 44 53 E
Morąg **152** 53 55N 19 56 E
Moral de Calatrava **157** 38 51N 3 33W
Moraleja **154** 40 6N 6 43W
Morales, Colombia **118** 2 45N 76 38W
Morales, Mexico **103** 24 21N 98 2W
Morales, L. **103** 23 35N 97 47W
Moranbah **230** 22 1 S 148 6 E
Morano Cálabro **165** 39 51N 16 8 E
Morant Cays **112** 17 22N 76 0W
Morant Pt. **112** 17 55N 76 12W
Morar L. **134** 56 57N 5 40W
Moratalla **157** 38 14N 1 49W
Moratuwa **201** 6 45N 79 55 E
Morava → **151** 48 10N 16 59 E
Moravian Hts. = Ceskomoravská Vrchovina **150** 49 30N 15 40 E
Moravica → **166** 43 52N 20 8 E
Moravice → **151** 49 50N 17 43 E
Moraviţa **166** 45 17N 21 14 E
Moravská Třebová **151** 49 45N 16 40 E
Moravské Budějovice **150** 49 4N 15 49 E
Morawa **229** 29 13 S 116 0 E
Morawhanna **119** 8 30N 59 40W
Moray Firth **134** 57 50N 3 30W
Morbach **147** 49 48N 7 7 E
Morbegno **162** 46 8N 9 34 E
Morbi **198** 22 50N 70 42 E
Morbihan □ **138** 47 55N 2 50W
Morcenx **140** 44 0N 0 55W
Morcillo **105** 24 10N 104 41W
Mordelles **138** 48 5N 1 52W
Morden **89** 49 15N 98 10W
Mordovian A.S.S.R.□ **179** 54 20N 44 30 E
Mordovo **179** 52 6N 40 50 E
Mordy **152** 52 13N 22 31 E
Møre og Romsdal fylke □ **171** 62 30N 8 0 E
Morea, Australia **231** 36 45 S 141 18 E
Morea, Greece **130** 37 45N 22 10 E
Morecambe **132** 54 5N 2 52W
Morecambe B. **132** 54 7N 3 0W
Moree **231** 29 28 S 149 54 E
Morehead **227** 8 41 S 141 41 E
Morelia **107** 19 42N 101 7W
Morell **81** 46 25N 62 42W
Morella, Australia **230** 23 0 S 143 52 E
Morella, Spain **156** 40 35N 0 5W
Morelos, Chihuahua, Mexico **101** 26 42N 107 40W
Morelos, Coahuila, Mexico **102** 28 25N 100 53W
Morelos, Quintana Roo, Mexico **111** 19 45N 88 47W
Morelos, Zacatecas, Mexico **105** 22 53N 102 37W
Morelos □ **107** 18 45N 99 0W
Morelos Cañada **109** 18 44N 97 25W
Morena, Sierra **155** 38 20N 4 0W
Moreni **170** 44 59N 25 36 E
Moreno **100** 28 30N 110 44W
Morero **123** 11 9 S 66 15W
Moreru → **123** 10 10 S 59 15W
Moresby I. **92** 52 30N 131 40W
Morestel **141** 45 40N 5 28 E
Moret **139** 48 22N 2 58 E
Moreton **230** 12 22 S 142 30 E
Moreton I. **231** 27 10 S 153 25 E
Moreuil **139** 49 46N 2 30 E
Morez **141** 46 31N 6 2 E
Morgan **232** 34 0 S 139 35 E
Morgan Vale **232** 33 10 S 140 32 E
Morgat **138** 48 15N 4 32W
Morgenzon **255** 26 45 S 29 36 E
Morges **148** 46 31N 6 29 E
Morghak **193** 29 7N 57 54 E
Morhange **139** 48 55N 6 38 E
Mori **162** 45 51N 10 59 E
Morialmée **143** 50 17N 4 35 E
Morice → **92** 54 12N 127 5W
Morice L. **92** 53 50N 127 40W
Morichal **118** 2 10N 70 34W
Morichal Largo → **119** 9 27N 62 25W
Moriguchi **221** 34 44N 135 34 E
Moriki **247** 12 52N 6 30 E
Morin-Heights **83** 45 54N 74 15W
Morinville **90** 53 49N 113 41W
Morioka **218** 39 45N 141 8 E
Moris **100** 28 8N 108 32W
Morisset **233** 33 6 S 151 30 E
Morlaàs **140** 43 21N 0 18W
Morlaix **138** 48 36N 3 52W
Morlanwelz **143** 50 28N 4 15 E
Mormanno **165** 39 53N 15 59 E
Mormant **139** 48 37N 2 52 E
Mornington, Vic., Australia **231** 38 15 S 145 5 E
Mornington, W. Austral., Australia **228** 17 31 S 126 6 E
Mornington, I. **126** 49 50 S 75 30W
Mornington I. **230** 16 30 S 139 30 E
Mórnos → **169** 38 30N 22 0 E
Moro **245** 10 50N 30 9 E
Moro G. **211** 6 30N 123 0 E
Morobe **227** 7 49 S 147 38 E
Morocco ■ **240** 32 0N 5 50W
Morococha **122** 11 40 S 76 5W
Morogoro **250** 6 50 S 37 40 E
Morogoro □ **250** 8 0 S 37 0 E
Moroleón **107** 20 8N 101 12W
Morombe **255** 21 45 S 43 22 E
Moron, Argentina **124** 34 39 S 58 37W
Morón, Cuba **112** 22 8N 78 39W
Morón de Almazán **156** 41 29N 2 27W
Morón de la Frontera **155** 37 6N 5 28W
Morona → **118** 4 40 S 77 10W
Morona-Santiago □ **118** 2 30 S 78 0W
Morondava **255** 20 17 S 44 17 E
Morondo **246** 8 57N 6 47W
Morones, Sa. de **105** 21 45N 103 10W
Morong **210** 14 41N 120 16 E
Moronou **246** 6 16N 4 59W
Morotai **207** 2 10N 128 30 E
Moroto **250** 2 28N 34 42 E
Moroto Summit **250** 2 30N 34 43 E
Morozov **167** 42 30N 25 10 E
Morozovsk **181** 48 25N 41 50 E
Morpeth **132** 55 11N 1 41W
Morphou **190** 35 2N 33 1 E
Morphou Bay **190** 35 15N 32 50 E
Morrelganj **202** 22 28N 89 51 E
Morrin **91** 51 40N 112 47W
Morrinhos, Ceara, Brazil **120** 3 14 S 40 7W
Morrinhos, Minas Gerais, Brazil **121** 17 45 S 49 10W
Morrinsville **234** 37 40 S 175 32 E
Morris **89** 49 25N 97 22W
Morris → **89** 49 21N 97 21W
Morris, Mt. **229** 26 9 S 131 4 E
Morrisburg **85** 44 55N 75 7W
Morro, Pta. **124** 27 6 S 71 0W
Morro, Pta. del **108** 19 51N 96 27W
Morro do Chapéu **121** 11 33 S 41 9W
Morros **120** 2 52 S 44 3W
Morrosquillo, Golfo de **112** 9 35N 75 40W
Mörrum **173** 56 12N 14 45 E
Mors **173** 56 50N 8 45 E
Morse **88** 50 25N 107 3W
Morshansk **179** 53 28N 41 50 E
Mörsil **172** 63 19N 13 40 E
Morson **86** 49 6N 94 19W
Mortagne **140** 45 28N 0 49W
Mortagne → **139** 48 33N 6 27 E
Mortagne-au-Perche **138** 48 31N 0 33 E
Mortain **138** 48 40N 0 57W
Mortara **162** 45 15N 8 43 E
Mortcha **243** 16 0N 21 10 E
Morteau **139** 47 3N 6 35 E
Morteros **124** 30 50 S 62 0W
Mortes, R. das → **121** 11 45 S 50 44W
Mortlach **88** 50 27N 106 4W
Mortlake **231** 38 5 S 142 50 E
Mortsel **143** 51 11N 4 27 E
Morundah **231** 34 57 S 146 19 E
Moruya **231** 35 58 S 150 3 E
Morvan, Mts. du **139** 47 5N 4 0 E
Morven, Australia **231** 26 22 S 147 5 E
Morven, N.Z. **235** 44 50 S 171 6 E
Morvern **134** 56 38N 5 44W
Morwell **231** 38 10 S 146 22 E
Moryn **152** 52 51N 14 22 E
Morzhovets, Ostrov **176** 66 44N 42 35 E
Mosalsk **178** 54 30N 34 55 E
Mosbach **147** 49 21N 9 9 E
Moščenice **163** 45 17N 14 16 E
Mosciano Sant' Ángelo **163** 42 42N 13 52 E
Moscos Is. **204** 14 0N 97 30 E
Moscow = Moskva **179** 55 45N 37 35 E
Mosel → **143** 50 22N 7 36 E
Moselle = Mosel → **143** 50 22N 7 36 E
Moselle □ **139** 48 59N 6 33 E
Moses Inlet **92** 51 47N 127 23W
Mosgiel **235** 45 53 S 170 21 E
Mosher **87** 48 42N 84 12W
Moshi **250** 3 22 S 37 18 E
Moshi □ **250** 3 22 S 37 18 E
Moshupa **254** 24 46 S 25 29 E
Mosina **152** 52 15N 16 50 E
Mosjøen **174** 65 51N 13 12 E
Moskenesøya **174** 67 58N 13 0 E
Moskenstraumen **174** 67 47N 12 45 E
Moskva **179** 55 45N 37 35 E
Moskva → **179** 55 5N 38 51 E
Moslavačka Gora **163** 45 40N 16 37 E
Mosley Cr. **92** 51 18N 124 50W
Mosomane **254** 24 2 S 26 19 E
Mosonmagyaróvár **151** 47 52N 17 18 E
Mošorin **166** 45 19N 20 4 E
Mospino **180** 47 52N 38 0 E
Mosquera **118** 2 35N 78 24W
Mosqueruela **156** 40 21N 0 27W
Mosquitia **112** 15 20N 84 10W

Mosquito B. 78 61 10N 78 0W
Mosquitos, Golfo de los 112 9 15N 81 10W
Moss 171 59 27N 10 40 E
Moss Vale 231 34 32 S 150 25 E
Mossaka 252 1 15 S 16 45 E
Mossâmedes 121 16 7 S 50 11W
Mossbank 88 49 56N 105 56W
Mossburn 235 45 41 S 168 15 E
Mosselbaai 254 34 11 S 22 8 E
Mossendjo 252 2 55 S 12 42 E
Mosses, Col des 148 46 25N 7 7 E
Mossgiel 231 33 15 S 144 5 E
Mossman 230 16 21 S 145 15 E
Mossoró 120 5 10 S 37 15W
Møsstrand 171 59 51N 8 4 E
Mossuril 251 14 58 S 40 42 E
Mossy → 88 54 5N 102 58W
Most 150 50 31N 13 38 E
Moştafáābād 193 33 39N 54 53 E
Mostaganem 241 35 54N 0 5 E
Mostar 166 43 22N 17 50 E
Mostardas 125 31 2 S 50 51W
Mostefa, Rass 241 36 55N 11 3 E
Mosterøy 171 59 5N 5 37 E
Mostiska 178 49 48N 23 4 E
Mosty 178 53 27N 24 38 E
Mosul = Al Mawşil 192 36 15N 43 5 E
Mosulpo 215 33 20N 126 17 E
Mosvatn 171 59 52N 8 5 E
Mota del Cuervo 156 39 30N 2 52W
Mota del Marqués 154 41 38N 5 11W
Motagua → 112 15 44N 88 14W
Motala 173 58 32N 15 1 E
Motegi 221 36 32N 140 11 E
Mothe, La, Rés. 83 48 46N 71 9W
Mothe-Achard, La 138 46 37N 1 40W
Motherwell 134 55 48N 4 0W
Motihari 199 26 30N 84 55 E
Motilla del Palancar 156 39 34N 1 55W
Motnik 163 46 14N 14 54 E
Motocurunya 119 4 24N 64 5W
Motovun 163 45 20N 13 50 E
Motozintla de Mendoza 110 15 22N 92 14W
Motril 157 36 31N 3 37W
Motru → 170 44 44N 22 59 E
Motte, L. la 82 48 20N 78 2W
Motte, La 141 44 20N 6 3 E
Motte-Chalançon, La 141 44 30N 5 21 E
Móttola 165 40 38N 17 0 E
Motu 234 38 18 S 177 40 E
Motueka 235 41 7 S 173 1 E
Motul 111 21 6N 89 17W
Motupena Pt. 227 6 30 S 155 10 E
Mouanda 252 1 28 S 13 7 E
Mouchalagane → 78 50 56N 68 41W
Moucontant 138 46 43N 0 36W
Moúdhros 168 39 50N 25 18 E
Mouding 216 25 20N 101 28 E
Moudjeria 246 17 50N 12 28W
Moudon 148 46 40N 6 49 E
Mougoundou 252 2 40 S 12 41 E
Mouila 252 1 50 S 11 0 E
Mouka 252 7 16N 21 52 E
Moulamein 231 35 3 S 144 1 E
Mould Bay 94 76 12N 119 25W
Moule 113 16 20N 61 22W
Moulins 140 46 35N 3 19 E
Moulmein 202 16 30N 97 40 E
Moulmeingyun 202 16 23N 95 16 E
Moulouya, O. → 241 35 5N 2 25W
Moúnda, Ákra 169 38 5N 20 45 E
Moundou 243 8 40N 16 10 E
Mounembé 252 3 20 S 12 32 E
Moung 204 12 46N 103 27 E
Moungoudi 252 2 45 S 11 46 E
Mount Albert 84 44 8N 79 19W
Mount Amherst 228 18 24 S 126 58 E
Mount Assiniboine Prov. Park 91 50 53N 115 39W
Mount Augustus 229 24 20 S 116 56 E
Mount Barker, S. Austral., Australia 232 35 5 S 138 52 E
Mount Barker, W. Austral., Australia 229 34 38 S 117 40 E
Mount Beauty 233 36 47 S 147 10 E
Mount Brydges 84 42 54N 81 29W
Mount Carleton Prov. Park 81 47 25N 66 55W
Mount Carmel 79 47 9N 53 29W
Mount Coolon 230 21 25 S 147 25 E
Mount Darwin 251 16 45 S 31 33 E
Mount Douglas 230 21 35 S 146 50 E
Mount Elizabeth 228 16 0 S 125 50 E
Mount Forest 84 43 59N 80 43W
Mount Gambier 232 37 50 S 140 46 E
Mount Garnet 230 17 37 S 145 6 E
Mount Hagen 227 5 52 S 144 16 E
Mount Hope, N.S.W., Australia 231 32 51 S 145 51 E
Mount Hope, S. Austral., Australia 231 34 7 S 135 23 E
Mount Howitt 231 26 31 S 142 16 E
Mount Isa 230 20 42 S 139 26 E
Mount Ive 232 32 25 S 136 5 E
Mount Keith 229 27 15 S 120 30 E
Mount Larcom 230 23 48 S 150 59 E
Mount Lofty Ra. 232 34 35 S 139 5 E
Mount Magnet 229 28 2 S 117 47 E
Mount Manara 232 32 29 S 143 58 E
Mount Margaret 231 26 54 S 143 21 E
Mount Maunganui 234 37 40 S 176 14 E
Mount Molloy 230 16 42 S 145 20 E
Mount Monger 229 31 0 S 122 0 E
Mount Morgan 230 23 40 S 150 25 E
Mount Moriah 79 48 58N 58 2W
Mount Mulligan 230 16 45 S 144 47 E
Mount Narryer 229 26 30 S 115 55 E
Mount Oxide Mine 230 19 30 S 139 29 E
Mount Pearl 79 47 31N 52 47W
Mount Perry 231 25 13 S 151 42 E
Mount Phillips 229 24 25 S 116 15 E
Mount Revelstoke Nat. Park 93 51 5N 118 30W
Mount Robson 76 52 56N 119 15W
Mount Robson Prov. Park 93 53 0N 119 0W
Mount Roskill 234 36 55 S 174 45 E
Mount Sandiman 229 24 25 S 115 30 E
Mount Somers 235 43 45 S 171 27 E
Mount Stewart 81 46 22N 62 52W
Mount Surprise 230 18 10 S 144 17 E
Mount Uniacke 81 44 54N 63 50W
Mount Vernon 229 24 9 S 118 2 E
Mount Victor 232 32 11 S 139 44 E
Mount Wellington 234 36 55 S 174 52 E
Mountain □ 210 17 20N 121 10 E
Mountain Park 91 52 50N 117 15W
Mountain View 91 49 8N 113 36W
Mountmellick 135 53 7N 7 20W
Moura, Australia 230 24 35 S 149 58 E
Moura, Brazil 119 1 32 S 61 38W
Moura, Portugal 155 38 7N 7 30W
Mourão 155 38 22N 7 22W
Mourdi Depression 243 18 10N 23 0 E
Mourdiah 246 14 35N 7 25W
Mourenx 140 43 23N 0 36W
Mouri 247 5 6N 1 14W
Mourilyan 230 17 35 S 146 3 E
Mourmelon-le-Grand 139 49 8N 4 22 E
Mourne → 135 54 45N 7 39W
Mourne Mts. 135 54 10N 6 0W
Mouscron 143 50 45N 3 12 E
Moussoro 243 13 41N 16 35 E
Mouthe 139 46 44N 6 12 E
Moutier 148 47 16N 7 21 E
Moûtiers 141 45 29N 6 31 E
Moutong 207 0 28N 121 13 E
Mouy 139 49 18N 2 20 E
Mouzáki 168 39 25N 21 37 E
Movano 102 26 42N 103 39W
Movas 100 28 10N 109 25W
Moville 135 55 11N 7 3W
Moxhe 143 50 38N 5 5 E
Moxico □ 253 12 0 S 20 30 E
Moxotó → 120 9 19 S 38 14W
Moy → 135 54 5N 8 50W
Moyahua 106 21 16N 103 10W
Moyale, Ethiopia 245 3 34N 39 4 E
Moyale, Kenya 250 3 30N 39 0 E
Moyamba 246 8 4N 12 30W
Moyen Atlas 241 32 0N 5 0W
Moyle □ 135 55 10N 6 15W
Moyo 206 8 10 S 117 40 E
Moyobamba 122 6 0 S 77 0W
Moyyero → 185 68 44N 103 42 E
Mozambique = Moçambique 251 15 3 S 40 42 E
Mozambique ■ 251 19 0 S 35 0 E
Mozambique Chan. 255 20 0 S 39 0 E
Mozdok 181 43 45N 44 48 E
Mozdūrān 193 36 9N 60 35 E
Mozhaysk 179 55 30N 36 2 E
Mozhga 182 56 26N 52 15 E
Mozhnābād 193 34 7N 60 6 E
Mozirje 163 46 22N 14 58 E
Mozyr 178 52 0N 29 15 E
Mpanda 250 6 23 S 31 1 E
Mpanda □ 250 6 23 S 31 40 E
Mpésoba 246 12 31N 5 39W
Mpika 251 11 51 S 31 25 E
Mpulungu 251 8 51 S 31 5 E
Mpwapwa 250 6 23 S 36 30 E
Mpwapwa □ 250 6 30 S 36 20 E
Mrągowo 152 53 52N 21 18 E
Mrakovo 182 52 43N 56 38 E
Mramor 166 43 20N 21 45 E
Mrimina 240 29 50N 7 9W
Mrkonjić Grad 166 44 26N 17 4 E
Mrkopalj 163 45 21N 14 52 E
Mrocza 152 53 16N 17 35 E
Msab, Oued en → 241 32 25N 5 20 E
Msaken 241 35 49N 10 33 E
Msambansovu 251 15 50 S 30 3 E
M'sila 241 35 46N 4 30 E
Msta → 178 58 25N 31 20 E
Mstislavl 178 54 0N 31 50 E
Mszana Dolna 152 49 41N 20 5 E
Mszczonów 152 51 58N 20 33 E
Mtama 251 10 17 S 39 21 E
Mtilikwe → 251 21 9 S 31 30 E
Mtsensk 179 53 25N 36 30 E
Mtskheta 181 41 52N 44 45 E
Mtwara-Mikindani 251 10 20 S 40 20 E
Mu → 202 21 56N 95 38 E
Mu Gia, Deo 204 17 40N 105 47 E
Mu Us Shamo 214 39 0N 109 0 E
Muacandalo 253 10 2 S 19 40 E
Muaná 120 1 25 S 49 15W
Muanda 253 6 0 S 12 20 E
Muang Chiang Rai 204 19 52N 99 50 E
Muang Lamphun 204 18 40N 99 2 E
Muang Pak Beng 204 19 54N 101 8 E
Muar 205 2 3N 102 34 E
Muarabungo 208 1 28 S 102 52 E
Muaraenim 208 3 40 S 103 50 E
Muarajuloi 209 0 12 S 114 3 E
Muarakaman 209 0 2 S 116 45 E
Muaratebo 208 1 30 S 102 26 E
Muaratembesi 208 1 42 S 103 8 E
Muaratewe 209 0 58 S 114 52 E
Mubarakpur 199 26 6N 83 18 E
Mubende 250 0 33N 31 22 E
Mubi 247 10 18N 13 16 E
Mubur, P. 205 3 20N 106 12 E
Mucajaí → 119 2 25N 60 52W
Mucajaí, Serra do 119 2 23N 61 10W
Mucari 253 9 30 S 16 54 E
Muchalat Inlet 92 49 38N 126 15W
Mücheln 146 51 18N 11 49 E
Muchinga Mts. 251 11 30 S 31 30 E
Muchkapskiy 179 51 52N 42 28 E
Muck 134 56 50N 6 15W
Muckadilla 231 26 35 S 148 23 E
Muco → 118 4 15N 70 21W
Mucoma 253 15 18 S 13 39 E
Muconda 253 10 31 S 21 15 E
Mucuim → 123 6 33 S 64 18W
Mucura 119 2 31 S 62 43W
Mucuri 121 18 0 S 39 36W
Mucurici 121 18 6 S 40 31W
Mucusso 254 18 1 S 21 25 E
Mudan Jiang → 215 46 20N 129 30 E
Mudanjiang 215 44 38N 129 30 E
Mudanya 180 40 25N 28 50 E
Muddy L. 88 52 19N 109 6W
Mudgee 231 32 32 S 149 31 E
Mudjatik → 77 56 1N 107 36W
Mudon 202 16 15N 97 44 E
Mudugh □ 256 7 0N 47 30 E
Muecate 251 14 55 S 39 40 E
Muêda 251 11 36 S 39 28 E
Muela, La 156 41 36N 1 7W
Mueller Ra. 228 18 18 S 126 46 E
Muende 251 14 28 S 33 0 E
Muenster 88 52 12N 105 0W
Muerto, Mar 110 16 10N 94 10W
Muertos, B. de los 99 23 55N 109 45W
Muertos, Punta de los 157 36 57N 1 54W
Mufindi □ 251 8 30 S 35 20 E
Mufu Shan 217 29 20N 114 30 E
Mufulira 251 12 32 S 28 15 E
Mufumbiro Range 250 1 25 S 29 30 E
Mugardos 154 43 27N 8 15W
Muge 155 39 3N 8 40W
Muge → 155 39 8N 8 44W
Múggia 163 45 36N 13 47 E
Mughayrā' 192 29 17N 37 41 E
Mugi 220 33 40N 134 25 E
Mugia 154 43 3N 9 10W
Mugila, Mts. 250 7 0 S 28 50 E
Muğla 177 37 15N 28 22 E
Müglizh 167 42 37N 25 32 E
Mugu 199 29 45N 82 30 E
Muhammad, Râs 191 27 44N 34 16 E
Muhammad Qol 244 20 53N 37 9 E
Muhammadabad 199 26 4N 83 25 E
Muharraqa = Sa'ad 189 31 28N 34 33 E
Muḥayriqah 194 23 59N 45 4 E
Muhesi → 250 7 0 S 35 20 E
Muheza □ 250 5 0 S 39 0 E
Mühldorf 147 48 14N 12 33 E
Mühlhausen 146 51 12N 10 29 E
Mühlig Hofmann fjella 13 72 30 S 5 0 E
Muhutwe 250 1 35 S 31 45 E
Muiden 142 52 20N 5 4 E
Muikamachi 219 37 15N 138 50 E
Muine Bheag 135 52 42N 6 57W
Muiños 154 41 58N 7 59W
Muir, L. 229 34 30 S 116 40 E
Mujeres, B. de 111 21 15N 86 46W
Mukachevo 178 48 27N 22 45 E
Mukah 206 2 55N 112 5 E
Mukawwa, Geziret 244 23 55N 35 53 E
Mukdahan 204 16 32N 104 43 E
Mukden = Shenyang 215 41 48N 123 27 E
Mukhtolovo 179 55 29N 43 15 E
Mukhtuya = Lensk 185 60 48N 114 55 E
Mukinbudin 229 30 55 S 118 5 E
Mukishi 251 8 30 S 24 44 E
Mukomuko 208 2 30 S 101 10 E
Mukomwenze 250 6 49 S 27 15 E
Mukry 183 37 54N 65 12 E
Muktsar 198 30 30N 74 30 E
Mukur 198 32 50N 67 42 E
Mukutawa → 89 53 10N 97 24W
Mukwela 251 17 0 S 26 40 E
Mula 157 38 3N 1 33W
Mula → 200 18 34N 74 21 E
Mula, La 101 29 13N 104 26W
Mulanay 210 13 31N 122 24 E
Mulange 250 3 40 S 27 10 E
Mulatos 100 28 39N 108 51W
Mulchén 124 37 45 S 72 20W
Mulde → 146 51 10N 12 48 E
Muleba 250 1 50 S 31 37 E
Muleba □ 250 2 0 S 31 30 E
Mulegns 149 46 32N 9 38 E
Mulejé 99 26 53N 112 1W
Mulga Valley 232 31 8 S 141 3 E
Mulgathing 231 30 15 S 134 8 E
Mulgrave 81 45 38N 61 31W
Mulgrave I. 227 10 5 S 142 10 E
Mulhacén 157 37 4N 3 20W
Mülheim 146 51 26N 6 53 E
Mulhouse 139 47 40N 7 20 E
Muli 216 27 52N 101 8 E
Muling 215 44 35N 130 10 E
Mull 134 56 27N 6 0W
Mullaittvu 201 9 15N 80 49 E
Mullengudgery 231 31 43 S 147 23 E
Muller, Pegunungan 209 0 30N 113 30 E
Mullet Pen. 135 54 10N 10 2W
Mullewa 229 28 29 S 115 30 E
Müllheim 147 47 48N 7 37 E
Mulligan → 230 26 40 S 139 0 E
Mullingar 135 53 31N 7 20W
Mullsjö 173 57 56N 13 55 E
Mullumbimby 231 28 30 S 153 30 E
Mulobezi 251 16 45 S 25 7 E
Mulshi L. 200 18 30N 73 48 E
Multai 198 21 50N 78 21 E
Multan 197 30 15N 71 36 E
Multé 110 17 41N 91 24W
Multrå 172 63 10N 17 24 E
Mulumbe, Mts. 251 8 40 S 27 30 E
Mulungushi Dam 251 14 48 S 28 48 E
Mulwad 244 18 45N 30 39 E
Mulwala 233 35 59 S 146 0 E
Mumbondo 253 10 9 S 14 15 E
Mumeng 227 7 1 S 146 37 E
Mumra 181 45 45N 47 41 E
Mun → 204 15 19N 105 30 E
Muna, Indonesia 207 5 0 S 122 30 E
Muna, Mexico 111 20 29N 89 43W
Munamagi 178 57 43N 27 4 E
Munawwar 199 32 47N 74 27 E
Münchberg 147 50 11N 11 48 E
Müncheberg 146 52 30N 14 9 E
München 147 48 8N 11 33 E
Munchen-Gladbach = Mönchengladbach 146 51 12N 6 23 E
Muncho Lake 76 59 0N 125 50W
Munchŏn 215 39 14N 127 19 E
Münchwilen 149 47 28N 8 59 E
Mundakayam 201 9 30N 76 50 E
Mundala 207 4 30 S 141 0 E
Mundare 90 53 35N 112 20W
Münden 146 51 25N 9 42 E
Mundiwindi 228 23 47 S 120 9 E
Mundo → 157 38 30N 2 15W
Mundo Novo 121 11 50 S 40 29W
Mundra 198 22 54N 69 48 E
Mundrabilla 229 31 52 S 127 51 E
Munducurus 119 4 47 S 58 16W
Munenga 253 10 2 S 14 41 E
Munera 157 39 2N 2 29W
Muneru → 201 16 45N 80 3 E
Mungallala 231 26 28 S 147 34 E
Mungallala Cr. → 231 28 53 S 147 5 E
Mungana 230 17 8 S 144 27 E
Mungaoli 198 24 24N 78 7 E
Mungari 251 17 12 S 33 30 E
Mungbere 250 2 36N 28 28 E
Munger 199 25 23N 86 30 E
Mungindi 231 28 58 S 149 1 E
Munhango 253 12 10 S 18 38 E
Munhango → 253 11 30 S 19 30 E
Munich = München 147 48 8N 11 33 E
Munjiye 244 18 47N 41 20 E
Munka-Ljungby 173 56 16N 12 58 E
Munkedal 173 58 28N 11 40 E
Munkfors 172 59 50N 13 30 E
Munku-Sardyk 185 51 45N 100 20 E
Münnerstadt 147 50 15N 10 11 E
Muñoz, Mexico 107 19 28N 98 12W

Munoz, Phil. **210** 15 43N 120 54 E
Muñoz Gamero, Pen. **126** 52 30 S 73 5 E
Munro **233** 37 56 S 147 11 E
Munroe L. **77** 59 13N 98 35W
Munsan **215** 37 51N 126 48 E
Munshiganj **202** 23 33N 90 32 E
Münsingen **148** 46 52N 7 32 E
Munson **91** 51 34N 112 45W
Munster, France **139** 48 2N 7 8 E
Munster, Niedersachsen, Germany **146** 52 59N 10 5 E
Münster, Nordrhein-Westfalen, Germany **146** 51 58N 7 37 E
Münster, Switz. **149** 46 30N 8 17 E
Munster □ **135** 52 20N 8 40W
Muntadgin **229** 31 45 S 118 33 E
Muntele Mare **170** 46 30N 23 12 E
Muntok **208** 2 5 S 105 10 E
Munyak **184** 43 30N 59 15 E
Munyama **251** 16 5 S 28 31 E
Muong Beng **204** 20 23N 101 46 E
Muong Boum **204** 22 24N 102 49 E
Muong Et **204** 20 49N 104 1 E
Muong Hai **204** 21 3N 101 49 E
Muong Hiem **204** 20 5N 103 22 E
Muong Houn **204** 20 8N 101 23 E
Muong Hung **204** 20 56N 103 53 E
Muong Kau **204** 15 6N 105 47 E
Muong Khao **204** 19 38N 103 32 E
Muong Khoua **204** 21 5N 102 31 E
Muong Liep **204** 18 29N 101 40 E
Muong May **204** 14 49N 106 56 E
Muong Ngeun **204** 20 36N 101 3 E
Muong Ngoi **204** 20 43N 102 41 E
Muong Nhie **204** 22 12N 102 28 E
Muong Nong **204** 16 22N 106 30 E
Muong Ou Tay **204** 22 7N 101 48 E
Muong Oua **204** 18 18N 101 20 E
Muong Peun **204** 20 13N 103 52 E
Muong Phalane **204** 16 39N 105 34 E
Muong Phieng **204** 19 6N 101 32 E
Muong Phine **204** 16 32N 106 2 E
Muong Sai **204** 20 42N 101 59 E
Muong Saiapoun **204** 18 24N 101 31 E
Muong Sen **204** 19 24N 104 8 E
Muong Sing **204** 21 11N 101 9 E
Muong Son **204** 20 27N 103 19 E
Muong Soui **204** 19 33N 102 52 E
Muong Va **204** 21 53N 102 19 E
Muong Xia **204** 20 19N 104 50 E
Muonio **174** 67 57N 23 40 E
Muotathal **149** 46 58N 8 46 E
Mupa **253** 16 5 S 15 50 E
Muping **215** 37 22N 121 36 E
Muqaddam, Wadi → **244** 18 4N 31 30 E
Muqdisho **256** 2 2N 45 25 E
Muqshin, W. → **195** 19 44N 55 14 E
Muquequete **253** 14 50 S 14 16 E
Mur → **150** 46 18N 16 53 E
Mur-de-Bretagne **138** 48 12N 3 0W
Mura → **163** 46 18N 16 53 E
Murakami **218** 38 14N 139 29 E
Murallón, Cuerro **126** 49 48 S 73 30W
Muralto **149** 46 11N 8 49 E
Muranda **250** 1 52 S 29 20 E
Murang'a **250** 0 45 S 37 9 E
Murashi **179** 59 30N 49 0 E
Murat **140** 45 7N 2 53 E
Murathüyüğü **190** 36 52N 36 55 E
Murau **150** 47 6N 14 10 E
Muravera **164** 39 25N 9 35 E
Murayama **218** 38 30N 140 25 E
Murban **195** 23 50N 53 45 E
Murça **154** 41 24N 7 28W
Murchison **235** 41 49 S 172 21 E
Murchison → **229** 27 45 S 114 0 E
Murchison, Mt. **13** 73 0 S 168 0 E
Murchison Falls = Kabarega Falls **250** 2 15N 31 30 E
Murchison House **229** 27 39 S 114 14 E
Murchison I. **86** 50 0N 88 21W
Murchison Mts. **235** 45 13 S 167 23 E
Murchison Ra. **230** 20 0 S 134 10 E
Murchison Rapids **251** 15 55 S 34 35 E
Murcia **157** 38 20N 1 10W
Murcia □ **157** 37 50N 1 30W
Murdoch Pt. **230** 14 37 S 144 55 E
Murdochville **80** 48 58N 65 30W
Mure, La **141** 44 55N 5 48 E
Mureş □ **170** 46 45N 24 40 E
Mureş → **170** 46 15N 20 13 E
Mureşul = Mureş → **170** 46 15N 20 13 E
Muret **140** 43 30N 1 20 E
Murfatlar **170** 44 10N 28 26 E
Murg **149** 47 6N 9 13 E
Murg → **147** 48 55N 8 10 E
Murgab **183** 38 10N 74 2 E
Murgeni **170** 46 12N 28 1 E
Murgenthal **148** 47 16N 7 50 E
Murgon **231** 26 15 S 151 54 E
Murgoo **229** 27 24 S 116 28 E
Muri **149** 47 17N 8 21 E
Muria **209** 6 36 S 110 53 E
Muriaé **121** 21 8 S 42 23W
Murias de Paredes **154** 42 52N 6 11W
Murici **120** 9 19 S 35 56W
Muriége **253** 9 58 S 21 11 E
Muriel L. **90** 54 9N 110 40W
Muriel Mine **251** 17 14 S 30 40 E
Murila **253** 10 44 S 20 20 E
Müritz See **146** 53 25N 12 40 E
Murka **250** 3 27 S 38 0 E
Murmansk **176** 68 57N 33 10 E
Murmerwoude **142** 53 18N 6 0 E
Murnau **147** 47 40N 11 11 E
Muro, France **141** 42 34N 8 54 E
Muro, Spain **156** 39 44N 3 3 E
Muro, C. de **141** 41 44N 8 37 E
Muro Lucano **165** 40 45N 15 30 E
Murom **179** 55 35N 42 3 E
Muroran **218** 42 25N 141 0 E
Muros **154** 42 45N 9 5W
Muros y de Noya, Ría de → **154** 42 45N 9 0W
Muroto **220** 33 18N 134 9 E
Muroto-Misaki **220** 33 15N 134 10 E
Murowana Goślina **152** 52 35N 17 0 E
Murphy L. **93** 52 3N 121 15W
Murrat **244** 18 51N 29 33 E
Murray →, Australia **232** 35 20 S 139 22 E
Murray →, Canada **76** 56 11N 120 45W
Murray, L. **227** 7 0 S 141 35 E
Murray Bridge **232** 35 6 S 139 14 E
Murray Downs **230** 21 4 S 134 40 E
Murray Harbour **81** 46 0N 62 28W
Murray River **81** 46 1N 62 37W
Murray Seascarp **225** 30 0N 135 0W
Murraysburg **254** 31 58 S 23 47 E
Murree **198** 33 56N 73 28 E
Murrin Murrin **229** 28 58 S 121 33 E
Murrumbidgee → **231** 34 43 S 143 12 E
Murrumburrah **231** 34 32 S 148 22 E
Murrurundi **231** 31 42 S 150 51 E
Mursala **208** 1 41N 98 28 E
Murshid **244** 21 40N 31 10 E
Murshidabad **199** 24 11N 88 19 E
Murska Sobota **163** 46 39N 16 12 E
Murtazapur **198** 20 40N 77 25 E
Murten **148** 46 56N 7 4 E
Murtensee **148** 46 56N 7 7 E
Murtle L. **93** 52 8N 119 38W
Murtoa **231** 36 35 S 142 28 E
Murtosa **154** 40 44N 8 40W
Muru → **122** 8 9 S 70 45W
Murungu **250** 4 12 S 31 10 E
Murupara **234** 38 28 S 176 42 E
Murwara **199** 23 46N 80 28 E
Murwillumbah **231** 28 18 S 153 27 E
Mürz → **150** 47 30N 15 25 E
Mürzzuschlag **150** 47 36N 15 41 E
Muş **177** 38 45N 41 30 E
Musa **252** 2 40N 19 18 E
Musa → **227** 9 3 S 148 55 E
Mûsa, G. **191** 28 33N 33 59 E
Musa Khel **197** 30 59N 69 52 E
Mûsá Qal'eh **197** 32 20N 64 50 E
Musairik, Wadi → **244** 19 30N 43 10 E
Musala **167** 42 13N 23 37 E
Musan **215** 42 12N 129 12 E
Musangu **251** 10 28 S 23 55 E
Musasa **250** 3 25 S 31 30 E
Musashino **221** 35 42N 139 34 E
Musay'īd **195** 25 0N 51 33 E
Musaymīr **194** 13 27N 44 37 E
Muscat = Masqat **195** 23 37N 58 36 E
Muscat & Oman = Oman ■ **195** 23 0N 58 0 E
Musel **154** 43 34N 5 42W
Musgrave Harbour **79** 49 27N 53 58W
Musgrave Ras. **229** 26 0 S 132 0 E
Mushaboom **81** 44 51N 62 32W
Mushie **252** 2 56 S 16 55 E
Mushin **247** 6 32N 3 21 E
Musi →, India **200** 16 41N 79 40 E
Musi →, Indonesia **208** 2 20 S 104 56 E
Muskeg → **76** 60 20N 123 20W
Muskeg L. **86** 49 0N 90 2W
Muskeg River **90** 53 55N 118 39W
Muskoka, L. **84** 45 0N 79 25W
Muskwa →, Alta., Canada **90** 56 15N 113 48W
Muskwa →, B.C., Canada **76** 58 47N 122 48W
Muskwa L. **90** 56 9N 114 38W
Muslīmiyah **192** 36 19N 37 12 E
Musmar **244** 18 13N 35 40 E
Musofu **251** 13 30 S 29 0 E
Musoma **250** 1 30 S 33 48 E
Musoma □ **250** 1 50 S 34 30 E
Musquanousse, L. **80** 50 22N 61 5W
Musquaro **80** 50 10N 61 3W
Musquaro, L. **78** 50 38N 61 5W
Musquash **81** 45 11N 66 19W
Musquodoboit Harbour **81** 44 50N 63 9W
Mussau I. **227** 1 30 S 149 40 E
Mussel Inlet **92** 52 53N 128 7W
Musselburgh **134** 55 57N 3 3W
Musselkanaal **142** 52 57N 7 0 E
Mussende **253** 10 32 S 16 5 E
Mussidan **140** 45 2N 0 22 E
Mussolo **253** 9 59 S 17 19 E
Mussomeli **164** 37 35N 13 43 E
Musson **143** 49 33N 5 42 E
Mussoorie **198** 30 27N 78 6 E
Mussuco **254** 17 2 S 19 3 E
Mustahil **256** 5 16N 44 45 E
Mustang **199** 29 10N 83 55 E
Musters, L. **126** 45 20 S 69 25W
Musudan **215** 40 50N 129 43 E
Muswellbrook **231** 32 16 S 150 56 E
Muszyna **151** 49 22N 20 55 E
Mût, Egypt **244** 25 28N 28 58 E
Mut, Turkey **190** 36 40N 33 28 E
Mutanda, Mozam. **255** 21 0 S 33 34 E
Mutanda, Zambia **251** 12 24 S 26 13 E
Mutaray **185** 60 56N 101 0 E
Mutare **251** 18 58 S 32 38 E
Mu'tariḑah, Al 'Urūq al **195** 21 15N 54 0 E
Muting **207** 7 23 S 140 20 E
Mutooroo **232** 32 26 S 140 55 E
Mutoto **253** 5 42 S 22 42 E
Mutshatsha **251** 10 35 S 24 20 E
Mutsu **218** 41 5N 140 55 E
Mutsu-Wan **218** 41 5N 140 55 E
Muttaburra **230** 22 38 S 144 29 E
Muttama **233** 34 46 S 148 8 E
Mutuáli **251** 14 55 S 37 0 E
Mutunópolis **121** 13 40 S 49 15W
Mututicachi **100** 30 45N 109 59W
Muvatupusha **201** 9 53N 76 35 E
Muweilih **191** 30 42N 34 19 E
Muxima **253** 9 33 S 13 58 E
Muy, Le **141** 43 28N 6 34 E
Muy Muy **112** 12 39N 85 36W
Muya **185** 56 27N 115 50 E
Muyinga **250** 3 14 S 30 33 E
Muyunkum, Peski **183** 44 12N 71 0 E
Muzaffarabad **199** 34 25N 73 30 E
Muzaffargarh **197** 30 5N 71 14 E
Muzaffarnagar **198** 29 26N 77 40 E
Muzaffarpur **199** 26 7N 85 23 E
Muzeze **253** 15 3 S 17 43 E
Muzhi **184** 65 25N 64 40 E
Muzillac **138** 47 35N 2 30W
Muzkol, Khrebet **183** 38 22N 73 20 E
Mvadhi-Ousyé **252** 1 13N 13 12 E
Mvam **252** 0 13 S 9 39 E
Mvôlô **245** 6 2N 29 53 E
Mvuma **251** 19 16 S 30 30 E
Mvurwi **251** 17 0 S 30 57 E
Mwadui **250** 3 26 S 33 32 E
Mwambo **251** 10 30 S 40 22 E
Mwandi **251** 17 30 S 24 51 E
Mwanza, Tanzania **250** 2 30 S 32 58 E
Mwanza, Zaïre **250** 7 55 S 26 43 E
Mwanza, Zambia **251** 16 58 S 24 28 E
Mwanza □ **250** 2 0 S 33 0 E
Mwaya **251** 9 32 S 33 55 E
Mweelrea **135** 53 37N 9 48W
Mweka **253** 4 50 S 21 34 E
Mwendjila **253** 7 12 S 18 51 E
Mwene **253** 6 35 S 22 27 E
Mwenezi → **251** 22 40 S 31 50 E
Mwenga **250** 3 1 S 28 28 E
Mweru, L. **251** 9 0 S 28 40 E
Mweza Range **251** 21 0 S 30 0 E
Mwilambwe **250** 8 7 S 25 0 E
Mwimbi **251** 8 38 S 31 39 E
Mwinilunga **251** 11 43 S 24 25 E
My Tho **205** 10 29N 106 23 E
Mya, O. → **241** 30 46N 4 54 E
Myajlar **198** 26 15N 70 20 E
Myanaung **202** 18 18N 95 22 E
Myaungmya **202** 16 30N 94 40 E
Mycenae = Mikínai **169** 37 43N 22 46 E
Myeik Kyunzu **204** 11 30N 97 30 E
Myingyan **202** 21 30N 95 20 E
Myitkyina **202** 25 24N 97 26 E
Myittha → **202** 23 12N 94 17 E
Myjava **151** 48 41N 17 37 E
Mymensingh **202** 24 45N 90 24 E
Myndus **169** 37 3N 27 14 E
Mynydd Du **133** 51 45N 3 45W
Mynzhilgi, Gora **183** 43 48N 68 51 E
Myrdal **171** 60 43N 7 10 E
Mýrdalsjökull **174** 63 40N 19 6W
Myrnam **90** 53 40N 111 14W
Myrtleford **233** 36 34 S 146 44 E
Mysen **171** 59 33N 11 20 E
Myslenice **152** 49 51N 19 57 E
Myślibórz **152** 52 55N 14 50 E
Mysłowice **152** 50 15N 19 12 E
Mysore **201** 12 17N 76 41 E
Mysore □ = Karnataka □ **201** 13 15N 77 0 E
Mystery Lake **90** 54 10N 114 55W
Mystishchi **179** 55 50N 37 50 E
Myszków **152** 50 45N 19 22 E
Myszyniec **152** 53 23N 21 21 E
Mythen **149** 47 2N 8 42 E
Mývatn **174** 65 36N 17 0W
Mze → **150** 49 46N 13 24 E
Mzimba **251** 11 55 S 33 39 E
Mzimvubu → **255** 31 38 S 29 33 E
Mzuzu **251** 11 30 S 33 55 E

N

N' Dioum **246** 16 31N 14 39W
Na-lang **202** 22 42N 97 33 E
Na Noi **204** 18 19N 100 43 E
Na Phao **204** 17 35N 105 44 E
Na Sam **204** 22 3N 106 37 E
Na San **204** 21 12N 104 2 E
Naab → **147** 49 1N 12 2 E
Naaldwijk **142** 51 59N 4 13 E
Na'am **245** 9 42N 28 27 E
Na'an **189** 31 53N 34 52 E
Naantali **175** 60 29N 22 2 E
Naarden **142** 52 18N 5 9 E
Naas **135** 53 12N 6 40W
Nababiep **254** 29 36 S 17 46 E
Nabadwip = Navadwip **199** 23 34N 88 20 E
Nabari **221** 34 37N 136 5 E
Nabawa **229** 28 30 S 114 48 E
Nabberu, L. **229** 25 30 S 120 30 E
Nabburg **147** 49 27N 12 11 E
Nabeul **241** 36 30N 10 44 E
Nabha **198** 30 26N 76 14 E
Nabīd **193** 29 40N 57 38 E
Nabire **207** 3 15 S 135 26 E
Nabisar **198** 25 8N 69 40 E
Nabisipi → **78** 50 14N 62 13W
Nabiswera **250** 1 27N 32 15 E
Nablus = Nābulus **189** 32 14N 35 15 E
Naboomspruit **255** 24 32 S 28 40 E
Nabq **191** 28 6N 34 25 E
Nabua **210** 13 24N 123 22 E
Nābulus **189** 32 14N 35 15 E
Nābulus □ **191** 32 20N 35 20 E
Nabunturan **211** 7 35N 125 58 E
Nacala-Velha **251** 14 32 S 40 34 E
Nacaome **112** 13 31N 87 30W
Nacaroa **251** 14 22 S 39 56 E
Nachako Res. **92** 53 42N 127 30W
Nachicapau, L. **78** 56 40N 68 5W
Nachikatsuura **221** 33 33N 135 58 E
Nachingwea **251** 10 23 S 38 49 E
Nachingwea □ **251** 10 30 S 38 30 E
Nachna **198** 27 34N 71 41 E
Náchod **151** 50 25N 16 8 E
Nachvak Fd. **78** 59 3N 63 45W
Nacka **172** 59 17N 18 12 E
Nackara **231** 32 48 S 139 12 E
Nackawic **81** 45 59N 67 17W
Nacmine **91** 51 28N 112 47W
Naco **100** 31 20N 109 56W
Nácori Chico **100** 29 37N 109 4W
Nácori Grande **100** 29 4N 110 3W
Nacozari de García **100** 30 25N 109 38W
Nadadores **102** 27 3N 101 36W
Nadadores → **102** 27 28N 100 43W
Nadern Harb. **92** 54 0N 132 36W
Nadi **244** 18 40N 33 41 E
Nadiad **198** 22 41N 72 56 E
Nadina → **92** 53 58N 126 30W
Nadina L. **92** 53 53N 127 2W
Nădlac **170** 46 10N 20 50 E
Nador **241** 35 14N 2 58W
Nadūshan **193** 32 2N 53 35 E
Nadvoitsy **176** 63 52N 34 14 E
Nadvornaya **180** 48 37N 24 30 E
Nadym **184** 65 35N 72 42 E
Nadym → **184** 66 12N 72 0 E
Nœrbø **171** 58 40N 5 39 E
Nœstved **172** 55 13N 11 44 E
Nafada **247** 11 8N 11 20 E
Näfels **149** 47 6N 9 4 E
Naftshahr **192** 34 0N 45 30 E
Nafūsah, Jabal **241** 32 12N 12 30 E
Nag Hammâdi **244** 26 2N 32 18 E
Naga, Cebu, Phil. **211** 10 13N 123 45 E
Naga, Luzon, Phil. **210** 13 38N 123 15 E
Naga, Zamboanga del S., Phil. **211** 7 46N 122 45 E
Naga, Kreb en **240** 24 12N 6 0W
Naga-Shima, Kagoshima, Japan **220** 32 10N 130 9 E
Naga-Shima, Yamaguchi, Japan **220** 33 49N 132 5 E
Nagagami → **87** 49 40N 84 40W
Nagagami L. **87** 49 25N 85 1W

Nagagamisis L. 87 49 28N 84 40W
Nagahama, Ehime, Japan 220 33 36N 132 29 E
Nagahama, Shiga, Japan 221 35 23N 136 16 E
Nagai 218 38 6N 140 2 E
Nagaland □ 202 26 0N 94 30 E
Nagambie 233 36 47 S 145 10 E
Nagano 221 36 40N 138 10 E
Nagano □ 221 36 15N 138 0 E
Nagaoka 219 37 27N 138 51 E
Nagappattinam 201 10 46N 79 51 E
Nagar Parkar 198 24 28N 70 46 E
Nagara → 221 35 40N 136 43 E
Nagari Hills 201 13 3N 79 45 E
Nagarjuna Sagar 201 16 35N 79 17 E
Nagas Pt. 92 52 12N 131 22W
Nagasaki 220 32 47N 129 50 E
Nagasaki □ 220 32 50N 129 40 E
Nagasin L. 87 47 48N 83 37W
Nagato 220 34 19N 131 5 E
Nagaur 198 27 15N 73 45 E
Nagbhir 200 20 34N 79 55 E
Nagercoil 201 8 12N 77 26 E
Nagina 199 29 30N 78 30 E
Nagīneh 193 34 20N 57 15 E
Nagir 199 36 12N 74 42 E
Nago 226 26 36N 128 0 E
Nagold 147 34 14N 57 2 E
Nagold → 147 48 52N 8 42 E
Nagoorin 230 24 17 S 151 15 E
Nagornyy 185 55 58N 124 57 E
Nagorsk 179 59 18N 50 48 E
Nagoya 221 35 10N 136 50 E
Nagpur 198 21 8N 79 10 E
Nagua 113 19 23N 69 50W
Nagyatád 151 46 14N 17 22 E
Nagyecsed 151 47 53N 22 24 E
Nagykanizsa 151 46 28N 17 0 E
Nagykörös 151 47 5N 19 48 E
Nagyléta 151 47 23N 21 55 E
Naha 226 26 13N 127 42 E
Nahalal 189 32 41N 35 12 E
Nahanni Butte 76 61 2N 123 31W
Nahanni Nat. Park 76 61 15N 125 0W
Nahariyya 189 33 1N 35 5 E
Nahāvand 193 34 10N 48 22 E
Nahe → 147 49 58N 7 57 E
Nahf 189 32 56N 35 18 E
Nahīya, Wadi → 244 28 55N 31 0 E
Nahlin 76 58 55N 131 38W
Nahud 244 18 12N 41 40 E
Nahuel Huapi, L. 126 41 0 S 71 32W
Nahuerachic 101 29 10N 108 5W
Naica 101 27 53N 105 31W
Naicam 88 52 30N 104 30W
Nā'ifah 188 19 59N 50 46 E
Naikoon Prov. Park 92 53 55N 131 55W
Naila 147 50 19N 11 43 E
Nain, Canada 78 56 34N 61 40W
Nā'īn, Iran 193 32 54N 53 0 E
Naini Tal 199 29 30N 79 30 E
Naintré 138 46 46N 0 29 E
Naipu 170 44 12N 25 47 E
Naira 207 4 28 S 130 0 E
Nairn, Canada 84 46 20N 81 35W
Nairn, U.K. 134 57 35N 3 54W
Nairobi 250 1 17 S 36 48 E
Naivasha 250 0 40 S 36 30 E
Naivasha, L. 250 0 48 S 36 20 E
Najac 140 44 14N 1 58 E
Najafābād 193 32 40N 51 15 E
Nájera 156 42 26N 2 48W
Najerilla → 156 42 32N 2 48W
Najibabad 198 29 40N 78 20 E
Najin 215 42 12N 130 15 E
Najmah 193 26 42N 50 6 E
Naju 215 35 3N 126 43 E
Naka → 221 36 20N 140 36 E
Nakadōri-Shima 219 32 57N 129 4 E
Nakalagba 250 2 50N 27 58 E
Nakama 220 33 56N 130 43 E
Nakaminato 221 36 21N 140 36 E
Nakamura 220 33 0N 133 0 E
Nakanai Mts. 227 5 40 S 151 0 E
Nakano 221 36 45N 138 22 E
Nakano-Shima 219 29 51N 129 52 E
Nakanojō 221 36 35N 138 51 E
Nakashibetsu 218 43 33N 144 59 E
Nakatsu 220 33 34N 131 15 E
Nakatsugawa 221 35 29N 137 30 E
Nakfa 245 16 40N 38 32 E
Nakhichevan A.S.S.R. □ 177 39 14N 45 30 E
Nakhl 191 29 55N 33 43 E
Nakhl-e Taqī 193 27 28N 52 36 E
Nakhodka 185 42 53N 132 54 E
Nakhon Nayok 204 14 12N 101 13 E
Nakhon Pathom 204 13 49N 100 3 E
Nakhon Phanom 204 17 23N 104 43 E
Nakhon Ratchasima 204 14 59N 102 12 E
Nakhon Sawan 204 15 35N 100 10 E
Nakhon Si Thammarat 205 8 29N 100 0 E
Nakhon Thai 204 17 5N 100 44 E
Nakina, B.C., Canada 76 59 12N 132 52W
Nakina, Ont., Canada 87 50 10N 86 40W
Nakło nad Notecią 152 53 9N 17 38 E
Nakodar 198 31 8N 75 31 E
Nakskov 173 54 50N 11 8 E
Näkten 172 62 48N 14 38 E
Naktong → 215 35 7N 128 57 E
Nakuru 250 0 15 S 36 4 E
Nakuru □ 250 0 15 S 35 5 E
Nakuru, L. 250 0 23 S 36 5 E
Nakusp 93 50 20N 117 45W
Nal → 197 25 20N 65 30 E
Nalchik 181 43 30N 43 33 E
Nälden 172 63 21N 14 14 E
Näldsjön 172 63 25N 14 15 E
Nalerigu 247 10 35N 0 25W
Nalgonda 200 17 6N 79 15 E
Nalhati 199 24 17N 87 52 E
Nalinnes 143 50 19N 4 27 E
Nallamalai Hills 201 15 30N 78 50 E
Nalón → 154 43 32N 6 4W
Nālūt 241 31 54N 11 0 E
Nam Can 205 8 46N 104 59 E
Nam Co 212 30 30N 90 45 E
Nam Dinh 204 20 25N 106 5 E
Nam Du, Hon 205 9 41N 104 21 E
Nam Ngum Dam 204 18 35N 102 34 E
Nam-Phan 205 10 30N 106 0 E
Nam Phong 204 16 42N 102 52 E
Nam Tha 204 20 58N 101 30 E
Nam Tok 204 14 21N 99 4 E
Namachire 253 11 26 S 22 43 E
Namacunde 254 17 18 S 15 50 E
Namak, Daryácheh-ye 193 34 30N 52 0 E
Namak, Kavir-e 193 34 30N 57 30 E
Namakan L. 86 48 27N 92 35W
Namakkal 201 11 13N 78 13 E
Namaland 254 24 30 S 17 0 E
Namangan 183 41 0N 71 40 E
Namapa 251 13 43 S 39 50 E
Namaqualand 254 30 0 S 18 0 E
Namasagali 250 1 2N 33 0 E
Namatanai 227 3 40 S 152 29 E
Namber 207 1 2 S 134 49 E
Nambour 231 26 32 S 152 58 E
Nambucca Heads 231 30 37 S 153 0 E
Namcha Barwa 212 29 40N 95 10 E
Namche Bazar 199 27 51N 86 47 E
Namchonjŏm 215 38 15N 126 26 E
Namêche 143 50 28N 5 0 E
Namecunda 251 14 54 S 37 37 E
Nameh 209 2 34N 116 21 E
Nameponda 251 15 50 S 39 50 E
Namerikawa 221 36 46N 137 20 E
Náměšť nad Oslavou 151 49 12N 16 10 E
Námestovo 151 49 24N 19 25 E
Nametil 251 15 40 S 39 21 E
Namew L., Sask., Canada 77 54 14N 101 56W
Namew L., Canada 89 54 10N 102 0W
Namhsan 202 22 48N 97 2 E
Nami 205 22 58N 97 10 E
Namib Desert = Namib-Woestyn 254 22 30 S 15 0 E
Namib-Woestyn 254 22 30 S 15 0 E
Namibe 253 15 7 S 12 11 E
Namibe □ 254 16 35 S 12 30 E
Namibia ■ 254 22 0 S 18 9 E
Namiquipa 101 29 15N 107 25W
Namkhan 202 23 50N 97 41 E
Namlea 207 3 18 S 127 5 E
Namoi → 231 30 12 S 149 30 E
Namous, O. en → 241 31 0N 0 15W
Nampō-Shotō 219 30 0N 140 0 E
Nampula 251 15 6N 39 15 E
Namrole 207 3 46 S 126 46 E
Namrun 190 37 8N 34 35 E
Namse Shankou 199 30 0N 82 25 E
Namsen → 174 64 27N 11 42 E
Namtay 185 62 43N 129 37 E
Namtu 202 23 5N 97 28 E
Namtumbo 251 10 30 S 36 4 E
Namu 92 51 52N 127 50W
Namuac 210 18 37N 121 10 E
Namucha Shank'ou 199 30 0N 82 28 E
Namur, Belgium 143 50 27N 4 52 E
Namur, Canada 82 45 54N 74 56W
Namur □ 143 50 17N 5 0 E
Namutoni 254 18 49 S 16 55 E
Namwala 253 15 44 S 26 30 E
Namwŏn 215 35 23N 127 23 E
Namysłów 152 51 6N 17 42 E
Nan 204 18 48N 100 46 E
Nan → 204 15 42N 100 9 E
Nan Shan 212 38 30N 99 0 E
Nan Xian 217 29 20N 112 22 E
Nana 170 44 17N 26 34 E
Nanaimo 92 49 10N 124 0W
Nanam 215 41 44N 129 40 E
Nanan 217 24 59N 118 21 E
Nanango 231 26 40 S 152 0 E
Nan'ao, China 217 23 28N 117 5 E
Nanao, Japan 219 37 0N 137 0 E
Nanbu 216 31 18N 106 3 E
Nanchang 217 28 42N 115 55 E
Nancheng 217 27 33N 116 35 E
Nanchital 109 18 4N 94 24W
Nanchong 216 30 43N 106 2 E
Nanchuan 216 29 9N 107 6 E
Nancy 139 48 42N 6 12 E
Nanda Devi 199 30 23N 79 59 E
Nandan, China 216 24 58N 107 29 E
Nandan, Japan 220 34 10N 134 42 E
Nanded 200 19 10N 77 20 E
Nandewar Ra. 231 30 15 S 150 35 E
Nandi □ 250 0 15N 35 0 E
Nandikotkur 201 15 52N 78 18 E
Nandura 198 20 52N 76 25 E
Nandurbar 198 21 20N 74 15 E
Nandyal 201 15 30N 78 30 E
Nanfeng, Guangdong, China 217 23 45N 111 47 E
Nanfeng, Jiangxi, China 217 27 12N 116 28 E
Nanga 229 26 7 S 113 45 E
Nanga-Eboko 247 4 41N 12 22 E
Nanga Parbat 199 35 10N 74 35 E
Nangade 251 11 5 S 39 36 E
Nangapinoh 209 0 20 S 111 44 E
Nangarhár □ 197 34 20N 70 0 E
Nangatayap 209 1 32 S 110 34 E
Nangeya Mts. 250 3 30N 33 30 E
Nangis 139 48 33N 3 0 E
Nangong 214 37 23N 115 22 E
Nangwarry 232 37 33 S 140 48 E
Nanhua 216 25 13N 101 21 E
Nanhuang 215 36 58N 121 48 E
Nanhui 217 31 5N 121 44 E
Nanika L. 92 53 47N 127 38W
Nanisivik 95 73 2N 84 33W
Nanjangud 201 12 6N 76 43 E
Nanjeko 251 15 31 S 23 30 E
Nanji Shan 217 27 27N 121 4 E
Nanjian 216 25 2N 100 25 E
Nanjiang 216 32 28N 106 51 E
Nanjing 217 24 25N 117 20 E
Nanjirinji 251 9 41 S 39 5 E
Nankana Sahib 198 31 27N 73 38 E
Nankang 217 25 40N 114 45 E
Nankoku 220 33 39N 133 44 E
Nanling 217 30 55N 118 20 E
Nanning 216 22 48N 108 20 E
Nannup 229 33 59 S 115 48 E
Nanpan Jiang → 216 25 10N 106 0 E
Nanpara 199 27 52N 81 33 E
Nanpi 214 38 2N 116 45 E
Nanping, Fujian, China 217 26 38N 118 10 E
Nanping, Henan, China 217 29 55N 112 3 E
Nanri Dao 217 25 15N 119 25 E
Nanripe 251 13 52 S 38 52 E
Nansei-Shotō 219 26 0N 128 0 E
Nansen Sd. 95 81 0N 91 0W
Nansio 250 2 3 S 33 4 E
Nant 140 44 1N 3 18 E
Nantes 138 47 12N 1 33W
Nanteuil-le-Haudouin 139 49 9N 2 48 E
Nantiat 140 46 1N 1 11 E
Nanton 91 50 21N 113 46W
Nantong 217 32 1N 120 52 E
Nantua 141 46 10N 5 35 E
Nanuku Passage 226 16 45 S 179 15W
Nanuque 121 17 50 S 40 21W
Nanutarra 228 22 32 S 115 30 E
Nanxiong 217 25 6N 114 15 E
Nanyang 217 33 11N 112 30 E
Nanyi Hu 217 31 5N 119 0 E
Nan'yō 220 34 3N 131 49 E
Nanyuan 214 39 44N 116 22 E
Nanyuki 250 0 2N 37 4 E
Nanzhang 217 31 45N 111 50 E
Náo, C. de la 157 38 44N 0 14 E
Naococane L. 78 52 50N 70 45W
Naoetsu 219 37 12N 138 10 E
Naogaon 202 24 52N 88 52 E
Naolinco de Victoria 108 19 39N 96 51W
Náousa 168 40 42N 22 9 E
Naozhou Dao 217 20 55N 110 20 E
Napanee 85 44 15N 77 0W
Napartokh B. 78 58 1N 62 19W
Nape 204 18 18N 105 6 E
Nape Pass = Keo Neua, Deo 204 18 23N 105 10 E
Napf 148 47 1N 7 56 E
Napier 234 39 30 S 176 56 E
Napier Broome B. 228 14 2 S 126 37 E
Napier Downs 228 17 11 S 124 36 E
Napier Pen. 230 12 4 S 135 43 E
Napierville 83 45 11N 73 25W
Napierville □ 83 45 10N 73 30W
Napinka 89 49 19N 100 50W
Naples = Nápoli 165 40 50N 14 17 E
Napo 216 23 22N 105 50 E
Napo □ 118 0 30 S 77 0W
Napo → 118 3 20 S 72 40W
Nápoli 165 40 50N 14 17 E
Nápoli, G. di 165 40 40N 14 10 E
Napopo 250 4 15N 28 0 E
Nappa Merrie 231 27 36 S 141 7 E
Naqâda 244 25 53N 32 42 E
Naqqāsh 193 35 40N 49 6 E
Nara, Japan 221 34 40N 135 49 E
Nara, Mali 246 15 10N 7 20W
Nara □ 221 34 30N 136 0 E
Nara, Canal 198 24 30N 69 20 E
Naracoorte 232 36 58 S 140 45 E
Naradhan 231 33 34 S 146 17 E
Naranjo 104 25 48N 108 31W
Naranjos 108 21 21N 97 41W
Narasapur 201 16 26N 81 40 E
Narasaropet 201 16 14N 80 4 E
Narathiwat 205 6 30N 101 48 E
Narayanganj 202 23 40N 90 33 E
Narayanpet 200 16 45N 77 30 E
Narbonne 140 43 11N 3 0 E
Narcea → 154 43 33N 6 44W
Nardīn 193 37 3N 55 59 E
Nardò 165 40 10N 18 0 E
Narembeen 229 32 7 S 118 24 E
Naretha 229 31 0 S 124 45 E
Narew 152 52 55N 23 31 E
Narew → 152 52 26N 20 41 E
Nari → 198 29 40N 68 0 E
Narindra, Helodranon' i 255 14 55 S 47 30 E
Narino □ 118 1 30N 78 0W
Narita 221 35 47N 140 19 E
Narmada → 198 21 38N 72 36 E
Narnaul 198 28 5N 76 11 E
Narni 163 42 30N 12 30 E
Naro, Ghana 246 10 22N 2 27W
Naro, Italy 164 37 18N 13 48 E
Naro Fominsk 179 55 23N 36 43 E
Narodnaya, G. 176 65 5N 60 0 E
Narok 250 1 55 S 33 52 E
Narok □ 250 1 20 S 36 30 E
Narón 154 43 32N 8 9W
Narooma 231 36 14 S 150 4 E
Narowal 197 32 6N 74 52 E
Narrabri 231 30 19 S 149 46 E
Narran → 231 28 37 S 148 12 E
Narrandera 231 34 42 S 146 31 E
Narraway → 90 55 44N 119 55W
Narrogin 229 32 58 S 117 14 E
Narromine 231 32 12 S 148 12 E
Narsampet 200 17 57N 79 58 E
Narsimhapur 199 22 54N 79 14 E
Nartkala 181 43 33N 43 51 E
Naruto, Kantō, Japan 220 34 11N 134 37 E
Narutō, Shikoku, Japan 221 35 36N 140 25 E
Naruto-Kaikyō 220 34 14N 134 39 E
Narva 178 59 23N 28 12 E
Narva → 178 59 27N 28 2 E
Narvacan 210 17 25N 120 28 E
Narvik 174 68 28N 17 26 E
Narvskoye Vdkhr. 178 59 18N 28 14 E
Narwana 198 29 39N 76 6 E
Naryan-Mar 176 68 0N 53 0 E
Naryilco 231 28 37 S 141 53 E
Narym 184 59 0N 81 30 E
Narymskoye 184 49 10N 84 15 E
Naryn 183 41 26N 75 58 E
Naryn → 183 40 52N 71 36 E
Nasa 174 66 29N 15 23 E
Nasarawa 247 8 32N 7 41 E
Năsăud 170 47 19N 24 29 E
Naşb, W. → 191 28 29N 34 31 E
Naseby 235 45 1 S 170 10 E
Naser, Buheirat en 244 23 0N 32 30 E
Nash Creek 81 47 56N 66 6W
Nashwaak Bridge 81 46 14N 66 37W
Nashwaaksis 81 45 59N 66 38W
Našice 166 45 32N 18 4 E
Nasielsk 152 52 35N 20 50 E
Nasik 200 19 58N 73 50 E
Nasipit 211 8 57N 125 19 E
Nasirabad 198 26 15N 74 45 E
Naskaupi → 78 53 47N 60 51W
Naso 165 38 8N 14 46 E
Naso Pt. 211 10 25N 121 57 E
Naşriān-e Pā'īn 192 32 52N 46 52 E
Nass → 76 55 0N 129 40W
Nassau 112 25 0N 77 20W
Nassau, Bahía 126 55 20 S 68 0W
Nasser, L. = Naser, Buheirat en 244 23 0N 32 30 E
Nasser City = Kôm Ombo 244 24 25N 32 52 E
Nassian 246 8 28N 3 28W
Nässjö 173 57 39N 14 42 E
Nastapoka → 78 56 55N 76 33W
Nastapoka, Is. 78 56 55N 76 50W

Nastopoka Is. 78 57 0N 77 0W
Nasugbu 210 14 5N 120 38 E
Näsum 173 56 10N 14 29 E
Näsviken 172 61 46N 16 52 E
Nata 254 20 12 S 26 12 E
Natagaima 118 3 37N 75 6W
Natal, Brazil 120 5 47 S 35 13W
Natal, Canada 91 49 43N 114 51W
Natal, Indonesia 208 0 35N 99 7 E
Natal □ 255 28 30 S 30 30 E
Natalinci 166 44 15N 20 49 E
Natalkuz L. 92 53 36N 125 20W
Naţanz 193 33 30N 51 55 E
Natashquan 80 50 14N 61 46W
Natashquan → 80 50 7N 61 50W
Natashquan-Est → 80 51 20N 61 40W
Natashquan Pt. 80 50 8N 61 40W
Naters 148 46 19N 8 0 E
Nathalia 231 36 1 S 145 13 E
Nathdwara 198 24 55N 73 50 E
Natimuk 231 36 42 S 142 0 E
Nation → 76 55 30N 123 32W
Natitingou 247 10 20N 1 26 E
Natividad, I. 99 27 52N 115 11W
Natogyi 202 21 25N 95 39 E
Natonin 210 17 6N 121 18 E
Nátora 100 28 56N 108 39W
Natron, L. 250 2 20 S 36 0 E
Natrûn, W. el. → 244 30 25N 30 13 E
Natuna Besar, Kepulauan 205 4 0N 108 15 E
Natuna Selatan, Kepulauan 205 2 45N 109 0 E
Naturaliste C. 230 40 50 S 148 15 E
Natya 232 34 57 S 143 13 E
Nau 183 40 9N 69 22 E
Nau Qala 198 34 5N 68 5 E
Naucelle 140 44 13N 2 20 E
Nauders 150 46 54N 10 30 E
Nauen 146 52 36N 12 52 E
Naughton 84 46 24N 81 12W
Naujan 210 13 20N 121 18 E
Naujoji Vilnia 178 54 48N 25 27 E
Naumburg 146 51 10N 11 48 E
Nā'ūr at Tunayb 191 31 48N 35 57 E
Nauru ■ 224 1 0 S 166 0 E
Nauru Is. 224 0 32 S 166 55 E
Naurzum 182 51 32N 64 34 E
Naushahra = Nowshera 197 34 0N 72 0 E
Nausori 226 18 2 S 178 32 E
Nauta 118 4 31 S 73 35W
Nautla 108 20 13N 96 47W
Nautla → 108 20 15N 96 47W
Nava 102 28 25N 100 45W
Nava del Rey 154 41 22N 5 6W
Navacerrada, Puerto de 154 40 47N 4 0W
Navachiste, B. de 104 25 26N 108 48W
Navadwip 199 23 34N 88 20 E
Navahermosa 155 39 41N 4 28W
Naval 211 11 34N 124 23 E
Navalcarnero 154 40 17N 4 5W
Navalmoral de la Mata 154 39 52N 5 33W
Navalvillar de Pela 155 39 9N 5 24W
Navan = An Uaimh 135 53 39N 6 40W
Navare 140 43 20N 1 20W
Navarino, I. 126 55 0 S 67 40W
Navarra □ 156 42 40N 1 40W
Navarre 140 43 15N 1 20W
Navarrenx 140 43 20N 0 45W
Navarrete 104 21 39N 105 7W
Navas del Marqués, Las 154 40 36N 4 20W
Navassa 113 18 30N 75 0W
Nave 162 45 35N 10 17 E
Naver → 134 58 34N 4 15W
Navia 154 43 35N 6 42W
Navia → 154 43 15N 6 50W
Navia de Suarna 154 42 58N 6 59W
Navidad 124 33 57 S 71 50W
Naviti 226 17 7 S 177 15 E
Navlya 178 52 53N 34 30 E
Navoi 183 40 9N 65 22 E
Navojoa 100 27 6N 109 26W
Navolato 104 24 47N 107 42W
Navolok 176 62 33N 39 57 E
Návpaktos 169 38 23N 21 50 E
Návplion 169 37 33N 22 50 E
Navrongo 247 10 51N 1 3W
Navsari 198 20 57N 72 59 E
Nawa Kot 198 28 21N 71 24 E
Nawabganj, Bangla. 202 24 35N 88 14 E
Nawabganj, Ut. P., India 199 26 56N 81 14 E
Nawabganj, Ut. P., India 199 28 32N 79 40 E
Nawabshah 197 26 15N 68 25 E
Nawada 199 24 50N 85 33 E
Nāwah 197 32 19N 67 53 E
Nawakot 199 27 55N 85 10 E
Nawalgarh 198 27 50N 75 15 E
Nawanshahr 199 32 33N 74 48 E
Nawapara 199 20 46N 82 33 E
Nawāsīf, Harrat 194 21 20N 42 10 E
Nawi 244 18 32N 30 50 E
Nawng Hpa 202 22 30N 98 30 E
Nawş, Ra's 195 17 15N 55 16 E
Náxos 169 37 8N 25 25 E
Nay 140 43 10N 0 18W
Nāy Band 193 27 20N 52 40 E
Naya → 118 3 13N 77 22W
Nayakhan 185 61 56N 159 0 E
Nayar 104 22 16N 104 28W
Nayar, Sa. de 104 22 0N 104 20W
Nayarit 98 32 20N 115 19W
Nayarit □ 104 22 0N 105 0W
Nayé 246 14 28N 12 12W
Nayong 216 26 50N 105 20 E
Nayoro 218 44 21N 142 28 E
Nayyāl, W. → 192 28 35N 39 4 E
Nazaré, Bahia, Brazil 121 13 2 S 39 0W
Nazaré, Goiás, Brazil 120 6 23 S 47 40W
Nazaré, Pará, Brazil 123 6 25 S 52 29W
Nazaré, Portugal 155 39 36N 9 4W
Nazareno 102 25 24N 103 26W
Nazareth = Nazerat 189 32 42N 35 17 E
Nazas 105 25 14N 104 8W
Nazas, R. → 105 25 45N 102 50W
Naze, The 133 51 53N 1 19 E
Nazerat 189 32 42N 35 17 E
Nāzīk 192 39 1N 45 4 E
Nazir Hat 202 22 35N 91 49 E
Nazko 92 53 1N 123 37W
Nazko → 92 53 7N 123 34W
Nazret 245 8 32N 39 22 E
Nazwá 195 22 56N 57 32 E
Nchanga 251 12 30 S 27 49 E
Ncheu 251 14 50 S 34 47 E
Ndala 250 4 45 S 33 15 E
Ndalatando 253 9 12 S 14 48 E
Ndali 247 9 50N 2 46 E
Ndareda 250 4 12 S 35 30 E
Ndélé 215 8 25N 20 36 E
Ndendé 252 2 22 S 11 23 E
Ndjamena 243 12 10N 14 59 E
Ndjolé 252 0 10 S 10 45 E
Ndola 251 13 0 S 28 34 E
Ndoto Mts. 250 2 0N 37 0 E
Ndoua, C. 226 22 24 S 166 56 E
Nduguti 250 4 18 S 34 41 E
Nea → 171 63 15N 11 0 E
Néa Epídhavros 169 37 40N 23 7 E
Néa Flippiás 168 39 12N 20 53 E
Néa Kallikrátia 168 40 21N 23 1 E
Néa Víssi 168 41 34N 26 33 E
Neagari 221 36 26N 136 25 E
Neagh, Lough 135 54 35N 6 25W
Neale L. 228 24 15 S 130 0 E
Neamţ □ 170 47 0N 26 20 E
Neápolis, Kozan, Greece 168 40 20N 21 24 E
Neápolis, Lakonia, Greece 169 36 27N 23 8 E
Neath 133 51 39N 3 49W
Neba, Î. 226 20 9 S 163 56 E
Nebbou 247 11 9N 1 51W
Nebine Cr. → 231 29 27 S 146 56 E
Nebit Dag 177 39 30N 54 22 E
Nebo 230 59 12N 32 25 E
Nebolchy 178 59 8N 33 18 E
Nébrodi, Monti 164 37 55N 14 50 E
Nechako → 93 53 30N 122 44W
Neckar → 147 49 31N 8 26 E
Necochea 124 38 30 S 58 50W
Nectar Brook 232 32 43 S 137 57 E
Nedelišće 163 46 23N 16 22 E
Neder Rijn → 142 51 57N 6 2 E
Nederbrakel 143 50 48N 3 46 E
Nederweert 143 51 17N 5 45 E
Nédha → 169 37 25N 21 45 E
Nedroma 241 35 1N 1 45W
Nedstrand 171 59 21N 5 49 E
Neede 142 52 8N 6 37 E
Needles, Pt. 234 36 3 S 175 25 E
Needles, The 133 50 39N 1 35W
Ñeembucú □ 124 27 0 S 58 0W
Neemuch = Nimach 198 24 30N 74 56 E
Neepawa 89 50 15N 99 30W
Neer 143 51 16N 5 59 E
Neerpelt 143 51 13N 5 26 E
Neft-chala = imeni 26 Bakinskikh Komissarov 177 39 19N 49 12 E
Nefta 241 33 53N 7 50 E
Neftah Sidi Boubekeur 241 35 1N 0 4 E
Neftegorsk 181 44 25N 39 45 E
Neftenbach 149 47 32N 8 41 E
Neftyannyye Kamni 177 40 20N 50 55 E
Negapatam = Nagappattinam 201 10 46N 79 51 E
Negba 189 31 40N 34 41 E
Negele 245 5 20N 39 36 E
Negev = Hanegev 189 30 50N 35 0 E
Negoiu 170 45 35N 24 32 E
Negombo 201 7 12N 79 50 E
Negotin 166 44 16N 22 37 E
Negotino 166 41 29N 22 9 E
Negra, La 124 23 46 S 70 18W
Negra, Peña 154 42 11N 6 30W
Negra, Pta., Maurit. 240 22 54N 16 18W
Negra, Pta., Peru 122 6 6 S 81 10W
Negra Pt. 210 18 40N 120 50 E
Negrais C. 202 16 0N 94 12 E
Negreira 154 42 54N 8 45W
Negreşti 170 46 50N 27 30 E
Négrine 241 34 30N 7 30 E
Negro →, Argentina 126 41 2 S 62 47W
Negro →, Bolivia 123 14 11 S 63 7W
Negro →, Brazil 119 3 0 S 60 0W
Negro →, Uruguay 125 33 24 S 58 22W
Negros 211 9 30N 122 40 E
Negru Vodă 170 43 47N 28 21 E
Neguac 81 47 15N 65 5W
Nehāvand 193 35 56N 49 31 E
Nehbandān 193 31 35N 60 5 E
Neheim-Hüsten 146 51 27N 7 58 E
Nehoiaşu 170 45 24N 26 20 E
Nei Monggol Zizhiqu □ 214 42 0N 112 0 E
Neidpath 88 50 12N 107 20W
Neijiang 216 29 35N 104 55 E
Neilburg 88 52 50N 109 38W
Neilrex 233 31 44 S 149 20 E
Neil's Harbour 81 46 48N 60 20W
Neiqiu 214 37 15N 114 30 E
Neira de Jusá 154 42 53N 7 14W
Neisse → 146 52 4N 14 46 E
Neiva 118 2 56N 75 18W
Neixiang 214 33 10N 111 52 E
Nejanilini L. 77 59 33N 97 48W
Nejapa de Madero 109 16 37N 95 59W
Nejo 245 9 30N 35 28 E
Nekā 193 36 39N 53 19 E
Nekemte 245 9 4N 36 30 E
Nêkheb 244 25 10N 32 48 E
Neksø 173 55 4N 15 8 E
Nelas 154 40 32N 7 52W
Nelaug 171 58 39N 8 40 E
Nelia 230 20 39 S 142 12 E
Nelidovo 178 56 13N 32 49 E
Nelkan 185 57 40N 136 4 E
Nellikuppam 201 11 46N 79 43 E
Nellore 201 14 27N 79 59 E
Nelma 185 47 39N 139 0 E
Nelson, Canada 93 49 30N 117 20W
Nelson, N.Z. 235 41 18 S 173 16 E
Nelson, U.K. 132 53 50N 2 14W
Nelson □ 235 42 11 S 172 15 E
Nelson → 77 54 33N 98 2W
Nelson, C., Australia 231 38 26 S 141 32 E
Nelson, C., Papua N. G. 227 9 0 S 149 20 E
Nelson, Estrecho 126 51 30 S 75 0W
Nelson Forks 76 59 30N 124 0W
Nelson House 77 55 47N 98 51W
Nelson L. 77 55 48N 100 7W
Nelson-Miramichi 81 46 59N 65 34W
Nelspruit 255 25 29 S 30 59 E
Néma 246 16 40N 7 15W
Neman → 178 55 25N 21 10 E
Neméa 169 37 49N 22 40 E
Nemegosenda L. 87 48 0N 83 7W
Nemeiben L. 77 55 20N 105 20W
Nemira 170 46 17N 26 19 E
Némiscachingue, L. 82 47 25N 74 30W
Nemiscau 78 51 18N 76 54W
Nemiscau, L. 78 51 25N 76 40W
Nemours 139 48 16N 2 40 E
Nemunas = Neman → 178 55 25N 21 10 E
Nemuro 218 43 20N 145 35 E
Nemuro-Kaikyō 218 43 30N 145 30 E
Nemuy 185 55 40N 136 9 E
Nen Jiang → 215 45 28N 124 30 E
Nenagh 135 52 52N 8 11W
Nenasi 205 3 9N 103 23 E
Nendiarene, Pte. 226 20 14 S 164 19 E
Nene → 132 52 38N 0 13 E
Nenjiang 213 49 10N 125 10 E
Neno 251 15 25 S 34 40 E
Nenusa, Kepulauan 207 4 45N 127 1 E
Néon Petrítsi 168 41 16N 23 15 E
Neópolis 120 10 18 S 36 35W
Neoskweskau 78 51 52N 74 17W
Nepal ■ 199 28 0N 84 30 E
Nepalganj 199 28 5N 81 40 E
Nephin 135 54 1N 9 21W
Nepisiguit → 81 47 37N 65 38W
Nepomuk 150 49 29N 13 35 E
Neptune 88 49 22N 104 4W
Néra → 166 44 48N 21 25 E
Nérac 140 44 8N 0 21 E
Nerastro, Sarīr 242 24 20N 20 37 E
Nerchinsk 185 52 0N 116 39 E
Nerchinskiy Zavod 185 51 20N 119 40 E
Nereju 170 45 43N 26 43 E
Nerekhta 179 57 26N 40 38 E
Néret L. 78 54 45N 70 44W
Neretva → 166 43 1N 17 27 E
Neretvanski Kanal 166 43 7N 17 10 E
Neringa 178 55 30N 21 5 E
Nerja 155 36 43N 3 55W
Nerl → 179 56 11N 40 34 E
Nerokoúrou 169 35 29N 24 3 E
Nerpio 157 38 11N 2 16W
Nerva 155 37 42N 6 30W
Nes, Iceland 174 65 53N 17 24W
Nes, Neth. 142 53 26N 5 47 E
Nes Ziyyona 189 31 56N 34 48W
Nesbyen 171 60 34N 9 35 E
Nesebŭr 167 42 41N 27 46 E
Nesflaten 171 59 38N 6 48 E
Neskaupstaður 174 65 9N 13 42W
Nesland 171 59 31N 7 59 E
Neslandsvatn 171 58 57N 9 10 E
Nesle 139 49 45N 2 53 E
Nesodden 171 59 48N 10 40 E
Nesque → 141 43 59N 4 59 E
Ness, Loch 134 57 15N 4 30W
Nesslau 149 47 14N 9 13 E
Nestaocano → 83 49 38N 73 28W
Nestor Falls 86 49 7N 93 56W
Nestórion Óros 168 40 24N 21 5 E
Néstos → 168 41 20N 24 35 E
Nesttun 171 60 19N 5 21 E
Nesvizh 178 53 14N 26 38 E
Netanya 189 32 20N 34 51 E
Nète → 143 51 7N 4 14 E
Nether Stowey 133 51 0N 3 10W
Netherbury 133 50 46N 2 45W
Netherdale 230 21 10 S 148 33 E
Netherlands ■ 142 52 0N 5 30 E
Netherlands Antilles ■ 118 12 15N 69 0W
Netherlands Guiana = Surinam ■ 119 4 0N 56 0W
Netley Gap 232 32 43 S 139 59 E
Neto → 165 39 13N 17 8 E
Netrakona 202 24 53N 90 47 E
Nettancourt 139 48 51N 4 57 E
Nettilling L. 95 66 30N 71 0W
Nettuno 164 41 29N 12 40 E
Netzahualcoyotl 110 17 42N 91 27W
Netzahualcóyotl, Presa 110 17 8N 93 35W
Neu-Isenburg 147 50 3N 8 42 E
Neu-Ulm 147 48 23N 10 2 E
Neubrandenburg 146 53 33N 13 17 E
Neubrandenburg □ 146 53 30N 13 20 E
Neubukow 146 54 1N 11 40 E
Neuburg 147 48 43N 11 11 E
Neuchâtel 148 47 0N 6 55 E
Neuchâtel □ 148 47 0N 6 55 E
Neuchâtel, Lac de 148 46 53N 6 50 E
Neudau 150 47 11N 16 6 E
Neudorf 88 50 43N 103 1W
Neuenegg 148 46 54N 7 18 E
Neuenhaus 146 52 30N 6 55 E
Neuf-Brisach 139 48 0N 7 30 E
Neufahrn 147 48 44N 12 11 E
Neufchâteau, Belgium 143 49 50N 5 25 E
Neufchâteau, France 139 48 21N 5 40 E
Neufchâtel 139 49 43N 1 30 E
Neufchâtel-sur-Aisne 139 49 26N 4 0 E
Neuhaus 146 53 16N 10 54 E
Neuhausen 149 47 41N 8 37 E
Neuillé-Pont-Pierre 138 47 33N 0 33 E
Neuilly-St-Front 139 49 10N 3 15 E
Neukalen 146 53 49N 12 48 E
Neumarkt 147 49 16N 11 28 E
Neumarkt-Sankt Veit 147 48 22N 12 30 E
Neumünster 146 54 4N 9 58 E
Neung-sur-Beuvron 139 47 30N 1 50 E
Neunkirchen, Austria 150 47 43N 16 4 E
Neunkirchen, Germany 147 49 23N 7 12 E
Neuquén 126 38 55 S 68 0 E
Neuquén □ 124 38 0 S 69 50W
Neuquén → 126 38 59 S 68 0W
Neuruppin 146 52 56N 12 48 E
Neusiedl 151 47 57N 16 50 E
Neusiedler See 151 47 50N 16 47 E
Neuss 146 51 12N 6 39 E
Neussargues-Moissac 140 45 9N 3 1 E
Neustadt, Canada 84 44 5N 81 0W
Neustadt, Baden-W., Germany 147 47 54N 8 13 E
Neustadt, Bayern, Germany 147 49 42N 12 10 E
Neustadt, Bayern, Germany 147 48 48N 11 47 E
Neustadt, Bayern, Germany 147 49 34N 10 37 E
Neustadt, Bayern, Germany 147 50 23N 11 0 E

Neustadt, Gera, Germany **146** 50 45N 11 43 E
Neustadt, Hessen, Germany **146** 50 51N 9 9 E
Neustadt, Niedersachsen, Germany **146** 52 30N 9 30 E
Neustadt, Potsdam, Germany **146** 52 50N 12 27 E
Neustadt, Rhld-Pfz., Germany **147** 49 21N 8 10 E
Neustadt, Schleswig-Holstein, Germany **146** 54 6N 10 49 E
Neustrelitz **146** 53 22N 13 4 E
Neutla **107** 20 42N 100 51W
Neuveville, La **148** 47 4N 7 6 E
Neuvic **140** 45 23N 2 16 E
Neuville, Belgium **143** 50 11N 4 32 E
Neuville, Rhône, France **141** 45 52N 4 51 E
Neuville, Vienne, France **138** 46 41N 0 15 E
Neuville-aux-Bois **139** 48 4N 2 3 E
Neuvy-le-Roi **138** 47 36N 0 36 E
Neuvy-St-Sépulchure **140** 46 35N 1 48 E
Neuvy-sur-Barangeon **139** 47 20N 2 15 E
Neuwerk **146** 53 55N 8 30 E
Neuwied **146** 50 26N 7 29 E
Neva → **176** 59 50N 30 30 E
Nevada, Sierra **157** 37 3N 3 15W
Nevada de Sta. Marta, Sa. **122** 10 55N 73 50W
Nevado, Cerro **124** 35 30 S 68 32W
Nevanka **185** 56 31N 98 55 E
Nevasa **200** 19 34N 75 0 E
Nevel **178** 56 0N 29 55 E
Nevele **143** 51 3N 3 33 E
Nevers **139** 47 0N 3 9 E
Nevertire **231** 31 50 S 147 44 E
Nevesinje **166** 43 14N 18 6 E
Neville **88** 49 58N 107 39W
Nevinnomyssk **181** 44 40N 42 0 E
Nevis **113** 17 0N 62 30W
Nevlunghavn **171** 55 58N 9 52 E
Nevrokop = Gotse Delchev **167** 41 43N 23 46 E
Nevyansk **182** 57 30N 60 13 E
New → **119** 3 20N 57 37W
New Amsterdam **119** 6 15N 57 36W
New Angledool **231** 29 5 S 147 55 E
New Brigden **91** 51 42N 110 29W
New Brighton **235** 43 29 S 172 43 E
New Britain **227** 5 50 S 150 20 E
New Brunswick □ **75** 46 50N 66 30W
New Bussa **247** 9 53N 4 31 E
New Caledonia = Nouvelle Calédonie **226** 21 0 S 165 0 E
New Carlisle **81** 48 1N 65 20W
New Castile = Castilla La Nueva **155** 39 45N 3 20W
New Delhi **198** 28 37N 77 13 E
New Denmark **81** 47 2N 67 38W
New Denver **93** 50 0N 117 25W
New England Ra. **231** 30 20 S 151 45 E
New Forest **133** 50 53N 1 40W
New Germany **81** 44 33N 64 43W
New Glasgow **81** 45 35N 62 36W
New Guinea **224** 4 0 S 136 0 E
New Hamburg **84** 43 23N 80 42W
New Hanover, Papua N. G. **227** 2 30 S 150 10 E
New Hanover, S. Africa **255** 29 22 S 30 31 E
New Harbour **81** 45 13N 61 29W
New Hazelton **76** 55 20N 127 30W
New Hebrides = Vanuatu ■ **224** 15 0 S 168 0 E
New Ireland **227** 3 20 S 151 50 E
New Liskeard **74** 47 31N 79 41W
New Norcia **229** 30 57 S 116 13 E
New Norfolk **230** 42 46 S 147 2 E
New Norway **91** 52 52N 112 57W
New Plymouth **234** 39 4 S 174 5 E
New Providence **112** 25 25N 78 35W
New Radnor **133** 52 15N 3 10W
New Richmond **80** 48 15N 65 45W
New Ross, Canada **81** 44 44N 64 27W
New Ross, Ireland **135** 52 24N 6 58W
New Sarepta **90** 53 16N 113 8W
New Siberian Is. = Novosibirskiye Ostrava **185** 75 0N 142 0 E
New South Wales □ **231** 33 0 S 146 0 E
New Springs **229** 25 49 S 120 1 E
New Washington **211** 11 39N 122 26 E
New Waterford **81** 46 13N 60 4W
New Westminster **93** 49 13N 122 55W
New World I. **79** 49 35N 54 40W
New Zealand ■ **235** 40 0 S 176 0 E
Newala **251** 10 58 S 39 18 E
Newala □ **251** 10 46 S 39 20 E
Newark-on-Trent **132** 53 6N 0 48W
Newboro L. **85** 44 38N 76 20W
Newbrook **90** 54 24N 112 57W
Newburgh **85** 44 19N 76 52W
Newbury **133** 51 24N 1 19W
Newcastle, Australia **231** 33 0 S 151 46 E
Newcastle, Canada **81** 47 1N 65 38W
Newcastle, S. Africa **255** 27 45 S 29 58 E
Newcastle, U.K. **135** 54 13N 5 54W
Newcastle Bridge **81** 46 5N 66 3W
Newcastle Emlyn **133** 52 2N 4 29W
Newcastle Ra. **228** 15 45 S 130 15 E
Newcastle-under-Lyme **132** 53 2N 2 15W
Newcastle-upon-Tyne **132** 54 59N 1 37W
Newcastle Waters **230** 17 30 S 133 28 E
Newdegate **229** 33 6 S 119 0 E
Newe Etan **189** 32 30N 35 32 E
Newe Sha'anan **189** 32 47N 34 59 E
Newe Zohar **189** 31 9N 35 21 E
Newell, L. **91** 50 26N 111 55W
Newfoundland **75** 48 30N 56 0W
Newfoundland □ **75** 53 0N 58 0W
Newgate **91** 49 2N 115 12W
Newham **133** 51 31N 0 2 E
Newhaven **133** 50 47N 0 4 E
Newman **228** 23 18 S 119 45 E
Newmarket, Canada **84** 44 3N 79 28W
Newmarket, Ireland **135** 52 13N 9 0W
Newmarket, U.K. **133** 52 15N 0 23 E
Newport, Canada **80** 48 16N 64 45W
Newport, Gwent, U.K. **133** 51 35N 3 0W
Newport, I. of W., U.K. **133** 50 42N 1 18W
Newport, Salop, U.K. **133** 52 47N 2 22W
Newquay **133** 50 24N 5 6W
Newry **135** 54 10N 6 20W
Newry & Mourne □ **135** 54 10N 6 15W
Newton Abbot **133** 50 32N 3 37W
Newton Boyd **231** 29 45 S 152 16 E
Newton Stewart **134** 54 57N 4 30W
Newtonmore **134** 57 4N 4 7W
Newtown, Canada **79** 49 12N 53 31W
Newtown, U.K. **133** 52 31N 3 19W
Newtownabbey **135** 54 40N 5 55W
Newtownabbey □ **135** 54 45N 6 0W
Newtownards **135** 54 37N 5 40W
Nexapa → **109** 18 7N 98 46W
Nexon **140** 45 41N 1 11 E
Nexpa **106** 18 3N 102 32W
Neya **179** 58 21N 43 49 E
Neyrīz **193** 29 15N 54 19 E
Neyshābūr **193** 36 10N 58 50 E
Neyyattinkara **201** 8 26N 77 5 E
Nezhin **178** 51 5N 31 55 E
Ngabang **209** 0 23N 109 55 E
Ngabordamlu, Tanjung **207** 6 56 S 134 11 E
N'Gage **253** 7 46 S 15 15 E
Ngaiphaipi **202** 22 14N 93 15 E
Ngambé **247** 5 48N 11 29 E
Ngami Depression **254** 20 30 S 22 46 E
Ngamo **251** 19 3 S 27 32 E
Nganglong Kangri **199** 33 0N 81 0 E
Nganjuk **209** 7 32 S 111 55 E
Ngao **204** 18 46N 99 59 E
Ngaoundéré **252** 7 15N 13 35 E
Ngapara **235** 44 57 S 170 46 E
Ngara **250** 2 29 S 30 40 E
Ngara □ **250** 2 29 S 30 40 E
Ngaruawahia **234** 37 42 S 175 11 E
Ngatapa **234** 38 32 S 177 45 E
Ngathainggyaung **202** 17 24N 95 5 E
Ngauruhoe, Mt. **234** 39 13 S 175 45 E
Ngawi **209** 7 24 S 111 26 E
Nggamea **226** 16 46 S 179 46W
Nghia Lo **204** 21 33N 104 28 E
Ngidinga **253** 5 37 S 15 17 E
Ngo **252** 2 29 S 15 45 E
N'Gola **253** 14 10 S 14 30 E
Ngoma **251** 13 8 S 33 45 E
Ngomahura **251** 20 26 S 30 43 E
Ngomba **251** 8 20 S 32 53 E
Ngop **245** 6 17N 30 9 E
Ngoring Hu **212** 34 55N 97 5 E
Ngorkou **246** 15 40N 3 41W
Ngorongoro **250** 3 11 S 35 32 E
Ngouri **243** 13 38N 15 22 E
Ngourti **243** 15 19N 13 12 E
Ngozi **250** 2 54 S 29 50 E
Ngudu **250** 2 58 S 33 25 E
Nguigmi **243** 14 20N 13 20 E
Ngukurr **230** 14 44 S 134 44 E
Ngunga **250** 3 37 S 33 37 E
Nguru **247** 12 56N 10 29 E
Nguru Mts. **250** 6 0 S 37 30 E
Nguyen Binh **204** 22 39N 105 56 E
Nha Trang **205** 12 16N 109 10 E
Nhacoongo **255** 24 18 S 35 14 E
Nhambiquara **123** 12 50 S 59 49W
Nhamundá **119** 2 14 S 56 43W
Nhamundá → **119** 2 12 S 56 41W
Nhangutazi, L. **255** 24 0 S 34 30 E
Nhecolândia **123** 19 17 S 56 58W
Nhill **231** 36 18 S 141 40 E
Nho Quan **204** 20 18N 105 45 E
Nhulunbuy **230** 12 10 S 137 20 E
Nhundo **253** 14 25 S 21 23 E
Nia-nia **250** 1 30N 27 40 E
Niafounké **246** 16 0N 4 5W
Niagara Falls **84** 43 7N 79 5W
Niagara-on-the-Lake **84** 43 15N 79 4W
Niah **206** 3 58N 113 46 E
Niamey **247** 13 27N 2 6 E
Nianforando **246** 9 37N 10 36W
Nianfors **172** 61 36N 16 46 E
Niangara **250** 3 42N 27 50 E
Nias **208** 1 0N 97 30 E
Niassa □ **251** 13 30 S 36 0 E
Nibāk **195** 24 25N 50 50 E
Nibbiano **162** 44 54N 9 20 E
Nibe **173** 56 59N 9 38 E
Nicapa Ostuacán **110** 17 22N 93 18W
Nicaragua ■ **112** 11 40N 85 30W
Nicaragua, Lago de **112** 12 0N 85 30W
Nicastro **165** 39 0N 16 18 E
Nicchehabin, Pta. **111** 19 47N 87 29W
Nice **141** 43 42N 7 14 E
Nichinan **220** 31 38N 131 23 E
Nicholás, Canal **112** 23 30N 80 5W
Nicholson **228** 18 2 S 128 54 E
Nicholson → **230** 17 31 S 139 36 E
Nicholson Ra. **229** 27 15 S 116 45 E
Nickerie □ **119** 4 0N 57 0W
Nickerie → **119** 5 58N 57 0W
Nicobar Is. **196** 9 0N 93 0 E
Nicoclí **118** 8 26N 76 48W
Nicola **93** 50 12N 120 40W
Nicola L. **93** 50 10N 120 32W
Nicolás Bravo, Durango, Mexico **105** 24 29N 104 45W
Nicolás Bravo, Quintana Roo, Mexico **111** 18 29N 89 20W
Nicolet **83** 46 17N 72 35W
Nicolls Town **112** 25 8N 78 0W
Nicopolis **169** 39 2N 20 37 E
Nicosia, Cyprus **190** 35 10N 33 25 E
Nicosia, Italy **165** 37 45N 14 22 E
Nicótera **165** 38 33N 15 57 E
Nicoya **112** 10 9N 85 27W
Nicoya, G. de **112** 10 0N 85 0W
Nicoya, Pen. de **112** 9 45N 85 40W
Nidau **148** 47 7N 7 15 E
Nidd → **132** 54 1N 1 32W
Nidda **146** 50 24N 9 2 E
Nidda → **147** 50 6N 8 34 E
Nido, Sa. del **101** 29 33N 106 48W
Nidwalden □ **149** 46 50N 8 25 E
Nidzica **152** 53 25N 20 28 E
Niebüll **146** 54 47N 8 49 E
Nied → **139** 49 23N 6 40 E
Niederaula **146** 50 48N 9 37 E
Niederbipp **148** 47 16N 7 42 E
Niederbronn **139** 48 57N 7 39 E
Niedere Tauern **150** 47 20N 14 0 E
Niedermarsberg **146** 51 28N 8 52 E
Niederösterreich □ **150** 48 25N 15 40 E
Niedersachsen □ **146** 52 45N 9 0 E
Niefang **252** 1 50N 10 14 E
Niel **143** 51 7N 4 20 E
Niellé **246** 10 5N 5 38W
Niem **252** 6 12N 15 14 E
Niemba **250** 5 58 S 28 24 E
Niemcza **152** 50 42N 16 47 E
Niemodlin **152** 50 38N 17 38 E
Niemur **232** 35 17 S 144 9 E
Nienburg **146** 52 38N 9 15 E
Niepołomice **152** 50 3N 20 13 E
Niers → **146** 51 45N 5 58 E
Niesen **148** 46 38N 7 39 E
Niesky **146** 51 18N 14 48 E
Nieszawa **152** 52 52N 18 50 E
Nieuw-Amsterdam, Neth. **142** 52 43N 6 52 E
Nieuw Amsterdam, Surinam **119** 5 53N 55 5W
Nieuw Beijerland **142** 51 49N 4 20 E
Nieuw-Dordrecht **142** 52 45N 6 59 E
Nieuw Loosdrecht **142** 52 12N 5 8 E
Nieuw Nickerie **119** 6 0N 56 59W
Nieuw-Schoonebeek **142** 52 39N 7 0 E
Nieuw-Vennep **142** 52 16N 4 38 E
Nieuw-Vossemeer **143** 51 34N 4 12 E
Nieuwe-Niedorp **142** 52 44N 4 54 E
Nieuwe-Pekela **142** 53 5N 6 58 E
Nieuwe-Schans **142** 53 11N 7 12 E
Nieuwendijk **142** 51 46N 4 55 E
Nieuwerkerken **143** 50 52N 5 12 E
Nieuwkoop **142** 52 9N 4 48 E
Nieuwleusen **142** 52 34N 6 17 E
Nieuwnamen **143** 51 18N 4 9 E
Nieuwolda **142** 53 15N 6 58 E
Nieuwpoort **143** 51 8N 2 45 E
Nieuwveen **142** 52 12N 4 46 E
Nieves, Mexico **105** 24 0N 103 1W
Nieves, Spain **154** 42 7N 8 26W
Nièvre □ **139** 47 10N 3 40 E
Nigata **220** 34 13N 132 39 E
Niğde **177** 38 0N 34 40 E
Nigel **255** 26 27 S 28 25 E
Nigel I. **92** 50 53N 127 43W
Niger □ **247** 10 0N 5 0 E
Niger ■ **247** 13 30N 10 0 E
Niger → **247** 5 33N 6 33 E
Nigeria ■ **247** 8 30N 8 0 E
Nightcaps **235** 45 57 S 168 2 E
Nigrīta **168** 40 56N 23 29 E
Nihtaur **199** 29 20N 78 23 E
Nii-Jima **221** 34 20N 139 15 E
Niigata **218** 37 58N 139 0 E
Niigata □ **219** 37 15N 138 45 E
Niihama **220** 33 55N 133 16 E
Niimi **220** 34 59N 133 28 E
Niitsu **218** 37 48N 139 7 E
Nījar **157** 36 53N 2 15W
Nijil **191** 30 32N 35 33 E
Nijkerk **142** 52 13N 5 30 E
Nijlen **143** 51 10N 4 40 E
Nijmegen **142** 51 50N 5 52 E
Nijverdal **142** 52 22N 6 28 E
Nīk Pey **193** 36 50N 48 10 E
Nike **247** 6 26N 7 29 E
Nikel **174** 69 24N 30 12 E
Nikiniki **207** 9 49 S 124 30 E
Nikītas **168** 40 13N 23 34 E
Nikki **247** 9 58N 3 12 E
Nikkō **221** 36 45N 139 35 E
Nikolayev **180** 46 58N 32 0 E
Nikolayevsk **179** 50 0N 45 35 E
Nikolayevsk-na-Amur **185** 53 8N 140 44 E
Nikolsk **179** 59 30N 45 28 E
Nikolskoye **185** 55 12N 166 0 E
Nikopol, Bulgaria **167** 43 43N 24 54 E
Nikopol, U.S.S.R. **180** 47 35N 34 25 E
Niksar **180** 40 31N 37 2 E
Nīkshahr **193** 26 15N 60 10 E
Nikšić **166** 42 50N 18 57 E
Nîl, Nahr en → **244** 30 10N 31 6 E
Nîl el Abyad → **245** 15 38N 32 31 E
Nîl el Azraq → **245** 15 38N 32 31 E
Nile = Nîl, Nahr en → **244** 30 10N 31 6 E
Nile □ **250** 2 0N 31 30 E
Nile Delta **244** 31 40N 31 0 E
Nilgiri Hills **201** 11 30N 76 30 E
Nilo Peçanha **121** 13 37 S 39 6W
Nilpena **232** 30 58 S 138 20 E
Niltepec **109** 16 34N 94 37W
Nimach **198** 24 30N 74 56 E
Nimbahera **198** 24 37N 74 45 E
Nîmes **141** 43 50N 4 23 E
Nimfaíon, Ákra- **168** 40 5N 24 20 E
Nimmitabel **231** 36 29 S 149 15 E
Nimneryskiy **185** 57 50N 125 10 E
Nimpkish → **92** 50 34N 126 58W
Nimpkish L. **92** 50 25N 126 59W
Nimpo L. **92** 52 20N 125 10W
Nimule **245** 3 32N 32 3 E
Nimún, Pta. **111** 20 46N 90 25W
Nin **163** 44 16N 15 12 E
Nīnawá **192** 36 25N 43 10 E
Ninda **253** 14 47 S 21 24 E
Nindigully **231** 28 21 S 148 50 E
Ninette **89** 49 24N 99 38W
Ninety Mile Beach, The **233** 38 15 S 147 24 E
Nineveh = Nīnawá **192** 36 25N 43 10 E
Ning Xian **214** 35 30N 107 58 E
Ningaloo **228** 22 41 S 113 41 E
Ning'an **215** 44 22N 129 20 E
Ningbo **217** 29 51N 121 28 E
Ningcheng **215** 41 32N 119 53 E
Ningde **217** 26 38N 119 23 E
Ningdu **217** 26 25N 115 59 E
Ninggang **217** 26 42N 113 55 E
Ningguo **217** 30 35N 119 0 E
Ninghai **217** 29 15N 121 27 E
Ninghua **217** 26 14N 116 45 E
Ningjin **214** 37 35N 114 57 E
Ningjing Shan **216** 30 0N 98 20 E
Ninglang **216** 27 20N 100 55 E
Ningling **214** 34 25N 115 22 E
Ningming **216** 22 8N 107 4 E
Ningnan **216** 27 5N 102 36 E
Ningpo = Ningbo **217** 29 51N 121 28 E
Ningqiang **216** 32 47N 106 15 E
Ningshan **216** 33 21N 108 21 E
Ningsia Hui A.R. = Ningxia Huizu Zizhiqu □ **214** 38 0N 106 0 E
Ningwu **214** 39 0N 112 18 E
Ningxia Huizu Zizhiqu □ **214** 38 0N 106 0 E
Ningxiang **217** 28 15N 112 30 E
Ningyang **214** 35 47N 116 45 E
Ningyuan **217** 25 37N 111 57 E
Ninh Binh **204** 20 15N 105 55 E

Ninh Giang 204 20 44N 106 24 E
Ninh Hoa 204 12 30N 109 7 E
Ninh Ma 204 12 48N 109 21 E
Ninove 143 50 51N 4 2 E
Nioaque 125 21 5 S 55 50W
Nioki 252 2 47 S 17 40 E
Nioman 78 50 25N 66 5W
Niono 246 14 15N 6 0W
Nioro du Rip 246 13 40N 15 50W
Nioro du Sahel 246 15 15N 9 30W
Niort 140 46 19N 0 29W
Nipa 227 6 9 S 143 29 E
Nipani 201 16 20N 74 25 E
Nipawin 88 53 20N 104 0W
Nipawin Prov. Park 88 54 0N 104 37W
Nipekamew → 88 54 59N 104 52W
Nipigon 86 49 0N 88 17W
Nipigon, L. 86 49 50N 88 30W
Nipigon B. 87 48 53N 87 50W
Nipin → 77 55 46N 108 35W
Nipishish L. 78 54 12N 60 45W
Nipisi L. 90 55 47N 114 57W
Nipissing L. 84 46 20N 80 0W
Nipissis → 78 50 30N 66 5W
Nipissis, L. 80 51 2N 66 10W
Nipisso, L. 80 50 52N 65 50W
Nipper's Harbour 79 49 48N 55 52W
Niquelândia 121 14 33 S 48 23W
Nīr 192 38 2N 47 59 E
Nira → 200 17 58N 75 8 E
Nirasaki 221 35 42N 138 27 E
Nirmal 200 19 3N 78 20 E
Nirmali 199 26 20N 86 35 E
Niš 166 43 19N 21 58 E
Nisa 155 39 30N 7 41W
Nişāb 192 14 25N 46 29 E
Nišava → 166 43 20N 21 46 E
Niscemi 165 37 8N 14 21 E
Nishi-Sonogi-Hantō 220 32 55N 129 45 E
Nishinomiya 221 34 45N 135 20 E
Nishin'omote 219 30 43N 130 59 E
Nishio 221 34 52N 137 3 E
Nishiwaki 220 34 59N 134 58 E
Nísíros 169 36 35N 27 12 E
Niskibi → 74 56 29N 88 9W
Nisko 152 50 35N 22 7 E
Nispen 143 51 29N 4 28 E
Nisporeny 170 47 4N 28 10 E
Nissafors 173 57 25N 13 37 E
Nissan → 173 56 40N 12 51 E
Nissedal 171 59 10N 8 30 E
Nisser 171 59 7N 8 28 E
Nissum Fjord 173 56 20N 8 11 E
Nistelrode 143 51 42N 5 34 E
Nisutlin → 76 60 14N 132 34W
Nitchequon 78 53 10N 70 58W
Niterói 121 22 52 S 43 0W
Nith →, Canada 84 43 12N 80 23W
Nith →, U.K. 134 55 20N 3 5W
Nitinat 92 48 56N 124 29W
Nitinat L. 92 48 45N 124 45W
Nitra 151 48 19N 18 4 E
Nitra → 151 47 46N 18 10 E
Nitsa → 182 57 29N 64 33 E
Nittedal 171 60 1N 10 57 E
Nittendau 147 49 12N 12 16 E
Niue I. 225 19 2 S 169 54W
Niulan Jiang → 216 27 30N 103 5 E
Niut 209 0 55N 110 6 E
Niutou Shan 217 29 5N 121 59 E
Niuzhuang 215 40 58N 122 28 E
Nivelles 143 50 35N 4 20 E
Nivernais 139 47 0N 3 40 E
Niverville 89 49 36N 97 3W
Nizam Sagar 200 18 10N 77 58 E
Nizamabad 200 18 45N 78 7 E
Nizamghat 202 28 20N 95 45 E
Nizhiye Sergi 182 56 40N 59 18 E
Nizhne Kolymsk 185 68 34N 160 55 E
Nizhne-Vartovskoye 184 60 56N 76 38 E
Nizhneangarsk 185 55 47N 109 30 E
Nizhnegorskiy 180 45 27N 34 38 E
Nizhneudinsk 185 54 54N 99 3 E
Nizhneyansk 185 71 26N 136 4 E
Nizhniy Lomov 179 53 34N 43 38 E
Nizhniy Novgorod = Gorkiy 179 56 20N 44 0 E
Nizhniy Pyandzh 183 37 12N 68 35 E
Nizhniy Tagil 182 57 55N 59 57 E
Nizhny Salda 182 58 8N 60 42 E
Nizhnyaya Tunguska → 185 64 20N 93 0 E
Nizké Tatry 151 48 55N 20 0 E
Nizuc, Pta. 111 21 2N 86 48W
Nizza Monferrato 162 44 46N 8 22 E
Njakwa 251 11 1 S 33 56 E
Njanji 251 14 25 S 31 46 E
Njinjo 251 8 48 S 38 54 E
Njombe 251 9 20 S 34 50 E
Njombe □ 251 9 20 S 34 49 E
Njombe → 250 6 56 S 35 6 E
Nkambe 247 6 35N 10 40 E
Nkana 251 12 50 S 28 8 E
Nkawkaw 247 6 36N 0 49W
Nkayi 251 19 41 S 29 20 E
Nkhota Kota 251 12 56 S 34 15 E
Nkolabona 252 1 14N 11 43 E
Nkone 252 1 2 S 22 20 E
Nkongsamba 247 4 55N 9 55 E
Nkunga 253 4 41 S 18 34 E
Nkurenkuru 254 17 42 S 18 32 E
Nkwanta 246 6 10N 2 10W
Nmaushahr 199 33 11N 74 15 E
Noakhali = Maijdi 202 22 48N 91 10 E
Nobel 84 45 25N 80 6W
Nobeoka 220 32 36N 131 41 E
Nōbi-Heiya 221 35 15N 136 45 E
Nobleford 91 49 53N 113 3W
Noblejas 156 39 58N 3 26W
Noce → 162 46 9N 11 4 E
Nocera Inferiore 165 40 45N 14 37 E
Nocera Terinese 165 39 2N 16 9 E
Nocera Umbra 163 43 8N 12 47 E
Nochistlán 105 21 22N 102 51W
Nochistlán, Sa. de 106 21 10N 103 5W
Nochixtlán, Sa. de 109 17 40N 97 10W
Noci 165 40 47N 17 7 E
Nockatunga 231 27 42 S 142 42 E
Nocrich 170 45 55N 24 26 E
Nocupétaro 107 18 48N 101 4W
Noda 221 35 56N 139 52 E
Noel 81 45 18N 63 45W
Noelville 84 46 8N 80 26W
Nogal Valley 256 8 35N 48 35 E
Nogales, Chihuahua, Mexico 100 31 10N 108 34W
Nogales, Sonora, Mexico 100 31 20N 110 56W
Nogales, Veracruz, Mexico 109 18 49N 97 10W
Nogat → 152 54 17N 19 17 E
Nōgata 220 33 48N 130 44 E
Nogent-en-Bassigny 139 48 0N 5 20 E
Nogent-le-Rotrou 138 48 20N 0 50 E
Nogent-sur-Seine 139 48 30N 3 30 E
Noggerup 229 33 32 S 116 5 E
Noginsk, Moskva, U.S.S.R. 179 55 50N 38 25 E
Noginsk, Sib., U.S.S.R. 185 64 30N 90 50 E
Nogoa → 230 23 40 S 147 55 E
Nogoyá 124 32 24 S 59 48W
Nógrád □ 151 48 0N 19 30 E
Nogueira de Ramuin 154 42 21N 7 43W
Noguera Pallaresa → 156 42 15N 1 0 E
Noguera Ribagorzana → 156 41 40N 0 43 E
Noh, L 111 18 38N 90 17W
Nohar 198 29 11N 74 49 E
Noing 211 5 40N 125 28 E
Noirclair, L. 80 50 38N 60 23W
Noire → 82 45 34N 76 57W
Noire, Mt. 138 48 11N 3 40W
Noirétable 140 45 48N 3 46 E
Noirmoutier 138 47 0N 2 15W
Noirmoutier, Î. de 138 46 58N 2 10W
Nojane 254 23 15 S 20 14 E
Nojima-Zaki 221 34 54N 139 53 E
Nok Kundi 197 28 50N 62 45 E
Nokaneng 254 19 40 S 22 17 E
Nokhtuysk 185 60 0N 117 45 E
Nokomis 88 51 35N 105 0W
Nokomis L. 77 57 0N 103 0W
Nokou 243 14 35N 14 47 E
Nol 173 57 56N 12 5 E
Nola, C.A.R. 252 3 35N 16 4 E
Nola, Italy 165 40 54N 14 29 E
Nolay 139 46 58N 4 35 E
Noli, C. di 162 44 12N 8 26 E
Nolinsk 182 57 28N 49 57 E
Noma Omuramba → 254 18 52 S 20 53 E
Noma-Saki 220 31 25N 130 7 E
Nomad 227 6 19 S 142 13 E
Noman L. 77 62 15N 108 55W
Nombre de Dios, Chihuahua, Mexico 101 28 41N 106 5W
Nombre de Dios, Durango, Mexico 105 23 51N 104 14W
Nombre de Dios, Panama 112 9 34N 79 28W
Nominingue 82 46 24N 75 2W
Nominingue, L. 82 46 26N 74 59W
Nomo-Zaki 220 32 35N 129 44 E
Nonacho L. 77 61 42N 109 40W
Nonancourt 138 48 47N 1 11 E
Nonant-le-Pin 138 48 42N 0 12 E
Nonda 230 20 40 S 142 28 E
Nong Chang 204 15 23N 99 51 E
Nong Het 204 19 29N 103 59 E
Nong Khai 204 17 50N 102 46 E
Nong'an 215 44 25N 125 5 E
Nonoava 101 27 28N 106 44W
Nonoava, R. → 101 27 29N 106 45W
Nonoc I. 211 9 51N 125 37 E
Nonthaburi 204 13 51N 100 34 E
Nontron 140 45 31N 0 40 E
Noonamah 228 12 40 S 131 4 E
Noondoo 231 28 35 S 148 30 E
Noonkanbah 228 18 30 S 124 50 E
Noord-Bergum 142 53 14N 6 1 E
Noord Brabant □ 143 51 40N 5 0 E
Noord Holland □ 142 52 30N 4 45 E
Noordbeveland 143 51 35N 3 50 E
Noordeloos 142 51 55N 4 56 E
Noordhollandsch Kanaal 142 52 55N 4 48 E
Noordhorn 142 53 16N 6 24 E
Noordoostpolder 142 52 45N 5 45 E
Noordwijk aan Zee 142 52 14N 4 26 E
Noordwijk-Binnen 142 52 14N 4 27 E
Noordwijkerhout 142 52 16N 4 30 E
Noordzee Kanaal 142 52 28N 4 35 E
Noorwolde 142 52 54N 6 8 E
Nootka 92 49 38N 126 38W
Nootka I. 92 49 32N 126 42W
Nóqui 253 5 55 S 13 30 E
Nora, Ethiopia 245 16 6N 40 4 E
Nora, Sweden 172 59 32N 15 2 E
Noranda 82 48 20N 79 0W
Norberg 172 60 4N 15 56 E
Nórcia 163 42 50N 13 5 E
Nord □ 139 50 15N 3 30 E
Nord, Grand L. du 80 50 54N 67 6W
Nord, Petit L. du 80 50 50N 67 10W
Nord-Ostsee Kanal 146 54 15N 9 40 E
Nord-Süd Kanal 146 53 0N 10 32 E
Nord-Trøndelag fylke □ 174 64 20N 12 0 E
Nordagutu 171 59 25N 9 20 E
Nordaustlandet 12 79 14N 23 0 E
Nordborg 173 55 5N 9 50 E
Nordby, Århus, Denmark 173 55 58N 10 32 E
Nordby, Ribe, Denmark 173 55 27N 8 24 E
Norddal 171 62 15N 7 14 E
Norddalsfjord 171 61 39N 5 23 E
Norddeich 146 53 37N 7 10 E
Nordegg 91 52 29N 116 5W
Norden 146 53 35N 7 12 E
Nordenham 146 53 29N 8 28 E
Norderhov 171 60 7N 10 17 E
Norderney 146 53 42N 7 15 E
Nordfjord 171 61 55N 5 30 E
Nordfriesische Inseln 146 54 40N 8 20 E
Nordhausen 146 51 29N 10 47 E
Nordhorn 146 52 27N 7 4 E
Nordjyllands Amtskommune □ 173 57 0N 10 0 E
Nordkapp, Norway 174 71 10N 25 44 E
Nordkapp, Svalbard 12 80 31N 20 0 E
Nordkinn 130 71 8N 27 40 E
Nordland fylke □ 174 65 40N 13 0 E
Nördlingen 147 48 50N 10 30 E
Nordrhein-Westfalen □ 146 51 45N 7 30 E
Nordstrand 146 54 27N 8 50 E
Nordvik 185 74 2N 111 32 E
Nore 171 60 10N 9 0 E
Nore → 135 52 40N 7 20W
Norefjell 171 60 16N 9 29 E
Norembega 74 48 59N 80 43W
Noresund 171 60 11N 9 37 E
Norfolk □ 132 52 39N 1 0 E
Norfolk Broads 132 52 30N 1 15 E
Norfolk I. 224 28 58 S 168 3 E
Norg 142 53 4N 6 28 E
Noria, La, Coahuila, Mexico 102 29 16N 102 22W
Noria, La, Sinaloa, Mexico 104 23 30N 106 18W
Noria, La, Tamaulipas, Mexico 103 23 31N 98 41W
Noria de San Pantaleón, La 105 23 40N 103 46W
Norias 105 24 22N 102 43W
Norilsk 185 69 20N 88 6 E
Norley 231 27 45 S 143 48 E
Norma, Mt. 230 20 55 S 140 42 E
Norman → 230 17 28 S 140 49 E
Norman Wells 94 65 17N 126 51W
Normanby 234 39 32 S 174 18 E
Normanby → 230 14 23 S 144 10 E
Normanby I. 227 10 55 S 151 5 E
Normandie 138 48 45N 0 10 E
Normandie, Collines de 138 48 55N 0 45W
Normandin 83 48 49N 72 31W
Normandy = Normandie 138 48 45N 0 10 E
Normanhurst, Mt. 229 25 4 S 122 30 E
Norman's Cove 79 47 33N 53 40W
Normanton 230 17 40 S 141 10 E
Normanville 232 35 27 S 138 18 E
Normétal 82 49 0N 79 22W
Norogachic 101 27 15N 107 7W
Norquay 89 51 53N 102 5W
Norquinco 126 41 51 S 70 55W
Norrahammar 173 57 43N 14 7 E
Norrbottens län □ 174 66 58N 20 0 E
Nørre Åby 173 55 27N 9 52 E
Nørre Nebel 173 55 47N 8 17 E
Nørresundby 173 57 5N 9 52 E
Norris Arm 79 49 5N 55 15W
Norris Point 79 49 31N 57 53W
Norrköping 173 58 37N 16 11 E
Norrtälje 172 59 46N 18 42 E
Norseman 229 32 8 S 121 43 E
Norsholm 173 58 31N 15 59 E
Norsk 185 52 30N 130 0 E
Norte, Meseta del 101 27 15N 104 20W
Norte, Pta. 126 42 5 S 63 46W
Norte de Santander □ 118 8 0N 73 0W
Nortelândia 123 14 25 S 56 48W
North → 78 57 30N 61 50W
North Andaman I. 196 13 15N 92 40 E
North Atlantic Ocean 128 30 0N 50 0W
North Aulatsivik I. 78 59 46N 64 5W
North Battleford 88 52 50N 108 17W
North Bay 84 46 20N 79 30W
North Belcher Is. 78 56 50N 79 50W
North Bend 93 49 50N 121 27W
North Berwick 134 56 4N 2 44W
North Buck L. 90 54 41N 112 32W
North Buganda □ 250 1 0N 32 0 E
North C., Canada 81 47 2N 60 20W
North C., N.Z. 234 34 23 S 173 4 E
North C., Papua N. G. 227 2 32 S 150 50 E
North Caribou L. 74 52 50N 90 40W
North Channel, Br. Is. 134 55 0N 5 30W
North Channel, Canada 84 46 0N 83 0W
North Cotabato □ 211 7 10N 125 0 E
North Dandalup 229 32 30 S 115 57 E
North Down □ 135 54 40N 5 45W
North Downs 133 51 17N 0 30 E
North East Frontier Agency = Arunachal Pradesh □ 202 28 0N 95 0 E
North East Providence Chan. 112 26 0N 76 0W
North Eastern □ 250 1 30N 40 0 E
North Esk → 134 56 44N 2 25W
North European Plain 130 55 0N 20 0 E
North Foreland 133 51 22N 1 28 E
North French → 87 51 10N 80 50W
North Frisian Is. = Nordfriesische Inseln 146 54 40N 8 20 E
North Gower 85 45 8N 75 43W
North Grant 81 45 40N 62 2W
North Hatley 83 45 17N 71 58W
North Head 81 44 46N 66 45W
North Henik L. 77 61 45N 97 40W
North Horr 250 3 20N 37 8 E
North I., Kenya 250 4 5N 36 5 E
North I., N.Z. 235 38 0 S 175 0 E
North Knife → 77 58 53N 94 45W
North Koel → 199 24 45N 83 50 E
North Korea ■ 215 40 0N 127 0 E
North Lakhimpur 202 27 14N 94 7 E
North Magnetic Pole 95 77 18N 101 48W
North Mashonaland □ 251 16 30 S 30 0 E
North Minch 134 58 5N 5 55W
North Nahanni → 76 62 15N 123 20W
North Ossetian A.S.S.R. □ 181 43 30N 44 30 E
North Pt. 81 47 5N 64 0W
North Pole 12 90 0N 0 0 E
North Portal 89 49 0N 102 33W
North Ram → 91 52 16N 114 38W
North Ronaldsay 134 59 20N 2 30W
North Rustico 81 46 27N 63 19W
North Saskatchewan → 88 53 15N 105 5W
North Sea 130 56 0N 4 0 E
North Sporades = Vorîai Sporádhes 169 39 15N 23 30 E
North Star 90 56 51N 117 38W
North Sydney 81 46 12N 60 15W
North Thompson → 93 50 40N 120 20W
North Twin I. 78 53 20N 80 0W
North Twin L. 79 49 16N 55 56W
North Tyne → 132 54 59N 2 7W
North Uist 134 57 40N 7 15W
North Vancouver 93 49 25N 123 3W
North Wabiskaw L. 90 56 0N 113 55W
North Walsham 132 52 49N 1 22 E
North West C. 228 21 45 S 114 9 E
North West Christmas I. Ridge 225 6 30N 165 0W
North West Frontier □ 197 34 0N 71 0 E

North West
Highlands **134** 57 35N 5 2W
North West
Providence
Channel **112** 26 0N 78 0W
North West River .. **78** 53 30N 60 10W
North West
Territories □ **94** 67 0N 110 0W
North Western □ **251** 13 30 S 25 30 E
North York Moors **132** 54 25N 0 50W
North Yorkshire □ **132** 54 15N 1 25W
Northallerton **132** 54 20N 1 26W
Northampton,
Australia **229** 28 27 S 114 33 E
Northampton, U.K. **133** 52 14N 0 54W
Northampton □ **133** 52 16N 0 55W
Northampton
Downs **230** 24 35 S 145 48 E
Northcliffe **229** 34 39 S 116 7 E
Northeim **146** 51 42N 10 0 E
Northern □, Malawi **251** 11 0 S 34 0 E
Northern □, Uganda **250** 3 5N 32 30 E
Northern □, Zambia **251** 10 30 S 31 0 E
Northern Circars **200** 17 30N 82 30 E
Northern Indian L. **77** 57 20N 97 20W
Northern Ireland □ **135** 54 45N 7 0W
Northern Light, L. **86** 48 15N 90 39W
Northern Marianas **224** 17 0N 145 0 E
Northern
Province □ **246** 9 15N 11 30W
Northern Samar □ **210** 12 30N 124 40 E
Northern
Territory □ **228** 16 0 S 133 0 E
Northland □ **234** 35 30 S 173 30 E
Northport **81** 45 56N 63 52W
Northumberland □ **132** 55 12N 2 0W
Northumberland, C. **232** 38 5 S 140 40 E
Northumberland Is. **230** 21 30 S 149 50 E
Northumberland Str. **81** 46 20N 64 0W
Northwest
Gander → **79** 48 55N 55 2W
Northwich **132** 53 16N 2 30W
Norton, Canada **81** 45 38N 65 42W
Norton, Zimbabwe **251** 17 52 S 30 40 E
Nortorf **146** 54 14N 9 47 E
Norway ■ **174** 63 0N 11 0 E
Norway House **89** 53 59N 97 50W
Norwegian B. **95** 77 30N 90 0W
Norwegian
Dependency □ **13** 66 0 S 15 0 E
Norwegian Sea **128** 66 0N 1 0 E
Norwich, Canada **84** 42 59N 80 36W
Norwich, U.K. **132** 52 38N 1 17 E
Norwood **85** 44 23N 77 59W
Noshiro **218** 40 12N 140 0 E
Nosok **184** 70 10N 82 20 E
Nosovka **178** 50 50N 31 37 E
Noss Hd. **134** 58 29N 3 4W
Nossa Senhora da
Glória **120** 10 14 S 37 25W
Nossa Senhora das
Dores **120** 10 29 S 37 13W
Nossa Senhora do
Livramento **123** 15 48 S 56 22W
Nossebro **173** 58 12N 12 43 E
Nossob → **254** 26 55 S 20 37 E
Nosy Boraha **255** 16 50 S 49 55 E
Nosy Varika **255** 20 35 S 48 32 E
Noteć → **152** 52 44N 15 26 E
Notengo, L. de **109** 16 12N 98 0W
Notigi Dam **77** 56 40N 99 10W
Notikewin → **90** 57 2N 117 38W
Notios Evvoïkos
Kólpos **169** 38 20N 24 0 E
Noto **165** 36 52N 15 4 E
Noto, G. di **165** 36 50N 15 10 E
Notodden **171** 59 35N 9 17 E
Notre-Dame **81** 46 18N 64 46W
Notre-Dame, Les **80** 48 10N 68 0W
Notre Dame B. **79** 49 45N 55 30W
Notre Dame de
Koartac =
Koartac **78** 60 55N 69 40W
Notre-Dame-de-la-
Doré **83** 48 43N 72 39W
Notre Dame de
Lourdes **89** 49 32N 98 33W
Notre-Dame-des-
Bois **83** 45 24N 71 4W
Notre Dame
d'Ivugivic =
Ivugivik **78** 62 24N 77 55W
Notre-Dame-du-
Bon-Conseil **83** 46 0N 72 21W
Notre Dame du Lac,
Ont., Canada **84** 46 18N 80 11W
Notre-Dame-du-Lac,
Qué., Canada **83** 47 36N 68 48W
Notre-Dame-du-
Laus **82** 46 5N 75 37W
Notre-Dame-du-
Nord **82** 47 36N 79 30W
Notre-Dame-du-
Portage **83** 47 46N 69 37W
Notsé **247** 7 0N 1 17 E
Nottawasaga B. **84** 44 35N 80 15W
Nottaway → **78** 51 22N 78 55W
Nøtterøy **171** 59 14N 10 24 E
Nottingham **132** 52 57N 1 10W
Nottingham □ **132** 53 10N 1 0W
Nottingham I. **95** 63 20N 77 55W
Nottingham Island **95** 63 6N 77 50W
Notukeu Cr. → **88** 49 56N 106 29W
Notwani → **254** 23 35 S 26 58 E
Nouâdhibou **240** 20 54N 17 0W
Nouâdhibou, Ras **240** 20 50N 17 0W
Nouakchott **246** 18 9N 15 58W
Noumea **226** 22 17 S 166 30 E
Noupoort **254** 31 10 S 24 57 E
Nouveau Comptoir **78** 53 0N 78 49W
Nouveau-Quebec,
Reg. **78** 56 0N 71 0W
Nouvelle **81** 48 8N 66 19W
Nouvelle → **81** 48 7N 66 19W
Nouvelle Calédonie **226** 21 0 S 165 0 E
Nouvelle France, C.
de **78** 62 27N 73 42W
Nouzonville **139** 49 48N 4 44 E
Nová Baňa **151** 48 28N 18 39 E
Nová Bystřice **150** 49 2N 15 8 E
Nova Cruz **120** 6 28 S 35 25W
Nova Era **121** 19 45 S 43 3W
Nova Esperança **125** 23 8 S 52 24W
Nova Friburgo **121** 22 16 S 42 30W
Nova Gaia **253** 10 10 S 17 35 E
Nova Gradiška **166** 45 17N 17 28 E
Nova Granada **121** 20 30 S 49 20W
Nova Iguaçu **121** 22 45 S 43 28W
Nova Iorque **120** 7 0 S 44 5W
Nova Lamego **246** 12 19N 14 11W
Nova Lima **125** 19 59 S 43 51W
Nova Lisboa =
Huambo **253** 12 42 S 15 54 E
Nova Lusitânia **251** 19 50 S 34 34 E
Nova Mambone **255** 21 0 S 35 3 E
Nova Mesto **163** 45 47N 15 12 E
Nova Paka **150** 50 29N 15 30 E
Nova Ponte **121** 19 8 S 47 41W
Nova Scotia □ **75** 45 10N 63 0W
Nova Sofala **255** 20 7 S 34 42 E
Nova Varoš **166** 43 29N 19 48 E
Nova Venécia **121** 18 45 S 40 24W
Nova Vida **123** 10 11 S 62 47W
Nova Zagora **167** 42 32N 25 59 E
Nova Zembla I. **95** 72 11N 74 50W
Novaci, Romania **170** 45 10N 23 42 E
Novaci, Yugoslavia **166** 41 5N 21 29 E
Noval Iorque **120** 6 48 S 44 0W
Novaleksandrovskaya
181 45 29N 41 17 E
Novannenskiy **179** 50 32N 42 39 E
Novar **84** 45 27N 79 15W
Novara **162** 45 27N 8 36 E
Novaya Kakhovka **180** 46 42N 33 27 E
Novaya Ladoga **176** 60 7N 32 16 E
Novaya Lyalya **182** 59 10N 60 35 E
Novaya Sibir, Os. **185** 75 10N 150 0 E
Novaya Zemlya **184** 75 0N 56 0 E
Nové Město **151** 48 45N 17 50 E
Nové Zámky **151** 48 0N 18 8 E
Novelda **157** 38 24N 0 45W
Novellara **162** 44 50N 10 43 E
Noventa Vicentina **163** 45 18N 11 30 E
Novgorod **178** 58 30N 31 25 E
Novgorod-Severskiy **178** 52 2N 33 10 E
Novi Bečej **166** 45 36N 20 10 E
Novi Grad **163** 45 19N 13 33 E
Novi Kneževa **166** 46 4N 20 8 E
Novi Krichim **167** 42 8N 24 31 E
Novi Lígure **162** 44 45N 8 47 E
Novi Pazar, Bulgaria **167** 43 25N 27 15 E
Novi Pazar,
Yugoslavia **166** 43 12N 20 28 E
Novi Sad **166** 45 18N 19 52 E
Novi Vinodolski **163** 45 10N 14 48 E
Novigrad **163** 44 10N 15 32 E
Noville **143** 50 4N 5 46 E
Novillero **104** 22 21N 105 39W
Novillo, Presa del **100** 29 10N 109 40W
Novo Acôrdo **120** 10 10 S 46 48W
Novo Aripuanã **119** 5 8 S 60 22W
Nôvo Cruzeiro **121** 17 29 S 41 53W
Nôvo Hamburgo **125** 29 37 S 51 7W
Novo Horizonte **121** 21 25 S 49 10W
Novo-Sergiyevskiy **182** 52 5N 53 38 E
Novo-Zavidovskiy **179** 56 32N 36 29 E
Novoakrainka **180** 48 25N 31 30 E
Novoalekseyevka **182** 50 8N 55 39 E
Novoaltaysk **184** 53 30N 84 0 E
Novoazovsk **180** 47 15N 38 4 E
Novobelitsa **178** 52 27N 31 2 E
Novobogatinskoye **181** 47 20N 51 11 E
Novocherkassk **181** 47 27N 40 5 E
Novodevichye **179** 53 37N 48 50 E
Novograd-Volynskiy **178** 50 34N 27 35 E
Novogrudok **178** 53 40N 25 50 E
Novokachalinsk **218** 45 5N 132 0 E
Novokayakent **181** 42 30N 47 52 E
Novokazalinsk **184** 45 48N 62 6 E
Novokhopersk **179** 51 5N 41 39 E
Novokuybyshevsk **182** 53 7N 49 58 E
Novokuznetsk **184** 53 45N 87 10 E
Novomirgorod **180** 48 45N 31 33 E
Novomoskovsk,
R.S.F.S.R.,
U.S.S.R. **179** 54 5N 38 15 E
Novomoskovsk,
Ukraine S.S.R.,
U.S.S.R. **180** 48 33N 35 17 E
Novoorsk **182** 51 21N 59 2 E
Novopolotsk **178** 55 32N 28 37 E
Novorossiysk **180** 44 43N 37 46 E
Novorybnoye **185** 72 50N 105 50 E
Novorzhev **178** 57 3N 29 25 E
Novoselitsa **180** 48 14N 26 15 E
Novoshakhtinsk **181** 47 46N 39 58 E
Novosibirsk **184** 55 0N 83 5 E
Novosibirskiye
Ostrava **185** 75 0N 142 0 E
Novosil **179** 52 59N 37 2 E
Novosokolniki **178** 56 33N 30 5 E
Novotroitsk **182** 51 10N 58 15 E
Novotroitskoye **183** 43 42N 73 46 E
Novotulskiy **179** 54 10N 37 43 E
Novouzensk **179** 50 32N 48 17 E
Novovolynsk **178** 50 45N 24 4 E
Novovyatsk **179** 58 24N 49 45 E
Novozybkov **178** 52 30N 32 0 E
Novska **166** 45 19N 17 0 E
Novvy Port **184** 67 40N 72 30 E
Novy Bug **180** 47 34N 32 29 E
Nový Bydzov **150** 50 14N 15 29 E
Novy Dwór
Mazowiecki **152** 52 26N 20 44 E
Nový Jičín **151** 49 30N 18 0 E
Novyy Afon **181** 43 7N 40 50 E
Novyy Oskol **179** 50 44N 37 55 E
Now Shahr **193** 36 40N 51 30 E
Nowa Deba **152** 50 26N 21 41 E
Nowa Huta **151** 50 5N 20 30 E
Nowa Nowa **233** 37 44 S 148 3 E
Nowa Ruda **152** 50 35N 16 30 E
Nowa Skalmierzyce **152** 51 43N 18 0 E
Nowa Sól **152** 51 48N 15 44 E
Nowbarān **193** 35 8N 49 42 E
Nowe **152** 53 41N 18 44 E
Nowe Miasteczko **152** 51 42N 15 42 E
Nowe Miasto **152** 51 38N 20 34 E
Nowe Miasto
Lubawskie **152** 53 27N 19 33 E
Nowe Warpno **152** 53 42N 14 18 E
Nowendoc **233** 31 32 S 151 44 E
Nowghāb **193** 33 53N 59 4 E
Nowgong **202** 26 20N 92 50 E
Nowingi **232** 34 33 S 142 15 E
Nowogard **152** 53 41N 15 10 E
Nowogród **152** 53 14N 21 53 E
Nowra **231** 34 53 S 150 35 E
Nowshera **197** 34 0N 72 0 E
Nowy Dwór,
Białystok, Poland **152** 53 40N 23 30 E
Nowy Dwór,
Gdańsk, Poland **152** 54 13N 19 7 E
Nowy Korczyn **152** 50 19N 20 48 E
Nowy Sącz **152** 49 40N 20 41 E
Nowy Sącz □ **152** 49 30N 20 30 E
Nowy Staw **152** 54 13N 19 2 E
Nowy Tomyśl **152** 52 19N 16 10 E
Noya **154** 42 48N 8 53W
Noyant **138** 47 30N 0 6 E
Noyers **139** 47 40N 4 0 E
Noyon, France **139** 49 34N 3 0 E
Noyon, Mongolia **214** 43 2N 102 4 E
Nozay **138** 47 34N 1 38W
Nsa, O. en → **241** 32 28N 5 24 E
Nsa, Plat. de **252** 2 26 S 15 20 E
Nsah **252** 2 23 S 15 19 E
Nsanje **251** 16 55 S 35 12 E
Nsawam **247** 5 50N 0 24W
Nsomba **251** 10 45 S 29 51 E
Nsopzup **202** 25 51N 97 30 E
Nsukka **247** 6 51N 7 29 E
Ntoum **252** 0 22N 9 47 E
Nu Jiang → **216** 29 58N 97 25 E
Nu Shan **216** 26 0N 99 20 E
Nuba Mts. =
Nubah, Jibalan **245** 12 0N 31 0 E
Nubah, Jibalan **245** 12 0N 31 0 E
Nûbîya, Es Sahrâ en **244** 21 30N 33 30 E
Ñuble □ **124** 37 0 S 72 0W
Nuboai **207** 2 10 S 136 30 E
Nubra → **199** 34 35N 77 35 E
Nueima → **189** 31 54N 35 25 E
Nueltin L. **77** 60 30N 99 30W
Nuenen **143** 51 29N 5 33 E
Nueva, I. **126** 55 13 S 66 30W
Nueva Antioquia **118** 6 5N 69 26W
Nueva Ciudad
Guerrero **102** 26 34N 99 15W
Nueva Coahuila **111** 17 55N 90 51W
Nueva Ecija □ **210** 15 35N 121 0 E
Nueva Esparta □ **119** 11 0N 64 0W
Nueva Gerona **112** 21 53N 82 49W
Nueva Imperial **126** 38 45 S 72 58W
Nueva Italia de Ruiz **106** 19 1N 102 6W
Nueva Palmira **124** 33 52 S 58 20W
Nueva Rosita **102** 27 57N 101 13W
Nueva San Salvador **112** 13 40N 89 18W
Nueva Vizcaya □ **210** 16 20N 121 20 E
Nuéve de Julio **124** 35 30 S 61 0W
Nuevitas **112** 21 30N 77 20W
Nuevo, Golfo **126** 43 0 S 64 30W
Nuevo Casas
Grandes **101** 30 25N 107 55W
Nuevo Ideal **104** 24 55N 105 7W
Nuevo Laredo **102** 27 30N 99 31W
Nuevo Leon □ **102** 25 40N 100 0W
Nuevo Morelos **103** 22 30N 99 12W
Nuevo Mundo,
Cerro **122** 21 55 S 66 53W
Nuevo Rocafuerte **118** 0 55 S 75 27W
Nuevo Urecho **106** 19 9N 101 52W
Nuevo Valle de
Moreno **107** 21 12N 101 25W
Nugget Pt. **235** 46 27 S 169 50 E
Nugrus, Gebel **244** 24 47N 34 35 E
Nugssuaq Pen. **95** 70 30N 53 0W
Nuhaka **234** 39 3 S 177 45 E
Nuits **139** 47 44N 4 12 E
Nuits-St-Georges **139** 47 10N 4 56 E
Nukey Bluff, Mt. **231** 32 26 S 135 29 E
Nukheila **244** 19 1N 26 21 E
Nukus **184** 42 20N 59 7 E
Nuland **142** 51 44N 5 26 E
Nules **156** 39 51N 0 9W
Nulki L. **92** 53 55N 124 7W
Nullagine → **228** 21 20 S 120 20 E
Nullarbor **229** 31 28 S 130 55 E
Nullarbor Plain **229** 30 45 S 129 0 E
Numalla, L. **231** 28 43 S 144 20 E
Numan **247** 9 29N 12 3 E
Numansdorp **142** 51 43N 4 26 E
Numaran **106** 20 15N 101 56W
Numata **221** 36 45N 139 4 E
Numatinna → **245** 7 38N 27 20 E
Numazu **221** 35 7N 138 51 E
Numbulwar **230** 14 15 S 135 45 E
Numfoor **207** 1 0 S 134 50 E
Numurkah **231** 36 5 S 145 26 E
Nunaksaluk I. **78** 55 49N 60 20W
Nuneaton **133** 52 32N 1 29W
Nungesser L. **86** 51 28N 93 30W
Nungo **251** 13 23 S 37 43 E
Nungwe **250** 2 48 S 32 2 E
Nunkini **111** 20 20N 90 11W
Nunkun **199** 33 57N 76 2 E
Nunspeet **142** 52 21N 5 45 E
Nuoro **164** 40 20N 9 20 E
Nuqayy, Jabal **241** 23 11N 19 30 E
Nuqūb **194** 14 59N 45 48 E
Nuquí **118** 5 42N 77 17W
Nur Dağı **190** 36 54N 35 39 E
Nur Dağları **190** 36 50N 36 23 E
Nūrābād **193** 27 47N 57 12 E
Nurata **183** 40 33N 65 41 E
Nuratau, Khrebet **183** 40 40N 66 30 E
Nure → **162** 45 3N 9 49 E
Nuremburg =
Nürnberg **147** 49 26N 11 5 E
Nūrestān **197** 35 30N 70 45 E
Nuri **100** 28 2N 109 22W
Nurina **229** 30 56 S 126 33 E
Nuriootpa **232** 34 27 S 139 0 E
Nurlat **182** 54 29N 50 45 E
Nürnberg **147** 49 26N 11 5 E
Nurran, L. =
Terewah, L. **231** 29 52 S 147 35 E
Nurrari Lakes **229** 29 1 S 130 5 E
Nurri **164** 39 43N 9 13 E
Nurzec → **152** 52 37N 22 25 E
Nusa Barung **209** 8 10 S 113 30 E
Nusa Kambangan **209** 7 40 S 108 10 E
Nusa Tenggara
Barat □ **209** 8 50 S 117 30 E
Nusa Tenggara
Timur □ **207** 9 30 S 122 0 E
Nusaybin **177** 37 3N 41 10 E
Nushki **197** 29 35N 66 0 E
Nut L. **88** 52 22N 103 42W
Nutak **78** 57 28N 61 59W
Nuth **143** 50 55N 5 53 E
Nutwood Downs **230** 15 49 S 134 10 E
Nuvuk Is. **78** 62 24N 78 3W
Nuwakot **199** 28 10N 83 55 E
Nuwara Eliya **201** 6 58N 80 48 E
Nuweiba' **191** 28 59N 34 39 E
Nuweveldberge **254** 32 10 S 21 45 E
Nuxco, L. **107** 17 10N 100 48W
Nuyts, C. **229** 32 2 S 132 21 E
Nuyts Arch. **231** 32 35 S 133 20 E
Nuzvid **200** 16 47N 80 53 E
Nxau-Nxau **254** 18 57 S 21 4 E
Nyaake **246** 4 52N 7 37W
Nyadal **172** 62 48N 17 59 E
Nyah West **231** 35 16 S 143 21 E
Nyahanga **250** 2 20 S 33 37 E

Nyahua **250** 5 25 S 33 23 E
Nyahururu **250** 0 2N 36 27 E
Nyainqentanglha Shan **212** 30 0N 90 0 E
Nyakanazi **250** 3 2 S 31 10 E
Nyakrom **247** 5 40N 0 50W
Nyâlâ **245** 12 2N 24 58 E
Nyamandhlovu **251** 19 55 S 28 16 E
Nyambiti **250** 2 48 S 33 27 E
Nyamwaga **250** 1 27 S 34 33 E
Nyandekwa **250** 3 57 S 32 32 E
Nyanding → **245** 8 40N 32 41 E
Nyandoma **176** 61 40N 40 12 E
Nyanga → **252** 2 58 S 10 15 E
Nyangana **254** 18 0 S 20 40 E
Nyanguge **250** 2 30 S 33 12 E
Nyankpala **247** 9 21N 0 58W
Nyanza, Burundi **250** 4 21 S 29 36 E
Nyanza, Rwanda **250** 2 20 S 29 42 E
Nyanza □ **250** 0 10 S 34 15 E
Nyarling → **76** 60 41N 113 23W
Nyasa, L. = Malawi, L. **251** 12 30 S 34 30 E
Nyaunglebin **202** 17 52N 96 42 E
Nyazepetrovsk **182** 56 3N 59 36 E
Nyazura **251** 18 40 S 32 16 E
Nyazwidzi → **251** 20 0 S 31 17 E
Nyborg **173** 55 18N 10 47 E
Nybro **173** 56 44N 15 55 E
Nyda **184** 66 40N 72 58 E
Nyeri **250** 0 23 S 36 56 E
Nyerol **245** 8 41N 32 1 E
Nyhem **172** 62 54N 15 37 E
Nyiel **245** 6 9N 31 13 E
Nyinahin **246** 6 43N 2 3W
Nyirbátor **151** 47 49N 22 9 E
Nyíregyháza **151** 47 58N 21 47 E
Nykarleby **174** 63 22N 22 31 E
Nykøbing, Sjælland, Denmark **172** 55 55N 11 40 E
Nykøbing, Storstrøm, Denmark **173** 54 56N 11 52 E
Nykøbing, Viborg, Denmark **173** 56 48N 8 51 E
Nyköping **173** 58 45N 17 0 E
Nykroppa **172** 59 37N 14 18 E
Nykvarn **172** 59 11N 17 25 E
Nyland **172** 63 1N 17 45 E
Nylstroom **255** 24 42 S 28 22 E
Nymagee **231** 32 7 S 146 20 E
Nymburk **150** 50 10N 15 1 E
Nynäshamn **172** 58 54N 17 57 E
Nyngan **231** 31 30 S 147 8 E
Nyon **148** 46 23N 6 14 E
Nyong → **247** 3 17N 9 54 E
Nyons **141** 44 22N 5 10 E
Nyora **233** 38 20 S 145 41 E
Nyord **172** 55 4N 12 13 E
Nyou **247** 12 42N 2 1W
Nysa **152** 50 30N 17 22 E
Nysa → **152** 52 4N 14 46 E
Nysted **173** 54 40N 11 44 E
Nytva **182** 57 56N 55 20 E
Nyūgawa **220** 33 56N 133 5 E
Nyunzu **250** 5 57 S 27 58 E
Nyurba **185** 63 17N 118 28 E
Nzega **250** 4 10 S 33 12 E
Nzega □ **250** 4 10 S 33 10 E
N'Zérékoré **246** 7 49N 8 48W
Nzeto **253** 7 10 S 12 52 E
Nzilo, Chutes de **251** 10 18 S 25 27 E
Nzubuka **250** 4 45 S 32 50 E

O

O-Shima, Fukuoka, Japan **220** 33 54N 130 25 E
Ō-Shima, Nagasaki, Japan **220** 34 29N 129 33 E
Ō-Shima, Shizuoka, Japan **221** 34 44N 139 24 E
Oak Bay **81** 45 14N 67 12W
Oak Hill **81** 45 20N 67 20W
Oak Lake **89** 49 46N 100 38W
Oak Point **89** 50 30N 98 1W
Oak River **89** 50 8N 100 26W
Oakan-Dake **218** 43 27N 144 10 E
Oakbank, Australia **231** 33 4 S 140 33 E
Oakbank, Canada **89** 49 57N 96 51W
Oakengates **132** 52 42N 2 29W
Oakey **231** 27 25 S 151 43 E
Oakham **132** 52 40N 0 43W
Oaklands **233** 35 34 S 146 10 E
Oakley Creek **233** 31 37 S 149 46 E
Oakover → **228** 20 15 S 119 10 E
Oakville **84** 43 27N 79 41W
Oamaru **235** 45 5 S 170 59 E
Ōamishirasato **221** 35 31N 140 18 E
Oarai **221** 36 21N 140 34 E
Oates Coast **13** 69 0 S 160 0 E
Oaxaca □ **109** 17 0N 96 30W
Oaxaca de Juárez **109** 17 3N 96 43W
Ob → **184** 66 45N 69 30 E
Oba **87** 49 4N 84 7W
Oba L. **87** 48 40N 84 16W
Obakamiga L. **87** 49 9N 85 9W
Obala **247** 4 9N 11 32 E
Obalski, L. **82** 48 43N 77 58W
Obama, Fukui, Japan **221** 35 30N 135 45 E
Obama, Nagasaki, Japan **220** 32 43N 130 13 E
Obamsca, L. **82** 50 24N 78 16W
Oban **134** 56 25N 5 30W
Obatanga Prov. Park **87** 48 20N 85 10W
Obbia **256** 5 25N 48 30 E
Obdam **142** 52 41N 4 55 E
Obed **90** 53 30N 117 10W
Obedjwan **82** 48 40N 74 56W
Ober-Aagau **148** 47 10N 7 45 E
Obera **125** 27 21 S 55 2W
Oberalppass **149** 46 39N 8 35 E
Oberalpstock **149** 46 45N 8 47 E
Oberammergau **147** 47 35N 11 3 E
Oberdrauburg **150** 46 44N 12 58 E
Oberengadin **149** 46 35N 9 55 E
Oberentfelden **148** 47 21N 8 2 E
Oberhausen **146** 51 28N 6 50 E
Oberkirch **147** 48 31N 8 5 E
Oberland **148** 46 30N 7 30 E
Obernai **139** 48 28N 7 30 E
Oberndorf **147** 48 17N 8 35 E
Oberon **231** 33 45 S 149 52 E
Oberösterreich □ **150** 48 10N 14 0 E
Oberpfälzer Wald **147** 49 30N 12 25 E
Obersiggenthal **149** 47 29N 8 18 E
Oberstdorf **147** 47 25N 10 16 E
Oberting **252** 0 22 S 9 46 E
Oberwil **148** 47 32N 7 33 E
Obi, Kepulauan **207** 1 23 S 127 45 E
Obiaruku **247** 5 51N 6 9 E
Óbidos, Brazil **119** 1 50 S 55 30W
Óbidos, Portugal **155** 39 19N 9 10W
Obihiro **218** 42 56N 143 12 E
Obilatu **207** 1 25 S 127 20 E
Obilnoye **181** 47 32N 44 30 E
Obing **147** 48 0N 12 25 E
Öbisfelde **146** 52 27N 10 57 E
Objat **140** 45 16N 1 24 E
Obluchye **185** 49 1N 131 4 E
Obninsk **179** 55 8N 36 37 E
Obo, C.A.R. **250** 5 20N 26 32 E
Obo, Ethiopia **245** 3 46N 38 52 E
Oboa, Mt. **250** 1 45N 34 45 E
Obock **245** 12 0N 43 20 E
Obonga L. **86** 49 57N 89 22W
Oborniki **152** 52 39N 16 50 E
Oborniki Śląskie **152** 51 17N 16 53 E
Obouya **252** 0 56 S 15 43 E
Oboyan **179** 51 13N 36 37 E
Obrenovac **166** 44 40N 20 11 E
Obrovac **163** 44 11N 15 41 E
Observatory Inlet **76** 55 10N 129 54W
Obshchi Syrt **130** 52 0N 53 0 E
Obskaya Guba **184** 69 0N 73 0 E
Obuasi **247** 6 17N 1 40W
Obubra **247** 6 8N 8 20 E
Obwalden □ **148** 46 55N 8 15 E
Obyachevo **182** 60 20N 49 37 E
Obzor **167** 42 50N 27 52 E
Ocamo → **119** 2 48N 65 14W
Ocampo, Chihuahua, Mexico **101** 28 11N 108 23W
Ocampo, Coahuila, Mexico **102** 27 20N 102 21W
Ocampo, Guanajuato, Mexico **107** 21 39N 101 30W
Ocampo, Tamaulipas, Mexico **103** 22 50N 99 20W
Ocaña, Colombia **118** 8 15N 73 20W
Ocaña, Spain **156** 39 55N 3 30W
Occidental, Cordillera, Colombia **118** 5 0N 76 0W
Occidental, Cordillera, Peru **122** 14 0 S 74 0W
Ocean, I. = Banaba **224** 0 45 S 169 50 E
Ocean Falls **92** 52 18N 127 48W
Ochagavia **156** 42 55N 1 5W
Ochamchire **181** 42 46N 41 32 E
Ochamps **143** 49 56N 5 16 E
Ocher **182** 57 53N 54 42 E
Ochiai **220** 35 1N 133 45 E
Ochil Hills **134** 56 14N 3 40W
Ochre River **89** 51 4N 99 47W
Ochsenfurt **147** 49 38N 10 3 E
Ochsenhausen **147** 48 4N 9 57 E
Ockelbo **172** 60 54N 16 45 E
Ocna Mureş **170** 46 23N 23 55 E
Ocna Sibiului **170** 45 52N 24 2 E
Ocnele Mari **170** 45 8N 24 18 E
Ocoña **122** 16 26 S 73 8W
Ocoña → **122** 16 28 S 73 8W
Ocosingo **110** 16 53N 92 6W
Ocotal **112** 13 41N 86 31W
Ocotepec **110** 17 13N 93 9W
Ocotlán **106** 20 21N 102 46W
Ocotlán de Morelos **109** 16 48N 96 40W
Ocozocoautla de Espinosa **110** 16 46N 93 22W
Ocquier **143** 50 24N 5 24 E
Ocreza → **155** 39 32N 7 50W
Ócsa **151** 47 17N 19 15 E
Octeville **138** 49 38N 1 40W
Ocuilan **107** 18 58N 99 25W
Ocumare del Tuy **118** 10 7N 66 46W
Ocuri **123** 18 45 S 65 50W
Oda, Ghana **247** 5 50N 0 51W
Oda, Ehime, Japan **220** 33 36N 132 53 E
Ōda, Shimane, Japan **220** 35 11N 132 30 E
Oda, Jebel **244** 20 21N 36 39 E
Ódáðahraun **174** 65 5N 17 0W
Ödåkra **172** 56 7N 12 45 E
Odate **218** 40 16N 140 34 E
Odawara **221** 35 20N 139 6 E
Odda **171** 60 3N 6 35 E
Odder **173** 55 58N 10 10 E
Oddur **256** 4 11N 43 52 E
Ödeborg **173** 58 32N 11 58 E
Odei → **77** 56 6N 96 54W
Odemira **155** 37 35N 8 40W
Odendaalsrus **254** 27 48 S 26 45 E
Odense **173** 55 22N 10 23 E
Odenwald **147** 49 40N 9 0 E
Oder → **146** 53 33N 14 38 E
Oderzo **163** 45 47N 12 29 E
Odessa, Ont., Canada **85** 44 17N 76 43W
Odessa, Sask., Canada **88** 50 17N 103 47W
Odessa, U.S.S.R. **180** 46 30N 30 45 E
Odiakwe **254** 20 12 S 25 17 E
Odiel → **155** 37 10N 6 55W
Odienné **246** 9 30N 7 34W
Odiongan **210** 12 24N 121 59 E
Odobeşti **170** 45 43N 27 4 E
Odolanów **152** 51 34N 17 40 E
O'Donnell **210** 15 21N 120 27 E
Odoorn **142** 52 51N 6 51 E
Odorheiul Secuiesc **170** 46 21N 25 21 E
Odoyevo **179** 53 56N 36 42 E
Odra →, Poland **152** 53 33N 14 38 E
Odra →, Spain **154** 42 14N 4 17W
Odweina **256** 9 25N 45 4 E
Odžaci **166** 45 30N 19 17 E
Odžak **166** 45 3N 18 18 E
Oedelem **143** 51 10N 3 21 E
Oegstgeest **142** 52 11N 4 29 E
Oeiras, Brazil **120** 7 0 S 42 8W
Oeiras, Portugal **155** 38 41N 9 18W
Oelsnitz **146** 50 24N 12 11 E
Oenpelli **228** 12 20 S 133 4 E
Ofanto → **165** 41 22N 16 13 E
Offa **247** 8 13N 4 42 E
Offaly □ **135** 53 15N 7 30W
Offenbach **147** 50 6N 8 46 E
Offenburg **147** 48 29N 7 56 E
Offerdal **172** 63 28N 14 0 E
Offida **163** 42 56N 13 40 E
Offranville **138** 49 52N 1 0 E
Ofidhousa **169** 36 33N 26 8 E
Ofotfjorden **174** 68 27N 16 40 E
Ofu **226** 14 11 S 169 41W
Ōfunato **218** 39 4N 141 43 E
Oga **218** 39 55N 139 50 E
Oga-Hantō **218** 39 58N 139 47 E
Ogaden **256** 7 30N 45 30 E
Ogahalla **87** 50 6N 85 51W
Ōgaki **221** 35 21N 136 37 E
Ogan → **208** 3 1 S 104 44 E
Ogascanane, L. **82** 47 5N 78 25W
Ogbomosho **247** 8 1N 4 11 E
Ogema **88** 49 35N 104 55W
Ogilvie Mts. **94** 65 0N 140 0W
Oglio → **162** 45 2N 10 39 E
Ogmore **230** 22 37 S 149 35 E
Ogna **171** 58 31N 5 48 E
Ognon → **139** 47 16N 5 28 E
Ogoja **247** 6 38N 8 39 E
Ogoki **87** 51 38N 85 58W
Ogoki → **87** 51 38N 85 57W
Ogoki L. **87** 50 50N 87 10W
Ogoki Res. **86** 50 45N 88 15W
Ogooué → **252** 1 0 S 10 0 E
Ōgori **220** 34 6N 131 24 E
Ogosta → **167** 43 48N 23 55 E
Ogowe = Ogooué → **252** 1 0 S 10 0 E
Ogr = Sharafa **245** 11 59N 27 7 E
Ograżden **166** 41 30N 22 50 E
Ogrein **244** 17 55N 34 50 E
Oguira, B. **104** 25 38N 108 58W
Ogulin **163** 45 16N 15 16 E
Ogun □ **247** 7 0N 3 0 E
Oguni **220** 33 11N 131 8 E
Oguta **247** 5 44N 6 44 E
Oğuzeli **190** 36 58N 37 27 E
Ogwashi-Uku **247** 6 15N 6 30 E
Ogwe **247** 5 0N 7 14 E
Ohai **235** 44 55 S 168 0 E
Ohakune **234** 39 24 S 175 24 E
Ōhara **221** 35 15N 140 23 E
Ohata **218** 41 24N 141 10 E
Ohau, L. **235** 44 15 S 169 53 E
Ohaupo **234** 37 56 S 175 20 E
Ohey **143** 50 26N 5 8 E
Ohiwa Harbour **234** 37 59 S 177 10 E
Ohre →, Czech. **150** 50 30N 14 10 E
Ohre →, Germany **146** 52 18N 11 47 E
Ohrid **166** 41 8N 20 52 E
Ohridsko, Jezero **166** 41 8N 20 52 E
Ohrigstad **255** 24 19 S 30 36 E
Öhringen **147** 49 11N 9 31 E
Ohuisa **100** 28 37N 109 48W
Oiapoque → **119** 4 8N 51 40W
Oikou **215** 38 35N 117 42 E
Oil Springs **84** 42 47N 82 7W
Oinousa **169** 38 33N 26 14 E
Oirschot **143** 51 30N 5 18 E
Oise □ **139** 49 28N 2 30 E
Oise → **139** 49 0N 2 4 E
Oisterwijk **143** 51 35N 5 12 E
Ōita **220** 33 14N 131 36 E
Ōita □ **220** 33 15N 131 30 E
Oiticica **120** 5 3 S 41 5W
Ojinaga **101** 29 34N 104 25W
Ojiya **219** 37 18N 138 48 E
Ojo Caliente, Aguascalientes, Mexico **105** 21 53N 102 15W
Ojo Caliente, Chihuahua, Mexico **101** 27 41N 105 12W
Ojo de Agua, Chiapas, Mexico **110** 17 11N 91 41W
Ojo de Agua, Sonora, Mexico **100** 30 4N 109 47W
Ojo de Federico **101** 31 1N 107 52W
Ojo de Laguna **101** 29 27N 106 23W
Ojo de Liebre, L. **99** 27 45N 114 15W
Ojocaliente **105** 22 34N 102 15W
Ojos del Salado, Cerro **124** 27 0 S 68 40W
Ojuelos **105** 23 5N 102 42W
Ojuelos de Jalisco **107** 21 52N 101 35W
Oka → **179** 56 20N 43 59 E
Okaba **207** 8 6 S 139 42 E
Okahandja **254** 22 0 S 16 59 E
Okahukura **224** 38 48 S 175 14 E
Okaihau **234** 35 19 S 173 47 E
Okak **78** 57 33N 61 58W
Okak Is. **78** 57 30N 61 30W
Okanagan L. **93** 50 0N 119 30W
Okanagan Mission **93** 49 45N 119 30W
Okanagan Mountain Prov. Park **93** 49 45N 119 30W
Okandja **252** 0 35 S 13 45 E
Okány **151** 46 52N 21 21 E
Okapa **227** 6 38 S 145 39 E
Okaputa **254** 20 5 S 17 0 E
Okara **197** 30 50N 73 31 E
Okarito **235** 43 15 S 170 9 E
Okato **234** 39 12 S 173 53 E
Okaukuejo **254** 19 10 S 16 0 E
Okavango Swamps **254** 18 45 S 22 45 E
Okawa **220** 33 9N 130 21 E
Okaya **221** 36 0N 138 10 E
Okayama **220** 34 40N 133 54 E
Okayama □ **220** 35 0N 133 50 E
Okazaki **221** 34 57N 137 10 E
Oke-Iho **247** 8 1N 3 18 E
Okehampton **133** 50 44N 4 1W
Okene **247** 7 32N 6 11 E
Oker → **146** 52 30N 10 22 E
Okha **185** 53 40N 143 0 E
Ókhi Óros **169** 38 5N 24 25 E
Okhotsk **185** 59 20N 143 10 E
Okhotsk, Sea of **185** 55 0N 145 0 E
Okhotskiy Perevoz **185** 61 52N 135 35 E
Okhotsko Kolymskoye **185** 63 0N 157 0 E
Oki-no-Shima **220** 32 44N 132 33 E
Oki-Shotō **220** 36 5N 133 15 E
Okiep **254** 29 39 S 17 53 E
Okigwi **247** 5 52N 7 20 E
Okija **247** 5 54N 6 55 E
Okinawa □ **226** 26 40N 128 0 E
Okinawa-Guntō **219** 26 40N 128 0 E
Okinawa-Jima **219** 26 32N 128 0 E
Okino-erabu-Shima **219** 27 21N 128 33 E
Okitipupa **247** 6 31N 4 50 E
Oknitsa **180** 48 25N 27 30 E
Okolo **250** 2 37N 31 8 E
Okonek **152** 53 32N 16 51 E
Okrika **247** 4 40N 7 10 E
Oktabrsk **177** 49 28N 57 25 E
Oktyabr **183** 43 41N 77 12 E
Oktyabrsk **179** 53 11N 48 40 E

Oktyabrskiy, Byelorussian S.S.R., U.S.S.R. 178 52 38N 28 53 E
Oktyabrskiy, R.S.F.S.R., U.S.S.R. 182 54 28N 53 28 E
Oktyabrskoy Revolyutsii, Os. 185 79 30N 97 0 E
Oktyabrskoye = Zhovtnevoye 180 46 54N 32 3 E
Oktyabrskoye 184 62 28N 66 3 E
Oku 226 26 35N 127 50 E
Ōkuchi 220 32 4N 130 37 E
Okulovka 178 58 25N 33 19 E
Okuru 235 43 55 S 168 55 E
Okushiri-Tō 218 42 15N 139 30 E
Okuta 247 9 14N 3 12 E
Okwa → 254 22 30 S 23 0 E
Ólafsfjörður 174 66 4N 18 39W
Ólafsvík 174 64 53N 23 43W
Olanchito 112 15 30N 86 30W
Öland 173 56 45N 16 38 E
Olargues 140 43 34N 2 53 E
Olary 231 32 18 S 140 19 E
Olascoaga 124 35 15 S 60 39W
Olavarría 124 36 55 S 60 20W
Oława 152 50 57N 17 20 E
Ólbia 164 40 55N 9 30 E
Ólbia, G. di 164 40 55N 9 35 E
Old Bahama Chan. = Bahama, Canal Viejo de 112 22 10N 77 30W
Old Castile = Castilla La Vieja 154 41 55N 4 0W
Old Castle 135 53 46N 7 10W
Old Cork 230 22 57 S 141 52 E
Old Crow 94 67 30N 140 5 E
Old Dongola 244 18 11N 30 44 E
Old Fort → 77 58 36N 110 24W
Old Perlican 79 48 5N 53 1W
Old Shinyanga 250 3 33 S 33 27 E
Old Wives L. 88 50 5N 106 0W
Oldbury 133 51 38N 2 30W
Oldeani 250 3 22 S 35 35 E
Oldenburg, Niedersachsen, Germany 146 53 10N 8 10 E
Oldenburg, Schleswig-Holstein, Germany 146 54 16N 10 53 E
Oldenzaal 142 52 19N 6 53 E
Oldham 132 53 33N 2 8W
Oldman → 91 49 57N 111 42W
Olds 91 51 50N 114 10W
O'Leary 81 46 42N 64 13W
Olecko 152 54 2N 22 31 E
Oléggio 162 45 36N 8 38 E
Oleiros 154 39 56N 7 56W
Olekma → 185 60 22N 120 42 E
Olekminsk 185 60 25N 120 30 E
Olen 143 51 9N 4 52 E
Olenegorsk 176 68 9N 33 18 E
Olenek 185 68 28N 112 18 E
Olenek → 185 73 0N 120 10 E
Olenino 178 56 15N 33 30 E
Oléron, Île d' 140 45 55N 1 15W
Oleśnica 152 51 13N 17 22 E
Olesno 152 50 51N 18 26 E
Olevsk 178 51 12N 27 39 E
Olga 185 43 50N 135 14 E
Olga, L. 82 49 47N 77 15W
Olga, Mt. 229 25 20 S 130 50 E
Olgastretet 12 78 35N 25 0 E
Ølgod 173 55 49N 8 36 E
Olhão 155 37 3N 7 48W
Olib 163 44 23N 14 44 E
Olib, I. 163 44 23N 14 44 E
Oliena 164 40 18N 9 22 E
Oliete 156 41 1N 0 41W
Olifants → 255 24 5 S 31 20 E
Olifantshoek 254 27 57 S 22 42 E
Ólimbos 169 35 44N 27 11 E
Ólimbos, Óros 168 40 6N 22 23 E
Olímpia 125 20 44 S 48 54W
Olimpo □ 124 20 30 S 58 45W
Olinalá 107 17 50N 98 51W
Olinda 120 8 1 S 34 51W
Olindiná 120 11 22 S 38 21W
Olite 156 42 29N 1 40W
Oliva, Argentina 124 32 0 S 63 38W
Oliva, Spain 157 38 58N 0 9W
Oliva, Punta del 154 43 37N 5 28W
Oliva de la Frontera 155 38 17N 6 54W
Olivares 156 39 46N 2 20W
Oliveira 121 20 39 S 44 50W
Oliveira de Azemeis 154 40 49N 8 29W
Oliveira dos Brejinhos 121 12 19 S 42 54W
Olivenza 155 38 41N 7 9W
Oliver 93 49 13N 119 37W
Oliver L. 77 56 56N 103 22W
Olivine Ra. 235 44 15 S 168 30 E
Olivone 149 46 32N 8 57 E
Olkhovka 181 49 48N 44 32 E
Olkusz 152 50 18N 19 33 E
Ollagüe 124 21 15 S 68 10W
Olloy 143 50 5N 4 36 E
Olmedo 154 41 20N 4 43W
Olmos 122 5 59 S 79 46W
Olofström 173 56 17N 14 32 E
Oloma 247 3 29N 11 19 E
Olomane → 78 50 14N 60 37W
Olombo 252 1 18 S 15 53 E
Olomouc 151 49 38N 17 12 E
Olonets 176 61 10N 33 0 E
Olongapo 210 14 50N 120 18 E
Oloron, Gave d' 140 43 33N 1 5W
Oloron-Ste-Marie 140 43 11N 0 38W
Olosega, I. 226 14 11 S 169 38W
Olot 156 42 11N 2 30 E
Olovo 166 44 8N 18 35 E
Olovyannaya 185 50 58N 115 35 E
Oloy → 185 66 29N 159 29 E
Olpe 146 51 2N 7 50 E
Olshanka 180 48 16N 30 58 E
Olshany 180 50 3N 35 53 E
Olst 142 52 20N 6 7 E
Olsztyn 152 53 48N 20 29 E
Olsztyn □ 152 54 0N 21 0 E
Olsztynek 152 53 34N 20 19 E
Olt □ 170 44 20N 24 30 E
Olt → 170 43 50N 24 40 E
Olten 148 47 21N 7 53 E
Olteniţa 170 44 7N 26 42 E
Oluta 109 17 55N 94 54W
Olutanga 211 7 26N 122 54 E
Olutanga I. 211 7 22N 122 52 E
Olvega 156 41 47N 2 0W
Olvera 155 36 55N 5 18W
Olympia 169 37 39N 21 39 E
Olympus, Mt. = Ólimbos, Óros 168 40 6N 22 23 E
Om → 184 54 59N 73 22 E
Om Hajer 245 14 20N 36 41 E
Om Koi 204 17 48N 98 22 E
Ōma 218 41 45N 141 5 E
Ōmachi 221 36 30N 137 50 E
Omae-Zaki 221 34 36N 138 14 E
Ōmagari 218 39 27N 140 29 E
Omagh 135 54 36N 7 20W
Omagh □ 135 54 35N 7 15W
Oman ■ 195 23 0N 58 0 E
Oman, G. of 193 24 30N 58 30 E
Omar Combon 256 3 10N 45 47 E
Omaruru 254 21 26 S 16 0 E
Omaruru → 254 22 7 S 14 15 E
Omate 122 16 45 S 71 0W
Ombai, Selat 207 8 30 S 124 50 E
Ombo 171 59 18N 6 0 E
Omboué 252 1 35 S 9 15 E
Ombrone → 162 42 39N 11 0 E
Omchi 241 21 22N 17 53 E
Omdurmân 245 15 40N 32 28 E
Ōme 221 35 47N 139 15 E
Omegna 162 45 52N 8 23 E
Omemee 85 44 18N 78 33W
Omeonga 250 3 40 S 24 22 E
Ometepe, Isla de 112 11 32N 85 35W
Ometepec 107 16 41N 98 25W
Ometepec → 107 16 30N 98 45W
Omez 189 32 22N 35 0 E
Omi-Shima, Ehime, Japan 220 34 15N 133 0 E
Ōmi-Shima, Yamaguchi, Japan 220 34 25N 131 9 E
Omihachiman 221 35 7N 136 3 E
Ominato 218 41 17N 141 10 E
Omineca → 76 56 3N 124 16W
Omiš 163 43 28N 16 40 E
Omišalj 163 45 13N 14 32 E
Omitara 254 22 16 S 18 2 E
Omitlán → 107 17 6N 99 34W
Ōmiya 221 35 54N 139 38 E
Ommanney B. 95 73 0N 101 0W
Omme Å → 173 55 56N 8 32 E
Ommen 142 52 31N 6 26 E
Ömnögovĭ □ 214 43 15N 104 0 E
Omo → 245 6 25N 36 10 E
Omolon → 185 68 42N 158 36 E
Omono-Gawa → 218 39 46N 140 3 E
Omsk 184 55 0N 73 12 E
Omsukchan 185 62 32N 155 48 E
Ōmu 218 44 34N 142 58 E
Omul, Vf. 170 45 27N 25 29 E
Omulew → 152 53 5N 21 33 E
Ōmura 220 32 56N 130 0 E
Omura-Wan 220 32 57N 129 52 E
Omurtag 167 43 8N 26 26 E
Ōmuta 220 33 0N 130 26 E
Omutninsk 182 58 45N 52 4 E
On 143 50 11N 5 18 E
On-Take 220 31 35N 130 39 E
Oña 156 42 43N 3 25W
Onakawana 87 50 36N 81 27W
Onaman → 87 49 59N 88 0W
Onaman L. 87 50 0N 87 26W
Onang 207 3 2 S 118 49 E
Onanole 89 50 37N 99 58W
Onaping 84 46 37N 81 25W
Onaping → 84 46 37N 81 18W
Onaping L. 87 47 3N 81 30W
Onarhā 197 35 30N 71 0 E
Onarheim 171 59 57N 5 35 E
Onatchiway, L. 83 49 3N 71 5W
Oñate 156 43 3N 2 25W
Onavas 100 28 31N 109 35W
Oncesti 170 43 56N 25 52 E
Oncócua 254 16 30 S 13 25 E
Onda 156 39 55N 0 17W
Ondaejin 215 41 34N 129 40 E
Ondangua 254 17 57 S 16 4 E
Ondárroa 156 43 19N 2 25W
Ondas → 121 12 8 S 45 0W
Ondava → 151 48 27N 21 48 E
Onderdijk 142 52 45N 5 8 E
Ondjiva 254 16 48 S 15 50 E
Ondo, Japan 220 34 11N 132 32 E
Ondo, Nigeria 247 7 4N 4 47 E
Ondo □ 247 7 0N 5 0 E
Öndörshil 214 45 13N 108 5 E
Öndverðarnes 174 64 52N 24 0W
Onega 176 64 0N 38 10 E
Onega → 176 63 58N 37 55 E
Onega, G. of = Onezhskaya Guba 176 64 30N 37 0 E
Onega, L. = Onezhskoye Ozero 176 62 0N 35 30 E
Onehunga 234 36 55 S 174 48 E
Onekotan, Ostrov 185 49 25N 154 45 E
Onema 250 4 35 S 24 30 E
Onerahi 234 35 45 S 174 22 E
Onezhskaya Guba 176 64 30N 37 0 E
Onezhskoye Ozero 176 62 0N 35 30 E
Ongarue 234 38 42 S 175 19 E
Ongea Levu 226 19 8 S 178 24W
Ongerup 229 33 58 S 118 28 E
Ongjin 215 37 56N 125 21 E
Ongkharak 204 14 8N 101 1 E
Ongniud Qi 215 43 0N 118 38 E
Ongoka 250 1 20 S 26 0 E
Ongole 201 15 33N 80 2 E
Ongon 214 45 41N 113 5 E
Onguren 185 53 38N 107 36 E
Onhaye 143 50 15N 4 50 E
Oni 181 42 33N 43 26 E
Onilahy → 255 23 34 S 43 45 E
Onion Lake 88 53 43N 110 0W
Onitsha 247 6 6N 6 42 E
Onmaka 202 22 17N 96 41 E
Ono, Fiji 226 18 55 S 178 29 E
Ono, Fukui, Japan 221 35 59N 136 29 E
Ono, Hyōgo, Japan 220 34 51N 134 56 E
Onoda 220 34 2N 131 25 E
Onomichi 220 34 25N 133 12 E
Onoway 90 53 42N 114 12W
Onpyŏng-ni 215 33 25N 126 55 E
Ons, Islas d' 154 42 23N 8 55W
Onsala 173 57 26N 12 0 E
Onslow 228 21 40 S 115 12 E
Onstwedde 142 53 2N 7 4 E
Ontake-San 221 35 53N 137 29 E
Ontaneda 154 43 12N 3 57W
Ontario □ 74 52 0N 88 10W
Ontario, L. 85 43 40N 78 0W
Onteniente 157 38 50N 0 35W
Ontur 157 38 38N 1 29W
Oodnadatta 231 27 33 S 135 30 E
Ooldea 229 30 27 S 131 50 E
Ooltgensplaat 143 51 41N 4 21 E
Oona River 92 53 57N 130 16W
Oordegem 143 50 58N 3 54 E
Oorindi 230 20 40 S 141 1 E
Oost-Vlaanderen □ 143 51 5N 3 50 E
Oost-Vlieland 142 53 18N 5 4 E
Oostakker 143 51 6N 3 46 E
Oostburg 143 51 19N 3 30 E
Oostduinkerke 143 51 7N 2 41 E
Oostelijk-Flevoland 142 52 31N 5 38 E
Oostende 143 51 15N 2 50 E
Oosterbeek 142 51 59N 5 51 E
Oosterdijk 142 52 44N 5 14 E
Oosterend, Friesland, Neth. 142 53 24N 5 23 E
Oosterend, Noord-Holland, Neth. 142 53 5N 4 52 E
Oosterhout, Noord-Brabant, Neth. 143 51 53N 5 50 E
Oosterhout, Noord-Brabant, Neth. 143 51 39N 4 47 E
Oosterschelde 143 51 33N 4 0 E
Oosterwolde 142 53 0N 6 17 E
Oosterzele 143 50 57N 3 48 E
Oostkamp 143 51 9N 3 14 E
Oostmalle 143 51 18N 4 44 E
Oostrozebekke 143 50 55N 3 21 E
Oostvleteven 143 50 56N 2 45 E
Oostvoorne 142 51 55N 4 5 E
Oostzaan 142 52 26N 4 52 E
Ootacamund 201 11 30N 76 44 E
Ootha 233 33 6 S 147 29 E
Ootmarsum 142 52 24N 6 54 E
Ootsa L. 92 53 50N 126 2W
Ootsa Lake 92 53 50N 126 5W
Opaka 167 43 28N 26 10 E
Opal 105 24 15N 102 18W
Opala, U.S.S.R. 185 51 58N 156 30 E
Opala, Zaïre 250 0 40 S 24 20 E
Opalenica 152 52 18N 16 24 E
Opan 167 42 13N 25 41 E
Opanake 201 6 35N 80 40 E
Opapa 234 39 47 S 176 42 E
Opasatica, L. 82 48 5N 79 18W
Opasatika 87 49 30N 82 50W
Opasatika → 87 50 25N 82 25W
Opasatika L. 87 49 4N 83 6W
Opasquia 77 53 16N 93 34W
Opataca, L. 82 50 22N 74 55W
Opatija 163 45 21N 14 17 E
Opatów 152 50 50N 21 27 E
Opava 151 49 57N 17 58 E
Opawica, L. 82 49 35N 75 55W
Opeinde 142 53 8N 6 4 E
Opémisca, L. 82 49 56N 74 52W
Open Bay Is. 235 43 51 S 168 51 E
Opeongo L. 85 45 42N 78 23W
Opglabbeek 143 51 3N 5 35 E
Ophthalmia Ra. 228 23 15 S 119 30 E
Opi 247 6 36N 7 28 E
Opichén 111 20 33N 89 51W
Opinaca → 78 52 15N 78 2W
Opinaca L. 78 52 39N 76 20W
Opiscoteo, L. 78 53 10N 68 10W
Opiskotish, L. 78 53 10N 67 50W
Oploo 143 51 37N 5 52 E
Opmeer 142 52 42N 4 57 E
Opobo 247 4 35N 7 34 E
Opochka 178 56 42N 28 45 E
Opocopa, L. 80 52 38N 66 35W
Opoczno 152 51 22N 20 18 E
Opodepe 100 29 55N 110 39W
Opol 211 8 31N 124 34 E
Opole 152 50 42N 17 58 E
Opole □ 152 50 40N 17 56 E
Opon = Capu-Lapu 211 10 20N 123 55 E
Opopeo 107 19 24N 101 36W
Oporto = Porto 154 41 8N 8 40W
Opotiki 234 38 1 S 177 19 E
Oppegård 171 59 48N 10 48 E
Oppenheim 147 49 50N 8 22 E
Opperdoes 142 52 45N 5 4 E
Óppido Mamertina 165 38 16N 15 59 E
Oppland fylke □ 171 61 15N 9 40 E
Oppstad 171 60 17N 11 40 E
Oprtalj 163 45 23N 13 50 E
Opua 234 35 19 S 174 9 E
Opunake 234 39 26 S 173 52 E
Opuzen 166 43 1N 17 34 E
Oquitoa 100 30 44N 111 41W
Or Yehuda 189 32 2N 34 50 E
Ora, Israel 189 30 55N 35 1 E
Ora, Italy 163 46 20N 11 19 E
Ora Banda 229 30 20 S 121 0 E
Oradea 170 47 2N 21 58 E
Öræfajökull 174 64 2N 16 39W
Orahovac 166 42 24N 20 40 E
Orahovica 166 45 35N 17 52 E
Orai 199 25 58N 79 30 E
Oraison 141 43 55N 5 55 E
Oran, Algeria 241 35 45N 0 39W
Oran, Argentina 124 23 10 S 64 20W
Orange, Australia 231 33 15 S 149 7 E
Orange, France 141 44 8N 4 47 E
Orange, C. 119 4 20N 51 30W
Orange Free State = Oranje Vrystaat □ 254 28 30 S 27 0 E
Orangeville 84 43 55N 80 5W
Orani 210 14 49N 120 32 E
Oranienburg 146 52 45N 13 15 E
Oranje → 254 28 41 S 16 28 E
Oranje Vrystaat □ 254 28 30 S 27 0 E
Oranjemund 254 28 38 S 16 29 E
Or'Aquiva 189 32 30N 34 54 E
Oras 210 12 9N 125 28 E
Orašje 166 45 1N 18 42 E
Orăştie 170 45 50N 23 10 E
Oraşul Stalin = Braşov 170 45 38N 25 35 E
Orava → 151 49 24N 19 20 E
Oravita 166 45 2N 21 43 E
Orawia 235 46 1 S 167 50 E
Oraya, La 122 11 32 S 75 54W
Orb → 140 43 17N 3 17 E
Orba → 162 44 53N 8 37 E
Ørbæk 173 55 17N 10 39 E
Orbe 148 46 43N 6 32 E
Orbec 138 49 1N 0 23 E
Orbetello 163 42 26N 11 11 E
Órbigo → 154 42 5N 5 42W
Orbost 231 37 40 S 148 29 E
Örbyhus 172 60 15N 17 43 E
Orcadas 13 60 44 S 44 37W
Orce 157 37 44N 2 28W

Orce → **157** 37 44N 2 28W
Orchies **139** 50 28N 3 14 E
Orchila, Isla **118** 11 48N 66 10W
Orco → **162** 45 10N 7 52 E
Orcopampa **122** 15 20 S 72 23W
Ord → **228** 15 33 S 138 15 E
Ord, Mt. **228** 17 20 S 125 34 E
Ordenes **154** 43 5N 8 29W
Ordos = Mu Us Shamo **214** 39 0N 109 0 E
Orduña, Álava, Spain **156** 42 58N 2 58 E
Orduña, Granada, Spain **157** 37 20N 3 30W
Ordzhonikidze, N. Ossetian A.S.S.R., U.S.S.R. **181** 43 0N 44 35 E
Ordzhonikidze, Ukraine S.S.R., U.S.S.R. **180** 47 39N 34 3 E
Ordzhonikidze, Uzbek S.S.R., U.S.S.R. **183** 41 21N 69 22 E
Ordzhonikidzeabad **183** 38 34N 69 1 E
Ore, Sweden **172** 61 8N 15 10 E
Ore, Zaïre **250** 3 17N 29 30 E
Ore Mts. = Erzgebirge **146** 50 25N 13 0 E
Orealla **119** 5 15N 57 23W
Orebić **166** 43 0N 17 11 E
Örebro **172** 59 20N 15 18 E
Örebro län □ **172** 59 27N 15 0 E
Öregrund **172** 60 21N 18 30 E
Öregrundsgrepen **172** 60 25N 18 15 E
Orekhov **180** 47 30N 35 48 E
Orekhovo-Zuyevo **179** 55 50N 38 55 E
Orel **179** 52 57N 36 3 E
Orel → **180** 48 30N 34 54 E
Orellana, Canal de **155** 39 2N 6 0W
Orellana, Pantano de **155** 39 5N 5 10W
Orellana la Vieja **155** 39 1N 5 32W
Oren **169** 37 3N 27 57 E
Orenburg **182** 51 45N 55 6 E
Orense **154** 42 19N 7 55W
Orense □ **154** 42 15N 7 51W
Orepuki **235** 46 19 S 167 46 E
Orestiás **168** 41 30N 26 33 E
Øresund **172** 55 45N 12 45 E
Oreti → **235** 46 28 S 168 14 E
Orford Ness **133** 52 6N 1 31 E
Orgaña **156** 42 13N 1 20 E
Orgaz **155** 39 39N 3 53W
Orgeyev **180** 47 24N 28 50 E
Orgon **141** 43 47N 5 3 E
Orgūn **197** 32 55N 69 12 E
Orhon Gol → **212** 49 30N 106 0 E
Oria **165** 40 30N 17 38 E
Orient **231** 28 7 S 142 50 E
Oriental **108** 19 22N 97 37W
Oriental, Cordillera, Bolivia **123** 17 0 S 66 0W
Oriental, Cordillera, Colombia **118** 6 0N 73 0W
Oriental, L. **109** 16 15N 94 36W
Oriente **124** 38 44 S 60 37W
Origny-Ste-Benoîte **139** 49 50N 3 30 E
Orihuela **157** 38 7N 0 55W
Orihuela del Tremedal **156** 40 33N 1 39W
Oriku **168** 40 20N 19 30 E
Orillia **84** 44 40N 79 24W
Orinduik **119** 4 40N 60 3W
Orinoco → **119** 9 15N 61 30W
Orissa □ **199** 20 0N 84 0 E
Oristano **164** 39 54N 8 35 E
Oristano, Golfo di **164** 39 50N 8 22 E
Orituco → **118** 8 45N 67 27W
Orizaba **109** 18 51N 97 6W
Orizare **167** 42 44N 27 39 E
Orizatlán **107** 21 11N 98 37W
Orizona **121** 17 3 S 48 18W
Ørje **171** 59 29N 11 39 E
Orjen **166** 42 35N 18 34 E
Orjiva **157** 36 53N 3 24W
Orkanger **171** 63 18N 9 52 E
Orkelljunga **173** 56 17N 13 17 E
Örkény **151** 47 9N 19 26 E
Orkla → **171** 63 18N 9 51 E
Orkney **254** 26 58 S 26 40 E
Orkney □ **134** 59 0N 3 0W
Orkney Is. **134** 59 0N 3 0W
Orla **152** 52 42N 23 20 E
Orlando, C. d' **165** 38 10N 14 43 E
Orléanais **139** 48 0N 2 0 E
Orléans **139** 47 54N 1 52 E
Orléans, Î. d' **83** 46 54N 70 58W
Orlice → **150** 50 5N 16 10 E
Orlické Hory **151** 50 15N 16 30 E
Orlik **185** 52 30N 99 55 E
Orlov **151** 49 17N 20 51 E
Orlov Gay **179** 50 56N 48 19 E
Orlovat **166** 45 14N 20 33 E
Ormara **197** 25 16N 64 33 E
Ormea **162** 44 9N 7 54 E
Ormília **168** 40 16N 23 39 E
Ormiston **88** 49 44N 105 24W
Ormoc **211** 11 0N 124 37 E
Ormond **234** 38 33 S 177 56 E
Ormondville **234** 40 5 S 176 19 E
Ormož **163** 46 25N 16 10 E
Ormstown **83** 45 8N 74 0W
Ornans **139** 47 7N 6 10 E
Orne □ **138** 48 40N 0 5 E
Orne → **138** 49 18N 0 15W
Orneta **152** 54 8N 20 9 E
Ørnhøj **173** 56 13N 8 34 E
Ornö **172** 59 4N 18 24 E
Örnsköldsvik **172** 63 17N 18 40 E
Oro **215** 40 1N 127 27 E
Oro, R. del → **104** 25 35N 105 3W
Orocué **118** 4 48N 71 20W
Orodo **247** 5 34N 7 4 E
Orol **154** 43 34N 7 39W
Oromocto **81** 45 54N 66 29W
Oromocto, L. **81** 45 36N 67 0W
Oron, Nigeria **247** 4 48N 8 14 E
Oron, Switz. **148** 46 34N 6 50 E
Orono **85** 43 59N 78 37W
Oropesa **154** 39 57N 5 10W
Oroqen Zizhiqi **213** 50 34N 123 43 E
Oroquieta **211** 8 32N 123 44 E
Orós **120** 6 15 S 38 55W
Orosei, G. di **164** 40 15N 9 40 E
Orosháza **151** 46 32N 20 42 E
Orote Pen. **226** 13 26N 144 38 E
Orotukan **185** 62 16N 151 42 E
Orrefors **173** 56 50N 15 45 E
Orroroo **231** 32 43 S 138 38 E
Orsa **172** 61 7N 14 37 E
Orsara di Púglia **165** 41 17N 15 16 E
Orsasjön **172** 61 7N 14 37 E
Orsha **178** 54 30N 30 25 E
Orsières **148** 46 2N 7 9 E
Orsk **182** 51 12N 58 34 E
Ørslev **172** 55 3N 11 56 E
Orsogna **163** 42 13N 14 17 E
Orşova **170** 44 41N 22 25 E
Ørsted **173** 56 30N 10 20 E
Orta, L. d' **162** 45 48N 8 21 E
Orta Nova **165** 41 20N 15 40 E
Orte **163** 42 28N 12 23 E
Ortegal, C. **154** 43 43N 7 52W
Orteguaza → **118** 0 43N 75 16W
Orthez **140** 43 29N 0 48W
Ortho **143** 50 8N 5 37 E
Ortigueira **154** 43 40N 7 50W
Ortiz, Chihuahua, Mexico **101** 28 15N 105 31W
Ortiz, Sonora, Mexico **100** 28 17N 110 43W
Ortles **162** 46 31N 10 33 E
Orto, Tokay **183** 42 20N 76 1 E
Ortón → **122** 10 50 S 67 0W
Ortona **163** 42 21N 14 24 E
Orūmīyeh **192** 37 40N 45 0 E
Orūmīyeh, Daryācheh-ye **192** 37 50N 45 30 E
Orune **164** 40 25N 9 20 E
Oruro **122** 18 0 S 67 9W
Oruro □ **122** 18 40 S 67 30W
Orust **173** 58 10N 11 40 E
Oruzgān □ **197** 33 30N 66 0 E
Orvault **138** 47 17N 1 38W
Orvieto **163** 42 43N 12 8 E
Orwell → **133** 52 2N 1 12 E
Oryakhovo **167** 43 40N 23 57 E
Orzinuovi **162** 45 24N 9 55 E
Orzyc → **152** 52 46N 21 14 E
Orzysz **152** 53 50N 21 58 E
Os **171** 60 9N 5 30 E
Osa **182** 57 17N 55 26 E
Osa → **152** 53 33N 18 46 E
Osa, Pen. de **112** 8 0N 84 0W
Ōsaka **221** 34 40N 135 30 E
Osaka □ **221** 34 30N 135 30 E
Ōsaka-Wan **221** 34 30N 135 18 E
Osan **215** 37 11N 127 4 E
Osawin → **87** 49 45N 85 19W
Osby **173** 56 23N 13 59 E
Oschatz **146** 51 17N 13 8 E
Oschersleben **146** 52 2N 11 13 E
Óschiri **164** 40 43N 9 7 E
Osečina **166** 44 23N 19 34 E
Ösel = Saaremaa **178** 58 30N 22 30 E
Osëry **179** 54 52N 38 28 E
Osgoode **85** 45 8N 75 36W
Osh **183** 40 37N 72 49 E
Oshawa **85** 43 50N 78 50W
Oshima **220** 33 55N 132 14 E
Oshmyany **178** 54 26N 25 52 E
Oshnovīyeh **192** 37 2N 45 6 E
Oshogbo **247** 7 48N 4 37 E
Oshtorīnān **193** 34 1N 48 38 E
Oshwe **252** 3 25 S 19 28 E
Osica de Jos **170** 44 14N 24 20 E
Osieczna **152** 51 55N 16 40 E
Osijek **166** 45 34N 18 41 E
Osilo **164** 40 45N 8 41 E
Osimo **163** 43 28N 13 30 E
Osintorf **178** 54 40N 30 39 E
Osipenko = Berdyansk **180** 46 45N 36 50 E
Osipovichi **178** 53 19N 28 33 E
Oskarshamn **173** 57 15N 16 27 E
Oskélanéo **82** 48 5N 75 15W
Oskol → **179** 49 6N 37 25 E
Osler **88** 52 22N 106 33W
Oslo **171** 59 55N 10 45 E
Oslob **211** 9 31N 123 26 E
Oslofjorden **171** 59 20N 10 35 E
Osmanabad **200** 18 5N 76 10 E
Osmancık **180** 40 45N 34 47 E
Osmaniye **177** 37 5N 36 10 E
Ösmo **172** 58 58N 17 55 E
Osnabrück **146** 52 16N 8 2 E
Osnaburgh L. **86** 51 12N 90 9W
Ośno Lubuskie **152** 52 28N 14 51 E
Oso, Sa. del **104** 26 13N 105 29W
Osoblaha **151** 50 17N 17 44 E
Osogovska Planina **166** 42 10N 22 30 E
Osor **162** 44 42N 14 24 E
Osorio **125** 29 53 S 50 17W
Osorno, Chile **126** 40 25 S 73 0W
Osorno, Spain **154** 42 24N 4 22W
Osorno □ **126** 40 34 S 73 9W
Osorno, Vol. **126** 41 0 S 72 30W
Osoyoos **93** 49 0N 119 30W
Osoyoos L. **93** 49 0N 119 27W
Ospika → **76** 56 20N 124 0W
Osprey Reef **230** 13 52 S 146 36 E
Oss **142** 51 46N 5 32 E
Ossa, Mt. **230** 41 52 S 146 3 E
Óssa, Oros **168** 39 47N 22 42 E
Ossa de Montiel **157** 38 58N 2 45W
Osse → **140** 44 7N 0 17 E
Ossendrecht **143** 51 24N 4 20 E
Ossokmanuan L. **78** 53 25N 65 0W
Ossora **185** 59 20N 163 13 E
Ostaboningue, L. **82** 47 9N 78 53W
Ostashkov **178** 57 4N 33 2 E
Oste → **146** 53 30N 9 12 E
Ostend = Oostende **143** 51 15N 2 50 E
Oster **178** 50 57N 30 53 E
Osterburg **146** 52 47N 11 44 E
Osterburken **147** 49 26N 9 25 E
Österbybruk **172** 60 13N 17 55 E
Österbymo **173** 57 49N 15 15 E
Östergötlands län □ **173** 58 35N 15 45 E
Osterholz-Scharmbeck **146** 53 14N 8 48 E
Østerild **173** 57 2N 8 51 E
Österkorsberga **173** 57 18N 15 6 E
Ostermundigen **148** 46 58N 7 30 E
Osterøya **171** 60 32N 5 30 E
Östersund **172** 63 10N 14 38 E
Østfold fylke □ **171** 59 25N 11 25 E
Ostfriesische Inseln **146** 53 45N 7 15 E
Ostfriesland **146** 53 20N 7 30 E
Óstia, Lido di **164** 41 43N 12 17 E
Ostiglía **163** 45 4N 11 9 E
Ostion, L. **109** 18 11N 94 38W
Ostra **163** 43 40N 13 5 E
Ostrava **151** 49 51N 18 18 E
Ostróda **152** 53 42N 19 58 E
Ostrog **178** 50 20N 26 30 E
Ostrogozhsk **179** 50 55N 39 7 E
Ostrogróg Szamotuły **152** 52 37N 16 33 E
Ostrołeka **152** 53 4N 21 32 E
Ostrołeka □ **152** 53 0N 21 30 E
Ostrov, Bulgaria **167** 43 40N 24 9 E
Ostrov, Romania **170** 44 6N 27 24 E
Ostrov, U.S.S.R. **178** 57 25N 28 20 E
Ostrów Lubelski **152** 51 29N 22 51 E
Ostrów Mazowiecka **152** 52 50N 21 51 E
Ostrów Wielkopolski **152** 51 36N 17 44 E
Ostrowiec-Świętokrzyski **152** 50 55N 21 22 E
Ostrozac **166** 43 43N 17 49 E
Ostrzeszów **152** 51 25N 17 52 E
Ostseebad-Kühlungsborn **146** 54 10N 11 40 E
Ostula **106** 18 30N 103 28W
Ostuni **165** 40 44N 17 34 E
O'Sullivan L. **87** 50 25N 87 2W
Osum → **167** 43 40N 24 50 E
Osumi → **168** 40 40N 20 10 E
Ōsumi-Hantō **220** 31 20N 130 55 E
Ōsumi-Kaikyō **219** 30 55N 131 0 E
Ōsumi-Shotō **219** 30 30N 130 0 E
Osuna **155** 37 14N 5 8W
Oswestry **132** 52 52N 3 3W
Oświecim **152** 50 2N 19 11 E
Ōta **221** 36 18N 139 22 E
Ota-Gawa → **220** 34 21N 132 18 E
Otago □ **235** 44 44 S 169 10 E
Otago Harb. **235** 45 47 S 170 42 E
Otago Pen. **235** 45 48 S 170 39 E
Otahuhu **234** 36 56 S 174 51 E
Ōtake **220** 34 12N 132 13 E
Ōtaki, Japan **221** 35 17N 140 15 E
Otaki, N.Z. **234** 40 45 S 175 10 E
Otane **234** 39 54 S 176 39 E
Otar **183** 43 32N 75 12 E
Otaru **218** 43 10N 141 0 E
Otaru-Wan = Ishikari-Wan **218** 43 25N 141 1 E
Otates **106** 20 55N 101 53W
Otatitlán **109** 18 12N 96 2W
Otautau **235** 46 9 S 168 1 E
Otava → **150** 49 26N 14 12 E
Otavalo **118** 0 13N 78 20W
Otavi **254** 19 40 S 17 24 E
Otchinjau **254** 16 30 S 13 56 E
Otelec **170** 45 36N 20 50 E
Otelnuk L. **78** 56 9N 68 12W
Otero de Rey **154** 43 6N 7 36W
Othonoí **168** 39 52N 19 22 E
Óthris, Óros **169** 39 4N 22 42 E
Otinapa **104** 24 11N 105 2W
Otira **235** 42 49 S 171 35 E
Otira Gorge **235** 42 53 S 171 33 E
Otish, Mts. **78** 52 22N 70 30W
Otjiwarongo **254** 20 30 S 16 33 E
Otmuchów **152** 50 28N 17 10 E
Otočac **163** 44 53N 15 12 E
Otoineppu **218** 44 44N 142 16 E
Oton **211** 10 42N 122 29 E
Otorohanga **234** 38 12 S 175 14 E
Otoskwin → **74** 52 13N 88 6W
Otosquen **89** 53 17N 102 1W
Ōtoyo **220** 33 43N 133 45 E
Otra → **171** 58 8N 8 1 E
Otranto **165** 40 9N 18 28 E
Otranto, C. d' **165** 40 7N 18 30 E
Otranto, Str. of **165** 40 15N 18 40 E
Otse **254** 25 2 S 25 45 E
Ōtsu **221** 35 0N 135 50 E
Ōtsuki **221** 35 36N 138 57 E
Otta **171** 61 46N 9 32 E
Otta → **171** 61 46N 9 31 E
Ottapalam **201** 10 46N 76 23 E
Ottawa = Outaouais → **83** 45 27N 74 8W
Ottawa **85** 45 27N 75 42W
Ottawa Is. **95** 59 35N 80 10W
Ottélé **247** 3 38N 11 19 E
Ottenby **173** 56 15N 16 24 E
Otter L. **77** 55 35N 104 39W
Otter Rapids, Ont., Canada **87** 50 11N 81 39W
Otter Rapids, Sask., Canada **77** 55 38N 104 44W
Otterberg **147** 49 30N 7 46 E
Otterndorf **146** 53 47N 8 52 E
Ottersheim **150** 48 21N 14 12 E
Otterup **173** 55 30N 10 22 E
Otterville **84** 42 55N 80 36W
Ottignies **143** 50 40N 4 33 E
Otto Beit Bridge **251** 15 59 S 28 56 E
Ottosdal **254** 26 46 S 25 59 E
Ottoshoop **254** 25 45 S 25 58 E
Ottsjö **172** 63 13N 13 2 E
Otu **247** 8 14N 3 22 E
Otukpa **247** 7 9N 7 41 E
Otumba **107** 19 42N 98 45W
Oturkpo **247** 7 16N 8 8 E
Otway, Bahía **126** 53 30 S 74 0W
Otway, C. **231** 38 52 S 143 30 E
Otwock **152** 52 5N 21 20 E
Ötz **150** 47 13N 10 53 E
Ötz → **150** 47 14N 10 50 E
Otzoloapan **107** 19 0N 100 16W
Ötztaler Alpen **150** 46 45N 11 0 E
Ou → **204** 20 4N 102 13 E
Ou Neua **204** 22 18N 101 48 E
Ou-Sammyaku **218** 39 20N 140 35 E
Ouaco **226** 20 50 S 164 29 E
Ouadâne **240** 20 50N 11 40W
Ouadda **252** 8 15N 22 20 E
Ouagadougou **247** 12 25N 1 30W
Ouagam **243** 14 22N 14 42 E
Ouahigouya **246** 13 31N 2 25W
Ouahila **240** 27 50N 5 0W
Ouahran = Oran **241** 35 45N 0 39W
Oualâta **246** 17 20N 6 55W
Ouallene **240** 24 41N 1 11 E
Ouanda Djallé **252** 8 55N 22 53 E
Ouandago **252** 7 13N 18 50 E
Ouango **252** 4 19N 22 30 E
Ouarâne **240** 21 0N 10 30W
Ouareau, L., Rés. **83** 46 17N 74 9W
Ouargla **241** 31 59N 5 16 E
Ouarkziz, Djebel **240** 28 50N 8 0W
Ouarzazate **240** 30 55N 6 50W
Ouasiemsca → **83** 49 0N 72 30W
Ouatagouna **247** 15 11N 0 43 E
Ouatere **252** 5 30N 19 8 E
Oubangi → **252** 1 0N 17 50 E
Oubarakai, O. → **241** 27 20N 9 0 E
Oubatche **226** 20 26 S 164 39 E
Ouche → **139** 47 6N 5 16 E
Oud-Beijerland **142** 51 50N 4 25 E
Oud-Gastel **143** 51 35N 4 28 E
Oud Turnhout **143** 51 19N 5 0 E
Ouddorp **142** 51 50N 3 57 E

Oude-Pekela 142 53 6N 7 0 E
Oude Rijn → 142 52 12N 4 24 E
Oudega 142 53 8N 6 0 E
Oudenaarde 143 50 50N 3 37 E
Oudenbosch 143 51 35N 4 32 E
Oudenburg 143 51 11N 3 1 E
Ouderkerk, Utrecht, Neth. 142 52 18N 4 55 E
Ouderkerk, Zuid-Holland, Neth. 142 51 56N 4 38 E
Oudeschild 142 53 2N 4 50 E
Oudewater 142 52 2N 4 52 E
Oudkarspel 142 52 43N 4 49 E
Oudon 138 47 22N 1 19W
Oudon → 138 47 38N 1 18 E
Oudtshoorn 254 33 35 S 22 14 E
Oued Zem 240 32 52N 6 34W
Ouégoa 226 20 20 S 164 26 E
Ouellé 246 7 26N 4 1W
Ouen, Î. 226 22 26 S 166 49 E
Ouenza 241 35 57N 8 4 E
Ouessa 246 11 4N 2 47W
Ouessant, Île d' 138 48 28N 5 6W
Ouesso 252 1 37N 16 5 E
Ouest, Pte. 80 49 52N 64 40W
Ouezzane 240 34 51N 5 35W
Ouffet 143 50 26N 5 28 E
Ouidah 247 6 25N 2 0 E
Ouistreham 138 49 17N 0 18W
Oujda 240 34 41N 1 55W
Oujeft 240 20 2N 13 0W
Ould Yenjé 246 15 38N 12 16W
Ouled Djellal 241 34 28N 5 2 E
Ouled Naïl, Mts. des 241 34 30N 3 30 E
Oulmès 240 33 17N 6 0W
Oulu 174 65 1N 25 29 E
Oulujärvi 174 64 25N 27 15 E
Oulujoki → 174 65 1N 25 30 E
Oulun lääni □ 174 64 36N 27 20 E
Oulx 162 45 2N 6 49 E
Oum Chalouba 243 15 48N 20 46 E
Oum-el-Bouaghi 241 35 55N 7 6 E
Oum el Ksi 240 29 4N 6 59W
Oum-er-Rbia, O. → 240 33 19N 8 21W
Oumè 246 6 21N 5 27W
Ounane, Dj. 241 25 4N 7 19 E
Ounasjoki → 174 66 31N 25 30 E
Ounguati 254 21 54 S 15 46 E
Ounianga-Kébir 243 19 4N 20 29 E
Ounianga Sérir 243 18 54N 19 51 E
Our → 143 49 55N 6 5 E
Ourcq → 139 49 1N 3 1 E
Oureg, Oued el → 241 32 34N 2 10 E
Ourém 120 1 33 S 47 6W
Ouricuri 120 7 53 S 40 5W
Ourinhos 125 23 0 S 49 54W
Ourique 155 37 38N 8 16W
Ouro Fino 125 22 16 S 46 25W
Ouro Prêto 125 20 20 S 43 30W
Ouro Sogui 246 15 36N 13 19W
Oursi 247 14 41N 0 27W
Ourthe → 143 50 29N 5 35 E
Ouse 230 42 38 S 146 42 E
Ouse →, E. Sussex, U.K. 133 50 43N 0 3 E
Ouse →, N. Yorks., U.K. 132 54 3N 0 7 E
Oust 140 42 52N 1 13 E
Oust → 138 47 35N 2 6W
Outaouais → 83 45 27N 74 8W
Outardes 83 50 20N 69 10W
Outardes → 83 49 24N 69 30W
Outat Oulad el Haj 241 33 22N 3 42W
Outer Hebrides 134 57 30N 7 40W
Outer I. 78 51 10N 58 35W
Outes 154 42 52N 8 55W
Outjo 254 20 5 S 16 7 E
Outlook 88 51 30N 107 0W
Outreau 139 50 40N 1 36 E
Ouvèze → 141 43 59N 4 51 E
Ouyen 231 35 1 S 142 22 E
Ouzouer-le-Marché 138 47 54N 1 32 E
Ovada 162 44 39N 8 40 E
Ovalau 226 17 40 S 178 48 E
Ovalle 124 30 33 S 71 18W
Ovar 154 40 51N 8 40W
Ovejas 118 9 32N 75 14W
Ovens 233 36 35 S 146 46 E
Overdinkel 142 52 14N 7 2 E
Overflakkee 142 51 44N 4 10 E
Overflowing → 89 53 8N 101 5W
Overijse 143 50 47N 4 32 E
Overijssel □ 142 52 25N 6 35 E
Overijsselsch Kanaal 142 52 31N 6 6 E
Overpelt 143 51 12N 5 20 E
Overum 173 58 0N 16 20 E
Ovidiopol 180 46 15N 30 30 E
Oviedo 154 43 25N 5 50W
Oviedo □ 154 43 20N 6 0W
Oviken 172 63 0N 14 23 E
Oviksfjällen 172 63 0N 13 49 E
Övör Hangay □ 214 45 0N 102 30 E
Ovoro 247 5 26N 7 16 E
Övre Sirdal 171 58 48N 6 43 E
Ovruch 178 51 25N 28 45 E
Owaka 235 46 27 S 169 40 E
Owase 221 34 7N 136 12 E
Owbeh 197 34 28N 63 10 E
Owen 232 34 15 S 138 32 E
Owen Falls 250 0 30N 33 5 E
Owen Mt. 235 41 35 S 172 33 E
Owen Sound 84 44 35N 80 55W
Owen Stanley Range 227 8 30 S 147 0 E
Owendo 252 0 17N 9 30 E
Owerri 247 5 29N 7 0 E
Owhango 234 39 0 S 175 23 E
Owikeno L. 92 51 40N 126 50W
Owl → 77 57 51N 92 44W
Owo 247 7 10N 5 39 E
Ox Mts. 135 54 6N 9 0W
Oxapampa 122 10 33 S 75 26W
Oxberg 172 61 7N 14 11 E
Oxbow 89 49 14N 102 10W
Oxelösund 173 58 43N 17 15 E
Oxford, Canada 81 45 44N 63 52W
Oxford, N.Z. 235 43 18 S 172 11 E
Oxford, U.K. 133 51 45N 1 15W
Oxford □ 133 51 45N 1 15W
Oxford L. 77 54 51N 95 37W
Oxía 169 38 16N 21 5 E
Oxílithos 169 38 35N 24 7 E
Oxkutzcab 111 20 18N 89 25W
Oxley 231 34 11 S 144 6 E
Oxus → = Pyandzh → 197 43 40N 59 1 E
Oya 206 2 55N 111 55 E
Oyabe 221 36 47N 136 56 E
Oyama, Canada 93 50 7N 119 22W
Oyama, Japan 221 36 18N 139 48 E
Oyana 220 32 32N 130 30 E
Oyapock → 119 4 8N 51 40W
Oyem 252 1 34N 11 31 E
Oyen 91 51 22N 110 28W
Öyeren 171 59 50N 11 15 E
Oykel → 134 57 55N 4 26W
Oymyakon 185 63 25N 142 44 E
Oyo 247 7 46N 3 56 E
Oyo □ 247 8 0N 3 30 E
Oyón 122 10 37 S 76 47W
Oyonnax 141 46 16N 5 40 E
Oyster River 92 49 53N 125 7W
Øystese 171 60 22N 6 9 E
Oytal 183 42 54N 73 17 E
Ōyūbari 218 43 1N 142 5 E
Ozamis 211 8 15N 123 50 E
Ózd 151 48 14N 20 15 E
Ozërnyy 182 51 8N 60 50 E
Ozieri 164 40 35N 9 0 E
Ozimek 152 50 41N 18 11 E
Ozorków 152 51 57N 19 16 E
Ozren 166 43 55N 18 29 E
Ozu, Ehime, Japan 220 33 30N 132 33 E
Ozu, Kumamoto, Japan 220 32 52N 130 52 E
Ozuluama 108 21 40N 97 51W
Ozumatlán, Sa. de 107 19 37N 101 5W
Ozun 170 45 47N 25 50 E

P

Pa 246 11 33N 3 19W
Pa-an 202 16 51N 97 40 E
Pa Mong Dam 204 18 0N 102 22 E
Paagoumène 226 20 29 S 164 11 E
Paal 143 51 2N 5 10 E
Paar → 147 48 13N 10 59 E
Paarl 254 33 45 S 18 56 E
Pab Hills 197 26 30N 66 45 E
Pabellón 105 22 10N 102 21W
Pabellón, Ensenada de 104 24 27N 107 36W
Pabianice 152 51 40N 19 20 E
Pabna 202 24 1N 89 18 E
Pabo 250 3 1N 32 10 E
Pabos Mills 80 48 19N 64 42W
Pacaás Novos, Serra dos 123 10 45 S 64 15W
Pacaipampa 122 5 35 S 79 39W
Pacaja → 120 1 56 S 50 50W
Pacajus 120 4 10 S 38 31W
Pacaraima, Sierra 119 4 0N 62 30W
Pacarán 122 12 50 S 76 3W
Pacaraos 122 11 12 S 76 42W
Pacasmayo 122 7 20 S 79 35W
Pacaudière, La 140 46 11N 3 52 E
Paceco 164 37 59N 12 32 E
Pachacamac 122 12 14 S 77 53W
Pacheco, Chihuahua, Mexico 101 30 6N 108 21W
Pacheco, Zacatecas, Mexico 105 24 6N 102 28W
Pachera 101 28 17N 107 24W
Pachhar 198 24 40N 77 42 E
Pachino 165 36 43N 15 4 E
Pachitea → 122 8 46 S 74 33W
Pachiza 122 7 16 S 76 46W
Pacho 118 5 8N 74 10W
Pachora 198 20 38N 75 29 E
Pachuca, Sa. de 107 20 40N 99 0W
Pachuca de Soto 107 20 7N 98 44W
Pacific 76 54 48N 128 28W
Pacific-Antarctic Basin 225 46 0 S 95 0W
Pacific-Antarctic Ridge 225 43 0 S 115 0W
Pacific Ocean 224 10 0N 140 0W
Pacific Rim Nat. Park 92 48 40N 124 45W
Pacitan 209 8 12 S 111 7 E
Packenham 85 45 22N 76 25W
Packsaddle 232 30 36 S 141 58 E
Pacofi 76 53 0N 132 30W
Pacov 150 49 27N 15 0 E
Pacquet 79 50 0N 55 53W
Pacsa 151 46 44N 17 2 E
Pacuí → 121 16 46 S 45 1W
Paczków 152 50 28N 17 0 E
Padaido, Kepulauan 207 1 5 S 138 0 E
Padang 208 1 0 S 100 20 E
Padangpanjang 208 0 40 S 100 20 E
Padangsidempuan 208 1 30N 99 15 E
Padangtikar 209 0 44 S 109 15 E
Padatchuang 202 19 46N 94 48 E
Padauari → 119 0 15 S 64 5W
Padborg 173 54 49N 9 21 E
Padcaya 123 21 52 S 64 48W
Paddockwood 88 53 30N 105 30W
Paderborn 146 51 42N 8 44 E
Padeşul 170 45 40N 22 22 E
Padilla, Bolivia 123 19 19 S 64 20W
Padilla, Mexico 103 24 1N 98 47W
Padina 170 44 50N 27 8 E
Padle 95 62 10N 97 5W
Padloping Island 95 67 0N 62 50W
Padma → 202 23 22N 90 32 E
Padmanabhapuram 201 8 16N 77 17 E
Pádova 163 45 24N 11 52 E
Padra 198 22 15N 73 7 E
Padrauna 199 26 54N 83 59 E
Padre Burgos 211 10 1N 125 0 E
Padrón 154 42 41N 8 39W
Padstow 132 50 33N 4 57W
Padua = Pádova 163 45 24N 11 52 E
Padul 155 37 1N 3 38W
Padula 165 40 20N 15 40 E
Padwa 200 18 27N 82 47 E
Paekakariki 234 40 59 S 174 58 E
Paengaroa 234 37 49 S 176 29 E
Paengnyong-do 215 37 57N 124 40 E
Paeroa 234 37 23 S 175 41 E
Paesana 162 44 40N 7 18 E
Paete 210 14 23N 121 29 E
Pag 163 44 30N 14 50 E
Paga 247 11 1N 1 8W
Pagadian 211 7 55N 123 30 E
Pagai Selatan 208 3 0 S 100 15W
Pagai Utara 208 2 35 S 100 0 E
Pagalu 237 1 25 S 5 36 E
Pagastikós Kólpos 168 39 15N 23 0 E
Pagatan 209 3 33 S 115 59 E
Paglieta 163 42 10N 14 30 E
Pagny-sur-Moselle 139 48 59N 6 2 E
Pago Pago 226 14 16 S 170 43W
Pagwa River 87 50 2N 85 14W
Pagwachuan → 87 50 12N 84 43W
Pahang → 205 3 30N 103 9 E
Pahiatua 234 40 27 S 175 50 E
Pai 204 19 19N 98 27 E
Paide 178 58 57N 25 31 E
Paignton 133 50 26N 3 33W
Paiján 122 7 42 S 79 20W
Päijänne, L. 175 61 30N 25 30 E
Paila, Sa. de la 102 26 7N 101 36W
Paimbœuf 138 47 17N 2 0W
Paimpol 138 48 48N 3 4W
Paimpont, L. 80 50 28N 61 34W
Painan 208 1 21 S 100 34 E
Paint Hills = Nouveau Comptoir 78 53 0N 78 49W
Paint I. 77 55 28N 97 57W
Pais Vasco 156 43 0N 2 30W
Paisley, Canada 84 44 18N 81 16W
Paisley, U.K. 134 55 51N 4 27W
Paita, N. Cal. 226 22 8 S 166 22 E
Paita, Peru 122 5 11 S 81 9W
Paiva → 154 41 4N 8 16W
Paiyegua, L. 111 19 13N 88 27W
Paizhou 217 30 12N 113 55 E
Pajapán 109 18 15N 94 42W
Pajares 154 43 1N 5 46W
Pajares, Puerto de 154 43 0N 5 46W
Pajarito, Sa. del 100 31 20N 111 5W
Pajaritos, Sierra de 104 20 59N 104 30W
Pajeczno 152 51 10N 19 0 E
Pak Lay 204 18 15N 101 27 E
Pak Phanang 205 8 21N 100 12 E
Pak Sane 204 18 22N 103 39 E
Pak Song 204 15 11N 106 14 E
Pak Suong 204 19 58N 102 15 E
Pakala 201 13 29N 79 8 E
Pakanbaru 208 0 30N 101 15 E
Pakaraima Mts. 119 6 0N 60 0W
Pakashkan L. 86 49 21N 90 15W
Pakenham, Australia 233 38 6 S 145 30 E
Pakenham, Canada 82 45 18N 76 18W
Pakhtakor 183 40 2N 65 46 E
Pakistan ■ 197 30 0N 70 0 E
Pakkading 204 18 19N 103 59 E
Pakokku 202 21 20N 95 0 E
Pakosc 152 52 48N 18 6 E
Pakowi L. 91 49 20N 111 0W
Pakpattan 197 30 25N 73 27 E
Pakrac 166 45 27N 17 12 E
Paks 151 46 38N 18 55 E
Pakse 204 15 5N 105 52 E
Paktīā □ 197 33 0N 69 15 E
Paktīkā □ 197 32 30N 69 0 E
Pakwach 250 2 28N 31 27 E
Pakwash L. 86 50 45N 93 30W
Pala, Chad 243 9 25N 15 5 E
Pala, Zaïre 250 6 45 S 29 30 E
Palabek 250 3 22N 32 33 E
Palafrugell 156 41 55N 3 10 E
Palagiano 165 40 35N 17 0 E
Palagonía 165 37 20N 14 43 E
Palagruža 163 42 24N 16 15 E
Palaiokastron 169 35 12N 26 18 E
Palaiokhóra 169 35 16N 23 39 E
Pálairos 169 38 45N 20 51 E
Palais, Le 138 47 20N 3 10W
Palakol 201 16 31N 81 46 E
Palam 200 19 0N 77 0 E
Palamás 168 39 26N 22 4 E
Palamós 156 41 50N 3 10 E
Palampur 198 32 10N 76 30 E
Palana, Australia 230 39 45 S 147 55 E
Palana, U.S.S.R. 185 59 10N 159 59 E
Palanan 210 17 8N 122 29 E
Palanan Bay 210 17 9N 122 27 E
Palanan Pt. 210 17 17N 122 30 E
Palandri 199 33 42N 73 40 E
Palangkaraya 209 2 16 S 113 56 E
Palani 201 10 30N 77 30 E
Palani Hills 201 10 14N 77 33 E
Palanpur 198 24 10N 72 25 E
Palapye 254 22 30 S 27 7 E
Palar → 201 12 27N 80 13 E
Palas 199 35 4N 73 14 E
Palatka 185 60 6N 150 54 E
Palau 102 27 53N 101 25W
Palavas 140 43 32N 3 56 E
Palawan 211 9 30N 118 30 E
Palawan □ 211 10 0N 119 0 E
Palawan Passage 211 10 0N 118 0 E
Palayankottai 201 8 45N 77 45 E
Palazzo San Gervásio 165 40 53N 15 58 E
Palazzolo Acreide 165 37 4N 14 54 E
Palca 122 19 7 S 69 9W
Paldiski 178 59 23N 24 9 E
Pale 166 43 50N 18 38 E
Palel 202 24 27N 94 2 E
Paleleh 207 1 10N 121 50 E
Palembang 208 3 0 S 104 50 E
Palena → 126 43 50 S 73 50W
Palena, L. 126 43 55 S 71 40W
Palencia 154 42 1N 4 34W
Palencia □ 154 42 31N 4 33W
Palenque 110 17 31N 91 58W
Palenque, Ruinas de 110 17 30N 91 59W
Palermo, Colombia 118 2 54N 75 26W
Palermo, Italy 164 38 8N 13 20 E
Palestine 189 32 0N 35 0 E
Palestrina 164 41 50N 12 52 E
Paletwa 202 21 10N 92 50 E
Palghat 201 10 46N 76 42 E
Palgrave, Mt. 228 23 22 S 115 58 E
Pali 198 25 50N 73 20 E
Palinit 210 12 15N 124 20 E
Palinuro, C. 165 40 1N 15 14 E
Paliseul 143 49 54N 5 8 E
Palitana 198 21 32N 71 49 E
Palizada 111 18 15N 92 5W
Palizzi 165 37 58N 15 59 E
Palk Bay 201 9 30N 79 15 E
Palk Strait 201 10 0N 79 45 E
Palkānah 192 35 49N 44 26 E
Palkonda 200 18 36N 83 48 E
Palkonda Ra. 201 13 50N 79 20 E
Palla Road = Dinokwe 254 23 29 S 26 37 E
Pallanza = Verbánia 162 45 56N 8 43 E
Pallasovka 179 50 4N 47 0 E
Palleru → 200 16 45N 80 2 E
Pallinup 229 34 0 S 117 55 E
Pallisa 250 1 12N 33 43 E
Palliser, C. 234 41 37 S 175 14 E
Palliser Bay 234 41 26 S 175 5 E
Pallu 198 28 59N 74 14 E

Palm Is. 230 18 40 S 146 35 E
Palma 251 10 46 S 40 29 E
Palma → 121 12 33 S 47 52W
Palma, B. de 157 39 30N 2 39 E
Palma, La, Guerrero, Mexico 107 17 6N 99 32W
Palma, La, Sinaloa, Mexico 104 26 1N 108 53W
Palma, La, Panama 112 8 15N 78 0W
Palma, La, Spain 155 37 21N 6 38W
Palma, L. 110 18 13N 93 49W
Palma de Mallorca 156 39 35N 2 39 E
Palma del Río 155 37 43N 5 17W
Palma di Montechiaro 164 37 12N 13 46 E
Palma Soriano 112 20 15N 76 0W
Palmaḩim 189 31 56N 34 44 E
Palmanova 163 45 54N 13 18 E
Palmar de Sepúlveda 104 25 43N 107 55W
Palmares 120 8 41 S 35 28W
Palmarito 118 7 37N 70 10W
Palmarola 164 40 57N 12 50 E
Palmarolle 82 48 40N 79 12W
Palmas 125 26 29 S 52 0W
Palmas, B. de las 99 23 40N 109 40W
Palmas, C. 246 4 27N 7 46W
Pálmas, G. di 164 39 0N 8 30 E
Palmas de Monte Alto 121 14 16 S 43 10W
Palmeira 121 25 25 S 50 0W
Palmeira dos Índios 120 9 25 S 36 37W
Palmeirais 120 6 0 S 43 0W
Palmeiras → 121 12 22 S 47 8W
Palmeirinhas, Pta. das 253 9 2 S 12 57 E
Palmela 155 38 32N 8 57W
Palmelo 121 17 20 S 48 27W
Palmer → 230 15 34 S 142 26 E
Palmer Arch. 13 64 15 S 65 0W
Palmer Land 13 73 0 S 60 0W
Palmerston 84 43 50N 80 51W
Palmerston North 235 40 21 S 175 39 E
Palmi 165 38 21N 15 51 E
Palmillas, Querétaro, Mexico 107 20 19N 99 55W
Palmillas, Tamaulipas, Mexico 103 23 18N 99 33W
Palmillas, Zacatecas, Mexico 105 22 39N 102 21W
Palmira, Argentina 124 32 59 S 68 34W
Palmira, Colombia 118 3 32N 76 16W
Palmyra = Tudmur 192 34 36N 38 15 E
Palmyra Is. 225 5 52N 162 5W
Palo 211 11 10N 124 59 E
Palo Blanco 102 26 45N 101 32W
Palo del Colle 165 41 4N 16 43 E
Paloma, La 124 30 35 S 71 0W
Palomar 87 48 10N 82 16W
Palomares 109 17 9N 95 4W
Palomas 103 22 28N 99 55W
Palombara Sabina 163 42 4N 12 45 E
Palompon 211 11 3N 124 23 E
Palopo 207 3 0 S 120 16 E
Palos, Cabo de 157 37 38N 0 40W
Palos, L. de 101 30 44N 106 29W
Palpa 122 14 30 S 75 15W
Palparara 230 24 47 S 141 28 E
Pålsboda 173 59 3N 15 22 E
Palu, Indonesia 207 1 0 S 119 52 E
Palu, Turkey 177 38 45N 40 0 E
Paluan 210 13 26N 120 29 E
Palwal 198 28 8N 77 19 E
Pama 247 11 19N 0 44 E
Pamanukan 209 6 16 S 107 49 E
Pamban I. 201 9 15N 79 20 E
Pambuhan 210 13 59N 123 5 E
Pamekasan 209 7 10 S 113 28 E
Pamiers 140 43 7N 1 39 E
Pamir → 183 37 1N 72 41 E
Pamirs 183 37 40N 73 0 E
Pampa, La □ 124 36 50 S 66 0W
Pampa de Agma 126 43 45 S 69 40W
Pampa de las Salinas 124 32 1 S 66 58W
Pampa Grande 123 18 5 S 64 6W
Pampa Hermosa 122 7 7 S 75 4W
Pampanga □ 210 15 4N 120 40 E
Pampanua 207 4 16 S 120 8 E
Pamparato 162 44 16N 7 54 E
Pampas, Argentina 124 35 0 S 63 0W
Pampas, Peru 122 12 20 S 74 50W
Pampas → 122 13 24 S 73 12W
Pamplona, Colombia 118 7 23N 72 39W
Pamplona, Phil. 210 18 31N 121 20 E
Pamplona, Spain 156 42 48N 1 38W
Pampoenpoort 254 31 3 S 22 40 E
Pamuk → 190 37 2N 34 49 E
Pan Xian 216 25 46N 104 38 E
Panabá 111 21 17N 88 16W
Panabo 211 7 19N 125 42 E
Panache, L. 84 46 15N 81 20W
Panagyurishte 167 42 30N 24 15 E
Panaitan 207 6 36 S 105 12 E
Panaji 201 15 25N 73 50 E
Panalachic 101 27 40N 107 23W
Panamá 112 9 0N 79 25W
Panama ■ 112 8 48N 79 55W
Panamá, Golfo de 112 8 4N 79 20W
Panama Canal 112 9 10N 79 37W
Panão 122 9 55 S 75 55W
Panaon I. 211 10 3N 125 13 E
Panare 205 6 51N 101 30 E
Panarea 165 38 38N 15 3 E
Panaro → 162 44 55N 11 25 E
Panarukan 209 7 42 S 113 56 E
Panay 211 11 10N 122 30 E
Panay, G. 211 11 0N 122 30 E
Pančevo 166 44 52N 20 41 E
Panciu 170 45 54N 27 8 E
Pancol 211 10 52N 119 25 E
Pancorbo, Paso 156 42 32N 3 5W
Pandan, Catanduanes, Phil. 210 14 3N 124 10 E
Pandan, Antiqe, Phil. 211 11 45N 122 10 E
Pandan Bay 211 11 43N 122 0 E
Pandegelang 207 6 25 S 106 0 E
Pandharpur 200 17 41N 75 20 E
Pandhurna 198 21 36N 78 35 E
Pandilla 156 41 32N 3 43W
Pando 125 34 44 S 56 0W
Pando □ 122 11 20 S 67 40W
Pando, L. = Hope, L. 231 28 24 S 139 18 E
Pandu 252 5 1N 19 16 E
Panevezys 178 55 42N 24 25 E
Panfilov 184 44 10N 80 0 E
Panfilovo 179 50 25N 42 46 E
Panga 250 1 52N 26 18 E
Pangaíon Óros 168 40 50N 24 0 E
Pangala 252 4 1 S 13 52 E
Pangalanes, Canal des 255 22 48 S 47 50 E
Pangani 250 5 25 S 38 58 E
Pangani □ 250 5 25 S 39 0 E
Pangani → 250 5 26 S 38 58 E
Panganiban 210 13 55N 124 18 E
Panganuran 211 8 2N 122 22 E
Pangasinan □ 210 15 55N 120 20 E
Pangfou = Bengbu 217 32 58N 117 20 E
Pangil 250 3 10 S 26 35 E
Pangkah, Tanjung 209 6 51 S 112 33 E
Pangkai 202 22 40N 98 40 E
Pangkajene 207 4 46 S 119 34 E
Pangkalanbrandan 208 4 1N 98 20 E
Pangkalanbuun 209 2 41 S 111 37 E
Pangkalansusu 208 4 2N 98 13 E
Pangkalpinang 208 2 0 S 106 0 E
Pangkoh 209 3 5 S 114 8 E
Panglao 211 9 35N 123 45 E
Panglao I. 211 9 35N 123 48 E
Pangmar 88 49 39N 104 40W
Pangong Tso 199 34 0N 78 20 E
Pangrango 207 6 46 S 107 1 E
Pangsau Pass 202 27 15N 96 10 E
Pangtara 202 20 57N 96 40 E
Panguipulli 126 39 38 S 72 20W
Pangutaran 211 6 18N 120 35 E
Pangutaran Group 211 6 18N 120 34 E
Pangutaran I. 211 6 18N 120 34 E
Pani Mines 198 22 29N 73 50 E
Pania-Mutombo 250 5 11 S 23 51 E
Panie, Mt. 226 20 36 S 164 46 E
Panipat 198 29 25N 77 2 E
Panitan 211 11 28N 122 46 E
Panjal Range 198 32 30N 76 50 E
Panjgur 197 27 0N 64 5 E
Panjim = Panaji 201 15 25N 73 50 E
Panjwai 198 31 26N 65 27 E
Pankshin 247 9 16N 9 25 E
Panmunjŏm 215 37 59N 126 38 E
Panna 199 24 40N 80 15 E
Panna Hills 199 24 40N 81 15 E
Panny → 90 57 8N 114 51W
Pano Lefkara 190 34 53N 33 20 E
Panorama 125 21 21 S 51 51W
Panruti 201 11 46N 79 35 E
Panshan 215 41 3N 122 2 E
Panshi 215 42 58N 126 5 E
Pantao 210 13 12N 123 20 E
Pantar 207 8 28 S 124 10 E
Pantelleria 164 36 52N 12 0 E
Pantepec 108 20 31N 97 56W
Pantha 202 23 55N 94 35 E
Pantin Sakan 202 18 38N 97 33 E
Pantón 154 42 31N 7 37W
Pánuco, Sinaloa, Mexico 104 23 25N 105 55W
Pánuco, Veracruz, Mexico 108 22 3N 98 10W
Pánuco → 108 22 16N 97 47W
Pánuco de Coronado 105 24 32N 104 20W
Panukulan 210 14 56N 121 49 E
Panyam 247 9 27N 9 8 E
Panyu 217 22 51N 113 20 E
Pao →, Anzoátegui, Venezuela 119 8 6N 64 17W
Pao →, Apure, Venezuela 118 8 33N 68 1W
Páola 165 39 21N 16 2 E
Paoting = Baoding 214 38 50N 115 28 E
Paot'ou = Baotou 214 40 32N 110 2 E
Paoua 252 7 9N 16 20 E
Papá 151 47 22N 17 30 E
Papagayo → 107 16 46N 99 43W
Papagayo, Golfo de 112 10 30N 85 50W
Papagni → 201 15 35N 77 45 E
Papakura 234 37 4 S 174 59 E
Papaloapán 109 18 9N 96 5W
Papaloapán → 109 18 42N 95 38W
Papantla de Olarte 108 20 27N 97 19W
Papar 206 5 45N 116 0 E
Papara 226 17 45 S 149 21W
Paparoa 235 36 6 S 174 16 E
Paparoa Range 235 42 5 S 171 35 E
Pápas, Ákra 169 38 13N 21 20 E
Papatoetoe 234 36 59 S 174 51 E
Papeete 226 17 32 S 149 34W
Papenburg 146 53 7N 7 25 E
Papenoo 226 17 30 S 149 25W
Paphos 190 34 46N 32 25 E
Papien Chiang = Da → 204 21 15N 105 20 E
Papigochic → 101 29 9N 109 40W
Papineau-Labelle, Parc Prov. 82 46 10N 75 15W
Papineauville 82 45 37N 75 1W
Paposo 124 25 0 S 70 30W
Papua, Gulf of 227 9 0 S 144 50 E
Papua New Guinea ■ 227 8 0 S 145 0 E
Papuča 163 44 22N 15 30 E
Papudo 124 32 29 S 71 27W
Papuk 166 45 30N 17 30 E
Papun 202 18 0N 97 30 E
Pará = Belém 120 1 20 S 48 30W
Pará □, Brazil 123 3 20 S 52 0W
Pará □, Surinam 119 40 0 S 53 0W
Parábita 165 40 3N 18 8 E
Paraburdoo 228 23 14 S 117 32 E
Paracale 210 14 17N 122 48 E
Paracas, Pen. 122 13 53 S 76 20W
Paracatu 121 17 10 S 46 50W
Paracatu → 121 16 30 S 45 4W
Parachilna 231 31 10 S 138 21 E
Parachinar 197 33 55N 70 5 E
Paracho de Verduzco 106 19 39N 102 4W
Paraćin 166 43 54N 21 27 E
Parácuaro 107 20 9N 100 46W
Paracuru 120 3 24 S 39 4W
Parada, Punta 122 15 22 S 75 11W
Paradas 155 37 18N 5 29W
Paradela 154 42 44N 7 37W
Paradip 199 20 15N 86 35 E
Paradis 82 48 15N 76 35W
Paradise → 78 53 27N 57 19W
Paradise Hill 88 53 32N 109 28W
Paradise Valley 91 53 2N 110 17W
Parado 209 8 42 S 118 30 E
Paradyz 152 51 19N 20 2 E
Paraguá →, Bolivia 123 13 34 S 61 53W
Paragua →, Venezuela 119 6 55N 62 55W
Paragua, La 119 6 50N 63 20W
Paraguaçu → 121 12 45 S 38 54W
Paraguaçu Paulista 125 22 22 S 50 35W
Paraguaipoa 118 11 21N 71 57W
Paraguaná, Pen. de 118 12 0N 70 0W
Paraguarí 124 25 36 S 57 0W
Paraguarí □ 124 26 0 S 57 10W
Paraguay ■ 124 23 0 S 57 0W
Paraguay → 124 27 18 S 58 38W
Paraíba = João Pessoa 120 7 10 S 34 52W
Paraíba □ 120 7 0 S 36 0W
Paraíba do Sul → 121 21 37 S 41 3W
Parainen 175 60 18N 22 18 E
Paraíso 110 18 24N 93 14W
Parak 193 27 38N 52 25 E
Parakhino Paddubye 178 58 26N 33 10 E
Parakou 247 9 25N 2 40 E
Parakylia 232 30 24 S 136 25 E
Paralimni 190 35 2N 33 58 E
Parálion-Astrous 169 37 25N 22 45 E
Paramakkudi 201 9 31N 78 39 E
Paramaribo 119 5 50N 55 10W
Parambu 120 6 13 S 40 43W
Paramillo, Nudo del 118 7 4N 75 55W
Paramirim 121 13 26 S 42 15W
Paramirim → 121 11 34 S 43 18W
Paramithiá 168 39 30N 20 35 E
Paramushir, Ostrov 185 50 24N 156 0 E
Paran → 189 30 20N 35 10 E
Paraná, Argentina 124 31 45 S 60 30W
Paraná, Brazil 121 12 30 S 47 48W
Paraná □ 125 24 30 S 51 0W
Paraná → 124 33 43 S 59 15W
Paranaguá 125 25 30 S 48 30W
Paranaíba → 121 20 6 S 51 4W
Paranapanema → 125 22 40 S 53 9W
Paranapiacaba, Serra do 125 24 31 S 48 35W
Paranavaí 125 23 4 S 52 56W
Parang, Jolo, Phil. 211 5 55N 120 54 E
Parang, Mindanao, Phil. 211 7 23N 124 16 E
Parangaba 120 3 45 S 38 33W
Parangippettai 201 11 30N 79 38 E
Paraparauma 234 40 57 S 175 3 E
Parapóla 169 36 55N 23 27 E
Paras 102 26 30N 99 31W
Paraspóri, Ákra 169 35 55N 27 15 E
Paratinga 121 12 40 S 43 10W
Paratoo 231 32 42 S 139 40 E
Parattah 230 42 22 S 147 23 E
Paraúna 121 16 55 S 50 26W
Paray-le-Monial 141 46 27N 4 7 E
Parbati → 198 25 50N 76 30 E
Parbatipur 202 25 39N 88 55 E
Parbhani 198 19 8N 76 52 E
Parchim 146 53 25N 11 50 E
Parczew 152 51 40N 22 52 E
Pardes Hanna 189 32 28N 34 57 E
Pardilla 154 41 33N 3 43W
Pardo 103 21 53N 100 51W
Pardo →, Bahia, Brazil 121 15 40 S 39 0W
Pardo →, Mato Grosso, Brazil 125 21 46 S 52 9W
Pardo →, Minas Gerais, Brazil 121 15 48 S 44 48W
Pardo →, São Paulo, Brazil 121 20 10 S 48 38W
Pardubice 150 50 3N 15 45 E
Pare 209 7 43 S 112 12 E
Pare □ 250 4 10 S 38 0 E
Pare Mts. 250 4 0 S 37 45 E
Parecis, Serra dos 123 13 0 S 60 0W
Paredes de Nava 154 42 9N 4 42W
Paredón 102 25 56N 100 58W
Pareh 192 38 52N 45 42 E
Parelhas 120 6 41 S 36 39W
Paren 185 62 30N 163 15 E
Parengarenga Harbour 234 34 31 S 173 0 E
Parent 82 47 55N 74 35W
Parent, Lac 82 48 31N 77 1W
Parentis-en-Born 140 44 21N 1 4W
Parepare 207 4 0 S 119 40 E
Parfino 178 57 59N 31 34 E
Parfuri 255 22 28 S 31 17 E
Parguba 176 62 20N 34 27 E
Parham 85 44 39N 76 43W
Paria, Golfo de 118 10 20N 62 0W
Paria, Pen. de 119 10 50N 62 30W
Pariaguán 119 8 51N 64 34W
Pariaman 208 0 47 S 100 11 E
Paricatuba 119 4 26 S 61 53W
Parigi, Java, Indonesia 209 7 42 S 108 29 E
Parigi, Sulawesi, Indonesia 207 0 50 S 120 5 E
Parika 119 6 50N 58 20W
Parima, Serra 119 2 30N 64 0W
Parinari 122 4 35 S 74 25W
Parincea 170 46 27N 27 9 E
Paring 170 45 20N 23 37 E
Parintins 119 2 40 S 56 50W
Paris, Canada 84 43 12N 80 25W
Paris, France 139 48 50N 2 20 E
Paris, Ville de □ 139 48 50N 2 20 E
Pariti 207 10 15 S 123 45 E
Park Rynie 255 30 25 S 30 45 E
Parkā Bandar 193 25 55N 59 35 E
Parkent 183 41 18N 69 40 E
Parkerview 88 51 21N 103 18W
Parkes 231 33 9 S 148 11 E
Parkhar 183 37 30N 69 34 E
Parkhill 84 43 15N 81 38W
Parks L. 87 49 27N 87 38W
Parkside 88 53 10N 106 33W
Parksville 92 49 20N 124 21W
Parlakimidi 200 18 45N 84 5 E
Parli 198 18 50N 76 35 E
Parma 162 44 50N 10 20 E
Parma → 162 44 56N 10 26 E
Parnaguá 120 10 10 S 44 38W
Parnaíba, Piauí, Brazil 120 2 54 S 41 47W
Parnaíba, São Paulo, Brazil 123 19 34 S 51 14W
Parnaíba → 120 3 0 S 41 50W
Parnamirim 120 8 5 S 39 34W
Parnarama 120 5 31 S 43 6W
Parnassós 169 38 35N 22 30 E
Parnassus 235 42 42 S 173 23 E
Párnis 169 38 14N 23 45 E
Párnon Óros 169 37 15N 22 45 E
Pärnu 178 58 28N 24 33 E
Parola 198 20 47N 75 7 E

Paroo → **231** 31 28 S 143 32 E
Páros **169** 37 5N 25 12 E
Parpaillon **141** 44 30N 6 40 E
Parral **124** 36 10 S 71 52W
Parramatta **231** 33 48 S 151 1 E
Parras, Sa. de **102** 25 24N 102 24W
Parras de la Fuente **102** 25 25N 102 11W
Parrett → **133** 51 7N 2 58W
Parrsboro **81** 45 30N 64 25W
Parry, C. **95** 70 20N 123 38W
Parry Is. **94** 77 0N 110 0W
Parry Sound **84** 45 20N 80 0W
Parsberg **147** 49 10N 11 43 E
Parseta → **152** 54 11N 15 34 E
Parsnip → **76** 55 10N 123 2W
Parson **93** 51 5N 116 37W
Parsons Pond, Newf., Canada **79** 49 59N 57 37W
Parson's Pond, Newf., Canada **79** 50 2N 57 43W
Parsons Ra. **230** 13 30 S 135 15 E
Partabpur **200** 20 0N 80 42 E
Partanna **164** 37 43N 12 51 E
Parthenay **138** 46 38N 0 16W
Partinico **164** 38 3N 13 6 E
Partridge → **87** 51 19N 80 18W
Partridge Pt. **79** 50 10N 56 10W
Partur **200** 19 40N 76 14 E
Paru →, Brazil **119** 1 33 S 52 38W
Parú →, Venezuela **118** 4 20N 66 27W
Paru de Oeste → **119** 1 30N 56 0W
Parubcan **210** 13 43N 123 45 E
Parucito → **118** 5 18N 65 59W
Parur **201** 10 13N 76 14 E
Paruro **122** 13 45 S 71 50W
Parvān □ **197** 35 0N 69 0 E
Parvatipuram **200** 18 50N 83 25 E
Parys **254** 26 52 S 27 29 E
Pas-de-Calais □ **139** 50 30N 2 30 E
Pasadena **79** 49 1N 57 36W
Pasaje, Ecuador **118** 3 23 S 79 50W
Pasaje, Mexico **105** 24 56N 103 51W
Pasaje → **124** 25 39 S 63 56W
Pasay **210** 14 33N 121 0 E
Paşcani **170** 47 14N 26 45 E
Pasco □ **122** 10 40 S 75 0W
Pasco, Cerro de **122** 10 45 S 76 10W
Pasewalk **146** 53 30N 14 0 E
Pasfield L. **77** 58 24N 105 20W
Pasha → **178** 60 29N 32 55 E
Pashiwari **199** 34 40N 75 10 E
Pashiya **182** 58 33N 58 26 E
Pashmakli = Smolyan **167** 41 36N 24 38 E
Pasighat **202** 28 4N 95 21 E
Pasing **147** 48 9N 11 27 E
Pasirian **209** 8 13 S 113 8 E
Paskūh **193** 27 34N 61 39 E
Pasłeka → **152** 54 26N 19 46 E
Pasley, C. **229** 33 52 S 123 35 E
Pašman **163** 43 58N 15 20 E
Pasmore → **232** 31 5 S 139 49 E
Pasni **197** 25 15N 63 27 E
Paso de Indios **126** 43 55 S 69 0W
Paso de los Libres **124** 29 44 S 57 10W
Paso de los Toros **124** 32 45 S 56 30W
Paso de Ovejas **108** 19 17N 96 26W
Paso del Macho **109** 18 58N 96 43W
Paso Flores **126** 40 35 S 70 38W
Pasorapa **123** 18 16 S 64 37W
Paspébiac **81** 48 3N 65 17W
Pasquel, Pta. **99** 25 31N 111 6W
Pasrur **198** 32 16N 74 43 E
Pass Island **79** 47 30N 56 12W
Passage Pt. **94** 73 29N 115 16W
Passage West **135** 51 52N 8 20W
Passau **147** 48 34N 13 27 E
Passendale **143** 50 54N 3 2 E
Passero, C. **165** 36 42N 15 8 E
Passi **211** 11 6N 122 38 E
Passo Fundo **125** 28 10 S 52 20W
Passos **121** 20 45 S 46 37W
Passow **146** 53 13N 14 10 E
Passwang **148** 47 22N 7 41 E
Passy **141** 45 55N 6 41 E
Pastaza □ **118** 2 0 S 77 0W
Pastaza → **118** 4 50 S 76 52W
Pastęk **152** 54 3N 19 41 E
Pasteur, L. **80** 50 13N 66 58W
Pasto **118** 1 13N 77 17W
Pastor Ortiz **107** 20 18N 101 35W
Pastora **103** 22 9N 100 3W
Pastoria **105** 22 28N 102 6W
Pastos Bons **120** 6 36 S 44 5W
Pastrana **156** 40 27N 2 53W
Pasuquin **210** 18 20N 120 37 E
Pasuruan **209** 7 40 S 112 44 E
Pasym **152** 53 48N 20 49 E
Pásztó **151** 47 52N 19 43 E
Patagonia **126** 45 0 S 69 0W
Patamban, Cerro **106** 19 45N 102 20W
Patambar **193** 29 45N 60 17 E
Patan, Gujarat, India **200** 17 22N 73 57 E
Patan, Maharashtra, India **198** 23 54N 72 14 E
Patani **207** 0 20N 128 50 E
Pataudi **198** 28 18N 76 48 E
Patay **139** 48 2N 1 40 E
Patchewollock **231** 35 22 S 142 12 E
Patea **234** 39 45 S 174 30 E
Pategi **247** 8 50N 5 45 E
Patensie **254** 33 46 S 24 49 E
Paternò **165** 37 34N 14 53 E
Paterson **233** 32 37 S 151 39 E
Paterson Inlet **235** 46 56 S 168 12 E
Paterson Ra. **228** 21 45 S 122 10 E
Paterswolde **142** 53 9N 6 34 E
Pathankot **198** 32 18N 75 45 E
Patharghata **202** 22 2N 89 58 E
Pathe **107** 19 57N 99 50W
Pathiu **205** 10 42N 99 19 E
Pathum Thani **204** 14 1N 100 32 E
Pati **209** 6 45 S 111 1 E
Patía **118** 2 4N 77 4W
Patía → **118** 2 13N 78 40W
Patiala **198** 30 23N 76 26 E
Patine Kouka **246** 12 45N 13 45W
Pativilca **122** 10 42 S 77 48W
Patkai Bum **202** 27 0N 95 30 E
Pátmos **169** 37 21N 26 36 E
Patna **199** 25 35N 85 12 E
Patnongon **211** 10 55N 122 0 E
Patonga **250** 2 45N 33 15 E
Patos **120** 6 55 S 37 16W
Patos, Lag. dos **125** 31 20 S 51 0 E
Patos de Minas **121** 18 35 S 46 32W
Patosi **168** 40 42N 19 38 E
Patquía **124** 25 30N 102 11W
Pátrai **169** 38 14N 21 47 E
Pátraikós, Kólpos **169** 38 17N 21 30 E
Patricio Lynch, I. **126** 48 35 S 75 30W
Patrick's Cove **79** 47 3N 54 7W
Patrie, La **83** 45 24N 71 15W
Patrocínio **121** 18 57 S 47 0W
Patta **250** 2 10 S 41 0 E
Pattada **164** 40 35N 9 7 E
Pattanapuram **201** 9 6N 76 50 E
Pattani **205** 6 48N 101 15 E
Patti, India **198** 31 17N 74 54 E
Patti, Italy **165** 38 8N 14 57 E
Pattoki **198** 31 5N 73 52 E
Pattukkattai **201** 10 25N 79 20 E
Patu **120** 6 6 S 37 38W
Patuakhali **202** 22 20N 90 25 E
Patuca → **112** 15 50N 84 18W
Patuca, Punta **112** 15 49N 84 14W
Pâturages **143** 50 25N 3 52 E
Pátzcuaro **107** 19 32N 101 36W
Pátzcuaro, L. de **107** 19 35N 101 35W
Pau **140** 43 19N 0 25W
Pau, Gave de **140** 43 33N 1 12W
Pau d' Arco **120** 7 30 S 49 22W
Pau dos Ferros **120** 6 7 S 38 10W
Paucartambo **122** 13 19 S 71 35W
Pauillac **140** 45 11N 0 46W
Pauini **122** 7 40 S 66 58W
Pauini → **119** 1 42 S 62 50W
Pauk **202** 21 27N 94 30 E
Paul I. **78** 56 30N 61 20W
Paul Isnard **119** 4 47N 54 1W
Paul-Sauvé, L. **82** 50 15N 78 20W
Paulatuk **94** 69 25N 124 0W
Paulau, L. de **111** 18 37N 91 15W
Paulhan **140** 43 33N 3 28 E
Paulis = Isiro **250** 2 53N 27 40 E
Paulista **120** 7 57 S 34 53W
Paulistana **120** 8 9 S 41 9W
Paulo Afonso **120** 9 21 S 38 15W
Paulo de Faria **121** 20 2 S 49 24W
Paulpietersburg **255** 27 23 S 30 50 E
Paungde **202** 18 29N 95 30 E
Pauni **199** 20 48N 79 40 E
Pausa **122** 15 16 S 73 22W
Pauto → **118** 5 9N 70 55W
Pāveh **192** 35 3N 46 22 E
Pavelets **179** 53 49N 39 14 E
Pavia **162** 45 10N 9 10 E
Pavlikeni **167** 43 14N 25 20 E
Pavlodar **184** 52 33N 77 0 E
Pavlograd **180** 48 30N 35 52 E
Pavlovo, Gorkiy, U.S.S.R. **179** 55 58N 43 5 E
Pavlovo, Yakut A.S.S.R., U.S.S.R. **185** 63 5N 115 25 E
Pavlovsk **179** 50 26N 40 5 E
Pavlovskaya **181** 46 17N 39 47 E
Pavlovskiy-Posad **179** 55 47N 38 42 E
Pavullo nel Frignano **162** 44 20N 10 50 E
Pawahku **202** 26 11N 98 40 E
Pawan → **209** 1 55 S 110 0 E
Paximádhia **169** 35 0N 24 35 E
Paxoí **168** 39 14N 20 12 E
Payakumbuh **208** 0 20 S 100 35 E
Payas **190** 36 46N 36 11 E
Payerne **148** 46 49N 6 56 E
Paymogo **155** 37 44N 7 21W
Payne Bay = Bellin **78** 60 0N 70 0W
Paynes Find **229** 29 15 S 117 42 E
Paynesville **246** 6 20N 10 45W
Pays Basque **140** 43 15N 1 0W
Paysandú **124** 32 19 S 58 8W
Paz → **112** 13 44N 90 10W
Paz, B. de la **99** 24 9N 110 25W
Paz, La, Entre Ríos, Argentina **124** 30 50 S 59 45W
Paz, La, San Luis, Argentina **124** 33 30 S 67 20W
Paz, La, Bolivia **122** 16 20 S 68 10W
Paz, La, Hond. **112** 14 20N 87 47W
Paz, La, Mexico **99** 24 10N 110 18W
Paz, La, Phil. **210** 15 26N 120 45 E
Paz, La □ **122** 15 30 S 68 0W
Paz Centro, La **112** 12 20N 86 41W
Pāzanān **193** 30 35N 49 59 E
Pazarcık **190** 36 16N 32 20 E
Pazardzhik **167** 42 12N 24 20 E
Pazin **163** 45 14N 13 56 E
Pazña **122** 18 36 S 66 55W
Pčinja → **166** 41 50N 21 45 E
Peace → **76** 59 0N 111 25W
Peace Point **76** 59 7N 112 27W
Peace River **90** 56 15N 117 18W
Peachland **93** 49 47N 119 45W
Peak, The **132** 53 24N 1 53W
Peak Downs **230** 22 14 S 148 0 E
Peak Downs Mine **230** 22 17 S 148 11 E
Peak Hill, N.S.W., Australia **231** 32 47 S 148 11 E
Peak Hill, W. Austral., Australia **229** 25 35 S 118 43 E
Peak Range **230** 22 50 S 148 20 E
Peake **232** 35 25 S 140 0 E
Peake Cr. → **231** 28 2 S 136 7 E
Pearl **86** 48 40N 88 40W
Pearl Banks **201** 8 45N 79 45 E
Pearse I. **76** 54 52N 130 14W
Peary Land **12** 82 40N 33 0W
Pebane **251** 17 10 S 38 8 E
Pebas **118** 3 10 S 71 46W
Pebble, I. **126** 51 20 S 59 40W
Peč **166** 42 40N 20 17 E
Peçanha **121** 18 33 S 42 34W
Péccioli **162** 43 32N 10 43 E
Pechea **170** 45 36N 27 49 E
Pechenezhin **180** 48 30N 24 48 E
Pechenga **176** 69 30N 31 25 E
Pechnezhskoye Vdkhr. **179** 50 0N 37 10 E
Pechora → **176** 68 13N 54 15 E
Pechorskaya Guba **176** 68 40N 54 0 E
Pechory **178** 57 48N 27 40 E
Pecica **170** 46 10N 21 3 E
Pečka **166** 44 18N 19 33 E
Pécora, C. **164** 39 28N 8 23 E
Pécs **151** 46 5N 18 15 E
Peddapalli **200** 18 40N 79 24 E
Peddapuram **200** 17 6N 8 13 E
Pedder, L. **230** 42 55 S 146 10 E
Pédernales, Dom. Rep. **113** 18 2N 71 44W
Pedernales, Mexico **101** 28 24N 107 6W
Pedhikos → **190** 35 10N 33 54 E
Pedirka **231** 26 40 S 135 14 E
Pedra Azul **121** 16 2 S 41 17W
Pedra Grande, Recifes de **121** 17 45 S 38 58W
Pedras Negras **123** 12 51 S 62 54W
Pedreiras **120** 4 32 S 44 40W
Pedrera, La **118** 1 18 S 69 43W
Pedriceña **105** 25 6N 103 47W
Pedro Afonso **120** 9 0 S 48 10W
Pedro Cays **112** 17 5N 77 48W
Pedro Chico **118** 1 4N 70 25W
Pedro de Valdivia **124** 22 55 S 69 38W
Pedro Escobedo **107** 20 30N 100 8W
Pedro Juan Caballero **125** 22 30 S 55 40W
Pedro Muñoz **157** 39 25N 2 56W
Pedrógão Grande **154** 39 55N 8 9W
Peduyim **189** 31 20N 34 37 E
Peebinga **232** 34 52 S 140 57 E
Peebles **134** 55 40N 3 12W
Peel **132** 54 14N 4 40W
Peel →, Australia **231** 30 50 S 150 29 E
Peel →, Canada **94** 67 0N 135 0W
Peelwood **233** 34 7 S 149 27 E
Peene → **146** 54 9N 13 46 E
Peera Peera Poolanna L. **231** 26 30 S 138 0 E
Peerless L. **90** 56 37N 114 40W
Peerless Lake **90** 56 40N 114 35W
Peers **90** 53 40N 116 0W
Pegasus Bay **235** 43 20 S 173 10 E
Peggau **150** 47 12N 15 21 E
Peggy's Cove **81** 44 30N 63 55W
Pegnitz **147** 49 45N 11 33 E
Pegnitz → **147** 49 29N 10 59 E
Pego **157** 38 51N 0 8W
Pegu **202** 17 20N 96 29 E
Pegu Yoma **202** 19 0N 96 0 E
Pehčevo **166** 41 41N 22 55 E
Pehuajó **124** 35 45 S 62 0W
Pei Xian **214** 34 44N 116 55 E
Peine, Chile **124** 23 45 S 68 8W
Peine, Germany **146** 52 19N 10 12 E
Peiss **147** 47 58N 11 47 E
Peissenberg **147** 47 48N 11 4 E
Peitz **146** 51 50N 14 23 E
Peixe **121** 12 0 S 48 40W
Peixe → **121** 21 31 S 51 58W
Peixoto de Azeredo → **123** 10 6 S 55 31W
Peize **142** 53 9N 6 30 E
Pek → **166** 44 45N 21 29 E
Pekalongan **209** 6 53 S 109 40 E
Pekan **205** 3 30N 103 25 E
Pékans → **80** 52 12N 66 49W
Peking = Beijing **214** 39 55N 116 20 E
Pelabuhan Kelang **205** 3 0N 101 23 E
Pelabuhan Ratu, Teluk **207** 7 5 S 106 30 E
Pelabuhanratu **207** 7 0 S 106 32 E
Pélagos **168** 39 17N 24 4 E
Pelaihari **209** 3 55 S 114 45 E
Pelat, Mont **141** 44 16N 6 42 E
Pełczyce **152** 53 3N 15 16 E
Peleaga **170** 45 22N 22 55 E
Pelechuco **122** 14 48 S 69 4W
Pelée, Mt. **113** 14 48N 61 0W
Pelee, Pt. **84** 41 54N 82 31W
Pelee I. **84** 41 47N 82 40W
Pelejo **122** 6 10 S 75 49W
Pelekech **250** 3 52N 35 8 E
Pelendria **190** 34 55N 33 0 E
Peleng **207** 1 20 S 123 30 E
Pelhřimov **150** 49 24N 15 12 E
Pélican, L. **78** 59 47N 73 35W
Pelican L. **89** 52 28N 100 20W
Pelican Narrows **77** 55 10N 102 56W
Pelican Portage **76** 55 51N 112 35W
Pelican Rapids **89** 52 45N 100 42W
Peljesac **166** 42 55N 17 25 E
Pella **168** 40 46N 22 23 E
Pélla □ **168** 40 52N 22 0 E
Péllaro **165** 38 1N 15 40 E
Pelletier Sta. **83** 47 33N 69 26W
Pellworm **146** 54 30N 8 40 E
Pelly **89** 51 52N 101 56W
Pelly → **94** 62 47N 137 19W
Pelly Bay **95** 68 38N 89 50W
Pelly Crossing **94** 62 49N 136 34W
Pelly L. **94** 66 0N 102 0W
Peloponnes = Pelopónnisos □ **169** 37 10N 22 0 E
Pelopónnisos □ **169** 37 10N 22 0 E
Peloritani, Monti **165** 38 2N 15 25 E
Peloro, C. **165** 38 15N 15 40 E
Pelorus Sound **235** 40 59 S 173 59 E
Pelotas **125** 31 42 S 52 23W
Pelòvo **167** 43 26N 24 17 E
Pelvoux, Massif de **141** 44 52N 6 20 E
Pelym → **182** 59 39N 63 26 E
Pemalang **209** 6 53 S 109 23 E
Pematangsiantar **208** 2 57N 99 5 E
Pemba, Mozam. **251** 12 58 S 40 30 E
Pemba, Tanzania **250** 5 0 S 39 45 E
Pemba, Zambia **251** 16 30 S 27 28 E
Pemba Channel **250** 5 0 S 39 37 E
Pemberton, Australia **229** 34 30 S 116 0 E
Pemberton, Canada **93** 50 25N 122 50W
Pembina →, Alta., Canada **90** 54 45N 114 17W
Pembina →, Man., Canada **89** 49 0N 98 12W
Pembroke, Canada **85** 45 50N 77 7W
Pembroke, U.K. **133** 51 41N 4 57W
Pembuang → **209** 3 24 S 112 33 E
Pen-y-Ghent **132** 54 10N 2 15W
Peña, La **104** 23 33N 105 23W
Peña, Sierra de la **156** 42 32N 0 45W
Peña de Francia, Sierra de **154** 40 32N 6 10W
Peña Nevada, Cerro **103** 23 46N 99 52W
Penafiel, Portugal **154** 41 12N 8 17W
Peñafiel, Spain **154** 41 35N 4 7W
Peñaflor **155** 37 43N 5 21W
Peñalara, Pico **154** 40 51N 3 57W
Penalva **120** 3 18 S 45 10W
Penamacôr **154** 40 10N 7 10W
Peñamiller **107** 21 3N 99 49W
Penang = Pinang **205** 5 25N 100 15 E
Penápolis **125** 21 30 S 50 0W
Peñaranda de Bracamonte **154** 40 53N 5 13W
Peñarroya-Pueblonuevo **155** 38 19N 5 16W
Peñas, C. de **154** 43 42N 5 52W
Penas, G. de **126** 47 0 S 75 0W
Peñas, Pta. **119** 11 17N 62 0W
Peñas de San Pedro **157** 38 44N 2 0W
Peñausende **154** 41 17N 5 52W
Pench'i = Benxi **215** 41 20N 123 48 E

Pencos 104 22 2N 105 26W
Pendálofon 168 40 14N 21 12 E
Pendelikón 169 38 10N 23 53 E
Pendembu 246 9 7N 12 14W
Pendências 120 5 15 S 36 43W
Pender B. 228 16 45 S 122 42 E
Pendzhikent 183 39 29N 67 37 E
Penedo 120 10 15 S 36 36W
Penetanguishene 84 44 50N 79 55W
Peng Xian 216 31 4N 103 32 E
Pengalengan 209 7 9 S 107 30 E
Penge, Kasai Or., Zaïre 250 5 30 S 24 33 E
Penge, Kivu, Zaïre 250 4 27 S 28 25 E
Penglai 215 37 48N 120 42 E
Pengshui 216 29 17N 108 12 E
Penguin 230 41 8 S 146 6 E
Pengxi 216 30 44N 105 45 E
Pengze 217 29 52N 116 32 E
Penhalonga 251 18 52 S 32 40 E
Penhold 91 52 8N 113 52W
Peniche 155 39 19N 9 22W
Penicuik 134 55 50N 3 14W
Penida 209 8 45 S 115 30 E
Peninsular Malaysia □ 205 4 0N 102 0 E
Peñíscola 156 40 22N 0 24 E
Penitente, Serra dos 120 8 45 S 46 20W
Penjamillo de Degollado 106 20 6N 101 54W
Pénjamo 106 20 26N 101 44W
Pénjamo, Sa. de 106 20 38N 101 47W
Penmarch 138 47 49N 4 21W
Penmarch, Pte. de 138 47 48N 4 22W
Pennabilli 163 43 50N 12 17 E
Pennant 88 50 32N 108 14W
Penne 163 42 28N 13 56 E
Penner → 201 14 35N 80 10 E
Penneshaw 232 35 44 S 137 56 E
Penniac 81 46 2N 66 34W
Pennine, Alpi 162 46 4N 7 30 E
Pennines 132 54 50N 2 20W
Pennino, Mte. 163 43 6N 12 54 E
Penny 93 53 51N 121 20W
Penny Highland 95 67 19N 66 20W
Penny Str. 95 76 30N 97 0W
Peno 178 57 2N 32 49 E
Penola 232 37 25 S 140 21 E
Peñoles 105 25 39N 104 30W
Peñón Blanco 105 24 47N 104 2W
Penonomé 112 8 31N 80 21W
Penrhyn Is. 225 9 0 S 158 30W
Penrith, Australia 231 33 43 S 150 38 E
Penrith, U.K. 132 54 40N 2 45W
Pensacola Mts. 13 84 0 S 40 0W
Pense 88 50 25N 104 59W
Penshurst 231 37 49 S 142 20 E
Pentecoste 120 3 48 S 39 17W
Pentecôte → 80 49 46N 67 10W
Pentecôte, L. 80 49 53N 67 20W
Penticton 93 49 30N 119 38W
Pentland 230 20 32 S 145 25 E
Pentland Firth 134 58 43N 3 10W
Pentland Hills 134 55 48N 3 25W
Peñuelas 105 21 43N 102 17W
Penukonda 201 14 5N 77 38 E
Penylan L. 77 61 50N 106 20W
Penza 179 53 15N 45 5 E
Penzance 133 50 7N 5 32W
Penzberg 147 47 46N 11 23 E
Penzhino 185 63 30N 167 55 E
Penzhinskaya Guba 185 61 30N 163 0 E
Penzlin 146 53 32N 13 6 E
Peotillos 103 22 30N 100 37W
Pepingen 143 50 46N 4 10 E
Pepinster 143 50 34N 5 47 E
Peqini 168 41 4N 19 44 E
Pera Hd. 230 12 55 S 141 37 E
Perabumilih 208 3 27 S 104 15 E
Perakhóra 169 38 2N 22 56 E
Perales de Alfambra 156 40 38N 1 0W
Perales del Puerto 154 40 10N 6 40W
Peralta 156 42 21N 1 49W
Pérama 169 35 20N 24 40 E
Perast 166 42 31N 18 47 E
Percé 80 48 31N 64 13W
Perche 138 48 31N 1 1 E
Perche, Collines du 138 48 30N 0 40 E
Percival Lakes 228 21 25 S 125 0 E
Percy 138 48 55N 1 11W
Percy Is. 230 21 39 S 150 16 E
Perdido → 126 42 55 S 67 0W
Perdido, Mte. 140 42 40N 0 5 E
Perdue 88 52 4N 107 33W
Perdue, Mt. 140 42 40N 0 5 E
Pereira 118 4 49N 75 43W
Pereira Barreto 121 20 38 S 51 7W
Perekerten 231 34 55 S 143 40 E
Perekop 180 46 10N 33 42 E
Perené → 122 11 9 S 74 14W
Perenjori 229 29 26 S 116 16 E
Pereslavl-Zalesskiy 179 56 45N 38 50 E
Pereyaslav Khmelnitskiy 178 50 3N 31 28 E
Perg 150 48 15N 14 38 E
Pergamino 124 33 52 S 60 30W
Pérgine Valsugano 163 46 4N 11 15 E
Pérgola 163 43 35N 12 50 E
Perhentian, Kepulauan 205 5 54N 102 42 E
Peri, L. 232 30 45 S 143 35 E
Periam 170 46 2N 20 59 E
Peribán de Ramos 106 19 32N 102 28W
Péribonca → 78 48 45N 72 5W
Péribonca, L. 83 50 1N 71 10W
Peribonka 83 48 46N 72 3W
Perico 124 24 20 S 65 5W
Pericos 104 25 3N 107 42W
Périers 138 49 11N 1 25W
Périgord 140 45 0N 0 40 E
Périgueux 140 45 10N 0 42 E
Perijá, Sierra de 118 9 30N 73 3W
Peristéra 169 39 15N 23 58 E
Perito Moreno 126 46 36 S 70 56W
Peritoró 120 4 20 S 44 18W
Perivol = Dragovishtitsa 166 42 22N 22 39 E
Periyakulam 201 10 5N 77 30 E
Periyar → 201 10 15N 76 10 E
Periyar, L. 201 9 25N 77 10 E
Perković 163 43 41N 16 10 E
Perla, La 101 28 18N 104 32W
Perlas, Arch. de las 112 8 41N 79 7W
Perlas, Punta de 112 12 30N 83 30W
Perleberg 146 53 5N 11 50 E
Perlevka 179 51 48N 38 57 E
Perlez 166 45 11N 20 22 E
Perm 182 58 0N 57 10 E
Përmeti 168 40 15N 20 21 E
Pernambuco = Recife 120 8 0 S 35 0W
Pernambuco □ 120 8 0 S 37 0W
Pernatty Lagoon 231 31 30 S 137 12 E
Pernik 166 42 35N 23 2 E
Peron, C. 229 25 30 S 113 30 E
Peron Is. 228 13 9 S 130 4 E
Peron Pen. 229 26 0 S 113 10 E
Péronne 139 49 55N 2 57 E
Péronnes 143 50 27N 4 9 E
Perosa Argentina 162 44 57N 7 11 E
Perote 108 19 34N 97 14W
Perote, Sa. de 106 19 33N 104 10W
Perouse Str., La 186 45 40N 142 0 E
Perow 76 54 35N 126 10W
Perpendicular Pt. 231 31 37 S 152 52 E
Perpignan 140 42 42N 2 53 E
Perros-Guirec 138 48 49N 3 28W
Perry River 95 67 43N 102 14W
Persberg 172 59 47N 14 15 E
Perseverancia 123 14 44 S 62 48W
Persia = Iran ■ 193 33 0N 53 0 E
Persian Gulf = Gulf, The 193 27 0N 50 0 E
Perstorp 172 56 10N 13 25 E
Perth, Australia 229 31 57 S 115 52 E
Perth, N.B., Canada 81 46 44N 67 42W
Perth, Ont., Canada 85 44 55N 76 15W
Perth, U.K. 134 56 24N 3 27W
Perthus, Le 140 42 30N 2 53 E
Pertuis 141 43 42N 5 30 E
Peru ■ 118 8 0 S 75 0W
Peru-Chile Trench 225 20 0 S 72 0W
Perúgia 163 43 6N 12 24 E
Perušić 163 44 40N 15 22 E
Péruwelz 143 50 31N 3 36 E
Pervomaysk, R.S.F.S.R., U.S.S.R. 179 54 56N 43 58 E
Pervomaysk, Ukraine S.S.R., U.S.S.R. 180 48 10N 30 46 E
Pervouralsk 182 56 55N 60 0 E
Perwez 143 50 38N 4 48 E
Pésaro 163 43 55N 12 53 E
Pesca, La 103 23 46N 97 47W
Pescadero, L. de 104 22 12N 105 20W
Pescara 163 42 28N 14 13 E
Pescara → 163 42 28N 14 13 E
Peschanokopskoye 181 46 14N 41 4 E
Péscia 162 43 54N 10 40 E
Pescina 163 42 0N 13 39 E
Peseux 148 46 59N 6 53 E
Peshawar 197 34 2N 71 37 E
Peshkopia 168 41 41N 20 25 E
Peshovka 182 59 4N 52 22 E
Peshtera 167 42 2N 24 18 E
Peski 179 51 14N 42 29 E
Peskovka 179 59 23N 52 20 E
Pêso da Régua 154 41 10N 7 47W
Pesqueira, Brazil 120 8 20 S 36 42W
Pesqueira, Mexico 100 29 23N 110 54W
Pesqueria 102 25 45N 100 4W
Pessac 140 44 48N 0 37W
Pessoux 143 50 17N 5 11 E
Pest □ 151 47 29N 19 5 E
Pestovo 178 58 33N 35 42 E
Pestravka 179 52 28N 49 57 E
Péta 169 39 10N 21 2 E
Petacalco, B. de 106 17 57N 102 5W
Petah Tiqwa 189 32 6N 34 53 E
Petalcingo 110 17 17N 92 27W
Petalídhion 169 36 57N 21 55 E
Petaling Jaya 205 3 4N 101 42 E
Petange 143 49 33N 5 55 E
Petatlán 107 17 31N 101 16W
Petauke 251 14 14 S 31 20 E
Petawawa 85 45 54N 77 17W
Petcacab 111 19 16N 88 12W
Petegem 143 50 59N 3 32 E
Petén Itzá, Lago 112 16 58N 89 50W
Peter 1st, I. 13 69 0 S 91 0W
Peter Pond L. 77 55 55N 108 44W
Peterbell 87 48 36N 83 21W
Peterborough, Australia 231 32 58 S 138 51 E
Peterborough, Canada 85 44 20N 78 20W
Peterborough, U.K. 133 52 35N 0 14W
Peterhead 134 57 30N 1 49W
Peters, L. 78 59 41N 70 53W
Peter's Mine 119 6 14N 59 20W
Petersfield 89 50 18N 96 58W
Petford 230 17 20 S 144 58 E
Petília Policastro 165 39 7N 16 48 E
Petit-Cap 80 48 3N 64 30W
Petit-de-Grat 81 45 30N 60 58W
Petit Étang 81 46 39N 60 58W
Petit Goâve 113 18 27N 72 51W
Petit-Mécatina, I. du 78 50 30N 59 25W
Petit-Quevilly, Le 138 49 26N 1 0 E
Petit-Rocher 81 47 46N 65 43W
Petit Saint Bernard, Col du 162 45 40N 6 52 E
Petitcodiac 81 45 57N 65 11W
Petite Baleine → 78 56 0N 76 45W
Petite-Cascapédia, Parc Prov. de la 80 48 30N 65 45W
Petite-Rivière 83 47 20N 70 33W
Petite Rivière Bridge 81 44 14N 64 27W
Petite Saguenay 83 48 15N 70 4W
Petitsikapau, L. 78 54 37N 66 25W
Petlacingo 109 18 5N 97 54W
Petlacotla 108 20 25N 97 54W
Petlad 198 22 30N 72 45 E
Peto 111 20 8N 88 55W
Petone 234 41 13 S 174 53 E
Petra, Jordan 189 30 20N 35 22 E
Petra, Spain 156 39 37N 3 6 E
Petra, Ostrova 12 76 15N 118 30 E
Petra Velikogo, Zaliv 218 42 40N 132 0 E
Petralia 165 37 49N 14 4 E
Petrel 157 38 30N 0 46W
Petrich 167 41 24N 23 13 E
Petrijanec 163 46 23N 16 17 E
Petrikov 178 52 11N 28 29 E
Petrila 170 45 29N 23 29 E
Petrinja 163 45 28N 16 18 E
Petrolândia 120 9 5 S 38 20W
Petrolia 84 42 54N 82 9W
Petrolina 120 9 24 S 40 30W
Petromagoúla 169 38 31N 23 0 E
Petropavlovsk 184 54 53N 69 13 E
Petropavlovsk-Kamchatskiy 185 53 3N 158 43 E
Petropavlovskiy = Akhtubinsk 181 48 13N 46 7 E
Petrópolis 121 22 33 S 43 9W
Petroşeni 170 45 28N 23 20 E
Petrova Gora 163 45 15N 15 45 E
Petrovac, Crna Gora, Yugoslavia 166 42 13N 18 57 E
Petrovac, Srbija, Yugoslavia 166 44 22N 21 26 E
Petrovaradin 166 45 16N 19 55 E
Petrovsk 179 52 22N 45 19 E
Petrovsk-Zabaykalskiy 185 51 20N 108 55 E
Petrovskoye = Svetlograd 181 45 25N 42 58 E
Petrovskoye 182 53 37N 56 23 E
Petrozavodsk 176 61 41N 34 20 E
Petrus Steyn 255 27 38 S 28 8 E
Petrusburg 254 29 4 S 25 26 E
Pettitts 233 34 56 S 148 10 E
Petty Harbour Long Pond 79 47 31N 52 58W
Petukhovka 178 53 42N 30 54 E
Peumo 124 34 21 S 71 12W
Peureulak 208 4 48N 97 45 E
Peusangan → 208 5 16N 96 51 E
Pevek 185 69 41N 171 19 E
Peveragno 162 44 20N 7 37 E
Peyrehorade 140 43 34N 1 7W
Peyruis 141 44 1N 5 56 E
Pézenas 140 43 28N 3 24 E
Pezinok 151 48 17N 17 17 E
Pfaffenhofen 147 48 31N 11 31 E
Pfäffikon 149 47 13N 8 46 E
Pfarrkirchen 147 48 25N 12 57 E
Pfeffenhausen 147 48 40N 11 58 E
Pforzheim 147 48 53N 8 43 E
Pfullendorf 147 47 55N 9 15 E
Pfungstadt 147 49 47N 8 36 E
Phala 254 23 45 S 26 50 E
Phalera = Phulera 198 26 52N 75 16 E
Phalodi 198 27 12N 72 24 E
Phalsbourg 139 48 46N 7 15 E
Phan 204 19 28N 99 43 E
Phan Rang 205 11 34N 109 0 E
Phan Ri = Hoa Da 205 11 16N 108 40 E
Phan Thiet 205 11 1N 108 9 E
Phanae 169 38 8N 25 57 E
Phanat Nikhom 204 13 27N 101 11 E
Phangan, Ko 205 9 45N 100 0 E
Phangnga 205 8 28N 98 30 E
Phanh Bho Ho Chi Minh 205 10 58N 106 40 E
Phanom Sarakham 204 13 45N 101 21 E
Pharenda 199 27 5N 83 17 E
Phatthalung 205 7 39N 100 6 E
Phayao 204 19 11N 99 55 E
Phelps L. 77 59 15N 103 15W
Phet Buri 204 13 1N 99 55 E
Phetchabun 204 16 25N 101 8 E
Phetchabun, Thiu Khao 204 16 0N 101 20 E
Phi Phi, Ko 205 7 45N 98 46 E
Phiafay 204 14 48N 106 0 E
Phibun Mangsahan 204 15 14N 105 14 E
Phichai 204 17 22N 100 10 E
Phichit 204 16 26N 100 22 E
Philippeville 143 50 12N 4 33 E
Philippi 168 41 1N 24 16 E
Philippi L. 230 24 20 S 138 55 E
Philippines ■ 210 12 0N 123 0 E
Philippolis 254 30 15 S 25 16 E
Philippopolis = Plovdiv 167 42 8N 24 44 E
Philipsburg 83 45 2N 73 5W
Philipstown 254 30 28 S 24 30 E
Phillip, I. 231 38 30 S 145 12 E
Phillott 231 27 53 S 145 50 E
Phimai 204 15 13N 102 30 E
Phitsanulok 204 16 50N 100 12 E
Phnom Dangrek 204 14 20N 104 0 E
Phnom Penh 205 11 33N 104 55 E
Phoenix Is. 224 3 30 S 172 0W
Phon 204 15 49N 102 36 E
Phon Tiou 204 17 53N 104 37 E
Phong → 204 16 23N 102 56 E
Phong Saly 204 21 42N 102 9 E
Phong Tho 204 22 32N 103 21 E
Phonhong 204 18 30N 102 25 E
Phonum 205 8 49N 98 48 E
Photharam 204 13 41N 99 51 E
Phra Chedi Sam Ong 204 15 16N 98 23 E
Phra Nakhon Si Ayutthaya 204 14 25N 100 30 E
Phra Thong, Ko 205 9 5N 98 17 E
Phrae 204 18 7N 100 9 E
Phrom Phiram 204 17 2N 100 12 E
Phu Dien 204 18 58N 105 31 E
Phu Loi 204 20 14N 103 14 E
Phu Ly 204 20 35N 105 50 E
Phu Tho 204 21 24N 105 13 E
Phuc Yen 204 21 16N 105 45 E
Phuket 205 7 52N 98 22 E
Phuket, Ko 205 8 0N 98 22 E
Phulbari 202 25 55N 90 2 E
Phulera 198 26 52N 75 16 E
Phun Phin 205 9 7N 99 12 E
Piacá 120 7 42 S 47 18W
Piacenza 162 45 2N 9 42 E
Piaçubaçu 120 10 24 S 36 25W
Piádena 162 45 8N 10 22 E
Pialba 231 25 20 S 152 45 E
Pian Cr. → 231 30 2 S 148 12 E
Piana 141 42 15N 8 34 E
Pianella 163 42 24N 14 5 E
Piangil 232 35 5 S 143 20 E
Pianoro 163 44 20N 11 20 E
Pianosa, Puglia, Italy 163 42 12N 15 44 E
Pianosa, Toscana, Italy 162 42 36N 10 4 E
Piapot 88 49 59N 109 8W
Piare → 163 45 32N 12 44 E
Pias 155 38 1N 7 29W
Piaseczno 152 52 5N 21 2 E
Piashti, L. 80 50 29N 62 52W
Piaski 152 51 8N 22 52 E
Piastów 152 52 12N 20 48 E
Piatã 121 13 9 S 41 48W
Piatra 170 43 51N 25 9 E
Piatra Neamţ 170 46 56N 26 21 E
Piatra Olt 170 44 22N 24 16 E
Piauí □ 120 7 0 S 43 0W
Piaui → 120 6 38 S 42 42W
Piave → 163 45 32N 12 44 E
Piaxtla, Pta 104 23 38N 106 50W
Piaxtla → 104 23 42N 106 49W
Piazza Ármerina 165 37 21N 14 20 E

Pibor → .... 245 7 35N 33 0 E
Pibor Post .... 245 6 47N 33 3 E
Pic → 87 48 36N 86 18W
Pic I. 87 48 43N 86 37W
Pica .... 122 20 35 S 69 25W
Picardías 103 25 19N 103 30W
Picardie .... 139 50 0N 2 15 E
Picardie, Plaine de .. 139 50 0N 2 0 E
Picardy = Picardie .. 139 50 0N 2 15 E
Piccadilly 79 48 34N 58 55W
Picerno .... 165 40 40N 15 37 E
Pich 111 19 31N 90 5W
Pichácic 101 28 8N 107 28W
Pichilemu .... 124 34 22 S 72 0W
Pichilingue 99 24 15N 110 20W
Pichincha, □ .... 118 0 10 S 78 40W
Pichucalco 110 17 31N 93 4W
Pickerel L. 86 48 40N 91 25W
Pickle Lake 86 51 30N 90 12W
Pico 240 38 28N 28 18W
Pico Truncado ..... 126 46 40 S 68 0W
Picos .... 120 7 5 S 41 28W
Picos Ancares,
Sierra de 154 42 51N 6 52W
Picota .... 122 6 54 S 76 24W
Picquigny .... 139 49 56N 2 10 E
Picton, Australia ... 231 34 12 S 150 34 E
Picton, Canada 85 44 1N 77 9W
Picton, N.Z. .... 235 41 18 S 174 3 E
Picton, I. .... 126 55 2 S 66 57W
Pictou 81 45 41N 62 42W
Pictou I. 81 45 49N 62 33W
Picture Butte 91 49 55N 112 45W
Picuí .... 120 6 31 S 36 21W
Picún Leufú .... 126 39 30 S 69 5W
Pidurutalagala ...... 201 7 10N 80 50 E
Pie I. 86 48 15N 89 6W
Piedad Cavadas, La . 106 20 21N 102 0W
Piedecuesta 118 6 59N 73 3W
Piedicavallo .... 162 45 41N 7 57 E
Piedmont =
Piemonte □ ...... 162 45 0N 7 30 E
Piedmonte d'Alife .. 165 41 22N 14 22 E
Piedra → 156 41 18N 1 47W
Piedra del Anguila .. 126 40 2 S 70 4W
Piedra Lais 118 3 10N 65 50W
Piedrabuena 155 39 0N 4 10W
Piedrahita 154 40 28N 5 23W
Piedras, R. de
las → .... 122 12 30 S 69 15W
Piedras Negras,
Coahuila, Mexico . 102 28 42N 100 31W
Piedras Negras,
Veracruz, Mexico 109 18 46N 96 11W
Piedras Pt. .... 211 10 11N 118 48 E
Piemonte □ .... 162 45 0N 7 30 E
Piensk .... 152 51 16N 15 2 E
Pier Millan .... 232 35 14 S 142 40 E
Pierceland 88 54 20N 109 46W
Piería □ .... 168 40 13N 22 25 E
Pierre .... 139 46 54N 5 13 E
Pierre Benite,
Barrage .... 141 45 42N 4 49 E
Pierrefeu .... 141 43 8N 6 9 E
Pierrefonds .... 139 49 20N 3 0 E
Pierrefontaine ...... 139 47 14N 6 32 E
Pierrefort .... 140 44 55N 2 50 E
Pierrelatte .... 141 44 23N 4 43 E
Pierreville 83 46 4N 72 49W
Pierson 89 49 11N 101 15W
Pieštany .... 151 48 38N 17 55 E
Piesting → .... 151 48 6N 16 40 E
Pieszyce .... 152 50 43N 16 33 E
Piet Retief .... 255 27 1 S 30 50 E
Pietarsaari =
Jakobstad .... 174 63 40N 22 43 E
Pietermaritzburg ... 255 29 35 S 30 25 E
Pietersburg .... 255 23 54 S 29 25 E
Pietraperzia .... 165 37 26N 14 8 E
Pietrasanta .... 162 43 57N 10 12 E
Pietrosu .... 170 47 12N 25 8 E
Pietrosul .... 170 47 35N 24 43 E
Pieve di Cadore ... 163 46 25N 12 22 E
Pieve di Teco ...... 162 44 3N 7 54 E
Pievepélago .... 162 44 12N 10 35 E
Pigádhia .... 169 35 30N 27 12 E
Pigadhítsa .... 168 39 59N 21 23 E
Pigeon I. .... 201 14 2N 74 20 E
Pigeon L., Alta.,
Canada 91 53 1N 114 2W
Pigeon L., Ont.,
Canada 85 44 27N 78 30W
Pigna .... 162 43 57N 7 40 E
Pigüe .... 124 37 36 S 62 25W
Pihani .... 199 27 36N 80 15 E
Pihuamo 106 19 15N 103 23W
Pijijiapan 110 15 42N 93 14W
Pijnacker .... 142 52 1N 4 26 E
Pikalevo .... 178 59 37N 34 0 E
Piketberg .... 254 32 55 S 18 40 E
Pikou .... 215 39 18N 122 22 E
Pikwitonei 77 55 35N 97 9W
Piła, Poland .... 152 53 10N 16 48 E
Pila, Spain 157 38 16N 1 11W
Piła □ .... 152 53 0N 17 0 E
Pila, La 103 22 3N 100 54W
Pilaía .... 168 40 32N 22 59 E
Pilani .... 198 28 22N 75 33 E
Pilão Arcado .... 120 10 9 S 42 26W
Pilar, Brazil .... 120 9 36 S 35 56W
Pilar, Paraguay ..... 124 26 50 S 58 20W
Pilares, Pta. 107 16 50N 99 52W
Pilares de Nacozari . 100 30 41N 109 17W
Pilas Group .... 211 6 45N 121 35 E
Pilawa .... 152 51 57N 21 32 E
Pilaya → .... 123 20 55 S 64 4W
Pilbara .... 228 21 15 S 118 16 E
Pilcaya 107 18 44N 99 40W
Pilcomayo → ...... 124 25 21 S 57 42W
Pílí, Greece .... 169 36 50N 27 15 E
Pili, Phil. .... 210 13 33N 123 19 E
Pilibhit .... 199 28 40N 79 50 E
Pilica → .... 152 51 52N 21 17 E
Pílion .... 168 39 27N 23 7 E
Pilis .... 151 47 17N 19 35 E
Pilisvörösvár .... 151 47 38N 18 56 E
Pilkhawa .... 198 28 43N 77 42 E
Pillaro .... 118 1 10 S 78 32W
Pílos .... 169 36 55N 21 42 E
Pilot Butte 88 50 28N 104 25W
Pilot Mound 89 49 15N 98 54W
Pilsen = Plzen ..... 150 49 45N 13 22 E
Pilštanj .... 163 46 8N 15 39 E
Pilzno .... 152 50 0N 21 16 E
Pimba .... 231 31 18 S 136 46 E
Pimenta Bueno ..... 123 11 35 S 61 10W
Pimentel .... 122 6 45 S 79 55W
Pin-Blanc, L. 82 46 45N 78 8W
Pina 156 41 29N 0 33W
Pinamalayan .... 210 13 2N 121 29 E
Pinang .... 205 5 25N 100 15 E
Pinar del Río 112 22 26N 83 40W
Pinaroo .... 232 35 17 S 140 53 E
Pinawa 89 50 9N 95 50W
Pincehely .... 151 46 41N 18 27 E
Pinchang .... 216 31 36N 107 3 E
Pincher Creek 91 49 30N 113 57W
Pinchi L. 76 54 38N 124 30W
Pîncota .... 166 46 20N 21 45 E
Pińczów .... 152 50 32N 20 32 E
Pind Dadan Khan .. 198 32 36N 73 7 E
Pindar .... 229 28 30 S 115 47 E
Pindaré → .... 120 3 17 S 44 47W
Pindaré Mirim .... 120 3 37 S 45 21W
Pindi Gheb .... 198 33 14N 72 21 E
Pindiga .... 247 9 58N 10 53 E
Pindobal .... 120 3 16 S 48 25W
Pindos Óros .... 168 40 0N 21 0 E
Pindus Mts. =
Pindos Óros ..... 168 40 0N 21 0 E
Pine → 77 58 50N 105 38W
Pine, C. 79 46 37N 53 32W
Pine Dock 89 51 38N 96 48W
Pine Falls 89 50 34N 96 11W
Pine Pass 76 55 25N 122 42W
Pine Point 76 60 50N 114 28W
Pine Portage 86 49 20N 88 26W
Pine Ridge .... 233 31 10 S 147 30 E
Pine River 89 51 45N 100 30W
Pinega → .... 176 64 8N 46 54 E
Pinehill .... 230 23 38 S 146 57 E
Pinerolo .... 162 44 47N 7 21 E
Pineto .... 163 42 36N 14 4 E
Pinetown .... 255 29 48 S 30 54 E
Pineview 93 53 50N 122 38W
Piney .... 139 48 22N 4 21 E
Ping → .... 204 15 42N 100 9 E
Pingaring .... 229 32 40 S 118 32 E
Pingba .... 216 26 23N 106 12 E
Pingchuan .... 216 27 35N 101 55 E
Pingding .... 214 37 47N 113 38 E
Pingdingshan .... 214 33 43N 113 27 E
Pingdong .... 217 22 39N 120 30 E
Pingdu .... 215 36 42N 119 59 E
Pingelly .... 229 32 32 S 117 5 E
Pingguo .... 216 23 19N 107 36 E
Pinghe .... 217 24 17N 117 21 E
Pinghu .... 217 30 40N 121 2 E
Pingjiang .... 217 28 45N 113 36 E
Pingle .... 217 24 40N 110 40 E
Pingli .... 216 32 27N 109 22 E
Pingliang .... 214 35 35N 106 31 E
Pinglu .... 214 39 31N 112 30 E
Pingluo .... 214 38 52N 106 30 E
Pingnan, Fujian,
China .... 217 26 55N 119 0 E
Pingnan,
Guangxi
Zhuangzu, China . 217 23 33N 110 22 E
Pingquan .... 215 41 1N 118 37 E
Pingrup .... 229 33 32 S 118 29 E
Pingtan .... 217 25 31N 119 47 E
Pingtang .... 216 25 49N 107 17 E
Pingüicas, Cerro 107 21 10N 99 42W
Pingwu .... 214 32 25N 104 30 E
Pingxiang,
Guangxi
Zhuangzu, China . 216 22 6N 106 46 E
Pingxiang, Jiangxi,
China .... 217 27 43N 113 48 E
Pingyao .... 214 37 12N 112 10 E
Pingyi .... 215 35 30N 117 35 E
Pingyin .... 214 36 20N 116 25 E
Pingyuan,
Guangdong,
China .... 217 24 37N 115 57 E
Pingyuan,
Shandong, China . 214 37 10N 116 22 E
Pingyuanjie .... 216 23 45N 103 48 E
Pinhal .... 125 22 10 S 46 46W
Pinheiro .... 120 2 31 S 45 5W
Pinhel 154 40 50N 7 1W
Pinhuá → .... 123 6 21 S 65 0W
Pini .... 208 0 10N 98 40 E
Piniós →, Ilía,
Greece .... 169 37 48N 21 20 E
Piniós →, Trikkala,
Greece .... 168 39 55N 22 10 E
Pinitos, Sa. de 100 31 8N 110 50W
Pinjarra .... 229 32 37 S 115 52 E
Pink → 77 56 50N 103 50W
Pinkafeld .... 151 47 22N 16 9 E
Pinlebu .... 202 24 5N 95 22 E
Pinnacles .... 229 28 12 S 120 26 E
Pinneberg .... 146 53 39N 9 48 E
Pino Hachado, Paso 126 38 39 S 70 54W
Pinos 105 22 18N 101 34W
Pinos, Sa. de 105 22 20N 101 30W
Pinos Puente 155 37 15N 3 45W
Pinotepa de Don
Luis 109 16 25N 97 55W
Pinrang .... 207 3 46 S 119 41 E
Pins, Î. des .... 226 22 37 S 167 30 E
Pins, Pte. aux 84 42 15N 81 51W
Pinsk .... 178 52 10N 26 1 E
Pintados .... 122 20 35 S 69 40W
Pintumba .... 229 31 30 S 132 12 E
Pintuyan .... 211 9 57N 125 15 E
Pinukpuk .... 210 17 35N 121 22 E
Pinware 79 51 37N 56 42W
Pinware → 79 51 39N 56 42W
Pinyang .... 217 27 42N 120 31 E
Pinyug .... 176 60 5N 48 0 E
Pinzolo .... 162 46 9N 10 45 E
Pio V. Corpuz ..... 211 11 55N 124 2 E
Pio XII .... 120 3 53 S 45 17W
Pioduran .... 210 13 2N 123 25 E
Piombino .... 162 42 54N 10 30 E
Piombino, Canale di 162 42 50N 10 25 E
Pioner, Os. .... 185 79 50N 92 0 E
Pionki .... 152 51 29N 21 28 E
Piorini → .... 119 3 23 S 63 30W
Piorini, L. .... 119 3 15 S 62 35W
Piotrków
Trybunalski ...... 152 51 23N 19 43 E
Piotrków
Trybunalski □ ... 152 51 30N 19 45 E
Piove di Sacco ..... 163 45 18N 12 1 E
Pip .... 193 26 45N 60 10 E
Pipar .... 198 26 25N 73 31 E
Piparia .... 198 22 45N 78 23 E
Pipéri .... 168 39 20N 24 19 E
Pipestone → 74 52 53N 89 23W
Pipestone Cr. →,
Man., Canada 89 49 38N 100 15W
Pipestone Cr. →,
Sask., Canada 77 49 42N 100 45W
Pipiriki .... 234 39 28 S 175 5 E
Pipmuacan, Rés. ... 83 49 45N 70 30W
Pippingarra .... 228 20 27 S 118 42 E
Pipriac 138 47 49N 1 58W
Piquet Carneiro .... 120 5 48 S 39 25W
Piquiri → .... 125 24 3 S 54 14W
Pīr Sohrāb .... 193 25 44N 60 54 E
Piracanjuba .... 121 17 18 S 49 1W
Piracicaba .... 125 22 45 S 47 40W
Piracuruca .... 120 3 50 S 41 50W
Piræus = Piraiévs .. 169 37 57N 23 42 E
Piraiévs .... 169 37 57N 23 42 E
Piraiévs □ .... 169 37 0N 23 30 E
Piráino .... 165 38 10N 14 52 E
Pirajuí .... 125 21 59 S 49 29W
Piran .... 163 45 31N 13 33 E
Pirané .... 124 25 42 S 59 6W
Piranhas .... 120 9 27 S 37 46W
Pirano = Piran .... 163 45 31N 13 33 E
Pirapemas .... 120 3 43 S 44 14W
Pirapora .... 121 17 20 S 44 56W
Piray → .... 123 16 32 S 63 45W
Pirdop .... 167 42 40N 24 10 E
Pires do Rio .... 121 17 18 S 48 17W
Pirganj .... 202 25 51N 88 24 E
Pírgos, Ilía, Greece . 169 37 40N 21 27 E
Pírgos, Messinia,
Greece .... 169 36 50N 22 16 E
Pirgovo .... 167 43 44N 25 43 E
Piriac-sur-Mer 138 47 22N 2 33W
Piribebuy .... 124 25 26 S 57 2W
Pirin Planina .... 167 41 40N 23 30 E
Pirineos .... 156 42 40N 1 0 E
Piripiri .... 120 4 15 S 41 46W
Piritu 118 9 23N 69 12W
Pirlerkondu .... 190 36 54N 32 29 E
Pirmasens .... 147 49 12N 7 30 E
Pirna .... 146 50 57N 13 57 E
Pirojpur .... 202 22 35N 90 1 E
Pirot .... 166 43 9N 22 39 E
Piru .... 207 3 4 S 128 12 E
Piryatin .... 178 50 15N 32 25 E
Pirýí .... 169 38 13N 25 59 E
Pisa .... 162 43 43N 10 23 E
Pisa → .... 152 53 14N 21 52 E
Pisa Ra. .... 235 44 52 S 169 12 E
Pisac .... 122 13 25 S 71 50W
Pisagua .... 122 19 40 S 70 15W
Pisarovina .... 163 45 35N 15 50 E
Pisciotta .... 165 40 7N 15 12 E
Pisco .... 122 13 50 S 76 12W
Piscu .... 170 45 30N 27 43 E
Písek .... 150 49 19N 14 10 E
Pishan .... 212 37 30N 78 33 E
Pishin Lora → .... 198 29 9N 64 55 E
Pising .... 207 5 8 S 121 53 E
Pissos 140 44 19N 0 49W
Piste 111 20 42N 88 35W
Pisticci .... 165 40 24N 16 33 E
Pistóia .... 162 43 57N 10 53 E
Pistol B. 77 62 25N 92 37W
Pistolet B. 79 51 35N 55 45W
Pisuerga → 154 41 33N 4 52W
Pisz .... 152 53 38N 21 49 E
Pital 111 18 33N 91 8W
Pitalito 118 1 51N 76 2W
Pitanga .... 121 24 46 S 51 44W
Pitangui .... 121 19 40 S 44 54 E
Pitarpunga, L. ..... 231 34 24 S 143 30 E
Pitcairn I. .... 225 25 5 S 130 5W
Pite älv → .... 174 65 20N 21 25 E
Piteå .... 174 65 20N 21 25 E
Piterka .... 179 50 41N 47 29 E
Piteşti .... 170 44 52N 24 54 E
Pithapuram .... 200 17 10N 82 15 E
Pithara .... 229 30 20 S 116 35 E
Píthion .... 168 41 24N 26 40 E
Pithiviers .... 139 48 10N 2 13 E
Pitigliano .... 163 42 38N 11 40 E
Pitlochry 134 56 43N 3 43W
Pitoco .... 211 10 8N 124 33 E
Pitrufquén .... 126 38 59 S 72 39W
Pitt I. 92 53 30N 129 50W
Pitt L. 93 49 25N 122 32W
Pittem .... 143 51 1N 3 13 E
Pittsworth .... 231 27 41 S 151 37 E
Pituri → .... 230 22 35 S 138 30 E
Piuí .... 121 20 28 S 45 58W
Pium .... 120 10 27 S 49 11W
Piura .... 122 5 15 S 80 38W
Piura □ .... 122 5 10 S 80 0W
Piva → .... 166 43 20N 18 50 E
Pivabiska → 87 50 13N 82 52W
Pivijay 118 10 28N 74 37W
Piwniczna .... 152 49 27N 20 42 E
Pixoyal 111 18 56N 90 37W
Piyai .... 168 39 17N 21 25 E
Pizarro 118 4 58N 77 22W
Pizol .... 149 46 57N 9 23 E
Pizzo .... 165 38 44N 16 10 E
Placentia 79 47 20N 54 0W
Placentia B. 79 47 0N 54 40W
Placer .... 211 11 52N 123 55 E
Placetas 112 22 15N 79 44W
Plačkovica .... 166 41 45N 22 30 E
Plaffeien .... 148 46 45N 7 17 E
Plaisance .... 140 43 36N 0 3 E
Pláka .... 168 40 0N 25 24 E
Plakenska Planina .. 166 41 14N 21 2 E
Plakhino .... 184 67 45N 86 5 E
Plamondon 90 54 51N 112 32W
Plan de las Hayas .. 108 19 45N 96 39W
Planá .... 150 49 50N 12 44 E
Plana Cays 113 22 38N 73 30W
Plancoët 138 48 32N 2 13W
Plandište .... 166 45 16N 21 10 E
Planeta Rica 118 8 25N 75 36W
Planina, Slovenija,
Yugoslavia ...... 163 46 10N 15 20 E
Planina, Slovenija,
Yugoslavia ...... 163 45 47N 14 19 E
Plaridel .... 211 8 37N 123 43 E
Plasencia 154 40 3N 6 8W
Plaški .... 163 45 4N 15 22 E
Plassen .... 172 61 9N 12 30 E
Plast .... 182 54 22N 60 50 E
Plaster Rock 81 46 53N 67 22W
Plastun .... 218 44 45N 136 19 E
Plata, La, Argentina 124 35 0 S 57 55W
Plata, La, Colombia 118 2 23N 75 53W
Plata, La, L. .... 126 44 55 S 71 50W
Plata, Río de la .... 124 34 45 S 57 30W
Platani → .... 164 37 23N 13 16 E
Plateau □ .... 247 8 0N 8 30 E
Plateros 105 23 13N 102 51W
Platí, Ákra .... 168 40 27N 24 0 E
Plato 118 9 47N 74 47W
Platte, Piz .... 149 46 30N 9 35 E
Plattling .... 147 48 46N 12 53 E

Plau 146 53 27N 12 16 E
Plauen 146 50 29N 12 9 E
Plav 166 42 38N 19 57 E
Plavinas 178 56 35N 25 46 E
Plavnica 166 42 20N 19 13 E
Plavsk 179 53 40N 37 18 E
Playa del Carmen 111 20 37N 87 4W
Playa Noriega, L. 100 29 4N 111 56W
Playa Vicente 109 17 50N 95 49W
Playgreen L. 89 54 0N 98 15W
Playón 104 25 16N 108 11W
Pleasant Bay 75 46 51N 60 48W
Pleasant Hills 233 35 28 S 146 50 E
Pleasant Pt. 235 44 16 S 171 9 E
Pleasantdale 88 52 35N 104 30W
Pléaux 140 45 8N 2 13 E
Pledger L. 87 50 53N 83 42W
Pleiku 204 13 57N 108 0 E
Plélan-le-Grand 138 48 0N 2 7W
Plémet 138 48 11N 2 36W
Pléneuf-Val-André 138 48 35N 2 32W
Pleniţa 170 44 14N 23 10 E
Plenty 88 51 47N 108 38W
Plenty → 230 23 25 S 136 31 E
Plenty, Bay of 234 37 45 S 177 0 E
Plesetsk 176 62 40N 40 10 E
Plessisville 83 46 14N 71 47W
Plestin-les-Grèves 138 48 40N 3 39W
Pleszew 152 51 53N 17 47 E
Pleternica 166 45 17N 17 48 E
Pletipi L. 78 51 44N 70 6W
Pleven 167 43 26N 24 37 E
Plevlja 166 43 21N 19 21 E
Plevna 85 44 58N 76 59W
Ploče 166 43 4N 17 26 E
Płock 152 52 32N 19 40 E
Płock □ 152 52 30N 19 45 E
Plöcken Passo 163 46 37N 12 57 E
Ploegsteert 143 50 44N 2 53 E
Ploëmeur 138 47 44N 3 26W
Ploërmel 138 47 55N 2 26W
Ploieşti 170 44 57N 26 5 E
Plomárion 169 38 58N 26 24 E
Plomb du Cantal 140 45 2N 2 48 E
Plombières 139 47 59N 6 27 E
Plomin 163 45 8N 14 10 E
Plön 146 54 8N 10 22 E
Plöner See 146 54 10N 10 22 E
Plonge, Lac La 77 55 8N 107 20W
Płońsk 152 52 37N 20 21 E
Płoty 152 53 48N 15 18 E
Plouaret 138 48 37N 3 28W
Plouay 138 47 55N 3 21W
Ploučnice → 150 50 46N 14 13 E
Ploudalmézeau 138 48 34N 4 41W
Plougasnou 138 48 42N 3 49W
Plouha 138 48 41N 2 57W
Plouhinee 138 48 0N 4 29W
Plovdiv 167 42 8N 24 44 E
Plum Coulee 89 49 11N 97 45W
Plumas 89 50 23N 99 5W
Plumtree 251 20 27 S 27 55 E
Plunge 178 55 53N 21 59 E
Plunkett 88 51 55N 105 27W
Pluvigner 138 47 46N 3 1W
Plymouth 133 50 23N 4 9W
Plymouth Sd. 133 50 20N 4 10W
Plympton 81 44 30N 65 55W
Plynlimon = Pumlumon Fawr 133 52 29N 3 47W
Plyussa 178 58 40N 29 20 E
Plyussa → 178 58 40N 29 0 E
Plzen 150 49 45N 13 22 E
Pniewy 152 52 31N 16 16 E
Pô 247 11 14N 1 5W
Po → 162 44 57N 12 4 E
Po, Foci del 163 44 55N 12 30 E
Po Hai = Bo Hai 215 39 0N 120 0 E
Pobé 247 7 0N 2 56 E
Pobeda 185 65 12N 146 12 E
Pobedino 185 49 51N 142 49 E
Pobedy Pik 184 40 45N 79 58 E
Pobiedziska 152 52 29N 17 11 E
Pobla de Lillet, La 156 42 16N 1 59 E
Pobla de Segur 156 42 15N 0 58 E
Pobladura de Valle 154 42 6N 5 44W
Pocatière, La 83 47 22N 70 2W
Počátky 150 49 15N 15 14 E
Pochep 178 52 58N 33 29 E
Pochinki 179 54 41N 44 59 E
Pochinok 178 54 28N 32 29 E
Pöchlarn 150 48 12N 15 12 E
Pochontas 76 53 10N 117 51W
Pochotitán 104 21 35N 104 43W
Poci 119 5 57N 61 29W
Pocinhos 120 7 4 S 36 3W
Pocito Casas 100 28 32N 111 6W
Poções 121 14 31 S 40 21W
Poconé 123 16 15 S 56 37W
Poços de Caldas 125 21 50 S 46 33W
Poddebice 152 51 54N 18 58 E
Poděbrady 150 50 9N 15 8 E
Podensac 140 44 40N 0 22W
Podgorač 166 45 27N 18 13 E
Podgorica = Titograd 166 42 30N 19 19 E
Podkamennaya Tunguska → 185 61 50N 90 13 E
Podlapac 163 44 37N 15 47 E
Podmokly 150 50 48N 14 10 E
Podoleni 170 46 46N 26 39 E
Podolínec 151 49 16N 20 31 E
Podolsk 179 55 25N 37 30 E
Podor 246 16 40N 15 2W
Podporozhy 176 60 55N 34 2 E
Podravska Slatina 166 45 42N 17 45 E
Podu Turcului 170 46 11N 27 25 E
Podujevo 166 42 54N 21 10 E
Poel 146 54 0N 11 25 E
Pofadder 254 29 10 S 19 22 E
Pogamasing 87 46 55N 81 50W
Poggiardo 165 40 3N 18 21 E
Poggibonsi 163 43 27N 11 8 E
Pogoanele 170 44 55N 27 0 E
Pogorzcla 152 51 50N 17 12 E
Pogoso 253 6 46 S 17 12 E
Pogradeci 168 40 57N 20 37 E
Pogranitšnyi 218 44 25N 131 24 E
Poh 207 0 46 S 122 51 E
Pohang 215 36 1N 129 23 E
Pohorelá 151 48 50N 20 2 E
Pohořelice 151 48 59N 16 31 E
Pohorje 163 46 30N 15 20 E
Poiana Mare 170 43 57N 23 5 E
Poiana Ruscăi, Munţii 170 45 45N 22 25 E
Poile, La 79 47 41N 58 24W
Poindimié 226 20 56 S 165 20 E
Poinsett, C. 13 65 42 S 113 18 E
Point Edward 84 43 0N 82 30W
Point Gatineau 82 45 28N 75 42W
Point L. 94 65 15N 113 4W
Point Leamington 79 49 20N 55 24W
Point Pass 232 34 5 S 139 5 E
Point Pedro 201 9 50N 80 15 E
Point Pelee Nat. Park 84 41 57N 82 31W
Point Sapin 81 46 58N 64 50W
Pointe-à-la-Frégate 80 49 12N 64 55W
Pointe-à-Maurier 80 50 20N 59 48W
Pointe-à-Pitre 113 16 10N 61 30W
Pointe au Baril Sta. 84 45 35N 80 23W
Pointe-au-Pic 83 47 38N 70 9W
Pointe-aux-Anglais 80 49 41N 67 10W
Pointe-aux-Outardes 83 49 3N 68 26W
Pointe-aux-Trembles 83 45 40N 73 30W
Pointe-Claire 83 45 26N 73 50W
Pointe du Bois 89 50 18N 95 33W
Pointe-Gatineau 85 45 28N 75 42W
Pointe-Lebel 83 49 10N 68 12W
Pointe Noire 253 4 48 S 11 53 E
Pointe-Parent 80 50 8N 61 47W
Pointe Verte 81 47 51N 65 46W
Poirino 162 44 55N 7 50 E
Poisonbush Ra. 228 22 30 S 121 30 E
Poisson-Blanc, L. du 82 46 0N 75 45W
Poissy 139 48 55N 2 0 E
Poitiers 138 46 35N 0 20 E
Poitou, Plaines et Seuil du 140 46 30N 0 1W
Poix 139 49 47N 2 0 E
Poix-Terron 139 49 38N 4 38 E
Pokataroo 231 29 30 S 148 36 E
Poko, Sudan 245 5 41N 31 55 E
Poko, Zaïre 250 3 7N 26 52 E
Pokrov 179 55 55N 39 7 E
Pokrovka 183 42 20N 78 0 E
Pokrovsk 185 61 29N 126 12 E
Pokrovsk-Uralskiy 182 60 10N 59 49 E
Pol 154 43 9N 7 20W
Pola = Pula 163 44 54N 13 57 E
Pola de Allande 154 43 16N 6 37W
Pola de Gordón, La 154 42 51N 5 41W
Pola de Lena 154 43 10N 5 49W
Pola de Siero 154 43 24N 5 39W
Pola de Somiedo 154 43 5N 6 15W
Polan 193 25 30N 61 10 E
Poland ■ 152 52 0N 20 0 E
Polanów 152 54 7N 16 41 E
Polar Sub-Glacial Basin 13 85 0 S 110 0 E
Polcura 124 37 17 S 71 43W
Połcyn Zdrój 152 53 47N 16 5 E
Polden Hills 133 51 7N 2 50W
Polemi 190 34 54N 32 30 E
Polessk 178 54 50N 21 8 E
Polesye 178 52 0N 28 10 E
Polevskoy 182 56 26N 60 11 E
Polewali 207 3 21 S 119 23 E
Polgar 151 47 54N 21 6 E
Pŏlgyo-ri 215 34 51N 127 21 E
Poli 252 8 34N 13 15 E
Políaigos 169 36 45N 24 38 E
Policastro, Golfo di 165 39 55N 15 35 E
Police 152 53 33N 14 33 E
Polička 151 49 43N 16 15 E
Polignano a Mare 165 41 0N 17 12 E
Poligny 139 46 50N 5 42 E
Políkhnitas 169 39 4N 26 10 E
Polillo 210 14 43N 121 56 E
Polillo Is. 210 14 56N 122 0 E
Polillo Strait 210 14 44N 121 51 E
Polinkin 111 19 9N 88 13W
Polis 190 35 2N 32 26 E
Polístena 165 38 25N 16 4 E
Políyiros 168 40 23N 23 25 E
Polkowice 152 51 29N 16 3 E
Polla 165 40 31N 15 27 E
Pollachi 201 10 35N 77 0 E
Pollensa 156 39 54N 3 1 E
Pollensa, B. de 156 39 53N 3 8 E
Póllica 165 40 13N 15 3 E
Pollino, Mte. 165 39 54N 16 13 E
Polna 178 58 31N 28 0 E
Polnovat 184 63 50N 65 54 E
Pologi 180 47 29N 36 15 E
Polonnoye 178 50 6N 27 30 E
Polotitlán 107 20 13N 99 49W
Polotsk 178 55 30N 28 50 E
Polski Trŭmbesh 167 43 20N 25 38 E
Polsko Kosovo 167 43 23N 25 38 E
Poltava 180 49 35N 34 35 E
Poltimore 82 45 47N 75 43W
Polunochnoye 176 60 52N 60 25 E
Polur 201 12 32N 79 11 E
Polyanovgrad 167 42 39N 26 59 E
Polyarny 176 69 8N 33 20 E
Polynesia 225 10 0 S 162 0W
Pom, L. de 111 18 35N 92 12W
Pomarance 162 43 18N 10 51 E
Pomarico 165 40 31N 16 33 E
Pomaro 106 18 20N 103 18W
Pombal, Brazil 120 6 45 S 37 50W
Pombal, Portugal 154 39 55N 8 40W
Pómbia 169 35 0N 24 51 E
Pomio 227 5 32 S 151 33 E
Pomona 102 25 43N 102 20W
Pomorie 167 42 32N 27 41 E
Pomoshnaya 180 48 13N 31 36 E
Pompei 165 40 45N 14 30 E
Pompey 139 48 50N 6 2 E
Pomuch 111 20 8N 90 11W
Ponape 224 6 55N 158 10 E
Ponask, L. 74 54 0N 92 41W
Ponass L. 88 52 16N 103 58W
Poncheville, L. 82 50 10N 76 55W
Poncin 141 46 6N 5 25 E
Poncitlán, Jalisco, Mexico 106 20 22N 102 55W
Poncitlán, Jalisco, Mexico 106 20 5N 103 30W
Pond Inlet 95 72 40N 77 0W
Pondicherry 201 11 59N 79 50 E
Pondoland 255 31 10 S 29 30 E
Pondooma 232 33 29 S 136 59 E
Pondrôme 143 50 6N 5 0 E
Ponds, I. of 78 53 27N 55 52W
Ponérihouen 226 21 5 S 165 24 E
Ponferrada 154 42 32N 6 35W
Pongo, Wadi → 245 8 42N 27 40 E
Poniatowa 152 51 11N 22 3 E
Poniec 152 51 48N 16 50 E
Ponikva 163 46 16N 15 26 E
Ponnaiyar → 201 11 50N 79 45 E
Ponnani 201 10 45N 75 59 E
Ponneri 201 13 20N 80 15 E
Ponnuru 201 16 5N 80 34 E
Ponoi 176 67 0N 41 0 E
Ponoi → 176 66 59N 41 17 E
Ponoka 91 52 42N 113 40W
Ponomarevka 182 53 19N 54 8 E
Ponorogo 209 7 52 S 111 27 E
Ponot 211 8 25N 123 0 E
Pons, France 140 45 35N 0 34W
Pons, Spain 156 41 55N 1 12 E
Ponsul → 155 39 40N 7 31W
Pont, Le 148 46 41N 6 20 E
Pont-à-Celles 143 50 30N 4 22 E
Pont-à-Mousson 139 48 54N 6 1 E
Pont-Audemer 138 49 21N 0 30 E
Pont-Aven 138 47 51N 3 47W
Pont Canavese 162 45 24N 7 33 E
Pont-de-Roide 139 47 23N 6 45 E
Pont-de-Salars 140 44 18N 2 44 E
Pont-de-Vaux 139 46 26N 4 56 E
Pont-de-Veyle 141 46 17N 4 53 E
Pont-l'Abbé 138 47 52N 4 15W
Pont-l'Évêque 138 49 18N 0 11 E
Pont-Rouge 83 46 45N 71 42W
Pont-St-Esprit 141 44 16N 4 40 E
Pont-sur-Yonne 139 48 18N 3 10 E
Ponta de Pedras 120 1 23 S 48 52W
Ponta Grossa 125 25 7 S 50 10W
Ponta Pora 125 22 20 S 55 35W
Pontacq 140 43 11N 0 8W
Pontailler 139 47 18N 5 24 E
Pontal → 120 9 8 S 40 12W
Pontalina 121 17 31 S 49 27W
Pontarlier 139 46 54N 6 20 E
Pontassieve 163 43 47N 11 25 E
Pontaubault 138 48 40N 1 20W
Pontaumur 140 45 52N 2 40 E
Pontcharra 141 45 26N 6 1 E
Pontchâteau 138 47 25N 2 5W
Ponte Alta, Serra do 121 19 42 S 47 40W
Ponte Alta do Norte 120 10 45 S 47 34W
Ponte Branca 123 16 27 S 52 40W
Ponte da Barca 154 41 48N 8 25W
Ponte de Sor 155 39 17N 7 57W
Ponte dell 'Olio 162 44 52N 9 39 E
Ponte di Legno 162 46 15N 10 30 E
Ponte do Lima 154 41 46N 8 35W
Ponte do Pungué 251 19 30 S 34 33 E
Ponte Leccia 141 42 28N 9 13 E
Ponte Macassar 207 9 30 S 123 58 E
Ponte nell' Alpi 163 46 10N 12 18 E
Ponte Nova 121 20 25 S 42 54W
Ponte San Martino 162 45 36N 7 47 E
Ponte San Pietro 162 45 42N 9 35 E
Pontebba 163 46 30N 13 17 E
Pontecorvo 164 41 28N 13 40 E
Pontedera 162 43 40N 10 37 E
Pontefract 132 53 42N 1 19W
Ponteix 88 49 46N 107 29W
Pontelandolfo 165 41 17N 14 41 E
Pontevedra, Negros, Phil. 211 10 22N 122 52 E
Pontevedra, Panay, Phil. 211 11 29N 122 50 E
Pontevedra, Spain 154 42 26N 8 40W
Pontevedra □ 154 42 25N 8 39W
Pontevedra, R. de → 154 42 22N 8 45W
Pontevico 162 45 16N 10 6 E
Pontiac, Parc 82 46 30N 76 30W
Pontian Kecil 205 1 29N 103 23 E
Pontianak 209 0 3 S 109 15 E
Pontine Is. = Ponziane, Isole 164 40 55N 13 0 E
Pontínia 164 41 25N 13 2 E
Pontivy 138 48 5N 3 0W
Pontoise 139 49 3N 2 5 E
Ponton → 76 58 27N 116 11W
Pontorson 138 48 34N 1 30W
Pontrémoli 162 44 22N 9 52 E
Pontresina 149 46 29N 9 48 E
Pontrieux 138 48 42N 3 10W
Ponts-de-Cé, Les 138 47 25N 0 30W
Pontypool, Canada 85 44 6N 78 38W
Pontypool, U.K. 133 51 42N 3 1W
Pontypridd 133 51 36N 3 21W
Ponza 164 40 55N 12 57 E
Ponziane, Isole 164 40 55N 13 0 E
Poochera 231 32 43 S 134 51 E
Poole 133 50 42N 1 58W
Pooley I. 92 52 45N 128 15W
Poona = Pune 200 18 29N 73 57 E
Poona Bayabao 211 7 56N 124 17 E
Poonamallee 201 13 3N 80 10 E
Pooncarie 231 33 22 S 142 31 E
Poonindie 232 34 34 S 135 54 E
Poopelloe, L. 231 31 40 S 144 0 E
Poopó 122 18 23 S 66 59W
Poopó, Lago de 122 18 30 S 67 35W
Poor Knights Is. 234 35 29 S 174 43 E
Popanyinning 229 32 40 S 117 2 E
Popayán 118 2 27N 76 36W
Poperinge 143 50 51N 2 42 E
Popigay 185 72 1N 110 39 E
Popilta, L. 231 33 10 S 141 42 E
Popina 167 44 7N 26 57 E
Popio, L. 231 33 10 S 141 52 E
Poplar →, Man., Canada 89 53 0N 97 19W
Poplar →, N.W.T., Canada 76 61 22N 121 52W
Poplar Point 89 50 4N 97 59W
Poplarfield 88 50 53N 97 36W
Popocatépetl, Volcán 109 19 2N 98 38W
Popokabaka 253 5 41 S 16 40 E
Pópoli 163 42 12N 13 50 E
Popondetta 227 8 48 S 148 17 E
Popovača 163 45 30N 16 41 E
Popovo 167 43 21N 26 18 E
Poppel 143 51 27N 5 2 E
Poprád 151 49 3N 20 18 E
Poprád → 151 49 38N 20 42 E
Poradaha 202 23 51N 89 1 E
Porali → 197 25 35N 66 26 E
Porangaba 122 8 48 S 70 36W
Porangahau 234 40 17 S 176 37 E
Porangatu 121 13 26 S 49 10W
Porbandar 198 21 44N 69 43 E
Porce → 118 7 28N 74 53W
Porcher I. 92 53 50N 130 30W
Porco 123 19 50 S 65 59W
Porcos → 121 12 42 S 45 7W
Porcuna 155 37 52N 4 11W
Porcupine 87 48 30N 81 11W
Porcupine → 77 59 11N 104 46W
Porcupine Plain 88 52 36N 103 15W
Pordenone 163 45 58N 12 40 E
Pordim 167 43 23N 24 51 E
Poreč 163 45 14N 13 36 E
Porecatu 121 22 43 S 51 24W

Poretskoye **179** 55 9N 46 21 E
Pori, Finland **175** 61 29N 21 48 E
Porí, Greece **169** 35 58N 23 13 E
Porjus **174** 66 57N 19 50 E
Porkhov **178** 57 45N 29 38 E
Porkkala **175** 59 59N 24 26 E
Porlamar **119** 10 57N 63 51W
Porlezza **162** 46 2N 9 8 E
Porma → **154** 42 49N 5 28W
Pornic **138** 47 7N 2 5W
Poronaysk **185** 49 13N 143 0 E
Póros **169** 37 30N 23 30 E
Poroshiri-Dake **218** 42 41N 142 52 E
Poroszló **151** 47 39N 20 40 E
Poroto Mts. **251** 9 0 S 33 30 E
Porpoise B. **13** 66 0 S 127 0 E
Porquerolles, Îles de **141** 43 0N 6 13 E
Porrentruy **148** 47 25N 7 6 E
Porreras **156** 39 31N 3 2 E
Porretta, Passo di **162** 44 2N 10 56 E
Porsangen **174** 70 40N 25 40 E
Porsgrunn **171** 59 10N 9 40 E
Port **139** 47 43N 6 4 E
Port Adelaide **232** 34 46 S 138 30 E
Port Alberni **92** 49 40N 124 50W
Port Albert **233** 38 42 S 146 42 E
Port Alfred, Canada **83** 48 18N 70 53W
Port Alfred, S. Africa **254** 33 36 S 26 55 E
Port Alice **92** 50 20N 127 25W
Port Alma **230** 23 38 S 150 53 E
Port Antonio **112** 18 10N 76 30W
Port Arthur = Lüshun **215** 38 45N 121 15 E
Port Arthur **230** 43 7 S 147 50 E
Port au Choix **79** 50 43N 57 22W
Port au Port **79** 48 33N 58 43W
Port au Port B. **79** 48 40N 58 50W
Port-au-Prince **113** 18 40N 72 20W
Port Augusta **231** 32 30 S 137 50 E
Port Augusta West **231** 32 29 S 137 29 E
Port Bell **250** 0 18N 32 35 E
Port Bergé Vaovao **255** 15 33 S 47 40 E
Port Blandford **79** 48 20N 54 10W
Port Bou **156** 42 25N 3 9 E
Port Bouët **246** 5 16N 3 57W
Port Bradshaw **230** 12 30 S 137 20 E
Port Broughton **232** 33 37 S 137 56 E
Port Burwell **84** 42 40N 80 48W
Port Campbell **232** 38 37 S 143 1 E
Port Canning **199** 22 23N 88 40 E
Port Carling **84** 45 7N 79 35W
Port-Cartier **80** 50 2N 66 50W
Port-Cartier-Ouest **80** 50 1N 66 52W
Port Chalmers **235** 45 49 S 170 30 E
Port Clements **92** 53 40N 132 10W
Port Colborne **84** 42 50N 79 10W
Port Coquitlam **93** 49 15N 122 45W
Port Credit **84** 43 33N 79 35W
Port Curtis **230** 23 57 S 151 20 E
Port-Daniel, Parc Prov. de **80** 48 11N 64 58W
Port Darwin, Australia **228** 12 24 S 130 45 E
Port Darwin, Falk. Is. **126** 51 50 S 59 0W
Port Davey **230** 43 16 S 145 55 E
Port-de-Bouc **141** 43 24N 4 59 E
Port-de-Paix **113** 19 50N 72 50W
Port Dickson **205** 2 30N 101 49 E
Port Douglas **230** 16 30 S 145 30 E
Port Dover **84** 42 47N 80 12W
Port Dufferin **81** 44 55N 62 23W
Port Edward **92** 54 12N 130 10W
Port Elgin, N.B., Canada **81** 46 3N 64 5W
Port Elgin, Ont., Canada **74** 44 25N 81 25W
Port Elizabeth **254** 33 58 S 25 40 E
Port Ellen **134** 55 38N 6 10W
Port-en-Bessin **138** 49 21N 0 45W
Port Erin **132** 54 5N 4 45W
Port Essington **228** 11 15 S 132 10 E
Port Etienne = Nouâdhibou **240** 20 54N 17 0W
Port Fairy **231** 38 22 S 142 12 E
Port Fitzroy **234** 36 8 S 175 20 E
Port Fouâd = Bûr Fuad **244** 31 15N 32 20 E
Port-Gentil **252** 0 40 S 8 50 E
Port Glasgow **134** 55 57N 4 40W
Port Greville **81** 45 24N 64 33W
Port Harcourt **247** 4 40N 7 10 E
Port Hardy **92** 50 41N 127 30W
Port Harrison = Inoucdjouac **78** 58 25N 78 15W
Port Hastings **81** 45 39N 61 24W
Port Hawkesbury **81** 45 36N 61 22W
Port Hedland **228** 20 25 S 118 35 E
Port Hood **81** 46 0N 61 32W
Port Hope **85** 43 56N 78 20W
Port Howe **81** 45 51N 63 45W
Port-Joinville **138** 46 45N 2 23W
Port Katon **181** 46 52N 38 46 E
Port Kembla **231** 34 52 S 150 49 E
Port-la-Nouvelle **140** 43 1N 3 3 E
Port Laoise **135** 53 2N 7 20W
Port-Leucate-Barcarès **140** 42 53N 3 3 E
Port Lincoln **232** 34 42 S 135 52 E
Port Loko **246** 8 48N 12 46W
Port Loring **84** 45 55N 80 0W
Port Lorne **81** 44 57N 65 16W
Port Louis, France **138** 47 42N 3 22W
Port Louis, Maur. **203** 20 10 S 57 30 E
Port Lyautey = Kenitra **240** 34 15N 6 40W
Port Macdonnell **232** 38 0 S 140 48 E
Port McNeill **92** 50 35N 127 5W
Port Macquarie **231** 31 25 S 152 25 E
Port Maria **112** 18 25N 77 5W
Port Medway **81** 44 8N 64 35W
Port Mellon **93** 49 32N 123 31W
Port-Menier **80** 49 51N 64 15W
Port Moody **93** 49 17N 122 51W
Port Morant **112** 17 54N 76 19W
Port Moresby **227** 9 24 S 147 8 E
Port Mourant **119** 6 15N 57 20W
Port Mouton **81** 43 58N 64 50W
Port Musgrave **230** 11 55 S 141 50 E
Port-Navalo **138** 47 34N 2 54W
Port Nelson **77** 57 3N 92 36W
Port Nicholson **234** 41 20 S 174 52 E
Port Nolloth **254** 29 17 S 16 52 E
Port Nouveau-Québec **78** 58 30N 65 59W
Port of Spain **113** 10 40N 61 31W
Port Pegasus **235** 47 12 S 167 41 E
Port Perry **85** 44 6N 78 56W
Port Phillip B. **231** 38 10 S 144 50 E
Port Pirie **231** 33 10 S 138 1 E
Port Pólnocny **152** 54 25N 18 42 E
Port Radium = Echo Bay **94** 66 5N 117 55W
Port Renfrew **92** 48 30N 124 20W
Port Roper **230** 14 45 S 135 47 E
Port Rowan **84** 42 40N 80 30W
Port Royal **81** 44 43N 65 36W
Port Safaga = Bûr Safâga **244** 26 43N 33 57 E
Port Said = Bûr Sa'îd **244** 31 16N 32 18 E
Port-St-Louis-du-Rhône **141** 43 23N 4 49 E
Port San Vicente **210** 18 30N 122 8 E
Port Saunders **79** 50 40N 57 18W
Port Severn **84** 44 48N 79 43W
Port Shepstone **255** 30 44 S 30 28 E
Port Simpson **76** 54 30N 130 20W
Port Stanley **84** 42 40N 81 10W
Port Sudan = Bûr Sûdân **244** 19 32N 37 9 E
Port Talbot **133** 51 35N 3 48W
Port Taufîq = Bûr Taufiq **244** 29 54N 32 32 E
Port-Vendres **140** 42 32N 3 8 E
Port Victoria **232** 34 30 S 137 29 E
Port Vladimir **176** 69 25N 33 6 E
Port Wakefield **232** 34 12 S 138 10 E
Port Weld **205** 4 50N 100 38 E
Portachuelo **123** 17 10 S 63 20W
Portadown **135** 54 27N 6 26W
Portage B. **89** 51 33N 98 50W
Portage La Prairie **89** 49 58N 98 18W
Portalegre **155** 39 19N 7 25W
Portalegre □ **155** 39 20N 7 40W
Portarlington **135** 53 10N 7 10W
Porteirinha **121** 15 44 S 43 2W
Portel, Brazil **120** 1 57 S 50 49W
Portel, Portugal **155** 38 19N 7 41W
Porter L., N.W.T., Canada **77** 61 41N 108 5W
Porter L., Sask., Canada **77** 56 20N 107 20W
Porterville **254** 33 0 S 18 57 E
Porthcawl **133** 51 28N 3 42W
Portile de Fier **170** 44 42N 22 30 E
Portimão **155** 37 8N 8 32W
Portland, N.S.W., Australia **231** 33 20 S 150 0 E
Portland, Vic., Australia **231** 38 20 S 141 35 E
Portland, Canada **85** 44 42N 76 12W
Portland, Bill of **133** 50 31N 2 27W
Portland, I. of **133** 50 32N 2 25W
Portland B. **231** 38 15 S 141 45 E
Portland Creek Pond **79** 50 11N 57 32W
Portland I. **234** 39 20 S 177 51 E
Portland Prom. **78** 58 40N 78 33W
Portneuf **83** 46 43N 71 55W
Portneuf → **83** 48 38N 69 5W
Portneuf, Parc Prov. de **83** 47 10N 72 25W
Pôrto, Brazil **120** 3 54 S 42 42W
Porto, Portugal **154** 41 8N 8 40W
Porto □ **154** 41 8N 8 20W
Porto, G. de **141** 42 17N 8 34 E
Pôrto Acre **122** 9 34 S 67 31W
Pôrto Alegre, Pará, Brazil **119** 4 22 S 52 44W
Pôrto Alegre, Rio Grande do Sul, Brazil **125** 30 5 S 51 10W
Porto Amboim = Gunza **253** 10 50 S 13 50 E
Porto Argentera **162** 44 15N 7 27 E
Porto Azzurro **162** 42 46N 10 24 E
Porto Botte **164** 39 3N 8 33 E
Pôrto Cajueiro **123** 11 3 S 55 53W
Porto Civitanova **163** 43 19N 13 44 E
Pôrto da Fôlha **120** 9 55 S 37 17W
Pôrto de Móz **120** 1 41 S 52 13W
Pôrto de Pedras **120** 9 10 S 35 17W
Pôrto des Meinacos **123** 12 33 S 53 7W
Porto Empédocle **164** 37 18N 13 30 E
Pôrto Esperança **123** 19 37 S 57 29W
Pôrto Esperidão **123** 15 51 S 58 28W
Pôrto Franco **120** 6 20 S 47 24W
Porto Garibaldi **163** 44 41N 12 14 E
Pôrto Grande **119** 0 42N 51 24W
Pôrto Jofre **123** 17 20 S 56 48W
Pórto Lágo **168** 40 58N 25 6 E
Porto Mendes **125** 24 30 S 54 15W
Pôrto Murtinho **123** 21 45 S 57 55W
Pôrto Nacional **120** 10 40 S 48 30W
Porto Novo **247** 6 23N 2 42 E
Porto Recanati **163** 43 26N 13 40 E
Porto San Giórgio **163** 43 11N 13 49 E
Pôrto Santana **119** 0 3 S 51 11W
Porto Santo Stefano **162** 42 26N 11 7 E
Pôrto São José **125** 22 43 S 53 10W
Pôrto Seguro **121** 16 26 S 39 5W
Porto Tolle **163** 44 57N 12 20 E
Porto Tórres **164** 40 50N 8 23 E
Pôrto União **125** 26 10 S 51 10W
Pôrto Válter **122** 8 15 S 72 40W
Porto-Vecchio **141** 41 35N 9 16 E
Pôrto Velho **123** 8 46 S 63 54W
Portobelo **112** 9 35N 79 42W
Portoferráio **162** 42 50N 10 20 E
Portogruaro **163** 45 47N 12 50 E
Portomaggiore **163** 44 41N 11 47 E
Portoscuso **164** 39 12N 8 22 E
Portovénere **162** 44 2N 9 50 E
Portoviejo **118** 1 7 S 80 28W
Portpatrick **134** 54 50N 5 7W
Portree **134** 57 25N 6 11W
Portrush **135** 55 13N 6 40W
Portsall **138** 48 37N 4 45W
Portsmouth, Domin. **113** 15 34N 61 27W
Portsmouth, U.K. **133** 50 48N 1 6W
Portsoy **134** 57 41N 2 41W
Porttipahta **174** 68 5N 26 40 E
Portugal ■ **154** 40 0N 7 0W
Portugalete **156** 43 19N 3 4W
Portuguesa □ **118** 9 10N 69 15W
Portuguese-Guinea = Guinea-Bissau ■ **246** 12 0N 15 0W
Portuguese Timor ■ = Timor **207** 9 0 S 125 0 E
Portumna **135** 53 5N 8 12W
Porvenir, Bolivia **122** 11 10 S 68 50W
Porvenir, Chile **126** 53 10 S 70 16W
Porvoo **175** 60 24N 25 40 E
Porzuna **155** 39 9N 4 9W
Posada → **164** 40 40N 9 45 E
Posadas, Argentina **125** 27 30 S 55 50W
Posadas, Spain **155** 37 47N 5 11W
Poschiavo **149** 46 19N 10 4 E
Posets **156** 42 39N 0 25 E
Poshan = Boshan **215** 36 28N 117 49 E
Posht-e-Badam **193** 33 2N 55 23 E
Posídhion, Ákra **168** 39 57N 23 30 E
Posidium **169** 35 30N 27 10 E
Poso **207** 1 20 S 120 55 E
Posoegroenoe **119** 4 23N 55 43W
Posong **215** 34 46N 127 5 E
Posse **121** 14 4 S 46 18W
Possel **252** 5 5N 19 10 E
Possession I. **13** 72 4 S 172 0 E
Pössneck **146** 50 42N 11 34 E
Postavy **178** 55 4N 26 50 E
Poste de la Baleine **78** 55 17N 77 45W
Poste Maurice Cortier **240** 22 14N 1 2 E
Postmasburg **254** 28 18 S 23 5 E
Postojna **163** 45 46N 14 12 E
Pótam **100** 27 36N 110 23W
Potamós, Andikíthira, Greece **169** 36 18N 22 58 E
Potamós, Kíthira, Greece **169** 36 15N 22 58 E
Potchefstroom **254** 26 41 S 27 7 E
Potcoava **170** 44 30N 24 39 E
Poté **121** 17 49 S 41 49W
Potelu, Lacul **170** 43 44N 24 20 E
Potenza **165** 40 40N 15 50 E
Potenza → **163** 43 27N 13 38 E
Potenza Picena **163** 43 22N 13 37 E
Poteriteri, L. **235** 46 5 S 167 10 E
Potes **154** 43 15N 4 42W
Potgietersrus **255** 24 10 S 28 55 E
Poti **181** 42 10N 41 38 E
Potiraguá **121** 15 36 S 39 53W
Potiskum **247** 11 39N 11 2 E
Potlogi **170** 44 34N 25 34 E
Potosí **123** 19 38 S 65 50W
Potosí □ **122** 20 31 S 67 0W
Potosí, B. **107** 17 35N 101 30W
Potosí, Cerro **103** 24 52N 100 13W
Pototan **211** 10 54N 122 38 E
Potrerillos **124** 26 30 S 69 30W
Potsdam **146** 52 23N 13 4 E
Potsdam □ **146** 52 40N 12 50 E
Pottenstein **147** 49 46N 11 25 E
Pottery Hill = Abû Ballas **244** 24 26N 27 36 E
Pouancé **138** 47 44N 1 10W
Pouce Coupé **76** 55 40N 120 10W
Pouch Cove **79** 47 46N 52 46W
Pouembout **226** 21 8 S 164 53 E
Pouilly **139** 47 18N 2 57 E
Poulaphouca Res. **135** 53 8N 6 30W
Pouldu, Le **138** 47 41N 3 36W
Poulin-de-Courval, L. **83** 48 52N 70 27W
Poum **226** 20 14 S 164 2 E
Poumadji **252** 5 56N 22 10 E
Pounga-Nganda **252** 2 58 S 10 51 E
Pourri, Mont **141** 45 32N 6 52 E
Pouso Alegre, Mato Grosso, Brazil **123** 11 46 S 57 16W
Pouso Alegre, Minas Gerais, Brazil **125** 22 14 S 45 57W
Poutrincourt, L. **83** 49 11N 74 7W
Pouzauges **138** 46 47N 0 50W
Povenets **176** 62 50N 34 50 E
Poverty Bay **234** 38 43 S 178 2 E
Povlen **166** 44 9N 19 44 E
Póvoa de Lanhosa **154** 41 33N 8 15W
Póvoa de Varzim **154** 41 25N 8 46W
Povorino **179** 51 12N 42 5 E
Povungnituk **78** 60 2N 77 10W
Povungnituk → **78** 60 3N 77 15W
Povungnituk, B. **78** 60 0N 77 30W
Povungnituk, Mts. de **78** 61 22N 75 5W
Powassan **84** 46 5N 79 25W
Powell L. **92** 50 2N 124 25W
Powell River **92** 49 50N 124 35W
Powys □ **133** 52 20N 3 20W
Poxoreu **123** 15 50 S 54 23W
Poyang Hu **217** 29 5N 116 20 E
Poyarkovo **185** 49 36N 128 41 E
Poysdorf **151** 48 40N 16 37 E
Poza de la Sal **156** 42 35N 3 31W
Poza Grande, La **99** 25 50N 112 5W
Poza Rica **108** 20 33N 97 27W
Požarevac **166** 44 35N 21 18 E
Pozas **103** 22 6N 100 52W
Pozas de Santa Ana **103** 22 48N 100 28W
Požega **166** 43 53N 20 2 E
Pozhva **182** 59 5N 56 5 E
Pozi **217** 23 30N 120 13 E
Poznań **152** 52 25N 16 55 E
Poznań □ **152** 52 50N 17 0 E
Pozo Alcón **157** 37 42N 2 56W
Pozo Almonte **122** 20 10 S 69 50W
Pozo Colorado **124** 23 30 S 58 45W
Pozo de Higueras **104** 22 19N 105 28W
Pozo Hondo **105** 23 30N 102 21W
Pozoblanco **155** 38 23N 4 51W
Pozorrubio **210** 16 7N 120 33 E
Pozos **107** 21 14N 100 29W
Pozuzo **122** 10 5 S 75 35W
Pozzallo **165** 36 44N 14 52 E
Pozzuoli **165** 40 46N 14 6 E
Pra → **247** 5 1N 1 37W
Prabuty **152** 53 47N 19 15 E
Prača **166** 43 47N 18 43 E
Prachatice **150** 49 1N 14 0 E
Prachin Buri **204** 14 0N 101 25 E
Prachuap Khiri Khan **205** 11 49N 99 48 E
Pradelles **140** 44 46N 3 52 E
Pradera **118** 3 25N 76 15W
Prades **140** 42 38N 2 23 E
Prado **121** 17 20 S 39 13W
Prado del Rey **155** 36 48N 5 33W
Præstø **172** 55 8N 12 2 E
Pragersko **163** 46 27N 15 42 E
Prague = Praha **150** 50 5N 14 22 E
Praha **150** 50 5N 14 22 E
Prahecq **140** 46 19N 0 26W
Prahita → **200** 19 0N 79 55 E
Prahova □ **170** 45 10N 26 0 E
Prahova → **170** 44 50N 25 50 E
Prahovo **166** 44 18N 22 39 E
Praid **170** 46 32N 25 10 E
Prainha, Amazonas, Brazil **123** 7 10 S 60 30W

Prainha, Pará, Brazil **119** 1 45 S 53 30W
Prairie **230** 20 50 S 144 35 E
Pramánda **168** 39 32N 21 8 E
Pran Buri **204** 12 23N 99 55 E
Prang **247** 8 1N 0 56W
Prapat **206** 2 41N 98 58 E
Praszka **152** 51 5N 18 31 E
Prata **121** 19 25 S 48 54W
Pratapgarh **198** 24 2N 74 40 E
Prática di Mare **164** 41 40N 12 26 E
Prätigau **149** 46 56N 9 44 E
Prato **162** 43 53N 11 5 E
Prátola Peligna **163** 42 7N 13 51 E
Pratovécchio **163** 43 44N 11 43 E
Prats-de-Mollo **140** 42 25N 2 27 E
Pratteln **148** 47 31N 7 41 E
Pravara → **200** 19 35N 74 45 E
Pravdinsk **179** 56 29N 43 28 E
Pravia **154** 43 30N 6 12W
Praxedis G. Guerrero **101** 31 22N 106 0W
Praya **209** 8 39 S 116 17 E
Pré-en-Pail **138** 48 28N 0 12W
Pré St. Didier **162** 45 45N 7 0 E
Precordillera **124** 30 0 S 69 1W
Predáppio **163** 44 7N 11 58 E
Predazzo **163** 46 19N 11 37 E
Predejane **166** 42 51N 22 9 E
Preeceville **88** 51 57N 102 40W
Préfailles **138** 47 9N 2 11W
Pregonero **118** 8 1N 71 46W
Pregrada **163** 46 11N 15 45 E
Preissac, L. **82** 48 20N 78 20W
Preko **163** 44 7N 15 14 E
Prelate **88** 50 51N 109 24W
Prelog **163** 46 18N 16 32 E
Premier **76** 56 4N 129 56W
Premuda **163** 44 20N 14 36 E
Prenj **166** 43 33N 17 53 E
Prenjasi **168** 41 6N 20 32 E
Prenzlau **146** 53 19N 13 51 E
Preobrazheniye **218** 42 54N 133 54 E
Prepansko Jezero **166** 40 55N 21 0 E
Přerov **151** 49 28N 17 27 E
Presanella **162** 46 13N 10 40 E
Prescott **85** 44 45N 75 30W
Prescott I. **92** 54 6N 130 37W
Preservation Inlet **235** 46 8 S 166 35 E
Preševo **166** 42 19N 21 39 E
Presicce **165** 39 53N 18 13 E
Presidencia de la Plaza **124** 27 0 S 29 50W
Presidencia Roque Saenz Peña **124** 26 45 S 60 30W
Presidente Epitácio **121** 21 56 S 52 6W
Presidente Hayes □ **124** 24 0 S 59 0W
Presidente Hermes **123** 11 17 S 61 55W
Presidente Prudente **125** 22 5 S 51 25W
Presidente Roxas **211** 11 26N 122 56 E
Presidios **104** 25 17N 105 38W
Presido → **104** 23 6N 106 17W
Preslav **167** 43 10N 26 52 E
Preslavska Planina **167** 43 10N 26 45 E
Prešov **151** 49 0N 21 15 E
Prespa **167** 41 44N 24 55 E
Prespa, L. = Prepansko Jezero **166** 40 55N 21 0 E
Presseger See **150** 46 37N 13 26 E
Prestbury **133** 51 54N 2 2W
Prestea **246** 5 22N 2 7W
Presteigne **133** 52 17N 3 0W
Přeštice **150** 49 34N 13 20 E
Presto **123** 18 55 S 64 56W
Preston **132** 53 46N 2 42W
Preston, C. **228** 20 51 S 116 12 E
Prestonpans **134** 55 58N 3 0W
Prestwick **134** 55 30N 4 38W
Prêto →, Amazonas, Brazil **119** 0 8 S 64 6W
Prêto →, Bahia, Brazil **120** 11 21 S 43 52W
Prêto do Igapó-Açu → **119** 4 26 S 59 48W
Pretoria **255** 25 44 S 28 12 E
Preuilly-sur-Claise **138** 46 51N 0 56 E
Préveza **169** 38 57N 20 47 E
Préveza □ **168** 39 20N 20 40 E
Priazovskoye **180** 46 44N 35 40 E
Pribilof Is. **12** 56 0N 170 0W
Priboj **166** 43 35N 19 32 E
Pribram **150** 49 41N 14 2 E
Price **80** 48 36N 68 7W
Price I. **92** 52 23N 128 41W
Prichalnaya **181** 48 57N 44 33 E
Priego **156** 40 26N 2 21W
Priego de Córdoba **155** 37 27N 4 12W
Priekule **178** 57 27N 21 45 E
Prien **147** 47 52N 12 20 E
Prieska **254** 29 40 S 22 42 E
Priestly **76** 54 8N 125 20W
Prieto Diaz **210** 13 2N 124 12 E
Prievidza **151** 48 46N 18 36 E
Prijedor **163** 44 58N 16 41 E
Prijepolje **166** 43 27N 19 40 E
Prikaspiyskaya Nizmennost **181** 47 0N 48 0 E
Prikumsk **180** 44 50N 44 10 E
Prilep **166** 41 21N 21 37 E
Priluki **178** 50 30N 32 24 E
Prime Seal I. **230** 40 3 S 147 43 E
Primeira Cruz **120** 2 30 S 43 26W
Primorsko **167** 42 15N 27 44 E
Primorsko-Akhtarsk **180** 46 2N 38 10 E
Primorskoye **180** 47 10N 37 38 E
Primrose L. **77** 54 55N 109 45W
Prince **88** 52 58N 108 23W
Prince Albert **88** 53 15N 105 50W
Prince Albert Mts. **13** 76 0 S 161 30 E
Prince Albert Nat. Park **88** 54 0N 106 25W
Prince Albert Pen. **94** 72 30N 116 0W
Prince Albert Sd. **94** 70 25N 115 0W
Prince Alfred C. **94** 74 20N 124 40W
Prince Charles I. **94** 67 47N 76 12W
Prince Charles Mts. **13** 72 0 S 67 0 E
Prince Edward I. □ **81** 46 20N 63 20W
Prince Edward Is. **203** 45 15 S 39 0 E
Prince Edward Island Nat. Pk. **81** 46 26N 63 12W
Prince Edward Pt. **85** 43 56N 76 52W
Prince George **93** 53 55N 122 50W
Prince Gustav Adolf Sea **94** 78 30N 107 0W
Prince of Wales I. **95** 73 0N 99 0W
Prince of Wales Is. **227** 10 40 S 142 10 E
Prince of Wales Str. **94** 73 0N 117 0W
Prince Patrick I. **94** 77 0N 120 0W
Prince Regent Inlet **95** 73 0N 90 0W
Prince Rupert **92** 54 20N 130 20W
Princenhage **143** 51 9N 4 45 E
Princesa Isabel **120** 7 44 S 38 0W
Princess Charlotte B. **230** 14 25 S 144 0 E
Princess Margaret Range **95** 80 30N 92 0W
Princess May Ranges **228** 15 30 S 125 30 E
Princess Royal Chan. **92** 53 0N 128 31W
Princess Royal I. **92** 53 0N 128 40W
Princeton **93** 49 27N 120 30W
Princeville **83** 46 10N 71 53W
Principe, I. de **237** 1 37N 7 27 E
Principe Chan. **92** 53 28N 130 0W
Principe da Beira **123** 12 20 S 64 30W
Prins Albert **254** 33 12 S 22 2 E
Prins Harald Kyst **13** 70 0 S 35 1 E
Prinsesse Astrid Kyst **13** 70 45 S 12 30 E
Prinsesse Ragnhild Kyst **13** 70 15 S 27 30 E
Prinzapolca **112** 13 20N 83 35W
Prior, C. **154** 43 34N 8 17W
Priozersk **176** 61 2N 30 7 E
Pripet = Pripyat → **178** 51 20N 30 9 E
Pripet Marshes = Polesye **178** 52 0N 28 10 E
Pripyat → **178** 51 20N 30 9 E
Prislop, Pasul **170** 47 37N 25 15 E
Pristen **179** 51 15N 36 44 E
Priština **166** 42 40N 21 13 E
Pritzwalk **146** 53 10N 12 11 E
Privas **141** 44 45N 4 37 E
Priverno **164** 41 29N 13 10 E
Privolzhsk **179** 57 23N 41 16 E
Privolzhskaya Vozvyshennost **179** 51 0N 46 0 E
Privolzhskiy **179** 51 25N 46 3 E
Privolzhye **179** 52 52N 48 33 E
Priyutnoye **181** 46 12N 43 40 E
Prizren **166** 42 13N 20 45 E
Prizzi **164** 37 44N 13 24 E
Prnjavor **166** 44 52N 17 43 E
Probolinggo **209** 7 46 S 113 13 E
Prochowice **152** 51 17N 16 20 E
Procida **164** 40 46N 14 0 E
Procter **93** 49 37N 116 57W
Proddatur **201** 14 45N 78 30 E
Proença-a-Nova **155** 39 45N 7 54W
Prof. Van Blommestein Meer **119** 4 45N 55 5W
Profondeville **143** 50 23N 4 52 E
Progreso, Coahuila, Mexico **102** 27 28N 101 4W
Progreso, Hidalgo, Mexico **107** 20 15N 99 12W
Progreso, Yucatán, Mexico **111** 21 17N 89 40W
Prokhladnyy **181** 43 50N 44 2 E
Prokletije **168** 42 30N 19 45 E
Prokopyevsk **184** 54 0N 86 45 E
Prokuplje **166** 43 16N 21 36 E
Proletarskaya **181** 46 42N 41 50 E
Prome = Pyè **202** 18 49N 95 13 E
Prophet → **76** 58 48N 122 40W
Propriá **120** 10 13 S 36 51W
Propriano **141** 41 41N 8 52 E
Proserpine **230** 20 21 S 148 36 E
Prosna **152** 51 1N 18 30 E
Prosperidad **211** 8 34N 125 52 E
Prostějov **151** 49 30N 17 9 E
Prostki **152** 53 42N 22 25 E
Proston **231** 26 8 S 151 32 E
Proszowice **152** 50 13N 20 16 E
Próti **169** 37 5N 21 32 E
Provadiya **167** 43 12N 27 30 E
Proven, Belgium **143** 50 54N 2 40 E
Prøven, Canada **95** 72 10N 55 8W
Provence **141** 43 40N 5 46 E
Providence Bay **84** 45 41N 82 15W
Providence C. **235** 45 59 S 166 29 E
Providencia **118** 0 28 S 76 28W
Providencia, I. de **112** 13 25N 81 26W
Provideniya **185** 64 23N 173 18W
Provins **139** 48 33N 3 15 E
Provost **91** 52 25N 110 20W
Prozor **166** 43 50N 17 34 E
Prudentópolis **121** 25 12 S 50 57W
Prud'homme **88** 52 20N 105 54W
Prudnik **152** 50 20N 17 38 E
Prüm **147** 50 14N 6 22 E
Pruszcz Gd. **152** 54 17N 18 40 E
Pruszków **152** 52 9N 20 49 E
Prut → **170** 46 3N 28 10 E
Pruzhany **178** 52 33N 24 28 E
Prvič **163** 44 55N 14 47 E
Prydz B. **13** 69 0 S 74 0 E
Przasnysz **152** 53 2N 20 45 E
Przedbórz **152** 51 6N 19 53 E
Przedecz **152** 52 20N 18 53 E
Przemyśl **152** 49 50N 22 45 E
Przeworsk **152** 50 6N 22 32 E
Przewóz **152** 51 28N 14 57 E
Przhevalsk **183** 42 30N 78 20 E
Przysuchla **152** 51 22N 20 38 E
Psakhná **169** 38 34N 23 35 E
Psará **169** 38 37N 25 38 E
Psathoúra **168** 39 30N 24 12 E
Psel → **180** 49 5N 33 20 E
Pserimos **169** 36 56N 27 12 E
Pskem → **183** 41 38N 70 1 E
Pskemskiy Khrebet **183** 42 0N 70 45 E
Pskent **183** 40 54N 69 20 E
Pskov **178** 57 50N 28 25 E
Psunj **166** 45 25N 17 19 E
Pszczyna **152** 49 59N 18 58 E
Pteleón **169** 39 3N 22 57 E
Ptich → **178** 52 9N 28 52 E
Ptolemaís **168** 40 30N 21 43 E
Ptuj **163** 46 28N 15 50 E
Ptujska Gora **163** 46 23N 15 47 E
Pu Xian **214** 36 24N 111 6 E
Pua **204** 19 11N 100 55 E
Puán, Argentina **124** 37 30 S 62 45W
Pu'an, China **216** 25 46N 104 57 E
Puan, S. Korea **215** 35 44N 126 44 E
Pubei **216** 22 16N 109 31 E
Pucacuro → **118** 3 20 S 74 58W
Pucallpa **122** 8 25 S 74 30W
Pucará, Bolivia **123** 18 43 S 64 11W
Pucará, Peru **122** 15 5 S 70 24W
Pucarani **122** 16 23 S 68 30W
Pucheng **217** 27 59N 118 31 E
Pucheni **170** 45 12N 25 17 E
Pucio Pt. **211** 11 46N 121 51 E
Pučišće **163** 43 22N 16 43 E
Puck **152** 54 45N 18 23 E
Pucka, Zatoka **152** 54 30N 18 40 E
Pucte **111** 18 13N 88 39W
Puding **216** 26 18N 105 44 E
Pudozh **176** 61 48N 36 32 E
Pudtol **210** 18 13N 121 22 E
Pudukkottai **201** 10 28N 78 47 E
Puebla **109** 19 3N 98 12W
Puebla □ **109** 18 50N 98 0W
Puebla, La **156** 39 46N 3 1 E
Puebla, Sa. de **107** 19 40N 98 0W
Puebla de Alcocer **155** 38 59N 5 14W
Puebla de Cazalla, La **155** 37 10N 5 20W
Puebla de Don Fadrique **157** 37 58N 2 25W
Puebla de Don Rodrigo **155** 39 5N 4 37W
Puebla de Guzmán **155** 37 37N 7 15W
Puebla de los Infantes, La **155** 37 47N 5 24W
Puebla de Montalbán, La **154** 39 52N 4 22W
Puebla de Sanabria **154** 42 4N 6 38W
Puebla de Trives **154** 42 20N 7 10W
Puebla del Caramiñal **154** 42 37N 8 56W
Pueblito de Allende **101** 26 59N 105 21W
Pueblo Hundido **124** 26 20 S 70 5W
Pueblo Nuevo, Durango, Mexico **104** 23 23N 105 23W
Pueblo Nuevo, Guanajuato, Mexico **107** 20 31N 101 22W
Pueblo Nuevo, Venezuela **118** 8 26N 71 26W
Pueblo Nuevo Solistahuacán **110** 17 6N 92 53W
Pueblo Viejo, L. **108** 22 10N 97 53W
Puelches **124** 38 5 S 65 51W
Puelén **124** 37 32 S 67 38W
Puente Alto **124** 33 32 S 70 35W
Puente de Ixtla **107** 18 37N 99 20W
Puente del Arzobispo **154** 39 48N 5 10W
Puente-Genil **155** 37 22N 4 47W
Puente la Reina **156** 42 40N 1 49W
Puente Nacional **108** 19 20N 96 26W
Puenteareas **154** 42 10N 8 28W
Puentedeume **154** 43 24N 8 10W
Puentes de Garcia Rodriguez **154** 43 27N 7 50W
Pu'er **216** 23 0N 101 15 E
Puerta, La **157** 38 22N 2 45W
Puerta Galera **210** 13 30N 120 57 E
Puerto Acosta **122** 15 32 S 69 15W
Puerto Aisén **126** 45 27 S 73 0W
Puerto Angel **109** 15 40N 96 29W
Puerto Armuelles **112** 8 20N 82 51W
Puerto Ayacucho **118** 5 40N 67 35W
Puerto Barrios **112** 15 40N 88 32W
Puerto Bermejo **124** 26 55 S 58 34W
Puerto Bermúdez **122** 10 20 S 75 0W
Puerto Bolívar **118** 3 19 S 79 55W
Puerto Cabello **118** 10 28N 68 1W
Puerto Cabezas **112** 14 0N 83 30W
Puerto Cabo Gracias á Dios **112** 15 0N 83 10W
Puerto Capaz = Jebba **240** 35 11N 4 43W
Puerto Carreño **118** 6 12N 67 22W
Puerto Castilla **112** 16 0N 86 0W
Puerto Chicama **122** 7 45 S 79 20W
Puerto Coig **126** 50 54 S 69 15W
Puerto Cortes, C. Rica **112** 8 55N 84 0W
Puerto Cortés, Hond. **112** 15 51N 88 0W
Puerto Cortés, Mexico **99** 24 28N 111 51W
Puerto Cumarebo **118** 11 29N 69 30W
Puerto de Lobos, B. **100** 30 25N 112 55W
Puerto de Santa María **155** 36 36N 6 13W
Puerto Deseado **126** 47 55 S 66 0W
Puerto Escondido **109** 15 50N 97 3W
Puerto Guaraní **123** 21 18 S 57 55W
Puerto Heath **122** 12 34 S 68 39W
Puerto Huitoto **118** 0 18N 74 3W
Puerto Inca **122** 9 22 S 74 54W
Puerto Juárez **111** 21 11N 86 49W
Puerto La Cruz **119** 10 13N 64 38W
Puerto Leguízamo **118** 0 12 S 74 46W
Puerto Limón **118** 3 23N 73 30W
Puerto Lobos **126** 42 0 S 65 3W
Puerto López **118** 4 5N 72 58W
Puerto Lumbreras **157** 37 34N 1 48W
Puerto Madero **110** 14 44N 92 25W
Puerto Madryn **126** 42 48 S 65 4W
Puerto Magdalena **99** 24 38N 112 9W
Puerto Maldonado **122** 12 30 S 69 10W
Puerto Manotí **112** 21 22N 76 50W
Puerto Mazarrón **157** 37 34N 1 15W
Puerto Mercedes **118** 1 11N 72 53W
Puerto Miraña **118** 1 20 S 70 19W
Puerto Montt **126** 41 28 S 73 0W
Puerto Morelos **111** 20 50N 86 52W
Puerto Nariño **118** 4 56N 67 48W
Puerto Natales **126** 51 45 S 72 15W
Puerto Nuevo **118** 5 53N 69 56W
Puerto Nutrias **118** 8 5N 69 18W
Puerto Ordaz **119** 8 16N 62 44W
Puerto Padre **112** 21 13N 76 35W
Puerto Páez **118** 6 13N 67 28W
Puerto Peñasco **100** 31 20N 113 33W
Puerto Pinasco **124** 22 36 S 57 50W
Puerto Pirámides **126** 42 35 S 64 20W
Puerto Plata **113** 19 48N 70 45W
Puerto Portillo **122** 9 45 S 72 42W
Puerto Princesa **211** 9 46N 118 45 E
Puerto Quellón **126** 43 7 S 73 37W
Puerto Quepos **112** 9 29N 84 6W
Puerto Real, Mexico **111** 18 46N 91 31W
Puerto Real, Spain **155** 36 33N 6 12W
Puerto Rico **122** 11 5 S 67 38W
Puerto Saavedra **126** 38 47 S 73 24W
Puerto Sastre **124** 22 2 S 57 55W
Puerto Siles **123** 12 48 S 65 5W
Puerto Suárez **123** 18 58 S 57 52W
Puerto Tejada **118** 3 14N 76 24W
Puerto Umbría **118** 0 52N 76 33W
Puerto Vallarta **106** 20 37N 105 15W
Puerto Varas **126** 41 19 S 72 59W
Puerto Villazón **123** 13 32 S 61 57W
Puerto Wilches **118** 7 21N 73 54W
Puertollano **155** 38 43N 4 7W
Puertomarin **154** 42 48N 7 36W
Puesto Cunambo **118** 2 10 S 76 0W
Pueyrredón, L. **126** 47 20 S 72 0W
Pugachev **179** 52 0N 48 49 E
Puge, China **216** 27 20N 102 31 E

Puge, Tanzania **250** 4 45 S 33 11 E
Puget-Théniers **141** 43 58N 6 53 E
Púglia □ **165** 41 0N 16 30 E
Pugo **210** 16 8N 121 31 E
Pugŏdong **215** 42 5N 130 0 E
Pugu **250** 6 55 S 39 4 E
Pūgūnzī **193** 25 49N 59 10 E
Pugwash **81** 45 51N 63 40W
Puha **234** 38 30 S 177 50 E
Pui **170** 45 30N 23 4 E
Puica **122** 15 0 S 72 33W
Puieşti **170** 46 25N 27 33 E
Puig Mayor, Mte. **156** 39 48N 2 47 E
Puigcerdá **156** 42 24N 1 50 E
Puigmal **156** 42 23N 2 7 E
Puisaye, Collines de **139** 47 34N 3 18 E
Puiseaux **139** 48 11N 2 30 E
Pujilí **118** 0 57 S 78 41W
Pujon-chosuji **215** 40 35N 127 35 E
Puka **168** 42 2N 19 53 E
Pukaki L. **235** 44 4 S 170 1 E
Pukapuka **225** 10 53 S 165 49W
Pukaskwa → **87** 48 0N 85 53W
Pukaskwa Nat. Park **87** 48 20N 86 0W
Pukatawagan **77** 55 45N 101 20W
Pukchin **215** 40 12N 125 45 E
Pukchŏng **215** 40 14N 128 10 E
Pukearuhe **234** 38 55 S 174 31 E
Pukekohe **234** 37 12 S 174 55 E
Puketeraki Ra. **235** 42 58 S 172 13 E
Pukeuri **235** 45 4 S 171 2 E
Pukou **217** 32 7N 118 38 E
Pula, Italy **164** 39 0N 9 0 E
Pula, Yugoslavia **163** 44 54N 13 57 E
Pulacayo **122** 20 25 S 66 41W
Pulawy **152** 51 23N 21 59 E
Pulgaon **198** 20 44N 78 21 E
Pulicat, L. **201** 13 40N 80 15 E
Puliyangudi **201** 9 11N 77 24 E
Pullabooka **233** 33 44 S 147 46 E
Pulmo, C. **99** 23 26N 109 25W
Pulog, Mt. **210** 16 40N 120 50 E
Púlpito, Pta. **99** 26 31N 111 28W
Púlpito do Sul **253** 15 46 S 12 0 E
Pułtusk **152** 52 43N 21 6 E
Pulupandan **211** 10 31N 122 48 E
Pumlumon Fawr **133** 52 29N 3 47W
Puna **123** 19 45 S 65 28W
Puná, I. **118** 2 55 S 80 5W
Punakha **202** 27 42N 89 52 E
Punalur **201** 9 0N 76 56 E
Punasar **198** 27 6N 73 6 E
Punata **123** 17 32 S 65 50W
Punch **199** 33 48N 74 4 E
Pune **200** 18 29N 73 57 E
Pungsan **215** 40 50N 128 9 E
Pungue, Ponte de **251** 19 0 S 34 0 E
Puning **217** 23 20N 116 12 E
Puningue, R. de → **107** 18 52N 100 40W
Punjab □, India **198** 31 0N 76 0 E
Punjab □, Pakistan **197** 30 0N 72 0 E
Punnichy **88** 51 23N 104 18W
Puno **122** 15 55 S 70 3W
Punt, La **149** 46 35N 9 56 E
Punta Abreojos **99** 26 42N 113 35W
Punta Allen **111** 19 48N 87 28W
Punta Alta **126** 38 53 S 62 4W
Punta Arenas **126** 53 10 S 71 0W
Punta Banda, C. **98** 31 45N 116 45W
Punta Cardón **118** 11 38N 70 14W
Punta Coles **122** 17 43 S 71 23W
Punta de Bombón **122** 17 10 S 71 48W
Punta de Díaz **124** 28 0 S 70 45W
Punta de Piedras **118** 10 54N 64 6W
Punta Delgado **126** 42 43 S 63 38W
Punta Prieta **98** 28 58N 114 17W
Puntabie **231** 32 12 S 134 13 E
Puntarenas **112** 10 0N 84 50W
Punto Fijo **118** 11 50N 70 13W
Puntzi L. **92** 52 12N 124 2W
Puqi **217** 29 40N 113 50 E
Puquio **122** 14 45 S 74 10W
Pur → **184** 67 31N 77 55 E
Purace, Vol. **118** 2 21N 76 23W
Puračić **166** 44 33N 18 28 E
Purari → **227** 7 49 S 145 0 E
Purbeck, Isle of **133** 50 40N 2 5W
Purcagua **107** 20 4N 100 28W
Purchena Tetica **157** 37 21N 2 21W
Purepero **106** 19 55N 102 1W
Puri **199** 19 50N 85 58 E
Purificación, Colombia **118** 3 51N 74 55W
Purificación, Mexico **106** 19 43N 104 38W
Purificación → **103** 23 58N 98 42W
Purísima, La, Baja Calif. S., Mexico **99** 26 10N 112 4W
Purísima, La, Coahuila, Mexico **102** 28 0N 101 20W
Purísima, La, Durango, Mexico **105** 24 14N 103 48W
Purmerend **142** 52 30N 4 58 E
Purna → **200** 19 6N 77 2 E
Purnia **199** 25 45N 87 31 E
Puruándiro **107** 20 5N 101 30W
Puruarán **107** 19 6N 101 32W
Purukcahu **209** 0 35 S 114 35 E
Puruliya **199** 23 17N 86 24 E
Purus → **119** 3 42 S 61 28W
Pŭrvomay **167** 42 8N 25 17 E
Purwakarta **209** 6 35 S 107 29 E
Purwodadi, Jawa, Indonesia **209** 7 7 S 110 55 E
Purwodadi, Jawa, Indonesia **209** 7 51 S 110 0 E
Purwokerto **209** 7 25 S 109 14 E
Purworejo **209** 7 43 S 110 2 E
Puryŏng **215** 42 0N 129 43 E
Pus → **200** 19 55N 77 55 E
Pusad **200** 19 56N 77 36 E
Pusan **215** 35 5N 129 0 E
Pushchino **185** 54 10N 158 0 E
Pushkin **178** 59 45N 30 25 E
Pushkino, R.S.F.S.R., U.S.S.R. **179** 51 16N 47 0 E
Pushkino, R.S.F.S.R., U.S.S.R. **179** 56 2N 37 49 E
Püspökladány **151** 47 19N 21 6 E
Pustoshka **178** 56 20N 29 30 E
Pustunich **111** 19 11N 90 26W
Puszczykowo **152** 52 18N 16 49 E
Put **111** 19 39N 89 25W
Putahow L. **77** 59 54N 100 40W
Putao **202** 27 28N 97 30 E
Putaruru **234** 38 2 S 175 50 E
Putbus **146** 54 19N 13 29 E
Puţeni **170** 45 49N 27 42 E
Putian **217** 25 23N 119 0 E
Putignano **165** 40 50N 17 5 E
Putina **122** 14 55 S 69 55W
Puting, Tanjung **209** 3 31 S 111 46 E
Putla → **109** 16 37N 97 38W
Putla de Guerrero **109** 17 2N 97 56W
Putlitz **146** 53 15N 12 3 E
Putna **170** 47 50N 25 33 E
Putna → **170** 45 42N 27 26 E
Putnok **151** 48 18N 20 26 E
Putorana, Gory **185** 69 0N 95 0 E
Putorino **234** 39 4 S 177 0 E
Putre **122** 18 12 S 69 35W
Puttalam Lagoon **201** 8 15N 79 45 E
Putte **143** 51 22N 4 24 E
Putten **142** 52 16N 5 36 E
Puttgarden **146** 54 28N 11 15 E
Puttur **201** 12 46N 75 12 E
Putty **233** 32 57 S 150 42 E
Putumayo → **118** 3 7 S 67 58W
Putuo **217** 29 56N 122 20 E
Putussibau **209** 0 50N 112 56 E
Puurs **143** 51 5N 4 17 E
Puy, Le **140** 45 3N 3 52 E
Puy-de-Dôme **140** 45 46N 2 57 E
Puy-de-Dôme □ **140** 45 47N 3 0 E
Puy-de-Sancy **140** 45 32N 2 48 E
Puy-Guillaume **140** 45 57N 3 29 E
Puy l'Évêque **140** 44 31N 1 9 E
Puyang **216** 35 40N 115 1 E
Puyehue **126** 40 40 S 72 37W
Puyjalon, L. **80** 50 30N 63 25W
Puylaurens **140** 43 35N 2 0 E
Puyo **118** 1 28 S 77 59W
Puyôo **140** 43 33N 0 56W
Pūzeh Rīg **193** 27 20N 58 40 E
Pwani □ **250** 7 0 S 39 0 E
Pweto **251** 8 25 S 28 51 E
Pwinbyu **202** 20 23N 94 40 E
Pwllheli **132** 52 54N 4 26W
Pya-ozero **176** 66 5N 30 58 E
Pyana → **179** 55 30N 46 0 E
Pyandzh **183** 37 14N 69 6 E
Pyandzh →, Afghan. **197** 43 40N 59 1 E
Pyandzh →, U.S.S.R. **183** 37 6N 68 20 E
Pyapon **202** 16 20N 95 40 E
Pyasina → **185** 73 30N 87 0 E
Pyatigorsk **181** 44 2N 43 6 E
Pyatikhatki **180** 48 28N 33 38 E
Pyaye **202** 19 12N 95 10 E
Pydna **168** 40 20N 22 34 E
Pyè **202** 18 49N 95 13 E
Pyinbauk **202** 19 10N 95 12 E
Pyinmana **202** 19 45N 96 12 E
Pyŏktong **215** 40 50N 125 50 E
Pyŏnggang **215** 38 24N 127 17 E
Pyŏngtaek **215** 37 1N 127 4 E
P'yŏngyang **215** 39 0N 125 45 E
Pyramids **244** 29 58N 31 9 E
Pyrenees = Pyrénées **140** 42 45N 0 18 E
Pyrénées **140** 42 45N 0 18 E
Pyrénées-Atlantiques □ **140** 43 15N 1 0W
Pyrénées-Orientales □ **140** 42 35N 2 26 E
Pyrzyce **152** 53 10N 14 55 E
Pyshchug **179** 58 57N 45 47 E
Pyshma → **182** 57 8N 66 18 E
Pytalovo **178** 57 5N 27 55 E
Pyttegga **171** 62 13N 7 42 E
Pyu **202** 18 30N 96 28 E
Pyzdry **152** 52 11N 17 42 E

Q

Qabalān **189** 32 8N 35 17 E
Qabātiyah **189** 32 25N 35 16 E
Qabr Hūd **195** 16 9N 49 34 E
Qādib, S. Yemen **195** 12 35N 54 2 E
Qādib, S. Yemen **195** 12 48N 53 57 E
Qa'el Jafr **191** 30 20N 36 25 E
Qa'emābād **193** 31 44N 60 2 E
Qā'emshahr **193** 36 30N 52 53 E
Qagan Nur **214** 43 30N 114 55 E
Qahar Youyi Zhongqi **214** 41 12N 112 40 E
Qahremānshahr **192** 34 19N 47 4 E
Qaidam Pendi **212** 37 0N 95 0 E
Qajarīyeh **193** 31 1N 48 22 E
Qal' at Shajwa **244** 25 2N 38 57 E
Qala-i-Jadid **198** 31 1N 66 25 E
Qala Yangi **198** 34 20N 66 30 E
Qalācheh **197** 35 30N 67 43 E
Qalansīyah **195** 12 41N 53 29 E
Qalāt **197** 32 15N 66 58 E
Qal'at al Akhḑar **192** 28 0N 37 10 E
Qal'at Bīshah **194** 20 0N 42 36 E
Qal'at Saura **244** 26 10N 38 40 E
Qal'at Sukkar **192** 31 51N 46 5 E
Qal'eh Darreh **192** 38 47N 47 2 E
Qal'eh-ye Best **197** 31 30N 64 21 E
Qal'eh-ye Now **197** 35 0N 63 5 E
Qal'eh-ye Panjeh **197** 37 0N 72 35 E
Qal'eh-ye Sarkari **197** 35 54N 67 17 E
Qal'eh-ye Valī **197** 35 46N 63 45 E
Qalqīlya **189** 32 12N 34 58 E
Qalyûb **244** 30 12N 31 11 E
Qam **189** 32 36N 35 43 E
Qamar, Ghubbat al **195** 16 20N 52 30 E
Qamar, Jabal al **195** 16 48N 53 15 E
Qamdo **216** 31 15N 97 6 E
Qamruddin Karez **197** 31 45N 68 20 E
Qāna **189** 33 12N 35 17 E
Qandahār **197** 31 32N 65 30 E
Qandahār □ **197** 31 0N 65 0 E
Qapān **193** 37 40N 55 47 E
Qâra **244** 29 38N 26 30 E
Qarā', Jabal al **195** 17 15N 54 15 E
Qara Qash → **199** 35 0N 78 30 E
Qara Tagh La = Kala Shank'ou **199** 35 42N 78 20 E
Qārah **192** 29 55N 40 3 E
Qarāvol **197** 37 14N 68 46 E
Qardud **245** 10 20N 29 56 E
Qareh → **192** 39 25N 47 22 E
Qareh Tekān **193** 36 38N 49 29 E
Qarqan He → **212** 39 30N 88 30 E
Qarrasa **245** 14 38N 32 5 E
Qartabā **190** 34 4N 35 50 E
Qaryat al Gharab **192** 31 27N 44 48 E
Qaryat al 'Ulyā **192** 27 33N 47 42 E
Qāsim **189** 32 59N 36 2 E
Qasr 'Amra **192** 31 48N 36 35 E
Qaşr Bū Hadi **241** 31 1N 16 45 E
Qaşr-e Qand **193** 26 15N 60 45 E
Qasr Farâfra **244** 27 0N 28 1 E
Qat Lesh **197** 34 40N 66 18 E
Qa'ţabah **194** 13 51N 44 42 E
Qatanā **190** 33 26N 36 4 E
Qaţānan, Ra's **195** 12 21N 53 33 E
Qatar ■ **195** 25 30N 51 15 E
Qatlīsh **193** 37 50N 57 19 E
Qatna **190** 34 50N 36 50 E
Qattâra **244** 30 12N 27 3 E
Qattâra, Munkhafed el **244** 29 30N 27 30 E
Qattâra Depression = Qattâra, Munkhafed el **244** 29 30N 27 30 E
Qawām al Ḩamzah **192** 31 43N 44 58 E
Qāyen **193** 33 40N 59 10 E
Qazvin **193** 36 15N 50 0 E
Qena **244** 26 10N 32 43 E
Qena, Wadi → **244** 26 12N 32 44 E
Qeshlāq **192** 34 55N 46 28 E
Qeshm **193** 26 55N 56 10 E
Qezi'ot **189** 30 52N 34 26 E
Qi Xian **214** 34 40N 114 48 E
Qian Gorlos **215** 45 5N 124 42 E
Qian Xian **214** 34 31N 108 15 E
Qiancheng **216** 27 12N 109 50 E
Qianjiang, Guangxi Zhuangzu, China **216** 23 38N 108 58 E
Qianjiang, Hubei, China **217** 30 24N 112 55 E
Qianjiang, Sichuan, China **216** 29 33N 108 47 E
Qianshan **217** 30 37N 116 35 E
Qianwei **216** 29 13N 103 56 E
Qianxi **216** 27 3N 106 3 E
Qianyang, Hunan, China **217** 27 18N 110 10 E
Qianyang, Shaanxi, China **214** 34 40N 107 8 E
Qianyang, Zhejiang, China **217** 30 11N 119 25 E
Qiaojia **216** 26 56N 102 58 E
Qibā' **192** 27 24N 44 20 E
Qichun **217** 30 18N 115 25 E
Qidong, Hunan, China **217** 26 49N 112 7 E
Qidong, Jiangsu, China **217** 31 48N 121 38 E
Qijiang **216** 28 57N 106 35 E
Qila Saifullāh **197** 30 45N 68 17 E
Qimen **217** 29 50N 117 42 E
Qin He → **214** 35 1N 113 22 E
Qin Jiang → **217** 26 15N 115 55 E
Qin Ling = Qinling Shandi **214** 33 50N 108 10 E
Qināb, W. → **195** 17 55N 49 59 E
Qin'an **214** 34 48N 105 40 E
Qing Xian **214** 38 35N 116 45 E
Qingcheng **215** 37 15N 117 40 E
Qingdao **215** 36 5N 120 20 E
Qingfeng **214** 35 52N 115 8 E
Qinghai □ **174** 36 0N 98 0 E
Qinghai Hu **212** 36 40N 100 10 E
Qinghecheng **215** 41 15N 124 30 E
Qinghemen **215** 41 48N 121 25 E
Qingjian **214** 37 8N 110 8 E
Qingjiang, Jiangsu, China **215** 33 30N 119 2 E
Qingjiang, Jiangxi, China **217** 28 4N 115 29 E
Qingliu **217** 26 11N 116 48 E
Qinglong **216** 25 49N 105 12 E
Qingping **216** 26 39N 107 47 E
Qingpu **217** 31 10N 121 6 E
Qingshui **214** 34 48N 106 8 E
Qingshuihe **214** 39 55N 111 35 E
Qingtian **217** 28 12N 120 15 E
Qingtongxia Shuiku **214** 37 50N 105 58 E
Qingxi **216** 27 8N 108 43 E
Qingxu **214** 37 34N 112 22 E
Qingyang, Anhui, China **217** 30 38N 117 50 E
Qingyang, Gansu, China **214** 36 2N 107 55 E
Qingyi Jiang → **216** 29 32N 103 44 E
Qingyuan, Guangdong, China **217** 23 40N 112 59 E
Qingyuan, Liaoning, China **215** 42 10N 124 55 E
Qingyuan, Zhejiang, China **217** 27 36N 119 3 E
Qingyun **215** 37 45N 117 20 E
Qingzhen **216** 26 31N 106 25 E
Qinhuangdao **215** 39 56N 119 30 E
Qinling Shandi **214** 33 50N 108 10 E
Qinshui **214** 35 40N 112 8 E
Qinyang **214** 35 7N 112 57 E
Qinyuan **214** 36 29N 112 20 E
Qinzhou **216** 21 58N 108 38 E
Qionghai **204** 19 15N 110 26 E
Qionglai **216** 30 25N 103 31 E
Qionglai Shan **216** 31 0N 102 30 E
Qiongshan **204** 19 51N 110 26 E
Qiongzhou Haixia **204** 20 10N 110 15 E
Qiqihar **213** 47 26N 124 0 E
Qirâiya, W. → **191** 30 27N 34 0 E
Qiryat 'Anavim **189** 31 49N 35 7 E
Qiryat Ata **189** 32 47N 35 6 E
Qiryat Bialik **189** 32 50N 35 5 E
Qiryat Gat **189** 31 32N 34 46 E
Qiryat Ḩayyim **189** 32 49N 35 4 E
Qiryat Mal'akhi **189** 31 44N 34 44 E
Qiryat Shemona **189** 33 13N 35 35 E
Qiryat Yam **189** 32 51N 35 4 E
Qishan, China **214** 34 25N 107 38 E
Qishan, Taiwan **217** 22 52N 120 25 E
Qishn **195** 15 26N 51 40 E
Qishon → **189** 32 49N 35 2 E
Qisrāyā **190** 34 55N 36 26 E
Qitai **212** 44 2N 89 35 E
Qitbīt, W. → **195** 19 15N 54 23 E
Qiubei **216** 24 2N 104 12 E
Qixia **215** 37 17N 120 52 E
Qiyang **217** 26 35N 111 50 E
Qizan, Si. Arabia **245** 16 57N 42 34 E
Qizān, Yemen **188** 17 0N 42 20 E
Qojūr **192** 36 12N 47 55 E
Qom **193** 34 40N 51 0 E
Qomsheh **193** 32 0N 51 55 E
Qondūz **197** 36 50N 68 50 E
Qondūz □ **197** 36 50N 68 50 E
Qu Jiang → **216** 30 1N 106 24 E
Qu Xian, Sichuan, China **216** 30 48N 106 58 E
Qu Xian, Zhejiang, China **217** 28 57N 118 54 E

Quackenbrück **146** 52 40N 7 59 E
Quadra I. **92** 50 10N 125 15W
Quairading **229** 32 0 S 117 21 E
Qualeup **229** 33 48 S 116 48 E
Qualicum Beach **92** 49 22N 124 26W
Quambatook **231** 35 49 S 143 34 E
Quambone **231** 30 57 S 147 53 E
Quan Long **205** 9 7N 105 8 E
Quandialla **231** 34 1 S 147 47 E
Quang Ngai **204** 15 13N 108 58 E
Quang Yen **204** 20 56N 106 52 E
Quannan **217** 24 45N 114 33 E
Quantock Hills **133** 51 8N 3 10W
Quanzhou, Fujian, China **217** 24 55N 118 34 E
Quanzhou, Guangxi Zhuangzu, China **217** 25 57N 111 5 E
Qu'Appelle **88** 50 33N 103 53W
Qu'Appelle → **88** 50 26N 101 19W
Quaraí **124** 30 15 S 56 20W
Quarré-les-Tombes **139** 47 21N 4 0 E
Quarryville **81** 46 50N 65 47W
Quartu Sant' Elena **164** 39 15N 9 10 E
Quathiaski Cove **92** 50 3N 125 12W
Quatsino **92** 50 30N 127 40W
Quatsino Sd. **92** 50 25N 127 58W
Qubab = Mishmar Ayyalon **189** 31 52N 34 57 E
Qūchān **193** 37 10N 58 27 E
Queanbeyan **231** 35 17 S 149 14 E
Québec **83** 46 52N 71 13W
Québec □ **75** 50 0N 70 0W
Quechultenango **107** 17 25N 99 13W
Quedlinburg **146** 51 47N 11 9 E
Queen Alexandra Ra. **13** 85 0 S 170 0 E
Queen Charlotte **92** 53 15N 132 2W
Queen Charlotte Bay **126** 51 50 S 60 40W
Queen Charlotte Is. **92** 53 20N 132 10W
Queen Charlotte Mts. **92** 53 5N 132 15W
Queen Charlotte Sd. **235** 41 10 S 174 15 E
Queen Charlotte Str. **92** 51 0N 128 0W
Queen Elizabeth Is. **95** 76 0N 95 0W
Queen Elizabeth Nat. Park **250** 0 0 30 0 E
Queen Mary Coast **13** 70 0 S 95 0 E
Queen Maud G. **94** 68 15N 102 30W
Queen Maud Ra. **13** 86 0 S 160 0W
Queens Chan. **228** 15 0 S 129 30 E
Queens Sd. **92** 51 57N 128 20W
Queenscliff **231** 38 16 S 144 39 E
Queensland □ **230** 22 0 S 142 0 E
Queenstown, Australia **230** 42 4 S 145 35 E
Queenstown, Canada **81** 45 41N 66 7W
Queenstown, N.Z. **235** 45 1 S 168 40 E
Queenstown, S. Africa **254** 31 52 S 26 52 E
Queguay Grande → **124** 32 9 S 58 9W
Queimadas **120** 11 0 S 39 38W
Quela **253** 9 10 S 16 56 E
Quelimane **251** 17 53 S 36 58 E
Quelpart = Cheju Do **215** 33 29N 126 34 E
Quemada, La **105** 22 26N 102 50W
Quemú-Quemú **124** 36 3 S 63 36W
Quequén **124** 38 30 S 58 30W
Querco **122** 13 50 S 74 52W
Queréndaro **107** 19 48N 100 53W
Querétaro, Baja Calif. S., Mexico **99** 25 25N 112 3W
Querétaro, Querétaro, Mexico **107** 20 36N 100 23W
Querétaro □ **107** 21 0N 99 55W
Querfurt **146** 51 22N 11 33 E
Querobabi **100** 30 3N 111 1W
Querqueville **138** 49 40N 1 42W
Quesada **157** 37 51N 3 4W
Queshan **214** 32 55N 114 2 E
Quesnel **93** 53 0N 122 30W
Quesnel → **93** 52 58N 122 29W
Quesnel L. **93** 52 30N 121 20W
Quesnoy, Le **139** 50 15N 3 38 E
Questembert **138** 47 40N 2 28W
Quetena **122** 22 10 S 67 25W
Quetico Prov. Park **86** 48 30N 91 45W
Quetrequile **126** 41 33 S 69 22W
Quetta **197** 30 15N 66 55 E
Quevedo **118** 1 2 S 79 29W
Quévillon, L. **82** 49 4N 76 57W
Quezaltenango **112** 14 50N 91 30W
Quezon □ **210** 14 40N 121 30 E
Quezon City **210** 14 38N 121 0 E
Qufār **192** 27 26N 41 37 E
Qui Nhon **204** 13 40N 109 13 E
Quiaca, La **124** 22 5 S 65 35W
Quibala **253** 10 46 S 14 59 E
Quibaxe **253** 8 24 S 14 27 E
Quibdo **118** 5 42N 76 40W
Quiberon **138** 47 29N 3 9W
Quíbor **118** 9 56N 69 37W
Quick **76** 54 36N 126 54W
Quickborn **146** 53 42N 9 52 E
Quiet L. **76** 61 5N 133 5W
Quiévrain **143** 50 24N 3 41 E
Quiindy **124** 25 58 S 57 14W
Quilá **104** 24 23N 107 13W
Quilán, C. **126** 43 15 S 74 30W
Quilchena **93** 50 10N 120 30W
Quilengues **253** 14 12 S 14 12 E
Quilimarí **124** 32 5 S 71 30W
Quilino **124** 30 14 S 64 29W
Quill Lake **88** 52 4N 104 15W
Quillabamba **122** 12 50 S 72 50W
Quillacollo **122** 17 26 S 66 17W
Quillagua **124** 21 40 S 69 40W
Quillaicillo **124** 31 17 S 71 40W
Quillan **140** 42 53N 2 10 E
Quillebeuf **138** 49 28N 0 30 E
Quillota **124** 32 54 S 71 16W
Quilmes **124** 34 43 S 58 15W
Quilon **201** 8 50N 76 38 E
Quilpie **231** 26 35 S 144 11 E
Quilpué **124** 33 5 S 71 33W
Quilua **251** 16 17 S 39 54 E
Quimbele **253** 6 17 S 16 41 E
Quimbonge **253** 8 36 S 18 30 E
Quime **122** 17 2 S 67 15W
Quimichis **104** 22 21N 105 32W
Quimilí **124** 27 40 S 62 30W
Quimper **138** 48 0N 4 9W
Quimperlé **138** 47 53N 3 33W
Quincemil **122** 13 15 S 70 40W
Quines **124** 32 13 S 65 48W
Quinga **251** 15 49 S 40 15 E
Quingey **139** 47 7N 5 52 E
Quiniluban Group **211** 11 27N 120 48 E
Quiñones **99** 24 22N 111 25W
Quintana de la Serena **155** 38 45N 5 40W
Quintana Roo **111** 20 52N 88 38W
Quintana Roo □ **111** 19 40N 88 30W
Quintanar de la Orden **156** 39 36N 3 5W
Quintanar de la Sierra **156** 41 57N 2 55W
Quintanar del Rey **157** 39 21N 1 56W
Quintero **124** 32 45 S 71 30W
Quintin **138** 48 26N 2 56W
Quinto **156** 41 25N 0 32W
Quinton **88** 51 23N 104 24W
Quinyambie **231** 30 15 S 141 0 E
Quinze, L. des **82** 47 35N 79 5W
Quípar → **157** 38 15N 1 40W
Quipungo **253** 14 37 S 14 40 E
Quiriego **100** 27 31N 109 16W
Quirihue **124** 36 15 S 72 35W
Quirimbo **253** 10 36 S 14 12 E
Quirindi **231** 31 28 S 150 40 E
Quirino □ **210** 16 15N 121 40 E
Quiriquire **118** 9 59N 63 13W
Quiroga, Mexico **107** 19 40N 101 32W
Quiroga, Spain **154** 42 28N 7 18W
Quiruvilca **122** 8 1 S 78 19W
Quissac **141** 43 55N 4 0 E
Quissanga **251** 12 24 S 40 28 E
Quitapa **253** 10 20 S 18 19 E
Quitilipi **124** 26 50 S 60 13W
Quito **118** 0 15 S 78 35W
Quitovac **100** 31 32N 112 42W
Quixadá **120** 4 55 S 39 0W
Quixaxe **251** 15 17 S 40 4 E
Quixeramobim **120** 5 12 S 39 17W
Quixinge **253** 9 52 S 14 23 E
Quizenga **253** 9 21 S 15 28 E
Qujing **216** 25 32N 103 41 E
Qul'ân, Jazâ'ir **244** 24 22N 35 31 E
Qumrān **189** 31 43N 35 27 E
Quneitra **189** 33 7N 35 48 E
Qunfudh **195** 16 39N 49 33 E
Quoin I. **228** 14 54 S 129 32 E
Quoin Pt. **254** 34 46 S 19 37 E
Quondong **231** 33 6 S 140 18 E
Quorn **231** 32 25 S 138 0 E
Qurein **245** 13 30N 34 50 E
Qurnat as Sawdā' **190** 34 18N 36 6 E
Qûs **244** 25 55N 32 50 E
Qusaybah **192** 34 24N 40 59 E
Quşay'ir **195** 14 55N 50 20 E
Quseir **244** 26 7N 34 16 E
Qūshchī **192** 37 59N 45 3 E
Qusrah **189** 32 5N 35 20 E
Quthing **255** 30 25 S 27 36 E
Qūţīābād **193** 35 47N 48 30 E
Quwayq → **190** 36 20N 37 10 E
Quwo **214** 35 38N 111 25 E
Quyang **214** 38 35N 114 40 E
Quynh Nhai **204** 21 49N 103 33 E
Quyon **82** 45 31N 76 14W
Quzi **214** 36 20N 107 20 E
Qytet Stalin **168** 40 47N 19 57 E

R

Ra, Ko **205** 9 13N 98 16 E
Råå **172** 56 0N 12 45 E
Raab **150** 48 21N 13 39 E
Raahe **174** 64 40N 24 28 E
Raalte **142** 52 23N 6 16 E
Raamsdonksveer **143** 51 43N 4 52 E
Ra'ananna **189** 32 12N 34 52 E
Raanes Pen. **95** 78 30N 85 45W
Raasay **134** 57 25N 6 4W
Raasay, Sd. of **134** 57 30N 6 8W
Rab **163** 44 45N 14 45 E
Raba **207** 8 36 S 118 55 E
Rába →, Hungary **152** 47 38N 17 38 E
Raba →, Poland **151** 50 8N 20 30 E
Rabaçal → **154** 41 30N 7 12W
Rabah **247** 13 5N 5 30 E
Rabai **250** 3 50 S 39 31 E
Rabaraba **227** 9 58 S 149 49 E
Rabastens, Hautes-Pyrénées, France **140** 43 25N 0 10 E
Rabastens, Tarn, France **140** 43 50N 1 43 E
Rabat, Malta **160** 35 53N 14 25 E
Rabat, Morocco **240** 34 2N 6 48W
Rabaul **227** 4 24 S 152 18 E
Rabbit → **76** 59 41N 127 12W
Rabbit Lake **88** 53 8N 107 46W
Rabbitskin → **76** 61 47N 120 42W
Rābigh **194** 22 50N 39 5 E
Rabka **152** 49 37N 19 59 E
Rābor **193** 29 17N 56 55 E
Rača **166** 44 14N 21 0 E
Răcale **165** 39 57N 18 6 E
Racalmuto **164** 37 25N 13 41 E
Răcăşdia **166** 44 59N 21 36 E
Racconigi **162** 44 47N 7 41 E
Race, C. **79** 46 40N 53 5W
Rach Gia **205** 10 5N 105 5 E
Raciąż **152** 52 46N 20 10 E
Racibórz **152** 50 7N 18 18 E
Racine L. **87** 48 2N 83 20W
Radama, Nosy **255** 14 0 S 47 47 E
Radama, Saikanosy **255** 14 16 S 47 53 E
Radan **166** 42 59N 21 29 E
Rădăuţi **170** 47 50N 25 59 E
Radbuza → **150** 49 35N 13 5 E
Räde **171** 59 21N 10 53 E
Radeburg **146** 51 6N 13 55 E
Radeče **163** 46 5N 15 14 E
Radekhov **178** 50 25N 24 32 E
Radew → **152** 54 2N 15 52 E
Radhanpur **198** 23 50N 71 38 E
Radiska → **166** 41 38N 20 37 E
Radisson **88** 52 30N 107 20W
Radium Hot Springs **91** 50 35N 116 2W
Radków **152** 50 30N 16 24 E
Radlin **152** 50 3N 18 29 E
Radna **166** 46 7N 21 41 E
Radnevo **167** 42 17N 25 58 E
Radnice **150** 49 51N 13 35 E
Radnor Forest **133** 52 17N 3 10W
Radolfzell **147** 47 44N 8 58 E
Radom **152** 51 23N 21 12 E
Radom □ **152** 51 30N 21 0 E
Radomir **166** 42 37N 23 4 E
Radomka → **152** 51 31N 21 11 E
Radomsko **152** 51 5N 19 28 E
Radomyshl **178** 50 30N 29 12 E
Radomysl Wielki **152** 50 14N 21 15 E
Radoszyce **152** 51 4N 20 15 E
Radoviš **166** 41 38N 22 28 E
Radovljica **163** 46 22N 14 12 E
Radstadt **150** 47 24N 13 28 E
Radstock **133** 51 17N 2 25W
Radstock, C. **231** 33 12 S 134 20 E
Răducăneni **170** 46 58N 27 54 E
Raduša **166** 42 7N 21 15 E
Radviliškis **178** 55 49N 23 33 E
Radville **88** 49 30N 104 15W
Radway **90** 54 4N 112 57W
Radymno **152** 49 59N 22 52 E
Radzanów **152** 52 56N 20 8 E
Radziejów **152** 52 40N 18 30 E
Radzymin **152** 52 25N 21 11 E
Radzyń Chełmiński **152** 53 23N 18 55 E
Radzyń Podlaski **152** 51 47N 22 37 E
Rae **76** 62 50N 116 3W
Rae Bareli **199** 26 18N 81 20 E
Rae Isthmus **95** 66 40N 87 30W
Raeren **143** 50 41N 6 7 E
Raeside, L. **229** 29 20 S 122 0 E
Raetihi **234** 39 25 S 175 17 E
Rafaela **124** 31 10 S 61 30W
Rafah **191** 31 18N 34 14 E
Rafai **250** 4 59N 23 58 E
Raffadali **164** 37 23N 13 29 E
Rafḩā **192** 29 35N 43 35 E
Rafsanjān **193** 30 30N 56 5 E
Raft Pt. **228** 16 4 S 124 26 E
Ragag **245** 10 59N 24 40 E
Ragang, Mt. **211** 7 43N 124 32 E
Ragay **210** 13 49N 122 47 E
Ragay G. **210** 13 30N 122 45 E
Ragged Mt. **229** 33 27 S 123 25 E
Raglan, Australia **230** 23 42 S 150 49 E
Raglan, N.Z. **234** 37 55 S 174 55 E
Ragunda **172** 63 6N 16 23 E
Ragusa **165** 36 56N 14 42 E
Raha **207** 4 55 S 123 0 E
Rahad, Nahr ed → **245** 14 28N 33 31 E
Rahad al Bardī **243** 11 20N 23 40 E
Rahaeng = Tak **204** 16 52N 99 8 E
Rahden **146** 52 26N 8 36 E
Raheita **245** 12 46N 43 4 E
Raḩīmah **193** 26 42N 50 4 E
Rahimyar Khan **197** 28 30N 70 25 E
Rāhjerd **193** 34 22N 50 22 E
Rahotu **234** 39 20 S 173 49 E
Rahum **100** 27 42N 110 30W
Raichur **201** 16 10N 77 20 E
Raiganj **199** 25 37N 88 10 E
Raigarh **199** 21 56N 83 25 E
Raighar **200** 19 51N 82 6 E
Raijua **207** 10 37 S 121 36 E
Railton **230** 41 25 S 146 28 E
Rainbow **232** 35 55 S 142 0 E
Rainbow Lake **76** 58 30N 119 23W
Rainy → **86** 48 43N 94 29W
Rainy L. **86** 48 42N 93 10W
Rainy River **86** 48 43N 94 29W
Raipur **199** 21 17N 81 45 E
Raj Nandgaon **199** 21 5N 81 5 E
Raja, Ujung **208** 3 40N 96 25 E
Raja Ampat, Kepulauan **207** 0 30 S 130 0 E
Rajahmundry **200** 17 1N 81 48 E
Rajajooseppi **174** 68 28N 28 29 E
Rajang → **206** 2 30N 112 0 E
Rajapalaiyam **201** 9 25N 77 35 E
Rajasthan □ **198** 26 45N 73 30 E
Rajasthan Canal **198** 28 0N 72 0 E
Rajauri **199** 33 25N 74 21 E
Rajbari **202** 23 47N 89 41 E
Rajgarh, Mad. P., India **198** 24 2N 76 45 E
Rajgarh, Raj., India **198** 28 40N 75 25 E
Rajgród **152** 53 42N 22 42 E
Rajhenburg **163** 46 1N 15 29 E
Rajkot **198** 22 15N 70 56 E
Rajmahal Hills **199** 24 30N 87 30 E
Rajpipla **198** 21 50N 73 30 E
Rajpura **198** 30 25N 76 32 E
Rajshahi **202** 24 22N 88 39 E
Rajshahi □ **199** 25 0N 89 0 E
Rakaia **235** 43 45 S 172 1 E
Rakaia → **235** 43 36 S 172 15 E
Rakan, Ra's **195** 26 10N 51 20 E
Rakaposhi **199** 36 10N 74 25 E
Rakata, Pulau **208** 6 10 S 105 20 E
Rakha **244** 18 25N 41 30 E
Rakhawt, W. → **195** 18 16N 51 50 E
Rakhneh-ye Jamshīdī **197** 34 22N 62 19 E
Rakhni **198** 30 4N 69 56 E
Rakhyūt **195** 16 44N 53 20 E
Rakitnoye **218** 45 36N 134 17 E
Rakitovo **167** 41 59N 24 5 E
Rakkestad **171** 59 25N 11 21 E
Rakoniewice **152** 52 10N 16 16 E
Rakops **254** 21 1 S 24 28 E
Rákospalota **151** 47 30N 19 5 E
Rakov **178** 53 58N 26 59 E
Rakovica **163** 44 59N 15 38 E
Rakovník **150** 50 6N 13 42 E
Rakovski **167** 42 21N 24 57 E
Rakvere **178** 59 30N 26 25 E
Raleigh **79** 51 34N 55 44W
Ralja **166** 44 33N 20 34 E
Ralston **91** 50 15N 111 10W
Ram →, Alta., Canada **91** 52 23N 115 25W
Ram →, N.W.T., Canada **76** 62 1N 123 41W
Rām Allāh **189** 31 55N 35 10 E
Ram Hd. **231** 37 47 S 149 30 E
Rama, Canada **88** 51 46N 103 0W
Rama, Israel **189** 32 56N 35 21 E
Rama, Nic. **112** 12 9N 84 15W
Ramacca **165** 37 24N 14 40 E
Ramachandrapuram **200** 16 50N 82 4 E
Ramah **78** 58 52N 63 15W
Ramah B. **78** 58 52N 63 13W
Ramales de la Victoria **156** 43 15N 3 28W
Ramalho, Serra do **121** 13 45 S 44 0W
Raman **205** 6 29N 101 18 E
Ramanathapuram **201** 9 25N 78 55 E
Ramanetaka, B. de **255** 14 13 S 47 52 E
Ramas C. **201** 15 5N 73 55 E
Ramat Gan **189** 32 4N 34 48 E
Ramat HaSharon **189** 32 7N 34 50 E
Ramatlhabama **254** 25 37 S 25 33 E
Ramban **199** 33 14N 75 12 E
Rambervillers **139** 48 20N 6 38 E
Rambi **226** 16 30 S 179 59W
Rambipuji **209** 8 12 S 113 37 E

Rambla, La **155** 37 37N 4 45W
Rambouillet .... **139** 48 40N 1 48 E
Ramdurg .... **201** 15 58N 75 22 E
Ramea **79** 47 31N 57 23W
Ramea Is. **79** 47 31N 57 22W
Ramechhap .... **199** 27 25N 86 10 E
Ramelau .... **207** 8 55 S 126 22 E
Ramenskoye .... **179** 55 32N 38 15 E
Ramgarh, Bihar, India .... **199** 23 40N 85 35 E
Ramgarh, Raj., India .... **198** 27 16N 75 14 E
Ramgarh, Raj., India .... **198** 27 30N 70 36 E
Rāmhormoz .... **193** 31 15N 49 35 E
Ramīān .... **193** 37 3N 55 16 E
Ramla .... **189** 31 55N 34 52 E
Ramlat Zalṭan .... **241** 28 30N 19 30 E
Ramlu .... **245** 13 32N 41 40 E
Ramme .... **173** 56 30N 8 11 E
Rammūn .... **189** 31 55N 35 17 E
Ramnad = Ramanathapuram **201** 9 25N 78 55 E
Ramnagar .... **199** 32 47N 75 18 E
Ramnäs .... **172** 59 46N 16 12 E
Ramon .... **179** 51 55N 39 21 E
Ramon, Har .... **189** 30 30N 34 38 E
Ramón Corona **105** 24 13N 103 37W
Ramonal **111** 18 25N 88 32W
Ramore **74** 48 30N 80 25W
Ramos **103** 22 50N 101 55W
Ramos Arizpe **102** 25 33N 100 58W
Ramoutsa .... **254** 24 50 S 25 52 E
Rampur, H.P., India **198** 31 26N 77 43 E
Rampur, Mad. P., India .... **198** 23 25N 73 53 E
Rampur, Orissa, India .... **199** 21 48N 83 58 E
Rampur, Ut. P., India .... **199** 28 50N 79 5 E
Rampur Hat .... **199** 24 10N 87 50 E
Rampura .... **198** 24 30N 75 27 E
Rāmsar .... **193** 36 53N 50 41 E
Ramsay I. **92** 52 33N 131 23W
Ramsel .... **143** 51 2N 4 50 E
Ramsey, Canada **87** 47 25N 82 20W
Ramsey, U.K. **132** 54 20N 4 21W
Ramsey L. **87** 47 13N 82 15W
Ramsgate .... **133** 51 20N 1 25 E
Ramshai .... **202** 26 44N 88 51 E
Ramsjö .... **172** 62 11N 15 37 E
Ramtek .... **199** 21 20N 79 15 E
Ramu → .... **227** 4 0 S 144 41 E
Ramvik .... **172** 62 49N 17 51 E
Ranaghat .... **199** 23 15N 88 35 E
Ranahu .... **198** 25 55N 69 45 E
Ranau .... **206** 6 2N 116 40 E
Rancagua .... **124** 34 10 S 70 50W
Rance .... **143** 50 9N 4 16 E
Rance → **138** 48 34N 1 59W
Rance, Barrage de la **138** 48 30N 2 3W
Rancharia .... **121** 22 15 S 50 55W
Rancheria → **76** 60 13N 129 7W
Ranchi .... **199** 23 19N 85 27 E
Rancho Conejo **99** 24 7N 111 1W
Rancho de Santiago **101** 28 21N 107 11W
Ranco, L. .... **126** 40 15 S 72 25W
Rancu .... **170** 44 32N 24 15 E
Rand .... **233** 35 33 S 146 32 E
Randan .... **140** 46 2N 3 21 E
Randazzo .... **165** 37 53N 14 56 E
Randers .... **173** 56 29N 10 1 E
Randers Fjord .... **173** 56 37N 10 20 E
Randfontein .... **255** 26 8 S 27 45 E
Random I. **79** 48 8N 53 44W
Randsfjorden .... **171** 60 15N 10 25 E
Råne älv → .... **174** 65 50N 22 20 E
Ranfurly, Canada **90** 53 25N 111 41W
Ranfurly, N.Z. .... **235** 45 7 S 170 6 E
Rangae .... **205** 6 19N 101 44 E
Rangamati .... **202** 22 38N 92 12 E
Rangataua .... **234** 39 26 S 175 28 E
Rangaunu B. .... **234** 34 51 S 173 15 E
Rångedala .... **173** 57 47N 13 9 E
Ranger L. **87** 46 52N 83 35W
Rangia .... **202** 26 28N 91 38 E
Rangiora .... **235** 43 19 S 172 36 E
Rangitaiki → .... **234** 37 54 S 176 49 E
Rangitata → .... **235** 43 45 S 171 15 E
Rangitikei → .... **234** 40 17 S 175 15 E
Rangitoto Range .... **234** 38 25 S 175 35 E
Rangkasbitung .... **207** 6 21 S 106 15 E
Rangoon .... **202** 16 45N 96 20 E
Rangpur .... **202** 25 42N 89 22 E
Rangsang .... **208** 1 20N 103 30 E
Rangsit .... **204** 13 59N 100 37 E
Ranibennur .... **201** 14 35N 75 30 E
Raniganj .... **199** 23 40N 87 5 E
Ranippettai .... **201** 12 56N 79 23 E
Rāniyah .... **192** 36 15N 44 53 E
Ranken → .... **230** 20 31 S 137 36 E
Rankin Inlet **95** 62 30N 93 0W
Rankins Springs .... **231** 33 49 S 146 14 E
Rannoch, L. **134** 56 41N 4 20W
Rannoch Moor **134** 56 38N 4 48W
Ranobe, Helodranon' i .... **255** 23 3 S 43 33 E
Ranohira .... **255** 22 29 S 45 24 E
Ranoke **87** 50 26N 81 35W
Ranomafana, Toamasina, Madag. .... **255** 18 57 S 48 50 E
Ranomafana, Toliara, Madag. .... **255** 24 34 S 47 0 E
Ranong .... **205** 9 56N 98 40 E
Rānsa .... **193** 33 39N 48 18 E
Ransiki .... **207** 1 30 S 134 10 E
Rantau .... **209** 2 56 S 115 9 E
Rantauprapat .... **208** 2 15N 99 50 E
Rantekombola .... **207** 3 15 S 119 57 E
Rantīs .... **189** 32 4N 35 3 E
Ranum .... **173** 56 54N 9 14 E
Ranyah, W. → .... **194** 21 18N 43 20 E
Raon l'Étape .... **139** 48 24N 6 50 E
Raoui, Erg er **240** 29 0N 2 0W
Raoyang .... **214** 38 15N 115 45 E
Rapa Iti .... **225** 27 35 S 144 20W
Rapallo .... **162** 44 21N 9 12 E
Rāpch .... **193** 25 40N 59 15 E
Raper, C. **95** 69 44N 67 6W
Rapid → **76** 59 15N 129 5W
Rapid City **89** 50 7N 100 2W
Rapide-Blanc **83** 47 48N 73 2W
Rapide-Sept **82** 47 46N 78 19W
Rapides des Joachims **82** 46 13N 77 43W
Rapla .... **178** 59 1N 24 52 E
Rapperswil .... **149** 47 14N 8 45 E
Rapu Rapu I. .... **210** 13 12N 124 9 E
Rarotonga .... **225** 21 30 S 160 0W
Ra's al' Ayn .... **192** 36 51N 40 4 E
Ra's al Khaymah .... **195** 25 50N 56 5 E
Ra's al Qaṣbah .... **191** 28 2N 34 38 E
Ra's al-Unuf .... **241** 30 25N 18 15 E
Ra's an Naqb .... **191** 30 0N 35 29 E
Ras Dashen .... **245** 13 8N 38 26 E
Ras el Ma **240** 34 26N 0 50W
Ras Mallap .... **244** 29 18N 32 50 E
Ra's Shamrah .... **190** 35 35N 35 45 E
Râs Timirist **246** 19 21N 16 30W
Rasa, Punta .... **126** 40 50 S 62 15W
Rascón **103** 21 58N 99 16W
Raseiniai .... **178** 55 25N 23 5 E
Rashad .... **245** 11 55N 31 0 E
Rashîd .... **244** 31 21N 30 22 E
Rashîd, Masabb .... **244** 31 22N 30 17 E
Rasht .... **193** 37 20N 49 40 E
Rasi Salai .... **204** 15 20N 104 9 E
Rasipuram .... **201** 11 30N 78 15 E
Raška .... **166** 43 19N 20 39 E
Rason, L. .... **229** 28 45 S 124 25 E
Raşova .... **170** 44 15N 27 55 E
Rasovo .... **167** 43 42N 23 17 E
Rasra .... **199** 25 50N 83 50 E
Rass el Oued .... **241** 35 57N 5 2 E
Rasskazovo .... **179** 52 35N 41 50 E
Rastatt .... **147** 48 50N 8 12 E
Rastu .... **170** 43 53N 23 16 E
Raszków .... **152** 51 43N 17 40 E
Rat → **89** 49 35N 97 10W
Rat Buri .... **204** 13 30N 99 54 E
Rat River **76** 61 7N 112 36W
Ratangarh .... **198** 28 5N 74 35 E
Raṭāwī .... **192** 30 38N 47 13 E
Rath .... **199** 25 36N 79 37 E
Rath Luirc **135** 52 21N 8 40W
Rathdrum **135** 52 57N 6 13W
Rathedaung .... **202** 20 29N 92 45 E
Rathenow .... **146** 52 38N 12 23 E
Rathkeale **135** 52 32N 8 57W
Rathlin I. **135** 55 18N 6 14W
Rathlin O'Birne I. **135** 54 40N 8 50W
Ratibor = Racibórz **152** 50 7N 18 18 E
Rätikon .... **150** 47 0N 9 55 E
Ratlam .... **198** 23 20N 75 0 E
Ratnagiri .... **200** 16 57N 73 18 E
Ratnapura .... **201** 6 40N 80 20 E
Rats, R. aux → **83** 48 53N 72 14W
Rattaphum .... **205** 7 8N 100 16 E
Ratten .... **150** 47 28N 15 44 E
Rattray Hd. **134** 57 38N 1 50W
Rättvik .... **172** 60 52N 15 7 E
Ratz, Mt. **76** 57 23N 132 12W
Ratzeburg .... **146** 53 41N 10 46 E
Raub .... **205** 3 47N 101 52 E
Rauch .... **124** 36 45 S 59 5W
Raufarhöfn **174** 66 27N 15 57W
Raufoss .... **171** 60 44N 10 37 E
Raukumara Ra. .... **234** 38 5 S 177 55 E
Raul Soares .... **121** 20 5 S 42 22W
Rauland .... **171** 59 43N 8 0 E
Rauma .... **175** 61 10N 21 30 E
Rauma → .... **171** 62 34N 7 43 E
Raundal .... **171** 60 40N 6 37 E
Raurkela .... **199** 22 14N 84 50 E
Rausu-Dake .... **218** 44 4N 145 7 E
Rava Russkaya .... **178** 50 15N 23 42 E
Ravānsar .... **192** 34 43N 46 40 E
Ravanusa .... **164** 37 16N 13 58 E
Rāvar .... **193** 31 20N 56 51 E
Ravels .... **143** 51 22N 5 0 E
Ravenna .... **163** 44 28N 12 15 E
Ravensburg .... **147** 47 48N 9 38 E
Ravenshoe .... **230** 17 37 S 145 29 E
Ravenstein .... **142** 51 47N 5 39 E
Ravensthorpe .... **229** 33 35 S 120 2 E
Ravenswood .... **230** 20 6 S 146 54 E
Ravensworth .... **233** 32 26 S 151 4 E
Ravi → .... **198** 30 35N 71 49 E
Ravna Gora .... **163** 45 24N 14 50 E
Ravna Reka .... **166** 43 59N 21 35 E
Rawa Mazowiecka .... **152** 51 46N 20 12 E
Rawalpindi .... **197** 33 38N 73 8 E
Rawāndūz .... **192** 36 40N 44 30 E
Rawang .... **205** 3 20N 101 35 E
Rawdon **83** 46 3N 73 40W
Rawene .... **234** 35 25 S 173 32 E
Rawicz .... **152** 51 36N 16 52 E
Rawka → .... **152** 52 9N 20 8 E
Rawlinna .... **229** 30 58 S 125 28 E
Rawlinson Range .... **229** 24 40 S 128 30 E
Rawson .... **126** 43 15 S 65 0W
Ray, C. **79** 47 33N 59 15W
Rayachoti .... **201** 14 4N 78 50 E
Rayadurg .... **201** 14 40N 76 50 E
Rayagada .... **200** 19 15N 83 20 E
Raychikhinsk .... **185** 49 46N 129 25 E
Rāyen .... **193** 29 34N 57 26 E
Rayevskiy .... **182** 54 4N 54 56 E
Rayleigh **93** 50 49N 120 17W
Raymond **91** 49 30N 112 35W
Raymond Terrace .... **233** 32 45 S 151 44 E
Raymore **88** 51 25N 104 31W
Rayón, Chiapas, Mexico **110** 17 12N 93 0W
Rayón, San Luis Potosí, Mexico **103** 21 51N 99 40W
Rayón, Sonora, Mexico **100** 29 43N 110 35W
Rayones **103** 25 1N 100 5W
Rayong .... **204** 12 40N 101 20 E
Raz, Pte. du **138** 48 2N 4 47W
Raza, Pta. **104** 21 2N 105 20W
Razan .... **193** 35 23N 49 2 E
Ražana .... **166** 44 6N 19 55 E
Ražanj .... **166** 43 40N 21 31 E
Razdelna .... **167** 43 13N 27 41 E
Razdel'naya .... **180** 46 50N 30 2 E
Razdolnoye, Ukraine S.S.R., U.S.S.R. .... **180** 45 46N 33 29 E
Razdolnoye, R.S.F.S.R., U.S.S.R. .... **218** 43 30N 131 52 E
Razeh .... **193** 32 47N 48 9 E
Razelm, Lacul .... **170** 44 50N 29 0 E
Razgrad .... **167** 43 33N 26 34 E
Razlog .... **167** 41 53N 23 28 E
Razmak .... **197** 32 45N 69 50 E
Razole .... **201** 16 36N 81 48 E
Ré, Île de **140** 46 12N 1 30W
Read Island **94** 69 12N 114 31W
Reading **133** 51 27N 0 57W
Real, Cordillera .... **122** 17 0 S 67 10W
Real del Castillo **98** 31 58N 116 19W
Realicó .... **124** 35 0 S 64 15W
Réalmont .... **140** 43 48N 2 10 E
Reata **102** 26 8N 101 5W
Rebais .... **139** 48 50N 3 10 E
Rebecca L. .... **229** 30 0 S 122 15 E
Rebeico **100** 28 53N 109 45W
Rebi .... **207** 6 23 S 134 7 E
Rebiana .... **242** 24 12N 22 10 E
Rebun-Tō .... **218** 45 23N 141 2 E
Recanati .... **163** 43 24N 13 32 E
Recaş .... **170** 45 46N 21 30 E
Recherche, Arch. of the .... **229** 34 15 S 122 50 E
Rechitsa .... **178** 52 13N 30 15 E
Recht .... **143** 50 20N 6 3 E
Recife .... **120** 8 0 S 35 0W
Recklinghausen .... **146** 51 36N 7 10 E
Reconquista .... **124** 29 10 S 59 45W
Recreio .... **123** 8 0 S 58 25W
Recreo .... **124** 29 25 S 65 10W
Recuay .... **122** 9 43 S 77 28W
Recz .... **152** 53 16N 15 31 E
Red → = Hong → .... **204** 20 17N 106 34 E
Red → **89** 50 24N 96 48W
Red Bay **78** 51 44N 56 25W
Red Cliffs .... **231** 34 19 S 142 11 E
Red Deer **91** 52 20N 113 50W
Red Deer →, Alta., Canada **91** 50 58N 110 0W
Red Deer →, Man., Canada **89** 52 53N 101 1W
Red Deer L., Alta., Canada **91** 52 43N 113 2W
Red Deer L., Man., Canada **89** 52 55N 101 20W
Red I. **79** 47 23N 54 10W
Red Indian L. **79** 48 35N 57 0W
Red L. **86** 51 3N 93 49W
Red Lake **86** 51 3N 93 49W
Red Lake Road **86** 49 59N 93 25W
Red Pass **93** 53 0N 119 0W
Red Rock, B.C., Canada **93** 53 42N 122 40W
Red Rock, Ont., Canada **86** 48 55N 88 15W
Red Rock's Pt. .... **229** 32 13 S 127 32 E
Red Sea .... **188** 25 0N 36 0 E
Red Sucker L. **77** 54 9N 93 40W
Red Tower Pass = Turnu Rosu Pasul **170** 45 33N 24 17 E
Reda .... **152** 54 40N 18 19 E
Rédange .... **143** 49 46N 5 52 E
Redberry L. **88** 52 45N 107 14W
Redbridge .... **133** 51 35N 0 7 E
Redcar **132** 54 37N 1 4W
Redcliff **91** 50 10N 110 50W
Redcliffe .... **231** 27 12 S 153 0 E
Redcliffe, Mt. .... **229** 28 30 S 121 30 E
Reddersburg .... **254** 29 41 S 26 10 E
Redditch **133** 52 18N 1 57W
Redditt **86** 49 59N 94 24W
Redenção .... **120** 4 13 S 38 43W
Redknife → **76** 61 14N 119 22W
Redmond .... **229** 34 55 S 117 40 E
Redon **138** 47 40N 2 6W
Redonda **113** 16 58N 62 19W
Redonda Bay **92** 50 17N 124 57W
Redonda Is. **92** 50 15N 124 50W
Redondela **154** 42 15N 8 38W
Redondo **155** 38 39N 7 37W
Redrock Pt. **76** 62 11N 115 2W
Redruth **133** 50 14N 5 14W
Redvers **89** 49 35N 101 40W
Redwater **90** 53 55N 113 6W
Redwillow → **90** 55 2N 119 18W
Ree, L. **135** 53 35N 8 0W
Reed, L. **77** 54 38N 100 30W
Reedy Creek .... **232** 36 58 S 140 2 E
Reefton, Australia .... **233** 34 15 S 147 27 E
Reefton, N.Z. .... **235** 42 6 S 171 51 E
Reforma **110** 17 56N 93 10W
Reforma de Pineda **109** 16 24N 94 28W
Reftele .... **173** 57 11N 13 35 E
Rega → .... **152** 54 10N 15 18 E
Regalbuto .... **165** 37 40N 14 38 E
Regar .... **183** 38 30N 68 14 E
Regavim .... **189** 32 32N 35 2 E
Regen .... **147** 48 58N 13 9 E
Regen → .... **147** 49 2N 12 6 E
Regeneração .... **120** 6 15 S 42 41W
Regensburg .... **147** 49 1N 12 7 E
Regensdorf .... **149** 47 26N 8 28 E
Réggio di Calábria .... **165** 38 7N 15 38 E
Réggio nell' Emilia .... **162** 44 42N 10 38 E
Regina, Canada **88** 50 27N 104 35W
Régina, Fr. Gui. **119** 4 19N 52 8W
Regina, Mexico **101** 28 22N 105 27W
Regina Beach **88** 50 47N 105 0W
Registro .... **125** 24 29 S 47 49W
Regocijo **104** 23 35N 105 11W
Reguengos de Monsaraz **155** 38 25N 7 32W
Rehar → .... **199** 23 55N 82 40 E
Rehoboth .... **254** 23 15 S 17 4 E
Rehovot .... **189** 31 54N 34 48 E
Rei-Bouba .... **252** 8 40N 14 15 E
Reichenbach, Germany .... **146** 50 36N 12 19 E
Reichenbach, Switz. **148** 46 38N 7 42 E
Reid .... **229** 30 49 S 128 26 E
Reid L. **88** 50 0N 108 9W
Reid Lake **92** 53 58N 123 6W
Reid River .... **230** 19 40 S 146 48 E
Reiden .... **148** 47 14N 7 59 E
Reigate **133** 51 14N 0 11W
Reillo **156** 39 54N 1 53W
Reims .... **139** 49 15N 4 0 E
Reina .... **189** 32 43N 35 18 E
Reina Adelaida, Arch. .... **126** 52 20 S 74 0W
Reinach, Aargau, Switz. .... **148** 47 14N 8 11 E
Reinach, Basel, Switz. .... **148** 47 29N 7 35 E
Reindeer → **77** 55 36N 103 11W
Reindeer I. **89** 52 30N 98 0W
Reindeer L. **77** 57 15N 102 15W
Reine, La **156** 48 50N 79 30W
Reinga, C. .... **234** 34 25 S 172 43 E
Reinland **89** 49 2N 97 52W
Reinosa **154** 43 2N 4 15W
Reinosa, Paso **154** 42 56N 4 10W
Reitdiep .... **142** 53 20N 6 20 E
Reitz .... **255** 27 48 S 28 29 E
Reivilo .... **254** 27 36 S 24 8 E
Rejmyra .... **173** 58 50N 15 55 E
Rejowiec Fabryczny **152** 51 5N 23 17 E
Reka → .... **163** 45 40N 14 0 E
Rekinniki .... **185** 60 51N 163 40 E
Rekovac .... **166** 43 51N 21 3 E
Reliance **77** 63 0N 109 20W
Rellano **101** 26 50N 104 29W

Remad, Oued → **241** 33 28N 1 20W
Rémalard **138** 48 26N 0 47 E
Remanso **120** 9 41 S 42 4W
Remarkable, Mt. **231** 32 48 S 138 10 E
Rembang **209** 6 42 S 111 21 E
Remchi **241** 35 2N 1 26W
Remedios, Colombia **118** 7 2N 74 41W
Remedios, Panama **112** 8 15N 81 50W
Remedios, Sa. de los **101** 26 56N 104 25W
Remeshk **193** 26 55N 58 50 E
Remetea **170** 46 45N 25 29 E
Remi Lake Prov. Park **87** 49 30N 82 15W
Remich **143** 49 32N 6 22 E
Rémigny **82** 47 46N 79 12W
Rémire **119** 4 53N 52 17W
Remiremont **139** 48 0N 6 36 E
Remo **245** 6 48N 41 20 E
Remontnoye **181** 46 34N 43 37 E
Remoulins **141** 43 55N 4 35 E
Remscheid **146** 51 11N 7 12 E
Ren Xian **214** 37 8N 114 40 E
Rena **171** 61 8N 11 20 E
Rena → **171** 61 8N 11 23 E
Renascença **118** 3 50 S 66 21W
Renata **93** 49 27N 118 7W
Rencontre East **79** 47 38N 55 12W
Rende **165** 39 19N 16 11 E
Rendeux **143** 50 14N 5 30 E
Rendína **169** 39 4N 21 58 E
Rendsburg **146** 54 18N 9 41 E
Rene **185** 66 2N 179 25W
Renews **79** 46 56N 52 56W
Renfrew, Canada **85** 45 30N 76 40W
Renfrew, U.K. **134** 55 52N 4 24W
Rengat **208** 0 30 S 102 45 E
Rengo **124** 34 24 S 70 50W
Renhua **217** 25 5N 113 40 E
Renhuai **216** 27 48N 106 24 E
Reni **180** 45 28N 28 15 E
Renigunta **201** 13 38N 79 30 E
Renison **87** 50 58N 81 7W
Renkum **142** 51 58N 5 43 E
Renmark **232** 34 11 S 140 43 E
Rennell Sd. **92** 53 23N 132 35W
Renner Springs T.O. **230** 18 20 S 133 47 E
Rennes **138** 48 7N 1 41W
Rennes, Bassin de **138** 48 12N 1 33W
Rennesøy **171** 59 6N 5 43 E
Rennie **89** 49 51N 95 33W
Rennison I. **92** 52 50N 129 20W
Reno → **163** 44 37N 12 17 E
Renqiu **214** 38 43N 116 5 E
Rentería **156** 43 19N 1 54W
Renwick **235** 41 30 S 173 51 E
Réo **246** 12 28N 2 35W
Réole, La **140** 44 35N 0 1W
Reotipur **199** 25 33N 83 45 E
Repalle **201** 16 2N 80 45 E
Répcelak **151** 47 24N 17 1 E
Repentigny **83** 45 44N 73 28W
Republiek **119** 5 30N 55 13W
Repulse B. **13** 64 30 S 99 30 E
Repulse Bay **95** 66 30N 86 30W
Requena, Peru **122** 5 5 S 73 52W
Requena, Spain **157** 39 30N 1 4W
Requena, Presa **107** 19 58N 99 17W
Resele **172** 63 20N 17 5 E
Resen **166** 41 5N 21 0 E
Reserve **88** 52 28N 102 39W
Resht = Rasht **193** 37 20N 49 40 E
Resistencia **124** 27 30 S 59 0W
Reşiţa **166** 45 18N 21 53 E
Resko **152** 53 47N 15 25 E
Resolute **95** 74 42N 94 54W
Resolution I., Canada **73** 61 30N 65 0W
Resolution I., N.Z. **235** 45 40 S 166 40 E
Resplandes **120** 6 17 S 45 13W
Resplendor **121** 19 20 S 41 15W
Ressano Garcia **255** 25 25 S 32 0 E
Rest Downs **233** 31 48 S 146 21 E
Restigouche → **81** 47 50N 67 0W
Reston **89** 49 33N 101 6W
Reszel **152** 54 4N 21 10 E
Retalhuleu **112** 14 33N 91 46W
Reteag **170** 47 10N 24 0 E
Retenue, Lac de **251** 11 0 S 27 0 E
Rethel **139** 49 30N 4 20 E
Rethem **146** 52 47N 9 25 E
Réthímnon **169** 35 18N 24 30 E
Réthímnon □ **169** 35 23N 24 28 E
Retie **143** 51 16N 5 5 E
Rétiers **138** 47 55N 1 25W
Retortillo **154** 40 48N 6 21W
Rétság **151** 47 58N 19 10 E
Reuland **143** 50 12N 6 8 E
Réunion **203** 22 0 S 56 0 E
Reus **156** 41 10N 1 5 E
Reusel **143** 51 21N 5 9 E
Reuss → **149** 47 16N 8 24 E
Reuterstadt Stavenhagen **146** 53 41N 12 54 E
Reutlingen **147** 48 28N 9 13 E
Reutte **150** 47 29N 10 42 E
Reuver **143** 51 17N 6 5 E
Reval = Tallinn **178** 59 22N 24 48 E
Revda **182** 56 48N 59 57 E
Revel **140** 43 28N 2 0 E
Revelganj **199** 25 50N 84 40 E
Revelstoke **93** 51 0N 118 10W
Reventazón **122** 6 10 S 80 58W
Revigny **139** 48 50N 5 0 E
Revilla Gigedo, Is. **225** 18 40N 112 0W
Revin **139** 49 55N 4 39 E
Revolyutsii, Pix **183** 38 31N 72 21 E
Revuè → **251** 19 50 S 34 0 E
Rewa **199** 24 33N 81 25 E
Rewa → **119** 3 19N 58 42W
Rewari **198** 28 15N 76 40 E
Rexton **81** 46 39N 64 52W
Rey **193** 35 35N 51 25 E
Rey, L. del **102** 27 1N 103 26W
Rey, Rio del → **247** 4 30N 8 48 E
Rey Malabo **247** 3 45N 8 50 E
Reyes **122** 14 19 S 67 23W
Reyhanlı **190** 36 16N 36 35 E
Reykjahlíð **174** 65 40N 16 55W
Reykjanes **174** 63 48N 22 40W
Reykjavík **174** 64 10N 21 57 E
Reynolds **89** 49 40N 95 55W
Reynolds Ra. **228** 22 30 S 133 0 E
Reynosa **102** 26 7N 98 18W
Reynosa Diaz **102** 26 12N 98 28W
Rezekne **178** 56 30N 27 17 E
Rezh **182** 57 23N 61 24 E
Rezovo **167** 42 0N 28 0 E
Reẓvān **193** 27 34N 56 6 E
Rgotina **166** 44 1N 22 17 E
Rhamnus **169** 38 12N 24 3 E
Rharis, O. → **241** 26 0N 5 4 E
Rhayader **133** 52 19N 3 30W
Rheden **142** 52 0N 6 3 E
Rhein **89** 51 25N 102 15W
Rhein → **146** 51 52N 6 20 E
Rhein-Main-Donau-Kanal **147** 49 1N 11 27 E
Rheinbach **146** 50 38N 6 54 E
Rheine **146** 52 17N 7 25 E
Rheineck **149** 47 28N 9 31 E
Rheinfelden **148** 47 32N 7 47 E
Rheinland-Pfalz □ **147** 50 0N 7 0 E
Rheinsberg **146** 53 6N 12 52 E
Rheinwaldhorn **149** 46 30N 9 3 E
Rhenen **142** 51 58N 5 33 E
Rheriss, Oued → **241** 30 50N 4 34W
Rheydt **146** 51 10N 6 24 E
Rhin = Rhein → **146** 51 52N 6 20 E
Rhinau **139** 48 19N 7 43 E
Rhine = Rhein → **146** 51 52N 6 20 E
Rhino Camp **250** 3 0N 31 22 E
Rhir, Cap **240** 30 38N 9 54W
Rhisnes **143** 50 31N 4 48 E
Rho **162** 45 31N 9 2 E
Rhodes = Ródhos **169** 36 15N 28 10 E
Rhodes' Tomb **251** 20 30 S 28 30 E
Rhodesia = Zimbabwe ■ **251** 20 0 S 30 0 E
Rhodope Mts. = Rhodopi Planina **167** 41 40N 24 20 E
Rhodopi Planina **167** 41 40N 24 20 E
Rhondda **133** 51 39N 3 30W
Rhône □ **141** 45 54N 4 35 E
Rhône → **141** 43 28N 4 42 E
Rhum **134** 57 0N 6 20W
Rhumney **133** 51 32N 3 7W
Rhyl **132** 53 19N 3 29W
Ri-Aba **247** 3 28N 8 40 E
Riachão **120** 7 20 S 46 37W
Riacho de Santana **121** 13 37 S 42 57W
Rialma **121** 15 18 S 49 34W
Riang **202** 27 31N 92 56 E
Riaño **154** 42 59N 5 0W
Rians **141** 43 37N 5 44 E
Riansares → **156** 39 32N 3 18W
Riasi **199** 33 10N 74 50 E
Riau □ **206** 0 0 102 35 E
Riau, Kepulauan **208** 0 30N 104 20 E
Riaza **156** 41 18N 3 30W
Riaza → **156** 41 42N 3 55W
Riba de Saelices **156** 40 55N 2 17W
Ribadavia **154** 42 17N 8 8W
Ribadeo **154** 43 35N 7 5W
Ribadesella **154** 43 30N 5 7W
Ribamar **120** 2 33 S 44 3W
Ribas **156** 42 19N 2 15 E
Ribas do Rio Pardo **123** 20 27 S 53 46W
Ribâţ **194** 14 18N 44 15 E
Ribble → **132** 54 13N 2 20W
Ribe **173** 55 19N 8 44 E
Ribeauvillé **139** 48 10N 7 20 E
Ribécourt **139** 49 30N 2 55 E
Ribeira **154** 42 36N 8 58W
Ribeira do Pombal **120** 10 50 S 38 32W
Ribeirão Prêto **125** 21 10 S 47 50W
Ribeiro Gonçalves **120** 7 32 S 45 14W
Ribemont **139** 49 47N 3 27 E
Ribera **164** 37 30N 13 13 E
Ribérac **140** 45 15N 0 20 E
Riberalta **123** 11 0 S 66 0W
Ribnica **163** 45 45N 14 45 E
Ribnitz-Damgarten **146** 54 14N 12 24 E
Ribstone Cr. → **91** 52 52N 110 5W
Ričany **150** 50 0N 14 40 E
Ricardo Flores Magón **101** 29 56N 106 57W
Riccarton **235** 43 32 S 172 37 E
Riccia **165** 41 30N 14 50 E
Riccione **163** 44 0N 12 39 E
Rice L. **85** 44 12N 78 10W
Riceton **88** 50 7N 104 19W
Riceys, Les **139** 47 59N 4 22 E
Rich **240** 32 16N 4 30W
Rich, C. **84** 44 43N 80 38W
Rich Valley **90** 53 51N 114 21W
Richan **86** 49 59N 92 49W
Richards Bay **255** 28 48 S 32 6 E
Richards I. **94** 68 0N 135 0W
Richards L. **77** 59 10N 107 10W
Richardson → **77** 58 25N 111 14W
Richardson Mts., Canada **94** 68 20N 135 45W
Richardson Mts., N.Z. **235** 44 49 S 168 34 E
Riche, C. **229** 34 36 S 118 47 E
Riche, Pte. **79** 50 42N 57 25W
Richelieu **138** 47 0N 0 20 E
Richibucto **81** 46 42N 64 54W
Richmond, N.S.W., Australia **231** 33 35 S 150 42 E
Richmond, Queens., Australia **230** 20 43 S 143 8 E
Richmond, Ont., Canada **85** 45 11N 75 50W
Richmond, Qué., Canada **83** 45 40N 72 9W
Richmond, N.Z. **235** 41 20 S 173 12 E
Richmond, S. Africa **255** 29 51 S 30 18 E
Richmond, N. Yorks., U.K. **132** 54 24N 1 43W
Richmond, Surrey, U.K. **133** 51 28N 0 18W
Richmond, Mt. **235** 41 32 S 173 22 E
Richmond, Ra. **231** 29 0 S 152 45 E
Richmond Hill **84** 43 52N 79 27W
Richmond Ra. **235** 41 32 S 173 22 E
Richmound **88** 50 27N 109 45W
Richterswil **149** 47 13N 8 43 E
Ricla **156** 41 31N 1 24W
Ricupe **253** 14 37 S 21 25 E
Ridā' **194** 14 25N 44 50 E
Riddarhyttan **172** 59 49N 15 33 E
Ridderkerk **142** 51 52N 4 35 E
Riddes **148** 46 11N 7 14 E
Ridge → **87** 50 25N 84 20W
Ridgedale **88** 53 0N 104 10W
Ridgelands **230** 23 16 S 150 17 E
Ridgetown **84** 42 26N 81 52W
Riding Mt. Nat. Park **89** 50 50N 100 0W
Ridley Mt. **229** 33 12 S 122 7 E
Ried **150** 48 14N 13 30 E
Riedlingen **147** 48 9N 9 28 E
Riel **143** 51 31N 5 1 E
Rienza → **163** 46 49N 11 47 E
Riesa **146** 51 19N 13 19 E
Riesco, I. **126** 52 55 S 72 40W
Riesi **165** 37 16N 14 4 E
Rieti **163** 42 23N 12 50 E
Rieupeyroux **140** 44 19N 2 12 E
Riez **141** 43 49N 6 6 E
Rifstangi **174** 66 32N 16 12W
Rift Valley □ **250** 0 20N 36 0 E
Rig Rig **243** 14 13N 14 25 E
Riga **178** 56 53N 24 8 E
Riga, G. of = Rīgas Jūras Līcis **178** 57 40N 23 45 E
Rīgān **193** 28 37N 58 58 E
Rīgas Jūras Līcis **178** 57 40N 23 45 E
Rigaud **83** 45 29N 74 18W
Rīgestān □ **197** 30 15N 65 0 E
Rignac **140** 44 25N 2 16 E
Rigolet **78** 54 10N 58 23W
Riihimäki **175** 60 45N 24 48 E
Riiser-Larsen-halvøya **13** 68 0 S 35 0 E
Rijau **247** 11 8N 5 17 E
Rijeka **163** 45 20N 14 21 E
Rijeka Crnojevica **166** 42 24N 19 1 E
Rijen **143** 51 35N 4 55 E
Rijkevorsel **143** 51 21N 4 46 E
Rijn → **142** 52 12N 4 21 E
Rijnsberg **142** 52 11N 4 27 E
Rijsbergen **143** 51 31N 4 41 E
Rijssen **142** 52 19N 6 30 E
Rijswijk **142** 52 4N 4 22 E
Rikā', W. ar → **194** 22 25N 44 50 E
Rike **245** 10 50N 39 53 E
Rikuzentakada **218** 39 0N 141 40 E
Rila **167** 42 7N 23 7 E
Rila Planina **166** 42 10N 23 0 E
Rilly **139** 49 11N 4 3 E
Rima → **247** 13 4N 5 10 E
Rimah, Wadi ar → **192** 26 5N 41 30 E
Rimavská Sobota **151** 48 22N 20 2 E
Rimbey **91** 52 35N 114 15W
Rimbo **172** 59 44N 18 21 E
Rimforsa **173** 58 6N 15 43 E
Rimi **247** 12 58N 7 43 E
Rímini **163** 44 3N 12 33 E
Rîmna → **170** 45 36N 27 3 E
Rîmnicu Sărat **170** 45 26N 27 3 E
Rîmnicu Vîlcea **170** 45 9N 24 21 E
Rimouski **83** 48 27N 68 30W
Rimouski → **83** 48 27N 68 32W
Rimouski, Parc Prov. de **83** 48 0N 68 15W
Rimouski-Est **83** 48 28N 68 31W
Rinca **207** 8 45 S 119 35 E
Rincón de Romos **105** 22 14N 102 18W
Rinconada **124** 22 26 S 66 10W
Rineanna **135** 52 42N 8 57W
Ringarum **173** 58 21N 16 26 E
Ringe **173** 55 13N 10 28 E
Ringgold Is. **226** 16 15 S 179 25W
Ringim **247** 12 13N 9 10 E
Ringkøbing **173** 56 5N 8 15 E
Ringsaker **171** 60 54N 10 45 E
Ringsjön **173** 55 55N 13 30 E
Ringsted **172** 55 25N 11 46 E
Ringvassøy **174** 69 56N 19 15 E
Rinía **169** 37 23N 25 13 E
Rinjani **209** 8 24 S 116 28 E
Rinteln **146** 52 11N 9 3 E
Río, Punta del **157** 36 49N 2 24W
Río Blanco **109** 18 50N 97 9W
Rio Branco, Brazil **122** 9 58 S 67 49W
Río Branco, Uruguay **125** 32 40 S 53 40W
Río Bravo, Coahuila, Mexico **102** 28 17N 100 55W
Río Bravo, Tamaulipas, Mexico **102** 25 59N 98 6W
Rio Brilhante **125** 21 48 S 54 33W
Río Bueno **126** 40 19 S 72 58W
Río Chico, Mexico **100** 28 21N 109 30W
Río Chico, Venezuela **118** 10 19N 65 59W
Rio Claro, Brazil **125** 22 19 S 47 35W
Rio Claro, Trin. & Tob. **113** 10 20N 61 25W
Río Colorado **126** 39 0 S 64 0W
Río Cuarto **124** 33 10 S 64 25W
Rio das Pedras **255** 23 8 S 35 28 E
Rio de Contas **121** 13 36 S 41 48W
Rio de Janeiro **125** 23 0 S 43 12W
Rio de Janeiro □ **125** 22 50 S 43 0W
Rio do Prado **121** 16 35 S 40 34W
Rio do Sul **125** 27 13 S 49 37W
Río Gallegos **126** 51 35 S 69 15W
Río Grande, Argentina **126** 53 50 S 67 45W
Río Grande, Bolivia **122** 20 51 S 67 17W
Rio Grande, Brazil **125** 32 0 S 52 20W
Río Grande, Mexico **105** 23 50N 103 2W
Río Grande, Nic. **112** 12 54N 83 33W
Rio Grande do Norte □ **120** 5 40 S 36 0W
Rio Grande do Sul □ **125** 30 0 S 53 0W
Río Hato **112** 8 22N 80 10W
Río Lagartos **111** 21 36N 88 10W
Río Laja **107** 21 12N 100 55W
Rio Largo **120** 9 28 S 35 50W
Rio Maior **155** 39 19N 8 57W
Rio Marina **162** 42 48N 10 25 E
Río Mayo **126** 45 40 S 70 15W
Río Mulatos **122** 19 40 S 66 50W
Río Muni = Mbini □ **252** 1 30N 10 0 E
Rio Negro, Brazil **125** 26 0 S 50 0W
Río Negro, Chile **126** 40 47 S 73 14W
Rio Negro, Pantanal do **123** 19 0 S 56 0W
Rio Pardo **125** 30 0 S 52 30W
Rio Pico **126** 44 0 S 70 22W
Rio Real **121** 11 28 S 37 56W
Río Segundo **124** 31 40 S 63 59W
Río Tercero **124** 32 15 S 64 8W
Rio Tinto, Brazil **120** 6 48 S 35 5W
Rio Tinto, Portugal **154** 41 11N 8 34W
Rio Verde **121** 17 50 S 51 0W
Rio Verde de Mato Grosso **123** 18 56 S 54 52W
Ríobamba **118** 1 50 S 78 45W
Ríohacha **118** 11 33N 72 55W
Rioja **122** 6 11 S 77 5W
Rioja, La **124** 29 20 S 67 0W
Rioja, La □, Argentina **124** 29 30 S 67 0W
Rioja, La □, Spain **156** 42 20N 2 20W
Riom **140** 45 54N 3 7 E
Riom-ès-Montagnes **140** 45 17N 2 39 E
Rion-des-Landes **140** 43 55N 0 56W

Riondel **93** 49 46N 116 51W
Rionegro **118** 6 9N 75 22W
Rionero in Vúlture **165** 40 55N 15 40 E
Rioni → **181** 42 5N 41 50 E
Rios **154** 41 58N 7 16W
Riosucio, Caldas, Colombia **118** 5 30N 75 40W
Ríosucio, Choco, Colombia **118** 7 27N 77 7W
Riou L. **77** 59 7N 106 25W
Ríoverde **103** 21 56N 99 59W
Rioz **139** 47 25N 6 4 E
Riozinho → **118** 2 55 S 67 7W
Riparia, Dora → **162** 45 7N 7 24 E
Ripatransone **163** 43 0N 13 45 E
Ripley **84** 44 4N 81 35W
Ripoll **156** 42 15N 2 13 E
Ripon, Canada **82** 45 45N 75 10W
Ripon, U.K. **132** 54 8N 1 31W
Riposto **165** 37 44N 15 12 E
Risalpur **198** 34 3N 71 59 E
Risan **166** 42 32N 18 42 E
Risaralda □ **118** 5 0N 76 10W
Riscle **140** 43 39N 0 5W
Rishā', W. ar → **192** 25 33N 44 5 E
Rishiri-Tō **218** 45 11N 141 15 E
Rishon le Ẓiyyon **189** 31 58N 34 48 E
Rishpon **189** 32 12N 34 49 E
Risle → **138** 49 26N 0 23 E
Rîsnov **170** 45 35N 25 27 E
Risør **171** 58 43N 9 13 E
Rissani **240** 31 18N 4 12W
Ritchie L. **80** 52 58N 66 1W
Riti **247** 7 57N 9 41 E
Ritidian Pt. **226** 13 39N 144 51 E
Riu **202** 28 19N 95 3 E
Riva Bella **138** 49 17N 0 18W
Riva del Garda **162** 45 53N 10 50 E
Riva Palacio **101** 28 33N 106 30W
Rivadavia, Buenos Aires, Argentina **124** 35 29 S 62 59W
Rivadavia, Mendoza, Argentina **124** 33 13 S 68 30W
Rivadavia, Salta, Argentina **124** 24 5 S 62 54W
Rivadavia, Chile **124** 29 57 S 70 35W
Rivarolo Canavese **162** 45 20N 7 42 E
Rivas **112** 11 30N 85 50W
Rive-de-Gier **141** 45 32N 4 37 E
River Cess **246** 5 30N 9 32W
River Hébert **81** 45 42N 64 23W
River John **81** 45 45N 63 3W
River Jordan **92** 48 26N 124 3W
River of Ponds **79** 50 32N 57 24W
River of Ponds L. **79** 50 30N 57 20W
River Valley **84** 46 35N 80 11W
Rivera **125** 31 0 S 55 50W
Rivercrest **89** 50 0N 97 3W
Riverdsale **254** 34 7 S 21 15 E
Riverhead **79** 46 58N 53 31W
Riverhurst **88** 50 55N 106 50W
Riverina **229** 29 45 S 120 40 E
Riverport **81** 44 18N 64 20W
Rivers **89** 50 2N 100 14W
Rivers □ **247** 5 0N 6 30 E
Rivers, L. of the **88** 49 49N 105 44W
Rivers Inlet **92** 51 42N 127 15W
Riverside-Albert **81** 45 42N 64 45W
Riversleigh **230** 19 5 S 138 40 E
Riverton, Australia **232** 34 10 S 138 46 E
Riverton, Canada **89** 51 1N 97 0W
Riverton, N.Z. **235** 46 21 S 168 0 E
Riverview Heights **81** 46 4N 64 48W
Rives **141** 45 21N 5 31 E
Rivesaltes **140** 42 47N 2 50 E
Riviera **162** 44 0N 8 30 E
Riviera di Levante **160** 44 23N 9 15 E
Riviera di Ponente **160** 43 50N 7 58 E
Rivière-à-la-Chaloupe **80** 50 17N 65 6W
Rivière-à-Pierre **83** 46 59N 72 11W
Rivière-au-Renard **80** 48 59N 64 23W
Rivière-aux-Rats **83** 47 13N 72 53W
Rivière-Bersimis **83** 48 56N 68 42W
Rivière-de-la-Chaloupe **80** 49 8N 62 32W
Rivière-du-Loup **83** 47 50N 69 30W
Rivière-Ouelle **83** 47 26N 70 1W
Rivière-Pentecôte **80** 49 57N 67 1W
Rivière-Pigou **80** 50 16N 65 35W
Rivière-Pilot **113** 14 26N 60 53W
Rivière-Portneuf **83** 48 38N 69 6W
Rivière-St-Jean **80** 50 17N 64 19W
Rivière-Ste.-Marguerite **80** 50 8N 66 37W
Rivière Verte **81** 47 19N 68 9W
Rivierre-au-Tonnère **80** 50 16N 64 47W
Rívoli **162** 45 3N 7 31 E
Rivoli B. **232** 37 32 S 140 3 E
Riwaka **235** 41 5 S 172 59 E
Rixensart **143** 50 43N 4 32 E
Riyadh = Ar Riyāḑ **192** 24 41N 46 42 E
Rizal, Cagayan, Phil. **210** 17 51N 121 21 E
Rizal, Nueva Ecija, Phil. **210** 15 43N 121 6 E
Rizal, Zamboanga del N., Phil. **211** 8 35N 123 26 E
Rize **177** 41 0N 40 30 E
Rizhao **215** 35 25N 119 30 E
Rizokarpaso **190** 35 35N 32 22 E
Rizzuto, C. **165** 38 54N 17 5 E
Rjukan **171** 59 54N 8 33 E
Rjuven **171** 59 9N 7 8 E
Rô **226** 21 22 S 167 50 E
Roa, Norway **171** 60 17N 10 37 E
Roa, Spain **154** 41 41N 3 56W
Road Town **113** 18 27N 64 37W
Roag, L. **134** 58 10N 6 55W
Roanne **141** 46 3N 4 4 E
Roatán **112** 16 18N 86 35W
Robb **90** 53 13N 116 58W
Robbins I. **230** 40 42 S 145 0 E
Robe →, Australia **228** 21 42 S 116 15 E
Robe →, Ireland **135** 53 38N 9 10W
Robe-Noire, L. de la **80** 50 42N 62 42W
Röbel **146** 53 24N 12 37 E
Robert's Arm **79** 49 29N 55 49W
Roberts Creek **93** 49 26N 123 38W
Robertsganj **199** 24 44N 83 4 E
Robertson, Australia **233** 34 37 S 150 36 E
Robertson, S. Africa **254** 33 46 S 19 50 E
Robertson I. **13** 65 15 S 59 30W
Robertson Ra. **228** 23 15 S 121 0 E
Robertsonville **83** 46 9N 71 13W
Robertsport **246** 6 45N 11 26W
Robertstown **232** 33 58 S 139 5 E
Robertville **81** 47 42N 65 46W
Roberval **83** 48 32N 72 15W
Robeson Ch. **12** 82 0N 61 30W
Robinson → **230** 16 3 S 137 16 E
Robinson Crusoe I. **225** 33 38 S 78 52W
Robinson Ranges **229** 25 40 S 119 0 E
Robinson River **230** 16 45 S 136 58 E
Robinvale **231** 34 40 S 142 45 E
Robla, La **154** 42 50N 5 41W
Roblin **89** 51 14N 101 21W
Roboré **123** 18 10 S 59 45W
Robsart **88** 49 23N 109 17W
Robson, Mt. **93** 53 10N 119 10W
Roc, Pointe du **138** 48 50N 1 37W
Roca, C. da **155** 38 40N 9 31W
Roca del Toro, Pta. **100** 31 20N 113 38W
Roca Partida, Pta. **109** 18 42N 95 10W
Rocanville **89** 50 23N 101 42W
Rocas, I. **120** 4 0 S 34 1W
Rocca d'Aspidé **165** 40 27N 15 10 E
Rocca San Casciano **163** 44 3N 11 45 E
Roccalbegna **163** 42 47N 11 30 E
Roccastrada **163** 43 0N 11 10 E
Roccella Iónica **165** 38 20N 16 24 E
Rocha **125** 34 30 S 54 25W
Rochdale **132** 53 36N 2 10W
Roche, La, France **141** 46 4N 6 19 E
Roche, La, Switz. **148** 46 42N 7 7 E
Roche-Bernard, La **138** 47 31N 2 19W
Roche-Canillac, La **140** 45 12N 1 57 E
Roche-en-Ardenne, La **143** 50 11N 5 35 E
Roche Percée **88** 49 4N 102 48W
Roche-sur-Yon, La **138** 46 40N 1 25W
Rochebaucourt **82** 48 41N 77 30W
Rochechouart **140** 45 50N 0 49 E
Rochedo **123** 19 57 S 54 52W
Rochefort, Belgium **143** 50 9N 5 12 E
Rochefort, France **140** 45 56N 0 57W
Rochefort-en-Terre **138** 47 42N 2 22W
Rochefoucauld, La **140** 45 44N 0 24 E
Rochelle, La **140** 46 10N 1 9W
Rocher River **76** 61 23N 112 44W
Rocherath **143** 50 26N 6 18 E
Roches → **80** 50 2N 66 55W
Rocheservière **138** 46 57N 1 30W
Rochester, Australia **232** 36 22 S 144 41 E
Rochester, Canada **90** 54 22N 113 27W
Rochester, U.K. **133** 51 22N 0 30 E
Rociana **155** 37 19N 6 35W
Rociu **170** 44 43N 25 2 E
Rock → **78** 60 7N 127 7W
Rock Creek **93** 49 4N 119 0W
Rock Flat **233** 36 21 S 149 13 E
Rock Island **83** 45 26N 73 34W
Rock Sound **112** 24 54N 76 12W
Rockall **130** 57 37N 13 42W
Rockanje **142** 51 52N 4 4 E
Rockefeller Plat. **13** 80 0 S 140 0W
Rockglen **88** 49 11N 105 57W
Rockhampton **230** 23 22 S 150 32 E
Rockhampton Downs **230** 18 57 S 135 10 E
Rockingham **229** 32 15 S 115 38 E
Rockingham B. **230** 18 5 S 146 10 E
Rockingham Forest **133** 52 28N 0 42W
Rockland **85** 45 33N 75 17W
Rockwood **84** 43 37N 80 8W
Rocky → **91** 53 8N 117 59W
Rocky Gully **229** 34 30 S 116 57 E
Rocky Harbour **79** 49 36N 57 55W
Rocky Island L. **87** 46 55N 83 0W
Rocky Lane **76** 58 31N 116 22W
Rocky Mountain House **91** 52 22N 114 55W
Rocky Mts. **76** 55 0N 121 0W
Rockyford **91** 51 14N 113 10W
Rocroi **139** 49 55N 4 30 E
Rod **197** 28 10N 63 5 E
Roda, La, Albacete, Spain **157** 39 13N 2 15W
Roda, La, Sevilla, Spain **155** 37 12N 4 46W
Rødberg **171** 60 17N 8 56 E
Rødby **173** 54 41N 11 23 E
Rødbyhavn **173** 54 39N 11 22 E
Roddickton **79** 50 51N 56 8W
Rødding **173** 55 23N 9 3 E
Rødekro **173** 55 4N 9 20 E
Roden **142** 53 8N 6 26 E
Rødenes **171** 59 35N 11 34 E
Rodenkirchen **146** 53 24N 8 26 E
Rodeo **105** 25 11N 104 4W
Roderick I. **92** 52 38N 128 22W
Rodez **140** 44 21N 2 33 E
Rodholívas **168** 40 55N 24 0 E
Rodhópi □ **168** 41 5N 25 30 E
Ródhos **169** 36 15N 28 10 E
Rodi Garganico **165** 41 55N 15 53 E
Rodna **170** 47 25N 24 50 E
Rodnei, Munţii **170** 47 35N 24 35 E
Rodney **84** 42 34N 81 41W
Rodney, C. **234** 36 17 S 174 50 E
Rodniki **179** 57 7N 41 47 E
Rodriguez **203** 19 45 S 63 20 E
Roe → **135** 55 10N 6 59W
Roebourne **228** 20 44 S 117 9 E
Roebuck B. **228** 18 5 S 122 20 E
Roebuck Plains **228** 17 56 S 122 28 E
Roer → **143** 51 12N 5 59 E
Roermond **143** 51 12N 6 0 E
Roes Welcome Sd. **95** 65 0N 87 0W
Roeselare **143** 50 57N 3 7 E
Rœulx **143** 50 31N 4 7 E
Rogachev **178** 53 8N 30 5 E
Rogaçica **166** 44 4N 19 40 E
Rogagua, L. **122** 13 43 S 66 50W
Rogaland fylke □ **171** 59 12N 6 20 E
Rogaška Slatina **163** 46 15N 15 42 E
Rogatec **163** 46 15N 15 46 E
Rogatica **166** 43 47N 19 0 E
Rogatin **178** 49 24N 24 36 E
Roger, L. **82** 47 50N 78 59W
Rogersville **81** 46 44N 65 26W
Roggan **78** 54 25N 79 32W
Roggan L. **78** 54 8N 77 50W
Roggel **143** 51 16N 5 56 E
Roggeveldberge **254** 32 10 S 20 10 E
Roggiano Gravina **165** 39 37N 16 9 E
Rogliano, France **141** 42 57N 9 30 E
Rogliano, Italy **165** 39 11N 16 20 E
Rogoaguado, L. **123** 13 0 S 65 30W
Rogowo **152** 52 43N 17 38 E
Rogozno **152** 52 45N 16 59 E
Rohan **138** 48 4N 2 45W
Rohault, L. **83** 49 23N 74 20W
Rohrbach **139** 49 3N 7 15 E
Rohri **197** 27 45N 68 51 E
Rohri Canal **198** 26 15N 68 27 E
Rohtak **198** 28 55N 76 43 E
Roi Et **204** 16 4N 103 40 E
Roisel **139** 49 58N 3 6 E
Rojas **124** 34 10 S 60 45W
Rojo, C. **108** 21 33N 97 20W
Rokan → **208** 2 0N 100 50 E
Rokeby **230** 13 39 S 142 40 E
Rokiskis **178** 55 55N 25 35 E
Rokitno **178** 50 57N 35 56 E
Rokycany **150** 49 43N 13 35 E
Roland **89** 49 22N 97 56W
Rolândia **125** 23 18 S 51 23W
Røldal **171** 59 47N 6 50 E
Rolde **142** 52 59N 6 39 E
Rollag **171** 60 2N 9 18 E
Rollands Plains **233** 31 17 S 152 42 E
Rolle **148** 46 28N 6 20 E
Rolleston, Australia **230** 24 28 S 148 35 E
Rolleston, N.Z. **235** 43 35 S 172 24 E
Rollet **82** 47 55N 79 15W
Rolling Hills **91** 50 13N 111 46W
Rollingstone **230** 19 2 S 146 24 E
Rom **245** 9 54N 32 16 E
Roma, Australia **231** 26 32 S 148 49 E
Roma, Italy **164** 41 54N 12 30 E
Romaine → **78** 50 18N 63 47W
Roman, Bulgaria **167** 43 8N 23 54 E
Roman, Romania **170** 46 57N 26 55 E
Roman, U.S.S.R. **185** 66 4N 112 14 E
Roman-Kosh, Gora **180** 44 37N 34 15 E
Romana, La **113** 18 27N 68 57W
Romanche → **141** 45 5N 5 43 E
Romang **207** 7 30 S 127 20 E
Români **191** 31 2N 32 39 E
Romania ■ **170** 46 0N 25 0 E
Romanija Planina **166** 43 50N 18 45 E
Romano, Cayo **112** 22 0N 77 30W
Romano di Lombardía **162** 45 32N 9 45 E
Romanovka = Bessarabka **180** 46 21N 28 58 E
Romans **141** 45 3N 5 3 E
Romanshorn **149** 47 33N 9 22 E
Romblon **210** 12 33N 122 17 E
Romblon □ **210** 12 30N 122 15 E
Romblon Pass **210** 12 27N 122 12 E
Rombo □ **250** 3 10 S 37 30 E
Rome = Roma **164** 41 54N 12 30 E
Romeleåsen **172** 55 34N 13 33 E
Romenay **141** 46 30N 5 1 E
Romerike **171** 60 7N 11 10 E
Romilly **139** 48 31N 3 44 E
Romîni **170** 44 59N 24 11 E
Romita **107** 20 52N 101 31W
Rommani **240** 33 31N 6 40W
Romney Marsh **133** 51 0N 1 0 E
Romny **178** 50 48N 33 28 E
Rømø **173** 55 10N 8 30 E
Romodan **178** 50 0N 33 15 E
Romodanovo **179** 54 26N 45 23 E
Romont **148** 46 42N 6 54 E
Romorantin-Lanthenay **139** 47 21N 1 45 E
Romsdalen **171** 62 25N 8 0 E
Ron **204** 17 53N 106 27 E
Rona **134** 57 33N 6 0W
Roncador, Cayos **112** 13 32N 80 4W
Roncador, Serra do **121** 12 30 S 52 30W
Roncesvalles, Paso **156** 43 1N 1 19W
Ronciglione **163** 42 18N 12 12 E
Ronco → **163** 44 24N 12 12 E
Ronda **155** 36 46N 5 12W
Ronda, Serranía de **155** 36 44N 5 3W
Rondane **171** 61 57N 9 50 E
Rondeau Prov. Park **84** 42 19N 81 51W
Rondón **118** 6 17N 71 6W
Rondônia **123** 10 52 S 61 57W
Rondônia □ **123** 11 0 S 63 0W
Rondonópolis **123** 16 28 S 54 38W
Rong Jiang → **216** 24 35N 109 20 E
Rong Xian, Guangxi Zhuangzu, China **217** 22 50N 110 31 E
Rong Xian, Sichuan, China **216** 29 23N 104 22 E
Rong'an **216** 25 14N 109 22 E
Rongchang **216** 29 20N 105 32 E
Ronge, L. la **77** 55 6N 105 17W
Ronge, La **77** 55 5N 105 20W
Rongjiang **216** 25 57N 108 28 E
Rongotea **234** 40 19 S 175 25 E
Rongshui **216** 25 5N 109 12 E
Ronne Ice Shelf **13** 78 0 S 60 0W
Ronneby **173** 56 12N 15 17 E
Ronsard, C. **229** 24 46 S 113 10 E
Ronse **143** 50 45N 3 35 E
Ronuro → **123** 11 56 S 53 33W
Roodeschool **142** 53 25N 6 46 E
Roompot **143** 51 37N 3 44 E
Roonui, Mt. **226** 17 49 S 149 12W
Roorkee **198** 29 52N 77 59 E
Roosendaal **143** 51 32N 4 29 E
Roosevelt → **123** 7 35 S 60 20W
Roosevelt, Mt. **76** 58 26N 125 20W
Roosevelt I. **13** 79 30 S 162 0W
Roosville **91** 49 0N 115 3W
Ropczyce **152** 50 4N 21 38 E
Roper → **230** 14 43 S 135 27 E
Roque Pérez **124** 35 25 S 59 24W
Roquebrou, La **140** 44 58N 2 12 E
Roquefort **140** 44 2N 0 20W
Roquefort-sur-Soulzon **140** 43 58N 2 59 E
Roquemaure **141** 44 3N 4 48 E
Roquetas **156** 40 50N 0 30 E
Roquevaire **141** 43 20N 5 36 E
Roraima □ **119** 2 0N 61 30W
Roraima, Mt. **119** 5 10N 60 40W
Rorketon **89** 51 24N 99 35W
Røros **171** 62 35N 11 23 E
Rorschach **149** 47 28N 9 30 E
Rørvik **174** 64 54N 11 15 E
Rosa **251** 9 33 S 31 15 E
Rosa, C. **241** 37 0N 8 16 E
Rosa, La **102** 25 33N 101 23W
Rosa, Monte **148** 45 57N 7 53 E
Rosa Anegados, Pta. **104** 21 17N 105 11W
Rosa Morada **104** 22 4N 105 4W
Rosa Morales **104** 25 22N 107 52W
Rosal **154** 41 57N 8 51W
Rosal de la Frontera **155** 37 59N 7 13W
Rosales, Mexico **101** 28 12N 105 33W
Rosales, Phil. **210** 15 54N 120 38 E
Rosalind **91** 52 47N 112 27W
Rosans **141** 44 24N 5 29 E

Rosario, Argentina 124 33 0 S 60 40W
Rosário, Brazil 120 3 0 S 44 15W
Rosario, Baja Calif. N., Mexico 98 30 1N 115 45W
Rosario, Baja Calif. S., Mexico 99 26 27N 111 38W
Rosario, Sinaloa, Mexico 104 22 58N 105 53W
Rosario, Paraguay 124 24 30 S 57 35W
Rosario, Phil. 211 8 24N 125 59 E
Rosario, R. del → 98 30 2N 115 48W
Rosario, Sa. del 105 25 36N 103 52W
Rosario, Villa del 118 10 19N 72 19W
Rosario de la Frontera 124 25 50 S 65 0W
Rosario de Lerma 124 24 59 S 65 35W
Rosario del Tala 124 32 20 S 59 10W
Rosário do Sul 125 30 15 S 54 55W
Rosário Oeste 123 14 50 S 56 25W
Rosarito, Baja Calif. N., Mexico 98 28 38N 114 4W
Rosarito, Baja Calif. N., Mexico 98 32 20N 117 2W
Rosarno 165 38 29N 15 59 E
Rosas 156 42 19N 3 10 E
Roscoff 138 48 44N 4 0W
Roscommon 135 53 38N 8 11W
Roscommon □ 135 53 40N 8 15W
Roscrea 135 52 58N 7 50W
Rose → 230 14 16 S 135 45 E
Rose Blanche 79 47 38N 58 45W
Rose Harbour 92 52 15N 131 10W
Rose Pt. 92 54 11N 131 39W
Rose Valley 88 52 19N 103 49W
Roseau 113 15 20N 61 24W
Rosebery 230 41 46 S 145 33 E
Rosebud 233 38 21 S 144 54 E
Rosebud → 91 51 25N 112 38W
Rosedale, Australia 230 24 38 S 151 53 E
Rosedale, Canada 93 49 10N 121 48W
Rosée 143 50 14N 4 41 E
Roseisle 89 49 30N 98 20W
Rosemary 91 50 46N 112 5W
Rosemère 83 45 38N 73 48W
Rosendaël 139 51 3N 2 24 E
Rosenheim 147 47 51N 12 9 E
Roseto degli Abruzzi 163 42 40N 14 2 E
Rosetown 88 51 35N 107 59W
Rosetta = Rashîd 244 31 21N 30 22 E
Rosewood, N.S.W., Australia 233 35 38 S 147 52 E
Rosewood, N. Terr., Australia 228 16 28 S 128 58 E
Rosewood, Queens., Australia 231 27 38 S 152 36 E
Rosh Haniqra, Kefar 189 33 5N 35 5 E
Rosh Pinna 189 32 58N 35 32 E
Roshkhvār 193 34 58N 59 37 E
Rosières 139 49 49N 2 43 E
Rosignano Marittimo 162 43 23N 10 28 E
Rosignol 119 6 15N 57 30W
Roşiori de Vede 170 44 9N 25 0 E
Rosita, La 102 28 24N 101 43W
Rositsa 167 43 57N 27 57 E
Rositsa → 167 43 10N 25 30 E
Roskilde 172 55 38N 12 3 E
Roskilde Amtskommune □ 172 55 35N 12 5 E
Roskilde Fjord 172 55 50N 12 2 E
Roslavl 178 53 57N 32 55 E
Roslyn 231 34 29 S 149 37 E
Rosmaninhal 155 39 44N 7 5W
Røsnœs 172 55 44N 10 55 E
Rosolini 165 36 49N 14 58 E
Rosporden 138 47 57N 3 50W
Ross, Australia 230 42 2 S 147 30 E
Ross, N.Z. 235 42 53 S 170 49 E
Ross Dependency □ 13 70 0 S 170 5W
Ross I. 13 77 30 S 168 0 E
Ross Ice Shelf 13 80 0 S 180 0 E
Ross on Wye 133 51 55N 2 34W
Ross River 94 62 30N 131 30W
Ross Sea 13 74 0 S 178 0 E
Rossa 149 46 23N 9 8 E
Rossan Pt. 135 54 42N 8 47W
Rossano Cálabro 165 39 36N 16 39 E
Rossburn 89 50 40N 100 49W
Rosseau 84 45 16N 79 39W
Rosseau L. 84 45 10N 79 35W
Rossel, C. 226 20 23 S 166 36 E
Rossignol, L., N.S., Canada 81 44 12N 65 10W
Rossignol, L., Qué., Canada 78 52 43N 73 40W
Rossland 93 49 6N 117 50W
Rosslare 135 52 17N 6 23W
Rosslau 146 51 52N 12 15 E
Rossmore 85 44 8N 77 23W
Rosso 246 16 40N 15 45W
Rossosh 181 50 15N 39 28 E
Rossport 87 48 50N 87 30W
Rossum 142 51 48N 5 20 E
Røssvatnet 174 65 45N 14 5 E
Rossville 230 15 48 S 145 15 E
Rostāq 197 37 7N 69 49 E
Rosthern 88 52 40N 106 20W
Rostock 146 54 4N 12 9 E
Rostock □ 146 54 10N 12 30 E
Rostov, Don, U.S.S.R. 181 47 15N 39 45 E
Rostov, Moskva, U.S.S.R. 179 57 14N 39 25 E
Rostrenen 138 48 14N 3 21W
Rosyth 134 56 2N 3 26W
Rota 155 36 37N 6 20W
Rotälven → 172 61 15N 14 3 E
Rotem 143 51 3N 5 45 E
Rotenburg 146 53 6N 9 24 E
Roth 147 49 15N 11 6 E
Rothaargebirge 144 51 0N 8 20 E
Rothenburg 149 47 6N 8 16 E
Rothenburg ob der Tauber 147 49 21N 10 11 E
Rother → 133 50 59N 0 40 E
Rotherham 132 53 26N 1 21W
Rothes 134 57 31N 3 12W
Rothesay, Canada 81 45 23N 66 0W
Rothesay, U.K. 134 55 50N 5 3W
Rothrist 148 47 18N 8 54 E
Roti 207 10 50 S 123 0 E
Roto 231 33 0 S 145 30 E
Roto Aira L. 234 39 3 S 175 45 E
Rotoehu L. 234 38 1 S 176 32 E
Rotoiti L. 235 41 51 S 172 49 E
Rotoma L. 234 38 2 S 176 35 E
Rotondella 165 40 10N 16 30 E
Rotoroa, L. 235 41 55 S 172 39 E
Rotorua 234 38 9 S 176 16 E
Rotorua, L. 234 38 5 S 176 18 E
Rotselaar 143 50 57N 4 42 E
Rott → 147 48 26N 13 26 E
Rotten → 148 46 18N 7 36 E
Rottenburg 147 48 28N 8 56 E
Rottenmann 150 47 31N 14 22 E
Rotterdam 142 51 55N 4 30 E
Rottnest I. 229 32 0 S 115 27 E
Rottumeroog 142 53 33N 6 34 E
Rottweil 147 48 9N 8 38 E
Rotuma 224 12 25 S 177 5 E
Roubaix 139 50 40N 3 10 E
Roudnice 150 50 25N 14 15 E
Rouen 138 49 27N 1 4 E
Rouge → 82 45 17N 74 10W
Rough Ridge 235 45 10 S 169 55 E
Rouillac 140 45 47N 0 4W
Rouleau 88 50 10N 104 56W
Round Hill, Alta., Canada 91 53 10N 112 38W
Round Hill, N.S., Canada 81 44 46N 65 24W
Round L., Newf., Canada 79 51 15N 56 32W
Round L., Ont., Canada 85 45 38N 77 30W
Round Mt. 231 30 26 S 152 16 E
Round Pond 79 48 11N 56 0W
Round Valley 90 53 21N 114 57W
Roura 119 4 44N 52 20W
Rousay 134 59 10N 3 2W
Rousse, L'Île 141 42 37N 8 57 E
Roussillon, Isère, France 141 45 24N 4 49 E
Roussillon, Pyrénées-Or., France 140 42 30N 2 35 E
Roussin, C. 226 21 20 S 167 59 E
Routhierville 80 48 11N 67 9W
Rouveen 142 52 37N 6 11 E
Rouvray, L. 83 49 18N 70 49W
Rouxville 254 30 25 S 26 50 E
Rouyn 82 48 20N 79 0W
Rovaniemi 174 66 29N 25 41 E
Rovato 162 45 34N 10 0 E
Rovenki 181 48 5N 39 21 E
Rovereto 162 45 53N 11 3 E
Rovigo 163 45 4N 11 48 E
Rovinari 170 44 56N 23 10 E
Rovinj 163 45 5N 13 40 E
Rovìra 118 4 15N 75 20W
Rovno 178 50 40N 26 10 E
Rovnoye 179 50 52N 46 3 E
Rovuma → 251 10 29 S 40 28 E
Row'ān 193 35 8N 48 51 E
Rowan L. 86 49 18N 93 32W
Rowena 231 29 48 S 148 55 E
Rowes 233 37 0 S 149 6 E
Rowley I. 95 69 6N 77 52W
Rowley Shoals 228 17 30 S 119 0 E
Roxa 246 11 15N 15 45W
Roxas, Capiz, Phil. 211 11 36N 122 49 E
Roxas, Isabela, Phil. 210 17 8N 121 36 E
Roxas, Mindoro, Phil. 210 12 35N 121 31 E
Roxas = Barbacan 211 10 20N 119 21 E
Roxborough Downs 230 22 30 S 138 45 E
Roxburgh 235 45 33 S 169 19 E
Roxen 173 58 30N 15 40 E
Roxton Falls 83 45 34N 72 31W
Roy Hill 228 22 37 S 119 58 E
Roya, Peña 156 40 25N 0 40W
Royalla 233 35 30 S 149 9 E
Royan 140 45 37N 1 2W
Roye 139 49 42N 2 48 E
Røyken 171 59 45N 10 23 E
Rožaj 166 42 50N 20 15 E
Różan 152 52 52N 21 25 E
Rozay 139 48 40N 2 56 E
Rozhishche 178 50 54N 25 15 E
Rozier, Le 140 44 13N 3 12 E
Rŏžnava 151 48 37N 20 35 E
Rozogi 152 53 48N 21 9 E
Rozoy-sur-Serre 139 49 40N 4 8 E
Rozwadów 152 50 37N 22 2 E
Rrësheni 168 41 47N 19 49 E
Rrogozhino 168 41 2N 19 50 E
Rtanj 166 43 45N 21 50 E
Rtishchevo 179 55 16N 43 50 E
Rúa 154 42 24N 7 6W
Ruacaná 254 17 20 S 14 12 E
Ruahine Ra. 234 39 55 S 176 2 E
Ruamahanga → 234 41 24 S 175 8 E
Ruapehu 234 39 17 S 175 35 E
Ruapuke I. 235 46 46 S 168 31 E
Ruâq, W. → 191 30 0N 33 49 E
Ruatoria 234 37 55 S 178 20 E
Ruaus, Wadi → 241 30 26N 15 24 E
Ruawai 234 36 8 S 173 59 E
Rub' al Khali 195 18 0N 48 0 E
Rubeho Mts. 250 6 50 S 36 25 E
Rubezhnoye 180 49 6N 38 25 E
Rubh a' Mhail 134 55 55N 6 10W
Rubha Hunish 134 57 42N 6 20W
Rubiataba 121 15 8 S 49 48W
Rubicone → 163 44 8N 12 28 E
Rubinéia 121 20 13 S 51 2W
Rubino 246 6 4N 4 18W
Rubio 118 7 43N 72 22W
Rubtsovsk 184 51 30N 81 10 E
Rubyvale 230 23 25 S 147 45 E
Rucava 178 56 9N 21 12 E
Rucheng 217 25 33N 113 38 E
Ruciane-Nida 152 53 40N 21 32 E
Rud 171 60 1N 10 1 E
Rūd Sar 193 37 8N 50 18 E
Ruda 173 57 6N 16 7 E
Ruda Śląska 152 50 16N 18 50 E
Rudall 232 33 43 S 136 17 E
Rūdbār 197 30 9N 62 36 E
Ruden 146 54 13N 13 47 E
Rüdersdorf 146 52 28N 13 48 E
Rudewa 251 10 7 S 34 40 E
Rudkøbing 173 54 56N 10 41 E
Rudna 152 51 30N 16 17 E
Rudnichnyy 182 59 38N 52 26 E
Rudnik, Bulgaria 167 42 36N 27 30 E
Rudnik, Poland 152 50 26N 22 15 E
Rudnik, Yugoslavia 170 44 7N 20 35 E
Rudnogorsk 185 57 15N 103 42 E
Rudnya 178 54 55N 31 7 E
Rudnyy 182 52 57N 63 7 E
Rudo 166 43 41N 19 23 E
Rudolf, Ostrov 184 81 45N 58 30 E
Rudolstadt 146 50 44N 11 20 E
Rudong 217 32 20N 121 12 E
Rudozem 167 41 29N 24 51 E
Rue 139 50 15N 1 40 E
Ruel 87 47 15N 81 28W
Ruelle 140 45 41N 0 14 E
Rufa'a 245 14 44N 33 22 E
Ruffec-Charente 140 46 2N 0 12 E
Rufiji □ 250 8 0 S 38 30 E
Rufiji → 250 7 50 S 39 15 E
Rufino 124 34 20 S 62 50W
Rufisque 246 14 40N 17 15W
Rufunsa 251 15 4 S 29 34 E
Rugao 217 32 23N 120 31 E
Rugby 133 52 23N 1 16W
Rügen 146 54 22N 13 25 E
Rugles 138 48 50N 0 40 E
Ruḥama 189 31 31N 34 43 E
Ruhea 202 26 10N 88 25 E
Ruhengeri 250 1 30 S 29 36 E
Ruhla 146 50 53N 10 21 E
Ruhland 146 51 27N 13 52 E
Ruhr → 146 51 25N 6 44 E
Ruhuhu → 251 10 31 S 34 34 E
Rui Barbosa 121 12 18 S 40 27W
Rui'an 217 27 47N 120 40 E
Ruichang 217 29 40N 115 39 E
Ruili 216 24 1N 97 43 E
Ruinen 142 52 46N 6 21 E
Ruinen A Kanaal 142 52 54N 7 8 E
Ruinerwold 142 52 44N 6 15 E
Ruisseau-Vert 83 49 4N 68 28W
Ruiz 104 21 57N 105 9W
Ruj 166 42 52N 22 42 E
Rujen 166 42 9N 22 30 E
Rujm Tal'at al Jamā'ah 191 30 24N 35 30 E
Ruk 198 27 50N 68 42 E
Rukwa □ 250 7 0 S 31 30 E
Rukwa L. 250 8 0 S 32 20 E
Rulhieres, C. 228 13 56 S 127 22 E
Rulles 143 49 43N 5 32 E
Rum Cay 112 23 40N 74 58W
Rum Jungle 228 13 0 S 130 59 E
Ruma 166 45 0N 19 50 E
Rumādah 194 13 34N 43 52 E
Rumāḥ 192 25 29N 47 10 E
Rumania = Romania ■ 170 46 0N 25 0 E
Rumaylah 192 30 47N 47 37 E
Rumaylah, 'Urūq ar 194 21 0N 47 30 E
Rumbalara 230 25 20 S 134 29 E
Rumbêk 245 6 54N 29 37 E
Rumbeke 143 50 56N 3 10 E
Rumburk 150 50 57N 14 32 E
Rumelange 143 49 27N 6 2 E
Rumia 152 54 37N 18 25 E
Rumilly 141 45 53N 5 56 E
Rumoi 218 43 56N 141 39W
Rumonge 250 3 59 S 29 26 E
Rumorosa, La 98 32 34N 116 6W
Rumsey 91 51 51N 112 48W
Rumula 230 16 35 S 145 20 E
Rumuruti 250 0 17N 36 32 E
Runan 214 33 0N 114 30 E
Runanga 235 42 25 S 171 15 E
Runcorn 132 53 20N 2 44W
Rungwa 250 6 55 S 33 32 E
Rungwa → 250 7 36 S 31 50 E
Rungwe 251 9 11 S 33 32 E
Rungwe □ 251 9 25 S 33 32 E
Runka 247 12 28N 7 20 E
Runn 172 60 30N 15 40 E
Ruoqiang 212 38 55N 88 10 E
Rupa 202 27 15N 92 21 E
Rupar 198 31 2N 76 38 E
Rupat 208 1 45N 101 40 E
Rupea 170 46 2N 25 13 E
Rupert → 78 51 29N 78 45W
Rupert B. 78 51 35N 79 0W
Rupert House = Fort Rupert 78 51 30N 78 40W
Rupsa 202 21 44N 89 30 E
Rupununi → 119 4 3N 58 35W
Rur → 146 51 20N 6 0 E
Rurrenabaque 122 14 30 S 67 32W
Rus → 157 39 30N 2 30W
Rusagonis 81 45 48N 66 37W
Rusambo 251 16 30 S 32 4 E
Rusape 251 18 35 S 32 8 E
Ruschuk = Ruse 167 43 48N 25 59 E
Ruse 167 43 48N 25 59 E
Ruşeţu 170 44 57N 27 14 E
Rush L. 87 47 47N 82 11W
Rush Lake 88 50 24N 107 24W
Rushan 215 36 56N 121 30 E
Rushden 133 52 17N 0 37W
Rushoon 79 47 21N 54 55W
Rushworth 233 36 32 S 145 1 E
Rusken 173 57 15N 14 20 E
Russas 120 4 55 S 37 50W
Russell, Canada 77 50 50N 101 20W
Russell, N.Z. 234 35 16 S 174 10 E
Russell I. 95 74 0N 98 25W
Russell L., Man., Canada 77 56 15N 101 30W
Russell L., N.W.T., Canada 76 63 5N 115 44W
Russellkonda 199 19 57N 84 42 E
Russi 163 44 21N 12 1 E
Russian S.F.S.R. □ 185 62 0N 105 0 E
Russkaya Polyana 184 53 47N 73 53 E
Russkoye Ustie 12 71 0N 149 0 E
Rust 151 47 49N 16 42 E
Rustam 198 34 25N 72 13 E
Rustam Shahr 198 26 58N 66 6 E
Rustavi 181 41 30N 45 0 E
Rustenburg 254 25 41 S 27 14 E
Ruswil 148 47 5N 8 8 E
Rutana 250 3 55 S 30 0 E
Rute 155 37 19N 4 23W
Ruteng 207 8 35 S 120 30 E
Rutherglen, Australia 233 36 5 S 146 29 E
Rutherglen, U.K. 134 55 50N 4 11W
Rüti 149 47 16N 8 51 E
Rutigliano 165 41 1N 17 0 E
Rutland Plains 230 15 38 S 141 43 E
Rutledge → 77 61 4N 112 0W
Rutledge L. 77 61 33N 110 47W
Rutshuru 250 1 13 S 29 25 E
Rutter 84 46 6N 80 40W
Ruurlo 142 52 5N 6 24 E
Ruvo di Púglia 165 41 7N 16 27 E
Ruvu 250 6 49 S 38 43 E
Ruvu → 250 6 23 S 38 52 E

Ruvuma □ . . . . 251 10 20 S 36 0 E
Ruwais . . . . 195 24 5N 52 50 E
Ruwenzori . . . . 250 0 30N 29 55 E
Ruyigi . . . . 250 3 29 S 30 15 E
Ruyuan . . . . 217 24 46N 113 16 E
Ruzayevka . . . . 179 54 4N 45 0 E
Růzhevo Konare . . . 167 42 23N 24 46 E
Ružomberok . . . . 151 49 3N 19 17 E
Rwanda ■ . . . . 250 2 0 S 30 0 E
Ry . . . . 173 56 5N 9 45 E
Ryakhovo . . . . 167 44 0N 26 18 E
Ryan, L. 134 55 0N 5 2W
Ryans B. 78 59 35N 64 3W
Ryazan . . . . 179 54 40N 39 40 E
Ryazhsk . . . . 179 53 45N 40 3 E
Rybache . . . . 184 46 40N 81 20 E
Rybachiy Poluostrov 176 69 43N 32 0 E
Rybachye . . . . 183 42 26N 76 12 E
Rybinskoye Vdkhr. . 179 58 30N 38 25 E
Rybnik . . . . 152 50 6N 18 32 E
Rybnitsa . . . . 180 47 45N 29 0 E
Rybnoye . . . . 179 54 45N 39 30 E
Rychwał . . . . 152 52 4N 18 10 E
Rycroft 90 55 45N 118 40W
Ryd . . . . 173 56 27N 14 42 E
Ryde 133 50 44N 1 9W
Rydöbruk . . . . 173 56 58N 13 7 E
Rydsnäs . . . . 173 57 47N 15 9 E
Rydułtowy . . . . 152 50 4N 18 23 E
Rydzyna . . . . 152 51 47N 16 39 E
Rye . . . . 133 50 57N 0 46 E
Rye → 132 54 12N 0 53W
Ryki . . . . 152 51 38N 21 56 E
Ryley 90 53 17N 112 26W
Rylsk . . . . 178 51 36N 34 43 E
Rylstone . . . . 231 32 46 S 149 58 E
Rymanów . . . . 152 49 35N 21 51 E
Ryn . . . . 152 53 57N 21 34 E
Ryōhaku-Sanchi . . . 221 36 9N 136 49 E
Ryōthu . . . . 218 38 5N 138 26 E
Rypin . . . . 152 53 3N 19 25 E
Ryūgasaki . . . . 221 35 54N 140 11 E
Ryūkyū Is. = Nansei-Shotō . . . 219 26 0N 128 0 E
Rzepin . . . . 152 52 20N 14 49 E
Rzeszów . . . . 152 50 5N 21 58 E
Rzeszów □ . . . . 152 50 0N 22 0 E
Rzhev . . . . 178 56 20N 34 20 E

S

Sa . . . . 204 18 34N 100 45 E
Sa Dec . . . . 205 10 20N 105 46 E
Sa-koi . . . . 202 19 54N 97 3 E
Sa'ad . . . . 189 31 28N 34 33 E
Sa'ādatābād, Fārs, Iran . . . . 193 30 10N 53 5 E
Sa'ādatābād, Kermān, Iran . . . 193 28 3N 55 53 E
Saale → . . . . 146 51 57N 11 56 E
Saaler Bodden . . . . 146 54 20N 12 25 E
Saalfeld . . . . 146 50 39N 11 21 E
Saalfelden . . . . 150 47 25N 12 51 E
Saane → . . . . 148 46 23N 7 18 E
Saar → . . . . 139 49 41N 6 32 E
Saarbrücken . . . . 147 49 15N 6 58 E
Saarburg . . . . 147 49 36N 6 32 E
Saaremaa . . . . 178 58 30N 22 30 E
Saarland □ . . . . 147 49 15N 7 0 E
Saarlouis . . . . 147 49 19N 6 45 E
Saas Fee . . . . 148 46 7N 7 56 E
Saas-Grund . . . . 148 46 7N 7 57 E
Sab 'Bi'ār . . . . 192 33 46N 37 41 E
Şaba 113 17 42N 63 26W
Sabac . . . . 166 44 48N 19 42 E
Sabadell . . . . 156 41 28N 2 7 E
Sabae . . . . 221 35 57N 136 11 E
Sabah □ . . . . 206 6 0N 117 0 E
Sabak Bernam . . . . 205 3 46N 100 58 E
Sabán 111 20 2N 88 35W
Sabana, La 107 16 49N 99 50W
Sábana de la Mar . . 113 19 7N 69 24W
Sabana Grande 105 24 30N 101 45W
Sábanalarga 118 10 38N 74 55W
Sabancuy 111 18 58N 91 11W
Sabang . . . . 208 5 50N 95 15 E
Sabangan . . . . 210 17 0N 120 55 E
Sabará . . . . 121 19 55 S 43 46W
Sabarania . . . . 207 2 5 S 138 18 E
Sabari → . . . . 200 17 35N 81 16 E
Sabasţiyah . . . . 189 32 17N 35 12 E
Sab'atayn, Ramlat as . . . . 194 15 30N 46 10 E
Sabáudia . . . . 164 41 17N 13 2 E
Sabaya . . . . 122 19 1 S 68 23W
Sabāyā, Jaz. . . . . 194 18 35N 41 3 E
Sabhah . . . . 241 27 9N 14 29 E
Sabhah □ . . . . 241 26 0N 14 0 E
Sabie . . . . 255 25 10 S 30 48 E
Sabinal 101 30 57N 107 30W
Sabinal, Punta del . . 157 36 43N 2 44W
Sabinas 102 27 51N 101 7W
Sabinas → 102 27 37N 100 42W
Sabinas Hidalgo 102 26 30N 100 10W
Sabinas Hidalgo → 102 26 50N 99 35W
Sabinópolis . . . . 121 18 40 S 43 6W
Sabinov . . . . 151 49 6N 21 5 E
Sabirabad . . . . 181 40 5N 48 30 E
Sabkhat Tāwurghā' . 241 31 48N 15 30 E
Sabkhet el Bardawîl 191 31 10N 33 15 E
Sablayan . . . . 210 12 50N 120 50 E
Sable, C. 81 43 29N 65 38W
Sable I. 75 44 0N 60 0W
Sable River 81 43 51N 65 3W
Sablé-sur-Sarthe . . . 138 47 50N 0 20W
Sables, R. aux → . . 84 46 13N 82 3W
Sables-d'Olonne, Les 140 46 30N 1 45W
Saboeiro . . . . 120 6 32 S 39 54W
Sabolev . . . . 185 54 20N 155 30 E
Sabor → 154 41 10N 7 7W
Sabou 246 12 1N 2 15W
Sabourin, L. 82 47 58N 77 41W
Sabrātah . . . . 241 32 47N 12 29 E
Sabria . . . . 241 33 22N 8 45 E
Sabrina Coast . . . . 13 68 0 S 120 0 E
Sabtang I. . . . . 210 20 19N 121 52 E
Sabugal 154 40 20N 7 5W
Sabulubek . . . . 208 1 36 S 98 40 E
Şabyā . . . . 194 17 9N 42 37 E
Sabzevār . . . . 193 36 15N 57 40 E
Sabzvārān . . . . 193 28 45N 57 50 E
Sacalum 111 20 29N 89 35W
Sacedón 156 40 29N 2 41W
Sachigo → 74 55 6N 88 58W
Sachigo, L. 74 53 50N 92 12W
Sachkhere . . . . 181 42 25N 43 28 E
Sachs Harbour 94 71 59N 125 15W
Sachseln . . . . 149 46 52N 8 15 E
Sacile . . . . 163 45 58N 12 30 E
Sacır → . . . . 190 36 46N 37 36 E
Säckingen . . . . 147 47 34N 7 56 E
Sackville 81 45 54N 64 22W
Sacramento, Brazil . 121 19 53 S 47 27W
Sacramento, Mexico 102 26 5N 101 20W
Sacratif, Cabo 157 36 42N 3 28W
Sacré-Coeur-de-Jésus 83 48 14N 69 48W
Săcueni . . . . 170 47 20N 22 5 E
Sada 154 43 22N 8 15W
Sada-Misaki-Hantō . 220 33 22N 132 1 E
Sádaba 156 42 19N 1 12W
Sadani . . . . 250 5 58 S 38 35 E
Sadao . . . . 205 6 38N 100 26 E
Sadaseopet . . . . 200 17 38N 77 59 E
Sadd el Aali . . . . 244 23 54N 32 54 E
Sade . . . . 247 11 22N 10 45 E
Şadh . . . . 195 17 3N 55 4 E
Sadimi . . . . 251 9 25 S 23 32 E
Sadiya . . . . 202 27 50N 95 40 E
Sado . . . . 218 38 0N 138 25 E
Sado → 155 38 29N 8 55W
Sadon . . . . 181 42 52N 43 58 E
Sœby . . . . 173 57 21N 10 30 E
Saelices 156 39 55N 2 49W
Safaga . . . . 244 26 42N 34 0 E
Şafaha . . . . 244 26 25N 39 0 E
Šafárikovo . . . . 151 48 25N 20 20 E
Safed Koh . . . . 197 34 0N 70 0 E
Säffle . . . . 172 59 8N 12 55 E
Saffron Walden . . . . 133 52 2N 0 15 E
Safi 240 32 18N 9 20W
Şafīābād . . . . 193 36 45N 57 58 E
Safīd Dasht . . . . 193 33 27N 48 11 E
Safīd Kūh . . . . 197 34 45N 63 0 E
Safonovo . . . . 178 55 4N 33 16 E
Safranbolu . . . . 180 41 15N 32 41 E
Safwān . . . . 192 30 7N 47 43 E
Sag Sag . . . . 227 5 32 S 148 23 E
Saga, Indonesia . . . 207 2 40 S 132 55 E
Saga, Kōchi, Japan . 220 33 5N 133 6 E
Saga, Saga, Japan . . 220 33 15N 130 16 E
Saga □ . . . . 220 33 15N 130 20 E
Sagae . . . . 218 38 22N 140 17 E
Sagaing □ . . . . 202 23 55N 95 56 E
Sagala 246 14 9N 6 38W
Sagami-Nada . . . . 221 34 58N 139 30 E
Sagami-Wan . . . . 221 35 15N 139 25 E
Sagamihara . . . . 221 35 33N 139 25 E
Saganaga L. 86 48 14N 90 52W
Saganash L. 87 49 4N 82 35W
Saganoseki . . . . 220 33 15N 131 53 E
Sagar . . . . 201 14 14N 75 6 E
Sagara . . . . 221 34 41N 138 12 E
Sagara, L. . . . . 250 5 20 S 31 0 E
Sagawa . . . . 220 33 28N 133 11 E
Sagay . . . . 211 10 57N 123 25 E
Sagīr, Zab as → . . 192 35 10N 43 20 E
Sagleipie 246 7 0N 8 52W
Saglek B. 78 58 30N 63 0W
Saglek Fd. 78 58 29N 63 15W
Saglouc 78 62 14N 75 38W
Sagō-ri . . . . 215 35 25N 126 49 E
Sagone . . . . 141 42 7N 8 42 E
Sagone, G. de . . . . 141 42 4N 8 40 E
Sagra, La 157 37 57N 2 35W
Sagres 155 37 0N 8 58W
Sagu . . . . 202 20 13N 94 46 E
Sagua la Grande . . . 112 22 50N 80 10W
Saguenay → 83 48 22N 71 0W
Sagunto 156 39 42N 0 18W
Sahaba . . . . 244 18 57N 30 25 E
Sahagún, Colombia . 118 8 57N 75 27W
Sahagún, Spain 154 42 18N 5 2W
Saham . . . . 189 32 42N 35 46 E
Saḩam al Jawlān . . . 189 32 45N 35 55 E
Sahand, Kūh-e . . . . 192 37 44N 46 27 E
Sahara . . . . 240 23 0N 5 0 E
Saḩara, G. . . . . 191 28 2N 34 8 E
Saharan Atlas . . . . 236 34 9N 3 29 E
Saharanpur . . . . 198 29 58N 77 33 E
Sahasinaka . . . . 255 21 49 S 47 49 E
Sahaswan . . . . 199 28 5N 78 45 E
Sahel, Canal du . . . 246 14 20N 6 0W
Sahibganj . . . . 199 25 12N 87 40 E
Sahiwal . . . . 197 30 45N 73 8 E
Şaḩneh . . . . 192 34 29N 47 41 E
Sahtaneh → 76 59 2N 122 28W
Sahuaripa 100 29 3N 109 14W
Sahuayo de Díaz . . . 106 20 4N 102 43W
Sahy . . . . 151 48 4N 18 55 E
Sai Buri . . . . 205 6 43N 101 45 E
Sai-Cinza . . . . 123 6 17 S 57 42W
Saibai I. . . . . 227 9 25 S 142 40 E
Sa'id Bundas . . . . 243 8 24N 24 48 E
Saïda . . . . 241 34 50N 0 11 E
Saīdābād, Kermān, Iran . . . . 193 29 30N 55 45 E
Sa'īdābād, Semnān, Iran . . . . 193 36 8N 54 11 E
Saïdia 241 35 5N 2 14W
Sa'idiyeh . . . . 193 36 20N 48 55 E
Saidor . . . . 227 5 40 S 146 29 E
Saidu . . . . 199 34 43N 72 24 E
Saignelégier . . . . 148 47 15N 7 0 E
Saignes . . . . 140 45 20N 2 31 E
Saigō . . . . 220 36 12N 133 20 E
Saijō, Ehime, Japan 220 33 55N 133 11 E
Saijō, Hiroshima, Japan . . . . 220 34 25N 132 45 E
Saiki . . . . 220 32 58N 131 51 E
Saillans . . . . 141 44 42N 5 12 E
Sailolof . . . . 207 1 7 S 130 46 E
Sain Alto 105 23 35N 103 15W
Şa'in Dezh . . . . 192 36 40N 46 25 E
St. Abb's Head . . . 134 55 55N 2 10W
St-Adalbert 83 46 51N 69 53W
St. Aegyd . . . . 150 47 52N 15 33 E
St-Affrique . . . . 140 43 57N 2 53 E
St-Agapitville 83 46 34N 71 26W
St-Agrève . . . . 141 45 0N 4 23 E
St-Aignan . . . . 138 47 16N 1 22 E
St. Alban's, Canada 79 47 51N 55 50W
St. Albans, U.K. . . . 133 51 44N 0 19W
St. Alban's Head . . . 133 50 34N 2 3W
St. Albert 90 53 37N 113 32W
St-Alexandre 83 47 41N 69 38W
St-Alexis-des-Monts 83 46 28N 73 8W
St-Amand . . . . 139 50 25N 3 26 E
St-Amand-en-Puisaye . . . . 139 47 32N 3 5 E
St-Amand-Mont-Rond . . . . 140 46 43N 2 30 E
St-Amarin . . . . 139 47 54N 7 0 E
St-Ambroise 83 48 33N 71 20W
St-Amour . . . . 141 46 26N 5 21 E
St-Anaclet 83 48 29N 68 26W
St-André 81 47 8N 67 45W
St-André-Avellin . . . 82 45 43N 75 3W
St-André-de-Cubzac 140 44 59N 0 26W
St-André-de-l'Eure . 138 48 54N 1 16 E
St-André-Est 83 45 34N 74 20W
St-André-les-Alpes . 141 43 58N 6 30 E
St. Andrews, N.B., Canada 81 45 7N 67 5W
St. Andrew's, Newf., Canada . . . 79 47 45N 59 15W
St. Andrews, N.Z. . . 235 44 33 S 171 10 E
St. Andrews, U.K. . 134 56 20N 2 48W
St-Anicet 83 45 8N 74 22W
St. Ann B. 81 46 22N 60 25W
St. Anne 138 49 43N 2 11W
St. Annes 89 49 40N 96 39W
St. Ann's Bay 112 18 26N 77 15W
St-Anselme, N.B., Canada 81 46 4N 64 43W
St-Anselme, Qué., Canada 83 46 37N 70 58W
St. Anthony, N.B., Canada 81 46 22N 64 45W
St. Anthony, Newf., Canada 79 51 22N 55 35W
St-Antonin 83 47 46N 69 29W
St-Antonin-Noble-Val . . . . 140 44 10N 1 45 E
St-Apolline 83 46 48N 70 12W
St. Arnaud . . . . 231 36 40 S 143 16 E
St. Arnaud Ra. . . . 235 42 1 S 172 53 E
St. Arthur 81 47 33N 67 46W
St. Asaph 132 53 15N 3 27W
St-Astier . . . . 140 45 8N 0 31 E
St-Aubert 83 47 11N 70 13W
St.-Aubin . . . . 148 46 54N 6 47 E
St-Aubin-du-Cormier 138 48 15N 1 26W
St-Augustin → 78 51 16N 58 40W
St-Augustin-Saguenay 79 51 13N 58 38W
St. Austell 133 50 20N 4 48W
St-Avold . . . . 139 49 6N 6 43 E
St-Barthélémy 83 46 11N 73 8W
St.-Barthélemy, I. . . 113 17 50N 62 50W
St-Basile 81 47 21N 68 14W
St-Basile-Sud 83 46 45N 71 49W
St. Bathans . . . . 235 44 53 S 169 50 E
St. Bathan's Mt. . . . 235 44 45 S 169 45 E
St. Bee's Hd. . . . . 132 54 30N 3 38 E
St. Benedict 88 52 34N 105 23W
St-Benoît-du-Sault . . 140 46 26N 1 24 E
St. Bernard, Col du Grand . . . . 148 45 53N 7 11 E
St.-Blaise . . . . 148 47 1N 6 59 E
St. Boniface 89 49 53N 97 5W
St-Bonnet . . . . 141 44 40N 6 5 E
St. Brendan's 79 48 52N 53 40W
St-Brévin-les-Pins . . 138 47 14N 2 10W
St-Brice-en-Coglès . . 138 48 25N 1 22W
St. Bride's 79 46 56N 54 10W
St. Bride's B. 133 51 48N 5 15W
St-Brieuc 138 48 30N 2 46W
St. Brieux 88 52 38N 104 54W
St-Bruno 83 48 28N 71 39W
St-Calais . . . . 138 47 55N 0 45 E
St-Casimir 83 46 40N 72 8W
St-Cast 138 48 37N 2 18W
St. Catharines 84 43 10N 79 15W
St. Catherine's Pt. . . 133 50 34N 1 18W
St-Céré . . . . 140 44 51N 1 54 E
St.-Cergue . . . . 148 46 27N 6 10 E
St-Cernin . . . . 140 45 5N 2 25 E
St-Césaire 83 45 25N 73 0W
St-Chamond . . . . 141 45 28N 4 31 E
St-Chély-d'Apcher . . 140 44 48N 3 17 E
St-Chinian . . . . 140 43 25N 2 56 E
St. Christopher 113 17 20N 62 40W
St-Chrysostôme 83 45 6N 73 46W
St-Ciers-sur-Gironde 140 45 17N 0 37W
St. Clair, L. 84 42 30N 82 45W
St-Claud . . . . 140 45 54N 0 28 E
St. Claude 89 49 40N 98 20W
St-Claude . . . . 141 46 22N 5 52 E
St-Clet 83 45 21N 74 13W
St-Cloud . . . . 138 48 51N 2 12 E
St-Coeur de Marie . . 83 48 39N 71 43W
St-Côme 83 46 16N 73 47W
St. Cricq, C. . . . . 229 25 17 S 113 6 E
St-Croix 81 45 34N 67 26W
St. Croix → 81 45 5N 67 6W
St-Cyprien . . . . 140 42 37N 3 0 E
St-Cyr . . . . 141 43 11N 5 43 E
St-Cyrille-de-L'Islet . 83 47 2N 70 17W
St. David's, Canada 79 48 12N 58 52W
St. David's, U.K. . . . 133 51 54N 5 16W
St. David's Head . . . 133 51 55N 5 16W
St-Denis . . . . 139 48 56N 2 22 E
St. Denis . . . . 203 20 52 S 55 27 E
St-Denis-d'Orques . . 138 48 2N 0 17W
St-Dié . . . . 139 48 17N 6 56 E
St-Dizier . . . . 139 48 40N 5 0 E
St-Donat-de-Montcalm 83 46 19N 74 13W
St-Egrève . . . . 141 45 14N 5 41 E
St-Eleanors 81 46 25N 63 49W
St. Elias Mts. 94 60 33N 139 28W
St.-Elie 119 4 49N 53 17W
St-Éloi 83 48 2N 69 14W
St-Élouthère 83 47 30N 69 15W
St-Éloy-les-Mines . . 140 46 10N 2 51 E
St-Émilion 140 44 53N 0 9W
St-Éphrem-de-Tring 83 46 2N 70 59W
St-Étienne . . . . 141 45 27N 4 22 E
St-Étienne-de-Tinée 141 44 16N 6 56 E
St. Eugène 85 45 30N 74 28W
St-Eusèbe 83 47 33N 68 55W
St. Eustache 89 49 59N 97 47W
St-Eustache 83 45 33N 73 54W
St. Eustatius 113 17 20N 63 0W
St-Fabien 83 48 18N 68 52W
St-Félicien 83 48 40N 72 25W
St-Félix-de-Valois . . 83 46 10N 73 26W
St-Florent . . . . 141 42 41N 9 18 E
St-Florent-sur-Cher . 139 46 59N 2 15 E
St-Florentin . . . . 139 48 0N 3 45 E
St-Flour . . . . 140 45 2N 3 6 E
St-Fons . . . . 141 45 42N 4 52 E
St. Francis, C. . . . . 254 34 14 S 24 49 E
St-Francis, L. 83 45 10N 74 22W
St-François 83 46 48N 70 49W
St-François → 83 46 7N 72 55W
St-François, L. 83 45 10N 74 22W
St-François-du-Lac . . 83 46 5N 72 50W
St. François Xavier . 89 49 55N 97 32W
St-Fulgence 83 48 27N 70 54W
St-Fulgent 138 46 50N 1 10W
St-Gabriel-de-Brandon 83 46 17N 73 24W

St-Gabriel-de-Gaspé 80 48 31N 64 32W
St-Gabriel-de-Rimouski 83 48 25N 68 10W
St-Gaudens 140 43 6N 0 44 E
St-Gédéon 83 48 30N 71 46W
St-Gédéon-de-Beauce 83 45 45N 70 40W
St-Gengoux-le-National 141 46 37N 4 40 E
St-Geniez-d'Olt 140 44 27N 2 58 E
St. George, Australia 231 28 1 S 148 30 E
St. George, N.B., Canada 81 45 11N 66 50W
St. George, Ont., Canada 84 43 15N 80 15W
St. George, C., Canada 79 48 30N 59 16W
St. George, C., Papua N. G. 227 4 49 S 152 53 E
St. George Ra. 228 18 40 S 125 0 E
St-Georges 143 50 37N 5 20 E
St. George's, Newf., Canada 79 48 26N 58 31W
St. Georges, Qué., Canada 74 46 42N 72 35W
St-Georges 83 46 8N 70 40W
St. Georges, Fr. Gui. 119 4 0N 52 0W
St. George's, Grenada 113 12 5N 61 43W
St. George's B. 79 48 24N 58 53W
Saint George's Channel 227 4 10 S 152 20 E
St. George's Channel 135 52 0N 6 0W
St-Georges-de-Cacouna 83 47 55N 69 30W
St-Georges-de-Didonne 140 45 36N 1 0W
St. Georges Head 231 35 12 S 150 42 E
St-Georges-Ouest 83 46 7N 70 40W
St.-Gérard 143 50 21N 4 44 E
St-Gérard 83 45 46N 71 25W
St-Germain 139 48 53N 2 5 E
St-Germain-de-Calberte 140 44 13N 3 48 E
St-Germain-de-Grantham 83 45 50N 72 34W
St-Germain-des-Fossés 140 46 12N 3 26 E
St-Germain-du-Plain 139 46 42N 4 58 E
St-Germain-Laval 141 45 50N 4 1 E
St-Germain-Lembron 140 45 27N 3 14 E
St-Gers 140 45 18N 0 37W
St-Gervais, Haute-Savoie, France 141 45 53N 6 42 E
St-Gervais, Puy-de-Dôme, France 140 46 4N 2 50 E
St-Gildas, Pte. de 138 47 8N 2 14W
St-Gilles-Croix-de-Vie 138 46 41N 1 55W
St-Gilles-du-Gard 141 43 40N 4 26 E
St.-Gingolph 148 46 24N 6 48 E
St-Girons 140 42 59N 1 8 E
St. Goar 147 50 12N 7 43 E
St-Godefroi 81 48 5N 65 6W
St-Gualtier 138 46 39N 1 26 E
St-Guénolé 138 47 49N 4 23W
St-Guillaume-d'Upton 83 45 53N 72 46W
St. Helena 129 15 55 S 5 44W
St. Helenabaai 254 32 40 S 18 10 E
St. Helens, Australia 230 41 20 S 148 15 E
St. Helens, U.K. 132 53 28N 2 44W
St. Helier 138 49 11N 2 6W
St-Henri 83 46 42N 71 4W
St-Hilaire 138 48 35N 1 7W
St-Hilarion 83 47 34N 70 24W
St-Hippolyte 139 47 20N 6 50 E
St-Hippolyte-du-Fort 140 43 58N 3 52 E
St-Honoré, Canada 83 48 32N 71 5W
St-Honoré, France 139 46 54N 3 50 E
St-Hubert 143 50 2N 5 23 E
St-Hubert-de-Témiscouata 83 47 49N 69 9W
St-Hyacinthe 83 45 40N 72 58W
St-Ignace 81 46 42N 65 5W
St. Ignace I. 87 48 45N 88 0W
St-Imier 148 47 9N 6 58 E
St-Isidore 83 45 20N 73 42W
St. Ives, Cambs., U.K. 133 52 20N 0 5W
St. Ives, Cornwall, U.K. 133 50 13N 5 29W
St-Jacques, N.B., Canada 81 47 26N 68 23W
St-Jacques, Qué., Canada 83 45 57N 73 34W
St-James 138 48 31N 1 20W
St. James-Assiniboia 89 49 54N 97 15W
St. Jean 83 45 20N 73 20W
St-Jean 141 45 30N 5 10 E
St-Jean →, Qué., Canada 78 50 17N 64 20W
St-Jean →, Qué., Canada 80 48 46N 64 26W
St-Jean, L. 83 48 40N 72 0W
St. Jean Baptiste 89 49 15N 97 20W
St-Jean-Baptiste-de-Restigouche 81 47 46N 67 13W
St-Jean-d'Angély 140 45 57N 0 31W
St-Jean-de-Dieu 83 48 0N 69 3W
St-Jean-de-Luz 140 43 23N 1 39W
St-Jean-de-Maurienne 141 45 16N 6 21 E
St-Jean-de-Monts 138 46 47N 2 4W
St-Jean-du-Gard 140 44 7N 3 52 E
St-Jean-en-Royans 141 45 1N 5 18 E
St-Jean-Port-Joli 83 47 15N 70 13W
St-Jérôme, Qué., Canada 83 48 26N 71 53W
St-Jérôme, Qué., Canada 83 45 47N 74 0W
St-Joachim 83 47 4N 70 50W
St-Joachim-de-Tourelle 80 49 9N 66 25W
St. John 81 45 20N 66 8W
St. John → 81 45 15N 66 4W
St. John, C. 79 50 0N 55 32W
St. John, L. 79 48 23N 54 41W
St. John B. 79 50 55N 57 9W
Saint John Harbour 81 45 15N 66 2W
St. John I. 79 50 49N 57 14W
St. John's, Antigua 113 17 6N 61 51W
St. John's, Canada 79 47 35N 52 40W
St.-Joseph 226 20 27 S 166 36 E
St. Joseph, I. 84 46 12N 83 58W
St. Joseph, L. 86 51 10N 90 35W
St-Joseph-de-Beauce 83 46 18N 70 53W
St-Joseph-de-la-Rivière-Bleue 83 47 26N 69 3W
St-Joseph-de-Sorel 83 46 2N 73 7W
St-Jovite 82 46 8N 74 38W
St-Jude 83 45 46N 72 59W
St-Juéry 140 43 55N 2 12 E
St-Julien 141 46 8N 6 5 E
St-Julien-Chapteuil 141 45 2N 4 4 E
St-Julien-du-Sault 139 48 1N 3 17 E
St-Junien 140 45 53N 0 55 E
St-Just-en-Chaussée 139 49 30N 2 25 E
St-Just-en-Chevalet 140 45 55N 3 50 E
St-Justin 140 43 59N 0 14W
St-Justine 83 46 24N 70 21W
St. Kilda, N.Z. 235 45 53 S 170 31 E
St. Kilda, U.K. 130 57 9N 8 34W
St. Kitts = St. Christopher 113 17 20N 62 40W
St. Kitts-Nevis ■ 113 17 20N 62 40W
St. Laurent 89 50 25N 97 58W
St-Laurent 119 5 29N 54 3W
St-Laurent-du-Pont 141 45 23N 5 45 E
St-Laurent-en-Grandvaux 141 46 35N 5 58 E
St. Lawrence, Australia 230 22 16 S 149 31 E
St. Lawrence, Canada 79 46 54N 55 23W
St. Lawrence → 75 49 30N 66 0W
St. Lawrence, Gulf of 75 48 25N 62 0W
St. Lazare 89 50 27N 101 18W
St.-Léger 143 49 37N 5 39 E
St-Léolin 81 47 46N 65 10W
St-Léon-le-Grand 80 48 23N 67 30W
St. Leonard 81 47 12N 67 58W
St-Léonard-de-Noblat 140 45 49N 1 29 E
St-Léonard-de-Portneuf 83 46 53N 71 55W
St. Lewis → 78 52 26N 56 11W
St-Lô 138 49 7N 1 5W
St Louis 81 46 53N 64 8W
St Louis 88 52 55N 105 49W
St-Louis 246 16 8N 16 27W
St-Louis, Mts 78 46 13N 73 36W
St-Louis-de-Kent 81 46 44N 64 58W
St-Loup-sur-Semouse 139 47 53N 6 16 E
St-Luc 83 45 22N 73 18W
St-Luc-de-Matane 80 48 48N 67 28W
St. Lucia ■ 113 14 0N 60 50W
St. Lucia, C. 255 28 32 S 32 29 E
St. Lucia, Lake 255 28 5 S 32 30 E
St. Lucia Channel 113 14 15N 61 0W
St-Ludger 83 45 45N 70 42W
St. Lunaire-Griquet 79 51 31N 55 28W
St. Maarten 113 18 0N 63 5W
St-Magloire 83 46 35N 70 17W
St-Maixent-l'École 140 46 24N 0 12W
St. Malo 89 49 19N 96 57W
St-Malo 138 48 39N 2 1W
St-Malo, G. de 138 48 50N 2 30W
St-Mandrier 141 43 4N 5 56 E
St-Marc 113 19 10N 72 41W
St-Marcellin 141 45 9N 5 20 E
St-Marcouf, Îs. 138 49 30N 1 10W
St. Margarets 81 46 54N 65 11W
St-Martin, Charente-Maritime, France 140 46 12N 1 22W
St-Martin, Pas-de-Calais, France 139 50 42N 1 38 E
St-Martin, I. 113 18 0N 63 0W
St. Martin L. 89 51 40N 98 30W
St-Martin-Vésubie 141 44 4N 7 15 E
St. Martins 81 45 22N 65 34W
St-Martory 140 43 9N 0 56 E
St. Mary → 91 49 37N 115 38W
St. Mary, Mt. 227 8 8 S 147 2 E
St. Mary B. 75 46 50N 53 50W
St. Mary Is. 201 13 20N 74 35 E
St. Mary Pk. 231 31 32 S 138 34 E
St. Mary Res. 91 49 20N 113 11W
St. Marys, Australia 230 41 35 S 148 11 E
St. Marys, Canada 84 43 20N 81 10W
St. Mary's, U.K. 133 49 55N 6 17W
St. Mary's, C. 79 46 50N 54 12W
St. Mary's Alpine Prov. Park 91 49 50N 116 25W
St. Marys Bay 81 44 25N 66 10W
St-Mathieu, Pte. de 138 48 20N 4 45W
St. Matthews, I. = Zadetkyi Kyun 205 10 0N 98 25 E
St. Matthias Grp. 227 1 30 S 150 0 E
St-Maur-des-Fossés 139 48 48N 2 30 E
St. Maurice 148 46 13N 7 0 E
St-Maurice → 83 46 21N 72 31W
St-Maurice, Parc Prov. du 83 47 5N 73 15W
St-Médard-de-Guizières 140 45 1N 0 4W
St-Méen-le-Grand 138 48 11N 2 12W
St. Michael's Mt. 133 50 7N 5 30W
St-Michel 141 45 15N 6 29 E
St-Michel-des-Saints 83 46 41N 73 55W
St-Mihiel 139 48 54N 5 30 E
St-Nazaire, Canada 83 45 44N 72 37W
St-Nazaire, France 138 47 17N 2 12W
St. Neots 133 52 14N 0 16W
St-Nicolas-de-Port 139 48 38N 6 18 E
St. Niklaus 148 46 10N 7 49 E
St-Noël 80 48 35N 67 50W
St. Norbert 89 49 46N 97 9W
St-Octave-de l'Aveniro 80 49 0N 66 33W
St-Omer, Canada 83 47 3N 69 43W
St-Omer, France 139 50 45N 2 15 E
St-Ouen 139 50 2N 2 7 E
St-Ours 83 45 53N 73 9W
St-Pacome 83 47 24N 69 58W
St-Palais 140 45 40N 1 8W
St-Pamphile 83 46 58N 69 48W
St-Pardoux-la-Rivière 140 45 29N 0 45 E
St. Pascal 83 47 32N 69 48W
St-Patrice, L. 82 46 22N 77 20W
St. Paul, Canada 90 54 0N 111 17W
St. Paul, Ind. Oc. 203 30 40 S 77 34 E
St-Paul → 78 51 27N 57 42W
St. Paul, I. 81 47 12N 60 9W
St-Paul-de-Fenouillet 140 42 50N 2 28 E
St-Paul-de-Montmigny 83 46 44N 70 22W
St-Paul-du-Nord 83 48 34N 69 14W
St-Paulin 83 46 25N 73 1W
St. Pauls 79 49 52N 57 49W
St-Péray 141 44 57N 4 50 E
St-Père-en-Retz 138 47 11N 2 2W
St. Peter Port 138 49 27N 2 31W
St. Peters, N.S., Canada 81 45 40N 60 53W
St. Peters, P.E.I., Canada 81 46 25N 62 35W
St-Philbert-de-Grand-Lieu 138 47 2N 1 39W
St-Philemon 83 46 41N 70 27W
St-Pie 83 45 30N 72 54W
St. Pierre, Canada 89 49 26N 96 59W
St. Pierre, Ind. Oc. 203 9 20 S 46 0 E
St Pierre 79 46 46N 56 12W
Saint-Pierre, I. 79 46 47N 56 11W
St-Pierre, L., Qué., Canada 83 50 8N 68 26W
St-Pierre, L., Qué., Canada 83 46 12N 72 52W
St-Pierre-d'Oléron 140 45 57N 1 19W
St-Pierre-Église 138 49 40N 1 24W
St-Pierre-en-Port 138 49 48N 0 30 E
St-Pierre et Miquelon □ 79 46 55N 56 10W
St-Pierre-le-Moûtier 139 46 47N 3 7 E
St.-Pierre-sur-Dives 138 49 2N 0 1W
St.-Pieters Leew 143 50 47N 4 16 E
St.-Pol 139 50 21N 2 20 E
St-Pol-de-Léon 138 48 41N 4 0W
St-Pol-sur-Mer 139 51 1N 2 20 E
St-Pons 140 43 30N 2 45 E
St-Pourçain-sur-Sioule 140 46 18N 3 18 E
St-Prime 83 48 35N 72 20W
St-Quay-Portrieux 138 48 39N 2 51W
St. Quentin 81 47 30N 67 23W
St-Quentin 139 49 50N 3 16 E
St-Rambert-d'Albon 141 45 17N 4 49 E
St-Raphaël, Canada 83 46 48N 70 45W
St-Raphaël, France 141 43 25N 6 46 E
St-Raymond 83 46 54N 71 50W
St-Rémi 83 45 16N 73 37W
St-Rémy-de-Provence 141 43 48N 4 50 E
St-Renan 138 48 26N 4 37W
St-Roch 83 47 18N 70 12W
St-Romuald 83 46 46N 71 20W
St-Saëns 138 49 41N 1 16 E
St-Sauveur 81 47 32N 65 20W
St-Sauveur-en-Puisaye 139 47 37N 3 12 E
St-Sauveur-le-Vicomte 138 49 23N 1 32W
St-Savin 140 46 34N 0 50 E
St-Savinien 140 45 53N 0 42W
St-Sébastien 83 45 47N 70 58W
St. Sebastien, Tanjon' i 255 12 26 S 48 44 E
St-Seine-l'Abbaye 139 47 26N 4 47 E
St-Sernin 140 43 54N 2 35 E
St-Servan-sur-Mer 138 48 38N 2 0W
St-Sever 140 43 46N 0 34W
St-Sever-Calvados 138 48 50N 1 3W
St-Siméon 83 47 51N 69 54W
St-Siméon-de-Bonaventure 81 48 5N 65 36W
St-Simon-de-Rimouski 83 48 12N 69 3W
St. Stephen 81 45 16N 67 17W
St-Sulpice-la-Pointe 140 43 46N 1 41 E
St-Sulpice-Laurière 140 46 3N 1 29 E
St-Thégonnec 138 48 31N 3 57W
St. Thomas 84 42 45N 81 10W
St-Tite 83 46 45N 72 34W
St-Tite-des-Caps 83 47 8N 70 47W
St-Tropez 141 43 17N 6 38 E
St. Troud = Sint Truiden 143 50 48N 5 10 E
St-Ulric 80 48 47N 67 42W
St-Urbain 83 47 33N 70 32W
St-Vaast-la-Hougue 138 49 35N 1 17W
St-Valéry 139 50 10N 1 38 E
St-Valéry-en-Caux 138 49 52N 0 43 E
St-Vallier 141 45 11N 4 50 E
St-Vallier-de-Thiey 141 43 42N 6 51 E
St-Varent 138 46 53N 0 13W
St-Vianney 80 48 37N 67 25W
St. Victor 88 49 26N 105 52W
St. Vincent, C. Verde Is. 128 18 0N 26 1W
St. Vincent, W. Indies 113 13 10N 61 10W
St. Vincent, G. 232 35 0 S 138 0 E
St. Vincent and the Grenadines ■ 113 13 0N 61 10W
St-Vincent-de-Tyrosse 140 43 39N 1 18W
St. Vincent Passage 113 13 30N 61 0W
St. Vincent's 79 46 48N 53 38W
St-Vith 143 50 17N 6 9 E
St. Walburg 88 53 39N 109 12W
St-Yrieux-la-Perche 140 45 31N 1 12 E
St-Yvon 80 49 10N 64 48W
St. Marys → 81 45 2N 61 53W
Ste-Adèle 83 45 57N 74 7W
Ste-Adresse 138 49 31N 0 5 E
Ste. Agathe 89 49 34N 97 11W
Ste-Agathe 83 46 23N 71 25W
Ste-Agathe-des-Monts 83 46 3N 74 17W
Ste-Angèle-de-Mérici 80 48 32N 68 5W
Ste-Anne, L. 80 50 0N 67 42W
Ste. Anne, Lac 90 53 42N 114 25W
Ste Anne de Beaupré 83 47 2N 70 58W
Ste-Anne-de-Madawaska 81 47 15N 68 2W
Ste-Anne-des-Monts 80 49 8N 66 30W
Ste-Anne-du-Lac 82 46 48N 75 25W
Ste-Blandine 83 48 22N 68 28W
Ste-Claire 83 46 36N 70 51W
Ste-Croix, Canada 83 46 38N 71 44W
Ste-Croix, Switz. 148 46 49N 6 34W
Ste-Énimie 140 44 22N 3 26 E
Ste-Famille 83 46 58N 70 58W
Ste-Félicité 80 48 54N 67 20W
Ste-Florence 80 48 16N 67 14W
Ste-Foy 83 46 47N 71 17W
Ste-Foy-la-Grande 140 44 50N 0 13 E
Ste-Françoise 83 48 6N 69 4W
Ste-Hermine 140 46 32N 1 4W
Ste-Livrade-sur-Lot 140 44 24N 0 36 E
Ste-Marguerite → 78 50 9N 66 36W
Ste Marie 113 14 48N 61 1W
Ste-Marie-aux-Mines 139 48 10N 7 12 E

Ste-Marie de la Madeleine **83** 46 26N 71 0W
Ste-Marthe-de-Gaspé **80** 49 12N 66 10W
Ste-Maure-de-Touraine **138** 47 7N 0 37 E
Ste-Maxime **141** 43 19N 6 39 E
Ste-Menehould **139** 49 5N 4 54 E
Ste-Mère-Église **138** 49 24N 1 19W
Ste-Monique **83** 48 44N 71 51W
Ste-Pudentienne **83** 45 28N 72 40W
Ste-Rose **113** 16 20N 61 45W
Ste.-Rose du Lac **89** 51 4N 99 30W
Ste-Sabine **83** 45 15N 73 2W
Ste-Thècle **83** 46 49N 72 31W
Saintes **140** 45 45N 0 37W
Saintes, Île des **113** 15 50N 61 35W
Saintes-Maries-de-la-Mer **141** 43 26N 4 26 E
Saintonge **140** 45 40N 0 50W
Sairecábur, Cerro **124** 22 43 S 67 54W
Sairs, L. **82** 46 49N 78 26W
Saitama □ **221** 36 25N 139 30 E
Saito **220** 32 3N 131 24 E
Sajama **122** 18 7 S 69 0W
Sajan **166** 45 50N 20 20 E
Sajószentpéter **151** 48 12N 20 44 E
Sajum **199** 33 20N 79 0 E
Sakai **221** 34 30N 135 30 E
Sakaide **220** 34 15N 133 50 E
Sakaiminato **220** 35 38N 133 11 E
Sakākah **192** 30 0N 40 8 E
Sakami, L. **78** 53 15N 77 0W
Sâkâne, 'Erg i-n **240** 20 30N 1 30W
Sakania **251** 12 43 S 28 30 E
Sakarya → **180** 41 7N 30 39 E
Sakashima-Guntō **219** 24 46N 124 0 E
Sakata **218** 38 55N 139 50 E
Sakchu **215** 40 23N 125 2 E
Sakeny → **255** 20 0 S 45 25 E
Sakété **247** 6 40N 2 45 E
Sakhalin, Ostrov **185** 51 0N 143 0 E
Sakhalinskiy Zaliv **185** 54 0N 141 0 E
Sakhi Gopal **199** 19 58N 85 50 E
Sakhnīn **189** 32 52N 35 12 E
Saki **180** 45 9N 33 34 E
Sakiai **178** 54 59N 23 0 E
Sakmara **182** 52 0N 55 20 E
Sakmara → **182** 51 46N 55 1 E
Sakołow Małopolski **152** 50 10N 22 9 E
Sakon Nakhon **204** 17 10N 104 9 E
Sakrand **198** 26 10N 68 15 E
Sakri **198** 21 2N 74 20 E
Sakskøbing **173** 54 49N 11 39 E
Saku **221** 36 17N 138 31 E
Sakuma **221** 35 3N 137 49 E
Sakura **221** 35 43N 140 14 E
Sakurai **221** 34 30N 135 51 E
Şal → **181** 47 31N 40 45 E
Šal'a, Czech. **151** 48 10N 17 50 E
Sala, Sweden **172** 59 58N 16 35 E
Sala Consilina **165** 40 23N 15 35 E
Sala-y-Gómez **225** 26 28 S 105 28W
Salaberry-de-Valleyfield **83** 45 15N 74 8W
Salada, L. **98** 32 20N 115 40W
Saladas **124** 28 15 S 58 40W
Saladillo **124** 35 40 S 59 55W
Salado →, Buenos Aires, Argentina **124** 35 44 S 57 22W
Salado →, La Pampa, Argentina **126** 37 30 S 67 0W
Salado →, Río Negro, Argentina **126** 41 34 S 65 3W
Salado →, Santa Fe, Argentina **124** 31 40 S 60 41W
Salado →, Oaxaca, Mexico **109** 17 55N 96 59W
Salado →, Tamaulipas, Mexico **102** 26 52N 99 19W
Salado, L. **100** 31 15N 113 12W
Salaga **247** 8 31N 0 31W
Sālah **190** 32 40N 36 45 E
Salaices **101** 27 2N 105 13W
Sălaj □ **170** 47 15N 23 0 E
Salala, Liberia **246** 6 42N 10 7W
Salala, Sudan **244** 21 17N 36 16 E
Salālah **195** 16 56N 53 59 E
Salamanca, Chile **124** 31 46 S 70 59W
Salamanca, Mexico **107** 20 34N 101 12W
Salamanca, Spain **154** 40 58N 5 39W
Salamanca □ **154** 40 57N 5 40W
Salāmatābād **192** 35 39N 47 50 E
Salamina **118** 5 25N 75 29W
Salamis, Cyprus **190** 35 11N 33 54 E
Salamis, Greece **169** 37 56N 23 30 E
Salar de Atacama **124** 23 30 S 68 25W
Salar de Uyuni **122** 20 30 S 67 45W
Sălard **170** 47 12N 22 3 E
Salas **154** 43 25N 6 15W
Salas de los Infantes **156** 42 2N 3 17W
Salatiga **209** 7 19 S 110 30 E
Salavat **182** 53 21N 55 55 E
Salaverry **122** 8 15 S 79 0W
Salawati **207** 1 7 S 130 52 E
Salay **211** 8 52N 124 47 E
Salayar **207** 6 7 S 120 30 E
Salazar → **156** 42 40N 1 20W
Salbris **139** 47 25N 2 3 E
Salcia **170** 43 56N 24 55 E
Salcombe **133** 50 14N 3 47W
Saldaña **154** 42 32N 4 48W
Saldanha **254** 33 0 S 17 58 E
Saldanhabaai **254** 33 6 S 18 0 E
Saldus **178** 56 38N 22 30 E
Sale, Australia **231** 38 6 S 147 6 E
Salé, Morocco **240** 34 3N 6 48W
Sale, U.K. **132** 53 26N 2 19W
Salekhard **176** 66 30N 66 35 E
Salem **201** 11 40N 78 11 E
Salemi **164** 37 49N 12 47 E
Salernes **141** 43 34N 6 15 E
Salerno **165** 40 40N 14 44 E
Salerno, G. di **165** 40 35N 14 45 E
Salfīt **189** 32 5N 35 11 E
Salford **132** 53 30N 2 17W
Salgir → **180** 45 38N 35 1 E
Salgótarján **151** 48 5N 19 47 E
Salgueiro **120** 8 4 S 39 6W
Salies-de-Béarn **140** 43 28N 0 56W
Şalif **194** 15 18N 42 41 E
Salin **202** 20 35N 94 40 E
Salina **165** 38 35N 14 50 E
Salina Cruz **109** 16 10N 95 12W
Salinas, Brazil **121** 16 10 S 42 10W
Salinas, Chile **124** 23 31 S 69 29W
Salinas, Ecuador **118** 2 10 S 80 58W
Salinas → **102** 25 54N 99 10W
Salinas, B. de **112** 11 4N 85 45W
Salinas, C. de **157** 39 16N 3 4 E
Salinas, Pampa de las **124** 31 58 S 66 42W
Salinas Ambargasta **124** 29 0 S 65 0W
Salinas de Hidalgo **103** 22 38N 101 43W
Salinas Grandes **124** 30 0 S 65 0W
Salinas Victoria **102** 25 58N 100 48W
Salinópolis **120** 0 40 S 47 20W
Salins **139** 46 57N 5 53 E
Salins-les-Bains **139** 46 58N 5 52 E
Salir **155** 37 14N 8 2W
Salisbury = Harare **251** 17 43 S 31 2 E
Salisbury, Australia **232** 34 46 S 138 40 E
Salisbury, Canada **81** 46 2N 65 3W
Salisbury, U.K. **133** 51 4N 1 48W
Salisbury I. **95** 63 30N 77 0W
Salisbury Plain **133** 51 13N 1 50W
Săliște **170** 45 45N 23 56 E
Salitre → **120** 9 29 S 40 39W
Salka **247** 10 20N 4 58 E
Salkhad **191** 32 30N 36 43 E
Sallent **156** 41 49N 1 54 E
Salles-Curan **140** 44 11N 2 48 E
Salling **173** 56 40N 8 55 E
Sallom Junction **244** 19 17N 37 6 E
Sally's Cove **79** 49 44N 57 56W
Salmās **192** 38 11N 44 47 E
Salmerón **156** 40 33N 2 29W
Salmo **93** 49 10N 117 20W
Salmon →, B.C., Canada **76** 54 3N 122 40W
Salmon →, N.B., Canada **81** 46 6N 65 56W
Salmon →, Qué., Canada **80** 49 25N 62 15W
Salmon Arm **93** 50 40N 119 15W
Salmon Gums **229** 32 59 S 121 38 E
Salmon Res. **79** 48 5N 56 0W
Salmon River **81** 44 3N 66 10W
Salo, Finland **175** 60 22N 23 10 E
Salò, Italy **162** 45 37N 10 32 E
Salobreña **155** 36 44N 3 35W
Salon-de-Provence **141** 43 39N 5 6 E
Salonica = Thessaloníki **168** 40 38N 22 58 E
Salonta **170** 46 49N 21 42 E
Salop = Shropshire □ **133** 52 36N 2 45W
Salor → **155** 39 39N 7 3W
Salou, Cabo **156** 41 3N 1 10 E
Salsacate **124** 31 20 S 65 5W
Salses **140** 42 50N 2 55 E
Salsette I. **200** 19 5N 72 50 E
Salsk **181** 46 28N 41 30 E
Salso → **165** 37 6N 13 55 E
Salsomaggiore **162** 44 48N 9 59 E
Salt → **76** 60 0N 112 25W
Salt Creek **232** 36 8 S 139 38 E
Salt Range **198** 32 30N 72 25 E
Salta **124** 24 57 S 65 25W
Salta □ **124** 24 48 S 65 30W
Saltabarranca **109** 18 36N 95 32W
Saltair **92** 48 57N 123 46W
Saltcoats, Canada **89** 51 5N 102 15W
Saltcoats, U.K. **134** 55 38N 4 47W
Saltee Is. **135** 52 7N 6 37W
Saltery Bay **92** 49 47N 124 10W
Saltfjorden **174** 67 15N 14 10 E
Saltholm **172** 55 38N 12 43 E
Salthólmavík **174** 65 24N 21 57W
Saltillo **102** 25 25N 101 0W
Salto, Argentina **124** 34 20 S 60 15W
Salto, Uruguay **124** 31 27 S 57 50W
Salto da Divisa **121** 16 0 S 39 57W
Salto de Agua **110** 17 37N 92 22W
Saltpond **247** 5 15N 1 3W
Saltsjöbaden **173** 59 15N 18 20 E
Saltspring **76** 48 54N 123 37W
Salûm **244** 31 31N 25 7 E
Salûm, Khâlig el **244** 31 30N 25 9 E
Salur **200** 18 27N 83 18 E
Salut, Îs. du **119** 5 15N 52 35W
Saluzzo **162** 44 39N 7 29 E
Salvacion **211** 9 56N 118 47 E
Salvación, B. **126** 50 50 S 75 10W
Salvador, Brazil **121** 13 0 S 38 30W
Salvador, Canada **88** 52 10N 109 32W
Salvaterra **120** 0 46 S 48 31W
Salvaterra de Magos **155** 39 1N 8 47W
Salvatierra **107** 20 13N 100 53W
Sálvora, Isla **154** 42 30N 8 58W
Salween → **202** 16 31N 97 37 E
Salyany **177** 39 10N 48 50 E
Salza → **150** 47 40N 14 43 E
Salzach → **150** 48 12N 12 56 E
Salzburg **150** 47 48N 13 2 E
Salzburg □ **150** 47 15N 13 0 E
Salzgitter **146** 52 13N 10 22 E
Salzwedel **146** 52 50N 11 11 E
Sam **252** 0 58N 11 16 E
Sam Neua **204** 20 29N 104 0 E
Sam Ngao **204** 17 18N 99 0 E
Sam Son **204** 19 44N 105 54 E
Sam Teu **204** 19 59N 104 38 E
Sama **182** 60 12N 60 22 E
Sama de Langreo **154** 43 18N 5 40W
Samachic **101** 27 17N 107 28W
Samacimbo **253** 13 33 S 16 59 E
Samagaltai **185** 50 36N 95 3 E
Samā'il **195** 23 40N 57 50 E
Samaipata **123** 18 9 S 63 52W
Samal **211** 7 5N 125 42 E
Samal I. **211** 7 3N 125 44 E
Samalayuca **101** 31 21N 106 28W
Samales Group **211** 6 0N 122 0 E
Samalkot **200** 17 3N 82 13 E
Samâlût **244** 28 20N 30 42 E
Samana **198** 30 10N 76 13 E
Samana Cay **113** 23 3N 73 45W
Samandağı **190** 36 5N 35 59 E
Samanga **251** 8 20 S 39 13 E
Samangán □ **197** 36 15N 68 3 E
Samangwa **250** 4 23 S 24 10 E
Samani **218** 42 7N 142 56 E
Samar **210** 12 0N 125 0 E
Samar □ **211** 11 50N 125 0 E
Samar Sea **210** 12 0N 124 30 E
Samara → **182** 53 10N 50 4 E
Samarai **227** 10 39 S 150 41 E
Samaria = Shōmrōn **189** 32 15N 35 13 E
Samarinda **209** 0 30 S 117 9 E
Samarkand **183** 39 40N 66 55 E
Sāmarrā **192** 34 12N 43 52 E
Samastipur **199** 25 50N 85 50 E
Samatan **140** 43 29N 0 55 E
Samaúma **123** 7 50 S 60 2W
Samba, Kashmir **199** 32 32N 75 10 E
Samba, Zaïre **250** 4 38 S 26 22 E
Samba Caju **253** 8 46 S 15 24 E
Sambaíba **120** 7 8 S 45 21W
Sambalpur **199** 21 28N 84 4 E
Sambar, Tanjung **209** 2 59 S 110 19 E
Sambas **209** 1 20N 109 20 E
Sambava **255** 14 16 S 50 10 E
Sambawizi **251** 18 24 S 26 13 E
Sambhal **199** 28 35N 78 37 E
Sambhar **198** 26 52N 75 6 E
Sambiase **165** 38 58N 16 16 E
Sambonifacio **162** 45 24N 11 16 E
Sambor, Cambodia **204** 12 46N 106 0 E
Sambor, U.S.S.R. **178** 49 30N 23 10 E
Sambre → **143** 50 27N 4 52 E
Sambro **81** 44 28N 63 36W
Sambuca di Sicilia **164** 37 39N 13 6 E
Samburu □ **250** 1 10N 37 0 E
Samchŏk **215** 37 30N 129 10 E
Samchonpo **215** 35 0N 128 6 E
Same **250** 4 2 S 37 38 E
Samedan **149** 46 32N 9 52 E
Samer **139** 50 38N 1 44 E
Samfya **251** 11 22 S 29 31 E
Samḫān, Jabal **195** 17 12N 54 55 E
Sámi **169** 38 15N 20 39 E
Samna **244** 25 12N 37 17 E
Samnah **192** 25 10N 37 15 E
Samnaun **149** 46 57N 10 22 E
Samnū **241** 27 15N 14 55 E
Samo Alto **124** 30 22 S 71 0W
Samobor **163** 45 47N 15 44 E
Samoëns **141** 46 5N 6 45 E
Samokov **167** 42 18N 23 35 E
Samoorombón, Bahía **124** 36 5 S 57 20W
Samorogouan **246** 11 21N 4 57W
Sámos, Greece **169** 37 45N 26 50 E
Samos, Spain **154** 42 44N 7 20W
Samoš, Yugoslavia **166** 45 13N 20 49 E
Samosir **208** 2 55N 98 50 E
Samotharáki **168** 39 48N 19 31 E
Samothráki **168** 40 28N 25 28 E
Samoylovka **179** 51 12N 43 43 E
Sampa **246** 8 0N 2 36W
Sampacho **124** 33 20 S 64 50W
Sampang **209** 7 11 S 113 13 E
Samper de Calanda **156** 41 11N 0 28W
Sampit **209** 2 34 S 113 0 E
Sampit → **209** 2 44 S 112 54 E
Sampit, Teluk **209** 3 5 S 113 3 E
Samrée **143** 50 13N 5 39 E
Samrong, Cambodia **204** 14 15N 103 30 E
Samrong, Thailand **204** 15 10N 100 40 E
Samsø **173** 55 50N 10 35 E
Samsø Bœlt **173** 55 45N 10 45 E
Samsonovo **183** 37 53N 65 15 E
Samsun **177** 41 15N 36 22 E
Samsun Dağı **169** 37 45N 27 10 E
Samtredia **181** 42 7N 42 24 E
Samui, Ko **205** 9 30N 100 0 E
Samur → **181** 41 53N 48 32 E
Samusole **251** 10 2 S 24 0 E
Samut Prakan **204** 13 32N 100 40 E
Samut Sakhon **204** 13 31N 100 13 E
Samut Songkhram → **204** 13 24N 100 1 E
Samwari **198** 28 30N 66 46 E
San **246** 13 15N 4 57W
San →, Cambodia **204** 13 32N 105 57 E
San →, Poland **152** 50 45N 21 51 E
San Adrián, C. de **154** 43 21N 8 50W
San Agustín **118** 1 53N 76 16W
San Agustín de Valle Fértil **124** 30 35 S 67 30W
San Ambrosio, Mexico **101** 27 37N 105 18W
San Ambrosio, Pac. Oc. **225** 26 28 S 79 53W
San Andrés, Mexico **105** 23 40N 101 56W
San Andres, Phil. **210** 13 19N 122 41 E
San Andrés → **98** 28 44N 114 16W
San Andrés, I. de **112** 12 42N 81 46W
San Andrés, L. de **103** 22 40N 97 52W
San Andrés Paxtlán **109** 16 13N 96 29W
San Andrés Solaga **109** 17 17N 96 13W
San Andrés Tuxtla **109** 18 27N 95 13W
San Antonio, Chile **124** 33 40 S 71 40W
San Antonio, Baja Calif. S., Mexico **99** 23 47N 110 1W
San Antonio, Campeche, Mexico **111** 18 28N 89 53W
San Antonio, Phil. **210** 14 57N 120 5 E
San Antonio, Venezuela **118** 3 30N 66 44W
San Antonio, C., Argentina **124** 36 15 S 56 40W
San Antonio, C., Cuba **112** 21 50N 84 57W
San Antonio, C. de **157** 38 48N 0 12 E
San Antonio, Pta. **98** 29 45N 115 43W
San Antonio Abad **157** 38 59N 1 19 E
San Antonio Bay **211** 8 38N 117 35 E
San Antonio de la Huerta **100** 28 38N 109 36W
San Antonio de las Alazanas **103** 25 16N 100 36W
San Antonio de los Baños **112** 22 54N 82 31W
San Antonio de los Cobres **124** 24 10 S 66 17W
San Antonio de Padua **105** 22 36N 103 50W
San Antonio del Mar **98** 31 5N 116 16W
San Antonio Oeste **126** 40 40 S 65 0W
San Antonio Rayón **103** 22 25N 98 25W
San Antonio Villalongín **107** 19 35N 100 45W
San Arcángelo **164** 40 14N 16 14 E
San Augustin, C. **211** 6 20N 126 13 E
San Baltasar Guelavila **109** 16 47N 96 20W
San Bartolo **103** 22 18N 100 4W
San Bartolo de Berrio **107** 21 37N 101 4W
San Bartolomé Loxicha **109** 15 58N 96 43W
San Bartolomeo in Galdo **165** 41 23N 15 2 E
San Benedetto **162** 45 2N 10 57 E
San Benedetto del Tronto **163** 42 57N 13 52 E

San Benito **104** 25 29N 107 51W
San Bernardino, Paso del **149** 46 28N 9 11 E
San Bernardino Str. **210** 13 0N 125 0 E
San Bernardo, Chile **124** 33 40 S 70 50W
San Bernardo, Durango, Mexico **104** 25 59N 105 33W
San Bernardo, Sonora, Mexico **100** 27 24N 108 50W
San Bernardo, I. de **118** 9 45N 75 50W
San Blas, Coahuila, Mexico **102** 27 25N 101 40W
San Blas, Nayarit, Mexico **104** 21 31N 105 16W
San Blas, Sinaloa, Mexico **104** 26 5N 108 46W
San Blas, Arch. de **112** 9 50N 78 31W
San Borja, Bolivia **122** 14 50 S 66 52W
San Borja, Mexico **98** 28 47N 113 55W
San Borjas, Sa. de **98** 28 42N 113 47W
San Buenaventura, Bolivia **122** 14 28 S 67 35W
San Buenaventura, Mexico **102** 27 5N 101 32W
San Carlos = Butuku-Luba **247** 3 29N 8 33 E
San Carlos, Argentina **124** 33 50 S 69 0W
San Carlos, Bolivia **123** 17 24 S 63 45W
San Carlos, Chile **124** 36 10 S 72 0W
San Carlos, Mexico **102** 29 1N 100 51W
San Carlos, Nic. **112** 11 12N 84 50W
San Carlos, Negros, Phil. **211** 10 29N 123 25 E
San Carlos, Pangasinan, Phil. **210** 15 55N 120 20 E
San Carlos, Uruguay **125** 34 46 S 54 58W
San Carlos, Amazonas, Venezuela **118** 1 55N 67 4W
San Carlos, Cojedes, Venezuela **118** 9 40N 68 36W
San Carlos, Sa. de **103** 24 40N 99 0W
San Carlos de Bariloche **126** 41 10 S 71 25W
San Carlos de la Rápita **156** 40 37N 0 35 E
San Carlos del Zulia **118** 9 1N 71 55W
San Cataldo **164** 37 30N 13 58 E
San Celoni **156** 41 42N 2 30 E
San Clara **89** 51 29N 101 26W
San Clemente, Chile **124** 35 30 S 71 29W
San Clemente, Spain **157** 39 24N 2 25W
San Constanzo **163** 43 46N 13 5 E
San Cristóbal, Argentina **124** 30 20 S 61 10W
San Cristóbal, Colombia **118** 2 18 S 73 2W
San Cristóbal, Dom. Rep. **113** 18 25N 70 6W
San Cristóbal, Venezuela **118** 16 50N 92 40W
San Cristóbal, B. **99** 27 23N 114 38W
San Cristóbal de la Barranca **106** 21 3N 103 26W
San Cristóbal de las Casas **110** 16 45N 92 38W
San Cristóbal Tepeojuma **109** 18 41N 98 27W
San Damiano d'Asti **162** 44 51N 8 4 E
San Daniele del Friuli **163** 46 10N 13 0 E
San Demétrio Corone **165** 39 34N 16 22 E
San Diego, Chihuahua, Mexico **101** 28 35N 105 34W
San Diego, Chihuahua, Mexico **101** 30 14N 108 0W
San Diego, San Luis Potosí, Mexico **103** 21 57N 100 4W
San Diego, C. **126** 54 40 S 65 10W
San Diego de la Unión **107** 21 28N 100 52W
San Dimas **104** 24 8N 105 58W
San Dionisio del Mar **109** 16 20N 94 45W
San Dionosio **211** 11 16N 123 6 E
San Donà di Piave **163** 45 38N 12 34 E
San Elpídio a Mare **163** 43 16N 13 41 E
San Emilio **210** 17 14N 120 37 E
San Estanislao **124** 24 39 S 56 26W
San Esteban, B. **104** 25 38N 109 14W
San Esteban, I. **100** 28 42N 112 36W
San Esteban de Gormaz **156** 41 34N 3 13W
San Fabian **210** 16 5N 120 25 E
San Felice sul Panaro **162** 44 51N 11 9 E
San Felipe, Chile **124** 32 43 S 70 42W
San Felipe, Colombia **118** 1 55N 67 6W
San Felipe, Baja Calif. N., Mexico **98** 31 0N 114 52W
San Felipe, Chihuahua, Mexico **101** 27 6N 104 58W
San Felipe, Chihuahua, Mexico **101** 27 20N 106 2W
San Felipe, Guanajuato, Mexico **107** 21 29N 101 13W
San Felipe, Yucatán, Mexico **111** 21 34N 88 14W
San Felipe, Phil. **210** 15 4N 120 4 E
San Felipe, Venezuela **118** 10 20N 68 44W
San Felipe Aztatán **104** 22 23N 105 24W
San Felipe de Híjar **106** 20 54N 104 44W
San Felipe Usila **109** 17 53N 96 33W
San Felíu de Guíxols **156** 41 45N 3 1 E
San Felíu de Llobregat **156** 41 23N 2 2 E
San Félix **225** 26 23 S 80 0W
San Fermin **105** 26 20N 104 49W
San Fermin, Pta. **98** 30 25N 114 40W
San Fernando, Chile **124** 34 30 S 71 0W
San Fernando, Chiapas, Mexico **110** 16 52N 93 13W
San Fernando, Tamaulipas, Mexico **103** 24 51N 98 10W
San Fernando, Cebu, Phil. **211** 10 10N 123 42 E
San Fernando, La Union, Phil. **210** 16 40N 120 23 E
San Fernando, Pampanga, Phil. **210** 15 5N 120 37 E
San Fernando, Tablas, Phil. **210** 12 18N 122 36 E
San Fernando, Spain **155** 36 28N 6 17W
San Fernando, Trin. & Tob. **113** 10 20N 61 30W
San Fernando → **103** 24 55N 97 40W
San Fernando de Apure **118** 7 54N 67 15W
San Fernando de Atabapo **118** 4 3N 67 42W
San Fernando di Púglia **165** 41 18N 16 5 E
San Francisco, Argentina **124** 31 30 S 62 5W
San Francisco, Bolivia **123** 15 16 S 65 31W
San Francisco, Coahuila, Mexico **102** 26 15N 102 50W
San Francisco, San Luis Potosí, Mexico **103** 21 40N 99 50W
San Francisco, San Luis Potosí, Mexico **103** 22 5N 99 53W
San Francisco, Sonora, Mexico **100** 30 48N 112 34W
San Francisco, Tamaulipas, Mexico **102** 25 21N 97 19W
San Francisco, Cebu, Phil. **211** 10 39N 124 23 E
San Francisco, Leyte, Phil. **211** 10 4N 125 9 E
San Francisco, Mindanao, Phil. **211** 8 30N 125 56 E
San Francisco, Paso de **124** 27 0 S 68 0W
San Francisco de Borja **101** 27 53N 106 41W
San Francisco de Conchos **101** 27 35N 105 19W
San Francisco de Macorís **113** 19 19N 70 15W
San Francisco del Mar **109** 16 14N 94 39W
San Francisco del Monte de Oro **124** 32 36 S 66 8W
San Francisco del Oro **101** 26 52N 105 51W
San Francisco del Rincón **106** 21 1N 101 51W
San Francisco Javier **157** 38 42N 1 26 E
San Francisco Solano, Pta. **118** 6 18N 77 29W
San Francisco Telixtlahuaca **109** 17 18N 96 54W
San Fratello **165** 38 1N 14 33 E
San Gabriel **118** 0 36N 77 49W
San Gabriel, Pta. **99** 28 26N 112 52W
San Gabriel Chilac **109** 18 19N 97 21W
San Gavino Monreale **164** 39 33N 8 47 E
San Gil **118** 6 33N 73 8W
San Gimignano **162** 43 28N 11 3 E
San Giórgio di Nogaro **163** 45 50N 13 13 E
San Giórgio Iónico **165** 40 27N 17 23 E
San Giovanni Bianco **162** 45 52N 9 40 E
San Giovanni in Fiore **165** 39 16N 16 42 E
San Giovanni in Persieceto **163** 44 39N 11 12 E
San Giovanni Rotondo **165** 41 41N 15 42 E
San Giovanni Valdarno **163** 43 32N 11 30 E
San Giuliano Terme **162** 43 45N 10 26 E
San Gottardo, Paso del **149** 46 33N 8 33 E
San Gregorio **125** 32 37 S 55 40W
San Guiseppe Iato **164** 37 57N 13 11 E
San Hipólito, B. **99** 26 57N 113 55W
San Ignacio, Bolivia **123** 16 20 S 60 55W
San Ignacio, Baja Calif. S., Mexico **99** 27 27N 112 51W
San Ignacio, Jalisco, Mexico **106** 20 45N 102 32W
San Ignacio, San Luis Potosí, Mexico **103** 23 12N 100 12W
San Ignacio, Sinaloa, Mexico **104** 23 55N 106 25W
San Ignacio, Sonora, Mexico **100** 30 42N 110 55W
San Ignacio, Paraguay **124** 26 52 S 57 3W
San Ignacio, L. **99** 26 54N 113 13W
San Ildefonso, Mexico **107** 20 10N 99 58W
San Ildefonso, Phil. **210** 15 5N 120 56 E
San Ildefonso, C. **210** 16 0N 122 1 E
San Isidro, Argentina **124** 34 29 S 58 31W
San Isidro, Coahuila, Mexico **102** 25 33N 102 26W
San Isidro, Coahuila, Mexico **102** 27 31N 102 22W
San Jacinto, Colombia **118** 9 50N 75 8W
San Jacinto, Phil. **210** 12 34N 123 44 E
San Javier, Misiones, Argentina **125** 27 55 S 55 5W
San Javier, Santa Fe, Argentina **124** 30 40 S 59 55W
San Javier, Beni, Bolivia **123** 14 34 S 64 42W
San Javier, Santa Cruz, Bolivia **123** 16 18 S 62 30W
San Javier, Chile **124** 35 40 S 71 45W
San Javier, Spain **157** 37 49N 0 50W
San Jeronimito **107** 17 33N 101 20W
San Jerónimo **105** 25 2N 102 11W
San Jerónimo, Sa. de **118** 8 0N 75 50W
San Jerónimo de Juárez **107** 17 8N 100 28W
San Jerónimo Taviche **109** 16 44N 96 35W
San Jerónimo Tecoatl **109** 18 9N 96 55W
San Joaquín, Bolivia **123** 13 4 S 64 49W
San Joaquín, Chihuahua, Mexico **101** 30 4N 107 47W
San Joaquín, Querétaro, Mexico **107** 20 30N 99 47W
San Joaquin, Phil. **211** 10 35N 122 8 E
San Joaquín, Venezuela **118** 10 16N 67 47W
San Joaquín → **123** 13 8 S 63 41W
San Jorge **124** 31 54 S 61 50W
San Jorge, Golfo **126** 46 0 S 66 0W
San Jorge, G. de **156** 40 50N 0 55W
San José, Bolivia **123** 17 53 S 60 50W
San José, C. Rica **112** 10 0N 84 2W
San José, Guat. **112** 14 0N 90 50W
San José, Chihuahua, Mexico **101** 28 47N 107 15W
San José, Sonora, Mexico **100** 27 32N 110 9W
San José, Sonora, Mexico **100** 30 42N 111 25W
San Jose, Luzon, Phil. **210** 15 45N 120 55 E
San Jose, Mindoro, Phil. **210** 12 27N 121 4 E
San José, Spain **157** 38 55N 1 18 E
San José, B. de **111** 18 40N 88 5W
San José, I. **99** 25 0N 110 38W
San José, Sa. **101** 28 51N 107 12W
San José Chiltepec **109** 17 57N 96 11W
San José de Feliciano **124** 30 26 S 58 46W
San José de Gracia, Baja Calif. S., Mexico **99** 26 34N 112 45W
San José de Gracia, Chihuahua, Mexico **101** 27 21N 106 18W
San José de Gracia, Jalisco, Mexico **106** 20 40N 102 35W
San José de Gracia, Sinaloa, Mexico **104** 26 8N 107 58W
San José de Gracia, Sonora, Mexico **100** 29 18N 110 38W
San José de Guaymas **100** 27 59N 110 54W
San José de Jáchal **124** 30 15 S 68 46W
San José de la Boca **104** 25 20N 105 47W
San José de la Popa **102** 26 11N 100 51W
San José de las Rusias **103** 23 34N 98 3W
San José de Mayo **124** 34 27 S 56 40W
San José de Ocune **118** 4 15N 70 20W
San José de Pimas **100** 28 44N 110 21W
San José de Raíces **103** 24 35N 100 14W
San José de Sextin **104** 26 7N 105 40W
San José de Uchapiamonas **122** 14 13 S 68 5W
San José del Cabo **99** 23 3N 109 41W
San José del Carmen **109** 17 52N 94 5W
San José del Guaviare **118** 2 35N 72 38W
San José do Anauá **119** 0 58N 61 22W
San José Iturbide **107** 21 0N 100 23W
San José Miahuatlán **109** 18 17N 97 17W
San Juan, Argentina **124** 31 30 S 68 30W
San Juan, Colombia **118** 8 46N 76 32W
San Juan, Chihuahua, Mexico **101** 26 54N 106 20W
San Juan, Sonora, Mexico **100** 31 8N 111 31W
San Juan, Ica, Peru **122** 15 22 S 75 7W
San Juan, Puno, Peru **122** 14 2 S 69 19W
San Juan, Luzon, Phil. **210** 16 40N 120 20 E
San Juan, Mindanao, Phil. **211** 8 25N 126 20 E
San Juan □, Argentina **124** 31 9 S 69 0W
San Juan □, Dom. Rep. **113** 18 45N 71 25W
San Juan →, Argentina **124** 32 20 S 67 25W
San Juan →, Bolivia **123** 21 2 S 65 19W
San Juan →, Colombia **118** 4 3N 77 27W
San Juan →, Tamaulipas, Mexico **102** 26 22N 98 51W
San Juan →, Veracruz, Mexico **109** 18 36N 95 40W
San Juan →, Nic. **112** 10 56N 83 42W
San Juan →, Venezuela **119** 10 14N 62 38W
San Juan, C. **252** 1 5N 9 20 E
San Juan, Volcán **104** 21 22N 104 58W
San Juan Atepec **109** 17 25N 96 32W
San Juan Bautista, Mexico **110** 16 24N 93 23W
San Juan Bautista, Paraguay **124** 26 37 S 57 6W
San Juan Bautista, Spain **157** 39 5N 1 31 E
San Juan Bautista, Llanuras de **100** 28 34N 111 44W
San Juan Bautista Sahcabchén **111** 19 53N 89 59W
San Juan Bautista Tuxtepec **109** 18 6N 96 7W
San Juan Bautista Valle Nacional **109** 17 47N 96 19W
San Juan de Guadelupe **105** 24 38N 102 44W
San Juan de los Lagos **106** 21 15N 102 18W
San Juan de los Morros **118** 9 55N 67 21W
San Juan de Sabinas **102** 27 55N 101 18W
San Juan del César **118** 10 46N 73 1W
San Juan del Norte **112** 10 58N 83 40W
San Juan del Norte, B. de **112** 11 0N 83 40W
San Juan del Puerto **155** 37 20N 6 50W
San Juan del Río, Durango, Mexico **105** 24 47N 104 27W
San Juan del Río, Querétaro, Mexico **107** 20 23N 100 0W
San Juan del Salado **103** 23 18N 101 56W
San Juan del Sur **112** 11 20N 85 51W
San Juan Evangelista **109** 17 54N 95 8W
San Juan Guichicovi **109** 16 58N 95 6W

San Juan Ixcaquixtla 109 18 27N 97 49W
San Juan Joconosco 107 19 18N 100 17W
San Juan Juquila Mixes 109 16 58N 95 55W
San Juan Lajarcia 109 16 31N 95 56W
San Juan Mixtepec 109 16 17N 96 26W
San Juan Nepomuceno 101 26 22N 107 26W
San Juan Quiahije 109 16 17N 97 20W
San Juan Teposcolula 109 17 33N 97 26W
San Juanico, B. 99 26 14N 112 27W
San Juanico, I. 104 21 43N 106 38W
San Juanito 101 28 44N 107 57W
San Julián, Argentina 126 49 15 S 67 45W
San Julian, Mexico 106 21 1N 102 10W
San Julian, Phil. 211 11 45N 125 27 E
San Just, Sierra de 156 40 45N 0 49W
San Justo 124 30 47 S 60 30W
San Kamphaeng 204 18 45N 99 8 E
San Lázaro 100 31 8N 110 38W
San Lázaro, C. 99 24 48N 112 19W
San Lázaro, Sa. 99 23 14N 109 49W
San Leonardo 156 41 51N 3 5W
San Lorenzo, Argentina 124 32 45 S 60 45W
San Lorenzo, Beni, Bolivia 123 15 22 S 65 48W
San Lorenzo, Tarija, Bolivia 123 21 26 S 64 47W
San Lorenzo, Ecuador 118 1 15N 78 50W
San Lorenzo, Chihuahua, Mexico 101 29 49N 107 6W
San Lorenzo, Coahuila, Mexico 102 25 32N 102 11W
San Lorenzo, Sinaloa, Mexico 104 24 23N 106 52W
San Lorenzo, Paraguay 124 25 20 S 57 32W
San Lorenzo, Venezuela 118 9 47N 71 4W
San Lorenzo, I., Mexico 98 28 38N 112 51W
San Lorenzo, I., Peru 122 12 7 S 77 15W
San Lorenzo, Mt. 126 47 40 S 72 20W
San Lorenzo → 104 24 15N 107 24W
San Lorenzo Cacaotepec 109 17 8N 96 48W
San Lorenzo de la Parrilla 156 39 51N 2 22W
San Lorenzo de Morunys 156 42 8N 1 35 E
San Lucas, Bolivia 123 20 5 S 65 7W
San Lucas, Baja Calif. S., Mexico 99 22 53N 109 54W
San Lucas, Baja Calif. S., Mexico 99 27 10N 112 14W
San Lucas, Durango, Mexico 105 22 33N 104 24W
San Lucas, Guanajuato, Mexico 107 20 18N 100 33W
San Lucas, C. 99 22 52N 109 53W
San Lucas Ojitlán 109 18 4N 96 23W
San Lúcido 165 39 18N 16 3 E
San Luis, Argentina 124 33 20 S 66 20W
San Luis, Cuba 112 22 17N 83 46W
San Luis, Guat. 112 16 14N 89 27W
San Luis □ 124 34 0 S 66 0W
San Luis, I. 98 29 58N 114 26W
San Luis, L. de 123 13 45 S 64 0W
San Luis, Salado de 103 24 10N 100 50W
San Luis, Sierra de 124 32 30 S 66 10W
San Luis Acatlán 107 16 48N 98 55W
San Luis de la Loma 107 17 18N 100 55W
San Luis de la Paz 107 21 18N 100 31W
San Luis del Cordero 105 25 26N 104 18W
San Luis Gonzaga, B. 98 29 48N 114 22W
San Luis Potosí 103 22 9N 100 59W
San Luis Potosí □ 103 22 30N 100 30W
San Luis Río Colorado 100 32 29N 114 48W
San Manuel 210 16 4N 120 40 E
San Marcial 100 28 31N 110 19W
San Marco Argentano 165 39 34N 16 8 E
San Marco dei Cavoti 165 41 20N 14 50 E
San Marco in Lámis 165 41 43N 15 38 E
San Marcos, Colombia 118 8 39N 75 8W
San Marcos, Guat. 112 14 59N 91 52W
San Marcos, Guerrero, Mexico 107 16 48N 99 21W
San Marcos, Jalisco, Mexico 106 20 47N 104 11W
San Marcos, Nayarit, Mexico 104 20 58N 105 23W
San Marcos, I. 99 27 13N 112 6W
San Marino 163 43 56N 12 25 E
San Marino ■ 163 43 56N 12 25 E
San Martin, Antarct. 13 68 11 S 67 0W
San Martín, Argentina 124 33 5 S 68 28W
San Martín, Colombia 118 3 42N 73 42W
San Martín, Mexico 105 22 14N 101 22W
San Martin → 123 13 8 S 63 43W
San Martín, L. 126 48 50 S 72 50W
San Martín Chalchicuautla 103 21 23N 98 39W
San Martín de Bolaños 105 21 29N 103 58W
San Martin de los Andes 126 40 10 S 71 20W
San Martín de Valdeiglesias 154 40 21N 4 24W
San Martín Hidalgo 106 20 27N 103 57W
San Martín Tuxtla, Volcán 109 18 33N 95 13W
San Martino de Calvi 162 45 57N 9 41 E
San Mateo, Mexico 105 22 53N 103 29W
San Mateo, Agusan del N., Phil. 211 8 48N 125 33 E
San Mateo, Isabela, Phil. 210 16 54N 121 33 E
San Mateo, Spain 156 40 28N 0 10 E
San Mateo del Mar 109 16 12N 95 0W
San Mateo Yucutindoo 109 16 43N 97 30W
San Matías 123 16 25 S 58 20W
San Matías, Golfo 126 41 30 S 64 0W
San Miguel = Linapacan 211 11 30N 119 52 E
San Miguel, El Salv. 112 13 30N 88 12W
San Miguel, Panama 112 8 27N 78 55W
San Miguel, Lanao del N., Phil. 211 9 3N 125 59 E
San Miguel, Lanao del S., Phil. 211 8 13N 124 14 E
San Miguel, Spain 157 39 3N 1 26 E
San Miguel, Venezuela 118 9 40N 65 11W
San Miguel →, Bolivia 123 13 52 S 63 56W
San Miguel →, S. Amer. 118 0 25N 76 30W
San Miguel, Pta. 99 28 58N 112 13W
San Miguel Canoa 108 19 9N 98 5W
San Miguel Chimalapa 109 16 43N 94 41W
San Miguel de Allende 107 20 55N 100 45W
San Miguel de Huachi 122 15 40 S 67 15W
San Miguel de la Paz 106 20 22N 102 40W
San Miguel de Salinas 157 37 59N 0 47W
San Miguel de Tucumán 124 26 50 S 65 20W
San Miguel del Monte 124 35 23 S 58 50W
San Miguel del Puerto 109 15 55N 96 10W
San Miguel el Alto 106 21 1N 102 21W
San Miguel Huautla Nochixtlán 109 17 44N 97 6W
San Miguel Is. 211 7 45N 118 28 E
San Miguel Sola de Vega 109 16 31N 96 59W
San Miguel Suchixtepec 109 16 5N 96 28W
San Miguel Talea de Castro 109 17 22N 96 15W
San Miguel Tequixtepec 109 18 3N 97 42W
San Miguel Totolapán 107 18 8N 100 23W
San Miguel Zapotitlán 104 25 56N 109 3W
San Miguelito 98 32 13N 116 54W
San Miniato 162 43 40N 10 50 E
San Narciso, Quezon, Phil. 210 13 34N 122 34 E
San Narciso, Zambales, Phil. 210 15 2N 120 3 E
San Nicolás, Guerrero, Mexico 107 16 26N 98 32W
San Nicolás, Tamaulipas, Mexico 103 24 41N 98 48W
San Nicolas, Phil. 210 18 10N 120 36 E
San Nicolás de Arriba 104 24 58N 105 25W
San Nicolás de la Joya 101 27 24N 106 14W
San Nicolás de los Arroyas 124 33 25 S 60 10W
San Nicolás de los Garzas 102 25 45N 100 18W
San Nicolás del Cañón 101 27 12N 106 24W
San Nicolás Tolentino 103 22 16N 100 34W
San Onofre 118 9 44N 75 32W
San Pablo, Bolivia 124 21 43 S 66 38W
San Pablo, Campeche, Mexico 111 19 7N 90 50W
San Pablo, Coahuila, Mexico 102 26 50N 101 56W
San Pablo, Zacatecas, Mexico 105 22 33N 102 6W
San Pablo, Isabela, Phil. 210 17 27N 121 48 E
San Pablo, Laguna, Phil. 210 14 11N 121 31 E
San Pablo Huitzo 109 17 15N 96 52W
San Pablo Huixtepec 109 16 50N 96 46W
San Pablo Tolimán 107 20 52N 99 54W
San Pablo Villa de Mitla 109 16 55N 96 24W
San Pantaleón 104 26 26N 108 4W
San Paolo di Civitate 165 41 44N 15 16 E
San Pascual 210 13 8N 122 59 E
San Pedro, Buenos Aires, Argentina 125 26 30 S 54 10W
San Pedro, Jujuy, Argentina 124 24 12 S 64 55W
San Pedro, Colombia 118 4 56N 71 53W
San-Pédro, Ivory C. 246 4 50N 6 33W
San Pedro, Baja Calif. S., Mexico 99 23 23N 110 12W
San Pedro, Chihuahua, Mexico 101 29 20N 104 56W
San Pedro, Chihuahua, Mexico 101 30 18N 107 39W
San Pedro, Michoacan, Mexico 107 20 18N 100 21W
San Pedro, Nuevo León, Mexico 102 25 56N 99 12W
San Pedro, Nuevo León, Mexico 102 25 22N 100 7W
San Pedro, Sinaloa, Mexico 104 24 48N 107 37W
San Pedro, Sonora, Mexico 100 27 1N 109 38W
San Pedro, Peru 122 14 49 S 74 5W
San Pedro □ 124 24 0 S 57 0W
San Pedro →, Chihuahua, Mexico 101 28 21N 105 25W
San Pedro →, Tabasco, Mexico 110 18 38N 92 29W
San Pedro, Pta., Chile 124 25 30 S 70 38W
San Pedro, Pta., Baja Calif. S., Mexico 99 27 13N 114 29W
San Pedro, Pta., Sonora, Mexico 100 28 3N 111 17W
San Pedro, Sa. de 104 21 5N 104 48W
San Pedro, Sierra de 155 39 18N 6 40W
San Pedro Almoloyan 107 21 37N 101 15W
San Pedro Amusgos 109 16 38N 98 5W
San Pedro Analco 106 21 8N 103 59W
San Pedro Comitancillo 109 16 31N 95 10W
San Pedro de Arimena 118 4 37N 71 42W
San Pedro de Atacama 124 22 55 S 68 15W
San Pedro de Chamella 104 22 52N 105 58W
San Pedro de Jujuy 124 24 12 S 64 55W
San Pedro de la Cueva 100 29 18N 109 44W
San Pedro de las Colonias 102 25 45N 102 59W
San Pedro de Lloc 122 7 15 S 79 28W
San Pedro de Macorís 113 18 30N 69 18W
San Pedro del Gallo 105 25 33N 104 18W
San Pedro del Norte 112 13 4N 84 33W
San Pedro del Paraná 124 26 43 S 56 13W
San Pedro del Pinatar 157 37 50N 0 50W
San Pedro el Alto 109 16 48N 97 3W
San Pedro Huamelula 109 16 2N 95 40W
San Pedro Lagunillas 104 21 13N 104 46W
San Pedro Mártir, Sa. de 98 30 45N 115 13W
San Pedro Mezquital → 104 21 53N 105 36W
San Pedro Mixtepec Juquila 109 16 0N 97 7W
San Pedro Ozumacun 109 17 40N 96 15W
San Pedro Pochutla 109 15 44N 96 28W
San Pedro Sula 112 15 30N 88 0W
San Pedro Tapanatepec 109 16 21N 94 12W
San Pedro Tidaá 109 17 20N 97 23W
San Pedro Totoltepec 107 19 18N 99 35W
San Pedro Tututepec 109 16 9N 97 38W
San Pedro Yeloixtlahuacán 109 18 7N 98 5W
San Pietro, I. 164 39 9N 8 17 E
San Pietro Vernótico 165 40 28N 18 0 E
San Quintín 98 30 29N 115 57W
San Quintín, B. 98 30 22N 115 55W
San Quintín, C. 98 30 21N 116 0W
San Rafael, Argentina 124 34 40 S 68 21W
San Rafael, Baja Calif. S., Mexico 99 27 10N 114 8W
San Rafael, Nuevo León, Mexico 103 25 1N 100 33W
San Rafael, San Luis Potosí, Mexico 103 22 37N 99 54W
San Rafael, Sonora, Mexico 100 28 34N 111 42W
San Rafael, Sonora, Mexico 100 31 15N 111 40W
San Rafael, Venezuela 118 10 58N 71 46W
San Rafael, B. de 98 28 30N 113 4W
San Ramón, Bolivia 123 13 17 S 64 43W
San Ramón, Peru 122 11 8 S 75 20W
San Ramón de la Nueva Orán 124 23 10 S 64 20W
San Remo 162 43 48N 7 47 E
San Román, B. 98 30 40N 116 3W
San Román, C. 118 12 12N 70 0W
San Roque, Argentina 124 28 25 S 58 45W
San Roque, Mexico 107 20 58N 101 51W
San Roque, Phil. 210 12 37N 124 52 E
San Roque, Spain 155 36 17N 5 21W
San Rosendo 124 37 16 S 72 43W
San Salvador, Bahamas 113 24 0N 74 40W
San Salvador, El Salv. 112 13 40N 89 10W
San Salvador, Mexico 105 24 31N 100 52W
San Salvador de Jujuy 124 24 10 S 64 48W
San Salvador el Seco 108 19 8N 97 39W
San Salvador I. 113 24 0N 74 32W
San Sebastián, Argentina 126 53 10 S 68 30W
San Sebastián, Jalisco, Mexico 106 21 26N 102 21W
San Sebastián, Jalisco, Mexico 106 20 47N 104 51W
San Sebastián, México, Mexico 107 19 44N 99 35W
San Sebastián, México, Mexico 107 20 10N 99 32W
San Sebastián, Spain 156 43 17N 1 58W
San Sebastián, Venezuela 118 9 57N 67 11W
San Sebastián Coatlán 109 16 12N 96 50W
San Sebastián Zinacatepec 109 18 20N 97 15W
San Serverino Marche 163 43 13N 13 10 E
San Stéfano di Cadore 163 46 34N 12 33 E
San Telmo 98 30 58N 116 6W
San Telmo, Pta. 106 18 19N 103 30W
San Teodoro 210 13 26N 121 1 E
San Tiburcio 105 24 8N 101 32W
San Valentin, Mte. 126 46 30 S 73 30W
San Vicente, Baja Calif. N., Mexico 98 31 20N 116 21W
San Vicente, Coahuila, Mexico 102 29 5N 100 55W
San Vicente, San Luis Potosí, Mexico 103 24 10N 100 55W
San Vicente → 98 31 19N 116 16W
San Vicente de Alcántara 155 39 22N 7 8W

San Vicente de Benítez **107** 17 18N 100 18W
San Vicente de la Barquera **154** 43 23N 4 29W
San Vicente del Caguán **118** 2 7N 74 46W
San Vicente Tancuayalab **103** 21 44N 98 34W
San Vincenzo . . . . . . **162** 43 6N 10 29 E
San Vito . . . . **164** 39 26N 9 32 E
San Vito, C. . . . . **164** 38 11N 12 41 E
San Vito al Tagliamento . . . . . **163** 45 55N 12 50 E
San Vito Chietino . . **163** 42 19N 14 27 E
San Vito dei Normanni . . . . **165** 40 40N 17 40 E
San Yanaro **118** 2 47N 69 42W
Saña, Peru . . . . **122** 6 54 S 79 36W
Sana', Yemen . . . . . . **194** 15 27N 44 12 E
Sana → . . . . **163** 45 3N 16 23 E
Sanaba **246** 12 25N 3 47W
Sanabria, La **154** 42 0N 6 30W
Şanāfīr . . . . **191** 27 56N 34 42 E
Sanaga → . . . . **247** 3 35N 9 38 E
Sanalona, Presa **104** 24 49N 107 7W
Sanām . . . . **194** 23 40N 44 45 E
Sanana . . . . **207** 2 5 S 125 59 E
Sanand . . . . **198** 22 59N 72 25 E
Sanandaj . . . . **192** 35 18N 47 1 E
Sanandita . . . . **124** 21 40 S 63 45W
Sanary . . . . **141** 43 7N 5 48 E
Sanāw . . . . **195** 17 50N 51 5 E
Sanawad . . . . **198** 22 11N 76 5 E
Sanbe-San . . . . **220** 35 6N 132 38 E
Sancergues . . . . **139** 47 10N 2 54 E
Sancerre . . . . **139** 47 20N 2 50 E
Sancerrois, Coll. du . **139** 47 20N 2 40 E
Sancha He → . . . . . **216** 26 48N 106 7 E
Sanchahe . . . . **215** 44 50N 126 2 E
Sánchez **113** 19 15N 69 36W
Sánchez Magallanes . **110** 18 17N 93 54W
Sanchor . . . . **198** 24 45N 71 55 E
Sanco Pt. . . . . **211** 8 15N 126 27 E
Sancoins . . . . **139** 46 47N 2 55 E
Sancti-Spíritus **112** 21 52N 79 33W
Sand →, Canada . . **90** 54 23N 111 2W
Sand →, S. Africa . **255** 22 25 S 30 5 E
Sand L. **86** 50 10N 94 35W
Sanda . . . . **221** 34 53N 135 14 E
Sandah . . . . **244** 20 35N 39 32 E
Sandakan . . . . **206** 5 53N 118 4 E
Sandalwood . . . . **232** 34 55 S 140 9 E
Sandanski . . . . **167** 41 35N 23 16 E
Sandaré **246** 14 40N 10 15W
Sanday **134** 59 15N 2 30W
Sandbank L. **87** 51 8N 82 41W
Sande, Møre og Romsdal, Norway . . . . **171** 62 15N 5 27 E
Sande, Sogn og Fjordane, Norway . . . . **171** 61 20N 5 47 E
Sandefjord . . . . **171** 59 10N 10 15 E
Sandeid . . . . **171** 59 33N 5 52 E
Sanderston . . . . **232** 34 46 S 139 15 E
Sandfly L. **77** 55 43N 106 6W
Sandgate . . . . **231** 27 18 S 153 3 E
Sandía . . . . **122** 14 10 S 69 30W
Sandnes . . . . **171** 58 50N 5 45 E
Sandness **134** 60 18N 1 38W
Sandoa . . . . **253** 9 41 S 23 0 E
Sandomierz . . . . **152** 50 40N 21 43 E
Sandona **118** 1 17N 77 28W
Sandongo . . . . **253** 15 30 S 21 28 E
Sandoval **102** 25 54N 97 40W
Sandoval, Boca de . . **103** 24 58N 97 32W
Sandover → . . . . . . **230** 21 43 S 136 32 E
Sandringham . . . . . . **132** 52 50N 0 30 E
Sandslån . . . . **172** 63 2N 17 49 E
Sandspit **92** 53 14N 131 49W
Sandstone . . . . **229** 27 59 S 119 16 E
Sandu . . . . **216** 26 0N 107 52 E
Sandvig . . . . **173** 55 18N 14 48 E
Sandviken . . . . **172** 60 38N 16 46 E
Sandwich, C. . . . . . . **230** 18 14 S 146 18 E
Sandwich B., Canada **78** 53 40N 57 15W
Sandwich B., S. Africa . . . . **254** 23 25 S 14 20 E
Sandy → **78** 55 30N 68 21W
Sandy Bight . . . . **229** 33 50 S 123 20 E
Sandy C., Queens., Australia . . . . **231** 24 42 S 153 15 E
Sandy C., Tas., Australia . . . . **230** 41 25 S 144 45 E
Sandy Cay **113** 23 13N 75 18W
Sandy Cove **79** 51 21N 56 40W
Sandy L., Alta., Canada **90** 53 47N 114 2W
Sandy L., Newf., Canada **79** 49 15N 57 0W
Sandy L., Ont., Canada **74** 53 2N 93 0W
Sandy Lake **74** 53 0N 93 15W
Sandy Narrows **77** 55 5N 103 4W
Sandy Point **81** 43 42N 65 19W
Sandybeach L. **86** 49 49N 92 21W
Sanford → . . . . **229** 27 22 S 115 53 E
Sang-i-Masha . . . . . . **198** 33 8N 67 27 E
Sanga . . . . **251** 12 22 S 35 21 E
Sanga → . . . . **252** 1 5 S 17 0 E
Sanga-Tolon . . . . **185** 61 50N 149 40 E
Sangamner . . . . **200** 19 37N 74 15 E
Sangar, Afghan. . . . . **198** 32 56N 65 30 E
Sangar, U.S.S.R. . . . **185** 64 2N 127 31 E
Sangar Sarai . . . . . . **198** 34 27N 70 35 E
Sangasangadalam . . . **209** 0 36 S 117 13 E
Sangay . . . . **118** 2 0 S 78 20W
Sange . . . . **250** 6 58 S 28 21 E
Sangeang . . . . **207** 8 12 S 119 6 E
Sangerhausen . . . . . . **146** 51 28N 11 18 E
Sanggan He → . . . . **214** 38 12N 117 15 E
Sanggau . . . . **209** 0 5N 110 30 E
Sangihe, Kepulauan **207** 3 0N 126 0 E
Sangihe, P. . . . . **207** 3 45N 125 30 E
Sangju . . . . **215** 36 25N 128 10 E
Sangkapura . . . . **209** 5 52 S 112 40 E
Sangkhla . . . . **204** 14 57N 98 28 E
Sangli . . . . **200** 16 55N 74 33 E
Sangmélina . . . . **247** 2 57N 12 1 E
Sangonera → **157** 37 59N 1 4W
Sangpang Bum . . . . . **202** 26 30N 95 50 E
Sangro → . . . . **163** 42 14N 14 32 E
Sangudo **90** 53 50N 114 54W
Sangue → . . . . **123** 11 1 S 58 39W
Sangüesa **156** 42 37N 1 17W
Sanguinaires, Îs. . . . . **141** 41 51N 8 36 E
Sangzhi . . . . **217** 29 25N 110 12 E
Sanhala **246** 10 3N 6 51W
Sāniyah . . . . **192** 33 49N 42 43 E
Sanje . . . . **250** 0 49 S 31 30 E
Sanjiang . . . . **216** 25 48N 109 37 E
Sanjo . . . . **218** 37 37N 138 57 E
Sankarankovil . . . . . . **201** 9 10N 77 35 E
Sankeshwar . . . . **201** 16 23N 74 32 E
Sankosh → . . . . **202** 26 24N 89 47 E
Sankt Andrä . . . . **150** 46 46N 14 50 E
Sankt Antönien . . . . . **149** 46 58N 9 48 E
Sankt Blasien . . . . . . **147** 47 47N 8 7 E
Sankt Gallen . . . . **149** 47 26N 9 22 E
Sankt Gallen □ . . . . **149** 47 25N 9 22 E
Sankt Gotthard P. = San Gottardo, Paso del . . . . **149** 46 33N 8 33 E
Sankt Ingbert . . . . . . **147** 49 16N 7 6 E
Sankt Johann, Salzburg, Austria . **150** 47 22N 13 12 E
Sankt Johann, Tirol, Austria . . . . **150** 47 30N 12 25 E
Sankt Margrethen . . **149** 47 28N 9 37 E
Sankt Moritz . . . . **149** 46 30N 9 50 E
Sankt Olof . . . . **173** 55 37N 14 8 E
Sankt Pölten . . . . **150** 48 12N 15 38 E
Sankt Valentin . . . . . **150** 48 11N 14 33 E
Sankt Veit . . . . **150** 46 54N 14 22 E
Sankt Wendel . . . . . . **147** 49 27N 7 9 E
Sankt Wolfgang . . . . **150** 47 43N 13 27 E
Sankuru → . . . . **253** 4 17 S 20 25 E
Sanlúcar de Barrameda **155** 36 46N 6 21W
Sanlúcar la Mayor . . **155** 37 26N 6 18W
Sanluri . . . . **164** 39 35N 8 55 E
Sanmaur **83** 47 54N 73 47W
Sanmenxia . . . . **214** 34 47N 111 12 E
Sanming . . . . **217** 26 15N 117 40 E
Sannan . . . . **221** 35 2N 135 1 E
Sannaspos . . . . **254** 29 6 S 26 34 E
Sannicandro Gargánico . . . . **165** 41 50N 15 34 E
Sannidal . . . . **171** 58 55N 9 15 E
Sannieshof . . . . **254** 26 30 S 25 47 E
Sannīn, J. . . . . **190** 33 57N 35 52 E
Sano . . . . **221** 36 19N 139 35 E
Sanok . . . . **152** 49 35N 22 10 E
Sanquhar **134** 55 21N 3 56W
Sansanding Dam **246** 13 48N 6 0W
Sansepolcro . . . . **163** 43 34N 12 8 E
Sansha . . . . **217** 26 58N 120 12 E
Sanshui . . . . **217** 23 10N 112 56 E
Sanski Most . . . . **163** 44 46N 16 40 E
Sansui . . . . **216** 26 58N 108 39 E
Santa . . . . **122** 8 59 S 78 40W
Sant' Ágata de Goti **165** 41 6N 14 30 E
Sant' Ágata di Militello . . . . **165** 38 2N 14 8 E
Santa Águeda **99** 27 19N 112 16W
Santa Ana, Beni, Bolivia . . . . **123** 13 50 S 65 40W
Santa Ana, Santa Cruz, Bolivia . . . . **123** 18 43 S 58 44W
Santa Ana, Santa Cruz, Bolivia . . . . **123** 16 37 S 60 43W
Santa Ana, Ecuador **118** 1 16 S 80 20W
Santa Ana, El Salv. . **112** 14 0N 89 31W
Santa Ana, Mexico . **100** 30 33N 111 7W
Sta. Ana . . . . **210** 18 28N 122 20 E
Santa Ana → **118** 9 30N 71 57W
Santa Ana Chiautempan **107** 19 19N 98 11W
Sant' Ángelo Lodigiano . . . . **162** 45 14N 9 25 E
Sant' Antíoco . . . . . . **164** 39 2N 8 30 E
Santa Apolonia **102** 25 39N 97 57W
Sant' Arcángelo di Romagna . . . . **163** 44 4N 12 26 E
Santa Bárbara, Colombia **118** 5 53N 75 35W
Santa Barbara, Hond. **112** 14 53N 88 14W
Santa Bárbara, Chihuahua, Mexico **101** 26 48N 105 49W
Santa Bárbara, Guanajuato, Mexico **107** 21 32N 101 22W
Santa Bárbara, Sonora, Mexico . . **100** 31 15N 110 46W
Santa Barbara, Phil. **211** 10 50N 122 32 E
Santa Bárbara, Spain . . . . **156** 40 42N 0 29 E
Santa Bárbara, Venezuela **118** 7 47N 71 10W
Santa Bárbara, B. de **100** 26 41N 109 39W
Santa Bárbara, Mt. . **157** 37 23N 2 50W
Santa Catalina **118** 10 36N 75 17W
Santa Catalina, I. . . . **99** 25 40N 110 47W
Santa Catarina, Baja Calif. N., Mexico **98** 29 42N 115 8W
Santa Catarina, Nuevo León, Mexico **102** 25 41N 100 28W
Santa Catarina □ . . . **125** 27 25 S 48 30W
Santa Catarina, I. de **125** 27 30 S 48 40W
Santa Catarina Juquila **109** 16 14N 97 18W
Santa Catarina Loxicha **109** 16 4N 96 46W
Santa Catarina Mechoacán **109** 16 20N 97 50W
Santa Catarina Tlaltempan **109** 18 37N 98 5W
Santa Caterina Villarmosa . . . . **165** 37 37N 14 1 E
Santa Cecília . . . . **125** 26 56 S 50 18W
Santa Clara, Cuba . . **112** 22 20N 80 0W
Santa Clara, Chihuahua, Mexico **101** 29 17N 107 1W
Santa Clara, Durango, Mexico . **105** 24 29N 103 21W
Santa Clara, Yucatán, Mexico . **111** 21 22N 89 1W
Santa Clara, Sa. de . **99** 27 10N 113 35W
Santa Clara de Olimar . . . . **125** 32 50 S 54 54W
Santa Clotilde . . . . . . **118** 2 33 S 73 45W
Santa Coloma de Farnés . . . . **156** 41 50N 2 39 E
Santa Coloma de Gramanet . . . . **156** 41 27N 2 13 E
Santa Comba **154** 43 2N 8 49W
Santa Croce Camerina . . . . **165** 36 50N 14 30 E
Santa Croce di Magliano . . . . **165** 41 43N 14 59 E
Santa Cruz, Argentina . . . . **126** 50 0 S 68 32W
Santa Cruz, Bolivia . **123** 17 43 S 63 10W
Santa Cruz, Brazil . . **120** 6 13 S 36 1W
Santa Cruz, Chile . . **124** 34 38 S 71 27W
Santa Cruz, C. Rica **112** 10 15N 85 35W
Santa Cruz, San Luis Potosí, Mexico **103** 23 16N 100 37W
Santa Cruz, Sonora, Mexico **100** 31 14N 110 35W
Santa Cruz, Peru . . . **122** 5 40 S 75 56W
Santa Cruz, Davao del S., Phil. . . . . **211** 6 50N 125 25 E
Santa Cruz, Laguna, Phil. . . . . **210** 14 20N 121 24 E
Santa Cruz, Mannduque, Phil. **210** 13 28N 122 2 E
Santa Cruz, Venezuela **119** 8 3N 64 27W
Santa Cruz □, Argentina . . . . **126** 49 0 S 70 0W
Santa Cruz □, Bolivia . . . . **123** 17 43 S 63 10W
Santa Cruz → . . . . . **126** 50 10 S 68 20W
Santa Cruz, Is. . . . . . **224** 10 30 S 166 0 E
Santa Cruz, I. **99** 25 17N 110 43W
Santa Cruz Cabrália **121** 16 17 S 39 2W
Santa Cruz de Mudela **157** 38 39N 3 28W
Sta. Cruz de Tenerife **240** 28 28N 16 15W
Santa Cruz del Norte **112** 23 9N 81 55W
Santa Cruz del Retamar **154** 40 8N 4 14W
Santa Cruz del Sur . **112** 20 44N 78 0W
Santa Cruz do Rio Pardo . . . . **125** 22 54 S 49 37W
Santa Cruz do Sul . . **125** 29 42 S 52 25W
Santa Cruz Tacache Mina **109** 17 51N 98 7W
Santa Cruz Zenzontepec **109** 16 33N 97 30W
Santa Domingo, Cay **112** 21 25N 75 15W
Santa Domingo del Pacífico **99** 25 32N 112 2W
Santa Elena, Argentina . . . . **124** 30 58 S 59 47W
Santa Elena, Ecuador . . . . **118** 2 16 S 80 52W
Santa Elena, Mexico **111** 20 20N 89 39W
Santa Elena, C. **112** 10 54N 85 56W
Sant' Eufémia, Golfo di . . . . **165** 38 50N 16 10 E
Santa Eulalia . . . . . . **157** 38 59N 1 32 E
Santa Fe, Argentina **124** 31 35 S 60 41W
Santa Fe, Mexico . . . **106** 20 12N 101 50W
Santa Fe, Nueva Viscaya, Phil. . . . . **210** 16 10N 120 57 E
Santa Fe, Tablas, Phil. . . . . **210** 12 10N 122 0 E
Santa Fe, Spain **155** 37 11N 3 43W
Santa Fé □ . . . . **124** 31 50 S 60 55W
Santa Filomena . . . . **120** 9 6 S 45 50W
Santa Gertrudis, Baja Calif. N., Mexico **99** 28 5N 113 4W
Santa Gertrudis, Chihuahua, Mexico **101** 27 49N 105 44W
Santa Helena . . . . . . **120** 2 14 S 45 18W
Santa Helena de Goiás . . . . **121** 17 53 S 50 35W
Santa Inês, Brazil . . **121** 13 17 S 39 48W
Santa Inés, Spain . . . **155** 38 32N 5 37W
Santa Inés, B. **99** 26 59N 111 59W
Santa Inés, I. . . . . . . **126** 54 0 S 73 0W
Santa Inés Ahuatempan **109** 18 25N 98 1W
Santa Inés del Monte **109** 16 56N 96 51W
Santa Isabel = Rey Malabo . . . . **247** 3 45N 8 50 E
Santa Isabel, Argentina . . . . **124** 36 10 S 66 54W
Santa Isabel, Brazil . **121** 11 45 S 51 30W
Santa Isabel, Pico . . **247** 3 36N 8 49 E
Santa Isabel do Araguaia . . . . **120** 6 7 S 48 19W
Santa Isabel do Morro . . . . **121** 11 34 S 50 40W
Santa Lucía, Corrientes, Argentina . . . . **124** 28 58 S 59 5W
Santa Lucía, San Juan, Argentina . . . . **124** 31 30 S 68 30W
Santa Lucia, Phil. . . **210** 17 7N 120 27 E
Santa Lucía, Spain . . **157** 37 35N 0 58W
Santa Lucía, Uruguay . . . . **124** 34 27 S 56 24W
Santa Lucía, Sa. de . **99** 27 0N 112 30W
Santa Lucia Monte Verde **109** 16 57N 97 40W
Santa Lucia Teotepec **109** 16 8N 97 13W
Santa Magdalena, I. **99** 24 55N 112 15W
Santa Margarita . . . . **124** 38 28 S 61 35W
Santa Margarita, I. . **99** 24 27N 111 50W
Santa Margarita, Sa. de **100** 30 4N 110 2W
Santa Margherita . . . **162** 44 20N 9 11 E
Santa María, Argentina . . . . **124** 26 40 S 66 0W
Santa Maria, Brazil . **125** 29 40 S 53 48W
Santa Maria, Ilocos S., Phil. . . . **210** 17 22N 120 29 E
Santa Maria, Isabela, Phil. . . . . . **210** 17 28N 121 45 E
Santa María, Spain . **156** 39 38N 2 47 E
Santa Maria, Switz. . **149** 46 36N 10 25 E
Santa Maria, Zambia . . . . **251** 11 5 S 29 58 E
Santa María →, Chihuahua, Mexico **101** 31 0N 107 14W
Santa María →, San Luis Potosí, Mexico **103** 21 37N 99 15W
Santa María, B. de . **104** 25 4N 108 6W
Santa María, Cabo de **155** 36 58N 7 53W
Santa María, L. de . **101** 31 7N 107 16W
Santa María Asunción Tlaxiaco **109** 17 16N 97 41W

Santa Maria Capua Vetere **165** 41 3N 14 15 E
Santa María Chimalapa **109** 16 55N 94 41W
Santa María Colotepec **109** 15 53N 96 55W
Santa Maria da Vitória **121** 13 24 S 44 12W
Santa María de Abajo **106** 21 25N 102 14W
Santa María de Cuevas **101** 27 55N 106 23W
Santa María de Ipire **119** 8 49N 65 19W
Santa María de los Ángeles **105** 22 11N 103 14W
Santa María de Otáez **104** 24 42N 106 0W
Santa Maria del Oro **104** 21 20N 104 35W
Santa María del Río **103** 21 48N 100 45W
Santa Maria di Leuca, C. **165** 39 48N 18 20 E
Santa Maria do Suaçuí **121** 18 12 S 42 25W
Santa Maria dos Marmelos **123** 6 7 S 61 51W
Santa María Ecatepec **109** 16 17N 95 53W
Santa María Huazolotitlán **109** 16 17N 97 56W
Santa María la Real de Nieva **154** 41 4N 4 24W
Santa María Natívitas **109** 17 39N 97 20W
Santa María Petapa **109** 16 50N 95 7W
Santa María Tonameca **109** 15 44N 96 33W
Santa María Zacatepec **109** 16 46N 98 0W
Santa María Zoquitlán **109** 16 33N 96 23W
Santa Marta, Colombia **118** 11 15N 74 13W
Santa Marta, Spain **155** 38 37N 6 39W
Santa Marta, Ría de **154** 43 44N 7 45W
Santa Marta, Sierra Nevada de **118** 10 55N 73 50W
Santa Marta Grande, C. **125** 28 43 S 48 50W
Santa Matilde **101** 27 8N 108 23W
Santa Maura = Levkás **169** 38 40N 20 43 E
Santa Mónica **102** 28 12N 100 37W
Santa Olalla, Huelva, Spain **155** 37 54N 6 14W
Santa Olalla, Toledo, Spain **154** 40 2N 4 25W
Sant' Onofrio **165** 38 42N 16 10 E
Santa Pola **157** 38 13N 0 35W
Santa Quitéria **120** 4 20 S 40 10W
Santa Rita, Jalisco, Mexico **106** 20 53N 102 22W
Santa Rita, Nuevo León, Mexico **103** 24 12N 100 30W
Santa Rita, Guarico, Venezuela **118** 8 8N 66 16W
Santa Rita, Zulia, Venezuela **118** 10 32N 71 32W
Santa Rita do Araquaia **123** 17 20 S 53 12W
Santa Rosa, La Pampa, Argentina **124** 36 40 S 64 17W
Santa Rosa, San Luis, Argentina **124** 32 21 S 65 10W
Santa Rosa, Bolivia **122** 10 36 S 67 20W
Santa Rosa, Brazil **125** 27 52 S 54 29W
Santa Rosa, Colombia **118** 3 32N 69 48W
Santa Rosa, Ecuador **118** 3 27 S 79 58W
Santa Rosa, Chihuahua, Mexico **101** 26 26N 107 27W
Santa Rosa, Nayarit, Mexico **104** 22 18N 104 24W
Santa Rosa, Querétaro, Mexico **107** 20 44N 100 27W
Santa Rosa, Quintana Roo, Mexico **111** 19 58N 88 53W
Santa Rosa, Sonora, Mexico **100** 27 52N 109 19W
Santa Rosa, Sonora, Mexico **100** 28 25N 109 8W
Santa Rosa, Tamaulipas, Mexico **103** 24 13N 97 52W
Santa Rosa, Peru **122** 14 30 S 70 50W
Santa Rosa, Phil. **210** 15 25N 120 57 E
Santa Rosa, Venezuela **118** 1 29N 66 55W
Santa Rosa, Presa **106** 20 55N 103 40W
Santa Rosa, Pta. **111** 19 28N 87 27W
Santa Rosa de Cabal **118** 4 52N 75 38W
Santa Rosa de Copán **112** 14 47N 88 46W
Santa Rosa de Osos **118** 6 39N 75 28W
Santa Rosa de Río Primero **124** 31 8 S 63 20W
Santa Rosa de Viterbo **118** 5 53N 72 59W
Santa Rosa del Palmar **123** 16 54 S 62 24W
Santa Rosalía, Baja Calif. S., Mexico **99** 27 19N 112 17W
Santa Rosalía, Sonora, Mexico **100** 29 7N 110 29W
Santa Rosalía, B. **98** 28 37N 114 13W
Santa Rosalía de Cuevas **101** 28 2N 106 28W
Santa Sofia **163** 43 57N 11 55 E
Santa Sylvina **124** 27 50 S 61 10W
Santa Tecla = Nueva San Salvador **112** 13 40N 89 18W
Santa Teresa, Argentina **124** 33 25 S 60 47W
Santa Teresa, Brazil **121** 19 55 S 40 36W
Santa Teresa, Nayarit, Mexico **104** 22 28N 104 44W
Santa Teresa, Tamaulipas, Mexico **103** 25 17N 97 51W
Santa Teresa, Venezuela **119** 4 43N 61 4W
Santa Teresa di Riva **165** 37 58N 15 21 E
Santa Teresa Gallura **164** 41 14N 9 12 E
Santa Vitória **121** 18 50 S 50 8W
Santa Vitória do Palmar **125** 33 32 S 53 25W
Santadi **164** 39 5N 8 42 E
Santahar **202** 24 48N 88 59 E
Santai **216** 31 5N 104 58 E
Santaluz **120** 11 15 S 39 22W
Santana **121** 13 2 S 44 5W
Santana, Coxilha de **125** 30 50 S 55 35W
Santana do Ipanema **120** 9 22 S 37 14W
Santana do Livramento **125** 30 55 S 55 30W
Santanayi **157** 39 20N 3 5 E
Santander, Colombia **118** 3 1N 76 28W
Santander, Phil. **211** 9 25N 123 20 E
Santander, Spain **154** 43 27N 3 51W
Santander □ **154** 43 25N 4 0W
Santander Jiménez **103** 24 13N 98 28W
Santarém, Brazil **119** 2 25 S 54 42W
Santarém, Portugal **155** 39 12N 8 42W
Santarém □ **155** 39 10N 8 40W
Santaren Channel **112** 24 0N 79 30W
Santéramo in Colle **165** 40 48N 16 45 E
Santerno → **163** 44 10N 11 38 E
Santhia **162** 45 20N 8 10 E
Santiago, Bolivia **123** 18 19 S 59 34W
Santiago, Brazil **125** 29 11 S 54 52W
Santiago, Chile **124** 33 24 S 70 40W
Santiago, Baja Calif. S., Mexico **99** 23 28N 109 43W
Santiago, Baja Calif. S., Mexico **99** 27 32N 112 49W
Santiago, Chiapas, Mexico **110** 16 38N 92 5W
Santiago, Sonora, Mexico **100** 29 27N 110 25W
Santiago, Panama **112** 8 0N 81 0W
Santiago, Peru **122** 14 11 S 75 43W
Santiago, Ilocos S., Phil. **210** 17 18N 120 27 E
Santiago, Isabela, Phil. **210** 16 41N 121 33 E
Santiago □ **124** 33 30 S 70 50W
Santiago →, Mexico **104** 25 11N 105 26W
Santiago →, Peru **118** 4 27 S 77 38W
Santiago, C. **126** 50 46 S 75 27W
Santiago, Punta de **247** 3 12N 8 40 E
Santiago, Serranía de **123** 18 25 S 59 25W
Santiago Astata **109** 15 59N 95 40W
Santiago Chazumba **109** 18 12N 97 40W
Santiago Choapan **109** 17 20N 95 57W
Santiago Comaltepec **109** 17 36N 96 34W
Santiago de Chuco **122** 8 9 S 78 11W
Santiago de Compostela **154** 42 52N 8 37W
Santiago de Cuba **112** 20 0N 75 49W
Santiago de la Peña **108** 20 57N 97 24W
Santiago de los Caballeros **113** 19 30N 70 40W
Santiago del Estero **124** 27 50 S 64 15W
Santiago del Estero □ **124** 27 40 S 63 15W
Santiago do Cacém **155** 38 1N 8 42W
Santiago Ixcuintla **104** 21 49N 105 13W
Santiago Ixtayutla **109** 16 35N 97 40W
Santiago Juxtlahuaca **109** 17 20N 98 1W
Santiago Lachiguiri **109** 16 41N 95 32W
Santiago Miahuatlán **109** 18 34N 97 26W
Santiago Miltepec **109** 17 59N 97 41W
Santiago Papasquiaro **104** 25 3N 105 25W
Santiago Pinotepa Nacional **109** 16 19N 98 1W
Santiago Tamazola **109** 17 42N 98 15W
Santiago Tulantepec **107** 20 2N 98 18W
Santiago Tuxtla **109** 18 28N 95 18W
Santiago Xanica **109** 16 0N 96 14W
Santiago Xonacatlán **108** 19 37N 97 36W
Santiago Yolomécatl **109** 17 28N 97 34W
Santiago Zacatepec **109** 17 11N 95 51W
Santiaguillo, L. de **105** 24 48N 104 48W
Santillana del Mar **154** 43 24N 4 6W
Säntis **149** 47 15N 9 22 E
Santisteban del Puerto **157** 38 17N 3 15W
Santo → **122** 8 56 S 78 37W
Santo Amaro **121** 12 30 S 38 43W
Santo Anastácio **125** 21 58 S 51 39W
Santo André **125** 23 39 S 46 29W
Santo Ângelo **125** 28 15 S 54 15W
Santo Antonio **123** 15 50 S 56 0W
Santo Antônio de Jesus **121** 12 58 S 39 16W
Santo Antônio do Içá **118** 3 5 S 67 57W
Santo Antônio do Leverger **123** 15 52 S 56 5W
Santo Corazón **123** 18 0 S 58 45W
Santo Domingo, Dom. Rep. **113** 18 30N 64 54W
Santo Domingo, Baja Calif. N., Mexico **99** 28 12N 114 2W
Santo Domingo, Coahuila, Mexico **102** 29 3N 102 18W
Santo Domingo, Durango, Mexico **105** 25 48N 104 28W
Santo Domingo, Oaxaca, Mexico **109** 16 28N 94 51W
Santo Domingo, San Luis Potosí, Mexico **103** 21 37N 100 46W
Santo Domingo, San Luis Potosí, Mexico **103** 22 18N 100 10W
Santo Domingo, San Luis Potosí, Mexico **103** 23 20N 101 44W
Santo Domingo, Tamaulipas, Mexico **102** 25 48N 98 19W
Santo Domingo, Nic. **112** 12 14N 84 59W
Santo Domingo → **109** 18 10N 96 8W
Santo Domingo, Pta. **99** 26 19N 112 42W
Santo Domingo Armenta **109** 16 18N 98 20W
Santo Domingo de la Calzada **156** 42 26N 2 57W
Santo Domingo de los Colorados **118** 0 15 S 79 9W
Santo Domingo Ixcatlán **109** 16 55N 97 32W
Santo Domingo Tehuantepec **109** 16 20N 95 14W
Santo Domingo Xagacia **109** 17 8N 96 17W
Santo Domingo Zanatepec **109** 16 29N 94 21W
Santo Nino I. **211** 11 55N 124 27 E
Santo Stéfano di Camastro **165** 38 1N 14 22 E
Santo Stino di Livenza **163** 45 45N 12 40 E
Santo Tirso **154** 41 21N 8 28W
Santo Tomás, Baja Calif. N., Mexico **98** 31 33N 116 24W
Santo Tomás, Chihuahua, Mexico **101** 28 41N 107 34W
Santo Tomás, Hidalgo, Mexico **107** 19 54N 98 34W
Santo Tomás, Peru **122** 14 26 S 72 8W
Santo Tomás, Pta. **98** 31 34N 116 42W
Santo Tomé **125** 28 40 S 56 5W
Santo Tomé de Guayana **119** 8 22N 62 40W
Santol **210** 16 47N 120 27 E
Santoña **154** 43 29N 3 27W
Santos **125** 24 0 S 46 20W
Santos, Sierra de los **155** 38 7N 5 12W
Santos Dumont **125** 22 55 S 43 10W
Santos Reyes Nopala **109** 16 6N 97 10W
Santos Reyes Pápalo **109** 17 49N 96 51W
Santpoort **142** 52 26N 4 39 E
Santuario **107** 20 39N 99 8W
Sānūr **189** 32 22N 35 15 E
Sanvignes-les-Mines **139** 46 40N 4 18 E
San'yō **220** 34 2N 131 5 E
Sanyuan **214** 34 35N 108 58 E
Sanyuki-Sammyaku **220** 34 5N 133 0 E
Sanza Pombo **253** 7 18 S 15 56 E
São Anastácio **125** 22 0 S 51 40W
São Bartolomeu de Messines **155** 37 15N 8 17W
São Benedito **120** 4 3 S 40 53W
São Bento **120** 2 42 S 44 50W
São Bento do Norte **120** 5 4 S 36 2W
São Borja **125** 28 39 S 56 0W
São Bras d'Alportel **155** 37 8N 7 37W
São Caitano **120** 8 21 S 36 6W
São Carlos **125** 22 0 S 47 50W
São Cristóvão **120** 11 1 S 37 15W
São Domingos **121** 13 25 S 46 19W
São Domingos do Maranhão **120** 5 42 S 44 22W
São Félix **121** 11 36 S 50 39W
São Francisco **121** 16 0 S 44 50W
São Francisco → **120** 10 30 S 36 24W
São Francisco do Maranhão **120** 6 15 S 42 52W
São Francisco do Sul **125** 26 15 S 48 36W
São Gabriel **125** 30 20 S 54 20W
São Gabriel da Palha **121** 18 47 S 40 39W
São Gonçalo **121** 22 48 S 43 5W
São Gotardo **121** 19 19 S 46 3W
Sao Hill **251** 8 20 S 35 12 E
São João da Boa Vista **125** 22 0 S 46 52W
São João da Pesqueira **154** 41 8N 7 24W
São João da Ponte **121** 15 56 S 44 1W
São João del Rei **121** 21 8 S 44 15W
São João do Araguaia **120** 5 23 S 48 46W
São João do Paraíso **121** 15 19 S 42 1W
São João do Piauí **120** 8 21 S 42 15W
São João dos Patos **120** 6 30 S 43 42W
São Joaquim da Barra **121** 20 35 S 47 53W
São José, B. de **120** 2 38 S 44 4W
São José da Laje **120** 9 1 S 36 3W
São José de Mipibu **120** 6 5 S 35 15W
São José do Peixe **120** 7 24 S 42 34W
São José do Rio Prêto **125** 20 50 S 49 20W
São José dos Campos **125** 23 7 S 45 52W
São Leopoldo **125** 29 50 S 51 10W
São Lourenço **121** 22 7 S 45 3W
São Lourenço → **123** 17 53 S 57 27W
São Lourenço, Pantanal do **123** 17 30 S 56 20W
São Luís **120** 2 39 S 44 15W
São Luís do Curu **120** 3 40 S 39 14W
São Luís Gonzaga **125** 28 25 S 55 0W
São Marcos → **121** 18 15 S 47 37W
São Marcos, B. de **120** 2 0 S 44 0W
São Martinho **154** 40 18N 8 8W
São Mateus **121** 18 44 S 39 50W
São Mateus → **121** 18 35 S 39 44W
São Miguel **240** 37 33N 25 27W
São Miguel do Araguaia **121** 13 19 S 50 13W
São Miguel dos Campos **120** 9 47 S 36 5W
São Nicolau → **120** 5 45 S 42 2W
São Paulo **125** 23 32 S 46 37W
São Paulo □ **125** 22 0 S 49 0W
Sao Paulo, I. **128** 0 50N 31 40W
São Paulo de Olivença **118** 3 27 S 68 48W
São Pedro do Sul **154** 40 46N 8 4W
São Rafael **120** 5 47 S 36 55W
São Raimundo das Mangabeiras **120** 7 1 S 45 29W
São Raimundo Nonato **120** 9 1 S 42 42W
São Romão **121** 16 22 S 45 4W
São Roque, C. de **120** 5 30 S 35 16W
São Sebastião, I. de **125** 23 50 S 45 18W
São Sebastião do Paraíso **125** 20 54 S 46 59W
São Simão **121** 18 56 S 50 30W
São Teotónio **155** 37 30N 8 42W
São Tomé, Atl. Oc. **237** 0 10N 6 39 E
São Tomé, Brazil **120** 5 58 S 36 4W
São Tomé, C. de **121** 22 0 S 40 59W
São Tomé & Principe ■ **253** 0 12N 6 39 E
São Vicente **125** 23 57 S 46 23W
São Vicente, Cabo de **155** 37 0N 9 0W
Saona, I. **113** 18 10N 68 40W
Saône → **139** 45 44N 4 50 E
Saône-et-Loire □ **139** 46 25N 4 50 E

Saonek **207** 0 22 S 130 55 E
Saoura, O. → **240** 29 0N 0 55W
Sápai **168** 41 2N 25 43 E
Sapão → **120** 11 1 S 45 32W
Saparua **207** 3 33 S 128 40 E
Sapé **120** 7 6 S 35 13W
Sapele **247** 5 50N 5 40 E
Sapiéntza **169** 36 45N 21 43 E
Sapone **247** 12 3N 1 35W
Saposoa **122** 6 55 S 76 45W
Sapozhok **179** 53 59N 40 41 E
Sappemeer **142** 53 10N 6 48 E
Sapporo **218** 43 0N 141 21 E
Sapri **165** 40 5N 15 37 E
Sapu Grande **211** 5 55N 125 16 E
Sapudi **209** 7 6 S 114 20 E
Saqqez **192** 36 15N 46 20 E
Sar Dasht **193** 32 32N 48 52 E
Sar-e Pol **197** 36 10N 66 0 E
Sar Gachīneh **193** 30 31N 51 31 E
Sar Planina **166** 42 10N 21 0 E
Sara, Phil. **211** 11 16N 123 1 E
Sara, Upp. Volta **246** 11 40N 3 53W
Sara Buri **204** 14 30N 100 55 E
Sarāb, Iran **192** 38 0N 47 30 E
Sarab, S. Yemen **195** 14 51N 48 31 E
Sarabadi **192** 33 1N 44 48 E
Sarabit el Khadim **191** 29 2N 33 25 E
Saragossa = Zaragoza **156** 41 39N 0 53W
Saraguro **118** 3 35 S 79 16W
Saraipali **199** 21 20N 82 59 E
Sarajevo **166** 43 52N 18 26 E
Saraktash **182** 51 47N 56 22 E
Saralu **170** 44 43N 28 10 E
Saramacca □ **119** 5 0N 56 0W
Saramacca → **119** 5 50N 55 55W
Saramati **202** 25 44N 95 2 E
Saran **244** 19 35N 40 30 E
Saran, G. **209** 0 30 S 111 25 E
Saranda, Albania **168** 39 52N 19 55 E
Saranda, Tanzania **250** 5 45 S 34 59 E
Sarandí del Yi **125** 33 18 S 55 38W
Sarandí Grande **124** 33 44 S 56 20W
Sarangani B. **211** 6 0N 125 13 E
Sarangani Is. **211** 5 25N 125 25 E
Sarangarh **199** 21 30N 83 5 E
Saransk **179** 54 10N 45 10 E
Sarapul **182** 56 28N 53 48 E
Sarāqib **190** 35 52N 36 47 E
Sarar Plain **256** 9 25N 46 17 E
Saratov **179** 51 30N 46 2 E
Saravane **204** 15 43N 106 25 E
Sarawak □ **206** 2 0N 113 0 E
Saraya **246** 12 50N 11 45W
Sarbāz **193** 26 38N 61 19 E
Sarbīsheh **193** 32 30N 59 40 E
Sårbogård **151** 46 50N 18 40 E
Sarca → **162** 45 52N 10 52 E
Sardalas **241** 25 50N 10 34 E
Sardarshahr **198** 28 30N 74 29 E
Sardegna **164** 39 57N 9 0 E
Sardhana **198** 29 9N 77 39 E
Sardinata **118** 8 5N 72 48W
Sardinia = Sardegna **164** 39 57N 9 0 E
Sardis **93** 49 8N 121 58W
Sārdūīyeh = Dar Mazār **193** 29 14N 57 20 E
Šarengrad **166** 45 14N 19 16 E
Sarėyamou **246** 16 7N 3 10W
Sargasso Sea **128** 27 0N 72 0W
Sargento, Pta. **100** 29 18N 112 23W
Sargodha **197** 32 10N 72 40 E
Sarh **243** 9 5N 18 23 E
Sarhro, Djebel **240** 31 6N 5 0W
Sārī **193** 36 30N 53 4 E
Sária **169** 35 54N 27 17 E
Sáric **100** 31 8N 111 23W
Saricumbe **253** 12 12 S 19 46 E
Sarida → **189** 32 4N 34 45 E
Sarikei **206** 2 8N 111 30 E
Sarina **230** 21 22 S 149 13 E
Sariñena **156** 41 47N 0 10W
Sarīr Tibasti **241** 22 50N 18 30 E
Saritaş Tepesi **190** 36 20N 32 38 E
Sariwŏn **215** 38 31N 125 46 E
Sariyer **167** 41 10N 29 3 E
Sark **138** 49 25N 2 20W
Sarkad **151** 46 47N 21 23 E
Sarlat-la-Canéda **140** 44 54N 1 13 E
Sărmaşu **170** 46 45N 24 13 E
Sarmi **207** 1 49 S 138 44 E
Sarmiento **126** 45 35 S 69 5W
Särna **172** 61 41N 13 8 E
Sarnano **163** 43 2N 13 17 E
Sarnen **148** 46 53N 8 13 E
Sarnia **84** 42 58N 82 23W
Sarno **165** 40 48N 14 35 E
Sarnowa **152** 51 39N 16 53 E
Sarny **178** 51 17N 26 40 E
Särö **173** 57 31N 11 57 E
Sarolangun **208** 2 19 S 102 42 E
Saronikós Kólpos **169** 37 45N 23 45 E
Saronno **162** 45 38N 9 2 E
Saros Körfezi **168** 40 30N 26 15 E
Sárospatak **151** 48 18N 21 33 E
Sarosul Romănesc **166** 45 34N 21 43 E
Sarova **179** 54 55N 43 19 E
Sarpsborg **171** 59 16N 11 12 E
Sarracín **156** 42 15N 3 45W
Sarralbe **139** 48 55N 7 1 E
Sarrat **210** 18 9N 120 39 E
Sarraz, La **148** 46 38N 6 30 E
Sarre = Saar → **139** 49 41N 6 32 E
Sarre, La **82** 48 45N 79 15W
Sarre-Union **139** 48 55N 7 4 E
Sarrebourg **139** 48 43N 7 3 E
Sarreguemines **139** 49 1N 7 4 E
Sarriá **154** 42 49N 7 29W
Sarrión **156** 40 9N 0 49W
Sarro **246** 13 40N 5 15W
Sarstedt **146** 52 13N 9 50 E
Sartène **141** 41 38N 8 58 E
Sarthe □ **138** 47 58N 0 10 E
Sarthe → **138** 47 33N 0 31W
Sartilly **138** 48 45N 1 28W
Sartynya **184** 63 22N 63 11 E
Sárvár **151** 47 15N 16 56 E
Sarvestān **193** 29 20N 53 10 E
Särvfjället **172** 62 42N 13 30 E
Sárviz → **151** 46 24N 18 41 E
Sary Ozek **183** 44 22N 77 59 E
Sary-Tash **183** 39 44N 73 15 E
Saryagach **183** 41 27N 69 9 E
Sarych, Mys. **180** 44 25N 33 45 E
Sarykolskiy Khrebet **183** 38 30N 74 30 E
Sarykopa, Ozero **182** 50 22N 64 6 E
Sarymoin, Ozero **182** 51 36N 64 30 E
Saryshagan **184** 46 12N 73 38 E
Sarzana **162** 44 5N 9 59 E
Sarzeau **138** 47 31N 2 48W
Sas van Gent **143** 51 14N 3 48 E
Sasa **189** 33 2N 35 23 E
Sásabe **100** 31 27N 111 31W
Sasabeneh **256** 7 59N 44 43 E
Sasaginnigak L. **89** 51 36N 95 39W
Sasaram **199** 24 57N 84 5 E
Sasayama **221** 35 4N 135 13 E
Sasca Montană **166** 44 50N 21 45 E
Sasebo **220** 33 10N 129 43 E
Saseginaga, L. **82** 47 6N 78 35W
Saser Mt. **199** 34 50N 77 50 E
Saskatchewan □ **77** 54 40N 106 0W
Saskatchewan → **89** 53 37N 100 40W
Saskatchewan Landing Prov. Park **88** 50 38N 107 59W
Saskatoon **88** 52 10N 106 38W
Saskylakh **185** 71 55N 114 1 E
Sasnovka **179** 56 20N 51 4 E
Sasolburg **255** 26 46 S 27 49 E
Sasovo **179** 54 25N 41 55 E
Sassandra **246** 5 0N 6 8W
Sassandra → **246** 4 58N 6 5W
Sássari **164** 40 44N 8 33 E
Sassenheim **142** 52 14N 4 31 E
Sassnitz **146** 54 29N 13 39 E
Sasso Marconi **163** 44 22N 11 12 E
Sassocorvaro **163** 43 47N 12 30 E
Sassoferrato **163** 43 26N 12 51 E
Sassuolo **162** 44 31N 10 47 E
Sástago **156** 41 19N 0 21W
Sastown **246** 4 45N 8 27W
Sasumua Dam **250** 0 45 S 36 40 E
Sasyk, Ozero **170** 45 45N 30 0 E
Sasykkul **183** 37 41N 73 11 E
Sata-Misaki **220** 30 59N 130 40 E
Satadougou **246** 12 25N 11 25W
Satara **200** 17 44N 73 58 E
Satevó **101** 27 57N 106 7W
Satipo **122** 11 15 S 74 25W
Satka **182** 55 3N 59 1 E
Satkania **202** 22 4N 92 3 E
Satkhira **202** 22 43N 89 8 E
Satmala Hills **200** 20 15N 74 40 E
Satna **199** 24 35N 80 50 E
Šator **163** 44 11N 16 37 E
Sátoraljaújhely **151** 48 25N 21 41 E
Satpura Ra. **198** 21 25N 76 10 E
Satrup **146** 54 39N 9 38 E
Satsuma-Hantō **220** 31 25N 130 25 E
Satsuna-Shotō **219** 30 0N 130 0 E
Sattahip **204** 12 41N 100 54 E
Sattenapalle **201** 16 25N 80 6 E
Satu Mare **170** 47 46N 22 55 E
Satui **209** 3 50 S 115 27 E
Satumare □ **170** 47 45N 23 0 E
Satun **205** 6 43N 100 2 E
Saturna **93** 48 47N 123 11W
Saturnina → **123** 12 15 S 58 10W
Saubosq, L. **80** 51 30N 64 53W
Sauce **124** 30 5 S 58 46W
Sauceda **102** 25 46N 101 19W
Saucillo **101** 28 1N 105 17W
Sauda **171** 59 40N 6 20 E
Saúde **120** 10 56 S 40 24W
Sauðarkrókur **174** 65 45N 19 40W
Saudi Arabia ■ **194** 26 0N 44 0 E
Sauerland **146** 51 0N 8 0 E
Saugeen → **84** 44 30N 81 22W
Saugues **140** 44 58N 3 32 E
Sauherad **171** 59 25N 9 15 E
Saujon **140** 45 41N 0 55W
Saül **119** 3 37N 53 12W
Saulgau **147** 48 4N 9 32 E
Saulieu **139** 47 17N 4 14 E
Saulnierville **81** 44 16N 66 8W
Sault **141** 44 6N 5 24 E
Sault-au-Moulton **83** 48 33N 69 15W
Sault aux Cochons → **83** 48 44N 69 4W
Sault Ste. Marie **84** 46 30N 84 20W
Saumlaki **207** 7 55 S 131 20 E
Saumur **138** 47 15N 0 5W
Saumur, L. **80** 51 16N 62 49W
Saunders C. **235** 45 53 S 170 45 E
Saunders I. **13** 57 48 S 26 28W
Saunders Point, Mt. **229** 27 52 S 125 38 E
Saurbœr, Borgarfjarðarsýsla, Iceland **174** 64 24N 21 35W
Saurbœr, Eyjafjarðarsýsla, Iceland **174** 65 27N 18 13W
Sauri **247** 11 42N 6 44 E
Saurimo **253** 9 40 S 20 12 E
Sautatá **118** 7 50N 77 4W
Sauvage, L. **82** 50 6N 74 30W
Sauveterre **140** 43 25N 0 57W
Sauz de Abajo **105** 24 42N 104 27W
Sauz de los Márquez **105** 22 7N 103 8W
Sauzé-Vaussais **140** 46 8N 0 8 E
Savá, Hond. **112** 15 32N 86 15W
Sava, Yugoslavia **163** 40 28N 17 32 E
Sava → **163** 44 50N 20 26 E
Savage I. = Niue I. **225** 19 2 S 169 54W
Savalou **247** 7 57N 1 58 E
Savane **251** 19 37 S 35 8 E
Savanna la Mar **112** 18 10N 78 10W
Savannakhet **204** 16 30N 104 49 E
Savant L. **86** 50 16N 90 44W
Savant Lake **86** 50 14N 90 40W
Savantvadi **201** 15 55N 73 54 E
Savanur **201** 14 59N 75 21 E
Savda **198** 21 9N 75 56 E
Savé **247** 8 2N 2 29 E
Save → **140** 43 47N 1 17 E
Sāveh **193** 35 2N 50 20 E
Savelugu **247** 9 38N 0 54W
Savenay **138** 47 20N 1 55W
Saverdun **140** 43 14N 1 34 E
Saverne **139** 48 39N 7 20 E
Savièse **148** 46 17N 7 22 E
Savigliano **162** 44 39N 7 40 E
Savigny-sur-Braye **138** 47 53N 0 49 E
Saviñao **154** 42 35N 7 38W
Savio → **163** 44 19N 12 20 E
Šavnik **166** 42 59N 19 10 E
Savognin **149** 46 36N 9 37 E
Savoie □ **141** 45 26N 6 35 E
Savona, Canada **93** 50 45N 120 50W
Savona, Italy **162** 44 19N 8 29 E
Savonlinna **176** 61 52N 28 53 E
Sävsjö **173** 57 20N 14 40 E
Sävsjøström **173** 57 1N 15 25 E
Savusavu **226** 16 34 S 179 15 E
Savusavu B. **226** 16 45 S 179 15 E
Sawahlunto **208** 0 40 S 100 52 E
Sawai **207** 3 0 S 129 5 E
Sawai Madhopur **198** 26 0N 76 25 E
Sawang Daen Din **204** 17 28N 103 28 E
Sawankhalok **204** 17 19N 99 50 E
Sawara **221** 35 55N 140 30 E
Sawdā, Jabal as **241** 28 51N 15 12 E
Sawel, Mt. **135** 54 48N 7 5W
Sawfajjin, W. → **241** 31 46N 14 30 E
Sawi **205** 10 14N 99 5 E
Sawmills **251** 19 30 S 28 2 E
Şawqirah **195** 18 7N 56 32 E
Sawqirah, Ghubbat **195** 18 35N 57 0 E
Sawu **207** 10 35 S 121 50 E
Sawu Sea **207** 9 30 S 121 50 E
Sawyerville **83** 45 20N 71 34W
Saxby → **230** 18 25 S 140 53 E
Saxon **148** 46 9N 7 11 E
Saxony, Lower = Niedersachsen □ **146** 52 45N 9 0 E
Say **247** 13 8N 2 22 E
Saya **247** 9 30N 3 18 E
Sayabec **80** 48 35N 67 41W
Sayaboury **204** 19 15N 101 45 E
Sayán **122** 11 8 S 77 12W
Sayan, Vostochnyy **185** 54 0N 96 0 E
Sayan, Zapadnyy **185** 52 30N 94 0 E
Sayasan **181** 42 56N 46 15 E
Saydā **190** 33 35N 35 25 E
Sayghān **197** 35 10N 67 55 E
Sayhan-Ovoo **214** 45 27N 103 54 E
Sayhandulaan **214** 44 40N 109 1 E
Sayḥut **195** 15 12N 51 10 E
Saynshand **214** 44 55N 110 11 E
Sayō **220** 34 59N 134 22 E
Sayula, Jalisco, Mexico **106** 19 52N 103 36W
Sayula, Sonora, Mexico **100** 29 22N 111 33W
Sayula, L. de **106** 20 3N 103 31W
Sayula de Alemán **109** 17 52N 94 57W
Saywūn **195** 15 56N 48 47 E
Sazan **168** 40 30N 19 20 E
Sázava → **150** 49 53N 14 24 E
Sazin **199** 35 35N 73 30 E
Sazlika → **167** 41 59N 25 50 E
Sbeïtla **241** 35 12N 9 7 E
Scaër **138** 48 2N 3 42W
Scafell Pikes **132** 54 26N 3 14W
Scalea **165** 39 49N 15 47 E
Scalpay **134** 57 51N 6 40W
Scandia **91** 50 20N 112 0W
Scandiano **162** 44 36N 10 40 E
Scandinavia **130** 64 0N 12 0 E
Scansano **163** 42 40N 11 20 E
Scapa Flow **134** 58 52N 3 6W
Scarborough, Trin. & Tob. **113** 11 11N 60 42W
Scarborough, U.K. **132** 54 17N 0 24W
Scargill **235** 42 56 S 172 58 E
Scarpe → **139** 50 31N 3 27 E
Scarsdale **232** 37 41 S 143 39 E
Şcatarie I. **81** 46 0N 59 44W
Sćedro **163** 43 6N 16 43 E
Sceptre **88** 50 51N 109 15W
Schaal See **146** 53 40N 10 57 E
Schaan **149** 47 10N 9 31 E
Schaesberg **143** 50 54N 6 0 E
Schaffen **143** 51 0N 5 5 E
Schaffhausen **149** 47 42N 8 39 E
Schaffhausen □ **149** 47 42N 8 36 E
Schagen **142** 52 49N 4 48 E
Schaijk **142** 51 44N 5 38 E
Schalkhaar **142** 52 17N 6 12 E
Schalkwijk **142** 52 0N 5 11 E
Schangnau **148** 46 50N 7 47 E
Schänis **149** 47 10N 9 3 E
Schärding **150** 48 27N 13 27 E
Scharhörn **146** 53 58N 8 24 E
Scharnitz **150** 47 23N 11 15 E
Scheessel **146** 53 10N 9 33 E
Schefferville **78** 54 48N 66 50W
Scheibbs **150** 48 1N 15 9 E
Schelde → **143** 51 15N 4 16 E
Scherfede **146** 51 32N 9 2 E
Scherpenheuvel **143** 50 58N 4 58 E
Scherpenisse **143** 51 33N 4 6 E
Scherpenzeel **142** 52 5N 5 30 E
Schesaplana **149** 47 5N 9 43 E
Schesslitz **147** 49 59N 11 2 E
Scheveningen **142** 52 6N 4 16 E
Schiedam **142** 51 55N 4 25 E
Schiermonnikoog **142** 53 30N 6 15 E
Schiers **149** 46 58N 9 41 E
Schifferstadt **147** 49 22N 8 23 E
Schifflange **143** 49 30N 6 1 E
Schijndel **143** 51 37N 5 27 E
Schiltigheim **139** 48 35N 7 45 E
Schio **163** 45 42N 11 21 E
Schipbeek **142** 52 14N 6 10 E
Schipluiden **142** 51 59N 4 19 E
Schirmeck **139** 48 29N 7 12 E
Schladming **150** 47 23N 13 41 E
Schlei → **146** 54 45N 9 52 E
Schleiden **146** 50 32N 6 26 E
Schleiz **146** 50 35N 11 49 E
Schleswig **146** 54 32N 9 34 E
Schleswig-Holstein □ **146** 54 10N 9 40 E
Schlieren **149** 47 26N 8 27 E
Schlüchtern **147** 50 20N 9 32 E
Schmalkalden **146** 50 43N 10 28 E
Schmölin **146** 50 54N 12 22 E
Schmölln **146** 53 15N 14 6 E
Schneeberg, Austria **150** 47 47N 15 48 E
Schneeberg, Germany **146** 50 35N 12 39 E
Schoenberg **143** 50 17N 6 16 E
Schönberg, Rostock, Germany **146** 53 50N 10 55 E
Schönberg, Schleswig-Holstein, Germany **146** 54 23N 10 20 E
Schönebeck **146** 52 2N 11 42 E
Schönenwerd **148** 47 23N 8 0 E
Schongau **147** 47 49N 10 54 E
Schöningen **146** 52 8N 10 57 E
Schoondijke **143** 51 21N 3 33 E
Schoonebeek **142** 52 39N 6 52 E
Schoonhoven **142** 51 57N 4 51 E
Schoorl **142** 52 42N 4 42 E
Schortens **146** 53 37N 7 51 E
Schoten **143** 51 16N 4 30 E
Schouten I. **230** 42 20 S 148 20 E
Schouwen **143** 51 43N 3 45 E
Schramberg **147** 48 12N 8 24 E
Schrankogl **150** 47 3N 11 7 E
Schreckhorn **148** 46 36N 8 7 E
Schreiber **87** 48 45N 87 20W
Schrobenhausen **147** 48 33N 11 16 E

Schruns **150** 47 5N 9 56 E
Schuler **91** 50 20N 110 6W
Schuls **149** 46 48N 10 18 E
Schumacher **87** 48 30N 81 16W
Schüpfen **148** 47 2N 7 24 E
Schüpfheim **148** 46 57N 8 2 E
Schwabach **147** 49 19N 11 3 E
Schwäbisch Gmünd **147** 48 49N 9 48 E
Schwäbisch Hall **147** 49 7N 9 45 E
Schwäbische Alb **147** 48 30N 9 30 E
Schwabmünchen **147** 48 11N 10 45 E
Schwanden **149** 46 58N 9 5 E
Schwandorf **147** 49 20N 12 7 E
Schwarmstedt **146** 52 41N 9 37 E
Schwarzach → **150** 46 56N 12 35 E
Schwärze **146** 52 50N 13 49 E
Schwarzenberg **146** 50 31N 12 49 E
Schwarzenburg **148** 46 49N 7 20 E
Schwarzwald **147** 48 0N 8 0 E
Schwaz **150** 47 20N 11 44 E
Schwedt **146** 53 4N 14 18 E
Schweinfurt **147** 50 3N 10 12 E
Schweizer Mittelland **148** 47 0N 7 15 E
Schweizer Reneke **254** 27 11 S 25 18 E
Schwerin **146** 53 37N 11 22 E
Schwerin □ **146** 53 35N 11 20 E
Schweriner See **146** 53 45N 11 26 E
Schwetzingen **147** 49 22N 8 35 E
Schwyz **149** 47 2N 8 39 E
Schwyz □ **149** 47 2N 8 39 E
Sciacca **164** 37 30N 13 3 E
Sciao **256** 3 26N 45 21 E
Scicli **165** 36 48N 14 41 E
Scie, La **79** 49 57N 55 36W
Scilla **165** 38 18N 15 44 E
Scilly, Isles of **133** 49 55N 6 15W
Ścinawa **152** 51 25N 16 26 E
Scione **168** 39 57N 23 36 E
Scone, Australia **231** 32 5 S 150 52 E
Scone, U.K. **134** 56 25N 3 26W
Scordia **165** 37 19N 14 50 E
Scoresbysund **12** 70 20N 23 0W
Scorno, Punta dello **164** 41 7N 8 23 E
Scotia Sea **13** 56 5 S 56 0W
Scotland **84** 43 1N 80 22W
Scotland □ **134** 57 0N 4 0W
Scotstown **83** 45 32N 71 17W
Scott, Antarct. **13** 77 0 S 165 0 E
Scott, Canada **88** 52 22N 108 50W
Scott, C. **228** 13 30 S 129 49 E
Scott Chan. **92** 50 45N 128 30W
Scott Glacier **13** 66 15 S 100 5 E
Scott I. **13** 67 0 S 179 0 E
Scott Inlet **95** 71 0N 71 0W
Scott Is. **92** 50 48N 128 40W
Scott-Jonction **83** 46 30N 71 4W
Scott L. **77** 59 55N 106 18W
Scott Reef **228** 14 0 S 121 50 E
Scottburgh **255** 30 15 S 30 47 E
Scottsdale **230** 41 9 S 147 31 E
Scugog, L. **85** 44 10N 78 55W
Scunthorpe **132** 53 35N 0 38W
Scuol **149** 46 48N 10 17 E
Scusciuban **256** 10 18N 50 12 E
Scutari = Üsküdar **177** 41 0N 29 5 E
Seabra **121** 12 25 S 41 46W
Seabrook, L. **229** 30 55 S 119 40 E
Seaford **233** 38 10 S 145 11 E
Seaforth **84** 43 35N 81 25W
Seager Wheeler L. **88** 54 17N 103 31W
Seahorse L. **80** 52 12N 65 48W
Seal → **77** 58 50N 97 30W
Seal Cove, N.B., Canada **81** 44 39N 66 51W
Seal Cove, Newf., Canada **79** 47 29N 56 4W
Seal Cove, Newf., Canada **79** 49 57N 56 22W
Seal L. **78** 54 20N 61 30W
Searchmont **87** 46 47N 84 3W
Seaspray **231** 38 25 S 147 15 E
Seaview Ra. **230** 18 40 S 145 45 E
Seaward Kaikouras, Mts. **235** 42 10 S 173 44 E
Seba Beach **90** 53 35N 114 47W
Sebangka **208** 0 7N 104 36 E
Sebastián Vizcaíno, B. **99** 28 0N 114 30W
Sebastopol = Sevastopol **180** 44 35N 33 30 E
Sebderat **245** 15 26N 36 42 E
Sebdou **241** 34 38N 1 19W
Sebeş **170** 45 58N 23 34 E
Sebeşului, Munţii **170** 45 36N 23 40 E
Sebezh **178** 56 14N 28 22 E
Sébi **246** 15 50N 4 12W
Şebinkarahisar **180** 40 22N 38 28 E
Sebiş **170** 46 23N 22 13 E
Sebkhet Te-n-Dghâmcha **246** 18 30N 15 55W
Sebkra Azzel Mati **240** 26 10N 0 43 E
Sebkra Mekerghene **240** 26 21N 1 30 E
Seblat **208** 3 14 S 101 38 E
Sebnitz **146** 50 58N 14 17 E
Sebou, Oued → **240** 34 16N 6 40W
Sebringville **84** 43 24N 81 4W
Sebta = Ceuta **240** 35 52N 5 18W
Sebuku **209** 3 30 S 116 25 E
Sebuku, Teluk **206** 4 0N 118 10 E
Sečanj **166** 45 25N 20 47 E
Secchia → **162** 44 4N 11 0 E
Sechelt **92** 49 25N 123 42W
Sechura **122** 5 39 S 80 50W
Sechura, Desierto de **122** 6 0 S 80 30W
Seclin **139** 50 33N 3 2 E
Secondigny **138** 46 37N 0 26W
Sečovce **151** 48 42N 21 40 E
Secretary I. **235** 45 15 S 166 56 E
Secunderabad **200** 17 28N 78 30 E
Sécure → **123** 15 10 S 64 52W
Sedan, Australia **232** 34 34 S 139 19 E
Sedan, France **139** 49 43N 4 57 E
Sedano **156** 42 43N 3 49W
Seddon **235** 41 40 S 174 7 E
Seddonville **235** 41 33 S 172 1 E
Sede Ya'aqov **189** 32 43N 35 7 E
Sedeh, Fārs, Iran **193** 30 45N 52 11 E
Sedeh, Khorāsān, Iran **193** 33 20N 59 14 E
Sederot **191** 31 32N 34 37 E
Sedgewick **91** 52 48N 111 41W
Sedhiou **246** 12 44N 15 30W
Sedičany **150** 49 40N 14 25 E
Sedico **163** 46 8N 12 6 E
Sedienie **167** 42 16N 24 33 E
Sedley **88** 50 10N 104 0W
Sedom **189** 31 5N 35 20 E
Sedova, Pik **184** 73 29N 54 58 E
Sedrata **241** 36 7N 7 31 E
Sedrun **149** 46 36N 8 47 E
Seduva **178** 55 45N 23 45 E
Sedziszów Małapolski **152** 50 5N 21 45 E
Seebad Ahlbeck **146** 53 56N 14 10 E
Seefeld **150** 47 19N 11 13 E
Seehausen **146** 52 52N 11 43 E
Seeheim **254** 26 50 S 17 45 E
Seekoe → **254** 30 18 S 25 1 E
Seelaw **146** 52 32N 14 22 E
Seeley's Bay **85** 44 29N 76 14W
Se'elim, Nahal **189** 31 21N 35 24 E
Sées **138** 48 38N 0 10 E
Seesen **146** 51 53N 10 10 E
Sefadu **246** 8 35N 10 58W
Séfeto **246** 14 8N 9 49W
Sefrou **240** 33 52N 4 52W
Sefton **235** 43 15 S 172 41 E
Sefuri-San **220** 33 28N 130 18 E
Sefwi Bekwai **246** 6 10N 2 25W
Seg-ozero **178** 63 0N 33 10 E
Segag **256** 7 39N 42 50 E
Segamat **205** 2 30N 102 50 E
Segarcea **170** 44 6N 23 43 E
Segbwema **246** 8 0N 11 0W
Seget **207** 1 24 S 130 58 E
Segezha **176** 63 44N 34 19 E
Seggueur, O. → **241** 32 4N 2 4 E
Segid **245** 16 55N 42 0 E
Segonzac **140** 45 36N 0 14W
Segorbe **156** 39 50N 0 30W
Ségou **246** 13 30N 6 16W
Segovia = Coco → **112** 15 0N 83 8W
Segovia, Colombia **118** 7 7N 74 42W
Segovia, Spain **154** 40 57N 4 10W
Segovia □ **154** 40 55N 4 10W
Segré **138** 47 40N 0 52W
Segre → **156** 41 40N 0 43 E
Séguéla **246** 7 55N 6 40W
Seguín **102** 25 27N 101 43W
Segundo → **124** 30 53 S 62 44W
Segura → **157** 38 6N 0 54W
Segura, Sierra de **157** 38 5N 2 45W
Seh Qal'eh **193** 33 40N 58 24 E
Sehitwa **254** 20 30 S 22 30 E
Sehore **198** 23 10N 77 5 E
Sehwan **197** 26 28N 67 53 E
Şeica Mare **170** 46 1N 24 7 E
Seikpyu **202** 20 54N 94 48 E
Seille →, Moselle, France **139** 49 7N 6 11 E
Seille →, Saône-et-Loire, France **141** 46 31N 4 57 E
Seilles **143** 50 30N 5 6 E
Sein, Î. de **138** 48 2N 4 52W
Seine → **138** 49 26N 0 26 E
Seine, B. de la **138** 49 40N 0 40W
Seine-et-Marne □ **139** 48 45N 3 0 E
Seine-Maritime □ **138** 49 40N 1 0 E
Seine-Saint-Denis □ **139** 48 58N 2 24 E
Seini **170** 47 44N 23 21 E
Seistan **193** 30 50N 61 0 E
Sejerø **172** 55 54N 11 9 E
Sejerø Bugt **172** 55 53N 11 15 E
Sejny **152** 54 6N 23 21 E
Seka **245** 8 10N 36 52 E
Sekayu **208** 2 51 S 103 51 E
Seke **250** 3 20 S 33 31 E
Seke-Banza **253** 5 20 S 13 16 E
Sekenke **250** 4 18 S 34 11 E
Seki **221** 35 29N 136 55 E
Sekigahara **221** 35 22N 136 28 E
Sekken Veøy **171** 62 45N 7 30 E
Sekondi-Takoradi **246** 4 58N 1 45W
Sekuma **254** 24 36 S 23 50 E
Selama **205** 5 12N 100 42 E
Selárgius **164** 39 14N 9 14 E
Selaru **207** 8 9 S 131 0 E
Selb **147** 50 9N 12 9 E
Selby **132** 53 47N 1 5W
Selca **163** 43 20N 16 50 E
Sele → **165** 40 27N 14 58 E
Selemdzha → **185** 51 42N 128 53 E
Selenge **252** 1 58 S 18 11 E
Selenge → **174** 49 25N 103 59 E
Selenica **168** 40 33N 19 39 E
Selenter See **146** 54 19N 10 26 E
Sélestat **139** 48 10N 7 26 E
Seletan, Tg. **209** 4 10 S 114 40 E
Seletin **170** 47 50N 25 12 E
Selevac **166** 44 28N 20 52 E
Sélibabi **246** 15 10N 12 15W
Seliger, Oz. **178** 57 15N 33 0 E
Şelim **181** 40 30N 42 46 E
Selîma, El Wâhât el **244** 21 22N 29 19 E
Selinda Spillway **254** 18 35 S 23 10 E
Selinoús **169** 37 35N 21 37 E
Selizharovo **178** 56 51N 33 27 E
Selje **171** 62 3N 5 22 E
Seljord **171** 59 30N 8 40 E
Selkirk, Man., Canada **89** 50 10N 96 55W
Selkirk, Ont., Canada **84** 42 49N 79 56W
Selkirk, U.K. **134** 55 33N 2 50W
Selkirk I. **89** 53 20N 99 6W
Selkirk Mts. **76** 51 15N 117 40W
Selles-sur-Cher **139** 47 16N 1 33 E
Sellières **139** 46 50N 5 32 E
Sellye **151** 45 52N 17 51 E
Selo **168** 41 10N 25 53 E
Selong **209** 8 39 S 116 32 E
Selongey **139** 47 36N 5 10 E
Selowandoma Falls **251** 21 15 S 31 50 E
Selpele **207** 0 1 S 130 5 E
Selsey Bill **133** 50 44N 0 47W
Seltz **139** 48 48N 8 4 E
Selu **207** 7 32 S 130 55 E
Sélune → **138** 48 38N 1 22W
Selva, Argentina **124** 29 50 S 62 0W
Selva, Italy **163** 46 33N 11 46 E
Selva, Spain **156** 41 13N 1 8 E
Selva, La **156** 42 0N 2 45 E
Selvas **122** 6 30 S 67 0W
Selwyn **230** 21 32 S 140 30 E
Selwyn L. **77** 60 0N 104 30W
Selwyn Ra. **230** 21 10 S 140 0 E
Seman → **168** 40 45N 19 50 E
Semans **88** 51 25N 104 44W
Semara **240** 26 48N 11 41W
Semarang **209** 7 0 S 110 26 E
Semau **207** 10 13 S 123 22 E
Sembabule **250** 0 4 S 31 25 E
Sembé **252** 1 39N 14 36 E
Sémé **246** 15 4N 13 41W
Semeih **245** 12 43N 30 53 E
Semenov **179** 56 43N 44 30 E
Semenovka, Ukraine S.S.R., U.S.S.R. **178** 52 8N 32 36 E
Semenovka, Ukraine S.S.R., U.S.S.R. **180** 49 37N 33 10 E
Semeru **209** 8 4 S 112 55 E
Semiluki **179** 51 41N 39 2 E
Semiozernoye **182** 52 22N 64 8 E
Semipalatinsk **184** 50 30N 80 10 E
Semirara I. **210** 12 4N 121 23 E
Semirara Is. **211** 12 0N 121 20 E
Semitau **209** 0 29N 111 57 E
Semiyarskoye **184** 50 55N 78 23 E
Semmering Pass **150** 47 41N 15 45 E
Semnān **193** 35 55N 53 25 E
Semnān □ **193** 36 0N 54 0 E
Semois → **143** 49 53N 4 44 E
Semporna **207** 4 30N 118 33 E
Semuda **209** 2 51 S 112 58 E
Semur-en-Auxois **139** 47 30N 4 20 E
Sena, Bolivia **122** 11 32 S 67 11W
Senā, Iran **193** 28 27N 51 36 E
Sena, Mozam. **251** 17 25 S 35 0 E
Sena → **122** 11 31 S 67 11W
Sena Madureira **122** 9 5 S 68 45W
Senador Pompeu **120** 5 40 S 39 20W
Senaja **206** 6 45N 117 3 E
Senanga **254** 16 2 S 23 14 E
Sendafa **245** 9 11N 39 3 E
Sendai, Kagoshima, Japan **220** 31 50N 130 20 E
Sendai, Miyagi, Japan **218** 38 15N 140 53 E
Sendai-Wan **218** 38 15N 141 0 E
Sendamangalam **201** 11 17N 78 17 E
Sendenhorst **146** 51 50N 7 49 E
Sendurjana **198** 21 32N 78 17 E
Senec **151** 48 12N 17 23 E
Sénécal, L. **80** 52 5N 63 20W
Senecu **101** 31 43N 106 23W
Seneffe **143** 50 32N 4 16 E
Senegal ■ **246** 14 30N 14 30W
Senegal → **246** 15 48N 16 32W
Senegambia **236** 12 45N 12 0W
Senekal **255** 28 30 S 27 36 E
Senftenberg **146** 51 30N 14 1 E
Senga Hill **251** 9 19 S 31 11 E
Senge Khambab = Indus → **197** 24 20N 67 47 E
Sengerema □ **250** 2 10 S 32 20 E
Sengiley **179** 53 58N 48 46 E
Sengkang **207** 4 8 S 120 1 E
Sengua → **251** 17 7 S 28 5 E
Senguerr → **126** 45 35 S 68 50W
Sénguio **107** 19 44N 100 21W
Senhor-do-Bonfim **120** 10 30 S 40 10W
Senica **151** 48 41N 17 25 E
Senigállia **163** 43 42N 13 12 E
Seniku **202** 25 32N 97 48 E
Senio → **163** 44 35N 12 15 E
Senise **164** 40 6N 16 15 E
Senj **163** 45 0N 14 58 E
Senja **174** 69 25N 17 30 E
Senlis **139** 49 13N 2 35 E
Senmonorom **204** 12 27N 107 12 E
Sennâr **245** 13 30N 33 35 E
Senne → **143** 50 42N 4 13 E
Senneterre **82** 48 25N 77 15W
Senniquelle **246** 7 19N 8 38W
Senno **178** 54 45N 29 43 E
Sennori **164** 40 49N 8 36 E
Seno **204** 16 35N 104 50 E
Senonches **138** 48 34N 1 2 E
Senorbì **164** 39 33N 9 8 E
Senožeče **163** 45 43N 14 3 E
Sens **139** 48 11N 3 15 E
Senta **166** 45 55N 20 3 E
Sentein **140** 42 53N 0 58 E
Sentery **250** 5 17 S 25 42 E
Sentier, Le **148** 46 37N 6 15 E
Sentispac **104** 21 49N 105 21W
Sento Sé **120** 9 40 S 41 18W
Sentolo **209** 7 55 S 110 13 E
Senya Beraku **247** 5 28N 0 31W
Senye **252** 1 34N 9 50 E
Seo de Urgel **156** 42 22N 1 23 E
Seohara **199** 29 15N 78 33 E
Seoni **199** 22 5N 79 30 E
Seoriuarayan **199** 21 45N 82 34 E
Seoul = Sŏul **215** 37 31N 126 58 E
Separation Point **78** 53 37N 57 25W
Sepīdān **193** 30 20N 52 5 E
Sepik → **227** 3 49 S 144 30 E
Sepo-ri **215** 38 57N 127 25 E
Sępólno Krajeńskie **152** 53 26N 17 30 E
Sepone **204** 16 45N 106 13 E
Sepopol **152** 54 16N 21 2 E
Sept-Îles **78** 50 13N 66 22W
Septemvri **167** 42 13N 24 6 E
Sepúlveda **154** 41 18N 3 45W
Sequart L. **80** 52 26N 63 47W
Sequeros **154** 40 31N 6 2W
Serafimovich **181** 49 36N 42 43 E
Seraing **143** 50 35N 5 32 E
Seraja **205** 2 41N 108 35 E
Seram **207** 3 10 S 129 0 E
Seram Laut, Kepulauan **207** 4 5 S 131 25 E
Seram Sea **207** 2 30 S 128 30 E
Serang **207** 6 8 S 106 10 E
Serasan **205** 2 29N 109 4 E
Seravezza **162** 43 59N 10 13 E
Serbâl, G. **191** 28 40N 33 39 E
Serbia = Srbija □ **166** 43 30N 21 0 E
Sercaia **170** 45 49N 25 9 E
Serdo **245** 11 56N 41 14 E
Serdobsk **179** 52 28N 44 10 E
Seredka **178** 58 12N 28 10 E
Seregno **162** 45 40N 9 12 E
Seremban **205** 2 43N 101 53 E
Serena, La, Chile **124** 29 55 S 71 10W
Serena, La, Spain **155** 38 45N 5 40W
Serengeti □ **250** 2 0 S 34 30 E
Serengeti Plain **250** 2 40 S 35 0 E
Sereth = Siret → **170** 47 58N 26 5 E
Sergach **179** 55 30N 45 30 E
Serge → **156** 41 54N 0 50 E
Sergino **184** 62 30N 65 38 E
Sergipe □ **120** 10 30 S 37 30W
Seria **206** 4 37N 114 23 E
Serian **206** 1 10N 110 31 E
Seriate **162** 45 42N 9 43 E
Seribu, Kepulauan **208** 5 36 S 106 33 E
Sérifontaine **139** 49 20N 1 45 E
Sérifos **169** 37 9N 24 30 E
Sérignan **140** 43 17N 3 17 E
Sérigny → **78** 56 47N 66 0W
Serik **190** 36 55N 31 7 E

Seringapatam Reef . **228** 13 38 S 122 5 E
Sermaize-les-Bains . . **139** 48 47N 4 54 E
Sermata . . . . **207** 8 15 S 128 50 E
Sérmide . . . . **163** 45 0N 11 17 E
Sernovodsk . . . . **182** 53 54N 51 16 E
Serny Zavod . . . . **184** 39 59N 58 50 E
Serock . . . . **152** 52 31N 21 4 E
Serón **157** 37 20N 2 29W
Serós . . . . **156** 41 27N 0 24 E
Serov . . . . **182** 59 29N 60 35 E
Serowe . . . . **254** 22 25 S 26 43 E
Serpa . . . . **155** 37 57N 7 38 E
Serpeddi, Punta . . . . **164** 39 19N 9 18 E
Serpentara . . . . **164** 39 8N 9 38 E
Serpentine . . . . **229** 32 23 S 115 58 E
Serpentine Lakes . . . **229** 28 30 S 129 10 E
Serpis → **157** 38 59N 0 9W
Serpukhov . . . . **179** 54 55N 37 28 E
Serra do Navio **119** 0 59N 52 3W
Serra San Bruno . . . **165** 38 31N 16 23 E
Serra Talhada . . . . . . **120** 7 59 S 38 18W
Serracapriola . . . . . . **165** 41 47N 15 12 E
Serradilla **154** 39 50N 6 9W
Sérrai . . . . **168** 41 5N 23 31 E
Sérrai □ . . . . **168** 41 5N 23 37 E
Serrakhis → . . . . . **190** 35 13N 32 55 E
Serramanna . . . . **164** 39 26N 8 56 E
Serrat, C. . . . . **241** 37 14N 9 10 E
Serre-Poncon,
Barrage de . . . . . . **141** 44 22N 6 20 E
Serres . . . . **141** 44 26N 5 43 E
Serrezuela . . . . **124** 30 40 S 65 20W
Serrinha . . . . **121** 11 39 S 39 0W
Serrita . . . . **120** 7 56 S 39 19W
Sersale . . . . **165** 39 1N 16 44 E
Sertã **154** 39 48N 8 6W
Sertânia . . . . **120** 8 5 S 37 20W
Sertanópolis . . . . **125** 23 4 S 51 2W
Sêrtar . . . . **216** 32 20N 100 41 E
Sertig . . . . **149** 46 44N 9 52 E
Serua . . . . **207** 6 18 S 130 1 E
Serui . . . . **207** 1 53 S 136 10 E
Serule . . . . **254** 21 57 S 27 20 E
Sérvia . . . . **168** 40 9N 21 58 E
Sesayap → . . . . **209** 3 36N 117 15 E
Sese Is. . . . . **250** 0 20 S 32 20 E
Sesepe . . . . **207** 1 30 S 127 59 E
Sesfontein . . . . **254** 19 7 S 13 39 E
Sesheke . . . . **254** 17 29 S 24 13 E
Sesia → . . . . **162** 45 5N 8 37 E
Sesimbra **155** 38 28N 9 6W
Sessa . . . . **253** 13 56 S 20 38 E
Sessa Aurunca . . . . . **164** 41 14N 13 55 E
Sestao **156** 43 18N 3 0W
Sesto S. Giovanni . . **162** 45 32N 9 14 E
Sestos . . . . **168** 40 16N 26 23 E
Sestri Levante . . . . . **162** 44 17N 9 22 E
Sestrières . . . . **162** 44 58N 6 56 E
Sestrunj . . . . **163** 44 10N 15 0 E
Sestu . . . . **164** 39 18N 9 6 E
Sesvenna . . . . **149** 46 42N 10 25 E
Setaka . . . . **220** 33 9N 130 28 E
Setana . . . . **218** 42 26N 139 51 E
Sète . . . . **140** 43 25N 3 42 E
Sete Lagôas . . . . **121** 19 27 S 44 16W
Sétif . . . . **241** 36 9N 5 26 E
Seto . . . . **221** 35 14N 137 6 E
Seton L. **93** 50 42N 122 8W
Seton Portage **93** 50 42N 122 17W
Setonaikai . . . . **220** 34 20N 133 30 E
Setsan . . . . **202** 16 3N 95 23 E
Settat **240** 33 0N 7 40W
Setté-Cama . . . . **252** 2 32 S 9 45 E
Séttimo Tor . . . . **162** 45 9N 7 46 E
Setting L. **77** 55 0N 98 38W
Settle **132** 54 5N 2 18W
Setto Calende . . . . . . **162** 45 44N 8 37 E
Setúbal **155** 38 30N 8 58W
Setúbal □ **155** 38 25N 8 35W
Setúbal, B. de **155** 38 40N 8 56W
Seugne → **140** 45 42N 0 32W
Seul, Lac-Rés. **86** 50 25N 92 30W
Seulimeum . . . . **208** 5 27N 95 15 E
Seuzach . . . . **149** 47 32N 8 49 E
Sevan . . . . **181** 40 33N 44 56 E
Sevan, Ozero . . . . . . **181** 40 30N 45 20 E
Sevastopol . . . . **180** 44 35N 33 30 E
Sevelen . . . . **149** 47 7N 9 30 E
Seven Emu . . . . **230** 16 20 S 137 8 E
Seven Islands B. **78** 59 25N 63 45W
Seven Sisters **76** 54 56N 128 10W
Seven Sisters Falls . . **89** 50 7N 96 2W
Seventy Mile House **93** 51 18N 121 23W
Sevenum . . . . **143** 51 25N 6 2 E
Sever → **155** 39 40N 7 32W
Sévérac-le-Château . **140** 44 20N 3 5 E
Severn →, Canada . **74** 56 2N 87 36W
Severn →, U.K. . . . **133** 51 35N 2 38W
Severn L. **74** 53 54N 90 48W
Severnaya Zemlya . . **185** 79 0N 100 0 E
Severnyye Uvaly . . . **176** 58 0N 48 0 E
Severo-Kurilsk . . . . . **185** 50 40N 156 8 E
Severo-Yeniseyskiy . **185** 60 22N 93 1 E
Severočeský □ . . . . . **150** 50 30N 14 0 E
Severodinsk . . . . **176** 64 27N 39 58 E
Severodonetsk . . . . . **181** 48 58N 38 30 E
Severomoravský □ . **151** 49 38N 17 40 E
Severomorsk . . . . **176** 69 5N 33 27 E
Severouralsk . . . . **182** 60 9N 59 57 E
Sevilla, Colombia . . . **118** 4 16N 75 57W
Sevilla, Spain **155** 37 23N 6 0W
Sevilla □ **155** 37 25N 5 30W
Seville = Sevilla **155** 37 23N 6 0W
Sevina **106** 19 38N 101 49W
Sevlievo . . . . **167** 43 2N 25 3 E
Sevnica . . . . **163** 46 2N 15 19 E
Sèvre-Nantaise → . **138** 47 12N 1 33W
Sèvre Niortaise → . **140** 46 18N 1 8W
Sevsk . . . . **178** 52 10N 34 30 E
Sewell, Canada **92** 53 47N 132 16W
Sewell, Chile . . . . **124** 34 10 S 70 23W
Sewer . . . . **207** 5 53 S 134 40 E
Sexbierum . . . . **142** 53 13N 5 29 E
Sexsmith **90** 55 21N 118 47W
Seybaplaya **111** 19 39N 90 40W
Seybaplaya, Pta. . . . **111** 19 39N 90 42W
Seychelles ■ . . . . **203** 5 0 S 56 0 E
Seyðisfjörður **174** 65 16N 14 0W
Seydvān . . . . **192** 38 34N 45 2 E
Seyé **111** 20 50N 89 22W
Seym → . . . . **178** 51 27N 32 34 E
Seymchan . . . . **185** 62 54N 152 30 E
Seymour . . . . **231** 37 0 S 145 10 E
Seymour Arm **93** 51 15N 118 57W
Seymour Inlet **92** 51 3N 127 0W
Seyne . . . . **141** 44 21N 6 22 E
Seyne-sur-Mer, La . . **141** 43 7N 5 52 E
Seyssel . . . . **141** 45 57N 5 50 E
Sežana . . . . **163** 45 43N 13 41 E
Sézanne . . . . **139** 48 40N 3 40 E
Sezze . . . . **164** 41 30N 13 3 E
Sfax . . . . **241** 34 49N 10 48 E
Sfîntu Gheorghe . . . . **170** 45 52N 25 48 E
Sha Xi → . . . . **217** 26 35N 118 0 E
Sha Xian . . . . **217** 26 23N 117 45 E
Shaanxi □ . . . . **214** 35 0N 109 0 E
Shaartuz . . . . **183** 37 16N 68 8 E
Shaba □ . . . . **250** 8 0 S 25 0 E
Shabla . . . . **167** 43 31N 28 32 E
Shabogamo L. **78** 53 15N 66 30W
Shabunda . . . . **250** 2 40 S 27 16 E
Shabuskwia L. **86** 51 15N 89 0W
Shabwah . . . . **194** 15 22N 47 1 E
Shache . . . . **212** 38 20N 77 10 E
Shackleton Ice Shelf **13** 66 0 S 100 0 E
Shackleton Inlet . . . . **13** 83 0 S 160 0 E
Shaddad . . . . **244** 21 25N 40 2 E
Shādegān . . . . **193** 30 40N 48 38 E
Shadi, China . . . . **217** 26 7N 114 47 E
Shadi, Kashmir . . . . . **199** 33 24N 77 14 E
Shadrinsk . . . . **182** 56 5N 63 32 E
Shādūf . . . . **190** 35 20N 37 25 E
Shaffa . . . . **247** 10 30N 12 6 E
Shaftesbury **133** 51 0N 2 12W
Shag Pt. . . . . **235** 45 29 S 170 52 E
Shagamu . . . . **247** 6 51N 3 39 E
Shagram . . . . **199** 36 24N 72 20 E
Shah Bunder . . . . **198** 24 13N 67 56 E
Shāh Jūy . . . . **197** 32 31N 67 25 E
Shahabad,
Andhra Pradesh,
India . . . . **200** 17 10N 76 54 E
Shahabad, Punjab,
India . . . . **198** 30 10N 76 55 E
Shahabad, Raj.,
India . . . . **198** 25 15N 77 11 E
Shahabad, Ut. P.,
India . . . . **199** 27 36N 79 56 E
Shahada . . . . **198** 21 33N 74 30 E
Shahadpur . . . . **198** 25 55N 68 35 E
Shahapur . . . . **201** 15 50N 74 34 E
Shahba . . . . **190** 32 52N 36 38 E
Shahdād . . . . **193** 30 30N 57 40 E
Shahdadkot . . . . **197** 27 50N 67 55 E
Shahe . . . . **214** 37 0N 114 32 E
Shahganj . . . . **199** 26 3N 82 44 E
Shaḩḩāt . . . . **242** 32 48N 21 54 E
Shahīdān . . . . **197** 36 42N 67 49 E
Shahjahanpur . . . . . . **199** 27 54N 79 57 E
Shahpur, Karnataka,
India . . . . **200** 16 40N 76 48 E
Shahpur, Mad. P.,
India . . . . **198** 22 12N 77 58 E
Shahpur, Pakistan . . **198** 28 46N 68 27 E
Shahpura . . . . **199** 23 10N 80 45 E
Shahr Kord . . . . **193** 32 15N 50 55 E
Shāhrakht . . . . **193** 33 38N 60 16 E
Shahrig . . . . **197** 30 15N 67 40 E
Shahukou . . . . **214** 40 20N 112 18 E
Shaibara . . . . **244** 25 26N 36 47 E
Shaikhabad . . . . **198** 34 2N 68 45 E
Shaim . . . . **182** 60 21N 64 10 E
Shajapur . . . . **198** 23 27N 76 21 E
Shakargarh . . . . **198** 32 17N 75 10 E
Shakawe . . . . **254** 18 28 S 21 49 E
Shakespeare I. **86** 49 38N 88 25W
Shakhristan . . . . **183** 39 47N 68 49 E
Shakhrisyabz . . . . **183** 39 3N 66 50 E
Shakhty . . . . **181** 47 40N 40 16 E
Shakhunya . . . . **179** 57 40N 46 46 E
Shaki . . . . **247** 8 41N 3 21 E
Shala, L. . . . . **245** 7 30N 38 30 E
Shalalth **93** 50 43N 122 13W
Shalkar Karashatau,
Ozero . . . . **182** 50 26N 61 12 E
Shalkar Yega Kara,
Ozero . . . . **182** 50 45N 60 54 E
Shallow Lake **84** 44 36N 81 5W
Shaluli Shan . . . . **216** 30 40N 99 55 E
Shalya . . . . **182** 57 17N 58 48 E
Shām . . . . **193** 26 39N 57 21 E
Sham, J. ash . . . . **195** 23 10N 57 5 E
Shamâl Dârfûr □ . . . **245** 15 0N 25 0 E
Shamâl Kordofân □ **245** 15 0N 30 0 E
Shamattawa **77** 55 51N 92 5W
Shamattawa → **74** 55 1N 85 23W
Shambe . . . . **245** 7 8N 30 46 E
Shambu . . . . **245** 9 32N 37 3 E
Shamgong Dzong . . . **202** 27 13N 90 35 E
Shamīl . . . . **193** 27 30N 56 55 E
Shamkhor . . . . **181** 40 50N 46 0 E
Shāmkūh . . . . **193** 35 47N 57 50 E
Shamli . . . . **198** 29 32N 77 18 E
Shamo = Gobi . . . . . **214** 44 0N 111 0 E
Shamo, L. . . . . **245** 5 45N 37 30 E
Shamrock **88** 50 10N 106 37W
Shan □ . . . . **202** 21 30N 98 30 E
Shan Xian . . . . **214** 34 50N 116 5 E
Shanan → . . . . **245** 8 0N 40 20 E
Shanchengzhen . . . . . **215** 42 20N 125 20 E
Shāndak . . . . **193** 28 28N 60 27 E
Shandong □ . . . . **215** 36 0N 118 0 E
Shandong Bandao . . **215** 37 0N 121 0 E
Shang Xian . . . . **214** 33 50N 109 58 E
Shangalowe . . . . **251** 10 50 S 26 30 E
Shangani → . . . . **251** 18 41 S 27 10 E
Shangbancheng . . . . . **215** 40 50N 118 1 E
Shangcai . . . . **217** 33 18N 114 14 E
Shangcheng . . . . **217** 31 47N 115 26 E
Shangchuan Dao . . . **217** 21 40N 112 50 E
Shangdu . . . . **214** 41 30N 113 30 E
Shanggao . . . . **217** 28 17N 114 55 E
Shanghai . . . . **217** 31 15N 121 26 E
Shanghang . . . . **217** 25 2N 116 23 E
Shanghe . . . . **215** 37 20N 117 10 E
Shangjin . . . . **217** 33 7N 110 3 E
Shanglin . . . . **216** 23 27N 108 33 E
Shangnan . . . . **214** 33 32N 110 50 E
Shangqiu . . . . **214** 34 26N 115 36 E
Shangrao . . . . **217** 28 25N 117 59 E
Shangshui . . . . **214** 33 42N 114 35 E
Shangsi . . . . **216** 22 8N 107 58 E
Shangyou . . . . **217** 25 48N 114 32 E
Shangzhi . . . . **215** 45 22N 127 56 E
Shanhetun . . . . **215** 44 33N 127 15 E
Shani . . . . **247** 10 14N 12 2 E
Shannon, Greenland **12** 75 10N 18 30W
Shannon, N.Z. . . . . . **234** 40 33 S 175 25 E
Shannon → **135** 52 35N 9 30W
Shannon L. **87** 49 48N 83 24W
Shansi = Shanxi □ . **214** 37 0N 112 0 E
Shantar, Ostrov
Bolshoy . . . . **185** 55 9N 137 40 E
Shantipur . . . . **199** 23 17N 88 25 E
Shantou . . . . **217** 23 18N 116 40 E
Shantung =
Shandong □ . . . . . . **215** 36 0N 118 0 E
Shanxi □ . . . . **214** 37 0N 112 0 E
Shanyang . . . . **214** 33 31N 109 55 E
Shanyin . . . . **214** 39 25N 112 56 E
Shaoguan . . . . **217** 24 48N 113 35 E
Shaowu . . . . **217** 27 22N 117 28 E
Shaoxing . . . . **217** 30 0N 120 35 E
Shaoyang, Hunan,
China . . . . **217** 26 59N 111 20 E
Shaoyang, Hunan,
China . . . . **217** 27 14N 111 25 E
Shapinsay **134** 59 2N 2 50W
Shaqrā', S. Yemen . **194** 13 22N 45 44 E
Shaqra', Si. Arabia . **192** 25 15N 45 16 E
Sharafa . . . . **245** 11 59N 27 7 E
Sharavati → . . . . . . **201** 14 20N 74 25 E
Sharbatāt, Ra's ash . **195** 17 56N 56 21 E
Sharbot Lake **85** 44 46N 76 41W
Shari . . . . **218** 43 55N 144 40 E
Sharjah = Ash
Shāriqah . . . . **195** 25 23N 55 26 E
Shark B. . . . . **229** 25 55 S 113 32 E
Sharm el Sheikh . . . . **191** 27 53N 34 18 E
Sharon, Plain of =
Hasharon . . . . **189** 32 12N 34 49 E
Sharp Pk. . . . . **211** 5 58N 125 31 E
Sharp Pt. . . . . **230** 10 58 S 142 43 E
Sharpe L. **77** 54 5N 93 40W
Sharq el Istiwa'iya □ **245** 5 0N 33 0 E
Sharya . . . . **179** 58 22N 45 20 E
Shasha . . . . **245** 6 29N 35 59 E
Shashemene . . . . **245** 7 13N 38 33 E
Shashi, Botswana . . . **255** 21 15 S 27 27 E
Shashi, China . . . . . . **217** 30 25N 112 14 E
Shashi → . . . . **251** 21 14 S 29 20 E
Shatsk . . . . **179** 54 0N 41 45 E
Shatura . . . . **179** 55 34N 39 31 E
Shaumyani . . . . **181** 41 22N 41 45 E
Shaunavon **88** 49 35N 108 25W
Shaw → . . . . **228** 20 21 S 119 17 E
Shaw I. . . . . **230** 20 30 S 149 2 E
Shawanaga **84** 45 31N 80 17W
Shawinigan **83** 46 35N 72 50W
Shawinigan Sud **83** 46 31N 72 45W
Shawville **82** 45 36N 76 30W
Shayib el Banat,
Gebel . . . . **244** 26 59N 33 29 E
Shaykh Sa'īd . . . . **192** 32 34N 46 17 E
Shaykh 'Uthmān . . . **194** 12 52N 44 59 E
Shaymak . . . . **183** 37 33N 74 50 E
Shchekino . . . . **179** 54 1N 37 34 E
Shcherbakov =
Andropov . . . . **179** 58 5N 38 50 E
Shchigri . . . . **179** 51 55N 36 58 E
Shchors . . . . **178** 51 48N 31 56 E
Shchuchiosk . . . . **184** 52 56N 70 12 E
Shchuchye . . . . **182** 55 12N 62 46 E
She Xian, Anhui,
China . . . . **217** 29 50N 118 25 E
She Xian, Hebei,
China . . . . **214** 36 30N 113 40 E
Shea **119** 2 48N 59 4W
Shebandowan **86** 48 38N 90 4W
Shebekino . . . . **179** 50 28N 36 54 E
Shebele, Wabi → . . **245** 2 0N 44 0 E
Shechem . . . . **189** 32 13N 35 21 E
Shediac **81** 46 14N 64 32W
Sheelin, Lough **135** 53 48N 7 20W
Sheep Haven **135** 55 12N 7 55W
Sheerness . . . . **133** 51 26N 0 47 E
Sheet Harbour **81** 44 56N 62 31W
Shefar'am . . . . **189** 32 48N 35 10 E
Sheffield **132** 53 23N 1 28W
Sheffield L. **79** 49 20N 56 34W
Shegaon . . . . **198** 20 48N 76 47 E
Sheguiandah **84** 45 54N 81 55W
Sheho **88** 51 35N 103 13W
Shehojele . . . . **245** 10 40N 35 9 E
Shehong . . . . **216** 30 54N 105 18 E
Shehuen → . . . . **126** 49 35 S 69 34W
Sheikhpura . . . . **199** 25 9N 85 53 E
Sheila **81** 47 29N 64 55W
Shek Hasan . . . . **245** 12 5N 35 58 E
Shekhupura . . . . **197** 31 42N 73 58 E
Sheki . . . . **181** 41 10N 47 5 E
Sheksna → . . . . **179** 59 0N 38 30 E
Shelburne, N.S.,
Canada **81** 43 47N 65 20W
Shelburne, Ont.,
Canada **84** 44 4N 80 15W
Shelburne B. . . . . **230** 11 50 S 142 50 E
Sheldrake **78** 50 20N 64 51W
Shelikhova, Zaliv . . . **185** 59 30N 157 0 E
Shell Lake **88** 53 19N 107 2W
Shell Lakes . . . . **229** 29 20 S 127 30 E
Shellbrook **88** 53 13N 106 24W
Shelley **93** 54 0N 122 37W
Shellharbour . . . . **231** 34 31 S 150 51 E
Shelling Rocks **135** 51 45N 10 35W
Shellmouth **89** 50 56N 101 29W
Shelon → . . . . **178** 58 10N 30 30 E
Shemakha . . . . **181** 40 38N 48 37 E
Shen Xian . . . . **214** 36 15N 115 40 E
Shenchi . . . . **214** 39 8N 112 10 E
Shencottah . . . . **201** 8 59N 77 18 E
Shendam . . . . **247** 8 49N 9 30 E
Shendî . . . . **245** 16 46N 33 22 E
Shendurni . . . . **200** 20 39N 75 36 E
Sheng Xian . . . . **217** 29 35N 120 50 E
Shengfang . . . . **214** 39 3N 116 42 E
Shëngjergji . . . . **168** 41 17N 20 10 E
Shëngjini . . . . **168** 41 50N 19 35 E
Shenjingzi . . . . **215** 44 40N 124 30 E
Shenmëria . . . . **168** 42 7N 20 13 E
Shenmu . . . . **214** 38 50N 110 29 E
Shennongjia . . . . **217** 31 43N 110 44 E
Shenqiu . . . . **214** 33 25N 115 5 E
Shenqiucheng . . . . . . **214** 33 24N 115 2 E
Shensi = Shaanxi □ **214** 35 0N 109 0 E
Shenyang . . . . **215** 41 48N 123 27 E
Shepetovka . . . . **178** 50 10N 27 10 E
Shephelah =
Hashefela . . . . **189** 31 30N 34 43 E
Shepparton . . . . **231** 36 23 S 145 26 E
Sheqi . . . . **214** 33 12N 112 57 E
Sher Khan Qala . . . . **198** 29 55N 66 20 E
Sher Qila . . . . **199** 36 7N 74 2 E
Sherada . . . . **245** 7 18N 36 30 E
Sherborne **133** 50 56N 2 31W
Sherbro I. **246** 7 30N 12 40W
Sherbrooke **83** 45 28N 71 57W
Sherda . . . . **241** 20 7N 16 46 E
Shereik . . . . **244** 18 44N 33 47 E
Sheridan L. **93** 51 31N 120 54W
Sherkot . . . . **199** 29 22N 78 35 E
Shërpūr, Afghan. . . . **197** 34 32N 69 10 E
Sherpur, Bangla. . . . . **202** 25 0N 90 0 E
Sherridon **77** 55 8N 101 5W
Sherwood Forest . . . **132** 53 5N 1 5W
Sherwood Park **90** 53 31N 113 19W

Sheslay **76** 58 17N 131 52W
Sheslay → **76** 58 48N 132 5W
Shethanei L. **77** 58 48N 97 50W
Shetland □ **134** 60 30N 1 30W
Shetland Is. **134** 60 30N 1 30W
Shevaroy Hills **201** 11 58N 78 12 E
Shewa □ **245** 9 33N 38 10 E
Shewa Gimira **245** 7 4N 35 51 E
Shibâm **195** 16 0N 48 36 E
Shibata **218** 37 57N 139 20 E
Shibecha **218** 43 17N 144 36 E
Shibetsu **218** 44 10N 142 23 E
Shibîn El Kôm **244** 30 31N 30 55 E
Shibîn el Qanâtir **244** 30 19N 31 19 E
Shibing **216** 27 2N 108 7 E
Shibogama L. **74** 53 35N 88 15W
Shibukawa **221** 36 29N 139 0 E
Shibushi **220** 31 25N 131 8 E
Shibushi-Wan **220** 31 24N 131 8 E
Shicheng **217** 26 22N 116 20 E
Shidād **194** 21 19N 40 3 E
Shidao **215** 36 50N 122 25 E
Shidian **216** 24 40N 99 5 E
Shido **220** 34 19N 134 10 E
Shiel, L. **134** 56 48N 5 32W
Shield, C. **230** 13 20 S 136 20 E
Shiga □ **221** 35 20N 136 0 E
Shigaib **243** 15 5N 23 35 E
Shigaraki **221** 34 57N 136 2 E
Shigu **216** 26 51N 99 56 E
Shiguaigou **214** 40 52N 110 15 E
Shihan, W. → **195** 17 24N 51 26 E
Shihchiachuangi = Shijiazhuang **214** 38 2N 114 28 E
Shiiba **220** 32 29N 131 4 E
Shijaku **168** 41 21N 19 33 E
Shijiazhuang **214** 38 2N 114 28 E
Shijiu Hu **217** 31 25N 118 50 E
Shikarpur, India **198** 28 17N 78 7 E
Shikarpur, Pakistan **197** 27 57N 68 39 E
Shiki Is. **226** 7 23N 151 52 E
Shikine-Jima **221** 34 19N 139 13 E
Shikoku **220** 33 30N 133 30 E
Shikoku □ **220** 33 30N 133 30 E
Shikoku-Sanchi **220** 33 30N 133 30 E
Shilabo **188** 6 22N 44 32 E
Shilda **182** 51 49N 59 47 E
Shiliguri **202** 26 45N 88 25 E
Shilka **185** 52 0N 115 55 E
Shilka → **185** 53 20N 121 26 E
Shillelagh **135** 52 46N 6 32W
Shillong **202** 25 35N 91 53 E
Shilo, Canada **89** 49 49N 99 38W
Shilo, Jordan **189** 32 4N 35 18 E
Shilong **217** 23 5N 113 52 E
Shilou **214** 37 0N 110 48 E
Shilovo **179** 54 25N 40 57 E
Shima-Hantō **221** 34 22N 136 45 E
Shimabara **220** 32 48N 130 20 E
Shimada **221** 34 49N 138 10 E
Shimane □ **220** 35 0N 132 30 E
Shimane-Hantō **220** 35 30N 133 0 E
Shimanovsk **185** 52 15N 127 30 E
Shimen **217** 29 35N 111 20 E
Shimenjie **217** 29 29N 116 48 E
Shimian **216** 29 17N 102 23 E
Shimizu **221** 35 0N 138 30 E
Shimo-Jima **220** 32 15N 130 7 E
Shimo-Koshiki-Jima **220** 31 40N 129 43 E
Shimoda **221** 34 40N 138 57 E
Shimodate **221** 36 20N 139 55 E
Shimoga **201** 13 57N 75 32 E
Shimoni **250** 4 38 S 39 20 E
Shimonita **221** 36 13N 138 47 E
Shimonoseki **220** 33 58N 131 0 E
Shimotsuma **221** 36 11N 139 58 E
Shimpuru Rapids **254** 17 45 S 19 55 E
Shimsha → **201** 13 15N 77 10 E
Shimsk **178** 58 15N 30 50 E
Shin, L. **134** 58 7N 4 30W
Shin-Tone → **221** 35 44N 140 51 E
Shinan **216** 22 44N 109 53 E
Shinano → **219** 36 50N 138 30 E
Shīndand **197** 33 12N 62 8 E
Shingbwiyang **202** 26 41N 96 13 E
Shingū **221** 33 40N 135 55 E
Shinji **220** 35 24N 132 54 E
Shinji Ko **220** 35 26N 132 57 E
Shinjō **218** 38 46N 140 18 E
Shinkafe **247** 13 8N 6 29 E
Shīnkay **197** 31 57N 67 26 E
Shinminato **221** 36 47N 137 4 E
Shinonoi **221** 36 35N 138 9 E
Shinshār **190** 34 36N 36 43 E
Shinshiro **221** 34 54N 137 30 E
Shinyanga **250** 3 45 S 33 27 E
Shinyanga □ **250** 3 50 S 34 0 E
Shio-no-Misaki **221** 33 25N 135 45 E
Shiogama **218** 38 19N 141 1 E
Shiojiri **221** 36 6N 137 58 E
Shipehenski Prokhod **167** 42 45N 25 15 E
Shiping **216** 23 45N 102 23 E
Shippegan **81** 47 45N 64 45W
Shippegan I. **81** 47 50N 64 38W
Shiqian **216** 27 32N 108 13 E
Shiqma, N. → **189** 31 37N 34 30 E
Shiquan **214** 33 5N 108 15 E
Shīr Kūh **193** 31 39N 54 3 E
Shirabad **183** 37 40N 67 1 E
Shirahama **221** 33 41N 135 20 E
Shirakawa, Fukushima, Japan **219** 37 7N 140 13 E
Shirakawa, Gifu, Japan **221** 36 17N 136 56 E
Shirane-San, Gumma, Japan **221** 36 48N 139 22 E
Shirane-San, Yamanashi, Japan **221** 35 42N 138 9 E
Shiraoi **218** 42 33N 141 21 E
Shīrāz **193** 29 42N 52 30 E
Shirbin **244** 31 11N 31 32 E
Shire → **251** 17 42 S 35 19 E
Shiretoko-Misaki **218** 44 21N 145 20 E
Shirigami-Misaki **218** 41 24N 140 12 E
Shirinab → **198** 30 15N 66 28 E
Shiringushi **179** 53 51N 42 46 E
Shiriya-Zaki **218** 41 25N 141 30 E
Shiroishi **218** 38 0N 140 37 E
Shirol **200** 16 47N 74 41 E
Shirpur **198** 21 21N 74 57 E
Shīrvān **193** 37 30N 57 50 E
Shirwa L. = Chilwa, L. **251** 15 15 S 35 40 E
Shishmanova **167** 42 58N 23 12 E
Shishou **217** 29 38N 112 22 E
Shisur **188** 17 30N 54 0 E
Shitai **217** 30 12N 117 25 E
Shivpuri **198** 25 26N 77 42 E
Shivta **189** 30 53N 34 40 E
Shixian **215** 43 5N 129 50 E
Shixing **217** 24 46N 114 5 E
Shiyan **217** 32 35N 110 45 E
Shiyata **244** 29 25N 25 7 E
Shizhu **216** 29 58N 108 7 E
Shizong **216** 24 50N 104 0 E
Shizuishan **214** 39 15N 106 50 E
Shizuoka **221** 35 0N 138 24 E
Shizuoka □ **221** 35 15N 138 40 E
Shklov **178** 54 16N 30 15 E
Shkoder = Shkodra **168** 42 6N 19 20 E
Shkodra **168** 42 6N 19 20 E
Shkodra □ **168** 42 25N 19 20 E
Shkumbini → **168** 41 5N 19 50 E
Shmidt, O. **185** 81 0N 91 0 E
Shō-Gawa → **221** 36 47N 137 4 E
Shoal L. **86** 49 33N 95 1W
Shoal Lake **89** 50 30N 100 35W
Shoals Prov. Park **87** 47 50N 83 50W
Shōbara **220** 34 51N 133 1 E
Shōdo-Shima **220** 34 30N 134 15 E
Shoeburyness **133** 51 31N 0 49 E
Shokpar **183** 43 49N 74 21 E
Sholapur = Solapur **200** 17 43N 75 56 E
Shologontsy **185** 66 13N 114 0 E
Shomera **189** 33 4N 35 17 E
Shōmrōn **189** 32 15N 35 13 E
Shoranur **201** 10 46N 76 19 E
Shorapur **201** 16 31N 76 48 E
Shortland I. **227** 7 0 S 155 45 E
Shoshong **254** 22 56 S 26 31 E
Shostka **178** 51 57N 33 32 E
Shou Xian **217** 32 37N 116 42 E
Shouchang **217** 29 18N 119 12 E
Shouguang **215** 37 52N 118 45 E
Shouning **217** 27 27N 119 31 E
Shouyang **214** 37 54N 113 8 E
Shpola **180** 49 1N 31 30 E
Shrewsbury **132** 52 42N 2 45W
Shrirampur **199** 22 44N 88 21 E
Shrirangapattana **201** 12 26N 76 43 E
Shropshire □ **133** 52 36N 2 45W
Shuangbai **216** 24 42N 101 38 E
Shuangcheng **215** 45 20N 126 15 E
Shuangfeng **217** 27 29N 112 11 E
Shuanggou **215** 34 2N 117 30 E
Shuangjiang **216** 23 26N 99 58 E
Shuangliao **215** 43 29N 123 30 E
Shuangshanzi **215** 40 20N 119 8 E
Shuangyang **215** 43 28N 125 40 E
Shuangyashan **213** 46 28N 131 5 E
Shu'b, Ra's **195** 12 30N 53 25 E
Shubenacadie **81** 45 5N 63 24W
Shucheng **217** 31 28N 116 57 E
Shu'eib, Wadi **189** 31 54N 35 38 E
Shuguri Falls **251** 8 33 S 37 22 E
Shuḩayr **195** 14 41N 49 23 E
Shuicheng **216** 26 38N 104 48 E
Shuiji **217** 27 13N 118 20 E
Shuiye **214** 36 7N 114 8 E
Shujalpur **198** 23 18N 76 46 E
Shukpa Kunzang **199** 34 22N 78 22 E
Shulan **215** 44 28N 127 0 E
Shule **212** 39 25N 76 3 E
Shumerlya **179** 55 30N 46 25 E
Shumikha **182** 55 10N 63 15 E
Shunchang **217** 26 54N 117 48 E
Shunde **217** 22 42N 113 14 E
Shungay **181** 48 30N 46 45 E
Shuo Xian **214** 39 20N 112 33 E
Shūr → **192** 28 30N 55 0 E
Shūr Āb **193** 34 23N 51 11 E
Shūr Gaz **193** 29 10N 59 20 E
Shūrāb, Iran **193** 33 43N 56 29 E
Shurab, U.S.S.R. **183** 40 3N 70 33 E
Shurchi **183** 37 59N 67 47 E
Shūrjestān **193** 31 24N 52 25 E
Shurkhua **202** 22 15N 93 38 E
Shurma **182** 56 58N 50 21 E
Shurugwi **251** 19 40 S 30 0 E
Shūsf **193** 31 50N 60 5 E
Shūshtar **193** 32 0N 48 50 E
Shuswap L. **93** 50 55N 119 3W
Shuwaykah **189** 32 20N 35 1 E
Shuya **179** 56 50N 41 28 E
Shuyang **215** 34 10N 118 42 E
Shuzenji **221** 34 58N 138 56 E
Shūzū **193** 29 52N 54 30 E
Shwaner, Pegunungan **209** 1 0 S 112 30 E
Shwebo **202** 22 30N 95 45 E
Shwegu **202** 24 15N 96 26 E
Shwegun **202** 17 9N 97 39 E
Shwenyaung **202** 20 46N 96 57 E
Shyok **199** 34 15N 78 12 E
Shyok → **199** 35 13N 75 53 E
Si Chon **205** 9 0N 99 54 E
Si Kiang = Xi Jiang → **217** 22 5N 113 20 E
Si Prachan **204** 14 37N 100 9 E
Si Racha **204** 13 10N 100 48 E
Si Xian **215** 33 30N 117 50 E
Siahan Range **197** 27 30N 64 40 E
Siak → **208** 1 13N 102 9 E
Siaksrindrapura **208** 0 51N 102 0 E
Sialkot **197** 32 32N 74 30 E
Sialsuk **202** 23 24N 92 45 E
Siam = Thailand ■ **204** 16 0N 102 0 E
Siam **232** 32 35 S 136 41 E
Sian = Xi'an **214** 34 15N 109 0 E
Sianori **104** 25 13N 106 47W
Siantan, P. **205** 3 10N 106 15 E
Siàpo → **118** 2 7N 66 28W
Sīāreh **193** 28 5N 60 14 E
Siargao **211** 9 52N 126 3 E
Siari, Kashmir **199** 34 55N 76 40 E
Siari, Phil. **211** 8 19N 122 58 E
Siari, I. **100** 26 58N 109 56W
Siasi **207** 5 34N 120 50 E
Siasi I. **211** 5 33N 120 51 E
Siassi **227** 5 40 S 147 51 E
Siátista **168** 40 15N 21 33 E
Siaton **211** 9 4N 123 2 E
Siau **207** 2 50N 125 25 E
Siauliai **178** 55 56N 23 15 E
Siaya □ **250** 0 0 34 20 E
Siazan **181** 41 3N 49 10 E
Sibâi, Gebel el **244** 25 45N 34 10 E
Sibang **252** 0 25N 9 31 E
Sibari **165** 39 47N 16 27 E
Sibay **182** 52 42N 58 39 E
Sibay I. **211** 11 51N 121 29 E
Şibaya, L. **255** 27 20 S 32 45 E
Šibenik **163** 43 48N 15 54 E
Siberia **186** 60 0N 100 0 E
Siberut **208** 1 30 S 99 0 E
Sibi **197** 29 30N 67 54 E
Sibil **207** 4 59 S 140 35 E
Sibiti **252** 3 38 S 13 19 E
Sibiu **170** 45 45N 24 9 E
Sibiu □ **170** 45 50N 24 15 E
Sibley Prov. Park **86** 48 30N 88 45W
Sibolga **208** 1 42N 98 45 E
Sibret **143** 49 58N 5 38 E
Sibsagar **202** 27 0N 94 36 E
Sibu **206** 2 18N 111 49 E
Sibuco **211** 7 20N 122 10 E
Sibuguey B. **211** 7 50N 122 45 E
Sibutu **211** 4 45N 119 30 E
Sibutu Group **211** 4 45N 119 20 E
Sibutu Passage **211** 4 50N 120 0 E
Sibuyan **210** 12 25N 122 40 E
Sibuyan Sea **210** 12 30N 122 20 E
Sicamous **93** 50 49N 119 0W
Sicapoo, Mt. **210** 18 1N 120 56 E
Sichuan □ **216** 31 0N 104 0 E
Sicilia **165** 37 30N 14 30 E
Sicilia □ **165** 37 30N 14 30 E
Sicilia, Canale di **164** 37 25N 12 30 E
Sicilian Channel = Sicilia, Canale di **164** 37 25N 12 30 E
Sicily = Sicilia **165** 37 30N 14 30 E
Sicuani **122** 14 21 S 71 10W
Şiculiana **164** 37 20N 13 23 E
Šid **166** 45 8N 19 14 E
Sidamo □ **245** 5 0N 37 50 E
Sidaouet **247** 18 34N 8 3 E
Siddeburen **142** 53 15N 6 52 E
Siddhapur **198** 23 56N 72 25 E
Siddipet **200** 18 0N 78 51 E
Sideburned L. **87** 47 45N 83 15W
Sidéradougou **246** 10 42N 4 12W
Siderno Marina **165** 38 16N 16 17 E
Sidheros, Ákra **169** 35 19N 26 19 E
Sidhirókastron **168** 41 13N 23 24 E
Sîdi Abd el Rahmân **244** 30 55N 29 44 E
Sîdi Barrâni **244** 31 38N 25 58 E
Sidi-bel-Abbès **241** 35 13N 0 39W
Sidi Bennour **240** 32 40N 8 25W
Sidi Haneish **244** 31 10N 27 35 E
Sidi Kacem **240** 34 11N 5 49W
Sidi Moussa, O. → **240** 26 58N 3 54 E
Sidi Omar **244** 31 24N 24 57 E
Sidi Slimane **240** 34 16N 5 56W
Sidi Smaïl **240** 32 50N 8 31W
Sidi 'Uzayz **242** 31 41N 24 55 E
Sidlaw Hills **134** 56 32N 3 10W
Sidley, Mt. **13** 77 2 S 126 2W
Sidmouth **133** 50 40N 3 13W
Sidmouth, C. **230** 13 25 S 143 36 E
Sidney, B.C., Canada **93** 48 39N 123 24W
Sidney, Man., Canada **89** 49 54N 99 4W
Sidoarjo **209** 7 27 S 112 43 E
Sidoktaya **202** 20 27N 94 15 E
Sidon = Saydā **190** 33 35N 35 25 E
Sidra, G. of = Surt, Khalīj **242** 31 40N 18 30 E
Siedlce **152** 52 10N 22 20 E
Siedlce □ **152** 52 0N 22 0 E
Sieg → **146** 50 46N 7 7 E
Siegburg **146** 50 48N 7 12 E
Siegen **146** 50 52N 8 2 E
Siem Pang **204** 14 7N 106 23 E
Siem Reap **204** 13 20N 103 52 E
Siena **163** 43 20N 11 20 E
Sieniawa **152** 50 11N 22 38 E
Sieradź **152** 51 37N 18 41 E
Sieraków **152** 52 39N 16 2 E
Sierck-les-Bains **139** 49 26N 6 20 E
Sierpc **152** 52 55N 19 43 E
Sierpe, Bocas de la **118** 10 0N 61 30W
Sierra Colorada **126** 40 35 S 67 50W
Sierra de Yeguas **155** 37 7N 4 52W
Sierra Gorda **124** 22 50 S 69 15W
Sierra Grande **126** 41 36 S 65 22W
Sierra Leone ■ **246** 9 0N 12 0W
Sierra Mojada **102** 27 18N 103 41W
Sierre **148** 46 17N 7 31 E
Sierrita de López **100** 29 23N 111 15W
Sif Fatima **241** 31 6N 8 41 E
Sífnos **169** 37 0N 24 45 E
Sifton **89** 51 21N 100 8W
Sifton Pass **76** 57 52N 126 15W
Sig **241** 35 32N 0 12W
Sigaboy **211** 6 39N 126 5 E
Sigdal **171** 60 4N 9 38 E
Sigean **140** 43 2N 2 58 E
Sighetul Marmatiei **170** 47 57N 23 52 E
Sighişoara **170** 46 12N 24 50 E
Sigira **195** 12 37N 54 20 E
Sigli **208** 5 25N 96 0 E
Siglufjörður **174** 66 12N 18 55W
Sigmaringen **147** 48 5N 9 13 E
Signakhi **181** 41 40N 45 57 E
Signau **148** 46 56N 7 45 E
Signy I. **13** 60 45 S 45 56W
Signy-l'Abbaye **139** 49 40N 4 25 E
Sigsig **118** 3 0 S 78 50W
Sigtuna **172** 59 36N 17 44 E
Sigüenza **156** 41 3N 2 40W
Siguiri **246** 11 31N 9 10W
Sigulda **178** 57 10N 24 55 E
Sigutlat L. **92** 52 57N 126 12W
Sihanoukville = Kompong Som **205** 10 38N 103 30 E
Sihaus **122** 8 40 S 77 40W
Sihochac **111** 19 30N 90 34W
Sihui **217** 23 20N 112 40 E
Si'īr **189** 31 35N 35 9 E
Siit **211** 5 59N 124 13 E
Sijarira Ra. **251** 17 36 S 27 45 E
Sijungjung **208** 0 42 S 100 58 E
Sikao **205** 7 34N 99 21 E
Sikar **198** 27 33N 75 10 E
Sikasso **246** 11 18N 5 35W
Sikhote Alin, Khrebet **185** 46 0N 136 0 E
Sikiá **168** 40 2N 23 56 E
Síkinos **169** 36 40N 25 8 E
Sikkani Chief → **76** 57 47N 122 15W
Sikkim □ **202** 27 50N 88 30 E
Siklós **151** 45 50N 18 19 E
Sikotu-Ko **218** 42 45N 141 25 E
Sil → **154** 42 27N 7 43W
Sila, La **165** 39 15N 16 35 E
Silacayoapan **109** 17 30N 98 9W
Silandro **162** 46 38N 10 48 E
Silanga **211** 11 1N 119 34 E
Silao **107** 20 56N 101 26W
Sīlat az Zahr **189** 32 19N 35 11 E
Silay **211** 10 47N 123 14 E
Silba **163** 44 24N 14 41 E
Silchar **202** 24 49N 92 48 E
Silcox **77** 57 12N 94 10W

Silenrieux . . . . **143** 50 14N 4 27 E
Sileru → . . . . **200** 17 49N 81 24 E
Silesia = Slask . . . . . **144** 51 0N 16 30 E
Silet . . . . **240** 22 44N 4 37 E
Silgarhi Doti . . . . **199** 29 15N 81 0 E
Silghat . . . . **202** 26 35N 93 0 E
Silifke . . . . **177** 36 22N 33 58 E
Siling Co . . . . **212** 31 50N 89 20 E
Silíqua . . . . **164** 39 20N 8 49 E
Silistra . . . . **167** 44 6N 27 19 E
Siljan . . . . **172** 60 55N 14 45 E
Silkeborg . . . . **173** 56 10N 9 32 E
Sillajhuay, Cordillera . . . . **122** 19 46 S 68 40W
Sillé-le-Guillaume . . **138** 48 10N 0 8W
Sillustani . . . . **122** 15 50 S 70 7W
Siltepec **110** 15 39N 92 17W
Silute . . . . **178** 55 21N 21 33 E
Silva Porto = Kuito **253** 12 22 S 16 55 E
Silvaplana . . . . **149** 46 28N 9 48 E
Silver Islet **86** 48 20N 88 45W
Silver Ridge **89** 50 48N 98 52W
Silver Star Prov. Park **93** 50 23N 119 5W
Silver Water **84** 45 52N 82 52W
Silvertip Mt. **93** 49 10N 121 13W
Silverton, Australia . **232** 31 52 S 141 10 E
Silverton, Canada . . **93** 49 57N 117 21W
Silves **155** 37 11N 8 26W
Silvi . . . . **163** 42 32N 14 5 E
Silvia **118** 2 37N 76 21W
Silvituc **111** 18 40N 90 16W
Silvolde . . . . **142** 51 55N 6 23 E
Silvretta Gruppe . . . **149** 46 50N 10 6 E
Silwa Bahari . . . . **244** 24 45N 32 55 E
Silwâd . . . . **189** 31 59N 35 15 E
Silz . . . . **150** 47 16N 10 56 E
Sim, C. **240** 31 26N 9 51W
Sim'ān, J. . . . . **190** 36 25N 36 53 E
Simanggang . . . . **206** 1 15N 111 32 E
Simao . . . . **216** 22 47N 101 5 E
Simão Dias . . . . **120** 10 44 S 37 49W
Simara I. . . . . **210** 12 48N 122 3 E
Simard, L. **82** 47 40N 78 40W
Sîmărtin . . . . **170** 46 19N 25 58 E
Simba . . . . **250** 2 10 S 37 36 E
Simbach . . . . **147** 48 16N 13 3 E
Simbo . . . . **250** 4 51 S 29 41 E
Simcoe **84** 42 50N 80 20W
Simcoe, L. **84** 44 25N 79 20W
Simenga . . . . **185** 62 42N 108 25 E
Simeto → . . . . **165** 37 25N 15 10 E
Simeulue . . . . **208** 2 45N 95 45 E
Simferopol . . . . **180** 44 55N 34 3 E
Sími . . . . **169** 36 35N 27 50 E
Simikot . . . . **199** 30 0N 81 50 E
Simití **118** 7 58N 73 57W
Simitli . . . . **166** 41 52N 23 7 E
Simla . . . . **198** 31 2N 77 9 E
Şimleu-Silvaniei . . . . **170** 47 17N 22 50 E
Simme → . . . . **148** 46 38N 7 25 E
Simmern . . . . **147** 49 59N 7 32 E
Simmie **88** 49 56N 108 6W
Simmons Pen. **95** 76 40N 89 7W
Simões . . . . **120** 7 36 S 40 49W
Simojärvi . . . . **174** 66 5N 27 3 E
Simojoki → . . . . **174** 65 35N 25 1 E
Simojovel de Allende **110** 17 12N 92 38W
Simonette → **90** 55 9N 118 15W
Simonhouse **89** 54 26N 101 23W
Simonstown . . . . **254** 34 14 S 18 26 E
Simontornya . . . . **151** 46 45N 18 33 E
Simpangkiri → . . . . **208** 2 50N 97 40 E
Simplício Mendes . . . **120** 7 51 S 41 54W
Simplon . . . . **148** 46 12N 8 4 E
Simplon Pass . . . . **148** 46 15N 8 0 E
Simplon Tunnel . . . . **148** 46 15N 8 7 E
Simpson **88** 51 27N 105 27W
Simpson Des. . . . . . . **230** 25 0 S 137 0 E
Simpson I. **87** 48 46N 87 41W
Simpson Pen. **95** 68 34N 88 45W
Simpungdong . . . . . . **215** 40 56N 129 29 E
Simrishamn . . . . **173** 55 33N 14 22 E
Simunjan . . . . **206** 1 25N 110 45 E
Simushir, Ostrov . . . **185** 46 50N 152 30 E
Sina → . . . . **200** 17 30N 75 55 E
Sinabang . . . . **208** 2 30N 96 24 E
Sinadogo . . . . **188** 5 50N 47 0 E
Sinai = Es Sînâ' . . . . **244** 29 0N 34 0 E
Sinai = Sînî □ . . . . . **191** 30 0N 34 0 E
Sinai, Mt. = Mûsa, G. . . . . **191** 28 33N 33 59 E
Sinai Peninsula . . . . . **191** 29 30N 34 0 E
Sinaia . . . . **170** 45 21N 25 38 E
Sinait . . . . **210** 17 52N 120 27 E
Sinako, Mt. . . . . **211** 7 30N 125 17 E
Sinaloa □ **104** 25 0N 107 30W
Sinaloa → **104** 25 18N 108 30W
Sinaloa de Leyva . . . **104** 25 50N 108 14W
Sinalunga . . . . **163** 43 12N 11 43 E
Sinan . . . . **216** 27 56N 108 13 E
Sînandrei . . . . **170** 45 52N 21 13 E
Sînâwan . . . . **241** 31 0N 10 37 E
Sinbaungwe . . . . **202** 19 43N 95 10 E
Sinbo . . . . **202** 24 46N 97 3 E
Sincé **118** 9 15N 75 9W
Sincelejo **118** 9 18N 75 24W
Sinchang . . . . **215** 40 7N 128 28 E
Sinchang-ni . . . . **215** 39 24N 126 8 E
Sinclair Mills **76** 54 5N 121 40W
Sinclair Pass **91** 50 40N 115 58W
Sincorá, Serra do . . . **121** 13 30 S 41 0W
Sind . . . . **198** 26 0N 68 30 E
Sind □ . . . . **197** 26 0N 69 0 E
Sind → . . . . **199** 34 18N 74 45 E
Sind Sagar Doab . . . **198** 32 0N 71 30 E
Sindal . . . . **173** 57 28N 10 10 E
Sindangan . . . . **211** 8 10N 123 5 E
Sindangan Bay . . . . . **211** 8 11N 122 50 E
Sindangbarang . . . . . **209** 7 27 S 107 1 E
Sinde . . . . **251** 17 28 S 25 51 E
Sinegorski . . . . **181** 48 0N 40 52 E
Sinelnikovo . . . . **180** 48 25N 35 30 E
Sines **155** 37 56N 8 51W
Sines, Cabo de **155** 37 58N 8 53W
Sineu . . . . **156** 39 38N 3 1 E
Sinewit, Mt. . . . . **227** 4 44 S 152 2 E
Sinfra **246** 6 35N 5 56W
Sing Buri . . . . **204** 14 53N 100 25 E
Singa . . . . **245** 13 10N 33 57 E
Singanallur . . . . **201** 11 2N 77 1 E
Singapore ■ . . . . **205** 1 17N 103 51 E
Singapore, Straits of **205** 1 15N 104 0 E
Singaraja . . . . **209** 8 6 S 115 10 E
Singatoka . . . . **226** 18 8 S 177 30 E
Singen . . . . **147** 47 45N 8 50 E
Singida . . . . **250** 4 49 S 34 48 E
Singida □ . . . . **250** 6 0 S 34 30 E
Singitikós Kólpos . . . **168** 40 6N 24 0 E
Singkaling Hkamti . . **202** 26 0N 95 39 E
Singkawang . . . . **209** 1 0N 108 57 E
Singleton . . . . **231** 32 33 S 151 0 E
Singleton, Mt. . . . . . **229** 29 27 S 117 15 E
Singö . . . . **172** 60 12N 18 45 E
Singoli . . . . **198** 25 0N 75 22 E
Singora = Songkhla **205** 7 13N 100 37 E
Singosan . . . . **215** 38 52N 127 25 E
Singuilucan **107** 19 58N 98 31W
Sinhung . . . . **215** 40 11N 127 34 E
Sînî □ . . . . **191** 30 0N 34 0 E
Siniátsikon, Óros . . . **168** 40 25N 21 35 E
Siniloan . . . . **210** 14 25N 121 27 E
Siniscóla . . . . **164** 40 35N 9 40 E
Sinj . . . . **163** 43 42N 16 39 E
Sinjai . . . . **207** 5 7 S 120 20 E
Sinjajevina, Planina . **166** 42 57N 19 22 E
Sinjār . . . . **192** 36 19N 41 52 E
Sinjil . . . . **189** 32 3N 35 15 E
Sinkat . . . . **244** 18 55N 36 49 E
Sinkiang Uighur = Xinjiang Uygur Zizhiqu □ . . . . **212** 42 0N 86 0 E
Sinmak . . . . **215** 38 25N 126 14 E
Sinnai . . . . **164** 39 18N 9 13 E
Sinnar . . . . **200** 19 48N 74 0 E
Sinni → . . . . **165** 40 9N 16 42 E
Sînnicolau Maré . . . . **166** 46 5N 20 39 E
Sinnuris . . . . **244** 29 26N 30 31 E
Sinoe, L. . . . . **170** 44 35N 28 50 E
Sinop . . . . **180** 42 1N 35 11 E
Sinoquipe **100** 30 10N 110 12W
Sinpo . . . . **215** 40 0N 128 13 E
Sins . . . . **149** 47 12N 8 24 E
Sinskoye . . . . **185** 61 8N 126 48 E
Sint-Amandsberg . . . **143** 51 4N 3 45 E
Sint Annaland . . . . . . **143** 51 36N 4 6 E
Sint Annaparoch . . . **142** 53 16N 5 40 E
Sint-Denijs . . . . **143** 50 45N 3 23 E
Sint Eustatius, I. . . . **113** 17 30N 62 59W
Sint-Genesius-Rode . **143** 50 45N 4 22 E
Sint-Gillis-Waas . . . . **143** 51 13N 4 6 E
Sint-Huibrechts-Lille **143** 51 13N 5 29 E
Sint-Katelinje-Waver **143** 51 5N 4 32 E
Sint-Kruis . . . . **143** 51 13N 3 15 E
Sint-Laureins . . . . . . **143** 51 14N 3 32 E
Sint Maarten, I. **113** 18 4N 63 4W
Sint-Michiels . . . . **143** 51 11N 3 15 E
Sint Nicolaasga . . . . . **142** 52 55N 5 45 E
Sint Niklaas . . . . **143** 51 10N 4 9 E
Sint Oedenrode . . . . . **143** 51 35N 5 29 E
Sint Pancras . . . . **142** 52 40N 4 48 E
Sint Philipsland . . . . **143** 51 37N 4 10 E
Sint Truiden . . . . **143** 50 48N 5 10 E
Sint Willebrord . . . . . **143** 51 33N 4 33 E
Sintaluta **88** 50 29N 103 27W
Sîntana . . . . **170** 46 20N 21 30 E
Sintang . . . . **209** 0 5N 111 35 E
Sintjohannesga . . . . . **142** 52 55N 5 52 E
Sintra **155** 38 47N 9 25W
Sinugif . . . . **256** 8 33N 48 59 E
Sinŭiju . . . . **215** 40 5N 124 24 E
Sinyukha → . . . . **180** 48 3N 30 51 E
Siocon . . . . **211** 7 40N 122 10 E
Siófok . . . . **151** 16 39 S 23 36 E
Sioma . . . . **254** 16 25 S 23 28 E
Sion . . . . **148** 46 14N 7 20 E
Sioux Lookout **86** 50 10N 91 50W
Sioux Narrows **86** 49 25N 94 10W
Sip Song Chau Thai **204** 21 30N 103 30 E
Şipalay . . . . **211** 9 45N 122 24 E
Šipan . . . . **166** 42 45N 17 52 E
Sipetzinco **107** 19 28N 98 18W
Siping . . . . **215** 43 8N 124 21 E
Sipiwesk L. **77** 55 5N 97 35W
Siple . . . . **13** 75 0 S 74 0 E
Sipocot . . . . **210** 13 46N 122 58 E
Sipora . . . . **208** 2 18 S 99 40 E
Siqueros **104** 23 19N 106 15W
Siquia → **112** 12 10N 84 20W
Siquijor . . . . **211** 9 12N 123 35 E
Siquijor □ . . . . **211** 9 11N 123 35 E
Siquijor I. . . . . **211** 9 11N 123 34 E
Siquirres **112** 10 6N 83 30W
Siquisique **118** 10 34N 69 42W
Sir Edward Pellew Group . . . . **230** 15 40 S 137 10 E
Sir Francis Drake, Mt. **92** 50 49N 124 48W
Sir Graham Moore Is. . . . . **228** 13 53 S 126 34 E
Sir Sandford, Mt. . . . **93** 51 40N 117 52W
Sira . . . . **201** 13 41N 76 49 E
Siracusa . . . . **165** 37 4N 15 17 E
Sirajganj . . . . **199** 24 25N 89 47 E
Sirakoro **246** 12 41N 9 14W
Sirasso **246** 9 16N 6 6W
Siraway . . . . **211** 7 34N 122 8 E
Sîrdān . . . . **193** 36 39N 49 12 E
Siret . . . . **170** 47 55N 26 5 E
Siret → . . . . **170** 47 58N 26 5 E
Şiria . . . . **170** 46 16N 21 38 E
Sirino, Monte . . . . . . **165** 40 7N 15 50 E
Sirkali = Sirkazhi . . **201** 11 15N 79 41 E
Sirkazhi . . . . **201** 11 15N 79 41 E
Sírna. . . . . **169** 36 22N 26 42 E
Sirnach . . . . **149** 47 28N 8 59 E
Şirohi . . . . **198** 24 52N 72 53 E
Široki Brijeg . . . . **166** 43 21N 17 36 E
Sironj . . . . **198** 24 5N 77 39 E
Síros . . . . **169** 37 28N 24 57 E
Sirrayn . . . . **194** 19 38N 40 36 E
Sirsa . . . . **198** 29 33N 75 4 E
Sirsi . . . . **201** 14 40N 74 49 E
Siruela **155** 38 58N 5 3W
Sisak . . . . **163** 45 30N 16 21 E
Sisaket . . . . **204** 15 8N 104 23 E
Sisal **111** 21 10N 90 2W
Sisante **157** 39 25N 2 12W
Sisargas, Islas **154** 43 21N 8 50W
Sishen . . . . **254** 27 47 S 22 59 E
Sishui, Henan, China . . . . **214** 34 48N 113 15 E
Sishui, Shandong, China . . . . **215** 35 42N 117 18 E
Sisipuk L. **77** 55 45N 101 50W
Sisoguichic **101** 27 48N 107 31W
Sisophon . . . . **204** 13 38N 102 59 E
Sissach . . . . **148** 47 27N 7 48 E
Sissonne . . . . **139** 49 34N 3 51 E
Sīstān va Balūchestān □ . . . **193** 27 0N 62 0 E
Sistema Central **154** 40 40N 5 55W
Sistema Iberico **156** 41 0N 2 10W
Sisteron . . . . **141** 44 12N 5 57 E
Sitamarhi . . . . **199** 26 37N 85 30 E
Sitapur . . . . **199** 27 38N 80 45 E
Siteki . . . . **255** 26 32 S 31 58 E
Sitges . . . . **156** 41 17N 1 47 E
Sithoniá . . . . **168** 40 0N 23 45 E
Sitía . . . . **169** 35 13N 26 6 E
Sítio da Abadia . . . . . **121** 14 48 S 46 16W
Sitoti . . . . **254** 23 15 S 23 40 E
Sitra . . . . **244** 28 40N 26 53 E
Sittang → . . . . **202** 17 10N 96 58 E
Sittard . . . . **143** 51 0N 5 52 E
Sittaung . . . . **202** 24 10N 94 35 E
Sittensen . . . . **146** 53 17N 9 32 E
Sittona . . . . **245** 14 25N 37 23 E
Sittwe . . . . **202** 20 18N 92 45 E
Situbondo . . . . **209** 7 45 S 114 0 E
Siuna **112** 13 37N 84 45W
Siuri . . . . **199** 23 50N 87 34 E
Sivaganga . . . . **201** 9 50N 78 28 E
Sivagiri . . . . **201** 9 16N 77 26 E
Sivakasi . . . . **201** 9 24N 77 47 E
Sivana . . . . **198** 28 37N 78 6 E
Sīvand . . . . **193** 30 5N 52 55 E
Sivas . . . . **177** 39 43N 36 58 E
Sivomaskinskiy . . . . . **176** 66 40N 62 35 E
Sivrihisar . . . . **177** 39 30N 31 35 E
Sivry . . . . **143** 50 10N 4 12 E
Sîwa . . . . **244** 29 11N 25 31 E
Sîwa, El Wâhât es . . **244** 29 10N 25 30 E
Siwalik Range . . . . . . **199** 28 0N 83 0 E
Siwan . . . . **199** 26 13N 84 21 E
Siyâl, Jazâ'ir . . . . **244** 22 49N 36 12 E
Sizewell . . . . **133** 52 13N 1 38 E
Siziwang Qi . . . . **214** 41 25N 111 40 E
Sjælland . . . . **172** 55 30N 11 30 E
Sjællands Odde . . . . **172** 56 0N 11 15 E
Själevad . . . . **172** 63 18N 18 36 E
Sjarinska Banja . . . . **166** 42 45N 21 38 E
Sjenica . . . . **166** 43 16N 20 0 E
Sjoa . . . . **171** 61 41N 9 33 E
Sjöbo . . . . **172** 55 37N 13 45 E
Sjösa . . . . **173** 58 47N 17 4 E
Sjumen = Kolarovgrad . . . . . **167** 43 18N 26 55 E
Skadarsko Jezero . . . **166** 42 10N 19 20 E
Skadovsk . . . . **180** 46 17N 32 52 E
Skagafjörður **174** 65 54N 19 35W
Skagastølstindane . . . **171** 61 28N 7 52 E
Skagen . . . . **173** 57 43N 10 35 E
Skagern . . . . **172** 59 0N 14 20 E
Skagerrak . . . . **173** 57 30N 9 0 E
Skala Podolskaya . . . **180** 48 50N 26 15 E
Skalat . . . . **178** 49 23N 25 55 E
Skalbmierz . . . . **152** 50 20N 20 25 E
Skalica . . . . **151** 48 50N 17 15 E
Skalni Dol = Kamenyak . . . . **167** 43 24N 26 57 E
Skals . . . . **173** 56 34N 9 24 E
Skanderborg . . . . **173** 56 2N 9 55 E
Skånevik . . . . **171** 59 43N 5 53 E
Skänninge . . . . **173** 58 24N 15 5 E
Skanör . . . . **172** 55 24N 12 50 E
Skantzoúra . . . . **169** 39 5N 24 6 E
Skara . . . . **173** 58 25N 13 30 E
Skaraborgs län □ . . . **173** 58 20N 13 30 E
Skardu . . . . **199** 35 20N 75 44 E
Skarrild . . . . **173** 55 58N 8 53 E
Skarszewy . . . . **152** 54 4N 18 25 E
Skaryszew . . . . **152** 51 19N 21 15 E
Skarzysko Kamienna **152** 51 7N 20 52 E
Skattungbyn . . . . **172** 61 10N 14 56 E
Skebokvarn . . . . **172** 59 7N 16 45 E
Skeena → **92** 54 9N 130 5W
Skeena Mts. **76** 56 40N 128 30W
Skegness . . . . **132** 53 9N 0 20 E
Skeldon **119** 5 55N 57 20W
Skellefte älv → . . . . **174** 64 45N 21 10 E
Skellefteå . . . . **174** 64 45N 20 58 E
Skelleftehamn . . . . . . **174** 64 47N 20 59 E
Skender Vakuf . . . . . **166** 44 29N 17 22 E
Skene . . . . **173** 57 30N 12 37 E
Skerries, The **132** 53 27N 4 40W
Skhíza . . . . **169** 36 41N 21 40 E
Skhoinoúsa . . . . **169** 36 53N 25 31 E
Ski . . . . **171** 59 43N 10 52 E
Skíathos . . . . **169** 39 12N 23 30 E
Skibbereen **135** 51 33N 9 16W
Skiddaw **132** 54 39N 3 9W
Skidegate **92** 53 15N 132 1W
Skien . . . . **171** 59 12N 9 35 E
Skierniewice . . . . **152** 51 58N 20 10 E
Skierniewice □ . . . . . **152** 52 0N 20 10 E
Skihist, Mt. **93** 50 12N 121 54W
Skikda . . . . **241** 36 50N 6 58 E
Skillingaryd . . . . **173** 57 27N 14 5 E
Skillinge . . . . **173** 55 30N 14 16 E
Skillingmark . . . . **172** 59 48N 12 1 E
Skinári, Ákra . . . . . . **169** 37 56N 20 40 E
Skipton, Australia . . **231** 37 39 S 143 40 E
Skipton, U.K. **132** 53 57N 2 1W
Skirmish Pt. . . . . **230** 11 59 S 134 17 E
Skiropoúla . . . . **169** 38 50N 24 21 E
Skíros . . . . **169** 38 55N 24 34 E
Skivarp . . . . **172** 55 26N 13 34 E
Skive . . . . **173** 56 33N 9 2 E
Skjåk . . . . **171** 61 52N 8 22 E
Skjálfandafljót → . . **174** 65 59N 17 25W
Skjálfandi **174** 66 5N 17 30W
Skjeberg . . . . **171** 59 12N 11 12 E
Skjern . . . . **173** 55 57N 8 30 E
Skoczów . . . . **152** 49 49N 18 45 E
Şkodje . . . . **171** 62 30N 6 43 E
Škofja Loka . . . . **163** 46 9N 14 19 E
Skoghall . . . . **172** 59 20N 13 30 E
Skoki . . . . **152** 52 40N 17 11 E
Skole . . . . **178** 49 3N 23 30 E
Skópelos . . . . **169** 39 9N 23 47 E
Skopin . . . . **179** 53 55N 39 32 E
Skopje . . . . **166** 42 1N 21 32 E
Skórcz . . . . **152** 53 47N 18 30 E
Skottfoss . . . . **171** 59 12N 9 30 E
Skovorodino . . . . **185** 54 0N 125 0 E
Skownan **89** 51 58N 99 35W
Skradin . . . . **163** 43 52N 15 53 E
Skreanäs . . . . **173** 56 52N 12 35 E
Skrwa → . . . . **152** 52 35N 19 32 E
Skull **135** 51 32N 9 40W
Skultorp . . . . **173** 58 24N 13 51 E
Skuodas . . . . **178** 56 21N 21 45 E
Skurup . . . . **172** 55 28N 13 30 E
Skutskär . . . . **173** 60 37N 17 25 E
Skvira . . . . **180** 49 44N 29 40 E
Skwierzyna . . . . **152** 52 33N 15 30 E
Skye **134** 57 15N 6 10W
Skyros = Skíros . . . . **169** 38 55N 24 34 E
Slagelse . . . . **172** 55 23N 11 19 E
Slagharen . . . . **142** 52 37N 6 34 E
Slamannon . . . . **232** 32 1 S 143 41 E
Slamet . . . . **209** 7 16 S 109 8 E
Slaney → **135** 52 52N 6 45W
Slangerup . . . . **172** 55 50N 12 11 E

Slânic **170** 45 14N 25 58 E
Slankamen **166** 45 8N 20 15 E
Slano **166** 42 48N 17 53 E
Slantsy **178** 59 7N 28 5 E
Slany **150** 50 13N 14 6 E
Slask **144** 51 0N 16 30 E
Slate Is. **87** 48 40N 87 0W
Slatina **170** 44 28N 24 22 E
Slave → **76** 61 18N 113 39W
Slave Coast **247** 6 0N 2 30 E
Slave Lake **90** 55 17N 114 43W
Slave Pt. **76** 61 11N 115 56W
Slavgorod **184** 53 1N 78 37 E
Slavinja **166** 43 9N 22 50 E
Slavkov **151** 49 10N 16 52 E
Slavnoye **178** 54 24N 29 15 E
Slavonska Požega **166** 45 20N 17 40 E
Slavonski Brod **166** 45 11N 18 0 E
Slavuta **178** 50 15N 27 2 E
Slavyanka **218** 42 53N 131 21 E
Slavyansk **180** 48 55N 37 36 E
Slavyansk-na-Kubani **180** 45 15N 38 11 E
Sława **152** 51 52N 16 2 E
Sławno **152** 54 20N 16 41 E
Sławoborze **152** 53 55N 15 42 E
Sleaford **132** 53 0N 0 22W
Sleaford B. **231** 34 55 S 135 45 E
Sleat, Sd. of **134** 57 5N 5 47W
Sleidinge **143** 51 8N 3 41 E
Sleman **209** 7 40 S 110 20 E
Slemon L. **76** 63 13N 116 4W
Ślesin **152** 52 22N 18 14 E
Sliedrecht **142** 51 50N 4 45 E
Slieve Aughty **135** 53 4N 8 30W
Slieve Bloom **135** 53 4N 7 40W
Slieve Donard **135** 54 10N 5 57W
Slieve Gullion **135** 54 8N 6 26W
Slieve Mish **135** 52 12N 9 50W
Slievenamon **135** 52 25N 7 37W
Sligo **135** 54 17N 8 28W
Sligo □ **135** 54 10N 8 35W
Sligo B. **135** 54 20N 8 40W
Slikkerveer **142** 51 53N 4 36 E
Slipje **143** 51 9N 2 51 E
Sliven **167** 42 42N 26 19 E
Slivnitsa **166** 42 50N 23 0 E
Sljeme **163** 45 57N 15 58 E
Slobodskoy **182** 58 40N 50 6 E
Slobozia, Argeş, Romania **170** 44 30N 25 14 E
Slobozia, Ialomiţa, Romania **170** 44 34N 27 23 E
Slocan **93** 49 48N 117 28W
Slocan L. **93** 49 50N 117 23W
Slochteren **142** 53 12N 6 48 E
Slöinge **173** 56 51N 12 42 E
Słomniki **152** 50 16N 20 4 E
Slonim **178** 53 4N 25 19 E
Slotermeer **142** 52 55N 5 38 E
Slough **133** 51 30N 0 35W
Slovakia = Slovensko □ **151** 48 30N 19 0 E
Slovakian Ore Mts. = Slovenské Rudohorie **151** 48 45N 20 0 E
Slovenia = Slovenija □ **163** 45 58N 14 30 E
Slovenija □ **163** 45 58N 14 30 E
Slovenj Gradec **163** 46 31N 15 5 E
Slovenska Bistrica **163** 46 24N 15 35 E
Slovenská Socialisticka Republika □ **151** 48 30N 10 0 E
Slovenské Rudohorie **151** 48 45N 20 0 E
Slovensko □ **151** 48 30N 19 0 E
Słubice **152** 52 22N 14 35 E
Sluch → **178** 51 37N 26 38 E
Sluis **143** 51 18N 3 23 E
Slunchev Bryag **167** 42 40N 27 41 E
Slunj **163** 45 6N 15 33 E
Słupca **152** 52 15N 17 52 E
Słupia → **152** 54 35N 16 51 E
Słupsk **152** 54 30N 17 3 E
Słupsk □ **152** 54 15N 17 30 E
Slurry **254** 25 49 S 25 42 E
Slutsk **178** 53 2N 27 31 E
Slyne Hd. **135** 53 25N 10 10W
Slyudyanka **185** 51 40N 103 40 E
Smålandsfarvandet **172** 55 10N 11 20 E
Smalandsstenar **173** 57 9N 13 24 E
Smalltree L. **77** 61 0N 105 0W
Smallwood Reservoir **75** 54 20N 63 10W
Smarje **163** 46 15N 15 34 E
Smart Syndicate Dam **254** 30 45 S 23 10 E
Smeaton **88** 53 30N 104 49W
Smederevo **166** 44 40N 20 57 E
Smederevska Palanka **166** 44 22N 20 58 E
Smela **180** 49 15N 31 58 E
Smidovich **185** 48 36N 133 49 E
Smigiel **152** 52 1N 16 32 E
Smilde **142** 52 58N 6 28 E
Smiley **88** 51 38N 109 29W
Smilyan **167** 41 29N 24 46 E
Smith **90** 55 10N 114 0W
Smith → **76** 59 34N 126 30W
Smith Arm **94** 66 15N 123 0W
Smith I. **78** 54 13N 58 18W
Smith Pen. **95** 77 12N 78 50W
Smith Sund **12** 78 30N 74 0W
Smithburne → **230** 17 3 S 140 57 E
Smithers **76** 54 45N 127 10W
Smithfield **255** 30 9 S 26 30 E
Smiths Cove **81** 44 37N 65 42W
Smiths Falls **85** 44 55N 76 0W
Smithton **230** 40 53 S 145 6 E
Smithtown **231** 30 58 S 152 48 E
Smithville **84** 43 6N 79 33W
Smoky → **90** 56 10N 117 21W
Smoky Bay **231** 32 22 S 134 13 E
Smoky Falls **87** 50 4N 82 10W
Smoky Lake **90** 54 10N 112 30W
Smøla **171** 63 23N 8 3 E
Smolensk **178** 54 45N 32 0 E
Smolikas, Óros **168** 40 9N 20 58 E
Smolník **151** 48 43N 20 44 E
Smolyan **167** 41 36N 24 38 E
Smooth Rock Falls **87** 49 17N 81 37W
Smoothrock L. **86** 50 30N 89 30W
Smoothstone L. **77** 54 40N 106 50W
Smorgon **178** 54 20N 26 24 E
Smulţi **170** 45 57N 27 44 E
Smyadovo **167** 43 2N 27 1 E
Smyrna = İzmir **177** 38 25N 27 8 E
Snaefell **132** 54 18N 4 26W
Snaefellsjökull **174** 64 45N 23 46W
Snake I. **231** 38 47 S 146 33 E
Snake L. **77** 55 32N 106 35W
Snaring **91** 53 5N 118 4W
Snarum **171** 60 1N 9 54 E
Snedsted **173** 56 55N 8 32 E
Sneek **142** 53 2N 5 40 E
Sneeker-meer **142** 53 2N 5 45 E
Snejbjerg **173** 56 8N 8 54 E
Snezhnoye **181** 48 0N 38 58 E
Sněžka **150** 50 41N 15 50 E
Snežnik **163** 45 36N 14 35 E
Sniadowo **152** 53 2N 22 0 E
Sniardwy, Jezioro **152** 53 48N 21 50 E
Snigirevka **180** 47 2N 32 49 E
Snina **151** 49 0N 22 9 E
Snipe L. **90** 55 7N 116 47W
Snizort, L. **134** 57 33N 6 28W
Snøhetta **171** 62 19N 9 16 E
Snonuten **171** 59 31N 6 50 E
Snoul **205** 12 4N 106 26 E
Snow Lake **77** 54 52N 100 3W
Snowbird L. **77** 60 45N 103 0W
Snowdon **132** 53 4N 4 8W
Snowdrift **77** 62 24N 110 44W
Snowdrift → **77** 62 24N 110 44W
Snowflake **89** 49 3N 98 39W
Snowtown **232** 33 46 S 138 14 E
Snowy → **231** 37 46 S 148 30 E
Snowy Mts. **231** 36 30 S 148 20 E
Snug Corner **113** 22 33N 73 52W
Snyatyn **180** 48 30N 25 50 E
Soacha **118** 4 35N 74 13W
Soahanina **255** 18 42 S 44 13 E
Soalala **255** 16 6 S 45 20 E
Soan → **198** 33 1N 71 44 E
Soanierana-Ivongo **255** 16 55 S 49 35 E
Sobat, Nahr → **245** 9 22N 31 33 E
Soběslav **150** 49 16N 14 45 E
Sobhapur **198** 22 47N 78 17 E
Sobinka **179** 56 0N 40 0 E
Sobo-Yama **220** 32 51N 131 22 E
Sobótka **152** 50 54N 16 44 E
Sobrado **154** 43 2N 8 2W
Sobral **120** 3 50 S 40 20W
Sobreira Formosa **155** 39 46N 7 51W
Soc Giang **204** 22 54N 106 1 E
Soc Trang **205** 9 37N 105 50 E
Soča → **163** 46 20N 13 40 E
Sochaczew **152** 52 15N 20 13 E
Sochi **181** 43 35N 39 40 E
Société, Is. de la **225** 17 0 S 151 0W
Society Is. = Société, Is. de la **225** 17 0 S 151 0W
Socoltenango **110** 16 13N 92 15W
Socompa, Portezuelo de **124** 24 27 S 68 18W
Soconusco, Sa. de **110** 15 30N 92 35W
Socorro, Colombia **118** 6 29N 73 16W
Socorro, Mexico **102** 26 56N 102 24W
Socorro, Phil. **211** 9 37N 125 58 E
Socotra **195** 12 30N 54 0 E
Socúellmos **157** 39 16N 2 47W
Soda Plains **199** 35 30N 79 0 E
Sodankylä **174** 67 29N 26 40 E
Söderfors **172** 60 23N 17 25 E
Söderhamn **172** 61 18N 17 10 E
Söderköping **172** 58 31N 16 20 E
Södermanlands län □ **172** 59 10N 16 30 E
Södertälje **172** 59 12N 17 39 E
Sodo **245** 7 0N 37 41 E
Södra Vi **173** 57 45N 15 45 E
Sodražica **163** 45 45N 14 39 E
Soekmekaar **255** 23 30 S 29 55 E
Soest, Germany **146** 51 34N 8 7 E
Soest, Neth. **142** 52 9N 5 19 E
Soestdijk **142** 52 11N 5 17 E
Sofádhes **168** 39 20N 22 4 E
Sofara **246** 13 59N 4 9W
Sofia = Sofiya **167** 42 45N 23 20 E
Sofia → **255** 15 27 S 47 23 E
Sofievka **180** 48 6N 33 55 E
Sofiiski **185** 52 15N 133 59 E
Sofikón **169** 37 47N 23 3 E
Sofiya **167** 42 45N 23 20 E
Sōfu-Gan **219** 29 49N 140 21 E
Sogakofe **247** 6 2N 0 39 E
Sogamoso **118** 5 43N 72 56W
Soğar **193** 25 53N 58 6 E
Sögel **146** 52 50N 7 32 E
Sogeri **227** 9 26 S 147 35 E
Sogn og Fjordane fylke □ **171** 61 40N 6 0 E
Sognefjorden **171** 61 10N 5 50 E
Sŏgwi-po **215** 33 13N 126 34 E
Soh **193** 33 26N 51 27 E
Sohâg **244** 26 33N 31 43 E
Sohano **227** 5 22 S 154 37 E
Sŏhori **215** 40 7N 128 23 E
Soignies **143** 50 35N 4 5 E
Sointula **92** 50 38N 127 0W
Soira, Mt. **245** 14 45N 39 30 E
Soissons **139** 49 25N 3 19 E
Sōja **220** 34 40N 133 45 E
Sojat **198** 25 55N 73 45 E
Sok → **182** 53 24N 50 8 E
Sokal **178** 50 31N 24 15 E
Söke **169** 37 48N 27 28 E
Sokelo **251** 9 55 S 24 36 E
Sokhós **168** 40 48N 23 22 E
Sokki, Oued In → **241** 29 30N 3 42 E
Sokna **171** 60 16N 9 50 E
Soknedal **171** 62 57N 10 13 E
Soko Banja **166** 43 40N 21 51 E
Sokodé **247** 9 0N 1 11 E
Sokol **179** 59 30N 40 5 E
Sokolac **166** 43 56N 18 48 E
Sokółka **152** 53 25N 23 30 E
Sokolo **246** 14 53N 6 8W
Sokolov **150** 50 12N 12 40 E
Sokołów Małpolski **151** 50 12N 22 7 E
Sokołów Podlaski **152** 52 25N 22 15 E
Sokoły **152** 52 59N 22 42 E
Sokoto **247** 13 2N 5 16 E
Sokoto □ **247** 12 30N 5 0 E
Sokoto → **247** 11 20N 4 10 E
Sokuluk **183** 42 52N 74 18 E
Sol Iletsk **182** 51 10N 55 0 E
Sola **171** 58 53N 5 36 E
Sola → **151** 50 4N 19 15 E
Solaf, W. → **191** 28 42N 33 41 E
Solai **250** 0 2N 36 12 E
Solana **210** 17 39N 121 41 E
Solana, La **157** 38 59N 3 14W
Solano **210** 16 31N 121 15 E
Solapur **200** 17 43N 75 56 E
Solares **154** 43 23N 3 43W
Solberga **173** 57 45N 14 43 E
Solca **170** 47 40N 25 50 E
Solec Kujawski **152** 53 5N 18 14 E
Soledad, Colombia **118** 10 55N 74 46W
Soledad, Mexico **102** 26 48N 101 42W
Soledad, Venezuela **119** 8 10N 63 34W
Soledad → **99** 25 17N 112 9W
Soledad, La **104** 24 46N 104 55W
Soledad de Doblado **109** 19 3N 96 25W
Soledad Diez Gutiérrez **103** 22 12N 100 57W
Solent, The **133** 50 45N 1 25W
Solenzara **141** 41 53N 9 23 E
Solesmes **139** 50 10N 3 30 E
Solfonn **171** 60 2N 6 57 E
Soligalich **179** 59 5N 42 10 E
Soligorsk **178** 52 51N 27 27 E
Solikamsk **182** 59 38N 56 50 E
Solila **255** 21 25 S 46 37 E
Solimões → = Amazonas → **119** 0 5 S 50 0W
Solingen **146** 51 10N 7 4 E
Solís **103** 23 15N 100 50W
Solis, Presa **107** 20 2N 100 37W
Sollebrunn **173** 58 8N 12 32 E
Sollefteå **172** 63 12N 17 20 E
Sollentuna **172** 59 26N 17 56 E
Sóller **156** 39 46N 2 43 E
Solling **146** 51 44N 9 36 E
Solna **172** 59 22N 18 1 E
Solnechnogorsk **179** 56 10N 36 57 E
Sologne **139** 47 40N 2 0 E
Solok **208** 0 45 S 100 40 E
Sololá **112** 14 49N 91 10 E
Solomon Is. ■ **224** 6 0 S 155 0 E
Solomon Sea **227** 7 0 S 150 0 E
Solomon's Pools = Birak Sulaymān **189** 31 42N 35 7 E
Solon **213** 46 32N 121 10 E
Solonópole **120** 5 44 S 39 1W
Solor **207** 8 27 S 123 0 E
Solotcha **179** 54 48N 39 53 E
Solothurn **148** 47 13N 7 32 E
Solothurn □ **148** 47 18N 7 40 E
Solotobe **183** 44 37N 66 3 E
Solsona **156** 42 0N 1 31 E
Solt **151** 46 45N 19 1 E
Solta **163** 43 24N 16 15 E
Solţānābād, Khorāsān, Iran **193** 34 13N 59 58 E
Solţānābād, Khorāsān, Iran **193** 36 29N 58 5 E
Solţānābād, Markazī, Iran **193** 35 31N 51 10 E
Soltau **146** 52 59N 9 50 E
Soltsy **178** 58 10N 30 30 E
Solund **171** 61 5N 4 50 E
Solunska Glava **166** 41 44N 21 31 E
Sölvesborg **173** 56 5N 14 35 E
Solvychegodsk **176** 61 21N 46 56 E
Solway Firth **132** 54 45N 3 38W
Solwezi **251** 12 11 S 26 21 E
Sōma **218** 37 40N 140 50 E
Somali Rep. ■ **256** 7 0N 47 0 E
Sombe Dzong **202** 27 13N 89 8 E
Sombernon **139** 47 20N 4 40 E
Sombor **166** 45 46N 19 9 E
Sombra **84** 42 43N 82 29W
Sombrerete **105** 23 38N 103 39W
Sombrero **113** 18 37N 63 30W
Someren **143** 51 23N 5 42 E
Somerset **89** 49 25N 98 39W
Somerset □ **133** 51 9N 3 0W
Somerset East **254** 32 42 S 25 35 E
Somerset I. **95** 73 30N 93 0W
Somerset West **254** 34 8 S 18 50 E
Someş → **170** 47 15N 23 45 E
Someşul Mare → **170** 47 18N 24 30 E
Somma Lombardo **162** 45 41N 8 42 E
Somma Vesuviana **165** 40 52N 14 23 E
Sommariva **231** 26 24 S 146 36 E
Sommatino **164** 37 20N 14 0 E
Somme □ **139** 50 0N 2 20 E
Somme, B. de la **138** 50 14N 1 33 E
Sommelsdijk **142** 51 46N 4 9 E
Sommen **173** 58 12N 15 0 E
Sommen, L. **173** 58 0N 15 15 E
Sommepy-Tahure **139** 49 15N 4 31 E
Sömmerda **146** 51 10N 11 8 E
Sommesous **139** 48 44N 4 12 E
Sommières **141** 43 47N 4 6 E
Somogy □ **151** 46 19N 17 30 E
Somogyszob **151** 46 18N 17 20 E
Somosomo Str. **226** 16 0 S 180 0 E
Somoto **112** 13 28N 86 37W
Sompolno **152** 52 26N 18 30 E
Somport, Paso **156** 42 48N 0 31W
Somport, Puerto de **156** 42 48N 0 31W
Somuncurá, Meseta de **126** 41 30 S 67 0W
Son, Neth. **143** 51 31N 5 30 E
Son, Norway **171** 59 32N 10 42 E
Son, Spain **154** 42 43N 8 58W
Son Ha **204** 15 3N 108 34 E
Son Hoa **204** 13 2N 108 58 E
Son La **204** 21 20N 103 50 E
Son Tay **204** 21 8N 105 30 E
Soná **112** 8 0N 81 20W
Sonamarg **199** 34 18N 75 21 E
Sonamukhi **199** 23 18N 87 27 E
Sonamura **202** 23 29N 91 15 E
Sŏnchŏn **215** 39 48N 124 55 E
Soncino **162** 45 24N 9 52 E
Sondags → **254** 33 44 S 25 51 E
Sóndalo **162** 46 20N 10 20 E
Sondar **199** 33 28N 75 56 E
Sønder Omme **173** 55 50N 8 54 E
Sønder Ternby **173** 57 31N 9 58 E
Sønderborg **173** 54 55N 9 49 E
Sonderjyllands Amtskommune □ **173** 55 10N 9 10 E
Sondershausen **146** 51 22N 10 50 E
Sóndrio **162** 46 10N 9 53 E
Sone **251** 17 23 S 34 55 E
Sonepur **199** 20 55N 83 50 E
Song **204** 18 28N 100 11 E
Song Cau **204** 13 27N 109 18 E
Song Xian **214** 34 12N 112 8 E
Songchŏn **215** 39 12N 126 15 E
Songea **251** 10 40 S 35 40 E
Songea □ **251** 10 30 S 36 0 E
Songeons **139** 49 32N 1 50 E
Songhua Hu **215** 43 35N 126 50 E
Songhua Jiang → **215** 47 45N 132 30 E
Songjiang **217** 31 1N 121 12 E
Songjin **215** 40 40N 129 10 E
Songjŏng-ni **215** 35 8N 126 47 E
Songkan **216** 28 35N 106 52 E
Songkhla **205** 7 13N 100 37 E
Songming **216** 25 12N 103 2 E

Songnim 215 38 45N 125 39 E
Songo 253 7 22 S 14 51 E
Songololo 253 5 42 S 14 2 E
Songpan 216 32 40N 103 30 E
Songtao 216 28 11N 109 10 E
Songwe 250 3 20 S 26 16 E
Songwe → 251 9 44 S 33 58 E
Songxi 217 27 31N 118 44 E
Songzi 217 30 12N 111 45 E
Sonid Youqi 214 42 45N 112 48 E
Sonipat 198 29 0N 77 5 E
Sonkel, Ozero 183 41 50N 75 12 E
Sonkovo 179 57 50N 37 5 E
Sonmiani 197 25 25N 66 40 E
Sonningdale 88 52 23N 107 44W
Sonnino 164 41 25N 13 13 E
Sono →, Goiás, Brazil 120 9 58 S 48 11W
Sono →, Minas Gerais, Brazil 121 17 2 S 45 32W
Sonobe 221 35 6N 135 28 E
Sonogno 149 46 22N 8 47 E
Sonora, Canada 81 45 4N 61 54W
Sonora, Mexico 98 32 18N 115 12W
Sonora □ 100 29 20N 110 40W
Sonora → 100 28 48N 111 49W
Sonora I. 92 50 22N 125 15W
Sonoyta 100 31 51N 112 50W
Sonoyta → 100 31 16N 113 26W
Sonoyta, Sa. de 100 31 54N 112 52W
Sŏnsan 215 36 14N 128 17 E
Sonsomate 112 13 43N 89 44W
Sonthofen 147 47 31N 10 16 E
Sooke 93 48 13N 123 43W
Sop Hao 204 20 33N 104 27 E
Sop Prap 204 17 53N 99 20 E
Sopachuy 123 19 29 S 64 31W
Sopi 207 2 34N 128 28 E
Sopo, Nahr → 245 8 40N 26 30 E
Sopot, Poland 152 54 27N 18 31 E
Sopot, Yugoslavia 166 44 29N 20 30 E
Sopotnica 166 41 23N 21 13 E
Sopron 151 47 45N 16 32 E
Sop's Arm 79 49 46N 56 56W
Sopur 199 34 18N 74 27 E
Sør-Rondane 13 72 0 S 25 0 E
Sør-Trøndelag fylke □ 171 63 0N 10 0 E
Sora 164 41 45N 13 36 E
Sorada 200 19 45N 84 26 E
Sorah 198 27 13N 68 56 E
Söråker 172 62 30N 17 32 E
Sorano 163 42 40N 11 42 E
Sorata 122 15 50 S 68 40W
Sorbas 157 37 6N 2 7W
Sordo → 109 16 30N 97 31W
Sorel 83 46 0N 73 10W
Sörenberg 148 46 50N 8 2 E
Sorento 231 38 22 S 144 47 E
Soreq, N. → 189 31 57N 34 43 E
Soresina 162 45 17N 9 51 E
Sorgono 164 40 1N 9 6 E
Sorgues 141 44 1N 4 53 E
Sorğun → 190 36 36N 34 20 E
Soria 156 41 43N 2 32W
Soria □ 156 41 46N 2 28W
Soriano 124 33 24 S 58 19W
Soriano nel Cimino 163 42 25N 12 14 E
Sorkh, Kuh-e 193 35 40N 58 30 E
Sorø, Denmark 172 55 26N 11 32 E
Soro, Guinea 246 10 9N 9 48W
Sorocaba 125 23 31 S 47 27W
Sorochinsk 182 52 26N 53 10 E
Soroki 180 48 8N 28 12 E
Soroksár 151 47 24N 19 9 E
Soron 199 27 55N 78 45 E
Sorong 207 0 55 S 131 15 E
Soroti 250 1 43N 33 35 E
Sørøya 174 70 40N 22 30 E
Sørøyane 171 62 25N 5 32 E
Sørøysundet 174 70 25N 23 0 E
Sorraia → 155 38 55N 8 53W
Sorrento 165 40 38N 14 23 E
Sorsele 174 65 31N 17 30 E
Sorso 164 40 50N 8 34 E
Sorsogon 210 13 0N 124 0 E
Sorsogon □ 210 12 50N 123 55 E
Sortavala 176 61 42N 30 41 E
Sortino 165 37 9N 15 1 E
Sorūbī 197 34 36N 69 43 E
Sorvizhi 179 57 52N 48 32 E
Sos 156 42 30N 1 13W
Sŏsan 215 36 47N 126 27 E
Soscumica, L. 82 50 15N 77 27W
Sosna → 179 52 42N 38 55 E
Sosnogorsk 176 63 37N 53 51 E
Sosnovka, R.S.F.S.R., U.S.S.R. 179 53 13N 41 24 E
Sosnovka, R.S.F.S.R., U.S.S.R. 185 54 9N 109 35 E
Sosnowiec 152 50 20N 19 10 E
Sospel 141 43 52N 7 27 E
Sostanj 163 46 23N 15 4 E
Sŏsura 215 42 16N 130 36 E
Sosva 182 59 10N 61 50 E
Sosva → 182 59 32N 62 20 E
Soteapan 109 18 14N 94 52W
Soto la Marina 103 23 46N 98 13W
Soto la Marina → 103 23 45N 97 45W
Soto y Amío 154 42 46N 5 53W
Sotteville-lès-Rouen 138 49 24N 1 5 E
Sotuta 111 20 36N 89 1W
Souanké 252 2 10N 14 3 E
Soucy 82 48 10N 75 30W
Soúdhas, Kólpos 169 35 25N 24 10 E
Soufflay 252 2 1N 14 54 E
Souflíon 168 41 12N 26 18 E
Sougne-Remouchamps 143 50 29N 5 42 E
Souillac 140 44 53N 1 29 E
Souk-Ahras 241 36 23N 7 57 E
Souk el Arba du Rharb 240 34 43N 5 59W
Soukhouma 204 14 38N 105 48 E
Sŏul 215 37 31N 126 58 E
Soulac-sur-Mer 140 45 30N 1 7W
Soultz 139 48 57N 7 52 E
Soumagne 143 50 37N 5 44 E
Sounding Cr. → 91 52 6N 110 28W
Sounding L. 91 52 8N 110 29W
Soúnion, Ákra 169 37 37N 24 1 E
Sour el Ghozlane 241 36 10N 3 45 E
Sources, Mt. aux 255 28 45 S 28 50 E
Sourdeval 138 48 43N 0 55W
Soure, Brazil 120 0 35 S 48 30W
Soure, Portugal 154 40 4N 8 38W
Souris, Man., Canada 77 49 40N 100 20W
Souris, P.E.I., Canada 81 46 21N 62 15W
Souris → 89 49 40N 99 34W
Soúrpi 169 39 6N 22 54 E
Sousa 120 6 45 S 38 10W
Sousel, Brazil 120 2 38 S 52 29W
Sousel, Portugal 155 38 57N 7 40W
Souss, O. → 240 30 27N 9 31W
Sousse 241 35 50N 10 38 E
Soustons 140 43 45N 1 19W
Souterraine, La 140 46 15N 1 30 E
South Africa, Rep. of, ■ 254 32 0 S 17 0 E
South America 114 10 0 S 60 0W
South Atlantic Ocean 129 20 0 S 10 0W
South Aulatsivik I. 78 56 45N 61 30W
South Australia □ 231 32 0 S 139 0 E
South Baymouth 84 45 33N 82 1W
South Bentinck Arm 92 52 7N 126 47W
South Branch 79 47 55N 59 2W
South Brook 79 49 26N 56 5W
South Buganda □ 250 0 15 S 31 30 E
South China Sea 205 10 0N 113 0 E
South Cotabato □ 211 6 0N 125 0 E
South Downs 133 50 53N 0 10W
South East C. 230 43 40 S 146 50 E
South-East Indian Rise 224 43 0 S 80 0 E
South East Is. 229 34 17 S 123 30 E
South Esk → 134 56 44N 3 3W
South Foreland 133 51 7N 1 23 E
South Georgia 13 54 30 S 37 0W
South Gillies 86 48 14N 89 42W
South Glamorgan □ 133 51 30N 3 20W
South Hd. 79 49 9N 58 22W
South Heart → 90 55 34N 116 11W
South Henik, L. 77 61 30N 97 30W
South Honshu Ridge 224 23 0N 143 0 E
South Horr 250 2 12N 36 56 E
South I., Kenya 250 2 35N 36 35 E
South I., N.Z. 235 44 0 S 170 0 E
South Invercargill 235 46 26 S 168 23 E
South Knife → 77 58 55N 94 37W
South Korea ■ 215 36 0N 128 0 E
South Magnetic Pole 13 65 36 S 139 24 E
South Mashonaland □ 251 18 0 S 31 30 E
South Molton 133 51 1N 3 50W
South Nahanni → 76 61 3N 123 21W
South Nation → 85 45 34N 75 6W
South Negril Pt. 112 18 14N 78 30W
South Orkney Is. 13 63 0 S 45 0W
South Pole 13 90 0 S 0 0
South Porcupine 87 48 30N 81 12W
South River 84 45 52N 79 23W
South Ronaldsay 134 58 46N 2 58W
South Sandwich Is. 129 57 0 S 27 0W
South Saskatchewan → 88 53 15N 105 5W
South Seal → 77 58 48N 98 8W
South Shetland Is. 13 62 0 S 59 0W
South Shields 132 54 59N 1 26W
South Taranaki Bight 234 39 40 S 174 5 E
South Thompson → 93 50 40N 120 20W
South Twin I. 78 53 7N 79 52W
South Twin L. 79 49 16N 55 47W
South Tyne → 132 54 46N 2 25W
South Uist 134 57 20N 7 15W
South Wabasca L. 90 55 55N 113 45W
South West Africa = Namibia ■ 254 22 0 S 18 9 E
South West C. 230 43 34 S 146 3 E
South West Port Moulton 81 43 54N 64 49W
South Yemen ■ 195 15 0N 48 0 E
South Yorkshire □ 132 53 30N 1 20W
Southampton, N.S., Canada 81 45 35N 64 15W
Southampton, Ont., Canada 84 44 30N 81 25W
Southampton, U.K. 133 50 54N 1 23W
Southampton I. 95 64 30N 84 0W
Southbank 92 54 2N 125 46W
Southbridge 235 43 48 S 172 16 E
Southeast Pacific Basin 225 16 30 S 92 0W
Southend 77 56 19N 103 22W
Southend-on-Sea 133 51 32N 0 42 E
Southern □, Malawi 251 15 0 S 35 0 E
Southern □, S. Leone 246 8 0N 12 30W
Southern □, Zambia 251 16 20 S 26 20 E
Southern Alps 235 43 41 S 170 11 E
Southern Cross 229 31 12 S 119 15 E
Southern Hills 229 32 15 S 122 40 E
Southern Indian L. 77 57 10N 98 30W
Southern Leyte □ 211 10 30N 125 10 E
Southern Ocean 13 62 0 S 60 0 E
Southern Uplands 134 55 30N 3 3W
Southey 88 50 56N 104 30W
Southland □ 235 45 51 S 168 13 E
Southport, Australia 231 27 58 S 153 25 E
Southport, U.K. 132 53 38N 3 1W
Southwestern Pacific Basin 224 42 0 S 170 0W
Southwold 133 52 19N 1 41 E
Soutpansberge 255 23 0 S 29 30 E
Souvigny 140 46 33N 3 10 E
Sovata 170 46 35N 25 3 E
Sovereign 88 51 31N 107 43W
Sovetsk, Lithuania, U.S.S.R. 178 55 6N 21 50 E
Sovetsk, R.S.F.S.R., U.S.S.R. 179 57 38N 48 53 E
Sovetskaya Gavan 185 48 50N 140 0 E
Sovicille 163 43 16N 11 12 E
Sovra 166 42 44N 17 34 E
Sowden L. 86 49 32N 91 12W
Sōya-Kaikyō = Perouse Str., La 186 45 40N 142 0 E
Sōya-Misaki 218 45 30N 142 0 E
Soyaló 110 16 54N 92 55W
Soyatita 104 25 45N 107 22W
Soyatlán, Jalisco, Mexico 106 19 38N 103 22W
Soyatlán, Jalisco, Mexico 106 20 18N 104 18W
Soyo 253 6 13 S 12 20 E
Sozh → 178 51 57N 30 48 E
Sozopol 167 42 23N 27 42 E
Spa 143 50 29N 5 53 E
Spain ■ 153 40 0N 5 0W
Spakenburg 142 52 15N 5 22 E
Spalding, Australia 231 33 30 S 138 37 E
Spalding, Canada 88 52 20N 104 30W
Spalding, U.K. 132 52 47N 0 9W
Spangereid 171 58 3N 7 9 E
Spaniard's Bay 79 47 38N 53 20W
Spanish 84 46 12N 82 20W
Spanish → 84 46 11N 82 19W
Spanish Town 112 18 0N 76 57W
Sparta = Spárti 169 37 5N 22 25 E
Spartel, C. 240 35 47N 5 56W
Spárti 169 37 5N 22 25 E
Spartivento, C., Calabria, Italy 165 37 56N 16 4 E
Spartivento, C., Sard., Italy 164 38 52N 8 50 E
Sparwood 91 49 44N 114 53W
Spas-Demensk 178 54 20N 34 0 E
Spas-Klepiki 179 55 10N 40 10 E
Spassk-Dalniy 185 44 40N 132 48 E
Spassk-Ryazanskiy 179 54 24N 40 25 E
Spátha, Akra 169 35 42N 23 43 E
Spatsizi → 76 57 42N 128 7W
Speed 232 35 21 S 142 27 E
Speer 149 47 12N 9 8 E
Speers 88 52 43N 107 34W
Speightstown 113 13 15N 59 39W
Speke Gulf 250 2 20 S 32 50 E
Spekholzerheide 143 50 51N 6 2 E
Spence Bay 95 69 32N 93 32W
Spencer, C. 232 35 20 S 136 53 E
Spencer B. 254 25 30 S 14 47 E
Spencer G. 232 34 0 S 137 20 E
Spencerville 85 44 51N 75 33W
Spences Bridge 93 50 25N 121 20W
Spenser Mts. 235 42 15 S 172 45 E
Sperkhiós → 169 38 57N 22 3 E
Sperling 89 49 30N 97 42W
Sperrin Mts. 135 54 50N 7 0W
Spessart 147 50 10N 9 20 E
Spétsai 169 37 15N 23 10 E
Spey → 134 57 26N 3 25W
Speyer 147 49 19N 8 26 E
Speyer → 147 49 19N 8 27 E
Spézia, La 162 44 8N 9 50 E
Spezzano Albanese 165 39 41N 16 19 E
Spiekeroog 146 53 45N 7 42 E
Spielfeld 163 46 43N 15 38 E
Spiez 148 46 40N 7 40 E
Spijk 142 53 24N 6 50 E
Spijkenisse 142 51 51N 4 20 E
Spíli 169 35 13N 24 31 E
Spilimbergo 163 46 7N 12 53 E
Spin Baldak = Qala-i-Jadid 198 31 1N 66 25 E
Spinazzola 165 40 58N 16 5 E
Spind 171 58 6N 6 53 E
Spineni 170 44 43N 24 37 E
Spirit River 90 55 45N 118 50W
Spiritwood 88 53 24N 107 33W
Spišská Nová Ves 151 48 58N 20 34 E
Spišské Podhradie 151 49 0N 20 48 E
Spital 150 47 42N 14 18 E
Spithead 133 50 43N 1 5W
Spittal 150 46 48N 13 31 E
Spitzbergen = Svalbard 12 78 0N 17 0 E
Split 163 43 31N 16 26 E
Split L. 77 56 8N 96 15W
Splitski Kanal 163 43 31N 16 20 E
Splügen 149 46 34N 9 21 E
Splügenpass 149 46 30N 9 20 E
Spoleto 163 42 46N 12 47 E
Sporádhes 169 39 0N 24 30 E
Sporyy Navolok, Mys. 184 75 50N 68 40 E
Spragge 84 46 15N 82 40W
Sprague 89 49 2N 95 38W
Spratly, I. 206 8 20N 112 0 E
Spree → 146 52 32N 13 13 E
Sprimont 143 50 30N 5 40 E
Spring Coulee 91 49 20N 113 3W
Spring Hill 233 33 23 S 149 9 E
Spring Valley 88 49 56N 105 24W
Springbok 254 29 42 S 17 54 E
Springdale 79 49 30N 56 6W
Springe 146 52 12N 9 35 E
Springfield, N.S., Canada 81 44 38N 64 52W
Springfield, Ont., Canada 84 42 50N 80 56W
Springfield, N.Z. 235 43 19 S 171 56 E
Springfontein 254 30 15 S 25 40 E
Springhill 75 45 40N 64 4W
Springhouse 93 51 56N 122 7W
Springhurst 231 36 10 S 146 31 E
Springs 255 26 13 S 28 25 E
Springside 88 51 21N 102 44W
Springsure 230 24 8 S 148 6 E
Springvale, Queens., Australia 230 23 33 S 140 42 E
Springvale, W. Austral., Australia 228 17 48 S 127 41 E
Springwater 88 51 58N 108 23W
Sproat L. 92 49 17N 125 2W
Spruce Grove 90 53 32N 113 55W
Spruce I. 89 53 5N 100 40W
Spruce Woods Prov. Park 89 49 43N 99 5W
Sprucedale 84 45 29N 79 28W
Spurn Hd. 132 53 34N 0 8 E
Spuž 166 42 32N 19 10 E
Spuzzum 93 49 37N 121 23W
Squamish 93 49 45N 123 10W
Squamish → 93 49 45N 123 8W
Square Islands 78 52 47N 55 47W
Squatec 83 47 53N 68 43W
Squaw Rapids 88 53 41N 103 21W
Squillace, Golfo di 165 38 43N 16 35 E
Squinzano 165 40 27N 18 1 E
Squires, Mt. 229 26 14 S 127 28 E
Sragen 209 7 26 S 111 2 E
Srbac 166 45 7N 17 30 E
Srbija □ 166 43 30N 21 0 E
Srbobran 166 45 32N 19 48 E
Sre Khtum 205 12 10N 106 52 E
Sre Umbell 205 11 8N 103 46 E
Srebrnica 166 44 10N 19 18 E
Sredinnyy Khrebet 185 57 0N 160 0 E
Sredinnyy Ra. 186 57 0N 160 0 E
Središče 163 46 24N 16 17 E
Sredna Gora 167 42 40N 24 20 E
Sredne Tambovskoye 185 50 55N 137 45 E
Srednekolymsk 185 67 27N 153 40 E
Srednevilyuysk 185 63 50N 123 5 E
Sredni Rodopi 167 41 40N 24 45 E
Śrem 152 52 6N 17 2 E

Sremska Mitrovica . . **166** 44 59N 19 33 E
Sremski Karlovci . . . **166** 45 12N 19 56 E
Srepok → . . . . **204** 13 33N 106 16 E
Sretensk . . . . **185** 52 10N 117 40 E
Sri Kalahasti . . . . **201** 13 45N 79 44 E
Sri Lanka ■ . . . . **201** 7 30N 80 50 E
Sriharikota, I. . . . . . . **201** 13 40N 80 20 E
Srikakulam . . . . **200** 18 14N 83 58 E
Srinagar . . . . **199** 34 5N 74 50 E
Sripur . . . . **202** 24 14N 90 30 E
Srirangam . . . . **201** 10 54N 78 42 E
Srivardhan . . . . **200** 18 4N 73 3 E
Srivilliputtur . . . . **201** 9 31N 77 40 E
Środa Śląska . . . . **152** 51 10N 16 36 E
Środa Wielkopolski . **152** 52 15N 17 19 E
Srokowo . . . . **152** 54 13N 21 31 E
Srpska Crnja . . . . **166** 45 38N 20 44 E
Srpska Itabej . . . . . . **166** 45 35N 20 44 E
Staaten → . . . . **230** 16 24 S 141 17 E
Staberhuk . . . . **146** 54 23N 11 18 E
Stabroek . . . . **143** 51 20N 4 22 E
Stad Delden . . . . **142** 52 16N 6 43 E
Stade . . . . **146** 53 35N 9 31 E
Staden . . . . **143** 50 59N 3 1 E
Staðarhólskirkja **174** 65 23N 21 58W
Städjan . . . . **172** 61 56N 12 52 E
Stadlandet . . . . **171** 62 10N 5 10 E
Stadskanaal . . . . **142** 53 4N 6 55 E
Stadthagen . . . . **146** 52 20N 9 14 E
Stadtlohn . . . . **146** 52 0N 6 52 E
Stadtroda . . . . **146** 50 51N 11 44 E
Stäfa . . . . **149** 47 14N 8 45 E
Stafafell **174** 64 25N 14 52W
Staffa **134** 56 26N 6 21W
Stafford **132** 52 49N 2 9W
Stafford □ **132** 52 53N 2 10W
Stagnone . . . . **164** 37 50N 12 28 E
Staines **133** 51 26N 0 30W
Stainz . . . . **150** 46 53N 15 17 E
Stakhanov . . . . **181** 48 35N 38 40 E
Stalač . . . . **166** 43 43N 21 28 E
Stalden . . . . **148** 46 14N 7 52 E
Stalingrad =
Volgograd . . . . **181** 48 40N 44 25 E
Staliniri =
Tskhinvali . . . . **181** 42 14N 44 1 E
Stalino = Donetsk . . **180** 48 0N 37 45 E
Stalinogorsk =
Novomoskovsk . . . **179** 54 5N 38 15 E
Stalowa Wola . . . . . . **152** 50 34N 22 3 E
Stalybridge **132** 53 29N 2 4W
Stamford, Australia . **230** 21 15 S 143 46 E
Stamford, U.K. **133** 52 39N 0 29W
Stančevo =
Kalipetrovo . . . . . . **167** 44 5N 27 14 E
Standard **91** 51 7N 112 59W
Standerton . . . . **255** 26 55 S 29 7 E
Stange . . . . **171** 60 43N 11 5 E
Stanger . . . . **255** 29 27 S 31 14 E
Stanhope . . . . **233** 36 27 S 144 59 E
Stanišić . . . . **166** 45 56N 19 10 E
Stanislav = Ivano-
Frankovsk . . . . **178** 48 40N 24 40 E
Stanisławów . . . . **152** 52 18N 21 33 E
Stanke Dimitrov . . . . **166** 42 17N 23 9 E
Stanley, Australia . . **230** 40 46 S 145 19 E
Stanley, N.B.,
Canada **81** 46 20N 66 44W
Stanley, Sask.,
Canada **77** 55 24N 104 22W
Stanley, Falk. Is. . . . **126** 51 40 S 59 51W
Stanley Res. . . . . **201** 11 50N 77 40 E
Stanovoy Khrebet . . **185** 55 0N 130 0 E
Stanovoy Ra. . . . . . . **186** 55 0N 130 0 E
Stans . . . . **149** 46 58N 8 21 E
Stansmore Ra. . . . . . **228** 21 23 S 128 33 E
Stanthorpe . . . . **231** 28 36 S 151 59 E
Stantsiya Karshi . . . . **183** 38 49N 65 47 E
Staphorst . . . . **142** 52 39N 6 12 E
Staporków . . . . **152** 51 9N 20 31 E
Star City **88** 52 50N 104 20W
Stara-minskaya . . . . . **181** 46 33N 39 0 E
Stara Moravica . . . . . **166** 45 50N 19 30 E
Stara Pazova . . . . **166** 45 0N 20 10 E
Stara Planina . . . . . . **167** 43 15N 23 0 E
Stara Zagora . . . . **167** 42 26N 25 39 E
Starachowice . . . . **152** 51 3N 21 2 E
Starashcherbinovskaya
181 46 40N 38 53 E
Staraya Russa . . . . . . **178** 57 58N 31 23 E
Starbuck **89** 49 46N 97 37W
Starbuck I. . . . . **225** 5 37 S 155 55W
Stargard . . . . **146** 53 29N 13 19 E
Stargard Szczeciński **152** 53 20N 15 0 E
Stari Bar . . . . **166** 42 7N 19 13 E
Stari Trg . . . . **163** 45 29N 15 7 E
Staritsa . . . . **178** 56 33N 35 0 E
Starnberg . . . . **147** 48 0N 11 20 E
Starnberger See . . . . **147** 47 55N 11 20 E
Starobelsk . . . . **181** 49 16N 39 0 E
Starodub . . . . **178** 52 30N 32 50 E
Starogard . . . . **152** 53 59N 18 30 E
Starokonstantinov . . **180** 49 48N 27 10 E
Starosielce . . . . **152** 53 8N 23 5 E
Start Pt. **133** 50 13N 3 38W
Stary Sącz . . . . **151** 49 33N 20 35 E
Staryy Biryuzyak . . . **181** 44 46N 46 50 E
Staryy Chartoriysk . . **178** 51 15N 25 54 E
Staryy Kheydzhan . . **185** 60 0N 144 50 E
Staryy Krym . . . . **180** 45 3N 35 8 E
Staryy Oskol . . . . **179** 51 19N 37 55 E
Stassfurt . . . . **146** 51 51N 11 34 E
Staszów . . . . **152** 50 33N 21 10 E
Staten, I. =
Estados, I. de Los **126** 54 40 S 64 30W
Stavanger . . . . **171** 58 57N 5 40 E
Stave Falls **93** 49 13N 122 22W
Stave L. **93** 49 22N 122 17W
Staveley . . . . **235** 43 40 S 171 32 E
Stavelot . . . . **143** 50 23N 5 55 E
Stavely **91** 50 10N 113 38W
Stavenisse . . . . **143** 51 35N 4 1 E
Staveren . . . . **142** 52 53N 5 22 E
Stavern . . . . **171** 59 0N 10 1 E
Stavre . . . . **172** 62 51N 15 19 E
Stavropol . . . . **181** 45 5N 42 0 E
Stavroúpolis . . . . **168** 41 12N 24 45 E
Stawell . . . . **231** 37 5 S 142 47 E
Stawell → . . . . **230** 20 20 S 142 55 E
Stawiski . . . . **152** 53 22N 22 9 E
Stawiszyn . . . . **152** 51 56N 18 4 E
Stayner **84** 44 25N 80 5W
Stębark . . . . **152** 53 30N 20 10 E
Stebleva . . . . **168** 41 18N 20 33 E
Steckborn . . . . **149** 47 44N 8 59 E
Steele, Mt. **94** 61 6N 140 23W
Steen River **76** 59 40N 117 12W
Steenbergen . . . . **143** 51 35N 4 19 E
Steenkool = Bintuni **207** 2 7 S 133 32 E
Steensby Inlet **95** 70 15N 78 35W
Steenvoorde . . . . **139** 50 48N 2 33 E
Steenwijk . . . . **142** 52 47N 6 7 E
Steep Pt. . . . . **229** 26 8 S 113 8 E
Steep Rock **89** 51 30N 98 48W
Ştefăneşti . . . . **170** 47 44N 27 15 E
Stefanie L. = Chew
Bahir . . . . **245** 4 40N 36 50 E
Stefansson Bay . . . . . **13** 67 20 S 59 8 E
Stefansson I. **94** 73 20N 105 45W
Steffisburg . . . . **148** 46 47N 7 38 E
Stege . . . . **172** 55 0N 12 18 E
Steiermark □ . . . . **150** 47 26N 15 0 E
Steigerwald . . . . **147** 49 45N 10 30 E
Stein . . . . **143** 50 58N 5 45 E
Steinbach **89** 49 32N 96 40W
Steinfort . . . . **143** 49 39N 5 55 E
Steinheim . . . . **146** 51 50N 9 6 E
Steinhuder Meer . . . . **146** 52 48N 9 20 E
Steinkjer . . . . **174** 63 59N 11 31 E
Stekene . . . . **143** 51 12N 4 2 E
Stellaland . . . . **254** 26 45 S 24 50 E
Stellarton **81** 45 32N 62 30W
Stellenbosch . . . . **254** 33 58 S 18 50 E
Stellendam . . . . **142** 51 49N 4 1 E
Stelvio, Paso dello . . **149** 46 32N 10 27 E
Stemshaug . . . . **171** 63 19N 8 44 E
Stendal . . . . **146** 52 36N 11 50 E
Stene . . . . **143** 51 12N 2 56 E
Stensele . . . . **174** 65 3N 17 8 E
Stenstorp . . . . **173** 58 17N 13 45 E
Stepanakert . . . . **177** 39 40N 46 25 E
Stephens Creek . . . . . **231** 31 50 S 141 30 E
Stephens I., Canada **92** 54 10N 130 45W
Stephens I., N.Z. . . . **235** 40 40 S 174 1 E
Stephenville **79** 48 31N 58 35W
Stephenville
Crossing **79** 48 30N 58 26W
Stepnica . . . . **152** 53 38N 14 36 E
Stepnoi = Elista . . . . **181** 46 16N 44 14 E
Stepnoye . . . . **182** 54 4N 60 26 E
Stepnyak . . . . **184** 52 50N 70 50 E
Steppe . . . . **186** 50 0N 50 0 E
Stereá Ellas □ . . . . . **169** 38 50N 22 0 E
Sterkstroom . . . . **254** 31 32 S 26 32 E
Sterlitamak . . . . **182** 53 40N 56 0 E
Şternberg . . . . **146** 53 42N 11 48 E
Šternberk . . . . **151** 49 45N 17 15 E
Stettin = Szczecin . . **152** 53 27N 14 27 E
Stettiner Haff . . . . . . **146** 53 50N 14 25 E
Stettler **91** 52 19N 112 40W
Stevens **87** 49 33N 85 49W
Stevenson L. **89** 53 55N 96 0W
Stevns Klint . . . . **172** 55 17N 12 28 E
Stewart, B.C.,
Canada **76** 55 56N 129 57W
Stewart, N.W.T.,
Canada **94** 63 19N 139 26W
Stewart, C. . . . . **230** 11 57 S 134 56 E
Stewart, I. . . . . **126** 54 50 S 71 15W
Stewart I. . . . . **235** 46 58 S 167 54 E
Stewart Valley **88** 50 36N 107 48W
Stewiacke **81** 45 9N 63 22W
Steynsburg . . . . **254** 31 15 S 25 49 E
Steyr . . . . **150** 48 3N 14 25 E
Steyr → . . . . **150** 48 17N 14 15 E
Steytlerville . . . . **254** 33 17 S 24 19 E
Stia . . . . **163** 43 48N 11 41 E
Stickney **81** 46 23N 67 34W
Stiens . . . . **142** 53 16N 5 46 E
Stigliano . . . . **165** 40 24N 16 13 E
Stigsnæs . . . . **172** 55 13N 11 18 E
Stigtomta . . . . **173** 58 47N 16 48 E
Stikine → **76** 56 40N 132 30W
Stilfontein . . . . **254** 26 50 S 26 50 E
Stilís . . . . **169** 38 55N 22 47 E
Stillwater . . . . **235** 42 27 S 171 20 E
Ştimfalías, L. . . . . . . **169** 37 51N 22 27 E
Štip . . . . **166** 41 42N 22 10 E
Stíra . . . . **169** 38 9N 24 14 E
Stiring-Wendel . . . . . **139** 49 12N 6 57 E
Stirling, Australia . . **230** 17 12 S 141 35 E
Stirling, Alta.,
Canada **91** 49 30N 112 30W
Stirling, Ont.,
Canada **85** 44 18N 77 33W
Stirling, N.Z. . . . . . . **235** 46 14 S 169 49 E
Stirling, U.K. **134** 56 7N 3 57W
Stirling Ra. . . . . **229** 34 23 S 118 0 E
Stittsville **85** 45 15N 75 55W
Stockach . . . . **147** 47 51N 9 1 E
Stockaryd . . . . **173** 57 19N 14 36 E
Stockerau . . . . **151** 48 24N 16 12 E
Stockholm, Canada . **89** 50 39N 102 18W
Stockholm, Sweden . **172** 59 20N 18 3 E
Stockholms län □ . . **172** 59 30N 18 20 E
Stockhorn . . . . **148** 46 42N 7 33 E
Stockport **132** 53 25N 2 11W
Stockton . . . . **233** 32 50 S 151 47 E
Stockton-on-Tees . . . **132** 54 34N 1 20W
Stockvik . . . . **172** 62 17N 17 23 E
Stoczek Łukowski . . **152** 51 58N 22 0 E
Stöde . . . . **172** 62 28N 16 35 E
Stogovo . . . . **166** 41 31N 20 38 E
Stoke . . . . **235** 41 19 S 173 14 E
Stoke-on-Trent **132** 53 1N 2 11W
Stokes Bay **84** 45 0N 81 28W
Stokes Pt. . . . . **230** 40 10 S 143 56 E
Stokes Ra. . . . . **228** 15 50 S 130 50 E
Stokkseyri **174** 63 50N 21 2W
Stokksnes **174** 64 14N 14 58W
Stolac . . . . **166** 43 8N 17 59 E
Stolberg . . . . **146** 50 48N 6 13 E
Stolbovaya,
R.S.F.S.R.,
U.S.S.R. . . . . **179** 55 10N 37 32 E
Stolbovaya,
R.S.F.S.R.,
U.S.S.R. . . . . **185** 64 50N 153 50 E
Stolbovoy, Ostrov . . **185** 56 44N 163 14 E
Stolbtsy . . . . **178** 53 30N 26 43 E
Stolin . . . . **178** 51 53N 26 50 E
Stolnici . . . . **170** 44 31N 24 48 E
Stolwijk . . . . **142** 51 59N 4 47 E
Ston . . . . **166** 42 51N 17 43 E
Stoneham **83** 47 0N 71 22W
Stonehaven **134** 56 58N 2 11W
Stonehenge . . . . **230** 24 22 S 143 17 E
Stoner **93** 53 38N 122 40W
Stonewall **89** 50 10N 97 19W
Stoney Creek **84** 43 14N 79 45W
Stony L., Man.,
Canada **77** 58 51N 98 40W
Stony L., Ont.,
Canada **85** 44 30N 78 0W
Stony Mountain **89** 50 5N 97 13W
Stony Plain **90** 53 32N 114 0W
Stony Rapids **77** 59 16N 105 50W
Stony Tunguska =
Tunguska,
Nizhnyaya → . . . **185** 65 48N 88 4 E
Stopnica . . . . **152** 50 27N 20 57 E
Stora Gla . . . . **172** 59 30N 12 30 E
Stora Karlsö . . . . **173** 57 17N 17 59 E
Stora Lulevatten . . . **174** 67 10N 19 30 E
Stora Sjöfallet . . . . . **174** 67 29N 18 40 E
Storavan . . . . **174** 65 45N 18 10 E
Støren . . . . **171** 63 28N 10 56 E
Store Bælt . . . . **173** 55 20N 11 0 E
Store Creek . . . . **231** 32 54 S 149 6 E
Store Heddinge . . . . **172** 55 18N 12 23 E
Støren . . . . **171** 63 3N 10 18 E
Storfjorden . . . . **171** 62 25N 6 30 E
Storkerson B. **94** 72 56N 124 50W
Storm B. . . . . **230** 43 10 S 147 30 E
Stormberg . . . . **254** 31 16 S 26 17 E
Stormsrivier . . . . **254** 33 59 S 23 52 E
Stormy L. **86** 49 23N 92 18W
Stornoway **134** 58 12N 6 23W
Storozhinets . . . . **180** 48 14N 25 45 E
Storsjö . . . . **172** 62 49N 13 5 E
Storsjöen, Hedmark,
Norway . . . . **171** 60 20N 11 40 E
Storsjöen, Hedmark,
Norway . . . . **171** 61 30N 11 14 E
Storsjön, Gävleborg,
Sweden . . . . **172** 60 35N 16 45 E
Storsjön, Jämtland,
Sweden . . . . **172** 62 50N 13 8 E
Storstrøms Amt. □ . **173** 54 50N 11 45 E
Storuman . . . . **174** 65 5N 17 10 E
Storvik . . . . **172** 60 35N 16 33 E
Stouffville **84** 43 58N 79 15W
Stoughton **88** 49 40N 103 0W
Stour →, Dorset,
U.K. **133** 50 48N 2 7W
Stour →,
Hereford & Worcs.,
U.K. **133** 52 25N 2 13W
Stour →, Kent,
U.K. . . . . **133** 51 15N 1 20 E
Stour →, Suffolk,
U.K. . . . . **133** 51 55N 1 5 E
Stourbridge **133** 52 28N 2 8W
Stout, L. **77** 52 0N 94 40W
Stowmarket . . . . **133** 52 11N 1 0 E
Strabane **135** 54 50N 7 28W
Strabane □ **135** 54 45N 7 25W
Stracin . . . . **166** 42 13N 22 2 E
Stradella . . . . **162** 45 4N 9 20 E
Strahan . . . . **230** 42 9 S 145 20 E
Strakonice . . . . **150** 49 15N 13 53 E
Straldzha . . . . **167** 42 35N 26 40 E
Stralsund . . . . **146** 54 17N 13 5 E
Strand, Norway . . . . **171** 61 17N 11 17 E
Strand, S. Africa . . . **254** 34 9 S 18 48 E
Stranda . . . . **171** 62 19N 6 58 E
Strandebarm . . . . **171** 60 17N 6 0 E
Strandvik . . . . **171** 60 9N 5 41 E
Strangford, L. **135** 54 30N 5 37W
Strängnäs . . . . **172** 59 23N 17 2 E
Stranraer, Canada . . **88** 51 43N 108 29W
Stranraer, U.K. **134** 54 54N 5 0W
Strasbourg, Canada . **88** 51 4N 104 55W
Strasbourg, France . **139** 48 35N 7 42 E
Strasburg . . . . **146** 53 30N 13 44 E
Strassen . . . . **143** 49 37N 6 4 E
Stratford, N.S.W.,
Australia . . . . **233** 32 7 S 151 55 E
Stratford, Vic.,
Australia . . . . **233** 37 59 S 147 7 E
Stratford, Canada . . **84** 43 23N 81 0W
Stratford, N.Z. . . . . . **234** 39 20 S 174 19 E
Stratford-on-Avon . . **133** 52 12N 1 42W
Strath Spey **134** 57 15N 3 40W
Strathalbyn . . . . **232** 35 13 S 138 53 E
Strathclyde □ **134** 56 0N 4 50W
Strathcona Prov.
Park **92** 49 38N 125 40W
Strathmore,
Australia . . . . **230** 17 50 S 142 35 E
Strathmore, Canada **91** 51 5N 113 18W
Strathmore, U.K. . . **134** 56 40N 3 4W
Strathnaver **93** 53 20N 122 33W
Strathpeffer **134** 57 35N 4 32W
Strathroy **84** 42 58N 81 38W
Strathy Pt. **134** 58 35N 4 0W
Stratton, Canada . . . **86** 48 41N 94 10W
Stratton, U.K. **132** 51 41N 1 45W
Straubing . . . . **147** 48 53N 12 35 E
Straumnes **174** 66 26N 23 8W
Strausberg . . . . **146** 52 40N 13 52 E
Strážnice . . . . **151** 48 54N 17 19 E
Streaky B. . . . . **231** 32 51 S 134 18 E
Streaky Bay . . . . **231** 32 48 S 134 13 E
Středočeský □ . . . . . **150** 49 55N 14 30 E
Středoslovenský □ . . **151** 48 30N 19 15 E
Streé . . . . **143** 50 17N 4 18 E
Streetsville **84** 43 35N 79 42W
Strehaia . . . . **170** 44 37N 23 10 E
Strelcha . . . . **167** 42 25N 24 19 E
Strelka . . . . **185** 58 5N 93 3 E
Streng → . . . . **204** 13 12N 103 37 E
Strésa . . . . **162** 45 52N 8 28 E
Strezhevoy . . . . **184** 60 42N 77 34 E
Stříbro . . . . **150** 49 44N 13 0 E
Strickland → . . . . **227** 7 35 S 141 36 E
Strijen . . . . **142** 51 45N 4 33 E
Strimón → . . . . **168** 40 46N 23 51 E
Strimonikós Kólpos . **168** 40 33N 24 0 E
Stroeder . . . . **126** 40 12 S 62 37W
Strofádhes . . . . **169** 37 15N 21 0 E
Strombacka . . . . **172** 61 58N 16 44 E
Strómboli . . . . **165** 38 48N 15 12 E
Strome **91** 52 48N 112 4W
Stromeferry **134** 57 20N 5 33W
Stromness **134** 58 58N 3 18W
Strömsnäsbruk . . . . . **173** 56 35N 13 45 E
Strömstad . . . . **172** 58 55N 11 15 E
Strömsund . . . . **174** 63 51N 15 33 E
Strongfield **88** 51 20N 106 35W
Stróngoli . . . . **165** 39 16N 17 2 E
Stronsay **134** 59 8N 2 38W
Stropkov . . . . **151** 49 13N 21 39 E
Stroud, Canada **84** 44 19N 79 37W
Stroud, U.K. **133** 51 44N 2 12W
Stroud Road . . . . **231** 32 18 S 151 57 E
Struer . . . . **173** 56 30N 8 35 E
Struga . . . . **166** 41 13N 20 44 E
Strugi Krasnyye . . . . **178** 58 21N 29 1 E
Strumica . . . . **166** 41 28N 22 41 E
Strumica → . . . . **166** 41 20N 22 22 E
Struthers **87** 48 41N 85 51W
Stryama . . . . **167** 42 16N 24 54 E
Stryi . . . . **178** 49 16N 23 48 E
Strzyków . . . . **152** 51 55N 19 33 E
Strzegom . . . . **152** 50 58N 16 20 E

Strzelce Krajeńskie 152 52 52N 15 33 E
Strzelce Opolskie 152 50 31N 18 18 E
Strzelecki Cr. → 231 29 37 S 139 59 E
Strzelin 152 50 46N 17 2 E
Strzelno 152 52 35N 18 9 E
Strzybnica 152 50 28N 18 48 E
Strzyzów 152 49 52N 21 47 E
Stuart → 76 54 0N 123 35W
Stuart L. 76 54 30N 124 30W
Stuart Mts. 235 45 2 S 167 39 E
Stuart Range 231 29 10 S 134 56 E
Stubbekøbing 173 54 53N 12 9 E
Stuben 150 47 10N 10 8 E
Studen Kladenets, Yazovir 167 41 37N 25 30 E
Studholme Junc. 235 44 42 S 171 9 E
Stugun 172 63 10N 15 40 E
Stühlingen 147 47 44N 8 26 E
Stull, L. 77 54 24N 92 34W
Stung Treng 204 13 31N 105 58 E
Stupart → 77 56 0N 93 25W
Stupino 179 54 57N 38 2 E
Sturgeon →, Ont., Canada 84 46 35N 80 11W
Sturgeon →, Sask., Canada 88 53 12N 105 52W
Sturgeon B. 89 52 0N 97 50W
Sturgeon Falls 84 46 25N 79 57W
Sturgeon L., Alta., Canada 90 55 6N 117 32W
Sturgeon L., Ont., Canada 85 44 28N 78 43W
Sturgeon L., Ont., Canada 86 50 0N 90 45W
Sturgeon L., Ont., Canada 86 48 29N 91 38W
Sturgis 88 51 56N 102 36W
Şturkö 173 56 5N 15 42 E
Štúrovo 151 47 48N 18 41 E
Sturt Cr. → 228 20 8 S 127 24 E
Sturt Creek 228 19 12 S 128 8 E
Sturts Meadows 232 31 18 S 141 42 E
Stutterheim 254 32 33 S 27 28 E
Stuttgart 147 48 46N 9 10 E
Stykkishólmur 174 65 2N 22 40W
Styr → 178 52 7N 26 35 E
Styria = Steiermark □ 150 47 26N 15 0 E
Su-no-Saki 221 34 58N 139 45 E
Su Xian 214 33 41N 116 59 E
Suakin 244 19 8N 37 20 E
Sual 210 16 4N 120 5 E
Suan 215 38 42N 126 22 E
Suapure → 118 6 48N 67 1W
Suaqui 100 29 12N 109 41W
Suaqui Grande 100 28 24N 109 54W
Suatá → 119 7 52N 65 22W
Subang 209 6 34 S 107 45 E
Subansiri → 202 26 48N 93 50 E
Subayhah 192 30 2N 38 50 E
Subi 205 2 58N 108 50 E
Subiaco 163 41 56N 13 5 E
Subotica 166 46 6N 19 49 E
Success 88 50 28N 108 6W
Suceava 170 47 38N 26 16 E
Suceava □ 170 47 37N 25 40 E
Suceava → 170 47 38N 26 16 E
Sucha-Beskidzka 152 49 44N 19 35 E
Suchan, Poland 152 53 18N 15 18 E
Suchan, U.S.S.R. 218 43 8N 133 9 E
Suchedniów 152 51 3N 20 49 E
Suchiapa 110 16 37N 93 5W
Suchiate → 110 14 33N 92 13W
Suchitoto 112 13 56N 89 0W
Suchou = Suzhou 217 31 19N 120 38 E
Süchow = Xuzhou 215 34 18N 117 10 E
Suchowola 152 53 33N 23 3 E
Sucilá 111 21 9N 88 19W
Sucio → 118 7 27N 77 7W
Suck → 135 53 17N 8 18W
Suckling, Mt. 227 9 49 S 148 53 E
Sucre, Bolivia 123 19 0 S 65 15W
Sucre, Colombia 118 8 49N 74 44W
Sucre □, Colombia 118 8 50N 75 40W
Sucre □, Venezuela 119 10 25N 63 30W
Sucuaro 118 4 34N 68 50W
Sućuraj 163 43 10N 17 8 E
Sucuriju 120 1 39N 49 57W
Sucuriú → 123 20 47 S 51 38W
Sud, Pte. 80 49 3N 62 14W
Sud-Ouest, Pte. du 80 49 23N 63 36W
Suda → 179 59 0N 37 40 E
Sudak 180 44 51N 34 57 E
Sudan ■ 245 15 0N 30 0 E
Suday 179 59 0N 43 0 E
Sudbury, Canada 84 46 30N 81 0W
Sudbury, U.K. 133 52 2N 0 44 E
Sûdd 245 8 20N 30 0 E
Suddie 119 7 8N 58 29W
Süderbrarup 146 54 38N 9 47 E
Süderlügum 146 54 50N 8 55 E
Süderoog-Sand 146 54 27N 8 30 E
Sudetan Mts. = Sudety 151 50 20N 16 45 E
Sudety 151 50 20N 16 45 E
Sudi 251 10 11 S 39 57 E
Sudirman, Pegunungan 207 4 30 S 137 0 E
Sudiţi 170 44 35N 27 38 E
Sudogda 179 55 55N 40 50 E
Sudr 244 29 40N 32 42 E
Sudzha 178 51 14N 35 17 E
Sueca 157 39 12N 0 21W
Suedala 172 55 30N 13 15 E
Suez = El Suweis 244 29 58N 32 31 E
Suez Canal = Suweis, Qanâl es 244 31 0N 32 20 E
Sûf 189 32 19N 35 49 E
Suffield 91 50 12N 111 10W
Suffolk □ 133 52 16N 1 0 E
Sufi-Kurgan 183 40 2N 73 30 E
Suga no-Sen 220 35 25N 134 25 E
Sugag 170 45 47N 23 37 E
Sugar L. 93 50 24N 118 30W
Sugbai Passage 211 5 22N 120 33 E
Suggi L. 88 54 22N 102 47W
Sugluk = Saglouc 78 62 14N 75 38W
Sugny 143 49 49N 4 54 E
Suhaia, L. 170 43 45N 25 15 E
Suhār 195 24 20N 56 40 E
Sühbaatar □ 214 45 30N 114 0 E
Suhl 146 50 35N 10 40 E
Suhl □ 146 50 37N 10 43 E
Suhr 148 47 22N 8 5 E
Sui Xian, Henan, China 214 34 25N 115 2 E
Sui Xian, Henan, China 217 31 42N 113 24 E
Suiá Missu → 123 11 13 S 53 15W
Suichang 217 28 29N 119 15 E
Suichuan 217 26 20N 114 32 E
Suide 214 37 30N 110 12 E
Suifenhe 215 44 25N 131 10 E
Suihua 213 46 32N 126 55 E
Suijiang 216 28 40N 103 59 E
Suining, Hunan, China 217 26 35N 110 10 E
Suining, Jiangsu, China 215 33 56N 117 58 E
Suining, Sichuan, China 216 30 26N 105 35 E
Suiping 214 33 10N 113 59 E
Suippes 139 49 8N 4 30 E
Suir → 135 52 15N 7 10W
Suita 221 34 45N 135 32 E
Suixi 217 21 19N 110 18 E
Suiyang, Guizhou, China 216 27 58N 107 18 E
Suiyang, Heilongjiang, China 215 44 30N 130 56 E
Suizhong 215 40 21N 120 20 E
Sujangarh 198 27 42N 74 31 E
Sujica 166 43 52N 17 11 E
Sukabumi 207 6 56 S 106 50 E
Sukadana, Kalimantan, Indonesia 209 1 10 S 110 0 E
Sukadana, Sumatera, Indonesia 208 5 5 S 105 33 E
Sukagawa 219 37 17N 140 23 E
Sukaraja 209 2 28 S 110 25 E
Sukarnapura = Jayapura 207 2 28 S 140 38 E
Sukchŏn 215 39 22N 125 35 E
Sukhindol 167 43 11N 25 10 E
Sukhinichi 178 54 8N 35 10 E
Sukhona → 176 60 30N 45 0 E
Sukhothai 204 17 1N 99 49 E
Sukhoy Log 182 56 55N 62 1 E
Sukhumi 181 43 0N 41 0 E
Sukkur 197 27 42N 68 54 E
Sukkur Barrage 198 27 40N 68 50 E
Sukma 200 18 24N 81 45 E
Sukovo 166 43 4N 22 37 E
Sukumo 220 32 56N 132 44 E
Sukunka → 76 55 45N 121 15W
Sul, Canal do 120 0 10 S 48 30W
Sula → 178 49 40N 32 41 E
Sula, Kepulauan 207 1 45 S 125 0 E
Sulaco → 112 15 2N 87 44W
Sulaiman Range 198 30 30N 69 50 E
Sulak → 181 43 20N 47 34 E
Sulam Tsor 189 33 4N 35 6 E
Sūlār 193 31 53N 51 54 E
Sulawesi □ 207 2 0 S 120 0 E
Sulechów 152 52 5N 15 40 E
Sulęcin 152 52 26N 15 10 E
Sulejów 152 51 26N 19 53 E
Sulejówek 152 52 13N 21 17 E
Sulgen 149 47 33N 9 7 E
Sulima 246 6 58N 11 32W
Sulina 170 45 10N 29 40 E
Sulingen 146 52 41N 8 47 E
Suliţa 170 47 39N 26 59 E
Sulitälma 174 67 17N 17 28 E
Sułkowice 152 49 50N 19 49 E
Sullana 122 4 52 S 80 39W
Sullivan 82 48 7N 77 50W
Sullivan Bay 92 50 55N 126 50W
Sullivan L. 91 52 0N 112 0W
Sully-sur-Loire 139 47 45N 2 20 E
Sulmierzyce 152 51 37N 17 32 E
Sulmona 163 42 3N 13 55 E
Sulphur Pt. 76 60 56N 114 48W
Sulsul 256 5 5N 44 50 E
Sultan 87 47 36N 82 47W
Sultan Kudarat □ 211 6 30N 124 10 E
Sultan sa Barongis 211 6 45N 124 35 E
Sultanpur 199 26 18N 82 4 E
Sultepec 107 18 52N 99 57W
Sultepec, Sa. de 107 18 45N 99 50W
Sultsa 176 63 27N 46 2 E
Sulu □ 211 5 30N 120 30 E
Sulu Arch. 211 6 0N 121 0 E
Sulu Sea 211 8 0N 120 0 E
Sululta 245 9 10N 38 43 E
Suluq 241 31 44N 20 14 E
Sulyukta 183 39 56N 69 34 E
Sulzbach 147 49 18N 7 4 E
Sulzbach-Rosenberg 147 49 30N 11 46 E
Sulzberger Ice Shelf 13 78 0 S 150 0 E
Sumalata 207 1 0N 122 31 E
Sumampa 124 29 25 S 63 29W
Sumatera □ 208 0 40N 100 20 E
Sumatra = Sumatera □ 208 0 40N 100 20 E
Sumba 207 9 45 S 119 35 E
Sumba, Selat 207 9 0 S 118 40 E
Sumbawa 206 8 26 S 117 30 E
Sumbawa Besar 206 8 30 S 117 26 E
Sumbawanga □ 250 8 0 S 31 30 E
Sumbe 253 11 10 S 13 48 E
Sumburgh Hd. 134 59 52N 1 17W
Sumdo 199 35 6N 78 41 E
Sumé 120 7 39 S 36 55W
Sumedang 209 6 52 S 107 55 E
Sümeg 151 46 59N 17 20 E
Sumenep 209 7 1 S 113 52 E
Sumgait 181 40 34N 49 38 E
Sumisu-Jima 221 31 27N 140 3 E
Sumiswald 148 47 2N 7 44 E
Summerford 79 49 29N 54 47W
Summerland 93 49 32N 119 41W
Summerside, Newf., Canada 79 48 59N 57 59W
Summerside, P.E.I., Canada 81 46 24N 63 47W
Summerville 79 48 27N 53 33W
Summit Lake 76 54 20N 122 40W
Sumner 235 43 35 S 172 48 E
Sumner L. 235 42 42 S 172 15 E
Sumoto 220 34 21N 134 54 E
Sumperk 151 49 59N 17 0 E
Sumprabum 202 26 33N 97 36 E
Sumy 178 50 57N 34 50 E
Sunagawa 218 43 29N 141 55 E
Sunan 215 39 15N 125 40 E
Sunart, L. 134 56 42N 5 43W
Sunbury 231 37 35 S 144 44 E
Sunchales 124 30 58 S 61 35W
Suncho Corral 124 27 55 S 63 27W
Sunchon 215 34 52N 127 31 E
Sunda, Selat 208 6 20 S 105 30 E
Sunda Is. 224 5 0 S 105 0 E
Sundarbans, The 202 22 0N 89 0 E
Sundargarh 199 22 4N 84 5 E
Sundays = Sondags → 254 33 44 S 25 51 E
Sundbyberg 172 59 22N 17 58 E
Sunderland, Canada 85 44 16N 79 4W
Sunderland, U.K. 132 54 54N 1 22W
Sundown 89 49 6N 96 16W
Sundre 91 51 49N 114 38W
Sundridge 84 45 45N 79 25W
Sunds 173 56 13N 9 1 E
Sundsjö 172 62 59N 15 9 E
Sundsvall 172 62 23N 17 17 E
Sung Hei 205 10 20N 106 2 E
Sungai Kolok 205 6 2N 101 58 E
Sungai Lembing 205 3 55N 103 3 E
Sungai Patani 205 5 37N 100 30 E
Sungaigerong 208 2 59 S 104 52 E
Sungailiat 208 1 51 S 106 8 E
Sungaipakning 206 1 19N 102 0 E
Sungaipenuh 208 2 1 S 101 20 E
Sungaitiram 209 0 45 S 117 8 E
Sungguminasa 207 5 17 S 119 30 E
Sunghua Chiang = Songhua Jiang → 215 47 45N 132 30 E
Sungikai 245 12 20N 29 51 E
Sungurlu 180 40 12N 34 21 E
Sunja 163 45 21N 16 35 E
Sunkar, Gora 183 44 15N 73 50 E
Sunndalsøra 171 62 40N 8 33 E
Sunne 172 59 52N 13 5 E
Sunnfjord 171 61 25N 5 18 E
Sunny Corner 81 46 57N 65 49W
Sunnybrae 81 45 24N 62 30W
Sunnyside 79 47 51N 53 55W
Sunshine 233 37 48 S 144 52 E
Suntar 185 62 15N 117 30 E
Sunwapta Pass 91 52 13N 117 10W
Sunyani 246 7 21N 2 22W
Suō-Nada 220 33 50N 131 30 E
Suoyarvi 176 62 12N 32 23 E
Supamo → 119 6 48N 61 50W
Supaul 199 26 10N 86 40 E
Supe 122 11 0 S 77 30W
Superior, L., N. Amer. 87 47 40N 87 0W
Superior, L., Mexico 109 16 20N 94 25W
Supetar 163 43 25N 16 32 E
Suphan Buri 204 14 14N 100 10 E
Supraśl 152 53 13N 23 19 E
Supriori, Kepulauan 207 1 0 S 136 0 E
Supung Sk. 215 40 35N 124 50 E
Sūq' Abs 194 16 0N 43 12 E
Suq al Jum'ah 241 32 58N 13 12 E
Sūq Suwayq 192 24 23N 38 27 E
Suqian 215 33 54N 118 8 E
Sūr 189 33 19N 35 16 E
Sura → 179 56 6N 46 0 E
Surab 197 28 25N 66 15 E
Surabaja = Surabaya 209 7 17 S 112 45 E
Surabaya 209 7 17 S 112 45 E
Surahammar 172 59 43N 16 13 E
Suraia 170 45 40N 27 25 E
Surakarta 209 7 35 S 110 48 E
Surakhany 181 40 25N 50 1 E
Şurandai 201 8 58N 77 26 E
Šurany 151 48 6N 18 10 E
Surat, Australia 231 27 10 S 149 6 E
Surat, India 198 21 12N 72 55 E
Surat Thani 205 9 6N 99 20 E
Suratgarh 198 29 18N 73 55 E
Suraz 152 52 57N 22 57 E
Surazh, Byelorussian S.S.R., U.S.S.R. 178 55 25N 30 44 E
Surazh, R.S.F.S.R., U.S.S.R. 178 53 5N 32 27 E
Surduc 170 47 15N 23 25 E
Surduc Pasul 170 45 21N 23 23 E
Surdulica 166 42 41N 22 11 E
Sûre → 143 49 44N 6 31 E
Surendranagar 198 22 45N 71 40 E
Surgères 140 46 7N 0 47W
Surgut 184 61 14N 73 20 E
Surhuisterveen 142 53 11N 6 10 E
Surianu 170 45 33N 23 31 E
Suriapet 200 17 10N 79 40 E
Şūrīf 189 31 40N 35 4 E
Surigao 211 9 47N 125 29 E
Surigao del Norte □ 211 10 0N 125 40 E
Surigao del Sur □ 211 8 45N 126 0 E
Surigao Strait 211 10 15N 125 23 E
Surin 204 14 50N 103 34 E
Surin Nua, Ko 205 9 30N 97 55 E
Surinam ■ 119 4 0N 56 0W
Suriname □ 119 5 30N 55 0W
Suriname → 119 5 50N 55 15W
Surkhandarya → 183 37 12N 67 20 E
Sūrmaq 193 31 3N 52 48 E
Surmene 181 41 0N 40 1 E
Surovikino 181 48 32N 42 55 E
Surprise, L. 82 49 20N 74 55W
Surprise L. 76 59 40N 133 15W
Surrey □ 133 51 16N 0 30W
Sursee 148 47 11N 8 6 E
Sursk 179 53 3N 45 40 E
Surt 241 31 11N 16 39 E
Surt, Al Hammadah al 241 30 0N 17 50 E
Surt, Khalīj 242 31 40N 18 30 E
Surtsey 174 63 20N 20 30W
Surubim 120 7 50 S 35 45W
Surud Ad 256 10 42N 47 9 E
Suruga-Wan 221 34 45N 138 30 E
Surumu → 119 3 22N 60 19W
Susa 162 45 8N 7 3 E
Suså → 172 55 20N 11 42 E
Sušac 163 42 46N 16 30 E
Susak 163 44 30N 14 18 E
Susaki 220 33 22N 133 17 E
Susamyr 183 42 12N 73 58 E
Susamyrtau, Khrebet 183 42 8N 73 15 E
Sūsangerd 193 31 35N 48 6 E
Susanino 185 52 50N 140 14 E
Susch 149 46 46N 10 5 E
Sušice 150 49 17N 13 30 E
Susong 217 30 10N 116 5 E
Susques 124 23 35 S 66 25W
Sussex 81 45 45N 65 37W
Sussex, E. □ 133 51 0N 0 20 E
Sussex, W. □ 133 51 0N 0 30W
Susteren 143 51 4N 5 51 E
Susticacán 105 22 36N 103 5W
Sustut → 76 56 20N 127 30W
Susuman 185 62 47N 148 10 E
Susunu 207 3 20 S 133 25 E
Susz 152 53 44N 19 20 E
Şuţeşti 170 45 13N 27 27 E

Sutherland, Australia **233** 34 2S 151 4E
Sutherland, S. Africa **254** 32 33S 20 40E
Sutherland Falls **235** 44 48S 167 46E
Sutivan **163** 43 23N 16 30E
Sutlej → **197** 29 23N 71 3E
Sutton, Ont., Canada **84** 44 18N 79 22W
Sutton, Qué., Canada **83** 45 6N 72 37W
Sutton, N.Z. **235** 45 34S 170 8E
Sutton → **74** 55 15N 83 45W
Sutton-in-Ashfield **132** 53 7N 1 20W
Suttor → **230** 21 36S 147 2E
Suttsu **218** 42 48N 140 14E
Suva **226** 18 6S 178 30E
Suva Gora **166** 41 45N 21 3E
Suva Planina **166** 43 10N 22 5E
Suva Reka **166** 42 21N 20 50E
Suvo Rudište **166** 43 17N 20 49E
Suvorov **179** 54 7N 36 30E
Suvorov Is. = Suwarrow Is. **225** 15 0S 163 0W
Suvorovo **167** 43 20N 27 35E
Suwa **221** 36 2N 138 8E
Suwa-Ko **221** 36 3N 138 5E
Suwałki **152** 54 8N 22 59E
Suwałki □ **152** 54 0N 22 30E
Suwannaphum **204** 15 33N 103 47E
Suwanose-Jima **219** 29 38N 129 43E
Suwarrow Is. **225** 15 0S 163 0W
Suwayq aş Şuqban **192** 31 32N 46 7E
Suweis, Khalîg el **244** 28 40N 33 0E
Suweis, Qanâl es **244** 31 0N 32 20E
Suwŏn **215** 37 17N 127 1E
Suykbulak **182** 50 25N 62 33E
Suyo **210** 16 59N 120 31E
Suzak **183** 44 9N 68 27E
Suzaka **221** 36 39N 138 19E
Suzdal **179** 56 29N 40 26E
Suze, La **138** 47 54N 0 2E
Suzhou **217** 31 19N 120 38E
Suzu **219** 37 25N 137 17E
Suzu-Misaki **219** 37 31N 137 21E
Suzuka **221** 34 55N 136 36E
Suzuka-Sam **221** 35 5N 136 30E
Suzzara **162** 45 0N 10 45E
Svalbard **12** 78 0N 17 0E
Svalbarð **174** 66 12N 15 43W
Svalöv **172** 55 57N 13 8E
Svanvik **174** 69 25N 30 3E
Svappavaara **174** 67 40N 21 3E
Svarstad **171** 59 27N 9 56E
Svartenhuk Pen. **95** 71 50N 54 30W
Svartisen **174** 66 40N 13 50E
Svartvik **172** 62 19N 17 24E
Svatovo **180** 49 35N 38 11E
Svay Chek **204** 13 48N 102 58E
Svay Rieng **205** 11 5N 105 48E
Sveio **171** 59 33N 5 23E
Svendborg **173** 55 4N 10 35E
Svene **171** 59 45N 9 31E
Svenljunga **173** 57 29N 13 5E
Svenstrup **173** 56 58N 9 50E
Sverdlovsk, R.S.F.S.R., U.S.S.R. **182** 56 50N 60 30E
Sverdlovsk, Ukraine S.S.R., U.S.S.R. **181** 48 5N 39 37E
Sverdrup Chan. **95** 79 56N 96 25W
Sverdrup Is. **95** 79 0N 97 0W
Svetac **163** 43 3N 15 43E
Sveti Ivan Zelina **163** 45 57N 16 16E
Sveti Jurij **163** 46 14N 15 24E
Sveti Lenart **163** 46 36N 15 48E
Sveti Nikola, Prokhad **166** 43 27N 22 6E
Sveti Nikole **166** 41 51N 21 56E
Sveti Rok **163** 40 1N 9 6E
Sveti Trojica **163** 46 37N 15 50E
Svetlaya **218** 46 33N 138 18E
Svetlogorsk **178** 52 38N 29 46E
Svetlograd **181** 45 25N 42 58E
Svetlovodsk **178** 49 2N 33 13E
Svetlyy **182** 50 48N 60 51E
Svetozarevo **166** 44 5N 21 15E
Svidník **151** 49 20N 21 37E
Svilaja Pl. **163** 43 49N 16 31E
Svilajnac **166** 44 15N 21 11E
Svilengrad **167** 41 49N 26 12E
Svir → **176** 60 30N 32 48E
Svishtov **167** 43 36N 25 23E
Svisloch **178** 53 3N 24 2E
Svitava → **151** 49 30N 16 37E
Svitavy **151** 49 47N 16 28E
Svobodnyy **185** 51 20N 128 0E
Svoge **167** 42 59N 23 23E
Svolvær **174** 68 15N 14 34E
Svratka → **151** 49 11N 16 38E
Svrljig **166** 43 25N 22 6E
Swa **202** 19 15N 96 17E
Swa Tende **253** 7 9S 17 7E
Swabian Alps = Schwäbische Alb **147** 48 30N 9 30E
Swakopmund **254** 22 37S 14 30E
Swale → **132** 54 5N 1 20W
Swalmen **143** 51 13N 6 2E
Swan →, Alta., Canada **90** 55 30N 115 18W
Swan →, Man., Canada **89** 52 30N 100 45W
Swan Hill **231** 35 20S 143 33E
Swan Hills **90** 54 42N 115 24W
Swan Islands **112** 17 22N 83 57W
Swan L. **89** 52 30N 100 40W
Swan Reach **232** 34 35S 139 37E
Swan River **89** 52 10N 101 16W
Swanage **133** 50 36N 1 59W
Swansea, Australia **231** 33 3S 151 35E
Swansea, U.K. **133** 51 37N 3 57W
Swar → **199** 34 40N 72 5E
Swartberge **254** 33 20S 22 0E
Swartruggens **254** 25 39S 26 42E
Swarzędz **152** 52 25N 17 4E
Swastika **74** 48 7N 80 6W
Swatow = Shantou **217** 23 18N 116 40E
Swaziland ■ **255** 26 30S 31 30E
Sweden ■ **174** 57 0N 15 0E
Swedru **247** 5 32N 0 41W
Swellendam **254** 34 1S 20 26E
Swider → **152** 52 6N 21 14E
Świdnica **152** 50 50N 16 30E
Świdnik **152** 51 13N 22 39E
Świdwin **152** 53 47N 15 49E
Świebodzice **152** 50 51N 16 20E
Świebodzin **152** 52 15N 15 31E
Świecie **152** 53 25N 18 30E
Świętokrzyskie, Góry **152** 51 0N 20 30E
Swift Current, Newf., Canada **79** 47 53N 54 12W
Swift Current, Sask., Canada **88** 50 20N 107 45W
Swiftcurrent → **88** 50 38N 107 44W
Swilly, L. **135** 55 12N 7 35W
Swindle, I. **92** 52 30N 128 35W
Swindon **133** 51 33N 1 47W
Swinemünde = Świnoujście **152** 53 54N 14 16E
Świnoujście **152** 53 54N 14 16E
Switzerland ■ **147** 46 30N 8 0E
Swords **135** 53 27N 6 15W
Syasstroy **178** 60 5N 32 15E
Sychevka **178** 55 59N 34 16E
Syców **152** 51 19N 17 40E
Sydenham → **84** 42 33N 82 25W
Sydney, Australia **231** 33 53S 151 10E
Sydney, Canada **81** 46 7N 60 7W
Sydney L. **86** 50 41N 94 25W
Sydney Mines **81** 46 18N 60 15W
Sydney River **81** 46 7N 60 13W
Sydprøven **12** 60 30N 45 35W
Syke **146** 52 55N 8 50E
Syktyvkar **176** 61 45N 50 40E
Sylhet **202** 24 54N 91 52E
Sylt **146** 54 50N 8 20E
Sylva → **182** 58 0N 56 54E
Sylvan L. **91** 52 21N 114 10W
Sylvan Lake **91** 52 20N 114 3W
Sylvania **88** 52 42N 104 0W
Sylvester **90** 55 0N 119 41W
Sym **184** 60 20N 88 18E
Symón **105** 24 42N 102 35W
Synnott Ra. **228** 16 30S 125 20E
Syrdarya **183** 40 50N 68 40E
Syrdarya → **184** 46 3N 61 0E
Syria ■ **192** 35 0N 38 0E
Syriam **202** 16 44N 96 19E
Syrian Desert **186** 31 0N 40 0E
Sysert **182** 56 29N 60 49E
Syul'dzhyukyor **185** 63 14N 113 32E
Syutkya **167** 41 50N 24 16E
Syzran **179** 53 12N 48 30E
Szabolcs-Szatmár □ **151** 48 2N 21 45E
Szamocin **152** 53 2N 17 7E
Szamos → **151** 48 7N 22 20E
Szaraz → **151** 46 28N 20 44E
Szarvas **151** 46 50N 20 38E
Szazhalombatta **151** 47 20N 18 58E
Szczawnica **151** 49 26N 20 30E
Szczebrzeszyn **152** 50 42N 22 59E
Szczecin **152** 53 27N 14 27E
Szczecin □ **152** 53 25N 14 32E
Szczecinek **152** 53 43N 16 41E
Szczekocimy **152** 50 38N 19 48E
Szczucin **152** 50 18N 21 4E
Szczuczyn **152** 53 36N 22 19E
Szczytno **152** 53 33N 21 0E
Szechwan = Sichuan □ **216** 31 0N 104 0E
Szécsény **151** 48 7N 19 30E
Szeged **151** 46 16N 20 10E
Szeghalom **151** 47 1N 21 10E
Székesfehérvár **151** 47 15N 18 25E
Szekszárd **151** 46 22N 18 42E
Szendrö **151** 48 24N 20 41E
Szentendre **151** 47 39N 19 4E
Szentes **151** 46 39N 20 21E
Szentgotthárd **151** 46 58N 16 19E
Szentlörinc **151** 46 3N 18 1E
Szerencs **151** 48 10N 21 12E
Szigetvár **151** 46 3N 17 46E
Szikszó **151** 48 12N 20 56E
Szkwa → **152** 53 11N 21 43E
Szlichtyngowa **152** 51 42N 16 15E
Szob **151** 47 48N 18 53E
Szolnok **151** 47 10N 20 15E
Szolnok □ **151** 47 15N 20 30E
Szombathely **151** 47 14N 16 38E
Szprotawa **152** 51 33N 15 35E
Sztum **152** 53 55N 19 1E
Sztutowo **152** 54 20N 19 15E
Szubin **152** 53 1N 17 45E
Szydłowiec **152** 51 15N 20 51E
Szypliszki **152** 54 17N 23 2E

T

't Harde **142** 52 24N 5 54E
't Zandt **142** 53 22N 6 46E
Ta Khli Khok **204** 15 18N 100 20E
Ta Lai **205** 11 24N 107 23E
Tabacal **124** 23 15S 64 15W
Tabaco **210** 13 22N 123 44E
Tabagné **246** 7 59N 3 4W
Ţâbah **192** 26 55N 42 38E
Tabajara **123** 8 56S 62 8W
Tabalos **122** 6 26S 76 37W
Tabango **211** 11 19N 124 22E
Tabar Is. **227** 2 50S 152 0E
Tabarca, Isla de **157** 38 17N 0 30W
Tabarka **241** 36 56N 8 46E
Ţabas, Khorāsān, Iran **193** 32 48N 60 12E
Ţabas, Khorāsān, Iran **193** 33 35N 56 55E
Tabasará, Serranía de **112** 8 35N 81 40W
Tabasco, Baja Calif. N., Mexico **98** 32 30N 114 50W
Tabasco, Zacatecas, Mexico **105** 21 52N 102 55W
Tabasco □ **110** 18 0N 92 40W
Tabatière, La **79** 50 50N 58 58W
Tabatinga, Serra da **120** 10 30S 44 0W
Tabayin **202** 22 42N 95 20E
Tabāzīn **193** 31 12N 57 54E
Tabelbala, Kahal de **240** 28 47N 2 0W
Taber **91** 49 47N 112 8W
Tabernas **157** 37 4N 2 26W
Tabernes de Valldigna **157** 39 5N 0 13W
Tabi **253** 8 10S 13 18E
Tabira **120** 7 35S 37 33W
Tablas **210** 12 25N 122 2E
Tablas Strait **210** 12 40N 121 48E
Table B. = Tafelbaai **254** 33 35S 18 25E
Table B. **78** 53 40N 56 25W
Table Mt. **254** 34 0S 18 22E
Table Top, Mt. **230** 23 24S 147 11E
Tableland **228** 17 16S 126 51E
Tabogon **211** 10 57N 124 2E
Tábor, Czech. **150** 49 25N 14 39E
Tabor, Israel **189** 32 42N 35 24E
Tabora **250** 5 2S 32 50E
Tabora □ **250** 5 0S 33 0E
Tabory **182** 58 31N 64 33E
Tabou **246** 4 30N 7 20W
Tabrīz **192** 38 7N 46 20E
Tabuelan **211** 10 49N 123 52E
Tabuenca **156** 41 42N 1 33W
Tabuk, Phil. **210** 17 24N 121 25E
Tabūk, Si. Arabia **191** 28 23N 36 36E
Tacámbaro de Codallos **107** 19 14N 101 28W
Tacaná, Volcán **110** 15 7N 92 6W
Tacheng **212** 46 40N 82 58E
Tachibana-Wan **220** 32 45N 130 7E
Tachick L. **92** 53 57N 124 12W
Tachikawa **221** 35 42N 139 25E
Tach'ing Shan = Daqing Shan **214** 40 40N 111 0E
Tachira **118** 8 7N 72 15E
Táchira □ **118** 8 7N 72 15W
Tachov **150** 49 47N 12 39E
Tácina → **165** 38 57N 16 55E
Tacloban **211** 11 15N 124 58E
Tacna **122** 18 0S 70 20W
Tacna □ **122** 17 40S 70 20W
Tacotalpa **110** 17 36N 92 49W
Tacotalpa → **110** 17 50N 92 52W
Tacualeche **105** 22 49N 102 25W
Tacuarembó **125** 31 45S 56 0W
Tacupeto **100** 28 49N 109 11W
Tacutu → **119** 3 1N 60 29W
Tademaït, Plateau du **241** 28 30N 2 30E
Tadent, O. → **241** 22 25N 6 40E
Tadjerdjeri, O. → **241** 26 0N 8 0W
Tadjerouna **241** 33 31N 2 3E
Tadjettaret, O. → **241** 21 20N 7 22E
Tadjmout, Oasis, Algeria **241** 33 52N 2 30E
Tadjmout, Saoura, Algeria **240** 25 37N 3 48E
Tadjoura **245** 11 50N 42 55E
Tadjoura, Golfe de **245** 11 50N 43 0E
Tadmor **235** 41 27S 172 45E
Tadotsu **220** 34 16N 133 45E
Tadoule, L. **77** 58 36N 98 20W
Tadoussac **83** 48 11N 69 42W
Tadzhik S.S.R. □ **183** 35 30N 70 0E
Taechŏn-ni **215** 36 21N 126 36E
Taegu **215** 35 50N 128 37E
Taegwan **215** 40 13N 125 12E
Taejŏn **215** 36 20N 127 28E
Tafalla **156** 42 30N 1 41W
Tafar **245** 6 52N 28 15E
Ţafas **189** 32 44N 36 5E
Tafassasset, O. → **241** 22 0N 9 57E
Tafelbaai **254** 33 35S 18 25E
Tafelney, C. **240** 31 3N 9 51W
Tafermaar **207** 6 47S 134 10E
Taffermit **240** 29 37N 9 15W
Tafí Viejo **124** 26 43S 65 17W
Tafīhān **193** 29 25N 52 39E
Tafiré **246** 9 4N 5 4W
Tafnidilt **240** 28 47N 10 58W
Tafraoute **240** 29 50N 8 58W
Taft, Iran **193** 31 45N 54 14E
Taft, Phil. **211** 11 57N 125 30E
Taga Dzong **202** 27 5N 89 55E
Tagana-an **211** 9 42N 125 35E
Taganrog **181** 47 12N 38 50E
Taganrogskiy Zaliv **180** 47 0N 38 30E
Tagânt **246** 18 20N 11 0W
Tagap Ga **202** 26 56N 96 13E
Tagapula I. **210** 12 4N 124 12E
Tagatay **210** 14 6N 120 56E
Tagauayan I. **211** 10 58N 121 13E
Tagbilaran **211** 9 39N 123 51E
Tage **227** 6 19S 143 20E
Tággia **162** 43 52N 7 50E
Taghrīfat **241** 29 5N 17 26E
Taghzout **240** 33 30N 4 49W
Tagish **76** 60 19N 134 16W
Tagish L. **76** 60 10N 134 20W
Tagkawayan **210** 13 58N 122 32E
Tagliacozzo **163** 42 4N 13 13E
Tagliamento → **163** 45 38N 13 5E
Táglio di Po **163** 45 0N 12 12E
Tagna **118** 2 24S 70 37W
Tago **211** 9 2N 126 13E
Tago, Mt. **211** 8 23N 125 5E
Tagomago, I. de **157** 39 2N 1 39E
Tagua, La **118** 0 3N 74 40W
Taguatinga **121** 12 16S 42 26W
Tagudin **210** 16 56N 120 27E
Tagula **227** 11 22S 153 15E
Tagula I. **227** 11 30S 153 30E
Tagum **211** 7 33N 125 53E
Tagus = Tajo → **155** 38 40N 9 24W
Tahakopa **235** 46 30S 169 23E
Tahala **241** 34 0N 4 28W
Tahan, Gunong **205** 4 34N 102 17E
Tahānah-ye sūr Gol. **197** 31 43N 67 53E
Tahara **221** 34 40N 137 16E
Tahat **241** 23 18N 5 33E
Tahdziú **111** 20 12N 88 57W
Tāherī **193** 27 43N 52 20E
Tahiti **226** 17 37S 149 27W
Tahora **234** 39 2S 174 49E
Tahoua **247** 14 57N 5 16E
Tahsis **92** 49 55N 126 40W
Tahta **244** 26 44N 31 32E
Tahuamanu → **122** 11 6S 67 36W
Tahulandang **207** 2 27N 125 23E
Tahuna **207** 3 38N 125 30E
Taï **246** 5 55N 7 30W
Tai Shan **215** 36 25N 117 20E
Tai Xian **217** 32 30N 120 7E
Tai'an **215** 36 12N 117 8E
Taibei **217** 25 4N 121 29E
Taibus Qi **214** 41 54N 115 22E
T'aichung = Taizhong **217** 24 12N 120 35E
Taidong **217** 22 43N 121 9E
Taieri → **235** 46 3S 170 12E
Taiga Madema **241** 23 46N 15 25E
Taigu **214** 37 28N 112 30E
Taihang Shan **214** 36 0N 113 30E
Taihape **234** 39 41S 175 48E
Taihe, Anhui, China **214** 33 20N 115 42E
Taihe, Jiangxi, China **217** 26 47N 114 52E
Taihu **217** 30 22N 116 20E
Taijiang **216** 26 39N 108 21E
Taikang **214** 34 5N 114 50E
Taikkyi **202** 17 20N 96 0E
Tailem Bend **232** 35 12S 139 29E
Tailfingen **147** 48 15N 9 1E
Taimyr = Taymyr, Poluostrov **185** 75 0N 100 0E

Taimyr, Oz. **185** 74 20N 102 0 E
Tain **134** 57 49N 4 4W
Tainan **217** 23 17N 120 18 E
Taínaron, Ákra **169** 36 22N 22 27 E
Tainggyo **202** 17 49N 94 29 E
Taining **217** 26 54N 117 9 E
Taintignies **143** 50 33N 3 22 E
Taiobeiras **121** 15 49 S 42 14W
T'aipei = Taibei **217** 25 4N 121 29 E
Taiping, China **217** 30 15N 118 6 E
Taiping, Malaysia **205** 4 51N 100 44 E
Taipingzhen **214** 33 35N 111 42 E
Taipu **120** 5 37 S 35 36W
Taisha **220** 35 24N 132 40 E
Taishan **217** 22 14N 112 41 E
Taishun **217** 27 30N 119 42 E
Taita □ **250** 4 0 S 38 30 E
Taita Hills **250** 3 25 S 38 15 E
Taitao, C. **126** 45 53 S 75 5W
Taitao, Pen. de **126** 46 30 S 75 0W
Taiwan ■ **217** 23 30N 121 0 E
Taiwan Shan **217** 23 40N 121 20 E
Taixing **217** 32 11N 120 0 E
Taïyetos Óros **169** 37 0N 22 23 E
Taiyib → **189** 31 55N 35 17 E
Taiyiba **189** 32 36N 35 27 E
Taiyuan **214** 37 52N 112 33 E
Taizhong **217** 24 12N 120 35 E
Taizhou **217** 32 28N 119 55 E
Taizhou Liedao **217** 28 30N 121 55 E
Ta'izz **194** 13 35N 44 2 E
Tājābād **193** 30 2N 54 24 E
Tajapuru, Furo do **120** 1 50 S 50 25W
Tajarḥī **241** 24 21N 14 28 E
Tajima **219** 37 12N 139 46 E
Tajimi **221** 35 19N 137 8 E
Tajo → **155** 38 40N 9 24W
Tajrīsh **193** 35 48N 51 25 E
Tājūrā **241** 32 51N 13 21 E
Tak **204** 16 52N 99 8 E
Takāb **192** 36 24N 47 7 E
Takachiho **220** 32 42N 131 18 E
Takada **219** 37 7N 138 15 E
Takahagi **219** 36 43N 140 45 E
Takahashi **220** 34 51N 133 39 E
Takaka **235** 40 51 S 172 50 E
Takamatsu **220** 34 20N 134 5 E
Takanabe **220** 32 8N 131 30 E
Takaoka **221** 36 47N 137 0 E
Takapau **234** 40 2 S 176 21 E
Takapuna **234** 36 47 S 174 47 E
Takasago **220** 34 45N 134 48 E
Takasaki **221** 36 20N 139 0 E
Takase **220** 34 7N 133 48 E
Takatsuki **221** 34 51N 135 37 E
Takaungu **250** 3 38 S 39 52 E
Takawa **220** 33 38N 130 51 E
Takayama **221** 36 18N 137 11 E
Takayama-Bonchi **221** 36 0N 137 18 E
Take-Shima **219** 30 49N 130 26 E
Takefu **221** 35 50N 136 10 E
Takehara **220** 34 21N 132 55 E
Takengon **208** 4 45N 96 50 E
Takeo, Cambodia **205** 10 59N 104 47 E
Takeo, Japan **220** 33 12N 130 1 E
Tåkern **173** 58 22N 14 45 E
Tākestān **193** 36 0N 49 40 E
Taketa **220** 32 58N 131 24 E
Takh **199** 33 6N 77 32 E
Takhār □ **197** 36 40N 70 0 E
Takhman **205** 11 29N 104 57 E
Taki **227** 6 29 S 155 52 E
Takikawa **218** 43 33N 141 54 E
Takiyuak L. **94** 65 30N 113 5W
Takla L. **76** 55 15N 125 45W
Takla Landing **76** 55 30N 125 50W
Takla Makan **186** 39 0N 83 0 E
Taku **220** 33 18N 130 3 E
Taku → **76** 58 30N 133 50W
Takua Pa **205** 7 18N 9 59 E
Takum **247** 7 18N 9 36 E
Takuma **220** 34 13N 133 40 E
Takundi **253** 4 45 S 16 34 E
Takuran **211** 7 51N 123 34 E
Takutu → **119** 3 1N 60 29W
Takysie Lake **92** 53 53N 125 53W
Tal Halāl **193** 28 54N 55 1 E
Tala, Mexico **106** 20 40N 103 42W
Tala, Uruguay **125** 34 21 S 55 46W
Talacogan **211** 8 32N 125 39 E
Talagante **124** 33 40 S 70 50W
Talaïnt **240** 29 41N 9 40W
Talak **247** 18 0N 5 0 E
Talakag **211** 8 16N 124 37 E
Talamanca, Cordillera de **112** 9 20N 83 20W
Talara **122** 4 38 S 81 18 E
Talas **183** 42 30N 72 13 E
Talas → **183** 44 0N 70 20 E
Talasea **227** 5 20 S 150 2 E
Talasskiy, Khrebet **183** 42 15N 72 0 E
Talâta **191** 30 36N 30 20 E
Talata Mafara **247** 12 38N 6 4 E
Talaud, Kepulauan **207** 4 30N 127 10 E
Talavera de la Reina **154** 39 55N 4 46W
Talawana **228** 22 51 S 121 9 E
Talawgyi **202** 25 4N 97 19 E
Talayan **211** 6 52N 124 24 E
Talbert, Sillon de **138** 48 53N 3 5W
Talbot, C. **228** 13 48 S 126 43 E
Talbot L. **89** 54 0N 99 55W
Talbragar → **231** 32 12 S 148 37 E
Talca **124** 35 28 S 71 40W
Talca □ **124** 35 20 S 71 46W
Talcahuano **124** 36 40 S 73 10W
Talcher **199** 21 0N 85 18 E
Talcho **247** 14 44N 3 28 E
Taldy Kurgan **184** 45 10N 78 45 E
Talesh **193** 37 58N 48 58 E
Ṭalesh, Kūhhā-ye **193** 39 0N 48 30 E
Talfīt **189** 32 5N 35 17 E
Talgar **183** 43 19N 77 15 E
Talgar, Pic **183** 43 5N 77 20 E
Talguharai **244** 18 19N 35 56 E
Tali Post **245** 5 55N 30 44 E
Taliabu **207** 1 45 S 125 0 E
Talibon **211** 10 9N 124 20 E
Talibong, Ko **205** 7 15N 99 23 E
Talikota **201** 16 29N 76 17 E
Talimardzhan **183** 38 23N 65 37 E
Talisay **211** 10 44N 122 58 E
Talisayan **211** 9 0N 124 55 E
Talitsa **182** 57 0N 63 43 E
Taliwang **206** 8 50 S 116 55 E
Tall **189** 33 0N 35 6 E
Tall 'Asūr **189** 31 59N 35 17 E
Tall Kalakh **190** 34 41N 36 15 E
Talla **244** 28 5N 30 43 E
Tallangatta **231** 36 15 S 147 19 E
Tallarook **231** 37 5 S 145 6 E
Tallawang **233** 32 12 S 149 28 E
Tällberg **172** 60 51N 15 2 E
Tallering Pk. **229** 28 6 S 115 37 E
Tallinn **178** 59 22N 24 48 E
Ṭallūzā **189** 32 17N 35 18 E
Tălmaciu **170** 45 38N 24 19 E
Talmest **240** 31 48N 9 21W
Talmont **140** 46 27N 1 37W
Talnoye **180** 48 50N 30 44 E
Taloda **198** 21 34N 74 11 E
Talodi **245** 10 35N 30 22 E
Talomo **211** 7 3N 125 32 E
Talovaya **179** 51 6N 40 45 E
Talpa de Allende **106** 20 23N 104 51W
Tālqān **197** 36 44N 69 33 E
Talsi **178** 57 10N 22 30 E
Talsinnt **241** 32 33N 3 27W
Taltal **124** 25 23 S 70 33W
Taltson → **76** 61 24N 112 46W
Taltson L. **77** 61 30N 110 15W
Talunkwan I. **92** 52 50N 131 45W
Talwood **231** 28 29 S 149 29 E
Talyawalka Cr. → **231** 32 28 S 142 22 E
Tam Chau **205** 10 48N 105 12 E
Tam Ky **204** 15 34N 108 29 E
Tam Quan **204** 14 35N 109 3 E
Tamala **229** 26 42 S 113 47 E
Tamalameque **118** 8 52N 73 49W
Tamale **247** 9 22N 0 50W
Taman **180** 45 14N 36 41 E
Tamana **220** 32 58N 130 32 E
Tamanar **240** 31 1N 9 46W
Tamano **220** 34 29N 133 59 E
Tamanrasset **241** 22 50N 5 30 E
Tamanrasset, O. → **240** 22 0N 2 0 E
Tamanthi **202** 25 19N 95 17 E
Tamar → **133** 50 33N 4 15W
Támara **118** 5 50N 72 10W
Tamarang **231** 31 27 S 150 5 E
Tamarite de Litera **156** 41 52N 0 25 E
Tamashima **220** 34 32N 133 40 E
Tamási **151** 46 40N 18 18 E
Tamaské **247** 14 49N 5 43 E
Tamasopo **103** 21 55N 99 24W
Tamaulipas □ **103** 24 0N 98 45W
Tamaulipas, Sa. de **103** 23 32N 98 31W
Tamazula, Durango, Mexico **104** 24 57N 106 57W
Tamazula, Sinaloa, Mexico **104** 25 28N 108 27W
Tamazula de Gordiano **106** 19 38N 103 15W
Tamazulapán, Sa. **109** 17 52N 97 30W
Tamazulapán del Progeso **109** 17 41N 97 34W
Tamazunchale **103** 21 16N 98 47W
Tamba-Dabatou **246** 11 50N 10 40W
Tambacounda **246** 13 45N 13 40W
Tambelan, Kepulauan **208** 1 0N 107 30 E
Tambellup **229** 34 4 S 117 37 E
Tambo, Australia **230** 24 54 S 146 14 E
Tambo, Peru **122** 12 57 S 74 1W
Tambo → **122** 10 42 S 73 47W
Tambo de Mora **122** 13 30 S 76 8W
Tambobamba **122** 13 54 S 72 8W
Tambohorano **255** 17 30 S 43 58 E
Tambopata → **122** 13 21 S 69 36W
Tambora **206** 8 12 S 118 5 E
Tamboritha, Mt. **233** 37 31 S 146 40 E
Tambov **179** 52 45N 41 28 E
Tambre → **154** 42 49N 8 53W
Tambuku **209** 7 8 S 113 40 E
Tambun Sigumbal **211** 6 5N 121 47 E
Tamburâ **245** 5 40N 27 25 E
Tâmchekket **246** 17 25N 10 40W
Tamdybulak **183** 41 46N 64 36 E
Tame **118** 6 28N 71 44W
Tameapa **104** 25 39N 107 22W
Tamega → **154** 41 5N 8 21W
Tamelelt **240** 31 50N 7 32W
Tamenglong **202** 25 0N 93 35 E
Tamerlanovka **183** 42 36N 69 17 E
Tamerza **241** 34 23N 7 58 E
Tames, L. de **108** 22 13N 98 5W
Tamesí →, Tamaulipas, Mexico **103** 22 13N 97 52W
Tamesí →, Mexico **103** 22 13N 97 52W
Tamiahua **108** 21 16N 97 27W
Tamiahua, L. de **108** 21 35N 97 35W
Tamil Nadu □ **201** 11 0N 77 0 E
Tamines **143** 50 26N 4 36 E
Tamluk **199** 22 18N 87 58 E
Tammerfors = Tampere **175** 61 30N 23 50 E
Tammisaari **175** 60 0N 23 26 E
Ṭammūn **189** 32 18N 35 23 E
Tämnaren **172** 60 10N 17 25 E
Tamo Abu, Pegunungan **206** 3 10N 115 0 E
Tampacan **103** 21 25N 98 44W
Tampamolón Corona **103** 21 34N 98 49W
Tampate **103** 21 42N 99 1W
Tampe Downs **228** 24 22 S 132 24 E
Tampere **175** 61 30N 23 50 E
Tampico **103** 22 13N 97 51W
Tampico Alto **108** 22 7N 97 48W
Tampin **205** 2 28N 102 13 E
Tamrah **194** 20 24N 45 25 E
Tamri **240** 30 49N 9 50W
Tamrida = Qādib **195** 12 35N 54 2 E
Tamsalu **178** 59 11N 26 8 E
Tamsweg **150** 47 7N 13 49 E
Tamuín **103** 21 59N 98 45W
Tamuín → **103** 21 59N 98 34W
Tamuja → **155** 39 38N 6 29W
Tamworth, Australia **231** 31 7 S 150 58 E
Tamworth, Canada **85** 44 29N 77 0W
Tamworth, U.K. **133** 52 38N 1 41W
Tamyang **215** 35 19N 126 59 E
Tan An **205** 10 32N 106 25 E
Tan-tan **240** 28 29N 11 1W
Tana **174** 70 26N 28 14 E
Tana → **250** 2 32 S 40 31 E
Tana, L. **245** 13 5N 37 30 E
Tana River **250** 2 0 S 39 30 E
Tanabe **221** 33 44N 135 22 E
Tanabi **121** 20 37 S 49 37W
Tanafjorden **174** 70 45N 28 25 E
Tanagro → **165** 40 35N 15 25 E
Tanahbala **208** 0 30 S 98 30 E
Tanahgrogot **209** 1 55 S 116 15 E
Tanahjampea **207** 7 10 S 120 35 E
Tanahmasa **208** 0 12 S 98 39 E
Tanahmerah **207** 6 5 S 140 16 E
Tanakura **219** 37 10N 140 20 E
Tanami **228** 19 59 S 129 43 E
Tanami Des. **228** 18 50 S 132 0 E
Tananarive = Antananarivo **255** 18 55 S 47 31 E
Tanannt **240** 31 54N 6 56W
Tánaro → **162** 45 1N 8 47 E
Tanauan, Batangas, Phil. **210** 14 5N 121 10 E
Tanauan, Leyte, Phil. **211** 11 7N 125 1 E
Tanaunella **164** 40 42N 9 45 E
Tanay **210** 14 30N 121 17 E
Tanba-Sanchi **221** 35 7N 135 48 E
Tancachacal **111** 18 40N 89 51W
Tancarville **138** 49 29N 0 28 E
Tancheng **215** 34 25N 118 20 E
Tanchŏn **215** 40 27N 128 54 E
Tancitaro **106** 19 20N 102 22W
Tancitaro, Pico de **106** 19 23N 102 13W
Tancoco **108** 21 17N 97 47W
Tanda, Ut. P., India **199** 26 33N 82 35 E
Tanda, Ut. P., India **199** 28 57N 78 56 E
Tanda, Ivory C. **246** 7 48N 3 10W
Tandag **211** 9 4N 126 9 E
Tandaia **251** 9 25 S 34 15 E
Tăndărei **170** 44 39N 27 40 E
Tandaué **254** 16 58 S 18 5 E
Tandil **124** 37 15 S 59 6W
Tandil, Sa. del **124** 37 30 S 59 0W
Tandlianwala **198** 31 3N 73 9 E
Tando Adam **197** 25 45N 68 40 E
Tandou L. **231** 32 40 S 142 5 E
Tandsbyn **172** 63 0N 14 45 E
Tandur **200** 19 11N 79 30 E
Tane-ga-Shima **219** 30 30N 131 0 E
Taneatua **234** 38 4 S 177 1 E
Tanen Tong Dan **204** 16 30N 98 30 E
Tanew → **152** 50 29N 22 16 E
Tanezrouft **240** 23 9N 0 11 E
Tang, Koh **205** 10 16N 103 7 E
Tang Krasang **204** 12 34N 105 3 E
Tanga **250** 5 5 S 39 2 E
Tanga □ **250** 5 20 S 38 0 E
Tanga Is. **227** 3 20 S 153 15 E
Tangail **202** 24 15N 89 55 E
Tangamandapio **106** 19 57N 102 26W
Tangancicuaro de Arista **106** 19 54N 102 8W
Tanganyika, L. **250** 6 40 S 30 0 E
Tangawan **211** 7 30N 122 20 E
Tanger **240** 35 50N 5 49W
Tangerang **207** 6 11 S 106 37 E
Tangerhütte **146** 52 26N 11 50 E
Tangermünde **146** 52 32N 11 57 E
Tanggu **215** 39 2N 117 40 E
Tanggula Shan **212** 32 40N 92 10 E
Tanghe **214** 32 47N 112 50 E
Tangier = Tanger **240** 35 50N 5 49W
Tangier **81** 44 48N 62 42W
Tangorin P.O. **230** 21 47 S 144 12 E
Tangshan **215** 39 38N 118 10 E
Tangtou **215** 35 28N 118 30 E
Tangub **211** 8 3N 123 44 E
Tanguiéta **247** 10 35N 1 21 E
Tangxi **217** 29 3N 119 25 E
Tangyan He → **216** 28 54N 108 19 E
Tanimbar, Kepulauan **207** 7 30 S 131 30 E
Taninges **141** 46 7N 6 36 E
Taniyama **220** 31 31N 130 31 E
Tanjay **211** 9 30N 123 5 E
Tanjong Malim **205** 3 42N 101 31 E
Tanjore = Thanjavur **201** 10 48N 79 12 E
Tanjung **209** 2 10 S 115 25 E
Tanjungbalai **208** 2 55N 99 44 E
Tanjungbatu **209** 2 23N 118 3 E
Tanjungkarang Telukbetung **208** 5 20 S 105 10 E
Tanjungpandan **209** 2 43 S 107 38 E
Tanjungpinang **208** 1 5N 104 30 E
Tanjungpriok **207** 6 8 S 106 55 E
Tanjungredeb **209** 2 9N 117 29 E
Tanjungselor **209** 2 55N 117 25 E
Tank **197** 32 14N 70 25 E
Tänndalen **172** 62 33N 12 18 E
Tannis Bugt **173** 57 40N 10 15 E
Tannu-Ola **185** 51 0N 94 0 E
Tano → **246** 5 7N 2 56W
Tanon Str. **211** 10 20N 123 30 E
Tanout **247** 14 50N 8 55 E
Tanque **102** 27 56N 102 13W
Tanque de Cundo **102** 28 15N 103 36W
Tanquinho **121** 11 58 S 39 6W
Tanta **244** 30 45N 30 57 E
Tantallon **89** 50 32N 101 50W
Tantoyuca **108** 21 21N 98 14W
Tantung = Dandong **215** 40 10N 124 20 E
Tantūra = Dor **189** 32 37N 34 55 E
Tanu I. **92** 52 46N 131 40W
Tanuku **200** 16 45N 81 44 E
Tanumshede **173** 58 42N 11 20 E
Tanunda **232** 34 30 S 139 0 E
Tanur **201** 11 1N 75 52 E
Tanus **140** 44 8N 2 19 E
Tanza **210** 14 41N 120 56 E
Tanzania ■ **250** 6 40 S 34 0 E
Tanzawa-Sanchi **221** 35 27N 139 0 E
Tanzilla → **76** 58 8N 130 43W
Tao Ko **205** 10 5N 99 52 E
Tao'an **215** 45 22N 122 40 E
Tao'er He → **215** 45 45N 124 5 E
Taohua Dao **217** 29 50N 122 20 E
Taole **214** 38 48N 106 40 E
Taormina **165** 37 52N 15 16 E
Taoudenni **240** 22 40N 3 55W
Taoudrart, Adrar **240** 24 25N 2 24 E
Taounate **240** 34 25N 4 41W
Taourirt, Algeria **240** 26 37N 0 20 E
Taourirt, Morocco **241** 34 25N 2 53W
Taouz **241** 30 53N 4 0W
Taoyuan, China **217** 28 55N 111 16 E
Taoyuan, Taiwan **217** 25 0N 121 13 E
Tapa **178** 59 15N 25 50 E
Tapa Shan = Daba Shan **216** 32 0N 109 0 E
Tapachula **110** 14 54N 92 17W
Tapah **205** 4 12N 101 15 E
Tapajós → **119** 2 24 S 54 41W
Tapaktuan **208** 3 15N 97 10 E
Tapalpa, Sa. de **106** 20 20N 103 50W
Tapalpán **106** 19 57N 103 48W
Tapanahoni → **119** 4 20N 54 25W
Tapanui **235** 45 56 S 169 18 E
Tapauá **123** 5 40 S 64 20W
Tapauá → **123** 5 40 S 64 21W
Tapaz **211** 11 16N 122 32 E
Tapeta **246** 6 29N 8 52W

Taphan Hin **204** 16 13N 100 26 E
Tapi → **198** 21 8N 72 41 E
Tapia **154** 43 34N 6 56W
Tapiantana Group **211** 6 20N 122 0 E
Tapijulapa **110** 17 28N 92 47W
Tapilon **211** 11 17N 124 2 E
Tapilula **110** 17 14N 93 2W
Tapini **227** 8 19 S 147 0 E
Tápiószele **151** 47 25N 19 55 E
Tapiraí **121** 19 52 S 46 1W
Tapirapé → **120** 10 41 S 50 38W
Tapirapecó, Serra **119** 1 10N 65 0W
Tapirapuã **123** 14 51 S 57 45W
Tapizuelas **100** 26 41N 108 53W
Taplan **232** 34 33 S 140 52 E
Tapoeripa **119** 5 22N 56 34W
Tapolca **151** 46 53N 17 29 E
Tapuaenuku, Mt. **235** 42 0 S 173 39 E
Tapul = Salvacion **211** 9 56N 118 47 E
Tapul Group **211** 5 35N 120 50 E
Tapun **202** 27 35N 96 22 E
Tapurucuará **119** 0 24 S 65 2W
Taqīābād **193** 35 33N 59 11 E
Ţaqţaq **192** 35 53N 44 35 E
Taquara **125** 29 36 S 50 46W
Taquari → **123** 19 15 S 57 17W
Taquaritinga **121** 21 24 S 48 30W
Tar Island **76** 57 3N 111 40W
Tara, Australia **231** 27 17 S 150 31 E
Tara, Canada **84** 44 28N 81 9W
Tara, Japan **220** 33 2N 130 11 E
Tara, U.S.S.R. **184** 56 55N 74 24 E
Tara, Zambia **251** 16 58 S 26 45 E
Tara →, U.S.S.R. **184** 56 42N 74 36 E
Tara →, Yugoslavia **166** 43 21N 18 51 E
Tara-Dake **220** 32 58N 130 6 E
Tarabagatay, Khrebet **184** 48 0N 83 0 E
Tarabuco **123** 19 10 S 64 57W
Tarābulus, Lebanon **190** 34 31N 35 50 E
Tarābulus, Libya **241** 32 49N 13 7 E
Tarachi **100** 28 52N 108 52W
Taradale **234** 39 33 S 176 53 E
Tarahouahout **241** 22 41N 5 59 E
Tarahumara, Sa. **101** 27 10N 107 15W
Tarakan **209** 3 20N 117 35 E
Tarakit, Mt. **250** 2 2N 35 10 E
Taralga **231** 34 26 S 149 52 E
Tarama-Jima **219** 24 39N 124 42 E
Taramakau → **235** 42 34 S 171 8 E
Tarana **233** 33 31 S 149 52 E
Taranagar **198** 28 43N 74 50 E
Taranaki □ **234** 39 5 S 174 51 E
Tarancón **156** 40 1N 3 1W
Taranga **198** 23 56N 72 43 E
Taranga Hill **198** 24 0N 72 40 E
Táranto **165** 40 30N 17 11 E
Táranto, G. di **165** 40 0N 17 15 E
Tarapacá **118** 2 56 S 69 46W
Tarapacá □ **124** 20 45 S 69 30W
Tarapoto **122** 6 30 S 76 20W
Taraquá **118** 0 6N 68 28W
Tarare **141** 45 54N 4 26 E
Tararua Range **234** 40 45 S 175 25 E
Tarascon, Ariège, France **140** 42 50N 1 37 E
Tarascon, Bouches-du-Rhône, France **141** 43 48N 4 39 E
Tarashcha **180** 49 30N 30 31 E
Tarat, Bj. **241** 26 13N 9 18 E
Tarata **122** 17 27 S 70 2W
Tarauacá **122** 8 6 S 70 48W
Tarauacá → **122** 6 42 S 69 48W
Taravo → **141** 41 42N 8 49 E
Tarawera **234** 39 2 S 176 36 E
Tarawera L. **234** 38 13 S 176 27 E
Tarawera Mt. **234** 38 14 S 176 32 E
Tarazona **156** 41 55N 1 43W
Tarazona de la Mancha **157** 39 16N 1 55W
Tarbat Ness **134** 57 52N 3 48W
Tarbela Dam **198** 34 8N 72 52 E
Tarbert, Strathclyde, U.K. **134** 55 55N 5 25W
Tarbert, W. Isles, U.K. **134** 57 54N 6 49W
Tarbes **140** 43 15N 0 3 E
Tarbrax **230** 21 7 S 142 26 E
Tarbū **241** 26 0N 15 5 E
Tarcento **163** 46 12N 13 12 E
Tarcoola **231** 30 44 S 134 36 E
Tarcoon **231** 30 15 S 146 43 E
Tardets-Sorholus **140** 43 8N 0 52W
Tardoire → **140** 45 52N 0 14 E
Taree **231** 31 50 S 152 30 E
Tarentaise **141** 45 30N 6 35 E
Taretán **106** 19 20N 101 55W
Tarf, Ras **240** 35 40N 5 11W
Tarf Shaqq al Abd **244** 26 50N 36 6 E
Ţarfā, Ra's aţ **194** 17 2N 42 22 E
Tarfa, Wadi el → **244** 28 25N 30 50 E
Tarfaya **240** 27 55N 12 55W
Targon **140** 44 44N 0 16W
Targuist **241** 34 59N 4 14W
Tărhăus **170** 46 40N 26 8 E
Tărhăus, Munţii **170** 46 39N 26 7 E
Tarhbalt **240** 30 39N 5 20W
Tarhit **240** 30 58N 2 0W
Tarhūnah **241** 32 27N 13 36 E
Tari **227** 5 54 S 142 59 E
Táriba **118** 7 49N 72 13W
Tarifa **155** 36 1N 5 36W
Tarija **124** 21 30 S 64 40W
Tarija □ **124** 21 30 S 63 30W
Tariku → **207** 2 55 S 138 26 E
Tarīm **195** 16 3N 49 0 E
Tarim He → **212** 39 30N 88 30 E
Tarim Pendi **212** 40 0N 84 0 E
Tarimbaro **107** 19 47N 101 8W
Tarime □ **250** 1 15 S 34 0 E
Tarimoro **107** 20 17N 100 45W
Taringo Downs **233** 32 13 S 145 33 E
Taritatu → **207** 2 54 S 138 27 E
Tarka → **254** 32 10 S 26 0 E
Tarkastad **254** 32 0 S 26 16 E
Tarkhankut, Mys **180** 45 25N 32 30 E
Tarko Sale **184** 64 55N 77 50 E
Tarkwa **246** 5 20N 2 0W
Tarlac **210** 15 29N 120 35 E
Tarlac □ **210** 15 30N 120 30 E
Tarlton Downs **230** 22 40 S 136 45 E
Tarm **173** 55 56N 8 31 E
Tarma **122** 11 25 S 75 45W
Tarn □ **140** 43 49N 2 8 E
Tarn → **140** 44 5N 1 6 E
Tarn-et-Garonne □ **140** 44 8N 1 20 E
Tarna → **151** 47 31N 19 59 E
Tårnby **172** 55 37N 12 36 E
Tarnica **151** 49 4N 22 44 E
Tarnobrzeg **152** 50 35N 21 41 E
Tarnobrzeg □ **152** 50 40N 22 0 E
Tarnogród **152** 50 22N 22 45 E
Tarnów **152** 50 3N 21 0 E
Tarnów □ **151** 50 0N 21 0 E
Tarnowskie Góry **152** 50 27N 18 54 E
Táro → **162** 45 0N 10 15 E
Taroom **231** 25 36 S 149 48 E
Taroudannt **240** 30 30N 8 52W
Tarp **146** 54 40N 9 25 E
Tarquínia **163** 42 15N 11 45 E
Tarqūmiyah **189** 31 35N 35 1 E
Tarragona **156** 41 5N 1 17 E
Tarragona □ **156** 41 0N 1 0 E
Tarrasa **156** 41 34N 2 1 E
Tárrega **156** 41 39N 1 9 E
Tarshiha = Me'ona **189** 33 1N 35 15 E
Tarso Emissi **241** 21 27N 18 36 E
Tarso Ourari **241** 21 27N 17 27 E
Tarsus **177** 36 58N 34 55 E
Tarsus → **190** 36 46N 34 52 E
Tartagal **124** 22 30 S 63 50W
Tartas **140** 43 50N 0 49W
Tartu **178** 58 20N 26 44 E
Tarţūs **190** 34 55N 35 55 E
Tarţūs □ **190** 35 0N 36 0 E
Tarumirim **121** 19 16 S 41 59W
Tarumizu **220** 31 29N 130 42 E
Tarussa **179** 54 44N 37 10 E
Tarutao, Ko **205** 6 33N 99 40 E
Tarutung **208** 2 0N 98 54 E
Tarvisio **163** 46 31N 13 35 E
Tarz Ulli **241** 25 32N 10 8 E
Tas-Buget **183** 44 46N 65 33 E
Taşağil **190** 36 55N 31 14 E
Tasahku **202** 27 33N 97 52 E
Tasāwah **241** 26 0N 13 30 E
Taschereau **82** 48 40N 78 40W
Taseko → **92** 52 4N 123 9W
Taseko L. **92** 51 15N 123 35W
Tasgaon **200** 17 2N 74 39 E
Tash-Kumyr **183** 41 40N 72 10 E
Ta'shan **245** 16 31N 42 33 E
Tashauz **184** 41 49N 59 58 E
Tashi Chho Dzong = Thimphu **202** 27 31N 89 45 E
T'ashihk'uerhkan **183** 37 47N 75 14 E
Tashkent **183** 41 20N 69 10 E
Tashtagol **184** 52 47N 87 53 E
Tasikmalaya **209** 7 18 S 108 12 E
Tåsjön **174** 64 15N 16 0 E
Taskan **185** 62 59N 150 20 E
Taskopru **180** 41 30N 34 15 E
Tasman → **235** 43 48 S 170 8 E
Tasman, Mt. **235** 43 34 S 170 12 E
Tasman B. **235** 40 59 S 173 25 E
Tasman Mts. **235** 41 3 S 172 25 E
Tasman Pen. **230** 43 10 S 148 0 E
Tasman Sea **224** 36 0 S 160 0 E
Tasmania □ **230** 42 0 S 146 30 E
Tăşnad **170** 47 30N 22 33 E
Tassialuk, L. **78** 59 3N 74 0W
Tassil Tin-Rerhoh **240** 20 5N 3 55 E
Tassili n-Ajjer **241** 25 47N 8 1 E
Tassili-Oua-n-Ahaggar **241** 20 41N 5 30 E
Tasty **183** 44 47N 69 7 E
Tasu **92** 52 45N 132 5W
Tasu Sd. **92** 52 47N 132 2W
Taşucu **190** 36 19N 33 52 E
Tata, Hungary **151** 47 37N 18 19 E
Tata, Morocco **240** 29 46N 7 56W
Tatabánya **151** 47 32N 18 25 E
Tatahouine **241** 32 57N 10 29 E
Tatamagouche **81** 45 43N 63 18W
Tatar A.S.S.R. □ **182** 55 30N 51 30 E
Tatarbunary **180** 45 50N 29 39 E
Tatarsk **184** 55 14N 76 0 E
Tatebayashi **221** 36 15N 139 32 E
Tatepusco **104** 21 20N 104 19W
Tateshina-Yama **221** 36 8N 138 11 E
Tateyama **221** 35 0N 139 50 E
Tathlina L. **76** 60 33N 117 39W
Tathlīth **194** 19 32N 43 30 E
Tathlīth, W. → **194** 20 35N 44 20 E
Tathra **231** 36 44 S 149 59 E
Tatinnai L. **77** 60 55N 97 40W
Tatla L. **92** 52 0N 124 20W
Tatlayoko L. **92** 51 35N 124 24W
Tatnam, C. **77** 57 16N 91 0W
Tatra = Tatry **152** 49 20N 20 0 E
Tatry **152** 49 20N 20 0 E
Tatsuno **220** 34 52N 134 33 E
Tatta **197** 24 42N 67 55 E
Tatton **93** 51 43N 121 22W
Tatuī **125** 23 25 S 47 53W
Tatuk, L. **92** 53 32N 124 14W
Tat'ung = Datong **214** 40 6N 113 18 E
Tatura **233** 36 29 S 145 16 E
Tatvan **177** 38 31N 42 15 E
Tau **226** 14 15 S 169 30W
Tauá **120** 6 1 S 40 26W
Taubaté **125** 23 0 S 45 36W
Tauberbischofsheim **147** 49 37N 9 40 E
Taucha **146** 51 22N 12 31 E
Tauern **150** 47 15N 12 40 E
Tauern-tunnel **150** 47 0N 13 12 E
Taufikia **245** 9 24N 31 37 E
Taumarunui **234** 38 53 S 175 15 E
Taumaturgo **122** 8 54 S 72 51W
Taung **254** 27 33 S 24 47 E
Taungdwingyi **202** 20 1N 95 40 E
Taunggyi **202** 20 50N 97 0 E
Taungtha **202** 21 12N 95 25 E
Taungup **202** 18 51N 94 14 E
Taungup Pass **202** 18 40N 94 45 E
Taunsa Barrage **198** 30 42N 70 50 E
Taunton **133** 51 1N 3 7W
Taunus **147** 50 15N 8 20 E
Taupo **234** 38 41 S 176 7 E
Taupo, L. **234** 38 46 S 175 55 E
Taurage **178** 55 14N 22 16 E
Tauranga **234** 37 42 S 176 11 E
Tauranga Harb. **234** 37 30 S 176 5 E
Tauri → **227** 8 8 S 146 8 E
Taurianova **165** 38 22N 16 1 E
Taurus Mts. = Toros Daglari **177** 37 0N 35 0 E
Tauste **156** 41 58N 1 18W
Tautira **226** 17 44 S 149 9W
Tauz **181** 41 0N 45 40 E
Tavaar **256** 3 6N 46 1 E
Tavannes **148** 47 13N 7 12 E
Tavda **182** 58 7N 65 8 E
Tavda → **182** 59 20N 63 28 E
Taverny **139** 49 2N 2 13 E
Taveta **250** 3 23 S 37 37 E
Taveuni **226** 16 51 S 179 58W
Tavignano → **141** 42 7N 9 33 E
Tavira **155** 37 8N 7 40W
Tavistock, Canada **84** 43 19N 80 50W
Tavistock, U.K. **133** 50 33N 4 9W
Tavolara **164** 40 55N 9 40 E
Távora → **154** 41 8N 7 35W
Tavoy **204** 14 2N 98 12 E
Taw → **133** 17 37 S 177 55 E
Tawau **206** 4 20N 117 55 E
Ţawī Şulaym **195** 22 33N 58 40 E
Tawitawi **211** 5 10N 120 0 E
Tawitawi □ **211** 5 0N 120 0 E
Tawitawi Group **211** 5 10N 120 15 E
Tawngche **202** 26 34N 95 38 E
Tāwurgha' **241** 32 1N 15 2 E
Taxco de Alarcón **107** 18 33N 99 36W
Taxila **198** 33 42N 72 52 E
Tay → **134** 56 37N 3 38W
Tay, Firth of **134** 56 25N 3 8W
Tay, L., Australia **229** 32 55 S 120 48 E
Tay, L., U.K. **134** 56 30N 4 10W
Tay Ninh **205** 11 20N 106 5 E
Tayabamba **122** 8 15 S 77 16W
Tayabas **210** 14 1N 121 35 E
Tayabas Bay **210** 13 45N 121 45 E
Tayahua **105** 22 5N 102 52W
Taylakovy **184** 59 13N 74 0 E
Taylor **76** 56 13N 120 40W
Taylor, Mt. **235** 43 30 S 171 20 E
Taymā **192** 27 35N 38 45 E
Taymyr, Poluostrov **185** 75 0N 100 0 E
Tayog **210** 16 2N 120 45 E
Tayoltita **104** 24 5N 105 56W
Tayport **134** 56 27N 2 52W
Ţayr Zibnā **189** 33 14N 35 23 E
Tayshet **185** 55 58N 98 1 E
Tayside □ **134** 56 25N 3 30W
Taytay, Palawan, Phil. **211** 10 45N 119 30 E
Taytay, Rizal, Phil. **210** 14 34N 121 8 E
Taytay Bay **211** 10 55N 119 35 E
Taz → **184** 67 32N 78 40 E
Taza **241** 34 16N 4 6W
Tāzah Khurmātū **192** 35 18N 44 20 E
Tazawa-Ko **218** 39 43N 140 40 E
Taze **202** 22 57N 95 24 E
Tazenakht **240** 30 35N 7 12W
Tazerbo **242** 25 45N 21 0 E
Tazin → **77** 60 26N 110 45W
Tazin L. **77** 59 44N 108 42W
Tazoult **241** 35 29N 6 11 E
Tazovskiy **184** 67 30N 78 44 E
Tbilisi **181** 41 43N 44 50 E
Tchad ■ **243** 12 30N 17 15 E
Tchad, L. **243** 13 30N 14 30 E
Tchaourou **247** 8 58N 2 40 E
Tch'eng-tou = Chengdu **216** 30 38N 104 2 E
Tchentlo L. **76** 55 15N 125 0W
Tchibanga **252** 2 45 S 11 0 E
Tchien **246** 5 59N 8 15W
Tchikala-Tcholohanga **253** 12 38 S 16 3 E
Tchin Tabaraden **247** 15 58N 5 56 E
Tchingou, Massif de **226** 20 54 S 165 0 E
Tchollirè **252** 8 24N 14 10 E
Tch'ong-k'ing = Chongqing **216** 29 35N 106 25 E
Tczew **152** 54 8N 18 50 E
Te Anau, L. **235** 45 15 S 167 45 E
Te Araroa **234** 37 39 S 178 25 E
Te Aroha **234** 37 32 S 175 44 E
Te Awamutu **234** 38 1 S 175 20 E
Te Kaha **234** 37 44 S 177 52 E
Te Karaka **234** 38 26 S 177 53 E
Te Kauwhata **234** 37 25 S 175 9 E
Te Kopuru **234** 36 2 S 173 56 E
Te Kuiti **234** 38 20 S 175 11 E
Te Puke **234** 37 46 S 176 22 E
Te Waewae B. **235** 46 13 S 167 33 E
Tea → **118** 0 30 S 65 9W
Tea Tree **230** 22 5 S 133 22 E
Teabo **111** 20 24N 89 17W
Teaca **170** 46 55N 24 30 E
Teacapán **104** 22 33N 105 45W
Teano **165** 41 15N 14 1 E
Teapa **110** 17 33N 92 57W
Teba **155** 36 59N 4 55W
Tebakang **206** 1 6N 110 30 E
Teberda **181** 43 30N 41 46 E
Tébessa **241** 35 22N 8 8 E
Tebicuary → **124** 26 36 S 58 16W
Tebingtinggi **208** 3 20N 99 9 E
Tebintingii **208** 1 0N 102 45 E
Tébourba **241** 36 49N 9 51 E
Téboursouk **241** 36 29N 9 10 E
Tebulos **181** 42 36N 45 17 E
Tecalitlan **106** 19 26N 103 15W
Tecamachalco **109** 18 53N 97 44W
Tecapulco **107** 18 29N 99 38W
Tecate **98** 32 34N 116 38W
Tech → **140** 42 36N 3 3 E
Techa → **182** 56 13N 62 58 E
Techaluta **106** 20 4N 103 33W
Techiman **246** 7 35N 1 58W
Techirghiol **170** 44 4N 28 32 E
Tecka **126** 7 35N 1 43W
Tecoanaga **107** 16 53N 99 24W
Tecoh **111** 20 55N 89 38W
Tecolotlán **106** 20 13N 104 3W
Tecolutilla **110** 18 17N 93 19W
Tecolutla → **108** 20 29N 97 0W
Tecomán **106** 18 55N 103 53W
Tecomate, L. **107** 16 42N 99 20W
Tecomaxtlahuaca **109** 17 21N 98 2W
Tecominoacán **110** 17 53N 93 32W
Tecorichic **101** 26 43N 106 43W
Tecoripa **100** 28 37N 109 57W
Tecozautla **107** 20 32N 99 38W
Tecpan de Galeana **107** 17 15N 100 41W
Tecpatán **110** 17 8N 93 18W
Tecuala **104** 22 23N 105 27W
Tecuci **170** 45 51N 27 27 E
Tecumseh **84** 42 19N 82 54W
Ted **256** 4 24N 43 55 E
Tedzhen **184** 37 23N 60 31 E
Tee Lake **82** 46 40N 79 0W
Teepee Creek **90** 55 22N 118 24W
Tees → **132** 54 36N 1 25W
Teesside **132** 54 37N 1 13W
Teeswater **84** 43 59N 81 17W
Tefé **119** 3 25 S 64 50W
Tefé → **119** 3 35 S 64 47W
Tegal **209** 6 52 S 109 8 E
Tegelen **143** 51 20N 6 9 E
Tegernsee **147** 47 43N 11 46 E
Teggiano **165** 40 24N 15 32 E

Teghra 199 25 30N 85 34 E
Tegid, L. 132 52 53N 3 38W
Tegina 247 10 5N 6 11 E
Tegucigalpa 112 14 5N 87 14W
Tehamiyam 244 18 20N 36 32 E
Tehilla 244 17 42N 36 6 E
Téhini 246 9 39N 3 40W
Tehrān 193 35 44N 51 30 E
Tehuacán 109 18 27N 97 23W
Tehuantepec, G. de 109 16 0N 94 50W
Tehuantepec → 109 16 10N 95 7W
Tehueco 104 26 17N 108 46W
Tehuipango 109 18 31N 97 4W
Tehuitzingo 109 18 21N 98 17W
Teich, Le 140 44 38N 0 59W
Teifi → 133 52 4N 4 14W
Teign → 133 50 41N 3 42W
Teignmouth 133 50 33N 3 30W
Teil, Le 141 44 33N 4 40 E
Teilleul, Le 138 48 32N 0 53W
Teiuş 170 46 12N 23 40 E
Teixeira 120 7 13 S 37 15W
Teixeira Pinto 246 12 3N 16 0W
Tejamén 104 24 48N 105 7W
Tejo → 155 38 40N 9 24W
Tejolocachic 101 28 46N 107 42W
Tejupilco de Hidalgo 107 18 54N 100 9W
Tekal de Venegas 111 21 1N 88 57W
Tekanto 111 21 1N 89 6W
Tekapo, L. 235 43 53 S 170 33 E
Tekax 111 20 12N 89 17W
Tekeli 183 44 50N 79 0 E
Tekeze → 245 14 20N 35 50 E
Tekija 166 44 42N 22 26 E
Tekirdağ 177 40 58N 27 30 E
Tekit 111 20 32N 89 20W
Tekkali 200 18 37N 84 15 E
Tekom 111 20 36N 88 16W
Tekouiât, O. → 240 22 25N 2 35 E
Tel Adashim 189 32 30N 35 17 E
Tel Aviv-Yafo 189 32 4N 34 48 E
Tel Lakhish 189 31 34N 34 51 E
Tel Megiddo 189 32 35N 35 11 E
Tel Mond 189 32 15N 34 56 E
Tela 112 15 40N 87 28W
Télagh 241 34 51N 0 32W
Telanaipura = Jambi 208 1 38 S 103 30 E
Telavi 181 42 0N 45 30 E
Telchac 111 21 12N 89 16W
Telchac Puerto 111 21 21N 89 16W
Telciu 170 47 25N 24 24 E
Telefomin 227 5 10 S 141 31 E
Telegraph Cove 92 50 32N 126 50W
Telegraph Cr. → 76 58 0N 131 10W
Telekhany 178 52 30N 25 46 E
Telemark fylke □ 171 59 25N 8 30 E
Telén 124 36 15 S 65 31W
Telen → 209 0 10 S 117 20 E
Teleneshty 170 47 35N 28 24 E
Teleng 193 25 47N 61 3 E
Teleño 154 42 23N 6 22W
Teleorman □ 170 44 0N 25 0 E
Teleorman → 170 44 15N 25 20 E
Teles Pires → 123 7 21 S 58 3W
Teletaye 247 16 31N 1 30 E
Telford 132 52 42N 2 31W
Telfs 150 47 19N 11 4 E
Telgte 146 51 59N 7 46 E
Télimélé 246 10 54N 13 2W
Telkwa 76 54 41N 127 5W
Téllez 107 19 59N 98 46W
Tellicherry 201 11 45N 75 30 E
Tellin 143 50 5N 5 13 E
Teloloapán 107 18 21N 99 51W
Teloloapán, Sa. de 107 18 20N 99 45W
Telpos Iz 176 63 35N 57 30 E
Telsen 126 42 30 S 66 50W
Telšiai 178 55 59N 22 14 E
Teltow 146 52 24N 13 15 E
Teluk Anson 205 4 3N 101 0 E
Teluk Intan = Teluk Anson 205 4 3N 101 0 E
Telukbutun 205 4 13N 108 12 E
Telukdalem 208 0 33N 97 50 E
Tema 247 5 41N 0 0 E
Temalacacingo 107 17 52N 98 41W
Temanggung 209 7 18 S 110 10 E
Temascal 109 18 14N 96 25W
Temascalcingo 107 19 55N 100 0W
Temascaltepec → 107 18 47N 100 41W
Temascaltepec de González 107 19 2N 100 3W
Temaverachi, Sa. 100 29 28N 109 22W
Temax 111 21 9N 88 56W
Tembe 250 0 16 S 28 14 E
Tembesi 208 1 43 S 103 6 E
Tembilahan 208 0 19 S 103 9 E
Tembladeras, L. 110 15 11N 92 50W
Temblador 119 8 59N 62 44W
Tembleque 156 39 41N 3 30W
Tembuland 255 31 35 S 28 0 E
Teme → 133 52 23N 2 15W
Temerloh 205 3 27N 102 25 E
Temir 184 49 21N 57 3 E
Temirtau, Kazakh S.S.R., U.S.S.R. 184 50 5N 72 56 E
Temirtau, R.S.F.S.R., U.S.S.R. 184 53 10N 87 30 E
Temiscamie → 78 50 59N 73 5W
Témiscaming 82 46 44N 79 5W
Témiscamingue, L. 82 47 10N 79 25W
Temma 230 41 12 S 144 48 E
Temnikov 179 54 40N 43 11 E
Temo → 164 40 20N 8 30 E
Temora 231 34 30 S 147 30 E
Temores 101 27 16N 108 15W
Temosachic 101 28 57N 107 51W
Temozón 111 20 48N 88 13W
Temperance Vale 81 46 4N 67 15W
Témpio Pausania 164 40 53N 9 6 E
Temple B. 230 12 15 S 143 3 E
Templeman, Mt. 93 50 42N 117 12W
Templemore 135 52 48N 7 50W
Templeton → 230 21 0 S 138 40 E
Templeuve 143 50 39N 3 17 E
Templin 146 53 8N 13 31 E
Tempoal 108 21 31N 98 23W
Tempoal → 108 21 47N 98 27W
Temryuk 180 45 15N 37 24 E
Temse 143 51 7N 4 13 E
Temska → 166 43 17N 22 33 E
Temuco 126 38 45 S 72 40W
Temuka 235 44 14 S 171 17 E
Ten Boer 142 53 16N 6 42 E
Ten Mile L. 79 51 6N 56 42W
Tena 118 0 59 S 77 49W
Tenabo 111 20 3N 90 14W
Tenacatita, B. 106 19 17N 104 50W
Tenali 201 16 15N 80 35 E
Tenamaxtlán 106 20 13N 104 10W
Tenampulco 108 20 10N 97 24W
Tenancingo de Degollado 107 18 58N 99 36W
Tenango, Sa. de 107 17 30N 99 10W
Tenango de Arista 107 19 7N 99 33W
Tenasserim 205 12 6N 99 3 E
Tenasserim □ 204 14 0N 98 30 E
Tenay 141 45 55N 5 30 E
Tenby 133 51 40N 4 42W
Tenda, Col di 162 44 7N 7 36 E
Tendaho 245 11 48N 40 54 E
Tende 141 44 5N 7 35 E
Tende, Col de 141 44 9N 7 32 E
Tendelti 245 13 1N 31 55 E
Tendjedi, Adrar 241 23 41N 7 32 E
Tendrara 241 33 3N 1 58W
Tendre, Mt. 148 46 35N 6 18 E
Teneida 244 25 30N 29 19 E
Tenejapa 110 16 49N 92 31W
Tenente Marques → 123 11 10 S 59 56W
Ténéré 247 19 0N 10 30 E
Ténéré, Erg du 243 17 35N 10 55 E
Tenerife 240 28 15N 16 35W
Ténès 241 36 31N 1 14 E
Tenexpa 107 17 11N 100 43W
Teng Xian, Guangxi Zhuangzu, China 217 23 21N 110 56 E
Teng Xian, Shandong, China 215 35 5N 117 10 E
Tengah □ 207 2 0 S 122 0 E
Tengah Kepulauan 209 7 5 S 118 15 E
Tengchong 216 25 0N 98 28 E
Tengchowfu = Penglai 215 37 48N 120 42 E
Tenggara □ 207 3 0 S 122 0 E
Tenggarong 209 0 24 S 116 58 E
Tenggol, P. 205 4 48N 103 41 E
Tengiz, Ozero 184 50 30N 69 0 E
Tenigerbad 149 46 42N 8 57 E
Tenixtepec 108 20 37N 97 9W
Tenkasi 201 8 55N 77 20 E
Tenke, Shaba, Zaïre 251 11 22 S 26 40 E
Tenke, Shaba, Zaïre 251 10 32 S 26 7 E
Tenkodogo 247 11 54N 0 19W
Tenna → 163 43 12N 13 47 E
Tennant Creek 230 19 30 S 134 15 E
Tenneville 143 50 6N 5 32 E
Tennsift, Oued → 240 32 3N 9 28W
Tenom 206 5 4N 115 57 E
Tenosique de Pino Suárez 110 17 29N 91 26W
Tenri 221 34 39N 135 49 E
Tenryū 221 34 52N 137 49 E
Tenryū-Gawa → 221 35 39N 137 48 E
Tent L. 77 62 25N 107 54W
Tenterfield 231 29 0 S 152 0 E
Tentzo, Sa. de 109 18 50N 98 15W
Teocaltiche 106 21 26N 102 35W
Teocelo 108 19 23N 96 58W
Teocuitatlán de Corona 106 20 7N 103 24W
Teófilo Otoni 121 17 50 S 41 30W
Teoloyucan 107 19 45N 99 10W
Teopisca 110 16 31N 92 29W
Teotepec, Cerro 107 17 27N 100 10W
Teotitlán del Camino 109 18 8N 97 5W
Tepa 207 7 52 S 129 31 E
Tepalcatepec 106 19 11N 102 51W
Tepalcatepec → 106 18 35N 101 59W
Tepalcingo 107 18 36N 98 51W
Tepatepec 107 20 14N 99 5W
Tepatitlán 110 17 50N 92 22W
Tepatitlán, Sa. de 106 20 50N 102 20W
Tepatitlán de Morelos 106 20 49N 102 44W
Tepatlaxco 109 19 4N 97 58W
Tepeaca 109 18 58N 97 54W
Tepeapulco 107 19 47N 98 33W
Tepechitlán 105 21 40N 103 20W
Tepecoacuilco de Trujano 107 18 18N 99 29W
Tepeguaje 103 23 30N 97 47W
Tepehuanes 104 25 21N 105 44W
Tepehuanes → 104 25 9N 105 27W
Tepehuanes, Sa. de 104 25 17N 106 0W
Tepeji del Río 107 19 54N 99 21W
Tepelena 168 40 17N 20 2 E
Tepequem, Serra 119 3 45N 61 45W
Tepetlixpa 107 19 2N 98 49W
Tepetongo 105 22 28N 103 9W
Tepetzintla 108 21 10N 97 50W
Tepexi de Rodríguez 109 18 35N 97 56W
Tepezalá 105 22 13N 102 10W
Tepic 104 21 30N 104 54W
Tepich 111 20 16N 88 16W
Teplice 150 50 40N 13 48 E
Teploklyuchenka 183 42 30N 78 30 E
Tepoca, C. 100 29 22N 112 27W
Tepotzotlán 107 19 43N 99 13W
Tepoztlán 107 18 59N 99 6W
Tepuxtepec, Presa de 107 20 3N 100 16W
Tequepa, B. 107 17 17N 101 5W
Tequesquitengo, L. de 107 18 37N 99 16W
Tequesquitlán 106 19 28N 104 38W
Tequila, Jalisco, Mexico 106 20 54N 103 47W
Tequila, Veracruz, Mexico 109 18 44N 97 4W
Tequisistlán → 109 16 29N 95 27W
Tequisquiapan 107 20 31N 99 52W
Ter → 156 42 0N 3 12 E
Ter Apel 142 52 53N 7 5 E
Téra 247 14 0N 0 45 E
Tera → 154 41 54N 5 44W
Teraina, I. 225 4 43N 160 25W
Téramo 163 42 40N 13 40 E
Terán 110 16 45N 93 10W
Terang 231 38 15 S 142 55 E
Terawhiti, C. 234 41 16 S 174 38 E
Terazit, Massif de 241 20 2N 8 30 E
Terborg 142 51 56N 6 22 E
Terceira 240 38 43N 27 13W
Tercero → 124 32 58 S 61 47W
Terdal 200 16 33N 75 3 E
Terebovlya 178 49 18N 25 44 E
Teregova 170 45 10N 22 16 E
Terek → 181 44 0N 47 30 E
Terek-Say 183 41 30N 71 11 E
Terence Bay 81 44 28N 63 43W
Terenos 123 20 26 S 54 50W
Tereshka → 179 51 48N 46 26 E
Teresina 120 5 9 S 42 45W
Teresinha 119 0 58N 52 2W
Terespol 152 52 5N 23 37 E
Terewah, L. 231 29 52 S 147 35 E
Terges → 155 37 49N 7 41W
Tergnier 139 49 40N 3 17 E
Terhazza 240 23 38N 5 22W
Terheijden 143 51 38N 4 45 E
Teridgerie Cr. → 231 30 25 S 148 50 E
Terifa 194 14 24N 43 48 E
Terlizzi 165 41 8N 16 32 E
Terme 180 41 11N 37 0 E
Termez 183 37 15N 67 15 E
Terminal Cobos 108 20 56N 97 22W
Términi Imerese 164 37 58N 13 42 E
Términos, L. de 111 18 37N 91 33W
Térmoli 163 42 0N 15 0 E
Ternate 207 0 45N 127 25 E
Terneuzen 143 51 20N 3 50 E
Terney 185 45 3N 136 37 E
Terni 163 42 34N 12 38 E
Ternitz 150 47 43N 16 2 E
Ternopol 178 49 30N 25 40 E
Terowie 231 32 27 S 147 52 E
Terra Nova 79 48 30N 54 13W
Terra Nova → 79 48 40N 54 0W
Terra Nova B. 13 74 50 S 164 40 E
Terra Nova Nat. Park 79 48 33N 53 58W
Terrace 76 54 30N 128 35W
Terrace Bay 87 48 47N 87 5W
Terracina 164 41 17N 13 12 E
Terralba 164 39 42N 8 38 E
Terranova = Ólbia 164 40 55N 9 30 E
Terranuova Bracciolini 163 43 31N 11 35 E
Terrasini Favarotta 164 38 10N 13 4 E
Terrasson 140 45 7N 1 19 E
Terrebonne 83 45 42N 73 38W
Terrecht 240 20 10N 0 10W
Terrenceville 79 47 40N 54 44W
Terrick Terrick 230 24 44 S 145 5 E
Terschelling 142 53 25N 5 20 E
Terskey Alatau, Khrebet 183 41 50N 77 0 E
Terter → 181 40 35N 47 22 E
Teruel 156 40 22N 1 8W
Teruel □ 156 40 48N 1 0W
Tervel 167 43 45N 27 28 E
Tervola 174 66 6N 24 49 E
Teryaweyna L. 231 32 18 S 143 22 E
Tešanj 166 44 38N 17 59 E
Teseney 245 15 5N 36 42 E
Tesha → 179 55 38N 42 9 E
Teshio 218 44 53N 141 44 E
Teshio-Gawa → 218 44 53N 141 45 E
Tešica 166 43 27N 21 45 E
Tesistán 106 20 47N 103 29W
Tesiyn Gol → 212 50 40N 93 20 E
Teslić 166 44 37N 17 54 E
Teslin 76 60 10N 132 43W
Teslin → 76 61 34N 134 35W
Teslin L. 76 60 15N 132 57W
Tesouro 123 16 4 S 53 34W
Tessalit 247 20 12N 1 0 E
Tessaoua 247 13 47N 7 56 E
Tessenderlo 143 51 4N 5 5 E
Tessin 146 54 2N 12 28 E
Tessit 247 15 13N 0 18 E
Test → 133 51 7N 1 30W
Testa del Gargano 165 41 50N 16 10 E
Teste, La 140 44 37N 1 8W
Têt 151 47 30N 17 33 E
Têt → 140 42 44N 3 2 E
Tetachuck L. 92 53 18N 125 55W
Tetas, Pta. 124 23 31 S 70 38W
Tete 251 16 13 S 33 33 E
Tete □ 251 15 15 S 32 40 E
Tête-à-la-Baleine 79 50 41N 59 20W
Tetela del Río 107 17 59N 100 5W
Teterev → 178 51 1N 30 5 E
Teteringen 143 51 37N 4 49 E
Teterow 146 53 45N 12 34 E
Teteven 167 42 58N 24 17 E
Tethul → 76 60 35N 112 12W
Tetillas 105 23 44N 102 55W
Tetitlán, Guerrero, Mexico 107 17 9N 100 38W
Tetitlán, Nayarit, Mexico 104 21 8N 104 36W
Tetiyev 180 49 22N 29 38 E
Tétouan 240 35 35N 5 21W
Tetovo 166 42 1N 21 2 E
Tetu L. 86 50 11N 95 2W
Tetuán = Tétouan 240 35 35N 5 21W
Tetyukhe Pristan 218 44 22N 135 48 E
Tetyushi 179 54 55N 48 49 E
Teuchitlán 106 20 41N 103 52W
Teuco → 124 25 35 S 60 11W
Teufen 149 47 24N 9 23 E
Teulada 164 38 59N 8 47 E
Teulon 89 50 23N 97 16W
Teun 207 6 59 S 129 8 E
Teutoburger Wald 144 52 5N 8 20 E
Tevere → 163 41 44N 12 14 E
Teverya 189 32 47N 35 32 E
Teviot → 134 55 21N 2 51W
Tewantin 231 26 27 S 153 3 E
Tewkesbury 133 51 59N 2 8W
Texada I. 92 49 40N 124 25W
Texas 231 28 49 S 151 9 E
Texcaltitlán 107 18 54N 99 55W
Texcoco, L. de 107 19 30N 99 0W
Texcoco de Mora 107 19 31N 98 53W
Texel 142 53 5N 4 50 E
Texisquiac 107 19 53N 99 12W
Texistepec 109 17 53N 94 47W
Teykovo 179 56 55N 40 30 E
Teyvareh 197 33 30N 64 24 E
Teza → 179 56 32N 41 53 E
Tezin 198 34 24N 69 30 E
Teziutlán 108 19 49N 97 21W
Tezoatlán de Segura y Luna 109 17 42N 97 49W
Tezontepec, Hidalgo, Mexico 107 19 53N 98 49W
Tezontepec, Hidalgo, Mexico 107 20 12N 99 16W
Tezpur 202 26 40N 92 45 E
Tezzeron L. 76 54 43N 124 30W
Tha-anne → 77 60 31N 94 37W
Tha Deua, Laos 204 17 57N 102 53 E
Tha Deua, Laos 204 19 26N 101 50 E
Tha Pla 204 17 48N 100 32 E
Tha Rua 204 14 34N 100 44 E
Tha Sala 205 8 40N 99 56 E

Tha Song Yang 204 17 34N 97 55 E
Thaba Putsoa 255 29 45 S 28 0 E
Thabana Ntlenyana 255 29 30 S 29 16 E
Thabazimbi 255 24 40 S 27 21 E
Thabeikkyin 202 22 53N 95 59 E
Thabor, Mt. 141 45 7N 6 34 E
Thai Binh 204 20 35N 106 1 E
Thai Hoa 204 19 20N 105 20 E
Thai Muang 205 8 24N 98 16 E
Thai Nguyen 204 21 35N 105 55 E
Thailand ■ 204 16 0N 102 0 E
Thailand, G. of 205 11 30N 101 0 E
Thakhek 204 17 25N 104 45 E
Thakurgaon 202 26 2N 88 34 E
Thal 197 33 28N 70 33 E
Thal Desert 198 31 10N 71 30 E
Thala 241 35 35N 8 40 E
Thalabarivat 204 13 33N 105 57 E
Thalkirch 149 46 39N 9 17 E
Thallon 231 28 39 S 148 49 E
Thalwil 149 47 17N 8 35 E
Thamarīt 195 17 39N 54 2 E
Thame → 133 51 35N 1 8W
Thames 234 37 7 S 175 34 E
Thames →, Canada 84 42 20N 82 25W
Thames →, U.K. 133 51 30N 0 35 E
Thames, Firth of 234 37 0 S 175 25 E
Thamesford 84 43 4N 81 0W
Thamesville 84 42 33N 81 59W
Thāmit, W. → 241 30 51N 16 14 E
Thamūd 195 17 18N 49 55 E
Than Uyen 204 22 0N 103 54 E
Thanbyuzayat 202 15 58N 97 44 E
Thane 200 19 12N 72 59 E
Thanesar 198 30 1N 76 52 E
Thanet, I. of 133 51 21N 1 20 E
Thangoo 228 18 10 S 122 22 E
Thangool 230 24 38 S 150 42 E
Thanh Hoa 204 19 48N 105 46 E
Thanh Hung 205 9 55N 105 43 E
Thanh Thuy 204 22 55N 104 51 E
Thanjavur 201 10 48N 79 12 E
Thann 139 47 48N 7 5 E
Thaon 139 48 15N 6 25 E
Thap Sakae 205 11 30N 99 37 E
Thap Than 204 15 27N 99 54 E
Thar Desert 198 28 0N 72 0 E
Tharad 198 24 30N 71 44 E
Thargomindah 231 27 58 S 143 46 E
Tharrawaddy 202 17 38N 95 48 E
Tharrawaw 202 17 41N 95 28 E
Tharthar, W. → 192 33 59N 43 12 E
Thasopoúla 168 40 49N 24 45 E
Thásos 168 40 40N 24 40 E
That Khe 204 22 16N 106 28 E
Thaton 202 16 55N 97 22 E
Thau, Étang de 140 43 23N 3 36 E
Thaungdut 202 24 30N 94 40 E
Thayetmyo 202 19 20N 95 10 E
Thayngen 149 47 49N 8 43 E
The Alberga → 231 27 6 S 135 33 E
The Bight 113 24 19N 75 24W
The Brothers 195 12 8N 53 10 E
The English
Company's Is. 230 11 50 S 136 32 E
The Entrance 233 33 21 S 151 30 E
The Frome → 231 29 8 S 137 54 E
The Grenadines, Is. 113 12 40N 61 20W
The Hamilton → 231 26 40 S 135 19 E
The Lynd 230 19 12 S 144 20 E
The Macumba → 231 27 52 S 137 12 E
The Neales → 231 28 8 S 136 47 E
The Oaks 233 34 3 S 150 34 E
The Officer → 229 27 46 S 132 30 E
The Pas 89 53 45N 101 15W
The Range 251 19 2 S 31 2 E
The Rock 231 35 15 S 147 2 E
The Salt Lake 231 30 6 S 142 8 E
The Stevenson → 231 27 6 S 135 33 E
The Warburton → 231 28 4 S 137 28 E
Thebes = Thívai 169 38 19N 23 19 E
Thebes 244 25 40N 32 35 E
Thedford 84 43 9N 81 51W
Theebine 231 25 57 S 152 34 E
Theil, Le 138 48 16N 0 42 E
Thekulthili L. 77 61 3N 110 0W
Thelon → 77 62 35N 104 3W
Thénezay 138 46 44N 0 2W
Thenia 241 36 44N 3 33 E
Thenon 140 45 9N 1 4 E
Theodore, Australia 230 24 55 S 150 3 E
Theodore, Canada 88 51 26N 102 55W
Thepha 205 6 52N 100 58 E
Thérain → 139 49 15N 2 27 E
Thermaïkos Kólpos 168 40 15N 22 45 E
Thermopylae P. 169 38 48N 22 35 E
Thesiger B. 94 71 30N 124 5W
Thesprotía □ 168 39 27N 20 22 E
Thessalía □ 168 39 30N 22 0 E
Thessalon 84 46 20N 83 30W
Thessaloníki 168 40 38N 22 58 E
Thessaloníki □ 168 40 45N 23 0 E
Thessaly =
Thessalía □ 168 39 30N 22 0 E
Thetford 133 52 25N 0 44 E
Thetford Mines 83 46 8N 71 18W
Theun → 204 18 19N 104 0 E
Theunissen 254 28 26 S 26 43 E
Theux 143 50 32N 5 49 E
Thevenard 231 32 9 S 133 38 E
Thévet, L. 80 51 50N 64 12W
Thiámis → 168 39 15N 20 6 E
Thiberville 138 49 8N 0 27 E
Thicket Portage 77 55 19N 97 42W
Thiel Mts. 13 85 15 S 91 0W
Thiene 163 45 42N 11 29 E
Thiérache 139 49 51N 3 45 E
Thiers 140 45 52N 3 33 E
Thies 246 14 50N 16 51W
Thiet 245 7 37N 28 49 E
Thika 250 1 1 S 37 5 E
Thille-Boubacar 246 16 31N 15 5W
Thillot, Le 139 47 53N 6 46 E
Thimân, W. → 191 28 4N 33 45 E
Thimphu 202 27 31N 89 45 E
þingvallavatn 174 64 11N 21 9W
Thio 226 21 37 S 166 14 E
Thionville 139 49 20N 6 10 E
Thíra 169 36 23N 25 27 E
Thirasía 169 36 26N 25 21 E
Thirsk 132 54 15N 1 20W
Thiruvarur 201 10 46N 79 38 E
Thistle I. 232 35 0 S 136 8 E
Thitgy 202 18 15N 96 13 E
Thithia 226 17 45 S 179 18W
Thitpokpin 202 19 24N 95 58 E
Thívai 169 38 19N 23 19 E
Thiviers 140 45 25N 0 54 E
Thizy 141 46 2N 4 18 E
þjórsá → 174 63 47N 20 48W
Thlewiaza →,
Man., Canada 77 59 43N 100 5W
Thlewiaza →,
N.W.T., Canada 77 60 29N 94 40W
Thmar Puok 204 13 57N 103 4 E
Tho Vinh 204 19 16N 105 42 E
Thoa → 77 60 31N 109 47W
Thoen 204 17 43N 99 12 E
Thoeng 204 19 41N 100 12 E
Thoissey 141 46 12N 4 48 E
Tholdi 199 35 5N 76 6 E
Tholen 143 51 32N 4 13 E
Thom Bay 95 70 9N 92 25W
Thomas, L. 231 26 4 S 137 58 E
Thomas Hubbard,
C. 95 82 0N 94 25W
Thommen 143 50 14N 6 5 E
Thompson, B.C.,
Canada 93 50 15N 121 24W
Thompson, Man.,
Canada 77 55 45N 97 52W
Thompson → 93 50 15N 121 24W
Thompson Landing 77 62 56N 110 40W
Thomson → 230 25 11 S 142 53 E
Thomson's Falls =
Nyahururu 250 0 2N 36 27 E
Thon Buri 205 13 43N 100 29 E
Thônes 141 45 54N 6 18 E
Thongwa 202 16 45N 96 33 E
Thonon-les-Bains 141 46 22N 6 29 E
Thonze 202 17 38N 95 47 E
Thorburn 81 45 34N 62 33W
Thorez 181 48 4N 38 34 E
Thorhild 90 54 10N 113 7W
þórisvatn 174 64 20N 18 55W
þorlákshöfn 174 63 51N 21 22W
Thornaby on Tees 132 54 36N 1 19W
Thornbury, Canada 84 44 34N 80 26W
Thornbury, N.Z. 235 46 17 S 168 9 E
Thornhill 93 54 12N 98 14W
Thornton-Beresfield 233 32 50 S 151 40 E
Thorold 84 43 7N 79 12W
Thorsby 90 53 14N 114 3W
þórshöfn 174 66 12N 15 20W
Thouarcé 138 47 17N 0 30W
Thouars 138 46 58N 0 15W
Thouin, C. 228 20 20 S 118 10 E
Thrace = Thráki □ 168 41 9N 25 30 E
Thráki □ 168 41 9N 25 30 E
Thrakikón Pélagos 168 40 30N 25 0 E
Three Hills 91 51 43N 113 15W
Three Hummock I. 230 40 25 S 144 55 E
Three Mile Plains 81 44 58N 64 7W
Three Points, C. 246 4 42N 2 6W
Three Rivers 229 25 10 S 119 5 E
Throssell, L. 229 27 33 S 124 10 E
Throssell Ra. 228 22 3 S 121 43 E
Thrun Pass 150 47 20N 12 25 E
Thuan Hoa 205 8 58N 105 30 E
Thubun Lakes 77 61 30N 112 0W
Thueyts 141 44 41N 4 9 E
Thuillies 143 50 18N 4 20 E
Thuin 143 50 20N 4 17 E
Thuir 140 42 38N 2 45 E
Thule, Antarct. 13 59 27 S 27 19W
Thule, Greenland 12 77 40N 69 0W
Thun 148 46 45N 7 38 E
Thundelarra 229 28 53 S 117 7 E
Thunder Bay 86 48 20N 89 15W
Thunder Cr. → 88 50 23N 105 32W
Thunersee 148 46 43N 7 39 E
Thung Song 205 8 10N 99 40 E
Thunkar 202 27 55N 91 0 E
Thuong Tra 204 16 2N 107 42 E
Thur → 149 47 32N 9 10 E
Thurgau □ 149 47 34N 9 10 E
Thüringer Wald 146 50 35N 11 0 E
Thurles 135 52 40N 7 53W
Thurloo Downs 231 29 15 S 143 30 E
Thurn P. 147 47 20N 12 25 E
Thursday I. 230 10 30 S 142 3 E
Thurso, Canada 82 45 36N 75 15W
Thurso, U.K. 134 58 34N 3 31W
Thurston I. 13 72 0 S 100 0W
Thury-Harcourt 138 49 0N 0 30W
Thusis 149 46 42N 9 26 E
Thutade L. 76 57 0N 126 55W
Thuy, Le 204 17 14N 106 49 E
Thyborøn 173 56 42N 8 12 E
Thylungra 231 26 4 S 143 28 E
Thyolo 251 16 7 S 35 5 E
Thysville = Mbanza
Ngungu 253 5 12 S 14 53 E
Ti-n-Barraouene,
O. → 247 18 40N 4 5 E
Ti-n-Medjerdam,
O. → 240 25 45N 1 30 E
Ti-n-Tarabine,
O. → 241 21 0N 7 25 E
Ti-n-Toumma 243 16 4N 12 40 E
Ti-n-Zaouatène 241 20 0N 2 55 E
Tia 231 31 10 S 150 34 E
Tiahuanacu 122 16 33 S 68 42W
Tian Shan 212 43 0N 84 0 E
Tianchang 217 32 40N 119 0 E
Tiandong 216 23 36N 107 8 E
Tian'e 216 25 1N 107 9 E
Tianguá 120 3 44 S 40 59W
Tianguistengo 107 20 44N 98 38W
Tianhe 216 24 48N 108 40 E
Tianjin 215 39 8N 117 10 E
Tiankoura 246 10 47N 3 17W
Tianlin 216 24 21N 106 12 E
Tianmen 217 30 39N 113 9 E
Tianquan 216 30 7N 102 43 E
Tianshui 214 34 32N 105 40 E
Tiantai 217 29 10N 121 2 E
Tianyang 216 23 42N 106 53 E
Tianzhen 214 40 24N 114 5 E
Tianzhu 216 26 54N 109 11 E
Tianzhuangtai 215 40 43N 122 5 E
Tiaret 241 35 20N 1 21 E
Tiarra 233 32 46 S 145 1 E
Tiassalé 246 5 58N 4 57W
Tibagi 125 24 30 S 50 24W
Tibagi → 125 22 47 S 51 1W
Tibati 247 6 22N 12 30 E
Tiber = Tevere → 163 41 44N 12 14 E
Tiberias, L. =
Kinneret, Yam 189 32 45N 35 35 E
Tibesti 241 21 0N 17 30 E
Tibet = Xizang □ 212 33 0N 85 0 E
Tibiri 247 13 34N 7 4 E
Ţibleş 170 47 32N 24 15 E
Tibnī 192 35 36N 39 50 E
Tibnīn 189 33 12N 35 24 E
Tibooburra 231 29 26 S 142 1 E
Tibro 173 58 28N 14 10 E
Tibugá, Golfo de 118 5 45N 77 20W
Tiburón, I. 100 29 0N 112 25W
Ticao I. 210 12 31N 123 42 E
Tichīt 246 18 21N 9 29W
Tichla 240 21 36N 14 58W
Ticho 245 7 50N 39 32 E
Ticino □ 149 46 20N 8 45 E
Ticino → 162 45 9N 9 14 E
Ticul 111 20 24N 89 32W
Tidaholm 173 58 12N 13 55 E
Tiddim 202 23 28N 93 45 E
Tide Head 81 47 59N 66 47W
Tideridjaouine,
Adrar 240 23 0N 2 15 E
Tidikelt 240 26 58N 1 30 E
Tidjikja 246 18 29N 11 35W
Tidore 207 0 40N 127 25 E
Tiébissou 246 7 9N 5 10W
Tiéboro 241 21 20N 17 7 E
Tiefencastel 149 46 40N 9 33 E
Tiel, Neth. 142 51 53N 5 26 E
Tiel, Senegal 246 14 55N 15 5W
Tieling 215 42 20N 123 55 E
Tielt 143 51 0N 3 20 E
Tien Shan 183 42 0N 80 0 E
Tien Yen 204 21 20N 107 24 E
Tienen 143 50 48N 4 57 E
Tiénigbé 246 8 11N 5 43W
Tientsin = Tianjin 215 39 8N 117 10 E
Tierp 172 60 20N 17 30 E
Tierra Amarilla 124 27 28 S 70 18W
Tierra Blanca,
Guanajuato,
Mexico 107 21 7N 100 57W
Tierra Blanca,
Veracruz, Mexico 109 18 27N 96 21W
Tierra Colorada,
Guerrero, Mexico 107 17 10N 99 35W
Tierra Colorada,
Tabasco, Mexico 110 17 56N 92 39W
Tierra de Barros 155 38 40N 6 30W
Tierra de Campos 154 42 10N 4 50W
Tierra del Fuego □ 126 54 0 S 67 45W
Tierra del Fuego, I.
Gr. de 126 54 0 S 69 0W
Tierralta 118 8 11N 76 4W
Tiétar → 154 39 50N 6 1W
Tieté → 125 20 40 S 51 35W
Tieyon 231 26 12 S 133 52 E
Tifarit 240 26 9N 10 33W
Tiflèt 240 33 54N 6 20W
Tiflis = Tbilisi 181 41 43N 44 50 E
Tifrah 189 31 19N 34 42 E
Tifu 207 3 39 S 126 24 E
Tiga, Î. 226 21 7 S 167 49 E
Tigaon 210 13 38N 123 30 E
Tigbauan 211 10 41N 122 27 E
Tigil 185 57 49N 158 40 E
Tignish 81 46 58N 64 2W
Tigray □ 245 13 35N 39 15 E
Tigre →, Peru 122 4 30 S 74 10W
Tigre →,
Venezuela 119 9 20N 62 30W
Tigris = Dijlah,
Nahr → 192 31 0N 47 25 E
Tiguentourine 241 27 52N 9 8 E
Tigveni 170 45 10N 24 31 E
Tigyaing 202 23 45N 96 10 E
Tigzerte, O. → 240 28 10N 9 37W
Tīh, Gebel el 244 29 32N 33 26 E
Tihāmah 194 22 0N 39 0 E
Tihodaine, Dunes de 241 25 15N 7 15 E
Tihuatlán 108 20 43N 97 32W
Tijesno 163 43 48N 15 39 E
Tījī 241 32 0N 11 18 E
Tijuana 98 32 32N 117 1W
Tikal 112 17 13N 89 24W
Tikamgarh 199 24 44N 78 50 E
Tikhoretsk 181 45 56N 40 5 E
Tikhvin 178 59 35N 33 30 E
Tikkadouine, Adrar 240 24 28N 1 30 E
Tiko 247 4 4N 9 20 E
Tikrīt 192 34 35N 43 37 E
Tiksi 185 71 40N 128 45 E
Tila 110 17 24N 92 29W
Tilamuta 207 0 32N 122 23 E
Tilapa 109 18 35N 98 33W
Tilapan 109 18 18N 95 47W
Tilburg 143 51 31N 5 6 E
Tilbury, Canada 84 42 17N 82 23W
Tilbury, U.K. 133 51 27N 0 24 E
Tilcara 124 23 36 S 65 23W
Tilemses 247 15 37N 4 44 E
Tilemsi, Vallée du 247 17 42N 0 15 E
Tilhar 199 28 0N 79 45 E
Tilia, O. → 240 27 32N 0 55 E
Tilichiki 185 60 27N 166 5 E
Tiligul → 180 47 4N 30 57 E
Tililane 240 27 49N 0 6W
Tilin 202 21 41N 94 6 E
Tílissos 169 35 2N 25 0 E
Till → 132 55 35N 2 3W
Tillabéri 247 14 28N 1 28 E
Tillberga 172 59 52N 16 39 E
Tillia 247 16 8N 4 47 E
Tillsonburg 84 42 53N 80 44W
Tílos 169 36 27N 27 27 E
Tilpa 231 30 57 S 144 24 E
Tilrhemt 241 33 9N 3 22 E
Tilsit = Sovetsk 178 55 6N 21 50 E
Tilston 89 49 23N 101 19W
Tilt → 134 56 50N 3 50W
Timagami L. 82 47 0N 80 10W
Timanskiy Kryazh 176 65 58N 50 5 E
Timareh 195 12 37N 54 17 E
Timaru 235 44 23 S 171 14 E
Timashevo 182 53 22N 51 9 E
Timashevsk 181 45 35N 39 0 E
Timau, Italy 163 46 35N 13 0 E
Timau, Kenya 250 0 4N 37 15 E
Timbákion 169 35 4N 24 45 E
Timbaúba 120 7 31 S 35 19W
Timbedgha 246 16 17N 8 16W
Timberlea 81 44 40N 63 45W
Timbío 118 2 20N 76 40W
Timbiqui 118 2 46N 77 42W
Timboon 231 38 30 S 142 58 E
Timbuktu =
Tombouctou 246 16 50N 3 0W
Timdjaouine 240 21 37N 4 30 E
Timellouline 241 29 22N 8 55 E
Timétrine
Montagnes 247 19 25N 1 0W
Timfi Óros 168 39 59N 20 45 E
Timfristós, Óros 169 38 57N 21 50 E
Timhadit 240 33 15N 5 4W
Tîmia 247 18 4N 8 40 E
Timimoun 241 29 14N 0 16 E

Timimoun, Sebkha de 240 28 50N 0 46 E
Timiş □ 170 45 40N 21 30 E
Timiş → 170 45 30N 21 0 E
Timişoara 170 45 43N 21 15 E
Timmins 87 48 28N 81 25W
Timok → 166 44 10N 22 40 E
Timon 120 5 8 S 42 52W
Timor 207 9 0 S 125 0 E
Timor □ 207 9 0 S 125 0 E
Timor Sea 228 10 0 S 127 0 E
Tin Alkoum 241 24 42N 10 17 E
Tin Gornai 247 16 38N 0 38W
Tin Gornaï → 247 20 30N 4 35 E
Tîna, Khalîg el 244 31 20N 32 42 E
Tinabog 210 12 1N 120 25 E
Tinaca Pt. 211 5 30N 125 25 E
Tinaco 118 9 42N 68 26W
Tinafak, O. → 241 27 10N 7 0 E
Tinaja, La, San Luis Potosí, Mexico 103 23 6N 100 51W
Tinaja, La, Veracruz, Mexico 109 18 45N 96 28W
Tinajas 103 23 55N 99 30W
Tinaquillo 118 9 55N 68 18W
Tinca 170 46 46N 21 58 E
Tinchebray 138 48 47N 0 45W
Tindivanam 201 12 15N 79 41 E
Tindouf 240 27 42N 8 10W
Tinee → 141 43 55N 7 11 E
Tineg 210 17 48N 120 56 E
Tineo 154 43 21N 6 27W
Tinerhir 240 31 29N 5 31W
Tinfouchi 240 28 52N 5 49W
Ting Jiang → 217 24 45N 116 35 E
Tingambato 107 19 5N 100 20W
Tinggi, Pulau 205 2 18N 104 7 E
Tingkawk Sakan 202 26 4N 96 44 E
Tinglayan 210 17 15N 121 9 E
Tinglev 173 54 57N 9 13 E
Tingo Maria 122 9 10 S 75 54W
Tingsryd 173 56 31N 15 0 E
Tinguindín 106 19 45N 102 29W
Tinh Bien 205 10 36N 104 57 E
Tinharé, I. de 121 13 30 S 38 58W
Tiniguiban 211 11 22N 119 30 E
Tinjoub 240 29 45N 5 40W
Tinkurrin 229 32 59 S 117 46 E
Tinnevelly = Tirunelveli 201 8 45N 77 45 E
Tinnoset 171 59 55N 9 3 E
Tinnsjø 171 59 55N 8 54 E
Tinogasta 124 28 5 S 67 32W
Tínos 169 37 33N 25 8 E
Tiñoso, C. 157 37 32N 1 6W
Tinsukia 202 27 29N 95 20 E
Tinta 122 14 3 S 71 20W
Tintagel 92 54 12N 125 35W
Tintigny 143 49 41N 5 31 E
Tintina 124 27 2 S 62 45W
Tintinara 232 35 48 S 140 2 E
Tinto → 155 37 12N 6 55W
Tinui 234 40 52 S 176 5 E
Tinum, Campeche, Mexico 111 19 59N 90 14W
Tinum, Yucatán, Mexico 111 20 46N 88 23W
Tinwald 235 43 55 S 171 43 E
Tioman, Pulau 205 2 50N 104 10 E
Tione di Trento 162 46 3N 10 44 E
Tior 245 6 26N 31 11 E
Tioulilin 240 27 1N 0 2W
Tipperary 135 52 28N 8 10W
Tipperary □ 135 52 37N 7 55W
Tipton 133 52 32N 2 4W
Tiptur 201 13 15N 76 26 E
Tiquicheo 107 18 53N 100 44W
Tiquié → 118 0 5N 68 25W
Tiracambu, Serra do 120 3 15 S 46 30W
Tiradero 110 17 48N 91 12W
Tirahart, O. → 240 23 45N 3 10 E
Tīrān, Iran 193 32 45N 51 8 E
Tīrān, Si. Arabia 191 27 57N 34 32 E
Tirana 168 41 18N 19 49 E
Tirana-Durrësi □ 168 41 35N 20 0 E
Tirano 162 46 13N 10 11 E
Tiraspol 180 46 55N 29 35 E
Tirat Karmel 189 32 46N 34 58 E
Tirat Yehuda 189 32 1N 34 56 E
Tirat Ẕevi 189 32 26N 35 31 E
Tiratimine 240 25 56N 3 37 E
Tirdout 247 16 7N 1 5W
Tire, Sa. del 106 19 50N 103 5W
Tirebolu 177 40 58N 38 45 E
Tiree 134 56 31N 6 55W
Tîrgovişte 170 44 55N 25 27 E
Tîrgu Frumos 170 47 12N 27 2 E
Tîrgu-Jiu 170 45 5N 23 19 E
Tîrgu Mureş 170 46 31N 24 38 E
Tîrgu Neamţ 170 47 12N 26 25 E
Tîrgu Ocna 170 46 16N 26 39 E
Tîrgu Secuiesc 170 46 0N 26 10 E
Tirich Mir 197 36 15N 71 55 E
Tiriola 165 38 57N 16 32 E
Tiripetío 107 19 33N 101 20W
Tiririca, Serra da 121 17 6 S 47 6W
Tiris 240 23 10N 13 20W
Tirlyanskiy 182 54 14N 58 35 E
Tirna → 200 18 4N 76 57 E
Tîrnava Mare → 170 46 15N 24 30 E
Tîrnava Mică → 170 46 17N 24 30 E
Tîrnăveni 170 46 19N 24 13 E
Tírnavos 168 39 45N 22 18 E
Tîrnova 170 45 23N 22 1 E
Tirodi 199 21 40N 79 44 E
Tirol □ 150 47 3N 10 43 E
Tiros 121 19 0 S 45 58W
Tirschenreuth 147 49 51N 12 20 E
Tirso → 164 39 52N 8 33 E
Tirso, L. del 164 40 8N 8 56 E
Tirua, Pt. 234 38 25 S 174 40 E
Tiruchchendur 201 8 30N 78 11 E
Tiruchchirappalli 201 10 45N 78 45 E
Tiruchengodu 201 11 23N 77 56 E
Tirumangalam 201 9 49N 77 58 E
Tirunelveli 201 8 45N 77 45 E
Tirupati 201 13 39N 79 25 E
Tiruppattur 201 12 30N 78 30 E
Tiruppur 201 11 5N 77 22 E
Tirutturaippundi 201 10 32N 79 41 E
Tiruvadaimarudur 201 11 2N 79 27 E
Tiruvallar 201 13 9N 79 57 E
Tiruvannamalai 201 12 15N 79 5 E
Tiruvettipuram 201 12 39N 79 33 E
Tiruvottiyur 201 13 10N 80 22 E
Tisa → 166 45 15N 20 17 E
Tisdale 88 52 50N 104 0W
Tisjön 172 60 56N 13 0 E
Tisnaren 172 58 58N 15 56 E
Tišnov 151 49 21N 16 25 E
Tisovec 151 48 41N 19 56 E
Tissemsilt 241 35 35N 1 50 E
Tissint 240 29 57N 7 16W
Tissø 172 55 35N 11 18 E
Tista → 202 25 23N 89 43 E
Tisza → 151 46 8N 20 2 E
Tiszaföldvár 151 47 0N 20 14 E
Tiszafüred 151 47 38N 20 50 E
Tiszalök 151 48 0N 21 10 E
Tiszavasvári 151 47 58N 21 18 E
Tit, Ahaggar, Algeria 241 23 0N 5 10 E
Tit, Tademait, Algeria 240 27 0N 1 29 E
Tit-Ary 185 71 55N 127 2 E
Titaguas 156 39 53N 1 6W
Titahi Bay 234 41 6 S 174 50 E
Titel 166 45 10N 20 18 E
Tithwal 199 34 21N 73 50 E
Titicaca, L. 122 15 30 S 69 30W
Titiwa 247 12 14N 12 53 E
Titlagarh 200 20 15N 83 11 E
Titlis 149 46 46N 8 27 E
Titograd 166 42 30N 19 19 E
Titov Veles 166 41 46N 21 47 E
Titova Korenica 163 44 45N 15 41 E
Titovo Užice 166 43 55N 19 50 E
Titule 250 3 15N 25 31 E
Titumate 118 8 19N 77 5W
Tivaouane 246 14 56N 16 45W
Tivat 166 42 28N 18 43 E
Tiveden 173 58 50N 14 30 E
Tiverton, N.S., Canada 81 44 23N 66 13W
Tiverton, Ont., Canada 84 44 16N 81 32W
Tiverton, U.K. 133 50 54N 3 30W
Tívoli 163 41 58N 12 45 E
Tiwī 194 22 45N 59 12 E
Tixbakab 111 21 5N 88 31W
Tixcacalcupul 111 20 32N 88 16W
Tixkokob 111 21 0N 89 24W
Tixmucuy 111 19 37N 90 16W
Tixtla de Guerrero 107 17 35N 99 26W
Tiyo 245 14 41N 40 15 E
Tizapán el Alto 106 20 10N 103 4W
Tizayuca 107 19 50N 98 59W
Tizga 240 32 1N 5 9W
Ti'zi N'Isli 240 32 28N 5 47W
Tizi-Ouzou 241 36 42N 4 3 E
Tizimín 111 21 9N 88 9W
Tiznados → 118 8 16N 67 47W
Tiznit 240 29 48N 9 45W
Tizoc 102 25 41N 101 59W
Tjeggelvas 174 66 37N 17 45 E
Tjeukemeer 142 52 53N 5 48 E
Tjirebon = Cirebon 209 6 45 S 108 32 E
Tjöme 171 59 8N 10 26 E
Tjonger Kanaal 142 52 52N 5 52 E
Tjörn 173 58 0N 11 35 E
Tkibuli 181 42 26N 43 0 E
Tkvarcheli 181 42 47N 41 42 E
Tlacochahuaya de Morelos 109 17 0N 96 34W
Tlacotalpan 109 18 37N 95 40W
Tlacotepec, Guerrero, Mexico 107 17 46N 99 59W
Tlacotepec, Puebla, Mexico 109 18 38N 97 37W
Tlacuitapa 106 21 14N 102 12W
Tlahualilo, Sa. de 102 26 34N 103 19W
Tlahualilo de Zaragoza 105 26 7N 103 27W
Tlahuelipa de Ocampo 107 20 8N 99 14W
Tlahuiltepa 107 20 58N 99 1W
Tlajomulco de Zúñiga 106 20 28N 103 27W
Tlalamantes de Abajo 101 26 54N 105 28W
Tlalchapa 107 18 24N 100 28W
Tlalixcoyan 109 18 48N 96 3W
Tlalnepantla, México, Mexico 107 19 33N 99 12W
Tlalnepantla, Morelos, Mexico 107 19 0N 98 59W
Tlalpan 107 19 17N 99 10W
Tlalpujahua 107 19 48N 100 10W
Tlaltenango de Sánchez Román 105 21 47N 103 19W
Tlaltizapán 107 18 41N 99 7W
Tlancualpican 109 18 26N 98 42W
Tlapa de Comonfort 107 17 33N 98 33W
Tlapacoyan 108 19 58N 97 13W
Tlapanala 109 18 41N 98 32W
Tlapaneco →, Guerrero, Mexico 107 17 5N 98 48W
Tlapaneco →, Mexico 107 18 4N 98 48W
Tlapehuala 107 18 13N 100 31W
Tlaquepaque 106 20 39N 103 19W
Tlatiaya 107 18 31N 100 15W
Tlaxcala 107 19 19N 98 14W
Tlaxcala □ 107 19 25N 98 10W
Tlaxcoapán 107 20 5N 99 13W
Tlaxico, Sa. de 109 17 25N 97 35W
Tlaxo de Morelos 107 19 37N 98 7W
Tlell 92 53 34N 131 56W
Tlemcen 241 34 52N 1 21W
Tleta Sidi Bouguedra 240 32 16N 9 59W
Tlumach 180 48 51N 25 0 E
Tłuszcz 152 52 25N 21 25 E
Tlyarata 181 42 9N 46 26 E
Tmassah 241 26 19N 15 51 E
Tnine d'Anglou 240 29 50N 9 50W
To Bong 204 12 45N 109 16 E
To-Shima 221 34 31N 139 17 E
Toad → 76 59 25N 124 57W
Toahayaná 101 26 8N 107 44W
Toamasina 255 18 10 S 49 25 E
Toamasina □ 255 18 0 S 49 0 E
Toay 124 36 43 S 64 38W
Toba 221 34 30N 136 51 E
Toba Inlet 92 50 25N 124 35W
Toba Kakar 197 31 30N 69 0 E
Toba Tek Singh 198 30 55N 72 25 E
Tobago 113 11 10N 60 30W
Tobarra 157 38 37N 1 44W
Tobelo 207 1 45N 127 56 E
Tobermorey 230 22 12 S 137 51 E
Tobermory, Canada 84 45 12N 81 40W
Tobermory, U.K. 134 56 37N 6 4W
Tobin, L. 228 21 45 S 125 49 E
Tobin L. 88 53 35N 103 30W
Tobique → 81 46 46N 67 42W
Toboali 208 3 0 S 106 25 E
Tobol 182 52 40N 62 39 E
Tobol → 182 58 10N 68 12 E
Toboli 207 0 38 S 120 5 E
Tobolsk 184 58 15N 68 10 E
Toboso 211 10 43N 123 31 E
Tobruk = Tubruq 242 32 7N 23 55 E
Toby Creek 93 50 20N 116 25W
Tocache Nuevo 122 8 9 S 76 26W
Tocantînia 120 9 33 S 48 22W
Tocantinópolis 120 6 20 S 47 25W
Tocantins → 120 1 45 S 49 10W
Toce → 162 45 56N 8 29 E
Tochigi 221 36 25N 139 45 E
Tochigi □ 221 36 45N 139 45 E
Tocina 155 37 37N 5 44W
Tocopilla 124 22 5 S 70 10W
Tocumbo 106 19 42N 102 32W
Tocumwal 231 35 51 S 145 31 E
Tocuyo → 118 11 3N 68 23W
Tocuyo de la Costa 118 11 2N 68 23W
Todd → 230 24 52 S 135 48 E
Todeli 207 1 38 S 124 34 E
Todenyang 250 4 35N 35 56 E
Todi, Italy 163 42 47N 12 24 E
Tödi, Switz. 149 46 48N 8 55 E
Todos los Santos, B. de 98 31 48N 116 42W
Todos os Santos, Baía de 121 12 48 S 38 38W
Todos Santos 99 23 27N 110 13W
Todtnau 147 47 50N 7 56 E
Toecé 247 11 50N 1 16W
Toetoes B. 235 46 42 S 168 41 E
Tofield 90 53 25N 112 40W
Tofino 92 49 11N 125 55W
Töfsingdalens nationalpark 172 62 15N 12 44 E
Toftlund 173 55 11N 9 2 E
Tōgane 221 35 33N 140 22 E
Togba 246 17 26N 10 12W
Togbo 252 6 0N 17 27 E
Toggenburg 149 47 16N 9 9 E
Togian, Kepulauan 207 0 20 S 121 50 E
Togliatti 179 53 32N 49 24 E
Togo 89 51 24N 101 35W
Togo ■ 247 6 15N 1 35 E
Togtoh 214 40 15N 111 10 E
Toguzak → 182 54 3N 62 44 E
Tōhoku □ 218 39 50N 141 45 E
Toi 221 34 54N 138 47 E
Toinya 245 6 17N 29 46 E
Tojo, Indonesia 207 1 20 S 121 15 E
Tōjō, Japan 220 34 53N 133 16 E
Tok → 182 52 46N 52 22 E
Toka 119 3 58N 59 17W
Tokaanu 234 38 58 S 175 46 E
Tokachi-Dake 218 43 17N 142 5 E
Tokachi-Gawa → 218 42 44N 143 42 E
Tokai 221 35 2N 136 55 E
Tokaj 151 48 8N 21 27 E
Tokala 207 1 30 S 121 40 E
Tōkamachi 219 37 8N 138 43 E
Tokanui 235 46 34 S 168 56 E
Tokara-Rettō 219 29 37N 129 43 E
Tokarahi 235 44 56 S 170 39 E
Tokashiki-Shima 219 26 11N 127 21 E
Tŏkchŏn 215 39 45N 126 18 E
Tokelau Is. 224 9 0 S 171 45W
Toki 221 35 18N 137 8 E
Tokmak 183 42 49N 75 15 E
Toko Ra. 230 23 5 S 138 20 E
Tokomaru Bay 234 38 8 S 178 22 E
Tokoname 221 34 53N 136 51 E
Tokoro-Gawa → 218 44 7N 144 5 E
Tokoroa 234 38 13 S 175 50 E
Tokorozawa 221 35 47N 139 28 E
Toktogul 183 41 50N 72 50 E
Tokuji 220 34 11N 131 42 E
Tokuno-Shima 219 27 56N 128 55 E
Tokushima 220 34 4N 134 34 E
Tokushima □ 220 34 15N 134 0 E
Tokuyama 220 34 3N 131 50 E
Tōkyō 221 35 45N 139 45 E
Tōkyō □ 221 35 40N 139 30 E
Tōkyō-Wan 221 35 25N 139 47 E
Tokzār 197 35 52N 66 26 E
Tol I. 226 7 20N 151 35 E
Tolbukhin 167 43 37N 27 49 E
Toledo, Phil. 211 10 23N 123 38 E
Toledo, Spain 154 39 50N 4 2W
Toledo, Montes de 155 39 33N 4 20W
Tolentino 163 43 12N 13 17 E
Tolga, Algeria 241 34 40N 5 22 E
Tolga, Norway 171 62 26N 11 1 E
Toliara 255 23 21 S 43 40 E
Toliara □ 255 21 0 S 45 0 E
Tolima □ 118 3 45N 75 15W
Tolima, Vol. 118 4 40N 75 19W
Tolimán 107 20 44N 99 27W
Tolitoli 207 1 5N 120 50 E
Tolkamer 142 51 52N 6 6 E
Tolkmicko 152 54 19N 19 31 E
Tollarp 173 55 55N 13 58 E
Tolmachevo 178 58 56N 29 51 E
Tolmezzo 163 46 23N 13 0 E
Tolmin 163 46 11N 13 45 E
Tolna 151 46 25N 18 48 E
Tolna □ 151 46 30N 18 30 E
Tolo 252 2 55 S 18 34 E
Tolo, Teluk 207 2 20 S 122 10 E
Tolochin 178 54 25N 29 42 E
Tolong Bay 211 9 20N 122 49 E
Tolosa 156 43 8N 2 5W
Tolox 155 36 41N 4 54W
Tolstoi 89 49 5N 96 49W
Toltén 126 39 13 S 74 14W
Toluca, Nevado de 107 19 8N 99 44W
Toluca de Lerdo 107 19 17N 99 40W
Tom Burke 255 23 5 S 28 4 E
Tom Price 228 22 40 S 117 48 E
Tomakomai 218 42 38N 141 36 E
Tomar 155 39 36N 8 25W
Tómaros Óros 168 39 29N 20 48 E
Tomás Barrón 122 17 35 S 67 31W
Tomaszów Mazowiecki 152 51 30N 19 57 E
Tomatlán 106 19 56N 105 15W
Tombador, Serra do 123 12 0 S 58 0W
Tombé 245 5 53N 31 40 E
Tombôco 253 6 48 S 13 18 E
Tombouctou 246 16 50N 3 0W
Tombua 254 15 55 S 11 55 E
Tomé 124 36 36 S 72 57W
Tomé-Açu 120 2 25 S 48 9W
Tomelilla 172 55 33N 13 58 E
Tomelloso 157 39 10N 3 2W
Tomiko L. 84 46 32N 79 49W
Tomil Harbor 226 9 30N 138 10 E
Tomingley 231 32 6 S 148 16 E

Tomini 207 0 30N 120 30 E
Tomini, Teluk 207 0 10 S 122 0 E
Tominian 246 13 17N 4 35W
Tomiño 154 41 59N 8 46W
Tomioka 221 37 20N 141 0 E
Tomkinson Ranges 229 26 11 S 129 5 E
Tommot 185 59 4N 126 20 E
Tomnavoulin 134 57 19N 3 18W
Tomnop Ta Suos 205 11 20N 104 15 E
Tomo, Colombia 118 2 38N 67 32W
Tomo, Japan 220 34 23N 133 23 E
Tomo → 118 5 20N 67 48W
Tomobe 221 36 20N 140 20 E
Tompkins 88 50 4N 108 47W
Tomsk 184 56 30N 85 5 E
Tomtabacken 173 57 30N 14 30 E
Tömuk 190 36 42N 34 23 E
Tonáchic 101 27 42N 107 4W
Tonalá, Chiapas, Mexico 110 16 4N 93 45W
Tonalá, Jalisco, Mexico 106 20 37N 103 14W
Tonalá → 110 18 13N 94 11W
Tonale, Passo del 162 46 15N 10 34 E
Tonami 221 36 40N 136 58 E
Tonantins 118 2 45 S 67 45W
Tonate 119 5 0N 52 28W
Tonaya 106 19 51N 103 58W
Tonbridge 133 51 12N 0 18 E
Tondano 207 1 35N 124 54 E
Tondela 154 40 31N 8 5W
Tønder 173 54 58N 8 50 E
Tondi 201 9 45N 79 4 E
Tondi Kiwindi 247 14 28N 2 2 E
Tondibi 247 16 39N 0 14W
Tonekābon 193 36 45N 51 12 E
Tong Xian 214 39 55N 116 35 E
Tonga ■ 224 19 50 S 174 30W
Tonga Trench 224 18 0 S 175 0W
Tongaat 255 29 33 S 31 9 E
Tongala 233 36 14 S 144 56 E
Tongaland 255 27 0 S 32 0 E
Tong'an 217 24 37N 118 8 E
Tongareva 225 9 0 S 158 0W
Tongbai 217 32 20N 113 23 E
Tongcheng, Anhui, China 217 31 4N 116 56 E
Tongcheng, Hubei, China 217 29 15N 113 50 E
Tongchŏn-ni 215 39 50N 127 25 E
Tongchuan 214 35 6N 109 3 E
Tongdao 216 26 10N 109 42 E
Tongeren 143 50 47N 5 28 E
Tonggu 217 28 31N 114 20 E
Tongguan 214 34 40N 110 25 E
Tonghai 216 24 10N 102 53 E
Tonghua 215 41 42N 125 58 E
Tongjiang 216 31 58N 107 11 E
Tongjosŏn Man 215 39 30N 128 0 E
Tongking, G. of 204 20 0N 108 0 E
Tongliang 216 29 50N 106 3 E
Tongliao 215 43 38N 122 18 E
Tongling 217 30 55N 117 48 E
Tonglu 217 29 45N 119 37 E
Tongnae 215 35 12N 129 5 E
Tongnan 216 30 9N 105 50 E
Tongobory 255 23 32 S 44 20 E
Tongoy 124 30 16 S 71 31W
Tongren 216 27 43N 109 11 E
Tongres = Tongeren 143 50 47N 5 28 E
Tongsa Dzong 202 27 31N 90 31 E
Tongue 134 58 29N 4 25W
Tongwei 214 35 0N 105 5 E
Tongxin 214 36 59N 105 58 E
Tongyang 215 39 9N 126 53 E
Tongyu 215 44 45N 123 4 E
Tongzi 216 28 9N 106 49 E
Tonila 106 19 26N 103 31W
Tonj 245 7 20N 28 44 E
Tonk 198 26 6N 75 54 E
Tonkin = Bac Phan 204 22 0N 105 0 E
Tonkin, G. of 204 20 0N 108 0 E
Tonlé Sap 204 13 0N 104 0 E
Tonnay-Charente 140 45 56N 0 55W
Tonneins 140 44 23N 0 19 E
Tonnerre 139 47 51N 3 59 E
Tönning 146 54 18N 8 57 E
Tono 218 39 19N 141 32 E
Tonoshō 220 34 29N 134 11 E
Tonosí 112 7 20N 80 20W
Tønsberg 171 59 19N 10 25 E
Tonstad 171 58 40N 6 45 E
Tonzang 202 23 36N 93 42 E
Tonzi 202 24 39N 94 57 E
Toolondo 232 36 58 S 141 58 E
Toompine 231 27 15 S 144 19 E
Toongi 233 32 28 S 148 30 E
Toonpan 230 19 28 S 146 48 E
Toora 231 38 39 S 146 23 E
Toora-Khem 185 52 28N 96 17 E
Toowoomba 231 27 32 S 151 56 E
Top of the World Prov. Park 91 50 0N 115 35W
Top-ozero 176 65 35N 32 0 E
Topalu 170 44 31N 28 3 E
Topia 104 25 13N 106 34W
Topki 184 55 20N 85 35 E
Topl'a → 151 48 45N 21 45 E
Topley 76 54 49N 126 18W
Toplica → 166 43 15N 21 49 E
Toplița 170 46 55N 25 20 E
Topocalma, Pta. 124 34 10 S 72 2W
Topola 166 44 17N 20 41 E
Topolčani 166 41 14N 21 56 E
Topoľčany 151 48 35N 18 12 E
Topoli 181 47 59N 51 38 E
Topolnitsa → 167 42 11N 24 18 E
Topolobampo 104 25 36N 109 3W
Topolovgrad 167 42 5N 26 20 E
Topolvǎtu Mare 166 45 46N 21 41 E
Toprakkale 190 37 5N 36 8 E
Topusko 163 45 18N 15 59 E
Toquepala 122 17 24 S 70 25W
Torá 156 41 49N 1 25 E
Tora Kit 245 11 2N 32 36 E
Toraka Vestale 255 16 20 S 43 58 E
Torata 122 17 23 S 70 1W
Torbay, Canada 79 47 40N 52 42W
Torbay, U.K. 133 50 26N 3 31W
Torch → 88 53 50N 103 5W
Tørdal 171 59 10N 8 45 E
Tordesillas 154 41 30N 5 0W
Tordoya 154 43 6N 8 36W
Töreboda 173 58 41N 14 7 E
Torey 185 50 33N 104 50 E
Torfajökull 174 63 54N 19 0W
Torgau 146 51 32N 13 0 E
Torgelow 146 53 40N 13 59 E
Torhout 143 51 5N 3 7 E
Tori 245 7 53N 33 35 E
Tori-Shima 219 30 29N 140 19 E
Torigni-sur-Vire 138 49 3N 0 58W
Torija 156 40 44N 3 2W
Torín 100 27 34N 110 14W
Toriñana, C. 154 43 3N 9 17W
Torino 162 45 4N 7 40 E
Torit 245 4 27N 32 31 E
Torkovichi 178 58 51N 30 21 E
Tormac 166 45 30N 21 30 E
Tormentine 75 46 6N 63 46W
Tormes → 154 41 18N 6 29W
Tornado Mt. 76 49 55N 114 40W
Torne älv → 174 65 50N 24 12 E
Torneå = Tornio 174 65 50N 24 12 E
Torneträsk 174 68 24N 19 15 E
Torngat Mts. 78 59 0N 63 40W
Tornio 174 65 50N 24 12 E
Tornionjoki → 174 65 50N 24 12 E
Tornquist 124 38 8 S 62 15W
Toro, Spain 154 41 35N 5 24W
Torö, Sweden 173 58 48N 17 50 E
Toro, Cerro del 124 29 10 S 69 50W
Törökszentmiklós 151 47 11N 20 27 E
Toroníos Kólpos 168 40 5N 23 30 E
Toronto, Australia 231 33 0 S 151 30 E
Toronto, Canada 84 43 39N 79 20W
Toropets 178 56 30N 31 40 E
Tororo 250 0 45N 34 12 E
Toros Dağlari 177 37 0N 35 0 E
Torotoro 123 18 7 S 65 46W
Torowie 231 33 8 S 138 55 E
Torpshammar 172 62 29N 16 20 E
Torquay, Australia 232 38 20 S 144 19 E
Torquay, Canada 88 49 9N 103 30W
Torquay, U.K. 133 50 27N 3 31W
Torquemada 154 42 2N 4 19W
Torralba de Calatrava 155 39 1N 3 44W
Torrão 155 38 16N 8 11W
Torre Annunziata 165 40 45N 14 26 E
Torre Blanca, R. → 107 21 6N 99 23W
Tôrre de Moncorvo 154 41 12N 7 8W
Torre del Greco 165 40 47N 14 22 E
Torre del Mar 155 36 44N 4 6W
Torre-Pacheco 157 37 44N 0 57W
Torre Pellice 162 44 49N 7 13 E
Torreblanca 156 40 14N 0 12 E
Torrecampo 155 38 29N 4 41W
Torrecilla en Cameros 156 42 15N 2 38W
Torredembarra 156 41 9N 1 24 E
Torredonjimeno 155 37 46N 3 57W
Torrejoncillo 154 39 54N 6 28W
Torrelaguna 156 40 50N 3 38W
Torrelavega 154 43 20N 4 5W
Torremaggiore 165 41 42N 15 17 E
Torremolinos 155 36 38N 4 30W
Torrens, L. 231 31 0 S 137 50 E
Torrens Cr. → 230 22 23 S 145 9 E
Torrens Creek 230 20 48 S 145 3 E
Torrente 157 39 27N 0 28W
Torrenueva 157 38 38N 3 22W
Torreón 102 25 33N 103 26W
Torreón de Cañas 104 26 23N 105 18W
Torreperogil 157 38 2N 3 17W
Torres 100 28 46N 110 20W
Torres Novas 155 39 27N 8 33W
Torres Strait 227 9 50 S 142 20 E
Torres Vedras 155 39 5N 9 15W
Torrevieja 157 37 59N 0 42W
Torridge → 133 50 51N 4 10W
Torridon, L. 134 57 35N 5 50W
Torrijos, Phil. 210 13 19N 122 5 E
Torrijos, Spain 154 39 59N 4 18W
Torrington 91 51 48N 113 35W
Torroella de Montgri 156 42 2N 3 8 E
Torrox 155 36 46N 3 57W
Torsås 173 56 24N 16 0 E
Torsby 172 60 7N 13 0 E
Torsill Mts. 95 65 0N 84 30W
Torsö 173 58 48N 13 45 E
Tórtoles de Esgueva 154 41 49N 4 2W
Tortona 162 44 53N 8 54 E
Tortoreto 163 42 50N 13 55 E
Tortorici 165 38 2N 14 48 E
Tortosa 156 40 49N 0 31 E
Tortosa, C. 156 40 41N 0 52 E
Tortosendo 154 40 15N 7 31W
Tortue, Î. de la 113 20 5N 72 57W
Tortuga, I. 99 27 26N 111 52W
Tortuga, La 119 11 0N 65 22W
Tortugas, L. 108 22 20N 98 7W
Torūd 193 35 25N 55 5 E
Torugart, Pereval 183 40 32N 75 24 E
Toruń 152 53 0N 18 39 E
Toruń □ 152 53 20N 19 0 E
Torup, Denmark 173 57 5N 9 5 E
Torup, Sweden 173 56 57N 13 5 E
Tory I. 135 55 17N 8 12W
Torysa → 151 48 39N 21 21 E
Torzhok 178 57 5N 34 55 E
Tosa 220 33 24N 133 23 E
Tosa-Shimizu 220 32 52N 132 58 E
Tosa-Wan 220 33 15N 133 30 E
Tosa-yamada 220 33 36N 133 38 E
Toscana 162 43 30N 11 5 E
Toscano, Arcipelago 162 42 30N 10 30 E
Tosco, C. 99 24 19N 111 43W
Tosno 178 59 38N 30 46 E
Tossa 156 41 43N 2 56 E
Tostado 124 29 15 S 61 50W
Tostedt 146 53 17N 9 42 E
Tosu 220 33 22N 130 31 E
Toszek 152 50 27N 18 32 E
Totak 171 59 40N 7 45 E
Totana 157 37 45N 1 30W
Totatiche 105 21 56N 103 27W
Toten 171 60 37N 10 53 E
Toteng 254 20 22 S 22 58 E
Tôtes 138 49 41N 1 3 E
Totimehuacán 109 18 58N 98 11W
Tótkomlós 151 46 24N 20 45 E
Totma 179 60 0N 42 40 E
Totnes 133 50 26N 3 41W
Totness 119 5 53N 56 19W
Totolcingo, L. 108 19 20N 97 37W
Totonicapán 112 14 58N 91 12W
Totora 123 17 42 S 65 9W
Tototlán 106 20 33N 102 48W
Totskoye 182 52 32N 52 45 E
Totten Glacier 13 66 45 S 116 10 E
Tottenham, Australia 231 32 14 S 147 21 E
Tottenham, Canada 84 44 1N 79 49W
Tottori 220 35 30N 134 15 E
Tottori □ 220 35 30N 134 12 E
Totutla 108 19 13N 96 56W
Touat 240 27 27N 0 30 E
Touba 246 8 22N 7 40W
Toubkal, Djebel 240 31 0N 8 0W
Touchwood 88 51 21N 104 9W
Toucy 139 47 44N 3 15 E
Tougan 246 13 11N 2 58W
Touggourt 241 33 6N 6 4 E
Tougué 246 11 25N 11 50W
Touho 226 20 47 S 165 14 E
Toukmatine 241 24 49N 7 11 E
Toul 139 48 40N 5 53 E
Toulepleu 246 6 32N 8 24W
Toulnustouc → 80 49 35N 68 24W
Toulnustouc Nord-Est. → 80 50 56N 67 44W
Toulon 141 43 10N 5 55 E
Toulouse 140 43 37N 1 27 E
Toummo 241 22 45N 14 8 E
Toummo Dhoba 241 22 30N 14 31 E
Toumodi 246 6 32N 5 4W
Tounassine, Hamada 240 28 48N 5 0W
Toungoo 202 19 0N 96 30 E
Touques → 138 49 22N 0 8 E
Touquet-Paris-Plage, Le 139 50 30N 1 36 E
Tour-du-Pin, La 141 45 33N 5 27 E
Touraine 138 47 20N 0 30 E
Tourane = Da Nang 204 16 4N 108 13 E
Tourcoing 139 50 42N 3 10 E
Tourine 240 22 23N 11 50W
Tournai 143 50 35N 3 25 E
Tournan-en-Brie 139 48 44N 2 46 E
Tournay 140 43 13N 0 13 E
Tournon 141 45 4N 4 50 E
Tournon-St-Martin 138 46 45N 0 58 E
Tournus 141 46 35N 4 54 E
Touros 120 5 12 S 35 28W
Tours 138 47 22N 0 40 E
Touside, Pic 241 21 1N 16 29 E
Touwsrivier 254 33 20 S 20 0 E
Tovar 118 8 20N 71 46W
Tovarkovskiy 179 53 40N 38 14 E
Tovdal 171 58 47N 8 10 E
Tovdalselva → 171 58 15N 8 5 E
Towada 218 40 37N 141 13 E
Towada-Ko 218 40 28N 140 55 E
Towamba 231 37 6 S 149 43 E
Towerhill Cr. → 230 22 28 S 144 35 E
Townshend I. 230 22 10 S 150 31 E
Townsville 230 19 15 S 146 45 E
Towyn 133 52 36N 4 5W
Toya-Ko 218 42 35N 140 51 E
Toyama 221 36 40N 137 15 E
Toyama □ 221 36 45N 137 30 E
Toyama-Wan 219 37 0N 137 30 E
Tōyō 220 33 26N 134 16 E
Toyohashi 221 34 45N 137 25 E
Toyokawa 221 34 48N 137 27 E
Toyonaka 221 34 50N 135 28 E
Toyooka 220 35 35N 134 48 E
Toyota 221 35 3N 137 7 E
Toyoura 220 34 6N 130 57 E
Toytepa 183 41 3N 69 20 E
Tozeur 241 33 56N 8 8 E
Tra On 205 9 58N 105 55 E
Trabancos → 154 41 36N 5 15W
Traben Trarbach 147 49 57N 7 7 E
Trabzon 180 41 0N 39 45 E
Tracadie 81 47 30N 64 55W
Tracy, N.B., Canada 81 45 41N 66 41W
Tracy, Qué., Canada 83 46 1N 73 9W
Tradate 162 45 43N 8 54 E
Tradovoye 218 43 17N 132 5 E
Trafalgar 233 38 14 S 146 12 E
Trafalgar, C. 155 36 10N 6 2W
Trāghān 241 26 0N 14 30 E
Tragowel 232 35 50 S 144 0 E
Traian 170 45 2N 28 15 E
Traiguén 126 38 15 S 72 41W
Trail 93 49 5N 117 40W
Trainor L. 76 60 24N 120 17W
Traíra → 118 1 4 S 69 26W
Tralee 135 52 16N 9 42W
Tralee B. 135 52 17N 9 55W
Tramelan 148 47 13N 7 7 E
Tramore 135 52 10N 7 10W
Tramping Lake 88 52 8N 108 57W
Tran Ninh, Cao Nguyen 204 19 30N 103 10 E
Tranås 173 58 3N 14 59 E
Trancas 124 26 11 S 65 20W
Tranche, La 140 46 20N 1 26W
Tranche-sur-Mer, La 138 46 20N 1 27W
Trancoso 154 40 49N 7 21W
Tranebjerg 173 55 51N 10 36 E
Tranemo 173 57 30N 13 20 E
Trang 205 7 33N 99 38 E
Trangahy 255 19 7 S 44 31 E
Trangan 207 6 40 S 134 20 E
Trangie 231 32 4 S 148 0 E
Trångsviken 172 63 19N 14 0 E
Trani 165 41 17N 16 24 E
Tranoroa 255 24 42 S 45 4 E
Tranquebar 201 11 1N 79 54 E
Tranqueras 125 31 13 S 55 45W
Trans Nzoia □ 250 1 0N 35 0 E
Transantarctic Mts. 13 85 0 S 170 0W
Transcona 89 49 55N 97 0W
Transilvania 170 46 19N 25 0 E
Transkei 255 32 15 S 28 15 E
Transtrand 172 61 6N 13 20 E
Transvaal □ 254 25 0 S 29 0 E
Transylvania = Transilvania 170 46 19N 25 0 E
Transylvanian Alps 130 45 30N 25 0 E
Trápani 164 38 1N 12 30 E
Traralgon 231 38 12 S 146 34 E
Traryd 173 56 35N 13 45 E
Trarza □ 246 17 30N 15 0W
Trás-os-Montes 253 10 17 S 19 5 E
Trasacco 163 41 58N 13 30 E
Trăscău, Munţii 170 46 14N 23 14 E
Trasimeno, L. 163 43 10N 12 5 E
Trat 205 12 14N 102 33 E
Traun 150 48 14N 14 15 E
Traunsee 150 47 55N 13 50 E
Traunstein 147 47 52N 12 40 E
Trävad 173 58 15N 13 5 E
Traveller's L. 231 33 20 S 142 0 E
Travemünde 146 53 58N 10 52 E
Travers, Mt. 235 42 1 S 172 45 E
Travers Res. 91 50 12N 112 51W
Traversay Is. 13 57 0 S 28 0W
Travnik 166 44 17N 17 39 E
Trayning 229 31 7 S 117 16 E
Trazo 154 43 0N 8 30W

Trbovlje .... 163 46 12N 15 5 E
Trébbia → .... 162 45 4N 9 41 E
Trebel → .... 146 53 55N 13 1 E
Třebíč .... 150 49 14N 15 55 E
Trebinje .... 166 42 44N 18 22 E
Trebisacce .... 165 39 52N 16 32 E
Trebišnica → ..... 166 42 47N 18 8 E
Trebišov .... 151 48 38N 21 41 E
Trebižat → .... 166 43 15N 17 30 E
Trebnje .... 163 45 54N 15 1 E
Třeboň .... 150 48 59N 14 48 E
Trebujena 155 36 52N 6 11W
Trecate .... 162 45 26N 8 42 E
Trece Martires ..... 210 14 20N 120 50 E
Tredegar 133 51 47N 3 16W
Tregaron 133 52 14N 3 56W
Trégastel-Plage 138 48 49N 3 31W
Tregnago .... 163 45 31N 11 10 E
Tregrosse Is. .... 230 17 41 S 150 43 E
Tréguier 138 48 47N 3 16W
Trégune 138 47 51N 3 51W
Treherne 89 49 38N 98 42W
Tréia .... 163 43 20N 13 20 E
Treignac .... 140 45 32N 1 48 E
Treinta y Tres ..... 125 33 16 S 54 17W
Treis .... 147 50 9N 7 19 E
Treklyano .... 166 42 33N 22 36 E
Trekveld .... 254 30 35 S 19 45 E
Trelde Næs .... 173 55 38N 9 53 E
Trelew .... 126 43 10 S 65 20W
Trelissac .... 140 45 11N 0 47 E
Trelleborg .... 172 55 20N 13 10 E
Trélon .... 139 50 5N 4 6 E
Tremblade, La 140 45 46N 1 8W
Tremblant, Mt. 82 46 16N 74 35W
Tremiti .... 163 42 8N 15 30 E
Tremp .... 156 42 10N 0 52 E
Trenche → 83 47 46N 72 53W
Trenčín .... 151 48 52N 18 4 E
Trenggalek .... 209 8 3 S 111 43 E
Trenque Lauquen .. 124 36 5 S 62 45W
Trent →, Canada .. 85 44 6N 77 34W
Trent →, U.K. 132 53 33N 0 44W
Trente et un Milles,
L. des 82 46 12N 75 49W
Trentino-Alto
Adige □ .... 162 46 30N 11 0 E
Trento .... 162 46 5N 11 8 E
Trenton, N.S.,
Canada 81 45 37N 62 38W
Trenton, Ont.,
Canada 85 44 10N 77 34W
Trepassey 79 46 43N 53 25W
Trepassey B. 79 46 37N 53 30W
Tréport, Le .... 138 50 3N 1 20 E
Trepuzzi .... 165 40 26N 18 4 E
Tres Arroyos ...... 124 38 26 S 60 20W
Três Corações ..... 125 21 44 S 45 15W
Três Lagoas .... 121 20 50 S 51 43W
Tres Lagos → ..... 126 49 35 S 71 25W
Tres Marías, Is. 104 21 25N 106 28W
Três Marias,
Represa .... 121 18 12 S 45 15W
Tres Montes, C. .... 126 46 50 S 75 30W
Tres Palos 107 16 50N 99 47W
Tres Palos, L. 107 16 45N 99 43W
Tres Picos 110 15 52N 93 32W
Três Pontas .... 121 21 23 S 45 29W
Tres Puentes ...... 124 27 50 S 70 15W
Tres Puntas, C. .... 126 47 0 S 66 0W
Três Rios .... 121 22 6 S 43 15W
Tres Valles 109 18 15N 96 8W
Tres Zapotes 109 18 28N 95 33W
Treska → .... 166 42 0N 21 20 E
Treskavika Planina . 166 43 40N 18 20 E
Trespaderne 156 42 47N 3 24W
Trets .... 141 43 27N 5 41 E
Treuchtlingen ...... 147 48 58N 10 55 E
Treuenbrietzen ..... 146 52 6N 12 51 E
Treuter Mts. 95 75 42N 82 30W
Trêve, L. la 82 49 56N 75 30W
Trevíglio .... 162 45 31N 9 35 E
Trevínca, Peña 154 42 15N 6 46W
Treviso .... 163 45 40N 12 15 E
Trévoux .... 141 45 57N 4 47 E
Treysa .... 146 50 55N 9 12 E
Trgovište .... 166 42 20N 22 10 E
Triabunna .... 230 42 30 S 147 55 E
Triánda .... 169 36 25N 28 10 E
Triang .... 205 3 15N 102 26 E
Triaucourt-en-
Argonne .... 139 48 59N 5 2 E
Tribsees .... 146 54 4N 12 46 E
Tribulation, C. ..... 230 16 5 S 145 29 E
Tribune 88 49 15N 103 49W
Tricárico .... 165 40 37N 16 9 E
Tricase .... 165 39 56N 18 20 E
Trichinopoly =
Tiruchchirappalli . 201 10 45N 78 45 E
Trichur .... 201 10 30N 76 18 E
Trida .... 231 33 1 S 145 1 E
Trier .... 147 49 45N 6 37 E
Trieste .... 163 45 39N 13 45 E
Trieste, G. di ...... 163 45 37N 13 40 E
Trieux → 138 48 50N 3 3W
Triggiano .... 165 41 4N 16 58 E
Triglav .... 163 46 21N 13 50 E
Trigno → .... 163 42 4N 14 48 E
Trigueros 155 37 24N 6 50W
Tríkeri .... 169 39 6N 23 5 E
Trikhonis, Límni ... 169 38 34N 21 30 E
Tríkkala .... 168 39 34N 21 47 E
Tríkkala □ .... 168 39 41N 21 30 E
Trikora, Puncak .... 207 4 15 S 138 45 E
Trilj .... 163 43 38N 16 42 E
Trillo 156 40 42N 2 35W
Trim 135 53 34N 6 48W
Trincheras 100 30 24N 111 32W
Trincomalee .... 201 8 38N 81 15 E
Trindade .... 121 16 40 S 49 30W
Trindade, I. .... 129 20 20 S 29 50W
Tring-Jonction 83 46 16N 70 59W
Trinidad, Bolivia ... 123 14 46 S 64 50W
Trinidad, Colombia . 118 5 25N 71 40W
Trinidad, Cuba 112 21 48N 80 0W
Trinidad, Uruguay . 124 33 30 S 56 50W
Trinidad, W. Indies . 113 10 30N 61 15W
Trinidad → 109 17 49N 95 9W
Trinidad, G. .... 126 49 55 S 75 25W
Trinidad, I. .... 126 39 10 S 62 0W
Trinidad, La .... 210 16 28N 120 35 E
Trinidad, Pta. 99 27 48N 112 46W
Trinidad &
Tobago ■ 113 10 30N 61 20W
Trinitápoli .... 165 41 22N 16 5 E
Trinitaria, La 110 16 7N 92 3W
Trinity 79 48 59N 53 55W
Trinity B. 79 48 20N 53 10W
Trino .... 162 45 10N 8 18 E
Trionto C. .... 165 39 38N 16 47 E
Triora .... 162 44 0N 7 46 E
Tripoli = Tarābulus,
Lebanon .... 190 34 31N 35 50 E
Tripoli = Tarābulus,
Libya .... 241 32 49N 13 7 E
Trípolis .... 169 37 31N 22 25 E
Tripura □ .... 202 24 0N 92 0 E
Triquet, L. 80 50 42N 59 47W
Trischen .... 146 54 3N 8 32 E
Tristan da Cunha ... 129 37 6 S 12 20W
Trivandrum .... 201 8 41N 77 0 E
Trivento .... 165 41 48N 14 31 E
Trnava .... 151 48 23N 17 35 E
Trobriand Is. ...... 227 8 30 S 151 0 E
Trochu 91 51 50N 113 13W
Trodely I. 78 52 15N 79 26W
Troezen .... 169 37 25N 23 15 E
Trogir .... 163 43 32N 16 15 E
Troglav .... 163 43 56N 16 36 E
Trøgstad .... 171 59 37N 11 16 E
Tróia .... 165 41 22N 15 19 E
Troilus, L. 78 50 50N 74 35W
Troina .... 165 37 47N 14 34 E
Trois Fourches, Cap
des 241 35 26N 2 58W
Trois-Pistoles 83 48 5N 69 10W
Trois-Riviéres 83 46 25N 72 34W
Troisvierges .... 143 50 8N 6 0 E
Troitsk .... 182 54 10N 61 35 E
Troitskiy .... 182 55 29N 37 18 E
Troitsko Pechorsk .. 176 62 40N 56 10 E
Trölladyngja 174 64 54N 17 16W
Trollhättan .... 173 58 17N 12 20 E
Trollheimen .... 171 62 46N 9 1 E
Trombetas → ...... 119 1 55 S 55 35W
Tromelin I. .... 203 15 52 S 54 25 E
Troms fylke □ ..... 174 68 56N 19 0 E
Tromsø .... 174 69 40N 18 56 E
Tronador .... 126 41 10 S 71 50W
Troncoso 105 22 37N 102 28W
Trondheim .... 171 63 36N 10 25 E
Trondheimsfjorden . 171 63 35N 10 30 E
Trönninge .... 173 56 37N 12 51 E
Trönö .... 172 61 22N 16 54 E
Tronto → .... 163 42 54N 13 55 E
Troon 134 55 33N 4 40W
Tropea .... 165 38 40N 15 53 E
Tropoja .... 168 42 23N 20 10 E
Trossachs, The 134 56 14N 4 24W
Trostan 135 55 4N 6 10W
Trostberg .... 147 48 2N 12 33 E
Trostyanets .... 178 50 33N 34 59 E
Trotternish 134 57 32N 6 15W
Trout → 76 61 19N 119 51W
Trout Creek 84 45 59N 79 22W
Trout L., N.W.T.,
Canada 76 60 40N 121 40W
Trout L., Ont.,
Canada 86 51 20N 93 15W
Trout Lake 93 50 35N 117 25W
Trout River 79 49 29N 58 8W
Trouville .... 138 49 21N 0 5 E
Trowbridge 133 51 18N 2 12W
Troy, Canada 81 45 42N 61 26W
Troy, Turkey ...... 168 39 57N 26 12 E
Troyan .... 167 42 57N 24 43 E
Troyes .... 139 48 19N 4 3 E
Trpanj .... 166 43 1N 17 15 E
Trstena .... 151 49 21N 19 37 E
Trstenik .... 166 43 36N 21 0 E
Trubchevsk .... 178 52 33N 33 47 E
Trucial States =
United Arab
Emirates ■ ...... 195 23 50N 54 0 E
Truite, L. à la 82 47 20N 78 20W
Trujillo, Colombia .. 118 4 10N 76 19W
Trujillo, Hond. 112 16 0N 86 0W
Trujillo, Peru ...... 122 8 6 S 79 0W
Trujillo, Spain 155 39 28N 5 55W
Trujillo, Venezuela . 118 9 22N 70 38W
Trujillo □ 118 9 25N 70 30W
Trujillo → 105 23 39N 103 8W
Truk .... 224 7 25N 151 46 E
Trŭn, Bulgaria ..... 166 42 51N 22 38 E
Trun, France .... 138 48 50N 0 2 E
Trun, Switz. .... 149 46 45N 8 59 E
Trundle .... 231 32 53 S 147 35 E
Trung-Phan .... 204 16 0N 108 0 E
Truro, Australia .... 232 34 24 S 139 9 E
Truro, Canada 81 45 21N 63 14W
Truro, U.K. 133 50 17N 5 2W
Truslove .... 229 33 20 S 121 45 E
Trustrup .... 173 56 20N 10 46 E
Trutnov .... 150 50 37N 15 54 E
Truyère → .... 140 44 38N 2 34 E
Tryavna .... 167 42 54N 25 25 E
Trzcianka .... 152 53 3N 16 25 E
Trzciel .... 152 52 23N 15 50 E
Trzcińsko Zdrój .... 152 52 58N 14 35 E
Trzebiatów .... 152 54 3N 15 18 E
Trzebiez .... 152 53 38N 14 31 E
Trzebinia-Siersza ... 152 50 11N 19 18 E
Trzebnica .... 152 51 20N 17 1 E
Trzemeszno .... 152 52 33N 17 48 E
Tržič .... 163 46 22N 14 18 E
Tsacha L. 92 53 3N 124 50W
Tsageri .... 181 42 39N 42 46 E
Tsamandás .... 168 39 46N 20 21 E
Tsaratanana .... 255 16 47 S 47 39 E
Tsaratanana, Mt. de 255 14 0 S 49 0 E
Tsarevo = Michurin 167 42 9N 27 51 E
Tsarichanka .... 180 48 55N 34 30 E
Tsaritsáni .... 168 39 53N 22 14 E
Tsau .... 254 20 8 S 22 22 E
Tsebrikovo .... 180 47 9N 30 10 E
Tselinograd .... 184 51 10N 71 30 E
Tsetserleg .... 212 47 36N 101 32 E
Tshabong .... 254 26 2 S 22 29 E
Tshane .... 254 24 5 S 21 54 E
Tshela .... 253 4 57 S 13 4 E
Tshesebe .... 255 21 51 S 27 32 E
Tshibeke .... 250 2 40 S 28 35 E
Tshibinda .... 250 2 23 S 28 43 E
Tshikapa .... 253 6 28 S 20 48 E
Tshilenge .... 250 6 17 S 23 48 E
Tshinsenda .... 251 12 20 S 28 0 E
Tshofa .... 250 5 13 S 25 16 E
Tshwane .... 254 22 24 S 22 1 E
Tsigara .... 254 20 22 S 25 54 E
Tsihombe .... 255 25 18 S 45 29 E
Tsimlyansk .... 181 47 40N 42 6 E
Tsimlyanskoye
Vdkhr. .... 181 48 0N 43 0 E
Tsinan = Jinan ..... 214 36 38N 117 1 E
Tsineng .... 254 27 5 S 23 5 E
Tsínga .... 168 41 23N 24 44 E
Tsinghai =
Qinghai □ .... 174 36 0N 98 0 E
Tsingtao = Qingdao 215 36 5N 120 20 E
Tsinjomitondraka ... 255 15 40 S 47 8 E
Tsiroanomandidy ... 255 18 46 S 46 2 E
Tsitsutl Pk. 92 52 43N 125 47W
Tsivilsk .... 179 55 50N 47 25 E
Tsivory .... 255 24 4 S 46 5 E
Tskhinvali .... 181 42 14N 44 1 E
Tsna → .... 179 54 55N 41 58 E
Tso Moriri, L. ..... 199 32 50N 78 20 E
Tsodilo Hill .... 254 18 49 S 21 43 E
Tsogttsetsiy .... 214 43 43N 105 35 E
Tsu .... 221 34 45N 136 25 E
Tsu L. 76 60 40N 111 52W
Tsuchiura .... 221 36 5N 140 15 E
Tsugaru-Kaikyō .... 218 41 35N 141 0 E
Tsukumi .... 220 33 4N 131 52 E
Tsukushi-Sanchi .... 220 33 25N 130 30 E
Tsumeb .... 254 19 9 S 17 44 E
Tsumis .... 254 23 39 S 17 29 E
Tsuna .... 220 34 28N 134 56 E
Tsuniah L. 92 51 33N 124 4W
Tsuno-Shima .... 220 34 21N 130 52 E
Tsuru .... 221 35 31N 138 57 E
Tsuruga .... 221 35 45N 136 2 E
Tsuruga-Wan ...... 221 35 50N 136 3 E
Tsurugi .... 221 36 29N 136 37 E
Tsurugi-San .... 220 33 51N 134 6 E
Tsurumi-Saki ...... 220 32 56N 132 5 E
Tsuruoka .... 218 38 44N 139 50 E
Tsurusaki .... 220 33 14N 131 41 E
Tsushima, Gifu,
Japan .... 221 35 10N 136 43 E
Tsushima, Nagasaki,
Japan .... 220 34 20N 129 20 E
Tsvetkovo .... 180 49 8N 31 33 E
Tu → .... 202 21 50N 96 15 E
Tua → 154 41 13N 7 26W
Tuai .... 234 38 47 S 177 10 E
Tuakau .... 234 37 16 S 174 59 E
Tual .... 207 5 38 S 132 44 E
Tuam 135 53 30N 8 50W
Tuamarina .... 235 41 25 S 173 59 E
Tuamotu Arch. ..... 225 17 0 S 144 0W
Tuamotu Ridge .... 225 20 0 S 138 0W
Tuanfeng .... 217 30 38N 114 52 E
Tuanxi .... 216 27 28N 107 8 E
Tuao .... 210 17 55N 122 22 E
Tuape 100 30 8N 110 42W
Tuapse .... 181 44 5N 39 10 E
Tuatapere .... 235 46 8 S 167 41 E
Tuban .... 209 6 54 S 112 3 E
Tubarão .... 125 28 30 S 49 0W
Tūbās .... 189 32 20N 35 22 E
Tubau .... 206 3 10N 113 40 E
Tubbergen .... 142 52 24N 6 48 E
Tübingen .... 147 48 31N 9 4 E
Tubize .... 143 50 42N 4 13 E
Tubruq .... 242 32 7N 23 55 E
Tubuaeran I. 225 3 51N 159 22W
Tubuai Is. .... 225 25 0 S 150 0W
Tuburan .... 211 6 39N 122 16 E
Tubutama 100 30 53N 111 29W
Tuc Trung .... 205 11 1N 107 12 E
Tucacas 118 10 48N 68 19W
Tucano .... 120 10 58 S 38 48W
Tuchang .... 217 24 59N 121 30 E
Tuchodi → 76 58 17N 123 42W
Tuchola .... 152 53 33N 17 52 E
Tuchów .... 152 49 54N 21 1 E
Tucumán □ .... 124 26 48 S 66 2W
Tucunaré .... 123 5 18 S 55 51W
Tucupido 118 9 17N 65 47W
Tucupita 119 9 2N 62 3W
Tucuruí .... 120 3 42 S 49 44W
Tuczno .... 152 53 13N 16 10 E
Tudela 156 42 4N 1 39W
Tudela de Duero ... 154 41 37N 4 39W
Tudmur .... 192 34 36N 38 15 E
Tudor, Lac 78 55 50N 65 25W
Tudora .... 170 47 31N 26 45 E
Tuel de González
Ortega 105 21 28N 103 29W
Tuella → 154 41 30N 7 12W
Tuen .... 231 28 33 S 145 37 E
Tueré → .... 120 2 48 S 50 59W
Tufi .... 227 9 8 S 149 19 E
Tugaske 88 50 52N 106 17W
Tuguegarao .... 210 17 35N 121 42 E
Tugur .... 185 53 44N 136 45 E
Tuitán 105 24 2N 104 15W
Tukangbesi,
Kepulauan .... 207 6 0 S 124 0 E
Tukarak I. 78 56 15N 78 45W
Tukayyid .... 192 29 47N 45 36 E
Tûkh .... 244 30 21N 31 12 E
Tukobo 246 5 1N 2 47W
Tūkrah .... 241 32 30N 20 37 E
Tuktoyaktuk 94 69 27N 133 2W
Tukums .... 178 57 2N 23 10 E
Tukuyu .... 251 9 17 S 33 35 E
Tula, Mexico 103 23 0N 99 43W
Tula, Nigeria ...... 247 9 51N 11 27 E
Tula, U.S.S.R. ...... 179 54 13N 37 38 E
Tula → 107 20 40N 99 30W
Tula de Allende 107 20 3N 99 21W
Tulak .... 197 33 55N 63 40 E
Tulancingo 107 20 5N 98 22W
Tulangbawang → .. 208 4 24 S 105 52 E
Tulbagh .... 254 33 16 S 19 6 E
Tulcán 118 0 48N 77 43W
Tulcea .... 170 45 13N 28 46 E
Tulcea □ .... 170 45 0N 29 0 E
Tulchin .... 180 48 41N 28 49 E
Tulcingo de Valle .. 109 18 3N 98 26W
Tūleh .... 193 34 35N 52 33 E
Tulemalu L. 77 62 58N 99 25W
Tulgheş .... 170 46 58N 25 45 E
Tuli, Indonesia ..... 207 1 24 S 122 26 E
Tuli, Zimbabwe .... 251 21 58 S 29 13 E
Tulija → 110 17 38N 92 22W
Tulimán 107 18 13N 99 4W
Ţūlkarm .... 189 32 19N 35 2 E
Tullamore, Australia 231 32 39 S 147 36 E
Tullamore, Ireland . 135 53 17N 7 30W
Tulle .... 140 45 16N 1 46 E
Tullibigeal .... 231 33 25 S 146 44 E
Tullins .... 141 45 18N 5 29 E
Tulln .... 150 48 20N 16 4 E
Tullow 135 52 48N 6 45W
Tullus .... 245 11 7N 24 31 E
Tully .... 230 17 56 S 145 55 E
Ţulmaythah .... 242 32 40N 20 55 E
Tulmur .... 230 22 40 S 142 20 E
Tulnici .... 170 45 51N 26 38 E
Tulovo .... 167 42 33N 25 32 E
Tulsequah 76 58 39N 133 35W
Tultitlán 107 19 39N 99 9W
Tulu Milki .... 245 9 55N 38 20 E

Tulu Welel 245 8 56N 34 47 E
Tulua 118 4 6N 76 11W
Tulúm 111 20 13N 87 28W
Tulun 185 54 32N 100 35 E
Tulungagung 209 8 5S 111 54 E
Tum 207 3 36S 130 21 E
Tuma 179 55 10N 40 30 E
Tuma → 112 13 6N 84 35W
Tumaco 118 1 50N 78 45W
Tumaco, Ensenada 118 1 55N 78 45W
Tumatumari 119 5 20N 58 55W
Tumauini 210 17 17N 121 49 E
Tumba 172 59 12N 17 48 E
Tumba, L. 252 0 50S 18 0 E
Tumbalá 110 17 18N 92 19W
Tumbarumba 231 35 44S 148 0 E
Tumbaya 124 23 50S 65 26W
Túmbes 122 3 37S 80 27W
Tumbes □ 122 3 50S 80 30W
Tumbiscatio del
Ruiz 106 18 31N 102 21W
Tumbwe 251 11 25S 27 15 E
Tumby Bay 232 34 21S 136 8 E
Tumd Youqi 214 40 30N 110 30 E
Tumen, China 215 43 0N 129 50 E
T'umen, N. Korea 215 42 55N 129 50 E
Tumen Jiang → 215 42 20N 130 35 E
Tumeremo 119 7 18N 61 30W
Tumiritinga 121 18 58S 41 38W
Tumkur 201 13 18N 77 6 E
Tummel, L. 134 56 43N 3 55W
Tump 197 26 7N 62 16 E
Tumpat 205 6 11N 102 10 E
Tumsar 199 21 26N 79 45 E
Tumu 246 10 56N 1 56W
Tumucumaque,
Serra 119 2 0N 55 0W
Tumupasa 122 14 9S 67 55W
Tumut 231 35 16S 148 13 E
Tumutuk 182 55 1N 53 19 E
Tunas, Sa. de las 101 29 40N 107 15W
Tunas de Zaza 112 21 39N 79 34W
Tunbridge Wells 133 51 7N 0 16 E
Tuncurry 231 32 17S 152 29 E
Tunduru 251 11 8S 37 25 E
Tunduru □ 251 11 5S 37 22 E
Tundzha → 167 41 40N 26 35 E
Tune 171 59 16N 11 2 E
Tunga → 201 15 0N 75 50 E
Tunga Pass 202 29 0N 94 14 E
Tungabhadra → 201 15 57N 78 15 E
Tungabhadra Dam 201 15 0N 75 50 E
Tungi 202 23 53N 90 24 E
Tungla 112 13 24N 84 21W
Tungnafellsjökull 174 64 45N 17 55W
Tungsten 76 61 57N 128 16W
Tungurahua □ 118 1 15S 78 35W
Tunguska,
Nizhnyaya → 185 65 48N 88 4 E
Tunguska,
Podkamennaya →
185 61 36N 90 18 E
Tuni 200 17 22N 82 36 E
Tunia 118 2 41N 76 31W
Tunis 241 36 50N 10 11 E
Tunis, Golfe de 241 37 0N 10 30 E
Tunisia ■ 241 33 30N 9 10 E
Tunja 118 5 33N 73 25W
Tunkás 111 20 54N 88 45W
Tunliu 214 36 13N 112 52 E
Tunnsjøen 174 64 45N 13 25 E
Tunulic → 78 58 57N 66 50W
Tunungayualok I. 78 56 0N 61 0W
Tunuyán 124 33 35S 69 0W
Tunuyán → 124 33 33S 67 30W
Tunxi 217 29 42N 118 25 E
Tuo Jiang → 216 28 50N 105 35 E
Tuoy-Khaya 185 62 32N 111 25 E
Tūp Āghāj 192 36 3N 47 50 E
Tupã 125 21 57S 50 28W
Tupaciguara 121 18 35S 48 42W
Tupik, R.S.F.S.R.,
U.S.S.R. 178 55 42N 33 22 E
Tupik, R.S.F.S.R.,
U.S.S.R. 185 54 26N 119 57 E
Tupinambaranas 119 3 0S 58 0W
Tupirama 120 8 58S 48 12W
Tupiratins 120 8 23S 48 8W
Tupitina 106 18 5N 102 44W
Tupiza 124 21 30S 65 40W
Tupižnica 166 43 43N 22 10 E
Tupper 76 55 32N 120 1W
Tupungato, Cerro 124 33 15S 69 50W
Tuquan 215 45 18N 121 38 E
Tuque, La 83 47 30N 72 50W
Túquerres 118 1 5N 77 37W
Tura, India 202 25 30N 90 16 E
Tura, U.S.S.R. 185 64 20N 100 17 E
Tura → 182 57 12N 66 56 E
Turaba, Wadi → 244 21 15N 41 32 E
Turabah 192 28 20N 43 15 E
Turagua, Serranía 119 7 20N 64 35W
Turaiyur 201 11 9N 78 38 E
Turakina 234 40 3S 175 16 E
Turakirae Hd. 234 41 26S 174 56 E
Tūrān, Iran 193 35 39N 56 42 E
Turan, U.S.S.R. 185 51 55N 95 0 E
Turayf 192 31 41N 38 39 E
Turbacz 151 49 30N 20 8 E
Turbe 166 44 15N 17 35 E
Turbenthal 149 47 27N 8 51 E
Turda 170 46 34N 23 47 E
Turégano 154 41 9N 4 1W
Turek 152 52 3N 18 30 E
Turen 118 9 17N 69 6W
Turfan = Turpan 212 43 58N 89 10 E
Turgay 182 49 38N 63 30 E
Turgay → 182 48 1N 62 45 E
Turgeon → 82 50 0N 78 56W
Turgeon, L. 82 49 2N 79 4W
Tŭrgovishte 167 43 17N 26 38 E
Turgutlu 177 38 30N 27 48 E
Turhal 180 40 24N 36 5 E
Turia → 157 39 27N 0 19W
Turiaçu 120 1 40S 45 19W
Turiaçu → 120 1 36S 45 19W
Turicachi 100 30 44N 109 32W
Turicato 107 19 9N 101 27W
Turiec → 151 49 7N 18 55 E
Turin = Torino 162 45 4N 7 40 E
Turin 91 49 58N 112 31W
Turinsk 182 58 3N 63 42 E
Turka 178 49 10N 23 2 E
Turkana □ 250 3 0N 35 30 E
Turkana, L. 250 3 30N 36 5 E
Turkestan 183 43 17N 68 16 E
Turkestanskiy,
Khrebet 183 39 35N 69 0 E
Túrkeve 151 47 6N 20 44 E
Turkey ■ 177 39 0N 36 0 E
Turkey Creek 228 17 2S 128 12 E
Turki 179 52 0N 43 15 E
Turkmen S.S.R. □ 184 39 0N 59 0 E
Turks Is. 113 21 20N 71 20W
Turks Island Passage 113 21 30N 71 30W
Turku 175 60 30N 22 19 E
Turkwe → 250 3 6N 36 6 E
Turnagain → 76 59 12N 127 35W
Turnagain, C. 234 40 28S 176 38 E
Turner 228 17 52S 128 16 E
Turner Pt. 230 11 47S 133 32 E
Turner Valley 91 50 40N 114 17W
Turnhout 143 51 19N 4 57 E
Türnitz 150 47 55N 15 29 E
Turnor L. 77 56 35N 108 35W
Turnour I. 92 50 36N 126 27W
Turnov 150 50 34N 15 10 E
Tŭrnovo 167 43 5N 25 41 E
Turnu Măgurele 170 43 46N 24 56 E
Turnu Rosu Pasul 170 45 33N 24 17 E
Turnu-Severin 170 44 39N 22 41 E
Turobin 152 50 50N 22 44 E
Tuross Head 233 36 3S 150 8 E
Turpan 212 43 58N 89 10 E
Turrës, Kalaja e 168 41 10N 19 28 E
Turriff 134 57 32N 2 28W
Tursāq 192 33 27N 45 47 E
Tursha 179 56 55N 47 36 E
Tursi 165 40 15N 16 27 E
Turtle → 86 48 51N 92 45W
Turtle Hd. I. 230 10 56S 142 37 E
Turtle Is. 211 6 7N 118 14 E
Turtle L. 88 53 36N 108 38W
Turtle Mt. Prov.
Park 89 49 3N 100 15W
Turtleford 88 53 23N 108 57W
Turua 234 37 14S 175 35 E
Turukhansk 185 65 21N 88 5 E
Turun ja Porin
lääni □ 175 60 27N 22 15 E
Turzovka 151 49 25N 18 35 E
Tuscánia 163 42 25N 11 53 E
Tuscany = Toscana 162 43 30N 11 5 E
Tuskar Rock 135 52 12N 6 10W
Tusket 81 43 52N 65 58W
Tusket → 81 43 41N 65 57W
Tustna 171 63 10N 8 5 E
Tuszyn 152 51 36N 19 33 E
Tutayev 179 57 53N 39 32 E
Tutepec 107 19 40N 99 8W
Tuticorin 201 8 50N 78 12 E
Tutin 166 43 0N 20 20 E
Tutóia 120 2 45S 42 20W
Tutong 206 4 47N 114 40 E
Tutova → 170 46 20N 27 30 E
Tutrakan 167 44 2N 26 40 E
Tutshi L. 76 59 56N 134 30W
Tuttlingen 147 47 59N 8 50 E
Tutuaca,
Chihuahua,
Mexico 101 28 1N 106 31W
Tutuaca,
Chihuahua,
Mexico 101 28 29N 108 12W
Tutuala 207 8 25S 127 15 E
Tutuila 226 14 19S 170 50W
Tutuko Mt. 235 44 35S 168 1 E
Tutye 232 35 12S 141 29 E
Tuva A.S.S.R. □ 185 51 30N 95 0 E
Tuvalu ■ 224 8 0S 178 0 E
Tuvutha 226 17 40S 178 48W
Tūwal 194 22 17N 39 6 E
Tuwaym 190 35 10N 36 32 E
Tuxcacuesco 106 19 44N 104 2W
Tuxcueca 106 20 10N 103 12W
Tuxford 88 50 34N 105 35W
Tuxpán, Jalisco,
Mexico 106 19 33N 103 24W
Tuxpan, Michoacan,
Mexico 107 19 34N 100 28W
Tuxpan, Nayarit,
Mexico 104 21 57N 105 18W
Tuxpan, Veracruz,
Mexico 108 20 57N 97 24W
Tuxpan → 108 20 59N 97 18W
Tuxtepec 107 19 52N 99 39W
Tuxtilla 109 18 14N 95 54W
Tuxtla Chico 110 14 57N 92 10W
Tuxtla Gutiérrez 110 16 45N 93 7W
Tuxtlas, Sa. de los 109 18 25N 95 0W
Tuy 154 42 3N 8 39W
Tuy An 204 13 17N 109 16 E
Tuy Duc 205 12 15N 107 27 E
Tuy Hoa 204 13 5N 109 10 E
Tuy Phong 205 11 14N 108 43 E
Tuya L. 76 59 7N 130 35W
Tuyen Hoa 204 17 50N 106 10 E
Tuyen Quang 204 21 50N 105 10 E
Tuymazy 182 54 36N 53 42 E
Tūysarkān 193 34 33N 48 27 E
Tuz Gölü 177 38 45N 33 30 E
Ţūz Khurmātū 192 34 56N 44 38 E
Tuzkan, Ozero 183 40 35N 67 28 E
Tuzla, Turkey 190 36 42N 35 6 E
Tuzla, Yugoslavia 166 44 34N 18 41 E
Tuzlov → 181 47 28N 39 45 E
Tvååker 173 57 4N 12 25 E
Tvedestrand 171 58 38N 8 58 E
Tvŭrditsa 167 42 42N 25 53 E
Twardogóra 152 51 23N 17 28 E
Tweed 85 44 29N 77 19W
Tweed → 134 55 42N 2 10W
Tweed Heads 231 28 10S 153 31 E
Tweedmuir 88 53 34N 105 57W
Tweedside 81 45 38N 67 1W
Tweedsmuir Prov.
Park 92 53 0N 126 20W
Twello 142 52 14N 6 6 E
Twelve Mile L. 88 49 29N 106 14W
Twillingate 79 49 42N 54 45W
Twin City 86 48 22N 89 25W
Twinnge 202 23 10N 96 2 E
Twistringen 146 52 48N 8 38 E
Two Creeks 90 54 18N 116 21W
Two Hills 90 53 43N 111 52W
Two Thumbs Ra. 235 43 45S 170 44 E
Twofold B. 231 37 8S 149 59 E
Tychy 152 50 9N 18 59 E
Tyczyn 152 49 58N 22 2 E
Tydal 171 63 4N 11 34 E
Tykocin 152 53 13N 22 46 E
Tyldal 171 62 8N 10 48 E
Týn nad Vltavou 150 49 13N 14 26 E
Tynda 185 55 10N 124 43 E
Tyndall 89 50 5N 96 40W
Tyne → 132 54 58N 1 28W
Tyne & Wear □ 132 54 55N 1 35W
Tyne Valley 81 46 35N 63 56W
Tynemouth 132 55 1N 1 27W
Tynset 171 62 17N 10 47 E
Tyre = Sūr 189 33 19N 35 16 E
Tyrifjorden 171 60 2N 10 8 E
Tyringe 172 56 9N 13 35 E
Tyristrand 171 60 5N 10 5 E
Tyrnyauz 181 43 21N 42 45 E
Tyrol = Tirol □ 150 47 3N 10 43 E
Tyrrell → 231 35 26S 142 51 E
Tyrrell, L. 231 35 20S 142 50 E
Tyrrell Arm 77 62 27N 97 30W
Tyrrell L. 77 63 7N 105 27W
Tyrrhenian Sea 158 40 0N 12 30 E
Tysfjorden 174 68 7N 16 25 E
Tysnes 171 60 1N 5 30 E
Tysnesøy 171 60 0N 5 35 E
Tyssedal 171 60 7N 6 35 E
Tystberga 173 58 51N 17 15 E
Tyub Karagan, M. 181 44 40N 50 19 E
Tyuleniy 181 44 28N 47 30 E
Tyulgan 182 52 22N 56 12 E
Tyumen 182 57 11N 65 29 E
Tyumen-Aryk 183 44 2N 67 1 E
Tyup 183 42 45N 78 20 E
Tywi → 133 51 48N 4 20W
Tzaneen 255 23 47S 30 9 E
Tzermíadhes
Neápolis 170 35 11N 25 29 E
Tzimol 110 16 16N 92 16W
Tzintzuntzán 107 19 37N 101 35W
Tzitzio 107 19 34N 100 55W
Tzoumérka, Óros 168 39 30N 21 26 E
Tzucacab 111 20 4N 89 3W
Tzukong = Zigong 216 29 15N 104 48 E
Tzummarum 142 53 14N 5 32 E

U

U Taphao 204 12 35N 101 0 E
Uacalla Iero 256 1 48N 42 38 E
Uachadi, Sierra 119 4 54N 65 18W
Uad Erni, O. → 240 26 45N 10 47W
Uainambi 118 1 43N 69 51W
Uanda 230 21 37S 144 55 E
Uanle Uen 256 2 37N 44 54 E
Uarsciek 256 2 28N 45 55 E
Uascen 256 4 11N 43 13 E
Uasin □ 250 0 30N 35 20 E
Uato-Udo 207 9 7S 125 36 E
Uatumã → 119 2 26S 57 37W
Uauá 120 9 50S 39 28W
Uaupés 118 0 8S 67 5W
Uaxactún 112 17 25N 89 29W
Uayamón 111 19 39N 90 25W
Uayma 111 20 44N 88 19W
Ub 166 44 28N 20 6 E
Ubá 125 21 8S 43 0W
Ubaitaba 121 14 18S 39 20W
Ubangi =
Oubangi → 252 1 0N 17 50 E
Ubaté 118 5 19N 73 49W
Ubauro 198 28 15N 69 45 E
Ubay 211 10 3N 124 28 E
'Ubaydīyah 194 13 7N 43 20 E
Ubaye → 141 44 28N 6 18 E
Ube 220 33 56N 131 15 E
Ubeda 157 38 3N 3 23W
Uberaba 121 19 50S 47 55W
Uberaba, L. 123 17 30S 57 50W
Uberlândia 121 19 0S 48 20W
Überlingen 147 47 46N 9 10 E
Ubiaja 247 6 41N 6 22 E
Ubolratna Phong, L. 204 16 45N 102 30 E
Ubombo 255 27 31S 32 4 E
Ubon Ratchathani 204 15 15N 104 50 E
Ubondo 250 0 55S 25 42 E
Ubort → 178 52 6N 28 30 E
Ubrique 155 36 41N 5 27W
Ubundu 250 0 22S 25 30 E
Ucareo, Sa. de 107 19 48N 100 36W
Ucayali → 122 4 30S 73 30W
Uccle 143 50 48N 4 22 E
Uchaly 182 54 19N 59 27 E
Uchi Lake 86 51 5N 92 35W
Uchiko 220 33 33N 132 39 E
Uchiura-Wan 218 42 25N 140 40 E
Uchiza 122 8 25S 76 20W
Uchte 146 52 29N 8 52 E
Uchterek 183 41 45N 73 12 E
Uchur → 185 58 48N 130 35 E
Ucluelet 92 48 57N 125 32W
Ucu 111 21 2N 89 45W
Ucuriş 170 46 41N 21 58 E
Uda → 185 54 42N 135 14 E
Udaipur 198 24 36N 73 44 E
Udaipur Garhi 199 27 0N 86 35 E
Udbina 163 44 31N 15 47 E
Uddeholm 172 60 1N 13 38 E
Uddel 142 52 15N 5 48 E
Uddevalla 173 58 21N 11 55 E
Uddjaur 174 65 25N 21 15 E
Uden 143 51 40N 5 37 E
Udgir 200 18 25N 77 5 E
Udhampur 199 33 0N 75 5 E
Udi 247 6 23N 7 21 E
Údine 163 46 5N 13 10 E
Udmurt A.S.S.R. □ 182 57 30N 52 30 E
Udon Thani 204 17 29N 102 46 E
Udumalaippettai 201 10 35N 77 15 E
Udupi 201 13 25N 74 42 E
Udvoy Balkan 167 42 50N 26 50 E
Udzungwa Range 251 9 30S 35 10 E
Ueckermünde 146 53 45N 14 1 E
Ueda 221 36 24N 138 16 E
Uedineniya, Os. 12 78 0N 85 0 E
Uel Scimbirro 256 2 23N 44 14 E
Uelen 185 66 10N 170 0W
Uelzen 146 53 0N 10 33 E
Ueno 221 34 45N 136 8 E
Uere → 252 3 45N 24 45 E
Uetendorf 148 46 47N 7 34 E
Ufa 182 54 45N 55 55 E
Ufa → 182 54 40N 56 0 E
Uffenheim 147 49 32N 10 15 E
Ugab → 254 20 55S 14 30 E
Ugalla → 250 5 8S 30 42 E
Ugamskiy, Khrebet 183 42 20N 70 30 E
Uganda ■ 250 2 0N 32 0 E
Ugchelen 142 52 11N 5 56 E
Ugento 165 39 55N 18 10 E
Ugep 247 5 53N 8 2 E
Ugie 255 31 10S 28 13 E
Ugijar 157 36 58N 3 7W
Ugine 141 45 45N 6 25 E
Ugla 244 25 40N 37 42 E
Uglegorsk 185 49 5N 142 2 E
Uglich 179 57 33N 38 20 E
Ugljane 163 43 35N 16 46 E
Ugolyak 185 64 33N 120 30 E

Ugra → **178** 54 30N 36 7 E
Ugûn Mûsa **191** 29 53N 32 40 E
Ugŭrchin **167** 43 6N 24 26 E
Uh → **151** 48 7N 21 25 E
Uherske Hradiště **151** 49 4N 17 30 E
Uhersky Brod **151** 49 1N 17 40 E
Úhlava → **150** 49 45N 13 24 E
Uíge **253** 7 30 S 14 40 E
Uige □ **253** 7 0 S 16 0 E
Ŭijŏngbu **215** 37 48N 127 0 E
Ŭiju **215** 40 15N 124 35 E
Uitenhage **254** 33 40 S 25 28 E
Uitgeest **142** 52 32N 4 43 E
Uithoorn **142** 52 14N 4 50 E
Uithuizen **142** 53 24N 6 41 E
Uitkerke **143** 51 18N 3 9 E
Uivuk, C. **78** 58 29N 62 34W
Újfehértó **151** 47 49N 21 41 E
Ujh → **199** 32 40N 75 30 E
Ujhani **199** 28 0N 79 6 E
Uji **221** 34 53N 135 48 E
Uji-guntō **219** 31 15N 129 25 E
Ujjain **198** 23 9N 75 43 E
Újpest **151** 47 32N 19 6 E
Újszász **151** 47 19N 20 7 E
Ujung Pandang **207** 5 10 S 119 20 E
Uka **185** 57 50N 162 0 E
Ukara I. **250** 1 50 S 33 0 E
Uke-Shima **219** 28 2N 129 14 E
Ukerewe □ **250** 2 0 S 32 30 E
Ukerewe I. **250** 2 0 S 33 0 E
Ukholovo **179** 53 47N 40 30 E
Ukhrul **202** 25 10N 94 25 E
Ukhta **176** 63 55N 54 0 E
Ukki Fort **199** 33 28N 76 54 E
Ukmerge **178** 55 15N 24 45 E
Ukrainian S.S.R. □ **180** 49 0N 32 0 E
Uksyanskoye **182** 55 57N 63 1 E
Uku **253** 11 24 S 14 22 E
Ukwi **254** 23 29 S 20 30 E
Ulaanbaatar **212** 47 55N 106 53 E
Ulaangom **212** 50 0N 92 10 E
Ulamambri **233** 31 19 S 149 23 E
Ulamba **251** 9 3 S 23 38 E
Ulan Bator = Ulaanbaatar **212** 47 55N 106 53 E
Ulan Ude **185** 51 45N 107 40 E
Ulanbel **183** 44 50N 71 7 E
Ulanga □ **251** 8 40 S 36 50 E
Ulanów **152** 50 30N 22 16 E
Ulaya, Morogoro, Tanzania **250** 7 3 S 36 55 E
Ulaya, Tabora, Tanzania **250** 4 25 S 33 30 E
Ulcinj **166** 41 58N 19 10 E
Ulco **254** 28 21 S 24 15 E
Ulefoss **171** 59 17N 9 16 E
Ulëza **168** 41 46N 19 57 E
Ulfborg **173** 56 16N 8 20 E
Ulft **142** 51 53N 6 23 E
Ulhasnagar **200** 19 15N 73 10 E
Ulinda **233** 31 35 S 149 30 E
Uljma **166** 45 2N 21 10 E
Ulla → **154** 42 39N 8 44W
Ulladulla **231** 35 21 S 150 29 E
Ullånger **172** 62 58N 18 10 E
Ullapool **134** 57 54N 5 10W
Ullared **173** 57 8N 12 42 E
Ulldecona **156** 40 36N 0 20 E
Ullswater **132** 54 35N 2 52W
Ullung-do **215** 37 30N 130 30 E
Ulm **147** 48 23N 10 0 E
Ulmarra **231** 29 37 S 153 4 E
Ulmeni **170** 45 4N 26 40 E
Ulonguè **251** 14 37 S 34 19 E
Ulricehamn **173** 57 46N 13 26 E
Ulrum **142** 53 22N 6 20 E
Ulsan **215** 35 20N 129 15 E
Ulsberg **171** 62 45N 9 59 E
Ulsteinvik **171** 62 21N 5 53 E
Ulster □ **135** 54 35N 6 30W
Ulstrem **167** 42 1N 26 27 E
Ultima **232** 35 30 S 143 18 E
Ulubaria **199** 22 31N 88 4 E
Uluguru Mts. **250** 7 15 S 37 40 E
Ulungur He → **212** 47 1N 87 24 E
Ulutau **184** 48 39N 67 1 E
Ulvenhout **143** 51 33N 4 48 E
Ulverston **132** 54 13N 3 7W
Ulverstone **230** 41 11 S 146 11 E
Ulvik **171** 60 35N 6 54 E
Ulya **185** 59 10N 142 0 E
Ulyanovsk **179** 54 20N 48 25 E
Ulyasutay **212** 47 56N 97 28 E
Umag **163** 45 26N 13 31 E
Umala **122** 17 25 S 68 5W
Umán, Mexico **111** 20 53N 89 45W
Uman, U.S.S.R. **180** 48 40N 30 12 E
Umanak **95** 70 58N 52 0W
Umarkhed **200** 19 37N 77 46 E
Umatac **226** 13 18N 144 39 E
Umba **176** 66 50N 34 20 E
Umbertide **163** 43 18N 12 20 E
Umboi I. **227** 5 40 S 148 0 E
Umbrella Mts. **235** 45 35 S 169 5 E
Umbria □ **163** 42 53N 12 30 E
Ume älv → **174** 63 45N 20 20 E
Umeå **174** 63 45N 20 20 E
Umera **207** 0 12 S 129 37 E
Umfreville L. **86** 50 18N 94 45W
Umfuli → **251** 17 30 S 29 23 E
Umgusa **251** 19 29 S 27 52 E
Umi **220** 33 34N 130 30 E
Umka **166** 44 40N 20 19 E
Umkomaas **255** 30 13 S 30 48 E
Umm ad Daraj, J. **191** 32 18N 35 48 E
Umm al Arānib **241** 26 10N 14 43 E
Umm al Qaywayn **195** 25 30N 55 35 E
Umm al Qittayn **191** 32 18N 36 40 E
Umm Arda **245** 15 17N 32 31 E
Umm Bāb **195** 25 12N 50 48 E
Umm Bel **245** 13 35N 28 0 E
Umm Dubban **245** 15 23N 32 52 E
Umm el Fahm **189** 32 31N 35 9 E
Umm 'Isheirât, G. **191** 28 21N 34 18 E
Umm Koweika **245** 13 10N 32 16 E
Umm Lajj **192** 25 0N 37 23 E
Umm Merwa **244** 18 4N 32 30 E
Umm Qays **189** 32 40N 35 41 E
Umm Rumah **244** 25 50N 36 30 E
Umm Ruwaba **245** 12 50N 31 20 E
Umm Sidr **245** 14 29N 25 10 E
Umm Thalwīwah **194** 21 9N 40 48 E
Ummanz **146** 54 29N 13 9 E
Umniati → **251** 16 49 S 28 45 E
Umpulo **253** 12 38 S 17 42 E
Umred **198** 20 51N 79 18 E
Umreth **198** 22 41N 73 4 E
Umshandige Dam **251** 20 10 S 30 40 E
Umtata **255** 31 36 S 28 49 E
Umuahia **247** 5 33N 7 29 E
Umvukwe Ra. **251** 16 45 S 30 45 E
Umzimvubu **255** 31 38 S 29 33 E
Umzingwane → **251** 22 12 S 29 56 E
Umzinto **255** 30 15 S 30 45 E
Una **198** 20 46N 71 8 E
Una → **163** 45 16N 16 55 E
Unac → **163** 44 30N 16 9 E
Uncastillo **156** 42 21N 1 8W
Uncía **122** 18 25 S 66 40W
Unden **173** 58 45N 14 25 E
Underbool **231** 35 10 S 141 51 E
Undersaker **172** 63 19N 13 21 E
Undersvik **172** 61 36N 16 20 E
Undredal **171** 60 57N 7 6 E
Unecha **178** 52 50N 32 37 E
Uneiuxi → **118** 0 37 S 65 34W
Ungarie **231** 33 38 S 146 56 E
Ungarra **232** 34 12 S 136 2 E
Ungava B. **95** 59 30N 67 30W
Ungava Pen. **78** 60 0N 74 0W
Ungeny **180** 47 11N 27 51 E
Unggi **215** 42 16N 130 28 E
Ungwatiri **245** 16 52N 36 10 E
Uni **182** 56 44N 51 47 E
União da Vitória **125** 26 13 S 51 5W
União dos Palmares **120** 9 10 S 36 2W
Uniejów **152** 51 59N 18 46 E
Unije **163** 44 40N 14 15 E
Unini → **119** 1 41 S 61 31W
Unión, La, Chile **126** 40 10 S 73 0W
Unión, La, Colombia **118** 1 35N 77 5W
Unión, La, El Salv. **112** 13 20N 87 50W
Unión, La, Chiapas, Mexico **110** 16 21N 90 54W
Unión, La, Guerrero, Mexico **106** 17 58N 101 49W
Unión, La, Peru **122** 9 43 S 76 45W
Unión, La, Spain **157** 37 38N 0 53W
Union, La □ **210** 16 30N 120 25 E
Union Bay **92** 49 35N 124 53W
Unión de San Antonio **106** 21 6N 101 58W
Unión de Tula **106** 19 58N 104 16W
Union I. **92** 50 0N 127 16W
Union of Soviet Socialist Republics ■ **185** 60 0N 100 0 E
Uniondale **254** 33 39 S 23 7 E
Unirea **170** 44 15N 27 35 E
United Arab Emirates ■ **195** 23 50N 54 0 E
United Kingdom ■ **131** 55 0N 3 0W
United States Range **95** 82 25N 68 0W
United States Trust Terr. of the Pacific Is. **224** 10 0N 160 0 E
Unity **88** 52 30N 109 5W
Universales, Mtes. **156** 40 18N 1 33W
University → **87** 47 55N 85 12W
Unjha **198** 23 46N 72 24 E
Unnao **199** 26 35N 80 30 E
Uno, Ilha **246** 11 15N 16 13W
Unst **134** 60 50N 0 55W
Unstrut → **146** 51 10N 11 48 E
Unter-engadin **149** 46 48N 10 20 E
Unterägeri **149** 47 8N 8 36 E
Unterkulm **148** 47 18N 8 7 E
Unterseen **148** 46 41N 7 50 E
Unterwaldner Alpen **149** 46 55N 8 15 E
Unuk → **76** 56 5N 131 3W
Ünye **180** 41 5N 37 15 E
Unzen-Dake **220** 32 45N 130 17 E
Unzha **179** 58 0N 44 0 E
Unzha → **179** 57 30N 43 40 E
Uors **149** 46 42N 9 12 E
Uozu **221** 36 48N 137 24 E
Upa → **151** 50 35N 16 15 E
Upata **119** 8 1N 62 24W
Upemba, L. **251** 8 30 S 26 20 E
Upernavik **12** 72 49N 56 20W
Upington **254** 28 25 S 21 15 E
Upleta **198** 21 46N 70 16 E
Upper Arrow L. **93** 50 30N 117 50W
Upper Austria = Oberösterreich □ **150** 48 10N 14 0 E
Upper Blackville **81** 46 39N 65 52W
Upper Campbell L. **92** 49 55N 125 39W
Upper Foster L. **77** 56 47N 105 20W
Upper Goose L. **86** 51 43N 92 43W
Upper Humber → **79** 49 11N 57 28W
Upper Hutt **234** 41 8 S 175 5 E
Upper Juba □ **256** 3 0N 43 0 E
Upper L. Erne **135** 54 14N 7 22W
Upper Manilla **233** 30 38 S 150 40 E
Upper Manitou L. **86** 49 24N 92 48W
Upper Musquodoboit **81** 45 10N 62 58W
Upper Sheikh **256** 9 56N 45 13 E
Upper Stewiacke **81** 45 13N 63 0W
Upper Taimyr → **185** 74 15N 99 48 E
*Upper Volta ■ **246** 12 0N 1 0W
Upphärad **173** 58 9N 12 19 E
Uppsala **172** 59 53N 17 38 E
Uppsala län □ **172** 60 0N 17 30 E
Upsala **86** 49 3N 90 28W
Upshi **199** 33 48N 77 52 E
Upstart, C. **230** 19 41 S 147 45 E
Upton **83** 45 39N 72 41W
Ur **192** 30 55N 46 25 E
Ura-Tyube **183** 39 55N 69 1 E
Urabá, Golfo de **118** 8 25N 76 53W
Uracara **122** 2 20 S 57 50W
Urach **147** 48 29N 9 25 E
Urad Qianqi **214** 40 40N 108 30 E
Uraga-Suidō **221** 35 13N 139 45 E
Urakawa **218** 42 9N 142 47 E
Ural → **182** 47 0N 51 48 E
Ural, Mt. **231** 33 21 S 146 12 E
Ural Mts. = Uralskie Gory **176** 60 0N 59 0 E
Uralla **231** 30 37 S 151 29 E
Uralsk **182** 51 20N 51 20 E
Uralskie Gory **176** 60 0N 59 0 E
Urambo **250** 5 4 S 32 0 E
Urambo □ **250** 5 0 S 32 0 E
Urana **233** 35 15 S 146 21 E
Urandangi **230** 21 32 S 138 14 E
Uranium City **77** 59 34N 108 37W
Uranquinty **231** 35 10 S 147 12 E
Uraricaá → **119** 3 20N 61 56W
Uraricuera → **119** 3 2N 60 30W
Uravakonda **201** 14 57N 77 12 E
Urawa **221** 35 50N 139 40 E
Uray **184** 60 5N 65 15 E
Uray'irah **193** 25 57N 48 53 E
Urbana, La **118** 7 8N 66 56W
Urbánia **163** 43 40N 12 31 E
Urbano Santos **120** 3 12 S 43 23W
Urbel → **156** 42 21N 3 40W
Urbino **163** 43 43N 12 38 E
Urbión, Picos de **156** 42 1N 2 52W
Urcos **122** 13 40 S 71 38W
Urda, Spain **155** 39 25N 3 43W
Urda, U.S.S.R. **181** 48 52N 47 23 E
Urdaneta **210** 15 59N 120 34 E
Urdinarrain **124** 32 37 S 58 52W
Urdos **140** 42 51N 0 35W
Urdzhar **184** 47 5N 81 38 E
Ure → **132** 54 20N 1 25W
Uren **179** 57 35N 45 55 E
Urengoy **184** 65 58N 28 25 E
Ures **100** 29 26N 110 24W
Ureshino **220** 33 6N 129 59 E
Urfa **177** 37 12N 38 50 E
Urfahr **150** 48 19N 14 17 E
Urgench **184** 41 40N 60 41 E
Urgut **183** 39 23N 67 15 E
Uri **199** 34 8N 74 2 E
Uri □ **149** 46 43N 8 35 E
Uriangato **107** 20 9N 101 11W
Uribante → **118** 7 25N 71 50W
Uribe **118** 3 13N 74 24W
Uribia **118** 11 43N 72 16W
Urim **189** 31 18N 34 32 E
Uriondo **124** 21 41 S 64 41W
Urique **101** 27 13N 107 55W
Urique → **101** 26 29N 107 58W
Urirotstock **149** 46 52N 8 32 E
Urk **142** 52 39N 5 36 E
Urlati **170** 44 59N 26 15 E
Urmia = Orūmīyeh **192** 37 40N 45 0 E
Urmia, L. = Orūmīyeh, Daryācheh-ye **192** 37 50N 45 30 E
Urner Alpen **149** 46 45N 8 45 E
Uroševac **166** 42 23N 21 10 E
Urrao **118** 6 20N 76 11W
Urshult **173** 56 31N 14 50 E
Ursula Chan. **92** 53 25N 128 55W
Ursulo Galván **108** 19 24N 96 21W
Ursus **152** 52 12N 20 53 E
Uruáchic **101** 27 52N 108 14W
Uruaçu **121** 14 30 S 49 10W
Uruana **121** 15 30 S 49 41W
Uruapan del Progreso **106** 19 25N 102 58W
Uruará → **119** 2 6 S 53 38W
Urubamba **122** 13 20 S 72 10W
Urubamba → **122** 10 43 S 73 48W
Urubaxi → **119** 0 31 S 64 50W
Urubu → **119** 2 55 S 58 25W
Uruçara **119** 2 32 S 57 45W
Uruçuí **120** 7 20 S 44 28W
Uruçuí, Serra do **120** 9 0 S 44 45W
Uruçuí Prêto → **120** 7 20 S 44 38W
Urucuia → **121** 16 8 S 45 5W
Urucurituba **119** 2 41 S 57 40W
Uruguai → **125** 26 0 S 53 30W
Uruguaiana **124** 29 50 S 57 0W
Uruguay ■ **124** 32 30 S 56 30W
Uruguay → **124** 34 12 S 58 18W
Urukthapel I. **226** 7 17N 134 25 E
Ürümqi **212** 43 45N 87 45 E
Urup → **181** 46 0N 41 10 E
Urup, Os. **185** 46 0N 151 0 E
Urutaí **121** 17 28 S 48 12W
Uryung-Khaya **185** 72 48N 113 23 E
Uryupinsk **179** 50 45N 41 58 E
Urzhum **179** 57 10N 49 56 E
Urziceni **170** 44 40N 26 42 E
Usa **220** 33 31N 131 21 E
Usa → **176** 65 57N 56 55 E
Uşak **177** 38 43N 29 28 E
Usakos **254** 22 0 S 15 31 E
Usborne, Mt. **126** 51 42 S 58 50W
Ušće **166** 43 30N 20 39 E
Usedom **146** 53 50N 13 55 E
Usfan **194** 21 58N 39 27 E
Ush-Tobe **184** 45 16N 78 0 E
Ushakova, O. **12** 82 0N 80 0 E
Ushant = Ouessant, Île d' **138** 48 28N 5 6W
Ushashi **250** 1 59 S 33 57 E
Ushat **245** 7 59N 29 28 E
Ushibuka **220** 32 11N 130 1 E
Ushuaia **126** 54 50 S 68 23W
Ushumun **185** 52 47N 126 32 E
Usk → **133** 51 37N 2 56W
Uskedal **171** 59 56N 5 53 E
Üsküdar **177** 41 0N 29 5 E
Uslar **146** 51 39N 9 39 E
Usmajac **106** 19 52N 103 34W
Usman **179** 52 5N 39 48 E
Usoke **250** 5 7 S 32 19 E
Usolye **182** 59 28N 56 31 E
Usolye Sibirskoye **185** 52 48N 103 40 E
Usoro **247** 5 33N 6 11 E
Uspallata, P. de **124** 32 37 S 69 22W
Uspanapa → **109** 17 58N 94 29W
Uspenskiy **184** 48 41N 72 43 E
Uspero **106** 19 2N 102 16W
Usquert **142** 53 24N 6 36 E
Ussel **140** 45 32N 2 18 E
Ussuri → **218** 48 27N 135 0 E
Ussuriysk **185** 43 48N 131 59 E
Ussurka **218** 45 12N 133 31 E
Ust-Aldan = Batamay **185** 63 30N 129 15 E
Ust Amginskoye = Khandyga **185** 62 42N 135 35 E
Ust-Bolsheretsk **185** 52 50N 156 15 E
Ust Buzulukskaya **179** 50 8N 42 11 E
Ust chaun **185** 68 47N 170 30 E
Ust-Donetskiy **181** 47 35N 40 55 E
Ust'-Ilga **185** 55 5N 104 55 E
Ust Ilimpeya = Yukti **185** 63 26N 105 42 E
Ust-Ilimsk **185** 58 3N 102 39 E
Ust Ishim **184** 57 45N 71 10 E
Ust-Kamchatsk **185** 56 10N 162 28 E
Ust-Kamenogorsk **184** 50 0N 82 36 E
Ust-Karenga **185** 54 25N 116 30 E
Ust Khayryuzova **185** 57 15N 156 45 E
Ust-Kut **185** 56 50N 105 42 E
Ust Kuyga **185** 70 1N 135 43 E
Ust-Labinsk **181** 45 15N 39 41 E
Ust Luga **178** 59 35N 28 20 E
Ust Maya **185** 60 30N 134 28 E
Ust-Mil **185** 59 40N 133 11 E
Ust-Nera **185** 64 35N 143 15 E
Ust-Nyukzha **185** 56 34N 121 37 E
Ust Olenek **185** 73 0N 119 48 E
Ust-Omchug **185** 61 9N 149 38 E
Ust Port **184** 69 40N 84 26 E

* *Renamed Burkina Faso*

Ust Tsilma **176** 65 25N 52 0 E
Ust-Tungir **185** 55 25N 120 36 E
Ust Urt = Ustyurt, Plato **184** 44 0N 55 0 E
Ust Usa **176** 66 0N 56 30 E
Ust-Uyskoye **182** 54 16N 63 54 E
Ust Vorkuta **184** 67 24N 64 0 E
Ustaoset **171** 60 30N 8 2 E
Ustaritz **140** 43 24N 1 27W
Uste **179** 59 35N 39 40 E
Uster **149** 47 22N 8 43 E
Ústí nad Labem **150** 50 41N 14 3 E
Ústí nad Orlicí **151** 49 58N 16 24 E
Ustica **164** 38 42N 13 10 E
Ustinov **182** 56 51N 53 14 E
Ustroń **151** 49 43N 18 48 E
Ustrzyki Dolne **152** 49 27N 22 40 E
Ustye **185** 57 46N 94 37 E
Ustyurt, Plato **184** 44 0N 55 0 E
Ustyuzhna **179** 58 50N 36 32 E
Usu **212** 44 27N 84 40 E
Usuki **220** 33 8N 131 49 E
Usulután **112** 13 25N 88 28W
Usumacinta → **110** 18 24N 92 38W
Usumbura = Bujumbura **250** 3 16 S 29 18 E
Usure **250** 4 40 S 34 22 E
Usva **182** 58 41N 57 37 E
Uta **207** 4 33 S 136 0 E
Utena **178** 55 27N 25 40 E
Ütersen **146** 53 40N 9 40 E
Utete **250** 8 0 S 38 45 E
Uthai Thani **204** 15 22N 100 3 E
Uthal **198** 25 44N 66 40 E
Utiariti **123** 13 0 S 58 10W
Utiel **156** 39 37N 1 11W
Utik L. **77** 55 15N 96 0W
Utikuma L. **90** 55 50N 115 30W
Utinga **121** 12 6 S 41 5W
Uto **220** 32 41N 130 40 E
Utrecht, Neth. **142** 52 5N 5 8 E
Utrecht, S. Africa **255** 27 38 S 30 20 E
Utrecht □ **142** 52 6N 5 7 E
Utrera **155** 37 12N 5 48W
Utsjoki **174** 69 51N 26 59 E
Utsunomiya **221** 36 30N 139 50 E
Uttar Pradesh □ **199** 27 0N 80 0 E
Uttaradit **204** 17 36N 100 5 E
Uttoxeter **132** 52 53N 1 50W
Utva → **182** 51 28N 52 40 E
Ütze **146** 52 28N 10 11 E
Uusikaupunki **175** 60 47N 21 25 E
Uva **182** 56 59N 52 13 E
Uvá → **118** 3 41N 70 3W
Uvac → **166** 43 35N 19 40 E
Uvarovo **179** 51 59N 42 14 E
Uvat **184** 59 5N 68 50 E
Uvelskiy **182** 54 26N 61 22 E
Uvinza **250** 5 5 S 30 24 E
Uvira **250** 3 22 S 29 3 E
Uvs Nuur **212** 50 20N 92 30 E
Uwa **220** 33 22N 132 31 E
Uwajima **220** 33 10N 132 35 E
'Uwayfi **195** 22 15N 56 59 E
Uweinat, Jebel **244** 21 54N 24 58 E
Uxbridge **84** 44 6N 79 7W
Uxin Qi **214** 38 50N 109 5 E
Uxmal, Ruinas **111** 20 22N 89 46W
Uyandi **185** 69 19N 141 0 E
Uyo **247** 5 1N 7 53 E
Uyu → **202** 24 51N 94 57 E
Uyuk **183** 43 36N 71 16 E
Uyuni **122** 20 28 S 66 47W
Uzbek S.S.R. □ **183** 41 30N 65 0 E
Uzen **177** 43 27N 53 10 E
Uzen, Bol. → **179** 50 0N 49 30 E
Uzen, Mal. → **179** 50 0N 48 30 E
Uzerche **140** 45 25N 1 34 E
Uzès **141** 44 1N 4 26 E
Uzgen **183** 40 46N 73 18 E
Uzh → **178** 51 15N 30 12 E
Uzhgorod **178** 48 36N 22 18 E
Uzlovaya **179** 54 0N 38 5 E
Uzun-Agach **183** 43 35N 76 20 E
Uzunköprü **167** 41 16N 26 43 E
Uzwil **149** 47 26N 9 9 E

V

V. Carranza, Presa **102** 27 30N 100 37W
Vaal → **254** 29 4 S 23 38 E
Vaaldam **255** 27 0 S 28 14 E
Vaals **143** 50 46N 6 1 E
Vaalwater **255** 24 15 S 28 8 E
Vaasa **174** 63 6N 21 38 E
Vaasan lääni □ **174** 63 2N 22 50 E
Vaassen **142** 52 17N 5 58 E
Vabre **140** 43 42N 2 24 E
Vác **151** 47 49N 19 10 E
Vacaria **125** 28 31 S 50 52W
Vaccarès, Étang de **141** 43 32N 4 34 E
Vach → **184** 60 45N 76 45 E
Vache, Î.-à- **113** 18 2N 73 35W
Väddö **172** 59 55N 18 50 E
Vadnagar **198** 23 47N 72 40 E
Vado Lígure **162** 44 16N 8 26 E
Vadodara **198** 22 20N 73 10 E
Vadsø **174** 70 3N 29 50 E
Vadstena **173** 58 28N 14 54 E
Vaduz **149** 47 8N 9 31 E
Værøy **174** 67 40N 12 40 E
Vagney **139** 48 1N 6 43 E
Vagnhärad **172** 58 57N 17 33 E
Vagos **154** 40 33N 8 42W
Váh → **151** 47 55N 18 0 E
Vahsel B. **13** 75 0 S 35 0W
Vaigach **184** 70 10N 59 0 E
Vaigai → **201** 9 15N 79 10 E
Vaiges **138** 48 2N 0 30W
Vaihingen **147** 48 55N 8 58 E
Vaijapur **200** 19 58N 74 45 E
Vaikam **201** 9 45N 76 25 E
Vailly Aisne **139** 49 25N 3 30 E
Vainillas, L. **110** 15 14N 92 53W
Vaippar → **201** 9 0N 78 25 E
Vaison **141** 44 14N 5 4 E
Vaitogi **226** 14 21 S 170 44W
Vajpur **198** 21 24N 73 17 E
Vakarel **167** 42 35N 23 40 E
Vakhsh → **183** 37 6N 68 18 E
Vaksdal **171** 60 29N 5 45 E
Vál **151** 47 22N 18 40 E
Val-Alain **83** 46 24N 71 45W
Val-Barrette **82** 46 30N 75 21W
Val Brillant **80** 48 32N 67 33W
Val Caron **84** 46 37N 81 1W
Val-d'Ajol, Le **139** 47 55N 6 30 E
Val-de-Marne □ **139** 48 45N 2 28 E
Val-des-Bois **82** 45 54N 75 35W
Val-d'Espoir **80** 48 31N 64 24W
Val-d'Oise □ **139** 49 5N 2 10 E
Val d'Or **82** 48 7N 77 47W
Val Marie **88** 49 15N 107 45W
Valadares **154** 41 5N 8 38W
Valadeces **102** 26 14N 98 40W
Valahia **170** 44 35N 25 0 E
Valais □ **148** 46 12N 7 45 E
Valais, Alpes du **148** 46 5N 7 35 E
Valandovo **166** 41 19N 22 34 E
Valašské Meziříčí **151** 49 29N 17 59 E
Valáxa **169** 38 50N 24 29 E
Vălcani **166** 46 0N 20 26 E
Valcheta **126** 40 40 S 66 8W
Valcourt **83** 45 29N 72 18W
Valdagno **163** 45 38N 11 18 E
Valdahon, Le **139** 47 8N 6 20 E
Valday **178** 57 58N 33 9 E
Valdayskaya Vozvyshennost **178** 57 0N 33 30 E
Valdeazogues → **155** 38 45N 4 55W
Valdemarsvik **173** 58 14N 16 40 E
Valdepeñas, Ciudad Real, Spain **155** 38 43N 3 25W
Valdepeñas, Jaén, Spain **155** 37 33N 3 47W
Valderaduey → **154** 41 31N 5 42W
Valderrobres **156** 40 53N 0 9 E
Valdés, Pen. **126** 42 30 S 63 45W
Valdes I. **93** 49 4N 123 39W
Valdez **118** 1 15N 79 0W
Valdivia, Chile **126** 39 50 S 73 14W
Valdivia, Colombia **118** 7 11N 75 27W
Valdivia □ **126** 40 0 S 73 0W
Valdobbiádene **163** 45 53N 12 0 E
Valdoviño **154** 43 36N 8 8W
Valdres **171** 60 55N 9 28 E
Vale **181** 41 30N 42 58 E
Valea lui Mihai **170** 47 32N 22 11 E
Valemount **93** 52 50N 119 15W
Valença, Brazil **121** 13 20 S 39 5W
Valença, Portugal **154** 42 1N 8 34W
Valença do Piauí **120** 6 20 S 41 45W
Valençay **139** 47 9N 1 34 E
Valence **141** 44 57N 4 54 E
Valence-d'Agen **140** 44 8N 0 54 E
Valencia, Phil. **211** 7 57N 125 3 E
Valencia, Spain **157** 39 27N 0 23W
Valencia, Venezuela **118** 10 11N 68 0W
Valencia □ **157** 39 20N 0 40W
Valencia, Albufera de **157** 39 20N 0 27W
Valencia, G. de **157** 39 30N 0 20 E
Valencia de Alcántara **155** 39 25N 7 14W
Valencia de Don Juan **154** 42 17N 5 31W
Valencia del Ventoso **155** 38 15N 6 29W
Valenciennes **139** 50 20N 3 34 E
Văleni **170** 44 15N 24 45 E
Valensole **141** 43 50N 5 59 E
Valentia Hr. **135** 51 56N 10 17W
Valentia I. **135** 51 54N 10 22W
Valentim, Sa. do **120** 6 0 S 43 30W
Valentin **218** 43 8N 134 17 E
Valenza **162** 45 2N 8 39 E
Våler **171** 60 41N 11 50 E
Valera **118** 9 19N 70 37W
Valerio **101** 27 39N 106 6W
Valga **178** 57 44N 26 0 E
Valguarnera Caropepe **165** 37 30N 14 22 E
Valinco, G. de **141** 41 40N 8 52 E
Valjevo **166** 44 18N 19 53 E
Valkenburg **143** 50 52N 5 50 E
Valkenswaard **143** 51 21N 5 29 E
Vall de Uxó **156** 39 49N 0 15W
Valla **172** 59 2N 16 20 E
Valladares **102** 26 53N 100 37W
Valladolid, Mexico **111** 20 41N 88 12W
Valladolid, Spain **154** 41 38N 4 43W
Valladolid □ **154** 41 38N 4 43W
Vallata **165** 41 3N 15 16 E
Valldemosa **156** 39 43N 2 37 E
Valle **171** 59 13N 7 33 E
Valle d'Aosta □ **162** 45 45N 7 22 E
Valle de Arán **156** 42 50N 0 55 E
Valle de Banderas **104** 20 49N 105 17W
Valle de Bravo **107** 19 11N 100 8W
Valle de Bravo, Presa **107** 19 10N 100 8W
Valle de Cabuérniga **154** 43 14N 4 18W
Valle de Guadalupe **106** 21 0N 102 37W
Valle de la Pascua **118** 9 13N 66 0W
Valle de las Palmas **98** 32 23N 116 47W
Valle de Olivos **101** 27 12N 106 17W
Valle de Santiago **107** 20 23N 101 12W
Valle de Suchil **105** 23 39N 103 54W
Valle de Topia **104** 25 13N 106 25W
Valle de Zaragoza **101** 27 28N 105 49W
Valle del Cauca □ **118** 3 45N 76 30W
Valle del Rosario **101** 27 19N 106 18W
Valle Fértil, Sierra del **124** 30 20 S 68 0W
Valle Hermoso **102** 25 41N 97 48W
Vallecas **154** 40 23N 3 41W
Vallecillo **102** 26 40N 99 58W
Valledupar **118** 10 29N 73 15W
Vallée-Jonction **83** 46 22N 70 55W
Vallejo **103** 23 7N 100 33W
Vallejo, Sa. de **104** 20 54N 105 17W
Vallenar **124** 28 30 S 70 50W
Valleraugue **140** 44 6N 3 39 E
Vallet **138** 47 10N 1 15W
Valletta **160** 35 54N 14 30 E
Valleyview, Alta., Canada **90** 55 5N 117 17W
Valleyview, B.C., Canada **93** 50 10N 120 13W
Valli di Comácchio **163** 44 40N 12 15 E
Vallimanca, Arroyo **124** 35 40 S 59 10W
Vallo della Lucánia **165** 40 14N 15 16 E
Vallon **141** 44 25N 4 23 E
Vallorbe **148** 46 42N 6 20 E
Valls **156** 41 18N 1 15 E
Vallsta **172** 61 31N 16 22 E
Valmaseda **156** 43 11N 3 12W
Valmiera **178** 57 37N 25 29 E
Valmont **138** 49 45N 0 30 E
Valmontone **164** 41 48N 12 55 E
Valmy **139** 49 5N 4 45 E
Valnera, Mte. **156** 43 9N 3 40W
Valognes **138** 49 30N 1 28W
Valona = Vlóra **168** 40 32N 19 28 E
Valongo **154** 41 8N 8 30W
Valora **86** 49 46N 91 13W
Valpaços **154** 41 36N 7 17W
Valparaíso, Chile **124** 33 2 S 71 40W
Valparaíso, Mexico **105** 22 46N 103 34W
Valparaíso □ **124** 33 2 S 71 40W
Valparaíso, Sa. **105** 23 0N 103 40W
Valpovo **166** 45 39N 18 25 E
Valréas **141** 44 24N 5 0 E
Valrita **87** 49 27N 82 33W
Vals **149** 46 39N 9 11 E
Vals → **254** 27 23 S 26 30 E
Vals, Tanjung **207** 8 26 S 137 25 E
Vals-les-Bains **141** 44 42N 4 24 E
Valsad **198** 20 40N 72 58 E
Valsbaai **254** 34 15 S 18 40 E
Valsequillo, Presa **109** 18 55N 98 10W
Valskog **172** 59 27N 15 57 E
Válta **168** 40 3N 23 25 E
Valtellina **162** 46 9N 9 55 E
Valuyki **179** 50 10N 38 5 E
Valverde del Camino **155** 37 35N 6 47W
Valverde del Fresno **154** 40 15N 6 51W
Vama **170** 47 34N 25 42 E
Vámos **169** 35 24N 24 13 E
Vamsadhara → **200** 18 21N 84 8 E
Van **177** 38 30N 43 0 E
Van Bruyssel **83** 47 56N 72 9W
Van Buren **81** 47 10N 67 55W
Van Canh **204** 13 37N 109 0 E
Van der Kloof Dam **254** 30 4 S 24 40 E
Van Diemen, C., N. Terr., Australia **228** 11 9 S 130 24 E
Van Diemen, C., Queens., Australia **230** 16 30 S 139 46 E
Van Diemen G. **228** 11 45 S 132 0 E
Van Gölü **177** 38 30N 43 0 E
Van Ninh **204** 12 42N 109 14 E
Van Reenen P. **255** 28 22 S 29 27 E
Van Rees, Pegunungan **207** 2 35 S 138 15 E
Van Tivu **201** 8 51N 78 15 E
Van Yen **204** 21 4N 104 42 E
Vananda **92** 49 46N 124 33W
Vanavara **185** 60 22N 102 16 E
Vancouver **93** 49 15N 123 10W
Vancouver, C. **229** 35 2 S 118 11 E
Vancouver I. **92** 49 50N 126 0W
Vancouver I. Ranges **92** 49 30N 125 40W
Vandavasi **201** 12 30N 79 30 E
Vandeloos Bay **201** 8 0N 81 45 E
Vanderbijlpark **255** 26 42 S 27 54 E
Vanderhoof **92** 54 0N 124 0W
Vanderlin I. **230** 15 44 S 137 2 E
Vandry **83** 47 52N 73 34W
Vandyke **230** 24 10 S 147 51 E
Vanegas **103** 23 52N 100 57W
Vänern **173** 58 47N 13 30 E
Vänersborg **173** 58 26N 12 19 E
Vang Vieng **204** 18 58N 102 32 E
Vanga **250** 4 35 S 39 12 E
Vangaindrano **255** 23 21 S 47 36 E
Vanguard **88** 49 55N 107 20W
Vanier **85** 45 27N 75 40W
Vanimo **227** 2 42 S 141 21 E
Vanivilasa Sagara **201** 13 45N 76 30 E
Vaniyambadi **201** 12 46N 78 44 E
Vankarem **185** 67 51N 175 50 E
Vankleek Hill **85** 45 32N 74 40W
Vanna **174** 70 6N 19 50 E
Vännäs **174** 63 58N 19 48 E
Vannes **138** 47 40N 2 47W
Vanoise, Massif de la **141** 45 25N 6 40 E
Vanrhynsdorp **254** 31 36 S 18 44 E
Vanrook **230** 16 57 S 141 57 E
Vans, Les **141** 44 25N 4 7 E
Vansbro **172** 60 32N 14 15 E
Vanscoy **88** 52 0N 106 59W
Vanse **171** 58 6N 6 41 E
Vansittart B. **228** 14 3 S 126 17 E
Vansittart I. **95** 65 50N 84 0W
Vanthli **198** 21 28N 70 25 E
Vanua Levu **224** 16 33 S 179 15 E
Vanuatu ■ **224** 15 0 S 168 0 E
Vanwyksvlei **254** 30 18 S 21 49 E
Vanylven **171** 62 5N 5 33 E
Vapnyarka **180** 48 32N 28 45 E
Vaquería **103** 25 8N 99 3W
Var □ **141** 43 27N 6 18 E
Var → **141** 43 39N 7 12 E
Vara **173** 58 16N 12 55 E
Varada → **201** 15 0N 75 40 E
Varades **138** 47 25N 1 1W
Varaita → **162** 44 49N 7 36 E
Varaldsøy **171** 60 6N 5 59 E
Varallo **162** 45 50N 8 13 E
Varanasi **199** 25 22N 83 0 E
Varangerfjorden **174** 70 3N 29 25 E
Varaždin **163** 46 20N 16 20 E
Varazze **162** 44 21N 8 36 E
Varberg **173** 57 6N 12 20 E
Vardar → **166** 40 35N 22 50 E
Varde **173** 55 38N 8 29 E
Varde Å **173** 55 35N 8 19 E
Varel **146** 53 23N 8 9 E
Varella, Mui **204** 12 54N 109 26 E
Varena **178** 54 12N 24 30 E
Varennes-sur-Allier **140** 46 19N 3 24 E
Vareš **166** 44 12N 18 23 E
Varese **162** 45 49N 8 50 E
Varese Lígure **162** 44 22N 9 33 E
Vårgårda **173** 58 2N 12 49 E
Vargem Bonita **121** 20 20 S 46 22W
Vargem Grande **120** 3 33 S 43 56W
Varginha **125** 21 33 S 45 25W
Vargön **173** 58 22N 12 20 E
Varhaug **171** 58 37N 5 41 E
Varillas **124** 24 0 S 70 10W
Våring **173** 58 30N 14 0 E
Värmeln **172** 59 35N 12 54 E
Värmlands län □ **172** 60 0N 13 20 E
Varna, Bulgaria **167** 43 13N 27 56 E
Varna, U.S.S.R. **182** 53 24N 60 58 E
Varna → **200** 16 48N 74 32 E
Värnamo **173** 57 10N 14 3 E
Varnsdorf **150** 50 55N 14 35 E
Värö **173** 57 16N 12 11 E
Vars **85** 45 21N 75 21W
Varsseveld **142** 51 56N 6 29 E
Varteig **171** 59 23N 11 12 E
Varvarin **166** 43 43N 21 20 E
Varzaneh **193** 32 25N 52 40 E
Várzea Alegre **120** 6 47 S 39 17W
Várzea da Palma **121** 17 36 S 44 44W
Várzea Grande **123** 15 39 S 56 8W

Varzi .... 162 44 50N 9 12 E
Varzo .... 162 46 12N 8 15 E
Varzy .... 139 47 22N 3 20 E
Vas □ .... 151 47 10N 16 55 E
Vasa .... 174 63 6N 21 38 E
Vasa Barris → .... 120 11 10 S 37 10W
Vásárosnamény .... 151 48 9N 22 19 E
Vascão → 155 37 31N 7 31W
Vaşcău .... 170 46 28N 22 30 E
Vascongadas 156 42 50N 2 45W
Väse .... 172 59 23N 13 52 E
Vāshīr .... 197 32 16N 63 51 E
Vasht = Khāsh .... 193 28 15N 61 15 E
Vasilevichi .... 178 52 15N 29 50 E
Vasilikón .... 169 38 25N 23 40 E
Vasilkov .... 178 50 7N 30 15 E
Vaslui .... 170 46 38N 27 42 E
Vaslui □ .... 170 46 30N 27 45 E
Väsman .... 172 60 9N 15 5 E
Vassar 89 49 10N 95 55W
Västerås .... 173 59 37N 16 38 E
Västerbottens län □ 174 64 58N 18 0 E
Västernorrlands län □ .... 172 63 30N 17 30 E
Västervik .... 173 57 43N 16 43 E
Västmanlands län □ 172 59 45N 16 20 E
Vasto .... 163 42 8N 14 40 E
Vasvár .... 151 47 3N 16 47 E
Vatan .... 139 47 4N 1 50 E
Vathí, Itháki, Greece .... 169 38 18N 20 40 E
Vathí, Sámos, Greece .... 169 37 46N 27 1 E
Váthia .... 169 36 29N 22 29 E
Vatican City ■ .... 163 41 54N 12 27 E
Vaticano, C. .... 164 38 40N 15 48 E
Vatili .... 190 35 6N 33 40 E
Vatin .... 166 45 12N 21 20 E
Vatnajökull 174 64 30N 16 48W
Vatnås .... 171 59 58N 9 37 E
Vatne .... 171 62 33N 6 38 E
Vatneyri 174 65 35N 24 0W
Vatoloha, Mt. .... 255 17 52 S 47 48 E
Vatomandry .... 255 19 20 S 48 59 E
Vatra-Dornei .... 170 47 22N 25 22 E
Vättern .... 173 58 25N 14 30 E
Vättis .... 149 46 55N 9 27 E
Vatulele .... 226 18 33 S 177 37 E
Vaucluse □ .... 141 44 3N 5 10 E
Vaucouleurs .... 139 48 37N 5 40 E
Vaud □ .... 148 46 35N 6 30 E
Vaulruz .... 148 46 38N 7 0 E
Vaupe □ 118 1 0N 71 0W
Vaupés → 118 0 2N 67 16W
Vauvert .... 141 43 42N 4 17 E
Vauxhall 91 50 5N 112 9W
Vavenby 93 51 36N 119 43W
Vavincourt .... 139 48 49N 5 12 E
Vavoua 246 7 23N 6 29W
Vaxholm .... 172 59 25N 18 20 E
Växjö .... 173 56 52N 14 50 E
Vaygach, Ostrov .. 184 70 0N 60 0 E
Vazovgrad .... 167 42 39N 24 45 E
Veadeiros .... 121 14 7 S 47 31W
Vechta .... 146 52 47N 8 18 E
Vechte → .... 142 52 34N 6 6 E
Vecilla, La 154 42 51N 5 27W
Vecsés .... 151 47 26N 19 19 E
Vedaranniyam .... 201 10 25N 79 50 E
Veddige .... 173 57 17N 12 20 E
Vedea → .... 170 44 0N 25 20 E
Vedia .... 124 34 30 S 61 31W
Vedra, I. del .... 157 38 52N 1 12 E
Vedrin .... 143 50 30N 4 52 E
Veendam .... 142 53 5N 6 52 E
Veenendaal .... 142 52 2N 5 34 E
Veerle .... 143 51 4N 4 59 E
Vefsna → .... 174 65 48N 13 10 E
Vega .... 174 65 40N 11 55 E
Vega, La, Dom. Rep. 113 19 20N 70 30W
Vega, La, Mexico .. 106 20 35N 103 51W
Vega, La, Peru .... 122 10 41 S 77 44W
Vega de Alatorre ... 108 20 2N 96 38W
Vegadeo 154 43 27N 7 4W
Vegafjorden .... 174 65 37N 12 0 E
Vegesack .... 146 53 10N 8 38 E
Veggli .... 171 60 3N 9 9 E
Veghel .... 143 51 37N 5 32 E
Vegorritis, Límni ... 168 40 45N 21 45 E
Vegreville 90 53 30N 112 5W
Vegusdal .... 171 58 32N 8 10 E
Veii .... 163 42 0N 12 24 E
Veitch .... 232 34 39 S 140 31 E
Vejen .... 173 55 30N 9 9 E
Vejer de la Frontera 155 36 15N 5 59W
Vejle .... 173 55 43N 9 30 E
Vejle Fjord .... 173 55 40N 9 50 E
Vela, La 118 11 27N 69 34W
Vela Luka .... 163 42 59N 16 44 E
Velanai I. .... 201 9 45N 79 45 E
Velardeña 105 25 4N 103 44W
Velas, C. 112 10 21N 85 52W
Velasco, Sierra de .. 124 29 20 S 67 10W
Velay, Mts. du .... 140 45 0N 3 40 E
Velddrif .... 254 32 42 S 18 11 E
Veldegem .... 143 51 7N 3 10 E
Velden .... 143 51 25N 6 10 E
Veldhoven .... 143 51 24N 5 25 E
Velebit Planina .... 163 44 50N 15 20 E
Velebitski Kanal ... 163 44 45N 14 55 E
Veleka → .... 167 42 4N 27 58 E
Velenje .... 163 46 23N 15 8 E
Velestínon .... 168 39 23N 22 43 E
Veleta, La 155 37 1N 3 22W
Vélez, Colombia ... 118 6 1N 73 41W
Velež, Yugoslavia .. 166 43 19N 18 2 E
Vélez Blanco 157 37 41N 2 5W
Vélez Málaga 155 36 48N 4 5W
Vélez Rubio 157 37 41N 2 5W
Velhas → .... 121 17 13 S 44 49W
Velika .... 166 45 27N 17 40 E
Velika Gorica .... 163 45 44N 16 5 E
Velika Gradište .... 166 44 46N 21 29 E
Velika Kapela .... 163 45 10N 15 5 E
Velika Kladuša .... 163 45 11N 15 48 E
Velika Morava → .166 44 43N 21 3 E
Velika Plana .... 166 44 20N 21 1 E
Velikaya → .... 178 57 48N 28 20 E
Velikaya Kema .... 218 45 30N 137 12 E
Velikaya Lepetikha .180 47 2N 33 58 E
Veliké Kapušany ... 151 48 34N 22 5 E
Velike Lašče .... 163 45 49N 14 45 E
Veliki Backa Kanal .166 45 45N 19 15 E
Veliki Jastrebac .... 166 43 25N 21 30 E
Veliki Popović .... 166 44 8N 21 18 E
Veliki Ustyug .... 176 60 47N 46 20 E
Velikiye Luki .... 178 56 25N 30 32 E
Velikonda Range ... 201 14 45N 79 10 E
Velikoye, Oz. .... 179 55 15N 40 10 E
Velingrad .... 167 42 4N 23 58 E
Velino, Mte. .... 163 42 10N 13 20 E
Velizh .... 178 55 36N 31 11 E
Velké Karlovice .... 151 49 20N 18 17 E
Velke Meziřici .... 150 49 21N 16 1 E
Vel'ký ostrov Žitný .151 48 5N 17 20 E
Vellar → .... 201 11 30N 79 36 E
Velletri .... 164 41 43N 12 43 E
Vellinge .... 172 55 29N 13 0 E
Vellore .... 201 12 57N 79 10 E
Velp .... 142 52 0N 5 59 E
Velsen-Noord .... 142 52 27N 4 40 E
Velsk .... 176 61 10N 42 5 E
Velten .... 146 52 40N 13 11 E
Veluwe Meer .... 142 52 24N 5 44 E
Velvendós .... 168 40 15N 22 6 E
Vembanad Lake .... 201 9 36N 76 15 E
Veme .... 171 60 14N 10 7 E
Ven .... 172 55 55N 12 45 E
Vena .... 173 57 31N 16 0 E
Venado Tuerto .... 124 33 50 S 62 0W
Venafro .... 165 41 28N 14 3 E
Venarey-les-Laumes 139 47 32N 4 26 E
Venaria .... 162 45 6N 7 39 E
Venčane .... 166 44 24N 20 28 E
Vence .... 141 43 43N 7 6 E
Vendas Novas 155 38 39N 8 27W
Vendée □ 138 46 50N 1 35W
Vendée → 138 46 20N 1 10W
Vendée, Collines de 138 46 35N 0 45W
Vendeuvre-sur-Barse139 48 14N 4 28 E
Vendôme .... 138 47 47N 1 3 E
Vendrell .... 156 41 10N 1 30 E
Vendsyssel .... 173 57 22N 10 0 E
Véneta, Laguna .... 163 45 23N 12 25 E
Véneto □ .... 163 45 40N 12 0 E
Venev .... 179 54 22N 38 17 E
Venézia .... 163 45 27N 12 20 E
Venézia, Golfo di .163 45 20N 13 0 E
Venezuela ■ 118 8 0N 65 0W
Venezuela, Golfo de118 11 30N 71 0W
Vengurla .... 201 15 53N 73 45 E
Vengurla Rocks .... 201 15 55N 73 22 E
Venice = Venézia .163 45 27N 12 20 E
Vénissieux .... 141 45 43N 4 53 E
Venkatagiri .... 201 14 0N 79 35 E
Venkatapuram .... 200 18 20N 80 30 E
Venlo .... 143 51 22N 6 11 E
Vennesla .... 171 58 15N 8 0 E
Venosta 82 45 52N 76 1W
Venraij .... 143 51 31N 6 0 E
Venta, La 110 18 5N 94 3W
Venta de Cardeña .. 155 38 16N 4 20W
Venta de San Rafael154 40 42N 4 12W
Ventana, La 103 23 0N 100 16W
Ventana, Sa. de la .. 124 38 0 S 62 30W
Ventanas 104 25 59N 106 49W
Ventersburg .... 254 28 7 S 27 9 E
Ventimíglia .... 162 43 50N 7 39 E
Ventnor 133 50 35N 1 12W
Ventosa, La 109 16 33N 94 57W
Ventotene .... 164 40 48N 13 25 E
Ventoux .... 141 44 10N 5 17 E
Ventspils .... 178 57 25N 21 32 E
Ventuarí → 118 3 58N 67 2W
Ventura, La 103 24 38N 100 54W
Venturosa, La 118 6 8N 68 48W
Venus B. .... 231 38 40 S 145 42 E
Venustiano Carranza, Chiapas, Mexico .110 16 21N 92 33W
Venustiano Carranza, Jalisco, Mexico 106 19 44N 103 47W
Vera, Argentina .... 124 29 30 S 60 20W
Vera, Spain 157 37 15N 1 51W
Veracruz 98 32 23N 115 6W
Veracruz □ 108 19 20N 96 40W
Veracruz Llave 108 19 12N 96 8W
Veraval .... 198 20 53N 70 27 E
Verbánia .... 162 45 56N 8 43 E
Verbicaro .... 165 39 46N 15 54 E
Verbier .... 148 46 6N 7 13 E
Vercelli .... 162 45 19N 8 25 E
Verchères 83 45 47N 73 21W
Verchovchevo .... 180 48 32N 34 10 E
Verde →, Argentina .... 126 41 56 S 65 5W
Verde →, Goiás, Brazil .... 121 19 11 S 50 44W
Verde →, Goiás, Brazil .... 121 18 1 S 50 14W
Verde →, Mato Grosso, Brazil .... 123 11 54 S 55 48W
Verde →, Mato Grosso, Brazil .... 123 21 25 S 56 20W
Verde →, Paraguay124 23 9 S 57 37W
Verde →, Chihuahua, Mexico 101 26 39N 107 11W
Verde →, Oaxaca, Mexico 109 15 59N 97 50W
Verde →, San Luis Potosí, Mexico 103 21 37N 99 15W
Verde, Cay 112 23 0N 75 5W
Verde Grande → .. 121 16 13 S 43 49W
Verde I. .... 210 13 33N 121 5 E
Verde I. Pass .... 210 13 34N 120 51 E
Verde Pequeno → .121 14 48 S 43 31W
Verden .... 146 52 58N 9 18 E
Verdhikoúsa .... 168 39 47N 21 59 E
Verdon → .... 141 43 43N 5 46 E
Verdon-sur-Mer, Le 140 45 33N 1 4W
Verdun .... 139 49 12N 5 24 E
Verdun-sur-le Doubs139 46 54N 5 0 E
Vereeniging .... 255 26 38 S 27 57 E
Veregin 89 51 35N 102 5W
Vérendrye, Parc Prov. de la 82 47 20N 76 40W
Vereshchagino .... 182 58 5N 54 40 E
Verga, C. 246 10 30N 14 10W
Vergara 156 43 9N 2 28W
Vergato .... 162 44 18N 11 8 E
Vergemont .... 230 23 33 S 143 1 E
Vergemont Cr. → .230 24 16 S 143 16 E
Vergt .... 140 45 2N 0 43 E
Verín 154 41 57N 7 27W
Veriña 154 43 32N 5 43W
Verkhnedvinsk .... 178 55 45N 27 58 E
Verkhneuralsk .... 182 53 53N 59 13 E
Verkhnevilyuysk ... 185 63 27N 120 18 E
Verkhneye Kalinino 185 59 54N 108 8 E
Verkhniy-Avzyan ... 182 53 32N 57 33 E
Verkhniy Baskunchak .... 181 48 14N 46 44 E
Verkhniy Tagil .... 182 57 22N 59 56 E
Verkhniy Ufaley ... 182 56 4N 60 14 E
Verkhniye Kigi .... 182 55 25N 58 37 E
Verkhnyaya Salda .. 182 58 2N 60 33 E
Verkhoturye .... 182 58 52N 60 48 E
Verkhovye .... 179 52 55N 37 15 E
Verkhoyansk .... 185 67 35N 133 25 E
Verkhoyansk Ra. .... 186 66 0N 129 0 E
Verkhoyanskiy Khrebet .... 185 66 0N 129 0 E
Verlo 88 50 19N 108 35W
Verma .... 171 62 21N 8 3 E
Vermenton .... 139 47 40N 3 42 E
Vermeulle, L. 78 54 43N 69 24W
Vermilion 90 53 20N 110 50W
Vermilion →, Alta., Canada 90 53 22N 110 51W
Vermilion →, Qué., Canada 83 47 38N 72 56W
Vermilion Bay 86 49 51N 93 34W
Vermilion Chutes 76 58 22N 114 51W
Vermilion L. 86 50 3N 92 13W
Vermilion Pass 93 51 15N 116 2W
Vernayez .... 148 46 8N 7 3 E
Verner 84 46 25N 80 8W
Verneuil-sur-Avre .. 138 48 45N 0 55 E
Vernier .... 148 46 13N 6 5 E
Vernon, Canada 93 50 20N 119 15W
Vernon, France .... 138 49 5N 1 30 E
Véroia .... 168 40 34N 22 12 E
Verolanuova .... 162 45 20N 10 5 E
Véroli .... 164 41 43N 13 24 E
Véron, L. 80 51 48N 65 7W
Verona, Canada 85 44 29N 76 42W
Verona, Italy .... 162 45 27N 11 0 E
Veropol .... 185 65 15N 168 40 E
Verriéres, Les .... 148 46 55N 6 28 E
Versailles .... 139 48 48N 2 8 E
Versalles .... 123 12 44 S 63 18W
Versoix .... 148 46 17N 6 10 E
Vert, C. 246 14 45N 17 30W
Vert I. 86 48 55N 88 3W
Verte, I. 83 48 2N 69 26W
Vertou 138 47 10N 1 28W
Vertus .... 139 48 54N 4 0 E
Verulam .... 255 29 38 S 31 2 E
Verviers .... 143 50 37N 5 52 E
Vervins .... 139 49 50N 3 53 E
Verwood 77 49 30N 105 40W
Verzej .... 163 46 34N 16 13 E
Vesdre → .... 143 50 36N 6 0 E
Veselí nad Lužnicí .. 150 49 12N 14 43 E
Veseliye .... 167 42 18N 27 38 E
Veselovskoye Vdkhr. .... 181 47 0N 41 0 E
Veshenskaya .... 181 49 35N 41 44 E
Vesle → .... 139 49 23N 3 38 E
Veslyana → .... 182 60 20N 54 0 E
Vesoul .... 139 47 40N 6 11 E
Vessigebro .... 173 56 58N 12 40 E
Vest-Agder fylke □ .171 58 30N 7 15 E
Vesta 112 9 43N 83 3W
Vestby .... 171 59 37N 10 45 E
Vesterålen .... 174 68 45N 15 0 E
Vestersche Veld .... 142 52 52N 6 9 E
Vestfjorden .... 174 67 55N 14 0 E
Vestfold fylke □ ... 171 59 15N 10 0 E
Vestmannaeyjar 174 63 27N 20 15W
Vestmarka .... 171 59 56N 11 59 E
Vestnes .... 171 62 39N 7 5 E
Vestone .... 162 45 43N 10 25 E
Vestsjœllands Amtskommune □ 172 55 30N 11 20 E
Vestspitsbergen .... 12 78 40N 17 0 E
Vestvågøy .... 174 68 18N 13 50 E
Vesuvio .... 165 40 50N 14 22 E
Vesuvius, Mt. = Vesuvio .... 165 40 50N 14 22 E
Vesyegonsk .... 179 58 40N 37 16 E
Veszprém .... 151 47 8N 17 57 E
Veszprém □ .... 151 47 5N 17 55 E
Vésztö .... 151 46 55N 21 16 E
Vetapalem .... 201 15 47N 80 18 E
Veteran 91 52 0N 111 7W
Vetlanda .... 173 57 24N 15 3 E
Vetluga .... 179 57 53N 45 45 E
Vetluzhskiy .... 179 57 17N 45 12 E
Vetovo .... 167 43 42N 26 16 E
Vetralia .... 163 42 20N 12 2 E
Vetren .... 167 42 15N 24 3 E
Vettore, Monte .... 163 42 49N 13 16 E
Veurne .... 143 51 5N 2 40 E
Vevey .... 148 46 28N 6 51 E
Vévi .... 168 40 47N 21 38 E
Veynes .... 141 44 32N 5 49 E
Veys .... 193 31 30N 49 0 E
Vézelise .... 139 48 30N 6 5 E
Vézère → .... 140 44 53N 0 53 E
Vezhen .... 167 42 50N 24 20 E
Vi Thanh .... 205 9 42N 105 26 E
Viacha .... 122 16 39 S 68 18W
Viadana .... 162 44 55N 10 30 E
Viana, Brazil .... 120 3 13 S 45 0W
Viana, Spain 156 42 31N 2 22W
Viana del Bollo 154 42 11N 7 6W
Viana do Alentejo .. 155 38 17N 7 59W
Viana do Castelo ... 154 41 42N 8 50W
Vianden .... 143 49 56N 6 12 E
Vianen .... 142 51 59N 5 5 E
Vianna do Castelo □ 154 41 50N 8 30W
Vianópolis .... 121 16 40 S 48 35W
Viar → 155 37 36N 5 50W
Viaréggio .... 162 43 52N 10 13 E
Viaur → .... 140 44 8N 1 58 E
Vibank 88 50 20N 103 56W
Vibo Valéntia .... 165 38 40N 16 5 E
Vibora, La 102 27 8N 103 3W
Viborg .... 173 56 27N 9 23 E
Viborillas 104 24 26N 106 13W
Vibraye .... 138 48 3N 0 44 E
Vic-en-Bigorre .... 140 43 24N 0 3 E
Vic-Fézensac .... 140 43 47N 0 19 E
Vic-sur-Cère .... 140 44 59N 2 38 E
Vic-sùr-Seille .... 139 48 45N 6 33 E
Vicam 100 27 35N 110 20W
Vicencio, L. de 107 19 20N 97 42W
Vicente Guerrero, Baja Calif. N., Mexico 98 30 45N 116 0W
Vicente Guerrero, Tlaxcala, Mexico .107 19 8N 98 10W
Vicenza .... 163 45 32N 11 31 E
Viceroy 88 49 28N 105 22W
Vich .... 156 41 58N 2 19 E
Vichada □ 118 5 0N 69 30W
Vichada → 118 4 55N 67 50W
Vichuga .... 179 57 12N 41 55 E

Vichy **140** 46 9N 3 26 E
Vico, L. di **163** 42 20N 12 10 E
Vico del Gargaro **165** 41 54N 15 57 E
Viçosa **120** 9 28 S 36 14W
Viçosa do Ceará **120** 3 34 S 41 5W
Vicosoprano **149** 46 22N 9 38 E
Victor **198** 21 0N 71 30 E
Victor, L. **80** 50 35N 61 50W
Victor Emanuel Ra. **227** 5 20 S 142 15 E
Victor Harbor **231** 35 30 S 138 37 E
Victoria, Argentina **124** 32 40 S 60 10W
Victoria, B.C., Canada **93** 48 30N 123 25W
Victoria, Newf., Canada **79** 47 46N 53 14W
Victoria, Chile **126** 38 13 S 72 20W
Victoria, Guinea **246** 10 50N 14 32W
Victoria, H.K. **217** 22 16N 114 15 E
Victoria, Ind. Oc. **203** 5 0 S 55 40 E
Victoria, Malaysia **206** 5 20N 115 14 E
Victoria, Mexico **107** 21 23N 100 12W
Victoria, Mindoro, Phil. **210** 13 12N 121 12 E
Victoria, Tarlac, Phil. **210** 15 35N 120 41 E
Victoria □ **232** 37 0 S 144 0 E
Victoria → **228** 15 10 S 129 40 E
Victoria, Grand L. **82** 47 31N 77 30W
Victoria, L., Australia **232** 33 57 S 141 15 E
Victoria, L., E. Afr. **250** 1 0 S 33 0 E
Victoria, La **118** 10 14N 67 20W
Victoria, Mt., Burma **202** 21 15N 93 55 E
Victoria, Mt., Papua N. G. **227** 8 55 S 147 32 E
Victoria & Albert Mts. **95** 80 45N 72 0W
Victoria Beach **89** 50 40N 96 35W
Victoria de Durango **105** 24 2N 104 40W
Victoria de las Tunas **112** 20 58N 76 59W
Victoria Falls **251** 17 58 S 25 52 E
Victoria Harbour **84** 44 45N 79 45W
Victoria I. **94** 71 0N 111 0W
Victoria Ld. **13** 75 0 S 160 0 E
Victoria Nile → **250** 2 14N 31 26 E
Victoria Peaks **211** 9 22N 118 20 E
Victoria Pk., Alta., Canada **91** 49 18N 114 8W
Victoria Pk., B.C., Canada **92** 50 3N 126 5W
Victoria Ra. **235** 42 12 S 172 7 E
Victoria Res. **79** 48 20N 57 27W
Victoria River Downs **228** 16 25 S 131 0 E
Victoria West **254** 31 25 S 23 4 E
Victorias **211** 10 54N 123 5 E
Victoriaville **83** 46 4N 71 56W
Victorica **124** 36 20 S 65 30W
Vicuña **124** 30 0 S 70 50W
Vicuña Mackenna **124** 33 53 S 64 25W
Vidauban **141** 43 25N 6 27 E
Vidigueira **155** 38 12N 7 48W
Vidin **166** 43 59N 22 50 E
Vidio, Cabo **154** 43 35N 6 14W
Vidisha **198** 23 28N 77 53 E
Vidöstern **173** 57 5N 14 0 E
Vidra **170** 45 56N 26 55 E
Viduša **166** 42 55N 18 21 E
Vidzy **178** 55 23N 26 37 E
Viechtach **147** 49 5N 12 53 E
Viedma **126** 40 50 S 63 0W
Viedma, L. **126** 49 30 S 72 30W
Vieira **154** 41 38N 8 8W
Vieja **103** 21 40N 100 35W
Viella **156** 42 43N 0 44 E
Vielsalm **143** 50 17N 5 54 E
Vienenburg **146** 51 57N 10 35 E
Vieng Pou Kha **204** 20 41N 101 4 E
Vienna = Wien **151** 48 12N 16 22 E
Vienna **84** 42 41N 80 48W
Vienne **141** 45 31N 4 53 E
Vienne □ **140** 46 30N 0 42 E
Vienne → **138** 47 13N 0 5 E
Vientiane **204** 17 58N 102 36 E
Vientos, Paso de los **113** 20 0N 74 0W
Vierlingsbeek **143** 51 36N 6 1 E
Viersen **146** 51 15N 6 23 E
Vierwaldstättersee **149** 47 0N 8 30 E
Vierzon **139** 47 13N 2 5 E
Viesca **103** 25 21N 102 48W
Vieste **164** 41 52N 16 14 E
Vietnam ■ **204** 19 0N 106 0 E
Vieux-Boucau-les-Bains **140** 43 48N 1 23W
Vif **141** 45 5N 5 41 E
Vigan **210** 17 35N 120 28 E
Vigan, Le **140** 44 0N 3 36 E
Vigévano **162** 45 18N 8 50 E
Vigia **120** 0 50 S 48 5W
Vigía Chico **111** 19 46N 87 35W
Vignacourt **139** 50 1N 2 15 E
Vignemale, Pic du **140** 42 47N 0 10W
Vigneulles **139** 48 59N 5 40 E
Vignola **162** 44 29N 11 0 E
Vigo **154** 42 12N 8 41W
Vigo, Ría de **154** 42 15N 8 45W
Vihiers **138** 47 10N 0 30W
Vijayadurg **200** 16 30N 73 25 E
Vijayawada **201** 16 31N 80 39 E
Vijfhuizen **142** 52 22N 4 41 E
Vikedal **171** 59 30N 5 55 E
Viken **173** 58 39N 14 20 E
Vikersund **171** 59 58N 10 2 E
Viking **91** 53 7N 111 50W
Vikna **174** 64 52N 10 57 E
Vikramasingapuram **201** 8 40N 76 47 E
Viksjö **172** 62 45N 17 26 E
Vikulovo **184** 56 50N 70 40 E
Vila da Maganja **251** 17 18 S 37 30 E
Vila de João Belo = Xai-Xai **255** 25 6 S 33 31 E
Vila de Manica **251** 18 58 S 32 59 E
Vila de Rei **155** 39 41N 8 9W
Vila do Bispo **155** 37 5N 8 53W
Vila do Chibuto **255** 24 40 S 33 33 E
Vila do Conde **154** 41 21N 8 45W
Vila Franca de Xira **155** 38 57N 8 59W
Vila Gamito **251** 14 12 S 33 0 E
Vila Gomes da Costa **255** 24 20 S 33 37 E
Vila Machado **251** 19 15 S 34 14 E
Vila Mouzinho **251** 14 48 S 34 25 E
Vila Nova de Foscôa **154** 41 5N 7 9W
Vila Nova de Ourém **155** 39 40N 8 35W
Vila Novo de Gaia **154** 41 4N 8 40W
Vila Pouca de Aguiar **154** 41 30N 7 38W
Vila Real **154** 41 17N 7 48W
Vila Real de Santo António **155** 37 10N 7 28W
Vila Vasco da Gama **251** 14 54 S 32 14 E
Vila Velha, Amapá, Brazil **119** 3 13N 51 13W
Vila Velha, Espirito Santo, Brazil **121** 20 20 S 40 17W
Vila Viçosa **155** 38 45N 7 27W
Vilaboa **154** 42 21N 8 39W
Vilaine → **138** 47 30N 2 27W
Vilanandro, Tanjona **255** 16 11 S 44 27 E
Vilanculos **255** 22 1 S 35 17 E
Vilar Formosa **154** 40 38N 6 45W
Vilareal □ **154** 41 36N 7 35W
Vilaseca-Salou **156** 41 7N 1 9 E
Vilcabamba, Cordillera **122** 13 0 S 73 0W
Vilcanchos **122** 13 40 S 74 25W
Vîlcea □ **170** 45 0N 24 10 E
Vileyka **178** 54 30N 26 53 E
Vilhelmina **174** 64 35N 16 39 E
Vilhena **123** 12 40 S 60 5W
Viliga **185** 61 36N 156 56 E
Viliya → **178** 55 54N 23 53 E
Viljandi **178** 58 28N 25 30 E
Vilkovo **180** 45 28N 29 32 E
Villa Abecia **124** 21 0 S 68 18W
Villa Ahumada **101** 30 37N 106 31W
Villa Aldama **108** 19 37N 97 13W
Villa Alta, Sa. de **109** 17 5N 96 0W
Villa Ana **124** 28 28 S 59 40W
Villa Ángela **124** 27 34 S 60 45W
Villa Azueta **109** 18 8N 95 40W
Villa Bella **123** 10 25 S 65 22W
Villa Bens = Tarfaya **240** 27 55N 12 55W
Villa Cañás **124** 34 0 S 61 35W
Villa Cisneros = Dakhla **240** 23 50N 15 53W
Villa Colón **124** 31 38 S 68 20W
Villa Constitución **124** 33 15 S 60 20W
Villa Corona **104** 23 52N 105 47W
Villa Coronado **101** 26 45N 105 10W
Villa Cuauhtémoc **108** 22 11N 97 50W
Villa de Álvarez **106** 19 15N 103 44W
Villa de Arriaga **103** 21 56N 101 20W
Villa de Comatitlán **110** 15 13N 92 35W
Villa de Cos **105** 23 17N 102 21W
Villa de Cura **118** 10 2N 67 29W
Villa de García **102** 25 49N 100 35W
Villa de Guadalupe **103** 23 22N 100 46W
Villa de María **124** 29 55 S 63 43W
Villa de Reyes **103** 21 48N 100 56W
Villa de Santiago **102** 25 27N 100 9W
Villa de Seris **100** 29 3N 110 57W
Villa del Pueblito **107** 20 32N 100 27W
Villa del Rosario **118** 10 19N 72 19W
Villa Dolores **124** 31 58 S 65 15W
Villa Escalante **107** 19 24N 101 39W
Villa Flores **110** 16 14N 93 14W
Villa Frontera **102** 26 56N 101 27W
Villa Garcia **105** 22 13N 101 57W
Villa Guerrero **105** 21 59N 103 36W
Villa Guillermina **124** 28 15 S 59 29W
Villa Hayes **124** 25 0 S 57 20W
Villa Hidalgo, Durango, Mexico **105** 26 16N 104 54W
Villa Hidalgo, Jalisco, Mexico **106** 21 40N 102 36W
Villa Hidalgó, San Luis Potosí, Mexico **103** 22 27N 100 42W
Villa Hidalgo, Zacatecas, Mexico **105** 22 21N 101 42W
Villa Insurgentes **99** 25 13N 111 48W
Villa Iris **124** 38 12 S 63 12W
Villa Juárez, Coahuila, Mexico **102** 27 37N 100 44W
Villa Juárez, Durango, Mexico **105** 25 30N 103 35W
Villa Juárez, San Luis Potosí, Mexico **103** 22 23N 100 16W
Villa López **101** 27 0N 105 2W
Villa Madero **107** 19 24N 101 16W
Villa María **124** 32 20 S 63 10W
Villa Matamoros **101** 26 47N 105 35W
Villa Mazán **124** 28 40 S 66 30W
Villa Minozzo **162** 44 21N 10 30 E
Villa Montes **124** 21 10 S 63 30W
Villa Morelos **107** 20 0N 101 25W
Villa Obregón **106** 21 7N 102 42W
Villa Ocampo, Argentina **124** 28 30 S 59 20W
Villa Ocampo, Mexico **104** 26 27N 105 31W
Villa Ojo de Agua **124** 29 30 S 63 44W
Villa Pesqueria **100** 29 8N 109 58W
Villa San Giovanni **165** 38 13N 15 38 E
Villa San José **124** 32 12 S 58 15W
Villa San Martín **124** 28 15 S 64 9W
Villa Santina **163** 46 25N 12 55 E
Villa Unión, Coahuila, Mexico **102** 28 15N 100 43W
Villa Unión, Durango, Mexico **105** 23 58N 104 2W
Villa Unión, Sinaloa, Mexico **104** 23 12N 106 14W
Villa Victoria **106** 18 47N 103 24W
Villa Victoria, Presa **107** 19 28N 100 2W
Villaba **211** 11 13N 124 24 E
Villablino **154** 42 57N 6 19W
Villacañas **156** 39 38N 3 20W
Villacarlos **156** 39 53N 4 17 E
Villacarriedo **156** 43 14N 3 48W
Villacarrillo **157** 38 7N 3 3W
Villacastín **154** 40 46N 4 25W
Villach **150** 46 37N 13 51 E
Villachuato **107** 20 10N 101 35W
Villaciado **164** 39 27N 8 45 E
Villada **154** 42 15N 4 59W
Villadiego **154** 42 31N 4 1W
Villadóssola **162** 46 4N 8 16 E
Villafeliche **156** 41 10N 1 30W
Villafranca **156** 42 17N 1 46W
Villafranca de los Barros **155** 38 35N 6 18W
Villafranca de los Caballeros **157** 39 26N 3 21W
Villafranca del Bierzo **154** 42 38N 6 50W
Villafranca del Cid **156** 40 26N 0 16W
Villafranca del Panadés **156** 41 21N 1 40 E
Villafranca di Verona **162** 45 20N 10 51 E
Villagarcía de Arosa **154** 42 34N 8 46W
Villagrán, Guanajuato, Mexico **107** 20 31N 100 59W
Villagrán, Tamaulipas, Mexico **103** 24 29N 99 29W
Villaguay **124** 32 0 S 59 0W
Villaharta **155** 38 9N 4 54W
Villahermosa, Mexico **110** 17 59N 92 55W
Villahermosa, Spain **157** 38 46N 2 52W
Villaines-la-Juhel **138** 48 21N 0 20W
Villajoyosa **157** 38 30N 0 12W
Villalba **154** 43 26N 7 40W
Villalba de Guardo **154** 42 42N 4 49W
Villalcampo, Pantano de **154** 41 31N 6 0W
Villaldama **102** 26 30N 100 26W
Villalón de Campos **154** 42 5N 5 4W
Villalpando **154** 41 51N 5 25W
Villaluenga **154** 40 2N 3 54W
Villamanán **154** 42 19N 5 35W
Villamartín **155** 36 52N 5 38W
Villamayor **156** 39 50N 2 59W
Villamblard **140** 45 2N 0 32 E
Villanova Monteleone **164** 40 30N 8 28 E
Villanueva, Colombia **118** 10 37N 72 59W
Villanueva, Mexico **105** 22 21N 102 53W
Villanueva de Castellón **157** 39 5N 0 31W
Villanueva de Córdoba **155** 38 20N 4 38W
Villanueva de la Fuente **157** 38 42N 2 42W
Villanueva de la Serena **155** 38 59N 5 50W
Villanueva de la Sierra **154** 40 12N 6 24W
Villanueva de los Castillejos **155** 37 30N 7 15W
Villanueva del Arzobispo **157** 38 10N 3 0W
Villanueva del Duque **155** 38 20N 5 0W
Villanueva del Fresno **155** 38 23N 7 10W
Villanueva y Geltrú **156** 41 13N 1 40 E
Villaodrid **154** 43 20N 7 11W
Villaputzu **164** 39 28N 9 33 E
Villar del Arzobispo **156** 39 44N 0 50W
Villar del Rey **155** 39 7N 6 50W
Villarcayo **156** 42 56N 3 34W
Villard-Bonnet **141** 45 14N 5 53 E
Villard-de-Lans **141** 45 3N 5 33 E
Villarino de los Aires **154** 41 18N 6 23W
Villarosa **165** 37 36N 14 9 E
Villarramiel **154** 42 2N 4 55W
Villarreal **156** 39 55N 0 3W
Villarrica, Chile **126** 39 15 S 72 15W
Villarrica, Paraguay **124** 25 40 S 56 30W
Villarrobledo **157** 39 18N 2 36W
Villarroya de la Sierra **156** 41 27N 1 46W
Villarrubia de los Ojos **157** 39 14N 3 36W
Villars **141** 46 0N 5 2 E
Villarta de San Juan **157** 39 15N 3 25W
Villasayas **156** 41 24N 2 39W
Villaseca de los Gamitos **154** 41 2N 6 7W
Villastar **156** 40 17N 1 9W
Villatobas **156** 39 54N 3 20W
Villavicencio, Argentina **124** 32 28 S 69 0W
Villavicencio, Colombia **118** 4 9N 73 37W
Villaviciosa **154** 43 32N 5 27W
Villazón **124** 22 0 S 65 35W
Ville-Marie **82** 47 20N 79 30W
Villebon, L. **82** 47 58N 77 17W
Villedieu **138** 48 50N 1 12W
Villefort **140** 44 28N 3 56 E
Villefranche **139** 47 19N 1 46 E
Villefranche-de-Lauragais **140** 43 25N 1 44 E
Villefranche-de-Rouergue **140** 44 21N 2 2 E
Villefranche-du-Périgord **140** 44 38N 1 5 E
Villefranche-sur-Saône **141** 45 59N 4 43 E
Villegrande **123** 18 30 S 64 10W
Villel **156** 40 14N 1 12W
Villemaur **139** 48 14N 3 40 E
Villemontel **82** 48 38N 78 22W
Villemur-sur-Tarn **140** 43 51N 1 31 E
Villena **157** 38 39N 0 52W
Villenauxe **139** 48 36N 3 30 E
Villenave **140** 44 46N 0 33W
Villeneuve, France **139** 48 42N 2 25 E
Villeneuve, Italy **162** 45 40N 7 10 E
Villeneuve, Switz. **148** 46 24N 6 56 E
Villeneuve-l'Archevêque **139** 48 14N 3 32 E
Villeneuve-lès-Avignon **141** 43 57N 4 49 E
Villeneuve-sur-Allier **140** 46 40N 3 13 E
Villeneuve-sur-Lot **140** 44 24N 0 42 E
Villeréal **140** 44 38N 0 45 E
Villers-Bocage **138** 49 3N 0 40W
Villers-Bretonneux **139** 49 50N 2 30 E
Villers-Cotterêts **139** 49 15N 3 4 E
Villers-le-Bouillet **143** 50 34N 5 15 E
Villers-le-Gambon **143** 50 11N 4 37 E
Villers-Outreaux **139** 50 2N 3 18 E
Villers-sur-Mer **138** 49 21N 0 2W
Villersexel **139** 47 33N 6 26 E
Villerupt **139** 49 28N 5 55 E
Villerville **138** 49 26N 0 5 E
Villiers **255** 27 2 S 28 36 E
Villingen **147** 48 4N 8 28 E
Villingen-Schwenningen **147** 48 3N 8 29 E
Villupuram **201** 11 59N 79 31 E
Vilna **90** 54 7N 111 55W
Vilnius **178** 54 38N 25 19 E
Vils **150** 47 33N 10 37 E
Vils → **147** 48 38N 13 11 E
Vilsbiburg **147** 48 27N 12 23 E
Vilshofen **147** 48 38N 13 11 E
Vilskutskogo, Proliv **185** 78 0N 103 0 E
Vilusi **166** 42 44N 18 34 E
Vilvoorde **143** 50 56N 4 26 E
Vilyuy → **185** 64 24N 126 26 E
Vilyuysk **185** 63 40N 121 35 E
Vimercate **162** 45 38N 9 25 E

Name	Page	Lat.	Long.
Vimiosa	154	41 35N	6 31W
Vimmerby	173	57 40N	15 55 E
Vimoutiers	138	48 57N	0 10 E
Vimperk	150	49 3N	13 46 E
Viña del Mar	124	33 0 S	71 30W
Vinaroz	156	40 30N	0 27 E
Vinces	118	1 32 S	79 45W
Vinchina	124	28 45 S	68 15W
Vindel älven →	174	63 55N	19 50 E
Vindeln	174	64 12N	19 43 E
Vinderup	173	56 29N	8 45 E
Vindhya Ra.	198	22 50N	77 0 E
Vinga	170	46 0N	21 14 E
Vingnes	171	61 7N	10 26 E
Vinh	204	18 45N	105 38 E
Vinh Linh	204	17 4N	107 2 E
Vinh Long	205	10 16N	105 57 E
Vinh Yen	204	21 21N	105 35 E
Vinhais	154	41 50N	7 0W
Vinica, Hrvatska, Yugoslavia	163	46 20N	16 9 E
Vinica, Slovenija, Yugoslavia	163	45 28N	15 16 E
Vinkeveen	142	52 13N	4 56 E
Vinkovci	166	45 19N	18 48 E
Vinnitsa	180	49 15N	28 30 E
Vinson Massif	13	78 35 S	85 25W
Vinstra	171	61 37N	9 44 E
Vintar	210	18 14N	120 39 E
Vinţu de Jos	170	46 0N	23 30 E
Viöl	146	54 32N	9 12 E
Violet Town	233	36 38 S	145 42 E
Vipava	163	45 51N	13 58 E
Vipiteno	163	46 55N	11 25 E
Viqueque	207	8 52 S	126 23 E
Vir, U.S.S.R.	183	37 45N	72 5 E
Vir, Yugoslavia	163	44 17N	15 3 E
Virac	210	13 30N	124 20 E
Virachei	204	13 59N	106 49 E
Virago Sd.	92	54 0N	132 30W
Virajpet = Virarajendrapet	201	12 10N	75 50 E
Viramgam	198	23 5N	72 0 E
Virarajendrapet	201	12 10N	75 50 E
Viravanallur	201	8 40N	77 30 E
Virden	89	49 50N	100 56W
Vire	138	48 50N	0 53W
Vire →	138	49 20N	1 7W
Virgem da Lapa	121	16 49 S	42 21W
Vírgenes, C., Argentina	126	52 19 S	68 21W
Vírgenes, C., Mexico	99	27 31N	112 21W
Virgin →	77	57 2N	108 17W
Virgin Is.	113	18 40N	64 30W
Virginia	254	28 8 S	26 55 E
Virginia Falls	76	61 38N	125 42W
Virginiatown	74	48 9N	79 36W
Virieu-le-Grand	141	45 51N	5 39 E
Virje	166	46 4N	16 59 E
Virovitica	166	45 51N	17 21 E
Virpazar	166	42 14N	19 6 E
Virserum	173	57 20N	15 35 E
Virton	143	49 35N	5 32 E
Virtsu	178	58 32N	23 33 E
Virú	122	8 25 S	78 45W
Virudunagar	201	9 30N	78 0 E
Vis	163	43 0N	16 10 E
Vis Kanal	163	43 4N	16 5 E
Visayan Sea	211	11 30N	123 30 E
Visby	173	57 37N	18 18 E
Viscount	88	51 57N	105 39W
Viscount Melville Sd.	94	74 10N	108 0W
Visé	143	50 44N	5 41 E
Višegrad	166	43 47N	19 17 E
Viseu, Brazil	120	1 10 S	46 5W
Viseu, Portugal	154	40 40N	7 55W
Viseu □	154	40 40N	7 55W
Vişeu de Sus	170	47 45N	24 25 E
Vishakhapatnam	200	17 45N	83 20 E
Vishera →	182	59 55N	56 25 E
Visikoi I.	13	56 43 S	27 15W
Visingsö	173	58 2N	14 20 E
Viskafors	173	57 37N	12 50 E
Vislanda	173	56 46N	14 30 E
Visnagar	198	23 45N	72 32 E
Višnja Gora	163	45 58N	14 45 E
Viso, Mte.	162	44 38N	7 5 E
Viso del Marqués	157	38 32N	3 34W
Visoko	166	43 58N	18 10 E
Visp	148	46 17N	7 52 E
Vispa →	148	46 9N	7 48 E
Visselhövede	146	52 59N	9 36 E
Vissoie	148	46 13N	7 36 E
Vistahermosa de Negrete	106	20 16N	102 29W
Vistonikos, Ormos	168	41 0N	25 7 E
Vistula = Wisła →	152	54 22N	18 55 E
Vit →	167	43 30N	24 30 E
Vitanje	163	46 25N	15 18 E
Vitebsk	178	55 10N	30 15 E
Viterbo	163	42 25N	12 8 E
Viti Levu	226	17 30 S	177 30 E
Vitiaz Str.	227	5 40 S	147 10 E
Vitigudino	154	41 1N	6 26W
Vitim	185	59 28N	112 35 E
Vitim →	185	59 26N	112 34 E
Vitína, Greece	169	37 40N	22 10 E
Vitina, Yugoslavia	166	43 17N	17 29 E
Vitória, Brazil	121	20 20 S	40 22W
Vitoria, Spain	156	42 50N	2 41W
Vitória da Conquista	121	14 51 S	40 51W
Vitória de São Antão	120	8 10 S	35 20W
Vitorino Friere	120	4 4 S	45 10W
Vitré	138	48 8N	1 12W
Vitry-le-François	139	48 43N	4 33 E
Vitsi, Óros	168	40 40N	21 25 E
Vitteaux	139	47 24N	4 30 E
Vittel	139	48 12N	5 57 E
Vittória	165	36 58N	14 30 E
Vittório Véneto	163	45 59N	12 18 E
Vitu Is.	227	4 50 S	149 25 E
Vivegnis	143	50 42N	5 39 E
Viver	156	39 55N	0 36W
Vivero	154	43 39N	7 38W
Viviers	141	44 30N	4 40 E
Vivonne, Australia	232	35 59 S	137 9 E
Vivonne, France	140	46 25N	0 15 E
Vivonne B.	232	35 59 S	137 9 E
Vizcaíno, Desierto de	99	28 0N	113 45W
Vizcaíno, Sa.	99	27 30N	114 30W
Vizcaya □	156	43 15N	2 45W
Vizianagaram	200	18 6N	83 30 E
Vizille	141	45 5N	5 46 E
Viziñada	163	45 20N	13 46 E
Viziru	170	45 0N	27 43 E
Viznaga	100	28 50N	111 15W
Vizovice	151	49 12N	17 56 E
Vizzini	165	37 9N	14 43 E
Vjosa →	168	40 37N	19 42 E
Vlaardingen	142	51 55N	4 21 E
Vlădeasa	170	46 47N	22 50 E
Vladicin Han	166	42 42N	22 1 E
Vladimir	179	56 15N	40 30 E
Vladimir Volynskiy	178	50 50N	24 18 E
Vladimirci	166	44 36N	19 45 E
Vladimirovac	166	45 1N	20 53 E
Vladimirovka, R.S.F.S.R., U.S.S.R.	181	48 27N	46 10 E
Vladimirovka, R.S.F.S.R., U.S.S.R.	181	44 45N	44 41 E
Vladimirovo	167	43 32N	23 22 E
Vladislavovka	180	45 15N	35 15 E
Vladivostok	185	43 10N	131 53 E
Vlamertinge	143	50 51N	2 49 E
Vlasenica	166	44 11N	18 59 E
Vlašić	166	44 19N	17 37 E
Vlašim	150	49 40N	14 53 E
Vlasinsko Jezero	166	42 44N	22 22 E
Vlasotinci	166	42 59N	22 7 E
Vleuten	142	52 6N	5 1 E
Vlieland	142	53 16N	4 55 E
Vliestroom	142	53 19N	5 8 E
Vlijmen	143	51 42N	5 14 E
Vlissingen	143	51 26N	3 34 E
Vlóra	168	40 32N	19 28 E
Vlóra □	168	40 12N	20 0 E
Vlorës, Gjiri i	168	40 29N	19 27 E
Vltava →	150	50 21N	14 30 E
Vo Dat	205	11 9N	107 31 E
Vobarno	162	45 38N	10 30 E
Voćin	166	45 37N	17 33 E
Vöcklabruck	150	48 1N	13 39 E
Vodice	163	43 47N	15 47 E
Vodňany	150	49 9N	14 11 E
Vodnjan	163	44 59N	13 52 E
Vogar	89	50 57N	98 39W
Vogelkop = Doberai, Jazirah	207	1 25 S	133 0 E
Vogelsberg	146	50 37N	9 15 E
Voghera	162	44 59N	9 1 E
Voh	226	20 58 S	164 42 E
Vohibinany	255	18 49 S	49 4 E
Vohimarina	255	13 25 S	50 0 E
Vohimena, Tanjon' i	255	25 36 S	45 8 E
Vohipeno	255	22 22 S	47 51 E
Voi	250	3 25 S	38 32 E
Void	139	48 40N	5 36 E
Voineşti, Iaşi, Romania	170	47 5N	27 27 E
Voineşti, Prahova, Romania	170	45 5N	25 14 E
Voiotía □	169	38 20N	23 0 E
Voiron	141	45 22N	5 35 E
Voisey B.	78	56 15N	61 50W
Voitsberg	150	47 3N	15 9 E
Voiviïs Límni	168	39 30N	22 45 E
Vojens	173	55 16N	9 18 E
Vojmsjön	174	64 55N	16 40 E
Vojnik	162	46 18N	15 19 E
Vojnió	163	45 19N	15 43 E
Vojvodina, Auton. Pokrajina □	166	45 20N	20 0 E
Vokhma	179	59 0N	46 45 E
Vokhma →	179	56 20N	46 20 E
Vokhtoga	179	58 46N	41 8 E
Volary	150	48 54N	13 52 E
Volcano Is.	224	25 0N	141 0 E
Volchansk	179	50 17N	36 58 E
Volchayevka	185	48 40N	134 30 E
Volchya →	180	48 0N	37 0 E
Volda	171	62 9N	6 5 E
Volendam	142	52 30N	5 4 E
Volga	179	57 58N	38 16 E
Volga →	181	48 30N	46 0 E
Volga Hts. = Privolzhskaya Vozvyshennost	179	51 0N	46 0 E
Volgodonsk	181	47 33N	42 5 E
Volgograd	181	48 40N	44 25 E
Volgogradskoye Vdkhr.	179	50 0N	45 20 E
Volgorechensk	179	57 28N	41 14 E
Volissós	169	38 29N	25 54 E
Volkach	147	49 52N	10 14 E
Volkerak	143	51 39N	4 18 E
Völkermarkt	150	46 39N	14 39 E
Volkhov	178	59 55N	32 15 E
Volkhov →	178	60 8N	32 20 E
Völklingen	147	49 15N	6 50 E
Volkovysk	178	53 9N	24 30 E
Volksrust	255	27 24 S	29 53 E
Vollenhove	142	52 40N	5 58 E
Vol'n'ansk	180	47 55N	35 29 E
Volnovakha	180	47 35N	37 30 E
Volochanka	185	71 0N	94 28 E
Volodarsk	179	56 12N	43 15 E
Vologda	179	59 10N	40 0 E
Volokolamsk	179	56 5N	35 57 E
Volokonovka	179	50 33N	37 52 E
Vólos	168	39 24N	22 59 E
Volosovo	178	59 27N	29 32 E
Volozhin	178	54 3N	26 30 E
Volsk	179	52 5N	47 22 E
Volta →	247	5 46N	0 41 E
Volta, L.	247	7 30N	0 15 E
Volta Blanche = White Volta →	247	9 10N	1 15W
Volta Redonda	125	22 31 S	44 5W
Voltaire, C.	228	14 16 S	125 35 E
Volterra	162	43 24N	10 50 E
Voltri	162	44 25N	8 43 E
Volturara Áppula	165	41 30N	15 2 E
Volturno →	165	41 1N	13 55 E
Volubilis	240	34 2N	5 33W
Volujak	166	43 53N	17 47 E
Vólvi, L.	168	40 40N	23 34 E
Volvo	231	31 41 S	143 57 E
Volzhsk	179	55 57N	48 23 E
Volzhskiy	181	48 56N	44 46 E
Vonda	88	52 19N	106 6W
Vondrozo	255	22 49 S	47 20 E
Vónitsa	169	38 53N	20 58 E
Voorburg	142	52 5N	4 24 E
Voorne Putten	142	51 52N	4 10 E
Voorst	142	52 10N	6 8 E
Voorthuizen	142	52 11N	5 36 E
Vopnafjörður	174	65 45N	14 40W
Vorarlberg □	150	47 20N	10 0 E
Vóras Óros	168	40 57N	21 45 E
Vorbasse	173	55 39N	9 6 E
Vorden	142	52 6N	6 19 E
Vorderrhein →	149	46 49N	9 25 E
Vordingborg	172	55 0N	11 54 E
Voreppe	141	45 18N	5 39 E
Voríai Sporádhes	169	39 15N	23 30 E
Vórios Evvoïkos Kólpos	169	38 45N	23 15 E
Vorkuta	176	67 48N	64 20 E
Vorma →	171	60 9N	11 27 E
Vorona →	179	51 22N	42 3 E
Voronezh, R.S.F.S.R., U.S.S.R.	179	51 40N	39 10 E
Voronezh, Ukraine S.S.R., U.S.S.R.	178	51 47N	33 28 E
Voronezh →	179	51 56N	37 17 E
Vorontsovo-Aleksandrovskoye = Zelenokumsk	181	44 24N	43 53 E
Voroshilovgrad	181	48 38N	39 15 E
Vorovskoye	185	54 30N	155 50 E
Vorselaar	143	51 12N	4 46 E
Vorskla →	180	48 50N	34 10 E
Vöru	178	57 48N	26 54 E
Vorukh	183	39 52N	70 35 E
Vorupør	173	56 58N	8 22 E
Vosges	139	48 20N	7 10 E
Vosges □	139	48 12N	6 20 E
Voskopoja	168	40 40N	20 33 E
Voskresensk	179	55 19N	38 43 E
Voskresenskoye	179	56 51N	45 30 E
Voss	171	60 38N	6 26 E
Vosselaar	143	51 19N	4 52 E
Vostochnyy Sayan	185	54 0N	96 0 E
Vostok I.	225	10 5 S	152 23W
Votice	150	49 38N	14 39 E
Votkinsk	182	57 0N	53 55 E
Votkinskoye Vdkhr.	176	57 30N	55 0 E
Vouga →	154	40 41N	8 40W
Vouillé	138	46 38N	0 10 E
Voulou	252	8 33N	22 36 E
Voulte-sur-Rhône, La	141	44 48N	4 46 E
Vouvray	138	47 25N	0 48 E
Vouvry	148	46 21N	6 51 E
Voúxa, Ákra	169	35 37N	23 32 E
Vouzela	154	40 43N	8 7W
Vouziers	139	49 22N	4 40 E
Voves	139	48 15N	1 38 E
Voxna	172	61 20N	15 40 E
Vozhe Oz.	176	60 45N	39 0 E
Vozhgaly	179	58 9N	50 11 E
Voznesenka	185	56 40N	95 3 E
Voznesensk	180	47 35N	31 21 E
Voznesenye	176	61 0N	35 45 E
Vráble	151	48 15N	18 16 E
Vraćevšnica	166	44 2N	20 34 E
Vrådal	171	59 20N	8 25 E
Vraka	168	42 8N	19 28 E
Vrakhnéïka	169	38 10N	21 40 E
Vrancea □	170	45 50N	26 45 E
Vrancei, Munţii	170	46 0N	26 30 E
Vrangelya, Ostrov	185	71 0N	180 0 E
Vranica	166	43 55N	17 50 E
Vranje	166	42 34N	21 54 E
Vranjska Banja	166	42 34N	22 1 E
Vranov	151	48 53N	21 40 E
Vransko	163	46 17N	14 58 E
Vratsa	167	43 13N	23 30 E
Vrbas	166	45 40N	19 40 E
Vrbas →	166	45 8N	17 29 E
Vrbnik	163	45 4N	14 40 E
Vrbovec	163	45 53N	16 28 E
Vrbovsko	163	45 24N	15 5 E
Vrchlabí	150	50 38N	15 37 E
Vrede	255	27 24 S	29 6 E
Vredefort	254	27 0 S	26 22 E
Vredenburg	254	32 51 S	18 0 E
Vredendal	254	31 41 S	18 35 E
Vreeswijk	142	52 1N	5 6 E
Vrena	173	58 54N	16 41 E
Vrgorac	166	43 12N	17 20 E
Vrhnika	163	45 58N	14 15 E
Vriddhachalam	201	11 30N	79 20 E
Vridi	246	5 15N	4 3W
Vries	142	53 5N	6 35 E
Vriezenveen	142	52 25N	6 38 E
Vrindavan	198	27 37N	77 40 E
Vrnograč	163	45 10N	15 57 E
Vrondádhes	169	38 25N	26 7 E
Vroomshoop	142	52 27N	6 34 E
Vrpolje	166	45 13N	18 24 E
Vršac	166	45 8N	21 18 E
Vrsacki Kanal	166	45 15N	21 0 E
Vryburg	254	26 55 S	24 45 E
Vryheid	255	27 45 S	30 47 E
Vsetín	151	49 20N	18 0 E
Vu Liet	204	18 43N	105 23 E
Vucha →	167	42 10N	24 26 E
Vučitrn	166	42 49N	20 59 E
Vught	143	51 38N	5 20 E
Vukovar	166	45 21N	18 59 E
Vulcan, Canada	91	50 25N	113 15W
Vulcan, Romania	170	45 23N	23 17 E
Vulcano	165	38 25N	14 58 E
Vŭlchedruma	167	43 42N	23 27 E
Vulci	163	42 23N	11 37 E
Vulkaneshty	180	45 35N	28 30 E
Vunduzi →	251	18 56 S	34 1 E
Vung Tau	205	10 21N	107 4 E
Vŭrbitsa	167	42 59N	26 40 E
Vurshets	167	43 15N	23 23 E
Vutcani	170	46 26N	27 59 E
Vuyyuru	201	16 28N	80 50 E
Vvedenka	182	54 0N	63 53 E
Vyara	198	21 8N	73 28 E
Vyasniki	179	56 10N	42 10 E
Vyatka →	182	56 30N	51 0 E
Vyatskiye Polyany	182	56 5N	51 0 E
Vyazemskiy	185	47 32N	134 45 E
Vyazma	178	55 10N	34 15 E
Vyborg	176	60 43N	28 47 E
Vychegda →	176	61 18N	46 36 E
Vychodné Beskydy	151	49 30N	22 0 E
Východočeský □	150	50 20N	15 45 E
Východoslovenský □	151	48 50N	21 0 E
Vyg-ozero	176	63 30N	34 0 E
Vyksa	179	55 19N	42 11 E
Vypin	201	10 10N	76 15 E
Vyrnwy, L.	132	52 48N	3 30W
Vyshniy Volochek	178	57 30N	34 30 E
Vyshzha = imeni 26 Bakinskikh Komissarov	177	39 22N	54 10 E
Vyškov	151	49 17N	17 0 E
Vysoké Mýto	151	49 58N	10 10 E
Vysokovsk	179	56 22N	36 30 E
Vysotsk	178	51 43N	26 32 E
Vyšší Brod	150	48 37N	14 19 E
Vytegra	176	61 0N	36 27 E

W

W.A.C. Bennett Dam 76 56 2N 122 6W
Wa 246 10 7N 2 25W
Waal → 142 51 59N 4 30 E
Waalwijk 143 51 42N 5 4 E
Waarschoot 143 51 10N 3 36 E
Waasmunster 143 51 6N 4 5 E
Wabag 227 5 32 S 143 40 E
Wabakimi L. 86 50 38N 89 45W
Wabamun 90 53 33N 114 28W
Wabana 75 47 40N 53 0W
Wabano → 83 48 20N 74 3W
Wabao, C. 226 21 35 S 167 53 E
Wabasca 90 55 57N 113 56W
Wabasca → 90 58 22N 115 20W
Wabaskang L. 86 50 26N 93 13W
Wabassi → 87 51 45N 86 20W
Wabatongushi L. 87 48 26N 84 13W
Wabawng 202 26 20N 97 25 E
Wabi → 245 7 45N 40 50 E
Wabigoon 86 49 43N 92 35W
Wabigoon L. 86 49 44N 92 44W
Wabimeig L. 87 51 28N 85 36W
Wabinosh L. 86 50 5N 89 0W
Wabowden 77 54 55N 98 38W
Wąbrzeźno 152 53 16N 18 57 E
Wabu Hu 217 32 20N 116 50 E
Wabuk Pt. 74 55 20N 85 5W
Wabush 80 52 55N 66 52W
Wachtebeke 143 51 11N 3 52 E
Wächtersbach 147 50 16N 9 18 E
Waco 78 51 27N 65 37W
Waconichi, L. 83 50 8N 74 0W
Wacouno → 80 50 54N 65 57W
Wad Ban Naqa 245 16 32N 33 9 E
Wad Banda 245 13 10N 27 56 E
Wad el Haddad 245 13 50N 33 30 E
Wad en Nau 245 14 10N 33 34 E
Wad Hamid 245 16 30N 32 45 E
Wâd Medanî 245 14 28N 33 30 E
Wad Thana 197 27 22N 66 23 E
Wadayama 220 35 19N 134 52 E
Waddân 241 29 9N 16 10 E
Waddân, Jabal 241 29 0N 16 15 E
Waddeneilanden 142 53 25N 5 10 E
Waddenzee 142 53 6N 5 10 E
Wadderin Hill 229 32 0 S 118 25 E
Waddington, Mt. 92 51 23N 125 15W
Waddinxveen 142 52 2N 4 40 E
Waddy Pt. 231 24 58 S 153 21 E
Wadena 88 51 57N 103 47W
Wädenswil 149 47 14N 8 40 E
Wadhams 92 51 30N 127 30W
Wâdî as Sîr 191 31 56N 35 49 E
Wâdî ash Shâṭi' 241 27 30N 15 0 E
Wâdî Banî Walîd 241 31 49N 14 0 E
Wadi Gemâl 244 24 35N 35 10 E
Wadi Halfa 244 21 53N 31 19 E
Wadian 217 32 42N 112 29 E
Wadim 195 22 40N 57 21 E
Wadlew 152 51 31N 19 23 E
Wadlin L. 90 57 44N 115 35W
Wadowice 152 49 52N 19 30 E
Waegwan 215 35 59N 128 23 E
Wafrah 192 28 33N 47 56 E
Wagenberg 143 51 40N 4 46 E
Wageningen, Neth. 142 51 58N 5 40 E
Wageningen, Surinam 119 5 50N 56 50W
Wager B. 95 65 26N 88 40W
Wager Bay 95 65 56N 90 49W
Wagga Wagga 231 35 7 S 147 24 E
Waghete 207 4 10 S 135 50 E
Wagin 229 33 17 S 117 25 E
Wagrowiec 152 52 48N 17 11 E
Wah 197 33 45N 72 40 E
Wahai 207 2 48 S 129 35 E
Wâḥid 191 30 48N 32 21 E
Wahnai 198 32 40N 65 50 E
Wahratta 232 31 58 S 141 50 E
Wai 200 17 56N 73 57 E
Wai, Koh 205 9 55N 102 55 E
Waiai → 235 46 12 S 167 38 E
Waiau 235 42 39 S 173 5 E
Waiau → 235 42 47 S 173 22 E
Waiawe Ganga → 201 6 15N 81 0 E
Waibeem 207 0 30 S 132 59 E
Waiblingen 147 48 49N 9 20 E
Waidhofen, Niederösterreich, Austria 150 48 49N 15 17 E
Waidhofen, Niederösterreich, Austria 150 47 57N 14 46 E
Waigeo 207 0 20 S 130 40 E
Waihao → 235 44 52 S 171 11 E
Waihao Downs 235 44 48 S 170 55 E
Waiheke Islands 234 36 48 S 175 6 E
Waihi 234 37 23 S 175 52 E
Waihola 235 46 1 S 170 8 E
Waihola L. 235 45 59 S 170 8 E
Waihou → 235 37 15 S 175 40 E
Waika 250 2 22 S 25 42 E
Waikabubak 207 9 45 S 119 25 E
Waikaia 235 45 44 S 168 51 E
Waikaka 235 45 55 S 169 1 E
Waikare, L. 234 37 26 S 175 13 E
Waikaremoana 234 38 42 S 177 12 E
Waikaremoana L. 234 38 49 S 177 9 E
Waikari 235 42 58 S 172 41 E
Waikato → 234 37 23 S 174 43 E
Waikerie 232 34 9 S 140 0 E
Waikiekie 234 35 57 S 174 16 E
Waikokopu 234 39 3 S 177 52 E
Waikouaiti 235 45 36 S 170 41 E
Waimangaroa 235 41 43 S 171 46 E
Waimarie 235 41 35 S 171 58 E
Waimate 235 44 45 S 171 3 E
Waimea Plain 235 45 55 S 168 35 E
Waimes 143 50 25N 6 7 E
Wainganga → 199 18 50N 79 55 E
Waingapu 207 9 35 S 120 11 E
Waingmaw 202 25 21N 97 26 E
Waini → 119 8 20N 59 50W
Wainuiomata 234 41 17 S 174 56 E
Wainwright 91 52 50N 110 50W
Waiotapu 234 38 21 S 176 25 E
Waiouru 234 39 28 S 175 41 E
Waipahi 235 46 6 S 169 15 E
Waipapa Pt. 235 46 40 S 168 51 E
Waipara 235 43 3 S 172 46 E
Waipawa 234 39 56 S 176 38 E
Waipiro 234 38 2 S 178 22 E
Waipu 234 35 59 S 174 29 E
Waipukurau 234 40 1 S 176 33 E
Wairakei 234 38 37 S 176 6 E
Wairarapa, L. 234 41 14 S 175 15 E
Wairau → 235 41 32 S 174 7 E
Wairio 235 45 59 S 168 3 E
Wairoa 234 39 3 S 177 25 E
Wairoa → 234 36 5 S 173 59 E
Waitaha 235 43 0 S 170 45 E
Waitaki → 235 44 56 S 171 7 E
Waitaki Plains 235 44 22 S 170 0 E
Waitara 234 38 59 S 174 15 E
Waitchie 232 35 22 S 143 8 E
Waitoa 234 37 37 S 175 35 E
Waitotara 234 39 49 S 174 44 E
Waiuku 234 37 15 S 174 45 E
Waiyevo 226 16 48 S 179 59W
Wajima 219 37 30N 137 0 E
Wajir 250 1 42N 40 5 E
Wajir □ 250 1 42N 40 20 E
Waka 252 1 1N 20 13 E
Wakasa 220 35 20N 134 24 E
Wakasa-Wan 221 35 40N 135 30 E
Wakatipu, L. 235 45 5 S 168 33 E
Wakaw 88 52 39N 105 44W
Wakayama 221 34 15N 135 15 E
Wakayama-ken □ 221 33 50N 135 30 E
Wake 220 34 48N 134 8 E
Wake I. 224 19 18N 166 36 E
Wakefield, Canada 82 45 38N 75 56W
Wakefield, N.Z. 235 41 24 S 173 5 E
Wakefield, U.K. 132 53 41N 1 31W
Wakeham 80 48 50N 64 34W
Wakeham Bay = Maricourt 78 56 34N 70 49W
Wakema 202 16 30N 95 11 E
Wakkanai 218 45 28N 141 35 E
Wakkerstroom 255 27 24 S 30 10 E
Wakomata L. 84 46 34N 83 22W
Wakool 231 35 28 S 144 23 E
Wakool → 231 35 5 S 143 33 E
Wakre 207 0 19 S 131 5 E
Waku 227 6 5 S 149 9 E
Wakuach L. 78 55 34N 67 32W
Walamba 251 13 30 S 28 42 E
Walamo 104 23 6N 106 13W
Wałbrzych 152 50 45N 16 18 E
Walbury Hill 133 51 22N 1 28W
Walcha 231 30 55 S 151 31 E
Walcha Road 233 30 55 S 151 24 E
Walcheren 143 51 30N 3 35 E
Wałcz 152 53 17N 16 27 E
Wald 149 47 17N 8 56 E
Waldbröl 146 50 52N 7 36 E
Waldburg Ra. 229 24 40 S 117 35 E
Waldeck, Canada 88 50 22N 107 36W
Waldeck, Germany 146 51 12N 9 4 E
Waldenburg 148 47 23N 7 45 E
Waldheim 88 52 39N 106 37W
Waldron 77 50 53N 102 35W
Waldshut 147 47 37N 8 12 E
Walembele 246 10 30N 1 58W
Walensee 149 47 7N 9 13 E
Walenstadt 149 47 8N 9 19 E
Wales □ 133 52 30N 3 30W
Wales I. 78 62 0N 72 30W
Walewale 247 10 21N 0 50W
Walgett 231 30 0 S 148 5 E
Walgreen Coast 13 75 15 S 105 0W
Walhachin 93 50 45N 120 59W
Walhalla 231 37 56 S 146 29 E
Walkaway 229 28 59 S 114 48 E
Walker L., Man., Canada 77 54 42N 95 57W
Walker L., Qué., Canada 78 50 20N 67 11W
Walkerston 230 21 11 S 149 8 E
Walkerton 84 44 10N 81 10W
Walla Walla 233 35 45 S 146 54 E
Wallabadah 230 17 57 S 142 15 E
Wallace 81 45 48N 63 29W
Wallaceburg 84 42 34N 82 23W
Wallacetown 235 46 21 S 168 19 E
Wallachia = Valahia 170 44 35N 25 0 E
Wallal 231 26 32 S 146 7 E
Wallal Downs 228 19 47 S 120 40 E
Wallambin, L. 229 30 57 S 117 35 E
Wallaroo 232 33 56 S 137 39 E
Wallasey 132 53 26N 3 2W
Walldürn 147 49 34N 9 23 E
Wallerawang 231 33 25 S 150 4 E
Wallhallow 230 17 50 S 135 50 E
Wallingford 132 51 40N 1 15W
Wallis & Futuna 224 13 18 S 176 10W
Wallisellen 149 47 25N 8 36 E
Wallsend, Australia 231 32 55 S 151 40 E
Wallsend, U.K. 132 54 59N 1 30W
Wallumbilla 231 26 33 S 149 9 E
Walmer 254 33 57 S 25 35 E
Walmsley, L. 77 63 25N 108 36W
Walney, Isle of 132 54 5N 3 15W
Walpeup 232 35 7 S 142 2 E
Walsall 133 52 36N 1 59W
Walsh 91 49 57N 110 3W
Walsh → 230 16 31 S 143 42 E
Walsh P.O. 230 16 40 S 144 0 E
Walshoutem 143 50 43N 5 4 E
Walsrode 146 52 51N 9 37 E
Waltair 200 17 44N 83 23 E
Waltershausen 146 50 53N 10 33 E
Waltham Sta. 82 45 57N 76 57W
Walton 81 45 14N 64 0W
Walu 202 26 28N 98 2 E
Walvisbaai 254 23 0 S 14 28 E
Walwa 233 35 59 S 147 44 E
Wamba, Kenya 250 0 58N 37 19 E
Wamba, Zaïre 250 2 10N 27 57 E
Wamena 207 4 4 S 138 57 E
Wamsasi 207 3 27 S 126 7 E
Wan Hat 202 20 14N 97 53 E
Wan Kinghao 202 21 34N 98 17 E
Wan Lai-kam 202 21 21N 98 22 E
Wan Tup 202 21 13N 98 42 E
Wan Xian 214 38 47N 115 7 E
Wana 197 32 20N 69 32 E
Wanaaring 231 29 38 S 144 9 E
Wanaka L. 235 44 33 S 169 7 E
Wan'an 217 26 26N 114 49 E
Wanapiri 207 4 30 S 135 59 E
Wanapitei → 84 46 2N 80 51W
Wanapitei L. 84 46 45N 80 40W
Wanbi 232 34 46 S 140 17 E
Wandaik 119 4 27N 59 35W
Wandanian 233 35 6 S 150 30 E
Wanderer 251 19 36 S 30 1 E
Wandoan 231 26 5 S 149 55 E
Wandre 143 50 40N 5 39 E
Wanfercée-Baulet 143 50 28N 4 35 E
Wanfu 215 40 8N 122 38 E
Wang → 204 17 8N 99 2 E
Wang Kai 245 9 3N 29 23 E
Wang Noi 204 14 13N 100 44 E
Wang Saphung 204 17 18N 101 46 E
Wang Thong 204 16 50N 100 26 E
Wanga 250 2 58N 29 12 E
Wangal 207 6 8 S 134 9 E
Wanganella 231 35 6 S 144 49 E
Wanganui 234 39 56 S 175 3 E
Wanganui →, N.I., N.Z. 234 39 55 S 175 4 E
Wanganui →, S.I., N.Z. 235 43 3 S 170 26 E
Wangaratta 231 36 21 S 146 19 E
Wangcang 216 32 18N 106 20 E
Wangdu 214 38 40N 115 7 E
Wangdu Phodrang 202 27 28N 89 54 E
Wangerooge 146 53 47N 7 52 E
Wangi 250 1 58 S 40 58 E
Wangiwangi 207 5 22 S 123 37 E
Wangjiang 217 30 10N 116 42 E
Wangmo 216 25 11N 106 5 E
Wangqing 215 43 12N 129 42 E
Wanham 90 55 44N 118 24W
Wankaner 198 22 35N 71 0 E
Wanless 89 54 11N 101 21W
Wannian 217 28 42N 117 4 E
Wanon Niwat 204 17 38N 103 46 E
Wanquan 214 40 50N 114 40 E
Wanrong 214 35 25N 110 50 E
Wanshan 216 27 30N 109 12 E
Wanshengchang 216 28 57N 106 53 E
Wanssum 143 51 32N 6 5 E
Wanstead 234 40 8 S 176 30 E
Wanxian 216 30 42N 108 20 E
Wanyin 202 20 23N 97 15 E
Wanyuan 216 32 4N 108 3 E
Wanzai 217 28 7N 114 30 E
Wanze 143 50 32N 5 13 E
Wapawekka L. 77 54 55N 104 40W
Wapella 89 50 16N 101 58W
Wapikopa L. 74 52 56N 87 53W
Wapiti → 90 55 5N 118 18W
Warabi 221 35 49N 139 41 E
Warangal 200 17 58N 79 35 E
Waratah 230 41 30 S 145 30 E
Waratah B. 231 38 54 S 146 5 E
Warburg, Canada 91 53 11N 114 19W
Warburg, Germany 146 51 29N 9 10 E
Warburton, W. Austral., Australia 229 26 8 S 126 35 E
Warburton, Australia 231 37 47 S 145 42 E
Warburton Ra. 229 25 55 S 126 28 E
Ward 235 41 49 S 174 11 E
Ward → 231 26 28 S 146 6 E
Ward Hunt, C. 227 8 2 S 148 10 E
Ward Hunt Str. 227 9 30 S 150 0 E
Warden 255 27 50 S 29 0 E
Wardha 198 20 45N 78 39 E
Wardlow 91 50 56N 111 31W
Wardner 91 49 25N 115 26W
Wards River 233 32 11 S 151 56 E
Ware 76 57 26N 125 41W
Waregem 143 50 53N 3 27 E
Waremme 143 50 43N 5 15 E
Waren 146 53 30N 12 41 E
Warendorf 146 51 57N 8 0 E
Warfield 93 49 6N 117 46W
Warialda 231 29 29 S 150 33 E
Wariap 207 1 30 S 134 5 E
Warin Chamrap 204 15 12N 104 53 E
Warka 152 51 47N 21 12 E
Warkopi 207 1 12 S 134 9 E
Warkworth 234 36 24 S 174 41 E
Warley 133 52 30N 2 0W
Warman 88 52 19N 106 30W
Warmbad, Namibia 254 28 25 S 18 42 E
Warmbad, S. Africa 255 24 51 S 28 19 E
Warmenhuizen 142 52 43N 4 44 E
Warmeriville 139 49 20N 4 13 E
Warmond 142 52 12N 4 30 E
Warnambool Downs 230 22 48 S 142 52 E
Warnemünde 146 54 9N 12 5 E
Warner 91 49 17N 112 12W
Warnes 123 17 30 S 63 10W
Warneton 143 50 45N 2 57 E
Warnow → 146 54 6N 12 9 E
Warnsveld 142 52 8N 6 14 E
Waroona 229 32 50 S 115 58 E
Warora 200 20 14N 79 1 E
Warracknabeal 232 36 9 S 142 26 E
Warragul 231 38 10 S 145 58 E
Warrawagine 228 20 51 S 120 42 E
Warrego → 231 30 24 S 145 21 E
Warrego Ra. 230 24 58 S 146 0 E
Warren, Australia 231 31 42 S 147 51 E
Warren, Canada 84 46 27N 80 18W
Warrender, C. 95 74 28N 81 46W
Warrenpoint 135 54 7N 6 15W
Warrenton 254 28 9 S 24 47 E
Warrenville 231 25 48 S 147 22 E
Warri 247 5 30N 5 41 E
Warrina 231 28 12 S 135 50 E
Warrington, N.Z. 235 45 43 S 170 35 E
Warrington, U.K. 132 53 25N 2 38W
Warrnambool 231 38 25 S 142 30 E
Warsa 207 0 47 S 135 55 E
Warsaw = Warszawa 152 52 13N 21 0 E
Warstein 146 51 26N 8 20 E
Warszawa 152 52 13N 21 0 E
Warszawa □ 152 52 30N 21 0 E
Warta 152 51 43N 18 38 E
Warta → 152 52 35N 14 39 E
Warthe = Warta → 152 52 35N 14 39 E
Waru 207 3 30 S 130 36 E
Warud 198 21 30N 78 16 E
Warwick, Australia 231 28 10 S 152 1 E
Warwick, U.K. 133 52 17N 1 36W
Warwick □ 133 52 20N 1 30W
Wasa 76 49 45N 115 50W
Wasaga Beach 84 44 31N 80 1W
Wasbank 255 28 15 S 30 9 E
Waseca 88 53 6N 109 28W
Wasekamio L. 77 56 45N 108 45W
Wash, The 132 52 58N 0 20 E
Washago 84 44 45N 79 20W
Washi L. 87 51 24N 87 2W
Washim 200 20 3N 77 0 E
Washuk 197 27 42N 64 45 E
Wasian 207 1 47 S 133 19 E
Wasilków 152 53 12N 23 13 E
Wasior 207 2 43 S 134 30 E
Waskada 89 49 6N 100 48W
Waskaiowaka, L. 77 56 33N 96 23W
Waskateena Beach 88 53 45N 105 15W
Waskatenau 90 54 7N 112 47W
Waskesiu L. 88 53 58N 106 12W
Waskesiu Lake 88 53 55N 106 5W
Wasm 244 18 2N 41 32 E
Wasmes 143 50 25N 3 50 E

Waspik 143 51 41N 4 57 E
Wassen 149 46 42N 8 36 E
Wassenaar 142 52 8N 4 24 E
Wasserburg 147 48 4N 12 15 E
Wasserkuppe 146 50 30N 9 56 E
Wassy 139 48 30N 4 58 E
Waswanipi 82 49 40N 76 29W
Waswanipi → 82 49 40N 76 25W
Waswanipi, L. 82 49 35N 76 40W
Watangpone 207 4 29 S 120 25 E
Water Park Pt. 230 22 56 S 150 47 E
Waterberg 255 24 14 S 28 0 E
Waterbury L. 77 58 10N 104 22W
Waterdown 84 43 20N 79 53W
Waterford, Canada 84 42 56N 80 17W
Waterford, Ireland 135 52 16N 7 8W
Waterford □ 135 52 10N 7 40W
Waterford Harb. 135 52 10N 6 58W
Waterhen L., Man., Canada 89 52 10N 99 40W
Waterhen L., Sask., Canada 77 54 28N 108 25W
Wateringen 142 52 2N 4 16 E
Waterloo, Belgium 143 50 43N 4 25 E
Waterloo, Ont., Canada 84 43 30N 80 32W
Waterloo, Qué., Canada 83 45 22N 72 32W
Waterloo, S. Leone 246 8 26N 13 8W
Watermeal-Boitsford 143 50 48N 4 25 E
Waterton Lakes Nat. Park 91 49 5N 114 15W
Waterton Park 91 49 3N 113 55W
Waterval-Boven 255 25 40 S 30 18 E
Waterville, N.S., Canada 81 45 3N 64 41W
Waterville, Qué., Canada 83 45 16N 71 54W
Watervliet 143 51 17N 3 38 E
Wates 209 7 51 S 110 10 E
Watford, Canada 84 42 57N 81 53W
Watford, U.K. 133 51 38N 0 23W
Wathaman → 77 57 16N 102 59W
Watheroo 229 30 15 S 116 0W
Wating 214 35 40N 106 38 E
Watîr, W. → 191 29 0N 34 40 E
Watou 143 50 51N 2 38 E
Watrous 88 51 40N 105 25W
Watsa 250 3 4N 29 30 E
Watshishou, L. 80 50 20N 60 50W
Watson, Australia 229 30 29 S 131 31 E
Watson, Canada 88 52 10N 104 30W
Watson Lake 76 60 6N 128 49W
Wattenwil 148 46 46N 7 30 E
Wattiwarriganna Cr. → 231 28 57 S 136 10 E
Wattwil 149 47 18N 9 6 E
Watuata = Batuata 207 6 12 S 122 42 E
Watubela, Kepulauan 207 4 28 S 131 35 E
Wau 227 7 21 S 146 47 E
Waubach 143 50 55N 6 3 E
Waubamik 84 45 27N 80 1W
Waubaushene 84 44 45N 79 42W
Waubra 231 37 21 S 143 39 E
Wauchope 231 31 28 S 152 45 E
Waugh 89 49 40N 95 11W
Wave Hill 228 17 32 S 131 0 E
Waveney → 133 52 24N 1 20 E
Waverley, Canada 81 44 47N 63 36W
Waverley, N.Z. 234 39 46 S 174 37 E
Wavre 143 50 43N 4 38 E
Wavreille 143 50 7N 5 15 E
Wâw 245 7 45N 28 1 E
Wâw al Kabîr 241 25 20N 16 43 E
Wâw an Nāmūs 241 24 55N 17 46 E
Wawa, Canada 87 47 59N 84 47W
Wawa, Nigeria 247 9 54N 4 27 E
Wawa, Sudan 244 20 30N 30 22 E
Wawagosic → 82 49 58N 79 6W
Wawanesa 89 49 36N 99 40W
Wawang L. 86 49 25N 90 34W
Wawoi → 227 7 48 S 143 16 E
Waxweiler 147 50 6N 6 22 E
Way, L. 229 26 45 S 120 16 E
Wayabula Rau 207 2 29N 128 17 E
Wayagamac, L. 83 47 21N 72 39W
Wayatinah 230 42 19 S 146 27 E
Wayi 245 5 8N 30 10 E
Waza 198 33 22N 69 22 E
Wazay 197 33 22N 69 26 E
Wāzin 241 31 58N 10 40 E
Wazirabad 198 32 30N 74 8 E
Wda → 152 53 25N 18 29 E
We, Indonesia 208 5 51N 95 18 E
Wé, Vanuatu 226 20 55 S 167 16 E
Weald, The 133 51 7N 0 9 E
Wear → 132 54 55N 1 22W
Webb 88 50 11N 108 12W
Webbwood 84 46 16N 81 52W
Weber 234 40 24 S 176 20 E
Webo = Nyaake 246 4 52N 7 37W
Weda 207 0 21N 127 50 E
Weda, Teluk 207 0 30N 127 50 E
Weddell I. 126 51 50 S 61 0W
Weddell Sea 13 72 30 S 40 0W
Wedderburn 231 36 26 S 143 33 E
Wedgeport 81 43 44N 65 59W
Wedza 251 18 40 S 31 33 E
Wee Elwah 233 32 2 S 145 14 E
Wee Waa 231 30 11 S 149 26 E
Weedon-Centre 83 45 42N 71 27W
Weekes 88 52 34N 102 52W
Weemelah 231 29 2 S 149 15 E
Weenen 255 28 48 S 30 7 E
Weener 146 53 10N 7 23 E
Weert 143 51 15N 5 43 E
Weesp 142 52 18N 5 2 E
Weggis 149 47 2N 8 26 E
Wegierska-Gorka 152 49 36N 19 7 E
Wegliniec 152 51 18N 15 10 E
Węgorzewo 152 54 13N 21 43 E
Węgrów 152 52 24N 22 0 E
Wehl 142 51 58N 6 13 E
Wei He →, Hebei, China 214 36 10N 115 45 E
Wei He →, Shaanxi, China 214 34 38N 110 15 E
Weichang 215 41 58N 117 49 E
Weichuan 214 34 20N 113 59 E
Weida 146 50 47N 12 3 E
Weiden 147 49 40N 12 10 E
Weifang 215 36 44N 119 7 E
Weihai 215 37 30N 122 6 E
Weilburg 146 50 28N 8 17 E
Weilheim 147 47 50N 11 9 E
Weimar 146 51 0N 11 20 E
Weinan 214 34 31N 109 29 E
Weinfelden 149 47 34N 9 6 E
Weingarten 147 47 49N 9 39 E
Weinheim 147 49 33N 8 40 E
Weining 216 26 50N 104 17 E
Weipa 230 12 40 S 141 50 E
Weir →, Australia 231 28 20 S 149 50 E
Weir →, Canada 77 56 54N 93 21W
Weir River 77 56 49N 94 6W
Weirdale 88 53 27N 105 15W
Weisen 149 46 42N 9 43 E
Weishan, Shandong, China 215 34 47N 117 5 E
Weishan, Yunnan, China 216 25 12N 100 20 E
Weissenburg 147 49 2N 10 58 E
Weissenfels 146 51 11N 12 0 E
Weisshorn 148 46 7N 7 43 E
Weissmies 148 46 8N 8 1 E
Weisstannen 149 46 59N 9 22 E
Weisswasser 146 51 30N 14 36 E
Weiswampach 143 50 8N 6 5 E
Wéitra 150 48 41N 14 54 E
Weixi 216 27 10N 99 10 E
Weixin 216 27 48N 105 3 E
Weiyuan 214 35 7N 104 10 E
Weiz 150 47 13N 15 39 E
Weizhou Dao 216 21 0N 109 5 E
Wejherowo 152 54 35N 18 12 E
Wekusko 77 54 30N 99 45W
Wekusko L. 77 54 40N 99 50W
Welbourn Hill 231 27 21 S 134 6 E
Welby 77 50 33N 101 29W
Weldon 88 53 1N 105 8W
Weldya 245 11 50N 39 34 E
Welega □ 245 9 25N 34 20 E
Welkenraedt 143 50 39N 5 58 E
Welkite 245 8 15N 37 42 E
Welkom 254 28 0 S 26 50 E
Welland 84 43 0N 79 15W
Welland → 132 52 43N 0 10W
Wellen 143 50 50N 5 21 E
Wellesley Is. 230 16 42 S 139 30 E
Wellin 143 50 5N 5 6 E
Wellingborough 133 52 18N 0 41W
Wellington, Australia 231 32 35 S 148 59 E
Wellington, B.C., Canada 92 49 13N 123 58W
Wellington, Newf., Canada 79 48 53N 53 58W
Wellington, Ont., Canada 85 43 57N 77 20W
Wellington, P.E.I., Canada 81 46 27N 64 0W
Wellington, N.Z. 234 41 19 S 174 46 E
Wellington, S. Africa 254 33 38 S 18 57 E
Wellington, Somerset, U.K. 133 50 58N 3 13W
Wellington, Salop, U.K. 132 52 42N 2 31W
Wellington □ 235 40 8 S 175 36 E
Wellington, I. 126 49 30 S 75 0W
Wellington, L. 231 38 6 S 147 20 E
Wellington Chan. 95 75 0N 93 0W
Wells, Canada 93 53 6N 121 36W
Wells, Norfolk, U.K. 132 52 57N 0 51 E
Wells, Somerset, U.K. 133 51 12N 2 39W
Wells Gray Prov. Park 93 52 30N 120 15W
Wells L. 229 26 44 S 123 15 E
Wellsford 234 36 16 S 174 32 E
Welmel, Wabi → 245 5 38N 40 47 E
Wełna → 152 52 46N 17 32 E
Welo 256 9 25N 48 55 E
Welo □ 245 11 50N 39 48 E
Wels 150 48 9N 14 1 E
Welsford 81 45 27N 66 20W
Welshpool 133 52 40N 3 9W
Welwyn 77 50 20N 101 30W
Wem 132 52 52N 2 45W
Wembere → 250 4 10 S 34 15 E
Wembley 90 55 9N 119 8W
Wemmel 143 50 55N 4 18 E
Wen Xian, Gansu, China 214 32 43N 104 36 E
Wen Xian, Henan, China 214 34 55N 113 5 E
Wenasaga → 86 50 38N 93 10W
Wenchang 204 19 38N 110 42 E
Wencheng 217 27 46N 120 4 E
Wenchi 246 7 46N 2 8W
Wenchow = Wenzhou 217 28 0N 120 38 E
Wenchuan 216 31 22N 103 35 E
Wendeng 215 37 15N 122 5 E
Wendesi 207 2 30 S 134 17 E
Wendo 245 6 40N 38 27 E
Wenduine 143 51 18N 3 5 E
Wenebegon → 87 46 53N 83 12W
Wenebegon L. 87 47 23N 83 6W
Weng'an 216 27 5N 107 25 E
Wengcheng 217 24 22N 113 50 E
Wengen 148 46 37N 7 55 E
Wengyuan 217 24 20N 114 9 E
Wenjiang 216 30 44N 103 55 E
Wenling 217 28 21N 121 20 E
Wenlock → 230 12 2 S 141 55 E
Wenshan 216 23 20N 104 18 E
Wenshang 214 35 45N 116 30 E
Wenshui, Guizhou, China 216 28 27N 106 28 E
Wenshui, Shanxi, China 214 37 26N 112 1 E
Wensu 212 41 15N 80 10 E
Wentworth, Australia 231 34 2 S 141 54 E
Wentworth, Canada 81 45 38N 63 33W
Wenut 207 3 11 S 133 19 E
Wenxi 214 35 20N 111 10 E
Wenzhou 217 28 0N 120 38 E
Wepener 254 29 42 S 27 3 E
Werbomont 143 50 23N 5 41 E
Werda 254 25 24 S 23 15 E
Werdau 146 50 45N 12 20 E
Werder, Ethiopia 256 6 58N 45 1 E
Werder, Germany 146 52 23N 12 56 E
Werdohl 146 51 15N 7 47 E
Wereilu 245 10 40N 39 28 E
Weri 207 3 10 S 132 38 E
Werkendam 142 51 50N 4 53 E
Werne 146 51 38N 7 38 E
Werneck 147 49 59N 10 6 E
Wernigerode 146 51 49N 10 45 E
Werra → 146 51 26N 9 39 E
Werribee 231 37 54 S 144 40 E
Werrimull 231 34 25 S 141 38 E
Werris Creek 231 31 18 S 150 38 E
Wersar 207 1 30 S 131 55 E
Wertach → 147 48 24N 10 53 E
Wertheim 147 49 44N 9 32 E
Wertingen 147 48 33N 10 41 E
Wervershoof 142 52 44N 5 10 E
Wervik 143 50 47N 3 3 E
Wesel 146 51 39N 6 34 E
Weser → 146 53 33N 8 30 E
Wesiri 207 7 30 S 126 30 E
Weslemkoon L. 85 45 2N 77 25W
Wesleyville 79 49 8N 53 36W
Wessel, C. 230 10 59 S 136 46 E
Wessel Is. 230 11 10 S 136 45 E
Wesselburen 146 54 11N 8 53 E
Wessem 143 51 11N 5 49 E
West Baines → 228 15 38 S 129 59 E
West Bengal □ 199 23 0N 88 0 E
West Bromwich 133 52 32N 2 1W
West Cape Howe 229 35 8 S 117 36 E
West End 112 26 41N 78 58W
West Falkland 126 51 40 S 60 0W
West Germany ■ 146 52 0N 9 0 E
West Glamorgan □ 133 51 40N 3 55W
West Ice Shelf 13 67 0 S 85 0 E
West Indies 113 15 0N 70 0W
West Looe 133 50 21N 4 29W
West Lorne 84 42 36N 81 36W
West Lunga → 251 13 6 S 24 39 E
West Magpie → 78 52 0N 65 0W
West Midlands □ 133 52 30N 1 55W
West Moors 132 50 49N 1 50W
West Nicholson 251 21 2 S 29 20 E
West Pt. 232 35 1 S 135 56 E
West Pokot □ 250 1 30N 35 15 E
West Poplar 88 49 0N 106 22W
West Road → 93 53 18N 122 53W
West Schelde → = Westerschelde → 143 51 25N 3 25 E
West Siberian Plain 186 62 0N 75 0 E
West Sussex □ 133 50 55N 0 30W
West-Terschelling 142 53 22N 5 13 E
West Thurlow I. 92 50 25N 125 35W
West-Vlaanderen □ 143 51 0N 3 0 E
West Wyalong 231 33 56 S 147 10 E
West Yorkshire □ 132 53 45N 1 40W
Westall Pt. 231 32 55 S 134 4 E
Westbourne 89 50 8N 98 35W
Westbury 230 41 30 S 146 51 E
Westerbork 142 52 51N 6 37 E
Westerland 146 54 51N 8 20 E
Western □, Kenya 250 0 30N 34 30 E
Western □, Uganda 250 1 45N 31 30 E
Western □, Zambia 251 15 15 S 24 30 E
Western Australia □ 234 25 0 S 118 0 E
Western Duck I. 84 45 45N 83 0W
Western Ghats 201 14 0N 75 0 E
Western Isles □ 134 57 30N 7 10W
Western Pen. 86 49 30N 94 50W
Western River 232 35 42 S 136 56 E
Western Sahara ■ 240 25 0N 13 0W
Western Samoa ■ 224 14 0 S 172 0W
Western Shore 81 44 32N 64 19W
Westerschelde → 143 51 25N 3 25 E
Westerstede 146 53 15N 7 55 E
Westervoort 142 51 58N 5 59 E
Westerwald 146 50 39N 8 0 E
Westfield 81 45 22N 66 14W
Westgat 143 51 39N 3 44 E
Westkapelle, Belgium 143 51 19N 3 19 E
Westkapelle, Neth. 143 51 31N 3 28 E
Westland □ 235 43 33 S 169 59 E
Westland Bight 235 42 55 S 170 5 E
Westlock 90 54 9N 113 55W
Westmalle 143 51 18N 4 42 E
Westmeath □ 135 53 30N 7 30W
Weston 206 5 10N 115 35 E
Weston I. 78 52 33N 79 36W
Weston-super-Mare 133 51 20N 2 59W
Westport, N.S., Canada 81 44 15N 66 22W
Westport, Newf., Canada 79 49 47N 56 38W
Westport, Ont., Canada 85 44 40N 76 25W
Westport, Ireland 135 53 44N 9 31W
Westport, N.Z. 235 41 46 S 171 37 E
Westray, Canada 89 53 36N 101 24W
Westray, U.K. 134 59 18N 3 0W
Westree 87 47 26N 81 34W
Westsyde 93 50 47N 120 21W
Westview 76 49 50N 124 31W
Westville 81 45 34N 62 43W
Wetar 207 7 30 S 126 30 E
Wetaskiwin 91 52 55N 113 24W
Wetlet 202 22 20N 95 53 E
Wetteren 143 51 0N 3 53 E
Wettingen 149 47 28N 8 20 E
Wetzikon 149 47 19N 8 48 E
Wetzlar 146 50 33N 8 30 E
Wevelgem 143 50 49N 3 12 E
Wewak 227 3 38 S 143 41 E
Wexford 135 52 20N 6 28W
Wexford □ 135 52 20N 6 25W
Wexford Harb. 135 52 20N 6 25W
Weyburn 88 49 40N 103 50W
Weyburn L. 76 63 0N 117 59W
Weyer 150 47 51N 14 40 E
Weyib → 245 7 15N 40 15 E
Weymouth, Canada 81 44 30N 66 1W
Weymouth, U.K. 133 50 36N 2 28W
Weymouth, C. 230 12 37 S 143 27 E
Wezemaal 143 50 57N 4 45 E
Wezep 142 52 28N 6 0 E
Whakamaru 234 38 23 S 175 50 E
Whakatane 234 37 57 S 177 1 E
Whale → 78 58 15N 67 40W
Whale Cove 77 62 11N 92 36W
Whales, B. of 13 78 0 S 165 0W
Whaletown 92 50 7N 125 2W
Whalsay 134 60 22N 1 0W
Whangamata 234 37 12 S 175 53 E
Whangamomona 234 39 8 S 174 44 E
Whangarei 234 35 43 S 174 21 E
Whangarei Harbour 234 35 45 S 174 28 E
Whangaroa Harb. 234 35 4 S 173 46 E
Wharanui 235 41 55 S 174 6 E
Wharfe → 132 53 55N 1 30W
Wharfedale 132 54 7N 2 4W
Whataroa 235 43 18 S 170 24 E
Whataroa → 235 43 7 S 170 16 E
Wheatley 84 42 6N 82 27W
Wheeler →, Qué., Canada 78 57 2N 67 13W
Wheeler →, Sask., Canada 77 57 25N 105 30W
Whernside 132 54 14N 2 24W
Whiskey Gap 91 49 0N 113 3W

Whiskey Jack L. **77** 58 23N 101 55W
Whistleduck Cr. → **230** 20 15 S 135 18 E
Whitbourne **79** 47 25N 53 32W
Whitby, Canada **85** 43 52N 78 56W
Whitby, U.K. **132** 54 29N 0 37W
White → **87** 48 33N 86 16W
White B. **79** 50 0N 56 35W
White Bear **88** 50 53N 108 13W
White Bear Res. ... **79** 48 10N 57 5W
White Cliffs .... **231** 30 50 S 143 10 E
White Fox **88** 53 27N 104 5W
White I. .... **234** 37 30 S 177 13 E
White L., Ont.,
Canada **85** 45 18N 76 31W
White L., Ont.,
Canada **87** 48 47N 85 37W
White Nile = Nîl el
Abyad → .... **245** 15 38N 32 31 E
White Nile Dam .... **245** 15 24N 32 30 E
White Otter L. **86** 49 5N 91 55W
White Owl L. **87** 47 10N 82 35W
White Pass **76** 59 40N 135 3W
White River,
Canada **87** 48 35N 85 20W
White River,
S. Africa .... **255** 25 20 S 31 0 E
White Rock **93** 49 2N 122 48W
White Russia =
Byelorussian
S.S.R. □ .... **178** 53 30N 27 0 E
White Sea = Beloye
More .... **176** 66 30N 38 0 E
White Volta → **247** 9 10N 1 15W
Whiteclay L. **86** 50 53N 88 45W
Whitecliffs .... **235** 43 26 S 171 55 E
Whitecourt **90** 54 10N 115 45W
Whitefish **84** 46 23N 81 19W
Whitefish Falls **84** 46 7N 81 44W
Whitefish L. **77** 62 41N 106 48W
Whitegull, L. **78** 55 27N 64 17W
Whitehaven **132** 54 33N 3 35W
Whitehorse **76** 60 43N 135 3W
Whitehorse, Vale of **133** 51 37N 1 30W
Whiteman Ra. ...... **227** 5 55 S 150 0 E
Whitemark .... **230** 40 7 S 148 3 E
Whitemouth **89** 49 57N 95 58W
Whitemouth → **89** 50 7N 96 2W
Whitemouth L. **89** 49 15N 95 40W
Whiteplains **246** 6 28N 10 40W
Whitesail, L. **76** 53 35N 127 45W
Whitesand → **88** 51 34N 102 56W
Whiteshell Prov.
Park **89** 50 0N 95 40W
Whiteside, Canal ... **126** 53 55 S 70 15W
Whiteswan Ls. **88** 54 5N 105 10W
Whitewater, Cr. → **86** 49 0N 108 0W
Whitewater L. **86** 50 50N 89 10W
Whitewood,
Australia .... **230** 21 28 S 143 30 E
Whitewood, Canada **89** 50 20N 102 20W
Whitfield .... **231** 36 42 S 146 24 E
Whithorn **134** 54 44N 4 25W
Whitianga .... **234** 36 47 S 175 41 E
Whitney **85** 45 31N 78 14W
Whitstable .... **133** 51 21N 1 2 E
Whitsunday I. ...... **230** 20 15 S 149 4 E
Whittlesea .... **231** 37 27 S 145 9 E
Wholdaia L. **77** 60 43N 104 20W
Whyalla .... **231** 33 2 S 137 30 E
Whycocomagh **81** 45 59N 61 7W
Whyjonta .... **231** 29 41 S 142 28 E
Wiarton **84** 44 40N 81 10W
Wiawso **246** 6 10N 2 25W
Wiazów .... **152** 50 50N 17 10 E
Wichabai **119** 2 57N 59 35W
Wichian Buri ...... **204** 15 39N 101 7 E
Wick **134** 58 26N 3 5W
Wicked Pt. **85** 43 52N 77 15W
Wickepin .... **229** 32 50 S 117 30 E
Wickham **83** 45 45N 72 30W
Wickham, C. ...... **230** 39 35 S 143 57 E
Wicklow **135** 53 0N 6 2W
Wicklow □ **135** 52 59N 6 25W
Wicklow Hd. **135** 52 59N 6 3W
Wicklow Mts. **135** 53 0N 6 30W
Widawa .... **152** 51 27N 18 51 E
Widawka .... **152** 51 7N 19 36 E
Widgiemooltha ..... **229** 31 30 S 121 34 E
Widnes **132** 53 22N 2 44W
Więcbork .... **152** 53 21N 17 30 E
Wiedenbrück ...... **146** 51 52N 8 15 E
Wiek .... **146** 54 37N 13 17 E
Wielbark .... **152** 53 24N 20 55 E
Wieleń .... **152** 52 53N 16 9 E
Wieliczka .... **152** 50 0N 20 5 E
Wieluń .... **152** 51 15N 18 34 E
Wien .... **151** 48 12N 16 22 E
Wiener Neustadt ... **151** 47 49N 16 16 E
Wieprz →,
Koszalin, Poland . **152** 54 26N 16 35 E
Wieprz →, Lublin,
Poland .... **152** 51 34N 21 49 E
Wierden .... **142** 52 22N 6 35 E
Wiers .... **143** 50 30N 3 32 E
Wieruszów .... **152** 51 19N 18 9 E
Wiesbaden .... **147** 50 7N 8 17 E
Wiesental .... **147** 49 15N 8 30 E
Wigan **132** 53 33N 2 38W
Wight, I. of **133** 50 40N 1 20W
Wigry, Jezioro ..... **152** 54 2N 23 8 E
Wigtown **134** 54 52N 4 27W
Wigtown B. **134** 54 46N 4 15W
Wijchen .... **142** 51 48N 5 44 E
Wijhe .... **142** 52 23N 6 8 E
Wijk bij Duurstede . **142** 51 59N 5 21 E
Wikwemikong **84** 45 48N 81 43W
Wil .... **149** 47 28N 9 3 E
Wilamowice .... **151** 49 55N 19 9 E
Wilangee .... **232** 31 28 S 141 20 E
Wilberforce **85** 45 2N 78 13W
Wilberforce, C. .... **230** 11 54 S 136 35 E
Wilcannia .... **231** 31 30 S 143 26 E
Wilcox **88** 50 6N 104 44W
Wildbad .... **147** 48 44N 8 32 E
Wildervank .... **142** 53 5N 6 52 E
Wildeshausen ...... **146** 52 54N 8 25 E
Wildgoose L. **87** 49 44N 87 11W
Wildhay → **90** 53 59N 117 20W
Wildhorn .... **148** 46 22N 7 21 E
Wildon .... **150** 46 52N 15 31 E
Wildspitze .... **150** 46 53N 10 53 E
Wildstrubel .... **148** 46 24N 7 32 E
Wildwood **90** 53 37N 115 14W
Wilga → .... **152** 51 52N 21 18 E
Wilgaroon .... **233** 30 52 S 145 42 E
Wilhelm II Coast ... **13** 68 0 S 90 0 E
Wilhelm Mt. .... **227** 5 50 S 145 1 E
Wilhelm-Pieck-Stadt
Guben .... **146** 51 59N 14 48 E
Wilhelmina, Geb. .. **119** 3 50N 56 30W
Wilhelmina Kanaal . **143** 51 36N 5 6 E
Wilhelmsburg,
Austria .... **150** 48 6N 15 36 E
Wilhelmsburg,
Germany .... **146** 53 28N 10 1 E
Wilhelmshaven ..... **146** 53 30N 8 9 E
Wilhelmstal .... **254** 21 58 S 16 21 E
Wilkes Land .... **13** 69 0 S 120 0 E
Wilkes Sub-Glacial
Basin .... **13** 75 0 S 130 0 E
Wilkie **88** 52 27N 108 42W
Wilkinson Lakes ... **229** 29 40 S 132 39 E
Willamulka .... **232** 33 55 S 137 52 E
Willandra Billabong
Creek → .... **231** 33 22 S 145 52 E
Willard **100** 28 58N 110 52W
Willard, Pta. **98** 29 50N 114 25W
Willaura .... **232** 37 31 S 142 45 E
Willbriggie .... **233** 34 28 S 146 2 E
Willebroek .... **143** 51 4N 4 22 E
Willemstad **113** 12 5N 69 0W
Willeroo .... **228** 15 14 S 131 37 E
William → **77** 59 8N 109 19W
William, Mt. .... **232** 37 17 S 142 35 E
William A. Switzer
Prov. Park **90** 53 30N 117 48W
William Creek ..... **231** 28 58 S 136 22 E
William L. **89** 53 54N 99 21W
Williambury .... **229** 23 45 S 115 12 E
Williams .... **229** 33 2 S 116 52 E
Williams L. **86** 51 48N 90 45W
Williams Lake **93** 52 10N 122 10W
Williamstown ...... **231** 37 51 S 144 52 E
Willingdon **90** 53 50N 112 8W
Willis Group .... **230** 16 18 S 150 0 E
Willisau .... **148** 47 7N 8 0 E
Williston .... **254** 31 20 S 20 53 E
Williston L. **76** 56 0N 124 0W
Willmore Wilderness
Park **90** 53 45N 119 30W
Willow Bunch **88** 49 20N 105 35W
Willow Bunch L. ... **88** 49 27N 105 27W
Willow L. **76** 62 10N 119 8W
Willow River **76** 54 6N 122 28W
Willow Tree .... **233** 31 40 S 150 45 E
Willow Wall, The .. **215** 42 10N 122 0 E
Willowbrook **88** 51 12N 102 48W
Willowlake → **76** 62 42N 123 8W
Willowmore .... **254** 33 15 S 23 30 E
Willows .... **230** 23 39 S 147 25 E
Wills, L. .... **228** 21 25 S 128 51 E
Wills Cr. → .... **230** 22 43 S 140 2 E
Willunga .... **232** 35 15 S 138 30 E
Wilmington .... **231** 32 39 S 138 7 E
Wilmot **81** 46 2N 62 30W
Wilpena Cr. → .... **231** 31 25 S 139 29 E
Wilrijk .... **143** 51 9N 4 22 E
Wilson →,
Queens.,
Australia .... **231** 27 38 S 141 24 E
Wilson →,
W. Austral.,
Australia .... **228** 16 48 S 128 16 E
Wilson Bluff .... **229** 31 41 S 129 0 E
Wilson Creek **92** 49 27N 123 43W
Wilson Landing **93** 50 0N 119 30W
Wilsons Beach **81** 44 56N 66 56W
Wilsons Promontory **231** 38 55 S 146 25 E
Wilster .... **146** 53 55N 9 23 E
Wilton **133** 51 5N 1 52W
Wilton → .... **230** 14 45 S 134 33 E
Wiltshire □ **133** 51 20N 2 0W
Wiltz .... **143** 49 57N 5 55 E
Wiluna .... **229** 26 36 S 120 14 E
Wimereux .... **139** 50 45N 1 37 E
Wimmera .... **231** 36 30 S 142 0 E
Wimmera → ...... **231** 36 8 S 141 56 E
Winagami L. **90** 55 37N 116 44W
Winagami Lake
Prov. Park **90** 55 37N 116 39W
Winam G. .... **250** 0 20 S 34 15 E
Winburg .... **254** 28 30 S 27 2 E
Winchelsea .... **232** 38 10 S 144 1 E
Winchester, Canada **85** 45 6N 75 21W
Winchester, N.Z. ... **235** 44 11 S 171 17 E
Winchester, U.K. .. **133** 51 4N 1 19W
Windemere L. **87** 47 58N 83 47W
Windermere **91** 50 28N 115 59W
Windermere, L. **132** 54 20N 2 57W
Windfall **90** 54 12N 116 13W
Windflower L. **76** 62 52N 118 30W
Windhoek .... **254** 22 35 S 17 4 E
Windigo → **83** 47 46N 73 19W
Windischgarsten .... **150** 47 42N 14 21 E
Windorah .... **230** 25 24 S 142 36 E
Windrush → **133** 51 48N 1 35W
Windsor, Australia . **231** 33 37 S 150 50 E
Windsor, N.S.,
Canada **81** 44 59N 64 5W
Windsor, Newf.,
Canada **79** 48 57N 55 40W
Windsor, Ont.,
Canada **84** 42 18N 83 0W
Windsor, Qué.,
Canada **83** 45 34N 72 0W
Windsor, N.Z. ..... **235** 44 59 S 170 49 E
Windsor, U.K. **133** 51 28N 0 36W
Windsorton .... **254** 28 16 S 24 44 E
Windthorst **88** 50 6N 102 50W
Windward Is.,
Atl. Oc. **113** 13 0N 63 0W
Windward Is.,
Pac. Oc. .... **225** 18 0 S 149 0W
Windward Passage
= Vientos, Paso
de los **113** 20 0N 74 0W
Windy L., N.W.T.,
Canada **77** 60 20N 100 2W
Windy L., Sask.,
Canada **88** 54 22N 102 35W
Winefred L. **90** 55 30N 110 30W
Winejok .... **245** 9 1N 27 30 E
Winfield **91** 52 58N 114 26W
Wingate Mts. ...... **228** 14 25 S 130 40 E
Wingen .... **231** 31 54 S 150 54 E
Wingene .... **143** 51 3N 3 17 E
Wingham, Australia **231** 31 48 S 152 22 E
Wingham, Canada .. **84** 43 55N 81 20W
Winisk **74** 55 20N 85 15W
Winisk → **74** 55 17N 85 5W
Winisk L. **74** 52 55N 87 22W
Winkler **89** 49 10N 97 56W
Winklern .... **150** 46 52N 12 52 E
Winneba **247** 5 25N 0 36W
Winnecke Cr. → .. **228** 18 35 S 131 34 E
Winning .... **228** 23 9 S 114 30 E
Winnipeg **89** 49 54N 97 9W
Winnipeg → **89** 50 38N 96 19W
Winnipeg, L. **89** 52 0N 97 0W
Winnipeg Beach **89** 50 30N 96 58W
Winnipegosis **89** 51 39N 99 55W
Winnipegosis L. **89** 52 30N 100 0W
Winokapau, L. **78** 53 15N 62 50W
Winschoten .... **142** 53 9N 7 3 E
Winsen .... **146** 53 21N 10 11 E
Winsum .... **142** 53 20N 6 32 E
Winter Harbour **92** 50 31N 128 2W
Winterberg .... **146** 51 12N 8 30 E
Wintering L. **87** 49 26N 87 16W
Winterswijk .... **142** 51 58N 6 43 E
Winterthur .... **149** 47 30N 8 44 E
Winterton **79** 47 58N 53 20W
Winton, Australia .. **230** 22 24 S 143 3 E
Winton, N.Z. ...... **235** 46 8 S 168 20 E
Wintzenheim .... **139** 48 4N 7 17 E
Wipper → .... **146** 51 17N 11 10 E
Wirral **132** 53 25N 3 0W
Wirraminna .... **232** 31 12 S 136 13 E
Wirrulla .... **231** 32 24 S 134 31 E
Wisbech .... **132** 52 39N 0 10 E
Wiseton **88** 51 19N 107 39W
Wishart **88** 51 33N 103 59W
Wishaw **134** 55 46N 3 55W
Wisła .... **151** 49 38N 18 53 E
Wisła → .... **152** 54 22N 18 55 E
Wisłok → .... **151** 50 13N 22 32 E
Wisłoka → .... **151** 50 27N 21 23 E
Wismar, Germany .. **146** 53 53N 11 23 E
Wismar, Guyana ... **119** 5 59N 58 18W
Wissant .... **139** 50 52N 1 40 E
Wissembourg ...... **139** 49 2N 7 57 E
Wissenkerke .... **143** 51 35N 3 45 E
Wistaria **92** 53 52N 126 22W
Wistoka → .... **152** 49 50N 21 28 E
Wisznice .... **152** 51 48N 23 13 E
Witbank .... **255** 25 51 S 29 14 E
Witdraai .... **254** 26 58 S 20 48 E
Witham → **132** 53 3N 0 8W
Withernsea .... **132** 53 43N 0 2 E
Withrow **91** 52 23N 114 30W
Witkowo .... **152** 52 26N 17 45 E
Witmarsum .... **142** 53 6N 5 28 E
Witney **133** 51 47N 1 29W
Witnossob → ..... **254** 26 55 S 20 37 E
Wittdün .... **146** 54 38N 8 23 E
Witten .... **146** 51 26N 7 19 E
Wittenberg .... **146** 51 51N 12 39 E
Wittenberge .... **146** 53 0N 11 44 E
Wittenburg .... **146** 53 30N 11 4 E
Wittenoom .... **228** 22 15 S 118 20 E
Wittingen .... **146** 52 43N 10 43 E
Wittlich .... **147** 50 0N 6 54 E
Wittmund .... **146** 53 39N 7 45 E
Wittow .... **146** 54 37N 13 21 E
Wittstock .... **146** 53 10N 12 30 E
Witzenhausen ...... **146** 51 20N 9 50 E
Wkra → .... **152** 52 27N 20 44 E
Władysławowo ..... **152** 54 48N 18 25 E
Wlen .... **152** 51 0N 15 39 E
Wlingi .... **209** 8 5 S 112 25 E
Włocławek .... **152** 52 40N 19 3 E
Włocławek □ ...... **152** 52 50N 19 10 E
Włodawa .... **152** 51 33N 23 31 E
Włoszczowa .... **152** 50 50N 19 55 E
Wodian .... **214** 32 50N 112 35 E
Wodonga .... **231** 36 5 S 146 50 E
Wodzisław Śląski ... **152** 50 1N 18 26 E
Woerden .... **142** 52 5N 4 54 E
Woerth .... **139** 48 57N 7 45 E
Woëvre, Plaine de la **139** 49 15N 5 45 E
Wognum .... **142** 52 40N 5 1 E
Wohlen .... **149** 47 21N 8 17 E
Woinbogoin .... **216** 32 51N 98 39 E
Wokam .... **207** 5 45 S 134 28 E
Wokha .... **202** 26 6N 94 16 E
Woking **76** 55 35N 118 50W
Wolbrom .... **152** 50 24N 19 45 E
Wołczyn .... **152** 51 1N 18 3 E
Woldegk .... **146** 53 27N 13 35 E
Wolf → **76** 60 17N 132 33W
Wolf Bay **80** 50 16N 60 8W
Wolf L. **76** 60 24N 131 40W
Wolfe I. **85** 44 7N 76 20W
Wolfenbüttel .... **146** 52 10N 10 33 E
Wolfenden **76** 52 0N 119 25W
Wolfheze .... **142** 52 0N 5 48 E
Wolfsberg .... **150** 46 50N 14 52 E
Wolfsburg .... **146** 52 27N 10 49 E
Wolfville **81** 45 5N 64 22W
Wolgast .... **146** 54 3N 13 46 E
Wolhusen .... **148** 47 4N 8 4 E
Wolin, Szczecin,
Poland .... **152** 54 0N 14 40 E
Wolin, Szczecin,
Poland .... **152** 53 50N 14 37 E
Wollaston, Islas .... **126** 55 40 S 67 30W
Wollaston L. **77** 58 7N 103 10W
Wollaston Pen. **94** 69 30N 115 0W
Wollogorang .... **230** 17 13 S 137 57 E
Wollongong .... **231** 34 25 S 150 54 E
Wolmaransstad ..... **254** 27 12 S 26 13 E
Wolmirstedt .... **146** 52 15N 11 35 E
Wołomin .... **152** 52 19N 21 15 E
Wołów .... **152** 51 20N 16 38 E
Wolseley, Australia . **232** 36 23 S 140 54 E
Wolseley, Canada .. **88** 50 25N 103 15W
Wolseley, S. Africa . **254** 33 26 S 19 7 E
Wolstenholme, C. ... **78** 62 35N 77 30W
Wolstenholme Fjord **95** 76 0N 70 0W
Wolsztyn .... **152** 52 8N 16 5 E
Wolvega .... **142** 52 52N 6 0 E
Wolverhampton **133** 52 35N 2 6W
Wommels .... **142** 53 6N 5 36 E
Wonarah .... **230** 19 55 S 136 20 E
Wonboyn .... **233** 37 15 S 149 55 E
Wonck .... **143** 50 46N 5 38 E
Wondai .... **231** 26 20 S 151 49 E
Wondelgem .... **143** 51 5N 3 44 E
Wonder Gorge ..... **251** 14 40 S 29 0 E
Wongalarroo L. ..... **231** 31 32 S 144 0 E
Wongan Hills ...... **229** 30 51 S 116 37 E
Wongawol .... **229** 26 5 S 121 55 E
Wŏnju .... **215** 37 22N 127 58 E
Wonosari .... **209** 7 58 S 110 36 E
Wonosobo .... **209** 7 22 S 109 54 E
Wŏnsan .... **215** 39 11N 127 27 E
Wonthaggi .... **231** 38 37 S 145 37 E
Woocalla .... **231** 31 42 S 137 12 E
Wood → **88** 50 8N 106 13W
Wood Buffalo Nat.
Park **76** 59 0N 113 41W
Wood Is. .... **228** 16 24 S 123 19 E
Wood L. **77** 55 17N 103 17W
Woodah I. .... **230** 13 27 S 136 10 E
Woodanilling ...... **229** 33 31 S 117 24 E
Woodbridge **84** 43 47N 79 36W

Woodburn **231** 29 6 S 153 23 E
Woodenbong **231** 28 24 S 152 39 E
Woodend **231** 37 20 S 144 33 E
Woodfibre **93** 49 41N 123 15W
Woodgreen **230** 22 26 S 134 12 E
Woodlands, Australia **229** 24 46 S 118 8 E
Woodlands, Canada **89** 50 12N 97 40W
Woodlark I. **227** 9 10 S 152 50 E
Woodpecker **93** 53 30N 122 40W
Woodridge **89** 49 20N 96 9W
Woodroffe, Mt. **229** 26 20 S 131 45 E
Woods, L., Australia **230** 17 50 S 133 30 E
Woods, L., Canada **78** 54 30N 65 13W
Woods, L. of the **86** 49 15N 94 45W
Woodside, S. Austral., Australia **232** 34 58 S 138 52 E
Woodside, Vic., Australia **233** 38 31 S 146 52 E
Woodstock, N.S.W., Australia **233** 33 45 S 148 53 E
Woodstock, Queens., Australia **230** 19 35 S 146 50 E
Woodstock, W. Austral., Australia **228** 21 41 S 118 57 E
Woodstock, N.B., Canada **81** 46 11N 67 37W
Woodstock, Ont., Canada **84** 43 10N 80 45W
Woodstock, U.K. **133** 51 51N 1 20W
Woodville **234** 40 20 S 175 53 E
Woody Point **79** 49 30N 57 55W
Woolamai, C. **231** 38 30 S 145 23 E
Woolgoolga **231** 30 6 S 153 11 E
Woombye **231** 26 40 S 152 55 E
Woomera **231** 31 30 S 137 10 E
Woonona **233** 34 21 S 150 54 E
Wooramel **229** 25 45 S 114 17 E
Wooramel ⟶ **229** 25 47 S 114 10 E
Wooroloo **229** 31 48 S 116 18 E
Worb **148** 46 56N 7 33 E
Worcester, S. Africa **254** 33 39 S 19 27 E
Worcester, U.K. **133** 52 12N 2 12W
Wörgl **150** 47 29N 12 3 E
Workington **132** 54 39N 3 34W
Worksop **132** 53 19N 1 9W
Workum **142** 52 59N 5 26 E
Wormerveer **142** 52 30N 4 46 E
Wormhoudt **139** 50 52N 2 28 E
Worms **147** 49 37N 8 21 E
Worsley **90** 56 31N 119 8W
Wörth **147** 49 1N 12 24 E
Wörther See **150** 46 37N 14 10 E
Worthing **133** 50 49N 0 21W
Wosi **207** 0 15 S 128 0 E
Woss Camp **92** 50 13N 126 35W
Woss L. **92** 50 7N 126 36W
Wottonville **83** 45 44N 71 48W
Wou-han = Wuhan **217** 30 31N 114 18 E
Woubrugge **142** 52 10N 4 39 E
Woudenberg **142** 52 5N 5 25 E
Woudsend **142** 52 56N 5 38 E
Wour **241** 21 14N 16 0 E
Wouw **143** 51 31N 4 23 E
Wowoni **207** 4 5 S 123 5 E
Woy Woy **231** 33 30 S 151 19 E
Wozniki **152** 50 35N 19 4 E
Wrangel I. **186** 71 0N 180 0 E
Wrath, C. **134** 58 38N 5 0W
Wrekin, The **132** 52 41N 2 35W
Wrexham **132** 53 5N 3 0W
Wriezen **146** 52 43N 14 9 E
Wright, Canada **93** 51 52N 121 40W
Wright, Phil. **211** 11 42N 125 2 E
Wrigley **94** 63 16N 123 37W
Wrocław **152** 51 5N 17 5 E
Wrocław □ **152** 51 0N 17 0 E
Wronki **152** 52 41N 16 21 E
Wrottesley, C. **94** 74 32N 121 33W
Wroxton **89** 51 14N 101 53W
Września **152** 52 21N 17 36 E
Wschowa **152** 51 48N 16 20 E
Wu Jiang ⟶ **216** 29 40N 107 20 E
Wu'an **214** 36 40N 114 15 E
Wubin **229** 30 6 S 116 37 E
Wubu **214** 37 28N 110 42 E
Wuchang **215** 44 55N 127 5 E
Wucheng **214** 37 12N 116 20 E
Wuchuan, Guangdong, China **217** 21 33N 110 43 E
Wuchuan, Guizhou, China **216** 28 25N 108 3 E
Wuchuan, Nei Mongol Zizhiqu, China **214** 41 5N 111 28 E
Wuday'ah **194** 17 2N 47 7 E
Wudi **215** 37 40N 117 35 E
Wuding **216** 25 24N 102 21 E
Wuding He ⟶ **214** 37 2N 110 23 E
Wudu **216** 33 22N 104 54 E
Wufeng **217** 30 12N 110 42 E
Wugang **217** 26 44N 110 35 E
Wugong Shan **217** 27 30N 114 0 E
Wuhan **217** 30 31N 114 18 E
Wuhe **215** 33 10N 117 50 E
Wuhsi = Wuxi **217** 31 33N 120 18 E
Wuhu **217** 31 22N 118 21 E
Wujiang **217** 31 10N 120 38 E
Wukari **247** 7 51N 9 42 E
Wulajie **215** 44 6N 126 33 E
Wulanbulang **214** 41 5N 110 55 E
Wulehe **247** 8 39N 0 0 E
Wulian **215** 35 40N 119 12 E
Wuliang Shan **216** 24 30N 100 40 E
Wuliaru **207** 7 27 S 131 0 E
Wuluk'omushih Ling **212** 36 25N 87 25 E
Wulumuchi = Ürümqi **212** 43 45N 87 45 E
Wum **247** 6 24N 10 2 E
Wuming **216** 23 12N 108 18 E
Wuning **217** 29 17N 115 5 E
Wunnummin L. **74** 52 55N 89 10W
Wunsiedel **147** 50 2N 12 0 E
Wunstorf **146** 52 26N 9 29 E
Wuntho **202** 23 55N 95 45 E
Wuping **217** 25 5N 116 5 E
Wuppertal, Germany **146** 51 15N 7 8 E
Wuppertal, S. Africa **254** 32 13 S 19 12 E
Wuqing **215** 39 23N 117 4 E
Würenlingen **149** 47 32N 8 16 E
Wurung **230** 19 13 S 140 38 E
Würzburg **147** 49 46N 9 55 E
Wurzen **146** 51 21N 12 45 E
Wushan, Gansu, China **214** 34 43N 104 53 E
Wushan, Sichuan, China **216** 31 7N 109 54 E
Wustrow **146** 54 4N 11 33 E
Wusuli Jiang = Ussuri ⟶ **218** 48 27N 135 0 E
Wutach ⟶ **147** 47 37N 8 15 E
Wutai **214** 38 40N 113 12 E
Wuting = Huimin **215** 37 27N 117 28 E
Wutong **217** 25 24N 110 4 E
Wutonghaolai **215** 42 50N 120 5 E
Wutongqiao **216** 29 22N 103 50 E
Wuustwezel **143** 51 23N 4 36 E
Wuwei, Anhui, China **217** 31 18N 117 54 E
Wuwei, Gansu, China **212** 37 57N 102 34 E
Wuxi, Jiangsu, China **217** 31 33N 120 18 E
Wuxi, Sichuan, China **216** 31 23N 109 35 E
Wuxiang **214** 36 49N 112 50 E
Wuxing **217** 30 51N 120 8 E
Wuxuan **216** 23 34N 109 38 E
Wuyang **214** 33 25N 113 35 E
Wuyi, Hebei, China **214** 37 46N 115 56 E
Wuyi, Zhejiang, China **217** 28 52N 119 50 E
Wuyi Shan **217** 27 0N 117 0 E
Wuyo **247** 10 23N 11 50 E
Wuyuan, Jiangxi, China **217** 29 15N 117 50 E
Wuyuan, Nei Mongol Zizhiqu, China **214** 41 2N 108 20 E
Wuzhai **214** 38 54N 111 48 E
Wuzhi Shan **204** 18 45N 109 45 E
Wuzhong **214** 38 2N 106 12 E
Wuzhou **217** 23 30N 111 18 E
Wyaaba Cr. ⟶ **230** 16 27 S 141 35 E
Wyalkatchem **229** 31 8 S 117 22 E
Wyandra **231** 27 12 S 145 56 E
Wyangala Res. **231** 33 54 S 149 0 E
Wyara, L. **231** 28 42 S 144 14 E
Wycheproof **231** 36 0 S 143 17 E
Wye ⟶ **133** 51 36N 2 40W
Wyemandoo, Mt. **229** 28 28 S 118 29 E
Wyk **146** 54 41N 8 33 E
Wymark **88** 50 7N 107 44W
Wymondham **133** 52 45N 0 42W
Wynberg **254** 34 2 S 18 28 E
Wynbring **231** 30 33 S 133 32 E
Wyndham, Australia **228** 15 33 S 128 3 E
Wyndham, N.Z. **235** 46 20 S 168 51 E
Wyniatt B. **94** 72 45N 110 30W
Wynndel **91** 49 11N 116 33W
Wynnum **231** 27 27 S 153 9 E
Wynyard, Australia **230** 41 5 S 145 44 E
Wynyard, Canada **88** 51 45N 104 10W
Wyola, L. **229** 29 8 S 130 17 E
Wyoming **84** 42 57N 82 7W
Wyong **231** 33 14 S 151 24 E
Wyrzysk **152** 53 10N 17 17 E
Wysoka **152** 53 13N 17 2 E
Wysokie **152** 50 55N 22 40 E
Wysokie Mazowieckie **152** 52 55N 22 30 E
Wyszków **152** 52 36N 21 25 E
Wyszogród **152** 52 23N 20 9 E

X

X-cán **111** 20 50N 87 43W
Xa-Muteba **253** 9 34 S 17 50 E
Xai-Xai **255** 25 6 S 33 31 E
Xainza **212** 30 58N 88 35 E
Xaltianguis **107** 17 4N 99 50W
Xambioá **120** 6 25 S 48 40W
Xangongo **254** 16 45 S 15 0 E
Xanten **146** 51 40N 6 27 E
Xánthi **168** 41 10N 24 58 E
Xánthi □ **168** 41 10N 24 58 E
Xapuri **122** 10 35 S 68 35W
Xar Moron He ⟶ **215** 43 25N 120 35 E
Xau, L. **254** 21 15 S 24 44 E
Xavantina **125** 21 15 S 52 48W
Xcacal **111** 20 37N 89 7W
Xcalak **111** 18 16N 87 50W
Xcupil **111** 19 39N 89 52W
Xhumo **254** 21 7 S 24 35 E
Xi Jiang ⟶ **217** 22 5N 113 20 E
Xi Xian, Henan, China **217** 32 20N 114 43 E
Xi Xian, Shanxi, China **214** 36 41N 110 58 E
Xia Xian **214** 35 8N 111 12 E
Xiachengzi **215** 44 40N 130 18 E
Xiachuan Dao **217** 21 40N 112 40 E
Xiaguan **216** 25 32N 100 16 E
Xiajiang **217** 27 30N 115 10 E
Xiajin **214** 36 56N 116 0 E
Xiamen **217** 24 25N 118 4 E
Xi'an **214** 34 15N 109 0 E
Xian Xian **214** 38 12N 116 6 E
Xianfeng **217** 29 40N 109 8 E
Xiang Jiang ⟶ **217** 28 55N 112 50 E
Xiangcheng, Henan, China **214** 33 29N 114 52 E
Xiangcheng, Henan, China **214** 33 50N 113 27 E
Xiangcheng, Sichuan, China **216** 28 53N 99 47 E
Xiangdu **216** 23 13N 106 58 E
Xiangfan **217** 32 2N 112 8 E
Xianghuang Qi **214** 42 2N 113 50 E
Xiangning **214** 35 58N 110 50 E
Xiangquan **214** 36 30N 113 1 E
Xiangshan **217** 29 29N 121 51 E
Xiangshui **215** 34 12N 119 33 E
Xiangtan **217** 27 51N 112 54 E
Xiangxiang **217** 27 43N 112 28 E
Xiangyang **217** 32 1N 112 8 E
Xiangyin **217** 28 38N 112 54 E
Xiangyun **216** 25 34N 100 35 E
Xiangzhou **216** 23 58N 109 40 E
Xianju **217** 28 51N 120 44 E
Xianning **217** 29 51N 114 16 E
Xianshui He ⟶ **216** 30 10N 100 59 E
Xianyang **214** 34 20N 108 40 E
Xianyou **217** 25 22N 118 38 E
Xiao Hinggan Ling **213** 49 0N 127 0 E
Xiao Xian **214** 34 15N 116 55 E
Xiaofeng **217** 30 35N 119 32 E
Xiaogan **217** 30 52N 113 55 E
Xiaojin **216** 30 59N 102 21 E
Xiaolan **217** 22 38N 113 13 E
Xiaoshan **217** 30 12N 120 18 E
Xiaoyi **214** 37 8N 111 48 E
Xiapu **217** 26 54N 119 59 E
Xiatil **111** 19 39N 88 29W
Xiawa **215** 42 35N 120 38 E
Xiayi **214** 34 15N 116 10 E
Xicalango, Pta. **111** 18 41N 91 56W
Xichang **216** 27 51N 102 19 E
Xichong **216** 30 57N 105 54 E
Xichú **107** 21 25N 100 4W
Xichuan **214** 33 0N 111 30 E
Xico **108** 19 25N 97 0W
Xicoténcatl **103** 23 0N 98 56W
Xicotepec de Juárez **108** 20 16N 97 57W
Xiemahe **217** 31 38N 111 12 E
Xieng Khouang **204** 19 17N 103 25 E
Xifei He ⟶ **214** 32 45N 116 40 E
Xifeng, Guizhou, China **216** 27 7N 106 42 E
Xifeng, Liaoning, China **215** 42 42N 124 45 E
Xifengzhen **214** 35 40N 107 40 E
Xigazê **212** 29 5N 88 45 E
Xihe **214** 34 2N 105 20 E
Xihua **214** 33 45N 114 30 E
Xiliao He ⟶ **215** 43 32N 123 35 E
Xilin **216** 24 30N 105 6 E
Xilitla **103** 21 20N 98 58W
Xilókastron **169** 38 4N 22 43 E
Xin Jiang ⟶ **217** 28 45N 116 35 E
Xin Xian **214** 38 22N 112 46 E
Xinavane **255** 25 2 S 32 47 E
Xinbin **215** 41 40N 125 2 E
Xincai **217** 32 43N 114 58 E
Xinchang **217** 29 28N 120 52 E
Xincheng, Guangxi Zhuangzu, China **216** 24 5N 108 39 E
Xincheng, Jiangxi, China **217** 26 48N 114 6 E
Xinfeng, Guangdong, China **217** 24 5N 114 16 E
Xinfeng, Jiangxi, China **217** 27 7N 116 11 E
Xinfeng, Jiangxi, China **217** 25 27N 114 58 E
Xing Xian **214** 38 27N 111 7 E
Xing'an, Guangxi Zhuangzu, China **217** 25 38N 110 40 E
Xingan, Jiangxi, China **217** 27 46N 115 20 E
Xingcheng **215** 40 40N 120 45 E
Xingguo **217** 26 21N 115 21 E
Xinghe **214** 40 55N 113 55 E
Xinghua **215** 32 58N 119 48 E
Xinghua Wan **217** 25 15N 119 20 E
Xinglong **215** 40 25N 117 30 E
Xingning **217** 24 3N 115 42 E
Xingping **214** 34 20N 108 28 E
Xingren **216** 25 24N 105 11 E
Xingshan **217** 31 15N 110 45 E
Xingtai **214** 37 3N 114 32 E
Xingu ⟶ **119** 1 30 S 51 53W
Xingyang **214** 34 45N 112 52 E
Xinhe **214** 37 30N 115 15 E
Xinhua **217** 27 42N 111 13 E
Xinhuang **216** 27 21N 109 12 E
Xinhui **217** 22 25N 113 0 E
Xiniás, L. **169** 39 2N 22 12 E
Xining **212** 36 34N 101 40 E
Xinjiang **214** 35 34N 111 11 E
Xinjiang Uygur Zizhiqu □ **212** 42 0N 86 0 E
Xinjie **216** 26 48N 101 15 E
Xinjin, Liaoning, China **215** 39 25N 121 58 E
Xinjin, Sichuan, China **216** 30 24N 103 47 E
Xinkai He ⟶ **215** 43 32N 123 35 E
Xinle **214** 38 25N 114 40 E
Xinlitun **215** 42 0N 122 8 E
Xinlong **216** 30 57N 100 12 E
Xinmin **215** 41 59N 122 50 E
Xinning **217** 26 28N 110 50 E
Xinping **216** 24 5N 101 59 E
Xinshao **217** 27 21N 111 26 E
Xintai **215** 35 55N 117 45 E
Xintian **217** 25 55N 112 13 E
Xinxiang **214** 35 18N 113 50 E
Xinxing **217** 22 35N 112 15 E
Xinyang **217** 32 6N 114 3 E
Xinye **217** 32 30N 112 21 E
Xinyi **217** 22 25N 111 0 E
Xinyu **217** 27 49N 114 58 E
Xinzhan **215** 43 50N 127 18 E
Xinzheng **214** 34 20N 113 45 E
Xinzhou **217** 30 50N 114 48 E
Xinzhu **217** 24 49N 120 57 E
Xiong Xian **214** 38 59N 116 8 E
Xiongyuecheng **215** 40 12N 122 5 E
Xiping, Henan, China **214** 33 22N 114 0 E
Xiping, Henan, China **214** 33 25N 111 8 E
Xiping, Zhejiang, China **217** 28 16N 119 29 E
Xique-Xique **120** 10 50 S 42 40W
Xiruá ⟶ **122** 6 3 S 67 50W
Xishui **217** 30 30N 115 15 E
Xituozhen **216** 30 22N 108 11 E
Xiuning **217** 29 45N 118 10 E
Xiuren **217** 24 27N 110 12 E
Xiushan **216** 28 25N 108 57 E
Xiushui **217** 29 2N 114 33 E
Xiuwen **216** 26 49N 106 32 E
Xiuyan **215** 40 18N 123 11 E
Xixabangma Feng **199** 28 20N 85 40 E
Xixia **217** 33 25N 111 29 E
Xixiang **216** 33 0N 107 44 E
Xizang □ **212** 33 0N 85 0 E
Xmaben **111** 19 13N 89 33W
Xochihuehuetlán **107** 17 55N 98 26W
Xochimilco **107** 19 15N 99 6W
Xochipala **107** 17 49N 99 37W
Xochistlahuaca **107** 16 47N 98 15W
Xochitlán **109** 18 42N 97 47W
Xpichil **111** 19 41N 88 25W
Xu Jiang ⟶ **217** 28 0N 116 25 E
Xuan Loc **205** 10 56N 107 14 E
Xuancheng **217** 30 56N 118 43 E
Xuan'en **217** 30 0N 109 30 E
Xuanhan **216** 31 18N 107 38 E
Xuanhua **214** 40 40N 115 2 E
Xuchang **214** 34 2N 113 48 E
Xuefeng Shan **217** 27 5N 110 35 E
Xuejiaping **217** 31 39N 110 16 E
Xul **111** 20 8N 89 32W
Xun Jiang ⟶ **217** 23 35N 111 30 E
Xun Xian **214** 35 42N 114 33 E
Xundian **216** 25 36N 103 15 E

Xunwu 217 24 54N 115 37 E
Xunyang 214 32 48N 109 22 E
Xunyi 214 35 8N 108 20 E
Xupu 217 27 53N 110 32 E
Xushui 214 39 2N 115 40 E
Xuwen 217 20 20N 110 10 E
Xuyen Moc 205 10 34N 107 25 E
Xuyong 216 28 10N 105 22 E
Xuzhou 215 34 18N 117 10 E

Y

Ya 'Bad 189 32 27N 35 10 E
Ya Xian 204 18 14N 109 29 E
Yaamba 230 23 8 S 150 22 E
Ya'an 216 29 58N 103 5 E
Yaapeet 231 35 45 S 142 3 E
Yabassi 247 4 30N 9 57 E
Yabba North 233 36 13 S 145 42 E
Yabelo 245 4 50N 38 8 E
Yablanitsa 167 43 2N 24 5 E
Yablonovy Khrebet 186 53 0N 114 0 E
Yablonovy Ra. = Yablonovy Khrebet 186 53 0N 114 0 E
Yabrai Shan 214 39 40N 103 0 E
Yabrūd 190 33 58N 36 39 E
Yacuiba 124 22 0 S 63 43W
Yacuma → 123 13 38 S 65 23W
Yadgir 200 16 45N 77 5 E
Yadrin 179 55 57N 46 12 E
Yagaba 247 10 14N 1 20W
Yagodnoye 185 62 33N 149 40 E
Yagoua 252 10 20N 15 13 E
Yaguas → 118 2 45 S 70 10W
Yagur 189 32 45N 35 4 E
Yaha 205 6 29N 101 8 E
Yahila 250 0 13N 24 28 E
Yahk 91 49 6N 116 10W
Yahualica 106 21 8N 102 51W
Yahuma 252 1 0N 23 10 E
Yaita 219 36 48N 139 56 E
Yaizu 221 34 52N 138 20 E
Yajalón 110 17 14N 92 20W
Yajiang 216 30 2N 100 57 E
Yajua 247 11 27N 12 49 E
Yakage 220 34 37N 133 35 E
Yakamba 252 2 42N 19 38 E
Yako 246 12 59N 2 15W
Yakoma 252 4 5N 22 27 E
Yakoruda 167 42 1N 23 39 E
Yakovlevka 218 44 26N 133 28 E
Yakshur Bodya 182 57 11N 53 7 E
Yaku-Shima 219 30 20N 130 30 E
Yakut A.S.S.R. □ 185 62 0N 130 0 E
Yakutsk 185 62 5N 129 50 E
Yala 205 6 33N 101 18 E
Yalahán, L. de 111 21 30N 87 15W
Yalbalgo 229 25 10 S 114 45 E
Yalboroo 230 20 50 S 148 40 E
Yale 93 49 34N 121 25W
Yalgoo 229 28 16 S 116 39 E
Yali 252 0 4N 21 3 E
Yaligimba 252 2 13N 22 56 E
Yalinga 252 6 33N 23 10 E
Yalkabul, Pta. 111 21 32N 88 37W
Yalleroi 230 24 3 S 145 42 E
Yaloke 252 5 19N 17 5 E
Yalong Jiang → 216 26 40N 101 55 E
Yalpukh, Oz. 170 45 30N 28 41 E
Yalta 180 44 30N 34 10 E
Yalu Chiang → 215 41 30N 126 30 E
Yalu Jiang → 215 40 0N 124 22 E
Yalutorovsk 184 56 41N 66 12 E
Yam Ha Melaḥ = Dead Sea 189 31 30N 35 30 E
Yam Kinneret 189 32 45N 35 35 E
Yamada 220 33 33N 130 49 E
Yamaga 220 33 1N 130 41 E
Yamagata 218 38 15N 140 15 E
Yamagata □ 218 38 30N 140 0 E
Yamagawa 220 31 12N 130 39 E
Yamaguchi 220 34 10N 131 32 E
Yamaguchi □ 220 34 20N 131 40 E
Yamal, Poluostrov 184 71 0N 70 0 E
Yamanaka 221 36 15N 136 22 E
Yamanashi □ 221 35 40N 138 40 E
Yamantau 176 54 20N 57 40 E
Yamantau, Gora 182 54 15N 58 6 E
Yamaska 83 46 0N 72 55W
Yamato 221 35 27N 139 25 E
Yamatotakada 221 34 31N 135 45 E
Yamazaki 220 35 0N 134 32 E
Yamba, N.S.W., Australia 231 29 26 S 153 23 E
Yamba, S. Austral., Australia 232 34 10 S 140 52 E
Yambah 230 23 10 S 133 50 E
Yambarran Ra. 228 15 10 S 130 25 E
Yambata 252 2 26N 21 58 E
Yâmbiô 245 4 35N 28 16 E
Yambol 167 42 30N 26 36 E
Yamdena 207 7 45 S 131 20 E
Yame 220 33 13N 130 35 E
Yamethin 202 20 29N 96 18 E
Yamil 247 12 53N 8 4 E
Yamma-Yamma, L. 231 26 16 S 141 20 E
Yampi Sd. 228 16 8 S 123 38 E
Yampol 180 48 15N 28 15 E
Yamrat 247 10 11N 9 55 E
Yamrukchal 167 42 44N 24 52 E
Yamuna → 198 25 30N 81 53 E
Yamzho Yumco 212 28 48N 90 35 E
Yan 247 10 5N 12 11 E
Yan → 201 9 0N 81 10 E
Yana → 185 71 30N 136 0 E
Yanac 231 36 8 S 141 25 E
Yanagawa 220 33 10N 130 24 E
Yanahara 220 34 58N 134 2 E
Yanai 220 33 58N 132 7 E
Yanam 200 16 47N 82 15 E
Yan'an 214 36 35N 109 26 E
Yanaul 182 56 25N 55 0 E
Yanbian 216 26 47N 101 31 E
Yanbu 'al Baḥr 192 24 0N 38 5 E
Yancannia 231 30 12 S 142 35 E
Yanchang 214 36 43N 110 1 E
Yancheng, Henan, China 214 33 35N 114 0 E
Yancheng, Jiangsu, China 215 33 23N 120 8 E
Yanchi 214 37 48N 107 20 E
Yanchuan 214 36 51N 110 10 E
Yanco 233 34 38 S 146 27 E
Yanco Cr. → 231 35 14 S 145 35 E
Yandal 229 27 35 S 121 10 E
Yandanooka 229 29 18 S 115 29 E
Yandaran 230 24 43 S 152 6 E
Yandé, Î. 226 20 3 S 163 49 E
Yandja 252 1 41 S 17 43 E
Yandongi 252 2 51N 22 16 E
Yandoon 202 17 0N 95 40 E
Yanfeng 216 25 52N 101 8 E
Yanfolila 246 11 11N 8 9W
Yang Xian 214 33 15N 107 30 E
Yanga 109 18 50N 96 48W
Yangambi 250 0 47N 24 20 E
Yangbi 216 25 41N 99 58 E
Yangcheng 214 35 28N 112 22 E
Yangch'ü = Taiyuan 214 37 52N 112 33 E
Yangchun 217 22 11N 111 48 E
Yanggao 214 40 21N 113 55 E
Yanggu 214 36 8N 115 43 E
Yangi-Yer 184 40 17N 68 48 E
Yangibazar 183 41 40N 70 53 E
Yangikishlak 183 40 25N 67 10 E
Yangiyul 183 41 0N 69 3 E
Yangjiang 217 21 50N 110 59 E
Yangliuqing 215 39 2N 117 5 E
Yangping 217 31 12N 111 25 E
Yangpingguan 214 32 58N 106 5 E
Yangquan 214 37 58N 113 31 E
Yangshan 217 24 30N 112 40 E
Yangshuo 217 24 48N 110 29 E
Yangtze Kiang = Chang Jiang → 217 31 48N 121 10 E
Yangxin 217 29 50N 115 12 E
Yangyang 215 38 4N 128 38 E
Yangyuan 214 40 1N 114 10 E
Yangzhou 217 32 21N 119 26 E
Yanhe 216 28 31N 108 29 E
Yanji 215 42 59N 129 30 E
Yanjin 216 28 5N 104 18 E
Yanjing 216 29 7N 98 33 E
Yanna 231 26 58 S 146 0 E
Yanonge 250 0 35N 24 38 E
Yanqi 212 42 5N 86 35 E
Yanqing 214 40 30N 115 58 E
Yanshan, Hebei, China 215 38 4N 117 22 E
Yanshan, Jiangxi, China 217 28 15N 117 41 E
Yanshan, Yunnan, China 216 23 35N 104 20 E
Yanshou 215 45 28N 128 22 E
Yantabulla 231 29 21 S 145 0 E
Yantai 215 37 34N 121 22 E
Yanting 216 31 11N 105 24 E
Yantra → 167 43 40N 25 37 E
Yanwa 216 27 35N 98 55 E
Yany Kurgan 183 43 55N 67 15 E
Yanyuan 216 27 25N 101 30 E
Yanzhou 214 35 35N 116 49 E
Yao, Chad 243 12 56N 17 33 E
Yao, Japan 221 34 32N 135 36 E
Yao Xian 214 34 55N 108 59 E
Yao Yai, Ko 205 8 0N 98 35 E
Yao'an 216 25 31N 101 18 E
Yaodu 216 32 45N 105 22 E
Yaoundé 247 3 50N 11 35 E
Yaowan 215 34 15N 118 3 E
Yap 224 9 31N 138 6 E
Yap Is. 226 9 30N 138 10 E
Yapen 207 1 50 S 136 0 E
Yapen, Selat 207 1 20 S 136 10 E
Yappar → 230 18 22 S 141 16 E
Yaqui 100 27 37N 110 40W
Yaqui, R. → 100 27 37N 110 39W
Yar 182 58 14N 52 5 E
Yar-Sale 184 66 50N 70 50 E
Yaracuy □ 118 10 20N 68 45W
Yaracuy → 118 10 33N 68 15W
Yaraka 230 24 53 S 144 3 E
Yaransk 179 57 22N 47 49 E
Yaratishky 178 54 3N 26 0 E
Yardea P.O. 231 32 23 S 135 32 E
Yare → 133 52 36N 1 28 E
Yarensk 176 61 10N 49 8 E
Yarfa 244 24 40N 38 35 E
Yarí → 118 0 20 S 72 20W
Yaritagua 118 10 5N 69 8W
Yarkand = Shache 212 38 20N 77 10 E
Yarker 85 44 23N 76 46W
Yarkhun → 199 36 17N 72 30 E
Yarmouth 81 43 50N 66 7W
Yarmūk → 189 32 42N 35 40 E
Yaroslavl 179 57 35N 39 55 E
Yarqa, W. → 191 30 0N 33 49 E
Yarra Yarra Lakes 229 29 40 S 115 45 E
Yarraden 230 14 17 S 143 15 E
Yarraloola 228 21 33 S 115 52 E
Yarram 231 38 29 S 146 9 E
Yarraman 231 26 50 S 152 0 E
Yarranvale 231 26 50 S 145 20 E
Yarras 231 31 25 S 152 20 E
Yarrawonga 233 36 0 S 146 0 E
Yarrow 93 49 5N 122 2W
Yarrowmere 230 21 27 S 145 53 E
Yarto 232 35 28 S 142 16 E
Yartsevo, R.S.F.S.R., U.S.S.R. 178 55 6N 32 43 E
Yartsevo, R.S.F.S.R., U.S.S.R. 185 60 20N 90 0 E
Yarumal 118 6 58N 75 24W
Yasawa 226 16 47 S 177 31 E
Yasawa Group 226 17 0 S 177 23 E
Yaselda → 178 52 7N 26 28 E
Yashbum 194 14 19N 46 56 E
Yashi 247 12 23N 7 54 E
Yashiro-Jima 220 33 55N 132 15 E
Yasin 199 36 24N 73 23 E
Yasinovataya 180 48 7N 37 57 E
Yasinski, L. 78 53 16N 77 35W
Yasothon 204 15 50N 104 10 E
Yass 231 34 49 S 148 54 E
Yasugi 220 35 26N 133 15 E
Yas'ur 189 32 54N 35 10 E
Yata → 123 10 29 S 65 26W
Yatağn 169 37 20N 28 10 E
Yates Pt. 235 44 29 S 167 49 E
Yathkyed L. 77 62 40N 98 0W
Yathong 233 32 37 S 145 33 E
Yatsuo 221 36 34N 137 8 E
Yatsushiro 220 32 30N 130 40 E
Yatsushiro-Kai 220 32 30N 130 25 E
Yatta Plateau 250 2 0 S 38 0 E
Yaṭṭah 189 31 27N 35 6 E
Yauca 122 15 39 S 74 35W
Yautepec 107 18 53N 99 4W
Yauya 122 8 59 S 77 17W
Yauyos 122 12 19 S 75 50W
Yaval 198 21 10N 75 42 E
Yavan 183 38 19N 69 2 E
Yavari → 122 4 21 S 70 2W
Yávaros 100 26 42N 109 31W
Yavatmal 200 20 20N 78 15 E
Yavne 189 31 52N 34 45 E
Yavorov 178 49 55N 23 20 E
Yawatahama 220 33 27N 132 24 E
Yawri B. 246 8 22N 13 0W
Yaxcabá 111 20 32N 88 50W
Yaxché 111 19 21N 88 11W
Yaxchilan, Ruinas de 110 16 54N 90 58W
Yaxi 216 27 33N 106 41 E
Yayama-Rettō 219 24 30N 123 40 E
Yazagyo 202 23 30N 94 6 E
Yazd 193 31 55N 54 27 E
Yazd □ 193 32 0N 55 0 E
Yazdān 197 33 30N 60 50 E
Ybbs 150 48 12N 15 4 E
Ydrim 194 14 20N 44 22 E
Ye Xian, Henan, China 214 33 35N 113 25 E
Ye Xian, Shandong, China 215 37 8N 119 57 E
Yea 233 37 14 S 145 26 E
Yealering 229 32 36 S 117 36 E
Yearinan 233 31 10 S 149 11 E
Yebbi-Souma 241 21 7N 17 54 E
Yechŏn 215 36 39N 128 27 E
Yecla 157 38 35N 1 5W
Yécora 100 28 20N 108 58W
Yecuatla 108 19 52N 96 45W
Yedashe 202 19 10N 96 20 E
Yedintsy 180 48 9N 27 18 E
Yeeda 228 17 31 S 123 38 E
Yeelanna 231 34 9 S 135 45 E
Yefremov 179 53 8N 38 3 E
Yegorlyk → 181 46 33N 41 40 E
Yegorlykskaya 181 46 35N 40 35 E
Yegoryevsk 179 55 27N 38 55 E
Yegros 124 26 20 S 56 25W
Yehuda, Midbar 189 31 35N 35 15 E
Yei 245 4 9N 30 40 E
Yei, Nahr → 245 6 15N 30 13 E
Yekumbe 252 1 2 S 23 27 E
Yelabuga 182 55 45N 52 4 E
Yelan 179 50 55N 43 43 E
Yelan-Kolenovski 179 51 16N 41 4 E
Yelandur 201 12 6N 77 0 E
Yelanskoye 185 61 25N 128 0 E
Yelarbon 231 28 33 S 150 38 E
Yelatma 179 55 0N 41 45 E
Yelcho, L. 126 43 18 S 72 18W
Yelets 179 52 40N 38 30 E
Yélimané 246 15 9N 10 34W
Yell 134 60 35N 1 5W
Yell Sd. 134 60 33N 1 15W
Yellamanchilli = Elamanchili 200 17 33N 82 50 E
Yellow Creek 88 52 45N 105 15W
Yellow Grass 88 49 48N 104 10W
Yellow Sea 215 35 0N 123 0 E
Yellowhead P. 93 52 53N 118 25W
Yellowknife 76 62 27N 114 29W
Yellowknife → 76 62 31N 114 19W
Yelnya 178 54 35N 33 15 E
Yelsk 178 51 50N 29 10 E
Yelvertoft 230 20 13 S 138 45 E
Yelwa 247 10 49N 4 41 E
Yemanzhelinsk 182 54 58N 61 18 E
Yembongo 252 3 12N 19 2 E
Yemen ■ 194 15 0N 44 0 E
Yen Bai 204 21 42N 104 52 E
Yenakiyevo 180 48 15N 38 15 E
Yenangyaung 202 20 30N 95 0 E
Yenanma 202 19 46N 94 49 E
Yenda 231 34 13 S 146 14 E
Yendéré 246 10 12N 4 59W
Yendi 247 9 29N 0 1W
Yengo 252 0 22N 15 29 E
Yenice 190 37 0N 35 4 E
Yeniköy 190 36 55N 33 16 E
Yenisafa 168 41 1N 24 57 E
Yenisey → 184 71 50N 82 40 E
Yeniseysk 185 58 27N 92 13 E
Yeniseyskiy Zaliv 184 72 20N 81 0 E
Yenne 141 45 43N 5 44 E
Yenotayevka 181 47 15N 47 0 E
Yenyuka 185 57 57N 121 15 E
Yeo, L. 229 28 0 S 124 30 E
Yeola 200 20 0N 74 30 E
Yeoval 233 32 47 S 148 9 E
Yeovil 133 50 57N 2 38W
Yepachic 101 28 26N 108 23W
Yepes 156 39 55N 3 39W
Yepómera 101 29 4N 107 51W
Yeppoon 230 23 5 S 150 47 E
Yeráki 169 37 0N 22 42 E
Yerbanis 105 24 45N 103 50W
Yerbent 184 39 30N 58 50 E
Yerbogachen 185 61 16N 108 0 E
Yerevan 181 40 10N 44 31 E
Yerilla 229 29 24 S 121 47 E
Yerla → 200 16 50N 74 30 E
Yermak 184 52 2N 76 55 E
Yermakovo 185 52 25N 126 20 E
Yermo 105 26 23N 104 1W
Yermolayevo 182 52 58N 56 12 E
Yerofey Pavlovich 185 54 0N 122 0 E
Yerseke 143 51 29N 4 3 E
Yershov 179 51 22N 48 16 E
Yerunaja, Cerro 122 10 16 S 76 55W
Yerushalayim 189 31 47N 35 10 E
Yerville 138 49 40N 0 53 E
Yes Tor 133 50 41N 3 59W
Yesagyo 202 21 38N 95 14 E
Yesan 215 36 41N 126 51 E
Yesca, La 104 21 19N 104 2W
Yesnogorsk 179 54 32N 37 38 E
Yessentuki 181 44 0N 42 53 E
Yessey 185 68 29N 102 10 E
Yeste 157 38 22N 2 19W
Yeu, I. d' 138 46 42N 2 20W
Yevlakh 181 40 39N 47 7 E
Yevpatoriya 180 45 15N 33 20 E
Yevstratovskiy 179 50 11N 39 45 E
Yeya → 181 46 40N 38 40 E
Yeysk 180 46 40N 38 12 E
Yezd = Yazd 193 31 55N 54 27 E
Yhati 124 25 45 S 56 35W
Yhú 125 25 0 S 56 0W
Yi → 124 33 7 S 57 8W
Yi 'Allaq, G. 191 30 22N 33 32 E
Yi He → 215 34 10N 118 8 E
Yi Xian, Anhui, China 217 29 55N 117 57 E
Yi Xian, Hebei, China 214 39 20N 115 30 E
Yi Xian, Liaoning, China 215 41 30N 121 22 E
Yialí 169 36 41N 27 11 E
Yi'allaq, G. 244 30 21N 33 31 E

Yialousa 190 35 32N 34 10 E
Yiáltra 169 38 51N 22 59 E
Yianisádhes 169 35 20N 26 10 E
Yiannitsa 168 40 46N 22 24 E
Yibin 216 28 45N 104 32 E
Yichang 217 30 40N 111 20 E
Yicheng, Henan, China 217 31 41N 112 12 E
Yicheng, Shanxi, China 214 35 42N 111 40 E
Yichuan 214 36 2N 110 10 E
Yichun, Heilongjiang, China 213 47 44N 128 52 E
Yichun, Jiangxi, China 217 27 48N 114 22 E
Yidhá 168 40 35N 22 53 E
Yidu, Hubei, China 217 30 25N 111 27 E
Yidu, Shandong, China 215 36 43N 118 28 E
Yidun 216 30 22N 99 21 E
Yihuang 217 27 30N 116 12 E
Yijun 214 35 28N 109 8 E
Yilan 217 24 51N 121 44 E
Yilehuli Shan 213 51 20N 124 20 E
Yiliang, Yunnan, China 216 27 38N 104 2 E
Yiliang, Yunnan, China 216 24 56N 103 11 E
Yilong 216 31 34N 106 23 E
Yimen 216 24 40N 102 10 E
Yimianpo 215 45 7N 128 2 E
Yinchuan 214 38 30N 106 15 E
Yindarlgooda, L. 229 30 40 S 121 52 E
Ying He → 214 32 30N 116 30 E
Ying Xian 214 39 32N 113 10 E
Yingcheng 217 30 56N 113 35 E
Yingde 217 24 10N 113 25 E
Yingjiang 216 24 41N 97 55 E
Yingjing 216 29 41N 102 52 E
Yingkou 215 40 37N 122 18 E
Yingshan, Henan, China 217 31 35N 113 50 E
Yingshan, Hubei, China 217 30 41N 115 32 E
Yingshan, Sichuan, China 216 31 4N 106 35 E
Yingshang 217 32 38N 116 12 E
Yining 212 43 58N 81 10 E
Yinjiang 216 28 1N 108 21 E
Yinnietharra 229 24 39 S 116 12 E
Yioúra, Attiki, Greece 168 39 23N 24 10 E
Yioúra, Thessalía, Greece 169 37 32N 24 40 E
Yipinglang 216 25 10N 101 52 E
Yirga Alem 245 6 48N 38 22 E
Yishan 216 24 28N 108 38 E
Yishui 215 35 47N 118 30 E
Ýthion 169 36 46N 22 34 E
Yitiaoshan 214 37 5N 104 2 E
Yitong 215 43 13N 125 20 E
Yiwu 217 29 20N 120 3 E
Yixing 217 31 21N 119 48 E
Yiyang, Henan, China 214 34 27N 112 10 E
Yiyang, Hunan, China 217 28 35N 112 18 E
Yiyang, Jiangxi, China 217 28 22N 117 20 E
Yizhang 217 25 27N 112 57 E
Yizheng 217 32 18N 119 10 E
Yizre'el 189 32 34N 35 19 E
Ylitornio 174 66 19N 23 39 E
Ylivieska 174 64 4N 24 28 E
Yngaren 173 58 50N 16 35 E
Ynykchanskiy 185 60 15N 137 35 E
Yobain 111 21 14N 89 7W
Yobuko 220 33 32N 129 54 E
Yochén 111 18 34N 89 52W
Yog Pt. 210 14 6N 124 12 E
Yogan 247 6 23N 1 30 E
Yogana 109 16 28N 96 48W
Yogyakarta 209 7 49 S 110 22 E
Yogyakarta □ 209 7 48 S 110 22 E
Yoho Nat. Park 93 51 25N 116 30W
Yojoa, L. de 112 14 53N 88 0W
Yŏju 215 37 20N 127 35 E
Yokadouma 252 3 26N 15 6 E
Yŏkaichiba 221 35 42N 140 33 E
Yokkaichi 221 35 0N 136 38 E
Yoko 247 5 32N 12 20 E
Yokohama 221 35 27N 139 28 E
Yokosuka 221 35 20N 139 40 E
Yokote 218 39 20N 140 30 E
Yola 247 9 10N 12 29 E
Yolaina, Cordillera de 112 11 30N 84 0W
Yolombo 252 1 36 S 23 12 E
Yombi 252 1 26 S 10 37 E
Yonago 220 35 25N 133 19 E
Yonaguni-Jima 219 24 27N 123 0 E
Yŏnan 215 37 55N 126 11 E
Yonezawa 218 37 57N 140 4 E
Yong Peng 205 2 0N 103 3 E
Yong Sata 205 7 8N 99 41 E
Yongampo 215 39 56N 124 23 E
Yong'an 217 25 59N 117 25 E
Yongcheng 214 33 55N 116 20 E
Yŏngchŏn 215 35 58N 128 56 E
Yongchuan 216 29 17N 105 55 E
Yongchun 217 25 16N 118 20 E
Yongdeng 214 36 38N 103 25 E
Yongding 217 24 43N 116 45 E
Yŏngdŏk 215 36 24N 129 22 E
Yŏngdŭngpo 215 37 31N 126 54 E
Yongfeng 217 27 20N 115 22 E
Yongfu 216 24 59N 109 59 E
Yonghe 214 36 46N 110 38 E
Yŏnghŭng 215 39 31N 127 18 E
Yongji 214 34 52N 110 28 E
Yŏngju 215 36 50N 128 40 E
Yongkang, Yunnan, China 216 24 9N 99 20 E
Yongkang, Zhejiang, China 217 28 55N 120 2 E
Yongnian 214 36 47N 114 29 E
Yongning, Guangxi Zhuangzu, China 216 22 44N 108 28 E
Yongning, Ningxia Huizu, China 214 38 15N 106 14 E
Yongping 216 25 27N 99 38 E
Yongqing 214 39 25N 116 28 E
Yongren 216 26 4N 101 40 E
Yongshan 216 28 11N 103 35 E
Yongsheng 216 26 38N 100 46 E
Yongshun 216 29 2N 109 51 E
Yongtai 217 25 49N 118 58 E
Yŏngwŏl 215 37 11N 128 28 E
Yongxin 217 26 58N 114 15 E
Yongxing 217 26 9N 113 8 E
Yongxiu 217 29 2N 115 42 E
Yonibana 246 8 30N 12 19W
Yonne □ 139 47 50N 3 40 E
Yonne → 139 48 23N 2 58 E
Yoqne'am 189 32 40N 35 6 E
Yoquivo, Chihuahua, Mexico 101 27 3N 107 29W
Yoquivo, Chihuahua, Mexico 101 28 5N 108 4W
York, Australia 229 31 52 S 116 47 E
York, U.K. 132 53 58N 1 7W
York → 80 48 49N 64 34W
York, C., Australia 230 10 42 S 142 31 E
York, C., Canada 95 76 30N 68 0W
York, Kap 12 75 55N 66 25W
York Sd. 228 14 50 S 125 5 E
Yorke Pen. 232 34 50 S 137 40 E
Yorkshire Wolds 132 54 0N 0 30W
Yorkton 89 51 11N 102 28W
Yornup 229 34 2 S 116 10 E
Yoro 112 15 9N 87 7W
Yoron-Jima 219 27 2N 128 26 E
Yos Sudarso, Pulau 207 8 0 S 138 30 E
Yoshii 220 33 16N 129 46 E
Yoshimatsu 220 32 0N 130 47 E
Yoshkar Ola 179 56 38N 47 55 E
Yŏsu 215 34 47N 127 45 E
Yotala 123 19 10 S 65 17W
Yotvata 189 29 55N 35 2 E
You Xian 217 27 1N 113 17 E
Youanmi 229 28 37 S 118 49 E
Youbou 92 48 53N 124 13W
Youghal 135 51 58N 7 51W
Youghal B. 135 51 55N 7 50W
Youkounkoun 246 12 35N 13 11W
Young, Australia 231 34 19 S 148 18 E
Young, Canada 88 51 47N 105 45W
Young, Uruguay 124 32 44 S 57 36W
Young Ra. 235 44 10 S 169 30 E
Younghusband, L. 231 30 50 S 136 5 E
Younghusband Pen. 232 36 0 S 139 25 E
Youngstown 91 51 35N 111 10W
Youssoufia 240 32 16N 8 31W
Youxi 217 26 10N 118 13 E
Youyang 216 28 47N 108 42 E
Youyu 214 40 10N 112 20 E
Yoweragabbie 229 28 14 S 117 39 E
Yowrie 233 36 17 S 149 46 E
Yozgat 177 39 51N 34 47 E
Ypané → 124 23 29 S 57 19W
Yport 138 49 45N 0 15 E
Ypres = Ieper 143 50 51N 2 53 E
Ysabel Chan. 227 2 0 S 150 0 E
Yssingeaux 141 45 9N 4 8 E
Ystad 172 55 26N 13 50 E
Ythan → 134 57 26N 2 12W
Ytterhogdal 172 62 12N 14 56 E
Ytyk-Kel 185 62 30N 133 45 E
Yu Shan 217 23 30N 120 58 E
Yu Xian, Hebei, China 214 39 50N 114 35 E
Yu Xian, Henan, China 214 34 10N 113 28 E
Yu Xian, Shanxi, China 214 38 5N 113 20 E
Yuan 'an 217 31 3N 111 34 E
Yuan Jiang →, Hunan, China 217 28 55N 111 50 E
Yuan Jiang →, Yunnan, China 216 22 20N 103 59 E
Yuanjiang, Hunan, China 217 28 47N 112 21 E
Yuanjiang, Yunnan, China 216 23 32N 102 0 E
Yuanli 217 24 29N 120 39 E
Yuanlin 217 23 58N 120 30 E
Yuanling 217 28 29N 110 22 E
Yuanmou 216 25 42N 101 53 E
Yuanqu 214 35 18N 111 40 E
Yuanyang, Henan, China 214 35 3N 113 58 E
Yuanyang, Yunnan, China 216 23 10N 102 43 E
Yuat → 227 4 10 S 143 52 E
Yūbari 218 43 4N 141 59 E
Yūbetsu 218 43 13N 144 5 E
Yucatán □ 111 20 50N 89 0W
Yucatán, Canal de 112 22 0N 86 30W
Yucatán, Península de 111 19 30N 89 0W
Yucheng 214 36 55N 116 32 E
Yuci 214 37 42N 112 46 E
Yucuyácua, Cerro 109 17 7N 97 40W
Yudino, R.S.F.S.R., U.S.S.R. 179 55 51N 48 55 E
Yudino, R.S.F.S.R., U.S.S.R. 184 55 10N 67 55 E
Yudu 217 25 59N 115 30 E
Yuendumu 228 22 16 S 131 49 E
Yueqing 217 28 9N 120 59 E
Yueqing Wan 217 28 5N 121 20 E
Yuexi, Anhui, China 217 30 50N 116 20 E
Yuexi, Sichuan, China 216 28 37N 102 26 E
Yueyang 217 29 21N 113 5 E
Yufu-Dake 220 33 17N 131 33 E
Yugan 217 28 43N 116 37 E
Yugoslavia ■ 161 44 0N 20 0 E
Yuhuan 217 28 9N 121 12 E
Yujiang 217 28 10N 116 43 E
Yukhnov 178 54 44N 35 15 E
Yūki 221 36 18N 139 53 E
Yukon Territory □ 94 63 0N 135 0W
Yukti 185 63 26N 105 42 E
Yukuhashi 220 33 44N 130 59 E
Yule → 228 20 41 S 118 17 E
Yuli 247 9 44N 10 12 E
Yulin, Guangxi Zhuangzu, China 217 22 40N 110 8 E
Yulin, Shaanxi, China 214 38 20N 109 30 E
Yülük Dağ 190 36 59N 33 50 E
Yuma, B. de 113 18 20N 68 35W
Yumali 232 35 32 S 139 45 E
Yumbe 250 3 28N 31 15 E
Yumbi 250 1 12 S 26 15 E
Yumbo 118 1 20 S 26 15 E
Yumen 212 39 50N 97 30 E
Yun Ho → 215 39 10N 117 10 E
Yun Xian, Hubei, China 217 32 50N 110 46 E
Yun Xian, Yunnan, China 216 24 27N 100 8 E
Yuna 229 28 20 S 115 0 E
Yunan 217 23 12N 111 30 E
Yuncheng, Henan, China 214 35 36N 115 57 E
Yuncheng, Shanxi, China 214 35 2N 111 0 E
Yunfu 217 22 50N 112 0 E
Yungas 123 17 0 S 66 0W
Yungay, Chile 124 37 10 S 72 5W
Yungay, Peru 122 9 2 S 77 45W
Yunhe 217 28 8N 119 33 E
Yunlin 217 23 42N 120 30 E
Yunling 216 27 0N 99 20 E
Yunlong 216 25 57N 99 13 E
Yunmeng 217 31 2N 113 43 E
Yunnan □ 216 25 0N 102 0 E
Yunomae 220 32 12N 130 59 E
Yunotso 220 35 5N 132 21 E
Yunquera de Henares 156 40 47N 3 11W
Yunta 231 32 34 S 139 36 E
Yunxi 214 33 0N 110 22 E
Yunxiao 217 23 59N 117 18 E
Yunyang 216 30 58N 108 54 E
Yuping 216 27 13N 108 56 E
Yupukarri 119 3 45N 59 20W
Yupyongdong 215 41 49N 128 53 E
Yuqing 216 27 13N 107 53 E
Yur 185 59 52N 137 41 E
Yurécuaro 106 20 20N 102 18W
Yurgao 184 55 42N 84 51 E
Yuria 182 59 22N 54 10 E
Yuribei 184 71 8N 76 58 E
Yurimaguas 122 5 55 S 76 7W
Yuriria 107 20 12N 101 9W
Yuriria, L. de 107 20 15N 101 6W
Yurya 179 59 1N 49 13 E
Yuryev-Polskiy 179 56 30N 39 40 E
Yuryevets 179 57 25N 43 2 E
Yuryuzan 182 54 27N 58 28 E
Yuscarán 112 13 58N 86 45W
Yushanzhen 216 29 28N 108 22 E
Yushe 214 37 4N 112 58 E
Yushu, Jilin, China 215 44 43N 126 38 E
Yushu, Qinghai, China 212 33 5N 96 55 E
Yutai 214 35 0N 116 45 E
Yutian 215 39 53N 117 45 E
Yuxi 216 24 30N 102 35 E
Yuyao 217 30 3N 121 10 E
Yuzawa 218 39 10N 140 30 E
Yuzha 179 56 34N 42 1 E
Yuzhno-Sakhalinsk 185 46 58N 142 45 E
Yuzhno-Surkhanskoye Vodokhranilishehe 183 37 53N 67 42 E
Yuzhno-Uralsk 182 54 26N 61 15 E
Yuzhnyy Ural 182 53 0N 58 0 E
Yvelines □ 139 48 40N 1 45 E
Yverdon 148 46 47N 6 39 E
Yvetot 138 49 37N 0 44 E
Yvonand 148 46 48N 6 44 E

Z

Zaachila 109 16 57N 96 45W
Zaalayskiy Khrebet 183 39 20N 73 0 E
Zaamslag 143 51 19N 3 55 E
Zaan → 142 52 25N 4 52 E
Zaandam 142 52 26N 4 49 E
Zab, Monts du 241 34 55N 5 0 E
Žabalj 166 45 21N 20 5 E
Žabari 166 44 22N 21 15 E
Zabarjad 244 23 40N 36 12 E
Zabaykalskiy 185 49 40N 117 25 E
Zabid 194 14 0N 43 10 E
Zabīd, W. → 194 14 7N 43 6 E
Ząbkowice Śląskie 152 50 35N 16 50 E
Žabljak 166 43 18N 19 7 E
Zabłudów 152 53 0N 23 19 E
Żabno 152 50 9N 20 53 E
Zābol 193 31 0N 61 32 E
Zābol □ 197 32 0N 67 0 E
Zābolī 193 27 10N 61 35 E
Zabré 247 11 12N 0 36W
Zabrze 152 50 18N 18 50 E
Zacapa 112 14 59N 89 31W
Zacapetec 107 18 39N 99 12W
Zacapoaxtla 108 19 53N 97 35W
Zacapu 106 19 50N 101 43W
Zacatal 111 18 36N 91 52W
Zacate 105 24 43N 102 48W
Zacatecas 105 22 47N 102 35W
Zacatecas □ 105 23 0N 103 0W
Zacatecas, Sa. de 105 23 25N 103 30W
Zacatecoluca 112 13 29N 88 51W
Zacatepec 108 19 16N 97 32W
Zacatlán 108 19 56N 97 58W
Zacatula 106 17 59N 102 9W
Zacoalco de Torres 106 20 14N 103 35W
Zacoalpan 107 16 45N 98 17W
Zacualpán 108 20 28N 98 22W
Zacualtipan 107 20 39N 98 36W
Zacualtipán, Sa. de 107 20 56N 98 42W
Zadar 163 44 8N 15 14 E
Zadawa 247 11 33N 10 19 E
Zadetkyi Kyun 205 10 0N 98 25 E
Zadonsk 179 52 25N 38 56 E
Zafarqand 193 33 11N 52 29 E
Zafora 169 36 5N 26 24 E
Zafra 155 38 26N 6 30W
Zafriya 189 31 59N 34 51 E
Żagań 152 51 39N 15 22 E
Zagazig 244 30 40N 31 30 E
Zāgheh 193 33 30N 48 42 E
Zaghouan 241 36 23N 10 10 E
Zaglivérion 168 40 36N 23 15 E
Zaglou 240 27 17N 0 3W
Zagnanado 247 7 18N 2 28 E
Zagorá, Greece 168 39 27N 23 6 E
Zagora, Morocco 240 30 22N 5 51W
Zagórów 152 52 10N 17 54 E
Zagorsk 179 56 20N 38 10 E
Zagórz 152 49 30N 22 14 E
Zagreb 163 45 50N 16 0 E
Zāgros, Kuhhā-ye 193 33 45N 47 0 E
Žagubica 166 44 15N 21 47 E
Zaguinaso 246 10 1N 6 14W
Zagyva → 151 47 5N 20 4 E
Zāhedān, Fārs, Iran 193 28 46N 53 52 E
Zāhedān, Sīstān va Balūchestān, Iran 193 29 30N 60 50 E
Zahirabad 200 17 43N 77 37 E

Zahlah 190 33 52N 35 50 E
Zahna 146 51 54N 12 47 E
Zahrez Chergui 240 35 0N 3 30 E
Zahrez Rharbi 240 34 50N 2 55 E
Zailiyskiy Alatau, Khrebet 183 43 5N 77 0 E
Zainsk 182 55 18N 52 4 E
Zaïr 240 29 47N 5 51W
Zaire □ 253 7 0 S 14 0 E
Zaïre ■ 253 3 0 S 23 0 E
Zaïre → 252 6 4 S 12 24 E
Zaječar 166 43 53N 22 18 E
Zakamensk 185 50 23N 103 17 E
Zakani 252 2 33N 23 16 E
Zakataly 181 41 38N 46 35 E
Zakavkazye 181 42 0N 44 0 E
Zākhū 192 37 10N 42 50 E
Zákinthos 169 37 47N 20 57 E
Zaklików 152 50 46N 22 7 E
Zakopane 152 49 18N 19 57 E
Zakroczym 152 52 26N 20 38 E
Zala 253 7 52 S 13 42 E
Zala □ 151 46 42N 16 50 E
Zala → 151 46 43N 17 16 E
Zalaegerszeg 151 46 53N 16 47 E
Zalakomár 151 46 33N 17 10 E
Zalalövö 151 46 51N 16 35 E
Zalamea de la Serena 155 38 40N 5 38W
Zalamea la Real 155 37 41N 6 38W
Zalău 170 47 12N 23 3 E
Zalazna 182 58 39N 52 31 E
Žalec 163 46 16N 15 10 E
Zaleshchiki 180 48 45N 25 45 E
Zalew Wislany 152 54 20N 19 50 E
Zalewo 152 53 50N 19 41 E
Zalīm 194 22 43N 42 10 E
Zalingei 243 12 51N 23 29 E
Zaliv Vislinskil = Zalew Wislany 152 54 20N 19 50 E
Zalţan, Jabal 241 28 46N 19 45 E
Zaltbommel 142 51 48N 5 15 E
Zambales □ 210 15 20N 120 10 E
Zambales Mts. 210 15 45N 120 5 E
Zambeke 250 2 8N 25 17 E
Zambeze → 251 18 55 S 36 4 E
Zambezi = Zambeze → 251 18 55 S 36 4 E
Zambezi 253 13 30 S 23 15 E
Zambezia □ 251 16 15 S 37 30 E
Zambia ■ 251 15 0 S 28 0 E
Zamboanga 211 6 59N 122 3 E
Zamboanga del Norte □ 211 8 0N 123 0 E
Zamboanga del Sur □ 211 7 40N 123 0 E
Zamboanguita 211 9 6N 123 12 E
Zambrano 118 9 45N 74 49W
Zambrów 152 52 59N 22 14 E
Zametchino 179 53 30N 42 30 E
Zamora, Ecuador 118 4 4 S 78 58W
Zamora, Spain 154 41 30N 5 45W
Zamora □ 154 41 30N 5 46W
Zamora-Chinchipe □ 118 4 15 S 78 50W
Zamora de Hidalgo 106 19 59N 102 16W
Zamość 152 50 43N 23 15 E
Zamość □ 152 50 40N 23 10 E
Zamuro, Sierra del 119 4 0N 62 30W
Zamzam, W. → 241 31 0N 14 30 E
Zan 247 9 26N 0 17W
Zanaga 252 2 48 S 13 48 E
Záncara → 157 39 18N 3 18W
Zandijk 142 52 28N 4 49 E
Zandvoort 142 52 22N 4 32 E
Zangābād 192 38 26N 46 44 E
Zangue → 251 17 50 S 35 21 E
Zanjan 193 36 40N 48 35 E
Zanjān □ 193 37 20N 49 30 E
Zannone 164 40 58N 13 2 E
Zante = Zákinthos 169 37 47N 20 57 E
Zanthus 229 31 2 S 123 34 E
Zanzibar 250 6 12 S 39 12 E
Zanzūr 241 32 55N 13 1 E
Zaouiet El-Kala = Bordj Omar Driss 241 28 10N 6 40 E
Zaouiet Reggane 240 26 32N 0 3 E
Zaoyang 217 32 10N 112 45 E
Zaozhuang 215 34 50N 117 35 E
Zapadna Morava → 166 43 38N 21 30 E
Zapadnaya Dvina 178 56 15N 32 3 E
Zapadnaya Dvina → 178 57 4N 24 3 E
Západné Beskydy 152 49 30N 19 0 E
Zapadni Rodopi 167 41 50N 24 0 E
Zapadočeský □ 150 49 35N 13 0 E
Západoslovenský □ 151 48 30N 17 30 E
Zapala 126 39 0 S 70 5W
Zapaleri, Cerro 124 22 49 S 67 11W
Zapatón → 155 39 0N 6 49W
Zape Chico 104 25 49N 105 47W
Zapiga 122 19 40 S 79 0W
Zapodnyy Sayan 185 52 30N 94 0 E
Zapolyarnyy 176 69 26N 30 51 E
Zapopán 106 20 43N 103 24W
Zaporozhye 180 47 50N 35 10 E
Zapotán 104 21 5N 104 52W
Zapotiltic 106 19 37N 103 26W
Zapotitlán 106 19 31N 103 44W
Zapotitlán, Sa. de 109 18 30N 97 37W
Zapotitlán Lagunas 109 17 38N 98 19W
Zapotitlán Tablas 107 17 13N 98 59W
Zapotlán del Rey 106 20 27N 102 55W
Zapotlanejo 106 20 38N 103 4W
Zapponeta 165 41 27N 15 57 E
Zaragoza, Colombia 118 7 30N 74 52W
Zaragoza, Chihuahua, Mexico 101 31 39N 106 20W
Zaragoza, Coahuila, Mexico 102 28 29N 100 55W
Zaragoza, Nuevo León, Mexico 103 23 58N 99 46W
Zaragoza, Oaxaca, Mexico 109 17 16N 97 5W
Zaragoza, Puebla, Mexico 108 19 46N 97 33W
Zaragoza, San Luis Potosí, Mexico 103 22 2N 100 44W
Zaragoza, Spain 156 41 39N 0 53W
Zaragoza □ 156 41 35N 1 0W
Zarand, Kermān, Iran 193 30 46N 56 34 E
Zarand, Markazī, Iran 193 35 18N 50 25 E
Zărandului, Munţii 170 46 14N 22 7 E
Zaranj 197 30 55N 61 55 E
Zarasai 178 55 40N 26 20 E
Zarate 124 34 7 S 59 0W
Zaraysk 179 54 48N 38 53 E
Zaraza 119 9 21N 65 19W
Zarca, La 105 25 50N 104 44W
Zāreh 193 35 7N 49 9 E
Zaria 247 11 0N 7 40 E
Zárkon 168 39 38N 22 6 E
Zarneh 192 33 55N 46 10 E
Żarów 152 50 56N 16 29 E
Zarqā' → 189 32 10N 35 37 E
Zarrīn 193 32 46N 54 37 E
Zaruma 118 3 40 S 79 38W
Żary 152 51 37N 15 10 E
Zarza, La 155 37 42N 6 51W
Zarza de Alange 155 38 49N 6 13W
Zarza de Granadilla 154 40 14N 6 3W
Zarzaïtine 241 28 15N 9 34 E
Zarzal 118 4 24N 76 4W
Zarzis 241 33 31N 11 2 E
Zas 154 43 4N 8 53W
Zashiversk 185 67 25N 142 40 E
Zaskar → 199 34 13N 77 20 E
Zaskar Mountains 199 33 15N 77 30 E
Zastron 254 30 18 S 27 7 E
Żatec 150 50 20N 13 32 E
Zator 152 49 59N 19 28 E
Zavala 166 42 50N 17 59 E
Zavāreh 193 33 29N 52 28 E
Zaventem 143 50 53N 4 28 E
Zavetnoye 181 47 13N 43 50 E
Zavidovići 166 44 27N 18 13 E
Zavitinsk 185 50 10N 129 20 E
Zavodoski 13 56 0 S 27 45W
Zavolzhsk 179 57 30N 42 10 E
Zavolzhye 179 56 37N 43 26 E
Zawadzkie 152 50 37N 18 28 E
Zawichost 152 50 48N 21 51 E
Zawidów 152 51 1N 15 1 E
Zawiercie 152 50 30N 19 24 E
Zāwiyat al Bayḑā 242 32 30N 21 40 E
Zāwiyat Masūs 242 31 35N 21 1 E
Zawyet Shammâs 244 31 30N 26 37 E
Zâwyet Um el Rakham 244 31 18N 27 1 E
Zâwyet Ungeîla 244 31 23N 26 42 E
Zāyā 192 33 33N 44 13 E
Zayarsk 185 56 12N 102 55 E
Zaymah 194 21 37N 40 6 E
Zaysan 184 47 28N 84 52 E
Zaysan, Oz. 184 48 0N 83 0 E
Zaytā 189 32 23N 35 2 E
Zayü 216 28 48N 97 27 E
Zāzamt, W. → 241 30 29N 14 30 E
Zazir, O. → 241 22 0N 5 40 E
Zázrivá 151 49 16N 19 7 E
Zbarazh 178 49 43N 25 44 E
Zbąszyń 152 52 14N 15 56 E
Zbąszynek 152 52 16N 15 51 E
Zblewo 152 53 56N 18 19 E
Zdolbunov 178 50 30N 26 15 E
Ždrelo 166 44 16N 21 28 E
Zduńska Wola 152 51 37N 18 59 E
Zduny 152 51 39N 17 21 E
Zealand Station 81 46 3N 66 56W
Zealandia 88 51 37N 107 45W
Zeballos 92 49 59N 126 50W
Zebediela 255 24 20 S 19 7 E
Zedelgem 143 51 8N 3 8 E
Zeebrugge 143 51 19N 3 12 E
Zeehan 230 41 52 S 145 25 E
Zeeland 143 51 41N 5 40 E
Zeeland □ 143 51 30N 3 50 E
Ze'elim 189 31 13N 34 32 E
Zeelst 143 51 25N 5 25 E
Zeerust 254 25 31 S 26 4 E
Zefat 189 32 58N 35 29 E
Zegdou 240 29 51N 4 45W
Zege 245 11 43N 37 18 E
Zegelsem 143 50 49N 3 43 E
Zégoua 246 10 32N 5 35W
Zehdenick 146 52 59N 13 20 E
Zeil, Mt. 228 23 30 S 132 23 E
Zeila 256 11 21N 43 30 E
Zeist 142 52 5N 5 15 E
Zeitz 146 51 3N 12 9 E
Zele 143 51 4N 4 2 E
Żelechów 152 51 49N 21 54 E
Zelega, W. → 191 29 7N 34 31 E
Zelengora 166 43 22N 18 30 E
Zelenika 166 42 27N 18 37 E
Zelenodolsk 179 55 55N 48 30 E
Zelenogradsk 178 54 53N 20 29 E
Zelenokumsk 181 44 24N 43 53 E
Zelënyy 181 48 6N 50 45 E
Zeleznik 166 44 43N 20 23 E
Zelhem 142 52 0N 6 21 E
Zell, Baden-W., Germany 147 47 42N 7 50 E
Zell, Rhld-Pfz., Germany 147 50 2N 7 11 E
Zell am See 150 47 19N 12 47 E
Zella Mehlis 146 50 40N 10 41 E
Zelów 152 51 28N 19 14 E
Zelzate 143 51 13N 3 47 E
Zembra, I. 241 37 5N 10 56 E
Zémio 250 5 2N 25 5 E
Zemlya Frantsa Iosifa 12 81 0N 55 0 E
Zemmora 241 35 44N 0 51 E
Zemmur 240 25 5N 12 0W
Zemoul, O. → 240 29 15N 7 0W
Zempoala 108 19 27N 96 23W
Zempoala, Pta. 108 19 28N 96 19W
Zemst 143 50 59N 4 28 E
Zemun 166 44 51N 20 25 E
Zendeh Jān 197 34 21N 61 45 E
Zengbe 247 5 46N 13 4 E
Zengcheng 217 23 13N 113 52 E
Zenica 166 44 10N 17 57 E
Zenina 241 34 30N 2 37 E
Zenon Park 88 53 4N 103 45W
Zentsūji 220 34 14N 133 47 E
Zenza do Itombe 253 9 16 S 14 13 E
Žepče 166 44 28N 18 2 E
Zeraf, Bahr ez → 245 9 42N 30 52 E
Zeravshan 183 39 10N 68 39 E
Zeravshanskiy, Khrebet 183 39 20N 69 0 E
Zerbst 146 51 59N 12 8 E
Zerhamra 240 29 58N 2 30W
Żerków 152 52 4N 17 32 E
Zermatt 148 46 2N 7 46 E
Zernez 149 46 42N 10 7 E
Zernograd 181 46 52N 40 19 E
Zerqani 168 41 30N 20 20 E
Zestafoni 181 42 6N 43 0 E
Zetel 146 53 25N 7 57 E
Zetten 142 51 56N 5 44 E
Zeulenroda 146 50 39N 12 0 E
Zeven 146 53 17N 9 19 E
Zevenaar 142 51 56N 6 5 E
Zevenbergen 143 51 38N 4 37 E
Zévio 162 45 23N 11 10 E
Zeya 185 53 48N 127 14 E
Zeya → 185 53 13N 127 35 E
Zeyne 190 36 25N 33 31 E
Zêzere → 155 39 28N 8 20W
Zghartā 190 34 21N 35 53 E
Zgierz 152 51 50N 19 27 E
Zgorzelec 152 51 10N 15 0 E
Zhabinka 178 52 13N 24 2 E
Zhailma 182 51 37N 61 33 E
Zhalanash 183 43 3N 78 38 E
Zhanadarya 183 44 45N 64 40 E
Zhanatas 183 43 35N 69 35 E
Zhangbei 214 41 10N 114 45 E
Zhangguangcai Ling 215 45 0N 129 0 E
Zhanghua 217 24 6N 120 29 E
Zhangjiakou 214 40 48N 114 55 E
Zhangping 217 25 17N 117 23 E
Zhangpu 217 24 8N 117 35 E
Zhangwu 215 42 43N 123 52 E
Zhangye 212 38 50N 100 23 E
Zhangzhou 217 24 30N 117 35 E
Zhanhua 215 37 40N 118 8 E
Zhanjiang 217 21 15N 110 20 E
Zhanyi 216 25 38N 103 48 E
Zhanyu 215 44 30N 122 30 E
Zhao Xian 214 37 43N 114 45 E
Zhao'an 217 23 41N 117 10 E
Zhaocheng 214 36 22N 111 38 E
Zhaojue 216 28 1N 102 49 E
Zhaoping 217 24 11N 110 48 E
Zhaoqing 217 23 0N 112 20 E
Zhaotong 216 27 20N 103 44 E
Zhaoyuan, Heilongjiang, China 215 45 27N 125 0 E
Zhaoyuan, Shandong, China 215 37 20N 120 23 E
Zharkol 182 49 57N 64 5 E
Zharkovskiy 178 55 56N 32 19 E
Zhashkov 180 49 15N 30 5 E
Zhashui 214 33 40N 109 8 E
Zhdanov 180 47 5N 37 31 E
Zhecheng 214 34 7N 115 20 E
Zhegao 217 31 46N 117 45 E
Zhejiang □ 217 29 0N 120 0 E
Zheleznodorozhny 176 62 35N 50 55 E
Zheleznogorsk 178 52 22N 35 23 E
Zheleznogorsk-Ilimskiy 185 56 34N 104 8 E
Zheltyye Vody 180 48 21N 33 31 E
Zhen an 216 33 27N 109 9 E
Zhenfeng 216 25 22N 105 40 E
Zheng'an 216 28 32N 107 27 E
Zhengding 214 38 8N 114 32 E
Zhenghe 217 27 20N 118 50 E
Zhengyang 217 32 37N 114 22 E
Zhengyangguan 217 32 30N 116 29 E
Zhengzhou 214 34 45N 113 34 E
Zhenhai 217 29 59N 121 42 E
Zhenjiang 217 32 11N 119 26 E
Zhenlai 215 45 50N 123 5 E
Zhenning 216 26 4N 105 45 E
Zhenping, Henan, China 217 33 10N 112 16 E
Zhenping, Shaanxi, China 216 31 59N 109 31 E
Zhenxiong 216 27 27N 104 50 E
Zhenyuan, Gansu, China 214 35 35N 107 30 E
Zhenyuan, Guizhou, China 216 27 4N 108 21 E
Zherdevka 179 51 56N 41 29 E
Zherong 217 27 15N 119 52 E
Zhetykol, Ozero 182 51 2N 60 54 E
Zhidan 214 36 48N 108 48 E
Zhigansk 185 66 48N 123 27 E
Zhigulevsk 179 53 28N 49 30 E
Zhijiang, Hubei, China 217 30 28N 111 45 E
Zhijiang, Hunan, China 216 27 27N 109 42 E
Zhijin 216 26 37N 105 45 E
Zhirnovsk 179 50 57N 44 49 E
Zhitomir 178 50 20N 28 40 E
Zhizdra 178 53 45N 34 40 E
Zhlobin 178 52 55N 30 0 E
Zhmerinka 180 49 2N 28 2 E
Zhodino 178 54 5N 28 17 E
Zhokhova, Ostrov 185 76 4N 152 40 E
Zhong Xian 216 30 21N 108 1 E
Zhongdian 216 27 48N 99 42 E
Zhongdong 216 22 48N 107 47 E
Zhongdu 216 24 40N 109 40 E
Zhongning 214 37 29N 105 40 E
Zhongshan, Guangdong, China 217 22 26N 113 20 E
Zhongshan, Guangxi Zhuangzu, China 217 24 29N 111 18 E
Zhongtiao Shan 214 35 0N 111 10 E
Zhongwei 214 37 30N 105 12 E
Zhongxiang 217 31 12N 112 34 E
Zhongyang 214 37 20N 111 11 E
Zhoucun 215 36 47N 117 48 E
Zhouning 217 27 12N 119 20 E
Zhoushan Dao 217 28 5N 122 10 E
Zhouzhi 214 34 10N 108 12 E
Zhovtnevoye 180 46 54N 32 3 E
Zhuanghe 215 39 40N 123 0 E
Zhuantobe 183 43 43N 78 18 E
Zhucheng 215 36 0N 119 27 E
Zhugqu 214 33 40N 104 30 E
Zhuhai 217 22 15N 113 30 E
Zhuji 217 29 40N 120 10 E
Zhukovka 178 53 35N 33 50 E
Zhumadian 217 32 59N 114 2 E
Zhuo Xian 214 39 28N 115 58 E
Zhuolu 214 40 20N 115 12 E
Zhuozi 214 41 0N 112 25 E
Zhupanovo 185 53 40N 159 52 E
Zhushan 217 32 15N 110 13 E
Zhuxi 217 32 25N 109 40 E
Zhuzhou 217 27 49N 113 12 E
Zi Shui → 217 28 40N 112 40 E
Zīārān 193 36 7N 50 32 E
Ziarat 198 30 25N 67 49 E
Zibo 215 36 47N 118 3 E
Zichang 214 37 18N 109 40 E
Zichem 143 51 2N 4 59 E
Zidarovo 167 42 20N 27 24 E
Ziębice 152 50 37N 17 2 E

Zielona Góra ...... **152** 51 57N 15 31 E
Zielona Góra □ .... **152** 51 57N 15 30 E
Zierikzee .... **143** 51 40N 3 55 E
Ziesar .... **146** 52 16N 12 19 E
Zifta .... **244** 30 43N 31 14 E
Zigazinskiy .... **182** 53 50N 57 20 E
Zigey .... **243** 14 43N 15 50 E
Zighrīn .... **190** 35 44N 35 54 E
Zigong .... **216** 29 15N 104 48 E
Zigui .... **217** 31 0N 110 40 E
Ziguinchor **246** 12 35N 16 20W
Zihuatanejo **107** 17 38N 101 33W
Zijin .... **217** 23 33N 115 8 E
Zikhron Ya'Aqov .. **189** 32 34N 34 56 E
Žilina .... **151** 49 12N 18 42 E
Zillah .... **241** 28 30N 17 33 E
Zillertaler Alpen ... **150** 47 6N 11 45 E
Zima .... **185** 54 0N 102 5 E
Zimane, Adrar in .. **240** 22 10N 4 30 E
Zimapán **107** 20 45N 99 21W
Zimapán, Sa. de ... **107** 20 45N 99 40W
Zimatlán de Álvarez **109** 16 52N 96 47W
Zimba .... **251** 17 20 S 26 11 E
Zimbabwe .... **251** 20 16 S 30 54 E
Zimbabwe ■ .... **251** 20 0 S 30 0 E
Zimnicea .... **170** 43 40N 25 22 E
Zimovniki .... **181** 47 10N 42 25 E
Zinacantán **110** 16 45N 92 42W
Zinal .... **148** 46 8N 7 38 E
Zinapécuaro **107** 19 52N 100 49W
Zinder .... **247** 13 48N 9 0 E
Zinga .... **251** 9 16 S 38 49 E
Zingem .... **143** 50 54N 3 40 E
Zingst .... **146** 54 24N 12 45 E
Ziniaré **247** 12 35N 1 18W
Zinkgruvan .... **173** 58 50N 15 6 E
Zinnowitz .... **146** 54 5N 13 54 E
Zionz L. **86** 51 25N 91 52W
Zipaquirá **118** 5 0N 74 0W
Zippori .... **189** 32 45N 35 16 E
Ziracuaretiro **106** 19 25N 101 55W
Zirahuén **106** 19 26N 101 44W
Zirándaro **107** 18 27N 100 59W
Zirc .... **151** 47 17N 17 42 E
Žiri .... **163** 46 5N 14 5 E
Žirje .... **163** 43 39N 15 42 E
Zirl .... **150** 47 17N 11 14 E
Zisterdorf .... **151** 48 33N 16 45 E
Zitácuaro **107** 19 24N 100 22W
Zitava ─► .... **151** 48 14N 18 21 E
Žitište .... **166** 45 30N 20 32 E
Zitlala **107** 17 38N 99 5W
Zítsa .... **168** 39 47N 20 40 E
Zittau .... **146** 50 54N 14 47 E
Zitundo .... **255** 26 48 S 32 47 E
Živinice .... **166** 44 27N 18 36 E
Ziway, L. .... **245** 8 0N 38 50 E
Zixi .... **217** 27 45N 117 4 E
Zixing .... **217** 25 59N 113 21 E
Ziyang, Shaanxi, China .... **216** 32 32N 108 31 E
Ziyang, Sichuan, China .... **216** 30 6N 104 40 E
Ziyun .... **216** 25 45N 106 5 E
Ziz, Oued ─► **241** 31 40N 4 15W
Zizhixian .... **217** 25 0N 111 47 E
Zizhong .... **216** 29 48N 104 47 E
Zlarin .... **163** 43 42N 15 49 E
Zlatar, Hrvatska, Yugoslavia .... **163** 46 5N 16 3 E
Zlatar, Srbija, Yugoslavia .... **166** 43 25N 19 47 E
Zlataritsa .... **167** 43 2N 25 55 E
Zlatibor .... **166** 43 45N 19 43 E
Zlatitsa .... **167** 42 41N 24 7 E
Zlatna .... **170** 46 8N 23 11 E
Zlatograd .... **167** 41 22N 25 7 E
Zlatoust .... **176** 55 10N 59 40 E
Zletovo .... **166** 41 59N 22 17 E
Zlin = Gottwaldov . **151** 49 14N 17 40 E
Zlītan .... **241** 32 32N 14 35 E
Złocieniec .... **152** 53 30N 16 1 E
Złoczew .... **152** 51 24N 18 35 E
Zlot .... **166** 44 1N 22 0 E
Złotoryja .... **152** 51 8N 15 55 E
Złotów .... **152** 53 22N 17 2 E
Złoty Stok .... **152** 50 27N 16 53 E
Zmeinogorsk .... **184** 51 10N 82 13 E
Żmigród .... **152** 51 28N 16 53 E
Zmiyev .... **180** 49 39N 36 27 E
Znamenka .... **180** 48 45N 32 30 E
Znamensk .... **178** 54 37N 21 17 E
Żnin .... **152** 52 51N 17 44 E
Znojmo .... **150** 48 50N 16 2 E
Zoar .... **254** 33 30 S 21 26 E
Zobeyrī .... **192** 34 10N 46 40 E
Zobia .... **250** 3 0N 25 59 E
Zoetermeer .... **142** 52 3N 4 30 E
Zofingen .... **148** 47 17N 7 56 E
Zogang .... **216** 29 55N 97 42 E
Zogno .... **162** 45 49N 9 41 E
Zogqên .... **216** 32 13N 98 47 E
Zohlaguna, Meseta de **111** 18 40N 89 35W
Zolder .... **143** 51 1N 5 19 E
Zollikofen .... **148** 47 0N 7 28 E
Zollikon .... **149** 47 21N 8 34 E
Zolochev .... **178** 49 45N 24 51 E
Zolotonosha .... **180** 49 39N 32 5 E
Zomba .... **251** 15 22 S 35 19 E
Zomergem .... **143** 51 7N 3 33 E
Zongo .... **252** 4 20N 18 35 E
Zongolica **109** 18 40N 96 59W
Zongolica, Sa. de ... **109** 18 20N 97 0W
Zonguldak .... **180** 41 28N 31 50 E
Zonhoven .... **143** 50 59N 5 23 E
Zontecomatlán **108** 20 46N 98 21W
Zorgo **247** 12 15N 0 35W
Zorita **155** 39 17N 5 39W
Zorleni .... **170** 46 14N 27 44 E
Zornitsa .... **167** 42 23N 26 58 E
Zorritos .... **122** 3 43 S 80 40W
Zory .... **152** 50 3N 18 44 E
Zorzor **246** 7 46N 9 28W
Zossen .... **146** 52 13N 13 28 E
Zottegam .... **143** 50 52N 3 48 E
Zou Xiang .... **214** 35 30N 116 58 E
Zouar .... **241** 20 30N 16 32 E
Zouérate **240** 22 44N 12 21W
Zousfana, O. ─► ... **240** 31 28N 2 17W
Zoushan Dao ...... **217** 30 5N 122 10 E
Zoutkamp .... **142** 53 20N 6 18 E
Zrenjanin .... **166** 45 22N 20 23 E
Zuarungu **247** 10 49N 0 46W
Zuba .... **247** 9 11N 7 12 E
Zubayr .... **194** 15 3N 42 10 E
Zubia **155** 37 8N 3 33W
Zubtsov .... **178** 56 10N 34 34 E
Zucualpan **107** 18 43N 99 47W
Zudáñez .... **123** 19 6 S 64 44W
Zuénoula **246** 7 34N 6 3W
Zuera **156** 41 51N 0 49W
Zuetina .... **241** 30 58N 20 7 E
Zufar .... **195** 17 40N 54 0 E
Zug .... **149** 47 10N 8 31 E
Zug □ .... **149** 47 9N 8 35 E
Zugdidi .... **181** 42 30N 41 55 E
Zugersee .... **149** 47 7N 8 35 E
Zugspitze .... **147** 47 25N 10 59 E
Zuid-Holland □ .... **142** 52 0N 4 35 E
Zuidbeveland ...... **143** 51 30N 3 50 E
Zuidbroek .... **142** 53 10N 6 52 E
Zuidelijk-Flevoland . **142** 52 22N 5 22 E
Zuidhorn .... **142** 53 15N 6 23 E
Zuidlaarder meer ... **142** 53 8N 6 42 E
Zuidlaren .... **142** 53 6N 6 42 E
Zuidwolde .... **142** 52 40N 6 26 E
Zújar **157** 37 34N 2 50W
Zújar ─► **155** 39 1N 5 47W
Zújar, Pantano del . **155** 38 55N 5 35W
Zula .... **245** 15 17N 39 40 E
Zulia □ **118** 10 0N 72 10W
Zulpich .... **146** 50 41N 6 38 E
Zululand .... **255** 43 19N 2 15 E
Zumaya **156** 43 19N 2 15W
Zumbo .... **251** 15 35 S 30 26 E
Zummo .... **247** 9 51N 12 59 E
Zumpango **107** 19 48N 99 6W
Zumpango, L. de ... **107** 19 46N 99 9W
Zumpango del Río . **107** 17 39N 99 30W
Zundert .... **143** 51 28N 4 39 E
Zungeru .... **247** 9 48N 6 8 E
Zunhua .... **215** 40 18N 117 58 E
Zunyi .... **216** 27 42N 106 53 E
Zuoquan .... **214** 37 5N 113 22 E
Zuozhou .... **216** 22 42N 107 27 E
Županja .... **166** 45 4N 18 43 E
Zuqar .... **245** 14 0N 42 40 E
Žur .... **166** 42 13N 20 34 E
Zura .... **182** 57 36N 53 24 E
Zurbātīyah .... **192** 33 9N 46 3 E
Zurich, Canada **84** 43 26N 81 37W
Zürich, Switz. ...... **149** 47 22N 8 32 E
Zürich □ .... **149** 47 26N 8 40 E
Zürichsee .... **149** 47 18N 8 40 E
Zuromin .... **152** 53 4N 19 51 E
Zuru .... **247** 11 20N 5 11 E
Zurzach .... **149** 47 35N 8 18 E
Žut .... **163** 43 52N 15 17 E
Zutendaal .... **143** 50 56N 5 35 E
Zutphen .... **142** 52 9N 6 12 E
Zuwārah .... **241** 32 58N 12 1 E
Zuyevka .... **179** 58 27N 51 10 E
Zūzan .... **193** 34 22N 59 53 E
Žužemberk .... **163** 45 52N 14 56 E
Zvenigorodka ...... **180** 49 4N 30 56 E
Zverinogolovskoye . **182** 54 23N 64 40 E
Zvezdets .... **167** 42 6N 27 26 E
Zvishavane .... **251** 20 17 S 30 2 E
Zvolen .... **151** 48 33N 19 10 E
Zvonce .... **166** 42 57N 22 34 E
Zvornik .... **166** 44 26N 19 7 E
Zwaag .... **142** 52 40N 5 4 E
Zwanenburg .... **142** 52 23N 4 45 E
Zwarte Meer .... **142** 52 38N 5 57 E
Zwarte Waler ...... **142** 52 39N 6 1 E
Zwartemeer .... **142** 52 43N 7 2 E
Zwartsluis .... **142** 52 39N 6 4 E
Zwedru = Tchien .. **246** 5 59N 8 15W
Zweibrücken .... **147** 49 15N 7 20 E
Zwenkau .... **146** 51 13N 12 19 E
Zwettl .... **150** 48 35N 15 9 E
Zwevegem .... **143** 50 48N 3 20 E
Zwickau .... **146** 50 43N 12 30 E
Zwiesel .... **147** 49 1N 13 14 E
Zwijnaarde .... **143** 51 0N 3 43 E
Zwijndrecht, Belgium .... **143** 51 13N 4 20 E
Zwijndrecht, Neth. . **142** 51 50N 4 39 E
Zwischenahn .... **146** 53 12N 8 1 E
Zwoleń .... **152** 51 21N 21 36 E
Zwolle .... **142** 52 31N 6 6 E
Żychlin .... **152** 52 15N 19 37 E
Zymoetz ─► **76** 54 33N 128 31W
Żyrardów .... **152** 52 3N 20 28 E
Zyrya .... **181** 40 20N 50 15 E
Zyryanka .... **185** 65 45N 150 51 E
Zyryanovsk .... **184** 49 43N 84 20 E
Żywiec .... **152** 49 42N 19 10 E